Sports Illustrated 2004 Almanac

By the Editors of Sports Illustrated

Sports Illustrated
2004
Almanac

First Edition
ISBN 1-931933-79-0

SPORTS ILLUSTRATED Executive Editor: Rob Fleder
SPORTS ILLUSTRATED Director, New Product Development: Bruce Kaufman

Sports Illustrated 2004 Almanac was prepared by
Bishop Books of New York City.

Cover photography credits :
Warren Sapp: Albert Dickson/TSN/Icon SMI
Tim Duncan: Manny Millan
Barry Bonds: John Biever

Back cover photography credits (left to right):
Carson Palmer: Peter Read Miller
Bode Miller: Bob Martin
LeBron James: Fernando Medina/NBAE via Getty Images

Spine photography credit: Bob Martin

Title page photography credit: John Biever

TIME INC. HOME ENTERTAINMENT

President . . . . Rob Gursha
Vice President, Branded Businesses . . . . David Arfine
Vice President, New Product Development . . . . Richard Fraiman
Executive Director, Marketing Services . . . . Carol Pittard
Director, Retail & Special Sales . . . . Tom Mifsud
Director of Finance . . . . Tricia Griffin
Marketing Director . . . . Kenneth Maehlum
Assistant Marketing Director . . . . Niki Whelan
Prepress Manager . . . . Emily Rabin
Marketing Manager . . . . Michelle Kuhr
Associate Book Production Manager . . . . Suzanne Janso

Special thanks: Bozena Bannett, Alex Bliss, Bernadette Corbie, Robert Dente, Gina Di Meglio, Anne-Michelle Gallero, Peter Harper, Robert Marasco, Natalie McCrea, Jonathan Polsky, Mary Jane Rigoroso, Steven Sandonato, Grace Sullivan

We welcome your comments and suggestions about Sports Illustrated Books. Please write to us at: Sports Illustrated Books, Attention: Book Editors, PO Box 11016, Des Moines, IA 50336-1016

If you would like to order any of our hardcover Collector's Edition books, please call us at 1-800-327-6388. (Monday through Friday, 7:00 a.m.–8:00 p.m. or Saturday, 7:00 a.m.–6:00 p.m. Central Time).

CONTENTS

SOURCES

In compiling the *Sports Illustrated 2004 Almanac*, the editors would like to extend their gratitude to the media relations offices of the following organizations for their help in providing information and materials relating to their sports: Major League Baseball; the Canadian Football League; the National Football League; the National Collegiate Athletic Association; the National Basketball Association; the National Hockey League; the Association of Tennis Professionals; the Women's Tennis Association; the U.S. Tennis Association; the U.S. Golf Association; the Ladies Professional Golf Association; the Professional Golfers Association; National Thoroughbred Racing Association; the U.S. Trotting Association; the Breeders' Cup; Churchill Downs; the New York Racing Association, Inc.; the Jockey's Guild, Inc.; Championship Auto Racing Teams; the National Hot Rod Association; the International Motor Sports Association; the National Association for Stock Car Auto Racing; the Professional Bowlers Association; the Ladies Professional Bowlers Tour; the United Soccer Leagues; Major League Soccer; the Women's United Soccer Association; the *Fédération Internationale de Football Association*; the U.S. Soccer Federation; the U.S. Olympic Committee; USA Track & Field; U.S. Swimming; U.S. Diving; U.S. Skiing; U.S. Figure Skating Association; the U.S. Chess Federation; U.S. Curling; the Iditarod Trail Committee; the International Game Fish Association; the USA Gymnastics; U.S. Handball Association; the Lacrosse Foundation; the American Power Boat Association; the Unlimited Hydroplane Racing Association; the Professional Rodeo Cowboys Association; U.S. Rowing; the American Amateur Softball Association; the U.S. Speed Skating ; U.S. Rugby Football Union; USA Triathlon; the National Archery Association; USA Wrestling; the U.S. Squash Racquets Association; the U.S. Polo Association; ABC Sports; and the U.S. Volleyball Association.

The following sources were consulted in gathering information:

Baseball   *The Baseball Encyclopedia*, Macmillan Publishing Co., 1990; *Total Baseball*, Viking Penguin, 1995; *Baseballistics*, St. Martin's Press, 1990; *The Book of Baseball Records*, Seymour Siwoff, publisher, 1991; *The Complete Baseball Record Book*, The Sporting News Publishing Co., 1992; *The Sporting News Baseball Guide*, The Sporting News Publishing Co., 1996; *The Sporting News Official Baseball Register*, The Sporting News Publishing Co., 1996; *National League Green Book—1994*, The Sporting News Publishing Co. 1993; *American League Red Book—1994*, The Sporting News Publishing Co., 1993; *The Scouting Report: 1996*, Harper Perennial, 1996.

Pro Football   *The Official 1997 National Football League Record & Fact Book*, The National Football League, 1997; *The Official National Football League Encyclopedia*, New American Library, 1990; *The Sporting News Football Guide*, The Sporting News Publishing Co., 1996; *The Sporting News Football Register*, The Sporting News Publishing Co., 1996; *The 1993 National Football League Record & Fact Book*, Workman Publishing, 1993; *The Football Encyclopedia*, David Neft and Richard Cohen, St. Martin's Press, 1991.

Pro Football Venues   *Ticketmaster*

College Football   *1997 NCAA Football*, The National Collegiate Athletic Association, 1997.

Pro Basketball   *The Official NBA Basketball Encyclopedia*, Villard Books, 1994; *The Sporting News Official NBA Guide*, The Sporting News Publishing Co., 1996; *The Sporting News Official NBA Register*, The Sporting News Publishing Co., 1996.

College Basketball   *1997 NCAA Basketball*, The National Collegiate Athletic Association, 1996.

Hockey *The National Hockey League Official Guide & Record Book 1997–98*, The National Hockey League, 1997; *The Sporting News Complete Hockey Book,* The Sporting News Publishing Co., 1993; *The Complete Encyclopedia of Hockey,* Visible Ink Press, 1993.

Tennis *1997 Official USTA Tennis Yearbook*, H.O. Zimman, Inc., 1997; *IBM/ATP Tour 1997 Player Guide*, Association of Tennis Professionals, 1997; *1997 Corel WTA Tour Media Guide*, Corel WTA Tour, 1997.

Golf *PGA Tour Book 1997*, PGA Tour Creative Services, 1997; *LPGA 1997 Player Guide*, LPGA Communications Department, 1997; *Senior PGA Tour Book 1997*, PGA Tour Creative Services, 1997; *USGA Yearbook 1997*, U.S. Golf Association, 1997.

Boxing *The Ring 1986–87 Record Book and Boxing Encyclopedia*, The Ring Publishing Corp., 1987. *Computer Boxing Update*, Ralph Citro, Inc., 1992; Bob Yalen, boxing statistician.

Horse Racing *The American Racing Manual 1994*, Daily Racing Form, Inc., 1994; *1994 Directory and Record Book*, The Thoroughbred Racing Association, 1994; *The Trotting and Pacing Guide 1994*, United States Trotting Association, 1994; *Breeders' Cup 1993 Statistics*, Breeders' Cup Limited, 1993; *NYRA Media Guide 1993*, The New York Racing Association, 1994; *The 120th Kentucky Derby Media Guide, 1994*, Churchill Downs Public Relations Dept., 1994; *The 120th Preakness Press Guide, 1994*, Maryland Jockey Club, 1994; *Harness Racing News,* Harness Racing Communications.

Motor Sports *The Official NASCAR Yearbook and Press Guide 1997*, UMI Publications, Inc., 1997; *1994 Indianapolis 500 Media Fact Book*, Indy 500 Publications, 1994; *IMSA Yearbook 1995 Season Review*, International Motor Sports Association, 1995; *1994 Winston Drag Racing Series Media Guide*, Sports Marketing Enterprises, 1994.

Bowling *1994 Professional Bowlers Association Press, Radio and Television Guide*, Professional Bowlers Association, Inc., 1994; *The Professional Women's Bowling Association Tour Guide 1997*.

Soccer *Rothmans Football Yearbook 1993–94*, Headline Book Publishing, 1993; *American Professional Soccer League 1992 Media Guide*, APSL Media Relations Department, 1992; *The European Football Yearbook*, Facer Publications Limited, 1988; *Soccer America,* Burling Communications; Dan Goldstein, editor of *Football Europe*.

NCAA Sports *1997–98 National Collegiate Championships*, The National Collegiate Athletic Association, 1998; *1993–94 National Directory of College Athletics,* Collegiate Directories Inc., 1993.

Olympics *The Complete Book of the Olympics*, Little, Brown and Co., 1991; *The Complete Book of the Summer Olympics,* Little, Brown and Co., 1996.

Track and Field *American Athletics Annual 1996*, The Athletics Congress/USA, 1996.

Swimming *6th World Swimming Championships Media Guide*, The World Swimming Championships Organizing Committee, 1991.

Skiing *U.S. Ski Team 1994 Media Guide / USSA Directory*, U.S. Ski Association, 1993; *Ski Racing Annual Competition Guide 1993–94*, Ski Racing International, 1993; *Ski Magazine's Encyclopedia of Skiing*, Harper & Row, 1974; *Caffe Lavazza Ski World Cup Press Kit*, Biorama, 1991.

In Ron #10 We Trust ©

The GOAT is DEAD!!

The Year In Sports

Chicago Cubs fans celebrate the team's first division title in 14 years

The Last Shall Be First

Dynasties tumbled, superstars stumbled and underdogs prevailed in a season of surprises both on and off the field of play

BY HANK HERSCH

IT WAS AN IMAGE of determination. Lance Armstrong lay sprawled on the asphalt, which he'd smacked after his bicycle's handlebar caught on a yellow cotton knapsack held in the hands of a young roadside spectator in the French Pyrenees. Less than a week remained in a taut Tour de France; less than 10 kilometers remained in the enervating climb to Luz-Ardiden. As rival Jan Ullrich of Germany slowed to allow Armstrong back into the race—reciprocating Armstrong's sportsmanlike gesture from the 2001 Tour—the 31-year-old Texan remounted, only to have his right foot slip off the pedal, causing him to fall crotch-first onto his top bar. Then i appeared: a look of fortitude and inten sity. "When I saw that," said Arm strong's personal coach, Chri Carmichael, who was watching on TV, " thought, This is going to be a goo thing, Lance rides much better when h has some emotion."

It was an unusual image as well. I resolutely overcoming his spill to pul away from Ullrich and gut out hi record-tying fifth consecutive victory i the Tour, Armstrong proved to be a rar sporting species in 2003: a dominant fig ure actually able to extend his domi nance. For was a year in which dynastie tumbled (the Los Angeles Lakers, th

Warren Sapp (rear) and the Tampa Bay Buccaneers began the year by wrapping up the first Super Bowl in franchise history.

U.S. women's soccer team), champions stumbled (Tiger Woods, the Miami Hurricanes) and idols were shockingly humbled (Kobe Bryant, Sammy Sosa). Their slippages, if only temporary, allowed unknowns to reach the summit (*Hello, Ben Curtis!*), controversial newcomers to steal headlines (MS. BURK GOES TO AUGUSTA) and stars in other sports to emerge ("...at the wire, it's Funny Cide!").

The passing of many of sport's trailblazing figures during the year served as further reminder of the inevitability of change. The deaths included Tex Schramm, 83, who as president and general manager of the Dallas Cowboys masterminded computerized scouting, scantily clad cheerleaders, instant replay, the wild-card playoff system and

AP PHOTO/ELISE AMENDOLA

what would become known as America's Team. And Mark McCormack, 72, who in 1960 made a handshake deal to represent Arnold Palmer, then during the next four decades became the most powerful agent in sports, capitalizing on the untapped marketing potential of stars. And George Plimpton, 76, who pulled back the curtain in books like *Paper Lion* and *Shadow Box* to reveal the lives of athletes as he became, if only for a short time, one himself. And Althea Gibson, 76, who left a sharecropper's shack in Silver, S.C., and blossomed into the queen of the lawns at Wimbledon and Forest Hills, the dominant tennis player in the 1950s and the first black to win a major championship. And Willie Shoemaker, 72, who rode four Kentucky Derby winners while, in the words of columnist Jim Murray, performing with "the effortless ease and grace of a guy born to do what he was doing." And Herb Brooks, 66, who coached the U.S. hockey team to its Miracle on Ice victory over the Soviet Union in 1980.

Brooks also coached the University of Minnesota and four NHL teams, one of which served as a beacon of consistency in 2003. The New Jersey Devils won their third Stanley Cup in nine seasons despite ranking among the most obscure outfits ever to have their names inscribed on the 111-year-old trophy. The Devils' biggest star, goalie Martin Brodeur, was brilliant in the playoffs, but not so brilliant that he could wrest the Conn Smythe Trophy for postseason MVP from his opposite number in the finals, Jean-Sebastien Giguere of the Anaheim Mighty Ducks. In Game 7, though, Brodeur needed only a second-period deflection by rookie right wing Michael Rupp—who scored his first playoff goal—to seize the NHL's most meaningful hardware, turning back 24 shots in New Jersey's decisive 3–0 victory.

As obscure as Rupp was, his *shadow* might have had a higher profile than golfer Ben Curtis before the British Open in July. A 26-year-old graduate of Kent State who still lived part-time in his parents' brick farmhouse in Ostrander, Ohio (pop. 405), Curtis had played only 14 PGA Tour events before the Open. He qualified for the field at Royal St. George's by finishing 13th earlier in the month at the Western Open in Chicago. "Ben doesn't show emotion and he doesn't say a whole lot," his father, Bob, said. "I mean, he's ranked 396 in the world. With Ben, it's always where he's playing next and what does he have to earn to keep his [Tour] card."

Coming down the stretch in the final round, four world-class talents stood poised to claim the claret jug: Woods, Vijay Singh, Davis Love III and Thomas Bjorn. Instead it went to the only player to break par (albeit by one shot), the self-taught Buckeye with the rumpled khakis and the unhurried rhythm to his swing. Curtis became the first golfer to win the first major tournament he entered since Francis Ouimet prevailed at the 1913 U.S. Open. "Right now, many people are probably saying, 'Well, he doesn't belong there,' but I know I do," he said of the fellowship of the jug. "So that's all that matters."

Curtis wasn't alone in his new sense of belonging, as each Grand Slam event crowned a first-time majors winner: Mike Weir at the Masters, Jim Furyk at the U.S. Open and Shaun Micheel at the PGA. Just as surprising was another development on the tour: For the first time since 1998, Tiger had gone Slamless. Though he would lead the Tour in prize money ($6,278,746) and in victories (five) down the stretch, Woods would endure a season full of interviews that included the words *slump* and *failure*. Yet in many ways those questions may have been preferable to the ones he got going into the Masters, which asked that he pick sides in the 10-month

Pujols had an All-Star season but he and the Cards fell short in the NL Central.

pitched battle between women's rights activist Martha Burk, who urged a tournament boycott because of Augusta National's male-only membership, and club chairman Hootie Johnson, who ham-handedly defended the status quo. Though several prominent members chose to resign, and the event was broadcast without commercials, only about 30 people turned out to protest during the tournament, leaving each side grounds to claim victory in what seemed likely to be the first of many skirmishes.

A storm of controversy enveloped baseball for a while, too. During a June game against the Tampa Bay Devil Rays at Wrigley Field, the slugging Sosa shattered his bat on a swing. Examining the splintered pieces, the umpires found evidence of a dirty little secret: cork. Suddenly, a charismatic 34-year-old Chicago Cubs outfielder—a surefire Hall of Famer who had belted 292 homers in the past five seasons—was in danger of having all of his accomplishments called into question. Major league baseball rounded up 76 of his bats and carted them off for X-rays.

Sosa explained that he used a corked bat only to put on a show during batting practice, and that he'd inadvertently grabbed it before going to the plate. He apologized for the mistake. He accepted his suspension for eight games (later reduced to seven). And when the other bats turned out to be clean, the editorial pages and talk-radio stations turned to other issues. Said Chicago manager Dusty Baker, "People are likely to give you a reprieve when you admit a mistake instead of trying to make excuses."

The amnesia in Chicago fans was especially acute this season, as Sosa and young righthanders Mark Prior and Kerry Wood led the Cubs on a tight pen-

nant chase down the stretch. Hope sprung eternal as the Cubs won the NL Central, holding off Houston and St. Louis, which was led by arguably the best player in baseball, Albert Pujols, who hit .359 with 43 home runs and 124 RBI. The Cubs then upset the Atlanta Braves to win their first postseason series since 1908. Over in the AL, the Boston Red Sox also reached the championship series, setting up a delicious possibility: that the two supposedly cursed teams would meet in the World Series and guarantee that at least *one* long-suffering legion of fans would have its prayers finally answered. Alas, the Cubs blew a three-games-to-one advantage against the Florida Marlins in the NLCS, with Prior and Wood absorbing the last two losses, and the Sox bungled a 5–2 eighth-inning lead in Game 7 against the New York Yankees, bowing in the 11th inning on a leadoff homer by third baseman Aaron Boone.

In horse racing, a modestly bred chestnut also went to the brink of ending a woeful streak while cashing in on a $5 million bonus. No thoroughbred had won the Triple Crown since Affirmed in 1978—and no gelding ever had. But after upsetting favored Empire Maker in the Kentucky Derby and romping to victory the Preakness, Funny Cide became the eighth horse in the last 25 years to have two wins entering the final leg. Alas, the three-year-old, and the Belmont crowd of 101,864, were denied a glimpse of history as Empire Maker struck back, covering the 1½-mile track in 2:28.26 to whip third-place Funny Cide by more than five lengths. "I've had bigger disappointments," said the gelding's trainer, Barclay Tagg, "but this was $5 million of disappointment."

What was a multimillion-dollar disappointment for certain fans of Manches-

Beckham scored three minutes into his Spanish league debut with Real Madrid.

ter United turned out to be a windfall for Real Madrid, as the Spanish club paid the British one a $41 million transfer fee to acquire David Beckham, arguably the most famous soccer player in the world. Joining the legendary team—which already boasts Ronaldo, Zinedine Zidane, Roberto Carlos, Luis Figo and Raul—Beckham would contribute as much to the marketing department as he would on the field. Sales of

Real merchandise spiked immediately after the signing of the talented and telegenic Beckham.

In the U.S., women's soccer was looking for a similar boost from the Women's World Cup, which was relocated to these shores from China due to the SARS outbreak. The domestic pro league, had folded on the eve of the tournament. A strong performance from the home team would surely revitalize interest in the women's game. The U.S. was eliminated in the semis by Germany, but there was still talk of reviving WUSA.

Earlier in the year, the Miami Hurricanes were looking to revive their late 1980s dynasty and repeat as national champions. They entered the Fiesta Bowl a heavy favorite over Ohio State. In his four-year career, quarterback Ken Dorsey had started 39 games and lost only one. But the Buckeyes had a gutty quarterback of their own in Craig Krenzel, and a defense that was not impressed by a Miami attack studded with NFL-caliber talent. "They couldn't

Clarett began the year with a national championship and ended it in controversy.

move the ball on the ground against us," said OSU end Darrion Scott. "We knew it, and they knew we knew it." The tense, hard-hitting title game—the best in the history of the Bowl Championship Series—ended in a 17-all tie as the Hurricanes' Todd Sievers hit a 40-yard field goal by with three seconds left. After a controversial interference call against Miami in the first overtime, the Buckeyes settled it in the second on tailback Maurice Clarett's five-yard TD run and a goal-line stand. The 'Canes' 34-game winning streak was over and, though he didn't know it at the time, Clarett's OSU

AP PHOTO/REED SAXON

career would not last another year. As the 2003–04 season got under way, he was suspended from the team for reportedly violating NCAA rules. In September, Clarett was attempting to make himself eligible for the NFL draft.

Like Miami football, the Connecticut women's basketball team saw an impressive winning streak come to an end. Their 70-game tear was snapped by Villanova in March, but the Huskies rebounded to seize a second straight crown behind star guard Diana Taurasi. In its storied basketball history, the Syracuse men's team had never won a title, falling just a Keith Smart jump shot short to Indiana in the 1987 final. But after coaching his alma mater to 20 or more wins in 25 of his 27 seasons, Jim Boeheim finally reached that promised land. Riding their 2–3 zone and getting 20 points, 10 rebounds and seven assists from 6'8" freshman Carmelo Anthony, the Orangemen defeated Kansas 81–78 in the final at New Orleans. Anthony, who has LIVE NOW/DIE LATER tattooed to his right biceps, then waved goodbye to Syracuse

and packed his bags for the NBA.

The Tampa Bay Buccaneers also entered the 2002–03 season without a title in their history, which began with a winless season in 1976. Team owner Malcolm Glazer hoped to change that in February 2002 by acquiring Jon Gruden as his coach, surrendering two first-round picks, two second-round picks and $8 million to get him. Super Bowl XXXVII in San Diego offered a clear-cut opportunity to evaluate the deal, as the Bucs' opponent, the Oakland Raiders, had been the peddler of Gruden's services. The payoff was decisive: a thorough 48–21 thrashing by Tampa Bay.

The San Antonio Spurs won the NBA title, defeating the New Jersey Nets in six games behind MVP Tim Duncan, who averaged 24.2 points, 17.0 rebounds, 5.3 assists and 5.3 blocks. Along the way, the Spurs ousted the Lakers four games to two in the Western Conference semifinals, ending Los Angeles's three-year stay at the summit. L.A. responded by signing two future Hall of Famers during the summer, Karl Malone and Gary Payton. But the excitement over their arrival was undercut by news of Bryant: On July 4, he surrendered to Eagle County, Colo., authorities, who later charged him with sexually assaulting a 19-year-old employee of a spa he had visited during the summer. While Bryant acknowledged that the two had had sex in his hotel room on June 30, he forcefully denied that the encounter was nonconsensual.

Bryant's trial most likely would not begin until spring 2004. By then, no doubt, there would be many more surprises in store.

Late October- November 2002

OCT 27 Emmitt Smith (above) celebrates after breaking Walter Payton's career rushing record during the Cowboys' 17–14 home loss to Seattle. With an 11-yard scamper in the fourth quarter, Smith surpasses Payton's total of 16,726 yards.

THIS MONTH'S SIGN OF THE
APOCALYPSE

A Colorado elementary school teacher who died at age 96 willed $40,729.88 to Ralphie, the buffalo mascot for the University of Colorado football team.

GO FIGURE

10 Wins through October of the 2002 season for golfer Annika Sorenstam, the first LPGA player since 1968 to win that many in a year.

256 Adults who competed in the first International Rock, Paper, Scissors Championships in Toronto.

2 Goalies in NHL history to get a shutout at a younger age than the Rangers' Dan Blackburn, who was 19 years 171 days old when he blanked Calgary on Nov. 7, 2002.

NOV 23 Running back Maurice Clarett (13) helps Ohio State to a 14–9 win in its annual grudge match with Michigan, giving the Buckeyes a 13–0 record and a shot at the national title.

NOV 23 In the fight of the year, Arturo Gatti (right) outslugs Micky Ward in Atlantic City to reverse the outcome of their memorable first bout, a controversial decision for Ward in May 2002.

THEY SAID IT

Jim Fassel, New York Giants coach, analyzing the team's prospects for success:

"In my opinion if we are going to have a good season, we have to put together more back-to-back wins."

DAVID E. KLUTHO

December 2002

DEC 14 Southern Cal quarterback Carson Palmer (above, 3) becomes the first West Coast player to win the Heisman Trophy since Marcus Allen in 1981. Palmer passes for 3,639 yards and 32 touchdowns during the season, guiding the Trojans to an 11–2 record and a fourth-place finish in the national rankings.

THEY SAID IT

Shaquille O'Neal, Lakers center, on solving the team's on-court problems: "I just want eight guys out there with me who want to play."

GO FIGURE

72 Straight losses by the women's basketball team at Division II Minnesota-Morris, an NCAA record, before a 56–40 win over Crown College on Dec. 10, 2002.

2.0 Rating ESPN2 drew for a Dec 12, 2002, high school basketball game featuring LeBron James, the network's highest rating in nearly two years.

3 U.S. skiers (Daron Rahlves, Marco Sullivan and Bode Miller) who finished in the top 10 of the Dec. 7, 2002, World Cup downhill in Colorado, the U.S.'s best showing since 1972.

DEC 23 SPORTS ILLUSTRATED readers meet new Boston Red Sox general manager Theo Epstein (above left), at 28 the youngest G.M. in the history of baseball.

DEC 15 With nine catches in the Colts' 28–23 win over the Browns, Indianapolis receiver Marvin Harrison has 127 receptions for the year, breaking the single-season record. He finishes with 143.

THIS MONTH'S SIGN OF THE
APOCALYPSE

Sylvester Stallone and Metro-Goldwyn Mayer Inc are planning to make *Rocky VI*.

January 2003

GO FIGURE

58 Living members of the Baseball Hall of Fame, as of January 2003.

74 Age of retired car dealership owner Jack Gosch, who on Jan. 6, 2003, stroked back-to-back holes in one, at the Sunrise Country Club in Rancho Mirage, Calif.

6 Consecutive losses in bowl games for Notre Dame's football team.

THEY SAID IT

Jack Nicholson, three-time Oscar winner and Lakers season-ticket holder, on discovering thespian talent: "There's probably not a better actor than Gary Payton."

JAN 3 Quarterback Craig Krenzel (below, 16) leads Ohio State to a 31–24 double-overtime victory over Miami in the Fiesta Bowl, delivering the Buckeyes their first national title in 33 years.

JAN 26 Wide receiver Joe Jurevicius (83) and the Tampa Bay Buccaneers stiff arm the Oakland Raiders in Super Bowl XXXVII in San Diego, running away with the NFL title in a 48–21 rout.

THIS MONTH'S SIGN OF THE
APOCALYPSE

The three female gymnasts banned by the Romanian Gymnastics Federation for appearing nude in an adult film were offered keys to the city by Bucharest mayor Traian Basescu.

DAVID CALLOW

JAN 25 Serena Williams defeats her sister Venus for the Australian Open title to complete a "Serena Slam" of victories in four straight Grand Slam events.

February 2003

THEY SAID IT

Hal McRae, former Devil Rays manager, on the upside of being dismissed after last season: "I'm not drinking nearly as much. I don't have any reason to drink."

FEB 9 Houston center Yao Ming (above) makes the All-Star Game in his first season in the NBA, scoring two points and grabbing two rebounds in the West's 155–145 double-overtime victory.

SIMON BRUTY/SPORTS ILLUSTRATED

GO **FIGURE**

5 Horses who shared the title role in the film *Seabiscuit*.

14 NBA players who attended the Bronx's DeWitt Clinton, more than any other high school.

806 1/2 Hours of coverage that NBC-owned networks will devote to the 2004 Olympics in Athens, up from the 441½ hours during the 2000 Games in Sydney.

THIS MONTH'S SIGN OF THE
APOCALYPSE

HBO is rebroadcasting the entire seven seasons of *Arli$$*.

FEB 15 Following an unprecedented 159–0 career at Iowa State, Cael Sanderson (above right) makes his international debut—and loses to Cuba's Yoel Romero.

KEVIN KANE/WIREIMAGE/ICON SMI

FEB 16 Michael Waltrip (above) beats inclement weather and a strong field to win his second Daytona 500 in three years.

March 2003

AP PHOTO/JOE CAVARETTA

MARCH 1 Roy Jones Jr. (above left) outpoints John Ruiz for the WBA title to become the first former middleweight champ in more than 100 years to win a piece of the heavyweight crown.

THEY SAID IT

Mo Vaughn, Mets first baseman, on changes in the game:

"Baseball's been played the same way for 200 years."

JOHN W. MCDONOUGH

MARCH 22 Gonzaga and Arizona (right) stage the NCAA tournament's most exciting game as they battle into double overtime, where the Zags miss a last-second runner, allowing the Wildcats to escape with a 96–95 victory.

V.J. LOVERO

MARCH 30 Anaheim manager Mike Scioscia (14) surveys his defending champion Angels during the pregame introductions for Opening Day 2003 at Edison Field. The season gets off on the wrong foot for the 2002 champs, though, as they are beaten 6–3 by the visiting Texas Rangers.

GO FIGURE

100 Miles added to the previously 1,100-mile Iditarod course after the starting point was moved 300 miles north of the traditional site, Wasilla, Alaska, which didn't have enough snow.

0 Votes that Pete Rose—one of 46 nominees on the ballot—received for induction into the Canadian Baseball Hall of Fame.

1,096 Offspring born to 1977 Triple Crown winner Seattle Slew, who died in May 2002 and whose final foal, an as-yet unnamed filly, was born in late winter 2003 at Swifty Farms in Indiana to dam May Day Ninety, a daughter of Alydar.

THIS MONTH'S SIGN OF THE
APOCALYPSE

The Reverend Jesse Jackson said he has evidence that the Masters is named for the "white male slave masters" who used the Augusta course.

April 2003

KEVORK DJANSEZIAN

APRIL 16 The Anaheim Ducks eliminate defending champ Detroit from the NHL playoffs.

KEVIN RIVOLI/AP

GO FIGURE

7 Winter athletic teams from the University of Indianapolis—men's basketball, swimming, wrestling and indoor track, and women's basketball, swimming and indoor track—that reached NCAA postseason championships, tying the Division II record set by UC Davis in 1998.

$14.3 million
Amount the Detroit Tigers will pay over the next three years to second baseman Damion Easley, whom they released in the spring of 2003, the most expensive contract ever eaten by a major league team.

23 Seasons since the ACC last failed to send a team to the regional finals of the NCAA men's basketball tournament; Duke and Maryland, the final two ACC teams in the 2003 tournament, lost in the Sweet 16.

APRIL 7 Sensational freshmen Carmelo Anthony (left) and Gerry McNamara lead Syracuse to the NCAA title, scoring 20 and 18 points, respectively, during the Orangemen's 81–78 triumph over Kansas in the final in New Orleans.

THIS MONTH'S SIGN OF THE APOCALYPSE

The fifth annual World Ice Golf Championship in Uummannaq, Greenland, was canceled because the weather was too nice.

AP PHOTO

THEY SAID IT

Erazem Lorbek, the 6' 10" forward from Slovenia, after dunking on a Michigan State teammate during practice:

"I took you to the school."

APRIL 27, Philadelphia righthander Kevin Millwood (above) throws a no-hitter against the San Francisco Giants at Veterans Stadium. Millwood strikes out 10 San Francisco batters while walking only three, and his teammates scrape together a run on four hits to give the Phillies a 1–0 win.

THEY SAID IT

Mark Grace, Diamondbacks 39-year-old first baseman, complaining to a stadium disc jockey about Sly & the Family Stone being played over the P.A. during batting practice: "How about something since we've been alive?"

MAY 25 Emulating his countryman Helio (Spiderman) Castroneves (above right), Gil de Ferran of Brazil (left) climbs the Brickyard netting to celebrate his Indy 500 win.

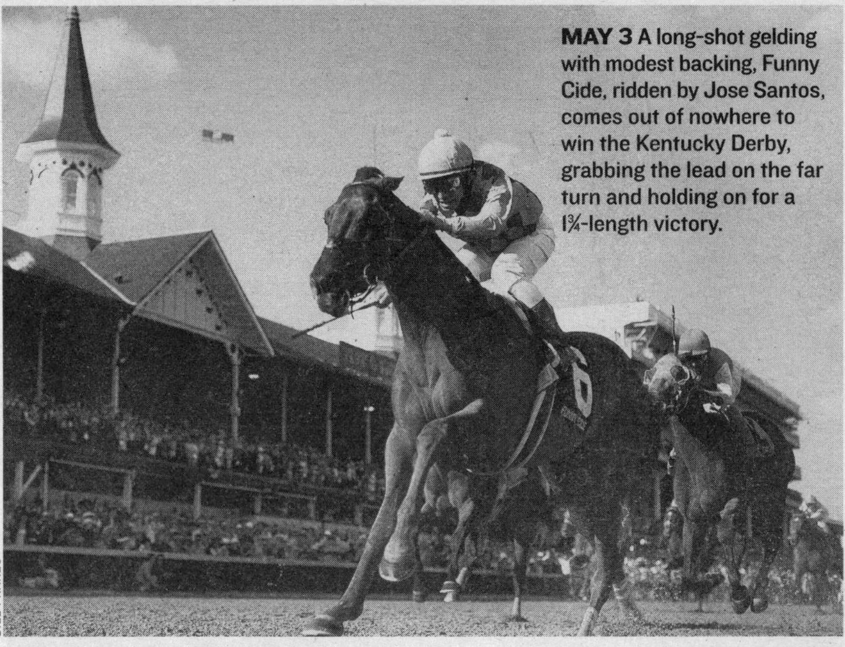

BILL FRAKES

MAY 3 A long-shot gelding with modest backing, Funny Cide, ridden by Jose Santos, comes out of nowhere to win the Kentucky Derby, grabbing the lead on the far turn and holding on for a 1¾-length victory.

JOHN MCCONNICO/AP

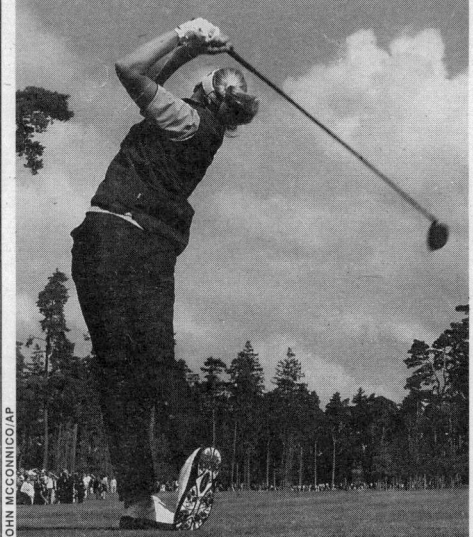

MAY 22 Annika Sorenstam (above) ruffles a few feathers by playing in the Colonial, but she shows that she is capable of making a PGA cut one day, shooting a first-round 71.

GO FIGURE

24 Consecutive three-pointers Robert Horry missed in the Lakers' final eight playoff games of 2003.

---

5 Straight sellouts at Waterfront Park in Trenton, for a total attendance of 41,093, during Yankee Derek Jeter's 2003 rehab assignment with the Double A Thunder.

---

3 Tenth-inning home runs hit by Cubs shortstop Alex Gonzalez in the first 10 days of May 2003.

---

11 Consecutive games in which Ottawa goalie Patrick Lalime allowed two or fewer goals, an NHL record.

June 2003

CHUCK SOLOMON

JUNE 13 Rocket to 300: Roger Clemens becomes the 21st pitcher with 300 career victories, striking out 10 batters and allowing just two runs in 6 ⅔ innings as New York beats the St. Louis Cardinals 5–2 at a sold-out Yankee Stadium.

JUNE 9 The New Jersey Devils down Anaheim in seven games and exult in their second Stanley Cup in four years.

THEY SAID IT

THIS MONTH'S SIGN OF THE
APOCALYPSE

The June 25, 2003, auction of Barry Bonds's 73rd home run ball was televised live by ESPN.

Sandra Day O'Connor, Supreme Court justice, whose son, Brian, 43, summitted Mount Everest in late spring 2003, despite her strenuous objections that the trip would be too risky: "So you can see how much my opinion matters when it really counts."

June 2003

BILL FRAKES

JUNE 7 Empire Maker (above) wins the Belmont by ¾ of a length, ruining the Triple Crown hopes of Funny Cide and Jose Santos, who finish 5¼ lengths behind, in third place. It is the second year in a row that a horse has its Triple Crown dream dashed at the Belmont.

THIS MONTH'S SIGN OF THE
APOCALYPSE

Police in Norway stopped a 94-year-old runner because they thought she had escaped from a nursing home.

JUNE 15 Tim Duncan (21), David Robinson (50) and the San Antonio Spurs defeat the New Jersey Nets for the NBA title. The victory is especially sweet for Robinson, who retires after the Finals.

DAVID E. KLUTHO

GO **FIGURE**

13 Home runs hit by the Angels in two games in Puerto Rico's Hiram Bithorn Stadium, tying the American League record for homers in consecutive games, set by the 1939 Yankees.

1 Set of twins—Kyle and Andy Boyll—who hit grand slam home runs in the seventh inning as North Central High of Farmersburg, Ind., beat Union High of Dugger 23–6.

10.8 Nielsen overnight rating for the telecast of the 2003 Belmont Stakes, the best overnight rating of any horse race since the 1990 Kentucky Derby.

JUNE 21 Lennox Lewis (above left) comes into his WBC heavyweight title defense against Vitali Klitschko looking puffy and out of shape, and he pays for it as the 6′ 8″ Klitschko rocks him repeatedly in the early rounds. Only a heavily bleeding cut over Klitschko's left eye—opened in Round 3 and worked thereafter by the champ—prevents Lewis from relinquishing his belt.

THEY **SAID IT**

Malik Rose, Spurs forward, after going 0 for 9 from the floor in Game 4 of the NBA Finals: "I was about two bricks short of a mansion."

July 2003

MARK J. TERRILL/AP

THEY SAID IT

John McEnroe, tennis Hall of Famer, on current ATP player Wayne Ferreira, who was leading a breakaway players' union: "Without even knowing what his points are, I'd say he has some good points."

JULY 18 Lakers superstar Kobe Bryant (8) is charged with sexual assault by Eagle County, Colo., authorities following a June 30 incident with a 19-year-old woman in a room at the Lodge & Spa at Cordillera, near Vail.

ROBERT LABERGE/GETTY IMAGES

JULY 27 Lance Armstrong (above) powers his way to a fifth straight Tour de France victory, tying Spain's Miguel Indurain for the most consecutive Tour wins. Armstrong promises to return in 2004 and attempt a record sixth straight triumph.

GO FIGURE

4 Goals by Landon Donovan on July 19 in a 5–0 win over Cuba, making him the fourth U.S. men's national soccer team player to score that many goals in a game.

44 1/2 Hot dogs eaten by 145-pound Takeru (Tsunami) Kobayashi, 25, in 12 minutes to win Nathan's Famous Hot Dog Eating contest for the third time.

20 Wimbledon titles for Martina Navratilova, who won the 2003 mixed doubles championship with Leander Paes, tying Billie Jean King's record for most titles at the tournament.

THIS MONTH'S SIGN OF THE
APOCALYPSE

David Beckham's July 1 physical exam for Real Madrid was broadcast on pay-per-view TV in Spain.

JULY 5 Reasserting her dominance on the WTA Tour after losing in the semifinals of the French Open, Serena Williams (right) defeats her sister Venus 4–6, 6–4, 6–2 to win the Wimbledon singles title for the second straight year. She defeated Venus in the 2002 final as well.

PHIL COLE/GETTY IMAGES

August 2003

ROBERT BECK

AUG 17 Ranked 169th in the world heading into the tournament, Shaun Micheel (left) wins the PGA Championship at Oak Hill. He shoots a 70 on Sunday to beat Chad Campbell by two strokes and secure his first victory on the PGA Tour.

AP PHOTO/JOHN AMIS

AUG 16 With 4:20 left in the first quarter of a preseason game against the Baltimore Ravens, Atlanta quarterback Michael Vick breaks his right fibula, souring the Falcons' playoff hopes and depriving the NFL of arguably its most exciting player for up to 10 weeks.

Ozzy Osbourne sang *TAKE ME OUT TO THE BALLGAME* at Wrigley Field on Aug. 17, 2003.

AUG 28 Sprinter Kelli White (1174) of the U.S. becomes the third woman to win both the 100 and 200 at the worlds, but her feat is later dimmed by positive drug tests.

THEY SAID IT

Barry Larkin, Red shortstop, on discussions about his future with the team, which had an interim manager and no G.M.: "We've decided to take a wait-and-see approach—mostly wait, because we don't know who to see."

DAVID BERGMAN

September 2003

AL BELLO/GETTY IMAGES

NICK WASS/AP

SEPT 7 Twenty-one-year-old Andy Roddick (above) delivers on his much-touted potential, winning the U.S. Open in straight sets over Spain's Juan Carlos Ferrero.

SEPT 14 Baltimore running back Jamal Lewis (right) sets a new NFL single-game rushing record, rumbling for 295 yards in the Ravens' 33–13 home shellacking of the Cleveland Browns.

THEY SAID IT

Darren Clarke, European Tour golfer, asked whether he had ever won tournaments in back-to-back weeks: "It's taken longer than five days to sober up, so probably not."

GO FIGURE

98 Consecutive races lost by Zippy Chippy, the losingest thoroughbred in history, after the 12-year-old gelding finished second by a length and a half to Short Notice at the Three County Fair in Northampton, Mass.

---

5 Straight season openers in which Arkansas running back Cedric Cobbs, who missed most of the 2000 season because of shoulder surgery, has scored a touchdown.

$309,000 Amount Georgia athletic boosters reportedly have spent since 1998 to refurbish and maintain the home of athletic director Vince Dooley.

THIS MONTH'S SIGN OF THE APOCALYPSE

Former NFL stars Lawrence Taylor and Jim McMahon will be the opposing coaches in the inaugural Lingerie Bowl, a tackle football game between models at halftime of Super Bowl XXXVIII.

SEPT 28 In his first season as manager of the team, Dusty Baker (below) leads the Chicago Cubs to their first division title in 14 years. The Cubs clinch the NL Central after a doubleheader sweep of the Pirates.

AP PHOTO/CHICAGO TRIBUNE, NUCCIO DINUZZO

October 2003

DAMIAN STRUMMEYER

OCT 16 Eternal rivals the New York Yankees and the Boston Red Sox stage a fall classic before the Fall Classic, battling each other to a Game 7 of the ALCS, which Aaron Boone (above) wins with a walkoff homer against Tim Wakefield in the bottom of the 11th inning.

THIS MONTH'S SIGN OF THE
APOCALYPSE

A 46-year-old Alabama man was charged with attempted murder after he allegedly fired a gun at his son while stewing over the Tide's loss to Arkansas.

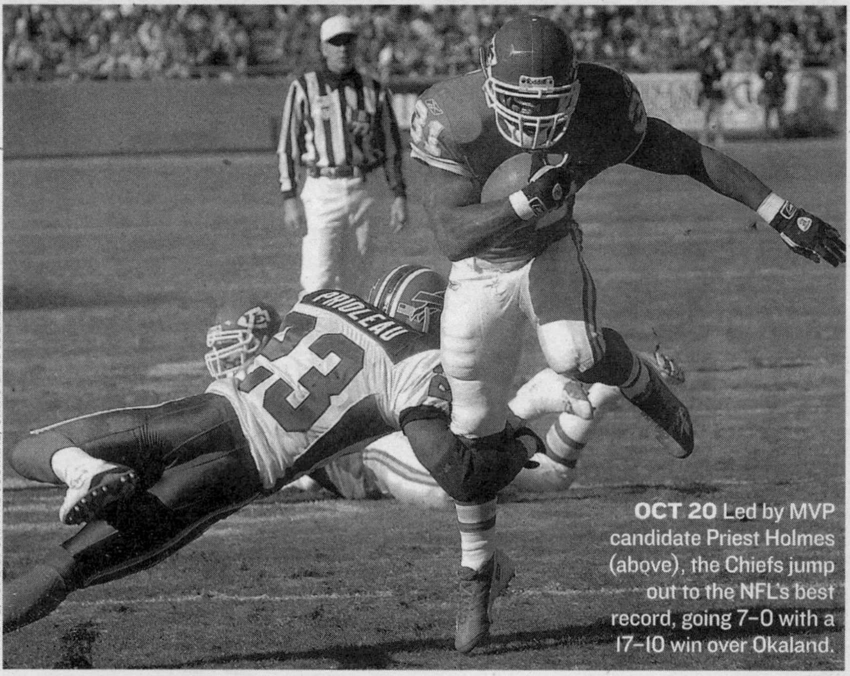

AP PHOTO/TOPEKA CAPITAL JOURNAL, CHRIS LANDSBERGER

OCT 20 Led by MVP candidate Priest Holmes (above), the Chiefs jump out to the NFL's best record, going 7–0 with a 17–10 win over Okaland.

AP PHOTO/PABLO MARTINEZ MONSIVAIS

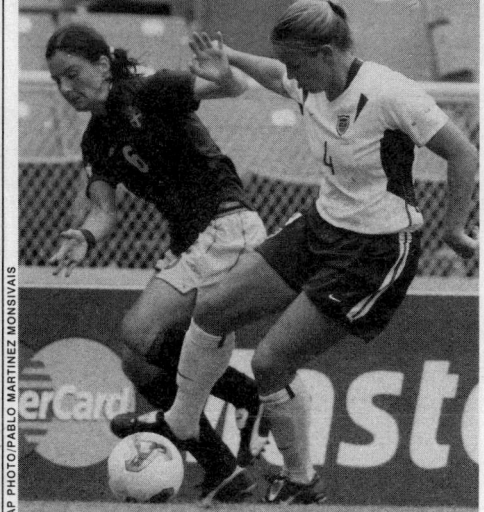

OCT 5 After getting by Sweden in the first round of the Women's World Cup, Cat Reddick (4) and the U.S. women's national team are eliminated by Germany in the semifinals 3–0.

GO FIGURE

3 Games in which Peyton Manning of the Colts has had a perfect quarterback rating of 158.3, more than anyone since the system was implemented in 1973.

$150 Expected retail price of LeBron James's first signature shoe, the Air Zoom Generation, which is "modeled after his Hummer H2."

3 Months of the regular season—April, May and June—in which the Marlins drew fewer than the 196,223 fans who attended their three home playoff games against the Cubs.

Late October 2003

BOB ROSATO

OCT 25 Employing their signature "small ball" attack, as exemplified by the speedy Juan Pierre (above), who squares to bunt in Game 5, the Florida Marlins defeat the heavily favored New York Yankees in six games to win the 2003 World Series.

THIS MONTH'S SIGN OF THE
APOCALYPSE

In an effort to exorcise the Curse of the Bambino, a 39-year-old Red Sox fan carried a 1918 photograph of Babe Ruth to the top of Mount Everest.

THEY SAID IT

Sarah Fisher, the IRL's only female racer, on her biggest driving problem: "I'm 22, and you have to be 25 to rent a car."

Baseball

The World Series
champion
Florida Marlins

Fish Story

Amid tall tales of curses and Yankee mystique, one yarn had the ring of truth: the Marlins' run to glory

BY MARK BECHTEL

FIVE OUTS. Less than two innings stood between baseball fans and the most improbable World Series in decades: the Cubs versus the Red Sox. Baseball's two most snakebitten franchises stood on the verge of meeting each other in the World Series, putting the Classic back into the Fall Classic. Chicago lore includes a curse placed on the team by a tavern owner whose goat, which he used to bring to the stadium to "goad" the opposition, was barred from Wrigley Field in 1945; and the Red Sox, whose sorry history hardly has to be recounted here, are allegedly laboring under the Curse of the Bambino, brought about by owner Harry Frazee's sale of Babe Ruth in 1918. Cursed or not, the Cubs haven't won a title since 1908, and Boston has gone without one since the Sultan of Swat left for the Big Apple.

In October 2003, both teams had golden chances to end all that. Both teams held a three-run lead with one out in the eighth inning of a potentially decisive game in the League Championship Series. And both teams blew it.

America's jones for nostalgia wasn't lost on the participants. "Everyone wants to see Cubs–Red Sox," said Florida Marlins reliever Chad Fox, whose team not only trailed the Cubs in that fateful eighth inning, but had also been down three games to one in the series to the luckless Chicago franchise. "But we're going to spoil that. Not in a cocky way, but we know what the fans want, what the media feel. But so what?"

That attitude carried the Marlins a long way. They knocked off the Cubs in dramatic fashion, then took care of the Yankees in six games to win their second title in seven years. Against the Cubs, Florida had to travel to Wrigley, trailing three games to two, and face Chicago's pair of aces, Mark Prior and Kerry Wood. Even long-suffering Cubs fans had to like their team's chances, two shots at a clinching victory with their best pitchers taking the mound. And in that unforgettable top-half of the eighth inning of Game 6, they were sitting pretty, holding a 3–0 lead with one out. Florida's Luis Castillo lifted a fly ball down the left field line; Cubs leftfielder Moises Alou drifted under the ball as it floated over foul territory toward the crowd. As he leaned into the crowd to make the catch, a young man wearing a Cubs cap and headphones beat him to it, preventing him from what surely would have been the second out of the inning. Castillo stayed alive and drew a walk, and the Marlins exploded for eight runs in the inning. "I kind of feel

bad for the guy," Alou said of the now infamous fan. "Every fan in every ballpark, the first reaction they have is they want a souvenir. They don't think about the outcome of the game or what could happen. Unfortunately, it happened. The guy saw a shot at having a baseball, and he went for it. Hopefully, he won't have to regret it for the rest of his life."

Whatever the fallout, the play instantly took its place in Cubs, and baseball, lore. (Before the first pitch of Game 7 was thrown, sitcom actor Kevin James had successfully pitched a movie about a fan who interferes with a play in a big game.) Still, the fan could have been let off the hook for good by Wood and the Cubs in Game 7, but the pitcher and his team could not get the job done as Florida rolled to a 9–6 win and advanced to the World Series.

Boston fans had a more traditional target for their ire. In a classic Game 7, manager

Beckett blanked the Yankees in Game 6, striking out nine, to win the MVP award.

Grady Little stuck with a tiring Pedro Martinez in the eighth with the Sox leading 5–2. The Yankees rallied for three runs and ultimately won it in the 11th on Aaron Boone's walkoff homer against Tim Wakefield. It was a fittingly dramatic conclusion for one of the most intense postseason series in baseball history.

After the teams split the opening games at Yankee Stadium, the action moved to Fenway Park. In the fourth inning of Game 3 Martinez hit New York's Karim Garcia with a pitch, the ball caroming off Garcia's back, just above his uniform number. That led to much posturing, shouting and gesturing, between the teams, including the unpleasant image of Martinez pointing at his noggin and then at New York's Jorge Posada, as if to warn him to watch his head at the plate. In the bottom of the inning, Manny Ramirez took offense to a high fastball from Roger Clemens—even though the pitch was over the plate—and the benches emptied. Martinez was standing off to the side minding his own business when 72-year-old Yankees coach Don Zimmer ran at him and threw a wild left hand. Martinez ducked the punch and pushed Zimmer to the ground. "When this series began, everyone knew it was going to be quite a battle," Little said after the game, which also featured a brawl between a couple of Yankees and a Fenway Park employee in the New York bullpen. "It was going to be very emotional, a lot of intensity. But I think we've upgraded it from a battle to a war."

Boston's presence on the battlefield with its eternal nemesis the Yankees came thanks to the wild card, and on the whole the regular season did little to bolster the traditionalists' argument that the wild card is ruining baseball. On Sept. 1, the top seven teams in the National League wild-card race were separated by a mere 3½ games. That pack of contenders contained a few erstwhile pretenders, like the Expos, Marlins and Cubs.

Chicago bounced back from a 95-loss season in 2002 thanks largely to its fireballing staff anchored by Wood and Prior, but there were bumps along the path to the Cubs's turnaround. Their biggest slugger, Sammy Sosa, got off to a slow start, and in early June made headlines for the wrong reasons. In a game against the Devil Rays, Sosa shattered his bat when he hit a slow roller to second base. The broken bat was corked, and Sosa was ejected.

Suddenly, the only player to hit 60 home runs in a season three times faced the distinct possibility that his entire legacy would be tarnished. He apologized, claiming that he only used the bat in practice to put on a show for the fans, and that he had taken it to the plate by mistake. Major League Baseball impounded 76 of his bats and X-rayed them all. None were corked, but he still found himself stigmatized. "It's a situation I've never been in before," Sosa said, "with the way people said things about me. What I learned from it is, it makes you stronger. I've

put it all behind me. When you're strong mentally and physically, you don't let anything bother you. I knew when I got healthy, I could still do the things I've always done." That meant hitting home runs; Sosa, who had six roundtrippers when he was busted, went on a tear, finishing the year with 40. The Cubs edged Houston (by one game) and St. Louis (three) to win their first division title since 1989.

The Marlins also improved significantly from their 2002 performance, and, like the Cubs, overcame a difficult start to do so. The team was listing along at 16–22 when owner Jeffrey Loria fired his manager, Jeff Torborg. The man he wanted to replace him, Jack McKeon, 72, was spending his time "in between jobs," as he called it, helping his grandson Zachary Booker, now a player at UNC-Wilmington. McKeon became the third-oldest person to manage a major league team, and the move raised the ire of commissioner Bud Selig, who criticized the Marlins for not considering a minority candidate.

While such criticism was warranted, McKeon defended his selection in typically lighthearted fashion, saying, "I am a minority. Senior citizens are a minority, aren't they? I'm not talking about race or religion. I'm talking about a section of society that is a minority." McKeon might have been old, but he was just what the young Marlins needed, a teacher. The team soon responded to him, finishing the year on a 75–49 tear and winning the hotly contested wild-card race.

A new manager also boosted the Royals, who got off to the season's most surprising start. Like the Cubs and Marlins, they were coming off a terrible season (62–100 in 2002), but behind surprisingly strong starting pitching they came out of the gate 16–3. Many of the players credited manager Tony Pena's loose attitude for the turnaround. "I give my players some freedom," said Pena, 46. "You need some space, room to make mistakes and correct yourself. I'm not going to scream at you, call you some kind of name or grab you by the chest."

The Royals players clearly appreciated Pena's approach. "He obviously remembers what it's like to play, what it's like to

DAMIAN STROHMEYER

would appear in only one game in the postseason. While his decisions concerning his team's bullpen may have been questionable, Epstein's preseason pickups paid immediate dividends. Embracing sabermetrics, which places an emphasis on on-base percentage, Epstein signed third baseman Bill Mueller, a journeyman with a good glove and a good eye, to be his everyday third baseman—even though the incumbent, Shea Hillenbrand, was coming off a season in which he hit .293 with 18 homers. The difference? Hillenbrand drew only 25 walks in 2002. Mueller went on to lead the AL in hitting with a .326 average, and produced a .398 on-base percentage. Epstein also signed David Ortiz from the Twins, and the slugger had a huge second half, finishing the season with 31 homers and a .288 average.

Epstein's emergence underscored a front-office trend: Teams are placing more emphasis on numbers than on old-fashioned, first-hand observations from scouts. (The Sox also hired stat guru Bill James as an advisor in the offseason.) Author Michael Lewis explored the development in *Moneyball*, his book about Oakland A's general manager Billy Beane. Beane gave Lewis unlimited access in 2002, and the book, which came out in the offseason, painted the G.M. as a boy wonder who was using statistical analysis to hoodwink his older counterparts on rival franchises. Needless to say, the book ruffled a few feathers. "All of us have our quirks and ways of doing things," one rival G.M. said. "It's presumptuous to think you do it better. If I were his owner, I'd be concerned. It goes beyond self-serving." But Beane's A's once again made the postseason, giving the upstart G.M. a measure of vindication.

Another baseball book that made waves came from noted author and Yankees left-hander David Wells. Titled *Perfect I'm Not,*

il and succeed," said reliever Jason rimsley. "He knows when guys need a ck in the ass and when they need a pat n the back." Alas, injuries to their pitch- g staff and the resurgence of the Twins, ho started slowly, pushed Kansas City out f the AL Central race.

The Royals might have been a factor in the ild-card race if not for the Boston Red Sox, ho gave the Yankees a run in the AL East, nd the Seattle Mariners, who won 93 games ut missed the playoffs by two. The Red Sox ised some eyebrows by hiring general man- ger Theo Epstein, a 28-year-old who ecame the youngest person in baseball his- ry to fill that position. Epstein decided to uild a bullpen by committee and eschew a oser, which led to some nervous moments Fenway Park. "I took care of that '28-Year- ld Theo Epstein' stuff," he said, "by becom- g 'Theo Epstein, the Guy Who Didn't now How to Build a Bullpen.' "

Epstein finally relented and got himself a oser in the summer, acquiring Byung- yun Kim from Arizona—although Kim

AP/DUANE BURLESON

Maroth had a rough season, but he found a measure of redemption at the very end.

the book contained, among other revelations, the news that Wells tossed his 1998 perfect game while "half drunk." The pitcher also asserted, much more believably, that 40 percent of major leaguers were on steroids. The book caused a predictable stir, but Wells put the distractions behind him and went 15–7, securing his 200th career victory on the final day of the season. (Yankees manager Joe Torre turned over the reins that day to Roger Clemens, letting the future Hall of Famer, who notched his 300th win and his 4,000th strikeout earlier in the season, play manager for a game. When Clemens came out of the dugout to remove Wells from the game, the lefty could only laugh.)

As compelling as baseball's pennant and wild-card races were, there was another race that generated nearly as much interest: Detroit's quest to avoid breaking the 1962 Mets' record for the most losses in a season. The Tigers set the pace early: They lost 9 games before they won one, and 17 before they won two. They ran off losing streaks of up to 11 games without blinking. They were

swept in a series 20 times and, heading in the last week of the season their recor stood at 38–118, within shouting distance the Mets mark of 120 losses (the Amazi won 40 that season). The Tigers ran off thre straight wins before losing to the Twins, gi ing them 119 losses on the season's penult mate day. At home against Minnesota the overcame an 8–0 deficit, winning the gam on a mad dash by Alex Sanchez in the nin inning. When he stormed home with tH winning run, Sanchez was mobbed by h teammates. The next day, Mike Maroth, wH became the majors' first 20-game loser sin 1980, beat the Twins 9–4 to prevent tH Tigers from matching New York's record f futility. "Believe it or not, I can look back this year with a smile on my face because how this season ended," said Maroth.

The Tigers' quest wasn't the season's on absurd storyline. On July 9, Pirates first bas man Randall Simon stood in the dugout du ing the Miller Park sausage races, in whic four people dressed as mascots for vario wieners (a hot dog, a Polish sausage, bratwurst and an Italian sausage) race duri the seventh inning stretch. As the costume figures passed by him, Simon could not resi the impulse to tap the Italian sausage wit his bat, knocking the woman inside to tH ground. Simon was fined and cited for diso derly conduct, and headline writers had field day: WURST BASE SCENARIO; THAT'S NC KOSHER; and WIENER BEANER were just a fe of the lines trotted out. Simon was later tra ed to the Cubs, but when he returned to M waukee in September he bought Italia sausages for an entire section of fans, an a of atonement that set him back $1,155.

Simon became a factor on the field, hi ting .333 in the postseason. But neither nor his teammates could solve Florida's 2 year-old Josh Beckett, who had 19 strik outs and two walks in 19⅓ innings in tH series. And he stymied the Yankees in tH World Series as well, tossing a six-h shutout in Game 6 to clinch the upset. "I a big relief," said Beckett, who was name MVP of the World Series. "I can't believ we don't have a game tomorrow. I can deer hunting now."

FOR THE RECORD·2003

Final Standings

National League

EASTERN DIVISION

Team	Won	Lost	Pct	GB	Home	Away
Atlanta	101	61	.623	—	55–26	46–35
Florida	91	71	.562	10	53–28	38–43
Philadelphia	86	76	.531	15	49–32	37–44
Montreal	83	79	.512	18	52–29	31–50
New York	66	95	.410	34½	34–46	32–49

CENTRAL DIVISION

Team	Won	Lost	Pct	GB	Home	Away
Chicago	88	74	.543	—	44–37	44–37
Houston	87	75	.537	1	48–33	39–42
St. Louis	85	77	.525	3	48–33	37–44
Pittsburgh	75	87	.463	13	39–42	36–45
Cincinnati	69	93	.426	19	35–46	34–47
Milwaukee	68	94	.420	20	31–50	37–44

WESTERN DIVISION

Team	Won	Lost	Pct	GB	Home	Away
San Francisco	100	61	.621	—	57–24	43–37
Los Angeles	85	77	.525	15½	46–35	39–42
Arizona	84	78	.519	16½	45–36	39–42
Colorado	74	88	.457	26½	49–32	25–56
San Diego	64	98	.395	36½	35–46	29–52

Wild-card team.

American League

EASTERN DIVISION

Team	Won	Lost	Pct	GB	Home	Away
New York	101	61	.623	—	50–32	51–29
†Boston	95	67	.586	6	53–28	42–39
Toronto	86	76	.531	15	41–40	45–36
Baltimore	71	91	.438	30	40–40	31–51
Tampa Bay	63	99	.389	38	36–45	27–54

CENTRAL DIVISION

Team	Won	Lost	Pct	GB	Home	Away
Minnesota	90	72	.556	—	48–33	42–39
Chicago	86	76	.531	4	51–30	35–46
Kansas City	83	79	.512	7	40–40	43–39
Cleveland	68	94	.420	22	38–43	30–51
Detroit	43	119	.265	47	23–58	20–61

WESTERN DIVISION

Team	Won	Lost	Pct	GB	Home	Away
Oakland	96	66	.593	—	57–24	39–42
Seattle	93	69	.574	3	50–31	43–38
Anaheim	77	85	.475	19	45–37	32–48
Texas	71	91	.438	25	43–38	28–53

2003 Playoffs

National League Division Playoffs

Sept 30	Florida 0 at San Francisco 2
Oct 1	Florida 9 at San Francisco 5
Oct 3	San Francisco 3 at Florida 4 (11 inn.)
Oct 4	San Francisco 6 at Florida 7

(Florida won series 3–1)

Sept 30	Chicago 4 at Atlanta 2
Oct 1	Chicago 3 at Atlanta 5
Oct 3	Atlanta 1 at Chicago 3
Oct 4	Atlanta 6 at Chicago 4
Oct 5	Chicago 5 at Atlanta 1

(Chicago won series 3–2)

National League Championship Series

Oct 7	Florida 9 at Chicago 8 (11 innings)
Oct 8	Florida 3 at Chicago 12
Oct 10	Chicago 5 at Florida 4 (11 innings)
Oct 11	Chicago 8 at Florida 3
Oct 12	Chicago 0 at Florida 4
Oct 14	Florida 8 at Chicago 3
Oct 15	Florida 9 at Chicago 6

(Florida won series 4–3)

GAME 1

												R	H	E
Florida	0	0	5	0	0	1	0	0	2	0	1	9	14	1
Chicago	4	0	0	0	0	2	0	0	2	0	0	8	11	1

W—Urbina. **L**—Guthrie. **SV**—Looper.
E—Fla: Gonzalez; Chi: Grudzielanek. **LOB**—Fla 8, Chi 5. **2B**—Fla: Castillo, Hollandsworth; Chi: A. Gonzalez, Simon, Miller, Lofton. **3B**—Fla. Conine, Pierre; Chi: Grudzielanek, Ramirez. **HR**—Fla: Rodriguez, Cabrera, Encarnacion, Lowell; Chi: Alou, A. Gonzalez, Sosa. **S**—Chi: Lofton. **SB**—Fla: Castillo, 2. **CS**—Fla: Pierre. **GIDP**—Chi: Alou. **T**—3:44. **A**—39,567.

Recap: Trailing 8–6 with two out in the bottom of the ninth, Chicago got a two-run homer from Sammy Sosa to send the game into extra innings. Sosa's heroics would go for naught, however, as Florida's Mike Lowell hit an 11th-inning pinch-hit homer to centerfield to win it for the Marlins.

GAME 2

										R	H	E
Florida	0	0	0	0	0	2	0	1	0	3	9	1
Chicago	2	3	3	0	3	1	0	0	x	12	16	1

W—Prior. **L**—Penny. **E**—Fla: Conine; Chi: Simon. **LOB**—Fla 8, Chi 8. **2B**—Fla: Encarnacion, Conine; Chi: Bako, Simon, Grudzielanek. **HR**—Fla: Lee, Cabrera; Chi: Sosa, Ramirez, Gonzalez 2. **S**—Chi: Prior. **SB**—Chi: Lofton. **GIDB**—Fla: Encarnacion **T**—3:02. **A**—39,562.

Recap: The Cubs chased Marlins starter Brad Penny in the third, touching him for seven runs on seven hits, including two home runs. Chicago added three more in the fifth to take an insurmountable 11–0 lead. Mark Prior pitched a solid seven innings for the win, striking out five batters and scattering eight hits.

National League Championship Series *(Cont.)*

GAME 3

Chicago	1	1	0	0	0	0	0	2	0	0	1	**5**	**12**	**0**
Florida	0	1	0	0	0	0	2	1	0	0	0	**4**	**10**	**0**

W—Borowski. **L**—Tejera. **SV**—Remlinger.
LOB—Chi 12, Fla. 12. **2B**—Chi: Alou; Fla: Gonzalez.
3B—Chi: Goodwin, Glanville. **HR**—Chi: Simon. **S**—Chi: Grudzielanek, Wood 2; Fla: Pierre, Mordecai, Castillo. **SB**—Fla: Pierre **GIDP**: Chi: Alou. **T**—4:16.
A—65,115.

Recap: Florida's Todd Hollandsworth scored Miguel Cabrera with a single in the bottom of the eighth to tie the game at 4–4, where it remained through the ninth. In the top of the 11th, the Cubs' Doug Glanville hit a triple, sending Kenny Lofton home with the winning run. Mike Remlinger closed the door in the bottom of the 11th.

GAME 4

Chicago	4	0	2	1	0	0	1	0	0	**8**	**8**	**0**
Florida	0	0	0	0	2	0	0	1	0	**3**	**6**	**1**

W—Clement. **L**—Willis. **E**—Fla: Rodriguez.
LOB—Chi 8, Fla 4. **2B**—Fla: Rodriguez. **HR**—Chi: Ramirez 2. **GIDP**—Fla: Cabrera. **HBP**—Fla: Lee
CS—Fla: Pierre. **T**—2:58. **A**—65,829.

Recap: Chicago third baseman Aramis Ramirez hit a grand slam—the first in Cubs playoff history—off Marlins starter Dontrelle Willis in the first inning, and the Cubs never looked back. Ramirez added a solo home run in the seventh and finished the game with six RBI.

GAME 5

Chicago	0	0	0	0	0	0	0	0	0	**0**	**2**	**0**
Florida	0	0	0	0	2	0	1	1	x	**4**	**8**	**0**

W—Beckett. **L**—Zambrano.
LOB—Chi 3, Fla 9. **HR**—Fla: Lowell, Rodriguez, Conine. **GIDP**—Fla: Lee. **HBP**—Fla: Cabrera. **T**—2:42. **A**—65,279.

Recap: Josh Beckett twirled a two-hit, complete game shutout, striking out 11 Cubs, and the Marlins got all of their runs on homers as Mike Lowell, Ivan Rodriguez and Jeff Conine all belted roundtrippers.

GAME 6

Florida	0	0	0	0	0	0	0	8	0	**8**	**9**	**0**
Chicago	1	0	0	0	0	1	1	0	0	**3**	**10**	**2**

W—Fox. **L**—Prior. **E**—Chi: Gonzalez, Grudzielanek.
LOB—Fla 6, Chi 7. **2B**—Fla: Pierre, Lee Mordecai; Chi: Sosa. **S**—Fla: Conine; Chi: Grudzielanek, Prior **GIDP**—Fla: Lee; Chi: Simon, Ramirez. **CS**—Fla: Pierre. **T**—3:00. **A**—39,577.

Recap: Despite Chicago's 95-year title drought, many observers, including Cubs manager Dusty Baker, insist that the team is not cursed. Game 6 of the 2003 NLCS qualified as more evidence for those in the opposite camp: With one out in the eighth and the Cubs leading 3–0, Mark Prior induced a foul fly down the left field line from Luis Castillo. As Chicago leftfielder Moises Alou drifted under it, a fan wearing headphones and a Cubs cap reached out and blocked the ball, preventing Alou from making the second out of the inning. Castillo walked, Chicago shortstop Alex Gonzalez later made an error, and the Cubs unraveled, giving up eight runs in the inning. They lost 8–3, missing their second straight opportunity to advance to the World Series for the first time since 1945.

GAME 7

Florida	3	0	0	0	3	1	2	0	0	**9**	**12**	**0**
Chicago	0	3	2	0	0	0	1	0	0	**6**	**6**	**0**

W—Penny. **L**—Wood. **SV**—Urbina. **LOB**—Fla 6, Chi 2. **2B**—Fla: Rodriguez, Gonzalez; Chi: Gonzalez.
3B—Fla: Pierre. **HR**—Fla: Cabrera; Chi: Wood, Alou, O'Leary. **HBP**—Chi: Sosa, Ramirez **SB**—Fla: Lee. **T**—3:11. **A**—39,574.

Recap: Florida centerfielder Juan Pierre foreshadowed the outcome of this one by leading off with a triple, but the road to that outcome was anything but straightforward. After giving up three runs in the first, Cubs pitcher Kerry Wood made amends by hitting a two-run homer to tie it in the second. The Cubs went ahead 5–3 in the third, only to lose that lead for good in the fifth. The Marlins advanced to the World Series for the second time in their 11-year history while the Cubs became the ninth team to lose a seven-game series after taking a three-games-to-one lead, and saw their title drought maddeningly extended.

American League Division Playoffs

Oct 1 ....Boston 4 at Oakland 5 (12 innings)
Oct 2 ....Boston 1 at Oakland 5
Oct 4 ....Oakland 1 at Boston 3 (11 innings)

Oct 5 ....Oakland 4 at Boston 5
Oct 6 ....Boston 4 at Oakland 3

(Boston won series 3–2)

Sept 30............Minnesota 3 at New York 1
Oct 2 ....Minnesota 1 at New York 4
Oct 4 ....New York 3 at Minnesota 1

Oct 5 ....New York 8 at Minnesota 1

(New York won series 3–1)

American League Championship Series

Oct 8 ....Boston 5 at New York 2
Oct 9 ....Boston 2 at New York 6
Oct 11 ....New York 4 at Boston 3
Oct 13 ....New York 2 at Boston 3

Oct 14 ....New York 4 at Boston 2
Oct 15 ....Boston 9 at New York 6
Oct 16 ....Boston 5 at New York 6 (11 innings)

(New York won series 4–3)

American League Championship Series *(Cont.)*

GAME 1

Boston	0	0	0	2	2	0	1	0	0	**5**	**13**	**0**
New York	0	0	0	0	0	0	2	0	0	**2**	**3**	**0**

W—Wakefield. **L**—Mussina. **SV**—Williamson.
LOB—Bos 10, NY 3. **2B**—NY: Posada. **HR**—Ortiz, Walker, Ramirez. **S**—NY: Matsui. **HBP**—Bos: Ortiz. **CS**—Bos: Jackson. **T**—3:20. **A**—56,281.

Recap: Tim Wakefield baffled the Yankees with his knuckleball, giving up just two hits and two runs in six innings, while the Red Sox much-maligned bullpen shut New York down in the final three innings. The Boston batters showed their power, taking Mike Mussina deep three times.

GAME 2

Boston	0	1	0	0	0	1	0	0	0	**2**	**10**	**1**
New York	0	2	1	0	1	0	2	0	x	**6**	**8**	**0**

W—Pettitte. **L**—Lowe. **E**—Bos: Jackson. **LOB**—Bos 8, NY 8. **2B**—Bos: Varitek; NY: Williams, Posada. **HR**—Bos: Varitek; NY: Johnson. **GIDP**—Bos: Kapler. **HBP**—NY: Boone, Soriano. **SB**—Bos: Nixon; NY Boone. **CS**—Bos: Kapler. **T**—3:05. **A**—56,295.

Recap: After struggling early, Yankees starter Andy Pettitte settled down to secure the win. Seven of Boston's first nine batters reached base, but the Sox got only one run in the first two innings. The Yanks picked up two in their half of the second, and put the game away in the seventh on a two-run double by catcher Jorge Posada.

GAME 3

New York	0	1	1	2	0	0	0	0	0	**4**	**7**	**0**
Boston	2	0	0	0	0	0	1	0	0	**3**	**6**	**0**

W—Clemens. **L**—Martinez. **SV**—Rivera.
LOB—NY 3, Bos, 3. **2B**—NY: Posada, Matsui; Bos: Walker. **HR**—NY: Jeter. **HBP**—NY: Garcia. **GIDP**—NY: Soriano, Matsui; Bos: Ramirez, Nixon. **CS**—Bos: Ramirez. **T**—3:09. **A**—34,209.

Recap: One of the most storied rivalries in sport added another chapter to its bitter legacy as Game 3 boiled over in the fourth inning. After giving up a run to fall behind 3–2, Red Sox starter Pedro Martinez hit Yankees rightfielder Karim Garcia with a pitch near the batter's head. The teams exchanged words from their respective dugouts and Martinez could be seen pointing at his head and then in the direction of the New York bench. In the next inning, after both teams had been warned by the umpires against retaliation, Boston rightfielder Manny Ramirez took issue with a high (but not inside) pitch from New York's Roger Clemens and strode toward the pitcher clutching his bat. Both benches cleared, and in the ensuing tussle, Yankees coach Don Zimmer, 72, charged at Martinez, who tossed him aside. When order was restored, Clemens struck out Ramirez, and the Yankees would hold on for a 4–3 win, but not before a late-inning scrape in the New York bullpen between a Fenway Park employee, Garcia and New York reliever Jeff Nelson.

GAME 4

New York	0	0	0	0	1	0	0	0	1	**2**	**6**	**1**
Boston	0	0	0	1	1	0	1	0	x	**3**	**6**	**0**

W—Wakefield. **L**—Mussina. **SV**—Williamson.
E—NY: Boone. **LOB**—NY 8, Bos 3 **2B**—NY: Jeter; Bos: Nixon **HR**—NY: Sierra; Bos: Walker, Nixon. **HBP**—NY: Dellucci; Bos: Walker. **GIDP**—Bos: Ortiz, Garciaparra. **SB**—NY: Dellucci. **CS**—Bos: Nixon 2. **T**—2:49. **A**—34,599.

Recap: A rainout one day earlier gave the teams more time to cool down after the hostilities of Game 3, and also changed the pitching rotations, allowing Boston to start Wakefield, who had won the opener in such impressive fashion. The knuckleballer delivered again, pitching seven strong innings while striking out eight and yielding only one run. Todd Walker and Trot Nixon homered for Boston.

GAME 5

New York	0	3	0	0	0	0	0	1	0	**4**	**7**	**1**
Boston	0	0	0	1	0	0	1	0	0	**2**	**6**	**2**

W—Wells. **L**—Lowe. **SV**—Rivera. **E**—NY: Soriano; Bos: Millar.
LOB—NY 7, Bos 7. **3B**—Bos: Walker. **HR**—Bos: Ramirez. **GIDP**—NY: Posada; Bos: Millar. **HBP**—Bos: Nixon. **CS**—NY: Boone. **T**—3:04. **A**—34,619.

Recap: David Wells produced a clutch performance on the mound for New York, holding the Red Sox to four hits and one run in seven innings. His teammates, meanwhile, jumped on Boston starter Derek Lowe in the second inning, getting RBI singles from Karim Garcia and Alfonso Soriano to go ahead 3–0. With Wells cruising, the Yankees held on for a 4–2 victory as Mariano Rivera pitched two innings for the save.

American League Championship Series (Cont.)

GAME 6

										R	H	E
Boston	0	0	4	0	0	0	3	0	2	**9**	**16**	**1**
New York	1	0	0	4	1	0	0	0	0	**6**	**12**	**2**

W—Embree. **L**—Contreras. **SV**—Williamson. **E**—Bos: Garciaparra; NY: Boone, Matsui. **LOB**—Bos 11, NY 8. **2B**—Bos: Mueller 2, Ramirez, Damon; NY: Johnson, Soriano. **3B**—Bos: Garciaparra. **HR**—Bos: Varitek, Nixon; NY: Giambi, Posada. **GIDP**—Bos: Mueller, Ramirez; NY: Johnson. **SB**—Bos: Damon; NY: Soriano 2, Jeter. **T**—3:57. **A**—56,277.

Recap: A back-and-forth affair saw Boston force a Game 7 matchup between future Hall of Famers Pedro Martinez and Roger Clemens at Yankee Stadium. Nomar Garciaparra snapped out of his postseason slump, going 4 for 5 and scoring two runs. Leading 7–6 in the ninth, Boston got a two-run homer from rightfielder Trot Nixon for the insurance runs that provided the final score.

GAME 7

												R	H	E
Boston	0	3	0	1	0	0	0	1	0	0	0	**5**	**11**	**0**
New York	0	0	0	0	1	0	1	3	0	0	1	**6**	**11**	**1**

W—Rivera. **L**—Wakefield. **E**—NY: Wilson. **LOB**—Bos 7, NY 8. **2B**—Bos: Varitek, Ortiz; NY: Matsui 2, Jeter, Posada. **HR**—Bos: Nixon, Millar, Ortiz; NY: Giambi 2, Boone. **GIDP**—Bos: Damon. **T**—3:56. **A**—56,279.

Recap: With Pedro Martinez and Roger Clemens

GAME 7 (CONT.)

taking the mound for their respective teams, and a trip to the World Series on the line, this game had all the makings of a classic—and the result exceeded the expectations. The Yankees won an 11-inning thriller that had a little bit of everything—brilliant pitching, clutch batting, excellent fielding, a stunning comeback and a walkoff homer. Indeed, Game 7 of the 2003 ALCS ranks with the New York Yankees' all time highlights, which is saying something, and it also extended the New York franchise's beguiling mastery over its New England counterpart.

Martinez won the battle of aces over Clemens, who was touched for six hits, two of them homers, and left the game in the fourth inning. The Boston righty appeared to be cruising to victory through seven innings, and the eighth began began well for the Sox as David Ortiz hit a first-pitch solo home run off reliever David Wells to give his team a 5–2 lead. But with one out in the Yankee half of the eighth, the game unraveled for Martinez and Boston. New York smacked three doubles and a single to tie the score at five, then turned to its closer, Mariano Rivera, who pitched three innings of scoreless relief (he would win the series MVP award). Third baseman Aaron Boone, who came on as a defensive replacement in the eighth, won it in the bottom of the 11th with a towering home run to left field off Tim Wakefield.

2003 World Series

Oct 18	Florida 3 at New York 2
Oct 19	Florida 1 at New York 6
Oct 21	New York 6 at Florida 1
Oct 22	New York 3 at Florida 4 (12 innings)
Oct 23	New York 4 at Florida 6
Oct 25	Florida 2 at New York 0

(Florida won series 4–2)

GAME 1

										R	H	E
Florida	1	0	0	0	2	0	0	0	0	**3**	**7**	**1**
New York	0	0	1	0	1	0	0	0	0	**2**	**9**	**0**

W—Penny. **L**—Wells. **SV**—Urbina. **E**—Fla: Cabrera. **LOB**—Fla 8, NY 9. **HR**—NY: Williams. **S**—Fla: Gonzalez, Rodriguez. **SB**—Fla: Castillo, Pierre; NY: Soriano, Posada. **HBP**—Fla: Pierre. **T**—3:43. **A**—55,769.

Recap: Employing their trademark "small ball" attack, the Marlins manufactured three runs and relied on pitchers Brad Penny, Dontrelle Willis and Ugueth Urbina to handcuff the New York offense. Florida centerfielder Juan Pierre led the Marlins speedy offense, scoring the first run of the game and driving in the other two.

GAME 2

										R	H	E
Florida	0	0	0	0	0	0	0	0	0	**1**	**6**	**0**
New York	3	1	0	2	0	0	0	0	x	**6**	**10**	**2**

W—Pettitte. **L**—Redman. **E**—NY: Boone 2. **LOB**—Fla 5, NY 6. **2B**—NY: Rivera, Johnson, Giambi. **HR**—NY: Matsui, Soriano. **GIDP**—Fla: Rodriguez, Cabrera. **HBP**—NY: Giambi. **CS**—Fla: Castillo; NY: Soriano, Posada. **T**—2:56. **A**—55,750.

GAME 2 (CONT.)

Recap: New York pitcher Andy Pettitte shut down the Marlins with a superb performance to help the Yankees even the series at one game apiece. Scattering six hits over 8⅔ innings, Pettitte did not allow a run until the ninth, and it was an unearned one at that. New York leftfielder Hideki Matsui staked his team to an early lead with a three-run homer in the first inning.

GAME 3

										R	H	E
New York	0	0	0	1	0	0	0	1	4	**6**	**6**	**1**
Florida	1	0	0	0	0	0	0	0	0	**1**	**8**	**0**

W—Mussina. **L**—Beckett. **SV**—Rivera. **E**—NY: Boone. **LOB**—NY 8, Fla 8. **2B**—NY: Jeter 2; Fla: Pierre, Gonzalez, Rodriguez. **HR**—NY: Boone, Williams. **S**— Fla: Cabrera. **HBP**—NY: Matsui, Jeter. **CS**—Fla: Pierre. **T**—3:21 (Plus rain delay totaling 39:00). **A**—65,731.

Recap: This one was closer than the final score suggests. Florida starter Josh Beckett, 23, pitched brilliantly, striking out 10 Yankees and yielding only two runs in 7⅓ innings, but the Yankees' Mike Mussina bettered him, giving up just one run while striking out nine in 7 innings. New York broke it open in the top of the ninth as Aaron Boone and Bernie Williams homered.

GAME 4

New York	0 1 0	0 0 0	0 0 2	0 0 0	**3**	**12**	**0**
Florida	3 0 0	0 0 0	0 0 0	0 0 1	**4**	**10**	**0**

W—Looper. **L**—Weaver. **LOB**—NY 10, Fla 7. **2B**—NY: Jeter, Williams; Fla: Rodriguez. **3B**—NY: Sierra. **HR**—Fla: Cabrera, Gonzalez. **S**—NY: Dellucci, Boone; Fla: Castillo, Pavano. **GIDP**—NY: Jeter 2. **T**—4:03. **A**—65,934.

Recap: Making what he said would be his last start, New York's Roger Clemens, 41, gave up three runs in the first before settling down and blanking the Marlins for six innings. The Yankees tied the game in the ninth on a two-out, two-run triple by pinch hitter Ruben Sierra. Florida reliever Braden Looper inherited a bases-loaded jam with one out in the 11th and got out of the inning. Alex Gonzalez won it in the 12th with a leadoff, walkoff home run to left against Jeff Weaver.

GAME 6TK

Florida	0 0 0	0 1 1	0 0 0	**2**	**7**	**0**
New York	0 0 0	0 0 0	0 0 0	**0**	**5**	**1**

W—Beckett. **L**—Pettitte. **E**—NY: Jeter. **LOB**—Fla 9, NY 5. **2B**—Fla: Lowell; NY: Williams, Posada. **S**—Fla: Encarnacion; NY: Boone. **GIDP**—NY: Williams, Johnson. **T**—2:57. **A**—55,773.

Recap: Twenty-three-year-old Josh Beckett twirled his second gem of the Series but unlike in Game 3, when he was a tough-luck loser, he came away with a masterly win this time, striking out nine Yankees, scattering five hits and not allowing a runner past second base in a complete-game shutout that delivered the Marlins their second championship in 11 years as a franchise. Beckett was named MVP of

GAME 5

New York	1 0 0	0 0 0	1 0 2	**4**	**12**	**1**
Florida	0 3 0	1 2 0	0 0 x	**6**	**9**	**1**

W—Penny. **L**—Contreras. **SV**—Urbina. **E**—NY: Wilson; Fla: Lee. **LOB**—NY 9, Fla 6. **2B**—NY: Wilson; Fla: Gonzalez 2, Conine, Pierre 2. **HR**—NY: Giambi. **S**—NY: Williams. **GIDP**—NY: Wilson; Fla: Lee. **CS**—Fla: Gonzalez. **T**—3:05. **A**—65,975.

Recap: Normally a clutch big-game pitcher, New York starter David Wells experienced back pain while warming up before this one, and manager Joe Torre nearly scratched him. Wells did make the start, but limped off the field after one inning, unable to continue. The Marlins jumped on reliever Jose Conteras, scoring three runs in the second, and got a solid seven innings from starter Brad Penny, who won his second game of the Series.

GAME 6 *(CONT.)*

the Series. The Marlins scraped out a run in the fifth on an RBI single by Luis Castillo, and took advantage of an error by New York shortstop Derek Jeter in the sixth to add a second, which came on a sacrifice fly from Juan Encarnacion. Florida manager Jack McKeon, 72, joins Bob Lemon (Yankees, 1978) as the only managers ever to take over a team after the season had begun and guide it to a World Series victory.

2003 World Series Composite Box Score

FLORIDA

BATTING	AB	R	H	HR	RBI	Avg
Conine	21	4	7	0	0	.333
Pierre	21	2	7	0	3	.333
Gonzalez	22	3	6	1	2	.273
Rodriguez	22	2	6	0	1	.273
Lowell	23	1	5	0	2	.217
Lee	24	2	5	0	2	.208
Encarnacion	11	1	2	0	1	.182
Cabrera	24	1	4	1	3	.167
Castillo	26	1	4	0	1	.154
Hollandsworth	2	0	0	0	0	.000
Pitchers	7	0	1	0	2	.143
Totals	203	17	47	2	17	.232

PITCHING	G	IP	H	BB	SO	ERA
Willis	3	3⅔	4	2	3	0.00
Pavano	2	9	8	1	6	1.00
Beckett (1–1)	2	16⅓	8	5	19	1.10
Penny (2–0)	2	12⅓	15	5	7	2.19
Fox	3	4	4	4	4	6.00
Urbina (2 SV)	3	3	2	3	2	6.00
Helling	1	2⅔	2	0	2	6.75
Looper	4	3⅔	6	0	4	9.82
Redman (0–1)	1	2⅓	5	2	2	15.43
Totals	6	56	54	22	49	3.21

NEW YORK

BATTING	AB	R	H	HR	RBI	Avg
Wilson	4	0	2	0	1	.500
Williams	25	5	10	2	5	.400
Jeter	26	5	9	0	2	.346
Johnson	17	3	5	0	0	.294
Garcia	14	1	4	0	0	.286
Matsui	23	1	6	1	4	.261
Sierra	4	0	1	0	2	.250
Giambi	17	2	4	1	1	.235
Soriano	22	2	5	1	2	.227
J. Rivera	6	0	1	0	1	.167
Posada	19	0	3	0	1	.158
Boone	21	1	3	1	2	.143
Flaherty	2	0	0	0	0	.000
Dellucci	2	1	0	0	0	.000
Pitchers	5	0	1	0	0	.200
Totals	207	21	54	6	21	.261

PITCHING	G	IP	H	BB	SO	ERA
Nelson	3	4	4	2	5	0.00
M. Rivera (1 SV)	2	4	2	0	4	0.00
Hammond	1	2	2	0	0	0.00
Pettitte (1–1)	2	15⅔	12	4	14	0.57
Mussina (1–0)	1	7	7	1	9	1.29
Wells (0–1)	2	8	6	2	1	3.38
Clemens	1	7	8	0	5	3.86
Contreras (0–1)	4	6⅓	5	5	10	5.68
Weaver (0–1)	1	1	1	0	0	9.00
Totals	6	55	47	14	48	2.13

National League Batting

BATTING AVERAGE

Albert Pujols, StL..............359
Todd Helton, Col..................358
Barry Bonds, SF...................341
Gary Sheffield, Atl 330
Edgar Renteria, StL...............330
Jason Kendall, Pitt 325
Marcus Giles, Atl..................316
Luis Castillo, Fla..................314
Mark Loretta, SD..................314
Mark Grudzielanek, Chi 314
Scott Podsednik, Mil 314

HITS

Albert Pujols, StL..................212
Todd Helton, Col...................209
Juan Pierre, Fla 204
Rafael Furcal, Atl...................194
Edgar Renteria, StL...............194
Jason Kendall, Pitt 191
Gary Sheffield, Atl 190
Luis Castillo, Fla 187
Orlando Cabrera, Mtl 186
Mark Loretta, SD 185

DOUBLES

Albert Pujols, StL...................51
Shawn Green, LA.....................49
Scott Rolen, StL......................49
Todd Helton, Col.....................49
Marcus Giles, Atl.....................49

TRIPLES

Rafael Furcal, Atl.....................10
Steve Finley, Ariz 10
Scott Podsednik, Mil 8
Kenny Lofton, Chi 8
Juan Pierre, Fla 7
D'Angelo Jimenez........................7

TRIPLES (CONT.)

Larry Walker, Col 7
Abraham Nunez, Pitt 7
Corey Patterson, Chi....................7

HOME RUNS

Jim Thome, Phil........................47
Barry Bonds, SF.......................45
Richie Sexson, Mil....................45
Albert Pujols, StL......................43
Javy Lopez, Atl 43
Sammy Sosa, Chi......................40
Jeff Bagwell, Hou......................39
Gary Sheffield, Atl 39
Jim Edmonds, StL......................39
Preston Wilson, Col....................36
Andruw Jones, Atl.................\..36

RUNS SCORED

Albert Pujols, StL.....................137
Todd Helton, Col......................135
Rafael Furcal, Atl.....................130
Gary Sheffield, Atl 126
Jim Thome, Phil.......................111
Barry Bonds, SF.......................111
Lance Berkman, Hou 110
Jeff Bagwell, Hou......................109
Chipper Jones, Atl 103
Craig Biggio, Hou.....................102

STOLEN BASES

Juan Pierre, Fla 65
Scott Podsednik, Mil 43
Dave Roberts, LA.......................40
Edgar Renteria, StL....................34
Kenny Lofton, Chi 30

RUNS BATTED IN

Preston Wilson, Col..................141
Gary Sheffield, Atl....................132
Jim Thome, Phil.......................131
Albert Pujols, StL......................124
Richie Sexson, Mil....................124
Todd Helton, Col......................117
Andruw Jones, Atl.....................116
Javy Lopez, Atl 109
Aramis Ramirez, Chi 106
Chipper Jones, Atl 106

SLUGGING PERCENTAGE

Barry Bonds, SF........................749
Albert Pujols, StL......................667
Todd Helton, Col.......................629
Jim Edmonds, StL......................617
Gary Sheffield, Atl 604

ON-BASE PERCENTAGE

Barry Bonds, SF........................529
Todd Helton, Col......................458
Albert Pujols, StL......................439
Larry Walker, Col 422
Gary Sheffield, Atl 419

BASES ON BALLS

Barry Bonds, SF........................148
Todd Helton, Col......................111
Jim Thome, Phil.......................111
Bobby Abreu, Phil.....................109
Lance Berkman, Hou 107

National League Pitching

EARNED RUN AVERAGE

Jason Schmidt, SF 2.34
Kevin Brown, LA 2.39
Mark Prior, Chi........................2.43
Brandon Webb, Ariz 2.84
Curt Schilling, Ariz 2.95
Hideo Nomo, LA 3.09
Carlos Zambrano, Chi.............3.11
Kerry Wood, Chi......................3.20
Livan Hernandez, Mtl..............3.20
Javier Vazquez, Mtl................3.24

SAVES

Eric Gagne, LA 55
John Smoltz, Atl 45
Billy Wagner, Hou 44
Tim Worrell, SF..........................38
Rocky Biddle, Mtl......................34
Joe Borowski, Chi 33
Ugueth Urbina, Fla....................32
Matt Mantei, Ariz 29
Mike Williams, Phil 28
Braden Looper, Fla 28

WINS

Russ Ortiz, Atl 21
Woody Williams, StL 18
Mark Prior, Chi 18
Sidney Ponson, SF....................17
Jason Schmidt, SF 17
Steve Trachsel, NY 16
Hideo Nomo, LA 16
Greg Maddux, Atl 16
Randy Wolf, Phil........................16
Three tied with 15.

GAMES PITCHED

Paul Quantrill, LA 89
Oscar Villarreal, Ariz 86
Ray King, Atl 80
Tom Martin, LA..........................80
Four tied with 78.

INNINGS PITCHED

Livan Hernandez, Mtl............233⅓
Javier Vazquez, Mtl 230⅔
Kevin Millwood, Phil 222
Woody Williams, StL 220⅔
Ben Sheets, Mil.....................220⅔

STRIKEOUTS

Kerry Wood, Chi......................266
Mark Prior, Chi 245
Javier Vazquez, Mtl.................241
Jason Schmidt, SF 208
Curt Schilling, Ariz 194
Kevin Brown, LA 185
Livan Hernandez, Mtl...............178
Hideo Nomo, LA 177
Randy Wolf, Phil.......................177
Brandon Webb, Ariz 172

COMPLETE GAMES

Livan Hernandez, Mtl...................8
Kevin Millwood, Phil 5
Jason Schmidt, SF 5
Matt Morris, StL..........................5
Three tied with 4.

SHUTOUTS

Jason Schmidt, SF 3
Matt Morris, StL...........................3
Kevin Millwood, Phil 3
Six tied with 2.

American League Batting

BATTING AVERAGE

Bill Mueller, Bos .... .326
Manny Ramirez, Bos............. .325
Derek Jeter, NY .... .324
Vernon Wells, Tor................. .317
Magglio Ordonez, Chi .... .317
Garret Anderson, Ana........... .315
A.J. Pierzynski, Minn............ .312
Ichiro Suzuki, Sea .... .312
Aubrey Huff, TB .... .311
Carlos Beltran, KC .... .307

HITS

Vernon Wells, Tor................. 215
Ichiro Suzuki, Sea 212
Michael Young, Tex 204
Garret Anderson, Ana........... 201
Aubrey Huff, TB 198
Alfonso Soriano, NY 198
Nomar Garciaparra, Bos 198
Magglio Ordonez, Chi 192
Manny Ramirez, Bos............. 185
Rocco Baldelli, TB 184

DOUBLES

Vernon Wells, Tor................. 49
Garret Anderson, Ana........... 49
Aubrey Huff, TB 47
Magglio Ordonez, Chi 46
Bill Mueller, Bos 45
Eric Hinske, Tor 45

TRIPLES

Cristian Guzman, Minn 14
Nomar Garciaparra, Bos 13
Carlos Beltran, KC 10

Four tied with nine.

HOME RUNS

Alex Rodriguez, Tex 47
Carlos Delgado, Tor 42
Frank Thomas, Chi................ 42
Jason Giambi, NY.................. 41
Rafael Palmeiro, Tex 38
Alfonso Soriano, NY 38
Manny Ramirez, Bos............. 37
Bret Boone, Sea................... 35
Aubrey Huff, TB 34
Vernon Wells, Tor................. 33

RUNS SCORED

Alex Rodriguez, Tex 124
Nomar Garciaparra, Bos 120
Vernon Wells, Tor................. 118
Manny Ramirez, Bos............. 117
Carlos Delgado, Tor 117
Alfonso Soriano, NY 114
Bret Boone, Sea................... 111
Ichiro Suzuki, Sea 111
Michael Young, Tex 106
Randy Winn, Sea 103
Johnny Damon, Bos 103

STOLEN BASES

Carl Crawford, TB 55
Alex Sanchez, Det 52
Carlos Beltran, KC 41
Alfonso Soriano, NY 35
Ichiro Suzuki, Sea 34

RUNS BATTED IN

Carlos Delgado, Tor 145
Alex Rodriguez, Tex 118
Vernon Wells, Tor................. 117
Bret Boone, Sea................... 117
Garret Anderson, Ana........... 116
Carlos Lee, Chi 113
Rafael Palmeiro, Tex 112
Jason Giambi, NY.................. 107
Aubrey Huff, TB 107
Miguel Tejada, Oak 106
Hideki Matsui, NY 106

SLUGGING PERCENTAGE

Alex Rodriguez, Tex .... .600
Carlos Delgado, Tor .... .593
David Ortiz, Bos................... .592
Manny Ramirez, Bos............. .587
Trot Nixon, Bos .... .578

ON-BASE PERCENTAGE

Manny Ramirez, Bos............. .427
Carlos Delgado, Tor .... .426
Jason Giambi, NY.................. .412
Edgar Martinez, Sea .... .406
Jorge Posada, NY................. .405

BASES ON BALLS

Jason Giambi, NY.................. 129
Carlos Delgado, Tor 109
Frank Thomas, Chi................ 100
Erubiel Durazo, Oak 100
Manny Ramirez, Bos............. 97

American League Pitching

EARNED RUN AVERAGE

Pedro Martinez, Bos 2.22
Tim Hudson, Oak................... 2.70
Esteban Loaiza, Chi.............. 2.90
Mark Mulder, Oak 3.13
Roy Halladay, Tor 3.25
Jamie Moyer, Sea 3.27
Barry Zito, Oak..................... 3.30
Mike Mussina, NY 3.40
Ryan Franklin, Sea............... 3.57
C.C. Sabathia, Clev 3.60

SAVES

Keith Foulke, Oak 43
Eddie Guardado, Minn 41
Mariano Rivera, NY 40
Jorge Julio, Balt 36
Troy Percival, Ana................ 33
Mike MacDougal, KC............. 27
Lance Carter, TB 26
Danys Baez, Clev 25
Scott Williamson, Bos 21
Armando Benitez, Sea........... 21

WINS

Roy Halladay, Tor 22
Andy Pettitte, NY.................. 21
Esteban Loaiza, Chi.............. 21
Jamie Moyer, Sea 21
Mike Mussina, NY 17
Derek Lowe, Bos 17
Roger Clemens, NY 17
Ramon Ortiz, Ana................. 16
Tim Hudson, Oak................... 16
Joel Pineiro, Sea 16

GAMES PITCHED

Scott Sauerbeck, Bos 79
Trever Miller, Tor.................. 79
Jamie Walker, Det................. 78
Jason Grimsley, KC 76
B.J. Ryan, Balt 76

SHUTOUTS

Tim Hudson, Oak................... 2
John Lackey, Ana.................. 2
Roy Halladay, Tor 2
Joel Pineiro, Sea 2
Jeff Suppan, Bos 2
Mark Mulder, Oak................. 2

STRIKEOUTS

Esteban Loaiza, Chi.............. 207
Pedro Martinez, Bos 206
Roy Halladay, Tor 204
Mike Mussina, NY 195
Roger Clemens, NY 190
Andy Pettitte, NY.................. 180
Bartolo Colon, Chi................ 173
Tim Wakefield, Bos 169
Johan Santana, Minn 169
Tim Hudson, Oak................... 162

INNINGS PITCHED

Roy Halladay, Tor 266
Bartolo Colon, Chi................ 242
Tim Hudson, Oak................... 240
Barry Zito, Oak..................... 231⅔
Mark Buehrle, Chi................. 230⅓

COMPLETE GAMES

Roy Halladay, Tor 9
Bartolo Colon, Chi................ 9
Mark Mulder, Oak................. 9
Barry Zito, Oak..................... 4
David Wells, NY 4

2003 Team Statistics

National League

TEAM BATTING	G	AB	R	H	2B	3B	HR	RBI	TB	BB	SO	SB	OBP	SLG	BA
Atlanta	162	5670	907	1608	321	31	235	872	2696	545	933	68	.349	.475	.284
St. Louis	162	5672	876	1580	342	32	196	827	2574	580	952	82	.350	.454	.279
Colorado	162	5518	853	1472	330	31	198	814	2458	619	1134	63	.344	.445	.267
Pittsburgh	162	5581	753	1492	275	45	163	711	2346	529	1049	86	.338	.420	.267
Florida	162	5490	751	1459	292	44	157	709	2310	515	978	150	.333	.421	.266
SF Giants	161	5456	755	1440	281	29	180	713	2319	593	980	53	.338	.425	.264
Arizona	162	5570	717	1467	303	47	152	696	2320	531	1006	76	.330	.417	.263
Houston	162	5583	805	1466	308	30	191	763	2407	557	1021	66	.336	.431	.263
Philadelphia	162	5543	791	1448	325	27	166	757	2325	651	1155	72	.343	.419	.261
San Diego	162	5531	678	1442	257	32	128	641	2147	565	1073	76	.333	.388	.261
Chicago	162	5519	724	1431	302	24	172	691	2297	492	1158	73	.323	.416	.259
Montreal	162	5437	711	1404	294	25	144	682	2180	522	990	100	.326	.401	.258
Milwaukee	162	5548	714	1423	266	24	196	685	2325	547	1221	99	.329	.419	.256
New York	161	5341	642	1317	262	24	124	607	1999	489	1035	70	.314	.374	.247
Cincinnati	162	5509	694	1349	239	21	182	669	2176	524	1326	80	.318	.395	.245
Los Angeles	162	5458	574	1328	260	25	124	544	2010	407	985	80	.303	.368	.243

TEAM PITCHING	W	L	ERA	CG	Sho	SV	Inn	H	R	ER	BB	SO
Los Angeles	85	77	3.16	3	17	58	1457⅔	1254	556	511	526	1289
San Francisco	100	61	3.73	7	10	43	1437⅓	1349	638	595	546	1006
Chicago	88	74	3.83	13	14	36	1456⅓	1304	683	619	617	1404
Arizona	84	78	3.84	7	11	42	1455	1379	685	621	526	1291
Houston	87	75	3.86	1	5	50	1450	1350	677	622	565	1139
Montreal	83	79	4.01	15	10	42	1437⅔	1467	716	640	463	1028
Florida	91	71	4.04	7	11	36	1445⅓	1415	692	648	530	1132
Philadelphia	86	76	4.04	9	13	33	1443⅔	1386	697	648	536	1060
Atlanta	101	61	4.10	4	7	51	1456⅓	1425	740	663	555	992
New York	66	95	4.48	3	10	38	1413⅓	1497	754	704	576	907
St. Louis	85	77	4.60	9	10	41	1463⅔	1544	796	748	508	969
Pittsburgh	75	87	4.64	7	10	44	1444⅓	1527	801	744	502	926
San Diego	64	98	4.87	2	10	31	1431⅓	1458	831	774	611	1091
Milwaukee	68	94	5.02	5	3	44	1452	1590	873	810	575	1034
Cincinnati	69	93	5.09	4	5	38	1446⅓	1578	886	818	590	932
Colorado	74	88	5.20	3	4	34	1420	1629	892	821	552	866

American League

TEAM BATTING	G	AB	R	H	2B	3B	HR	RBI	TB	BB	SO	SB	OBP	SLG	BA
Boston	162	5769	961	1667	371	40	238	932	2832	620	943	88	.360	.491	.289
Toronto	162	5661	894	1580	357	33	190	853	2573	546	1081	37	.349	.455	.279
Minnesota	162	5655	801	1567	318	45	155	755	2440	512	1027	94	.341	.431	.277
Kansas City	162	5568	836	1526	288	39	162	781	2378	476	926	120	.336	.427	.274
New York	163	5605	877	1518	304	14	230	845	2540	684	1042	98	.356	.453	.271
Seattle	162	5561	795	1509	290	33	139	759	2282	586	989	108	.344	.410	.271
Anaheim	162	5487	736	1473	276	33	150	687	2265	476	838	129	.330	.413	.268
Baltimore	163	5665	743	1516	277	24	152	695	2297	431	902	89	.323	.405	.268
Texas	162	5664	826	1506	274	36	239	799	2569	488	1052	65	.330	.454	.266
Tampa Bay	162	5654	715	1501	298	38	137	678	2286	420	1030	142	.320	.404	.265
Chicago	162	5487	791	1445	303	19	220	766	2446	519	916	77	.331	.446	.263
Cleveland	162	5572	699	1413	296	26	158	660	2235	466	1062	86	.316	.401	.254
Oakland	162	5497	768	1398	317	24	176	742	2291	556	898	48	.327	.417	.254
Detroit	162	5466	591	1312	201	39	153	553	2050	443	1099	98	.300	.375	.240

TEAM PITCHING	W	L	ERA	CG	Sho	SV	Inn	H	R	ER	BB	SO
Oakland	96	66	3.63	16	14	48	1441⅔	1336	643	582	499	1018
Seattle	93	69	3.76	8	14	38	1441	1340	637	602	466	1001
New York	101	61	4.02	8	12	49	1462	1512	716	653	375	1119
Chicago	86	76	4.17	12	4	36	1431	1364	715	663	518	1056
Cleveland	68	94	4.21	5	7	34	1459⅓	1477	778	682	501	943
Anaheim	77	85	4.38	5	9	39	1431⅓	1444	743	680	486	980
Minnesota	90	72	4.41	7	8	45	1462	1526	758	716	402	997
Boston	95	67	4.48	5	6	36	1464⅔	1503	809	729	488	1141
Toronto	86	76	4.69	14	6	36	1435	1560	826	748	485	984
Baltimore	71	91	4.76	9	3	41	1449⅔	1529	820	767	526	981
Tampa Bay	63	99	4.93	7	7	30	1436⅔	1454	852	787	639	877
Kansas City	83	79	5.05	7	10	36	1438⅔	1569	867	808	566	865
Detroit	43	119	5.30	3	5	27	1438⅔	1616	928	847	557	764
Texas	71	91	5.67	4	3	43	1433⅓	1625	969	903	603	1009

National League Team-by-Team Statistical Leaders

Arizona Diamondbacks

BATTING	G	AB	R	H	2B	3B	HR	RBI	TB	BB	SO	SB	OBP	SLG	BA
Luis Gonzalez	156	579	92	176	46	4	26	104	308	94	67	5	.402	.532	.304
Steve Finley	147	516	82	148	24	10	22	70	258	57	94	15	.363	.500	.287
A. Cintron	117	448	70	142	26	6	13	51	219	29	33	2	.359	.489	.317
Junior Spivey	106	365	52	93	22	2	13	50	158	33	95	4	.326	.433	.255
Shea Hillenbrand	85	330	40	88	18	1	17	59	159	17	44	0	.302	.482	.267
Craig Counsell	89	303	40	71	6	3	3	21	92	41	32	11	.328	.304	.234
M Kata	78	288	42	74	16	5	7	29	121	25	53	3	.315	.420	.257
Danny Bautista	88	284	29	78	16	3	4	36	112	21	50	3	.330	.394	.275
L. Overbay	86	254	23	70	20	0	4	28	35	67	1	0	.365	.402	.276
C. Moeller	78	239	29	64	17	1	7	29	104	23	59	1	.335	.435	.268
Rod Barajas	80	220	19	48	15	0	3	28	72	14	43	0	.265	.327	.218
Carlos Baerga	105	207	31	71	13	0	4	39	96	18	20	1	.396	.464	.343
Quinton McCracken	115	203	17	46	5	2	0	18	55	15	34	5	.276	.271	.227
R. Hammock	65	195	30	55	10	8	28	93	17	44	3	2	.343	.477	.282
Dave Dellucci	70	165	18	40	11	3	2	19	63	19	45	9	.328	.382	.242

PITCHING	W–L	ERA	G	GS	SV	INN	H	ER	BB	SO
J. Valverde	2-1	2.15	54	0	10	50.1	24	12	26	71
O. Villarreal	10-7	2.57	86	1	0	98.0	80	28	46	80
Matt Mantei	5-4	2.62	50	0	29	55.0	37	16	18	68
B. Webb	10-9	2.84	29	28	0	180.2	140	57	68	172
Curt Schilling	8-9	2.95	24	24	0	168.0	144	55	32	194
Miguel Batista	10-9	3.54	36	29	0	193.1	197	76	60	142
S. Randolph	8-1	4.05	50	0	0	60.0	50	27	43	50
Randy Johnson	6-8	4.26	18	18	0	114.0	125	54	27	125
Elmer Dessens	8-8	5.07	34	30	0	175.2	212	99	57	113

Atlanta Braves

BATTING	G	AB	R	H	2B	3B	HR	RBI	TB	BB	SO	SB	OBP	SLG	BA
Rafael Furcal	156	664	130	194	35	10	15	61	294	60	76	25	.352	.443	.292
Andruw Jones	156	595	101	165	28	2	36	116	305	53	125	4	.338	.513	.277
Gary Sheffield	155	576	126	190	37	2	39	132	348	86	55	18	.419	.604	.330
Chipper Jones	153	555	103	169	33	2	27	106	287	94	83	2	.402	.517	.305
Marcus Giles	145	551	101	174	49	2	21	69	290	59	80	14	.390	.526	.316
Vinny Castilla	147	542	65	150	28	3	22	76	250	26	86	1	.310	.461	.277
Javy Lopez	129	457	89	150	29	3	43	109	314	33	90	0	.378	.687	.328
Robert Fick	126	409	52	110	26	1	11	80	171	42	47	1	.335	.418	.269
Mark DeRosa	103	266	40	70	14	0	6	22	102	16	49	1	.316	.383	.263
Julio Franco	103	197	28	58	12	2	5	31	89	25	43	0	.372	.452	.294
Darren Bragg	104	162	21	39	5	1	0	9	46	13	38	2	.305	.284	.241
H. Blanco	55	151	11	30	8	0	1	13	41	10	21	0	.252	.272	.199

PITCHING	W–L	ERA	G	GS	SV	INN	H	ER	BB	SO
John Smoltz	0-2	1.12	62	0	45	64.1	48	8	8	73
R. King	3-4	3.51	80	0	0	59.0	46	23	27	43
Russ Ortiz	21-7	3.81	34	34	0	212.1	177	90	102	149
Mike Hampton	14-8	3.84	31	31	0	190.0	186	81	78	110
Greg Maddux	16-11	3.96	36	36	0	218.1	225	96	33	124
Horacio Ramirez	12-4	4.00	29	29	0	182.1	181	81	72	100
R. Hernandez	5-3	4.35	66	0	0	60.0	61	29	43	45
T. Hodges	3-3	4.66	52	1	0	65.2	69	34	31	66
Shane Reynolds	11-9	5.43	30	29	0	167.1	191	101	59	94

Chicago Cubs

BATTING	G	AB	R	H	2B	3B	HR	RBI	TB	BB	SO	SB	OBP	SLG	BA
Kenny Lofton	56	208	39	68	13	4	3	20	98	18	22	12	.381	.471	.327
Mark Grudzielanek	121	481	73	151	38	1	3	38	200	30	64	6	.366	.416	.314
Corey Patterson	83	329	49	98	17	7	13	55	168	15	77	16	.329	.511	.298
Tom Goodwin	87	171	26	49	10	0	-1	12	62	11	33	19	.328	.363	.287
Eric Karros	114	336	37	96	16	1	12	40	150	28	46	1	.340	.446	.286
R. Martinez	108	293	30	83	16	1	3	34	110	24	50	0	.333	.375	.283
Moises Alou	151	565	83	158	35	1	22	91	261	63	67	3	.357	.462	.280
Sammy Sosa	137	517	99	144	22	0	40	103	286	62	143	0	.358	.553	.279
Aramis Ramirez	63	232	31	60	7	1	15	39	114	17	31	1	.314	.491	.259
Damian Miller	114	352	34	82	19	1	9	36	130	39	91	1	.310	.369	.233
Paul Bako	70	188	19	43	13	0	0	17	62	22	47	0	.311	.330	.229
Alex Gonzalez	152	536	71	122	37	0	20	59	219	47	123	3	.295	.409	.218
Troy O'Leary	93	174	18	38	9	0	5	26	62	14	31	3	.275	.356	.218
Hee Seop Choi	80	202	31	44	17	0	8	28	85	37	71	-1	.350	.421	.218

Chicago Cubs (Cont.)

PITCHING	W–L	ERA	G	GS	SV	INN	H	ER	BB	SO
Mark Prior	18–6	2.43	30	40	0	211.1	183	57	50	245
Joe Borowski	2–2	2.63	68	0	33	68.1	53	20	19	66
Mark Guthrie	2–3	2.74	65	0	0	42.2	40	13	22	24
Carlos Zambrano	13–11	3.11	32	32	0	214.0	188	74	94	168
Kerry Wood	14–11	3.20	32	32	0	211.0	152	75	100	266
Kyle Farnsworth	3–2	3.30	77	0	0	76.1	53	28	36	92
Mike Remlinger	6–5	3.65	73	0	0	69.0	54	28	39	83
Matt Clement	14–12	4.11	32	32	0	201.2	169	92	79	171
Shawn Estes	8–11	5.73	29	28	0	152.1	182	97	83	103
Antonio Alfonseca	3–1	5.83	60	0	0	66.1	76	43	27	51
Juan Cruz	2–7	6.05	25	6	0	61.0	66	41	28	65

Cincinnati Reds

BATTING	G	AB	R	H	2B	3B	HR	RBI	TB	BB	SO	SB	OBP	SLG	BA
Jose Guillen	91	315	52	106	21	1	23	63	198	17	63	1	.385	.629	.337
Sean Casey	147	573	71	167	19	3	14	80	234	51	58	4	.350	.408	.291
D'Angelo Jimenez	73	290	34	84	13	2	7	31	122	34	43	7	.365	.421	.290
Barry Larkin	70	241	39	68	16	1	2	18	92	22	32	2	.345	.382	.282
Aaron Boone	106	403	61	110	19	3	18	65	189	35	74	15	.339	.469	.273
Austin Kerns	82	292	39	77	11	0	15	58	133	41	68	5	.364	.455	.264
Juan Castro	113	320	28	81	14	1	9	33	124	18	58	2	.290	.388	.253
Ken Griffey Jr.	53	166	34	41	12	1	13	26	94	27	44	1	.370	.566	.247
Ruben Mateo	74	207	16	50	9	0	3	18	68	12	53	0	.290	.329	.242
Ray Olmedo	79	230	24	55	6	1	0	17	63	13	46	1	.280	.274	.239
Jason LaRue	118	379	52	87	23	1	16	50	160	33	111	3	.321	.422	.230
Kelly Stinnett	60	179	14	41	13	0	3	19	63	13	51	0	.294	.352	.229
Wily Mo Pena	80	165	20	36	6	1	5	16	59	12	53	3	.283	.358	.218
Reggie Taylor	100	180	17	39	5	2	5	19	63	11	68	7	.266	.350	.217
Adam Dunn	116	381	70	82	12	1	27	57	177	74	126	8	.354	.465	.215

PITCHING	W–L	ERA	G	GS	SV	INN	H	ER	BB	SO
Kent Mercker	0–2	2.35	49	0	0	38.1	31	10	25	41
Felix Heredia	5–2	3.00	57	0	1	72.0	61	24	28	41
Scott Williamson	5–3	3.19	42	0	21	42.1	34	15	25	53
S. Sullivan	6–0	3.62	50	0	0	49.2	39	20	26	43
Gabe White	3–0	3.93	34	0	0	34.1	36	15	6	23
Chris Reitsma	9–5	4.29	57	3	12	84.0	92	40	19	53
Paul Wilson	8–10	4.64	28	28	0	166.2	190	86	50	93
John Riedling	2–3	4.90	55	8	1	101.0	107	55	47	65
Danny Graves	4–15	5.33	30	26	2	169.0	204	100	41	60
Jimmy Haynes	2–12	6.30	18	18	0	94.1	118	66	57	49
Ryan Dempster	3–7	6.54	22	20	0	115.2	134	84	70	84

Colorado Rockies

BATTING	G	AB	R	H	2B	3B	HR	RBI	TB	BB	SO	SB	OBP	SLG	BA
Todd Helton	160	583	135	209	49	5	33	117	367	11	72	0	.458	.630	.358
Jay Payton	157	600	93	181	32	5	28	89	307	43	77	6	.354	.512	.302
Larry Walker	143	454	86	129	25	7	16	79	216	98	87	7	.422	.476	.284
Preston Wilson	155	600	94	169	43	1	36	141	322	54	139	14	.343	.537	.282
Rafael Belliard	116	447	73	124	31	2	8	50	183	49	71	7	.351	.409	.277
Greg Norton	114	179	19	47	15	0	6	31	80	16	47	2	.325	.447	.263
Chris Stynes	138	443	71	113	31	3	11	73	183	48	76	3	.335	.413	.255
Juan Uribe	87	316	45	80	19	3	10	33	135	17	60	7	.297	.427	.253
J. Hernandez	69	257	33	61	6	1	8	27	93	27	95	1	.308	.362	.237
Charles Johnson	108	356	49	82	20	0	20	61	162	49	84	1	.320	.455	.230
Bobby Estalella	46	140	17	28	7	0	7	21	56	19	55	2	.294	.400	.200

PITCHING	W–L	ERA	G	GS	SV	INN	H	ER	BB	SO
Brian Fuentes	3–3	2.75	75	0	4	75.1	64	23	34	82
Steve Reed	5–3	3.27	67	0	0	63.1	59	23	26	39
Javier Lopez	4–1	3.70	75	0	1	58.1	58	24	12	40
Justin Speier	3–1	4.05	72	0	9	73.1	73	33	23	66
Shawn Chacon	11–8	4.60	23	23	0	137.0	124	70	58	93
Darren Oliver	13–11	5.04	33	32	0	180.1	201	101	61	88
Jason Jennings	12–13	5.11	32	32	0	181.1	212	103	88	119
Jose Jimenez	2–10	5.22	63	7	20	101.2	137	59	32	45
Denny Stark	3–3	5.83	17	13	0	78.2	98	51	33	30
Aaron Cook	4–6	6.02	43	16	0	124.0	160	83	57	43
Scott Elarton	4–4	6.27	11	10	0	51.2	73	36	20	20
Nelson Cruz	3–5	7.21	20	7	0	53.2	65	43	11	38

Florida Marlins

BATTING	G	AB	R	H	2B	3B	HR	RBI	TB	BB	SO	SB	OBP	SLG	BA
Luis Castillo	152	595	99	187	19	6	6	39	236	63	60	21	.381	.397	.314
Juan Pierre	162	668	100	204	28	7	1	41	249	55	35	65	.361	.373	.305
Ivan Rodriguez	144	511	90	152	36	3	16	85	242	55	92	10	.369	.474	.297
Mike Lowell	130	492	76	136	27	1	32	105	261	56	78	3	.350	.530	.276
Derrek Lee	155	539	91	146	31	2	31	92	274	88	131	21	.379	.508	.271
Juan Encarnacion	156	601	80	162	37	6	19	94	268	37	82	19	.313	.446	.270
M. Cabrera	87	314	39	84	21	3	12	62	147	25	84	0	.325	.468	.268
Alex Gonzalez	150	528	52	135	33	6	18	77	234	33	106	0	.313	.443	.256
Todd Hollandsworth	93	228	32	58	23	3	3	20	96	22	55	2	.317	.421	.254
Mike Redmond	59	125	12	30	7	1	0	11	39	7	16	0	.302	.312	.240
Jeff Conine	25	84	13	20	3	0	5	15	38	13	10	0	.337	.452	.238

PITCHING	W–L	ERA	G	GS	SV	INN	H	ER	BB	SO
Ugueth Urbina	3–0	1.41	33	0	6	38.1	23	6	13	37
Josh Beckett	9–8	3.04	24	23	0	142.0	132	48	56	152
Dontrelle Willis	14–6	3.30	27	27	0	160.2	148	59	58	142
Mark Redmond	14–9	3.59	29	29	0	190.2	172	76	61	151
Braden Looper	6–4	3.68	74	0	28	80.2	82	33	29	56
Tommy Phelps	3–2	4.00	27	7	0	63.0	70	28	23	43
Tim Spooneybarger	1–2	4.07	33	0	0	42.0	27	19	11	32
Brad Penny	14–10	4.13	32	32	0	196.1	195	90	56	138
Carl Pavano	12–13	4.30	33	32	0	201.0	204	96	49	133
Michael Tejera	3–4	4.67	50	6	2	81.0	82	42	36	58
A. Almanza	4–5	6.08	51	0	0	50.1	59	34	25	49

Houston Astros

BATTING	G	AB	R	H	2B	3B	HR	RBI	TB	BB	SO	SB	OBP	SLG	BA
Richard Hidalgo	141	514	91	159	43	4	28	88	294	58	104	9	.384	.572	.309
Jeff Kent	130	505	77	150	39	1	22	93	257	39	85	6	.351	.509	.297
M. Ensberg	127	385	69	112	15	1	25	60	204	48	60	7	.377	.530	.291
Lance Berkman	153	538	110	155	35	6	25	93	277	107	108	5	.412	.515	.288
Jeff Bagwell	160	605	109	168	28	2	39	100	317	88	119	11	.373	.524	.278
Craig Biggio	153	628	102	166	44	2	15	62	259	57	116	8	.350	.412	.264
Geoff Blum	123	420	51	110	19	0	10	52	159	20	50	0	.295	.379	.262
Adam Everett	128	287	51	99	18	3	8	51	147	28	66	8	.320	.380	.256
Jose Vizcaino	91	189	14	47	7	3	3	26	69	8	22	0	.281	.365	.249
Orlando Merced	123	212	20	49	17	2	3	26	79	15	33	3	.283	.373	.231
Brad Ausmus	143	450	43	103	12	2	4	47	131	46	66	5	.303	.291	.229

PITCHING	W–L	ERA	G	GS	SV	INN	H	ER	BB	SO
Billy Wagner	1–4	1.78	78	0	44	86.0	52	17	23	105
Octavio Dotel	6–4	2.48	76	0	4	87.0	53	24	31	97
Roy Oswalt	10–5	2.97	21	21	0	127.1	116	42	29	108
Brad Lidge	6–3	3.60	78	0	1	85.0	60	34	42	97
Tim Redding	10–14	3.68	33	32	0	176.0	179	72	65	116
Ricky Stone	6–4	3.69	65	0	1	83.0	76	34	31	47
Wade Miller	14–13	4.13	33	33	0	187.0	168	86	77	161
Ron Villone	6–6	4.13	19	19	0	106.2	91	49	48	91
Pete Munro	3–4	4.67	40	2	0	54.0	63	28	26	27
Kirk Saarloos	2–1	4.93	36	4	0	49.1	55	27	17	43
J. Robertson	15–9	5.10	32	31	0	160.2	180	91	64	99

Los Angeles Dodgers

BATTING	G	AB	R	H	2B	3B	HR	RBI	TB	BB	SO	SB	OBP	SLG	BA
Brian Jordan	66	224	28	67	9	0	6	28	94	23	30	1	.372	.420	.299
J. Cabrera	128	347	43	98	32	2	6	37	152	17	62	6	.332	.438	.282
Shawn Green	160	611	84	171	49	2	19	85	281	68	112	6	.355	.460	.280
Paul Lo Duca	147	568	64	155	34	2	7	52	214	44	54	0	.345	.377	.273
Cesar Izturis	158	558	47	140	21	6	1	40	176	25	70	10	.282	.315	.251
Dave Roberts	107	388	56	97	6	5	2	16	119	43	39	40	.331	.307	.250
Alex Cora	148	477	39	119	24	3	4	34	161	16	59	4	.287	.338	.249
Fred McGriff	86	297	32	74	14	0	13	40	127	31	66	0	.322	.428	.249
Adrian Beltre	158	559	50	134	30	2	23	80	237	37	103	2	.290	.424	.240
Mike Kincade	88	162	25	35	7	0	5	14	57	13	38	1	.335	.352	.216
Rickey Henderson	30	72	7	15	1	0	2	5	22	11	16	3	.321	.306	.208
Jeromy Burnitz	61	230	25	47	4	0	13	32	90	14	57	4	.252	.391	.204

Los Angeles Dodgers *(Cont.)*

PITCHING	W–L	ERA	G	GS	SV	INN	H	ER	BB	SO
Eric Gagne	2–3	1.20	77	0	55	82.1	37	11	20	137
Paul Quantrill	2–5	1.75	89	0	1	77.1	61	15	15	44
Guillermo Mota	6–3	1.97	76	0	1	105.0	78	23	26	99
Wilson Alvarez	6–2	2.37	21	12	1	95.0	80	25	23	82
Kevin Brown	14–9	2.39	32	32	0	211.0	184	56	56	185
Paul Shuey	6–4	3.00	62	0	0	69.0	50	23	33	60
Hideo Nomo	16–13	3.90	33	33	0	218.1	175	75	98	177
Tom Martin	1–2	3.53	80	0	0	51.0	36	20	24	41
Kazuhisa Ishii	9–7	3.86	27	27	0	147.0	129	63	101	140
Darren Dreifort	4–4	4.03	10	10	0	60.1	58	27	25	67
Odalis Perez	12–12	4.52	30	30	0	185.1	191	93	46	141
Andy Ashby	3–10	5.18	21	12	0	73.0	90	42	17	41

Milwaukee Brewers

BATTING	G	AB	R	H	2B	3B	HR	RBI	TB	BB	SO	SB	OBP	SLG	BA
S. Podsednik	154	558	100	175	29	8	9	58	247	56	91	43	.379	.443	.314
Geoff Jenkins	124	487	81	144	30	2	28	95	262	58	120	0	.375	.538	.296
Alex Sanchez	43	163	15	46	10	3	0	10	62	7	28	8	.316	.380	.282
Grady Clark	128	315	33	86	21	1	6	40	127	21	40	13	.330	.403	.273
Richie Sexon	162	606	97	165	28	2	45.	124	332	98	151	2	.379	.548	.272
Eddie Perez	107	350	26	95	17	1	11	45	147	17	47	0	.304	.420	.271
Wes Helms	134	476	56	124	21	0	23	67	214	43	131	0	.330	.450	.261
Eric Young	109	404	71	105	18	1	15	31	170	48	34	25	.344	.421	.260
Keith Ginter	127	358	51	92	15	2	14	44	153	37	87	1	.352	.427	.257
John Vander Wal	117	327	50	84	25	1	14	45	153	46	104	1	.350	.468	.257
Keith Osik	80	241	22	60	12	0	2	21	78	31	44	0	.342	.324	.249
Royce Clayton	146	483	49	110	16	1	11	39	161	49	92	5	.301	.333	.228

PITCHING	W–L	ERA	G	GS	SV	INN	H	ER	BB	SO
Danny Kolb	1–2	1.96	37	0	21	41.1	34	9	19	39
Doug Davis	3–2	2.58	8	8	0	52.1	49	15	21	35
V. de los Santos	3–3	4.13	45	0	1	48.0	38	22	22	35
Leo Estrella	7–3	4.36	58	0	3	66.0	75	32	21	25
Ben Sheets	11–13	4.45	34	34	0	220.2	232	109	43	157
Mike DeJean	4–7	4.87	58	0	18	64.2	69	35	27	54
W. Obermueller	2–5	5.07	12	11	0	65.2	81	37	25	34
Matt Kinney	10–13	5.19	33	31	0	190.2	201	110	80	152
Brooks Kieschnick	1–1	5.26	42	0	0	53.0	66	31	13	39
W. Franklin	10–13	5.50	36	34	0	194.2	201	119	94	116
Glendon Rusch	1–12	6.42	32	19	1	123.1	171	88	45	93

Montreal Expos

BATTING	G	AB	R	H	2B	3B	HR	RBI	TB	BB	SO	SB	OBP	SLG	BA
Vladimir Guerrero	112	394	71	130	20	3	25	78	231	63	53	9	.426	.586	.330
Jose Vidro	144	509	77	158	36	0	15	65	239	69	50	3	.397	.470	.310
Orlando Cabrera	162	626	95	186	47	2	17	80	288	52	64	24	.347	.460	.297
Wil Cordero	130	436	57	121	27	0	16	71	196	49	90	1	.354	.450	.278
Brad Wilkerson	146	504	78	135	34	4	19	77	234	89	155	13	.380	.464	.268
Jamey Carroll	105	227	31	59	10	1	1	10	74	19	39	5	.323	.326	.260
Endy Chavez	141	483	66	121	25	5	5	47	171	31	59	18	.294	.354	.251
Henry Mateo	100	154	29	37	3	1	0	7	42	11	38	11	.304	.273	.240
Jose Macias	111	272	31	65	15	2	4	22	96	11	45	4	.273	.353	.239
Ron Calloway	126	340	36	81	17	1	9	52	127	20	80	9	.282	.374	.238
B. Schneider	108	335	34	77	26	1	9	46	132	37	75	0	.309	.394	.230
Michael Barrett	70	226	33	47	9	2	10	30	90	21	37	0	.280	.398	.208
Fernando Tatis	53	175	15	34	6	0	2	15	46	18	40	2	.281	.263	.194

PITCHING	W–L	ERA	G	GS	SV	INN	H	ER	BB	SO
Luis Ayala	10–3	2.92	65	0	5	71.0	65	23	13	66
Joey Eischen	2–2	3.06	70	0	1	53.0	57	18	13	40
Livan Hernandez	15–10	3.20	33	33	0	233.1	225	83	57	178
Javier Vasquez	13–12	3.24	34	34	0	230.2	198	83	57	241
Scott Stewart	3–1	3.98	51	0	0	43.0	52	19	13	29
Tomo Ohka	10–12	4.16	34	34	0	199.0	233	92	45	118
Zach Day	9–8	4.18	23	23	0	131.1	132	61	59	61
C. Vargas	6–8	4.34	23	20	0	114.0	111	55	41	62
Rocky Biddle	5–8	4.65	73	0	34	71.2	71	37	40	54
T.J. Tucker	2–3	4.73	45	7	0	80.0	90	42	20	41

New York Mets

BATTING	G	AB	R	H	2B	3B	HR	RBI	TB	BB	SO	SB	OBP	SLG	BA
Jose Reyes	69	274	47	84	12	4	5	32	119	13	36	13	.334	.434	.307
Jason Phillips	119	403	45	120	25	0	11	58	178	39	50	0	.373	.442	.298
Cliff Floyd	108	365	57	106	25	2	18	68	189	51	66	3	.376	.518	.290
Mike Piazza	68	234	37	67	13	0	11	34	113	35	40	0	.377	.483	.286
Jeromy Burnitz	65	234	38	64	18	0	18	45	136	21	55	1	.344	.581	.274
Timo Perez	127	346	32	93	21	0	4	42	126	18	29	5	.301	.364	.269
Roger Cedeno	141	484	70	129	25	4	7	37	183	38	86	14	.320	.378	.267
Roberto Alomar	73	263	34	69	17	1	2	22	94	29	40	6	.336	.357	.262
Ty Wigginton	156	573	73	146	36	6	11	71	227	46	124	12	.318	.396	.255
Vance Wilson	96	268	28	65	9	1	8	39	100	15	56	1	.293	.373	.243
Joe McEwing	119	278	31	67	11	0	1	16	81	25	57	3	.309	.291	.241
Tony Clark	125	254	29	59	13	0	16	43	120	24	23	0	.300	.472	.232
Raul Gonzalez	107	217	28	50	12	2	2	21	72	27	34	3	.317	.332	.230
Rey Sanchez	56	174	11	36	3	1	0	12	41	8	18	1	.240	.236	.207

PITCHING	W–L	ERA	G	GS	SV	INN	H	ER	BB	SO
David Weathers	1–6	3.08	77	0	7	87.2	87	30	40	75
Armando Benitez	3–3	3.10	45	0	21	49.1	41	17	24	50
Dan Wheeler	1–3	3.71	35	0	2	51.0	49	21	17	35
Steve Trachsel	16–10	3.78	33	33	0	204.2	204	86	65	111
Jae Weong Seo	9–12	3.82	32	31	0	188.1	193	80	46	110
Al Leiter	15–9	3.99	30	30	0	180.2	176	80	94	139
Tom Glavine	9–14	4.52	32	32	0	183.1	205	92	66	82
Mike Stanton	2–7	4.57	50	0	5	45.1	37	23	19	34
Aaron Heilman	2–7	6.75	14	13	0	65.1	79	49	41	51

Philadelphia Phillies

BATTING	G	AB	R	H	2B	3B	HR	RBI	TB	BB	SO	SB	OBP	SLG	BA
Mike Lieberthal	131	508	68	159	30	1	13	80	230	38	59	0	.373	.453	.313
Marlon Byrd	135	495	86	150	28	4	7	45	207	44	94	11	.366	.418	.303
Bobby Abreu	158	577	99	173	35	1	20	101	270	109	126	22	.409	.468	.300
Placido Polanco	122	492	87	142	30	3	14	63	220	42	38	14	.352	.447	.289
Jim Thome	159	578	111	154	30	3	47	131	331	111	182	0	.385	.573	.266
Tomas Perez	125	298	39	79	18	1	5	33	114	23	54	0	.316	.383	.265
Jimmy Rollins	156	628	85	165	42	6	8	62	243	54	113	20	.320	.387	.263
Ricky Ledee	121	255	37	63	15	2	13	46	121	34	59	0	.334	.475	.247
Chase Utley	43	134	13	32	10	1	2	21	50	11	22	2	.322	.373	.239
Pat Burrell	146	522	57	109	31	4	21	64	211	72	142	0	.309	.404	.209
David Bell	85	297	32	58	14	0	4	37	84	41	40	0	.296	.283	.195

PITCHING	W–L	ERA	G	GS	SV	INN	H	ER	BB	SO
Rheal Cormier	8–0	1.70	65	0	1	84.2	54	16	25	67
Terry Adams	1–4	2.65	66	0	0	68.0	68	20	23	51
Dan Plesac	2–1	2.70	58	0	2	33.1	29	10	11	37
Turk Wendell	3–3	3.38	56	0	1	64.0	54	24	28	27
Vincente Padilla	14–12	3.62	32	32	0	208.2	196	84	62	133
A. Telemaco	1–4	3.97	8	8	0	45.1	41	20	11	29
Kevin Millwood	14–12	4.01	35	35	0	222.0	210	99	68	169
Randy Wolf	16–10	4.23	33	33	0	200.0	176	94	78	177
Brett Myers	14–9	4.43	32	32	0	193.0	205	95	76	143
Carlos Silva	3–1	4.43	62	1	1	87.1	92	43	37	48
Brandon Duckworth	4–7	4.94	24	18	0	93.0	98	51	44	68
Jose Mesa	5–7	6.52	61	0	24	58.0	71	42	31	45

Pittsburgh Pirates

BATTING	G	AB	R	H	2B	3B	HR	RBI	TB	BB	SO	SB	OBP	SLG	BA
Tike Redman	56	230	36	76	16	5	3	19	111	14	18	7	.374	.483	.330
Jason Kendall	150	587	84	191	29	3	6	58	244	49	40	8	.399	.416	.325
Brian Giles	105	388	70	116	30	4	16	70	202	85	48	0	.430	.521	.299
Matt Stairs	121	305	49	89	20	1	20	57	171	45	64	0	.389	.561	.292
Reggie Sanders	130	453	74	129	27	4	31	87	257	38	110	15	.345	.567	.285
A. Ramirez	96	375	44	105	27	1	12	67	168	25	68	1	.330	.448	.280
Kenny Lofton	84	339	58	94	19	4	9	26	148	28	29	18	.333	.437	.277
Randall Simon	91	307	34	84	14	0	10	51	128	12	30	0	.305	.417	.274
Bob Mackowiak	77	174	20	47	4	4	6	19	77	15	53	6	.342	.443	.270
Craig Wilson	116	309	49	81	15	4	18	48	158	35	89	3	.360	.511	.262
Jack Wilson	150	558	58	143	21	3	9	62	197	36	74	5	.303	.353	.256
A. Nunez	118	311	37	77	8	7	4	35	111	26	53	9	.310	.357	.248
Jeff Reboulet	93	261	37	63	10	2	3	25	86	27	47	2	.321	.330	.241
J. Hernandez	58	193	19	43	9	1	3	21	63	16	56	1	.282	.326	.223

PITCHING	W–L	ERA	G	GS	SV	INN	H	ER	BB	SO
Kip Wells	10–9	3.28	31	31	0	197.1	171	72	76	147
Jeff Suppan	10–7	3.57	21	21	0	141.0	147	56	31	78
J. Tavarez	3–3	3.66	64	0	11	83.2	75	34	27	39
Scott Sauerbeck	3–4	4.05	53	0	0	40.0	30	18	25	32
Brian Meadows	2–1	4.72	34	7	1	76.1	91	40	11	38
S. Torres	7–5	4.76	41	16	2	121.0	128	64	42	84
Jeff D'Amico	9–16	4.77	29	29	0	175.1	204	93	42	100
Kris Benson	5–9	4.97	18	18	0	105.0	127	58	36	68
Joe Beimel	1–3	5.05	18	18	0	62.1	69	35	33	42
Josh Fogg	10–9	5.26	26	26	0	142.0	166	83	40	71
Mike Williams	1–3	6.27	40	0	25	37.1	42	26	22	20

St. Louis Cardinals

BATTING	G	AB	R	H	2B	3B	HR	RBI	TB	BB	SO	SB	OBP	SLG	BA
Albert Pujols	157	591	137	212	51	1	43	124	394	79	65	5	.439	.667	.359
Edgar Renteria	157	587	96	194	47	1	13	100	282	65	54	34	.394	.480	.330
J.D. Drew	100	287	60	83	13	3	15	42	147	36	48	2	.374	.513	.289
Scott Rolen	154	559	98	160	49	1	28	104	295	82	104	13	.382	.528	.286
Eduardo Perez	105	253	47	72	16	0	11	41	121	29	53	5	.365	.478	.285
Bo Hart	77	296	46	82	13	5	4	28	117	12	64	3	.317	.395	.277
Jim Edmonds	137	447	89	123	32	2	39	89	276	77	127	1	.385	.617	.275
Tino Martinez	138	476	66	130	25	2	15	69	204	53	71	1	.352	.429	.273
Orlando Palmeiro	141	317	37	86	13	1	3	33	110	32	31	3	.336	.347	.271
Mike Matheny	141	441	43	111	18	2	8	47	157	44	81	1	.320	.356	.252
Fernando Vina	61	259	35	65	14	4	4	23	99	11	24	4	.309	.382	.251
K. Robinson	116	208	19	52	6	3	1	16	67	8	27	6	.281	.322	.250
Miguel Cairo	92	261	41	64	15	2	5	32	98	13	30	4	.289	.375	.245

PITCHING	W–L	ERA	G	GS	SV	INN	H	ER	BB	SO
Jason Isringhausen	0–1	2.36	40	0	22	42.0	31	11	18	41
Cal Eldred	7–4	3.74	62	0	8	67.1	62	28	31	67
Matt Morris	11–8	3.76	27	27	0	172.1	164	72	39	120
Sterling Hitchcock	5–1	3.79	8	6	0	38.0	34	16	14	32
Steve Kline	5–5	3.82	78	0	3	63.2	56	27	30	31
Woody Williams	18–9	3.87	34	33	0	220.2	220	95	55	153
G. Stephenson	7–13	4.59	32	27	0	174.1	167	89	60	91
Danny Haren	3–7	5.08	14	14	0	72.2	84	41	22	43
Brett Tomko	13–9	5.28	33	32	0	202.2	252	119	57	114
Jason Simontacchi	9–5	5.56	46	16	1	126.1	153	78	41	74
Jeff Fassero	1–7	5.68	62	6	3	77.2	93	49	34	55

San Diego Padres

BATTING	G	AB	R	H	2B	3B	HR	RBI	TB	BB	SO	SB	OBP	SLG	BA
Mark Loretta	154	589	74	185	28	4	13	72	260	54	62	5	.372	.441	.314
Sean Burroughs	146	517	62	148	27	6	7	58	208	44	75	7	.352	.402	.286
Phil Nevin	59	226	30	63	8	0	13	46	110	21	44	2	.339	.487	.279
Rondell White	115	413	49	115	17	3	18	66	192	25	71	1	.330	.465	.278
Lou Merloni	65	151	20	41	7	2	1	17	55	22	33	2	.362	.364	.272
Gary Matthews Jr.	103	306	50	83	19	1	4	22	116	34	66	12	.346	.379	.271
Xavier Nady	110	307	50	99	17	1	9	39	145	24	74	6	.321	.391	.267
Mark Kotsay	128	482	64	128	28	4	7	38	185	56	82	6	.343	.384	.266
B. Buchanan	115	198	29	52	10	2	8	29	90	24	51	6	.346	.455	.263
Ramon Vazquez	116	422	56	110	17	4	3	30	144	52	88	10	.342	.341	.261
Ryan Klesko	121	397	47	100	18	0	21	67	181	65	83	2	.354	.456	.252
Gary Bennett	96	307	26	73	15	0	2	42	94	24	48	3	.296	.306	.238

PITCHING	W–L	ERA	G	GS	SV	INN	H	ER	BB	SO
Rod Beck	3–2	1.78	36	0	20	35.1	25	7	11	32
S. Linebrink	2–1	2.82	43	0	0	60.2	55	19	22	51
Matt Herges	2–2	2.86	40	0	3	44.0	40	14	20	40
Adam Eaton	9–12	4.08	31	31	0	183.0	173	83	68	146
Jake Peavy	12–11	4.11	32	32	0	194.2	173	89	82	156
Brian Lawrence	10–15	4.19	33	33	0	210.2	206	98	57	116
B. Villafuerte	0–2	4.20	31	0	2	40.2	39	19	26	24
Mike Matthews	6–4	4.45	77	0	0	64.2	65	32	29	44
Jay Witasick	3–7	4.53	46	0	2	45.2	42	23	25	42
L. Hackman	2–2	5.17	65	0	0	76.2	78	44	36	48
Oliver Perez	4–7	5.38	19	19	0	103.2	103	62	65	117
Kevin Jarvis	4–8	5.87	16	16	0	92.0	113	60	32	49
Jaret Wright	1–5	8.37	39	0	2	47.1	69	44	28	41

San Francisco Giants

BATTING	G	AB	R	H	2B	3B	HR	RBI	TB	BB	SO	SB	OBP	SLG	BA
Barry Bonds	130	390	111	133	22	1	45	90	292	148	58	7	.529	.749	.341
Andres Galarraga	110	272	36	82	15	0	12	42	133	19	61	1	.352	.489	.301
Marquis Grissom	149	587	82	176	33	3	20	79	275	20	82	11	.322	.468	.300
Ray Durham	110	410	61	117	30	5	8	33	181	50	82	7	.366	.441	.285
Benito Santiago	108	401	53	112	21	2	11	56	170	29	69	0	.329	.424	.279
Rich Aurelia	129	505	65	140	26	1	13	58	207	36	82	2	.325	.410	.277
J.T. Snow	103	330	48	90	18	3	8	51	138	55	55	1	.387	.418	.273
Y. Torreabla	66	200	22	52	10	2	4	29	78	14	39	1	.312	.390	.260
Edgardo Alfonzo	142	514	56	133	25	2	13	81	201	58	41	5	.334	.391	.259
Neifi Perez	120	328	27	84	19	4	1	31	114	14	23	3	.285	.348	.256
Jose Cruz Jr.	158	539	90	135	26	1	20	68	223	102	121	5	.366	.414	.250
Pedro Feliz	95	235	31	58	9	3	16	48	121	10	53	2	.278	.515	.247

PITCHING	W–L	ERA	G	GS	SV	INN	H	ER	BB	SO
Jason Schmidt	17–5	2.34	29	29	0	207.2	152	54	46	208
Tim Worrell	4–4	2.87	76	0	38	78.1	74	25	28	65
Felix Rodriguez	8–2	3.10	68	0	2	61.0	59	21	29	46
J. Williams	7–5	3.30	21	21	0	131.0	116	48	49	88
Scott Eyre	2–1	3.32	74	0	1	57.0	60	21	26	35
Kevin Correia	3–1	3.66	10	7	0	39.1	41	16	18	28
Sidney Ponson	3–6	3.71	10	10	0	68.0	64	28	18	34
K. Ainsworth	5–4	3.82	11	11	0	66.0	66	28	26	48
Jim Brower	8–5	3.96	51	5	2	100.0	90	44	39	65
Kirk Rueter	10–5	4.53	27	27	0	147.0	170	74	47	41
Damian Moss	9–7	4.70	21	20	0	115.0	121	60	63	57
Jesse Foppert	8–9	5.03	23	21	0	111.0	103	62	69	101

American League Team-by-Team Statistical Leaders

Anaheim Angels

BATTING	G	AB	R	H	2B	3B	HR	RBI	TB	BB	SO	SB	OBP	SLG	BA
Garret Anderson	159	638	80	201	49	4	29	116	345	31	83	6	.345	.541	.315
Brad Fullmer	63	206	32	63	9	2	9	35	103	26	31	5	.387	.500	.306
Chone Figgins	71	240	34	71	9	4	0	27	88	20	38	13	.345	.367	.296
Jeff DaVanon	123	330	56	93	16	1	12	43	147	42	59	17	.360	.445	.282
Benjie Molina	119	409	37	115	24	0	14	71	181	13	31	1	.304	.443	.281
Tim Salmon	148	528	78	145	35	4	19	72	245	77	93	3	.374	.464	.275
Eric Owens	111	241	29	65	6	0	1	20	74	10	24	11	.300	.307	.269
Adam Kennedy	143	449	71	121	17	1	13	49	179	44	73	22	.344	.399	.269
Scott Speizio	158	521	69	138	36	7	16	83	236	46	66	6	.326	.453	.265
David Eckstein	120	452	59	114	22	1	3	31	147	36	45	16	.325	.325	.252
Troy Glaus	91	319	53	79	17	2	16	50	148	46	73	7	.343	.464	.248
Shawn Wooten	98	272	25	66	8	0	7	32	95	24	45	0	.303	.349	.243

PITCHING	W–L	ERA	G	GS	SV	INN	H	ER	BB	SO
Brenden Donnelly	2–2	1.58	63	0	3	74.0	55	13	24	79
Ben Weber	5–1	2.69	62	0	0	80.1	84	24	22	46
Scot Shields	5–6	2.85	44	13	1	148.1	138	47	38	111
Francisco Rodriguez	8–3	3.03	59	0	2	86.0	50	29	35	95
Troy Percival	0–5	3.47	52	0	33	49.1	33	19	23	48
Jarrod Washburn	10–15	4.43	32	32	0	207.1	205	102	54	118
John Lackey	10–16	4.63	33	33	0	204.0	223	105	66	151
Ramon Ortiz	16–13	5.20	32	32	0	180.0	209	104	63	94
Kevin Appier	7–7	5.63	19	19	0	92.2	105	58	36	50
Aaron Sele	7–11	5.77	25	25	0	121.2	135	78	58	53

Baltimore Orioles

BATTING	G	AB	R	H	2B	3B	HR	RBI	TB	BB	SO	SB	OBP	SLG	BA
Melvin Mora	96	344	68	109	17	1	15	48	173	49	71	6	.418	.503	.317
Larry Bigbee	83	287	43	87	15	1	9	31	131	29	60	1	.365	.456	.303
Luis Matos	109	439	70	133	23	3	13	45	201	28	90	15	.353	.458	.303
B.J. Surhoff	93	319	32	94	20	0	5	41	129	29	29	2	.353	.404	.295
Jeff Conine	124	493	75	143	33	3	15	80	227	37	60	5	.338	.460	.290
Jay Gibbons	160	625	80	173	39	2	23	100	285	49	89	0	.330	.456	.277
Brook Fordyce	108	348	28	95	12	2	6	31	129	19	44	2	.311	.371	.273
Jerry Hairston Jr.	58	218	25	59	12	2	2	21	81	23	25	14	.353	.372	.271
Brian Roberts	112	460	65	124	22	4	5	41	169	46	58	23	.337	.366	.270
David Segui	67	224	26	59	10	1	5	25	86	26	47	1	.341	.384	.263
Deivi Cruz	152	548	61	137	24	2	14	65	207	13	49	1	.269	.378	.258
Geronimo Gil	54	169	22	40	4	0	3	16	53	12	34	0	.299	.314	.237
Tony Batista	161	631	76	148	20	1	26	99	248	28	102	4	.270	.393	.235
Gary Matthews Jr.	41	162	21	33	12	1	2	20	53	9	29	0	.250	.327	.204

PITCHING	W–L	ERA	G	GS	SV	INN	H	ER	BB	SO
Kerry Ligtenberg	4–2	3.34	68	0	0	59.1	60	22	14	47
B.J. Ryan	4–1	3.40	76	0	0	50.1	42	19	27	63
Sidney Ponson	14–6	3.77	21	21	0	148.0	147	62	43	100
Eric DuBose	3–6	3.79	17	10	0	73.2	60	31	25	44
Pat Hentgen	7–8	4.09	28	22	1	160.2	150	73	58	100
Jason Johnson	10–10	4.18	32	32	0	189.2	216	88	80	118
Jorge Julio	0–7	4.38	64	0	36	61.2	60	30	34	52
H. Carrasco	2–6	4.93	40	0	1	38.1	40	21	20	27
Buddy Groom	1–3	5.36	60	0	1	45.1	58	27	14	34
Rick Helling	7–8	5.71	24	24	0	138.2	156	88	40	86
Rodrigo Lopez	7–10	5.82	26	26	0	147.0	188	95	43	103
Travis Driskill	3–5	6.00	20	0	1	48.0	62	32	9	33
Damian Moss	1–5	6.22	10	9	0	50.2	63	35	29	22
Omar Daal	4–11	6.34	19	17	0	93.2	134	66	30	53

Boston Red Sox

BATTING	G	AB	R	H	2B	3B	HR	RBI	TB	BB	SO	SB	OBP	SLG	BA
Bill Mueller	146	524	85	171	45	5	19	85	283	59	77	1	.398	.540	.326
Manny Ramirez	154	569	117	185	36	1	37	104	334	97	94	3	.427	.587	.325
Trot Nixon	134	441	81	135	24	6	28	87	255	65	96	4	.396	.578	.306
Shea Hillenbrand	49	185	20	56	17	0	3	38	82	7	26	1	.335	.443	.303
Nomar Garciaparra	156	658	120	198	37	13	28	105	345	39	61	19	.345	.524	.301
Gabe Kapler	68	158	29	46	11	1	4	23	71	14	23	4	.349	.449	.291
David Ortiz	128	448	79	129	39	2	31	101	265	58	83	0	.369	.592	.288
Todd Walker	144	587	92	166	38	4	13	85	251	48	54	1	.333	.428	.283
Kevin Millar	148	544	83	150	30	1	25	96	257	60	108	3	.348	.472	.276
Johnny Damon	145	608	103	166	32	6	12	67	246	68	74	30	.345	.405	.273
Jason Varitek	142	451	63	123	31	1	25	85	231	51	106	3	.351	.512	.273
D. Jackson	109	161	34	42	7	0	1	13	52	8	28	16	.294	.323	.261
Doug Mirabelli	62	163	23	42	13	0	6	18	73	11	36	0	.307	.448	.258

PITCHING	W–L	ERA	G	GS	SV	INN	H	ER	BB	SO
Pedro Martinez	14–4	2.22	29	29	0	186.2	147	46	47	206
Byung-Hyun Kim	8–5	3.18	49	5	16	79.1	70	28	18	69
Mike Timlin	6–4	3.55	72	0	2	83.2	77	33	9	65
Tim Wakefield	11–7	4.09	35	33	1	202.1	193	92	71	169
Brandon Lyon	4–6	4.12	49	0	9	59.0	73	27	19	50
Alan Embree	4–1	4.25	65	0	1	55.0	49	26	16	45
Derek Lowe	17–7	4.47	33	33	0	203.1	216	101	72	110
John Burkett	12–9	5.15	32	30	0	181.2	202	104	47	107
Casey Fossum	6–5	5.47	19	14	1	79.0	82	48	34	63
Jeff Suppan	3–4	5.57	11	10	0	63.0	70	39	20	32
Scott Williamson	0–1	6.20	24	0	0	20.1	20	14	9	21
Ramiro Mendoza	3–5	6.75	37	5	0	66.2	98	50	20	36

Chicago White Sox

BATTING	G	AB	R	H	2B	3B	HR	RBI	TB	BB	SO	SB	OBP	SLG	BA
Magglio Ordonez	160	606	95	192	46	3	29	99	331	57	73	9	.380	.546	.317
Carl Everett	73	256	40	77	14	0	10	41	121	22	36	4	.377	.473	.301
Carlos Lee	158	623	100	181	35	1	31	113	311	37	91	18	.331	.499	.291
Aaron Rowand	934	157	22	45	8	0	6	24	71	7	21	0	.327	.452	.287
Sandy Alomar Jr.	75	194	22	52	12	0	5	26	79	4	17	0	.281	.407	.268
Frank Thomas	153	546	87	146	35	0	42	105	307	100	115	0	.390	.562	.267
Joe Crede	151	536	68	140	31	2	19	75	232	32	75	1	.308	.433	.261
Tony Graffanino	90	250	51	65	15	3	7	23	107	24	37	8	.331	.428	.260
D'Angelo Jimenez	73	271	35	69	11	5	7	26	111	32	46	4	.332	.410	.255
Roberto Alomar	67	253	42	64	11	1	3	17	86	30	37	6	.330	.340	.253
Miguel Olivo	114	317	37	75	19	1	6	27	114	19	80	6	.287	.360	.237
Jose Valentin	144	503	79	119	26	2	28	74	233	54	114	8	.313	.463	.237
Paul Konerko	137	444	49	104	19	0	18	65	177	43	50	0	.305	.399	.234
Brian Daubach	95	183	26	42	11	0	6	21	71	34	54	1	.352	.388	.230

PITCHING	W–L	ERA	G	GS	SV	INN	H	ER	BB	SO
Damaso Marte	4–2	1.58	71	0	11	79.2	50	14	34	87
Esteban Loaiza	21–9	2.90	34	34	0	226.1	196	73	56	207
Tom Gordon	7–6	3.16	66	0	12	74.0	57	26	31	91
Bartolo Colon	15–13	3.87	34	34	0	242.0	223	104	67	173
Mark Buehrle	14–14	4.14	35	35	0	230.0	250	106	61	119
Jon Garland	12–13	4.51	32	32	0	191.2	188	96	74	108
Billy Koch	5–5	5.77	55	0	11	53.0	59	34	28	42
Dan Wright	1–7	6.15	20	15	1	86.1	91	59	46	47

Cleveland Indians

BATTING	G	AB	R	H	2B	3B	HR	RBI	TB	BB	SO	SB	OBP	SLG	BA
Milton Bradley	101	377	61	121	34	2	10	56	189	64	73	17	.421	.501	.321
V. Martinez	49	159	15	46	4	0	1	16	53	13	21	1	.345	.333	.289
Jody Gerut	127	480	66	134	33	2	22	75	237	35	70	4	.336	.494	.279
Shane Spencer	64	210	23	57	10	0	8	26	91	81	52	2	.328	.433	.271
Coco Crisp	99	414	55	110	15	6	3	27	146	23	51	15	.302	.353	.266
Ellis Burks	55	198	27	52	11	1	6	28	83	27	46	1	.360	.419	.263
Casey Blake	152	557	80	143	35	0	17	67	229	38	109	7	.312	.411	.257
Travis Hafner	91	291	35	74	19	3	14	40	141	22	81	2	.327	.485	.254
Ben Broussard	116	386	53	96	21	3	16	55	171	32	75	5	.312	.443	.249
Matt Lawton	99	374	57	93	19	0	15	53	157	47	47	10	.343	.420	.249
Josh Bard	91	303	25	74	13	1	8	36	113	22	53	0	.293	.373	.244
Omar Vizquel	64	250	43	61	13	2	1	19	84	29	20	8	.321	.336	.244
J. Peralta	77	242	24	55	10	1	4	21	79	20	65	1	.295	.326	.227
John McDonald	82	214	21	46	9	1	1	14	60	11	31	3	.258	.280	.215
B. Phillips	112	370	36	77	18	1	6	33	115	14	77	4	.242	.311	.208

PITCHING	W–L	ERA	G	GS	SV	INN	H	ER	BB	SO
R. Betancourt	2–2	2.13	33	0	1	38.0	27	9	13	36
David Riske	2–2	2.29	68	0	8	74.2	52	19	20	82
Jack Cressend	2–1	2.51	33	0	0	43.0	40	12	9	28
C.C. Sabathia	13–9	3.60	30	30	0	197.2	190	79	66	141
J. Stanford	1–3	3.60	13	8	0	50.0	48	20	16	30
Cliff Lee	3–3	3.61	9	9	0	52.1	41	21	20	44
B. Anderson	9–10	3.71	24	24	0	148.0	162	61	32	72
Dannys Baez	2–9	3.81	73	0	25	75.2	65	32	23	66
Jason Boyd	3–1	4.30	44	0	0	52.1	38	25	26	31
Jake Westbrook	7–10	4.33	34	22	0	133.0	142	64	56	58
Jason Davis	8–11	4.68	27	27	0	165.1	172	86	47	85
Terry Mulholland	3–4	4.91	45	3	0	99.0	117	54	37	42
Billy Traber	6–9	5.24	33	18	0	111.2	132	65	40	88
R. Rodriguez	3–9	5.73	15	15	0	81.2	89	52	28	41

Detroit Tigers

BATTING	G	AB	R	H	2B	3B	HR	RBI	TB	BB	SO	SB	OBP	SLG	BA
Dimitri Young	155	562	78	167	34	7	29	85	302	58	130	2	.372	.537	.297
Alex Sanchez	101	394	43	114	13	5	1	22	140	18	46	44	.320	.355	.289
Warren Morris	97	346	37	94	13	2	6	37	129	23	42	4	.316	.373	.272
Kevin Witt	93	270	25	71	9	0	10	26	110	15	68	1	.301	.407	.263
Carlos Pena	131	452	51	112	21	6	18	50	199	53	123	4	.332	.440	.248
Craig Monroe	128	425	51	102	18	1	23	70	191	27	89	4	.287	.449	.240
Eric Munson	99	313	28	75	9	0	18	50	138	55	61	3	.312	.441	.240
Bobby Higginson	130	469	61	110	13	4	14	15	173	59	73	8	.320	.369	.235
R. Santiago	141	444	41	100	18	1	2	29	126	33	66	10	.292	.284	.225
Omar Infante	69	221	24	49	6	1	0	8	57	18	37	6	.278	.258	.222
Andres Torres	59	168	23	37	4	3	1	9	50	10	35	5	.263	.298	.220
Shane Halter	114	360	33	78	5	2	12	30	123	27	77	2	.269	.342	.217
Brandon Inge	104	330	32	67	15	3	8	30	112	24	79	4	.265	.339	.203

PITCHING	W–L	ERA	G	GS	SV	INN	H	ER	BB	SO
Jamie Walker	4–3	3.32	78	0	3	65.0	61	24	17	45
Nate Cornejo	6–17	4.67	32	32	0	194.2	236	101	58	46
C. Spurling	1–3	4.68	66	0	3	77.0	78	40	22	38
Steve Sparks	0–6	4.72	42	0	2	89.2	95	47	34	49
N. Robertson	1–2	5.44	8	8	0	44.2	55	27	23	33
Chris Mears	1–3	5.44	29	3	5	41.1	50	25	11	21
Matt Roney	1–9	5.45	45	11	0	100.2	102	61	48	47
J. Bonderman	6–19	5.56	33	28	0	162.0	193	100	58	108
Mike Maroth	9–21	5.73	33	33	0	193.1	231	123	50	87
W. Ledezma	3–7	5.79	34	8	0	84.0	99	54	35	49
Gary Knots	3–8	6.04	20	18	0	95.1	111	64	47	51
F. German	2–4	6.04	45	0	5	44.2	47	30	45	41
Adam Bernero	1–12	6.08	18	17	0	100.2	104	68	41	54

Kansas City Royals

BATTING	G	AB	R	H	2B	3B	HR	RBI	TB	BB	SO	SB	OBP	SLG	BA
Carlos Beltran	141	521	102	160	14	10	26	100	272	72	81	41	.389	.522	.307
Raul Ibanez	152	608	95	179	33	5	18	90	276	49	81	8	.345	.454	.294
Mike Sweeney	108	392	62	115	18	1	16	83	183	64	56	3	.391	.467	.293
Joe Randa	131	502	80	146	31	1	16	72	227	41	61	1	.348	.452	.291
Angel Berroa	158	567	92	163	28	-7	17	73	256	29	100	21	.338	.451	.287
Aaron Guiel	99	354	63	98	30	0	15	52	173	27	63	3	.346	.489	.277
Ken Harvey	135	485	50	129	30	0	13	64	191	29	94	2	.313	.408	.266
Michael Tucker	104	389	61	102	20	5	13	55	171	39	88	8	.331	.440	.262
Desi Relaford	141	500	70	127	27	5	8	59	188	40	70	20	.315	.376	.254
Mike DiFelice	62	189	29	48	16	1	3	25	75	9	30	1	.299	.397	.254
Brent Mayne	113	372	39	91	17	1	6	36	128	32	59	0	.307	.344	.245
Carlos Febles	74	196	31	46	5	0	0	11	51	13	30	8	.299	.260	.235

PITCHING	W–L	ERA	G	GS	SV	INN	H	ER	BB	SO
Darrell May	10–8	3.77	35	32	0	210.0	197	88	53	115
Jeremy Affeldt	7–6	3.93	36	18	4	126.0	126	55	38	98
B. Anderson	5–1	3.99	7	7	0	49.2	50	22	11	15
Mike MacDougal	3–5	4.08	68	0	27	64.0	64	29	32	57
Jimmy Gobble	4–5	4.61	9	9	0	52.2	56	27	15	31
R. Hernandez	7–5	4.61	16	16	0	91.2	87	47	37	48
D.J. Carrasco	6–5	4.82	50	2	2	80.1	82	43	40	57
Jose Lima	8–3	4.91	14	14	0	73.1	80	40	26	32
Jason Grimsley	2–6	5.16	76	0	0	75.0	88	43	36	58
Kyle Snyder	1–6	5.17	15	15	0	85.1	94	49	21	39
Paul Abbott	1–2	5.29	10	8	0	47.2	47	28	26	32
Chris George	9–6	7.11	18	18	0	93.2	120	74	44	39

Minnesota Twins

BATTING	G	AB	R	H	2B	3B	HR	RBI	TB	BB	SO	SB	OBP	SLG	BA
Shannon Stewart	65	270	43	87	22	0	6	38	127	25	36	3	.384	.470	.322
A.J. Pierzynski	137	487	63	152	35	3	11	74	26	24	55	3	.360	.464	.312
Jacque Jones	136	517	76	157	33	1	16	69	240	21	105	13	.333	.464	.304
Doug Mientkiewicz	142	487	67	146	38	1	11	65	219	74	55	4	.393	.450	.300
Corey Koskie	131	469	76	137	29	2	14	69	212	77	113	11	.393	.452	.292
Matt LeCroy	107	345	39	99	19	0	17	64	169	25	82	0	.342	.490	.287
Cristian Guzman	143	534	78	143	15	14	3	53	195	30	79	18	.311	.365	.268
Luis Rivas	135	475	69	123	16	9	8	43	181	30	65	17	.308	.381	.259
Bobby Kielty	75	238	40	60	13	0	9	32	100	42	56	6	.370	.420	.252
Chris Gomez	58	175	14	44	9	3	1	15	62	7	13	2	.279	.354	.251
Dustan Mohr	121	348	50	87	22	0	10	36	139	33	106	5	.314	.399	.250
Torii Hunter	154	581	83	145	31	4	26	102	262	50	106	6	.312	.451	.250
Denny Hocking	83	188	22	45	10	2	3	22	68	15	37	0	.291	.362	.239

PITCHING	W–L	ERA	G	GS	SV	INN	H	ER	BB	SO
LaTroy Hawkins	9–3	1.86	74	0	2	77.1	69	16	15	75
Eddie Guardado	3–5	2.89	66	0	41	65.1	50	21	14	60
Johan Santana	12–3	3.07	45	18	0	158.1	127	54	47	169
Juan Rincon	5–6	3.68	58	0	0	85.2	74	35	38	63
Brad Radke	14–10	4.49	33	33	0	212.1	242	106	28	120
Kenny Rogers	13–8	4.57	33	31	0	195.0	227	99	50	116
Kyle Lohse	14–11	4.61	33	33	0	201.0	211	103	45	130
J.C. Romero	2–0	5.00	73	0	0	63.0	66	35	42	50
Rick Reed	6–12	5.07	27	21	0	135.0	155	76	29	71
Joe Mays	8–8	6.30	31	21	0	130.0	159	91	39	50

New York Yankees

BATTING	G	AB	R	H	2B	3B	HR	RBI	TB	BB	SO	SB	OBP	SLG	BA
Derek Jeter	119	482	87	156	25	3	10	52	217	43	88	11	.393	.450	.324
Karim Garcia	52	151	17	46	5	0	6	21	69	9	32	0	.342	.457	.305
Alfonso Soriano	156	682	114	198	36	5	38	91	358	38	130	35	.338	.525	.290
Hideki Matsui	153	623	82	179	42	1	16	106	271	63	86	2	.353	.435	.287
Nick Johnson	96	324	60	92	19	0	14	47	153	70	57	5	.422	.472	.284
Jorge Posada	142	481	83	135	24	0	30	101	249	93	110	2	.405	.518	.281
Ruben Sierra	63	174	19	48	8	1	6	31	76	13	20	1	.323	.437	.276
Juan Rivera	57	173	22	46	14	0	7	26	81	10	27	0	.304	.468	.266
Bernie Williams	119	445	77	117	19	1	15	64	183	71	61	5	.367	.411	.263
Raul Mondesi	98	361	56	93	23	3	16	49	170	38	66	17	.330	.471	.258
Aaron Boone	54	189	31	48	13	0	6	31	79	11	30	8	.302	.418	.254
Robin Ventura	89	283	31	71	13	0	9	42	111	40	62	0	.344	.392	.251
Jason Giambi	156	535	97	134	25	0	41	107	282	129	140	2	.412	.527	.250
Todd Zeile	66	816	29	39	8	0	6	23	65	24	36	0	.294	.349	.210

PITCHING	W–L	ERA	G	GS	SV	INN	H	ER	BB	SO
Mariano Rivera	5–2	1.66	64	0	40	70.2	61	13	10	63
Chris Hammond	3–2	2.86	62	0	1	63.0	65	20	11	45
Jose Contreras	7–2	3.30	18	9	0	71.0	52	26	30	72
Mike Mussina	17–8	3.40	31	31	0	214.2	192	81	40	195
Antonio Osuna	2–5	3.73	48	0	0	50.2	58	21	20	47
Roger Clemens	17–9	3.91	33	33	0	211.2	199	92	58	190
Andy Pettitte	21–8	4.02	33	33	0	208.1	227	93	50	180
David Wells	15–7	4.14	31	30	0	213.0	242	98	20	101
Sterling Hitchcock	1–3	5.44	27	1	0	49.2	57	30	18	36
Jeff Weaver	7–9	5.99	32	24	0	159.1	211	106	47	93

Oakland Athletics

BATTING	G	AB	R	H	2B	3B	HR	RBI	TB	BB	SO	SB	OBP	SLG	BA
Eric Chavez	156	588	94	166	39	5	29	101	302	62	89	8	.350	.514	.282
Miguel Tejada	162	636	98	177	42	0	27	106	300	53	65	10	.336	.472	.278
Ramon Hernandez	140	483	70	132	24	1	21	78	221	33	79	0	.331	.458	.273
Jose Guillen	45	170	25	45	7	1	8	23	78	7	32	0	.311	.459	.265
Eric Byrnes	121	414	64	109	27	9	12	51	190	42	71	10	.333	.459	.263
Erubiel Durazo	154	537	92	139	29	0	21	77	231	100	105	1	.374	.430	.259
Scott Hatteberg	147	541	63	137	34	0	12	61	207	66	53	0	.342	.383	.253
Mark Ellis	154	553	78	137	31	5	9	52	205	48	94	6	.313	.371	.248
Chris Singleton	120	306	38	75	24	1	1	36	104	26	55	7	.301	.340	.245
Terrence Long	140	486	64	119	22	2	14	61	187	31	67	4	.293	.385	.245
Jermaine Dye	65	221	28	38	6	0	4	20	56	25	42	1	.261	.253	.172

PITCHING	W–L	ERA	G	GS	SV	INN	H	ER	BB	SO
Keith Foulke	9–1	2.08	72	0	43	86.2	57	20	20	88
Tim Hudson	16–7	2.70	34	34	0	240.0	197	72	61	162
Chad Bradford	7–4	3.04	72	0	2	77.0	67	26	30	62
Mark Mulder	15–9	3.13	26	26	0	186.2	180	65	40	128
R. Rincon	8–4	3.25	64	0	0	55.1	45	20	32	40
Barry Zito	14–12	3.30	35	35	0	231.2	186	85	88	146
John Halama	3–5	4.22	35	13	0	108.2	117	51	36	51
Ted Lilly	12–10	4.34	32	31	0	178.1	179	86	58	147
Rich Harden	5–4	4.46	15	13	0	74.2	72	37	40	67
Jim Mecir	2–3	5.59	41	0	1	37.0	40	23	16	25

Seattle Mariners

BATTING	G	AB	R	H	2B	3B	HR	RBI	TB	BB	SO	SB	OBP	SLG	BA
Ichiro Suzuki	159	679	111	212	29	8	13	62	296	36	69	34	.352	.436	.312
Randy Winn	157	600	103	177	37	4	11	75	255	41	108	23	.346	.425	.295
Bret Boone	159	622	111	183	35	5	35	117	333	68	125	16	.366	.535	.294
Rey Sanchez	46	170	22	50	5	1	0	11	57	8	21	1	.330	.335	.294
Edgar Martinez	145	497	72	146	25	0	24	98	243	92	95	0	.406	.489	.294
Carlos Guillen	109	388	63	107	19	3	7	52	153	52	64	4	.359	.394	.276
John Olerud	152	539	64	145	35	0	10	83	210	84	67	0	.372	.390	.269
Mike Cameron	147	534	74	135	31	5	18	76	230	70	137	17	.344	.431	.253
Willie Bloomquist	89	196	30	49	7	2	1	14	63	19	39	4	.317	.321	.250
Dan Wilson	96	316	32	76	15	2	4	43	107	15	52	0	.272	.339	.241
Ben Davis	80	246	25	58	18	0	6	42	94	18	61	0	.284	.382	.236
Mark McLemore	99	309	34	72	15	2	2	37	97	38	71	5	.318	.314	.233
Jeff Cirillo	87	258	24	53	11	0	2	23	70	24	32	1	.284	.271	.205

PITCHING	W–L	ERA	G	GS	SV	INN	H	ER	BB	SO
Shigetoshi Hasegawa	2–4	1.48	63	0	16	73.0	62	12	18	32
Rafael Soriano	3–0	1.53	40	0	1	53.0	30	9	12	68
Julio Mateo	4–0	3.15	50	0	1	85.2	69	30	13	71
Jamie Moyer	21–7	3.27	33	33	0	215.0	199	78	66	129
Ryan Franklin	11–13	3.57	32	32	0	212.0	199	84	61	99
Joel Pineiro	16–11	3.78	32	32	0	211.2	192	89	76	151
Kaz Sasaki	1–2	4.05	35	0	10	33.1	31	15	15	29
Arthur Rhodes	3–3	4.17	67	0	3	54.0	53	25	18	48
Freddy Garcia	12–14	4.51	33	33	0	201.1	196	101	71	144
Gil Meche	15–13	4.59	32	32	0	186.1	187	95	63	130

Tampa Bay Devil Rays

BATTING	G	AB	R	H	2B	3B	HR	RBI	TB	BB	SO	SB	OBP	SLG	BA
Aubrey Huff	162	636	91	198	47	3	34	107	353	53	80	2	.367	.555	.311
Rocco Baldelli	156	637	89	184	32	8	11	78	265	30	128	27	.326	.416	.289
Carl Crawford	151	630	80	177	18	9	5	55	228	26	102	55	.309	.362	.281
Travis Lee	145	542	75	149	37	3	19	70	249	64	97	6	.348	.459	.275
Ben Grieve	117	433	58	119	13	4	15	53	185	35	88	10	.333	.427	.275
M. Anderson	145	482	59	130	27	3	6	67	181	41	60	19	.328	.376	.270
Damian Rolls	107	373	43	95	20	0	7	46	136	19	84	11	.301	.365	.255
Toby Hall	130	463	50	117	23	0	12	47	176	23	49	0	.295	.380	.253
Al Martin	100	238	19	60	12	2	3	26	85	17	51	2	.306	.357	.252
Ben Grieve	55	165	28	38	7	0	4	17	57	32	41	0	.371	.345	.230

PITCHING	W–L	ERA	G	GS	SV	INN	H	ER	BB	SO
Al Levine	3–5	2.90	36	0	0	49.2	45	18	18	25
Chad Gaudin	2–0	3.60	15	3	0	40.0	37	16	16	23
Travis Harper	4–8	3.77	61	0	1	93.0	86	39	31	64
J. Gonzalez	6–11	3.91	25	25	0	156.1	131	68	69	97
Victor Zambrano	12–10	4.21	34	28	0	188.1	165	88	106	132
Lance Carter	7–5	4.33	62	0	26	79.0	72	38	19	47
Jesus Colome	3–7	4.50	54	0	2	74.0	69	37	46	69
Jorge Sosa	5–12	4.62	29	19	0	128.2	137	66	60	72
Seth McClung	4–1	5.35	12	5	0	38.2	33	25	25	25
Rob Bell	5–4	5.52	19	18	0	101.0	103	62	39	44
Joe Kennedy	3–12	6.13	32	22	1	133.2	167	91	47	77
D. Brazelton	1–6	6.89	10	10	0	48.1	57	37	23	24

Texas Rangers

BATTING	G	AB	R	H	2B	3B	HR	RBI	TB	BB	SO	SB	OBP	SLG	BA
Michael Young	160	666	106	204	33	9	14	72	297	36	103	13	.339	.446	.306
Hank Blalock	143	567	89	170	33	3	29	90	296	-44	.97	2	.350	.522	.300
Alex Rodriguez	161	607	124	181	30	6	47	118	364	87	126	17	.396	.600	.298
Juan Gonzalez	82	327	49	96	17	1	24	70	187	14	73	1	.329	.572	.294
Carl Everett	74	270	53	74	13	3	18	51	147	31	48	4	.356	.544	.274
Doug Glanville	52	195	22	53	5	0	4	14	70	6	25	4	.294	.359	.272
Rafael Palmeiro	154	561	92	146	21	2	38	112	285	84	77	2	.359	.508	.260
Mark Teixeira	146	529	66	137	29	5	26	84	254	44	120	1	.331	.480	.259
Einar Diaz	101	334	30	86	14	1	4	35	114	9	32	3	.294	.341	.257
Laynce Nix	53	184	25	47	10	0	8	30	81	9	53	3	.289	.440	.255
Todd Greene	62	205	25	47	10	1	10	20	89	2	47	0	.243	.434	.229
Shane Spencer	55	185	16	42	10	0	4	23	64	27	40	0	.329	.346	.227
R. Christenson	60	165	22	29	7	0	2	16	42	15	44	2	.255	.255	.176

PITCHING	W–L	ERA	G	GS	SV	INN	H	ER	BB	SO
Francisco Cordero	5–8	2.94	73	0	15	82.2	70	27	38	90
Brian Shouse	0–1	3.10	62	0	1	61.0	62	21	14	40
Ron Mahay	3–3	3.18	35	0	0	45.1	33	16	20	38
E. Ramirez	3–1	3.86	34	0	0	49.0	46	21	9	41
Ugueth Urbina	3–1	4.19	39	0	26	38.2	33	18	18	41
John Thomson	13–14	4.85	35	35	0	217.0	234	117	49	136
R.A. Dickey	9–8	5.09	38	13	1	116.2	135	66	38	94
Aaron Fultz	1–3	5.21	64	0	0	67.1	75	39	27	53
Joaquin Benoit	8–5	5.49	25	17	0	105.0	99	64	51	87
Ismael Valdes	8–8	6.10	22	22	0	115.0	148	78	29	47
Ryan Drese	2–4	6.85	11	8	0	46.0	61	35	24	26
Tony Mounce	1–5	7.11	11	11	0	50.2	65	40	25	30
Colby Lewis	10–9	7.30	26	26	0	127.0	163	103	70	88
Jay Powell	3–0	7.82	51	0	0	58.2	75	51	34	40

Toronto Blue Jays

BATTING	G	AB	R	H	2B	3B	HR	RBI	TB	BB	SO	SB	OBP	SLG	BA
Vernon Wells	161	678	118	215	49	5	35	117	373	42	80	4	.359	.550	.317
Greg Myers	121	329	51	101	19	0	15	52	165	37	57	0	.374	.502	.307
Carlos Delgado	161	570	117	172	38	1	42	145	338	109	137	0	.426	.593	.302
Frank Catalanotto	133	489	83	146	34	6	.13	59	231	35	62	2	.351	.472	.299
Shannon Stewart	71	303	47	89	22	2	7	35	136	27	30	1	.347	.449	.294
Reed Johnson	114	412	79	121	21	2	10	52	176	20	67	5	.353	.427	.294
Mike Bordick	102	343	39	94	18	2	5	54	131	33	60	3	.340	.382	.274
Orlando Hudson	142	474	54	127	21	6	9	57	187	39	87	5	.328	.395	.268
Josh Phelps	119	396	57	106	18	1	20	66	186	39	115	1	.358	.470	.268
Chris Woodward	104	349	49	91	22	2	7	45	138	28	72	1	.316	.395	.261
Tom Wilson	96	256	37	66	19	0	5	35	100	28	80	0	.331	.391	.258
Dave Berg	61	161	26	41	6	1	4	18	61	11	34	0	.301	.379	.255
Eric Hinske	124	449	74	109	45	3	12	63	196	59	104	12	.329	.437	.243
Bobby Kielty	62	189	31	44	13	1	4	25	71	29	36	2	.342	.376	.233

PITCHING	W–L	ERA	G	GS	SV	INN	H	ER	BB	SO
J. Kershner	3–3	3.17	40	0	0	54.0	43	19	15	32
Roy Halladay	22–7	3.25	36	36	0	266.0	253	96	32	204
A. Lopez	1–3	3.42	72	0	14	73.2	58	28	34	64
Kelvim Escobar	13–9	4.29	41	26	4	180.1	189	86	78	159
Josh Towers	8–1	4.48	14	8	1	64.1	67	32	7	42
Trever Miller	2–2	4.61	79	0	4	52.2	46	27	28	44
Pete Walker	2–2	4.88	23	7	0	55.1	59	30	24	29
Doug Davis	4–6	5.00	12	11	0	54.0	70	30	26	25
M. Hendrickson	9–9	5.51	30	30	0	158.1	207	97	40	76
Jeff Tam	0–4	5.64	44	0	1	44.2	58	28	25	26
Cliff Politte	1–5	5.66	54	0	12	49.1	52	31	17	40
Cory Lidle	12–15	5.75	31	31	0	192.2	216	123	60	112
T. Sturtze	7–6	5.94	40	8	0	89.1	107	59	43	54

The World Series

Results

1903	Boston (A) 5, Pittsburgh (N) 3
1904	No series
1905	New York (N) 4, Philadelphia (A) 1
1906	Chicago (A) 4, Chicago (N) 2
1907	Chicago (N) 4, Detroit (A) 0; 1 tie
1908	Chicago (N) 4, Detroit (A) 1
1909	Pittsburgh (N) 4, Detroit (A) 3
1910	Philadelphia (A) 4, Chicago (N) 1
1911	Philadelphia (A) 4, New York (N) 2
1912	Boston (A) 4, New York (N) 3; 1 tie
1913	Philadelphia (A) 4, New York (N) 1
1914	Boston (N) 4, Philadelphia (A) 0
1915	Boston (A) 4, Philadelphia (N) 1
1916	Boston (A) 4, Brooklyn (N) 1
1917	Chicago (A) 4, New York (N) 2
1918	Boston (A) 4, Chicago (N) 2
1919	Cincinnati (N) 5, Chicago (A) 3
1920	Cleveland (A) 5, Brooklyn (N) 2
1921	New York (N) 5, New York (A) 3
1922	New York (N) 4, New York (A) 0; 1 tie
1923	New York (A) 4, New York (N) 2
1924	Washington (A) 4, New York (N) 3
1925	Pittsburgh (N) 4, Washington (A) 3
1926	St. Louis (N) 4, New York (A) 3
1927	New York (A) 4, Pittsburgh (N) 0
1928	New York (A) 4, St. Louis (N) 0
1929	Philadelphia (A) 4, Chicago (N) 1
1930	Philadelphia (A) 4, St. Louis (N) 2
1931	St. Louis (N) 4, Philadelphia (A) 3
1932	New York (A) 4, Chicago (N) 0
1933	New York (N) 4, Washington (A) 1
1934	St. Louis (N) 4, Detroit (A) 3
1935	Detroit (A) 4, Chicago (N) 2
1936	New York (A) 4, New York (N) 2
1937	New York (A) 4, New York (N) 1
1938	New York (A) 4, Chicago (N) 0
1939	New York (A) 4, Cincinnati (N) 0
1940	Cincinnati (N) 4, Detroit (A) 3
1941	New York (A) 4, Brooklyn (N) 1
1942	St. Louis (N) 4, New York (A) 1
1943	New York (A) 4, St. Louis (N) 1
1944	St. Louis (N) 4, St. Louis (A) 2
1945	Detroit (A) 4, Chicago (N) 3
1946	St. Louis (N) 4, Boston (A) 3
1947	New York (A) 4, Brooklyn (N) 3
1948	Cleveland (A) 4, Boston (N) 2
1949	New York (A) 4, Brooklyn (N) 1
1950	New York (A) 4, Philadelphia (N) 0
1951	New York (A) 4, New York (N) 2
1952	New York (A) 4, Brooklyn (N) 3
1953	New York (A) 4, Brooklyn (N) 2
1954	New York (N) 4, Cleveland (A) 0
1955	Brooklyn (N) 4, New York (A) 3
1956	New York (A) 4, Brooklyn (N) 3
1957	Milwaukee (N) 4, New York (A) 3
1958	New York (A) 4, Milwaukee (N) 3
1959	Los Angeles (N) 4, Chicago (A) 2
1960	Pittsburgh (N) 4, New York (A) 3
1961	New York (A) 4, Cincinnati (N) 1
1962	New York (A) 4, San Francisco (N) 3
1963	Los Angeles (N) 4, New York (A) 0
1964	St. Louis (N) 4, New York (A) 3
1965	Los Angeles (N) 4, Minnesota (A) 3
1966	Baltimore (A) 4, Los Angeles (N) 0
1967	St. Louis (N) 4, Boston (A) 3
1968	Detroit (A) 4, St. Louis (N) 3
1969	New York (N) 4, Baltimore (A) 1
1970	Baltimore (A) 4, Cincinnati (N) 1
1971	Pittsburgh (N) 4, Baltimore (A) 3
1972	Oakland (A) 4, Cincinnati (N) 3
1973	Oakland (A) 4, New York (N) 3
1974	Oakland (A) 4, Los Angeles (N) 1
1975	Cincinnati (N) 4, Boston (A) 3
1976	Cincinnati (N) 4, New York (A) 0
1977	New York (A) 4, Los Angeles (N) 2
1978	New York (A) 4, Los Angeles (N) 2
1979	Pittsburgh (N) 4, Baltimore (A) 3
1980	Philadelphia (N) 4, Kansas City (A) 2
1981	Los Angeles (N) 4, New York (A) 2
1982	St. Louis (N) 4, Milwaukee (A) 3
1983	Baltimore (A) 4, Philadelphia (N) 1
1984	Detroit (A) 4, San Diego (N) 1
1985	Kansas City (A) 4, St. Louis (N) 3
1986	New York (N) 4, Boston (A) 3
1987	Minnesota (A) 4, St. Louis (N) 3
1988	Los Angeles (N) 4, Oakland (A) 1
1989	Oakland (A) 4, San Francisco (N) 0
1990	Cincinnati (N) 4, Oakland (A) 0
1991	Minnesota (A) 4, Atlanta (N) 3
1992	Toronto (A) 4, Atlanta (N) 2
1993	Toronto (A) 4, Philadelphia (N) 2
1994	Series canceled due to players' strike.
1995	Atlanta (N) 4, Cleveland (A) 2
1996	New York (A) 4, Atlanta (N) 2
1997	Florida (N) 4, Cleveland (A) 3
1998	New York (A) 4, San Diego (N) 0
1999	New York (A) 4, Atlanta (N) 0
2000	New York (A) 4 , New York (N) 1
2001	Arizona (N) 4, New York (A) 3
2002	Anaheim (A) 4, San Francisco (N) 3
2003	Florida (N) 4, New York (A) 2

Most Valuable Players

1955	Johnny Podres, Bklyn	1981	Ron Cey, LA; Steve Yeager, LA;
1956	Don Larsen, NY (A)		Pedro Guerrero, LA
1957	Lew Burdette, Mil	1982	Darrell Porter, StL
1958	Bob Turley, NY (A)	1983	Rick Dempsey, Balt
1959	Larry Sherry, LA	1984	Alan Trammell, Det
1960	Bobby Richardson, NY (A)	1985	Bret Saberhagen, KC
1961	Whitey Ford, NY (A)	1986	Ray Knight, NY (N)
1962	Ralph Terry, NY (A)	1987	Frank Viola, Minn
1963	Sandy Koufax, LA	1988	Orel Hershiser, LA
1964	Bob Gibson, StL	1989	Dave Stewart, Oak
1965	Sandy Koufax, LA	1990	Jose Rijo, Cin
1966	Frank Robinson, Balt	1991	Jack Morris, Minn
1967	Bob Gibson, StL	1992	Pat Borders, Tor
1968	Mickey Lolich, Det	1993	Paul Molitor, Tor
1969	Donn Clendenon, NY (N)	1994	Series canceled due to strike.
1970	Brooks Robinson, Balt	1995	Tom Glavine, Atl
1971	Roberto Clemente, Pitt	1996	John Wetteland, NY (A)
1972	Gene Tenace, Oak	1997	Livan Hernandez, Fla
1973	Reggie Jackson, Oak	1998	Scott Brosius, NY (A)
1974	Rollie Fingers, Oak	1999	Mariano Rivera, NY (A)
1975	Pete Rose, Cin	2000	Derek Jeter, NY (A)
1976	Johnny Bench, Cin	2001	Randy Johnson, Ariz
1977	Reggie Jackson, NY (A)		Curt Schilling, Ariz
1978	Bucky Dent, NY (A)	2002	Troy Glaus, Ana
1979	Willie Stargell, Pitt	2003	Josh Beckett, Fla
1980	Mike Schmidt, Phil		

Career Batting Leaders (Minimum 40 at bats)

GAMES

Yogi Berra	75
Mickey Mantle	65
Elston Howard	54
Hank Bauer	53
Gil McDougald	53
Phil Rizzuto	52
Joe DiMaggio	51
Frankie Frisch	50
Pee Wee Reese	44
Roger Maris	41
Babe Ruth	41

AT BATS

Yogi Berra	259
Mickey Mantle	230
Joe DiMaggio	199
Frankie Frisch	197
Gil McDougald	190
Hank Bauer	188
Phil Rizzuto	183
Elston Howard	171
Pee Wee Reese	169
Roger Maris	152

HITS

Yogi Berra	71
Mickey Mantle	59
Frankie Frisch	58
Joe DiMaggio	54
Pee Wee Reese	46
Hank Bauer	46
Phil Rizzuto	45
Gil McDougald	45
Lou Gehrig	43
Eddie Collins	42
Babe Ruth	42
Elston Howard	42

BATTING AVERAGE

Bobby Brown	.439
Paul Molitor	.418
Pepper Martin	.418
Hal McRae	.400
Lou Brock	.391
Marquis Grissom	.390
Thurman Munson	.373
George Brett	.373
Pat Borders	.372
Hank Aaron	.364

HOME RUNS

Mickey Mantle	18
Babe Ruth	15
Yogi Berra	12
Duke Snider	11
Reggie Jackson	10
Lou Gehrig	10
Frank Robinson	8
Bill Skowron	8
Joe DiMaggio	8
Goose Goslin	7
Hank Bauer	7
Gil McDougald	7

RUNS BATTED IN

Mickey Mantle	40
Yogi Berra	39
Lou Gehrig	35
Babe Ruth	33
Joe DiMaggio	30
Bill Skowron	29
Duke Snider	26
Reggie Jackson	24
Bill Dickey	24
Hank Bauer	24
Gil McDougald	24

RUNS

Mickey Mantle	42
Yogi Berra	41
Babe Ruth	37
Lou Gehrig	30
Joe DiMaggio	27
Derek Jeter	27
Roger Maris	26
Elston Howard	25
Gil McDougald	23
Jackie Robinson	22

STOLEN BASES

Lou Brock	14
Eddie Collins	14
Frank Chance	10
Davey Lopes	10
Phil Rizzuto	10
Honus Wagner	9
Frankie Frisch	9
Johnny Evers	8
Kenny Lofton	8
Roberto Alomar	7
Joe Tinker	7
Pepper Martin	7
Joe Morgan	7
Rickey Henderson	7

Career Batting Leaders *(Cont.)*

TOTAL BASES

Mickey Mantle	123
Yogi Berra	117
Babe Ruth	96
Lou Gehrig	87
Joe DiMaggio	84
Duke Snider	79
Hank Bauer	75
Reggie Jackson	74
Frankie Frisch	74
Gil McDougald	72

SLUGGING AVERAGE

Reggie Jackson	.755
Babe Ruth	.744
Lou Gehrig	.731
Bobby Brown	.707
Lenny Dykstra	.700
Al Simmons	.658
Lou Brock	.655
Pepper Martin	.636
Paul Molitor	.636
Joe Harris	.625

STRIKEOUTS

Mickey Mantle	54
Elston Howard	37
Duke Snider	33
Derek Jeter	33
Babe Ruth	30
David Justice	30
Gil McDougald	29
Bill Skowron	26
Bernie Williams	26
Hank Bauer	25
Reggie Jackson	24
Bob Meusel	24
Jorge Posada	24

Career Pitching Leaders

GAMES

Whitey Ford	22
Mariano Rivera	20
Mike Stanton	19
Jeff Nelson	16
Rollie Fingers	16
Allie Reynolds	15
Bob Turley	15
Clay Carroll	14
Clem Labine	13
Mark Wohlers	13

LOSSES

Whitey Ford	8
Eddie Plank	5
Schoolboy Rowe	5
Joe Bush	5
Rube Marquard	5
Christy Mathewson	5

COMPLETE GAMES

Christy Mathewson	10
Chief Bender	9
Bob Gibson	8
Red Ruffing	7
Whitey Ford	7
George Mullin	6
Eddie Plank	6
Art Nehf	6
Waite Hoyt	6

INNINGS PITCHED

Whitey Ford	146
Christy Mathewson	101⅔
Red Ruffing	85⅔
Chief Bender	85
Waite Hoyt	83¾
Bob Gibson	81
Art Nehf	79
Allie Reynolds	77
Jim Palmer	65
Catfish Hunter	63

SAVES

Mariano Rivera	9
Rollie Fingers	6
Allie Reynolds	4
Johnny Murphy	4
John Wetteland	4
Robb Nen	4

STRIKEOUTS

Whitey Ford	94
Bob Gibson	92
Allie Reynolds	62
Sandy Koufax	61
Red Ruffing	61
Chief Bender	59
George Earnshaw	56
John Smoltz	52
Waite Hoyt	49
Christy Mathewson	48
Roger Clemens	48

*EARNED RUN AVERAGE

Jack Billingham	0.35
Harry Brecheen	0.83
Babe Ruth	0.87
Sherry Smith	0.89
Sandy Koufax	0.95
Hippo Vaughn	1.00
Monte Pearson	1.01
Christy Mathewson	1.06
Mariano Rivera	1.16
Babe Adams	1.29

WINS

Whitey Ford	10
Bob Gibson	7
Red Ruffing	7
Allie Reynolds	7
Lefty Gomez	6
Chief Bender	6
Waite Hoyt	6
Jack Coombs	5
Three Finger Brown	5
Herb Pennock	5
Christy Mathewson	5
Vic Raschi	5
Catfish Hunter	5

SHUTOUTS

Christy Mathewson	4
Three Finger Brown	3
Whitey Ford	3
Bill Hallahan	2
Lew Burdette	2
Bill Dinneen	2
Sandy Koufax	2
Allie Reynolds	2
Art Nehf	2
Bob Gibson	2

BASES ON BALLS

Whitey Ford	34
Allie Reynolds	32
Art Nehf	32
Jim Palmer	31
Bob Turley	29
Paul Derringer	27
Red Ruffing	27
Don Gullett	26
Burleigh Grimes	26
Vic Raschi	25

*Minimum 25 innings pitched.

Alltime Team Rankings (by championships)

Team	W	L	Appearances	Pct.	Most Recent	Last Championship
New York Yankees	26	13	39	.666	2003	2000
Phil/KC/Oakland Athletics	9	5	14	.643	1990	1989
St. Louis Cardinals	9	6	15	.600	1987	1982
Brooklyn/LA Dodgers	6	12	18	.333	1988	1988
Pittsburgh Pirates	5	2	7	.714	1979	1979
Cincinnati Reds	5	4	9	.556	1990	1990
Boston Red Sox	5	4	9	.556	1986	1918
New York/San Francisco Giants	5	12	17	.294	2002	1954
Detroit Tigers	4	5	9	.444	1984	1984
Washington/Minnesota Twins	3	3	6	.500	1991	1991
St. Louis/Baltimore Orioles	3	4	7	.429	1983	1983
Boston/Milwaukee/Atlanta Braves	3	6	9	.333	1999	1995
Florida Marlins	2	0	2	1.000	2003	2003
Toronto Blue Jays	2	0	2	1.000	1993	1993
New York Mets	2	2	4	.500	2000	1986
Chicago White Sox	2	2	4	.500	1959	1917
Cleveland Indians	2	3	5	.400	1997	1948
Chicago Cubs	2	8	10	.200	1945	1908
Anaheim Angels	1	0	1	1.000	2002	2002
Arizona Diamondbacks	1	0	1	1.000	2001	2001
Kansas City Royals	1	1	2	.500	1985	1985
Philadelphia Phillies	1	4	5	.200	1993	1980
Seattle/Milwaukee Brewers	0	1	1	.000	1982	—
San Diego Padres	0	2	2	.000	1998	—

League Championship Series

National League

1969	New York (E) 3, Atlanta (W) 0
1970	Cincinnati (W) 3, Pittsburgh (E) 0
1971	Pittsburgh (E) 3, San Francisco (W) 1
1972	Cincinnati (W) 3, Pittsburgh (E) 2
1973	New York (E) 3, Cincinnati (W) 2
1974	Los Angeles (W) 3, Pittsburgh (E) 1
1975	Cincinnati (W) 3, Pittsburgh (E) 0
1976	Cincinnati (W) 3, Philadelphia (E) 0
1977	Los Angeles (W) 3, Philadelphia (E) 1
1978	Los Angeles (W) 3, Philadelphia (E) 1
1979	Pittsburgh (E) 3, Cincinnati (W) 0
1980	Philadelphia (E) 3, Houston (W) 2
1981	Los Angeles (W) 3, Montreal (E) 2
1982	St. Louis (E) 3, Atlanta (W) 0
1983	Philadelphia (E) 3, Los Angeles (W) 1
1984	San Diego (W) 3, Chicago (E) 2
1985	St. Louis (E) 4, Los Angeles (W) 2
1986	New York (E) 4, Houston (W) 2
1987	St. Louis (E) 4, San Francisco (W) 3
1988	Los Angeles (W) 4, New York (E) 3
1989	San Francisco (W) 4, Chicago (E) 1
1990	Cincinnati (W) 4, Pittsburgh (E) 2
1991	Atlanta (W) 4, Pittsburgh (E) 3
1992	Atlanta (W) 4, Pitsburgh (E) 3
1993	Philadelphia (E) 4, Atlanta (W) 2
1994	Playoffs canceled due to players' strike.
1995	Atlanta (E) 4, Cincinnati (C) 0
1996	Atlanta (E) 4, St. Louis (C) 3
1997	Florida (wc) 4, Atlanta (E) 2
1998	San Diego (W) 4, Atlanta (E) 2
1999	Atlanta (E) 4, New York (wc) 2
2000	New York (wc) 4, St. Louis (C) 1
2001	Arizona (W) 4, Atlanta (E) 2
2002	San Francisco (wc) 4, St. Louis (C) 1
2003	Florida Marlins (wc) 4, Chicago (C) 3

American League

1969	Baltimore (E) 3, Minnesota (W) 0
1970	Baltimore (E) 3, Minnesota (W) 0
1971	Baltimore (E) 3, Oakland (W) 0
1972	Oakland (W) 3, Detroit (E) 2
1973	Oakland (W) 3, Baltimore (E) 2
1974	Oakland (W) 3, Baltimore (E) 1
1975	Boston (E) 3, Oakland (W) 0
1976	New York (E) 3, Kansas City (W) 2
1977	New York (E) 3, Kansas City (W) 2
1978	New York (E) 3, Kansas City (W) 1
1979	Baltimore (E) 3, California (W) 1
1980	Kansas City (W) 3, New York (E) 0
1981	New York (E) 3, Oakland (W) 0
1982	Milwaukee (E) 3, California (W) 2
1983	Baltimore (E) 3, Chicago (W) 1
1984	Detroit (E) 3, Kansas City (W) 0
1985	Kansas City (W) 4, Toronto (E) 3
1986	Boston (E) 4, California (W) 3
1987	Minnesota (W) 4, Detroit (E) 1
1988	Oakland (W) 4, Boston (E) 0
1989	Oakland (W) 4, Toronto (E) 1
1990	Oakland (W) 4, Boston (E) 0
1991	Minnesota (W) 4, Toronto (E) 1
1992	Toronto (E) 4, Oakland (W) 2
1993	Toronto (E) 4, Chicago (W) 2
1994	Playoffs canceled due to players' strike.
1995	Cleveland (C) 4, Seattle (W) 2
1996	New York (E) 4, Baltimore (wc) 1
1997	Cleveland (C) 4, Baltimore (E) 2
1998	New York (E) 4, Cleveland (C) 2
1999	New York (E) 4, Boston (wc) 1
2000	New York (E) 4, Seattle (wc) 2
2001	New York (E) 4, Seattle (W) 1
2002	Anaheim (wc) 4, Minnesota (C) 1
2003	New York (E) 4, Boston 3

NLCS Most Valuable Player

1977........Dusty Baker, LA	1986........Mike Scott, Hou	1995........Mike Devereaux, Atl
1978........Steve Garvey, LA	1987........Jeffrey Leonard, SF	1996........Javier Lopez, Atl
1979........Willie Stargell, Pitt	1988........Orel Hershiser, LA	1997........Livan Hernandez, Fla
1980........Manny Trillo, Phil	1989........Will Clark, SF	1998........Sterling Hitchcock, SD
1981........Burt Hooton, LA	1990........R. Myers/R. Dibble, Cin	1999........Eddie Perez, Atl
1982........Darrell Porter, StL	1991........Steve Avery, Atl	2000........Mike Hampton, NY
1983........Gary Matthews, Phil	1992........John Smoltz, Atl	2001........Craig Counsell, Ariz
1984........Steve Garvey, SD	1993........Curt Schilling, Phil	2002........Benito Santiago, SF
1985........Ozzie Smith, StL	1994........Playoffs canceled	2003........Ivan Rodriguez, Fla

ALCS Most Valuable Player

1980........Frank White, KC	1988........Dennis Eckersley, Oak	1996........Bernie Williams, NY
1981........Graig Nettles, NY	1989........Rickey Henderson, Oak	1997........Marquis Grissom, Clev
1982........Fred Lynn, Calif	1990........Dave Stewart, Oak	1998........David Wells, NY
1983........Mike Boddicker, Balt	1991........Kirby Puckett, Minn	1999........Orlando Hernandez, NY
1984........Kirk Gibson, Det	1992........Roberto Alomar, Tor	2000........David Justice, NY
1985........George Brett, KC	1993........Dave Stewart, Tor	2001........Andy Pettitte, NY
1986........Marty Barrett, Bos	1994........Playoffs canceled	2002........Adam Kennedy, Ana
1987........Gary Gaetti, Minn	1995........Orel Hershiser, Clev	2003........Mariano Rivera, NY

Divisional Playoffs

National League

1995 ....Atlanta (E) 3, Colorado (wc) 1
Cincinnati (C) 3, Los Angeles (W) 0
1996 ....St. Louis (C) 3, San Diego (W) 0
Atlanta (E) 3, Los Angeles (wc) 0
1997 ....Atlanta (E) 3, Houston (C) 0
Florida (wc) 3, San Francisco (W) 0
1998 ....San Diego (W) 3, Houston (C) 1
Atlanta (E) 3, Chicago (wc) 0
1999 ....Atlanta (E) 3, Houston (C) 1
New York (wc) 3, Arizona (W) 1
2000 ....St. Louis (C) 3, Atlanta (E) 0
New York (wc) 3, San Francisco (W) 1
2001 ....Atlanta (E) 3, Houston (C) 0
Arizona (W) 3, St. Louis (wc) 2
2002 ....St. Louis (C) 3, Arizona (W) 0
San Francisco (wc) 3, Atlanta (E) 2
2003 ....Chicago (C) 3, Atlanta (E) 2
Florida (wc) 3, San Francisco (W) 1

American League

1995 ....Cleveland (C) 3, Boston (E) 0
Seattle (W) 3, New York (wc) 2
1996 ....Baltimore (wc) 3, Cleveland (C) 1
New York (E) 3, Texas (W) 1
1997 ....Baltimore (E) 3, Seattle (W) 1
Cleveland (C) 3, New York (wc) 2
1998 ....New York (E) 3, Texas (W) 0
Cleveland (C) 3, Boston (wc) 1
1999 ....New York (E) 3, Texas (W) 1
Boston (wc) 3, Cleveland (C) 2
2000 ....New York (E) 3, Oakland (W) 2
Seattle (wc) 3, Chicago (C) 0
2001 ....Seattle (W) 3, Cleveland (wc) 2
New York (E) 3, Oakland (wc) 2
2002 ....Minnesota (C) 3, Oakland (W) 2
Anaheim (wc) 3, New York (E) 1
2003 ....New York (E) 3, Minnesota (C) 1
Boston (wc) 3, Oakland (W) 2

The All-Star Game

Results

Date	Winner	Score	Site	Date	Winner	Score	Site
7-6-33	American	4–2	Comiskey Park, Chi	7-14-53	National	5–1	Crosley Field, Cin
7-10-34	American	9–7	Polo Grounds, NY	7-13-54	American	11–9	Municipal Stadium, Clev
7-8-35	American	4–1	Municipal Stadium, Clev	7-12-55	National	6–5	County Stadium, Mil
7-7-36	National	4–3	Braves Field, Bos	7-10-56	National	7–3	Griffith Stadium, Wash
7-7-37	American	8–3	Griffith Stadium, Wash	7-9-57	American	6–5	Busch Stadium, StL
7-6-38	National	4–1	Crosley Field, Cin	7-8-58	American	4–3	Memorial Stadium, Balt
7-11-39	American	3–1	Yankee Stadium, NY	7-7-59	National	5–4	Forbes Field, Pitt
7-10-40	National	4–0	Sportsman's Park, StL	8-3-59	American	5–3	Memorial Coliseum, LA
7-8-41	American	7–5	Briggs Stadium, Det	7-11-60	National	5–3	Municipal Stadium, KC
7-6-42	American	3–1	Polo Grounds, NY	7-13-60	National	6–0	Yankee Stadium, NY
7-13-43	American	5–3	Shibe Park, Phil	7-11-61	National	5–4	Candlestick Park, SF
7-11-44	National	7–1	Forbes Field, Pitt	7-31-61	Tie*	1–1	Fenway Park, Bos
1945	No game due to wartime travel restrictions.			7-10-62	National	3–1	D.C. Stadium, Wash
7-9-46	American	12–0	Fenway Park, Bos	7-30-62	American	9–4	Wrigley Field, Chi
7-8-47	American	2–1	Wrigley Field, Chi	7-9-63	National	5–3	Municipal Stadium, Clev
7-13-48	American	5–2	Sportsman's Park, StL	7-7-64	National	7–4	Shea Stadium, NY
7-12-49	American	11–7	Ebbets Field, Bklyn	7-13-65	National	6–5	Metro. Stadium, Minn
7-11-50	National	4–3	Comiskey Park, Chi	7-12-66	National	2–1	Busch Stadium, StL
7-10-51	National	8–3	Briggs Stadium, Det	7-11-67	National	2–1	Anaheim Stadium, Cal
7-8-52	National	3–2	Shibe Park, Phil	7-9-68	National	1–0	Astrodome, Hou

*Game called because of rain after nine innings.

Results (Cont.)

Date	Winner	Score	Site	Date	Winner	Score	Site
7-23-69	National	9–3	R.F.K. Stadium, Wash.	7-12-88	American	2–1	Riverfront Stadium, Cin
7-14-70	National	5–4	Riverfront Stadium, Cin	7-11-89	American	5–3	Anaheim Stadium, Cal
7-13-71	American	6–4	Tiger Stadium, Det	7-10-90	American	2–0	Wrigley Field, Chi
7-25-72	National	4–3	Atlanta Stadium, Atl	7-9-91	American	4–2	SkyDome, Tor
7-24-73	National	7–1	Royals Stadium, KC	7-14-92	American	13–6	Jack Murphy Stadium, SD
7-23-74	National	7–2	Three Rivers Stadium, Pitt	7-13-93	American	9–3	Camden Yards, Balt
7-15-75	National	6–3	County Stadium, Mil	7-12-94	National	8–7	Three Rivers Stadium, Pitt
7-13-76	National	7–1	Veterans Stadium, Phil	7-11-95	National	3–2	The Ballpark in Arlington, Tex
7-19-77	National	7–5	Yankee Stadium, NY				
7-11-78	National	7–3	Jack Murphy Stadium, SD	7-9-96	National	6–0	Veterans Stadium, Phil
7-17-79	National	7–6	Kingdome, Sea	7-8-97	American	3–1	Jacobs Field, Clev
7-8-80	National	4–2	Dodger Stadium, LA	7-7-98	American	13–8	Coors Field, Col
8-9-81	National	5–4	Municipal Stadium, Clev	7-13-99	American	4–1	Fenway Park, Bos
7-13-82	National	4–1	Olympic Stadium, Mtl	7-11-00	American	6–3	Turner Field, Atl
7-6-83	American	13–3	Comiskey Park, Chi	7-10-01	American	4–1	Safeco Field, Sea
7-10-84	National	3–1	Candlestick Park, SF	7-9-02	Tie (11 inn)	7–7	Miller Park, Milwaukee
7-16-85	National	6–1	Metrodome, Minn	7-15-03	American	7–6	Comiskey Park, Chicago
7-15-86	American	3–2	Astrodome, Hou				
7-14-87	National	2–0	Oakland Coliseum, Oak				

Most Valuable Players

1962	Maury Wills, LA	NL	1976	George Foster, Cin	NL	1992	Ken Griffey Jr., Sea	AL
	Leon Wagner, LA	AL	1977	Don Sutton, LA	NL	1993	Kirby Puckett, Minn	AL
1963	Willie Mays, SF	NL	1978	Steve Garvey, LA	NL	1994	Fred McGriff, Atl	NL
1964	Johnny Callison, Phil	NL	1979	Dave Parker, Pitt	NL	1995	Jeff Conine, Fla	NL
1965	Juan Marichal, SF	NL	1980	Ken Griffey, Cin	NL	1996	Mike Piazza, LA	NL
1966	Brooks Robinson, Balt	AL	1981	Gary Carter, Mtl	NL	1997	Sandy Alomar, Clev	AL
1967	Tony Perez, Cin	NL	1982	Dave Concepcion, Cin	NL	1998	Roberto Alomar, Balt	AL
1968	Willie Mays, SF	NL	1983	Fred Lynn, Calif	AL	1999	Pedro Martinez, Bos	AL
1969	Willie McCovey, SF	NL	1984	Gary Carter, Mtl	NL	2000	Derek Jeter, NY	AL
1970	Carl Yastrzemski, Bos	AL	1985	LaMarr Hoyt, SD	NL	2001	Cal Ripken Jr., Balt	AL
1971	Frank Robinson, Balt	AL	1986	Roger Clemens, Bos	AL	2002	None selected	
1972	Joe Morgan, Cin	NL	1987	Tim Raines, Mtl	NL	2003	Garret Anderson, Ana	AL
1973	Bobby Bonds, SF	NL	1988	Terry Steinbach, Oak	AL			
1974	Steve Garvey, LA	NL	1989	Bo Jackson, KC	AL			
1975	Bill Madlock, Chi	NL	1990	Julio Franco, Tex	AL			
	Jon Matlack, NY	NL	1991	Cal Ripken Jr., Balt	AL			

The Regular Season

Most Valuable Players

NATIONAL LEAGUE

Year	Name and Team	Position	Noteworthy
1911	Wildfire Schulte, Chi	Outfield	21 HR†, 121 RBI†, .300
1912	*Larry Doyle, NY	Second base	10 HR, 90 RBI, .330
1913	Jake Daubert, Bklyn	First base	52 RBI, .350†
1914	*Johnny Evers, Bos	Second base	FA .976†, .279
1915–23	No selection		
1924	Dazzy Vance, Bklyn	Pitcher	28†–6, 2.16 ERA†, 262 K†
1925	Rogers Hornsby, StL	Second base, Manager	39 HR†, 143 RBI†, .403†
1926	*Bob O'Farrell, StL	Catcher	7 HR, 68 RBI; .293
1927	*Paul Waner, Pitt	Outfield	237 hits†, 131 RBI†, .380†
1928	*Jim Bottomley, StL	First base	31 HR†, 136 RBI†, .325
1929	*Rogers Hornsby, Chi	Second base	39 HR, 149 RBI, 156 runs†, .380
1930	No selection		
1931	*Frankie Frisch, StL	Second base	4 HR, 82 RBI, 28 SB†, .311
1932	Chuck Klein, Phil	Outfield	38 HR†, 137 RBI, 226 hits†, .348
1933	*Carl Hubbell, NY	Pitcher	23†–12, 1.66 ERA†, 10 SO†
1934	*Dizzy Dean, StL	Pitcher	30†–7, 2.66 ERA, 195 K†
1935	*Gabby Hartnett, Chi	Catcher	13 HR, 91 RBI, .344
1936	*Carl Hubbell, NY	Pitcher	26†–6, 2.31 ERA†
1937	Joe Medwick, StL	Outfield	31 HR‡, 154 RBI†, 111 runs†, .374†
1938	Ernie Lombardi, Cin	Catcher	19 HR, 95 RBI, .342†
1939	*Bucky Walters, Cin	Pitcher	27†–11, 2.29 ERA†, 137 K‡
1940	*Frank McCormick, Cin	First base	19 HR, 127 RBI, 191 hits†, .309
1941	*Dolph Camilli, Bklyn	First base	34 HR†, 120 RBI†, .285

*Played for pennant or, after 1968, division winner. †Led league. ‡Tied for league lead.

Most Valuable Players *(Cont.)*
NATIONAL LEAGUE *(Cont.)*

Year	Name and Team	Position	Noteworthy
1942	*Mort Cooper, StL	Pitcher	22†–7, 1.78 ERA†, 10 SO†
1943	*Stan Musial, StL	Outfield	13 HR, 81 RBI, 220 hits†, .357†
1944	*Marty Marion, StL	Shortstop	FA .972†, 63 RBI
1945	*Phil Cavarretta, Chi	First base	6 HR, 97 RBI, .355†
1946	*Stan Musial, StL	First base, Outfield	103 RBI, 124 runs†, 228 hits†, .365†
1947	Bob Elliott, Bos	Third base	22 HR, 113 RBI, .317
1948	Stan Musial, StL	Outfield	39 HR, 131 RBI†, .376†
1949	*Jackie Robinson, Bklyn	Second base	16 HR, 124 RBI, 37 SB†, .342†
1950	*Jim Konstanty, Phil	Pitcher	16–7, 22 saves†, 2.66 ERA
1951	Roy Campanella, Bklyn	Catcher	33 HR, 108 RBI, .325
1952	Hank Sauer, Chi	Outfield	37 HR‡, 121 RBI†, .270
1953	*Roy Campanella, Bklyn	Catcher	41 HR, 142 RBI†, .312
1954	*Willie Mays, NY	Outfield	41 HR, 110 RBI, 13 3B†, .345†
1955	*Roy Campanella, Bklyn	Catcher	32 HR, 107 RBI, .318
1956	*Don Newcombe, Bklyn	Pitcher	27†–7, 3.06 ERA
1957	*Hank Aaron, Mil	Outfield	44 HR†, 132 RBI†, .322
1958	Ernie Banks, Chi	Shortstop	47 HR†, 129 RBI†, .313
1959	Ernie Banks, Chi	Shortstop	45 HR, 143 RBI†, .304
1960	Dick Groat, Pitt	Shortstop	2 HR, 50 RBI, .325†
1961	*Frank Robinson, Cin	Outfield	37 HR, 124 RBI, .323
1962	Maury Wills, LA	Shortstop	104 SB†, 208 hits, .299, GG
1963	*Sandy Koufax, LA	Pitcher	25†–5, 1.88 ERA†, 306 K†
1964	*Ken Boyer, StL	Third Base	24 HR, 119 RBI†, .295
1965	Willie Mays, SF	Outfield	52 HR†, 112 RBI, .317, GG
1966	Roberto Clemente, Pitt	Outfield	29 HR, 119 RBI, 202 hits, .317, GG
1967	*Orlando Cepeda, StL	First base	25 HR, 111 RBI†, .325
1968	*Bob Gibson, StL	Pitcher	22–9, 1.12 ERA†, 268 K†, 13 SO†, GG
1969	Willie McCovey, SF	First base	45 HR†, 126 RBI†, .320
1970	*Johnny Bench, Cin	Catcher	45 HR†, 148 RBI†, .293, GG
1971	Joe Torre, StL	Third base	24 HR, 137 RBI†, .363†
1972	*Johnny Bench, Cin	Catcher	40 HR†, 125 RBI†, .270, GG
1973	Pete Rose, Cin	Outfield	5 HR, 64 RBI, .338†, 230 hits†
1974	*Steve Garvey, LA	First base	21 HR, 111 RBI, 200 hits, .312, GG
1975	*Joe Morgan, Cin	Second base	17 HR, 94 RBI, 67 SB, .327, GG
1976	*Joe Morgan, Cin	Second base	27 HR, 111 RBI, 60 SB, .320, GG
1977	George Foster, Cin	Outfield	52 HR†, 149 RBI†, .320
1978	Dave Parker, Pitt	Outfield	30 HR, 117 RBI, .334†, GG
1979	Keith Hernandez, StL	First base	11 HR, 105 RBI, 210 hits, .344†, GG
	*Willie Stargell, Pitt	First base	32 HR, 82 RBI, .281
1980	*Mike Schmidt, Phil	Third base	48 HR†, 121 RBI†, .286, GG
1981	Mike Schmidt, Phil	Third base	31 HR†, 91 RBI†, 78 runs†, .316, GG
1982	*Dale Murphy, Atl	Outfield	36 HR, 109 RBI‡, .281, GG
1983	Dale Murphy, Atl	Outfield	36 HR, 121 RBI†, .302, GG
1984	*Ryne Sandberg, Chi	Second base	19 HR, 84 RBI, 114 runs†, .314, GG
1985	*Willie McGee, StL	Outfield	10 HR, 82 RBI, 18 3B†, .353†, GG
1986	Mike Schmidt, Phil	Third base	37 HR†, 119 RBI†, .290, GG
1987	Andre Dawson, Chi	Outfield	49 HR†, 137 RBI†, .287, GG
1988	*Kirk Gibson, LA	Outfield	25 HR, 76 RBI, 106 runs, .290
1989	*Kevin Mitchell, SF	Outfield	47 HR†, 125 RBI†, .291
1990	*Barry Bonds, Pitt	Outfield	33 HR, 114 RBI, .301
1991	*Terry Pendleton, Atl	Third base	23 HR, 86 RBI, .319†
1992	Barry Bonds, Pitt	Outfield	34 HR, 103 RBI, .311
1993	Barry Bonds, SF	Outfield	46 HR†, 123 RBI†, .336
1994	Jeff Bagwell, Hou	First base	39 HR, 116 RBI†, .368
1995	*Barry Larkin, Cin	Shortstop	15 HR, 66 RBI, 51 SB, .319
1996	*Ken Caminiti, SD	Third base	40 HR, 130 RBI, .326
1997	Larry Walker, Col	Outfield	49 HR†, 130 RBI, .452 OBA†, .366, GG
1998	Sammy Sosa, Chi	Outfield	66 HR, 158 RBI†, 134 runs†, 416 TB†, .308
1999	*Chipper Jones, Atl	Third Base	45 HR, 110 RBI, 116 runs, .319
2000	*Jeff Kent, SF	Second Base	33 HR, 125 RBI, 114 runs, .334
2001	Barry Bonds, SF	Outfield	73 HR†, 137 RBI, 177 BB†, .328, .863 SLG†
2002	Barry Bonds, SF	Outfield	46 HR, 110 RBI, .582 OBP, 198 BB†, .370

*Played for pennant or, after 1968, division winner. †Led league. ‡Tied for league lead.

Most Valuable Players *(Cont.)*

AMERICAN LEAGUE

Year	Name and Team	Position	Noteworthy
1911	Ty Cobb, Det	Outfield	8 HR, 144 RBI†, 24 3B†, .420†
1912	*Tris Speaker, Bos	Outfield	10 HR‡, 98 RBI, 53 2B†, .383
1913	Walter Johnson, Wash	Pitcher	36†–7, 1.09 ERA†, 11 SO†, 243 K†
1914	*Eddie Collins, Phil	Second base	2 HR, 85 RBI, 122 runs†, .344
1915–21	No selection		
1922	George Sisler, StL	First base	8 HR, 105 RBI, 246 hits†, .420†
1923	*Babe Ruth, NY	Outfield	41 HR†, 131 RBI†, .393
1924	*Walter Johnson, Wash	Pitcher	23†–7, 2.72 ERA†, 158 K†
1925	*Roger Peckinpaugh, Wash	Shortstop	4 HR, 64 RBI, .294
1926	George Burns, Clev	First base	114 RBI, 216 hits‡, 64 2B†, .358
1927	*Lou Gehrig, NY	First base	47 HR, 175 RBI†, 52 2B†, .373
1928	Mickey Cochrane, Phil	Catcher	10 HR, 57 RBI, .293
1929	No selection		
1930	No selection		
1931	*Lefty Grove, Phil	Pitcher	31†–4, 2.06 ERA†, 175 K†
1932	Jimmie Foxx, Phil	First base	58 HR†, 169 RBI†, 151 runs†, .364
1933	Jimmie Foxx, Phil	First base	48 HR†, 163 RBI†, .356†
1934	*Mickey Cochrane, Det	Catcher	2 HR, 76 RBI, .320
1935	*Hank Greenberg, Det	First base	36 HR‡, 170 RBI†, 203 hits, .328
1936	*Lou Gehrig, NY	First base	49 HR†, 152 RBI, 167 runs†, .354
1937	Charlie Gehringer, Det	Second base	14 HR, 96 RBI, 133 runs, .371†
1938	Jimmie Foxx, Phil	First base	50 HR, 175 RBI†, .349†
1939	*Joe DiMaggio, NY	Outfield	30 HR, 126 RBI, .381†
1940	*Hank Greenberg, Det	Outfield	41 HR†, 150 RBI†, 50 2B†, .340
1941	*Joe DiMaggio, NY	Outfield	30 HR, 125 RBI†, .357
1942	*Joe Gordon, NY	Second base	18 HR, 103 RBI, .322
1943	*Spud Chandler, NY	Pitcher	20†–4, 1.64 ERA†, 5 SO‡
1944	Hal Newhouser, Det	Pitcher	29†–9, 2.22 ERA†, 187 K†
1945	*Hal Newhouser, Det	Pitcher	25†–9, 1.81 ERA†, 8 SO†, 212 K†
1946	*Ted Williams, Bos	Outfield	38 HR, 123 RBI, 142 runs†, .342
1947	*Joe DiMaggio, NY	Outfield	20 HR, 97 RBI, .315
1948	*Lou Boudreau, Clev	Shortstop	18 HR, 106 RBI, .355
1949	Ted Williams, Bos	Outfield	43 HR†, 159 RBI‡, 150 runs†, .343
1950	*Phil Rizzuto, NY	Shortstop	125 runs, 200 hits, .324
1951	*Yogi Berra, NY	Catcher	27 HR, 88 RBI, .294
1952	Bobby Shantz, Phil	Pitcher	24†–7, 2.48 ERA
1953	Al Rosen, Clev	Third base	43 HR†, 145 RBI†, 115 runs†, .336
1954	Yogi Berra, NY	Catcher	22 HR, 125 RBI, .307
1955	*Yogi Berra, NY	Catcher	27 HR, 108 RBI, .272
1956	*Mickey Mantle, NY	Outfield	52 HR†, 130 RBI†, 132 runs†, .353†
1957	*Mickey Mantle, NY	Outfield	34 HR, 94 RBI, 121 runs†, .365
1958	Jackie Jensen, Bos	Outfield	35 HR, 122 RBI†, .286
1959	*Nellie Fox, Chi	Second base	2 HR, 70 RBI, .306, GG
1960	*Roger Maris, NY	Outfield	39 HR, 112 RBI†, .283, GG
1961	*Roger Maris, NY	Outfield	61 HR†, 142 RBI†, .269
1962	*Mickey Mantle, NY	Outfield	30 HR, 89 RBI, .321, GG
1963	*Elston Howard, NY	Catcher	28 HR, 85 RBI, .287, GG
1964	Brooks Robinson, Balt	Third base	28 HR, 118 RBI†, .317, GG
1965	*Zoilo Versalles, Minn	Shortstop	126 runs†, 45 2B‡, 12 3B‡, GG
1966	*Frank Robinson, Balt	Outfield	49 HR†, 122 RBI†, 122 runs†, .316†
1967	*Carl Yastrzemski, Bos	Outfield	44 HR†, 121 RBI†, 112 runs†, .326‡, GG
1968	*Denny McLain, Det	Pitcher	31†–6, 1.96 ERA, 280 K
1969	*Harmon Killebrew, Minn	Third base, First base	49 HR†, 140 RBI†, .276
1970	*Boog Powell, Balt	First base	35 HR, 114 RBI, .297
1971	*Vida Blue, Oak	Pitcher	24–8, 1.82 ERA†, 8 SO†, 301 K
1972	Dick Allen, Chi	First base	37 HR†, 113 RBI†, .308
1973	*Reggie Jackson, Oak	Outfield	32 HR†, 117 RBI†, 99 runs†, .293
1974	Jeff Burroughs, Tex	Outfield	25 HR, 118 RBI†, .301
1975	*Fred Lynn, Bos	Outfield	21 HR, 105 RBI, 103 runs†, .331, GG
1976	*Thurman Munson, NY	Catcher	17 HR, 105 RBI, .302
1977	Rod Carew, Minn	First base	100 RBI, 128 runs†, 239 hits†, .388†
1978	Jim Rice, Bos	Outfield, DH	46 HR†, 139 RBI†, 213 hits‡, .315
1979	*Don Baylor, Calif	Outfield, DH	36 HR, 139 RBI†, 120 runs†, .296
1980	*George Brett, KC	Third base	24 HR, 118 RBI, .390†
1981	*Rollie Fingers, Mil	Pitcher	6–3, 28 saves†, 1.04 ERA

Most Valuable Players *(Cont.)*

AMERICAN LEAGUE *(Cont.)*

Year	Name and Team	Position	Noteworthy
1982	*Robin Yount, Mil	Shortstop	29 HR, 114 RBI, 210 hits†, .331, GG
1983	*Cal Ripken Jr., Balt	Shortstop	27 HR, 102 RBI, 121 runs†, 211 hits†, .318
1984	*Willie Hernandez, Det	Pitcher	9–3, 32 saves, 1.92 ERA
1985	Don Mattingly, NY	First base	35 HR, 145 RBI†, 48 2B†, .324, GG
1986	*Roger Clemens, Bos	Pitcher	24†–4, 2.48 ERA†, 238 K
1987	George Bell, Tor	Outfield	47 HR, 134 RBI†, .308
1988	*Jose Canseco, Oak	Outfield	42 HR†, 124 RBI†, 40 SB, .307
1989	Robin Yount, Mil	Outfield	21 HR, 103 RBI, 101 runs, .318
1990	*Rickey Henderson, Oak	Outfield	28 HR, 119 runs†, 65 SB†, .325
1991	Cal Ripken Jr., Balt	Shortstop	34 HR, 114 RBI, .323
1992	Dennis Eckersley, Oak	Pitcher	7–1, 1.91 ERA, 51 saves
1993	Frank Thomas, Chi	First base	41 HR, 128 RBI, .317
1994	Frank Thomas, Chi	First base	38 HR, 101 RBI, .353
1995	*Mo Vaughn, Bos	First base	39 HR, 126 RBI, .300
1996	*Juan Gonzalez, Tex	Outfield	47 HR, 144 RBI, .314
1997	*Ken Griffey Jr., Sea	Outfield	56 HR†, 125 runs†, 393 TB†, 147 RBI†, .304
1998	*Juan Gonzalez, Tex	Outfield	45 HR, 157 RBI†, 50 2B†, .318
1999	*Ivan Rodriguez, Tex	Catcher	35 HR, 113 RBI, 116 runs, .332, GG
2000	*Jason Giambi, Oak	First Base	43 HR, 137 RBI, .333
2001	*Ichiro Suzuki, Sea	Outfield	.350†, 242 H†, 127 R, 56 SB†
2002	*Miguel Tejada, Oak	Shortstop	34 HR, 131 RBI, .308

*Played for pennant or, after 1968, division winner. †Led league. ‡Tied for league lead.

Notes: 2B=doubles; 3B=triples; FA=fielding average; GG=won Gold Glove, award begun in 1957; K=strikeouts; SO=shutouts; SB=stolen bases; TB=total bases.

Rookies of the Year

NATIONAL LEAGUE

Year	Name and Team
1947*	Jackie Robinson, Bklyn (1B)
1948*	Alvin Dark, Bos (SS)
1949	Don Newcombe, Bklyn (P)
1950	Sam Jethroe, Bos (OF)
1951	Willie Mays, NY (OF)
1952	Joe Black, Bklyn (P)
1953	Junior Gilliam, Bklyn (2B)
1954	Wally Moon, StL (OF)
1955	Bill Virdon, StL (OF)
1956	Frank Robinson, Cin (OF)
1957	Jack Sanford, Phil (P)
1958	Orlando Cepeda, SF (1B)
1959	Willie McCovey, SF (1B)
1960	Frank Howard, LA (OF)
1961	Billy Williams, Chi (OF)
1962	Ken Hubbs, Chi (2B)
1963	Pete Rose, Cin (2B)
1964	Dick Allen, Phil (3B)
1965	Jim Lefebvre, LA (2B)
1966	Tommy Helms, Cin (2B)
1967	Tom Seaver, NY (P)
1968	Johnny Bench, Cin (C)
1969	Ted Sizemore, LA (2B)
1970	Carl Morton, Mtl(P)
1971	Earl Williams, Atl (C)
1972	Jon Matlack, NY (P)
1973	Gary Matthews, SF (OF)
1974	Bake McBride, StL (OF)
1975	John Montefusco, SF (P)
1976	Pat Zachry, Cin (P)
	Butch Metzger, SD (P)
1977	Andre Dawson, Mtl (OF)
1978	Bob Horner, Atl (3B)
1979	Rick Sutcliffe, LA (P)
1980	Steve Howe, LA (P)
1981	Fernando Valenzuela, LA (P)
1982	Steve Sax, LA (2B)
1983	Darryl Strawberry, NY (OF)

*Just one selection for both leagues.

AMERICAN LEAGUE

Year	Name and Team
1949	Roy Sievers, StL (OF)
1950	Walt Dropo, Bos (1B)
1951	Gil McDougald, NY (3B)
1952	Harry Byrd, Phil (P)
1953	Harvey Kuenn, Det (SS)
1954	Bob Grim, NY (P)
1955	Herb Score, Clev (P)
1956	Luis Aparicio, Chi (SS)
1957	Tony Kubek, NY (OF, SS)
1958	Albie Pearson, Wash (OF)
1959	Bob Allison, Wash (OF)
1960	Ron Hansen, Balt (SS)
1961	Don Schwall, Bos (P)
1962	Tom Tresh, NY (SS)
1963	Gary Peters, Chi (P)
1964	Tony Oliva, Minn (OF)
1965	Curt Blefary, Balt (OF)
1966	Tommie Agee, Chi (OF)
1967	Rod Carew, Minn (2B)
1968	Stan Bahnsen, NY (P)
1969	Lou Piniella, KC (OF)
1970	Thurman Munson, NY (C)
1971	Chris Chambliss, Clev (1B)
1972	Carlton Fisk, Bos (C)
1973	Al Bumbry, Balt (OF)
1974	Mike Hargrove, Tex (1B)
1975	Fred Lynn, Bos (OF)
1976	Mark Fidrych, Det (P)
1977	Eddie Murray, Balt (DH)
1978	Lou Whitaker, Det (2B)
1979	Alfredo Griffin, Tor (SS)
	John Castino, Minn (3B)
1980	Joe Charboneau, Clev (OF)
1981	Dave Righetti, NY (P)
1982	Cal Ripken Jr., Balt (SS)
1983	Ron Kittle, Chi (OF)
1984	Alvin Davis, Sea (1B)

Rookies of the Year *(Cont.)*

NATIONAL LEAGUE *(Cont.)*

1984	Dwight Gooden, NY (P)
1985	Vince Coleman, StL (OF)
1986	Todd Worrell, StL (P)
1987	Benito Santiago, SD (C)
1988	Chris Sabo, Cin (3B)
1989	Jerome Walton, Chi (OF)
1990	Dave Justice, Atl (OF)
1991	Jeff Bagwell, Hou (3B)
1992	Eric Karros, LA (1B)
1993	Mike Piazza, LA (C)
1994	Raul Mondesi, LA (OF)
1995	Hideo Nomo, LA (P)
1996	Todd Hollandsworth, LA (OF)
1997	Scott Rolen, Phil (3B)
1998	Kerry Wood, Chi (P)
1999	Scott Williamson, Cin (P)
2000	Rafael Furcal, Atl (SS)
2001	Albert Pujols, StL (OF)
2002	Jason Jennings, Col (P)

AMERICAN LEAGUE *(Cont.)*

1985	Ozzie Guillen, Chi (SS)
1986	Jose Canseco, Oak (OF)
1987	Mark McGwire, Oak (1B)
1988	Walt Weiss, Oak (SS)
1989	Gregg Olson, Balt (P)
1990	Sandy Alomar Jr, Clev (C)
1991	Chuck Knoblauch, Minn (2B)
1992	Pat Listach, Mil (SS)
1993	Tim Salmon, Calif (OF)
1994	Bob Hamelin, KC (DH)
1995	Marty Cordova, Minn (OF)
1996	Derek Jeter, NY (SS)
1997	Nomar Garciaparra, Bos (SS)
1998	Ben Grieve, Oak (OF)
1999	Carlos Beltran, KC (OF)
2000	Kazuhiro Sasaki, Sea (P)
2001	Ichiro Suzuki, Sea (OF)
2002	Eric Hinske, Tor (3B)

Cy Young Award

Year	W–L	Sv	ERA	Year	W–L	Sv	ERA
1956....*Don Newcombe, Bklyn (NL)	27–7	0	3.06	1962....Don Drysdale, LA (NL)	25–9	1	2.83
1957....Warren Spahn, Mil (NL)	21–11	3	2.69	1963....*Sandy Koufax, LA (NL)	25–5	0	1.88
1958....Bob Turley, NY (AL)	21–7	1	2.97	1964....Dean Chance, LA (AL)	20–9	4	1.65
1959....Early Wynn, Chi (AL)	22–10	0	3.17	1965....Sandy Koufax, LA (NL)	26–8	2	2.04
1960....Vernon Law, Pitt (NL)	20–9	0	3.08	1966....Sandy Koufax, LA (NL)	27–9	0	1.73
1961....Whitey Ford, NY (AL)	25–4	0	3.21				

NATIONAL LEAGUE

Year	W–L	Sv	ERA
1967.....Mike McCormick, SF	22–10	0	2.85
1968.....*Bob Gibson, StL	22–9	0	1.12
1969.....Tom Seaver, NY	25–7	0	2.21
1970.....Bob Gibson, StL	23–7	0	3.12
1971.....Ferguson Jenkins, Chi	24–13	0	2.77
1972.....Steve Carlton, Phil	27–10	0	1.97
1973.....Tom Seaver, NY	19–10	0	2.08
1974.....Mike Marshall, LA	15–12	21	2.42
1975.....Tom Seaver, NY	22–9	0	2.38
1976.....Randy Jones, SD	22–14	0	2.74
1977.....Steve Carlton, Phil	23–10	0	2.64
1978.....Gaylord Perry, SD	21–6	0	2.72
1979.....Bruce Sutter, Chi	6–6	37	2.23
1980.....Steve Carlton, Phil	24–9	0	2.34
1981.....Fernando Valenzuela, LA	13–7	0	2.48
1982.....Steve Carlton, Phil	23–11	0	3.10
1983.....John Denny, Phil	19–6	0	2.37
1984.....†Rick Sutcliffe, Chi	16–1	0	2.69
1985.....Dwight Gooden, NY	24–4	0	1.53
1986.....Mike Scott, Hou	18–10	0	2.22
1987.....Steve Bedrosian, Phil	5–3	40	2.83
1988.....Orel Hershiser, LA	23–8	1	2.26
1989.....Mark Davis, SD	4–3	44	1.85
1990.....Doug Drabek, Pitt	22–6	0	2.76
1991.....Tom Glavine, Atl	20–11	0	2.55
1992.....Greg Maddux, Chi	20–11	0	2.18
1993.....Greg Maddux, Atl	20–10	0	2.36
1994.....Greg Maddux, Atl	16–6	0	1.56
1995.....Greg Maddux, Atl	19–2	0	1.63
1996.....John Smoltz, Atl	24–8	0	2.94
1997.....Pedro Martinez, Mtl	17–8	0	1.90
1998.....Tom Glavine, Atl	20–6	0	2.47
1999.....Randy Johnson, Ariz	17–9	0	2.48
2000.....Randy Johnson, Ariz	19–7	0	2.64
2001.....Randy Johnson, Ariz	21–6	0	2.49
2002.....Randy Johnson, Ariz	24–5	0	2.32

AMERICAN LEAGUE

Year	W–L	Sv	ERA
1967.....Jim Lonborg, Bos	22–9	0	3.16
1968.....*Denny McLain, Det	31–6	0	1.96
1969.....Denny McLain, Det	24–9	0	2.80
	Mike Cuellar, Balt	23–11	0	2.38
1970.....Jim Perry, Minn	24–12	0	3.03
1971.....*Vida Blue, Oak	24–8	0	1.82
1972.....Gaylord Perry, Clev	24–16	1	1.92
1973.....Jim Palmer, Balt	22–9	1	2.40
1974.....Catfish Hunter, Oak	25–12	0	2.49
1975.....Jim Palmer, Balt	23–11	1	2.09
1976.....Jim Palmer, Balt	22–13	0	2.51
1977.....Sparky Lyle, NY	13–5	26	2.17
1978.....Ron Guidry, NY	25–3	0	1.74
1979.....Mike Flanagan, Balt	23–9	0	3.08
1980.....Steve Stone, Balt	25–7	0	3.23
1981.....*Rollie Fingers, Mil	6–3	28	1.04
1982.....Pete Vuckovich, Mil	18–6	0	3.34
1983.....LaMarr Hoyt, Chi	24–10	0	3.66
1984.....*Willie Hernandez, Det	9–3	32	1.92
1985.....Bret Saberhagen, KC	20–6	0	2.87
1986.....*Roger Clemens, Bos	24–4	0	2.48
1987.....Roger Clemens, Bos	20–9	0	2.97
1988.....Frank Viola, Minn	24–7	0	2.64
1989.....Bret Saberhagen, KC	23–6	0	2.16
1990.....Bob Welch, Oak	27–6	0	2.95
1991.....Roger Clemens, Bos	18–10	0	2.62
1992.....*Dennis Eckersley, Oak	7–1	51	1.91
1993.....Jack McDowell, Chi	22–10	0	3.37
1994.....David Cone, KC	16–4	0	2.94
1995.....Randy Johnson, Sea	18–2	0	2.48
1996.....Pat Hentgen, Tor	20–10	0	3.22
1997.....Roger Clemens, Tor	21–7	0	2.05
1998.....Roger Clemens, Tor	20–6	0	2.65
1999.....Pedro Martinez, Bos	23–4	0	1.55
2000.....Pedro Martinez, Bos	18–6	0	1.74
2001.....Roger Clemens, NY	20–3	0	3.51
2002.....Barry Zito, Oak	23–5	0	2.75

*Won the MVP and Cy Young awards in the same season.

†NL games only. Sutcliffe pitched 15 games with Cleveland before being traded to the Cubs.

Career Individual Batting

GAMES

Pete Rose	3562
Carl Yastrzemski	3308
Hank Aaron	3298
*Rickey Henderson	3081
Ty Cobb	3034
Stan Musial	3026
Eddie Murray	3026
Cal Ripken Jr.	3001
Willie Mays	2992
Dave Winfield	2973
Rusty Staub	2951
Brooks Robinson	2896
Robin Yount	2856
Al Kaline	2834
Harold Baines	2830
Eddie Collins	2826
Reggie Jackson	2820
Frank Robinson	2808
Honus Wagner	2792
Tris Speaker	2789

AT BATS

Pete Rose	14053
Hank Aaron	12364
Carl Yastrzemski	11988
Cal Ripken Jr.	11551
Ty Cobb	11429
Eddie Murray	11336
Robin Yount	11008
Dave Winfield	11003
Stan Musial	10972
*Rickey Henderson	10961
Willie Mays	10881
Paul Molitor	10835
Brooks Robinson	10654
Honus Wagner	10427
George Brett	10349
Lou Brock	10332
Cap Anson	10278
Luis Aparicio	10230
Tris Speaker	10208
Al Kaline	10116

HOME RUNS

Hank Aaron	755
Babe Ruth	714
Willie Mays	660
*Barry Bonds	658
Frank Robinson	586
Mark McGwire	583
Harmon Killebrew	573
Reggie Jackson	563
Mike Schmidt	548
*Sammy Sosa	539
Mickey Mantle	536
Jimmie Foxx	534
*Rafael Palmeiro	528
Ted Williams	521
Willie McCovey	521
Eddie Mathews	512
Ernie Banks	512
Mel Ott	511
Eddie Murray	504
Lou Gehrig	493

* Active in 2003.

HITS

Pete Rose	4256
Ty Cobb	4189
Hank Aaron	3771
Stan Musial	3630
Tris Speaker	3515
Carl Yastrzemski	3419
Cap Anson	3418
Honus Wagner	3415
Paul Molitor	3319
Eddie Collins	3313
Willie Mays	3283
Eddie Murray	3255
Nap Lajoie	3251
Cal Ripken Jr.	3184
George Brett	3154
Paul Waner	3152
Robin Yount	3142
Tony Gwynn	3141
Dave Winfield	3110
*Rickey Henderson	3055

BATTING AVERAGE (5,000 AB)

Ty Cobb	.367
Rogers Hornsby	.358
Ed Delahanty	.346
Tris Speaker	.345
Ted Williams	.344
Billy Hamilton	.344
Dan Brouthers	.342
Jesse Burkett	.342
Babe Ruth	.342
Harry Heilmann	.342
Willie Keeler	.341
Bill Terry	.341
George Sisler	.340
Lou Gehrig	.340
Jesse Burkett	.338
Tony Gwynn	.338
Nap Lajoie	.338
Al Simmons	.334
Paul Waner	.333
Eddie Collins	.333

RUNS

*Rickey Henderson	2295
Ty Cobb	2245
Babe Ruth	2174
Hank Aaron	2174
Pete Rose	2165
Willie Mays	2062
Cap Anson	1996
Stan Musial	1949
*Barry Bonds	1941
Lou Gehrig	1888
Tris Speaker	1881
Mel Ott	1859
Frank Robinson	1829
Eddie Collins	1820
Carl Yastrzemski	1816
Ted Williams	1798
Paul Molitor	1782
Charlie Gehringer	1774
Jimmie Foxx	1751
Honus Wagner	1740

DOUBLES

Tris Speaker	793
Pete Rose	746
Stan Musial	725
Ty Cobb	724
George Brett	665
Nap Lajoie	657
Carl Yastrzemski	646
Honus Wagner	640
Hank Aaron	624
Paul Molitor	605
Paul Waner	604
Cal Ripken Jr.	603
Robin Yount	583
Cap Anson	581
Wade Boggs	578
Charlie Gehringer	574
Eddie Murray	560
Tony Gwynn	543
*Rafael Palmeiro	543
Harry Heilmann	542

TRIPLES

Sam Crawford	312
Ty Cobb	297
Honus Wagner	252
Jake Beckley	244
Roger Connor	233
Tris Speaker	223
Fred Clarke	223
Dan Brouthers	206
Joe Kelley	194
Paul Waner	190
Bid McPhee	189
Eddie Collins	187
Ed Delahanty	185
Sam Rice	184
Jesse Burkett	182
Edd Roush	182
Ed Konetchy	182
Buck Ewing	178
Rabbit Maranville	177
Stan Musial	177

BASES ON BALLS

*Rickey Henderson	2190
*Barry Bonds	2070
Babe Ruth	2062
Ted Williams	2019
Joe Morgan	1865
Carl Yastrzemski	1845
Mickey Mantle	1735
Mel Ott	1708
Eddie Yost	1614
Darrell Evans	1605
Stan Musial	1599
Pete Rose	1566
Harmon Killebrew	1559
Lou Gehrig	1508
Mike Schmidt	1507
Eddie Collins	1503
Willie Mays	1463
Jimmie Foxx	1452
Eddie Mathews	1444
Frank Robinson	1420

Career Individual Batting *(Cont.)*

RUNS BATTED IN		STOLEN BASES		TOTAL BASES	
Hank Aaron	2297	*Rickey Henderson	1406	Hank Aaron	6856
Babe Ruth	2213	Lou Brock	938	Stan Musial	6134
Cap Anson	2076	Billy Hamilton	912	Willie Mays	6066
Lou Gehrig	1995	Ty Cobb	892	Ty Cobb	5854
Stan Musial	1951	Tim Raines	808	Babe Ruth	5793
Ty Cobb	1937	Vince Coleman	752	Pete Rose	5752
Jimmie Foxx	1922	Eddie Collins	744	Carl Yastrzemski	5539
Eddie Murray	1917	Arlie Latham	739	Eddie Murray	5397
Willie Mays	1903	Max Carey	738	Frank Robinson	5373
Mel Ott	1860	Honus Wagner	722	*Barry Bonds	5253
Carl Yastrzemski	1844	Joe Morgan	689	Dave Winfield	5221
Ted Williams	1839	Willie Wilson	668	Cal Ripken Jr.	5168
Dave Winfield	1833	Tom Brown	657	Tris Speaker	5101
Al Simmons	1827	Bert Campaneris	649	Lou Gehrig	5060
Frank Robinson	1812	Otis Nixon	620	George Brett	5044
*Barry Bonds	1742	George Davis	616	Mel Ott	5041
Honus Wagner	1732	Dummy Hoy	594	*Rafael Palmeiro	4983
Reggie Jackson	1702	Maury Wills	586	Jimmie Foxx	4956
Cal Ripken Jr.	1695	George Van Haltren	583	Ted Williams	4884
*Rafael Palmeiro	1687	Ozzie Smith	580	Honus Wagner	4862

SLUGGING AVERAGE (5,000 AB)		ON-BASE PERCENTAGE (5,000 AB)		STRIKEOUTS	
Babe Ruth	.690	Ted Williams	.481	Reggie Jackson	2597
Ted Williams	.634	Babe Ruth	.469	Jose Canseco	1942
Lou Gehrig	.632	Lou Gehrig	.442	*Andres Galarraga	2000
Jimmie Foxx	.609	*Barry Bonds	.433	*Sammy Sosa	1975
Hank Greenberg	.605	*Frank Thomas	.428	Willie Stargell	1936
*Barry Bonds	.602	Jimmie Foxx	.425	Mike Schmidt	1883
*Manny Ramirez	.598	Ty Cobb	.424	Tony Perez	1867
Mark McGwire	.588	Rogers Hornsby	.424	*Fred McGriff	1863
Joe DiMaggio	.579	*Edgar Martinez	.423	Dave Kingman	1816
Rogers Hornsby	.577	Mickey Mantle	.420	Bobby Bonds	1757
*Mike Piazza	.572	Jesse Burkett	.417	Dale Murphy	1748
*Frank Thomas	.568	Tris Speaker	.417	Lou Brock	1730
*Jim Thome	.568	Stan Musial	.416	Mickey Mantle	1710
*Larry Walker	.567	Wade Boggs	.415	Harmon Killebrew	1699
Albert Belle	.564	*Manny Ramirez	.413	Chili Davis	1698
*Juan Gonzalez	.563	*Jeff Bagwell	.411	Dwight Evans	1697
*Ken Griffey Jr.	.562	*Jim Thome	.411	*Rickey Henderson	1694
Johnny Mize	.562	Mel Ott	.410	Dave Winfield	1686
Stan Musial	.559	Mickey Cochrane	.409	Gary Gaetti	1602
Willie Mays	.557	Hank Greenberg	.409	Mark McGwire	1596
Mickey Mantle	.557				

The 30–30 Club (30 HR, 30 SB in single season)

Year		HR	SB	Year		HR	SB
1922	Kenny Williams, StL	39	37	1993	Sammy Sosa, ChiC	33	36
1956	Willie Mays, NYG	36	40	1995	Barry Bonds, SF	33	31
1957	Willie Mays, NYG	35	38	1995	Sammy Sosa, ChiC	36	34
1963	Hank Aaron, Mil	44	31	1996	Barry Bonds, SF	42	40
1969	Bobby Bonds, SF	32	45	1996	Ellis Burks, Col	40	32
1970	Tommy Harper, Mil	31	38	1996	Barry Larkin, Cin	33	36
1973	Bobby Bonds, SF	39	43	1996	Dante Bichette, Col	31	31
1975	Bobby Bonds, NYY	32	30	1997	Larry Walker, Col	49	33
1977	Bobby Bonds, Cal	37	41	1997	Jeff Bagwell, Hou	43	31
1978	Bobby Bonds, Chi/Tex	31	43	1997	Raul Mondesi, LA	30	32
1983	Dale Murphy, Atl	36	30	1997	Barry Bonds, SF	40	37
1987	Joe Carter, Clev	32	31	1998	Alex Rodriguez, Sea	42	46
1987	Eric Davis, Cin	37	50	1998	Shawn Green, Tor	35	35
1987	Darryl Strawberry, NYM	39	36	1999	Jeff Bagwell, Hou	42	30
1987	Howard Johnson, NYM	36	32	1999	Raul Mondesi, LA	33	36
1988	Jose Canseco, Oak	42	40	2000	Preston Wilson, Fla	31	36
1989	Howard Johnson, NYM	36	41	2001	Vladimir Guerrero, Mtl	34	37
1990	Ron Gant, Atl	32	33	2001	Jose Cruz Jr., Tor	34	32
1990	Barry Bonds, Pitt	33	52	2001	Bobby Abreu, Phil	31	36
1991	Ron Gant, Atl	32	34	2002	Alfonso Soriano, NY	39	41
1991	Howard Johnson, NYM	38	30	2002	Vladimir Guerrero, Mtl	39	40
1992	Barry Bonds, Pitt	34	39	2003	Alfonso Soriano, NY	38	35

*Active in 2003.

Career Individual Pitching

GAMES

*Jesse Orosco	1251
Dennis Eckersley	1071
Hoyt Wilhelm	1070
*Dan Plesac	1064
Kent Tekulve	1050
*John Franco	1036
Lee Smith	1022
Goose Gossage	1002
Lindy McDaniel	987
Mike Jackson	960
Rollie Fingers	944
Gene Garber	931
Cy Young	906
Sparky Lyle	899
Jim Kaat	898
*Mike Stanton	885
Paul Assenmacher	884
Jeff Reardon	880
Don McMahon	874
Phil Niekro	864

LOSSES

Cy Young	316
Pud Galvin	308
Nolan Ryan	292
Walter Johnson	279
Phil Niekro	274
Gaylord Perry	265
Don Sutton	256
Jack Powell	254
Eppa Rixey	251
Bert Blyleven	250
Bobby Mathews	248
Robin Roberts	245
Warren Spahn	245
Steve Carlton	244
Early Wynn	244
Jim Kaat	237
Frank Tanana	236
Gus Weyhing	232
Tommy John	231
Bob Friend	230
Ted Lyons	230

EARNED RUN AVERAGE (2,000 IP)

Ed Walsh	1.82
Addie Joss	1.89
Al Spalding	2.04
Three Finger Brown	2.06
John Ward	2.10
Christy Mathewson	2.13
Tommy Bond	2.14
Rube Waddell	2.16
Walter Johnson	2.17
Ed Reulbach	2.28
Will White	2.28
Eddie Plank	2.35
Larry Corcoran	2.36
Eddie Cicotte	2.38
Candy Cummings	2.39
Doc White	2.39
Nap Rucker	2.42
George Bradley	2.43
Jim McCormick	2.43
Chief Bender	2.46

INNINGS PITCHED

Cy Young	7356⅔
Pud Galvin	5941⅓
Walter Johnson	5914⅔
Phil Niekro	5404⅓
Nolan Ryan	5386
Gaylord Perry	5350⅓
Don Sutton	5282⅓
Warren Spahn	5243⅔
Steve Carlton	5217⅓
Grover Alexander	5190
Kid Nichols	5056⅓
Tim Keefe	5047⅓
Bert Blyleven	4970
Bobby Mathews	4956
Mickey Welch	4802
Tom Seaver	4782⅔
Christy Mathewson	4780⅔
Tommy John	4710⅓
Robin Roberts	4688⅔
Early Wynn	4564

WINNING PERCENTAGE**

Al Spalding	.796
Spud Chandler	.717
*Pedro Martinez	.713
Whitey Ford	.690
Dave Foutz	.690
Bob Caruthers	.688
Don Gullett	.686
Lefty Grove	.680
Joe Wood	.671
*Randy Johnson	.669
Vic Raschi	.667
Larry Corcoran	.665
Christy Mathewson	.665
Sam Leever	.660
*Roger Clemens	.660
Sal Maglie	.658
*Andy Pettitte	.656
Dick McBride	.656
Sandy Koufax	.655
Johnny Allen	.654

SHUTOUTS

Walter Johnson	110
Grover Alexander	90
Christy Mathewson	79
Cy Young	76
Eddie Plank	69
Warren Spahn	63
Nolan Ryan	61
Tom Seaver	61
Bert Blyleven	60
Don Sutton	58
Pud Galvin	57
Ed Walsh	57
Bob Gibson	56
Three Finger Brown	55
Steve Carlton	55
Jim Palmer	53
Gaylord Perry	53
Juan Marichal	52
Rube Waddell	50
Vic Willis	50

WINS

Cy Young	511
Walter Johnson	417
Grover Alexander	373
Christy Mathewson	373
Pud Galvin	365
Warren Spahn	363
Kid Nichols	361
Tim Keefe	342
Steve Carlton	329
John Clarkson	328
Eddie Plank	326
Nolan Ryan	324
Don Sutton	324
Phil Niekro	318
Gaylord Perry	314
Tom Seaver	311
*Roger Clemens	310
Charley Radbourn	309
Mickey Welch	307
Lefty Grove	300
Early Wynn	300

SAVES

Lee Smith	478
*John Franco	424
Dennis Eckersley	390
Jeff Reardon	367
*Trevor Hoffman	352
Randy Myers	347
Rollie Fingers	341
John Wetteland	330
*Roberto Hernandez	320
Rick Aguilera	318
*Robb Nen	314
Tom Henke	311
Goose Gossage	310
Jeff Montgomery	304
Doug Jones	303
Bruce Sutter	300
*Rod Beck	286
*Mariano Rivera	283
*Troy Percival	283
Todd Worrell	256

COMPLETE GAMES

Cy Young	749
Pud Galvin	639
Tim Keefe	554
Walter Johnson	531
Kid Nichols	531
Mickey Welch	525
Bobby Mathews	525
Charley Radbourn	489
John Clarkson	485
Tony Mullane	468
Jim McCormick	466
Gus Weyhing	448
Grover Alexander	437
Christy Mathewson	434
Jack Powell	422
Eddie Plank	410
Will White	394
Amos Rusie	392
Vic Willis	388
Tommy Bond	386

* Active in 2003. ** Minumum 100 victories.

Career Individual Pitching (Cont.)

STRIKEOUTS		BASES ON BALLS	
Nolan Ryan	5714	Nolan Ryan	2795
Steve Carlton	4136	Steve Carlton	1833
*Roger Clemens	4099	Phil Niekro	1809
*Randy Johnson	3871	Early Wynn	1775
Bert Blyleven	3701	Bob Feller	1764
Tom Seaver	3640	Bobo Newsom	1732
Don Sutton	3574	Amos Rusie	1704
Gaylord Perry	3534	Charlie Hough	1665
Walter Johnson	3509	Gus Weyhing	1566
Phil Niekro	3342	Red Ruffing	1541
Ferguson Jenkins	3192	Bump Hadley	1442
Bob Gibson	3117	Warren Spahn	1434
Jim Bunning	2855	Earl Whitehill	1431
Mickey Lolich	2832	Tony Mullane	1408
Cy Young	2803	Sad Sam Jones	1396
Frank Tanana	2773	Jack Morris	1390
*Greg Maddux	2765	Tom Seaver	1390
*David Cone	2668	Gaylord Perry	1379
*Chuck Finley	2610	*Roger Clemens	1379
Warren Spahn	2583	Bobby Witt	1375

Alltime Winningest Managers

CAREER

	W	L	Pct	Yrs		W	L	Pct	Yrs
Connie Mack	3755	3967	.486	53	Gene Mauch	1907	2044	.483	26
John McGraw	2810	1987	.586	33	Bill McKechnie	1904	1737	.523	25
Sparky Anderson	2238	1855	.547	26	*Joe Torre	1745	1543	.531	22
Bucky Harris	2168	2228	.493	29	Ralph Houk	1627	1539	.514	20
Joe McCarthy	2155	1346	.616	24	Fred Clarke	1609	1189	.575	19
Walter Alston	2063	1634	.558	23	Dick Williams	1592	1474	.519	21
*Tony LaRussa	2042	1821	.529	25	Tommy Lasorda	1589	1434	.526	20
Leo Durocher	2015	1717	.540	24	Earl Weaver	1506	1080	.582	17
*Bobby Cox	1967	1513	.565	22	Clark Griffith	1491	1367	.522	20
Casey Stengel	1942	1868	.510	25	Miller Huggins	1431	1149	.555	17

REGULAR SEASON

	W	L	Pct	Yrs		W	L	Pct	Yrs
Connie Mack	3731	3948	.486	53	Gene Mauch	1902	2037	.483	26
John McGraw	2784	1959	.587	33	Bill McKechnie	1896	1723	.524	25
Sparky Anderson	2194	1834	.545	26	*Joe Torre	1680	1509	.527	22
Bucky Harris	2157	2218	.493	29	Ralph Houk	1619	1531	.514	20
Joe McCarthy	2125	1333	.615	24	Fred Clarke	1602	1181	.576	19
Walter Alston	2040	1613	.558	23	Dick Williams	1571	1451	.520	21
*Tony LaRussa	2009	1789	.529	25	Tommy Lasorda	1558	1404	.526	20
Leo Durocher	2008	1709	.540	24	Clark Griffith	1491	1367	.522	20
*Bobby Cox	1906	1465	.565	22	Earl Weaver	1480	1060	.583	17
Casey Stengel	1905	1842	.508	25	Miller Huggins	1413	1134	.555	17

WORLD SERIES

	W	L	T	Pct	App	WS		W	L	T	Pct	App	WS
Casey Stengel	37	26	0	.587	10	7	Bucky Harris	11	10	0	.524	3	2
Joe McCarthy	30	13	0	.698	9	7	Billy Southworth	11	11	0	.500	4	2
John McGraw	26	28	2	.482	9	2	Earl Weaver	11	13	0	.458	4	1
Connie Mack	24	19	0	.558	8	5	*Bobby Cox	11	18	0	.379	5	1
*Joe Torre	21	11	0	.657	6	4	Whitey Herzog	10	11	0	.476	3	1
Walter Alston	20	20	0	.500	7	4	Bill Carrigan	8	2	0	.800	2	2
Miller Huggins	18	15	1	.544	6	3	Cito Gaston	8	4	0	.667	2	2
Sparky Anderson	16	12	0	.571	5	3	Danny Murtaugh	8	6	0	.571	2	2
Tommy Lasorda	12	11	0	.522	4	2	Tom Kelly	8	6	0	.571	2	2
Dick Williams	12	14	0	.462	4	2	Ralph Houk	8	8	0	.500	3	2
Frank Chance	11	9	1	.548	4	2	Bill McKechnie	8	14	0	.364	4	2

*Active in 2003.

Individual Batting (Single Season)

HITS

George Sisler, 1920............257
Lefty O'Doul, 1929..............254
Bill Terry, 1930....................254
Al Simmons, 1925...............253
Rogers Hornsby, 1922........250
Chuck Klein, 1930 250
Ty Cobb, 1911 248
George Sisler, 1922.............246
Ichiro Suzuki, 2001 242
Heinie Manush, 1928..........241
Babe Herman, 1930 241

BATTING AVERAGE

Hugh Duffy, 1894............... .440
Tip O'Neill, 1887 .... .435
Ross Barnes, 1876 .... .429
Nap Lajoie, 1901 .... .426
Willie Keeler, 1897............. .424
Rogers Hornsby, 1924........ .424
George Sisler, 1922........... .420
Ty Cobb, 1911 .... .420
Fred Dunlap, 1884............. .412
Ed Delahanty, 1899 .... .410

DOUBLES

Earl Webb, 1931 67
George Burns, 1926 64
Joe Medwick, 1936...............64
Hank Greenberg, 1934..........63
Paul Waner, 1932 62
Charlie Gehringer, 1936 60
Tris Speaker, 1923................59
Chuck Klein, 1930 59
Todd Helton, 2000 59
Billy Herman, 1936 57
Billy Herman, 1935 57
Carlos Delgado, 2000............57

TOTAL BASES

Babe Ruth, 1921..................457
Rogers Hornsby, 1922.........450
Lou Gehrig, 1927.................447
Chuck Klein, 1930 445
Jimmie Foxx, 1932...............438
Stan Musial, 1948................429
Sammy Sosa, 2001..............425
Hack Wilson, 1930...............423
Chuck Klein, 1932................420
Luis Gonzalez, 2001............419
Lou Gehrig, 1930.................419

TRIPLES

Chief Wilson, 1912.................36
Dave Orr, 1886 31
Heinie Reitz, 1894.................31
Perry Werden, 1893...............29
Harry Davis, 1897 28
George Davis, 1893................27
Sam Thompson, 1894...........27
Jimmy Williams, 1899 27
John Reilly, 1890 26
George Treadway, 1894.........26
Joe Jackson, 1912.................26
Sam Crawford, 1914..............26
Kiki Cuyler, 1925....................26

HOME RUNS

Barry Bonds, 2001.................73
Mark McGwire, 1998 70
Sammy Sosa, 1998................66
Mark McGwire, 1999 65
Sammy Sosa, 2001................64
Sammy Sosa, 1999................63
Roger Maris, 1961 61
Babe Ruth, 1927....................60
Babe Ruth, 1921....................59
Jimmie Foxx, 1932................58
Hank Greenberg, 1938..........58
Mark McGwire, 1997 58

RUNS BATTED IN

Hack Wilson, 1930................190
Lou Gehrig, 1931..................184
Hank Greenberg, 1937........183
Lou Gehrig, 1927..................175
Jimmie Foxx, 1938................175
Lou Gehrig, 1930..................174
Babe Ruth, 1921...................171
Chuck Klein, 1930 170
Hank Greenberg, 1935........170
Jimmie Foxx, 1932...............169

STRIKEOUTS

Bobby Bonds, 1970...............189
Jose Hernandez, 2002 188
Bobby Bonds, 1969............187
Preston Wilson, 2000...........187
Rob Deer, 1987 186
Jose Hernandez, 2001 185
Jim Thome, 2001..................185
Pete Incaviglia, 1986 185
Cecil Fielder, 1990...............182
Jim Thome, 2003 182

RUNS

Billy Hamilton, 1894 192
Tom Brown, 1891..................177
Babe Ruth, 1921...................177
Tip O'Neill, 1887 167
Lou Gehrig, 1936..................167
Billy Hamilton, 1895..............166
Willie Keeler, 1894................165
Joe Kelley, 1894 165
Arlie Latham, 1887................163
Babe Ruth, 1928...................163
Lou Gehrig, 1931..................163

STOLEN BASES

Hugh Nicol, 1887.................138
Rickey Henderson, 1982 130
Arlie Latham, 1887...............129
Lou Brock, 1974 118
Charlie Comiskey, 1887......117
John Ward, 1887 111
Billy Hamilton, 1889..............111
Billy Hamilton, 1891..............111
Vince Coleman, 1985 110
Arlie Latham, 1888................109
Vince Coleman, 1987 109

BASES ON BALLS

Barry Bonds, 2002...............198
Barry Bonds, 2001................177
Babe Ruth, 1923...................170
Ted Williams, 1947 162
Ted Williams, 1949 162
Mark McGwire, 1998 162
Ted Williams, 1946 156
Eddie Yost, 1956 151
Eddie Joost, 1949.................149
Jeff Bagwell, 1999 149

SLUGGING AVERAGE

Barry Bonds, 2001............ .863
Babe Ruth, 1920.................. .847
Babe Ruth, 1921................. .846
Barry Bonds, 2002............. .799
Babe Ruth, 1927................. .772
Lou Gehrig, 1927................ .765
Babe Ruth, 1923................. .764
Rogers Hornsby, 1925......... .756
Mark McGwire, 1998 .... .752
Jeff Bagwell, 1994 .... .750

Individual Pitching (Single Season)

GAMES

Mike Marshall, 1974	106
Kent Tekulve, 1979	94
Mike Marshall, 1973	92
Kent Tekulve, 1978	91
Wayne Granger, 1969	90
Mike Marshall, 1979	90
Kent Tekulve, 1987	90
Steve Kline, 2001	89
Mark Eichhorn, 1987	89
Paul Quantrill, 2003	89

GAMES STARTED

Will White, 1879	75
Jim Galvin, 1883	75
Jim McCormick, 1880	74
Charley Radbourn, 1884	73
Guy Hecker, 1884	73
Jim Galvin, 1884	72
John Clarkson, 1889	72
Bill Hutchison, 1892	71
John Clarkson, 1885	70
Matt Kilroy, 1887	69

INNINGS PITCHED

Will White, 1878	680.0
Charley Radbourn, 1884	678.2
Guy Hecker, 1884	670.2
Jim McCormick, 1880	657.2
Jim Galvin, 1883	656.1
Jim Galvin, 1884	636.1
Charley Radbourn, 1883	632.1
Bill Hutchison, 1892	627.0
John Clarkson, 1885	623.0
Jim Devlin, 1876	622.0

WINS

Charley Radbourn, 1884	59
John Clarkson, 1885	53
Guy Hecker, 1884	52
John Clarkson, 1889	49
Charley Radbourn, 1883	48
Charlie Buffinton, 1884	48
Al Spalding, 1876	47
John Ward, 1879	47
Jim Galvin, 1883	46
Jim Galvin, 1884	46
Matt Kilroy, 1887	46

LOSSES

John Coleman, 1883	48
Will White, 1880	42
Larry McKeon, 1884	41
George Bradley, 1879	40
Jim McCormick, 1879	40
Henry Porter, 1888	37
Kid Carsey, 1891	37
George Cobb, 1892	37
Stump Weidman, 1886	36
Bill Hutchison, 1892	36

WINNING PERCENTAGE

Roy Face, 1959	.947
Johnny Allen, 1937	.938
Greg Maddux, 1995	.905
Randy Johnson, 1995	.900
Ron Guidry, 1978	.893
Freddie Fitzsimmons, 1940	.889
Lefty Grove, 1931	.886
Bob Stanley, 1978	.882
Preacher Roe, 1951	.880
Fred Goldsmith, 1880	.875
Tom Seaver, 1981	.875

SAVES

Bobby Thigpen, 1990	57
John Smoltz, 2002	55
Eric Gagne, 2003	55
Randy Myers, 1993	53
Trevor Hoffman, 1998	53
Eric Gagne, 2002	52
Dennis Eckersley, 1992	51
Rod Beck, 1998	51
Mariano Rivera, 2001	50
Dennis Eckersley, 1990	48
Rod Beck, 1993	48
Jeff Shaw, 1998	48

EARNED RUN AVERAGE

Tim Keefe, 1880	0.86
Dutch Leonard, 1914	0.96
Three Finger Brown, 1906	1.04
Bob Gibson, 1968	1.12
Christy Mathewson, 1909	1.14
Walter Johnson, 1913	1.14
Jack Pfiester, 1907	1.15
Addie Joss, 1908	1.16
Carl Lundgren, 1907	1.17
Denny Driscoll, 1882	1.21

SHUTOUTS

George Bradley, 1876	16
Grover Alexander, 1916	16
Jack Coombs, 1910	13
Bob Gibson, 1968	13
Jim Galvin, 1884	12
Ed Morris, 1886	12
Grover Alexander, 1915	12
Tommy Bond, 1879	11
Charley Radbourn, 1884	11
Dave Foutz, 1886	11
Christy Mathewson, 1908	11
Ed Walsh, 1908	11
Walter Johnson, 1913	11
Sandy Koufax, 1963	11
Dean Chance, 1964	11

COMPLETE GAMES

Will White, 1879	75
Charley Radbourn, 1884	73
Jim McCormick, 1880	72
Jim Galvin, 1883	72
Guy Hecker, 1884	72
Jim Galvin, 1884	71
Tim Keefe, 1883	68
John Clarkson, 1885	68
John Clarkson, 1889	68
Bill Hutchison, 1892	67

STRIKEOUTS

Matt Kilroy, 1886	513
Toad Ramsey, 1886	499
Hugh Daily, 1884	483
Dupee Shaw, 1884	451
Charley Radbourn, 1884	441
Charlie Buffinton, 1884	417
Guy Hecker, 1884	385
Nolan Ryan, 1973	383
Sandy Koufax, 1965	382
Bill Sweeney, 1884	374

BASES ON BALLS

Amos Rusie, 1890	289
Mark Baldwin, 1889	274
Amos Rusie, 1892	267
Amos Rusie, 1891	262
Mark Baldwin, 1890	249
Jack Stivetts, 1891	232
Mark Baldwin, 1891	227
Phil Knell, 1891	226
Bob Barr, 1890	219
Amos Rusie, 1893	218

Manager of the Year

NATIONAL LEAGUE

1983	Tommy Lasorda, LA
1984	Jim Frey, Chi
1985	Whitey Herzog, StL
1986	Hal Lanier, Hou
1987	Buck Rodgers, Mtl
1988	Tommy Lasorda, LA
1989	Don Zimmer, Chi
1990	Jim Leyland, Pitt
1991	Bobby Cox, Atl
1992	Jim Leyland, Pitt
1993	Dusty Baker, SF
1994	Felipe Alou, Mtl
1995	Don Baylor, Col
1996	Bruce Bochy, SD
1997	Dusty Baker, SF
1998	Larry Dierker, Hou
1999	Jack McKeon, Cin
2000	Dusty Baker, SF
2001	Larry Bowa, Phil
2002	Tony La Russa

AMERICAN LEAGUE

1983	Tony La Russa, Chi
1984	Sparky Anderson, Det
1985	Bobby Cox, Tor
1986	John McNamara, Bos
1987	Sparky Anderson, Det
1988	Tony La Russa, Oak
1989	Frank Robinson, Balt
1990	Jeff Torborg, Chi
1991	Tom Kelly, Minn
1992	Tony La Russa, Oak
1993	Gene Lamont, Chi
1994	Buck Showalter, NY
1995	Lou Piniella, Sea
1996	Joe Torre, NY/Johnny Oates, Tex
1997	Davey Johnson, Balt
1998	Joe Torre, NY
1999	Jimy Williams, Bos
2000	Jerry Manuel, Chi
2001	Lou Piniella, Sea
2002	Mike Scioscia, Ana

Individual Batting (Single Game)

MOST RUNS

7	Guy Hecker, Lou	Aug 15, 1886

MOST HITS

7	Wilbert Robinson, Balt	June 10, 1892
	Rennie Stennett, Pitt	Sept 16, 1975

MOST HOME RUNS

4	Bobby Lowe, Bos (N)	May 30, 1894
	Ed Delahanty, Phil	July 13, 1896
	Lou Gehrig, NY (A)	June 3, 1932
	Gil Hodges, Bklyn	Aug 31, 1950
	Joe Adcock, Mil (N)	July 31, 1954
	Rocky Colavito, Clev	June 10, 1959
	Willie Mays, SF	April 30, 1961
	Mike Schmidt, Phil	April 17, 1976
	Bob Horner, Atl	July 6, 1986
	Mark Whiten, StL	Sept 7, 1993
	Mike Cameron, Sea	May 2, 2002
	Shawn Green, LA	May 23, 2002
	Carlos Delgado, Tor	Sept 25, 2003

MOST GRAND SLAMS

2	Tony Lazzeri, NY (A)	May 24, 1936
	Jim Tabor, Bos (A)	July 4, 1939
	Rudy York, Bos (A)	July 27, 1946
	Jim Gentile, Balt	May 9, 1961
	Tony Cloninger, Atl	July 3, 1966
	Jim Northrup, Det	June 24, 1968
	Frank Robinson, Balt	June 26, 1970
	Robin Ventura, Chi (A)	Sept 4, 1995
	Chris Hoiles, Balt	Aug 14, 1998
	Fernando Tatis, StL	Apr 23, 1999
	N. Garciaparra, Bos	May 10, 1999
	Bill Mueller, Bos	July 29, 2003

MOST RBIs

12	Jim Bottomley, StL	Sept 16, 1924
	Mark Whiten, StL	Sept 7, 1993

Individual Batting (Single Inning)

MOST RUNS

3	Tommy Burns, Chi (N)	Sept 6, 1883, 7th inning
	Ned Williamson, Chi (N)	Sept 6, 1883, 7th inning
	Sammy White, Bos (A)	June 18, 1953, 7th inning

MOST HITS

3	Tommy Burns, Chi (N)	Sept 6, 1883, 7th inning
	Fred Pfeiffer, Chi (N)	Sept 6, 1883, 7th inning
	Ned Williamson, Chi (N)	Sept 6, 1883, 7th inning
	Gene Stephens, Bos (A)	June 18, 1953, 7th inning

MOST RBIs

8	Fernando Tatis, StL	Apr 23, 1999, 3rd inning

Note: All single-game hitting records for a nine-inning game.

Individual Pitching (Single Game)

MOST INNINGS PITCHED

26 .....Leon Cadore, Bklyn   May 1, 1920, tie 1–1
        Joe Oeschger, Bos (N)   May 1, 1920, tie 1–1

MOST RUNS ALLOWED

24 .....Al Travers, Det   May 18, 1912

MOST HITS ALLOWED

36 .....Jack Wadsworth, Lou   Aug 17, 1894

MOST STRIKEOUTS

20 .....Roger Clemens, Bos   April 29, 1986
20 .....Roger Clemens, Bos   Sept 18, 1996
20 .....Kerry Wood, Chi (N)   May 6, 1998
20 .....Randy Johnson, Ariz   May 8, 2001

MOST WALKS ALLOWED

16 .....Bill George, NY (N)   May 30, 1887
        George Van Haltren,   June 27, 1887
        Chi (N)
        Henry Gruber, Clev   Apr 19, 1890
        Bruno Haas, Phil (A)   June 2, 1915

MOST WILD PITCHES

6 .......J.R. Richard, Hou   April 10, 1979
        Phil Niekro, Atl   Aug 14, 1979
        Bill Gullickson, Mtl   April 10, 1982

Individual Pitching (Single Inning)

MOST RUNS ALLOWED

13 .....Lefty O'Doul, Bos (A)   July 7, 1923

MOST WALKS ALLOWED

8 ....Dolly Gray, Wash   Aug 28, 1909

MOST WILD PITCHES

4 ....Walter Johnson, Wash   Sept 21, 1914
        Phil Niekro, Atl   Aug 14, 1979

Miscellaneous

LONGEST GAME, BY INNINGS

26 .....Brooklyn 1, Boston 1   May 1, 1920

LONGEST NINE-INNING GAME, BY TIME

4:27...Los Angeles 11, San Francisco 10 Oct 5, 2001

Baseball Hall of Fame

Players

	Position	Career	Selected		Position	Career	Selected
Hank Aaron	OF	1954–76	1982	Orlando Cepeda	1B	1958–74	1999
Grover Alexander	P	1911–30	1938	Frank Chance	1B	1898–1914	1946
Cap Anson	1B	1876–97	1939	Oscar Charleston*	OF		1976
Luis Aparicio	SS	1956–73	1984	Jack Chesbro	P	1899–1909	1946
Luke Appling	SS	1930–50	1964	Fred Clarke	OF	1894–1915	1945
Richie Ashburn	OF	1948–62	1995	John Clarkson	P	1882–94	1963
Earl Averill	OF	1929–41	1975	Roberto Clemente	OF	1955–72	1973
Frank Baker	3B	1908–22	1955	Ty Cobb	OF	1905–28	1936
Dave Bancroft	SS	1915–30	1971	Mickey Cochrane	C	1925–37	1947
Ernie Banks	SS-1B	1953–71	1977	Eddie Collins	2B	1906–30	1939
Jake Beckley	1B	1888–1907	1971	Jimmy Collins	3B	1895–1908	1945
Cool Papa Bell*	OF		1974	Earle Combs	OF	1924–35	1970
Johnny Bench	C	1967–83	1989	Roger Connor	1B	1880–97	1976
Chief Bender	P	1903–25	1953	Stan Coveleski	P	1912–28	1969
Yogi Berra	C	1946–65	1972	Sam Crawford	OF	1899–1917	1957
Jim Bottomley	1B	1922–37	1974	Joe Cronin	SS	1926–45	1956
Lou Boudreau	SS	1938–52	1970	Candy Cummings	P	1872–77	1939
Roger Bresnahan	C	1897–1915	1945	Kiki Cuyler	OF	1921–38	1968
George Brett	3B	1973–93	1999	Ray Dandridge*	3B		1987
Lou Brock	OF	1961–79	1985	George Davis	SS	1890–1909	1998
Dan Brouthers	1B	1879–1904	1945	Leon Day*	P		1995
Three Finger Brown	P	1903–16	1949	Dizzy Dean	P	1930–47	1953
Jim Bunning	P	1955–71	1996	Ed Delahanty	OF	1888–1903	1945
Jesse Burkett	OF	1890–1905	1946	Bill Dickey	C	1928–46	1954
Roy Campanella	C	1948–57	1969	Martin Dihigo*	P-OF		1977
Rod Carew	1B-2B	1967–85	1991	Joe DiMaggio	OF	1936–51	1955
Max Carey	OF	1910–29	1961	Larry Doby	OF	1947–59	1998
Steve Carlton	P	1965–88	1994	Bobby Doerr	2B	1937–51	1986
Gary Carter	C	1974–92	2003	Don Drysdale	P	1956–69	1984

Note: Career dates indicate first and last appearances in the majors.

*Elected on the basis of his career in the Negro leagues.

Baseball Hall of Fame (Cont.)

Players (Cont.)

	Position	Career	Selected		Position	Career	Selected
Hugh Duffy	OF	1888–1906	1945	Eddie Mathews	3B	1952–68	1978
Johnny Evers	2B	1902–29	1939	Christy Mathewson	P	1900–16	1936
Buck Ewing	C	1880–97	1946	Willie Mays	OF	1951–73	1979
Red Faber	P	1914–33	1964	Bill Mazeroski	2B	1956–72	2001
Bob Feller	P	1936–56	1962	Tommy McCarthy	OF	1884–96	1946
Rick Ferrell	C	1929–47	1984	Willie McCovey	1B	1959–80	1986
Rollie Fingers	P	1968–85	1992	Joe McGinnity	P	1899–1908	1946
Carlton Fisk	C	1969–93	2000	Bid McPhee	2B	1882–99	2000
Elmer Flick	OF	1898–1910	1963	Joe Medwick	OF	1932–48	1968
Whitey Ford	P	1950–67	1974	Johnny Mize	1B	1936–53	1981
Bill Foster*	P		1996	Joe Morgan	2B	1963–84	1990
Nellie Fox	2B	1947–65	1997	Eddie Murray	1B	1977–97	2003
Jimmie Foxx	1B	1925–45	1951	Stan Musial	OF-1B	1941–63	1969
Frankie Frisch	2B	1919–37	1947	Hal Newhouser	P	1939–55	1992
Pud Galvin	P	1879–92	1965	Kid Nichols	P	1890–1906	1949
Lou Gehrig	1B	1923–39	1939	Phil Niekro	P	1964–87	1997
Charlie Gehringer	2B	1924–42	1949	Jim O'Rourke	OF	1876–1904	1945
Bob Gibson	P	1959–75	1981	Mel Ott	OF	1926–47	1951
Josh Gibson*	C		1972	Satchel Paige*	P	1948–65	1971
Lefty Gomez	P	1930–43	1972	Jim Palmer	P	1965–84	1990
Goose Goslin	OF	1921–38	1968	Herb Pennock	P	1912–34	1948
Hank Greenberg	1B	1930–47	1956	Tony Perez	1B	1964–86	2000
Burleigh Grimes	P	1916–34	1964	Gaylord Perry	P	1962–83	1991
Lefty Grove	P	1925–41	1947	Eddie Plank	P	1901–17	1946
Chick Hafey	OF	1924–37	1971	Kirby Puckett	OF	1984–95	2001
Jesse Haines	P	1918–37	1970	Charley Radbourn	P	1880–91	1939
Billy Hamilton	OF	1888–1901	1961	Pee Wee Reese	SS	1940–58	1984
Gabby Hartnett	C	1922–41	1955	Sam Rice	OF	1915–35	1963
Harry Heilmann	OF	1914–32	1952	Eppa Rixey	P	1912–33	1963
Billy Herman	2B	1931–47	1975	Phil Rizzuto	SS	1941–56	1994
Harry Hooper	OF	1909–25	1971	Robin Roberts	P	1948–66	1976
Rogers Hornsby	2B	1915–37	1942	Brooks Robinson	3B	1955–77	1983
Waite Hoyt	P	1918–38	1969	Frank Robinson	OF	1956–76	1982
Carl Hubbell	P	1928–43	1947	Jackie Robinson	2B	1947–56	1962
Catfish Hunter	P	1965–79	1987	Joe (Bullet) Rogan*	P		1998
Monte Irvin*	OF	1949–56	1973	Edd Roush	OF	1913–31	1962
Reggie Jackson	OF	1967–87	1993	Red Ruffing	P	1924–47	1967
Travis Jackson	SS	1922–36	1982	Amos Rusie	P	1889–1901	1977
Ferguson Jenkins	P	1965–83	1991	Babe Ruth	OF	1914–35	1936
Hugh Jennings	SS	1891–1918	1945	Nolan Ryan	P	1966–93	1999
Judy Johnson*	3B		1975	Ray Schalk	C	1912–29	1955
Walter Johnson	P	1907–27	1936	Mike Schmidt	3B	1972–89	1995
Addie Joss	P	1902–10	1978	Red Schoendienst	2B	1945–63	1989
Al Kaline	OF	1953–74	1980	Tom Seaver	P	1967–86	1992
Tim Keefe	P	1880–93	1964	Joe Sewell	SS	1920–33	1977
Willie Keeler	OF	1892–1910	1939	Al Simmons	OF	1924–44	1953
George Kell	3B	1943–57	1983	George Sisler	1B	1915–30	1939
Joe Kelley	OF	1891–1908	1971	Enos Slaughter	OF	1938–59	1985
George Kelly	1B	1915–32	1973	Hilton Smith*	P		2001
King Kelly	C	1878–93	1945	Ozzie Smith	SS	1978–96	2002
Harmon Killebrew	1B-3B	1954–75	1984	Duke Snider	OF	1947–64	1980
Ralph Kiner	OF	1946–55	1975	Warren Spahn	P	1942–65	1973
Chuck Klein	OF	1928–44	1980	Al Spalding	P	1871–78	1939
Sandy Koufax	P	1955–66	1972	Tris Speaker	OF	1907–28	1937
Nap Lajoie	2B	1896–1916	1937	Willie Stargell	OF-1B	1962–82	1988
Tony Lazzeri	2B	1926–39	1991	Turkey Stearns*	CF		2000
Bob Lemon	P	1941–58	1976	Don Sutton	P	1966–88	1998
Buck Leonard*	1B		1977	Bill Terry	1B	1923–36	1954
Fred Lindstrom	3B	1924–36	1976	Sam Thompson	OF	1885–1906	1974
Pop Lloyd*	SS-1B		1977	Joe Tinker	SS	1902–16	1946
Ernie Lombardi	C	1931–47	1986	Pie Traynor	3B	1920–37	1948
Ted Lyons	P	1923–46	1955	Dazzy Vance	P	1915–35	1955
Mickey Mantle	OF	1951–68	1974	Arky Vaughan	SS	1932–48	1985
Heinie Manush	OF	1923–39	1964	Rube Waddell	P	1897–1910	1946
Rabbit Maranville	SS-2B	1912–35	1954	Honus Wagner	SS	1897–1917	1936
Juan Marichal	P	1960–75	1983	Bobby Wallace	SS	1894–1918	1953
Rube Marquard	P	1908–25	1971	Ed Walsh	P	1904–17	1946

*Elected on the basis of his career in the Negro leagues.

Players (Cont.)

	Position	Career	Selected
Lloyd Waner	OF	1927–45	1967
Paul Waner	OF	1926–45	1952
John Ward	2B-P	1878–94	1964
Mickey Welch	P	1880–92	1973
Willie Wells*	SS	1924–49	1997
Zach Wheat	OF	1909–27	1959
Hoyt Wilhelm	P	1952–72	1985
Billy Williams	OF	1959–76	1987
Ted Williams	OF	1939–60	1966
Vic Willis	P	1898–1910	1995
Hack Wilson	OF	1923–34	1979
Dave Winfield	OF	1973–95	2001
Early Wynn	P	1939–63	1972
Carl Yastrzemski	OF	1961–83	1989
Cy Young	P	1890–1911	1937
Ross Youngs	OF	1917–26	1972
Robin Yount	SS	1974–93	1999

Pioneers/Executives (Cont.)

	Selected
Happy Chandler (commissioner)	1982
Charles Comiskey (manager-executive)	1939
Rube Foster (player-manager-executive)	1981
Ford Frick (commissioner-executive)	1970
Warren Giles (executive)	1979
Will Harridge (executive)	1972
William Hulbert (executive)	1995
Ban Johnson (executive)	1937
Kenesaw M. Landis (commissioner)	1944
Larry MacPhail (executive)	1978
Lee MacPhail Jr. (executive)	1998
Branch Rickey (manager-executive)	1967
Al Spalding (player-executive)	1939
Bill Veeck (owner)	1991
George Weiss (executive)	1971
George Wright (player-manager)	1937
Harry Wright (player-manager-executive)	1953
Tom Yawkey (executive)	1980

Umpires

	Selected
Al Barlick	1989
Nestor Chylak	1999
Jocko Conlan	1974
Tom Connolly	1953
Billy Evans	1973
Cal Hubbard	1976
Bill Klem	1953
Bill McGowan	1992

Managers

	Managed	Selected
Walt Alston	1954–76	1983
Sparky Anderson	1970–94	2000
Leo Durocher	1939–73	1994
Clark Griffith	1901–20	1946
Bucky Harris	1924–56	1975
Ned Hanlon	1899–1907	1996
Miller Huggins	1913–29	1964
Tommy Lasorda	1977–96	1997
Al Lopez	1951–69	1977
Connie Mack	1894–1950	1937
Joe McCarthy	1926–50	1957
John McGraw	1899–1932	1937
Bill McKechnie	1915–46	1962
Wilbert Robinson	1902–31	1945
Frank Selee	1890–1905	1999
Casey Stengel	1934–65	1966
Earl Weaver	1968–82, 85–86	1996

Pioneers/Executives

	Selected
Ed Barrow (manager-executive)	1953
Morgan Bulkeley (executive)	1937
Alexander Cartwright (executive)	1938
Henry Chadwick (writer-executive)	1938

*Elected on the basis of his career in the Negro leagues.

Notable Achievements

No-Hit Games, Nine Innings or More

NATIONAL LEAGUE

Date	Pitcher and Game
1876......July 15	George Bradley, StL vs Hart 2–0
1880......June 12	John Richmond, Wor vs Clev 1–0 (perfect game)
June 17	Monte Ward, Prov vs Buff 5–0 (perfect game)
Aug 19	Larry Corcoran, Chi vs Bos 6–0
Aug 20	Pud Galvin, Buff vs Wor 1–0
1882......Sept 20	Larry Corcoran, Chi vs Wor 5–0
Sept 22	Tim Lovett, Bklyn vs NY 4–0
1883......July 25	Hoss Radbourn, Prov vs Clev 8–0
Sept 13	Hugh Daily, Clev vs Phil 1–0
1884......June 27	Larry Corcoran, Chi vs Prov 6–0
Aug 4	Pud Galvin, Buff vs Det 18–0
1885......July 27	John Clarkson, Chi vs Prov 4–0
Aug 29	Charles Ferguson, Phil vs Prov 1–0
1891......July 31	Amos Rusie, NY vs Bklyn 6–0
June 22	Tom Lovett, Bklyn vs NY 4–0
1892......Aug 6	Jack Stivetts, Bos vs Bklyn 11–0
Aug 22	Alex Sanders, Lou vs Balt 6–2

Date	Pitcher and Game
1892......Oct 15	Bumpus Jones, Cin vs Pitt 7–1 (first major league game)
1893......Aug 16	Bill Hawke, Balt vs Wash 5–0
1897......Sept 18	Cy Young, Clev vs Cin 6–0
1898......Apr 22	Ted Breitenstein, Cin vs Pitt 11–0
Apr 22	Jim Hughes, Balt vs Bos 8–0
July 8	Frank Donahue, Phil vs Bos 5–0
Aug 21	Walter Thornton, Chi vs Bklyn 2–0
1899......May 25	Deacon Phillippe, Lou vs NY 7–0
Aug 7	Vic Willis, Bos vs Wash 7–1
1900......July 12	Noodles Hahn, Cin vs Phil 4–0
1901......July 15	Christy Mathewson, NY vs StL 5–0
1903......Sept 18	Chick Fraser, Phil vs Chi 10–0
1904......June 11	Bob Wicker, Chi at NY 1–0 (hit in 10th; won in 12th)
1905......June 13	Christy Mathewson, NY vs Chi 1–0
1906......May 1	John Lush, Phil vs Bklyn 6–0
July 20	Mal Eason, Bklyn vs StL 2–0

No-Hit Games, Nine Innings or More *(Cont.)*
NATIONAL LEAGUE *(Cont.)*

Date	Pitcher and Game	Date	Pitcher and Game
1906......Aug 1	Harry McIntire, Bklyn vs Pitt 0–1 (hit in 11th; lost in 13th)	1965......Sept 9	Sandy Koufax, LA vs Chi 1–0 (perfect game)
1907......May 8	Frank Pfeffer, Bos vs Cin 6–0	1967......June 18	Don Wilson, Hou vs Atl 2–0
Sept 20	Nick Maddox, Pitt vs Bklyn 2–1	1968......July 29	George Culver, Cin vs Phil 6–1
1908......July 4	George Wiltse, NY vs Phil 1–0 (10 innings)	Sept 17	Gaylord Perry, SF vs StL 1–0
		Sept 18	Ray Washburn, StL vs SF 2–0
Sept 5	Nap Rucker, Bklyn vs Bos 6–0	1969......Apr 17	Bill Stoneman, Mtl vs Phil 7–0
1909......Apr 15	Leon Ames, NY vs Bklyn 0–3 (hit in 10th; lost in 13th)	Apr 30	Jim Maloney, Cin vs Hou 10–0
		May 1	Don Wilson, Hou vs Cin 4–0
1912......Sept 6	Jeff Tesreau, NY vs Phil 3–0	Aug 19	Ken Holtzman, Chi vs Atl 3–0
1914......Sept 9	George Davis, Bos vs Phil 7–0	Sept 20	Bob Moose, Pitt vs NY 4–0
1915......Apr 15	Rube Marquard, NY vs Bklyn 2–0	1970......June 12	Dock Ellis, Pitt vs SD 2–0
Aug 31	Jimmy Lavender, Chi vs NY 2–0	July 20	Bill Singer, LA vs Phil 5–0
1916......June 16	Tom Hughes, Bos vs Pitt 2–0	1971......June 3	Ken Holtzman, Chi vs Cin 1–0
1917......May 2	Jim Vaughn, Chi vs Cin 0–1 (hit in 10th; lost in 10th)	June 23	Rick Wise, Phil vs Cin 4–0
		Aug 14	Bob Gibson, StL vs Pitt 11–0
May 2	Fred Toney, Cin vs Chi 1–0 (10 innings)	1972......Apr 16	Burt Hooton, Chi vs Phil 4–0
		Sept 2	Milt Pappas, Chi vs SD 8–0
1919......May 11	Hod Eller, Cin vs StL 6–0	Oct 2	Bill Stoneman, Mtl vs NY 7–0
1922......May 7	Jesse Barnes, NY vs Phil 6–0	1973......Aug 5	Phil Niekro, Atl vs SD 9–0
1924......July 17	Jesse Haines, StL vs Bos 5–0	1975......Aug 24	Ed Halicki, SF vs NY 6–0
1925......Sept 13	Dazzy Vance, Bklyn vs Phil 10–1	1976......July 9	Larry Dierker, Hou vs Mtl 6–0
1929......May 8	Carl Hubbell, NY vs Pitt 1–0	Aug 9	John Candelaria, Pitt vs LA 2–0
1934......Sept 21	Paul Dean, StL vs Bklyn 3–0	Sept 29	John Montefusco, SF vs Atl 9–0
1938......June 11	Johnny Vander Meer, Cin vs Bos 3–0	1978......Apr 16	Bob Forsch, StL vs Phil 5–0
		June 16	Tom Seaver, Cin vs StL 4–0
June 15	Johnny Vander Meer, Cin vs Bklyn 6–0	1979......Apr 7	Ken Forsch, Hou vs Atl 6–0
		1980......June 27	Jerry Reuss, LA vs SF 8–0
1940......Apr 30	Tex Carleton, Bklyn vs Cin, 3–0	1981......May 10	Charlie Lea, Mtl vs SF 4–0
1941......Aug 30	Lon Warneke, StL vs Cin 2–0	Sept 26	Nolan Ryan, Hou vs LA 5–0
1944......Apr 27	Jim Tobin, Bos vs Bklyn 2–0	1983......Sept 26	Bob Forsch, StL vs Mtl 3–0
May 15	Clyde Shoun, Cin vs Bos 1–0	1986......Sept 25	Mike Scott, Hou vs SF 2–0
1946......Apr 23	Ed Head, Bklyn vs Bos 5–0	1988......Sept 16	Tom Browning, Cin vs LA 1–0 (perfect game)
1947......June 18	Ewell Blackwell, Cin vs Bos 6–0		
1948......Sept 9	Rex Barney, Bklyn vs NY 2–0	1990......June 29	Fernando Valenzuela, LA vs StL 6–0
1950......Aug 11	Vern Bickford, Bos vs Bklyn 7–0	1990......Aug 15	Terry Mulholland, Phil vs SF 6–0
1951......May 6	Cliff Chambers, Pitt vs Bos 3–0	1991......May 23	Tommy Greene, Phil vs Mtl 2–0
1952......June 19	Carl Erskine, Bklyn vs Chi 5–0	July 26	Mark Gardner, Mtl vs LA 0–1 (hit in 10th, lost in 10th)
1954......June 12	Jim Wilson, Mil vs Phil 2–0		
1955......May 12	Sam Jones, Chi vs Pitt 4–0	July 28	Dennis Martinez, Mtl vs LA 2–0 (perfect game)
1956......May 12	Carl Erskine, Bklyn vs NY 3–0		
Sept 25	Sal Maglie, Bklyn vs Phil 5–0	Sept 11	Kent Mercker (6), Mark Wohlers (2), and Alejandro Pena (1), Atl vs SD 1–0
1959......May 26	Harvey Haddix, Pitt vs Mil 0–1 (hit in 13th; lost in 13th)		
		1992......Aug 17	Kevin Gross, LA vs SF 2–0
1960......May 15	Don Cardwell, Chi vs StL 4–0	1993......Sept 8	Darryl Kile, Hou vs NY 7–1
Aug 18	Lew Burdette, Mil vs Phil 1–0	1994......Apr 8	Kent Mercker, Atl vs LA 6–0
Sept 16	Warren Spahn, Mil vs Phil 4–0	1995......June 3	Pedro Martinez, Mtl vs SD 1–0 (perfect through nine, hit in 10th)
1961......Apr 28	Warren Spahn, Mil vs SF 1–0		
1962......June 30	Sandy Koufax, LA vs NY 5–0	July 14	Ramon Martinez, LA vs Fla 7–0
1963......May 11	Sandy Koufax, LA vs SF 8–0	1996......May 11	Al Leiter, Fla vs Col 11–0
May 17	Don Nottebart, Hou vs Phil 4–1	Sept 17	Hideo Nomo, LA vs Col 9–0
June 15	Juan Marichal, SF vs Hou 1–0	1997......June 10	Kevin Brown, Fla vs SF 9–0
1964......Apr 23	Ken Johnson, Hou vs Cin 0–1	July 12	Francisco Cordova (9) and Ricardo Rincon (1), Pitt vs Col 3–0
June 4	Sandy Koufax, LA vs Phil 3–0		
June 21	Jim Bunning, Phil vs NY 6–0 (perfect game)	1999......June 25	Jose Jimenez, StL vs Ariz 1–0
		2001......May 12	A.J. Burnett, Fla vs SD 3–0
1965......June 14	Jim Maloney, Cin vs NY 0–1 (hit in 11th; lost in 11th)	Sept 3	Bud Smith, StL vs SD 4–0
		2003......June 11	R. Oswalt (1), P. Munro (2.2), K. Saarloos (1.1), B. Lidge (2), O. Dotel (1), B. Wagner (1), Hou vs NYY 8–0
Aug 19	Jim Maloney, Cin vs Chi 1–0 (10 innings)		
		April 27	Kevin Millwood, Phil vs SF 1–0

Note: Includes the games struck from the official record book on Sept. 4, 1991, when baseball's committee on statistical accuracy voted to define no-hitters as games of nine innings or more that end with a team getting no hits.

No-Hit Games, Nine Innings or More *(Cont.)*

AMERICAN LEAGUE

Date	Pitcher and Game
1901......May 9	Earl Moore, Clev vs Chi 2–4 (hit in 10th; lost in 10th)
1902......Sept 20	Jimmy Callahan, Chi vs Det 3–0
1904......May 5	Cy Young, Bos vs Phil 3–0 (perfect game)
Aug 17	Jesse Tannehill, Bos vs Chi 6–0
1905......July 22	Weldon Henley, Phil vs StL 6–0
Sept 6	Frank Smith, Chi vs Det 15–0
Sept 27	Bill Dinneen, Bos vs Chi 2–0
1908......June 30	Cy Young, Bos vs NY 8–0
Sept 18	Bob Rhoades, Clev vs Bos 2–1
Sept 20	Frank Smith, Chi vs Phil 1–0
1908......Oct 2	Addie Joss, Clev vs Chi 1–0 (perfect game)
1910......Apr 20	Addie Joss, Clev vs Chi 1–0
May 12	Chief Bender, Phil vs Clev 4–0
Aug 30	Tom Hughes, NY vs Clev 0–5 (hit in 10th; lost in 11th)
1911......July 29	Joe Wood, Bos vs StL 5–0
Aug 27	Ed Walsh, Chi vs Bos 5–0
1912......July 4	George Mullin, Det vs StL 7–0
Aug 30	Earl Hamilton, StL vs Det 5–1
1914......May 14	Jim Scott, Chi vs Wash 0–1 (hit in 10th; lost in 10th)
May 31	Joe Benz, Chi vs Clev 6–1
1916......June 21	George Foster, Bos vs NY 2–0
Aug 26	Joe Bush, Phil vs Clev 5–0
Aug 30	Dutch Leonard, Bos vs StL 4–0
1917......Apr 14	Ed Cicotte, Chi vs StL 11–0
Apr 24	George Mogridge, NY vs Bos 2–1
May 5	Ernie Koob, StL vs Chi 1–0
May 6	Bob Groom, StL vs Chi 3–0
June 23	Ernie Shore, Bos vs Wash 4–0 (perfect game)
1918......June 3	Dutch Leonard, Bos vs Det 5–0
1919......Sept 10	Ray Caldwell, Clev vs NY 3–0
1920......July 1	Walter Johnson, Wash vs Bos 1–0
1922......Apr 30	Charlie Robertson, Chi vs Det 2–0 (perfect game)
1923......Sept 4	Sam Jones, NY vs Phil 2–0
Sept 7	Howard Ehmke, Bos vs Phil 4–0
1926......Aug 21	Ted Lyons, Chi vs Bos 6–0
1931......Apr 29	Wes Ferrell, Clev vs StL 9–0
Aug 8	Bob Burke, Wash vs Bos 5–0
1934......Sept 18	Bobo Newsom, StL vs Bos 1–2 (hit in 10th; lost in 10th)
1935......Aug 31	Vern Kennedy, Chi vs Clev 5–0
1937......June 1	Bill Dietrich, Chi vs StL 8–0
1938......Aug 27	Mtle Pearson, NY vs Clev 13–0
1940......Apr 16	Bob Feller, Clev vs Chi 1–0 (opening day)
1945......Sept 9	Dick Fowler, Phil vs StL 1–0
1946......Apr 30	Bob Feller, Clev vs NY 1–0
1947......July 10	Don Black, Clev vs Phil 3–0
Sep 3	Bill McCahan, Phil vs Wash 3–0
1948......June 30	Bob Lemon, Clev vs Det 2–0
1951......July 1	Bob Feller, Clev vs Det 2–1
July 12	Allie Reynolds, NY vs Clev 1–0
Sept 28	Allie Reynolds, NY vs Bos 8–0
1952......May 15	Virgil Trucks, Det vs Wash 1–0
Aug 25	Virgil Trucks, Det vs NY 1–0
1953......May 6	Bobo Holloman, StL vs Phil 6–0 (first major league start)
1956......July 14	Mel Parnell, Bos vs Chi 4–0

Date	Pitcher and Game
1966......Oct 8	Don Larsen, NY (A) vs Bklyn (N) 2–0 (World Series) (perfect game)
1957......Aug 20	Bob Keegan, Chi vs Wash 6–0
1958......July 20	Jim Bunning, Det vs Bos 3–0
Sept 20	Hoyt Wilhelm, Balt vs NY 1–0
1962......May 5	Bo Belinsky, LA vs Balt 2–0
June 26	Earl Wilson, Bos vs LA 2–0
Aug 1	Bill Monbouquette, Bos vs Chi 1–0
Aug 26	Jack Kralick, Minn vs KC 1–0
1965......Sept 16	Dave Morehead, Bos vs Clev 2–0
1966......June 10	Sonny Siebert, Clev vs Wash 2–0
1967......Apr 30	Steve Barber (8⅔) and Stu Miller (⅓), Balt vs Det 1–2
Aug 25	Dean Chance, Minn vs Clev 2–1
Sept 10	Joel Horlen, Chi vs Det 6–0
1968......Apr 27	Tom Phoebus, Balt vs Bos 6–0
May 8	Catfish Hunter, Oak vs Minn 4–0 (perfect game)
1969......Aug 13	Jim Palmer, Balt vs Oak 8–0
1970......July 3	Clyde Wright, Cal vs Oak 4–0
Sept 21	Vida Blue, Oak vs Minn 6–0
1973......Apr 27	Steve Busby, KC vs Det 3–0
May 15	Nolan Ryan, Cal vs KC 3–0
July 15	Nolan Ryan, Cal vs Det 6–0
July 30	Jim Bibby, Tex vs Oak 6–0
1974......June 19	Steve Busby, KC vs Mil 2–0
July 19	Dick Bosman, Clev vs Oak 4–0
Sept 28	Nolan Ryan, Cal vs Minn 4–0
1975......June 1	Nolan Ryan, Cal vs Balt 1–0
Sept 28	Vida Blue (5), Glenn Abbott and Paul Lindblad (1), Rollie Fingers (2), Oak vs Cal 5–0
1976......July 28	John Odom (5) and Francisco Barrios (4), Chi vs Oak 2–1
1977......May 14	Jim Colborn, KC vs Tex 6–0
May 30	Dennis Eckersley, Clev vs Cal 1–0
Sept 22	Bert Blyleven, Tex vs Cal 6–0
1981......May 15	Len Barker, Clev vs Tor 3–0 (perfect game)
1983......July 4	Dave Righetti, NY vs Bos 4–0
Sept 29	Mike Warren, Oak vs Chi 3–0
1984......Apr 7	Jack Morris, Det vs Chi 4–0
Sept 30	Mike Witt, Cal vs Tex 1–0 (perfect game)
1986......Sept 19	Joe Cowley, Chi vs Cal 7–1
1987......Apr 15	Juan Nieves, Mil vs Balt 7–0
1990......Apr 11	Mark Langston (7), Mike Witt (2), Cal vs Sea 1–0
June 2	Randy Johnson, Sea vs Det 2–0
June 11	Nolan Ryan, Tex vs Oak 5–0
June 29	Dave Stewart, Oak vs Tor 5–0
1990......July 1	Andy Hawkins, NY vs Chi 0–4 (pitched eight of nine-innning game)
Sept 2	Dave Stieb, Tor vs Clev 3–0
1991......May 1	Nolan Ryan, Tex vs Tor 3–0
July 13	Bob Milacki (6), Mike Flanagan (1), Mark Williamson (1), and Gregg Olson (1), Balt vs Oak 2–0
Aug 11	Wilson Alvarez, Chi vs Balt 7–0
Aug 26	Bret Saberhagen, KC vs Chi 7–0
1993......Apr 22	Chris Bosio, Sea vs Bos 7–0
Sept 4	Jim Abbott, NY vs Clev 4–0

No-Hit Games, Nine Innings or More *(Cont.)*

AMERICAN LEAGUE *(Cont.)*

Date	Pitcher and Game	Date	Pitcher and Game
1994......Apr 27	Scott Erickson, Minn vs Mil 6–0	1999......July 18	David Cone, NY vs Mtl 6–0
July 28	Kenny Rogers, Texas vs Cal 4–0		(perfect game)
	(perfect game)	Sept 11	Eric Milton, Minn vs Ana 7–0
1996......May 14	Dwight Gooden, NY vs Sea 2–0	2001......Apr 4	Hideo Nomo, Bos vs Balt 3–0
1998......May 17	David Wells, NY vs Minn 4–0	2002......Apr 27	Derek Lowe, Bos vs TB 10–0
	(perfect game)		

Longest Hitting Streaks

NATIONAL LEAGUE

Player and Team	Year	G
Willie Keeler, Balt	1897	44
Pete Rose, Cin	1978	44
Bill Dahlen, Chi	1894	42
Tommy Holmes, Bos	1945	37
Billy Hamilton, Phil	1894	36
Luis Castillo, Fla	2002	35
Fred Clarke, Lou	1895	35
Benito Santiago, SD	1987	34
George Davis, NY	1893	33
Rogers Hornsby, StL	1922	32

AMERICAN LEAGUE

Player and Team	Year	G
Joe DiMaggio, NY	1941	56
George Sisler, StL	1922	41
Ty Cobb, Det	1911	40
Paul Molitor, Mil	1987	39
Ty Cobb, Det	1917	35
Ty Cobb, Det	1912	34
George Sisler, StL	1925	34
John Stone, Det	1930	34
George McQuinn, StL	1938	34
Dom DiMaggio, Bos	1949	34

Triple Crown Hitters

NATIONAL LEAGUE

Player and Team	Year	HR	RBI	BA
Paul Hines, Prov	1878	4	50	.358
Hugh Duffy, Bos	1894	18	145	.438
Heinie Zimmerman*, Chi	1912	14	103	.372
Rogers Hornsby, StL	1922	42	152	.401
	1925	39	143	.403
Chuck Klein, Phil	1933	28	120	.368
Joe Medwick, StL	1937	31	154	.374

*Zimmerman ranked first in RBIs as calculated by Ernie Lanigan, but only third as calculated by Information Concepts Inc.

AMERICAN LEAGUE

Player and Team	Year	HR	RBI	BA
Nap Lajoie, Phil	1901	14	125	.422
Ty Cobb, Det	1909	9	115	.377
Jimmie Foxx, Phil	1933	48	163	.356
Lou Gehrig, NY	1934	49	165	.363
Ted Williams, Bos	1942	36	137	.356
	1947	32	114	.343
Mickey Mantle, NY	1956	52	130	.353
Frank Robinson, Balt	1966	49	122	.316
Carl Yastrzemski, Bos	1967	44	121	.326

THEY SAID IT

Steve Smith, Rangers coach, on the art of hitting pop-ups to the catcher in fungo: "I just pretend I'm back in my playing days with the bases loaded and two out."

Triple Crown Pitchers

NATIONAL LEAGUE				
Player and Team	Year	W	L	SO	ERA
Tommy Bond, Bos	1877	40	17	170	2.11
Hoss Radbourn, Prov	1884	60	12	441	1.38
Tim Keefe, NY	1888	35	12	333	1.74
John Clarkson, Bos	1889	49	19	284	2.73
Amos Rusie, NY	1894	36	13	195	2.78
Christy Mathewson, NY	1905	31	8	206	1.27
	1908	37	11	259	1.43
Grover Alexander, Phil	1915	31	10	241	1.22
	1916	33	12	167	1.55
	1917	30	13	201	1.86
Hippo Vaughn, Chi	1918	22	10	148	1.74
Grover Alexander, Chi	1920	27	14	173	1.91
Dazzy Vance, Bklyn	1924	28	6	262	2.16
Bucky Walters, Cin	1939	27	11	137	2.29
Sandy Koufax, LA	1963	25	5	306	1.88
	1965	26	8	382	2.04
	1966	27	9	317	1.73
Steve Carlton, Phil	1972	27	10	310	1.97
Dwight Gooden, NY	1985	24	4	268	1.53
Randy Johnson, Ariz	2002	24	5	334	2.32

AMERICAN LEAGUE				
Player and Team	Year	W	L	SO	ERA
Cy Young, Bos	1901	33	10	158	1.62
Rube Waddell, Phil	1905	26	11	287	1.48
Walter Johnson, Wash	1913	36	7	303	1.09
	1918	23	13	162	1.27
	1924	23	7	158	2.72
Lefty Grove, Phil	1930	28	5	209	2.54
	1931	31	4	175	2.06
Lefty Gomez, NY	1934	26	5	158	2.33
	1937	21	11	194	2.33
Hal Newhouser, Det	1945	25	9	212	1.81
Roger Clemens, Tor	1997	21	7	292	2.05
	1998	20	6	271	2.64
Pedro Martinez, Bos	1999	23	4	313	2.07

Consecutive Games Played, 500 or More Games

Cal Ripken Jr.	2,632	Sandy Alomar Sr.	648
Lou Gehrig	2,130	Eddie Brown	618
Everett Scott	1,307	Miguel Tejada	599
Steve Garvey	1,207	Roy McMillan	585
Billy Williams	1,117	George Pinckney	577
Joe Sewell	1,103	Steve Brodie	574
Stan Musial	895	Aaron Ward	565
Eddie Yost	829	Alex Rodriguez	546
Gus Suhr	822	Candy LaChance	540
Nellie Fox	798	Buck Freeman	535
Pete Rose	745	Fred Luderus	533
Dale Murphy	740	Clyde Milan	511
Richie Ashburn	730	Charlie Gehringer	511
Ernie Banks	717	Vada Pinson	508
Pete Rose	678	Tony Cuccinello	504
Earl Averill	673	Charlie Gehringer	504
Frank McCormick	652	Omar Moreno	503

Unassisted Triple Plays

Player and Team	Date	Pos	Opp	Opp Batter
Neal Ball, Clev	7-19-09	SS	Bos	Amby McConnell
Bill Wambsganss, Clev	10-10-20	2B	Bklyn	Clarence Mitchell
George Burns, Bos	9-14-23	1B	Clev	Frank Brower
Ernie Padgett, Bos	10-6-23	SS	Phil	Walter Holke
Glenn Wright, Pitt	5-7-25	SS	StL	Jim Bottomley
Jimmy Cooney, Chi	5-30-27	SS	Pitt	Paul Waner
Johnny Neun, Det	5-31-27	1B	Clev	Homer Summa
Ron Hansen, Wash	7-30-68	SS	Clev	Joe Azcue
Mickey Morandini, Phil	9-20-92	2B	Pitt	Jeff King
John Valentin, Bos	7-15-94	SS	Minn	Marc Newfield
Randy Velarde, Oak	5-29-00	2B	NYY	Shane Spencer
Rafael Furcal, Atl	8-10-03	SS	StL	Woody Williams

Pennant Winners

Year	Team	Manager	W	L	Pct	GA
1900	Brooklyn	Ned Hanlon	82	54	.603	4½
1901	Pittsburgh	Fred Clarke	90	49	.647	7½
1902	Pittsburgh	Fred Clarke	103	36	.741	27½
1903	Pittsburgh	Fred Clarke	91	49	.650	6½
1904	New York	John McGraw	106	47	.693	13
1905	New York	John McGraw	105	48	.686	9
1906	Chicago	Frank Chance	116	36	.763	20
1907	Chicago	Frank Chance	107	45	.704	17
1908	Chicago	Frank Chance	99	55	.643	1
1909	Pittsburgh	Fred Clarke	110	42	.724	6½
1910	Chicago	Frank Chance	104	50	.675	13
1911	New York	John McGraw	99	54	.647	7½
1912	New York	John McGraw	103	48	.682	10
1913	New York	John McGraw	101	51	.664	12½
1914	Boston	George Stallings	94	59	.614	10½
1915	Philadelphia	Pat Moran	90	62	.592	7
1916	Brooklyn	Wilbert Robinson	94	60	.610	2½
1917	New York	John McGraw	98	56	.636	10
1918	Chicago	Fred Mitchell	84	45	.651	10½
1919	Cincinnati	Pat Moran	96	44	.686	9
1920	Brooklyn	Wilbert Robinson	93	61	.604	7
1921	New York	John McGraw	94	59	.614	4
1922	New York	John McGraw	93	61	.604	7
1923	New York	John McGraw	95	58	.621	4½
1924	New York	John McGraw	93	60	.608	1½
1925	Pittsburgh	Bill McKechnie	95	58	.621	8½
1926	St. Louis	Rogers Hornsby	89	65	.578	2
1927	Pittsburgh	Donie Bush	94	60	.610	1½
1928	St. Louis	Bill McKechnie	95	59	.617	2
1929	Chicago	Joe McCarthy	98	54	.645	10½
1930	St. Louis	Gabby Street	92	62	.597	2
1931	St. Louis	Gabby Street	101	53	.656	13
1932	Chicago	Charlie Grimm	90	64	.584	4
1933	New York	Bill Terry	91	61	.599	5
1934	St. Louis	Frankie Frisch	95	58	.621	2
1935	Chicago	Charlie Grimm	100	54	.649	4
1936	New York	Bill Terry	92	62	.597	5
1937	New York	Bill Terry	95	57	.625	3
1938	Chicago	Gabby Hartnett	89	63	.586	2
1939	Cincinnati	Bill McKechnie	97	57	.630	4½
1940	Cincinnati	Bill McKechnie	100	53	.654	12
1941	Brooklyn	Leo Durocher	100	54	.649	2½
1942	St. Louis	Billy Southworth	106	48	.688	2
1943	St. Louis	Billy Southworth	105	49	.682	18
1944	St. Louis	Billy Southworth	105	49	.682	14½
1945	Chicago	Charlie Grimm	98	56	.636	3
1946	St. Louis*	Eddie Dyer	98	58	.628	2
1947	Brooklyn	Burt Shotton	94	60	.610	5
1948	Boston	Billy Southworth	91	62	.595	6½
1949	Brooklyn	Burt Shotton	97	57	.630	1
1950	Philadelphia	Eddie Sawyer	91	63	.591	2
1951	New York†	Leo Durocher	98	59	.624	1
1952	Brooklyn	Chuck Dressen	96	57	.627	4½
1953	Brooklyn	Chuck Dressen	105	49	.682	13
1954	New York	Leo Durocher	97	57	.630	5
1955	Brooklyn	Walt Alston	98	55	.641	13½
1956	Brooklyn	Walt Alston	93	61	.604	1
1957	Milwaukee	Fred Haney	95	59	.617	8
1958	Milwaukee	Fred Haney	92	62	.597	8
1959	Los Angeles‡	Walt Alston	88	68	.564	2
1960	Pittsburgh	Danny Murtaugh	95	59	.617	7
1961	Cincinnati	Fred Hutchinson	93	61	.604	4
1962	San Francisco#	Al Dark	103	62	.624	1
1963	Los Angeles	Walt Alston	99	63	.611	6
1964	St. Louis	Johnny Keane	93	69	.574	1
1965	Los Angeles	Walt Alston	97	65	.599	2

Pennant Winners (Cont.)

Year	Team	Manager	W	L	Pct	GA
1966	Los Angeles	Walt Alston	95	67	.586	1½
1967	St. Louis	Red Schoendienst	101	60	.627	10½
1968	St. Louis	Red Schoendienst	97	65	.599	9
1969	New York (E)††	Gil Hodges	100	62	.617	8
1970	Cincinnati (W)††	Sparky Anderson	102	60	.630	14½
1971	Pittsburgh (E)††	Danny Murtaugh	97	65	.599	7
1972	Cincinnati (W)††	Sparky Anderson	95	59	.617	10½
1973	New York (E)††	Yogi Berra	82	79	.509	1½
1974	Los Angeles (W)††	Walt Alston	102	60	.630	4
1975	Cincinnati (W)††	Sparky Anderson	108	54	.667	20
1976	Cincinnati (W)††	Sparky Anderson	102	60	.630	10
1977	Los Angeles (W)††	Tommy Lasorda	98	64	.605	10
1978	Los Angeles (W)††	Tommy Lasorda	95	67	.586	2½
1979	Pittsburgh (E)††	Chuck Tanner	98	64	.605	2
1980	Philadelphia (E)††	Dallas Green	91	71	.562	1
1981	Los Angeles (W)††	Tommy Lasorda	63	47	.573	**
1982	St. Louis (E)††	Whitey Herzog	92	70	.568	3
1983	Philadelphia (E)††	Pat Corrales/ Paul Owens	90	72	.556	6
1984	San Diego (W)††	Dick Williams	92	70	.568	12
1985	St. Louis (E)††	Whitey Herzog	101	61	.623	3
1986	New York (E)††	Dave Johnson	108	54	.667	21½
1987	St. Louis (E)††	Whitey Herzog	95	67	.586	3
1988	Los Angeles (W)††	Tommy Lasorda	94	67	.584	7
1989	San Francisco (W)††	Roger Craig	92	70	.568	3
1990	Cincinnati (W)††	Lou Piniella	91	71	.562	5
1991	Atlanta (W)††	Bobby Cox	94	68	.580	1
1992	Atlanta (W)††	Bobby Cox	98	64	.605	8
1993	Philadelphia (E)††	Jim Fregosi	97	65	.599	3
1994	Season ended Aug. 11 due to players' strike.					
1995	Atlanta (E)††	Bobby Cox	90	54	.625	21
1996	Atlanta (E)††	Bobby Cox	96	66	.593	8
1997	Florida (wc)††	Jim Leyland	92	70	.568	-9
1998	San Diego (W)††	Bruce Bochy	98	64	.605	9½
1999	Atlanta Braves (E)††	Bobby Cox	103	59	.636	6½
2000	New York Mets (wc)††	Bobby Valentine	94	68	.580	-6½
2001	Arizona (W)††	Bob Brenly	92	70	.568	2
2002	San Francisco (wc)††	Dusty Baker	95	66	.590	-2½
2003	Florida (wc)††	Jack McKeon	91	71	.562	-10

*Defeated Brooklyn, two games to none, in playoff for pennant. †Defeated Brooklyn, two games to one, in playoff for pennant. ‡Defeated Milwaukee, two games to none, in playoff for pennant. #Defeated Los Angeles, two games to one, in playoff for pennant. ††Won Championship Series. **First half 36–21; second half 27–26, in season split by strike; defeated Houston in playoff for Western Division title.

THEY SAID IT

Jeff Bagwell, Astros first baseman, on a power slump in which he had gone without a home run in 35 games: "I'm Ichiro without speed and without the batting average."

Leading Batsmen

Year	Player and Team	BA	Year	Player and Team	BA
1900	Honus Wagner, Pitt	.381	1952	Stan Musial, StL	.336
1901	Jesse Burkett, StL	.382	1953	Carl Furillo, Bklyn	.344
1902	Ginger Beaumtl, Pitt	.357	1954	Willie Mays, NY	.345
1903	Honus Wagner, Pitt	.355	1955	Richie Ashburn, Phil	.338
1904	Honus Wagner, Pitt	.349	1956	Hank Aaron, Mil	.328
1905	Cy Seymour, Cin	.377	1957	Stan Musial, StL	.351
1906	Honus Wagner, Pitt	.339	1958	Richie Ashburn, Phil	.350
1907	Honus Wagner, Pitt	.350	1959	Hank Aaron, Mil	.355
1908	Honus Wagner, Pitt	.354	1960	Dick Groat, Pitt	.325
1909	Honus Wagner, Pitt	.339	1961	Roberto Clemente, Pitt	.351
1910	Sherry Magee, Phil	.331	1962	Tommy Davis, LA	.346
1911	Honus Wagner, Pitt	.334	1963	Tommy Davis, LA	.326
1912	Heinie Zimmerman, Chi	.372	1964	Roberto Clemente, Pitt	.339
1913	Jake Daubert, Bklyn	.350	1965	Roberto Clemente, Pitt	.329
1914	Jake Daubert, Bklyn	.329	1966	Matty Alou, Pitt	.342
1915	Larry Doyle, NY	.320	1967	Roberto Clemente, Pitt	.357
1916	Hal Chase, Cin	.339	1968	Pete Rose, Cin	.335
1917	Edd Roush, Cin	.341	1969	Pete Rose, Cin	.348
1918	Zach Wheat, Bklyn	.335	1970	Rico Carty, Atl	.366
1919	Edd Roush, Cin	.321	1971	Joe Torre, StL	.363
1920	Rogers Hornsby, StL	.370	1972	Billy Williams, Chi	.333
1921	Rogers Hornsby, StL	.397	1973	Pete Rose, Cin	.338
1922	Rogers Hornsby, StL	.401	1974	Ralph Garr, Atl	.353
1923	Rogers Hornsby, StL	.384	1975	Bill Madlock, Chi	.354
1924	Rogers Hornsby, StL	.424	1976	Bill Madlock, Chi	.339
1925	Rogers Hornsby, StL	.403	1977	Dave Parker, Pitt	.338
1926	Bubbles Hargrave, Cin	.353	1978	Dave Parker, Pitt	.334
1927	Paul Waner, Pitt	.380	1979	Keith Hernandez, StL	.344
1928	Rogers Hornsby, Bos	.387	1980	Bill Buckner, Chi	.324
1929	Lefty O'Doul, Phil	.398	1981	Bill Madlock, Pitt	.341
1930	Bill Terry, NY	.401	1982	Al Oliver, Mtl	.331
1931	Chick Hafey, StL	.349	1983	Bill Madlock, Pitt	.323
1932	Lefty O'Doul, Bklyn	.368	1984	Tony Gwynn, SD	.351
1933	Chuck Klein, Phil	.368	1985	Willie McGee, StL	.353
1934	Paul Waner, Pitt	.362	1986	Tim Raines, Mtl	.334
1935	Arky Vaughan, Pitt	.385	1987	Tony Gwynn, SD	.370
1936	Paul Waner, Pitt	.373	1988	Tony Gwynn, SD	.313
1937	Joe Medwick, StL	.374	1989	Tony Gwynn, SD	.336
1938	Ernie Lombardi, Cin	.342	1990	Willie McGee, StL	.335
1939	Johnny Mize, StL	.349	1991	Terry Pendleton, Atl	.319
1940	Debs Garms, Pitt	.355	1992	Gary Sheffield, SD	.330
1941	Pete Reiser, Bklyn	.343	1993	Andres Galarraga, Col	.370
1942	Ernie Lombardi, Bos	.330	1994	Tony Gwynn, SD	.394
1943	Stan Musial, StL	.357	1995	Tony Gwynn, SD	.368
1944	Dixie Walker, Bklyn	.357	1996	Tony Gwynn, SD	.353
1945	Phil Cavarretta, Chi	.355	1997	Tony Gwynn, SD	.372
1946	Stan Musial, StL	.365	1998	Larry Walker, Col	.363
1947	Harry Walker, StL-Phil	.363	1999	Larry Walker, Col	.379
1948	Stan Musial, StL	.376	2000	Todd Helton, Col	.372
1949	Jackie Robinson, Bklyn	.342	2001	Larry Walker, Col	.350
1950	Stan Musial, StL	.346	2002	Barry Bonds, SF	.370
1951	Stan Musial, StL	.355	2003	Albert Pujols, StL	.359

Leaders in Runs Scored

Year	Player and Team	Runs	Year	Player and Team	Runs
1900	Roy Thomas, Phil	131	1953	Duke Snider, Bklyn	132
1901	Jesse Burkett, StL	139	1954	Stan Musial, StL	120
1902	Honus Wagner, Pitt	105		Duke Snider, Bklyn	120
1903	Ginger Beaumont, Pitt	137	1955	Duke Snider, Bklyn	126
1904	George Browne, NY	99	1956	Frank Robinson, Cin	122
1905	Mike Donlin, NY	124	1957	Hank Aaron, Mil	118
1906	Honus Wagner, Pitt	103	1958	Willie Mays, SF	121
	Frank Chance, Chi	103	1959	Vada Pinson, Cin	131
1907	Spike Shannon, NY	104	1960	Bill Bruton, Mil	112
1908	Fred Tenney, NY	101	1961	Willie Mays, SF	129
1909	Tommy Leach, Pitt	126	1962	Frank Robinson, Cin	134
1910	Sherry Magee, Phil	110	1963	Hank Aaron, Mil	121
1911	Jimmy Sheckard, Chi	121	1964	Dick Allen, Phil	125
1912	Bob Bescher, Cin	120	1965	Tommy Harper, Cin	126
1913	Tommy Leach, Chi	99	1966	Felipe Alou, Atl	122
	Max Carey, Pitt	99	1967	Hank Aaron, Atl	113
1914	George Burns, NY	100		Lou Brock, StL	113
1915	Gavvy Cravath, Phil	89	1968	Glenn Beckert, Chi	98
1916	George Burns, NY	105	1969	Bobby Bonds, SF	120
1917	George Burns, NY	103		Pete Rose, Cin	120
1918	Heinie Groh, Cin	88	1970	Billy Williams, Chi	137
1919	George Burns, NY	86	1971	Lou Brock, StL	126
1920	George Burns, NY	115	1972	Joe Morgan, Cin	122
1921	Rogers Hornsby, StL	131	1973	Bobby Bonds, SF	131
1922	Rogers Hornsby, StL	141	1974	Pete Rose, Cin	110
1923	Ross Youngs, NY	121	1975	Pete Rose, Cin	112
1924	Frankie Frisch, NY	121	1976	Pete Rose, Cin	130
	Rogers Hornsby, StL	121	1977	George Foster, Cin	124
1925	Kiki Cuyler, Pitt	144	1978	Ivan DeJesus, Chi	104
1926	Kiki Cuyler, Pitt	113	1979	Keith Hernandez, StL	116
1927	Lloyd Waner, Pitt	133	1980	Keith Hernandez, StL	111
	Rogers Hornsby, NY	133	1981	Mike Schmidt, Phil	78
1928	Paul Waner, Pitt	142	1982	Lonnie Smith, StL	120
1929	Rogers Hornsby, Chi	156	1983	Tim Raines, Mtl	133
1930	Chuck Klein, Phil	158	1984	Ryne Sandberg, Chi	114
1931	Bill Terry, NY	121	1985	Dale Murphy, Atl	118
	Chuck Klein, Phil	121	1986	Von Hayes, Phil	107
1932	Chuck Klein, Phil	152		Tony Gwynn, SD	107
1933	Pepper Martin, StL	122	1987	Tim Raines, Mtl	123
1934	Paul Waner, Pitt	122	1988	Brett Butler, SF	109
1935	Augie Galan, Chi	133	1989	Howard Johnson, NY	104
1936	Arky Vaughan, Pitt	122		Will Clark, SF	104
1937	Joe Medwick, StL	111		Ryne Sandberg, Chi	104
1938	Mel Ott, NY	116	1990	Ryne Sandberg, Chi	116
1939	Billy Werber, Cin	115	1991	Brett Butler, LA	112
1940	Arky Vaughan, Pitt	113	1992	Barry Bonds, Pitt	109
1941	Pete Reiser, Bklyn	117	1993	Lenny Dykstra, Phil	143
1942	Mel Ott, NY	118	1994	Jeff Bagwell, Hou	104
1943	Arky Vaughan, Bklyn	112	1995	Craig Biggio, Hou	123
1944	Bill Nicholson, Chi	116	1996	Ellis Burks, Col	142
1945	Eddie Stanky, Bklyn	128	1997	Craig Biggio, Hou	146
1946	Stan Musial, StL	124	1998	Sammy Sosa, Chi	134
1947	Johnny Mize, NY	137	1999	Jeff Bagwell, Hou	143
1948	Stan Musial, StL	135	2000	Jeff Bagwell, Hou	152
1949	Pee Wee Reese, Bklyn	132	2001	Sammy Sosa, Chi	146
1950	Earl Torgeson, Bos	120	2002	Sammy Sosa, Chi	122
1951	Stan Musial, StL	124	2003	Albert Pujols, StL	137
	Ralph Kiner, Pitt	124			
1952	Stan Musial, StL	105			
	Solly Hemus, StL	105			

Leaders in Hits

Year	Player and Team	Hits	Year	Player and Team	Hits
1900	Willie Keeler, Bklyn	208	1954	Don Mueller, NY	212
1901	Jesse Burkett, StL	228	1955	Ted Kluszewski, Cin	192
1902	Ginger Beaumont, Pitt	194	1956	Hank Aaron, Mil	200
1903	Ginger Beaumont, Pitt	209	1957	Red Schoendienst, NY-Mil	200
1904	Ginger Beaumont, Pitt	185	1958	Richie Ashburn, Phil	215
1905	Cy Seymour, Cin	219	1959	Hank Aaron, Mil	223
1906	Harry Steinfeldt, Chi	176	1960	Willie Mays, SF	190
1907	Ginger Beaumont, Bos	187	1961	Vada Pinson, Cin	208
1908	Honus Wagner, Pitt	201	1962	Tommy Davis, LA	230
1909	Larry Doyle, NY	172	1963	Vada Pinson, Cin	204
1910	Honus Wagner, Pitt	178	1964	Roberto Clemente, Pitt	211
	Bobby Byrne, Pitt	178		Curt Flood, StL	211
1911	Doc Miller, Bos	192	1965	Pete Rose, Cin	209
1912	Heinie Zimmerman, Chi	207	1966	Felipe Alou, Atl	218
1913	Gavvy Cravath, Phil	179	1967	Roberto Clemente, Pitt	209
1914	Sherry Magee, Phil	171	1968	Felipe Alou, Atl	210
1915	Larry Doyle, NY	189		Pete Rose, Cin	210
1916	Hal Chase, Cin	184	1969	Matty Alou, Pitt	231
1917	Heinie Groh, Cin	182	1970	Pete Rose, Cin	205
1918	Charlie Hollocher, Chi	161		Billy Williams, Chi	205
1919	Ivy Olson, Bklyn	164	1971	Joe Torre, StL	230
1920	Rogers Hornsby, StL	218	1972	Pete Rose, Cin	198
1921	Rogers Hornsby, StL	235	1973	Pete Rose, Cin	230
1922	Rogers Hornsby, StL	250	1974	Ralph Garr, Atl	214
1923	Frankie Frisch, NY	223	1975	Dave Cash, Phil	213
1924	Rogers Hornsby, StL	227	1976	Pete Rose, Cin	215
1925	Jim Bottomley, StL	227	1977	Dave Parker, Pitt	215
1926	Eddie Brown, Bos	201	1978	Steve Garvey, LA	202
1927	Paul Waner, Pitt	237	1979	Garry Templeton, StL	211
1928	Freddy Lindstrom, NY	231	1980	Steve Garvey, LA	200
1929	Lefty O'Doul, Phil	254	1981	Pete Rose, Phil	140
1930	Bill Terry, NY	254	1982	Al Oliver, Mtl	204
1931	Lloyd Waner, Pitt	214	1983	Jose Cruz, Hou	189
1932	Chuck Klein, Phil	226		Andre Dawson, Mtl	189
1933	Chuck Klein, Phil	223	1984	Tony Gwynn, SD	213
1934	Paul Waner, Pitt	217	1985	Willie McGee, StL	216
1935	Billy Herman, Chi	227	1986	Tony Gwynn, SD	211
1936	Joe Medwick, StL	223	1987	Tony Gwynn, SD	218
1937	Joe Medwick, StL	237	1988	Andres Galarraga, Mtl	184
1938	Frank McCormick, Cin	209	1989	Tony Gwynn, SD	203
1939	Frank McCormick, Cin	209	1990	Brett Butler, SF	192
1940	Stan Hack, Chi	191		Lenny Dykstra, Phil	192
	Frank McCormick, Cin	191	1991	Terry Pendleton, Atl	187
1941	Stan Hack, Chi	186	1992	Terry Pendleton, Atl	199
1942	Enos Slaughter, StL	188		Andy Van Slyke, Pitt	199
1943	Stan Musial, StL	220	1993	Lenny Dykstra, Phil	194
1944	Stan Musial, StL	197	1994	Tony Gwynn, SD	165
	Phil Cavarretta, Chi	197	1995	Dante Bichette, Col	197
1945	Tommy Holmes, Bos	224		Tony Gwynn, SD	197
1946	Stan Musial, StL	228	1996	Lance Johnson, NY	227
1947	Tommy Holmes, Bos	191	1997	Tony Gwynn, SD	220
1948	Stan Musial, StL	230	1998	Dante Bichette, Col	219
1949	Stan Musial, StL	207	1999	Luis Gonzalez, Ariz	206
1950	Duke Snider, Bklyn	199	2000	Todd Helton, Col	216
1951	Richie Ashburn, Phil	221	2001	Rich Aurilia, SF	206
1952	Stan Musial, StL	194	2002	Vladimir Guerrero	206
1953	Richie Ashburn, Phil	205	2003	Albert Pujols, StL	212

Home Run Leaders

Year	Player and Team	HR	Year	Player and Team	HR
1900	Herman Long, Bos	12	1949	Ralph Kiner, Pitt	54
1901	Sam Crawford, Cin	16	1950	Ralph Kiner, Pitt	47
1902	Tommy Leach, Pitt	6	1951	Ralph Kiner, Pitt	42
1903	Jimmy Sheckard, Bklyn	9	1952	Ralph Kiner, Pitt	37
1904	Harry Lumley, Bklyn	9		Hank Sauer, Chi	37
1905	Fred Odwell, Cin	9	1953	Eddie Mathews, Mil	47
1906	Tim Jordan, Bklyn	12	1954	Ted Kluszewski, Cin	49
1907	Dave Brain, Bos	10	1955	Willie Mays, NY	51
1908	Tim Jordan, Bklyn	12	1956	Duke Snider, Bklyn	43
1909	Red Murray, NY	7	1957	Hank Aaron, Mil	44
1910	Fred Beck, Bos	10	1958	Ernie Banks, Chi	47
	Wildfire Schulte, Chi	10	1959	Eddie Mathews, Mil	46
1911	Wildfire Schulte, Chi	21	1960	Ernie Banks, Chi	41
1912	Heinie Zimmerman, Chi	14	1961	Orlando Cepeda, SF	46
1913	Gavvy Cravath, Phil	19	1962	Willie Mays, SF	49
1914	Gavvy Cravath, Phil	19	1963	Hank Aaron, Mil	44
1915	Gavvy Cravath, Phil	24		Willie McCovey, SF	44
1916	Dave Robertson, NY	12	1964	Willie Mays, SF	47
	Cy Williams, Chi	12	1965	Willie Mays, SF	52
1917	Dave Robertson, NY	12	1966	Hank Aaron, Atl	44
	Gavvy Cravath, Phil	12	1967	Hank Aaron, Atl	39
1918	Gavvy Cravath, Phil	8	1968	Willie McCovey, SF	36
1919	Gavvy Cravath, Phil	12	1969	Willie McCovey, SF	45
1920	Cy Williams, Phil	15	1970	Johnny Bench, Cin	45
1921	George Kelly, NY	23	1971	Willie Stargell, Pitt	48
1922	Rogers Hornsby, StL	42	1972	Johnny Bench, Cin	40
1923	Cy Williams, Phil	41	1973	Willie Stargell, Pitt	44
1924	Jack Fournier, Bklyn	27	1974	Mike Schmidt, Phil	36
1925	Rogers Hornsby, StL	39	1975	Mike Schmidt, Phil	38
1926	Hack Wilson, Chi	21	1976	Mike Schmidt, Phil	38
1927	Hack Wilson, Chi	30	1977	George Foster, Cin	52
	Cy Williams, Phil	30	1978	George Foster, Cin	40
1928	Hack Wilson, Chi	31	1979	Dave Kingman, Chi	48
	Jim Bottomley, StL	31	1980	Mike Schmidt, Phil	48
1929	Chuck Klein, Phil	43	1981	Mike Schmidt, Phil	31
1930	Hack Wilson, Chi	56	1982	Dave Kingman, NY	37
1931	Chuck Klein, Phil	31	1983	Mike Schmidt, Phil	40
1932	Chuck Klein, Phil	38	1984	Dale Murphy, Atl	36
	Mel Ott, NY	38		Mike Schmidt, Phil	36
1933	Chuck Klein, Phil	28	1985	Dale Murphy, Atl	37
1934	Ripper Collins, StL	35	1986	Mike Schmidt, Phil	37
	Mel Ott, NY	35	1987	Andre Dawson, Chi	49
1935	Wally Berger, Bos	34	1988	Darryl Strawberry, NY	39
1936	Mel Ott, NY	33	1989	Kevin Mitchell, SF	47
1937	Mel Ott, NY	31	1990	Ryne Sandberg, Chi	40
	Joe Medwick, StL	31	1991	Howard Johnson, NY	38
1938	Mel Ott, NY	36	1992	Fred McGriff, SD	35
1939	Johnny Mize, StL	28	1993	Barry Bonds, SF	46
1940	Johnny Mize, StL	43	1994	Matt Williams, SF	43
1941	Dolph Camilli, Bklyn	34	1995	Dante Bichette, Col	40
1942	Mel Ott, NY	30	1996	Andres Galarraga, Col	47
1943	Bill Nicholson, Chi	29	1997	Larry Walker, Col	49
1944	Bill Nicholson, Chi	33	1998	Mark McGwire, StL	70
1945	Tommy Holmes, Bos	28	1999	Mark McGwire, StL	65
1946	Ralph Kiner, Pitt	23	2000	Sammy Sosa, Chi	50
1947	Ralph Kiner, Pitt	51	2001	Barry Bonds, SF	73
	Johnny Mize, NY	51	2002	Sammy Sosa, Chi	49
1948	Ralph Kiner, Pitt	40	2003	Jim Thome, Phil	47
	Johnny Mize, NY	40			

Runs Batted In Leaders

Year	Player and Team	RBI	Year	Player and Team	RBI
1900	Elmer Flick, Phil	110	1952	Hank Sauer, Chi	121
1901	Honus Wagner, Pitt	126	1953	Roy Campanella, Bklyn	142
1902	Honus Wagner, Pitt	91	1954	Ted Kluszewski, Cin	141
1903	Sam Mertes, NY	104	1955	Duke Snider, Bklyn	136
1904	Bill Dahlen, NY	80	1956	Stan Musial, StL	109
1905	Cy Seymour, Cin	121	1957	Hank Aaron, Mil	132
1906	Jim Nealon, Pitt	83	1958	Ernie Banks, Chi	129
	Harry Steinfeldt, Chi	83	1959	Ernie Banks, Chi	143
1907	Sherry Magee, Phil	85	1960	Hank Aaron, Mil	126
1908	Honus Wagner, Pitt	109	1961	Orlando Cepeda, SF	142
1909	Honus Wagner, Pitt	100	1962	Tommy Davis, LA	153
1910	Sherry Magee, Phil	123	1963	Hank Aaron, Mil	130
1911	Wildfire Schulte, Chi	121	1964	Ken Boyer, StL	119
1912	Heinie Zimmerman, Chi	103	1965	Deron Johnson, Cin	130
1913	Gavvy Cravath, Phil	128	1966	Hank Aaron, Atl	127
1914	Sherry Magee, Phil	103	1967	Orlando Cepeda, StL	111
1915	Gavvy Cravath, Phil	115	1968	Willie McCovey, SF	105
1916	Heinie Zimmerman, Chi-NY	83	1969	Willie McCovey, SF	126
1917	Heinie Zimmerman, NY	102	1970	Johnny Bench, Cin	148
1918	Sherry Magee, Phil	76	1971	Joe Torre, StL	137
1919	Hi Myers, Bklyn	73	1972	Johnny Bench, Cin	125
1920	George Kelly, NY	94	1973	Willie Stargell, Pitt	119
	Rogers Hornsby, StL	94	1974	Johnny Bench, Cin	129
1921	Rogers Hornsby, StL	126	1975	Greg Luzinski, Phil	120
1922	Rogers Hornsby, StL	152	1976	George Foster, Cin	121
1923	Irish Meusel, NY	125	1977	George Foster, Cin	149
1924	George Kelly, NY	136	1978	George Foster, Cin	120
1925	Rogers Hornsby, StL	143	1979	Dave Winfield, SD	118
1926	Jim Bottomley, StL	120	1980	Mike Schmidt, Phil	121
1927	Paul Waner, Pitt	131	1981	Mike Schmidt, Phil	91
1928	Jim Bottomley, StL	136	1982	Dale Murphy, Atl	109
1929	Hack Wilson, Chi	159		Al Oliver, Mtl	109
1930	Hack Wilson, Chi	190	1983	Dale Murphy, Atl	121
1931	Chuck Klein, Phil	121	1984	Gary Carter, Mtl	106
1932	Don Hurst, Phil	143		Mike Schmidt, Phil	106
1933	Chuck Klein, Phil	120	1985	Dave Parker, Cin	125
1934	Mel Ott, NY	135	1986	Mike Schmidt, Phil	119
1935	Wally Berger, Bos	130	1987	Andre Dawson, Chi	137
1936	Joe Medwick, StL	138	1988	Will Clark, SF	109
1937	Joe Medwick, StL	154	1989	Kevin Mitchell, SF	125
1938	Joe Medwick, StL	122	1990	Matt Williams, SF	122
1939	Frank McCormick, Cin	128	1991	Howard Johnson, NY	117
1940	Johnny Mize, StL	137	1992	Darren Daulton, Phil	109
1941	Dolph Camilli, Bklyn	120	1993	Barry Bonds, SF	123
1942	Johnny Mize, NY	110	1994	Jeff Bagwell, Hou	116
1943	Bill Nicholson, Chi	128	1995	Dante Bichette, Col	128
1944	Bill Nicholson, Chi	122	1996	Andres Galarraga, Col	150
1945	Dixie Walker, Bklyn	124	1997	Andres Galarraga, Col	140
1946	Enos Slaughter, StL	130	1998	Sammy Sosa, Chi	158
1947	Johnny Mize, NY	138	1999	Mark McGwire, StL	147
1948	Stan Musial, StL	131	2000	Todd Helton, Col	147
1949	Ralph Kiner, Pitt	127	2001	Sammy Sosa, Chi	160
1950	Del Ennis, Phil	126	2002	Lance Berkman, Hou	128
1951	Monte Irvin, NY	121	2003	Preston Wilson, Col	141

Leading Base Stealers

Year	Player and Team	SB	Year	Player and Team	SB
1900	George Van Haltren, NY	45	1950	Sam Jethroe, Bos	35
	Patsy Donovan, StL	45	1951	Sam Jethroe, Bos	35
1901	Honus Wagner, Pitt	48	1952	Pee Wee Reese, Bklyn	30
1902	Honus Wagner, Pitt	43	1953	Bill Bruton, Mil	26
1903	Jimmy Sheckard, Bklyn	67	1954	Bill Bruton, Mil	34
	Frank Chance, Chi	67	1955	Bill Bruton, Mil	35
1904	Honus Wagner, Pitt	53	1956	Willie Mays, NY	40
1905	Billy Maloney, Chi	59	1957	Willie Mays, NY	38
	Art Devlin, NY	59	1958	Willie Mays, SF	31
1906	Frank Chance, Chi	57	1959	Willie Mays, SF	27
1907	Honus Wagner, Pitt	61	1960	Maury Wills, LA	50
1908	Honus Wagner, Pitt	53	1961	Maury Wills, LA	35
1909	Bob Bescher, Cin	54	1962	Maury Wills, LA	104
1910	Bob Bescher, Cin	70	1963	Maury Wills, LA	40
1911	Bob Bescher, Cin	80	1964	Maury Wills, LA	53
1912	Bob Bescher, Cin	67	1965	Maury Wills, LA	94
1913	Max Carey, Pitt	61	1966	Lou Brock, StL	74
1914	George Burns, NY	62	1967	Lou Brock, StL	52
1915	Max Carey, Pitt	36	1968	Lou Brock, StL	62
1916	Max Carey, Pitt	63	1969	Lou Brock, StL	53
1917	Max Carey, Pitt	46	1970	Bobby Tolan, Cin	57
1918	Max Carey, Pitt	58	1971	Lou Brock, StL	64
1919	George Burns, NY	40	1972	Lou Brock, StL	63
1920	Max Carey, Pitt	52	1973	Lou Brock, StL	70
1921	Frankie Frisch, NY	49	1974	Lou Brock, StL	118
1922	Max Carey, Pitt	51	1975	Davey Lopes, LA	77
1923	Max Carey, Pitt	51	1976	Davey Lopes, LA	63
1924	Max Carey, Pitt	49	1977	Frank Taveras, Pitt	70
1925	Max Carey, Pitt	46	1978	Omar Moreno, Pitt	71
1926	Kiki Cuyler, Pitt	35	1979	Omar Moreno, Pitt	77
1927	Frankie Frisch, StL	48	1980	Ron LeFlore, Mtl	97
1928	Kiki Cuyler, Chi	37	1981	Tim Raines, Mtl	71
1929	Kiki Cuyler, Chi	43	1982	Tim Raines, Mtl	78
1930	Kiki Cuyler, Chi	37	1983	Tim Raines, Mtl	90
1931	Frankie Frisch, StL	28	1984	Tim Raines, Mtl	75
1932	Chuck Klein, Phil	20	1985	Vince Coleman, StL	110
1933	Pepper Martin, StL	26	1986	Vince Coleman, StL	107
1934	Pepper Martin, StL	23	1987	Vince Coleman, StL	109
1935	Augie Galan, Chi	22	1988	Vince Coleman, StL	81
1936	Pepper Martin, StL	23	1989	Vince Coleman, StL	65
1937	Augie Galan, Chi	23	1990	Vince Coleman, StL	77
1938	Stan Hack, Chi	16	1991	Marquis Grissom, Mtl	76
1939	Stan Hack, Chi	17	1992	Marquis Grissom, Mtl	78
	Lee Handley, Pitt	17	1993	Chuck Carr, Fla	58
1940	Lonny Frey, Cin	22	1994	Craig Biggio, Hou	39
1941	Danny Murtaugh, Phil	18	1995	Quilvio Veras, Fla	56
1942	Pete Reiser, Bklyn	20	1996	Eric Young, Col	53
1943	Arky Vaughan, Bklyn	20	1997	Tony Womack, Pitt	60
1944	Johnny Barrett, Pitt	28	1998	Tony Womack, Pitt	58
1945	Red Schoendienst, StL	26	1999	Tony Womack, Ariz	72
1946	Pete Reiser, Bklyn	34	2000	Luis Castillo, Fla	62
1947	Jackie Robinson, Bklyn	29	2001	Juan Pierre, Col	46
1948	Richie Ashburn, Phil	32	2002	Luis Castillo, Fla	48
1949	Jackie Robinson, Bklyn	37	2003	Juan Pierre, Fla	65

Leading Pitchers—Winning Percentage

Year	Pitcher and Team	W	L	Pct	Year	Pitcher and Team	W	L	Pct
1900	Jesse Tannehill, Pitt	20	6	.769	1953	Carl Erskine, Bklyn	20	6	.769
1901	Jack Chesbro, Pitt	21	10	.677	1954	Johnny Antonelli, NY	21	7	.750
1902	Jack Chesbro, Pitt	28	6	.824	1955	Don Newcombe, Bklyn	20	5	.800
1903	Sam Leever, Pitt	25	7	.781	1956	Don Newcombe, Bklyn	27	7	.794
1904	Joe McGinnity, NY	35	8	.814	1957	Bob Buhl, Mil	18	7	.720
1905	Sam Leever, Pitt	20	5	.800	1958	Warren Spahn, Mil	22	11	.667
1906	Ed Reulbach, Chi	19	4	.826		Lew Burdette, Mil	20	10	.667
1907	Ed Reulbach, Chi	17	4	.810	1959	Roy Face, Pitt	18	1	.947
1908	Ed Reulbach, Chi	24	7	.774	1960	Ernie Broglio, StL	21	9	.700
1909	Christy Mathewson, NY	25	6	.806	1961	Johnny Podres, LA	18	5	.783
	Howie Camnitz, Pitt	25	6	.806	1962	Bob Purkey, Cin	23	5	.821
1910	King Cole, Chi	20	4	.833	1963	Ron Perranoski, LA	16	3	.842
1911	Rube Marquard, NY	24	7	.774	1964	Sandy Koufax, LA	19	5	.792
1912	Claude Hendrix, Pitt	24	9	.727	1965	Sandy Koufax, LA	26	8	.765
1913	Bert Humphries, Chi	16	4	.800	1966	Juan Marichal, SF	25	6	.806
1914	Bill James, Bos	26	7	.788	1967	Dick Hughes, StL	16	6	.727
1915	Grover Alexander, Phil	31	10	.756	1968	Steve Blass, Pitt	18	6	.750
1916	Tom Hughes, Bos	16	3	.842	1969	Tom Seaver, NY	25	7	.781
1917	Ferdie Schupp, NY	21	7	.750	1970	Bob Gibson, StL	23	7	.767
1918	Claude Hendrix, Chi	19	7	.731	1971	Don Gullett, Cin	16	6	.727
1919	Dutch Ruether, Cin	19	6	.760	1972	Gary Nolan, Cin	15	5	.750
1920	Burleigh Grimes, Bklyn	23	11	.676	1973	Tommy John, LA	16	7	.696
1921	Bill Doak, StL	15	6	.714	1974	Andy Messersmith, LA	20	6	.769
1922	Pete Donohue, Cin	18	9	.667	1975	Don Gullett, Cin	15	4	.789
1923	Dolf Luque, Cin	27	8	.771	1976	Steve Carlton, Phil	20	7	.741
1924	Emil Yde, Pitt	16	3	.842	1977	John Candelaria, Pitt	20	5	.800
1925	Bill Sherdel, StL	15	6	.714	1978	Gaylord Perry, SD	21	6	.778
1926	Ray Kremer, Pitt	20	6	.769	1979	Tom Seaver, Cin	16	6	.727
1927	Larry Benton, Bos-NY	17	7	.708	1980	Jim Bibby, Pitt	19	6	.760
1928	Larry Benton, NY	25	9	.735	1981*	Tom Seaver, Cin	14	2	.875
1929	Charlie Root, Chi	19	6	.760	1982	Phil Niekro, Atl	17	4	.810
1930	Freddie Fitzsimmons, NY	19	7	.731	1983	John Denny, Phil	19	6	.760
1931	Paul Derringer, StL	18	8	.692	1984	Rick Sutcliffe, Chi	16	1	.941
1932	Lon Warneke, Chi	22	6	.786	1985	Orel Hershiser, LA	19	3	.864
1933	Ben Cantwell, Bos	20	10	.667	1986	Bob Ojeda, NY	18	5	.783
1934	Dizzy Dean, StL	30	7	.811	1987	Dwight Gooden, NY	15	7	.682
1935	Bill Lee, Chi	20	6	.769	1988	David Cone, NY	20	3	.870
1936	Carl Hubbell, NY	26	6	.813	1989	Mike Bielecki, Chi	18	7	.720
1937	Carl Hubbell, NY	22	8	.733	1990	Doug Drabeck, Pitt	22	6	.786
1938	Bill Lee, Chi	22	9	.710	1991	John Smiley, Pitt	20	8	.714
1939	Paul Derringer, Cin	25	7	.781		Jose Rijo, Cin	15	6	.714
1940	Freddie Fitzsimmons, Bklyn	16	2	.889	1992	Bob Tewksbury, StL	16	5	.762
1941	Elmer Riddle, Cin	19	4	.826	1993	Tom Glavine, Atl	22	6	.786
1942	Larry French, Bklyn	15	4	.789	1994	Ken Hill, Mtl	16	5	.762
1943	Mort Cooper, StL	21	8	.724	1995	Greg Maddux, Atl	19	2	.905
1944	Ted Wilks, StL	17	4	.810	1996	John Smoltz, Atl	24	8	.750
1945	Harry Brecheen, StL	15	4	.789	1997	Denny Neagle, Atl	20	5	.800
1946	Murray Dickson, StL	15	6	.714	1998	John Smoltz, Atl	17	3	.850
1947	Larry Jansen, NY	21	5	.808	1999	Mike Hampton, Hou	22	4	.846
1948	Harry Brecheen, StL	20	7	.741	2000	Randy Johnson, Ariz	19	7	.730
1949	Preacher Roe, Bklyn	15	6	.714	2001	Curt Schilling, Ariz	22	6	.786
1950	Sal Maglie, NY	18	4	.818	2002	Randy Johnson, Ariz	24	5	.828
1951	Preacher Roe, Bklyn	22	3	.880	2003	Jason Schmidt, SF	17	5	.773
1952	Hoyt Wilhelm, NY	15	3	.833					

*1981 percentages based on 10 or more victories. Note: Percentages based on 15 or more victories in all other years.

Leading Pitchers—Earned Run Average

Year	Player and Team	ERA	Year	Player and Team	ERA
1900	Rube Waddell, Pitt	2.37	1952	Hoyt Wilhelm, NY	2.43
1901	Jesse Tannehill, Pitt	2.18	1953	Warren Spahn, Mil	2.10
1902	Jack Taylor, Chi	1.33	1954	Johnny Antonelli, NY	2.29
1903	Sam Leever, Pitt	2.06	1955	Bob Friend, Pitt	2.84
1904	Joe McGinnity, NY	1.61	1956	Lew Burdette, Mil	2.71
1905	Christy Mathewson, NY	1.27	1957	Johnny Podres, Bklyn	2.66
1906	Three Finger Brown, Chi	1.04	1958	Stu Miller, SF	2.47
1907	Jack Pfiester, Chi	1.15	1959	Sam Jones, SF	2.82
1908	Christy Mathewson, NY	1.43	1960	Mike McCormick, SF	2.70
1909	Christy Mathewson, NY	1.14	1961	Warren Spahn, Mil	3.01
1910	George McQuillan, Phil	1.60	1962	Sandy Koufax, LA	2.54
1911	Christy Mathewson, NY	1.99	1963	Sandy Koufax, LA	1.88
1912	Jeff Tesreau, NY	1.96	1964	Sandy Koufax, LA	1.74
1913	Christy Mathewson, NY	2.06	1965	Sandy Koufax, LA	2.04
1914	Bill Doak, StL	1.72	1966	Sandy Koufax, LA	1.73
1915	Grover Alexander, Phil	1.22	1967	Phil Niekro, Atl	1.87
1916	Grover Alexander, Phil	1.55	1968	Bob Gibson, StL	1.12
1917	Grover Alexander, Phil	1.83	1969	Juan Marichal, SF	2.10
1918	Hippo Vaughn, Chi	1.74	1970	Tom Seaver, NY	2.81
1919	Grover Alexander, Chi	1.72	1971	Tom Seaver, NY	1.76
1920	Grover Alexander, Chi	1.91	1972	Steve Carlton, Phil	1.98
1921	Bill Doak, StL	2.58	1973	Tom Seaver, NY	2.08
1922	Rosy Ryan, NY	3.00	1974	Buzz Capra, Atl	2.28
1923	Dolf Luque, Cin	1.93	1975	Randy Jones, SD	2.24
1924	Dazzy Vance, Bklyn	2.16	1976	John Denny, StL	2.52
1925	Dolf Luque, Cin	2.63	1977	John Candelaria, Pitt	2.34
1926	Ray Kremer, Pitt	2.61	1978	Craig Swan, NY	2.43
1927	Ray Kremer, Pitt	2.47	1979	J.R. Richard, Hou	2.71
1928	Dazzy Vance, Bklyn	2.09	1980	Don Sutton, LA	2.21
1929	Bill Walker, NY	3.08	1981	Nolan Ryan, Hou	1.69
1930	Dazzy Vance, Bklyn	2.61	1982	Steve Rogers, Mtl	2.40
1931	Bill Walker, NY	2.26	1983	Atlee Hammaker, SF	2.25
1932	Lon Warneke, Chi	2.37	1984	Alejandro Pena, LA	2.48
1933	Carl Hubbell, NY	1.66	1985	Dwight Gooden, NY	1.53
1934	Carl Hubbell, NY	2.30	1986	Mike Scott, Hou	2.22
1935	Cy Blanton, Pitt	2.59	1987	Nolan Ryan, Hou	2.76
1936	Carl Hubbell, NY	2.31	1988	Joe Magrane, StL	2.18
1937	Jim Turner, Bos	2.38	1989	Scott Garrelts, SF	2.28
1938	Bill Lee, Chi	2.66	1990	Danny Darwin, Hou	2.21
1939	Bucky Walters, Cin	2.29	1991	Dennis Martinez, Mtl	2.39
1940	Bucky Walters, Cin	2.48	1992	Bill Swift, SF	2.08
1941	Elmer Riddle, Cin	2.24	1993	Greg Maddux, Atl	2.36
1942	Mort Cooper, StL	1.77	1994	Greg Maddux, Atl	1.56
1943	Howie Pollet, StL	1.75	1995	Greg Maddux, Atl	1.63
1944	Ed Heusser, Cin	2.38	1996	Kevin Brown, Fla	1.89
1945	Hank Borowy, Chi	2.14	1997	Pedro Martinez, Mtl	1.90
1946	Howie Pollet, StL	2.10	1998	Greg Maddux, Atl	1.98
1947	Warren Spahn, Bos	2.33	1999	Randy Johnson, Ariz	2.48
1948	Harry Brecheen, StL	2.24	2000	Kevin Brown, LA	2.58
1949	Dave Koslo, NY	2.50	2001	Randy Johnson, Ariz	2.49
1950	Jim Hearn, StL-NY	2.49	2002	Randy Johnson, Ariz	2.32
1951	Chet Nichols, Bos	2.88	2003	Jason Schmidt, SF	2.34

Note: Based on 10 complete games through 1950, then 154 innings until National League expanded in 1962, when it became 162 innings. In strike-shortened 1981, one inning per game required.

Leading Pitchers—Strikeouts

Year	Player and Team	SO	Year	Player and Team	SO
1900	Rube Waddell, Pitt	133	1952	Warren Spahn, Bos	183
1901	Noodles Hahn, Cin	233	1953	Robin Roberts, Phil	198
1902	Vic Willis, Bos	226	1954	Robin Roberts, Phil	185
1903	Christy Mathewson, NY	267	1955	Sam Jones, Chi	198
1904	Christy Mathewson, NY	212	1956	Sam Jones, Chi	176
1905	Christy Mathewson, NY	206	1957	Jack Sanford, Phil	188
1906	Fred Beebe, Chi-StL	171	1958	Sam Jones, StL	225
1907	Christy Mathewson, NY	178	1959	Don Drysdale, LA	242
1908	Christy Mathewson, NY	259	1960	Don Drysdale, LA	246
1909	Orval Overall, Chi	205	1961	Sandy Koufax, LA	269
1910	Christy Mathewson, NY	190	1962	Don Drysdale, LA	232
1911	Rube Marquard, NY	237	1963	Sandy Koufax, LA	306
1912	Grover Alexander, Phil	195	1964	Bob Veale, Pitt	250
1913	Tom Seaton, Phil	168	1965	Sandy Koufax, LA	382
1914	Grover Alexander, Phil	214	1966	Sandy Koufax, LA	317
1915	Grover Alexander, Phil	241	1967	Jim Bunning, Phil	253
1916	Grover Alexander, Phil	167	1968	Bob Gibson, StL	268
1917	Grover Alexander, Phil	200	1969	Ferguson Jenkins, Chi	273
1918	Hippo Vaughn, Chi	148	1970	Tom Seaver, NY	283
1919	Hippo Vaughn, Chi	141	1971	Tom Seaver, NY	289
1920	Grover Alexander, Chi	173	1972	Steve Carlton, Phil	310
1921	Burleigh Grimes, Bklyn	136	1973	Tom Seaver, NY	251
1922	Dazzy Vance, Bklyn	134	1974	Steve Carlton, Phil	240
1923	Dazzy Vance, Bklyn	197	1975	Tom Seaver, NY	243
1924	Dazzy Vance, Bklyn	262	1976	Tom Seaver, NY	235
1925	Dazzy Vance, Bklyn	221	1977	Phil Niekro, Atl	262
1926	Dazzy Vance, Bklyn	140	1978	J.R. Richard, Hou	303
1927	Dazzy Vance, Bklyn	184	1979	J.R. Richard, Hou	313
1928	Dazzy Vance, Bklyn	200	1980	Steve Carlton, Phil	286
1929	Pat Malone, Chi	166	1981	Fernando Valenzuela, LA	180
1930	Bill Hallahan, StL	177	1982	Steve Carlton, Phil	286
1931	Bill Hallahan, StL	159	1983	Steve Carlton, Phil	275
1932	Dizzy Dean, StL	191	1984	Dwight Gooden, NY	276
1933	Dizzy Dean, StL	199	1985	Dwight Gooden, NY	268
1934	Dizzy Dean, StL	195	1986	Mike Scott, Hou	306
1935	Dizzy Dean, StL	182	1987	Nolan Ryan, Hou	270
1936	Van Lingle Mungo, Bklyn	238	1988	Nolan Ryan, Hou	228
1937	Carl Hubbell, NY	159	1989	Jose DeLeon, StL	201
1938	Clay Bryant, Chi	135	1990	David Cone, NY	233
1939	Claude Passeau, Phil-Chi	137	1991	David Cone, NY	241
	Bucky Walters, Cin	137	1992	John Smoltz, Atl	215
1940	Kirby Higbe, Phil	137	1993	Jose Rijo, Cin	227
1941	Johnny Vander Meer, Cin	202	1994	Andy Benes, SD	189
1942	Johnny Vander Meer, Cin	186	1995	Hideo Nomo, LA	236
1943	Johnny Vander Meer, Cin	174	1996	John Smoltz, Atl	276
1944	Bill Voiselle, NY	161	1997	Curt Schilling, Phil	319
1945	Preacher Roe, Pitt	148	1998	Curt Schilling, Phil	300
1946	Johnny Schmitz, Chi	135	1999	Randy Johnson, Ariz	364
1947	Ewell Blackwell, Cin	193	2000	Randy Johnson, Ariz	347
1948	Harry Brecheen, StL	149	2001	Randy Johnson, Ariz	372
1949	Warren Spahn, Bos	151	2002	Randy Johnson, Ariz	334
1950	Warren Spahn, Bos	191	2003	Kerry Wood, Chi	266
1951	Warren Spahn, Bos	164			
	Don Newcombe, Bklyn	164			

Leading Pitchers—Saves

Year	Player and Team	SV	Year	Player and Team	SV
1947	Hugh Casey, Bklyn	18	1976	Rawly Eastwick, Cin	26
1948	Harry Gumpert, Cin	17	1977	Rollie Fingers, SD	35
1949	Ted Wilks, StL	9	1978	Rollie Fingers, SD	37
1950	Jim Konstanty, Phil	22	1979	Bruce Sutter, Chi	37
1951	Ted Wilks, StL, Pitt	13	1980	Bruce Sutter, Chi	28
1952	Al Brazle, StL	16	1981	Bruce Sutter, StL	25
1953	Al Brazle, StL	18	1982	Bruce Sutter, StL	36
1954	Jim Hughes, Bklyn	24	1983	Lee Smith, Chi	29
1955	Jack Meyer, Phil	16	1984	Bruce Sutter, StL	45
1956	Clem Labine, Bklyn	19	1985	Jeff Reardon, Mtl	41
1957	Clem Labine, Bklyn	17	1986	Todd Worrell, StL	36
1958	Roy Face, Pitt	20	1987	Steve Bedrosian, Phil	40
1959	Lindy McDaniel, StL	15	1988	John Franco, Cin	39
	Don McMahon, Mil	15	1989	Mark Davis, SD	44
1960	Lindy McDaniel, StL	26	1990	John Franco, NY	33
1961	Stu Miller, SF	17	1991	Lee Smith, StL	47
	Roy Face, Pitt	17	1992	Lee Smith, StL	42
1962	Roy Face, Pitt	28	1993	Randy Myers, Chi	53
1963	Lindy McDaniel, Chi	22	1994	John Franco, NY	30
1964	Hal Woodeshick, Hou	23	1995	Randy Myers, Chi	38
1965	Ted Abernathy, Chi	31	1996	Jeff Brantley, Cin	44
1966	Phil Regan, LA	21		Todd Worrell, LA	44
1967	Ted Abernathy, Cin	28	1997	Jeff Shaw, Cin	42
1968	Phil Regan, Chi, LA	25	1998	Trevor Hoffman, SD	53
1969	Fred Gladding, Hou	29	1999	Ugueth Urbina, Mtl	41
1970	Wayne Granger, Cin	35	2000	Antonio Alfonseca, Fla	45
1971	Dave Giusti, Pitt	30	2001	Robb Nen, SF	45
1972	Clay Carroll, Cin	37	2002	John Smoltz, Atl	55
1973	Mike Marshall, Mtl	13	2003	Eric Gagne, LA	55
1974	Mike Marshall, LA	21			
1975	Al Hrabosky, StL	22			
	Rawly Eastwick, Cin	22			

THEY SAID IT

Ozzie Guillen, Marlins third base coach, on the inexplicable (to him) popularity of baseball's richest team: "You go to the moon, and you'll find someone who's a Yankee fan."

American League

Pennant Winners

Year	Team	Manager	W	L	Pct	GA
1901	Chicago	Clark Griffith	83	53	.610	4
1902	Philadelphia	Connie Mack	83	53	.610	5
1903	Boston	Jimmy Collins	91	47	.659	14½
1904	Boston	Jimmy Collins	95	59	.617	1½
1905	Philadelphia	Connie Mack	92	56	.622	2
1906	Chicago	Fielder Jones	93	58	.616	3
1907	Detroit	Hughie Jennings	92	58	.613	1½
1908	Detroit	Hughie Jennings	90	63	.588	½
1909	Detroit	Hughie Jennings	98	54	.645	3½
1910	Philadelphia	Connie Mack	102	48	.680	14½
1911	Philadelphia	Connie Mack	101	50	.669	13½
1912	Boston	Jake Stahl	105	47	.691	14
1913	Philadelphia	Connie Mack	96	57	.627	6½
1914	Philadelphia	Connie Mack	99	53	.651	8½
1915	Boston	Bill Carrigan	101	50	.669	2½
1916	Boston	Bill Carrigan	91	63	.591	2
1917	Chicago	Pants Rowland	100	54	.649	9
1918	Boston	Ed Barrow	75	51	.595	2½
1919	Chicago	Kid Gleason	88	52	.629	3½
1920	Cleveland	Tris Speaker	98	56	.636	2
1921	New York	Miller Huggins	98	55	.641	4½
1922	New York	Miller Huggins	94	60	.610	1
1923	New York	Miller Huggins	98	54	.645	16
1924	Washington	Bucky Harris	92	62	.597	2
1925	Washington	Bucky Harris	96	55	.636	8½
1926	New York	Miller Huggins	91	63	.591	3
1927	New York	Miller Huggins	110	44	.714	19
1928	New York	Miller Huggins	101	53	.656	2½
1929	Philadelphia	Connie Mack	104	46	.693	18
1930	Philadelphia	Connie Mack	102	52	.662	8
1931	Philadelphia	Connie Mack	107	45	.704	13½
1932	New York	Joe McCarthy	107	47	.695	13
1933	Washington	Joe Cronin	99	53	.651	7
1934	Detroit	Mickey Cochrane	101	53	.656	7
1935	Detroit	Mickey Cochrane	93	58	.616	3
1936	New York	Joe McCarthy	102	51	.667	19½
1937	New York	Joe McCarthy	102	52	.662	13
1938	New York	Joe McCarthy	99	53	.651	9½
1939	New York	Joe McCarthy	106	45	.702	17
1940	Detroit	Del Baker	90	64	.584	1
1941	New York	Joe McCarthy	101	53	.656	17
1942	New York	Joe McCarthy	103	51	.669	9
1943	New York	Joe McCarthy	98	56	.636	13½
1944	St. Louis	Luke Sewell	89	65	.578	1
1945	Detroit	Steve O'Neill	88	65	.575	1½
1946	Boston	Joe Cronin	104	50	.675	12
1947	New York	Bucky Harris	97	57	.630	12
1948	Cleveland†	Lou Boudreau	97	58	.626	1
1949	New York	Casey Stengel	97	57	.630	1
1950	New York	Casey Stengel	98	56	.636	3
1951	New York	Casey Stengel	98	56	.636	5
1952	New York	Casey Stengel	95	59	.617	2
1953	New York	Casey Stengel	99	52	.656	8½
1954	Cleveland	Al Lopez	111	43	.721	8
1955	New York	Casey Stengel	96	58	.623	3
1956	New York	Casey Stengel	97	57	.630	9
1957	New York	Casey Stengel	98	56	.636	8
1958	New York	Casey Stengel	92	62	.597	10
1959	Chicago	Al Lopez	94	60	.610	5
1960	New York	Casey Stengel	97	57	.630	8
1961	New York	Ralph Houk	109	53	.673	8
1962	New York	Ralph Houk	96	66	.593	5
1963	New York	Ralph Houk	104	57	.646	10½
1964	New York	Yogi Berra	99	63	.611	1
1965	Minnesota	Sam Mele	102	60	.630	7
1966	Baltimore	Hank Bauer	97	63	.606	9

Pennant Winners (Cont.)

Year	Team	Manager	W	L	Pct	GA
1967	Boston	Dick Williams	92	70	.568	1
1968	Detroit	Mayo Smith	103	59	.636	12
1969	Baltimore (E)‡	Earl Weaver	109	53	.673	19
1970	Baltimore (E)‡	Earl Weaver	108	54	.667	15
1971	Baltimore (E)‡	Earl Weaver	101	57	.639	12
1972	Oakland (W)‡	Dick Williams	93	62	.600	5½
1973	Oakland (W)‡	Dick Williams	94	68	.580	6
1974	Oakland (W)‡	Al Dark	90	72	.556	5
1975	Boston (E)‡	Darrell Johnson	95	65	.594	4½
1976	New York (E)‡	Billy Martin	97	62	.610	10½
1977	New York (E)‡	Billy Martin	100	62	.617	2½
1978	New York (E)†‡	Billy Martin, Bob Lemon	100	63	.613	1
1979	Baltimore (E)‡	Earl Weaver	102	57	.642	8
1980	Kansas City (W)‡	Jim Frey	97	65	.599	14
1981	New York (E)‡	Gene Michael/Bob Lemon	59	48	.551	#
1982	Milwaukee (E)‡	Buck Rodgers, Harvey Kuenn	95	67	.586	1
1983	Baltimore (E)‡	Joe Altobelli	98	64	.605	6
1984	Detroit (E)‡	Sparky Anderson	104	58	.642	15
1985	Kansas City (W)‡	Dick Howser	91	71	.562	1
1986	Boston (E)‡	John McNamara	95	66	.590	5½
1987	Minnesota (W)‡	Tom Kelly	85	77	.525	2
1988	Oakland (W)‡	Tony La Russa	104	58	.642	13
1989	Oakland (W)‡	Tony La Russa	99	63	.611	7
1990	Oakland (W)‡	Tony La Russa	103	59	.636	9
1991	Minnesota (W)‡	Tom Kelly	95	67	.586	8
1992	Toronto†	Cito Gaston	96	66	.593	4
1993	Toronto‡	Cito Gaston	95	67	.586	7
1994	Season ended Aug. 11 due to players' strike.					
1995	Cleveland (C)‡	Mike Hargrove	100	44	.694	30
1996	New York (E)‡	Joe Torre	92	70	.568	4
1997	Cleveland (C)‡	Mike Hargrove	86	75	.534	6
1998	New York (E)‡	Joe Torre	114	48	.704	22
1999	New York (E)‡	Joe Torre	98	64	.605	4
2000	New York (E)‡	Joe Torre	87	74	.540	2½
2001	New York (E)‡	Joe Torre	95	65	.594	13½
2002	Anaheim (wc)‡	Mike Scioscia	99	63	.611	-4
2003	New York (E)‡	Joe Torre	101	61	.623	6

†Defeated Boston in one-game playoff. ‡Won championship series.
#First half 34–22; second half 25–26, in season split by strike; defeated Milwaukee in playoff for Eastern Divison title.

Leading Batsmen

Year	Player and Team	BA	Year	Player and Team	BA
1901	Nap Lajoie, Phil	.422	1923	Harry Heilmann, Det	.403
1902	Ed Delahanty, Wash	.376	1924	Babe Ruth, NY	.378
1903	Nap Lajoie, Clev	.355	1925	Harry Heilmann, Det	.393
1904	Nap Lajoie, Clev	.381	1926	Heinie Manush, Det	.378
1905	Elmer Flick, Clev	.306	1927	Harry Heilmann, Det	.398
1906	George Stone, StL	.358	1928	Goose Goslin, Wash	.379
1907	Ty Cobb, Det	.350	1929	Lew Fonseca, Clev	.369
1908	Ty Cobb, Det	.324	1930	Al Simmons, Phil	.381
1909	Ty Cobb, Det	.377	1931	Al Simmons, Phil	.390
1910	Nap Lajoie, Clev*	.383	1932	Dale Alexander, Det-Bos	.367
1911	Ty Cobb, Det	.420	1933	Jimmie Foxx, Phil	.356
1912	Ty Cobb, Det	.410	1934	Lou Gehrig, NY	.363
1913	Ty Cobb, Det	.390	1935	Buddy Myer, Wash	.349
1914	Ty Cobb, Det	.368	1936	Luke Appling, Chi	.388
1915	Ty Cobb, Det	.369	1937	Charlie Gehringer, Det	.371
1916	Tris Speaker, Clev	.386	1938	Jimmie Foxx, Bos	.349
1917	Ty Cobb, Det	.383	1939	Joe DiMaggio, NY	.381
1918	Ty Cobb, Det	.382	1940	Joe DiMaggio, NY	.352
1919	Ty Cobb, Det	.384	1941	Ted Williams, Bos	.406
1920	George Sisler, StL	.407	1942	Ted Williams, Bos	.356
1921	Harry Heilmann, Det	.394	1943	Luke Appling, Chi	.328
1922	George Sisler, StL	.420	1944	Lou Boudreau, Clev	.327

*League president Ban Johnson declared Ty Cobb batting champion with a .385 average, beating Lajoie's .384. However, subsequent research has led to the revision of Lajoie's average to .383 and Cobb's to .382.

Leading Batsmen *(Cont.)*

Year	Player and Team	BA	Year	Player and Team	BA
1945	Snuffy Stirnweiss, NY	.309	1975	Rod Carew, Minn	.359
1946	Mickey Vernon, Wash	.353	1976	George Brett, KC	.333
1947	Ted Williams, Bos	.343	1977	Rod Carew, Minn	.388
1948	Ted Williams, Bos	.369	1978	Rod Carew, Minn	.333
1949	George Kell, Det	.343	1979	Fred Lynn, Bos	.333
1950	Billy Goodman, Bos	.354	1980	George Brett, KC	.390
1951	Ferris Fain, Phil	.344	1981	Carney Lansford, Bos	.336
1952	Ferris Fain, Phil	.327	1982	Willie Wilson, KC	.332
1953	Mickey Vernon, Wash	.337	1983	Wade Boggs, Bos	.361
1954	Bobby Avila, Clev	.341	1984	Don Mattingly, NY	.343
1955	Al Kaline, Det	.340	1985	Wade Boggs, Bos	.368
1956	Mickey Mantle, NY	.353	1986	Wade Boggs, Bos	.357
1957	Ted Williams, Bos	.388	1987	Wade Boggs, Bos	.363
1958	Ted Williams, Bos	.328	1988	Wade Boggs, Bos	.366
1959	Harvey Kuenn, Det	.353	1989	Kirby Puckett, Minn	.339
1960	Pete Runnels, Bos	.320	1990	George Brett, KC	.329
1961	Norm Cash, Det	.361	1991	Julio Franco, Tex	.341
1962	Pete Runnels, Bos	.326	1992	Edgar Martinez, Sea	.343
1963	Carl Yastrzemski, Bos	.321	1993	John Olerud, Tor	.363
1964	Tony Oliva, Minn	.323	1994	Paul O'Neill, NY	.359
1965	Tony Oliva, Minn	.321	1995	Edgar Martinez, Sea	.356
1966	Frank Robinson, Balt	.316	1996	Alex Rodriguez, Sea	.358
1967	Carl Yastrzemski, Bos	.326	1997	Frank Thomas, Chi	.347
1968	Carl Yastrzemski, Bos	.301	1998	Bernie Williams, NY	.339
1969	Rod Carew, Minn	.332	1999	Nomar Garciaparra, Bos	.357
1970	Alex Johnson, Cal	.329	2000	Nomar Garciaparra, Bos	.372
1971	Tony Oliva, Minn	.337	2001	Ichiro Suzuki, Sea	.350
1972	Rod Carew, Minn	.318	2002	Manny Ramirez, Bos	.349
1973	Rod Carew, Minn	.350	2003	Bill Mueller, Bos	.326
1974	Rod Carew, Minn	.364			

Leaders in Runs Scored

Year	Player and Team	Runs	Year	Player and Team	Runs
1901	Nap Lajoie, Phil	145	1936	Lou Gehrig, NY	167
1902	Dave Fultz, Phil	110	1937	Joe DiMaggio, NY	151
1903	Patsy Dougherty, Bos	108	1938	Hank Greenberg, Det	144
1904	Patsy Dougherty, Bos-NY	113	1939	Red Rolfe, NY	139
1905	Harry Davis, Phil	92	1940	Ted Williams, Bos	134
1906	Elmer Flick, Clev	98	1941	Ted Williams, Bos	135
1907	Sam Crawford, Det	102	1942	Ted Williams, Bos	141
1908	Matty McIntyre, Det	105	1943	George Case, Wash	102
1909	Ty Cobb, Det	116	1944	Snuffy Stirnweiss, NY	125
1910	Ty Cobb, Det	106	1945	Snuffy Stirnweiss, NY	107
1911	Ty Cobb, Det	147	1946	Ted Williams, Bos	142
1912	Eddie Collins, Phil	137	1947	Ted Williams, Bos	125
1913	Eddie Collins, Phil	125	1948	Tommy Henrich, NY	138
1914	Eddie Collins, Phil	122	1949	Ted Williams, Bos	150
1915	Ty Cobb, Det	144	1950	Dom DiMaggio, Bos	131
1916	Ty Cobb, Det	113	1951	Dom DiMaggio, Bos	113
1917	Donie Bush, Det	112	1952	Larry Doby, Clev	104
1918	Ray Chapman, Clev	84	1953	Al Rosen, Clev	115
1919	Babe Ruth, Bos	103	1954	Mickey Mantle, NY	129
1920	Babe Ruth, NY	158	1955	Al Smith, Clev	123
1921	Babe Ruth, NY	177	1956	Mickey Mantle, NY	132
1922	George Sisler, StL	134	1957	Mickey Mantle, NY	121
1923	Babe Ruth, NY	151	1958	Mickey Mantle, NY	127
1924	Babe Ruth, NY	143	1959	Eddie Yost, Det	115
1925	Johnny Mostil, Chi	135	1960	Mickey Mantle, NY	119
1926	Babe Ruth, NY	139	1961	Mickey Mantle, NY	132
1927	Babe Ruth, NY	158		Roger Maris, NY	132
1928	Babe Ruth, NY	163	1962	Albie Pearson, LA	115
1929	Charlie Gehringer, Det	131	1963	Bob Allison, Minn	99
1930	Al Simmons, Phil	152	1964	Tony Oliva, Minn	109
1931	Lou Gehrig, NY	163	1965	Zoilo Versalles, Minn	126
1932	Jimmie Foxx, Phil	151	1966	Frank Robinson, Balt	122
1933	Lou Gehrig, NY	138	1967	Carl Yastrzemski, Bos	112
1934	Charlie Gehringer, Det	134	1968	Dick McAuliffe, Det	95
1935	Lou Gehrig, NY	125			

Leaders in Runs Scored *(Cont.)*

Year	Player and Team	Runs	Year	Player and Team	Runs
1969	Reggie Jackson, Oak	123	1988	Wade Boggs, Bos	128
1970	Carl Yastrzemski, Bos	125	1989	Rickey Henderson, NY-Oak	113
1971	Don Buford, Balt	99		Wade Boggs, Bos	113
1972	Bobby Murcer, NY	102	1990	Rickey Henderson, Oak	119
1973	Reggie Jackson, Oak	99	1991	Paul Molitor, Mil	133
1974	Carl Yastrzemski, Bos	93	1992	Tony Phillips, Det	114
1975	Fred Lynn, Bos	103	1993	Rafael Palmeiro, Tex	124
1976	Roy White, NY	104	1994	Frank Thomas, Chi	106
1977	Rod Carew, Minn	128	1995	Albert Belle, Clev	121
1978	Ron LeFlore, Det	126		Edgar Martinez, Sea	121
1979	Don Baylor, Cal	120	1996	Alex Rodriguez, Sea	141
1980	Willie Wilson, KC	133	1997	Ken Griffey Jr., Sea	125
1981	Rickey Henderson, Oak	89	1998	Derek Jeter, NY	127
1982	Paul Molitor, Mil	136	1999	Roberto Alomar, Clev	138
1983	Cal Ripken, Balt	121	2000	Johnny Damon, KC	136
1984	Dwight Evans, Bos	121	2001	Alex Rodriguez, Tex	133
1985	Rickey Henderson, NY	146	2002	Alfonso Soriano, NY	128
1986	Rickey Henderson, NY	130	2003	Alex Rodriguez, Tex	124
1987	Paul Molitor, Mil	114			

Leaders in Hits

Year	Player and Team	Hits	Year	Player and Team	Hits
1901	Nap Lajoie, Phil	229	1943	Dick Wakefield, Det	200
1902	Piano Legs Hickman, Bos-Clev	194	1944	Snuffy Stirnweiss, NY	205
1903	Patsy Dougherty, Bos	195	1945	Snuffy Stirnweiss, NY	195
1904	Nap Lajoie, Clev	211	1946	Johnny Pesky, Bos	208
1905	George Stone, StL	187	1947	Johnny Pesky, Bos	207
1906	Nap Lajoie, Clev	214	1948	Bob Dillinger, StL	207
1907	Ty Cobb, Det	212	1949	Dale Mitchell, Clev	203
1908	Ty Cobb, Det	188	1950	George Kell, Det	218
1909	Ty Cobb, Det	216	1951	George Kell, Det	191
1910	Nap Lajoie, Clev	227	1952	Nellie Fox, Chi	192
1911	Ty Cobb, Det	248	1953	Harvey Kuenn, Det	209
1912	Ty Cobb, Det	227	1954	Nellie Fox, Chi	201
1913	Joe Jackson, Clev	197		Harvey Kuenn, Det	201
1914	Tris Speaker, Bos	193	1955	Al Kaline, Det	200
1915	Ty Cobb, Det	208	1956	Harvey Kuenn, Det	196
1916	Tris Speaker, Clev	211	1957	Nellie Fox, Chi	196
1917	Ty Cobb, Det	225	1958	Nellie Fox, Chi	187
1918	George Burns, Phil	178	1959	Harvey Kuenn, Det	198
1919	Ty Cobb, Det	191	1960	Minnie Minoso, Chi	184
	Bobby Veach, Det	191	1961	Norm Cash, Det	193
1920	George Sisler, StL	257	1962	Bobby Richardson, NY	209
1921	Harry Heilmann, Det	237	1963	Carl Yastrzemski, Bos	183
1922	George Sisler, StL	246	1964	Tony Oliva, Minn	217
1923	Charlie Jamieson, Clev	222	1965	Tony Oliva, Minn	185
1924	Sam Rice, Wash	216	1966	Tony Oliva, Minn	191
1925	Al Simmons, Phil	253	1967	Carl Yastrzemski, Bos	189
1926	George Burns, Clev	216	1968	Bert Campaneris, Oak	177
	Sam Rice, Wash	216	1969	Tony Oliva, Minn	197
1927	Earle Combs, NY	231	1970	Tony Oliva, Minn	204
1928	Heinie Manush, StL	241	1971	Cesar Tovar, Minn	204
1929	Dale Alexander, Det	215	1972	Joe Rudi, Oak	181
	Charlie Gehringer, Det	215	1973	Rod Carew, Minn	203
1930	Johnny Hodapp, Clev	225	1974	Rod Carew, Minn	218
1931	Lou Gehrig, NY	211	1975	George Brett, KC	195
1932	Al Simmons, Phil	216	1976	George Brett, KC	215
1933	Heinie Manush, Wash	221	1977	Rod Carew, Minn	239
1934	Charlie Gehringer, Det	214	1978	Jim Rice, Bos	213
1935	Joe Vosmik, Clev	216	1979	George Brett, KC	212
1936	Earl Averill, Clev	232	1980	Willie Wilson, KC	230
1937	Beau Bell, StL	218	1981	Rickey Henderson, Oak	135
1938	Joe Vosmik, Bos	201	1982	Robin Yount, Mil	210
1939	Red Rolfe, NY	213	1983	Cal Ripken Jr., Balt	211
1940	Rip Radcliff, StL	200	1984	Don Mattingly, NY	207
	Barney McCosky, Det	200	1985	Wade Boggs, Bos	240
	Doc Cramer, Bos	200	1986	Don Mattingly, NY	238
1941	Cecil Travis, Wash	218	1987	Kirby Puckett, Minn	207
1942	Johnny Pesky, Bos	205		Kevin Seitzer, KC	207

Leaders in Hits (Cont.)

Year	Player and Team	Hits	Year	Player and Team	Hits
1988	Kirby Puckett, Minn	234	1996	Paul Molitor, Minn	225
1989	Kirby Puckett, Minn	215	1997	Nomar Garciaparra, Bos	209
1990	Rafael Palmeiro, Tex	191	1998	Alex Rodriguez, Sea	213
1991	Paul Molitor, Mil	216	1999	Derek Jeter, NY	219
1992	Kirby Puckett, Minn	210	2000	Darin Erstad, Ana	240
1993	Paul Molitor, Tor	211	2001	Ichiro Suzuki, Sea	242
1994	Kenny Lofton, Clev	160	2002	Alfonso Soriano, NY	209
1995	Lance Johnson, Chi	186	2003	Vernon Wells, Tor	215

Home Run Leaders

Year	Player and Team	HR	Year	Player and Team	HR
1901	Nap Lajoie, Phil	13	1955	Mickey Mantle, NY	37
1902	Socks Seybold, Phil	16	1956	Mickey Mantle, NY	52
1903	Buck Freeman, Bos	13	1957	Roy Sievers, Wash	42
1904	Harry Davis, Phil	10	1958	Mickey Mantle, NY	42
1905	Harry Davis, Phil	8	1959	Rocky Colavito, Clev	42
1906	Harry Davis, Phil	12		Harmon Killebrew, Wash	42
1907	Harry Davis, Phil	8	1960	Mickey Mantle, NY	40
1908	Sam Crawford, Det	7	1961	Roger Maris, NY	61
1909	Ty Cobb, Det	9	1962	Harmon Killebrew, Minn	48
1910	Jake Stahl, Bos	10	1963	Harmon Killebrew, Minn	45
1911	Frank Baker, Phil	9	1964	Harmon Killebrew, Minn	49
1912	Frank Baker, Phil	10	1965	Tony Conigliaro, Bos	32
	Tris Speaker, Bos	10	1966	Frank Robinson, Balt	49
1913	Frank Baker, Phil	13	1967	Harmon Killebrew, Minn	44
1914	Frank Baker, Phil	9		Carl Yastrzemski, Bos	44
1915	Braggo Roth, Chi-Clev	7	1968	Frank Howard, Wash	44
1916	Wally Pipp, NY	12	1969	Harmon Killebrew, Minn	49
1917	Wally Pipp, NY	9	1970	Frank Howard, Wash	44
1918	Babe Ruth, Bos	11	1971	Bill Melton, Chi	33
	Tilly Walker, Phil	11	1972	Dick Allen, Chi	37
1919	Babe Ruth, Bos	29	1973	Reggie Jackson, Oak	32
1920	Babe Ruth, NY	54	1974	Dick Allen, Chi	32
1921	Babe Ruth, NY	59	1975	Reggie Jackson, Oak	36
1922	Ken Williams, StL	39		George Scott, Mil	36
1923	Babe Ruth, NY	41	1976	Graig Nettles, NY	32
1924	Babe Ruth, NY	46	1977	Jim Rice, Bos	39
1925	Bob Meusel, NY	33	1978	Jim Rice, Bos	46
1926	Babe Ruth, NY	47	1979	Gorman Thomas, Mil	45
1927	Babe Ruth, NY	60	1980	Reggie Jackson, NY	41
1928	Babe Ruth, NY	54		Ben Oglivie, Mil	41
1929	Babe Ruth, NY	46	1981	Tony Armas, Oak	22
1930	Babe Ruth, NY	49	1981	Dwight Evans, Bos	22
1931	Babe Ruth, NY	46		Bobby Grich, Cal	22
	Lou Gehrig, NY	46		Eddie Murray, Balt	22
1932	Jimmie Foxx, Phil	58	1982	Reggie Jackson, Cal	39
1933	Jimmie Foxx, Phil	48		Gorman Thomas, Mil	39
1934	Lou Gehrig, NY	49	1983	Jim Rice, Bos	39
1935	Jimmie Foxx, Phil	36	1984	Tony Armas, Bos	43
	Hank Greenberg, Det	36	1985	Darrell Evans, Det	40
1936	Lou Gehrig, NY	49	1986	Jesse Barfield, Tor	40
1937	Joe DiMaggio, NY	46	1987	Mark McGwire, Oak	49
1938	Hank Greenberg, Det	58	1988	Jose Canseco, Oak	42
1939	Jimmie Foxx, Bos	35	1989	Fred McGriff, Tor	36
1940	Hank Greenberg, Det	41	1990	Cecil Fielder, Det	51
1941	Ted Williams, Bos	37	1991	Jose Canseco, Oak	44
1942	Ted Williams, Bos	36		Cecil Fielder, Det	44
1943	Rudy York, Det	34	1992	Juan Gonzalez, Tex	43
1944	Nick Etten, NY	22	1993	Juan Gonzalez, Tex	46
1945	Vern Stephens, StL	24	1994	Ken Griffey Jr., Sea	40
1946	Hank Greenberg, Det	44	1995	Albert Belle, Clev	50
1947	Ted Williams, Bos	32	1996	Mark McGwire, Oak	52
1948	Joe DiMaggio, NY	39	1997	Ken Griffey Jr., Sea	56
1949	Ted Williams, Bos	43	1998	Ken Griffey Jr., Sea	56
1950	Al Rosen, Clev	37	1999	Ken Griffey Jr., Sea	48
1951	Gus Zernial, Chi-Phil	33	2000	Troy Glaus, Ana	47
1952	Larry Doby, Clev	32	2001	Alex Rodriguez, Tex	52
1953	Al Rosen, Clev	43	2002	Alex Rodriguez, Tex	57
1954	Larry Doby, Clev	32	2003	Alex Rodriguez, Tex	47

Runs Batted In Leaders

Year	Player and Team	RBI	Year	Player and Team	RBI
1907	Ty Cobb, Det	116	1955	Ray Boone, Det	116
1908	Ty Cobb, Det	108		Jackie Jensen, Bos	116
1909	Ty Cobb, Det	107	1956	Mickey Mantle, NY	130
1910	Sam Crawford, Det	120	1957	Roy Sievers, Wash	114
1911	Ty Cobb, Det	144	1958	Jackie Jensen, Bos	122
1912	Frank Baker, Phil	133	1959	Jackie Jensen, Bos	112
1913	Frank Baker, Phil	126	1960	Roger Maris, NY	112
1914	Sam Crawford, Det	104	1961	Roger Maris, NY	142
1915	Sam Crawford, Det	112	1962	Harmon Killebrew, Minn	126
	Bobby Veach, Det	112	1963	Dick Stuart, Bos	118
1916	Del Pratt, StL	103	1964	Brooks Robinson, Balt	118
1917	Bobby Veach, Det	103	1965	Rocky Colavito, Clev	108
1918	Bobby Veach, Det	78	1966	Frank Robinson, Balt	122
1919	Babe Ruth, Bos	114	1967	Carl Yastrzemski, Bos	121
1920	Babe Ruth, NY	137	1968	Ken Harrelson, Bos	109
1921	Babe Ruth, NY	171	1969	Harmon Killebrew, Minn	140
1922	Ken Williams, StL	155	1970	Frank Howard, Wash	126
1923	Babe Ruth, NY	131	1971	Harmon Killebrew, Minn	119
1924	Goose Goslin, Wash	129	1972	Dick Allen, Chi	113
1925	Bob Meusel, NY	138	1973	Reggie Jackson, Oak	117
1926	Babe Ruth, NY	145	1974	Jeff Burroughs, Tex	118
1927	Lou Gehrig, NY	175	1975	George Scott, Mil	109
1928	Babe Ruth, NY	142	1976	Lee May, Balt	109
	Lou Gehrig, NY	142	1977	Larry Hisle, Minn	119
1929	Al Simmons, Phil	157	1978	Jim Rice, Bos	139
1930	Lou Gehrig, NY	174	1979	Don Baylor, Cal	139
1931	Lou Gehrig, NY	184	1980	Cecil Cooper, Mil	122
1932	Jimmie Foxx, Phil	169	1981	Eddie Murray, Balt	78
1933	Jimmie Foxx, Phil	163	1982	Hal McRae, KC	133
1934	Lou Gehrig, NY	165	1983	Cecil Cooper, Mil	126
1935	Hank Greenberg, Det	170		Jim Rice, Bos	126
1936	Hal Trosky, Clev	162	1984	Tony Armas, Bos	123
1937	Hank Greenberg, Det	183	1985	Don Mattingly, NY	145
1938	Jimmie Foxx, Bos	175	1986	Joe Carter, Clev	121
1939	Ted Williams, Bos	145	1987	George Bell, Tor	134
1940	Hank Greenberg, Det	150	1988	Jose Canseco, Oak	124
1941	Joe DiMaggio, NY	125	1989	Ruben Sierra, Tex	119
1942	Ted Williams, Bos	137	1990	Cecil Fielder, Det	132
1943	Rudy York, Det	118	1991	Cecil Fielder, Det	133
1944	Vern Stephens, StL	109	1992	Cecil Fielder, Det	124
1945	Nick Etten, NY	111	1993	Albert Belle, Clev	129
1946	Hank Greenberg, Det	127	1994	Kirby Puckett, Minn	112
1947	Ted Williams, Bos	114	1995	Albert Belle, Clev	126
1948	Joe DiMaggio, NY	155		Mo Vaughn, Bos	126
1949	Ted Williams, Bos	159	1996	Albert Belle, Clev	148
	Vern Stephens, Bos	159	1997	Ken Griffey Jr., Sea	147
1950	Walt Dropo, Bos	144	1998	Juan Gonzales, Tex	157
	Vern Stephens, Bos	144	1999	Manny Ramirez, Clev	165
1951	Gus Zernial, Chi-Phil	129	2000	Edgar Martinez, Sea	145
1952	Al Rosen, Clev	105	2001	Bret Boone, Sea	141
1953	Al Rosen, Clev	145	2002	Alex Rodriguez, Tex	142
1954	Larry Doby, Clev	126	2003	Carlos Delgado, Tor	145

Note: Runs Batted In not compiled before 1907; officially adopted in 1920.

Leading Base Stealers

Year	Player and Team	SB	Year	Player and Team	SB
1901	Frank Isbell, Chi	48	1912	Clyde Milan, Wash	88
1902	Topsy Hartsel, Phil	54	1913	Clyde Milan, Wash	75
1903	Harry Bay, Clev	46	1914	Fritz Maisel, NY	74
1904	Elmer Flick, Clev	42	1915	Ty Cobb, Det	96
	Harry Bay, Clev	42	1916	Ty Cobb, Det	68
1905	Danny Hoffman, Phil	46	1917	Ty Cobb, Det	55
1906	Elmer Flick, Clev	39	1918	George Sisler, StL	45
	John Anderson, Wash	39	1919	Eddie Collins, Chi	33
1907	Ty Cobb, Det	49	1920	Sam Rice, Wash	63
1908	Patsy Dougherty, Chi	47	1921	George Sisler, StL	35
1909	Ty Cobb, Det	76	1922	George Sisler, StL	51
1910	Eddie Collins, Phil	81	1923	Eddie Collins, Chi	49
1911	Ty Cobb, Det	83			

Leading Base Stealers *(Cont.)*

Year	Player and Team	SB	Year	Player and Team	SB
1924	Eddie Collins, Chi	42	1964	Luis Aparicio, Balt	57
1925	John Mostil, Chi	43	1965	Bert Campaneris, KC	51
1926	John Mostil, Chi	35	1966	Bert Campaneris, KC	52
1927	George Sisler, StL	27	1967	Bert Campaneris, KC	55
1928	Buddy Myer, Bos	30	1968	Bert Campaneris, Oak	62
1929	Charlie Gehringer, Det	27	1969	Tommy Harper, Sea	73
1930	Marty McManus, Det	23	1970	Bert Campaneris, Oak	42
1931	Ben Chapman, NY	61	1971	Amos Otis, KC	52
1932	Ben Chapman, NY	38	1972	Bert Campaneris, Oak	52
1933	Ben Chapman, NY	27	1973	Tommy Harper, Bos	54
1934	Bill Werber, Bos	40	1974	Bill North, Oak	54
1935	Bill Werber, Bos	29	1975	Mickey Rivers, Cal	70
1936	Lyn Lary, StL	37	1976	Bill North, Oak	75
1937	Bill Werber, Phil	35	1977	Freddie Patek, KC	53
	Ben Chapman, Wash-Bos	35	1978	Ron LeFlore, Det	68
1938	Frank Crosetti, NY	27	1979	Willie Wilson, KC	83
1939	George Case, Wash	51	1980	Rickey Henderson, Oak	100
1940	George Case, Wash	35	1981	Rickey Henderson, Oak	56
1941	George Case, Wash	33	1982	Rickey Henderson, Oak	130
1942	George Case, Wash	44	1983	Rickey Henderson, Oak	108
1943	George Case, Wash	61	1984	Rickey Henderson, Oak	66
1944	Snuffy Stirnweiss, NY	55	1985	Rickey Henderson, NY	80
1945	Snuffy Stirnweiss, NY	33	1986	Rickey Henderson, NY	87
1946	George Case, Clev	28	1987	Harold Reynolds, Sea	60
1947	Bob Dillinger, StL	34	1988	Rickey Henderson, NY	93
1948	Bob Dillinger, StL	28	1989	Rickey Henderson, NY-Oak	77
1949	Bob Dillinger, StL	20	1990	Rickey Henderson, Oak	65
1950	Dom DiMaggio, Bos	15	1991	Rickey Henderson, Oak	58
1951	Minnie Minoso, Clev-Chi	31	1992	Kenny Lofton, Clev	66
1952	Minnie Minoso, Chi	22	1993	Kenny Lofton, Clev	70
1953	Minnie Minoso, Chi	25	1994	Kenny Lofton, Clev	60
1954	Jackie Jensen, Bos	22	1995	Kenny Lofton, Clev	54
1955	Jim Rivera, Chi	25	1996	Kenny Lofton, Clev	75
1956	Luis Aparicio, Chi	21	1997	Brian Hunter, Det	74
1957	Luis Aparicio, Chi	28	1998	Rickey Henderson, Oak	66
1958	Luis Aparicio, Chi	29	1999	Brian Hunter, Sea	44
1959	Luis Aparicio, Chi	56	2000	Johnny Damon, KC	46
1960	Luis Aparicio, Chi	51	2001	Ichiro Suzuki, Sea	56
1961	Luis Aparicio, Chi	53	2002	Alfonso Soriano, NY	41
1962	Luis Aparicio, Chi	31	2003	Carl Crawford, TB	55
1963	Luis Aparicio, Balt	40			

Leading Pitchers—Winning Percentage

Year	Pitcher and Team	W	L	Pct	Year	Pitcher and Team	W	L	Pct
1901	Clark Griffith, Chi	24	7	.774	1925	Stan Coveleski, Wash	20	5	.800
1902	Bill Bernhard, Phil-Clev	18	5	.783	1926	George Uhle, Clev	27	11	.711
1903	Earl Moore, Clev	22	7	.759	1927	Waite Hoyt, NY	22	7	.759
1904	Jack Chesbro, NY	41	12	.774	1928	General Crowder, StL	21	5	.808
1905	Jess Tannehill, Bos	22	9	.710	1929	Lefty Grove, Phil	20	6	.769
1906	Eddie Plank, Phil	19	6	.760	1930	Lefty Grove, Phil	28	5	.848
1907	Wild Bill Donovan, Det	25	4	.862	1931	Lefty Grove, Phil	31	4	.886
1908	Ed Walsh, Chi	40	15	.727	1932	Johnny Allen, NY	17	4	.810
1909	George Mullin, Det	29	8	.784	1933	Lefty Grove, Phil	24	8	.750
1910	Chief Bender, Phil	23	5	.821	1934	Lefty Gomez, NY	26	5	.839
1911	Chief Bender, Phil	17	5	.773	1935	Eldon Auker, Det	18	7	.720
1912	Smoky Joe Wood, Bos	34	5	.872	1936	Monte Pearson, NY	19	7	.731
1913	Walter Johnson, Wash	36	7	.837	1937	Johnny Allen, Clev	15	1	.938
1914	Chief Bender, Phil	17	3	.850	1938	Red Ruffing, NY	21	7	.750
1915	Smoky Joe Wood, Bos	15	5	.750	1939	Lefty Grove, Bos	15	4	.789
1916	Eddie Cicotte, Chi	15	7	.682	1940	Schoolboy Rowe, Det	16	3	.842
1917	Reb Russell, Chi	15	5	.750	1941	Lefty Gomez, NY	15	5	.750
1918	Sad Sam Jones, Bos	16	5	.762	1942	Ernie Bonham, NY	21	5	.808
1919	Eddie Cicotte, Chi	29	7	.806	1943	Spud Chandler, NY	20	4	.833
1920	Jim Bagby, Clev	31	12	.721	1944	Tex Hughson, Bos	18	5	.783
1921	Carl Mays, NY	27	9	.750	1945	Hal Newhouser, Det	25	9	.735
1922	Joe Bush, NY	26	7	.788	1946	Boo Ferriss, Bos	25	6	.806
1923	Herb Pennock, NY	19	6	.760	1947	Allie Reynolds, NY	19	8	.704
1924	Walter Johnson, Wash	23	7	.767					

Leading Pitchers—Winning Percentage *(Cont.)*

Year	Pitcher and Team	W	L	Pct	Year	Pitcher and Team	W	L	Pct
1948	Jack Kramer, Bos	18	5	.783	1976	Bill Campbell, Minn	17	5	.773
1949	Ellis Kinder, Bos	23	6	.793	1977	Paul Splittorff, KC	16	6	.727
1950	Vic Raschi, NY	21	8	.724	1978	Ron Guidry, NY	25	3	.893
1951	Bob Feller, Clev	22	8	.733	1979	Mike Caldwell, Mil	16	6	.727
1952	Bobby Shantz, Phil	24	7	.774	1980	Steve Stone, Balt	25	7	.781
1953	Ed Lopat, NY	16	4	.800	1981*	Pete Vuckovich, Mil	14	4	.778
1954	Sandy Consuegra, Chi	16	3	.842	1982	Pete Vuckovich, Mil	18	6	.750
1955	Tommy Byrne, NY	16	5	.762		Jim Palmer, Balt	15	5	.750
1956	Whitey Ford, NY	19	6	.760	1983	Richard Dotson, Chi	22	7	.759
1957	Dick Donovan, Chi	16	6	.727	1984	Doyle Alexander, Tor	17	6	.739
	Tom Sturdivant, NY	16	6	.727	1985	Ron Guidry, NY	22	6	.786
1958	Bob Turley, NY	21	7	.750	1986	Roger Clemens, Bos	24	4	.857
1959	Bob Shaw, Chi	18	6	.750	1987	Roger Clemens, Bos	20	9	.690
1960	Jim Perry, Clev	18	10	.643	1988	Frank Viola, Minn	24	7	.774
1961	Whitey Ford, NY	25	4	.862	1989	Bret Saberhagen, KC	23	6	.793
1962	Ray Herbert, Chi	20	9	.690	1990	Bob Welch, Oak	27	6	.818
1963	Whitey Ford, NY	24	7	.774	1991	Scott Erickson, Minn	20	8	.714
1964	Wally Bunker, Balt	19	5	.792	1992	Mike Mussina, Balt	18	5	.783
1965	Mudcat Grant, Minn	21	7	.750	1993	Jimmy Key, NY	18	6	.750
1966	Sonny Siebert, Clev	16	8	.667	1994	Jimmy Key, NY	17	4	.810
1967	Joel Horlen, Chi	19	7	.731	1995	Randy Johnson, Sea	18	2	.900
1968	Denny McLain, Det	31	6	.838	1996	Charles Nagy, Clev	17	5	.773
1969	Jim Palmer, Balt	16	4	.800	1997	Randy Johnson, Sea	20	4	.833
1970	Mike Cuellar, Balt	24	8	.750	1998	David Wells, NY	18	4	.818
1971	Dave McNally, Balt	21	5	.808	1999	Pedro Martinez, Bos	23	4	.852
1972	Catfish Hunter, Oak	21	7	.750	2000	Tim Hudson, Oak	20	6	.769
1973	Catfish Hunter, Oak	21	5	.808	2001	Roger Clemens, NY	20	3	.870
1974	Mike Cuellar, Balt	22	10	.688	2002	Pedro Martinez, Bos	20	4	.833
1975	Mike Torrez, Balt	20	9	.690	2003	Roy Halladay, Tor	22	7	.759

*1981 percentages based on 10 or more victories. Note: Percentages based on 15 or more victories in all other years.

Leading Pitchers—Earned Run Average

Year	Player and Team	ERA	Year	Player and Team	ERA
1913	Walter Johnson, Wash	1.14	1946	Hal Newhouser, Det	1.94
1914	Dutch Leonard, Bos	1.01	1947	Spud Chandler, NY	2.46
1915	Smoky Joe Wood, Bos	1.49	1948	Gene Bearden, Clev	2.43
1916	Babe Ruth, Bos	1.75	1949	Mel Parnell, Bos	2.78
1917	Eddie Cicotte, Chi	1.53	1950	Early Wynn, Clev	3.20
1918	Walter Johnson, Wash	1.27	1951	Saul Rogovin, Det-Chi	2.78
1919	Walter Johnson, Wash	1.49	1952	Allie Reynolds, NY	2.07
1920	Bob Shawkey, NY	2.46	1953	Ed Lopat, NY	2.43
1921	Red Faber, Chi	2.47	1954	Mike Garcia, Clev	2.64
1922	Red Faber, Chi	2.80	1955	Billy Pierce, Chi	1.97
1923	Stan Coveleski, Clev	2.76	1956	Whitey Ford, NY	2.47
1924	Walter Johnson, Wash	2.72	1957	Bobby Shantz, NY	2.45
1925	Stan Coveleski, Wash	2.84	1958	Whitey Ford, NY	2.01
1926	Lefty Grove, Phil	2.51	1959	Hoyt Wilhelm, Balt	2.19
1927	Wilcy Moore, NY#	2.28	1960	Frank Baumann, Chi	2.68
1928	Garland Braxton, Wash	2.52	1961	Dick Donovan, Wash	2.40
1929	Lefty Grove, Phil	2.81	1962	Hank Aguirre, Det	2.21
1930	Lefty Grove, Phil	2.54	1963	Gary Peters, Chi	2.33
1931	Lefty Grove, Phil	2.06	1964	Dean Chance, LA	1.65
1932	Lefty Grove, Phil	2.84	1965	Sam McDowell, Clev	2.18
1933	Monte Pearson, Clev	2.33	1966	Gary Peters, Chi	1.98
1934	Lefty Gomez, NY	2.33	1967	Joe Horlen, Chi	2.06
1935	Lefty Grove, Bos	2.70	1968	Luis Tiant, Clev	1.60
1936	Lefty Grove, Bos	2.81	1969	Dick Bosman, Wash	2.19
1937	Lefty Gomez, NY	2.33	1970	Diego Segui, Oak	2.56
1938	Lefty Grove, Bos	3.07	1971	Vida Blue, Oak	1.82
1939	Lefty Grove, Bos	2.54	1972	Luis Tiant, Bos	1.91
1940	Bob Feller, Clev†	2.62	1973	Jim Palmer, Balt	2.40
1941	Thornton Lee, Chi	2.37	1974	Catfish Hunter, Oak	2.49
1942	Ted Lyons, Chi	2.10	1975	Jim Palmer, Balt	2.09
1943	Spud Chandler, NY	1.64	1976	Mark Fidrych, Det	2.34
1944	Dizzy Trout, Det	2.12	1977	Frank Tanana, Cal	2.54
1945	Hal Newhouser, Det	1.81			

Leading Pitchers—Earned Run Average (Cont.)

Year	Player and Team	ERA	Year	Player and Team	ERA
1978	Ron Guidry, NY	1.74	1991	Roger Clemens, Bos	2.62
1979	Ron Guidry, NY	2.78	1992	Roger Clemens, Bos	2.41
1980	Rudy May, NY	2.47	1993	Kevin Appier, KC	2.56
1981	Steve McCatty, Oak	2.32	1994	Steve Ontiveros, Oak	2.65
1982	Rick Sutcliffe, Clev	2.96	1995	Randy Johnson, Sea	2.48
1983	Rick Honeycutt, Tex	2.42	1996	Juan Guzman, Tor	2.93
1984	Mike Boddicker, Balt	2.79	1997	Roger Clemens, Tor	2.05
1985	Dave Stieb, Tor	2.48	1998	Roger Clemens, Tor	2.64
1986	Roger Clemens, Bos	2.48	1999	Pedro Martinez, Bos	2.07
1987	Jimmy Key, Tor	2.76	2000	Pedro Martinez, Bos	1.74
1988	Allan Anderson, Minn	2.45	2001	Freddy Garcia, Sea	3.05
1989	Bret Saberhagen, KC	2.16	2002	Pedro Martinez, Bos	2.26
1990	Roger Clemens, Bos	1.93	2003	Pedro Martinez, Bos	2.22

Note: Based on 10 complete games through 1950, then 154 innings until the American League expanded in 1961, when it became 162 innings. In strike-shortened 1981, one inning per game required. Earned runs not tabulated in American League prior to 1913.

#Wilcy Moore pitched only six complete games—he started 12—in 1927 but was recognized as leader because of 213 innings pitched. †Ernie Bonham, New York, had 1.91 ERA and 10 complete games in 1940 but appeared in only 12 games and 99 innings, and Bob Feller was recognized as leader.

Leading Pitchers—Strikeouts

Year	Player and Team	SO	Year	Player and Team	SO
1901	Cy Young, Bos	159	1945	Hal Newhouser, Det	212
1902	Rube Waddell, Phil	210	1946	Bob Feller, Clev	348
1903	Rube Waddell, Phil	301	1947	Bob Feller, Clev	196
1904	Rube Waddell, Phil	349	1948	Bob Feller, Clev	164
1905	Rube Waddell, Phil	286	1949	Virgil Trucks, Det	153
1906	Rube Waddell, Phil	203	1950	Bob Lemon, Clev	170
1907	Rube Waddell, Phil	226	1951	Vic Raschi, NY	164
1908	Ed Walsh, Chi	269	1952	Allie Reynolds, NY	160
1909	Frank Smith, Chi	177	1953	Billy Pierce, Chi	186
1910	Walter Johnson, Wash	313	1954	Bob Turley, Balt	185
1911	Ed Walsh, Chi	255	1955	Herb Score, Clev	245
1912	Walter Johnson, Wash	303	1956	Herb Score, Clev	263
1913	Walter Johnson, Wash	243	1957	Early Wynn, Clev	184
1914	Walter Johnson, Wash	225	1958	Early Wynn, Chi	179
1915	Walter Johnson, Wash	203	1959	Jim Bunning, Det	201
1916	Walter Johnson, Wash	228	1960	Jim Bunning, Det	201
1917	Walter Johnson, Wash	188	1961	Camilo Pascual, Minn	221
1918	Walter Johnson, Wash	162	1962	Camilo Pascual, Minn	206
1919	Walter Johnson, Wash	147	1963	Camilo Pascual, Minn	202
1920	Stan Coveleski, Clev	133	1964	Al Downing, NY	217
1921	Walter Johnson, Wash	143	1965	Sam McDowell, Clev	325
1922	Urban Shocker, StL	149	1966	Sam McDowell, Clev	225
1923	Walter Johnson, Wash	130	1967	Jim Lonborg, Bos	246
1924	Walter Johnson, Wash	158	1968	Sam McDowell, Clev	283
1925	Lefty Grove, Phil	116	1969	Sam McDowell, Clev	279
1926	Lefty Grove, Phil	194	1970	Sam McDowell, Clev	304
1927	Lefty Grove, Phil	174	1971	Mickey Lolich, Det	308
1928	Lefty Grove, Phil	183	1972	Nolan Ryan, Cal	329
1929	Lefty Grove, Phil	170	1973	Nolan Ryan, Cal	383
1930	Lefty Grove, Phil	209	1974	Nolan Ryan, Cal	367
1931	Lefty Grove, Phil	175	1975	Frank Tanana, Cal	269
1932	Red Ruffing, NY	190	1976	Nolan Ryan, Cal	327
1933	Lefty Gomez, NY	163	1977	Nolan Ryan, Cal	341
1934	Lefty Gomez, NY	158	1978	Nolan Ryan, Cal	260
1935	Tommy Bridges, Det	163	1979	Nolan Ryan, Cal	223
1936	Tommy Bridges, Det	175	1980	Len Barker, Clev	187
1937	Lefty Gomez, NY	194	1981	Len Barker, Clev	127
1938	Bob Feller, Clev	240	1982	Floyd Bannister, Sea	209
1939	Bob Feller, Clev	246	1983	Jack Morris, Det	232
1940	Bob Feller, Clev	261	1984	Mark Langston, Sea	204
1941	Bob Feller, Clev	260	1985	Bert Blyleven, Clev-Minn	206
1942	Bobo Newsom, Wash, Tex Hughson, Bos	113	1986	Mark Langston, Sea	245
1943	Allie Reynolds, Clev	151	1987	Mark Langston, Sea	262
1944	Hal Newhouser, Det	187	1988	Roger Clemens, Bos	291
			1989	Nolan Ryan, Tex	301

Leading Pitchers—Strikeouts (Cont.)

Year	Player and Team	SO	Year	Player and Team	SO
1990	Nolan Ryan, Tex	232	1997	Roger Clemens, Tor	292
1991	Roger Clemens, Bos	241	1998	Roger Clemens, Tor	271
1992	Randy Johnson, Sea	241	1999	Pedro Martinez, Bos	313
1993	Randy Johnson, Sea	308	2000	Pedro Martinez, Bos	284
1994	Randy Johnson, Sea	204	2001	Hideo Nomo, Bos	220
1995	Randy Johnson, Sea	294	2002	Pedro Martinez, Bos	239
1996	Roger Clemens, Bos	257	2003	Esteban Loaiza, Chi	207

Leading Pitchers—Saves

Year	Player and Team	SV	Year	Player and Team	SV
1947	Joe Page, NY	17	1976	Sparky Lyle, NY	23
1948	Russ Christopher, Clev	17	1977	Bill Campbell, Bos	31
1949	Joe Page, NY	29	1978	Goose Gossage, NY	27
1950	Mickey Harris, Wash	15	1979	Mike Marshall, Minn	32
1951	Ellis Kinder, Bos	14	1980	Dan Quisenberry, KC	33
1952	Harry Dorish, Chi	11	1981	Rollie Fingers, Mil	28
1953	Ellis Kinder, Bos	27	1982	Dan Quisenberry, KC	35
1954	Johnny Sain, NY	22	1983	Dan Quisenberry, KC	35
1955	Ray Narleski, Clev	19	1984	Dan Quisenberry, KC	44
1956	George Zuverink, Bal	16	1985	Dan Quisenberry, KC	37
1957	Bob Grim, NY	19	1986	Dave Righetti, NY	46
1958	Ryne Duren, NY	20	1987	Tom Henke, Tor	34
1959	Turk Lown, Chi	15	1988	Dennis Eckersley, Oak	45
1960	Mike Fornieles, Bos	14	1989	Jeff Russell, Tex	38
	Johnny Klippstein, Clev	14	1990	Bobby Thigpen, Chi	57
1961	Luis Arroyo, NY	29	1991	Bryan Harvey, Cal	46
1962	Dick Radatz, Bos	24	1992	Dennis Eckersley, Oak	51
1963	Stu Miller, Bal	27	1993	Jeff Montgomery, KC	45
1964	Dick Radatz, Bos	29		Duane Ward, Tor	45
1965	Ron Kline, Wash	29	1994	Lee Smith, Bal	33
1966	Jack Aker, KC	32	1995	Jose Mesa, Clev	46
1967	Minnie Rojas, Cal	27	1996	John Wetteland, NY	43
1968	Al Worthington, Minn	18	1997	Randy Myers, Balt	45
1969	Ron Perranoski, Minn	31	1998	Tom Gordon, Bos	46
1970	Ron Perranoski, Minn	34	1999	Mariano Rivera, NY	45
1971	Ken Sanders, Mil	31	2000	Todd Jones, Det	42
1972	Sparky Lyle, NY	35	2001	Mariano Rivera, NY	50
1973	John Hiller, Det	38	2002	Eddie Guardado, Minn	45
1974	Terry Forster, Chi	24	2003	Keith Foulke, Oak	43
1975	Goose Gossage, Chi	26			

The Commissioners of Baseball

Kenesaw Mountain Landis ....Elected Nov. 12, 1920. Served until his death on Nov. 25, 1944.
Happy Chandler ....Elected April 24, 1945. Served until July 15, 1951.
Ford Frick ....Elected Sept. 20, 1951. Served until Nov. 16, 1965.
William Eckert ....Elected Nov. 17, 1965. Served until Dec. 20, 1968.
Bowie Kuhn ....Elected Feb. 8, 1969. Served until Sept. 30, 1984.
Peter Ueberroth ....Elected March 3, 1984. Took office Oct. 1, 1984. Served through March 31, 1989.
A. Bartlett Giamatti ....Elected Sept. 8, 1988. Took office April 1, 1989. Served until his death on Sept. 1, 1989.
Francis Vincent Jr. ....Appointed Acting Commissioner Sept. 2, 1989. Elected Commissioner Sept. 13, 1989. Served through Sept. 7, 1992.
Allan H. (Bud) Selig ....Elected chairman of the executive council and given the powers of interim commissioner on Sept. 9, 1992. Unanimously elected Commissioner July 9, 1998.

Pro Football

Chucky's Revenge

The Super Bowl played like a horror film for the Raiders, who watched their old coach come back to rout them

BY HANK HERSCH

THE GAMBLE SEEMED to both mortgage the future and bankrupt the present: two first-round draft choices, a pair of second-round picks and $8 million in cash. But for Malcolm Glazer, owner of the Tampa Bay Buccaneers, it was a reasonable sum for a shot at outstripping his franchise's inglorious past. So in February 2002, after bungled attempts to bring in two-time Super Bowl winner Bill Parcells and University of Florida mastermind Steve Spurrier to guide the team, Glazer ponied up his picks and bucks to Oakland Raiders owner Al Davis for his coach—or, more accurately, the right to negotiate with his coach. Without once speaking to 38-year-old Jon Gruden directly, Glazer was willing to pay so dearly for him that 11 months later the NFL would legislate against such deals for coaches. "Jon's special," said Malcolm's son Joel, Tampa Bay's executive vice president. "When you're dealing with special, sometimes you do special things."

Special. The youngest coach in the league, Gruden accepted Glazer's five-year, $17.5 million offer to return to his hometown, then propelled the Bucs to the first Super Bowl appearance in their 26-year history. Special. At Super Bowl XXXVII in San Diego, Gruden faced the Raiders team he had spent four years restoring to prominence with his boundless energy and incessant cajoling. Special. The finale pitted Oakland's league-leading offense, orchestrated by regular-season MVP Rich Gannon, against Tampa Bay's league-leading D, spearheaded by defensive player of the year Derrick Brooks. It would be the first time that a No. 1-ranked offense faced a No. 1 defense for the championship.

Special might not be the most apt description of the Bucs' 48–21 victory in the game, but it certainly applied to their defense's effort. Tampa Bay intercepted Gannon a Super Bowl–record five times—with free safety Dexter Jackson, the game's MVP, making two of the picks. The Bucs D also sacked Gannon five times, allowed only 19 rushing yards and scored three

BOB ROSATO

touchdowns, matching the total of the vaunted Oakland attack. A franchise that began life in the NFL with 26 consecutive defeats had crested the league's summit. "We have a great defense," Gruden said afterward. "Not good—great."

While fans will remember this season for Gruden's ascent, there were several other memorable stories in 2002, including that of a 33-year-old Dallas Cowboys running back, lately reduced to banging out hard yardage behind a rebuilt offensive line on a struggling team—and getting hammered for it, both literally and figuratively. Pundits and critics used words like ancient and finished and selfish to sting Emmitt Smith as he marched toward Walter Payton's career rushing record of 16,726 yards.

Much to the chagrin of opposing defenses, Williams found a happy home in Miami.

For his part, the rugged No. 22 said that his ability, not his age, was the only thing to consider in any discussion about whether or not he should retire. And he still believed in his ability.

Smith came to Dallas from the University of Florida in 1990 as the 17th pick in the draft, and while other star backs ended their careers—Barry Sanders, Terrell Davis, Robert Smith, Jamal Anderson—he soldiered on, enduring concussions, bone chips and a broken hand while gaining 1,000 yards in a record 11 consecutive seasons. "When it comes to the game," he said, "I don't know how any man can fix his lips

AL TIELEMANS

Harrison ran down the record for receptions in a season. Harrison snagged 143 passes to shatter Herman Moore's seven-year-old record by 20 and become the first player to catch more than 100 passes in four straight seasons. Never one to break off a route, or a one-liner for that matter—"I'm not into talking because that's never won any football games," he says—Harrison received far less attention for his spectacular exploits than his fellow All-Pro wideout, Terrell Owens of the San Francisco 49ers.

The more, ahem, demonstrative Owens celebrated one of his league-high 13 touchdown catches by pulling a pen out of his sock and signing an autograph in the middle of a Monday night game. He capped another scoring play by borrowing a cheerleader's pom-poms and performing an end-zone shimmy. Owens's theatrics created controversy that almost obscured his standing among the league's elite players.

Another player who took his rightful place among the league's elite was running back Ricky Williams. After three unhappy seasons in New Orleans, Williams was traded to Miami, where he made an immediate impact, rushing for a league-best 1,853 yards and averaging 4.8 yards per carry. Despite Williams' performance, and that of defensive end Jason Taylor, who led the league with 18.5 sacks, the Dolphins (9–7) fell victim to their seemingly annual December swoon, losing their last two games and missing the playoffs.

There were signs in the season's opening week that the league—and especially its officials—would have a rocky season. Teams averaged a record 49.3 points in 16 games in Week 1, six of which went into overtime or were decided in the final minute. The most bizarre of those final minutes was in Cleveland, where Browns

and say I'm selfish."

Needing 93 yards to break the record, Smith faced the Seattle Seahawks on Oct. 27 at Texas Stadium. He had averaged about 60 yards a game in his first seven games. "You're not going to get it today," Seattle defensive tackle Chad Eaton told Smith during the coin toss. But by early in the fourth quarter, Smith had gained 83 yards. On second down at the Cowboys' 30-yard line, he burst through a seam, stumbled over a defender's arm, kept his balance and chugged on into history as seemingly everyone in the stadium captured the moment with their flashbulb cameras. A five-minute ceremony followed his 11-yard scamper for the record, and then Smith returned to the field and capped the Dallas drive with a touchdown, extending his record career total to 150. By season's end, Smith held the NFL records for career rushing yards (17,160), attempts (4,052) and touchdowns (153). But also by season's end, Smith's future with the Cowboys seemed uncertain after Dallas owner Jerry Jones lured the 61-year-old Parcells out of retirement with a four-year, $17 million contract.

While Smith chased Payton's record, Indianapolis Colts wide receiver Marvin

McNair overcame a rash of nagging injuries to lead the Titans to the AFC championship game against Oakland.

JOHN BIEVER

linebacker Dwayne Rudd, thinking he had clinched a 39–37 victory over the Chiefs with a sack, tossed his helmet 15 yards downfield as time expired. Kansas City quarterback Trent Green, however, had lateraled the ball before Rudd's hit, keeping the play alive and converting Rudd's celebratory heave into a 15-yard unsportsmanlike conduct penalty. (No player on the field is allowed to remove his headgear while the game is on.) That gave Kansas City kicker Morten Andersen a shot at a 30-yard field goal, which he nailed for the win.

After the cries for Rudd's unhelmeted head died down, the expansion Browns rallied to reach the playoffs for the first time in their three seasons of existence. The league's powerhouse during that time, however, saw its electrifying attack short-circuit in 2002. With quarterback Kurt Warner bothered by an injured right thumb and then a broken right pinky, the defending NFC champion St. Louis Rams—a.k.a. the Greatest Show on Turf—stumbled to an 0–5 start. Despite some prestidigitation from third-string quarterback Marc Bulger, 25, who led the team to five straight wins, the Rams lost their grip on the offensive elixir that had carried them to two straight championship games, and finished at 7–9. Their opponent in Supe XXXVI, the New England Patriots, also missed the postseason cut, though little blame could be attached to their signal caller, 25-year-old Tom Brady, who threw for 3,764 yards in his first full season.

Young quarterbacks like Bulger and Brady were all the rage in 2002. The No. 1 pick in the draft, David Carr of Fresno State, immediately showed his mettle when he guided the Houston Texans to a win in their franchise debut, a 19–10 upset of the already hated Cowboys in Houston's new $417 million Xanadu, Reliant Park. (As the season wore on Carr showed enough mettle

for a medal, absorbing a league-record 76 sacks.) Taking over for Vinny Testaverde, 26-year-old Chad Pennington of the Jets conjured up images of Joe Montana with his pinpoint passing (a league-leading .689 completion percentage and 104.2 efficiency rating) and Joe Namath with his cool in the clutch: New York was 8–4 under Pennington after a 1–3 start. Said Testaverde after the Jets' 41–0 waxing of the Colts in the wild-card round, "Chad's very deserving of those comparisons."

In Atlanta, second-year southpaw Michael Vick, 22, proved he was no ordinary Joe, either. With a throwing arm that ranked with the league's strongest, Vick also flashed 4.3 speed, uncanny elusiveness in the backfield and the open-field wizardry of a latter-day Gale Sayers. In a 34–34 tie with the Pittsburgh Steelers in Week 10, Vick connected for three first down passes on third-and-22 or longer, rallied the Falcons from a 17-point deficit and scored the final points on a scintillating 11-yard scramble. "If you put him in a six-by-six cell with 11 guys, it'd take them an hour to touch him," said Green Bay quarterback Brett Favre, who would get a bitter taste of Vick's talent in a 27–7 wild-card loss at Lambeau Field, the Packers' first home playoff defeat

BOB ROSATO

in the 82-year history of the franchise.

The other NFC first rounder really put the wild in wild-card. Despite blowing a 24-point second-half lead and trailing 39–38 with only seconds remaining, the New York Giants had a chance to beat the 49ers with a 41-yard field goal on the game's final play. But a bad snap by 42-year-old Trey Junkin forced holder Matt Allen to abort the attempt, then scramble and heave a pass toward guard Rich Seubert. Seubert, who had been declared an eligible receiver before the game, was dragged down by a Niners defender before the ball arrived. The referees flagged another Giants lineman for being downfield on the chaotic play, but, perhaps thinking Seubert was also ineligible, failed to call pass interference when Seubert was pulled down. That call, which should have been made, would have offset the other penalty and given New York another shot at a winning kick. Commissioner Paul Tagliabue called it the worst officiating blunder he'd seen in his 13 years in office, but the 2002 season, right through Supe XXXVII, was full of similarly blown calls and confusion over rules governing instant replay and the field of play.

In the divisional playoffs, Vick and the Falcons would fall 20–6 to the Philadelphia Eagles and their double-threat quarterback, Donovan McNabb, who was suiting up for the first time since he broke his right fibula in Week 11. Though McNabb had accounted for the bulk of his team's offense at the time of his injury, the Eagles rallied to win five of their last six regular-season

games without him, a gritty display that helped Philadelphia's Andy Reid win the coach of the year award. But in the conference championship the Bucs traveled to frigid Philly and shackled McNabb and the Eagles 27–10.

The Raiders, meanwhile, were churning through the AFC bracket, dumping the Jets and then the Tennessee Titans and their rugged, versatile quarterback, Steve McNair. Fueling the Raider drive were record-setting receivers Jerry Rice and Tim Brown, a dominant offensive line and the savvy of Gannon, who had passed for a league-leading 4,689 yards during the regular season. Gruden's successor in Oakland, former offensive coordinator Bill Callahan, increasingly abandoned all notions of offensive balance in favor of an all-pass all-the-time approach.

But before the kickoff in San Diego, Oakland declared All-Pro center Barret Robbins ineligible for the game after he missed curfew the night before, then went AWOL. His absence didn't help, but far more damaging to the Raiders was Gruden's intimate knowledge of their offense, which he had helped construct. Though Gannon had thrown only 10 interceptions in 618 regular-season passes, the Buccaneers' defensive backfield read him as if he were a first-grade primer. "It was uncanny" said strong safety John Lynch. "I was never involved in a game where we were so ready for what the other team ran."

Behind the running of Michael Pittman (125 yards on 29 carries) and the solid play of quarterback Brad Johnson (215 yards passing, two TDs) the Bucs' normally tepid offense outgained the Raiders', 365–269. In all, it was a remarkable performance for a coach known as Chucky (after a menacing toy figure in a horror film series) because of his intense and often malevolent facial expressions. "Coach Gruden came from heaven," said Malcolm Glazer of the youngest-ever Super Bowl winner, "and brought us to heaven."

2002 NFL Final Standings

American Football Conference

EAST DIVISION

	W	L	T	Pct	Pts	OP
NY Jets	9	7	0	.562	359	336
New England	9	7	0	.562	381	346
Miami	9	7	0	.562	378	301
Buffalo	8	8	0	.500	379	397

NORTH DIVISION

	W	L	T	Pct	Pts	OP
Pittsburgh	10	5	1	.656	390	345
†Cleveland	9	7	0	.562	344	320
Baltimore	7	9	0	.438	316	354
Cincinnati	2	14	0	.125	279	456

SOUTH DIVISION

	W	L	T	Pct	Pts	OP
Tennessee	11	5	0	.688	367	324
†Indianapolis	10	6	0	.625	349	313
Jacksonville	6	10	0	.375	328	315
Houston	4	12	0	.250	213	356

WEST DIVISION

	W	L	T	Pct	Pts	OP
Oakland	11	5	0	.688	450	304
Denver	9	7	0	.562	392	344
San Diego	8	8	0	.500	333	367
Kansas City	8	8	0	.500	467	399

† Wild-card team.

National Football Conference

EAST DIVISION

	W	L	T	Pct	Pts	OP
Philadelphia	12	4	0	.750	415	241
†NY Giants	10	6	0	.625	320	279
Washington	7	9	0	.438	307	365
Dallas	5	11	0	.312	217	329

NORTH DIVISION

	W	L	T	Pct	Pts	OP
Green Bay	12	4	0	.750	398	328
Minnesota	6	10	0	.375	390	442
Chicago	4	12	0	.250	281	379
Detroit	3	13	0	.188	306	451

SOUTH DIVISION

	W	L	T	Pct	Pts	OP
Tampa Bay	12	4	0	.750	346	196
†Atlanta	9	6	1	.594	402	314
New Orleans	9	7	0	.562	432	388
Carolina	7	9	0	.438	258	302

WEST DIVISION

	W	L	T	Pct	Pts	OP
San Francisco	10	6	0	.625	367	351
St. Louis	7	9	0	.438	316	369
Seattle	7	9	0	.438	355	369
Arizona	5	11	0	.312	262	417

† Wild-card team.

2002–03 NFL Playoffs

AFC FIRST ROUND	AFC DIVISIONAL PLAYOFF	AFC CHAMPIONSHIP	NFC CHAMPIONSHIP	NFC DIVISIONAL PLAYOFF	NFC FIRST ROUND

SUPER BOWL XXXVII

January 26, 2003

Indianapolis 0
NY Jets 41

NY Jets 10

Oakland 41

Oakland 30

Oakland 21
TAMPA BAY 48

Cleveland 33
Pittsburgh 36

Pittsburgh 31

Tennessee 24

Tennessee 34 (ot)

Atlanta 27
Green Bay 7

Atlanta 6

Philadelphia 10

Philadelphia 20

San Francisco 6

Tampa Bay 27

Tampa Bay 31

NY Giants 38
San Francisco 39

NFL Playoff Box Scores

AFC Wild-card Games

Indianapolis 0   0   0   0— 0
NY Jets .... 7 17 10 7—41

FIRST QUARTER

NY Jets: Anderson 56 pass from Pennington (Hall kick), 4:10. Drive: 77 yards, 5 plays.

SECOND QUARTER

NY Jets: FG Hall 41, 0:52. Drive: 46 yards, 9 plays.
NY Jets: Jordan 1 run (Hall kick), 5:19. Drive: 39 yards, 7 plays.
NY Jets: Moss 4 pass from Pennington (Hall kick), 14:23. Drive: 42 yards, 6 plays.

THIRD QUARTER

NY Jets: FG Hall 39, 1:32. Drive: -1 yard, 4 plays.
NY Jets: Baker 3 pass from Pennington (Hall kick), 13:16. Drive: 74 yards, 11 plays.

FOURTH QUARTER

NY Jets: Jordan 1 run (Hall kick), 10:01. Drive: 64 yards, 13 plays.

A: 78,524; T: 2:58.

Cleveland .... 7 10 7 9—33
Pittsburgh .... 0 7 7 22—36

FIRST QUARTER

Cleveland: Green 1 run (Dawson kick), 1:16. Drive: 80 yards, 4 plays.

SECOND QUARTER

Cleveland: Northcutt 32 pass from Holcomb (Dawson kick), 0:22. Drive: 32 yards, 1 play.
Pittsburgh: Randle El 66 punt return (Reed kick), 5:25.
Cleveland: FG Dawson 31, 14:11. Drive: 45 yards, 10 plays.

THIRD QUARTER

Cleveland: Northcutt 15 pass from Holcomb (Dawson kick), 2:49. Drive: 14 yards, 3 plays.
Pittsburgh: Burress 6 pass from Maddox (Reed kick), 11:10. Drive: 71 yards, 10 plays.

FOURTH QUARTER

Cleveland: FG Dawson 24, 0:08. Drive: 64 yards, 8 plays.
Pittsburgh: Tuman 3 pass from Maddox (Reed kick), 2:32. Drive: 65 yards, 6 plays.
Cleveland: Davis 22 pass from Holcomb (two-pt conversion failed), 4:43. Drive: 61 yards, 5 plays.
Pittsburgh: Ward 5 pass from Maddox (Reed kick), 11:54. Drive: 77 yards, 10 plays.
Pittsburgh: Fuamatu-Ma'afala 3 run (Tuman pass from Randle El for two-pt conversion), 14:06. Drive: 61 yards, 6 plays.

A: 62,595; T: 3:24.

NFC Wild-card Games

Atlanta .... 14 10 3 0—27
Green Bay .... 0 0 7 0— 7

FIRST QUARTER

Atlanta: Jefferson 10 pass from Vick (Feely kick), 5:43. Drive: 76 yards, 10 plays.
Atlanta: Ulmer 1 return of blocked punt (Feely kick), 8:22.

SECOND QUARTER

Atlanta: Duckett 6 run (Feely kick), 2:54. Drive: 21 yards, 4 plays.
Atlanta: FG Feely 22, 15:00. Drive: 90 yards, 16 plays.

THIRD QUARTER

Green Bay: Driver 14 pass from Favre (Longwell kick), 4:34. Drive: 73 yards, 10 plays.
Atlanta: FG Feely 23, 11:17. Drive: 73 yards, 12 plays.

A: 65,358; T: 3:11.

NY Giants .... 7 21 10 0—38
San Francisco .... 7 7 8 17—39

FIRST QUARTER

San Francisco: Owens 76 pass from Garcia (Chandler kick), 5:01. Drive: 76 yards, 1 play.
NY Giants: Toomer 12 pass from Collins (Bryant kick), 14:42. Drive: 65 yards, 11 plays.

SECOND QUARTER

NY Giants: Shockey 2 pass from Collins (Bryant kick), 2:41. Drive: 61 yards, 5 plays.
San Francisco: Barlow 1 run (Chandler kick), 8:55. Drive: 69 yards, 10 plays.
NY Giants: Toomer 8 pass from Collins (Bryant kick), 12:11. Drive: 8 yards, 1 play.
NY Giants: Toomer 24 pass from Collins (Bryant kick), 14:50. Drive: 56 yards, 5 plays.

THIRD QUARTER

NY Giants: Barber 6 run (Bryant kick), 5:07. Drive: 54 yards, 6 plays.
NY Giants: FG Bryant 21, 10:33. Drive: 63 yards, 9 plays.
San Francisco: Owens 26 pass from Garcia (Owens pass from Garcia for two-pt conversion), 12:57. Drive: 70 yards, 7 plays.

FOURTH QUARTER

San Francisco: Garcia 14 run (Owens pass from Garcia for two-pt conversion), 0:05. Drive 27 yards, 3 plays.
San Francisco: FG Chandler 25, 7:11. Drive: 74 yards, 15 plays.
San Francisco: Streets 13 pass from Garcia (two-pt conversion failed,) time 14:00. Drive: 68 yards 9 plays.
A: 66, 318; T: 3:38.

AFC Divisional Games

Pittsburgh 0	13	7	11	0—31
Tennessee..........14	0	14	3	3—34

FIRST QUARTER

Tennessee: McNair 8 run (Nedney kick), 3:59. Drive: 52 yards, 7 plays.
Tennessee: George 1 run (Nedney kick), 14:43. Drive: 76 yards, 16 plays.

SECOND QUARTER

Pittsburgh: Ward 8 pass from Maddox (Reed kick), 5:31. Drive: 8 yards, 2 plays.
Pittsburgh: FG Reed 30, 8:13. Drive: 47 yards, 5 plays.
Pittsburgh: FG Reed 39, 15:00. Drive: 61 yards, 8 plays.

THIRD QUARTER

Pittsburgh: Zereoue 31 run (Reed kick), 0:23. Drive: 31 yards, 1 play.
Tennessee: Wycheck 7 pass from McNair (Nedney kick), 5:23. Drive: tktktktktktkt
Tennessee: Kinney 2 pass from McNair (Nedney kick), 10:22. Drive: 58 yards, 8 plays.

FOURTH QUARTER

Pittsburgh: Ward 21 pass from Maddox (Burress pass from Ward for two-pt conversion), 4:51. Drive: 65 yards, 6 plays.
Pittsburgh: FG Reed 40, 6:30. Drive: 35 yards, 5 plays.
Tennessee: FG Nedney 42, 9:20. Drive: 34 yards, 7 plays.

OVERTIME

Tennesee: FG Nedney 26, 2:15. Drive 61 yards, 5 plays.

A: 68,809; T: 3:41.

NY Jets................3	7	0	0—10
Oakland...............3	7	7	13—30

FIRST QUARTER

NY Jets: FG Hall 38, 4:02. Drive: 45 yards, 8 plays.
Oakland: FG Janikowski 29, 9:12. Drive: 53 yards, 9 plays.

SECOND QUARTER

Oakland: Crockett 1 run (Janikowski kick), 1:16. Drive: 27 yards, 6 plays.
NY Jets: Sowell 1 pass from Pennington (Hall kick), 14:38. Drive: 81 yards, 16 plays.

THIRD QUARTER

Oakland: Porter 29 pass from Gannon (Janikowski kick), 10:36. Drive: 45 yards, 2 plays.

FOURTH QUARTER

Oakland: Rice 9 pass from Gannon (Janikowski kick), 0:45. Drive: 65 yards, 4 plays.
Oakland: FG Janikowski 34, 7:05. Drive: 46 yards, 7 plays.
Oakland: FG Janikowski 31, 12:18. Drive: 37 yards, 8 plays.

A: 62,600; T: 3:15.

NFC Divisional Games

Atlanta 0	6	0	0— 6
Philadelphia.........10	3	0	7—20

FIRST QUARTER

Philadelphia: Taylor 39 int. return (Akers kick), 7:02.
Philadelphia: FG Akers 34, 11:13. Drive: 47 yards, 6 plays.

SECOND QUARTER

Philadelphia: FG Akers 39, 4:55. Drive: 65 yards, 9 plays.
Atlanta: FG Feely 34, 10:50. Drive: 61 yards, 13 plays.
Atlanta: FG Feely 52, 15:00. Drive: 45 yards, 10 plays.

FOURTH QUARTER

Philadelphia: Thrash 35 pass from McNabb (Akers kick), 8:34. Drive: tktktktt tktktktktk tktk.

A: 66,452; T: 3:06.

San Francisco........3	3	0	0— 6
Tampa Bay.............7	21	3	0—31

FIRST QUARTER

Tampa Bay: Alstott 2 run (Gramatica kick), 8:26. Drive: 74 yards, 12 plays.
San Francisco: FG Chandler 24, 14:43. Drive: 63 yards, 12 plays.

SECOND QUARTER

Tampa Bay: Jurevicius 20 pass from B. Johnson (Gramatica kick), 5:33. Drive: 77 yards, 11 plays.
San Francisco: FG Chandler 40, 6:26. Drive: 24 yards, 5 plays.
Tampa Bay: Dudley 12 pass from B. Johnson (Gramatica kick), 7:36. Drive: 52 yards, 2 plays.
Tampa Bay: Alstott 2 run (Gramatica kick), 14:10. Drive: 26 yards, 4 plays.

THIRD QUARTER

Tampa Bay: FG Gramatica 19, 6:32. Drive: 36 yards, 10 plays.

A: 65,599; T: 3:01.

AFC Championship

Tennessee	7	10	7	0—24
Oakland................	14	10	3	14—41

FIRST QUARTER

Oakland: Porter 3 pass from Gannon (Janikowski kick), 4:01. Drive: 69 yards, 7 plays.
Tennessee: Bennett 33 pass from McNair (Nedney kick), 9:01. Drive: 74 yards, 9 plays.
Oakland: Garner 12 pass from Gannon (Janikowski kick), 12:13. Drive: 85 yards, 7 plays.

SECOND QUARTER

Tennessee: FG Nedney 29, 2:21. Drive: 62 yards, 10 plays.
Tennessee: McNair 9 run (Nedney kick), 12:13. Drive: 55 yards, 11 plays.
Oakland: Jolley 1 pass from Gannon (Janikowski kick), 14:00. Drive: 16 yards, 2 plays.
Oakland: FG Janikowski 43, 15:00. Drive: 14 yards, 5 plays.

THIRD QUARTER

Oakland: FG Janikowski 32, 10:31.
Tennessee: McNair 13 run (Hentrich kick), 14:29. Drive: 67 yards, 8 plays.

FOURTH QUARTER

Oakland: Gannon 2 run (Janikowski kick), 3:33. Drive: 66 yards, 9 plays.
Oakland: Crockett 7 run (Janikowski kick), 11:35. Drive: 69 yards, 10 plays.

A: 62,544; T: 3:23.

NFC Championship

Tampa Bay	10	7	3	7—27
Philadelphia............	7	3	0	0—10

FIRST QUARTER

Philadelphia: Staley 20 run (Akers kick), 0:52. Drive: 26 yards, 2 plays.
Tampa Bay: FG Gramatica 48, 5:02. Drive: 37 yards, 9 plays.
Tampa Bay: Alstott 1 run (Gramatica kick), 14:20. Drive: 96 yards, 7 plays.

SECOND QUARTER

Philadelphia: FG Akers 30, 6:56. Drive: 26 yards, 8 plays.
Tampa Bay: K. Johnson 9 pass from B. Johnson (Gramatica kick), 12:32. Drive: 80 yards, 12 plays.

THIRD QUARTER

Tampa Bay: FG Gramatica 27, 13:58. Drive: 43 yards, 8 plays.

FOURTH QUARTER

Tampa Bay: Barber 92 int. return (Gramatica kick), 11:48.

A: 66,713; T: 3:12.

Super Bowl Box Score

Oakland...................	3	0	6	12—21
Tampa Bay	3	17	14	14—48

FIRST QUARTER

Oakland: FG Janikowski 40, 4:20. Drive: 14 yards, 7 plays. Key plays: C. Woodson 12 int. return to Tampa Bay 36; Brown 9 pass from Gannon on third-and-2 to Tampa Bay 19. **Oakland 3–0.**
Tampa Bay: FG Gramatica 31, 7:09. Drive: 58 yards, 9 plays. Key plays: Jurevicius 23 pass from B. Johnson on third-and-10 to Oakland 37; Pittman 23 run to Oakland 14. **3–3.**

SECOND QUARTER

Tampa Bay: FG Gramatica 43, 3:44. Drive: 26 yards, 9 plays. Key plays: Jackson 9 int. return to Tampa Bay 49; K. Johnson 9 pass from B. Johnson on third-and-9 to Oakland 39. **Tampa Bay 6–3.**
Tampa Bay: Alstott 2 run (Gramatica kick), 8:36. Drive: 27 yards, 4 plays. Key plays: Williams 25 punt return to Oakland 27; Pittman 19 run to Oakland 2. **Tampa Bay 13–3.**
Tampa Bay: McCardell 5 pass from B. Johnson (Gramatica kick), 14:30. Drive: 77 yards, 10 plays. Key plays: Alstott 16 pass from B. Johnson to Oakland 42; Alstott 12 pass from B. Johnson to Oakland 5. **Tampa Bay 20–3.**

THIRD QUARTER

Tampa Bay: McCardell 8 pass from B. Johnson (Gramatica kick), 9:30. Drive: 89 yards, 14 plays. Key play: Jurevicius 33 pass from B. Johnson to Oakland 14. **Tampa Bay 27–3.**
Tampa Bay: Smith 44 int. return (Gramatica kick), 10:13. **Tampa Bay 34–3.**
Oakland: Porter 39 pass from Gannon (two-pt conversion failed), 12:46. Drive: 82 yards, 8 plays. Key play: Jolley 25 pass from Gannon on third-and-11 to Oakland 42. **Tampa Bay 34–9.**

FOURTH QUARTER

Oakland: Johnson 13 return of blocked punt (two-pt conversion failed), 0:44. **Tampa Bay 34–15.**
Oakland: Rice 48 pass from Gannon (two-pt conversion failed), 8:54. Drive: 78 yards, 8 plays. Key play: Jolley 14 pass from Gannon on third-and-7 to Tampa Bay 45. **Tampa Bay 34–21.**
Tampa Bay: Brooks 44 int. return (Gramatica kick), 13:42. **Tampa Bay 41–21.**
Tampa Bay: Smith 50 int. return (Gramatica kick), 14:58. **Tampa Bay 48–21.**

Team Statistics

	Oakland	Tampa Bay
FIRST DOWNS	11	24
Rushing	1	6
Passing	9	15
Penalty	1	3
THIRD DOWN EFF	7–16	6–15
FOURTH DOWN EFF	0–0	0–1
TOTAL NET YARDS	269	365
Total plays	60	76
Avg gain	4.5	4.8
NET YARDS RUSHING	19	150
Rushes	11	42
Avg per rush	1.7	3.6
NET YARDS PASSING	250	215
Completed–Att	24–44	18–34
Yards per pass	5.7	6.3
Sacked–yards lost	5–22	0–0
Had intercepted	5	1
PUNTS–Avg	5–39.0	4–38.8
TOTAL RETURN YARDS	41	197
Punt returns	3–29	1–25
Kickoff returns	9–149	4–90
Interceptions	1–12	5–172
PENALTIES–Yds	7–51	5–41
FUMBLES–Lost	1–0	1–0
TIME OF POSSESSION	22:46	37:14

Passing

OAKLAND

	Comp	Att	Yds	Int	TD
Gannon	24	44	272	5	2

TAMPA BAY

	Comp	Att	Yds	Int	TD
B. Johnson	18	34	215	1	2

Rushing

OAKLAND

	No.	Yds	Lg	TD
Garner	7	10	4	0
Crockett	2	6	4	0
Gannon	2	3	2	0

TAMPA BAY

	No.	Yds	Lg	TD
Pittman	29	124	24	0
Alstott	10	15	5	1
B. Johnson	1	10	10	0
Stecker	1	1	1	0
Tupa	1	0	0	0

Receiving

OAKLAND

	No.	Yds	Lg	TD
Rice	5	77	48	1
Porter	4	62	39	1
Jolley	5	59	25	0
Garner	7	51	9	0
Brown	1	9	9	0
Ritchie	1	7	7	0
Wheatley	1	7	7	0

TAMPA BAY

	No.	Yds	Lg	TD
Jurevicius	4	78	33	0
K. Johnson	6	69	18	0
Alstott	5	43	16	0
McCardell	2	13	8	2
Dilger	1	12	12	0

Defense

OAKLAND

	Tck	Ast	Int	Sack
Barton	8	5	0	0
C. Woodson	8	0	1	0
Romanowski	7	3	0	0
Smith	7	4	0	0
R. Woodson	7	1	0	0
Dorsett	6	2	0	0
Coleman	4	1	0	0
James	4	0	0	0
Parrella	3	1	0	0
Cooper	2	1	0	0
Harris	2	1	0	0
Johnson	2	0	0	0
Brown	1	0	0	0
Crockett	1	0	0	0
Ioane	1	0	0	0
Treu	1	0	0	0

TAMPA BAY

	Tck	Ast	Int	Sack
Quarles	7	0	0	0
Kelly	5	3	0	0
Rice	5	0	0	2
Smith	5	0	2	0
Ivy	4	0	0	0
Spires	3	0	0	1
Wyms	3	0	0	1
Barber	2	2	0	0
Barnes	2	0	0	0
Brooks	2	1	1	0
Howell	2	0	0	0
Jackson	2	0	2	0
Sapp	2	0	0	1
Webster	2	1	0	0
Golden	1	0	0	0
Jurevicius	1	0	0	0
Phillips	1	0	0	0
Singleton	1	0	0	0

2002 Associated Press All-Pro Team

OFFENSE

Terrell Owens, San Francisco	Wide Receiver
Marvin Harrison, Indianapolis	Wide Receiver
Jeremy Shockey, NY Giants	Tight End
Lincoln Kennedy, Oakland	Tackle
Jonathan Ogden, Baltimore	Tackle
Alan Faneca, Pittsburgh	Guard
Will Shields, Kansas City	Guard
Barret Robbins, Oakland	Center
Rich Gannon, Oakland	Quarterback
Ricky Williams, Miami	Running Back
Priest Holmes, Kansas City	Running Back

DEFENSE

Jason Taylor, Miami	Defensive End
Simeon Rice, Tampa Bay	Defensive End
Kris Jenkins, Carolina	Tackle
Warren Sapp, Tampa Bay	Tackle
Joey Porter, Pittsburgh	Outside Linebacker
Derrick Brooks, Tampa Bay	Outside Linebacker
Zach Thomas, Miami	Inside Linebacker
Brian Urlacher, Chicago	Inside Linebacker
Patrick Surtain, Miami	Cornerback
Troy Vincent, Philadelphia	Cornerback
Brian Dawkins, Philadelphia	Saftey
Rod Woodson, Oakland	Saftey

SPECIALISTS

Adam Vinatieri, New England	Kicker
Todd Sauerbrun, Carolina	Punter
Michael Lewis, New Orleans	Kick Returner

2002 AFC Team-by-Team Results

BALTIMORE RAVENS (7–9)

7	at Carolina	10
0	TAMPA BAY	25
34	DENVER	23
26	at Cleveland	21
20	at Indianapolis	22
17	JACKSONVILLE	10
18	PITTSBURGH	31
17	at Atlanta	20
38	CINCINNATI	27
7	at Miami	26
13	TENNESSEE	12
27	at Cincinnati	23
25	NEW ORLEANS	37
23	at Houston	19
13	CLEVELAND	14
31	at Pittsburgh	34
316		354

BUFFALO BILLS (8–8)

31	NY JETS	37(OT)
45	at Minnesota	39 (OT)
23	at Denver	28
33	CHICAGO	27 (OT)
31	OAKLAND	49
31	at Houston	24
23	at Miami	10
24	DETROIT	17
7	NEW ENGLAND	38
16	at Kansas City	17
13	at NY Jets	31
38	MIAMI	21
17	at New England	27
20	SAN DIEGO	13
0	at Green Bay	10
27	CINCINNATI	9
379		397

CINCINNATI BENGALS (2–14)

6	SAN DIEGO	34
7	at Cleveland	20
3	at Atlanta	30
7	TAMPA BAY	35
21	at Indianapolis	28
7	PITTSBURGH	34
24	TENNESSEE	30
38	at Houston	3
27	at Baltimore	38
20	CLEVELAND	27
21	at Pittsburgh	29
23	BALTIMORE	27
31	at Carolina	52
15	JACKSONVILLE	29
20	NEW ORLEANS	13
9	at Buffalo	27
279		456

CLEVELAND BROWNS (9–7)

39	KANSAS CITY	40	27	at Cincinnati	20
20	CINCINNATI	7	24	at New Orleans	15
31	at Tennessee OT	28	6	CAROLINA	13
13	at Pittsburgh	16(ot	21	at Jacksonville	20
21	BALTIMORE	26	23	INDIANAPOLIS	28
3	at Tampa Bay	17	14	at Baltimore	13
34	HOUSTON	17	24	ATLANTA	16
24	at NY Jets	21	344		320
20	PITTSBURGH	23			

DENVER BRONCOS (9–7)

23	ST. LOUIS	16
24	at San Francisco	14
28	BUFFALO	23
23	at Baltimore	34
26	SAN DIEGO	9
22	MIAMI	24
37	at Kansas City	34 (OT)
24	at New England	16
10	OAKLAND	34
31	at Seattle	9
20	INDIANAPOLIS	23 (OT)
27	at San Diego	30 (OT)
13	at NY Jets	19
31	KANSAS CITY	24
16	at Oakland	28
37	ARIZONA	7
392		**344**

HOUSTON TEXANS (4–12)

19	DALLAS	10
3	at San Diego	24
3	INDIANAPOLIS	23
17	at Philadelphia	35
24	BUFFALO	31
17	at Cleveland	34
21	at Jacksonville	19
3	CINCINNATI	38
10	at Tennessee	17
tk	JACKSONVILLE	24
16	NY GIANTS	14
3	at Indianapolis	19
24	at Pittsburgh	6
19	BALTIMORE	23
10	at Washington	26
3	TENNESEE	13
213		**356**

INDIANAPOLIS COLTS (10–6)

28	at Jacksonville	25
13	MIAMI	21
23	at Houston	3
28	CINCINNATI	21
22	BALTIMORE	20
10	at Pittsburgh	28
21	at Washington	26
15	TENNESSEE	23
35	at Philadelphia	13
20	DALLAS	3
23	at Denver	20 (OT)
19	HOUSTON	3
17	at Tennessee	27
28	at Cleveland	23
27	NY GIANTS	44
20	JACKSONVILLE	13
349		**313**

JACKSONVILLE JAGUARS (6–10)

25	INDIANAPOLIS	28
23	at Kansas City	16
28	NY JETS	3
28	PHILADELPHIA	25
14	at Tennessee	23
10	at Baltimore	17
19	HOUSTON	21
17	at NY Giants	24
26	WASHINGTON	7
24	at Houston	21
19	at Dallas	21
23	PITTSBURGH	25
20	CLEVELAND	21
29	at Cincinnati	15
10	TENNESSEE	28
13	at Indianapolis	20
328		**315**

KANSAS CITY CHIEFS (8–8)

40	at Cleveland	39
16	JACKSONVILLE	23
38	at New England	41 (OT)
48	MIAMI	30
29	at NY Jets	25
34	at San Diego	35
34	DENVER	37 (OT)
20	OAKLAND	10
13	at San Francisco	17
17	BUFFALO	16
32	at Seattle	39
49	ARIZONA	0
49	ST. LOUIS	10
24	at Denver	31
24	SAN DIEGO	22
0	at Oakland	24
467		**399**

MIAMI DOLPHINS (9–7)

49	DETROIT	21
21	at Indianapolis	13
30	NY JETS	3
30	at Kansas City	48
26	NEW ENGLAND	13
24	at Denver	22
10	BUFFALO	23
10	at Green Bay	24
10	at NY Jets	13
26	BALTIMORE	7
30	SAN DIEGO	3
21	at Buffalo	38
27	CHICAGO	9
23	OAKLAND	17
17	at Minnesota	20
24	at New England	27 (OT)
378		**301**

NEW ENGLAND PATRIOTS (9–7)

30	PITTSBURGH	14
44	at NY Jets	7
41	KANSAS CITY	38 (OT)
14	at San Diego	21
13	at Miami	26
10	GREEN BAY	28
16	DENVER	24
38	at Buffalo	7
33	at Chicago	30
20	at Oakland	27
24	MINNESOTA	17
20	at Detroit	12
27	BUFFALO	17
7	at Tennessee	24
17	NY JETS	30
27	MIAMI	24 (OT)
381		**346**

NEW YORK JETS (9–7))

37	at Buffalo	31 (OT)
7	NEW ENGLAND	44
3	at Miami	30
3	at Jacksonville	28
25	Kansas City	29
20	MINNESOTA	7
21	CLEVELAND	24
44	at San Diego	13
13	MIAMI	10
31	at Detroit	14
31	BUFFALO	13
20	at Oakland	26
19	DENVER	13
13	at Chicago	20
30	at New England	17
42	GREEN BAY	17
359		**336**

OAKLAND RAIDERS (11–5)

31	SEATTLE	17
30	at Pittsburgh	17
52	TENNESSEE	25
49	at Buffalo	31
13	at St. Louis	28
21	SAN DIEGO	27 (OT)
10	at Kansas City	20
20	SAN FRANCISCO	23 (OT)
34	at Denver	10
27	NEW ENGLAND	20
41	at Arizona	20
26	NY JETS	20
27	at San Diego	7
17	at Miami	23
28	DENVER	16
24	KANSAS CITY	0
450		**304**

PITTSBURGH STEELERS (10-5-1)

14	at New England	30
17	OAKLAND	30
16	CLEVELAND	13 (OT)
29	at New Orleans	32
34	at Cincinnati	7
28	INDIANAPOLIS	10
31	at Baltimore	18
23	at Cleveland	20
34	ATLANTA	34 (OT)
23	at Tennessee	31
29	Cincinnati	21
25	at Jacksonville	23
6	HOUSTON	24
30	CAROLINA	14
17	at Tampa Bay	7
34	BALTIMORE	31
390		**345**

SAN DIEGO CHARGERS (8-8)

34	at Cincinnati	6
24	HOUSTON	3
23	at Arizona	15
21	NEW ENGLAND	14
9	at Denver	26
35	KANSAS CITY	34
27	at Oakland	21 (OT)
13	NY JETS	44
24	at St. Louis	28
20	San Francisco	17 (OT)
3	at Miami	30
30	DENVER	27 (OT)
7	OAKLAND	27
13	at Buffalo	20
22	at Kansas City	24
28	SEATTLE	31 (OT)
333		**367**

TENNESSEE TITANS (11-5)

27	PHILADELPHIA	24
13	at Dallas	21
28	CLEVELAND	31 (OT)
25	at Oakland	52
14	WASHINGTON	31
23	JACKSONVILLE	14
30	at Cincinnati	24
23	at Indianapolis	15
17	HOUSTON	10
31	PITTSBURGH	23
12	at Baltimore	13
32	at NY Giants	29 (OT)
27	INDIANAPOLIS	17
24	NEW ENGLAND	7
28	at Jacksonville	10
13	at Houston	3
367		**324**

2002 NFC Team-by-Team Results

ARIZONA CARDINALS (5-11)

23	at Washington	31
24	at Seattle	13
15	SAN DIEGO	23
21	NY Giants	7
16	at Carolina	13
9	DALLAS	6 (OT)
28	at San Francisco	38
14	ST. LOUIS	27
6	SEATTLE	27
14	at Philadelphia	38
20	OAKLAND	41
0	at Kansas City	49
23	DETROIT	20 (OT)
28	at St. Louis	30
14	SAN FRANCISCO	17
7	at Denver	37
262		**417**

ATLANTA FALCONS (9-6-1)

34	at Green Bay	37 (OT)
13	CHICAGO	14
30	CINCINNATI	3
6	TAMPA BAY	20
17	at NY Giants	10
30	CAROLINA	0
37	at New Orleans	35
20	BALTIMORE	17
34	at Pittsburgh	34 (OT)
24	New Orleans	17
41	at Carolina	0
30	at Minnesota	24 (OT)
10	at Tampa Bay	34
24	SEATTLE	30 (OT)
36	DETROIT	15
16	at Cleveland	24
402		**314**

CAROLINA PANTHERS (7-9)

10	BALTIMORE	7
31	DETROIT	7
21	at Minnesota	14
14	at Green Bay	17
13	ARIZONA	16
13	at Dallas	14
0	at Atlanta	30
9	TAMPA BAY	12
24	NEW ORLEANS	34
10	at Tampa Bay	23
0	ATLANTA	41
13	at Cleveland	6
52	CINCINNATI	31
14	at Pittsburgh	30
24	CHICAGO	14
10	at New Orleans	6
258		**302**

CHICAGO BEARS (4-12)

27	MINNESOTA	23
14	at Atlanta	13
23	NEW ORLEANS	29
27	at Buffalo	33 (OT)
21	GREEN BAY	34
20	at Detroit	23 (OT)
7	at Minnesota	25
13	PHILADELPHIA	19
30	NEW ENGLAND	33
16	at St. Louis	21
20	DETROIT	17 (OT)
20	at Green Bay	30
9	at Miami	27
20	NY JETS	13
14	at Carolina	24
0	TAMPA BAY	15
281		**379**

DALLAS COWBOYS (5-11)

10	at Houston	19
21	TENNESSEE	13
13	at Philadelphia	44
13	at St. Louis	10
17	NY GIANTS	21
14	CAROLINA	13
6	at Arizona	9 (OT)
14	SEATTLE	17
7	at Detroit	9
3	at Indianapolis	20
21	JACKSONVILLE	19
27	WASHINGTON	20
27	SAN FRANCISCO	31
7	at NY Giants	37
3	PHILADELPHIA	27
14	at Washington	20
217		**329**

DETROIT LIONS (3-13)

21	at Miami	49
7	at Carolina	31
31	GREEN BAY	37
26	NEW ORLEANS	21
24	at Minnesota	31
23	CHICAGO	20 (OT)
17	at Buffalo	24
9	DALLAS	7
14	at Green Bay	40
14	NY JETS	31
17	at Chicago	20 (OT)
12	NEW ENGLAND	20
20	at Arizona	23 (OT)
20	TAMPA BAY	23
15	at Atlanta	36
36	MINNESOTA	38
306		**451**

2002 NFC Team-by-Team Results *(Cont.)*

GREEN BAY PACKERS (12–4)

37	ATLANTA	34 (OT)
20	at New Orleans	35
37	at Detroit	31
17	CAROLINA	14
34	at Chicago	21
28	at New England	10
30	WASHINGTON	9
24	MIAMI	10
40	DETROIT	14
21	at Minnesota	31
7	at Tampa Bay	21
30	CHICAGO	20
26	MINNESOTA	22
20	at San Francisco	14
10	BUFFALO	0
17	at NY Jets	42
398		**328**

MINNESOTA VIKINGS (6–10)

23	at Chicago	27
39	BUFFALO	45 (OT)
14	CAROLINA	21
23	at Seattle	48
31	DETROIT	24
7	at NY Jets	20
25	CHICAGO	7
24	at Tampa Bay	38
20	NY GIANTS	27
31	GREEN BAY	21
17	at New England	24
24	ATLANTA	30 (OT)
22	at Green Bay	26
32	at New Orleans	31
20	MIAMI	17
38	at Detroit	36
390		**442**

NEW ORLEANS SAINTS (9–7)

26	at Tampa Bay	20 (OT)
35	GREEN BAY	20
29	at Chicago	23
21	at Detroit	26
32	PITTSBURGH	29
43	at Washington	27
35	SAN FRANCISCO	27
35	ATLANTA	37
34	at Carolina	24
17	at ATLANTA	24
15	CLEVELAND	24
23	TAMPA BAY	20
37	at Baltimore	25
31	MINNESOTA	32
13	at Cincinnati	20
6	CAROLINA	10
432		**388**

NEW YORK GIANTS (10–6)

13	SAN FRANCISCO	16
26	at St. Louis	21
9	SEATTLE	6
7	at Arizona	21
21	at Dallas	17
10	ATLANTA	17
3	at Philadelphia	17
24	JACKSONVILLE	17
27	at Minnesota	20
19	WASHINGTON	17
14	at Houston	16
29	TENNESSEE	32 (OT)
27	at Washington	21
37	DALLAS	7
44	at Indianapolis	27
10	PHILADELPHIA	7 (OT)
324		**279**

PHILADELPHIA EAGLES (12–4)

24	at Tennessee	27
37	at Washington	7
44	DALLAS	13
35	HOUSTON	17
25	at Jacksonville	28
20	TAMPA BAY	10
17	NY GIANTS	3
19	at Chicago	13
13	INDIANAPOLIS	35
38	ARIZONA	14
38	at San Francisco	17
10	ST. LOUIS	3
27	at Seattle	20
34	WASHINGTON	21
27	at Dallas	3
7	at NY Giants	10 (OT)
415		**241**

ST. LOUIS RAMS (7–9)

16	at Denver	23
21	NY GIANTS	26
14	at Tampa Bay	26
10	DALLAS	13
13	at San Francisco	37
28	OAKLAND	13
37	SEATTLE	20
27	at Arizona	14
28	SAN DIEGO	24
21	CHICAGO	16
17	at Washington	20
3	at Philadelphia	10
10	at Kansas City	49
30	ARIZONA	28
10	at Seattle	30
31	SAN FRANCISCO	20
316		**369**

SAN FRANCISCO 49ERS (10–6)

16	at NY Giants	13
14	DENVER	24
20	WASHINGTON	10
37	ST. LOUIS	13
28	at Seattle	21
27	at New Orleans	35
38	ARIZONA	28
23	at Oakland	20 (OT)
17	Kansas City	13
17	at San Diego	20 (OT)
17	PHILADELPHIA	38
31	SEATTLE	24
31	at Dallas	27
14	GREEN BAY	20
17	at Arizona	14
20	at St. Louis	
367		**351**

SEATTLE SEAHAWKS (7–9)

17	at Oakland	31
13	ARIZONA	24
6	at NY Giants	9
48	MINNESOTA	23
21	SAN FRANCISCO	28
20	at St. Louis	37
17	at Dallas	14
3	WASHINGTON	14
27	at Arizona	6
9	DENVER	31
39	KANSAS CITY	32
24	at San Francisco	31
20	PHILADELPHIA	27
30	at Atlanta	24 (OT)
30	ST.LOUIS	10
31	at San Diego	28 (OT)
355		**369**

TAMPA BAY BUCCANEERS (12–4)

20	NEW ORLEANS	26 (OT)
25	at Baltimore	0
26	St. Louis	14
35	at Cincinnati	7
20	at Atlanta	6
17	Cleveland	3
10	at Philadelphia	20
12	at Carolina	9
38	MINNESOTA	24
23	CAROLINA	10
21	GREEN BAY	7
20	at New Orleans	23
34	at Atlanta	10
23	at Detroit	20
7	PITTSBURGH	17
15	at Chicago	0
346		**196**

WASHINGTON REDSKINS (7–9)

31	ARIZONA	23
7	PHILADELPHIA	37
10	at San Francisco	20
31	at Tennessee	14
27	NEW ORLEANS	43
9	at Green Bay	30
26	INDIANAPOLIS	21
14	at Seattle	3
7	at Jacksonville	26
17	at NY Giants	19
20	ST. LOUIS	17
20	at Dallas	27
21	NY GIANTS	27
21	at Philadelphia	34
26	HOUSTON	10
20	DALLAS	14
307		**365**

American Football Conference
Scoring

TOUCHDOWNS	TD	Rush	Rec	Ret	2PT	Pts	KICKING	PAT	FG	Lg	Pts
Holmes, KC	24	21	3	0	0	144	Janikowski, Oak	50/50	26/33	51	128
Williams, Mia	17	16	1	0	0	102	Elam, Den	42/43	26/36	55	120
Portis, Den	17	15	2	0	0	102	Vinatieri, NE	36/36	27/30	57	117
Tomlinson, SD	15	14	1	0	0	90	Andersen, KC	51/51	22/26	50	117
George, Tenn	14	12	2	0	1	86	Hollis, Buff	40/40	25/33	54	115
Henry, Buff	14	13	1	0	0	84	Mare, Mia	42/43	24/31	53	114
Ward, Pitt	12	0	12	0	3	78	Nedney, Tenn	36/36	25/31	53	111
Harrison, Ind	11	0	11	0	1	68	Hall, NYJ	35/37	24/31	46	107
Garner, Oak	11	7	4	0	0	66	Vanderjagt, Ind	34/34	23/31	54	103
Moulds, Buff	10	0	10	0	0	60	Dawson, Clev	34/35	22/28	52	100

Passing

	Att	Comp	Pct Comp	Yds	Avg Gain	TD	Pct TD	Int	Pct Int	Lg	Rating Pts
Pennington, NYJ	275	399	68.9	3120	7.82	22	5.5	6	1.5	47	104.2
Gannon, Oak	418	618	67.6	4689	7.59	26	4.2	10	1.6	75	97.3
Green, KC	287	470	61.1	3690	7.85	26	5.5	13	2.8	99	92.6
Manning, Ind	392	591	66.3	4200	7.11	27	4.6	19	3.2	69	88.8
Bledsoe, Buff	375	610	61.5	4359	7.15	24	3.9	15	2.5	73	86.0
Brady, NE	373	601	62.1	3764	6.26	28	4.7	14	2.3	49	85.7
Brunell, Jax	245	416	58.9	2788	6.70	17	4.1	7	1.7	79	85.7
Griese, Den	291	436	66.7	3214	7.37	15	3.4	15	3.4	82	85.6
Fiedler, Mia	179	292	61.3	2024	6.93	14	4.8	9	3.1	59	85.2
Maddox, Pitt	234	377	62.1	2836	7.52	20	5.3	16	4.2	72	85.2

Pass Receiving

RECEPTIONS	No.	Yds	Avg	Lg	TD	YARDS	No.	Yds	Avg	Lg	TD
Harrison, Ind	143	1722	12.0	69	11	Harrison, Ind	143	1722	12.0	69	11
Ward, Pitt	112	1329	11.9	72	12	Ward, Pitt	112	1329	11.9	72	12
Moulds, Buff	100	1287	12.9	70	10	Burress, Pitt	78	1325	17.0	62	7
Brown, NE	97	890	9.2	38	3	Moulds, Buff	100	1287	12.9	70	10
Price, Buff	94	1252	13.3	73	9	Coles, NYJ	89	1264	14.2	43	5
Rice, Oak	92	1211	13.2	75	7	Price, Buff	94	1252	13.3	73	9
Garner, Oak	91	941	10.3	69	4	Rice, Oak	92	1211	13.2	75	7
Coles, NYJ	89	1264	14.2	43	5	Johnson, Cin	69	1166	16.9	72	5
Smith, Den	89	1027	11.5	46	5	Smith, Jax	80	1027	12.8	47	7
Brown, Oak	81	930	11.5	45	2	Smith, Den	89	1027	11.5	46	5

Rushing / Total Yards from Scrimmage

	Att	Yds	Avg	Lg	TD	Total Yards from Scrimmage	Total	Rush	Rec
Williams, Mia	383	1853	4.8	63	16	Holmes, KC	2287	1615	672
Tomlinson, SD	372	1683	4.5	76	14	Williams, Mia	2216	1853	363
Holmes, KC	313	1615	5.2	56	21	Tomlinson, SD	2172	1683	489
Portis, Den	273	1508	5.5	59	15	Garner, Oak	1903	962	941
Henry, Buff	325	1438	4.4	34	13	Portis, Den	1872	1508	364
Lewis, Balt	308	1327	4.3	75	6	Lewis, Balt	1769	1327	442
Taylor, Jax	287	1314	4.6	63	8	Henry, Buff	1747	1438	309
Dillon, Cin	314	1311	4.2	67	7	Harrison, Ind	1732	10	1722
George, Tenn	343	1165	3.4	35	12	Taylor, Jax	1722	1314	408
Martin, NYJ	261	1094	4.2	35	7	Dillon, Cin	1609	1311	298

Interceptions / Sacks

	No.	Yds	Lg	TD	Sacks	
Woodson, Oak	8	225	98	2	Taylor, Mia	18.5
Five tied with six.					Freeney, Ind	13
					Coleman, Oak	11
					Abraham, NYJ	10
					Carter, Tenn	10

American Football Conference (Cont.)

Punting

	No.	Yds	Avg	Net Avg	TB	In 20	Lg	Blk	Ret	Ret Avg
Hanson, Jax	81	3583	44.2	37.6	10	27	64	0	39	8.7
Moorman, Buff	66	2844	43.1	36.0	7	18	84	0	29	10.1
Lechler, Oak	53	2251	42.5	32.7	12	18	70	0	18	15.3
Hentrich, Tenn	65	2725	41.9	33.9	5	28	56	0	28	13.9
Gardocki, Clev	81	3388	41.8	35.3	6	27	59	0	42	9.7

Punt Returns

	No.	Yds	Avg	Lg	TD
Moss, NYJ	25	413	16.5	63	2
Brightful, Balt	15	241	16.1	95	1
Northcutt, Clev	25	367	14.7	87	2
Hall, KC	29	390	13.4	90	2
Shaw, Jax	25	310	12.4	69	1

Kickoff Returns

	No.	Yds	Avg	Lg	TD
Faulk, NE	26	725	27.9	87	2
Kasper, Den	15	393	26.2	56	0
Morton, NYJ	58	1509	26.0	98	2
Droughns, Den	20	516	25.8	53	0
Bennett, Cin	49	1231	25.1	94	1

National Football Conference

Scoring

TOUCHDOWNS	TD	Rush	Rec	Ret	2PT	Pts
Alexander, Sea	18	16	2	0	0	108
McAllister, NO	16	13	3	0	0	96
Owens, SF	14	1	13	0	0	84
Barber, NYG	11	11	0	0	0	66
Williams, Minn	11	11	0	0	0	66
Culpepper, Minn	10	10	0	0	1	62
Faulk, StL	10	8	2	0	0	60
Hearst, SF	9	8	1	0	1	56

Four tied with 54.

KICKING	PAT	FG	Lg	Pts
Feely, Atl	42/43	32/40	52	138
Akers, Phil	43/43	30/34	51	133
Carney, NO	37/37	31/35	48	130
Gramatica, TB	32/32	32/39	53	128
Longwell, GB	44/44	28/34	49	128
Bryant, NYG	30/32	26/32	47	108
Lindell, Sea	38/38	23/29	52	107
Hanson, Det	31/31	23/28	49	100
Edinger, Chi	29/29	22/28	53	95
Wilkins, StL	37/37	19/25	47	94

Passing

	Att	Comp	Pct Comp	Yds	Avg Gain	TD	Pct TD	Int	Pct Int	Lg	Rating Pts
Johnson, TB	281	451	62.3	3049	6.76	22	4.9	6	1.3	76	92.9
Hasselbeck, Sea	267	419	63.7	3075	7.34	15	3.6	10	2.4	49	87.8
McNabb, Phil	211	361	58.4	2289	6.34	17	4.7	6	1.7	59	86.0
Garcia, SF	328	528	62.1	3344	6.33	21	4.0	10	1.9	76	85.6
Favre, GB	341	551	61.9	3658	6.64	27	4.9	16	2.9	85	85.6
Collins, NYG	335	545	61.5	4073	7.47	19	3.5	14	2.6	82	85.4
Vick, Atl	231	421	54.9	2936	6.97	16	3.8	8	1.9	74	81.6
Brooks, NO	283	528	53.6	3572	6.77	27	5.1	15	2.8	64	80.1
Miller, Chi	180	314	57.3	1944	6.19	13	4.1	9	2.9	54	77.5
Peete, Car	223	381	58.5	2630	6.91	15	3.9	14	3.7	69	77.4

Pass Receiving

RECEPTIONS	No.	Yds	Avg	Lg	TD
Moss, Minn	106	1347	12.7	60	7
Owens, SF	100	1300	13.0	76	13
Booker, Chi	97	1183	12.2	54	6
Holt, StL	91	1302	14.3	58	4
Horn, NO	88	1312	14.9	63	7
Toomer, NYG	82	1343	16.4	82	8
Faulk, StL	80	537	6.7	40	2
Bruce, StL	79	1075	13.6	34	7
Robinson, Sea	78	1240	15.9	83	5
Johnson, TB	76	1088	14.3	76	5

YARDS	Yds	No.	Avg	Lg	TD
Moss, Minn	106	1347	12.7	60	7
Toomer, NYG	82	1343	16.4	82	8
Horn, NO	88	1312	14.9	63	7
Holt, StL	91	1302	14.3	58	4
Owens, SF	100	1300	13.0	76	13
Robinson, Sea	78	1240	15.9	83	5
Booker, Chi	97	1183	12.2	54	6
Johnson, TB	76	1088	14.3	76	5
Bruce, StL	79	1075	13.6	34	7
Driver, GB	70	1064	15.2	85	9

National Football Conference (Cont.)

Rushing

	Att	Yds	Avg	Lg	TD
McAllister, NO	325	1388	4.3	62	13
Barber, NYG	304	1387	4.6	70	11
Bennett, Minn	255	1296	5.1	85	5
Green, GB	286	1240	4.3	43	7
Alexander, Sea	295	1175	4.0	58	16
Staley, Phil	269	1029	3.8	57	5
Stewart, Det	231	1021	4.4	56	4
Smith, Dall	254	975	3.8	30	5
Hearst, SF	215	972	4.5	40	8
Faulk, StL	212	953	4.5	44	8

Total Yards from Scrimmage

	Total	Rush	Rec
Barber, NYG	1984	1387	597
McAllister, NO	1740	1388	352
Bennett, Minn	1647	1296	351
Alexander, Sea	1635	1175	460
Green, GB	1633	1240	393
Staley, Phil	1570	1029	541
Faulk, StL	1490	953	537
Moss, Minn	1398	51	1347
Owens, SF	1379	79	1300
Stewart, Det	1354	1021	333

Interceptions

	No.	Yds	Lg	TD
Kelly, TB	8	68	31	0
Sharper, GB	7	233	89	1
Parrish, SF	7	204	60	0

Seven tied with five.

Sacks

Rice, TB	15.5
Douglas, Phil	12.5
Carter, SF	12.5

Three tied with 12.

Punting

	No.	Yds	Avg	Net Avg	TB	In 20	Lg	Blk	Ret	Ret Yds
Sauerbrun, Car	104	4735	45.5	37.5	12	31	67	0	63	8.8
Player, Ariz	88	3864	43.9	35.0	10	28	58	0	42	13.0
Landeta, Phil	52	2229	42.9	34.6	7	19	63	0	20	14.4
Tupa, TB	90	3856	42.8	35.4	12	30	71	0	42	10.3
Maynard, Chi	87	3679	42.3	37.4	2	26	75	0	46	8.4

Punt Returns

	No.	Yds	Avg	Lg	TD
Williams, SF	20	336	16.8	89	1
Lewis, NO	44	625	14.2	83	1
Mitchell, Phil	46	567	12.3	76	1
Galloway, Dall	15	181	12.1	71	0
Rossum, Atl	24	288	12.0	36	0

Kickoff Returns

	No.	Yds	Avg	Lg	TD
Jenkins, Ariz	20	559	28.0	95	1
Mitchell, Phil	43	1162	27.0	57	0
Drummond, Det	40	1039	26.0	91	0
Lewis, NO	70	1807	25.8	97	2
Stecker, TB	37	934	25.2	67	0

2002 NFL Team Leaders

AFC Total Offense

	Total Yds	Yds Rush	Yds Pass	Time of Poss	Pts/ Game
Oakland	6237	1762	4475	31:22	28.1
Denver	6090	2266	3824	30:29	24.5
Kansas City	6000	2378	3622	28:57	29.2
Pittsburgh	5952	2120	3832	32:47	24.4
Indianapolis	5616	1561	4055	30:52	21.8
Buffalo	5591	1596	3995	30:56	23.7
Miami	5392	2502	2890	31:24	23.6
San Diego	5325	2137	3188	29:57	20.8
Tennessee	5272	1952	3320	32:47	22.9
Cincinnati	5206	1730	3476	28:55	17.4
New England	5085	1508	3577	29:11	23.8
NY Jets	5036	1618	3418	28:52	22.4
Cleveland	5027	1615	3412	29:45	21.5
Jacksonville	4851	2089	2762	28:39	20.5
Baltimore	4639	1792	2847	27:47	19.8
Houston	3572	1347	2225	28:06	13.3

AFC Total Defense

	Opp Total Yds	Opp Yds Rush	Opp Yds Pass	PA/ Game
Miami	4656	1554	3102	18.8
Denver	4826	1489	3337	21.5
Pittsburgh	4835	1375	3460	21.6
Indianapolis	4909	1992	2917	19.6
Tennessee	4964	1424	3540	20.3
Oakland	4979	1453	3526	19.0
Buffalo	5189	2122	3067	24.8
Houston	5230	2089	3141	22.3
Cincinnati	5265	2006	3259	28.5
Jacksonville	5335	2071	3264	19.7
Cleveland	5347	2078	3269	20.0
Baltimore	5353	1762	3591	22.1
New England	5377	2198	3179	21.6
NY Jets	5463	1973	3490	21.0
San Diego	6034	1739	4295	22.9
Kansas City	6248	2067	4181	24.9

NFC Total Offense

	Total Yds	Yds Rush	Yds Pass	Time of Poss	Pts/ Game
Minnesota	6192	2507	3685	31:30	24.4
NY Giants	5826	1875	3951	31:26	20.0
Seattle	5818	1740	4078	28:55	22.2
San Francisco	5701	2244	3457	32:00	22.9
Philadelphia	5604	2220	3384	31:10	25.9
Green Bay	5560	1933	3627	31:50	24.9
St. Louis	5559	1405	4154	30:38	19.8
Atlanta	5534	2367	3167	32:02	25.1
New Orleans	5205	1767	3438	28:44	27.0
Washington	5143	1889	3254	29:36	19.2
Tampa Bay	5002	1557	3445	31:43	21.6
Arizona	4563	1823	2740	28:41	16.4
Detroit	4471	1477	2994	25:44	19.1
Chicago	4395	1344	3051	27:42	17.6
Dallas	4375	1754	2621	28:04	13.6
Carolina	4280	1586	2694	29:20	16.1

NFC Total Defense

	Opp Total Yds	Opp Yds Rush	Opp Yds Pass	PA/ Game
Tampa Bay	4044	1554	2490	12.3
Carolina	4646	1653	2993	18.9
Philadelphia	4754	1660	3094	15.1
Washington	4787	1754	3033	22.8
NY Giants	4949	1830	3119	17.4
Green Bay	4985	1998	2987	20.5
St. Louis	5025	1816	3209	23.1
San Francisco	5158	1652	3506	21.9
Dallas	5267	1818	3449	20.6
Atlanta	5334	2047	3287	19.6
Chicago	5606	2076	3530	23.7
Minnesota	5769	1666	4103	27.6
New Orleans	5796	1991	3805	24.3
Seattle	5852	2441	3411	23.1
Arizona	6020	2146	3874	26.1
Detroit	6117	1967	4150	28.2

Takeaways/Giveaways

American Football Conference

	Takeaways Int	Fum	Total	Giveaways Int	Fum	Total	Net Diff
Kansas City	18	13	31	13	2	15	16
Jacksonville	14	13	27	9	6	15	12
Oakland	21	10	31	10	9	19	12
New England	18	11	29	14	10	24	5
NY Jets	15	8	23	10	9	19	4
Tennessee	18	11	29	15	10	25	4
San Diego	17	10	27	16	8	24	3
Miami	21	9	30	15	15	30	0
Pittsburgh	19	17	36	22	14	36	0
Baltimore	25	6	31	14	18	32	-1
Cleveland	17	12	29	22	9	31	-2
Indianapolis	10	17	27	19	13	32	-5
Denver	9	13	22	20	7	27	-5
Houston	10	11	21	15	14	29	-8
Buffalo	10	9	19	15	16	31	-12
Cincinnati	9	11	20	22	13	35	-15

National Football Conference

	Takeaways Int	Fum	Total	Giveaways Int	Fum	Total	Net Diff
Green Bay	24	21	45	16	12	28	17
Tampa Bay	31	7	38	10	11	21	17
Philadelphia	15	22	37	11	13	24	13
Atlanta	24	15	39	12	15	27	12
San Francisco	19	8	27	10	7	17	10
New Orleans	20	18	38	15	15	30	8
Seattle	19	11	30	16	12	28	2
NY Giants	11	14	25	14	13	27	-2
Dallas	19	10	29	16	18	34	-5
Chicago	9	19	28	18	17	35	-7
Detroit	10	14	24	25	6	31	-7
Carolina	17	16	33	22	18	40	-7
Arizona	17	8	25	22	13	35	-10
Washington	14	12	26	20	20	40	-14
Minnesota	16	7	23	23	18	41	-18
St. Louis	12	14	26	27	18	45	-19

Conference Rankings

American Football Conference

	Offense Total	Rush	Pass	Defense Total	Rush	Pass
Baltimore	15	8	14	12	7	14
Buffalo	6	13	3	7	15	2
Cincinnati	10	10	8	9	10	6
Cleveland	13	12	10	11	13	8
Denver	2	3	5	2	4	9
Houston	16	16	16	8	14	4
Indianapolis	5	14	2	4	9	1
Jacksonville	14	6	15	10	12	7
Kansas City	3	2	6	16	11	15
Miami	7	1	13	1	5	3
New England	11	15	7	13	16	5
NY Jets	12	11	9	14	8	11
Oakland	1	9	1	6	3	12
Pittsburgh	4	5	4	3	1	10
San Diego	8	4	12	15	6	16
Tennessee	9	7	11	5	2	13

National Football Conference

	Offense Total	Rush	Pass	Defense Total	Rush	Pass
Arizona	12	8	14	15	15	14
Atlanta	8	2	11	10	13	8
Carolina	16	12	15	2	3	3
Chicago	14	16	12	11	14	12
Dallas	15	10	16	9	8	10
Detroit	13	14	13	16	10	16
Green Bay	6	5	5	6	12	2
Minnesota	1	1	4	12	5	15
New Orleans	9	9	8	13	11	13
NY Giants	2	7	3	5	9	6
Philadelphia	5	4	9	3	4	5
St. Louis	7	15	1	7	7	7
San Francisco	4	3	6	8	2	11
Seattle	3	11	2	14	16	9
Tampa Bay	11	13	7	1	1	1
Washington	10	6	10	4	6	4

Baltimore Ravens

SCORING	Rush	TD Rec	Ret	PAT	FG	S	Pts
Stover	0	0	0	33/33	21/25	0	96
J. Lewis	6	1	0	0	0	0	42
Heap	0	6	0	1	0	0	38
T. Taylor	0	6	0	0	0	0	36

RUSHING	No.	Yds	Avg	Lg	TD
J. Lewis	308	1327	4.3	75	6
C. Taylor	33	122	3.7	17	0

PASSING	Att	Comp	Pct Comp	Yds	Avg Gain	TD	Int	Rating Pts
Blake	295	165	55.9	2084	7.06	13	11	77.3
Redman	182	97	53.3	1034	5.68	7	3	76.1

RECEIVING	No.	Yds	Avg	Lg	TD
Heap	68	836	12.3	43	6
T. Taylor	61	869	14.2	64	6
J. Lewis	47	442	9.4	77t	1
Stokley	24	357	14.9	35t	2
C. Taylor	14	129	9.2	20t	2

INTERCEPTIONS: Reed, 5

PUNTING	No.	Yds	Avg	Net Avg	TB	In 20	Lg	Blk
Zastudil	81	3368	41.6	33.7	5	31	61	2

SACKS: Boulware, 7

Cincinnati Bengals

SCORING	Rush	TD Rec	Ret	PAT	FG	S	Pts
Rackers	0	0	0	30/32	15/18	0	75
Dillon	7	0	0	0	0	0	42
Warrick	0	6	0	0	0	0	36
C. Johnson	0	5	0	0	0	0	30
Kitna	4	0	0	0	0	0	24

RUSHING	No.	Yds	Avg	Lg	TD
Dillon	314	1311	4.2	67t	7
Bennett	33	155	4.7	29	0
Ru. Johnson	17	67	3.9	13	0

PASSING	Att	Comp	Pct Comp	Yds	Avg Gain	TD	Int	Rating Pts
Kitna	473	294	62.2	3178	6.72	16	16	79.1
Frerotte	85	44	51.8	437	5.14	1	5	46.1
A. Smith	33	12	36.4	117	3.55	0	1	34.5

RECEIVING	No.	Yds	Avg	Lg	TD
C. Johnson	69	1166	16.9	72t	5
Warrick	53	606	11.4	37t	6
Dugans	47	421	9.0	31	0
Dillon	43	298	6.9	19	0
Houshmandzadeh	41	492	12.0	31	1

INTERCEPTIONS: Hawkins and Kaesviharn, 2

PUNTING	No.	Yds	Avg	Net Avg	TB	In 20	Lg	Blk
Harris	65	2608	40.1	31.4	4	11	57	1

SACKS: J. Smith, 6.5

Buffalo Bills

SCORING	Rush	TD Rec	Ret	PAT	FG	S	Pts
Hollis	0	0	0	40/40	25/33	0	115
Henry	13	1	0	0	0	0	84
Moulds	0	10	0	0	0	0	60
P. Price	0	9	0	0	0	0	54

RUSHING	No.	Yds	Avg	Lg	TD
Henry	325	1438	4.4	34	13

PASSING	Att	Comp	Pct Comp	Yds	Avg Gain	TD	Int	Rating Pts
Bledsoe	610	375	61.5	4359	7.15	24	15	86.0

RECEIVING	No.	Yds	Avg	Lg	TD
Moulds	100	1287	12.9	70t	10
P. Price	94	1252	13.3	73t	9
Centers	43	388	9.0	25	0
Henry	43	309	7.2	26t	1
Reed	37	514	13.9	42	2

INTERCEPTIONS: Clements, 6

PUNTING	No.	Yds	Avg	Net Avg	TB	In 20	Lg	Blk
Moorman	66	2844	43.1	36.0	7	18	84	1

SACKS: Schobel, 8.5

Cleveland Browns

SCORING	Rush	TD Rec	Ret	PAT	FG	S	Pts
P. Dawson	0	0	0	34/35	22/28	0	100
Northcutt	1	5	2	1	0	0	50
Morgan	0	7	0	1	0	0	44
Davis	0	6	1	0	0	0	42
Green	6	0	0	0	0	0	36
K. Johnson	0	4	0	0	0	0	24

RUSHING	No.	Yds	Avg	Lg	TD
Green	243	887	3.7	64t	6
White	106	470	4.4	54	3
Northcutt	8	104	13.0	36t	1

PASSING	Att	Comp	Pct Comp	Yds	Avg Gain	TD	Int	Rating Pts
Couch	443	273	61.6	2842	6.42	18	18	76.8
Holcomb	106	64	60.4	790	7.45	8	4	92.9

RECEIVING	No.	Yds	Avg	Lg	TD
K. Johnson	67	703	10.5	30t	4
White	63	452	7.2	33	0
Morgan	56	964	17.2	78t	7
Northcutt	38	601	15.8	43t	5
Davis	37	420	11.4	31	6
Campbell	25	179	7.2	26	3

INTERCEPTIONS: Little, 4

PUNTING	No.	Yds	Avg	Net Avg	TB	In 20	Lg	Blk
Gardocki	81	3399	41.8	35.3	6	27	59	0

SACKS: Word, 8

Denver Broncos

SCORING

	TD			PAT	FG	S	Pts
	Rush	Rec	Ret				
Elam	0	0	0	42/43	26/36	0	120
Portis	15	2	0	0	0	0	102
Smith	0	5	0	0	0	0	30
Anderson	2	2	0	0	0	0	24
Sharpe	0	3	0	0	0	0	18

RUSHING

	No.	Yds	Avg	Lg	TD
Portis	273	1508	5.5	59	15
Anderson	84	386	4.6	32	2
Gary	37	147	4.0	26	1
Griese	37	107	2.9	13	1

PASSING

	Att	Comp	Pct Comp	Yds	Avg Gain	TD	Int	Rating Pts
Griese	436	291	66.7	3214	7.37	15	15	85.6
Beuerlein	117	68	58.1	925	7.91	6	5	82.7

RECEIVING

	No.	Yds	Avg	Lg	TD
Smith	89	1027	11.5	46	5
McCaffrey	69	903	13.1	69t	2
Sharpe	61	686	11.2	82t	3
Lelie	35	525	15.0	48	2
Portis	33	264	11.0	66t	2

INTERCEPTIONS: O'Neal, 5

PUNTING

	No.	Yds	Avg	Net Avg	TB	In 20	Lg	Blk
Knorr	24	906	37.8	34.1	2	8	59	0
Rouen	29	1239	42.7	31.7	4	6	63	2

SACKS: Pryce, 9

Houston Texans

SCORING

	TD			PAT	FG	S	Pts
	Rush	Rec	Ret				
K. Brown	0	0	0	20/20	17/24	0	71
Bradford	0	6	0	0	0	0	36
Carr	3	0	0	0	0	0	18
Miller	0	3	0	0	0	0	18
Wells	3	0	0	0	0	0	18

RUSHING

	No.	Yds	Avg	Lg	TD
Wells	197	529	2.7	37	3
Allen	155	519	3.3	32	0
Carr	59	282	4.8	20	3

PASSING

	Att	Comp	Pct Comp	Yds	Avg Gain	TD	Int	Rating Pts
Carr	444	233	52.5	2592	5.84	9	15	62.8

RECEIVING

	No.	Yds	Avg	Lg	TD
Miller	51	613	12.0	42	3
Allen	47	302	6.4	21	0
Bradford	45	697	15.5	81	6
Gaffney	41	483	11.8	27	1
Dawson	21	286	13.6	28	0

INTERCEPTIONS: Glenn, 5

PUNTING

	No.	Yds	Avg	Net Avg	TB	In 20	Lg	Blk
Stanley	114	4720	41.4	36.8	6	36	62	2

SACKS: Posey, 8

Indianapolis Colts

SCORING

	TD			PAT	FG	S	Pts
	Rush	Rec	Ret				
Vanderjagt	0	0	0	34/34	23/31	0	103
Harrison	0	11	0	1	0	0	68
Mungrow	8	0	0	0	0	0	48
Pollard	0	6	0	1	0	0	38
Wayne	0	4	0	0	0	0	24
James	2	1	0	1	0	0	20

RUSHING

	No.	Yds	Avg	Lg	TD
James	277	989	3.6	20	2
Mungrow	97	336	3.5	49	8
Manning	38	148	3.9	13	2

PASSING

	Att	Comp	Pct Comp	Yds	Avg Gain	TD	Int	Rating Pts
Manning	591	392	66.3	4200	7.11	27	19	88.8

RECEIVING

	No.	Yds	Avg	Lg	TD
Harrison	143	1722	12.0	69	11
James	61	354	5.8	23	1
Wayne	49	716	14.6	49	4
Ismail	44	462	10.5	42t	3
Pollard	43	478	11.1	41t	6

INTERCEPTIONS: Peterson, 3

PUNTING

	No.	Yds	Avg	Net Avg	TB	In 20	Lg	Blk
H. Smith	66	2672	40.5	34.9	9	26	69	1

SACKS: Freeney, 13

Jacksonville Jaguars

SCORING

	TD			PAT	FG	S	Pts
	Rush	Rec	Ret				
Mack	9	0	0	0	0	0	54
Taylor	8	0	0	2	0	0	52
J. Smith	0	7	0	1	0	0	44
Seder	0	0	0	11/11	8/12	0	35
Epstein	0	0	0	13/13	5/9	0	28

RUSHING

	No.	Yds	Avg	Lg	TD
Taylor	287	1314	4.6	63t	8
Mack	98	436	4.4	23	9
Brunell	43	207	4.8	27	0
Garrard	25	139	5.6	41t	2

PASSING

	Att	Comp	Pct Comp	Yds	Avg Gain	TD	Int	Rating Pts
Brunell	416	245	58.9	2788	6.70	17	7	85.7
Garrard	46	23	50.0	231	5.02	1	2	53.8

RECEIVING

	No.	Yds	Avg	Lg	TD
J. Smith	80	1027	12.8	47	7
Taylor	49	408	8.3	72	0
Shaw	44	525	11.9	48	1
Brady	43	461	10.7	42t	4
Mitchell	25	246	9.8	45	2

INTERCEPTIONS: McCree, 6

PUNTING

	No.	Yds	Avg	Net Avg	TB	In 20	Lg	Blk
Hanson	81	3583	44.2	37.6	10	27	64	0

SACKS: Henderson and Stroud, 6.5

Kansas City Chiefs

SCORING		TD					
	Rush	Rec	Ret	PAT	FG	S	Pts
Holmes	21	3	0	0	0	0	144
Andersen	0	0	0	51/51	22/26	0	117
Boerigter	0	8	0	0	0	0	48
Gonzalez	0	7	0	0	0	0	42
Hall	0	3	3	0	0	0	36

RUSHING	No.	Yds	Avg	Lg	TD
Holmes	313	1615	5.2	56	21
Green	31	225	7.3	24	1

PASSING	Att	Comp	Pct Comp	Yds	Avg Gain	TD	Int	Rating Pts
Green	470	287	61.1	3690	7.85	26	13	92.6
Collins	6	5	83.3	73	12.2	1	0	156.9

RECEIVING	No.	Yds	Avg	Lg	TD
Holmes	70	672	9.6	64t	3
Gonzalez	63	773	12.3	42t	7
Kennison	53	906	17.1	64	2
Morton	29	397	13.7	30	1
Boerigter	20	420	21.0	99t	8
Hall	20	322	16.1	75t	3

INTERCEPTIONS: Wesley, 6

PUNTING	No.	Yds	Avg	Net Avg	TB	In 20	Lg	Blk
Stryzinski	64	2422	37.8	31.2	6	15	56	1

SACKS: Hicks, 9

Miami Dolphins

SCORING		TD					
	Rush	Rec	Ret	PAT	FG	S	Pts
Mare	0	0	0	42/43	24/31	0	114
R. Williams	16	1	0	0	0	0	102
McMichael	0	4	0	0	0	0	24

RUSHING	No.	Yds	Avg	Lg	TD
R. Williams	383	1853	4.8	63t	16
Minor	44	180	4.1	23	2
Lucas	36	126	3.5	17	2
Edwards	20	107	5.4	19	1

PASSING	Att	Comp	Pct Comp	Yds	Avg Gain	TD	Int	Rating Pts
Fiedler	292	179	61.3	2024	6.93	14	9	85.2
Lucas	160	92	57.5	1045	6.53	4	6	69.9

RECEIVING	No.	Yds	Avg	Lg	TD
Chambers	52	734	14.1	59t	3
R. Williams	47	363	7.7	52	1
McMichael	39	484	12.4	45	4
Konrad	34	233	6.9	19	3
McKnight	29	528	18.2	77	2

INTERCEPTIONS: Surtain, 6

PUNTING	No.	Yds	Avg	Net Avg	TB	In 20	Lg	Blk
Royals	69	2772	40.2	34.5	6	5	56	0

SACKS: Taylor, 18.5

New England Patriots

SCORING		TD					
	Rush	Rec	Ret	PAT	FG	S	Pts
Vinatieri	0	0	0	36/36	27/30	0	117
A. Smith	6	2	0	1	0	0	50
Fauria	0	7	0	1	0	0	44
Faulk	2	3	2	0	0	0	42
Patten	0	5	0	0	0	0	30
Brown	0	3	0	1	0	0	20

RUSHING	No.	Yds	Avg	Lg	TD
A. Smith	252	982	3.9	42t	6
Faulk	52	271	5.2	45t	2
Brady	42	110	2.6	15	1

PASSING	Att	Comp	Pct Comp	Yds	Avg Gain	TD	Int	Rating Pts
Brady	601	373	62.1	3764	6.26	28	14	85.7

RECEIVING	No.	Yds	Avg	Lg	TD
Brown	97	890	9.2	38	3
Patten	61	825	13.5	39	5
Branch	43	489	11.4	49t	3
Faulk	37	379	10.2	36t	3
A. Smith	31	243	7.8	35	2
Fauria	27	253	9.4	33	7

INTERCEPTIONS: Buckley and Law, 4

PUNTING	No.	Yds	Avg	Net Avg	TB	In 20	Lg	Blk
Walter	70	2723	38.9	33.3	9	19	55	1

SACKS: McGinest and Seymour, 5.5

New York Jets

SCORING		TD					
	Rush	Rec	Ret	PAT	FG	S	Pts
Hall	0	0	0	35/37	24/31	0	107
Chrebet	0	9	0	0	0	0	54
Martin	7	0	0	1	0	0	44
Moss	0	4	2	0	0	0	36
Becht	0	5	0	1	0	0	32
Coles	0	5	0	1	0	0	32

RUSHING	No.	Yds	Avg	Lg	TD
Martin	261	1094	4.2	35	7
Jordan	84	316	3.8	61t	3

PASSING	Att	Comp	Pct Comp	Yds	Avg Gain	TD	Int	Rating Pts
Penn'ton	399	275	68.9	3120	7.82	22	6	104.2
Testaverde	83	54	65.1	499	6.01	3	3	78.3

RECEIVING	No.	Yds	Avg	Lg	TD
Coles	89	1264	14.2	43	5
Chrebet	51	691	13.5	37	9
Martin	49	362	7.4	28	0
Anderson	45	257	5.7	15	1
Moss	30	433	14.4	47	4
Becht	28	243	8.7	21	5

INTERCEPTIONS: D. Abraham, 4

PUNTING	No.	Yds	Avg	Net Avg	TB	In 20	Lg	Blk
Turk	63	2584	41.0	34.9	9	13	65	0

SACKS: J. Abraham, 10

Oakland Raiders

SCORING	Rush	Rec	Ret	PAT	FG	S	Pts
		TD					
Janikowski	0	0	0	50/50	26/33	0	128
Garner	7	4	0	0	0	0	66
Porter	0	9	0	2	0	0	58
Crockett	8	0	0	0	0	0	48
Rice	0	7	0	0	0	0	42

RUSHING	No.	Yds	Avg	Lg	TD
Garner	182	962	5.3	36t	7
Wheatley	108	419	3.9	36	2
Gannon	50	156	3.1	24	3
Crockett	40	118	3.0	33	8

PASSING	Att	Comp	Pct Comp	Yds	Avg Gain	TD	Int	Rating Pts
Gannon	618	418	67.6	4689	7.59	26	10	97.3

RECEIVING	No.	Yds	Avg	Lg	TD
Rice	92	1211	13.2	75	7
Garner	91	941	10.3	69t	4
Brown	81	930	11.5	41	2
Porter	51	688	13.5	36	9
Jolley	32	409	12.8	33	2

INTERCEPTIONS: R. Woodson, 8

PUNTING	No.	Yds	Avg	Net Avg	TB	In 20	Lg	Blk
Lechler	53	2251	42.5	32.7	12	18	70	0
Stemke	5	212	42.4	31.8	0	1	56	1

SACKS: R. Coleman, 11.0

San Diego Chargers

SCORING	Rush	Rec	Ret	PAT	FG	S	Pts
		TD					
Tomlinson	14	1	0	0	0	0	90
Christie	0	0	0	35/36	18/26	0	89
Conway	2	5	0	0	0	0	42
Caldwell	0	3	0	1	0	0	20

RUSHING	No.	Yds	Avg	Lg	TD
Tomlinson	372	1683	4.5	76	14
Brees	38	130	3.4	15	1
Fletcher	26	128	4.9	15	1

PASSING	Att	Comp	Pct Comp	Yds	Avg Gain	TD	Int	Rating Pts
Brees	526	320	60.8	3284	6.24	17	16	76.9
Flutie	11	3	27.3	64	5.82	0	0	51.3

RECEIVING	No.	Yds	Avg	Lg	TD
Tomlinson	79	489	6.2	30	1
Conway	57	852	14.9	52t	5
Dwight	50	623	12.5	42	2
Alexander	45	510	11.3	32	1
Caldwell	22	208	9.5	26	3
McCrary	22	96	4.4	25	3

INTERCEPTIONS: Edwards, 5

PUNTING	No.	Yds	Avg	Net Avg	TB	In 20	Lg	Blk
Bennett	87	3540	40.7	34.3	6	31	63	2

SACKS: Johnson, 6.5

Pittsburgh Steelers

SCORING	Rush	Rec	Ret	PAT	FG	S	Pts
		TD					
Ward	0	12	0	3	0	0	78
Peterson	0	0	0	25/26	12/21	0	61
Reed	0	0	0	10/11	17/19	0	61
Bettis	9	0	0	0	0	0	54
Burress	0	7	0	1	0	0	44
Zereoue	4	0	0	0	0	0	24

RUSHING	No.	Yds	Avg	Lg	TD
Zereoue	193	762	3.9	42	4
Bettis	187	666	3.6	41t	9
Stewart	43	191	4.4	28t	2
Ward	12	142	11.8	39	0
Randle El	19	134	7.1	24	0

PASSING	Att	Comp	Pct Comp	Yds	Avg Gain	TD	Int	Rating Pts
Maddox	377	234	62.1	2836	7.52	20	16	85.2
Stewart	166	109	65.7	1155	6.96	6	6	82.8

RECEIVING	No.	Yds	Avg	Lg	TD
Ward	112	1329	11.9	72t	12
Burress	78	1325	17.0	62t	7
Randle El	47	489	10.4	36	2
Zereoue	42	341	8.1	54	0
Mathis	23	218	9.5	22	2

INTERCEPTIONS: Porter and Alexander, 4

PUNTING	No.	Yds	Avg	Net Avg	TB	In 20	Lg	Blk
Miller	55	2267	41.2	32.5	5	14	62	1
Rouen	7	316	45.1	38.7	1	1	55	0

SACKS: Gildon and Porter, 9

Tennessee Titans

SCORING	Rush	Rec	Ret	PAT	FG	S	Pts
		TD					
Nedney	0	0	0	36/36	25/31	0	111
George	12	2	0	1	0	0	86
Mason	0	5	0	0	0	0	30
K. Dyson	0	4	0	0	0	0	24
Simon	1	3	0	0	0	0	24
McNair	3	0	0	1	0	0	20

RUSHING	No.	Yds	Avg	Lg	TD
George	343	1165	3.4	35	12
McNair	82	440	5.4	26	3
Holcombe	47	242	5.1	39	0

PASSING	Att	Comp	Pct Comp	Yds	Avg Gain	TD	Int	Rating Pts
McNair	492	301	61.2	3387	6.88	22	15	84.0

RECEIVING	No.	Yds	Avg	Lg	TD
Mason	79	1012	12.8	40	5
Dyson	41	460	11.2	40	4
Wycheck	40	346	8.7	19	2
George	36	255	7.1	14t	2
Bennett	33	478	14.5	53	2

INTERCEPTIONS: Schulters, 6

PUNTING	No.	Yds	Avg	Net Avg	TB	In 20	Lg	Blk
Hentrich	65	2725	41.9	33.9	5	28	56	1

SACKS: Carter, 10

Arizona Cardinals

SCORING

	TD						
	Rush	Rec	Ret	PAT	FG	S	Pts
Gramatica	0	0	0	29/29	15/21	0	74
Shipp	6	3	0	0	0	0	54
Kasper	0	3	0	0	0	0	18
Makovicka	0	3	0	0	0	0	18

RUSHING

	No.	Yds	Avg	Lg	TD
Shipp	188	834	4.4	56	6
T. Jones	138	511	3.7	58t	2
Plummer	46	283	6.2	34t	2

PASSING

	Att	Comp	Pct Comp	Yds	Avg Gain	TD	Int	Rating Pts
Plummer	530	284	53.6	2972	5.61	18	20	65.7
McCown	18	7	38.9	66	3.67	0	2	10.2

RECEIVING

	No.	Yds	Avg	Lg	TD
F. Jones	44	358	8.1	24	1
Shipp	38	413	10.9	80t	3
Sanders	34	400	11.8	37	2
Boston	32	512	16.0	34	1
McAddley	25	362	14.5	42	1
Jenkins	21	250	11.9	65t	1

INTERCEPTIONS: Wilson, 4

PUNTING

	No.	Yds	Avg	Net Avg	TB	In 20	Lg	Blk
Player	88	3864	43.9	35.0	10	28	58	1

SACKS: Vanden Bosch, 3.5

Carolina Panthers

SCORING

	TD						
	Rush	Rec	Ret	PAT	FG	S	Pts
Graham	0	0	0	21/21	13/18	0	60
L. Smith	7	0	0	0	0	0	42
Brown	4	1	0	0	0	0	30
S. Smith	0	3	2	0	0	0	30
Walls	0	4	0	0	0	0	24
Muhammad	0	3	0	0	0	0	18

RUSHING

	No.	Yds	Avg	Lg	TD
L. Smith	209	737	3.5	59	7
Brown	102	360	3.5	24	4
Goings	50	188	3.8	20	0
Hoover	31	129	4.2	11	0

PASSING

	Att	Comp	Pct Comp	Yds	Avg Gain	TD	Int	Rating Pts
Peete	381	223	58.5	2630	6.90	15	14	77.4
Fasani	44	15	34.1	171	3.89	0	4	8.8
Weinke	38	17	44.7	180	4.74	0	3	26.2

RECEIVING

	No.	Yds	Avg	Lg	TD
Muhammad	63	823	13.1	42	3
S. Smith	54	872	16.1	69	3
L. Smith	20	167	8.4	58	0
Walls	19	241	12.7	27	4

INTERCEPTIONS: Minter, 4

PUNTING

	No.	Yds	Avg	Net Avg	TB	In 20	Lg	Blk
S'rbrun	104	4735	45.5	37.5	12	31	67	1

Atlanta Falcons

SCORING

	TD						
	Rush	Rec	Ret	PAT	FG	S	Pts
Feely	0	0	0	42/43	32/40	0	138
Dunn	7	2	0	0	0	0	54
Vick	8	0	0	0	0	0	48
Finneran	0	6	0	0	0	0	36
Crumpler	0	5	0	0	0	0	30
Duckett	4	0	0	0	0	0	24

RUSHING

	No.	Yds	Avg	Lg	TD
Dunn	230	927	4.0	59t	7
Vick	113	777	6.9	46t	8
Duckett	130	507	3.9	33	4
Christian	31	119	3.8	16	3

PASSING

	Att	Comp	Pct Comp	Yds	Avg Gain	TD	Int	Rating Pts
Vick	421	231	54.9	2936	6.97	16	8	81.6
D. Johnson	57	37	64.9	448	7.86	2	3	78.7

RECEIVING

	No.	Yds	Avg	Lg	TD
Finneran	56	838	15.0	47	6
Dunn	50	377	7.5	31t	2
Crumpler	36	455	12.6	33	5
Jefferson	27	394	14.6	63	1
Gaylor	25	385	15.4	74t	3

INTERCEPTIONS: Carpenter and Bolden, 4

PUNTING

	No.	Yds	Avg	Net Avg	TB	In 20	Lg	Blk
Mohr	67	2804	41.9	38.7	5	21	59	0

SACKS: Kerney, 10.5

SACKS: Peppers, 12

Chicago Bears

SCORING

	TD						
	Rush	Rec	Ret	PAT	FG	S	Pts
Edinger	0	0	0	29/29	22/28	0	95
Booker	0	6	0	0	0	0	36
Thomas	6	0	0	0	0	0	36
White	0	4	0	0	0	0	24

RUSHING

	No.	Yds	Avg	Lg	TD
Thomas	214	721	3.4	34	6
L. Johnson	103	329	3.2	23	1
Burris	15	104	6.9	17	0
Peterson	19	101	5.3	14	1

PASSING

	Att	Comp	Pct Comp	Yds	Avg Gain	TD	Int	Rating Pts
Miller	314	180	57.3	1944	6.19	13	9	77.5
Chandler	161	103	64.0	1023	6.35	4	4	79.8
Burris	51	18	35.3	207	4.06	3	5	28.4

RECEIVING

	No.	Yds	Avg	Lg	TD
Booker	97	1183	12.2	54	6
White	51	656	12.9	76t	4
Thomas	24	163	6.8	19	0
M. Robinson	21	244	11.6	45t	3
Davis	20	193	9.7	37	3

INTERCEPTIONS: M. Brown, 3

PUNTING

	No.	Yds	Avg	Net Avg	TB	In 20	Lg	Blk
Maynard	87	3679	42.3	37.4	2	26	75	0

SACKS: Colvin, 10.5

Dallas Cowboys

SCORING

SCORING	Rush	TD Rec	Ret	PAT	FG	S	Pts
Cundiff	0	0	0	25/25	12/19	0	61
Bryant	0	6	0	0	0	0	36
Galloway	0	6	0	0	0	0	36
Smith	5	0	0	0	0	0	30

RUSHING

RUSHING	No.	Yds	Avg	Lg	TD
Smith	254	975	3.8	30	5
Hambrick	79	317	4.0	18	1
Wiley	22	168	7.6	46t	1

PASSING

PASSING	Att	Comp	Pct Comp	Yds	Avg Gain	TD	Int	Rating Pts
Hutchinson	250	127	50.8	1555	6.22	7	8	66.3
Carter	221	125	56.6	1465	6.63	7	8	72.3

RECEIVING

RECEIVING	No.	Yds	Avg	Lg	TD
Galloway	61	908	14.9	80t	6
Bryant	44	733	16.7	78t	6
McGee	23	294	12.8	58	1
D. Scott	22	218	9.9	17t	1

INTERCEPTIONS: Ro. Williams and Ross, 5

PUNTING

PUNTING	No.	Yds	Avg	Net Avg	TB	In 20	Lg	Blk
Filipovic	65	2640	40.6	31.5	6	14	60	1
Knorr	47	1928	41.0	35.1	4	11	56	0

SACKS: Ellis, 7.5

Green Bay Packers

SCORING

SCORING	Rush	TD Rec	Ret	PAT	FG	S	Pts
Longwell	0	0	0	44/44	28/24	0	128
Driver	0	9	0	0	0	0	54
Green	7	2	0	0	0	0	54
Franks	7	0	0	0	0	0	42
Henderson	1	3	0	0	0	0	24

RUSHING

RUSHING	No.	Yds	Avg	Lg	TD
Green	286	1240	4.3	43	7
Fisher	70	283	4.0	28	2
Davenport	39	184	4.7	43	1

PASSING

PASSING	Att	Comp	Pct Comp	Yds	Avg Gain	TD	Int	Rating Pts
Favre	551	341	61.9	3658	6.64	27	16	85.6
Pederson	28	19	67.9	134	4.79	1	0	90.5

RECEIVING

RECEIVING	No.	Yds	Avg	Lg	TD
Driver	70	1064	15.2	85t	9
Green	57	393	6.9	23t	2
Glenn	56	817	14.6	49	2
Franks	54	442	8.2	20t	7
Henderson	26	168	6.5	17	3
J. Walker	23	319	13.9	30	1

INTERCEPTIONS: Sharper, 7

PUNTING

PUNTING	No.	Yds	Avg	Net Avg	TB	In 20	Lg	Blk
Bidwell	79	3296	41.7	35.7	6	26	57	0

SACKS: Gbaha-Biamila, 12

Detroit Lions

SCORING

SCORING	Rush	TD Rec	Ret	PAT	FG	S	Pts
Hanson	0	0	0	31/31	23/28	0	100
Stewart	4	2	0	0	0	0	36
Schroeder	0	5	0	1	0	0	32
Hakim	0	3	1	0	0	0	24

RUSHING

RUSHING	No.	Yds	Avg	Lg	TD
Stewart	231	1021	4.4	56	4
Schlesinger	49	139	2.8	17	2
Cason	26	107	4.1	40	1

PASSING

PASSING	Att	Comp	Pct Comp	Yds	Avg Gain	TD	Int	Rating Pts
Harrington	429	215	50.1	2294	5.38	12	16	59.9
McMahon	147	62	42.2	874	5.95	7	9	52.4

RECEIVING

RECEIVING	No.	Yds	Avg	Lg	TD
Stewart	46	333	7.2	52t	2
Hakim	37	541	14.6	64t	3
Schroeder	36	595	16.5	46	5
Schlesinger	35	263	7.5	43	0
Ricks	27	339	12.6	49	3

INTERCEPTIONS: Claiborne, 3

PUNTING

PUNTING	No.	Yds	Avg	Net Avg	TB	In 20	Lg	Blk
Jett	91	3838	42.2	38.0	7	29	57	0

SACKS: Edwards, 6.5

Minnesota Vikings

SCORING

SCORING	Rush	TD Rec	Ret	PAT	FG	S	Pts
Anderson	0	0	0	36/37	18/23	0	90
M. Williams	11	0	0	0	0	0	66
Culpepper	10	0	0	1	0	0	62
Moss	0	7	0	0	0	0	42
Bennett	5	1	0	0	0	0	36
Bates	4	0	0	0	0	0	24

RUSHING

RUSHING	No.	Yds	Avg	Lg	TD
Bennett	255	1296	5.1	85t	5
Culpepper	106	609	5.7	38	10
M. Williams	84	414	4.9	44	11

PASSING

PASSING	Att	Comp	Pct Comp	Yds	Avg Gain	TD	Int	Rating Pts
Culpepper	549	333	60.7	3853	7.02	18	23	75.3

RECEIVING

RECEIVING	No.	Yds	Avg	Lg	TD
Moss	106	1347	12.7	60	7
Bates	50	689	13.8	59	4
Kleinsasser	37	393	10.6	39	1
Bennett	37	351	9.5	45t	1
Chamberlain	34	389	11.4	61	0
M. Williams	27	251	9.3	36	0

INTERCEPTIONS: Biekert, 4

PUNTING

PUNTING	No.	Yds	Avg	Net Avg	TB	In 20	Lg	Blk
Rich'son	62	2472	39.9	35.3	6	21	59	1

SACKS: Johnstone 7.0

New Orleans Saints

SCORING

	Rush	TD Rec	Ret	PAT	FG	S	Pts
Carney	0	0	0	37/37	31/35	0	130
McAllister	13	3	0	0	0	0	96
Stallworth	0	8	0	0	0	0	48
Horn	0	7	0	1	0	0	44
Pathon	0	4	0	0	0	0	24

RUSHING

	No.	Yds	Avg	Lg	TD
McAllister	325	1388	4.3	62	13
Brooks	62	253	4.1	21	2

PASSING

	Att	Comp	Pct Comp	Yds	Avg Gain	TD	Int	Rating Pts
Brooks	528	283	53.6	3572	6.77	27	15	80.1
Delhomme	10	8	80.0	113	11.3	0	0	113.8

RECEIVING

	No.	Yds	Avg	Lg	TD
Horn	88	1312	14.9	63	7
McAllister	47	352	7.5	30	3
Pathon	43	523	12.2	64	4
Stallworth	42	594	14.1	57t	8
Reed	21	360	17.1	54	3

INTERCEPTIONS: Thomas and S. Knight, 5

PUNTING

	No.	Yds	Avg	Net Avg	TB	In 20	Lg	Blk
Gowin	61	2553	41.9	36.9	6	15	59	0
D. Johnson	8	307	38.4	34.8	0	1	55	0

SACKS: Howard, 8

Philadelphia Eagles

SCORING

	Rush	TD Rec	Ret	PAT	FG	S	Pts
Akers	0	0	0	43/43	30/34	0	133
Staley	5	3	0	1	0	0	50
Thrash	2	6	0	0	0	0	48
Pinkston	0	7	0	0	0	0	42
McNabb	6	0	0	0	0	0	36
Freeman	0	4	0	0	0	0	24

RUSHING

	No.	Yds	Avg	Lg	TD
Staley	269	1029	3.8	57	5
McNabb	63	460	7.3	40t	6
Levens	75	411	5.5	47t	1
Westbrook	46	193	4.2	18	0

PASSING

	Att	Comp	Pct Comp	Yds	Avg Gain	TD	Int	Rating Pts
McNabb	361	211	58.4	2289	6.34	17	6	86.0
Feeley	154	86	55.8	1011	6.56	6	5	75.4
Detmer	28	19	67.9	224	8.00	2	0	115.8

RECEIVING

	No.	Yds	Avg	Lg	TD
Pinkston	60	798	13.3	42t	7
Thrash	52	635	12.2	39t	6
Staley	51	541	10.6	45	3
Freeman	46	600	13.0	59t	4
C. Lewis	42	398	9.5	30	3

INTERCEPTIONS: Taylor, 5

PUNTING

	No.	Yds	Avg	Net Avg	TB	In 20	Lg	Blk
Landeta	52	2229	42.9	34.6	7	19	63	0
Johnson	14	523	37.4	27.7	2	4	53	0
Baker	13	445	34.2	29.8	1	2	44	0

SACKS: H. Douglas, 12.5

New York Giants

SCORING

	Rush	TD Rec	Ret	PAT	FG	S	Pts
Bryant	0	0	0	30/32	26/32	0	108
Barber	11	0	0	0	0	0	66
Toomer	0	8	0	0	0	0	48
Dayne	3	0	0	0	0	0	18
Stackhouse	0	3	0	0	0	0	18

RUSHING

	No.	Yds	Avg	Lg	TD
Barber	304	1387	4.6	70	11
Dayne	125	428	3.4	30t	3

PASSING

	Att	Comp	Pct Comp	Yds	Avg Gain	TD	Int	Rating Pts
Collins	545	335	61.5	4073	7.47	19	14	85.4

RECEIVING

	No.	Yds	Avg	Lg	TD
Toomer	82	1343	16.4	82t	8
Shockey	74	894	12.1	30	2
Barber	69	597	8.7	38	0
Hilliard	27	386	14.3	38	2
Dixon	22	377	17.1	33	2
Campbell	22	175	8.0	27	1

INTERCEPTIONS: Sehorn, Peterson and Williams, 2

PUNTING

	No.	Yds	Avg	Net Avg	TB	In 20	Lg	Blk
M. Allen	63	2326	36.9	32.5	4	20	65	0
Rouen	8	333	41.6	33.0	2	1	55	0

SACKS: Strahan, 11

St. Louis Rams

SCORING

	Rush	TD Rec	Ret	PAT	FG	S	Pts
Wilkins	0	0	0	37/37	19/25	0	94
Faulk	8	2	0	0	0	0	60
Bruce	0	7	0	0	0	0	42
Holt	0	4	0	0	0	0	24
Proehl	0	4	0	0	0	0	24

RUSHING

	No.	Yds	Avg	Lg	TD
Faulk	212	953	4.5	44	8
Gordon	65	228	3.5	29	1

PASSING

	Att	Comp	Pct Comp	Yds	Avg Gain	TD	Int	Rating Pts
Warner	220	144	65.5	1431	6.50	3	11	67.4
Bulger	214	138	64.5	1826	8.53	14	6	101.5
Martin	195	124	63.6	1216	6.24	7	10	71.7

RECEIVING

	No.	Yds	Avg	Lg	TD
Holt	91	1302	14.3	58	4
Faulk	80	537	6.7	40	2
Bruce	79	1075	13.6	34t	7
Proehl	43	466	10.8	33	4
Conwell	34	419	12.3	52	2
Gordon	30	278	9.3	25	2

INTERCEPTIONS: Herring, 3

PUNTING

	No.	Yds	Avg	Net Avg	TB	In 20	Lg	Blk
Berger	72	3020	41.9	32.7	10	26	64	0

SACKS: Little, 12.0145

San Francisco 49ers

SCORING

SCORING	Rush	Rec	Ret	PAT	FG	S	Pts
Owens	1	13	0	0	0	0	84
Cortez	0	0	0	25/25	18/24	0	79
Hearst	8	1	0	1	0	0	54
Chandler	0	0	0	14/14	8/12	0	38
Barlow	4	1	0	0	0	0	30
Streets	0	5	0	0	0	0	30

RUSHING	No.	Yds	Avg	Lg	TD
Hearst	215	972	4.5	40	8
Barlow	145	675	4.7	35	4
Garcia	73	353	4.8	21t	3

PASSING	Att	Comp	Pct Comp	Yds	Avg Gain	TD	Int	Rating Pts
Garcia	528	328	62.1	3344	6.33	21	10	85.6
Rattay	43	26	60.5	232	5.40	2	0	90.5

RECEIVING	No.	Yds	Avg	Lg	TD
Owens	100	1300	13.0	76t	13
Streets	72	756	10.5	47t	5
Hearst	48	317	6.6	16	1
E. Johnson	36	321	8.9	38	0
Stokes	32	332	10.4	51	1

INTERCEPTIONS: Parrish, 7

PUNTING	No.	Yds	Avg	Net Avg	TB	In 20	Lg	Blk
Baker	42	1688	40.2	32.0	3	12	51	0
LaFleur	22	805	36.6	30.8	1	5	60	1

SACKS: Carter, 12.5

Tampa Bay Buccaneers

SCORING	Rush	Rec	Ret	PAT	FG	S	Pts
Gramatica	0	0	0	32/32	32/39	0	128
Alstott	5	2	0	0	0	0	42
McCardell	0	6	0	0	0	0	36
K. Johnson	0	5	0	2	0	0	34
Brooks	0	0	4	0	0	0	24
Jurevicius	0	4	0	0	0	0	24

RUSHING	No.	Yds	Avg	Lg	TD
Pittman	204	718	3.5	21	1
Alstott	146	548	3.8	32	5
Stecker	28	174	6.2	59	0

PASSING	Att	Comp	Pct Comp	Yds	Avg Gain	TD	Int	Rating Pts
B. Johnson	451	281	62.3	3049	6.76	22	6	92.9
R. Johnson	88	57	64.8	536	6.09	1	2	75.8
King	27	10	37.0	80	2.96	0	1	30.0

RECEIVING	No.	Yds	Avg	Lg	TD
K. Johnson	76	1088	14.3	76t	5
McCardell	61	670	11.0	65t	6
Pittman	59	477	8.1	64	0
Jurevicius	37	423	11.4	26	4
Alstott	35	242	6.9	44t	2
Dilger	34	329	9.7	40	2

INTERCEPTIONS: Kelly, 8

PUNTING	No.	Yds	Avg	Net Avg	TB	In 20	Lg	Blk
Tupa	90	3856	42.8	35.4	12	30	71	0

SACKS: Rice, 15.5

Seattle Seahawks

SCORING	Rush	Rec	Ret	PAT	FG	S	Pts
Alexander	16	2	0	0	0	0	108
Lindell	0	0	0	38/38	23/29	0	107
Robinson	0	5	0	0	0	0	30
Jackson	0	4	0	0	0	0	24
Stevens	0	3	0	0	0	0	18

RUSHING	No.	Yds	Avg	Lg	TD
Alexander	295	1175	4.0	58	16
Hasselbeck	40	202	5.1	21	1
Morris	32	153	4.8	24	0

PASSING	Att	Comp	Pct Comp	Yds	Avg Gain	TD	Int	Rating Pts
Hasselbeck	419	266	63.7	3075	7.34	15	10	87.8
Dilfer	168	94	56.0	1182	7.04	4	6	71.1

RECEIVING	No.	Yds	Avg	Lg	TD
Robinson	78	1240	15.9	83	5
Jackson	62	877	14.1	48	4
Alexander	59	460	7.8	80t	2
Engram	50	619	12.4	38	0
Mili	43	508	11.8	49	2
Stevens	26	252	9.7	29	3

INTERCEPTIONS: Tongue, 5

PUNTING	No.	Yds	Avg	Net Avg	TB	In 20	Lg	Blk
Feagles	61	2542	41.7	37.0	4	22	58	0

SACKS: Randle, 7

Washington Redskins

SCORING	Rush	Rec	Ret	PAT	FG	S	Pts
Tuthill	0	0	0	20/21	10/16	0	50
Davis	7	1	0	0	0	0	48
Gardner	0	8	0	0	0	0	48
Thompson	0	4	0	0	0	0	24
Cortez	0	0	0	9/9	5/8	0	24

RUSHING	No.	Yds	Avg	Lg	TD
Davis	207	820	4.0	33	7
Watson	116	534	4.6	24	1
Betts	65	307	4.7	27	1

PASSING	Att	Comp	Pct Comp	Yds	Avg Gain	TD	Int	Rating Pts
Matthews	237	124	52.3	1251	5.28	11	6	72.6
Ramsey	227	117	51.5	1539	6.78	9	8	71.8
Wuerffel	92	58	63.0	719	7.82	3	6	70.9

RECEIVING	No.	Yds	Avg	Lg	TD
Gardner	71	1006	14.2	43t	8
Thompson	53	773	14.6	47	4
Watson	32	253	7.9	62t	1
Davis	23	142	6.2	14t	1
McCants	21	256	12.2	32	2

INTERCEPTIONS: Smoot, 4

PUNTING	No.	Yds	Avg	Net Avg	TB	In 20	Lg	Blk
Barker	48	1924	40.1	30.0	5	13	63	0
Jarrett	20	771	38.6	30.5	2	5	74	1

SACKS: Arrington, 11

First two rounds of the 68th annual NFL Draft held April 26–27 in New York City.

First Round

Team	Selection	Position
1. ....Cincinnati	Carson Palmer, USC	QB
2. ....Detroit	Charles Rogers, Michigan St	WR
3. ....Houston	Andre Johnson, Miami (FL)	WR
4. ....NY Jets (from Chicago)	DeWayne Robertson, Kentucky	DT
5. ....Dallas	Terence Newman, Kansas St	CB
6. ....New Orleans (from Arizona)	Jonathan Sullivan, Georgia	DT
7. ....Jacksonville	Byron Leftwich, Marshall	QB
8. ....Carolina	Jordan Gross, Utah	OT
9. ....Minnesota (passed on 7&8)	Kevin Williams, Oklahoma St	DT
10. ......Baltimore	Terrell Suggs, Arizona St	DE
11. ......Seattle	Marcus Trufant Washington St	CB
12. ......St. Louis	Jimmy Kennedy, Penn St	DT
13. ......New England (from Wash)	Ty Warren, Texas A&M	DT
14. ......Chicago (from Buff)	Michael Haynes, Penn St	DE
15. ......Philadelphia (from SD)	Jerome McDougal, Miami (FL)	DE
16. ......Pittsburgh (from KC)	Troy Polamalu, Southern Cal	S
17. ......Arizona (from NO)	Bryant Johnson, Penn St	WR
18. ......Arizona (from Mia)	Calvin Pace, Wake Forest	DE
19. ......Baltimore (from NE)	Kyle Boller, California	QB
20. ......Denver	George Foster, Georgia	OT
21. ......Cleveland	Jeff Faine, Notre Dame	C
22. ......Chicago (from NY Jets)	Rex Grossman, Florida	QB
23. ......Buffalo (from Atlanta)	Willis McGahee, Miami (FL)	RB
24. ......Indianapolis	Dallas Clark, Iowa	TE
25. ......NY Giants	William Joseph, Miami (FL)	DT
26. ......San Francisco	Kwame Harris, Stanford	OT
27. ......Kansas City (from Pitt)	Larry Johnson, Penn St	RB
28. ......Tennessee	Andre Wolfolk, Oklahoma	CB
29. ......Green Bay	Nick Barnett, Oregon St	LB
30. ......San Diego (from Phil)	Sammy Davis, Texas A&M	CB
31. ......Oakland	Nnamdi Asomugha, California	CB
32. ......Oakland (from TB)	Tyler Brayton, Colorado	DE

Second Round

Team	Selection	Position
33. ......Cincinnati	Eric Steinbach, Iowa	OG
34. ......Detroit	Boss Bailey, Georgia	LB
35. ......Chicago	Charles Tillman, Louisiana-Lafayette	CB
36. ......New England	Eugene Wilson, Illinois	CB
37. ......New Orleans (from Arizona)	Jon Stinchcomb, Georgia	OT
38. ......Dallas	Al Johnson, Wisconsin	C
39. ......Jacksonville	Rashean Mathis, Bethune-Cookman	S
40. ......Minnesota	E.J. Henderson, Maryland	LB
41. ......Houston (from Balt)	Bennie Joppru, Michigan	TE
42. ......Seattle	Ken Hamlin, Arkansas	S
43.......St. Louis	Pisa Tinoisamoa, Hawaii	LB
44. ......Washington	Taylor Jacobs, Florida	WR
45. ......New England (from Car)	Bethel Johnson, Texas A&M	WR
46. ......San Diego	Drayton Florence, Tuskegee	CB
47. ......Kansas City	Kawika Mitchell, S Florida	LB
48. ......Buffalo	Chris Kelsay, Nebraska	DE
49. ......Miami	Eddie Moore, Tennessee	LB
50. ......Carolina (from NE)	Bruce Nelson, Iowa	C
51. ......Denver	Terry Pierce, Kansas St	LB
52. ......Cleveland	Chaun Thompson, W Texas A&M	LB
53. ......NY Jets	Victor Hobson, Michigan	LB
54. ......Arizona (from NO)	Anquan Boldin, Florida St	WR
55. ......Atlanta	Bryan Scott, Penn St	S
56. ......NY Giants	Osi Umenyiora, Troy St	DE
57. ......San Francisco	Anthony Adams, Penn St	NT
58. ......Indianapolis	Mike Doss, Ohio St	S
59. ......Pittsburgh	Alonzo Jackson, Florida St	DE
60. ......Tennessee	Tyrone Calico, Middle Tenn St	WR
61. ......Philadelphia	L.J. Smith, Rutgers	TE
62. ......San Diego (from GB)	Terrence Kiel, Texas A&M	S
63. ......Oakland	Teyo Johnson, Stanford	WR
64. ......Tampa Bay	DeWayne White, Louisville	DE

THEY SAID IT

Randy Moss, Vikings receiver, on former teammate Cris Carter, who left HBO's **Inside the NFL** *to sign with the Dolphins: "I love it. And I think a lot of football teams he's been making comments about will love it too."*

Final Standings

	W	L	T	Pct	Pts	OP
Frankfurt*	6	4	0	.600	252	182
Rhein*	6	4	0	.600	189	188
Scotland	6	4	0	.600	303	190
Barcelona	5	5	0	.500	150	221
Amsterdam	4	6	0	.400	230	273
Berlin	3	7	0	.300	248	318

*Clinched World Bowl 2003 berth.

2003 World Bowl

June 14, 2003, in Glasgow

Rhein Fire	3	6	0	7—16
Frankfurt Galaxy	11	14	7	3—35

FIRST QUARTER

Frankfurt: FG Hilbert 53, 12:05.
Frankfurt: Lewis 1 run (Kleinmann kick), 5:42.
Rhein: FG France 39, 0:56.

SECOND QUARTER

Frankfurt: Lester 20 pass from Gray (Kleinmann kick), 9:53.
Rhein: FG Anderbrugge 31, 3:42.
Frankfurt: Gillespie 29 run (Kleinmann kick), 2:06.
Rhein: FG Anderbrugge 27, 0:00.

THIRD QUARTER

Frankfurt: Tate 1 run (Kleinmann kick), 3:13.

FOURTH QUARTER

Frankfurt: FG Kleinmann 34, 4:37.
Rhein: Blakley 5 pass from Greisen (Anderbrugge kick), 1:55.
A: 28,138. T: 2:40.

NFL Europe Individual Leaders

PASSING

	Att	Comp	Pct Comp	Yds	Avg Gain	TD	Pct TD	Int	Pct Int	Lg	Rating Pts
Nall, Scotland	258	151	58.5	2050	7.95	18	7.0	7	2.7	52	95.9
Stambaugh, Berlin	254	169	66.5	1759	6.93	13	5.1	6	2.4	80t	93.6
Hill, Amsterdam	356	220	61.8	2256	6.34	13	3.7	5	1.4	56	86.3
Burford, Barcelona	175	102	58.3	1054	6.02	8	4.6	3	1.7	59t	83.8
Brown, Frankfurt	196	112	57.1	1402	7.15	5	2.6	5	2.6	43	77.4

RECEIVING

RECEPTIONS	No.	Yds	Avg	Lg	TD
Hatchette, Amsterdam	61	790	13.0	36	7
Lester, Frankfurt	45	678	15.1	61t	6
McMullen, Amsterdam	40	316	7.9	24	2
Simonton, Scotland	39	382	9.8	40	2
Thurmon, Berlin	37	412	11.1	80t	5
Skaggs, Amsterdam	37	401	10.8	35t	5

YARDS	Yds	No.	Avg	Lg	TD
Hatchette, Amsterdam	790	61	13.0	36	7
Lester, Frankfurt	678	45	15.1	61t	6
Baker, Frankfurt	671	35	19.2	82t	7
Shepherd, Scotland	518	29	17.9	49	4
Minardi, Scotland	470	29	16.2	34t	5

RUSHING

	Att	Yds	Avg	Lg	TD
Simonton, Scotland	162	871	5.4	70	8
Denson, Rhein	128	725	5.7	31	3
Lewis, Frankfurt	160	669	4.2	25	8
Allen, Berlin	102	635	6.2	39	3
Hicks, Scotland	74	546	7.4	93t	4

Other Statistical Leaders

Points (TDs)	Simonton, Scotland	60
Points (Kicking)	Hart, Scotland	64
Yards from Scrimmage	Simonton, Scotland	1253
Interceptions	Barnes, Frankfurt	
	Unertl, Frankfurt	4
Sacks	Williams, Berlin	10.5
Punting Avg	Murphy, Barcelona	42.4
Punt Return Avg	Newson, Rhein	17.2
Kickoff Return Avg	Newson, Rhein	28.7

2002 Canadian Football League

EASTERN DIVISION

	W	L	T	OL	Pts	Pct	PF	PA
†Montreal	13	5	0	1	27	.750	577	408
*Toronto	8	10	0	0	16	.444	344	482
Hamilton	7	11	0	1	15	.417	427	524
Ottawa	4	14	0	2	10	.278	356	550

WESTERN DIVISION

	W	L	T	OL	Pts	Pct	PF	PA
†Edmonton	13	5	0	0	26	.722	516	450
*Winnipeg	12	6	0	0	24	.667	566	421
*B.C.	10	8	0	0	20	.556	480	399
*Saskatchewan	8	10	0	2	18	.500	435	393
Calgary	6	12	0	2	14	.389	438	512

†Clinched division title.

*Clinched playoff berth.

OL=Overtime losses.

Regular Season Statistical Leaders

Points (TDs)	Pringle, Montreal	102
Points (Kicking)	Fleming, Edmonton	183
Rushing Yards	Jenkins, Toronto	1484
Passing Yards	Jones, Winnipeg	4545
Receiving Yards	Vaughn, Edmonton	1497
Receptions	Vaughn, Edmonton	98

2002 Playoff Results

FIRST ROUND

TORONTO 24, Saskatchewan 14
WINNIPEG 30, British Columbia 3

SEMI-FINALS

MONTREAL 35, Toronto 18
EDMONTON 33, Winnipeg 30

Home team in caps.

2002 Grey Cup Championship

Nov. 24, 2002, at Edmonton, Alberta

Montreal Alouettes	1	10	0	14—25
Edmonton Eskimos	0	0	10	6—16

A: 62,531.

THEY SAID IT

Michael Vick, Falcons quarterback,
on the secret of his success:
"I have two weapons—my legs, my
arm and my brains."

The Super Bowl

Results

	Date	Winner (Share)	Loser (Share)	Score	Site (Attendance)
I	1-15-67	Green Bay ($15,000)	Kansas City ($7,500)	35–10	Los Angeles (61,946)
II	1-14-68	Green Bay ($15,000)	Oakland ($7,500)	33–14	Miami (75,546)
III	1-12-69	NY Jets ($15,000)	Baltimore ($7,500)	16–7	Miami (75,389)
IV	1-11-70	Kansas City ($15,000)	Minnesota ($7,500)	23–7	New Orleans (80,562)
V	1-17-71	Baltimore ($15,000)	Dallas ($7,500)	16–13	Miami (79,204)
VI	1-16-72	Dallas ($15,000)	Miami ($7,500)	24–3	New Orleans (81,023)
VII	1-14-73	Miami ($15,000)	Washington ($7,500)	14–7	Los Angeles (90,182)
VIII	1-13-74	Miami ($15,000)	Minnesota ($7,500)	24–7	Houston (71,882)
IX	1-12-75	Pittsburgh ($15,000)	Minnesota ($7,500)	16–6	New Orleans (80,997)
X	1-18-76	Pittsburgh ($15,000)	Dallas ($7,500)	21–17	Miami (80,187)
XI	1-9-77	Oakland ($15,000)	Minnesota ($7,500)	32–14	Pasadena (103,438)
XII	1-15-78	Dallas ($18,000)	Denver ($9,000)	27–10	New Orleans (75,583)
XIII	1-21-79	Pittsburgh ($18,000)	Dallas ($9,000)	35–31	Miami (79,484)
XIV	1-20-80	Pittsburgh ($18,000)	Los Angeles ($9,000)	31–19	Pasadena (103,985)
XV	1-25-81	Oakland ($18,000)	Philadelphia ($9,000)	27–10	New Orleans (76,135)
XVI	1-24-82	San Francisco ($18,000)	Cincinnati ($9,000)	26–21	Pontiac, MI (81,270)
XVII	1-30-83	Washington ($36,000)	Miami ($18,000)	27–17	Pasadena (103,667)
XVIII	1-22-84	LA Raiders ($36,000)	Washington ($18,000)	38–9	Tampa (72,920)
XIX	1-20-85	San Francisco ($36,000)	Miami ($18,000)	38–16	Stanford (84,059)
XX	1-26-86	Chicago ($36,000)	New England ($18,000)	46–10	New Orleans (73,818)
XXI	1-25-87	NY Giants ($36,000)	Denver ($18,000)	39–20	Pasadena (101,063)
XXII	1-31-88	Washington ($36,000)	Denver ($18,000)	42–10	San Diego (73,302)
XXIII	1-22-89	San Francisco ($36,000)	Cincinnati ($18,000)	20–16	Miami (75,129)
XXIV	1-28-90	San Francisco ($36,000)	Denver ($18,000)	55–10	New Orleans (72,919)
XXV	1-27-91	NY Giants ($36,000)	Buffalo ($18,000)	20–19	Tampa (73,813)
XXVI	1-26-92	Washington ($36,000)	Buffalo ($18,000)	37–24	Minneapolis (63,130)
XXVII	1-31-93	Dallas ($36,000)	Buffalo ($18,000)	52–17	Pasadena (98,374)
XXVIII	1-30-94	Dallas ($38,000)	Buffalo ($23,500)	30–13	Atlanta (72,817)
XXIX	1-29-95	San Francisco ($42,000)	San Diego ($26,000)	49–26	Miami (74,107)
XXX	1-28-96	Dallas ($42,000)	Pittsburgh ($27,000)	27–17	Tempe, AZ (76,347)
XXXI	1-26-97	Green Bay ($48,000)	New England ($29,000)	35–21	New Orleans (72,301)
XXXII	1-25-98	Denver ($48,000)	Green Bay ($27,500)	31–24	San Diego (68,912)
XXXIII	1-31-99	Denver ($53,000)	Atlanta ($32,500)	34–19	Miami (74,803)
XXXIV	1-30-00	St. Louis ($58,000)	Tennessee ($33,000)	23–16	Atlanta (72,625)
XXXV	1-28-01	Baltimore ($58,000)	NY Giants ($34,500)	34–7	Tampa (71,921)
XXXVI	2-3-02	New England ($63,000)	St. Louis ($34,500)	20–17	New Orleans (72,922)
XXXVII	1-26-03	Tampa Bay ($64,000)	Oakland (35,000)	48–21	San Diego (67,603)

Most Valuable Players

Super Bowl	Player/ Team	Position	Super Bowl	Player/ Team	Position
I	Bart Starr, GB	QB	XIX	Joe Montana, SF	QB
II	Bart Starr, GB	QB	XX	Richard Dent, Chi	DE
III	Joe Namath, NYJ	QB	XXI	Phil Simms, NYG	QB
IV	Len Dawson, KC	QB	XXII	Doug Williams, Wash	QB
V	Chuck Howley, Dall	LB	XXIII	Jerry Rice, SF	WR
VI	Roger Staubach, Dall	QB	XXIV	Joe Montana, SF	QB
VII	Jake Scott, Mia	S	XXV	Ottis Anderson, NYG	RB
VIII	Larry Csonka, Mia	RB	XXVI	Mark Rypien, Wash	QB
IX	Franco Harris, Pitt	RB	XXVII	Troy Aikman, Dall	QB
X	Lynn Swann, Pitt	WR	XXVIII	Emmitt Smith, Dall	RB
XI	Fred Biletnikoff, Oak	WR	XXIX	Steve Young, SF	QB
XII	Randy White, Dall	DT	XXX	Larry Brown, Dall	DB
	Harvey Martin, Dall	DE	XXXI	Desmond Howard, GB	KR
XIII	Terry Bradshaw, Pitt	QB	XXXII	Terrell Davis, Den	RB
XIV	Terry Bradshaw, Pitt	QB	XXXIII	John Elway, Den	QB
XV	Jim Plunkett, Oak	QB	XXXIV	Kurt Warner, StL	QB
XVI	Joe Montana, SF	QB	XXXV	Ray Lewis, Balt	LB
XVII	John Riggins, Wash	RB	XXXVI	Tom Brady, NE	QB
XVIII	Marcus Allen, Rai	RB	XXXVII	Dexter Jackson, TB	S

Composite Standings

	W	L	Pct	Pts	Opp Pts
San Francisco 49ers	5	0	1.000	188	89
Baltimore Ravens	1	0	1.000	34	7
Chicago Bears	1	0	1.000	46	10
New York Jets	1	0	1.000	16	7
Tampa Bay Buccaneers	1	0	1.000	48	21
Pittsburgh Steelers	4	1	.800	120	100
Green Bay Packers	3	1	.750	127	76
Oakland/LA Raiders	3	2	.600	132	114
New York Giants	2	1	.667	66	73
Dallas Cowboys	5	3	.625	221	132
Washington Redskins	3	2	.600	122	103
Baltimore Colts	1	1	.500	23	29
Kansas City Chiefs	1	1	.500	33	42
Miami Dolphins	2	3	.400	74	103
Denver Broncos	2	4	.333	115	206
Los Angeles/St. Louis Rams	1	2	.333	59	67
New England Patriots	1	2	.333	51	98
Philadelphia Eagles	0	1	.000	10	27
San Diego Chargers	0	1	.000	26	49
Atlanta Falcons	0	1	.000	19	34
Tennesse Titans	0	1	.000	16	23
Cincinnati Bengals	0	2	.000	37	46
Buffalo Bills	0	4	.000	73	139
Minnesota Vikings	0	4	.000	34	95

Career Leaders update

Passing

	GP	Att	Comp	Pct Comp	Yds	Avg Gain	TD	Pct TD	Int	Pct Int	Lg	Rating Pts
Joe Montana, SF	4	122	83	68.0	1142	9.36	11	9.0	0	0.0	44	127.8
Jim Plunkett, Rai	2	46	29	63.0	433	9.41	4	8.7	0	0.0	t80	122.8
Terry Bradshaw, Pitt	4	84	49	58.3	932	11.10	9	10.7	4	4.8	t75	112.8
Troy Aikman, Dall	3	80	56	70.0	689	8.61	5	6.3	1	1.3	t56	111.9
Bart Starr, GB	2	47	29	61.7	452	9.62	3	6.4	1	2.1	t62	106.0
Kurt Warner, StL	2	89	52	58.4	779	8.75	3	3.4	1	1.1	t73	93.8
Brett Favre, GB	2	69	39	56.5	502	7.28	5	7.2	1	1.4	t81	97.7
Roger Staubach, Dall	4	98	61	62.2	734	7.49	8	8.2	4	4.1	t45	95.4
Len Dawson, KC	2	44	28	63.6	353	8.02	2	4.5	2	4.5	t46	84.8
Bob Griese, Mia	3	41	26	63.4	295	7.20	1	2.4	2	4.9	t28	72.7

Note: Minimum 40 attempts.

Rushing

	GP	Yds	Att	Avg	Lg	TD
Franco Harris, Pitt	4	354	101	3.5	25	4
Larry Csonka, Mia	3	297	57	5.2	9	2
Emmitt Smith, Dall	3	289	70	4.1	38	5
Terrell Davis, Den	2	259	75	4.1	15	3
John Riggins, Wash	2	230	64	3.6	43	2
Timmy Smith, Wash	1	204	22	9.3	58	2
Thurman Thomas, Buff	4	204	52	3.9	31	4
Roger Craig, SF	3	198	52	3.8	18	2
Marcus Allen, Rai	1	191	20	9.6	t74	2
Tony Dorsett, Dall	2	162	31	5.2	29	1

Receiving

	GP	No.	Yds	Avg	Lg	TD
Jerry Rice, SF	4	33	589	17.9	48t	8
Andre Reed, Buff	4	27	323	11.9	40	0
Roger Craig, SF	3	20	212	10.6	40	2
Thurman Thomas, Buff	4	20	144	7.2	24	0
Jay Novacek, Dall	3	17	178	10.5	23	2
Lynn Swann, Pitt	4	16	364	22.8	64t	3
Michael Irvin, Dall	3	16	256	16.0	25	2
Chuck Foreman, Minn	3	15	139	9.3	26	0
Cliff Branch, Rai	3	14	181	12.9	50	3
Preston Pearson, Balt-Pitt-Dall	5	12	105	8.8	14	0
Don Beebe, Buff-GB	5	12	171	14.3	43	2
Kenneth Davis, Buff	4	12	72	6.0	19	0
Antonio Freeman, GB	2	12	231	19.3	81t	3
Torry Holt, StL	2	12	158	13.2	32	1

Single-Game Leaders

Scoring

	Pts
Roger Craig: XIX, San Francisco vs Miami (1 R, 2 P)	18
Jerry Rice: XXIV, San Francisco vs Denver (3 P); XXIX, SF vs San Diego (3 P)	18
Ricky Watters: XXIX, San Francisco vs San Diego (1 R, 2 P)	18
Terrell Davis: XXXII, Denver vs Green Bay (3 R)	18

Rushing Yards

	Yds
Timmy Smith: XXII, Washington vs Denver	204
Marcus Allen: XVIII, LA Raiders vs Washington	191
John Riggins: XVII, Washington vs Miami	166
Franco Harris: IX, Pittsburgh vs Minnesota	158
Terrell Davis: XXXII, Denver vs Green Bay	157
Larry Csonka: VIII, Miami vs Minnesota	145
Clarence Davis: XI, Oakland vs Minnesota	137
Thurman Thomas: XXV, Buffalo vs NY Giants	135
Emmitt Smith: XXVIII, Dallas vs Buffalo	132
Michael Pittman: XXXVII, Tampa Bay vs Oakland	124

Receptions

	No.
Dan Ross: XVI, Cincinnati vs San Francisco	11
Jerry Rice: XXIII, San Francisco vs Cincinnati	11
Tony Nathan: XIX, Miami vs San Francisco	10
Jerry Rice: XXIX, San Francisco vs San Diego	10
Andre Hastings: XXX, Pittsburgh vs Dallas	10
Ricky Sanders: XXII, Washington vs Denver	9
Antonio Freeman: XXXII, Green Bay vs Denver	9
Six tied with eight.	

Touchdown Passes

	No.
Steve Young: XXIX, San Francisco vs San Diego	6
Joe Montana: XXIV, San Francisco vs Denver	5
Terry Bradshaw: XIII, Pittsburgh vs Dallas	4
Doug Williams: XXII, Washington vs Denver	4
Troy Aikman: XXVII, Dallas vs Buffalo	4
Five tied with three.	

Passing Yards

	Yds
Kurt Warner: XXXIV, St. Louis vs Tennessee	414
Kurt Warner: XXXVI, St. Louis vs New England	365
Joe Montana: XXIII, San Francisco vs Cincinnati	357
Doug Williams: XXII, Washington vs Denver	340
John Elway: XXXIII, Denver vs Atlanta	336
Joe Montana: XIX, San Francisco vs Miami	331
Steve Young: XXIX, San Francisco vs San Diego	325
Terry Bradshaw: XIII, Pittsburgh vs Dallas	318
Dan Marino: XIX, Miami vs San Francisco	318
Terry Bradshaw: XIV, Pittsburgh vs LA Rams	309

Receiving Yards

	Yds
Jerry Rice: XXIII, San Francisco vs Cincinnati	215
Ricky Sanders: XXII, Washington vs Denver	193
Isaac Bruce: XXXIV, St. Louis vs Tennessee	162
Lynn Swann: X, Pittsburgh vs Dallas	161
Andre Reed: XXVII, Buffalo vs Dallas	152
Rod Smith: XXXIII, Denver vs Atlanta	152
Jerry Rice: XXIX, San Francisco vs San Diego	149
Jerry Rice: XXIV, San Francisco vs Denver	148
Max McGee: I, Green Bay vs Kansas City	138

NFL Playoff History

1933
NFL championship Chicago Bears 23, NY Giants 21

1934
NFL championship NY Giants 30, Chicago Bears 13

1935
NFL championship Detroit 26, NY Giants 7

1936
NFL championship Green Bay 21, Boston 6

1937
NFL championship Washington 28, Chicago Bears 21

1938
NFL championship NY Giants 23, Green Bay 17

1939
NFL championship Green Bay 27, NY Giants 0

1940
NFL championship Chicago Bears 73, Washington 0

1941
W. div. playoff Chicago Bears 33, Green Bay 14
NFL championship Chicago Bears 37, NY Giants 9

1942
NFL championship Washington 14, Chicago Bears 6

1943
E. div. playoff Washington 28, NY Giants 0
NFL championship Chicago Bears 41, Washington 21

1944
NFL championship Green Bay 14, NY Giants 7

1945
NFL championship Cleveland 15, Washington 14

1946
NFL championship Chicago Bears 24, NY Giants 14

1947
E. div. playoff Philadelphia 21, Pittsburgh 0
NFL championship Chi Cardinals 28, Philadelphia 21

1948
NFL championship Philadelphia 7, Chi Cardinals 0

1949
NFL championship Philadelphia 14, Los Angeles 0

1950
Am. Conf. playoff Cleveland 8, NY Giants 3
Nat. Conf. playoff Los Angeles 24, Chicago Bears 14
NFL championship Cleveland 30, Los Angeles 28

1951
NFL championship Los Angeles 24, Cleveland 17

1952
Nat. Conf. playoff	Detroit 31, Los Angeles 21
NFL championship	Detroit 17, Cleveland 7

1953
NFL championship	Detroit 17, Cleveland 16

1954
NFL championship	Cleveland 56, Detroit 10

1955
NFL championship	Cleveland 38, Los Angeles 14

1956
NFL championship	NY Giants 47, Chicago Bears 7

1957
W. Conf. playoff	Detroit 31, San Francisco 27
NFL championship	Detroit 59, Cleveland 14

1958
E. Conf. playoff	NY Giants 10, Cleveland 0
NFL championship	Baltimore 23, NY Giants 17

1959
NFL championship	Baltimore 31, NY Giants 16

1960
NFL championship	Philadelphia 17, Green Bay 13
AFL championship	Houston 24, LA Chargers 16

1961
NFL championship	Green Bay 37, NY Giants 0
AFL championship	Houston 10, San Diego 3

1962
NFL championship	Green Bay 16, NY Giants 7
AFL championship	Dallas Texans 20, Houston 17

1963
NFL championship	Chicago 14, NY Giants 10
AFL E. div. playoff	Boston 26, Buffalo 8
AFL championship	San Diego 51, Boston 10

1964
NFL championship	Cleveland 27, Baltimore 0
AFL championship	Buffalo 20, San Diego 7

1965
NFL W. Conf. playoff	Green Bay 13, Baltimore 10
NFL championship	Green Bay 23, Cleveland 12
AFL championship	Buffalo 23, San Diego 0

1966
NFL championship	Green Bay 34, Dallas 27
AFL championship	Kansas City 31, Buffalo 7

1967
NFL E. Conf. championship	Dallas 52, Cleveland 14
NFL W. Conf. championship	Green Bay 28, Los Angeles 7
NFL championship	Green Bay 21, Dallas 17
AFL championship	Oakland 40, Houston 7

1968
NFL E. Conf. championship	Cleveland 31, Dallas 20
NFL W. Conf. championship	Baltimore 24, Minnesota 14
NFL championship	Baltimore 34, Cleveland 0

1968 *(Cont.)*
AFL W. div. playoff	Oakland 41, Kansas City 6
AFL championship	NY Jets 27, Oakland 23

1969
NFL E. Conf. championship	Cleveland 38, Dallas 14
NFL W. Conf. championship	Minnesota 23, Los Angeles 20
NFL championship	Minnesota 27, Cleveland 7
AFL div. playoffs	Kansas City 13, NY Jets 6
	Oakland 56, Houston 7
AFL championship	Kansas City 17, Oakland 7

1970
AFC div. playoffs	Baltimore 17, Cincinnati 0
	Oakland 21, Miami 14
AFC championship	Baltimore 27, Oakland 17
NFC div. playoffs	Dallas 5, Detroit 0
	San Francisco 17, Minnesota 14
NFC championship	Dallas 17, San Francisco 10

1971
AFC div. playoffs	Miami 27, Kansas City 24
	Baltimore 20, Cleveland 3
AFC championship	Miami 21, Baltimore 0
NFC div. playoffs	Dallas 20, Minnesota 12
	San Francisco 24, Washington 20
NFC championship	Dallas 14, San Francisco 3

1972
AFC div. playoffs	Pittsburgh 13, Oakland 7
	Miami 20, Cleveland 14
AFC championship	Miami 21, Pittsburgh 17
NFC div. playoffs	Dallas 30, San Francisco 28
	Washington 16, Green Bay 3
NFC championship	Washington 26, Dallas 3

1973
AFC div. playoffs	Oakland 33, Pittsburgh 14
	Miami 34, Cincinnati 16
AFC championship	Miami 27, Oakland 10
NFC div. playoffs	Minnesota 27, Washington 20
	Dallas 27, Los Angeles 16
NFC championship	Minnesota 27, Dallas 10

1974
AFC div. playoffs	Oakland 28, Miami 26
	Pittsburgh 32, Buffalo 14
AFC championship	Pittsburgh 24, Oakland 13
NFC div. playoffs	Minnesota 30, St Louis 14
	Los Angeles 19, Washington 10
NFC championship	Minnesota 14, Los Angeles 10

1975
AFC div. playoffs	Pittsburgh 28, Baltimore 10
	Oakland 31, Cincinnati 28
AFC championship	Pittsburgh 16, Oakland 10
NFC div. playoffs	Los Angeles 35, St Louis 23
	Dallas 17, Minnesota 14
NFC championship	Dallas 37, Los Angeles 7

1976
AFC div. playoffs	Oakland 24, New England 21
	Pittsburgh 40, Baltimore 14
AFC championship	Oakland 24, Pittsburgh 7
NFC div. playoffs	Minnesota 35, Washington 20
	Los Angeles 14, Dallas 12
NFC championship	Minnesota 24, Los Angeles 13

1977

AFC div. playoffs	Denver 34, Pittsburgh 21
	Oakland 37, Baltimore 31
AFC championship	Denver 20, Oakland 17
NFC div. playoffs	Dallas 37, Chicago 7
	Minnesota 14, Los Angeles 7
NFC championship	Dallas 23, Minnesota 6

1978

AFC 1st-rd. playoff	Houston 17, Miami 9
AFC div. playoffs	Houston 31, New England 14
	Pittsburgh 33, Denver 10
AFC championship	Pittsburgh 34, Houston 5
NFC 1st-rd. playoff	Atlanta 14, Philadelphia 13
NFC div. playoffs	Dallas 27, Atlanta 20
	Los Angeles 34, Minnesota 10
NFC championship	Dallas 28, Los Angeles 0

1979

AFC 1st-rd. playoff	Houston 13, Denver 7
AFC div. playoffs	Houston 17, San Diego 14
	Pittsburgh 34, Miami 14
AFC championship	Pittsburgh 27, Houston 13
NFC 1st-rd. playoff	Philadelphia 27, Chicago 17
NFC div. playoffs	Tampa Bay 24, Philadelphia 17
	Los Angeles 21, Dallas 19
NFC championship	Los Angeles 9, Tampa Bay 0

1980

AFC 1st-rd. playoff	Oakland 27, Houston 7
AFC div. playoffs	San Diego 20, Buffalo 14
	Oakland 14, Cleveland 12
AFC championship	Oakland 34, San Diego 27
NFC 1st-rd. playoff	Dallas 34, Los Angeles 13
NFC div. playoffs	Philadelphia 31, Minnesota 16
	Dallas 30, Atlanta 27
NFC championship	Philadelphia 20, Dallas 7

1981

AFC 1st-rd. playoff	Buffalo 31, NY Jets 27
AFC div. playoffs	San Diego 41, Miami 38
	Cincinnati 28, Buffalo 21
AFC championship	Cincinnati 27, San Diego 7
NFC 1st-rd. playoff	NY Giants 27, Philadelphia 21
NFC div. playoffs	Dallas 38, Tampa Bay 0
	San Francisco 38, NY Giants 24
NFC championship	San Francisco 28, Dallas 27

1982

AFC 1st-rd. playoffs	Miami 28, New England 13
	LA Raiders 27, Cleveland 10
	NY Jets 44, Cincinnati 17
	San Diego 31, Pittsburgh 28
AFC div. playoffs	NY Jets 17, LA Raiders 14
	Miami 34, San Diego 13
AFC championship	Miami 14, NY Jets 0
NFC 1st-rd. playoffs	Washington 31, Detroit 7
	Green Bay 41, St Louis 16
	Minnesota 30, Atlanta 24
	Dallas 30, Tampa Bay 17
NFC div. playoffs	Washington 21, Minnesota 7
	Dallas 37, Green Bay 26
NFC championship	Washington 31, Dallas 17

1983

AFC 1st-rd. playoff	Seattle 31, Denver 7
AFC div. playoffs	Seattle 27, Miami 20
	LA Raiders 38, Pittsburgh 10
AFC championship	LA Raiders 30, Seattle 14
NFC 1st-rd. playoff	LA Rams 24, Dallas 17 .

1983 *(Cont.)*

NFC div. playoffs	San Francisco 24, Detroit 23
	Washington 51, LA Rams 7
NFC championship	Washington 24, San Francisco 21

1984

AFC 1st-rd. playoff	Seattle 13, LA Raiders 7
AFC div. playoffs	Miami 31, Seattle 10
	Pittsburgh 24, Denver 17
AFC championship	Miami 45, Pittsburgh 28
NFC 1st-rd. playoff	NY Giants 16, LA Rams 13
NFC div. playoffs	San Francisco 21, NY Giants 10
	Chicago 23, Washington 19
NFC championship	San Francisco 23, Chicago 0

1985

AFC 1st-rd. playoff	New England 26, NY Jets 14
AFC div. playoffs	Miami 24, Cleveland 21
	New England 27, LA Raiders 20
AFC championship	New England 31, Miami 14
NFC 1st-rd. playoff	NY Giants 17, San Francisco 3
NFC div. playoffs	LA Rams 20, Dallas 0
	Chicago 21, NY Giants 0
NFC championship	Chicago 24, LA Rams 0

1986

AFC 1st-rd. playoff	NY Jets 35, Kansas City 15
AFC div. playoffs	Cleveland 23, NY Jets 20
	Denver 22, New England 17
AFC championship	Denver 23, Cleveland 20
NFC 1st-rd. playoff	Washington 19, LA Rams 7
NFC div playoffs	Washington 27, Chicago 13
	NY Giants 49, San Francisco 3
NFC championship	NY Giants 17, Washington 0

1987

AFC 1st-rd. playoff	Houston 23, Seattle 20
AFC div. playoffs	Cleveland 38, Indianapolis 21
	Denver 34, Houston 10
AFC championship	Denver 38, Cleveland 33
NFC 1st-rd. playoff	Minnesota 44, New Orleans 10
NFC div playoffs	Minnesota 36, San Francisco 24
	Washington 21, Chicago 17
NFC championship	Washington 17, Minnesota 10

1988

AFC 1st-rd. playoff	Houston 24, Cleveland 23
AFC div. playoffs	Cincinnati 21, Seattle 13
	Buffalo 17, Houston 10
AFC championship	Cincinnati 21, Buffalo 10
NFC 1st-rd. playoff	Minnesota 28, LA Rams 17
NFC div. playoffs	Chicago 20, Philadelphia 12
	San Francisco 34, Minnesota 9
NFC championship	San Francisco 28, Chicago 3

1989

AFC 1st-rd. playoff	Pittsburgh 26, Houston 23
AFC div. playoffs	Cleveland 34, Buffalo 30
	Denver 24, Pittsburgh 23
AFC championship	Denver 37, Cleveland 21
NFC 1st-rd. playoff	LA Rams 21, Philadelphia 7
NFC div. playoffs	LA Rams 19, NY Giants 13
	San Francisco 41, Minnesota 13
NFC championship	San Francisco 30, LA Rams 3

1990

AFC 1st-rd. playoffs	Miami 17, Kansas City 16
	Cincinnati 41, Houston 14
AFC div. playoffs	Buffalo 44, Miami 34
	LA Raiders 20, Cincinnati 10
AFC championship	Buffalo 51, LA Raiders 3
NFC 1st-rd. playoffs	Chicago 16, New Orleans 6

1990 (Cont.)

NFC 1st-rd. playoffs	Washington 20, Philadelphia 6
NFC div. playoffs	NY Giants 31, Chicago 3
	San Francisco 28, Washington 10
NFC championship	NY Giants 15, San Francisco 13

1991

AFC 1st-rd. playoffs	Houston 17, NY Jets 10
	Kansas City 10, LA Raiders 6
AFC div. playoffs	Denver 26, Houston 24
	Buffalo 37, Kansas City 14
AFC championship	Buffalo 10, Denver 7
NFC 1st-rd. playoffs	Atlanta 27, New Orleans 20
	Dallas 17, Chicago 13
NFC div. playoffs	Washington 24, Atlanta 7
	Detroit 38, Dallas 6
NFC championship	Washington 41, Detroit 10

1992

AFC 1st-rd. playoffs	San Diego 17, Kansas City 0
	Buffalo 41, Houston 38 (OT)
AFC div. playoffs	Buffalo 24, Pittsburgh 3
	Miami 31, San Diego 0
AFC championship	Buffalo 29, Miami 10
NFC 1st-rd. playoffs	Washington 24, Minnesota 7
	Philadelphia 36, New Orleans 20
NFC div. playoffs	San Francisco 20, Washington 13
	Dallas 34, Philadelphia 10
NFC championship	Dallas 30, San Francisco 20

1993

AFC 1st-rd. playoffs	LA Raiders 42, Denver 24
	Kansas City 27, Pittsburgh 24 (OT)
AFC div. playoffs	Buffalo 29, LA Raiders 23
	Kansas City 28, Houston 20
AFC championship	Buffalo 30, Kansas City 13
NFC 1st-rd. playoffs	NY Giants 17, Minnesota 10
	Green Bay 28, Detroit 24
NFC div. playoffs	San Francisco 44, NY Giants 3
	Dallas 27, Green Bay 17
NFC championship	Dallas 38, San Francisco 21

1994

AFC 1st-rd. playoffs	Miami 27, Kansas City 17
	Cleveland 20, New England 13
AFC div. playoffs	San Diego 22, Miami 21
	Pittsburgh 29, Cleveland 9
AFC championship	San Diego 17, Pittsburgh 13
NFC 1st-rd. playoffs	Green Bay 16, Detroit 12
	Chicago 35, Minnesota 18
NFC div. playoffs	Dallas 35, Green Bay 9
	San Francisco 44, Chicago 15
NFC championship	San Francisco 38, Dallas 28

1995

AFC 1st-rd. playoffs	Buffalo 37, Miami 22
	Indianapolis 35, San Diego 20
AFC div. playoffs	Pittsburgh 40, Buffalo 21
	Indianapolis 10, Kansas City 7
AFC championship	Pittsburgh 20, Indianapolis 16
NFC 1st-rd. playoffs	Philadelphia 58, Detroit 37
	Green Bay 37, Atlanta 20
NFC div. playoffs	Dallas 30, Philadelphia 11
	Green Bay 27, San Francisco 17
NFC championship	Dallas 38, Green Bay 27

1996

AFC 1st-rd. playoffs	Jacksonville 30, Buffalo 27
	Pittsburgh 42, Indianapolis 14
AFC div. playoffs	Jacksonville 30, Denver 27
	New England 28, Pittsburgh 3
AFC championship	New England 20, Jacksonville 6
NFC 1st-rd. playoffs	Dallas 40, Minnesota 15
	San Francisco 14, Philadelphia 0
NFC div. playoffs	Green Bay 35, San Francisco 14
	Carolina 26, Dallas 17
NFC championship	Green Bay 30, Carolina 13

1997

AFC 1st-rd. playoffs	Denver 42, Jacksonville 17
	New England 17, Miami 3
AFC div. playoffs	Denver 14, Kansas City 0
	Pittsburgh 7, New England 6
AFC championship	Denver 24, Pittsburgh 21
NFC 1st-rd. playoffs	Minnesota 23, NY Giants 22
	Tampa Bay 20, Detroit 10
NFC div. playoffs	Green Bay 21, Tampa Bay 7
	San Francisco 38, Minnesota 22
NFC championship	Green Bay 23, San Francisco 10

1998

AFC 1st-rd. playoffs	Miami 24, Buffalo 17
	Jacksonville 25, New England 10
AFC div. playoffs	Denver 38, Miami 3
	NY Jets 34, Jacksonville 24
AFC championship	Denver 23, NY Jets 10
NFC 1st-rd. playoffs	Arizona 20, Dallas 7
	San Francisco 30, Green Bay 27
NFC div. playoffs	Atlanta 20, San Francisco 18
	Minnesota 41, Arizona 21
NFC championship	Atlanta 30, Minnesota 27 (ot)

1999

AFC 1st-rd. playoffs	Tennessee 22, Buffalo 16
	Miami 20, Seattle 17
AFC div. playoffs	Jacksonville 62, Miami 7
	Tennessee 19, Indianapolis 16
AFC championship	Tennessee 33, Jacksonville 14
NFC 1st-rd. playoffs	Washington 27, Detroit 13
	Minnesota 27, Dallas 10
NFC div. playoffs	Tampa Bay 14, Washington 13
	St Louis 49, Minnesota 37
NFC championship	St Louis 11, Tampa Bay 6

2000

AFC 1st-rd. playoffs	Baltimore 21, Denver 3
	Miami 23, Indianapolis 17 (ot)
AFC div. playoffs	Baltimore 24, Tennessee 10
	Oakland 27, Miami 0
AFC championship	Baltimore 16, Oakland 3
NFC 1st-rd. playoffs	New Orleans 31, St. Louis 28
	Philadelphia 21, Tampa Bay 3
NFC div. playoffs	NY Giants 20, Philadelphia 10
	Minnesota 34, New Orleans 16
NFC championship	NY Giants 41, Minnesota 0

2001

AFC 1st-rd. playoffs	Oakland 38, NY Jets 24
	Baltimore 20, Miami 3
AFC div. playoffs	New England 16, Oakland 13(ot)
	Pittsburgh 27, Baltimore 10
AFC championship	New England 24, Pittsburgh 17
NFC 1st-rd. playoffs	Philadelphia 31, Tampa Bay 9
	Green Bay 25, San Francisco 15
NFC div. playoffs	Philadelphia 33, Chicago 19
	St. Louis 45, Green Bay 17
NFC championship	St. Louis 29, Philadelphia 24

2002

AFC 1st-rd. playoffs	NY Jets 41, Indianapolis 0
	Pittsburgh 36, Cleveland 33
AFC div. playoffs	Tennessee 34, Pittsburgh 31 (ot)
	Oakland 30, NY Jets 10
AFC championship	Oakland 41, Tennessee 24
NFC 1st-rd. playoffs	Atlanta 27, Green Bay 7
	San Francisco 39, NY Giants 38
NFC div. playoffs	Phialdelphia 20, Atlanta 6
	Tampa Bay 31, San Francisco 6
NFC championship	Tampa Bay 27, Philadelphia 10

Career Leaders

Scoring

	Yrs	TD	FG	PAT	Pts
†Gary Anderson	21	0	494	741	2,223
†Morten Andersen	21	0	486	695	2,153
George Blanda	26	9	335	943	2,002
Norm Johnson	18	0	366	638	1,736
Nick Lowery	18	0	383	562	1,711
Jan Stenerud	19	0	373	580	1,699
Eddie Murray	19	0	352	539	1,595
Al Del Greco	17	0	347	543	1,584
Pat Leahy	18	0	304	558	1,470
Jim Turner	16	1	304	521	1,439
Matt Bahr	17	0	300	522	1,422
Mark Moseley	16	0	300	482	1,382
Jim Bakken	17	0	282	534	1,380
Fred Cox	15	0	282	519	1,365
Lou Groza	17	1	234	641	1,349
†John Carney	15	0	321	368	1,331
†Steve Christie	13	0	299	399	1,296
Jim Breech	14	0	243	517	1,246
Pete Stoyanovich	12	0	272	420	1,236
†Matt Stover	12	0	288	366	1,230

Rushing

	Yrs	Att	Yds	Avg	Lg	TD
†Emmitt Smith	13	4,052	17,162	4.2	75	150
Walter Payton	13	3,838	16,726	4.4	76	110
Barry Sanders	10	3,062	15,269	5.0	85	99
Eric Dickerson	11	2,996	13,259	4.4	85	90
Tony Dorsett	12	2,936	12,739	4.3	99	77
Jim Brown	9	2,359	12,312	5.2	80	106
Marcus Allen	16	3,022	12,243	4.1	61	123
Franco Harris	13	2,949	12,120	4.1	75	91
Thurman Thomas	13	2,877	12,074	4.2	80	66
†Jerome Bettis	10	2,873	11,542	4.0	71	62
John Riggins	14	2,916	11,352	3.9	66	104
O.J. Simpson	11	2,404	11,236	4.7	94	61
†Marshall Faulk	9	2,367	10,395	4.4	71	87
†Curtis Martin	8	2,604	10,361	4.0	70	71
Ricky Watters	9	2,550	10,325	4.1	57	77
Ottis Anderson	14	2,562	10,273	4.0	76	81
Earl Campbell	8	2,187	9,407	4.3	81	74
†Terry Allen	12	2,152	8,614	4.0	55	73
Jim Taylor	10	1,941	8,597	4.4	84	83
Joe Perry	14	1,737	8,378	4.8	78	53

Touchdowns

	Yrs	Rush	Rec	Ret	Total TD
†Jerry Rice	18	10	192	1	203
†Emmitt Smith	13	153	11	0	164
Marcus Allen	16	123	21	1	145
†Cris Carter	15	0	130	1	131
Jim Brown	9	106	20	0	126
Walter Payton	13	110	15	0	125
†Marshall Faulk	9	87	33	0	120
John Riggins	14	104	12	0	116
Lenny Moore	12	63	48	2	113
Barry Sanders	10	99	10	0	109
Don Hutson	11	3	99	3	105
Steve Largent	14	1	100	0	101
†Tim Brown	15	1	97	3	101
Franco Harris	13	91	9	0	100
Eric Dickerson	11	90	6	0	96
Jim Taylor	10	83	10	0	93
Tony Dorsett	12	77	13	1	91
Bobby Mitchell	11	18	65	8	91
Ricky Watters	10	78	13	0	91

Two tied with 90.

Combined Yards Gained

	Yrs	Total	Rush	Rec	Int Ret	Punt Ret	Kickoff Ret	Fum Ret
†Jerry Rice	18	22,248	645	21,597	0	0	6	0
†Brian Mitchell	13	21,987	1,947	2,298	0	4,845	12,897	5
Walter Payton	13	21,803	16,726	4,538	0	0	539	0
†Emmitt Smith	13	20,101	17,162	2,939	0	0	0	0
†Tim Brown	15	18,867	190	14,167	0	3,272	1,235	3
Barry Sanders	10	18,308	15,269	2,921	0	0	118	0
Herschel Walker	12	18,168	8,225	4,859	0	0	5,084	0
Marcus Allen	16	17,648	12,243	5,411	0	0	0	-6
†Eric Metcalf	13	17,230	2,392	5,572	0	3,453	5,813	0
Thurman Thomas	13	16,532	12,074	4,458	0	0	0	0
†Marshall Faulk	9	16,410	10,395	5,984	0	0	18	13
Tony Dorsett	12	16,326	12,739	3,554	0	0	0	33
Henry Ellard	16	15,718	50	13,777	0	1,527	364	0
Irving Fryar	17	15,594	242	12,785	0	2055	505	7
Jim Brown	9	15,459	12,312	2,499	0	0	648	0
Eric Dickerson	11	15,411	13,259	2,137	0	0	0	15
Glyn Milburn	9	14,911	817	1,322	0	2,984	9,788	0
James Brooks	12	14,910	7,962	3,621	0	565	2,762	0
Ricky Watters	10	14,891	10,643	4,248	0	0	0	0
Franco Harris	13	14,622	12,120	2,287	0	0	233	-18

† Active in 2002.

Career Leaders (Cont.)

Passing

PASSING EFFICIENCY*

	Yrs	Att	Comp	Pct Comp	Yds	Avg Gain	TD	Pct TD	Int	Pct Int	Rating Pts
†Kurt Warner	5	1,623	1,083	66.7	14,082	8.68	101	6.2	64	3.9	98.2
Steve Young	15	4,149	2,667	64.3	33,124	7.98	232	5.6	107	2.6	96.8
Joe Montana	15	5,391	3,409	63.2	40,551	7.52	273	5.1	139	2.6	92.3
†Jeff Garcia	4	1,968	1,224	62.2	13,704	6.96	95	4.8	43	2.2	89.9
†Brett Favre	12	5,993	3,652	60.9	42,285	7.06	314	5.2	188	3.1	86.7
Dan Marino	17	8,358	4,967	59.4	61,361	7.34	420	5.0	252	3.0	86.4
†Peyton Manning	5	2,817	1,749	62.1	20,618	7.32	138	4.9	100	3.6	85.9
†Rich Gannon	14	3,913	2,367	60.5	26,945	6.89	171	4.4	98	2.5	85.3
†Mark Brunell	9	3,561	2,142	60.2	25,309	7.11	142	4.0	86	2.4	85.1
†Brad Johnson	11	2,831	1,747	61.7	19,428	6.86	114	4.0	74	2.6	84.6
Jim Kelly	11	4,779	2,874	60.1	35,467	7.42	237	5.0	175	3.7	84.4
†Trent Green	5	1,743	1,006	57.7	12,977	7.45	82	4.7	53	3.0	84.2
†Brian Griese	5	1,678	1,044	62.2	11,763	7.01	71	4.2	53	3.2	84.1
Roger Staubach	11	2,958	1,685	57.0	22,700	7.67	153	5.2	109	3.7	83.4
Neil Lomax	8	3,153	1,817	57.6	22,771	7.22	136	4.3	90	2.9	82.7
Sonny Jurgensen	18	4,262	2,433	57.1	32,224	7.56	255	6.0	189	4.4	82.6
Len Dawson	19	3,741	2,136	57.1	28,711	7.67	239	6.4	183	4.9	82.6
Ken Anderson	16	4,475	2,654	59.3	32,838	7.34	197	4.4	160	3.6	81.9
Bernie Kosar	12	3,365	1,994	59.3	23,301	6.92	124	3.7	87	2.6	81.8
†Steve McNair	8	2,780	1,634	58.8	19,422	7.00	108	3.9	76	2.7	81.7

*1,500 or more attempts. The passer ratings are based on performance standards established for completion percentage, interception percentage, touchdown percentage and average gain. Passers are allocated points according to how their marks compare with those standards.

YARDS

	Yrs	Att	Comp	Pct Comp	Yds		Yrs	Att	Comp	Pct Comp	Yds
Dan Marino	17	8,358	4,967	59.4	61,361	Boomer Esiason	14	5,205	2,969	57.0	37,920
John Elway	16	7,250	4,123	56.9	51,475	Jim Kelly	11	4,779	2,874	60.1	35,467
Warren Moon	17	6,823	3,988	58.5	49,325	Jim Everett	12	4,923	2,841	57.7	34,837
Fran Tarkenton	18	6,467	3,686	57.0	47,003	Jim Hart	19	5,076	2,593	51.1	34,665
Dan Fouts	15	5,604	3,297	58.8	43,040	Steve DeBerg	17	4,746	2,924	61.6	34,241
†Brett Favre	12	5,993	3,652	60.9	42,285	†Drew Bledsoe	10	5,128	2,919	56.9	34,016
Joe Montana	15	5,391	3,409	63.2	40,551	John Hadl	16	4,687	2,363	50.4	33,503
Johnny Unitas	18	5,186	2,830	54.6	40,239	Phil Simms	14	4,647	2,576	55.4	33,462
†Vinny Testaverde	16	5,732	3,211	56.0	39,558	Steve Young	15	4,149	2,667	64.3	33,124
Dave Krieg	19	5,311	3,105	58.5	38,147	Troy Aikman	12	4,715	2,898	61.5	32,942

TOUCHDOWNS

	No.		No.		No.
Dan Marino	420	Boomer Esiason	247	Jim Hart	209
Fran Tarkenton	342	John Hadl	244	Randall Cunningham	207
†Brett Favre	314	†Vinny Testaverde	244	Jim Everett	203
John Elway	300	Len Dawson	239	Phil Simms	199
Warren Moon	291	Jim Kelly	237	Ken Anderson	197
Johnny Unitas	290	George Blanda	236	Joe Ferguson	196
Joe Montana	273	Steve Young	232	Bobby Layne	196
Dave Krieg	261	John Brodie	214	Norm Snead	196
Sonny Jurgensen	255	Terry Bradshaw	212	Steve DeBerg	196
Dan Fouts	254	Y.A. Tittle	212	Ken Stabler	194

† Active in 2002.

Career Leaders *(Cont.)*

Receiving

RECEPTIONS

	Yrs	No.	Yds	Avg	Lg	TD		Yrs	No.	Yds	Avg	Lg	TD
†Jerry Rice	18	1,456	21,597	14.8	96	192	†Shannon Sharpe	14	753	9,290	12.3	82	54
†Cris Carter	16	1,101	13,899	12.6	80	130	Michael Irvin	12	750	11,904	15.9	87	65
†Tim Brown	15	1,018	14,167	13.9	80	97	Charlie Joiner	18	750	12,146	16.2	87	65
Andre Reed	16	951	13,198	13.9	83	87	Andre Rison	12	743	10,205	13.7	80	84
Art Monk	16	940	12,721	13.5	79	68	Gary Clark	11	699	10,856	15.5	84	65
Irving Fryar	17	851	12,785	15.0	80	84	†Terance Mathis	13	689	8,809	12.8	81	63
Steve Largent	14	819	13,089	16.0	74	100	†Herman Moore	12	670	9,174	13.7	93	62
Henry Ellard	16	814	13,777	16.9	81	65	†Marvin Harrison	7	665	8,800	13.2	78	73
†Larry Centers	13	808	6,691	8.3	54	27	†Jimmy Smith	10	664	9,287	14.0	75	51
James Lofton	16	764	14,004	18.3	80	75	Ozzie Newsome	13	662	7,980	12.1	74	47

YARDS

†Jerry Rice	21,597	Art Monk	12,721	Harold Jackson	10,372
James Lofton	14,004	Charlie Joiner	12,146	Lance Alworth	10,266
Henry Ellard	13,777	†Tim Brown	14,167	Andre Rison	10,205
Andre Reed	13,198	Michael Irvin	11,904	Drew Hill	9,831
Steve Largent	13,089	Don Maynard	11,834	†Isaac Bruce	9,480
†Cris Carter	13,899	Gary Clark	10,856	†Rob Moore	9,368
Irving Fryar	12,785	Stanley Morgan	10,716		

Sacks

Reggie White	198.0	Chris Doleman	150.5
†Bruce Smith	195.0	Richard Dent	137.5
Kevin Greene	160.0		

Note: Officially compiled since 1982.

Interceptions

	Yrs	No.	Yds	Avg	Lg	TD
Paul Krause	16	81	1185	14.6	81	3
Emlen Tunnell	14	79	1282	16.2	55	4
Rod Woodson	16	69	1465	21.2	98	17
Dick (Night Train) Lane	14	68	1207	17.8	80	5
Ken Riley	15	65	596	9.2	66	5

Punting

	Yrs	No.	Yds	Avg	Lg	Blk
Sammy Baugh	16	338	15,245	45.1	85	9
Tommy Davis	11	511	22,833	44.7	82	2
Yale Lary	11	503	22,279	44.3	74	4
†Darren Bennett	8	689	30,340	44.0	66	3
†Tom Rouen	10	656	28,795	43.9	76	7

Note: 250 or more punts.

Punt Returns

	Yrs	No.	Yds	Avg	Lg	TD
George McAfee	8	112	1431	12.8	74	2
Jack Christiansen	8	85	1084	12.8	89	8
Claude Gibson	5	110	1381	12.6	85	3
Bill Dudley	9	124	1515	12.2	96	3
Rick Upchurch	9	248	3008	12.1	92	8
†Desmond Howard	11	244	2895	11.9	95	8

Note: 75 or more returns.

Kickoff Returns

	Yrs	No.	Yds	Avg	Lg	TD
Gale Sayers	7	91	2781	30.6	103	6
Lynn Chandnois	7	92	2720	29.6	93	3
Abe Woodson	9	193	5538	28.7	105	5
Claude (Buddy) Young	6	90	2514	27.9	104	2
Travis Williams	5	102	2801	27.5	105	6

Note: 75 or more returns.

† Active in 2002.

Single-Season Leaders
Scoring

POINTS

	Year	TD	PAT	FG	Pts
Paul Hornung, GB	1960	15	41	15	176
Gary Anderson, Minn	1998	0	59	35	164
Mark Moseley, Wash	1983	0	62	33	161
Marshall Faulk, StL	2000	26	0	0	156
Gino Cappelletti, Bos	1964	7	38	25	155
Emmitt Smith, Dall	1995	25	0	0	150
Chip Lohmiller, Wash	1991	0	56	31	149
Gino Cappelletti, Bos	1961	8	48	17	147
Paul Hornung, GB	1961	10	41	15	146
Jim Turner, NYJ	1968	0	43	34	145
John Kasay, Car	1996	0	34	37	145
Mike Vanderjagt	1999	0	34	38	145
John Riggins, Wash	1983	24	0	0	144
Kevin Butler, Chi	1985	0	51	31	144
Olindo Mare, Mia	1999	0	27	39	144
Priest Holmes	2002	24	0	0	144

Note: Cappelletti's 1964 total includes a two-point conversion.

TOUCHDOWNS

	Year	Rush	Rec	Ret	Total
Marshall Faulk, StL	2000	18	8	0	26
Emmitt Smith, Dall	1995	25	0	0	25
John Riggins, Wash	1983	24	0	0	24
Priest Holmes, KC	2002	21	3	0	24
O.J. Simpson, Buff	1975	16	7	0	23
Jerry Rice, SF	1987	1	22	0	23
Terrell Davis, Den	1998	21	2	0	23
Gale Sayers, Chi	1965	14	6	2	22
Emmitt Smith, Dall	1994	21	1	0	22

FIELD GOALS

	Year	Att	No.
Olindo Mare, Mia	1999	46	39
John Kasay, Car	1996	45	37
Cary Blanchard, Ind	1996	40	36
Al Del Greco, Tenn	1998	39	36
Gary Anderson, Minn	1998	35	35
Jeff Jaeger, LA Raiders	1993	44	35
Ali Haji-Sheikh, NYG	1983	42	35
Matt Stover, Balt	2000	39	35

Six tied with 34.

Rushing

YARDS GAINED

	Year	Att	Yds	Avg
Eric Dickerson, LA Rams	1984	379	2105	5.6
Barry Sanders, Det	1997	335	2053	6.1
Terrell Davis, Den	1998	392	2008	5.1
O.J. Simpson, Buff	1973	332	2003	6.0
Earl Campbell, Hou	1980	373	1934	5.2
Jim Brown, Clev	1963	291	1883	6.4
Barry Sanders, Det	1994	331	1883	5.7
Ricky Williams, Mia	2002	383	1853	4.8
Walter Payton, Chi	1977	339	1852	5.5
Jamal Anderson, Atl	1998	410	1846	4.5
Eric Dickerson, LA Rams	1986	404	1821	4.5
O.J. Simpson, Buff	1975	329	1817	5.5
Eric Dickerson, LA Rams	1983	390	1808	4.6

AVERAGE GAIN

	Year	Avg
Beattie Feathers, Chi	1934	8.44
Randall Cunningham, Phil	1990	7.98
Michael Vick, Atl	2002	6.88
Bobby Douglass, Chi	1972	6.87

Minimum 100 attempts.

TOUCHDOWNS

	Year	No.
Emmitt Smith, Dall	1995	25
John Riggins, Wash	1983	24
Priest Holmes, KC	2002	24
Emmitt Smith, Dall	1994	21
Joe Morris, NYG	1985	21
Terry Allen, Wash	1996	21
Terrell Davis, Den	1998	21

Passing

YARDS GAINED

	Year	Att	Comp	Pct	Yds
Dan Marino, Mia	1984	564	362	64.2	5084
Kurt Warner, StL	2001	546	375	68.7	4830
Dan Fouts, SD	1981	609	360	59.1	4802
Dan Marino, Mia	1986	623	378	60.7	4746
Dan Fouts, SD	1980	589	348	59.1	4715
Warren Moon, Hou	1991	655	404	61.7	4690
Warren Moon, Hou	1990	584	362	62.0	4689
Rich Gannon, Oak	2002	618	418	67.6	4689
Neil Lomax, StL Cards	1984	560	345	61.6	4614
Drew Bledsoe, NE	1994	691	400	57.9	4555

PASSER RATING

	Year	Rat.
Steve Young, SF	1994	112.8
Joe Montana, SF	1989	112.4
Milt Plum, Clev	1960	110.4
Sammy Baugh, Wash	1945	109.9
Kurt Warner, Rams	1999	109.2

TOUCHDOWNS

	Year	No.
Dan Marino, Mia	1984	48
Dan Marino, Mia	1986	44
Kurt Warner, StL	1999	41
Brett Favre, GB	1995	38

Four tied with 36.

Single-Season Leaders *(Cont.)*
Receiving

RECEPTIONS

	Year	No.	Yds
Marvin Harrison, Ind	2002	143	1722
Herman Moore, Det	1995	123	1686
Cris Carter, Minn	1994	122	1256
Jerry Rice, SF	1995	122	1848
Cris Carter, Minn	1995	122	1371
Isaac Bruce, Rams	1995	119	1781
Jimmy Smith, Jax	1999	116	1636
Marvin Harrison, Ind	1999	115	1663
Rod Smith, Den	2001	113	1343
Sterling Sharpe, GB	1993	112	1274
Jerry Rice, SF	1994	112	1499
Jimmy Smith, Jax	2001	112	1373
Hines Ward, Pitt	2002	112	1329

YARDS GAINED

	Year	Yds
Jerry Rice, SF	1995	1848
Isaac Bruce, Rams	1995	1781
Charley Hennigan, Hou	1961	1746
Marvin Harrison, Ind	2002	1722
Herman Moore, Det	1995	1686

TOUCHDOWNS

	Year	No.
Jerry Rice, SF	1987	22
Mark Clayton, Mia	1984	18
Sterling Sharpe, GB	1994	18

Six tied with 17.

All-Purpose Yards

	Year	Run	Rec	Ret	Total
Michael Lewis, NO	2002	15	200	2432	2647
Lionel James, SD	1985	516	1027	992	2535
Terry Metcalf, StL Cards	1975	816	378	1268	2462
Mack Herron, NE	1974	824	474	1146	2444
Gale Sayers, Chi	1966	1231	447	762	2440
Marshall Faulk, Rams	1999	1381	1048	0	2429
Timmy Brown, Phil	1963	841	487	1100	2428
Barry Sanders, Det	1997	2053	305	0	2358
Tim Brown, Rai	1988	50	725	1542	2317
Marcus Allen, Rai	1985	1759	555	–6	2308
Timmy Brown, Phil	1962	545	849	912	2306
Edgerrin James, Ind	2000	1709	594	0	2303

Punting

	Year	No.	Yds	Avg
Sammy Baugh, Wash	1940	35	1799	51.4
Yale Lary, Det	1963	35	1713	48.9
Sammy Baugh, Wash	1941	30	1462	48.7
Yale Lary, Det	1961	52	2516	48.4
Sammy Baugh, Wash	1942	37	1783	48.2

Interceptions

	Year	No.
Dick (Night Train) Lane, Rams	1952	14
Dan Sandifer, Wash	1948	13
Spec Sanders, NY Yanks	1950	13
Lester Hayes, Oak	1980	13

Nine tied with 12.

Sacks

	Year	No.
Michael Strahan, NYG	2001	22.5
Mark Gastineau, NYJ	1984	22
Reggie White, Phil	1987	21
Chris Doleman, Minn	1989	21
Lawrence Taylor, NYG	1986	20.5

Punt Returns

	Year	Avg
Herb Rich, Balt Colts	1950	23.0
Jack Christiansen, Det	1952	21.5
Dick Christy, NY Titans	1961	21.3
Bob Hayes, Dall	1968	20.8

Kickoff Returns

	Year	Avg
Travis Williams, GB	1967	41.1
Gale Sayers, Chi	1967	37.7
Ollie Matson, Chi Cards	1958	35.5
Jim Duncan, Balt Colts	1970	35.4
Lynn Chandnois, Pitt	1952	35.2

Single-Game Leaders

Scoring

POINTS

	Date	Pts
Ernie Nevers, Chi Cards vs Chi	11-28-29	40
Dub Jones, Clev vs Chi	11-25-51	36
Gale Sayers, Chi vs SF	12-12-65	36
Paul Hornung, GB vs Balt Colts	10-8-61	33

On Thanksgiving Day, 1929, Nevers scored all the Cardinals' points on six rushing TDs and four PATs. The Cards defeated Red Grange and the Bears, 40–6. Jones and Sayers each rushed for four touchdowns and scored two more on returns in their teams' victories. Hornung scored four touchdowns and kicked 6 PATs and a field goal in a 45-7 win over the Colts.

FIELD GOALS

	Date	No.
Jim Bakken, StL Cards vs Pitt	9-24-67	7
Rich Karlis, Minn vs Rams	11-5-89	7
Chris Boniol, Dall vs GB	11-18-96	7

Fourteen players tied with 6 FGs each.
Bakken was 7 for 9, Karlis and Boniol 7 for 7.

Single-Game Leaders *(Cont.)*
Scoring *(Cont.)*
TOUCHDOWNS

	Date	No.
Ernie Nevers, Chi Cards vs Chi	11-28-29	6
Dub Jones, Clev vs Chi	11-25-51	6
Gale Sayers, Chi vs SF	12-12-65	6
Bob Shaw, Chi Cards vs Balt Colts	10-2-50	5
Jim Brown, Clev vs Balt Colts	11-1-59	5
Abner Haynes, Dall Texans vs Oak	11-26-61	5
Billy Cannon, Hou vs NY Titans	12-10-61	5
Cookie Gilchrist, Buff vs NYJ	12-8-63	5
Paul Hornung, GB vs Balt Colts	12-12-65	5
Kellen Winslow, SD vs Oak	11-22-81	5
Jerry Rice, SF vs Atl	10-14-90	5
James Stewart, Jax vs Phil	10-12-97	5
Shaun Alexander, Sea vs Minn	9-29-02	5

Rushing

YARDS GAINED

	Date	Yds
Corey Dillon, Cin vs Den	10-22-00	278
Walter Payton, Chi vs Minn	11-20-77	275
O.J. Simpson, Buff vs Det	11-25-76	273
Shaun Alexander, Sea vs Oak	11-11-01	266
Mike Anderson, Den vs NO	12-3-00	251

CARRIES

	Date	No.
Jamie Morris, Wash vs Cin	12-17-88	45
Butch Woolfolk, NYG vs Phil	11-20-83	43
James Wilder, TB vs GB	9-30-84	43
James Wilder, TB vs Pitt	10-30-83	42
Terrell Davis, Den vs Buff	10-26-97	42

TOUCHDOWNS

	Date	No.
Ernie Nevers, Chi Cards vs Chi	11-28-29	6
Jim Brown, Clev vs Balt Colts	11-1-59	5
Cookie Gilchrist, Buff vs NYJ	12-8-63	5
James Stewart, Jax vs Phil	10-12-97	5

Passing

YARDS GAINED

	Date	Yds
N. Van Brocklin, Rams vs NY Yanks	9-28-51	554
Warren Moon, Hou vs KC	12-16-90	527
Boomer Esiason, Ariz vs Wash	11-10-96	522
Dan Marino, Mia vs NYJ	10-23-88	521
Phil Simms, NYG vs Cin	10-13-85	513

COMPLETIONS

	Date	No.
Drew Bledsoe, NE vs Minn	11-13-94	45
Rich Gannon, Oak vs Pitt	9-15-02	43
Richard Todd, NYJ vs SF	9-21-80	42
Vinny Testaverde, NYJ vs Sea	12-6-98	42
Warren Moon, Hou vs Dall	11-10-91	41
Ken Anderson, Cin vs SD	12-20-82	40
Phil Simms, NYG vs Cin	10-13-85	40
Brad Johnson, TB vs Chi	11-18-01	40

TOUCHDOWNS

	Date	No.
Sid Luckman, Chi vs NYG	11-14-43	7
Adrian Burk, Phil vs Wash	10-17-54	7
George Blanda, Hou vs NY Titans	11-19-61	7
Y. A. Tittle, NYG vs Wash	10-28-62	7
Joe Kapp, Minn vs Balt Colts	9-28-69	7

Receiving

YARDS GAINED

	Date	Yds
Flipper Anderson, Rams vs NO	11-26-89	336
Stephone Paige, KC vs SD	12-22-85	309
Jim Benton, Clev vs Det	11-22-45	303
Cloyce Box, Det vs Balt Colts	12-3-50	302
Jimmy Smith, Jax vs Balt Ravens	9-10-00	291

RECEPTIONS

	Date	No.
Terrell Owens, SF vs Chi	12-17-00	20
Tom Fears, Rams vs GB	12-3-50	18
Clark Gaines, NYJ vs SF	9-21-80	17
Sonny Randle, StL Cards vs NYG	11-4-62	16
Jerry Rice, SF vs Rams		16
Keenan McCardell, Jax vs Rams	10-20-96	16
Troy Brown, NE vs KC	9-22-02	16

Five tied with 15.

Single-Game Leaders (Cont.)

Receiving (Cont.)

TOUCHDOWNS

	Date	No.
Bob Shaw, Chi Cards vs Balt Colts	10-2-50	5
Kellen Winslow, SD vs Oak	11-22-81	5
Jerry Rice, SF vs Atl	10-14-90	5

All-Purpose Yards

	Date	Yds
Glyn Milburn, Den vs Sea	12-10-95	404
Billy Cannon, Hou vs NY Titans	12-10-61	373
Tyrone Hughes, NO vs LA Rams	10-23-94	347
Lionel James, SD vs LA Rai	11-10-85	345
Timmy Brown, Phil vs StL Cards	12-16-62	341

Longest Plays

RUSHING	Opponent	Year	Yds
Tony Dorsett, Dall	Minn	1983	99
Andy Uram, GB	Chi Cards	1939	97
Bob Gage, Pitt	Chi	1949	97
Jim Spavital, Balt Colts	GB	1950	96
Bob Hoernschemeyer, Det	NY Yanks	1950	96
Garrison Hearst, SF	NYJ	1998	96
Corey Dillon, Cin	Det	2001	96

PASSING	Opponent	Year	Yds
Frank Filchock to Andy Farkas, Wash	Pitt	1939	99
George Izo to Bobby Mitchell, Wash	Clev	1963	99
Karl Sweetan to Pat Studstill, Det	Balt Colts	1966	99
Sonny Jurgensen to Gerry Allen, Wash	Chi	1968	99
Jim Plunkett to Cliff Branch, LA Rai	Wash	1983	99
Ron Jaworski to Mike Quick, Phil	Atl	1985	99
Stan Humphries to Tony Martin, SD	Sea	1994	99
Brett Favre to Robert Brooks, GB	Chi	1995	99
Trent Green to Marc Boerigter, KC	SD	2002	99

FIELD GOALS	Opponent	Year	Yds
Tom Dempsey, NO	Det	1970	63
Jason Elam, Den	Jax	1998	63
Steve Cox, Clev	Cin	1984	60
Morten Andersen, NO	Chi	1991	60

PUNTS	Opponent	Year	Yds
Steve O'Neal, NYJ	Den	1969	98
Joe Lintzenich, Chi	NYG	1931	94
Shawn McCarthy, NE	Buff	1991	93
Randall Cunningham, Phil	NYG	1989	91

INTERCEPTION RETURNS	Opponent	Year	Yds
Vencie Glenn, SD	Den	1987	103
Louis Oliver, Mia	Buff	1992	103
Seven players tied at 102.			

KICKOFF RETURNS	Opponent	Year	Yds
Al Carmichael, GB	Chi	1956	106
Noland Smith, KC	Den	1967	106
Roy Green, StL Cards	Dall	1979	106

PUNT RETURNS	Opponent	Year	Yds
Robert Bailey, LA Rams	NO	1994	103
Gil LeFebvre, Cin	Brooklyn	1933	98
Charlie West, Minn	Wash	1968	98
Dennis Morgan, Dall	StL Cards	1974	98
Terance Mathis, NYJ	Dall	1990	98

YET ANOTHER SIGN OF THE APOCALYPSE

A Tampa Bay Buccaneers fan purchased season tickets in four sections of Raymond James Stadium so that he could watch each quarter from a different angle.

Rushing

Year	Player, Team	Att	Yards	Avg	TD	Year	Player, Team	Att	Yards	Avg	TD
1932	Cliff Battles, Bos	148	576	3.9	3	1972	O.J. Simpson, Buff, AFC	292	1251	4.3	6
1933	Jim Musick, Bos	173	809	4.7	5		Larry Brown, Wash, NFC	285	1216	4.3	8
1934	Beattie Feathers, Chi	101	1004	9.9	8	1973	O.J. Simpson, Buff, AFC	332	2003	6.0	12
1935	Doug Russell, Chi Cards	140	499	3.6	0		John Brockington, GB, NFC	265	1144	4.3	3
1936	Alphonse Leemans, NY	206	830	4.0	2	1974	Otis Armstrong, Den, AFC	263	1407	5.3	9
1937	Cliff Battles, Wash	216	874	4.0	5		Lawrence McCutcheon, LA, NFC	236	1109	4.7	3
1938	Byron White, Pitt	152	567	3.7	4	1975	O.J. Simpson, Buff, AFC	329	1817	5.5	16
1939	Bill Osmanski, Chi	121	699	5.8	7		Jim Otis, StL, NFC	269	1076	4.0	5
1940	Byron White, Det	146	514	3.5	5	1976	O.J. Simpson, Buff, AFC	290	1503	5.2	8
1941	Clarence Manders, Bklyn	111	486	4.4	5		Walter Payton, Chi, NFC	311	1390	4.5	13
1942	Bill Dudley, Pitt	162	696	4.3	5	1977	Walter Payton, Chi, NFC	339	1852	5.5	14
1943	Bill Paschal, NY	147	572	3.9	10		Mark van Eeghen, Oak, AFC	324	1273	3.9	7
1944	Bill Paschal, NY	196	737	3.8	9	1978	Earl Campbell, Hou, AFC	302	1450	4.8	13
1945	Steve Van Buren, Phil	143	832	5.8	15		Walter Payton, Chi, NFC	333	1395	4.2	11
1946	Bill Dudley, Pitt	146	604	4.1	3	1979	Earl Campbell, Hou, AFC	368	1697	4.6	19
1947	Steve Van Buren, Phil	217	1008	4.6	13		Walter Payton, Chi, NFC	369	1610	4.4	14
1948	Steve Van Buren, Phil	201	945	4.7	10	1980	Earl Campbell, Hou, AFC	373	1934	5.2	13
1949	Steve Van Buren, Phil	263	1146	4.4	11		Walter Payton, Chi, NFC	317	1460	4.6	6
1950	Marion Motley, Clev	140	810	5.8	3	1981	George Rogers, NO, NFC	378	1674	4.4	13
1951	Eddie Price, NY	271	971	3.6	7		Earl Campbell, Hou, AFC	361	1376	3.8	10
1952	Dan Towler, LA	156	894	5.7	10	1982	Freeman McNeil, NY Jets, AFC	151	786	5.2	6
1953	Joe Perry, SF	192	1018	5.3	10		Tony Dorsett, Dall, NFC	177	745	4.2	5
1954	Joe Perry, SF	173	1049	6.1	8	1983	Eric Dickerson, LA Rams, NFC	390	1808	4.6	18
1955	Alan Ameche, Balt	213	961	4.5	9		Curt Warner, Sea, AFC	335	1449	4.3	13
1956	Rick Casares, Chi	234	1126	4.8	12	1984	Eric Dickerson, LA Rams, NFC	379	2105	5.6	14
1957	Jim Brown, Clev	202	942	4.7	9		Earnest Jackson, SD, AFC	296	1179	4.0	8
1958	Jim Brown, Clev	257	1527	5.9	17	1985	Marcus Allen, LA Raiders, AFC	380	1759	4.6	11
1959	Jim Brown, Clev	290	1329	4.6	14		Gerald Riggs, Atl, NFC	397	1719	4.3	10
1960	Jim Brown, Clev, NFL	215	1257	5.8	9	1986	Eric Dickerson, LA Rams, NFC	404	1821	4.5	11
	Abner Haynes, Dall Texans, AFL	156	875	5.6	9		Curt Warner, Sea, AFC	319	1481	4.6	13
1961	Jim Brown, Clev, NFL	305	1408	4.6	8	1987	Charles White, LA Rams, NFC	324	1374	4.2	11
	Billy Cannon, Hou, AFL	200	948	4.7	6		Eric Dickerson, Ind, AFC	223	1011	4.5	5
1962	Jim Taylor, GB, NFL	272	1474	5.4	19	1988	Eric Dickerson, Ind, AFC	388	1659	4.3	14
	Cookie Gilchrist, Buff, AFL	214	1096	5.1	13		Herschel Walker, Dall, NFC	361	1514	4.2	5
1963	Jim Brown, Clev, NFL	291	1863	6.4	12	1989	Christian Okoye, KC, AFC	370	1480	4.0	12
	Clem Daniels, Oak, AFL	215	1099	5.1	3		Barry Sanders, Det, NFC	280	1470	5.3	14
1964	Jim Brown, Clev, NFL	280	1446	5.2	7	1990	Barry Sanders, Det, NFC	255	1304	5.1	13
	Cookie Gilchrist, Buff, AFL	230	981	4.3	6		Thurman Thomas, Buff, AFC	271	1297	4.8	11
1965	Jim Brown, Clev, NFL	289	1544	5.3	17	1991	Emmitt Smith, Dall, NFC	365	1563	4.3	12
	Paul Lowe, SD, AFL	222	1121	5.0	7		Thurman Thomas, Buff, AFC	288	1407	4.9	7
1966	Jim Nance, Bos, AFL	299	1458	4.9	11	1992	Emmitt Smith, Dall, NFC	373	1713	4.6	18
	Gale Sayers, Chi, NFL	229	1231	5.4	8		Barry Foster, Pitt, AFC	390	1690	4.3	11
1967	Jim Nance, Bos, AFL	269	1216	4.5	7	1993	Emmitt Smith, Dall, NFC	283	1486	5.3	9
	Leroy Kelly, Clev, NFL	235	1205	5.1	11		T. Thomas, Buff, AFC	355	1315	3.7	6
1968	Leroy Kelly, Clev, NFL	248	1239	5.0	16	1994	Barry Sanders, Det, NFC	331	1883	5.7	7
	Paul Robinson, Cin, AFL	238	1023	4.3	8		Chris Warren, Sea, AFC	333	1545	4.6	9
1969	Gale Sayers, Chi, NFL	236	1032	4.4	8						
	Dickie Post, SD, AFL	182	873	4.8	6						
1970	Larry Brown, Wash, NFC	237	1125	4.7	5						
	Floyd Little, Den, AFC	209	901	4.3	3						
1971	Floyd Little, Den, AFC	284	1133	4.0	6						
	John Brockington, GB, NFC	216	1105	5.1	4						

Rushing *(Cont.)*

Year	Player, Team	Att	Yards	Avg	TD
1995	Emmitt Smith, Dall, NFC	377	1773	4.7	25
	Curtis Martin, NE, AFC	368	1487	4.0	14
1996	Barry Sanders, Det, NFC	307	1553	5.1	11
	Terrell Davis, Den, AFC	345	1538	4.5	13
1997	Barry Sanders, Det, NFC	335	2053	6.1	11
	Terrell Davis, Den, AFC	369	1730	4.7	15
1998	Terrell Davis, Den, AFC	392	2008	5.1	21
	Jamal Anderson, Atl, NFC	410	1846	4.5	14
1999	Edgerrin James, Ind, AFC	369	1553	4.2	13
	Stephen Davis, Wash, NFC	290	1405	4.8	17
2000	Edgerrin James, Ind, AFC	387	1709	4.4	13
	Robert Smith, Minn, NFC	295	1521	5.2	7
2001	Priest Holmes, Kan, AFC	327	1555	4.8	8
	Stephen Davis, Wash, NFC	356	1432	4.0	5
2002	Ricky Williams, Mia, AFC	383	1853	4.8	16
	Deuce McAllister, NO, NFC	325	1388	4.3	13

Passing*

Year	Player, Team	Att	Comp	Yards	TD	Int
1932	Arnie Herber, GB	101	37	639	9	9
1933	Harry Newman, NY	136	53	973	11	17
1934	Arnie Herber, GB	115	42	799	8	12
1935	Ed Danowski, NY	113	57	794	10	9
1936	Arnie Herber, GB	173	77	1239	11	13
1937	Sammy Baugh, Wash	171	81	1127	8	14
1938	Ed Danowski, NY	129	70	848	7	8
1939	Parker Hall, Clev	208	106	1227	9	13
1940	Sammy Baugh, Wash	177	111	1367	12	10
1941	Cecil Isbell, GB	206	117	1479	15	11
1942	Cecil Isbell, GB	268	146	2021	24	14
1943	Sammy Baugh, Wash	239	133	1754	23	19
1944	Frank Filchock, Wash	147	84	1139	13	9
1945	Sammy Baugh, Wash	182	128	1669	11	4
	Sid Luckman, Chi	217	117	1725	14	10
1946	Bob Waterfield, LA	251	127	1747	18	17
1947	Sammy Baugh, Wash	354	210	2938	25	15
1948	Tommy Thompson, Phil	246	141	1965	25	11
1949	Sammy Baugh, Wash	255	145	1903	18	14
1950	Norm Van Brocklin, LA	233	127	2061	18	14
1951	Bob Waterfield, LA	176	88	1566	13	10
1952	Norm Van Brocklin, LA	205	113	1736	14	17
1953	Otto Graham, Clev	258	167	2722	11	9
1954	Norm Van Brocklin, LA	260	139	2637	13	21
1955	Otto Graham, Clev	185	98	1721	15	8
1956	Ed Brown, Chi	168	96	1667	11	12
1957	Tommy O'Connell, Clev	110	63	1229	9	8
1958	Eddie LeBaron, Wash	145	79	1365	11	10
1959	Charlie Conerly, NY	194	113	1706	14	4
1960	Milt Plum, Clev, NFL	250	151	2297	21	5
	Jack Kemp, LA, AFL	406	211	3018	20	25
1961	George Blanda, Hou, AFL	362	187	3330	36	22
	Milt Plum, Clev, NFL	302	177	2416	18	10
1962	Len Dawson, Dall, AFL	310	189	2759	29	17
	Bart Starr, GB, NFL	285	178	2438	12	9
1963	Y.A. Tittle, NY, NFL	367	221	3145	36	14
	Tobin Rote, SD, AFL	286	170	2510	20	17
1964	Len Dawson, KC, AFL	354	199	2879	30	18
	Bart Starr, GB, NFL	272	163	2144	15	4
1965	Rudy Bukich, Chi, NFL	312	176	2641	20	9
	John Hadl, SD, AFL	348	174	2798	20	21
1966	Bart Starr, GB, NFL	251	156	2257	14	3
	Len Dawson, KC, AFL	284	159	2527	26	10
1967	Sonny Jurgensen, Wash, NFL	508	288	3747	31	16
	Daryle Lamonica, Oakland, AFL	425	220	3228	30	20
1968	Len Dawson, KC, AFL	224	131	2109	17	9
	Earl Morrall, Balt, NFL	317	182	2909	26	17
1969	Sonny Jurgensen, Wash, NFL	442	274	3102	22	15
	Greg Cook, Cin, AFL	197	106	1854	15	11
1970	John Brodie, SF, NFC	378	223	2941	24	10
	Daryle Lamonica, Oak, AFC	356	179	2516	22	15
1971	Roger Staubach, Dall, NFC	211	126	1882	15	4
	Bob Griese, Mia, AFC	263	145	2089	19	9
1972	Norm Snead, NY, NFC	325	196	2307	17	12
	Earl Morrall, Mia, AFC	150	83	1360	11	7
1973	Roger Staubach, Dall, NFC	286	179	2428	23	15
	Ken Stabler, Oak, AFC	260	163	1997	14	10
1974	Ken Anderson, Cin, AFC	328	213	2667	18	10
	Sonny Jurgensen, Wash, NFC	167	107	1185	11	5
1975	Ken Anderson, Cin, AFC	377	228	3169	21	11
	Fran Tarkenton, Minn, NFC	425	273	2994	25	13
1976	Ken Stabler, Oak, AFC	291	194	2737	27	17
	James Harris, LA, NFC	158	91	1460	8	6
1977	Bob Griese, Mia, AFC	307	180	2252	22	13
	Roger Staubach, Dall, NFC	361	210	2620	18	9
1978	Roger Staubach, Dall, NFC	413	231	3190	25	16
	Terry Bradshaw, Pitt, AFC	368	207	2915	28	20
1979	Roger Staubach, Dall, NFC	461	267	3586	27	11
	Dan Fouts, SD, AFC	530	332	4082	24	24
1980	Brian Sipe, Clev, AFC	554	337	4132	30	14
	Ron Jaworski, Phi, NFC	451	257	3529	27	12
1981	Ken Anderson, Cin, AFC	479	300	3754	29	10
	Joe Montana, SF, NFC	488	311	3565	19	12
1982	Ken Anderson, Cin, AFC	309	218	2495	12	9
	Joe Theismann, Wash, NFC	252	161	2033	13	9
1983	Steve Bartkowski, Atl, NFC	432	274	3167	22	5
	Dan Marino, Mia AFC	296	173	2210	20	6
1984	Dan Marino, Mia, AFC	564	362	5084	48	17
	Joe Montana, SF, NFC	432	279	3630	28	10
1985	Ken O'Brien, NY, AFC	488	297	3888	25	8
	Joe Montana, SF, NFC	494	303	3653	27	13

Passing *(Cont.)*

Year	Player, Team	Att	Comp	Yards	TD	Int	Year	Player, Team	Att	Comp	Yards	TD	Int
1986	Tommy Kramer, Minn, NFC	372	208	3000	24	10	1995	Brett Favre, GB, NFC	570	359	4413	38	13
	Dan Marino, Mia, AFC	623	378	4746	44	23		Jeff Blake, Cin, AFC	567	326	3822	28	17
1987	Joe Montana, SF, NFC	398	266	3054	31	13	1996	Vinny Testaverde, Balt, AFC	549	325	4177	33	19
	Bernie Kosar, Clev, AFC	389	241	3033	22	9		Brett Favre, GB, NFC	543	325	3899	39	13
1988	Boomer Esiason, Cin, AFC	388	223	3572	28	14	1997	Steve Young, SF, NFC	356	241	3029	19	6
	Wade Wilson, Minn, NFC	332	204	2746	15	9		Mark Brunell, Jax, AFC	435	264	3281	18	7
1989	Joe Montana, SF, NFC	386	271	3521	26	8	1998	Randall Cunningham, Minn, NFC	425	259	3704	34	10
	Boomer Esiason, Cin, AFC	455	258	3525	28	11		Vinny Testaverde, NYJ, AFC	421	259	3256	29	7
1990	Jim Kelly, Buffalo, AFC	346	219	2829	24	9	1999	Kurt Warner, StL, NFC	499	325	4353	41	13
	Phil Simms, NY, NFC	311	184	2284	15	4		Peyton Manning, Ind, AFC	533	331	4135	26	15
1991	Steve Young, SF, NFC	279	180	2517	17	8	2000	Trent Green, StL, NFC	240	145	2063	16	5
	Jim Kelly, Buff, AFC	474	304	3844	33	17		Brian Griese, Den, AFC	336	216	2688	19	4
1992	Steve Young, SF, NFC	402	268	3465	25	7	2001	Kurt Warner, StL, NFC	546	375	4830	36	22
	Warren Moon, Hou, AFC	346	224	2521	18	12		Rich Gannon, Oak, AFC	549	361	3828	27	9
1993	Steve Young, SF, NFC	462	314	4023	29	16	2002	Brad Johnson, TB, NFC	451	281	3049	22	6
	John Elway, Den, AFC	551	348	4030	25	10		Chad Pennington, NYJ, AFC	399	275	3120	22	6
1994	Steve Young, SF, NFC	461	324	3969	35	10							
	Dan Marino, Mia, AFC	615	385	4453	30	17							

*Since 1973, the annual passing leaders have been determined by a passer rating system that compares individual performances to a fixed performance standard.

Pass Receiving*

Year	Player, Team	No.	Yds	Avg	TD	Year	Player, Team	No.	Yds	Avg	TD
1932	Ray Flaherty, NY	21	350	16.7	3	1962	Lionel Taylor, Den, AFL	77	908	11.8	4
1933	John Kelly, Brooklyn	22	246	11.2	3		Bobby Mitchell, Wash, NFL	72	1384	19.2	11
1934	Joe Carter, Phil	16	238	14.9	4	1963	Lionel Taylor, Den, AFL	78	1101	14.1	10
	Morris Badgro, NY	16	206	12.9	1		Bobby Joe Conrad, St. Louis, NFL	73	967	13.2	10
1935	Tod Goodwin, NY	26	432	16.6	4	1964	Charley Hennigan, Houston, AFL	101	1546	15.3	8
1936	Don Hutson, GB	34	536	15.8	8		Johnny Morris, Chi, NFL	93	1200	12.9	10
1937	Don Hutson, GB	41	552	13.5	7	1965	Lionel Taylor, Den, AFL	85	1131	13.3	6
1938	Gaynell Tinsley, Chi Cards	41	516	12.6	1		Dave Parks, SF, NFL	80	1344	16.8	12
1939	Don Hutson, GB	34	846	24.9	6	1966	Lance Alworth, SD, AFL	73	1383	18.9	13
1940	Don Looney, Phil	58	707	12.2	4		Charley Taylor, Wash, NFL	72	1119	15.5	12
1941	Don Hutson, GB	58	738	12.7	10	1967	George Sauer, NY, AFL	75	1189	15.9	6
1942	Don Hutson, GB	74	1211	16.4	17		Charley Taylor, Wash, NFL	70	990	14.1	9
1943	Don Hutson, GB	47	776	16.5	11	1968	Clifton McNeil, SF, NFL	71	994	14.0	7
1944	Don Hutson, GB	58	866	14.9	9		Lance Alworth, SD, AFL	68	1312	19.3	10
1945	Don Hutson, GB	47	834	17.7	9	1969	Dan Abramowicz, NO, NFL	73	1015	13.9	7
1946	Jim Benton, LA	63	981	15.6	6		Lance Alworth, SD, AFL	64	1003	15.7	4
1947	Jim Keane, Chi	64	910	14.2	10	1970	Dick Gordon, Chi, NFC	71	1026	14.5	13
1948	Tom Fears, LA	51	698	13.7	4		Marlin Briscoe, Buff, NFL	57	1036	18.2	8
1949	Tom Fears, LA	77	1013	13.2	9	1971	Fred Biletnikoff, Oak, AFC	61	929	15.2	9
1950	Tom Fears, LA	84	1116	13.3	7		Bob Tucker, NY, NFC	59	791	13.4	4
1951	Elroy Hirsch, LA	66	1495	22.7	17	1972	Harold Jackson, Phil, NFC	62	1048	16.9	4
1952	Mac Speedie, Clev	62	911	14.7	5		Fred Biletnikoff, Oak, AFC	58	802	13.8	7
1953	Pete Pihos, Phil	63	1049	16.7	10	1973	Harold Carmichael, Phil, NFC	67	1116	16.7	9
1954	Pete Pihos, Phil	60	872	14.5	10		Fred Willis, Hou, AFC	57	371	6.5	1
	Billy Wilson, SF	60	830	13.8	5	1974	Lydell Mitchell, Balt, AFC	72	544	7.6	2
1955	Pete Pihos, Phil	62	864	13.9	7		Charles Young, Phil, NFC	63	696	11.0	3
1956	Billy Wilson, SF	60	889	14.8	5						
1957	Billy Wilson, SF	52	757	14.6	6						
1958	Raymond Berry, Balt	56	794	14.2	9						
	Pete Retzlaff, Phil	56	766	13.7	2						
1959	Raymond Berry, Balt	66	959	14.5	14						
1960	Lionel Taylor, Den, AFL	92	1235	13.4	12						
	Raymond Berry, Balt, NFL	74	1298	17.5	10						
1961	Lionel Taylor, Den, AFL	100	1176	·11.8	4						
	Jim Phillips, LA, NFL	78	1092	14.0	5						

*Most catches.

Pass Receiving *(Cont.)*

Year	Player, Team	No.	Yds	Avg	TD
1975	Chuck Foreman, Minn, NFC	73	691	9.5	9
	Reggie Rucker, Clev, AFC	60	770	12.8	3
	Lydell Mitchell, Balt, AFC	60	544	9.1	4
1976	MacArthur Lane, KC, AFC	66	686	10.4	1
	Drew Pearson, Dall, NFC	58	806	13.9	6
1977	Lydell Mitchell, Balt, AFC	71	620	8.7	4
	Ahmad Rashad, Minn, NFC	51	681	13.4	2
1978	Rickey Young, Minn, NFC	88	704	8.0	5
	Steve Largent, Sea, AFC	71	1168	16.5	8
1979	Joe Washington, Balt, AFC	82	750	9.1	3
	Ahmad Rashad, Minn, NFC	80	1156	14.5	9
1980	Kellen Winslow, SD, AFC	89	1290	14.5	9
	Earl Cooper, SF, NFC	83	567	6.8	4
1981	Kellen Winslow, SD, AFC	88	1075	12.2	10
	Dwight Clark, SF, NFC	85	1105	13.0	4
1982	Dwight Clark, SF, NFC	60	913	15.2	5
	Kellen Winslow, SD, AFC	54	721	13.4	6
1983	Todd Christensen, LA, AFC	92	1247	13.6	12
	Roy Green, StL, NFC	78	1227	15.7	14
	Charlie Brown, Wash, NFC	78	1225	15.7	8
	Earnest Gray, NY, NFC	78	1139	14.6	5
1984	Art Monk, Wash, NFC	106	1372	12.9	7
	Ozzie Newsome, Clev, AFC	89	1001	11.2	5
1985	Roger Craig, SF, NFC	92	1016	11.0	6
	Lionel James, SD, AFC	86	1027	11.9	6
1986	Todd Christensen, LA Rai, AFC	95	1153	12.1	8
	Jerry Rice, SF, NFC	86	1570	18.3	15
1987	J.T. Smith, StL Card, NFC	91	1117	12.3	8
	Al Toon, NY, AFC	68	976	14.4	5
1988	Al Toon, NY, AFC	93	1067	11.5	5
	Henry Ellard, LA Rams, NFC	86	1414	16.4	10
1989	Sterling Sharpe, GB, NFC	90	1423	15.8	12
	Andre Reed, Buff, AFC	88	1312	14.9	9
1990	Jerry Rice, SF, NFC	100	1502	15.0	13
	Haywood Jeffries, Hou, AFC	74	1048	14.2	8
	Drew Hill, Hou, AFC	74	1019	13.8	5
1991	Haywood Jeffries, Hou, AFC	100	1181	11.8	7
	Michael Irvin, Dall, NFC	93	1523	16.4	8
1992	Sterling Sharpe, GB, NFC	108	1461	13.5	13
	Haywood Jeffries, Hou, AFC	90	913	10.1	9
1993	Sterling Sharpe, GB, NFC	112	1274	11.4	11
	Reggie Langhorne, Ind, AFC	85	1038	12.2	3
1994	Cris Carter, Minn, NFC	122	1256	10.3	7
	Ben Coates, NE, AFC	96	1174	12.2	7
1995	Herman Moore, Det, NFC	123	1686	13.7	14
	Carl Pickens, Cin, AFC	99	1234	12.5	17
1996	Jerry Rice, SF, NFC	108	1254	11.6	8
	Carl Pickens, Cin, AFC	100	1180	11.8	12
1997	Herman Moore, Det, NFC	104	1293	12.4	8
	Tim Brown, Oak, AFC	104	1408	13.5	5
1998	Frank Sanders, Ariz, NFC	89	1145	12.9	3
	O.J. McDuffie, Mia, AFC	90	1050	11.7	7
1999	Mushin Muhammad, Car, NFC	96	1253	13.1	8
	Jimmy Smith, Jax, AFC	116	1636	14.1	6
2000	Mushin Muhammad, Car, NFC	102	1183	11.6	6
	Marvin Harrison, Ind, AFC	102	1413	13.9	14
2001	Rod Smith, Den, AFC	113	1343	11.9	11
	Keyshawn Johnson, TB, NFC	106	1266	11.9	1
2002	Marvin Harrison, Ind, AFC	143	1722	12.0	11
	Randy Moss, Minn, NFC	106	1347	12.7	7

THEY SAID IT

Mike Holmgren, Seahawks coach, offering insight into the nature of momentum: "When it's going, it just kind of goes, and when it's not going, it kind of stops."

Scoring

Year	Player, Team	TD	FG	PAT	TP
1932	Earl Clark, Portsmouth	6	3	10	55
1933	Ken Strong, NY	6	5	13	64
	Glenn Presnell, Ports	6	6	10	64
1934	Jack Manders, Chi	3	10	31	79
1935	Earl Clark, Det	6	1	16	55
1936	Earl Clark, Det	7	4	19	73
1937	Jack Manders, Chi	5	18	15	69
1938	Clarke Hinkle, GB	7	3	7	58
1939	Andy Farkas, Wash	11	0	2	68
1940	Don Hutson, GB	7	0	15	57
1941	Don Hutson, GB	12	1	20	95
1942	Don Hutson, GB	17	1	33	138
1943	Don Hutson, GB	12	3	36	117
1944	Don Hutson, GB	9	0	31	85
1945	Steve Van Buren, Phil	18	0	2	110
1946	Ted Fritsch, GB	10	9	13	100
1947	Pat Harder, Chicago Cards	7	7	39	102
1948	Pat Harder, Chicago Cards	6	7	53	110
1949	Pat Harder, Chicago Cards	8	3	45	102
	Gene Roberts, NY	17	0	0	102
1950	Doak Walker, Det	11	8	38	128
1951	Elroy Hirsch, LA	17	0	0	102
1952	Gordy Soltau, SF	7	6	34	94
1953	Gordy Soltau, SF	6	10	48	114
1954	Bobby Walston, Phil	11	4	36	114
1955	Doak Walker, Det	7	9	27	96
1956	Bobby Layne, Det	5	12	33	99
1957	Sam Baker, Wash	1	14	29	77
	Lou Groza, Clev	0	15	32	77
1958	Jim Brown, Clev	18	0	0	108
1959	Paul Hornung, GB	7	7	31	94
1960	Paul Hornung, GB, NFL	15	15	41	176
	Gene Mingo, Den, AFL	6	18	33	123
1961	Gino Cappelletti, Bos, AFL	8	17	48	147
	Paul Hornung, GB, NFL	10	15	41	146
1962	Gene Mingo, Den, AFL	4	27	32	137
	Jim Taylor, GB, NFL	19	0	0	114
1963	Gino Cappelletti, Bos, AFL	2	22	35	113
	Don Chandler, NY, NFL	0	18	52	106
1964	Gino Cappelletti, Bos, AFL	7	25	36	155
	Lenny Moore, Balt, NFL	20	0	0	120
1965	Gale Sayers, Chi, NFL	22	0	0	132
	Gino Cappelletti, Bos, AFL	9	17	27	132
1966	Gino Cappelletti, Bos, AFL	6	16	35	119
	Bruce Gossett, LA, NFL	0	28	29	113
1967	Jim Bakken, StL, NFL	0	27	36	117
	George Blanda, Oak, AFL	0	20	56	116
1968	Jim Turner, NY, AFL	0	34	43	145
	Leroy Kelly, Clev, NFL	20	0	0	120
1969	Jim Turner, NY, AFL	0	32	33	129
	Fred Cox, Minn, NFL	0	26	43	121
1970	Fred Cox, Minn, NFC	0	30	35	125
	Jan Stenerud, KC, AFC	0	30	26	116
1971	Garo Yepremian, Mia, AFC	0	28	33	117
	Curt Knight, Wash, NFC	0	29	27	114
1972	Chester Marcol, GB, NFC	0	33	29	128
	Bobby Howfield, NY AFC	0	27	40	121
1973	David Ray, LA, NFC	0	30	40	130
	Roy Gerela, Pitt, AFC	0	29	36	123
1974	Chester Marcol, GB, NFC	0	25	19	94
	Roy Gerela, Pitt, AFC	0	20	33	93
1975	O.J. Simpson, Buff, AFC	23	0	0	138
	Chuck Foreman, Minn, NFC	22	0	0	132
1976	Toni Linhart, Balt, AFC	0	20	49	109
	Mark Moseley, Wash, NFC	0	22	31	97
1977	Errol Mann, Oak, AFC	0	20	39	99
	Walter Payton, Chi, NFC	16	0	0	96
1978	Frank Corral, LA, NFC	0	29	31	118
	Pat Leahy, NY, AFC	0	22	41	107
1979	John Smith, NE, AFC	0	23	46	115
	Mark Moseley, Wash, NFC	0	25	39	114
1980	John Smith, NE, AFC	0	26	51	129
	Ed Murray, Det, NFC	0	27	35	116
1981	Ed Murray, Det, NFC	0	25	46	121
	Rafael Septien, Dall, NFC	0	27	40	121
	Jim Breech, Cin, AFC	0	22	49	115
	Nick Lowery, KC, AFC	0	26	37	115
1982	Marcus Allen, LA, AFC	14	0	0	84
	Wendell Tyler, LA, NFC	13	0	0	78
1983	Mark Moseley, Wash, NFC	0	33	62	161
	Gary Anderson, Pitt, AFC	0	27	38	119
1984	Ray Wersching, SF, NFC	0	25	56	131
	Gary Anderson, Pitt, AFC	0	24	45	117
1985	Kevin Butler, Chi, NFC	0	31	51	144
	Gary Anderson, Pitt, AFC	0	33	40	139
1986	Tony Franklin, NE, AFC	0	32	44	140
	Kevin Butler, Chi, NFC	0	28	36	120
1987	Jerry Rice, SF, NFC	23	0	0	138
	Jim Breech, Cin, AFC	0	24	25	97
1988	Scott Norwood, Buff, AFC	0	32	33	129
	Mike Cofer, SF, NFC	0	27	40	121
1989	Mike Cofer, SF, NFC	0	29	49	136
	David Treadwell, Den, AFC	0	27	39	120
1990	Nick Lowery, KC, AFC	0	34	37	139
	Chip Lohmiller, Wash, NFC	0	30	41	131
1991	Chip Lohmiller, Wash, NFC	0	31	56	149
	Pete Stoyanovich, Mia, AFC	0	31	28	121
1992	Pete Stoyanovich, Mia, AFC	0	30	34	124
	Morten Anderson, NO, NFC	0	29	33	120
	Chip Lohmiller, Wash, NFC	0	30	30	120
1993	Jeff Jaeger, Rai, AFC	0	35	27	132
	Jason Hanson, Det, NFC	0	34	28	130
1994	John Carney, SD, AFC	0	34	33	135
	Fuad Reveiz, Minn, NFC	0	34	30	132
	Emmitt Smith, Dall, NFC	22	0	0	132
1995	Emmitt Smith, Dall, NFC	25	0	0	150
	Norm Johnson, Pitt, AFC	0	34	39	141
1996	John Kasay, Car, NFC	0	37	34	145
	Cary Blanchard, Ind, AFC	0	36	27	135
1997	Richie Cunningham, Dall, NFC	0	34	24	126
	Mike Hollis, Jax, AFC	0	41	31	134
1998	Gary Anderson, Minn, NFC	0	35	59	164
	Steve Christie, Buff, AFC	0	33	41	140
1999	Jeff Wilkins, StL, NFC	0	20	28	124
	Mike Vanderjagt, Ind, AFC	0	34	38	145
2000	Marshall Faulk, StL, NFC	26	0	0	156
	Matt Stover, Balt, AFC	0	35	30	135
2001	Marshall Faulk, StL, NFC	21	0	2	128
	Mike Vanderjagt, Ind, AFC	0	28	41	125
2002	Jay Feely, Atl, NFC	0	32	43	138
	Priest Holmes, KC, AFC	24	0	0	144

Pro Bowl Alltime Results

Date	Result
1-15-39	NY Giants 13, Pro All-Stars 10
1-14-40	Green Bay 16, NFL All-Stars 7
12-29-40	Chi Bears 28, NFL All-Stars 14
1-4-42	Chi Bears 35, NFL All-Stars 24
12-27-42	NFL All-Stars 17, Washington 14
1-14-51	A. Conf. 28, N. Conf. 27
1-12-52	N. Conf. 30, A. Conf. 13
1-10-53	N. Conf. 27, A. Conf. 7
1-17-54	East 20, West 9
1-16-55	West 26, East 19
1-15-56	East 31, West 30
1-13-57	West 19, East 10
1-12-58	West 26, East 7
1-11-59	East 28, West 21
1-17-60	West 38, East 21
1-15-61	West 35, East 31
1-7-62	AFL West 47, East 27
1-14-62	NFL West 31, East 30
1-13-63	AFL West 21, East 14
1-13-63	NFL East 30, West 20
1-12-64	NFL West 31, East 17
1-19-64	AFL West 27, East 24
1-10-65	NFL West 34, East 14
1-16-65	AFL West 38, East 14
1-15-66	AFL All-Stars 30, Buffalo 19
1-15-66	NFL East 36, West 7
1-21-67	AFL East 30, West 23
1-22-67	NFL East 20, West 10
1-21-68	AFL East 25, West 24
1-21-68	NFL West 38, East 20
1-19-69	AFL West 38, East 25
1-19-69	NFL West 10, East 7
1-17-70	AFL West 26, East 3
1-18-70	NFL West 16, East 13
1-24-71	NFC 27, AFC 6
1-23-72	AFC 26, NFC 13
1-21-73	AFC 33, NFC 28
1-20-74	AFC 15, NFC 13
1-20-75	NFC 17, AFC 10
1-26-76	NFC 23, AFC 20
1-17-77	AFC 24, NFC 14
1-23-78	NFC 14, AFC 13
1-29-79	NFC 13, AFC 7
1-27-80	NFC 37, AFC 27
2-1-81	NFC 21, AFC 7
1-31-82	AFC 16, NFC 13
2-6-83	NFC 20, AFC 19
1-29-84	NFC 45, AFC 3
1-27-85	AFC 22, NFC 14
2-2-86	NFC 28, AFC 24
2-1-87	AFC 10, NFC 6
2-7-88	AFC 15, NFC 6
1-29-89	NFC 34, AFC 3
2-4-90	NFC 27, AFC 21
2-3-91	AFC 23, NFC 21
2-2-92	NFC 21, AFC 15
2-7-93	AFC 23, NFC 20
2-6-94	NFC 17, AFC 3
2-5-95	AFC 41, NFC 13
2-4-96	NFC 20, AFC 13
2-2-97	AFC 26, NFC 23
2-1-98	AFC 29, NFC 24
2-7-99	AFC 23, NFC 10
2-6-00	NFC 51, AFC 31
2-4-01	AFC 38, NFC 17
2-9-02	AFC 38, NFC 30
2-2-03	AFC 45, NFC 20

Chicago All-Star Game* Results

Date	Result (Attendance)
8-31-34	Chi Bears 0, All-Stars 0 (79,432)
8-29-35	Chi Bears 5, All-Stars 0 (77,450)
9-3-36	All-Stars 7, Detroit 7 (76,000)
9-1-37	All-Stars 6, Green Bay 0 (84,560)
8-31-38	All-Stars 28, Washington 16 (74,250)
8-30-39	NY Giants 9, All-Stars 0 (81,456)
8-29-40	Green Bay 45, All-Stars 28 (84,567)
8-28-41	Chi Bears 37, All-Stars 13 (98,203)
8-28-42	Chi Bears 21, All-Stars 0 (101,100)
8-25-43	All-Stars 27, Washington 7 (48,471)
8-30-44	Chi Bears 24, All-Stars 21 (48,769)
8-30-45	Green Bay 19, All-Stars 7 (92,753)
8-23-46	All-Stars 16, Los Angeles 0 (97,380)
8-22-47	All-Stars 16, Chi Bears 0 (105,840)
8-20-48	Chi Cardinals 28, All-Stars 0 (101,220)
8-12-49	Philadelphia 38, All-Stars 0 (93,780)
8-11-50	All-Stars 17, Philadelphia 7 (88,885)
8-17-51	Cleveland 33, All-Stars 0 (92,180)
8-15-52	Los Angeles 10, All-Stars 7 (88,316)
8-14-53	Detroit 24, All-Stars 10 (93,818)
8-13-54	Detroit 31, All-Stars 6 (93,470)
8-12-55	All-Stars 30, Cleveland 27 (75,000)
8-10-56	Cleveland 26, All-Stars 0 (75,000)
8-9-57	NY Giants 22, All-Stars 12 (75,000)
8-15-58	All-Stars 35, Detroit 19 (70,000)
8-14-59	Baltimore 29, All-Stars 0 (70,000)
8-12-60	Baltimore 32, All-Stars 7 (70,000)
8-4-61	Philadelphia 28, All-Stars 14 (66,000)
8-3-62	Green Bay 42, All-Stars 20 (65,000)
8-2-63	All-Stars 20, Green Bay 17 (65,000)
8-7-64	Chicago 28, All-Stars 17 (65,000)
8-6-65	Cleveland 24, All-Stars 16 (68,000)
8-5-66	Green Bay 38, All-Stars 0 (72,000)
8-4-67	Green Bay 27, All-Stars 0 (70,934)
8-2-68	Green Bay 34, All-Stars 17 (69,917)
8-1-69	NY Jets 26, All-Stars 24 (74,208)
7-31-70	Kansas City 24, All-Stars 3 (69,940)
7-30-71	Baltimore 24, All-Stars 17 (52,289)
7-28-72	Dallas 20, All-Stars 7 (54,162)
7-27-73	Miami 14, All-Stars 3 (54,103)
1974	No game
8-1-75	Pittsburgh 21, All-Stars 14 (54,103)
7-23-76	Pittsburgh 24, All-Stars 0 (52,895)

*Discontinued.

YET ANOTHER SIGN OF THE APOCALYPSE

A Wisconsin couple have arranged to have their infant daughter baptized at Lambeau Field.

Most Career Wins

Coach	Yrs	Teams	Regular Season				Career			
			W	L	T	Pct	W	L	T	Pct
Don Shula	33	Colts, Dolphins	328	156	6	.676	347	173	6	.665
George Halas	40	Bears	318	148	31	.671	324	151	31	.671
Tom Landry	29	Cowboys	250	162	6	.605	270	178	6	.601
Curly Lambeau	33	Packers, Cardinals, Redskins	226	132	22	.624	229	134	22	.623
Chuck Noll	23	Steelers	193	148	1	.566	209	156	1	.572
Chuck Knox	22	Rams, Bills, Seahawks	186	147	1	.558	193	158	1	.550
†Dan Reeves	21	Broncos, Giants, Falcons	187	155	2	.546	198	164	2	.546
Paul Brown	21	Browns, Bengals	166	100	6	.621	170	108	6	.609
Bud Grant	18	Vikings	158	96	5	.620	168	108	5	.607
†M. Schottenheimer	16	Browns, Chiefs, Redskins, Chargers	161	101	1	.614	166	112	1	.597
Marv Levy	17	Chiefs, Bills	143	112	0	.561	154	120	0	.562
Steve Owen	23	Giants	151	100	17	.595	153	108	17	.581
Bill Parcells	15	Giants, Patriots, Jets	138	100	1	.579	149	106	1	.582
Joe Gibbs	12	Redskins	124	60	0	.674	140	65	0	.683
Hank Stram	17	Chiefs, Saints	131	97	10	.571	136	100	10	.573
Weeb Ewbank	20	Colts, Jets	130	129	7	.502	134	130	7	.507
Mike Ditka	14	Bears, Saints	121	95	0	.560	127	101	0	.557
Jim Mora	15	Saints, Colts	125	106	0	.541	125	112	0	.527
George Seifert	10	49ers, Panthers	114	62	0	.648	124	67	0	.649
Sid Gillman	18	Rams, Chargers, Oilers	122	99	7	.550	123	104	7	.541

†Active in 2002.

Top Winning Percentages

	W	L	T	Pct		W	L	T	Pct
Vince Lombardi	105	35	6	.740	Don Shula	347	173	6	.665
John Madden	112	39	7	.731	George Seifert	124	67	0	.649
Joe Gibbs	140	65	0	.683	Curly Lambeau	229	134	22	.623
George Allen	118	54	5	.681	Bill Walsh	102	63	1	.617
George Halas	324	151	31	.671	†Bill Cowher	116	74	1	.610

Note: Minimum 100 victories.

†Active in 2002.

Alltime Number-One Draft Choices

Year	Team	Selection	Position
1936	Philadelphia	Jay Berwanger, Chicago	HB
1937	Philadelphia	Sam Francis, Nebraska	FB
1938	Cleveland	Corbett Davis, Indiana	FB
1939	Chicago Cardinals	Ki Aldrich, Texas Christian	C
1940	Chicago Cardinals	George Cafego, Tennessee	HB
1941	Chicago Bears	Tom Harmon, Michigan	HB
1942	Pittsburgh	Bill Dudley, Virginia	HB
1943	Detroit	Frank Sinkwich, Georgia	HB
1944	Boston	Angelo Bertelli, Notre Dame	QB
1945	Chicago Cardinals	Charley Trippi, Georgia	HB
1946	Boston	Frank Dancewicz, Notre Dame	QB
1947	Chicago Bears	Bob Fenimore, Oklahoma A&M	HB
1948	Washington	Harry Gilmer, Alabama	QB
1949	Philadelphia	Chuck Bednarik, Pennsylvania	C
1950	Detroit	Leon Hart, Notre Dame	E
1951	New York Giants	Kyle Rote, Southern Methodist	HB
1952	Los Angeles	Bill Wade, Vanderbilt	QB
1953	San Francisco	Harry Babcock, Georgia	E
1954	Cleveland	Bobby Garrett, Stanford	QB
1955	Baltimore	George Shaw, Oregon	QB
1956	Pittsburgh	Gary Glick, Colorado A&M	DB
1957	Green Bay	Paul Hornung, Notre Dame	HB
1958	Chicago Cardinals	King Hill, Rice	QB
1959	Green Bay	Randy Duncan, Iowa	QB
1960	Los Angeles	Billy Cannon, Louisiana St	RB
1961	Minnesota	Tommy Mason, Tulane	RB
	Buffalo (AFL)	Ken Rice, Auburn	G

Year	Team	Player	Pos
1962	Washington	Ernie Davis, Syracuse	RB
	Oakland (AFL)	Roman Gabriel, N Carolina St	QB
1963	LA Rams	Terry Baker, Oregon St	QB
	Kansas City (AFL)	Buck Buchanan, Grambling	DT
1964	San Francisco	Dave Parks, Texas Tech	E
	Boston (AFL)	Jack Concannon, Boston College	QB
1965	NY Giants	Tucker Frederickson, Auburn	RB
	Houston (AFL)	Lawrence Elkins, Baylor	E
1966	Atlanta	Tommy Nobis, Texas	LB
	Miami (AFL)	Jim Grabowski, Illinois	RB
1967	Baltimore	Bubba Smith, Michigan St	DT
1968	Minnesota	Ron Yary, Southern California	T
1969	Buffalo (AFL)	O.J. Simpson, Southern California	RB
1970	Pittsburgh	Terry Bradshaw, Louisiana Tech	QB
1971	New England	Jim Plunkett, Stanford	QB
1972	Buffalo	Walt Patulski, Notre Dame	DE
1973	Houston	John Matuszak, Tampa	DE
1974	Dallas	Ed Jones, Tennessee St	DE
1975	Atlanta	Steve Bartkowski, California	QB
1976	Tampa Bay	Lee Roy Selmon, Oklahoma	DE
1977	Tampa Bay	Ricky Bell, Southern California	RB
1978	Houston	Earl Campbell, Texas	RB
1979	Buffalo	Tom Cousineau, Ohio St	LB
1980	Detroit	Billy Sims, Oklahoma	RB
1981	New Orleans	George Rogers, South Carolina	RB
1982	New England	Kenneth Sims, Texas	DT
1983	Baltimore	John Elway, Stanford	QB
1984	New England	Irving Fryar, Nebraska	WR
1985	Buffalo	Bruce Smith, Virginia Tech	DE
1986	Tampa Bay	Bo Jackson, Auburn	RB
1987	Tampa Bay	Vinny Testaverde, Miami (FL)	QB
1988	Atlanta	Aundray Bruce, Auburn	LB
1989	Dallas	Troy Aikman, UCLA	QB
1990	Indianapolis	Jeff George, Illinois	QB
1991	Dallas	Russell Maryland, Miami (FL)	DT
1992	Indianapolis	Steve Emtman, Washington	DT
1993	New England	Drew Bledsoe, Washington St	QB
1994	Cincinnati	Dan Wilkinson, Ohio St	DT
1995	Cincinnati	Ki-Jana Carter, Penn St	RB
1996	New York Jets	Keyshawn Johnson, Southern California	WR
1997	St Louis	Orlando Pace, Ohio St	OT
1998	Indianapolis	Peyton Manning, Tennessee	QB
1999	Cleveland	Tim Couch, Kentucky	QB
2000	Cleveland	Courtney Brown, Penn St	DE
2001	Atlanta	Michael Vick, Virginia Tech	QB
2002	Houston	David Carr, Fresno St	QB
2003	Cincinnati	Carson Palmer, Southern California	QB

From 1947 through 1958, the first selection in the draft was a bonus pick, awarded to the winner of a random draw. That club, in turn, forfeited its last-round draft choice. The winner of the bonus choice was eliminated from future draws. The system was abolished after 1958, by which time all clubs had received a bonus choice.

Members of the Pro Football Hall of Fame

Herb Adderley
George Allen
Marcus Allen
Lance Alworth
Doug Atkins
Morris (Red) Badgro
Lem Barney
Cliff Battles
Sammy Baugh
Chuck Bednarik
Bert Bell
Bobby Bell
Raymond Berry

Elvin Bethea
Charles W. Bidwill Sr.
Fred Biletnikoff
George Blanda
Mel Blount
Terry Bradshaw
Jim Brown
Paul Brown
Roosevelt Brown
Willie Brown
Buck Buchanan
Nick Buoniconti
Dick Butkus

Earl Campbell
Tony Canadeo
Joe Carr
Dave Casper
Guy Chamberlin
Jack Christiansen
Earl (Dutch) Clark
George Connor
Jimmy Conzelman
Lou Creekmur
Larry Csonka
Al Davis
Willie Davis

Len Dawson
Joe DeLamielleure
Eric Dickerson
Dan Dierdorf
Mike Ditka
Art Donovan
Tony Dorsett
John (Paddy) Driscoll
Bill Dudley
Albert Glen (Turk) Edwards
Weeb Ewbank
Tom Fears
Jim Finks
Ray Flaherty
Len Ford
Dan Fortmann
Dan Fouts
Frank Gatski
Bill George
Joe Gibbs
Frank Gifford
Sid Gillman
Otto Graham
Harold (Red) Grange
Bud Grant
Joe Greene
Forrest Gregg
Bob Griese
Lou Groza
Joe Guyon
George Halas
Jack Ham
Dan Hampton
John Hannah
Franco Harris
Mike Haynes
Ed Healey
Mel Hein
Ted Hendricks
Wilbur (Pete) Henry
Arnie Herber
Bill Hewitt
Clarke Hinkle
Elroy (Crazylegs) Hirsch
Paul Hornung
Ken Houston
Cal Hubbard
Sam Huff
Lamar Hunt
Don Hutson
Jimmy Johnson
John Henry Johnson
Charlie Joiner
David (Deacon) Jones
Stan Jones
Henry Jordan
Sonny Jurgensen
Jim Kelly
Leroy Kelly
Walt Kiesling
Frank (Bruiser) Kinard

Paul Krause
Earl (Curly) Lambeau
Jack Lambert
Tom Landry
Dick (Night Train) Lane
Jim Langer
Willie Lanier
Steve Largent
Yale Lary
Dante Lavelli
Bobby Layne
Alphonse (Tuffy) Leemans
Marv Levy
Bob Lilly
Larry Little
James Lofton
Vince Lombardi
Howie Long
Ronnie Lott
Sid Luckman
William Roy (Link) Lyman
Tom Mack
John Mackey
Tim Mara
Wellington Mara
Gino Marchetti
George Preston Marshall
Ollie Matson
Don Maynard
George McAfee
Mike McCormack
Tommy McDonald
Hugh McElhenny
Johnny (Blood) McNally
Mike Michalske
Wayne Millner
Bobby Mitchell
Ron Mix
Joe Montana
Lenny Moore
Marion Motley
Mike Munchak
Anthony Munoz
George Musso
Bronko Nagurski
Joe Namath
Earle (Greasy) Neale
Ernie Nevers
Ozzie Newsome
Ray Nitschke
Chuck Noll
Leo Nomellini
Merlin Olsen
Jim Otto
Steve Owen
Alan Page
Clarence (Ace) Parker
Jim Parker
Walter Payton
Joe Perry
Pete Pihos

Hugh (Shorty) Ray
Dan Reeves
Mel Renfro
John Riggins
Jim Ringo
Andy Robustelli
Art Rooney
Dan Rooney
Pete Rozelle
Bob St. Clair
Gale Sayers
Joe Schmidt
Tex Schramm
Lee Roy Selmon
Billy Shaw
Art Shell
Don Shula
O.J. Simpson
Mike Singletary
Jackie Slater
Jackie Smith
John Stallworth
Bart Starr
Roger Staubach
Ernie Stautner
Jan Stenerud
Dwight Stephenson
Hank Stram
Ken Strong
Joe Stydahar
Lynn Swann
Fran Tarkenton
Charley Taylor
Jim Taylor
Lawrence Taylor
Jim Thorpe
Y.A. Tittle
George Trafton
Charley Trippi
Emlen Tunnell
Clyde (Bulldog) Turner
Johnny Unitas
Gene Upshaw
Norm Van Brocklin
Steve Van Buren
Doak Walker
Bill Walsh
Paul Warfield
Bob Waterfield
Mike Webster
Arnie Weinmeister
Randy White
Dave Wilcox
Bill Willis
Larry Wilson
Kellen Winslow
Alex Wojciechowicz
Willie Wood
Ron Yary
Jack Youngblood

Champions of Other Leagues

Canadian Football League Grey Cup

Year	Results	Site	Attendance
1909	U of Toronto 26, Parkdale 6	Toronto	3,807
1910	U of Toronto 16, Hamilton Tigers 7	Hamilton	12,000
1911	U of Toronto 14, Toronto 7	Toronto	13,687
1912	Hamilton Alerts 11, Toronto 4	Hamilton	5,337
1913	Hamilton Tigers 44, Parkdale 2	Hamilton	2,100
1914	Toronto 14, U of Toronto 2	Toronto	10,500
1915	Hamilton Tigers 13, Toronto RAA 7	Toronto	2,808
1916–19	No game	—	—
1920	U of Toronto 16, Toronto 3	Toronto	10,088
1921	Toronto 23, Edmonton 0	Toronto	9,558
1922	Queen's U 13, Edmonton 1	Kingston	4,700
1923	Queen's U 54, Regina 0	Toronto	8,629
1924	Queen's U 11, Balmy Beach 3	Toronto	5,978
1925	Ottawa Senators 24, Winnipeg 1	Ottawa	6,900
1926	Ottawa Senators 10, Toronto U 7	Toronto	8,276
1927	Balmy Beach 9, Hamilton Tigers 6	Toronto	13,676
1928	Hamilton Tigers 30, Regina 0	Hamilton	4,767
1929	Hamilton Tigers 14, Regina 3	Hamilton	1,906
1930	Balmy Beach 11, Regina 6	Toronto	3,914
1931	Montreal AAA 22, Regina 0	Montreal	5,112
1932	Hamilton Tigers 25, Regina 6	Hamilton	4,806
1933	Toronto 4, Sarnia 3	Sarnia	2,751
1934	Sarnia 20, Regina 12	Toronto	8,900
1935	Winnipeg 18, Hamilton Tigers 12	Hamilton	6,405
1936	Sarnia 26, Ottawa RR 20	Toronto	5,883
1937	Toronto 4, Winnipeg 3	Toronto	11,522
1938	Toronto 30, Winnipeg 7	Toronto	18,778
1939	Winnipeg 8, Ottawa 7	Ottawa	11,738
1940	Ottawa 12, Balmy Beach 5	Ottawa	1,700
1940	Ottawa 8, Balmy Beach 2	Toronto	4,998
1941	Winnipeg 18, Ottawa 16	Toronto	19,065
1942	Toronto RCAF 8, Winnipeg RCAF 5	Toronto	12,455
1943	Hamilton F Wild 23, Winnipeg RCAF 14	Toronto	16,423
1944	Montreal St H-D Navy 7, Hamilton F Wild 6	Hamilton	3,871
1945	Toronto 35, Winnipeg 0	Toronto	18,660
1946	Toronto 28, Winnipeg 6	Toronto	18,960
1947	Toronto 10, Winnipeg 9	Toronto	18,885
1948	Calgary 12, Ottawa 7	Toronto	20,013
1949	Montreal Als 28, Calgary 15	Toronto	20,087
1950	Toronto 13, Winnipeg 0	Toronto	27,101
1951	Ottawa 21, Saskatchewan 14	Toronto	27,341
1952	Toronto 21, Edmonton 11	Toronto	27,391
1953	Hamilton Ticats 12, Winnipeg 6	Toronto	27,313
1954	Edmonton 26, Montreal 25	Toronto	27,321
1955	Edmonton 34, Montreal 19	Vancouver	39,417
1956	Edmonton 50, Montreal 27	Toronto	27,425
1957	Hamilton 32, Winnipeg 7	Toronto	27,051
1958	Winnipeg 35, Hamilton 28	Vancouver	36,567
1959	Winnipeg 21, Hamilton 7	Toronto	33,133
1960	Ottawa 16, Edmonton 6	Vancouver	38,102
1961	Winnipeg 21, Hamilton 14	Toronto	32,651
1962	Winnipeg 28, Hamilton 27	Toronto	32,655
1963	Hamilton 21, British Columbia 10	Vancouver	36,545
1964	British Columbia 34, Hamilton 24	Toronto	32,655
1965	Hamilton 22, Winnipeg 16	Toronto	32,655
1966	Saskatchewan 29, Ottawa 14	Vancouver	36,553
1967	Hamilton 24, Saskatchewan 1	Ottawa	31,358
1968	Ottawa 24, Calgary 21	Toronto	32,655
1969	Ottawa 29, Saskatchewan 11	Montreal	33,172
1970	Montreal 23, Calgary 10	Toronto	32,669
1971	Calgary 14, Toronto 11	Vancouver	34,484
1972	Hamilton 13, Saskatchewan 10	Hamilton	33,993
1973	Ottawa 22, Edmonton 18	Toronto	36,653
1974	Montreal 20, Edmonton 7	Vancouver	34,450
1975	Edmonton 9, Montreal 8	Calgary	32,454

Canadian Football League Grey Cup *(Cont.)*

Year	Results	Site	Attendance
1976	Ottawa 23, Saskatchewan 20	Toronto	53,467
1977	Montreal 41, Edmonton 6	Montreal	68,318
1978	Edmonton 20, Montreal 13	Toronto	54,695
1979	Edmonton 17, Montreal 9	Montreal	65,113
1980	Edmonton 48, Hamilton 10	Toronto	54,661
1981	Edmonton 26, Ottawa 23	Montreal	52,478
1982	Edmonton 32, Toronto 16	Toronto	54,741
1983	Toronto 18, British Columbia 17	Vancouver	59,345
1984	Winnipeg 47, Hamilton 17	Edmonton	60,081
1985	British Columbia 37, Hamilton 24	Montreal	56,723
1986	Hamilton 39, Edmonton 15	Vancouver	59,621
1987	Edmonton 38, Toronto 36	Vancouver	59,478
1988	Winnipeg 22, British Columbia 21	Ottawa	50,604
1989	Saskatchewan 43, Hamilton 40	Toronto	54,088
1990	Winnipeg 50, Edmonton 11	Vancouver	46,968
1991	Toronto 36, Calgary 21	Winnipeg	51,985
1992	Calgary 24, Winnipeg 10	Toronto	45,863
1993	Edmonton 33, Winnipeg 23	Calgary	50,035
1994	British Columbia 26, Baltimore 23	Vancouver	55,097
1995	Baltimore 37, Calgary 20	Regina, Saskatchewan	52,564
1996	Toronto 43, Edmonton 37	Hamilton, Ontario	38,595
1997	Toronto 47, Saskatchewan 23	Edmonton	60,431
1998	Calgary 26, Hamilton 24	Winnipeg	34,157
1999	Hamilton 32, Calgary 21	Vancouver	45,118
2000	British Columbia 28, Montreal 26	Calgary	43,822
2001	Calgary 27, Winnipeg 19	Montreal	65,255
2002	Montreal 25, Edmonton 16	Edmonton	62,531

In 1909, Earl Grey, the Governor-General of Canada, donated a trophy for the Rugby Football Championship of Canada. The trophy, which subsequently became known as the Grey Cup, was originally open only to teams registered with the Canada Rugby Union. Since 1954, it has been awarded to the winner of the Canadian Football League's championship game.

AMERICAN FOOTBALL LEAGUE I

Year	Champion	Record
1926	Philadelphia Quakers	7-2

AMERICAN FOOTBALL LEAGUE II

Year	Champion	Record
1936	Boston Shamrocks	8-3
1937	LA Bulldogs	8-0

AMERICAN FOOTBALL LEAGUE III

Year	Champion	Record
1940	Columbus Bullies	8-1-1
1941	Columbus Bullies	5-1-2

ALL-AMERICAN FOOTBALL CONFERENCE

Year	Championship Game
1946	Cleveland 14, NY Yankees 9
1947	Cleveland 14, NY Yankees 3
1948	Cleveland 49, Buffalo 7
1949	Cleveland 21, San Francisco 7

WORLD FOOTBALL LEAGUE

Year	World Bowl Championship
1974	Birmingham 22, Florida 21
1975	Disbanded midseason

UNITED STATES FOOTBALL LEAGUE

Year	Championship Game
1983	Michigan 24, Philadelphia 22
1984	Philadelphia 23, Arizona 3
1985	Baltimore 28, Oakland 24

NFL EUROPE

Year	Champion	Record
1991	London	9-1-0
1992	Sacramento	8-2-0
1995	Frankfurt	6-4-0
1996	Scotland	7-3-0
1997	Barcelona	5-5-0
1998	Rhein	7-3-0
1999	Frankfurt	6-4-0
2000	Rhein	7-3-0
2001	Berlin	6-4-0
2002	Berlin	6-4-0
2003	Frankfurt	6-4-0

Known as World League of American Football until 1998.

DAVID BERGMAN

College Football

Craig Krenzel of
national champion
Ohio State

Tempest in Tempe

Miami cried foul, but Ohio State won the national championship—its first since 1968—in a Fiesta Bowl thriller

BY B.J. SCHECTER

THE BALL FELL harmlessly to the ground in the back of the end zone, setting off a joyous celebration. The Miami Hurricanes had just won their second straight national championship, extending their winning streak to 35 games with a thrilling overtime win. Players, coaches, photographers and fans started to storm the field from the Miami sideline. Undiluted joy. On the other sideline, despair. The Hurricanes had just defeated a determined and resilient Ohio State team.

Or so they thought.

There in the back of the end zone was a yellow flag. While the field was cleared of would-be celebrators, the referees convened at the goal line. Back judge Terry Porter had thrown the flag, calling pass interference against Miami cornerback Glenn Sharpe. It was a questionable call, especially when you considered the situation and the borderline nature of the infraction. But then Miami had benefitted from a similarly dubious pass interference call earlier in the game. These things have a

way of evening out, but try telling that to the Hurricanes faithful: This call came on fourth down in the first overtime, with Miami leading 24–17. The Buckeyes were down to their last chance, and quarterback Craig Krenzel lofted a pass intended for Chris Gamble in the corner of the end zone. Sharpe and Gamble appeared to get there at the same time and, initially, the referees made no call. Porter waited a good four seconds—"replaying it in my mind. . . . I wanted to make doubly sure it was the right call," he said—before throwing the flag and giving Ohio State a second life.

Both sides experienced a measure of disbelief. Krenzel, who had thrown his helmet to the ground in disgust after the play, dislodging some of its padding, began feverishly stuffing the padding back in so he could continue to play. Miami coaches and players reacted bitterly. "They let us play all day," said Hurricanes secondary coach Mark Stoops, "then he makes a touch call. There's not another official in the history of the game that would make that call."

Ohio State did not waste its second chance. Krenzel scored the equalizer on a one-yard plunge three plays later, then, under NCAA overtime rules, it was the Ohio State offense's turn again from the Miami 25-yard line. The Buckeyes came right back out and churned to the Hurricanes' goal line, freshman tailback Maurice Clarett slicing in for the touchdown from five yards out: Ohio State 31, Miami 24.

The Hurricanes lined up at the Ohio State 25 needing a touchdown to stay alive. They marched to the Buckeyes' two-yard line, where they had first-and-goal. But Ohio State's defense had limited Miami's high-octane offense all night, and they were

Clarett dashed five yards for the winning touchdown in the Fiesta Bowl.

not about to give in now. On the game's final play, Buckeyes linebacker Cie Grant barreled through the line untouched and got to Hurricanes quarterback Ken Dorsey, who threw up a desperation pass as Grant hauled him to the ground. The ball fell incomplete, taking with it Miami's 34-game winning streak and the Hurricanes' hopes of becoming the first team since Nebraska in 1995 to repeat as national champs.

Dorsey, a senior who had come into the game with a record of 38–1 as a starter, was inconsolable. He knelt on the field and buried his helmet in his hands while Ohio State players exulted all around him. It was the Buckeyes' first national championship since 1968. As they had done all season, the Buckeyes overcame long odds (they were 13-point underdogs in the title game) and flouted expectations. Second-year coach Jim Tressel had put together an efficient game plan, focusing on ball-control and team play. As he accepted the national championship trophy, Tressel addressed the Ohio State faithful, saying, "We've always had the best damn band in the land, and now we've got the best damn team in the land."

And who could argue? The Buckeyes had limited Miami, which averaged 42 points a game during the season, to 17 points in regulation time, the final three coming on a last-second 40-yard field goal. Ohio State led 17–7 in the third quarter, outrushed the Hurricanes 145 to 65, and possessed the ball for nearly three minutes more than Miami. The Hurricanes may have had more individual talent, and many teams had better athletes, but the Buckeyes, who came together and made big plays when they needed them the most, were undeniably the best team in the country this season. Miami may have been flashier and more potent, but no team performed better in the clutch, when the game was on the line, than the Buckeyes. Ohio State made first downs on two fourth-down situations in overtime in the Fiesta Bowl—including a sensational, game-turning fourth-and-14 conversion on a pass by Krenzel to Michael Jenkins—and saved its regular season with a game-winning touchdown in the closing minutes against Purdue. The Buckeyes always made the plays

they needed to make to win games, and they've got the 14–0 record to prove it.

From the moment All-America safety Mike Doss shocked his teammates and coaches by deciding to return for his senior season instead of entering the NFL draft, Ohio State, it seems, became that oldest of sports clichés, the team of destiny. The underappreciated Krenzel quietly and confidently commanded the offense, and the Buckeyes found a star in true freshman running back Clarett, who, despite his penchant for off-the-field controversy, provided the spark that lit Ohio State's championship fuse. (Clarett said at one point that he was considering leaving school for the pros and challenging the NFL rule that prohibited him from doing so; and four days before the Fiesta Bowl, he publicly expressed his anger

DAMIAN STROHMEYER

Dorsey finished his Miami career with a 38–2 record as a starter, then signed with the NFL's 49ers.

at Ohio State officials over a mixup involving paperwork that would have allowed him to fly back to Ohio to attend the funeral of a friend.)

And the Buckeye defense, well, it was the bomb. Let's face it, the Buckeyes had a good offense that became downright ordinary without Clarett, who missed four games with a shoulder injury, but their defense was arguably the best in the nation. No team stopped the run better than Ohio State, a fact the Buckeyes demonstrated in Tempe by shutting down Miami's star running back Willis McGahee (67 yards on 20 carries before leaving the game with a torn ACL in the fourth quarter). Doss and middle linebacker Matt Wilhelm were the unit's stars, but linemen Darrion Scott, Will Smith, Kenny Peterson and Will Anderson did all the dirty work in overpowering Miami's highly touted offensive line in the Fiesta Bowl.

Most fans and pundits expected a blowout—in Miami's favor—from the title game, but what they got was one of the greatest games in college football history: two undefeated teams battling into overtime. It was a fitting end to an exciting season that saw defending champion Miami pick up where it left off in 2001, despite losing 12 players to the NFL, including its entire secondary, most of its offensive line and All-America running back Clinton Portis. Making matters worse, Portis's replacement, Frank Gore, was lost for the season when he blew out his knee during spring practice. But in came McGahee, who seized the opportunity and rushed for more than 1,600 yards. And the depleted secondary and offensive line? It took all of two games before those units were regarded among the nation's best.

"We all knew we had it in us," said Hurricanes cornerback Maurice Sikes. "We are on scholarship too. We just had to wait our turn. That's how it works here at Miami. Did anyone expect Willis McGahee to run for more than 1,500 yards? That's what you do here. When your time comes you have to step up."

While Miami wasn't quite as dominant as it had been in 2001, it rode the steady leadership of Dorsey and the game-breaking ability of sophomore tight end Kellen Winslow Jr. to go 12–0. The Hurricanes were both lucky and good: They nearly lost to Florida State in October, escaping with a 28–27 victory after the Seminoles' last-second field goal attempt sailed wide left. Lowly Rutgers threw a scare into the Hurricanes for three quarters, and Pitt gave the Hurricanes a run for their money before losing 28–21. But Miami ran the table and, after it outscored Virginia Tech 56–45 in the regular-season finale, was poised to repeat as national champion. Then came Ohio State. "The only people who thought we could win this game were in our locker room," said Buckeyes reserve defensive end Simon Fraser. That proved to be enough.

As exciting as the Fiesta Bowl was, the race for the Heisman Trophy was nearly as compelling and wild. At the beginning of the season, leading contenders seemed to fall by the bunch, and as late as November no clear favorite had emerged. Miami's Dorsey and McGahee were in the mix, but they would compete for votes. Then, just when it seemed that the winner would take the trophy by default more than merit, along came a handful of unlikely candidates.

Penn State running back Larry Johnson had been quietly piling up yards all season, but when he rushed for 863 of them in a three-game stretch, he got the nation's attention. He finished the season with 2,015 yards and set an NCAA record with 8.02 yards per carry. Iowa quarterback Brad Banks engineered the Hawkeyes' surprising 11–1 run and, after passing for 2,369 yards and 25 touchdowns and rushing for 387 yards and five scores, he too earned a trip to New York City.

But the biggest out-of-nowhere candidate was Southern Cal's Carson Palmer. A fifth-year senior, Palmer had had a rollercoaster career with the Trojans. But he became more and more comfortable in USC offensive coordinator Norm Chow's wide-open scheme, and after a 3–2 start, Palmer and Southern Cal were rolling. In a

season, Notre Dame coach Tyrone Willingham helped his team reestablish itself as a national power, leading the Irish to a 10–3 record. Watching the team grasp the West Coast offense so quickly made Notre Dame fans look forward to the future, when Willingham presumably will be able to bring even better players to South Bend. Maryland (11–3) proved it wasn't a one-year wonder by winning 10 of its final 11 games and destroying Tennessee in the Peach Bowl. Sugar Bowl champion Georgia (13–1), N.C. State (11–3), Iowa (11–2) and USC (11–2) were the biggest surprises, while Florida (8–5) and Florida State (9–5) struggled for the first time in nearly a decade.

Dennis Franchione led probation-saddled Alabama to a 9–3 record then bolted for Texas A&M, which fired R.C. Slocum, the winningest coach in Aggies history, after a 6–6 season. And Mike Price led Washington State to its first Pac-10 title since 1998, then bolted for Alabama. But his career with the Crimson Tide ended before it began, as Price was dismissed in May after engaging in wht the university termed "questionable conduct" during a trip to Florida.

That bit of unpleasantness, however, took none of the shine off of several terrific performances in 2002, two of which were especially outstanding: In a game against Texas Tech in September, Iowa State's Seneca Wallace made an astounding 12-yard touchdown run that featured so much zigzagging it actually covered more than 60 yards. A few weeks later Kentucky, playing at home, kicked a field goal in the closing seconds for an apparent victory. The Wildcats even doused coach Guy Morris with Gatorade in celebration, only to see LSU complete a Hail Mary to win the game as time expired.

At the end, Ohio State was the only undefeated team left. As they exited the field in Sun Devil Stadium after the Fiesta Bowl, the Buckeyes sang the school fight song, *Carmen Ohio*, with thousands of fans. So take a bow, Ohio State, the college football nation sings your praise.

nationally televised game against Notre Dame, which boasted the No. 2 pass defense in the country, Palmer carved up the Fighting Irish. He threw for 425 yards and four touchdowns in a 44–13 rout, increasing his season totals to 3,639 yards and 32 touchdowns, including 2,006 yards and 23 TDs in his last six games.

Largely due to a preponderance of East Coast voters, it had been 21 years since a player from a West Coast school won the Heisman. But Palmer's ascendancy could not be denied, and voters awarded him the trophy by a margin that wasn't as close as expected. The quarterback even avoided the Heisman jinx by passing for a workmanlike 303 yards and a touchdown in Southern Cal's 38–17 romp over Iowa in the Orange Bowl.

The 2002 season will be remembered for the resurgence of a few prominent programs and the sagging of a few others. In his first

Final Polls

Associated Press

		Record	Pts	Head Coach	SI Preseason Rank
1.	Ohio St (71)	14–0	1775	Jim Tressel	12
2.	Miami [FL]	12–1	1693	Larry Coker	2
3.	Georgia	13–1	1598	Mark Richt	10
4.	Southern Cal	11–2	1590	Pete Carroll	21
5.	Oklahoma	12–2	1476	Bob Stoops	1
6.	Texas	11–2	1363	Mack Brown	4
7.	Kansas St	11–2	1356	Bill Snyder	32
8.	Iowa	11–2	1334	Kirk Ferentz	40
9.	Michigan	10–3	1182	Lloyd Carr	20
10.	Washington St	10–3	1085	Mike Price	7
11.	Alabama	10–3	988	Dennis Franchione	31
12.	N Carolina St	11–3	943	Chuck Amato	26
13.	Maryland	11–3	844	Ralph Friedgen	16
14.	Auburn	9–4	821	Tommy Tuberville	23
15.	Boise St	12–1	692	Dan Hawkins	46
16.	Penn St	9–4	675	Joe Paterno	25
17.	Notre Dame	10–3	657	Tyrone Willingham	39
18.	Virginia Tech	10–4	544	Frank Beamer	15
19.	Pittsburgh	9–4	520	Walt Harris	45
20.	Colorado	9–5	307	Gary Barnett	6
21.	Florida St	9–5	291	Bobby Bowden	5
22.	Virginia	9–5	250	Al Groh	51
23.	Texas Christian	10–2	231	Gary Patterson	75
24.	Marshall	11–2	201	Bob Pruett	17
25.	W Virginia	9–4	195	Rich Rodriguez	67

Note: As voted by a panel of 72 sportswriters and broadcasters following bowl games (1st-place votes in parentheses).

USA Today/ESPN

		Pts	SI Preseason Rank			Pts	SI Preseason Rank
1.	Ohio St (61)	1525	12	14.	Virginia Tech	644	15
2.	Miami [FL]	1451	2	15.	Penn St	619	25
3.	Georgia	1378	10	16.	Auburn	579	23
4.	Southern Cal	1362	21	17.	Notre Dame	525	39
5.	Oklahoma	1244	1	18.	Pittsburgh	486	45
6.	Kansas St	1230	32	19.	Marshall	333	17
7.	Texas	1140	4	20.	W Virginia	297	67
8.	Iowa	1105	40	21.	Colorado	291	6
9.	Michigan	1011	20	22.	Texas Christian	274	75
10.	Washington St	932	7	23.	Florida St	219	5
11.	N Carolina St	876	26	24.	Florida	145	8
12.	Boise St	808	46	25.	Virginia	141	51
13.	Maryland	803	16				

Note: As voted by a panel of 60 Division I-A head coaches; 25 points for 1st, 24 for 2nd, etc. (1st-place votes in parentheses).

Bowls and Playoffs

NCAA Division I-A Bowl Results

Date	Bowl	Result	Payout/Team ($)	Attendance
12-17-02	New Orleans	N Texas 24, Cincinnati 19	750,000	19,024
12-18-02	GMAC	Marshall 38, Louisville 15	750,000	40,646
12-23-02	Tangerine	Texas Tech 55, Clemson 15	750,000	21,689
12-25-02	Las Vegas	UCLA 27, New Mexico 13	800,000	30,324
12-25-02	Hawaii	Tulane 36, Hawaii 28	750,000	35,513
12-26-02	Motor City	Boston College 51, Toledo 25	780,000	51,872
12-26-02	Insight	Pittsburgh 38, Oregon St 13	750,000	40,533
12-27-02	Houston	Oklahoma St 33, Southern Miss 23	750,000	44,687
12-27-02	Independence	Mississippi 27, Nebraska 23	1.2 million	46,096
12-27-02	Holiday	Kansas St 34, Arizona St 27	2 million	58,717

NCAA Division I-A Bowl Results *(Cont.)*

Date	Bowl	Result	Payout/Team ($)	Attendance
12-28-02	Alamo	Wisconsin 31, Colorado 28 (OT)	1.35 million	50,690
12-28-02	Contintental Tire	Virginia 48, W Virginia 22	750,000	73,535
12-30-02	Music City	Minnesota 29, Arkansas 14	750,000	39,183
12-30-02	Seattle	Wake Forest 38, Oregon 17	1 million	38,241
12-31-02	Humanitarian	Boise St 34, Iowa St 16	750,000	30,446
12-31-02	Sun	Purdue 34, Washington 24	1.35 million	48,917
12-31-02	Silicon Valley	Fresno St 30, Georgia Tech 21	750,000	10,142
12-31-02	Liberty	Texas Christian 17, Colorado St 3	1.3 million	55,207
12-31-02	Peach	Maryland 30, Tennessee 3	2 million	68,330
12-31-02	San Francisco	Virginia Tech 20, Air Force 13	800,000	25,966
1-1-03	Cotton	Texas 35, Louisiana St 20	3 million	70,817
1-1-03	Outback	Michigan 38, Florida 30	2.55 million	65,101
1-1-03	Gator	N Carolina St 28, Notre Dame 6	1.6 million	73,491
1-1-03	Capital One	Auburn 13, Penn St 9	5.125 million	66,334
1-1-03	Rose	Oklahoma 34, Washington St 14	13.5 million	86,848
1-1-03	Sugar	Georgia 26, Florida St 13	13.5 million	74,269
1-2-03	Orange	Southern Cal 38, Iowa 17	13.5 million	75,971
1-3-03	Fiesta	Ohio St 31, Miami (FL) 24 [2 OT]	13.5 million	77,502

NCAA Division I-AA Championship Box Score

Western Kentucky	7	10	7	10 —34
McNeese St	0	6	8	0 —14

FIRST QUARTER
WK: Johnson 16 pass from Michael (Martinez kick), 9:36

SECOND QUARTER
WK: Frazier 55 run (Martinez kick), 14:51
M: FG Marino 30, 7:32.
WK: FG Martinez 40, 4:55.
M: FG Marino 24, :07.

THIRD QUARTER
WK: Frazier 14 run (Martinez kick), 11:03.
M: Lawton 15 pass from Pendarvis (Hamilton pass for two-pt conversion), 3:49.

FOURTH QUARTER
WK: Michael 2 run (Martinez kick), 13:49.
WK: FG Martinez 23, 2:51.

	WESTERN KENTUCKY	McNEESE ST
First downs	13	26
Rushed–yards	50–235	34–149
Passing yards	185	268
Sacked–yards lost	1–8	3–18
Return yards	103	105
Passes	6-10-0	25-48-3
Punts	6–37.3	6–35.5
Fumbles-lost	1–1	2–0
Penalties-yards	7–38	6–35
Time of possession	30:18	29:42

Att: 12,360.

Small College Championship Summaries

NCAA DIVISION II

First round: Valdosta St 24, Catawba 7; Carson-Newman 40, Fayetteville St 27; UC-Davis 24, Central Washington 6; Texas A&M-Kingsville 58, Nebraska Kearney 40; Grand Valley St 62, C.W. Post 13; Indiana (PA) 27, Saginaw Valley St 23; NW Missouri St 45, Minnesota Duluth 41; Northern Colorado 49, Central Missouri St 28.

Quarterfinals: Valdosta St 31, Carson-Newman 28; Texas A&M-Kingsville 27, UC-Davis 20 [OT]; Grand Valley St 62, Indiana (PA) 21; Northern Colorado 23, NW Missouri St 12.

Semifinals: Valdosta St 21, Texas A&M-Kingsville 12; Grand Valley St 44, Northern Colorado 7.

Championship: 12-14-02 Florence, AL

Valdosta St	3	3	7	11—24
Grand Valley St	14	3	7	7—31

NCAA DIVISION III

First round: Wheaton (IL) 42, Alma 14; Wittenberg 34, Hanover 33; Wabash 42, MacMurray 7; Brockport St 16, Springfield 0; John Carroll 27, Hobart 7; Muhlenberg 56, UMass-Dartmouth 6; Wartburg 45, Lake Forest 0; Coe 21, WI-La Crosse 18; St. John's (MN) 31, Redlands 24; King's (PA) 28, Salisbury 0; Washington and Jefferson 24, Christopher Newport 10; Trinity (TX) 48, Mary Hardin-Baylor 38.

NCAA DIVISION III *(CONT.)*

Second Round: Mount Union 42, Wheaton 21; Wabash 25, Wittenberg 14; Brockport St 15, Rowan 12; John Carroll 21, Muhlenberg 10; Linfield 52, Wartburg 15; St. John's 45, Coe 14; Bridgewater (VA) 19, King's 17; Trinity 45, Washington and Jefferson 10.

Quarterfinals: Mount Union 45, Wabash 16; John Carroll 16, Brockport St 10 [OT]; St. John's 21, Linfield 14; Trinity 38, Bridgewater 32.

Semifinals: Mount Union 57, John Carroll 19; Trinity 41, St. John's 34.

Championship: 12-21-02 Salem, VA

Mount Union	7	21	7	13—48
Trinity	0	0	7	0—7

NAIA CHAMPIONSHIP

12-21-02 Hardin County, TN

Carroll	7	14	0	7—28
Georgetown (KY)	7	0	0	0—7

Awards

Heisman Memorial Trophy

Player, School	Class	Pos	1st	2nd	3rd	Total
Carson Palmer, Southern Cal	Sr	QB	242	224	154	1328
Brad Banks, Iowa	Sr	QB	199	173	152	1095
Larry Johnson, Penn St	Sr	RB	108	130	142	726
Willis McGahee, Miami (FL)	So	RB	101	118	121	660
Ken Dorsey, Miami (FL)	Sr	QB	122	89	99	643

Note: Former Heisman winners and the media vote, with ballots allowing for three names (3 points for 1st, 2 for 2nd, 1 for 3rd).

Other Awards

Maxwell Award (Player)..Larry Johnson, Penn St, RB
Sporting News Player of the Year ....Carson Palmer, Southern Cal, QB
Walter Camp Player of the Year ....Larry Johnson, Penn St, RB
Chuck Bednarik Award (Defense) .........................E.J. Henderson, Maryland, LB
Vince Lombardi/Rotary Award (Lineman/LB) ....Terrell Suggs, Arizona St, DL
Outland Trophy (Interior Lineman).........................Rien Long, Washington St, DL
Davey O'Brien Award (QB)...Brad Banks, Iowa, QB
Unitas Golden Arm Award (Senior QB)............Carson Palmer, Southern Cal, QB
Doak Walker Award (RB) ....Larry Johnson, Penn St, RB
Biletnikoff Award (WR)..Charles Rogers, Michigan St WR
Butkus Award (Linebacker) ..................................E.J. Henderson, Maryland, LB
Jim Thorpe Award (Defensive Back)................Terence Newman, Kansas St, DB
Associated Press Player of the Year ....Brad Banks, Iowa, QB
Walter Payton Award (Div I-AA Player)...............Tony Romo, Eastern Illinois, QB
Harlon Hill Trophy (Div II Player)..........................Curt Anes, Grand Valley St, QB
Gagliardi Trophy (Div III Player)....................................Dan Pugh, Mt. Union, RB

Coaches' Awards

Walter Camp Award ....Kirk Ferentz, Iowa
Eddie Robinson Award (Div I-AA) ....Tommy Tate, McNeese St
Bobby Dodd Award ....Jim Tressel, Ohio St
Bear Bryant Award ....Jim Tressel, Ohio St

AFCA COACHES OF THE YEAR

Division I-A ....Jim Tressel, Ohio St
Division I-AA...Jack Harbaugh, Western Kentucky
Division II...Brian Kelly, Grand Valley St
Division III..Larry Kehres, Mt. Union

Football Writers Association of America All-America Team

OFFENSE

QB........Carson Palmer, Southern Cal, Sr
RB........Larry Johnson, Penn St, Sr
RB........Willis McGahee, Miami, So,
WR.......Charles Rogers, Michigan St, Jr
WR.......Reggie Williams, Washington, So
TE.......Dallas Clark, Iowa, Jr
OL.......Shawn Andrews, Arkansas, So
OL.......Derrick Dockery, Texas, Sr
OL.......Jordan Gross, Utah, Sr
OL.......Bruce Nelson, Iowa, Sr
OL.......Brett Romberg, Miami, Sr
K ....Nate Kaeding, Iowa, Jr
KR........Derek Abney, Kentucky, Jr

DEFENSE

DL ....Michael Haynes, Penn St, Sr
DL ....Rien Long, Washington St, Jr
DL ....David Pollack, Georgia, So
DL ....Terrell Suggs, Arizona St, Jr
LB .......E.J. Henderson, Maryland, Sr
LB ....Teddy Lehman, Oklahoma, Jr
LB ....Matt Wilhelm, Ohio St, Sr
DB.......Mike Doss, Ohio St, Sr
DB.......Terence Newman, Kansas St, Sr
DB.......Troy Polamalu, Southern Cal, Sr
DB.......Shane Walton, Notre Dame, Sr
P ....Andy Groom, Ohio St, Sr

Division I-A

ATLANTIC COAST CONFERENCE

	Conference		Full Season		
	W	L	W	L	Pct
Florida St	7	1	9	5	.643
Maryland	6	2	11	3	.786
Virginia	6	2	9	5	.643
N Carolina St	5	3	11	3	.786
Clemson	4	4	7	6	.538
Georgia Tech	4	4	7	6	.538
Wake Forest	3	5	7	6	.538
N Carolina	1	7	3	9	.250
Duke	0	8	2	10	.167

BIG EAST CONFERENCE

	Conference		Full Season		
	W	L	W	L	Pct
Miami (FL)	7	0	12	1	.923
W Virginia	6	1	9	4	.692
Pittsburgh	5	2	9	4	.692
Boston College	3	4	9	4	.692
Virginia Tech	3	4	10	4	.714
Syracuse	2	5	4	8	.333
Temple	2	5	4	8	.333
Rutgers	0	7	1	11	.083

BIG TEN CONFERENCE

	Conference		Full Season		
	W	L	W	L	Pct
Iowa	8	0	11	2	.846
Ohio St	8	0	14	0	1.000
Michigan	6	2	10	3	.769
Penn St	5	3	9	4	.692
Illinois	4	4	5	7	.417
Purdue	4	4	7	6	.538
Minnesota	3	5	8	5	.615
Michigan St	2	6	4	8	.333
Wisconsin	2	6	8	6	.571
Indiana	1	7	3	9	.250
Northwestern	1	7	3	9	.250

BIG 12 CONFERENCE

	Conference		Full Season		
NORTH	W	L	W	L	Pct
*Colorado	7	1	9	5	.643
Kansas St	6	2	11	2	.846
Iowa St	4	4	7	7	.500
Nebraska	3	5	7	7	.500
Missouri	2	6	5	7	.417
Kansas	0	8	2	10	.167
SOUTH					
*Oklahoma	6	2	12	2	.857
Texas	6	2	11	2	.846
Oklahoma St	5	3	8	5	.615
Texas Tech	5	3	9	5	.643
Texas A&M	3	5	6	6	.500
Baylor	1	7	3	9	.250

*Full season record includes Big 12 Championship Game in which Oklahoma defeated Colorado 29–7 on Dec. 7.

Division I-A *(Cont.)*

CONFERENCE USA

	Conference		Full Season		
	W	L	W	L	Pct
Cincinnati	6	2	7	7	.500
Texas Christian	6	2	10	2	.833
Louisville	5	3	7	6	.538
Southern Mississippi	5	3	7	6	.538
E Carolina	4	4	4	8	.333
Tulane	4	4	8	5	.615
Alabama-Birmingham	4	4	5	7	.417
Houston	3	5	5	7	.417
Memphis	2	6	3	9	.250
Army	1	7	1	11	.083

MID-AMERICAN ATHLETIC CONFERENCE

	Conference		Full Season		
EAST	W	L	W	L	Pct
*Marshall	7	1	11	2	.846
Central Florida	6	2	7	5	.583
Miami (OH)	5	3	7	5	.583
Ohio University	4	4	4	8	.333
Akron	3	5	4	8	.333
Kent St	1	7	3	9	.250
Buffalo	0	8	1	11	.083
WEST					
*Toledo	7	1	9	5	.643
Northern Illinois	7	1	8	4	.667
Bowling Green	6	2	9	3	.750
Ball St	4	4	6	6	.500
Western Michigan	3	5	4	8	.333
Central Michigan	2	6	4	8	.333
Eastern Michigan	1	7	3	9	.250

*Full season record includes MAC Championship Game in which Marshall defeated Toledo 49–45 on Dec 7.

MOUNTAIN WEST CONFERENCE

	Conference		Full Season		
	W	L	W	L	Pct
Colorado St	6	1	10	4	.714
New Mexico	5	2	7	7	.500
Air Force	4	3	8	5	.615
San Diego St	4	3	4	9	.308
Nevada–Las Vegas	3	4	5	7	.417
Utah	3	4	5	6	.455
Brigham Young	2	5	5	7	.417
Wyoming	1	6	2	10	.167

PACIFIC 10 CONFERENCE

	Conference		Full Season		
	W	L	W	L	Pct
Southern California	7	1	11	2	.846
Washington St	7	1	10	3	.769
Arizona St	5	3	8	6	.571
California	4	4	7	5	.583
Oregon St	4	4	8	5	.615
UCLA	4	4	8	5	.615
Washington	4	4	7	6	.538
Oregon	3	5	7	6	.538
Arizona	1	7	4	8	.333
Stanford	1	7	2	9	.182

Division I-A *(Cont.)*

SOUTHEASTERN CONFERENCE

EAST	Conference W	L	Full Season W	L	Pct
*Georgia	7	1	13	1	.929
Florida	6	2	8	5	.615
Tennessee	5	3	8	5	.615
Kentucky	3	5	7	5	.583
S Carolina	3	5	5	7	.417
Vanderbilt	0	8	2	10	.167
WEST					
*Alabama	6	2	10	3	.769
Arkansas	5	3	9	5	.643
Auburn	5	3	9	4	.692
Louisiana St	5	3	8	5	.615
Mississippi	3	5	7	6	.538
Mississippi St	0	8	3	9	.250

*Full season record includes SEC Championship Game in which Georgia defeated Arkansas 30–3, on Dec. 7.

SUN BELT CONFERENCE

	Conference W	L	Full Season W	L	Pct
N Texas	6	0	8	5	.615
New Mexico St	5	1	7	5	.583
Arkansas St	3	3	6	7	.462
Middle Tennessee St	2	4	4	8	.333
Louisiana-Lafayette	2	4	3	9	.250
Louisiana-Monroe	2	4	3	9	.250
Idaho	1	5	2	10	.167

WESTERN ATHLETIC CONFERENCE

	Conference W	L	Full Season W	L	Pct
Boise St	8	0	12	1	.923
Hawaii	7	1	10	4	.714
Fresno St	6	2	9	5	.643
Nevada	4	4	5	7	.417
San Jose St	4	4	6	7	.462
Louisiana Tech	3	5	4	8	.333
Rice	3	5	4	7	.364
Southern Methodist	3	5	3	9	.250
Texas–El Paso	1	7	2	10	.167
Tulsa	1	7	1	11	.083

INDEPENDENTS

	Full Season W	L	Pct
S Florida	9	2	.818
Notre Dame	10	3	.769
Connecticut	6	6	.500
Utah St	4	7	.364
Troy St	4	8	.333
Navy	2	10	.167

Division I-AA
ATLANTIC 10 CONFERENCE

	Conference		Full Season		
	W	L	W	L	Pct
Maine	7	2	11	3	.786
Northeastern	7	2	10	3	.769
Villanova	6	3	11	4	.733
Massachusetts	6	3	8	4	.667
William & Mary	5	4	6	5	.545
Delaware	4	5	6	6	.500
Hofstra	4	5	6	6	.500
Richmond	4	5	4	7	.364
James Madison	3	6	5	7	.417
New Hampshire	2	7	3	8	.273
Rhode Island	1	8	3	9	.250

BIG SKY CONFERENCE

	Conference		Full Season		
	W	L	W	L	Pct
Idaho St	5	2	8	3	.727
Montana	5	2	11	3	.786
Montana St	5	2	7	6	.538
Eastern Washington	3	4	6	5	.545
Northern Arizona	3	4	6	5	.545
Portland St	3	4	6	5	.545
Sacramento St	3	4	5	7	.417
Weber St	1	6	3	8	.273

BIG SOUTH CONFERENCE

	Conference		Full Season		
	W	L	W	L	Pct
Gardner-Webb	3	0	9	1	.900
Elon	2	1	4	7	.364
Liberty	1	2	2	9	.182
Charleston Southern	0	3	4	8	.333

GATEWAY COLLEGIATE ATHLETIC CONFERENCE

	Conference		Full Season		
	W	L	W	L	Pct
Western Kentucky	7	1	12	3	.800
Western Illinois	6	2	11	2	.846
Illinois St	4	3	6	5	.545
Youngstown St	4	3	7	4	.636
Indiana St	3	4	5	7	.417
Northern Iowa	2	5	5	6	.455
Southern Illinois	2	5	4	8	.333
SW Missouri St	1	6	4	7	.364

IVY LEAGUE

	Conference		Full Season		
	W	L	W	L	Pct
Pennsylvania	7	0	9	1	.900
Harvard	6	1	7	3	.700
Princeton	4	3	6	4	.600
Yale	4	3	6	4	.600
Cornell	3	4	4	6	.400
Brown	2	5	2	8	.200
Dartmouth	2	5	3	7	.300
Columbia	0	7	1	9	.100

METRO ATLANTIC ATHLETIC CONFERENCE

	Conference		Full Season		
	W	L	W	L	Pct
Duquesne	8	0	11	1	.917
Fairfield	5	3	5	6	.455
Marist	5	3	7	4	.636
St. Peters	5	3	6	5	.545
Iona	4	4	5	6	.455
Siena	3	5	3	7	.300
Canisius	2	6	2	9	.182
La Salle	2	6	2	9	.182
St. John's	2	6	2	8	.200

Division I-AA *(Cont.)*

MID-EASTERN ATHLETIC CONFERENCE

	Conference		Full Season		
	W	L	W	L	Pct
Bethune-Cookman	7	1	11	2	.846
Florida A&M	5	3	7	5	.583
Hampton	5	3	7	5	.583
Morgan St	5	3	7	5	.583
Howard	4	4	6	5	.545
S Carolina St	4	4	7	5	.583
Delaware St	2	6	4	8	.333
N Carolina A&T	2	6	4	8	.333
Norfolk St	2	6	5	6	.455

NORTHEAST CONFERENCE

	Conference		Full Season		
	W	L	W	L	Pct
Albany	6	1	8	4	.667
Sacred Heart	5	2	7	3	.700
Stony Brook	5	2	8	2	.800
Wagner	4	3	7	4	.636
Central Connecticut St	3	4	5	6	.455
Monmouth	2	5	2	8	.200
Robert Morris	2	5	3	7	.300
St. Francis (PA)	1	6	2	8	.200

OHIO VALLEY CONFERENCE

	Conference		Full Season		
	W	L	W	L	Pct
Eastern Illinois	5	1	8	4	.667
Murray St	5	1	7	5	.583
Eastern Kentucky	4	2	8	4	.667
SE Missouri St	4	2	8	4	.667
Tennessee Tech	2	4	5	7	.417
Tennessee St	1	5	2	10	.167
Tennessee-Martin	0	6	2	10	.167

PATRIOT LEAGUE

	Conference		Full Season		
	W	L	W	L	Pct
Fordham	6	1	10	3	.769
Colgate	6	1	9	3	.750
Lafayette	5	2	7	5	.583
Lehigh	4	3	8	4	.667
Towson	3	4	6	5	.545
Georgetown	2	5	5	6	.455
Holy Cross	2	5	4	8	.333
Bucknell	0	7	2	9	.182

PIONEER CONFERENCE

	Conference		Full Season		
NORTH	W	L	W	L	Pct
*Dayton	4	0	11	1	.917
San Diego	3	1	5	5	.500
Butler	2	2	4	6	.400
Drake	1	3	5	6	.455
Valparaiso	0	4	1	10	.091
SOUTH					
*Morehead St	3	0	9	3	.750
Davidson	2	1	7	3	.700
Austin Peay	1	2	7	5	.583
Jacksonville	0	3	3	7	.300

*Full season record includes Pioneer Conference Championship in which Dayton def. Morehead St 28–0 on Nov. 25.

Division I-AA *(Cont.)*

SOUTHERN CONFERENCE

	Conference		Full Season		
	W	L	W	L	Pct
Georgia Southern	7	1	11	3	.786
Appalachian St	6	2	8	4	.667
Furman	6	2	8	4	.667
Wofford	6	2	9	3	.750
Virginia Military	3	5	6	6	.500
Western Carolina	3	5	5	6	.455
E Tennessee St	2	6	4	8	.333
Chattanooga	2	6	2	10	.167
The Citadel	1	7	3	9	.250

SOUTHLAND CONFERENCETK

	Conference		Full Season		
	W	L	W	L	Pct
McNeese St	6	0	13	2	.867
Northwestern St	4	2	9	4	.692
Nicholls St	3	3	7	4	.636
Stephen F. Austin	3	3	6	5	.545
Jacksonville St	2	4	5	6	.455
Sam Houston St	2	4	4	7	.364
SW Texas St	1	5	4	7	.364

SOUTHWESTERN ATHLETIC CONFERENCE

	Conference		Full Season		
EASTERN	W	L	W	L	Pct
*Alabama A&M	6	1	8	4	.667
Jackson St	5	2	7	4	.636
Alcorn St	3	4	6	5	.545
Mississippi Valley St	3	4	5	6	.455
Alabama St	2	5	6	6	.500
WESTERN					
*Grambling	6	1	11	2	.846
Southern	5	2	6	6	.500
Texas Southern	3	4	4	7	.364
Arkansas–Pine Bluff	2	5	3	8	.273
Prairie View A&M	0	7	1	10	.091

*Full season record includes SWAC Championship Game in which Grambling defeated Alabama A&M 31–19 on Dec. 14.

INDEPENDENTS

	Full Season		
	W	L	Pct
St. Mary's (CA)	6	6	.500
Florida International	5	6	.455
Samford	4	7	.364
Cal Poly	3	8	.273
Florida Atlantic	2	9	.182
Savannah St	1	9	.100
Southern Utah	1	10	.091
Morris Brown	1	11	.083

Division I-A

SCORING

	Class	GP	TD	XP	FG	Pts	Pts/Game
Brock Forsey, Boise St	Sr	12	29	0	0	174	14.50
Willis McGahee, Miami	So	12	27	0	0	162	13.50
Larry Johnson, Penn St	Sr	12	23	0	0	140	11.67
Josh Harris, Bowling Green	Jr	12	22	1	0	134	11.17
Chance Harridge, Air Force	Jr	12	22	0	0	132	11.00
Nick Calaycay, Boise St	Sr	9	0	59	11	92	10.22
Art Brown, E Carolina	Jr	10	17	0	0	102	10.20
Lee Suggs, Virginia Tech	Sr	13	22	0	0	132	10.15
Michael Turner, Northern Illinois	Jr	12	20	0	0	120	10.00
Maurice Clarett, Ohio St	Fr	10	16	0	0	96	9.60
Terry Caulley, Connecticut	Fr	10	16	0	0	96	9.60

FIELD GOALS

	Class	GP	FGA	FG	Pct	FG/Game
Nick Browne, Texas Christian	Jr	11	28	22	.786	2.00
Mike Nugent, Ohio St	So	13	26	24	.923	1.85
Drew Dunning, Washington St	Jr	12	32	22	.688	1.83
Jeff Babcock, Colorado St	So	13	31	23	.742	1.77
John Anderson, Washington	Sr	12	30	21	.700	1.75

TOTAL OFFENSE

			Rushing		Passing			Total Offense	
	Class	GP	Car	Net	Att	Yds	Yds	Yds/Play	Yds/Game
Byron Leftwich, Marshall	Sr	12	37	-1	491	4268	4267	8.08	355.6
Kliff Kingsbury, Texas Tech	Sr	14	102	-114	712	5017	4903	6.02	350.2
Cody Pickett, Washington	Jr	13	86	-185	612	4458	4273	6.12	328.7
Timmy Chang, Hawaii	So	14	39	-17	624	4474	4457	6.72	318.4
Ryan Schneider, Central Florida	Jr	12	37	-89	430	3770	3681	7.88	306.8
Luke McCown, Louisiana Tech	Jr	12	61	30	550	3539	3569	6.31	297.4
Zack Threadgill, Nevada	Sr	12	62	116	451	3418	3534	6.89	294.5
Carson Palmer, Southern Cal	Sr	13	50	-122	489	3942	3820	7.09	293.8
Jose Fuentes, Utah St	Sr	11	57	-104	454	3268	3164	6.19	287.6
Adam Hall, San Diego St	Jr	11	64	-110	452	3253	3143	6.09	285.7

RUSHING

	Class	GP	Car	Yds	TD	Avg	Yds/Game
Larry Johnson, Penn St	Sr	12	251	2015	8.03	20	167.92
Michael Turner, Northern Illinois	Jr	12	338	1915	5.67	19	159.58
Chris Brown, Colorado	Jr	12	275	1744	6.34	18	145.33
Willis McGahee, Miami	So	12	262	1686	6.44	27	140.50
Steven Jackson, Oregon St	So	12	300	1657	5.52	15	138.00
Marcus Merriweather, Ball St	Sr	12	332	1618	4.87	12	134.83
Quentin Griffin, Oklahoma	Sr	13	257	1740	6.77	14	133.85
Avon Cobourne, W Virginia	Sr	12	310	1593	5.14	15	132.75
Joffrey Reynolds, Houston	Sr	12	316	1545	4.89	11	128.75
Brock Forsey, Boise St	Sr	12	271	1533	5.66	23	127.75

PASSING EFFICIENCY

	Class	GP	Att	Comp	Pct Comp	Yds	Yds/Att	TD	Int	Rating Pts
Brad Banks, Iowa	Sr	12	258	155	60.08	2369	9.18	25	4	166.1
Byron Leftwich, Marshall	Sr	11	447	309	69.13	4019	8.99	26	9	159.8
Brian Jones, Toledo	Sr	13	382	270	70.68	3115	8.16	21	7	153.7
Ryan Schneider, Central Florida	Jr	12	430	265	61.63	3770	8.77	31	16	151.6
Jason Gesser, Washington St	Sr	12	368	219	59.51	3169	8.61	27	11	150.1
Carson Palmer, Southern Cal	Sr	12	458	288	62.88	3639	7.95	32	10	148.3
Craig Krenzel, Ohio St	Sr	13	228	141	61.84	1988	8.72	12	5	148.1
Ken Dorsey, Miami	Sr	12	350	194	55.43	3073	8.78	26	10	148.0
Matt Schaub, Virginia	Jr	13	396	272	68.69	2794	7.06	27	7	146.9
Scott McBrien, Maryland	Jr	13	265	151	56.98	2377	8.97	15	10	143.5

Note: Minimum 15 attempts per game.

Division I-A *(Cont.)*

RECEPTIONS PER GAME

	Class	GP	No.	Yds	TD	R/Game
Nate Burleson, Nevada	Sr	12	138	1629	12	11.50
J.R. Tolver, San Diego St	Sr	13	128	1785	13	9.85
Kassim Osgood, San Diego St	Sr	13	108	1552	8	8.31
Rashaun Woods, Oklahoma St	Jr	12	98	1531	16	8.17
Taylor Stubblefield, Purdue	So	9	70	697	0	7.78

RECEIVING YARDS PER GAME

	Class	GP	No.	Yds	TD	Yds/Game
J.R. Tolver, San Diego St	Sr	13	128	1785	13	137.31
Nate Burleson, Nevada	Sr	12	138	1629	12	135.75
Rashaun Woods, Oklahoma St	Jr	12	98	1531	16	127.58
Kassim Osgood, San Diego St	Sr	13	108	1552	8	119.38
Reggie Williams, Washington	So	12	89	1390	11	115.83

ALL-PURPOSE RUNNERS

	Class	GP	Rush	Rec	PR	KOR	Yds	Yds/Game
Larry Johnson, Penn State	Sr	13	2087	349	0	219	2655	204.23
Michael Turner, Northern Illinois	Jr	12	1915	100	0	269	2284	190.33
Robbie Mixon, Central Michigan	Sr	12	1361	253	0	524	2138	178.17
Jason Wright, Northwestern	Jr	12	1234	266	0	513	2013	167.75
Brock Forsey, Boise St	Sr	13	1611	282	0	234	2127	163.62

INTERCEPTIONS

	Class	GP	No.	Int/Game
Jim Leonhard, Wisconsin	So	14	11	.79
Jason David, Wash St	Jr	10	7	.70
Gerald Jones, San Jose St	Jr	12	8	.67
Jason Goss, TCU	Sr	12	8	.67

Three tied with .62

PUNTING

	Class	No.	Avg
Matt Payne, BYU	So	51	47.59
Mark Mariscal, Colorado	Sr	67	47.55
Glenn Pakulak, Kentucky	Sr	66	45.58
Andy Groom, Ohio St	Sr	60	44.95
Donnie Jones, LSU	Jr	64	43.95

Note: Minimum of 3.6 per game.

PUNT RETURNS

	Class	No.	Yds	TD	Avg
Dan Sheldon, Northern IL	So	21	477	3	22.71
Aris Comeaux, Army	Sr	12	233	2	19.42
Cody Cardwell, SMU	Sr	27	467	1	17.30
DeJuan Groce, Nebraska	Sr	43	732	4	17.02
Lynaris Elpheage, Tulane	Jr	28	463	1	16.54

Note: Minimum 1.2 per game.

KICKOFF RETURNS

	Class	No.	Yds	TD	Avg
Charles Pauley, San Jose St	Sr	31	978	2	31.55
Broderick Clark, Louisville	Fr	31	897	2	28.94
LaShaun Ward, California	Sr	28	809	1	28.89
Jason Wright, Northwestern	Jr	18	513	1	28.50
Nathan Jones, Rutgers	Jr	26	736	2	28.31

Note: Minimum of 1.2 per game.

Division I-A Team Single-Game Highs

RUSHING AND PASSING

Rushing and passing yards: 508—Andrew Walter, Arizona St, QB, Oct 19 (vs. Oregon)
Rushing and passing plays: 78—Kliff Kingsbury, Texas Tech, QB, Oct 19 (vs. Missouri)
Rushing plays: 48—Tanardo Sharps, Temple, RB, Nov 16 (vs. Rutgers)
Net rushing yards: 377—Robbie Mixon, Central Mich., RB, Nov 2 (vs. Eastern Mich.)
Passes attempted: 70—Kliff Kingsbury, Texas Tech, QB, Oct 19 (vs. Missouri)
Passes completed: 49—Kliff Kingsbury, Texas Tech. QB, Oct 19 (vs. Missouri)
 49—Kliff Kingsbury, Texas Tech, QB, Oct 5 (vs. Texas A&M)
Passing yards: 536—Andrew Walter, Arizona St, QB, Oct 19 (vs. Oregon)

RECEIVING AND RETURNS

Passes caught: 19—Nate Burleson, Nevada, WR, Nov 9 (vs. Texas–El Paso)
Receiving yards: 296—J.R. Tolver, San Diego St, WR, Sep 14 (vs. Arizona St)
Punt return yards: 169—Cody Cardwell, SMU, WR, Nov 16 (vs. Texas–El Paso)
Kickoff return yards: 243—Kwane Doster, Vanderbilt, TB, Sep 21 (vs. Mississippi)

Division I-AA

SCORING

	Class	GP	TD	XP	FG	Pts	Pts/Game
T.J. Stallings, Morgan St.	Sr	12	23	0	0	144	12.00
Dale Jennings, Butler	Sr	10	20	0	0	120	12.00
Chaz Williams, Georgia Southern	So	14	27	0	0	162	11.57
Gary Jones, Albany (NY)	Jr	12	23	0	0	138	11.50
J.R. Taylor, Eastern Illinois	Sr	12	18	0	0	112	9.33

FIELD GOALS

	Class	GP	FGA	FG	Pct	FG/Game
M. Hoambrecker, Northern Iowa	Sr	11	28	25	.893	2.27
Justin Langan, Western Illinois	So	13	27	20	.741	1.54
Jesse Obert, Dayton	Sr	12	23	17	.739	1.42
Matt Fordyce, Fordham	Sr	13	26	18	.692	1.38
Chris Snyder, Montana	Jr	14	32	19	.594	1.36

TOTAL OFFENSE

			Rushing		Passing		Total Offense		
	Class	GP	Car	Net	Att	Yds	Yds	Yds/Play	Yds/Game
Bruce Eugene, Grambling	So	13	137	535	543	4483	5018	7.38	386.0
Ira Vandever, Drake	Sr	11	127	415	361	3239	3654	7.49	332.2
Brian Mann, Dartmouth	Sr	10	118	393	423	2913	3306	6.11	330.6
Robert Kent, Jackson St	Jr	11	118	179	395	3386	3565	6.95	324.1
David Maechi, Valparaiso	Jr	11	132	223	390	3326	3549	6.80	322.6

RUSHING

	Class	GP	Car	Yds	Avg	TD	Yds/Game
Jay Bailey, Austin Peay	Sr	12	319	1687	5.29	18	140.58
J.R. Taylor, Eastern Illinois	Sr	12	254	1522	5.99	18	126.83
Gary Jones, Albany	Jr	12	231	1509	6.53	22	125.75
Verondre Barnes, Liberty	So	11	221	1304	5.90	5	118.55
P.J. Mays, Youngstown St	Sr	11	255	1284	5.04	11	116.73

PASSING EFFICIENCY

	Class	GP	Att	Comp	Pct Comp	Yds	Yds/Att	TD	Int	Rating Pts
Eric Rasmussen, San Diego	Jr	10	279	170	60.93	2473	8.86	25	1	164.2
Billy Napier, Furman	Sr	12	276	189	68.48	2475	8.97	16	8	157.1
Ira Vandever, Drake	Sr	11	361	205	56.79	3239	8.97	32	11	155.3
Russ Michna, Western Illinois	Jr	13	330	189	57.27	3037	9.20	23	5	154.5
Jack Tomco, SE Missouri St	Jr	12	372	242	65.05	3132	8.42	29	16	152.9

Note: Minimum 15 attempts per game.

RECEPTIONS PER GAME

	Class	GP	No.	Yds	TD	R/G
Chas Gessner, Brown	Sr	10	114	1166	11	11.40
Carl Morris, Harvard	Sr	10	90	1288	8	9.00
Rob Milanese, Penn	Sr	10	85	1112	8	8.50
Aryvia Holmes, Samford	Sr	10	84	1158	9	8.40
Jay Barnard, Dartmouth	Jr	10	83	899	8	8.30

RECEIVING YARDS PER GAME

	Class	GP	No.	Yds	TD	Yds/G
T. Douglas, Grambling	Jr	12	92	1704	18	142.0
Carl Morris, Harvard	Sr	10	90	1288	8	128.8
Willie Ponder, SE MO St	Sr	12	87	1453	15	121.1
Chas Gessner, Brown	Sr	10	114	1166	11	116.6
Aryvia Holmes, Samford	Sr	10	84	1158	9	115.8

INTERCEPTIONS

	Class	GP	No.	Yds	TD	Int/G
R. Mathis, B-Cookman	Sr	13	14	455	3	1.1
Mark Kasmer, Dayton	Sr	12	11	157	2	.92
Antwan Hill, Alabama St	So	12	10	199	1	.83
C. Oaks, Robert Morris	Jr	10	7	130	2	.70
C. Blackshear, C Conn St	So	10	7	204	1	.70
Chad King, Stony Brook	Jr	10	7	109	1	.70
Mike Devore, St. John's (NY)	Jr	10	7	45	0	.70

PUNTING

	Class	No.	Avg
Mark Gould, Northern Arizona	Jr	62	48.18
Mike Scifres, Western Illinois	Sr	53	48.02
Brent Barth, Virginia Military	Sr	64	47.38
Eddie Johnson, Idaho St	Sr	51	46.22
David Beckford, Alabama St	Sr	57	43.95

Division I-AA (Cont)

ALL-PURPOSE RUNNERS

	Class	GP	Rush	Rec	PR	KOR	Yds	Yds/Game
Stephan Lewis, New Hampshire	Sr	11	1152	419	13	645	2229	202.64
Andre Raymond, Eastern Illinois	Jr	12	612	672	112	872	2268	189.00
Jay Bailey, Austin Peay	Sr	12	1687	85	0	381	2153	179.42
Ari Confesor, Holy Cross	Jr	12	113	721	322	841	1997	166.42
Fred Amey, Cal St–Sacramento	So	11	31	989	278	514	1812	164.73

Division II

SCORING

	Class	GP	TD	XP	FG	Pts	Pts/Game
David Kircus, Grand Valley St	Sr	14	35	1	0	212	15.14
Ian Smart, C.W. Post	Sr	12	30	0	0	180	15.00
Ben Nelson, St. Cloud St	Sr	11	23	0	0	138	12.55
Kegan Coleman, Central Missouri St	So	12	24	0	0	144	12.00
DaMarcus Blount, N Alabama	Fr	11	20	0	0	120	10.91

FIELD GOALS

	Class	GP	FGA	FG	Pct	FG/Game
Henrik Juul-Nielsen, Nebraska-Kearney	Sr	11	24	20	83.3	1.82
Andrew Keippela, Western Oregon	So	9	23	14	60.9	1.56
J.W. Boren, Tarleton St	Sr	11	25	17	68.0	1.55
Austin Wellock, Ashland	Fr	11	19	15	78.9	1.36
Keith Witt, S Dakota St	Fr	10	25	13	52.0	1.30

TOTAL OFFENSE

	Class	GP	Yds	Yds/Game
Andrew Webb, Fort Lewis	Jr	11	4245	385.91
Dusty Burk, Truman	Sr	11	3441	312.82
Josh Chapman, MO Southern St	Sr	11	3408	309.82
Zak Hill, Central Washington	Jr	9	2692	299.11
Brett Gilliland, W Alabama	Jr	11	3213	292.10

RUSHING

	Class	GP	Car	Yds	TD	Yds/Game
Ian Smart, C.W. Post	Sr	12	287	2023	30	168.63
LeVar Ammons, Quincy	So	10	249	1650	13	165.00
Darrin Davis, Southern Conn St	Sr	11	327	1620	15	147.33
Mike Miller, Nebraska-Kearney	So	11	333	1600	13	145.50
Robert Campbell, Findlay	Jr	11	341	1575	16.	143.20

PASSING EFFICIENCY

	Class	GP	Att	Comp	Pct Comp	Yds	TD	Int	Rating Pts
Curt Anes, Grand Valley St	Sr	14	414	278	67.2	3692	47	6	176.6
Brian Eyerman, Indiana (PA)	Sr	12	290	173	59.7	2724	36	7	174.7
Ricky Fritz, Minnesota-Duluth	Sr	12	287	160	55.8	2760	34	13	166.6
Ryan Flanigan, UC–Davis	Jr	12	253	166	65.6	2397	20	10	163.4
Zak Hill, Central Washington	Jr	9	308	209	67.9	2694	22	7	160.4

Note: Minimum 15 attempts per game.

RECEPTIONS PER GAME

	Class	GP	No.	Yds	TD	Rec/G
Andrew Blakley, Truman	Sr	11	96	965	6	8.70
Gerald Gales, W Alabama	Jr	11	96	994	4	8.70
Chris Brewer, Fort Lewis	So	11	85	1274	18	7.70
Mark Green, SW Baptist	Jr	11	85	1014	4	7.70
Jamal Allen, Fort Lewis	Sr	11	80	939	5	7.30

RECEIVING YARDS PER GAME

	Class	GP	No.	Yds	TD	Yds/G
Chris Brewer, Fort Lewis	So	11	85	1274	18	115.8
N. Lewis, S Arkansas	So	11	65	1239	14	112.6
Nate Washington, Tiffin	So	10	53	1120	11	112.0
Ryshaun Ward, Concord	Sr	11	67	1214	11	110.4
Kyle Henderson, W Alabama	Sr	11	58	1190	14	108.2

Division II *(Cont.)*

INTERCEPTIONS

	Class	GP	No.	Yds	Int/ Game
Nicholas Murray, Johnson Smith	Jr	10	10	97	1.0
Rico Cody, Fort Valley St	Sr	11	10	73	0.9
Jon Arnold, California (PA)	Jr	11	9	48	0.8
Ryan Bowers, Presbyterian	Sr	11	9	43	0.8
Jamel Jackson, Catawba	Jr	9	7	130	0.8

PUNTING

	Class	No.	Avg
Michael Koenen, Western Wash	So	43	44.4
Sean McNicholas, Edinboro	Sr	58	44.2
Eric Roth, Washburn	Sr	53	42.5
Jeff Williams, Adams St	Fr	65	42.3
Daniel de la Corte, Fort Lewis	So	53	41.8
Ryan Wettstein, Northern Michigan	Jr	60	41.8

Note: Minimum 3.6 per game.

Division III

SCORING

	Class	GP	TD	XP	FG	Pts	Pts/Game
Dan Pugh, Mount Union	Sr	14	41	2	0	250	17.86
David Russell, Linfield	Sr	11	30	0	0	180	16.36
Fredrick Jackson, Coe	Sr	12	29	0	0	174	14.50
Greg Wood, Worcester St	Jr	11	26	1	0	158	14.36
Ryan Soule, Hartwick	Sr	10	22	0	0	132	13.20

FIELD GOALS

	Class	GP	FGA	FG	Pct	FG/Game
Ben Lambert, Washington (MO)	So	10	21	15	71.4	1.50
Alex Espinoza, California Luteran	Jr	9	19	13	68.4	1 44
Christopher Reed, Muhlenberg	Sr	12	21	16	76.2	1.33
Pat Dunne, Lake Forest	Sr	11	22	14	63.6	1.27

Three tied with 1.20.

TOTAL OFFENSE

	Class	GP	Yds	Yds/Game
Adam King, Howard Payne	So	10	3613	361.3
Tom Stetzer, WI-Platteville	Jr	9	3136	348.4
Eli Grant, Case Reserve	Jr	10	3192	319.2
Dan Cole, RPI	Jr	10	3173	317.3
Roy Hampton, Trinity (TX)	Sr	14	4418	315.6

RUSHING

	Class	GP	Car	Yds	TD	Yds/Game
Aaron Stepka, Colby	So	8	293	1370	11	171.3
David McNeal, Merchant Marine	Jr	11	338	1860	17	169.1
Randal Baker, Carthage	Sr	10	286	1680	16	168.0
Dan Pugh, Mount Union	Sr	14	384	2300	35	164.3
Luke Hagel, Ripon	Sr	10	265	1616	19	161.6

PASSING EFFICIENCY

	Class	GP	Att	Comp	Pct Comp	Yds	TD	Int	Rating Pts
Roy Hampton, Trinity (TX)	Sr	14	397	260	65.5	4095	43	6	184.9
Rob Adamson, Mount Union	Sr	11	231	139	60.2	2424	30	9	183.4
Eli Grant, Case Reserve	Jr	10	345	220	63.8	3265	33	7	170.8
Matt Trickey, Ripon	So	10	217	126	58.1	2228	23	13	167.3
Mike Donnenwerth, Simpson	Jr	10	258	158	61.2	2318	22	5	161.0

Note: Minimum 15 attempts per game.

Division III (Cont.)

RECEPTIONS PER GAME

	Class	GP	No.	Yds	TD	Rec/Game
Luis Uresti, Sul Ross St.	Sr	9	87	1082	4	9.7
Conrad Singh, Hampden-Sydney	Jr	10	86	831	5	8.6
Blake Elliott, St. John's (MN)	Jr	14	120	1484	22	8.6
Jim Raptis, Chicago	Jr	9	77	983	4	8.6
Dwayne Tawney, Whitworth	Jr	10	83	1226	8	8.3
Mark Boehms, Alma	Sr	11	91	1116	11	8.3

RECEIVING YARDS PER GAME

	Class	GP	No.	Yds	TD	Yds/Game
Ryan Soule, Hartwick	Sr	10	76	1550	20	155.0
Lewis Howes, Principia	So	9	71	1218	10	135.3
Matt Kent, WI-Platteville	Jr	9	65	1139	13	126.6
Dwayne Tawney, Whitworth	Jr	10	83	1226	8	122.6
Nick Bublavi, Catholic	So	10	62	1206	14	120.6

INTERCEPTIONS

	Class	GP	No.	Yds	Int/G
Jeff Thomas, Redlands	Sr	10	13	127	1.3
James Patrick, Stillman	Jr	10	11	146	1.1
David Simpson, Alma	Sr	11	12	134	1.1
Kyle Hausler, Capital	Fr	10	10	158	1.0

Five tied with 0.9.

PUNTING

	Class	No.	Avg
Scott Verhalen, E Texas Baptist	Jr	39	43.3
Cory Ohnesorge, Occidental	Fr	39	42.2
Sean Lipscomb, Redlands	Sr	45	41.7
Dusty Lehr, Juniata	Sr	48	40.0
Philip Stuebs, Martin Luther	Jr	34	39.9

Note: Minimum 3.6 per game.

2002 NCAA Division I-A Team Leaders

Offense

SCORING

	GP	Pts	Avg
Boise St.	13	593	45.62
Kansas St.	13	582	44.77
Bowling Green	12	490	40.83
Miami (FL)	13	527	40.54
Oklahoma	14	541	38.64
Texas Tech	14	537	38.36
Iowa	13	484	37.23
Hawaii	14	502	35.86
Southern Cal	13	465	35.77
California	12	427	35.58

RUSHING

	GP	Car	Yds	Avg	TD	Yds/Game
Air Force	13	786	4001	5.1	41	307.8
W Virginia	13	714	3687	5.2	39	283.6
Navy	12	652	3249	5.0	34	270.8
Nebraska	14	724	3762	5.2	29	268.7
Kansas St.	13	655	3433	5.2	53	264.1
Rice	11	606	2725	4.5	24	247.7
Wake Forest	13	718	3135	4.4	33	241.2
Ohio	12	649	2878	4.4	30	239.8
Colorado	14	652	3259	5.0	28	232.8
Penn St.	13	526	2972	5.7	36	228.6

TOTAL OFFENSE

	GP	Plays	Yds	Avg	TD*	Yds/Game
Boise St.	13	950	6519	6.86	79	501.46
Hawaii	14	1039	6939	6.68	66	495.64
Marshall	13	991	6439	6.50	59	495.31
Texas Tech	14	1155	6835	5.92	71	488.21
Toledo	14	1033	6611	6.40	66	472.21
Miami (FL)	13	887	6056	6.83	70	465.85
Purdue	13	1034	5879	5.69	51	452.23
Southern California	13	1009	5840	5.79	60	449.23
Bowling Green	12	898	5387	6.00	65	448.92
Illinois	12	915	5356	5.85	43	446.33

*Defensive and special teams TDs not included.

Offense (Cont.)

PASSING

	GP	Att	Comp	Yds	Pct Comp	Yds/Att	TD	Int	Yds/Game
Texas Tech	14	770	515	5444	66.88	7.07	50	15	388.9
Hawaii	14	731	407	5406	55.68	7.40	35	26	386.1
Marshall	13	575	383	4804	66.61	8.35	35	15	369.5
Washington	13	621	372	4501	59.90	7.25	28	14	346.2
San Diego St	13	584	352	4302	60.27	7.37	24	10	330.9
Central Florida	12	442	270	3837	61.09	8.68	31	17	319.8
Utah St	11	487	258	3388	52.98	6.96	21	16	308.0
Southern California	13	494	313	3988	63.36	8.07	33	10	306.8
Arizona St	14	558	306	4254	54.84	7.62	31	16	303.9
Louisiana Tech	12	527	305	3633	57.87	6.89	19	19	302.8

Single-Game Highs

Points Scored: 77—Kentucky, Sept 7 (vs Texas–El Paso).
Net Rushing Yards: 536—W Virginia, Sept 28 (vs E Carolina).
Passing Yards: 559—Arizona St, Oct 19 (vs Oregon).
Rushing and Passing Yards: 733—Marshall, Oct 12 (vs Buffalo).
Fewest Rushing and Passing Yards Allowed: 60—Oklahoma, Oct 19 (vs Iowa St).

Defense

SCORING

	GP	Pts	Avg
Kansas St	13	154	11.8
Ohio St	14	183	13.1
N Texas	13	192	14.8
Georgia	14	212	15.1
Alabama	13	200	15.4
Oklahoma	14	216	15.4
Maryland	14	228	16.3
Texas	13	212	16.3
Notre Dame	13	217	16.7
N Carolina St	14	238	17.0

TOTAL DEFENSE

	GP	Plays	Yds	Avg	Yds/Game
Texas Christian	12	799	2882	3.61	240.25
Kansas St	13	864	3237	3.75	249.00
Alabama	13	764	3345	4.38	257.31
Troy St	12	784	3322	4.24	276.83
Tennessee	13	840	3703	4.41	284.85
Southern Cal	13	842	3704	4.40	284.92
Miami (FL)	13	935	3705	3.96	285.00
Louisiana St	13	825	3728	4.52	286.77
N Texas	13	870	3778	4.34	290.62
Oklahoma	14	928	4104	4.42	293.14

RUSHING

	GP	Car	Yds	Avg	TD	Yds/Game
Texas Christian	12	393	778	1.98	9	64.8
Kansas St	13	446	904	2.03	7	69.5
Ohio St	14	418	1088	2.60	5	77.7
Alabama	13	390	1042	2.67	10	80.2
Iowa	13	416	1065	2.56	17	81.9
Southern Cal	13	388	1081	2.79	9	83.2
S Florida	11	420	959	2.28	8	87.2
Washington St	13	453	1134	2.50	11	87.2
Oregon St	13	479	1225	2.56	13	94.2
Notre Dame	13	439	1238	2.82	11	95.2

TURNOVER MARGIN

		Turnovers Gained			Turnovers Lost			Margin/
	GP	Fum	Int	Total	Fum	Int	Total	Game
S Florida	11	14	22	36	10	5	15	1.91
Tulane	13	21	22	43	11	10	21	1.69
California	12	21	15	36	8	10	18	1.50
W Virginia	13	15	19	34	6	9	15	1.46
Southern Cal	13	19	17	36	8	10	18	1.38
Wake Forest	13	21	13	34	10	6	16	1.38
Oklahoma	14	12	24	36	6	11	17	1.36
Texas	13	13	22	35	6	12	18	1.31
Wisconsin	14	13	22	35	9	8	17	1.29
TCU	12	20	22	42	14	13	27	1.25

PASSING EFFICIENCY

	GP	Att	Comp	Yds	Pct Comp	Yds/Att	TD	Pct TD	Int	Pct Int	Rating Pts
Miami (FL)	13	353	163	1556	46.18	4.41	8	2.27	12	3.40	83.91
Texas Christian	12	406	158	2105	38.92	5.18	16	3.94	22	5.42	84.62
Kansas State	13	418	191	2333	45.69	5.58	11	2.63	20	4.78	91.70
Southern Mississippi	13	379	177	2195	46.70	5.79	6	1.58	16	4.22	92.13
Louisiana State	13	361	163	1985	45.15	5.50	13	3.60	17	4.71	93.85
Oregon St	13	456	222	2591	48.68	5.68	10	2.19	20	4.39	94.89
Texas	13	400	192	2147	48.00	5.37	17	4.25	22	5.50	96.11
Marshall	13	366	175	2099	47.81	5.73	10	2.73	15	4.10	96.79
Oklahoma	14	432	206	2594	47.69	6.00	13	3.01	24	5.56	96.96
Notre Dame	13	452	223	2662	49.34	5.89	12	2.65	21	4.65	98.24

National Champions

Year	Champion	Record	Bowl Game	Head Coach
1883	Yale	8-0-0	No bowl	Ray Tompkins (Captain)
1884	Yale	9-0-0	No bowl	Eugene L. Richards (Captain)
1885	Princeton	9-0-0	No bowl	Charles DeCamp (Captain)
1886	Yale	9-0-1	No bowl	Robert N. Corwin (Captain)
1887	Yale	9-0-0	No bowl	Harry W. Beecher (Captain)
1888	Yale	13-0-0	No bowl	Walter Camp
1889	Princeton	10-0-0	No bowl	Edgar Poe (Captain)
1890	Harvard	11-0-0	No bowl	George A. Stewart/George C. Adams
1891	Yale	13-0-0	No bowl	Walter Camp
1892	Yale	13-0-0	No bowl	Walter Camp
1893	Princeton	11-0-0	No bowl	Tom Trenchard (Captain)
1894	Yale	16-0-0	No bowl	William C. Rhodes
1895	Pennsylvania	14-0-0	No bowl	George Woodruff
1896	Princeton	10-0-1	No bowl	Garrett Cochran
1897	Pennsylvania	15-0-0	No bowl	George Woodruff
1898	Harvard	11-0-0	No bowl	W. Cameron Forbes
1899	Harvard	10-0-1	No bowl	Benjamin H. Dibblee
1900	Yale	12-0-0	No bowl	Malcolm McBride
1901	Michigan	11-0-0	Won Rose	Fielding Yost
1902	Michigan	11-0-0	No bowl	Fielding Yost
1903	Princeton	11-0-0	No bowl	Art Hillebrand
1904	Pennsylvania	12-0-0	No bowl	Carl Williams
1905	Chicago	11-0-0	No bowl	Amos Alonzo Stagg
1906	Princeton	9-0-1	No bowl	Bill Roper
1907	Yale	9-0-1	No bowl	Bill Knox
1908	Pennsylvania	11-0-1	No bowl	Sol Metzger
1909	Yale	10-0-0	No bowl	Howard Jones
1910	Harvard	8-0-1	No bowl	Percy Houghton
1911	Princeton	8-0-2	No bowl	Bill Roper
1912	Harvard	9-0-0	No bowl	Percy Houghton
1913	Harvard	9-0-0	No bowl	Percy Houghton
1914	Army	9-0-0	No bowl	Charley Daly
1915	Cornell	9-0-0	No bowl	Al Sharpe
1916	Pittsburgh	8-0-0	No bowl	Pop Warner
1917	Georgia Tech	9-0-0	No bowl	John Heisman
1918	Pittsburgh	4-1-0	No bowl	Pop Warner
1919	Harvard	9-0-1	Won Rose	Bob Fisher
1920	California	9-0-0	Won Rose	Andy Smith
1921	Cornell	8-0-0	No bowl	Gil Dobie
1922	Cornell	8-0-0	No bowl	Gil Dobie
1923	Illinois	8-0-0	No bowl	Bob Zuppke
1924	Notre Dame	10-0-0	Won Rose	Knute Rockne
1925	Alabama (H)	10-0-0	Won Rose	Wallace Wade
	Dartmouth (D)	8-0-0	No bowl	Jesse Hawley
1926	Alabama (H)	9-0-1	Tied Rose	Wallace Wade
	Stanford (D)(H)	10-0-1	Tied Rose	Pop Warner
1927	Illinois	7-0-1	No bowl	Bob Zuppke
1928	Georgia Tech (H)	10-0-0	Won Rose	Bill Alexander
	Southern Cal (D)	9-0-1	No bowl	Howard Jones
1929	Notre Dame	9-0-0	No bowl	Knute Rockne
1930	Notre Dame	10-0-0	No bowl	Knute Rockne
1931	Southern Cal	10-1-0	Won Rose	Howard Jones
1932	Southern Cal (H)	10-0-0	Won Rose	Howard Jones
	Michigan (D)	8-0-0	No bowl	Harry Kipke
1933	Michigan	7-0-1	No bowl	Harry Kipke
1934	Minnesota	8-0-0	No bowl	Bernie Bierman
1935	Minnesota (H)	8-0-0	No bowl	Bernie Bierman
	Southern Methodist (D)	12-1-0	Lost Rose	Matty Bell
1936	Minnesota	7-1-0	No bowl	Bernie Bierman
1937	Pittsburgh	9-0-1	No bowl	Jock Sutherland
1938	Texas Christian (AP)	11-0-0	Won Sugar	Dutch Meyer
	Notre Dame (D)	8-1-0	No bowl	Elmer Layden
1939	Southern Cal (D)	8-0-2	Won Rose	Howard Jones
	Texas A&M (AP)	11-0-0	Won Sugar	Homer Norton
1940	Minnesota	8-0-0	No bowl	Bernie Bierman
1941	Minnesota	8-0-0	No bowl	Bernie Bierman
1942	Ohio St	9-1-0	No bowl	Paul Brown

Year	Champion	Record	Bowl Game	Head Coach
1943	Notre Dame	9-1-0	No bowl	Frank Leahy
1944	Army	9-0-0	No bowl	Red Blaik
1945	Army	9-0-0	No bowl	Red Blaik
1946	Notre Dame	8-0-1	No bowl	Frank Leahy
1947	Notre Dame	9-0-0	No bowl	Frank Leahy
	Michigan*	10-0-0	Won Rose	Fritz Crisler
1948	Michigan	9-0-0	No bowl	Bennie Oosterbaan
1949	Notre Dame	10-0-0	No bowl	Frank Leahy
1950	Oklahoma	10-1-0	Lost Sugar	Bud Wilkinson
1951	Tennessee	10-1-0	Lost Sugar	Bob Neyland
1952	Michigan St	9-0-0	No bowl	Biggie Munn
1953	Maryland	10-1-0	Lost Orange	Jim Tatum
1954	Ohio St	10-0-0	Won Rose	Woody Hayes
	UCLA (UPI)	9-0-0	No bowl	Red Sanders
1955	Oklahoma	11-0-0	Won Orange	Bud Wilkinson
1956	Oklahoma	10-0-0	No bowl	Bud Wilkinson
1957	Auburn	10-0-0	No bowl	Shug Jordan
	Ohio St (UPI)	9-1-0	Won Rose	Woody Hayes
1958	Louisiana St	11-0-0	Won Sugar	Paul Dietzel
1959	Syracuse	11-0-0	Won Cotton	Ben Schwartzwalder
1960	Minnesota	8-2-0	Lost Rose	Murray Warmath
1961	Alabama	11-0-0	Won Sugar	Bear Bryant
1962	Southern Cal	11-0-0	Won Rose	John McKay
1963	Texas	11-0-0	Won Cotton	Darrell Royal
1964	Alabama	10-1-0	Lost Orange	Bear Bryant
1965	Alabama	9-1-1	Won Orange	Bear Bryant
	Michigan St (UPI)	10-1-0	Lost Rose	Duffy Daugherty
1966	Notre Dame	9-0-1	No bowl	Ara Parseghian
1967	Southern Cal	10-1-0	Won Rose	John McKay
1968	Ohio St	10-0-0	Won Rose	Woody Hayes
1969	Texas	11-0-0	Won Cotton	Darrell Royal
1970	Nebraska	11-0-1	Won Orange	Bob Devaney
	Texas (UPI)	10-1-0	Lost Cotton	Darrell Royal
1971	Nebraska	13-0-0	Won Orange	Bob Devaney
1972	Southern Cal	12-0-0	Won Rose	John McKay
1973	Notre Dame	11-0-0	Won Sugar	Ara Parseghian
	Alabama (UPI)	11-1-0	Lost Sugar	Bear Bryant
1974	Oklahoma	11-0-0	No bowl	Barry Switzer
	Southern Cal (UPI)	10-1-1	Won Rose	John McKay
1975	Oklahoma	11-1-0	Won Orange	Barry Switzer
1976	Pittsburgh	12-0-0	Won Sugar	Johnny Majors
1977	Notre Dame	11-1-0	Won Cotton	Dan Devine
1978	Alabama	11-1-0	Won Sugar	Bear Bryant
	Southern Cal (UPI)	12-1-0	Won Rose	John Robinson
1979	Alabama	12-0-0	Won Sugar	Bear Bryant
1980	Georgia	12-0-0	Won Sugar	Vince Dooley
1981	Clemson	12-0-0	Won Orange	Danny Ford
1982	Penn St	11-1-0	Won Sugar	Joe Paterno
1983	Miami (FL)	11-1-0	Won Orange	Howard Schnellenberger
1984	Brigham Young	13-0-0	Won Holiday	LaVell Edwards
1985	Oklahoma	11-1-0	Won Orange	Barry Switzer
1986	Penn St	12-0-0	Won Fiesta	Joe Paterno
1987	Miami (FL)	12-0-0	Won Orange	Jimmy Johnson
1988	Notre Dame	12-0-0	Won Fiesta	Lou Holtz
1989	Miami (FL)	11-1-0	Won Sugar	Dennis Erickson
1990	Colorado	11-1-1	Won Orange	Bill McCartney
	Georgia Tech (UPI)	11-0-1	Won Citrus	Bobby Ross
1991	Miami (FL)	12-0-0	Won Orange	Dennis Erickson
	Washington (CNN)	12-0-0	Won Rose	Don James
1992	Alabama	13-0-0	Won Sugar	Gene Stallings
1993	Florida St	12-1-0	Won Orange	Bobby Bowden
1994	Nebraska	13-0-0	Won Orange	Tom Osborne
1995	Nebraska	12-0-0	Won Fiesta	Tom Osborne
†1996	Florida	12–1	Won Sugar	Steve Spurrier
1997	Michigan	12–0	Won Rose	Lloyd Carr
	Nebraska (ESPN)	13–0	Won Orange	Tom Osborne
1998	Tennessee	13–0	Won Fiesta	Phillip Fulmer

National Champions (Cont.)

Year	Champion	Record	Bowl Game	Head Coach
1999	Florida St	12–0	Won Sugar	Bobby Bowden
2000	Oklahoma	13–0	Won Orange	Bob Stoops
2001	Miami (FL)	12–0	Won Rose	Larry Coker
2002	Ohio St	14–0	Won Fiesta	Jim Tressel

*The AP, which had voted Notre Dame No. 1, took a second vote, giving the national title to Michigan after its 49–0 win over Southern Cal in the Rose Bowl.   Note: Selectors: Helms Athletic Foundation (H) 1883–1935, The Dickinson System (D) 1924–40, The Associated Press (AP) 1936–present, United Press International (UPI) 1958–90, *USA Today*/CNN (CNN) 1991–96, and *USA Today*/ESPN (ESPN) 1997–present. †In 1996 the NCAA introduced overtime to break ties.

Results of Major Bowl Games

Rose Bowl

1-1-02	Michigan 49, Stanford 0
1-1-16	Washington St 14, Brown 0
1-1-17	Oregon 14, Pennsylvania 0
1-1-18	Mare Island 19, Camp Lewis 7
1-1-19	Great Lakes 17, Mare Island 0
1-1-20	Harvard 7, Oregon 6
1-1-21	California 28, Ohio St 0
1-2-22	Washington & Jefferson 0, California 0
1-1-23	Southern Cal 14, Penn St 3
1-1-24	Navy 14, Washington 14
1-1-25	Notre Dame 27, Stanford 10
1-1-26	Alabama 20, Washington 19
1-1-27	Alabama 7, Stanford 7
1-2-28	Stanford 7, Pittsburgh 6
1-1-29	Georgia Tech 8, California 7
1-1-30	Southern Cal 47, Pittsburgh 14
1-1-31	Alabama 24, Washington St 0
1-1-32	Southern Cal 21, Tulane 12
1-2-33	Southern Cal 35, Pittsburgh 0
1-1-34	Columbia 7, Stanford 0
1-1-35	Alabama 29, Stanford 13
1-1-36	Stanford 7, Southern Methodist 0
1-1-37	Pittsburgh 21, Washington 0
1-1-38	California 13, Alabama 0
1-2-39	Southern Cal 7, Duke 3
1-1-40	Southern Cal 14, Tennessee 0
1-1-41	Stanford 21, Nebraska 13
1-1-42	Oregon St 20, Duke 16
1-1-43	Georgia 9, UCLA 0
1-1-44	Southern Cal 29, Washington 0
1-1-45	Southern Cal 25, Tennessee 0
1-1-46	Alabama 34, Southern Cal 14
1-1-47	Illinois 45, UCLA 14
1-1-48	Michigan 49, Southern Cal 0
1-1-49	Northwestern 20, California 14
1-2-50	Ohio St 17, California 14
1-1-51	Michigan 14, California 6
1-1-52	Illinois 40, Stanford 7
1-1-53	Southern Cal 7, Wisconsin 0
1-1-54	Michigan St 28, UCLA 20
1-1-55	Ohio St 20, Southern Cal 7
1-2-56	Michigan St 17, UCLA 14
1-1-57	Iowa 35, Oregon St 19
1-1-58	Ohio St 10, Oregon 7
1-1-59	Iowa 38, California 12
1-1-60	Washington 44, Wisconsin 8
1-2-61	Washington 17, Minnesota 7
1-1-62	Minnesota 21, UCLA 3
1-1-63	Southern Cal 42, Wisconsin 37
1-1-64	Illinois 17, Washington 7

1-1-65	Michigan 34, Oregon St 7
1-1-66	UCLA 14, Michigan St 12
1-2-67	Purdue 14, Southern Cal 13
1-1-68	Southern Cal 14, Indiana 3
1-1-69	Ohio St 27, Southern Cal 16
1-1-70	Southern Cal 10, Michigan 3
1-1-71	Stanford 27, Ohio St 17
1-1-72	Stanford 13, Michigan 12
1-1-73	Southern Cal 42, Ohio St 17
1-1-74	Ohio St 42, Southern Cal 21
1-1-75	Southern Cal 18, Ohio St 17
1-1-76	UCLA 23, Ohio St 10
1-1-77	Southern Cal 14, Michigan 6
1-2-78	Washington 27, Michigan 20
1-1-79	Southern Cal 17, Michigan 10
1-1-80	Southern Cal 17, Ohio St 16
1-1-81	Michigan 23, Washington 6
1-1-82	Washington 28, Iowa 0
1-1-83	UCLA 24, Michigan 14
1-2-84	UCLA 45, Illinois 9
1-1-85	Southern Cal 20, Ohio St 17
1-1-86	UCLA 45, Iowa 28
1-1-87	Arizona St 22, Michigan 15
1-1-88	Michigan St 20, Southern Cal 17
1-2-89	Michigan 22, Southern Cal 14
1-1-90	Southern Cal 17, Michigan 10
1-1-91	Washington 46, Iowa 34
1-1-92	Washington 34, Michigan 14
1-1-93	Michigan 38, Washington 31
1-1-94	Wisconsin 21, UCLA 16
1-2-95	Penn St 38, Oregon 20
1-1-96	Southern Cal 41, Northwestern 32
1-1-97	Ohio St 20, Arizona St 17
1-1-98	Michigan 21, Washington St 16
1-1-99	Wisconsin 38, UCLA 31
1-1-00	Wisconsin 17, Stanford 9
1-1-01	Washington 34, Purdue 24
1-3-02	Miami 37, Nebraska 14
1-1-03	Oklahoma 34, Washington St 14

City: Pasadena. Stadium: Rose Bowl, capacity 96,576.
Playing Sites: Tournament Park (1902, 1916–22), Rose Bowl (1923–41, since 1943), Duke Stadium, Durham, NC (1942).

Orange Bowl

1-1-35	Bucknell 26, Miami (FL) 0
1-1-36	Catholic 20, Mississippi 19
1-1-37	Duquesne 13, Mississippi St 12
1-1-38	Auburn 6, Michigan St 0
1-2-39	Tennessee 17, Oklahoma 0

Note: The Fiesta, Orange, Rose and Sugar Bowls constitute the Bowl Alliance, formed in 1995. The Alliance holds eight berths: one each for the champions of the ACC, Big 10, Big 12, Big East, Pac 10 and SEC, and two at-large, reserved for any Division I-A team with at least nine wins and ranked in the top 12 of the BCS rankings. Of the eight teams, the two highest-ranked go to the Fiesta Bowl in 2003, and the Sugar Bowl in 2004. Once these four BCS matches have been set conferences may place the remaining qualified teams in the other bowls. Teams that have won at least six games against Division I-A teams qualify.

Orange Bowl *(Cont.)*

1-1-40 ....Georgia Tech 21, Missouri 7
1-1-41 ....Mississippi St 14, Georgetown 7
1-1-42 ....Georgia 40, Texas Christian 26
1-1-43 ....Alabama 37, Boston College 21
1-1-44 ....Louisiana St 19, Texas A&M 14
1-1-45 ....Tulsa 26, Georgia Tech 12
1-1-46 ....Miami (FL) 13, Holy Cross 6
1-1-47 ....Rice 8, Tennessee 0
1-1-48 ....Georgia Tech 20, Kansas 14
1-1-49 ....Texas 41, Georgia 28
1-2-50 ....Santa Clara 21, Kentucky 13
1-1-51 ....Clemson 15, Miami (FL) 14
1-1-52 ....Georgia Tech 17, Baylor 14
1-1-53 ....Alabama 61, Syracuse 6
1-1-54 ....Oklahoma 7, Maryland 0
1-1-55 ....Duke 34, Nebraska 7
1-2-56 ....Oklahoma 20, Maryland 6
1-1-57 ....Colorado 27, Clemson 21
1-1-58 ....Oklahoma 48, Duke 21
1-1-59 ....Oklahoma 21, Syracuse 6
1-1-60 ....Georgia 14, Missouri 0
1-2-61 ....Missouri 21, Navy 14
1-1-62 ....Louisiana St 25, Colorado 7
1-1-63 ....Alabama 17, Oklahoma 0
1-1-64 ....Nebraska 13, Auburn 7
1-1-65 ....Texas 21, Alabama 17
1-1-66 ....Alabama 39, Nebraska 28
1-2-67 ....Florida 27, Georgia Tech 12
1-1-68 ....Oklahoma 26, Tennessee 24
1-1-69 ....Penn St 15, Kansas 14
1-1-70 ....Penn St 10, Missouri 3
1-1-71 ....Nebraska 17, Louisiana St 12
1-1-72 ....Nebraska 38, Alabama 6
1-1-73 ....Nebraska 40, Notre Dame 6
1-1-74 ....Penn St 16, Louisiana St 9
1-1-75 ....Notre Dame 13, Alabama 11
1-1-76 ....Oklahoma 14, Michigan 6
1-1-77 ....Ohio St 27, Colorado 10
1-2-78 ....Arkansas 31, Oklahoma 6
1-1-79 ....Oklahoma 31, Nebraska 24
1-1-80 ....Oklahoma 24, Florida St 7
1-1-81 ....Oklahoma 18, Florida St 17
1-1-82 ....Clemson 22, Nebraska 15
1-1-83 ....Nebraska 21, Louisiana St 20
1-2-84 ....Miami (FL) 31, Nebraska 30
1-1-85 ....Washington 28, Oklahoma 17
1-1-86 ....Oklahoma 25, Penn St 10
1-1-87 ....Oklahoma 42, Arkansas 8
1-1-88 ....Miami (FL) 20, Oklahoma 14
1-2-89 ....Miami (FL) 23, Nebraska 3
1-1-90 ....Notre Dame 21, Colorado 6
1-1-91 ....Colorado 10, Notre Dame 9
1-1-92 ....Miami (FL) 22, Nebraska 0
1-1-93 ....Florida St 27, Nebraska 14
1-1-94 ....Florida St 18, Nebraska 16
1-1-95 ....Nebraska 24, Miami (FL) 17
1-1-96 ....Florida St 31, Notre Dame 26
12-31-96 ....Nebraska 41, Virginia Tech 21
1-2-98 ....Nebraska 42, Tennessee 17
1-2-99 ....Florida 31, Syracuse 10
1-1-00 ....Michigan 35, Alabama 34 (ot)
1-3-01 ....Oklahoma 13, Florida St 2
1-2-02 ....Florida 56, Maryland 23
1-2-03 ....Southern Cal 38, Iowa 17

City: Miami. Stadium: Pro Player Stadium, capacity 75,192.
Playing Sites: Orange Bowl (1935–96), Pro Player Stadium
(since 1996).

Sugar Bowl

1-1-35 ....Tulane 20, Temple 14
1-1-36 ....Texas Christian 3, Louisiana St 2
1-1-37 ....Santa Clara 21, Louisiana St 14
1-1-38 ....Santa Clara 6, Louisiana St 0
1-2-39 ....Texas Christian 15, Carnegie Tech 7
1-1-40 ....Texas A&M 14, Tulane 13
1-1-41 ....Boston Col 19, Tennessee 13
1-1-42 ....Fordham 2, Missouri 0
1-1-43 ....Tennessee 14, Tulsa 7
1-1-44 ....Georgia Tech 20, Tulsa 18
1-1-45 ....Duke 29, Alabama 26
1-1-46 ....Oklahoma St 33, St. Mary's (CA) 13
1-1-47 ....Georgia 20, N Carolina 10
1-1-48 ....Texas 27, Alabama 7
1-1-49 ....Oklahoma 14, N Carolina 6
1-2-50 ....Oklahoma 35, Louisiana St 0
1-1-51 ....Kentucky 13, Oklahoma 7
1-1-52 ....Maryland 28, Tennessee 13
1-1-53 ....Georgia Tech 24, Mississippi 7
1-1-54 ....Georgia Tech 42, W Virginia 19
1-1-55 ....Navy 21, Mississippi 0
1-2-56 ....Georgia Tech 7, Pittsburgh 0
1-1-57 ....Baylor 13, Tennessee 7
1-1-58 ....Mississippi 39, Texas 7
1-1-59 ....Louisiana St 7, Clemson 0
1-1-60 ....Mississippi 21, Louisiana St 0
1-2-61 ....Mississippi 14, Rice 6
1-1-62 ....Alabama 10, Arkansas 3
1-1-63 ....Mississippi 17, Arkansas 13
1-1-64 ....Alabama 12, Mississippi 7
1-1-65 ....Louisiana St 13, Syracuse 10
1-1-66 ....Missouri 20, Florida 18
1-2-67 ....Alabama 34, Nebraska 7
1-1-68 ....Louisiana St 20, Wyoming 13
1-1-69 ....Arkansas 16, Georgia 2
1-1-70 ....Mississippi 27, Arkansas 22
1-1-71 ....Tennessee 34, Air Force 13
1-1-72 ....Oklahoma 40, Auburn 22
12-31-72 ....Oklahoma 14, Penn St 0
12-31-73 ....Notre Dame 24, Alabama 23
12-31-74 ....Nebraska 13, Florida 10
12-31-75 ....Alabama 13, Penn St 6
1-1-77 ....Pittsburgh 27, Georgia 3
1-2-78 ....Alabama 35, Ohio St 6
1-1-79 ....Alabama 14, Penn St 7
1-1-80 ....Alabama 24, Arkansas 9
1-1-81 ....Georgia 17, Notre Dame 10
1-1-82 ....Pittsburgh 24, Georgia 20
1-1-83 ....Penn St 27, Georgia 23
1-2-84 ....Auburn 9, Michigan 7
1-1-85 ....Nebraska 28, Louisiana St 10
1-1-86 ....Tennessee 35, Miami (FL) 7
1-1-87 ....Nebraska 30, Louisiana St 15
1-1-88 ....Syracuse 16, Auburn 16
1-2-89 ....Florida St 13, Auburn 7
1-1-90 ....Miami (FL) 33, Alabama 25
1-1-91 ....Tennessee 23, Virginia 22
1-1-92 ....Notre Dame 39, Florida 28
1-1-93 ....Alabama 34, Miami (FL) 13
1-1-94 ....Florida 41, West Virginia 7
1-2-95 ....Florida St 23, Florida 17
12-31-95 ....Virginia Tech 28, Texas 10
1-2-97 ....Florida 52, Florida St 20
1-1-98 ....Florida St 31, Ohio St 14
1-1-99 ....Ohio St 24, Texas A&M 14
1-4-00 ....Florida St 46, Virginia Tech 29
1-2-01 ....Miami (FL) 37, Florida 20

Sugar Bowl *(Cont.)*

1-1-02 ....Louisiana St 47, Illinois 34
1-1-03 ....Georgia 26, Florida St 13
City: New Orleans. Stadium: Louisiana Superdome, capacity 76,791.
Playing Sites: Tulane Stadium (1935–74), Louisiana Superdome (since 1975).

Cotton Bowl

1-1-37 ....Texas Christian 16, Marquette 6
1-1-38 ....Rice 28, Colorado 14
1-2-39 ....St. Mary's (CA) 20, Texas Tech 13
1-1-40 ....Clemson 6, Boston Col 3
1-1-41 ....Texas A&M 13, Fordham 12
1-1-42 ....Alabama 29, Texas A&M 21
1-1-43 ....Texas 14, Georgia Tech 7
1-1-44 ....Texas 7, Randolph Field 7
1-1-45 ....Oklahoma St 34, Texas Christian 0
1-1-46 ....Texas 40, Missouri 27
1-1-47 ....Arkansas 0, Louisiana St 0
1-1-48 ....Southern Methodist 13, Penn St 13
1-1-49 ....Southern Methodist 21, Oregon 13
1-2-50 ....Rice 27, N Carolina 13
1-1-51 ....Tennessee 20, Texas 14
1-1-52 ....Kentucky 20, Texas Christian 7
1-1-53 ....Texas 16, Tennessee 0
1-1-54 ....Rice 28, Alabama 6
1-1-55 ....Georgia Tech 14, Arkansas 6
1-2-56 ....Mississippi 14, Texas Christian 13
1-1-57 ....Texas Christian 28, Syracuse 27
1-1-58 ....Navy 20, Rice 7
1-1-59 ....Texas Christian 0, Air Force 0
1-1-60 ....Syracuse 23, Texas 14
1-2-61 ....Duke 7, Arkansas 6
1-1-62 ....Texas 12, Mississippi 7
1-1-63 ....Louisiana St 13, Texas 0
1-1-64 ....Texas 28, Navy 6
1-1-65 ....Arkansas 10, Nebraska 7
1-1-66 ....Louisiana St 14, Arkansas 7
12-31-66 ....Georgia 24, Southern Methodist 9
1-1-68 ....Texas A&M 20, Alabama 16
1-1-69 ....Texas 36, Tennessee 13
1-1-70 ....Texas 21, Notre Dame 17
1-1-71 ....Notre Dame 24, Texas 11
1-1-72 ....Penn St 30, Texas 6
1-1-73 ....Texas 17, Alabama 13
1-1-74 ....Nebraska 19, Texas 3
1-1-75 ....Penn St 41, Baylor 20
1-1-76 ....Arkansas 31, Georgia 10
1-1-77 ....Houston 30, Maryland 21
1-2-78 ....Notre Dame 38, Texas 10
1-1-79 ....Notre Dame 35, Houston 34
1-1-80 ....Houston 17, Nebraska 14
1-1-81 ....Alabama 30, Baylor 2
1-1-82 ....Texas 14, Alabama 12
1-1-83 ....SMU 7, Pittsburgh 3
1-2-84 ....Georgia 10, Texas 9
1-1-85 ....Boston Col 45, Houston 28
1-1-86 ....Texas A&M 36, Auburn 16
1-1-87 ....Ohio St 28, Texas A&M 12
1-1-88 ....Texas A&M 35, Notre Dame 10
1-2-89 ....UCLA 17, Arkansas 3
1-1-90 ....Tennessee 31, Arkansas 27
1-1-91 ....Miami (FL) 46, Texas 3
1-1-92 ....Florida St 10, Texas A&M 2
1-1-93 ....Notre Dame 28, Texas A&M 3
1-1-94 ....Notre Dame 24, Texas A&M 21
1-2-95 ....Southern Cal 55, Texas Tech 14
1-1-96 ....Colorado 38, Oregon 6

Cotton Bowl *(Cont.)*

1-1-97 ....Brigham Young 19, Kansas St 15
1-1-98 ....UCLA 29, Texas A&M 23
1-1-99 ....Texas 38, Mississippi St 11
1-1-00 ....Arkansas 27, Texas 6
1-1-01 ....Kansas St 35, Tennessee 21
1-1-02 ....Oklahoma 10, Arkansas 3
1-1-03 ....Texas 35, Louisiana St 20
City: Dallas. Stadium: Cotton Bowl, capacity 68,252.

Sun Bowl

1-1-36 ....Hardin-Simmons 14, New Mexico St 14
1-1-37 ....Hardin-Simmons 34, UTEP 6
1-1-38 ....W Virginia 7, Texas Tech 6
1-2-39 ....Utah 26, New Mexico 0
1-1-40 ....Catholic 0, Arizona St 0
1-1-41 ....Case Reserve 26, Arizona St 13
1-1-42 ....Tulsa 6, Texas Tech 0
1-1-43 ....2nd Air Force 13, Hardin-Simmons 7
1-1-44 ....Southwestern (TX) 7, New Mexico 0
1-1-45 ....Southwestern (TX) 35, New Mexico 0
1-1-46 ....New Mexico 34, Denver 24
1-1-47 ....Cincinnati 18, Virginia Tech 6
1-1-48 ....Miami (OH) 13, Texas Tech 12
1-1-49 ....W Virginia 21, UTEP 12
1-2-50 ....UTEP 33, Georgetown 20
1-1-51 ....W Texas St 14, Cincinnati 13
1-1-52 ....Texas Tech 25, Pacific 14
1-1-53 ....Pacific 26, Southern Miss 7
1-1-54 ....UTEP 37, Southern Miss 14
1-1-55 ....UTEP 47, Florida St 20
1-2-56 ....Wyoming 21, Texas Tech 14
1-1-57 ....George Washington 13, UTEP 0
1-1-58 ....Louisville 34, Drake 20
12-31-58 ....Wyoming 14, Hardin-Simmons 6
12-31-59 ....New Mexico St 28, N Texas 8
12-31-60 ....New Mexico St 20, Utah St 13
12-30-61 ....Villanova 17, Wichita St 9
12-31-62 ....W Texas St 15, Ohio 14
12-31-63 ....Oregon 21, Southern Methodist 14
12-26-64 ....Georgia 7, Texas Tech 0
12-31-65 ....UTEP 13, Texas Christian 12
12-24-66 ....Wyoming 28, Florida St 20
12-30-67 ....UTEP 14, Mississippi 7
12-28-68 ....Auburn 34, Arizona 10
12-20-69 ....Nebraska 45, Georgia 6
12-19-70 ....Georgia Tech 17, Texas Tech 9
12-18-71 ....Louisiana St 33, Iowa St 15
12-30-72 ....N Carolina 32, Texas Tech 28
12-29-73 ....Missouri 34, Auburn 17
12-28-74 ....Mississippi St 26, N Carolina 24
12-26-75 ....Pittsburgh 33, Kansas 19
1-2-77 ....Texas A&M 37, Florida 14
12-31-77 ....Stanford 24, Louisiana St 14
12-23-78 ....Texas 42, Maryland 0
12-22-79 ....Washington 14, Texas 7
12-27-80 ....Nebraska 31, Mississippi St 17
12-26-81 ....Oklahoma 40, Houston 14
12-25-82 ....N Carolina 26, Texas 10
12-24-83 ....Alabama 28, Southern Methodist 7
12-22-84 ....Maryland 28, Tennessee 27
12-28-85 ....Georgia 13, Arizona 13
12-25-86 ....Alabama 28, Washington 6
12-25-87 ....Oklahoma St 35, W Virginia 33
12-24-88 ....Alabama 29, Army 28
12-30-89 ....Pittsburgh 31, Texas A&M 28
12-31-90 ....Michigan St 17, Southern Cal 16
12-31-91 ....UCLA 6, Illinois 3
12-31-92 ....Baylor 20, Arizona 15

Sun Bowl *(Cont.)*

12-24-93 ....Oklahoma 41, Texas Tech 10
12-30-94 ....Texas 35, N Carolina 31
12-29-95 ....Iowa 38, Washington 18
12-31-96 ....Stanford 38, Michigan St 0
12-31-97 ....Arizona 17, Iowa 7
12-31-98 ....Texas Christian 28, Southern Cal 19
12-31-99 ....Oregon 24, Minnesota 20
12-29-00 ....Wisconsin 21, UCLA 20
12-31-01 ....Washington St 33, Purdue 27
12-31-02 ....Purdue 34, Washington 24

City: El Paso. Stadium: Sun Bowl, capacity 51,270.

Name Changes: Sun Bowl (1936–86; 94–), John Hancock Sun Bowl (1987–88), John Hancock Bowl (1989–93).

Playing Sites: Kidd Field (1936–62), Sun Bowl (since 1963).

Gator Bowl

1-1-46 ....Wake Forest 26, S Carolina 14
1-1-47 ....Oklahoma 34, N Carolina St 13
1-1-48 ....Maryland 20, Georgia 20
1-1-49 ....Clemson 24, Missouri 23
1-2-50 ....Maryland 20, Missouri 7
1-1-51 ....Wyoming 20, Washington & Lee 7
1-1-52 ....Miami (FL) 14, Clemson 0
1-1-53 ....Florida 14, Tulsa 13
1-1-54 ....Texas Tech 35, Auburn 13
12-31-54 ....Auburn 33, Baylor 13
12-31-55 ....Vanderbilt 25, Auburn 13
12-29-56 ....Georgia Tech 21, Pittsburgh 14
12-28-57 ....Tennessee 3, Texas A&M 0
12-27-58 ....Mississippi 7, Florida 3
1-2-60 ....Arkansas 14, Georgia Tech 7
12-31-60 ....Florida 13, Baylor 12
12-30-61 ....Penn St 30, Georgia Tech 15
12-29-62 ....Florida 17, Penn St 7
12-28-63 ....N Carolina 35, Air Force 0
1-2-65 ....Florida St 36, Oklahoma 19
12-31-65 ....Georgia Tech 31, Texas Tech 21
12-31-66 ....Tennessee 18, Syracuse 12
12-30-67 ....Penn St 17, Florida St 17
12-28-68 ....Missouri 35, Alabama 10
12-27-69 ....Florida 14, Tennessee 13
1-2-71 ....Auburn 35, Mississippi 28
12-31-71 ....Georgia 7, N Carolina 3
12-30-72 ....Auburn 24, Colorado 3
12-29-73 ....Texas Tech 28, Tennessee 19
12-30-74 ....Auburn 27, Texas 3
12-29-75 ....Maryland 13, Florida 0
12-27-76 ....Notre Dame 20, Penn St 9
12-30-77 ....Pittsburgh 34, Clemson 3
12-29-78 ....Clemson 17, Ohio St 15
12-28-79 ....N Carolina 17, Michigan 15
12-29-80 ....Pittsburgh 37, S Carolina 9
12-28-81 ....N Carolina 31, Arkansas 27
12-30-82 ....Florida St 31, W Virginia 12
12-30-83 ....Florida 14, Iowa 6
12-28-84 ....Oklahoma St 21, S Carolina 14
12-30-85 ....Florida St 34, Oklahoma St 23
12-27-86 ....Clemson 27, Stanford 21
12-31-87 ....Louisiana St 30, S Carolina 13
1-1-89 ....Georgia 34, Michigan St 27
12-30-89 ....Clemson 27, W Virginia 7
1-1-91 ....Michigan 35, Mississippi 3
12-29-91 ....Oklahoma 48, Virginia 14
12-31-92 ....Florida 27, N Carolina St 10
12-31-93 ....Alabama 24, North Carolina 10
12-30-94 ....Tennessee 45, Virginia Tech 23
1-1-96 ....Syracuse 41, Clemson 0
1-1-97 ....N Carolina 20, W Virginia 13
1-1-98 ....N Carolina 42, Viginia Tech 13
1-1-99 ....Georgia Tech 35, Notre Dame 28

Gator Bowl (Cont.)

1-1-00 ....Miami 27, Georgia Tech 13
1-1-01 ....Virginia Tech 41, Clemson 20
1-1-02 ....Florida St 30, Virginia Tech 17
1-1-03 ....N Carolina St 28, Notre Dame 6

City: Jacksonville, FL. Stadium: Alltel Stadium, capacity 76,976.

Florida Citrus Bowl

1-1-47 ....Catawba 31, Maryville (TN) 6
1-1-48 ....Catawba 7, Marshall 0
1-1-49 ....Murray St 21, Sul Ross St 21
1-2-50 ....St. Vincent 7, Emory & Henry 6
1-1-51 ....Morris Harvey 35, Emory & Henry 14
1-1-52 ....Stetson 35, Arkansas St 20
1-1-53 ....E Texas St 33, Tennessee Tech 0
1-1-54 ....E Texas St 7, Arkansas St 7
1-1-55 ....NE-Omaha 7, Eastern Kentucky 6
1-2-56 ....Juniata 6, Missouri Valley 6
1-1-57 ....W Texas St 20, Southern Miss 13
1-1-58 ....E Texas St 10, Southern Miss 9
12-27-58 ....E Texas St 26, Missouri Valley 7
1-1-60 ....Middle Tennessee St 21, Presbyterian 12
12-30-60 ....Citadel 27, Tennessee Tech 0
12-29-61 ....Lamar 21, Middle Tennessee St 14
12-22-62 ....Houston 49, Miami (OH) 21
12-28-63 ....Western Kentucky 27, Coast Guard 0
12-12-64 ....E Carolina 14, Massachusetts 13
12-11-65 ....E Carolina 31, Maine 0
12-10-66 ....Morgan St 14, W Chester 6
12-16-67 ....TN-Martin 25, W Chester 8
12-27-68 ....Richmond 49, Ohio 42
12-26-69 ....Toledo 56, Davidson 33
12-28-70 ....Toledo 40, William & Mary 12
12-28-71 ....Toledo 28, Richmond 3
12-29-72 ....Tampa 21, Kent St 18
12-22-73 ....Miami (OH) 16, Florida 7
12-21-74 ....Miami (OH) 21, Georgia 10
12-20-75 ....Miami (OH) 20, S Carolina 7
12-18-76 ....Oklahoma St 49, Brigham Young 21
12-23-77 ....Florida St 40, Texas Tech 17
12-23-78 ....N Carolina St 30, Pittsburgh 17
12-22-79 ....Louisiana St 34, Wake Forest 10
12-20-80 ....Florida 35, Maryland 20
12-19-81 ....Missouri 19, Southern Miss 17
12-18-82 ....Auburn 33, Boston Col 26
12-17-83 ....Tennessee 30, Maryland 23
12-22-84 ....Georgia 17, Florida St 17
12-28-85 ....Ohio St 10, Brigham Young 7
1-1-87 ....Auburn 16, Southern Cal 7
1-1-88 ....Clemson 35, Penn St 10
1-2-89 ....Clemson 13, Oklahoma 6
1-1-90 ....Illinois 31, Virginia 21
1-1-91 ....Georgia Tech 45, Nebraska 21
1-1-92 ....California 37, Clemson 13
1-1-93 ....Georgia 21, Ohio State 14
1-1-94 ....Penn State 31, Tennessee 13
1-2-95 ....Alabama 24, Ohio St 17
1-1-96 ....Tennessee 20, Ohio St 14
1-1-97 ....Tennessee 48, Northwestern 28
1-1-98 ....Florida 21, Penn St 6
1-1-99 ....Michigan 45, Arkansas 31
1-1-00 ....Michigan St 37, Florida 34
1-1-01 ....Michigan 31, Auburn 28
1-1-02 ....Tennessee 45, Michigan 17
1-1-03 ....Auburn 13, Penn St 9

City: Orlando, FL. Stadium: Florida Citrus Bowl, capacity 70,000.

Name Change: Tangerine Bowl (1947–82).

Playing Sites: Tangerine Bowl (1947–72, 1974–82); Florida Field, Gainesville (1973); Orlando Stadium/Florida Citrus Bowl-Orlando (since 1983).

Liberty Bowl

12-19-59 ....Penn St 7, Alabama 0
12-17-60 ....Penn St 41, Oregon 12
12-16-61 ....Syracuse 15, Miami (FL) 14
12-15-62 ....Oregon St 6, Villanova 0
12-21-63 ....Mississippi St 16, N Carolina St 12
12-19-64 ....Utah 32, W Virginia 6
12-18-65 ....Mississippi 13, Auburn 7
12-10-66 ....Miami (FL) 14, Virginia Tech 7
12-16-67 ....N Carolina St 14, Georgia 7
12-14-68 ....Mississippi 34, Virginia Tech 17
12-13-69 ....Colorado 47, Alabama 33
12-12-70 ....Tulane 17, Colorado 3
12-20-71 ....Tennessee 14, Arkansas 13
12-18-72 ....Georgia Tech 31, Iowa St 30
12-17-73 ....N Carolina St 31, Kansas 18
12-16-74 ....Tennessee 7, Maryland 3
12-22-75 ....Southern Cal 20, Texas A&M 0
12-20-76 ....Alabama 36, UCLA 6
12-19-77 ....Nebraska 21, N Carolina 17
12-23-78 ....Missouri 20, Louisiana St 15
12-22-79 ....Penn St 9, Tulane 6
12-27-80 ....Purdue 28, Missouri 25
12-30-81 ....Ohio St 31, Navy 28
12-29-82 ....Alabama 21, Illinois 15
12-29-83 ....Notre Dame 19, Boston Col 18
12-27-84 ....Auburn 21, Arkansas 15
12-27-85 ....Baylor 21, Louisiana St 7
12-29-86 ....Tennessee 21, Minnesota 14
12-29-87 ....Georgia 20, Arkansas 17
12-28-88 ....Indiana 34, S Carolina 10
12-28-89 ....Mississippi 42, Air Force 29
12-27-90 ....Air Force 23, Ohio St 11
12-29-91 ....Air Force 38, Mississippi St 15
12-31-92 ....Mississippi 13, Air Force 0
12-28-93 ....Louisville 18, Michigan St 7
12-31-94 ....Illinois 30, E Carolina 0
12-30-95 ....East Carolina 19, Stanford 13
12-27-96 ....Syracuse 30, Houston 17
12-31-97 ....Southern Miss 41, Pittsburgh 7
12-31-98 ....Tulane 41, Brigham Young 27
12-31-99 ....Southern Miss 23, Colorado St 17
12-29-01 ....Colorado St 22, Louisville 17
12-31-01 ....Louisville 28, Brigham Young 10
12-31-02 ....Texas Christian 17, Colorado St 3

City: Memphis (since 1965). Stadium: Liberty Bowl Memorial Stadium, capacity 62,921.

Playing Sites: Philadelphia (Municipal Stadium, 1959–63), Atlantic City (Convention Center, 1964).

Bluebonnet Bowl

12-19-59 ....Clemson 23, Texas Christian 7
12-17-60 ....Texas 3, Alabama 3
12-16-61 ....Kansas 33, Rice 7
12-22-62 ....Missouri 14, Georgia Tech 10
12-21-63 ....Baylor 14, LSU 7
12-19-64 ....Tulsa 14, Mississippi 7
12-18-65 ....Tennessee 27, Tulsa 6
12-17-66 ....Texas 19, Mississippi 0
12-23-67 ....Colorado 31, Miami (FL) 21
12-31-68 ....Southern Methodist 28, Oklahoma 27
12-31-69 ....Houston 36, Auburn 7
12-31-70 ....Alabama 24, Oklahoma 24
12-31-71 ....Colorado 29, Houston 17
12-30-72 ....Tennessee 24, Louisiana St 17
12-29-73 ....Houston 47, Tulane 7
12-23-74 ....N Carolina St 31, Houston 31
12-27-75 ....Texas 38, Colorado 21
12-31-76 ....Nebraska 27, Texas Tech 24
12-31-77 ....Southern Cal 47, Texas A&M 28
12-31-78 ....Stanford 25, Georgia 22
12-31-79 ....Purdue 27, Tennessee 22

Bluebonnet Bowl *(Cont.)*

12-31-80 ....N Carolina 16, Texas 7
12-31-81 ....Michigan 33, UCLA 14
12-31-82 ....Arkansas 28, Florida 24
12-31-83 ....Oklahoma St 24, Baylor 14
12-31-84 ....W Virginia 31, Texas Christian 14
12-31-85 ....Air Force 24, Texas 16
12-31-86 ....Baylor 21, Colorado 9
12-31-87 ....Texas 32, Pittsburgh 27

City: Houston. Playing sites: Rice Stadium (1959–67; 1985–86), Astrodome (1968–84, 1987).

Name change: Astro-Bluebonnet Bowl (1968–76). Bowl was discontinued after 1987.

Peach Bowl

12-30-68 ....Louisiana St 31, Florida St 27
12-30-69 ....W Virginia 14, S Carolina 3
12-30-70 ....Arizona St 48, N Carolina 26
12-30-71 ....Mississippi 41, Georgia Tech 18
12-29-72 ....N Carolina St 49, W Virginia 13
12-28-73 ....Georgia 17, Maryland 16
12-28-74 ....Vanderbilt 6, Texas Tech 6
12-31-75 ....W Virginia 13, N Carolina St 10
12-31-76 ....Kentucky 21, N Carolina 0
12-31-77 ....N Carolina St 24, Iowa St 14
12-25-78 ....Purdue 41, Georgia Tech 21
12-31-79 ....Baylor 24, Clemson 18
1-2-81 ....Miami (FL) 20, Virginia Tech 10
12-31-81 ....W Virginia 26, Florida 6
12-31-82 ....Iowa 28, Tennessee 22
12-30-83 ....Florida St 28, N Carolina 3
12-31-84 ....Virginia 27, Purdue 24
12-31-85 ....Army 31, Illinois 29
12-31-86 ....Virginia Tech 25, N Carolina St 24
1-2-88 ....Tennessee 27, Indiana 22
12-31-88 ....N Carolina St 28, Iowa 23
12-30-89 ....Syracuse 19, Georgia 18
12-29-90 ....Auburn 27, Indiana 23
1-1-92 ....E Carolina 37, N Carolina St 34
1-2-93 ....N Carolina 21, Mississippi St 17
12-31-93 ....Clemson 14, Kentucky 13
1-1-95 ....N Carolina St 28, Mississippi St 24
12-30-95 ....Virginia 34, Georgia 27
12-28-96 ....Louisiana St 10, Clemson 7
1-2-98 ....Auburn 21, Clemson 17
12-31-98 ....Georgia 35, Virginia 33
12-30-99 ....Mississippi St 17, Clemson 7
12-29-00 ....Louisiana St 28, Georgia Tech 14
12-31-01 ....N Carolina 16, Auburn 10
12-31-02 ....Maryland 30, Tennessee 3

City: Atlanta. Stadium: Georgia Dome, capacity 71,500. Playing Sites: Grant Field (1968–70), Atlanta–Fulton County Stadium (1971–92), Georgia Dome (since 1993).

Fiesta Bowl

12-27-71 ....Arizona St 45, Florida St 38
12-23-72 ....Arizona St 49, Missouri 35
12-21-73 ....Arizona St 28, Pittsburgh 7
12-28-74 ....Oklahoma St 16, Brigham Young 6
12-26-75 ....Arizona St 17, Nebraska 14
12-25-76 ....Oklahoma 41, Wyoming 7
12-25-77 ....Penn St 42, Arizona St 30
12-25-78 ....Arkansas 10, UCLA 10
12-25-79 ....Pittsburgh 16, Arizona 10
12-26-80 ....Penn St 31, Ohio St 19
1-1-82 ....Penn St 26, Southern Cal 10
1-1-83 ....Arizona St 32, Oklahoma 21
1-2-84 ....Ohio St 28, Pittsburgh 23
1-1-85 ....UCLA 39, Miami (FL) 37
1-1-86 ....Michigan 27, Nebraska 23
1-2-87 ....Penn St 14, Miami (FL) 10

Fiesta Bowl *(Cont.)*

1-1-88 ....Florida St 31, Nebraska 28
1-2-89 ....Notre Dame 34, W Virginia 21
1-1-90 ....Florida St 41, Nebraska 17
1-1-91 ....Louisville 34, Alabama 7
1-1-92 ....Penn St 42, Tennessee 17
1-1-93 ....Syracuse 26, Colorado 22
1-1-94 ....Arizona 29, Miami (FL) 0
1-2-95 ....Colorado 41, Notre Dame 24
1-2-96 ....Nebraska 62, Florida 24
1-1-97 ....Penn St 38, Texas 15
12-31-97 ....Kansas St 35, Syracuse 18
1-4-99 ....Tennessee 23, Florida St 16
1-2-00 ....Nebraska 31, Tennessee 21
1-1-01 ....Oregon St 41, Notre Dame 9
1-1-02 ....Oregon 38, Colorado 16
1-3-03 ....Ohio St 31, Miami (FL) 24 [2 OT]

City: Tempe, AZ. Stadium: Sun Devil Stadium, capacity 73,471.

Independence Bowl

12-13-76 ....McNeese St 20, Tulsa 16
12-17-77 ....Louisiana Tech 24, Louisville 14
12-16-78 ....E Carolina 35, Louisiana Tech 13
12-15-79 ....Syracuse 31, McNeese St 7
12-13-80 ....Southern Miss 16, McNeese St 14
12-12-81 ....Texas A&M 33, Oklahoma St 16
12-11-82 ....Wisconsin 14, Kansas St 3
12-10-83 ....Air Force 9, Mississippi 3
12-15-84 ....Air Force 23, Virginia Tech 7
12-21-85 ....Minnesota 20, Clemson 13
12-20-86 ....Mississippi 20, Texas Tech 17
12-19-87 ....Washington 24, Tulane 12
12-23-88 ....Southern Miss 38, UTEP 18
12-16-89 ....Oregon 27, Tulsa 24
12-15-90 ....Louisiana Tech 34, Maryland 34
12-29-91 ....Georgia 24, Arkansas 15
12-31-92 ....Wake Forest 39, Oregon 35
12-31-93 ....Virginia Tech 45, Indiana 20
12-28-94 ....Virginia 20, Texas Christian 10
12-29-95 ....Louisiana St 45, Michigan St 26
12-31-96 ....Auburn 32, Army 29
12-28-97 ....Louisiana St 27, Notre Dame 9
12-31-98 ....Mississippi 35, Texas Tech 18
12-31-99 ....Mississippi 27, Oklahoma 25
12-31-00 ....Mississippi St 43, Texas A&M 41
12-27-01 ....Alabama 14, Iowa St 13
12-27-02 ....Mississippi 27, Nebraska 23

City: Shreveport, LA. Stadium: Independence Stadium, capacity 50,459.

All-American Bowl

12-22-77 ....Maryland 17, Minnesota 7
12-20-78 ....Texas A&M 28, Iowa St 12
12-29-79 ....Missouri 24, S Carolina 14
12-27-80 ....Arkansas 34, Tulane 15
12-31-81 ....Mississippi St 10, Kansas 0
12-31-82 ....Air Force 36, Vanderbilt 28
12-22-83 ....W Virginia 20, Kentucky 16
12-29-84 ....Kentucky 20, Wisconsin 19
12-31-85 ....Georgia Tech 17, Michigan St 14
12-31-86 ....Florida St 27, Indiana 13
12-22-87 ....Virginia 22, Brigham Young 16
12-29-88 ....Florida 14, Illinois 10
12-28-89 ....Texas Tech 49, Duke 21
12-28-90 ....N Carolina St 31, Southern Miss. 27

City: Birmingham, AL. Stadium: Legion Field.
Name Change: Hall of Fame Classic (1977–84). Bowl was discontinued after 1990.

Holiday Bowl

12-22-78 ....Navy 23, Brigham Young 16
12-21-79 ....Indiana 38, Brigham Young 37
12-19-80 ....Brigham Young 46, SMU 45
12-18-81 ....Brigham Young 38, Washington St 36
12-17-82 ....Ohio St 47, Brigham Young 17
12-23-83 ....Brigham Young 21, Missouri 17
12-21-84 ....Brigham Young 24, Michigan 17
12-22-85 ....Arkansas 18, Arizona St 17
12-30-86 ....Iowa 39, San Diego St 38
12-30-87 ....Iowa 20, Wyoming 19
12-30-88 ....Oklahoma St 62, Wyoming 14
12-29-89 ....Penn St 50, Brigham Young 39
12-29-90 ....Texas A&M 65, Brigham Young 14
12-30-91 ....Iowa 13, Brigham Young 13
12-30-92 ....Hawaii 27, Illinois 17
12-30-93 ....Ohio St 28, Brigham Young 21
12-30-94 ....Michigan 24, Colorado St 14
12-29-95 ....Kansas St 54, Colorado St 21
12-30-96 ....Colorado 33, Washington 21
12-29-97 ....Colorado St 35, Missouri 24
12-30-98 ....Arizona 23, Nebraska 20
12-29-99 ....Kansas St 24, Washington 20
12-29-00 ....Oregon 35, Texas 30
12-28-01 ....Texas 47, Washington 43
12-27-02 ....Kansas St 34, Arizona St 27

City: San Diego. Stadium: Qualcomm Stadium, capacity 70,000.

Las Vegas Bowl

12-19-81 ....Toledo 27, San Jose St 25
12-18-82 ....Fresno St 29, Bowling Green 28
12-17-83 ....Northern Illinois 20, Cal St–Fullerton 13
12-15-84 ....UNLV 30, Toledo 13*
12-14-85 ....Fresno St 51, Bowling Green 7
12-13-86 ....San Jose St 37, Miami (OH) 7
12-12-87 ....Eastern Michigan 30, San Jose St 27
12-10-88 ....Fresno St 35, Western Michigan 30
12-9-89 ....Fresno St 27, Ball St 6
12-8-90 ....San Jose St 48, Central Michigan 24
12-14-91 ....Bowling Green 28, Fresno St 21
12-18-92 ....Bowling Green 35, Nevada 34
12-17-93 ....Utah St 42, Ball St 33
12-15-94 ....UNLV 52, Central Michigan 24
12-14-95 ....Toledo 40, Nevada 37
12-19-96 ....Nevada 18, Ball St 15
12-19-97 ....Oregon 41, Air Force 13
12-19-98 ....N Carolina 20, San Diego St 13
12-18-99 ....Utah 17, Fresno St 16
12-21-00 ....UNLV 31, Arkansas 14
12-25-01 ....Utah 10, Southern Cal 6
12-25-02 ....UCLA 27, New Mexico 13

* Toledo won later by forfeit.

City: Las Vegas (since 1992). Stadium: Sam Boyd Silver Bowl Stadium, capacity 40,000.
Name change: California Bowl (1981–91).
Playing sites: Fresno, CA (Bulldog Stadium, 1981–91), Las Vegas.

Aloha Bowl

12-25-82 ....Washington 21, Maryland 20
12-26-83 ....Penn St 13, Washington 10
12-29-84 ....Southern Methodist 27, Notre Dame 20
12-28-85 ....Alabama 24, Southern Cal 3
12-27-86 ....Arizona 30, N Carolina 21
12-25-87 ....UCLA 20, Florida 16
12-25-88 ....Washington St 24, Houston 22
12-25-89 ....Michigan St 33, Hawaii 13
12-25-90 ....Syracuse 28, Arizona 0
12-25-91 ....Georgia Tech 18, Stanford 17
12-25-92 ....Kansas 23, Brigham Young 20

Aloha Bowl (Cont.)

12-25-93 ....Colorado 41, Fresno St 30
12-25-94 ....Boston College 12, Kansas St 7
12-25-95 ....Kansas 51, UCLA 30
12-25-96 ....Navy 42, California 38
12-25-97 ....Washington 51, Michigan St 23
12-25-98 ....Colorado 51, Oregon 43
12-25-99 ....Wake Forest 23, Arizona St 3
12-25-00 ....Boston College 31, Arizona St 17

City: Honolulu. Stadium: Aloha Stadium. Bowl was discontinued after 2000.

Freedom Bowl

12-16-84 ....Iowa 55, Texas 17
12-30-85 ....Washington 20, Colorado 17
12-30-86 ....UCLA 31, Brigham Young 10
12-30-87 ....Arizona St 33, Air Force 28
12-29-88 ....Brigham Young 20, Colorado 17
12-29-90 ....Colorado St 32, Oregon 31
12-30-91 ....Tulsa 28, San Diego St 17
12-29-92 ....Fresno St 24, Southern Cal 7
12-30-93 ....Southern Cal 28, Utah 21
12-29-94 ....Utah 16, Arizona 13

City: Anaheim. Stadium: Anaheim Stadium. Bowl was discontinued after 1994.

Outback Bowl

12-23-86 ....Boston College 27, Georgia 24
1-2-88 ....Michigan 28, Alabama 24
1-2-89 ....Syracuse 23, Louisiana St 10
1-1-90 ....Auburn 31, Ohio St 14
1-1-91 ....Clemson 30, Illinois 0
1-1-92 ....Syracuse 24, Ohio St 17
1-1-93 ....Tennessee 38, Boston College 23
1-1-94 ....Michigan 42, N Carolina St 7
1-2-95 ....Wisconsin 34, Duke 20
1-1-96 ....Penn St 43, Auburn 14
1-1-97 ....Alabama 17, Michigan 14
1-1-98 ....Georgia 33, Wisconsin 6
1-1-99 ....Penn St 26, Kentucky 14
1-1-00 ....Georgia 28, Purdue 25
1-1-01 ....S Carolina 24, Ohio St 7
1-1-02 ....S Carolina 31, Ohio St 28
1-1-03 ....Michigan 38, Florida 30

City: Tampa. Stadium: Raymond James Stadium, capacity 75,000. Name change: Hall of Fame Bowl (1986–95).

Insight.com Bowl

12-31-89 ....Arizona 17, N Carolina St 10
12-31-90 ....California 17, Wyoming 15
12-31-91 ....Indiana 24, Baylor 0
12-29-92 ....Washington St 31, Utah 28
12-29-93 ....Kansas St 52, Wyoming 17
12-29-94 ....Brigham Young 31, Oklahoma 6
12-27-95 ....Texas Tech 55, Air Force 41
12-27-96 ....Wisconsin 38, Utah 10
12-27-97 ....Arizona 20, New Mexico 14
12-26-98 ....Missouri 34, W Virginia 31
12-31-99 ....Colorado 62, Boston College 28
12-28-00 ....Iowa St 37, Pittsburgh 29
12-29-01 ....Syracuse 26, Kansas St 3
12-26-02 ....Pittsburgh 38, Oregon St 13

City: Tucson. Stadium: Arizona Stadium, capacity 55,883. Name change: Copper Bowl 1989–97.

Tangerine Bowl

12-28-90 ....Florida St 24, Penn St 17
12-28-91 ....Alabama 30, Colorado 25
1-1-93 ....Stanford 24, Penn St 3
1-1-94 ....Boston College 31, Virginia 13
1-2-95 ....S Carolina 24, W Virginia 21
12-30-95 ....N Carolina 20, Arkansas 10
12-27-96 ....Miami (FL) 31, Virginia 21
12-29-97 ....Georgia Tech 35, W Virginia 30
12-29-98 ....Miami (FL) 46, N Carolina St 23
12-30-99 ....Illinois 62, Virginia 21
12-28-00 ....N Carolina St 38, Minnesota 30
12-20-01 ....Pittsburgh 34, N Carolina St 19
12-23-02 ....Texas Tech 55, Clemson 15

City: Miami. Stadium: Pro-Player Stadium, capacity 75,192. Name change: Blockbuster Bowl (1990–93), Carquest Bowl (1994–97), Micron PC Bowl (1998–00).

Alamo Bowl

12-31-93 ....California 37, Iowa 3
12-31-94 ....Washington St 10, Baylor 3
12-28-95 ....Texas A&M 22, Michigan 20
12-29-96 ....Iowa 27, Texas Tech 0
12-30-97 ....Purdue 33, Oklahoma St 20
12-29-98 ....Purdue 37, Kansas St 34
12-28-99 ....Penn St 24, Texas A&M 0
12-30-00 ....Nebraska 66, Northwestern 17
12-29-01 ....Iowa 16, Texas Tech 13
12-28-02 ....Wisconsin 31, Colorado 28 (OT)

City: San Antonio, TX. Stadium: Alamodome, capacity 67,000.

YET ANOTHER SIGN OF THE APOCALYPSE

USC players and coaches asked for autographs from O.J. Simpson when he showed up at a Trojans practice a few days before the 2003 Orange Bowl.

1936

		Record	Coach
1.	Minnesota	7-1-0	Bernie Bierman
2.	Louisiana St	9-0-1	Bernie Moore
3.	Pittsburgh	7-1-1	Jack Sutherland
4.	Alabama	8-0-1	Frank Thomas
5.	Washington	7-1-1	Jimmy Phelan
6.	Santa Clara	7-1-0	Buck Shaw
7.	Northwestern	7-1-0	Pappy Waldorf
8.	Notre Dame	6-2-1	Elmer Layden
9.	Nebraska	7-2-0	Dana X. Bible
10.	Pennsylvania	7-1-0	Harvey Harman
11.	Duke	9-1-0	Wallace Wade
12.	Yale	7-1-0	Ducky Pond
13.	Dartmouth	7-1-1	Red Blaik
14.	Duquesne	7-2-0	John Smith
15.	Fordham	5-1-2	Jim Crowley
16.	Texas Christian	8-2-2	Dutch Meyer
17.	Tennessee	6-2-2	Bob Neyland
18.	Arkansas	7-3-0	Fred Thomsen
19.	Navy	6-3-0	Tom Hamilton
20.	Marquette	7-1-0	Frank Murray

1937

		Record	Coach
1.	Pittsburgh	9-0-1	Jack Sutherland
2.	California	9-0-1	Stub Allison
3.	Fordham	7-0-1	Jim Crowley
4.	Alabama	9-0-0	Frank Thomas
5.	Minnesota	6-2-0	Bernie Bierman
6.	Villanova	8-0-1	Clipper Smith
7.	Dartmouth	7-0-2	Red Blaik
8.	Louisiana St	9-1-0	Bernie Moore
9.	Notre Dame	6-2-1	Elmer Layden
	Santa Clara	8-0-0	Buck Shaw
11.	Nebraska	6-1-2	Biff Jones
12.	Yale	6-1-1	Ducky Pond
13.	Ohio St	6-2-0	Francis Schmidt
14.	Holy Cross	8-0-2	Eddie Anderson
	Arkansas	6-2-2	Fred Thomsen
16.	Texas Christian	4-2-2	Dutch Meyer
17.	Colorado	8-0-0	Bunnie Oakes
18.	Rice	5-3-2	Jimmy Kitts
19.	N Carolina	7-1-1	Ray Wolf
20.	Duke	7-2-1	Wallace Wade

1938

		Record	Coach
1.	Texas Christian	10-0-0	Dutch Meyer
2.	Tennessee	10-0-0	Bob Neyland
3.	Duke	9-0-0	Wallace Wade
4.	Oklahoma	10-0-0	Tom Stidham
5.	#Notre Dame	8-1-0	Elmer Layden
6.	Carnegie Tech	7-1-0	Bill Kern
7.	Southern Cal	8-2-0	Howard Jones
8.	Pittsburgh	8-2-0	Jack Sutherland
9.	Holy Cross	8-1-0	Eddie Anderson
10.	Minnesota	6-2-0	Bernie Bierman
11.	Texas Tech	10-0-0	Pete Cawthon
12.	Cornell	5-1-1	Carl Snavely
13.	Alabama	7-1-1	Frank Thomas
14.	California	10-1-0	Stub Allison
15.	Fordham	6-1-2	Jim Crowley
16.	Michigan	6-1-1	Fritz Crisler
17.	Northwestern	4-2-2	Pappy Waldorf

1938 (Cont.)

		Record	Coach
18.	Villanova	8-0-1	Clipper Smith
19.	Tulane	7-2-1	Red Dawson
20.	Dartmouth	7-2-0	Red Blaik

#Selected No. 1 by the Dickinson System.

1939

		Record	Coach
1.	Texas A&M	10-0-0	Homer Norton
2.	Tennessee	10-0-0	Bob Neyland
3.	#Southern Cal	7-0-2	Howard Jones
4.	Cornell	8-0-0	Carl Snavely
5.	Tulane	8-0-1	Red Dawson
6.	Missouri	8-1-0	Don Faurot
7.	UCLA	6-0-4	Babe Horrell
8.	Duke	8-1-0	Wallace Wade
9.	Iowa	6-1-1	Eddie Anderson
10.	Duquesne	8-0-1	Buff Donelli
11.	Boston College	9-1-0	Frank Leahy
12.	Clemson	8-1-0	Jess Neely
13.	Notre Dame	7-2-0	Elmer Layden
14.	Santa Clara	5-1-3	Buck Shaw
15.	Ohio St	6-2-0	Francis Schmidt
16.	Georgia Tech	7-2-0	Bill Alexander
17.	Fordham	6-2-0	Jim Crowley
18.	Nebraska	7-1-1	Biff Jones
19.	Oklahoma	6-2-1	Tom Stidham
20.	Michigan	6-2-0	Fritz Crisler

#Selected No. 1 by the Dickinson System.

1940

		Record	Coach
1.	Minnesota	8-0-0	Bernie Bierman
2.	Stanford	9-0-0	C. Shaughnessy
3.	Michigan	7-1-0	Fritz Crisler
4.	Tennessee	10-0-0	Bob Neyland
5.	Boston College	10-0-0	Frank Leahy
6.	Texas A&M	8-1-0	Homer Norton
7.	Nebraska	8-1-0	Biff Jones
8.	Northwestern	6-2-0	Pappy Waldorf
9.	Mississippi St	9-0-1	Allyn McKeen
10.	Washington	7-2-0	Jimmy Phelan
11.	Santa Clara	6-1-1	Buck Shaw
12.	Fordham	7-1-0	Jim Crowley
13.	Georgetown	8-1-0	Jack Hagerty
14.	Pennsylvania	6-1-1	George Munger
15.	Cornell	6-2-0	Carl Snavely
16.	SMU	8-1-1	Matty Bell
17.	Hard.-Simmons	9-0-0	Abe Woodson
18.	Duke	7-2-0	Wallace Wade
19.	Lafayette	9-0-0	Hooks Mylin
20.	—		

Only 19 teams selected.

1941

		Record	Coach
1.	Minnesota	8-0-0	Bernie Bierman
2.	Duke	9-0-0	Wallace Wade
3.	Notre Dame	8-0-1	Frank Leahy
4.	Texas	8-1-1	Dana X. Bible
5.	Michigan	6-1-1	Fritz Crisler
6.	Fordham	7-1-0	Jim Crowley
7.	Missouri	8-1-0	Don Faurot
8.	Duquesne	8-0-0	Buff Donelli
9.	Texas A&M	9-1-0	Homer Norton
10.	Navy	7-1-1	Swede Larson
11.	Northwestern	5-3-0	Pappy Waldorf
12.	Oregon St	7-2-0	Lon Stiner
13.	Ohio St	6-1-1	Paul Brown
14.	Georgia	8-1-1	Wally Butts
15.	Pennsylvania	7-1-1	George Munger
16.	Mississippi St	8-1-1	Allyn McKeen
17.	Mississippi	6-2-1	Harry Mehre
18.	Tennessee	8-2-0	John Barnhill
19.	Washington St	6-4-0	Babe Hollingbery
20.	Alabama	8-2-0	Frank Thomas

1942

		Record	Coach
1.	Ohio St	9-1-0	Paul Brown
2.	Georgia	10-1-0	Wally Butts
3.	Wisconsin	8-1-1	H. Stuhldreher
4.	Tulsa	10-0-0	Henry Frnka
5.	Georgia Tech	9-1-0	Bill Alexander
6.	Notre Dame	7-2-2	Frank Leahy
7.	Tennessee	8-1-1	John Barnhill
8.	Boston College	8-1-0	Denny Myers
9.	Michigan	7-3-0	Fritz Crisler
10.	Alabama	7-3-0	Frank Thomas
11.	Texas	8-2-0	Dana X. Bible
12.	Stanford	6-4-0	Marchie Schwartz
13.	UCLA	7-3-0	Babe Horrell
14.	William & Mary	9-1-1	Carl Voyles
15.	Santa Clara	7-2-0	Buck Shaw
16.	Auburn	6-4-1	Jack Meagher
17.	Washington St	6-2-2	Babe Hollingbery
18.	Mississippi St	8-2-0	Allyn McKeen
19.	Minnesota	5-4-0	George Hauser
	Holy Cross	5-4-1	Ank Scanlon
	Penn St	6-1-1	Bob Higgins

1943

		Record	Coach
1.	Notre Dame	9-1-0	Frank Leahy
2.	Iowa Pre-Flight	9-1-0	Don Faurot
3.	Michigan	8-1-0	Fritz Crisler
4.	Navy	8-1-0	Billick Whelchel
5.	Purdue	9-0-0	Elmer Burnham
6.	Great Lakes	10-2-0	Tony Hinkle
7.	Duke	8-1-0	Eddie Cameron
8.	Del Monte P-F	7-1-0	Bill Kern
9.	Northwestern	6-2-0	Pappy Waldorf
10.	March Field	9-1-0	Paul Schissler
11.	Army	7-2-1	Red Blaik
12.	Washington	4-0-0	Ralph Welch
13.	Georgia Tech	7-3-0	Bill Alexander

1943 (Cont.)

		Record	Coach
14.	Texas	7-1-0	Dana X. Bible
15.	Tulsa	6-0-1	Henry Frnka
16.	Dartmouth	6-1-0	Earl Brown
17.	Bainbridge NTS	7-0-0	Joe Maniaci
18.	Colorado College	7-0-0	Hal White
19.	Pacific	7-2-0	Amos A. Stagg
20.	Pennsylvania	6-2-1	George Munger

1944

		Record	Coach
1.	Army	9-0-0	Red Blaik
2.	Ohio St	9-0-0	Carroll Widdoes
3.	Randolph Field	11-0-0	Frank Tritico
4.	Navy	6-3-0	Oscar Hagberg
5.	Bainbridge NTS	9-0-0	Joe Maniaci
6.	Iowa Pre-Flight	10-1-0	Jack Meagher
7.	Southern Cal	7-0-2	Jeff Cravath
8.	Michigan	8-2-0	Fritz Crisler
9.	Notre Dame	8-2-0	Ed McKeever
10.	March Field	7-1-2	Paul Schissler
11.	Duke	5-4-0	Eddie Cameron
12.	Tennessee	8-0-1	John Barnhill
13.	Georgia Tech	8-2-0	Bill Alexander
	Norman P-F	6-0-0	John Gregg
15.	Illinois	5-4-1	Ray Eliot
16.	El Toro Marines	8-1-0	Dick Hanley
17.	Great Lakes	9-2-1	Paul Brown
18.	Fort Pierce	9-0-0	Hamp Pool
19.	St. Mary's P-F	4-4-0	Jules Sikes
20.	2nd Air Force	7-2-1	Bill Reese

1945

		Record	Coach
1.	Army	9-0-0	Red Blaik
2.	Alabama	9-0-0	Frank Thomas
3.	Navy	7-1-1	Oscar Hagberg
4.	Indiana	9-0-1	Bo McMillan
5.	Oklahoma A&M	8-0-0	Jim Lookabaugh
6.	Michigan	7-3-0	Fritz Crisler
7.	St. Mary's (CA)	7-1-0	Jimmy Phelan
8.	Pennsylvania	6-2-0	George Munger
9.	Notre Dame	7-2-1	Hugh Devore
10.	Texas	9-1-0	Dana X. Bible
11.	Southern Cal	7-3-0	Jeff Cravath
12.	Ohio St	7-2-0	Carroll Widdoes
13.	Duke	6-2-0	Eddie Cameron
14.	Tennessee	8-1-0	John Barnhill
15.	Louisiana St	7-2-0	Bernie Moore
16.	Holy Cross	8-1-0	John DeGrosa
17.	Tulsa	8-2-0	Henry Frnka
18.	Georgia	8-2-0	Wally Butts
19.	Wake Forest	4-3-1	Peahead Walker
20.	Columbia	8-1-0	Lou Little

1946

		Record	Coach
1.	Notre Dame	8-0-1	Frank Leahy
2.	Army	9-0-1	Red Blaik
3.	Georgia	10-0-0	Wally Butts
4.	UCLA	10-0-0	B. LaBrucherie

Note: Except where indicated with an asterisk, the polls from 1936 through 1964 were taken before the bowl games and those from 1965 through the present were taken after the bowl games.

1946 (Cont.)

		Record	Coach
5.	Illinois	7-2-0	Ray Eliot
6.	Michigan	6-2-1	Fritz Crisler
7.	Tennessee	9-1-0	Bob Neyland
8.	Louisiana St	9-1-0	Bernie Moore
9.	N Carolina	8-1-0	Carl Snavely
10.	Rice	8-2-0	Jess Neely
11.	Georgia Tech	8-2-0	Bobby Dodd
12.	Yale	7-1-1	Howard Odell
13.	Pennsylvania	6-2-0	George Munger
14.	Oklahoma	7-3-0	Jim Tatum
15.	Texas	8-2-0	Dana X. Bible
16.	Arkansas	6-3-1	John Barnhill
17.	Tulsa	9-1-0	J.O. Brothers
18.	N Carolina St	8-2-0	Beattie Feathers
19.	Delaware	9-0-0	Bill Murray
20.	Indiana	6-3-0	Bo McMillan

1947

		Record	Coach
1.	Notre Dame	9-0-0	Frank Leahy
2.	#Michigan	9-0-0	Fritz Crisler
3.	SMU	9-0-1	Matty Bell
4.	Penn St	9-0-0	Bob Higgins
5.	Texas	9-1-0	Blair Cherry
6.	Alabama	8-2-0	Red Drew
7.	Pennsylvania	7-0-1	George Munger
8.	Southern Cal	7-1-1	Jeff Cravath
9.	N Carolina	8-2-0	Carl Snavely
10.	Georgia Tech	9-1-0	Bobby Dodd
11.	Army	5-2-2	Red Blaik
12.	Kansas	8-0-2	George Sauer
13.	Mississippi	8-2-0	Johnny Vaught
14.	William & Mary	9-1-0	Rube McCray
15.	California	9-1-0	Pappy Waldorf
16.	Oklahoma	7-2-1	Bud Wilkinson
17.	N Carolina St	5-3-1	Beattie Feathers
18.	Rice	6-3-1	Jess Neely
19.	Duke	4-3-2	Wallace Wade
20.	Columbia	7-2-0	Lou Little

#The AP, which had voted Notre Dame No. 1 before the
bowl games, took a second vote, giving the title to Michigan after its 49–0 win over Southern Cal in the Rose Bowl.

1948

		Record	Coach
1.	Michigan	9-0-0	Bennie Oosterbaan
2.	Notre Dame	9-0-1	Frank Leahy
3.	N Carolina	9-0-1	Carl Snavely
4.	California	10-0-0	Pappy Waldorf
5.	Oklahoma	9-1-0	Bud Wilkinson
6.	Army	8-0-1	Red Blaik
7.	Northwestern	7-2-0	Bob Voigts
8.	Georgia	9-1-0	Wally Butts
9.	Oregon	9-1-0	Jim Aiken
10.	SMU	8-1-1	Matty Bell
11.	Clemson	10-0-0	Frank Howard
12.	Vanderbilt	8-2-1	Red Sanders
13.	Tulane	9-1-0	Henry Frnka
14.	Michigan St	6-2-2	Biggie Munn
15.	Mississippi	8-1-0	Johnny Vaught
16.	Minnesota	7-2-0	Bernie Bierman
17.	William & Mary	6-2-2	Rube McCray
18.	Penn St	7-1-1	Bob Higgins
19.	Cornell	8-1-0	Lefty James
20.	Wake Forest	6-3-0	Peahead Walker

1949

		Record	Coach
1.	Notre Dame	10-0-0	Frank Leahy
2.	Oklahoma	10-0-0	Bud Wilkinson
3.	California	10-0-0	Pappy Waldorf
4.	Army	9-0-0	Red Blaik
5.	Rice	9-1-0	Jess Neely
6.	Ohio St	6-1-2	Wes Fesler
7.	Michigan	6-2-1	Bennie Oosterbaan
8.	Minnesota	7-2-0	Bernie Bierman
9.	Louisiana St	8-2-0	Gaynell Tinsley
10.	Pacific	11-0-0	Larry Siemering
11.	Kentucky	9-2-0	Bear Bryant
12.	Cornell	8-1-0	Lefty James
13.	Villanova	8-1-0	Jim Leonard
14.	Maryland	8-1-0	Jim Tatum
15.	Santa Clara	7-2-1	Len Casanova
16.	N Carolina	7-3-0	Carl Snavely
17.	Tennessee	7-2-1	Bob Neyland
18.	Princeton	6-3-0	Charlie Caldwell
19.	Michigan St	6-3-0	Biggie Munn
20.	Missouri	7-3-0	Don Faurot
	Baylor	8-2-0	Bob Woodruff

1950

		Record	Coach
1.	Oklahoma	10-0-0	Bud Wilkinson
2.	Army	8-1-0	Red Blaik
3.	Texas	9-1-0	Blair Cherry
4.	Tennessee	10-1-0	Bob Neyland
5.	California	9-0-1	Pappy Waldorf
6.	Princeton	9-0-0	Charlie Caldwell
7.	Kentucky	10-1-0	Bear Bryant
8.	Michigan St	8-1-0	Biggie Munn
9.	Michigan	5-3-1	Bennie Oosterhaan
10.	Clemson	8-0-1	Frank Howard
11.	Washington	8-2-0	Howard Odell
12.	Wyoming	9-0-0	Bowden Wyatt
13.	Illinois	7-2-0	Ray Eliot
14.	Ohio St	6-3-0	Wes Fesler
15.	Miami (FL)	9-0-1	Andy Gustafson
16.	Alabama	9-2-0	Red Drew
17.	Nebraska	6-2-1	Bill Glassford
18.	Washington & Lee	8-2-0	George Barclay
19.	Tulsa	9-1-1	J.O. Brothers
20.	Tulane	6-2-1	Henry Frnka

1951

		Record	Coach
1.	Tennessee	10-0-0	Bob Neyland
2.	Michigan St	9-0-0	Biggie Munn
3.	Maryland	9-0-0	Jim Tatum
4.	Illinois	8-0-1	Ray Eliot
5.	Georgia Tech	10-0-1	Bobby Dodd
6.	Princeton	9-0-0	Charlie Caldwell
7.	Stanford	9-1-0	Chuck Taylor
8.	Wisconsin	7-1-1	Ivy Williamson
9.	Baylor	8-1-1	George Sauer
10.	Oklahoma	8-2-0	Bud Wilkinson
11.	Texas Christian	6-4-0	Dutch Meyer
12.	California	8-2-0	Pappy Waldorf
13.	Virginia	8-1-0	Art Guepe
14.	San Francisco	9-0-0	Joe Kuharich
15.	Kentucky	7-4-0	Bear Bryant
16.	Boston University	6-4-0	Buff Donelli
17.	UCLA	5-3-1	Red Sanders
18.	Washington St	7-3-0	Forest Evashevski

1951 (Cont.)

		Record	Coach
19.	Holy Cross	8-2-0	Eddie Anderson
20.	Clemson	7-2-0	Frank Howard

1952

		Record	Coach
1.	Michigan St	9-0-0	Biggie Munn
2.	Georgia Tech	11-0-0	Bobby Dodd
3.	Notre Dame	7-2-1	Frank Leahy
4.	Oklahoma	8-1-1	Bud Wilkinson
5.	Southern Cal	9-1-0	Jess Hill
6.	UCLA	8-1-0	Red Sanders
7.	Mississippi	8-0-2	Johnny Vaught
8.	Tennessee	8-1-1	Bob Neyland
9.	Alabama	9-2-0	Red Drew
10.	Texas	8-2-0	Ed Price
11.	Wisconsin	6-2-1	Ivy Williamson
12.	Tulsa	8-1-1	J.O. Brothers
13.	Maryland	7-2-0	Jim Tatum
14.	Syracuse	7-2-0	Ben Schwartzwalder
15.	Florida	7-3-0	Bob Woodruff
16.	Duke	8-2-0	Bill Murray
17.	Ohio St	6-3-0	Woody Hayes
18.	Purdue	4-3-2	Stu Holcomb
19.	Princeton	8-1-0	Charlie Caldwell
20.	Kentucky	5-4-2	Bear Bryant

1953

		Record	Coach
1.	Maryland	10-0-0	Jim Tatum
2.	Notre Dame	9-0-1	Frank Leahy
3.	Michigan St	8-1-0	Biggie Munn
4.	Oklahoma	8-1-1	Bud Wilkinson
5.	UCLA	8-1-0	Red Sanders
6.	Rice	8-2-0	Jess Neely
7.	Illinois	7-1-1	Ray Eliot
8.	Georgia Tech	8-2-1	Bobby Dodd
9.	Iowa	5-3-1	Forest Evashevski
10.	W Virginia	8-1-0	Art Lewis
11.	Texas	7-3-0	Ed Price
12.	Texas Tech	10-1-0	DeWitt Weaver
13.	Alabama	6-2-3	Red Drew
14.	Army	7-1-1	Red Blaik
15.	Wisconsin	6-2-1	Ivy Williamson
16.	Kentucky	7-2-1	Bear Bryant
17.	Auburn	7-2-1	Shug Jordan
18.	Duke	7-2-1	Bill Murray
19.	Stanford	6-3-1	Chuck Taylor
20.	Michigan	6-3-0	Bennie Oosterbaan

1954

		Record	Coach
1.	Ohio St	9-0-0	Woody Hayes
2.	#UCLA	9-0-0	Red Sanders
3.	Oklahoma	10-0-0	Bud Wilkinson
4.	Notre Dame	9-1-0	Terry Brennan
5.	Navy	7-2-0	Eddie Erdelatz
6.	Mississippi	9-1-0	Johnny Vaught
7.	Army	7-2-0	Red Blaik
8.	Maryland	7-2-1	Jim Tatum
9.	Wisconsin	7-2-0	Ivy Williamson
10.	Arkansas	8-2-0	Bowden Wyatt

1954 (Cont.)

		Record	Coach
11.	Miami (FL)	8-1-0	Andy Gustafson
12.	W Virginia	8-1-0	Art Lewis
13.	Auburn	7-3-0	Shug Jordan
14.	Duke	7-2-1	Bill Murray
15.	Michigan	6-3-0	Bennie Oosterbaan
16.	Virginia Tech	8-0-1	Frank Moseley
17.	Southern Cal	8-3-0	Jess Hill
18.	Baylor	7-3-0	George Sauer
19.	Rice	7-3-0	Jess Neely
20.	Penn St	7-2-0	Rip Engle

#Selected No. 1 by UP.

1955

		Record	Coach
1.	Oklahoma	10-0-0	Bud Wilkinson
2.	Michigan St	8-1-0	Duffy Daugherty
3.	Maryland	10-0-0	Jim Tatum
4.	UCLA	9-1-0	Red Sanders
5.	Ohio St	7-2-0	Woody Hayes
6.	Texas Christian	9-1-0	Abe Martin
7.	Georgia Tech	8-1-1	Bobby Dodd
8.	Auburn	8-1-1	Shug Jordan
9.	Notre Dame	8-2-0	Terry Brennan
10.	Mississippi	9-1-0	Johnny Vaught
11.	Pittsburgh	7-3-0	John Michelosen
12.	Michigan	7-2-0	Bennie Oosterbaan
13.	Southern Cal	6-4-0	Jess Hill
14.	Miami (FL)	6-3-0	Andy Gustafson
15.	Miami (OH)	9-0-0	Ara Parseghian
16.	Stanford	6-3-1	Chuck Taylor
17.	Texas A&M	7-2-1	Bear Bryant
18.	Navy	6-2-1	Eddie Erdelatz
19.	W Virginia	8-2-0	Art Lewis
20.	Army	6-3-0	Red Blaik

1956

		Record	Coach
1.	Oklahoma	10-0-0	Bud Wilkinson
2.	Tennessee	10-0-0	Bowden Wyatt
3.	Iowa	8-1-0	Forest Evashevski
4.	Georgia Tech	9-1-0	Bobby Dodd
5.	Texas A&M	9-0-1	Bear Bryant
6.	Miami (FL)	8-1-1	Andy Gustafson
7.	Michigan	7-2-0	Bennie Oosterbaan
8.	Syracuse	7-1-0	Ben Schwartzwalder
9.	Michigan St	7-2-0	Duffy Daugherty
10.	Oregon St	7-2-1	Tommy Prothro
11.	Baylor	8-2-0	Sam Boyd
12.	Minnesota	6-1-2	Murray Warmath
13.	Pittsburgh	7-2-1	John Michelosen
14.	Texas Christian	7-3-0	Abe Martin
15.	Ohio St	6-3-0	Woody Hayes
16.	Navy	6-1-2	Eddie Erdelatz
17.	Geo Washington	7-1-1	Gene Sherman
18.	Southern Cal	8-2-0	Jess Hill
19.	Clemson	7-1-2	Frank Howard
20.	Colorado	7-2-1	Dallas Ward
	Penn St	6-2-1	Rip Engle

1957

		Record	Coach
1.	Auburn	10-0-0	Shug Jordan
2.	#Ohio St	8-1-0	Woody Hayes
3.	Michigan St	8-1-0	Duffy Daugherty
4.	Oklahoma	9-1-0	Bud Wilkinson
5.	Navy	8-1-1	Eddie Erdelatz
6.	Iowa	7-1-1	Forest Evashevski
7.	Mississippi	8-1-1	Johnny Vaught
8.	Rice	7-3-0	Jess Neely
9.	Texas A&M	8-2-0	Bear Bryant
10.	Notre Dame	7-3-0	Terry Brennan
11.	Texas	6-3-1	Darrell Royal
12.	Arizona St	10-0-0	Dan Devine
13.	Tennessee	7-3-0	Bowden Wyatt
14.	Mississippi St	6-2-1	Wade Walker
15.	N Carolina St	7-1-2	Earle Edwards
16.	Duke	6-2-2	Bill Murray
17.	Florida	6-2-1	Bob Woodruff
18.	Army	7-2-0	Red Blaik
19.	Wisconsin	6-3-0	Milt Brunt
20.	VMI	9-0-1	John McKenna

#Selected No. 1 by UP.

1958

		Record	Coach
1.	Louisiana St	10-0-0	Paul Dietzel
2.	Iowa	7-1-1	Forest Evashevski
3.	Army	8-0-1	Red Blaik
4.	Auburn	9-0-1	Shug Jordan
5.	Oklahoma	9-1-0	Bud Wilkinson
6.	Air Force	9-0-1	Ben Martin
7.	Wisconsin	7-1-1	Milt Bruhn
8.	Ohio St	6-1-2	Woody Hayes
9.	Syracuse	8-1-0	Ben Schwartzwalder
10.	Texas Christian	8-2-0	Abe Martin
11.	Mississippi	8-2-0	Johnny Vaught
12.	Clemson	8-2-0	Frank Howard
13.	Purdue	6-1-2	Jack Mollenkopf
14.	Florida	6-3-1	Bob Woodruff
15.	S Carolina	7-3-0	Warren Giese
16.	California	7-3-0	Pete Elliott
17.	Notre Dame	6-4-0	Terry Brennan
18.	SMU	6-4-0	Bill Meek
19.	Oklahoma St	7-3-0	Cliff Speegle
20.	Rutgers	8-1-0	John Stiegman

1959

		Record	Coach
1.	Syracuse	10-0-0	Ben Schwartzwalder
2.	Mississippi	9-1-0	Johnny Vaught
3.	Louisiana St	9-1-0	Paul Dietzel
4.	Texas	9-1-0	Darrell Royal
5.	Georgia	9-1-0	Wally Butts
6.	Wisconsin	7-2-0	Milt Bruhn
7.	Texas Christian	8-2-0	Abe Martin
8.	Washington	9-1-0	Jim Owens
9.	Arkansas	8-2-0	Frank Broyles
10.	Alabama	7-1-2	Bear Bryant
11.	Clemson	8-2-0	Frank Howard

1959 (Cont.)

		Record	Coach
12.	Penn St	8-2-0	Rip Engle
13.	Illinois	5-3-1	Ray Eliot
14.	Southern Cal	8-2-0	Don Clark
15.	Oklahoma	7-3-0	Bud Wilkinson
16.	Wyoming	9-1-0	Bob Devaney
17.	Notre Dame	5-5-0	Joe Kuharich
18.	Missouri	6-4-0	Dan Devine
19.	Florida	5-4-1	Bob Woodruff
20.	Pittsburgh	6-4-0	John Michelosen

1960

		Record	Coach
1.	Minnesota	8-1-0	Murray Warmath
2.	Mississippi	9-0-1	Johnny Vaught
3.	Iowa	8-1-0	Forest Evashevski
4.	Navy	9-1-0	Wayne Hardin
5.	Missouri	9-1-0	Dan Devine
6.	Washington	9-1-0	Jim Owens
7.	Arkansas	8-2-0	Frank Broyles
8.	Ohio St	7-2-0	Woody Hayes
9.	Alabama	8-1-1	Bear Bryant
10.	Duke	7-3-0	Bill Murray
11.	Kansas	7-2-1	Jack Mitchell
12.	Baylor	8-2-0	John Bridgers
13.	Auburn	8-2-0	Shug Jordan
14.	Yale	9-0-0	Jordan Oliver
15.	Michigan St	6-2-1	Duffy Daugherty
16.	Penn St	6-3-0	Rip Engle
17.	New Mexico St	10-0-0	Warren Woodson
18.	Florida	8-2-0	Ray Graves
19.	Syracuse	7-2-0	Ben Schwartzwalder
	Purdue	4-4-1	Jack Mollenkopf

1961

		Record	Coach
1.	Alabama	10-0-0	Bear Bryant
2.	Ohio St	8-0-1	Woody Hayes
3.	Texas	9-1-0	Darrell Royal
4.	Louisiana St	9-1-0	Paul Dietzel
5.	Mississippi	9-1-0	Johnny Vaught
6.	Minnesota	7-2-0	Murray Warmath
7.	Colorado	9-1-0	Sonny Grandelius
8.	Michigan St	7-2-0	Duffy Daugherty
9.	Arkansas	8-2-0	Frank Broyles
10.	Utah St	9-0-1	John Ralston
11.	Missouri	7-2-1	Dan Devine
12.	Purdue	6-3-0	Jack Mollenkopf
13.	Georgia Tech	7-3-0	Bobby Dodd
14.	Syracuse	7-3-0	Ben Schwartzwalder
15.	Rutgers	9-0-0	John Bateman
16.	UCLA	7-3-0	Bill Barnes
17.	Rice	7-3-0	Jess Neely
	Penn St	7-3-0	Rip Engle
	Arizona	8-1-1	Jim LaRue
20.	Duke	7-3-0	Bill Murray

1962

		Record	Coach
1.	Southern Cal	10-0-0	John McKay
2.	Wisconsin	8-1-0	Milt Bruhn
3.	Mississippi	9-0-0	Johnny Vaught
4.	Texas	9-0-1	Darrell Royal
5.	Alabama	9-1-0	Bear Bryant
6.	Arkansas	9-1-0	Frank Broyles
7.	Louisiana St	8-1-1	Charlie McClendon
8.	Oklahoma	8-2-0	Bud Wilkinson
9.	Penn St	9-1-0	Rip Engle
10.	Minnesota	6-2-1	Murray Warmath

11–20: UPI

		Record	Coach
11.	Georgia Tech	7-2-1	Bobby Dodd
12.	Missouri	7-1-2	Dan Devine
13.	Ohio St	6-3-0	Woody Hayes
14.	Duke	8-2-0	Bill Murray
	Washington	7-1-2	Jim Owens
16.	Northwestern	7-2-0	Ara Parseghian
	Oregon St	8-2-0	Tommy Prothro
18.	Arizona St	7-2-1	Frank Kush
	Miami (FL)	7-3-0	Andy Gustafson
	Illinois	2-7-0	Pete Elliott

1963

		Record	Coach
1.	Texas	10-0-0	Darrell Royal
2.	Navy	9-1-0	Wayne Hardin
3.	Illinois	7-1-1	Pete Elliott
4.	Pittsburgh	9-1-0	John Michelosen
5.	Auburn	9-1-0	Shug Jordan
6.	Nebraska	9-1-0	Bob Devaney
7.	Mississippi	7-0-2	Johnny Vaught
8.	Alabama	8-2-0	Bear Bryant
9.	Oklahoma	8-2-0	Bud Wilkinson
10.	Michigan St	6-2-1	Duffy Daugherty

11–20: UPI

		Record	Coach
11.	Mississippi St	6-2-2	Paul Davis
12.	Syracuse	8-2-0	Ben Schwartzwalder
13.	Arizona St	8-1-0	Frank Kush
14.	Memphis St	9-0-1	Billy J. Murphy
15.	Washington	6-4-0	Jim Owens
16.	Penn St	7-3-0	Rip Engle
	Southern Cal	7-3-0	John McKay
	Missouri	7-3-0	Dan Devine
19.	N Carolina	8-2-0	Jim Hickey
20.	Baylor	7-3-0	John Bridgers

1964

		Record	Coach
1.	Alabama	10-0-0	Bear Bryant
2.	Arkansas	10-0-0	Frank Broyles
3.	Notre Dame	9-1-0	Ara Parseghian
4.	Michigan	8-1-0	Bump Elliott
5.	Texas	9-1-0	Darrell Royal
6.	Nebraska	9-1-0	Bob Devaney
7.	Louisiana St	7-2-1	Charlie McClendon
8.	Oregon St	8-2-0	Tommy Prothro
9.	Ohio St	7-2-0	Woody Hayes
10.	Southern Cal	7-3-0	John McKay

1964 *(Cont.)*

11–20: UPI

		Record	Coach
11.	Florida St	8-1-1	Bill Peterson
12.	Syracuse	7-3-0	Ben Schwartzwalder
13.	Princeton	9-0-0	Dick Colman
14.	Penn St	6-4-0	Rip Engle
	Utah	8-2-0	Ray Nagel
16.	Illinois	6-3-0	Pete Elliott
	New Mexico	9-2-0	Bill Weeks
18.	Tulsa	8-2-0	Glenn Dobbs
19.	Missouri	6-3-1	Dan Devine
20.	Mississippi	5-4-1	Johnny Vaught
	Michigan St	4-5-1	Duffy Daugherty

1965

		Record	Coach
1.	Alabama	9-1-1	Bear Bryant
2.	#Michigan St	10-1-0	Duffy Daugherty
3.	Arkansas	10-1-0	Frank Broyles
4.	UCLA	8-2-1	Tommy Prothro
5.	Nebraska	10-1-0	Bob Devaney
6.	Missouri	8-2-1	Dan Devine
7.	Tennessee	8-1-2	Doug Dickey
8.	Louisiana St	8-3-0	Charlie McClendon
9.	Notre Dame	7-2-1	Ara Parseghian
10.	Southern Cal	7-2-1	John McKay

11–20: UPI

		Record	Coach
11.	Texas Tech	8-2-0	J.T. King
12.	Ohio St	7-2-0	Woody Hayes
13.	Florida	7-3-0	Ray Graves
14.	Purdue	7-2-1	Jack Mollenkopf
15.	Georgia	6-4-0	Vince Dooley
16.	Tulsa	8-2-0	Glenn Dobbs
17.	Mississippi	6-4-0	Johnny Vaught
18.	Kentucky	6-4-0	Charlie Bradshaw
19	Syracuse	7-3-0	Ben Schwartzwalder
20.	Colorado	6-2-2	Eddie Crowder

#Selected No. 1 by UPI.

1966*

		Record	Coach
1.	Notre Dame	9-0-1	Ara Parseghian
2.	Michigan St	9-0-1	Duffy Daugherty
3.	Alabama	10-0-0	Bear Bryant
4.	Georgia	9-1-0	Vince Dooley
5.	UCLA	9-1-0	Tommy Prothro
6.	Nebraska	9-1-0	Bob Devaney
7.	Purdue	8-2-0	Jack Mollenkopf
8.	Georgia Tech	9-1-0	Bobby Dodd
9.	Miami (FL)	7-2-1	Charlie Tate
10.	SMU	8-2-0	Hayden Fry

11–20: UPI

		Record	Coach
11.	Florida	8-2-0	Ray Graves
12.	Mississippi	8-2-0	Johnny Vaught
13.	Arkansas	8-2-0	Frank Broyles
14.	Tennessee	7-3-0	Doug Dickey
15.	Wyoming	9-1-0	Lloyd Eaton
16.	Syracuse	8-2-0	Ben Schwartzwalder
17.	Houston	8-2-0	Bill Yeoman
18.	Southern Cal	7-3-0	John McKay
19.	Oregon St	7-3-0	Dee Andros
20.	Virginia Tech	8-1-1	Jerry Claiborne

Note: Except where indicated with an asterisk, the polls from 1936 through 1964 were taken before the bowl games and those from 1965 through the present were taken after the bowl games. Additionally, the AP ranked only ten teams in its polls from 1962–67; positions 11–20 from those years are from the UPI poll.

1967*

		Record	Coach
1.	Southern Cal	9-1-0	John McKay
2.	Tennessee	9-1-0	Doug Dickey
3.	Oklahoma	9-1-0	Chuck Fairbanks
4.	Indiana	9-1-0	John Pont
5.	Notre Dame	8-2-0	Ara Parseghian
6.	Wyoming	10-0-0	Lloyd Eaton
7.	Oregon St	7-2-1	Dee Andros
8.	Alabama	8-1-1	Bear Bryant
9.	Purdue	8-2-0	Jack Mollenkopf
10.	Penn St	8-2-0	Joe Paterno

11–20: UPI†

11.	UCLA	7-2-1	Tommy Prothro
12.	Syracuse	8-2-0	Ben Schwartzwalder
13.	Colorado	8-2-0	Eddie Crowder
14.	Minnesota	8-2-0	Murray Warmath
15.	Florida St	7-2-1	Bill Peterson
16.	Miami (FL)	7-3-0	Charlie Tate
17.	N Carolina St	8-2-0	Earle Edwards
18.	Georgia	7-3-0	Vince Dooley
19.	Houston	9-2-0	Bill Yeoman
20.	Arizona St	8-2-0	Frank Kush

†UPI ranked Penn St 11th and did not rank Alabama, which was on probation.

1968

		Record	Coach
1.	Ohio St	10-0-0	Woody Hayes
2.	Penn St	11-0-0	Joe Paterno
3.	Texas	9-1-1	Darrell Royal
4.	Southern Cal	9-1-1	John McKay
5.	Notre Dame	7-2-1	Ara Parseghian
6.	Arkansas	10-1-0	Frank Broyles
7.	Kansas	9-2-0	Pepper Rodgers
8.	Georgia	8-1-2	Vince Dooley
9.	Missouri	8-3-0	Dan Devine
10.	Purdue	8-2-0	Jack Mollenkopf
11.	Oklahoma	7-4-0	Chuck Fairbanks
12.	Michigan	8-2-0	Bump Elliott
13.	Tennessee	8-2-1	Doug Dickey
14.	SMU	8-3-0	Hayden Fry
15.	Oregon St	7-3-0	Dee Andros
16.	Auburn	7-4-0	Shug Jordan
17.	Alabama	8-3-0	Bear Bryant
18.	Houston	6-2-2	Bill Yeoman
19.	Louisiana St	8-3-0	Charlie McClendon
20.	Ohio	10-1-0	Bill Hess

1969

		Record	Coach
1.	Texas	11-0-0	Darrell Royal
2.	Penn St	11-0-0	Joe Paterno
3.	Southern Cal	10-0-1	John McKay
4.	Ohio St	8-1-0	Woody Hayes
5.	Notre Dame	8-2-1	Ara Parseghian
6.	Missouri	9-2-0	Dan Devine
7.	Arkansas	9-2-0	Frank Broyles
8.	Mississippi	8-3-0	Johnny Vaught
9.	Michigan	8-3-0	Bo Schembechler
10.	Louisiana St	9-1-0	Charlie McClendon

1969 *(Cont.)*

		Record	Coach
11.	Nebraska	9-2-0	Bob Devaney
12.	Houston	9-2-0	Bill Yeoman
13.	UCLA	8-1-1	Tommy Prothro
14.	Florida	9-1-1	Ray Graves
15.	Tennessee	9-2-0	Doug Dickey
16.	Colorado	8-3-0	Eddie Crowder
17.	W Virginia	10-0-1	Jim Carlen
18.	Purdue	8-2-0	Jack Mollenkopf
19.	Stanford	7-2-1	John Ralston
20.	Auburn	8-3-0	Shug Jordan

1970

		Record	Coach
1.	Nebraska	11-0-1	Bob Devaney
2.	Notre Dame	10-1-0	Ara Parseghian
3.	#Texas	10-1-0	Darrell Royal
4.	Tennessee	11-0-1	Bill Battle
5.	Ohio St	9-1-0	Woody Hayes
6.	Arizona St	11-0-0	Frank Kush
7.	Louisiana St	9-3-0	Charlie McClendon
8.	Stanford	9-3-0	John Ralston
9.	Michigan	9-1-0	Bo Schembechler
10.	Auburn	9-2-0	Shug Jordan
11.	Arkansas	9-2-0	Frank Broyles
12.	Toledo	12-0-0	Frank Lauterbur
13.	Georgia Tech	9-3-0	Bud Carson
14.	Dartmouth	9-0-0	Bob Blackman
15.	Southern Cal	6-4-1	John McKay
16.	Air Force	9-3-0	Ben Martin
17.	Tulane	8-4-0	Jim Pittman
18.	Penn St	7-3-0	Joe Paterno
19.	Houston	8-3-0	Bill Yeoman
20.	Oklahoma	7-4-1	Chuck Fairbanks
	Mississippi	7-4-0	Johnny Vaught

#Selected No. 1 by UPI.

1971

		Record	Coach
1.	Nebraska	13-0-0	Bob Devaney
2.	Oklahoma	11-1-0	Chuck Fairbanks
3.	Colorado	10-2-0	Eddie Crowder
4.	Alabama	11-1-0	Bear Bryant
5.	Penn St	11-1-0	Joe Paterno
6.	Michigan	11-1-0	Bo Schembechler
7.	Georgia	11-1-0	Vince Dooley
8.	Arizona St	11-1-0	Frank Kush
9.	Tennessee	10-2-0	Bill Battle
10.	Stanford	9-3-0	John Ralston
11.	Louisiana St	9-3-0	Charlie McClendon
12.	Auburn	9-2-0	Shug Jordan
13.	Notre Dame	8-2-0	Ara Parseghian
14.	Toledo	12-0-0	John Murphy
15.	Mississippi	10-2-0	Billy Kinard
16.	Arkansas	8-3-1	Frank Broyles
17.	Houston	9-3-0	Bill Yeoman
18.	Texas	8-3-0	Darrell Royal
19.	Washington	8-3-0	Jim Owens
20.	Southern Cal	6-4-1	John McKay

1972

		Record	Coach
1.	Southern Cal	12-0-0	John McKay
2.	Oklahoma	11-1-0	Chuck Fairbanks
3.	Texas	10-1-0	Darrell Royal
4.	Nebraska	9-2-1	Bob Devaney
5.	Auburn	10-1-0	Shug Jordan
6.	Michigan	10-1-0	Bo Schembechler
7.	Alabama	10-2-0	Bear Bryant
8.	Tennessee	10-2-0	Bill Battle
9.	Ohio St	9-2-0	Woody Hayes
10.	Penn St	10-2-0	Joe Paterno
11.	Louisiana St	9-2-1	Charlie McClendon
12.	N Carolina	11-1-0	Bill Dooley
13.	Arizona St	10-2-0	Frank Kush
14.	Notre Dame	8-3-0	Ara Parseghian
15.	UCLA	8-3-0	Pepper Rodgers
16.	Colorado	8-4-0	Eddie Crowder
17.	N Carolina St	8-3-1	Lou Holtz
18.	Louisville	9-1-0	Lee Corso
19.	Washington St	7-4-0	Jim Sweeney
20.	Georgia Tech	7-4-1	Bill Fulcher

1973

		Record	Coach
1.	Notre Dame	11-0-0	Ara Parseghian
2.	Ohio St	10-0-1	Woody Hayes
3.	Oklahoma	10-0-1	Barry Switzer
4.	#Alabama	11-1-0	Bear Bryant
5.	Penn St	12-0-0	Joe Paterno
6.	Michigan	10-0-1	Bo Schembechler
7.	Nebraska	9-2-1	Tom Osborne
8.	Southern Cal	9-2-1	John McKay
9.	Arizona St	11-1-0	Frank Kush
	Houston	11-1-0	Bill Yeoman
11.	Texas Tech	11-1-0	Jim Carlen
12.	UCLA	9-2-0	Pepper Rodgers
13.	Louisiana St	9-3-0	Charlie McClendon
14.	Texas	8-3-0	Darrell Royal
15.	Miami (OH)	11-0-0	Bill Mallory
16.	N Carolina St	9-3-0	Lou Holtz
17.	Missouri	8-4-0	Al Onofrio
18.	Kansas	7-4-1	Don Fambrough
19.	Tennessee	8-4-0	Bill Battle
20.	Maryland	8-4-0	Jerry Claiborne
	Tulane	9-3-0	Bennie Ellender

#Selected No. 1 by UPI.

1974

		Record	Coach
1.	Oklahoma	11-0-0	Barry Switzer
2.	#Southern Cal	10-1-1	John McKay
3.	Michigan	10-1-0	Bo Schembechler
4.	Ohio St	10-2-0	Woody Hayes
5.	Alabama	11-1-0	Bear Bryant
6.	Notre Dame	10-2-0	Ara Parseghian
7.	Penn St	10-2-0	Joe Paterno
8.	Auburn	10-2-0	Shug Jordan
9.	Nebraska	9-3-0	Tom Osborne
10.	Miami (OH)	10-0-1	Dick Crum
11.	N Carolina St	9-2-1	Lou Holtz
12.	Michigan St	7-3-1	Denny Stolz

1974 (Cont.)

		Record	Coach
13.	Maryland	8-4-0	Jerry Claiborne
14.	Baylor	8-4-0	Grant Teaff
15.	Florida	8-4-0	Doug Dickey
16.	Texas A&M	8-3-0	Emory Ballard
17.	Mississippi St	9-3-0	Bob Tyler
	Texas	8-4-0	Darrell Royal
19.	Houston	8-3-1	Bill Yeoman
20.	Tennessee	7-3-2	Bill Battle

#Selected No. 1 by UPI.

1975

		Record	Coach
1.	Oklahoma	11-1-0	Barry Switzer
2.	Arizona St	12-0-0	Frank Kush
3.	Alabama	11-1-0	Bear Bryant
4.	Ohio St	11-1-0	Woody Hayes
5.	UCLA	9-2-1	Dick Vermeil
6.	Texas	10-2-0	Darrell Royal
7.	Arkansas	10-2-0	Frank Broyles
8.	Michigan	8-2-2	Bo Schembechler
9.	Nebraska	10-2-0	Tom Osborne
10.	Penn St	9-3-0	Joe Paterno
11.	Texas A&M	10-2-0	Emory Bellard
12.	Miami (OH)	11-1-0	Dick Crum
13.	Maryland	9-2-1	Jerry Claiborne
14.	California	8-3-0	Mike White
15.	Pittsburgh	8-4-0	Johnny Majors
16.	Colorado	9-3-0	Bill Mallory
17.	Southern Cal	8-4-0	John McKay
18.	Arizona	9-2-0	Jim Young
19.	Georgia	9-3-0	Vince Dooley
20.	W Virginia	9-3-0	Bobby Bowden

1976

		Record	Coach
1.	Pittsburgh	12-0-0	Johnny Majors
2.	Southern Cal	11-1-0	John Robinson
3.	Michigan	10-2-0	Bo Schembechler
4.	Houston	10-2-0	Bill Yeoman
5.	Oklahoma	9-2-1	Barry Switzer
6.	Ohio St	9-2-1	Woody Hayes
7.	Texas A&M	10-2-0	Emory Bellard
8.	Maryland	11-1-0	Jerry Claiborne
9.	Nebraska	9-3-1	Tom Osborne
10.	Georgia	10-2-0	Vince Dooley
11.	Alabama	9-3-0	Bear Bryant
12.	Notre Dame	9-3-0	Dan Devine
13.	Texas Tech	10-2-0	Steve Sloan
14.	Oklahoma St	9-3-0	Jim Stanley
15.	UCLA	9-2-1	Terry Donahue
16.	Colorado	8-4-0	Bill Mallory
17.	Rutgers	11-0-0	Frank Burns
18.	Kentucky	9-3-0	Fran Curci
19.	Iowa St	8-3-0	Earle Bruce
20.	Mississippi St	9-2-0	Bob Tyler

1977

		Record	Coach
1.	Notre Dame	11-1-0	Dan Devine
2.	Alabama	11-1-0	Bear Bryant
3.	Arkansas	11-1-0	Lou Holtz
4.	Texas	11-1-0	Fred Akers
5.	Penn St	11-1-0	Joe Paterno
6.	Kentucky	10-1-0	Fran Curci
7.	Oklahoma	10-2-0	Barry Switzer
8.	Pittsburgh	9-2-1	Jackie Sherrill
9.	Michigan	10-2-0	Bo Schembechler
10.	Washington	10-2-0	Don James
11.	Ohio St	9-3-0	Woody Hayes
12.	Nebraska	9-3-0	Tom Osborne
13.	Southern Cal	8-4-0	John Robinson
14.	Florida St	10-2-0	Bobby Bowden
15.	Stanford	9-3-0	Bill Walsh
16.	San Diego St	10-1-0	Claude Gilbert
17.	N Carolina	8-3-1	Bill Dooley
18.	Arizona St	9-3-0	Frank Kush
19.	Clemson	8-3-1	Charley Pell
20.	Brigham Young	9-2-0	LaVell Edwards

1978

		Record	Coach
1.	Alabama	11-1-0	Bear Bryant
2.	#Southern Cal	12-1-0	John Robinson
3.	Oklahoma	11-1-0	Barry Switzer
4.	Penn St	11-1-0	Joe Paterno
5.	Michigan	10-2-0	Bo Schembechler
6.	Clemson	11-1-0	Charley Pell
7.	Notre Dame	9-3-0	Dan Devine
8.	Nebraska	9-3-0	Tom Osborne
9.	Texas	9-3-0	Fred Akers
10.	Houston	9-3-0	Bill Yeoman
11.	Arkansas	9-2-1	Lou Holtz
12.	Michigan St	8-3-0	Darryl Rogers
13.	Purdue	9-2-1	Jim Young
14.	UCLA	8-3-1	Terry Donahue
15.	Missouri	8-4-0	Warren Powers
16.	Georgia	9-2-1	Vince Dooley
17.	Stanford	8-4-0	Bill Walsh
18.	N Carolina St	9-3-0	Bo Rein
19.	Texas A&M	8-4-0	Emory Bellard (4–2)
			Tom Wilson (4–2)
20.	Maryland	9-3-0	Jerry Claiborne

#Selected No. 1 by UPI.

1979

		Record	Coach
1.	Alabama	12-0-0	Bear Bryant
2.	Southern Cal	11-0-1	John Robinson
3.	Oklahoma	11-1-0	Barry Switzer
4.	Ohio St	11-1-0	Earle Bruce
5.	Houston	11-1-0	Bill Yeoman
6.	Florida St	11-1-0	Bobby Bowden
7.	Pittsburgh	11-1-0	Jackie Sherrill
8.	Arkansas	10-2-0	Lou Holtz
9.	Nebraska	10-2-0	Tom Osborne
10.	Purdue	10-2-0	Jim Young
11.	Washington	10-1-0	Don James
12.	Texas	9-3-0	Fred Akers
13.	Brigham Young	11-1-0	LaVell Edwards
14.	Baylor	8-4-0	Grant Teaff
15.	N Carolina	8-3-1	Dick Crum
16.	Auburn	8-3-0	Doug Barfield
17.	Temple	10-2-0	Wayne Hardin

1979 *(Cont.)*

		Record	Coach
18.	Michigan	8-4-0	Bo Schembechler
19.	Indiana	8-4-0	Lee Corso
20.	Penn St	8-4-0	Joe Paterno

1980

		Record	Coach
1.	Georgia	12-0-0	Vince Dooley
2.	Pittsburgh	11-1-0	Jackie Sherrill
3.	Oklahoma	10-2-0	Barry Switzer
4.	Michigan	10-2-0	Bo Schembechler
5.	Florida St	10-2-0	Bobby Bowden
6.	Alabama	10-2-0	Bear Bryant
7.	Nebraska	10-2-0	Tom Osborne
8.	Penn St	10-2-0	Joe Paterno
9.	Notre Dame	9-2-1	Dan Devine
10.	N Carolina	11-1-0	Dick Crum
11.	Southern Cal	8-2-1	John Robinson
12.	Brigham Young	12-1-0	LaVell Edwards
13.	UCLA	9-2-0	Terry Donahue
14.	Baylor	10-2-0	Grant Teaff
15.	Ohio St	9-3-0	Earle Bruce
16.	Washington	9-3-0	Don James
17.	Purdue	9-3-0	Jim Young
18.	Miami (FL)	9-3-0	H. Schnellenberger
19.	Mississippi St	9-3-0	Emory Bellard
20.	SMU	8-4-0	Ron Meyer

1981

		Record	Coach
1.	Clemson	12-0-0	Danny Ford
2.	Texas	10-1-1	Fred Akers
3.	Penn St	10-2-0	Joe Paterno
4.	Pittsburgh	11-1-0	Jackie Sherrill
5.	SMU	10-1-0	Ron Meyer
6.	Georgia	10-2-0	Vince Dooley
7.	Alabama	9-2-1	Bear Bryant
8.	Miami (FL)	9-2-0	H. Schnellenberger
9.	N Carolina	10-2-0	Dick Crum
10.	Washington	10-2-0	Don James
11.	Nebraska	9-3-0	Tom Osborne
12.	Michigan	9-3-0	Bo Schembechler
13.	Brigham Young	11-2-0	LaVell Edwards
14.	Southern Cal	9-3-0	John Robinson
15.	Ohio St	9-3-0	Earle Bruce
16.	Arizona St	9-2-0	Darryl Rogers
17.	W Virginia	9-3-0	Don Nehlen
18.	Iowa	8-4-0	Hayden Fry
19.	Missouri	8-4-0	Warren Powers
20.	Oklahoma	7-4-1	Barry Switzer

1982

		Record	Coach
1.	Penn St	11-1-0	Joe Paterno
2.	SMU	11-0-1	Bobby Collins
3.	Nebraska	12-1-0	Tom Osborne
4.	Georgia	11-1-0	Vince Dooley
5.	UCLA	10-1-1	Terry Donahue
6.	Arizona St	10-2-0	Darryl Rogers
7.	Washington	10-2-0	Don James
8.	Clemson	9-1-1	Danny Ford
9.	Arkansas	9-2-1	Lou Holtz
10.	Pittsburgh	9-3-0	Foge Fazio
11.	Louisiana St	8-3-1	Jerry Stovall
12.	Ohio St	9-3-0	Earle Bruce

1982 *(Cont.)*

		Record	Coach
13.	Florida St	9-3-0	Bobby Bowden
14.	Auburn	9-3-0	Pat Dye
15.	Southern Cal	8-3-0	John Robinson
16.	Oklahoma	8-4-0	Barry Switzer
17.	Texas	9-3-0	Fred Akers
18.	N Carolina	8-4-0	Dick Crum
19.	W Virginia	9-3-0	Don Nehlen
20.	Maryland	8-4-0	Bobby Ross

1983

		Record	Coach
1.	Miami (FL)	11-1-0	H. Schnellenberger
2.	Nebraska	12-1-0	Tom Osborne
3.	Auburn	11-1-0	Pat Dye
4.	Georgia	10-1-1	Vince Dooley
5.	Texas	11-1-0	Fred Akers
6.	Florida	9-2-1	Charlie Pell
7.	Brigham Young	11-1-0	LaVell Edwards
8.	Michigan	9-3-0	Bo Schembechler
9.	Ohio St	9-3-0	Earle Bruce
10.	Illinois	10-2-0	Mike White
11.	Clemson	9-1-1	Danny Ford
12.	SMU	10-2-0	Bobby Collins
13.	Air Force	10-2-0	Ken Hatfield
14.	Iowa	9-3-0	Hayden Fry
15.	Alabama	8-4-0	Ray Perkins
16.	W Virginia	9-3-0	Don Nehlen
17.	UCLA	7-4-1	Terry Donahue
18.	Pittsburgh	8-3-1	Foge Fazio
19.	Boston College	9-3-0	Jack Bicknell
20.	E Carolina	8-3-0	Ed Emory

1984

		Record	Coach
1.	Brigham Young	13-0-0	LaVell Edwards
2.	Washington	11-1-0	Don James
3.	Florida	9-1-1	Chas Pell (0-1-1) Galen Hall (9-0)
4.	Nebraska	10-2-0	Tom Osborne
5.	Boston College	10-2-0	Jack Bicknell
6.	Oklahoma	9-2-1	Barry Switzer
7.	Oklahoma St	10-2-0	Pat Jones
8.	SMU	10-2-0	Bobby Collins
9.	UCLA	9-3-0	Terry Donahue
10.	Southern Cal	10-3-0	Ted Tollner
11.	S Carolina	10-2-0	Joe Morrison
12.	Maryland	9-3-0	Bobby Ross
13.	Ohio St	9-3-0	Earle Bruce
14.	Auburn	9-4-0	Pat Dye
15.	Louisiana St	8-3-1	Bill Arnsparger
16.	Iowa	8-4-1	Hayden Fry
17.	Florida St	7-3-2	Bobby Bowden
18.	Miami (FL)	8-5-0	Jimmy Johnson
19.	Kentucky	9-3-0	Jerry Claiborne
20.	Virginia	8-2-2	George Welsh

1985

		Record	Coach
1.	Oklahoma	11-1-0	Barry Switzer
2.	Michigan	10-1-1	Bo Schembechler
3.	Penn St	11-1-0	Joe Paterno
4.	Tennessee	9-1-2	Johnny Majors
5.	Florida	9-1-1	Galen Hall
6.	Texas A&M	10-2-0	Jackie Sherrill
7.	UCLA	9-2-1	Terry Donahue
8.	Air Force	12-1-0	Fisher DeBerry

1985 *(Cont.)*

		Record	Coach
9.	Miami (FL)	10-2-0	Jimmy Johnson
10.	Iowa	10-2-0	Hayden Fry
11.	Nebraska	9-3-0	Tom Osborne
12.	Arkansas	10-2-0	Ken Hatfield
13.	Alabama	9-2-1	Ray Perkins
14.	Ohio St	9-3-0	Earle Bruce
15.	Florida St	9-3-0	Bobby Bowden
16.	Brigham Young	11-3-0	LaVell Edwards
17.	Baylor	9-3-0	Grant Teaff
18.	Maryland	9-3-0	Bobby Ross
19.	Georgia Tech	9-2-1	Bill Curry
20.	Louisiana St	9-2-1	Bill Arnsparger

1986

		Record	Coach
1.	Penn St	12-0-0	Joe Paterno
2.	Miami (FL)	11-1-0	Jimmy Johnson
3.	Oklahoma	11-1-0	Barry Switzer
4.	Arizona St	10-1-1	John Cooper
5.	Nebraska	10-2-0	Tom Osborne
6.	Auburn	10-2-0	Pat Dye
7.	Ohio St	10-3-0	Earle Bruce
8.	Michigan	11-2-0	Bo Schembechler
9.	Alabama	10-3-0	Ray Perkins
10.	Louisiana St	9-3-0	Bill Arnsparger
11.	Arizona	9-3-0	Larry Smith
12.	Baylor	9-3-0	Grant Teaff
13.	Texas A&M	9-3-0	Jackie Sherrill
14.	UCLA	8-3-1	Terry Donahue
15.	Arkansas	9-3-0	Ken Hatfield
16.	Iowa	9-3-0	Hayden Fry
17.	Clemson	8-2-2	Danny Ford
18.	Washington	8-3-1	Don James
19.	Boston College	9-3-0	Jack Bicknell
20.	Virginia Tech	9-2-1	Bill Dooley

1987

		Record	Coach
1.	Miami (FL)	12-0-0	Jimmy Johnson
2.	Florida St	11-1-0	Bobby Bowden
3.	Oklahoma	11-1-0	Barry Switzer
4.	Syracuse	11-0-1	Dick MacPherson
5.	Louisiana St	10-1-1	Mike Archer
6.	Nebraska	10-2-0	Tom Osborne
7.	Auburn	9-1-2	Pat Dye
8.	Michigan St	9-2-1	George Perles
9.	UCLA	10-2-0	Terry Donahue
10.	Texas A&M	10-2-0	Jackie Sherrill
11.	Oklahoma St	10-2-0	Pat Jones
12.	Clemson	10-2-0	Danny Ford
13.	Georgia	9-3-0	Vince Dooley
14.	Tennessee	10-2-1	Johnny Majors
15.	S Carolina	8-4-0	Joe Morrison
16.	Iowa	10-3-0	Hayden Fry
17.	Notre Dame	8-4-0	Lou Holtz
18.	Southern Cal	8-4-0	Larry Smith
19.	Michigan	8-4-0	Bo Schembechler
20.	Arizona St	7-4-1	John Cooper

1988

		Record	Coach
1.	Notre Dame	12-0-0	Lou Holtz
2.	Miami (FL)	11-1-0	Jimmy Johnson
3.	Florida St	11-1-0	Bobby Bowden
4.	Michigan	9-2-1	Bo Schembechler
5.	W Virginia	11-1-0	Don Nehlen
6.	UCLA	10-2-0	Terry Donahue
7.	Southern Cal	10-2-0	Larry Smith
8.	Auburn	10-2-0	Pat Dye
9.	Clemson	10-2-0	Danny Ford
10.	Nebraska	11-2-0	Tom Osborne
11.	Oklahoma St	10-2-0	Pat Jones
12.	Arkansas	10-2-0	Ken Hatfield
13.	Syracuse	10-2-0	Dick MacPherson
14.	Oklahoma	9-3-0	Barry Switzer
15.	Georgia	9-3-0	Vince Dooley
16.	Washington St	9-3-0	Dennis Erickson
17.	Alabama	9-3-0	Bill Curry
18.	Houston	9-3-0	Jack Pardee
19.	Louisiana St	8-4-0	Mike Archer
20.	Indiana	8-3-1	Bill Mallory

†1989

		Record	Coach
1.	Miami (FL)	11-1-0	Dennis Erickson
2.	Notre Dame	12-1-0	Lou Holtz
3.	Florida St	10-2-0	Bobby Bowden
4.	Colorado	11-1-0	Bill McCartney
5.	Tennessee	11-1-0	Johnny Majors
6.	Auburn	10-2-0	Pat Dye
7.	Michigan	10-2-0	Bo Schembechler
8.	Southern Cal	9-2-1	Larry Smith
9.	Alabama	10-2-0	Bill Curry
10.	Illinois	10-2-0	John Mackovic
11.	Nebraska	10-2-0	Tom Osborne
12.	Clemson	10-2-0	Danny Ford
13.	Arkansas	10-2-0	Ken Hatfield
14.	Houston	9-2-0	Jack Pardee
15.	Penn St	8-3-1	Joe Paterno
16.	Michigan St	8-4-0	George Perles
17.	Pittsburgh	8-3-1	Mike Gottfried
18.	Virginia	10-3-0	George Welsh
19.	Texas Tech	9-3-0	Spike Dykes
20.	Texas A&M	8-4-0	R.C. Slocum
21.	W Virginia	8-3-1	Don Nehlen
22.	Brigham Young	10-3-0	LaVell Edwards
23.	Washington	8-4-0	Don James
24.	Ohio St	8-4-0	John Cooper
25.	Arizona	8-4-0	Dick Tomey

1990

		Record	Coach
1.	Colorado	11-1-1	Bill McCartney
2.	#Georgia Tech	11-0-1	Bobby Ross
3.	Miami (FL)	10-2-0	Dennis Erickson
4.	Florida St	10-2-0	Bobby Bowden
5.	Washington	10-2-0	Don James
6.	Notre Dame	9-3-0	Lou Holtz
7.	Michigan	9-3-0	Gary Moeller
8.	Tennessee	9-2-2	Johnny Majors
9.	Clemson	10-2-0	Ken Hatfield
10.	Houston	10-1-0	John Jenkins
11.	Penn St	9-3-0	Joe Paterno
12.	Texas	10-2-0	David McWilliams
13.	Florida	9-2-0	Steve Spurrier
14.	Louisville	10-1-1	H. Schnellenberger
15.	Texas A&M	9-3-1	R.C. Slocum

1990 (Cont.)

		Record	Coach
16.	Michigan St	8-3-1	George Perles
17.	Oklahoma	8-3-0	Gary Gibbs
18.	Iowa	8-4-0	Hayden Fry
19.	Auburn	8-3-1	Pat Dye
20.	Southern Cal	8-4-1	Larry Smith
21.	Mississippi	9-3-0	Billy Brewer
22.	Brigham Young	10-3-0	LaVell Edwards
23.	Virginia	8-4-0	George Welsh
24.	Nebraska	9-3-0	Tom Osborne
25.	Illinois	8-4-0	John Mackovic

#Selected No. 1 by UPI.

1991

		Record	Coach
1.	Miami (FL)	12-0-0	Dennis Erickson
2.	#Washington	12-0-0	Don James
3.	Penn St	11-2-0	Joe Paterno
4.	Florida St	11-2-0	Bobby Bowden
5.	Alabama	11-1-0	Gene Stallings
6.	Michigan	10-2-0	Gary Moeller
7.	Florida	10-2-0	Steve Spurrier
8.	California	10-2-0	Bruce Snyder
9.	E Carolina	11-1-0	Bill Lewis
10.	Iowa	10-1-1	Hayden Fry
11.	Syracuse	10-2-0	Paul Pasqualoni
12.	Texas A&M	10-2-0	R.C. Slocum
13.	Notre Dame	10-3-0	Lou Holtz
14.	Tennessee	9-3-0	Johnny Majors
15.	Nebraska	9-2-1	Tom Osborne
16.	Oklahoma	9-3-0	Gary Gibbs
17.	Georgia	9-3-0	Ray Goff
18.	Clemson	9-2-1	Ken Hatfield
19.	UCLA	9-3-0	Terry Donahue
20.	Colorado	8-3-1	Bill McCartney
21.	Tulsa	10-2-0	David Rader
22.	Stanford	8-4-0	Dennis Green
23.	Brigham Young	8-3-2	LaVell Edwards
24.	N Carolina St	9-3-0	Dick Sheridan
25.	Air Force	10-3-0	Fisher DeBerry

#Selected No. 1 by *USA Today*/ CNN.

1992

		Record	Coach
1.	Alabama	13-0-0	Gene Stallings
2.	Florida St	11-1-0	Bobby Bowden
3.	Miami	11-1-0	Dennis Erickson
4.	Notre Dame	10-1-1	Lou Holtz
5.	Michigan	9-0-3	Gary Moeller
6.	Syracuse	10-2-0	Paul Pasqualoni
7.	Texas A&M	12-1-0	R.C. Slocum
8.	Georgia	10-2-0	Ray Goff
9.	Stanford	10-3-0	Bill Walsh
10.	Florida	9-4-0	Steve Spurrier
11.	Washington	9-3-0	Don James
12.	Tennessee	9-3-0	Johnny Majors
13.	Colorado	9-2-1	Bill McCartney
14.	Nebraska	9-3-0	Tom Osborne
15.	Washington St	9-3-0	Mike Price
16.	Mississippi	9-3-0	Billy Brewer
17.	N Carolina St	9-3-1	Dick Sheridan
18.	Ohio St	8-3-1	John Cooper
19.	N Carolina	9-3-0	Mack Brown
20.	Hawaii	11-2-0	Bob Wagner
21.	Boston College	8-3-1	Tom Coughlin
22.	Kansas	8-4-0	Glen Mason
23.	Mississippi St	7-5-0	Jackie Sherrill
24.	Fresno St	9-4-0	Jim Sweeney
25.	Wake Forest	8-4-0	Bill Dooley

1993

		Record	Coach
1.	Florida St	12-1-0	Bobby Bowden
2.	Notre Dame	11-1-0	Lou Holtz
3.	Nebraska	11-1-0	Tom Osborne
4.	Auburn	11-0-0	Terry Bowden
5.	Florida	11-2-0	Steve Spurrier
6.	Wisconsin	10-1-1	Barry Alvarez
7.	W Virginia	11-1-0	Don Nehlen
8.	Penn St	10-2-0	Joe Paterno
9.	Texas A&M	10-2-0	R.C. Slocum
10.	Arizona	10-2-0	Dick Tomey
11.	Ohio St	10-1-1	John Cooper
12.	Tennessee	9-2-1	Phil Fulmer
13.	Boston College	9-3-0	Tom Coughlin
14.	Alabama	9-3-1	Gene Stallings
15.	Miami	9-3-0	Dennis Erickson
16.	Colorado	8-3-1	Bill McCartney
17.	Oklahoma	9-3-0	Gary Gibbs
18.	UCLA	8-4-0	Terry Donahue
19.	N Carolina	10-3-0	Mack Brown
20.	Kansas St	9-2-1	Bill Snyder
21.	Michigan	8-4-0	Gary Moeller
22.	Virginia Tech	9-3-0	Frank Beamer
23.	Clemson	9-3-0	Ken Hatfield
24.	Louisville	9-3-0	H. Schnellenberger
25.	California	9-4-0	Keith Gilbertson

1994

		Record	Coach
1.	Nebraska	13-0-0	Tom Osborne
2.	Penn St	12-0-0	Joe Paterno
3.	Colorado	11-1-0	Bill McCartney
4.	Florida St	10-1-1	Bobby Bowden
5.	Alabama	12-1-0	Gene Stallings
6.	Miami (FL)	10-2-0	Dennis Erickson
7.	Florida	10-2-1	Steve Spurrier
8.	Texas A&M	10-0-1	R.C. Slocum
9.	Auburn	9-1-1	Terry Bowden
10.	Utah	10-2-0	Ron McBride
11.	Oregon	9-4-0	Rich Brooks
12.	Michigan	8-4-0	Gary Moeller
13.	Southern Cal	8-3-1	John Robinson
14.	Ohio St	9-4-0	John Cooper
15.	Virginia	9-3-0	George Welsh
16.	Colorado St	10-2-0	Sonny Lubick
17.	N Carolina St	9-3-0	Mike O'Cain
18.	Brigham Young	10-3-0	LaVell Edwards
19.	Kansas St	9-3-0	Bill Snyder
20.	Arizona	8-4-0	Dick Tomey
21.	Washington St	8-4-0	Mike Price
22.	Tennessee	8-4-0	Phillip Fulmer
23.	Boston College	7-4-1	Dan Henning
24.	Mississippi St	8-4-0	Jackie Sherrill
25.	Texas	8-4-0	John Mackovic

1995

		Record	Coach
1.	Nebraska	12-0-0	Tom Osborne
2.	Florida	12-1-0	Steve Spurrier
3.	Tennessee	11-1-0	Phillip Fulmer
4.	Florida St	10-2-0	Bobby Bowden
5.	Colorado	10-2-0	Rick Neuheisel
6.	Ohio St	11-2-0	John Cooper
7.	Kansas St	10-2-0	Bill Snyder
8.	Northwestern	10-2-0	Gary Barnett
9.	Kansas	10-2-0	Glen Mason
10.	Virginia Tech	10-2-0	Frank Beamer
11.	Notre Dame	9-3-0	Lou Holtz
12.	Southern Cal	9-2-1	John Robinson

†In 1989 the AP expanded its final poll to 25 teams.

*In 1996 the NCAA introduced overtime to break ties.

1995 *(Cont.)*

		Record	Coach
13.	Penn St	9-3-0	Joe Paterno
14.	Texas	10-2-1	John Mackovic
15.	Texas A&M	9-3-0	S.C. Slocum
16.	Virginia	9-4-0	George Welsh
17.	Michigan	9-4-0	Lloyd Carr
18.	Oregon	9-3-0	Mike Bellotti
19.	Syracuse	9-3-0	Paul Pasqualoni
20.	Miami (FL)	8-3-0	Butch Davis
21.	Alabama	8-3-0	Gene Stallings
22.	Auburn	8-4-0	Terry Bowden
23.	Texas Tech	9-3-0	Spike Dykes
24.	Toledo	11-0-1	Gary Pinkel
25.	Iowa	8-4-0	Hayden Fry

1996

		Record*	Coach
1.	Florida	12–1	Steve Spurrier
2.	Ohio St	11–1	John Cooper
3.	Florida St	11–1	Bobby Bowden
4.	Arizona St	11–1	Bruce Snyder
5.	Brigham Young	14–1	LaVell Edwards
6.	Nebraska	11–2	Tom Osborne
7.	Penn St	11–2	Joe Paterno
8.	Colorado	10–2	Rick Neuheisel
9.	Tennessee	10–2	Phillip Fulmer
10.	N Carolina	10–2	Mack Brown
11.	Alabama	10–3	Gene Stallings
12.	Louisiana St	10–2	Gerry DiNardo
13.	Virginia Tech	10–2	Frank Beamer
14.	Miami (FL)	9–3	Butch Davis
15.	Northwestern	9–3	Gary Barnett
16.	Washington	9–3	Jim Lambright
17.	Kansas St	9–3	Bill Snyder
18.	Iowa	9–3	Hayden Fry
19.	Notre Dame	8–3	Lou Holtz
20.	Michigan	8–4	Lloyd Carr
21.	Syracuse	9–3	Paul Pasqualoni
22.	Wyoming	10–2	Joe Tiller
23.	Texas	8–5	John Mackovic
24.	Auburn	8–4	Terry Bowden
25.	Army	10–2	Bob Sutton

1997

		Record	Coach
1.	Michigan	12–0	Lloyd Carr
2.	Nebraska	13–0	Tom Osborne
3.	Florida St	11–1	Bobby Bowden
4.	Florida	10–2	Steve Spurrier
5.	UCLA	10–2	Bob Toledo
6.	N Carolina	11–1	Mack Brown
7.	Tennessee	11–2	Phillip Fulmer
8.	Kansas St	11–1	Bill Snyder
9.	Washington St	10–2	Mike Price
10.	Georgia	10–2	Jim Donnan
11.	Auburn	10–3	Terry Bowden
12.	Ohio St	10–3	John Cooper
13.	Louisiana St	9–3	Gerry DiNardo
14.	Arizona St	8–3	Bruce Snyder
15.	Purdue	9–3	Joe Tiller
16.	Penn St	9–3	Joe Paterno
17.	Colorado St	11–2	Sonny Lubick
18.	Washington	8–4	Jim Lambright
19.	Southern Mississippi	9–3	Jeff Bower
20.	Texas A&M	9–4	R. C. Slocum
21.	Syracuse	9–4	Paul Pasqualoni
22.	Mississippi	8–4	Tommy Tuberville
23.	Missouri	7–5	Larry Smith
24.	Oklahoma St	8–4	Bob Simmons
25.	Georgia Tech	7–5	George O'Leary

1998

		Record	Coach
1.	Tennessee	13-0	Phillip Fulmer
2.	Ohio St	11-1	John Cooper
3.	Florida St	11-2	Bobby Bowden
4.	Arizona	12-1	Dick Tomey
5.	Florida	10-2	Steve Spurrier
6.	Wisconsin	11-1	Barry Alvarez
7.	Tulane	12-0	Tommy Bowden
8.	UCLA	10-2	Bob Toledo
9.	Georgia Tech	10-2	George O'Leary
10.	Kansas St	11-2	Bill Snyder
11.	Texas A&M	11-3	R.C. Slocum
12.	Michigan	10-3	Lloyd Carr
13.	Air Force	12-1	Fisher DeBerry
14.	Georgia	9-3	Jim Donnan
15.	Texas	9-3	Mack Brown
16.	Arkansas	9-3	Houston Nutt
17.	Penn St	9-3	Joe Paterno
18.	Virginia	9-3	George Welsh
19.	Nebraska	9-4	Frank Solich
20.	Miami (FL)	9-3	Butch Davis
21.	Missouri	8-4	Larry Smith
22.	Notre Dame	9-3	Bob Davie
23.	Virginia Tech	9-3	Frank Beamer
24.	Purdue	9-4	Joe Tiller
25.	Syracuse	8-4	Paul Pasqualoni

1999

		Record	Coach
1.	Florida St	12-0	Bobby Bowden
2.	Virginia Tech	11-1	Frank Beamer
3.	Nebraska	12-1	Frank Solich
4.	Wisconsin	10-2	Barry Alvarez
5.	Michigan	10-2	Lloyd Carr
6.	Kansas St	11-1	Bill Snyder
7.	Michigan St	10-2	Nick Saban
8.	Alabama	10-3	Mike DuBose
9.	Tennessee	9-3	Phillip Fulmer
10.	Marshall	13-0	Bob Pruett
11.	Penn St	10-3	Joe Paterno
12.	Florida	9-4	Steve Spurrier
13.	Mississippi St	10-2	Jackie Sherrill
14.	Southern Miss	9-3	Jeff Bower
15.	Miami (FL)	9-4	Butch Davis
16.	Georgia	8-4	Jim Donnan
17.	Arkansas	8-4	Houston Nutt
18.	Minnesota	8-4	Glen Mason
19.	Oregon	9-3	Mike Bellotti
20.	Georgia Tech	8-4	Goerge O'Leary
21.	Texas	9-5	Mack Brown
22.	Mississippi	8-4	David Cutcliffe
23.	Texas A&M	8-4	R.C. Slocum
24.	Illinois	8-4	Ron Turner
25.	Purdue	7-5	Joe Tiller

2000

		Record	Coach
1.	Oklahoma	13-0	Bob Stoops
2.	Miami (FL)	11-1	Butch Davis
3.	Washington	11-1	Rick Neuheisel
4.	Oregon St	11-1	Dennis Erickson
5.	Florida St	11-2	Bobby Bowden
6.	Virginia Tech	11-1	Frank Beamer
7.	Oregon	10-2	Mike Belotti
8.	Nebraska	10-2	Frank Solich
9.	Kansas St	11-3	Bill Snyder
10.	Florida	10-3	Steve Spurrier
11.	Michigan	9-3	Lloyd Carr
12.	Texas	9-3	Mack Brown
13.	Purdue	8-4	Joe Tiller

2000 (Cont.)

		Record	Coach
14.	Colorado St	10-2	Sonny Lubeck
15.	Notre Dame	9-3	Bob Davie
16.	Clemson	9-3	Tommy Bowden
17.	Georgia Tech	9-3	George O'Leary
18.	Auburn	9-4	Tommy Tuberville
19.	S Carolina	8-4	Lou Holtz
20.	Georgia	8-4	Jim Donnan
21.	Texas Christian	10-2	Dennis Franchione
22.	Louisiana State	8-4	Nick Saban
23.	Wisconsin	9-4	Barry Alvarez
24.	Mississippi St	8-4	Jackie Sherrill
25.	Iowa St	9-3	Dan McCarney

2001

		Record	Coach
1.	Miami (FL)	12-0	Larry Coker
2.	Oregon	11-1	Mike Belotti
3.	Florida	10-2	Steve Spurrier
4.	Tennessee	11-2	Phillip Fulmer
5.	Texas	11-2	Mack Brown
6.	Oklahoma	11-2	Bob Stoops
7.	Louisiana St	10-3	Nick Saban
8.	Nebraska	11-2	Frank Solich
9.	Colorado	10-3	Gary Barnett
10.	Washington St	10-2	Mike Price
11.	Maryland	10-2	Ralph Friedgen
12.	Illinois	10-2	Ron Turner
13.	S Carolina	9-3	Lou Holtz
14.	Syracuse	10-3	Paul Pasqualoni
15.	Florida St	8-4	Bobby Bowden
16.	Stanford	9-3	Tyrone Willingham
17.	Louisville	11-2	John Smith
18.	Virginia Tech	8-4	Frank Beamer
19.	Washington	8-4	Rick Neuheisel
20.	Michigan	8-4	Lloyd Carr
21.	Boston College	8-4	Tom O'Brien
22.	Georgia	8-4	Mark Richt
23.	Toledo	10-2	Tom Amstutz
24.	Georgia Tech	8-5	George O'Leary
25.	Brigham Young	12-2	Gary Crowton

2002

		Record	Coach
1.	Ohio St	14-0	Jim Tressel
2.	Miami (FL)	12-1	Larry Coker
3.	Georgia	13-1	Mark Richt
4.	Southern Cal	11-2	Pete Carroll
5.	Oklahoma	12-2	Bob Stoops
6.	Texas	11-2	Mack Brown
7.	Kansas St	11-2	Bill Snyder
8.	Iowa	11-2	Kirk Ferentz
9.	Michigan	10-3	Lloyd Carr
10.	Washington St	10-3	Mike Price
11.	Alabama	10-3	Dennis Franchione
12.	N Carolina St	11-3	Chuck Amato
13.	Maryland	11-3	Ralph Friedgen
14.	Auburn	9-4	Tommy Tuberville
15.	Boise St	12-1	Dan Hawkins
16.	Penn St	9-4	Joe Paterno
17.	Notre Dame	10-3	Tyrone Willingham
18.	Virginia Tech	10-4	Frank Beamer
19.	Pittsburgh	9-4	Walt Harris
20.	Colorado	9-5	Gary Barnett
21.	Florida St	9-5	Bobby Bowden
22.	Virginia	9-5	Al Groh
23.	Texas Christian	10-2	Gary Patterson
24.	Marshall	11-2	Bob Pruett
25.	W Virginia	9-4	Rich Rodriguez

NCAA Divisional Championships

Division I-AA

Year	Winner	Runner-Up	Score
1978	Florida A&M	Massachusetts	35–28
1979	Eastern Kentucky	Lehigh	30–7
1980	Boise St	Eastern Kentucky	31–29
1981	Idaho St	Eastern Kentucky	34–23
1982	Eastern Kentucky	Delaware	17–14
1983	Southern Illinois	Western Carolina	43–7
1984	Montana St	Louisiana Tech	19–6
1985	Georgia Southern	Furman	44–42
1986	Georgia Southern	Arkansas St	48–21
1987	NE Louisiana	Marshall	43–42
1988	Furman	Georgia Southern	17–12
1989	Georgia Southern	Stephen F. Austin St	37–34
1990	Georgia Southern	NV-Reno	36–13
1991	Youngstown St	Marshall	25–17
1992	Marshall	Youngstown St	31–28
1993	Youngstown St	Marshall	17–5
1994	Youngstown St	Boise St	28–14
1995	Montana	Marshall	22–20
1996	Marshall	Montana	49–29
1997	Youngstown St	McNesse St	10–9
1998	Massachusetts	Georgia Southern	55–43
1999	Georgia Southern	Youngstown St	59–24
2000	Georgia Southern	Montana	27–25
2001	Montana	Furman	13–6
2002	Western Kentucky	McNeese St	34–14

Division II

Year	Winner	Runner-Up	Score
1973	Louisiana Tech	Western Kentucky	34–0
1974	Central Michigan	Delaware	54–14
1975	Northern Michigan	Western Kentucky	16–14
1976	Montana St	Akron	24–13
1977	Lehigh	Jacksonville St	33–0
1978	Eastern Illinois	Delaware	10–9
1979	Delaware	Youngstown St	38–21
1980	Cal Poly SLO	Eastern Illinois	21–13
1981	SW Texas St	N Dakota St	42–13
1982	SW Texas St	UC–Davis	34–9
1983	N Dakota St	Central St (OH)	41–21
1984	Troy St	N Dakota St	18–17
1985	N Dakota St	N Alabama	35–7
1986	N Dakota St	S Dakota	27–7
1987	Troy St	Portland St	31–17
1988	N Dakota St	Portland St	35–21
1989	Mississippi College	Jacksonville St	3–0
1990	N Dakota St	Indiana (PA)	51–11
1991	Pittsburg St	Jacksonville St	23–6
1992	Jacksonville St	Pittsburg St	17–13
1993	N Alabama	Indiana (PA)	41–34
1994	N Alabama	Texas A&M–Kingsville	16–10
1995	N Alabama	Pittsburg St	27–7
1996	Northern Colorado	Carson-Newman	23–14
1997	Northern Colorado	New Haven	51–0
1998	NW Missouri St	Carson-Newman	24–6
1999	NW Missouri St	Carson-Newman	58–52 (OT)
2000	Delta St	Bloomsburg	63–34
2001	Grand Valley St	N Dakota	17–14
2002	Grand Valley St	Valdosta St	31–24

Division III

Year	Winner	Runner-Up	Score
1973	Wittenberg	Juniata	41–0
1974	Central (IA)	Ithaca	10–8
1975	Wittenberg	Ithaca	28–0
1976	St. John's (MN)	Towson St	31–28
1977	Widener	Wabash	39–36
1978	Baldwin-Wallace	Wittenberg	24–10
1979	Ithaca	Wittenberg	14–10
1980	Dayton	Ithaca	63–0
1981	Widener	Dayton	17–10
1982	W Georgia	Augustana (IL)	14–0
1983	Augustana (IL)	Union (NY)	21–17
1984	Augustana (IL)	Central (IA)	21–12

Division III (Cont.)

Year	Winner	Runner-Up	Score
1985	Augustana (IL)	Ithaca	20–7
1986	Augustana (IL)	Salisbury St	31–3
1987	Wagner	Dayton	19–3
1988	Ithaca	Central (IA)	39–24
1989	Dayton	Union (NY)	17–7
1990	Allegheny	Lycoming	21–14 (OT)
1991	Ithaca	Dayton	34–20
1992	WI-LaCrosse	Washington & Jefferson	16–12
1993	Mount Union	Rowan	34–24
1994	Albion	Washington & Jefferson	38–15
1995	WI-LaCrosse	Rowan	36–7
1996	Mount Union	Rowan	56–24
1997	Mount Union	Lycoming	61–12
1998	Mount Union	Rowan	44–24
1999	Pacific Lutheran	Rowan	42–13
2000	Mount Union	St. John's	10–7
2001	Mount Union	Bridgewater	30–27
2002	Mount Union	Trinity (TX)	48–7

NAIA Divisional Championships

Division I

Year	Winner	Runner-Up	Score
1956	St. Joseph's (IN)/ Montana St		0–0
1957	Pittsburg St (KS)	Hillsdale (MI)	27–26
1958	NE Oklahoma	Northern Arizona	19–13
1959	Texas A&I	Lenoir-Rhyne (NC)	20–7
1960	Lenoir-Rhyne (NC)	Humboldt St (CA)	15–14
1961	Pittsburg St (KS)	Linfield (OR)	12–7
1962	Central St (OK)	Lenoir-Rhyne (NC)	28–13
1963	St. John's (MN)	Prairie View (TX)	33–27
1964	Concordia-Moorhead/ Sam Houston		7–7
1965	St. John's (MN)	Linfield (OR)	33–0
1966	Waynesburg (PA)	WI-Whitewater	42–21
1967	Fairmont St (WV)	Eastern Washington	28–21
1968	Troy St (MI)	Texas A&I	43–35
1969	Texas A&I	Concordia-Moorhead (MN)	32–7
1970	Texas A&I	Wofford (SC)	48–7
1971	Livingston (AL)	Arkansas Tech	14–12
1972	E Texas St	Carson-Newman (TN)	21–18
1973	Abilene Christian	Elon (NC)	42–14
1974	Texas A&I	Henderson St (AR)	34–23
1975	Texas A&I	Salem (WV)	37–0
1976	Texas A&I	Central Arkansas	26–0
1977	Abilene Christian	SW Oklahoma	24–7
1978	Angelo St (TX)	Elon (NC)	34–14
1979	Texas A&I	Central St (OK)	20–14
1980	Elon (NC)	NE Oklahoma	17–10
1981	Elon (NC)	Pittsburg St	3–0
1982	Central St (OK)	Mesa (CO)	14–11
1983	Carson-Newman (TN)	Mesa (CO)	36–28
1984	Carson-Newman (TN)/Central Arkansas		19–19
1985	Central Arkansas/ Hillsdale (MI)		10–10
1986	Carson-Newman (TN)	Cameron (OK)	17–0
1987	Cameron (OK)	Carson-Newman (TN)	30–2
1988	Carson-Newman (TN)	Adams St (CO)	56–21
1989	Carson-Newman (TN)	Emporia St (KS)	34–20
1990	Central St (OH)	Mesa St (CO)	38–16
1991	Central Arkansas	Central St (OH)	19–16
1992	Central St (OH)	Gardner-Webb (NC)	19–16
1993	E Central (OH)	Glenville St (WV)	49–35
1994	Northeastern St (OK)	Arkansas–Pine Bluff	13–12
1995	Central St (OH)	Northeastern St (OK)	37–7
1996	SW Oklahoma St	Montana Tech	33–31
1997	Findlay (OH)	Willamette (OR)	14–7
1998	Azusa Pacific	Olivet Nazarene	17–14
1999	Northwestern Oklahoma St	Georgetown (KY)	34–26
2000	Georgetown (KY)	Northwestern Oklahoma St	20–0
2001	Georgetown (KY)	Sioux Falls	49–27
2002	Carroll (MN)	Georgetown (KY)	28–7

Division II

Year	Winner	Runner-Up	Score
1970	Westminster (PA)	Anderson (IN)	21–16
1971	California Lutheran	Westminster (PA)	30–14
1972	Missouri Southern	Northwestern (IA)	21–14
1973	Northwestern (IA)	Glenville St (WV)	10–3
1974	Texas Lutheran	Missouri Valley	42–0
1975	Texas Lutheran	California Lutheran	34–8
1976	Westminster (PA)	Redlands (CA)	20–13
1977	Westminster (PA)	California Lutheran	17–9
1978	Concordia-Moorhead (MN)	Findlay (OH)	7–0
1979	Findlay (OH)	Northwestern (IA)	51–6
1980	Pacific Lutheran	Wilmington (OH)	38–10
1981	Austin Coll./ Conc.-Moorhead (MN)		24–24
1982	Linfield (OR)	William Jewell (MO)	33–15
1983	Northwestern (IA)	Pacific Lutheran	25–21
1984	Linfield (OR)	Northwestern (IA)	33–22
1985	WI-La Crosse	Pacific Lutheran	24–7
1986	Linfield (OR)	Baker (KS)	17–0
1987	Pacific Lutheran	WI-Stevens Point*	16–16
1988	Westminster (PA)	WI-La Crosse	21–14
1989	Westminster (PA)	WI-La Crosse	51–30
1990	Peru St (NE)	Westminster (PA)	17–7
1991	Georgetown (KY)	Pacific Lutheran	28–20
1992	Findlay (OH)	Linfield (OR)	26–13
1993	Pacific Lutheran (WA)	Westminster (PA)	50–20
1994	Westminster (PA)	Pacific Lutheran	27–7
1995	Findlay (OH)/ Central Washington		21–21
1996	Sioux Falls (SD)	Western Washington	47–25

*Forfeited 1987 season due to use of an ineligible player.   †In 1997 the NAIA consolidated its two divisions into one.

Awards

Heisman Memorial Trophy

Awarded to the best college player by the Downtown Athletic Club of New York City. The trophy is named after John W. Heisman, who coached Georgia Tech to the national championship in 1917 and later served as DAC athletic director.

Year	Winner, College, Position	Winner's Season Statistics	Runner-Up, College
1935	Jay Berwanger, Chicago, HB	Rush: 119 Yds: 577 TD: 6	Monk Meyer, Army
1936	Larry Kelley, Yale, E	Rec: 17 Yds: 372 TD: 6	Sam Francis, Nebraska
1937	Clint Frank, Yale, HB	Rush: 157 Yds: 667 TD: 11	Byron White, Colorado
1938	†Davey O'Brien, Texas Christian, QB	Att/Comp: 194/110 Yds: 1733 TD: 19	Marshall Goldberg, Pittsburgh
1939	Nile Kinnick, Iowa, HB	Rush: 106 Yds: 374 TD: 5	Tom Harmon, Michigan
1940	Tom Harmon, Michigan, HB	Rush: 191 Yds: 852 TD: 16	John Kimbrough, Texas A&M
1941	†Bruce Smith, Minnesota, HB	Rush: 98 Yds: 480 TD: 6	Angelo Bertelli, Notre Dame
1942	Frank Sinkwich, Georgia, HB	Att/Comp: 166/84 Yds: 1392 TD: 10	Paul Governali, Columbia
1943	Angelo Bertelli, Notre Dame, QB	Att/Comp: 36/25 Yds: 511 TD: 10	Bob Odell, Pennsylvania
1944	Les Horvath, Ohio State, QB	Rush: 163 Yds: 924 TD: 12	Glenn Davis, Army
1945	*†Doc Blanchard, Army, FB	Rush: 101 Yds: 718 TD: 13	Glenn Davis, Army
1946	Glenn Davis, Army, HB	Rush: 123 Yds: 712 TD: 7	Charley Trippi, Georgia
1947	†John Lujack, Notre Dame, QB	Att/Comp: 109/61 Yds: 777 TD: 9	Bob Chappius, Michigan
1948	*Doak Walker, Southern Methodist, HB	Rush: 108 Yds: 532 TD: 8	Charlie Justice, N Carolina
1949	†Leon Hart, Notre Dame, E	Rec: 19 Yds: 257 TD: 5	Charlie Justice, N Carolina
1950	*Vic Janowicz, Ohio St, HB	Att/Comp: 77/32 Yds: 561 TD: 12	Kyle Rote, Southern Methodist
1951	Dick Kazmaier, Princeton, HB	Rush: 149 Yds: 861 TD: 9	Hank Lauricella, Tennessee
1952	Billy Vessels, Oklahoma, HB	Rush: 167 Yds: 1072 TD: 17	Jack Scarbath, Maryland
1953	John Lattner, Notre Dame, HB	Rush: 134 Yds: 651 TD: 6	Paul Giel, Minnesota
1954	Alan Ameche, Wisconsin, FB	Rush: 146 Yds: 641 TD: 9	Kurt Burris, Oklahoma
1955	Howard Cassady, Ohio St, HB	Rush: 161 Yds: 958 TD: 15	Jim Swink, Texas Christian
1956	Paul Hornung, Notre Dame, QB	Att/Comp: 111/59 Yds: 917 TD: 3	Johnny Majors, Tennessee
1957	John David Crow, Texas A&M, HB	Rush: 129 Yds: 562 TD: 10	Alex Karras, Iowa
1958	Pete Dawkins, Army, HB	Rush: 78 Yds: 428 TD: 6	Randy Duncan, Iowa

Heisman Memorial Trophy (Cont.)

Year	Winner, College, Position	Winner's Season Statistics	Runner-Up, College
1959	Billy Cannon, Louisiana St, HB	Rush: 139 Yds: 598 TD: 6	Rich Lucas, Penn St
1960	Joe Bellino, Navy, HB	Rush: 168 Yds: 834 TD: 18	Tom Brown, Minnesota
1961	Ernie Davis, Syracuse, HB	Rush: 150 Yds: 823 TD: 15	Bob Ferguson, Ohio St
1962	Terry Baker, Oregon St, QB	Att/Comp: 203/112 Yds: 1738 TD: 15	Jerry Stovall, Louisiana St
1963	*Roger Staubach, Navy, QB	Att/Comp: 161/107 Yds: 1474 TD: 7	Billy Lothridge, Georgia Tech
1964	John Huarte, Notre Dame, QB	Att/Comp: 205/114 Yds: 2062 TD: 16	Jerry Rhome, Tulsa
1965	Mike Garrett, Southern Cal, HB	Rush: 267 Yds: 1440 TD: 16	Howard Twilley, Tulsa
1966	Steve Spurrier, Florida, QB	Att/Comp: 291/179 Yds: 2012 TD: 16	Bob Griese, Purdue
1967	Gary Beban, UCLA, QB	Att/Comp: 156/87 Yds: 1359 TD: 8	O.J. Simpson, Southern Cal
1968	O.J. Simpson, Southern Cal, HB	Rush: 383 Yds: 1880 TD: 23	Leroy Keyes, Purdue
1969	Steve Owens, Oklahoma, FB	Rush: 358 Yds: 1523 TD: 23	Mike Phipps, Purdue
1970	Jim Plunkett, Stanford, QB	Att/Comp: 358/191 Yds: 2715 TD: 18	Joe Theismann, Notre Dame
1971	Pat Sullivan, Auburn, QB	Att/Comp: 281/162 Yds: 2012 TD: 20	Ed Marinaro, Cornell
1972	Johnny Rodgers, Nebraska, FL	Rec: 55 Yds: 942 TD: 17	Greg Pruitt, Oklahoma
1973	John Cappelletti, Penn St, HB	Rush: 286 Yds: 1522 TD: 17	John Hicks, Ohio St
1974	*Archie Griffin, Ohio St, HB	Rush: 256 Yds: 1695 TD: 12	Anthony Davis, Southern Cal
1975	Archie Griffin, Ohio St, HB	Rush: 262 Yds: 1450 TD: 4	Chuck Muncie, California
1976	†Tony Dorsett, Pittsburgh, HB	Rush: 370 Yds: 2150 TD: 23	Ricky Bell, Southern Cal
1977	Earl Campbell, Texas, FB	Rush: 267 Yds: 1744 TD: 19	Terry Miller, Oklahoma St
1978	*Billy Sims, Oklahoma, HB	Rush: 231 Yds: 1762 TD: 20	Chuck Fusina, Penn St
1979	Charles White, Southern Cal, HB	Rush: 332 Yds: 1803 TD: 19	Billy Sims, Oklahoma
1980	George Rogers, S Carolina, HB	Rush: 324 Yds: 1894 TD: 14	Hugh Green, Pittsburgh
1981	Marcus Allen, Southern Cal, HB	Rush: 433 Yds: 2427 TD: 23	Herschel Walker, Georgia
1982	*Herschel Walker, Georgia, HB	Rush: 335 Yds: 1752 TD: 17	John Elway, Stanford
1983	Mike Rozier, Nebraska, HB	Rush: 275 Yds: 2148 TD: 29	Steve Young, Brigham Young
1984	Doug Flutie, Boston College, QB	Att/Comp: 396/233 Yds: 3454 TD: 27	Keith Byars, Ohio St
1985	Bo Jackson, Auburn, HB	Rush: 278 Yds: 1786 TD: 17	Chuck Long, Iowa
1986	Vinny Testaverde, Miami (FL), QB	Att/Comp: 276/175 Yds: 2557 TD: 26	Paul Palmer, Temple
1987	Tim Brown, Notre Dame, WR	Rec: 39 Yds: 846 TD: 7	Don McPherson, Syracuse
1988	*Barry Sanders, Oklahoma St, RB	Rush: 344 Yds: 2628 TD: 39	Rodney Peete, Southern Cal
1989	*Andre Ware, Houston, QB	Att/Comp: 578/365 Yds: 4699 TD: 46	Anthony Thompson, Indiana
1990	*Ty Detmer, Brigham Young, QB	Att/Comp: 562/361 Yds: 5188 TD: 41	Raghib Ismail, Notre Dame
1991	*Desmond Howard, Michigan, WR	Rec: 61 Yds: 950 TD: 23	Casey Weldon, Florida St
1992	Gino Torretta, Miami (FL), QB	Att/Comp: 402/228 Yds: 3060 TD: 19	Marshall Faulk, San Diego St
1993	†Charlie Ward, Florida St, QB	Att/Comp: 380/264 Yds: 3032 TD: 27	Heath Shuler, Tennessee
1994	Rashaan Salaam, Colorado, RB	Rush: 298 Yds: 2055 TD: 24	Ki-Jana Carter, Penn St
1995	Eddie George, Ohio State, RB	Rush: 303 Yds: 1826 TD: 23	Tommie Frazier, Nebraska
1996	†Danny Wuerffel, Florida, QB	Att/Comp: 360/207 Yds: 3625 TD: 39	Troy Davis, Iowa St
1997	*Charles Woodson, Michigan, CB/WR	7 interceptions; Rec: 11 Yds: 231 TD: 4	Peyton Manning, Tennessee
1998	Ricky Williams, Texas, RB	Rush: 361 Yds: 2124 TD: 28	Michael Bishop, Kansas St
1999	Ron Dayne, Wisconsin, RB	Rush: 303 Yds: 1834 TD: 19	Joe Hamilton, Georgia Tech
2000	Chris Weinke, Florida St, QB	Att/Comp: 431/266 Yds: 4167 TD: 33	Josh Heupel, Oklahoma
2001	Eric Crouch, Nebraska, QB	Att/Comp: 189/105 Yds: 1510 TD: 7; Rush: 1115 Yds, 18 TD	Rex Grossman, Florida
2002	Carson Palmer, Southern Cal, QB	Att/Comp: 450/228 Yds: 3639 TD: 32	Brad Banks, Iowa

*Juniors (all others seniors).   †Winners who played for national championship teams the same year.

Note: Former Heisman winners and national media cast votes, with ballots allowing for three names (3 points for first, 2 for second and 1 for third).

Maxwell Award

Given to the nation's outstanding college football player by the Maxwell Football Club of Philadelphia.

Year	Player, College, Position	Year	Player, College, Position
1937	Clint Frank, Yale, HB	1970	Jim Plunkett, Stanford, QB
1938	Davey O'Brien, Texas Christian, QB	1971	Ed Marinaro, Cornell, RB
1939	Nile Kinnick, Iowa, HB	1972	Brad Van Pelt, Michigan St, DB
1940	Tom Harmon, Michigan, HB	1973	John Cappelletti, Penn St, RB
1941	Bill Dudley, Virginia, HB	1974	Steve Joachim, Temple, QB
1942	Paul Governali, Columbia, QB	1975	Archie Griffin, Ohio St, RB
1943	Bob Odell, Pennsylvania, HB	1976	Tony Dorsett, Pittsburgh, RB
1944	Glenn Davis, Army, HB	1977	Ross Browner, Notre Dame, DE
1945	Doc Blanchard, Army, FB	1978	Chuck Fusina, Penn St, QB
1946	Charley Trippi, Georgia, HB	1979	Charles White, Southern Cal, RB
1947	Doak Walker, Southern Meth, HB	1980	Hugh Green, Pittsburgh, DE
1948	Chuck Bednarik, Pennsylvania, C	1981	Marcus Allen, Southern Cal, RB
1949	Leon Hart, Notre Dame, E	1982	Herschel Walker, Georgia, RB
1950	Reds Bagnell, Pennsylvania, HB	1983	Mike Rozier, Nebraska, RB
1951	Dick Kazmaier, Princeton, HB	1984	Doug Flutie, Boston College, QB
1952	John Lattner, Notre Dame, HB	1985	Chuck Long, Iowa, QB
1953	John Lattner, Notre Dame, HB	1986	Vinny Testaverde, Miami (FL), QB
1954	Ron Beagle, Navy, E	1987	Don McPherson, Syracuse, QB
1955	Howard Cassady, Ohio St, HB	1988	Barry Sanders, Oklahoma St, RB
1956	Tommy McDonald, Oklahoma, HB	1989	Anthony Thompson, Indiana, RB
1957	Bob Reifsnyder, Navy, T	1990	Ty Detmer, Brigham Young, QB
1958	Pete Dawkins, Army, HB	1991	Desmond Howard, Michigan, WR
1959	Rich Lucas, Penn St, QB	1992	Gino Torretta, Miami (FL), QB
1960	Joe Bellino, Navy, HB	1993	Charlie Ward, Florida St, QB
1961	Bob Ferguson, Ohio St, FB	1994	Kerry Collins, Penn St, QB
1962	Terry Baker, Oregon St, QB	1995	Eddie George, Ohio St, RB
1963	Roger Staubach, Navy, QB	1996	Danny Wuerffel, Florida, QB
1964	Glenn Ressler, Penn St, C	1997	Peyton Manning, Tennessee, QB
1965	Tommy Nobis, Texas, LB	1998	Ricky Williams, Texas, RB
1966	Jim Lynch, Notre Dame, LB	1999	Ron Dayne, Wisconsin, RB
1967	Gary Beban, UCLA, QB	2000	Drew Brees, Purdue, QB
1968	O.J. Simpson, Southern Cal, RB	2001	Ken Dorsey, Miami (FL), QB
1969	Mike Reid, Penn St, DT	2002	Larry Johnson, Penn St, RB

Davey O'Brien National Quarterback Award

Given to the top quarterback in the nation by the Davey O'Brien Educational and Charitable Trust of Fort Worth. Named for Texas Christian Hall of Fame quarterback Davey O'Brien (1936–38).

Year	Player, College	Year	Player, College
1981	Jim McMahon, Brigham Young	1992	Gino Torretta, Miami (FL)
1982	Todd Blackledge, Penn St	1993	Charlie Ward, Florida St
1983	Steve Young, Brigham Young	1994	Kerry Collins, Penn St
1984	Doug Flutie, Boston College	1995	Danny Wuerffel, Florida
1985	Chuck Long, Iowa	1996	Danny Wuerffel, Florida
1986	Vinny Testaverde, Miami (FL)	1997	Peyton Manning, Tennessee
1987	Don McPherson, Syracuse	1998	Michael Bishop, Kansas St
1988	Troy Aikman, UCLA	1999	Joe Hamilton, Georgia Tech
1989	Andre Ware, Houston	2000	Chris Weinke, Florida St
1990	Ty Detmer, Brigham Young	2001	Eric Crouch, Nebraska
1991	Ty Detmer, Brigham Young	2002	Brad Banks, Iowa

Note: Originally honored the outstanding football player in the Southwest as follows: 1977—Earl Campbell, Texas, RB; 1978—Billy Sims, Oklahoma, RB; 1979—Mike Singletary, Baylor, LB; 1980—Mike Singletary, Baylor, LB.

Vince Lombardi/Rotary Award

Given to the outstanding college lineman of the year, the award is sponsored by the Rotary Club of Houston.

Year	Player, College, Position	Year	Player, College, Position
1970	Jim Stillwagon, Ohio St, MG	1985	Tony Casillas, Oklahoma, NG
1971	Walt Patulski, Notre Dame, DE	1986	Cornelius Bennett, Alabama, LB
1972	Rich Glover, Nebraska, MG	1987	Chris Spielman, Ohio St, LB
1973	John Hicks, Ohio St, OT	1988	Tracy Rocker, Auburn, DT
1974	Randy White, Maryland, DT	1989	Percy Snow, Michigan St, LB
1975	Lee Roy Selmon, Oklahoma, DT	1990	Chris Zorich, Notre Dame, NG
1976	Wilson Whitley, Houston, DT	1991	Steve Emtman, Washington, DT
1977	Ross Browner, Notre Dame, DE	1992	Marvin Jones, Florida St, LB
1978	Bruce Clark, Penn St, DT	1993	Aaron Taylor, Notre Dame, OT
1979	Brad Budde, Southern Cal, G	1994	Warren Sapp, Miami (FL), DT
1980	Hugh Green, Pittsburgh, DE	1995	Orlando Pace, Ohio St, OT
1981	Kenneth Sims, Texas, DT	1996	Orlando Pace, Ohio St, OT
1982	Dave Rimington, Nebraska, C	1997	Grant Wistrom, Nebraska, DE
1983	Dean Steinkuhler, Nebraska, G	1998	Dat Nguyen, Texas A&M, LB
1984	Tony Degrate, Texas, DT		

Lombardi Award (Cont.)

Year	Player, College, Position	Year	Player, College, Position
1999	Corey Moore, Virginia Tech, DE	2001	Julius Peppers, N Carolina, DE
2000	Jamal Reynolds, Florida St, DE	2002	Terrell Suggs, Arizona St, DL

Outland Trophy

Given to the outstanding interior lineman, selected by the Football Writers Association of America.

Year	Player, College, Position	Year	Player, College, Position
1946	George Connor, Notre Dame, T	1975	Lee Roy Selmon, Oklahoma, DT
1947	Joe Steffy, Army, G	1976	Ross Browner, Notre Dame, DE
1948	Bill Fischer, Notre Dame, G	1977	Brad Shearer, Texas, DT
1949	Ed Bagdon, Michigan St, G	1978	Greg Roberts, Oklahoma, G
1950	Bob Gain, Kentucky, T	1979	Jim Ritcher, N Carolina St, C
1951	Jim Weatherall, Oklahoma, T	1980	Mark May, Pittsburgh, OT
1952	Dick Modzelewski, Maryland, T	1981	Dave Rimington, Nebraska, C
1953	J.D. Roberts, Oklahoma, G	1982	Dave Rimington, Nebraska, C
1954	Bill Brooks, Arkansas, G	1983	Dean Steinkuhler, Nebraska, G
1955	Calvin Jones, Iowa, G	1984	Bruce Smith, Virginia Tech, DT
1956	Jim Parker, Ohio St, G	1985	Mike Ruth, Boston College, NG
1957	Alex Karras, Iowa, T	1986	Jason Buck, Brigham Young, DT
1958	Zeke Smith, Auburn, G	1987	Chad Hennings, Air Force, DT
1959	Mike McGee, Duke, T	1988	Tracy Rocker, Auburn, DT
1960	Tom Brown, Minnesota, G	1989	Mohammed Elewonibi, Brigham Young, G
1961	Merlin Olsen, Utah St, T	1990	Russell Maryland, Miami (FL), DT
1962	Bobby Bell, Minnesota, T	1991	Steve Emtman, Washington, DT
1963	Scott Appleton, Texas, T	1992	Will Shields, Nebraska, G
1964	Steve DeLong, Tennessee, T	1993	Rob Waldrop, Arizona, NG
1965	Tommy Nobis, Texas, G	1994	Zach Wiegert, Nebraska, G
1966	Loyd Phillips, Arkansas, T	1995	Jonathan Ogden, UCLA, OT
1967	Ron Yary, Southern Cal, T	1996	Orlando Pace, Ohio St, OT
1968	Bill Stanfill, Georgia, T	1997	Aaron Taylor, Nebraska, G
1969	Mike Reid, Penn St, DT	1998	Kris Farris, UCLA, OL
1970	Jim Stillwagon, Ohio St, MG	1999	Chris Samuels, Alabama, OL
1971	Larry Jacobson, Nebraska, DT	2000	John Henderson, Tennessee, DT
1972	Rich Glover, Nebraska, MG	2001	Bryant McKinnie, Miami (FL), OT
1973	John Hicks, Ohio St, OT	2002	Rien Long, Washington St, DL
1974	Randy White, Maryland, DE		

Butkus Award

Given to the top collegiate linebacker, the award was established by the Downtown Athletic Club of Orlando and named for college Hall of Famer Dick Butkus of Illinois.

Year	Player, College	Year	Player, College
1985	Brian Bosworth, Oklahoma	1995	Kevin Hardy, Illinois
1986	Brian Bosworth, Oklahoma	1996	Matt Russell, Colorado
1987	Paul McGowan, Florida St	1997	Andy Katzenmoyer, Ohio St
1988	Derrick Thomas, Alabama	1998	Chris Claiborne, Southern Cal
1989	Percy Snow, Michigan St	1999	LaVar Arrington, Penn St
1990	Alfred Williams, Colorado	2000	Dan Morgan, Miami (FL)
1991	Erick Anderson, Michigan	2001	Rocky Calmus, Oklahoma
1992	Marvin Jones, Florida St	2002	E.J. Henderson, Maryland
1993	Trev Alberts, Nebraska		
1994	Dana Howard, Illinois		

Jim Thorpe Award

Given to the best defensive back of the year, the award is presented by the Jim Thorpe Athletic Club of Oklahoma City.

Year	Player, College	Year	Player, College
1986	Thomas Everett, Baylor	1994	Chris Hudson, Colorado
1987	Bennie Blades, Miami (FL)	1995	Greg Myers, Colorado St
	Rickey Dixon, Oklahoma	1996	Lawrence Wright, Florida
1988	Deion Sanders, Florida St	1997	Charles Woodson, Michigan
1989	Mark Carrier, Southern Cal	1998	Antoine Winfield, Ohio St
1990	Darryl Lewis, Arizona	1999	Tyrone Carter, Minnesota
1991	Terrell Buckley, Florida St	2000	Jamar Fletcher, Wisconsin
1992	Deon Figures, Colorado	2001	Roy Williams, Oklahoma
1993	Antonio Langham, Alabama	2002	Terence Newman, Kansas St

Walter Payton Player of the Year Award

Given to the top Division I-AA player as voted by Division I-AA sports information directors. Sponsored by Sports Network.

Year	Player, College, Position
1987	Kenny Gamble, Colgate, RB
1988	Dave Meggett, Towson St, RB
1989	John Friesz, Idaho, QB
1990	Walter Dean, Grambling, RB
1991	Jamie Martin, Weber St, QB
1992	Michael Payton, Marshall, QB
1993	Doug Nussmeier, Idaho, QB
1994	Steve McNair, Alcorn St, QB

Year	Player, College, Position
1995	Dave Dickenson, Montana, QB
1996	Archie Amerson, Northern Arizona, RB
1997	Brian Finneran, Villanova, WR
1998	Jerry Azumah, New Hampshire, RB
1999	Adrian Peterson, Georgia Southern, RB
2000	Louis Ivory, Furman, RB
2001	Brian Westbrook, Villanova, RB
2002	Tony Romo, Eastern Ilinois, QB

NCAA Division I-A Individual Records

Career

SCORING

Most Points Scored: 468—Travis Prentice, Miami (OH), 1996–99
Most Points Scored per Game: 12.1—Marshall Faulk, San Diego St, 1991–93
Most Touchdowns Scored: 73—Travis Prentice, Miami (OH), 1996–99
Most Touchdowns Scored per Game: 2.0—Marshall Faulk, San Diego St, 1991–93
Most Touchdowns Scored, Rushing: 73—Travis Prentice, Miami (OH), 1996–99
Most Touchdowns Scored, Passing: 121—Ty Detmer, Brigham Young, 1988–91
Most Touchdowns Scored, Receiving: 50—Troy Edwards, Louisiana Tech, 1996–98
Most Touchdowns Scored, Interception Returns: 5—Ken Thomas, San Jose St, 1979–82; Jackie Walker, Tennessee, 1969–71; Deltha O'Neal, California, 1996–99
Most Touchdowns Scored, Punt Returns: 7—Johnny Rodgers, Nebraska, 1970–72; Jack Mitchell, Oklahoma, 1946–48; David Allen, Kansas St, 1997–99
Most Touchdowns Scored, Kickoff Returns: 6—Anthony Davis, Southern Cal, 1972–74

TOTAL OFFENSE

Most Plays: 1,917—Antwaan Randle El, Indiana, 1998–01
Most Plays per Game: 48.5—Doug Gaynor, Long Beach St, 1984–85
Most Yards Gained: 14,665—Ty Detmer, Brigham Young, 1988–91 (15,031 passing, -366 rushing)
Most Yards Gained per Game: 382.4—Tim Rattay, Louisiana Tech, 1997–99
Most 300+ Yard Games: 33 —Ty Detmer, Brigham Young, 1988–91

RUSHING

Most Rushes: 1,215—Steve Bartalo, Colorado St, 1983–86 (4813 yds)
Most Rushes per Game: 34.0—Ed Marinaro, Cornell, 1969–71
Most Yards Gained: 6,397—Ron Dayne, Wisconsin, 1996–99
Most Yards Gained per Game: 174.6—Ed Marinaro, Cornell, 1969–71

RUSHING (CONT.)

Most 100+ Yard Games: 33—Tony Dorsett, Pittsburgh, 1973–76; Archie Griffin, Ohio St, 1972–75
Most 200+ Yard Games: 11—Marcus Allen, Southern Cal, 1978–81; Ricky Williams, Texas, 1995–98; Ron Dayne, Wisconsin, 1996–99

PASSING

Highest Passing Efficiency Rating: 163.6—Danny Wuerffel, Florida, 1993–96 (1,170 attempts, 708 completions, 42 interceptions, 10,875 yards, 114 touchdown passes)
Most Passes Attempted: 1,679—Chris Redman, Louisville, 1996–99
Most Passes Attempted per Game: 47.0—Tim Rattay, Louisiana Tech, 1997–99
Most Passes Completed: 1,031—Chris Redman, Louisville, 1996–99
Most Passes Completed per Game: 30.8—Tim Rattay, Louisiana Tech, 1997–99
*Highest Completion Percentage: 67.1—Tim Couch, Kentucky, 1996–98
Most Yards Gained: 15,031—Ty Detmer, Brigham Young, 1988–91
Most Yards Gained per Game: 386.2—Tim Rattay, Louisiana Tech, 1997–99

*Minimum 1,000 attempts.

RECEIVING

Most Passes Caught: 300—Arnold Jackson, Louisville, 1997–00
Most Passes Caught per Game: 10.5—Emmanuel Hazard, Houston, 1989–90
Most Yards Gained: 5,005—Trevor Insley, Nevada, 1996–99
Most Yards Gained per Game: 140.9—Alex Van Dyke, Nevada, 1994–95
Highest Average Gain per Reception: 25.7—Wesley Walker, California, 1973–75

Career *(Cont.)*

ALL-PURPOSE RUNNING

Most Plays: 1,347—Steve Bartalo, Colorado St, 1983–86 (1,215 rushes, 132 receptions)
Most Yards Gained: 7,206—Ricky Williams, Texas, 1995–98 (6,279 rushing, 927 receiving)
Most Yards Gained per Game: 237.8—Ryan Benjamin, Pacific, 1990–92
Highest Average Gain per Play: 17.4—Anthony Carter, Michigan, 1979–82

INTERCEPTIONS

Most Passes Intercepted: 29—Al Brosky, Illinois, 1950–52
Most Passes Intercepted per Game: 1.1—Al Brosky, Illinois, 1950–52
Most Yards on Interception Returns: 501—Terrell Buckley, Florida St, 1989–91
Highest Average Gain per Interception: 26.5—Tom Pridemore, W Virginia, 1975–77

SPECIAL TEAMS

Highest Punt Return Average: 23.6—Jack Mitchell, Oklahoma, 1946–48
Highest Kickoff Return Average: 35.1—Anthony Davis, Southern Cal, 1972–74
Highest Average Yards per Punt: 46.3—Todd Sauerbrun, W Virginia, 1991–94
Note: 150–249 punts.

Single Season

SCORING

Most Points Scored: 234—Barry Sanders, Oklahoma St, 1988
Most Points Scored per Game: 21.3—Barry Sanders, Oklahoma St, 1988
Most Touchdowns Scored: 39—Barry Sanders, Oklahoma St, 1988
Most Touchdowns Scored, Rushing: 37—Barry Sanders, Oklahoma St, 1988
Most Touchdowns Scored, Passing: 54—David Klingler, Houston, 1990
Most Touchdowns Scored, Receiving: 27—Troy Edwards, Louisiana Tech, 1998
Most Touchdowns Scored, Interception Returns: 4—Deltha O'Neal, California, 1999
Most Touchdowns Scored, Punt Returns: 4—Santana Moss, Miami (FL), 2000; David Allen, Kansas St, 1998; Quinton Spotwood, Syracuse, 1997; Tinker Keck, Cincinnati, 1997; James Henry, Southern Miss, 1987; Golden Richards, Brigham Young, 1971; Cliff Branch, Colorado, 1971
Most Touchdowns Scored, Kickoff Returns: 3—Leland McElroy, Texas A&M, 1993; Terance Mathis, New Mexico, 1989; Willie Gault, Tennessee, 1980; Anthony Davis, Southern Cal, 1974; Stan Brown, Purdue, 1970; Forrest Hall, San Francisco, 1946

TOTAL OFFENSE

Most Plays: 704—David Klingler, Houston, 1990
Most Yards Gained: 5,221—David Klingler, Houston, 1990
Most Yards Gained per Game: 474.6—David Klingler, Houston, 1990
Most 300+ Yard Games: 12—Ty Detmer, Brigham Young, 1990

RUSHING

Most Rushes: 403—Marcus Allen, Southern Cal, 1981
Most Rushes per Game: 39.6—Ed Marinaro, Cornell, 1971
Most Yards Gained: 2,628—Barry Sanders, Oklahoma St, 1988
Most Yards Gained per Game: 238.9—Barry Sanders, Oklahoma St, 1988
Most 100+ Yard Games: 11—By 14 players, most recently Ahman Green, Nebraska, 1997

PASSING

Highest Passing Efficiency Rating: 183.3—Shaun King, Tulane, 1998 (328 attempts, 223 completions, 6 interceptions, 3,232 yards, 36 TD passes)
Most Passes Attempted: 643—David Klingler, Houston, 1990
Most Passes Attempted per Game: 58.5—David Klingler, Houston, 1990
Most Passes Completed: 400—Tim Couch, Kentucky, 1998
Most Passes Completed per Game: 36.4—Tim Couch, Kentucky, 1998
Highest Completion Percentage: 73.6—Daunte Culpepper, Central Florida, 1998
Most Yards Gained: (12 games) 5,188—Ty Detmer, Brigham Young, 1990; (11 games) 5,140—David Klingler, Houston, 1990
Most Yards Gained per Game: 467.3—David Klingler, Houston, 1990

RECEIVING

Most Passes Caught: 142—Emmanuel Hazard, Houston, 1989
Most Passes Caught per Game: 13.4—Howard Twilley, Tulsa, 1965
Most Yards Gained: 2,060—Trevor Insley, Nevada, 1999
Most Yards Gained per Game: 187.3—Trevor Insley, Nevada, 1999
Highest Average Gain per Reception: 27.9—Elmo Wright, Houston, 1968 (min. 30 receptions)

ALL-PURPOSE RUNNING

Most Plays: 432—Marcus Allen, Southern Cal, 1981
Most Yards Gained: 3,250—Barry Sanders, Oklahoma St, 1988
Most Yards Gained per Game: 295.5—Barry Sanders, Oklahoma St, 1988
Highest Average Gain per Play: 18.5—Henry Bailey, UNLV, 1992

NCAA Division I-A Individual Records (Cont.)

Single Season (Cont.)

INTERCEPTIONS

Most Passes Intercepted: 14 — Al Worley, Washington, 1968
Most Yards on Interception Returns: 302 — Charles Phillips, Southern Cal, 1974
Highest Average Gain per Interception: 50.6 — Norm Thompson, Utah, 1969

SPECIAL TEAMS

Highest Punt Return Average: 25.9 — Bill Blackstock, Tennessee, 1951
Highest Kickoff Return Average: 40.1 — Paul Allen, Brigham Young, 1961
Highest Average Yards per Punt: 50.3 — Chad Kessler, Louisiana St, 1997

Single Game

SCORING

Most Points Scored: 48—Howard Griffith, Illinois, 1990 (vs Southern Illinois)
Most Field Goals: 7—Dale Klein, Nebraska, 1985 (vs Missouri); Mike Prindle, Western Michigan, 1984 (vs Marshall)
Most Extra Points (Kick): 13—Derek Mahoney, Fresno St, 1991 (vs New Mexico); Terry Leiweke, Houston, 1968 (vs Tulsa)
Most Extra Points (2-Pts): 6—Jim Pilot, New Mexico St, 1961 (vs Hardin-Simmons)

TOTAL OFFENSE

Most Yards Gained: 732—David Klingler, Houston, 1990 (vs Arizona St)

RUSHING

Most Yards Gained: 406—LaDainian Tomlinson, Texas Christian, 1999 (vs UTEP)
Most Touchdowns Rushed: 8—Howard Griffith, Illinois, 1990 (vs Southern Illinois)

PASSING

Most Passes Completed: 55—Rusty LaRue, Wake Forest, 1995 (vs Duke); Drew Brees, Purdue, 1998 (vs Wisconsin)
Most Yards Gained: 716—David Klingler, Houston, 1990 (vs Arizona St)
Most Touchdown Passes: 11—David Klingler, Houston, 1990 [vs Eastern Washington (I-AA)]

RECEIVING

Most Passes Caught: 23—Randy Gatewood, UNLV, 1994 (vs Idaho)
Most Yards Gained: 405—Troy Edwards, Louisiana Tech, 1998 (vs Nebraska)
Most Touchdown Catches: 6—Tim Delaney, San Diego St, 1969 (vs New Mexico St)

NCAA Division I-AA Individual Records

Career

SCORING

Most Points Scored: 544—Brian Westbrook, Villanova, 1998-01
Most Touchdowns Scored: 89—Brian Westbrook, Villanova, 1998-01
Most Touchdowns Scored, Rushing: 84—Adrian Peterson, Georgia Southern, 1998-01
Most Touchdowns Scored, Passing: 139—Willie Totten, Mississippi Valley, 1982-85
Most Touchdowns Scored, Receiving: 50—Jerry Rice, Mississippi Valley, 1981-84

RUSHING

Most Rushes: 1,124—Charles Roberts, Cal St-Sacramento, 1997-00
Most Rushes per Game: 38.2—Arnold Mickens, Butler, 1994-95
Most Yards Gained: 6,559—Adrian Peterson, Georgia Southern, 1998-01
Most Yards Gained per Game: 190.7—Arnold Mickens, Butler, 1994-95

PASSING

Highest Passing Efficiency Rating: 170.8—Shawn Knight, William & Mary, 1991-94
Most Passes Attempted: 1,680—Marcus Brady, Cal St—Northridge, 1998-01; Steve McNair, Alcorn St, 1991-94
Most Passes Completed: 1,039—Marcus Brady, Cal St—Northridge, 1998-01
Most Passes Completed per Game: 26.5—Chris Sanders, Chattanooga, 1999-00
Highest Completion Percentage: 67.3—Dave Dickenson, Montana, 1992-95
Most Yards Gained: 14,496—Steve McNair, Alcorn St, 1991-94
Most Yards Gained per Game: 350.0—Neil Lomax, Portland St, 1978-80

RECEIVING

Most Passes Caught: 317—Jacquay Nunnally, Florida A&M, 1997-00
Most Yards Gained: 4,693—Jerry Rice, Mississippi Valley, 1981-84
Most Yards Gained per Game: 116.9—Derrick Ingram, Alabama–Birmingham, 1993-94
Highest Average Gain per Reception: 24.3—John Taylor, Delaware St, 1982-85

Single Season

SCORING

Most Points Scored: 176—Brian Westbrook, Villanova, 2001
Most Touchdowns Scored: 29—Adrian Peterson, Georgia Southern, 1999; Brian Westbrook, Villanova, 2001
Most Touchdowns Scored, Rushing: 28—Adrian Peterson, Georgia Southern, 1999
Most Touchdowns Scored, Passing: 56—Willie Totten, Mississippi Valley, 1984
Most Touchdowns Scored, Receiving: 27—Jerry Rice, Mississippi Valley, 1984

RUSHING

Most Rushes: 409—Arnold Mickens, Butler, 1994
Most Rushes per Game: 40.9—Arnold Mickens, Butler, 1994
Most Yards Gained: 2,260—Charles Roberts, Cal St–Sacramento, 1998
Most Yards Gained per Game: 225.5—Arnold Mickens, Butler, 1994

PASSING

Highest Passing Efficiency Rating: 204.6—Shawn Knight, William & Mary, 1993
Most Passes Attempted: 577—Joe Lee, Towson, 1999
Most Passes Completed: 324—Willie Totten, Mississippi Valley, 1984
Most Passes Completed per Game: 32.4—Willie Totten, Mississippi Valley, 1984
Highest Completion Percentage: 70.6—Giovanni Carmazzi, Hofstra, 1997
Most Yards Gained: 4,863—Steve McNair, Alcorn St, 1994
Most Yards Gained per Game: 455.7—Willie Totten, Mississippi Valley, 1984

RECEIVING

Most Passes Caught: 120—Stephen Campbell, Brown, 2000
Most Yards Gained: 1,712—Eddie Conti, Delaware, 1998
Most Yards Gained per Game: 168.2—Jerry Rice, Mississippi Valley, 1984
Highest Average Gain per Reception: 28.9—Mikhael Ricks, Stephen F. Austin, 1997; (min. 35 receptions)

Single Game

SCORING

Most Points Scored: 42—Jesse Burton, McNeese St, 1998 (vs Southern Utah); Archie Amerson, Northern Arizona, 1996 (vs Weber St)
Most Field Goals: 8—Goran Lingmerth, Northern Arizona, 1986 (vs Idaho)

RUSHING

Most Yards Gained: 437—Maurice Hicks, N Carolina A&T, 2001 (vs Morgan St)
Most Touchdowns Rushed: 7—Archie Amerson, Northern Arizona, 1996 (vs Weber St)

PASSING

Most Passes Completed: 48—Clayton Millis, Cal St–Northridge, 1995 (vs St. Mary's [CA])
Most Yards Gained: 624—Jamie Martin, Weber St, 1991 (vs Idaho St)
Most Touchdown Passes: 9—Willie Totten, Mississippi Valley, 1984 (vs Kentucky St)

RECEIVING

Most Passes Caught: 24—Chas Gessner, Brown, 2002, (vs Rhode Island); Jerry Rice, Mississippi Valley, 1983 (vs Southern–BR)
Most Yards Gained: 376—Kassim Osgood, Cal Poly, 2000 (vs Northern Iowa)
Most Touchdown Catches: 6—Cos DeMatteo, Chattanooga, 2000 (vs Mississippi Valley)

NCAA Division II Individual Records

Career

SCORING

Most Points Scored: 570—Ian Smart, C.W. Post, 1999–2002
Most Touchdowns Scored: 95—Ian Smart, C.W. Post, 1999–2002
Most Touchdowns Scored, Rushing: 94—Ian Smart, C.W. Post, 1999–2002
Most Touchdowns Scored, Passing: 116—Chris Hatcher, Valdosta St, 1991–94
Most Touchdowns Scored, Receiving: 76—David Kircus, Grand Valley St, 1999–2002

RUSHING

Most Rushes: 1,131—Josh Ranek, S Dakota St, 1997–01
Most Rushes per Game: 29.8—Bernie Peeters, Luther, 1968–71
Most Yards Gained: 6,958—Brian Shay, Emporia St, 1995–98
Most Yards Gained per Game: 183.4—Anthony Gray, Western NM, 1997–98

Career *(Cont.)*

PASSING

Highest Passing Efficiency Rating: 190.8—Dusty Bonner, Valdosta St, 2000–01
Most Passes Attempted: 1,719—Bob McLaughlin, Lock Haven, 1992–95
Most Passes Completed: 1,001—Chris Hatcher, Valdosta St, 1991–94
Most Passes Completed per Game: 25.7—Chris Hatcher, Valdosta St, 1991–94
Highest Completion Percentage: 72.7—Dusty Bonner, Valdosta St, 2000–01
Most Yards Gained: 11,213—Justin Coleman, Nebraska–Kearney, 1997–00
Most Yards Gained per Game: 323.7—Dusty Bonner, Valdosta St, 2000–01

RECEIVING

Most Passes Caught: 323—Clarence Coleman, Ferris St, 1998–01
Most Yards Gained: 4,983—Clarence Coleman, Ferris St, 1998–01
Most Yards Gained per Game: 160.8—Chris George, Glenville St, 1993–94
Highest Average Gain per Reception: 22.8—Tyrone Johnson, Western St (CO), 1990–93

Single Season

SCORING

Most Points Scored: 212—David Kircus, Grand Valley St, 2002
Most Touchdowns Scored: 35—David Kircus, Grand Valley St, 2002
Most Touchdowns Scored, Rushing: 33—Ian Smart, C.W. Post, 2001
Most Touchdowns Scored, Passing: 54—Dusty Bonner, Valdosta St, 2000
Most Touchdowns Scored, Receiving: 35—David Kircus, Grand Valley St, 2002

RUSHING

Most Rushes: 385—Joe Gough, Wayne St (MI), 1994
Most Rushes per Game: 38.6—Mark Perkins, Hobart, 1968
Most Yards Gained: 2,653—Kavin Gailliard, American International, 1999
Most Yards Gained per Game: 222.0—Anthony Gray, Western New Mexico, 1997

PASSING

Highest Passing Efficiency Rating: 221.63—Curt Anes, Grand Valley St, 2001
Most Passes Attempted: 544—Lance Funderburk, Valdosta St, 1995
Most Passes Completed: 356—Lance Funderburk, Valdosta St, 1995
Most Passes Completed per Game: 32.4—Lance Funderburk, Valdosta St, 1995
Highest Completion Percentage: 74.7—Chris Hatcher, Valdosta St, 1994
Most Yards Gained: 4,189—Wilkie Perez, Glenville St, 1997
Most Yards Gained per Game: 393.4—Grady Benton, W Texas A&M, 1994

RECEIVING

Most Passes Caught: 119—Brad Bailey, W Texas A&M, 1994
Most Yards Gained: 1,876—Chris George, Glenville St, 1993
Most Yards Gained per Game: 187.6—Chris George, Glenville St, 1993
Highest Average Gain per Reception: 32.5—Tyrone Johnson, Western St, 1991 (min. 30 receptions)

Single Game

SCORING

Most Points Scored: 48—Paul Zaeske, N Park, 1968 (vs N Central); Junior Wolf, Panhandle St, 1958 (vs St. Mary [KS])
Most Field Goals: 6—Steve Huff, Central Missouri St, 1985 (vs SE Missouri St)

RUSHING

Most Yards Gained: 405—Alvon Brown, Kentucky St, 2000 (vs Kentucky Wesleyan)
Most Touchdowns Rushed: 8—Junior Wolf, Panhandle St, 1958 (vs St. Mary [KS])

PASSING

Most Passes Completed: 56—Jarrod DeGeorgia, Wayne St (NE), 1996 (vs Drake)
Most Yards Gained: 642—Wilkie Perez, Glenville St, 1997, (vs Concord)
Most Touchdowns Passed: 10—Bruce Swanson, N Park, 1968 (vs N Central)

RECEIVING

Most Passes Caught: 23—Chris George, Glenville St, 1994 (vs WV Wesleyan); Barry Wagner, Alabama A&M, 1989 (vs Clark Atlanta)
Most Yards Gained: 401—Kevin Ingram, W Chester, 1998 (vs Clarion)
Most Touchdown Catches: 8—Paul Zaeske, N Park, 1968 (vs N Central)

Career

SCORING

Most Points Scored: 562—R.J. Bowers, Grove City, 1997–00
Most Touchdowns Scored: 92—R.J. Bowers, Grove City, 1997–00
Most Touchdowns Scored, Rushing: 91—R.J. Bowers, Grove City, 1997–00
Most Touchdowns Scored, Passing: 148—Justin Peery, Westminster (MO), 1996–99
Most Touchdowns Scored, Receiving: 75—Scott Pingel, Westminster (MO), 1996–99

RUSHING

Most Rushes: 1,190—Steve Tardif, Maine Maritime, 1996–99
Most Rushes per Game: 32.7—Chris Sizemore, Bridgewater (VA), 1972–74
Most Yards Gained: 7,353—R.J. Bowers, Grove City, 1997–00
Most Yards Gained per Game: 183.8—R.J. Bowers, Grove City, 1997–00

PASSING

Highest Passing Efficiency Rating: 194.2—Bill Borchert, Mount Union, 1994–97
Most Passes Attempted: 1,696—Kirk Baumgartner, WI–Stevens Point, 1986–89
Most Passes Completed: 1,012—Justin Peery, Westminster (MO), 1996–99
Most Passes Completed per Game: 25.9—Justin Peery, Westminster (MO), 1996–99
Highest Completion Percentage: 67.0—Gary Smeck, Mount Union, 1997–00
Most Yards Gained: 13,262—Justin Peery, Westminster (MO), 1996–99
Most Yards Gained per Game: 340.1—Justin Peery, Westminster (MO), 1996–99

RECEIVING

Most Passes Caught: 436—Scott Pingel, Westminster (MO), 1996–99
Most Yards Gained: 6,108—Scott Pingel, Westminster (MO), 1996–99
Most Yards Gained per Game: 156.6—Scott Pingel, Westminster (MO), 1996–99
Highest Average Gain per Reception: 22.9—Kirk Aikens, Hartwick, 1995–98

Single Season

SCORING

Most Points Scored: 250—Dan Pugh, Mount Union, 2002
Most Points Scored per Game: 20.8—James Regan, Pomona-Pitzer, 1997
Most Touchdowns Scored: 41—Dan Pugh Mount Union, 2002
Most Touchdowns Scored, Rushing: 35—Dan Pugh, Mount Union, 2002
Most Touchdowns Scored, Passing: 54—Justin Peery, Westminster (MO), 1999
Most Touchdowns Scored, Receiving: 26—Scott Pingel, Westminster (MO), 1998

RUSHING

Most Rushes: 380—Mike Birosak, Dickinson, 1989
Most Rushes per Game: 38.0—Mike Birosak, Dickinson, 1989
Most Yards Gained: 2,385—Dante Brown, Marietta, 1996

PASSING

Highest Passing Efficiency Rating: 225.0—Mike Simpson, Eureka, 1994
Most Passes Attempted: 527—Kirk Baumgartner, WI–Stevens Point, 1988
Most Passes Completed: 329—Justin Peery, Westminster (MO), 1999
Most Passes Completed per Game: 32.9—Justin Peery, Westminster (MO), 1999
Highest Completion Percentage: 72.9—Jim Ballard, Mount Union, 1993
Most Yards Gained: 4,501—Justin Peery, Westminster (MO), 1998
Most Yards Gained per Game: 450.1—Justin Peery, Westminster (MO), 1998

RECEIVING

Most Passes Caught: 136—Scott Pingel, Westminster (MO), 1999
Most Yards Gained: 2,157—Scott Pingel, Westminster, (MO), 1998
Most Yards Gained per Game: 215.7—Scott Pingel, Westminster, (MO), 1998
Highest Average Gain per Reception: 26.9—Marty Redlawsk, Concordia (IL), 1985

Single Game

SCORING

Most Field Goals: 6—Jim Hever, Rhodes, 1984 (vs Millsaps)

PASSING

Most Passes Completed: 51—Scott Kello, Sul Ross St, 2002 (vs Howard Payne)
Most Yards Gained: 731—Zamir Amin, Menlo, 2000 (vs California Lutheran)
Most Touchdown Passes: 9—Joe Zarlinga, Ohio Northern, 1998 (vs Capital)

RUSHING

Most Yards Gained: 441—Dante Brown, Marietta, 1996 (vs Baldwin-Wallace)
Most Touchdowns Rushed: 8—Carey Bender, Coe, 1994 (vs Beloit)

RECEIVING

Most Passes Caught: 23—Sean Munroe, Mass-Boston, 1992 (vs Mass-Maritime)
Most Yards Gained: 418—Lewis Howes, Principia, 2002 (vs Martin Luther)
Most Touchdown Catches: 7—Matt Perceval, Wesleyan (CT), 1998 (vs Middlebury)

Career

Scoring

POINTS (KICKERS)	Years	Pts
Roman Anderson, Houston	1988–91	423
Carlos Huerta, Miami (FL)	1988–91	397
Jason Elam, Hawaii	1988–92	395
Derek Schmidt, Florida St	1984–87	393
Kris Brown, Nebraska	1995–98	388

POINTS (NON-KICKERS)	Years	Pts
Travis Prentice, Miami (OH)	1996–99	468
Ricky Williams, Texas	1995–98	452
Brock Forsey, Boise St	1999–02	408
Anthony Thompson, Indiana	1986–89	394
Ron Dayne, Wisconsin	1996–99	378

POINTS PER GAME (NON-KICKERS)	Years	Pts/Game
Marshall Faulk, San Diego St	1991–93	12.1
Ed Marinaro, Cornell	1969–71	11.8
Bill Burnett, Arkansas	1968–70	11.3
Steve Owens, Oklahoma	1967–69	11.2
Eddie Talboom, Wyoming	1948–50	10.8

Total Offense

YARDS GAINED	Years	Yds
Ty Detmer, Brigham Young	1988–91	14,665
Tim Rattay, Louisiana Tech	1997–99	12,618
Kliff Kingsbury, Texas Tech	1999–02	12,263
Chris Redman, Louisville	1996–99	12,129
Drew Brees, Purdue	1997–00	11,815

YARDS PER GAME	Years	Yds/Game
Tim Rattay, Louisiana Tech	1997–99	382.4
Chris Vargas, Nevada	1992–93	320.9
Ty Detmer, Brigham Young	1988–91	318.8
Daunte Culpepper, Central Florida	1996–98	313.5
Mike Perez, San Jose St	1986–87	309.1

Rushing

YARDS GAINED	Years	Yds
Ron Dayne, Wisconsin	1996–99	6,397
Ricky Williams, Texas	1995–98	6,279
Tony Dorsett, Pittsburgh	1973–76	6,082
Charles White, Southern Cal	1976–79	5,598
Travis Prentice, Miami (OH)	1996–99	5,596

YARDS PER GAME	Years	Yds/Game
Ed Marinaro, Cornell	1969–71	174.6
O.J. Simpson, Southern Cal	1967–68	164.4
Herschel Walker, Georgia	1980–82	159.4
LeShon Johnson, Northern Illinois	1992–93	150.6
Ron Dayne, Wisconsin	1996–99	148.8

TOUCHDOWNS RUSHING	Years	TD
Travis Prentice, Miami (OH)	1996–99	73
Ricky Williams, Texas	1995–98	72
Anthony Thompson, Indiana	1986–89	64
Ron Dayne, Wisconsin	1996–99	63
Eric Crouch, Nebraska	1998–01	59

Passing

PASSING EFFICIENCY	Years	Rating
Danny Wuerffel, Florida	1993–96	163.6
Ty Detmer, Brigham Young	1988–91	162.7
Steve Sarkisian, Brigham Young	1995–96	162.0
Billy Blanton, San Diego St	1993–96	157.1
Jim McMahon, Brigham Young	1977–78, 80–81	156.9

Note: Minimum 500 completions.

YARDS GAINED	Years	Yds
Ty Detmer, Brigham Young	1988–91	15,031
Tim Rattay, Louisiana Tech	1997–99	12,746
Chris Redman, Louisville	1996–99	12,541
Kliff Kingsbury, Texas Tech	1999–02	12,429
Todd Santos, San Diego St	1984–87	11,425

COMPLETIONS	Years	Comp
Kliff Kingsbury, Texas Tech	1999–02	1,231
Chris Redman, Louisville	1996–99	1,031
Tim Rattay, Louisiana Tech	1997–99	1,015
Ty Detmer, Brigham Young	1988–91	958
Drew Brees, Purdue	1997–00	942

TOUCHDOWNS PASSING	Years	TD
Ty Detmer, Brigham Young	1988–91	121
Tim Rattay, Louisiana Tech	1997–99	115
Danny Wuerffel, Florida	1993–96	114
Chad Pennington, Marshall	1997–99	100
Kliff Kingsbury, Texas Tech	1999–02	95

Receiving

CATCHES	Years	No.
Arnold Jackson, Louisville	1997–00	300
Trevor Insley, Nevada	1996–99	298
Geoff Noisy, Nevada	1995–98	295
Troy Edwards, Louisiana Tech	1996–98	280
Aaron Turner, Pacific	1989–92	266

CATCHES PER GAME	Years	No./Game
Emmanuel Hazard, Houston	1989–90	10.5
Alex Van Dyke, Nevada	1994–95	10.3
Howard Twilley, Tulsa	1963–65	10.0
Jason Phillips, Houston	1987–88	9.4
Troy Edwards, Louisiana Tech	1996–98	8.2
Bryan Reeves, Nevada	1992–93	8.2

YARDS GAINED	Years	Yds
Trevor Insley, Nevada	1996–99	5,005
Marcus Harris, Wyoming	1993–96	4,518
Ryan Yarborough, Wyoming	1990–93	4,357
Troy Edwards, Louisiana Tech	1996–98	4,352
Aaron Turner, Pacific	1989–92	4,345

TOUCHDOWN CATCHES	Years	TD
Troy Edwards, Louisiana Tech	1996–98	50
Aaron Turner, Pacific	1989–92	43
Ryan Yarborough, Wyoming	1990–93	42
Marcus Harris, Wyoming	1993–96	38
Clarkston Hines, Duke	1986–89	38

Career (Cont.)

All-Purpose Running

YARDS GAINED	Years	Yds
Ricky Williams, Texas	1996–98	7,206
Napoleon McCallum, Navy	1981–85	7,172
Darrin Nelson, Stanford	1977–78, 80–81	6,885
Kevin Faulk, Louisiana St	1995–98	6,833
Ron Dayne, Wisconsin	1996–99	6,701

YARDS PER GAME	Years	Yds/Game
Ryan Benjamin, Pacific	1990–92	237.8
Sheldon Canley, San Jose St	1988–90	205.8
Howard Stevens, Louisville	1971–72	193.7
O.J. Simpson, Southern Cal	1967–68	192.9
Alex Van Dyke, Nevada	1994–95	188.5

Interceptions

PLAYER/SCHOOL	Years	Int
Al Brosky, Illinois	1950–52	29
John Provost, Holy Cross	1972–74	27
Martin Bayless, Bowling Green	1980–83	27
Tom Curtis, Michigan	1967–69	25
Tony Thurman, Boston Col	1981–84	25
Tracy Saul, Texas Tech	1989–92	25

Punting Average

PLAYER/SCHOOL	Years	Avg
Todd Sauerbrun, W Virginia	1991–94	46.3
Reggie Roby, Iowa	1979–82	45.6
Greg Montgomery, Michigan St	1985–87	45.4
Tom Tupa, Ohio St	1984–87	45.2
Barry Helton, Colorado	1984–87	44.9

Note: 150–249 punts.

Punt Return Average

PLAYER/SCHOOL	Years	Avg
Jack Mitchell, Oklahoma	1946–48	23.6
Gene Gibson, Cincinnati	1949–50	20.5
Eddie Macon, Pacific	1949–51	18.9
Jackie Robinson, UCLA	1939–40	18.8
Bobby Dillon, Texas	1949–51	17.7
Mike Fuller, Auburn	1972–74	17.7

Note: At least 30 returns.

Kickoff Return Average

PLAYER/SCHOOL	Years	Avg
Anthony Davis, Southern Cal	1972–74	35.1
Eric Booth, Southern Miss	1994–97	32.4
Overton Curtis, Utah St	1957–58	31.0
Fred Montgomery, New Mexico St	1991–92	30.5
Altie Taylor, Utah St	1966–68	29.3

Note: At least 30 returns.

Single Season

Scoring

POINTS	Year	Pts
Barry Sanders, Oklahoma St	1988	234
Brock Forsey, Boise St	2002	192
Troy Edwards, Louisiana Tech	1998	188
Mike Rozier, Nebraska	1983	174
Lydell Mitchell, Penn St	1971	174

FIELD GOALS	Year	FG
John Lee, UCLA	1984	29
Paul Woodside, W Virginia	1982	28
Luis Zendejas, Arizona St	1983	28
Fuad Reveiz, Tennessee	1982	27
Sebastian Janikowski, Florida St	1998	27

Two tied with 26.

All-Purpose Running

YARDS GAINED	Year	Yds
Barry Sanders, Oklahoma St	1988	3,250
Ryan Benjamin, Pacific	1991	2,995
Troy Edwards, Louisiana Tech	1998	2,794
Mike Pringle, Fullerton St	1989	2,690
Larry Johnson, Penn St	2002	2,655

All-Purpose Running (Cont.)

YARDS PER GAME	Year	Yds/Game
Barry Sanders, Oklahoma St	1988	295.5
Ryan Benjamin, Pacific	1991	249.6
Byron (Whizzer) White, Colorado	1937	246.3
Mike Pringle, Fullerton St	1989	244.6
Paul Palmer, Temple	1986	239.4

Total Offense

YARDS GAINED	Year	Yds
David Klingler, Houston	1990	5,221
Ty Detmer, Brigham Young	1990	5,022
Kliff Kingsbury, Texas Tech	2002	4,903
Tim Rattay, Louisiana Tech	1998	4,840
Andre Ware, Houston	1989	4,661

YARDS PER GAME	Year	Yds/Game
David Klingler, Houston	1990	474.6
Andre Ware, Houston	1989	423.7
Ty Detmer, Brigham Young	1990	418.5
Tim Rattay, Louisiana Tech	1998	403.3
Mike Maxwell, Nevada	1995	402.6

Single Season (*Cont.*)

Rushing

YARDS GAINED

	Year	Yds
Barry Sanders, Oklahoma St	1988	2,628
Marcus Allen, Southern Cal	1981	2,342
Troy Davis, Iowa St	1996	2,185
LaDainian Tomlinson, Texas Christian	2000	2,158
Mike Rozier, Nebraska	1983	2,148

YARDS PER GAME

	Year	Yds/Game
Barry Sanders, Oklahoma St	1988	238.9
Marcus Allen, Southern Cal	1981	212.9
Ed Marinaro, Cornell	1971	209.0
Troy Davis, Iowa St	1996	198.6
LaDainian Tomlinson, Texas Christian	2000	196.2

TOUCHDOWNS RUSHING

	Year	TD
Barry Sanders, Oklahoma St	1988	37
Mike Rozier, Nebraska	1983	29
Willis McGahee, Miami (FL)	2002	28
Ricky Williams, Texas	1998	27
Lee Suggs, Virginia Tech	2000	27
Brock Forsey, Boise St	2002	26

Passing

PASSING EFFICIENCY

	Year	Rating
Shaun King, Tulane	1998	183.3
Michael Vick, Virginia Tech	1999	180.4
Danny Wuerffel, Florida	1995	178.4
Jim McMahon, Brigham Young	1980	176.9
Ty Detmer, Brigham Young	1989	175.6

YARDS GAINED

	Year	Yds
Ty Detmer, Brigham Young	1990	5,188
David Klingler, Houston	1990	5,140
Kliff Kingsbury, Texas Tech	2002	5,017
Tim Rattay, Louisiana Tech	1998	4,943
Andre Ware, Houston	1989	4,699

COMPLETIONS

	Year	Att	Comp
Kliff Kingsbury, Texas Tech	2002	712	479
Tim Couch, Kentucky	1998	553	400
Tim Rattay, Louisiana Tech	1998	559	380
David Klingler, Houston	1990	643	374
Andre Ware, Houston	1989	578	365

Passing (*Cont.*)

TOUCHDOWNS PASSING

	Year	TD
David Klingler, Houston	1990	54
Jim McMahon, Brigham Young	1980	47
Andre Ware, Houston	1989	46
Tim Rattay, Louisiana Tech	1998	46
Kliff Kingsbury, Texas Tech	2002	45

Receiving

CATCHES

	Year	GP	No.
Emmanuel Hazard, Houston	1989	11	142
Troy Edwards, Louisiana Tech	1998	12	140
Nate Burleson, Nevada	2002	12	138
Howard Twilley, Tulsa	1965	10	134
Trevor Insley, Nevada	1999	11	134

CATCHES PER GAME

	Year	No.	No./Game
Howard Twilley, Tulsa	1965	134	13.4
Emmanuel Hazard, Houston	1989	142	12.9
Trevor Insley, Nevada	1999	134	12.2
Troy Edwards, Louisiana Tech	1998	140	11.7
Alex Van Dyke, Nevada	1995	129	11.7

YARDS GAINED

	Year	Yds
Trevor Insley, Nevada	1999	2,060
Troy Edwards, Louisiana Tech	1998	1,996
Alex Van Dyke, Nevada	1995	1,854
J.R. Tolver, San Diego St	2002	1,785
Howard Twilley, Tulsa	1965	1,779

TOUCHDOWN CATCHES

	Year	TD
Troy Edwards, Louisiana Tech	1998	27
Randy Moss, Marshall	1997	25
Emmanuel Hazard, Houston	1989	22
Desmond Howard, Michigan	1991	19
Ashley Lelie, Hawaii	2001	19

Single Game

Scoring

POINTS

	Opponent	Year	Pts
Howard Griffith, Illinois	Southern Illinois	1990	48
Marshall Faulk, San Diego St	Pacific	1991	44
Jim Brown, Syracuse	Colgate	1956	43
Showboat Boykin, Mississippi	Mississippi St	1951	42
Fred Wendt, UTEP*	New Mexico St	1948	42

*UTEP was Texas Mines in 1948.

FIELD GOALS

	Opponent	Year	FG
Dale Klein, Nebraska	Missouri	1985	7
Mike Prindle, Western Michigan	Marshall	1984	7

Note: 14 tied with 6.
Klein's distances were 32-22-43-44-29-43-43. Prindle's distances were 32-44-42-23-48-41-27.

Single Game (Cont.)

Total Offense

YARDS GAINED	Opponent	Year	Yds
David Klingler, Houston	Arizona St	1990	732
Matt Vogler, TCU	Houston	1990	696
Brian Lindgren, Idaho	Middle Tenn St	2001	657
David Klingler, Houston	Texas Christian	1990	625
Scott Mitchell, Utah	Air Force	1988	625

Passing

YARDS GAINED	Opponent	Year	Yds
David Klingler, Houston	Arizona St	1990	716
Matt Vogler, TCU	Houston	1990	690
Brian Lindgren, Idaho	Middle Tenn St	2001	637
Scott Mitchell, Utah	Air Force	1988	631
Jeremy Leach, New Mexico	Utah	1989	622

COMPLETIONS	Opponent	Year	Comp
Drew Brees, Purdue	Wisconsin	1998	55
Rusty LaRue, Wake Forest	Duke	1995	55
Rusty LaRue, Wake Forest	NC St	1995	50
Brian Lindgren, Idaho	Middle Tenn St	2001	49
Kliff Kingsbury, Texas Tech	Missouri	2002	49
Kliff Kingsbury, Texas Tech	Texas A&M	2002	49

TOUCHDOWNS PASSING	Opponent	Year	TD
David Klingler, Houston	E Wash	1990	11

Note: Klingler's TD passes were 5-48-29-7-3-7-40-10-7-8-51.

Rushing

YARDS GAINED	Opponent	Year	Yds
LaDainian Tomlinson	UTEP	1999	406
Tony Sands, Kansas, Texas Christian	Missouri	1991	396
Marshall Faulk, San Diego St	Pacific	1991	386
Troy Davis, Iowa St	Missouri	1996	378
Anthony Thompson, Indiana	Wisconsin	1989	377
Robbie Mixon, Central Michigan	Eastern Mich	2002	377

TOUCHDOWNS RUSHING	Opponent	Year	TD
Howard Griffith, Illinois	Southern Illinois	1990	8

Note: Griffith's TD runs were 5-51-7-41-5-18-5-3.

Receiving

CATCHES	Opponent	Year	No.
Randy Gatewood, UNLV	Idaho	1994	23
Jay Miller, Brigham Young	New Mexico	1973	22
Troy Edwards, La. Tech	Nebraska	1998	21
Chris Daniels, Purdue	Michigan St	1999	21
Rick Eber, Tulsa	Idaho St	1967	20
Kenny Christian, Eastern Michigan	Temple	2000	20

YARDS GAINED	Opponent	Year	Yds
Troy Edwards, Louisiana Tech	Nebraska	1998	405
Randy Gatewood, UNLV	Idaho	1994	363
Chuck Hughes, UTEP*	N Texas St	1965	349
Nate Burleson, Nevada	San Jose St	2001	326
Rick Eber, Tulsa	Idaho St	1967	322

*UTEP was Texas Western in 1965.

TOUCHDOWN CATCHES	Opponent	Year	TD
Tim Delaney, San Diego St	New Mex. St	1969	6

Note: Delaney's TD catches were 2-22-34-31-30-9.

Longest Plays (since 1941)

PASSING	Opponent	Year	Yds
Fred Owens to Jack Ford, Portland	St. Mary's (CA)	1947	99
Bo Burris to Warren McVea, Houston	Washington St	1966	99
Colin Clapton to Eddie Jenkins, Holy Cross	Boston U	1970	99
Terry Peel to Robert Ford, Houston	Syracuse	1970	99
Terry Peel to Robert Ford, Houston	San Diego St	1972	99
Cris Collinsworth to Derrick Gaffney, Florida	Rice	1977	99
Scott Ankrom to James Maness, Texas Christian	Rice	1984	99
Gino Toretta to Horace Copeland, Miami (FL)	Arkansas	1991	99
John Paci to Thomas Lewis, Indiana	Penn St	1993	99
Troy DeGar to Wes Caswell, Tulsa	Oklahoma	1996	99
Drew Brees to Vinny Sutherland, Purdue	Northwestern	1999	99
Dan Urban to Justin McCariens, Northern Illinois	Ball St	2000	99
Jason Johnson to Brandon Marshall, Arizona	Idaho	2001	99

RUSHING	Opponent	Year	Yd
Gale Sayers, Kansas	Nebraska	1963	99
Max Anderson, Arizona St	Wyoming	1967	99
Ralph Thompson, W Texas St	Wichita St	1970	99
Kelsey Finch, Tennessee	Florida	1977	99
Eric Vann, Kansas	Oklahoma	1997	99

FIELD GOALS	Opponent	Year	Yds
Steve Little, Arkansas	Texas	1977	67
Russell Erxleben, Texas	Rice	1977	67
Joe Williams, Wichita St	Southern IL	1978	67
Martin Gramatica, Kansas St	Northern IL	1998	65
Tony Franklin, Texas A&M	Baylor	1976	65

PUNTS	Opponent	Year	Yds
Pat Brady, Nevada*	Loyola (CA)	1950	99
George O'Brien, Wisconsin	Iowa	1952	96
John Hadl, Kansas	Oklahoma	1959	94
Carl Knox, Texas Christian	Oklahoma St	1947	94
Preston Johnson, SMU	Pittsburgh	1940	94

*Nevada was Nevada-Reno in 1950.

DIVISION I-A WINNINGEST TEAMS
Alltime Winning Percentage

	Yrs	W	L	T	Pct	GP	Bowl Record
Notre Dame	114	791	250	42	.750	1,083	13-12-0
Michigan	124	823	269	36	.746	1,128	17-16-0
Alabama	108	754	284	43	.717	1,081	29-19-3
Oklahoma	108	725	282	53	.709	1,060	22-12-1
Texas	110	766	306	33	.708	1,105	20-20-2
Ohio St	113	745	292	53	.708	1,090	15-19-0
Nebraska	113	771	308	40	.707	1,119	20-21-0
Tennessee	106	726	299	52	.698	1,077	23-20-0
Penn St	116	753	322	41	.693	1,116	23-12-2
Southern Cal	110	695	296	54	.691	1,045	26-15-0
Florida St	56	409	194	17	.673	620	18-11-2
Boise St	35	271	134	2	.668	407	3-0-0
Washington	113	632	347	50	.639	1,029	14-14-1
Georgia	109	662	367	54	.636	1,083	20-15-3
Miami (OH)	114	611	342	44	.635	997	5-2-0
Miami (FL)	76	496	283	19	.634	798	15-12-0
Louisiana St	109	636	368	47	.628	1,051	16-17-1
Arizona St	90	502	303	24	.620	829	10-8-1
Auburn	110	626	374	47	.620	1047	15-12-2
Florida	96	582	354	40	.617	976	13-16-0
Colorado	113	630	384	36	.617	1,050	11-14-0
Central Michigan	102	519	317	36	.616	872	0-2-0
Army	113	622	393	51	.607	1,066	2-2-0
Texas A&M	108	623	396	48	.606	1,067	13-14-0
UCLA	84	499	323	37	.603	859	12-10-1

Note: Includes bowl games.

Alltime Victories

Michigan	823	Georgia	662	W Virginia	615
Notre Dame	791	Syracuse	652	Pittsburgh	612
Nebraska	771	Louisiana St	636	Miami (OH)	611
Texas	766	Washington	632	Arkansas	610
Alabama	754	Colorado	630	Minnesota	599
Penn St	753	Auburn	626	Virginia Tech	597
Ohio St	745	Texas A&M	623	Clemson	585
Tennessee	726	Army	622	Florida	582
Oklahoma	725	N Carolina	619	Navy	581
Southern Cal	695	Georgia Tech	616	Mississippi	573

NUMBER ONE VS NUMBER TWO

The No. 1 and No. 2 teams, according to the Associated Press Poll, have met 33 times, including 13 bowl games, since the poll's inception in 1936. The No. 1 teams have a 20-11-2 record in these matchups. Notre Dame (4-3-2) has played in nine of the games.

Date	Results	Stadium
10-9-43	No. 1 Notre Dame 35, No. 2 Michigan 12	Michigan (Ann Arbor)
11-20-43	No. 1 Notre Dame 14, No. 2 Iowa Pre-Flight 13	Notre Dame (South Bend)
12-2-44	No. 1 Army 23, No. 2 Navy 7	Municipal (Baltimore)
11-10-45	No. 1 Army 48, No. 2 Notre Dame 0	Yankee (New York)
12-1-45	No. 1 Army 32, No. 2 Navy 13	Municipal (Philadelphia)
11-9-46	No. 1 Army 0, No. 2 Notre Dame 0	Yankee (New York)
1-1-63	No. 1 Southern Cal 42, No. 2 Wisconsin 37 (Rose Bowl)	Rose Bowl (Pasadena)
10-12-63	No. 2 Texas 28, No. 1 Oklahoma 7	Cotton Bowl (Dallas)
1-1-64	No. 1 Texas 28, No. 2 Navy 6 (Cotton Bowl)	Cotton Bowl (Dallas)
11-19-66	No. 1 Notre Dame 10, No. 2 Michigan St 10	Spartan (E Lansing)
9-28-68	No. 1 Purdue 37, No. 2 Notre Dame 22	Notre Dame (South Bend)
1-1-69	No. 1 Ohio St 27, No. 2 Southern Cal 16 (Rose Bowl)	Rose Bowl (Pasadena)
12-6-69	No. 1 Texas 15, No. 2 Arkansas 14	Razorback (Fayetteville)
11-25-71	No. 1 Nebraska 35, No. 2 Oklahoma 31	Owen Field (Norman)
1-1-72	No. 1 Nebraska 38, No. 2 Alabama 6 (Orange Bowl)	Orange Bowl (Miami)
1-1-79	No. 2 Alabama 14, No. 1 Penn St 7 (Sugar Bowl)	Sugar Bowl (New Orleans)
9-26-81	No. 1 Southern Cal 28, No. 2 Oklahoma 24	Coliseum (Los Angeles)
1-1-83	No. 2 Penn St 27, No. 1 Georgia 23 (Sugar Bowl)	Sugar Bowl (New Orleans)

NUMBER ONE VS NUMBER TWO *(Cont.)*

Date	Results	Stadium
10-19-85	No. 1 Iowa 12, No. 2 Michigan 10	Kinnick (Iowa City)
9-27-86	No. 2 Miami (FL) 28, No. 1 Oklahoma 16	Orange Bowl (Miami)
1-2-87	No. 2 Penn St 14, No. 1 Miami (FL) 10 (Fiesta Bowl)	Sun Devil (Tempe)
11-21-87	No. 2 Oklahoma 17, No. 1 Nebraska 7	Memorial (Lincoln)
1-1-88	No. 2 Miami (FL) 20, No. 1 Oklahoma 14 (Orange Bowl)	Orange Bowl (Miami)
11-26-88	No. 1 Notre Dame 27, No. 2 Southern Cal 10	Coliseum (Los Angeles)
9-16-89	No. 1 Notre Dame 24, No. 2 Michigan 19	Michigan (Ann Arbor)
11-16-91	No. 2 Miami (FL) 17, No. 1 Florida St 16	Campbell (Tallahassee)
1-1-93	No. 2 Alabama 34, No. 1 Miami (FL) 13 (Sugar Bowl)	Superdome (New Orleans)
11-13-93	No. 2 Notre Dame 31, No. 1 Florida St 24	Notre Dame (South Bend)
1-1-94	No. 1 Florida St 18, No. 2 Nebraska 16 (Orange Bowl)	Orange Bowl (Miami)
1-2-96	No. 1 Nebraska 62, No. 2 Florida 24 (Fiesta Bowl)	Sun Devil (Tempe)
11-30-96	No. 2 Florida St 24, No. 1 Florida 21	Campbell (Tallahassee)
1-4-99	No. 1 Tennessee 23, No. 2 Florida St 16 (Fiesta Bowl)	Sun Devil (Tempe)
1-4-00	No. 1 Florida St 46, No. 2 Virginia Tech 29 (Sugar Bowl)	Superdome (New Orleans)
1-3-03	No. 2 Ohio St 31, Miami (FL) 24 [2OT] (Fiesta Bowl)	Sun Devil (Tempe)

LONGEST DIVISION I-A WINNING STREAKS

Wins	Team	Yrs	Ended by	Score
47	Oklahoma	1953–57	Notre Dame	7–0
39	Washington	1908–14	Oregon St	0–0
37	Yale	1890–93	Princeton	6–0
37	Yale	1887–89	Princeton	10–0
35	Toledo	1969–71	Tampa	21–0
34	Miami	2000–03	Ohio St	31–24 (2ot)
34	Pennsylvania	1894–96	Lafayette	6–4
31	Oklahoma	1948–50	Kentucky	13–7
31	Pittsburgh	1914–18	Cleveland Naval Reserve	10–9
31	Pennsylvania	1896–98	Harvard	10–0
30	Texas	1968–70	Notre Dame	24–11

LONGEST DIVISION I-A UNBEATEN STREAKS

No.	W	T	Team	Yrs	Ended by	Score
63	59	4	Washington	1907–17	California	27–0
56	55	1	Michigan	1901–05	Chicago	2–0
50	46	4	California	1920–25	Olympic Club	15–0
48	47	1	Oklahoma	1953–57	Notre Dame	7–0
48	47	1	Yale	1885–89	Princeton	10–0
47	42	5	Yale	1879–85	Princeton	6–5
44	42	2	Yale	1894–96	Princeton	24–6
42	39	3	Yale	1904–08	Harvard	4–0
39	37	2	Notre Dame	1946–50	Purdue	28–14
37	36	1	Oklahoma	1972–75	Kansas	23–3
37	37	0	Yale	1890–93	Princeton	6–0
35	35	0	Toledo	1969–71	Tampa	21–0
35	34	1	Minnesota	1903–05	Wisconsin	16–12
34	34	0	Miami	2000–03	Ohio St	31–24 (2ot)
34	33	1	Nebraska	1912–16	Kansas	7–3
34	34	0	Pennsylvania	1894–96	Lafayette	6–4
34	32	2	Princeton	1884–87	Harvard	12–0
34	29	5	Princeton	1877–82	Harvard	1–0
33	30	3	Tennessee	1926–30	Alabama	18–6
33	31	2	Georgia Tech	1914–18	Pittsburgh	32–0
33	30	3	Harvard	1911–15	Cornell	10–0
32	31	1	Nebraska	1969–71	UCLA	20–17
32	30	2	Army	1944–47	Columbia	21–20
32	31	1	Harvard	1898–1900	Yale	28–0
31	30	1	Penn St	1967–70	Colorado	41–13
31	30	1	San Diego St	1967–70	Long Beach St	27–11
31	29	2	Georgia Tech	1950–53	Notre Dame	27–14
31	31	0	Oklahoma	1948–50	Kentucky	13–7
31	31	0	Pittsburgh	1914–18	Cleveland Naval	10–9
31	31	0	Pennsylvania	1896–98	Harvard	10–0

Note: Includes bowl games.

LONGEST DIVISION I-A LOSING STREAKS

Losses		Seasons	Ended Against	Score
34	Northwestern	1979–82	Northern Illinois	31–6
28	Virginia	1958–61	William & Mary	21–6
28	Kansas St	1945–48	Arkansas St	37–6
27	New Mexico St	1988–90	Cal St–Fullerton	43–9
27	Eastern Michigan	1980–82	Kent St	9–7

MOST-PLAYED DIVISION I-A RIVALRIES

GP	Opponents (Series Leader Listed First)	Record	First Game	GP	Opponents (Series Leader Listed First)	Record	First Game
112	Minnesota-Wisconsin	58-46-8	1890	100	Clemson–S Carolina	60-36-4	1896
111	Missouri-Kansas	52-50-9	1891	100	Kansas–Kansas St	61-34-5	1902
109	Nebraska-Kansas	85-21-3	1892	99	Mississippi–Miss St	56-37-6	1901
109	Texas–Texas A&M	70-34-5	1894	99	N Carolina–Wake Forest	65-31-2	1888
107	Miami (OH)-Cincinnati	57-43-7	1888	98	Michigan–Ohio St	56-37-6	1897
107	N Carolina–Virginia	†56-47-4	1892	98	Tennessee-Kentucky	66-23-9	1893
106	Auburn-Georgia	51-47-8	1892	97	Oklahoma-Kansas	63-28-6	1903
106	Oregon–Oregon St	53-43-10	1894	97	Georgia–Georgia Tech	54-38-5	1893
105	Purdue-Indiana	64-35-6	1891	97	Nebraska–Iowa St	80-15-2	1896
105	Stanford-California	54-40-11	1892	97	Texas-Oklahoma	55-37-5	1900
103	Baylor–Texas Christian*	49-47-7	1899	97	Oklahoma–Oklahoma St	74-16-7	1904
103	Army-Navy	49-47-7	1890				
102	Utah–Utah St	70-28-4	1892				

*Have not met since 1995.
†Disputed series record: Virginia claims N Carolina leads series 54-49-4 based on a forfeited game in 1956.

NCAA Coaches' Records

ALLTIME WINNINGEST DIVISION I-A COACHES

Coach (Alma Mater)	Colleges Coached	Yrs	W	L	T	Pct
Knute Rockne (Notre Dame '14)†	Notre Dame 1918–30	13	105	12	5	.881
Frank W. Leahy (Notre Dame '31)†	Boston Col 1939–40; Notre Dame 1941–43, 1946–53	13	107	13	9	.864
George W. Woodruff (Yale 1889)†	Pennsylvania 1892–01; Illinois 1903; Carlisle 1905	12	142	25	2	.846
Barry Switzer (Arkansas '60)	Oklahoma 1973–88	16	157	29	4	.837
Tom Osborne (Hastings '59)†	Nebraska 1973–98	25	255	49	3	.836
Percy D. Haughton (Harvard 1899)†	Cornell 1899–1900; Harvard 1908–16; Columbia 1923–24	13	96	17	6	.832
Bob Neyland (Army '16)†	Tennessee 1926–34, 1936–40, 1946–52	21	173	31	12	.829
Fielding Yost (W Virginia 1895)†	Ohio Wesleyan 1897; Nebraska 1898; Kansas 1899; Stanford 1900; Michigan 1901–23, 1925–26	29	196	36	12	.828
Bud Wilkinson (Minnesota '37)†	Oklahoma 1947–63	17	145	29	4	.826
Jock Sutherland (Pittsburgh '18)†	Lafayette 1919–23; Pittsburgh 1924–38	20	144	28	14	.812
Bob Devaney (Alma, MI '39)†	Wyoming 1957–61; Nebraska 1962–72	16	136	30	7	.806
*Phillip Fulmer (Tennessee '71)	Tennessee 1992–	11	103	25	0	.805
Frank W. Thomas (Notre Dame '23)†	Tenn.-Chattanooga 1925–28; Alabama 1931–42, 1944–46	19	141	33	9	.795
Henry L. Williams (Yale 1891)†	Army 1891; Minnesota 1900–21	23	141	34	12	.786
Gil Dobie (Minnesota '02)†	N Dakota St 1906–07; Washington 1908-16; Navy 1917–19; Cornell 1920–35; Boston College 1936–38	33	180	45	15	.781
Bear Bryant (Alabama '36)†	Maryland 1945, Kentucky 1946–53, Texas A&M 1954–57, Alabama 1958–82	38	323	85	17	.780

*Active in 2002. †Hall of Fame member.
Note: Minimum 10 years as head coach at Division I institutions; record at four-year colleges only; bowl games included; ranked by percentage, ties computed as half won, half lost.

ALLTIME WINNINGEST DIVISION I-A COACHES *(Cont.)*
By Victories

	Yrs	W	L	T	Pct		Yrs	W	L	T	Pct
*Joe Paterno	37	336	100	3	.769	Bo Schembechler	27	234	65	8	.775
*Bobby Bowden	37	332	96	4	.773	Hayden Fry	37	232	178	10	.564
Paul (Bear) Bryant	38	323	85	17	.780	Jess Neely	40	207	176	19	.539
Glenn (Pop) Warner	44	319	106	32	.733	Warren Woodson	31	203	95	14	.673
Amos Alonzo Stagg	57	314	199	35	.605	Don Nehlen	30	202	128	8	.609
LaVell Edwards	29	257	100	3	.718	Vince Dooley	25	201	77	10	.715
Tom Osborne	25	255	49	3	.836	Eddie Anderson	39	201	128	15	.606
Woody Hayes	33	238	72	10	.759	*Active in 2002.					
*Lou Holtz	31	238	120	7	.662						

Most Bowl Victories

	W	L	T		W	L	T
*Joe Paterno	20	10	1	Barry Switzer	8	5	0
*Bobby Bowden	18	7	1	*Jackie Sherrill	8	6	0
Paul (Bear) Bryant	15	12	2	Darrell Royal	8	7	1
Jim Wacker	13	2	0	Vince Dooley	8	10	2
*Lou Holtz	12	8	2	Pat Dye	7	2	1
Tom Osborne	12	13	0	Bob Devaney	7	3	0
Don James	10	5	0	Dan Devine	7	3	0
John Vaught	10	8	0	Earle Bruce	7	5	0
Bobby Dodd	9	4	0	Charlie McClendon	7	6	0
Johnny Majors	9	7	0	Hayden Fry	7	9	1
*John Robinson	8	1	0	LaVell Edwards	7	14	1
Terry Donahue	8	4	1	*Active in 2002.			

WINNINGEST ACTIVE DIVISION I-A COACHES
By Percentage

Coach, College	Yrs	W	L	T	Pct#	Bowls		
						W	L	T
Bob Pruett, Marshall	7	80	13	0	.860	5	1	0
Phillip Fulmer, Tennessee	11	103	25	0	.805	6	5	0
Bobby Bowden, Florida St	37	332	96	4	.773	18	7	1
Joe Paterno, Penn St	37	336	100	3	.769	20	10	1
Lloyd Carr, Michigan	8	76	23	0	.768	5	3	0
R. C. Slocum, Texas A&M	14	123	47	2	.721	3	8	0
Dennis Erickson, Oregon St	17	144	56	1	.719	5	5	0
Bill Snyder, Kansas St	14	116	51	1	.694	6	4	0
Rick Neuheisel, Washington	8	66	30	0	.688	4	3	0
Dennis Franchione, Texas A&M	20	155	73	2	.678	5	2	0

#Bowl games included in overall record. Ties computed as half win, half loss..
Note: Minimum five years as Division I-A head coach; record at four-year colleges only.

YET ANOTHER SIGN OF THE APOCALYPSE

Florida State canceled two days of classes during the 2002 football season because of concerns about campus congestion brought on by a Thursday night home game against Clemson.

WINNINGEST ACTIVE DIVISION I-A COACHES *(Cont.)*
By Victories

Joe Paterno, Penn St 336	Frank Beamer, Virginia Tech 159
Bobby Bowden, Florida St 332	Dennis Franchione, Alabama 155
Lou Holtz, S Carolina 238	Fisher DeBerry, Air Force 149
Jackie Sherrill, Mississippi St 178	Dennis Erickson, Oregon St 144
Ken Hatfield, Rice 159	Paul Pasqualoni, Syracuse 129
	Mike Price, Washington St 129

WINNINGEST ACTIVE DIVISION I-AA COACHES
By Percentage

Coach, College	Yrs	W	L	T	Pct*
Mike Kelly, Dayton 22		206	41	1	.833
Greg Gattuso, Duquesne 10		82	25	0	.766
Al Bagnoli, Pennsylvania 21		163	51	0	.762
Pete Richardson, Southern 15		126	47	1	.727
Roy Kidd, Eastern Kentucky 39		315	123	8	.715
Joe Gardi, Hofstra 13		105	42	2	.711
Billy Joe, Florida A&M 29		228	94	4	.706
Joe Taylor, Hampton 20		153	64	4	.701
Walt Hameline, Wagner 22		157	71	2	.687
Joe Walton, Robert Morris 9		61	28	1	.683

*Playoff games included.

Note: Minimum five years as a Division I-A and/or Division I-AA head coach; record at four-year colleges only.

By Victories

Roy Kidd, Eastern Kentucky 315	Al Bagnoli, Pennsylvania 163
Billy Joe, Florida A&M 228	Walt Hameline, Wagner 157
Mike Kelly, Dayton 206	Jimmye Laycock, William & Mary 154
Ron Randleman, Sam Houston St 205	Joe Taylor, Hampton 153
Bill Hayes, N Carolina A&T 195	Andy Talley, Villanova 152

WINNINGEST ACTIVE DIVISION II COACHES
By Percentage

Coach, College	Yrs	W	L	T	Pct*
Chuck Broyles, Pittsburg St (KS) 13		131	26	2	.834
Ken Sparks, Carson-Newman 23		223	52	2	.809
John Luckhardt, California (PA) 18		143	42	2	.770
Brian Kelly, Grand Valley St 12		104	34	2	.750
Bob Biggs, UC–Davis 10		90	30	1	.748
Danny Hale, Bloomsburg 15		121	44	1	.732
Peter Yetten, Bentley 15		108	40	1	.728
Frank Cignetti, Indiana (PA) 21		176	69	1	.718
Dale Lennon, N Dakota 6		48	21	0	.696
Kent Schoolfield, Fort Valley St 6		48	21	0	.696

*Ties computed as half win, half loss. Playoff games included.

Note: Minimum five years as a college head coach; record at four-year colleges only.

By Victories

Ken Sparks, Carson-Newman 223	Gary Howard, Central Oklahoma 162
Willard Bailey, Virginia Union 205	Mel Tjeerdsma, NW Missouri St 147
Bud Elliott, Eastern New Mexico 193	John Luckhardt, California (PA) 143
Frank Cignetti, Indiana (PA) 176	Jerry Vandergriff, Angelo St 138
Dennis Douds, E Stroudsburg 170	Monte Cater, Shepherd 137

WINNINGEST ACTIVE DIVISION III
By Percentage

Coach, College	Yrs	W	L	T	Pct*
Larry Kehres, Mount Union	17	192	17	3	.913
Joe Fincham, Wittenberg	7	73	9	0	.890
Dick Farley, Williams	16	108	17	3	.856
Rich Kacmarynski, Central (IA)	6	57	10	0	.851
Rick Willis, Wartburg	6	53	10	0	.841
Chris Creighton, Wabash	6	52	10	0	.839
Bill Zwaan, Widener	6	54	14	0	.794
John Gagliardi, St. John's (MN)	54	400	114	11	.772
E. J. Mills, Amherst	6	37	11	0	.771
Frosty Westering, Pacific Lutheran	38	299	93	7	.758

*Ties computed as half won, half lost. Playoff games included.

Note: Minimum five years as a college head coach; record at four-year colleges only.

By Victories

John Gagliardi, St John's (MN)	400	Tom Gilburg, Franklin & Marshall	160
Frosty Westering, Pacific Lutheran	299	Eric Hamilton, College of New Jersey	159
Frank Girardi, Lycoming	232	Lou Wacker, Emory & Henry	155
Peter Mazzaferro, Bridgewater (MA)	197	Wayne Perry, Hanover	150
Larry Kehres, Mount Union	192	Rick Giancola, Montclair St	139

NAIA Coaches' Records

WINNINGEST ACTIVE NAIA COACHES
By Percentage

Coach, College	Yrs	W	L	T	Pct*
Bill Cronin, Georgetown (KY)	6	64	10	0	.865
Ted Kessinger, Bethany (KS)	27	214	53	1	.800
Hank Biesiot, Dickinson St (ND)	28	191	68	1	.737
Carl Poelker, McKendree (IL)	21	140	60	1	.699
Bob Young, Sioux Falls (SD)	21	149	67	3	.687
Geno DeMarco, Geneva (PA)	10	71	35	0	.670
Larry Wilcox, Benedictine (KS)	24	168	85	0	.664
Vic Wallace, Lambuth (TN)	21	145	79	4	.645
Orv Otten, Northwestern (IA)	8	54	30	0	.643
Todd Sturdy, St. Ambrose (IA)	8	52	29	0	.642

*Playoff games included.

Note: Minimum five years as a collegiate head coach and includes record against four-year institutions only.

By Victories

Ted Kessinger, Bethany (KS)	214	Vic Wallace, Lambuth (TN)	145
Hank Biesiot, Dickinson St (ND)	191	Carl Poelker, McKendree (IL)	140
Larry Wilcox, Benedictine (KS)	168	Jim Dennison, Walsh (OH)	135
Kevin Donley, St. Francis (IN)	155	Fran Schwenk, Doane (NE)	110
Bob Young, Sioux Falls (SD)	149	Bob Green, Montana Tech	95

David Robinson
of the NBA champion
San Antonio Spurs

Pro Basketball

JOHN W. MCDONOUGH

Going in Style

The league said goodbye to Michael Jordan, John Stockton and David Robinson, the last of whom went out with a second NBA title

BY STEPHEN CANNELLA

SPORTS PSYCHOLOGISTS, self-help gurus and a certain Los Angeles–based Zen master preach that living in the moment is the key to happiness, inner peace and swished free throws. It's sound advice, but even the most disciplined Buddhist monk would have had difficulty focusing on the here and now during the 2002–03 NBA season. The temptations of the past and future were too great.

On one hand there was the haze of nostalgia surrounding the final tours of three of the league's brightest stars. Michael Jordan and David Robinson announced before the season that they would retire when it ended, and as they took their last laps around the league they were honored at every stop. (Jordan's final appearances were greeted with decidedly more hoopla, which was precisely how Robinson, humble to the end, wanted it.) Then, in a move that surprised no one, John Stockton followed suit shortly after the Utah Jazz were eliminated from the Western Conference playoffs, ending his 19-year career and his incomparable partnership with Karl Malone. Just like that, three of the 50 greatest players in NBA history were gone.

When fans weren't reliving the glory days of His Airness, the Admiral and the league's alltime assists leader, they were fixating on a player who wouldn't even debut as a professional until the following season. With all due respect to Robinson's San Antonio Spurs, who defeated the New Jersey Nets in six artless games to win their second NBA title in five years, their unlikely championship run was little more than a distraction from the LeBron James hype machine. It's no stretch to say that the 18-year-old point guard from St. Vincent–St. Mary High School in Akron, Ohio, was the most talked-about player around the league, whether the topic of conversation was his Magic Johnson–like game, his megawatt smile, his $90 million Nike endorsement contract or his expensive tastes in vintage jerseys and motor vehicles. After James put on a so-so performance (21 points) in a January tournament game at UCLA's Pauley Pavilion,

Duncan won both the regular-season and Finals MVP awards.

Bill Walton, who broadcast the game to a national audience in ESPN, pronounced, "I still believe LeBron James would start on any NBA team today."

So it was easy to view the 2002–03 season the way some poeple look back on the Eisenhower years, as the bland period between two rollicking eras. The Finals matchup between the Spurs and the Nets typified the season, providing precious little to capture the nation's attention. To begin with, there was no marquee team involved, the Spurs having eliminated the Los Angeles Lakers, with their superstar tandem of Shaq and Kobe, and the Dallas Mavericks, with their appealing assemblage of international talent, including Dirk Nowitzki of Germany, Steve Nash of Canada and reserve Eduardo Najera of Mexico, en route to the Finals. The Sacramento Kings, who won the Pacific Division by nine games, lost star forward Chris Webber to a knee injury in the playoffs and lost to Dallas in the second round. The Boston Celtics and the Philadelphia 76ers bowed out in the Eastern Conference semifinals, and the big-market New York Knicks missed the playoffs altogether. There was no must-see leading man, such as the Lakers' Shaquille O'Neal or Dallas owner Mark Cuban, for fans to rally behind or rail against. And there was no overarching drama, such as the Lakers' pursuit of a four-peat, to lend the occasion historic gravity.

It was no surprise, then, that the Spurs-Nets matchup drew the lowest television ratings for an NBA Finals in 27 years. The series featured all the up and down action of the Battle of the Somme. The Spurs and the Nets combined to average 169.8 points per game, the third-lowest total in Finals history, and neither team shot well consistently. San Antonio executed coach Gregg Popovich's game plans to perfection and did a spectacular job of getting back on defense to stonewall New Jersey's fast-break offense.

Jason Kidd, the league's preeminent point guard and the focal point of the Nets' offense, was forced to operate mostly in a half-court set rather than in the open floor, where's he's most comfortable and dangerous. The Nets shot only 37.0% in the series

ANDREW D. BERNSTEIN / NBAE/ GETTY IMAGES

and averaged a modest 8.5 points per outing. But he turned back the clock in San Antonio's series-clinching, 88–77 win, scoring 13 points and pulling down 17 rebounds. "My last game, streamers flying, world champions," he said afterward. "How could you write a better script than this? I've had some ups and downs in my career, but I'm gonna end on the highest of highs."

It was a rare moment of ebullience from a member of the Spurs, who to a man reflected the even-keeled image of their superstar, Tim Duncan. The laconic seven-footer, who was named the regular-season MVP after averaging 23.3 points and 12.9 rebounds per game, was his metronomic self in the Finals, averaging 24.2 points, 17 rebounds and 5.3 assists. Duncan's stamp—from his sound fundamental play to his squeaky-clean, low-gloss image—was all over the Spurs' championship, and he carted off the Finals MVP award following a command performance in Game 6 (21 points, 20 rebounds, 10 assists and eight blocked shots) that cemented his reputation as one of the greatest big men the game has ever seen. Afterward a reporter asked him if he realized how close he was to a quadruple double. "No, I didn't," he said with a disinterested shrug. "That's cool."

Some would argue that dispatching the Nets was a mere formality for the Spurs, that they cleared the toughest hurdle on the road to the championship two rounds earlier, when they downed Los Angeles in six games. The Lakers spent the first half of the season in a fog, losing 19 of their first 30 games. O'Neal missed the first 12 games of the season after a September operation on his arthritic right big toe that could have—nay, *should* have—been done early in the offseason. The Big Aristotle was now the Big Aristoe-tle, and he struggled for weeks to get

and Kidd, who led the team in scoring (19.7 ppg), got little help from his supporting cast. Forward Kenyon Martin, for example, picked up a stomach flu and all but disappeared as the series wound down. He turned the ball over eight times in New Jersey's 93–83 Game 5 loss, then shot a horrid 3-for-23 from the field in the deciding Game 6.

Kidd's uncertain future (there was speculation that he would sign with San Antonio as a free agent after the season, but he ended up re-signing with New Jersey) was yet another factor sapping attention from the Finals themselves. On the other hand, the storybook finish to Robinson's career did lend the series some verve. Limited by injuries for much of the year, the Admiral had played in only 64 regular-season games back into the flow after his return. By the All-Star break the Lakers were a bickering, disharmonious group and even coach Phil Jackson, the maestro of superstar egos, had to wonder if the Lakers could make beautiful music again. With a record of 24–23, the team was a long shot to make the playoffs, much less win a fourth straight championship.

Things began to turn for LA in February, when guard Kobe Bryant embarked upon a torrid scoring streak. Bryant single-handedly dragged the Lakers back into the playoff hunt by scoring 40 or more points in nine straight games and 35 or more in 13 straight. (Only Wilt Chamberlain has a longer run of 35-point games.) The streak established Bryant, 24, as the heir to Jordan's mantle as the league's top clutch performer and most explosive scorer. More important for the Lakers, who went 11–2 during that stretch, Bryant's heroics got their season back on track. They won 11 of their last 13 games and charged into the postseason as the fifth seed in the Western Conference.

Los Angeles eliminated the Minnesota Timberwolves—who lost in the first round of the playoffs for a record seventh straight season—in six games before falling to the Spurs. Shortly after his team was eliminated, O'Neal announced he would dedicate himself to an offseason workout regimen and pledged to arrive in training camp ready for another title run. The Lakers also reloaded their lineup, signing veteran All-Stars Karl Malone and Gary Payton with an eye toward reclaiming the NBA title. But Bryant put that plan, as well as his own future, in jeopardy during the summer, when he became involved with a woman in a Colorado hotel room and got hit with a sexual assault charge. The case was scheduled for a preliminary hearing in the fall.

Bryant's future aside, O'Neal had other significant obstacles in his pursuit of a fourth ring. There was Duncan, of course, and Shaq gained a new rival—both in the paint and in the off-court competitions for endorsements and the public's imagination—in the outsized person of Houston Rockets' rookie center Yao Ming of China. When the Rockets chose Yao with the first pick in the 2002 draft, many observers questioned whether the 21-year-old could succeed in the NBA. Yao quickly put those worries to rest, averaging a respectable 13.5 points, 8.2 rebounds and 1.8 blocks per game in his first season. In his first head-to-head showdown with Shaq, in January, the 7' 5" Yao blocked three of O'Neal's shots in the first quarter.

Yao complemented his surprisingly high skill level with a winning personality and a charismatic smile, and he quickly became a worldwide sensation. Fan voting installed him (over Shaq) as the starting center for the Western Conference All-Star team. By mid-season, Houston's home attendance had shot up by more than 2,000 fans per game, and the Rockets became one of the league's best draws on the road. NBA games were broadcast by no fewer than 12 television networks in Yao's homeland, and China's favorite son popped up in a number of memorable U.S. TV commercials.

Yao wasn't the only young star on the rise. Orlando Magic guard Tracy McGrady, 24, led the the league in scoring (32.1 ppg) and nearly led his team to an upset of the top-seeded Pistons in the first round of the playoffs. (McGrady averaged 31.7 points in the series, but Detroit rallied from a three-games-to-one deficit and won in seven.) At age 27, the Timberwolves' Kevin Garnett has sealed his status among the game's elite. He led the NBA with six triple-doubles, averaged 23 points and 13.4 rebounds a game and, along with Bryant, was a contender for the MVP award that went to Duncan.

The emergence of these players was a welcome shot in the arm for the NBA. According to a midseason poll conducted by SPORTS ILLUSTRATED, fan interest in the league was dropping steadily; 62.1% of those polled said they were "not at all interested in the NBA." That trend isn't likely to be reversed by Jordan's departure. At age 40 Jordan showed flashes of his former briliance—he averaged 20.0 points per game and scored more than 40 three times—but for the second straight year he was unable to lead the Washington Wizards into the playoffs.

The NBA, and Cleveland fans, could hardly wait for the arrival of James.

Much of the good will of Jordan's final year—the ceremony honoring him at the All-Star Game, the ovations at every stop on his farewell tour—evaporated shortly after the season ended. In May, with rumors swirling that many Wizards players had strained relationships with Jordan, owner Abe Pollin asked His Airness not to return to his job as the team's president of basketball operations. The decision shocked Jordan, who had hoped to continue climbing the ranks of the organization. It also suggested that Jordan may find success more elusive in an executive's suite than it was on the court.

Jordan wasn't the only high-profile figure to get his walking papers. In a dizzying start to the offseason, seven teams hired new coaches in June. The Detroit Pistons, made the most surprising move, firing Rick Carlisle, the 2002 Coach of the Year and winner of two straight division titles, and replacing him with former 76ers coach Larry Brown, whose team was eliminated by the Pistons in the playoffs. Former Knicks coach Jeff Van Gundy left the broadcasters' booth to coach the Rockets. Former Chicago Bulls coach Tim Floyd landed with the New Orleans Hornets.

The Cleveland Cavaliers also made a coaching change, hiring former Hornets coach Paul Silas to mentor young LeBron James. The Cavaliers tied the Denver Nuggets for the league's worst record (17–65) and haven't won a playoff series since 1993. But from the moment the Cavs won the NBA draft lottery on May 22—there was never any doubt that they would take hometown hero James with the first pick—interest surged in Cleveland. There was a rush for Cavaliers season tickets,

FERNANDO MEDINA / NBAE/ GETTY IMAGES

and more than 10,000 people packed Gund Arena on draft night to watch the event on TV. "LeBron is like one in a billion," Cavaliers forward Darius Miles said. "Like there was Magic Johnson, now there's LeBron James. It comes once every couple decades."

With the physical maturity and skills of a much older player, James has the ability to thrive in the NBA—provided the trappings of stardom don't weigh him down. He was investigated by the Ohio High School Athletic Association after he was seen driving a $50,000 Hummer around Akron (he insisted his mother, Gloria, bought it for him), and he later forfeited some of his high school eligibility because he accepted several vintage basketball jerseys as a gift from a local merchant.

By the time he was drafted in June, however, those events were speed bumps in King James's past. His future—and that of the evolving NBA—were all that mattered.

NBA Final Standings

Eastern Conference

ATLANTIC DIVISION

Team	W	L	Pct	GB
New Jersey	49	33	.598	—
Philadelphia	48	34	.585	1
Boston	44	38	.537	5
Orlando	42	40	.512	7
Washington	37	45	.451	12
New York	37	45	.451	12
Miami	25	57	.305	24

CENTRAL DIVISION

Team	W	L	Pct	GB
Detroit	50	32	.610	—
Indiana	48	34	.585	2
New Orleans	47	35	.573	3
Milwaukee	42	40	.512	8
Atlanta	35	47	.427	15
Chicago	30	52	.366	20
Toronto	24	58	.293	26
Cleveland	17	65	.207	33

Western Conference

MIDWEST DIVISION

Team	W	L	Pct	GB
San Antonio	60	22	.732	—
Dallas	60	22	.732	0
Minnesota	51	31	.622	9
Utah	47	35	.573	13
Houston	43	39	.524	17
Memphis	28	54	.341	32
Denver	17	65	.207	43

PACIFIC DIVISION

Team	W	L	Pct	GB
Sacramento	59	23	.720	—
L.A. Lakers	50	32	.610	9
Portland	50	32	.610	9
Phoenix	44	38	.537	15
Seattle	40	42	.488	19
Golden State	38	44	.463	21
L.A. Clippers	27	55	.329	32

2003 NBA Playoffs

EASTERN CONFERENCE

WESTERN CONFERENCE

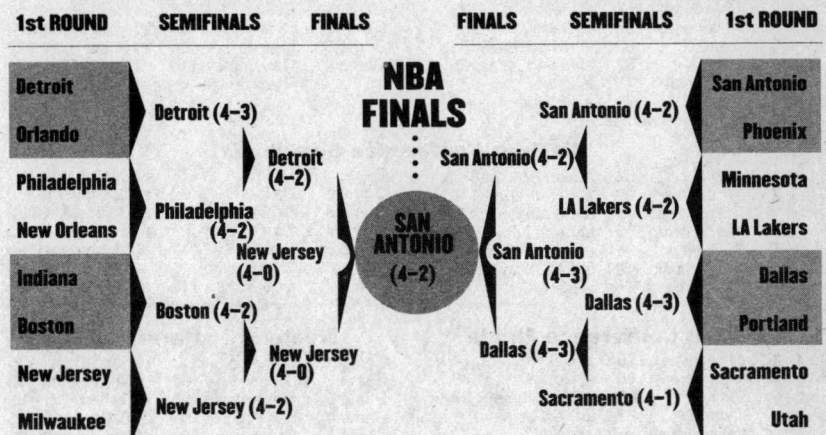

2003 NBA Playoff Results

Eastern Conference First Round

Game 1	Orlando	99	at Detroit	94
Game 2	Orlando	77	at Detroit	89
Game 3	Detroit	80	at Orlando	89
Game 4	Detroit	92	at Orlando	100
Game 5	Orlando	67	at Detroit	98
Game 6	Detroit	103	at Orlando	88
Game 7	Orlando	93	at Detroit	103

Detroit won series 4–3.

Game 1	Milwaukee	96	at New Jersey	109
Game 2	Milwaukee	88	at New Jersey	85
Game 3	New Jersey	103	at Milwaukee	101
Game 4	New Jersey	114	at Milwaukee	119 (ot)
Game 5	Milwaukee	83	at New Jersey	80
Game 6	New Jersey	113	at Milwaukee	101

New Jersey won series 4–2.

Game 1	Boston	103	at Indiana	100
Game 2	Boston	77	at Indiana	89
Game 3	Indiana	83	at Boston	101
Game 4	Indiana	92	at Boston	102
Game 5	Boston	88	at Indiana	93 (ot)
Game 6	Indiana	90	at Boston	110

Boston won series 4–2.

Game 1	New Orleans	90	at Philadelphia	98
Game 2	New Orleans	85	at Philadelphia	90
Game 3	Philadelphia	85	at New Orleans	99
Game 4	Philadelphia	96	at New Orleans	87
Game 5	New Orleans	93	at Philadelphia	91
Game 6	Philadelphia	107	at New Orleans	103

Philadelphia won series 4–2.

Western Conference First Round

Game 1	Phoenix	96	at San Antonio	95(ot)
Game 2	Phoenix	76	at San Antonio	84
Game 3	San Antonio	99	at Phoenix	86
Game 4	San Antonio	84	at Phoenix	86
Game 5	Phoenix	82	at San Antonio	94
Game 6	San Antonio	87	at Phoenix	85

San Antonio won series 4–2.

Game 1	Utah	90	at Sacramento	96
Game 2	Utah	95	at Sacramento	108
Game 3	Sacramento	104	at Utah	107
Game 4	Sacramento	99	at Utah	82
Game 5	Utah	91	at Sacramento	111

Sacramento won series 4–1.

Game 1	Portland	86	at Dallas	96
Game 2	Portland	99	at Dallas	103
Game 3	Dallas	115	at Portland	103
Game 4	Dallas	79	at Portland	98
Game 5	Portland	103	at Dallas	99
Game 6	Dallas	103	at Portland	125
Game 7	Portland	95	at Dallas	107

Dallas won series 4–3.

Game 1	LA Lakers	117	at Minnesota	98
Game 2	LA Lakers	91	at Minnesota	119
Game 3	Minnesota	114	at LA Lakers	110 (ot)
Game 4	Minnesota	97	at LA Lakers	102
Game 5	LA Lakers	120	at Minnesota	90
Game 6	Minnesota	85	at LA Lakers	101

LA Lakers won series 4–2.

Eastern Conference Semifinals

Game 1	Philadelphia	87	at Detroit	98
Game 2	Philadelphia	97	at Detroit	104
Game 3	Detroit	83	at Philadelphia	93
Game 4	Detroit	82	at Philadelphia	95
Game 5	Philadelphia	77	at Detroit	78
Game 6	Detroit	93	at Philadelphia	89

Detroit won series 4–2.

Game 1	Boston	93	at New Jersey	97
Game 2	Boston	95	at New Jersey	97
Game 3	New Jersey	94	at Boston	76
Game 4	New Jersey	110	at Boston	101

New Jersey won series 4–0.

Western Conference Semifinals

Game 1	LA Lakers	82	at San Antonio	87
Game 2	LA Lakers	95	at San Antonio	114
Game 3	San Antonio	95	at LA Lakers	110
Game 4	San Antonio	95	at LA Lakers	99
Game 5	LA Lakers	94	at San Antonio	96
Game 6	San Antonio	110	at LA Lakers	82

San Antonio won series 4–2.

Game 1	Dallas	113	at Sacramento	124
Game 2	Dallas	132	at Sacramento	110
Game 3	Sacramento	137	at Dallas	141 (2 ot)
Game 4	Sacramento	99	at Dallas	83
Game 5	Dallas	112	at Sacramento	93
Game 6	Sacramento	115	at Dallas	109
Game 7	Dallas	112	at Sacramento	99

Dallas won series 4–3.

Eastern Conference Finals

Game 1	New Jersey	76	at Detroit	74
Game 2	New Jersey	88	at Detroit	86
Game 3	New Jersey	86	at New Jersey	97
Game 4	Detroit	82	at New Jersey	102

New Jersey won series 4–0.

Western Conference Finals

Game 1	Dallas	113	at San Antonio	110
Game 2	Dallas	106	at San Antonio	119
Game 3	San Antonio	96	at Dallas	83
Game 4	San Antonio	102	at Dallas	95
Game 5	Dallas	103	at San Antonio	91
Game 6	San Antonio	90	at Dallas	78

San Antonio won series 4–2.

Finals

Game 1	New Jersey	89	at San Antonio	101
Game 2	New Jersey	87	at San Antonio	85
Game 3	San Antonio	84	at New Jersey	79
Game 4	San Antonio	76	at New Jersey	77
Game 5	San Antonio	93	at New Jersey	83
Game 6	New Jersey	77	at San Antonio	88

San Antonio won series 4–2.

NBA Finals Composite Box Score

NEW JERSEY NETS

Player	GP	FG%	3FG%	FT%	Rebounds Off	Rebounds Total	A	Stl	TO	BS	Ppg	Hi
Kidd	6	36.4	27.0	83.3	14	37	47	7	18	1	19.7	30
Martin	6	34.3	0.0	66.7	15	60	13	10	22	14	14.7	23
Jefferson	6	41.7	0.0	79.2	8	39	11	8	14	2	13.2	19
Kittles	6	37.7	30.4	80.0	6	25	8	11	3	3	10.8	21
Harris	6	30.6	33.3	78.9	7	16	7	2	6	0	6.5	15
Williams	5	42.3	—	75.0	10	21	4	1	1	7	5.6	10
Rogers	6	32.3	37.5	83.3	4	10	3	0	5	0	4.7	11
Collins	6	33.3	0.0	80.0	15	28	6	4	5	3	3.7	7
Mutombo	6	50.0	—	100.0	7	17	0	3	5	8	2.3	4
Johnson	5	55.6	50.0	—	0	1	1	1	3	0	2.2	4
Scalabrine	1	—	—	—	0	1	0	0	0	0	0.0	0
Totals	**6**	**37.0**	**27.7**	**78.4**	**86**	**255**	**100**	**47**	**85**	**38**	**82.0**	**89**

SAN ANTONIO SPURS

Player	GP	FG%	3FG%	FT%	Rebounds Off	Rebounds Total	A	Stl	TO	BS	Ppg	Hi
Duncan	6	49.5	0.0	68.5	23	102	32	6	23	32	24.2	32
Parker	6	38.6	42.9	60.9	2	19	25	2	11	1	14.0	26
Robinson	6	61.1	—	70.0	15	44	4	7	3	11	10.8	14
Jackson	6	37.7	35.7	50.0	4	25	16	7	26	2	10.3	17
Ginobili	6	34.8	21.4	81.0	9	27	12	13	10	3	8.7	12
Rose	6	44.2	0.0	100.0	10	23	4	3	11	3	7.7	14
Claxton	6	56.0	—	75.0	1	6	9	4	4	4	6.2	13
Bowen	6	23.3	28.6	100.0	2	19	5	4	4	2	3.3	6
Kerr	4	75.0	100.0	50.0	1	1	2	1	0	0	2.0	6
Willis	5	33.3	—	100.0	7	9	0	0	3	1	1.6	6
Totals	**6**	**43.2**	**32.0**	**70.5**	**74**	**275**	**109**	**47**	**99**	**59**	**87.8**	**101**

NBA Finals Box Scores

Game 1

NEW JERSEY 89

NJ	Min	FG M-A	FT M-A	Reb O-T	A	PF	S	TO	TP
Kidd	44	4-17	1-2	0-8	10	1	2	3	10
Kittles	30	2-7	3-4	2-3	2	1	0	1	8
Jefferson	36	5-10	5-6	0-4	1	3	2	3	15
Martin	33	10-24	1-2	4-12	2	6	1	1	21
Collins	31	1-4	3-4	4-9	3	4	0	0	5
Harris	24	4-10	6-7	0-1	0	1	0	0	15
Rogers	21	5-10	0-0	1-2	1	3	0	0	11
Williams	11	2-5	0-0	2-4	0	4	0	0	4
Mutombo	6	0-1	0-0	0-2	0	2	0	0	0
Johnson	4	0-1	0-0	0-0	0	1	0	0	0
Totals	240	33-89	19-25	13-45	19	26	5	8	89

Percentages: FG—.371, FT—.760. 3-pt goals: 4-13, .308 (Kidd 1-5, Kittles 1-3, Martin 0-1, Harris 1-2, Rogers 1-2). Team rebounds: 11. Blocked shots: 5 (Kidd, Martin 2, Williams, Mutombo).

SAN ANTONIO 101

SA	Min	FG M-A	FT M-A	Reb O-T	A	PF	S	TO	TP
Jackson	42	5-15	2-5	1-3	5	3	2	3	12
Parker	40	6-14	3-4	0-3	5	0	1	2	16
Duncan	44	11-17	10-14	3-20	6	1	3	1	32
Bowen	26	2-3	0-0	0-2	1	4	0	1	6
Robinson	27	6-8	2-3	2-6	1	2	0	0	14
Ginobili	28	3-8	0-0	1-7	3	3	0	3	7
Rose	24	5-11	2-2	3-6	2	5	1	2	12
Claxton	8	1-3	0-0	0-0	1	2	0	0	2
Ferry	1	0-0	0-0	0-0	0	0	0	0	0
Totals	240	39-79	19-28	10-47	24	20	7	12	101

Percentages: FG—.494, FT—.679. 3-pt goals: 4-10, .400 (Jackson 0-4, Parker 1-2, Bowen 2-2, Ginobili 1-2). Team rebounds: 8. Blocked shots: 12 (Duncan 7, Robinson 4, Claxton).

A: 18,797. Officials: Bavetta, Crawford, DeRosa.

Game 2

NEW JERSEY 87

NJ	Min	FG M-A	FT M-A	Reb O-T	A	PF	S	TO	TP
Kidd	42	11-24	6-8	4-7	3	1	0	4	30
Kittles	21	3-7	1-2	1-4	1	1	3	1	8
Jefferson	39	3-10	2-2	1-3	3	3	2	3	8
Martin	33	6-16	2-2	3-5	4	5	2	1	14
Collins	34	3-6	0-0	1-4	1	2	1	1	6
Harris	27	5-8	0-0	2-7	1	1	1	1	10
Mutombo	20	2-3	0-0	1-4	0	3	0	0	4
Rogers	18	2-8	2-2	2-5	2	4	0	1	7
Johnson	6	0-1	0-0	0-0	1	1	0	0	0
Totals	240	35-83	13-16	15-39	16	21	9	13	87

Percentages: FG—.422, FT—.813. 3-pt goals: 4-11, .364 (Kidd 2-4, Kittles 1-2, Collins 0-1, Harris 0-1, Rogers 1-3). Team rebounds:5. Blocked shots: 5 (Martin 2, Mutombo 3).

SAN ANTONIO 85

SA	Min	FG M-A	FT M-A	Reb O-T	A	PF	S	TO	TP
Parker	41	9-17	3-4	1-5	5	3	0	1	21
Jackson	40	6-10	0-0	0-2	3	2	2	7	16
Duncan	43	8-19	3-10	2-12	3	3	0	4	19
Bowen	26	1-2	0-0	0-5	0	1	0	2	3
Robinson	33	3-6	4-6	4-8	1	0	2	1	10
Ginobili	29	1-6	2-2	4-6	3	4	1	3	4
Rose	19	3-4	1-1	2-3	1	1	1	2	7
Claxton	7	2-2	1-2	0-0	0	0	0	1	5
Kerr	1	0-1	0-0	1-2	0	1	2	0	0
Willis	1	0-1	0-0	1-2	0	0	0	0	0
Totals	240	33-68	14-25	14-43	17	16	6	21	85

Percentages: FG—.485, FT—.560. 3-pt goals: 5-13, .385 (Parker 0-2, Jackson 4-7, Duncan 0-1, Bowen 1-1, Ginobili 0-2). Team rebounds: 10. Blocked shots: 7 (Parker, Jackson, Duncan 3, Robinson 2).

A: 18,797. Officials: Crawford, Delaney, Salvatore.

Game 3

SAN ANTONIO 84

SA	Min	FG M-A	FT M-A	Reb O-T	A	PF	S	TO	TP
Parker	43	9-21	4-8	1-3	6	0	0	1	26
Jackson	36	2-7	2-4	0-6	2	3	1	4	7
Duncan	45	6-13	9-12	3-16	7	3	1	5	21
Bowen	32	0-5	0-0	1-4	0	3	1	1	0
Robinson	26	1-6	6-8	1-3	0	2	1	0	8
Ginobili	28	3-6	2-3	2-2	4	2	4	1	8
Rose	22	4-7	0-0	0-2	0	2	1	3	8
Claxton	5	2-2	0-0	0-1	0	1	1	1	4
Willis	3	1-1	0-0	1-1	0	1	0	1	2
Totals	240	43-83	14-19	14-42	22	27	13	13	103

Percentages: FG—.418, FT—.657. 3-pt goals: 5-10, .500 (Parker 4-6, Jackson 1-2, Bowen 0-2). Team rebounds:15. Blocked shots: 8 (Duncan 3, Bowen 2, Ginobili 2, Rose).

NEW JERSEY 79

NJ	Min	FG M-A	FT M-A	Reb O-T	A	PF	S	TO	TP
Kidd	42	6-19	0-0	2-3	11	3	2	4	12
Kittles	34	8-16	2-3	1-4	1	2	3	0	21
Martin	42	8-18	7-8	2-11	0	5	4	5	23
Jefferson	36	3-11	0-0	2-9	0	2	2	1	6
Collins	25	0-3	0-0	4-5	1	6	0	3	0
Harris	22	1-6	4-4	1-1	3	2	1	2	7
Mutombo	18	1-1	0-0	1-3	0	3	1	1	2
Rogers	11	0-3	2-2	0-2	0	2	0	2	2
Johnson	6	2-2	0-0	0-1	0	0	0	0	4
Williams	4	1-2	0-0	1-1	0	0	0	0	2
Totals	240	30-82	15-17	14-41	17	26	13	18	79

Percentages: FG—.370, FT—.882. 3-pt goals: 4-13, .308 (Kidd 0-5, Kittles 3-5, Martin 0-1, Harris 1-2). Team rebounds: 10. Blocked shots: 5 (Kittles 2, Martin 2, Collins).

A: 19,280. Officials: Garretson, Javie, Nies.

Game 4

SAN ANTONIO 76

SA	Min	FG M-A	FT M-A	Reb O-T	A	PF	S	TO	TP
Parker	31	1-12	1-2	0-4	3	3	0	2	3
Jackson	28	1-9	2-3	2-4	3	3	1	2	5
Bowen	40	2-9	0-0	1-7	1	2	2	0	5
Duncan	39	10-23	3-3	8-17	2	4	1	3	23
Robinson	24	4-5	6-7	3-7	1	6	1	0	14
Ginobili	28	3-10	2-3	1-2	1	1	4	1	10
Claxton	17	3-6	4-4	1-3	2	1	1	0	10
Willis	16	2-7	2-2	5-5	0	3	0	2	6
Rose	15	0-9	0-0	1-4	0	3	0	1	0
Kerr	1	0-0	0-0	0-0	1	0	0	0	0
Ferry	1	0-0	0-0	0-0	0	0	0	0	0
Totals	240	26-...	...	...	...	...	...	...	76

Percentages: FG—.289, FT—.833. 3-pt goals: 4-18, .222 (Parker 0-2, Jackson 1-4, Bowen 1-5, Ginobili 2-6, Willis 0-1). Team rebounds: 12. Blocked shots: 10 (Jackson, Duncan 7, Robinson 1, Willis).

NEW JERSEY 77

NJ	Min	FG M-A	FT M-A	Reb O-T	A	PF	S	TO	TP
Kidd	47	5-18	6-6	3-8	9	3	0	5	16
Kittles	35	2-10	0-0	1-6	1	0	1	0	4
Martin	40	7-16	6-12	5-13	3	5	1	5	20
Jefferson	40	8-15	2-4	1-10	1	1	0	3	18
Collins	10	0-0	0-0	2-2	1	4	1	0	0
Mutombo	21	1-3	2-2	2-3	0	3	2	1	4
Williams	17	2-6	4-5	2-7	1	3	0	0	8
Harris	15	1-1	0-0	3-4	3	1	1	0	4
Rogers	11	2-5	0-0	0-0	0	2	0	1	4
Johnson	4	1-1	0-0	0-0	0	0	0	0	3
Totals	240	45-92	13-16	14-41	27	22	5	8	107

Percentages: FG—.359, FT—.690. 3-pt goals: 1-9, .111 (Kidd 0-4, Kittles 0-4, Johnson 1-1). Team rebounds: 9. Blocked shots: 13 (Martin 3, Jefferson 2, Collins, Mutombo 3, Williams 4).

A: 19,280. Officials: Callahan, Fryer, Rush.

NBA Finals Box Scores (Cont.)

Game 5

SAN ANTONIO 93

SA	Min	FG M–A	FT M–A	Reb O–T	A	PF	S	TO	TP
Parker	33	5–13	3–5	0–2	4	3	1	2	14
Jackson	32	2–7	0–0	1–7	3	2	0	4	5
Duncan	46	10–18	9–10	3–17	4	3	1	6	29
Bowen	29	1–4	2–2	0–1	1	4	0	0	4
Robinson	20	2–4	2–2	1–3	0	6	3	1	6
Rose	29	6–9	2–2	2–3	1	2	0	1	14
Ginobili	26	4–8	4–4	0–3	0	5	2	1	12
Claxton	15	1–4	1–2	0–1	2	4	2	0	3
Kerr	9	2–2	1–2	1–1	0	0	1	0	6
Willis	1	0–0	0–0	0–1	0	0	0	0	0
Totals	240	33–69	24–29	8–39	15	29	10	15	93

Percentages: FG—.478, FT—.828. 3-pt goals: 3–9, .333 (Parker 1–2, Jackson 1–4, Bowen 0–2, Kerr 1–1). Team rebounds: 8. Blocked shots: 9 (Duncan 4, Robinson 2, Ginobili 1, Claxton).

NEW JERSEY 83

NJ	Min	FG M–A	FT M–A	Reb O–T	A	PF	S	TO	TP
Kidd	48	10–23	5–6	3–7	7	2	2	2	29
Kittles	34	3–9	2–2	1–4	1	3	1	1	8
Martin	38	2–8	0–0	1–9	3	5	1	8	4
Jefferson	37	5–11	9–11	2–6	4	4	2	1	19
Collins	26	1–3	5–6	4–5	0	5	1	0	7
Williams	23	4–9	2–3	4–7	0	4	0	0	10
Harris	22	1–7	3–4	0–1	0	0	0	1	5
Mutombo	7	0–1	0–0	1–2	0	2	0	0	0
Rogers	5	0–3	1–2	1–1	0	0	0	1	1
Totals	240	26–74	27–34	17–42	15	25	7	16	83

Percentages: FG—.351, FT—.794. 3-pt goals: 4–16, .250 (Kidd 4–10, Kittles 0–3, Martin 0–1, Rogers 0–2). Team rebounds: 7. Blocked shots: 5 (Kittles, Martin 3, Williams).
A: 19,280. Officials: Bavetta, Crawford, Salvatore.

Game 6

NEW JERSEY 77

NJ	Min	FG M–A	FT M–A	Reb O–T	A	PF	S	TO	TP
Kidd	42	8–20	2–2	2–4	7	4	1	0	21
Kittles	34	5–12	4–4	0–4	2	2	3	0	16
Jefferson	41	6–15	1–1	2–7	2	5	0	3	13
Martin	39	3–23	0–0	0–10	1	3	1	2	6
Collins	25	2–5	0–0	0–3	0	4	1	1	4
Williams	16	2–4	0–0	1–1	2	4	1	1	4
Harris	15	0–1	2–4	1–2	0	1	0	1	2
Mutombo	10	1–1	2–2	2–3	0	1	0	1	4
Rogers	8	1–2	0–0	0–0	0	1	0	0	3
Johnson	8	2–4	0–0	0–0	0	0	1	2	4
Slay	1	0–0	0–0	0–0	0	0	0	0	0
Scalabrine	1	0–0	0–0	0–1	0	0	0	0	0
Totals	240	30–87	11–13	8–35	14	25	8	11	77

Percentages: FG—.345, FT—.846. 3-pt goals: 6–21, .286 (Kidd 3–9, Kittles 2–6, Jefferson 0–1, Martin 0–2, Harris 0–1, Rogers 1–1, Johnson 0–1). Team rebounds: 11. Blocked shots: 5 (Martin 2, Collins, Williams, Mutombo).

SAN ANTONIO 88

SA	Min	FG M–A	FT M–A	Reb O–T	A	PF	S	TO	TP
Jackson	35	7–13	0–0	0–3	0	3	1	6	17
Parker	24	2–6	0–0	0–2	2	0	0	3	4
Duncan	46	9–19	3–5	4–20	10	2	0	4	21
Bowen	18	1–7	0–0	0–0	2	0	1	0	2
Robinson	31	6–8	1–4	4–17	1	2	0	1	13
Ginobili	33	2–8	7–9	1–7	1	3	2	1	11
Claxton	23	5–8	3–4	0–1	4	2	0	2	13
Rose	18	1–3	3–3	2–5	0	1	0	2	5
Kerr	9	1–1	0–0	0–0	1	0	0	2	2
Ferry	1	0–0	0–0	0–0	0	0	0	0	0
Smith	1	0–1	0–0	0–0	0	0	0	0	0
Willis	1	0–0	0–0	0–0	0	0	0	0	0
Totals	240	34–74	17–25	11–55	20	14	4	19	88

Percentages: FG—.459, FT—.680. 3-pt goals: 3–15, .200 (Jackson 0–1, Duncan 0–1, Bowen 0–2, Ginobili 0–4, Smith 0–1). Team rebounds: 6. Blocked shots: 13 (Duncan 8, Robinson 2, Claxton 1, Rose 2).
A: 18,797. Officials: Crawford, Delaney, Garretson.

All-NBA Teams

FIRST TEAM	SECOND TEAM	THIRD TEAM
G Kobe Bryant, LA Lakers	Jason Kidd, New Jersey	Stephon Marbury, Phoenix
G Tracy McGrady, Orlando	Allen Iverson, Philadelphia	Steve Nash, Dallas
C Shaquille O'Neal, LA Lakers	Ben Wallace, Detroit	Jermaine O'Neal, Indiana
F Kevin Garnett, Minnesota	Dirk Nowitzki, Dallas	Paul Pierce, Boston
F Tim Duncan, San Antonio	Chris Webber, Sacramento	Jamal Mashburn, New Orleans

All-Defensive Team

FIRST TEAM	SECOND TEAM
G Doug Christie, Sacramento	Jason Kidd, New Jersey
G Kobe Bryant, LA Lakers	Eric Snow, Philadelphia
F/C Ben Wallace, Detroit	Shaquille O'Neal, LA Lakers
F Tim Duncan, San Antonio	Bruce Bowen, San Antonio
F Kevin Garnett, Minnesota	Ron Artest, Indiana

All-Rookie Teams

FIRST TEAM	SECOND TEAM
Yao Ming, Houston	Emanuel Ginobili, San Antonio
Amare Stoudemire, Phoenix	Gordan Giricek, Orlando
Caron Butler, Miami	Carlos Boozer, Cleveland
Drew Gooden, Orlando	Jay Williams, Chicago
Nene Hilario, Denver	J.R. Bremer, Boston

Scoring

	GP	Pts	Avg
Tracy McGrady, Orl	75	2,407	32.1
Kobe Bryant, LAL	82	2,461	30.0
Allen Iverson, Phil	82	2,262	27.6
Shaquille O'Neal, LAL	67	1,841	27.5
Paul Pierce, Bos	79	2,048	25.9
Dirk Nowitzki, Dall	80	2,011	25.1
Tim Duncan, SA	81	1,884	23.3
Chris Webber, Sac	67	1,542	23.0
Kevin Garnett, Minn	82	1,883	23.0
Ray Allen, Sea	76	1,713	22.5
Allan Houston, NY	82	1,845	22.5

Assists

	GP	Assists	Avg
Jason Kidd, NJ	80	711	8.9
Jason Williams, Mem	76	631	8.3
Gary Payton, Mil	80	663	8.3
Stephon Marbury, Phoe	81	654	8.1
John Stockton, Utah	82	629	7.7
Jamaal Tinsley, Ind	73	548	7.5
Jason Terry, Atl	81	600	7.4
Steve Nash, Dall	82	598	7.3
Andre Miller, LAC	80	537	6.7
Eric Snow, Phil	82	544	6.6

Free-Throw Percentage

	FTA	FTM	Pct
Allan Houston, NY	363	395	.919
Ray Allen, Sea	316	345	.916
Steve Nash, Dall	308	339	.909
Troy Hudson, Minn	208	231	.900
Reggie Miller, Ind	207	230	.900
Jason Terry, Atl	259	292	.887
Dirk Nowitzki, Dall	483	548	.881
Chauncey Billups, Det	318	362	.878
Jerry Stackhouse, Wash	455	518	.878
Darrell Armstrong, Orl	165	188	.878

Steals

	GP	Steals	Avg
Allen Iverson, Phil	82	225	2.74
Ron Artest, Ind	69	159	2.30
Shawn Marion, Phoe	81	185	2.28
Doug Christie, Sac	80	180	2.25
Jason Kidd, NJ	80	179	2.24
Kobe Bryant, LAL	82	181	2.21
Paul Pierce, Bos	79	139	1.76
Caron Butler, Mia	78	137	1.76
Steve Francis, Hou	81	141	1.74
Jamaal Tinsley, Ind	73	125	1.71

Rebounds

	GP	Reb	Avg
Ben Wallace, Det	73	1,126	15.4
Kevin Garnett, Minn	82	1,102	13.4
Tim Duncan, SA	81	1,043	12.9
Jermaine O'Neal, Ind	77	796	10.3
Brian Grant, Mia	82	837	10.2
Troy Murphy, GS	79	806	10.2
Dirk Nowitzki, Dall	80	791	9.9
Shawn Marion, Phoe	81	773	9.5
Jerome Williams, Tor	71	650	9.2
P.J. Brown, NO	78	701	9.0
Donyell Marshall, Chi	78	699	9.0

Field-Goal Percentage

	FGA	FGM	Pct
Eddy Curry, Chi	335	573	.585
Shaquille O'Neal, LAL	695	1,211	.574
Carlos Boozer, Clev	331	618	.536
P.J. Brown, NO	319	601	.531
Radoslav Nesterovic, Minn	400	762	.525
Nene, Den	321	619	.519
Tim Duncan, SA	714	1,392	.513
Matt Harpring, Utah	521	1,020	.511
Pau Gasol, Mem	569	1,116	.510
Brian Grant, Mia	344	676	.509

Three-Point Field-Goal Percentage

	3FGM	3FGA	Pct
Bruce Bowen, SA	101	229	.441
Michael Redd, Mil	182	416	.438
Wesley Person, Mem	100	231	.433
David Wesley, NO	134	316	.424
Wally Szczerbiak, Minn	61	145	.421
Steve Nash, Dall	111	269	.413
Matt Harpring, Utah	66	160	.413
Anthony Peeler, Minn	87	212	.410
Mike Bibby, Sac	56	137	.409
Eddie Jones, Mia	98	241	.407
Jon Barry, Det	87	214	.407

Blocked Shots

	GP	BS	Avg
Theo Ratliff, Atl	81	262	3.23
Ben Wallace, Det	73	230	3.15
Tim Duncan, SA	81	237	2.93
Elton Brand, LAC	62	158	2.55
Adonal Foyle, GS	82	205	2.50
Shaquille O'Neal, LAL	67	159	2.37
Jermaine O'Neal, Ind	77	178	2.31
Andrei Kirilenko, Utah	80	175	2.19
Shawn Bradley, Dall	81	170	2.10
Erick Dampier, GS	82	154	1.88
Zydrunas Ilgauskas, Clev	81	152	1.88
Keon Clark, Sac	80	150	1.88

NBA Team Statistics

Offense

Team	FG Pct	3FG Pct	FTPct	Rebound Avg Off	Total	A	TO	Stl	Scoring Avg
Dallas	45.3	38.1	82.9	11.1	42.1	22.4	11.1	8.1	103.0
Golden St	44.1	34.4	77.8	15.7	46.7	20.9	15.2	7.2	102.4
Sacramento	46.4	38.1	74.6	11.0	44.5	24.8	14.3	9.0	101.7
LA Lakers	45.1	35.5	73.4	13.2	44.3	23.3	14.1	7.8	100.4
Milwaukee	35.6	38.3	77.6	10.7	39.5	22.2	12.2	7.6	99.5
Orlando	43.6	35.7	77.7	11.7	40.9	20.4	13.9	8.5	98.5
Minnesota	46.6	36.8	77.0	11.7	43.6	25.2	13.3	6.7	98.1
Memphis	45.2	36.5	73.9	11.5	41.6	23.1	14.8	7.9	97.5
Indiana	44.0	33.9	76.6	12.2	44.2	23.3	14.0	8.5	96.8
Philadelphia	44.8	31.1	77.5	12.7	42.2	21.6	14.1	10.3	96.8
New York	44.1	38.3	81.5	10.3	39.2	21.9	13.6	7.1	95.8
San Antonio	46.2	35.4	72.5	11.4	42.6	19.9	15.4	7.7	95.8
Phoenix	44.4	34.3	74.2	12.8	42.5	21.0	14.2	8.1	95.5
New Jersey	44.1	33.2	75.7	12.1	42.9	23.0	14.4	8.7	95.4
Portland	46.0	33.0	74.5	12.1	41.1	22.7	14.4	8.8	95.2
Chicago	44.5	35.0	72.2	12.0	43.0	21.7	16.2	7.4	95.0
Utah	46.8	35.0	74.5	12.4	41.5	25.6	15.9	8.6	94.7
Atlanta	44.4	35.2	79.3	11.4	42.6	20.5	15.9	7.5	94.1
New Orleans	43.5	37.6	76.8	13.4	43.6	22.0	14.0	8.0	93.9
Houston	44.0	34.6	76.8	12.5	43.8	18.4	14.6	7.2	93.8
LA Clippers	43.7	33.1	75.0	12.3	42.3	19.6	15.2	7.0	93.8
Boston	41.5	33.4	74.2	10.3	40.5	19.2	13.5	8.8	92.7
Seattle	43.8	35.3	74.4	11.7	40.8	21.6	12.5	8.3	92.1
Washington	44.0	31.2	77.8	11.2	40.4	19.7	12.6	7.6	91.5
Cleveland	42.3	32.7	74.7	13.6	44.6	20.9	17.4	7.8	91.4
Detroit	43.0	35.8	77.1	10.8	40.6	19.8	12.7	6.8	91.4
Toronto	42.7	34.4	71.8	12.5	41.2	19.3	13.5	7.4	90.9
Miami	41.3	31.6	76.5	11.6	41.6	18.3	13.4	7.2	85.6
Denver	41.1	27.8	70.0	13.6	42.4	21.2	17.4	8.7	84.2

Defense (Opponent's Statistics)

Team	FG Pct	3FG Pct	FTPct	Rebound Avg. Off	Total	A	TO	Stl	Scoring Avg
Detroit	43.8	34.4	74.6	10.5	41.3	18.3	13.4	6.9	87.7
New Jersey	42.7	35.9	74.9	11.4	41.4	19.6	15.8	8.4	90.2
San Antonio	42.7	33.9	76.8	12.6	40.9	19.0	14.3	8.1	90.4
Miami	43.7	35.3	75.1	10.6	42.2	18.1	12.6	7.6	90.6
New Orleans	43.8	33.8	76.6	11.1	40.0	19.9	14.1	7.9	91.8
Houston	43.3	34.7	77.5	11.9	40.6	20.5	12.7	8.1	92.3
Utah	43.4	34.9	75.9	12.3	38.2	19.5	15.3	8.8	92.3
Seattle	44.7	34.4	74.2	11.4	41.5	20.8	14.1	6.1	92.3
Denver	44.3	37.0	75.7	10.5	40.3	21.5	16.3	9.1	92.4
Portland	45.0	34.1	76.4	11.1	39.1	22.7	14.7	8.3	92.5
Washington	44.2	36.1	77.1	11.6	41.4	21.7	13.6	7.5	92.5
Boston	43.5	33.1	74.9	11.4	45.0	22.2	15.3	7.5	93.1
Indiana	42.8	34.0	76.7	12.3	42.2	20.7	14.7	7.6	93.3
Phoenix	43.8	32.0	76.5	12.6	42.9	22.2	15.1	7.8	94.4
Philadelphia	45.2	35.5	76.0	11.1	40.3	22.1	16.5	7.8	94.5
Dallas	43.8	34.0	72.7	12.7	45.5	21.7	15.3	6.7	95.2
Sacramento	42.0	32.0	74.1	14.0	45.8	21.4	14.6	8.3	95.2
Minnesota	43.7	34.6	75.2	11.9	41.7	22.8	13.0	7.0	96.0
Toronto	46.1	37.5	75.9	11.9	43.6	21.1	13.2	7.4	96.8
New York	45.7	34.0	77.1	11.4	43.3	21.1	13.8	7.7	97.2
Atlanta	43.6	35.9	76.0	13.1	42.6	21.6	12.4	9.0	97.6
Orlando	45.5	33.4	76.7	11.8	43.5	22.4	15.7	7.8	98.4
Milwaukee	45.8	37.5	74.5	12.4	43.4	23.1	13.6	6.6	99.3
Chicago	43.9	32.3	74.9	13.6	45.0	23.8	14.2	9.4	100.1
Memphis	46.0	36.3	75.9	13.7	44.9	24.3	14.3	8.7	100.7
Cleveland	45.3	35.8	77.2	11.4	41.7	24.1	13.6	9.8	101.0
Golden St	45.2	37.2	75.6	14.7	43.8	23.6	13.2	8.7	103.6

Atlanta Hawks

Player	GP	MPG	FG%	3Pt%	FT%	OFF	DEF	Total	APG	SPG	BPG	TO	PF	PPG
			Field Goals			Rebounds								
Glenn Robinson	69	37.6	.432	.342	.876	1.20	5.40	6.60	3.0	1.32	.38	3.59	2.70	20.8
S. Abdur-Rahim	81	38.1	.478	.350	.841	2.20	6.20	8.40	3.0	1.07	.47	2.62	3.00	19.9
Jason Terry	81	38.0	.428	.371	.887	.50	3.00	3.40	7.4	1.56	.17	3.07	2.20	17.2
Dion Glover	76	24.9	.427	.354	.784	.80	2.90	3.70	1.9	.93	.20	1.42	1.90	9.7
Theo Ratliff	81	31.1	.464	.000	.720	1.90	5.60	7.50	.9	.69	3.23	1.69	3.30	8.7
Ira Newble	73	26.5	.495	.381	.778	1.20	2.50	3.70	1.4	.68	.36	.95	2.40	7.7
Chris Crawford	5	7.6	.615	.333	.875	.60	.80	1.40	.2	.40	.60	.40	1.40	4.8
Alan Henderson	82	18.2	.468	.000	.638	1.90	3.00	4.90	.5	.40	.39	.74	2.00	4.8
Nazr Mohammed	35	12.7	.421	.000	.634	1.30	2.30	3.70	.2	.46	.60	.71	2.30	4.6
Emanual Davis	24	14.2	.364	.241	.773	.20	1.60	1.80	1.5	.50	.08	1.04	1.20	3.7
Dan Dickau	50	10.3	.412	.361	.808	.20	.70	.90	1.7	.28	.04	1.06	1.30	3.7
Darvin Ham	75	12.3	.447	.000	.481	1.00	1.10	2.00	.5	.21	.25	.87	1.70	2.4
J. Jackson	53	10.5	.364	.100	.727	.40	.70	1.10	1.4	.36	.11	.64	1.00	2.3
Matt Maloney	14	7.4	.320	.333	.600	.10	.40	.50	1.2	.29	.00	.36	.60	1.7
Hawks	82	242.7	.444	.352	.793	11.4	31.2	42.6	20.5	7.5	5.8	16.7	21.7	94.1
Opponents	82	242.7	.436	.359	.760	11.4	31.2	42.6	21.6	9.0	5.0	13.0	20.3	97.6

Boston Celtics

Player	GP	MPG	FG%	3Pt%	FT%	OFF	DEF	Total	APG	SPG	BPG	TO	PF	PPG
			Field Goals			Rebounds								
Paul Pierce	79	39.2	.416	.302	.802	1.30	6.00	7.30	4.4	1.76	.78	3.65	2.90	25.9
Antoine Walker	78	41.5	.388	.323	.615	1.30	5.90	7.20	4.8	1.49	.40	3.33	2.80	20.1
Tony Delk	67	28.0	.416	.395	.782	.60	2.90	3.50	2.2	1.07	.15	1.03	1.90	9.8
Eric Williams	82	28.7	.442	.336	.750	1.70	2.90	4.70	1.7	1.05	.23	1.18	2.90	9.1
J.R. Bremer	64	23.5	.369	.353	.766	.30	2.00	2.30	2.6	.59	.05	.92	1.30	8.3
Tony Battie	67	25.1	.539	.200	.746	2.20	4.30	6.50	.7	.49	1.21	.72	2.90	7.3
Walter McCarty	82	23.8	.414	.367	.622	.80	2.70	3.50	1.3	.95	.34	.82	2.30	6.1
Vin Baker	52	18.1	.478	.000	.673	1.70	2.10	3.80	.6	.42	.58	1.17	2.80	5.2
Mark Blount	81	17.3	.432	.000	.727	1.40	2.40	3.80	.7	.52	.84	1.27	2.30	5.0
Bimbo Coles	14	19.7	.333	.219	.833	.30	1.40	1.70	2.1	.49	.11	.80	1.70	4.4
Kedrick Brown	51	13.1	.357	.077	.625	.90	1.90	2.70	.4	.67	.25	.45	1.30	2.8
Grant Long	41	11.9	.386	.000	.783	.60	1.40	2.00	.6	.22	.02	.46	1.50	1.8
Bruno Sundov	26	5.3	.250	.250	.000	.30	.80	1.10	.3	.23	.12	.35	.90	1.2
Celtics	82	241.8	.415	.334	.742	10.4	30.1	40.5	19.2	8.8	3.7	14.0	21.4	92.7
Opponents	82	241.8	.435	.331	.749	11.4	33.5	45.0	22.2	7.5	4.5	16.0	21.9	93.1

Chicago Bulls

Player	GP	MPG	FG%	3Pt%	FT%	OFF	DEF	Total	APG	SPG	BPG	TO	PF	PPG
			Field Goals			Rebounds								
Jalen Rose		40.9	.406	.370	.854	.80	3.50	4.30	4.8	.88	.28	3.48	3.30	22.1
Donyell Marshall	78	30.5	.459	.379	.756	3.00	6.00	9.00	1.8	1.22	1.09	1.73	3.00	13.4
Marcus Fizer	38	21.3	.465	.167	.657	2.10	3.60	5.70	1.3	.37	.45	1.50	2.30	11.7
Jamal Crawford	24.9	.413	.355	.806	.30	2.10	2.30	4.2	.96	.31	1.68	1.60	10.7
Eddy Curry	81	19.4	.585	.000	.624	1.40	2.90	4.40	.5	.22	.77	1.69	2.80	10.5
Jay Williams	75	26.1	.399	.322	.640	.40	2.20	2.60	4.7	1.15	.23	2.28	2.40	9.5
Tyson Chandler	75	24.4	.531	.000	.608	2.30	4.60	6.90	1.0	.49	1.41	1.80	2.90	9.2
Eddie Robinson	64	21.2	.492	.214	.810	1.20	1.90	3.10	1.0	.97	.20	.81	1.90	5.7
Lonny Baxter	55	12.4	.466	.000	.680	1.20	1.80	3.00	.3	.16	.40	.84	2.50	4.8
Trenton Hassell	82	24.4	.367	.325	.745	.60	2.70	3.10	1.8	.55	.74	1.01	2.40	4.2
Rick Brunson	17	11.5	.460	.667	.833	.20	.90	1.10	2.1	.59	.18	1.00	1.20	3.5
Corie Blount	50	16.7	.485	.000	.571	1.40	2.70	4.10	1.0	.66	.38	.86	2.40	3.0
Fred Hoiberg	63	12.4	.389	.238	.820	.20	2.00	2.20	1.1	.63	.08	.40	.90	2.3
Dalibor Bagaric	10	7.6	.308	.000	.750	.70	1.30	2.00	.4	.30	.30	.50	1.10	1.9
Roger Mason Jr.	17	6.6	.355	.333	1.000	.10	.60	.70	.7	.24	.00	.29	1.20	1.8
Bulls	82	243.0	.445	.350	.722	12.0	31.0	43.0	21.7	7.4	5.6	16.9	24.7	95.0
Opponents	82	243.0	.439	.323	.749	13.6	31.4	45.0	23.8	9.4	5.0	14.7	21.9	100.1

Cleveland Cavaliers

Player	GP	MPG	FG%	3Pt%	FT%	OFF	DEF	Total	APG	SPG	BPG	TO	PF	PPG
			Field Goals			**Rebounds**								
Ricky Davis	79	39.6	.410	.363	.748	1.20	3.70	4.90	5.5	1.58	.46	3.51	2.30	20.6
Z. Ilgauskas	81	30.0	.441	.000	.781	3.00	4.60	7.50	1.6	.69	1.88	2.59	3.40	17.2
Dajuan Wagner	47	29.5	.369	.316	.800	.40	1.30	1.70	2.8	.81	.15	1.81	2.30	13.4
Carlos Boozer	81	25.3	.536	.000	.771	2.50	5.00	7.50	1.3	.73	.62	1.27	2.80	10.0
Jumaine Jones	80	27.6	.434	.354	.687	1.30	3.70	5.10	1.4	.84	.28	1.34	2.20	9.8
Darius Miles	67	30.0	.410	.000	.594	1.70	3.70	5.40	2.6	1.00	1.03	2.66	2.40	9.2
Smush Parker	66	16.7	.402	.322	.831	.40	1.40	1.80	2.5	.73	.18	2.02	1.60	6.2
Chris Mihm	52	15.6	.404	.000	.724	1.80	2.70	4.40	.5	.35	.73	.92	2.40	5.9
Milt Palacio	80	24.7	.418	.216	.747	.60	2.30	2.90	3.2	.85	.20	1.64	2.10	5.0
Tierre Brown	15	11.2	.458	.000	.786	.50	1.50	2.00	2.6	.87	.00	1.47	.60	4.3
DeSagana Diop	80	11.8	.351	.000	.367	.80	1.90	2.70	.5	.41	1.01	.70	1.90	1.5
Michael Stewart	47	5.3	.378	.000	.667	.40	.80	1.20	.1	.04	.32	.21	.90	.8
Cavaliers	**82**	**241.8**	**.422**	**.327**	**.747**	**13.6**	**31.0**	**44.6**	**20.9**	**7.8**	**6.4**	**18.3**	**22.7**	**91.4**
Opponents	**82**	**241.8**	**.453**	**.358**	**.772**	**11.4**	**30.4**	**41.7**	**24.0**	**9.8**	**6.0**	**14.2**	**20.8**	**101.0**

Dallas Mavericks

Player	GP	MPG	FG%	3Pt%	FT%	OFF	DEF	Total	APG	SPG	BPG	TO	PF	PPG
			Field Goals			**Rebounds**								
Dirk Nowitzki	17	42.5	.479	.443	.912	.90	10.60	11.50	2.2	1.24	.94	2.35	3.10	25.3
Nick Van Exel	20	33.6	.460	.393	.703	.90	2.50	3.40	4.1	.60	.00	1.95	2.40	19.5
Michael Finley	20	41.1	.435	.412	.864	1.30	4.50	5.80	3.0	1.30	.60	1.55	2.30	18.3
Steve Nash	20	36.5	.447	.487	.873	.80	2.80	3.50	7.3	.85	.05	2.55	2.40	16.1
Raef LaFrentz	20	24.6	.433	.200	.842	1.80	2.60	4.40	.3	.55	2.15	.70	4.30	8.0
Eduardo Najera	19	20.7	.453	.000	.792	1.90	2.00	3.90	.8	.74	.21	.84	2.80	6.1
Raja Bell	17	17.9	.548	.462	.550	.80	2.20	3.00	1.6	.29	.00	.35	2.40	5.7
Walt Williams	15	15.1	.395	.341	1.000	.80	2.10	2.90	1.0	.33	.80	1.13	1.90	5.7
T. Abdul-Wahad	8	9.9	.300	.000	.875	1.40	1.40	2.80	.9	.00	.00	.13	.80	3.1
Shawn Bradley	17	14.5	.400	.000	.750	1.40	2.50	3.80	.3	.18	.82	.88	2.80	2.9
Adrian Griffin	15	8.7	.415	.333	1.000	1.10	1.80	2.90	.5	.27	.00	.60	1.60	2.5
Evan Eschmeyer	5	6.4	.500	.000	.000	.40	.60	1.00	.4	.60	.20	.00	1.60	1.2
Mavericks	**20**	**242.5**	**.450**	**.397**	**.829**	**11.2**	**30.9**	**42.1**	**20.4**	**6.1**	**5.2**	**12.5**	**24.3**	**104.1**
Opponents	**20**	**242.5**	**.454**	**.348**	**.753**	**13.0**	**33.4**	**46.4**	**23.1**	**6.9**	**4.5**	**13.7**	**22.1**	**104.7**

Denver Nuggets

Player	GP	MPG	FG%	3Pt%	FT%	OFF	DEF	Total	APG	SPG	BPG	TO	PF	PPG
			Field Goals			**Rebounds**								
Juwan Howard	77	35.5	.450	.500	.803	2.40	5.20	7.60	3.0	1.00	.35	2.45	3.10	18.4
Nene	80	28.2	.519	.000	.578	2.60	3.50	6.10	1.9	1.59	.81	2.26	3.70	10.5
S. Williams	78	24.1	.394	.356	.765	.30	1.90	2.20	3.4	.99	.08	1.46	1.80	8.0
Rodney White	72	21.7	.408	.239	.784	.60	2.40	3.00	1.7	.63	.44	2.17	1.90	9.0
Donnell Harvey	77	20.9	.446	.143	.670	1.60	3.70	5.30	1.3	.62	.35	1.60	2.60	7.9
Marcus Camby	29	21.2	.410	.400	.660	2.60	4.60	7.20	1.6	.69	1.38	.93	2.40	7.6
Vincent Yarbrough	59	23.4	.393	.269	.790	.60	2.10	2.70	2.2	.97	.56	1.37	2.50	6.9
Devin Brown	10	9.3	.343	.000	.750	.80	1.00	1.80	.7	.40	.10	.90	1.40	3.0
Jeff Trepagnier	8	12.1	.425	.500	1.000	1.00	1.00	2.00	.8	1.00	.00	1.00	.60	5.6
Chris Andersen	59	15.4	.400	.000	.550	1.80	2.80	4.60	.5	.51	1.02	1.02	1.50	5.2
Junior Harrington	82	24.4	.362	.250	.652	.50	2.50	3.00	3.4	.98	.18	1.91	3.00	5.1
Nikoloz Tskitishvili	81	16.3	.293	.243	.738	.80	1.40	2.20	1.1	.38	.36	1.04	1.70	3.9
Ryan Bowen	62	16.1	.492	.286	.659	1.30	1.30	2.50	.9	1.05	.47	.69	1.30	3.6
John Crotty	12	15.0	.341	.308	.600	.10	1.20	1.30	2.4	.25	.00	.75	1.30	3.4
Adam Harrington	19	5.8	.297	.357	.750	.10	.40	.40	.6	.11	.05	.11	.40	1.6
Predrag Savovic	27	9.5	.312	.154	.724	.30	.60	.90	.8	.52	.04	.78	1.20	3.1
Nuggets	**82**	**240.6**	**.411**	**.278**	**.699**	**13.6**	**28.8**	**42.4**	**21.2**	**8.7**	**5.2**	**18.5**	**25.1**	**84.2**
Opponents	**82**	**240.6**	**.443**	**.370**	**.757**	**10.5**	**29.8**	**40.3**	**21.5**	**9.1**	**6.6**	**17.1**	**21.8**	**92.4**

Detroit Pistons

Player	GP	MPG	FG%	3Pt%	FT%	OFF	DEF	Total	APG	SPG	BPG	TO	PF	PPG
Richard Hamilton	82	32.2	.443	.269	.833	1.10	2.80	3.90	2.5	.78	.16	2.44	3.00	19.7
Chauncey Billups	74	31.4	.421	.392	.878	.50	3.20	3.70	3.9	.85	.20	1.81	1.80	16.2
Clifford Robinson	81	34.9	.398	.336	.676	1.00	2.90	3.90	3.3	1.07	1.09	1.95	3.20	12.2
Corliss Williamson	82	25.1	.453	.182	.790	1.80	2.60	4.40	1.3	.54	.33	1.54	2.90	12.0
Chucky Atkins	65	21.5	.361	.355	.816	.30	1.20	1.50	2.7	.42	.06	1.18	1.70	7.1
Jon Barry	80	18.4	.450	.407	.860	.40	1.80	2.30	2.6	.79	.18	1.01	1.30	6.9
Mehmet Okur	72	19.0	.426	.339	.733	1.60	3.00	4.70	1.0	.35	.54	.92	2.30	6.9
Ben Wallace	73	39.4	.481	.167	.450	4.00	11.40	15.40	1.6	1.42	3.15	1.21	2.50	6.9
Zeljko Rebraca	30	16.3	.552	.000	.792	.90	2.20	3.10	.3	.20	.57	.97	2.60	6.6
Tayshaun Prince	42	10.4	.449	.426	.647	.10	1.00	1.10	.6	.24	.33	.50	.60	3.3
Michael Curry	78	19.9	.402	.296	.800	.20	1.40	1.60	1.3	.56	.05	.55	2.10	3.0
Danny Manning	13	6.8	.406	.375	.833	.50	.80	1.40	.5	.69	.23	.54	.80	2.6
Hubert Davis	43	7.6	.392	.333	.833	.10	.70	.80	.7	.12	.00	.26	.50	1.8
Don Reid	1	10.0	.000	.000	.500	.00	.00	.00	.0	.00	.00	.00	4.00	1.0
Pepe Sanchez	9	4.1	.000	.000	.000	.40	.20	.70	.9	.56	.00	.22	.30	.0
Pistons	**82**	**242.7**	**.430**	**.358**	**.771**	**10.8**	**29.8**	**40.6**	**19.8**	**6.8**	**5.7**	**13.5**	**21.3**	**91.4**
Opponents	**82**	**242.7**	**.438**	**.344**	**.746**	**10.5**	**30.8**	**41.3**	**18.3**	**6.9**	**4.3**	**14.0**	**23.2**	**87.7**

Golden State Warriors

Player	GP	MPG	FG%	3Pt%	FT%	OFF	DEF	Total	APG	SPG	BPG	TO	PF	PPG
Antawn Jamison	82	39.3	.470	.311	.789	2.40	4.70	7.00	1.9	.93	.55	2.16	2.40	22.2
Gilbert Arenas	82	35.0	.431	.348	.791	1.20	3.50	4.70	6.3	1.51	.21	3.54	3.20	18.3
Jason Richardson	82	32.9	.410	.368	.764	1.40	3.30	4.60	3.0	1.10	.28	2.18	2.50	15.6
Troy Murphy	79	31.8	.451	.214	.841	2.90	7.30	10.20	1.3	.82	.38	1.41	3.10	11.7
Earl Boykins	68	19.4	.429	.377	.865	.50	.80	1.30	3.3	.56	.06	1.07	1.10	8.8
Erick Dampier	82	24.1	.496	.000	.698	3.00	3.60	6.60	.7	.33	1.88	1.37	3.00	8.2
Bob Sura	55	20.5	.412	.329	.696	1.10	2.00	3.00	3.2	.82	.04	1.49	2.00	7.3
Mike Dunleavy Jr.	82	15.9	.403	.347	.780	.80	1.80	2.60	1.3	.65	.23	1.05	1.50	5.7
Adonal Foyle	82	21.8	.536	.000	.673	2.10	3.80	6.00	.5	.49	2.50	.89	2.60	5.4
Chris Mills	21	12.5	.368	.280	.889	.90	1.50	2.40	1.0	.33	.14	.48	1.40	4.8
Danny Fortson	17	13.1	.370	.000	.655	1.60	2.60	4.30	.7	.53	.00	.88	2.50	3.5
Oscar Torres	17	6.4	.444	.538	.700	.20	.50	.70	.2	.24	.12	.47	.50	3.1
Jiri Welsch	37	6.3	.253	.250	.759	.30	.40	.80	.7	.22	.05	.51	.90	1.6
Dean Oliver	15	6.2	.241	.167	.875	.10	.50	1.10	1.5	.47	.00	.67	.60	1.5
A.J. Guyton	2	4.5	.000	.000	.000	.00	.00	.00	1.0	.50	.00	.50	.00	.0
Guy Rucker	3	1.3	.000	.000	.000	.00	.30	.30	.3	.00	.00	.00	.30	.0
Warriors	**82**	**240.9**	**.441**	**.344**	**.778**	**15.7**	**31.0**	**46.7**	**20.9**	**7.2**	**6.2**	**15.8**	**21.8**	**102.4**
Opponents	**82**	**240.9**	**.452**	**.372**	**.756**	**14.7**	**29.1**	**43.8**	**23.6**	**8.7**	**6.0**	**13.7**	**23.6**	**103.6**

Houston Rockets

Player	GP	MPG	FG%	3Pt%	FT%	OFF	DEF	Total	APG	SPG	BPG	TO	PF	PPG
Steve Francis	81	41.0	.435	.354	.800	2.00	4.20	6.20	6.2	1.74	.51	3.69	3.10	21.0
Cuttino Mobley	73	41.7	.434	.352	.858	1.00	3.20	4.20	2.8	1.30	.49	2.27	2.50	17.5
Yao Ming	82	29.0	.498	.500	.811	2.40	5.80	8.20	1.7	.38	1.79	2.11	2.80	13.5
James Posey	58	28.4	.439	.326	.826	.90	3.90	4.80	1.8	1.33	.16	1.34	2.30	9.3
Glen Rice	62	24.7	.429	.398	.759	.50	2.00	2.50	1.0	.37	.08	.89	1.60	9.0
Eddie Griffin	77	24.5	.400	.333	.617	1.80	4.20	6.00	1.1	.68	1.44	.99	1.80	8.6
Maurice Taylor	67	20.6	.432	.000	.725	1.40	2.10	3.60	1.0	.33	.33	1.49	2.30	8.4
Kelvin Cato	73	17.1	.520	.000	.532	1.80	4.10	5.90	.3	.52	1.16	.77	2.40	4.5
Moochie Norris	82	16.8	.406	.244	.684	.50	1.50	1.90	2.4	.67	.05	1.05	.90	4.4
Terence Morris	49	12.9	.466	.219	.786	.80	1.80	2.60	.5	.16	.35	.59	.70	3.7
Jason Collier	13	8.0	.472	.000	1.000	.90	1.30	2.20	.1	.15	.08	.15	.80	2.8
Juaquin Hawkins	58	11.8	.385	.417	.500	.30	1.10	1.30	.8	.50	.10	.50	1.00	2.3
Bostjan Nachbar	14	5.5	.355	.200	.500	.20	.60	.80	.2	.14	.14	.43	.90	2.1
Tito Maddox	9	3.9	.250	.000	.625	.10	.70	.80	.6	.33	.11	.33	.40	1.
Rockets	**82**	**243.0**	**.440**	**.346**	**.768**	**12.5**	**31.3**	**43.8**	**18.4**	**7.2**	**6.0**	**15.6**	**19.5**	**93.8**
Opponents	**82**	**243.0**	**.433**	**.347**	**.775**	**11.9**	**28.7**	**40.6**	**20.5**	**8.1**	**4.7**	**13.2**	**21.9**	**92.3**

Indiana Pacers

Player	GP	MPG	FG% Field Goals	3Pt%	FT%	OFF Rebounds	DEF	Total	APG	SPG	BPG	TO	PF	PPG
Jermaine O'Neal...	77	37.2	.484	.333	.731	2.60	7.70	10.30	2.0	.86	2.31	2.34	3.60	20.8
Ron Artest............	69	33.6	.428	.336	.736	1.50	3.80	5.20	2.9	2.30	.72	2.10	3.50	15.5
Brad Miller	73	31.1	.493	.313	.818	2.50	5.70	8.30	2.6	.89	.59	1.62	2.80	13.1
Reggie Miller	70	30.2	.441	.355	.900	.30	2.20	2.50	2.4	.89	.06	.94	1.30	12.6
Al Harrington	82	30.1	.434	.283	.770	1.90	4.30	6.20	1.5	.87	.40	1.99	3.40	12.2
Jamaal Tinsley......	73	30.6	.396	.277	.714	.80	2.80	3.60	7.5	1.71	.25	2.63	2.80	7.8
Ron Mercer..........	72	23.2	.409	.188	.802	.40	1.70	2.10	1.6	.68	.19	.75	1.70	7.7
Jonathan Bender..	46	17.8	.441	.358	.714	.90	2.00	2.90	.9	.17	1.22	.91	1.90	6.6
Erick Strickland.....	71	18.0	.429	.388	.805	.30	1.70	2.00	2.9	.54	.10	1.38	1.60	6.5
Austin Croshere....	49	12.9	.411	.391	.815	.80	2.30	3.20	1.1	.12	.27	.57	1.00	5.1
Tim Hardaway	10	12.7	.367	.355	.500	.10	1.40	1.50	2.4	.90	.00	1.10	.80	4.9
Jamison Brewer....	10	8.0	.529	.000	.444	.50	.40	.90	1.8	.20	.10	.60	1.10	2.2
Jeff Foster............	77	10.4	.360	.000	.540	1.50	2.10	3.60	.7	.36	.27	.44	1.30	2.1
Primoz Brezec	22	5.0	.395	.000	.600	.60	.50	1.00	.2	.09	.18	.32	.70	1.9
Fred Jones............	19	6.1	.375	.286	.750	.20	.30	.50	.3	.32	.05	.32	.70	1.2
Pacers	**82**	**242.7**	**.441**	**.339**	**.766**	**12.2**	**32.0**	**44.2**	**23.3**	**8.5**	**5.4**	**14.8**	**22.1**	**96.8**
Opponents.........	**82**	**242.7**	**.428**	**.340**	**.767**	**12.3**	**30.0**	**42.2**	**20.7**	**7.6**	**6.3**	**15.3**	**23.5**	**93.3**

Los Angeles Clippers

Player	GP	MPG	FG% Field Goals	3Pt%	FT%	OFF Rebounds	DEF	Total	APG	SPG	BPG	TO	PF	PPG
Elton Brand	62	39.6	.502	.000	.685	4.60	6.80	11.30	2.5	1.15	2.55	2.60	3.30	18.5
Corey Maggette ..	64	31.3	.444	.350	.802	1.20	3.80	5.00	1.9	.86	.25	2.30	3.00	16.8
Lamar Odom	49	34.3	.439	.326	.777	1.20	5.40	6.70	3.6	.86	.84	2.86	3.70	14.6
Andre Miller	80	36.4	.406	.213	.795	1.10	2.90	4.00	6.7	1.24	.14	2.58	2.50	13.6
M. Olowokandi......	36	38.0	.427	.000	.657	1.60	7.50	9.10	1.3	.50	2.19	2.72	3.10	12.3
Eric Piatkowski	62	21.9	.471	.398	.828	.70	1.80	2.50	1.1	.53	.15	.90	1.50	9.7
Q. Richardson	59	23.2	.372	.308	.685	1.70	3.10	4.80	.9	.59	.17	1.08	1.60	9.4
Marko Jaric	66	20.9	.401	.319	.752	.50	1.90	2.40	2.9	1.47	.17	1.56	1.90	7.4
Keyon Dooling......	55	17.6	.389	.360	.772	.20	1.10	1.30	1.6	.44	.11	1.09	1.70	6.4
Cherokee Parks ...	30	21.6	.503	.500	.605	1.50	2.90	4.40	.7	.53	.67	.60	1.70	6.3
Melvin Ely	52	15.4	.495	.000	.703	1.20	2.10	3.30	.3	.19	.62	.96	1.80	4.5
Tremaine Fowlkes..	37	15.5	.438	.222	.847	1.10	1.70	2.80	.6	.68	.05	.54	1.70	4.4
Zhizhi Wang	41	10.0	.383	.340	.724	.60	1.20	1.90	.2	.20	.24	.76	1.00	4.4
Sean Rooks	70	19.2	.421	.000	.810	.80	2.30	3.10	1.0	.49	.63	.94	2.50	4.2
Chris Wilcox	46	10.4	.521	.000	.500	.70	1.60	2.30	.5	.15	.26	.57	1.40	3.7
Clippers..............	**82**	**240.9**	**.437**	**.331**	**.750**	**12.3**	**30.0**	**42.3**	**19.6**	**7.0**	**5.6**	**15.7**	**21.8**	**93.8**
Opponents.........	**82**	**240.9**	**.447**	**.365**	**.774**	**12.8**	**30.0**	**42.8**	**22.4**	**8.0**	**5.1**	**14.1**	**22.5**	**97.9**

Los Angeles Lakers

Player	GP	MPG	FG% Field Goals	3Pt%	FT%	OFF Rebounds	DEF	Total	APG	SPG	BPG	TO	PF	PPG
Kobe Bryant	82	41.5	.451	.383	.843	1.30	5.60	6.90	5.9	2.21	.82	3.51	2.70	30.0
Shaquille O'Neal ...	67	37.8	.574	.000	.622	3.90	7.20	11.10	3.1	.57	2.37	2.93	3.40	27.5
Derek Fisher	82	34.5	.437	.401	.800	.50	2.40	2.90	3.6	1.13	.18	1.15	2.40	10.5
Rick Fox	76	28.7	.422	.375	.754	.80	3.40	4.30	3.3	.91	.18	1.59	2.80	9.0
Devean George ...	71	22.7	.390	.371	.790	1.30	2.70	4.00	1.3	.79	.54	.92	2.50	6.9
Robert Horry.........	80	29.3	.387	.288	.769	2.30	4.20	6.40	2.9	1.20	.76	1.40	3.10	6.5
S Medvedenko	58	10.7	.434	.000	.721	1.10	1.30	2.40	.3	.19	.14	.64	2.00	4.4
Samaki Walker	67	18.6	.420	.000	.653	1.70	3.80	5.50	1.0	.30	.82	.84	2.10	4.4
Brian Shaw	72	12.5	.387	.349	.667	.30	1.40	1.70	1.4	.44	.18	.75	.90	3.5
Mark Madsen	54	14.5	.423	.000	.590	1.60	1.40	2.90	.7	.28	.35	.50	2.10	3.2
Kareem Rush.........	76	11.5	.393	.279	.696	.30	.90	1.20	.9	.13	.14	.83	.90	3.0
Jannero Pargo.......	34	10.1	.398	.292	1.000	.30	.80	1.10	1.1	.38	.06	.68	1.30	2.5
Tracy Murray	31	6.2	.324	.211	.778	.20	.60	.70	.4	.16	.10	.45	.70	2.0
Soumaila Samake ..	13	5.9	.417	.000	1.000	.80	1.00	1.80	.3	.00	.38	.15	1.00	1.7
Lakers	**82**	**243.0**	**.451**	**.356**	**.734**	**13.1**	**31.1**	**44.3**	**23.3**	**7.8**	**5.7**	**14.5**	**22.9**	**100.4**
Opponents...........	**82**	**243.0**	**.443**	**.380**	**.760**	**11.7**	**30.4**	**42.1**	**21.4**	**7.9**	**3.8**	**14.5**	**23.4**	**98.0**

Memphis Grizzlies

Player	GP	MPG	Field Goals		FT%	Rebounds			APG	SPG	BPG	TO	PF	PPG
			FG%	3Pt%		OFF	DEF	Total						
Pau Gasol	82	36.0	.510	.100	.736	2.30	6.40	8.80	2.8	.41	1.80	2.60	2.70	19.0
Mike Miller	16	22.5	.510	.500	.806	.40	3.10	3.40	1.9	.38	.31	1.63	2.10	12.8
Jason Williams	76	31.7	.388	.354	.840	.30	2.50	2.80	8.3	1.20	.13	2.21	1.70	12.1
Lorenzen Wright	70	28.3	.454	.000	.659	2.40	5.10	7.50	1.1	.73	.77	1.57	3.00	11.4
Wesley Person	66	29.4	.456	.433	.814	.40	2.50	2.90	1.7	.64	.29	.85	1.00	11.0
Shane Battier	78	30.6	.483	.398	.828	1.60	2.80	4.40	1.3	1.31	1.13	.87	2.70	9.7
Stromile Swift	67	22.1	.481	.000	.722	1.70	4.00	5.70	.7	.82	1.55	1.48	2.30	9.7
Mike Batiste	75	16.6	.422	.222	.784	1.10	2.30	3.40	.7	.56	.21	.92	1.60	6.4
Earl Watson	79	17.3	.435	.341	.721	.60	1.50	2.10	2.8	1.13	.18	1.11	1.70	5.5
Michael Dickerson	6	14.5	.417	.364	1.000	.20	.80	1.00	1.3	.83	.17	1.00	2.70	4.8
Chris Owens	1	6.0	.667	.000	.000	1.00	.00	1.00	.0	.00	.00	1.00	.00	4.0
Brevin Knight	55	16.9	.425	.250	.541	.30	1.20	1.50	4.2	1.25	.04	1.71	2.20	3.9
Ryan Humphrey	13	9.4	.343	.000	.455	.30	2.00	2.30	.3	.38	.15	.15	1.40	2.2
Robert Archibald	12	6.0	.300	.000	.389	.50	.90	1.40	.3	.00	.25	.58	.80	1.6
Cezary Trybanski	15	5.7	.250	.000	.400	.40	.50	.90	.1	.00	.40	.53	.90	.9
Grizzlies	**82**	**243.0**	**.452**	**.365**	**.739**	**11.5**	**30.1**	**41.6**	**23.1**	**7.9**	**6.1**	**15.4**	**20.5**	**97.5**
Opponents	**82**	**243.0**	**.460**	**.363**	**.759**	**13.7**	**31.2**	**44.9**	**24.3**	**8.7**	**5.2**	**14.8**	**21.7**	**100.7**

Miami Heat

Player	GP	MPG	Field Goals		FT%	Rebounds			APG	SPG	BPG	TO	PF	PPG
			FG%	3Pt%		OFF	DEF	Total						
Eddie Jones	47	38.1	.423	.407	.822	.70	4.10	4.80	3.7	1.36	.66	1.81	2.90	18.5
Caron Butler	78	36.6	.416	.318	.824	1.70	3.40	5.10	2.7	1.76	.40	2.46	2.90	15.4
Brian Grant	82	32.2	.509	.000	.771	2.90	7.30	10.20	1.3	.77	.57	1.57	3.70	10.3
Malik Allen	80	29.0	.424	.000	.802	1.70	3.60	5.30	.7	.46	.98	1.60	2.90	9.6
Travis Best	72	25.1	.396	.330	.854	.40	1.70	2.00	3.5	.61	.10	1.47	2.40	8.4
Mike James	78	22.1	.373	.294	.732	.30	1.60	1.90	3.2	.82	.06	1.38	2.30	7.8
Rasual Butler	72	21.0	.362	.292	.731	.40	2.20	2.60	1.3	.29	.60	1.07	1.50	7.5
Eddie House	55	18.6	.387	.300	.861	.30	1.50	1.80	1.6	.80	.02	.84	1.30	7.5
Vladimir Stepania	79	20.2	.433	.000	.530	2.70	4.30	7.00	.3	.57	.51	.87	2.10	5.6
LaPhonso Ellis	55	14.3	.382	.252	.758	.80	2.10	2.90	.3	.27	.27	.56	1.60	5.0
Sean Lampley	35	13.9	.434	.000	.695	.70	1.60	2.40	.9	.20	.09	.71	1.20	4.8
Anthony Carter	49	18.6	.356	.000	.660	.20	1.40	1.70	4.1	.92	.10	1.65	1.40	4.1
Sean Marks	23	9.7	.373	.000	.667	.30	1.20	1.50	.1	.22	.26	.61	1.60	2.3
Ken Johnson	16	9.8	.405	.000	.333	.30	1.80	2.00	.0	.06	.75	.38	1.30	2.0
Heat	**82**	**241.8**	**.412**	**.316**	**.765**	**11.6**	**30.0**	**41.6**	**18.3**	**7.2**	**4.0**	**14.2**	**22.6**	**85.6**
Opponents	**82**	**241.8**	**.437**	**.353**	**.751**	**10.6**	**31.5**	**42.2**	**18.1**	**7.6**	**5.3**	**14.3**	**20.4**	**90.6**

Milwaukee Bucks

Player	GP	MPG	Field Goals		FT%	Rebounds			APG	SPG	BPG	TO	PF	PPG
			FG%	3Pt%		OFF	DEF	Total						
Sam Cassell	78	34.6	.470	.362	.861	.70	3.70	4.40	5.8	1.13	.18	2.27	2.80	19.7
Gary Payton	80	40.1	.454	.297	.710	1.00	3.20	4.20	8.3	1.66	.25	2.34	2.30	20.4
Michael Redd	82	28.2	.469	.438	.805	1.20	3.30	4.50	1.4	1.22	.16	.90	1.70	15.1
Desmond Mason	80	34.5	.449	.292	.749	1.90	4.60	6.50	2.0	.84	.40	1.44	2.60	14.3
Tim Thomas	80	29.5	.443	.366	.780	1.20	3.70	4.90	1.3	.88	.61	1.66	3.20	13.3
Toni Kukoc	63	27.0	.432	.361	.706	1.10	3.20	4.20	3.7	1.29	.46	1.94	2.10	11.6
Anthony Mason	65	32.6	.486	.000	.718	1.40	5.00	6.40	3.2	.49	.18	1.22	2.30	7.2
Jason Caffey	51	17.5	.456	.000	.651	1.30	2.10	3.50	.7	.37	.29	1.10	2.40	5.8
Marcus Haislip	39	11.3	.431	.250	.684	.50	.80	1.40	.2	.18	.46	.54	1.40	4.1
Dan Gadzuric	49	15.5	.483	.000	.518	1.30	2.70	4.00	.2	.45	1.06	.55	2.60	3.4
Ervin Johnson	69	17.0	.452	.000	.682	1.70	2.60	4.30	.3	.49	.91	.49	2.60	2.2
Joel Przybilla	32	17.1	.391	.000	.500	1.50	3.00	4.50	.4	.31	1.41	.59	2.70	1.5
Jamal Sampson	5	1.6	.000	.000	.000	.20	.20	.40	.2	.20	.00	.00	.00	.0
Bucks	**82**	**242.7**	**.457**	**.383**	**.776**	**10.7**	**28.9**	**39.5**	**22.2**	**7.6**	**4.2**	**12.7**	**22.2**	**99.5**
Opponents	**82**	**242.7**	**.458**	**.375**	**.745**	**12.5**	**31.0**	**43.4**	**23.1**	**6.6**	**4.1**	**14.4**	**20.5**	**99.3**

Minnesota Timberwolves

Player	GP	MPG	Field Goals		FT%	Rebounds			APG	SPG	BPG	TO	PF	PPG
			FG%	3Pt%		OFF	DEF	Total						
Kevin Garnett 82		40.5	.502	.282	.751	3.00	10.50	13.40	6.0	1.38	1.57	2.79	2.40	23.0
Wally Szczerbiak ..52		35.3	.481	.421	.867	1.00	3.60	4.60	2.6	.85	.42	1.67	2.40	17.6
Troy Hudson 79		32.9	.428	.365	.900	.50	1.80	2.30	5.7	.76	.09	2.30	2.00	14.2
R. Nesterovic 77		30.4	.525	.000	.642	1.90	4.60	6.50	1.5	.51	1.51	1.29	3.30	11.2
Kendall Gill 82		25.2	.422	.322	.764	.60	2.40	3.00	1.9	.95	.18	1.32	2.10	8.7
Anthony Peeler 82		27.4	.414	.410	.780	.50	2.50	2.90	3.0	.88	.16	1.00	2.00	7.7
Joe Smith 54		20.7	.460	.000	.779	2.10	2.90	5.00	.7	.26	1.02	.80	3.20	7.5
Rod Strickland 47		20.3	.432	.091	.738	.40	1.60	2.00	4.6	.98	.13	1.62	1.20	6.8
Gary Trent 80		15.3	.535	.000	.594	1.30	2.30	3.60	1.0	.40	.29	.74	1.80	6.0
Marc Jackson 77		13.5	.438	1.000	.765	1.10	1.80	2.90	.5	.31	.39	.77	1.80	5.5
Reggie Slater 26		5.4	.540	.000	.600	.70	.50	1.20	.2	.23	.04	.35	1.20	3.1
Loren Woods 38		9.3	.382	.333	.778	.70	1.80	2.50	.5	.26	.34	.61	1.00	2.1
Mike Wilks 46		15.0	.338	.286	.787	.40	1.10	1.50	2.0	.59	.09	.61	1.50	3.2
Igor Rakocevic 42		5.8	.379	.417	.806	.10	.30	.40	.8	.10	.00	.55	.60	1.9
Timberwolves ...82		**241.5**	**.466**	**.368**	**.770**	**11.7**	**31.9**	**43.6**	**25.2**	**6.7**	**5.3**	**13.7**	**20.8**	**98.1**
Opponents..........82		**241.5**	**.437**	**.347**	**.752**	**11.9**	**29.8**	**41.7**	**22.8**	**7.0**	**4.9**	**13.6**	**20.6**	**96.0**

New Jersey Nets

Player	GP	MPG	Field Goals		FT%	Rebounds			APG	SPG	BPG	TO	PF	PPG
			FG%	3Pt%		OFF	DEF	Total						
Jason Kidd 80		37.4	.414	.341	.841	1.40	4.90	6.30	8.9	2.24	.31	3.70	1.60	18.7
Kenyon Martin 81		34.1	.470	.209	.653	2.10	6.20	8.30	2.4	1.27	.91	2.49	3.80	16.7
R. Jefferson 80		36.0	.501	.250	.743	1.90	4.60	6.40	2.5	1.00	.55	1.95	2.70	15.5
Kerry Kittles 65		30.0	.467	.356	.785	.80	3.10	3.90	2.6	1.55	.46	.85	1.70	13.0
Lucious Harris 77		25.6	.413	.346	.804	.80	2.20	3.00	2.0	.69	.10	.92	1.20	10.3
Rodney Rogers 68		19.2	.402	.333	.756	.90	3.00	3.90	1.6	.74	.46	1.34	2.80	7.0
Aaron Williams 81		19.7	.453	.000	.785	1.70	2.40	4.10	1.1	.33	.70	1.05	2.50	6.2
D. Mutombo 24		21.4	.374	.000	.727	2.30	4.10	6.40	.8	.17	1.54	1.42	2.30	5.8
Jason Collins 81		23.5	.414	.000	.763	1.70	2.90	4.50	1.1	.58	.54	1.05	3.10	5.7
Anthony Johnson...66		12.8	.446	.371	.689	.20	1.00	1.20	1.3	.56	.08	.62	1.40	4.1
Brian Scalabrine ...59		12.3	.402	.359	.833	.70	1.70	2.40	.8	.27	.31	.78	1.30	3.1
Tamar Slay 36		7.6	.379	.280	.700	.20	.60	.90	.4	.39	.08	.56	.90	2.6
B. Armstrong 17		4.1	.333	.167	.833	.00	.20	.20	.1	.18	.06	.29	.50	1.4
Chris Childs 12		8.8	.300	.167	.667	.30	.20	.40	1.3	.67	.08	.50	1.40	1.3
Donny Marshall 3		2.0	.000	.000	.000	.00	1.00	1.00	.0	.00	.00	.33	.00	.0
Nets...................82		**240.9**	**.441**	**.332**	**.757**	**12.1**	**30.8**	**42.9**	**23.0**	**8.7**	**4.6**	**14.8**	**21.6**	**95.4**
Opponents..........82		**240.9**	**.427**	**.359**	**.749**	**11.4**	**30.0**	**41.4**	**19.6**	**8.5**	**5.2**	**16.6**	**22.9**	**90.1**

New Orleans Hornets

Player	GP	MPG	Field Goals		FT%	Rebounds			APG	SPG	BPG	TO	PF	PPG
			FG%	3Pt%		OFF	DEF	Total						
Jamal Mashburn...82		40.5	.422	.389	.848	.80	5.30	6.10	5.6	1.01	.21	2.80	2.40	21.6
Baron Davis 50		37.8	.416	.350	.710	1.10	2.60	3.70	6.4	1.82	.44	2.80	3.00	17.1
David Wesley 73		37.1	.433	.424	.781	.50	1.90	2.40	3.4	1.49	.12	1.81	2.40	16.7
P.J. Brown 78		33.4	.531	.000	.836	3.10	5.90	9.00	1.9	.86	1.03	1.26	2.60	10.7
Jamaal Magloire ..82		29.8	.480	.000	.717	3.20	5.70	8.80	1.1	.60	1.35	1.93	3.40	10.3
C. Alexander.......66		20.6	.382	.333	.808	.60	1.20	1.80	1.2	.47	.09	1.03	1.90	7.9
Kenny Anderson...23		18.6	.427	.143	.789	.50	1.70	2.20	3.2	.95	.08	1.23	1.70	6.1
Robert Pack..........28		15.7	.403	.000	.745	.40	1.40	1.80	2.9	.89	.00	1.43	1.30	5.2
George Lynch.......81		18.5	.409	.354	.554	1.70	2.60	4.40	1.3	.81	.23	.64	1.70	4.5
Jerome Moiso 51		12.6	.520	.000	.659	1.20	2.30	3.50	.4	.37	.86	.90	1.70	4.0
Robert Traylor.......69		12.3	.443	.333	.648	1.60	2.20	3.80	.7	.65	.54	.77	2.20	3.9
Stacey Augmon....70		12.3	.411	.000	.750	.40	1.30	1.70	1.0	.39	.13	.57	1.10	3.0
Randy Livingston....2		6.0	.500	.000	1.000	.00	.00	.00	.5	.00	.00	.00	.00	3.0
Bryce Drew..........13		6.1	.296	.429	.000	.30	.70	1.00	.8	.15	.00	.23	.20	1.5
Kirk Haston..........12		4.8	.118	.000	.500	.00	.60	.60	.3	.00	.42	.58	.80	.5
Hornets 82		**242.7**	**.435**	**.376**	**.768**	**13.4**	**30.2**	**43.6**	**22.0**	**8.0**	**4.8**	**14.8**	**21.6**	**93.9**
Opponents...........82		**242.7**	**.438**	**.338**	**.766**	**11.1**	**28.9**	**40.0**	**19.9**	**7.9**	**5.2**	**14.6**	**21.4**	**91.8**

New York Knicks

Player	GP	MPG	Field Goals		FT%	Rebounds			APG	SPG	BPG	TO	PF	PPG
			FG%	3Pt%		OFF	DEF	Total						
Allan Houston .....:..82		37.9	.445	.396	.919	.30	2.50	2.80	2.7	.66	.09	2.17	2.30	22.5
Latrell Sprewell 74		38.6	.403	.372	.794	.60	3.20	3.90	4.5	1.38	.30	2.32	1.80	16.4
Kurt Thomas 81		31.8	.483	.667	.750	2.00	5.90	7.90	2.0	1.00	1.20	1.70	4.20	14.0
Howard Eisley.....82		27.4	.417	.389	.848	.30	2.00	2.30	5.4	.87	.11	1.82	2.70	9.1
S Anderson..........82		21.1	.462	.371	.732	.80	2.30	3.10	1.1	.89	.24	1.39	2.20	8.4
O. Harrington........74		25.0	.508	.000	.820	2.20	4.20	6.40	.8	.16	.31	1.22	3.10	7.7
Charlie Ward 66		22.2	.399	.378	.774	.40	2.30	2.70	4.6	1.18	.17	1.44	2.20	7.2
C. Weatherspoon..79		25.6	.449	.000	.768	2.70	4.90	7.60	.9	.87	.46	.80	2.20	6.6
Lee Nailon 38		10.7	.442	.000	.824	.80	1.00	1.80	.7	.16	.08	.84	1.20	5.5
Michael Doleac...75		13.9	.426	.000	.783	.90	2.10	2.90	.6	.21	.21	.65	2.00	4.4
Lavor Postell........12		8.2	.368	.286	.867	.10	.30	.30	.3	.17	.00	.58	.80	3.6
Travis Knight........32		9.0	.385	.000	.769	.60	1.40	1.90	.4	.25	.28	.31	1.40	1.9
Frank Williams 21		8.0	.273	.375	.667	.10	.70	.90	1.6	.33	.10	.81	1.00	1.3
Knicks 82		**242.1**	**.441**	**.383**	**.815**	**10.3**	**29.0**	**39.2**	**22.0**	**7.1**	**3.1**	**14.0**	**23.0**	**95.9**
Opponents.........82		**242.1**	**.457**	**.340**	**.771**	**11.4**	**31.9**	**43.3**	**21.1**	**7.7**	**3.8**	**14.4**	**19.9**	**97.2**

Orlando Magic

Player	GP	MPG	Field Goals		FT%	Rebounds			APG	SPG	BPG	TO	PF	PPG
			FG%	3Pt%		OFF	DEF	Total						
Tracy McGrady 75		39.4	.457	.386	.793	1.60	4.90	6.50	5.5	1.65	.79	2.60	2.10	32.1
Grant Hill...............29		29.1	.492	.250	.819	1.40	5.70	7.10	4.2	.97	.45	2.90	1.60	14.5
Gordan Giricek 76		28.3	.436	.341	.820	.50	2.70	3.10	1.8	.68	.11	1.91	2.10	12.3
Drew Gooden 70		26.8	.457	.292	.712	2.30	4.20	6.50	1.2	.76	.50	2.14	2.50	12.5
Pat Garrity............81		31.9	.419	.396	.830	.90	2.90	3.80	1.5	.77	.25	.95	3.10	10.7
Darrell Armstrong..82		28.7	.409	.336	.878	1.10	2.50	3.60	3.9	1.65	.16	1.95	2.00	9.4
Shawn Kemp 79		20.7	.418	.000	.742	1.90	3.80	5.70	.7	.84	.42	1.29	3.00	6.8
Jacque Vaughn 80		21.1	.448	.235	.776	.30	1.20	1.50	2.9	.80	.03	1.21	2.10	5.9
Horace Grant.........5		17.0	.520	.000	.000	.40	1.20	1.60	1.4	.60	.00	.20	1.00	5.2
Andrew DeClercq...77		17.2	.534	.000	.644	1.80	2.60	4.40	.7	.51	.47	1.09	3.40	4.7
Pat Burke 62		12.6	.382	.143	.690	.90	1.40	2.40	.4	.31	.40	.76	1.60	4.3
Steven Hunter.......33		13.5	.544	.000	.409	1.20	1.70	2.80	.2	.27	1.09	.45	1.70	3.9
Chris Whitney 51		20.6	.355	.305	.826	.10	1.30	1.30	2.8	.57	.04	1.39	1.80	7.0
Jeryl Sasser 75		13.7	.309	.295	.679	.90	1.60	2.50	.9	.60	.16	.52	1.20	2.6
Olumide Oyedeji...27		5.4	.435	.000	.636	.40	1.50	1.90	.2	.19	.11	.19	1.10	1.0
Magic...................82		**241.5**	**.436**	**.357**	**.777**	**11.7**	**29.2**	**40.9**	**20.4**	**8.5**	**3.7**	**14.4**	**23.0**	**98.5**
Opponents.........82		**241.5**	**.455**	**.334**	**.767**	**11.8**	**31.7**	**43.5**	**22.4**	**7.8**	**5.0**	**16.4**	**22.2**	**98.4**

Philadelphia 76ers

Player	GP	MPG	Field Goals		FT%	Rebounds			APG	SPG	BPG	TO	PF	PPG
			FG%	3Pt%		OFF	DEF	Total						
Allen Iverson.........82		42.5	.414	.277	.774	.80	3.40	4.20	5.5	2.74	.16	3.49	1.80	27.6
Keith Van Horn 74		31.6	.482	.369	.804	2.10	4.90	7.10	1.3	.85	.41	2.03	3.40	15.9
Eric Snow..............82		37.9	.452	.219	.858	.90	2.80	3.70	6.6	1.62	.13	2.37	2.90	12.9
Kenny Thomas......66		30.0	.465	.000	.746	2.80	5.20	8.00	1.7	.94	.42	1.76	2.60	10.1
Derrick Coleman...64		27.2	.448	.328	.784	2.40	4.70	7.00	1.4	.83	1.08	1.50	2.70	9.4
Aaron McKie 29		29.7	.429	.330	.836	.80	3.60	4.40	3.5	1.64	.11	1.36	2.20	9.0
Todd MacCulloch..42		19.3	.517	.000	.671	1.60	3.10	4.70	.5	.45	.76	.83	2.50	7.1
Greg Buckner 75		20.2	.465	.273	.802	1.00	1.90	2.90	1.3	.96	.21	.83	2.70	6.0
Brian Skinner........77		17.9	.550	.000	.602	1.80	3.00	4.80	.2	.61	.69	.81	2.30	6.0
Tyrone Hill 56		24.1	.422	.000	.675	2.30	4.70	7.00	.7	.82	.46	1.21	3.10	5.6
Monty Williams......21		13.1	.425	.000	.750	.60	1.60	2.10	1.2	.57	.24	.81	1.60	4.4
John Salmons.......64		7.9	.414	.323	.743	.30	.70	.90	.7	.27	.09	.45	.80	2.1
Efthimios Rentzias...35		4.1	.339	.500	.889	.30	.50	.70	.2	.17	.06	.11	.60	1.5
Kenny Satterfield...39		12.9	.301	.179	.680	.40	.70	1.10	1.7	.51	.05	1.10	.90	3.4
76ers 82		**242.1**	**.448**	**.311**	**.775**	**12.7**	**29.5**	**42.2**	**21.6**	**10.3**	**3.5**	**14.8**	**22.0**	**96.8**
Opponents.........82		**242.1**	**.452**	**.354**	**.760**	**11.1**	**29.3**	**40.3**	**22.1**	**7.8**	**6.4**	**17.1**	**23.0**	**94.5**

Phoenix Suns

Player	GP	MPG	FG%	3Pt%	FT%	OFF	DEF	Total	APG	SPG	BPG	TO	PF	PPG
			Field Goals			Rebounds								
Stephon Marbury	81	40.0	.439	.301	.803	.70	2.60	3.20	8.1	1.33	.25	3.25	2.50	22.3
Shawn Marion	81	41.6	.452	.387	.851	2.50	7.10	9.50	2.4	2.28	1.17	1.94	2.60	21.2
A. Stoudemire	82	31.3	.472	.200	.661	3.00	5.70	8.80	1.0	.76	1.06	2.30	3.30	13.5
A. Hardaway	58	30.6	.447	.356	.794	1.10	3.30	4.40	4.1	1.14	.45	2.50	2.60	10.6
Joe Johnson	82	27:5	.397	.366	.774	.70	2.50	3.20	2.6	.76	.23	1.32	1.70	9.8
Casey Jacobsen	72	15.9	.373	.315	.686	.40	.80	1.20	1.0	.49	.08	.76	1.30	5.1
Jake Tsakalidis	33	16.5	.452	.000	.672	1.40	2.30	3.70	.4	.18	.52	.79	2.40	4.9
Tom Gugliotta	27	16.6	.455	.000	1.000	.90	2.80	3.70	1.1	.52	.19	1.15	1.30	4.8
Bo Outlaw	80	22.5	.550	.000	.621	1.70	2.90	4.60	1.4	.63	.89	.95	2.40	4.7
Scott Williams	69	12.6	.411	.000	.786	1.00	1.80	2.80	.3	.39	.30	.46	2.30	4.0
Jake Voskuhl	65	14.6	.564	.000	.667	1.50	2.00	3.50	.6	.28	.45	.74	2.60	3.8
Dan Langhi	60	9.0	.401	.290	.600	.30	1.10	1.50	.4	.25	.10	.27	1.00	3.1
Randy Brown	32	8.2	.372	.000	.750	.10	.70	.80	1.1	.53	.06	.53	1.10	1.3
Alton Ford	11	2.8	.333	.000	.333	.00	.50	.50	.1	.00	.00	.18	.60	.6
Suns	**82**	**241.5**	**.443**	**.343**	**.742**	**12.8**	**29.8**	**42.5**	**21.0**	**8.1**	**4.9**	**14.7**	**22.0**	**95.5**
Opponents	**82**	**241.5**	**.438**	**.320**	**.766**	**12.6**	**30.3**	**42.9**	**22.2**	**7.8**	**5.5**	**16.0**	**21.5**	**94.4**

Portland Trail Blazers

Player	GP	MPG	FG%	3Pt%	FT%	OFF	DEF	Total	APG	SPG	BPG	TO	PF	PPG
			Field Goals			Rebounds								
Rasheed Wallace	74	36.3	.471	.358	.735	1.50	5.90	7.40	2.1	.95	1.04	1.89	3.00	18.1
Bonzi Wells	75	31.9	.441	.292	.722	1.30	3.90	5.30	3.3	1.64	.24	2.87	2.90	15.2
Derek Anderson	76	33.6	.427	.350	.859	.70	2.80	3.50	4.3	1.18	.21	1.68	1.90	13.9
Scottie Pippen	64	29.9	.444	.286	.818	.90	3.50	4.30	4.5	1.64	.39	2.56	2.30	10.8
Zach Randolph	77	16.9	.513	.000	.758	1.80	2.60	4.50	.5	.55	.18	.81	1.80	8.4
Ruben Patterson	78	21.2	.492	.150	.627	1.50	1.80	3.40	1.3	.94	.37	1.50	2.10	8.3
Dale Davis	78	29.3	.541	.000	.633	3.00	4.20	7.20	1.2	.65	.90	.91	2.40	7.4
D. Stoudamire	59	22.3	.376	.386	.791	.70	1.90	2.60	3.5	.66	.10	1.39	1.10	6.9
Arvydas Sabonis	78	15.5	.476	.500	.787	1.10	3.20	4.30	1.8	.78	.63	.96	1.80	6.1
Jeff McInnis	75	17.5	.444	.171	.746	.30	1.00	1.30	2.3	.28	.03	1.00	1.60	5.8
Antonio Daniels	67	14.2	.452	.305	.855	.20	.90	1.10	1.3	.49	.13	.48	.60	3.7
Qyntel Woods	53	6.3	.500	.333	.350	.30	.70	1.00	.2	.28	.02	.43	.70	2.4
Charles Smith	3	4.3	.250	.000	.750	.00	.00	.00	.3	.33	.00	.33	1.00	1.7
Chris Dudley	3	3.7	.000	.000	.000	.00	.70	.70	.0	.00	.00	.00	1.00	.0
R. Boumtje-Boumtje	2	2.5	.000	.000	.000	.50	.00	.50	.5	.50	.00	.00	.00	.0
Blazers	**82**	**242.1**	**.460**	**.330**	**.745**	**12.1**	**29.0**	**41.1**	**22.7**	**8.8**	**3.9**	**15.2**	**19.9**	**95.2**
Opponents	**82**	**242.1**	**.450**	**.341**	**.764**	**11.1**	**28.0**	**39.1**	**22.7**	**8.3**	**4.8**	**15.5**	**20.4**	**92.5**

Sacramento Kings

Player	GP	MPG	FG%	3Pt%	FT%	OFF	DEF	Total	APG	SPG	BPG	TO	PF	PPG
			Field Goals			Rebounds								
Chris Webber	67	39.1	.461	.238	.607	2.40	8.10	10.50	5.4	1.58	1.31	3.21	3.00	23.0
Predrag Stojakovic	72	34.0	.481	.382	.875	.80	4.70	5.50	2.0	1.00	.07	1.40	2.00	19.2
Mike Bibby	55	33.4	.470	.409	.861	.60	2.10	2.70	5.2	1.31	.15	2.31	1.70	15.9
Bobby Jackson	59	28.4	.464	.379	.846	1.00	2.70	3.70	3.1	1.20	.05	1.80	2.10	15.2
Vlade Divac	80	29.8	.466	.240	.713	2.00	5.20	7.20	3.4	1.04	1.31	1.90	3.00	9.9
Doug Christie	80	33.9	.479	.395	.810	.80	3.50	4.30	4.7	2.25	.46	1.80	2.30	9.4
Jim Jackson	63	20.8	.442	.451	.855	1.30	2.80	4.20	1.9	.49	.06	1.27	2.10	7.7
Keon Clark	80	22.3	.501	.000	.656	1.70	3.90	5.60	1.0	.48	1.88	1.18	2.80	6.7
Hidayet Turkoglu	67	17.5	.422	.372	.800	.50	2.30	2.80	1.3	.37	.18	.75	1.90	6.7
Gerald Wallace	47	12.1	.492	.250	.527	.80	1.90	2.70	.5	.51	.32	.94	1.40	4.7
Damon Jones	49	14.5	.381	.364	.741	.20	1.20	1.40	1.6	.37	.08	.47	.90	4.6
Scot Pollard	23	14.1	.460	.000	.605	2.00	2.60	4.60	.3	.57	.65	.65	2.20	4.5
L. Funderburke	27	8.5	.444	.000	.588	.60	1.40	2.00	.3	.04	.41	.22	.90	2.7
Mateen Cleaves	12	4.6	.261	1.000	.750	.10	.60	.70	.8	.17	.00	1.17	.50	1.3
Kings	**82**	**241.8**	**.464**	**.381**	**.746**	**11.0**	**33.5**	**44.5**	**24.8**	**9.0**	**5.6**	**14.5**	**20.3**	**101.7**
Opponents	**82**	**241.8**	**.420**	**.320**	**.741**	**14.0**	**31.9**	**45.8**	**21.5**	**8.3**	**4.3**	**15.4**	**19.9**	**95.2**

San Antonio Spurs

Player	GP	MPG	Field Goals		FT%	Rebounds		Total	APG	SPG	BPG	TO	PF	PPG
			FG%	3Pt%		OFF	DEF							
Tim Duncan	81	39.3	.513	.273	.710	3.20	9.70	12.90	3.9	.68	2.93	3.06	2.90	23.3
Tony Parker	82	33.8	.464	.337	.755	.40	2.20	2.60	5.3	.87	.05	2.41	2.10	15.5
Stephen Jackson	80	28.2	.435	.320	.760	.80	2.80	3.60	2.3	1.56	.38	2.20	2.50	11.8
Malik Rose	79	24.5	.459	.400	.791	1.90	4.50	6.40	1.6	.72	.51	2.15	2.60	10.4
David Robinson	64	26.2	.469	.000	.710	2.50	5.40	7.90	1.0	.81	1.73	1.30	2.00	8.5
Emanuel Ginobili	69	20.7	.438	.345	.737	.70	1.70	2.30	2.0	1.39	.25	1.45	2.50	7.6
Bruce Bowen	82	31.3	.466	.441	.404	.70	2.20	2.90	1.4	.80	.51	.88	2.40	7.1
Steve Smith	53	19.5	.388	.331	.833	.40	1.50	1.90	1.3	.53	.17	.81	1.50	6.8
Speedy Claxton	30	15.7	.462	.000	.684	.70	1.10	1.90	2.5	.73	.23	1.17	1.40	5.8
Kevin Willis	71	11.8	.479	.000	.614	1.20	2.00	3.20	.3	.28	.28	.85	1.70	4.2
Steve Kerr	75	12.7	.430	.395	.882	.20	.60	.80	.9	.36	.04	.47	.70	4.0
Danny Ferry	64	9.4	.355	.350	.769	.30	.90	1.20	.3	.11	.14	.42	.90	1.9
Mengke Bateer	12	3.8	.235	.333	.000	.20	.70	.80	.3	.00	.00	.50	1.20	.8
Spurs	82	241.8	.462	.354	.725	11.5	31.2	42.6	20.0	7.7	6.5	15.8	20.4	95.8
Opponents	82	241.8	.427	.339	.768	12.5	28.3	40.9	19.0	8.1	5.2	15.0	23.4	90.4

Seattle SuperSonics

Player	GP	MPG	Field Goals		FT%	Rebounds		Total	APG	SPG	BPG	TO	PF	PPG
			FG%	3Pt%		OFF	DEF							
Ray Allen	29	41.3	.441	.351	.920	1.70	3.90	5.60	5.9	1.59	.10	2.79	2.40	24.5
Rashard Lewis	77	39.5	.452	.346	.820	2.00	4.60	6.50	1.7	1.29	.45	1.86	2.70	18.1
Brent Barry	75	33.1	.458	.403	.795	.60	3.40	4.00	5.1	1.51	.20	1.89	2.70	10.3
V. Radmanovic	72	26.5	.410	.355	.706	1.10	3.40	4.50	1.3	.89	.31	1.39	1.90	10.1
P. Drobnjak	82	24.2	.412	.353	.791	1.40	2.50	3.90	1.0	.59	.46	.79	2.20	9.4
Kevin Ollie	29	26.6	.441	1.000	.759	.40	2.40	2.90	3.8	1.10	.03	1.24	1.80	8.0
Jerome James	51	15.0	.478	.000	.587	1.50	2.70	4.20	.5	.24	1.61	1.47	3.30	5.4
Vitaly Potapenko	26	15.5	.441	.000	.759	1.00	2.50	3.40	.2	.35	.31	.96	1.80	4.0
Reggie Evans	20.4	20.4	.471	.000	.519	2.50	4.10	6.60	.5	.57	.16	.78	2.60	3.2
Elden Campbell	15	12.3	.333	.000	.762	.90	1.70	2.60	.6	.60	.53	.53	1.80	3.2
Calvin Booth	47	12.2	.437	.000	.723	.70	1.60	2.30	.3	.23	.70	.47	1.60	2.9
Ansu Sesay	45	10.0	.383	.000	.571	.80	.90	1.60	.5	.31	.11	.56	1.40	2.1
Ronald Murray	2	10.0	.400	.000	.000	.00	1.50	1.50	1.0	.00	.00	2.00	.00	2.0
Joseph Forte	17	5.1	.286	.000	.667	.20	.40	.60	.6	.24	.00	.59	.40	1.4
Sonics	82	242.1	.437	.353	.744	11.7	29.1	40.8	21.6	8.3	3.6	13.2	20.9	92.1
Opponents	82	242.1	.447	.344	.742	11.4	30.0	41.5	20.8	6.1	5.0	14.7	20.4	92.3

Toronto Raptors

Player	GP	MPG	Field Goals		FT%	Rebounds		Total	APG	SPG	BPG	TO	PF	PPG
			FG%	3Pt%		OFF	DEF							
Vince Carter	43	34.2	.467	.344	.806	1.40	3.00	4.40	3.3	1.12	.95	1.72	2.80	20.6
Voshon Lenard	63	30.6	.402	.365	.804	.80	2.60	3.40	2.3	.94	.33	1.63	2.50	14.3
Morris Peterson	82	36.0	.392	.337	.789	1.20	3.20	4.40	2.3	1.07	.39	1.56	2.80	14.1
Antonio Davis	53	35.7	.407	.000	.771	2.50	5.80	8.20	2.5	.43	1.17	2.23	2.80	13.9
Alvin Williams	75	33.8	.438	.329	.782	.70	2.40	3.10	5.3	1.42	.27	1.64	2.20	13.2
Lindsey Hunter	29	23.2	.351	.318	.723	.50	1.50	2.00	2.4	1.21	.17	1.97	1.70	9.7
Jerome Williams	71	33.0	.499	.167	.555	3.30	5.90	9.20	1.3	1.63	.37	1.38	2.80	9.7
Rafer Alston	47	20.9	.415	.392	.685	.40	1.80	2.30	4.1	.81	.32	1.83	2.60	7.8
Jelani McCoy	67	20.4	.491	.000	.548	1.40	3.90	5.30	.6	.42	.90	1.43	2.40	6.8
Damone Brown	5	23.0	.314	.000	.750	.60	2.40	3.00	.6	.20	.00	1.20	2.80	5.6
Mamadou N'diaye	22	16.5	.448	.000	.723	1.30	2.40	3.70	.3	.36	1.45	.95	2.60	5.5
Michael Bradley	67	19.6	.481	.167	.522	2.40	3.70	6.10	1.0	.24	.48	1.13	1.90	5.0
Greg Foster	29	18.6	.385	.250	.813	1.00	2.50	3.50	.4	.03	.31	1.03	2.80	4.2
Chris Jefferies	63	13.1	.387	.333	.674	.30	.80	1.20	.4	.37	.31	.88	1.10	3.9
Nate Huffman	7	10.9	.360	.000	.625	1.30	2.00	3.30	.7	.14	.43	.43	1.90	3.3
Art Long	7	11.4	.360	.500	.200	1.10	1.70	2.90	.6	.43	.43	1.57	1.90	2.9
Maceo Baston	16	6.6	.600	.000	.833	.30	1.20	1.40	.0	.25	.69	.38	1.00	2.5
Zendon Hamilton	3	4.0	.400	.000	1.000	.30	1.00	1.30	.0	.33	.00	.33	.70	2.0
Raptors	82	241.5	.427	.343	.718	12.5	28.7	41.2	19.3	7.4	4.8	14.4	21.5	90.9
Opponents	82	241.5	.461	.375	.759	11.9	31.7	43.6	21.1	7.4	5.0	13.7	20.8	96.8

Utah Jazz

Player	GP	MPG	FG%	3Pt%	FT%	OFF	DEF	Total	APG	SPG	BPG	TO	PF	PPG
			Field Goals			**Rebounds**								
Karl Malone 81		36.2	.462	.214	.763	1.40	6.40	7.80	4.7	1.68	.38	2.59	2.50	20.6
Matt Harpring 78		32.8	.511	.413	.792	2.40	4.20	6.60	1.7	.94	.22	2.05	2.80	17.6
Andrei Kirilenko ...80		27.7	.491	.325	.800	1.80	3.40	5.30	1.7	1.48	2.19	1.70	2.30	12.0
John Stockton 82		27.7	.483	.363	.826	.60	1.80	2.50	7.7	1.67	.20	2.22	2.20	10.8
Calbert Cheaney .81		29.0	.499	.400	.580	.90	2.60	3.50	2.0	.80	.16	1.33	2.80	8.6
Scott Padgett 82		16.1	.402	.338	.757	1.00	2.30	3.30	1.0	.50	.29	.85	1.80	5.7
Jarron Collins 22		19.1	.442	.000	.710	1.50	1.30	2.70	.6	.23	.27	.86	3.20	5.5
Greg Ostertag 81		23.8	.518	.000	.510	2.20	4.00	6.20	.7	.25	1.81	1.28	2.90	5.4
Mark Jackson 82		17.9	.398	.284	.763	.40	1.70	2.10	4.6	.59	.04	1.85	1.10	4.7
T. Massenburg......58		13.7	.448	.000	.774	1.00	1.70	2.70	.3	.29	.33	.86	2.50	4.7
D. Stevenson 61		12.5	.401	.333	.691	.40	1.00	1.40	.7	.36	.13	.80	.90	4.6
Carlos Arroyo 44		6.5	.459	.429	.818	.30	.30	.60	1.2	.27	.02	.68	.60	2.8
John Amaechi 50		9.5	.314	.000	.481	.50	1.00	1.50	.4	.28	.14	.68	1.00	2.0
Jazz....................82		**241.2**	**.468**	**.349**	**.745**	**12.5**	**29.0**	**41.5**	**25.6**	**8.6**	**5.7**	**16.8**	**22.4**	**94.7**
Opponents..........82		**241.2**	**.434**	**.349**	**.745**	**12.5**	**25.9**	**38.2**	**19.5**	**8.8**	**5.2**	**15.9**	**23.8**	**92.3**

Washington Wizards

Player	GP	MPG	FG%	3Pt%	FT%	OFF	DEF	Total	APG	SPG	BPG	TO	PF	PPG
			Field Goals			**Rebounds**								
Jerry Stackhouse...70		39.2	.409	.290	.878	.90	2.80	3.70	4.5	.93	.40	2.76	1.90	21.5
Michael Jordan...82		37.0	.445	.291	.821	.90	5.20	6.10	3.8	1.50	.48	2.11	2.10	20.0
Larry Hughes.....67		31.9	.467	.367	.731	1.00	3.60	4.60	3.1	1.28	.36	2.03	2.20	12.8
Tyronn Lue............75		26.5	.433	.341	.875	.30	1.70	2.00	3.5	.63	.01	1.03	2.00	8.6
Christian Laettner...76		29.1	.494	.125	.833	1.50	5.10	6.60	3.1	1.08	.53	1.14	2.70	8.3
Kwame Brown.....80		22.2	.446	.000	.668	1.60	3.70	5.30	.7	.63	1.00	1.38	2.00	7.4
Juan Dixon............42		15.4	.384	.298	.804	.30	1.40	1.70	1.0	.62	.07	1.00	1.30	6.4
B. Haywood.........81		23.8	.510	.000	.633	2.40	2.60	5.00	.4	.40	1.47	.80	2.80	6.2
Etan Thomas........38		13.5	.492	.000	.638	1.80	2.50	4.30	.1	.21	.61	.87	1.70	4.8
Bryon Russell 70		19.8	.353	.329	.768	.60	2.40	3.00	1.0	1.00	.10	.79	1.90	4.5
Jahidi White..........16		14.4	.472	.000	.680	2.30	2.30	4.60	.1	.06	.75	.56	2.10	4.2
Jared Jeffries......20		14.6	.476	.500	.552	1.30	1.60	2.90	.8	.40	.25	1.05	1.40	4.0
Bobby Simmons ...36		10.5	.393	.000	.914	.90	1.20	2.10	.6	.28	.08	.77	1.40	3.3
Anthony Goldwire...5		6.8	.571	1.000	.800	.00	.60	.60	.2	.00	.00	.80	.20	2.6
Charles Oakley....42		12.2	.418	.000	.824	.90	1.70	2.50	1.0	.31	.14	.50	2.10	1.8
Brian Cardinal........5		3.0	.250	.000	1.000	.60	.40	1.00	.2	.00	.00	.20	.00	.8
Wizards..............82		**241.8**	**.440**	**.312**	**.779**	**11.2**	**29.2**	**40.4**	**19.7**	**7.6**	**4.8**	**13.4**	**20.0**	**91.5**
Opponents..........82		**241.8**	**.442**	**.362**	**.771**	**11.6**	**29.8**	**41.4**	**21.7**	**7.5**	**4.4**	**14.3**	**22.0**	**92.5**

2003 NBA Draft

The 2003 NBA Draft was held on June 26 in New York City.

First Round
1. LeBron James, Cleveland
2. Darko Milicic, Detroit
3. Carmelo Anthony, Denver
4. Chris Bosh, Toronto
5. Dwyane Wade, Miami
6. Chris Kaman, LA Clippers
7. Kirk Hinrich, Chicago
8. T.J. Ford, Milwaukee
9. Mike Sweetney, New York
10. Jarvis Hayes, Washington
11. Mickael Pietrus, Golden State
12. Nick Collison, Seattle
13. Marcus Banks, Memphis (from Houston; to Boston)
14. Luke Ridnour, Seattle (from Mil)
15. Reece Gaines, Orlando
16. Troy Bell, Boston(to Memphis)
17. Zarko Cabarkapa, Phoenix
18. David West, New Orleans
19. Aleksandar Pavlovic, Utah (to Orl)
20. Dahntay Jones, Boston (from Phil, to Memphis)
21. Boris Diaw-Riffiod, Atlanta (from Indiana)
22. Zoran Planinic, New Jersey
23. Travis Outlaw, Portland
24. Brian Cook, LA Lakers
25. Carlos Delfino, Detroit
26. Ndudi Ebi, Minnesota
27. Kendrick Perkins, Memphis
28. Leandrinho Barbosa, San Antonio (to Phoenix)
29. Josh Howard, Dallas

Second Round
30. Maciej Lampe, New York
31. Jason Kapono, Cleveland
32. Luke Walton, LA Lakers (from Toronto)
33. Jerome Beasley, Miami
34. Sofoklis Schortsanitis, LAC
35. Szymon Szewczyk, Milwaukee (from Memphis)
36. Mario Austin, Chicago
37. Travis Hansen, Atlanta
38. Steve Blake, Washington
39. Slavko Vranes, New York
40. Derrick Zimmerman, GS
41. Willie Green, Seattle (to Phil)
42. Zaur Pachulia, Orlando
43. Keith Bogans, Mil (to Orl)
44. Malick Badiane, Houston
45. Matt Bonner, Chicago (from Phoenix, to Toronto)
46. Sani Becirovic, Denver (from Boston)
47. Maurice Williams, Utah
48. James Lang, New Orleans
49. James Jones, Indiana
50. Paccelis Morlende, Phil (to Seattle)
51. Kyle Korver, New Jersey (to Philadelphia)
52. Remon Van de Hare, Toronto (from LA Lakers)
53. Tommy Smith, Chicago (from Detroit via Miami)
54. Nedzad Sinanovic, Portland
55. Rick Rickert, Minnesota
56. Brandon Hunter, Boston
57. Xue Yuyang, Dallas (to Denver)
58. Andreas Glyniadakis, Detroit (from San Antonio)

Women's National Basketball Association

Final Standings

EASTERN CONFERENCE

Team	W	L	Pct	GB
†Detroit	25	9	.735	—
*Charlotte	18	16	.529	7
*Connecticut	18	16	.529	7
*Cleveland	17	17	.500	8
Indiana	16	18	.471	9
New York	16	18	.471	9
Washington	9	25	.265	16

WESTERN CONFERENCE

Team	W	L	Pct	GB
†Los Angeles	24	10	.706	—
*Houston	20	14	.588	4
*Sacramento	19	15	.559	5
*Minnesota	18	16	.529	6
Seattle	18	16	.529	6
San Antonio	12	22	.353	12
Phoenix	8	26	.235	16

†Clinched conference title.   *Clinched playoff berth.

2003 Playoffs

FIRST ROUND

EASTERN CONFERENCE

Game 1......Cleveland 74 at Detroit 76
Game 2......Detroit 59 at Cleveland 66
Game 3......Cleveland 63 at Detroit 77
Detroit won series 2–1.

Game 1......Connecticut 68 at Charlotte 66
Game 2......Charlotte 62 at Connecticut 68
Connecticut won series 2–0.

WESTERN CONFERENCE

Game 1......Minnesota 74 at Los Angeles 72
Game 2......Los Angeles 80 at Minnesota 69
Game 3......Minnesota 64 at Los Angeles 74
Los Angeles won series 2–1.

Game 1......Sacramento 65 at Houston 59
Game 2......Houston 69 at Sacramento 48
Game 3......Sacramento 70 at Houston 68
Sacramento won series 2–1.

EASTERN CONFERENCE FINALS

Game 1......Connecticut 63 at Detroit 73
Game 2......Detroit 79 at Connecticut 73
Detroit won series 2–0.

WESTERN CONFERENCE FINALS

Game 1......Sacramento 77 at Los Angeles 69
Game 2......Los Angeles 79 at Sacramento 54
Game 3......Sacramento 63 at Los Angeles 66
Los Angeles won series 2–1.

WNBA FINALS

Game 1..........Los Angeles 75 at Detroit 63
Game 2..........Detroit 62 at Los Angeles 61
Game 3..........Los Angeles 78 at Detroit 83
Detroit won series 2–1.

THEY SAID IT

Jerome James, SuperSonics center, responding to coach Nate McMillan's charges that he is selfish: "I don't have the first clue who he is talking about, because all I worry about is Jerome."

NBA Champions

Season	Winner	Series	Runner-Up	Winning Coach	Finals MVP
1946–47	Philadelphia	4–1	Chicago	Eddie Gottlieb	—
1947–48	Baltimore	4–2	Philadelphia	Buddy Jeannette	—
1948–49	Minneapolis	4–2	Washington	John Kundla	—
1949–50	Minneapolis	4–2	Syracuse	John Kundla	—
1950–51	Rochester	4–3	New York	Les Harrison	—
1951–52	Minneapolis	4–3	New York	John Kundla	—
1952–53	Minneapolis	4–1	New York	John Kundla	—
1953–54	Minneapolis	4–3	Syracuse	John Kundla	—
1954–55	Syracuse	4–3	Ft Wayne	Al Cervi	—
1955–56	Philadelphia	4–1	Ft Wayne	George Senesky	—
1956–57	Boston	4–3	St Louis	Red Auerbach	—
1957–58	St Louis	4–2	Boston	Alex Hannum	—
1958–59	Boston	4–0	Minneapolis	Red Auerbach	—
1959–60	Boston	4–3	St Louis	Red Auerbach	—
1960–61	Boston	4–1	St Louis	Red Auerbach	—
1961–62	Boston	4–3	LA Lakers	Red Auerbach	—
1962–63	Boston	4–2	LA Lakers	Red Auerbach	—
1963–64	Boston	4–1	San Francisco	Red Auerbach	—
1964–65	Boston	4–1	LA Lakers	Red Auerbach	—
1965–66	Boston	4–3	LA Lakers	Red Auerbach	—
1966–67	Philadelphia	4–2	San Francisco	Alex Hannum	—
1967–68	Boston	4–2	LA Lakers	Bill Russell	—
1968–69	Boston	4–3	LA Lakers	Bill Russell	Jerry West, LA
1969–70	New York	4–3	LA Lakers	Red Holzman	Willis Reed, NY
1970–71	Milwaukee	4–0	Baltimore	Larry Costello	Kareem Abdul-Jabbar, Mil
1971–72	LA Lakers	4–1	New York	Bill Sharman	Wilt Chamberlain, LA
1972–73	New York	4–1	LA Lakers	Red Holzman	Willis Reed, NY
1973–74	Boston	4–3	Milwaukee	Tommy Heinsohn	John Havlicek, Bos
1974–75	Golden State	4–0	Washington	Al Attles	Rick Barry, GS
1975–76	Boston	4–2	Phoenix	Tommy Heinsohn	JoJo White, Bos
1976–77	Portland	4–2	Philadelphia	Jack Ramsay	Bill Walton, Port
1977–78	Washington	4–3	Seattle	Dick Motta	Wes Unseld, Wash
1978–79	Seattle	4–1	Washington	Lenny Wilkens	Dennis Johnson, Sea
1979–80	LA Lakers	4–2	Philadelphia	Paul Westhead	Magic Johnson, LA
1980–81	Boston	4–2	Houston	Bill Fitch	Cedric Maxwell, Bos
1981–82	LA Lakers	4–2	Philadelphia	Pat Riley	Magic Johnson, LA
1982–83	Philadelphia	4–0	LA Lakers	Billy Cunningham	Moses Malone, Phil
1983–84	Boston	4–3	LA Lakers	K.C. Jones	Larry Bird, Bos
1984–85	LA Lakers	4–2	Boston	Pat Riley	Kareem Abdul-Jabbar, LA
1985–86	Boston	4–2	Houston	K.C. Jones	Larry Bird, Bos
1986–87	LA Lakers	4–2	Boston	Pat Riley	Magic Johnson, LA
1987–88	LA Lakers	4–3	Detroit	Pat Riley	James Worthy, LA
1988–89	Detroit	4–0	LA Lakers	Chuck Daly	Joe Dumars, Det
1989–90	Detroit	4–1	Portland	Chuck Daly	Isiah Thomas, Det
1990–91	Chicago	4–1	LA Lakers	Phil Jackson	Michael Jordan, Chi
1991–92	Chicago	4–2	Portland	Phil Jackson	Michael Jordan, Chi
1992–93	Chicago	4–2	Phoenix	Phil Jackson	Michael Jordan, Chi
1993–94	Houston	4–3	New York	Rudy Tomjanovich	Hakeem Olajuwon, Hou
1994–95	Houston	4–0	Orlando	Rudy Tomjanovich	Hakeem Olajuwon, Hou
1995–96	Chicago	4–2	Seattle	Phil Jackson	Michael Jordan, Chi
1996–97	Chicago	4–2	Utah	Phil Jackson	Michael Jordan, Chi
1997–98	Chicago	4–2	Utah	Phil Jackson	Michael Jordan, Chi
1998–99	San Antonio	4–1	New York	Gregg Popovich	Tim Duncan, SA
1999–00	LA Lakers	4–2	Indiana	Phil Jackson	Shaquille O'Neal, LA
2000–01	LA Lakers	4–1	Philadelphia	Phil Jackson	Shaquille O'Neal, LA
2001–02	LA Lakers	4–0	New Jersey	Phil Jackson	Shaquille O'Neal, LA
2002–03	San Antonio	4–2	New Jersey	Gregg Popovich	Tim Duncan, SA

NBA Awards

Most Valuable Player: Maurice Podoloff Trophy

Season	Player, Team	GP	Field Goals		3-Pt FG		Free Throws		Rebounds		A	Stl	BS	Avg
			FGM	Pct	FGM	Pct	FTM	Pct	Off	Total				
1955–56	Bob Pettit, StL	72	646	42.9	–	–	557	73.6	–	1,164	189	–	–	25.7
1956–57	Bob Cousy, Bos	64	478	37.8	–	–	363	82.1	–	309	478	–	–	20.6
1957–58	Bill Russell, Bos	69	456	44.2	–	–	230	51.9	–	1,564	202	–	–	16.6
1958–59	Bob Pettit, StL	72	719	43.8	–	–	667	75.9	–	1,182	221	–	–	29.2
1959–60	Wilt Chamberlain, Phil	72	1,065	46.1	–	–	577	58.2	–	1,941	168	–	–	37.6
1960–61	Bill Russell, Bos	78	532	42.6	–	–	258	55.0	–	1,868	264	–	–	16.9
1961–62	Bill Russell, Bos	76	575	45.7	–	–	286	59.5	–	1,891	341	–	–	18.9
1962–63	Bill Russell, Bos	78	511	43.2	–	–	287	55.5	–	1,843	348	–	–	16.8
1963–64	Oscar Robertson, Cin	79	840	48.3	–	–	800	85.3	–	783	868	–	–	31.4
1964–65	Bill Russell, Bos	78	429	43.8	–	–	244	57.3	–	1,878	410	–	–	14.1
1965–66	Wilt Chamberlain, Phil	79	1,074	54.0	–	–	501	51.3	–	1,943	414	–	–	33.5
1966–67	Wilt Chamberlain, Phil	81	785	68.3	–	–	386	44.1	–	1,957	630	–	–	24.1
1967–68	Wilt Chamberlain, Phil	82	819	59.5	–	–	354	38.0	–	1,952	702	–	–	24.3
1968–69	Wes Unseld, Balt	82	427	47.6	–	–	277	60.5	–	1,491	213	–	–	13.8
1969–70	Willis Reed, NY	81	702	50.7	–	–	351	75.6	–	1,126	161	–	–	21.7
1970–71	Kareem Abdul-Jabbar, Mil	82	1,063	57.7	–	–	470	69.0	–	1,311	272	–	–	31.7
1971–72	Kareem Abdul-Jabbar, Mil	81	1,159	57.4	–	–	504	68.9	–	1,346	370	–	–	34.8
1972–73	Dave Cowens, Bos	82	740	45.2	–	–	204	77.9	–	1,329	333	–	–	20.5
1973–74	Kareem Abdul-Jabbar, Mil	81	948	53.9	–	–	295	70.2	287	1,178	386	112	283	27.0
1974–75	Bob McAdoo, Buff	82	1,095	51.2	–	–	641	80.5	307	1,155	179	92	174	34.5
1975–76	Kareem Abdul-Jabbar, LA	82	914	52.9	–	–	447	70.3	272	1,383	413	119	338	27.7
1976–77	Kareem Abdul-Jabbar, LA	82	888	57.9	–	–	376	70.1	266	1,090	319	101	261	26.2
1977–78	Bill Walton, Port	58	460	52.2	–	–	177	72.0	118	766	291	60	146	18.9
1978–79	Moses Malone, Hou	82	716	54.0	–	–	599	73.9	587	1,444	147	79	119	24.8
1979–80	Kareem Abdul-Jabbar, LA	82	835	60.4	0	00.0	364	76.5	190	886	371	81	280	24.8
1980–81	Julius Erving, Phil	82	794	52.1	4	22.2	422	78.7	244	657	364	173	147	24.6
1981–82	Moses Malone, Hou	81	945	51.9	0	00.0	630	76.2	558	1,188	142	76	125	31.1
1982–83	Moses Malone, Phil	78	654	50.1	0	00.0	600	76.1	445	1,194	101	89	157	24.5
1983–84	Larry Bird, Bos	79	758	49.2	18	24.7	374	88.8	181	796	520	144	69	24.2
1984–85	Larry Bird, Bos	80	918	52.2	56	42.7	403	88.2	164	842	531	129	98	28.7
1985–86	Larry Bird, Bos	82	796	49.6	82	42.3	441	89.6	190	805	557	166	51	25.8
1986–87	Magic Johnson, LA Lakers	80	683	52.2	8	20.5	535	84.8	122	504	977	138	36	23.9
1987–88	Michael Jordan, Chi	82	1,069	53.5	7	13.2	723	84.1	139	449	485	259	131	35.0
1988–89	Magic Johnson, LA Lakers	77	579	50.9	59	31.4	513	91.1	111	607	988	138	22	22.5
1989–90	Magic Johnson, LA Lakers	79	546	48.0	106	38.4	567	89.0	128	522	907	132	34	22.3
1990–91	Michael Jordan, Chi	82	990	53.9	29	31.2	571	85.1	118	492	453	223	83	31.5
1991–92	Michael Jordan, Chi	80	943	51.9	27	27.0	491	83.2	91	511	489	182	75	30.1
1992–93	Charles Barkley, Phoe	76	716	52.0	67	30.5	445	76.5	237	928	385	119	74	25.6
1993–94	Hakeem Olajuwon, Hou	80	894	52.8	8	42.1	388	71.6	229	955	287	128	297	27.3
1994–95	David Robinson, SA	81	788	53.0	6	30.0	656	77.4	234	877	236	134	262	27.6
1995–96	Michael Jordan, Chi	82	916	49.5	111	42.7	548	83.4	148	543	352	180	42	30.4
1996–97	Karl Malone, Utah	82	864	55.0	0	00.0	521	75.5	193	809	368	113	48	27.4
1997–98	Michael Jordan, Chi	82	881	46.5	30	23.8	565	78.4	130	475	283	141	45	28.7
1998–99	Karl Malone, Utah	49	393	49.3	0	00.0	378	78.8	107	463	201	62	28	23.8
1999–00	Shaquille O'Neal, LA Lakers	79	956	57.4	0	00.0	432	52.4	336	1078	299	36	239	29.7
2000–01	Allen Iverson, Phil	71	762	42.0	98	32.0	585	81.4	50	273	325	78	20	31.1
2001–02	Tim Duncan, SA	82	764	50.8	1	10.0	560	79.9	268	1042	307	61	203	25.5
2002–03	Tim Duncan, SA	81	714	51.3	6	27.3	450	71.0	260	1045	316	55	237	23.3

Coach of the Year: Arnold (Red) Auerbach Trophy

1962–63...Harry Gallatin, StL	1976–77...Tom Nissalke, Hou	1990–91...Don Chaney, Hou
1963–64...Alex Hannum, SF	1977–78...Hubie Brown, Atl	1991–92...Don Nelson, GS
1964–65...Red Auerbach, Bos	1978–79...Cotton Fitzsimmons, KC	1992–93...Pat Riley, NY
1965–66...Dolph Schayes, Phil	1979–80...Bill Fitch, Bos	1993–94...Lenny Wilkens, Atl
1966–67...Johnny Kerr, Chi	1980–81...Jack McKinney, Ind	1994–95...Del Harris, LA Lakers
1967–68...Richie Guerin, StL	1981–82...Gene Shue, Wash	1995–96...Phil Jackson, Chi
1968–69...Gene Shue, Balt	1982–83...Don Nelson, Mil	1996–97...Pat Riley, Mia
1969–70...Red Holzman, NY	1983–84...Frank Layden, Utah	1997–98...Larry Bird, Ind
1970–71...Dick Motta, Chi	1984–85...Don Nelson, Mil	1998–99...Mike Dunleavy, Port
1971–72...Bill Sharman, LA	1985–86...Mike Fratello, Atl	1999–00...Glenn (Doc) Rivers, Orl
1972–73...Tom Heinsohn, Bos	1986–87...Mike Schuler, Port	2000–01...Larry Brown, Phil
1973–74...Ray Scott, Det	1987–88...Doug Moe, Den	2001–02...Rick Carlisle, Det
1974–75...Phil Johnson, KC-Oma	1988–89....Cotton Fitzsimmons, Phoe	2002–03...Gregg Popovich, SA
1975–76...Bill Fitch, Clev	1989–90....Pat Riley, LA Lakers	

Note: Award named after Auerbach in 1986.

Rookie of the Year: Eddie Gottlieb Trophy

1952–53...Don Meineke, FW
1953–54...Ray Felix, Balt
1954–55...Bob Pettit, Mil
1955–56...Maurice Stokes, Roch
1956–57...Tom Heinsohn, Bos
1957–58...Woody Sauldsberry, Phil
1958–59...Elgin Baylor, Minn
1959–60...Wilt Chamberlain, Phil
1960–61...Oscar Robertson, Cin
1961–62...Walt Bellamy, Chi
1962–63...Terry Dischinger, Chi
1963–64...Jerry Lucas, Cin
1964–65...Willis Reed, NY
1965–66...Rick Barry, SF
1966–67...Dave Bing, Det
1967–68...Earl Monroe, Balt
1968–69...Wes Unseld, Balt
1969–70...K. Abdul-Jabbar, Mil

1970–71...Dave Cowens, Bos
Geoff Petrie, Port
1971–72...Sidney Wicks, Port
1972–73...Bob McAdoo, Buff
1973–74...Ernie DiGregorio, Buff
1974–75...Keith Wilkes, GS
1975–76...Alvan Adams, Phoe
1976–77...Adrian Dantley, Buff
1977–78...Walter Davis, Phoe
1978–79...Phil Ford, KC
1979–80...Larry Bird, Bos
1980–81...Darrell Griffith, Utah
1981–82...Buck Williams, NJ
1982–83...Terry Cummings, SD
1983–84...Ralph Sampson, Hou
1984–85...Michael Jordan, Chi
1985–86...Patrick Ewing, NY
1986–87...Chuck Person, Ind

1987–88...Mark Jackson, NY
1988–89...Mitch Richmond,.GS
1989–90...David Robinson, SA
1990–91...Derrick Coleman, NJ
1991–92...Larry Johnson, Char
1992–93...Shaquille O'Neal, Orl
1993–94...Chris Webber, GS
1994–95...J. Kidd, Dall/G. Hill, Det
1995–96...Damon Stoudamire, Tor
1996–97...Allen Iverson, Phil
1997–98...Tim Duncan, SA
1998–99...Vince Carter, Tor
1999–00...Steve Francis, Hou
Elton Brand, Chi
2000–01 ..Mike Miller, Orl
2001–02...Pau Gasol, Mem
2002–03 ..Amare Stoudemire, Phoe

Defensive Player of the Year

1982–83...Sidney Moncrief, Mil
1983–84...Sidney Moncrief, Mil
1984–85...Mark Eaton, Utah
1985–86...Alvin Robertson, SA
1986–87...Michael Cooper, Lakers
1987–88...Michael Jordan, Chi
1988–89...Mark Eaton, Utah

1989–90...Dennis Rodman, Det
1990–91...Dennis Rodman, Det
1991–92...David Robinson, SA
1992–93...Hakeem Olajuwon, Hou
1993–94...Hakeem Olajuwon, Hou
1994–95...Dikembe Mutombo, Den
1995–96...Gary Payton, Sea

1996–97...Dikembe Mutombo, Den
1997–98...Dikembe Mutombo, Atl
1998–99...Alonzo Mourning, Mia
1999–00...Alonzo Mourning, Mia
2000–01...Dikembe Mutombo, Phil
2001–02...Ben Wallace, Det
2002–03...Ben Wallace, Det

Sixth Man Award

1982–83...Bobby Jones, Phil
1983–84...Kevin McHale, Bos
1984–85...Kevin McHale, Bos
1985–86...Bill Walton, Bos
1986–87...Ricky Pierce, Mil
1987–88...Roy Tarpley, Dall
1988–89...Eddie Johnson, Phoe

1989–90...Ricky Pierce, Mil
1990–91...Detlef Schrempf, Ind
1991–92...Detlef Schrempf, Ind
1992–93...Cliff Robinson, Port
1993–94...Dell Curry, Char
1994–95...Anthony Mason, NY
1995–96...Tony Kukoc, Chi

1996–97...John Starks, NY
1997–98...Danny Manning, Phoe
1998–99...Darrell Armstrong, Orl
1999–00...Rodney Rogers, Phoe
2000–01...Aaron McKie, Phil
2001–02...Corliss Williamson, Det
2002–03...Bobby Jackson, Sac

J. Walter Kennedy Citizenship Award

1974–75...Wes Unseld, Wash
1975–76...Slick Watts, Sea
1976–77...Dave Bing, Wash
1977–78...Bob Lanier, Det
1978–79...Calvin Murphy, Hou
1979–80...Austin Carr, Clev
1980–81...Mike Glenn, NY
1981–82...Kent Benson, Det
1982–83...Julius Erving, Phil
1983–84...Frank Layden, Utah

1984–85...Dan Issel, Den
1985–86...Michael Cooper, Lakers
Rory Sparrow, NY
1986–87...Isiah Thomas, Det
1987–88...Alex English, Den
1988–89...Thurl Bailey, Utah
1989–90...Glenn Rivers, Atl
1990–91...Kevin Johnson, Phoe
1991–92...Magic Johnson, Lakers
1992–93...Terry Porter, Port

1993–94...Joe Dumars, Det
1994–95...Joe O'Toole, Atl
1995–96...Chris Dudley, Port
1996–97...P.J. Brown, Mia
1997–98...Steve Smith, Atl
1998–99...Brian Grant, Port
1999–00...Vlade Divac, Sac
2000–01...Dikembe Mutombo, Phil
2001–02...Alonzo Mourning, Mia
2002–03...David Robinson, SA

Most Improved Player

1985–86...Alvin Robertson, SA
1986–87...Dale Ellis, Sea
1987–88...Kevin Duckworth, Port
1988–89...Kevin Johnson, Phoe
1989–90...Rony Seikaly, Mia
1990–91...Scott Skiles, Orl

1991–92...Pervis Ellison, Wash
1992–93...Chris Jackson, Den
1993–94...Don MacLean, Wash
1994–95...Dana Barros, Phil
1995–96.....Gheorghe Muresan, Wash
1996–97...Isaac Austin, Mia

1997–98...Alan Henderson, Atl
1998–99...Darrell Armstrong, Orl
1999–00...Jalen Rose, Ind
2000–01...Tracy McGrady, Orl
2001–02...Jermaine O'Neal, Ind
2002–03...Gilbert Arenas, GS

Executive of the Year

1972–73...Joe Axelson, KC-Oma
1973–74...Eddie Donovan, Buff
1974–75...Dick Vertlieb, GS
1975–76...Jerry Colangelo, Phoe
1976–77...Ray Patterson, Hou
1977–78...Angelo Drossos, SA
1978–79...Bob Ferry, Wash
1979–80...Red Auerbach, Bos
1980–81...Jerry Colangelo, Phoe
1981–82...Bob Ferry, Wash
1982–83...Zollie Volchok, Sea

1983–84...Frank Layden, Utah
1984–85...Vince Boryla, Den
1985–86...Stan Kasten, Atl
1986–87...Stan Kasten, Atl
1987–88...Jerry Krause, Chi
1988–89...Jerry Colangelo, Phoe
1989–90...Bob Bass, SA
1990–91...Bucky Buckwalter, Port
1991–92...Wayne Embry, Clev
1992–93...Jerry Colangelo, Phoe
1993–94...Bob Whitsitt, Sea

1994–95...Jerry West, LA Lakers
1995–96...Jerry Krause, Chi
1996–97...Bob Bass, Char
1997–98...Wayne Embry, Clev
1998–99...Geoff Petrie, Sac
1999–00...John Gabriel, Orl
2000–01...Geoff Petrie, Sac
2001–02...Rod Thorn, NJ
2002–03...Joe Dumars, Det

Sponsored by *The Sporting News*.

Scoring

MOST POINTS, CAREER

	Pts	Avg
Kareem Abdul-Jabbar	38,387	24.6
Karl Malone	36,374	25.4
Wilt Chamberlain	31,419	30.1
Michael Jordan	32,292	30.1
Moses Malone	27,409	20.6
Elvin Hayes	27,313	21.0
Hakeem Olajuwon	26,946	21.8
Oscar Robertson	26,710	25.7
Dominique Wilkins	26,669	24.8
John Havlicek	26,395	20.8

MOST POINTS, SEASON

Wilt Chamberlain, Phil	4,029	1961–62
Wilt Chamberlain, SF	3,586	1962–63
Michael Jordan, Chi	3,041	1986–87
Wilt Chamberlain, Phil	3,033	1960–61
Wilt Chamberlain, SF	2,948	1963–64
Michael Jordan, Chi	2,868	1987–88
Bob McAdoo, Buff	2,831	1974–75
Rick Barry, SF	2,775	1966–67
Michael Jordan, Chi	2,753	1989–90
Elgin Baylor, LA	2,719	1962–63

HIGHEST SCORING AVERAGE, CAREER

Michael Jordan	30.1	990 games
Wilt Chamberlain	30.1	1,045 games
Shaquille O'Neal	27.6	742 games
Elgin Baylor	27.4	846 games
Jerry West	27.0	932 games
Allen Iverson	27.0	487 games
Bob Pettit	26.4	792 games
George Gervin	26.2	791 games
Oscar Robertson	25.7	1,040 games
Karl Malone	25.4	1,434 games

Note: Minimum 400 games.

HIGHEST SCORING AVERAGE, SEASON

Wilt Chamberlain, Phil	50.4	1961–62
Wilt Chamberlain, SF	44.8	1962–63
Wilt Chamberlain, Phil	38.4	1960–61
Wilt Chamberlain, Phil	37.6	1959–60
Michael Jordan, Chi	37.1	1986–87
Wilt Chamberlain, SF	36.9	1963–64
Rick Barry, SF	35.6	1966–67
Michael Jordan, Chi	35.0	1987–88
Elgin Baylor, LA	34.8	1960–61

Note: Minimum 70 games.

MOST POINTS, GAME

	Player, Team	Opp	Date
100	Wilt Chamberlain, Phil	NY	3/2/62
78	Wilt Chamberlain, Phil	LA	12/8/61
73	Wilt Chamberlain, Phil	Chi	1/13/62
73	Wilt Chamberlain, SF	NY	11/16/62
73	David Thompson, Den	Det	4/9/78
72	Wilt Chamberlain, SF	LA	11/3/62
71	David Robinson, SA	LAC	4/24/94
71	Elgin Baylor, LA	NY	11/15/60
70	Wilt Chamberlain, SF	Syr	3/10/63
69	Michael Jordan, Chi	Clev	3/28/90

Field-Goal Percentage

Highest FG Percentage, Career: .599—Artis Gilmore
Highest FG Percentage, Season: .727—Wilt
  Chamberlain, LA Lakers, 1972–73 (426/586)

Free Throws

HIGHEST FREE-THROW PERCENTAGE, CAREER

Mark Price	.904
Rick Barry	.900
Calvin Murphy	.892
Scott Skiles	.889
Larry Bird	.886
Reggie Miller	.886

Note: Minimum 1200 free throws made.

HIGHEST FREE-THROW PERCENTAGE, SEASON

Calvin Murphy, Hou	.958	1980–81
Mahmoud Abdul-Rauf, Den	.956	1993–94
Jeff Hornacek, Utah	.950	1999–00
Mark Price, Clev	.948	1992–93
Mark Price, Clev	.947	1991–92

MOST FREE THROWS MADE, CAREER

	No.	Yrs	Pct
Karl Malone	9,619	18	.742
Moses Malone	8,531	19	.769
Oscar Robertson	7,694	14	.838
Jerry West	7,160	14	.814
Michael Jordan	7,327	15	.835

Three-Point Field Goals

Most Three-Point Field-Goals, Career: 2,330—Reggie
  Miller
Highest Three-Point Field-Goal Percentage, Career:
  .454—Steve Kerr
Most Three-Point Field Goals, Season: 267—Dennis
  Scott, Orl, 1995–96
Highest Three-Point Field-Goal Percentage, Season:
  .524—Steve Kerr, Chi, 1994–95
Most Three-Point Field Goals, Game: 12—Kobe
  Bryant, LA Lakers vs Seattle, 1/7/03

Note: First year of shot: 1979–80.

Steals

Most Steals, Career: 3,265—John Stockton
Most Steals, Season: 301—Alvin Robertson, San
  Antonio, 1985–86
Most Steals, Game: 11—Kendall Gill, New Jersey vs
  Miami, 4/3/99; Larry Kenon, San Antonio
  vs Kansas City, 12/26/76

Rebounds

MOST REBOUNDS, CAREER

	No.	Yrs	Avg
Wilt Chamberlain	23,924	14	22.9
Bill Russell	21,620	13	22.5
Kareem Abdul-Jabbar	17,440	20	11.4
Elvin Hayes	16,279	16	12.5
Moses Malone	16,212	19	12.2
Robert Parish	14,715	21	9.1
Nate Thurmond	14,464	14	15.0
Walt Bellamy	14,241	14	13.7
Karl Malone	14,601	18	10.2
Wes Unseld	13,769	13	14.0

Rebounds (Cont.)
MOST REBOUNDS, SEASON

Wilt Chamberlain, Phil	2,149	1960–61
Wilt Chamberlain, Phil	2,052	1961–62
Wilt Chamberlain, Phil	1,957	1966–67
Wilt Chamberlain, Phil	1,952	1967–68
Wilt Chamberlain, SF	1,946	1962–63
Wilt Chamberlain, Phil	1,943	1965–66
Wilt Chamberlain, Phil	1,941	1959–60
Bill Russell, Bos	1,930	1963–64
Bill Russell, Bos	1,878	1964–65
Bill Russell, Bos	1,868	1960–61

MOST REBOUNDS, GAME

	Player, Team	Opp	Date
55	Wilt Chamberlain, Phil	Bos	11/24/60
51	Bill Russell, Bos	Syr	2/5/60
49	Bill Russell, Bos	Phil	11/16/57
49	Bill Russell, Bos	Det	3/11/65
45	Wilt Chamberlain, Phil	Syr	2/6/60
45	Wilt Chamberlain, Phil	LA	1/21/61

Assists
MOST ASSISTS, CAREER

John Stockton	15, 806
Mark Jackson	10, 215
Magic Johnson	10,141
Oscar Robertson	9,887
Isiah Thomas	9,061

Assists (Cont.)
MOST ASSISTS, SEASON

John Stockton, Utah	1,164	1990–91
John Stockton, Utah	1,134	1989–90
John Stockton, Utah	1,128	1987–88
John Stockton, Utah	1,126	1991–92
Isiah Thomas, Det	1,123	1984–85

MOST ASSISTS, GAME: 30—Scott Skiles, Orlando vs Denver, 12/30/90

Blocked Shots
MOST BLOCKED SHOTS, CAREER

Hakeem Olajuwon	3,830
Kareem Abdul-Jabbar	3,189
Mark Eaton	3,064
David Robinson	2,954
Patrick Ewing	2,894

MOST BLOCKED SHOTS, SEASON

Mark Eaton, Utah	456	1984–85
Manute Bol, Wash	397	1985–86
Elmore Smith, LA	393	1973–74

MOST BLOCKED SHOTS, GAME: 17—Elmore Smith, LA Lakers vs Portland, 10/28/73

Scoring
MOST POINTS, CAREER

	Pts	Yrs	Avg
Michael Jordan	5,987	13	33.4
Kareem Abdul-Jabbar	5,762	18	24.3
Karl Malone	4,519	18	26.3
Jerry West	4,457	13	29.1
Larry Bird	3,897	12	23.8
John Havlicek	3,776	13	22.0
Hakeem Olajuwon	3,755	15	25.9
Magic Johnson	3,701	13	19.5
Elgin Baylor	3,623	12	27.0
Scottie Pippen	3,619	15	17.7

*HIGHEST SCORING AVERAGE, CAREER

	Avg	Games
Michael Jordan	33.4	179
Allen Iverson	30.6	57
Jerry West	29.1	153
Shaquille O'Neal	28.1	136
Elgin Baylor	27.0	134
George Gervin	27.0	59
Karl Malone	26.3	172
Hakeem Olajuwon	25.9	145
Bob Pettit	25.5	88
Dominique Wilkins	25.4	55

*Minimum of 25 games.

Scoring (Cont.)
MOST POINTS, GAME

	Player, Team	Opp	Date
†63	Michael Jordan, Chi	Bos	4/20/86
61	Elgin Baylor, LA	Bos	4/14/62
56	Wilt Chamberlain, Phil	Syr	3/22/62
56	Michael Jordan, Chi	Mia	4/29/92
56	Charles Barkley, Phoe	GS	5/4/94
55	Rick Barry, SF	Phil	4/18/67
55	Michael Jordan, Chi	Clev	5/1/88
55	Michael Jordan, Chi	Phoe	4/16/95
55	Michael Jordan, Chi	Wash	4/27/97

†Double overtime game.

Rebounds
MOST REBOUNDS, CAREER

	No.	Yrs	Avg
Bill Russell	4,104	13	24.9
Wilt Chamberlain	3,913	13	24.5
Kareem Abdul-Jabbar	2,481	18	10.5
Karl Malone	1,877	18	10.9
Wes Unseld	1,777	12	14.9

MOST REBOUNDS, GAME

	Player, Team	Opp	Date
41	Wilt Chamberlain, Phil	Bos	4/5/67
40	Bill Russell, Bos	Phil	3/23/58
40	Bill Russell, Bos	StL	3/29/60
*40	Bill Russell, Bos	LA	4/18/62

Three tied at 39.
*Overtime game.

Assists

MOST ASSISTS, CAREER

	No.	Games
Magic Johnson	2,346	190
John Stockton	1,839	182
Larry Bird	1,062	164
Scottie Pippen	1,035	204
Michael Jordan	1,022	179

MOST ASSISTS, GAME

Player, Team		Opp	Date
24	Magic Johnson, LAL	Pho	5/15/84
24	John Stockton, Utah	LAL	5/17/88
23	Magic Johnson, LAL	Port	5/3/85
22	Doc Rivers, Atl	Bos	5/16/88
Four tied at 21.			

Games played

Kareem Abdul-Jabbar	237
Scottie Pippen	204
Danny Ainge	193
Magic Johnson	190
Robert Parish	184

Appearances

John Stockton	19
Kareem Abdul-Jabbar	18
Karl Malone	18
Robert Parish	16
Dolph Schayes	15
Clyde Drexler	15
Tree Rollins	15
Jerome Kersey	15
Hakeem Olajuwon	15

NBA Season Leaders

Scoring

1946–47	Joe Fulks, Phil	1389	1975–76	Bob McAdoo, Buff	31.1
1947–48	Max Zaslofsky, Chi	1007	1976–77	Pete Maravich, NO	31.1
1948–49	George Mikan, Minn	1698	1977–78	George Gervin, SA	27.2
1949–50	George Mikan, Minn	1865	1978–79	George Gervin, SA	29.6
1950–51	George Mikan, Minn	1932	1979–80	George Gervin, SA	33.1
1951–52	Paul Arizin, Phil	1674	1980–81	Adrian Dantley, Utah	30.7
1952–53	Neil Johnston, Phil	1564	1981–82	George Gervin, SA	32.3
1953–54	Neil Johnston, Phil	1759	1982–83	Alex English, Den	28.4
1954–55	Neil Johnston, Phil	1631	1983–84	Adrian Dantley, Utah	30.6
1955–56	Bob Pettit, StL	1849	1984–85	Bernard King, NY	32.9
1956–57	Paul Arizin, Phil	1817	1985–86	Dominique Wilkins, Atl	30.3
1957–58	George Yardley, Det	2001	1986–87	Michael Jordan, Chi	37.1
1958–59	Bob Pettit, StL	2105	1987–88	Michael Jordan, Chi	35.0
1959–60	Wilt Chamberlain, Phil	2707	1988–89	Michael Jordan, Chi	32.5
1960–61	Wilt Chamberlain, Phil	3033	1989–90	Michael Jordan, Chi	33.6
1961–62	Wilt Chamberlain, Phil	4029	1990–91	Michael Jordan, Chi	31.5
1962–63	Wilt Chamberlain, SF	3586	1991–92	Michael Jordan, Chi	30.1
1963–64	Wilt Chamberlain, SF	2948	1992–93	Michael Jordan, Chi	32.6
1964–65	Wilt Chamberlain, SF-Phil	2534	1993–94	David Robinson, SA	29.8
1965–66	Wilt Chamberlain, Phil	2649	1994–95	Shaquille O'Neal, Orl	29.3
1966–67	Rick Barry, SF	2775	1995–96	Michael Jordan, Chi	30.4
1967–68	Dave Bing, Det	2142	1996–97	Michael Jordan, Chi	29.6
1968–69	Elvin Hayes, SD	2327	1997–98	Michael Jordan, Chi	28.7
1969–70	Jerry West, LA	*31.2	1998–99	Allen Iverson, Phil	26.8
1970–71	Kareem Abdul-Jabbar, Mil	31.7	1999–00	Shaquille O'Neal, LA Lakers	29.7
1971–72	Kareem Abdul-Jabbar, Mil	34.8	2000–01	Allen Iverson, Phil	31.1
1972–73	Nate Archibald, KC-Oma	34.0	2001–02	Allen Iverson, Phil	31.4
1973–74	Bob McAdoo, Buff	30.6	2002–03	Tracy McGrady, Orl	32.1
1974–75	Bob McAdoo, Buff	34.5			

*Based on per game average since 1969–70.

Rebounding

1950–51	Dolph Schayes, Syr	1080	1962–63	Wilt Chamberlain, SF	1946
1951–52	Larry Foust, FW	880	1963–64	Bill Russell, Bos	1930
	Mel Hutchins, Mil	880	1964–65	Bill Russell, Bos	1878
1952–53	George Mikan, Minn	1007	1965–66	Wilt Chamberlain, Phil	1943
1953–54	Harry Gallatin, NY	1098	1966–67	Wilt Chamberlain, Phil	1957
1954–55	Neil Johnston, Phil	1085	1967–68	Wilt Chamberlain, Phil	1952
1955–56	Bob Pettit, StL	1164	1968–69	Wilt Chamberlain, LA	1712
1956–57	Maurice Stokes, Roch	1256	1969–70	Elvin Hayes, SD	*16.9
1957–58	Bill Russell, Bos	1564	1970–71	Wilt Chamberlain, LA	18.2
1958–59	Bill Russell, Bos	1612	1971–72	Wilt Chamberlain, LA	19.2
1959–60	Wilt Chamberlain, Phil	1941	1972–73	Wilt Chamberlain, LA	18.6
1960–61	Wilt Chamberlain, Phil	2149	1973–74	Elvin Hayes, Capital	18.1
1961–62	Wilt Chamberlain, Phil	2052	1974–75	Wes Unseld, Wash	14.8

Rebounding (Cont.)

Season	Player	Avg	Season	Player	Avg
1975–76	Kareem Abdul-Jabbar, LA	16.9	1989–90	Hakeem Olajuwon, Hou	14.0
1976–77	Bill Walton, Port	14.4	1990–91	David Robinson, SA	13.0
1977–78	Len Robinson, NO	15.7	1991–92	Dennis Rodman, Det	18.7
1978–79	Moses Malone, Hou	17.6	1992–93	Dennis Rodman, Det	18.3
1979–80	Swen Nater, SD	15.0	1993–94	Dennis Rodman, SA	17.3
1980–81	Moses Malone, Hou	14.8	1994–95	Dennis Rodman, SA	16.8
1981–82	Moses Malone, Hou	14.7	1995–96	Dennis Rodman, Chi	14.9
1982–83	Moses Malone, Phil	15.3	1996–97	Dennis Rodman, Chi	16.1
1983–84	Moses Malone, Phil	13.4	1997–98	Dennis Rodman, Chi	15.0
1984–85	Moses Malone, Phil	13.1	1998–99	Chris Webber, Sac	13.0
1985–86	Bill Laimbeer, Det	13.1	1999–00	Dikembe Mutombo, Atl	14.1
1986–87	Charles Barkley, Phil	14.6	2000–01	Dikembe Mutombo, Atl	13.5
1987–88	Michael Cage, LA Clippers	13.0	2001–02	Ben Wallace, Det	13.0
1988–89	Hakeem Olajuwon, Hou	13.5	2002–03	Ben Wallace, Det	15.4

*Based on per game average since 1969–70.

Assists

Season	Player	Total	Season	Player	Avg
1946–47	Ernie Calverly, Prov	202	1975–76	Don Watts, Sea	8.1
1947–48	Howie Dallmar, Phil	120	1976–77	Don Buse, Ind	8.5
1948–49	Bob Davies, Roch	321	1977–78	Kevin Porter, NJ-Det	10.2
1949–50	Dick McGuire, NY	386	1978–79	Kevin Porter, Det	13.4
1950–51	Andy Phillip, Phil	414	1979–80	Micheal Richardson, NY	10.1
1951–52	Andy Phillip, Phil	539	1980–81	Kevin Porter, Wash	9.1
1952–53	Bob Cousy, Bos	547	1981–82	Johnny Moore, SA	9.6
1953–54	Bob Cousy, Bos	578	1982–83	Magic Johnson, LA	10.5
1954–55	Bob Cousy, Bos	557	1983–84	Magic Johnson, LA	13.1
1955–56	Bob Cousy, Bos	642	1984–85	Isiah Thomas, Det	13.9
1956–57	Bob Cousy, Bos	478	1985–86	Magic Johnson, LA Lakers	12.6
1957–58	Bob Cousy, Bos	463	1986–87	Magic Johnson, LA Lakers	12.2
1958–59	Bob Cousy, Bos	557	1987–88	John Stockton, Utah	13.8
1959–60	Bob Cousy, Bos	715	1988–89	John Stockton, Utah	13.6
1960–61	Oscar Robertson, Cin	690	1989–90	John Stockton, Utah	14.5
1961–62	Oscar Robertson, Cin	899	1990–91	John Stockton, Utah	14.2
1962–63	Guy Rodgers, SF	825	1991–92	John Stockton, Utah	13.7
1963–64	Oscar Robertson, Cin	868	1992–93	John Stockton, Utah	12.0
1964–65	Oscar Robertson, Cin	861	1993–94	John Stockton, Utah	12.6
1965–66	Oscar Robertson, Cin	847	1994–95	John Stockton, Utah	12.3
1966–67	Guy Rodgers, Chi	908	1995–96	John Stockton, Utah	11.2
1967–68	Wilt Chamberlain, Phil	702	1996–97	Mark Jackson, Ind	11.4
1968–69	Oscar Robertson, Cin	772	1997–98	Rod Strickland, Wash	10.1
1969–70	Len Wilkens, Sea	*9.1	1998–99	Jason Kidd, Phoe	10.8
1970–71	Norm Van Lier, Cin	10.1	1999–00	Jason Kidd, Phoe	10.1
1971–72	Jerry West, LA	9.7	2000–01	Jason Kidd, Phoe	9.8
1972–73	Nate Archibald, KC-Oma	11.4	2001–02	Andre Miller, Clev	10.9
1973–74	Ernie DiGregorio, Buff	8.2	2002–03	Jason Kidd, NJ	8.9
1974–75	Kevin Porter, Wash	8.0			

*Based on per game average since 1969–70.

Field-Goal Percentage

Season	Player	Pct	Season	Player	Pct
1946–47	Bob Feerick, Wash	40.1	1967–68	Wilt Chamberlain, Phil	59.5
1947–48	Bob Feerick, Wash	34.0	1968–69	Wilt Chamberlain, LA	58.3
1948–49	Arnie Risen, Roch	42.3	1969–70	Johnny Green, Cin	55.9
1949–50	Alex Groza, Ind	47.8	1970–71	Johnny Green, Cin	58.7
1950–51	Alex Groza, Ind	47.0	1971–72	Wilt Chamberlain, LA	64.9
1951–52	Paul Arizin, Phil	44.8	1972–73	Wilt Chamberlain, LA	72.7
1952–53	Neil Johnston, Phil	45.2	1973–74	Bob McAdoo, Buff	54.7
1953–54	Ed Macauley, Bos	48.6	1974–75	Don Nelson, Bos	53.9
1954–55	Larry Foust, FW	48.7	1975–76	Wes Unseld, Wash	56.1
1955–56	Neil Johnston, Phil	45.7	1976–77	Kareem Abdul-Jabbar, LA	57.9
1956–57	Neil Johnston, Phil	44.7	1977–78	Bobby Jones, Den	57.8
1957–58	Jack Twyman, Cin	45.2	1978–79	Cedric Maxwell, Bos	58.4
1958–59	Ken Sears, NY	49.0	1979–80	Cedric Maxwell, Bos	60.9
1959–60	Ken Sears, NY	47.7	1980–81	Artis Gilmore, Chi	67.0
1960–61	Wilt Chamberlain, Phil	50.9	1981–82	Artis Gilmore, Chi	65.2
1961–62	Walt Bellamy, Chi	51.9	1982–83	Artis Gilmore, SA	62.6
1962–63	Wilt Chamberlain, SF	52.8	1983–84	Artis Gilmore, SA	63.1
1963–64	Jerry Lucas, Cin	52.7	1984–85	James Donaldson, LA Clippers	63.7
1964–65	Wilt Chamberlain, SF-Phil	51.0	1985–86	Steve Johnson, SA	63.2
1965–66	Wilt Chamberlain, Phil	54.0	1986–87	Kevin McHale, Bos	60.4
1966–67	Wilt Chamberlain, Phil	68.3	1987–88	Kevin McHale, Bos	60.4

Field-Goal Percentage (Cont.)

1988–89	Dennis Rodman, Det	59.5	1996–97	Gheorghe Muresan, Wash	60.4
1989–90	Mark West, Phoe	62.5	1997–98	Shaquille O'Neal, LA Lakers	58.4
1990–91	Buck Williams, Port	60.2	1998–99	Shaquille O'Neal, LA Lakers	57.6
1991–92	Buck Williams, Port	60.4	1999–00	Shaquille O'Neal, LA Lakers	57.4
1992–93	Cedric Ceballos, Phoe	57.6	2000–01	Shaquille O'Neal, LA Lakers	57.2
1993–94	Shaquille O'Neal, Orl	59.9	2001–02	Shaquille O'Neal, LA Lakers	57.9
1994–95	Chris Gatling, GS	63.3	2002–03	Eddy Curry, Chi	58.5
1995–96	Gheorghe Muresan, Wash	58.4			

Free-Throw Percentage

1946–47	Fred Scolari, Wash	81.1	1975–76	Rick Barry, GS	92.3
1947–48	Bob Feerick, Wash	78.8	1976–77	Ernie DiGregorio, Buff	94.5
1948–49	Bob Feerick, Wash	85.9	1977–78	Rick Barry, GS	92.4
1949–50	Max Zaslofsky, Chi	84.3	1978–79	Rick Barry, Hou	94.7
1950–51	Joe Fulks, Phil	85.5	1979–80	Rick Barry, Hou	93.5
1951–52	Bob Wanzer, Roch	90.4	1980–81	Calvin Murphy, Hou	95.8
1952–53	Bill Sharman, Bos	85.0	1981–82	Kyle Macy, Phoe	89.9
1953–54	Bill Sharman, Bos	84.4	1982–83	Calvin Murphy, Hou	92.0
1954–55	Bill Sharman, Bos	89.7	1983–84	Larry Bird, Bos	88.8
1955–56	Bill Sharman, Bos	86.7	1984–85	Kyle Macy, Phoe	90.7
1956–57	Bill Sharman, Bos	90.5	1985–86	Larry Bird, Bos	89.6
1957–58	Dolph Schayes, Syr	90.4	1986–87	Larry Bird, Bos	91.0
1958–59	Bill Sharman, Bos	93.2	1987–88	Jack Sikma, Mil	92.2
1959–60	Dolph Schayes, Syr	89.2	1988–89	Magic Johnson, LA Lakers	91.1
1960–61	Bill Sharman, Bos	92.1	1989–90	Larry Bird, Bos	93.0
1961–62	Dolph Schayes, Syr	89.6	1990–91	Reggie Miller, Ind	91.8
1962–63	Larry Costello, Syr	88.1	1991–92	Mark Price, Clev	94.7
1963–64	Oscar Robertson, Cin	85.3	1992–93	Mark Price, Clev	94.8
1964–65	Larry Costello, Phil	87.7	1993–94	Mahmoud Abdul-Rauf, Den	95.6
1965–66	Larry Siegfried, Bos	88.1	1994–95	Spud Webb, Sac	93.4
1966–67	Adrian Smith, Cin	90.3	1995–96	Mahmoud Abdul-Rauf, Den	93.0
1967–68	Oscar Robertson, Cin	87.3	1996–97	Mark Price, GS	90.6
1968–69	Larry Siegfried, Bos	86.4	1997–98	Chris Mullin, Ind	93.9
1969–70	Flynn Robinson, Mil	89.8	1998–99	Reggie Miller, Ind	91.5
1970–71	Chet Walker, Chi	85.9	1999–00	Jeff Hornacek, Utah	95.0
1971–72	Jack Marin, Balt	89.4	2000–01	Reggie Miller, Ind	92.8
1972–73	Rick Barry, GS	90.2	2001–02	Reggie Miller, Ind	91.1
1973–74	Ernie DiGregorio, Buff	90.2	2002–03	Allan Houston, NY	91.9
1974–75	Rick Barry, GS	90.4			

Three-Point Field-Goal Percentage

1979–80	Fred Brown, Sea	44.3	1992–93	B.J. Armstrong, Chi	45.3
1980–81	Brian Taylor, SD	38.3	1993–94	Tracy Murray, Por	45.9
1981–82	Campy Russell, NY	43.9	1994–95	Steve Kerr, Chi	52.4
1982–83	Mike Dunleavy, SA	34.5	1995–96	Tim Legler, Wash	52.2
1983–84	Darrell Griffith, Utah	36.1	1996–97	Kevin Gamble, Sac	48.2
1984–85	Byron Scott, LA Lakers	43.3	1997–98	Dale Ellis, Sea	46.0
1985–86	Craig Hodges, Mil	45.1	1998–99	Dell Curry, Char	47.6
1986–87	Kiki Vandeweghe, Por	48.1	1999–00	Hubert Davis, Dall	49.1
1987–88	Craig Hodges, Mil-Phoe	49.1	2000–01	Brent Barry, Sea	47.6
1988–89	Jon Sundvold, Mia	52.2	2001–02	Steve Smith, SA	47.2
1989–90	Steve Kerr, Clev	50.7	2002–03	Bruce Bowen, SA	44.1
1990–91	Jim Les, Sac	46.1			
1991–92	Dana Barros, Sea	44.6			

Steals

1973–74	Larry Steele, Por	2.68	1989–90	Michael Jordan, Chi	2.77
1974–75	Rick Barry, GS	2.85	1990–91	Alvin Robertson, Mil	3.04
1975–76	Don Watts, Sea	3.18	1991–92	John Stockton, Utah	2.98
1976–77	Don Buse, Ind	3.47	1992–93	Michael Jordan, Chi	2.83
1977–78	Ron Lee, Phoe	2.74	1993–94	Nate McMillan, Sea	2.96
1978–79	M.L. Carr, Det	2.46	1994–95	Scottie Pippen, Chi	2.94
1979–80	Micheal Richardson, NY	3.23	1995–96	Gary Payton, Sea	2.85
1980–81	Magic Johnson, LA	3.43	1996–97	Mookie Blaylock, Atl	2.72
1981–82	Magic Johnson, LA	2.67	1997–98	Mookie Blaylock, Atl	2.61
1982–83	Micheal Richardson, GS-NJ	2.84	1998–99	Kendall Gill, NJ	2.68
1983–84	Rickey Green, Utah	2.65	1999–00	Eddie Jones, Char	2.67
1984–85	Micheal Richardson, NJ	2.96	2000–01	Allen Iverson, Phil	2.51
1985–86	Alvin Robertson, SA	3.67	2001–02	Allen Iverson, Phil	2.80
1986–87	Alvin Robertson, SA	3.21	2002–03	Allen Iverson, Phil	2.74
1987–88	Michael Jordan, Chi	3.16			
1988–89	John Stockton, Utah	3.21			

Blocked Shots

1973–74	Elmore Smith, LA	4.85	1988–89	Manute Bol, GS	4.31
1974–75	Kareem Abdul-Jabbar, Mil	3.26	1989–90	Hakeem Olajuwon, Hou	4.59
1975–76	Kareem Abdul-Jabbar, LA	4.12	1990–91	Hakeem Olajuwon, Hou	3.95
1976–77	Bill Walton, Port	3.25	1991–92	David Robinson, SA	4.49
1977–78	George Johnson, NJ	3.38	1992–93	Hakeem Olajuwon, Hou	4.17
1978–79	Kareem Abdul-Jabbar, LA	3.95	1993–94	Dikembe Mutombo, Den	4.10
1979–80	Kareem Abdul-Jabbar, LA	3.41	1994–95	Dikembe Mutombo, Den	3.91
1980–81	George Johnson, SA	3.39	1995–96	Dikembe Mutombo, Den	4.49
1981–82	George Johnson, SA	3.12	1996–97	Shawn Bradley, NJ	3.40
1982–83	Wayne Rollins, Atl	4.29	1997–98	Marcus Camby, Tor	3.65
1983–84	Mark Eaton, Utah	4.28	1998–99	Alonzo Mourning, Mia	3.91
1984–85	Mark Eaton, Utah	5.56	1999–00	Alonzo Mourning, Mia	3.72
1985–86	Manute Bol, Wash	4.96	2000–01	Theo Ratliff, Phil/Atl	3.74
1986–87	Mark Eaton, Utah	4.06	2001–02	Ben Wallace, Det	3.48
1987–88	Mark Eaton, Utah	3.71	2002–03	Theo Ratliff, Atl	3.23

NBA All-Star Game Results

Year	Result	Site	Winning Coach	Most Valuable Player
1951	East 111, West 94	Boston	Joe Lapchick	Ed Macauley, Bos
1952	East 108, West 91	Boston	Al Cervi	Paul Arizin, Phil
1953	West 79, East 75	Ft Wayne	John Kundla	George Mikan, Minn
1954	East 98, West 93 (OT)	New York	Joe Lapchick	Bob Cousy, Bos
1955	East 100, West 91	New York	Al Cervi	Bill Sharman, Bos
1956	West 108, East 94	Rochester	Charley Eckman	Bob Pettit, StL
1957	East 109, West 97	Boston	Red Auerbach	Bob Cousy, Bos
1958	East 130, West 118	St Louis	Red Auerbach	Bob Pettit, StL
1959	West 124, East 108	Detroit	Ed Macauley	B. Pettit, StL/ E. Baylor, Minn
1960	East 125, West 115	Philadelphia	Red Auerbach	Wilt Chamberlain, Phil
1961	West 153, East 131	Syracuse	Paul Seymour	Oscar Robertson, Cin
1962	West 150, East 130	St Louis	Fred Schaus	Bob Pettit, StL
1963	East 115, West 108	Los Angeles	Red Auerbach	Bill Russell, Bos
1964	East 111, West 107	Boston	Red Auerbach	Oscar Robertson, Cin
1965	East 124, West 123	St Louis	Red Auerbach	Jerry Lucas, Cin
1966	East 137, West 94	Cincinnati	Red Auerbach	Adrian Smith, Cin
1967	West 135, East 120	San Francisco	Fred Schaus	Rick Barry, SF
1968	East 144, West 124	New York	Alex Hannum	Hal Greer, Phil
1969	East 123, West 112	Baltimore	Gene Shue	Oscar Robertson, Cin
1970	East 142, West 135	Philadelphia	Red Holzman	Willis Reed, NY
1971	West 108, East 107	San Diego	Larry Costello	Lenny Wilkens, Sea
1972	West 112, East 110	Los Angeles	Bill Sharman	Jerry West, LA
1973	East 104, West 84	Chicago	Tom Heinsohn	Dave Cowens, Bos
1974	West 134, East 123	Seattle	Larry Costello	Bob Lanier, Det
1975	East 108, West 102	Phoenix	K.C. Jones	Walt Frazier, NY
1976	East 123, West 109	Philadelphia	Tom Heinsohn	Dave Bing, Wash
1977	West 125, East 124	Milwaukee	Larry Brown	Julius Erving, Phil
1978	East 133, West 125	Atlanta	Billy Cunningham	Randy Smith, Buff
1979	West 134, East 129	Detroit	Lenny Wilkens	David Thompson, Den
1980	East 144, West 135 (OT)	Washington	Billy Cunningham	George Gervin, SA
1981	East 123, West 120	Cleveland	Billy Cunningham	Nate Archibald, Bos
1982	East 120, West 118	New Jersey	Bill Fitch	Larry Bird, Bos
1983	East 132, West 123	Los Angeles	Billy Cunningham	Julius Erving, Phil
1984	East 154, West 145 (OT)	Denver	K.C. Jones	Isiah Thomas, Det
1985	West 140, East 129	Indiana	Pat Riley	Ralph Sampson, Hou
1986	East 139, West 132	Dallas	K.C. Jones	Isiah Thomas, Det
1987	West 154, East 149 (OT)	Seattle	Pat Riley	Tom Chambers, Sea
1988	East 138, West 133	Chicago	Mike Fratello	Michael Jordan, Chi
1989	West 143, East 134	Houston	Pat Riley	Karl Malone, Utah
1990	East 130, West 113	Miami	Chuck Daly	Magic Johnson, LA Lakers
1991	East 116, West 114	Charlotte	Chris Ford	Charles Barkley, Phil
1992	West 153, East 113	Orlando	Don Nelson	Magic Johnson, LA Lakers
1993	West 135, East 132	Salt Lake City	Paul Westphal	K. Malone/ J. Stockton ,Utah
1994	East 127, West 118	Minneapolis	Lenny Wilkens	Scottie Pippen, Chi
1995	West 139, East 112	Phoenix	Paul Westphal	Mitch Richmond, Sac
1996	East 129, West 118	San Antonio	Phil Jackson	Michael Jordan, Chi
1997	East 132, West 120	Cleveland	Doug Collins	Glen Rice, Char
1998	East 135, West 114	New York	Larry Bird	Michael Jordan, Chi
1999	Cancelled due to lockout.			
2000	West 137, East 126	Oakland	Phil Jackson	O'Neal, Lakers/T. Duncan, SA
2001	East 111, West 110	Washington	Larry Brown	Allen Iverson, Phil
2002	West 135, East 120	Philadelphia	Don Nelson	Kobe Bryant, LA Lakers
2003	West 155, East 145 (2OT)	Atlanta	Rick Adelman	Kevin Garnett, Minn

Contributors

Senda Abbott (1984)
Forest C. (Phog) Allen (1959)
Clair F. Bee (1967)
Danny Biasone (2000)
Walter A. Brown (1965)
John W. Bunn (1964)
Bob Douglas (1971)
Al Duer (1981)
Wayne Embry (1999)
Clifford Fagan (1983)
Harry A. Fisher (1973)
Larry Fleisher (1991)
Edward Gottlieb (1971)
Luther H. Gulick (1959)
Lester Harrison (1979)
Chick Hearn (2003)
Ferenc Hepp (1980)

Edward J. Hickox (1959)
Paul D. (Tony) Hinkle (1965)
Ned Irish (1964)
R. William Jones (1964)
J. Walter Kennedy (1980)
Meadowlark Lemon (2003)
Emil S. Liston (1974)
Earl Lloyd (2003)
John B. McLendon (1978)
Bill Mokray (1965)
Ralph Morgan (1959)
Frank Morgenweck (1962)
James Naismith (1959)
Peter F. Newell (1978)
C.M. Newton (2000)
John J. O'Brien (1961)
Larry O'Brien (1991)

Harold G. Olsen (1959)
Maurice Podoloff (1973)
H. V. Porter (1960)
William A. Reid (1963)
Elmer Ripley (1972)
Lynn W. St. John (1962)
Abe Saperstein (1970)
Arthur A. Schabinger (1961)
Amos Alonzo Stagg (1959)
Boris Stankovic (1991)
Edward Steitz (1983)
Chuck Taylor (1968)
Oswald Tower (1959)
Arthur L. Trester (1961)
Clifford Wells (1971)
Lou Wilke (1982)
Fred Zollner (1999)

Players

Kareem Abdul-Jabbar (1995)
Nate (Tiny) Archibald (1991)
Paul J. Arizin (1977)
Thomas B. Barlow (1980)
Rick Barry (1987)
Elgin Baylor (1976)
John Beckman (1972)
Walt Bellamy (1993)
Sergei Belov (1992)
Dave Bing (1990)
Larry Bird (1998)
Carol Blazejowski (1994)
Bennie Borgmann (1961)
Bill Bradley (1982)
Joseph Brennan (1974)
Al Cervi (1984)
Wilt Chamberlain (1978)
Charles (Tarzan) Cooper (1976)
Kresimir Cosic (1996)
Bob Cousy (1970)
Dave Cowens (1991)
Joan Crawford (1997)
Billy Cunningham (1986)
Denise Curry (1997)
Bob Davies (1969)
Forrest S. DeBernardi (1961)
Dave DeBusschere (1982)
H.G. (Dutch) Dehnert (1968)
Anne Donovan (1995)
Paul Endacott (1971)
Alex English (1997)
Julius Erving (1993)
Harold (Bud) Foster (1964)
Walter (Clyde) Frazier (1987)
Max (Marty) Friedman (1971)
Joe Fulks (1977)
Lauren (Laddie) Gale (1976)
Harry (the Horse) Gallatin (1991)
William Gates (1989)
George Gervin (1996)
Tom Gola (1975)
Gail Goodrich (1996)

Hal Greer (1981)
Robert (Ace) Gruenig (1963)
Clifford O. Hagan (1977)
Victor Hanson (1960)
John Havlicek (1983)
Connie Hawkins (1992)
Elvin Hayes (1990)
Marques Haynes (1998)
Tom Heinsohn (1986)
Nat Holman (1964)
Robert J. Houbregs (1987)
Bailey Howell (1997)
Chuck Hyatt (1959)
Dan Issel (1993)
Harry (Buddy) Jeannette (1994)
Earvin (Magic) Johnson (2002)
William C. Johnson (1976)
D. Neil Johnston (1990)
K.C. Jones (1989)
Sam Jones (1983)
Edward (Moose) Krause (1975)
Bob Kurland (1961)
Bob Lanier (1992)
Joe Lapchick (1966)
Nancy Lieberman-Cline (1996)
Clyde Lovellette (1988)
Jerry Lucas (1979)
Angelo (Hank) Luisetti (1959)
C. Edward Macauley (1960)
Moses Malone (2001)
Peter P. Maravich (1987)
Slater Martin (1981)
Bob McAdoo (2000)
Branch McCracken (1960)
Jack McCracken (1962)
Bobby McDermott (1988)
Dick McGuire (1993)
Kevin McHale (1999)
Dino Meneghin (2003)
Ann Meyers (1993)
George L. Mikan (1959)
Vern Mikkelsen (1995)

Cheryl Miller (1995)
Earl Monroe (1990)
Calvin Murphy (1993)
Charles (Stretch) Murphy (1960)
H. O. (Pat) Page (1962)
Robert Parish (2003)
Drazen Petrovic (2002)
Bob Pettit (1970)
Andy Phillip (1961)
Jim Pollard (1977)
Frank Ramsey (1981)
Willis Reed (1981)
Arnie Risen (1998)
Oscar Robertson (1979)
John S. Roosma (1961)
Bill Russell (1974)
John (Honey) Russell (1964)
Adolph Schayes (1972)
Ernest J. Schmidt (1973)
John J. Schommer (1959)
Barney Sedran (1962)
Uljana Semjonova (1993)
Bill Sharman (1975)
Christian Steinmetz (1961)
Lusia Harris Stewart (1992)
Isiah Thomas (2000)
David Thompson (1996)
John A. (Cat) Thompson (1962)
Nate Thurmond (1984)
Jack Twyman (1982)
Wes Unseld (1988)
Robert (Fuzzy) Vandivier (1974)
Edward A. Wachter (1961)
Bill Walton (1993)
Robert F. Wanzer (1987)
Jerry West (1979)
Nera White (1992)
Lenny Wilkens (1989)
John R. Wooden (1960)
James Worthy (2003)
George (Bird) Yardley (1996)

Coaches

Harold Anderson (1984)
Red Auerbach (1968)
Leon Barmore (2003)
Sam Barry (1978)
Ernest A. Blood (1960)
Larry Brown (2002)
Howard G. Cann (1967)

H. Clifford Carlson (1959)
Lou Carnesecca (1992)
Ben Carnevale (1969)
Pete Carril (1997)
Everett Case (1981)
John Chaney (2001)
Jody Conradt (1998)

Denny Crum (1994)
Chuck Daly (1994)
Everett S. Dean (1966)
Antonio Diaz-Miguel (1997)
Edgar A. Diddle (1971)
Bruce Drake (1972)

Note: Year of election in parentheses.

Coaches *(Cont.)*

Clarence Gaines (1981)
Jack Gardner (1983)
Amory T. (Slats) Gill (1967)
Aleksandr Gomelsky (1995)
Alex Hannum (1998)
Marv Harshman (1984)
Don Haskins (1997)
Edgar S. Hickey (1978)
Howard A. Hobson (1965)
Red Holzman (1986)
Hank Iba (1968)
Alvin F. (Doggie) Julian (1967)
Frank W. Keaney (1960)
George E. Keogan (1961)
Bob Knight (1991)
Mike Krzyzewski (2001)

John Kundla (1995)
Ward L. Lambert (1960)
Harry Litwack (1975)
Kenneth D. Loeffler (1964)
A.C. (Dutch) Lonborg (1972)
Arad A. McCutchan (1980)
Al McGuire (1992)
Frank McGuire (1976)
Walter E. Meanwell (1959)
Raymond J. Meyer (1978)
Ralph Miller (1988)
Billie Moore (1999)
Aleksandar Nikolic (1998)
Lute Olson (2002
Jack Ramsay (1992)
Cesare Rubini (1994)

Adolph F. Rupp (1968)
Leonard D. Sachs (1961)
Everett F. Shelton (1979)
Dean Smith (1982)
Pat Summitt (2000)
Fred R. Taylor (1985)
Bertha Teague (1984)
John Thompson (1999)
Margaret Wade (1984)
Stanley H. Watts (1985)
Lenny Wilkens (1998)
John R. Wooden (1972)
Morgan Wooten (2000)
Phil Woolpert (1992)
Kay Yow (2002)

Referees

James E. Enright (1978)
George T. Hepbron (1960)
George Hoyt (1961)
Matthew P. Kennedy (1959)
Lloyd Leith (1982)
Zigmund J. Mihalik (1985)

John P. Nucatola (1977)
Ernest C. Quigley (1961)
J. Dallas Shirley (1979)
Earl Strom (1995)
David Tobey (1961)
David H. Walsh (1961)

Teams

Buffalo Germans (1961)
First Team (1959)
Harlem Globetrotters (2002)
Original Celtics (1959)
Renaissance (1963)

ABA Champions

Year	Champion	Series	Runner-up	Winning Coach
1968	Pittsburgh Pipers	4–3	New Orleans Bucs	Vince Cazetta
1969	Oakland Oaks	4–1	Indiana Pacers	Alex Hannum
1970	Indiana Pacers	4–2	Los Angeles Stars	Bob Leonard
1971	Utah Stars	4–3	Kentucky Colonels	Bill Sharman
1972	Indiana Pacers	4–2	New York Nets	Bob Leonard
1973	Indiana Pacers	4–3	Kentucky Colonels	Bob Leonard
1974	New York Nets	4–1	Utah Stars	Kevin Loughery
1975	Kentucky Colonels	4–1	Indiana Pacers	Hubie Brown
1976	New York Nets	4–2	Denver Nuggets	Kevin Loughery

ABA Postseason Awards

Most Valuable Player

1967–68	Connie Hawkins, Pitt
1968–69	Mel Daniels, Ind
1969–70	Spencer Haywood, Den
1970–71	Mel Daniels, Ind
1971–72	Artis Gilmore, Ken
1972–73	Billy Cunningham, Car
1973–74	Julius Erving, NY
1974–75	Julius Erving, NY
	George McGinnis, Ind
1975–76	Julius Erving, NY

Rookie of the Year

1967–68	Mel Daniels, Minn
1968–69	Warren Armstrong, Oak
1969–70	Spencer Haywood, Den
1970–71	Charlie Scott, Vir
	Dan Issel, Ken
1971–72	Artis Gilmore, Ken
1972–73	Brian Taylor, NY
1973–74	Swen Nater, SA
1974–75	Marvin Barnes, StL
1975–76	David Thompson, Den

Coach of the Year

1967–68	Vince Cazetta, Pitt
1968–69	Alex Hannum, Oak
1969–70	Bill Sharman, LA
	Joe Belmont, Den
1970–71	Al Bianchi, Vir
1971–72	Tom Nissalke, Dall
1972–73	Larry Brown, Car
1973–74	Babe McCarthy, Ken
	Joe Mullaney, Utah
1974–75	Larry Brown, Den
1975–76	Larry Brown, Den

ABA Season Leaders

Scoring

	GP	Pts	Avg
1967–68...Connie Hawkins, Pitt	70	1875	26.8
1968–69...Rick Barry, Oak	35	1190	34.0
1969–70...Spencer Haywood, Den	84	2519	30.0
1970–71...Dan Issel, Ken	83	2480	29.4
1971–72...Charlie Scott, Vir	73	2524	34.6
1972–73...Julius Erving, Vir	71	2268	31.9
1973–74...Julius Erving, NY	84	2299	27.4
1974–75...George McGinnis, Ind	79	2353	29.8
1975–76...Julius Erving, NY	84	2462	29.3

Rebounds

1967–68................Mel Daniels, Minn	15.6
1968–69................Mel Daniels, Ind	16.5
1969–70................Spencer Haywood, Den	19.5
1970–71................Mel Daniels, Ind	18.0
1971–72................Artis Gilmore, Ken	17.8
1972–73................Artis Gilmore, Ken	17.5
1973–74................Artis Gilmore, Ken	18.3
1974–75................Swen Nater, SA	16.4
1975–76................Artis Gilmore, Ken	15.5

Assists

1967–68................Larry Brown, NO	6.5
1968–69................Larry Brown, Oak	7.1
1969–70................Larry Brown, Wash	7.1
1970–71................Bill Melchionni, NY	8.3
1971–72................Bill Melchionni, NY	8.4
1972–73................Bill Melchionni, NY	7.5
1973–74................Al Smith, Den	8.2
1974–75................Mack Calvin, Den	7.7
1975–76................Don Buse, Ind	8.2

Steals

1973–74................Ted McClain, Car	2.98
1974–75................Brian Taylor, NY	2.80
1975–76................Don Buse, Ind	4.12

Blocked Shots

1973–74................Caldwell Jones, SD	4.00
1974–75................Caldwell Jones, SD	3.24
1975–76................Billy Paultz, SA	3.05

World Championship of Basketball

Year	Winner	Runner-Up	Score	Site
1950 ....Argentina	United States	†	Rio de Janeiro
1954 ....United States	Brazil	†	Rio de Janeiro
1959 ....Brazil	United States	†	Santiago, Chile
1963 ....Brazil	Yugoslavia	†	Rio de Janeiro
1967 ....Soviet Union	Yugoslavia	†	Montevideo, Uruguay
1970 ....Yugoslavia	Brazil	†	Ljubljana, Yugoslavia
1974 ....Soviet Union	Yugoslavia	†	San Juan
1978 ....Yugoslavia	Soviet Union	82–81 (OT)	Manila
1982 ....Soviet Union	United States	95–94	Cali, Colombia
1986 ....United States	Soviet Union	87–85	Madrid
1990 ....Yugoslavia	Soviet Union	92–75	Buenos Aires
1994* ....United States	Russia	137–91	Toronto
1998 ....Yugoslavia	Russia	64–62	Athens
2002 ....Yugoslavia	Argentina	84–77 (OT)	Indianapolis

*U.S. professionals began competing in 1994. In 1998, a labor dispute resulted in a boycott of the World Championship by NBA stars; the U.S. roster was filled by members of the CBA and European professional leagues and college players.
†Result determined by overall record in final round of competition.

THEY SAID IT

Yao Ming, Rockets center and media darling, identifying his favorite English words: "Last question."

College Basketball

Carmelo Anthony
of national champion
Syracuse

Jim Dandy

With a pair of freshman leading the way, Syracuse delivered Jim Boeheim his first NCAA title in 27 years as coach of the Orangemen

BY B.J. SCHECTER

THREE DAYS BEFORE his team was to play Kansas for the 2003 national championship, Syracuse coach Jim Boeheim was at peace. Sprawled out on the bed in his New Orleans hotel room, Boeheim talked about how basketball was no longer everything in his life, and explained at length that as much as he wanted to win a national title, it wouldn't make or break him. As he spoke about the biggest heartbreak of his coaching career—a loss to Indiana in the 1987 championship, during which the Hoosiers' Keith Smart sank a game-winning jumper in the final seconds—Boeheim's four-year-old son, Jimmy, came running in from an adjacent room, bounced on the bed and dived into his father's arms. The smile on his face told the story of the new and improved Jim Boeheim.

"Over the years I have thought about [the Indiana game] a lot," said Boeheim. "We were so close. So close. I wish we would have won that game, but would my life really be much different if that shot hadn't gone in? I don't think so. I never thought Marv Levy would have been a bet-

ter coach if he had won one of those Super Bowls. I don't think Dan Marino would have been a better quarterback had he won a championship. And I know I won't be a better coach if I win one."

Boeheim finally did win a coveted championship, as his Orangemen produced an impressive 81–78 victory over the Jayhawks in New Orleans. Given that Syracuse hadn't even made the NCAA tournament the previous year, and that the Orangemen weren't ranked in the preseason polls, the appearance in the title game alone speaks volumes about Boeheim's coaching ability. Now that he'd finally won the big one, does his ranking among the alltime greats change at all? That question remains open for debate, but what's indisputable is that Boeheim is a changed man.

For years, Boeheim had been one of the most underappreciated and misunderstood coaches in the nation. Much of it was the coach's own doing as his whining, scowling and complaining had become as synonymous with Syracuse basketball as the Carrier Dome. But from the day that Boeheim met Juli Greene at a Kentucky Derby party

RICH CLARKSON/ NCAA PHOTOS

in 1995, Boeheim's world was turned upside down. They clicked immediately, and were married 1½ years later. They now have three children. "For years I used to get scared when basketball season was over," said Boeheim. "I was always afraid I wasn't going to have anything to do and would spend most of my free time at the driving range. Now I have a lot of things to do."

Those things included changing diapers, getting involved in charities and enjoying a life outside of basketball. Boeheim became more relaxed, and more approachable. The changes may or may not have made Boeheim a better coach, but they certainly made him more enjoyable to be around. "He's basically a very shy guy who's finally reached a comfort level," said former Big East Commissioner Dave Gavitt, a longtime friend of Boeheim.

As a coach with 25 20-win seasons, Boeheim could say without question that his 2002–03 team, the one that would finally deliver him his first national title, wasn't his most talented group ever. It wasn't even close. But this team was certainly his most enjoyable. With two superb freshman—All-America Carmelo Anthony and unflappable point guard Gerry McNamara—and a corps of players who understood their roles, the Orangemen ascended to heights that even Boeheim didn't think were attainable at the beginning of the season. "I

have to be honest," he said. "In October, I didn't think we were very good."

It all started with Anthony, the versatile and supremely talented 6'8" forward who came into the season with LeBron James–like hype and exceeded it. As Anthony adjusted to the college game, he became more and more dominant—and the Orangemen got better and better. Anthony was also the calming presence that the Orangemen needed. Despite occasionally taking upwards of 25 shots a game, he was unselfish, didn't walk around with an air of arrogance and played the game with an infectious enthusiasm. "There are times I know I could have been selfish and scored 40," said Anthony, "but that's not what's best for the team."

It was essentially a foregone conclusion that Anthony would bolt for the pros at the end of the season, but he didn't cause the chemistry problems that one-year wonders often do. In the final against Kansas, Anthony was, simply put, the best player on the floor. He scored from the outside, from the inside, off the dribble and off the break. His final line—20 points, 10 rebounds and seven assists—was impressive, but even more amazing was the poise he exhibited. Early in the game he was laughing after a call didn't go his way and he had the demeanor of someone playing a Sunday game at the park, not a freshman trying to lead his team to a national championship.

Kansas had no answer for Anthony, who stretched the defense and cleared the way for McNamara to drain six three-pointers in the first half. "We tried not to double off McNamara," said Kansas forward Nick Collison, "but when Anthony gets the ball, everyone's got to give help."

After beating Texas in the national semifinals, Syracuse assistant Mike Hopkins spent all night breaking down film of Kansas and came to a conclusion: "There's no way they can cover 'Melo one-on-one," Hopkins said. "They have to go zone. There's no way [Keith] Langford can check 'Melo. They don't want to get into foul trouble; that's why we have to attack."

Hopkins was right. Langford, who was arguably Kansas's most dangerous offensive player in the tournament after Collison, started out on Anthony but quickly got into foul trouble. He played just 23 minutes, and though he scored 19 points, he fouled out with 5:36 remaining. What's more, Syracuse was able to control the tempo, jumping out to an 18-point lead in the first half and not allowing Kansas to score in bunches off transition.

All in all, it was quite a performance from the Orangemen. In addition to Anthony's prodcution, McNamara's long-range three-pointer clinic produced 18 points. Boeheim's boys were equally impressive on the other side of the ball, too, using their vaunted 2–3 zone to clog the middle and force turnovers. Indeed,

when Kansas cut the lead to single digits and threatened to tie the score late in the game, Orangeman class sophomore forward Hakim Warrick came out of nowhere to block Michael Lee's three-point attempt with 1.5 seconds remaining and preserve the victory.

As he left the court, Anthony embraced his brother, Justus, who then yelled what many Orangemen fans were thinking: "Ain't nothing left for him to do." A similar statement could hold true for Boeheim: he has nothing left to prove, to himself or anyone else.

Kansas coach Roy Williams, for his part, entered the season with much to prove. Though he had made it to three Final Fours, Williams had yet to win a national title despite being favored to do so on numerous occasions. And after the Jayhawks lost to eventual champion Maryland in the semis in 2002, some Kansas fans wondered if Williams would ever bring a national championship to Lawrence. Yet with Collison and star guard Kirk Hinrich returning for the 2002–03 season, Kansas fans had to like their chances.

The Jayhawks stumbled early in the season, and after losing to Oregon in December they were 3–3. Following that game, Williams met with Collison, who had only scored seven points, and tried to take the blame. But Collison would hear nothing of it, saying, "You and I both know if I'd have played a better game, we would have won. I promise you, I'll never let that happen again."

Collison made good on his vow, and by the end of the season, the Jayhawks were one of the pre-tournament favorites. In the West regional semifinal against Duke, Collison turned in one of the best performances of the tournament, scoring 33 points and pulling down 19 rebounds in a 69–65 victory. After Kentucky and Arizona failed to make the Final Four, the planets seemed to be aligning for Kansas. Fans in Lawrence could be forgiven for thinking that this, finally, was their year.

A 33-point trouncing of Marquette in the national semifinals did nothing to diminish this feeling, but then came the final in New Orleans, where Syracuse's freshman got the best of the Kansas seniors and Williams, and the Jayhawk faithful, were once again left heartbroken. Seven days later, Williams added insult to injury—at least as far as Kansas fans were concerned—by saying yes to Dean Smith and North Carolina three years after turning down that coaching job.

"Other than serious injury or death to my family, I've never had anything more difficult than what I've been through this afternoon with my team, and telling those 13 young men that I was leaving them," Williams said. "I was a Tar Heel born. When I die, I'll be a Tar Heel dead. But in the middle, I have been Tar Heel and Jayhawk bred, and I am so, so happy and proud of that."

Elsewhere in college basketball there wasn't as much for coaches, players or fans to be proud of. A series of scandals right before March Madness put a damper on the excitement of the tournament. Jim Harrick was suspended (and eventually resigned) from Georgia after former guard Tony Cole alleged he used Harrick's credit card to buy a television, and that the coach's son paid bills for him, and arranged for him to receive an A in a course he said he never attended. As a result, the school pulled the Bulldogs out of the SEC and NCAA tournaments. Another set of Bulldogs, from Fresno State, also got itself banned from the

DARREN CARROLL

Collison performed brilliantly in the NCAAs, but he and Kansas fell short in the final.

NCAA tournament following accusations of academic fraud under former coach Jerry Tarkanian. And at St. Bonaventure, the players voted to forfeit their final two games in response to the Atlantic 10 conference's barring the Bonnies from competing in the conference tournament for using an ineligible player (school president Robert Wickenheiser and coach Jan van Breda Kolff departed in the wake of the incident). Things did not improve in the off-season, as Iowa State's Larry Eustachy resigned following reports that he went on drinking binges at student parties after games at Missouri and Kansas State.

The picture was much rosier in the women's game, where Connecticut showed its mettle by repeating as national champion. This one was the toughest to win of the Huskies' four titles. UConn lost four starters from the 2001–02 title team, and coach Geno Auriemma expected to endure some growing pains. He wasn't sure a repeat was possible, but he wasn't about to tell his team that.

During the first week of practice Auriemma realized that he was going to have to push this group harder. "What am I supposed to tell these guys? 'It's a rebuilding year at Connecticut . . . it's OK to lose?'" he said. "If I do that, I'm being somewhat disrespectful to them." Instead,

Strother, a freshman, rose to the occasion in the championship game, scoring 17 points.

Auriemma made it clear that he wasn't willing to drop the bar, telling his squad, "Listen, I know this isn't last year's team. But I don't give a damn, we're winning the national championship!"

The Huskies won games at a regular clip during the regular season, but it wasn't as easy as it appeared. They had one superstar in junior All-America guard Diana Taurasi, but few other players with any big-game experience. Considered by many to be the best player in the history of the women's game, Taurasi did enough to keep UConn on a winning track, but Auriemma was becoming increasingly concerned about his team's reliance on their star.

In January, Connecticut topped Louisiana Tech's record 54-game winning streak with a victory over Georgetown. The next game, with Taurasi a non-factor because of foul trouble (she would score a season-low four points), the young Huskies came of age with an impressive 72–53 win over Notre Dame in South Bend. Then, UConn won at Duke, which had been ranked No. 1 all season, and never looked back.

The streak reached 70 games before the Huskies fell to Villanova in the championship game of the Big East tournament, but the loss may have been a blessing in disguise. "Maybe what it did was give us a sense of, 'Look, we are starting to let things slip a little bit.' We needed to be slapped in the face with reality in a huge game by a team we have beat for 10 straight years, every single year." said Auriemma.

Taurasi also realized that she needed to be more aggressive in the NCAA tournament. She promptly picked up her game, increasing her scoring average from 16.3 points a game in the regular season to 25.8 in the tournament, and came up big when her team needed it the most. In the national semifinal against Texas, the Huskies trailed by nine points with 12:55 remaining and six with 3:14 left. That's when Taurasi took over, scoring 11 of her 26 points in the final 8:55 to lead Connecticut to a 71–69 victory over the Longhorns. What was the difference in the game? "We have Diana, and they don't," said Auriemma.

In the championship game against Tennessee, Taurasi was again spectacular, scoring a game-high 28 points, but the difference may have been freshman Ann Strother, who scored 17 points, including three of UConn's 10 three-pointers in the 73–68 victory. What began as a season of uncertainty ended with a fourth national championship for the Huskies. Asked for the key to this improbable title, Auriemma immediately pointed to Taurasi.

"I would venture to say no one has [won a national championship] the way she has," said Auriemma. "It's never been done like this." Added Huskies assistant Chris Dailey, "It's almost scary to think about, isn't it? I mean what else could she do?"

Scarier still, at least for the Huskies' opponents, is that Taurasi has one more year of eligibility.

NCAA Championship Game Box Score

Syracuse 81

SYRACUSE	Min	FG M–A	FT M–A	Reb O–T	A	PF	TP
Warrick	31	2–4	2–4	0–2	1	3	6
Anthony	37	7–16	3–4	4–10	7	2	20
Forth	24	3–4	0–1	1–3	0	5	6
McNamara	34	6–13	0–0	0–0	1	2	18
Duany	13	4–6	1–2	3–4	0	3	11
Pace	21	4–9	0–0	1–8	2	2	8
Edelin	27	4–10	4–6	0–2	2	1	12
McNeil	13	0–1	0–0	2–5	0	4	0
Totals	200	30–63	10–17	11–34	13	22	81

Percentages: FG—.476, FT—.588. 3-pt goals: 11–18, .611 (Anthony 3–5, McNamara 6–10, Duany 2–3). Team rebounds: 2. Blocked shots: 7 (Warrick 2, Forth 3, McNeil 2). Turnovers: 17 (Warrick 3, Anthony 3, McNamara 3, Duany 2, Pace 2, Edelin 2, McNeil 2). Steals: 10 (Edelin 3, Pace 3, Anthony, Forth, McNamara, Duany).

Halftime: Syracuse 53, Kansas 42.   A: 54,524.

Kansas 78

KANSAS	Min	FG M–A	FT M–A	Reb O–T	A	PF	TP
Collison	40	8–14	3–10	8–21	3	5	19
Langford	23	7–9	5–10	2–2	0	5	19
Graves	37	7–13	2–7	11–16	3	2	16
Hinrich	38	6–20	1–1	1–2	4	1	16
Miles	34	1–5	0–0	1–6	7	1	2
Lee	23	2–8	0–0	1–1	1	1	5
Nash	5	0–2	1–2	0–1	0	1	1
Totals	200	31–71	12–30	24–49	18	16	78

Percentages: FG—.437, FT—.400. 3-pt goals: 4–20, .200 (Langford 0–1, Hinrich 3–12, Miles 0–2, Lee 1–5). Team rebounds: 3. Blocked shots: 4 (Collison 3, Hinrich). Turnovers: 18 (Collison 5, Miles 4, Langford 3, Hinrich 3, Graves 2, Lee). Steals: 9 (Collison 3, Lee 2, Langford, Graves, Hinrich, Miles).

Officials: Dick Cartmell, Gerald Boudreaux, Reggie Cofer.

Final AP Top 25

Poll taken before NCAA Tournament.

1. Kentucky (70)	29–3
2. Arizona (1)	25–3
3. Oklahoma	24–6
4. Pittsburgh	26–4
5. Texas	22–6
6. Kansas	25–7
7. Duke	24–6
8. Wake Forest	24–5
9. Marquette	23–5
10. Florida	24–7
11. Illinois	24–6
12. Xavier	25–5
13. Syracuse	24–5
14. Louisville	24–6
15. Creighton	29–4
16. Dayton	25–5
17. Maryland	19–9
18. Stanford	23–8
19. Memphis	23–6
20. Mississippi St	21–9
21. Wisconsin	22–7
22. Notre Dame	22–9
23. Connecticut	21–9
24. Missouri	21–10
25. Georgia	19–8

National Invitation Tournament Scores

Opening round: College of Charleston 71, Kent St 66; Providence 67, Richmond 49; Temple 98, Drexel 59; Boston College 90, Fairfield 78; Siena 74, Villanova 59; Western Michigan 63, IL-Chicago 62; Iowa St 76, Wichita St 65; Iowa 62, Valparaiso 60.
First round: Wyoming 78, Eastern Washington 71; N Carolina 83, DePaul 72; Georgetown 70, Tennessee 60; Providence 68, College of Charleston 64; Temple 75, Boston College 62; Rhode Island 61, Seton Hall 60; Minnesota 65, St. Louis 52; Hawaii 85, UNLV 68; St. John's 62, Boston University 57; Virginia 89, Brown 73; Alabama-Birmingham 82, Louisiana-Lafayette 80; Siena 68, Western Michigan 62; Iowa 54, Iowa St 53; Georgia Tech 72, Ohio St 58; San Diego St 67, UCSB 62; Texas Tech 66, Nevada 54.
Second round: N Carolina 90, Wyoming 74; Georgetown 67; Providence 58; Temple 61; Rhode Island 53; Minnesota 84, Hawaii 70; St. John's 73, Virginia 63; Alabama-Birmingham 80, Siena 71; Georgia Tech 79, Iowa 78; Texas Tech 57, San Diego St 48.
Third round: Georgetown 79, N Carolina 74; Minnesota 63, Temple 58; St. John's 79, Alabama-Birmingham 71; Texas Tech 80, Georgia Tech 72.
Semifinals: Georgetown 88, Minnesota 74; St. John's 64, Texas Tech 63.
Consolation Game: Texas Tech 71, Minnesota 61.
Championship Game: St. John's 70, Georgetown 67.

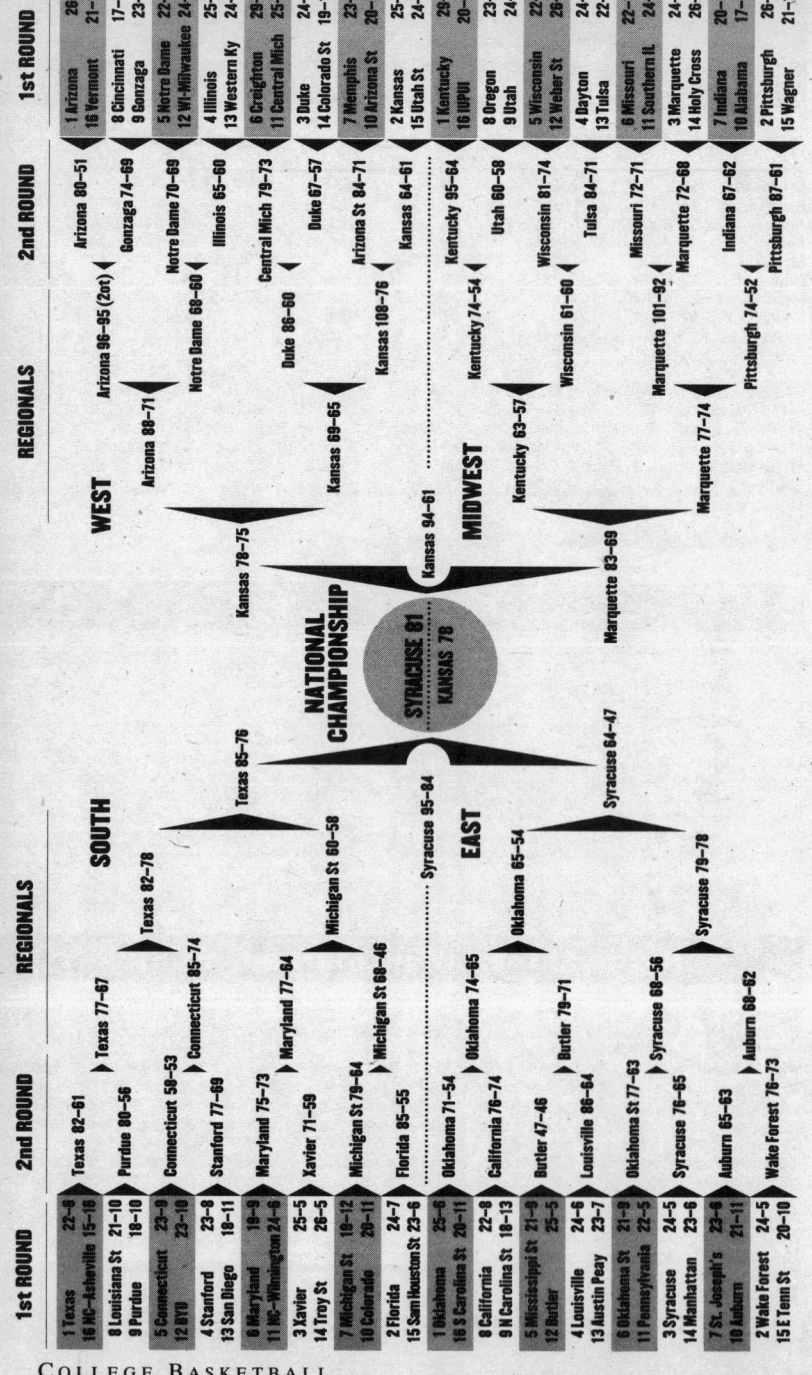

America East

	Conference			All Games		
	W	L	Pct	W	L	Pct
Boston University	13	3	.813	20	11	.645
†Vermont	11	5	.688	21	12	.636
Hartford	10	6	.625	17	13	.567
Binghamton	9	7	.563	14	13	.519
Northeastern	8	8	.500	16	15	.516
Maine	8	8	.500	14	16	.467
Stony Brook	7	9	.438	13	16	.448
Albany	3	13	.188	7	21	.250
New Hampshire	3	13	.188	5	23	.179

Atlantic Coast

	Conference			All Games		
	W	L	Pct	W	L	Pct
Wake Forest	13	3	.813	25	6	.806
†Duke	12	5	.706	26	7	.788
Maryland	11	5	.688	21	10	.677
N Carolina St	9	8	.529	18	13	.581
Georgia Tech	7	9	.438	15	15	.500
N Carolina	6	10	.375	19	16	.528
Virginia	6	10	.375	16	15	.516
Clemson	5	11	.313	15	13	.536
Florida St	4	12	.250	14	15	.483

Atlantic Sun

	Conference			All Games		
	W	L	Pct	W	L	Pct
†Troy St	14	2	.875	26	6	.813
Mercer	14	2	.875	23	6	.793
Central Florida	11	5	.688	21	11	.656
Jacksonville St	10	6	.625	20	9	.690
Samford	9	7	.563	13	15	.464
Georgia St	8	8	.500	14	15	.483
Jacksonville	8	8	.500	13	16	.448
Stetson	4	12	.250	6	20	.231
Florida Atlantic	3	13	.188	7	21	.250
Gardner Webb	2	14	.125	5	24	.172
Campbell	1	15	.063	5	22	.185

Atlantic 10

	Conference			All Games		
	W	L	Pct	W	L	Pct
EAST						
St. Joseph's	12	4	.750	23	7	.767
Rhode Island	10	6	.625	20	11	.645
Temple	10	6	.625	18	16	.514
Massachusetts	6	10	.375	12	18	.400
Fordham	3	13	.188	4	24	.143
St. Bonaventure	1	15	.063	7	22	.241
WEST						
Xavier	15	1	.938	26	6	.813
†Dayton	14	2	.875	25	6	.806
Richmond	10	6	.625	16	13	.552
LaSalle	6	10	.375	13	16	.448
George Washington	5	11	.313	12	17	.414
Duquesne	4	12	.250	10	20	.333

Big East

	Conference			All Games		
	W	L	Pct	W	L	Pct
EAST						
Connecticut	10	6	.625	23	10	.697
Boston College	10	6	.625	19	12	.594
Providence	8	8	.500	18	14	.563
Villanova	8	8	.500	15	16	.484
St. John's	7	9	.438	21	13	.600
Miami (FL)	4	12	.250	11	17	.393
Virginia Tech	4	12	.250	11	18	.379
WEST						
Syracuse	13	3	.813	30	5	.857
†Pittsburgh	13	3	.813	28	5	.848
Notre Dame	10	6	.625	24	10	.706
Seton Hall	10	6	.625	17	13	.567
Georgetown	6	10	.375	19	15	.543
W Virginia	5	11	.313	14	15	.483
Rutgers	4	12	.250	12	16	.429

Big Sky

	Conference			All Games		
	W	L	Pct	W	L	Pct
†Weber St	14	0	1.000	26	6	.813
Eastern Washington	9	5	.643	18	13	.581
Idaho St	7	7	.500	15	14	.517
Montana	7	7	.500	13	17	.433
Northern Arizona	6	8	.429	15	13	.517
Sacramento St	5	9	.357	12	17	.414
Montana St	5	9	.357	11	16	.393
Portland St	3	11	.214	5	22	.185

Big South

	Conference			All Games		
	W	L	Pct	W	L	Pct
Winthrop	11	3	.786	20	10	.667
Charleston Southern	8	6	.571	14	14	.500
Liberty	8	6	.571	14	15	.483
Elon	8	6	.571	12	15	.444
†UNC-Asheville	7	7	.500	15	17	.469
Radford	6	8	.429	10	20	.333
Coastal Carolina	5	9	.357	13	15	.464
High Point	3	11	.214	7	20	.259
Birm'ham Southern	0	0	—	19	9	.679

Big 10

	Conference			All Games		
	W	L	Pct	W	L	Pct
Wisconsin	12	4	.750	24	8	.750
†Illinois	11	5	.688	25	7	.781
Purdue	10	6	.625	19	11	.633
Michigan St	10	6	.625	22	13	.629
Michigan	10	6	.625	17	13	.567
Indiana	8	8	.500	21	13	.618
Minnesota	8	8	.500	19	14	.559
Ohio St	7	9	.433	17	15	.531
Iowa	7	9	.438	17	14	.515
Northwestern	3	13	.188	12	17	.414
Penn St	2	14	.125	7	21	.250

† Conference tourney winner.
Note: Standings based on regular-season conference play only; overall records include all tournament play.

Big 12

	Conference			All Games		
	W	L	Pct	W	L	Pct
Kansas	14	2	.875	30	8	.789
Texas	13	3	.813	26	7	.788
†Oklahoma	12	4	.750	27	7	.794
Oklahoma St	10	6	.625	22	10	.688
Colorado	9	7	.563	20	12	.625
Missouri	9	7	.563	22	11	.667
Texas Tech	6	10	.375	22	13	.629
Texas A&M	6	10	.375	14	14	.500
Iowa St	5	11	.313	17	14	.531
Baylor	5	11	.313	14	14	.500
Kansas St	4	12	.250	13	17	.433
Nebraska	3	13	.188	11	19	.367

Big West

	Conference			All Games		
	W	L	Pct	W	L	Pct
Santa Barbara	14	4	.778	18	14	.563
UC–Irvine	13	5	.722	20	9	.690
†Utah St	12	6	.667	23	9	.719
Cal Poly	10	8	.556	16	13	.552
Idaho	9	9	.500	13	15	.464
Cal St–Northridge	8	10	.444	14	15	.483
Cal St–Fullerton	8	10	.444	10	19	.345
Pacific	7	11	.389	12	16	.429
UC–Riverside	5	13	.278	6	18	.250
Long Beach St	4	14	.222	5	22	.185

Colonial

	Conference			All Games		
	W	L	Pct	W	L	Pct
†UNC-Wilmington	15	3	.833	24	7	.774
Va. Commonwealth	12	6	.667	18	10	.643
Drexel	12	8	.667	19	12	.613
George Mason	11	7	.611	16	12	.571
Delaware	9	9	.500	15	14	.517
Old Dominion	9	9	.500	12	15	.444
James Madison	8	10	.444	13	17	.433
William & Mary	7	11	.389	12	16	.429
Hofstra	6	12	.333	8	21	.276
Towson	1	17	.056	4	24	.143

Conference USA

	Conference			All Games		
AMERICAN	W	L	Pct	W	L	Pct
Marquette	14	2	.875	27	6	.818
†Louisville	11	5	.688	25	7	.781
Cincinnati	9	7	.563	17	12	.586
St. Louis	9	7	.563	16	14	.533
DePaul	8	8	.500	16	13	.552
Charlotte	8	8	.500	13	16	.448
E Carolina	3	13	.188	12	15	.444
NATIONAL						
Memphis	13	3	.813	23	7	.767
AL-Birmingham	8	8	.500	21	13	.618
Tulane	8	8	.500	16	15	.516
S Florida	7	9	.438	15	14	.517
Houston	6	10	.375	8	20	.286
Southern Miss	5	11	.313	13	16	.448
Texas Christian	3	13	.188	9	19	.321

Horizon League

	Conference			All Games		
	W	L	Pct	W	L	Pct
Butler	14	2	.875	27	6	.818
†WI-Milwaukee	13	3	.813	24	8	.750
IL-Chicago	12	4	.750	21	9	.700
Detroit	9	7	.563	18	12	.600
Loyola Chicago	9	7	.563	15	16	.484
Wright St	4	12	.250	10	18	.357
WI–Green Bay	4	12	.250	10	20	.333
Youngstown St	4	12	.250	9	20	.310
Cleveland St	3	13	.188	8	22	.267

Ivy League

	Conference			All Games		
	W	L	Pct	W	L	Pct
Pennsylvania	14	0	1.000	22	6	.786
Brown	12	2	.857	17	12	.586
Princeton	10	4	.714	16	11	.593
Yale	8	6	.571	14	13	.519
Harvard	4	10	.286	12	15	.444
Cornell	4	10	.286	9	18	.333
Dartmouth	4	10	.286	8	19	.296
Columbia	0	14	.000	2	25	.074

Metro Atlantic

	Conference			All Games		
	W	L	Pct	W	L	Pct
†Manhattan	14	4	.778	23	7	.767
Fairfield	13	5	.722	19	12	.613
Siena	12	6	.667	21	11	.636
Niagara	12	6	.667	17	12	.586
Iona	11	7	.611	17	12	.586
Marist	8	10	.444	13	16	.448
Rider	7	11	.389	12	16	.429
Canisius	6	12	.333	10	18	.357
St. Peter's	6	12	.333	10	19	.345
Loyola (MD)	1	17	.056	4	24	.143

Mid-American

	Conference			All Games		
EAST	W	L	Pct	W	L	Pct
Kent St	12	6	.667	21	10	.677
Miami (OH)	11	7	.611	13	15	.464
Akron	9	9	.500	14	14	.500
Marshall	9	9	.500	14	15	.483
Ohio	8	10	.444	14	16	.467
Buffalo	2	16	.111	5	23	.179
WEST						
†Central Michigan	14	4	.778	25	7	.781
Northern Illinois	11	7	.611	17	14	.548
Western Michigan	10	8	.556	20	11	.625
Eastern Michigan	8	10	.444	14	14	.500
Bowling Green	8	10	.444	13	16	.448
Ball St	8	10	.444	12	17	.414
Toledo	7	11	.389	13	16	.448

Mid-Continent

	Conference			All Games		
	W	L	Pct	W	L	Pct
Valparaiso	12	2	.857	20	11	.645
Oakland	10	4	.714	17	11	.607
†Indiana-Purdue	10	4	.714	20	14	.588
Oral Roberts	9	5	.643	18	10	.643
MO–Kansas City	7	7	.500	9	20	.310
Southern Utah	5	9	.357	11	17	.393
Western Illinois	3	11	.214	7	21	.250
Chicago St	0	14	.000	3	27	.100

Mid-Eastern Athletic

	Conference			All Games		
	W	L	Pct	W	L	Pct
†S Carolina St	15	3	.833	20	11	.645
Hampton	13	5	.722	19	11	.633
Delaware St	13	5	.722	15	12	.556
Florida A&M	11	7	.611	17	12	.586
Coppin St	11	7	.611	11	17	.393
Norfolk St	10	8	.556	14	15	.483
Howard	9	9	.500	13	17	.433
Morgan St	6	12	.333	7	22	.241
Bethune Cookman	5	13	.278	8	22	.267
MD-Eastern Shore	5	13	.278	5	23	.179
N Carolina A&T	1	17	.056	1	26	.037

Missouri Valley

	Conference			All Games		
	W	L	Pct	W	L	Pct
Southern Illinois	16	2	.889	24	7	.774
†Creighton	15	3	.833	29	5	.853
Wichita St	12	6	.667	18	12	.600
SW Missouri St	12	6	.667	17	12	.586
Evansville	8	10	.444	12	16	.429
Bradley	8	10	.444	12	18	.400
Northern Iowa	7	11	.389	11	17	.393
Drake	5	13	.278	10	20	.333
Illinois St	5	13	.278	8	21	.276
Indiana St	2	16	.111	7	24	.226

Mountain West

	Conference			All Games		
	W	L	Pct	W	L	Pct
Utah	11	3	.786	25	8	.758
Brigham Young	11	3	.786	23	9	.719
Nevada–Las Vegas	8	6	.571	21	11	.656
Wyoming	8	6	.571	21	11	.656
San Diego St	6	8	.429	16	14	.533
†Colorado St	5	9	.357	19	14	.576
New Mexico	4	10	.286	10	18	.357
Air Force	3	11	.214	12	16	.429

Northeast

	Conference			All Games		
	W	L	Pct	W	L	Pct
†Wagner	14	4	.778	21	11	.656
Monmouth (NJ)	13	5	.722	15	13	.536
Central Conn	12	6	.667	15	13	.536
Quinnipiac	10	8	.556	17	12	.586
St. Francis (PA)	10	8	.556	14	14	.500
Fairleigh Dickinson	9	9	.500	15	14	.517
St. Francis (NY)	9	9	.500	14	16	.467
Robert Morris	7	11	.389	10	17	.370
LIU–Brooklyn	7	11	.389	9	19	.321
Mt. St. Mary's	6	12	.333	11	16	.407
Sacred Heart	6	12	.333	8	21	.276
MD-Balt County	5	13	.278	7	20	.259

Ohio Valley

	Conference			All Games		
	W	L	Pct	W	L	Pct
†Austin Peay	13	3	.813	23	8	.742
Morehead St	13	3	.813	20	9	.690
Tennessee Tech	11	5	.688	20	12	.625
Murray St	9	7	.563	17	12	.586
Eastern Illinois	9	7	.563	14	15	.483
Tennessee-Martin	7	9	.438	14	14	.500
Eastern Kentucky	5	11	.313	11	17	.393
SE Missouri St	5	11	.313	11	19	.367
Tennessee St	0	16	.000	2	25	.074

Pac 10

	Conference			All Games		
	W	L	Pct	W	L	Pct
Arizona	17	1	.944	28	4	.875
Stanford	14	4	.778	24	9	.727
California	13	5	.722	22	9	.710
Arizona St	11	7	.611	20	12	.625
†Oregon	10	8	.556	23	10	.697
Oregon St	6	12	.333	13	15	.464
Southern California	6	12	.333	13	17	.433
UCLA	6	12	.333	10	19	.345
Washington	5	13	.278	10	17	.370
Washington St	2	16	.111	7	20	.259

Patriot League

	Conference			All Games		
EAST	W	L	Pct	W	L	Pct
†Holy Cross	13	1	.929	26	5	.839
American	9	5	.643	16	14	.533
Colgate	9	5	.643	14	14	.500
Lehigh	8	6	.571	16	12	.571
Bucknell	7	7	.500	14	15	.483
Lafayette	6	8	.429	13	16	.448
Navy	4	10	.286	8	20	.286
Army	0	14	.000	5	22	.185

†Conference tourney winner.

Southeastern

EAST	Conference			All Games		
	W	L	Pct	W	L	Pct
†Kentucky	16	0	1.000	32	4	.889
Florida	12	4	.750	25	8	.758
Georgia	11	5	.688	19	8	.704
Tennessee	9	7	.563	17	12	.586
S Carolina	5	11	.313	12	16	.429
Vanderbilt	3	13	.188	11	18	.379
WEST						
Mississippi St	9	7	.563	21	10	.677
Louisiana St	8	8	.500	21	11	.656
Auburn	8	8	.500	22	12	.647
Alabama	7	9	.438	17	12	.586
Mississippi	4	12	.250	14	15	.483
Arkansas	4	12	.250	9	19	.321

Southern

NORTH	Conference			All Games		
	W	L	Pct	W	L	Pct
Appalachian St	11	5	.688	19	10	.655
†E Tennessee St	11	5	.688	20	11	.645
Davidson	11	5	.688	17	10	.630
Western Carolina	6	10	.375	9	19	.321
Virginia Military	3	13	.188	10	20	.333
WEST						
Charleston	13	3	.813	25	8	.758
TN-Chattanooga	11	5	.688	21	9	.700
Georgia Southern	8	8	.500	16	13	.552
Wofford	8	8	.500	14	15	.483
Furman	8	8	.500	14	17	.452
The Citadel	3	13	.188	8	20	.286

Southland

	Conference			All Games		
	W	L	Pct	W	L	Pct
†Sam Houston St	17	3	.850	23	7	.767
Stephen F. Austin	16	4	.800	21	8	.724
Texas-Arlington	13	7	.650	16	13	.552
SW Texas St	11	9	.550	17	12	.586
McNeese St	10	10	.500	15	14	.517
Lamar	10	10	.500	13	14	.481
Louisiana-Monroe	10	10	.500	12	16	.429
SE Louisiana	9	11	.450	11	16	.407
Texas–San Antonio	7	13	.350	10	17	.370
Northwestern St	6	14	.300	6	21	.222
Nicholls St	1	19	.050	3	25	.107

Southwestern Athletic

	Conference			All Games		
	W	L	Pct	W	L	Pct
Prairie View	14	4	.778	17	12	.586
Mississippi Valley St	13	5	.722	15	14	.517
†Texas Southern	11	7	.611	18	13	.581
Alabama St	11	7	.611	14	15	.483
Alcorn St	10	8	.556	14	19	.424
Grambling	9	9	.500	12	18	.400
Jackson St	9	9	.500	10	18	.357
Southern	5	13	.278	9	20	.310
Alabama A&M	4	14	.222	8	19	.296
Arkansas–Pine Bluff	4	14	.222	4	24	.143

Sun Belt

EAST	Conference			All Games		
	W	L	Pct	W	L	Pct
†Western Kentucky	12	2	.857	24	9	.727
Midd Tenn St	9	5	.643	16	14	.533
AR–Little Rock	8	6	.571	19	11	.633
Arkansas St	6	8	.429	13	15	.464
Florida Int'l	1	13	.071	8	21	.276
WEST						
La.-Lafayette	12	3	.800	20	10	.667
New Mexico St	9	6	.600	20	9	.690
Denver	7	8	.467	17	15	.531
New Orleans	7	8	.467	15	14	.517
S Alabama	7	8	.467	14	14	.500
N Texas	2	13	.133	7	21	.250

West Coast

	Conference			All Games		
	W	L	Pct	W	L	Pct
Gonzaga	12	2	.857	24	9	.727
†San Diego	10	4	.714	18	12	.600
San Francisco	9	5	.643	15	14	.517
Pepperdine	7	7	.500	15	13	.536
St. Mary's (CA)	6	8	.429	15	15	.500
Santa Clara	4	10	.286	13	15	.464
Portland	4	10	.286	11	17	.393
Loyola Marymount	4	10	.286	11	20	.355

Western Athletic

	Conference			All Games		
	W	L	Pct	W	L	Pct
Fresno St	13	5	.722	20	8	.714
†Tulsa	12	6	.667	23	10	.697
Rice	11	7	.611	19	10	.655
Southern Methodist	11	7	.611	17	13	.567
Nevada	11	7	.611	18	14	.563
Hawaii	9	9	.500	18	13	.563
Louisiana Tech	9	9	.500	12	15	.444
Boise St	7	11	.389	13	16	.448
San Jose St	4	14	.222	7	21	.250
Texas–El Paso	3	15	.167	6	24	.200

Independents

	All Games		
	W	L	Pct
Centenary	14	14	.500
TX A&M–Corpus Christi	14	15	.483
TX–Pan American	10	20	.333
IU–PU Fort Wayne	9	21	.300
Lipscomb	8	20	.286
Morris Brown	8	20	.286
Savannah St	3	24	.111

†Conference tourney winner.

Scoring

	Class	GP	FG	3FG	FT	Pts	Avg
Ruben Douglas, New Mexico	Sr	28	218	94	253	783	28.0
Henry Domercant, Eastern Illinois	Sr	29	252	84	222	810	27.9
Mike Helms, Oakland	Jr	28	241	74	196	752	26.9
Michael Watson, Missouri–Kansas City	Jr	29	247	118	128	740	25.5
Troy Bell, Boston College	Sr	31	224	106	227	781	25.2
Keydren Clark, St. Peter's	Fr	29	231	109	151	722	24.9
Luis Flores, Manhattan	Jr	30	231	56	221	739	24.6
Chris Williams, Ball St	Sr	30	226	64	220	736	24.5
Mike Sweetney, Georgetown	Jr	34	264	0	248	776	22.8
Kevin Martin, Western Carolina	So	24	161	50	174	546	22.8
Willie Green, Detroit	Sr	30	244	37	153	678	22.6
Ricky Minard, Morehead St	Jr	29	225	54	149	653	22.5
Chris Kaman, Central Michigan	Jr	31	244	0	206	694	22.4
Seth Doliboa, Wright St	Jr	28	217	67	124	625	22.3
Marcus Hatten, St. John's (NY)	Sr	34	277	56	146	756	22.2
Carmelo Anthony, Syracuse	Fr	35	277	56	168	778	22.2
Andrew Wisniewski, Centenary (LA)	Jr	28	207	53	150	617	22.0
Andre Emmett, Texas Tech	Jr	34	297	11	136	741	21.8
Ron Williamson, Howard	Sr	30	197	104	152	650	21.7
Julius Jenkins, Georgia Southern	Sr	27	213	74	84	584	21.6
Darshan Luckie, St. Francis (PA)	Fr	28	201	46	157	605	21.6
Dwyane Wade, Marquette	Jr	33	251	14	194	710	21.5
Brandon Hunter, Ohio	Sr	30	217	11	199	644	21.5
Jermaine Hall, Wagner	Sr	32	273	7	133	686	21.4
Marques Green, St. Bonaventure	Jr	27	182	94	116	574	21.3

FIELD-GOAL PERCENTAGE

	Class	GP	FG	FGA	Pct
Adam Mark, Belmont	Jr	28	199	297	67.0
Ricky White, Maine	Sr	24	131	198	66.2
Matt Nelson, Colorado St	So	31	205	319	64.3
Armond Williams, IL-Chicago	Jr	30	168	263	63.9
Michael Harris, Rice	So	28	172	276	62.3
Chris Kaman, Central Michigan	Jr	31	244	392	62.2
David Gruber, Northern Iowa	Jr	28	141	231	61.0
Ike Diogu, Arizona St	Fr	32	209	344	60.8
Omar Bartlett, Jacksonville St	Sr	30	178	293	60.8
Jason Keep, San Diego	Sr	30	195	323	60.4

Note: Minimum 5 made per game.

FREE-THROW PERCENTAGE

	Class	GP	FT	FTA	Pct
Steve Drabyn, Belmont	Jr	29	78	82	95.1
Matt Logie, Lehigh	Sr	28	91	96	94.8
Hollis Price, Oklahoma	Sr	34	130	140	92.9
Brian Dux, Canisius	Sr	28	115	125	92.0
J.J. Redick, Duke	Fr	33	102	111	91.9
Tim Parker, Chattanooga	Sr	30	78	85	91.8
Dwayne Byfield, Monmouth	So	28	72	79	91.1
Gerry McNamara, Syracuse	Fr	35	90	99	90.9
Kyle Korver, Creighton	Sr	34	109	120	90.8
Jeb Ivey, Portland St	Sr	27	69	76	90.8

Note: Minimum 2.5 made per game.

REBOUNDS

	Class	GP	Reb	Avg
Brandon Hunter, Ohio	Sr	30	378	12.6
Amien Hicks, Morris Brown	Sr	24	298	12.4
Adam Sonn, Belmont	Sr	29	352	12.1
Chris Kaman, Central Michigan	Jr	31	373	12.0
David West, Xavier	Sr	32	379	11.8
Louis Truscott, Houston	Sr	28	315	11.3
Emeka Okafor, Connecticut	So	33	370	11.2
Kenny Adeleke, Hofstra	So	29	320	11.0
James Singleton, Murray St	Sr	29	320	11.0
James Thomas, Texas	Jr	33	363	11.0

ASSISTS

	Class	GP	A	Avg
Martell Bailey, IL-Chicago	Jr	30	244	8.1
Marques Green, St. Bonaventure	Jr	27	216	8.0
T.J. Ford, Texas	So	33	254	7.7
Elliott Prasse-Freeman, Harvard	Sr	27	207	7.7
Antawn Doby, Long Island	Sr	26	193	7.4
Richard Little, VMI	Jr	30	216	7.2
Steve Blake, Maryland	Sr	31	221	7.1
Chris Thomas, Notre Dame	So	34	236	6.9
Raymond Felton, N Carolina	Fr	35	236	6.7
Luke Ridnour, Oregon	Jr	33	218	6.6

*Includes games played in tournaments.

THREE-POINT FIELD-GOAL PERCENTAGE

	Class	GP	FG	FGA	Pct
Jeff Schiffner, Pennsylvania	Jr	28	74	150	49.3
Kyle Korver, Creighton	Sr	34	129	269	48.0
Terrence Woods, Florida A&M	Jr	28	139	304	45.7
Chez Marks, Morehead St	Sr	29	82	180	45.6
Tyson Dorsey, Samford	Jr	27	75	165	45.5
Tim Keller, Air Force	So	28	78	173	45.1
Pat Carroll, St. Joseph's	So	30	76	169	45.0
Dedrick Dye, Wagner	Sr	32	96	217	44.2
Jimmy Boykin, Coppin St	Jr	28	72	163	44.2
Brett Blizzard, UNC-Wilmington	Sr	31	109	247	44.1

Note: Minimum 1.5 made per game.

BLOCKED SHOTS

	Class	GP	BS	Avg
Emeka Okafor, Connecticut	So	33	156	4.7
Nick Billings, Binghamton	So	27	117	4.3
Justin Rowe, Maine	Sr	25	105	4.2
Deng Gai, Fairfield	So	25	96	3.8
Robert Battle, Drexel	Sr	31	116	3.7
Kyle Davis, Auburn	Jr	34	124	3.6
Kendrick Moore, Oral Roberts	Sr	28	94	3.4
David Harrison, Colorado	So	32	106	3.3
Mike Sweetney, Georgetown	Jr	34	109	3.2
Chris Kaman, Central Michigan	Jr	31	98	3.2

THREE-POINT FIELD GOALS MADE PER GAME

	Class	GP	FG	Avg
Terrence Woods, Florida A&M	Jr	28	139	5.0
Demon Brown, Charlotte	Jr	29	137	4.7
Michael Watson, MO–Kansas City	Jr	29	118	4.1
Brad Boyd, Louisiana-Lafayette	Jr	27	104	3.9
Kyle Korver, Creighton	Sr	34	129	3.8
Keydren Clark, St. Peter's	Fr	29	109	3.8
Shawn Hall, Appalachian St	Sr	28	103	3.7

Five tied with 3.5

STEALS

	Class	GP	S	Avg
Alexis McMillan, Stetson	Sr	22	87	4.0
Zakee Wadood, E Tenn St	Jr	29	93	3.2
Jay Heard, Jacksonville St	Sr	30	95	3.2
Eric Bush, Alabama-Birmingham	Sr	34	106	3.1
Marcus Hatten, St. John's	Sr	34	100	2.9
Rawle Marshall, Oakland	So	28	80	2.9
Marcus Banks, UNLV	Sr	32	91	2.8
Tim Pickett, Florida St	Jr	29	82	2.8
Demetrice Williams, S Alabama	Sr	28	76	2.7
Robby Collum, Western Michigan	Sr	31	83	2.7

Single-Game Highs

POINTS

54......Michael Watson, Missouri–Kansas City, Feb 22 (vs Oral Roberts)
53 .....Antawn Doby, Long Island, Feb 22 (vs St. Francis)
52 .....Ron Williamson, Howard, Jan 21 (vs N Carolina A&T)

REBOUNDS

26 .....Brandon Hunter, Ohio, Jan 8 (vs Akron)
24......Erroyl Bing, E Carolina, Jan 25 (vs S Florida)
24 .....Brandon Hunter, Ohio, Dec 31 (vs St. Bonaventure)

ASSISTS

17 .....Antawn Doby, Long Island, Dec 15 (vs St. Francis [NY])
17......Zakee Smith, Cal St–Fullerton, Dec 4 (vs Pepperdine)
16 .....Malcolm Campbell, Alabama St, Feb 10 (vs Mississippi Valley)
16 .....Blake Stepp, Gonzaga, Dec 20 (vs Long Beach St)

THREE-POINT FIELD GOALS

12 .....Terrence Woods, Florida A&M, Mar 1 (vs Coppin St)
11 .....Terrence Woods, Florida A&M, Feb 1 (vs N Carolina A&T)
11 .....Ron Williamson, Howard, Jan 21 (vs N Carolina A&T)

STEALS

10 .....Marcus Hatten, St. John's (NY), Feb 18 (vs Syracuse)
10 .....Joseph Frazier, Cal St–Northridge, Dec 7 (vs Bethany [CA])
10 .....Rawle Marshall, Oakland, Dec 2 (vs Texas A&M)

BLOCKED SHOTS

11......David Harrison, Colorado, Mar 8 (vs Nebraska)
11 .....Jordan Cornette, Notre Dame, Nov 17 (vs Belmont)

Four tied with 10.

NCAA Men's Division I Team Leaders

SCORING OFFENSE

	GP	W	L	Pts	Avg
Arizona	32	28	4	2725	85.2
Appalachian St	29	19	10	2434	83.9
Kansas	38	30	8	3141	82.7
E Tenn St	31	20	11	2543	82.0
Louisville	32	25	7	2612	81.6
Oregon	33	23	10	2689	81.5
Morehead St	29	20	9	2355	81.2
Chattanooga	30	21	9	2435	81.2
Duke	33	26	7	2677	81.1
Davidson	27	17	10	2180	80.7

SCORING DEFENSE

	GP	W	L	Pts	Avg
Air Force	28	12	16	1596	57.0
Miami (OH)	28	13	15	1643	58.7
Holy Cross	31	26	5	1821	58.7
Bucknell	29	14	15	1706	58.8
Pittsburgh	33	28	5	1955	59.2
Wisconsin	32	24	8	1899	59.3
St. Joseph's	30	23	7	1784	59.5
Mississippi St	31	21	10	1852	59.7

Three tied at 60.0.

SCORING MARGIN

	Off	Def	Mar
Kansas	82.7	66.9	15.8
Pittsburgh	74.9	59.2	15.7
Arizona	85.2	70.7	14.5
Creighton	79.1	64.8	14.3
Kentucky	77.3	64.1	13.1
Illinois	74.6	61.6	13.1
Maryland	79.7	66.7	13.0
Louisville	81.6	68.7	13.0
Holy Cross	70.3	58.7	11.6

Two tied with 11.5.

FIELD-GOAL PERCENTAGE

	FG	FGA	Pct
Morehead St	854	1674	51.0
Pittsburgh	893	1766	50.6
Colorado St	876	1733	50.5
Central Michigan	864	1714	50.4
Creighton	974	1956	49.8
Kansas	1182	2393	49.4
Stephen F. Austin	753	1534	49.1
Kentucky	1026	2102	48.8
Maine	827	1697	48.7
Akron	761	1562	48.7

FIELD-GOAL PERCENTAGE DEFENSE

	FG	FGA	Pct
St. Joseph's	609	1639	37.2
Illinois	657	1741	37.7
Maryland	704	1864	37.8
Connecticut	817	2157	37.9
Syracuse	878	2253	39.0
Pittsburgh	682	1750	39.0
Florida St	650	1662	39.1
Sam Houston St	676	1727	39.1
Lamar	621	1577	39.4
Oklahoma St	699	1775	39.4

FREE-THROW PERCENTAGE

	FT	FTA	Pct
Manhattan	560	711	78.8
Providence	496	636	77.9
Marist	442	568	77.8
Davidson	413	531	77.8
Oregon	530	685	77.4
Marquette	585	759	77.1
N Carolina St	488	634	77.0
Marshall	468	609	76.8
Eastern Illinois	453	590	76.8
Central Michigan	601	789	76.2

THREE-POINT FIELD GOALS MADE PER GAME

	GP	FG	Avg
Mississippi Valley	29	299	10.3
St. Bonaventure	27	271	10.1
Davidson	27	269	10.0
Troy St	32	312	9.8
Missouri–Kansas City	29	272	9.4
Charleston	33	308	9.3
Samford	28	258	9.2
Baylor	28	254	9.1
Pennsylvania	28	251	9.0
Oregon	33	291	8.8

REBOUNDING MARGIN

	GP	REB	Opp REB	Margin /G
Wake Forest	31	1292	993	+9.6
Kansas	38	1589	1288	7.9
Holy Cross	31	1131	887	7.9
Vermont	33	1295	1052	7.4
Utah St	33	1154	923	7.0
Texas	33	1386	1158	6.9
DePaul	29	1075	875	6.9
Davidson	27	1110	926	6.8
Mercer	29	1171	977	6.7
Pittsburgh	33	1203	984	6.6

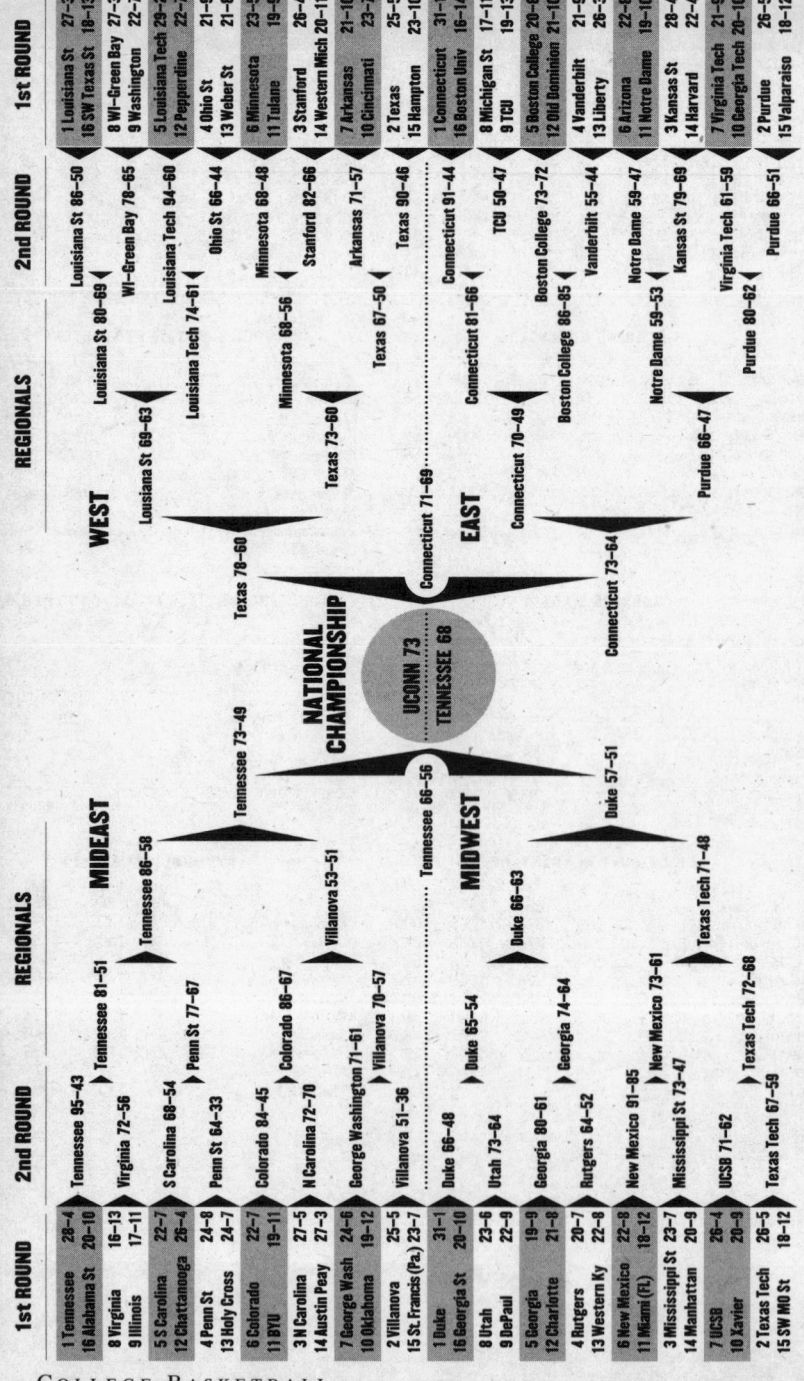

1st ROUND

1 Tennessee 28–4
16 Alabama St 20–10
8 Virginia 16–13
9 Illinois 17–11
5 S Carolina 22–7
12 Chattanooga 26–4
4 Penn St 24–8
13 Holy Cross 24–7
6 Colorado 22–7
11 BYU 19–11
3 N Carolina 27–5
14 Austin Peay 23–7
7 George Wash 24–6
10 Oklahoma 19–12
2 Villanova 25–5
15 St.Francis (Pa.) 23–7

1 Duke 31–1
16 Georgia St 20–10
8 Utah 23–6
9 DePaul 22–9
5 Georgia 19–9
12 Charlotte 21–8
4 Rutgers 20–7
13 Western Ky 22–8
6 New Mexico 22–8
11 Miami (Fl) 18–12
3 Mississippi St 23–7
14 Manhattan 20–9
7 UCSB 26–4
10 Xavier 20–9
2 Texas Tech 26–5
15 SW MO St 18–12

2nd ROUND

Tennessee 95–43
Tennessee 81–51
Virginia 72–56
S Carolina 68–54
Penn St 77–67
Penn St 64–33
Colorado 84–45
Colorado 86–67
N Carolina 72–70
George Washington 71–61
Villanova 70–57
Villanova 51–36

Duke 66–48
Duke 65–54
Utah 73–64
Georgia 80–61
Georgia 74–64
Rutgers 64–52
New Mexico 91–85
New Mexico 73–61
Mississippi St 73–47
Texas Tech 72–68
UCSB 71–62
Texas Tech 67–59

REGIONALS

MIDEAST

Tennessee 86–58

Villanova 53–51

Tennessee 73–49

MIDWEST

Duke 66–63

Texas Tech 71–48

Duke 57–51

NATIONAL CHAMPIONSHIP

Tennessee 66–56

UCONN 73
TENNESSEE 68

REGIONALS

WEST

Louisiana St 80–69

Louisiana Tech 74–61

Louisiana St 69–63

Texas 73–60

Texas 78–60

EAST

Connecticut 81–66

Boston College 86–85

Connecticut 70–49

Purdue 66–47

Connecticut 71–69

Connecticut 73–64

2nd ROUND

Louisiana St 86–50
WI–Green Bay 78–65
Louisiana Tech 94–60
Ohio St 66–44
Minnesota 68–48
Stanford 82–66
Arkansas 71–57
Texas 90–46

Connecticut 91–44
TCU 50–47
Boston College 73–72
Vanderbilt 55–44
Notre Dame 59–47
Kansas St 79–69
Virginia Tech 61–59
Purdue 66–51

1st ROUND

1 Louisiana St 27–3
16 SW Texas St 18–13
8 WI–Green Bay 27–3
9 Washington 22–7
5 Louisiana Tech 29–2
12 Pepperdine 22–7
4 Ohio St 21–9
13 Weber St 21–8
6 Minnesota 23–5
11 Tulane 19–9
3 Stanford 26–4
14 Western Mich 20–11
7 Arkansas 21–10
10 Cincinnati 23–7
2 Texas 25–5
15 Hampton 23–10

1 Connecticut 31–1
16 Boston Univ 16–14
8 Michigan St 17–11
9 TCU 19–13
5 Boston College 20–8
12 Old Dominion 21–10
4 Vanderbilt 21–9
13 Liberty 26–3
6 Arizona 22–8
11 Notre Dame 19–10
3 Kansas St 28–4
14 Harvard 22–4
7 Virginia Tech 21–9
10 Georgia Tech 20–10
2 Purdue 26–5
15 Valparaiso 18–12

Connecticut 73

Connecticut	Min	FG M-A	FT M-A	Reb O-T	A	PF	TP
Taurasi	37	8-15	8-8	1-4	1	2	28
Conlon	39	3-7	2-4	0-4	6	2	11
Moore	35	2-5	0-0	1-4	3	2	4
Turner	21	5-7	0-0	1-1	1	3	10
Strother	32	6-11	2-2	0-3	3	2	17
Battle	12	0-3	0-0	0-0	1	0	0
Crockett	24	1-1	1-2	2-6	0	5	3
Totals	200	25-49	13-16	5-22	15	16	73

Percentages: FG—.510, FT—.813. 3-pt goals: 10–21, .476 (Taurasi 4–9, Conlon 3–5, Strother 3–7). Team rebounds: 2. Blocked shots: 1 (Taurasi). Turnovers: 11 (Taurasi 3, Moore 3, Turner 2, Strother 1, Battle 1, Crockett 1). Steals: 4 (Conlon 2, Battle 2).

Halftime: Connecticut 35, Tennessee 30.
A: 28,210. Officials: Mattingly, Barlow, Dean.

Tennessee 68

Tennessee	Min	FG M-A	FT M-A	Reb O-T	A	PF	TP
Butts	17	2-4	0-0	1-1	2	3	4
G. Jackson	35	6-14	3-6	6-9	4	3	15
Lawson	40	5-13	5-5	1-5	5	1	18
Moore	25	2-4	0-0	1-2	1	1	5
Ely	25	3-6	0-0	0-2	0	1	6
Zolman	11	0-0	0-0	1-2	0	2	0
B. Jackson	20	4-10	2-2	1-5	0	3	13
Robinson	17	1-2	1-6	4-8	1	2	3
McDaniel	6	1-3	0-0	1-2	0	2	2
Fluker	4	1-1	0-0	1-1	0	0	2
Totals	200	25-57	11-19	20-40	13	18	68

Percentages: FG—.439, FT—.579. 3-pt goals: 7–18, .389 (G. Jackson 0-2, Lawson 3-8, Moore 1-1, B. Jackson). Team rebounds: 3. Blocked shots: 1 (G. Jackson). Turnovers: 15 (Butts 1, G. Jackson 2, Lawson 3, Moore 1, Ely 2, Zolman 1, B. Jackson 3, Robinson 1, Team 1). Steals: 7 (Butts 1, Lawson 1, Morre 3, Ely 1, Zolman 1).

SCORING

Player and Team	Class	GP	TFG	3FG	FT	Pts	Avg
Chandi Jones, Houston	Jr	28	275	52	168	770	27.5
Molly Creamer, Bucknell	Sr	28	239	62	219	759	27.1
La Toya Thomas, Mississippi St	Sr	31	297	18	182	794	25.6
Tiffany Webb, Wright St	So	28	246	50	132	674	24.1
Kelly Mazzante, Penn St	Jr	35	292	98	155	837	23.9
Jocelyn Penn, S Carolina	Sr	30	282	14	138	716	23.9
Allison Curtin, Tulsa	Sr	30	231	56	174	692	23.1
Alana Beard, Duke	Jr	37	294	24	201	813	22.0
Shanika Freeman, Jacksonville St	So	29	212	21	184	629	21.7
Hana Peljito, Harvard	Jr	24	178	24	130	510	21.3
Shalayna Johnson, Uof Md Baltimore County	Sr	23	179	72	53	483	21.0
Tamara James, Miami (FL)	Fr	31	238	19	155	650	21.0
Nikki Reddick, Coastal Carolina	Jr	27	171	83	135	560	20.7
Lindsay Whalen, Minnesota	Jr	31	225	34	155	639	20.6
Tamara Bowie, Ball St	Sr	30	237	28	116	618	20.6

Sorry, Wrong Number

Looking into wire transfers received by Louisville center Marvin Stone, NCAA investigators mistakenly called 53-year-old Marvin Stone, a project engineer in Atlanta. The elder Stone (no relation) received a $450 transfer from a relative in Lousiville on Nov. 15, 2002, which prompted a call from NCAA representative Deana Garner. "I had a thousand things running through my head," said Stone. "All I do is watch college basketball. What did the NCAA want with me? You're not going to confuse us. He's 6' 10", and I'm 5' 7"."

FIELD-GOAL PERCENTAGE

Player and Team	Class	GP	FG	FGA	Pct
Courtney Coleman, Ohio St	Sr	32	184	278	66.2
Janel McCarville, Minnesota	So	30	155	236	65.7
C. Anderson, Vanderbilt	Sr	32	217	341	63.6
Gerlonda Hardin, Austin Peay	Jr	31	198	312	63.5
Jocelyn Penn, S Carolina	Sr	30	282	449	62.8
Beth Swink, St. Francis (PA)	So	31	199	318	62.6
Michelle Smith, UAB	Sr	26	151	242	62.4
Shawntinice Polk, Arizona	Fr	31	218	358	60.9
Liene Jansone, Siena	Jr	33	234	388	60.3
Khara Smith, Depaul	Fr	32	181	301	60.1

Note: Minimum 5 made per game.

REBOUNDS

Player and Team	Class	GP	Reb	Avg
Jennifer Butler, Massachusetts	Sr	28	412	14.7
Angela Buckner, Wichita St	Jr	28	366	13.1
Cheryl Ford, Louisiana Tech	Sr	34	438	12.9
Ashlee Kelly, Quinnipiac	Jr	28	338	12.1
Tori Talbert, SW Texas St	So	32	385	12.0
Alex Cook, Northern Iowa	So	30	360	12.0
Rosalee Mason, Manhattan	Jr	30	342	11.4
Amie Williams, Jackson St	Jr	29	318	11.0
Jamie Gray, Evansville	Jr	27	296	11.0

Two tied with 10.8.

FREE-THROW PERCENTAGE

Player and Team	Class	GP	FT	FTA	Pct
Jill Marano, La Salle	So	29	88	93	94.6
Kandi Brown, Morehead St	Jr	28	104	111	93.7
Kim McDonough, St. Peter's	Sr	28	81	88	92.0
Erin Thorn, Brigham Young	Sr	31	87	95	91.6
Carey Sauer, San Francisco	Jr	29	112	123	91.1
Molly McDowell, Southern IL	Sr	27	113	125	90.4
Casey Rost, Western Mich	So	32	121	134	90.3
Jen Perugini, Youngstown St	So	28	81	91	89.0
Katie Houlehan, Missouri–KC	So	28	72	81	88.9
Jennifer Youngblood, N Illinois	Jr	28	70	79	88.6

Note: Minimum 2.5 made per game.

ASSISTS

Player and Team	Class	GP	A	Avg
La'Terrica Dobin, Northwestern St	Jr	28	298	10.6
Latesha Lee, Jackson St	Jr	29	214	7.4
Laura Ingham, Nevada	Sr	29	212	7.3
Ashley McElhiney, Vanderbilt	Sr	30	219	7.3
Ivelina Vrancheva, Florida Int'l	Jr	30	217	7.2
Yolanda Paige, W Virginia	So	28	199	7.1
Jess Cichowicz, James Madison	Sr	28	194	6.9
Sara Nord, Louisville	Jr	29	199	6.9
Cricket Williams, San Jose St	Jr	28	192	6.9
Cristina Ciocan, S Carolina	Jr	31	207	6.7

THREE-POINT FIELD-GOAL PERCENTAGE

Player and Team	Class	GP	FG	FGA	Pct
Sinnamonn Garrett, New Mex St	Jr	28	68	137	49.6
Jess Hansen, UCSB	Sr	32	67	142	47.2
Kate Bulger, W Virginia	Jr	28	77	164	47.0
Lindsay Bowen, Michigan St	Fr	29	77	166	46.4
Laura Spanheimer, Creighton	So	33	77	168	45.8
Sara Potts, Kentucky	So	27	74	163	45.4
Caity Matter, Ohio St	So	32	106	235	45.1
Kara Lawson, Tennessee	So	38	77	171	45.0
Angela Davidson, NW St	Sr	27	54	123	43.9
Katie Davis, Villanova	Sr	34	104	237	43.9

Note: Minimum 1.5 made per game.

BLOCKED SHOTS

Player and Team	Class	GP	BS	Avg
Amie Williams, Jackson St	Jr	29	152	5.2
Sandora Irvin, Texas Christian	So	33	128	3.9
Christen Roper, Hawaii	Sr	30	110	3.7
Amy Collins, Stephen F. Austin	Sr	28	91	3.3
Alyssa Shriver, Tulsa	Sr	30	96	3.2
Sonja Brown, Southern Miss	Sr	28	89	3.2
Ugo Oha, George Washington	Jr	32	93	2.9
Hollie Tyler, Montana	So	30	86	2.9
Teana McKiver, Tulane	Sr	29	80	2.8
Brooke McAfee, IUPUI	Fr	28	75	2.7

NCAA Men's Division II Individual Leaders

SCORING

Player and Team	Class	GP	TFG	3FG	FT	Pts	Avg
Ron Christy, Teikyo Post	Jr	29	295	64	134	788	27.2
Alexus Foyle, BYU-Hawaii	Sr	23	261	11	81	614	26.7
Jerome Beasley, N Dakota	Sr	29	293	33	153	772	26.6
Tim Black, Barton	Sr	28	215	63	221	714	25.5
Patrick Pope, St. Augustine's	Sr	27	204	65	212	685	25.4
Ben Dewar, Lake Superior St	Sr	26	190	69	173	622	23.9
Spencer Ross, Queens (NC)	Jr	33	256	56	220	788	23.9
Robbie Ballard, Emporia St	Sr	27	226	95	83	630	23.3
Wykeen Kelly, Salem International	Sr	30	216	91	168	691	23.0
Rod Edwards, Ouachita Baptist	Jr	28	193	91	167	644	23.0

NCAA Men's Division II Individual Leaders *(Cont.)*

REBOUNDS

Player and Team	Class	GP	Reb	Avg
Billy McDaniel, AR-Monticello	Fr	27	345	12.8
Gordon James, Bridgeport	Jr	30	379	12.6
Fred Hooks, Humboldt St	Jr	29	353	12.2
Brian Atkins, Concord	Jr	28	320	11.4
Dwight Windom, Lincoln Memorial	Sr	29	324	11.2
Kenyon Booker, Shaw	Sr	30	333	11.1
Danny Jones, Tarleton St	Sr	33	364	11.0
Marcus West, Mt. Olive	Jr	28	306	10.9
Ramzee Stanton, West Chester	Sr	30	326	10.9
Jayson Williams, Lane	Jr	28	303	10.8
Jakim Donaldson, Edinboro	So	27	291	10.8

ASSISTS

Player and Team	Class	GP	A	Avg
Clayton Smith, Metro St	Sr	33	274	8.3
Wayne Hinton, Johnson Smith	Sr	29	237	8.2
Marlon Parmer, Kentucky Wesleyan	Sr	35	286	8.2
Josh Mueller, S Dakota	So	28	227	8.1
Jamie Holden, St. Joseph's (IN)	Jr	26	207	8.0
Aaron Smith, Columbia Union	Sr	27	194	7.2
Cornelius McMurray, Bowie St	Sr	33	228	6.9
Deshawn Bowman, Columbus St	Jr	31	206	6.6
Joe Bakhoun, Oklahoma PH	Sr	25	164	6.6
Ryan Luckman, Bloomsburg	Sr	26	170	6.5

FIELD-GOAL PERCENTAGE

Player and Team	Class	GP	FG	FGA	Pct
Anthony Greenup, Shaw	Jr	30	172	242	71.1
Maxie Stamps, Drury	Jr	23	125	189	66.1
Jon Smith, Bowie St	Jr	35	201	306	65.7
Ramzee Stanton, West Chester	Sr	30	254	402	63.2
Phil Sellers, St. Rose	Sr	25	208	333	62.5
Josh Buettner, Michigan Tech	So	32	187	302	61.9
Ronald Thompson, Morehouse	Jr	25	125	202	61.9
Paul Tonkovich, Caldwell	Sr	26	159	258	61.6
Jon Shepherd, Northeastern St	Sr	35	201	327	61.5
Demond Perris, Emporia St	Jr	28	150	246	61.0

Note: Minimum 5 made per game.

FREE-THROW PERCENTAGE

Player and Team	Class	GP	FT	FTA	Pct
Aaron Farley, Harding	Sr	30	137	146	93.8
Derek Paben, S Dakota	Jr	28	78	85	91.8
Robbie Ballard, Emporia St	Sr	27	83	91	91.2
Drew Carlson, Minnesota St–Mankato	Sr	27	83	91	91.2
Germayne Forbes, W Georgia	Jr	28	82	90	91.1
Rico Grier, Pfeiffer	So	29	80	88	90.9
Kelvin Parker, NW Missouri St	Jr	31	96	106	90.6
Cris Brunson, Southern IN	So	32	105	116	90.5
Jacob Fahl, Southwest St	Sr	28	113	125	90.4
Jamar Love, Incarnate Word	Sr	28	111	123	90.2

Note: Minimum 2.5 made per game.

NCAA Women's Division II Individual Leaders

SCORING

Player and Team	Class	GP	TFG	3FG	FT	Pts	Avg
Tysell Bozeman, Felician	Fr	27	420	31	145	1016	37.6
Monica Tokoro, Cal St–Los Angeles	So	26	258	22	115	653	25.1
Heather Garay, Cal St–Bakersfield	Sr	30	277	0	173	727	24.2
Dani Thomas, Southampton	Sr	28	210	67	168	655	23.4
Mandy Koupal, S Dakota	Jr	32	262	40	176	740	23.1
Shannon Donnelly, Cal St–Stanislaus	Sr	28	233	1	145	612	21.9
Tara Newnam, Southeastern Oklahoma	Sr	25	199	3	124	525	21.0
Naomi Mobley, Shaw	Sr	31	250	6	144	650	21.0
Melissa McKavish, Slippery Rock	Sr	26	183	38	134	538	20.7
Stephanie Heid, Hillsdale	Sr	29	230	26	108	594	20.5

REBOUNDS

Player and Team	Class	GP	Reb	Avg
Naomi Mobley, Shaw	Sr	31	454	14.6
Litreece Hurn, Lane	So	26	375	14.4
I. Stojkovic, Western New Mex	Jr	25	328	13.1
Georgia Gordon, New York Tech	Sr	27	353	13.1
Germaletta Dyson, Paine	Fr	26	337	13.0
Heather Lawrence, Harding	Sr	27	334	12.4
Cherelle Payne, CW Post	Jr	25	308	12.3
H. Garay, Cal St–Bakersfield	Sr	30	357	11.9
S. Donnelly, Cal St–Stanislaus	Sr	28	333	11.9
Mandy Koupal, S Dakota	Jr	32	380	11.9
Amy Swan, Georgian Court	Sr	27	320	11.9

ASSISTS

Player and Team	Class	GP	A	Avg
Kelly West, W Liberty St	Jr	32	302	9.4
Jess Hambley, St. Michael's	Jr	29	222	7.7
Ebony Vincent, Wayne St (MI)	Jr	29	222	7.7
Jamie Blakely, Emporia St	Sr	31	220	7.1
Nickie Randall, Bellarmine	Sr	31	216	7.0
Kim Abts, Cal St–Chico	So	26	176	6.8
Monica Tokoro, Cal St–LA	So	26	170	6.5
Jen Gwin, Gannon	So	26	168	6.5
Liz Leonard, Bentley	Sr	35	226	6.5
Martina McCloud, Tuskegee	Sr	29	186	6.4

FIELD-GOAL PERCENTAGE

Player and Team	Class	GP	FGA	FG	Pct
Melissa Pater, S Dakota St	Sr	35	267	411	65.0
Lindsey Dietz, Minnesota-Duluth	Fr	30	186	294	63.3
Melanie Carter, Abilene Christian	Jr	29	172	276	62.3
Martha Brinker, St. Mary's (TX)	Jr	29	167	268	62.3
Becky Siembak, California (PA)	Jr	35	257	427	61.6
Helen Young, Pitt-Johnstown	Sr	28	186	304	61.2
Catreia Shaw, Clayton St	Sr	27	166	272	61.0
Jessica Guarneri, Wingate	Sr	28	217	356	61.0
Sarah Wright, Bentley	Sr	36	181	300	60.3
Andriette Roberts, Clark Atlanta	Jr	27	136	226	60.2

Note: Minimum 5 made per game.

FREE-THROW PERCENTAGE

Player and Team	Class	GP	FTA	FT	Pct
Mary Kacic, Dowling	Sr	31	118	128	92.2
Amanda Davied, Pittsburg St	Sr	28	113	126	89.7
Renee Gagnier, Concord	Jr	26	102	114	89.5
Nickie Randall, Bellarmine	Sr	31	99	112	88.4
Andrea Patterson, Eckerd	Sr	28	113	129	87.6
Becky Mowen, N Dakota	Sr	32	126	144	87.5
Kristin Creswell, Pitt-Johnstown	Jr	28	112	128	87.5
Lyndsey Hawkins, Ouach. Bapt.	Jr	27	123	141	87.2
Lauren Meyer, Georgian Court	So	28	109	126	86.5
Haley Hobson, Midwestern St	Fr	30	76	88	86.4
Randi Johnson, Lake Superior St	So	28	76	88	86.4

Note: Minimum 2.5 made per game.

NCAA Men's Division III Individual Leaders

SCORING

Player and Team	Class	GP	TFG	3FG	FT	Pts	Avg
Patrick Glover, Johnson St	Sr	26	269	37	188	763	29.3
Rich Melzer, WI-River Falls	Jr	26	284	0	163	731	28.1
Willie Chandler, Misericordia	Sr	28	251	93	135	730	26.1
Derek Reich, Chicago	Sr	25	221	38	156	636	25.4
Adam Turner, Bard	Fr	21	191	35	114	531	25.3
Robert Hennigan, Emerson	Jr	25	184	101	154	623	24.9
Shawn Jones, Westfield St	Sr	25	215	43	141	614	24.6
Rohan Russell, Johnson & Wales	Jr	25	190	92	136	608	24.3
Steve Wood, Grinnell	Jr	25	206	60	136	608	24.3
Ray Robinson, Waynesburg	Sr	25	217	73	95	602	24.1

REBOUNDS

Player and Team	Class	GP	Reb	Avg
Jed Johnson, Maine Maritime	Sr	25	414	16.6
Joe Corbett, Hobart	Sr	23	331	14.4
Anthony Fitzgerald, Villa Julie	Fr	25	337	13.5
Darren Pugh, Lebanon Valley	Sr	26	324	12.5
Jon Schwadron, Dickinson	Sr	25	303	12.1
Derek Suttles, MacMurray	Jr	24	284	11.8
Craig Coupe, Tufts	So	25	285	11.4
Matt Beacom, Pitt-Bradford	Sr	29	328	11.3
Patrick Glover, Johnson St	Sr	26	294	11.3
Perry Davis, Buffalo St	Jr	27	303	11.2
Kyle McNamar, Curry	Sr	25	280	11.2

FIELD-GOAL PERCENTAGE

Player and Team	Class	GP	FG	FGA	Pct
Aaron Marshall, St. Lawrence	So	27	206	305	67.5
Gian Paul Gonzalez, Messiah	Fr	22	144	218	66.1
Ryan Hodges, Cal Lutheran	Jr	25	129	197	65.5
Omar Warthen, Neumann	Sr	29	149	229	65.1
John Thomas, Fontbonne	Sr	25	128	198	64.6
Bryan Nelson, Wooster	Sr	31	221	341	64.4
Tim Dworak, WI-Oshkosh	Sr	32	283	446	63.5
Kwesi Liverpool, York (NY)	Fr	24	128	202	63.4
Keith Davis, Savannah A&D	Jr	27	206	327	63.0
Mark Gabriel, Haverford	So	18	141	227	62.1
Andy Larkin, Rochester	Jr	27	139	224	62.1

Note: Minimum 5 made per game.

ASSISTS

Player and Team	Class	GP	A	Avg
Tennyson Whitted, Ramapo	Sr	30	253	8.4
Michael Crotty, Williams	Jr	32	245	7.7
Jesse Farrell, Trinity (CT)	So	24	176	7.3
Cliff Foster, La Roche	Jr	26	173	6.7
Paul Russo, Emory & Henry	Sr	26	171	6.6
Travis Magnusson, ME-Farmington	Fr	25	163	6.5
Evan Fowler, Mary Washington	Jr	29	187	6.4
Labeeb Abdullah, Savannah A&D	Sr	26	167	6.4
Trevelle Boyd, E Texas Baptist	Sr	26	163	6.3
Tim Gaspar, UMass-Dartmouth	Sr	27	167	6.2

FREE-THROW PERCENTAGE

Player and Team	Class	GP	FT	FTA	Pct
Nick Wilkins, Coe	So	26	66	69	95.7
Matt Larson, Linfield	So	25	99	108	91.7
Sean Fleming, Clark (MA)	Sr	24	109	120	90.8
Aaron Faulkner, St. Norbert	So	23	77	85	90.6
Victor Garcia, Knox	Sr	21	114	126	90.5
Steve King, Fontbonne	Sr	24	81	90	90.0
Nick Bennett, WI-Stevens Pt	So	24	62	69	89.9
B. Constantine, Wm. Paterson	Jr	25	77	86	89.5
Ryan Connor, Salem St	Jr	28	90	101	89.1
Bryan Nelson, Wooster	Sr	31	193	218	88.5

Note: Minimum 2.5 made per game.

NCAA Women's Division III Individual Leaders

SCORING

Player and Team	Class	GP	TFG	3FG	FT	Pts	Avg
Tiffany Trent, Cazenovia	Jr	23	208	35	165	616	26.8
Amy Campion, Salisbury	Sr	28	241	59	140	681	24.3
Doris Zimmerman, Wilson	Sr	28	256	7	136	65	23.4
Amy Meggers, Buena Vista	Jr	27	232	41	110	615	22.8
Heather Francouer, Oglethorpe	Sr	26	190	23	188	591	22.7
Melody Bongiorno, Chapman	Jr	27	219	23	141	602	22.3
Rebecca Segert, Merchant Marine	Jr	22	144	48	152	488	22.2
Kelly Heil, Ohio Wesleyan	So	28	222	50	110	604	21.6
Tanasha Ellis, E Texas Baptist	Sr	25	195	0	148	538	21.5
Angel Hall, Anderson (IN)	Jr	27	182	103	108	575	21.3

REBOUNDS

Player and Team	Class	GP	Reb	Avg
Andreen Gilpin, UMass-Boston	Sr	26	408	15.7
Janice Coppolino, Framingham St.	Sr	23	360	15.7
Whitney Bull, Wilkes	Sr	24	323	13.5
Siobhan Zerilla, Wilmington (OH)	So	29	381	13.1
Kristin Bhiary, St. Joseph's (LI)	Sr	27	350	13.0
Erica Dabney, Mary Baldwin	Fr	26	337	13.0
Becky Worsham, Trinity (DC)	Fr	26	335	12.9
Cheryl Kulesa, Rutgers-Camden	Sr	28	340	12.1
Kelly Weismuller, Brooklyn	Fr	24	288	12.0
Julia Knights, Maine Maritime	Fr	27	323	12.0
Shelly Ulfig, Alma	Sr	26	311	12.0

FIELD-GOAL PERCENTAGE

Player and Team	Class	GP	FG	FGA	Pct
Kelly Weismuller, Brooklyn	Fr	24	205	296	69.3
Alicia Davis, Loras	Jr	29	174	257	67.7
Jessica Justice, Mt. Holyoke	Sr	26	158	244	64.8
Kathy Darling, Johns Hopkins	Sr	28	206	322	64.0
Lindsey Chappell, Earlham	Jr	24	159	250	63.6
Danielle Fitzpatrick, Brandeis	Jr	21	138	217	63.6
Elizabeth Klotz, Fontbonne	Jr	25	178	286	62.2
Olivia Zurek, Bates	So	26	146	251	58.2
Tanasha Ellis, E Texas Baptist	Sr	25	195	338	57.7
Tara Rausch, Wilmington (OH)	Jr	29	232	403	57.6

Note: Minimum 5 made per game.

ASSISTS

Player and Team	Class	GP	A	Avg
A. Poppleton, Notre Dame (MD)	Sr	27	226	8.4
Diana Esterkamp, Otterbein	Jr	25	182	7.3
Megan Woodruff, Wilmington (OH)	Sr	29	209	7.2
Maggie Allenn, Mt. St. Vincent	Jr	25	160	6.4
Leslie Livingstone, Misericordia	Sr	28	174	6.2
Bernice Amadeo, New Jersey City	So	25	155	6.2
Diana Olaya, Lehman	Sr	24	148	6.2
Brooke Johnson, Peace	Jr	25	154	6.2
Evita Estevez, Emmanuel (MA)	Fr	30	178	5.9

Four tied with 5.8.

FREE-THROW PERCENTAGE

Player and Team	Class	GP	FT	FTA	Pct
Angel Hall, Anderson (IN)	Jr	27	108	118	91.5
Jessica Gates, Muskingum	Sr	26	83	93	89.2
Brandi Cochran, Hollins	So	26	115	129	89.1
M. Woodruff, Wilmington (OH)	Sr	29	137	154	89.0
Katie Robinson, Swarthmore	Jr	27	99	113	87.6
Nikki Bablik, Bethany (WV)	So	26	67	77	87.0
Michelle Bedard, Endicott	Sr	26	75	87	86.2
Abby Pyzik, Lynchburg	Jr	26	68	79	86.1
Melody Bongiorno, Chapman	Jr	27	141	164	86.0
E. Kelley, Colorado College	Sr	23	172	201	85.6

Note: Minimum 2.5 made per game.

YET ANOTHER SIGN OF THE APOCALYPSE

A woman sued a Lexington, Ky., surgeon and University of Kentucky sports booster because he cauterized "UK" onto her uterus before removing it in a hysterectomy.

NCAA Men's Division I Championship Results

NCAA Final Four Results

Year	Winner	Score	Runner-up	Third Place	Fourth Place	Winning Coach
1939	Oregon	46–33	Ohio St	*Oklahoma	*Villanova	Howard Hobson
1940	Indiana	60–42	Kansas	*Duquesne	*Southern Cal	Branch McCracken
1941	Wisconsin	39–34	Washington St	*Pittsburgh	*Arkansas	Harold Foster
1942	Stanford	53–38	Dartmouth	*Colorado	*Kentucky	Everett Dean
1943	Wyoming	46–34	Georgetown	*Texas	*DePaul	Everett Shelton
1944	Utah	42–40 (OT)	Dartmouth	*Iowa St	*Ohio St	Vadal Peterson
1945	Oklahoma St	49–45	NYU	*Arkansas	*Ohio St	Hank Iba
1946	Oklahoma St	43–40	N Carolina	Ohio St	California	Hank Iba
1947	Holy Cross	58–47	Oklahoma	Texas	CCNY	Alvin Julian
1948	Kentucky	58–42	Baylor	Holy Cross	Kansas St	Adolph Rupp
1949	Kentucky	46–36	Oklahoma St	Illinois	Oregon St	Adolph Rupp
1950	CCNY	71–68	Bradley	N Carolina St	Baylor	Nat Holman
1951	Kentucky	68–58	Kansas St	Illinois	Oklahoma St	Adolph Rupp
1952	Kansas	80–63	St. John's (NY)	Illinois	Santa Clara	Forrest Allen
1953	Indiana	69–68	Kansas	Washington	Louisiana St	Branch McCracken
1954	La Salle	92–76	Bradley	Penn St	Southern Cal	Kenneth Loeffler
1955	San Francisco	77–63	La Salle	Colorado	Iowa	Phil Woolpert
1956	San Francisco	83–71	Iowa	Temple	Southern Meth	Phil Woolpert
1957	N Carolina	54–53 (3OT)	Kansas	San Francisco	Michigan St	Frank McGuire
1958	Kentucky	84–72	Seattle	Temple	Kansas St	Adolph Rupp
1959	California	71–70	W Virginia	Cincinnati	Louisville	Pete Newell
1960	Ohio St	75–55	California	Cincinnati	NYU	Fred Taylor
1961	Cincinnati	70–65 (OT)	Ohio St	Vacated‡	Utah	Edwin Jucker
1962	Cincinnati	71–59	Ohio St	Wake Forest	UCLA	Edwin Jucker
1963	Loyola (IL)	60–58 (OT)	Cincinnati	Duke	Oregon St	George Ireland
1964	UCLA	98–83	Duke	Michigan	Kansas St	John Wooden
1965	UCLA	91–80	Michigan	Princeton	Wichita St	John Wooden
1966	UTEP	72–65	Kentucky	Duke	Utah	Don Haskins
1967	UCLA	79–64	Dayton	Houston	N Carolina	John Wooden
1968	UCLA	78–55	N Carolina	Ohio St	Houston	John Wooden
1969	UCLA	92–72	Purdue	Drake	N Carolina	John Wooden
1970	UCLA	80–69	Jacksonville	New Mexico St	St. Bonaventure	John Wooden
1971	UCLA	68–62	Vacated‡	Vacated‡	Kansas	John Wooden
1972	UCLA	81–76	Florida St	N Carolina	Louisville	John Wooden
1973	UCLA	87–66	Memphis St	Indiana	Providence	John Wooden
1974	N Carolina St	76–64	Marquette	UCLA	Kansas	Norm Sloan
1975	UCLA	92–85	Kentucky	Louisville	Syracuse	John Wooden
1976	Indiana	86–68	Michigan	UCLA	Rutgers	Bob Knight
1977	Marquette	67–59	N Carolina	UNLV	NC-Charlotte	Al McGuire
1978	Kentucky	94–88	Duke	Arkansas	Notre Dame	Joe Hall
1979	Michigan St	75–64	Indiana St	DePaul	Penn	Jud Heathcote
1980	Louisville	59–54	Vacated‡	Purdue	Iowa	Denny Crum
1981	Indiana	63–50	N Carolina	Virginia	Louisiana St	Bob Knight
1982	N Carolina	63–62	Georgetown	*Houston	*Louisville	Dean Smith
1983	N Carolina St	54–52	Houston	*Georgia	*Louisville	Jim Valvano
1984	Georgetown	84–75	Houston	*Kentucky	*Virginia	John Thompson
1985	Villanova	66–64	Georgetown	St. John's (NY)	Vacated‡	Rollie Massimino
1986	Louisville	72–69	Duke	*Kansas	*Louisiana St	Denny Crum
1987	Indiana	74–73	Syracuse	*UNLV	*Providence	Bob Knight
1988	Kansas	83–79	Oklahoma	*Arizona	*Duke	Larry Brown
1989	Michigan	80–79 (OT)	Seton Hall	*Duke	*Illinois	Steve Fisher
1990	UNLV	103–73	Duke	*Arkansas	*Georgia Tech	Jerry Tarkanian
1991	Duke	72–65	Kansas	*UNLV	*N Carolina	Mike Krzyzewski
1992	Duke	71–51	Michigan	*Cincinnati	*Indiana	Mike Krzyzewski
1993	N Carolina	77–71	Michigan	*Kansas	*Kentucky	Dean Smith
1994	Arkansas	76–72	Duke	*Arizona	*Florida	Nolan Richardson
1995	UCLA	89–78	Arkansas	*N Carolina	*Oklahoma St	Jim Harrick
1996	Kentucky	76–67	Syracuse	Vacated‡	Mississippi St	Rick Pitino
1997	Arizona	84–79 (OT)	Kentucky	*Minnesota	*N Carolina	Lute Olson
1998	Kentucky	78–69	Utah	*Stanford	*N Carolina	Tubby Smith
1999	Connecticut	77–74	Duke	*Michigan St	*Ohio St	Jim Calhoun
2000	Michigan St	89–76	Florida	*Wisconsin	*N Carolina	Tom Izzo
2001	Duke	82–72	Arizona	*Maryland	*Michigan St	Mike Krzyzewski
2002	Maryland	64–52	Indiana	*Kansas	*Oklahoma	Gary Williams
2003	Syracuse	81–78	Kansas	*Texas	*Marquette	Jim Boeheim

*Tied for third place. ‡Student-athletes representing St. Joseph's (PA) in 1961, Villanova in 1971, Western Kentucky in 1971, UCLA in 1980, Memphis State in 1985 and Massachusetts in 1996 were declared ineligible subsequent to the tournament. Under NCAA rules, the teams' and ineligible student-athletes' records were deleted, and the teams' places in the standings were vacated.

NCAA Final Four MVPs

Year	Winner, School	GP	Field Goals		3-Pt FG		Free Throws		Reb	A	Stl	BS	Avg
			FGM	Pct	FGA	FGM	FTM	Pct					
1939	....None selected												
1940	....Marv Huffman, Indiana	2	7	—	—	—	4	—	—	—	—	—	9.0
1941	....John Kotz, Wisconsin	2	8	—	—	—	6	—	—	—	—	—	11.0
1942	....Howard Dallmar, Stanford	2	8	—	—	—	4	66.7	—	—	—	—	10.0
1943	....Ken Sailors, Wyoming	2	10	—	—	—	8	72.7	—	—	—	—	14.0
1944	....Arnie Ferrin, Utah	2	11	—	—	—	6	—	—	—	—	—	14.0
1945	....Bob Kurland, Oklahoma St	2	16	—	—	—	5	—	—	—	—	—	18.5
1946	....Bob Kurland, Oklahoma St	2	21	—	—	—	10	66.7	—	—	—	—	26.0
1947	....George Kaftan, Holy Cross	2	18	—	—	—	12	70.6	—	—	—	—	24.0
1948	....Alex Groza, Kentucky	2	16	—	—	—	5	—	—	—	—	—	18.5
1949	....Alex Groza, Kentucky	2	19	—	—	—	14	—	—	—	—	—	26.0
1950	....Irwin Dambrot, CCNY	2	12	42.9	—	—	4	50.0	—	—	—	—	14.0
1951	....None selected												
1952	....Clyde Lovellette, Kansas	2	24	—	—	—	18	—	—	—	—	—	33.0
1953	....*B.H. Horn, Kansas	2	17	—	—	—	17	—	—	—	—	—	25.5
1954	....Tom Gola, La Salle	2	12	—	—	—	14	—	—	—	—	—	19.0
1955	....Bill Russell, San Francisco	2	19	—	—	—	9	—	—	—	—	—	23.5
1956	....*Hal Lear, Temple	2	32	—	—	—	16	—	—	—	—	—	40.0
1957	....*Wilt Chamberlain, Kansas	2	18	51.4	—	—	19	70.4	25	—	—	—	32.5
1958	....*Elgin Baylor, Seattle	2	18	34.0	—	—	12	75.0	41	—	—	—	24.0
1959	....*Jerry West, West Virginia	2	22	66.7	—	—	22	68.8	25	—	—	—	33.0
1960	....Jerry Lucas, Ohio State	2	16	66.7	—	—	3	100.0	23	—	—	—	17.5
1961	....*Jerry Lucas, Ohio State	2	20	71.4	—	—	16	94.1	25	—	—	—	28.0
1962	....Paul Hogue, Cincinnati	2	23	63.9	—	—	12	63.2	38	—	—	—	29.0
1963	....Art Heyman, Duke	2	18	41.0	—	—	15	68.2	19	—	—	—	25.5
1964	....Walt Hazzard, UCLA	2	11	55.0	—	—	8	66.7	10	—	—	—	15.0
1965	....*Bill Bradley, Princeton	2	34	63.0	—	—	19	95.0	24	—	—	—	43.5
1966	....*Jerry Chambers, Utah	2	25	53.2	—	—	20	83.3	35	—	—	—	35.0
1967	....Lew Alcindor, UCLA	2	14	60.9	—	—	11	45.8	38	—	—	—	19.5
1968	....Lew Alcindor, UCLA	2	22	62.9	—	—	9	90.0	34	—	—	—	26.5
1969	....Lew Alcindor, UCLA	2	23	67.7	—	—	16	64.0	41	—	—	—	31.0
1970	....Sidney Wicks, UCLA	2	15	71.4	—	—	9	60.0	34	—	—	—	19.5
1971	....*†Howard Porter, Villanova	2	20	48.8	—	—	7	77.8	24	—	—	—	23.5
1972	....Bill Walton, UCLA	2	20	69.0	—	—	17	73.9	41	—	—	—	28.5
1973	....Bill Walton, UCLA	2	28	82.4	—	—	4	40.0	30	—	—	—	29.0
1974	....David Thompson, NC State	2	19	51.4	—	—	11	78.6	17	—	—	—	24.5
1975	....Richard Washington, UCLA	2	23	54.8	—	—	8	72.7	20	—	—	—	27.0
1976	....Kent Benson, Indiana	2	17	50.0	—	—	7	63.6	18	—	—	—	20.5
1977	....Butch Lee, Marquette	2	11	34.4	—	—	8	100.0	6	2	1	1	15.0
1978	....Jack Givens, Kentucky	2	28	65.1	—	—	8	66.7	17	4	1	3	32.0
1979	....Earvin Johnson, Michigan St	2	17	68.0	—	—	19	86.4	17	3	0	2	26.5
1980	....Darrell Griffith, Louisville	2	23	62.2	—	—	11	68.8	7	15	0	2	28.5
1981	....Isiah Thomas, Indiana	2	14	56.0	—	—	9	81.8	4	9	3	4	18.5
1982	....James Worthy, N Carolina	2	20	74.1	—	—	2	28.6	8	9	0	4	21.0
1983	....*Akeem Olajuwon, Houston	2	16	55.2	—	—	9	64.3	40	3	2	5	20.5
1984	....Patrick Ewing, Georgetown	2	8	57.1	—	—	2	100.0	18	1	1	15	9.0
1985	....Ed Pinckney, Villanova	2	8	57.1	—	—	12	75.0	15	6	3	0	14.0
1986	....Pervis Ellison, Louisville	2	15	60.0	—	—	6	75.0	24	2	3	1	18.0
1987	....Keith Smart, Indiana	2	14	63.6	1	0	7	77.8	7	7	0	2	17.5
1988	....Danny Manning, Kansas	2	25	55.6	1	0	6	66.7	17	4	8	9	28.0
1989	....Glen Rice, Michigan	2	24	49.0	16	7	4	100.0	16	1	0	3	29.5
1990	....Anderson Hunt, UNLV	2	19	61.3	16	9	2	50.0	4	9	1	1	24.5
1991	....Christian Laettner, Duke	2	12	54.5	1	1	21	91.3	17	2	1	2	23.0
1992	....Bobby Hurley, Duke	2	10	41.7	12	7	8	80.0	3	11	0	3	17.5
1993	....Donald Williams, N Carolina	2	15	65.2	14	10	10	100.0	4	2	2	0	25.0
1994	....Corliss Williamson, Arkansas	2	21	50.0	0	0	10	71.4	21	8	4	3	26.0
1995	....Ed O'Bannon, UCLA	2	16	45.7	8	3	10	76.9	25	3	7	1	22.5
1996	....Tony Delk, Kentucky	2	15	41.7	16	8	6	54.6	9	2	3	2	22.0
1997	....Miles Simon, Arizona	2	17	45.9	10	3	17	77.3	8	6	0	1	27.0
1998	....Jeff Sheppard, Kentucky	2	16	55.2	10	4	7	77.8	10	7	4	0	21.5
1999	....Richard Hamilton, Connecticut	2	20	51.3	7	3	8	72.7	12	4	2	1	25.5
2000	....Mateen Cleaves, Michigan St	2	8	44.4	4	3	10	83.3	6	5	2	0	14.5
2001	....Shane Battier, Duke	2	13	50.0	12	5	12	70.6	19	8	2	6	21.5
2002	....Juan Dixon, Maryland	2	16	59.3	15	7	12	80.0	8	5	7	0	25.5
2003	....Carmelo Anthony, Syracuse	2	19	54.3	6	9	9	81.1	24	8	4	0	26.5

*Not a member of the championship-winning team.   †Record later vacated.

Best NCAA Tournament Single-Game Scoring Performances

Player and Team	Year	Round	FG	3FG	FT	TP
Austin Carr, Notre Dame vs Ohio	1970	1st	25	—	11	61
Bill Bradley, Princeton vs Wichita St	1965	C*	22	—	14	58
Oscar Robertson, Cincinnati vs Arkansas	1958	C	21	—	14	56
Austin Carr, Notre Dame vs Kentucky	1970	2nd	22	—	8	52
Austin Carr, Notre Dame vs Texas Christian	1971	1st	20	—	12	52
David Robinson, Navy vs Michigan	1987	1st	22	0	6	50
Elvin Hayes, Houston vs Loyola (IL)	1968	1st	20	—	9	49
Hal Lear, Temple vs SMU	1956	C*	17	—	14	48
Austin Carr, Notre Dame vs Houston	1971	C	17	—	13	47
Dave Corzine, DePaul vs Louisville	1978	2nd	18	—	10	46

C=regional third place; C*=third-place game.

NIT Championship Results

Year	Winner	Score	Runner-up	Year	Winner	Score	Runner-up
1938	Temple	60–36	Colorado	1972	Maryland	100–69	Niagara
1939	Long Island U	44–32	Loyola (IL)	1973	Virginia Tech	92–91 (OT)	Notre Dame
1940	Colorado	51–40	Duquesne	1974	Purdue	97–81	Utah
1941	Long Island U	56–42	Ohio U	1975	Princeton	80–69	Providence
1942	W Virginia	47–45	W Kentucky	1976	Kentucky	71–67	NC-Charlotte
1943	St. John's (NY)	48–27	Toledo	1977	St. Bonaventure	94–91	Houston
1944	St. John's (NY)	47–39	DePaul	1978	Texas	101–93	N Carolina St
1945	DePaul	71–54	Bowling Green	1979	Indiana	53–52	Purdue
1946	Kentucky	46–45	Rhode Island	1980	Virginia	58–55	Minnesota
1947	Utah	49–45	Kentucky	1981	Tulsa	86–84 (OT)	Syracuse
1948	St. Louis	65–52	NYU	1982	Bradley	67–58	Purdue
1949	San Francisco	48–47	Loyola (IL)	1983	Fresno St	69–60	DePaul
1950	CCNY	69–61	Bradley	1984	Michigan	83–63	Notre Dame
1951	BYU	62–43	Dayton	1985	UCLA	65–62	Indiana
1952	La Salle	75–64	Dayton	1986	Ohio St	73–63	Wyoming
1953	Seton Hall	58–46	St. John's (NY)	1987	Southern Miss	84–80	La Salle
1954	Holy Cross	71–62	Duquesne	1988	Connecticut	72–67	Ohio St
1955	Duquesne	70–58	Dayton	1989	St. John's (NY)	73–65	St. Louis
1956	Louisville	93–80	Dayton	1990	Vanderbilt	74–72	St. Louis
1957	Bradley	84–83	Memphis St	1991	Stanford	78–72	Oklahoma
1958	Xavier (OH)	78–74 (OT)	Dayton	1992	Virginia	81–76	Notre Dame
1959	St. John's (NY)	76–71 (OT)	Bradley	1993	Minnesota	62–61	Georgetown
1960	Bradley	88–72	Providence	1994	Villanova	80–73	Vanderbilt
1961	Providence	62–59	St. Louis	1995	Virginia Tech	65–64 (OT)	Marquette
1962	Dayton	73–67	St. John's (NY)	1996	Nebraska	60–56	St. Joseph's
1963	Providence	81–66	Canisius	1997	Michigan	82–73	Florida St
1964	Bradley	86–54	New Mexico	1998	Minnesota	79–72	Penn St
1965	St. John's (NY)	55–51	Villanova	1999	California	61–60	Clemson
1966	BYU	97–84	NYU	2000	Wake Forest	71–61	Notre Dame
1967	Southern Illinois	71–56	Marquette	2001	Tulsa	79–60	Alabama
1968	Dayton	61–48	Kansas	2002	Memphis	72–62	S Carolina
1969	Temple	89–76	Boston College	2003	St. John's	70–67	Georgetown
1970	Marquette	65–53	St. John's (NY)				
1971	N Carolina	84–66	Georgia Tech				

NCAA Men's Division I Season Leaders

Scoring Average

Year	Player and Team	Ht	Class	GP	FG	3FG	FT	Pts	Avg
1948	Murray Wier, Iowa	5-9	Sr	19	152	—	95	399	21.0
1949	Tony Lavelli, Yale	6-3	Sr	30	228	—	215	671	22.4
1950	Paul Arizin, Villanova	6-3	Sr	29	260	—	215	735	25.3
1951	Bill Mlkvy, Temple	6-4	Sr	25	303	—	125	731	29.2
1952	Clyde Lovellette, Kansas	6-9	Sr	28	315	—	165	795	28.4
1953	Frank Selvy, Furman	6-3	Jr	25	272	—	194	738	29.5
1954	Frank Selvy, Furman	6-3	Sr	29	427	—	355	1209	41.7
1955	Darrell Floyd, Furman	6-1	Jr	25	344	—	209	897	35.9
1956	Darrell Floyd, Furman	6-1	Sr	28	339	—	268	946	33.8
1957	Grady Wallace, S Carolina	6-4	Sr	29	336	—	234	906	31.2
1958	Oscar Robertson, Cincinnati	6-5	So	28	352	—	280	984	35.1
1959	Oscar Robertson, Cincinnati	6-5	Jr	30	331	—	316	978	32.6
1960	Oscar Robertson, Cincinnati	6-5	Sr	30	369	—	273	1011	33.7
1961	Frank Burgess, Gonzaga	6-1	Sr	26	304	—	234	842	32.4
1962	Billy McGill, Utah	6-9	Sr	26	394	—	221	1009	38.8
1963	Nick Werkman, Seton Hall	6-3	Jr	22	221	—	208	650	29.5
1964	Howard Komives, Bowling Green	6-1	Sr	23	292	—	260	844	36.7

Scoring Average *(Cont.)*

Year	Player and Team	Ht	Class	GP	FG	3FG	FT	Pts	Avg
1965	Rick Barry, Miami (FL)	6-7	Sr	26	340	—	293	973	37.4
1966	Dave Schellhase, Purdue	6-4	Sr	24	284	—	213	781	32.5
1967	Jim Walker, Providence	6-3	Sr	28	323	—	205	851	30.4
1968	Pete Maravich, Louisiana St	6-5	So	26	432	—	274	1138	43.8
1969	Pete Maravich, Louisiana St	6-5	Jr	26	433	—	282	1148	44.2
1970	Pete Maravich, Louisiana St	6-5	Sr	31	522	—	337	1381	44.5
1971	Johnny Neumann, Mississippi	6-6	So	23	366	—	191	923	40.1
1972	Dwight Lamar, Southwestern Louisiana	6-1	Jr	29	429	—	196	1054	36.3
1973	William Averitt, Pepperdine	6-1	Sr	25	352	—	144	848	33.9
1974	Larry Fogle, Canisius	6-5	So	25	326	—	183	835	33.4
1975	Bob McCurdy, Richmond	6-7	Sr	26	321	—	213	855	32.9
1976	Marshall Rodgers, TX-Pan American	6-2	Sr	25	361	—	197	919	36.8
1977	Freeman Williams, Portland St	6-4	Jr	26	417	—	176	1010	38.8
1978	Freeman Williams, Portland St	6-4	Sr	27	410	—	149	969	35.9
1979	Lawrence Butler, Idaho St	6-3	Sr	27	310	—	192	812	30.1
1980	Tony Murphy, Southern-BR	6-3	Sr	29	377	—	178	932	32.1
1981	Zam Fredrick, S Carolina	6-2	Sr	27	300	—	181	781	28.9
1982	Harry Kelly, Texas Southern	6-7	Jr	29	336	—	190	862	29.7
1983	Harry Kelly, Texas Southern	6-7	Sr	29	333	—	169	835	28.8
1984	Joe Jakubick, Akron	6-5	Sr	27	304	—	206	814	30.1
1985	Xavier McDaniel, Wichita St	6-8	Sr	31	351	—	142	844	27.2
1986	Terrance Bailey, Wagner	6-2	Jr	29	321	—	212	854	29.4
1987	Kevin Houston, Army	5-11	Sr	29	311	63	268	953	32.9
1988	Hersey Hawkins, Bradley	6-3	Sr	31	377	87	284	1125	36.3
1989	Hank Gathers, Loyola Marymount	6-7	Jr	31	419	0	177	1015	32.7
1990	Bo Kimble, Loyola Marymount	6-5	Sr	32	404	92	231	1131	35.3
1991	Kevin Bradshaw, U.S. Int'l	6-6	Sr	28	358	60	278	1054	37.6
1992	Brett Roberts, Morehead St	6-8	Sr	29	278	66	193	815	28.1
1993	Greg Guy, TX-Pan American	6-1	Jr	19	189	67	111	556	29.3
1994	Glenn Robinson, Purdue	6-8	Jr	34	368	79	215	1030	30.3
1995	Kurt Thomas, Texas Christian	6-9	Sr	27	288	3	202	781	28.9
1996	Kevin Granger, Texas Southern	6-3	Sr	24	194	30	230	648	27.0
1997	Charles Jones, LIU-Brooklyn	6-3	Jr	30	338	109	118	903	30.1
1998	Charles Jones, LIU-Brooklyn	6-3	Sr	30	326	116	101	869	29.0
1999	Alvin Young, Niagara	6-3	Sr	29	253	65	157	728	25.1
2000	Courtney Alexander, Fresno St	6-6	Sr	27	252	58	107	669	24.8
2001	Ronnie McCollum, Centenary	6-4	Sr	27	244	85	214	787	29.1
2002	Jason Conley, Virginia Military	6-5	Fr	28	285	79	171	820	29.3
2003	Ruben Douglas, New Mexico	6-5	Sr	28	218	94	253	783	28.0

Rebounds

Year	Player and Team	Ht	Class	GP	Reb	Avg
1951	Ernie Beck, Pennsylvania	6-4	So	27	556	20.6
1952	Bill Hannon, Army	6-3	So	17	355	20.9
1953	Ed Conlin, Fordham	6-5	So	26	612	23.5
1954	Art Quimby, Connecticut	6-5	Jr	26	588	22.6
1955	Charlie Slack, Marshall	6-5	Jr	21	538	25.6
1956	Joe Holup, George Washington	6-6	Sr	26	604	†.256
1957	Elgin Baylor, Seattle	6-6	Jr	25	508	†.235
1958	Alex Ellis, Niagara	6-5	Sr	25	536	†.262
1959	Leroy Wright, Pacific	6-8	Jr	26	652	†.238
1960	Leroy Wright, Pacific	6-8	Sr	17	380	†.234
1961	Jerry Lucas, Ohio St	6-8	Jr	27	470	†.198
1962	Jerry Lucas, Ohio St	6-8	Sr	28	499	†.211
1963	Paul Silas, Creighton	6-7	Sr	27	557	20.6
1964	Bob Pelkington, Xavier (OH)	6-7	Sr	26	567	21.8
1965	Toby Kimball, Connecticut	6-8	Sr	23	483	21.0
1966	Jim Ware, Oklahoma City	6-8	Sr	29	607	20.9
1967	Dick Cunningham, Murray St	6-10	Jr	22	479	21.8
1968	Neal Walk, Florida	6-10	Jr	25	494	19.8
1969	Spencer Haywood, Detroit	6-8	So	22	472	21.5
1970	Artis Gilmore, Jacksonville	7-2	Jr	28	621	22.2
1971	Artis Gilmore, Jacksonville	7-2	Sr	26	603	23.2
1972	Kermit Washington, American	6-8	Jr	23	455	19.8
1973	Kermit Washington, American	6-8	Sr	22	439	20.0
1974	Marvin Barnes, Providence	6-9	Sr	32	597	18.7
1975	John Irving, Hofstra	6-9	So	21	323	15.4
1976	Sam Pellom, Buffalo	6-8	So	26	420	16.2
1977	Glenn Mosley, Seton Hall	6-8	Sr	29	473	16.3
1978	Ken Williams, N Texas St	6-7	Sr	28	411	14.7
1979	Monti Davis, Tennessee St	6-7	Jr	26	421	16.2
1980	Larry Smith, Alcorn St	6-8	Sr	26	392	15.1
1981	Darryl Watson, Miss Valley	6-7	Sr	27	379	14.0

Rebounds (Cont.)

Year	Player and Team	Ht	Class	GP	Reb	Avg
1982	LaSalle Thompson, Texas	6-10	Jr	27	365	13.5
1983	Xavier McDaniel, Wichita St	6-7	So	28	403	14.4
1984	Akeem Olajuwon, Houston	7-0	Jr	37	500	13.5
1985	Xavier McDaniel, Wichita St	6-8	Sr	31	460	14.8
1986	David Robinson, Navy	6-11	Jr	35	455	13.0
1987	Jerome Lane, Pittsburgh	6-6	So	33	444	13.5
1988	Kenny Miller, Loyola (IL)	6-9	Fr	29	395	13.6
1989	Hank Gathers, Loyola (CA)	6-7	Jr	31	426	13.7
1990	Anthony Bonner, St. Louis	6-8	Sr	33	456	13.8
1991	Shaquille O'Neal, Louisiana St	7-1	So	28	411	14.7
1992	Popeye Jones, Murray St	6-8	Sr	30	431	14.4
1993	Warren Kidd, Middle Tenn St	6-9	Sr	26	386	14.8
1994	Jerome Lambert, Baylor	6-8	Jr	24	355	14.8
1995	Kurt Thomas, Texas Christian	6-9	Sr	27	393	14.6
1996	Marcus Mann, Mississippi Valley	6-8	Sr	29	394	13.6
1997	Tim Duncan, Wake Forest	6-11	Sr	31	457	14.7
1998	Ryan Perryman, Dayton	6-7	Sr	33	412	12.5
1999	Ian McGinnis, Dartmouth	6-8	So	26	317	12.2
2000	Darren Phillips, Fairfield	6-7	Sr	29	405	14.0
2001	Chris Marcus, Western Kentucky	7-1	Jr	31	374	12.1
2002	Jeremy Bishop, Quinnipiac	6-6	Jr	29	347	12.0
2003	Brandon Hunter, Ohio	6-7	Sr	30	378	12.6

†From 1956–1962, title was based on highest individual recoveries out of total by both teams in all games.

Assists

Year	Player and Team	Class	GP	A	Avg
1984	Craig Lathen, IL-Chicago	Jr	29	274	9.45
1985	Rob Weingard, Hofstra	Sr	24	228	9.50
1986	Mark Jackson, St. John's (NY)	Jr	36	328	9.11
1987	Avery Johnson, Southern-BR	Jr	31	333	10.74
1988	Avery Johnson, Southern-BR	Sr	30	399	13.30
1989	Glenn Williams, Holy Cross	Sr	28	278	9.93
1990	Todd Lehmann, Drexel	Sr	28	260	9.29
1991	Chris Corchiani, N Carolina St	Sr	31	299	9.65
1992	Van Usher, Tennessee Tech	Sr	29	254	8.76
1993	Sam Crawford, New Mex St	Sr	34	310	9.12
1994	Jason Kidd, California	So	30	272	9.06
1995	Nelson Haggerty, Baylor	Sr	28	284	10.10
1996	Raimonds Miglinieks, UC-Irvine	Sr	27	230	8.52
1997	Kenny Mitchell, Dartmouth	Sr	26	203	7.81
1998	Ahlon Lewis, Arizona St	Sr	32	294	9.19
1999	Doug Gottlieb, Oklahoma St	Jr	34	299	8.79
2000	Mark Dickel, UNLV	Sr	31	280	9.03
2001	Markus Carr, Cal St–Northridge	Jr	32	286	8.94
2002	T.J. Ford, Texas	Fr	33	273	8.27
2003	Martell Bailey, IL-Chicago	Jr	30	244	8.13

Blocked Shots

Year	Player and Team	Class	GP	BS	Avg
1986	David Robinson, Navy	Jr	35	207	5.91
1987	David Robinson, Navy	Sr	32	144	4.50
1988	Rodney Blake, St. Joseph's (PA)	Sr	29	116	4.00
1989	Alonzo Mourning, Georgetown	Fr	34	169	4.97
1990	Kenny Green, Rhode Island	Sr	26	124	4.77
1991	Shawn Bradley, Brigham Young	Fr	34	177	5.21
1992	Shaquille O'Neal, Louisiana St	Jr	30	157	5.23
1993	Theo Ratliff, Wyoming	Jr	28	124	4.43
1994	Grady Livingston, Howard	Jr	26	115	4.42
1995	Keith Closs, Central Conn St	Fr	26	139	5.35
1996	Keith Closs, Central Conn St	So	28	178	6.36
1997	Adonal Foyle, Colgate	Jr	28	180	6.43
1998	Jerome James, Florida A&M	Sr	27	125	4.63
1999	Tarvis Williams, Hampton	Jr	27	135	5.00
2000	Ken Johnson, Ohio St	Sr	30	161	5.37
2001	Tarvis Williams, Hampton	Sr	32	147	4.59
2002	Wojciech Myrda, LA-Monroe	Sr	32	172	5.38
2003	Emeka Okafor, Connecticut	So	33	156	4.73

Steals

Year	Player and Team	Class	GP	S	Avg
1986	Darron Brittman, Chicago St	Sr	28	139	4.96
1987	Tony Fairley, Charleston Sou	Sr	28	114	4.07
1988	Aldwin Ware, Florida A&M	Sr	29	142	4.90
1989	Kenny Robertson, Cleveland St	Jr	28	111	3.96

Steals (Cont.)

Year	Player and Team	Class	GP	S	Avg
1990	Ronn McMahon, E Washington	Sr	29	130	4.48
1991	Van Usher, Tennessee Tech	Jr	28	104	3.71
1992	Victor Snipes, NE Illinois	So	25	86	3.44
1993	Jason Kidd, California	Fr	29	110	3.80
1994	Shawn Griggs, SW Louisiana	Sr	30	120	4.00
1995	Roderick Anderson, Texas	Sr	30	101	3.37
1996	Pointer Williams, McNeese St	Sr	27	118	4.37
1997	Joel Hoover, MD-Eastern Shore	Fr	28	90	3.21
1998	Bonzi Wells, Ball St	Sr	29	103	3.55
1999	Shawnta Rogers, George Wash	Sr	29	103	3.55
2000	Carl Williams, Liberty	Sr	28	107	3.82
2001	Greedy Daniels, Texas Christian	Jr	25	108	4.32
2002	Desmond Cambridge, AL A&M	Sr	29	160	5.52
2003	Alexis McMillan, Stetson	Sr	22	87	3.95

Single Game Records

SCORING HIGHS VS NON-DIVISION I OPPONENT

Pts	Player and Team vs Opponent	Date
72	Kevin Bradshaw, U.S. Int'l vs Loyola Marymount	1-5-91
69	Pete Maravich, Louisiana St vs Alabama	2-7-70
68	Calvin Murphy, Niagara vs Syracuse	12-7-68
66	Jay Handlan, Washington & Lee vs Furman	2-17-51
66	Pete Maravich, Louisiana St vs Tulane	2-10-69
66	Anthony Roberts, Oral Roberts vs N Carolina A&T	2-19-77
65	Anthony Roberts, Oral Roberts vs Oregon	3-9-77
65	Scott Haffner, Evansville vs Dayton	2-18-89
64	Pete Maravich, Louisiana St vs Kentucky	2-21-70
63	Johnny Neumann, Mississippi vs Louisiana St	1-30-71
63	Hersey Hawkins, Bradley vs Detroit	2-22-88

SCORING HIGHS VS NON-DIVISION I OPPONENT

Pts	Player and Team vs Opponent	Date
100	Frank Selvy, Furman vs Newberry	2-13-54
85	Paul Arizin, Villanova vs Philadelphia NAMC	2-12-49
81	Freeman Williams, Portland St vs Rocky Mountain	2-3-78
73	Bill Mlkvy, Temple vs Wilkes	3-3-51
71	Freeman Williams, Portland St vs Southern Oregon	2-9-77

REBOUNDING HIGHS BEFORE 1973

Reb	Player and Team vs Opponent	Date
51	Bill Chambers, William & Mary vs Virginia	2-14-53
43	Charlie Slack, Marshall vs Morris Harvey	1-12-54
42	Tom Heinsohn, Holy Cross vs Boston College	3-1-55
40	Art Quimby, Connecticut vs Boston U	1-11-55
39	Maurice Stokes, St. Francis (PA) vs John Carroll	1-28-55
39	Dave DeBusschere, Detroit vs Central Michigan	1-30-60
39	Keith Swagerty, Pacific vs UC-Santa Barbara	3-5-65

REBOUNDING HIGHS SINCE 1973*

Reb	Player and Team vs Opponent	Date
35	Larry Abney, Fresno St vs Southern Methodist	2-17-00
34	David Vaughn, Oral Roberts vs Brandeis	1-8-73
32	Jervaughn Scales, Southern-BR vs Grambling	2-7-94
32	Durand Macklin, Louisiana St vs Tulane	11-26-76
31	Jim Bradley, Northern Illinois vs WI-Milwaukee	2-19-73
31	Calvin Natt, NE Louisiana vs Georgia Southern	12-29-76

ASSISTS

A	Player and Team vs Opponent	Date
22	Tony Fairley, Baptist vs Armstrong St	2-9-87
22	Avery Johnson, Southern-BR vs Texas Southern	1-25-88
22	Sherman Douglas, Syracuse vs Providence	1-28-89
21	Mark Wade, UNLV vs Navy	12-29-86
21	Kelvin Scarborough, New Mexico vs Hawaii	2-13-87
21	Anthony Manuel, Bradley vs UC-Irvine	12-19-87
21	Avery Johnson, Southern-BR vs Alabama St	1-16-88

Single Game Records *(Cont.)*

STEALS

S	Player and Team vs Opponent	Date
13	Mookie Blaylock, Oklahoma vs Centenary	12-12-87
13	Mookie Blaylock, Oklahoma vs Loyola Marymount	12-17-88
12	Kenny Robertson, Cleveland St vs Wagner	12-3-88
12	Terry Evans, Oklahoma vs Florida A&M	1-27-93
12	Richard Duncan, Middle Tenn St vs Eastern Kentucky	2-20-99
12	Greedy Daniels, Texas Christian vs AR–Pine Bluff	12-30-00
12	Jehiel Lewis, Navy vs Bucknell	1-12-02

BLOCKED SHOTS

BS	Player and Team vs Opponent	Date
14	David Robinson, Navy vs NC–Wilmington	1-4-86
14	Shawn Bradley, Brigham Young vs Eastern Kentucky	12-7-90
14	Roy Rogers, Alabama vs Georgia	2-10-96
14	Loren Woods, Arizona vs Oregon	2-3-00
13	Kevin Roberson, Vermont vs New Hampshire	1-9-92
13	Jim McIlvaine, Marquette vs Northeastern (IL)	12-9-92
13	Keith Closs, Central Conn. St vs St. Francis (PA)	12-21-94
13	D'or Fischer, Northwestern St vs SW Texas St	1-22-01
13	Wojciech Myrda, LA–Monroe vs Texas–San Antonio	1-17-02

Single Season Records

POINTS

Player and Team	Year	GP	FG	3FG	FT	Pts
Pete Maravich, Louisiana St	1970	31	522	—	337	1381
Elvin Hayes, Houston	1968	33	519	—	176	1214
Frank Selvy, Furman	1954	29	427	—	355	1209
Pete Maravich, Louisiana St	1969	26	433	—	282	1148
Pete Maravich, Louisiana St	1968	26	432	—	274	1138
Bo Kimble, Loyola Marymount	1990	32	404	92	231	1131
Hersey Hawkins, Bradley	1988	31	377	87	284	1125
Austin Carr, Notre Dame	1970	29	444	—	218	1106
Austin Carr, Notre Dame	1971	29	430	—	241	1101
Otis Birdsong, Houston	1977	36	452	—	186	1090

SCORING AVERAGE

Player and Team	Year	GP	FG	3FG	FT	Pts	Avg
Pete Maravich, Louisiana St	1970	31	522	337	1381		44.5
Pete Maravich, Louisiana St	1969	26	433	282	1148		44.2
Pete Maravich, Louisiana St	1968	26	432	274	1138		43.8
Frank Selvy, Furman	1954	29	427	355	1209		41.7
Johnny Neumann, Mississippi	1971	23	366	191	923		40.1
Freeman Williams, Portland St	1977	26	417	176	1010		38.8
Billy McGill, Utah	1962	26	394	221	1009		38.8
Calvin Murphy, Niagara	1968	24	337	242	916		38.2
Austin Carr, Notre Dame	1970	29	444	218	1106		38.1
Austin Carr, Notre Dame	1971	29	430	241	1101		38.0

REBOUNDS

Player and Team	Year	GP	Reb	Player and Team	Year	GP	Reb
Walt Dukes, Seton Hall	1953	33	734	Artis Gilmore, Jacksonville	1970	28	621
Leroy Wright, Pacific	1959	26	652	Tom Gola, La Salle	1955	31	618
Tom Gola, La Salle	1954	30	652	Ed Conlin, Fordham	1953	26	612
Charlie Tyra, Louisville	1956	29	645	Art Quimby, Connecticut	1955	25	611
Paul Silas, Creighton	1964	29	631	Bill Russell, San Francisco	1956	29	609
Elvin Hayes, Houston	1968	33	624	Jim Ware, Oklahoma City	1966	29	607

REBOUND AVERAGE BEFORE 1973

Player and Team	Year	GP	Reb	Avg
Charlie Slack, Marshall	1955	21	538	25.6
Leroy Wright, Pacific	1959	26	652	25.1
Art Quimby, Connecticut	1955	25	611	24.4
Charlie Slack, Marshall	1956	22	520	23.6
Ed Conlin, Fordham	1953	26	612	23.5

REBOUND AVERAGE SINCE 1973*

Player and Team	Year	GP	Reb	Avg
Kermit Washington, American	1973	22	439	20.0
Marvin Barnes, Providence	1973	30	571	19.0
Marvin Barnes, Providence	1974	32	597	18.7
Pete Padgett, NV–Reno	1973	26	462	17.8
Jim Bradley, Northern Illinois	1973	24	426	17.8

*Freshmen became eligible for varsity play in 1973.

Single Season Records (Cont.)

ASSISTS

Player and Team	Year	GP	A	Player and Team	Year	GP	A
Mark Wade, UNLV	1987	38	406	Sherman Douglas, Syracuse	1989	38	326
Avery Johnson, Southern-BR	1988	30	399	Sam Crawford, New Mex. St	1993	34	310
Anthony Manuel, Bradley	1988	31	373	Greg Anthony, UNLV	1991	35	310
Avery Johnson, Southern-BR	1987	31	333	Reid Gettys, Houston	1984	37	309
Mark Jackson, St. John's (NY)	1986	32	328	Carl Golston, Loyola (IL)	1985	33	305

ASSIST AVERAGE

Player and Team	Year	GP	A	Avg	Player and Team	Year	GP	A	Avg
Avery Johnson, Southern-BR	1988	30	399	13.3	Chris Corchiani, N Carolina St	1991	31	299	9.6
Anthony Manuel, Bradley	1988	31	373	12.0	Tony Fairley, Charleston So.*	1987	28	270	9.6
Avery Johnson, Southern-BR	1987	31	333	10.7	Tyrone Bogues, Wake Forest	1987	29	276	9.5
Mark Wade, UNLV	1987	38	406	10.7	Ron Weingard, Hofstra	1985	24	228	9.5
Nelson Haggerty, Baylor	1995	28	284	10.1	Craig Neal, Georgia Tech	1988	32	303	9.5
Glenn Williams, Holy Cross	1989	28	278	9.9	*Formerly Baptist.				

FIELD-GOAL PERCENTAGE

Player and Team	Year	GP	FG	FGA	Pct
Steve Johnson, Oregon St	1981	28	235	315	74.6
Dwayne Davis, Florida	1989	33	179	248	72.2
Keith Walker, Utica	1985	27	154	216	71.3
Steve Johnson, Oregon St	1980	30	211	297	71.0
Adam Mark, Belmont	2002	26	150	212	70.8
Oliver Miller, Arkansas	1991	38	254	361	70.4
Alan Williams, Princeton	1987	25	163	232	70.3
Mark McNamara, California	1982	27	231	329	70.2
Warren Kidd, Middle Tennessee St	1991	30	173	247	70.0
Pete Freeman, Akron	1991	28	175	250	70.0

Based on qualifiers for annual championship.

FREE-THROW PERCENTAGE

Player and Team	Year	GP	FT	FTA	Pct
Craig Collins, Penn St	1985	27	94	98	95.9
Steve Drabyn, Belmont	2003	29	78	82	95.1
Rod Foster, UCLA	1982	27	95	100	95.0
Clay McKnight, Pacific	2000	24	74	78	94.9
Matt Logie, Lehigh	2003	28	91	96	94.8
Danny Basile, Marist	1994	27	84	89	94.4
Carlos Gibson, Marshall	1978	28	84	89	94.4
Jim Barton, Dartmouth	1986	26	65	69	94.2
Gary Buchanan, Villanova	2001	31	97	103	94.2
Jack Moore, Nebraska	1982	27	123	131	93.9

Based on qualifiers for annual championship.

THREE-POINT FIELD-GOAL PERCENTAGE

Player and Team	Year	GP	3FG	3FGA	Pct
Glenn Tropf, Holy Cross	1988	29	52	82	63.4
Sean Wightman, Western Michigan	1992	30	48	76	63.2
Keith Jennings, E Tennessee St	1991	33	84	142	59.2
Dave Calloway, Monmouth (NJ)	1989	28	48	82	58.5
Steve Kerr, Arizona	1988	38	114	199	57.3
Reginald Jones, Prairie View	1987	28	64	112	57.1
Jim Cantamessa, Siena	1998	29	66	117	56.4
Joel Tribelhorn, Colorado St	1989	33	76	135	56.3
Mike Joseph, Bucknell	1988	28	65	116	56.0
Brian Jackson, Evansville	1995	27	53	95	55.8
Amory Sanders, SE Missouri St	2001	24	53	95	55.8

Based on qualifiers for annual championship.

Single Season Records (Cont.)

STEALS

Player and Team	Year	GP	S
Desmond Cambridge, Alabama A&M	2002	29	160
Mookie Blaylock, Oklahoma	1988	39	150
Aldwin Ware, Florida A&M	1988	29	142
Darron Brittman, Chicago St	1986	28	139
John Linehan, Providence	2002	31	139

BLOCKED SHOTS

Player and Team	Year	GP	BS
David Robinson, Navy	1986	35	207
Adonal Foyle, Colgate	1997	28	180
Keith Closs, Central Conn St	1996	28	178
Shawn Bradley, BYU	1991	34	177
Wojiech Myrda, LA–Monroe	2002	32	172

STEAL AVERAGE

Player and Team	Year	GP	S	Avg
D. Cambridge, Alabama A&M	2002	29	160	5.52
Darron Brittman, Chicago St	1986	28	139	4.96
Aldwin Ware, Florida A&M	1988	29	142	4.90
John Linehan, Providence	2002	31	139	4.48
Ronn McMahon, E Washington	1990	29	130	4.48

BLOCKED-SHOT AVERAGE

Player and Team	Year	GP	BS	Avg
Adonal Foyle, Colgate	1997	28	180	6.43
Keith Closs, Central Conn St	1996	28	178	6.36
David Robinson, Navy	1986	35	207	5.91
Adonal Foyle, Colgate	1996	29	165	5.69
Wojiech Myrda, LA-Monroe	2002	32	172	5.37

Career Records

POINTS

Player and Team	Ht	Final Year	GP	FG	3FG*	FT	Pts
Pete Maravich, Louisiana St	6-5	1970	83	1387	—	893	3667
Freeman Williams, Portland St	6-4	1978	106	1369	—	511	3249
Lionel Simmons, La Salle	6-7	1990	131	1244	56	673	3217
Alphonso Ford, Mississippi Valley	6-2	1993	109	1121	333	590	3165
Harry Kelly, Texas Southern	6-7	1983	110	1234	—	598	3066
Hersey Hawkins, Bradley	6-3	1988	125	1100	118	690	3008
Oscar Robertson, Cincinnati	6-5	1960	88	1052	—	869	2973
Danny Manning, Kansas	6-10	1988	147	1216	10	509	2951
Alfredrick Hughes, Loyola (IL)	6-5	1985	120	1226	—	462	2914
Elvin Hayes, Houston	6-8	1968	93	1215	—	454	2884
Larry Bird, Indiana St	6-9	1979	94	1154	—	542	2850
Otis Birdsong, Houston	6-4	1977	116	1176	—	480	2832
Kevin Bradshaw, Bethune-Cookman, U.S. Int'l	6-6	1991	111	1027	132	618	2804
Allan Houston, Tennessee	6-6	1993	128	902	346	651	2801
Hank Gathers, Southern Cal, Loyola Marymount	6-7	1990	117	1127	0	469	2723
Reggie Lewis, Northeastern	6-7	1987	122	1043	30 (1)	592	2708
Daren Queenan, Lehigh	6-5	1988	118	1024	29	626	2703
Byron Larkin, Xavier (OH)	6-3	1988	121	1022	51	601	2696
David Robinson, Navy	7-1	1987	127	1032	1	604	2669
Wayman Tisdale, Oklahoma	6-9	1985	104	1077	—	507	2661

*Listed is the number of three-pointers scored since it became the national rule in 1987; the number in the parentheses is number scored prior to 1987—these counted as three points in the game but counted as two-pointers in the national rankings. The three-pointers in the parentheses are not included in total points.

SCORING AVERAGE

Player and Team	Final Year	GP	FG	FT	Pts	Avg
Pete Maravich, Louisiana St	1968	83	1387	893	3667	44.2
Austin Carr, Notre Dame	1971	74	1017	526	2560	34.6
Oscar Robertson, Cincinnati	1960	88	1052	869	2973	33.8
Calvin Murphy, Niagara	1970	77	947	654	2548	33.1
Dwight Lamar, Southwestern Louisiana	1973	57	768	326	1862	32.7
Frank Selvy, Furman	1954	78	922	694	2538	32.5
Rick Mount, Purdue	1970	72	910	503	2323	32.3
Darrell Floyd, Furman	1956	71	868	545	2281	32.1
Nick Werkman, Seton Hall	1964	71	812	649	2273	32.0
Willie Humes, Idaho St	1971	48	565	380	1510	31.5
William Averitt, Pepperdine	1973	49	615	311	1541	31.4
Elgin Baylor, Coll. of Idaho, Seattle	1958	80	956	588	2500	31.3
Elvin Hayes, Houston	1968	93	1215	454	2884	31.0
Freeman Williams, Portland St	1978	106	1369	511	3249	30.7
Larry Bird, Indiana St	1979	94	1154	542	2850	30.3

Career Records (Cont.)

REBOUNDS BEFORE 1973

Player and Team	Final Year	GP	Reb
Tom Gola, La Salle	1955	118	2201
Joe Holup, George Washington	1956	104	2030
Charlie Slack, Marshall	1956	88	1916
Ed Conlin, Fordham	1955	102	1884
Dickie Hemric, Wake Forest	1955	104	1802

REBOUNDS SINCE 1973*

Player and Team	Final Year	GP	Reb
Tim Duncan, Wake Forest	1997	128	1570
Derrick Coleman, Syracuse	1990	143	1537
Malik Rose, Drexel	1996	120	1514
Ralph Sampson, Virginia	1983	132	1511
Pete Padgett, NV-Reno	1976	104	1464

ASSISTS

Player and Team	Final Year	GP	A
Bobby Hurley, Duke	1993	140	1076
Chris Corchiani, N Carolina St	1991	124	1038
Ed Cota, N Carolina	2000	138	1030
Keith Jennings, E Tennessee St	1991	127	983
Sherman Douglas, Syracuse	1989	138	960

FIELD-GOAL PERCENTAGE

Player and Team	Final Year	FG	FGA	Pct
Steve Johnson, Oregon St	1981	828	1222	67.8
Michael Bradley, Kentucky/Villanova	2001	441	651	67.7
Murray Brown, Florida St	1980	566	847	66.8
Lee Campbell, SW Missouri St	1990	411	618	66.5
Warren Kidd, Middle Tennessee St	1993	496	747	66.4

Note: Minimum 400 field goals and 4 FG made per game.

FREE-THROW PERCENTAGE

Player and Team	Final Year	FT	FTA	Pct
Greg Starrick, Kentucky; Southern Illinois	1972	341	375	90.9
Jack Moore, Nebraska	1982	446	495	90.1
Steve Henson, Kansas St	1990	361	401	90.0
Steve Alford, Indiana	1987	535	596	89.8
Bob Lloyd, Rutgers	1967	543	605	89.8

Note: Minimum 300 free throws made.

*Freshmen became eligible for varsity play in 1973.

THEY SAID IT

Tom Izzo, Michigan State basketball coach, after being asked whether he wakes up at night believing his team will suddenly live up to his preseason expectations: "Yeah, I do. But sometimes I wake up and think Halle Berry is right around the corner, too."

Career Records (Cont.)

THREE-POINT FIELD GOALS MADE

Player and Team	Final Year	GP	3FG
Curtis Staples, Virginia	1998	122	413
Keith Veney, Lamar; Marshall	1997	111	409
Doug Day, Radford	1993	117	401
Ronnie Schmitz, MO–Kansas City	1993	112	378
Mark Alberts, Akron	1993	103	375

THREE-POINT FIELD-GOAL PERCENTAGE

Player and Team	Final Year	3FG	3FGA	Pct
Tony Bennett, WI–Green Bay	1992	290	584	49.7
David Olson, Eastern Illinois	1992	262	562	46.6
Ross Land, Northern Arizona	2000	308	664	46.4
Dan Dickau, Washington/Gonzaga	2002	215	465	46.2
Sean Jackson, Ohio/Princeton	1992	243	528	46.0

Note: Minimum 200 3-point field goals and 2.0 3FG/G.

STEALS

Player and Team	Final Year	GP	S
John Linehan, Providence	2002	122	385
Eric Murdock, Providence	1991	117	376
Pepe Sanchez, Temple	2000	116	365
Cookie Belcher, Nebraska	2001	131	353
Kevin Braswell, Georgetown	2002	128	349

BLOCKED SHOTS

Player and Team	Final Year	GP	BS
Wojciech Myrda, Louisiana-Monroe	2002	115	535
Adonal Foyle, Colgate	1997	87	492
Tim Duncan, Wake Forest	1997	128	481
Alonzo Mourning, Georgetown	1992	120	453
Tarvis Williams, Hampton	2001	114	452

NCAA Men's Division I Team Leaders

Division I Team Alltime Wins

Team	First Year	Yrs	W	L	T
Kentucky	1903	100	1849	572	1
N Carolina	1911	93	1808	666	0
Kansas	1899	105	1801	753	0
Duke	1906	98	1706	775	0
St. John's (NY)	1908	96	1661	763	0
Temple	1895	107	1607	874	0
Syracuse	1901	102	1602	737	0
Pennsylvania	1897	103	1555	876	2
Indiana	1901	103	1540	825	0
Notre Dame	1898	98	1529	838	1
UCLA	1920	84	1520	672	0
Oregon St	1902	102	1517	1067	0
Utah	1909	95	1492	775	0
Princeton	1901	103	1475	896	0
Purdue	1897	105	1453	849	0
Washington	1896	101	1444	980	0

Note: Minimum of 25 years in Division I.

Division I Alltime Winning Percentage

Team	First Year	Yrs	W	L	T	Pct
Kentucky	1903	100	1849	572	1	.764
N Carolina	1911	93	1808	666	0	.731
UNLV	1959	45	925	363	0	.718
Kansas	1899	105	1801	753	0	.705
Duke	1906	98	1706	775	0	.688
St. John's (NY)	1908	96	1661	763	0	.685
Syracuse	1901	102	1602	737	0	.685
UCLA	1920	84	1520	672	0	.678
Western Kentucky	1915	84	1466	723	0	.670
Utah	1909	95	1492	775	0	.658
Indiana	1901	103	1540	825	0	.651
Arkansas	1924	80	1377	742	0	.650
Temple	1895	107	1607	874	0	.648
Louisville	1912	89	1431	778	0	.648
Notre Dame	1898	98	1529	838	1	.646

NCAA Men's Division I Winning Streaks

Longest—Full Season

Team	Games	Years	Ended by
UCLA	88	1971–74	Notre Dame (71–70)
San Francisco	60	1955–57	Illinois (62–33)
UCLA	47	1966–68	Houston (71–69)
UNLV	45	1990–91	Duke (79–77)
Texas	44	1913–17	Rice (24–18)
Seton Hall	43	1939–41	LIU-Brooklyn (49–26)
LIU-Brooklyn	43	1935–37	Stanford (45–31)
UCLA	41	1968–69	Southern Cal (46–44)
Marquette	39	1970–71	Ohio St (60–59)
Cincinnati	37	1962–63	Wichita St (65–64)
N Carolina	37	1957–58	W Virginia (75–64)

Longest—Regular Season

Team	Games	Years	Ended by
UCLA	76	1971–74	Notre Dame (71–70)
Indiana	57	1975–77	Toledo (59–57)
Marquette	56	1970–72	Detroit (70–49)
Kentucky	54	1952–55	Georgia Tech (59–58)
San Francisco	51	1955–57	Illinois (62–33)
Pennsylvania	48	1970–72	Temple (57–52)
Ohio State	47	1960–62	Wisconsin (86–67)
Texas	44	1913–17	Rice (24–18)
UCLA	43	1966–68	Houston (71–69)
LIU-Brooklyn	43	1935–37	Stanford (45–31)
Seton Hall	42	1939–41	LIU-Brooklyn (49–26)

Longest—Home Court

Team	Games	Years	Team	Games	Years
Kentucky	129	1943–55	Lamar	80	1978–84
St. Bonaventure	99	1948–61	Long Beach St	75	1968–74
UCLA	98	1970–76	UNLV	72	1974–78
Cincinnati	86	1957–64	Arizona	71	1987–92
Marquette	81	1967–73	Cincinnati	68	1972–78
Arizona	81	1945–51	Western Kentucky	67	1949–55

NCAA Men's Division I Winningest Coaches

Active Coaches

WINS

Coach and Team	W
James Phelan, Mt. St. Mary's (MD)	830
Bob Knight, Texas Tech	809
Lefty Driesell, Georgia St	786
Lou Henson, New Mexico St	762
Eddie Sutton, Oklahoma St	724
John Chaney, Temple	692
Lute Olson, Arizona	690
Mike Krzyzewski, Duke	663
Jim Boeheim, Syracuse	653
Jim Calhoun, Connecticut	647

Note: Minimum 5 years as a Division I head coach; includes record at 4-year colleges only.

WINNING PERCENTAGE

Coach and Team	Yrs	W	L	Pct
Roy Williams, Kansas	15	418	101	.805
Jim Boeheim, Syracuse	27	653	226	.743
Lute Olson, Arizona	30	690	240	.742
Rick Majerus, Utah	19	407	142	.741
Mike Krzyzewski, Duke	28	663	234	.739
Bob Huggins, Cincinnati	22	517	184	.738
Rick Pitino, Louisville	17	396	144	.733
Bob Knight, Texas Tech	37	809	311	.722
John Chaney, Temple	31	692	269	.720
Tom Izzo, Michigan St	8	189	78	.708

Note: Minimum 5 years as a Division I head coach; includes record at 4-year colleges only.

Alltime Winningest Men's Division I Coaches

	W
Dean Smith (N Carolina)	879
Adolph Rupp (Kentucky)	876
Jim Phelan (Mt. St. Mary's)	830
Bob Knight (Army, Indiana, Texas Tech)	809
Lefty Driesell (Davidson, Maryland, James Madison, Georgia St)	786
Jerry Tarkanian (Long Beach St, UNLV, Fresno St)	778
Hank Iba (NW Missouri St, Colorado, Oklahoma St)	767
Lou Henson (Hardin-Simmons, New Mexico St, Illinois)	762
Ed Diddle (Western Kentucky)	759
Phog Allen (Baker, Kansas, Haskell, Central Missouri St, Kansas)	746
Norm Stewart (Northern Iowa, Missouri)	731
Eddie Sutton (Creighton, Arkansas, Kentucky, Oklahoma St)	724
Ray Meyer (DePaul)	724
Don Haskins (UTEP)	719
John Chaney (Cheyney St, Temple)	692
Denny Crum (Louisville)	675

Note: Minimum 10 head coaching seasons in Division I.

Alltime Winningest Men's Division I Coaches *(Cont.)*
WINNING PERCENTAGE

Coach (Team, Years)	Yrs	W	L	Pct
Clair Bee (Rider 29–31, LIU-Brooklyn 32–45, 46–51)	21	412	87	.826
Adolph Rupp (Kentucky 31–72)	41	876	190	.822
Roy Williams (Kansas 89–)	15	418	101	.805
John Wooden (Indiana St 47–48, UCLA 49–75)	29	664	162	.804
John Kresse (Charleston 80–02)	23	560	143	.797
Jerry Tarkanian (Long Beach St 69–73, UNLV 74–92, Fresno St 95–02)	31	778	202	.794
Dean Smith (N Carolina 62–97)	36	879	254	.776
Harry Fisher (Columbia 07–16, Army 22–23, 25)	13	147	44	.770
Frank Keaney (Rhode Island 21–48)	27	387	117	.768
George Keogan (St. Louis 16, Allegheny 19, Valparaiso 20–21, Notre Dame 24–43)	24	385	117	.767
Jack Ramsay (St. Joseph's [PA] 56–66)	11	231	71	.765
Vic Bubas (Duke 60–69)	10	213	67	.761
Charles (Chick) Davies (Duquesne 25–43, 47–48)	21	314	106	.748
Ray Mears (Wittenberg 57–62, Tennessee 63–77)	21	399	135	.747
Jim Boeheim (Syracuse 77–)	27	653	226	.743
Lute Olson (Long Beach St 73–74, Iowa 74–83, Arizona 83–)	30	690	240	.742
Rick Majerus (Marquette 84–86, Ball St 88–89, Utah 90–)	19	407	142	.741
Al McGuire (Belmont Abbey 58–64, Marquette 65–77)	20	405	143	.739
Everett Case (N Carolina St 47–64)	18	376	133	.739
Phog Allen (Baker 06–08, Kansas 08–09, Haskell 09, Cent MO St 13–19, Kansas 20–56)	48	746	264	.739
Mike Krzyzewski (Army 76–80, Duke 81–)	28	663	234	.739

Note: Minimum 10 head coaching seasons in Division I.

NCAA Women's Division I Championship Results

Year	Winner	Score	Runner-up	Winning Coach
1982	Louisiana Tech	76–62	Cheyney	Sonja Hogg
1983	Southern Cal	69–67	Louisiana Tech	Linda Sharp
1984	Southern Cal	72–61	Tennessee	Linda Sharp
1985	Old Dominion	70–65	Georgia	Marianne Stanley
1986	Texas	97–81	Southern Cal	Jody Conradt
1987	Tennessee	67–44	Louisiana Tech	Pat Summitt
1988	Louisiana Tech	56–54	Auburn	Leon Barmore
1989	Tennessee	76–60	Auburn	Pat Summitt
1990	Stanford	88–81	Auburn	Tara VanDerveer
1991	Tennessee	70–67 (OT)	Virginia	Pat Summitt
1992	Stanford	78–62	Western Kentucky	Tara VanDerveer
1993	Texas Tech	84–82	Ohio State	Marsha Sharp
1994	N Carolina	60–59	Louisiana Tech	Sylvia Hatchell
1995	Connecticut	70–64	Tennessee	Geno Auriemma
1996	Tennessee	83–65	Georgia	Pat Summitt
1997	Tennessee	68–59	Old Dominion	Pat Summitt
1998	Tennessee	93–75	Louisiana Tech	Pat Summitt
1999	Purdue	62–45	Duke	Carolyn Peck
2000	Connecticut	71–52	Tennessee	Geno Auriemma
2001	Notre Dame	68–66	Purdue	Muffet McGraw
2002	Connecticut	82–70	Oklahoma	Geno Auriemma
2003	Connecticut	73–68	Tennessee	Geno Auriemma

NCAA Women's Division I Alltime Individual Leaders

Single-Game Records
SCORING HIGHS

Pts	Player and Team vs Opponent	Year
60	Cindy Brown, Long Beach St vs San Jose St	1987
58	Kim Perrot, SW Louisiana vs SE Louisiana	1990
58	Lorri Bauman, Drake vs SW Missouri St	1984
56	Jackie Stiles, SW Missouri St vs Evansville	2000
55	Patricia Hoskins, Mississippi Valley vs Southern-BR	1989
55	Patricia Hoskins, Mississippi Valley vs Alabama St	1989
54	Anjinea Hopson, Grambling vs Jackson St	1994
54	Mary Lowry, Baylor vs Texas	1994
54	Wanda Ford, Drake vs SW Missouri St	1986

Three tied with 53.

Single-Game Records *(Cont.)*
REBOUNDS

Reb	Player and Team vs Opponent	Year
40	Deborah Temple, Delta St vs AL-Birmingham	1983
37	Rosina Pearson, Bethune-Cookman vs Florida Memorial	1985
33	Maureen Formico, Pepperdine vs Loyola (CA)	1985
31	Darlene Beale, Howard vs S Carolina St	1987
30	Cindy Bonforte, Wagner vs Queens (NY)	1983
30	Kayone Hankins, New Orleans vs. Nicholls St	1994
30	Wanda Ford, Drake vs Eastern Illinois	1985
30	Jennifer Butler, Massachusetts vs Florida	2003

Three tied with 29.

ASSISTS

A	Player and Team vs Opponent	Year
23	Michelle Burden, Kent St vs Ball St	1991
22	Shawn Monday, Tennessee Tech vs Morehead St	1988
22	Veronica Pettry, Loyola (IL) vs Detroit	1989
22	Tine Freil, Pacific vs Wichita St	1991
21	Tine Freil, Pacific vs Fresno St	1992
21	Amy Bauer, Wisconsin vs Detroit	1989
21	Neacole Hall, Alabama St vs Southern-BR	1989

Six tied with 20.

Single Season Records
POINTS

Player and Team	Year	GP	FG	3FG	FT	Pts
Jackie Stiles, SW Missouri St	2001	35	365	65	267	1062
Cindy Brown, Long Beach St	1987	35	362	—	250	974
Genia Miller, Cal St-Fullerton	1991	33	376	0	217	969
Sheryl Swoopes, Texas Tech	1993	34	356	32	211	955
Andrea Congreaves, Mercer	1992	28	353	77	142	925
Wanda Ford, Drake	1986	30	390	—	139	919
Chamique Holdsclaw, Tennessee	1998	39	370	9	166	915
Barbara Kennedy, Clemson	1982	31	392	—	124	908
Patricia Hoskins, Mississippi Valley	1989	27	345	13	205	908
LaTaunya Pollard, Long Beach St	1983	31	376	—	155	907

SEASON SCORING AVERAGE

Player and Team	Year	GP	FG	3FG	FT	Pts	Avg
Patricia Hoskins, Mississippi Valley	1989	27	345	13	205	908	33.6
Andrea Congreaves, Mercer	1992	28	353	77	142	925	33.0
Deborah Temple, Delta St	1984	28	373	—	127	873	31.2
Andrea Congreaves, Mercer	1993	26	302	51	150	805	31.0
Wanda Ford, Drake	1986	30	390	—	139	919	30.6
Anucha Browne, Northwestern	1985	28	341	—	173	855	30.5
LeChandra LeDay, Grambling	1988	28	334	36	146	850	30.4
Jackie Stiles, SW MIssouri St	2001	35	365	65	267	1062	30.3
Kim Perrot, Southwestern Louisiana	1990	28	308	95	128	839	30.0
Tina Hutchinson, San Diego St	1984	30	383	—	132	898	29.9
Jan Jensen, Drake	1991	30	358	6	166	888	29.6
Genia Miller, Cal St-Fullerton	1991	33	376	0	217	969	29.4
Barbara Kennedy, Clemson	1982	31	392	—	124	908	29.3
LaTaunya Pollard, Long Beach St	1983	31	376	—	155	907	29.3
Lisa McMullen, Alabama St	1991	28	285	126	119	815	29.1

Single Season Records *(Cont.)*

Player and Team	Year	GP	Reb	Player and Team	Year	GP	Reb
Wanda Ford, Drake	1985	30	534	Rosina Pearson, Beth.-Cookman	1985	26	480
Wanda Ford, Drake	1986	30	506	Patricia Hoskins, Miss Valley	1987	28	476
Anne Donovan, Old Dominion	1983	35	504	Cheryl Miller, Southern Cal	1985	30	474
Darlene Jones, Miss Valley	1983	31	487	Darlene Beale, Howard	1987	29	459
Melanie Simpson, Okla. City	1982	37	481	Olivia Bradley, W Virginia	1985	30	458

REBOUND AVERAGE

Player and Team	Year	GP	Reb	Avg
Rosina Pearson, Bethune-Cookman	1985	26	480	18.5
Wanda Ford, Drake	1985	30	534	17.8
Katie Beck, E Tennessee St	1988	25	441	17.6
DeShawne Blocker, E Tennessee St	1994	26	450	17.3
Patricia Hoskins, Mississippi Valley	1987	28	476	17.0
Wanda Ford, Drake	1986	30	506	16.9
Patricia Hoskins, Mississippi Valley	1989	27	440	16.3
Joy Kellogg, Oklahoma City	1984	23	373	16.2
Deborah Mitchell, Mississippi Coll.	1983	28	447	16.0
Cheryl Miller, Southern California	1985	30	474	15.8

FIELD-GOAL PERCENTAGE

Player and Team	Year	GP	FG	FGA	Pct
Myndee Larsen, Southern Utah	1998	28	249	344	72.4
Chantelle Anderson, Vanderbilt	2001	34	292	404	72.3
Deneka Knowles, Southeastern La.	1996	26	199	276	72.1
Barbara Farris, Tulane	1998	27	151	210	71.9
Renay Adams, Tennessee Tech	1991	30	185	258	71.7
Regina Days, Georgia Southern	1986	27	234	332	70.5
Kim Wood, WI-Green Bay	1994	27	188	271	69.4
Kelly Lyons, Old Dominion	1990	31	308	444	69.4
Alisha Hill, Howard	1995	28	194	281	69.0
Ruth Riley, Notre Dame	1999	31	198	290	68.3

Based on qualifiers for annual championship.

FREE-THROW PERCENTAGE

Player and Team	Year	GP	FT	FTA	Pct
Ginny Doyle, Richmond	1992	29	96	101	95.0
Jill Marano, La Salle	2003	29	88	93	94.6
Sue Bird, Connecticut	2002	39	98	104	94.2
Paula Corder-King, SE Missouri St	1999	28	111	118	94.1
Kandi Brown, Morehead St	2003	28	104	111	93.7
Linda Cyborski, Delaware	1991	29	74	79	93.7
Kandi Brown, Morehead St	2002	29	74	79	93.7
Paula Corder-King, SE Missouri St	2000	27	69	74	93.2
Jennifer Howard, N Carolina St	1994	27	118	127	92.9
Keely Feeman, Cincinnati	1986	30	76	82	92.7

Based on qualifiers for annual championship.

Career Records
POINTS

Player and Team	Yrs	GP	Pts
Jackie Stiles, SW Missouri St	1997–01	129	3393
Patricia Hoskins, Mississippi Valley	1985–89	110	3122
Lorri Bauman, Drake	1981–84	120	3115
Chamique Holdsclaw, Tennessee	1995–99	148	3025
Cheryl Miller, Southern Cal	1983–86	128	3018
Cindy Blodgett, Maine	1994–98	118	3005
Valorie Whiteside, Appalachian St	1984–88	116	2944
Joyce Walker, Louisiana St	1981–84	117	2906
Sandra Hodge, New Orleans	1981–84	107	2860
Andrea Congreaves, Mercer	1989–93	108	2796

SCORING AVERAGE

Player and Team	Yrs	GP	FG	3FG	FT	Pts	Avg
Patricia Hoskins, Mississippi Valley	1985–89	110	1196	24	706	3122	28.4
Sandra Hodge, New Orleans	1981–84	107	1194	—	472	2860	26.7
Jackie Stiles, SW Missouri St	1997–01	129	1160	221	852	3393	26.3
Lorri Bauman, Drake	1981–84	120	1104	—	907	3115	26.0
Andrea Congreaves, Mercer	1989–93	108	1107	153	429	2796	25.9
Cindy Blodgett, Maine	1994–98	118	1055	219	676	3005	25.5
Valorie Whiteside, Appalachian St	1984–88	116	1153	0	638	2944	25.4
Joyce Walker, Louisiana St	1981–84	117	1259	—	388	2906	24.8
Tarcha Hollis, Grambling	1988–91	85	904	3	247	2058	24.2
Korie Hlede, Duquesne	1994–98	109	1045	162	379	2631	24.1

NCAA Men's Division II Championship Results

Year	Winner	Score	Runner-up	Third Place	Fourth Place
1957	Wheaton (IL)	89–65	Kentucky Wesleyan	Mount St Mary's (MD)	Cal St-Los Angeles
1958	S Dakota	75–53	St. Michael's	Evansville	Wheaton (IL)
1959	Evansville	83–67	SW Missouri St	N Carolina A&T	Cal St-Los Angeles
1960	Evansville	90–69	Chapman	Kentucky Wesleyan	Cornell College
1961	Wittenberg	42–38	SE Missouri St	S Dakota St	Mount St Mary's (MD)
1962	Mount St Mary's (MD)	58–57 (OT)	Cal St-Sacramento	Southern Illinois	Nebraska Wesleyan
1963	S Dakota St	44–42	Wittenberg	Oglethorpe	Southern Illinois
1964	Evansville	72–59	Akron	N Carolina A&T	Northern Iowa
1965	Evansville	85–82 (OT)	Southern Illinois	N Dakota	St Michael's
1966	Kentucky Wesleyan	54–51	Southern Illinois	Akron	N Dakota
1967	Winston-Salem	77–74	SW Missouri St	Kentucky Wesleyan	Illinois St
1968	Kentucky Wesleyan	63–52	Indiana St	Trinity (TX)	Ashland
1969	Kentucky Wesleyan	75–71	SW Missouri St	†Vacated	Ashland
1970	Philadelphia Textile	76–65	Tennessee St	UC-Riverside	Buffalo St
1971	Evansville	97–82	Old Dominion	†Vacated	Kentucky Wesleyan
1972	Roanoke	84–72	Akron	Tennessee St	Eastern Mich
1973	Kentucky Wesleyan	78–76 (OT)	Tennessee St	Assumption	Brockport St
1974	Morgan St	67–52	SW Missouri St	Assumption	New Orleans
1975	Old Dominion	76–74	New Orleans	Assumption	TN-Chattanooga
1976	Puget Sound	83–74	TN-Chattanooga	Eastern Illinois	Old Dominion
1977	TN-Chattanooga	71–62	Randolph-Macon	N Alabama	Sacred Heart
1978	Cheyney	47–40	WI-Green Bay	Eastern Illinois	Central Florida
1979	N Alabama	64–50	WI-Green Bay	Cheyney	Bridgeport
1980	Virginia Union	80–74	New York Tech	Florida Southern	N Alabama
1981	Florida Southern	73–68	Mount St Mary's (MD)	Cal Poly-SLO	WI-Green Bay
1982	District of Columbia	73–63	Florida Southern	Kentucky Wesleyan	Cal St-Bakersfield
1983	Wright St	92–73	District of Columbia	*Cal St-Bakersfield	*Morningside
1984	Central Missouri St	81–77	St. Augustine's	*Kentucky Wesleyan	*N Alabama
1985	Jacksonville St	74–73	S Dakota St	*Kentucky Wesleyan	*Mount St. Mary's (MD)
1986	Sacred Heart	93–87	SE Missouri St	*Cheyney	*Florida Southern
1987	Kentucky Wesleyan	92–74	Gannon	*Delta St	*Eastern Montana
1988	Lowell	75–72	AK-Anchorage	Florida Southern	Troy St
1989	N Carolina Central	73–46	SE Missouri St	UC-Riverside	Jacksonville St
1990	Kentucky Wesleyan	93–79	Cal St-Bakersfield	N Dakota	Morehouse
1991	N Alabama	79–72	Bridgeport (CT)	*Cal St-Bakersfield	*Virginia Union
1992	Virginia Union	100–75	Bridgeport (CT)	*Cal St-Bakersfield	*California (PA)

*Indicates tied for third. †Student-athletes representing American International in 1969 and Southwestern Louisiana in 1971 were declared ineligible subsequent to the tournament. Under NCAA rules, the teams' and ineligible student-athletes' records were deleted, and the teams' places in the final standings were vacated.

NCAA Men's Division II Championship Results *(Cont.)*

Year	Winner	Score	Runner-up	Third Place	Fourth Place
1993	Cal St-Bakersfield	85–72	Troy St (AL)	*New Hampshire Coll	*Wayne St (MI)
1994	Cal St-Bakersfield	92–86	Southern Indiana	*New Hampshire Coll	*Washburn
1995	Southern Indiana	71–63	UC–Riverside	*Norfolk St	*Indiana (PA)
1996	Fort Hays St	70–63	Northern Kentucky	*California (PA)	*Virginia Union
1997	Cal St-Bakersfield	57–56	Northern Kentucky	*Lynn	*Salem-Teikyo
1998	UC-Davis	83–77	Kentucky Wesleyan	*St. Rose	*Virginia Union
1999	Kentucky Wesleyan	75–60	Metropolitan St	*Truman St	*Florida Southern
2000	Metropolitan St	97–79	Kentucky Wesleyan	*Missouri Southern	*Seattle Pacific
2001	Kentucky Wesleyan	72–63	Washburn	*Western Washington	*Tampa
2002	Metropolitan St	80–72	Kentucky Wesleyan	*Shaw	*Indiana (PA)
2003	Northeastern St (OK)	75–64	vacated	*Bowie St	*Queens (NC)

NCAA Men's Division II Alltime Individual Leaders

SINGLE-GAME SCORING HIGHS

Pts	Player and Team vs Opponent	Date
113	Bevo Francis, Rio Grande vs Hillsdale	1954
84	Bevo Francis, Rio Grande vs Alliance	1954
82	Bevo Francis, Rio Grande vs Bluffton	1954
80	Paul Crissman, Southern Cal Col vs Pacific Christian	1966
77	William English, Winston-Salem vs Fayetteville St	1968

Single Season Records
SCORING AVERAGE

Player and Team	Year	GP	FG	FT	Pts	Avg
Bevo Francis, Rio Grande	1954	27	444	367	1255	46.5
Earl Glass, Mississippi Industrial	1963	19	322	171	815	42.9
Earl Monroe, Winston-Salem	1967	32	509	311	1329	41.5
John Rinka, Kenyon	1970	23	354	234	942	41.0
Willie Shaw, Lane	1964	18	303	121	727	40.4

REBOUND AVERAGE

Player and Team	Year	GP	Reb	Avg
Tom Hart, Middlebury	1956	21	620	29.5
Tom Hart, Middlebury	1955	22	649	29.5
Frank Stronczek, American Int'l	1966	26	717	27.6
R.C. Owens, College of Idaho	1954	25	677	27.1
Maurice Stokes, St Francis (PA)	1954	26	689	26.5

ASSISTS

Player and Team	Year	GP	A
Steve Ray, Bridgeport	1989	32	400
Steve Ray, Bridgeport	1990	33	385
Tony Smith, Pfeiffer	1992	35	349
Jim Ferrer, Bentley	1989	31	309
Rob Paternostro, New Hamp. Coll.	1995	33	309

ASSIST AVERAGE

Player and Team	Year	GP	A	Avg
Steve Ray, Bridgeport	1989	32	400	12.5
Steve Ray, Bridgeport	1990	33	385	11.7
Demetri Beekman, Assumption	1993	23	264	11.5
Ernest Jenkins, NM Highlands	1995	27	291	10.8
Brian Gregory, Oakland	1989	28	300	10.7

FIELD-GOAL PERCENTAGE

Player and Team	Year	Pct
Todd Linder, Tampa	1987	75.2
Maurice Stafford, N Alabama	1984	75.0
Matthew Cornegay, Tuskegee	1982	74.8
Brian Moten, W Georgia	1992	73.4
Ed Phillips, Alabama A&M	1968	73.3

FREE-THROW PERCENTAGE

Player and Team	Year	Pct
Paul Cluxton, Northern Kentucky	1997	100.0
Tomas Rimkus, Pace	1997	95.6
C.J. Cowgill, Chaminade	2001	95.0
Billy Newton, Morgan St	1976	94.4
Kent Andrews, McNeese St	1968	94.4

Career Records
POINTS

Player and Team	Yrs	Pts
Travis Grant, Kentucky St	1969–72	4045
Bob Hopkins, Grambling	1953–56	3759
Tony Smith, Pfeiffer	1989–92	3350
Earnest Lee, Clark Atlanta	1984–87	3298
Joe Miller, Alderson-Broaddus	1954–57	3294

Career Records (Cont.)

CAREER SCORING AVERAGE

Player and Team	Yrs	GP	Pts	Avg
Travis Grant, Kentucky St	1969–72	121	4045	33.4
John Rinka, Kenyon	1967–70	99	3251	32.8
Florindo Vieira, Quinnipiac	1954–57	69	2263	32.8
Willie Shaw, Lane	1961–64	76	2379	31.3
Mike Davis, Virginia Union	1966–69	89	2758	31.0

REBOUND AVERAGE

Player and Team	Yrs	GP	Reb	Avg
Tom Hart, Middlebury	1953, 55–56	63	1738	27.6
Maurice Stokes, St. Francis (PA)	1953–55	72	1812	25.2
Frank Stronczek, American Int'l	1965–67	62	1549	25.0
Bill Thieben, Hofstra	1954–56	76	1837	24.2
Hank Brown, Lowell Tech	1965–67	49	1129	23.0

ASSISTS

Player and Team	Yrs	A
Demetri Beekman, Assumption	1990–93	1044
Adam Kaufman, Edinboro	1998–01	936
Rob Paternostro, New Hamp. Coll.	1992–95	919
Gallagher Driscoll, St. Rose	1989–92	878
Tony Smith, Pfeiffer	1989–92	828

ASSIST AVERAGE

Player and Team	Yrs	GP	A	Avg
Steve Ray, Bridgeport	1989–90	65	785	12.1
Demetri Beekman, Assumption	1990–93	119	1044	8.8
Ernest Jenkins, NM Highlands	1992–95	84	699	8.3
Adam Kaufman, Edinboro	1998–01	116	936	8.1
Mark Benson, Texas A&I	1989–91	86	674	7.8

Note: Minimum 550 Assists.

FIELD-GOAL PERCENTAGE

Player and Team	Yrs	Pct
Todd Linder, Tampa	1984–87	70.8
Tom Schurfranz, Bellarmine	1989–92	70.2
Chad Scott, California (PA)	1991–94	70.0
Ed Phillips, Alabama, A&M	1968–71	68.9
Ulysses Hackett, SC-Spartanburg	1990–92	67.9

Note: Minimum 400 FGM.

FREE-THROW PERCENTAGE

Player and Team	Yrs	Pct
Paul Cluxton, Northern Kentucky	1994–97	93.5
Kent Andrews, McNeese St	1967–69	91.6
Jon Hagen, Mankato St	1963–65	90.0
Dave Reynolds, Davis & Elkins	1986–89	89.3
Michael Shue, Lock Haven	1994–97	88.5

Note: Minimum 250 FTM.

NCAA Men's Division III Championship Results

Year	Winner	Score	Runner-up	Third Place	Fourth Place
1975	LeMoyne-Owen	57–54	Glassboro St	Augustana (IL)	Brockport St
1976	Scranton	60–57	Wittenberg	Augustana (IL)	Plattsburgh St
1977	Wittenberg	79–66	Oneonta St	Scranton	Hamline
1978	North Park	69–57	Widener	Albion	Stony Brook
1979	North Park	66–62	Potsdam St	Franklin & Marshall	Centre
1980	North Park	83–76	Upsala	Wittenberg	Longwood
1981	Potsdam St	67–65 (OT)	Augustana (IL)	Ursinus	Otterbein
1982	Wabash	83–62	Potsdam St	Brooklyn	Cal St-Stanislaus
1983	Scranton	64–63	Wittenberg	Roanoke	WI–Whitewater
1984	WI–Whitewater	103–86	Clark (MA)	DePauw	Upsala
1985	North Park	72–71	Potsdam St	Nebraska Wesleyan	Widener
1986	Potsdam St	76–73	LeMoyne-Owen	Nebraska Wesleyan	Jersey City St
1987	North Park	106–100	Clark (MA)	Wittenberg	Stockton St
1988	Ohio Wesleyan	92–70	Scranton	Nebraska Wesleyan	Hartwick
1989	WI–Whitewater	94–86	Trenton St	Southern Maine	Centre
1990	Rochester	43–42	DePauw	Washington (MD)	Calvin
1991	WI–Platteville	81–74	Franklin & Marshall	Otterbein	Ramapo (NJ)
1992	Calvin	62–49	Rochester	WI–Platteville	Jersey City St
1993	Ohio Northern	71–68	Augustana	Mass–Dartmouth	Rowan
1994	Lebanon Valley Coll	66–59 (OT)	New York University	Wittenberg	St Thomas (MN)
1995	WI–Platteville	69–55	Manchester	Rowan	Trinity (CT)
1996	Rowan	100–93	Hope (MI)	Illinois Wesleyan	Franklin & Marshall
1997	Illinois Wesleyan	89–86	Nebraska Wesleyan	Williams	Alvernia
1998	WI–Platteville	69–56	Hope (MI)	Williams	Wilkes
1999	WI–Platteville	76–75 (2 OT)	Hampden-Sydney	William Paterson	Connecticut Coll.
2000	Calvin	79–74	WI-Eau Claire	Salem St	Franklin & Marshall
2001	Catholic	76–62	William Paterson	*Illinois Wesleyan	*Ohio Northern
2002	Otterbein	102–83	Elizabethtown	Carthage	Rochester
2003	Williams	67–65	Gustavus Adolphus	Wooster	Hampden Sydney

NCAA Men's Division III Alltime Individual Leaders

SINGLE-GAME SCORING HIGHS

Pts	Player and Team vs Opponent	Year
77	Jeff Clement, Grinnell vs Illinois College	1998
69	Steve Diekmann, Grinnell vs Simpson	1995
63	Joe DeRoche, Thomas vs St. Joseph's (ME)	1988
62	Shannon Lilly, Bishop vs Southwest Assembly of God	1983
61	Steve Honderd, Calvin vs Kalamazoo	1993
61	Dana Wilson, Husson vs Ricker	1974
61	Joshua Metzger, Wisconsin Lutheran vs Grinnell	2000

Single Season Records

SCORING AVERAGE

Player and Team	Year	GP	FG	FT	Pts	Avg
Steve Diekmann, Grinnell	1995	20	223	162	745	37.3
Rickey Sutton, Lyndon St	1976	14	207	93	507	36.2
Shannon Lilly, Bishop	1983	26	345	218	908	34.9
Dana Wilson, Husson	1974	20	288	122	698	34.9
Rickey Sutton, Lyndon St	1977	16	223	112	558	34.9

REBOUND AVERAGE

Player and Team	Year	GP	Reb	Avg
Joe Manley, Bowie St	1976	29	579	20.0
Fred Petty, New Hampshire College	1974	22	436	19.8
Larry Williams, Pratt	1977	24	457	19.0
Charles Greer, Thomas	1977	17	318	18.7
Larry Parker, Plattsburgh St	1975	23	430	18.7

ASSISTS

Player and Team	Year	GP	A
Robert James, Kean	1989	29	391
Tennyson Whitted, Ramapo	2002	29	319
Ricky Spicer, WI-Whitewater	1989	31	295
Joe Marcotte, New Jersey Tech	1995	30	292
Andre Bolton, Chris. Newport	1996	30	289

ASSIST AVERAGE

Player and Team	Year	GP	A	Avg
Robert James, Kean	1989	29	391	13.5
Albert Kirchner, Mt. St. Vincent	1990	24	267	11.1
Tennyson Whitted, Ramapo	2002	29	319	11.0
Ron Torgalski, Hamilton	1989	26	275	10.6
Louis Adams, Rust	1989	22	227	10.3

FIELD-GOAL PERCENTAGE

Player and Team	Year	Pct
Travis Weiss, St. John's (MN)	1994	76.6
Pete Metzelaars, Wabash	1982	75.3
Tony Rychlec, Mass. Maritime	1981	74.9
Tony Rychlec, Mass. Maritime	1982	73.1
Russ Newnan, Menlo	1991	73.0

FREE-THROW PERCENTAGE

Player and Team	Year	Pct
Korey Coon, IL Wesleyan	2000	96.3
Chanse Young, Manchester	1998	95.6
Andy Enfield, Johns Hopkins	1991	95.3
Nick Wilkins, Coe	2003	95.7
Chris Carideo, Widener	1992	95.2
Yudi Teichman, Yeshiva	1989	95.2

Career Records

POINTS

Player and Team	Yrs	Pts
Andre Foreman, Salisbury St	1989–92	2940
Lamont Strothers, Chris. Newport	1988–91	2709
Matt Hancock, Colby	1987–90	2678
Scott Fitch, Geneseo St	1990–94	2634
Greg Grant, Trenton St	1987–89	2611

CAREER SCORING AVERAGE

Player and Team	Yrs	GP	Avg
Dwain Govan, Bishop	1974–75	55	32.8
Dave Russell, Shepherd	1974–75	60	30.6
Rickey Sutton, Lyndon St	1976–79	80	29.7
John Atkins, Knoxville	1976–78	70	28.7
Steve Petnik, Windham	1974–77	76	27.6

REBOUND AVERAGE

Player and Team	Yrs	GP	Reb	Avg
Larry Parker, Plattsburgh St	1975–78	85	1482	17.4
Charles Greer, Thomas	1975–77	58	926	16.0
Willie Parr, LeMoyne-Owen	1974–76	76	1182	15.6
Michael Smith, Hamilton	1989–92	107	1632	15.2
Dave Kufeld, Yeshiva	1977–80	81	1222	15.1

ASSIST AVERAGE

Player and Team	Yrs	Avg
Phil Dixon, Shenandoah	1993–96	8.6
Steve Artis, Chris. Newport	1990–93	8.1
David Genovese, Mt. St. Vincent	1992–95	7.5
Kevin Root, Eureka	1989–91	7.1
Dennis Jacobi, Bowdoin	1989–92	7.1

The Stanley Cup champion New Jersey Devils

Hockey

Sympathy for the Devils

The New Jersey Devils won their third Stanley Cup in nine years—so why can't they get any respect from NHL fans?

BY B.J. SCHECTER

THE NEW JERSEY DEVILS are walking, talking, skating, shooting evidence that you don't have to be flashy to be successful in hockey. Though they play just across the Hudson River from the bright-lights-on-Broadway New York Rangers, the Devils are a world apart from that high-rolling, low-achieving outfit. The Devils don't get the fan support they deserve (they failed to sell out several playoff games) and they play in a nondescript arena built on top of a swamp. Their style of play often matches that arena, miring opponents and paying spectators alike in a sleep-inducing swamp of low-scoring, defensive hockey. But no one can argue with the Devils' success, which reached new heights in 2002–03 after a thrilling 3–0 win over the Anaheim Mighty Ducks in Game 7 of the Stanley Cup finals. The victory brought New Jersey its third championship in nine years.

In Detroit, home of the Red Wings, such feats bring the city to a weeklong standstill of celebration. In New Jersey, they have

parade in a parking lot and get on with business as usual. Perhaps that's because Devils president Lou Lamoriello has such a keen eye for hard-nosed, hard-working players who are more interested in winning than in personal accolades. When New Jersey star center Bobby Holik signed a $9 million-a-year deal with the Rangers, Lamoriello didn't panic. He watched a player he'd been grooming for some time, John Madden, who earns $1.5 million per season, blossom into one of the best centers in the league.

"I think John was the key to our success all year," said Devils goalie Martin Brodeur, one of the Devils' few recognizable stars. "When Holik left, a lot of people were asking the question: 'Who is going to be the guy?' John came in and took it to heart to be the best player out there every night and compete really hard."

Though the Devils often scored less than Bill Gates at the junior prom, they didn't need a lot of goals to win, thanks to their defensive style and to Brodeur. While Anaheim's Jean-Sébastien Giguere stole

PHOTO BY ELSA/GETTY IMAGES/NHLI

the spotlight with his spectacular play during the early rounds of the playoffs—and took home the Conn Smythe Trophy as the MVP of the postseason—it was the steady Brodeur who excelled in the finals. Brodeur produced three shutouts in the finals—running his playoff total to a single-season record seven—and reaffirmed himself as the top goaltender in the NHL.

The series began with a pair of 3–0 shutouts by Brodeur at the Meadowlands and it appeared that the Devils might sweep the Ducks, who were appearing in their first Stanley Cup. But Anaheim showed some resiliency by winning Games 3 and 4 in overtime at home to tie the series. In the

Center stage: the indefatigable Madden picked up where Holik left off.

first period of Game 5, Madden received a cut on his left cheek from the skate of Anaheim's Adam Oates. The fiery Devils center bled all over the ice and required 16 stitches before he could resume playing. To that point, the series had been played with a sportsmanship that bordered on the genteel. Madden's injury changed that. As Devils center Scott Gomez put it, "Everyone had been kind of polite, and the series wasn't that rough. It definitely needed some blood."

Apparently, the bloodletting loosened

Giguere's white-hot goaltending carried the unheralded Ducks to the Stanley Cup finals.

up the goal scorers, who had been MIA until then. In the series' first 248 minutes of action, there had been a total of 12 goals and three shutouts. In the first 52 minutes and 52 seconds of Game 5, there were nine goals, and the series now pulsed with energy. New Jersey won 6–3 and, more importantly, rattled Giguere, who had been nearly impenetrable. "I'm sure Anaheim disagrees," said Gomez. "but this was good for hockey. You put nine goals on the board, you get people talking."

In Game 6, all the talk was about the thundering hit laid on Paul Kariya by Devils defenseman Scott Stevens. The 6'1", 215-pound Stevens leveled the 5'10", 180-pound Kariya in the second period, leaving the Ducks captain lying on the ice for two min-

utes. Kariya was helped to the Anaheim dressing room, and when he got his bearings, he turned to team physician Craig Milhouse and said, "Let's go."

"After that hit," said Ducks forward Dan Bylsma, "he looked like a guy who really wanted the puck." No one would have faulted Kariya, who has a history of concussions, for wanting nothing to do with the puck, or the remainder of the game, after absorbing such a hit, but he returned to the ice, determined to make an immediate impact. Three minutes later, Kariya picked up the puck, bolted down the left wing and fired a shot past Brodeur. "It was inspiring after [Kariya's] problems with concussions," said Ducks forward Steve Thomas after Anaheim's 5–2 victory. "But you're not going to keep a guy like that in the dressing room in Game 6 of the Stanley Cup finals."

The series, alas, returned to its opening

form in Game 7, as the Devils clamped down their neutral zone trap again and won in another 3–0 blanking. Perhaps appropriately, the series took on a different character in the Continental Airlines Arena, hard by the New Jersey Turnpike, than it did in Anaheim, home of Disneyland. It was certainly no thrill ride for the Ducks, who were outscored 15–3 in the four games in Jersey.

As perhaps the most anonymous group of champions in NHL history skated around the ice at Continental Airlines Arena with the Stanley Cup, Devils coach Pat Burns couldn't help but stand back and smile. It was the first championship for the three-time coach of the year, who had been out of the game for two years. Burns had been passed over for several other NHL coaching jobs, so he did not hesitate to crow to the media about his accomplishment. "I was out of the game for two years, and I read a lot of articles by a lot of people sitting right here, some of them saying I was done and I was never going to get back in the game and I wasn't the style of coach that people wanted," Burns said. "[But Lamoriello] believed in me."

More importantly, the Devils believed in themselves. Sure, they play a staid brand of hockey and may never be mentioned in the same breath with the greatest teams in NHL history, but they'll take it. "Well, three cups in nine years is something special," said veteran defenseman Ken Daneyko. "For us, we don't care about the Rodney Dangerfield mentality."

Though the Ducks fell short of winning they Cup, they earned the respect of the league with an impressive run in the playoffs, thanks largely to the stellar play of Giguere, who stepped up his play during the second half of the season. Anaheim toppled the giants of the Western Conference in the playoffs, sweeping the defending-champion Red Wings in the first round then downing the top-seeded Stars in six games in round two.

Giguere, nicknamed Jiggy by his teammates, set the tone in Game 1 at Detroit by making 63 saves in a 2–1 triple-overtime victory. In the first overtime, Red Wings forward Luc Robitaille blasted a shot off the crossbar, causing the goal judge to light the lamp. But Giguere was so sure that the puck hadn't gone in, he bolted out of his crease and gave the safe sign to the officials and the hostile crowd. Replays proved that Giguere was correct, and he seemed to get stronger after that. "That was outstanding," said Ducks goalie consultant Francois Allaire, a longtime coach of Giguere's. "He made 20 saves in the first overtime, maybe the best goaltending I'd seen since Patrick Roy stopped 13 in overtime [in Game 3 of the '86 Eastern Conference finals against the Rangers]. But when Jiggy waved off that goal, he was telling the world that he had no fear. That gave our team a good feeling."

Giguere's confidence rose with each game and so did the feeling of invincibility of his teammates. After eliminating Dallas, the Ducks swept the red-hot Minnesota Wild—and most of their success could be attributed to the fantastic play of Giguere. "[It] was the best sustained stretch of goaltending I've ever seen," said Ducks veteran defenseman Keith Carney. "I've played with some good goalies, but this run has been remarkable, especially given the intensity and pressure of the playoffs."

The Minnesota Wild, in just their third season, seemed to thrive on the pressure of big games, especially in the playoffs. In the first round, the Wild trailed the Colorado Avalanche three games to one but rallied to win the next three games, including two in Denver, and take the series. In the second round against Vancouver the Wild did it again. Down three games to one, the NHL's lowest-salaried team ($21.5 million), won the final three games of the series, outscoring the Canucks 16–5 during that span. It was the first time a team recovered from a 3–1 deficit in two playoff series in the same season.

After saying hello to the newly competitive Wild in the playoffs, the NHL said goodbye to legendary goalie Patrick Roy, who retired after 18 seasons with the Canadiens and Avalanche. Roy, who backstopped four Stanley Cup champions, left as the NHL's all-time winningest goalie

Selanne left San Jose for a stacked Colorado team.

agents both, could reunite. Kariya and Selanne share the same agent, and after that phone call, they contacted him and told him they had decided they wanted to play together on a team with a realistic shot at the Stanley Cup—even if it meant earning less money.

"We both said, 'Forget about the money, where's the place we want to play?'" said Kariya. "Colorado jumped out at us." Kariya ended up signing a one-year, $1.2 million deal, and Selanne, who turned down a $6.5 million option to stay in San Jose, agreed to a one-year $5.8 million contract. It's easy to see why

(551 regular-season victories, 151 playoff wins). He also won three Veniza Trophies as the league's best goalie and was a three-time winner of the Conn Smythe Trophy given to the most valuable player of the playoffs. Roy helped make the butterfly style the predominant goaltending mode in the league, and set the standard by which all other goalies of his generation were judged.

The Avalanche lost a first-ballot Hall of Famer in Roy, but they significantly upgraded their roster by signing two of the most coveted free agents in the market during the offseason. Colorado landed All-Stars Teemu Selanne and Kariya, who have been best friends since their days as teammates with the Ducks from 1996–2001. Ever since Selanne was traded to the Sharks in March 2001, the two have wanted to play together again. At midnight on June 30, Kariya picked up the phone and called his buddy to talk about how the pair, free

Colorado was so attractive to the two players. With reigning Hart Trophy winner Peter Forsberg (29 goals, 77 assists) and high-scoring forwards Joe Sakic (26 goals, 32 assists) and Milan Hejduk (50 goals, 48 assists) the Avalanche are suddenly the prohibitive favorites to win the 2004 Stanley Cup. "There is so much talent here," Kariya said. "To play with guys like Joe Sakic and Peter Forsberg and Rob Blake and Adam Foote and guys like that, it's a once-in-a-lifetime opportunity. Added Selanne, "This organization has a history of winning the Stanley Cup. That's why this is so thrilling."

Unlike the fans in New Jersey, the rabid Colorado faithful will be satisfied with nothing less than the Stanley Cup in '04. But as the Devils proved, talent is only one among several qualities required to hoist the most recognizable trophy in North American sports. The others? Heart, selflessness, desire, great goaltending—and a little bit of luck.

NHL Final Standings

Eastern Conference

NORTHEAST DIVISION

	GP	W	L	T	OTL	Pts	GF	GA
Ottawa	82	52	21	8	1	113	263	182
Toronto	82	44	28	7	3	98	236	208
Boston	82	36	31	11	4	87	245	237
Montreal	82	30	35	8	9	77	206	234
Buffalo	82	27	37	10	8	72	190	219

ATLANTIC DIVISION

	GP	W	L	T	OTL	Pts	GF	GA
New Jersey	82	46	20	10	6	108	216	166
Philadelphia	82	45	20	13	4	107	211	166
NY Islanders	82	35	34	11	2	83	224	231
NY Rangers	82	32	36	10	4	78	210	231
Pittsburgh	82	27	44	6	5	65	189	255

SOUTHEAST DIVISION

	GP	W	L	T	OTL	Pts	GF	GA
Tampa Bay	82	36	25	16	5	93	219	210
Washington	82	39	29	8	6	92	224	220
Atlanta	82	31	39	7	5	74	226	284
Florida	82	24	36	13	9	70	176	237
Carolina	82	22	43	11	6	61	171	240

Western Conference

CENTRAL DIVISION

	GP	W	L	T	OTL	Pts	GF	GA
Detroit	82	48	20	10	4	110	269	203
St. Louis	82	41	24	11	6	99	253	222
Chicago	82	30	33	13	6	79	207	226
Nashville	82	27	35	13	7	74	183	206
Columbus	82	29	42	8	3	69	213	263

NORTHWEST DIVISION

	GP	W	L	T	OTL	Pts	GF	GA
Colorado	82	42	19	13	8	105	251	194
Vancouver	82	45	23	13	1	104	264	208
Minnesota	82	42	29	10	1	95	198	178
Edmonton	82	36	26	11	9	92	231	230
Calgary	82	29	36	13	4	75	186	228

PACIFIC DIVISION

	GP	W	L	T	OTL	Pts	GF	GA
Dallas	82	46	17	15	4	111	245	169
Anaheim	82	40	27	9	6	95	203	193
Los Angeles	82	33	37	6	6	78	203	221
Phoenix	82	31	35	11	5	78	204	230
San Jose	82	28	37	9	8	73	214	239

OTL=overtime loss; worth 1 pt.

2003 Stanley Cup Playoffs

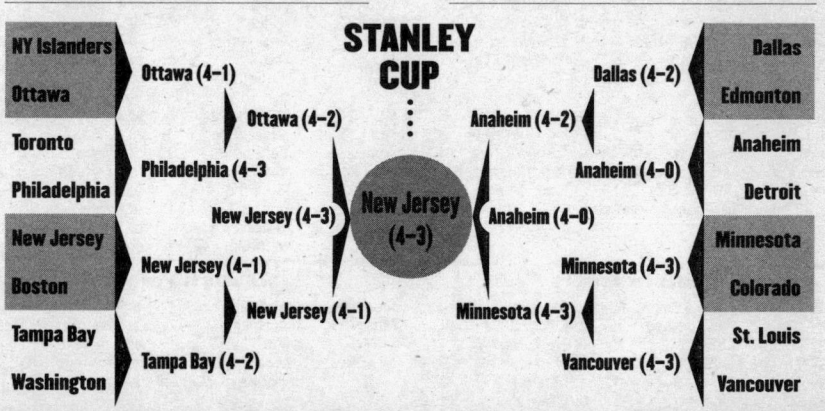

EASTERN CONFERENCE

QUARTERFINALS | SEMIFINALS | CONFERENCE FINAL

NY Islanders
Ottawa — Ottawa (4-1)
— Ottawa (4-2)
Toronto
Philadelphia — Philadelphia (4-3)
— New Jersey (4-3)
New Jersey
Boston — New Jersey (4-1)
— New Jersey (4-1)
Tampa Bay
Washington — Tampa Bay (4-2)

STANLEY CUP — New Jersey (4-3)

WESTERN CONFERENCE

CONFERENCE FINAL | SEMIFINALS | QUARTERFINALS

Dallas (4-2) — Dallas
Edmonton
Anaheim (4-2) — Anaheim (4-0) — Anaheim
Detroit
Anaheim (4-0)
Minnesota (4-3) — Minnesota — Minnesota
Colorado
Minnesota (4-3)
Vancouver (4-3) — St. Louis
Vancouver

Stanley Cup Playoff Results

Conference Quarterfinals

EASTERN CONFERENCE

April 9	NY Islanders	3	at Ottawa	0
April 12	NY Islanders	0	at Ottawa	3
April 14	Ottawa	3	at NY Islanders	2†

April 16	Ottawa	3	at NY Islanders	1
April 17	NY Islanders	1	at Ottawa	4

Ottawa won series 4–1.

Conference Quarterfinals *(Cont.)*

EASTERN CONFERENCE *(Cont.)*

April 9	Boston	1	at New Jersey	2	
April 11	Boston	2	at New Jersey	4	
April 13	New Jersey	3	at Boston	0	
April 15	New Jersey	1	at Boston	5	
April 17	Boston	1	at New Jersey	4	

New Jersey won series 4–1.

April 9	Toronto	5	at Philadelphia	3	
April 11	Toronto	1	at Philadelphia	4	
April 14	Philadelphia	3	at Toronto	4†	
April 16	Philadelphia	3	at Toronto	2•	

April 10	Washington	3	at Tampa Bay	0	
April 12	Washingotn	6	at Tampa Bay	3	
April 15	Tampa Bay	4	at Washington	3*	
April 16	Tampa Bay	3	at Washington	1	
April 18	Washington	1	at Tampa Bay	2	
April 20	Tampa Bay	2	at Washington	1•	

Tampa Bay won series 4–2.

April 19	Toronto	1	at Philadelphia	4	
April 21	Philadelphia	1	at Toronto	2†	
April 22	Toronto	1	at Philadelphia	6	

Philadelphia won series 4–3.

WESTERN CONFERENCE

April 9	Edmonton	2	at Dallas	1	
April 11	Edmonton	1	at Dallas	6	
April 13	Dallas	2	at Edmonton	3	
April 15	Dallas	3	at Edmonton	1	
April 17	Edmonton	2	at Dallas	5	
April 19	Dallas	3	at Edmonton	2	

Dallas won series 4–2.

April 10	Anaheim	2	at Detroit	1•	
April 12	Anaheim	3	at Detroit	2	
April 14	Detroit	1	at Anaheim	2	
April 16	Detroit	2	at Anaheim	3*	

Anaheim won series 4–0.

April 10	Minnesota	4	at Colorado	2	
April 12	Minnesota	2	at Colorado	3	
April 14	Colorado	3	at Minnesota	0	
April 16	Colorado	3	at Minnesota	1	
April 19	Minnesota	3	at Colorado	2	
April 21	Colorado	2	at Minnesota	3*	
April 22	Minnesota	3	at Colorado	2*	

Minnesota won series 4–3.

April 10	St. Louis	6	at Vancouver	0	
April 12	St. Louis	1	at Vancouver	3	
April 14	Vancouver	1	at St. Louis	3	
April 16	Vancouver	1	at St. Louis	4	
April 18	St. Louis	3	at Vancouver	5	
April 20	Vancouver	4	at St. Louis	3	
April 22	St. Louis	1	at Vancouver	4	

Vancouver won series 4–3.

Conference Semifinals

EASTERN CONFERENCE

April 25	Philadelphia	2	at Ottawa	4	
April 27	Philadelphia	2	at Ottawa	0	
April 29	Ottawa	3	at Philadelphia	2*	
May 1	Ottawa	0	at Philadelphia	1	
May 3	Philadelphia	2	at Ottawa	5	
May 5	Ottawa	5	at Philadelphia	1	

Ottawa won series 4–2.

April 24	Tampa Bay	0	at New Jersey	3	
April 26	Tampa Bay	2	at New Jersey	3*	
April 28	New Jersey	3	at Tampa Bay	4	
April 30	New Jersey	3	at Tampa Bay	1	
May 2	Tampa Bay	1	at New Jersey	2•	

New Jersey won series 4–1.

WESTERN CONFERENCE

April 24	Anaheim	4	at Dallas	3#	
April 26	Anaheim	3	at Dallas	2*	
April 28	Dallas	2	at Anaheim	1	
April 30	Dallas	0	at Anaheim	1	
May 3	Anaheim	1	at Dallas	4	
May 5	Dallas	3	at Anaheim	4	

Anaheim won series 4–2.

April 25	Minnesota	3	at Vancouver	4*	
April 27	Minnesota	3	at Vancouver	2	
April 29	Vancouver	3	at Minnesota	2	
May 2	Vancouver	3	at Minnesota	2*	
May 5	Minnesota	7	at Vancouver	2	
May 7	Vancouver	1	at Minnesota	5	
May 8	Minnesota	4	at Vancouver	2	

Minnesota won series 4–3.

Eastern Finals

May 10	New Jersey	2	at Ottawa	3*	
May 13	New Jersey	4	at Ottawa	1	
May 15	Ottawa	0	at New Jersey	1	
May 17	Ottawa	2	at New Jersey	5	
May 19	New Jersey	1	at Ottawa	3	
May 21	Ottawa	2	at New Jersey	1*	
May 23	New Jersey	3	at Ottawa	2	

New Jersey won series 4–3.

Western Finals

May 10	Anaheim	1	at Minnesota	0†	
May 12	Anaheim	2	at Minnesota	0	
May 14	Minnesota	0	at Anaheim	4	
May 16	Minnesota	1	at Anaheim	2	

Anaheim won series 4–0.

Stanley Cup Finals

May 27	Anaheim	0	at New Jersey	3	
May 29	Anaheim	0	at New Jersey	3	
May 31	New Jersey	2	at Anaheim	3*	
June 2	New Jersey	0	at Anaheim	1*	

June 5	Anaheim	3	at New Jersey	6	
June 7	New Jersey	2	at Anaheim	5	
June 9	Anaheim	0	at New Jersey	3	

New Jersey won series 4–3.

*Overtime game. †Double overtime game. •Triple overtime game. #Quintuple overtime game.

Game 1

```
Anaheim..........0      0      0—0
New Jersey......0      1      2—3
```

FIRST PERIOD

Scoring: None. Penalties: McKenzie, NJ (charging), 9:17; White, NJ (cross-checking), 14:01; Carney, Ana (roughing), 18:10.

SECOND PERIOD

Scoring: 1, New Jersey, Friesen (Brylin, Gionta), 1:45. Penalties: None.

THIRD PERIOD

Scoring: 2, New Jersey, Marshall (Elias, Gomez), 5:34. 3, New Jersey, Friesen (White), e.n., 19:38. Penalties: None

Shots on goal: Anaheim—4-4-8—16. New Jersey—6-15-9—30. Power-play opportunities: Ana 0 of 2, NJ 0 of 1. Goalies: Ana, Giguere (29 shots, 27 saves); NJ, Brodeur (16 shots, 16 saves). A: 19,040.

Referees: Watson, Marouelli. Linesmen: Murphy, Nowak.

Game 2

```
Anaheim..........0      0      0—0
New Jersey......0      2      1—3
```

FIRST PERIOD

Scoring: None. Penalties: Pahlsson, Ana (interference), 6:10; LeClerc, Ana (hooking), 18:24.

SECOND PERIOD

Scoring: 1, New Jersey, Elias (Tverdovsky, Gomez) (pp), 4:42. 2, New Jersey, Gomez (Tverdovsky, Elias), 12:11. Penalties: Elias, New Jersey (holding stick), 2:23; Sykora, Ana (holding), 3:19.

THIRD PERIOD

Scoring: 3, New Jersey, Friesen (Gionta, Niedermayer), 4:22. Penalties: Carney, Ana (high sticking), 0:27; McKenzie, NJ (interference), 8:29; Stevens, NJ (holding), 19:19.

Shots on goal: Ana—7-2-7—16. NJ—7-6-12—25. Power-play opportunities: Ana 0-of-3; NJ 1-of-4. Goalies: Ana, Giguere (25 shots, 22 saves); NJ, Brodeur (16 shots, 16 saves). A: 19,040.

Referees: McCreary, Devorski. Linesmen: Murphy, Nowak.

Game 3

```
New Jersey...........0      1      1      0—2
Anaheim................0      2      0      1—3
```

FIRST PERIOD

Scoring: None. Penalties: Thomas, Ana (cross-checking), 0:15; LeClerc, Ana (slashing major), 3:58; Brylin, NJ (holding stick), 8:04; Salei, Ana (hooking), 8:04; Rafalski, NJ (hooking), 18:29.

SECOND PERIOD

Scoring: 1, Anaheim, Chouinard (Ozolinsh), 3:39. 2, New Jersey, Elias (Langenbrunner, Rafalski), 14:02. 3, Anaheim, Ozolinsh (Giguere), 14:47. Penalties: Sykora, Ana, (hooking), 19:31.

THIRD PERIOD

Scoring: 4, New Jersey, Gomez (Marshall, Elias), 9:11. Penalties: Salei, Ana (hooking), 3:15; Gionta, New Jersey (slashing), 10:35.

OVERTIME

Scoring: 5, Anaheim, Salei (Oates), 6:59. Penalties: None.

Shots on goal: NJ—8-12-8-3—31. Ana—9-9-10-5—33. Power-play opportunities: NJ 0-of-4; Ana 0-of-2. Goalies: NJ, Brodeur (33 shots, 30 saves); Ana, Giguere (31 shots, 29 saves). A: 17,174. Referees: McCreary, Marouelli. Linesmen: Lazarowich, Wheler.

Game 4

```
New Jersey...........0      0      0      0—0
Anaheim................0      0      0      1—1
```

FIRST PERIOD

Scoring: None. Penalties: Sauer, Ana (interference), 5:54; Niedermayer, NJ (holding), 7:15; Bylsma, Ana (interference), 16:46.

SECOND PERIOD

Scoring: None. Penalties: Niedermayer, Ana (hooking), 8:50.

THIRD PERIOD

Scoring: None. Penalties: None.

OVERTIME

Scoring: 1, Anaheim, Thomas (Pahlsson, Ozolinsh), 0:39. Penalties: None.

Shots on goal: NJ—10-8-7-1—26. Ana—7-8-9-2—26. Power-play opportunities: NJ 0-of-3; Ana 0-of-1. Goalies: NJ, Brodeur (26 shots, 25 saves); Ana, Giguere (26 shots, 26 saves). A: 17,174.

Referees: Watson, Marouelli. Linesmen: Lazarowich, Wheler.

Game 5

Anaheim	2	1	0—3
New Jersey	2	2	2—6

FIRST PERIOD

Scoring: 1, Anaheim, Sykora (Oates), 0:42. 2, New Jersey, Rheaume (Stevenson, Brylin), 3:35; 3, New Jersey, Elias (Rafalski, Gomez) (pp). 4, Anaheim, Rucchin (Sykora, Kariya), 12:50. Penalties: Niedermayer, NJ (roughing), 4:34; Oates, Ana (roughing), 4:34; Carney, Ana (tripping), 7:03; Stevenson, NJ (roughing), 14:36; LeClerc, Ana (roughing), 17:50.

SECOND PERIOD

Scoring: 5, New Jersey, Gionta (Pandolfo, Niedermayer), 3:12. 6, Anaheim, Pahlson (Niedermayer, Carney), 6:35. 7, Pandolfo (Gionta, Stevens), 9:02. Penalties: Oates, Ana (high sticking), 0:18; Chistov, Ana (high sticking), 6:39.

THIRD PERIOD

Scoring: 8, New Jersey, Langenbrunner (Rupp, Niedermayer), 5:39. 9, New Jersey, Langenbrunner (Gionta), 12:52. Penalties: Salei, Ana (roughing), 11:52; Marshall, New Jersey (roughing), 11:52.

Shots on goal: Ana—12-7-4—23. NJ—11-13-13—37. Power-play opportunities: Ana 0-of-1; NJ 1-of-4. Goalies: Ana, Giguere (37 shots, 31 saves); NJ, Brodeur (23 shots, 20 saves). A: 19, 040.

Referees: McCreary, Devorski. Linesmen: Murphy, Nowak.

Game 6

New Jersey	0	1	1—2
Anaheim	3	1	1—5

FIRST PERIOD

Scoring: 1, Anaheim, Rucchin (Kariya, Sykora), 4:26. 2, Anaheim, Rucchin (LeClerc, Niedermayer), 13:42. 3, Anaheim, Thomas (Kariya, Carney) (pp) 15:59. Penalties: Elias, NJ (interference), 8:55; Langenbrunner, NJ (roughing) (served by Gomez), 14:24; Salei, Ana (roughing), 14:24; Kariya, Ana (tripping), 18:39.

SECOND PERIOD

Scoring: 4, New Jersey, Pandolfo (Madden, Gionta), 2:18. 5, Anaheim, Kariya (Sykora, Oates), 17:15. Penalties: Langenbrunner, NJ (hooking), 6:26; Stevenson, NJ (slashing), 18:27

THIRD PERIOD

Scoring: 6, Anaheim, Sykora (Chistov, Havelid) (pp) 3:57. 7, Marshall, New Jersey (Rafalski, Elias) (pp), 10:46. Penalties: Stevenson, NJ (roughing double minor), 1:15; Krog, Ana (high sticking), 6:26; Pahlson, Ana (tripping), 9:32; Rheaume, NJ (clipping), 14:45; Marshall, NJ (tripping), 18:51; White, NJ (roughing), 19:59; Thomas, Ana (slashing), 19:59.

Shots on goal: NJ—9-10-9—28; Ana—9-10-5—24. Power-play opportunities: NJ 1-of-3; Ana 2-of-8. Goalies: NJ, Brodeur (22 shots, 17 saves), Schwab (2 shots, 2 saves); Ana, Giguere (28 shots, 26 saves). A: 17, 174.

Referees: Watson, Marouelli. Linesmen: Lazarowich, Wheler.

Game 7

Anaheim	0	0	0—0
New Jersey	0	2	1—3

FIRST PERIOD

Scoring: None. Penalties: Stevenson, NJ (boarding), 17:31.

SECOND PERIOD

Scoring: 1, New Jersey, Rupp (Niedermayer, White), 2:22; 2, New Jersey, Friesen (Rupp, Niedermayer), 12:18. Penalties: Niedermayer, Ana (interference), 3:58.

THIRD PERIOD

Scoring: 3, New Jersey, Friesen (Rupp), 16:16. Penalties: LeClerc, Ana (cross checking), 16:45.

Shots on goal: Ana—5-9-10—24; NJ—7-12-6—25. Power-play opportunities: Ana 0-of-1; NJ 0-of-2. Goalies: Ana, Giguere (25 shots, 22 saves); NJ, Brodeur (24 shots, 24 saves). A: 19,040.

Referees: McCreary, Marouelli. Linesmen: Lazarowich, Murphy.

Individual Playoff Leaders

Scoring

POINTS

Player and Team	GP	G	A	Pts	+/-	PM	Player and Team	GP	G	A	Pts	+/-	PM
J. Langenbrunner, NJ	24	11	7	18	11	16	Doug Weight, StL	7	5	8	13	0	2
S. Niedermayer, NJ	24	2	16	18	11	16	Adam Oates, Ana	21	4	9	13	2	6
M. Gaborik, Minn	18	9	8	17	2	6	Petr Sykora, Ana	21	4	9	13	3	12
John Madden, NJ	24	6	10	16	10	2	S. Zholtok, Minn	18	2	11	13	-7	4
Marian Hossa, Ott	18	5	11	16	-1	6	M. St. Louis, TB	11	7	5	12	5	0
Mike Modano, Dall	12	5	10	15	2	4	Jay Pandolfo, NJ	24	6	6	12	9	2
Jeff Friesen, NJ	24	10	4	14	10	6	Paul Kariya, Ana	21	6	6	12	0	6
M. Naslund, Van	14	5	9	14	-6	18	Scott Gomez, NJ	24	3	9	12	3	2
Sergei Zubov, Dall	12	4	10	14	2	4							
Wes Walz, Minn	18	7	6	13	5	14							
A. Brunette, Minn	18	7	6	13	-3	4							
Patrik Elias, NJ	24	5	8	13	5	26							

Individual Playoff Leaders *(Cont.)*

GOALS

Player and Team	GP	G
J. Langenbrunner, NJ	24	11
Jeff Friesen, NJ	24	10
M. Gaborik, MIN	18	9
Six tied with 7.		

POWER PLAY GOALS

Player and Team	GP	PP
Doug Weight, STL	7	5
M. Gaborik, MIN	18	4
A. Brunette, MIN	18	4
Ed Jovanovski, VAN	14	4
D. Alfredsson, OTT	18	4

ASSISTS

Player and Team	GP	A
S. Niedermayer, NJ	24	16
Marian Hossa, OTT	18	11
S. Zholtok, MIN	18	11
John Madden, NJ	24	10
Mike Modano, DAL	12	10
Sergei Zubov, DAL	12	10

GAME-WINNING GOALS

Player and Team	GP	GW
J. Langenbrunner, NJ	24	4
Jeff Friesen, NJ	24	4
Steve Thomas, Ana	21	3
Martin St. Louis, TB	11	3

SHORT-HANDED GOALS

Player and Team	GP	SH
Martin St. Louis, TB	11	2
Wes Walz, Minn	18	2
Rob Niedermayer, Ana	21	2

PLUS/MINUS

Player and Team	GP	+/–
Scott Stevens, NJ	24	14
J. Langenbrunner, NJ	24	11
Scott Niedermayer, NJ	24	11
Two tied with 10.		

Goaltending (Minimum 420 minutes)

GOALS AGAINST AVERAGE

Player and Team	GP	W - L - T	Avg
J. Giguere, ANH	21	15 - 6 - 0	1.62
M. Brodeur, NJ	24	16 - 8 - 0	1.65
P. Lalime, OTT	18	11 - 7 - 0	1.82
Marty Turco, DAL	12	6 - 6 - 0	1.88
M. Fernandez, MIN	9	3 - 4 - 0	1.96

SAVE PERCENTAGE

Player and Team	GP	W-L-T	GAA	GA	SV	SV%	SA
J. Giguere, Ana	21	15-6-0	1.62	38	659	.945	697
M. Brodeur, NJ	24	16-8-0	1.65	41	581	.934	622
M. Fernandez, Minn	9	3-4-0	1.96	18	235	.929	253
Olaf Kolzig, Wash	6	2-4-0	2.08	14	178	.927	192
P. Lalime, Ott	18	11-7-0	1.82	34	415	.924	449

NHL Awards

Award	Player and Team
Hart Trophy (MVP)	Peter Forsberg, Col
Calder Trophy (top rookie)	Barret Jackman, StL
Vezina Trophy (top goaltender)	Martin Brodeur, NJ
Norris Trophy (top defenseman)	Nicklas Lidstrom, Det
Lady Byng Trophy (for gentlemanly play)	Alexander Mogilny, Det
Adams Award (top coach)	Jacques Lemaire, Minn

Award	Player and Team
Selke Trophy (top defensive forward)	Jere Lehtinen, Dall
Jennings Trophy (goaltender on club allowing fewest goals)	Roman Cechmanek/ Robert Esche, Phil Martin Brodeur, NJ
Conn Smythe Trophy (playoff MVP)	Jean-Sebastien Giguere, Ana

Individual Regular Season Leaders

Scoring

POINTS

Player and Team	GP	G	A	Pts	+/–	PM
P. Forsberg, COL	75	29	77	106	52	70
M. Naslund, VAN	82	48	56	104	6	52
Joe Thornton, BOS	77	36	65	101	12	109
Milan Hejduk, COL	82	50	48	98	52	32
Todd Bertuzzi, VAN	82	46	51	97	2	144
Pavol Demitra, STL	78	36	57	93	0	32
Glen Murray, BOS	82	44	48	92	9	64
Mario Lemieux, PIT	67	28	63	91	-25	43
Dany Heatley, ATL	77	41	48	89	-8	58
Z. Palffy, LA	76	37	48	85	22	47
Mike Modano, DAL	79	28	57	85	34	30
S. Fedorov, DET	80	36	47	83	15	52
Paul Kariya, ANH	82	25	56	81	-3	48
Marian Hossa, OTT	80	45	35	80	8	34
A. Mogilny, TOR	73	33	46	79	4	12
D. Alfredsson, OTT	78	27	52	79	15	42
V. Prospal, TB	80	22	57	79	9	53
V. Lecavalier, TB	80	34	44	78	0	39
A. Kovalev, NYR/PIT	78	37	40	77	-9	70
Jaromir Jagr, WAS	75	36	41	77	5	38

GOALS

Player and Team	GP	G
Milan Hejduk, Col	82	50
M. Naslund, Van	82	48
Todd Bertuzzi, Van	82	46
Marian Hossa, Ott	80	45
Glen Murray, Bos	82	44

POWER PLAY GOALS

Player and Team	GP	PP
Todd Bertuzzi, VAN	82	25
M. Naslund, VAN	82	24
Dany Heatley, ATL	77	19
Milan Hejduk, COL	82	18
Mats Sundin, TOR	75	16

GAME-WINNING GOALS

Player and Team	GP	GW
Markus Nasland, Van	82	12
Sergei Fedorov, Det	80	11
Marian Hossa, Ott	80	10
Jaromir Jagr, Wash	75	9
Michal Handzus, Phil	82	9
Alexander Mogilny, Tor	73	9

SHORT-HANDED GOALS

Player and Team	GP	SHG
Shawn Bates, NYI	74	6
Brian Rolston, BOS	81	5
M. Rucinsky, STL	61	4
Matt Cooke, VAN	82	4
Curtis Brown, BUF	74	4
Kirk Maltby, DET	82	4

ASSISTS

Player and Team	GP	A
P. Forsberg, Col	75	77
Joe Thornton, Bos	77	65
Mario Lemieux, Pitt	67	63
Pavol Demitra, StL	78	57
Mike Modano, Dall	79	57
V. Prospal, TB	80	57
Brad Richards, TB	80	57

PLUS/MINUS

Player and Team	GP	+/–
P. Forsberg, Col	75	52
Milan Hejduk, Col	82	52
N. Lidstrom, Det	82	40
Jere Lehtinen, Dall	80	39
D. Hatcher, Dall	82	37

Goaltending
(Minimum 25 games)

GOALS AGAINST AVERAGE

Player and Team	GP	W-L-T	GAA	TGA
Marty Turco, DAL	55	31-10-10	1.72	92
R. Cechmanek, PHI	58	33-15-10	1.83	102
D. Roloson, MIN	50	23-16-8	2.00	98
M. Brodeur, NJ	73	41-23-9	2.02	147
P. Lalime, OTT	67	39-20-7	2.16	142

SAVE PERCENTAGE

Player and Team	GP	W-L-T	GA	SA	Pct
Marty Turco, DAL	55	31-10-10	92	1359	.932
D. Roloson, MIN	50	23-16-8	98	1334	.927
R. Cechmanek, PHI	58	33-15-10	102	1368	.925
M. Fernandez, MIN	35	19-13-2	74	972	.924
Ed Belfour, TOR	62	37-20-5	141	1816	.922

WINS

Player and Team	GP	GAA	W	L	T
M. Brodeur, NJ	73	2.02	41	23	9
P. Lalime, OTT	67	2.16	39	20	7
Ed Belfour, TOR	62	2.26	37	20	5
Patrick Roy, COL	63	2.18	35	15	13
J. Giguere, ANH	65	2.30	34	22	6
Curtis Joseph, DET	61	2.49	34	19	6

SHUTOUTS

Player and Team	GP	W	L	T	SO
M. Brodeur, NJ	73	41	23	9	9
P. Lalime, OTT	67	39	20	7	8
J. Giguere, ANH	65	34	22	6	8
J. Thibault, CHI	62	26	28	7	8
Ed Belfour, TOR	62	37	20	5	7
Marty Turco, DAL	55	31	10	10	7

NHL Team-by-Team Statistical Leaders

Anaheim Mighty Ducks

SCORING

Player	GP	G	A	Pts	+/-	PM
Paul Kariya	82	25	56	81	-3	48
Petr Sykora	82	34	25	59	-7	24
Steve Rucchin	82	20	38	58	-14	12
Adam Oates	67	9	36	45	-1	16
S Ozolinsh	82	12	32	44	-6	56
Niclas Havelid	82	11	22	33	5	30
Steve Thomas	81	14	16	30	10	53
Stan Chistov	79	12	18	30	4	54
Mike LeClerc	57	9	19	28	-8	34
Jason Krog	67	10	15	25	1	12
Keith Carney	81	4	18	22	8	65
R Niedermayer	66	10	12	22	-10	57
A McDonald	46	10	11	21	-1	14
P Kjellberg	76	8	11	19	-9	16
S Pahlsson	34	4	11	15	10	18
Ruslan Salei	61	4	8	12	2	78
F Olausson	44	2	6	8	0	22
V Vishnevski	80	2	6	8	-8	76
M Chouinard	70	3	4	7	-9	40
Dan Blysma	39	1	4	5	-1	12
Alexei Smirnov	44	3	2	5	-1	18
Lance Ward	65	3	2	5	-6	121
Kevin Sawyer	31	2	1	3	-2	115
Kurt Sauer	80	1	2	3	-23	74
Mike Brown	16	1	1	2	0	44
Rob Valicevic	10	1	0	1	1	2

GOALTENDING

Player	GP	Mins	Avg	W	L	T	SO
J.S. Giguere	65	3775	2.30	34	22	6	8
Martin Gerber	22	1203	1.94	6	11	3	1
Team total	82	4978	2.22	40	33	9	9

Atlanta Thrashers

SCORING

Player	GP	G	A	Pts	+/-	PM
Dany Heatley, R	77	41	48	89	-8	58
Slava Kozlov, R	79	21	49	70	-10	66
Ilya Kovalchuk, L	81	38	29	67	-23	57
Marc Savard, C	57	16	31	47	-11	77
Patrik Stefan, C	71	13	21	34	-10	12
Yannick Tremblay, D	75	8	22	30	-27	32
Tony Hrkac, C	80	9	17	26	-16	14
Shawn McEachern, L	46	10	16	26	-27	28
Frantisek Kaberle, D	79	7	19	26	-19	32
Andy Sutton, D	53	3	18	21	-8	114
Lubos Bartecko, R	37	7	9	16	3	8
Daniel Tjarnqvist, D	75	3	12	15	-20	26
Brad Tapper, R	35	10	4	14	2	23
Dan Snyder, C	36	10	4	14	-4	34
Pascal Rheaume, C	56	4	9	13	-8	24
Richard Smehlik, D	43	2	9	11	-4	16
Chris Tamer, D	72	1	9	10	-10	118
Per Svartvadet, L	62	1	7	8	-11	8
Jeff Cowan, L	66	3	5	8	-15	115
Mark Hartigan, C	23	5	2	7	-8	6
Jeff Odgers, R	74	2	4	6	-13	171
Mike Weaver, D	40	0	5	5	-5	20

GOALTENDING

Player	GP	Mins	Avg	W	L	T	SO
Pasi Nurminen	52	2856	2.88	21	19	5	2
Byron Defoe	17	895	4.36	5	11	1	0
Milan Hnilicka	21	1097	3.56	4	13	1	0
Frederic Cassivi	2	123	5.36	1	1	0	0
Team total	82	4971	3.36	31	44	7	2

Boston Bruins
SCORING

Player	GP	G	A	Pts	+/–	PM
Joe Thornton, C	77	36	65	101	12	109
Glen Murray, R	82	44	48	92	9	64
Brian Rolston, C	81	27	32	59	1	32
Mike Knuble, L	75	30	29	59	18	45
Jozef Stumple, C	78	14	37	51	0	12
P.J. Axelsson, L	66	17	19	36	8	24
Nick Boynton, D	78	7	17	24	8	99
Jonathan Girard, D	73	6	16	22	4	21
Michal Grosek, L	63	2	18	20	2	71
Marty McInnis, R	77	9	10	19	-11	38
Martin Lapointe, R	59	8	10	18	-19	87
Ivan Huml, L	41	6	11	17	3	30
Hal Gill, D	76	4	13	17	21	56
Sean O'Donnell, D	70	1	15	16	8	76
Rob Zamuner, L	55	10	6	16	2	18
Sergei Samsonov, L	8	5	6	11	8	2
P.J. Stock, C	71	1	9	10	-5	160
Don Sweeney, D	67	3	5	8	-1	24
Sean Brown, D	69	1	5	6	-6	117
Lee Goren, R	14	2	1	3	-2	7
Andy Hilbert, C	14	0	3	3	-1	7

GOALTENDING

Player	GP	Mins	Avg	W	L	T	SO
Steve Shields	36	2112	2.76	12	13	9	0
John Grahame	23	1352	2.71	11	9	2	1
Jeff Hackett	18	991	3.21	8	9	0	1
Tim Thomas	4	220	3.01	3	1	0	0
Andrew Raycroft	5	300	2.40	2	3	0	0
Team total	82	4975	2.82	36	35	11	2

Buffalo Sabres
SCORING

Player	GP	G	A	Pts	+/–	PM
M. Satan, LW	79	26	50	76	-3	20
C. Gratton, C	66	15	29	44	-5	86
J.P. Dumont, RW	76	14	21	35	-14	44
Ales Kotalik, RW	68	21	14	35	-2	30
Stu Barnes, C	68	11	21	32	-13	20
Curtis Brown, C	74	15	16	31	4	40
Taylor Pyatt, LW	78	14	14	28	-8	38
Jochen Hecht, LW	49	10	16	26	4	30
Tim Connolly, C	80	12	13	25	-28	32
D. Kalinin, D	65	8	13	21	-7	57
A. Zhitnik, D	70	3	18	21	-5	85
B. Campbell, D	65	2	17	19	-8	20
Adam Mair, C	79	6	11	17	-4	146
J. Patrick, D	69	4	12	16	-3	26
H. Tallinder, D	46	3	10	13	-3	28
D. Briere, C	14	7	5	12	1	12
M. Afinogenov, RW	35	5	6	11	-12	21
V. Varada, RW	44	7	4	11	-2	23
R. Warrener, D	50	0	9	9	1	63
Eric Boulton, LW	58	1	5	6	1	178
J. Botterill, LW	17	1	4	5	1	14
Jay McKee, D	59	0	5	5	-16	49
R. Fitzpatrick, D	36	1	3	4	-7	16
Chris Taylor, C	11	1	2	3	-1	2
J. Woolley, D	14	0	3	3	-1	29
Denis Hamel, RW	25	2	0	2	-4	17

GOALTENDING

Player	GP	Mins	Avg	W	L	T	SO
Martin Biron	54	3170	2.56	17	28	6	4
Ryan Miller	15	912	2.63	6	8	1	1
Mika Noronen	16	891	2.42	4	9	3	1
Team total	82	4973	2.55	27	45	10	6

Calgary Flames
SCORING

Player	GP	G	A	Pts	+/–	PM
J. Iginla, RW	75	35	32	67	-10	49
Craig Conroy, C	79	22	37	59	-4	36
Chris Drury, LW	80	23	30	53	-9	33
M. Gelinas, LW	81	21	31	52	-3	51
Toni Lydman, D	81	6	20	26	-7	28
S. Yelle, C	82	10	15	25	-10	50
O. Saprykin, LW	52	8	15	23	5	46
Chris Clark, RW	81	10	12	22	-11	126
Dave Lowry, LW	34	5	14	19	4	22
R. Niedermayer, C	54	8	10	18	-13	42
Bob Boughner, D	69	3	14	17	5	126
J. Leopold, D	58	4	10	14	-15	12
D. Gauthier, D	72	1	11	12	5	99
Robyn Regehr, D	76	0	12	12	-9	87
Blake Sloan, RW	67	2	8	10	-5	28
Scott Nichol, C	68	5	5	10	-7	149

SCORING (CONT.)

Player	GP	G	A	Pts	+/–	PM
M. Johansson, C	46	4	5	9	-15	12
Petr Buzek, D	44	3	5	8	-6	14
C. Kobasew, RW	23	4	2	6	-3	8
Craig Berube, LW	55	2	4	6	-6	100
Steve Begin, C	50	3	1	4	-7	51
A. Ference, D	16	0	4	4	1	6
Jamie Wright, LW	19	2	2	4	1	12
Blair Betts, C	9	1	3	4	3	0
S. Donovan, RW	13	1	2	3	-2	7
Marc Savard, C	10	1	2	3	-3	8
Micki Dupont, D	16	1	2	3	-5	4
S. Montador, D	50	1	1	2	-9	114

GOALTENDING

Player	GP	Mins	Avg	W	L	T	SO
Roman Turek	65	3822	2.57	27	29	9	4
Jamie McLennan	22	1165	2.99	2	11	4	0
Team total	82	4987	2.67	29	40	13	4

NHL Team-by-Team Statistical Leaders *(Cont.)*

Carolina Hurricanes

SCORING

Player	GP	G	A	Pts	+/-	PM
Jeff O'Neill, RW	82	30	31	61	-21	38
Ron Francis, C	82	22	35	57	-22	30
R. Brind'Amour, C	48	14	23	37	-9	37
Sean Hill, D	82	5	24	29	4	141
Erik Cole, LW	53	14	13	27	1	72
Jan Hlavac, LW	52	9	15	24	-9	22
J. Vasicek, C	57	10	10	20	-19	33
B. Battaglia, LW	70	5	14	19	-17	90
Craig Adams, RW	81	6	12	18	-10	71
Kevyn Adams, C	77	9	9	18	-8	57
Sami Kapanen, LW	43	6	12	18	-17	12
Bret Hedican, D	72	3	14	17	-24	75
J. Svoboda, RW	48	3	11	14	-5	32
Ryan Bayda, LW	25	4	10	14	-5	16
David Tanabe, D	68	3	10	13	-26	24
N. Wallin, D	77	2	8	10	-19	71
Aaron Ward, D	77	3	6	9	-22	90
Glen Wesley, D	63	1	7	8	-5	40
B. St. Jacques, D	18	2	5	7	-3	12
Tomas Kurka, LW	14	3	2	5	1	2
Jeff Daniels, LW	59	0	4	4	-8	8
C. MacDonald, C	35	1	3	4	-3	20
J. Boulerice, RW	48	2	1	3	-2	108
Tomas Malec, D	41	0	2	2	-5	43

GOALTENDING

Player	GP	Mins	Avg	W	L	T	SO
Kevin Weekes	51	2965	2.55	14	24	9	5
Arturs Irbe	34	1884	3.18	7	24	2	0
P. DesRochers	2	123	3.41	1	1	0	0
Team total	82	4972	2.81	22	49	11	5

Colorado Avalanche

SCORING

Player	GP	G	A	Pts	+/-	PM
P. Forsberg, LW	75	29	77	106	52	70
Milan Hejduk, RW	82	50	48	98	52	32
Alex Tanguay, LW	82	26	41	67	34	36
Joe Sakic, C	58	26	32	58	4	24
S. Reinprecht, C	77	18	33	51	-6	18
Derek Morris, D	75	11	37	48	16	68
Rob Blake, D	79	17	28	45	20	57
G. de Vries, D	82	6	26	32	15	70
Adam Foote, D	78	11	20	31	30	88
Radim Vrbata, RW	66	11	19	30	E	16
M. Skoula, D	81	4	21	25	11	68
D. McAmmond, LW	41	10	8	18	1	10
Eric Messier, LW	72	4	10	14	-2	16
Dan Hinote, RW	60	6	4	10	4	49
Mike Keane, LW	65	5	5	10	E	34
Serge Aubin, LW	66	4	6	10	-2	64
Jeff Shantz, C	74	3	6	9	-12	35
V. Nedorost, C	42	4	5	9	8	20
Riku Hahl, C	42	3	4	7	3	12
B. Battaglia, LW	13	1	5	6	-2	10
Scott Parker, RW	43	1	3	4	6	82
Brad Larsen, LW	6	0	3	3	3	2
B. Marchment, D	14	0	3	3	4	33
Bryan Muir, D	32	0	2	2	3	19
C. McAllister, D	14	0	1	1	6	26
D.J. Smith, D	34	1	0	1	2	55

GOALTENDING

Player	GP	Mins	Avg	W	L	T	SO
Patrick Roy	63	3769	2.18	35	15	13	5
David Aebischer	27	1235	2.43	7	12	0	1
Team total	82	5904	2.24	42	27	13	6

Chicago Blackhawks

SCORING

Player	GP	G	A	Pts	+/-	PM
S. Sullivan, RW	82	26	35	61	15	42
A. Zhamnov, C	74	15	43	58	E	70
Eric Daze, LW	54	22	22	44	10	14
Kyle Calder, LW	82	15	27	42	-6	40
T. Arnason, C	82	19	20	39	7	20
Theo Fleury, RW	54	12	21	33	-7	77
S. Berezin, LW	66	18	13	31	-3	8
Phil Housley, D	57	6	23	29	7	24
Mark Bell, LW	82	14	15	29	E	113
N. Dempsey, D	67	5	23	28	-7	26
A. Nikolishin, C	60	6	15	21	-3	26
Chris Simon, LW	61	12	6	18	-4	125
Steve Thomas, RW	69	4	13	17	E	51
Jon Klemm, D	70	2	14	16	-9	44
A. Karpovtsev, D	40	4	10	14	-8	12
Steve Poapst, D	75	2	11	13	14	50
M. Eastwood, C	53	2	10	12	-6	24
Lyle Odelein, D	65	7	4	11	7	76
Igor Korolev, C	48	4	5	9	-1	30
S. McCarthy, D	57	1	4	5	-1	23
J. Strudwick, D	48	2	3	5	-4	87

GOALTENDING

Player	GP	Mins	Avg	W	L	T	SO
Jocelyn Thibault	62	3650	2.37	26	28	7	8
Michael Leighton	8	447	2.82	2	3	2	1
Steve Passmore	11	617	3.70	2	5	2	0
Craig Anderson	6	270	4.00	0	3	2	0
Team total	82	4984	2.66	30	39	13	9

Columbus Blue Jackets

SCORING

Player	GP	G	A	Pts	+/-	PM
Ray Whitney, LW	81	24	52	76	-26	22
A. Cassels, C	79	20	48	68	-4	30
G. Sanderson, LW	82	34	33	67	-4	34
D. Vyborny, RW	79	20	26	46	12	16
J. Spacek, D	81	9	36	45	-23	70
M. Sillinger, C	75	18	25	43	-21	52
Rick Nash, LW	74	17	22	39	-27	78
Tyler Wright, C	70	19	11	30	-25	113
G. Marshall, RW	66	8	20	28	-8	71
L. Pirjeta, LW	51	11	10	21	-4	12
D. Walser, D	53	4	13	17	-9	34
R. Klesla, D	72	2	14	16	-22	71
Sean Pronger, C	78	7	6	13	-26	72
L. Richardson, D	82	0	13	13	-16	73
E. Knutsen, C	31	5	4	9	-15	10
M. Davidsson, RW	34	4	5	9	-12	18
H. Hyvonen, RW	36	4	5	9	-11	22
D. Westcott, D	39	0	7	7	-3	77
Jody Shelley, LW	68	1	4	5	-5	249
David Ling, RW	35	3	2	5	-6	86
Tomi Kallio, RW	12	1	2	3	-7	8
D. Van Impe, D	14	1	1	2	-6	10
J. Allison, D	48	0	1	1	-15	90
J. Grand-Pierre, D	41	1	0	1	-6	64
S. Lachance, D	61	0	1	1	-20	46

GOALTENDING

Player	GP	Mins	Avg	W	L	T	S
Marc Dennis	77	4511	3.09	27	41	8	5
J.F. Labbe	11	451	3.59	2	4	0	0
Team total	82	4962	3.13	29	45	8	5

Dallas Stars

SCORING

Player	GP	G	A	Pts	+/–	PM
Mike Modano, C	79	28	57	85	34	30
Sergei Zubov, D	82	11	44	55	21	26
Bill Guerin, RW	64	25	25	50	5	113
J. Lehtinen, RW	80	31	17	48	39	20
Jason Arnott, C	72	23	24	47	9	51
B. Morrow, LW	71	21	22	43	20	134
P. Turgeon, LW	65	12	30	42	4	18
Scott Young, RW	79	23	19	42	24	30
Ulf Dahlen, RW	63	17	20	37	11	14
Darryl Sydor, D	81	5	31	36	22	40
Niko Kapanen, C	82	5	29	34	25	44
D. Hatcher, D	82	8	22	30	37	106
P. Boucher, D	80	7	20	27	28	94
Rob DiMaio, RW	69	10	9	19	18	76
M. Malhotra, LW	59	3	7	10	-2	42
S. Robidas, D	76	3	7	10	15	35
Stu Barnes, C	13	2	5	7	2	8
Steve Ott, C	26	3	4	7	6	31
C. Lemieux, RW	32	2	4	6	-9	14
R. Matvichuk, D	68	1	5	6	1	58
Kirk Muller, C	55	1	5	6	-6	18
S. Pellerin, LW	20	1	3	4	-3	8
Aaron Downey, RW	43	1	1	2	1	69

GOALTENDING

Player	GP	Mins	Avg	W	L	T	SO
Marty Turco	55	3203	1.72	31	10	10	7
Ron Tugnutt	31	1701	2.47	15	10	5	4
Corey Hirsch	2	97	2.46	0	1	0	0
Team total	82	5001	1.99	46	21	15	11

Detroit Red Wings

SCORING

Player	GP	G	A	Pts	+/–	PM
S. Fedorov, C	80	36	47	83	15	52
Brett Hull, RW	82	37	39	76	11	22
B. Shanahan, LW	78	30	38	68	5	103
N. Lidstrom, D	82	18	44	62	40	38
P. Datsyuk, C	64	12	39	51	20	16
H. Zetterberg, LW	79	22	22	44	6	8
I. Larionov, C	74	10	33	43	-7	48
T. Holmstrom, LW	74	20	20	40	11	62
Kirk Maltby, LW	82	14	23	37	17	91
Kris Draper, C	82	14	21	35	6	82
L. Robitaille, LW	81	11	20	31	4	50
J. Woolley, D	62	6	17	23	12	22
D. McCarty, RW	73	13	9	22	10	138
C. Chelios, D	66	2	17	19	4	78
M. Dandenault, D	74	4	15	19	25	64
B. Devereaux, C	61	3	9	12	4	16
Dmitri Bykov, D	71	2	10	12	1	43
Sean Avery, C	39	5	6	11	7	120
S. Yzerman, C	16	2	6	8	6	8
P. Boileau, D	25	2	6	8	8	14
M. Schneider, D	13	2	5	7	2	16
Jiri Fischer, D	15	1	5	6	E	16
J. Williams, C	16	3	3	6	3	2
M. Kuznetsov, D	53	0	3	3	E	54
Jesse Wallin, D	32	0	1	1	-2	19

GOALTENDING

Player	GP	Mins	Avg	W	L	T	SO
Curtis Joseph	61	3566	2.49	34	19	6	5
Manny Legace	25	1406	2.18	14	5	4	0
Team total	82	4972	2.40	48	24	10	5

Edmonton Oilers

SCORING

Player	GP	G	A	Pts	+/–	PM
Ryan Smyth, LW	66	27	34	61	5	67
T. Marchant, C	77	20	40	60	13	48
Anson Carter, RW	68	25	30	55	-11	20
Mike York, LW	71	22	29	51	-8	10
Mike Comrie, C	69	20	31	51	-18	90
S. Horcoff, C	78	12	21	33	10	55
Ethan Moreau, LW	78	14	17	31	-7	112
M. Reasoner, C	70	11	20	31	19	28
Ales Hemsky, RW	59	6	24	30	5	14
Eric Brewer, D	80	8	21	29	-11	45
J. Niinimaa, D	63	4	24	28	-7	66
Steve Staios, D	76	5	21	26	13	96
J. Chimera, LW	66	14	9	23	-2	36
Dan Cleary, RW	57	4	13	17	5	31
G. Laraque, RW	64	6	7	13	-4	110

Player	GP	G	A	Pts	+/–	PM
F. Pisani, RW	35	8	5	13	9	10
Jason Smith, D	68	4	8	12	5	64
B. Swanson, C	44	2	10	12	-7	10
Radek Dvorak, RW	12	4	4	8	-3	14
S. Ferguson, D	78	3	5	8	11	120
A. Semenov, D	46	1	6	7	-7	58
Jiri Dopita, C	21	1	5	6	-4	11
Cory Cross, D	11	2	3	5	3	8
B. Isbister, LW	13	3	2	5	E	9
Jani Rita, LW	12	3	1	4	2	0
Ales Pisa, D	48	1	3	4	11	24

GOALTENDING TK TK

Player	GP	Mins	Avg	W	L	T	SO
Tommy Salo	65	3814	2.71	29	27	8	4
Jussi Markkanen	22	1180	2.59	7	8	3	3
Team total	82	4994	2.68	36	35	11	7

Florida Panthers
SCORING

Player	GP	G	A	Pts	+/-	PM
Olli Jokinen, C	81	36	29	65	-17	79
V. Kozlov, RW	74	22	34	56	-8	18
K. Huselius, LW	78	20	23	43	-6	20
M. Nilson, LW	82	15	19	34	2	31
I. Novoseltsev, RW	78	10	17	27	-16	30
S. Ozolinsh, D	51	7	19	26	-16	40
Valeri Bure, RW	46	5	21	26	-11	10
N. Hagman, LW	80	8	15	23	-8	20
S. Weiss, C	77	6	15	21	-13	17
J. Bednar, LW	52	5	13	18	-2	14
J. Bouwmeester, D	82	4	12	16	-29	14
Matt Cullen, C	30	6	6	12	-4	22
A. Lilja, D	56	4	8	12	8	56
Ivan Majesky, D	82	4	8	12	-18	92
M. Biron, D	34	1	8	9	-18	14
Brad Ference, D	60	2	6	8	2	118
S. Matteau, LW	52	4	4	8	-9	27
Ryan Johnson, C	58	2	5	7	-13	26
D. Yushkevich, D	23	1	6	7	-12	14
D. Shvidki, RW	23	4	2	6	-7	12
P. Worrell, LW	63	2	3	5	-14	193
Lance Ward, D	36	3	1	4	-4	78
B. Ritchie, C	30	0	3	3	-4	19
Igor Ulanov, D	56	1	1	2	7	39

GOALTENDING

Player	GP	Mins	Avg	W	L	T	SO
Roberto Longo	65	3628	2.71	20	34	7	6
Yani Hurme	28	1376	2.88	4	11	6	1
Team total	82	5004	2.76	24	45	13	7

Minnesota Wild
SCORING

Player	GP	G	A	Pts	+/-	PM
M. Gaborik, RW	81	30	35	65	12	46
C. Ronning, C	80	17	31	48	-6	24
P. Dupuis, LW	80	20	28	48	17	44
A. Brunette, LW	82	18	28	46	-10	30
S. Zholtok, C	78	16	26	42	1	18
Wes Walz, C	80	13	19	32	11	63
A. Laaksonen, LW	82	15	16	31	4	26
Filip Kuba, D	78	8	21	29	E	29
Jim Dowd, C	78	8	17	25	-1	31
Richard Park, RW	81	14	10	24	-3	16
P. Bouchard, C	50	7	13	20	1	18
A. Zyuzin, D	66	4	12	16	-7	34
B. Bombardir, D	58	1	14	15	15	16
W. Mitchell, D	69	2	12	14	13	84
L. Sekeras, D	60	2	9	11	-12	30
J. Stevenson, LW	32	5	6	11	6	69
Nick Schultz, D	75	3	7	10	11	23
Matt Johnson, LW	60	3	5	8	-8	201
Bill Muckalt, RW	8	5	3	8	5	6
D. Hendrickson, C	28	1	5	6	-3	8
J. Marshall, LW	45	1	5	6	4	69
S. Veilleux, C	38	3	2	5	-6	23
Brad Brown, D	57	0	1	1	-1	90

GOALTENDING

Player	GP	Mins	Avg	W	L	T	SO
Dwayne Roloson	50	2945	2.00	23	16	8	4
Manny Fernandez	35	1979	2.24	19	13	2	2
Dieter Kochan	1	60	5.00	0	1	0	0
Team total	82	4984	2.13	42	30	10	6

Los Angeles Kings
SCORING

Player	GP	G	A	Pts	+/-	PM
Z. Palffy, RW	76	37	48	85	22	47
M. Schneider, D	65	14	29	43	E	57
J. Modry, D	82	13	25	38	-13	68
B. Smolinski, C	58	18	20	38	-1	18
D. Armstrong, C	66	12	26	38	5	30
E. Belanger, C	62	16	19	35	-5	26
A. Frolov, LW	79	14	17	31	12	34
J. Allison, C	26	6	22	28	9	22
L. Visnovsky, D	57	8	16	24	2	28
I. Laperriere, RW	73	7	12	19	-9	122
A. Deadmarsh, RW	20	13	4	17	2	21
M. Eloranta, LW	75	5	12	17	-15	56
E. Rasmussen, LW	57	4	12	16	-1	28
B. Chartrand, C	62	8	6	14	-10	33
Steve Heinze, RW	27	5	7	12	-5	12
Joe Corvo, D	50	5	7	12	2	14
C. Johnson, LW	70	3	6	9	-13	22
M. Cammalleri, C	28	5	3	8	-4	22
Aaron Miller, D	49	1	5	6	-7	24
M. Norstrom, D	82	0	6	6	E	49
Brad Norton, D	53	3	3	6	1	97
Jared Aulin, C	17	2	2	4	-3	0
D. Yushkevich, D	42	0	3	3	-4	24

GOALTENDING

Player	GP	Mins	Avg	W	L	T	SO
Felix Potvin	42	2367	2.66	17	20	3	3
Jamie Storr	39	2027	2.55	12	19	2	3
Kristobal Huet	12	542	2.33	4	4	1	1
Team total	82	4926	2.58	33	43	6	7

Montreal Canadiens
SCORING

Player	GP	G	A	Pts	+/-	PM
Saku Koivu, C	82	21	50	71	5	72
R. Zednik, RW	80	31	19	50	4	79
Y. Perreault, C	73	24	22	46	-11	30
Jan Bulis, LW	82	16	24	40	9	30
A. Markov, D	79	13	24	37	13	34
Doug Gilmour, C	61	11	19	30	-6	36
P. Brisebois, D	73	4	25	29	-14	32
A. Dackell, RW	73	7	18	25	-5	24
D. Audette, RW	54	11	12	23	-7	19
Oleg Petrov, RW	53	7	16	23	-2	16
Joe Juneau, C	72	6	16	22	-10	20
Craig Rivet, D	82	7	15	22	1	71
Randy McKay, RW	75	6	13	19	-14	72
Mike Ribeiro, C	52	5	12	17	-3	6
Chad Kilger, LW	60	9	7	16	-4	21
M. Czerkawski, RW	43	5	9	14	-7	16
N. Sundstrom, RW	33	5	9	14	3	8
P. Traverse, D	65	0	13	13	-9	24
Marcel Hossa, LW	34	6	7	13	3	14
S. Quintal, D	67	5	5	10	-4	70
Karl Dykhuis, D	65	1	4	5	-5	34
Jason Ward, RW	8	3	2	5	3	0
F. Bouillon, D	20	3	1	4	-1	2

GOALTENDING

Player	GP	Mins	Avg	W	L	T	SO
Jose Theodore	57	3419	2.90	20	31	6	2
Jeff Hackett	18	1063	2.54	7	8	2	0
Mathieu Garon	8	482	1.99	3	5	0	2
Team total	82	4964	2.73	30	44	8	4

Nashville Predators

SCORING

Player	GP	G	A	Pts	+/–	PM
D. Legwand, C	64	17	31	48	-2	34
K. Timonen, D	72	6	34	40	-3	46
A. Johansson, LW	56	20	17	37	-4	22
D. Arkhipov, C	79	11	24	35	-18	32
S. Hartnell, LW	82	12	22	34	-3	101
Andy Delmore, D	71	18	16	34	-17	28
Scott Walker, RW	60	15	18	33	2	58
V. Orszagh, RW	78	16	16	32	-1	38
Adam Hall, RW	79	16	12	28	-8	31
V. Yachmenev, LW	62	5	15	20	7	12
Rem Murray, C	53	6	13	19	1	18
Jason York, D	74	4	15	19	13	52
Greg Johnson, C	38	8	9	17	7	22
Clarke Wilm, C	82	5	11	16	-11	36
K. Skrastins, D	82	3	10	13	-18	44
D. Pederson, C	43	4	6	10	2	39
Mark Eaton, D	50	2	7	9	1	22
Cale Hulse, D	80	2	6	8	-11	121
Martin Erat, LW	27	1	7	8	-9	14
Bill Houlder, D	82	2	4	6	-2	46
V. Fiddler, C	19	4	2	6	2	14
B. Gilchrist, LW	41	1	2	3	-11	14
Reid Simpson, LW	26	0	1	1	-4	56

GOALTENDING

Player	GP	Mins	Avg	W	L	T	SO
Tomas Vokoun	69	3974	2.20	25	31	11	3
Mike Dunham	15	819	3.15	2	9	2	0
Jan Lasak	3	90	3.32	0	1	0	0
Team total	82	4981	2.42	27	42	13	3

New Jersey Devils

SCORING

Player	GP	G	A	Pts	+/–	PM
Patrik Elias, C	81	28	29	57	17	22
Scott Gomez, C	80	13	42	55	17	48
J. Langenbrunner, RW	78	22	33	55	17	65
Jeff Friesen, LW	81	23	28	51	23	26
J. Nieuwendyk, C	80	17	28	45	10	56
John Madden, C	80	19	22	41	13	26
B. Rafalski, D	79	3	37	40	18	14
S. Niedermayer, D	81	11	28	39	23	62
Brian Gionta, RW	58	12	13	25	5	23
S. Stevens, D	81	4	16	20	18	41
T. Stevenson, RW	77	7	13	20	7	115
S. Brylin, C	52	11	8	19	-2	16
Jay Pandolfo, LW	68	6	11	17	12	23
O. Tverdovsky, D	50	5	8	13	2	22
Colin White, D	72	5	8	13	19	98
Jim McKenzie, LW	76	4	8	12	3	88
Jiri Bicek, C	44	5	6	11	7	25
Ken Daneyko, D	69	2	7	9	6	33
C. Berglund, LW	38	4	5	9	3	20
Michael Rupp, RW	26	5	3	8	E	21
T. Albelin, D	37	1	6	7	10	6
P. Rheaume, C	21	4	1	5	3	8

GOALTENDING

Player	GP	Mins	Avg	W	L	T	SO
Martin Brodeur	73	4374	2.02	41	23	9	9
Corey Schwab	11	614	1.47	5	3	1	1
Team total	82	4988	1.95	46	25	10	10

New York Islanders

SCORING

Player	GP	G	A	Pts	+/–	PM
A. Yashin, C	81	26	39	65	-12	32
Jason Blake, RW	81	25	30	55	16	58
Mark Parrish, RW	81	23	25	48	-12	28
D. Scatchard, C	81	27	18	45	9	108
Shawn Bates, C	74	13	29	42	-9	52
Michael Peca, C	66	13	29	42	-4	43
R. Hamrlik, D	73	9	32	41	21	87
A. Aucoin, D	73	8	27	35	-5	70
Arron Asham, RW	78	15	19	34	1	57
Jason Wiemer, C	81	9	19	28	5	116
K. Jonsson, D	71	8	18	26	-8	24
Oleg Kvasha, LW	69	12	14	26	4	44
B. Isbister, LW	53	10	13	23	-9	34
M. Weinhandl, RW	47	6	17	23	-2	10
M. Timander, D	80	3	13	16	-2	24
R. Martinek, D	66	2	11	13	14	26
C. Lapointe, C	66	6	6	12	-3	20
J. Niinimaa, D	13	1	5	6	-3	14
Eric Cairns, D	60	1	4	5	-7	124
Raffi Torres, LW	17	0	5	5	E	10
S. Butenschon, D	37	0	4	4	-6	26
J. Mapletoft, C	11	2	2	4	-1	2
Steve Webb, RW	49	1	0	1	-5	75

GOALTENDING

Player	GP	Mins	Avg	W	L	T	SO
Chris Osgood	37	1993	2.92	17	14	4	2
Garth Snow	43	2390	2.31	16	17	5	1
Rick DiPietro	10	585	2.97	2	5	2	0
Team total	82	4968	2.63	35	36	11	3

New York Rangers

SCORING

Player	GP	G	A	Pts	+/–	PM
Petr Nedved, LW	78	27	31	58	-4	64
Eric Lindros, RW	81	19	34	53	5	141
Tom Poti, D	80	11	37	48	-6	60
Mark Messier, C	78	18	22	40	-2	30
M. Barnaby, LW	79	14	22	36	9	142
Bobby Holik, C	64	16	19	35	-1	50
Pavel Bure, RW	39	19	11	30	4	16
Brian Leetch, D	51	12	18	30	-3	20
Radek Dvorak, RW	63	6	21	27	-3	16
M. Samuelsson, RW	58	8	14	22	E	32
J. Lundmark, C	55	8	11	19	-3	16
V. Malakhov, D	71	3	14	17	-7	52
S. McCarthy, RW	82	6	9	15	-4	81
D. Kasparaitis, D	80	3	11	14	5	85
R. Petrovicky, LW	66	5	9	14	-12	77
A. Kovalev, RW	24	10	3	13	2	20
B. Mironov, D	36	3	9	12	3	34
Rem Murray, C	32	6	6	12	-3	4
D. Purinton, D	58	3	9	12	-2	161
J. Bouchard, D	27	5	7	12	6	14
Rico Fata, RW	36	2	4	6	-1	6
Anson Carter, RW	11	1	4	5	E	6
D. LaCouture, LW	24	1	4	5	4	0
Cory Cross, D	26	0	4	4	13	16
Ted Donato, LW	49	2	1	3	-1	6
S. Lefebvre, D	35	0	2	2	-7	10

GOALTENDING

Player	GP	Mins	Avg	W	L	T	SO
Mike Dunham	43	2467	2.29	19	17	5	5
Dan Blackburn	32	1762	3.17	8	16	4	1
Mike Richter	13	694	2.94	5	6	1	0
Team total	82	4962	2.70	32	40	10	6

Ottawa Senators
SCORING

Player	GP	G	A	Pts	+/-	PM
Marian Hossa, RW	80	45	35	80	8	34
D. Alfredsson, RW	78	27	52	79	15	42
Todd White, C	80	25	35	60	19	28
M. Havlat, LW	67	24	35	59	20	30
Radek Bonk, LW	70	22	32	54	6	36
Wade Redden, D	76	10	35	45	23	70
Zdeno Chara, D	74	9	30	39	29	116
Mike Fisher, C	74	18	20	38	13	54
M. Arvedson, LW	80	16	20	36	13	48
S. Van Allen, C	78	12	20	32	17	66
K. Rachunek, D	58	4	25	29	23	30
P. Schaefer, LW	75	6	17	23	11	32
Jason Spezza, C	33	7	14	21	-3	8
C. Phillips, D	78	3	16	19	7	71
P. Schastlivy, LW	33	9	10	19	3	4
A. Volchenkov, D	57	3	13	16	-4	40
Jody Hull, RW	70	3	8	11	-3	14
Chris Neil, RW	68	6	4	10	8	147
Shane Hnidy, D	67	0	8	8	-1	130
B. Smolinski, C	10	3	5	8	1	2
V. Varada, RW	11	2	6	8	3	8
C. Leschyshyn, D	54	1	6	7	11	18
B. Pothier, D	14	2	4	6	11	6
S. Martins, C	14	2	3	5	3	10

GOALTENDING

Player	GP	Mins	Avg	W	L	T	SO
Patrick Lalime	67	3943	2.16	39	20	7	8
Martin Prusek	18	935	2.38	12	2	1	0
Ray Emery	3	85	1.42	1	0	0	0
Team total	82	4963	2.19	52	22	8	8

Philadelphia Flyers
SCORING

Player	GP	G	A	Pts	+/-	PM
J. Roenick, C	79	27	32	59	20	75
Mark Recchi, RW	79	20	32	52	E	35
K. Primeau, C	80	19	27	46	4	93
M. Handzus, C	82	23	21	44	13	46
Kim Johnsson, D	82	10	29	39	11	38
E. Desjardins, D	79	8	24	32	30	35
John LeClair, LW	35	18	10	28	10	16
Simon Gagne, LW	46	9	18	27	20	16
Marty Murray, C	76	11	15	26	-1	13
D. Brashear, LW	80	8	17	25	5	161
J. Williams, RW	41	8	16	24	15	22
E. Weinrich, D	81	2	18	20	16	40
R. Somik, RW	60	8	10	18	9	10
Tony Amonte, RW	13	7	8	15	12	2
Sami Kapanen, LW	28	4	9	13	-1	6
D. Seidenberg, D	58	4	9	13	8	20
Pavel Brendl, RW	42	5	7	12	8	4
M. Ragnarsson, D	43	2	6	8	5	32
E. Chouinard, C	28	4	4	8	2	8
C. Therien, D	67	1	6	7	10	36
Todd Fedoruk, LW	63	1	5	6	1	105
Joe Sacco, RW	34	1	5	6	E	20
T. Warriner, LW	13	2	3	5	2	6
Paul Ranheim, LW	28	0	4	4	-4	6
D. Yushkevich, D	18	2	2	4	7	8
Dan McGillis, D	24	0	3	3	7	20
J. Vandermeer, D	24	2	1	3	9	27

GOALTENDING

Player	GP	Mins	Avg	W	L	T	SO
R. Cechmanek	58	3350	1.83	33	15	10	6
Robert Esche	30	1638	2.20	12	9	3	2
Team total	82	4988	1.95	45	24	13	8

Phoenix Coyotes
SCORING

Player	GP	G	A	Pts	+/-	PM
Mike Johnson, RW	82	23	40	63	9	47
Shane Doan, C	82	21	37	58	3	86
L. Nagy, LW	80	22	35	57	17	92
D. Langkow, C	82	20	32	52	20	56
D. Briere, C	68	17	29	46	-21	50
Tony Amonte, RW	59	13	23	36	-12	26
T. Numminen, D	78	6	24	30	E	30
B. Radivojevic, RW	79	12	15	27	-2	63
Paul Mara, D	73	10	15	25	-7	78
Danny Markov, D	64	4	16	20	2	36
Ramzi Abid, LW	30	10	8	18	1	30
Deron Quint, D	51	7	10	17	-5	20
Brian Savage, LW	43	6	10	16	-4	22
C. Lemieux, RW	36	6	8	14	-3	30
L. Wilson, RW	31	6	8	14	1	26
K. Buchberger, RW	79	3	9	12	E	109
Todd Simpson, D	66	2	7	9	7	135
R. Suchy, D	77	1	8	9	2	18
O. Vaananen, D	67	2	7	9	1	82
Brad May, LW	20	3	4	7	3	32
Paul Ranheim, LW	40	3	4	7	-4	10
Jan Hrdina, C	4	0	4	4	3	8
Jeff Taffe, C	20	3	1	4	-4	4
D. Berehowsky, D	7	1	2	3	E	27
A. Nazarov, LW	59	3	0	3	-9	135

GOALTENDING

Player	GP	Mins	Avg	W	L	T	SO
Brian Boucher	45	2544	3.02	15	20	8	0
Sean Burke	22	1248	2.11	12	6	2	2
Zac Bierk	16	884	2.17	4	9	1	1
Patrick DesRochers	4	175	3.77	0	3	0	0
J.M. Pelletier	2	119	3.04	0	2	0	0
Team total	82	4970	2.67	31	40	11	3

Pittsburgh Penguins
SCORING

Player	GP	G	A	Pts	+/-	PM
M. Lemieux, C	67	28	63	91	-25	43
A. Kovalev, RW	54	27	37	64	-11	50
M. Straka, LW	60	18	28	46	-18	12
D. Tarnstrom, D	61	7	34	41	-11	50
Jan Hrdina, C	57	14	25	39	1	34
A. Morozov, LW	27	9	16	25	-3	16
V. Nieminen, LW	75	9	12	21	-25	93
R. Robitaille, C	41	5	12	17	5	8
W. Primeau, C	70	5	11	16	-30	55
Rico Fata, RW	27	5	8	13	-6	10
Milan Kraft, C	31	7	5	12	-8	10
Tomas Surovy, LW	26	4	7	11	E	10
S. McKenna, LW	79	9	1	10	-18	128
M. Rozsival, D	53	4	6	10	-5	40
S. Donovan, RW	52	4	5	9	-6	30
M. Bergevin, D	69	2	5	7	-9	36
A. Daigle, RW	33	4	3	7	-10	8
J. Laukkanen, D	17	1	6	7	-3	4
K. Manderville, C	82	2	5	7	-22	46
Ian Moran, D	70	0	7	7	-17	46
Eric Meloche, RW	13	5	1	6	-2	4
Michal Sivek, C	38	3	3	6	-5	14
G. Lefebvre, LW	12	2	4	6	1	0
M. Johansson, C	12	1	5	6	1	4
Hans Jonsson, D	63	1	4	5	-23	36
R. Lintner, D	19	3	2	5	-9	10
A. Ference, D	22	1	3	4	-16	36
D. LaCouture, LW	44	2	2	4	-8	72
Jamie Pushor, D	76	3	1	4	-28	76

GOALTENDING

Player	GP	Mins	Avg	W	L	T	SO
Johan Hedberg	41	2410	3.14	14	22	4	1
Sebastien Caron	24	1408	2.64	7	14	2	2
J.S. Aubin	21	1132	3.13	6	13	0	1
Team total	82	4950	2.99	27	49	6	4

St. Louis Blues
SCORING

Player	GP	G	A	Pts	+/-	PM
P. Demitra, C	78	36	57	93	E	32
Al MacInnis, D	80	16	52	68	22	61
C. Stillman, LW	79	24	43	67	12	56
Doug Weight, C	70	15	52	67	-6	52
S. Mellanby, RW	80	26	31	57	1	176
K. Tkachuk, LW	56	31	24	55	1	139
E. Boguniecki, RW	80	22	27	49	22	38
Petr Cajanek, C	51	9	29	38	16	20
A. Khavanov, D	81	8	25	33	-1	48
Dallas Drake, RW	80	20	10	30	-7	66
M. Rucinsky, LW	61	16	14	30	-1	38
B. Jackman, D	82	3	16	19	23	190
Shjon Podein, LW	68	4	6	10	7	28
B. Salvador, D	71	2	8	10	7	95
C. Laflamme, D	47	0	9	9	1	45
Tyson Nash, LW	66	6	3	9	E	114
Jamal Mayers, RW	15	2	5	7	1	8
S. Dubinsky, C	28	0	6	6	3	4
Reed Low, RW	79	2	4	6	3	234
S. Martins, C	28	3	3	6	-8	18
T. Koivisto, D	22	2	4	6	1	10
M. Eastwood, C	17	1	3	4	1	8
Jeff Finley, D	64	1	3	4	-2	46
C. Pronger, D	5	1	3	4	-2	10

GOALTENDING

Player	GP	Mins	Avg	W	L	T	SO
Brent Johnson	38	2042	2.47	16	13	5	2
Fred Brathwaite	30	1615	2.75	12	9	4	2
Curtis Sanford	8	397	1.96	5	1	0	1
Chris Osgood	9	532	3.05	4	3	2	2
Reinhard Divis	2	83	0.73	2	0	0	0
Tom Barrasso	6	293	3.27	1	4	0	1
Cody Rudkowsky	1	30	0.00	1	0	0	0
Team total	82	4992	2.58	41	30	11	8

San Jose Sharks
SCORING

Player	GP	G	A	Pts	+/-	PM
T. Selanne, RW	82	28	36	64	-6	30
V. Damphousse, C	82	23	38	61	-13	66
P. Marleau, C	82	28	29	57	-10	33
Marco Sturm, LW	82	28	20	48	9	16
Owen Nolan, RW	61	22	20	42	-5	91
Mike Ricci, C	75	11	23	34	-12	53
Mike Rathje, D	82	7	22	29	-19	48
Scott Hannan, D	81	3	19	22	E	61
S. Thornton, LW	41	9	12	21	-7	41
Jim Fahey, D	43	1	19	20	-3	33
Todd Harvey, RW	76	3	16	19	5	74
Adam Graves, LW	82	9	9	18	-14	32
Dan McGillis, D	37	3	13	16	-6	30
J. Cheechoo, RW	66	9	7	16	-5	39
Mark Smith, C	75	4	11	15	1	64
Brad Stuart, D	36	4	10	14	-6	46
N. Dimitrakos, RW	21	6	7	13	-7	8
N. Sundstrom, RW	47	2	10	12	-4	22
B. Marchment, D	67	2	9	11	-2	108
A. McCauley, C	16	3	7	10	-2	4
Kyle McLaren, D	33	0	8	8	-10	30
M. Ragnarsson, D	25	1	7	8	2	30
Jeff Jillson, D	26	0	6	6	-7	9
Matt Bradley, RW	46	2	3	5	-1	37
Lynn Loyns, C	19	3	0	3	-4	19
Rob Davison, D	15	1	2	3	4	22
M. Zalesak, RW	10	1	2	3	-2	0

GOALTENDING

Player	GP	Mins	Avg	W	L	T	SO
Evgeni Nabakov	55	3227	2.71	19	28	8	3
Miikka Kirprusoff	22	1199	3.25	5	14	0	1
Vesa Toskala	11	537	2.35	4	3	1	1
Team total	82	4963	2.81	28	45	9	5

Tampa Bay Lightning

SCORING

Player	GP	G	A	Pts	+/–	PM
V. Prospal, LW	80	22	57	79	9	53
V. Lecavalier, C	80	34	44	78	E	39
B. Richards, C	80	17	57	74	3	24
M. St. Louis, RW	82	33	37	70	10	32
Dan Boyle, D	77	13	40	53	9	44
F. Modin, LW	76	17	23	40	7	43
D. Andreychuk, LW	72	20	14	34	-12	34
R. Fedotenko, RW	76	18	14	32	-7	44
Pavel Kubina, D	75	3	19	22	-7	78
Ben Clymer, RW	65	6	12	18	-2	57
Andre Roy, LW	62	10	7	17	E	119
B. Lukowich, D	70	1	14	15	4	46
Cory Sarich, D	82	5	9	14	-3	63
Tim Taylor, C	82	4	8	12	-13	38
Nolan Pratt, D	67	1	7	8	-6	35
A. Svitov, C	63	4	4	8	-4	58
S. Keefe, RW	37	2	5	7	-1	24
N. Alexeev, RW	37	4	2	6	-6	8
Stan Neckar, D	70	1	4	5	-6	43
J. Cullimore, D	28	1	3	4	3	31
C. Dingman, LW	51	2	1	3	-11	91
J. Olvestad, RW	37	0	3	3	-2	16

GOALTENDING

Player	GP	Mins	Avg	W	L	T	SO
Nikolai Khabibulin	65	3787	2.47	30	22	11	4
John Grahame	17	914	2.23	6	5	4	2
Kevin Hodson	7	283	2.55	0	3	1	0
Team total	82	5094	2.43	36	30	16	6

Toronto Maple Leafs

SCORING

Player	GP	G	A	Pts	+/–	PM
A. Mogilny, RW	73	33	46	79	4	12
Mats Sundin, C	75	37	35	72	1	58
T. Kaberle, D	82	11	36	47	20	30
Nik Antropov, LW	72	16	29	45	11	124
R. Svehla, D	82	7	38	45	13	46
R. Reichel, C	81	12	30	42	7	26
Darcy Tucker, LW	77	10	26	36	-7	119
M. Renberg, LW	67	14	21	35	5	36
J. Hoglund, LW	79	13	19	32	2	12
Tie Domi, RW	79	15	14	29	-1	171
Travis Green, C	75	12	12	24	2	67
Bryan McCabe, D	75	6	18	24	9	135
T. Fitzgerald, RW	66	4	13	17	10	57
Jyrki Lumme, D	73	6	11	17	10	46
S. Corson, LW	46	7	8	15	-5	49
A. McCauley, C	64	6	9	15	3	16
Owen Nolan, RW	14	7	5	12	2	16
Aki Berg, D	78	4	7	11	3	28
Paul Healey, LW	44	3	7	10	8	16
Wade Belak, D	55	3	6	9	-2	196
Gary Roberts, LW	14	5	3	8	-2	10
Karel Pilar, D	17	3	4	7	-7	12
A. Ponikarovsky, RW	13	0	3	3	4	11
Ric Jackman, D	42	0	2	2	-10	41

GOALTENDING

Player	GP	Mins	Avg	W	L	T	SO
Ed Belfour	62	3738	2.26	37	20	5	7
Trevor Kidd	19	1143	3.10	6	10	2	0
Mikael Tellqvist	3	86	2.79	1	1	0	0
Team Total	82	4957	2.46	44	31	7	7

Vancouver Canucks

SCORING

Player	GP	G	A	Pts	+/–	PM
M. Naslund, LW	82	48	56	104	6	52
T. Bertuzzi, RW	82	46	51	97	2	144
B. Morrison, C	82	25	46	71	18	36
E. Jovanovski, D	67	6	40	46	19	113
Matt Cooke, C	82	15	27	42	21	82
T. Linden, RW	71	19	22	41	-1	30
Henrik Sedin, C	78	8	31	39	9	38
Brent Sopel, D	81	7	30	37	-15	23
Daniel Sedin, LW	79	14	17	31	8	34
Sami Salo, D	79	9	21	30	9	10
Trent Klatt, RW	82	16	13	29	10	8
M. Ohlund, D	59	2	27	29	1	42
T. Letowski, C	78	11	14	25	8	36
A. Chubarov, C	62	7	13	20	4	6
Marek Malik, D	69	7	11	18	23	52
M. Lindgren, C	54	5	9	14	-2	18
T. Warriner, LW	30	4	6	10	E	22
Bryan Allen, D	48	5	3	8	8	73
Murray Baron, D	78	2	4	6	13	62
Brandon Reid, C	7	2	3	5	4	0
Jarkko Ruutu, LW	36	2	2	4	-7	66
D. Langdon, LW	45	0	1	1	-2	143

GOALTENDING

Player	GP	Mins	Avg	W	L	T	SO
Dan Cloutier	57	3377	2.42	33	16	7	2
Peter Skudra	23	1192	2.72	9	5	6	1
Alexander Auld	7	382	1.57	3	3	0	1
Team total	82	4973	2.42	45	24	13	4

Washington Capitals

SCORING

Player	GP	G	A	Pts	+/–	PM
Jaromir Jagr, RW	75	36	41	77	5	38
Robert Lang, C	82	22	47	69	12	22
S. Gonchar, D	82	18	49	67	13	52
M. Nylander, C	71	17	39	56	9	36
Peter Bondra, RW	76	30	26	56	-3	52
Kip Miller, LW	72	12	38	50	-1	18
D. Zubrus, RW	63	13	22	35	15	43
Jeff Halpern, C	82	13	21	34	6	88
Mike Grier, RW	82	15	17	32	-14	36
S. Konowalchuk, LW	77	15	15	30	3	71
Ivan Ciernik, LW	47	8	10	18	6	24
Ken Klee, D	70	1	16	17	22	89
C. Johansson, D	82	3	12	15	9	22
Brendan Witt, D	69	2	9	11	12	106
B. Sutherby, C	72	2	9	11	7	93
S. Berezin, LW	9	5	4	9	10	4
Jason Doig, D	55	3	5	8	-3	108
G. Metropolit, C	23	2	3	5	4	6
A. Salomonsson, RW	32	1	4	5	-1	14
Rick Berry, D	43	2	1	3	-3	87
J. Kwiatkowski, D	34	0	3	3	1	12
Stephen Peat, RW	27	1	0	1	-3	57
J. Fortin, D	33	0	1	1	-3	22

GOALTENDING

Player	GP	Mins	Avg	W	L	T	SO
Olaf Kolzig	66	3894	2.40	33	25	6	4
S. Charpentier	17	859	2.79	5	7	1	0
Craig Billington	5	217	4.70	1	3	1	0
Team total	82	4970	2.57	39	35	8	4

2003 NHL Draft

First Round

The opening round of the 2002 NHL draft was held on June 22 in Toronto, Ont.

Team	Selection	Position	Team	Selection	Position
1.....Pittsburgh	Marc-Andre Fleury	G	16...St. Jose	Steve Bernier	F
2.....Carolina	Eric Staal	F	17...New Jersey	Zach Parise	F
3.....Florida	Nathan Horton	F	18...Washington	Eric Fehr	F
4.....Columbus	Nikolai Zherdev	F	19...Anaheim	Ryan Getzlaf	F
5.....Buffalo	Thomas Vanek	F	20...Minnesota	Brent Burns	F
6.....St. Jose	Milan Michalek	F	21...Boston	Mark Stuart	D
7.....Nashville	Ryan Suter	D	22...Edmonton	Marc-Antoine Pouliot	F
8.....Atlanta	Braydon Coburn	D	23...Vancouver	Ryan Kesler	F
9.....Calgary	Dion Phaneuf	D	24...Philadelphia	Mike Richards	F
10...Montreal	Andrei Kostitsyn	F	25...Florida	Anthony Stewart	F
11...Buffalo	Keith Ballard	D	26...Los Angeles	Brian Boyle	F
12...NY Rangers	Hugh Jessiman	F	27...Los Angeles	Jeff Tambellini	F
13...Los Angeles	Dustin Brown	F	28...Anaheim	Corey Perry	F
14...Chicago	Brent Seabrook	D	29...Ottawa	Patrick Eaves	F
15...NY Islanders	Robert Nilsson	F	30...St. Louis	Shawn Belle	D

FOR THE RECORD·Year by Year

The Stanley Cup

Awarded annually to the team that wins the NHL's best-of-seven final-round playoffs. The Stanley Cup is the oldest trophy competed for by professional athletes in North America. It was donated in 1893 by Frederick Arthur, Lord Stanley of Preston.

Results

1892–93.....Montreal A.A.A.	1900–01.....Winnipeg Victorias	1907–08.....Montreal Wanderers
1893–94.....Montreal A.A.A.	1901–02.....Winnipeg Victorias (Jan)	1908–09.....Ottawa Senators
1894–95.....Montreal Victorias	1901–02.....Montreal A.A.A. (Mar)	1909–10.....Montreal Wanderers
1895–96.....Winnipeg Victorias (Feb)	1902–03.....Montreal A.A.A. (Feb)	1910–11.....Ottawa Senators
1895–96.....Montreal Victorias (Dec)	1902–03.....Ottawa Silver Seven (Mar)	1911–12.....Quebec Bulldogs
1896–97.....Montreal Victorias	1903–04.....Ottawa Silver Seven	1912–13.....Quebec Bulldogs
1897–98.....Montreal Victorias	1904–05.....Ottawa Silver Seven	1913–14.....Toronto Blueshirts
1898–99.....Montreal Victorias (Feb)	1905–06.....Ottawa Silver Seven (Feb)	1914–15.....Vancouver Millionaires
1898–99.....Montreal Shamrocks (Mar)	1905–06.....Montreal Wanderers (Mar)	1915–16.....Montreal Canadiens
1899–1900...Montreal Shamrocks	1906–07.....Kenora Thistles (Jan)	1916–17.....Seattle Metropolitans
	1906–07.....Montreal Wanderers (Mar)	

NHL WINNERS AND FINALISTS

Season	Champion	Finalist	GP in Final
1917–18.....................Toronto Arenas		Vancouver Millionaires	5
1918–19.....................No decision*		No decision*	5
1919–20.....................Ottawa Senators		Seattle Metropolitans	5
1920–21.....................Ottawa Senators		Vancouver Millionaires	5
1921–22.....................Toronto St. Pats		Vancouver Millionaires	5
1922–23.....................Ottawa Senators		Vancouver Maroons, Edmonton Eskimos	2, 4
1923–24.....................Montreal Canadiens		Vancouver Maroons, Calgary Tigers	2, 2
1924–25.....................Victoria Cougars		Montreal Canadiens	4
1925–26.....................Montreal Maroons		Victoria Cougars	4
1926–27.....................Ottawa Senators		Boston Bruins	4
1927–28.....................New York Rangers		Montreal Maroons	5
1928–29.....................Boston Bruins		New York Rangers	2
1929–30.....................Montreal Canadiens		Boston Bruins	2
1930–31.....................Montreal Canadiens		Chicago Blackhawks	5
1931–32.....................Toronto Maple Leafs		New York Rangers	3
1932–33.....................New York Rangers		Toronto Maple Leafs	4
1933–34.....................Chicago Blackhawks		Detroit Red Wings	4
1934–35.....................Montreal Maroons		Toronto Maple Leafs	3

NHL WINNERS AND FINALISTS (CONT.)

Season	Champion	Finalist	GP in Final
1935–36	Detroit Red Wings	Toronto Maple Leafs	4
1936–37	Detroit Red Wings	New York Rangers	5
1937–38	Chicago Blackhawks	Toronto Maple Leafs	4
1938–39	Boston Bruins	Toronto Maple Leafs	5
1939–40	New York Rangers	Toronto Maple Leafs	6
1940–41	Boston Bruins	Detroit Red Wings	4
1941–42	Toronto Maple Leafs	Detroit Red Wings	7
1942–43	Detroit Red Wings	Boston Bruins	4
1943–44	Montreal Canadiens	Chicago Blackhawks	4
1944–45	Toronto Maple Leafs	Detroit Red Wings	7
1945–46	Montreal Canadiens	Boston Bruins	5
1946–47	Toronto Maple Leafs	Montreal Canadiens	6
1947–48	Toronto Maple Leafs	Detroit Red Wings	4
1948–49	Toronto Maple Leafs	Detroit Red Wings	4
1949–50	Detroit Red Wings	New York Rangers	7
1950–51	Toronto Maple Leafs	Montreal Canadiens	5
1951–52	Detroit Red Wings	Montreal Canadiens	4
1952–53	Montreal Canadiens	Boston Bruins	5
1953–54	Detroit Red Wings	Montreal Canadiens	7
1954–55	Detroit Red Wings	Montreal Canadiens	7
1955–56	Montreal Canadiens	Detroit Red Wings	5
1956–57	Montreal Canadiens	Boston Bruins	5
1957–58	Montreal Canadiens	Boston Bruins	6
1958–59	Montreal Canadiens	Toronto Maple Leafs	5
1959–60	Montreal Canadiens	Toronto Maple Leafs	4
1960–61	Chicago Blackhawks	Detroit Red Wings	6
1961–62	Toronto Maple Leafs	Chicago Blackhawks	6
1962–63	Toronto Maple Leafs	Detroit Red Wings	5
1963–64	Toronto Maple Leafs	Detroit Red Wings	7
1964–65	Montreal Canadiens	Chicago Blackhawks	7
1965–66	Montreal Canadiens	Detroit Red Wings	6
1966–67	Toronto Maple Leafs	Montreal Canadiens	6
1967–68	Montreal Canadiens	St. Louis Blues	4
1968–69	Montreal Canadiens	St. Louis Blues	4
1969–70	Boston Bruins	St. Louis Blues	4
1970–71	Montreal Canadiens	Chicago Blackhawks	7
1971–72	Boston Bruins	New York Rangers	6
1972–73	Montreal Canadiens	Chicago Blackhawks	6
1973–74	Philadelphia Flyers	Boston Bruins	6
1974–75	Philadelphia Flyers	Buffalo Sabres	6
1975–76	Montreal Canadiens	Philadelphia Flyers	4
1976–77	Montreal Canadiens	Boston Bruins	4
1977–78	Montreal Canadiens	Boston Bruins	6
1978–79	Montreal Canadiens	New York Rangers	5
1979–80	New York Islanders	Philadelphia Flyers	6
1980–81	New York Islanders	Minnesota North Stars	5
1981–82	New York Islanders	Vancouver Canucks	4
1982–83	New York Islanders	Edmonton Oilers	4
1983–84	Edmonton Oilers	New York Islanders	5
1984–85	Edmonton Oilers	Philadelphia Flyers	5
1985–86	Montreal Canadiens	Calgary Flames	6
1986–87	Edmonton Oilers	Philadelphia Flyers	7
1987–88	Edmonton Oilers	Boston Bruins	4
1988–89	Calgary Flames	Montreal Canadiens	6
1989–90	Edmonton Oilers	Boston Bruins	5
1990–91	Pittsburgh Penguins	Minnesota North Stars	6
1991–92	Pittsburgh Penguins	Chicago Blackhawks	4
1992–93	Montreal Canadiens	Los Angeles Kings	5
1993–94	New York Rangers	Vancouver Canucks	7
1994–95	New Jersey Devils	Detroit Red Wings	4
1995–96	Colorado Avalanche	Florida Panthers	4
1996–97	Detroit Red Wings	Philadelphia Flyers	4
1997–98	Detroit Red Wings	Washington Capitals	4
1998–99	Dallas Stars	Buffalo Sabres	6
1999–00	New Jersey Devils	Dallas Stars	6

NHL WINNERS AND FINALISTS (CONT.)

Season	Champion	Finalist	GP in Final
2000–01	Colorado Avalanche	New Jersey Devils	7
2001–02	Detroit Red Wings	Carolina Hurricanes	5
2002–03	New Jersey Devils	Anaheim Mighty Ducks	7

*In 1919 the Montreal Canadiens traveled to meet Seattle, the PCHL champions. After 5 games had been played—the teams were tied at 2 wins and 1 tie—the series was called off by the local Department of Health because of the influenza epidemic and the death of Canadiens defenseman Joe Hall from influenza.

Conn Smythe Trophy

Awarded to the Most Valuable Player of the Stanley Cup playoffs, as selected by the Professional Hockey Writers Association. The trophy is named after the former coach, general manager, president and owner of the Toronto Maple Leafs.

1965	Jean Beliveau, Mtl
1966	Roger Crozier, Det
1967	Dave Keon, Tor
1968	Glenn Hall, StL
1969	Serge Savard, Mtl
1970	Bobby Orr, Bos
1971	Ken Dryden, Mtl
1972	Bobby Orr, Bos
1973	Yvan Cournoyer, Mtl
1974	Bernie Parent, Phil
1975	Bernie Parent, Phil
1976	Reggie Leach, Phil
1977	Guy Lafleur, Mtl
1978	Larry Robinson, Mtl
1979	Bob Gainey, Mtl
1980	Bryan Trottier, NYI
1981	Butch Goring, NYI
1982	Mike Bossy, NYI
1983	Bill Smith, NYI
1984	Mark Messier, Edm
1985	Wayne Gretzky, Edm
1986	Patrick Roy, Mtl
1987	Ron Hextall, Phil
1988	Wayne Gretzky, Edm
1989	Al MacInnis, Cgy
1990	Bill Ranford, Edm
1991	Mario Lemieux, Pitt
1992	Mario Lemieux, Pitt
1993	Patrick Roy, Mtl
1994	Brian Leetch, NYR
1995	Claude Lemieux, NJ
1996	Joe Sakic, Col
1997	Mike Vernon, Det
1998	Steve Yzerman, Det
1999	Joe Nieuwendyk, Dall
2000	Scott Stevens, NJ
2001	Patrick Roy, Col
2002	Nicklas Lidstrom, Det
2003	J.-S. Giguere, Ana

Alltime Stanley Cup Playoff Leaders

Points

	Yrs	GP	G	A	Pts
Wayne Gretzky, four teams	16	208	122	260	382
*Mark Messier, Edm, NYR	18	236	109	186	295
Jari Kurri, four teams	15	200	106	127	233
Glenn Anderson, four teams	15	225	93	121	214
Paul Coffey, six teams	16	198	59	137	196
*Doug Gilmour, seven teams	18	182	60	128	188
*Brett Hull, Cal, StL, Dall, Det	18	190	100	85	185
Bryan Trottier, NYI, Pitt	17	221	71	113	184
Ray Bourque, Bos, Col	21	214	41	139	180
Jean Beliveau, Mtl	17	162	79	97	176
Denis Savard, Chi, Mtl	16	169	66	109	175
*Steve Yzerman, Det	18	181	67	109	176
*Mario Lemieux, Pitt	9	107	76	96	172
Denis Potvin, NYI	14	185	56	108	164
Mike Bossy, NYI	10	129	85	75	160
Gordie Howe, Det, Hart	20	157	68	92	160
Bobby Smith, Minn, Mtl	13	184	64	96	160
Sergei Fedorov, Det	12	158	49	111	160
*Al MacInnis, Cgy, StL	19	177	39	121	160
*Claude Lemieux, four teams	17	233	80	77	158

*Active in 2002–03 season.

Goals

	Yrs	GP	G
Wayne Gretzky, four teams	17	208	122
*Mark Messier, Edm, NYR	18	236	109
Jari Kurri, five teams	15	200	106
*Brett Hull, Cgy, StL, Dall, Det	18	190	100
Glenn Anderson, four teams	15	225	93
Mike Bossy, NYI	10	129	85
Maurice Richard, Mtl	15	133	82
*Claude Lemieux, Mtl, NJ, Col	17	233	80
Jean Beliveau, Mtl	17	162	79
*Mario Lemieux, Pitt	9	107	76

*Active in 2002–03.

Assists

	Yrs	GP	A
Wayne Gretzky, four teams	17	208	260
*Mark Messier, Edm, NYR	18	236	186
Ray Bourque, Bos, Col	21	214	139
Paul Coffey, six teams	16	198	137
*Doug Gilmour, five teams	18	182	128
Jari Kurri, five teams	15	196	127
Glenn Anderson, four teams	15	225	121
*Al MacInnis, Cgy, StL	18	177	120
Larry Robinson, Mtl, LA	20	227	116
Larry Murphy, six teams	20	215	115
Bryan Trottier, NYI, Pitt	17	221	113

*Active in 2002–03.

Alltime Stanley Cup Playoff Goaltending Leaders

WINS	W	L	Pct
*Patrick Roy, Mtl, Col	151	94	.616
Grant Fuhr, five teams	92	50	.648
Billy Smith, LA, NYI	88	36	.710
*Martin Brodeur, NJ	83	56	.597
*Ed Belfour, Chi, SJ, Dall	82	61	.573
Ken Dryden, Mtl	80	32	.714
Mike Vernon, four teams	77	56	.579
Jacques Plante, five teams	71	37	.657
Andy Moog, four teams	68	57	.544
*Tom Barrasso, four teams	61	54	.530

*Active in 2002–03 season.

SHUTOUTS	GP	W	SO
*Patrick Roy, Mtl, Col	247	151	23
*Martin Brodeur, NJ	139	83	20
Clint Benedict, Ott, Mtl M	48	25	15
*Curtis Joseph, StL, Edm, Tor	122	58	15
Jacques Plante, five teams	112	71	14
Turk Broda, Tor	101	58	13
Terry Sawchuk, Det, LA	106	54	12
Dominik Hasek, Buff, Det	97	53	12

GOALS AGAINST AVG	Avg
*Martin Brodeur, NJ	1.84
George Hainsworth, Mtl, Tor	1.93
Turk Broda, Tor	1.98
Dominik Hasek, Edm, Tor, Buff	2.03
*Ed Belfour, Chi, Dall	2.17

Note: At least 50 games played.
*Active in 2002–03.

Alltime Stanley Cup Playoff Wins

TEAM	W	L	Pct	TEAM	W	L	Pct
Montreal	387	255	.603	New Jersey†	106	82	.564
Detroit	251	230	.522	Buffalo	99	110	.474
Toronto	245	262	.483	Calgary*	69	87	.442
Boston	239	260	.479	Washington	69	85	.448
Chicago	188	218	.463	Los Angeles	65	101	.392
NY Rangers	183	195	.484	Vancouver	63	85	.426
Philadelphia	167	154	.520	Carolina§	35	49	.417
St. Louis	137	161	.460	San Jose	29	38	.433
Dallas#	136	133	.506	Phoenix††	28	63	.308
Edmonton	135	90	.600	Ottawa	28	34	.452
NY Islanders	132	98	.574	Anaheim	19	17	.528
Colorado**	116	97	.545	Florida	13	18	.419
Pittsburgh	109	99	.524	Tampa Bay	7	10	.412

*Atlanta Flames 1972–80. †Colorado Rockies 1976–82. #Minnesota North Stars 1967–93. **Quebec Nordiques 1979–95. ††Winnipeg Jets 1979–96. §Hartford Whalers 1979–97. Note: Teams ranked by playoff victories.

Stanley Cup Playoff Coaching Records

Coach	Team	Yrs	Series			Series Games	Games			Cups	Pct
				W	L	Games	W	L	T		
Glen Sather	Edm	10	27	21	6	*126	89	37	0	4	.706
Toe Blake	Mtl	13	23	18	5	119	82	37	0	8	.689
Scott Bowman	Five teams	28	68	49	19	353	223	130	0	9	.632
Bob Hartley	Col	4	13	10	3	80	49	31	0	1	.613
Hap Day	Tor	9	14	10	4	80	49	31	0	5	.613
Al Arbour	StL, NYI	16	42	30	12	209	123	86	0	4	.589
†Ken Hitchcock	Dall, Phil	6	16	11	5	93	53	40	0	1	.570
Mike Keenan	five teams	11	28	18	10	160	91	69	0	1	.569
Fred Shero	Phil, NYR	8	21	15	6	108	61	47	0	2	.565
†Jacques Lemaire	Mtl, NJ, Minn	7	18	12	6	101	57	44	0	1	.564

*Does not include suspended game, May 24, 1988. †Active in 2002–03.
Note: Coaches ranked by winning percentage. Minimum: 65 games.

The 10 Longest Overtime Games

Date	Result	OT	Scorer	Series	Series Winner
3-24-36	Det 1 vs Mtl M 0	116:30	Mud Bruneteau	SF	Det
4-3-33	Tor 1 vs Bos 0	104:46	Ken Doraty	SF	Tor
5-4-00	Phil 2 vs Pitt 1	92:01	Keith Primeau	CSF	Phil
4-24-03	Ana 4 vs Dall 3	80:48	Petr Sykora	CSF	Ana
4-24-96	Pitt 3 vs Wash 2	79:15	Petr Nedved	CQF	Pitt
3-23-43	Tor 3 vs Det 2	70:18	Jack McLean	SF	Det
3-28-30	Mtl 2 vs NYR 1	68:52	Gus Rivers	SF	Mtl
4-18-87	NYI 3 vs Wash 2	68:47	Pat LaFontaine	DSF	NYI
4-27-94	Buff 1 vs NJ 0	65:43	Dave Hannan	CQF	NJ
3-27-51	Mtl 3 vs Det 2	61:09	Maurice Richard	SF	Mtl

Hart Memorial Trophy

Awarded annually "to the player adjudged to be the most valuable to his team." The original trophy was donated by Dr. David A. Hart, father of Cecil Hart, former manager-coach of the Montreal Canadiens. In the 1980s Wayne Gretzky won the award nine times.

Year	Winner	Key Statistics	Runner-Up
1924	Frank Nighbor, Ott	10 goals, 3 assists in 20 games	Sprague Cleghorn, Mtl
1925	Billy Burch, Ham	20 goals, 4 assists in 27 games	Howie Morenz, Mtl
1926	Nels Stewart, Mtl M	42 points in 36 games	Sprague Cleghorn, Mtl
1927	Herb Gardiner, Mtl	12 points in 44 games as defenseman	Bill Cook, NYR
1928	Howie Morenz, Mtl	33 goals, 18 assists	Roy Worters, Pitt
1929	Roy Worters, NYA	1.21 goals against, 13 shutouts	Ace Bailey, Tor
1930	Nels Stewart, Mtl M	39 goals, 16 assists	Lionel Hitchman, Bos
1931	Howie Morenz, Mtl	28 goals, 23 assists	Eddie Shore, Bos
1932	Howie Morenz, Mtl	24 goals, 25 assists	Ching Johnson, NYR
1933	Eddie Shore, Bos	27 assists in 48 games as defenseman	Bill Cook, NYR
1934	Aurel Joliat, Mtl	27 points	Lionel Conacher, Chi
1935	Eddie Shore, Bos	26 assists in 48 games as defenseman	Charlie Conacher, Tor
1936	Eddie Shore, Bos	16 assists in 46 games as defenseman	Hooley Smith, Mtl M
1937	Babe Siebert, Mtl	28 points	Lionel Conacher, Mtl M
1938	Eddie Shore, Bos	17 points in 47 games as defenseman	Paul Thompson, Chi
1939	Toe Blake, Mtl	led NHL in points (47)	Syl Apps, Tor
1940	Ebbie Goodfellow, Det	28 points	Syl Apps, Tor
1941	Bill Cowley, Bos	led NHL in assists (45) and points (62)	Dit Clapper, Bos
1942	Tom Anderson, Bos	41 points	Syl Apps, Tor
1943	Bill Cowley, Bos	led NHL in assists (45)	Doug Bentley, Chi
1944	Babe Pratt, Tor	57 points in 50 games	Bill Cowley, Bos
1945	Elmer Lach, Mtl	led NHL in assists (54) and points (80)	Maurice Richard, Mtl
1946	Max Bentley, Chi	61 points in 47 games	Gaye Stewart, Tor
1947	Maurice Richard, Mtl	led NHL in goals (45); 26 assists	Milt Schmidt, Bos
1948	Buddy O'Connor, NYR	60 points in 60 games	Frank Brimsek, Bos
1949	Sid Abel, Det	28 goals, 26 assists	Bill Durnan, Mtl
1950	Charlie Rayner, NYR	6 shutouts	Ted Kennedy, Tor
1951	Milt Schmidt, Bos	61 points in 62 games	Maurice Richard, Mtl
1952	Gordie Howe, Det	led NHL in goals (47) and points (86)	Elmer Lach, Mtl
1953	Gordie Howe, Det	led NHL in goals (49) and points (95)	Al Rollins, Chi
1954	Al Rollins, Chi	5 shutouts	Red Kelly, Det
1955	Ted Kennedy, Tor	52 points	Harry Lumley, Tor
1956	Jean Beliveau, Mtl	led NHL in goals (47) and points (88)	Tod Sloan, Tor
1957	Gordie Howe, Det	led NHL in goals (44) and points (89)	Jean Beliveau, Mtl
1959	Andy Bathgate, NYR	74 points in 70 games	Gordie Howe, Det
1960	Gordie Howe, Det	45 assists, 73 points	Bobby Hull, Chi
1961	Bernie Geoffrion, Mtl	50 goals, 95 points	Johnny Bower, Tor
1962	Jacques Plante, Mtl	42 wins, 2.37 goals against avg.	Doug Harvey, NYR
1963	Gordie Howe, Det	47 assists, 73 points	Stan Mikita, Chi
1964	Jean Beliveau, Mtl	50 assists, 78 points	Bobby Hull, Chi
1965	Bobby Hull, Chi	39 goals, 32 assists	Norm Ullman, Det
1966	Bobby Hull, Chi	led NHL in goals (54) and points (97)	Jean Beliveau, Mtl
1967	Stan Mikita, Chi	led NHL in assists (62) and points (97)	Ed Giacomin, NYR
1968	Stan Mikita, Chi	40 goals, 47 assists	Jean Beliveau, Mtl
1969	Phil Esposito, Bos	led NHL in assists (77) and points (126)	Jean Beliveau, Mtl
1970	Bobby Orr, Bos	led NHL in assists (87) and points (120)	Tony Esposito, Chi
1971	Bobby Orr, Bos	102 assists, 139 points	Tony Esposito, Chi
1972	Bobby Orr, Bos	80 assists, 117 points	Ken Dryden, Mtl
1973	Bobby Clarke, Phil	67 assists, 104 points	Phil Esposito, Bos
1974	Phil Esposito, Bos	led NHL in goals (68) and points (145)	Bernie Parent, Phil
1975	Bobby Clarke, Phil	89 assists, 116 points	Rogatien Vachon, LA
1976	Bobby Clarke, Phil	89 assists, 119 points	Denis Potvin, NYI
1977	Guy Lafleur, Mtl	led NHL in assists (80) and points (136)	Bobby Clarke, Phil
1978	Guy Lafleur, Mtl	led NHL in goals (60) and points (132)	Bryan Trottier, NYI
1979	Bryan Trottier, NYI	led NHL in assists (87) and points (134)	Guy Lafleur, Mtl
1980	Wayne Gretzky, Edm	51 goals, 86 assists	Marcel Dionne, LA
1981	Wayne Gretzky, Edm	led NHL in assists (109) and points (164)	Mike Liut, StL
1982	Wayne Gretzky, Edm	NHL-record 92 goals and 212 points	Bryan Trottier, NYI
1983	Wayne Gretzky, Edm	led NHL in goals (71) and points (196)	Pete Peeters, Bos
1984	Wayne Gretzky, Edm	led NHL in goals (87) and points (205)	Rod Langway, Wash
1985	Wayne Gretzky, Edm	led NHL in goals (73) and points (208)	Dale Hawerchuk, Winn
1986	Wayne Gretzky, Edm	NHL-record 163 assists and 215 points	Mario Lemieux, Pitt

Hart Memorial Trophy *(Cont.)*

Year	Winner	Key Statistics	Runner-Up
1987	Wayne Gretzky, Edm	led NHL in assists (121) and points (183)	Ray Bourque, Bos
1988	Mario Lemieux, Pitt	led NHL in goals (70) and points (168)	Grant Fuhr, Edm
1989	Wayne Gretzky, LA	114 assists, 168 points	Mario Lemieux, Pitt
1990	Mark Messier, Edm	84 assists, 129 points	Ray Bourque, Bos
1991	Brett Hull, StL	led NHL in goals (86); 131 points	Wayne Gretzky, LA
1992	Mark Messier, NYR	72 assists, 107 points	Patrick Roy, Mtl
1993	Mario Lemieux, Pitt	69 goals, 91 assists in 60 games	Doug Gilmour, Tor
1994	Sergei Fedorov, Det	56 goals, 64 assists	Dominik Hasek, Buff
1995	Eric Lindros, Phil	29 goals, 41 assists in 46 games	Jaromir Jagr, Pitt
1996	Mario Lemieux, Pitt	led NHL in goals (69) and points (161)	Mark Messier, NYR
1997	Dominik Hasek, Buff	5 shutouts, 2.27 goals against avg.	Paul Kariya, Ana
1998	Dominik Hasek, Buff	13 shutouts, 2.09 goals against avg.	Jaromir Jagr, Pitt
1999	Jaromir Jagr, Pitt	44 goals, 127 points	Alexei Yashin, Ott
2000	Chris Pronger, StL	62 points, +52 plus/minus rating	Jaromir Jagr, Pitt
2001	Joe Sakic, Col	118 points, +45 plus/minus rating	Mario Lemieux, Pitt
2002	Jose Theodore, Mtl	2.11 goals against avg./7 shutouts	Jarome Iginla, Cal
2003	Peter Forsberg, Col	77 assists, +52 plus/minus rating	Markus Naslund, Van

Art Ross Trophy

Awarded annually "to the player who leads the league in scoring points at the end of the regular season." The trophy was presented to the NHL in 1947 by Arthur Howie Ross, former manager-coach of the Boston Bruins. The tie-breakers, in order, are as follows: (1) player with most goals, (2) player with fewer games played, (3) player scoring first goal of the season. Bobby Orr is the only defenseman in NHL history to win this trophy, and he won it twice (1970 and 1975).

Year	Winner	Pts	Year	Winner	Pts
1919	Newsy Lalonde, Mtl	44	1957	Gordie Howe, Det	89
1920	Joe Malone, Que	30	1958	Dickie Moore, Mtl	84
1921	Newsy Lalonde, Mtl	48	1959	Dickie Moore, Mtl	96
1922	Punch Broadbent, Ott	41	1960	Bobby Hull, Chi	81
1923	Babe Dye, Tor	46	1961	Bernie Geoffrion, Mtl	95
1924	Cy Denneny, Ott	37	1962	Bobby Hull, Chi	84
1925	Babe Dye, Tor	23	1963	Gordie Howe, Det	86
1926	Nels Stewart, Mtl M	44	1964	Stan Mikita, Chi	89
1927	Bill Cook, NYR	42	1965	Stan Mikita, Chi	87
1928	Howie Morenz, Mtl	37	1966	Bobby Hull, Chi	97
1929	Ace Bailey, Tor	51	1967	Stan Mikita, Chi	97
1930	Cooney Weiland, Bos	32	1968	Stan Mikita, Chi	87
1931	Howie Morenz, Mtl	73	1969	Phil Esposito, Bos	126
1932	Harvey Jackson, Tor	51	1970	Bobby Orr, Bos	120
1933	Bill Cook, NYR	53	1971	Phil Esposito, Bos	152
1934	Charlie Conacher, Tor	50	1972	Phil Esposito, Bos	133
1935	Charlie Conacher, Tor	57	1973	Phil Esposito, Bos	130
1936	Sweeney Schriner, NYA	45	1974	Phil Esposito, Bos	145
1937	Sweeney Schriner, NYA	46	1975	Bobby Orr, Bos	135
1938	Gordie Drillon, Tor	52	1976	Guy Lafleur, Mtl	125
1939	Toe Blake, Mtl	47	1977	Guy Lafleur, Mtl	136
1940	Milt Schmidt, Bos	52	1978	Guy Lafleur, Mtl	132
1941	Bill Cowley, Bos	62	1979	Bryan Trottier, NYI	134
1942	Bryan Hextall, NYR	56	1980	Marcel Dionne, LA	137
1943	Doug Bentley, Chi	73	1981	Wayne Gretzky, Edm	164
1944	Herb Cain, Bos	82	1982	Wayne Gretzky, Edm	212
1945	Elmer Lach, Mtl	80	1983	Wayne Gretzky, Edm	196
1946	Max Bentley, Chi	61	1984	Wayne Gretzky, Edm	205
1947	*Max Bentley, Chi	72	1985	Wayne Gretzky, Edm	208
1948	Elmer Lach, Mtl	61	1986	*Wayne Gretzky, Edm	215
1949	Roy Conacher, Chi	68	1987	Wayne Gretzky, Edm	183
1950	Ted Lindsay, Det	78	1988	Mario Lemieux, Pitt	168
1951	Gordie Howe, Det	86	1989	Mario Lemieux, Pitt	199
1952	Gordie Howe, Det	86	1990	Wayne Gretzky, LA	142
1953	Gordie Howe, Det	95	1991	Wayne Gretzky, LA	163
1954	Gordie Howe, Det	81	1992	Mario Lemieux, Pitt	131
1955	Bernie Geoffrion, Mtl	75	1993	Mario Lemieux, Pitt	160
1956	Jean Beliveau, Mtl	88	1994	Wayne Gretzky, LA	130
			1995	Jaromir Jagr, Pitt	70

Art Ross Trophy (Cont.)

1996	Mario Lemieux, Pitt	161		2000	Jaromir Jagr, Pitt	96
1997	Mario Lemieux, Pitt	122		2001	Jaromir Jagr, Pitt	121
1998	Jaromir Jagr, Pitt	102		2002	Jarome Iginla, Cgy	96
1999	Jaromir Jagr, Pitt	127		2003	Peter Forsberg, Col	106

Note: Listing includes scoring leaders prior to inception of Art Ross Trophy in 1947–48.

Lady Byng Memorial Trophy

Awarded annually "to the player adjudged to have exhibited the best type of sportsmanship and gentlemanly conduct combined with a high standard of playing ability." Lady Byng, who first presented the trophy in 1925, was the wife of Canada's Governor-General. She donated a second trophy in 1936 after the first was given permanently to Frank Boucher of the New York Rangers, who won it seven times in eight seasons. Stan Mikita, one of the league's most penalized players during his early years in the NHL, won the trophy twice late in his career (1967 and 1968).

1925	Frank Nighbor, Ott	1952	Sid Smith, Tor	1979	Bob MacMillan, Atl
1926	Frank Nighbor, Ott	1953	Red Kelly, Det	1980	Wayne Gretzky, Edm
1927	Billy Burch, NYA	1954	Red Kelly, Det	1981	Rick Kehoe, Pitt
1928	Frank Boucher, NYR	1955	Sid Smith, Tor	1982	Rick Middleton, Bos
1929	Frank Boucher, NYR	1956	Earl Reibel, Det	1983	Mike Bossy, NYI
1930	Frank Boucher, NYR	1957	Andy Hebenton, NYR	1984	Mike Bossy, NYI
1931	Frank Boucher, NYR	1958	Camille Henry, NYR	1985	Jari Kurri, Edm
1932	Joe Primeau, Tor	1959	Alex Delvecchio, Det	1986	Mike Bossy, NYI
1933	Frank Boucher, NYR	1960	Don McKenney, Bos	1987	Joe Mullen, Cgy
1934	Frank Boucher, NYR	1961	Red Kelly, Tor	1988	Mats Naslund, Mtl
1935	Frank Boucher, NYR	1962	Dave Keon, Tor	1989	Joe Mullen, Cgy
1936	Doc Romnes, Chi	1963	Dave Keon, Tor	1990	Brett Hull, StL
1937	Marty Barry, Det	1964	Ken Wharram, Chi	1991	Wayne Gretzky, LA
1938	Gordie Drillon, Tor	1965	Bobby Hull, Chi	1992	Wayne Gretzky, LA
1939	Clint Smith, NYR	1966	Alex Delvecchio, Det	1993	Pierre Turgeon, NYI
1940	Bobby Bauer, Bos	1967	Stan Mikita, Chi	1994	Wayne Gretzky, LA
1941	Bobby Bauer, Bos	1968	Stan Mikita, Chi	1995	Ron Francis, Pitt
1942	Syl Apps, Tor	1969	Alex Delvecchio, Det	1996	Paul Kariya, Ana
1943	Max Bentley, Chi	1970	Phil Goyette, StL	1997	Paul Kariya, Ana
1944	Clint Smith, Chi	1971	John Bucyk, Bos	1998	Ron Francis, Pitt
1945	Billy Mosienko, Chi	1972	Jean Ratelle, NYR	1999	Wayne Gretzky, NYR
1946	Toe Blake, Mtl	1973	Gilbert Perreault, Buff	2000	Pavol Demitra, StL
1947	Bobby Bauer, Bos	1974	John Bucyk, Bos	2001	Joe Sakic, Col
1948	Buddy O'Connor, NYR	1975	Marcel Dionne, Det	2002	Ron Francis, Car
1949	Bill Quackenbush, Det	1976	Jean Ratelle, NYR-Bos	2003	Alexander Mogilny, Det
1950	Edgar Laprade, NYR	1977	Marcel Dionne, LA		
1951	Red Kelly, Det	1978	Butch Goring, LA		

James Norris Memorial Trophy

Awarded annually "to the defense player who demonstrates throughout the season the greatest all-around ability in the position." James Norris was the former owner-president of the Detroit Red Wings. Bobby Orr holds the record for most consecutive times winning the award (eight, 1968–1975).

1954	Red Kelly, Det	1971	Bobby Orr, Bos	1988	Ray Bourque, Bos
1955	Doug Harvey, Mtl	1972	Bobby Orr, Bos	1989	Chris Chelios, Mtl
1956	Doug Harvey, Mtl	1973	Bobby Orr, Bos	1990	Ray Bourque, Bos
1957	Doug Harvey, Mtl	1974	Bobby Orr, Bos	1991	Ray Bourque, Bos
1958	Doug Harvey, Mtl	1975	Bobby Orr, Bos	1992	Brian Leetch, NYR
1959	Tom Johnson, Mtl	1976	Denis Potvin, NYI	1993	Chris Chelios, Chi
1960	Doug Harvey, Mtl	1977	Larry Robinson, Mtl	1994	Ray Bourque, Bos
1961	Doug Harvey, Mtl	1978	Denis Potvin, NYI	1995	Paul Coffey, Det
1962	Doug Harvey, NYR	1979	Denis Potvin, NYI	1996	Chris Chelios, Chi
1963	Pierre Pilote, Chi	1980	Larry Robinson, Mtl	1997	Brian Leetch, NYR
1964	Pierre Pilote, Chi	1981	Randy Carlyle, Pitt	1998	Rob Blake, LA
1965	Pierre Pilote, Chi	1982	Doug Wilson, Chi	1999	Al MacInnis, StL
1966	Jacques Laperriere, Mtl	1983	Rod Langway, Wash	2000	Chris Pronger, StL
1967	Harry Howell, NYR	1984	Rod Langway, Wash	2001	Nicklas Lidstrom, Det
1968	Bobby Orr, Bos	1985	Paul Coffey, Edm	2002	Nicklas Lidstrom, Det
1969	Bobby Orr, Bos	1986	Paul Coffey, Edm	2003	Nicklas Lidstrom, Det
1970	Bobby Orr, Bos	1987	Ray Bourque, Bos		

Calder Memorial Trophy

Awarded annually "to the player selected as the most proficient in his first year of competition in the National Hockey League." Frank Calder was a former NHL president. Sergei Makarov, who won the award in 1989–90, was the oldest recipient of the trophy, at 31. Players are no longer eligible for the award if they are 26 or older as of September 15th of the season in question.

1933 ....Carl Voss, Det	1957 ....Larry Regan, Bos	1981 ....Peter Stastny, Que
1934 ....Russ Blinko, Mtl M	1958 ....Frank Mahovlich, Tor	1982 ....Dale Hawerchuk, Winn
1935 ....Dave Schriner, NYA	1959 ....Ralph Backstrom, Mtl	1983 ....Steve Larmer, Chi
1936 ....Mike Karakas, Chi	1960 ....Bill Hay, Chi	1984 ....Tom Barrasso, Buff
1937 ....Syl Apps, Tor	1961 ....Dave Keon, Tor	1985 ....Mario Lemieux, Pitt
1938 ....Cully Dahlstrom, Chi	1962 ....Bobby Rousseau, Mtl	1986 ....Gary Suter, Cgy
1939 ....Frank Brimsek, Bos	1963 ....Kent Douglas, Tor	1987 ....Luc Robitaille, LA
1940 ....Kilby MacDonald, NYR	1964 ....Jacques Laperriere, Mtl	1988 ....Joe Nieuwendyk, Cgy
1941 ....Johnny Quilty, Mtl	1965 ....Roger Crozier, Det	1989 ....Brian Leetch, NYR
1942 ....Grant Warwick, NYR	1966 ....Brit Selby, Tor	1990 ....Sergei Makarov, Cgy
1943 ....Gaye Stewart, Tor	1967 ....Bobby Orr, Bos	1991 ....Ed Belfour, Chi
1944 ....Gus Bodnar, Tor	1968 ....Derek Sanderson, Bos	1992 ....Pavel Bure, Van
1945 ....Frank McCool, Tor	1969 ....Danny Grant, Minn	1993 ....Teemu Selanne, Winn
1946 ....Edgar Laprade, NYR	1970 ....Tony Esposito, Chi	1994 ....Martin Brodeur, NJ
1947 ....Howie Meeker, Tor	1971 ....Gilbert Perreault, Buff	1995 ....Peter Forsberg, Que
1948 ....Jim McFadden, Det	1972 ....Ken Dryden, Mtl	1996 ....Daniel Alfredsson, Ott
1949 ....Pentti Lund, NYR	1973 ....Steve Vickers, NYR	1997 ....Bryan Berard, NYI
1950 ....Jack Gelineau, Bos	1974 ....Denis Potvin, NYI	1998 ....Sergei Samsonov, Bos
1951 ....Terry Sawchuk, Det	1975 ....Eric Vail, Atl	1999 ....Chris Drury, Col
1952 ....Bernie Geoffrion, Mtl	1976 ....Bryan Trottier, NYI	2000 ....Scott Gomez, NJ
1953 ....Gump Worsley, NYR	1977 ....Willi Plett, Atl	2001 ....Evgeni Nabakov, SJ
1954 ....Camille Henry, NYR	1978 ....Mike Bossy, NYI	2002 ....Dany Heatley, Atl
1955 ....Ed Litzenberger, Chi	1979 ....Bobby Smith, Minn	2003 ....Barret Jackman, StL
1956 ....Glenn Hall, Det	1980 ....Ray Bourque, Bos	

Vezina Trophy

Awarded annually "to the goalkeeper adjudged to be the best at his position." The trophy is named after Georges Vezina, an outstanding goalie for the Montreal Canadiens who collapsed during a game on November 28, 1925, and died four months later of tuberculosis. The general managers of the NHL teams vote on the award.

1927 ....George Hainsworth, Mtl	1958 ....Jacques Plante, Mtl	1980 ....Bob Sauve, Buff
1928 ....George Hainsworth, Mtl	1959 ....Jacques Plante, Mtl	Don Edwards, Buff
1929 ....George Hainsworth, Mtl	1960 ....Jacques Plante, Mtl	1981 ....Richard Sevigny, Mtl
1930 ....Tiny Thompson, Bos	1961 ....Johnny Bower, Tor	Denis Herron, Mtl
1931 ....Roy Worters, NYA	1962 ....Jacques Plante, Mtl	Michel Larocque, Mtl
1932 ....Charlie Gardiner, Chi	1963 ....Glenn Hall, Chi	1982 ....Billy Smith, NYI
1933 ....Tiny Thompson, Bos	1964 ....Charlie Hodge, Mtl	1983 ....Pete Peeters, Bos
1934 ....Charlie Gardiner, Chi	1965 ....Terry Sawchuk, Tor	1984 ....Tom Barrasso, Buff
1935 ....Lorne Chabot, Chi	Johnny Bower, Tor	1985 ....Pelle Lindbergh, Phil
1936 ....Tiny Thompson, Bos	1966 ....Gump Worsley, Mtl	1986 ....John Vanbiesbrouck,
1937 ....Normie Smith, Det	Charlie Hodge, Mtl	NYR
1938 ....Tiny Thompson, Bos	1967 ....Glenn Hall, Chi	1987 ....Ron Hextall, Phil
1939 ....Frank Brimsek, Bos	Rogie Vachon, Mtl	1988 ....Grant Fuhr, Edm
1940 ....Dave Kerr, NYR	1969 ....Jacques Plante, StL	1989 ....Patrick Roy, Mtl
1941 ....Turk Broda, Tor	Glenn Hall, StL	1990 ....Patrick Roy, Mtl
1942 ....Frank Brimsek, Bos	1970 ....Tony Esposito, Chi	1991 ....Ed Belfour, Chi
1943 ....Johnny Mowers, Det	1971 ....Ed Giacomin, NYR	1992 ....Patrick Roy, Mtl
1944 ....Bill Durnan, Mtl	Gilles Villemure, NYR	1993 ....Ed Belfour, Chi
1945 ....Bill Durnan, Mtl	1972 ....Tony Esposito, Chi	1994 ....Dominik Hasek, Buff
1946 ....Bill Durnan, Mtl	Gary Smith, Chi	1995 ....Dominik Hasek, Buff
1947 ....Bill Durnan, Mtl	1973 ....Ken Dryden, Mtl	1996 ....Jim Carey, Wash
1948 ....Turk Broda, Tor	1974 ....Bernie Parent, Phil	1997 ....Dominik Hasek, Buff
1949 ....Bill Durnan, Mtl	Tony Esposito, Chi	1998 ....Dominik Hasek, Buff
1950 ....Bill Durnan, Mtl	1975 ....Bernie Parent, Phil	1999 ....Dominik Hasek, Buff
1951 ....Al Rollins, Tor	1976 ....Ken Dryden, Mtl	2000 ....Olaf Kolzig, Wash
1952 ....Terry Sawchuk, Det	1977 ....Ken Dryden, Mtl	2001 ....Dominik Hasek, Buff
1953 ....Terry Sawchuk, Det	Michel Larocque, Mtl	2002 ....Jose Theodore, Mtl
1954 ....Harry Lumley, Tor	1978 ....Ken Dryden, Mtl	2003 ....Martin Brodeur, NJ
1955 ....Terry Sawchuk, Det	Michel Larocque, Mtl	
1956 ....Jacques Plante, Mtl	1979 ....Ken Dryden, Mtl	
1957 ....Jacques Plante, Mtl	Michel Larocque, Mtl	

Selke Trophy

Awarded annually "to the forward who best excels in the defensive aspects of the game." The trophy is named after Frank J. Selke, the architect of the Montreal Canadians dynasty that won five consecutive Stanley Cups in the late '50s. The winner is selected by a vote of the Professional Hockey Writers Association.

1978........Bob Gainey, Mtl	1987........Dave Poulin, Phil	1996........Sergei Fedorov, Det
1979........Bob Gainey, Mtl	1988........Guy Carbonneau, Mtl	1997........Michael Peca, Buff
1980........Bob Gainey, Mtl	1989........Guy Carbonneau, Mtl	1998........Jere Lehtinen, Dall
1981........Bob Gainey, Mtl	1990........Rick Meagher, StL	1999........Jere Lehtinen, Dall
1982........Steve Kasper, Bos	1991........Dirk Graham, Chi	2000........Steve Yzerman, Det
1983........Bobby Clarke, Phil	1992........Guy Carbonneau, Mtl	2001........John Madden, NJ
1984........Doug Jarvis, Wash	1993........Doug Gilmour, Tor	2002........Michael Peca, NYI
1985........Craig Ramsay, Buff	1994........Sergei Fedorov, Det	2003........Jere Lehtinen, Dall
1986........Troy Murray, Chi	1995........Ron Francis, Pitt	

Adams Award

Awarded annually "to the NHL coach adjudged to have contributed the most to his team's success." The trophy is named in honor of Jack Adams, longtime coach and general manager of the Detroit Red Wings. The winner is selected by a vote of the National Hockey League Broadcasters' Association.

1974.....Fred Shero, Phil	1984:....Bryan Murray, Wash	1994.....Jacques Lemaire, NJ
1975.....Bob Pulford, LA	1985.....Mike Keenan, Phil	1995.....Marc Crawford, Que
1976.....Don Cherry, Bos	1986.....Glen Sather, Edm	1996.....Scotty Bowman, Det
1977.....Scott Bowman, Mtl	1987.....Jacques Demers, Det	1997.....Ted Nolan, Buff
1978.....Bobby Kromm, Det	1988:....Jacques Demers, Det	1998.....Pat Burns, Bos
1979.....Al Arbour, NYI	1989.....Pat Burns, Mtl	1999.....Jacques Martin, Ott
1980.....Pat Quinn, Phil	1990.....Bob Murdoch, Winn	2000.....Joel Quenneville, StL
1981.....Red Berenson, StL	1991.....Brian Sutter, StL	2001.....Bill Barber, Phil
1982.....Tom Watt, Winn	1992.....Pat Quinn, Van	2002.....Bob Francis, Phoe
1983.....Orval Tessier, Chi	1993.....Pat Burns, Tor	2003.....Jacques Lemaire, Minn

THEY SAID IT

Ed Jovanovski, Canucks defenseman, on his improvement since being acquired from Florida in '99: "When I got traded here it turned my career around 360 degrees."

Alltime Point Leaders

	Player	Yrs	GP	G	A	Pts	Pts/game
1.	Wayne Gretzky, Edm, LA, StL, NYR	20	1487	894	1963	2857	1.921
2.	Gordie Howe, Det, Hart	26	1767	801	1049	1850	1.047
3.	*Mark Messier, Edm, NYR, Van	24	1680	676	1168	1844	1.098
4.	Marcel Dionne, Det, LA, NYR	18	1348	731	1040	1771	1.314
5.	*Ron Francis, Hart, Pitt, Car	22	1651	536	1222	1758	1.065
6.	*Mario Lemieux, Pitt	15	879	682	1010	1692	1.925
7.	*Steve Yzerman, Det	20	1378	660	1010	1670	1.212
8.	Phil Esposito, Chi, Bos, NYR	18	1282	717	873	1590	1.240
9.	Ray Bourque, Bos, Col	22	1612	410	1169	1579	.980
10.	Paul Coffey, eight teams	21	1409	396	1135	1531	1.087
11.	Stan Mikita, Chi	22	1394	541	926	1467	1.052
12.	Bryan Trottier, NYI, Pitt	18	1279	524	901	1425	1.114
13.	*Doug Gilmour, seven teams	20	1474	450	964	1414	.959
14.	Dale Hawerchuk, Winn, Buff, StL, Phil	16	1188	518	891	1409	1.186
15.	Adam Oates, Det, StL, Bos, Wash, Phil, Ana	18	1277	339	1072	1402	1.098

*Active in 2002–03.

Alltime Goal-Scoring Leaders

	Player	Yrs	GP	G	G/game
1.	Wayne Gretzky, Edm, LA, StL, NYR	20	1487	894	.601
2.	Gordie Howe, Det, Hart	26	1767	801	.453
3.	Marcel Dionne, Det, LA, NYR	18	1348	731	.542
4.	Phil Esposito, Chi, Bos, NYR	18	1282	717	.559
5.	*Brett Hull, Cal, StL, Dall, Det	18	1183	716	.605
6.	Mike Gartner, Wash, Minn, NYR, Tor, Phoe	19	1432	708	.494
7.	*Mario Lemieux, Pitt	15	879	682	.776
8.	*Mark Messier, Edm, NYR, Van	24	1680	676	.402
9.	*Steve Yzerman, Det.	20	1378	660	.479
10.	*Luc Robitaille, LA, Pitt, NYR, Det	17	1286	631	.491

*Active in 2002–03.

Alltime Assist Leaders

	Player	Yrs	GP	A	A/game
1.	Wayne Gretzky, Edm, LA, StL, NYR	20	1487	1963	1.320
2.	Ray Bourque, Bos, Col	22	1612	1169	.725
3.	*Ron Francis, Hart, Pitt, Car	22	1651	1222	.740
4.	Paul Coffey, eight teams	21	1409	1135	.806
5.	*Mark Messier, Edm, NYR, Van	24	1680	1168	.695
6.	*Adam Oates, Det, StL, Bos, Wash	18	1277	1072	.840
7.	Gordie Howe, Det, Hart	26	1767	1049	.594
8.	Marcel Dionne, Det, LA, NYR	18	1348	1040	.771
9.	*Steve Yzerman, Det	20	1378	1010	.733
10.	*Mario Lemieux, Pitt	15	879	1010	1.150

*Active player in 2002–03.

Alltime Penalty Minutes Leaders

	Player	Yrs	GP	PIM	Min/game
1.	Dave Williams, Tor, Van, Det, LA, Hart	14	962	3966	4.12
2.	Dale Hunter, Que, Wash, Col	19	1407	3565	2.53
3.	Marty McSorley, Pitt, Edm, LA, NYR, SJ, Bos	17	961	3381	3.52
4.	Bob Probert, Det, Chi	16	935	3300	3.53
5.	*Tie Domi, Tor, NYR, Winn	14	863	3198	3.71
6.	*Rob Ray, Buff, Ott	14	894	3193	3.57
7.	*Craig Berube, Phil, Tor, Cgy, Wash, NYI	17	1054	3149	2.99
8.	Tim Hunter, Cgy, Que, Van, SJ	16	815	3146	3.86
9.	Chris Nilan, Mtl, NYR, Bos	13	688	3043	4.42
10.	*Rick Tocchet, Phil, Pitt, LA, Bos, Wash, Phoe	18	1144	2974	2.60

*Active in 2002–03.

Goaltending Records

ALLTIME WIN LEADERS

Goaltender	W	L	T	Pct
*Patrick Roy, Mtl, Col	551	315	131	.618
Terry Sawchuk, five teams	447	330	173	.562
Jacques Plante, five teams	434	246	147	.614
Tony Esposito, Mtl, Chi	423	306	152	.566
Glenn Hall, Det, Chi, StL	407	327	163	.545
Grant Fuhr, six teams	403	295	114	.567
*Ed Belfour, Chi, SJ, Dall, Tor	401	262	105	.591
Mike Vernon, Cgy, Det, SJ, Fla	385	273	92	.575
*Curtis Joseph, StL, Edm, Tor, Det	380	279	87	.568
John Vanbiesbrouck, five teams	374	346	119	.517

*Active in 2002–03.

ACTIVE GOALTENDING LEADERS

Goaltender	W	L	T	Pct
Martin Brodeur, NJ	365	191	94	.634
Chris Osgood, Det	274	152	58	.626
Patrick Roy, Mtl, Col	551	315	131	.618
Patrick Lalime, Pitt, Ott	142	89	25	.604
Ed Belfour, Chi, SJ, Dall	401	262	105	.591
Roman Turek, Dall, StL, Cgy	153	104	43	.582
Curtis Joseph, StL, Edm, Tor	380	279	87	.568
Tom Barrasso, Buff, Pitt, Ott, Tor	369	277	86	.563
Mike Richter, NYR	301	258	73	.534
Olaf Kolzig, Wash	215	185	54	.533

Note: Ranked by winning percentage; minimum 250 games played. All players active in 2002–03.

ALLTIME SHUTOUT LEADERS

Goaltender	Team	Yrs	GP	SO
Terry Sawchuk	Det, Bos, Tor, LA, NYR	21	971	103
George Hainsworth	Mtl, Tor	11	465	94
Glenn Hall	Det, Chi, StL	18	906	84
Jacques Plante	Mtl, NYR, StL, Tor, Bos	18	837	82
Tiny Thompson	Bos, Det	12	553	81
Alex Connell	Ott, Det, NYA, Mtl M	12	417	81
Tony Esposito	Mtl, Chi	16	886	76
Lorne Chabot	NYR, Tor, Mtl, Chi, Mtl M, NYA	11	411	73
Harry Lumley	Det, NYR, Chi, Tor, Bos	16	804	71
Roy Worters	Pitt Pir, NYA, *Mtl	12	484	67

*Played 1 game for Canadiens in 1929–30, not a shutout.

ALLTIME GOALS AGAINST AVERAGE LEADERS (PRE-1950)

Goaltender	Team	Yrs	GP	GA	GAA
George Hainsworth	Mtl, Tor	11	465	937	1.91
Alex Connell	Ott, Det, NYA, Mtl M	12	417	830	1.91
Chuck Gardiner	Chi	7	316	664	2.02
Lorne Chabot	NYR, Tor, Mtl, Chi, Mtl M, NYA	11	411	861	2.04
Tiny Thompson	Bos, Det	12	553	1183	2.08

ALLTIME GOALS AGAINST AVERAGE LEADERS (POST-1950)

Goaltender	Team	Yrs	GP	GA	GAA
*Martin Brodeur	NJ	11	665	1419	2.19
Dominik Hasek	Chi, Buff, Det	12	581	1254	2.23
Ken Dryden	Mtl	8	397	870	2.24
*Roman Turek	Dall, StL, Cgy	7	310	694	2.30
Jacques Plante	Mtl, NYR, StL, Tor, Bos	18	837	1965	2.38

*Active in 2002–03.

Note: Minimum 250 games played. Goals against average equals goals against per 60 minutes played.

Coaching Records

Coach	Team	Seasons	W	L	T	Pct
Scott Bowman	five teams	1967–87, 91–	1244	583	314	.654
Toe Blake	Mtl	1955–68	500	255	159	.634
Fred Shero	Phil, NYR	1971–81	390	225	119	.612
*Glen Sather	Edm, NYR	1979–89, 93–94, 2003–	475	281	114	.611
Emile Francis	NYR, StL	1965–77, 81–83	388	273	117	.574
Billy Reay	Tor, Chi	1957–59, 63–77	542	385	175	.571
*Pat Burns	Mtl, Tor, Bos, NJ	1988–2001, 2002–	458	334	139	.567
*Marc Crawford	Que, Col, Van	1994–	326	240	93	.565
Al Arbour	StL, NYI	1970–94	781	577	248	.564
Bryan Murray	Wash, Det, Fla	1981–98	484	368	123	.559
*Pat Quinn	Phil, LA, Van, Tor	1978–	571	436	144	.559

Note: Minimum 600 regular-season games. Ranked by percentage.

Impostor on Ice

In July 2003, after a five-month manhunt that involved the NHL, FBI, Secret Service and law enforcement agencies from four states, Elander Mark Lachney, a 35-year-old from Denham Springs, La., was apprehended for allegedly impersonating Blues winger Keith Tkachuk. In 1995, Lachney—who is 5'11", weighs 180 pounds and "doesn't look like he works out," according to a police source—was sentenced to four years in prison on two counts of filing fals public records while impersonating the 6' 2", 227-pound Tkachuk. Authorities suspected Lachney was at it again in February 2003 when Tkachuk was called by his bank regarding a request for a credit card in his name to be mailed to Louisiana. Lachney, who police say left messages for them saying, "You can't get me, I'm too smart," later allegedly secured $10,000 in loans using the aliases of Tkachuk, Rangers defenseman Brian Leetch and Flyers center Jeremy Roenick. When he was arrested, he had Louisiana driver's licenses in the names of all three players. He was charged with bank fraud and identity theft, both felonies. Tkachuk said he's "happy the thing is over."

Goals

Player	Season	GP	G	Player	Season	GP	G
Wayne Gretzky, Edm	1981–82	80	92	Wayne Gretzky, Edm	1982–83	80	71
Wayne Gretzky, Edm	1983–84	74	87	Brett Hull, StL	1991–92	73	70
Brett Hull, StL	1990–91	78	86	Mario Lemieux, Pitt	1987–88	77	70
Mario Lemieux, Pitt	1988–89	76	85	Bernie Nicholls, LA	1988–89	79	70
Alexander Mogilny, Buff	1992–93	77	76	Mario Lemieux, Pitt	1992–93	60	69
Phil Esposito, Bos	1970–71	78	76	Mario Lemieux, Pitt	1995–96	70	69
Teemu Selanne, Winn	1992–93	84	76	Mike Bossy, NYI	1978–79	80	69
Wayne Gretzky, Edm	1984–85	80	73	Phil Esposito, Bos	1973–74	78	68
Brett Hull, StL	1989–90	80	72	Jari Kurri, Edm	1985–86	78	68
Jari Kurri, Edm	1984–85	73	71	Mike Bossy, NYI	1980–81	79	68

Assists

Player	Season	GP	A	Player	Season	GP	A
Wayne Gretzky, Edm	1985–86	80	163	Wayne Gretzky, LA	1989–90	73	102
Wayne Gretzky, Edm	1984–85	80	135	Bobby Orr, Bos	1970–71	78	102
Wayne Gretzky, Edm	1982–83	80	125	Mario Lemieux, Pitt	1987–88	77	98
Wayne Gretzky, LA	1990–91	78	122	Adam Oates, Bos	1992–93	84	97
Wayne Gretzky, Edm	1986–87	79	121	Doug Gilmour, Tor	1992–93	83	95
Wayne Gretzky, Edm	1981–82	80	120	Pat LaFontaine, Buff	1992–93	84	95
Wayne Gretzky, Edm	1983–84	74	118	Mario Lemieux, Pitt	1985–86	79	93
Mario Lemieux, Pitt	1988–89	76	114	Peter Stastny, Que	1981–82	80	93
Wayne Gretzky, LA	1988–89	78	114	Wayne Gretzky, LA	1993–94	81	92
Wayne Gretzky, Edm	1987–88	64	109	Mario Lemieux, Pitt	1995–96	70	92
Wayne Gretzky, Edm	1980–81	80	109	Ron Francis, Pitt	1995–96	77	92

Points

Player	Season	G	A	Pts	Player	Season	G	A	Pts
Wayne Gretzky, Edm	1985–86	52	163	215	Wayne Gretzky, LA	1990–91	41	122	163
Wayne Gretzky, Edm	1981–82	92	120	212	Mario Lemieux, Pitt	1995–96	69	92	161
Wayne Gretzky, Edm	1984–85	73	135	208	Mario Lemieux, Pitt	1992–93	69	91	160
Wayne Gretzky, Edm	1983–84	87	118	205	Steve Yzerman, Det	1988–89	65	90	155
Mario Lemieux, Pitt	1988–89	85	114	199	Phil Esposito, Bos	1970–71	76	76	152
Wayne Gretzky, Edm	1982–83	71	125	196	Bernie Nicholls, LA	1988–89	70	80	150
Wayne Gretzky, Edm	1986–87	62	121	183	Wayne Gretzky, Edm	1987–88	40	109	149
Mario Lemieux, Pitt	1987–88	70	98	168	Pat LaFontaine, Buff	1992–93	53	95	148
Wayne Gretzky, LA	1988–89	54	114	168	Mike Bossy, NYI	1981–82	64	83	147
Wayne Gretzky, Edm	1980–81	55	109	164	Phil Esposito, Bos	1973–74	68	77	145

Points per Game

Player	Season	GP	Pts	Avg	Player	Season	GP	Pts	Avg
Wayne Gretzky, Edm	1983–84	74	205	2.77	Mario Lemieux, Pitt	1987–88	77	168	2.18
Wayne Gretzky, Edm	1985–86	80	215	2.69	Wayne Gretzky, LA	1988–89	78	168	2.15
Mario Lemieux, Pitt	1992–93	60	160	2.67	Wayne Gretzky, LA	1990–91	78	163	2.09
Wayne Gretzky, Edm	1981–82	80	212	2.65	Mario Lemieux, Pitt	1989–90	59	123	2.08
Mario Lemieux, Pitt	1988–89	76	199	2.62	Wayne Gretzky, Edm	1980–81	80	164	2.05
Wayne Gretzky, Edm	1984–85	80	208	2.60	Mario Lemieux, Pitt	1991–92	64	131	2.05
Wayne Gretzky, Edm	1982–83	80	196	2.45	Bill Cowley, Bos	1943–44	36	71	1.97
Wayne Gretzky, Edm	1987–88	64	149	2.33	Phil Esposito, Bos	1970–71	78	152	1.95
Wayne Gretzky, Edm	1986–87	79	183	2.32	Wayne Gretzky, LA	1989–90	73	142	1.95
Mario Lemieux, Pitt	1995–96	70	161	2.30	Steve Yzerman, Det	1988–89	80	155	1.94

Note: Minimum 50 points in one season.

Goals per Game

Player	Season	GP	G	Avg
Joe Malone, Mtl	1917–18	20	44	2.20
Cy Denneny, Ott	1917–18	22	36	1.64
Newsy Lalonde, Mtl	1917–18	14	23	1.64
Joe Malone, Que	1919–20	24	39	1.63
Newsy Lalonde, Mtl	1919–20	23	36	1.57
Joe Malone, Ham	1920–21	20	30	1.50
Babe Dye, Ham-Tor	1920–21	24	35	1.46
Cy Denneny, Ott	1920–21	24	34	1.42
Reg Noble, Tor	1917–18	20	28	1.40
Newsy Lalonde, Mtl	1920–21	24	33	1.38

Note: Minimum 20 goals in one season.

Assists per Game

Player	Season	GP	A	Avg
Wayne Gretzky, Edm	1985–86	80	163	2.04
Wayne Gretzky, Edm	1987–88	64	109	1.70
Wayne Gretzky, Edm	1984–85	80	135	1.69
Wayne Gretzky, Edm	1983–84	74	118	1.59
Wayne Gretzky, Edm	1982–83	80	125	1.56
Wayne Gretzky, LA	1990–91	78	122	1.56
Wayne Gretzky, Edm	1986–87	79	121	1.53
Mario Lemieux, Pitt	1992–93	60	91	1.52
Wayne Gretzky, Edm	1981–82	80	120	1.50
Mario Lemieux, Pitt	1988–89	76	114	1.50

Note: Minimum 35 assists in one season.

Shutout Leaders

	Season	SO	Length of Schedule
George Hainsworth, Mtl	1928–29	22	44
Alex Connell, Ott	1925–26	15	36
Alex Connell, Ott	1927–28	15	44
Hal Winkler, Bos	1927–28	15	44
Tony Esposito, Chi	1969–70	15	76
George Hainsworth, Mtl	1926–27	14	44
Clint Benedict, Mtl M	1926–27	13	44
Alex Connell, Ott	1926–27	13	44
George Hainsworth, Mtl	1927–28	13	44
John Roach, NYR	1928–29	13	44
Roy Worters, NYA	1928–29	13	44
Harry Lumley, Tor	1953–54	13	70
Dominik Hasek, Buff	1997–98	13	82
Tiny Thompson, Bos	1928–29	12	44
Lorne Chabot, Tor	1928–29	12	44
Chuck Gardiner, Chi	1930–31	12	44
Terry Sawchuk, Det	1951–52	12	70
Terry Sawchuk, Det	1953–54	12	70
Terry Sawchuk, Det	1954–55	12	70
Glenn Hall, Det	1955–56	12	70
Bernie Parent, Phil	1973–74	12	78
Bernie Parent, Phil	1974–75	12	80
Lorne Chabot, NYR	1927–28	11	44

	Season	SO	Length of Schedule
Harry Holmes, Det	1927–28	11	44
Clint Benedict, Mtl M	1928–29	11	44
Joe Miller, Pitt Pirates	1928–29	11	44
Tiny Thompson, Bos	1932–33	11	48
Terry Sawchuck, Det	1950–51	11	70
Dominik Hasek, Buff	2000–01	11	82
Lorne Chabot, NYR	1926–27	10	44
Roy Worters, Pitt Pirates	1927–28	10	44
Clarence Dolson, Det	1928–29	10	44
John Roach, Det	1932–33	10	48
Chuck Gardiner, Chi	1933–34	10	48
Tiny Thompson, Bos	1935–36	10	48
Frank Brimsek, Bos	1938–39	10	48
Bill Durnan, Mtl	1948–49	10	60
Gerry McNeil, Mtl	1952–53	10	70
Harry Lumley, Tor	1952–53	10	70
Tony Esposito, Chi	1973–74	10	78
Ken Dryden, Mtl	1976–77	10	80
Martin Brodeur, NJ	1996–97	10	82
Martin Brodeur, NJ	1997–98	10	82
Roman Cechmanek, Phil	2000–01	10	82
Byron Dafoe, Bos	1998–99	10	82

Wins

	Season	Record
Bernie Parent, Phil	1973–74	47-13-12
Bernie Parent, Phil	1974–75	44-14-9
Terry Sawchuk, Det	1950–51	44-13-13
Terry Sawchuk, Det	1951–52	44-14-12
Tom Barasso, Pitt	1992–93	43-14-5
Ed Belfour, Chi	1990–91	43-19-7
Martin Brodeur, NJ	1997–98	43-17-8
Martin Brodeur, NJ	1999–00	43-20-8
Jacques Plante, Mtl	1955–56	42-12-10
Jacques Plante, Mtl	1961–62	42-14-14
Ken Dryden, Mtl	1975–76	42-10-8
Mike Richter, NYR	1993–94	42-12-6
Roman Turek, StL	1999–00	42-15-9
Martin Brodeur, NJ	2000–01	42-17-11

Goals Against Average

(PRE-1950)

	Season	GP	GAA
George Hainsworth, Mtl	1928–29	44	0.92
George Hainsworth, Mtl	1927–28	44	1.05
Alex Connell, Ott	1925–26	36	1.12
Tiny Thompson, Bos	1928–29	44	1.18
Roy Worters, NYA	1928–29	38	1.21

(POST-1950)

	Season	GP	GAA
Marty Turco, Dall	2002–03	55	1.7287
Tony Esposito, Chi	1971–72	48	1.7698
Al Rollins, Tor	1950–51	40	1.7744
Ron Tugnutt, Ott	1998–99	43	1.7943
Roman Cechmanek	2002–03	58	1.8280

Single-Game Records

Goals

	Date	G
Joe Malone, Que vs Tor	1-31-20	7
Newsy Lalonde, Mtl vs Tor	1-10-20	6
Joe Malone, Que vs Ott	3-10-20	6
Corb Denneny, Tor vs Ham	1-26-21	6
Cy Denneny, Ott vs Ham	3-7-21	6
Syd Howe, Det vs NYR	2-3-44	6
Red Berenson, StL vs Phil	11-7-68	6
Darryl Sittler, Tor vs Bos	2-7-76	6

Assists

	Date	A
Billy Taylor, Det vs Chi	3-16-47	7
Wayne Gretzky, Edm vs Wash	2-15-80	7
Wayne Gretzky, Edm vs Chi	12-11-85	7
Wayne Gretzky, Edm vs Que	2-14-86	7

Note: 24 tied with 6.

Points

	Date	G	A	Pts
Darryl Sittler, Tor vs Bos	2-7-76	6	4	10
Maurice Richard, Mtl vs Det	12-28-44	5	3	8
Bert Olmstead, Mtl vs Chi	1-9-54	4	4	8
Tom Bladon, Phil vs Clev	12-11-77	4	4	8
Bryan Trottier, NYI vs NYR	12-23-78	5	3	8
Peter Stastny, Que vs Wash	2-22-81	4	4	8
Anton Stastny, Que vs Wash	2-22-81	3	5	8
Wayne Gretzky, Edm vs NJ	11-19-83	3	5	8
Wayne Gretzky, Edm vs Minn	1-4-84	4	4	8
Paul Coffey, Edm vs Det	3-14-86	2	6	8
Mario Lemieux, Pitt vs StL	10-15-88	2	6	8
Bernie Nicholls, LA vs Tor	12-1-88	2	6	8
Mario Lemieux, Pitt vs NJ	12-31-88	5	3	8

NHL Season Leaders

Points

eason	Player and Club	Pts	Season	Player and Club	Pts
1917–18	Joe Malone, Mtl	44	1956–57	Gordie Howe, Det	89
1918–19	Newsy Lalonde, Mtl	30	1957–58	Dickie Moore, Mtl	84
1919–20	Joe Malone, Que	48	1958–59	Dickie Moore, Mtl	96
1920–21	Newsy Lalonde, Mtl	41	1959–60	Bobby Hull, Chi	81
1921–22	Punch Broadbent, Ott	46	1960–61	Bernie Geoffrion, Mtl	95
1922–23	Babe Dye, Tor	37	1961–62	Andy Bathgate, NY	84
1923–24	Cy Denneny, Ott	23		Bobby Hull, Chi	84
1924–25	Babe Dye, Tor	44	1962–63	Gordie Howe, Det	86
1925–26	Nels Stewart, Mtl M	42	1963–64	Stan Mikita, Chi	89
1926–27	Bill Cook, NY	37	1964–65	Stan Mikita, Chi	87
1927–28	Howie Morenz, Mtl	51	1965–66	Bobby Hull, Chi	97
1928–29	Ace Bailey, Tor	32	1966–67	Stan Mikita, Chi	97
1929–30	Cooney Weiland, Bos	73	1967–68	Stan Mikita, Chi	87
1930–31	Howie Morenz, Mtl	51	1968–69	Phil Esposito, Bos	126
1931–32	Harvey Jackson, Tor	53	1969–70	Bobby Orr, Bos	120
1932–33	Bill Cook, NY	50	1970–71	Phil Esposito, Bos	152
1933–34	Charlie Conacher, Tor	52	1971–72	Phil Esposito, Bos	133
1934–35	Charlie Conacher, Tor	57	1972–73	Phil Esposito, Bos	130
1935–36	Sweeney Schriner, NYA	45	1973–74	Phil Esposito, Bos	145
1936–37	Sweeney Schriner, NYA	46	1974–75	Bobby Orr, Bos	135
1937–38	Gord Drillon, Tor	52	1975–76	Guy Lafleur, Mtl	125
1938–39	Hector Blake, Mtl	47	1976–77	Guy Lafleur, Mtl	136
1939–40	Milt Schmidt, Bos	52	1977–78	Guy Lafleur, Mtl	132
1940–41	Bill Cowley, Bos	62	1978–79	Bryan Trottier, NYI	134
1941–42	Bryan Hextall, NY	54	1979–80	Marcel Dionne, LA	137
1942–43	Doug Bentley, Chi	73		Wayne Gretzky, Edm	137
1943–44	Herb Cain, Bos	82	1980–81	Wayne Gretzky, Edm	164
1944–45	Elmer Lach, Mtl	80	1981–82	Wayne Gretzky, Edm	212
1945–46	Max Bentley, Chi	61	1982–83	Wayne Gretzky, Edm	196
1946–47	Max Bentley, Chi	72	1983–84	Wayne Gretzky, Edm	205
1947–48	Elmer Lach, Mtl	61	1984–85	Wayne Gretzky, Edm	208
1948–49	Roy Conacher, Chi	68	1985–86	Wayne Gretzky, Edm	215
1949–50	Ted Lindsay, Det	78	1986–87	Wayne Gretzky, Edm	183
1950–51	Gordie Howe, Det	86	1987–88	Mario Lemieux, Pitt	168
1951–52	Gordie Howe, Det	86	1988–89	Mario Lemieux, Pitt	199
1952–53	Gordie Howe, Det	95	1989–90	Wayne Gretzky, LA	142
1953–54	Gordie Howe, Det	81	1990–91	Wayne Gretzky, LA	163
1954–55	Bernie Geoffrion, Mtl	75	1991–92	Mario Lemieux, Pitt	131
1955–56	Jean Beliveau, Mtl	88	1992–93	Mario Lemieux, Pitt	160

Points (Cont.)

Season	Player and Club	Pts	Season	Player and Club	Pts
1993–94	Wayne Gretzky, LA	130	1998–99	Jaromir Jagr, Pitt	127
1994–95	Jaromir Jagr, Pitt	70	1999–00	Jaromir Jagr, Pitt	96
1995–96	Mario Lemieux, Pitt	161	2000–01	Jaromir Jagr, Pitt	121
1996–97	Mario Lemieux, Pitt	122	2001–02	Jarome Iginla, Cal	96
1997–98	Jaromir Jagr, Pitt	102	2002–03	Peter Forsberg, Col	106

Goals

Season	Player and Club	G	Season	Player and Club	G
1917–18	Joe Malone, Mtl	44	1960–61	Bernie Geoffrion, Mtl	50
1918–19	Odie Cleghorn, Mtl	23	1961–62	Bobby Hull, Chi	50
1919–20	Joe Malone, Que	39	1962–63	Gordie Howe, Det	38
1920–21	Babe Dye, Ham-Tor	35	1963–64	Bobby Hull, Chi	43
1921–22	Punch Broadbent, Ott	32	1964–65	Norm Ullman, Det	42
1922–23	Babe Dye, Tor	26	1965–66	Bobby Hull, Chi	54
1923–24	Cy Denneny, Ott	22	1966–67	Bobby Hull, Chi	52
1924–25	Babe Dye, Tor	38	1967–68	Bobby Hull, Chi	44
1925–26	Nels Stewart, Mtl	34	1968–69	Bobby Hull, Chi	58
1926–27	Bill Cook, NY	33	1969–70	Phil Esposito, Bos	43
1927–28	Howie Morenz, Mtl	33	1970–71	Phil Esposito, Bos	76
1928–29	Ace Bailey, Tor	22	1971–72	Phil Esposito, Bos	66
1929–30	Cooney Weiland, Bos	43	1972–73	Phil Esposito, Bos	55
1930–31	Bill Cook, NY	30	1973–74	Phil Esposito, Bos	68
1931–32	Charlie Conacher, Tor	34	1974–75	Phil Esposito, Bos	61
	Bill Cook, NY	34	1975–76	Guy Lafleur, Mtl	56
1932–33	Bill Cook, NY	28	1976–77	Steve Shutt, Mtl	60
1933–34	Charlie Conacher, Tor	32	1977–78	Guy Lafleur, Mtl	60
1934–35	Charlie Conacher, Tor	36	1978–79	Mike Bossy, NYI	69
1935–36	Charlie Conacher, Tor	23	1979–80	Charlie Simmer, LA	56
	Bill Thoms, Tor	23		Blaine Stoughton, Hart	56
1936–37	Larry Aurie, Det	23	1980–81	Mike Bossy, NYI	68
	Nels Stewart, Bos-NYA	23	1981–82	Wayne Gretzky, Edm	92
1937–38	Gord Drill, Tor	26	1982–83	Wayne Gretzky, Edm	71
1938–39	Roy Conacher, Bos	26	1983–84	Wayne Gretzky, Edm	87
1939–40	Bryan Hextall, NY	24	1984–85	Wayne Gretzky, Edm	73
1940–41	Bryan Hextall, NY	26	1985–86	Jari Kurri, Edm	68
1941–42	Lynn Patrick, NY	32	1986–87	Wayne Gretzky, Edm	62
1942–43	Doug Bentley, Chi	43	1987–88	Mario Lemieux, Pitt	70
1943–44	Doug Bentley, Chi	38	1988–89	Mario Lemieux, Pitt	85
1944–45	Maurice Richard, Mtl	50	1989–90	Brett Hull, StL	72
1945–46	Gaye Stewart, Tor	37	1990–91	Brett Hull, StL	78
1946–47	Maurice Richard, Mtl	50	1991–92	Brett Hull, StL	70
1947–48	Ted Lindsay, Det	33	1992–93	Alexander Mogilny, Buff	76
1948–49	Sid Abel, Det	28		Teemu Selanne, Winn	76
1949–50	Maurice Richard, Mtl	43	1993–94	Pavel Bure, Van	60
1950–51	Gordie Howe, Det	43	1994–95	Peter Bondra, Wash	34
1951–52	Gordie Howe, Det	47	1995–96	Mario Lemieux, Pitt	69
1952–53	Gordie Howe, Det	49	1996–97	Keith Tkachuk, Phoe	52
1953–54	Maurice Richard, Mtl	37	1997–98	Teemu Selanne, Ana	52
1954–55	Bernie Geoffrion, Mtl	38		Peter Bondra, Wash	52
	Maurice Richard, Mtl	38	1998–99	Teemu Selanne, Ana	47
1955–56	Jean Beliveau, Mtl	47	1999–00	Pavel Bure, Fla	58
1957–58	Dickie Moore, Mtl	36	2000–01	Pavel Bure, Fla	59
1956–57	Gordie Howe, Det	44	2001–02	Jarome Iginla, Cal	52
1958–59	Jean Beliveau, Mtl	45	2002–03	Milan Hejduk, Col	50
1959–60	Bobby Hull, Chi	39			
	Bronco Horvath, Bos	39			

Assists

Season	Player and Club	A	Season	Player and Club	A
1917–18	statistic not kept		1963–64	Andy Bathgate, NY-Tor	58
1918–19	Newsy Lalonde, Mtl	9	1964–65	Stan Mikita, Chi	59
1919–20	Corbett Denneny, Tor	12	1965–66	Stan Mikita, Chi	48
1920–21	Louis Berlinquette, Mtl	9		Bobby Rousseau, Mtl	48
1921–22	Punch Broadbench, Ott	14		Jean Beliveau, Mtl	48
1922–23	Babe Dye, Tor	11	1966–67	Stan Mikita, Chi	62
1923–24	Billy Boucher, Mtl	6	1967–68	Phil Esposito, Bos	49
1924–25	Cy Denneny, Ott	15	1968–69	Phil Esposito, Bos	77
1925–26	Cy Denneny, Ott	12	1969–70	Bobby Orr, Bos	87
1926–27	Dick Irvin, Chi	18	1970–71	Bobby Orr, Bos	102
1927–28	Howie Morenz, Mtl	18	1971–72	Bobby Orr, Bos	80
1928–29	Frank Boucher, NY	16	1972–73	Phil Esposito, Bos	75
1929–30	Frank Boucher, NY	36	1973–74	Bobby Orr, Bos	89
1930–31	Joe Primeau, Tor	36	1974–75	Bobby Clarke, Phil	89
1931–32	Joe Primeau, Tor	37		Bobby Orr, Bos	89
1932–33	Frank Boucher, NY	28	1975–76	Bobby Clarke, Phil	89
1933–34	Joe Primeau, Tor	32	1976–77	Guy Lafleur, Mtl	80
1934–35	Art Chapman, NYA	28	1977–78	Bryan Trottier, NYI	77
1935–36	Art Chapman, NYA	28	1978–79	Bryan Trottier, NYI	87
1936–37	Syl Apps, Tor	29	1979–80	Wayne Gretzky, Edm	86
1937–38	Syl Apps, Tor	29	1980–81	Wayne Gretzky, Edm	109
1938–39	Bill Cowley, Bos	34	1981–82	Wayne Gretzky, Edm	120
1939–40	Milt Schmidt, Bos	30	1982–83	Wayne Gretzky, Edm	125
1940–41	Bill Cowley, Bos	45	1983–84	Wayne Gretzky, Edm	118
1941–42	Phil Watson, NY	37	1984–85	Wayne Gretzky, Edm	135
1942–43	Bill Cowley, Bos	45	1985–86	Wayne Gretzky, Edm	163
1943–44	Clint Smith, Chi	49	1986–87	Wayne Gretzky, Edm	121
1944–45	Elmer Lach, Mtl	54	1987–88	Wayne Gretzky, Edm	109
1945–46	Elmer Lach, Mtl	34	1988–89	Wayne Gretzky, LA	114
1946–47	Billy Taylor, Det	46		Mario Lemieux, Pitt	114
1947–48	Doug Bentley, Chi	37	1989–90	Wayne Gretzky, LA	102
1948–49	Doug Bentley, Chi	43	1990–91	Wayne Gretzky, LA	122
1949–50	Ted Lindsay, Det	55	1991–92	Wayne Gretzky, LA	90
1950–51	Gordie Howe, Det	43	1992–93	Adam Oates, Bos	97
	Ted Kennedy, Tor	43	1993–94	Wayne Gretzky, LA	92
1951–52	Elmer Lach, Mtl	50	1994–95	Ron Francis, Pitt	48
1952–53	Gordie Howe, Det	46	1995–96	Mario Lemieux, Pitt	92
1953–54	Gordie Howe, Det	48		Ron Francis, Pitt	92
1954–55	Bert Olmstead, Mtl	48	1996–97	Mario Lemieux, Pitt	72
1955–56	Bert Olmstead, Mtl	56	1997–98	Jaromir Jagr, Pitt	67
1956–57	Ted Lindsay, Det	55		Wayne Gretzky, NYR	67
1957–58	Henri Richard, Mtl	52	1998–99	Jaromir Jagr, Pitt	83
1958–59	Dickie Moore, Mtl	55	1999–00	Mark Recchi, Phil	63
1959–60	Bobby Hull, Chi	42	2000–01	Jaromir Jagr, Pitt	69
1960–61	Jean Beliveau, Mtl	58		Adam Oates, Wash	69
1961–62	Andy Bathgate, NY	56	2001–02	Adam Oates, Wash	57
1962–63	Henri Richard, Mtl	50	2002–03	Peter Forsberg, Col	77

THEY SAID IT

Paul Maurice, Hurricanes coach, on when goalie Kevin Weekes, who was out with postconcussion syndrome, would take an NHL-mandated neurological test to determine his return date: "I don't know. He's busy studying for it."

Goals Against Average

Season	Goaltender and Club	GP	Min	GA	SO	Avg
1917–18	Georges Vezina, Mtl	21	1282	84	1	3.93
1918–19	Clint Benedict, Ott	18	1113	53	2	2.86
1919–20	Clint Benedict, Ott	24	1444	64	5	2.66
1920–21	Clint Benedict, Ott	24	1457	75	2	3.09
1921–22	Clint Benedict, Ott	24	1508	84	2	3.34
1922–23	Clint Benedict, Ott	24	1478	54	4	2.19
1923–24	Georges Vezina, Mtl	24	1459	48	3	1.97
1924–25	Georges Vezina, Mtl	30	1860	56	5	1.81
1925–26	Alex Connell, Ott	36	2251	42	15	1.12
1926–27	Clint Benedict, Mtl M	43	2748	65	13	1.42
1927–28	George Hainsworth, Mtl	44	2730	48	13	1.05
1928–29	George Hainsworth, Mtl	44	2800	43	22	0.92
1929–30	Tiny Thompson, Bos	44	2680	98	3	2.19
1930–31	Roy Worters, NYA	44	2760	74	8	1.61
1931–32	Chuck Gardiner, Chi	48	2989	92	4	1.85
1932–33	Tiny Thompson, Bos	48	3000	88	11	1.76
1933–34	Wilf Cude, Det-Mtl	30	1920	47	5	1.47
1934–35	Lorne Chabot, Chi	48	2940	88	8	1.80
1935–36	Tiny Thompson, Bos	48	2930	82	10	1.68
1936–37	Normie Smith, Det	48	2980	102	6	2.05
1937–38	Tiny Thompson, Bos	48	2970	89	7	1.80
1938–39	Frank Brimsek, Bos	43	2610	68	10	1.56
1939–40	Dave Kerr, NYR	48	3000	77	8	1.54
1940–41	Turk Broda, Tor	48	2970	99	5	2.00
1941–42	Frank Brimsek, Bos	47	2930	115	3	2.35
1942–43	Johnny Mowers, Det	50	3010	124	6	2.47
1943–44	Bill Durnan, Mtl	50	3000	109	2	2.18
1944–45	Bill Durnan, Mtl	50	3000	121	1	2.42
1945–46	Bill Durnan, Mtl	40	2400	104	4	2.60
1946–47	Bill Durnan, Mtl	60	3600	138	4	2.30
1947–48	Turk Broda, Tor	60	3600	143	5	2.38
1948–49	Bill Durnan, Mtl	60	3600	126	10	2.10
1949–50	Bill Durnan, Mtl	64	3840	141	8	2.20
1950–51	Al Rollins, Tor	40	2367	70	5	1.77
1951–52	Terry Sawchuk, Det	70	4200	133	12	1.90
1952–53	Terry Sawchuk, Det	63	3780	120	9	1.90
1953–54	Harry Lumley, Tor	69	4140	128	13	1.86
1954–55	Harry Lumley, Tor	69	4140	134	8	1.94
	Terry Sawchuk, Det	68	4060	132	12	1.94
1955–56	Jacques Plante, Mtl	64	3840	119	7	1.86
1956–57	Jacques Plante, Mtl	61	3660	123	9	2.02
1957–58	Jacques Plante, Mtl	57	3386	119	9	2.11
1958–59	Jacques Plante, Mtl	67	4000	144	9	2.16
1959–60	Jacques Plante, Mtl	69	4140	175	3	2.54
1960–61	Johnny Bower, Tor	58	3480	145	2	2.50
1961–62	Jacques Plante, Mtl	70	4200	166	4	2.37
1962–63	Jacques Plante, Mtl	56	3320	138	5	2.49
1963–64	Johnny Bower, Tor	51	3009	106	5	2.11
1964–65	Johnny Bower, Tor	34	2040	81	3	2.38
1965–66	Johnny Bower, Tor	35	1998	75	3	2.25
1966–67	Glenn Hall, Chi	32	1664	66	2	2.38
1967–68	Gump Worsley, Mtl	40	2213	73	6	1.98
1968–69	Jacques Plante, StL	37	2139	70	5	1.96
1969–70	Ernie Wakely, StL	30	1651	58	4	2.11
1970–71	Jacques Plante, Tor	40	2329	73	4	1.88
1971–72	Tony Esposito, Chi	48	2780	82	9	1.77
1972–73	Ken Dryden, Mtl	54	3165	119	6	2.26
1973–74	Bernie Parent, Phil	73	4314	136	12	1.89
1974–75	Bernie Parent, Phil	68	4041	137	12	2.03
1975–76	Ken Dryden, Mtl	62	3580	121	8	2.03
1976–77	Michael Larocque, Mtl	26	1525	53	4	2.09
1977–78	Ken Dryden, Mtl	52	3071	105	5	2.05
1978–79	Ken Dryden, Mtl	47	2814	108	5	2.30
1979–80	Bob Sauve, Buff	32	1880	74	4	2.36
1980–81	Richard Sevigny, Mtl	33	1777	71	2	2.40
1981–82	Denis Herron, Mtl	27	1547	68	3	2.64
1982–83	Pete Peeters, Bos	62	3611	142	8	2.36
1983–84	Pat Riggin, Wash	41	2299	102	4	2.66

Goals Against Average (Cont.)

Season	Goaltender and Club	GP	Min	GA	SO	Avg
1984–85	Tom Barrasso, Buff	54	3248	144	5	2.66
1985–86	Bob Froese, Phil	51	2728	116	5	2.55
1986–87	Brian Hayward, Mtl	37	2178	102	1	2.81
1987–88	Pete Peeters, Wash	35	1896	88	2	2.78
1988–89	Patrick Roy, Mtl	48	2744	113	4	2.47
1989–90	Patrick Roy, Mtl	54	3173	134	3	2.53
	Mike Liut, Hart-Wash	37	2161	91	4	2.53
1990–91	Ed Belfour, Chi	74	4127	170	4	2.47
1991–92	Patrick Roy, Mtl	67	3935	155	5	2.36
1992–93	*Felix Potvin, Tor	48	2781	116	2	2.50
1993–94	Dominik Hasek, Buff	58	3358	109	7	1.95
1994–95	Dominik Hasek, Buff	41	2416	85	5	2.11
1995–96	Ron Hextall, Phil	53	3102	112	4	2.17
	Chris Osgood, Det	50	2933	106	5	2.17
1996–97	Martin Brodeur, NJ	67	3838	120	10	1.88
1997–98	Ed Belfour, Dall	61	3581	112	9	1.88
1998–99	Ron Tugnutt, Ott	43	2508	75	3	1.79
1999–00	Brian Boucher, Phil	35	2038	65	4	1.91
2000–01	Marty Turco, Dall	26	1266	40	3	1.90
2001–02	Patrick Roy, Col	63	3774	122	9	1.94
2002–03	Marty Turco, Dall	55	3193	92	7	1.72

*Rookie.

Penalty Minutes

Season	Player and Club	GP	PIM	Season	Player and Club	GP	PIM
1918–19	Joe Hall, Mtl	17	85	1961–62	Lou Fontinato, Mtl	54	167
1919–20	Cully Wilson, Tor	23	79	1962–63	Howie Young, Det	64	273
1920–21	Bert Corbeau, Mtl	24	86	1963–64	Vic Hadfield, NYR	69	151
1921–22	Sprague Cleghorn, Mtl	24	63	1964–65	Carl Brewer, Tor	70	177
1922–23	Billy Boucher, Mtl	24	52	1965–66	Reggie Fleming, Bos-NYR	69	166
1923–24	Bert Corbeau, Tor	24	55	1966–67	John Ferguson, Mtl	67	177
1924–25	Billy Boucher, Mtl	30	92	1967–68	Barclay Plager, StL	49	153
1925–26	Bert Corbeau, Tor	36	121	1968–69	Forbes Kennedy, Phil-Tor	77	219
1926–27	Nels Stewart, Mtl M	44	133	1969–70	Keith Magnuson, Chi	76	213
1927–28	Eddie Shore, Bos	44	165	1970–71	Keith Magnuson, Chi	76	291
1928–29	Red Dutton, Mtl M	44	139	1971–72	Brian Watson, Pitt	75	212
1929–30	Joe Lamb, Ott	44	119	1972–73	Dave Schultz, Phil	76	259
1930–31	Harvey Rockburn, Det	42	118	1973–74	Dave Schultz, Phil	73	348
1931–32	Red Dutton, NYA	47	107	1974–75	Dave Schultz, Phil	76	472
1932–33	Red Horner, Tor	48	144	1975–76	Steve Durbano, Pitt-KC	69	370
1933–34	Red Horner, Tor	42	126	1976–77	Dave Williams, Tor	77	338
1934–35	Red Horner, Tor	46	125	1977–78	Dave Schultz, LA-Pitt	74	405
1935–36	Red Horner, Tor	43	167	1978–79	Dave Williams, Tor	77	298
1936–37	Red Horner, Tor	48	124	1979–80	Jimmy Mann, Winn	72	287
1937–38	Red Horner, Tor	47	82	1980–81	Dave Williams, Van	77	343
1938–39	Red Horner, Tor	48	85	1981–82	Paul Baxter, Pitt	76	409
1939–40	Red Horner, Tor	30	87	1982–83	Randy Holt, Wash	70	275
1940–41	Jimmy Orlando, Det	48	99	1983–84	Chris Nilan, Mtl	76	338
1941–42	Jimmy Orlando, Det	48	81	1984–85	Chris Nilan, Mtl	77	358
1942–43	Jimmy Orlando, Det	40	89	1985–86	Joey Kocur, Det	59	377
1943–44	Mike McMahon, Mtl	42	98	1986–87	Tim Hunter, Cgy	73	361
1944–45	Pat Egan, Bos	48	86	1987–88	Bob Probert, Det	74	398
1945–46	Jack Stewart, Det	47	73	1988–89	Tim Hunter, Cgy	75	375
1946–47	Gus Mortson, Tor	60	133	1989–90	Basil McRae, Minn	66	351
1947–48	Bill Barilko, Tor	57	147	1990–91	Bob Ray, Buff	66	350
1948–49	Bill Ezinicki, Tor	52	145	1991–92	Mike Peluso, Chi	63	408
1949–50	Bill Ezinicki, Tor	67	144	1992–93	Marty McSorley, LA	81	399
1950–51	Gus Mortson, Tor	60	142	1993–94	Tie Domi, Winn	81	347
1951–52	Gus Kyle, Bos	69	127	1994–95	Enrico Ciccone, TB	41	225
1952–53	Maurice Richard, Mtl	70	112	1995–96	Matthew Barnaby, Buff	73	335
1953–54	Gus Mortson, Chi	68	132	1996–97	Gino Odjick, Van	70	371
1954–55	Fern Flaman, Bos	70	150	1997–98	Donald Brashear, Van	77	372
1955–56	Lou Fontinato, NYR	70	202	1998–99	Rob Ray, Buff	76	261
1956–57	Gus Mortson, Chi	70	147	1999–00	Denny Lambert, Atl	73	219
1957–58	Lou Fontinato, NYR	70	152	2000–01	Matthew Barnaby, TB	76	265
1958–59	Ted Lindsay, Chi	70	184	2001–02	Peter Worrell, Fla	79	354
1959–60	Carl Brewer, Tor	67	150	2002–03	Jody Shelley, Clb	68	249
1960–61	Pierre Pilote, Chi	70	165				

NHL All-Star Game

First played in 1947, this game was scheduled before the start of the regular season and used to match the defending Stanley Cup Champions against a squad made up of the league All-stars from other teams. In 1966 the games were moved to mid-season, although there was no game that year. The format changed to a conference versus conference showdown in 1969.

Results

Year	Site	Score	MVP	Attendance
1947	Toronto	All-Stars 4, Toronto 3	None named	14,169
1948	Chicago	All-Stars 3, Toronto 1	None named	12,794
1949	Toronto	All-Stars 3, Toronto 1	None named	13,541
1950	Detroit	Detroit 7, All-Stars 1	None named	9,166
1951	Toronto	1st team 2, 2nd team 2	None named	11,469
1952	Detroit	1st team 1, 2nd team 1	None named	10,680
1953	Montreal	All-Stars 3, Montreal 1	None named	14,153
1954	Detroit	All-Stars 2, Detroit 2	None named	10,689
1955	Detroit	Detroit 3, All-Stars 1	None named	10,111
1956	Montreal	All-Stars 1, Montreal 1	None named	13,095
1957	Montreal	All-Stars 5, Montreal 3	None named	13,003
1958	Montreal	Montreal 6, All-Stars 3	None named	13,989
1959	Montreal	Montreal 6, All-Stars 1	None named	13,818
1960	Montreal	All-Stars 2, Montreal 1	None named	13,949
1961	Chicago	All-Stars 3, Chicago 1	None named	14,534
1962	Toronto	Toronto 4, All-Stars 1	Eddie Shack, Tor	14,236
1963	Toronto	All-Stars 3, Toronto 3	Frank Mahovlich, Tor	14,034
1964	Toronto	All-Stars 3, Toronto 2	Jean Beliveau, Mtl	14,232
1965	Montreal	All-Stars 5, Montreal 2	Gordie Howe, Det	13,529
1967	Montreal	Montreal 3, All-Stars 0	Henri Richard, Mtl	14,284
1968	Toronto	Toronto 4, All-Stars 3	Bruce Gamble, Tor	15,753
1969	Montreal	East 3, West 3	Frank Mahovlich, Det	16,260
1970	St Louis	East 4, West 1	Bobby Hull, Chi	16,587
1971	Boston	West 2, East 1	Bobby Hull, Chi	14,790
1972	Minnesota	East 3, West 2	Bobby Orr, Bos	15,423
1973	NY Rangers	East 5, West 4	Greg Polis, Pitt	16,986
1974	Chicago	West 6, East 4	Garry Unger, StL	16,426
1975	Montreal	Wales 7, Campbell 1	Syl Apps Jr, Pitt	16,080
1976	Philadelphia	Wales 7, Campbell 5	Pete Mahovlich, Mtl	16,436
1977	Vancouver	Wales 4, Campbell 3	Rick Martin, Buff	15,607
1978	Buffalo	Wales 3, Campbell 2 (OT)	Billy Smith, NYI	16,433
1980	Detroit	Wales 6, Campbell 3	Reg Leach, Phil	21,002
1981	Los Angeles	Campbell 4, Wales 1	Mike Liut, StL	15,761
1982	Washington	Wales 4, Campbell 2	Mike Bossy, NYI	18,130
1983	NY Islanders	Campbell 9, Wales 3	Wayne Gretzky, Edm	15,230
1984	NJ Devils	Wales 7, Campbell 6	Don Maloney, NYR	18,939
1985	Calgary	Wales 6, Campbell 4	Mario Lemieux, Pitt	16,825
1986	Hartford	Wales 4, Campbell 3 (OT)	Grant Fuhr, Edm	15,100
1988	St Louis	Wales 6, Campbell 5 (OT)	Mario Lemieux, Pitt	17,878
1989	Edmonton	Campbell 9, Wales 5	Wayne Gretzky, LA	17,503
1990	Pittsburgh	Wales 12, Campbell 7	Mario Lemieux, Pitt	16,236
1991	Chicago	Campbell 11, Wales 5	Vince Damphousse, Tor	18,472
1992	Philadelphia	Campbell 10, Wales 6	Brett Hull, StL	17,380
1993	Montreal	Wales 16, Campbell 6	Mike Gartner, NYR	17,137
1994	NY Rangers	East 9, West 8	Mike Richter, NYR	18,200
1996	Boston	East 5, West 4	Ray Bourque, Bos	17,565
1997	San Jose	East 11, West 7	Mark Recchi, Mtl	17,565
1998	Vancouver	N America 8, World 7	Teemu Selanne, Ana (World)	18,422
1999	Tampa Bay	N America 8, World 6	Wayne Gretzky, NYR (N America)	19,758
2000	Toronto	World 9, N America 4	Pavel Bure, Fla (World)	19,300
2001	Denver	N America 14, World 12	Bill Guerin, Bos (N America)	18,646
2002	Los Angeles	World 8, N America 5	Eric Daze, Chi (N America)	18,118
2003	Sunrise, Fla.	West 6, East 5 (shootout)	Dany Heatley, Atl (East)	19,250

Note: The Challenge Cup, a series between the NHL All-Stars and the Soviet Union, was played instead of the All-Star Game in 1979. Eight years later, Rendez-Vous '87, a two-game series matching the Soviet Union and the NHL All-Stars, replaced the All-Star Game. The 1995 NHL All-Star game was cancelled due to a labor dispute. The 1998 NHL All-Star game, billed as a preview to the 1998 Winter Olympics in Nagano, Japan, matched North Amercian-born All-Stars and All-Stars born elsewhere.

Hockey Hall of Fame

Located in Toronto, the Hockey Hall of Fame was officially opened on August 26, 1961. The current chairman is William C. Hay. There are, at present, 306 members of the Hockey Hall of Fame—209 players, 84 "builders," and 14 on-ice officials. (One member, Alan Eagleson, resigned from the Hall 3-25-98.) To be eligible, player and referee/linesman candidates should have been out of the game for three years, but the Hall's Board of Directors can make exceptions.

Players

Sid Abel (1969)
Jack Adams (1959)
Charles (Syl) Apps (1961)
George Armstrong (1975)
Irvine (Ace) Bailey (1975)
Donald H. (Dan) Bain (1945)
Hobey Baker (1945)
Bill Barber (1990)
Marty Barry (1965)
Andy Bathgate (1978)
Bobby Bauer (1996)
Jean Beliveau (1972)
Clint Benedict (1965)
Douglas Bentley (1964)
Max Bentley (1966)
Hector (Toe) Blake (1966)
Leo Boivin (1986)
Dickie Boon (1952)
Mike Bossy (1991)
Emile (Butch) Bouchard (1966)
Frank Boucher (1958)
George (Buck) Boucher (1960)
Johnny Bower (1976)
Russell Bowie (1945)
Frank Brimsek (1966)
Harry L. (Punch) Broadbent
    (1962)
Walter (Turk) Broda (1967)
John Bucyk (1981)
Billy Burch (1974)
Harry Cameron (1962)
Gerry Cheevers (1985)
Francis (King) Clancy (1958)
Aubrey (Dit) Clapper (1947)
Bobby Clarke (1987)
Sprague Cleghorn (1958)
Neil Colville (1967)
Charlie Conacher (1961)
Lionel Conacher (1994)
Roy Conacher (1998)
Alex Connell (1958)
Bill Cook (1952)
Fred (Bun) Cook (1995)
Arthur Coulter (1974)
Yvan Cournoyer (1982)
Bill Cowley (1968)
Samuel (Rusty) Crawford (1962)
Jack Darragh (1962)
Allan M. (Scotty) Davidson
    (1950)
Clarence (Hap) Day (1961)
Alex Delvecchio (1977)
Cy Denneny (1959)
Marcel Dionne (1992)
Gordie Drillon (1975)
Charles Drinkwater (1950)
Ken Dryden (1983)

Woody Dumart (1992)
Thomas Dunderdale (1974)
Bill Durnan (1964)
Mervyn A. (Red) Dutton (1958)
Cecil (Babe) Dye (1970)
Phil Esposito (1984)
Tony Esposito (1988)
Arthur F. Farrell (1965)
Bernie Federko (2002)
Viacheslav Fetisov (2001)
Ferdinand (Fern) Flaman (1990)
Frank Foyston (1958)
Frank Frederickson (1958)
Grant Fuhr (2003)
Bill Gadsby (1970)
Bob Gainey (1992)
Chuck Gardiner (1945)
Herb Gardiner (1958)
Jimmy Gardner (1962)
Mike Gartner (2001)
Bernie (Boom Boom) Geoffrion
    (1972)
Eddie Gerard (1945)
Ed Giacomin (1987)
Rod Gilbert (1982)
Clark Gilles (2002)
Hamilton (Billy) Gilmour (1962)
Frank (Moose) Goheen (1952)
Ebenezer R. (Ebbie)
    Goodfellow (1963)
Michel Goulet (1998)
Mike Grant (1950)
Wilfred (Shorty) Green (1962)
Wayne Gretzky (1999)
Si Griffis (1950)
George Hainsworth (1961)
Glenn Hall (1975)
Joe Hall (1961)
Doug Harvey (1973)
Dale Hawerchuk (2001)
George Hay (1958)
William (Riley) Hern (1962)
Bryan Hextall (1969)
Harry (Hap) Holmes (1972)
Tom Hooper (1962)
George (Red) Horner (1965)
Miles (Tim) Horton (1977)
Gordie Howe (1972)
Syd Howe (1965)
Harry Howell (1979)
Bobby Hull (1983)
John (Bouse) Hutton (1962)
Harry M. Hyland (1962)
James (Dick) Irvin (1958)
Harvey (Busher) Jackson
    (1971)
Ernest (Moose) Johnson (1952)

Ivan (Ching) Johnson (1958)
Tom Johnson (1970)
Aurel Joliat (1947)
Gordon (Duke) Keats (1958)
Leonard (Red) Kelly (1969)
Ted (Teeder) Kennedy (1966)
Dave Keon (1986)
Jari Kurri (2001)
Elmer Lach (1966)
Guy Lafleur (1988)
Pat LaFonaine (2003)
Edouard (Newsy) Lalonde (1950)
Rod Langway (2002)
Jacques Laperriere (1987)
Guy LaPointe (1993)
Edgar Laprade (1993)
Reed Larson (1996)
Jean (Jack) Laviolette (1962)
Hugh Lehman (1958)
Jacques Lemaire (1984)
Mario Lemieux (1997)
Percy LeSueur (1961)
Herbert A. Lewis (1989)
Ted Lindsay (1966)
Harry Lumley (1980)
Lanny McDonald (1992)
Frank McGee (1945)
Billy McGimsie (1962)
George McNamara (1958)
Duncan (Mickey) MacKay (1952)
Frank Mahovlich (1981)
Joe Malone (1950)
Sylvio Mantha (1960)
Jack Marshall (1965)
Fred G. (Steamer) Maxwell
    (1962)
Stan Mikita (1983)
Dicky Moore (1974)
Patrick (Paddy) Moran (1958)
Howie Morenz (1945)
Billy Mosienko (1965)
Joe Mullen (2000)
Frank Nighbor (1947)
Reg Noble (1962)
Herbert (Buddy) O'Connor (1988)
Harry Oliver (1967)
Bert Olmstead (1985)
Bobby Orr (1979)
Bernie Parent (1984)
Brad Park (1988)
Lester Patrick (1947)
Lynn Patrick (1980)
Gilbert Perreault (1990)
Tommy Phillips (1945)
Pierre Pilote (1975)
Didier (Pit) Pitre (1962)
Jacques Plante (1978)

Players *(Cont.)*

Denis Potvin (1991)
Walter (Babe) Pratt (1966)
Joe Primeau (1963)
Marcel Pronovost (1978)
Bob Pulford (1991)
Harvey Pulford (1945)
Hubert (Bill) Quackenbush (1976)
Frank Rankin (1961)
Jean Ratelle (1985)
Claude (Chuck) Rayner (1973)
Kenneth Reardon (1966)
Henri Richard (1979)
Maurice (Rocket) Richard (1961)
George Richardson (1950)
Gordon Roberts (1971)
Larry Robinson (1995)
Art Ross (1945)
Blair Russel (1965)
Ernest Russell (1965)
Jack Ruttan (1962)
Borje Salming (1996)
Denis Savard (2000)
Serge Savard (1986)
Terry Sawchuk (1971)
Fred Scanlan (1965)
Milt Schmidt (1961)
Dave (Sweeney) Schriner (1962)
Earl Seibert (1963)
Oliver Seibert (1961)
Eddie Shore (1947)
Steve Shutt (1993)
Albert C. (Babe) Siebert (1964)
Harold (Bullet Joe) Simpson (1962)
Daryl Sittler (1989)
Alfred E. Smith (1962)
Billy Smith (1993)
Clint Smith (1991)
Reginald (Hooley) Smith (1972)
Thomas Smith (1973)
Allan Stanley (1981)
Russell (Barney) Stanley (1962)
Peter Stastny (1998)
John (Black Jack) Stewart (1964)
Nels Stewart (1962)
Bruce Stuart (1961)
Hod Stuart (1945)
Frederic (Cyclone) (O.B.E.)
  Taylor (1947)
Cecil R. (Tiny) Thompson
  (1959)
Vladislav Tretiak (1989)
Harry J. Trihey (1950)
Bryan Trottier (1997)
Norm Ullman (1982)
Georges Vezina (1945)
Jack Walker (1960)
Marty Walsh (1962)
Harry Watson (1994)
Harry E. Watson (1962)
Ralph (Cooney) Weiland (1971)

Players *(Cont.)*

Harry Westwick (1962)
Fred Whitcroft (1962)
Gordon (Phat) Wilson (1962)
Lorne (Gump) Worsley (1980)
Roy Worters (1969)

Builders

Charles Adams (1960)
Weston W. Adams (1972)
Thomas (Frank) Ahearn (1962)
John (Bunny) Ahearne (1977)
Montagu Allan (C.V.O.) (1945)
Keith Allen (1992)
Al Arbour (1996)
Harold Ballard (1977)
David Bauer (1989)
John Bickell (1978)
Scott Bowman (1991)
George V. Brown (1961)
Walter A. Brown (1962)
Frank Buckland (1975)
Walter L. Bush (2000)
Jack Butterfield (1980)
Frank Calder (1947)
Angus D. Campbell (1964)
Clarence Campbell (1966)
Joe Cattarinich (1977)
Bob Cole (1996)
Joseph (Leo) Dandurand (1963)
Francis Dilio (1964)
George S. Dudley (1958)
James A. Dunn (1968)
Robert Alan Eagleson (1989–98*)
Sergio Gambucci (1996)
Emile Francis (1982)
Jack Gibson (1976)
Tommy Gorman (1963)
Frank Griffiths (1993)
William Hanley (1986)
Charles Hay (1974)
James C. Hendy (1968)
Foster Hewitt (1965)
William Hewitt (1947)
Fred J. Hume (1962)
Mike Ilitch (2003)
George (Punch) Imlach (1984)
Tommy Ivan (1974)
William M. Jennings (1975)
Bob Johnson (1992)
Gordon W. Juckes (1979)
John Kilpatrick (1960)
Brian Kilrea (2003)
Seymour Knox III (1993)
George Leader (1969)
Robert LeBel (1970)
Thomas F. Lockhart (1965)
Paul Loicq (1961)
Frederic McLaughlin (1963)
John Mariucci (1985)

Builders *(Cont.)*

Frank Mathers (1992)
John (Jake) Milford (1984)
Hartland Molson (1973)
Scotty Morrison (1999)
Mngr. Athol (Pere) Murray (1998)
Roger Neilson (2002)
Francis Nelson (1947)
Bruce A. Norris (1969)
James Norris, Sr. (1958)
James D. Norris (1962)
William M. Northey (1947)
John O'Brien (1962)
Brian O'Neill (1994)
Fred Page (1993)
Craig Patrick (1996)
Frank Patrick (1958)
Allan W. Pickard (1958)
Rudy Pilous (1985)
Norman (Bud) Poile (1990)
Samuel Pollock (1978)
Donat Raymond (1958)
John Robertson (1947)
Claude C. Robinson (1947)
Philip D. Ross (1976)
Gunther Sabetzki (1995)
Glen Sather (1997)
Frank J. Selke (1960)
Harry Sinden (1983)
Frank D. Smith (1962)
Conn Smythe (1958)
Edward M. Snider (1988)
Lord Stanley of Preston
  (G.C.B.) (1945)
James T. Sutherland (1947)
Anatoli V. Tarasov (1974)
Bill Torrey (1995)
Lloyd Turner (1958)
William Tutt (1978)
Carl Potter Voss (1974)

Referees/Linesmen

Fred C. Waghorn (1961)
Arthur Wirtz (1971)
Bill Wirtz (1976)
John A. Ziegler, Jr. (1987)
Neil Armstrong (1991)
John Ashley (1981)
William L. Chadwick (1964)
John D'Amico (1993)
Chaucer Elliott (1961)
George Hayes (1988)
Robert W. Hewitson (1963)
Fred J. (Mickey) Ion (1961)
Matt Pavelich (1987)
Mike Rodden (1962)
J. Cooper Smeaton (1961)
Roy (Red) Storey (1967)
Frank Udvari (1973)
Andy van Hellemond (1999)

Note: Year of election to the Hall of Fame is in parentheses after the member's name.
*Eagleson resigned from Hall March 25, 1998.

Tennis

AP PHOTO/BILL KOSTROUN

**U.S. Open champion
Andy Roddick**

Youth Movement

Led by 21-year-old U.S. Open champ Andy Roddick, young players gave the men's tour a much-needed boost

BY B.J. SCHECTER

Ever since he burst onto the pro tour as a brash 18-year-old in 2000, Andy Roddick has had expectations and hype draped around his neck like a lead weight. As women's tennis has boosted its profile in recent years, thanks to Serena and Venus Williams, who dominate on and off the court, the men's game has taken a back seat, sorely needing a superstar. Roddick was supposed to be that superstar, but he needed time to develop and grow up.

Sure, Roddick showed flashes of brilliance at times, but despite his obvious talent and power, he was still just a kid. His immaturity occasionally showed in the form oncourt meltdowns. And without a Grand Slam title to his name, Roddick caused some fans to wonder whether he would ever blossom.

But he was smarter and more mentally tough than his critics gave him credit for. He refused to get discouraged, and before Wimbledon he hired Brad Gilbert to be his coach. The change was immediately notice-able, as Gilbert did for Roddick what he had done for Andre Agassi several years before—touched up the rough edges and molded a good player into a great one.

Soon after hiring Gilbert, Roddick made it to the semifinals at Wimbledon. Still, even though he had won 100 matches faster than Sampras and Agassi had, Roddick needed to win a Grand Slam to shed the label of great American tennis hope. And what better place to do it than at the U.S. Open.

In a rain-filled Open, Roddick made it to the semifinals with relative ease, but it looked like his run might end there. He had lost the first two sets to Argentina's David Nalbandian and faced a match point in the third set tiebreaker. Roddick reached back for everything he had and hit a 138-mph ace to win the point. He ended up winning the set. Nalbandian appeared deflated and, seizing the opportunity, Roddick closed out the match less than an hour later.

He was even more brilliant in the final,

BOB MARTIN

where he made a resounding statement that this stage was his, soundly beat ing the world's No. 1 player, Juan Carlos Ferrero of Spain, 6–3, 7–6, 6–3. It seemed that America's great hope had arrived. After winning the match, Roddick collapsed to his knees, put his hands over his face and started to cry. Seeking his coach and family members in the stands, Roddick's registerd disbelief.

But he quickly got used to the idea of himself as a Grand Slam champion. He was playful in the postmatch press conference, grabbing the microphone before anyone could ask any questions and saying, "No more, 'What's it feel like to be the future of American tennis?' crap!" But several hours after it was over, disbelief seem to set back in. "Did I really win this thing?" Roddick asked. "Was the scoreboard really right?" he said, returning to the court and sitting in a line judge's chair.

Roddick had won first slam in his 219th match as a professional, far sooner than Agassi, who didn't make it to his first Grand Slam final until his 225th match, and didn't win one until his 348th. More importantly, Roddick showed he was a complete player and possessed much more than a big serve. Gilbert taught Roddick patience, helped him improve his backhand immeasurably and helped Roddick understand that the only expectations that really mattered were his own. "The more you play, the more you learn," Roddick said. "You don't have all the answers when you come out here at 18."

In recent seasons the women of tennis didn't seem to have an answer for Serena and Venus Williams, who had won every U.S. Open since 1999 and were finalists in five of the previous six majors. But with Serena (knee surgery) and Venus (abdominal strain) both forced to withdraw from the 2003 tournament that streak would end. Jennifer Capriati joked that the Open winner would have an asterisk next two her name, and the 27-year-old American seemed like a perfect candidate to win it.

In the semifinals, however, she ran into Belgium's Justine Henin-Hardenne, who rallied from a 6–4, 5–3 deficit in what would turn out to be the match of the year. Henin-Hardenne took the second set 7–5, and trailed 5–2 in the third before winning 7–6. After the 183-minute match, Henin-Hardenne doubled over in pain and couldn't carry her racquets to the locker room. She received I.V. treatments afterward and didn't return to her hotel room until 3 a.m.

In the final Henin-Hardenne faced her countrywoman, Kim Clijsters, who despite never winning a Grand Slam had taken over the No. 1 ranking from Serena Williams. Despite being barely able to walk less than 24 hours earlier, Henin-Hardenne dominated Clijsters in exactly the same fashion as she had in the French Open final in June. When the last ball was struck at Arthur Ashe stadium, Henin-Hardenne had secured her second Slam of the year with a 7–5, 6–2 victory.

Henin-Hardenne reached that final at Roland Garros by defeating Serena Williams, who endured a frustrating French Open. The younger of the two Williams stars was booed during the semis for challenging a few calls, and she came to Wimbledon on a mission to prove that she was still the best player in the world. Venus, who was criticized for not putting enough time into her tennis, was also eager to show that her game hadn't slipped. The sisters were on another crash course to meet in the final until Venus aggravated an abdominal injury in the semifinals against Clijsters. Venus was overcome with pain, and Serena urged her to withdraw, telling her she had nothing to prove. But Venus persevered and won the match, setting up another all-Williams final.

At first, Venus balked at playing in the final; then when she announced that she would compete, conspiracy theorists came out in full, doubting the legitimacy of the competiton between the sisters. When Serena, down 4–5 and facing a double break point in the first set, tried a weak drop-shot they pointed to it as Exhibit A. But Serena wasn't going to give the Wimbledon plate to her older sister because Venus was injured. She showed fire in the second and third sets, tried to ignore her sister's pain and won her fifth Grand Slam over Venus in the last two years. "I was telling myself, This is Wimbledon," Serena said. "God knows if I would get this opportunity again. If anything, I fought harder."

Though the men's draw at Wimbledon was devoid of such drama, a new star was born. After top-seed and defending champion Lleyton Hewitt lost in the first round and Agassi went down in the fourth, the door was open for Roddick to win his first Slam or for Tim Henman to become the first British male to win the tournament since 1936. Henman lost to Sebastien Grosjean in the quarterfinals and Roddick was was swept 7-6, 6–3, 6–3 by Switzerland's Roger Federer.

Federer's serve and volleying and return of serve were flawless. After the defeat a frustrated Roddick said, "Maybe I can play like that sometime." Federer cruised past Mark Philippoussis in the final. He, along with Roddick and the 23-year-old gave the men's game a much-need infusion of youth. Add Nalbandian, Guillermo Coria and Hewitt, who are all in their 20s, and the men appear to have solid young players who will create rivalries for years to come. "It's certainly shaping up to be a pretty good group, huh?" said Roddick after the U.S. Open. "We're all pretty close."

Lately, Agassi has been pretty close to a sure thing at the Australian Open. He won titles Down Under in 2000 and 2001 then missed the 2002 tournament with a wrist injury. In 2003, the 32-year-old Agassi increased his winning streak at the Australian to 21 straight matches with an impressive 6–2, 6–2, 6–1 victory over Germany's Rainer Schuettler in the final. "I feel like I'm half Australian," Agassi joked afterward.

On the women's side, it was an All-Williams final for the fourth consecutive Grand Slam. And once again Serena prevailed, winning her fourth consecutive major, a feat quickly dubbed the Serena Slam. In women's doubles, Venus and Serena won again, dominating Paola Suarez and Virginia Ruano to win the title. At the trophy presentation Suarez, in yet another testament to the Williams sisters' dominance of the sport, said, "Next year I hope Venus and Serena don't play, so we can win the tournament."

The sentiment has existed on the women's tour for several years now. When healthy, the Williams sisters are by far the best two players in the game. But in the men's game there was an important changing of the guard. Roddick finally inherited the torch as the star of American men's tennis, and with a formidable group of twentysomethings to battle him in every Slam, there was new hope for the men's game.

2003 Grand Slam Champions

Australian Open
Men's Singles

	Winner	Runner-up	Score
Quarterfinals	Andy Roddick	Jounes El Aynaoui	4–6, 7–6 (7-5), 4–6, 6–4, 21–19
	Rainer Schuettler	David Nalbandian	6–3, 5–7, 6–1, 6–0
	Wayne Ferreira	Juan Carlos Ferrero	7–6 (7-4), 7–6 (7-5), 6–1
	Andre Agassi	Sebastien Grosjean	6–3, 6–2, 6–2,
Semifinals	Rainer Schuettler	Andy Roddick	7–5, 2–6, 6–3, 6–3
	Andre Agassi	Wayne Ferreira	6–2, 6–2, 6–3
Final	Andre Agassi	Rainer Schuettler	6–2, 6–2, 6–1

Women's Singles

	Winner	Runner-up	Score
Quarterfinals	Justine Henin-Hardenne	Virginia Ruano Pasqual	6–2, 6–2
	Venus Williams	Daniela Hantuchova	6–4, 6–3
	Serena Williams	Meghann Shaughnessy	6–2, 6–2
	Kim Clijsters	Anastasia Myskina	6–2, 6–4
Semifinals	Serena Williams	Kim Clijsters	4–6, 6–3, 7–5
	Venus Williams	Justine Henin-Hardenne	6–3, 6–3
Final	Serena Williams	Venus Williams	7–6 (7-4), 3–6, 6–4

Doubles

	Winner	Runner-up	Score
Men's Final	Michael Llodra/ Fabrice Santoro	Mark Knowles/ Daniel Nestor	6–4, 3–6, 6–3
Women's Final	Serena Williams/ Venus Williams	Virginia Ruano Pasqual/ Paola Suarez	4–6, 6–4, 6–3
Mixed Final	Leander Paes/ Martina Navratilova	Todd Woodbridge/ Eleni Daniilidou	6–4, 7–5

French Open
Men's Singles

	Winner	Runner-up	Score
Quarterfinals	Albert Costa	Tommy Robredo	2–6, 3–6, 6–4, 7–5, 6–2
	Juan Carlos Ferrero	F. Gonzalez	6–1, 3–6, 6–1, 5–7, 6–4
	Martin Verkerk	Carlos Moya	6–3, 6–4, 5–7, 4–6, 8–6
	Guillermo Coria	Andre Agassi	4–6, 6–3, 6–2, 6–4
Semifinals	Juan Carlos Ferrero	Albert Costa	6–3, 7–6 (7-5), ret.
	Martin Verkerk	Guillermo Coria	7–6 (7-4), 6–4, 7–6 (7-0
Final	Juan Carlos Ferrero	Martin Verkerk	6–1, 6–3, 6–2

Women's Singles

	Winner	Runner-up	Score
Quarterfinals	Serena Williams	Amelie Mauresmo	6–1, 6–2
	Justine Henin-Hardenne	Chandra Rubin	6–3, 6–2
	N. Petrova	V. Zvonareva	6–1, 4–6, 6–3
	Kim Clijsters	C. Martinez	6–2, 6–1
Semifinals	Justine Henin-Hardenne	Serena Williams	6–2, 4–6, 7–5
	Kim Clijsters	N. Petrova	7–5, 6–1
Final	Justine Henin-Hardenne	Kim Clijsters	6–0, 6–4

French Open *(Cont.)*

Doubles

	Winner	Runner-Up	Score
Men's Final	Bob Bryan/ Mike Bryan	Paul Haarhuis/ Yevgeny Kafelnikov	7–6 (7-3), 6–3
Women's Final	Kim Clijsters/ Ai Sugiyama	Virginia Ruano Pasqual/ Paola Suarez	6–7 (5-7), 6–2, 9–7
Mixed Final	Lisa Raymond/ Mike Bryan	Elena Likhovtseva/ Mahesh Bhupathi	6–3, 6–4

Wimbledon

Men's Singles

	Winner	Runner-Up	Score
Quarterfinals	Sebastien Grosjean	Tim Henman	7–6 (10-8), 3–6, 6–3, 6–4
	Andy Roddick	Jonas Bjorkman	6–4, 6–2, 6–4,
	Mark Philippoussis	Alexander Popp	4–6, 4–6, 6–3, 6–3, 8–6
	Roger Federer	Sjeng Schalken	6–3, 6–4, 6–4
Semifinals	Roger Federer	Andy Roddick	7–6 (8-6), 6–3, 6–3
	Mark Philippoussis	Sebastien Grosjean	7–6 (7-3), 6–3, 6–3
Final	Roger Federer	Mark Philippoussis	7–6 (7-5), 6–2, 7–6 (7-3)

Women's Singles

	Winner	Runner-Up	Score
Quarterfinals	Serena Williams	Jennifer Capriati	2–6, 6–2, 6–3
	Justine Henin-Hardenne	Svetlana Kuznetsova	6–2, 6–2
	Venus Williams	Lindsay Davenport	6–2, 2–6, 6–1
	Kim Clijsters	Silvia Farina Elia	5–7, 6–0
Semifinals	Serena Williams	Justine Henin-Hardenne	6–3, 6–2
	Venus Williams	Kim Clijsters	4–6, 6–3, 6–1
Final	Serena Williams	Venus Williams	4–6, 6–4, 6–2

Doubles

	Winner	Runner-Up	Score
Men's Final	Jonas Bjorkman/ Todd Woodbridge	Mahesh Bhupathi/ Max Mirnyi	3–6, 6–3, 7–6 (7-4), 6–3
Women's Final	Kim Clijsters/ Ai Sugiyama	Virginia Ruano Pascual/ Paola Suarez	6–4, 6–4
Mixed Final	Laender Paes/ Martina Navratilova	Andy Ram/ Anastassia Rodionova	6–3, 6–3

U.S. Open

Men's Singles

	Winner	Runner-Up	Score
Quarterfinals	Andre Agassi	Guillermo Coria	6–4, 6–3, 7–5
	Andy Roddick	Sjeng Schalken	6–4, 6–2, 6–3
	Juan Carlos Ferrero	Lleyton Hewitt	4–6, 6–3, 7–6 (7-5), 6–1
	David Nalbandian	Younes El Aynaoui	7–6 (7-2), 6–2, 3–6, 7–5
Semifinals	Juan Carlos Ferrero	Andre Agassi	6–4, 6–3, 3–6, 6–4
	Andy Roddick	David Nalbandian	6–7 (4-7), 3–6, 7–6 (9-7), 6–1, 6–3
Final	Andy Roddick	Juan Carlos Ferrero	6–3, 7–6 (7-2), 6–3

U.S. Open *(Cont.)*

Women's Singles

	Winner	Runner-Up	Score
Quarterfinals	Kim Clijsters	Amelie Mauresmo	6–1, 6–4
	Jennifer Capriati	Francesca Schiavone	6–1, 6–3
	Lindsay Davenport	Paola Suarez	6–4, 6–0
	Justine Henin-Hardenne	Anastasia Myskina	6–2, 6–3
Semifinals	Kim Clijsters	Lindsay Davenport	6–2, 6–3
	Justine Henin-Hardenne	Jennifer Capriati	4–6, 7–5, 7–6 (7-4)
Final	Justine Henin-Hardenne	Kim Clijsters	7–5, 6–1

Doubles

	Winner	Runner-Up	Score
Men's Final	Jonas Bjorkman/ Todd Woodbridge	Bob Bryan/ Mike Bryan	5–7, 6–0, 7–5
Women's Final	Virginia Ruano Pascual/ Paola Suarez	Svetlana Kuznetsova/ Martina Navratilova	6–2, 6–3
Mixed Final	Katarina Srebotnik/ Bob Bryan	Lina Krasnoroutskaya/ Daniel Nestor	5–7, 7–5, 7–6 (10-5)

Major Tournament Results

Men's Tour (late 2002)

Date	Tournament	Site	Winner	Runner-Up	Score
Oct 7–13	CA Trophy Tournament	Vienna	Roger Federer	Jiri Novak	6–4, 6–1, 3–6, 6–4
Oct 7–13	Lyon Grand Prix	Lyon, France	Paul-Henri Mathieu	Gustavo Kuerten	4–6, 6–3, 6–1
Oct 21–27	Swiss Indoors	Basel, Switzerland	David Nalbandian	Fernando Gonzalez	6–4, 6–3, 6–2
Oct 21–27	St. Petersburg Open	St. Petersburg, Russia	Sebastien Grosjean	Mikhail Youzhny	7–5, 6–4
Oct 21–27	Stockholm Open	Stockholm	Paradorn Srichaphan	Marcelo Rios	6–7 (2), 6–0, 6–3, 6–2
Oct 28–Nov 3	Paris Masters	Paris	Marat Safin	Lleyton Hewitt	7–6 (7-4), 6–0, 6–4
Nov 11–17	Tennis Masters Cup	Shanghai	Lleyton Hewitt	Juan Carlos Ferrero	7–5, 7–5, 2–6, 2–6, 6–4

Men's Tour (Through September 7, 2003)

Date	Tournament	Site	Winner	Runner-Up	Score
Dec 30–Jan 5	Qatar Open	Doha, Qatar	Stafen Koubek	Jan-Michael Gambill	6–4, 6–4
Jan 12–26	Australian Open	Melbourne	Andre Agassi	Rainer Schuettler	6–2, 6–2, 6–1
Feb 10–16	Marseille Open	Marseille, France	Roger Federer	Jonas Bjorkman	6–2, 7–6 (8-6)
Feb 17–23	ABN/Amro Tournament	Rotterdam, Amsterdam	Max Mirnyi	Raemon Sluiter	7–6 (7-3), 6–4
Feb 17–23	Kroger St. Jude	Memphis	Taylor Dent	Andy Roddick	6–1, 6–4
Feb 24–Mar 2	Dubai Open	Dubai, UAE	Roger Federer	Jiri Novak	6–1, 7–6 (7-2)
Mar 10–16	Pacific Life Open	Indian Wells, California	Lleyton Hewitt	Gustavo Kuerten	6–1, 6–1
Mar 19–31	NASDAQ 100 Open	Miami	Andre Agassi	Carlos Moya	6–3, 6–3
Apr 8–13	Estoril Open	Estoril, Portugal	Nikolay Davydenko	Agustin Calleri	6–4, 6–3
Apr 14–20	Monte Carlo Masters	Monte Carlo	Juan Carlos Ferrero	Guillermo Coria	6–2, 6–2
Apr 28–May 4	BMW Open	Munich	Roger Federer	Jarkko Nieminen	6–1, 6–4
May 5–11	Italian Masters	Rome	Felix Mantilla	Roger Federer	7–5, 6–2, 7–6 (10-8)
May 12–18	Hamburg Masters	Hamburg	Guillermo Coria	Agustin Calleri	6–3, 6–4, 6–4

Men's Tour (Through September 7, 2003) *(Cont.)*

Date	Tournament	Site	Winner	Runner-Up	Score
May 26– Jun 8	French Open	Paris	Juan Carlos Ferrero	Martin Verkerk	6–1, 6–3, 6–2
June 9–15	Gerry Weber Open	Halle, Germany	Roger Federer	Nicholas Kiefer	6–1, 6–3
June 16–22	Ordina Open	'S-Hertog'bosch Netherlands	Sjeng Schalken	Arnaud Clement	6–3, 6–4
Jun 23–Jul 6	Wimbledon	Wimbledon	Roger Federer	Mark Philippoussis	7–6 (7-5), 6–2, 7–6 (7-3)
July 7–13	Swiss Open	Gstaad, Switzerland	Jiri Novak	Roger Federer	5–7, 6–3, 6–3, 1–6, 6–3
July 14–20	Mercedes Cup	Stuttgart, Germany	Guillermo Coria	Tommy Robredo	6–2, 6–2, 6–1
July 21–27	Generali Open	Kitzbuhel, Austria	Guillermo Coria	Nicolas Massu	6–1, 6–4, 6–2
July 21–27	RCA Championships	Indianapolis	Andy Roddick	P. Srichaphan	7–6 (7-2), 6–4
Aug 4–10	Tennis Masters Series	Montreal	Andy Roddick	David Nalbandian	6–1, 6–3
Jul 28-Aug.3	Legg Mason Classic	Wash., D.C.	Tim Henman	F. Gonzalez	6–3, 6–4
Aug 25– Sept 7	U.S. Open	New York City	Andy Roddick	Juan Carlo Ferrero	6–3, 7–6 (7-2), 6–3

Women's Tour (Late 2002)

Date	Tournament	Site	Winner	Runner-Up	Score
Sept 23–29	Sparkassen Cup	Leipzig, Germany	Serena Williams	Anastasia Myskina	6–3, 6–2
Sep 30–Oct 6	Ladies Kremlin Cup	Moscow	M. Maleeva	L. Davenport	5–7, 6–3, 7–6 (4)
Sep 30–Oct 6	Japan Open	Tokyo	Jill Craybas	Silvja Talaja	2–6, 6–4, 6–4
Oct 14–20	Swisscom Challenge	Zurich	Patty Schnyder	L. Davenport	6–7 (5), 7–6 (8), 6–3
Oct 21–27	Generali Ladies Open	Linz, Aust.	Justine Henin	Alexandra Stevenson	6–3, 6–0
Nov 4–10	Sanex Championships	Los Angeles	Kim Clijsters	Serena Williams	7–5, 6–3

Women's Tour (Through September 7, 2003)

Date	Tournament	Site	Winner	Runner-Up	Score
Jan 5–11	Adidas International	Sydney	Kim Clijsters	L. Davenport	6–4, 6–3
Jan 12–25	Australian Open	Melbourne	Serena Williams	Venus Williams	7–6 (7-4), 3–6, 6–4
Jan 26–Feb 2	Pan Pacific Open	Tokyo	L. Davenport	Monica Seles	6–7 (6-8), 6–1, 6–2
Feb 3–9	Open Gaz de France	Paris	Serena Williams	Amelie Mauresmo	6–3, 6–2
Feb 10–16	Qatar Open	Doha, Qatar	Anastasia Myskina	Elena Likhovtseva	6–3, 6–1
Mar 6–16	Pacific Life Open	Indian Wells, California	Kim Clijsters	Lindsay Davenport	6–4, 7–5
Mar 19–29	NASDAQ-100 Open	Miami	Serena Williams	Jennifer Capriati	4–6, 6–4, 6–1
Apr 7–13	Family Circle Cup	Charleston, S Carolina	Justine Henin-Hardenne	Serena Williams	6–3, 6–4
Apr 14–20	Bausch & Lomb Championships	Amelia Island, Florida	Elena Dementieva	Lindsay Davenport	4–6, 7–5, 6–3
Apr 28–May 4	J&s Cup	Warsaw	Amelie Mauresmo	Venus Williams	6–7 (6-8), 6–0, 3–0, ret.
May 5–11	German Open	Berlin	Justine Henin-Hardenne	Kim Clijsters	6–4, 4–6, 7–5
May 12–18	Italia Masters	Rome	Kim Clijsters	Amelie Mauresmo	3–6, 7–6 (7-3), 6–0
May 19–24	Int'l de Strasbourg	Strasbourg, France	Silvia Farina Elia	Karolina Sprem	6–3, 4–6, 6–4
May 26–Jun 7	French Open	Paris	Justine Henin-Hardenne	Kim Clijsters	6–0, 6–4
June 17–23	Hastings Direct Int'l Championships	Eastbourne, England	Chanda Rubin	Conchita Martinez	6–4, 3–6, 6–4
Jun 23–July 6	Wimbledon	Wimbledon	Serena Williams	Venus Williams	4–6, 6–4, 6–2
July 21–27	Bank of the West	Stanford	Kim Clijster	Jennifer Capriati	4–6, 6–4, 6–2
July 28–Aug 3	Acura Classic	San Diego	J. H.-Hardenne	Kim Clijsters	3–6, 6–2, 6–3
Aug 4–10	JP Morgan Chase Open	Los Angeles	Kim Clijsters	L. Davenport	6–1, 3–6, 6–1
Aug 11–17	AT&T Canada Cup	Toronto	Justine Henin-Hardenne	Lina Krasnoroutskaya	6–1, 6–0
Aug 17–23	Pilot Pen Int'l	New Haven,CT	Jennifer Capriati	L. Davenport	6–2, 4–0, ret.
Aug 26–Sep7	U.S. Open	New York City	Justine Henin-Hardenne	Kim Clijsters	7–5, 6–1

2002 Singles Leaders

Men

Rank	Player	Tournament Wins	Match Record	Earnings ($)
1.	Lleyton Hewitt	5	61–15	4,619,386
2.	Andre Agassi	5	53–12	2,186,006
3.	Marat Safin	1	56–26	1,719,408
4.	Juan Carlos Ferrero	2	48–25	2,761,498
5.	Carlos Moya	4	59–21	1,772,314
6.	Roger Federer	3	58–22	1,995,027
7.	Jiri Novak	0	53–26	1,454,130
8.	Tim Henman	1	50–19	1,194,899
9.	Albert Costa	1	35–22	1,434,439
10.	Andy Roddick	2	56–22	1,060,878

Note: Compiled by the ATP Tour, through 2002 season.
Note: Prize money reflects both singles and doubles.

Women

Rank	Player	Ranking Points	Earnings ($)
1.	Serena Williams	6080.00	3,935,668
2.	Venus Williams	5140.00	2,583,571
3.	Jennifer Capriati	3796.00	2,217,935
4.	Kim Clijsters	3557.00	1,754,376
5.	J. Henin-Hardenne	3218.00	1,213,093
6.	Amelie Mauresmo	3068.00	1,073,807
7.	Monica Seles	2952.00	1,096,630
8.	D. Hantuchova	2667.75	1,188,379
9.	Jelena Dokic	2506.00	918,633
10.	Martina Hingis	2348.00	1,467,584

Note: Compiled by the WTA, as of Dec 16, 2002.
Note: Prize money reflects singles play only.

New Kid on the Block

They keep coming, a new one every month it seems, all of them young and stinging the ball and filling the sport with surprise. They're always sweet to see, so refreshing: After Maria Sharapova, two months past her 16th birthday, served her final ace to polish off 11th-seeded Jelena Dokic in straight sets in late June 2003, she dropped her racket onto the grass of Wimbledon's Court 1 in disbelief, her golden hair swaying in the sunlight. She clasped her hands as if in prayer and raised them to the sky.

Few pros are as demonstrative: Sharapova barks at herself after each point, clenches her fist on each stroll to the service line, squeals with each shot. Fewer still show such happiness. How long will it last? As Sharapova blew kisses, Dokic hoisted her bag and hurried away.

Remember Dokic? Four years ago she was that same blonde girl, two months past her 16th birthday, when she rocked Wimbledon by upsetting world No. 1 Martina Hingis in the first round. Two other girls burst through then too—18-year-old Alexandra Stevenson and 17-year-old Mirjana Lucic, both of whom advanced to the semifinals. In 2003, Stevenson lost in the first round, as she has at almost every Grand Slam event since the summer of 1999. Lucic isn't even in the WTA media guide anymore.

Dokic sits through her press conferences now and speaks in a voice full of weariness, unimpressed by the questions. Her father is no longer a part of her tennis life. "We'll see," Dokic says when asked about Sharapova. "We've seen a lot of players come and go."

Despite occasional setbacks, Sharapova is one of tennis's hottest properties. She was born in Siberia, but at two her family moved to Sochi to flee radioactive fallout from the Chernobyl disaster. When she was six, her father, Uri, had her playing a tournament in Moscow, where Martina Navratilova recommended Nick Bollettieri's Academy in Florida. Two years later Maria and her father arrived in Miami, then journeyed to Bollettieri's uninvited. A coach took her on court; Sharapova knocked his hat off with her first stroke. "Then I hit a few [more] balls, and he called Nick right away," Sharapova says.

She now works with Robert Lansdorp, legendary coach of Tracy Austin, Lindsay Davenport and Pete Sampras. . . .

Sharapova had never advanced past the first round of a Grand Slam event until Wimbledon 2003, but she carries herself with unusual maturity. She laughs off the photographers, says she finds modeling boring, doesn't fight the damning Anna Kournikova comparison. "Right now it might be my looks or my grunts [attracting the attention], but in a few years, if I become a great player, it's not going to be about my looks or my grunts," she says. "It's going to be about how I became a champion."

Sharapova dispatched Ashley Harkleroad, 21st-seeded Elena Bovina and Dokic before falling to Kuznetsova. "I'm expecting to win," Sharapova said. "I can't go to a tournament thinking, Yeah, I'm going to get my ass kicked today, so I might as well just leave. I mean, I'm very happy and I'm very surprised. Yes, I'm very young; I'm 16, and I'm in the fourth round at Wimbledon? How odd is that?"

Not so odd anymore. The 2003 Wimbledon was full of girls who had flashed and faded. While Sharapova charmed reporters with her laugh and walked past the people pointing at her on the grounds at Wimbledon, Dokic huddled with her boyfriend in the players' restaurant and ate undisturbed. Hingis sat at a table in the sun, retired at 22 and grinning as well-wishers stopped by. She had won Wimbledon at 16, but no, Hingis said, she didn't miss the tour. "I got out at the right time," Hingis said, happier even than the girl who just got in.

—S.L. Price

National Team Competition

2002 Davis Cup World Group Final

Russia def. France 3–2, Nov. 29–Dec. 1, 2001 in Paris
    Marat Safin (Rus) def. Paul-Henri Mathieu (Fra) 6–4, 3–6, 6–1, 6–4
    Sebastien Grosjean (Fra) def. Yevgeny Kafelnikov (Rus) 7–6 (3), 6–3, 6–0
    Escude and Santoro (Fra) def. Kafelnikov and Safin (Rus) 6–3, 3–6, 5–7, 6–3, 6–4
    Marat Safin (Rus) def. Sebastien Grosjean (Fra) 6–3, 6–2, 7–6 (11-9)
    Mikhail Youzhny (Rus) def. Paul-Henri Mathieu (Fra) 3–6, 2–6, 6–3, 7–5, 6–4

2003 Davis Cup World Group Tournament

FIRST ROUND

Croatia def. United States 4–1
France def. Romania 4–1
Australia def. Great Britain 4–1
Argentina def. Germany 5–0
Switzerland def. Netherlands 3–2
Sweden def. Brazil 3–2
Czech Republic def. Russia 3–2
Spain def. Belgium 5–0

QUARTERFINAL ROUND

Switzerland def. France 3–2
Australia def. Sweden 3–0
Spain def. Croatia 5–0
Argentina def. Russia 5–0

SEMIFINALS

Australia def. Switzerland 3–2
    Lleyton Hewitt (Aus) def. Michel Kratochvil
    (Sui), 6–4, 6–4, 6–1
    Roger Federer (Sui) def. Mark Philippoussis (Aus)
    6–3, 6–4, 7–6 (7-3)
    Arthurs and Woodbridge (Aus) def. Federer and
    Rosset (Aus) 4–6, 7–6 (7-5), 5–7, 6–4, 6–4
    Lleyton Hewitt (Aus) def. Roger Federer (Sui)
    5–7, 2–6, 7–6 (7-4), 7–5, 6–1
    Michel Kratochvil (Sui) def. Todd Woodbridge
    (Aus) 6–4, ret.

Spain def. Argentina, 3–2
    Juan Carlos Ferrero (Esp) def. Gaston Gaudio (Arg),
    6–4, 6–0
    Carlos Moya (Esp) def. Mariano Zabaleta (Arg),
    5–7, 2–6, 6–2, 6–0, 6–1
    Arnold and Calleri (Arg) def. Corretja and Costa (Esp)
    6–3, 1–6, 6–4, 6–2
    Agustin Calleri (Arg) def. Juan Carlos Ferrero (Esp)
    6–4, 7–5, 6–1
    Carlos Moya (Esp) def. Gaston Gaudio (Arg)
    6–1, 6–4, 6–2

FINAL: Australia versus Spain to be held Nov. 28–30.

2003 Federation Cup World Group Tournament

FIRST ROUND

United States def. Czech Rep. 5–0
Italy def. Sweden 3–2
Belgium def. Austria 5–0
Slovak Rep. def. Germany 3–2
Slovenia def. Argentina 3–2
Russia def. Croatia 4–1
Spain def. Australia 3–2
France def. Colombia 5–0

QUARTERFINALS

United States def. Italy 5–0
Belgium def. Slovak Rep. 5–0
Russia def. Slovenia 5–0
France def. Spain 4–1

Note: Semifinals to be held Nov 19–20, in Russia.

Grand Slam Tournaments

MEN

Australian Championships

Year	Winner	Finalist	Score
1905	Rodney Heath	A. H. Curtis	4–6, 6–3, 6–4, 6–4
1906	Tony Wilding	H. A. Parker	6–0, 6–4, 6–4
1907	Horace M. Rice	H. A. Parker	6–3, 6–4, 6–4
1908	Fred Alexander	A. W. Dunlop	3–6, 3–6, 6–0, 6–2, 6–3
1909	Tony Wilding	E. F. Parker	6–1, 7–5, 6–2
1910	Rodney Heath	Horace M. Rice	6–4, 6–3, 6–2
1911	Norman Brookes	Horace M. Rice	6–1, 6–2, 6–3
1912	J. Cecil Parke	A. E. Beamish	3–6, 6–3, 1–6, 6–1, 7–5
1913	E. F. Parker	H. A. Parker	2–6, 6–1, 6–2, 6–3
1914	Pat O'Hara Wood	G. L. Patterson	6–4, 6–3, 5–7, 6–1
1915	Francis G. Lowe	Horace M. Rice	4–6, 6–1, 6–1, 6–4
1916–18	No tournament		
1919	A. R. F. Kingscote	E. O. Pockley	6–4, 6–0, 6–3
1920	Pat O'Hara Wood	Ron Thomas	6–3, 4–6, 6–8, 6–1, 6–3
1921	Rhys H. Gemmell	A. Hedeman	7–5, 6–1, 6–4
1922	Pat O'Hara Wood	Gerald Patterson	6–0, 3–6, 3–6, 6–3, 6–2
1923	Pat O'Hara Wood	C. B. St John	6–1, 6–1, 6–3
1924	James Anderson	R. E. Schlesinger	6–3, 6–4, 3–6, 5–7, 6–3
1925	James Anderson	Gerald Patterson	11–9, 2–6, 6–2, 6–3
1926	John Hawkes	J. Willard	6–1, 6–3, 6–1
1927	Gerald Patterson	John Hawkes	3–6, 6–4, 3–6, 18–16, 6–3
1928	Jean Borotra	R. O. Cummings	6–4, 6–1, 4–6, 5–7, 6–3
1929	John C. Gregory	R. E. Schlesinger	6–2, 6–2, 5–7, 7–5
1930	Gar Moon	Harry C. Hopman	6–3, 6–1, 6–3
1931	Jack Crawford	Harry C. Hopman	6–4, 6–2, 2–6, 6–1
1932	Jack Crawford	Harry C. Hopman	4–6, 6–3, 3–6, 6–3, 6–1
1933	Jack Crawford	Keith Gledhill	2–6, 7–5, 6–3, 6–2
1934	Fred Perry	Jack Crawford	6–3, 7–5, 6–1
1935	Jack Crawford	Fred Perry	2–6, 6–4, 6–4, 6–4
1936	Adrian Quist	Jack Crawford	6–2, 6–3, 4–6, 3–6, 9–7
1937	Vivian B. McGrath	John Bromwich	6–3, 1–6, 6–0, 2–6, 6–1
1938	Don Budge	John Bromwich	6–4, 6–2, 6–1
1939	John Bromwich	Adrian Quist	6–4, 6–1, 6–3
1940	Adrian Quist	Jack Crawford	6–3, 6–1, 6–2
1941–45	No tournament		
1946	John Bromwich	Dinny Pails	5–7, 6–3, 7–5, 3–6, 6–2
1947	Dinny Pails	John Bromwich	4–6, 6–4, 3–6, 7–5, 8–6
1948	Adrian Quist	John Bromwich	6–4, 3–6, 6–3, 2–6, 6–3
1949	Frank Sedgman	Ken McGregor	6–3, 6–3, 6–2
1950	Frank Sedgman	Ken McGregor	6–3, 6–4, 4–6, 6–1
1951	Richard Savitt	Ken McGregor	6–3, 2–6, 6–3, 6–1
1952	Ken McGregor	Frank Sedgman	7–5, 12–10, 2–6, 6–2
1953	Ken Rosewall	Mervyn Rose	6–0, 6–3, 6–4
1954	Mervyn Rose	Rex Hartwig	6–2, 0–6, 6–4, 6–2
1955	Ken Rosewall	Lew Hoad	9–7, 6–4, 6–4
1956	Lew Hoad	Ken Rosewall	6–4, 3–6, 6–4, 7–5
1957	Ashley Cooper	Neale Fraser	6–3, 9–11, 6–4, 6–2
1958	Ashley Cooper	Mal Anderson	7–5, 6–3, 6–4
1959	Alex Olmedo	Neale Fraser	6–1, 6–2, 3–6, 6–3
1960	Rod Laver	Neale Fraser	5–7, 3–6, 6–3, 8–6, 8–6
1961	Roy Emerson	Rod Laver	1–6, 6–3, 7–5, 6–4
1962	Rod Laver	Roy Emerson	8–6, 0–6, 6–4, 6–4
1963	Roy Emerson	Ken Fletcher	6–3, 6–3, 6–1
1964	Roy Emerson	Fred Stolle	6–3, 6–4, 6–2
1965	Roy Emerson	Fred Stolle	7–9, 2–6, 6–4, 7–5, 6–1
1966	Roy Emerson	Arthur Ashe	6–4, 6–8, 6–2, 6–3
1967	Roy Emerson	Arthur Ashe	6–4, 6–1, 6–1
1968	Bill Bowrey	Juan Gisbert	7–5, 2–6, 9–7, 6–4
1969*	Rod Laver	Andres Gimeno	6–3, 6–4, 7–5

*Became Open (amateur and professional) in 1969.

MEN (Cont.)
Australian Championships (Cont.)

Year	Winner	Finalist	Score
1970	Arthur Ashe	Dick Crealy	6–4, 9–7, 6–2
1971	Ken Rosewall	Arthur Ashe	6–1, 7–5, 6–3
1972	Ken Rosewall	Mal Anderson	7–6, 6–3, 7–5
1973	John Newcombe	Onny Parun	6–3, 6–7, 7–5, 6–1
1974	Jimmy Connors	Phil Dent	7–6, 6–4, 4–6, 6–3
1975	John Newcombe	Jimmy Connors	7–5, 3–6, 6–4, 7–5
1976	Mark Edmondson	John Newcombe	6–7, 6–3, 7–6, 6–1
1977 (Jan)	Roscoe Tanner	Guillermo Vilas	6–3, 6–3, 6–3
1977 (Dec)	Vitas Gerulaitis	John Lloyd	6–3, 7–6, 5–7, 3–6, 6–2
1978	Guillermo Vilas	John Marks	6–4, 6–4, 3–6, 6–3
1979	Guillermo Vilas	John Sadri	7–6, 6–3, 6–2
1980	Brian Teacher	Kim Warwick	7–5, 7–6, 6–3
1981	Johan Kriek	Steve Denton	6–2, 7–6, 6–7, 6–4
1982	Johan Kriek	Steve Denton	6–3, 6–3, 6–2
1983	Mats Wilander	Ivan Lendl	6–1, 6–4, 6–4
1984	Mats Wilander	Kevin Curren	6–7, 6–4, 7–6, 6–2
1985 (Dec)	Stefan Edberg	Mats Wilander	6–4, 6–3, 6–3
1987 (Jan)	Stefan Edberg	Pat Cash	6–3, 6–4, 3–6, 5–7, 6–3
1988	Mats Wilander	Pat Cash	6–3, 6–7, 3–6, 6–1, 8–6
1989	Ivan Lendl	Miloslav Mecir	6–2, 6–2, 6–2
1990	Ivan Lendl	Stefan Edberg	4–6, 7–6, 5–2, ret.
1991	Boris Becker	Ivan Lendl	1–6, 6–4, 6–4, 6–4
1992	Jim Courier	Stefan Edberg	6–3, 3–6, 6–4, 6–2
1993	Jim Courier	Stefan Edberg	6–2, 6–1, 2–6, 7–5
1994	Pete Sampras	Todd Martin	7–6, 6–4, 6–4
1995	Andre Agassi	Pete Sampras	4–6, 6–1, 7–6, 6–4
1996	Boris Becker	Michael Chang	6–2, 6–4, 2–6, 6–2
1997	Pete Sampras	Carlos Moya	6–2, 6–3, 6–3
1998	Petr Korda	Marcelo Ríos	6–2, 6–2, 6–2
1999	Yevgeny Kafelnikov	Thomas Enqvist	4–6, 6–0, 6–3, 7–6
2000	Andre Agassi	Yevgeny Kafelnikov	3–6, 6–3, 6–2, 6–4
2001	Andre Agassi	Arnaud Clement	6–4, 6–2, 6–2
2002	Thomas Johansson	Marat Safin	3–6, 6–4, 6–4, 7–6 (7–4)
2003	Andre Agassi	Rainer Schuettler	6–2, 6–2, 6–1

French Championships

Year	Winner	Finalist	Score
1925†	Rene Lacoste	Jean Borotra	7–5, 6–1, 6–4
1926	Henri Cochet	Rene Lacoste	6–2, 6–4, 6–3
1927	Rene Lacoste	Bill Tilden	6–4, 4–6, 5–7, 6–3, 11–9
1928	Henri Cochet	Rene Lacoste	5–7, 6–3, 6–1, 6–3
1929	Rene Lacoste	Jean Borotra	6–3, 2–6, 6–0, 2–6, 8–6
1930	Henri Cochet	Bill Tilden	3–6, 8–6, 6–3, 6–1
1931	Jean Borotra	Claude Boussus	2–6, 6–4, 7–5, 6–4
1932	Henri Cochet	Giorgio de Stefani	6–0, 6–4, 4–6, 6–3
1933	Jack Crawford	Henri Cochet	8–6, 6–1, 6–3
1934	Gottfried von Cramm	Jack Crawford	6–4, 7–9, 3–6, 7–5, 6–3
1935	Fred Perry	Gottfried von Cramm	6–3, 3–6, 6–1, 6–3
1936	Gottfried von Cramm	Fred Perry	6–0, 2–6, 6–2, 2–6, 6–0
1937	Henner Henkel	Henry Austin	6–1, 6–4, 6–3
1938	Don Budge	Roderick Menzel	6–3, 6–2, 6–4
1939	Don McNeill	Bobby Riggs	7–5, 6–0, 6–3
1940	No tournament		
1941‡	Bernard Destremau	n/a	n/a
1942‡	Bernard Destremau	n/a	n/a
1943‡	Yvon Petra	n/a	n/a
1944‡	Yvon Petra	n/a	n/a
1945‡	Yvon Petra	Bernard Destremau	7–5, 6–4, 6–2
1946	Marcel Bernard	Jaroslav Drobny	3–6, 2–6, 6–1, 6–4, 6–3
1947	Joseph Asboth	Eric Sturgess	8–6, 7–5, 6–4
1948	Frank Parker	Jaroslav Drobny	6–4, 7–5, 5–7, 8–6
1949	Frank Parker	Budge Patty	6–3, 1–6, 6–1, 6–4
1950	Budge Patty	Jaroslav Drobny	6–1, 6–2, 3–6, 5–7, 7–5
1951	Jaroslav Drobny	Eric Sturgess	6–3, 6–3, 6–3
1952	Jaroslav Drobny	Frank Sedgman	6–2, 6–0, 3–6, 6–4

MEN *(Cont.)*
French Championships *(Cont.)*

Year	Winner	Finalist	Score
1953	Ken Rosewall	Vic Seixas	6–3, 6–4, 1–6, 6–2
1954	Tony Trabert	Arthur Larsen	6–4, 7–5, 6–1
1955	Tony Trabert	Sven Davidson	2–6, 6–1, 6–4, 6–2
1956	Lew Hoad	Sven Davidson	6–4, 8–6, 6–3
1957	Sven Davidson	Herbie Flam	6–3, 6–4, 6–4
1958	Mervyn Rose	Luis Ayala	6–3, 6–4, 6–4
1959	Nicola Pietrangeli	Ian Vermaak	3–6, 6–3, 6–4, 6–1
1960	Nicola Pietrangeli	Luis Ayala	3–6, 6–3, 6–4, 4–6, 6–3
1961	Manuel Santana	Nicola Pietrangeli	4–6, 6–1, 3–6, 6–0, 6–2
1962	Rod Laver	Roy Emerson	3–6, 2–6, 6–3, 9–7, 6–2
1963	Roy Emerson	Pierre Darmon	3–6, 6–1, 6–4, 6–4
1964	Manuel Santana	Nicola Pietrangeli	6–3, 6–1, 4–6, 7–5
1965	Fred Stolle	Tony Roche	3–6, 6–0, 6–2, 6–3
1966	Tony Roche	Istvan Gulyas	6–1, 6–4, 7–5
1967	Roy Emerson	Tony Roche	6–1, 6–4, 2–6, 6–2
1968*	Ken Rosewall	Rod Laver	6–3, 6–1, 2–6, 6–2
1969	Rod Laver	Ken Rosewall	6–4, 6–3, 6–4
1970	Jan Kodes	Zeljko Franulovic	6–2, 6–4, 6–0
1971	Jan Kodes	Ilie Nastase	8–6, 6–2, 2–6, 7–5
1972	Andres Gimeno	Patrick Proisy	4–6, 6–3, 6–1, 6–1
1973	Ilie Nastase	Nikki Pilic	6–3, 6–3, 6–0
1974	Bjorn Borg	Manuel Orantes	6–7, 6–0, 6–1, 6–1
1975	Bjorn Borg	Guillermo Vilas	6–2, 6–3, 6–4
1976	Adriano Panatta	Harold Solomon	6–1, 6–4, 4–6, 7–6
1977	Guillermo Vilas	Brian Gottfried	6–0, 6–3, 6–0
1978	Bjorn Borg	Guillermo Vilas	6–1, 6–1, 6–3
1979	Bjorn Borg	Victor Pecci	6–3, 6–1, 6–7, 6–4
1980	Bjorn Borg	Vitas Gerulaitis	6–4, 6–1, 6–2
1981	Bjorn Borg	Ivan Lendl	6–1, 4–6, 6–2, 3–6, 6–1
1982	Mats Wilander	Guillermo Vilas	1–6, 7–6, 6–0, 6–4
1983	Yannick Noah	Mats Wilander	6–2, 7–5, 7–6
1984	Ivan Lendl	John McEnroe	3–6, 2–6, 6–4, 7–5, 7–5
1985	Mats Wilander	Ivan Lendl	3–6, 6–4, 6–2, 6–2
1986	Ivan Lendl	Mikael Pernfors	6–3, 6–2, 6–4
1987	Ivan Lendl	Mats Wilander	7–5, 6–2, 3–6, 7–6
1988	Mats Wilander	Henri Leconte	7–5, 6–2, 6–1
1989	Michael Chang	Stefan Edberg	6–1, 3–6, 4–6, 6–4, 6–2
1990	Andres Gomez	Andre Agassi	6–3, 2–6, 6–4, 6–4
1991	Jim Courier	Andre Agassi	3–6, 6–4, 2–6, 6–1, 6–4
1992	Jim Courier	Petr Korda	7–5, 6–2, 6–1
1993	Sergi Bruguera	Jim Courier	6–4, 2–6, 6–2, 3–6, 6–3
1994	Sergi Bruguera	Alberto Berasategui	6–3, 7–5, 2–6, 6–1
1995	Thomas Muster	Michael Chang	7–5, 6–2, 6–4
1996	Yevgeny Kafelnikov	Michael Stich	7–6, 7–5, 7–6
1997	Gustavo Kuerten	Sergi Bruguera	6–3, 6–4, 6–2
1998	Carlos Moya	Alex Corretja	6–3, 7–5, 6–3
1999	Andre Agassi	Andrei Medvedev	1–6, 2–6, 6–4, 6–3, 6–4
2000	Gustavo Kuerten	Magnus Norman	6–2, 6–3, 2–6, 7–6
2001	Gustavo Kuerten	Alex Corretja	6–7, 7–5, 6–2, 6–0
2002	Albert Costa	Juan Carlos Ferrero	6–1, 6–0, 4–6, 6–3
2003	Juan Carlos Ferrero	Martin Verkerk	6–1, 6–3, 6–2

*Became Open (amateur and professional) in 1968 but closed to contract professionals in 1972.

†1925 was the first year that entries were accepted from all countries.‡From 1941 to 1945 the event was called Tournoi de France and was closed to all foreigners.

Wimbledon Championships

Year	Winner	Finalist	Score
1877	Spencer W. Gore	William C. Marshall	6–1, 6–2, 6–4
1878	P. Frank Hadow	Spencer W. Gore	7–5, 6–1, 9–7
1879	John T. Hartley	V. St Leger Gould	6–2, 6–4, 6–2
1880	John T. Hartley	Herbert F. Lawford	6–0, 6–2, 2–6, 6–3
1881	William Renshaw	John T. Hartley	6–0, 6–2, 6–1
1882	William Renshaw	Ernest Renshaw	6–1, 2–6, 4–6, 6–2, 6–2
1883	William Renshaw	Ernest Renshaw	2–6, 6–3, 6–3, 4–6, 6–3

MEN *(Cont.)*

Wimbledon Championship *(Cont.)*

Year	Winner	Finalist	Score
1884	William Renshaw	Herbert F. Lawford	6–0, 6–4, 9–7
1885	William Renshaw	Herbert F. Lawford	7–5, 6–2, 4–6, 7–5
1886	William Renshaw	Herbert F. Lawford	6–0, 5–7, 6–3, 6–4
1887	Herbert F. Lawford	Ernest Renshaw	1–6, 6–3, 3–6, 6–4, 6–4
1888	Ernest Renshaw	Herbert F. Lawford	6–3, 7–5, 6–0
1889	William Renshaw	Ernest Renshaw	6–4, 6–1, 3–6, 6–0
1890	William J. Hamilton	William Renshaw	6–8, 6–2, 3–6, 6–1, 6–1
1891	Wilfred Baddeley	Joshua Pim	6–4, 1–6, 7–5, 6–0
1892	Wilfred Baddeley	Joshua Pim	4–6, 6–3, 6–3, 6–2
1893	Joshua Pim	Wilfred Baddeley	3–6, 6–1, 6–3, 6–2
1894	Joshua Pim	Wilfred Baddeley	10–8, 6–2, 8–6
1895	Wilfred Baddeley	Wilberforce V. Eaves	4–6, 2–6, 8–6; 6–2, 6–3
1896	Harold S. Mahoney	Wilfred Baddeley	6–2, 6–8, 5–7, 8–6, 6–3
1897	Reggie F. Doherty	Harold S. Mahoney	6–4, 6–4, 6–3
1898	Reggie F. Doherty	H. Laurie Doherty	6–3, 6–3, 2–6, 5–7, 6–1
1899	Reggie F. Doherty	Arthur W. Gore	1–6, 4–6, 6–2, 6–3, 6–3
1900	Reggie F. Doherty	Sidney H. Smith	6–8, 6–3, 6–1, 6–2
1901	Arthur W. Gore	Reggie F. Doherty	4–6, 7–5, 6–4, 6–4
1902	H. Laurie Doherty	Arthur W. Gore	6–4, 6–3, 3–6, 6–0
1903	H. Laurie Doherty	Frank L. Riseley	7–5, 6–3, 6–0
1904	H. Laurie Doherty	Frank L. Riseley	6–1, 7–5, 8–6
1905	H. Laurie Doherty	Norman E. Brookes	8–6, 6–2, 6–4
1906	H. Laurie Doherty	Frank L. Riseley	6–4, 4–6, 6–2, 6–3
1907	Norman E. Brookes	Arthur W. Gore	6–4, 6–2, 6–2
1908	Arthur W. Gore	H. Roper Barrett	6–3, 6–2, 4–6, 3–6, 6–4
1909	Arthur W. Gore	M. J. G. Ritchie	6–8, 1–6, 6–2, 6–2, 6–2
1910	Anthony F. Wilding	Arthur W. Gore	6–4, 7–5, 4–6, 6–2
1911	Anthony F. Wilding	H. Roper Barrett	6–4, 4–6, 2–6, 6–2 ret
1912	Anthony F. Wilding	Arthur W. Gore	6–4, 6–4, 4–6, 6–4
1913	Anthony F. Wilding	Maurice E. McLoughlin	8–6, 6–3, 10–8
1914	Norman E. Brookes	Anthony F. Wilding	6–4, 6–4, 7–5
1915–18	No tournament		
1919	Gerald L. Patterson	Norman E. Brookes	6–3, 7–5, 6–2
1920	Bill Tilden	Gerald L. Patterson	2–6, 6–3, 6–2, 6–4
1921	Bill Tilden	Brian I. C. Norton	4–6, 2–6, 6–1, 6–0, 7–5
1922	Gerald L. Patterson	Randolph Lycett	6–3, 6–4, 6–2
1923	Bill Johnston	Francis T. Hunter	6–0, 6–3, 6–1
1924	Jean Borotra	Rene Lacoste	6–1, 3–6, 6–1, 3–6, 6–4
1925	Rene Lacoste	Jean Borotra	6–3, 6–3, 4–6, 8–6
1926	Jean Borotra	Howard Kinsey	8–6, 6–1, 6–3
1927	Henri Cochet	Jean Borotra	4–6, 4–6, 6–3, 6–4, 7–5
1928	Rene Lacoste	Henri Cochet	6–1, 4–6, 6–4, 6–2
1929	Henri Cochet	Jean Borotra	6–4, 6–3, 6–4
1930	Bill Tilden	Wilmer Allison	6–3, 9–7, 6–4
1931	Sidney B. Wood Jr	Francis X. Shields	walkover
1932	Ellsworth Vines	Henry Austin	6–4, 6–2, 6–0
1933	Jack Crawford	Ellsworth Vines	4–6, 11–9, 6–2, 2–6, 6–4
1934	Fred Perry	Jack Crawford	6–3, 6–0, 7–5
1935	Fred Perry	Gottfried von Cramm	6–2, 6–4, 6–4
1936	Fred Perry	Gottfried von Cramm	6–1, 6–1, 6–0
1937	Don Budge	Gottfried von Cramm	6–3, 6–4, 6–2
1938	Don Budge	Henry Austin	6–1, 6–0, 6–3
1939	Bobby Riggs	Elwood Cooke	2–6, 8–6, 3–6, 6–3, 6–2
1940–45	No tournament		
1946	Yvon Petra	Geoff E. Brown	6–2, 6–4, 7–9, 5–7, 6–4
1947	Jack Kramer	Tom P. Brown	6–1, 6–3, 6–2
1948	Bob Falkenburg	John Bromwich	7–5, 0–6, 6–2, 3–6, 7–5
1949	Ted Schroeder	Jaroslav Drobny	3–6, 6–0, 6–3, 4–6, 6–4
1950	Budge Patty	Frank Sedgman	6–1, 8–10, 6–2, 6–3
1951	Dick Savitt	Ken McGregor	6–4, 6–4, 6–4
1952	Frank Sedgman	Jaroslav Drobny	4–6, 6–3, 6–2, 6–3
1953	Vic Seixas	Kurt Nielsen	9–7, 6–3, 6–4
1954	Jaroslav Drobny	Ken Rosewall	13–11, 4–6, 6–2, 9–7
1955	Tony Trabert	Kurt Nielsen	6–3, 7–5, 6–1
1956	Lew Hoad	Ken Rosewall	6–2, 4–6, 7–5, 6–4
1957	Lew Hoad	Ashley Cooper	6–2, 6–1, 6–2
1958	Ashley Cooper	Neale Fraser	3–6, 6–3, 6–4, 13–11

MEN *(Cont.)*
Wimbledon Championships *(Cont.)*

Year	Winner	Finalist	Score
1959	Alex Olmedo	Rod Laver	6–4, 6–3, 6–4
1960	Neale Fraser	Rod Laver	6–4, 3–6, 9–7, 7–5
1961	Rod Laver	Chuck McKinley	6–3, 6–1, 6–4
1962	Rod Laver	Martin Mulligan	6–2, 6–2, 6–1
1963	Chuck McKinley	Fred Stolle	9–7, 6–1, 6–4
1964	Roy Emerson	Fred Stolle	6–4, 12–10, 4–6, 6–3
1965	Roy Emerson	Fred Stolle	6–2, 6–4, 6–4
1966	Manuel Santana	Dennis Ralston	6–4, 11–9, 6–4
1967	John Newcombe	Wilhelm Bungert	6–3, 6–1, 6–1
1968*	Rod Laver	Tony Roche	6–3, 6–4, 6–2
1969	Rod Laver	John Newcombe	6–4, 5–7, 6–4, 6–4
1970	John Newcombe	Ken Rosewall	5–7, 6–3, 6–2, 3–6, 6–1
1971	John Newcombe	Stan Smith	6–3, 5–7, 2–6, 6–4, 6–4
1972	Stan Smith	Ilie Nastase	4–6, 6–3, 6–3, 4–6, 7–5
1973	Jan Kodes	Alex Metreveli	6–1, 9–8, 6–3
1974	Jimmy Connors	Ken Rosewall	6–1, 6–1, 6–4
1975	Arthur Ashe	Jimmy Connors	6–1, 6–1, 5–7, 6–4
1976	Bjorn Borg	Ilie Nastase	6–4, 6–2, 9–7
1977	Bjorn Borg	Jimmy Connors	3–6, 6–2, 6–1, 5–7, 6–4
1978	Bjorn Borg	Jimmy Connors	6–2, 6–2, 6–3
1979	Bjorn Borg	Roscoe Tanner	6–7, 6–1, 3–6, 6–3, 6–4
1980	Bjorn Borg	John McEnroe	1–6, 7–5, 6–3, 6–7, 8–6
1981	John McEnroe	Bjorn Borg	4–6, 7–6, 7–6, 6–4
1982	Jimmy Connors	John McEnroe	3–6, 6–3, 6–7, 7–6, 6–4
1983	John McEnroe	Chris Lewis	6–2, 6–2, 6–2
1984	John McEnroe	Jimmy Connors	6–1, 6–1, 6–2
1985	Boris Becker	Kevin Curren	6–3, 6–7, 7–6, 6–4
1986	Boris Becker	Ivan Lendl	6–4, 6–3, 7–5
1987	Pat Cash	Ivan Lendl	7–6, 6–2, 7–5
1988	Stefan Edberg	Boris Becker	4–6, 7–6, 6–4, 6–2
1989	Boris Becker	Stefan Edberg	6–0, 7–6, 6–4
1990	Stefan Edberg	Boris Becker	6–2, 6–2, 3–6, 3–6, 6–4
1991	Michael Stich	Boris Becker	6–4, 7–6, 6–4
1992	Andre Agassi	Goran Ivanisevic	6–7, 6–4, 6–4, 1–6, 6–4
1993	Pete Sampras	Jim Courier	7–6, 7–6, 3–6, 6–3
1994	Pete Sampras	Goran Ivanisevic	7–6, 7–6, 6–0
1995	Pete Sampras	Boris Becker	6–7, 6–2, 6–4, 6–2
1996	Richard Krajicek	MaliVai Washington	6–3, 6–4, 6–3
1997	Pete Sampras	Cedric Pioline	6–4, 6–2, 6–4
1998	Pete Sampras	Goran Ivanisevic	6–7, 7–6, 6–4, 3–6, 6–2
1999	Pete Sampras	Andre Agassi	6–3, 6–4, 7–5
2000	Pete Sampras	Patrick Rafter	6–7, 7–6, 6–4, 6–2
2001	Goran Ivanisevic	Patrick Rafter	6–3, 3–6, 6–3, 2–6, 9–7
2002	Lleyton Hewitt	David Nalbandian	6–1, 6–3, 6–2
2003	Roger Federer	Mark Philippoussis	7–6 (7-5), 6–2, 7–6 (7-3)

*Became Open (amateur and professional) in 1968 but closed to contract professionals in 1972.

Note: Prior to 1922 the tournament was run on a challenge-round system. The previous year's winner "stood out"of an All Comers event, which produced a challenger to play him for the title.

United States Championships

Year	Winner	Finalist	Score
1881	Richard D. Sears	W.E. Glyn	6–0, 6–3, 6–2
1882	Richard D. Sears	C.M. Clark	6–1, 6–4, 6–0
1883	Richard D. Sears	James Dwight	6–2, 6–0, 9–7
1884	Richard D. Sears	H.A. Taylor	6–0, 1–6, 6–0, 6–2
1885	Richard D. Sears	G.M. Brinley	6–3, 4–6, 6–0, 6–3
1886	Richard D. Sears	R.L. Beeckman	4–6, 6–1, 6–3, 6–4
1887	Richard D. Sears	H.W. Slocum Jr	6–1, 6–3, 6–2
1888‡	H. W. Slocum Jr	H.A. Taylor	6–4, 6–1, 6–0
1889	H. W. Slocum Jr	Q.A. Shaw	6–3, 6–1, 4–6, 6–2
1890	Oliver S. Campbell	H.W. Slocum Jr	6–2, 4–6, 6–3, 6–1
1891	Oliver S. Campbell	Clarence Hobart	2–6, 7–5, 7–9, 6–1, 6–2
1892	Oliver S. Campbell	Frederick H. Hovey	7–5, 3–6, 6–3, 7–5
1893‡	Robert D. Wrenn	Frederick H. Hovey	6–4, 3–6, 6–4, 6–4

MEN *(Cont.)*
United States Championships *(Cont.)*

Year	Winner	Finalist	Score
1894	Robert D. Wrenn	M.F. Goodbody	6–8, 6–1, 6–4, 6–4
1895	Frederick H. Hovey	Robert D. Wrenn	6–3, 6–2, 6–4
1896	Robert D. Wrenn	Frederick H. Hovey	7–5, 3–6, 6–0, 1–6, 6–1
1897	Robert D. Wrenn	Wilberforce V. Eaves	4–6, 8–6, 6–3, 2–6, 6–2
1898‡	Malcolm D. Whitman	Dwight F. Davis	3–6, 6–2, 6–2, 6–1
1899	Malcolm D. Whitman	J. Parmly Paret	6–1, 6–2, 3–6, 7–5
1900	Malcolm D. Whitman	William A. Larned	6–4, 1–6, 6–2, 6–2
1901‡	William A. Larned	Beals C. Wright	6–2, 6–8, 6–4, 6–4
1902	William A. Larned	Reggie F. Doherty	4–6, 6–2, 6–4, 8–6
1903	H. Laurie Doherty	William A. Larned	6–0, 6–3, 10–8
1904‡	Holcombe Ward	William J. Clothier	10–8, 6–4, 9–7
1905	Beals C. Wright	Holcombe Ward	6–2, 6–1, 11–9
1906	William J. Clothier	Beals C. Wright	6–3, 6–0, 6–4
1907‡	William A. Larned	Robert LeRoy	6–2, 6–2, 6–4
1908	William A. Larned	Beals C. Wright	6–1, 6–2, 8–6
1909	William A. Larned	William J. Clothier	6–1, 6–2, 5–7, 1–6, 6–1
1910	William A. Larned	Thomas C. Bundy	6–1, 5–7, 6–0, 6–8, 6–1
1911	William A. Larned	Maurice E. McLoughlin	6–4, 6–4, 6–2
1912†	Maurice E. McLoughlin	Bill Johnson	3–6, 2–6, 6–2, 6–4, 6–2
1913	Maurice E. McLoughlin	Richard N. Williams	6–4, 5–7, 6–3, 6–1
1914	Richard N. Williams	Maurice E. McLoughlin	6–3, 8–6, 10–8
1915	Bill Johnston	Maurice E. McLoughlin	1–6, 6–0, 7–5, 10–8
1916	Richard N. Williams	Bill Johnston	4–6, 6–4, 0–6, 6–2, 6–4
1917#	R.L. Murray	N. W. Niles	5–7, 8–6, 6–3, 6–3
1918	R.L. Murray	Bill Tilden	6–3, 6–1, 7–5
1919	Bill Johnston	Bill Tilden	6–4, 6–4, 6–3
1920	Bill Tilden	Bill Johnston	6–1, 1–6, 7–5, 5–7, 6–3
1921	Bill Tilden	Wallace F. Johnson	6–1, 6–3, 6–1
1922	Bill Tilden	Bill Johnston	4–6, 3–6, 6–2, 6–3, 6–4
1923	Bill Tilden	Bill Johnston	6–4, 6–1, 6–4
1924	Bill Tilden	Bill Johnston	6–1, 9–7, 6–2
1925	Bill Tilden	Bill Johnston	4–6, 11–9, 6–3, 4–6, 6–3
1926	Rene Lacoste	Jean Borotra	6–4, 6–0, 6–4
1927	Rene Lacoste	Bill Tilden	11–9, 6–3, 11–9
1928	Henri Cochet	Francis T. Hunter	4–6, 6–4, 3–6, 7–5, 6–3
1929	Bill Tilden	Francis T. Hunter	3–6, 6–3, 4–6, 6–2, 6–4
1930	John H. Doeg	Francis X. Shields	10–8, 1–6, 6–4, 16–14
1931	Ellsworth Vines	George M. Lott Jr	7–9, 6–3, 9–7, 7–5
1932	Ellsworth Vines	Henri Cochet	6–4, 6–4, 6–4
1933	Fred Perry	Jack Crawford	6–3, 11–13, 4–6, 6–0, 6–1
1934	Fred Perry	Wilmer L. Allison	6–4, 6–3, 1–6, 8–6
1935	Wilmer L. Allison	Sidney B. Wood Jr	6–2, 6–2, 6–3
1936	Fred Perry	Don Budge	2–6, 6–2, 8–6, 1–6, 10–8
1937	Don Budge	Gottfried von Cramm	6–1, 7–9, 6–1, 3–6, 6–1
1938	Don Budge	Gene Mako	6–3, 6–8, 6–2, 6–1
1939	Bobby Riggs	Welby Van Horn	6–4, 6–2, 6–4
1940	Don McNeill	Bobby Riggs	4–6, 6–8, 6–3, 6–3, 7–5
1941	Bobby Riggs	Francis Kovacs II	5–7, 6–1, 6–3, 6–3
1942	Ted Schroeder	Frank Parker	8–6, 7–5, 3–6, 4–6, 6–2
1943	Joseph R. Hunt	Jack Kramer	6–3, 6–8, 10–8, 6–0
1944	Frank Parker	William F. Talbert	6–4, 3–6, 6–3, 6–3
1945	Frank Parker	William F. Talbert	14–12, 6–1, 6–2
1946	Jack Kramer	Tom P. Brown	9–7, 6–3, 6–0
1947	Jack Kramer	Frank Parker	4–6, 2–6, 6–1, 6–0, 6–3
1948	Pancho Gonzales	Eric W. Sturgess	6–2, 6–3, 14–12
1949	Pancho Gonzales	Ted Schroeder	16–18, 2–6, 6–1, 6–2, 6–4
1950	Arthur Larsen	Herbie Flam	6–3, 4–6, 5–7, 6–4, 6–3
1951	Frank Sedgman	Vic Seixas	6–4, 6–1, 6–1
1952	Frank Sedgman	Gardnar Mulloy	6–1, 6–2, 6–3
1953	Tony Trabert	Vic Seixas	6–3, 6–2, 6–3
1954	Vic Seixas	Rex Hartwig	3–6, 6–2, 6–4, 6–4
1955	Tony Trabert	Ken Rosewall	9–7, 6–3, 6–3
1956	Ken Rosewall	Lew Hoad	4–6, 6–2, 6–3, 6–3

MEN (Cont.)
United States Championships (Cont.)

Year	Winner	Finalist	Score
1957	Mal Anderson	Ashley J. Cooper	10–8, 7–5, 6–4
1958	Ashley J. Cooper	Mal Anderson	6–2, 3–6, 4–6, 10–8, 8–6
1959	Neale Fraser	Alex Olmedo	6–3, 5–7, 6–2, 6–4
1960	Neale Fraser	Rod Laver	6–4, 6–4, 9–7
1961	Roy Emerson	Rod Laver	7–5, 6–3, 6–2
1962	Rod Laver	Roy Emerson	6–2, 6–4, 5–7, 6–4
1963	Rafael Osuna	Frank Froehling III	7–5, 6–4, 6–2
1964	Roy Emerson	Fred Stolle	6–4, 6–2, 6–4
1965	Manuel Santana	Cliff Drysdale	6–2, 7–9, 7–5, 6–1
1966	Fred Stolle	John Newcombe	4–6, 12–10, 6–3, 6–4
1967	John Newcombe	Clark Graebner	6–4, 6–4, 8–6
1968*	Arthur Ashe	Tom Okker	14–12, 5–7, 6–3, 3–6, 6–3
1968**	Arthur Ashe	Bob Lutz	4–6, 6–3, 8–10, 6–0, 6–4
1969	Rod Laver	Tony Roche	7–9, 6–1, 6–3, 6–2
1969**	Stan Smith	Bob Lutz	9–7, 6–3, 6–1
1970	Ken Rosewall	Tony Roche	2–6, 6–4, 7–6, 6–3
1971	Stan Smith	Jan Kodes	3–6, 6–3, 6–2, 7–6
1972	Ilie Nastase	Arthur Ashe	3–6, 6–3, 6–7, 6–4, 6–3
1973	John Newcombe	Jan Kodes	6–4, 1–6, 4–6, 6–2, 6–3
1974	Jimmy Connors	Ken Rosewall	6–1, 6–0, 6–1
1975	Manuel Orantes	Jimmy Connors	6–4, 6–3, 6–3
1976	Jimmy Connors	Bjorn Borg	6–4, 3–6, 7–6, 6–4
1977	Guillermo Vilas	Jimmy Connors	2–6, 6–3, 7–6, 6–0
1978	Jimmy Connors	Bjorn Borg	6–4, 6–2, 6–2
1979	John McEnroe	Vitas Gerulaitis	7–5, 6–3, 6–3
1980	John McEnroe	Bjorn Borg	7–6, 6–1, 6–7, 5–7, 6–4
1981	John McEnroe	Bjorn Borg	4–6, 6–2, 6–4, 6–3
1982	Jimmy Connors	Ivan Lendl	6–3, 6–2, 4–6, 6–4
1983	Jimmy Connors	Ivan Lendl	6–3, 6–7, 7–5, 6–0
1984	John McEnroe	Ivan Lendl	6–3, 6–4, 6–1
1985	Ivan Lendl	John McEnroe	7–6, 6–3, 6–4
1986	Ivan Lendl	Miloslav Mecir	6–4, 6–2, 6–0
1987	Ivan Lendl	Mats Wilander	6–7, 6–0, 7–6, 6–4
1988	Mats Wilander	Ivan Lendl	6–4, 4–6, 6–3, 5–7, 6–4
1989	Boris Becker	Ivan Lendl	7–6, 1–6, 6–3, 7–6
1990	Pete Sampras	Andre Agassi	6–4, 6–3, 6–2
1991	Stefan Edberg	Jim Courier	6–2, 6–4, 6–0
1992	Stefan Edberg	Pete Sampras	3–6, 6–4, 7–6, 6–2
1993	Pete Sampras	Cedric Pioline	6–4, 6–4, 6–3
1994	Andre Agassi	Michael Stich	6–1, 7–6, 7–5
1995	Pete Sampras	Andre Agassi	6–4, 6–3, 4–6, 7–5
1996	Pete Sampras	Michael Chang	6–1, 6–4, 7–6
1997	Patrick Rafter	Greg Rusedski	6–3, 6–2, 4–6, 7–5
1998	Patrick Rafter	Mark Philippoussis	6–3, 3–6, 6–2, 6–0
1999	Andre Agassi	Todd Martin	6–4, 6–7, 6–7, 6–3, 6–2
2000	Marat Safin	Pete Sampras	6–4, 6–3, 6–3
2001	Lleyton Hewitt	Pete Sampras	7–6, 6–1, 6–1
2002	Pete Sampras	Andre Agassi	6–3, 6–4, 5–7, 6–4
2003	Andy Roddick	Juan Carlos Ferrero	6–3, 7–6 (7-2), 6–3

‡No challenge round played.*Became Open (amateur and professional) in 1968.†Challenge round abolished; #National Patriotic Tournament.**Amateur event held.

WOMEN
Australian Championships

Year	Winner	Finalist	Score
1922	Margaret Molesworth	Esna Boyd	6–3, 10–8
1923	Margaret Molesworth	Esna Boyd	6–1, 7–5
1924	Sylvia Lance	Esna Boyd	6–3, 3–6, 6–4
1925	Daphne Akhurst	Esna Boyd	1–6, 8–6, 6–4
1926	Daphne Akhurst	Esna Boyd	6–1, 6–3
1927	Esna Boyd	Sylvia Harper	5–7, 6–1, 6–2
1928	Daphne Akhurst	Esna Boyd	7–5, 6–2
1929	Daphne Akhurst	Louise Bickerton	6–1, 5–7, 6–2
1930	Daphne Akhurst	Sylvia Harper	10–8, 2–6, 7–5

WOMEN *(Cont.)*
Australian Championships *(Cont.)*

Year	Winner	Finalist	Score
1931	Coral Buttsworth	Margorie Crawford	1–6, 6–3, 6–4
1932	Coral Buttsworth	Kathrine Le Messurier	9–7, 6–4
1933	Joan Hartigan	Coral Buttsworth	6–4, 6–3
1934	Joan Hartigan	Margaret Molesworth	6–1, 6–4
1935	Dorothy Round	Nancye Wynne Bolton	1–6, 6–1, 6–3
1936	Joan Hartigan	Nancye Wynne Bolton	6–4, 6–4
1937	Nancye Wynne Bolton	Emily Westacott	6–3, 5–7, 6–4
1938	Dorothy Bundy	D. Stevenson	6–3, 6–2
1939	Emily Westacott	Nell Hopman	6–1, 6–2
1940	Nancye Wynne Bolton	Thelma Coyne	5–7, 6–4, 6–0
1941–45	No tournament		
1946	Nancye Wynne Bolton	Joyce Fitch	6–4, 6–4
1947	Nancye Wynne Bolton	Nell Hopman	6–3, 6–2
1948	Nancye Wynne Bolton	Marie Toomey	6–3, 6–1
1949	Doris Hart	Nancye Wynne Bolton	6–3, 6–4
1950	Louise Brough	Doris Hart	6–4, 3–6, 6–4
1951	Nancye Wynne Bolton	Thelma Long	6–1, 7–5
1952	Thelma Long	H. Angwin	6–2, 6–3
1953	Maureen Connolly	Julia Sampson	6–3, 6–2
1954	Thelma Long	J. Staley	6–3, 6–4
1955	Beryl Penrose	Thelma Long	6–4, 6–3
1956	Mary Carter	Thelma Long	3–6, 6–2, 9–7
1957	Shirley Fry	Althea Gibson	6–3, 6–4
1958	Angela Mortimer	Lorraine Coghlan	6–3, 6–4
1959	Mary Carter-Reitano	Renee Schuurman	6–2, 6–3
1960	Margaret Smith	Jan Lehane	7–5, 6–2
1961	Margaret Smith	Jan Lehane	6–1, 6–4
1962	Margaret Smith	Jan Lehane	6–0, 6–2
1963	Margaret Smith	Jan Lehane	6–2, 6–2
1964	Margaret Smith	Lesley Turner	6–3, 6–2
1965	Margaret Smith	Maria Bueno	5–7, 6–4, 5–2 ret.
1966	Margaret Smith	Nancy Richey	Default
1967	Nancy Richey	Lesley Turner	6–1, 6–4
1968	Billie Jean King	Margaret Smith	6–1, 6–2
1969*	Margaret Smith Court	Billie Jean King	6–4, 6–1
1970	Margaret Smith Court	Kerry Melville Reid	6–3, 6–1
1971	Margaret Smith Court	Evonne Goolagong	2–6, 7–6, 7–5
1972	Virginia Wade	Evonne Goolagong	6–4, 6–4
1973	Margaret Smith Court	Evonne Goolagong	6–4, 7–5
1974	Evonne Goolagong	Chris Evert	7–6, 4–6, 6–0
1975	Evonne Goolagong	Martina Navratilova	6–3, 6–2
1976	Evonne Goolagong Cawley	Renata Tomanova	6–2, 6–2
1977 (Jan)	Kerry Melville Reid	Dianne Balestrat	7–5, 6–2
1977 (Dec)	Evonne Goolagong Cawley	Helen Gourlay	6–3, 6–0
1978	Chris O'Neil	Betsy Nagelsen	6–3, 7–6
1979	Barbara Jordan	Sharon Walsh	6–3, 6–3
1980	Hana Mandlikova	Wendy Turnbull	6–0, 7–5
1981	Martina Navratilova	Chris Evert Lloyd	6–7, 6–4, 7–5
1982	Chris Evert Lloyd	Martina Navratilova	6–3, 2–6, 6–3
1983	Martina Navratilova	Kathy Jordan	6–2, 7–6
1984	Chris Evert Lloyd	Helena Sukova	6–7, 6–1, 6–3
1985 (Dec)	Martina Navratilova	Chris Evert Lloyd	6–2, 4–6, 6–2
1987 (Jan)	Hana Mandlikova	Martina Navratilova	7–5, 7–6
1988	Steffi Graf	Chris Evert	6–1, 7–6
1989	Steffi Graf	Helena Sukova	6–4, 6–4
1990	Steffi Graf	Mary Joe Fernandez	6–3, 6–4
1991	Monica Seles	Jana Novotna	5–7, 6–3, 6–1
1992	Monica Seles	Mary Joe Fernandez	6–2, 6–3
1993	Monica Seles	Steffi Graf	4–6, 6–3, 6–2
1994	Steffi Graf	Arantxa Sánchez Vicario	6–0, 6–2
1995	Mary Pierce	Arantxa Sánchez Vicario	6–3, 6–2
1996	Monica Seles	Anke Huber	6–4, 6–1
1997	Martina Hingis	Mary Pierce	6–2, 6–2
1998	Martina Hingis	Conchita Martinez	6–3, 6–3
1999	Martina Hingis	Amelie Mauresmo	6–2, 6–3
2000	Lindsay Davenport	Martina Hingis	6–1, 7–5

WOMEN (Cont.)

Australian Championships (Cont.)

Year	Winner	Finalist	Score
2001	Jennifer Capriati	Martina Hingis	6–4, 6–3
2002	Jennifer Capriati	Martina Hingis	4–6, 7–6 (9–7), 6–2
2003	Serena Williams	Venus Williams	7–6 (7-4), 3–6, 6–4

*Became Open (amateur and professional) in 1969.

French Championships

Year	Winner	Finalist	Score
1925†	Suzanne Lenglen	Kathleen McKane	6–1, 6–2
1926	Suzanne Lenglen	Mary K. Browne	6–1, 6–0
1927	Kea Bouman	Irene Peacock	6–2, 6–4
1928	Helen Wills	Eileen Bennett	6–1, 6–2
1929	Helen Wills	Simone Mathieu	6–3, 6–4
1930	Helen Wills Moody	Helen Jacobs	6–2, 6–1
1931	Cilly Aussem	Betty Nuthall	8–6, 6–1
1932	Helen Wills Moody	Simone Mathieu	7–5, 6–1
1933	Margaret Scriven	Simone Mathieu	6–2, 4–6, 6–4
1934	Margaret Scriven	Helen Jacobs	7–5, 4–6, 6–1
1935	Hilde Sperling	Simone Mathieu	6–2, 6–1
1936	Hilde Sperling	Simone Mathieu	6–3, 6–4
1937	Hilde Sperling	Simone Mathieu	6–2, 6–4
1938	Simone Mathieu	Nelly Landry	6–0, 6–3
1939	Simone Mathieu	Jadwiga Jedrzejowska	6–3, 8–6
1940–45	No tournament		
1946	Margaret Osborne	Pauline Betz	1–6, 8–6, 7–5
1947	Patricia Todd	Doris Hart	6–3, 3–6, 6–4
1948	Nelly Landry	Shirley Fry	6–2, 0–6, 6–0
1949	Margaret Osborne duPont	Nelly Adamson	7–5, 6–2
1950	Doris Hart	Patricia Todd	6–4, 4–6, 6–2
1951	Shirley Fry	Doris Hart	6–3, 3–6, 6–3
1952	Doris Hart	Shirley Fry	6–4, 6–4
1953	Maureen Connolly	Doris Hart	6–2, 6–4
1954	Maureen Connolly	Ginette Bucaille	6–4, 6–1
1955	Angela Mortimer	Dorothy Knode	2–6, 7–5, 10–8
1956	Althea Gibson	Angela Mortimer	6–0, 12–10
1957	Shirley Bloomer	Dorothy Knode	6–1, 6–3
1958	Zsuzsi Kormoczi	Shirley Bloomer	6–4, 1–6, 6–2
1959	Christine Truman	Zsuzsi Kormoczi	6–4, 7–5
1960	Darlene Hard	Yola Ramirez	6–3, 6–4
1961	Ann Haydon	Yola Ramirez	6–2, 6–1
1962	Margaret Smith	Lesley Turner	6–3, 3–6, 7–5
1963	Lesley Turner	Ann Haydon Jones	2–6, 6–3, 7–5
1964	Margaret Smith	Maria Bueno	5–7, 6–1, 6–2
1965	Lesley Turner	Margaret Smith	6–3, 6–4
1966	Ann Jones	Nancy Richey	6–3, 6–1
1967	Francoise Durr	Lesley Turner	4–6, 6–3, 6–4
1968*	Nancy Richey	Ann Jones	5–7, 6–4, 6–1
1969	Margaret Smith Court	Ann Jones	6–1, 4–6, 6–3
1970	Margaret Smith Court	Helga Niessen	6–2, 6–4
1971	Evonne Goolagong	Helen Gourlay	6–3, 7–5
1972	Billie Jean King	Evonne Goolagong	6–3, 6–3
1973	Margaret Smith Court	Chris Evert	6–7, 7–6, 6–4
1974	Chris Evert	Olga Morozova	6–1, 6–2
1975	Chris Evert	Martina Navratilova	2–6, 6–2, 6–1
1976	Sue Barker	Renata Tomanova	6–2, 0–6, 6–2
1977	Mima Jausovec	Florenza Mihai	6–2, 6–7, 6–1
1978	Virginia Ruzici	Mima Jausovec	6–2, 6–2
1979	Chris Evert Lloyd	Wendy Turnbull	6–2, 6–0
1980	Chris Evert Lloyd	Virginia Ruzici	6–0, 6–3
1981	Hana Mandlikova	Sylvia Hanika	6–2, 6–4
1982	Martina Navratilova	Andrea Jaeger	7–6, 6–1
1983	Chris Evert Lloyd	Mima Jausovec	6–1, 6–2
1984	Martina Navratilova	Chris Evert Lloyd	6–3, 6–1
1985	Chris Evert Lloyd	Martina Navratilova	6–3, 6–7, 7–5

WOMEN (Cont.)
French Championships (Cont.)

Year	Winner	Finalist	Score
1986	Chris Evert Lloyd	Martina Navratilova	2–6, 6–3, 6–3
1987	Steffi Graf	Martina Navratilova	6–4, 4–6, 8–6
1988	Steffi Graf	Natalia Zvereva	6–0, 6–0
1989	Arantxa Sánchez Vicario	Steffi Graf	7–6, 3–6, 7–5
1990	Monica Seles	Steffi Graf	7–6, 6–4
1991	Monica Seles	Arantxa Sánchez Vicario	6–3, 6–4
1992	Monica Seles	Steffi Graf	6–2, 3–6, 10–8
1993	Steffi Graf	Mary Joe Fernandez	4–6, 6–2, 6–4
1994	Arantxa Sánchez Vicario	Mary Pierce	6–4, 6–4
1995	Steffi Graf	Arantxa Sánchez Vicario	7–5, 4–6, 6–0
1996	Steffi Graf	Arantxa Sánchez Vicario	6–3, 6–7 (4–7), 10–8
1997	Iva Majoli	Martina Hingis	6–4, 6–2
1998	Arantxa Sánchez Vicario	Monica Seles	7–6 (7–5), 0–6, 6–2
1999	Steffi Graf	Martina Hingis	4–6, 7–5, 6–2
2000	Mary Pierce	Conchita Martinez	6–2, 7–5
2001	Jennifer Capriati	Kim Clijsters	1–6, 6–4, 12–10
2002	Serena Williams	Venus Williams	7–5, 6–3
2003	Justine Henin-Hardenne	Kim Clijsters	6–0, 6–4

†1925 was the first year that entries were accepted from all countries. *Became Open (amateur and professional) in 1968 but closed to contract professionals in 1972.

Wimbledon Championships

Year	Winner	Finalist	Score
1884	Maud Watson	Lilian Watson	6–8, 6–3, 6–3
1885	Maud Watson	Blanche Bingley	6–1, 7–5
1886	Blanche Bingley	Maud Watson	6–3, 6–3
1887	Charlotte Dod	Blanche Bingley	6–2, 6–0
1888	Charlotte Dod	Blanche Bingley Hillyard	6–3, 6–3
1889	Blanche Bingley Hillyard	n/a	n/a
1890	Lena Rice	n/a	n/a
1891	Charlotte Dod	n/a	n/a
1892	Charlotte Dod	Blanche Bingley Hillyard	6–1, 6–1
1893	Charlotte Dod	Blanche Bingley Hillyard	6–8, 6–1, 6–4
1894	Blanche Bingley Hillyard	n/a	n/a
1895	Charlotte Cooper	n/a	
1896	Charlotte Cooper	Mrs. W. H. Pickering	6–2, 6–3
1897	Blanche Bingley Hillyard	Charlotte Cooper	5–7, 7–5, 6–2
1898	Charlotte Cooper	n/a	n/a
1899	Blanche Bingley Hillyard	Charlotte Cooper	6–2, 6–3
1900	Blanche Bingley Hillyard	Charlotte Cooper	4–6, 6–4, 6–4
1901	Charlotte Cooper Sterry	Blanche Bingley Hillyard	6–2, 6–2
1902	Muriel Robb	Charlotte Cooper Sterry	7–5, 6–1
1903	Dorothea Douglass	n/a	n/a
1904	Dorothea Douglass	Charlotte Cooper Sterry	6–0, 6–3
1905	May Sutton	Dorothea Douglass	6–3, 6–4
1906	Dorothea Douglass	May Sutton	6–3, 9–7
1907	May Sutton	Dorothea Douglass Lambert Chambers	6–1, 6–4
1908	Charlotte Cooper Sterry	n/a	n/a
1909	Dora Boothby	n/a	n/a
1910	Dorothea Douglass Lambert Chambers	Dora Boothby	6–2, 6–2
1911	Dorothea Douglass Lambert Chambers	Dora Boothby	6–0, 6–0
1912	Ethel Larcombe	n/a	n/a
1913	Dorothea Douglass Lambert Chambers		
1914	Dorothea Douglass Lambert Chambers	Ethel Larcombe	7–5, 6–4
1915–18	No tournament		
1919	Suzanne Lenglen	Dorothea Douglass Lambert Chambers	10–8, 4–6, 9–7
1920	Suzanne Lenglen	Dorothea Douglass Lambert Chambers	6–3, 6–0
1921	Suzanne Lenglen	Elizabeth Ryan	6–2, 6–0

WOMEN *(Cont.)*
Wimbledon Championships *(Cont.)*

Year	Winner	Finalist	Score
1922	Suzanne Lenglen	Molla Mallory	6–2, 6–0
1923	Suzanne Lenglen	Kathleen McKane	6–2, 6–2
1924	Kathleen McKane	Helen Wills	4–6, 6–4, 6–2
1925	Suzanne Lenglen	Joan Fry	6–2, 6–0
1926	Kathleen McKane Godfree	Lili de Alvarez	6–2, 4–6, 6–3
1927	Helen Wills	Lili de Alvarez	6–2, 6–4
1928	Helen Wills	Lili de Alvarez	6–2, 6–3
1929	Helen Wills	Helen Jacobs	6–1, 6–2
1930	Helen Wills Moody	Elizabeth Ryan	6–2, 6–2
1931	Cilly Aussem	Hilde Kranwinkel	7–5, 7–5
1932	Helen Wills Moody	Helen Jacobs	6–3, 6–1
1933	Helen Wills Moody	Dorothy Round	6–4, 6–8, 6–3
1934	Dorothy Round	Helen Jacobs	6–2, 5–7, 6–3
1935	Helen Wills Moody	Helen Jacobs	6–3, 3–6, 7–5
1936	Helen Jacobs	Hilde Kranwinkel Sperling	6–2, 4–6, 7–5
1937	Dorothy Round	Jadwiga Jedrzejowska	6–2, 2–6, 7–5
1938	Helen Wills Moody	Helen Jacobs	6–4, 6–0
1939	Alice Marble	Kay Stammers	6–2, 6–0
1940–45	No tournament		
1946	Pauline Betz	Louise Brough	6–2, 6–4
1947	Margaret Osborne	Doris Hart	6–2, 6–4
1948	Louise Brough	Doris Hart	6–3, 8–6
1949	Louise Brough	Margaret Osborne duPont	10–8, 1–6, 10–8
1950	Louise Brough	Margaret Osborne duPont	6–1, 3–6, 6–1
1951	Doris Hart	Shirley Fry	6–1, 6–0
1952	Maureen Connolly	Louise Brough	6–4, 6–3
1953	Maureen Connolly	Doris Hart	8–6, 7–5
1954	Maureen Connolly	Louise Brough	6–2, 7–5
1955	Louise Brough	Beverly Fleitz	7–5, 8–6
1956	Shirley Fry	Angela Buxton	6–3, 6–1
1957	Althea Gibson	Darlene Hard	6–3, 6–2
1958	Althea Gibson	Angela Mortimer	8–6, 6–2
1959	Maria Bueno	Darlene Hard	6–4, 6–3
1960	Maria Bueno	Sandra Reynolds	8–6, 6–0
1961	Angela Mortimer	Christine Truman	4–6, 6–4, 7–5
1962	Karen Hantze Susman	Vera Sukova	6–4, 6–4
1963	Margaret Smith	Billie Jean Moffitt	6–3, 6–4
1964	Maria Bueno	Margaret Smith	6–4, 7–9, 6–3
1965	Margaret Smith	Maria Bueno	6–4, 7–5
1966	Billie Jean King	Maria Bueno	6–3, 3–6, 6–1
1967	Billie Jean King	Ann Haydon Jones	6–3, 6–4
1968*	Billie Jean King	Judy Tegart	9–7, 7–5
1969	Ann Haydon Jones	Billie Jean King	3–6, 6–3, 6–2
1970	Margaret Smith Court	Billie Jean King	14–12, 11–9
1971	Evonne Goolagong	Margaret Smith Court	6–4, 6–1
1972	Billie Jean King	Evonne Goolagong	6–3, 6–3
1973	Billie Jean King	Chris Evert	6–0, 7–5
1974	Chris Evert	Olga Morozova	6–0, 6–4
1975	Billie Jean King	Evonne Goolagong Cawley	6–0, 6–1
1976	Chris Evert	Evonne Goolagong Cawley	6–3, 4–6, 8–6
1977	Virginia Wade	Betty Stove	4–6, 6–3, 6–1
1978	Martina Navratilova	Chris Evert	2–6, 6–4, 7–5
1979	Martina Navratilova	Chris Evert Lloyd	6–4, 6–4
1980	Evonne Goolagong Cawley	Chris Evert Lloyd	6–1, 7–6
1981	Chris Evert Lloyd	Hana Mandlikova	6–2, 6–2
1982	Martina Navratilova	Chris Evert Lloyd	6–1, 3–6, 6–2
1983	Martina Navratilova	Andrea Jaeger	6–0, 6–3
1984	Martina Navratilova	Chris Evert Lloyd	7–6, 6–2
1985	Martina Navratilova	Chris Evert Lloyd	4–6, 6–3, 6–2
1986	Martina Navratilova	Hana Mandlikova	7–6, 6–3
1987	Martina Navratilova	Steffi Graf	7–5, 6–3
1988	Steffi Graf	Martina Navratilova	5–7, 6–2, 6–1
1989	Steffi Graf	Martina Navratilova	6–2, 6–7, 6–1

WOMEN (Cont.)

Wimbledon Championships (Cont.)

Year	Winner	Finalist	Score
1990	Martina Navratilova	Zina Garrison	6–4, 6–1
1991	Steffi Graf	Gabriela Sabatini	6–4, 3–6, 8–6
1992	Steffi Graf	Monica Seles	6–2, 6–1
1993	Steffi Graf	Jana Novotna	7–6, 1–6, 6–4
1994	Conchita Martinez	Martina Navratilova	6–4, 3–6, 6–3
1995	Steffi Graf	Arantxa Sánchez Vicario	4–6, 6–1, 7–5
1996	Steffi Graf	Arantxa Sánchez Vicario	6–3, 7–5
1997	Martina Hingis	Jana Novotna	2–6, 6–3, 6–3
1998	Jana Novotna	Nathalie Tauziat	6–4, 7–6
1999	Lindsay Davenport	Steffi Graf	6–4, 7–5
2000	Venus Williams	Lindsay Davenport	6–3, 7–6
2001	Venus Williams	Justine Henin	6–1, 3–6, 6–0
2002	Serena Williams	Venus Williams	7–6 (7–4), 6–3
2003	Serena Williams	Venus Williams	4–6, 6–4, 6–2

*Became Open (amateur and professional) in 1968 but closed to contract professionals in 1972.

Note: Prior to 1922 the tournament was run on a challenge-round system. The previous year's winner "stood out" of an All-Comers event, which produced a challenger to play her for the title.

United States Championships

Year	Winner	Finalist	Score
1887	Ellen Hansell	Laura Knight	6–1, 6–0
1888	Bertha L. Townsend	Ellen Hansell	6–3, 6–5
1889	Bertha L. Townsend	Louise Voorhes	7–5, 6–2
1890	Ellen C. Roosevelt	Bertha L. Townsend	6–2, 6–2
1891	Mabel Cahill	Ellen C. Roosevelt	6–4, 6–1, 4–6, 6–3
1892	Mabel Cahill	Elisabeth Moore	5–7, 6–3, 6–4, 4–6, 6–2
1893	Aline Terry	Alice Schultze	6–1, 6–3
1894	Helen Hellwig	Aline Terry	7–5, 3–6, 6–0, 3–6, 6–3
1895	Juliette Atkinson	Helen Hellwig	6–4, 6–2, 6–1
1896	Elisabeth Moore	Juliette Atkinson	6–4, 4–6, 6–2, 6–2
1897	Juliette Atkinson	Elisabeth Moore	6–3, 6–3, 4–6, 3–6, 6–3
1898	Juliette Atkinson	Marion Jones	6–3, 5–7, 6–4, 2–6, 7–5
1899	Marion Jones	Maud Banks	6–1, 6–1, 7–5
1900	Myrtle McAteer	Edith Parker	6–2, 6–2, 6–0
1901	Elisabeth Moore	Myrtle McAteer	6–4, 3–6, 7–5, 2–6, 6–2
1902**	Marion Jones	Elisabeth Moore	6–1, 1–0, ret.
1903	Elisabeth Moore	Marion Jones	7–5, 8–6
1904	May Sutton	Elisabeth Moore	6–1, 6–2
1905	Elisabeth Moore	Helen Homans	6–4, 5–7, 6–1
1906	Helen Homans	Maud Barger-Wallach	6–4, 6–3
1907	Evelyn Sears	Carrie Neely	6–3, 6–2
1908	Maud Barger-Wallach	Evelyn Sears	6–3, 1–6, 6–3
1909	Hazel Hotchkiss	Maud Barger-Wallach	6–0, 6–1
1910	Hazel Hotchkiss	Louise Hammond	6–4, 6–2
1911	Hazel Hotchkiss	Florence Sutton	8–10, 6–1, 9–7
1912†	Mary K. Browne	Eleanora Sears	6–4, 6–2
1913	Mary K. Browne	Dorothy Green	6–2, 7–5
1914	Mary K. Browne	Marie Wagner	6–2, 1–6, 6–1
1915	Molla Bjurstedt	Hazel Hotchkiss Wightman	4–6, 6–2, 6–0
1916	Molla Bjurstedt	Louise Hammond Raymond	6–0, 6–1
1917‡	Molla Bjurstedt	Marion Vanderhoef	4–6, 6–0, 6–2
1918	Molla Bjurstedt	Eleanor Goss	6–4, 6–3
1919	Hazel Hotchkiss Wightman	Marion Zinderstein	6–1, 6–2
1920	Molla Bjurstedt Mallory	Marion Zinderstein	6–3, 6–1
1921	Molla Bjurstedt Mallory	Mary K. Browne	4–6, 6–4, 6–2
1922	Molla Bjurstedt Mallory	Helen Wills	6–3, 6–1
1923	Helen Wills	Molla Bjurstedt Mallory	6–2, 6–1
1924	Helen Wills	Molla Bjurstedt Mallory	6–1, 6–3
1925	Helen Wills	Kathleen McKane	3–6, 6–0, 6–2
1926	Molla Bjurstedt Mallory	Elizabeth Ryan	4–6, 6–4, 9–7
1927	Helen Wills	Betty Nuthall	6–1, 6–4
1928	Helen Wills	Helen Jacobs	6–2, 6–1
1929	Helen Wills	Phoebe Holcroft Watson	6–4, 6–2
1930	Betty Nuthall	Anna McCune Harper	6–1, 6–4
1931	Helen Wills Moody	Eileen Whitingstall	6–4, 6–1
1932	Helen Jacobs	Carolin Babcock	6–2, 6–2
1933	Helen Jacobs	Helen Wills Moody	8–6, 3–6, 3–0, ret.
1934	Helen Jacobs	Sarah Palfrey	6–1, 6–4

WOMEN *(Cont.)*

United States Championships *(Cont.)*

Year	Winner	Finalist	Score
1935	Helen Jacobs	Sarah Palfrey Fabyan	6–2, 6–4
1936	Alice Marble	Helen Jacobs	4–6, 6–3, 6–2
1937	Anita Lizane	Jadwiga Jedrzejowska	6–4, 6–2
1938	Alice Marble	Nancye Wynne	6–0, 6–3
1939	Alice Marble	Helen Jacobs	6–0, 8–10, 6–4
1940	Alice Marble	Helen Jacobs	6–2, 6–3
1941	Sarah Palfrey Cooke	Pauline Betz	7–5, 6–2
1942	Pauline Betz	Louise Brough	4–6, 6–1, 6–4
1943	Pauline Betz	Louise Brough	6–3, 5–7, 6–3
1944	Pauline Betz	Margaret Osborne	6–3, 8–6
1945	Sarah Palfrey Cooke	Pauline Betz	3–6, 8–6, 6–4
1946	Pauline Betz	Patricia Canning	11–9, 6–3
1947	Louise Brough	Margaret Osborne	8–6, 4–6, 6–1
1948	Margaret Osborne duPont	Louise Brough	4–6, 6–4, 15–13
1949	Margaret Osborne duPont	Doris Hart	6–4, 6–1
1950	Margaret Osborne duPont	Doris Hart	6–4, 6–3
1951	Maureen Connolly	Shirley Fry	6–3, 1–6, 6–4
1952	Maureen Connolly	Doris Hart	6–3, 7–5
1953	Maureen Connolly	Doris Hart	6–2, 6–4
1954	Doris Hart	Louise Brough	6–8, 6–1, 8–6
1955	Doris Hart	Patricia Ward	6–4, 6–2
1956	Shirley Fry	Althea Gibson	6–3, 6–4
1957	Althea Gibson	Louise Brough	6–3, 6–2
1958	Althea Gibson	Darlene Hard	3–6, 6–1, 6–2
1959	Maria Bueno	Christine Truman	6–1, 6–4
1960	Darlene Hard	Maria Bueno	6–4, 10–12, 6–4
1961	Darlene Hard	Ann Haydon	6–3, 6–4
1962	Margaret Smith	Darlene Hard	9–7, 6–4
1963	Maria Bueno	Margaret Smith	7–5, 6–4
1964	Maria Bueno	Carole Graebner	6–1, 6–0
1965	Margaret Smith	Billie Jean Moffitt	8–6, 7–5
1966	Maria Bueno	Nancy Richey	6–3, 6–1
1967	Billie Jean King	Ann Haydon Jones	11–9, 6–4
1968*	Virginia Wade	Billie Jean King	6–4, 6–4
1968#	Margaret Smith Court	Maria Bueno	6–2, 6–2
1969	Margaret Smith Court	Nancy Richey	6–2, 6–2
1969#	Margaret Smith Court	Virginia Wade	4–6, 6–3, 6–0
1970	Margaret Smith Court	Rosie Casals	6–2, 2–6, 6–1
1971	Billie Jean King	Rosie Casals	6–4, 7–6
1972	Billie Jean King	Kerry Melville	6–3, 7–5
1973	Margaret Smith Court	Evonne Goolagong	7–6, 5–7, 6–2
1974	Billie Jean King	Evonne Goolagong	3–6, 6–3, 7–5
1975	Chris Evert	Evonne Goolagong Cawley	5–7, 6–4, 6–2
1976	Chris Evert	Evonne Goolagong Cawley	6–3, 6–0
1977	Chris Evert	Wendy Turnbull	7–6, 6–2
1978	Chris Evert	Pam Shriver	7–6, 6–4
1979	Tracy Austin	Chris Evert Lloyd	6–4, 6–3
1980	Chris Evert Lloyd	Hana Mandlikova	5–7, 6–1, 6–1
1981	Tracy Austin	Martina Navratilova	1–6, 7–6, 7–6
1982	Chris Evert Lloyd	Hana Mandlikova	6–3, 6–1
1983	Martina Navratilova	Chris Evert Lloyd	6–1, 6–3
1984	Martina Navratilova	Chris Evert Lloyd	4–6, 6–4, 6–4
1985	Hana Mandlikova	Martina Navratilova	7–6, 1–6, 7–6
1986	Martina Navratilova	Helena Sukova	6–3, 6–2
1987	Martina Navratilova	Steffi Graf	7–6, 6–1
1988	Steffi Graf	Gabriela Sabatini	6–3, 3–6, 6–1
1989	Steffi Graf	Martina Navratilova	3–6, 6–4, 6–2
1990	Gabriela Sabatini	Steffi Graf	6–2, 7–6
1991	Monica Seles	Martina Navratilova	7–6, 6–1
1992	Monica Seles	Arantxa Sánchez Vicario	6–3, 6–2
1993	Steffi Graf	Helena Sukova	6–3, 6–3
1994	Arantxa Sánchez Vicario	Steffi Graf	1–6, 7–6, 6–4
1995	Steffi Graf	Monica Seles	7–6, 0–6, 6–3
1996	Steffi Graf	Monica Seles	7–5, 7–4
1997	Martina Hingis	Venus Williams	6–0, 6–4
1998	Lindsay Davenport	Martina Hingis	6–3, 7–5
1999	Serena Williams	Martina Hingis	6–3, 7–6
2000	Venus Williams	Lindsay Davenport	6–4, 7–5
2001	Venus Williams	Serena Williams	6–2, 6–4

WOMEN *(Cont.)*
United States Championships *(Cont.)*

Year	Winner	Finalist	Score
2002	Serena Williams	Venus Williams	6-4, 6-3
2003	Justine Henin-Hardenne	Kim Clijsters	7-5, 6-1

**Five-set final abolished; †Challenge round abolished. *Became Open (amateur and professional) in 1968. ‡National Patriotic Tournament; #Amateur event held.

Grand Slams

Singles

Don Budge, 1938
Maureen Connolly, 1953
Rod Laver, 1962, 1969
Margaret Smith Court, 1970
Steffi Graf, 1988

Doubles

Frank Sedgman and Ken McGregor, 1951
Martina Navratilova and Pam Shriver, 1984
Maria Bueno and two partners: Christine Truman
(Australian), Darlene Hard (French, Wimbledon
and U.S. Championships), 1960
Martina Hingis and two partners: Mirjana Lucic
(Australian), Jana Novotna (French, Wimbledon
and U.S. Championships), 1998

Mixed Doubles

Margaret Smith and Ken Fletcher, 1963
Owen Davidson and two partners: Lesley Turner
(Australian), Billie Jean King (French, Wimbledon
and U.S. Championships), 1967

Alltime Grand Slam Champions

MEN

Player	Aus. S-D-M	French S-D-M	Wim. S-D-M	U.S. S-D-M	Total
Roy Emerson	6-3-0	2-6-0	2-3-0	2-4-0	28
John Newcombe	2-5-0	0-3-0	3-6-0	2-3-1	25
Frank Sedgman	2-2-2	0-2-2	1-3-2	2-2-2	22
Bill Tilden	†	0-0-1	3-1-0	7-5-4	21
Rod Laver	3-4-0	2-1-1	4-1-2	2-0-0	20
John Bromwich	2-8-1	0-0-0	0-2-2	0-3-1	19
Jean Borotra	1-1-1	1-5-2	2-3-1	0-0-1	18
Fred Stolle	0-3-1	1-2-0	0-2-3	1-3-2	18
Ken Rosewall	4-3-0	2-2-0	0-2-0	2-2-1	18
Neale Fraser	0-3-1	0-3-0	1-2-0	2-3-3	18
Adrian Quist	3-10-0	0-1-0	0-2-0	0-1-0	17
John McEnroe	0-0-0	0-0-1	3-4-0	4-5-0	17
Jack Crawford	4-4-3	1-1-1	1-1-1	0-0-0	17
*Mark Woodforde	0-2-2	0-1-1	0-6-1	0-3-1	17

†Did not compete.

WOMEN

Player	Aus. S-D-M	French S-D-M	Wim. S-D-M	U.S. S-D-M	Total
Margaret Smith Court	11-8-2	5-4-4	3-2-5	5-5-8	62
Martina Navratilova	3-8-1	2-7-2	9-7-4	4-9-2	58
Billie Jean King	1-0-1	1-1-2	6-10-4	4-5-4	39
Doris Hart	1-1-2	2-5-3	1-4-5	2-4-5	35
Helen Wills Moody	†	4-2-0	8-3-1	7-4-2	31
Louise Brough	1-1-0	0-3-0	4-5-4	1-8-3	30**
Margaret Osborne duPont	†	2-3-0	1-5-1	3-8-6	29**
Elizabeth Ryan	†	0-4-0	0-12-7	0-1-2	26
Steffi Graf	4-0-0	6-0-0	7-1-0	5-0-0	23
Pam Shriver	0-7-0	0-4-1	0-5-0	0-5-0	22
Chris Evert	2-0-0	7-2-0	3-1-0	6-0-0	21
Darlene Hard	†	1-3-2	0-4-3	2-6-0	21
Suzanne Lenglen	†	2-2-2#	6-6-3	0-0-0	21
Nancye Wynne Bolton	6-10-4	0-0-0	0-0-0	0-0-0	20
Maria Bueno	0-1-0	0-1-1	3-5-0	4-4-0	19
Thelma Coyne Long	2-12-4	0-0-1	0-0-0	0-0-0	19

*Active player. †Did not compete. #Suzanne Lenglen also won four singles titles at the French Championships before 1925, when competition was first opened to entries from all nations.**From 1940–45, with competition in the U.S. Championships thinned due to wartime constraints, Louise Brough Clapp also won four doubles titles (1942–45) and one mixed doubles title (1942); and Margaret Osborne duPont won five doubles titles (1941–45) and three mixed doubles titles (1943–45).

Alltime Grand Slam Singles Champions

MEN

Player	Aus.	French	Wim.	U.S.	Total
Pete Sampras	2	0	7	5	14
Roy Emerson	6	2	2	2	12
Bjorn Borg	0	6	5	0	11
Rod Laver	3	2	4	2	11
Bill Tilden	†	0	3	7	10
Jimmy Connors	1	0	2	5	8
Ivan Lendl	2	3	0	3	8
Fred Perry	1	1	3	3	8
Ken Rosewall	4	2	0	2	8
*Andre Agassi	4	1	1	2	8
Henri Cochet	†	4	2	1	7
Rene Lacoste	†	3	2	2	7
Bill Larned	†	†	0	7	7
John McEnroe	0	0	3	4	7
John Newcombe	2	0	3	2	7
Willie Renshaw	†	†	7	†	7
Dick Sears	†	†	0	7	7

*Active player. †Did not compete.

WOMEN

Player	Aus.	French	Wim.	U.S.	Total
Margaret Smith Court	11	5	3	5	24
Steffi Graf	4	6	7	5	22
Helen Wills Moody	†	4	8	7	19
Chris Evert	2	7	3	6	18
Martina Navratilova	3	2	9	4	18
Billie Jean King	1	1	6	4	12
Maureen Connolly	1	2	3	3	9
*Monica Seles	4	3	0	2	9
Suzanne Lenglen	†	2#	6	0	8
Molla Bjurstedt Mallory	†	†	0	8	8
Maria Bueno	0	0	3	4	7
Evonne Goolagong	4	1	2	0	7
Dorothea D.L. Chambers	†	†	7	0	7
Nancye Wynne Bolton	6	0	0	0	6
Louise Brough	1	0	4	1	6
Margaret Osborne duPont	†	2	1	3	6
Doris Hart	1	2	1	2	6
Blanche Bingley Hillyard	†	†	6	†	6
*Serena Williams	1	1	2	2	6

*Active player. †Did not compete.
#Suzanne Lenglen also won four singles titles at the French Championships before 1925, when competition was first opened to entries from all nations.

National Team Competition

Davis Cup

the 1898 U.S. Championships. A Davis Cup meeting between two countries is known as a tie and is a three-day event consisting of two singles matches, followed by one doubles match and then two more singles matches. The United States boasts the greatest number of wins (31), followed by Australia (20).

Year	Winner	Finalist	Site	Score
1900	United States	Great Britain	Boston	3–0
1901	No tournament			
1902	United States	Great Britain	New York	3–2
1903	Great Britain	United States	Boston	4–1
1904	Great Britain	Belgium	Wimbledon	5–0
1905	Great Britain	United States	Wimbledon	5–0
1906	Great Britain	United States	Wimbledon	5–0
1907	Australasia	Great Britain	Wimbledon	3–2
1908	Australasia	United States	Melbourne	3–2
1909	Australasia	United States	Sydney	5–0
1910	No tournament			
1911	Australasia	United States	Christchurch, NZ	5–0
1912	Great Britain	Australasia	Melbourne	3–2
1913	United States	Great Britain	Wimbledon	3–2
1914	Australasia	United States	New York	3–2
1915–18	No tournament			
1919	Australasia	Great Britain	Sydney	4–1
1920	United States	Australasia	Auckland, NZ	5–0
1921	United States	Japan	New York	5–0
1922	United States	Australasia	New York	4–1
1923	United States	Australasia	New York	4–1
1924	United States	Australia	Philadelphia	5–0
1925	United States	France	Philadelphia	5–0
1926	United States	France	Philadelphia	4–1
1927	France	United States	Philadelphia	3–2
1928	France	United States	Paris	4–1
1929	France	United States	Paris	3–2
1930	France	United States	Paris	4–1
1931	France	Great Britain	Paris	3–2
1932	France	United States	Paris	3–2
1933	Great Britain	France	Paris	3–2
1934	Great Britain	United States	Wimbledon	4–1
1935	Great Britain	United States	Wimbledon	5–0
1936	Great Britain	Australia	Wimbledon	3–2
1937	United States	Great Britain	Wimbledon	4–1
1938	United States	Australia	Philadelphia	3–2
1939	Australia	United States	Philadelphia	3–2
1940–45	No tournament			
1946	United States	Australia	Melbourne	5–0
1947	United States	Australia	New York	4–1
1948	United States	Australia	New York	5–0
1949	United States	Australia	New York	4–1
1950	Australia	United States	New York	4–1
1951	Australia	United States	Sydney	3–2
1952	Australia	United States	Adelaide	4–1
1953	Australia	United States	Melbourne	3–2
1954	United States	Australia	Sydney	3–2
1955	Australia	United States	New York	5–0
1956	Australia	United States	Adelaide	5–0
1957	Australia	United States	Melbourne	3–2
1958	United States	Australia	Brisbane	3–2
1959	Australia	United States	New York	3–2
1960	Australia	Italy	Sydney	4–1
1961	Australia	Italy	Melbourne	5–0
1962	Australia	Mexico	Brisbane	5–0
1963	United States	Australia	Adelaide	3–2
1964	Australia	United States	Cleveland	3–2
1965	Australia	Spain	Sydney	4–1
1966	Australia	India	Melbourne	4–1
1967	Australia	Spain	Brisbane	4–1
1968	United States	Australia	Adelaide	4–1
1969	United States	Romania	Cleveland	5–0
1970	United States	W Germany	Cleveland	5–0
1971	United States	Romania	Charlotte, NC	3–2
1972	United States	Romania	Bucharest	3–2

Davis Cup (Cont.)

Year	Winner	Finalist	Site	Score
1973	Australia	United States	Cleveland	5–0
1974	South Africa	India	*	walkover
1975	Sweden	Czechoslovakia	Stockholm	3–2
1976	Italy	Chile	Santiago	4–1
1977	Australia	Italy	Sydney	3–1
1978	United States	Great Britain	Palm Springs	4–1
1979	United States	Italy	San Francisco	5–0
1980	Czechoslovakia	Italy	Prague	4–1
1981	United States	Argentina	Cincinnati	3–1
1982	United States	France	Grenoble, France	4–1
1983	Australia	Sweden	Melbourne	3–2
1984	Sweden	United States	Göteborg, Sweden	4–1
1985	Sweden	W Germany	Munich	3–2
1986	Australia	Sweden	Melbourne	3–2
1987	Sweden	India	Göteborg, Sweden	5–0
1988	West Germany	Sweden	Göteborg, Sweden	4–1
1989	West Germany	Sweden	Stuttgart	3–2
1990	United States	Australia	St. Petersburg	3–2
1991	France	United States	Lyon	3–1
1992	United States	Switzerland	Fort Worth, TX	3–1
1993	Germany	Australia	Dusseldorf	4–1
1994	Sweden	Russia	Moscow	4–1
1995	United States	Russia	Moscow	3–2
1996	France	Sweden	Malmö, Sweden	3–2
1997	Sweden	United States	Göteborg, Sweden	5–0
1998	Sweden	Italy	Milan	4–1
1999	Australia	France	Nice, France	3–2
2000	Spain	Australia	Barcelona	3–1
2001	France	Australia	Melbourne	3–2
2003	Russia	France	Paris	3–2

*India refused to play the final in protest over South Africa's governmental policy of apartheid.
Note: Prior to 1972 the challenge-round system was in effect, with the previous year's winner "standing out" of the competition until the finals. A straight 16-nation tournament has been held since 1981.

Federation Cup

The Federation Cup was started in 1963 by the International Lawn Tennis Federation (now the ITF). Until 1991 all entrants gathered at one site at one time for a tournament that was concluded within one week. Since 1995 the Fed Cup, as it is now called, has been contested in three rounds by a World Group of eight nations. A meeting between two countries now consists of five matches: four singles and one doubles. The United States has the most wins (15), followed by Australia (7).

Year	Winner	Finalist	Site	Score
1963	United States	Australia	London	2–1
1964	Australia	United States	Philadelphia	2–1
1965	Australia	United States	Melbourne	2–1
1966	United States	W Germany	Turin	3–0
1967	United States	Great Britain	W Berlin	2–0
1968	Australia	Netherlands	Paris	3–0
1969	United States	Australia	Athens	2–1
1970	Australia	Great Britain	Freiburg	3–0
1971	Australia	Great Britain	Perth	3–0
1972	South Africa	Great Britain	Johannesburg	2–1
1973	Australia	South Africa	Bad Homburg	3–0
1974	Australia	United States	Naples	2–1
1975	Czechoslovakia	Australia	Aix-en-Provence	3–0
1976	United States	Australia	Philadelphia	2–1
1977	United States	Australia	Eastbourne, G.B.	2–1
1978	United States	Australia	Melbourne	2–1
1979	United States	Australia	Madrid	3–0
1980	United States	Australia	W Berlin	3–0
1981	United States	Great Britain	Nagoya	3–0
1982	United States	W Germany	Santa Clara, CA	3–0
1983	Czechoslovakia	W Germany	Zurich	2–1
1984	Czechoslovakia	Australia	Sao Paulo	2–1
1985	Czechoslovakia	United States	Tokyo	2–1
1986	United States	Czechoslovakia	Prague	3–0
1987	W Germany	United States	Vancouver	2–1

Federation Cup (Cont.)

Year	Winner	Finalist	Site	Score
1988	Czechoslovakia	USSR	Melbourne	2–1
1989	United States	Spain	Tokyo	3–0
1990	United States	USSR	Atlanta	2–1
1991	Spain	United States	Nottingham	2–1
1992	Germany	Spain	Frankfurt	2–1
1993	Spain	Australia	Frankfurt	3–0
1994	Spain	United States	Frankfurt	3–0
1995	Spain	United States	Valencia, Spain	3–2
1996	United States	Spain	Atlantic City	5–0
1997	France	Netherlands	Hertogenbosch, Neth.	4–1
1998	Spain	Switzerland	Geneva	3–2
1999	United States	Russia	Palo Alto, California	4–1
2000	United States	Spain	Las Vegas, Nevada	5–0
2001	Belgium	Russia	Barcelona	2–1
2002	Slovak Republic	Spain	Maspalomas, C. Isles	3–1

Rankings

ATP Computer Year-End Top 10
MEN

1973
1. Ilie Nastase
2. John Newcombe
3. Jimmy Connors
4. Tom Okker
5. Stan Smith
6. Ken Rosewall
7. Manuel Orantes
8. Rod Laver
9. Jan Kodes
10. Arthur Ashe

1974
1. Jimmy Connors
2. John Newcombe
3. Bjorn Borg
4. Rod Laver
5. Guillermo Vilas
6. Tom Okker
7. Arthur Ashe
8. Ken Rosewall
9. Stan Smith
10. Ilie Nastase

1975
1. Jimmy Connors
2. Guillermo Vilas
3. Bjorn Borg
4. Arthur Ashe
5. Manuel Orantes
6. Ken Rosewall
7. Ilie Nastase
8. John Alexander
9. Roscoe Tanner
10. Rod Laver

1976
1. Jimmy Connors
2. Bjorn Borg
3. Ilie Nastase
4. Manuel Orantes
5. Raul Ramirez
6. Guillermo Vilas
7. Adriano Panatta
8. Harold Solomon
9. Eddie Dibbs
10. Brian Gottfried

1977
1. Jimmy Connors
2. Guillermo Vilas
3. Bjorn Borg
4. Vitas Gerulaitis
5. Brian Gottfried
6. Eddie Dibbs
7. Manuel Orantes
8. Raul Ramirez
9. Ilie Nastase
10. Dick Stockton

1978
1. Jimmy Connors
2. Bjorn Borg
3. Guillermo Vilas
4. John McEnroe
5. Vitas Gerulaitis
6. Eddie Dibbs
7. Brian Gottfried
8. Raul Ramirez
9. Harold Solomon
10. Corrado Barazzutti

1979
1. Bjorn Borg
2. Jimmy Connors
3. John McEnroe
4. Vitas Gerulaitis
5. Roscoe Tanner
6. Guillermo Vilas
7. Arthur Ashe
8. Harold Solomon
9. Jose Higueras
10. Eddie Dibbs

1980
1. Bjorn Borg
2. John McEnroe
3. Jimmy Connors
4. Gene Mayer
5. Guillermo Vilas
6. Ivan Lendl
7. Harold Solomon
8. Jose–Luis Clerc
9. Vitas Gerulaitis
10. Eliot Teltscher

1981
1. John McEnroe
2. Ivan Lendl
3. Jimmy Connors
4. Bjorn Borg
5. Jose–Luis Clerc
6. Guillermo Vilas
7. Gene Mayer
8. Eliot Teltscher
9. Vitas Gerulaitis
10. Peter McNamara

ATP Computer Year-End Top 10
MEN (CONT.)

1982
1 ....John McEnroe
2 ....Jimmy Connors
3 ....Ivan Lendl
4 ....Guillermo Vilas
5 ....Vitas Gerulaitis
6 ....Jose–Luis Clerc
7 ....Mats Wilander
8 ....Gene Mayer
9 ....Yannick Noah
10 ..Peter McNamara

1983
1 ....John McEnroe
2 ....Ivan Lendl
3 ....Jimmy Connors
4 ....Mats Wilander
5 ....Yannick Noah
6 ....Jimmy Arias
7 ....Jose Higueras
8 ....Jose–Luis Clerc
9 ....Kevin Curren
10 ..Gene Mayer

1984
1 ....John McEnroe
2 ....Jimmy Connors
3 ....Ivan Lendl
4 ....Mats Wilander
5 ....Andres Gomez
6 ....Anders Jarryd
7 ....Henrik Sundstrom
8 ....Pat Cash
9 ....Eliot Teltscher
10 ..Yannick Noah

1985
1 ....Ivan Lendl
2 ....John McEnroe
3 ....Mats Wilander
4 ....Jimmy Connors
5 ....Stefan Edberg
6 ....Boris Becker
7 ....Yannick Noah
8 ....Anders Jarryd
9 ....Miloslav Mecir
10 ..Kevin Curren

1986
1 ....Ivan Lendl
2 ....Boris Becker
3 ....Mats Wilander
4 ....Yannick Noah
5 ....Stefan Edberg
6 ....Henri Leconte
7 ....Joakim Nystrom
8 ....Jimmy Connors
9 ....Miloslav Mecir
10 ..Andres Gomez

1987
1 ....Ivan Lendl
2 ....Stefan Edberg
3 ....Mats Wilander
4 ....Jimmy Connors
5 ....Boris Becker
6 ....Miloslav Mecir
7 ....Pat Cash
8 ....Yannick Noah
9 ....Tim Mayotte
10 ..John McEnroe

1988
1 ....Mats Wilander
2 ....Ivan Lendl
3 ....Andre Agassi
4 ....Boris Becker
5 ....Stefan Edberg
6 ....Kent Carlsson
7 ....Jimmy Connors
8 ....Jakob Hlasek
9 ....Henri Leconte
10 ...Tim Mayotte

1989
1 ....Ivan Lendl
2 ....Boris Becker
3 ....Stefan Edberg
4 ....John McEnroe
5 ....Michael Chang
6 ....Brad Gilbert
7 ....Andre Agassi
8 ....Aaron Krickstein
9 ....Alberto Mancini
10 ..Jay Berger

1990
1 ....Stefan Edberg
2 ....Boris Becker
3 ....Ivan Lendl
4 ....Andre Agassi
5 ....Pete Sampras
6 ....Andres Gomez
7 ....Thomas Muster
8 ....Emilio Sanchez
9 ....Goran Ivanisevic
10 ..Brad Gilbert

1991
1 ....Stefan Edberg
2 ....Jim Courier
3 ....Boris Becker
4 ....Michael Stich
5 ....Ivan Lendl
6 ....Pete Sampras
7 ....Guy Forget
8 ....Karel Novacek
9 ....Petr Korda
10 ..Andre Agassi

1992
1 ....Jim Courier
2 ....Stefan Edberg
3 ....Pete Sampras
4 ....Goran Ivanisevic
5 ....Boris Becker
6 ....Michael Chang
7 ....Petr Korda
8 ....Ivan Lendl
9 ....Andre Agassi
10 ..Richard Krajicek

1993
1 ....Pete Sampras
2 ....Michael Stich
3 ....Jim Courier
4 ....Sergi Bruguera
5 ....Stefan Edberg
6 ....Andrei Medvedev
7 ....Goran Ivanisevic
8 ....Michael Chang
9 ....Thomas Muster
10 ..Cedric Pioline

1994
1 ....Pete Sampras
2 ....Andre Agassi
3 ....Boris Becker
4 ....Sergi Bruguera
5 ....Goran Ivanisevic
6 ....Michael Chang
7 ....Stefan Edberg
8 ....Alberto Berasategui
9 ....Michael Stich
10 ..Todd Martin

1995
1 ....Pete Sampras
2 ....Andre Agassi
3 ....Thomas Muster
4 ....Boris Becker
5 ....Michael Chang
6 ....Yevgeny Kafelnikov
7 ....Thomas Enqvist
8 ....Jim Courier
9 ....Wayne Ferreira
10 ...Goran Ivanisevic

1996
1 ....Pete Sampras
2 ....Michael Chang
3 ....Yevgeny Kafelnikov
4 ....Goran Ivanisevic
5 ....Thomas Muster
6 ....Boris Becker
7 ....Richard Krajicek
8 ....Andre Agassi
9 ....Thomas Enqvist
10 ...Wayne Ferreira

ATP Computer Year-End Top 10

MEN *(CONT.)*

1997
1 ....Pete Sampras
2 ....Patrick Rafter
3 ....Michael Chang
4 ....Jonas Bjorkman
5 ....Yevgeny Kafelnikov
6 ....Greg Rusedski
7 ....Carlos Moya
8 ....Sergei Bruguera
9 ....Thomas Muster
10..Marcelo Ríos

1998
1 ....Pete Sampras
2 ....Marcelo Rios
3 ....Alex Corretja
4 ....Patrick Rafter
5 ....Carlos Moya
6 ....Andre Agassi
7 ....Tim Henman
8 ....Karol Kucera
9 ...Greg Rusedski
10..Richard Krajicek

1999
1 ....Andre Agassi
2 ....Yevgeny Kafelnikov
3 ....Pete Sampras
4 ....Thomas Enqvist
5 ....Gustavo Kuerten
6 ....Nicolas Kiefer
7 ....Todd Martin
8 ....Nicolas Lapentti
9 ....Marcelo Rios
10 ..Richard Krajicek

2000
1 ....Gustavo Kuerten
2 ....Marat Safin
3 ...Pete Sampras
4 ....Magnus Norman
5 ....Yevgeny Kafelnikov
6 ....Andre Agassi
7 ....Lleyton Hewitt
8 ....Alex Corretja
9 ....Thomas Enqvist
10 ..Tim Henman

2001
1 ....Lleyton Hewitt
2 ....Gustavo Kuerten
3 ....Andre Agassi
4 ....Yevgeny Kafelnikov
5 ....Juan Carlos Ferrero
6 ....Sebastien Grosjean
7 ....Patrick Rafter
8 ....Tommy Haas
9 ....Tim Henman
10 ..Pete Sampras

2002
1 ....Lleyton Hewitt
2 ....Andre Agassi
3 ....Marat Safin
4 ....Juan Carlos Ferrero
5 ....Carlos Moya
6 ....Roger Federer
7 ....Jiri Novak
8 ....Tim Henman
9 ....Albert Costa
10 ..Andy Roddick

WTA Computer Year-End Top 10

WOMEN

1973
1 ....Margaret Smith
      Court
2 ....Billie Jean King
3 ....Evonne Goolagong
4 ....Chris Evert
5 ....Rosie Casals
6 ....Virginia Wade
7 ....Kerry Reid
8 ....Nancy Gunter
9 ....Julie Heldman
10..Helga Masthoff

1974
1 ....Billie Jean King
2 ....Evonne Goolagong
3 ....Chris Evert
4 ....Virginia Wade
5 ....Julie Heldman
6 ....Rosie Casals
7 ....Kerry Reid
8 ....Olga Morozova
9 ....Lesley Hunt
10..Francoise Durr

1975
1 ....Chris Evert
2 ....Billie Jean King
3 ....Evonne Goolagong
      Cawley
4 ....Martina Navratilova
5 ....Virginia Wade
6 ....Margaret Smith
      Court
7 ....Olga Morozova
8 ....Nancy Gunter
9 ....Francoise Durr
10..Rosie Casals

1976
1 ....Chris Evert
2 ....Evonne Goolagong
      Cawley
3 ...Virginia Wade
4 ....Martina Navratilova
5 ....Sue Barker
6 ....Betty Stove
7 ....Dianne Balestrat
8 ....Mima Jausovec
9 ....Rosie Casals
10...Francoise Durr

1977
1 ....Chris Evert
2 ...Billie Jean King
3 ....Martina Navratilova
4 ....Virginia Wade
5 ....Sue Barker
6 ...Rosie Casals
7 ....Betty Stove
8 ...Dianne Balestrat
9 ....Wendy Turnbull
10...Kerry Reid

1978
1 ....Martina Navratilova
2 ....Chris Evert
3 ....Evonne Goolagong
      Cawley
4 ....Virginia Wade
5 ....Billie Jean King
6 ....Tracy Austin
7 ....Wendy Turnbull
8 ....Kerry Reid
9 ....Betty Stove
10...Dianne Balestrat

1979
1 ....Martina Navratilova
2 ....Chris Evert Lloyd
3 ....Tracy Austin
4 ....Evonne Goolagong
      Cawley
5 ....Billie Jean King
6 ....Dianne Balestrat
7 ....Wendy Turnbull
8 ....Virginia Wade
9 ....Kerry Reid
10...Sue Barker

1980
1 ....Chris Evert Lloyd
2 ....Tracy Austin
3 ....Martina Navratilova
4 ....Hana Mandlikova
5 ....Evonne Goolagong
      Cawley
6 ....Billie Jean King
7 ....Andrea Jaeger
8 ....Wendy Turnbull
9 ....Pam Shriver
10...Greer Stevens

1981
1 ....Chris Evert Lloyd
2 ....Tracy Austin
3 ....Martina Navratilova
4 ....Andrea Jaeger
5 ....Hana Mandlikova
6 ....Sylvia Hanika
7 ....Pam Shriver
8 ....Wendy Turnbull
9 ....Bettina Bunge
10...Barbara Potter

1982
1 ....Martina Navratilova
2 ....Chris Evert Lloyd
3 ....Andrea Jaeger
4 ....Tracy Austin
5 ....Wendy Turnbull
6 ....Pam Shriver
7 ....Hana Mandlikova
8 ....Barbara Potter
9 ....Bettina Bunge
10...Sylvia Hanika

1983
1 ....Martina Navratilova
2 ....Chris Evert Lloyd
3 ....Andrea Jaeger
4 ....Pam Shriver
5 ....Sylvia Hanika
6 ....Jo Durie
7 ....Bettina Bunge
8 ....Wendy Turnbull
9 ....Tracy Austin
10...Zina Garrison

1984
1 ....Martina Navratilova
2 ....Chris Evert Lloyd
3 ....Hana Mandlikova
4 ....Pam Shriver
5 ....Wendy Turnbull
6 ....Manuela Maleeva
7 ....Helena Sukova
8 ....Claudia Kohde-
      Kilsch
9 ....Zina Garrison
10...Kathy Jordan

WTA Computer Year-End Top 10 (Cont.)
WOMEN (CONT.)

1985
1 ....Martina Navratilova
2 ....Chris Evert Lloyd
3 ....Hana Mandlikova
4 ....Pam Shriver
5 ....Claudia Kohde-
      Kilsch
6 ....Steffi Graf
7 ....Manuela Maleeva
8 ....Zina Garrison
9 ....Helena Sukova
10...Bonnie Gadusek

1986
1 ....Martina Navratilova
2 ....Chris Evert Lloyd
3 ....Pam Shriver
4 ....Hana Mandlikova
5 ....Helena Sukova
6 ....Pam Shriver
7 ....Claudia Kohde-
      Kilsch
8 ....Manuela Maleeva
9 ....Kathy Rinaldi
10...Gabriela Sabatini

1987
1 ....Steffi Graf
2 ....Martina Navratilova
3 ....Chris Evert
4 ....Pam Shriver
5 ....Hana Mandlikova
6 ....Gabriela Sabatini
7 ....Helena Sukova
8 ....Manuela Maleeva
9 ....Zina Garrison
10...Claudia Kohde-
      Kilsch

1988
1 ....Steffi Graf
2 ....Martina Navratilova
3 ....Chris Evert
4 ....Gabriela Sabatini
5 ....Pam Shriver
6 ....Manuela Maleeva-
      Fragniere
7 ....Natalia Zvereva
8 ....Helena Sukova
9 ....Zina Garrison
10...Barbara Potter

1989
1 ....Steffi Graf
2 ....Martina Navratilova
3 ....Gabriela Sabatini
4 ....Zina Garrison
5 ....A.S. Vicario
6 ....Monica Seles
7 ....Conchita Martinez
8 ....Helena Sukova
9 ....Manuela Maleeva-
      Fragniere
10...Chris Evert*

1990
1 ....Steffi Graf
2 ....Monica Seles
3 ....Martina Navratilova
4 ....Mary Joe Fernandez
5 ....Gabriela Sabatini
6 ....Katerina Maleeva
7 ....A.S. Vicario
8 ....Jennifer Capriati
9 ....M. Maleeva-Fragniere
10...Zina Garrison

1991
1 ....Monica Seles
2 ....Steffi Graf
3 ....Gabriela Sabatini
4 ....Martina Navratilova
5 ....Arantxa Sánchez
      Vicario
6 ....Jennifer Capriati
7 ....Jana Novotna
8 ....Mary Joe Fernandez
9 ....Conchita Martinez
10...M. Maleeva-Fragniere

1992
1 ....Monica Seles
2 ....Steffi Graf
3 ....Gabriela Sabatini
4 ....Arantxa Sánchez
      Vicario
5 ....Martina Navratilova
6 ....Mary Joe Fernandez
7 ....Jennifer Capriati
8 ....Conchita Martinez
9 ....M. Maleeva-Fragniere
10 ..Jana Novotna

1993
1 ....Steffi Graf
2 ....Arantxa Sánchez
      Vicario
3 ....Martina Navratilova
4 ....Conchita Martinez
5 ....Gabriela Sabatini
6 ....Jana Novotna
7 ....Mary Joe Fernandez
8 ....Monica Seles
9 ....Jennifer Capriati
10 ..Anke Huber

1994
1 ....Steffi Graf
2 ....Arantxa Sánchez
      Vicario
3 ....Conchita Martinez
4 ....Jana Novotna
5 ....Mary Pierce
6 ....Lindsay Davenport
7 ....Gabriela Sabatini
8 ....Martina Navratilova
9 ....Kimiko Date
10 ..Natasha Zvereva

1995
1 ....Steffi Graf (co-No. 1)
1 ....Monica Seles
      (co-No. 1)
2 ....Conchita Martinez
3 ....A: S.Vicario
4 ....Kimiko Date
5 ....Mary Pierce
6 ....Magdalena Maleeva
7 ....Gabriela Sabatini
8 ....Mary Joe Fernandez
9 ....Iva Majoli
10 ..Anke Huber

1996
1 ....Steffi Graf
2 ....Monica Seles
3 ....Jana Novotna
4 ....Lindsay Davenport
5 ....Martina Hingis
6 ....Stephanie de Ville
7 ....Tamarine
      Tanasugarn
8 ....Anke Huber
9 ....Conchita Martinez
10 ..Julie Halard-
      Decugis

1997
1 ....Martina Hingis
2 ....Jana Novotna
3 ....Lindsay Davenport
4 ....Amanda Coetzer
5 ....Monica Seles
6 ....Iva Majoli
7 ....Mary Pierce
8 ....Irina Spirlea
9 ....Arantxa Sánchez
Vicario
10 ...Mary Joe Fernandez

1998
1 ....Lindsay Davenport
2 ....Martina Hingis
2 ....Jana Novotna
4 ....A.S. Vicario
5 ....Venus Williams
6 ....Monica Seles
7 ....Mary Pierce
8 ....Conchita Martinez
9 ....Steffi Graf
10...Nathalie Tauziat

1999
1 ....Martina Hingis
2 ....Lindsay Davenport
3 ....Venus Williams
4 ....Serena Williams
5 ....Mary Pierce
6 ....Monica Seles
7 ....Nathalie Tauziat
8 ....Barbara Schett
9 ....J. Halard-Decugis
10 ..Amelie Mauresmo

2000
1 ....Martina Hingis
2 ....Lindsay Davenport
3 ....Venus Williams
4 ....Monica Seles
5 ....Conchita Martinez
6 ....Serena Williams
7 ....Mary Pierce
8 ....Anna Kournikova
9 ....Arantxa
      Sánchez Vicario
10 ..Nathalie Tauziat

2001
1 ....Lindsay Davenport
2 ....Jennifer Capriati
3 ....Venus Williams
4 ....Martina Hingis
5 ....Kim Clijsters
6 ....Serena Williams
7 ....Justine Henin
8 ....Jelena Dokic
9 ....Amelie Mauresmo
10 ..Monica Seles

2002
1 ....Serena Williams
2 ....Venus Williams
3 ....Jennifer Capriati
4 ....Kim Clijsters
5 ....Justine Henin
6 ....Amelie Mauresmo
7 ....Monica Seles
8 ....Daniela Hantuchova
9 ....Jelena Dokic
10 ..Martina Hingis

*When Chris Evert announced her retirement at the 1989 United States Open, she was ranked fourth in the world. That was her last official series tournament.

Prize Money

Top 25 Men's Career Prize Money Leaders

Note: From arrival of Open tennis in 1968 through December 9, 2002.

	Earnings ($)
Pete Sampras	43,280,489
Andre Agassi	25,658,496
Boris Becker	25,080,956
Yevgeny Kafelnikov	23,202,345
Ivan Lendl	21,262,417
Stefan Edberg	20,630,941
Goran Ivanisevic	19,748,638
Michael Chang	19,070,332
Jim Courier	14,033,132
Gustavo Kuerten	13,456,299
Michael Stich	12,590,152
John McEnroe	12,539,622
Thomas Muster	12,224,410
Sergi Bruguera	11,632,199
Patrick Rafter	11,103,311
Lleyton Hewitt	10,862,801
Petr Korda	10,448,450
Richard Krajicek	9,977,484
Alex Corretja	9,828,939
Thomas Enqvist	9,784,703
Marcelo Rios	9,404,181
Wayne Ferreira	9,227,992
Jonas Bjorkman	9,114,985
Todd Woodbridge	8,688,899
Jimmy Connors	8,641,040

Top 25 Women's Career Prize Money Leaders

Note: From arrival of Open tennis in 1968 through October 6, 2003.

	Earnings ($)
Steffi Graf	21,895,277
Martina Navratilova	20,888,793
Martina Hingis	18,344,660
Arantxa Sánchez Vicario	16,917,312
Lindsay Davenport	16,120,654
Monica Seles	14,815,095
Venus Williams	12,901,130
Serena Williams	12,291,030
Jana Novotna	11,249,134
Conchita Martinez	10,589,990
Chris Evert	8,896,195
Gabriela Sabatini	8,785,850
Jennifer Capriati	7,977,644
Natasha Zvereva	7,792,503
Mary Pierce	6,700,645
Nathalie Tauziat	6,649,907
Kim Clijsters	6,461,044
Helena Sukova	6,391,245
Amanda Coetzer	5,528,360
Pam Shriver	5,460,566
Justine Henin-Hardenne	5,460,514
Mary Joe Fernandez	5,258,471
Lisa Raymond	5,001,618
Anke Huber	4,768,292
Gigi Fernandez	4,681,906

THEY SAID IT

Andy Roddick, 20-year-old U.S. tennis player, responding to a female reporter who asked him if he enjoys being the "new sex symbol" of tennis: "Do you want to go to dinner later?"

Open Era Overall Wins

Men's Career Leaders—Singles Titles Won

The top tournament-winning men from the institution of Open tennis in 1968 through Oct 8, 2003.

	W		W
Jimmy Connors	109	Thomas Muster	44
Ivan Lendl	94	Stefan Edberg	41
John McEnroe	77	Stan Smith	39
Pete Sampras	64	Michael Chang	34
Bjorn Borg	62	Arthur Ashe	33
Guillermo Vilas	62	Mats Wilander	33
Andre Agassi	58	John Newcombe	32
Ilie Nastase	57	Manuel Orantes	32
Boris Becker	49	Ken Rosewall	32
Rod Laver	47	Tom Okker	31

Women's Career Leaders—Singles Titles Won

The top tournament-winning women from the institution of Open tennis in 1968 through Oct. 8, 2003.

	W		W
Martina Navratilova	167	Tracy Austin	29
Chris Evert	157	Arantxa Sánchez Vicario	29
Steffi Graf	108	Venus Williams	28
Evonne Goolagong Cawley	88	Hana Mandlikova	27
Margaret Smith Court	79	Gabriela Sabatini	27
Billie Jean King	67	Nancy Richey	25
Virginia Wade	55	Jana Novotna	24
Monica Seles	53	Serena Williams	23
Martina Hingis	40	Kerry Melville Reid	22
Lindsay Davenport	37		
Conchita Martinez	32		

Annual ATP/WTA Champions

Men—ATP Tour World Championship

Year	Player	Year	Player
1970	Stan Smith	1986 (Dec)	Ivan Lendl
1971	Ilie Nastase	1987	Ivan Lendl
1972	Ilie Nastase	1988	Boris Becker
1973	Ilie Nastase	1989	Stefan Edberg
1974	Guillermo Vilas	1990	Andre Agassi
1975	Ilie Nastase	1991	Pete Sampras
1976	Manuel Orantes	1992	Boris Becker
1977	Not held	1993	Michael Stich
1978	Jimmy Connors	1994	Pete Sampras
1979	John McEnroe	1995	Boris Becker
1980	Bjorn Borg	1996	Pete Sampras
1981	Bjorn Borg	1997	Pete Sampras
1982	Ivan Lendl	1998	Alex Corretja
1983	Ivan Lendl	1999	Pete Sampras
1984	John McEnroe	2000	Gustavo Kuerten
1985	John McEnroe	2001	Lleyton Hewitt
1986 (Jan)	Ivan Lendl	2002	Lleyton Hewitt

Note: Event held twice in 1986. *Since 1984 the final has been best-of-five sets.

Women—WTA Tour Championship

Year	Player	Year	Player
1972	Chris Evert	1987	Steffi Graf
1973	Chris Evert	1988	Gabriela Sabatini
1974	Evonne Goolagong	1989	Steffi Graf
1975	Chris Evert	1990	Monica Seles
1976	Evonne Goolagong Cawley	1991	Monica Seles
1977	Chris Evert	1992	Monica Seles
1978	Martina Navratilova	1993	Steffi Graf
1979	Martina Navratilova	1994	Gabriela Sabatini
1980	Tracy Austin	1995	Steffi Graf
1981	Martina Navratilova	1996	Steffi Graf
1982	Sylvia Hanika	1997	Jana Novotna
1983	Martina Navratilova	1998	Martina Hingis
1984*	Martina Navratilova	1999	Lindsay Davenport
1985	Martina Navratilova	2000	Martina Hingis
1986 (Mar)	Martina Navratilova	2001	Serena Williams
1986 (Nov)	Martina Navratilova	2002	Kim Clijsters

YET ANOTHER SIGN OF THE APOCALYPSE

The father of a 16-year-old tennis player in France was arrested under suspicion of slipping a fatigue-inducing drug into the water bottles of his son's opponents.

Pauline Betz Addie (1965)
George T. Adee (1964)
Fred B. Alexander (1961)
Wilmer L. Allison (1963)
Manuel Alonso (1977)
Malcolm Anderson (2000)
Arthur Ashe (1985)
Juliette Atkinson (1974)
H.W. Bunny Austin (1997)
Tracy Austin (1992)
Lawrence A. Baker Sr. (1975)
Maud Barger-Wallach (1958)
Angela Mortimer Barrett (1993)
Boris Becker (2003)
Karl Behr (1969)
Bjorn Borg (1987)
Jean Borotra (1976)
Lesley Turner Bowrey (1997)
Maureen Connolly Brinker (1968)
John Bromwich (1984)
Norman Everard Brookes (1977)
Mary K. Browne (1957)
Jacques Brugnon (1976)
J. Donald Budge (1964)
Maria E. Bueno (1978)
May Sutton Bundy (1956)
Mabel E. Cahill (1976)
Rosie Casals (1996)
Oliver S. Campbell (1955)
Malcolm Chace (1961)
Dorothea Douglass
  Chambers (1981)
Philippe Chatrier (1992)
Louise Brough Clapp (1967)
Clarence Clark (1983)
Joseph S. Clark (1955)
William J. Clothier (1956)
Henri Cochet (1976)
Arthur W. (Bud) Collins Jr. (1994)
Jimmy Connors (1998)
Ashley Cooper (1991)
Margaret Smith Court (1979)
Gottfried von Cramm (1977)
Jack Crawford (1979)
Joseph F. Cullman III (1990)
Allison Danzig (1968)
Sarah Palfrey Danzig (1963)
Herman David (1998)
Dwight F. Davis (1956)
Charlotte Dod (1983)
John H. Doeg (1962)
Lawrence Doherty (1980)

Reginald Doherty (1980)
Jaroslav Drobny (1983)
Margaret Osborne duPont
  (1967)
Francoise Durr (2003)
James Dwight (1955)
Roy Emerson (1982)
Pierre Etchebaster (1978)
Chris Evert (1995)
Robert Falkenburg (1974)
Neale Fraser (1984)
Shirley Fry-Irvin (1970)
Charles S. Garland (1969)
Althea Gibson (1971)
Kathleen McKane Godfree
  (1978)
Richard A. Gonzales (1968)
Evonne Goolagong Cawley
  (1988)
Bryan M. Grant Jr. (1972)
David Gray (1985)
Clarence Griffin (1970)
King Gustaf V of Sweden
  (1980)
Harold H. Hackett (1961)
Ellen Forde Hansell (1965)
Darlene R. Hard (1973)
Doris J. Hart (1969)
Gladys M. Heldman (1979)
W.E. (Slew) Hester Jr. (1981)
Bob Hewitt (1992)
Lew Hoad (1980)
Harry Hopman (1978)
Fred Hovey (1974)
Joseph R. Hunt (1966)
Lamar Hunt (1993)
Francis T. Hunter (1961)
Helen Hull Jacobs (1962)
William Johnston (1958)
Ann Haydon Jones (1985)
Perry Jones (1970)
Robert Kelleher (2000)
Billie Jean King (1987)
Jan Kodes (1990)
John A. Kramer (1968)
Rene Lacoste (1976)
Al Laney (1979)
William A. Larned (1956)
Arthur D. Larsen (1969)
Rod G. Laver (1981)
Ivan Lendl (2001)
Suzanne Lenglen (1978)

Dorothy Round Little (1986)
George M. Lott Jr. (1964)
Gene Mako (1973)
Molla Bjurstedt Mallory (1958)
Hana Mandlikova (1994)
Alice Marble (1964)
Alastair B. Martin (1973)
Dan Maskell (1996)
William McChesney Martin (1982)
John McEnroe (1999)
Ken McGregor (1999)
Chuck McKinley (1986)
Maurice McLoughlin (1957)
Frew McMillan (1992)
W. Donald McNeill (1965)
Elisabeth H. Moore (1971)
Gardnar Mulloy (1972)
R. Lindley Murray (1958)
Julian S. Myrick (1963)
Ilie Nastase (1991)
Martina Navratilova (2000)
John D. Newcombe (1986)
Arthur C. Nielsen Sr (1971)
Alex Olmedo (1987)
Rafael Osuna (1979)
Mary Ewing Outerbridge (1981)
Frank A. Parker (1966)
Gerald Patterson (1989)
Budge Patty (1977)
Theodore R. Pell (1966)
Fred Perry (1975)
Tom Pettitt (1982)
Nicola Pietrangeli (1986)
Adrian Quist (1984)
Dennis Ralston (1987)
Ernest Renshaw (1983)
William Renshaw (1983)
Vincent Richards (1961)
Nancy Richey (2003)
Bobby Riggs (1967)
Helen Wills Moody Roark
  (1959)
Anthony D. Roche (1986)
Ellen C. Roosevelt (1975)
Mervyn Rose (2001)
Ken Rosewall (1980)
Elizabeth Ryan (1972)
Manuel Santana (1984)
Richard Savitt (1976)
Frederick R. Schroeder (1966)
Eleonora Sears (1968)
Richard D. Sears (1955)

Frank Sedgman (1979)
Pancho Segura (1984)
Vic Seixas Jr. (1971)
Francis X. Shields (1964)
Betty Nuthall Shoemaker (1977)
Pam Shriver (2002)
Henry W. Slocum Jr. (1955)
Stan Smith (1987)
Fred Stolle (1985)
William F. Talbert (1967)
Bill Tilden (1959)
Lance Tingay (1982)
Ted Tinling (1986)
Brian Tobin (2003)

Bertha Townsend Toulmin
  (1974)
Tony Trabert (1970)
James H. Van Alen (1965)
John Van Ryn (1963)
Guillermo Vilas (1991)
Ellsworth Vines (1962)
Virginia Wade (1989)
Marie Wagner (1969)
Holcombe Ward (1956)
Watson Washburn (1965)
Malcolm D. Whitman (1955)
Hazel Hotchkiss Wightman
  (1957)

Mats Wilander (2002)
Anthony Wilding (1978)
Richard Norris Williams II
  (1957)
Major Walter Clopton Wingfield
  (1997)
Sidney B. Wood (1964)
Robert D. Wrenn (1955)
Beals C. Wright (1956)

Note: Years in parentheses are dates of induction.

THEY SAID IT

Martina Navratilova, tennis legend and gay activist, on Damir Dokic, WTA pro Jelena Dokic's father, who said he might kill himself if he found out his daughter was a lesbian: "It's a good thing I'm not his daughter then . . . . [Actually] maybe it's too bad I'm not."

Golf

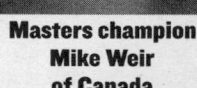

Masters champion
Mike Weir
of Canada

First Time's a Charm

That was the case for this year's PGA major winners, each of whom had never won a Grand Slam event before

BY STEPHEN CANNELLA

After six years of domination by a certain Nike-clad terminator, the golf world belonged to an unlikely collection of no-namers, trailblazers, hellraisers and one very precocious ninth-grader in 2003. Four new names—Mike Weir, Jim Furyk, Ben Curtis and Shaun Micheel—were added to the list of golfers who have won a major championship, the first time the Grand Slams were swept by rookie major winners since 1969. In May, at the Bank of America Colonial in Ft. Worth, Tex., Annika Sorenstam became the first woman to tee off in a PGA event in 58 years. It wasn't quite a Jackie Robinson moment, but the LPGA's best player held her own against the men and did her gender proud.

Whether women's rights activist Martha Burk did the same earlier in the year is open to debate. Burk helped turn the Masters into a circus with her lengthy and loud protest against the Augusta National Golf Club's men-only membership policy. While Burk railed against one of golf's musty traditions, the sport's future dawned in the person of amateur Michelle Wie, who exploded on the scene with a ninth-place finish at the Kraft Nabisco Championship, one of the LPGA's majors. Only 13 years old, Wie threatened to make Tiger Woods look like a late-bloomer.

Ah yes, Tiger. It's not that Woods faded into obscurity at the ripe old age of 27, though he did disappear for a monthlong, mind-clearing sabbatical in September. After notching his Tour-leading fifth victory of the year at the WGC-American Express Championship in October, Woods entered the schedule's stretch holding the top spot in the world rankings and on the PGA money list.

Still, the routinely transcendent Woods failed to capture a major championship for the first time since 1998, and he had little more than a passing role in the year's biggest stories. It didn't start out that way. Tiger went into the Masters seeking an unprecedented third straight victory at Augusta. A long course (7,290-yards) made squishy and slow by torrents of rain in the days before the tournament made him the prohibitive favorite.

Sorenstam played the Colonial for personal, not political, reasons.

The rain was appropriate, given the black cloud that had hovered over hallowed Augusta National for months. In July 2002, Burk, the chairwoman of National Council of Women's Organizations, sent a letter to Augusta chairman Hootie Johnson requesting that women be admitted to the club. Johnson refused, saying his was a private organization that would never bow to public presssure.

During the ensuing months the Martha and Hootie spat devolved into an embarrassing spectacle of hardheaded grandstanding from both sides. Many golfers were criticized for not taking a strong stand against Augusta's exclusionary tradition. A few weeks before the tournament, Woods, who had been urged to boycott the event in a *New York Times* editorial, told reporters, "I think [the Masters] has become not just about a golf tournament anymore."

With protesters and camera crews everywhere, rain washed out the opening round. When play finally began with a 36-hole marathon on Masters Friday, Woods stumbled out of the gate and came within a stroke of missing the cut for the first time in 103 tournaments.

Canada's Mike Weir quietly took the lead with a second-round 68. Weir, 32, had two victories earlier in the year, at the Nissan Open and the Bob Hope Classic, but he was best known—if he was known at all—for collapsing against Woods in the final round of the 1999 PGA Championship. Weir began the final round in second place, two strokes behind leader Jeff Maggert.

Woods, for his part, had climbed back into contention with a blistering third-round 66 that put him four strokes off the lead. More drama unfolded on Sunday, but Woods wasn't part of it. His final-round charge fell apart when he double-bogeyed the third hole. Maggert also fell flat on Sunday.

That left Weir and 35-year-old journeyman Len Mattiace, who eagled the par-5 13th on Sunday to complete an astonishing climb from eighth place to first. Par on the final hole would have given Mattiace a vise grip on the tournament, but his errant drive and subsequent bogey on 18 left the door open for Weir. The Canadian calmly sank a molar-grinding seven-foot putt on 18 to complete a round of 68 and force a playoff for the green jacket.

Neither golfer distinguished himself on the extra hole. Weir missed a six-foot putt for par. Mattiace hammered his par attempt 18 feet past the hole, then missed again. Weir's tap-in gave him his first bogey of the day—and the green jacket. (No one had ever won a Masters playoff with a bogey.) He became the first Canadian to win a major and the first lefty to do so in 40 years. All in the midst of the Martha-Hootie engendered distractions.

The Colonial is usually one of the Tour's sleepier stops, but Sorenstam's presence

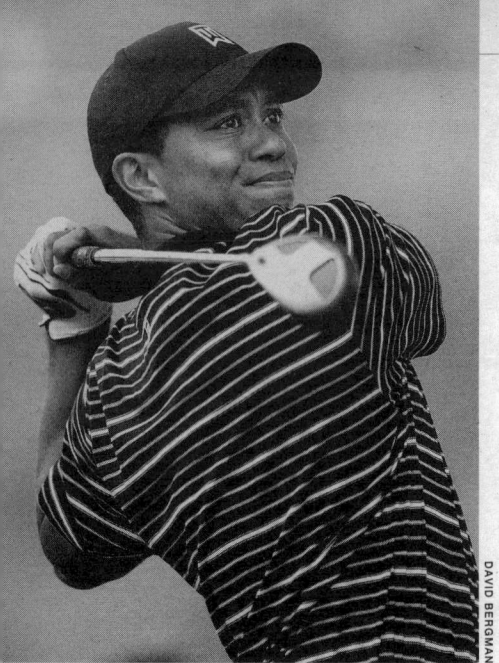

DAVID BERGMAN

Woods won five tournaments and led the PGA money list down the stretch, yet could still consider 2003 a substandard year.

A year removed from playing on the Hooters Tour, Curtis, a self-taught and self-coached grinder, calmly withstood charges from some of golf's elite in the final round. He bested Singh and Thomas Bjornby by a stroke and Woods and Davis Love III by two. On one of the world's most difficult courses Curtis was the only player to finish the tournament below par. He became the first golfer to win the first major in which he played since Francis Ouimet won the 1913 U.S. Open.

Weir and Curtis's out-of-the-blue heroics bookended Jim Furyk's surprisingly easy U.S. Open win—Furyk tied the Open record by shooting an eight-under 272—so the unexpected was expected at the year's final major. Still, Shaun Micheel's two-shot PGA Championship victory at grueling, rough-choked Oak Hill Country Club was a jolt.

Micheel, 34, had never finished higher than third in a PGA event. But on a weekend when the thickly-grown rough frazzled the world's best golfers, Micheel's unspectacular but consistent tee work and solid putting was enough to gain victory.

With their efforts to Tiger-proof courses with difficult rough and hazardous tree placement, PGA officials have introduced a new democracy to the sport. Woods made news with public allegations that many players are also assisted by illegal, technically-enhanced drivers. This may have been sour grapes provoked by his "drought" of Grand Slam victories, the fact that he no longer easily outdrives his competition and his loyalty to Nike equipment, which many players feel is inferior to other brands. In any case, the PGA will institute voluntary equipment testing in 2004.

Club manufacturers are already drooling over the thought of Wie one day using their products. She's years from becoming a pro, but her picture-perfect swing, 300-yard drives and uncanny poise have already earned her the mantle as the Next Tiger. The golf world will be anxious to see if the current Tiger returns to form in 2004.

made it a media madhouse as well. In February, the 32-year-old Swede announced that she would enter the tournament on a sponsor's exemption. Her motivations were personal, not political. There are no Tour bylaws forbidding women from competition; the LPGA's best player, like any elite athlete, was simply looking to challenge herself.

Still, a woman's presence in the field didn't sit well with many male players, some of whom—Vijay Singh, most notably—lashed out in pig-headed, chauvinistic fashion. Sorenstam ignored such nonsense and played with composure and grace. She shot 71 and 74 in the first two rounds. It wasn't enough to make the cut (she missed by four shots), and her flawed short game was more harshly exposed than it is on the LPGA tour, but it was an entirely respectable performance. "Give her five more tournaments," said Tour veteran Esteban Toledo, who finished ninth. "She could make a cut."

Ohio native Ben Curtis, 26, couldn't do that in May when he played the Memorial tournament in Dublin, only 15 miles from his hometown of Ostrander. But two months later he stood tall at the Royal St. George's Golf Club, winning the British Open.

Men's Majors

The Masters
Augusta National GC (par 72; 7,290 yds); Augusta, GA, April 10–13

Player	Score	Earnings ($)
Mike Weir #	70-68-75-68—281	1,080,000
Len Mattiace	73-74-69-65—281	648,000
Phil Mickelson	73-70-72-68—283	408,000
Jim Furyk	73-72-71-68—284	288,000
Jeff Maggert	72-73-66-75—286	240,000
Ernie Els	79-66-72-70—287	208,500
Vijay Singh	73-71-70-73—287	208,500
Jonathan Byrd	74-71-71-72—288	162,000
Mark O'Meara	76-71-70-71—288	162,000
Jose Maria Olazabal	73-71-71-73—288	162,000
David Toms	71-73-70-74—288	162,000
Scott Verplank	76-73-70-69—288	162,000
Tim Clark	72-75-71-71—289	120,000
Retief Goosen	73-74-72-70—289	120,000
Rich Beem	74-72-71-73—290	$93,000
Angel Cabrera	76-71-71-72—290	$93,000
K.J. Choi	76-69-72-73—290	$93,000
Paul Lawrie	72-72-73-73—290	$93,000
Davis Love III	77-71-71-71—290	$93,000
Tiger Woods	76-73-66-75—290	$93,000

#Won in a playoff

U.S. Open
Olympia Fields CC, North Course (par 70; 7,190 yds); Olympia Fields, IL, June 12–15

Player	Score	Earnings ($)
Jim Furyk	67-66-67-72—272	1,080,000
Stephen Leaney	67-68-68-72—275	650,000
Kenny Perry	72-71-69-67—279	341,367
Mike Weir	73-67-68-71—279	341,367
Fredrik Jacobson	69-67-73-71—280	185,934
Nick Price	71-65-69-75—280	185,934
Justin Rose	70-71-70-69—280	185,934
David Toms	72-67-70-71—280	185,934
Ernie Els	69-70-69-72—280	185,934
Padraig Harrington	69-72-72-68—281	124,936
Jonathan Kaye	70-70-72-69—281	124,936
Cliff Kresge	69-70-72-70—281	124,936
Billy Mayfair	69-71-67-74—281	124,936
Scott Verplank	76-67-68-70—281	124,936
Tim Petrovic	69-70-70-73—282	93,359
Eduardo Romero	70-66-70-76—282	93,359
Hidemichi Tanaka	69-71-71-71—282	93,359
Jonathan Byrd	69-66-71-76—282	93,359
Tom Byrum	69-69-71-73—282	93,359

Eight players tied at 283

British Open
Royal St. George's GC (par 71; 7,106 yds); Sandwich, England, July 17–20

Player	Score	Earnings ($)
Ben Curtis	72-72-70-69—283	1,112,720
Vijay Singh	75-70-69-70—284	548,412
Thomas Bjorn	73-70-69-72—284	548,412
Tiger Woods	73-72-69-71—285	294,076
Davis Love III	69-72-72-72—285	294,076
Fredrik Jacobson	70-76-70-70—286	213,801
Brian Davis	77-73-68-68—286	213,801
Nick Faldo	76-74-67-70—287	155,383
Kenny Perry	74-70-70-73—287	155,383
Phillip Price	74-72-69-73—288	108,093
Gary Evans	71-75-70-74—288	108,093
Sergio Garcia	73-71-70-74—288	108,093
Hennie Otto	68-76-75-69—288	108,093
Retief Goosen	73-75-71-69—288	108,093
Pierre Fulke	77-72-67-73—289	78,420
Chad Campbell	74-71-72-72—289	78,420
Stuart Appleby	75-71-71-72—289	78,420
Tom Watson	71-77-73-69—290	66,763
Ernie Els	78-68-72-72—290	66,763
Greg Norman	69-79-74-68—290	66,763
Mathias Gronberg	71-74-73-72—290	66,763

PGA Championship
Oak Hill CC, East Course (par 70; 7,134 yds), Rochester, NY, August 14–17

Player	Score	Earnings ($)
Shaun Micheel	69-68-69-70—276	1,080,000
Chad Campbell	69-72-65-72—278	648,000
Tim Clark	72-70-68-69—279	408,000
Alex Cejka	74-69-68-69—280	288,000
Ernie Els	71-70-70-71—282	214,000
Jay Haas	74-69-69-70—282	214,000
Loren Roberts	70-73-70-71—284	175,667
Mike Weir	68-71-70-75—284	175,667
Fred Funk	69-73-70-72—284	175,667
Charles Howell III	70-72-70-73—285	135,500
Kenny Perry	75-72-70-68—285	135,500
Billy Andrade	67-72-72-74—285	135,500
Niclas Fasth	76-70-71-68—285	135,500
Tim Herron	69-72-74-71—286	98,250
Scott McCarron	74-70-71-71—286	98,250
Rod Pampling	66-74-73-73—286	98,250
Robert Gamez	70-73-70-73—286	98,250
Toshi Izawa	71-72-71-73—287	73,000
Rocco Mediate	72-74-71-70—287	73,000
Kevin Sutherland	69-74-71-73—287	73,000
Carlos Franco	73-73-69-72—287	73,000
Jim Furyk	72-74-69-72—287	73,000

Late 2002 PGA Tour Events

Tournament	Final Round	Winner	Score/ Under Par	Earnings ($)
Walt Disney World Golf Classic	Oct 20	Bob Burns	263/–25	666,000
The Buick Challenge	Oct 27	Jonathan Byrd	261/–27	666,000
The Tour Championship	Nov 3	Vijay Singh	268/–12	900,000
Southern Farm Bureau Classic	Nov 3	Luke Donald	201/–15	468,000
Hyundai Team Matches	Nov 17	Rich Beem/Peter Lonard	2 & 1	100,000 each
Franklin Templeton Shootout	Nov 24	Rocco Mediate/Lee Janzen	185/–31	250,000 each
PGA Grand Slam of Golf	Nov 27	Tiger Woods	127/–17	400,000
The Skins Game	Dec 1	Mark O'Meara	8 skins	405,000
Target World Challenge	Dec 8	Padraig Harrington	268/–20	1,000,000

2003 PGA Tour Events

Tournament	Final Round	Winner	Score/ Under Par	Earnings ($)
Mercedes Championships	Jan 12	Ernie Els	261/–31	1,000,000
Sony Open in Hawaii	Jan 19	Ernie Els*	264/–16	810,000
Phoenix Open	Jan 26	Vijay Singh	261/–23	720,000
Bob Hope Chrysler Classic	Feb 2	Mike Weir	330/–30	810,000
AT&T Pebble Beach National Pro-Am	Feb 9	David Love III	274/–14	900,000
Buick Invitational	Feb 16	Tiger Woods	272/–16	810,000
Nissan Open	Feb 23	Mike Weir*	275/–9	810,000
WGC: Accenture Match Play Champ.	Mar 2	Tiger Woods	2 & 1	1,005,000
Chrysler Classic of Tucson	Mar 2	Frank Lickliter II	269/–19	540,000
Ford Championship	Mar 9	Scott Hoch*	271/–17	900,000
Honda Classic	Mar 16	Justin Leonard	264/–24	900,000
Bay Hill Invitational	Mar 23	Tiger Woods	269/–19	810,000
The Players Championship	Mar 30	Davis Love III	271/–17	1,170,000
BellSouth Classic	Apr 6	Ben Crane	272/–16	720,000
The Masters	Apr 13	Mike Weir*	281/–7	1,080,000
The Heritage	Apr 20	Davis Love III*	271/–13	810,000
Shell Houston Open	Apr 27	Fred Couples	267/–21	810,000
HP Classic of New Orleans	May 4	Steve Flesch*	267/–21	900,000
Wachovia Championship	May 11	David Toms	278/–10	1,080,000
EDS Byron Nelson Classic	May 18	Vijay Singh	265/–15	1,008,000
Bank of America Colonial	May 25	Kenny Perry	261/–19	900,000
Memorial Tournament	June 1	Kenny Perry	275/–13	900,000
FBR Capital Open	June 8	Rory Sabbatini	270/–14	810,000
U.S. Open	June 15	Jim Furyk	272/–8	1,080,000
Buick Classic	June 22	Jonathan Kaye*	271/–13	900,000
FedEx St. Jude Classic	June 29	David Toms	264/–20	810,000
Western Open	July 6	Tiger Woods	267/–21	810,000
Greater Milwaukee Open	July 13	Kenny Perry	268/–12	630,000
British Open	July 20	Ben Curtis	283/–1	1,100,000
B.C. Open	July 20	Craig Stadler	267/–21	540,000
Greater Hartford Open	July 27	Peter Jacobsen	266/–14	720,000
Buick Open	Aug 3	Jim Furyk	267/–21	720,000
The International	Aug 10	Davis Love III	+46‡	900,000
PGA Championship	Aug 17	Shaun Micheel	276/–4	1,080,000
WGC-NEC Invitational	Aug 24	Darren Clarke	268/–12	1,050,000
Reno-Tahoe Open	Aug 24	Kirk Triplett	271/–17	540,000
Deutsche Bank Championship	Sep 1	Adam Scott	264/–20	900,000
Bell Canadian Open	Sep 7	Bob Tway*	272/–8	756,000
John Deere Classic	Sep 14	Vijay Singh	268/–16	630,000
84 Lumber Classic of Pennsylvania	Sep 21	J.L. Lewis	266/–22	720,000
Valero Texas Open	Sep 28	Tommy Armour III	254/–26	630,000
WGC-American Express Champ.	Oct 5	Tiger Woods	274/–6	1,050,000
Southern Farm Bureau Classic	Oct 5	John Huston	268/–20	540,000

* Won playoff. ‡ Revised Stableford scoring.

Women's Majors

Kraft Nabisco Championship
Mission Hills CC; Rancho Mirage, CA
(par 72; 6,460 yds) March 27–30

layer	Score	Earnings ($)
Annika Sorenstam	70-71-71-68—280	225,000
P. Meunier-Lebouc	70-68-70-73—281	240,000
Annika Sorenstam	68-72-71-71—282	146,120
Lorena Ochoa	71-70-74-68—283	106,000
Laura Davies	70-75-69-70—284	82,000
Beth Daniel	75-74-68-70—287	51,200
Catriona Matthew	71-74-72-70—287	51,200
Maria Hjorth	72-72-73-70—287	51,200
Laura Diaz	76-71-69-71—287	51,200
Jennifer Rosales	74-70-72-72—288	35,600
*Michelle Wie	72-74-66-76—288	
Cristie Kerr	74-71-74-71—290	29,160
Rosie Jones	71-75-72-72—290	29,160
Woo-Soon Ko	74-73-70-73—290	29,160
Juli Inkster	75-74-66-75—290	29,160
Catrin Nilsmark	71-78-73-69—291	22,080
Dawn Coe-Jones	72-74-72-73—291	22,080
Dorothy Delasin	71-71-76-73—291	22,080
Karen Stupples	71-71-76-73—291	22,080
Se Ri Pak	71-72-71-77—291	22,080
Hee-Won Han	73-74-75-70—292	19,040

*Amateur

McDonald's LPGA Championship
DuPont CC; Wilmington, DE
(par 71; 6,408 yds) June 5–8

Player	Score	Earnings ($)
Annika Sorenstam#	70-64-72-72—278	240,000
Grace Park	69-72-70-67—278	147,934
Rosie Jones	73-68-72-71—284	85,718
Rachel Teske	69-70-74-71—284	85,718
Beth Daniel	71-71-70-72—284	85,718
Young-A Yang	73-74-69-69—285	41,873
Joanne Mills	68-73-75-69—285	41,873
Young Kim	70-73-72-70—285	41,873
Becky Morgan	73-70-70-72—285	41,873
Kate Golden	72-70-68-75—285	41,873
P. Meunier-Lebouc	75-69-72-70—286	24,037
Jennifer Rosales	74-68-74-70—286	24,037
Suzann Pettersen	70-71-75-70—286	24,037
Angela Jerman	73-72-69-72—286	24,037
Jeong Jang	72-73-69-72—286	24,037
Akiko Fukushima	72-68-74-72—286	24,037
Michele Redman	74-70-69-73—286	24,037
Wendy Ward	68-69-75-74—286	24,037
Hee-Won Han	67-69-74-76—286	24,037

Seven players tied at 287

#Won in a playoff

U.S. Women's Open
Pumpkin Ridge GC; North Plains, OR
(par 71; 6,509 yds) July 3–6

Player	Score	Earnings ($)
Hilary Lunke#	71-69-68-75—283	560,000
Kelly Robbins	74-69-71-69—283	275,839
Angela Stanford	70-70-69-74—283	275,839
Annika Sorenstam	72-72-67-73—284	150,994
*Aree Song	70-73-68-74—285	
Jeong Jang	73-69-69-75—286	115,333
Mhairi McKay	66-70-75-75—286	115,333
Juli Inkster	69-71-74-73—287	97,363
Rosie Jones	70-72-73-73—288	90,241
Grace Park	72-76-73-68—289	79,243
Suzann Pettersen	76-69-69-75—289	79,243
Donna Andrews	69-72-72-77—290	71,362
Jennifer Rosales	74-69-76-73—292	56,500
Lorena Ochoa	71-75-72-74—292	56,500
Cristie Kerr	72-73-73-74—292	56,500
Rachel Teske	71-73-72-76—292	56,500
P. Meunier-Lebouc	73-69-74-76—292	56,500
Laura Diaz	71-71-74-76—292	56,500
Natalie Gulbis	73-69-72-78—292	56,500
Yuri Fudoh	74-72-75-72—293	43,491
Beth Daniel	73-69-77-74—293	43,491

#Won in a playoff
*Amateur

Weetabix Women's British Open
Royal Lytham & St. Annes GC; Lytham St.
Annes, Eng. (par 72; 6,308 yds) July 31–August 3

Player	Score	Earnings ($)
Annika Sorenstam	68-72-68-70—278	254,880
Se Ri Pak	69-69-69-72—279	159,300
Grace Park	74-65-71-70—280	99,563
Karrie Webb	67-72-70-71—280	99,563
P. Meunier-Lebouc	70-69-67-76—282	71,685
V. Goetze-Ackerman	73-71-68-71—283	58,941
Wendy Ward	67-71-69-76—283	58,941
Sophie Gustafson	73-69-71-71—284	50,976
Young Kim	73-70-72-70—285	46,197
Gloria Park	70-75-69-72—286	39,825
Candie Kung	73-71-69-73—286	39,825
Karen Stupples	69-74-70-74—287	33,453
Paula Marti	71-70-70-76—287	33,453
Lynnette Brooky	70-74-75-69—288	25,727
Laura Diaz	73-74-71-70—288	25,727
Jeong Jang	76-69-72-71—288	25,727
Cristie Kerr	74-71-71-72—288	25,727
Beth Daniel	74-71-67-76—288	25,727
Hee-Won Han	75-71-70-73—289	19,913
Laura Davies	75-70-70-74—289	19,913
Lorie Kane	69-75-70-75—289	19,913
Becky Morgan	72-70-71-76—289	19,913
Heather Bowie	70-66-74-79—289	19,913

Late 2002 LPGA Tour Events

Tournament	Final Round	Winner	Score/ Under Par	Earnings ($)
Sports Today CJ Nine Bridges Classic...Oct 27		Se Ri Pak	213/–3	225,000
Cisco World Ladies Championship ....Nov 3		Grace Park	1-up	153,000
Mizuno Classic...Nov 10		Annika Sorenstam	201/–15	169,500
ADT Championship ....Nov 24		Annika Sorenstam	275/–13	215,000tk

2003 LPGA Tour Events

Tournament	Final Round	Winner	Score/ Under Par	Earnings ($)
Takefuji Classic ....Mar 2		Annika Sorenstam*	196/–14	135,000
Welch's/Fry's Championship..................Mar 16		Wendy Doolan	259/–21	120,000
Safeway Ping ....Mar 23		Se Ri Pak	265/–23	150,000
Kraft Nabisco Championship ....Mar 30		Patricia Meunier-Lebouc	281/–7	240,000
Office Depot Championship ....Apr 6		Annika Sorenstam	211/–5	225,000
Takefuji Classic ....Apr 19		Candie Kung	204/–12	165,000
Chick-fil-A Charity Championship ....Apr 27		Se Ri Pak*	200/–16	202,500
Michelob Light Open at Kingsmill...........May 4		Grace Park	275/–9	240,000
Asahi Ryokuken Int'l Champ. at Mt. Vintage May 11		Rosie Jones	273/–15	195,000
LPGA Corning Classic ....May 25		Juli Inkster	264/–24	150,000
Kellogg-Keebler Classic..............................June 1		Annika Sorenstam	199/–17	180,000
McDonald's LPGA Championship ....June 8		Annika Sorenstam*	278/–6	240,000
Giant Eagle LPGA Classic ....June 15		Rachel Teske*	204/–12	150,000
Wegman's Rochester LPGA ....June 22		Rachel Teske	277/–11	180,000
ShopRite LPGA Classic ....June 29		Angela Stanford	197/–16	195,000
U.S. Women's Open.................................July 6		Hilary Lunke*	283/–1	560,000
Canadian Women's Open......................July 13		Beth Daniel	275/–13	195,000
Sybase Big Apple Classic ....July 20		Hee-Won Han*	199/–17	142,500
Evian Masters...July 27		Juli Inkster	267/–21	315,000
Women's British Open ....Aug 3		Annika Sorenstam	278/–10	254,880
Wendy's Championship for Children ......Aug 10		Hee-Won Han*	199/–17	165,000
Jamie Farr Kroger Classic ....Aug 17		Se Ri Pak	271/–13	150,000
Wachovia Classic....................................Aug 24		Candie Kung	274/–14	180,000
State Farm Classic ....Aug 31		Candie Kung	202/–14	180,000
John Q. Hammons Hotel Classic ....Sep 7		Karrie Webb	200/–10	150,000
Safeway Classic ....Sep 28		Annika Sorenstam	201/–15	180,000
Longs Drugs Challenge ....Oct 5		Helen Alfredsson	275/–13	150,000

* Won in playoff.

Late 2002 Senior Tour Events

Tournament	Final Round	Winner	Score/ Under Par	Earnings ($)
SBC Championship	Oct 20	Dana Quigley	201/–2	217,500
Senior TOUR Championship	Oct 27	Tom Watson	274/–5	440,000
Our Lucaya Senior Slam	Nov 10	Fuzzy Zoeller	138/–6	300,000
Hyundai Team Matches	Nov 17	Allen Doyle/Dana Quigley	2 & 1	100,000 each

2003 Senior Tour Events

Tournament	Final Round	Winner	Score/ Under Par	Earnings ($)
MasterCard Championship	Feb 2	Dana Quigley	198/–18	250,000
Royal Caribbean Classic#	Feb 9	Dave Barr	207/–9	217,500
ACE Group Classic	Feb 16	Vicente Fernandez	202/–14	240,000
Verizon Classic	Feb 23	Bruce Fleisher	205/–8	240,000
MasterCard Classic	Mar 9	David Eger	204/–12	300,000
SBC Classic	Mar 16	Tom Purtzer	135/–9	225,000
Toshiba Senior Classic	Mar 23	Rodger Davis	197/–16	232,500
Emerald Coast Classic#	Apr 20	Bob Gilder	193/–17	217,500
Liberty Mutual Legends of Golf	April 27	Bruce Lietzke	206/–10	350,000
Bruno's Memorial Classic	May 4	Tom Jenkins	200/–16	210,000
Kinko's C;assic of Austin	May 11	Hale Irwin*	208/–8	240,000
Bayer Advantage Celebrity Pro-Am	May 18	Jay Sigel	205/–11	240,000
Columbus Southern Open	May 25	Morris Hatalsky	198/–12	225,000
Music City Champ. at Gaylord Opryland	June 1	Jim Ahern	196/–20	210,000
Senior PGA Championship	June 8	John Jacobs	276/–4	360,000
Farmers Charity Classic	June 22	Doug Tewell*	201/–15	225,000
U.S. Senior Open	June 29	Bruce Lietzke	277/–7	470,000
Ford Senior Players Championship	July 13	Craig Stadler	271/–17	375,000
Senior British Open	July 27	Tom Watson	263/–17	255,731
FleetBoston Classic	Aug 3	Allen Doyle	198/–15	225,000
3M Championship	Aug 10	Wayne Levi	205/–11	262,500
Long Island Classic	Aug 17	Jim Thorpe	195/–15	225,000
Allianz Championship	Aug 24	Tom Pooley	200/–13	225,000
Jeld-Wen Tradition	Aug 31	Tom Watson	273/–15	330,000
Kroger Classic	Sep 7	Gil Morgan	200/–16	225,000
Constellation Energy Classic	Sep 14	Larry Nelson	207/–9	225,000
SAS Championship	Sep 21	D.A. Weibring	203/–13	270,000
Greater Hickory Classic at Rock Barn	Sep 28	Craig Stadler	201/–15	225,000

*Won in playoff.

THEY SAID IT

Paul Azinger, PGA golfer, on fellow pro Phil Mickelson, who failed in his tryout as a pitcher with the Triple-A Toldeo Mud Hens: "The last time I batted was in Little League, and that's the speed he was throwing."

U.S. Amateur Results*

Tournament	Final Round	Winner	Score	Runner-Up
Women's Amateur Public Links	June 22	Michelle Wie	1-up	V. Nirapathpongporn
Men's Amateur Public Links	July 19	Brandt Snedeker	10 & 9	Dayton Rose
Girls' Junior Amateur	July 26	Sukjin-Lee Wuesthoff	1-up	In-Bee Park
Boys' Junior Amateur	July 26	Brian Harman	5 & 4	Jordan Cox
Women's Amateur	Aug 10	V. Nirapathpongporn	2 & 1	Jane Park
Men's Amateur	Aug 24	Nick Flanagan	37 holes	Casey Wittenberg
Senior Men	Sep 11	Kemp Richardson	19 holes	Frank Abbott
Senior Women	Sep 11	Marlene Streit	23 holes	Nancy Fitzgerald

*Results through 10/9/03

International Results*

Tournament	Final Round	Winner	Score	Runner-Up
Walker Cup	Sep 7	Great Britain/Ireland	12½–11½	United States
Solheim Cup	Sep 14	Europe	17½–10½	United States

*Results through 10/9/03

PGA Tour Final 2002 Money Leaders

Name	Events	Best Finish	Scoring Average*	Money ($)
Tiger Woods	18	1 (5)	68.13	6,912,625
Phil Mickelson	26	1 (2)	70.11	4,311,971
Vijay Singh	28	1 (2)	68.68	3,756,563
David Toms	27	2 (3)	69.69	3,459,739
Ernie Els	18	1 (2)	68.76	3,291,895
Jerry Kelly	29	1 (2)	70.52	2,946,889
Rich Beem	30	1 (2)	71.40	2,938,365
Justin Leonard	26	1 (1)	70.15	2,738,235
Charles Howell III	32	1 (1)	70.28	2,702,747
Retief Goosen	15	1 (1)	69.18	2,617,004

*Adjusted for average score of field in each tournament entered.

LPGA Tour Final 2002 Money Leaders

Name	Events	Best Finish	Scoring Average	Money ($)
Annika Sorenstam	23	1 (11)	68.70	2,863,904
Se Ri Pak	24	1 (5)	69.85	1,722,281
Juli Inkster	20	1 (2)	70.82	1,154,349
Mi Hyun Kim	28	1 (2)	71.16	1,049,993
Karrie Webb	21	1 (2)	70.33	1,009,760
Grace Park	28	1 (1)	70.99	861,943
Laura Diaz	25	1 (2)	70.93	843,790
Carin Koch	25	2 (3)	70.91	785,817
Rachel Teske	27	1 (2)	71.49	779,329
Rosie Jones	24	2 (1)	70.76	722,412

Senior Tour Final 2002 Money Leaders

Name	Events	Best Finish	Scoring Average	Money ($)
Hale Irwin	27	1 (4)	68.93	3,028,304
Bob Gilder	34	1 (4)	70.26	2,367,637
Bruce Fleisher	31	1 (1)	69.73	1,860,534
Tom Kite	23	1 (3)	69.64	1,631,930
Doug Tewell	27	1 (2)	69.85	1,579,988
Dana Quigley	35	1 (2)	70.50	1,569,972
Bruce Lietzke	22	1 (3)	69.96	1,527,676
Tom Watson	14	1 (1)	69.57	1,522,437
Jim Thorpe	32	1 (1)	70.28	1,511,591
Morris Hatalsky	24	1 (1)	69.85	1,391,044

Top Banana

It's time to acknowledge what has become stupefyingly obvious: The tournament that used to be called the Crosby, after the great crooner Bing, has become, for all practical purposes, the Murray, after the man who gave a scalp massage this year to a female spectator on the 15th tee and hit the Pebble Beach sign with a well-flung banana. Bill Murray is a multisport comedian. He oversees promotions as co-owner of a couple of minor-league baseball teams, and he's done play-by-play on a Cubs broadcast. But it's his annual appearances at the AT&T Pebble Beach National Pro-Am that provide spiritual refreshment.

On that hallowed ocen-kissed course Murray plays golf like nobody else, but like golf was a *game* meant for *playing*. And people find this irresistible. At Pebble Beach even Tiger Woods gets eclipsed by *Caddyshack's* Carl Spackler. How else to explain that advance ticket sales for this year, when Woods was out and Murray in, outstripped last year, when Murray missed but Tiger played?

You could call Murray the Meadowlark Lemon of golf, except the Globetrotters had more set pieces. Murray flies blind and flirts shamelessly. "Stick with us," he told two women this year. "Maybe we'll find some beer and wine." Later he scored a blue scarf from a female fan and wore it around his waist the rest of the round. When eight teenagers in sombreros joined his gallery, Murray cocked an eyebrow and said, "Are you here for the closing ceremonies?" Then he added, "I thought we tightened up our borders." Saturday was Murray's banana day: He tossed a peel at his pro partner, Scott Simpson, on the 1st tee, which incited Simpson and the rest of the foursome, actor Andy Garcia and pro Paul Stankowski, to throw bananas back. This is

not, you see, a man who demands quiet on the course. "You!" Murray said suddenly, pointing to a white-haired woman watching him on the 10th tee on Thursday. "I need you in my posse!"

That's not exactly an exclusive group. The working-class kind from Willamette, Ill., is the Pied Piper of Pebble Beach. Kevin Costner had 25 fans behind him as he came off the 14th tee on Thursday. Murray, playing just behind him, had at least 10 times that number.

What makes the scene even more delicious is that the golf establishment once opposed Murray even being in the Murray. In their defense, PGA honchos circa 1992 were unprepared for a golfer wearing bib overalls and a hat shaped like the Hubert Humphrey Metrodome. Early on, Mujrray pulled an elderly woman out of the gallery, danced with her in a bunker, then tossed her in the sand. In '93 he yelled "Hurry up!" at former vice president Dan Quayle as Quayle was about to hit a shot. That brought the wrath of then PGA Tour commissioner Deane Beman, who blasted Murray's behavior as "inappropriate" and "detrimental" to the tournament. Murray responded by likening the Tour to "a Nazi state" and demanded Beman's resignation, calling him "just another screwhead too big for his britches." For once he wasn't kidding. "Bill almost didn't come back after the first year," says Simpson. "Now he's embraced."

That's putting it mildly. On Friday, when Murray hit his ball into the rough on the 16th hole, a middle-aged woman stretched out next to it. Murray promptly pounced on her, gyrating spasmodically. A moment later he helped her to her feet. "You all right?" Murray asked.

"I am now," the woman said, speaking for sports fans everywhere.

—Gary Van Sickle

Men's Golf

THE MAJOR TOURNAMENTS
The Masters

Year	Winner	Score	Runner-Up	Year	Winner	Score	Runner-Up
1934	Horton Smith	284	Craig Wood	1972	Jack Nicklaus	286	Bruce Crampton
1935	Gene Sarazen* (144)	282	Craig Wood (149)				Bobby Mitchell
	(only 36-hole playoff)						Tom Weiskopf
1936	Horton Smith	285	Harry Cooper	1973	Tommy Aaron	283	J.C. Snead
1937	Byron Nelson	283	Ralph Guldahl	1974	Gary Player	278	Tom Weiskopf
1938	Henry Picard	285	Ralph Guldahl				Dave Stockton
			Harry Cooper	1975	Jack Nicklaus	276	Johnny Miller
1939	Ralph Guldahl	279	Sam Snead				Tom Weiskopf
1940	Jimmy Demaret	280	Lloyd Mangrum	1976	Ray Floyd	271	Ben Crenshaw
1941	Craig Wood	280	Byron Nelson	1977	Tom Watson	276	Jack Nicklaus
1942	Byron Nelson* (69)	280	Ben Hogan (70)	1978	Gary Player	277	Hubert Green
1943–45	No tournament						Rod Funseth
1946	Herman Keiser	282	Ben Hogan				Tom Watson
1947	Jimmy Demaret	281	Byron Nelson	1979	Fuzzy Zoeller* (4–3)†	280	Ed Sneed (4–4)
			Frank Stranahan				Tom Watson (4–4)
1948	Claude Harmon	279	Cary Middlecoff	1980	Seve Ballesteros	275	Gibby Gilbert
1949	Sam Snead	282	Johnny Bulla				Jack Newton
			Lloyd Mangrum	1981	Tom Watson	280	Johnny Miller
1950	Jimmy Demaret	283	Jim Ferrier				Jack Nicklaus
1951	Ben Hogan	280	Skee Riegel	1982	Craig Stadler* (4)	284	Dan Pohl (5)
1952	Sam Snead	286	Jack Burke Jr.	1983	Seve Ballesteros	280	Ben Crenshaw
1953	Ben Hogan	274	Ed Oliver Jr.				Tom Kite
1954	Sam Snead* (70)	289	Ben Hogan (71)	1984	Ben Crenshaw	277	Tom Watson
1955	Cary Middlecoff	279	Ben Hogan	1985	Bernhard Langer	282	Curtis Strange
1956	Jack Burke Jr.	289	Ken Venturi				Seve Ballesteros
1957	Doug Ford	282	Sam Snead				Ray Floyd
1958	Arnold Palmer	284	Doug Ford	1986	Jack Nicklaus	279	Greg Norman
			Fred Hawkins				Tom Kite
1959	Art Wall Jr.	284	Cary Middlecoff	1987	Larry Mize* (4–3)	285	Seve Ballesteros (5)
1960	Arnold Palmer	282	Ken Venturi				Greg Norman (4–4)
1961	Gary Player	280	Charles R. Coe	1988	Sandy Lyle	281	Mark Calcavecchia
			Arnold Palmer	1989	Nick Faldo* (5–3)	283	Scott Hoch (5–4)
1962	Arnold Palmer* (68)	280	Gary Player (71)	1990	Nick Faldo* (4–4)	278	Ray Floyd (4–x)
			D. Finsterwald (77)	1991	Ian Woosnam	277	José María Olazábal
1963	Jack Nicklaus	286	Tony Lema	1992	Fred Couples	275	Ray Floyd
1964	Arnold Palmer	276	Dave Marr	1993	Bernhard Langer	277	Chip Beck
			Jack Nicklaus	1994	José María Olazábal	279	Tom Lehman
1965	Jack Nicklaus	271	Arnold Palmer	1995	Ben Crenshaw	274	Davis Love III
			Gary Player	1996	Nick Faldo	276	Greg Norman
1966	Jack Nicklaus* (70)	288	Tommy Jacobs (72)	1997	Tiger Woods	270	Tom Kite
			Gay Brewer Jr. (78)	1998	Mark O'Meara	279	David Duval
1967	Gay Brewer Jr.	280	Bobby Nichols				Fred Couples
1968	Bob Goalby	277	Roberto DeVicenzo	1999	José María Olazábal	280	Davis Love III
1969	George Archer	281	Billy Casper	2000	Vijay Singh	278	Ernie Els
			George Knudson	2001	Tiger Woods	272	David Duval
			Tom Weiskopf	2002	Tiger Woods	276	Retief Goosen
1970	Billy Casper* (69)	279	Gene Littler (74)	2003	Mike Weir	281	Len Mattiace
1971	Charles Coody	279	Johnny Miller				
			Jack Nicklaus				

*Winner in playoff. Playoff scores are in parentheses. †Playoff cut from 18 holes to sudden death.
Note: Played at Augusta National Golf Club, Augusta, GA.

United States Open Championship

Year	Winner	Score	Runner-Up	Site
1895	Horace Rawlins	†173	Willie Dunn	Newport GC, Newport, RI
1896	James Foulis	†152	Horace Rawlins	Shinnecock Hills GC, Southampton, NY
1897	Joe Lloyd	†162	Willie Anderson	Chicago GC, Wheaton, IL
1898	Fred Herd	328	Alex Smith	Myopia Hunt Club, Hamilton, MA
1899	Willie Smith	315	George Low	Baltimore CC, Baltimore
			Val Fitzjohn	
			W.H. Way	
1900	Harry Vardon	313	John H. Taylor	Chicago GC, Wheaton, IL
1901	Willie Anderson* (85)	331	Alex Smith (86)	Myopia Hunt Club, Hamilton, MA
1902	Laurie Auchterlonie	307	Stewart Gardner	Garden City GC, Garden City, NY
1903	Willie Anderson* (82)	307	David Brown (84)	Baltusrol GC, Springfield, NJ
1904	Willie Anderson	303	Gil Nicholls	Glen View Club, Golf, IL
1905	Willie Anderson	314	Alex Smith	Myopia Hunt Club, Hamilton, MA
1906	Alex Smith	295	Willie Smith	Onwentsia Club, Lake Forest, IL
1907	Alex Ross	302	Gil Nicholls	Philadelphia Cricket Club, Chestnut Hill, PA
1908	Fred McLeod* (77)	322	Willie Smith (83)	Myopia Hunt Club, Hamilton, MA
1909	George Sargent	290	Tom McNamara	Englewood GC, Englewood, NJ
1910	Alex Smith* (71)	298	John McDermott (75)	Philadelphia Cricket Club, Chestnut Hill, PA
			Macdonald Smith (77)	
1911	John McDermott* (80)	307	Mike Brady (82)	Chicago GC, Wheaton, IL
			George Simpson (85)	
1912	John McDermott	294	Tom McNamara	CC of Buffalo, Buffalo
1913	Francis Ouimet* (72)	304	Harry Vardon (77)	The Country Club, Brookline, MA
			Edward Ray (78)	
1914	Walter Hagen	290	Chick Evans	Midlothian CC, Blue Island, IL
1915	Jerry Travers	297	Tom McNamara	Baltusrol GC, Springfield, NJ
1916	Chick Evans	286	Jock Hutchison	Minikahda Club, Minneapolis
1917–18	No tournament			
1919	Walter Hagen* (77)	301	Mike Brady (78)	Brae Burn CC, West Newton, MA
1920	Edward Ray	295	Harry Vardon	Inverness CC, Toledo
			Jack Burke	
			Leo Diegel	
			Jock Hutchison	
1921	Jim Barnes	289	Walter Hagen	Columbia CC, Chevy Chase, MD
			Fred McLeod	
1922	Gene Sarazen	288	John L. Black	Skokie CC, Glencoe, IL
			Bobby Jones	
1923	Bobby Jones* (76)	296	Bobby Cruickshank (78)	Inwood CC, Inwood, NY
1924	Cyril Walker	297	Bobby Jones	Oakland Hills CC, Birmingham, MI
1925	W. MacFarlane* (75–72)	291	Bobby Jones (75–73)	Worcester CC, Worcester, MA
1926	Bobby Jones	293	Joe Turnesa	Scioto CC, Columbus, OH
1927	Tommy Armour* (76)	301	Harry Cooper (79)	Oakmont CC, Oakmont, PA
1928	Johnny Farrell* (143)	294	Bobby Jones (144)	Olympia Fields CC, Matteson, IL
1929	Bobby Jones* (141)	294	Al Espinosa (164)	Winged Foot GC, Mamaroneck, NY
1930	Bobby Jones	287	Macdonald Smith	Interlachen CC, Hopkins, MN
1931	Billy Burke* (149–148)	292	George Von Elm	Inverness Club, Toledo
			(149–149)	
1932	Gene Sarazen	286	Phil Perkins	Fresh Meadows CC, Flushing, NY
			Bobby Cruickshank	
1933	Johnny Goodman	287	Ralph Guldahl	North Shore CC, Glenview, IL
1934	Olin Dutra	293	Gene Sarazen	Merion Cricket Club, Ardmore, PA
1935	Sam Parks Jr.	299	Jimmy Thompson	Oakmont CC, Oakmont, PA
1936	Tony Manero	282	Harry Cooper	Baltusrol GC (Upper Course), Springfield, NJ
1937	Ralph Guldahl	281	Sam Snead	Oakland Hills CC, Birmingham, MI
1938	Ralph Guldahl	284	Dick Metz	Cherry Hills CC, Denver
1939	Byron Nelson* (68–70)	284	Craig Wood (68–73)	Philadelphia CC, Philadelphia
			Denny Shute (76)	
1940	Lawson Little* (70)	287	Gene Sarazen (73)	Canterbury GC, Cleveland
1941	Craig Wood	284	Denny Shute	Colonial Club, Fort Worth
1942–45	No tournament			
1946	Lloyd Mangrum* (72–72)	284	Vic Ghezzi (72–73)	Canterbury GC, Cleveland
			Byron Nelson (72–73)	

Men's Golf *(Cont)*

United States Open Championship *(Cont.)*

Year	Winner	Score	Runner-Up	Site
1947	Lew Worsham* (69)	282	Sam Snead (70)	St. Louis CC, Clayton, MO
1948	Ben Hogan	276	Jimmy Demaret	Riviera CC, Los Angeles
1949	Cary Middlecoff	286	Sam Snead, Clayton Heafner	Medinah CC, Medinah, IL
1950	Ben Hogan* (69)	287	Lloyd Mangrum (73), George Fazio (75)	Merion GC, Ardmore, PA
1951	Ben Hogan	287	Clayton Heafner	Oakland Hills CC, Birmingham, MI
1952	Julius Boros	281	Ed Oliver	Northwood CC, Dallas
1953	Ben Hogan	283	Sam Snead	Oakmont CC, Oakmont, PA
1954	Ed Furgol	284	Gene Littler	Baltusrol GC (Lower Course), Springfield, NJ
1955	Jack Fleck* (69)	287	Ben Hogan (72)	Olympic Club (Lower Course), San Francisco
1956	Cary Middlecoff	281	Ben Hogan, Julius Boros	Oak Hill, Rochester, NY
1957	Dick Mayer* (72)	282	Cary Middlecoff (79)	Inverness Club, Toledo
1958	Tommy Bolt	283	Gary Player	Southern Hills CC, Tulsa
1959	Billy Casper	282	Bob Rosburg	Winged Foot GC, Mamaroneck, NY
1960	Arnold Palmer	280	Jack Nicklaus	Cherry Hills CC, Denver
1961	Gene Littler	281	Bob Goalby, Doug Sanders	Oakland Hills CC, Birmingham, MI
1962	Jack Nicklaus* (71)	283	Arnold Palmer (74)	Oakmont CC, Oakmont, PA
1963	Julius Boros* (70)	293	Jacky Cupit (73), Arnold Palmer (76)	The Country Club, Brookline, MA
1964	Ken Venturi	278	Tommy Jacobs	Congressional CC, Bethesda, MD
1965	Gary Player* (71)	282	Kel Nagle (74)	Bellerive CC, St. Louis
1966	Billy Casper* (69)	278	Arnold Palmer (73)	Olympic Club (Lake Course), San Francisco
1967	Jack Nicklaus	275	Arnold Palmer	Baltusrol GC (Lower Course), Springfield, NJ
1968	Lee Trevino	275	Jack Nicklaus	Oak Hill CC, Rochester, NY
1969	Orville Moody	281	Deane Beman, Al Geiberger, Bob Rosburg	Champions GC (Cypress Creek Course), Houston
1970	Tony Jacklin	281	Dave Hill	Hazeltine GC, Chaska, MN
1971	Lee Trevino* (68)	280	Jack Nicklaus (71)	Merion GC (East Course), Ardmore, PA
1972	Jack Nicklaus	290	Bruce Crampton	Pebble Beach GL, Pebble Beach, CA
1973	Johnny Miller	279	John Schlee	Oakmont CC, Oakmont, PA
1974	Hale Irwin	287	Forrest Fezler	Winged Foot GC, Mamaroneck, NY
1975	Lou Graham* (71)	287	John Mahaffey (73)	Medinah CC, Medinah, IL
1976	Jerry Pate	277	Tom Weiskopf, Al Geiberger	Atlanta Athletic Club, Duluth, GA
1977	Hubert Green	278	Lou Graham	Southern Hills CC, Tulsa
1978	Andy North	285	Dave Stockton, J.C. Snead	Cherry Hills CC, Denver
1979	Hale Irwin	284	Gary Player, Jerry Pate	Inverness Club, Toledo
1980	Jack Nicklaus	272	Isao Aoki	Baltusrol GC (Lower Course), Springfield, NJ
1981	David Graham	273	George Burns, Bill Rogers	Merion GC, Ardmore, PA
1982	Tom Watson	282	Jack Nicklaus	Pebble Beach GL, Pebble Beach, CA
1983	Larry Nelson	280	Tom Watson	Oakmont CC, Oakmont, PA
1984	Fuzzy Zoeller* (67)	276	Greg Norman (75)	Winged Foot GC, Mamaroneck, NY
1985	Andy North	279	Dave Barr, T.C. Chen, Denis Watson	Oakland Hills CC, Birmingham, MI
1986	Ray Floyd	279	Lanny Wadkins, Chip Beck	Shinnecock Hills GC, Southampton, NY
1987	Scott Simpson	277	Tom Watson	Olympic Club (Lake Course), San Francisco
1988	Curtis Strange* (71)	278	Nick Faldo (75)	The Country Club, Brookline, MA
1989	Curtis Strange	278	Chip Beck, Mark McCumber, Ian Woosnam	Oak Hill CC, Rochester, NY
1990	Hale Irwin* (74) (3)	280	Mike Donald (74) (4)	Medinah CC, Medinah, IL
1991	Payne Stewart* (75)	282	Scott Simpson (77)	Hazeltine GC, Chaska, MN
1992	Tom Kite	285	Jeff Sluman	Pebble Beach GL, Pebble Beach, CA
1993	Lee Janzen	272	Payne Stewart	Baltusrol GC, Springfield, NJ
1994	Ernie Els*	279	Loren Roberts, Colin Montgomerie	Oakmont CC, Oakmont, PA

United States Open Championship (Cont.)

Year	Winner	Score	Runner-Up	Site
1995	Corey Pavin	280	Greg Norman	Shinnecock Hills GC, Southampton, NY
1996	Steve Jones	278	Davis Love III	Oakland Hills CC, Birmingham, MI
			Tom Lehman	
1997	Ernie Els	276	Colin Montgomerie	Congressional CC, Bethesda, MD
1998	Lee Janzen	280	Payne Stewart	The Olympic Club, San Francisco
1999	Payne Stewart	279	Phil Mickelson	Pinehurst Resort and CC, Pinehurst, NC
2000	Tiger Woods	272	Miguel Angel Jiménez	Pebble Beach GL, Pebble Beach, CA
			Ernie Els	
2001	Retief Goosen* (70)	276	Mark Brooks (72)	Southern Hills CC, Tulsa
2002	Tiger Woods	277	Phil Mickelson	Bethpage Black Course, Bethpage, NY
2003	Jim Furyk	272	Stephen Leaney	Olympia Fields CC, Olympia Fields, IL

*Winner in playoff. Playoff scores are in parentheses. The 1990 playoff went to one hole of sudden death after an 18-hole playoff. In the 1994 playoff, Montgomerie was eliminated after 18 playoff holes, and Els beat Roberts on the 20th.
†Before 1898, 36 holes. From 1898 on, 72 holes.

British Open

Year	Winner	Score	Runner-Up	Site
1860†	Willie Park	174	Tom Morris Sr.	Prestwick, Scotland
1861‡	Tom Morris Sr.	163	Willie Park	Prestwick, Scotland
1862	Tom Morris Sr.	163	Willie Park	Prestwick, Scotland
1863	Willie Park	168	Tom Morris Sr.	Prestwick, Scotland
1864	Tom Morris, Sr.	160	Andrew Strath	Prestwick, Scotland
1865	Andrew Strath	162	Willie Park	Prestwick, Scotland
1866	Willie Park	169	David Park	Prestwick, Scotland
1867	Tom Morris Sr.	170	Willie Park	Prestwick, Scotland
1868	Tom Morris Jr.	154	Tom Morris Sr.	Prestwick, Scotland
1869	Tom Morris Jr.	157	Tom Morris Sr.	Prestwick, Scotland
1870	Tom Morris Jr.	149	David Strath	Prestwick, Scotland
			Bob Kirk	
1871	No tournament			
1872	Tom Morris Jr.	166	David Strath	Prestwick, Scotland
1873	Tom Kidd	179	Jamie Anderson	St. Andrews, Scotland
1874	Mungo Park	159	No record	Musselburgh, Scotland
1875	Willie Park	166	Bob Martin	Prestwick, Scotland
1876	Bob Martin#	176	David Strath	St. Andrews, Scotland
1877	Jamie Anderson	160	Bob Pringle	Musselburgh, Scotland
1878	Jamie Anderson	157	Robert Kirk	Prestwick, Scotland
1879	Jamie Anderson	169	Andrew Kirkaldy	St. Andrews, Scotland
			James Allan	
1880	Robert Ferguson	162	No record	Musselburgh, Scotland
1881	Robert Ferguson	170	Jamie Anderson	Prestwick, Scotland
1882	Robert Ferguson	171	Willie Fernie	St. Andrews, Scotland
1883	Willie Fernie*	159	Robert Ferguson	Musselburgh, Scotland
1884	Jack Simpson	160	Douglas Rolland	Prestwick, Scotland
			Willie Fernie	
1885	Bob Martin	171	Archie Simpson	St. Andrews, Scotland
1886	David Brown	157	Willie Campbell	Musselburgh, Scotland
1887	Willie Park Jr.	161	Bob Martin	Prestwick, Scotland
1888	Jack Burns	171	Bernard Sayers	St. Andrews, Scotland
			David Anderson	
1889	Willie Park Jr.* (158)	155	Andrew Kirkaldy (163)	Musselburgh, Scotland
1890	John Ball	164	Willie Fernie	Prestwick, Scotland
1891	Hugh Kirkaldy	166	Andrew Kirkaldy	St. Andrews, Scotland
			Willie Fernie	
1892	Harold Hilton	**305	John Ball	Muirfield, Scotland
			Hugh Kirkaldy	
1893	William Auchterlonie	322	John E. Laidlay	Prestwick, Scotland
1894	John H. Taylor	326	Douglas Rolland	Royal St. George's, England
1895	John H. Taylor	322	Alexander Herd	St. Andrews, Scotland
1896	Harry Vardon* (157)	316	John H. Taylor (161)	Muirfield, Scotland
1897	Harold Hilton	314	James Braid	Hoylake, England
1898	Harry Vardon	307	Willie Park Jr.	Prestwick, Scotland
1899	Harry Vardon	310	Jack White	Royal St. George's, England
1900	John H. Taylor	309	Harry Vardon	St. Andrews, Scotland
1901	James Braid	309	Harry Vardon	Muirfield, Scotland
1902	Alexander Herd	307	Harry Vardon	Hoylake, England

British Open (Cont.)

Year	Winner	Score	Runner-Up	Site
1903	Harry Vardon	300	Tom Vardon	Prestwick, Scotland
1904	Jack White	296	John H. Taylor	Royal St. George's, England
1905	James Braid	318	John H. Taylor	St. Andrews, Scotland
			Rolland Jones	
1906	James Braid	300	John H. Taylor	Muirfield, Scotland
1907	Arnaud Massy	312	John H. Taylor	Hoylake, England
1908	James Braid	291	Tom Ball	Prestwick, Scotland
1909	John H. Taylor	295	James Braid	Deal, England
			Tom Ball	
1910	James Braid	299	Alexander Herd	St. Andrews, Scotland
1911	Harry Vardon	303	Arnaud Massy	Royal St. George's, England
1912	Ted Ray	295	Harry Vardon	Muirfield, Scotland
1913	John H. Taylor	304	Ted Ray	Hoylake, England
1914	Harry Vardon	306	John H. Taylor	Prestwick, Scotland
1915–19	No tournament			
1920	George Duncan	303	Alexander Herd	Deal, England
1921	Jock Hutchison* (150)	296	Roger Wethered (159)	St. Andrews, Scotland
1922	Walter Hagen	300	George Duncan	Royal St. George's, England
			Jim Barnes	
1923	Arthur G. Havers	295	Walter Hagen	Troon, Scotland
1924	Walter Hagen	301	Ernest Whitcombe	Hoylake, England
1925	Jim Barnes	300	Archie Compston	Prestwick, Scotland
			Ted Ray	
1926	Bobby Jones	291	Al Watrous	Royal Lytham & St. Annes, England
1927	Bobby Jones	285	Aubrey Boomer	St. Andrews, Scotland
1928	Walter Hagen	292	Gene Sarazen	Royal St. George's, England
1929	Walter Hagen	292	Johnny Farrell	Muirfield, Scotland
1930	Bobby Jones	291	Macdonald Smith	Hoylake, England
			Leo Diegel	
1931	Tommy Armour	296	Jose Jurado	Carnoustie, Scotland
1932	Gene Sarazen	283	Macdonald Smith	Prince's, England
1933	Denny Shute* (149)	292	Craig Wood (154)	St. Andrews, Scotland
1934	Henry Cotton	283	Sidney F. Brews	Royal St. George's, England
1935	Alfred Perry	283	Alfred Padgham	Muirfield, Scotland
1936	Alfred Padgham	287	James Adams	Hoylake, England
1937	Henry Cotton	290	Reginald A. Whitcombe	Carnoustie, Scotland
1938	Reginald A. Whitcombe	295	James Adams	Royal St. George's, England
1939	Richard Burton	290	Johnny Bulla	St. Andrews, Scotland
1940–45	No tournament			
1946	Sam Snead	290	Bobby Locke	St. Andrews, Scotland
			Johnny Bulla	
1947	Fred Daly	293	Reginald W. Horne	Hoylake, England
			Frank Stranahan	
1948	Henry Cotton	294	Fred Daly	Muirfield, Scotland
1949	Bobby Locke* (135)	283	Harry Bradshaw (147)	Royal St. George's, England
1950	Bobby Locke	279	Roberto DeVicenzo	Troon, Scotland
1951	Max Faulkner	285	Tony Cerda	Portrush, Ireland
1952	Bobby Locke	287	Peter Thomson	Royal Lytham & St. Annes, England
1953	Ben Hogan	282	Frank Stranahan	Carnoustie, Scotland
			Dai Rees	
			Peter Thomson	
			Tony Cerda	
1954	Peter Thomson	283	Sidney S. Scott	Royal Birkdale, England
			Dai Rees	
			Bobby Locke	
1955	Peter Thomson	281	John Fallon	St. Andrews, Scotland
1956	Peter Thomson	286	Flory Van Donck	Hoylake, England
1957	Bobby Locke	279	Peter Thomson	St. Andrews, Scotland
1958	Peter Thomson* (139)	278	Dave Thomas (143)	Royal Lytham & St. Annes, England
1959	Gary Player	284	Fred Bullock	Muirfield, Scotland
			Flory Van Donck	
1960	Kel Nagle	278	Arnold Palmer	St. Andrews, Scotland
1961	Arnold Palmer	284	Dai Rees	Royal Birkdale, England
1962	Arnold Palmer	276	Kel Nagle	Troon, Scotland

British Open *(Cont.)*

Year	Winner	Score	Runner-Up	Site
1963	Bob Charles* (140)	277	Phil Rodgers (148)	Royal Lytham & St. Annes, England
1964	Tony Lema	279	Jack Nicklaus	St. Andrews, Scotland
1965	Peter Thomson	285	Brian Huggett	Southport, England
			Christy O'Connor	
1966	Jack Nicklaus	282	Doug Sanders	Muirfield, Scotland
			Dave Thomas	
1967	Robert DeVicenzo	278	Jack Nicklaus	Hoylake, England
1968	Gary Player	289	Jack Nicklaus	Carnoustie, Scotland
			Bob Charles	
1969	Tony Jacklin	280	Bob Charles	Royal Lytham & St. Annes, England
1970	Jack Nicklaus* (72)	283	Doug Sanders (73)	St. Andrews, Scotland
1971	Lee Trevino	278	Lu Liang Huan	Royal Birkdale, England
1972	Lee Trevino	278	Jack Nicklaus	Muirfield, Scotland
1973	Tom Weiskopf	276	Johnny Miller	Troon, Scotland
1974	Gary Player	282	Peter Oosterhuis	Royal Lytham & St. Annes, England
1975	Tom Watson* (71)	279	Jack Newton (72)	Carnoustie, Scotland
1976	Johnny Miller	279	Jack Nicklaus	Royal Birkdale, England
			Seve Ballesteros	
1977	Tom Watson	268	Jack Nicklaus	Turnberry, Scotland
1978	Jack Nicklaus	281	Ben Crenshaw	St. Andrews, Scotland
			Tom Kite	
			Ray Floyd	
			Simon Owen	
1979	Seve Ballesteros	283	Ben Crenshaw	Royal Lytham & St. Annes, England
			Jack Nicklaus	
1980	Tom Watson	271	Lee Trevino	Muirfield, Scotland
1981	Bill Rogers	276	Bernhard Langer	Royal St. George's, England
1982	Tom Watson	284	Nick Price	Troon, Scotland
			Peter Oosterhuis	
1983	Tom Watson	275	Andy Bean	Royal Birkdale, England
1984	Seve Ballesteros	276	Tom Watson	St. Andrews, Scotland
			Bernhard Langer	
1985	Sandy Lyle	282	Payne Stewart	Royal St. George's, England
1986	Greg Norman	280	Gordon Brand	Turnberry, Scotland
1987	Nick Faldo	279	Paul Azinger	Muirfield, Scotland
			Rodger Davis	
1988	Seve Ballesteros	273	Nick Price	Royal Lytham & St. Annes, England
1989††	Mark Calcavecchia* (4-3-3-3)	275	Wayne Grady (4-4-4-4)	Troon, Scotland
			Greg Norman (3-3-4-x)	
1990	Nick Faldo	270	Payne Stewart	St. Andrews, Scotland
			Mark McNulty	
1991	Ian Baker-Finch	272	Mike Harwood	Royal Birkdale, England
1992	Nick Faldo	272	John Cook	Muirfield, Scotland
1993	Greg Norman	267	Nick Faldo	Royal St. George's, England
1994	Nick Price	268	Jesper Parnevik	Turnberry, Scotland
1995	John Daly* (4-3-4-4)	282	C. Rocca (5-4-7-3)	St. Andrews, Scotland
1996	Tom Lehman	271	Mark McCumber	Royal Lytham & St. Annes, England
			Ernie Els	
1997	Justin Leonard	272	Jesper Parnevik	Troon, Scotland
			Darren Clarke	
1998	Mark O'Meara* (4-4-5-4)	280	Brian Watts (5-4-5-5)	Southport, England
1999	Paul Lawrie* (5-4-3-3)	290	Jean Van de Velde (6-4-3-5)	Carnoustie GC, Carnoustie,
			Justin Leonard (5-4-4-5)	Scotland
2000	Tiger Woods	269	Thomas Bjorn	St. Andrews, Scotland
			Ernie Els	
2001	David Duval	274	Niclas Fasth	Royal Lytham & St. Annes, England
2002	Ernie Els*	278	Stuart Appleby	Muirfield, Scotland
2003	Ben Curtis	283	Vijay Singh	Royal St. George's, England

*Winner in playoff. Playoff scores are in parentheses. †The first event was open only to professional golfers.
‡The second annual open was open to amateurs and pros. #Tied, but refused playoff.
**Championship extended from 36 to 72 holes. ††Playoff cut from 18 holes to 4 holes.

PGA Championship

Year	Winner	Score	Runner-Up	Site
1916	Jim Barnes	1 up	Jock Hutchison	Siwanoy CC, Bronxville, NY
1917–18	No tournament			
1919	Jim Barnes	6 & 5	Fred McLeod	Engineers CC, Roslyn, NY
1920	Jock Hutchison	1 up	J. Douglas Edgar	Flossmoor CC, Flossmoor, IL
1921	Walter Hagen	3 & 2	Jim Barnes	Inwood CC, Far Rockaway, NY
1922	Gene Sarazen	4 & 3	Emmet French	Oakmont CC, Oakmont, PA
1923	Gene Sarazen	1 up 38 holes	Walter Hagen	Pelham CC, Pelham, NY
1924	Walter Hagen	2 up	Jim Barnes	French Lick CC, French Lick, IN
1925	Walter Hagen	6 & 5	William Mehlhorn	Olympia Fields CC, Olympia Fields, IL
1926	Walter Hagen	5 & 3	Leo Diegel	Salisbury GC, Westbury, NY
1927	Walter Hagen	1 up	Joe Turnesa	Cedar Crest CC, Dallas
1928	Leo Diegel	6 & 5	Al Espinosa	Five Farms CC, Baltimore
1929	Leo Diegel	6 & 4	Johnny Farrell	Hillcrest CC, Los Angeles
1930	Tommy Armour	1 up	Gene Sarazen	Fresh Meadow CC, Flushing, NY
1931	Tom Creavy	2 & 1	Denny Shute	Wannamoisett CC, Rumford, RI
1932	Olin Dutra	4 & 3	Frank Walsh	Keller GC, St. Paul
1933	Gene Sarazen	5 & 4	Willie Goggin	Blue Mound CC, Milwaukee
1934	Paul Runyan	1 up	Craig Wood	Park CC, Williamsville, NY
1935	Johnny Revolta	5 & 4 38 holes	Tommy Armour	Twin Hills CC, Oklahoma City
1936	Denny Shute	3 & 2	Jimmy Thomson	Pinehurst CC, Pinehurst, NC
1937	Denny Shute	1 up 37 holes	Harold McSpaden	Pittsburgh FC, Aspinwall, PA
1938	Paul Runyan	8 & 7	Sam Snead	Shawnee CC, Shawnee-on-Delaware, PA
1939	Henry Picard	1 up 37 holes	Byron Nelson	Pomonok CC, Flushing, NY
1940	Byron Nelson	1 up	Sam Snead	Hershey CC, Hershey, PA
1941	Vic Ghezzi	1 up 38 holes	Byron Nelson	Cherry Hills CC, Denver
1942	Sam Snead	2 & 1	Jim Turnesa	Seaview CC, Atlantic City
1943	No tournament			
1944	Bob Hamilton	1 up	Byron Nelson	Manito G & CC, Spokane, WA
1945	Byron Nelson	4 & 3	Sam Byrd	Morraine CC, Dayton
1946	Ben Hogan	6 & 4	Ed Oliver	Portland CC, Portland, OR
1947	Jim Ferrier	2 & 1	Chick Harbert	Plum Hollow CC, Detroit
1948	Ben Hogan	7 & 6	Mike Turnesa	Norwood Hills CC, St. Louis
1949	Sam Snead	3 & 2	Johnny Palmer	Hermitage CC, Richmond
1950	Chandler Harper	4 & 3	Henry Williams Jr.	Scioto CC, Columbus, OH
1951	Sam Snead	7 & 6	Walter Burkemo	Oakmont CC, Oakmont, PA
1952	Jim Turnesa	1 up	Chick Harbert	Big Spring CC, Louisville
1953	Walter Burkemo	2 & 1	Felice Torza	Birmingham CC, Birmingham, MI
1954	Chick Harbert	4 & 3	Walter Burkemo	Keller GC, St. Paul
1955	Doug Ford	4 & 3	Cary Middlecoff	Meadowbrook CC, Detroit
1956	Jack Burke	3 & 2	Ted Kroll	Blue Hill CC, Boston
1957	Lionel Hebert	2 & 1	Dow Finsterwald	Miami Valley CC, Dayton
1958	Dow Finsterwald	276	Billy Casper	Llanerch CC, Havertown, PA
1959	Bob Rosburg	277	Jerry Barber Doug Sanders	Minneapolis GC, St. Louis Park, MN
1960	Jay Hebert	281	Jim Ferrier	Firestone CC, Akron
1961	Jerry Barber* (67)	277	Don January (68)	Olympia Fields CC, Olympia Fields, IL
1962	Gary Player	278	Bob Goalby	Aronimink GC, Newton Square, PA
1963	Jack Nicklaus	279	Dave Ragan Jr.	Dallas Athletic Club, Dallas
1964	Bobby Nichols	271	Jack Nicklaus Arnold Palmer	Columbus CC, Columbus, OH
1965	Dave Marr	280	Billy Casper Jack Nicklaus	Laurel Valley CC, Ligonier, PA
1966	Al Geiberger	280	Dudley Wysong	Firestone CC, Akron
1967	Don Massengale* (69)	281	Don January (71)	Columbine CC, Littleton, CO
1968	Julius Boros	281	Bob Charles Arnold Palmer	Pecan Valley CC, San Antonio
1969	Ray Floyd	276	Gary Player	NCR CC, Dayton
1970	Dave Stockton	279	Arnold Palmer Bob Murphy	Southern Hills CC, Tulsa

PGA Championship (Cont.)

Year	Winner	Score	Runner-Up	Site
1971 ....Jack Nicklaus		281	Billy Casper	PGA Nat'l GC, Palm Beach Gardens, FL
1972 ....Gary Player		281	Tommy Aaron	Oakland Hills CC, Birmingham, MI
			Jim Jamieson	
1973 ....Jack Nicklaus		277	Bruce Crampton	Canterbury GC, Cleveland
1974 ....Lee Trevino		276	Jack Nicklaus	Tanglewood GC, Winston-Salem, NC
1975 ....Jack Nicklaus		276	Bruce Crampton	Firestone CC, Akron
1976 ....Dave Stockton		281	Ray Floyd	Congressional CC, Bethesda, MD
			Don January	
1977† ....Lanny Wadkins* (4-4-4)		282	Gene Littler (4-4-5)	Pebble Beach GL, Pebble Beach, CA
1978 ....John Mahaffey* (4–3)		276	Jerry Pate (4–4)	Oakmont CC, Oakmont, PA
			Tom Watson (4–5)	
1979 ....David Graham* (4-4-2)		272	Ben Crenshaw (4-4-4)	Oakland Hills CC, Birmingham, MI
1980 ....Jack Nicklaus		274	Andy Bean	Oak Hill CC, Rochester, NY
1981 ....Larry Nelson		273	Fuzzy Zoeller	Atlanta Athletic Club, Duluth, GA
1982 ....Raymond Floyd		272	Lanny Wadkins	Southern Hills CC, Tulsa
1983 ....Hal Sutton		274	Jack Nicklaus	Riviera CC, Pacific Palisades, CA
1984 ....Lee Trevino		273	Gary Player	Shoal Creek, Birmingham, AL
			Lanny Wadkins	
1985 ....Hubert Green		278	Lee Trevino	Cherry Hills CC, Denver
1986 ....Bob Tway		276	Greg Norman	Inverness CC, Toledo
1987 ....Larry Nelson* (4)		287	Lanny Wadkins (5)	PGA Natl GC, Palm Beach Gardens, FL
1988 ....Jeff Sluman		272	Paul Azinger	Oak Tree GC, Edmond, OK
1989 ....Payne Stewart		276	Mike Reid	Kemper Lakes GC, Hawthorn Woods, IL
1990 ....Wayne Grady		282	Fred Couples	Shoal Creek, Birmingham, AL
1991 ....John Daly		276	Bruce Lietzke	Crooked Stick GC, Carmel, IN
1992 ....Nick Price		278	Jim Gallagher Jr.	Bellerive CC, St. Louis
1993 ....Paul Azinger* (4–4)		272	Greg Norman (4–5)	Inverness CC, Toledo
1994 ....Nick Price		269	Corey Pavin	Southern Hills CC, Tulsa
1995 ....Steve Elkington* (3)		267	Colin Montgomerie (4)	Riviera CC, Pacific Palisades, CA
1996 ....Mark Brooks* (3)		277	Kenny Perry (x)	Valhalla GC, Louisville
1997 ....Davis Love III		269	Justin Leonard	Winged Foot GC, Mamaroneck, NY
1998 ....Vijay Singh		271	Steve Stricker	Sahalee CC, Redmond, WA
1999 ....Tiger Woods		277	Sergio Garcia	Medinah CC, Medinah, IL
2000 ....Tiger Woods* (3-4-5)		270	Bob May (4-4-x)	Valhalla GC, Louisville
2001 ....David Toms		265	Phil Mickelson	Atlanta AC, Duluth, GA
2002 ....Rich Beem		278	Tiger Woods	Hazeltine National GC, Shaska, MN
2003 ....Shaun Micheel		276	Chad Campbell	Oak Hill CC, Rochester, NY

*Winner in playoff. Playoff scores are in parentheses. †Playoff changed from 18 holes to sudden death.

Alltime Major Championship Winners

	Masters	U.S. Open	British Open	PGA Champ.	U.S. Amateur	British Amateur	Total
†Jack Nicklaus 6		4	3	5	2	0	20
Bobby Jones......................0		4	3	0	5	1	13
Walter Hagen.....................0		2	4	5	0	0	11
*Tiger Woods......................3		2	1	2	3	0	11
Ben Hogan.........................2		4	1	2	0	0	9
†Gary Player 3		1	3	2	0	0	9
John Ball 0		0	1	0	0	8	9
†Arnold Palmer 4		1	2	0	1	0	8
†Tom Watson 2		1	5	0	0	0	8
Harold Hilton.....................0		0	2	0	1	4	7
Gene Sarazen....................1		2	1	3	0	0	7
Sam Snead 3		0	1	3	0	0	7
Harry Vardon 0		1	6	0	0	0	7

*Active PGA player. †Active Senior PGA player.

Alltime Multiple Professional Major Winners

MASTERS

Jack Nicklaus 6
Arnold Palmer.............4
Jimmy Demaret 3
Nick Faldo 3
Gary Player 3
Sam Snead 3
Tiger Woods 3
Seve Ballesteros........2
Ben Crenshaw............2
Ben Hogan 2
Bernhard Langer 2
Byron Nelson..............2
José María Olazábal ...2
Horton Smith 2
Tom Watson 2

U.S. OPEN

Willie Anderson 4
Ben Hogan 4
Bobby Jones 4
Jack Nicklaus 4

U.S. OPEN (Cont.)

Hale Irwin 3
Julius Boros 2
Billy Casper 2
Ernie Els 2
Ralph Guldahl 2
Walter Hagen 2
Lee Janzen.................2
John McDermott 2
Cary Middlecoff 2
Andy North 2
Gene Sarazen 2
Alex Smith 2
Payne Stewart 2
Curtis Strange 2
Lee Trevino.................2
Tiger Woods 2

BRITISH OPEN

Harry Vardon 6
James Braid 5
J.H. Taylor 5

BRITISH OPEN (Cont.)

Peter Thomson 5
Tom Watson 5
Walter Hagen 4
Bobby Locke 4
Tom Morris Sr..............4
Tom Morris Jr. 4
Willie Park 4
Jamie Anderson 3
Seve Ballesteros 3
Henry Cotton 3
Nick Faldo 3
Robert Ferguson 3
Bobby Jones 3
Jack Nicklaus 3
Gary Player.................3
Harold Hilton 2
Bob Martin 2
Greg Norman 2
Arnold Palmer.............2
Willie Park Jr. 2
Lee Trevino.................2

PGA CHAMPIONSHIP

Walter Hagen 5
Jack Nicklaus 5
Gene Sarazen 3
Sam Snead..................3
Jim Barnes 2
Leo Diegel 2
Raymond Floyd 2
Ben Hogan 2
Byron Nelson 2
Larry Nelson 2
Gary Player.................2
Paul Runyan 2
Denny Shute 2
Dave Stockton 2
Lee Trevino 2
Tiger Woods 2

THE PGA TOUR

Most Career Wins*

	Wins		Wins		Wins
Sam Snead	82	Billy Casper	51	Tiger Woods	39
Jack Nicklaus	73	Walter Hagen	44	Lloyd Mangrum	36
Ben Hogan	64	Cary Middlecoff	40	Horton Smith	32
Arnold Palmer	62	Gene Sarazen	39	Harry Cooper	31
Byron Nelson	52	Tom Watson	39	Jimmy Demaret	31

* Through 10/3/03

Season Money Leaders

	Earnings ($)		Earnings ($)		Earnings ($)
1934 ...Paul Runyan	6,767.00	1957 ...Dick Mayer	65,835.00	1980 ...Tom Watson	530,808.33
1935 ...Johnny Revolta	9,543.00	1958 ...Arnold Palmer	42,607.50	1981 ...Tom Kite	375,698.84
1936 ...Horton Smith	7,682.00	1959 ...Art Wall	53,167.60	1982 ...Craig Stadler	446,462.00
1937 ...Harry Cooper	14,138.69	1960 ...Arnold Palmer	75,262.85	1983 ...Hal Sutton	426,668.00
1938 ...Sam Snead	19,534.49	1961 ...Gary Player	64,540.45	1984 ...Tom Watson	476,260.00
1939 ...Henry Picard	10,303.00	1962 ...Arnold Palmer	81,448.33	1985 ...Curtis Strange	542,321.00
1940 ...Ben Hogan	10,655.00	1963 ...Arnold Palmer	128,230.00	1986 ...Greg Norman	653,296.00
1941 ...Ben Hogan	18,358.00	1964 ...Jack Nicklaus	113,284.50	1987 ...Curtis Strange	925,941.00
1942 ...Ben Hogan	13,143.00	1965 ...Jack Nicklaus	140,752.14	1988 ...Curtis Strange	1,147,644.00
1943 ...No statistics compiled		1966 ...Billy Casper	121,944.92	1989 ...Tom Kite	1,395,278.00
1944 ...Byron Nelson*	37,967.69	1967 ...Jack Nicklaus	188,998.08	1990 ...Greg Norman	1,165,477.00
1945 ...Byron Nelson*	63,335.66	1968 ...Billy Casper	205,168.67	1991 ...Corey Pavin	979,430.00
1946 ...Ben Hogan	42,556.16	1969 ...Frank Beard	164,707.11	1992 ...Fred Couples	1,344,188.00
1947 ...Jimmy Demaret	27,936.83	1970 ...Lee Trevino	157,037.63	1993 ...Nick Price	1,478,557.00
1948 ...Ben Hogan	32,112.00	1971 ...Jack Nicklaus	244,490.50	1994 ...Nick Price	1,499,927.00
1949 ...Sam Snead	31,593.83	1972 ...Jack Nicklaus	320,542.26	1995 ...Greg Norman	1,654,959.00
1950 ...Sam Snead	35,758.83	1973 ...Jack Nicklaus	308,362.10	1996 ...Tom Lehman	1,780,159.00
1951 ...Lloyd Mangrum	26,088.83	1974 ...Johnny Miller	353,021.59	1997 ...Tiger Woods	2,066,833.00
1952 ...Julius Boros	37,032.97	1975 ...Jack Nicklaus	298,149.17	1998 ...David Duval	2,591,031.00
1953 ...Lew Worsham	34,002.00	1976 ...Jack Nicklaus	266,438.57	1999 ...Tiger Woods	6,616,585.00
1954 ...Bob Toski	65,819.81	1977 ...Tom Watson	310,653.16	2000 ...Tiger Woods	9,188,321.00
1955 ...Julius Boros	63,121.55	1978 ...Tom Watson	362,428.93	2001 ...Tiger Woods	5,687,777.00
1956 ...Ted Kroll	72,835.83	1979 ...Tom Watson	462,636.00	2002 ...Tiger Woods	6,912,625.00

* War bonds. Note: Total money listed from 1968 through 1974. Official money listed from 1975 on.

Career Money Leaders*

	Player	Earnings ($)
1.	Tiger Woods	39,382,598
2.	Davis Love II	25,591,946
3.	Vijay Singh	24,388,523
4.	Phil Mickelson	23,646,350
5.	Nick Price	18,819,927
6.	Jim Furyk	18,672,197
7.	Ernie Els	18,535,527
8.	Scott Hoch	17,216,624
9.	David Toms	16,463,734
10	David Duval	16,235,305
11	Justin Leonard	15,915,559
12	Mark Calcavecchia	15,659,067
13	Hal Sutton	15,145,667
14	Fred Couples	15,070,065
15	Jeff Sluman	14,310,426
16	Tom Lehman	14,038,977
17	Greg Norman	13,931,929
18	Kenny Perry	13,721,988
19	Brad Faxon	13,549,795
20	Mark O'Meara	13,143,679
21	Loren Roberts	13,010,425
22	Fred Funk	12,742,430
23	Paul Azinger	12,649,495
24	Mike Weir	12,642,708
25	Bob Estes	12,078,029
26	John Huston	12,034,999
27	Bob Tway	11,910,533
28	Payne Stewart	11,737,008
29	Jay Haas	11,485,390
30	Lee Janzen	11,252,000
31	John Cook	11,084,705
32	Rocco Mediate	10,996,130
33	Tom Kite	10,920,309
34	Jeff Maggert	10,742,125
35	Scott Verplank	10,626,942
36	Chris DiMarco	10,514,935
37	Corey Pavin	10,220,841
38	Kirk Triplett	10,117,890
39	Steve Elkington	10,018,932
40	Billy Mayfair	9,972,813
41	Tom Watson	9,881,778
42	Jesper Parnevik	9,740,697
43	Craig Stadler	9,593,493
44	Stuart Appleby	9,378,347
45	Stewart Cink	9,298,043
46	Steve Lowery	9,051,377
47	Robert Allenby	8,801,721
48	Billy Andrade	8,647,832
49	Duffy Waldorf	8,590,789
50	Jerry Kelly	8,548,984

*Through 10/5/03.

Year by Year Statistical Leaders

SCORING AVERAGE

Year	Player	Avg
1980	Lee Trevino	69.73
1981	Tom Kite	69.80
1982	Tom Kite	70.21
1983	Raymond Floyd	70.61
1984	Calvin Peete	70.56
1985	Don Pooley	70.36
1986	Scott Hoch	70.08
1987	David Frost	70.09
1988	Greg Norman	69.38
1989	Payne Stewart	69.485†
1990	Greg Norman	69.10
1991	Fred Couples	69.59
1992	Fred Couples	69.38
1993	Greg Norman	68.90
1994	Greg Norman	68.81
1995	Greg Norman	69.06
1996	Tom Lehman	69.32
1997	Nick Price	68.98
1998	David Duval	69.13
1999	Tiger Woods	68.43
2000	Tiger Woods	67.79
2001	Tiger Woods	68.81
2002	Tiger Woods	68.13

Note: Scoring average per round, with adjustments made at each round for the field's course scoring average.

DRIVING DISTANCE

Year	Player	Yds
1980	Dan Pohl	274.3
1981	Dan Pohl	280.1
1982	Bill Calfee	275.3
1983	John McComish	277.4
1984	Bill Glasson	276.5
1985	Andy Bean	278.2
1986	Davis Love III	285.7
1987	John McComish	283.9
1988	Steve Thomas	284.6
1989	Ed Humenik	280.9
1990	Tom Purtzer	279.6
1991	John Daly	288.9
1992	John Daly	283.4

DRIVING DISTANCE (Cont.)

Year	Player	Yds
1993	John Daly	288.9
1994	Davis Love III	283.8
1995	John Daly	289.0
1996	John Daly	288.8
1997	John Daly	302.0
1998	John Daly	299.4
1999	John Daly	305.6
2000	John Daly	301.4
2001	John Daly	306.7
2002	John Daly	306.8

Note: Average computed by charting distance of two tee shots on a predetermined par-four or par-five hole (one on front nine, one on back nine).

DRIVING ACCURACY

Year	Player	Pct
1980	Mike Reid	79.5
1981	Calvin Peete	81.9
1982	Calvin Peete	84.6
1983	Calvin Peete	81.3
1984	Calvin Peete	77.5
1985	Calvin Peete	80.6
1986	Calvin Peete	81.7
1987	Calvin Peete	83.0
1988	Calvin Peete	82.5
1989	Calvin Peete	82.6
1990	Calvin Peete	83.7
1991	Hale Irwin	78.3
1992	Doug Tewell	82.3
1993	Doug Tewell	82.5
1994	David Edwards	81.6
1995	Fred Funk	81.3
1996	Fred Funk	78.7
1997	Allen Doyle	80.8
1998	Bruce Fleisher	81.4
1999	Fred Funk	80.2
2000	Fred Funk	79.7
2001	Joe Durant	81.1
2002	Fred Funk	81.2

Note: Percentage of fairways hit on number of par-four and par-five holes played; par-three holes excluded.

GREENS IN REGULATION

Year	Player	Avg
1980	Jack Nicklaus	72.1
1981	Calvin Peete	73.1
1982	Calvin Peete	72.4
1983	Calvin Peete	71.4
1984	Andy Bean	72.1
1985	John Mahaffey	71.9
1986	John Mahaffey	72.0
1987	Gil Morgan	73.3
1988	John Adams	73.9
1989	Bruce Lietzke	72.6
1990	Doug Tewell	70.9
1991	Bruce Lietzke	73.3
1992	Tim Simpson	74.0
1993	Fuzzy Zoeller	73.6
1994	Bill Glasson	73.0
1995	Lenny Clements	72.3
1996	Fred Couples	71.8
	Mark O'Meara	71.8
1997	Tom Lehman	72.7
1998	Hal Sutton	71.3
1999	Tiger Woods	71.4
2000	Tiger Woods	75.2
2001	Tom Lehman	74.5
2002	Tiger Woods	74.0

Note: Average of greens reached in regulation out of total holes played; hole is considered hit in regulation if any part of the ball rests on the putting surface in two shots less than the hole's par—a par-5 hit in two shots is one green in regulation.

PUTTING

Year	Player	Avg
1980	Jerry Pate	28.81
1981	Alan Tapie	28.70
1982	Ben Crenshaw	28.65
1983	Morris Hatalsky	27.96
1984	Gary McCord	28.57
1985	Craig Stadler	28.627†
1986	Greg Norman	1.736
1987	Ben Crenshaw	1.743
1988	Don Pooley	1.729
1989	Steve Jones	1.734

† Number had to be carried to extra decimal place to determine winner.

Year by Year Statistical Leaders (Cont.)

PUTTING (Cont.)

1990	Larry Rinker	1.7467†	1995	Jim Furyk	1.708
1991	Jay Don Blake	1.7326†	1996	Brad Faxon	1.709
1992	Mark O'Meara	1.731	1997	Don Pooley	1.718
1993	David Frost	1.739	1998	Rick Fehr	1.722
1994	Loren Roberts	1.737	1999	Brad Faxon	1.723

2000	Brad Faxon	1.704
2001	David Frost	1.708
2002	Bob Heintz	1.682

Note: Average number of putts taken on greens reached in regulation; prior to 1986, based on average number of putts per 18 holes.

SAND SAVES

1980	Bob Eastwood	65.4	1988	Greg Powers	63.5
1981	Tom Watson	60.1	1989	Mike Sullivan	66.0
1982	Isao Aoki	60.2	1990	Paul Azinger	67.2
1983	Isao Aoki	62.3	1991	Ben Crenshaw	64.9
1984	Peter Oosterhuis	64.7	1992	Mitch Adcock	66.9
1985	Tom Purtzer	60.8	1993	Ken Green	64.4
1986	Paul Azinger	63.8	1994	Corey Pavin	65.4
1987	Paul Azinger	63.2	1995	Billy Mayfair	68.6

1996	Gary Rusnak	64.0
1997	Bob Estes	70.3
1998	Keith Fergus	71.0
1999	Jeff Sluman	67.3
2000	Fred Couples	67.0
2001	Franklin Langham	68.9
2002	J. Olazabal	64.9

Note: Percentage of up-and-down efforts from greenside sand traps only—fairway bunkers excluded.

PAR BREAKERS

1980	Tom Watson	.213	1984	Craig Stadler	.220
1981	Bruce Lietzke	.225	1985	Craig Stadler	.218
1982	Tom Kite	.2154†	1986	Greg Norman	.248
1983	Tom Watson	.211	1987	Mark Calcavecchia	.221

1988	Ken Green	.236
1989	Greg Norman	.224
1990	Greg Norman	.219

Note: Average based on total birdies and eagles scored out of total holes played. Discontinued as an official category after 1990.

EAGLES

1980	Dave Eichelberger	16	1987	Phil Blackmar	20
1981	Bruce Lietzke	12	1988	Ken Green	21
1982	Tom Weiskopf	10	1989	Lon Hinkle	14
	J.C. Snead	10		Duffy Waldorf	14
	Andy Bean	10	1990	Paul Azinger	14
1983	Chip Beck	15	1991	Andy Bean	15
1984	Gary Hallberg	15	1992	Dan Forsman	18
1985	Larry Rinker	14	1993	Davis Love III	15
1986	Joey Sindelar	16	1994	Davis Love III	18

1995	Kelly Gibson	16
1996	Tom Watson	97.2
1997	Tiger Woods	104.1
1998	Davis Love III	83.3
1999	Vijay Singh	104.8
2000	Tiger Woods	72.0
2001	Phil Mickelson	73.8
2002	John Daly	78.4

Note: Total of eagles scored 1980–1995. Since 1996 winner determined by number of holes played per eagle.

BIRDIES

1980	Andy Bean	388	1988	Dan Forsman	465
1981	Vance Heafner	388	1989	Ted Schulz	415
1982	Andy Bean	392	1990	Mike Donald	401
1983	Hal Sutton	399	1991	Scott Hoch	446
1984	Mark O'Meara	419	1992	Jeff Sluman	417
1985	Joey Sindelar	411	1993	John Huston	426
1986	Joey Sindelar	415	1994	Brad Bryant	397
1987	Dan Forsman	409	1995	Steve Lowery	410

1996	Fred Couples	4.20
1997	Tiger Woods	4.25
1998	David Duval	4.29
1999	Tiger Woods	4.46
2000	Tiger Woods	4.92
2001	Phil Mickelson	4.49
2002	Tiger Woods	4.47

Note: Total of birdies scored 1980–95. Since 1996, winner determined by average number of birdies per round.

ALL-AROUND

1987	Dan Pohl	170	1993	Gil Morgan	252
1988	Payne Stewart	170	1994	Bob Estes	227
1989	Paul Azinger	250	1995	Justin Leonard	323
1990	Paul Azinger	162	1996	Fred Couples	214
1991	Scott Hoch	283	1997	Bill Glasson	282
1992	Fred Couples	256	1998	John Huston	151

1999	Tiger Woods	120
2000	Tiger Woods	113
2001	Phil Mickelson	174
2002	Phil Mickelson	259

Note: Sum of the places of standing from the other statistical categories; the player with the number closest to zero leads.

† Number had to be carried to extra decimal place to determine winner.

PGA Player of the Year Award

1948 ....Ben Hogan	1966 ....Billy Casper	1984 ....Tom Watson
1949 ....Sam Snead	1967 ....Jack Nicklaus	1985 ....Lanny Wadkins
1950 ....Ben Hogan	1968 ....Not awarded	1986 ....Bob Tway
1951 ....Ben Hogan	1969 ....Orville Moody	1987 ....Paul Azinger
1952 ....Julius Boros	1970 ....Billy Casper	1988 ....Curtis Strange
1953 ....Ben Hogan	1971 ....Lee Trevino	1989 ....Tom Kite
1954 ....Ed Furgol	1972 ....Jack Nicklaus	1990 ....Wayne Levi
1955 ....Doug Ford	1973 ....Jack Nicklaus	1991 ....Fred Couples
1956 ....Jack Burke	1974 ....Johnny Miller	1992 ....Fred Couples
1957 ....Dick Mayer	1975 ....Jack Nicklaus	1993 ....Nick Price
1958 ....Dow Finsterwald	1976 ....Jack Nicklaus	1994 ....Nick Price
1959 ....Art Wall	1977 ....Tom Watson	1995 ....Greg Norman
1960 ....Arnold Palmer	1978 ....Tom Watson	1996 ....Tom Lehman
1961 ....Jerry Barber	1979 ....Tom Watson	1997 ....Tiger Woods
1962 ....Arnold Palmer	1980 ....Tom Watson	1998 ....David Duval
1963 ....Julius Boros	1981 ....Bill Rogers	1999 ....Tiger Woods
1964 ....Ken Venturi	1982 ....Tom Watson	2000 ....Tiger Woods
1965 ....Dave Marr	1983 ....Hal Sutton	2001 ....Tiger Woods
		2002 ....Tiger Woods

Vardon Trophy: Scoring Average

Year	Winner	Avg	Year	Winner	Avg	Year	Winner	Avg
1937	Harry Cooper	*500	1962	Arnold Palmer	70.27	1983	Raymond Floyd	70.61
1938	Sam Snead	520	1963	Billy Casper	70.58	1984	Calvin Peete	70.56
1939	Byron Nelson	473	1964	Arnold Palmer	70.01	1985	Don Pooley	70.36
1940	Ben Hogan	423	1965	Billy Casper	70.85	1986	Scott Hoch	70.08
1941	Ben Hogan	494	1966	Billy Casper	70.27	1987	Don Pohl	70.25
1942–46	No award		1967	Arnold Palmer	70.18	1988	Chip Beck	69.46
1947	Jimmy Demaret	69.90	1968	Billy Casper	69.82	1989	Greg Norman	69.49
1948	Ben Hogan	69.30	1969	Dave Hill	70.34	1990	Greg Norman	69.10
1949	Sam Snead	69.37	1970	Lee Trevino	70.64	1991	Fred Couples	69.59
1950	Sam Snead	69.23	1971	Lee Trevino	70.27	1992	Fred Couples	69.38
1951	Lloyd Mangrum	70.05	1972	Lee Trevino	70.89	1993	Nick Price	69.11
1952	Jack Burke	70.54	1973	Bruce Crampton	70.57	1994	Greg Norman	68.81
1953	Lloyd Mangrum	70.22	1974	Lee Trevino	70.53	1995	Steve Elkington	69.62
1954	E.J. Harrison	70.41	1975	Bruce Crampton	70.51	1996	Tom Lehman	69.32
1955	Sam Snead	69.86	1976	Don January	70.56	1997	Nick Price	68.98
1956	Cary Middlecoff	70.35	1977	Tom Watson	70.32	1998	David Duval	69.13
1957	Dow Finsterwald	70.30	1978	Tom Watson	70.16	1999	Tiger Woods	68.43
1958	Bob Rosburg	70.11	1979	Tom Watson	70.27	2000	Tiger Woods	67.79
1959	Art Wall	70.35	1980	Lee Trevino	69.73	2001	Tiger Woods	68.81
1960	Billy Casper	69.95	1981	Tom Kite	69.80	2002	Tiger Woods	68.13
1961	Arnold Palmer	69.85	1982	Tom Kite	70.21			

*Point system used, 1937–41.

Note: As of 1988, based on minimum of 60 rounds per year. Adjusted for average score of field in tournaments entered.

Alltime PGA Tour Records*

Scoring

90 HOLES

324—(65-61-67-66-65) by Joe Durant, at four courses, La Quinta, CA, to win the 2001 Bob Hope Classic (36 under par).

72 HOLES

254—(64-62-63-65) by Tommy Armour III, at LaCantera GC, San Antonio, TX, to win the 2003 Valero Texas Open (26 under par).

54 HOLES, OPENING ROUNDS

189—(64-62-63) by John Cook, at the TPC at Southwind, Memphis, en route to winning the 1996 St. Jude Classic.

189—(65-60-64) Mark Calcavecchia, at the TPC at Scottsdale, Scottsdale, AZ, en route to winning the 2001 Phoenix Open.

54 HOLES, OPENING ROUNDS (Cont.)

189—(64-62-63) by Tommy Armour III, at LaCantera GC, San Antonio, TX, en route to winning the 2003 Valero Texas Open.

54 HOLES, CONSECUTIVE ROUNDS

189—(63-63-63) by Chandler Harper in the last three rounds to win the 1954 Texas Open at Brackenridge Park GC, San Antonio.

189—(64-62-63) by John Cook, at the TPC at Southwind, Memphis, in the first three rounds en route to winning the 1996 St. Jude Classic.

189—(65-60-64) Mark Calcavecchia, at the TPC at Scottsdale, Scottsdale, AZ, in the first three rounds en route to winning the 2001 Phoenix Open.

Alltime PGA Tour Records *(Cont.)**

Scoring *(Cont.)*

54 HOLES, CONSECUTIVE ROUNDS *(Cont.)*

189—(64-62-63) by Tommy Armour III, at LaCantera GC, San Antonio, TX, in the first three rounds en route to winning the 2003 Valero Texas Open.

36 HOLES, OPENING ROUNDS

125—(64–61) by Tiger Woods, in the 2000 World Golf Championships/ NEC Invitational, which he won, at Firestone CC, Akron.

125—(65–60) by Mark Calcavecchia, in the 2001 Phoenix Open, which he won, at TPC at Scottsdale, Scottsdale, AZ.

36 HOLES, CONSECUTIVE ROUNDS

125—(64–61) by Gay Brewer, in the middle rounds of the 1967 Pensacola Open, which he won, at Pensacola CC, Pensacola, FL.

125—(63–62) by Ron Streck, in the last two rounds to win the 1978 Texas Open at Oak Hills CC, San Antonio.

125—(62–63) by Blaine McCallister, in the middle two rounds of the 1988 Hardee's Golf Classic, which he won at Oakwood CC, Coal Valley, IL.

125—(62–63) by John Cook, in the middle two rounds of the 1996 St. Jude Classic, which he won at the TPC at Southwind, Memphis.

125—(62–63) by John Cook, in the fourth and fifth rounds in winning the 1997 Bob Hope Chrysler Classic at Indian Wells CC, Indian Hills, CA.

125—(64–61) by Tiger Woods, in the first two rounds of the 2000 World Golf Championship/ NEC Invitational, which he won, at Firestone CC, Akron.

125—(65–60) by Mark Calcavecchia, in the first two rounds of the 2001 Phoenix Open, which he won, at TPC at Scottsdale, Scottsdale, AZ.

125—(62-63) by Tommy Armour III, in the middle two rounds of the 2003 Valero Texas Open, which he won at LaCantera GC, San Antonio, TX.

18 HOLES

59—by Al Geiberger, at Colonial Country Club, Memphis, in second round in winning the 1977 Memphis Classic.

59—by Chip Beck, at Sunrise Golf Club, Las Vegas, in third round of the 1991 Las Vegas Invitational.

59—by David Duval, on the Palmer Course at PGA West, La Quinta, CA, in the fifth round of the 1999 Bob Hope Chrysler Classic.

9 HOLES

27—by Mike Souchak, at Brackenridge Park GC, San Antonio, on par-35 second nine of first round in the 1955 Texas Open.

27—by Andy North, at En-Joie GC, Endicott, NY, on par-34 second nine of first round in the 1975 BC Open.

27—by Billy Mayfair, at Warwick Hills, Grand Blanc, MI, on par-36 back nine of fourth round, 2001 Buick Open.

MOST CONSECUTIVE ROUNDS UNDER 70

19—Byron Nelson in 1945.

Scoring *(Cont.)*

MOST BIRDIES IN A ROW

8—Bob Goalby, at Pasadena GC, St. Petersburg, FL, during fourth round in winning the 1961 St Petersburg Open.

8—Fuzzy Zoeller, at Oakwood CC, Coal Valley, IL, during first round of 1976 Quad Cities Open.

8—Dewey Arnette, at Warwick Hills GC, Grand Blanc, MI, during first round of the 1987 Buick Open.

8—Edward Fryatt, at the Blue Course of the Doral Resort and Spa, Miami, during second round of the 2000 Doral-Ryder Open.

MOST BIRDIES IN A ROW TO WIN

5—Jack Nicklaus, to win 1978 Jackie Gleason Inverrary Classic (last 5 holes).

Wins

MOST CONSECUTIVE YEARS WINNING AT LEAST ONE TOURNAMENT

17—Jack Nicklaus, 1962–78.

17—Arnold Palmer, 1955–71.

16—Billy Casper, 1956–71.

MOST CONSECUTIVE WINS

11—Byron Nelson, from Miami Four Ball, March 8–11, 1945, through Canadian Open, August 2–4, 1945.

MOST WINS IN A SINGLE EVENT

8—Sam Snead, Greater Greensboro Open, 1938, 1946, 1949, 1950, 1955, 1956, 1960, and 1965.

MOST CONSECUTIVE WINS IN A SINGLE EVENT

4—Walter Hagen, PGA Championships, 1924–27.

4—Gene Sarazen, Miami Open, 1926, (schedule change) 1928–30.

4—Tiger Woods, Bay Hill Invitational, 2000–03.

MOST WINS IN A CALENDAR YEAR

18—Byron Nelson, 1945

MOST YEARS BETWEEN WINS

15 yrs, 5 mos—Butch Baird, 1961–76.

MOST YEARS FROM FIRST WIN TO LAST

28 yrs, 11 mos, 20 days—Raymond Floyd, 1963–92.

YOUNGEST WINNERS

19 yrs, 10 mos—John McDermott, 1911 U.S. Open.

OLDEST WINNER

52 yrs, 10 mos—Sam Snead, 1965 Greater Greensboro Open.

WIDEST WINNING MARGIN: STROKES

16—Bobby Locke, 1948 Chicago Victory National

*Through 10/3/03

THE MAJOR TOURNAMENTS

LPGA Championship

Year	Winner	Score	Runner-Up	Site
1955	Beverly Hanson† (4 & 3)	220	Louise Suggs	Orchard Ridge CC, Ft Wayne, IN
1956	Marlene Hagge*	291	Patty Berg	Forest Lake CC, Detroit
1957	Louise Suggs	285	Wiffi Smith	Churchill Valley CC, Pittsburgh
1958	Mickey Wright	288	Fay Crocker	Churchill Valley CC, Pittsburgh
1959	Betsy Rawls	288	Patty Berg	Sheraton Hotel CC, French Lick, IN
1960	Mickey Wright	292	Louise Suggs	Sheraton Hotel CC, French Lick, IN
1961	Mickey Wright	287	Louise Suggs	Stardust CC, Las Vegas
1962	Judy Kimball	282	Shirley Spork	Stardust CC, Las Vegas
1963	Mickey Wright	294	Mary Lena Faulk Mary Mills Louise Suggs	Stardust CC, Las Vegas
1964	Mary Mills	278	Mickey Wright	Stardust CC, Las Vegas
1965	Sandra Haynie	279	Clifford A. Creed	Stardust CC, Las Vegas
1966	Gloria Ehret	282	Mickey Wright	Stardust CC, Las Vegas
1967	Kathy Whitworth	284	Shirley Englehorn	Pleasant Valley CC, Sutton, MA
1968	Sandra Post*	294	Kathy Whitworth (75)	Pleasant Valley CC, Sutton, MA
1969	Betsy Rawls	293	Susie Berning Carol Mann	Concord GC, Kiameshia Lake, NY
1970	Shirley Englehorn*	285	Kathy Whitworth (78)	Pleasant Valley CC, Sutton, MA
1971	Kathy Whitworth	288	Kathy Ahern	Pleasant Valley CC, Sutton, MA
1972	Kathy Ahern	293	Jane Blalock	Pleasant Valley CC, Sutton, MA
1973	Mary Mills	288	Betty Burfeindt	Pleasant Valley CC, Sutton, MA
1974	Sandra Haynie	288	JoAnne Carner	Pleasant Valley CC, Sutton, MA
1975	Kathy Whitworth	288	Sandra Haynie	Pine Ridge GC, Baltimore
1976	Betty Burfeindt	287	Judy Rankin	Pine Ridge GC, Baltimore
1977	Chako Higuchi	279	Pat Bradley Sandra Post Judy Rankin	Bay Tree Golf Plantation, N Myrtle Beach, SC
1978	Nancy Lopez	275	Amy Alcott	Jack Nicklaus GC, Kings Island, OH
1979	Donna Caponi	279	Jerilyn Britz	Jack Nicklaus GC, Kings Island, OH
1980	Sally Little	285	Jane Blalock	Jack Nicklaus GC, Kings Island, OH
1981	Donna Caponi	280	Jerilyn Britz Pat Meyers	Jack Nicklaus GC, Kings Island, OH
1982	Jan Stephenson	279	JoAnne Carner	Jack Nicklaus GC, Kings Island, OH
1983	Patty Sheehan	279	Sandra Haynie	Jack Nicklaus GC, Kings Island, OH
1984	Patty Sheehan	272	Beth Daniel Pat Bradley	Jack Nicklaus GC, Kings Island, OH
1985	Nancy Lopez	273	Alice Miller	Jack Nicklaus GC, Kings Island, OH
1986	Pat Bradley	277	Patty Sheehan	Jack Nicklaus GC, Kings Island, OH
1987	Jane Geddes	275	Betsy King	Jack Nicklaus GC, Kings Island, OH
1988	Sherri Turner	281	Amy Alcott	Jack Nicklaus GC, Kings Island, OH
1989	Nancy Lopez	274	Ayako Okamoto	Jack Nicklaus GC, Kings Island, OH
1990	Beth Daniel	280	Rosie Jones	Bethesda CC, Bethesda, MD
1991	Meg Mallon	274	Pat Bradley Ayako Okamoto	Bethesda CC, Bethesda, MD
1992	Betsy King	267	Karen Noble	Bethesda CC, Bethesda, MD
1993	Patty Sheehan	275	Lauri Merten	Bethesda CC, Bethesda, MD
1994	Laura Davies	279	Alice Ritzman	DuPont CC, Wilmington, DE
1995	Kelly Robbins	274	Laura Davies	DuPont CC, Wilmington, DE
1996	Laura Davies	213†	Julie Piers	DuPont CC, Wilmington, DE
1997	Chris Johnson*	281	Leta Lindley	DuPont CC, Wilmington, DE
1998	Se Ri Pak	273	Donna Andrews	DuPont CC, Wilmington, DE
1999	Juli Inkster	268	Liselotte Neumann	DuPont CC, Wilmington, DE
2000	Juli Inkster*	281	Stefania Croce	DuPont CC, Wilmington, DE
2001	Karrie Webb	270	Laura Diaz	DuPont CC, Wilmington, DE
2002	Se Ri Pak	279	Beth Daniel	DuPont CC, Wilmington, DE
2003	Annika Sorenstam*	278	Grace Park	DuPont CC, Wilmington, DE

*Won in playoff. †Won match-play final. #Shortened due to rain.

U.S. Women's Open

Year	Winner	Score	Runner-Up	Site
1946	Patty Berg	5 & 4	Betty Jameson	Spokane CC, Spokane, WA
1947	Betty Jameson	295	Sally Sessions	Starmount Forest CC, Greensboro, NC
			Polly Riley	
1948	Babe Zaharias	300	Betty Hicks	Atlantic City CC, Northfield, NJ
1949	Louise Suggs	291	Babe Zaharias	Prince George's G & CC, Landover, MD
1950	Babe Zaharias	291	Betsy Rawls	Rolling Hills CC, Wichita, KS
1951	Betsy Rawls	293	Louise Suggs	Druid Hills GC, Atlanta
1952	Louise Suggs	284	Marlene Bauer	Bala GC, Philadelphia
			Betty Jameson	
1953	Betsy Rawls* (71)	302	Jackie Pung (77)	CC of Rochester, Rochester, NY
1954	Babe Zaharias	291	Betty Hicks	Salem CC, Peabody, MA
1955	Fay Crocker	299	Mary Lena Faulk	Wichita CC, Wichita, KS
			Louise Suggs	
1956	Kathy Cornelius* (75)	302	Barbara McIntire (82)	Northland CC, Duluth, MN
1957	Betsy Rawls	299	Patty Berg	Winged Foot GC, Mamaroneck, NY
1958	Mickey Wright	290	Louise Suggs	Forest Lake CC, Detroit
1959	Mickey Wright	287	Louise Suggs	Churchill Valley CC, Pittsburgh
1960	Betsy Rawls	292	Joyce Ziske	Worcester CC, Worcester, MA
1961	Mickey Wright	293	Betsy Rawls	Baltusrol GC (Lower Course), Springfield, NJ
1962	Murle Breer	301	Jo Ann Prentice	Dunes GC, Myrtle Beach, SC
			Ruth Jessen	
1963	Mary Mills	289	Sandra Haynie	Kenwood CC, Cincinnati
			Louise Suggs	
1964	Mickey Wright* (70)	290	Ruth Jessen (72)	San Diego CC, Chula Vista, CA
1965	Carol Mann	290	Kathy Cornelius	Atlantic City CC, Northfield, NJ
1966	Sandra Spuzich	297	Carol Mann	Hazeltine Natl GC, Chaska, MN
1967	Catherine LaCoste	294	Susie Berning	Hot Springs GC (Cascades Course),
			Beth Stone	Hot Springs, VA
1968	Susie Berning	289	Mickey Wright	Moslem Springs GC, Fleetwood, PA
1969	Donna Caponi	294	Peggy Wilson	Scenic Hills CC, Pensacola, FL
1970	Donna Caponi	287	Sandra Haynie	Muskogee CC, Muskogee, OK
			Sandra Spuzich	
1971	JoAnne Carner	288	Kathy Whitworth	Kahkwa CC, Erie, PA
1972	Susie Berning	299	Kathy Ahern	Winged Foot GC, Mamaroneck, NY
			Pam Barnett	
			Judy Rankin	
1973	Susie Berning	290	Gloria Ehret	CC of Rochester, Rochester, NY
			Shelley Hamlin	
1974	Sandra Haynie	295	Carol Mann	La Grange CC, La Grange, IL
			Beth Stone	
1975	Sandra Palmer	295	JoAnne Carner	Atlantic City CC, Northfield, NJ
			Sandra Post	
			Nancy Lopez	
1976	JoAnne Carner* (76)	292	Sandra Palmer (78)	Rolling Green CC, Springfield, PA
1977	Hollis Stacy	292	Nancy Lopez	Hazeltine Natl GC, Chaska, MN
1978	Hollis Stacy	289	JoAnne Carner	CC of Indianapolis, Indianapolis
			Sally Little	
1979	Jerilyn Britz	284	Debbie Massey	Brooklawn CC, Fairfield, CT
			Sandra Palmer	
1980	Amy Alcott	280	Hollis Stacy	Richland CC, Nashville
1981	Pat Bradley	279	Beth Daniel	La Grange CC, La Grange, IL
1982	Janet Anderson	283	Beth Daniel	Del Paso CC, Sacramento
			Sandra Haynie	
			Donna White	
			JoAnne Carner	
1983	Jan Stephenson	290	JoAnne Carner	Cedar Ridge CC, Tulsa
			Patty Sheehan	
1984	Hollis Stacy	290	Rosie Jones	Salem CC, Peabody, MA
1985	Kathy Baker	280	Judy Dickinson	Baltusrol GC (Upper Course), Springfield, NJ
1986	Jane Geddes* (71)	287	Sally Little (73)	NCR GC, Dayton
1987	Laura Davies* (71)	285	Ayako Okamoto (73)	Plainfield CC, Plainfield, NJ
			JoAnne Carner (74)	
1988	Liselotte Neumann	277	Patty Sheehan	Baltimore CC, Baltimore
1989	Betsy King	278	Nancy Lopez	Indianwood G & CC, Lake Orion, MI
1990	Betsy King	284	Patty Sheehan	Atlanta Athletic Club, Duluth, GA
1991	Meg Mallon	283	Pat Bradley	Colonial Club, Fort Worth

U.S. Women's Open (Cont.)

Year	Winner	Score	Runner-Up	Site
1992	Patty Sheehan* (72)	280	Juli Inkster	Oakmont CC, Oakmont, PA
1993	Lauri Merten	280	Donna Andrew	Crooked Stick, Carmel, IN
			Helen Alfredsson	
1994	Patty Sheehan	277	Tammie Green	Indianwood G & CC, Lake Orion, MI
1995	Annika Sorenstam	278	Meg Mallon	The Broadmoor GC, Colorado Springs, CO
1996	Annika Sorenstam	272	Kris Tschetter	Pine Needles GC, Southern Pines, NC
1997	Alison Nicholas	274	Nancy Lopez	Pumpkin Ridge CC, North Plains, OR
1998	Se Ri Pak†	290	Jenny Chuasiriporn	Blackwolf Run Golf Resort, Kohler, WI
1999	Juli Inkster	272	Sherri Turner	Old Waverly GC, West Point, MS
2000	Karrie Webb	282	Cristie Kerr	Merit GC, Libertyville, IL
			Meg Mallon	
2001	Karrie Webb	273	Se Ri Pak	Pine Needles GC, Southern Pines, NC
2002	Juli Inkster	276	Annika Sorenstam	Prairie Dunes CC, Hutchinson, KS
2003	Hilary Lunke*	283	Kelly Robbins	Pumpkin Ridge GC, North Plains, OR

* Winner in playoff; 18-hole playoff scores are in parentheses. † Winner on second hole of sudden death after 18-hole playoff ended in a tie.

Nabisco Championship

Year	Winner	Score	Runner-Up	Year	Winner	Score	Runner-Up
1972	Jane Blalock	213	Carol Mann	1989	Juli Inkster	279	Tammie Green
			Judy Rankin				JoAnne Carner
1973	Mickey Wright	284	Joyce Kazmierski	1990	Betsy King	283	Kathy Postlewait
1974	Jo Ann Prentice*	289	Jane Blalock				Shirley Furlong
			Sandra Haynie	1991	Amy Alcott	273	Dottie Mochrie
1975	Sandra Palmer	283	Kathy McMullen	1992	Dottie Mochrie*	279	Juli Inkster
1976	Judy Rankin	285	Betty Burfeindt	1993	Helen Alfredsson	284	Amy Benz
1977	Kathy Whitworth	289	JoAnne Carner				Tina Barrett
			Sally Little				Betsy King
1978	Sandra Post*	283	Penny Pulz	1994	Donna Andrews	276	Laura Davies
1979	Sandra Post	276	Nancy Lopez	1995	Nanci Bowen	285	Susie Redman
1980	Donna Caponi	275	Amy Alcott	1996	Patti Sheehan	281	Kelly Robbins
1981	Nancy Lopez	277	Carolyn Hill				Meg Mallon
1982	Sally Little	278	Hollis Stacy				Annika Sörenstam
			Sandra Haynie	1997	Betsy King	276	Kris Tschetter
1983	Amy Alcott	282	Beth Daniel	1998	Pat Hurst	281	Helen Dobson
			Kathy Whitworth	1999	Dottie Pepper	269	Meg Mallon
1984	Juli Inkster*	280	Pat Bradley	2000	Karrie Webb	274	Dottie Pepper
1985	Alice Miller	275	Jan Stephenson	2001	Annika Sorenstam	281	five players
1986	Pat Bradley	280	Val Skinner	2002	Annika Sorenstam	280	Liselotte Neumann
1987	Betsy King*	283	Patty Sheehan	2003	P. Meunier-Lebouc	281	Annika Sorenstam
1988	Amy Alcott	274	Colleen Walker				

*Winner in sudden-death playoff. Note: Designated fourth major in 1983; played at Mission Hills CC, Rancho Mirage, CA.

du Maurier Classic

Year	Winner	Score	Runner-Up	Site
1973	Jocelyne Bourassa*	214	Sandra Haynie	Montreal GC, Montreal
			Judy Rankin	
1974	Carole Jo Callison	208	JoAnne Carner	Candiac GC, Montreal
1975	JoAnne Carner*	214	Carol Mann	St. George's CC, Toronto
1976	Donna Caponi*	212	Judy Rankin	Cedar Brae G & CC, Toronto
1977	Judy Rankin	214	Pat Meyers	Lachute G & CC, Montreal
			Sandra Palmer	
1978	JoAnne Carner	278	Hollis Stacy	St. George's CC, Toronto
1979	Amy Alcott	285	Nancy Lopez	Richelieu Valley CC, Montreal
1980	Pat Bradley	277	JoAnne Carner	St. George's CC, Toronto
1981	Jan Stephenson	278	Nancy Lopez	Summerlea CC, Dorion, Quebec
			Pat Bradley	
1982	Sandra Haynie	280	Beth Daniel	St. George's CC, Toronto
1983	Hollis Stacy	277	JoAnne Carner	Beaconsfield GC, Montreal
			Alice Miller	
1984	Juli Inkster	279	Ayako Okamoto	St. George's G & CC, Toronto
1985	Pat Bradley	278	Jane Geddes	Beaconsfield CC, Montreal
1986	Pat Bradley*	276	Ayako Okamoto	Board of Trade CC, Toronto
1987	Jody Rosenthal	272	Ayako Okamoto	Islesmere GC, Laval, Quebec
1988	Sally Little	279	Laura Davies	Vancouver GC, Coquitlam, British Columbia
1989	Tammie Green	279	Pat Bradley	Beaconsfield GC, Montreal
			Betsy King	

du Maurier Classic (Cont.)

Year	Winner	Score	Runner-Up	Site
1990	Cathy Johnston	276	Patty Sheehan	Westmount G & CC, Kitchener, Ontario
1991	Nancy Scranton	279	Debbie Massey	Vancouver GC, Coquitlam, British Columbia
1992	Sherri Steinhauer	277	Judy Dickinson	St. Charles CC, Winnipeg, Manitoba
1993	Brandie Burton	277	Betsy King	London Hunt and CC, London, Ontario
1994	Martha Nause	279	Michelle McGann	Ottawa Hunt and GC, Ottawa, Ont.
1995	Jenny Lidback	280	Liselotte Neumann	Beaconsfield GC, Pointe-Claire, Quebec
1996	Laura Davies	277	Nancy Lopez Karrie Webb	Edmonton CC, Edmonton, Alberta
1997	Colleen Walker	278	Liselotte Neumann	Glen Abbey GC, Oakville, Ontario
1998	Brandie Burton	270	Annika Sorenstam	Essex G & CC, Windsor, Ontario
1999	Karrie Webb	277	Laura Davies	Priddis Greens G & CC, Calgary, Alberta
2000	Meg Mallon	282	Rosie Jones	Royal Ottawa GC, Aylmer, Quebec

*Winner in sudden-death playoff. Note: Designated third major in 1979; discontinued in 2001.

Women's British Open

Year	Winner	Score	Runner-Up	Site
2001	Se Ri Pak	277	Mi Hyun Kim	Sunningdale GC, Berkshire, England
2002	Karrie Webb	273	Michelle Ellis Paula Marti	Turnberry GC, Ailsa, Scotland
2003	Annika Sorenstam	278	Se Ri Pak	Royal Lytham & St. Annes, England

Note: Designated fourth major in 2001.

Alltime Major Championship Winners

	LPGA	U.S. Open	Nabisco	Brit. Open	‡du Maurier	#Titleholders	†Western	U.S. Am	Brit. Am	Total
Patty Berg	0	1	0	0	0	7	7	1	0	16
Mickey Wright	4	4	0	0	0	2	3	0	0	13
Louise Suggs	1	2	0	0	0	4	4	1	1	13
Babe Zaharias	0	3	0	0	0	3	4	1	1	12
*Juli Inkster	2	2	2	0	1	0	0	3	0	10
Betsy Rawls	2	4	0	0	0	0	2	0	0	8
*JoAnne Carner	0	2	0	0	0	0	0	5	0	7
Kathy Whitworth	3	0	0	0	0	2	1	0	0	6
Pat Bradley	1	1	1	0	3	0	0	0	0	6
*Patty Sheehan	3	2	1	0	0	0	0	0	0	6
Glenna Vare	0	0	0	0	0	0	0	6	0	6
*Betsy King	1	2	3	0	0	0	0	0	0	6
*Annika Sorenstam	1	2	2	1	0	0	0	0	0	6

*Active LPGA player.
#Major from 1937–1972. †Major from 1937–1967. ‡Major from 1979–2000.

Alltime Multiple Professional Major Winners

LPGA

Mickey Wright	4
Nancy Lopez	3
Patty Sheehan	3
Kathy Whitworth	3
Donna Caponi	2
Sandra Haynie	2
Mary Mills	2
Betsy Rawls	2
Laura Davies	2
Juli Inkster	2
Se Ri Pak	2

U.S. OPEN

Betsy Rawls	4
Mickey Wright	4
Susie Maxwell Berning	3

U.S. OPEN (Cont.)

Hollis Stacy	3
Babe Zaharias	3
JoAnne Carner	2
Donna Caponi	2
Betsy King	2
Patty Sheehan	2
Louise Suggs	2
Annika Sorenstam	2
Karrie Webb	2
Juli Inkster	2

NABISCO/DINAH SHORE

Amy Alcott	3
Betsy King	3
Juli Inkster	2
Annika Sorenstam	2

DU MAURIER

Pat Bradley	3
Brandie Burton	2
JoAnne Carner	2

TITLEHOLDERS

Patty Berg	7
Louise Suggs	4
Babe Zaharias	3
Dorothy Kirby	2
Marilynn Smith	2
Kathy Whitworth	2
Mickey Wright	2

WESTERN OPEN

Patty Berg	7
Louise Suggs	4
Babe Zaharias	4
Mickey Wright	3
June Beebe	2
Opal Hill	2
Betty Jameson	2
Betsy Rawls	2

THE LPGA TOUR

Most Career Wins†

	Wins		Wins		Wins
Kathy Whitworth	88	*JoAnne Carner	43	Pat Bradley	31
Mickey Wright	82	Sandra Haynie	42	*Juli Inkster	30
Patty Berg	60	Babe Zaharias	41	*Amy Alcott	29
Louise Suggs	58	Carol Mann	38	*Karrie Webb	29
Betsy Rawls	55	*Patty Sheehan	35	Jane Blalock	27
Nancy Lopez	48	*Betsy King	34	Judy Rankin	26
*Annika Sorenstam	45	*Beth Daniel	33		

*Active player.

Season Money Leaders

		Earnings ($)			Earnings ($)			Earnings ($)
1950	Babe Zaharias	14,800	1968	Kathy Whitworth	48,379	1986	Pat Bradley	492,021
1951	Babe Zaharias	15,087	1969	Carol Mann	49,152	1987	Ayako Okamoto	466,034
1952	Betsy Rawls	14,505	1970	Kathy Whitworth	30,235	1988	Sherri Turner	350,851
1953	Louise Suggs	19,816	1971	Kathy Whitworth	41,181	1989	Betsy King	654,132
1954	Patty Berg	16,011	1972	Kathy Whitworth	65,063	1990	Beth Daniel	863,578
1955	Patty Berg	16,492	1973	Kathy Whitworth	82,864	1991	Pat Bradley	763,118
1956	Marlene Hagge	20,235	1974	JoAnne Carner	87,094	1992	Dottie Mochrie	693,335
1957	Patty Berg	16,272	1975	Sandra Palmer	76,374	1993	Betsy King	595,992
1958	Beverly Hanson	12,639	1976	Judy Rankin	150,734	1994	Laura Davies	687,201
1959	Betsy Rawls	26,774	1977	Judy Rankin	122,890	1995	Annika Sorenstam	666,533
1960	Louise Suggs	16,892	1978	Nancy Lopez	189,814	1996	Karrie Webb	1,002,000
1961	Mickey Wright	22,236	1979	Nancy Lopez	197,489	1997	Annika Sorenstam	1,236,789
1962	Mickey Wright	21,641	1980	Beth Daniel	231,000	1998	Annika Sorenstam	1,092,748
1963	Mickey Wright	31,269	1981	Beth Daniel	206,998	1999	Karrie Webb	1,591,959
1964	Mickey Wright	29,800	1982	JoAnne Carner	310,400	2000	Karrie Webb	1,876,853
1965	Kathy Whitworth	28,658	1983	JoAnne Carner	291,404	2001	Annika Sorenstam	2,105,868
1966	Kathy Whitworth	33,517	1984	Betsy King	266,771	2002	Annika Sorenstam	2,863,904
1967	Kathy Whitworth	32,937	1985	Nancy Lopez	416,472			

Career Money Leaders†

	Earnings ($)		Earnings ($)		Earnings ($)
1. Annika Sorenstam	12,915,374	11. Pat Bradley	5,746,685	21. Mi-Hyun Kim	3,654,581
2. Karrie Webb	9,428,825	12. Patty Sheehan	5,513,409	22. Rachel Teske	3,621,810
3. Juli Inkster	8,663,981	13. Kelly Robbins	5,378,705	23. Chris Johnson	3,538,265
4. Beth Daniel	7,754,968	14. Nancy Lopez	5,320,876	24. D. Ammaccapane	3,512,176
5. Betsy King	7,489,881	15. Lorie Kane	4,889,433	25. Michele Redman	3,475,068
6. Rosie Jones	7,157,601	16. Liselotte Neumann	4,605,718	26. Donna Andrews	3,448,586
7. Se Ri Pak	7,111,010	17. Sherri Steinhauer	3,974,074	27. Amy Alcott	3,408,074
8. Meg Mallon	6,962,374	18. Tammie Green	3,935,962	28. Pat Hurst	3,251,731
9. Dottie Pepper	6,764,220	19. Jane Geddes	3,805,553	29. Michelle McGann	3,242,998
10. Laura Davies	6,403,543	20. Brandie Burton	3,764,982	30. Helen Alfredsson	3,124,494

LPGA Player of the Year

1966	Kathy Whitworth	1979	Nancy Lopez	1992	Dottie Mochrie
1967	Kathy Whitworth	1980	Beth Daniel	1993	Betsy King
1968	Kathy Whitworth	1981	JoAnne Carner	1994	Beth Daniel
1969	Kathy Whitworth	1982	JoAnne Carner	1995	Annika Sörenstam
1970	Sandra Haynie	1983	Patty Sheehan	1996	Laura Davies
1971	Kathy Whitworth	1984	Betsy King	1997	Annika Sorenstam
1972	Kathy Whitworth	1985	Nancy Lopez	1998	Annika Sorenstam
1973	Kathy Whitworth	1986	Pat Bradley	1999	Karrie Webb
1974	JoAnne Carner	1987	Ayako Okamoto	2000	Karrie Webb
1975	Sandra Palmer	1988	Nancy Lopez	2001	Annika Sorenstam
1976	Judy Rankin	1989	Betsy King	2002	Annika Sorenstam
1977	Judy Rankin	1990	Beth Daniel		
1978	Nancy Lopez	1991	Pat Bradley		

†Through 10/13/03.

Vare Trophy: Best Scoring Average

	Avg			Avg			Avg
1953.......Patty Berg	75.00	1970.......Kathy Whitworth	72.26	1987.......Betsy King	71.14
1954.......Babe Zaharias	75.48	1971.......Kathy Whitworth	72.88	1988.......Colleen Walker	71.26
1955.......Patty Berg	74.47	1972.......Kathy Whitworth	72.38	1989.......Beth Daniel	70.38
1956.......Patty Berg	74.57	1973.......Judy Rankin	73.08	1990.......Beth Daniel	70.54
1957.......Louise Suggs	74.64	1974.......JoAnne Carner	72.87	1991.......Pat Bradley	70.76
1958.......Beverly Hanson	74.92	1975.......JoAnne Carner	72.40	1992.......Dottie Mochrie	70.80
1959.......Betsy Rawls	74.03	1976.......Judy Rankin	72.25	1993.......Nancy Lopez	70.83
1960.......Mickey Wright	73.25	1977.......Judy Rankin	72.16	1994.......Beth Daniel	70.90
1961.......Mickey Wright	73.55	1978.......Nancy Lopez	71.76	1995.......Annika Sorenstam	71.00
1962.......Mickey Wright	73.67	1979.......Nancy Lopez	71.20	1996.......Annika Sorenstam	70.47
1963.......Mickey Wright	72.81	1980.......Amy Alcott	71.51	1997.......Karrie Webb	70.00
1964.......Mickey Wright	72.46	1981.......JoAnne Carner	71.75	1998.......Annika Sorenstam	69.99
1965.......Kathy Whitworth	72.61	1982.......JoAnne Carner	71.49	1999.......Karrie Webb	69.43
1966.......Kathy Whitworth	72.60	1983.......JoAnne Carner	71.41	2000.......Karrie Webb	70.05
1967.......Kathy Whitworth	72.74	1984.......Patty Sheehan	71.40	2001.......Annika Sorenstam	69.42
1968.......Carol Mann	72.04	1985.......Nancy Lopez	70.73	2002.......Annika Sorenstam	68.70
1969.......Kathy Whitworth	72.38	1986.......Pat Bradley	71.10		

Alltime LPGA Tour Records†

Scoring

72 HOLES

261—(71-61-63-66) by Se Ri Pak to win at the Highland Meadows CC, Sylvania, OH, in the 1998 Jamie Farr Kroger Classic (23 under par).

261—(65-59-69-68) by Annika Sorenstam to win at the Moon Valley CC, Phoenix, in the 2001 Standard Register PING (27 under par).

54 HOLES

193—(66-61-66) by Karrie Webb to lead at the Walnut Hills CC, East Lansing, MI, in the 2000 Oldsmobile Classic (23 under par).

193—(65-59-69) by Annika Sorenstam to lead at the Moon Valley CC, Phoenix, in the 2001 Standard Register PING (23 under par)

36 HOLES

124—(65-59) by Annika Sorenstam to lead at the Moon Valley CC, Phoenix, in the 2001 Standard Register PING (20 under par).

18 HOLES

59—by Annika Sorenstam at the Moon Valley CC, Phoenix, in the second round in winning the 2001 Standard Register PING (13 under par).

9 HOLES

28—by Mary Beth Zimmerman at Rail GC, 1984 Rail Charity Golf Classic, Springfield, IL (par 36). Zimmerman shot 64.

28—by Pat Bradley at Green Gables CC, Denver, 1984 Columbia Savings Classic (par 35). Bradley shot 65.

28—by Muffin Spencer-Devlin at Knollwood CC, Elmsford, NY, in winning the 1985 MasterCard International Pro-Am (par 35). Spencer-Devlin shot 64.

28—by Peggy Kirsch at Squaw Creek CC, Vienna, OH, in the 1991 Phar-Mor (par 35).

28—by Renee Heiken at Highland Meadows CC, Sylvania, OH, in the 1996 Jamie Farr Kroger Classic (par 34).

†Through 10/13/03.

Scoring (Cont.)

9 HOLES (Cont.)

28—by Annika Sorenstam at the Moon Valley CC, Phoenix, in the 2001 Standard Register PING (par 36).

28—by Danielle Ammaccapane at Highland Meadows GC, Sylvania, OH, in the 2002 Jamie Farr Kroger Classic (par 34)

28—by Young Kim at Dell Urich GC, Tucson, AZ, in the 2003 Welch's/Fry's Championship (par 35)

28—by Chris Johnson at Highland Meadows GC, Sylvania, OH, in the 2003 Jamie Farr Kroger Classic (par 34)

MOST CONSECUTIVE ROUNDS UNDER 70

11—Annika Sorenstam, in 2002.

MOST BIRDIES IN A ROW

9—Beth Daniel at Onion Creek Club in Austin, in the second round of the 1999 Philips Invitational. Daniel shot 62 (8 under par).

Wins

MOST CONSECUTIVE WINS IN SCHEDULED EVENTS

4—Mickey Wright, in 1962.

4—Mickey Wright, in 1963.

4—Kathy Whitworth, in 1969.

4—Annika Sorenstam in 2001.

MOST CONSECUTIVE WINS IN ENTERED TOURNAMENTS

5—Nancy Lopez, in 1978.

MOST WINS IN A CALENDAR YEAR

13—Mickey Wright, in 1963.

WIDEST WINNING MARGIN, STROKES

14—Louise Suggs, 1949 U.S. Women's Open.

14—Cindy Mackey, 1986 MasterCard Int'l Pro-Am.

U.S. Senior Open

Year	Winner	Score	Runner-Up	Site
1980	Roberto DeVicenzo	285	William C. Campbell	Winged Foot GC, Mamaroneck, NY
1981	Arnold Palmer* (70)	289	Bob Stone (74)	Oakland Hills CC, Birmingham, MI
			Billy Casper (77)	
1982	Miller Barber	282	Gene Littler	Portland GC, Portland, OR
			Dan Sikes, Jr.	
1983	Billy Casper* (75) (3)	288	Rod Funseth (75) (4)	Hazeltine GC, Chaska, MN
1984	Miller Barber	286	Arnold Palmer	Oak Hill CC, Rochester, NY
1985	Miller Barber	285	Roberto DeVicenzo	Edgewood Tahoe GC, Stateline, NV
1986	Dale Douglass	279	Gary Player	Scioto CC, Columbus, OH
1987	Gary Player	270	Doug Sanders	Brooklawn CC, Fairfield, CT
1988	Gary Player* (68)	288	Bob Charles (70)	Medinah CC, Medinah, IL
1989	Orville Moody	279	Frank Beard	Laurel Valley GC, Ligonier, PA
1990	Lee Trevino	275	Jack Nicklaus	Ridgewood CC, Paramus, NJ
1991	Jack Nicklaus (65)	282	Chi Chi Rodriguez (69)	Oakland Hills CC, Birmingham, MI
1992	Larry Laoretti	275	Jim Colbert	Saucon Valley CC, Bethlehem, PA
1993	Jack Nicklaus	278	Tom Weiskopf	Cherry Hills CC, Englewood, CO
1994	Simon Hobday	274	Jim Albus	Pinehurst Resort & CC, Pinehurst, NC
1995	Tom Weiskopf	275	Jack Nicklaus	Congressional CC, Bethesda, MD
1996	Dave Stockton	277	Hale Irwin	Canterbury CC, Beachwood, OH
1997	Graham Marsh	280	Hale Irwin	Olympia Fields CC, Olympia Fields, IL
1998	Hale Irwin	285	Vicente Fernandez	Riviera CC, Pacific Palisades, CA
1999	Dave Eichelberger	281	Ed Dougherty	Des Moines G & CC, Des Moines, IA
2000	Hale Irwin	267	Bruce Fleisher	Saucon Valley CC, Bethlehem, PA
2001	Bruce Fleisher	280	Isao Aoki	Salem CC, Peabody, MA
			Gil Morgan	
2002	Don Pooley*	274	Tom Watson	Caves Valley GC, Owings Mill, MD
2003	Bruce Lietzke	277	Tom Watson	Inverness GC, Toledo, OH

*Winner in playoff. Playoff scores are in parentheses. The 1983 playoff went to one hole of sudden death after an 18-hole playoff.

SENIOR TOUR
Season Money Leaders

	Earnings ($)		Earnings ($)		Earnings ($)
1980...Don January	44,100	1988...Bob Charles	533,929	1996...Jim Colbert	1,627,890
1981...Miller Barber	83,136	1989...Bob Charles	725,887	1997...Hale Irwin	2,449,420
1982...Miller Barber	106,890	1990...Lee Trevino	1,190,518	1998...Hale Irwin	2,861,945
1983...Don January	237,571	1991...Mike Hill	1,065,657	1999...Bruce Fleisher	2,515,705
1984...Don January	328,597	1992...Lee Trevino	1,027,002	2000...Larry Nelson	2,708,005
1985...Peter Thomson	386,724	1993...Dave Stockton	1,175,944	2001...Allen Doyle	2,553,582
1986...Bruce Crampton	454,299	1994...Dave Stockton	1,402,519	2002...Hale Irwin	3,028,304
1987...Chi Chi Rodriguez	509,145	1995...Jim Colbert	1,444,386		

Career Money Leaders†

	Earnings ($)		Earnings ($)		Earnings ($)
1. Hale Irwin	18,413,235	11. Isao Aoki	8,661,016	21. J.C. Snead	6,936,110
2. Gil Morgan	12,568,466	12. Raymond Floyd	8,636,897	22. Bob Murphy	6,874,920
3. Jim Colbert	11,184,384	13. Jim Dent	8,520,456	23. Dale Douglass	6,864,085
4. Larry Nelson	10,496,595	14. George Archer	8,314,648	24. Tom Wargo	6,733,391
5. Bruce Fleisher	10,394,772	15. Mike Hill	8,119,490	25. Chi Chi Rodriguez	6,634,738
6. Dave Stockton	10,075,282	16. Jay Sigel	7,963,876	26. Tom Jenkins	6,569,249
7. Lee Trevino	9,687,963	17. Graham Marsh	7,472,572	27. Vicente Fernandez	6,565,476
8. Dana Quigley	9,038,584	18. Jim Thorpe	7,243,613	28. John Bland	6,207,725
9. Bob Charles	8,874,820	19. Bruce Summerhays	7,052,639	29. Mike McCullough	6,049,957
10. Allen Doyle	8,778,936	20. John Jacobs	6,976,707	30. Jim Albus	5,993,544

Most Career Wins†

	Wins		Wins
Hale Irwin	38	Bruce Crampton	20
Lee Trevino	29	Jim Colbert	20
Miller Barber	24	Gary Player	19
Bob Charles	23	George Archer	19
Don January	22	Mike Hill	18
Chi Chi Rodriguez	22	Larry Nelson	17
Gil Morgan	22	Bruce Fleisher	16

†Through 10/19/03.

MAJOR MEN'S AMATEUR CHAMPIONSHIPS

U.S. Amateur

Year	Winner	Score	Runner-Up	Site
1895	Charles B. Macdonald	12 & 11	Charles E. Sands	Newport GC, Newport, RI
1896	H.J. Whigham	8 & 7	J.G Thorp	Shinnecock Hills GC, Southampton, NY
1897	H.J. Whigham	8 & 6	W. Rossiter Betts	Chicago GC, Wheaton, IL
1898	Findlay S. Douglas	5 & 3	Walter B. Smith	Morris County GC, Morristown, NJ
1899	H.M. Harriman	3 & 2	Findlay S. Douglas	Onwentsia Club, Lake Forest, IL
1900	Walter Travis	2 up	Findlay S. Douglas	Garden City GC, Garden City, NY
1901	Walter Travis	5 & 4	Walter E. Egan	CC of Atlantic City, NJ
1902	Louis N. James	4 & 2	Eben M. Byers	Glen View Club, Golf, IL
1903	Walter Travis	5 & 4	Eben M. Byers	Nassau CC, Glen Cove, NY
1904	H. Chandler Egan	8 & 6	Fred Herreshoff	Baltusrol GC, Springfield, NJ
1905	H. Chandler Egan	6 & 5	D.E. Sawyer	Chicago GC, Wheaton, IL
1906	Eben M. Byers	2 up	George S. Lyon	Englewood GC, Englewood, NJ
1907	Jerry Travers	6 & 5	Archibald Graham	Euclid Club, Cleveland, OH
1908	Jerry Travers	8 & 7	Max H. Behr	Garden City GC, Garden City, NY
1909	Robert A. Gardner	4 & 3	H. Chandler Egan	Chicago GC, Wheaton, IL
1910	William C. Fownes Jr.	4 & 3	Warren K. Wood	The Country Club, Brookline, MA
1911	Harold Hilton	1 up	Fred Herreshoff	The Apawamis Club, Rye, NY
1912	Jerry Travers	7 & 6	Charles Evans Jr.	Chicago GC, Wheaton, IL
1913	Jerry Travers	5 & 4	John G. Anderson	Garden City GC, Garden City, NY
1914	Francis Ouimet	6 & 5	Jerry Travers	Ekwanok CC, Manchester, VT
1915	Robert A. Gardner	5 & 4	John G. Anderson	CC of Detroit, Grosse Pt. Farms, MI
1916	Chick Evans	4 & 3	Robert A. Gardner	Merion Cricket Club, Haverford, PA
1917–18	No tournament			
1919	S. Davidson Herron	5 & 4	Bobby Jones	Oakmont CC, Oakmont, PA
1920	Chick Evans	7 & 6	Francis Ouimet	Engineers' CC, Roslyn, NY
1921	Jesse P. Guilford	7 & 6	Robert A. Gardner	St. Louis CC, Clayton, MO
1922	Jess W. Sweetser	3 & 2	Chick Evans	The Country Club, Brookline, MA
1923	Max R. Marston	1 up	Jess W. Sweetser	Flossmoor CC, Flossmoor, IL
1924	Bobby Jones	9 & 8	George Von Elm	Merion Cricket Club, Ardmore, PA
1925	Bobby Jones	8 & 7	Watts Gunn	Oakmont CC, Oakmont, PA
1926	George Von Elm	2 & 1	Bobby Jones	Baltusrol GC, Springfield, NJ
1927	Bobby Jones	8 & 7	Chick Evans	Minikahda Club, Minneapolis
1928	Bobby Jones	10 & 9	T. Phillip Perkins	Brae Burn CC, West Newton, MA
1929	Harrison R. Johnston	4 & 3	Dr. O.F. Willing	Del Monte G & CC, Pebble Beach, CA
1930	Bobby Jones	8 & 7	Eugene V. Homans	Merion Cricket Club, Ardmore, PA
1931	Francis Ouimet	6 & 5	Jack Westland	Beverly CC, Chicago, IL
1932	C. Ross Somerville	2 & 1	John Goodman	Baltimore CC, Timonium, MD
1933	George T. Dunlap Jr.	6 & 5	Max R. Marston	Kenwood CC, Cincinnati, OH
1934	Lawson Little	8 & 7	David Goldman	The Country Club, Brookline, MA
1935	Lawson Little	4 & 2	Walter Emery	The Country Club, Cleveland, OH
1936	John W. Fischer	1 up	Jack McLean	Garden City GC, Garden City, NY
1937	John Goodman	2 up	Raymond E. Billows	Alderwood CC, Portland, OR
1938	William P. Turnesa	8 & 7	B. Patrick Abbott	Oakmont CC, Oakmont, PA
1939	Marvin H. Ward	7 & 5	Raymond E. Billows	North Shore CC, Glenview, IL
1940	Richard D. Chapman	11 & 9	W. McCullough Jr.	Winged Foot GC, Mamaroneck, NY
1941	Marvin H. Ward	4 & 3	B. Patrick Abbott	Omaha Field Club, Omaha, NE
1942–45	No tournament			
1946	Ted Bishop	1 up	Smiley L. Quick	Baltusrol GC, Springfield, NJ
1947	Skee Riegel	2 & 1	John W. Dawson	Del Monte G & CC, Pebble Beach, CA
1948	William P. Turnesa	2 & 1	Raymond E. Billows	Memphis CC, Memphis, TN
1949	Charles R. Coe	11 & 10	Rufus King	Oak Hill CC, Rochester, NY
1950	Sam Urzetta	1 up	Frank Stranahan	Minneapolis GC, Minneapolis, MN
1951	Billy Maxwell	4 & 3	Joseph F. Gagliardi	Saucon Valley CC, Bethlehem, PA
1952	Jack Westland	3 & 2	Al Mengert	Seattle GC, Seattle, WA
1953	Gene Littler	1 up	Dale Morey	Oklahoma City G & CC, Oklahoma City
1954	Arnold Palmer	1 up	Robert Sweeny	CC of Detroit, Grosse Pt. Farms, MI
1955	E. Harvie Ward Jr.	9 & 8	William Hyndman III	CC of Virginia, Richmond, VA
1956	E. Harvie Ward Jr.	5 & 4	Charles Kocsis	Knollwood Club, Lake Forest, IL
1957	Hillman Robbins Jr.	5 & 4	Dr. Frank M. Taylor	The Country Club, Brookline, MA
1958	Charles R. Coe	5 & 4	Tommy Aaron	Olympic Club, San Francisco, CA
1959	Jack Nicklaus	1 up	Charles R. Coe	Broadmoor GC, Colorado Springs, CO
1960	Deane Beman	6 & 4	Robert W. Gardner	St. Louis CC, Clayton, MO
1961	Jack Nicklaus	8 & 6	H. Dudley Wysong	Pebble Beach GL, Pebble Beach, CA

U.S. Amateur (Cont.)

Year	Winner	Score	Runner-Up	Site
1962	Labron E. Harris Jr.	1 up	Downing Gray	Pinehurst CC, Pinehurst, NC
1963	Deane Beman	2 & 1	Richard H. Sikes	Wakonda Club, Des Moines, IA
1964	William C. Campbell	1 up	Edgar M. Tutwiler	Canterbury GC, Cleveland, OH
1965	Robert J. Murphy Jr.	291	Robert B. Dickson	Southern Hills, CC, Tulsa
1966	Gary Cowan	285-75	Deane Beman	Merion GC, Ardmore, PA
1967	Robert B. Dickson	285	Marvin Giles III	Broadmoor GC, Colorado Springs
1968	Bruce Fleisher	284	Marvin Giles III	Scioto CC, Columbus, OH
1969	Steven N. Melnyk	286	Marvin Giles III	Oakmont CC, Oakmont, PA
1970	Lanny Wadkins	279	Tom Kite	Waverley CC, Portland, OR
1971	Gary Cowan	280	Eddie Pearce	Wilmington CC, Wilmington DE
1972	Marvin Giles III	285	two tied	Charlotte CC, Charlotte, NC
1973	Craig Stadler	6 & 5	David Strawn	Inverness Club, Toledo
1974	Jerry Pate	2 & 1	John P. Grace	Ridgewood CC, Ridgewood, NJ
1975	Fred Ridley	2 up	Keith Fergus	CC of Virginia, Richmond
1976	Bill Sander	8 & 6	C. Parker Moore Jr.	Bel Air CC, Los Angeles
1977	John Fought	9 & 8	Doug Fischesser	Aronimink GC, Newton Square, PA
1978	John Cook	5 & 4	Scott Hoch	Plainfield CC, Plainfield, NJ
1979	Mark O'Meara	8 & 7	John Cook	Canterbury GC, Cleveland
1980	Hal Sutton	9 & 8	Bob Lewis	CC of North Carolina, Pinehurst, NC
1981	Nathaniel Crosby	1 up	Brian Lindley	Olympic Club, San Francisco
1982	Jay Sigel	8 & 7	David Tolley	The Country Club, Brookline, MA
1983	Jay Sigel	8 & 7	Chris Perry	North Shore CC, Glenview, IL
1984	Scott Verplank	4 & 3	Sam Randolph	Oak Tree GC, Edmond, OK
1985	Sam Randolph	1 up	Peter Persons	Montclair GC, West Orange, NJ
1986	Buddy Alexander	5 & 3	Chris Kite	Shoal Creek, Shoal Creek, AL
1987	Bill Mayfair	4 & 3	Eric Rebmann	Jupiter Hills Club, Jupiter, FL
1988	Eric Meeks	7 & 6	Danny Yates	Va. Hot Springs G & CC, VA
1989	Chris Patton	3 & 1	Danny Green	Merion GC, Ardmore, PA
1990	Phil Mickelson	5 & 4	Manny Zerman	Cherry Hills CC, Englewood, CO
1991	Mitch Voges	7 & 6	Manny Zerman	The Honors Course, Ooltewah, TN
1992	Justin Leonard	8 & 7	Tom Scherrer	Muirfield Village GC, Dublin, OH
1993	John Harris	5 & 3	Danny Ellis	Champions GC, Houston
1994	Tiger Woods	2 up	Trip Kuehne	TPC-Sawgrass, Ponte Vedre, FL
1995	Tiger Woods	2 up	Buddy Marucci	Newport Country Club, Newport, RI
1996	Tiger Woods	38 holes	Steve Scott	Pumpkin Ridge GC, Cornelius, OR
1997	Matthew Kuchar	2 & 1	Joel Kribel	Cog Hill G & CC, Lemont, IL
1998	Hank Kuehne	2 & 1	Tom McKnight	Oak Hill CC, Rochester, NY
1999	David Gossett	9 & 8	Sung Yoon Kim	Pebble Beach GL, Pebble Beach, CA
2000	Jeff Quinney	39 holes	James Driscoll	Baltusrol GC, Upper Springfield, NJ
2001	Bubba Dickerson	1 up	Robert Hamilton	East Lake CC, Atlanta
2002	Ricky Barnes	2 & 1	Hunter Mahan	Oakland Hills CC, Bloomfield Hills, MI
2003	Nick Flanagan	37 holes	Frank Abbott	East Lake CC, Atlanta

Note: All stroke play from 1965 to 1972.

U.S. Junior Amateur

1948...Dean Lind	1962...Jim Wiechers	1976...Madden Hatcher III	1990...Mathew Todd
1949...Gay Brewer	1963...Gregg McHatton	1977...Willie Wood Jr.	1991...Tiger Woods
1950...Mason Rudolph	1964...Johnny Miller	1978...Don Hurter	1992...Tiger Woods
1951...Tommy Jacobs	1965...James Masserio	1979...Jack Larkin	1993...Tiger Woods
1952...Don Bisplinghoff	1966...Gary Sanders	1980...Eric Johnson	1994...Terry Noe
1953...Rex Baxter	1967...John Crooks	1981...Scott Erickson	1995...D. Scott Hailes
1954...Foster Bradley	1968...Eddie Pearce	1982...Rich Marik	1996...Shane McMenamy
1955...William Dunn	1969...Aly Trompas	1983...Tim Straub	1997...Jason Allred
1956...Harlan Stevenson	1970...Gary Koch	1984...Doug Martin	1998...James Oh
1957...Larry Beck	1971...Mike Brannan	1985...Charles Rymer	1999...Hunter Mahan
1958...Buddy Baker	1972...Bob Byman	1986...Brian Montgomery	2000...Matthew Rosenfeld
1959...Larry Lee	1973...Jack Renner	1987...Brett Quigley	2001...Henry Liaw
1960...Bill Tindall	1974...David Nevatt	1988...Jason Widener	2002...Charlie Beljan
1961...Charles McDowell	1975...Brett Mullin	1989...David Duval	2003...Brian Harman

Mid-Amateur Championship

1981...Jim Holtgrieve	1987...Jay Sigel	1993...Jeff Thomas	1999...Danny Green
1982...William Hoffer	1988...David Eger	1994...Tim Jackson	2000...Greg Puga
1983...Jay Sigel	1989...James Taylor	1995...Jerry Courville Jr.	2001...Tim Jackson
1984...Mike Podolak	1990...Jim Stuart	1996...John Miller	2002...George Zahringer
1985...Jay Sigel	1991...Jim Stuart	1997...Ken Bakst	2003...Nathan Smith
1986...Bill Loeffler	1992...Danny Yates	1998...John Miller	

British Amateur

Year	Winner
887	H. G. Hutchinson
1888	John Ball
1889	J.E. Laidlay
1890	John Ball
1891	J.E. Laidlay
1892	John Ball
1893	Peter Anderson
1894	John Ball
1895	L.M.B. Melville
1896	F.G. Tait
1897	A.J.T. Allan
1898	F.G. Tait
1899	John Ball
1900	H.H. Hilton
1901	H.H. Hilton
1902	C. Hutchings
1903	R. Maxwell
1904	W.J. Travis
1905	A.G. Barry
1906	James Robb
1907	John Ball
1908	E.A. Lassen
1909	R. Maxwell
1910	John Ball
1911	H.H. Hilton
1912	John Ball
1913	H.H. Hilton
1914	J.L.C. Jenkins
1915–19	not held
1920	C.J.H. Tolley
1921	W.I. Hunter
1922	E.W.E. Holderness
1923	R.H. Wethered
1924	E.W.E. Holderness
1925	R. Harris
1926	Jess Sweetser
1927	Dr. W. Tweddell
1928	T.P. Perkins
1929	C.J.H. Tolley
1930	Robert T. Jones Jr
1931	E. Martin Smith
1932	J. DeForest
1933	M. Scott
1934	W. Lawson Little
1935	W. Lawson Little
1936	H. Thomson
1937	R. Sweeney Jr
1938	C.R. Yates
1939	A.T. Kyle
1940–45	not held
1946	J. Bruen
1947	Willie D. Turnesa
1948	Frank R. Stranahan
1949	S.M. McReady
1950	Frank R. Stranahan
1951	Richard D. Chapman
1952	E.H. Ward
1953	J.B. Carr
1954	D.W. Bachli
1955	J.W. Conrad
1956	J.C. Beharrel
1957	R. Reid Jack
1958	J.B. Carr
1959	Deane Beman
1960	J.B. Carr
1961	M. Bonallack
1962	R. Davies
1963	M. Lunt
1964	C. Clark
1965	M. Bonallack
1966	C.R. Cole
1967	R. Dickson
1968	M. Bonallack
1969	M. Bonallack
1970	M. Bonallack
1971	Steve Melnyk
1972	Trevor Homer
1973	R. Siderowf
1974	Trevor Homer
1975	M. Giles
1976	R. Siderowf
1977	P. McEvoy
1978	P. McEvoy
1979	J. Sigel
1980	D. Evans
1981	P. Ploujoux
1982	M. Thompson
1983	A. Parkin
1984	J.M. Olazabal
1985	G. McGimpsey
1986	D. Curry
1987	P. Mayo
1988	C. Hardin
1989	S. Dodd
1990	R. Muntz
1991	G. Wolstenholme
1992	S. Dundas
1993	I. Pyman
1994	L. James
1995	G. Sherry
1996	W. Bladon
1997	C. Watson
1998	Sergio Garcia
1999	Graeme Storm
2000	Mikko Ilonen
2001	Michael Hoey
2002	Alejandro Larrazabal
2003	Gary Wolstenholme

Amateur Public Links

Year	Winner
1922	Edmund R. Held
1923	Richard J. Walsh
1924	Joseph Coble
1925	Raymond J. McAuliffe
1926	Lester Bolstad
1927	Carl F. Kauffmann
1928	Carl F. Kauffmann
1929	Carl F. Kauffmann
1930	Robert E. Wingate
1931	Charles Ferrera
1932	R.L. Miller
1933	Charles Ferrera
1934	David A. Mitchell
1935	Frank Strafaci
1936	B. Patrick Abbott
1937	Bruce N. McCormick
1938	Al Leach
1939	Andrew Szwedko
1940	Robert C. Clark
1941	William M. Welch Jr
1942–45	not held
1946	Smiley L. Quick
1947	Wilfred Crossley
1948	Michael R. Ferentz
1949	Kenneth J. Towns
1950	Stanley Bielat
1951	Dave Stanley
1952	Omer L. Bogan
1953	Ted Richards Jr
1954	Gene Andrews
1955	Sam D. Kocsis
1956	James H. Buxbaum
1957	Don Essig III
1958	Daniel D. Sikes Jr
1959	William A. Wright
1960	Verne Callison
1961	Richard H. Sikes
1962	Richard H. Sikes
1963	Robert Lunn
1964	William McDonald
1965	Arne Dokka
1966	Lamont Kaser
1967	Verne Callison
1968	Gene Towry
1969	John M. Jackson Jr
1970	Robert Risch
1971	Fred Haney
1972	Bob Allard
1973	Stan Stopa
1974	Charles Barenaba
1975	Randy Barenaba
1976	Eddie Mudd
1977	Jerry Vidovic
1978	Dean Prince
1979	Dennis Walsh
1980	Jodie Mudd
1981	Jodie Mudd
1982	Billy Tuten
1983	Billy Tuten
1984	Bill Malley
1985	Jim Sorenson
1986	Bill Mayfair
1987	Kevin Johnson
1988	Ralph Howe III
1989	Tim Hobby
1990	Michael Combs
1991	David Berganio Jr
1992	Warren Schulte
1993	David Berganio Jr
1994	Guy Yamamoto
1995	Chris Wollmann
1996	Tim Hogarth
1997	Tim Clark
1998	Trevor Immelman
1999	Hunter Haas
2000	D.J. Trahan
2001	Chez Reavie
2002	Ryan Moore
2003	Brandt Snedeker

U.S. Senior Golf

1955 ....J. Wood Platt	1971 ....Tom Draper	1987 ....John Richardson
1956 ....Frederick J. Wright	1972 ....Lewis W. Oehmig	1988 ....Clarence Moore
1957 ....J. Clark Espie	1973 ....William Hyndman III	1989 ....Bo Williams
1958 ....Thomas C. Robbins	1974 ....Dale Morey	1990 ....Jackie Cummings
1959 ....J. Clark Espie	1975 ....William F. Colm	1991 ....Bill Bosshard
1960 ....Michael Cestone	1976 ....Lewis W. Oehmig	1992 ....Clarence Moore
1961 ....Dexter H. Daniels	1977 ....Dale Morey	1993 ....Joe Ungvary
1962 ....Merrill L. Carlsmith	1978 ...........K.K. Compton	1994 ....O. Gordon Brewer
1963 ....Merrill L. Carlsmith	1979 ....William C. Campbell	1995 ....James Stahl Jr.
1964 ....William D. Higgins	1980 ....William C. Campbell	1996 ....O. Gordon Brewer
1965 ....Robert B. Kiersky	1981 ....Ed Updegraff	1997 ....Cliff Cunningham
1966 ....Dexter H. Daniels	1982 ....Alton Duhon	1998 ....Bill Shean Jr.
1967 ....Ray Palmer	1983 ....William Hyndman III	1999 ....Bill Ploeger
1968 ....Curtis Person Sr.	1984 ....Bob Rawlins	2000 ....Bill Shean Jr.
1969 ....Curtis Person Sr.	1985 ....Lewis W. Oehmig	2001 ....Kemp Richardson
1970 ....Gene Andrews	1986 ....Bo Williams	2002 ....Greg Reynolds
		2003 ....Kemp Richardson

Note: Event is for amateur golfers at least 55 years of age.

MAJOR WOMEN'S AMATEUR CHAMPIONSHIPS

U.S. Women's Amateur

Year	Winner	Score	Runner-Up	Site
1895 ....Mrs. Charles S. Brown		132	Nellie Sargent	Meadow Brook Club, Hempstead, NY
1896 ....Beatrix Hoyt		2 & 1	Mrs. Arthur Turnure	Morris Couty GC, Morristown, NJ
1897 ....Beatrix Hoyt		5 & 4	Nellie Sargent	Essex County Club, Manchester, MA
1898 ....Beatrix Hoyt		5 &3	Maude Wetmore	Ardsley Club, Ardsley-on-Hudson, NY
1899 ....Ruth Underhill		2 & 1	Margaret Fox	Philadelphia CC, Philadelphia, PA
1900 ....Frances C. Griscom		6 & 5	Margaret Curtis	Shinnecock Hills GC, Shinnecock Hills, NY
1901 ....Genevieve Hecker		5 &3	Lucy Herron	Baltusrol GC, Springfield, NJ
1902 ....Genevieve Hecker		4 &3	Louisa A. Wells	The Country Club, Brookline, MA
1903 ....Bessie Anthony		7 &6	J. Anna Carpenter	Chicago GC, Wheaton, IL
1904 ....Georgianna M. Bishop		5 &3	Mrs. E.F. Sanford	Merion Cricket Club, Haverford, PA
1905 ....Pauline Mackay		1 up	Margaret Curtis	Morris County GC, Convent, NJ
1906 ....Harriot S. Curtis		2 & 1	Mary B. Adams	Brae Burn CC, West Newton, MA
1907 ....Margaret Curtis		7 &6	Harriot S. Curtis	Midlothian CC, Blue Island, IL
1908 ....Katherine C. Harley		6 &5	Mrs. T.H. Polhemus	Chevy Chase Club, Chevy Chase, MD
1909 ....Dorothy I. Campbell		3 &2	Nonna Barlow	Merion Cricket Club, Haverford, PA
1910 ....Dorothy I. Campbell		2 & 1	Mrs. G.M. Martin	Homewood CC, Flossmoor, IL
1911 ....Margaret Curtis		5 &3	Lillian B. Hyde	Baltusrol GC, Springfield, NJ
1912 ....Margaret Curtis		3 &2	Nonna Barlow	Essex County Club, Manchester, MA
1913 ....Gladys Ravenscroft		2 up	Marion Hollins	Wilmington CC, Wilmington, DE
1914 ....Katherine Harley		1 up	Elaine V. Rosenthal	Nassau CC, Glen Cove, NY
1915 ....Florence Vanderbeck		3 &2	Margaret Gavin	Onwentsia Club, Lake Forest, IL
1916 ....Alexa Stirling		2 & 1	Mildred Caverly	Belmont Springs CC, Waverley, MA
1917–18 .....No tournament				
1919...........Alexa Stirling		6 & 5	Margaret Gavin	Shawnee CC, Shawnee-on-Delaware, PA
1920 ....Alexa Stirling		5 & 4	Dorothy Campbell	Mayfield CC, Cleveland
1921 ....Marion Hollins		5 & 4	Alexa Stirling	Hollywood GC, Deal, NJ
1922..............Glenna Collett		5 &4	Margaret Gavin	Greenbriar GC, White Sulphur Springs, WV
1923 ....Edith Cummings		3 &2	Alexa Stirling	Westchester-Biltmore CC, Rye, NY
1924 ....Dorothy Campbell		7 &6	Mary K. Browne	Rhode Island CC, Nyatt, RI
1925 ....Glenna Collett		9 &8	Alexa Stirling	St. Louis CC, Clayton, MO
1926 ....Helen Stetson		3 &1	Elizabeth Goss	Merion Cricket Club, Ardmore, PA
1927 ....Miiriam Burns Horn		5 &4	Maureen Orcutt	Cherry Valley Club, Garden City, NY
1928 ....Glenna Collett		13 & 12	Virginia Van Wie	Va. Hot Springs G & TC, Hot Springs, VA
1929 ....Glenna Collett		4 &3	Leona Pressler	Oakland Hills CC, Birmingham, MI
1930 ....Glenna Collett		6 &5	Virginia Van Wie	Los Angeles CC, Beverly Hills, CA
1931 ....Helen Hicks		2 & 1	Glenna Collet Vare	CC of Buffalo, Williamsville, NY
1932 ....Virginia Van Wie		10 &8	Glenna Collet Vare	Salem CC, Peabody, MA
1933 ....Virginia Van Wie		4 &3	Helen Hicks	Exmoor CC, Highland Park, IL
1934 ....Virginia Van Wie		2 & 1	Dorothy Traung	Whitemarsh Valley CC, Chestnut Hill, PA
1935 ....Glenna Collett Vare		3 &2	Patty Berg	Interlachen CC, Hopkins, MN
1936 ....Pamela Barton		4 &3	Maureen Orcutt	Canoe Brook CC, Summit, NJ
1937 ....Estelle Lawson		7 &6	Patty Berg	Memphis CC, Memphis, TN
1938 ....Patty Berg		6 &5	Estelle Lawson	Westmoreland CC, Wilmette, IL

U.S. Women's Amateur (Cont.)

Year	Winner	Score	Runner-Up	Site
1939	Betty Jameson	3 & 2	Dorothy Kirby	Wee Burn Club, Darien, CT
1940	Betty Jameson	6 & 5	Jane S. Cothran	Del Monte G & CC, Pebble Beach, CA
1941	Elizabeth Hicks	5 & 3	Helen Sigel	The Country Club, Brookline, MA
1942–45	No tournament			
1946	Babe Zaharias	11 & 9	Clara Sherman	Southern Hills CC, Tulsa
1947	Louise Suggs	2 up	Dorothy Kirby	Franklin Hills CC, Franklin, MI
1948	Grace S. Lenczyk	4 & 3	Helen Sigel	Del Monte G & CC, Pebble Beach, CA
1949	Dorothy Porter	3 & 2	Dorothy Kielty	Merion GC, Ardmore, PA
1950	Beverly Hanson	6 & 4	Mae Murray	Atlanta AC, Atlanta
1951	Dorothy Kirby	2 & 1	Claire Doran	Town & CC, St. Paul
1952	Jacqueline Pung	2 & 1	Shirley McFedters	Waverley CC, Portland, OR
1953	Mary Lena Faulk	3 & 2	Polly Riley	Rhode Island CC, West Barrington, RI
1954	Barbara Romack	4 & 2	Mickey Wright	Allegheny CC, Sewickley, PA
1955	Patricia A. Lesser	7 & 6	Jane Nelson	Myers Park CC, Charlotte
1956	Marlene Stewart	2 & 1	JoAnne Gunderson	Meridian Hills CC, Indianapolis
1957	JoAnne Gunderson	8 & 6	Ann Casey Johnstone	Del Paso CC, SacramentoA
1958	Anne Quast	3 & 2	Barbara Romack	Wee Burn CC, Darien, CT
1959	Barbara McIntire	4 & 3	Joanne Goodwin	Congressional CC, Washington, D.C.
1960	JoAnne Gunderson	6 & 5	Jean Ashley	Tulsa CC, Tulsa
1961	Anne Quast Decker	14 & 13	Phyllis Preuss	Tacoma G & CC, Tacoma, WA
1962	JoAnne Gunderson	9 & 8	Anne Baker	CC of Rochester, Rochester, NY
1963	Anne Quast Decker	2 & 1	Peggy Conley	Taconic GC, Williamstown, MA
1964	Barbara McIntire	3 & 2	JoAnne Gunderson	Prairie Dunes CC, Hutchinson, KS
1965	Jean Ashley	5 & 4	Anne Quast Decker	Lakewood CC, Denver
1966	JoAnne Gunderson	1 up	Marlene Stewart Streit	Sewickley Heights CC, Sewickley, PA
1967	Mary Lou Dill	5 & 4	Jean Ashley	Annandale CC, Pasadena
1968	JoAnne Gunderson Carner	5 & 4	Anne Quast Decker	Birmingham CC, Birmingham, MI
1969	Catherine Lacoste	3 & 2	Shelley Hamling	Las Colinas C, Irving, TX
1970	Martha Wilkinson	3 & 2	Cynthia Hall	Wee Burn CC, Darien, CT
1971	Laura Baugh	1 up	Beth Barry	Atlanta CC, Atlanta
1972	Mary Budke	5 & 4	Cynthia Hill	St. Louis CC, St. Louis
1973	Carol Semple	1 up	Anne Quast Decker	Montclair GC, Montclair, NJ
1974	Cynthia Hill	5 & 4	Carol Semple	Broadmoor GC, Seattle
1975	Beth Daniel	3 & 2	Donna Horton	Brae Burn CC, West Newton, MA
1976	Donna Horton	2 & 1	Marianne Bretton	Del Paso CC, Sacramento
1977	Beth Daniel	3 & 1	Cathy Sherk	Cincinnati CC, Cincinnati
1978	Cathy Sherk	4 & 3	Judith Oliver	Sunnybrook GC, Plymouth Meeting, PA
1979	Carolyn Hill	7 & 6	Patty Sheehan	Memphis CC, Memphis
1980	Juli Inkster	2 up	Patti Rizzo	Prairie Dunes CC, Hutchinson, KS
1981	Juli Inkster	1 up	Lindy Goggin	Waverley CC, Portland, OR
1982	Juli Inkster	4 & 3	Cathy Hanlon	Broadmoor GC, Colorado Springs, CO
1983	Joanne Pacillo	2 & 1	Sally Quinlan	Canoe Brook CC, Summit, NJ
1984	Deb Richard	1 up	Kimberly Williams	Broadmoor GC, Seattle
1985	Michiko Hattori	5 & 4	Cheryl Stacy	Fox Chapel GC, Pittsburgh
1986	Kay Cockerill	9 & 7	Kathleen McCarthy	Pasatiempo GC, Santa Cruz, CA
1987	Kay Cockerill	3 & 2	Tracy Kerdyk	Rhode Island CC, Barrington, RI
1988	Pearl Sinn	6 & 5	Karen Noble	Minikahda Club, Minneapolis
1989	Vicki Goetze	4 & 3	Brandie Burton	Pinehurst CC (No. 2), Pinehurst, NC
1990	Pat Hurst	37 holes	Stephanie Davis	Canoe Brook CC, Summit, NJ
1991	Amy Fruhwirth	5 & 4	Heidi Voorhees	Prairie Dunes CC, Hutchinson, KN
1992	Vicki Goetz	1 up	Annika Sorensteam	Kemper Lakes GC, Hawthorne Hills, IL
1993	Jill McGill	1 up	Sarah Ingram	San Diego CC, Chula Vista, CA
1994	Wendy Ward	2 & 1	Jill McGill	The Homestead, Hot Springs, WV
1995	Kelli Kuehne	4 & 3	Anne-Marie Knight	The Country Club, Brookline, MA
1996	Kelli Kuehne	2 & 1	Marisa Baena	Firethorn GC, Lincoln, NE
1997	Silvia Cavalleri	5 & 4	Robin Burke	Brae Burn CC, West Newton, MA
1998	Grace Park	7 & 6	Jenny Chuasiriporn	Barton Hills CC, Ann Arbor, MI
1999	Dorothy Delasin	4 & 3	Jimin Kang	Biltmore Forest CC, Asheville, NC
2000	Marcy Newton	8 & 7	Laura Myerscough	Waverley CC, Portland, OR
2001	Meredith Duncan	37 holes	Nicole Perrot	Flint Hills GC, Wichita, KA
2002	Becky Lucidi	3 & 2	Brandi Jackson	Sleepy Hollow CC, Scarborough, NY
2003	Virada Nirapathpongporn	2 & 1	Jane Park	Philadelphia CC, Gladwyne, PA

U.S. Girls' Junior Amateur

1949 ....Marlene Bauer	1968 ....Peggy Harmon	1987 ....Michelle McGann
1950 ....Patricia Lesser	1969 ....Hollis Stacy	1988 ....Jamille Jose
1951 ....Arlene Brooks	1970 ....Hollis Stacy	1989 ....Brandie Burton
1952 ....Mickey Wright	1971 ....Hollis Stacy	1990 ....Sandrine Mendiburu
1953 ....Millie Meyerson	1972 ....Nancy Lopez	1991 ....Emilee Klein
1954 ....Margaret Smith	1973 ....Amy Alcott	1992 ....Jamie Koizumi
1955 ....Carole Jo Kabler	1974 ....Nancy Lopez	1993 ....Kellee Booth
1956 ....JoAnne Gunderson	1975 ....Dayna Benson	1962 ....Maureen Orcutt
1957 ....Judy Eller	1976 ....Pilar Dorado	1963 ....Sis Choate
1958 ....Judy Eller	1977 ....Althea Tome	1994 ....Kelli Kuehne
1959 ....Judy Rand	1978 ....Lori Castillo	1995 ....Marcy Newton
1960 ....Carol Sorenson	1979 ....Penny Hammel	1996 ....Dorothy Delasin
1961 ....Mary Lowell	1980 ....Laurie Rinker	1997 ....Beth Bauer
1962 ....Mary Lou Daniel	1981 ....Kay Cornelius	1998 ....Leigh Anne Hardin
1963 ....Janis Ferraris	1982 ....Heather Farr	1999 ....Aree Wongluekiet
1964 ....Peggy Conley	1983 ....Kim Saiki	2000 ....Lisa Ferrero
1965 ....Gail Sykes	1984 ....Cathy Mockett	2001 ....Nicole Perrot
1966 ....Claudia Mayhew	1985 ....Dana Lofland	2002 ....In-Bee Park
1967 ....Elizabeth Story	1986 ....Pat Hurst	2003 ....Sukjin-Lee Wuesthoff

Women's British Amateur

1893 ....Lady Margaret Scott	1929 ....Miss J. Wethered	1966 ....E. Chadwick
1894 ....Lady Margaret Scott	1930 ....Miss D. Fishwick	1967 ....E. Chadwick
1895 ....Lady Margaret Scott	1931 ....Miss E. Wilson	1968 ....B. Varangot
1896 ....Miss Pascoe	1932 ....Miss E. Wilson	1975 ....C. Lacoste
1897 ....Miss E.C. Orr	1933 ....Miss E. Wilson	1976 ....D. Oxley
1898 ....Miss L. Thomson	1934 ....Mrs. A.M. Holm	1977 ....A. Uzielli
1899 ....Miss M. Hezlet	1935 ....Miss W. Morgan	1978 ....E. Kennedy
1900 ....Miss Adair	1936 ....Miss P. Barton	1979 ....M. Madill
1901 ....Miss Graham	1937 ....Miss J. Anderson	1980 ....A. Quast
1902 ....Miss M. Hezlet	1938 ....Mrs. A.M. Holm	1981 ............I.C. Robertson
1903 ....Miss Adair	1939 ....Miss P. Barton	1982 ....K. Douglas
1904 ....Miss L. Dod	1940–45 ....not held	1983 ....J. Thornhill
1905 ....Miss B. Thompson	1946 ..........G.W. Hetherington	1984 ....J. Rosenthal
1906 ....Mrs. Kennon	1947 ....B. Zaharias	1985 ....L. Beman
1907 ....Miss M. Hezlet	1948 ....L. Suggs	1986 ....M. McGuire
1908 ....Miss M. Titterton	1949 ....F. Stephens	1987 ....J. Collingham
1909 ....Miss D. Campbell	1950 ....Vicomtesse de Saint	1988 ....J. Furby
1910 ....Miss Grant Suttie	Sauveur	1989 ....H. Dobson
1911 ....Miss D. Campbell	1951 ..........P.J. MacCann	1990 ....J. Hall
1912 ....Miss G. Ravenscroft	1952 ....M. Paterson	1991 ....V. Michaud
1913 ....Miss M. Dodd	1953 ....M. Stewart	1992 ....P. Pedersen
1914 ....Miss C. Leitch	1954 ....F. Stephens	1993 ....Catriona Lambert
1915–19 ....not held	1955 ....J. Valentine	1994 ....Emma Duggleby
1920 ....Miss C. Leitch	1956 ....M. Smith	1995 ....Julie Hall
1921 ....Miss C. Leitch	1957 ....P. Garvey	1996 ....Kelli Kuehne
1922 ....Miss J. Wethered	1958 ....J. Valentine	1997 ....Alison Rose
1923 ....Miss D. Chambers	1959 ....E. Price	1998 ....K. Rostron
1924 ....Miss J. Wethered	1960 ....B. McIntyre	1999 ....Marine Monnet
1925 ....Miss J. Wethered	1961 ....M. Spearman	2000 ....Rebecca Hudson
1926 ....Miss C. Leitch	1962 ....M. Spearman	2001 ....Rebecca Hudson
1927 ....Miss Thion de la	1963 ....B. Varangot	2002 ....Rebecca Hudson
Chaume	1964 ....C. Sorenson	2003 ....Elisa Serramia
1928 ....Miss N. Le Blan	1965 ....B. Varangot	

Women's Amateur Public Links

1977 ....Kelly Fuiks	1986 ....Cindy Schreyer	1996 ....Heather Graff
1978 ....Kelly Fuiks	1987 ....Tracy Kerdyk	1997 ....Jo Jo Robertson
1979 ....Lori Castillo	1988 ....Pearl Sinn	1998 ....Amy Spooner
1980 ....Lori Castillo	1989 ....Pearl Sinn	1999 ....Jody Niemann
1981 ....Mary Enright	1990 ....Cathy Mockett	2000 ....Catherine Cartwright
1982 ....Nancy Taylor	1991 ....Tracy Hanson	2001 ....Candie Kung
1983 ....Kelli Antolock	1992 ....Amy Fruhwirth	2002 ....Annie Thurman
1984 ....Heather Farr	1993 ....Connie Masterson	2003 ....Michelle Wie
1985 ....Danielle	1994 ....Jill McGill	
Ammaccapane	1995 ....Jo Jo Robertson	

U.S. Senior Women's Amateur

1964 ....Loma Smith	1977 ....Dorothy Porter	1990 ....Anne Sander
1965 ....Loma Smith	1978 ....Alice Dye	1991 ....Phyllis Preuss
1966 ....Maureen Orcutt	1979 ....Alice Dye	1992 ....Rosemary Thompson
1967 ....Marge Mason	1980 ....Dorothy Porter	1993 ....Anne Sander
1968 ....Carolyn Cudone	1981 ....Dorothy Porter	1994 ....Marlene Streit
1969 ....Carolyn Cudone	1982 ....Edean Ihlanfeldt	1995 ....Jean Smith
1970 ....Carolyn Cudone	1983 ....Dorothy Porter	1996 ....Gayle Borthwick
1971 ....Carolyn Cudone	1984 ....Constance Guthrie	1997 ....Nancy Fitzgerald
1972 ....Carolyn Cudone	1985 ....Marlene Streit	1998 ....Gayle Borthwick
1973 ....Gwen Hibbs	1986 ....Connie Guthrie	1999 ....C. Semple Thompson
1974 ....Justine Cushing	1987 ....Anne Sander	2000 ....C. Semple Thompson
1975 ....Alberta Bower	1988 ....Lois Hodge	2001 ....C. Semple Thompson
1976 ....Cecile H. Maclaurin	1989 ....Anne Sander	2002 ....C. Semple Thompson
		2003 ....Marlene Streit

Women's Mid-Amateur Championship

1987 ....Cindy Scholefield	1993 ....Sarah Ingram	1999 ....Alissa Herron
1988 ....Martha Lang	1994 ....Sarah Ingram	2000 ....Ellen Port
1989 ....Robin Weiss	1995 ....Ellen Port	2001 ....Laura Shanahan
1990 ....C. Semple Thompson	1996 ....Ellen Port	2002 ....Kathy Hartwiger
1991 ....Sarah LeBrun Ingram	1997 ....C. Semple Thompson	2003 ....Amber Marsh
1992 ....M. Marney-McInerney	1998 ....Virginia Derby Grimes	

International Golf

Ryder Cup Matches

Year	Results	Site
1927	United States 9½, Great Britain 2½	Worcester CC, Worcester, MA
1929	Great Britain 7, United States 5	Moortown GC, Leeds, England
1931	United States 9, Great Britain 3	Scioto CC, Columbus, OH
1933	Great Britain 6½, United States 5½	Southport and Ainsdale Courses, Southport, England
1935	United States 9, Great Britain 3	Ridgewood CC, Ridgewood, NJ
1937	United States 8, Great Britain 4	Southport and Ainsdale Courses, Southport, England
1939–1945	No tournament	
1947	United States 11, Great Britain 1	Portland GC, Portland, OR
1949	United States 7, Great Britain 5	Ganton GC, Scarborough, England
1951	United States 9½, Great Britain 2½	Pinehurst CC, Pinehurst, NC
1953	United States 6½, Great Britain 5½	Wentworth Club, Surrey, England
1955	United States 8, Great Britain 4	Thunderbird Ranch & CC, Palm Springs, CA
1957	Great Britain 7½, United States 4½	Lindrick GC, Yorkshire, England
1959	United States 8½, Great Britain 3½	Eldorado CC, Palm Desert, CA
1961	United States 14½, Great Britain 9½	Royal Lytham & St. Annes GC, St Anne's-on-the-Sea, England
1963	United States 23, Great Britain 9	East Lake CC, Atlanta
1965	United States 19½, Great Britain 12½	Royal Birkdale GC, Southport, England
1967	United States 23½, Great Britain 8½	Champions GC, Houston
1969	United States 16, Great Britain 16	Royal Birkdale GC, Southport, England
1971	United States 18½, Great Britain 13½	Old Warson CC, St. Louis
1973	United States 19, Great Britain 13	Hon Co of Edinburgh Golfers, Muirfield, Scotland
1975	United States 21, Great Britain 11	Laurel Valley GC, Ligonier, PA
1977	United States 12½, Great Britain 7½	Royal Lytham & St. Annes GC, St. Annes-on-the-Sea, England
1979	United States 17, Europe 11	Greenbrier, White Sulphur Springs, WV
1981	United States 18½, Europe 9½	Walton Heath GC, Surrey, England
1983	United States 14½, Europe 13½	PGA National GC, Palm Beach Gardens, FL
1985	Europe 16½, United States 11½	Belfry GC, Sutton Coldfield, England
1987	Europe 15, United States 13	Muirfield GC, Dublin, OH
1989	Europe 14, United States 14	Belfry GC, Sutton Coldfield, England
1991	United States 14½, Europe 13½	Ocean Course, Kiawah Island, SC
1993	United States 15, Europe 13	Belfry GC, Sutton Coldfield, England
1995	Europe 14½, United States 13½	Oak Hill CC, Rochester, NY
1997	Europe 14½, United States 13½	Valderrama GC, Sotogrande, Spain
1999	United States 14½, Europe 13½	The Country Club, Brookline, MA
2002	Europe 15½, Unites States 12½	Belfry GC, Sutton Coldfield, England

Team matches held every odd year between U.S. professionals and those of Great Britain/Europe. Team members selected on basis of finishes in PGA and European tour events. Match in 2001 canceled due to 9/11 terrorist attacks.

Walker Cup Matches

Year	Results	Site
1922	United States 8, Great Britain 4	Nat'l Golf Links of America, Southampton, NY
1923	United States 6, Great Britain 5	St. Andrews, Scotland
1924	United States 9, Great Britain 3	Garden City GC, Garden City, NY
1926	United States 6, Great Britain 5	St. Andrews, Scotland
1928	United States 11, Great Britain 1	Chicago GC, Wheaton, IL
1930	United States 10, Great Britain 2	Royal St. George GC, Sandwich, England
1932	United States 8, Great Britain 1	The Country Club, Brookline, MA
1934	United States 9, Great Britain 2	St. Andrews, Scotland
1936	United States 9, Great Britain 0	Pine Valley GC, Clementon, NJ
1938	Great Britain 7, United States 4	St. Andrews, Scotland
1940–46	No tournament	
1947	United States 8, Great Britain 4	St. Andrews, Scotland
1949	United States 10, Great Britain 2	Winged Foot GC, Mamaroneck, NY
1951	United States 6, Great Britain 3	Birkdale GC, Southport, England
1953	United States 9, Great Britain 3	The Kittansett Club, Marion, MA
1955	United States 10, Great Britain 2	St. Andrews, Scotland
1957	United States 8, Great Britain 3	Minikahda Club, Minneapolis
1959	United States 9, Great Britain 3	Muirfield, Scotland
1961	United States 11, Great Britain 1	Seattle GC, Seattle
1963	United States 12, Great Britain 8	Ailsa Course, Turnberry, Scotland
1965	Great Britain 11, United States 11	Baltimore CC, Five Farms, Baltimore, MD
1967	United States 13, Great Britain 7	Royal St. George's GC, Sandwich, England
1969	United States 10, Great Britain 8	Milwaukee CC, Milwaukee, WI
1971	Great Britain 13, United States 11	St. Andrews, Scotland
1973	United States 14, Great Britain 10	The Country Club, Brookline, MA
1975	United States 15½, Great Britain 8½	St. Andrews, Scotland
1977	United States 16, Great Britain 8	Shinnecock Hills GC, Southampton, NY
1979	United States 15½, Great Britain 8½	Muirfield, Scotland
1981	United States 15, Great Britain 9	Cypress Point Club, Pebble Beach, CA
1983	United States 13½, Great Britain 10½	Royal Liverpool GC, Hoylake, England
1985	United States 13, Great Britain 11	Pine Valley GC, Pine Valley, NJ
1987	United States 16½, Great Britain 7½	Sunningdale GC, Berkshire, England
1989	Great Britain 12½, United States 11½	Peachtree Golf Club, Atlanta
1991	United States 14, Great Britain 10	Portmarnock GC, Dublin, Ireland
1993	United States 19, Great Britain 5	Interlachen CC, Edina, MN
1995	Great Britain/Ireland 14, United States 10	Royal Porthcawl, Porthcawl, Wales
1997	United States 18, Great Britain/Ireland 6	Quaker Ridge GC, Scarsdale, NY
1999	Great Britain/Ireland 15, United States 9	Nairn GC, Nairn, Scotland
2001	Great Britain/Ireland 15, United States 9	Ocean Forest GC, Sea Island, GA
2003	Great Britain/Ireland 12½, United States 11½	Ganton GC, Ganton, England

Men's amateur team competition every other year between United States and Great Britain/Ireland. U.S. team members selected by USGA.

Solheim Cup Matches

Year	Results	Site
1990	United States 11½, Europe 4½	Lake Nona GC, Orlando, FL
1992	Europe 11½, United States 6½	Dalmahoy Hotel GC, Edinburgh
1994	United States 13, Europe 7	The Greenbriar, White Sulpher Springs, WV
1996	United States 17, Europe 11	Marriot St Pierre Hotel & CC, Chepstow, Wales
1998	United States 16, Europe 12	Muirfield Village GC, Dublin, OH
2000	Europe 14½, United States, 11½	Loch Lomond GC, Luss, Scotand
2002	United States 15½, Europe 12½	Interlachen CC, Minneapolis, MN
2003	Europe 17½, United States 10½	Barseback G&CC, Malmo, Sweden

Team matches held every other year between U.S. professionals and those of Europe. Team members selected on basis of finishes in LPGA and European tour events.

Curtis Cup Matches

Year	Results	Site
1932	United States 5½, British Isles 3½	Wentworth GC, Wentworth, England
1934	United States 6½, British Isles 2½	Chevy Chase Club, Chevy Chase, MD
1936	United States 4½, British Isles 4½	King's Course, Gleneagles, Scotland
1938	United States 5½, British Isles 3½	Essex CC, Manchester, MA
1940–46	No tournament	
1948	United States 6½, British Isles 2½	Birkdale GC, Southport, England
1950	United States 7½, British Isles 1½	CC of Buffalo, Williamsville, NY

Curtis Cup Matches (Cont.)

Year	Results	Site
1952	British Isles 5, United States 4	Muirfield, Scotland
1954	United States 6, British Isles 3	Merion GC, Ardmore, PA
1956	British Isles 5, United States 4	Prince's GC, Sandwich Bay, England
1958	British Isles 4½, United States 4½	Brae Burn CC, West Newton, Mass.
1960	United States 6½, British Isles 2½	Lindrick GC, Worksop, England
1962	United States 8, British Isles 1	Broadmoor CG, Colorado Springs,CO
1964	United States 10½, British Isles 7½	Royal Porthcawl GC, Porthcawl, South Wales
1966	United States 13, British Isles 5	Va. Hot Springs G & TC, Hot Springs, VA
1968	United States 10½, British Isles 7½	Royal County Down GC, Newcastle, N. Ire.
1970	United States 11½, British Isles 6½	Brae Burn CC, West Newton, MA
1972	United States 10, British Isles 8	Western Gailes, Ayrshire, Scotland
1974	United States 13, British Isles 5	San Francisco GC, San Francisco
1976	United States 11½, British Isles 6½	Royal Lytham & St. Annes GC, England
1978	United States 12, British Isles 6	Apawamis Club, Rye, NY
1980	United States 13, British Isles 5	St. Pierre G & CC, Chepstow, Wales
1982	United States 14½, British Isles 3½	Denver CC, Denver
1984	United States 9½, British Isles 8½	Muirfield, Scotland
1986	British Isles 13, United States 5	Prairie Dunes CC, Hutchinson, KS
1988	British Isles 11, United States 7	Royal St. George's GC, Sandwich, England
1990	United States 14, British Isles 4	Somerset Hills CC, Bernardsville, NJ
1992	Great Britain/Ireland 10, United States 8	Royal Liverpool GC, Hoylake, England
1994	Great Britain/Ireland 9, United States 9	The Honors Course, Ooltewah, TN
1996	Great Britain/Ireland 11½, United States 6½	Killarney Golf & Fishing Club, Killarney, Ireland
1998	United States 10, Great Britain/Ireland 8	The Minikahda Club, Minneapolis
2000	United States 10, Great Britain/Ireland 8	Ganton GC, North Yorkshire, England
2002	United States 11, Great Britain/Ireland 7	Fox Chapel GC, Pittsburgh, PA

Women's amateur team competition every other year between the United States and Great Britain/Ireland. U.S. team members selected by USGA.

Boxing

**Shane Mosley and
Oscar De La Hoya
battle in Las Vegas**

Heavy Muddle

Lacking stars and quality matchups, especially among the heavyweights, boxing continued to lose its punch

BY STEPHEN CANNELLA

THESE ARE NOT banner days for boxing, particularly in the heavyweight division. Elite fighters with the punch to put opponents on the canvas and the personality to put fans in the seats are a rarity. Matchups between them are even rarer. As 2003 drew to a close the three major heavyweight belts were held by a graybeard champion (Lennox Lewis) drifting toward retirement; a light heavyweight (Roy Jones Jr.) who took the title from a pug named John Ruiz despite being 33 pounds lighter than Ruiz; and a run-of-the-mill puncher (Chris Byrd) with almost zero box office appeal. Ali, Frazier and Foreman they weren't.

Forget about matchups with panache and crossover appeal. Cobbling together any sort of title bout was an ordeal in 2003. Take the buildup to Lewis's successful (sort of) defense of his WBC belt in June, which was bizarre even by boxing's circusy standards. With visions of a huge payday bobbing and weaving in his head, Lewis—who had been absent from the ring since the previous summer—spent the early part of the year stumping for a rematch against the fighter formerly known as Iron Mike.

While Tyson hemmed and hawed in the pre-fight negotiations, Vitali Klitschko—a former kickboxing champion and, with a record of 32–1, the WBC's top contender—argued loudly that he should be the one fighting Lewis. The Ukrainian appeared to get his wish when Tyson backed away from Lewis's challenge. Alas, the Lewis-Klitschko matchup fell apart in April when the two camps couldn't agree on how to split the event's international broadcast rights.

So the champ moved on to Plan C: a bout against little-known Canadian Kirk Johnson on June 21 at the Staples Center in Los Angeles. Two weeks before the fight, however, Johnson pulled out with a torn chest muscle. Left scrambling, promoters and HBO executives hastily elevated Klitschko, who had been scheduled to fight Cedric Boswell earlier in the evening, from the undercard to the night's main event.

Thus in spite of itself, a heavyweight division starved for quality cards ended up with the fight that fans deserved to see. At 6'8",

Klitschko (right) led Lewis on all three judges' cards when the fight was stopped.

the 31-year-old Klitschko presented an unusual opponent for the 6'5" Lewis, who was used to (literally) looking down at his foes in the ring. Still, Klitschko's stilted upright style, lack of ring polish and questionable heart—he refused to come out for the 10th round of his 2000 WBO title defense against Chris Byrd because of a torn rotator cuff—had most fight afficionados expecting an easy win for Lewis.

The Englishman apparently bought the hype. He weighed in at a doughy 256½ pounds, three pounds more than he'd been for any of his previous 43 fights, and from the opening bell he looked slouchy and unprepared. Instead of a rout, fans were treated to a wildly entertaining slugfest. And since this was a high-profile heavyweight bout, there was also a controversial and unsatisfying conclusion.

Klitschko charged the champ early, keeping him off balance with an onslaught of left jabs. Late in the second round Klitschko caught Lewis with a long, looping right hand. Clearly shellshocked by Klitschko's unex-

pectedly spirited attack, Lewis staggered back to his corner when the round ended.

The champ regrouped, and in the third he opened a gash over Klitschko's left eye. The challenger gamely held his ground and continued to land punches, but Lewis smartly worked the wound. As the fight wore on creeks of blood poured down Klitschko's face, and by the end of the sixth round his eye looked more like an internal organ than an external one. Disregarding the fact that Klitschko had clearly outboxed the champion—he led on all three judges' scorecards—ring doctor Paul Wallace stopped the fight.

Lewis had a TKO, Klitschko had a nasty cut that would take 60 stitches to close, and the heavyweight division had yet another disputed outcome. "I don't know why the doctor stopped the fight," said Klitschko, who was talking rematch before he left the ring. "I could still see everything."

Lewis also bemoaned the stoppage, saying he was denied the chance at a knockout and a convincing victory. But three months shy of his 38th birthday, Lewis looked old, sluggish and uninspired. The victory was a Pyrrhic one: Instead of cementing his legacy as an elite heavyweight, he emerged with his stature and reputation diminished. In the wake of the fight there was a chorus of calls for Lewis to step aside.

He got the message. Klitschko healed quickly and demanded a December rematch. But the champ, who had also discussed a possible showdown with Roy Jones Jr., announced in August that he wouldn't fight again in 2003. He also hinted that he was close to hanging up the gloves for good.

While Lewis's star faded in the likely twilight of his career, junior welterweight Micky Ward retired in the glow of a rivalry that typified boxing at its best. In June, he and Arturo Gatti fought the final installment of an action-packed trilogy that began with a classic free-for-all in May 2002. On that night Ward won a razor-thin decision after 10 furious rounds. In the rematch six months later Gatti sent his rival flying into a turnbuckle with a savage third-round right, shattering Ward's eardrum. The valiant Ward somehow stayed on his feet for the rest of the bout, finally losing on points.

The two 142-pounders met for an early-summer rubbermatch in Atlantic City. Ward announced beforehand that the fight would be his last, and when the bell rang, he—and Gatti—fought like it, pounding each other with abandon. In the third round, Ward developed double vision; by the end of the fight he was choosing from at least three Gattis in his line of sight. Gatti broke his right hand in the fourth, and was essentially a one-armed fighter for the remainder of the bout.

Both fighters soldiered on, and Gatti was awarded a unanimous decision after 10 frenetic rounds. The loss was the 14th of Ward's career (against 38 wins), but the 37-year-old left the stage with his head held high. His three battles with Gatti—all of them non-title bouts—were reminders of how gripping the sport can be when two evenly-matched gladiators engage each other with heart, passion, and mutual respect. Before the final round in Atlantic City Ward and Gatti embraced. They repeated the gesture after both received treatment at the Atlantic City Medical Center. "I got great respect for him," Gatti said.

"But I'm glad I won't see him anymore."

In September, Shane Mosley renewed acquaintances with Oscar De La Hoya, whom he had outpointed for the WBC welterweight title in 2000. De La Hoya, the reigning WBA and WBC super-welterweight champion, had rebounded from that devastating loss and rehabilitated his career with four straight wins heading into the Mosley fight. Sugar Shane, for his part, lost the belt to Vernon Forrest soon after taking it from De La Hoya, and was more than two years removed from his last victory when the bell rang for his rematch with the Golden Boy.

A crowd of more than 16,000 at the MGM Grand in Las Vegas saw the two fighters cautiously battle to a draw during the first eight rounds. But Mosley began to take over in the ninth, and by the 12th round De La Hoya was clearly winded and wobbly. Even though De La Hoya landed more punches in the fight (221 to Mosley's 127) all three judges gave Sugar Shane the final four rounds and awarded him a 115–113 decision.

De La Hoya had said before the fight that he would retire if he failed to retain his titles, and the loss, the third of his career, may well have cost him a place in the boxing pantheon. He was incensed by the decision, and said that his lawyers would launch an investigation into the judges' scoring.

His accusations of malfeasance at the scorers' table were met with raised eyebrows, but De La Hoya certainly had the means to cover any legal fees he might incur. He was guaranteed $17.5 million for his efforts, versus $4.5 million for Mosley. Such are the benefits of being one of the few active fighters with a name recognizable outside of boxing circles.

Jones Jr., who outboxes every opponent regardless of weight, ended the year as the clear pound-for-pound king of the sport. But the next candidate for savior of a sport that is fast losing mainstream appeal could be Klitschko. He's intelligent and well-spoken (he has a Ph.D. in sports science) and, as he proclaimed after his loss to Lewis, "I showed everybody I have heart."

In a lackluster heavyweight class, that may be all it takes to be a champion.

Current Champions

Division	Weight Limit	WBA Champion	WBC Champion	IBF Champion
Heavyweight	None	Roy Jones Jr.	Lennox Lewis	Chris Byrd
Cruiserweight	190	Jean-Marc Mormeck	Wayne Braithwaite	James Toney
Light Heavyweight	175	Silvio Branco	Antonio Tarver	Antonio Tarver
Super Middleweight	168	Anthony Mundine	Markus Beyer	Sven Ottke
Middleweight	160	William Joppy	Bernard Hopkins	Bernard Hopkins
Junior Middleweight	154	Alejandro Garcia	Shane Mosley	Ronald Wright
Welterweight	147	Jose Rivera	Ricardo Mayorga	Cory Spinks
Junior Welterweight	140	Vivian Harris	Kostya Tszyu	Kostya Tszyu
Lightweight	135	Leonard Dorin	Floyd Mayweather	Paul Spadafora
Junior Lightweight	130	Yodsanan Nanthachai	Jesus Chavez	Carlos Hernandez
Featherweight	126	Derrick Gainer	Erik Morales	Juan Manuel Marquez
Junior Featherweight	122	Mahyar Monshipour	Oscar Larios	Manny Pacquiao
Bantamweight	118	Johnny Bredahl	Veeraphol Sahaprom	Rafael Marquez
Junior Bantamweight	115	Alexander Munoz	Masanori Tokuyama	Luis Perez
Flyweight	112	Eric Morel	Pongsaklek Wonjongkam	Irene Pacheco
Junior Flyweight	108	Rosendo Alvarez	Jorge Arce	Jose Victor Burgos
Strawweight	105	Noel Arambulent	Jose Aguirre	Daniel Reyes

Note: WBC=World Boxing Council; WBA=World Boxing Association; IBF=International Boxing Federation.
Champions as of Sept. 16, 2002

Championship and Major Fights of 2002 and 2003

Abbreviations: WBC=World Boxing Council; WBA= World Boxing Association; IBF=International Boxing Federation; KO=knockout; TKO=technical knockout; UD=unanimous decision; SD=split decision; DQ=disqualification; MD=majority decision; TD=technical decision.

Heavyweight

Date	Winner	Loser	Result	Title	Site
Dec 14	Chris Byrd	Evander Holyfield	UD	IBF	Atlantic City
Mar 1	Roy Jones Jr.	John Ruiz	UD	WBA	Las Vegas
June 21	Lennox Lewis	Vitali Klitschko	TKO 6	WBC	Los Angeles
Sept 20	Chris Byrd	Fres Oquendo	UD	IBF	Uncasville, Conn.

Cruiserweight

Date	Winner	Loser	Result	Title	Site
Oct 11	Wayne Braithwaite	Vincenzo Cantatore	TKO 10	WBC	Campione d'Italia, Italy
Feb 21	Wayne Braithwaite	Ravea Springs	TKO 4	WBC	Miami
Mar 1	Jean-Marc Mormeck	Alexander Gurov	TKO 8	WBA	Las Vegas
April 26	James Toney	Vassiliy Girov	UD	IBF	Mashantucket, Conn.

Light Heavyweight

Date	Winner	Loser	Result	Title	Site
Mar 8	Mehdi Sahnoune	Bruno Girard	TKO 7	WBA	Marseille
Apr 26	Antonio Tarver	Montell Griffin	UD	WBC/IBF	Mashantucket, Conn.
Oct 10	Silvio Branco	Mehdi Sahnoune	TKO 11	WBA	Marseille

Super Middleweight

Date	Winner	Loser	Result	Title	Site
Sept. 6	Eric Lucas	Omar Sheika	UD	WBC	Montreal
Nov 16	Sven Ottke	Rudy Markussen	UD	IBF	Nuremberg
Mar 15	Sven Ottke	Byron Mitchell	Split	WBA/IBF	Berlin
April 5	Markus Beyer	Eric Lucas	Split	WBC	Leipzig, Germany
June 14	Sven Ottke	David Starie	UD	WBA/IBF	Magdeburg, Germany
Aug 16	Markus Beyer	Danny Green	DQ 5	WBC	Nurburgring, Germany
Sept 3	Anthony Mundine	Antwun Echols	UD	WBA	Sydney
Sept 6	Sven Ottke	Mads Larsen	MD	WBA/IBF	Erfurt, Germany

Middleweight

Date	Winner	Loser	Result	Title	Site
Oct 10	William Joppy	Naotaka Hozumi	TKO 10	WBA	Tokyo
Mar 29	Bernard Hopkins	Morrade Hakkar	TKO 8	WBC/WBA/IBF	Philadelphia

Junior Middleweight (Super Welterweight)

Date	Winner	Loser	Result	Title	Site
Mar 1	Alejandro Garcia	Santiago Samaniego	TKO 3	WBA	Las Vegas
Mar 1	Ronald Wright	Juan C. Candelo	UD	IBF	Las Vegas
May 3	Oscar De La Hoya	Luis Campas	TKO 7	WBC/WBA	Las Vegas
May 9	Javier Castillejo	Diego Castillo	TKO 1	WBC	Leganes, Spain
Sept 13	Shane Mosley	Oscar De La Hoya	UD	WBC/WBA	Las Vegas
Sept 20	Alejandro Garcia	Rhoshii Wells	TKO 10	WBA	Uncasville, Conn.

Welterweight

Date	Winner	Loser	Result	Title	Site
Jan 25	Ricardo Mayorga	Vernon Forrest	TKO 3	WBC/WBA	Temecula, Calif.
Mar 22	Cory Spinks	Michele Piccirillo	UD	IBF	Campione d'Italia, Italy
Sept 13	Jose Antonio Rivera	Michel Trabant	MD	WBA	Berlin

Junior Welterweight (Super Lightweight)

Date	Winner	Loser	Result	Title	Site
Oct 19	Vivian Harris	Diosbelys Hurtado	TKO 2	WBA	Houston
Jan 19	Kostya Tszyu	James Leija	TKO 6	WBC/WBA/IBF	Melbourne
July 12	Vivian Harris	Souleymane M'Baye	UD	WBA	Las Vegas

Lightweight

Date	Winner	Loser	Result	Title	Site
Nov 9	Paul Spadafora	Dennis Holbaek	UD	IBF	Chester, W Va.
Dec 7	Floyd Mayweather	Jose Luis Castillo	UD	WBC	Las Vegas
April 19	Floyd Mayweather	Victoriano Sosa	UD	WBC	Fresno, Calif.
May 17	Leonard Dorin/Paul Spadafora		DRAW	WBA/IBF	Pittsburgh

Junior Lightweight (Super Featherweight)

Date	Winner	Loser	Result	Title	Site
Dec 5	Yodsanan Nanthachai	Lamont Pearson	TKO 9	WBA	Bangkok
Jan 13	S. Singmanassak	Choi Yong-Soo	UD	WBC	Tokyo
Feb 1	Carlos Hernandez	David Santos	Tech D 8	IBF	Las Vegas
Mar 15	Acelino Freitas	Juan Carlos Ramirez	TKO 4	WBA	Chicago
Aug 9	Acelino Freitas	Jorge Barrios	TKO 12	WBA	Miami
Aug 15	Jesus Chavez	S. Singmanassak	UD	WBC	Austin, Tex.
Oct 4	Carlos Hernandez	Steve Forbes	Tech D 10	IBF	Los Angeles

Featherweight

Date	Winner	Loser	Result	Title	Site
Nov 16	Erik Morales	Paulie Ayala	UD	WBC	Las Vegas
Feb 1	Juan Manuel Marquez	Manuel Medina	TKO 7	IBF	Las Vegas
Feb 22	Erik Morales	Eddie Croft	TKO 3	WBC	Mexico City
April 12	Derrick Gainer	Oscar Leon	Split	WBA	Las Vegas
May 3	Erik Morales	Fernando Velardez	TKO 5	WBC	Las Vegas
Sept 26	Chris John	Oscar Leon	UD	WBA	Bali

Junior Featherweight (Super Bantamweight)

Date	Winner	Loser	Result	Title	Site
Oct 9	Salim Medjkoune	Osamu Sato	UD	WBA	Tokyo
Oct 26	Manny Pacquiao	F. Rakkiatgym	TKO 1	IBF	Davao City, Philippines
Nov 1	Oscar Larios	Willie Jorrin	TKO 1	WBC	Sacramento, Calif.
April 4	Salim Medjkoune	Vincenzo Gigliotti	UD	WBA	Clermont-Ferrand, Fra.
April 26	Oscar Larios	Shigeru Nakazato	UD	WBC	Tokyo
July 4	Mahyar Monshipour	Salim Medjkoune	KO 12	WBA	Poitiers, France
July 26	Manny Pacquiao	Emmanuel Lucero	TKO 3	IBF	Los Angeles
Sept 7	Oscar Larios	Kozo Ishii	TKO 2	WBC	Nagoya, Japan

Bantamweight

Date	Winner	Loser	Result	Title	Site
Nov 8	Johnny Bredahl	Rafael (Leo) Gamez	UD	WBA	Copenhagen
Feb 15	Rafael Marquez	Tim Austin	TKO 8	IBF	Las Vegas
May 1	Veerapol Sahaprom	Hugo Dianzo	UD	WBC	Bangkok
Oct 4	Veerapol Sahaprom	Toshiaki Nishioka	Split Draw	WBC	Tokyo
Oct 4	Hideki Todaka	Rafael (Leo) Gamez	UD	WBA	Tokyo
Oct 4	Rafael Marquez	Mauricio Pastrana	UD	IBF	Los Angeles

Junior Bantamweight (Super Flyweight)

Date	Winner	Loser	Result	Title	Site
Dec 20	Masamori Tokuyama	Gerry Penalosa	Split	WBC	Osaka
Jan 4	Luis Perez	Felix Machado	Split	IBF	Washington, D.C.
June 23	Masamori Tokuyama	Katsushige Kawashima	UD	WBC	Yokohama
Oct 4	Alexander Munoz	Hidenobu Honda	UD	WBA	Tokyo

Flyweight

Date	Winner	Loser	Result	Title	Site
Sept 6	P. Wonjongkam	Jesus Martinez	UD	WBC	Rangsit, Thailand
Oct 12	Eric Morel	Denkaosaen Kaovichit	TKO 11	WBA	Anaheim, Calif.
Nov 26	P. Wonjongkam	Hidenobu Honda	UD	WBC	Osaka
Nov 29	Irene Pacheco	Alejandro Montiel	UD	IBF	El Paso, Tex.
June 6	P. Wonjongkam	Randy Mangubat	UD	WBC	Songkhla, Thailand
June 28	Eric Morel	Isidro Garcia	UD	WBA	Bayamon, Puerto Rico
Sept 27	Irene Pacheco	Damaen Kelly	TKO 6	IBF	Barranquillla, Colombia

Junior Flyweight

Date	Winner	Loser	Result	Title	Site
Nov 16	Jorge Arce	Augustin Luna	TKO 3	WBC	Las Vegas
Feb 15	Jose Victor Burgos	Alex Sanchez	TKO 12	IBF	Las Vegas
Feb 22	Jorge Arce	Ernesto Castro	KO 1	WBC	Mexico City
Mar 31	Rosendo Alvarez	Beibis Mendoza	MD	WBA	Little Rock, Ark.
May 3	Jorge Arce	Melchor Cob Castor	Tech D 6	WBC	Las Vegas

Strawweight (Mini Flyweight)

Date	Winner	Loser	Result	Title	Site
Oct 19	Jose Aguirre	Juan Palacios	Split	WBC	Tabasco, Mexico
Dec 20	Noel Arambulet	Keitaro Hoshino	MD	WBA	Osaka
Feb 22	Jose Aguirre	Juan Alfonso Keb	TKO 7	WBC	Mexico City
Mar 22	Miguel Barrera	Roberto Leyba	KO 3	IBF	Las Vegas
May 31	Edgar Cardenas	Miguel Barrera	KO 10	IBF	Tijuana, Mexico
June 23	Jose Aguirre	Keitaro Hoshino	TKO 12	WBC	Yokohama
July 12	Noel Arambulet	Yutaka Niida	Split	WBA	Yokohama
Oct 4	Daniel Reyes	Edgar Cardenas	TKO 6	IBF	Los Angeles

World Champions

Sanctioning bodies: the National Boxing Association (NBA), the New York State Athletic Commission (NY), the World Boxing Association (WBA), the World Boxing Council (WBC), and the International Boxing Federation (IBF).

Heavyweights
(Weight: Unlimited)

Champion	Reign	Champion	Reign	Champion	Reign
John L. Sullivan*	1885–92	Joe Frazier* NY	1968–70	Evander Holyfield*	1990–92
James J. Corbett*	1892–97	Jimmy Ellis WBA	1968–70	Lennox Lewis WBC	1993–95
Bob Fitzsimmons*	1897–99	Joe Frazier*	1970–73	Riddick Bowe*	1992–93
James J. Jeffries*	1899–05†	George Foreman*	1973–74	Evander Holyfield*	1993–94
Marvin Hart*	1905–06	Muhammad Ali*	1974–78	Michael Moorer*	1994
Tommy Burns*	1906–08	Leon Spinks*	1978	George Foreman*	1994–95
Jack Johnson*	1908–15	Ken Norton WBC	1978	Oliver McCall WBC	1995
Jess Willard*	1915–19	Larry Holmes WBC	1978–80	Frank Bruno WBC	1995–96
Jack Dempsey*	1919–26	Muhammad Ali*	1978–79†	Bruce Seldon WBA	1995–96
Gene Tunney*	1926–28†	John Tate WBA	1979–80	Mike Tyson WBA	1996
Max Schmeling*	1930–32	Mike Weaver WBA	1980–82	Michael Moorer IBF	1996–97
Jack Sharkey*	1932–33	Larry Holmes*	1980–85	Shannon Briggs*	1997–98
Primo Carnera*	1933–34	Michael Dokes WBA	1982–83	Lennox Lewis* WBC	1997–01
Max Baer*	1934–35	Gerrie Coetzee WBA	1983–84	E. Holyfield WBA, IBF	1996–99
James J. Braddock*	1935–37	Tim Witherspoon WBC	1984	Lennox Lewis	1999–01
Joe Louis*	1937–49†	Pinklon Thomas WBC	1984–86	E. Holyfield WBA	2000–01
Ezzard Charles*	1949–51	Greg Page WBA	1984–85	John Ruiz WBA	2001–03
Jersey Joe Walcott*	1951–52	Michael Spinks*	1985–87	Hasim Rahman*	
Rocky Marciano*	1952–56†	Tim Witherspoon WBA	1986	WBC, IBF	2001
Floyd Patterson*	1956–59	Trevor Berbick WBC	1986	Chris Byrd IBF	2002–
Ingemar Johansson*	1959–60	Mike Tyson WBC	1986–87	Roy Jones Jr.. WBA	2003–
Floyd Patterson*	1960–62	James Smith WBA	1986–87	Lennox Lewis*	
Sonny Liston*	1962–64	Tony Tucker IBF	1987	WBC	2001–
Muhammad Ali*	1964–70†	Mike Tyson*	1987–90		
Ernie Terrell WBA	1965–67	Buster Douglas*	1990		

Cruiserweights
(Weight Limit: 190 pounds)

Champion	Reign	Champion	Reign	Champion	Reign
Marvin Camel* WBC	1980	Ricky Parkey IBF	1986–87	Orlin Norris WBA	1993–95
Carlos De Leon* WBC	1980–82	E. Holyfield* WBA, IBF	1987–88	Nate Miller WBA	1995–97
Ossie Ocasio WBA	1982–84	Evander Holyfield*	1988†	M. Dominguez* WBC	1996–98
S.T. Gordon* WBC	1982–83	Toufik Belbouli WBA	1989	A. Washington IBF	1996–97
Carlos De Leon* WBC	1983–85	Robert Daniels WBA	1989–91	Uriah Grant IBF	1997
Marvin Camel IBF	1983–84	Carlos De Leon* WBC	1989–90	Imamu Mayfield IBF	1997–98
Lee Roy Murphy IBF	1984–86	Glenn McCrory IBF	1989–90	Fabrice Tiozzo WBA	1997–00
Piet Crous WBA	1984–85	Jeff Lampkin IBF	1990	J.C. Gomez* WBC	1998–02†
Alfonso Ratliff* WBC	1985	M. Duran* WBC	1990–91	Arthur Williams IBF	1998–99
Dwight Braxton WBA	1985–86	Bobby Czyz WBA	1991–92†	Vassiliy Girov* IBF	1999–03
Bernard Benton* WBC	1985–86	Anaclet Wamba* WBC	1991–95†	James Toney* IBF	2003–
Carlos De Leon* WBC	1986–88	James Pritchard IBF	1991	Virgil Hill WBA	2000–02
Evander Holyfield* WBA	1986–88	James Warring IBF	1991–92	Wayne Braithwaite WBC	2002–
		Alfred Cole IBF	1992–96	J.M. Mormeck WBA	2002–

*Lineal champion.
†Champion relinquished title to retire or switch weight classes, or had title stripped by boxing organization.

Light Heavyweights
(Weight Limit: 175 pounds)

Champion	Reign	Champion	Reign	Champion	Reign
Jack Root*	1903	Harold Johnson NBA	1961	Virgil Hill* WBA	1987–91
George Gardner*	1903	Harold Johnson*	1962–63	Pr Charles Williams IBF	1987–93
Bob Fitzsimmons*	1903–05	Willie Pastrano*	1963–65	Thomas Hearns WBC	1987†
Jack O'Brien*	1905–12†	Jose Torres*	1965–66	Donny Lalonde WBC	1987–88
Jack Dillon*	1914–16	Dick Tiger*	1966–68	Sugar Ray Leonard WBC	1988
Battling Levinsky*	1916–20	Bob Foster*	1968–74†	Dennis Andries WBC	1989
Georges Carpentier*	1920–22	Vicente Rondon WBA	1971–72	Jeff Harding WBC	1989–90
Battling Siki*	1922–23	John Conteh WBC	1974–77	Dennis Andries WBC	1990–91
Mike McTigue*	1923–25	Victor Galindez* WBA	1974–78	Thomas Hearns* WBA	1991–92
Paul Berlenbach*	1925–26	Miguel A. Cuello WBC	1977–78	Jeff Harding WBC	1991–94
Jack Delaney*	1926–27†	Mate Parlov WBC	1978	Iran Barkley* WBA	1992
Jimmy Slattery NBA	1927	Mike Rossman* WBA	1978–79	Virgil Hill* WBA	1992–97
Tommy Loughran*	1927–29†	Victor Galindez* WBA	1979	Henry Maske IBF	1993–96
Maxie Rosenbloom*	1930–34	Marvin Johnson* WBC	1978–79	Mike McCallum WBC	1994–95
George Nichols NBA	1932	M.S. Muhammad* WBC	1979–81	Fabrice Tiozzo WBC	1995–96
Bob Godwin NBA	1933	Marvin Johnson WBA	1979–80	D. Michalczewski* IBF	1997†
Bob Olin*	1934–35	E.M. Muhammad* WBA	1980–81	Roy Jones Jr. WBC, WBA	1997–03
John Henry Lewis*	1935–38†	Michael Spinks* WBA	1981–83	William Guthrie IBF	1997–98
Melio Bettina	1939	Dwight Qawi WBC	1981–83	Reggie Johnson IBF	1998–99
Billy Conn*	1939–40†	Michael Spinks*	1983–85†	Roy Jones Jr.*	1999–03
Anton Christoforidis	1941	J. B. Williamson WBC	1985–86	Bruno Girard WBA	2001–03
Gus Lesnevich*	1941–48	Slobodan Kacar IBF	1985–86	Mehdi Sahnoune WBA	2003
Freddie Mills*	1948–50	Marvin Johnson* WBA	1986–87	Silvio Branco WBA	2003–
Joey Maxim*	1950–52	Dennis Andries WBC	1986–87	Antonio Tarver WBC,	
Archie Moore*	1952–62†	Bobby Czyz IBF	1986–87	IBF	2003–
		Leslie Stewart WBA	1987		

Super Middleweights
(Weight Limit: 168 pounds)

Champion	Reign	Champion	Reign	Champion	Reign
Murray Sutherland* IBF	1984	Iran Barkley IBF	1992	Richie Woodhall WBC	1998–99
Chong-Pal Park* IBF	1984–87	Nigel Benn WBC	1992–96	Sven Ottke IBF	1998–
Chong-Pal Park* WBA	1987–88	James Toney IBF	1992–94	Byron Mitchell* WBA	1999–00
G. Rocchigiani IBF	1988–89	Michael Nunn* WBA	1992–94	Markus Beyer WBC	1999–00
F. Obelmejias* WBA	1988–89	Steve Little* WBA	1994	Bruno Girard* WBA	2000–01†
Sugar Ray Leonard WBC	1988–90†	Frank Liles* WBA	1994–99	Glenn Catley WBC	2000–01
In-Chul Baek* WBA	1989–90	Roy Jones Jr. IBF	1994–96	Eric Lucas WBC	2000–03
Lindell Holmes IBF	1990–91	Thulane Malinga WBC	1996	Byron Mitchell WBA	2000–03
Chris Tiozzo* WBA	1990–91	V. Nardiello WBC	1996	Sven Ottke IBF	2003†
Mauro Galvano WBC	1990–92	Robin Reid WBC	1996–97	Anthony Mundine WBA	2003–
Victor Cordova* WBA	1991	Charles Brewer IBF	1997–98	Markus Beyer WBC	2003–
Darrin Van Horn IBF	1991–92	Thulane Malinga WBC	1997–98		

*Lineal champion. †Champion retired or relinquished title.

Middleweights
(Weight Limit: 160 pounds)

Champion	Reign	Champion	Reign	Champion	Reign
Jack Dempsey*	1884–91	Jake La Motta*	1949–51	Sugar Ray Leonard*	1987†
Bob Fitzsimmons*	1891–97†	Sugar Ray Robinson*	1951	Frank Tate IBF	1987–88
Kid McCoy	1897–98	Randy Turpin*	1951	Sumbu Kalambay WBA	1987–89
Tommy Ryan*	1898–07†	Sugar Ray Robinson*	1951–52†	Thomas Hearns* WBC	1987–88
Stanley Ketchel*	1908	Bobo Olson*	1953–55	Iran Barkley* WBC	1988–89
Billy Papke*	1908	Sugar Ray Robinson*	1955–57	Michael Nunn IBF	1988–91
Stanley Ketchel*	1908–10†	Gene Fullmer*	1957	Roberto Duran* WBC	1989–90†
Frank Klaus*	1913	Sugar Ray Robinson*	1957	Michael Nunn* IBF	1991
George Chip*	1913–14	Carmen Basilio*	1957–58	Mike McCallum WBA	1989–91
Al McCoy*	1914–17	Sugar Ray Robinson*	1958–60	Julian Jackson WBC	1990–93
Mike O'Dowd*	1917–20	Gene Fullmer NBA	1959–62	James Toney* IBF	1991–93†
Johnny Wilson*	1920–23	Paul Pender*	1960–61	Reggie Johnson WBA	1992–94
Harry Greb*	1923–26	Terry Downes*	1961–62	Roy Jones Jr.* IBF	1993–95†
Tiger Flowers*	1926	Paul Pender*	1962–63†	G. McClellan WBC	1993–95†
Mickey Walker*	1926–31†	Dick Tiger WBA	1962–63	Jorge Castro IBF	1994–95
Gorilla Jones*	1931–32	Dick Tiger*	1963	Shinji Takehara WBA	1995–96
Marcel Thil*	1932–37	Joey Giardello*	1963–65	Jullian Jackson WBC	1995
Fred Apostoli*	1937–39	Dick Tiger*	1965–66	Quincy Taylor WBC	1995–96
Al Hostak NBA	1938	Emile Griffith*	1966–67	Bernard Hopkins* IBF	1994–
Solly Krieger NBA	1938–39	Nino Benvenuti*	1967	Keith Holmes WBC	1996–98
Al Hostak NBA	1939–40	Emile Griffith*	1967–68	William Joppy WBA	1996–97
Ceferino Garcia*	1939–40	Nino Benvenuti*	1968–70	J.C. Green WBA	1997
Ken Overlin*	1940–41	Carlos Monzon*	1970–77†	William Joppy WBA	1998–01
Tony Zale NBA	1940–41	Rodrigo Valdez WBC	1974–76	Hassine Cherifi WBC	1998–99
Billy Soose*	1941	Rodrigo Valdez*	1977–78	Keith Holmes WBA	1999–00
Tony Zale*	1941–47	Hugo Corro*	1978–79	Felix Trinidad WBA	2001
Rocky Graziano*	1947–48	Vito Antuofermo*	1979–80	Bernard Hopkins*	2001–
Tony Zale*	1948	Alan Minter*	1980	William Joppy WBA	2001–
Marcel Cerdan*	1948–49	Marvin Hagler*	1980–87		

Junior Middleweights
(Weight Limit: 154 pounds)

Champion	Reign	Champion	Reign	Champion	Reign
Emile Griffith (EBU)	1962–63	Sugar Ray Leonard*	1981–82†	Simon Brown* WBC	1993–94
Dennis Moyer*	1962–63	Tadashi Mihara WBA	1981–82	Terry Norris* WBC	1994
Ralph Dupas*	1963	Davey Moore WBA	1982–83	Luis Santana* WBC	1995–95
Sandro Mazzinghi*	1963–65	Thomas Hearns* WBC	1982–84	Vincent Pettway IBF	1994–95
Nino Benvenuti*	1965–66	Roberto Duran WBA	1983–84	Paul Vaden IBF	1995
Ki-Soo Kim*	1966–68	Mark Medal IBF	1984	Carl Daniels WBA	1995
Sandro Mazzinghi*	1968	Thomas Hearns*	1984–86†	Terry Norris* WBC	1995–97
Freddie Little*	1969–70	Mike McCallum* WBA	1984–87†	Terry Norris* IBF	1995–96†
Carmelo Bossi*	1970–71	Carlos Santos IBF	1984–86	L. Boudouani WBA	1996–99
Koichi Wajima*	1971–74	Buster Drayton IBF	1986–87	Raul Marquez IBF	1997
Oscar Albarado*	1974–75	Duane Thomas WBC	1986–87	Keith Mullings* WBC	1997–99
Koichi Wajima*	1975	Matthew Hilton IBF	1987–88	Yori Boy Campas IBF	1997–98
Miguel de Oliveira WBC	1975–76	Lupe Aquino WBC	1987	Fernando Vargas IBF	1998–00
Jae-Do Yuh*	1975–76	Gianfranco Rosi WBC	1987–88	F. Javier Castillejo* WBC	1999–01
Elisha Obed WBC	1975–76	Julian Jackson WBA	1987–90	David Reid WBA	1999–00
Koichi Wajima*	1976	Donald Curry WBC	1988–89	Felix Trinidad WBA	2000–01
Jose Duran*	1976	Robert Hines IBF	1988–89	Felix Trinidad WBA, IBF	2001†
Eckhard Dagge WBC	1976–77	Darrin Van Horn IBF	1989	Oscar De La Hoya*	
Miguel Angel Castellini*	1976–77	Rene Jacquot WBC	1989	WBC	2001–03
Eddie Gazo*	1977–78	John Mugabi* WBC	1989–90	Fernando Vargas WBA	2001–02
Rocky Mattioli WBC	1977–79	Gianfranco Rosi IBF	1989–94	Ronald Wright IBF	2001–
Masashi Kudo*	1978–79	Terry Norris* WBC	1990–93	Oscar De La Hoya*	
Maurice Hope WBC	1979–81	Gilbert Dele WBA	1991	WBC/WBA	2002–03
Ayub Kalule*	1979–81	Vinny Pazienza WBA	1991–92	Shane Mosley* WBC	2003–
Wilfred Benitez WBC	1981–82	Julio C. Vasquez WBA	1992–95	Alejandro Garcia WBA	2003–

*Lineal champion.
†Champion relinquished title to retire or switch weight classes, or had title stripped by boxing organization.

Welterweights
(Weight Limit: 147 pounds)

Champion	Reign	Champion	Reign	Champion	Reign
Paddy Duffy*	1888–90†	Barney Ross*	1935–38	Sugar Ray Leonard*	1980–82†
Mysterious Billy Smith*	1892–94	Henry Armstrong*	1938–40	Donald Curry* WBA	1983–85
Tommy Ryan*	1894–98†	Fritzie Zivic*	1940–41	Milton McCrory WBC	1983–85
Mysterious Billy Smith*	1898–1900	Red Cochrane*	1941–46	Donald Curry*	1985–86
Rube Ferns*	1900	Marty Servo*	1946	Lloyd Honeyghan*	1986–87
Matty Matthews*	1900–01	Sugar Ray Robinson*	1946–51†	Jorge Vaca* WBC	1987–88
Rube Ferns*	1901	Johnny Bratton	1951	Lloyd Honeyghan* WBC	1988–89
Joe Walcott*	1901–04	Kid Gavilan*	1951–54	Mark Breland WBA	1987
The Dixie Kid*	1904–05†	Johnny Saxton*	1954–55	Marlon Starling WBA	1987–88
Honey Mellody*	1906–07	Tony DeMarco*	1955	Tomas Molinares WBA	1988–89
Mike Sullivan*	1907–08†	Carmen Basilio*	1955–56	Simon Brown IBF	1988–91
Jimmy Gardner*	1908†	Johnny Saxton*	1956	Mark Breland WBA	1989–90
Jimmy Clabby*	1910–1†	Carmen Basilio*	1956–57†	Marlon Starling* WBC	1989–90
Waldemar Holberg*	1914	Virgil Akins*	1958	Aaron Davis WBA	1990–91
Tom McCormick*	1914	Don Jordan*	1958–60	Maurice Blocker* WBC	1990–91
Matt Wells*	1914–15	Kid Paret*	1960–61	Meldrick Taylor WBA	1991–92
Mike Glover*	1915	Emile Griffith*	1961	Simon Brown* WBC	1991
Jack Britton*	1915	Kid Paret*	1961–62	Buddy McGirt* WBC	1991–93
Ted "Kid" Lewis*	1915–16	Emile Griffith*	1962–63	Felix Trinidad IBF	1993–00
Jack Britton*	1916–17	Luis Rodriguez*	1963	Pernell Whitaker* WBC	1993–97
Ted "Kid" Lewis*	1917–19	Emile Griffith*	1963–66†	Crisanto Espana WBA	1992–94
Jack Britton*	1919–22	Curtis Cokes*	1966–69	Ike Quartey WBA	1994–97†
Mickey Walker*	1922–26	Jose Napoles*	1969–70	Oscar De La Hoya* WBC	1997–99
Pete Latzo*	1926–27	Billy Backus*	1970–71	James Page WBA	1998–01
Joe Dundee*	1927–29	Jose Napoles*	1971–75	Felix Trinidad* IBF, WBC	1999–00†
Jackie Fields*	1929–30	Hedgemon Lewis NY	1972–73	Shane Mosley* WBC	2000–02
Young Jack Thompson*	1930	Angel Espada WBA	1975–76	Andrew Lewis WBA	2001–02
Tommy Freeman*	1930–31	John H. Stracey*	1975–76	Vernon Forrest IBF	2001
Young Jack Thompson*	1931	Carlos Palomino*	1976–79	Vernon Forrest* WBC	2001–03
Lou Brouillard*	1931–32	Pipino Cuevas WBA	1976–80	Ricardo Mayorga WBA	2002
Jackie Fields*	1932–33	Wilfredo Benitez*	1979	Ricardo Mayorga* WBC	2003–
Young Corbett III*	1933	Sugar Ray Leonard*	1979–80	Michele Piccirillo IBF	2002–03
Jimmy McLarnin*	1933–34	Roberto Duran*	1980	Cory Spinks IBF	2003–
Barney Ross*	1934	Thomas Hearns WBA	1980–81	Jose Rivera WBA	2003–
Jimmy McLarnin*	1934–35				

Junior Welterweights
(Weight Limit: 140 pounds)

Champion	Reign	Champion	Reign	Champion	Reign
Pinkey Mitchell*	1922–25	M. Velasquez WBC	1976	Juan Coggi WBA	1991
Red Herring	1925	S. Muangsurin WBC	1976–78	Edwin Rosario WBA	1991–92
Mushy Callahan*	1926–30	A. Cervantes WBA	1977–80	Rafael Pineda IBF	1991–92
Jack (Kid) Berg*	1930–31	Sang-Hyun Kim WBC	1978–80	Akinobu Hiranaka WBA	1992
Tony Canzoneri*	1931–32	Saoul Mamby WBC	1980–82	Pernell Whitaker IBF	1992–93†
Johnny Jadick*	1932–33	Aaron Pryor* WBA	1980–83	Charles Murray IBF	1993–94
Sammy Fuller	1932–33	Leroy Haley WBC	1982–83	Jake Rodriguez IBF	1994–95
Battling Shaw*	1933	Aaron Pryor* IBF	1983–85†	Juan Coggi WBA	1993–94
Tony Canzoneri*	1933	Bruce Curry WBC	1983–84	Frankie Randall* WBC	1994
Barney Ross*	1933–35†	Johnny Bumphus WBA	1984	Frankie Randall WBA	1994–96
Tippy Larkin*	1946	Bill Costello WBC	1984–85	Juan Coggi WBA	1996
Carlos Ortiz*	1959–60	Gene Hatcher WBA	1984–85	Julio César Chávez* WBC	1994–96
Duilio Loi*	1960–62	Ubaldo Sacco WBA	1985–86	Kostya Tszyu IBF	1995–97
Eddie Perkins*	1962	Lonnie Smith* WBC	1985–86	Frankie Randall WBA	1996–97
Duilio Loi*	1962–63†	Patrizio Oliva WBA	1986–87	Oscar De La Hoya* WBC	1996–97†
Roberto Cruz WBA	1963	Gary Hinton IBF	1986	Khalid Rahilou WBA	1997–98
Eddie Perkins*	1963–65	Rene Arredondo* WBC	1986	Vincent Phillips* IBF	1997–99
Carlos Hernandez*	1965–66	Tsuyoshi Hamada WBC	1986–87	Sharmba Mitchell WBA	1998–01
Sandro Lopopolo*	1966–67	Joe Louis Manley IBF	1986–87	Kostya Tszyu WBC	1998–
Paul Fujii*	1967–68	Terry Marsh IBF	1987	Terronn Millett* IBF	1999–00
Nicolino Loche*	1968–72	Juan Coggi WBA	1987–90	Zab Judah* IBF	2000–01
Pedro Adigue WBC	1968–70	Rene Arredondo WBC	1987	Kostya Tszyu*†	
Bruno Arcari WBC	1970–74	R. Mayweather* WBC	1987–89	WBA/WBC	2001–03
Alfonso Frazer*	1972	James McGirt IBF	1988	Kostya Tszyu*	2001–
Antonio Cervantes*	1972–76	Meldrick Taylor IBF	1988–90	Kostya Tszyu* WBC/IBF	2003–
Perico Fernandez WBC	1974–75	Julio César Chávez* WBC	1989–94	Vivian Harris WBA	2003–
S. Muangsurin WBC	1975–76	Julio César Chávez* IBF	1990–91		
Wilfred Benitez*	1976–79†	Loreto Garza WBA	1990–91		

Lightweights
(Weight Limit: 135 pounds)

Champion	Reign	Champion	Reign	Champion	Reign
Jack McAuliffe*	1886–94†	James Carter*	1954–55	Vinny Pazienza IBF	1987–88
Kid Lavigne*	1896–99	Wallace Smith*	1955–56	Greg Haugen IBF	1988–89
Frank Erne*	1899–1902	Joe Brown*	1956–62	P. Whitaker* WBC, IBF	1989–90
Joe Gans*	1902–04	Carlos Ortiz*	1962–65	Edwin Rosario WBA	1989–90
Jimmy Britt*	1904–05	Ismael Laguna*	1965	Juan Nazario WBA	1990
Battling Nelson*	1905–06	Carlos Ortiz*	1965–68	P. Whitaker* WBA, WBC	1990–92†
Joe Gans*	1906–08	Carlos Teo Cruz*	1968–69	Pernell Whitaker* IBF	1991–92†
Battling Nelson*	1908–10	Mando Ramos*	1969–70	Julio César Chávez IBF	1990–91
Ad Wolgast*	1910–12	Ismael Laguna*	1970	Edwin Rosario WBA	1991–92
Willie Ritchie*	1912–14	Ken Buchanan*	1970–72	Julio César Chávez WBC	1990–92
Freddie Welsh*	1915–17	Roberto Duran*	1972–79†	Miguel Gonzalez WBC	1992–95
Benny Leonard*	1917–25†	Chango Carmona WBC	1972	Joey Gamache WBA	1992–93
Jimmy Goodrich*	1925	Rodolfo Gonzalez WBC	1972–74	Dingaan Thobela WBA	1993
Rocky Kansas*	1925–26	Ishimatsu Suzuki WBC	1974–76	Fred Pendleton* IBF	1993–94
Sammy Mandell*	1926–30	Estaban DeJesus WBC	1976–78	Orzubek Nazarov WBA	1993–98
Al Singer*	1930	Jim Watt WBC*	1979–81	Rafael Ruelas* IBF	1994–95
Tony Canzoneri*	1930–33	Ernesto Espana WBA	1979–80	Oscar De La Hoya* IBF	1995†
Barney Ross*	1933–35†	Hilmer Kenty WBA	1980–81	Phillip Holiday IBF	1995–97
Tony Canzoneri*	1935–36	Sean O'Grady WBA	1981	Jean B. Mendy* WBC	1996–97
Lou Ambers*	1936–38	Claude Noel WBA	1981	Steve Johnston* WBC	1997–98
Henry Armstrong*	1938–39	Alexis Arguello* WBC	1981–82†	Shane Mosley IBF	1997–99†
Lou Ambers*	1939–40	Arturo Frias WBA	1981–82	Jean B. Mendy WBA	1998–99
Sammy Angott NBA	1940–41	Ray Mancini* WBA	1982–84	Cesar Bazan* WBC	1998–99
Lew Jenkins*	1940–41	Alexis Arguello	1982–83	Steve Johnston* WBC	1999–00
Sammy Angott*	1941–42†	Edwin Rosario WBC	1983–84	Julien Lorcy WBA	1999
Beau Jack* NY	1942–43	Choo Choo Brown IBF	1984	Stefano Zoff WBA	1999
Bob Montgomery* NY	1943	L. Bramble* WBA	1984–86	Paul Spadafora IBF	1999–
Sammy Angott NBA	1943–44	Jose Luis Ramirez WBC	1984–85	Gilbert Serrano WBA	1999–00
Beau Jack* NY	1943–44	Harry Arroyo IBF	1984–85	T. Hatakeyama WBA	2000–01
Bob Montgomery* NY	1944–47	Jimmy Paul IBF	1985–86	Jose Luis Castillo* WBC	2000–02
Juan Zurita NBA	1944–45	Hector Camacho WBC	1985–86	Julien Lorcy WBA	2001
Ike Williams*	1947–51	Greg Haugen IBF	1986–87	Raul Balbi WBA	2001
James Carter*	1951–52	Edwin Rosario* WBA	1986–87	F. Mayweather* WBC	2002–
Lauro Salas*	1952	Julio César Chávez* WBC	1987–88	Leonard Dorin WBA	2002–
James Carter*	1952–54	Jose Luis Ramirez WBC	1987–88		
Paddy DeMarco*	1954	Julio César Chávez*	1988–89†		

Junior Lightweights
(Weight Limit: 130 pounds)

Champion	Reign	Champion	Reign	Champion	Reign
Johnny Dundee*	1921–23	Alexis Arguello WBC	1978–80	Brian Mitchell IBF	1991
Jack Bernstein*	1923	Yasutsune Uehara*	1980–81	Genaro Hernandez WBA	1991–95
Johnny Dundee*	1923–24	Rafael Limon WBC	1980–81	James Leija* WBC	1994
Steve (Kid) Sullivan*	1924–25	C. Boza-Edwards WBC	1981	Juan Molina IBF	1991–95
Mike Ballerino*	1925	Samuel Serrano*	1981–83	Gabriel Ruelas* WBC	1994–95
Tod Morgan*	1925–29	R. Navarrete WBC	1981–82	Eddie Hopson IBF	1995
Benny Bass*	1929–31	Rafael Limon WBC	1982	Tracy Patterson IBF	1995
Kid Chocolate*	1931–33	Bobby Chacon WBC	1982–83	Azumah Nelson* WBC	1995–97
Frankie Klick*	1933–34†	Roger Mayweather* WBC	1983–84	Choi Yong-Soo WBA	1995–98
Sandy Saddler*	1949–50†	Hector Camacho WBC	1983–84	Arturo Gatti IBF	1995–98†
Harold Gomes*	1959–60	Rocky Lockridge*	1984–85	Genaro Hernandez* WBC	1997–98
Gabriel (Flash) Elorde*	1960–67	Hwan-Kil Yuh IBF	1984–85	Roberto Garcia IBF	1998–99
Yoshiaki Numata*	1967	Julio César Chávez WBC	1984–87	Floyd Mayweather* WBC	1998–01†
Hiroshi Kobayashi*	1967–71	Lester Ellis IBF	1985	T. Hatakeyama WBA	1998–99
Rene Barrientos WBC	1969–70	Wilfredo Gomez*	1985–86	Lakva Sim WBA	1999
Yoshiaki Numata WBC	1970–71	Barry Michael IBF	1985–87	Diego Corrales IBF	1999–01
Alfredo Marcano*	1971–72	Alfredo Layne* WBA	1986	Jong Kwon Baek WBA	1999–00
R. Arredondo WBC	1971–74	Brian Mitchell* WBA	1986–91†	Joel Casamayor WBA	2000–02
Ben Villaflor*	1972–73	Rocky Lockridge IBF	1987–88	Steve Forbes IBF	2000–02†
Kuniaki Shibata*	1973	Azumah Nelson* WBC	1988–94	Acelino Freitas* WBA	2002–
Ben Villaflor*	1973–76	Tony Lopez IBF	1988–89	Y. Nantchachai WBA	2002–
Kuniaki Shibata WBC	1974–75	Juan Molina IBF	1989–90	S. Singmanassak WBC	2002–03
Alfredo Escalera WBC	1975–78	Tony Lopez IBF	1990–91	Jesus Chavez WBC	2003–
Samuel Serrano*	1976–80	Joey Gamache WBA	1991	Carlos Hernandez IBF	2003–

Featherweights
(Weight Limit: 126 pounds)

Champion	Reign
Torpedo Billy Murphy*	1890
Young Griffo*	1890–92†
George Dixon*	1892–97
Solly Smith*	1897–98
Dave Sullivan*	1898
George Dixon*	1898–1900
Terry McGovern*	1900–01
Young Corbett II*	1901–03†
Abe Attell*	1903–04
Tommy Sullivan*	1904–05†
Abe Attell*	1906–12
Johnny Kilbane*	1912–23
Eugene Criqui*	1923
Johnny Dundee*	1923–24†
"Kid" Kaplan*	1925–26†
Tony Canzoneri*	1927–28
Andre Routis*	1928–29
Battling Battalino*	1929–32†
Tommy Paul NBA	1932–33
Kid Chocolate NY	1932–33†
Freddie Miller NBA	1933–36
Mike Beloise NY	1936–37
Petey Sarron NBA	1936–37
Maurice Holtzer	1937–38
Henry Armstrong*	1937–38†
Joey Archibald* NY	1938–39
Leo Rodak NBA	1938–39
Joey Archibald	1939–40
Petey Scalzo NBA	1940–41
Harry Jeffra*	1940–41
Joey Archibald*	1941
Richie Lamos NBA	1941
Chalky Wright*	1941–42
Jackie Wilson NBA	1941–43
Willie Pep*	1942–48
Jackie Callura NBA	1943
Phil Terranova NBA	1943–44
Sal Bartolo NBA	1944–46

Champion	Reign
Sandy Saddler*	1948–49
Willie Pep*	1949–50
Sandy Saddler*	1950–57†
Kid Bassey*	1957–59
Davey Moore*	1959–63
Sugar Ramos*	1963–64
Vicente Saldivar*	1964–67†
Paul Rojas WBA	1968
Jose Legra WBC	1968–69
Shozo Saijyo WBA	1968–71
J. Famechon* WBC	1969–70
Vicente Saldivar* WBC	1970
Kuniaki Shibata* WBC	1970–72
Antonio Gomez WBA	1971–72
C. Sanchez* WBC	1972
Ernesto Marcel WBA	1972–74
Jose Legra* WBC	1972–73
Eder Jofre* WBC	1973–74†
Ruben Olivares WBA	1974
Bobby Chacon WBC	1974–75
Alexis Arguello* WBA	1974–76†
Ruben Olivares WBA	1975
Poison Kotey WBC	1975–76
Danny Lopez* WBC	1976–80
Rafael Ortega WBA	1977
Cecilio Lastra WBA	1977–78
Eusebio Pedroza* WBA	1978–85
S. Sanchez* WBC	1980–82†
Juan LaPorte WBC	1982–84
Wilfredo Gomez WBC	1984
Min-Keun Oh IBF	1984–85
Azumah Nelson WBC	1984–88
Barry McGuigan* WBA	1985–86
Ki Young Chung IBF	1985–86
Steve Cruz* WBA	1986–87
Antonio Rivera IBF	1986–88
A. Esparragoza* WBA	1987–91

Champion	Reign
Calvin Grove IBF	1988
Jorge Paez IBF	1988–91
Jeff Fenech WBC	1988–90†
Marcos Villasana WBC	1990–91
Paul Hodkinson WBC	1991–93
Troy Dorsey IBF	1991
Manuel Medina IBF	1991–93
Yung Kyun Park* WBA	1991–93
Gregorio Vargas WBC	1993
Tom Johnson IBF	1993–97†
Eloy Rojas* WBA	1993–96
Kevin Kelley WBC	1993–95
A. Gonzalez WBC	1995
Manuel Medina WBC	1995–95
Luisito Espinosa WBC	1995–99
Wilfredo Vazquez* WBA	1996–98
Hector Lizarraga IBF	1997–98
Naseem Hamed* WBO	1998†
Naseem Hamed*	1998–01
Freddy Norwood WBA	1998
Manuel Medina WBC	1998–99
Antonio Cermeno WBA	1998–99
Cesar Soto WBC	1999
Freddy Norwood WBA	1999–00
Naseem Hamed* WBC	1999†
Paul Ingle IBF	1999–00
Guty Espadas WBC	2000–01
Erik Morales WBC	2000–02
Derrick Gainer WBA	2000–
Mbulelo Botile IBF	2001
Frankie Toledo IBF	2001
Manuel Medina IBF	2001–02
Marco A. Barrera*	2001–
Johnny Tapia IBF	2002
Marco A. Barrera* WBC	2002†
Erik Morales WBC	2002–
Juan Marquez IBF	2003–

Junior Featherweights
(Weight Limit: 122 pounds)

Champion	Reign
Jack (Kid) Wolfe*	1922–23
Carl Duane*	1923–24
Rigoberto Riasco* WBC	1976
R. Kobayashi* WBC	1976
Dong-Kyun Yum* WBC	1976–77
Wilfredo Gomez* WBC	1977–83†
Soo-Hwan Hong WBA	1977–78
Ricardo Cardona WBA	1978–80
Leo Randolph WBA	1980
Sergio Palma WBA	1980–82
Leonardo Cruz WBA	1982–84
Jaime Garza* WBC	1983
Bobby Berna IBF	1983–84
Loris Stecca WBA	1984
Seung-Il Suh IBF	1984–85
Victor Callejas WBA	1984–86
Juan Meza* WBC	1984–85
Ji-Won Kim IBF	1985–86
Lupe Pintor* WBC	1985–86
S. Payakaroon* WBC	1986–87

Champion	Reign
Seung-Hoon Lee IBF	1987–88
Louie Espinoza WBA	1987
Jeff Fenech* WBC	1987†
Julio Gervacio WBA	1987–88
Daniel Zaragoza* WBC	1988–90
Jose Sanabria IBF	1988–89
B. Pinango WBA	1988
J.J. Estrada WBA	1988–89
Fabrice Benichou IBF	1989–90
Jesus Salud WBA	1989–90
Welcome Ncita IBF	1990–92
Paul Banke* WBC	1990
Luis Mendoza WBA	1990–91
Raul Perez WBA	1992
Pedro Decima* WBC	1990–91
K. Hatanaka* WBC	1991
Daniel Zaragoza* WBC	1991–92
Thiery Jacob* WBC	1992
Tracy Patterson* WBC	1992–94

Champion	Reign
Kennedy McKinney IBF	1993–94
Wilfredo Vasquez WBA	1992–95
Vuyani Bungu IBF	1994–99†
H. Acero* Sanchez WBC	1994–95
Antonio Cermeno WBA	1995–98†
Daniel Zaragoza* WBC	1995–97
Erik Morales* WBC	1997–00†
Enrique Sanchez WBA	1998
Nestor Garza WBA	1998–00
Benedict Ledwaba IBF	1999–01
Clarence Adams WBA	2000–01†
Willie Jorrin WBC	2000–02
Manny Pacquiao IBF	2001–
Yober Ortega WBA	2001–02
Y. Sithyodthong WBA	2002
Osamu Sato WBA	2002
Salim Medjkoune WBA	2002–03
Mahyar Monshipour WBA	2003–
Oscar Larios WBC	2002–

*Lineal champion.

†Champion relinquished title to retire or switch weight classes, or had title stripped by boxing organization.

Bantamweights
(Weight Limit: 118 pounds)

Champion	Reign	Champion	Reign	Champion	Reign
Spider Kelly	1887	Sixto Escobar*	1938–39†	Daniel Zaragoza WBC	1985
Hughey Boyle	1887–88	Georgie Pace NBA	1939–40	Miguel Lora WBC	1985–88
Spider Kelly	1889	Lou Salica*	1940–42	Gaby Canizales*	1986
Chappie Moran	1889–90	Manuel Ortiz*	1942–47	Bernardo Pinango*	1986–87†
George Dixon	1890–91	Harold Dade*	1947	W. Vasquez WBA	1987–88
Pedlar Palmer	1895–99	Manuel Ortiz*	1947–50	Kevin Seabrooks* IBF	1987–88
Terry McGovern*	1899–00†	Vic Toweel*	1950–52	Kaokor Galaxy WBA	1988
Harry Harris	1901	Jimmy Carruthers*	1952–54†	Moon Sung-Kil WBA	1988–89
Harry Forbes*	1901–03	Robert Cohen*	1954–56	Kaokor Galaxy WBA	1989
Frankie Neil*	1903–04	Paul Macias NBA	1955–57	Raul Perez WBC	1988–91
Joe Bowker*	1904–05†	Mario D'Agata*	1956–57	O. Canizales* IBF	1988–95†
Jimmy Walsh*	1905–06†	Alphonse Halimi*	1957–59	Luisito Espinosa WBA	1989–91
Owen Moran*	1907–08	Joe Becerra*	1959–60†	Israel Contreras WBA	1991–92
Monte Attell	1909–10	Eder Jofre*	1961–65	Eddie Cook WBA	1992–93
Frankie Conley	1910–11	Fighting Harada*	1965–68	Greg Richardson WBC	1991
Johnny Coulon*	1910–14	Lionel Rose*	1968–69	J. Tatsuyoshi, WBC	1991–92
Kid Williams*	1914–17	Ruben Olivares*	1969–70	Victor Rabanales WBC	1992–93
Kewpie Ertle	1915	Chucho Castillo*	1970–71	Jung-Il Byun WBC	1993
Pete Herman*	1917–20	Ruben Olivares*	1971–72	Jorge Julio WBA	1993
Joe Lynch*	1920–21	Rafael Herrera*	1972	Yasuei Yakushiji WBC	1993–95
Pete Herman*	1921	Enrique Pinder*	1972–73	Junior Jones WBA	1994
Johnny Buff*	1921–22	Romeo Anaya*	1973	John M. Johnson WBA	1994
Joe Lynch*	1922–24	Arnold Taylor*	1973–74	D. Chuvatana WBA	1994–95
Abe Goldstein*	1924	Rafael Herrera WBC	1973–74	V. Sahaprom* WBA	1995–96
Cannonball Martin*	1924–25	Soo-Hwan Hong*	1974–75	W. McCullough WBC	1995–96
Phil Rosenberg*	1925–27†	Rodolfo Martinez WBC	1974–76	Harold Mestre IBF	1995
Bud Taylor NBA	1927–28	Alfonso Zamora*	1975–77	Mbulelo Botile IBF	1995–97
Bushy Graham NY	1928–29	Carlos Zarate* WBC	1976–79	Nana Konadu* WBA	1996–98
Panama Al Brown*	1929–35	Jorge Lujan	1977–80	S. Singmanassak WBC	1996–97
Sixto Escobar NBA	1934–35	Lupe Pintor* WBC	1979–83†	Tim Austin IBF	1997–03
Baltazar Sangchilli*	1935–36	Julian Solis	1980	J.Tatsuyoshi WBC	1997–98
Lou Salica NBA	1935	Jeff Chandler*	1980–84	Johnny Tapia* WBA	1998–99
Sixto Escobar NBA	1935–36	Albert Davila WBC	1983–85	V. Sahaprom* WBC	1998–
Tony Marino*	1936	Richard Sandoval*	1984–86	Paulie Ayala* WBA	1999–01†
Sixto Escobar*	1936–37	Satoshi Shingaki IBF	1984–85	Eidy Moya WBA	2001–02
Harry Jeffra*	1937–38	Jeff Fenech IBF	1985	Johnny Bredahl WBA	2002–
				Rafael Marquez IBF	2003

Junior Bantamweights
(Weight Limit: 115 pounds)

Champion	Reign	Champion	Reign	Champion	Reign
Rafael Orono* WBC	1980–81	Sugar Rojas* WBC	1987–88	Harold Grey IBF	1996
Chul-Ho Kim* WBC	1981–82	Ellyas Pical IBF	1987–89	Danny Romero IBF	1996–97
Gustavo Ballas WBA	1981	Giberto Roman* WBC	1988–89	Gerry Penalosa* WBC	1997–98
Rafael Pedroza WBA	1981–82	Juan Polo Perez IBF	1989–90	Johnny Tapia IBF	1997–99†
Jiro Watanabe WBA	1982–84	Nana Konadu* WBC	1989–90	Satoshi Iida WBA	1997–98
Rafael Orono* WBC	1982–83	Sung-Kil Moon* WBC	1990–93	In-Joo Cho* WBC	1998–00
Payao Poontarat* WBC	1983–84	Robert Quiroga IBF	1990–93	Jesus Rojas WBA	1998–99
Joo-Do Chun IBF	1983–85	Julio Borboa IBF	1993–94	Mark Johnson IBF	1999–00
Jiro Watanabe*	1984–86	Katsuya Onizuka WBA	1993–94	Hideki Todaka WBA	1999–00
Kaosai Galaxy WBA	1984	Lee Hyung-Chul WBA	1994–95	Felix Machado IBF	2000–03
Ellyas Pica IBF	1985–86	Jose Luis Bueno* WBC	1993–94	M. Tokuyama* WBC	2000–
Cesar Polanco IBF	1986	H. Kawashima* WBC	1994–97	Leo Gamez WBA	2000–01
Gilberto Roman* WBC	1986–87	Harold Grey IBF	1994–95	Celes Kobayashi WBA	2001–02
Ellyas Pical IBF	1986	Alimi Goitia WBA	1995–96	Alexander Munoz WBA	2002–
Santos Laciar* WBC	1987	Yokthai Sith-Oar WBA	1996–97	Luis Perez IBF	2003–
Tae-Il Chang IBF	1987	Carlos Salazar IBF	1995–96		

*Lineal champion.
†Champion relinquished title to retire or switch weight classes, or had title stripped by boxing organization.

Flyweights
(Weight Limit: 112 pounds)

Champion	Reign
Sid Smith*	1913
Bill Ladbury*	1913–14
Percy Jones*	1914†
Joe Symonds*	1914–16
Jimmy Wilde*	1916–23
Pancho Villa*	1923–25†
Fidel La Barba*	1925–27†
Frenchy Belanger* NBA	1927–28
Izzy Schwartz NY	1927–29
Frankie Genaro* NBA	1928–29
Spider Pladner* NBA	1929
Frankie Genaro* NBA	1929–31
Midget Wolgast NY	1930–35
Young Perez* NBA	1931–32
Jackie Brown* NBA	1932–35
Benny Lynch*	1935–38†
Small Montana NY	1935–37
Peter Kane*	1938–43
Little Dado NY	1938–40
Jackie Paterson*	1943–48
Rinty Monaghan*	1948–50†
Terry Allen*	1950
Dado Marino*	1950–52
Yoshio Shirai*	1952–54
Pascual Perez*	1954–60
Pone Kingpetch*	1960–62
Masahiko Harada*	1962–63
Pone Kingpetch*	1963
Hiroyuki Ebihara*	1963–64
Pone Kingpetch*	1964–65
Salvatore Burrini*	1965–66
H. Accavallo WBA	1966–68
Walter McGowan*	1966
Chartchai Chionoi*	1966–69
Efren Torres*	1969–70
Hiroyuki Ebihara WBA	1969

Champion	Reign
B. Villacampo WBA	1969–70
Chartchai Chionoi*	1970
B. Chartvanchai WBA	1970
Masao Ohba WBA	1970–73
Erbito Salavarria*	1970–73†
B. Gonzalez WBA	1972
V. Borkorsor WBC	1972–73†
Venice Borkorsor*	1973†
Chartchai Chionoi WBA	1973–74
B. Gonzalez* WBA	1973–74
Shoji Oguma* WBC	1974–75
S. Hanagata WBA	1974–75
Miguel Canto* WBC	1975–79
Erbito Salavarria WBA	1975–76
Alfonso Lopez WBA	1976
G. Espadas WBA	1976–78
B. Gonzalez WBA	1978–79
Chan-Hee Park* WBC	1979–80
Luis Ibarra WBA	1979–80
Tae-Shik Kim WBA	1980
Shoji Oguma* WBC	1980–81
Peter Mathebula WBA	1980–81
Santos Laciar WBA	1981
Antonio Avelar* WBC	1981–82
Luis Ibarra WBA	1981
Juan Herrera WBA	1981–82
P. Cardona* WBC	1982
Santos Laciar WBA	1982–85
Freddie Castillo* WBC	1982
E. Mercedes* WBC	1982–83
Charlie Magri* WBC	1983
Frank Cedeno* WBC	1983–84
Soon-Chun Kwon IBF	1983–85
Koji Kobayashi* WBC	1984
Gabriel Bernal* WBC	1984
Sot Chitalada* WBC	1984–88

Champion	Reign
Hilario Zapate WBA	1985–87
Chong-Kwan Chung IBF	1985–86
Bi-Won Chung IBF	1986
Hi-Sup Shin IBF	1986–87
Dodie Penalosa IBF	1987
Fidel Bassa WBA	1987–89
Choi-Chang Ho IBF	1987–88
Rolando Bohol IBF	1988
Yong-Kang Kim* WBC	1988–89
Duke McKenzie IBF	1988–89
Sot Chitalada* WBC	1989–91
Dave McAuley IBF	1989–92
Jesus Rojas WBA	1989–90
Yul-Woo Lee WBA	1990
L. Tamakuma WBA	1990–91
M. Kittikasem* WBC	1991–92
Yuri Arbachakov* WBC	1992–97
Yong Kang Kim WBA	1991–92
Rodolfo Blanco IBF	1992–93
P. Sithbangprachan IBF	1993–95
David Griman WBA	1992–94
S.S. Ploenchit WBA	1994–96
Francisco Tejedor IBF	1995
Danny Romero IBF	1995–96
Mark Johnson IBF	1996–99†
Jose Bonilla WBA	1996–98
Chatchai Sasakul* WBC	1997–98
Hugo Soto WBA	1998–99
Manny Pacquiao* WBC	1998–99
Leo Gamez WBA	1999
Irene Pacheco IBF	1999–
S. Pisnurachan WBA	1999–00
M. Sinsurat* WBC	1999–00
Malcolm Tunacao* WBC	2000–01
Eric Morel WBA	2000–
P. Wonjongkam* WBC	2001–

Junior Flyweights
(Weight Limit: 108 pounds)

Champion	Reign	Champion	Reign	Champion	Reign
Franco Udella WBC	1975	Dodie Penalosa IBF	1983–86	H. Gonzalez* WBC, IBF	1994–95
Jaime Rios WBA	1975–76	Francisco Quiroz WBA	1984–85	Choi Hi-Yong WBA	1995–96
Luis Estaba* WBC	1975–78	Joey Olivo WBA	1985	S. Sor Jaturong WBC, IBF	1995–96
Juan Guzman WBA	1976	Myung-Woo Yuh* WBA	1985–91	Carlos Murillo WBA	1996
Yoko Gushiken WBA	1976–81	Jum-Hwan Choi IBF	1986–88	Keiji Yamaguchi WBA	1996
Freddy Castillo* WBC	1978	Tacy Macalos IBF	1988–89	Michael Carbajal IBF	1996–97
Sor Vorasingh* WBC	1978	German Torres WBC	1988–89	Saman Jaturong* WBC	1995–99
Sung-Jun Kim* WBC	1978–80	Yul-Woo Lee WBC	1989	Phichitchor Siriwat WBA	1996–00
Shigeo Nakajima* WBC	1980	M. Kittikasem IBF	1989–90	Mauricio Pastrana IBF	1997–98†
Hilario Zapata* WBC	1980–82	H. Gonzalez WBC	1989–90	Will Grigsby IBF	1998–99
Pedro Flores WBA	1981	Michael Carbajal IBF	1990–94	Ricardo Lopez IBF	1999–02
Hwan-Jin Kim WBA	1981	R. Pascua WBC	1990	Yo-Sam Choi* WBC	1999–02
Katsuo Tokashiki WBA	1981–83	M. C. Castro WBC	1991	Beibis Mendoza WBA	2000–01
Amado Urzua* WBC	1982	H. Gonzalez WBC	1991–93	Rosendo Alvarez WBA	2001–
Tadashi Tomori* WBC	1982	Hirokia Ioka* WBA	1991–92	Jorge Arce* WBC	2002–
Hilario Zapata* WBC	1982–83	Myung-Woo Yuh* WBA	1993†	Jose Burgos IBF	2003–
Jung-Koo Chang* WBC	1983–88†	Michael Carbajal* WBC	1993–94		
Lupe Madera WBA	1983–84	Leo Gamez WBA	1993–95		

Strawweights
(Weight Limit: 105 pounds)

Champion	Reign	Champion	Reign	Champion	Reign
Kyung-Yun Lee* IBF	1987	Ricardo Lopez* WBC	1990–98†	Songkram Popaoin WBA	1999
Hiroki Ioka* WBC	1987–88	Hi-Yong Choi WBA	1991–92	Noel Arambulet WBA	1999–00
Leo Gamez WBA	1988–89	Manny Melchor IBF	1992	Jose Aguirre* WBC	2000–
S. Sithnaruepol IBF	1988–89	Hideyuki Ohashi WBA	1992–93	Joma Gamboa WBA	2000
N. Kiatwanchai* WBC	1988–89	R.S. Voraphin IBF	1992–96	Keitaro Hoshino WBA	2000–01
Bong-Jun Kim WBA	1989–91	Chana Porpaoin WBA	1993–95	Chana Porpaoin WBA	2001
Nico Thomas IBF	1989	Rosendo Alvarez WBA	1995–98	Roberto Leyva IBF	2001–02
Eric Chavez IBF	1989–90	R. Sor Vorapin WBA	1996–97	Yutaka Niida WBA	2001†
Jum-Hwan Choi* WBC	1989–90	Zolani Petelo* IBF	1997–00†	Miguel Barrera IBF	2002–03
Hideyuki Ohashi* WBC	1990	W. Chor Charoen WBC	1998–00	Edgar Cardenas IBF	2003
F. Lookmingkwan IBF	1990–92	R. Lopez* WBA, WBC	1998–99†	Noel Arambulet WBA	2002–
				Daniel Reyes IBF	2003–

*Lineal champion.
†Champion relinquished title to retire or switch weight classes, or had title stripped by boxing organization.

Alltime Career Leaders

Total Bouts

ame	Years Active	Bouts	Name	Years Active	Bouts
Len Wickwar	1928–47	463	Maxie Rosenbloom	1923–39	299
Jack Britton	1905–30	350	Harry Greb	1913–26	298
Johnny Dundee	1910–32	333	Young Stribling	1921–33	286
Billy Bird	1920–48	318	Battling Levinsky	1910–29	282
George Marsden	1928–46	311	Ted (Kid) Lewis	1909–29	279

Note: Based on records in *The Ring Record Book* and *Boxing Encyclopedia*.

Most Knockouts

Name	Years Active	KOs	Name	Years Active	KOs
Archie Moore	1936–63	130	Sandy Saddler	1944–56	103
Young Stribling	1921–33	126	Sam Langford	1902–26	102
Billy Bird	1920–48	125	Henry Armstrong	1931–45	100
George Odwell	1930–45	114	Jimmy Wilde	1911–23	98
Sugar Ray Robinson	1940–65	110	Len Wickwar	1928–47	93

Note: Based on records in *The Ring Record Book* and *Boxing Encyclopedia*.

Punch Drunk Love

Of the dozen trainers Iron Mike Tyson has employed during his 18-year career, few have lasted long and none have left happily. They wind up getting either dumped, banished, marginalized, verbally battered or all of the above. Only Trainer No. 1, Cus D'Amato, bowed out with dignity, and he had to die to gain that distinction.

It isn't easy trying to harness the power of an entity only slightly less stable than nitroglycerin. And yet during the winter of 2003 in Las Vegas, Freddie Roach, Trainer No. 12, said he was thankful for the chance to be preparing the faded 36-year-old ex-champ for a scheduled Feb. 22 bout with Clifford Etienne in Memphis. "The challenge is to bring Mike back to something like what he once was," said Roach, who'd spent seven weeks trying to iron out Mike's kinks. "The challenge is to get inside his head."

Even as he spoke, though, Roach realized that Tyson's head is not a place that's easily broached. In the days leading up to the fight, Tyson showed up to train with a tattoo etched over the left side of his face and complained about back pain. (Asked if the tattoo hurt, Tyson, an authority in these matters, said, "No, there's not too many nerves in your face.") On two days that week, Tyson didn't show up at all. Nor did he respond to a dozen phone messages from Roach. As rumors that Tyson was on a partying binge and suffering a "mental meltdown" circulated, Roach sat in the dark. "Mike went from being a great guy to somebody who withdrew into a shell," Roach said on Friday. "I'd heard all the horror stories, but this is just crazy."

In some ways it was just business as usual. It's not that Tyson's trainers aren't credible; it's that to get to him they must wade though a sea of flunkies. "If, by chance, a trainer reaches Mike," says one veteran cornerman, "he's faced with a guy who's not a model of rationality."

Roach was supposed to be different, a mild, gritty ex-pug who has trained 16 world champions and would go toe-to-toe for what he believed. "Freddie was a world-class fighter who put his whole heart into the game," says trainer Joe Goossen. "If you don't, he lets you know."

Roach, 42, joined Team Tyson on Dec. 26, 2002, after agreeing to a $150,000 fee—a substandard 5% of Tyson's $3 million purse. If there was no fight, there would be no pay. He left the stable of 19 pros he trains at his L.A. gym, moved in with his mother in Vegas and set to work. Tyson had been out of the ring since June, when he was knocked out by Lennox Lewis in eight rounds. "Mike boxed for the first three minutes," Roach says. "Then he gave up."

Roach hoped that that humiliation would make Tyson train diligently. And for a while the fighter did, meeting Roach for roadwork at 5:30 a.m., showing up for every workout, scrapping his entourage. He even reperfected the left jab-pivot-left hook, a combination he used in the late 1980s when he was training with Kevin Rooney. "I was getting through to Mike," Roach insists. "He obeyed my orders."

A moment of truth came one day during a sparring session. In the final round, Tyson suddenly bent over and vomited. "After Mike was done puking, I told him to finish the round," recalls Roach. "He glared at me and said, 'F--- you.' I said, 'No, f--- you, Mike. Let's finish.'" Tyson did. "If you let Mike be the bully, he will," Roach says. "Don't give Mike control, and he'll give you respect."

For a while, maybe. While promoters debated whether to cancel the fight, Roach knew less about Tyson's status than a fan browsing the Web. Finally, Roach reached Tyson, who told him he had the flu and planned to pull out. The fight was dead. Roach would receive nothing. Then Tyson mumbled a few words of thanks and hung up.

—Franz Lidz

The fight ended up going off after all and, with Roach in his corner, Tyson dispatched Etienne in 49 seconds.—Ed.

World Heavyweight Championship Fights

Date	Winner	Wgt	Loser	Wgt	Result	Site
Sept 7, 1892	James J. Corbett*	178	John L. Sullivan	212	KO 21	New Orleans
Jan 25, 1894	James J. Corbett*	184	Charley Mitchell	158	KO 3	Jacksonville
Mar 17, 1897	Bob Fitzsimmons*	167	James J. Corbett	183	KO 14	Carson City, NV
June 9, 1899	James J. Jeffries*	206	Bob Fitzsimmons	167	KO 11	Coney Island, NY
Nov 3, 1899	James J. Jeffries*	215	Tom Sharkey	183	Ref 25	Coney Island, NY
Apr 6, 1900	James J. Jeffries*	n/a	Jack Finnegan	n/a	KO 1	Detroit
May 11, 1900	James J. Jeffries*	218	James J. Corbett	188	KO 23	Coney Island, NY
Nov 15, 1901	James J. Jeffries*	211	Gus Ruhlin	194	TKO 6	San Francisco
July 25, 1902	James J. Jeffries*	219	Bob Fitzsimmons	172	KO 8	San Francisco
Aug 14, 1903	James J. Jeffries*	220	James J. Corbett	190	KO 10	San Francisco
Aug 25, 1904	James J. Jeffries*	219	Jack Munroe	186	TKO 2	San Francisco
July 3, 1905	Marvin Hart*	190	Jack Root	171	KO 12	Reno
Feb 23, 1906	Tommy Burns*	180	Marvin Hart	188	Ref 20	Los Angeles
Oct 2, 1906	Tommy Burns*	n/a	Jim Flynn	n/a	KO 15	Los Angeles
Nov 28, 1906	Tommy Burns*	172	Jack O'Brien	163½	Draw 20	Los Angeles
May 8, 1907	Tommy Burns*	180	Jack O'Brien	167	Ref 20	Los Angeles
Jul 4, 1907	Tommy Burns*	181	Bill Squires	180	KO 1	Colma, CA
Dec 2, 1907	Tommy Burns*	177	Gunner Moir	204	KO 10	London
Feb 10, 1908	Tommy Burns*	n/a	Jack Palmer	n/a	KO 4	London
Mar 17, 1908	Tommy Burns*	n/a	Jem Roche	n/a	KO 1	Dublin
Apr 18, 1908	Tommy Burns*	n/a	Jewey Smith	n/a	KO 5	Paris
June 13, 1908	Tommy Burns*	184	Bill Squires	183	KO 8	Paris
Aug 24, 1908	Tommy Burns*	181	Bill Squires	184	KO 13	Sydney
Sept 2, 1908	Tommy Burns*	183	Bill Lang	187	KO 6	Melbourne
Dec 26, 1908	Jack Johnson*	192	Tommy Burns	168	TKO 14	Sydney
Mar 10, 1909	Jack Johnson*	n/a	Victor McLaglen	n/a	ND 6	Vancouver
May 19, 1909	Jack Johnson*	205	Jack O'Brien	161	ND 6	Philadelphia
June 30, 1909	Jack Johnson*	207	Tony Ross	214	ND 6	Pittsburgh
Sept 9, 1909	Jack Johnson*	209	Al Kaufman	191	ND 10	San Francisco
Oct 16, 1909	Jack Johnson*	205½	Stanley Ketchel	170¼	KO 12	Colma, CA
July 4, 1910	Jack Johnson*	208	James J. Jeffries	227	KO 15	Reno
July 4, 1912	Jack Johnson*	195½	Jim Flynn	175	TKO 9	Las Vegas
Dec 19, 1913	Jack Johnson*	n/a	Jim Johnson	n/a	Draw 10	Paris
June 27, 1914	Jack Johnson*	221	Frank Moran	203	Ref 20	Paris
Apr 5, 1915	Jess Willard*	230	Jack Johnson	205½	KO 26	Havana
Mar 25, 1916	Jess Willard*	225	Frank Moran	203	ND 10	New York City
July 4, 1919	Jack Dempsey*	187	Jess Willard	245	TKO 4	Toledo, OH
Sept 6, 1920	Jack Dempsey*	185	Billy Miske	187	KO 3	Benton Harbor, MI
Dec 14, 1920	Jack Dempsey*	188¼	Bill Brennan	197	KO 12	New York City
July 2, 1921	Jack Dempsey*	188	Georges Carpentier	172	KO 4	Jersey City
July 4, 1923	Jack Dempsey*	188	Tommy Givvons	175½	Ref 15	Shelby, MT
Sept 14, 1923	Jack Dempsey*	192½	Luis Firpo	216½	KO 2	New York City
Sept 23, 1926	Gene Tunney*	189½	Jack Dempsey	190	UD 10	Philadelphia
Sept 22, 1927	Gene Tunney*	189½	Jack Dempsey	192½	UD 10	Chicago
July 26, 1928	Gene Tunney*	192	Tom Heeney	203½	TKO 11	New York City
June 12, 1930	Max Schmeling*	188	Jack Sharkey	197	DQ 4	New York City
July 3, 1931	Max Schmeling*	189	Young Stribling	186½	TKO 15	Cleveland
June 21, 1932	Jack Sharkey*	205	Max Schmeling	188	Split 15	Long Island City
June 29, 1933	Primo Carnera*	260½	Jack Sharkey	201	KO 6	Long Island City
Oct 22, 1933	Primo Carnera*	259½	Paulino Uzcudun	229¼	UD 15	Rome
Mar 1, 1934	Primo Carnera*	270	Tommy Loughran	184	UD 15	Miami
June 14, 1934	Max Baer*	209½	Primo Carnera	263¼	TKO 11	Long Island City
June 13, 1935	James J. Braddock*	193¾	Max Baer	209½	UD 15	Long Island City
June 22, 1937	Joe Louis*	197¼	James J. Braddock	197	KO 8	Chicago
Aug 30, 1937	Joe Louis*	197	Tommy Farr	204¼	UD 15	New York City
Feb 23, 1938	Joe Louis*	200	Nathan Mann	193½	KO 3	New York City
Apr 1, 1938	Joe Louis*	202½	Harry Thomas	196	KO 5	Chicago
June 22, 1938	Joe Louis*	198¼	Max Schmeling	193	KO 1	New York City
Jan 25, 1939	Joe Louis*	200¼	John Henry Lewis	180¾	KO 1	New York City
Apr 17, 1939	Joe Louis*	201¼	Jack Roper	204¾	KO 1	Los Angeles
June 28, 1939	Joe Louis*	200¾	Tony Galento	233¾	TKO 4	New York City
Sept 20, 1939	Joe Louis*	200	Bob Pastor	183	KO 11	Detroit
Feb 9, 1940	Joe Louis*	203	Arturo Godoy	202	Split 15	New York City
Mar 29, 1940	Joe Louis*	201½	Johnny Paychek	187½	KO 2	New York City
June 20, 1940	Joe Louis*	199	Arturo Godoy	201¼	TKO 8	New York City
Dec 16, 1940	Joe Louis*	202¼	Al McCoy	180¾	TKO 6	Boston
Jan 31, 1941	Joe Louis*	202½	Red Burman	188	KO 5	New York City

Date	Winner	Wgt	Loser	Wgt	Result	Site
Feb 17, 1941	Joe Louis*	203½	Gus Dorazio	193½	KO 2	Philadelphia
Mar 21, 1941	Joe Louis*	202	Abe Simon	254½	TKO 13	Detroit
Apr 8, 1941	Joe Louis*	203½	Tony Musto	199½	TKO 9	St Louis
May 23, 1941	Joe Louis*	201½	Buddy Baer	237½	DQ 7	Washington, D.C.
June 18, 1941	Joe Louis*	199½	Billy Conn	174	KO 13	New York City
Sept 29, 1941	Joe Louis*	202¼	Lou Nova	202½	TKO 6	New York City
Jan 9, 1942	Joe Louis*	206¾	Buddy Baer	250	KO 1	New York City
Mar 27, 1942	Joe Louis*	207½	Abe Simon	255½	KO 6	New York City
June 9, 1946	Joe Louis*	207	Billy Conn	187	KO 8	New York City
Sept 18, 1946	Joe Louis*	211	Tami Mauriello	198½	KO 1	New York City
Dec 5, 1947	Joe Louis*	211½	Jersey Joe Walcott	194½	Split 15	New York City
June 25, 1948	Joe Louis*	213½	Jersey Joe Walcott	194¾	KO 11	New York City
June 22, 1949	Ezzard Charles*	181¾	Jersey Joe Walcott	195½	UD 15	Chicago
Aug 10, 1949	Ezzard Charles*	180	Gus Lesnevich	182	TKO 8	New York City
Oct 14, 1949	Ezzard Charles*	182	Pat Valentino	188½	KO 8	San Francisco
Aug 15, 1950	Ezzard Charles*	183¼	Freddie Beshore	184½	TKO 14	Buffalo
Sept 27, 1950	Ezzard Charles*	184½	Joe Louis	218	UD 15	New York City
Dec 5, 1950	Ezzard Charles*	185	Nick Barone	178½	KO 11	Cincinnati
Jan 12, 1951	Ezzard Charles*	185	Lee Oma	193	TKO 10	New York City
Mar 7, 1951	Ezzard Charles*	186	Jersey Joe Walcott	193	UD 15	Detroit
May 30, 1951	Ezzard Charles*	182	Joey Maxim	181½	UD 15	Chicago
July 18, 1951	Jersey Joe Walcott*	194	Ezzard Charles	182	KO 7	Pittsburgh
June 5, 1952	Jersey Joe Walcott*	196	Ezzard Charles	191½	UD 15	Philadelphia
Sept 23, 1952	Rocky Marciano*	184	Jersey Joe Walcott	196	KO 13	Philadelphia
May 15, 1953	Rocky Marciano*	184½	Jersey Joe Walcott	197¾	KO 1	Chicago
Sept 24, 1953	Rocky Marciano*	185	Roland LaStarza	184¾	TKO 11	New York City
June 17, 1954	Rocky Marciano*	187½	Ezzard Charles	185½	UD 15	New York City
Sept 17, 1954	Rocky Marciano*	187	Ezzard Charles	192½	KO 8	New York City
May 16, 1955	Rocky Marciano*	189	Don Cockell	205	TKO 9	San Francisco
Sept 21, 1955	Rocky Marciano*	188¼	Archie Moore	188	KO 9	New York City
Nov 30, 1956	Floyd Patterson*	182¼	Archie Moore	187¾	KO 5	Chicago
July 29, 1957	Floyd Patterson*	184	Tommy Jackson	192½	TKO 10	New York City
Aug 22, 1957	Floyd Patterson*	187¼	Pete Rademacher	202	KO 6	Seattle
Aug 18, 1958	Floyd Patterson*	184½	Roy Harris	194	TKO 13	Los Angeles
May 1, 1959	Floyd Patterson*	182½	Brian London	206	KO 11	Indianapolis
June 26, 1959	Ingemar Johansson*	196	Floyd Patterson	182	TKO 3	New York City
June 20, 1960	Floyd Patterson*	190	Ingemar Johansson	194¾	KO 5	New York City
Mar 13, 1961	Floyd Patterson*	194¾	Ingemar Johansson	206½	KO 6	Miami Beach
Dec 4, 1961	Floyd Patterson*	188½	Tom McNeeley	197	KO 4	Toronto
Sept 25, 1962	Sonny Liston*	214	Floyd Patterson	189	KO 1	Chicago
July 22, 1963	Sonny Liston*	215	Floyd Patterson	194½	KO 1	Las Vegas
Feb 25, 1964	Cassius Clay*	210½	Sonny Liston	218	TKO 7	Miami Beach
Mar 5, 1965	Ernie Terrell	199	Eddie Machen	192	UD 15	Chicago
May 25, 1965	Muhammad Ali*	206	Sonny Liston	215¼	KO 1	Lewiston, ME
Nov 1, 1965	Ernie Terrell	206	George Chuvalo	209	UD 15	Toronto
Nov 22, 1965	Muhammad Ali*	210	Floyd Patterson	196¾	TKO 12	Las Vegas
Mar 29, 1966	Muhammad Ali*	214½	George Chuvalo	216	UD 15	Toronto
May 21, 1966	Muhammad Ali*	201½	Henry Cooper	188	TKO 6	London
June 28, 1966	Ernie Terrell	209½	Doug Jones	187½	UD 15	Houston
Aug 6, 1966	Muhammad Ali*	209½	Brian London	201½	KO 3	London
Sept 10, 1966	Muhammad Ali*	203½	Karl Mildenberger	194¼	TKO 12	Frankfurt
Nov 14, 1966	Muhammad Ali*	212¾	Cleveland Williams	210½	TKO 3	Houston
Feb 6, 1967	Muhammad Ali*	212¼	Ernie Terrell	212½	UD 15	Houston
Mar 22, 1967	Muhammad Ali*	211½	Zora Folley	202½	KO 7	New York City
Mar 4, 1968	Joe Frazier	204½	Buster Mathis	243½	TKO 11	New York City
Apr 27, 1968	Jimmy Ellis	197	Jerry Quarry	195	Maj 15	Oakland
June 24, 1968	Joe Frazier NY	203½	Manuel Ramos	208	TKO 2	New York City
Aug 14, 1968	Jimmy Ellis	198	Floyd Patterson	188	Ref 15	Stockholm
Dec 10, 1968	Joe Frazier NY	203	Oscar Bonavena	207	UD 15	Philadelphia
Apr 22, 1969	Joe Frazier NY	204½	Dave Zyglewicz	190½	KO 1	Houston
June 23, 1969	Joe Frazier NY	203½	Jerry Quarry	198½	TKO 8	New York City
Feb 16, 1970	Joe Frazier NY	205	Jimmy Ellis	201	TKO 5	New York City
Nov 18, 1970	Joe Frazier	209	Bob Foster	188	KO 2	Detroit
Mar 8, 1971	Joe Frazier*	205½	Muhammad Ali	215	UD 15	New York City
Jan 15, 1972	Joe Frazier*	215½	Terry Daniels	195	TKO 4	New Orleans
May 26, 1972	Joe Frazier*	217½	Ron Stander	218	TKO 5	Omaha
Jan 22, 1973	George Foreman*	217½	Joe Frazier	214	TKO 2	Kingston, Jam.

World Heavyweight Championship Fights *(Cont.)*

Date	Winner	Wgt	Loser	Wgt	Result	Site
Sept 1, 1973	George Foreman*	219½	Jose Roman	196½	KO 1	Tokyo
Mar 26, 1974	George Foreman*	224¼	Ken Norton	212¼	TKO 2	Caracas
Oct 30, 1974	Muhammad Ali*	216½	George Foreman	220	KO 8	Kinshasa, Zaire
Mar 24, 1975	Muhammad Ali*	223½	Chuck Wepner	225	TKO 15	Cleveland
May 16, 1975	Muhammad Ali*	224½	Ron Lyle	219	TKO 11	Las Vegas
July 1, 1975	Muhammad Ali*	224½	Joe Bugner	230	UD 15	Kuala Lumpur, Malay.
Oct 1, 1975	Muhammad Ali*	224½	Joe Frazier	215	TKO 15	Manila
Feb 20, 1976	Muhammad Ali*	226	Jean Pierre Coopman	206	KO 5	San Juan
Apr 30, 1976	Muhammad Ali*	230	Jimmy Young	209	UD 15	Landover, MD
May 24, 1976	Muhammad Ali*	230	Richard Dunn	206½	TKO 5	Munich
Sept 28, 1976	Muhammad Ali*	221	Ken Norton	217½	UD 15	New York City
May 16, 1977	Muhammad Ali*	221¼	Alfredo Evangelista	209¼	UD 15	Landover, MD
Sept 29, 1977	Muhammad Ali*	225	Earnie Shavers	211¼	UD 15	New York City
Feb 15, 1978	Leon Spinks*	197¼	Muhammad Ali	224¼	Split 15	Las Vegas
June 9, 1978	Larry Holmes	209	Ken Norton	220	Split 15	Las Vegas
Sept 15, 1978	Muhammad Ali*	221	Leon Spinks	201	UD 15	New Orleans
Nov 10, 1978	Larry Holmes*	214	Alfredo Evangelista	208¼	KO 7	Las Vegas
Mar 23, 1979	Larry Holmes*	214	Osvaldo Ocasio	207	TKO 7	Las Vegas
June 22, 1979	Larry Holmes*	215	Mike Weaver	202	TKO 12	New York City
Sept 28, 1979	Larry Holmes*	210	Earnie Shavers	211	TKO 11	Las Vegas
Oct 20, 1979	John Tate	240	Gerrie Coetzee	222	UD 15	Pretoria
Feb 3, 1980	Larry Holmes *	213½	Lorenzo Zanon	215	TKO 6	Las Vegas
Mar 31, 1980	Mike Weaver	232	John Tate	232	KO 15	Knoxville
Mar 31, 1980	Larry Holmes*	211	Leroy Jones	254½	TKO 8	Las Vegas
July 7, 1980	Larry Holmes*	214¼	Scott LeDoux	226	TKO 7	Minneapolis
Oct 2, 1980	Larry Holmes*	211¼	Muhammad Ali	217½	TKO 11	Las Vegas
Oct 25, 1980	Mike Weaver	210	Gerrie Coetzee	226½	KO 13	Sun City, S.A.
Apr 11, 1981	Larry Holmes*	215	Trevor Berbick	215½	UD 15	Las Vegas
June 12, 1981	Larry Holmes*	212¼	Leon Spinks	200¼	TKO 3	Detroit
Oct 3, 1981	Mike Weaver	215	James Quick Tillis	209	UD 15	Rosemont, IL
Nov 6, 1981	Larry Holmes*	213¼	Renaldo Snipes	215¾	TKO 11	Pittsburgh
June 11, 1982	Larry Holmes*	212½	Gerry Cooney	225½	TKO 13	Las Vegas
Nov 26, 1982	Larry Holmes*	217½	Tex Cobb	234¼	UD 15	Houston
Dec 10, 1982	Michael Dokes	216	Mike Weaver	209¾	TKO 1	Las Vegas
Mar 27, 1983	Larry Holmes*	221	Lucien Rodriguez	209	UD 12	Scranton, PA
May 20, 1983	Michael Dokes	223	Mike Weaver	218½	Draw 15	Las Vegas
May 20, 1983	Larry Holmes*	213	Tim Witherspoon	219½	Split 12	Las Vegas
Sept 10, 1983	Larry Holmes*	223	Scott Frank	211¼	TKO 5	Atlantic City
Sept 23, 1983	Gerrie Coetzee	215	Michael Dokes	217	KO 10	Richfield, OH
Nov 25, 1983	Larry Holmes*	219	Marvis Frazier	200	TKO 1	Las Vegas
Mar 9, 1984	Tim Witherspoon	220¼	Greg Page	239½	Maj 12	Las Vegas
Aug 31, 1984	Pinklon Thomas	216	Tim Witherspoon	217	Maj 12	Las Vegas
Nov 9, 1984	Larry Holmes* IBF	221½	James Smith	227	TKO 12	Las Vegas
Dec 1, 1984	Greg Page	236½	Gerrie Coetzee	218	KO 8	Sun City, S.A.
Mar 15, 1985	Larry Holmes*	223½	David Bey	233¼	TKO 10	Las Vegas
Apr 29, 1985	Tony Tubbs	229	Greg Page	239½	UD 15	Buffalo
May 20, 1985	Larry Holmes*	224¼	Carl Williams	215	UD 15	Las Vegas
June 15, 1985	Pinklon Thomas	220¼	Mike Weaver	221¼	KO 8	Las Vegas
Sept 21, 1985	Michael Spinks*	200	Larry Holmes	221½	UD 15	Las Vegas
Jan 17, 1986	Tim Witherspoon	227	Tony Tubbs	229	Maj 15	Atlanta
Mar 22, 1986	Trevor Berbick	218½	Pinklon Thomas	222¾	UD 15	Las Vegas
Apr 19, 1986	Michael Spinks*	205	Larry Holmes	223	Split 15	Las Vegas
July 19, 1986	Tim Witherspoon	234¾	Frank Bruno	228	TKO 11	Wembley, Eng.
Sept 6, 1986	Michael Spinks*	201	Steffen Tangstad	214¾	TKO 4	Las Vegas
Nov 22, 1986	Mike Tyson	221¼	Trevor Berbick	218½	TKO 2	Las Vegas
Dec 12, 1986	James Smith	228½	Tim Witherspoon	233½	TKO 1	New York City
Mar 7, 1987	Mike Tyson	219	James Smith	233	UD 12	Las Vegas
May 30, 1987	Mike Tyson	218¾	Pinklon Thomas	217¾	TKO 6	Las Vegas
May 30, 1987	Tony Tucker	222¼	Buster Douglas	227¼	TKO 10	Las Vegas
June 15, 1987	Michael Spinks*	208¾	Gerry Cooney	238	TKO 5	Atlantic City
Aug 1, 1987	Mike Tyson	221	Tony Tucker	221	UD 12	Las Vegas
Oct 16, 1987	Mike Tyson	216	Tyrell Biggs	228¾	TKO 7	Atlantic City
Jan 22, 1988	Mike Tyson	215¾	Larry Holmes	225¾	TKO 4	Atlantic City
Mar 20, 1988	Mike Tyson	216¼	Tony Tubbs	238¼	KO 2	Tokyo
June 27, 1988	Mike Tyson*	218¼	Michael Spinks	212¼	KO 1	Atlantic City
Feb 25, 1989	Mike Tyson*	218	Frank Bruno	228	TKO 5	Las Vegas
July 21, 1989	Mike Tyson*	219¼	Carl Williams	218	TKO 1	Atlantic City

Date	Winner	Wgt	Loser	Wgt	Result	Site
Feb 10, 1990	Buster Douglas*	231½	Mike Tyson	220½	KO 10	Tokyo
Oct 25, 1990	Evander Holyfield*	208	Buster Douglas	246	KO 3	Las Vegas
Apr 19, 1991	Evander Holyfield*	212	George Foreman	257	UD 12	Atlantic City
Nov 23, 1991	Evander Holyfield*	210	Bert Cooper	215	TKO 7	Atlanta
June 19, 1992	Evander Holyfield*	210	Larry Holmes	233	UD 12	Las Vegas
Nov 13, 1992	Riddick Bowe*	235	Evander Holyfield	205	UD 12	Las Vegas
Feb 6, 1993	Riddick Bowe*	243	Michael Dokes	244	KO 1	New York City
May 8, 1993	Lennox Lewis	235	Tony Tucker	235	UD 12	Las Vegas
May 22, 1993	Riddick Bowe*	244	Jesse Ferguson	224	KO 2	Washington, D.C.
Oct 2, 1993	Lennox Lewis	229	Frank Bruno	233	KO 7	London
Nov 6, 1993	Evander Holyfield*	217	Riddick Bowe	246	Split 12	Las Vegas
Apr 22, 1994	Michael Moorer*	214	Evander Holyfield	214	Split 12	Las Vegas
May 6, 1994	Lennox Lewis	235	Phil Jackson	218	TKO 8	Atlantic City
Nov 6, 1994	George Foreman*	250	Michael Moorer	222	KO 10	Las Vegas
Mar 11, 1995	Riddick Bowe	241	Herbie Hide	214	KO 6	Las Vegas
Apr 8, 1995	Oliver McCall	231	Larry Holmes	236	UD 12	Las Vegas
Apr 8, 1995	Bruce Seldon	236	Tony Tucker	243	TKO 7	Las Vegas
Apr 22, 1995	George Foreman*	256	Axel Schulz	221	Split 12	Las Vegas
Jun 17, 1995	Riddick Bowe	243	Jorge Luis Gonzalez	237	KO 6	Las Vegas
Aug 19, 1995	Bruce Seldon	234	Joe Hipp	233	TKO 10	Las Vegas
Sept 2, 1995	Frank Bruno	247¾	Oliver McCall	234¾	UD 12	London
Dec 9, 1995	Frans Botha	237	Axel Shulz	223	Split 12	Stuttgart
Mar 16, 1996	Mike Tyson	220	Frank Bruno	247	TKO 3	Las Vegas
June 22, 1996	Michael Moorer	222¼	Axel Shulz	222¾	Split 12	Dortmund, Ger.
Sept 7, 1996	Mike Tyson	219	Bruce Seldon	229	TKO 1	Las Vegas
Nov 3, 1996	George Foreman*	253	Crawford Grimsley		UD 12	Tokyo
Nov 9, 1996	Evander Holyfied	215	Mike Tyson	222	TKO 11	Las Vegas
Feb 7, 1997	Lennox Lewis	251	Oliver McCall	237	TKO 5	Las Vegas
Apr 26, 1997	George Foreman*	253	Lou Savarese		Split 12	Atlantic City
June 28, 1997	Evander Holyfied	218	Mike Tyson	218	DQ 4	Las Vegas
Oct 4, 1997	Lennox Lewis	244	Andrew Golota	244	TKO 1	Atlantic City
Nov 8, 1997	Evander Holyfield	214	Michael Moorer	223	TKO 8	Las Vegas
Nov 22, 1997	Shannon Briggs*		George Foreman		MD 12	Atlantic City
Mar 28, 1998	Lennox Lewis*	243	Shannon Briggs	228	TKO 5	Atlantic City
Mar 13, 1999	Evander Holyfield	215	Lennox Lewis*	246	Draw 12	New York City
Nov 13, 1999	Lennox Lewis*	242	Evander Holyfield	217	UD 12	Las Vegas
Apr 29, 2000	Lennox Lewis*	247	Michael Grant	250	KO 2	New York
July 15, 2000	Lennox Lewis*	250	Frans Botha	236	TKO 2	London
Aug 12, 2000	Evander Holyfield	221	John Ruiz	224	UD 12	Las Vegas
Nov 11, 2000	Lennox Lewis*	249	David Tua	245	UD 12	Las Vegas
Mar 3, 2001	John Ruiz	227	Evander Holyfield	217	UD 12	Las Vegas
Apr 22, 2001	Hasim Rahman*	238	Lennox Lewis	253½	KO 5	Brakpan, S Africa
Nov 17, 2001	Lennox Lewis*	246½	Hasim Rahman	236	KO 4	Las Vegas
Dec 15, 2001	John Ruiz	232	Evander Holyfield	219	Draw 12	Mashantucket, CT
June 8, 2002	Lennox Lewis*	249¼	Mike Tyson	234½	KO 8	Memphis, TN
July 27, 2002	John Ruiz	233	Kirk Johnson	238	DQ 10	Las Vegas
Dec 14, 2002	Chris Byrd	214	Evander Holyfield	220	UD 12	Atlantic City
Mar 1, 2003	Roy Jones Jr.	193	John Ruiz	226	UD 12	Las Vegas
June 21, 2003	Lennox Lewis*	256½	Vitali Klitschko	248	TKO 6	Los Angeles
Sept 20, 2003	Chris Byrd	211½	Fres Oquendo	224	UD 12	Uncasville, CT

*Lineal champion. KO=knockout; TKO=technical knockout; UD=unanimous decision; Split=split decision; Ref=referee's decision; MD=majority decision; DQ=disqualification; ND=no decision.

Year	Fighter	Year	Fighter	Year	Fighter
1928	Gene Tunney	1935	Barney Ross	1940	Billy Conn
1929	Tommy Loughran	1936	Joe Louis	1941	Joe Louis
1930	Max Schmeling	1937	Henry Armstrong	1942	Ray Robinson
1932	Jack Sharkey	1938	Joe Louis	1943	Fred Apostoli
1934	T. Canzoneri/B. Ross	1939	Joe Louis	1944	Beau Jack

Note: No award in 1933; no fight of the year named until 1945

Year	Fighter	Fight	Winner	Site
1945	Willie Pep	Rocky Graziano–Freddie Cochrane	Rocky Graziano	New York City
1946	Tony Zale	Tony Zale–Rocky Graziano	Tony Zale	New York City
1947	Gus Lesnevich	Rocky Graziano–Tony Zale	Rocky Graziano	Chicago
1948	Ike Williams	Marcel Cerdan–Tony Zale	Marcel Cerdan	Jersey City
1949	Ezzard Charles	Willie Pep–Sandy Saddler	Willie Pep	New York City
1950	Ezzard Charles	Jake LaMotta–Laurent Dauthuille	Jake LaMotta	Detroit
1951	Ray Robinson	Jersey Joe Walcott–Ezzard Charles	Jersey Joe Walcott	Pittsburgh
1952	Rocky Marciano	Rocky Marciano–Jersey Joe Walcott	Rocky Marciano	Philadelphia
1953	Carl Olson	Rocky Marciano–Roland LaStarza	Rocky Marciano	New York City
1954	Rocky Marciano	Rocky Marciano–Ezzard Charles	Rocky Marciano	New York City
1955	Rocky Marciano	Carmen Basilio–Tony DeMarco	Carmen Basilio	Boston
1956	Floyd Patterson	Carmen Basilio–Johnny Saxton	Carmen Basilio	Syracuse
1957	Carmen Basilio	Carmen Basilio–Ray Robinson	Carmen Basilio	New York City
1958	Ingemar Johansson	Ray Robinson–Carmen Basilio	Ray Robinson	Chicago
1959	Ingemar Johansson	Gene Fullmer–Carmen Basilio	Gene Fullmer	San Francisco
1960	Floyd Patterson	Floyd Patterson–Ingemar Johansson	Floyd Patterson	New York City
1961	Joe Brown	Joe Brown–Dave Charnley	Joe Brown	London
1962	Dick Tiger	Joey Giardello–Henry Hank	Joey Giardello	Philadelphia
1963	Cassius Clay	Cassius Clay–Doug Jones	Cassius Clay	New York City
1964	Emile Griffith	Cassius Clay–Sonny Liston	Cassius Clay	Miami Beach
1965	Dick Tiger	Floyd Patterson–George Chuvalo	Floyd Patterson	New York City
1966	No award	Jose Torres–Eddie Cotton	Jose Torres	Las Vegas
1967	Joe Frazier	Nino Benvenuti–Emile Griffith	Nino Benvenuti	New York City
1968	Nino Benvenuti	Dick Tiger–Frank DePaula	Dick Tiger	New York City
1969	Jose Napoles	Joe Frazier–Jerry Quarry	Joe Frazier	New York City
1970	Joe Frazier	Carlos Monzon–Nino Benvenuti	Carlos Monzon	Rome
1971	Joe Frazier	Joe Frazier–Muhammad Ali	Joe Frazier	New York City
1972	Muhammad Ali / Carlos Monzon	Bob Foster–Chris Finnegan	Bob Foster	London
1973	George Foreman	George Foreman–Joe Frazier	George Foreman	Kingston, Jam.
1974	Muhammad Ali	Muhammad Ali–George Foreman	Muhammad Ali	Kinshasa, Zaire
1975	Muhammad Ali	Muhammad Ali–Joe Frazier	Muhammad Ali	Manila
1976	George Foreman	George Foreman–Ron Lyle	George Foreman	Las Vegas
1977	Carlos Zarate	Joe Young–George Foreman	Joe Young	San Juan
1978	Muhammad Ali	Leon Spinks–Muhammad Ali	Leon Spinks	Las Vegas
1979	Ray Leonard	Danny Lopez–Mike Ayala	Danny Lopez	San Antonio
1980	Thomas Hearns	Saad Muhammad–Yaqui Lopez	Saad Muhammad	McAfee, NJ
1981	Ray Leonard / Salvador Sanchez	Ray Leonard–Tommy Hearns	Ray Leonard	Las Vegas
1982	Larry Holmes	Bobby Chacon–Rafael Limon	Bobby Chacon	Sacramento
1983	Marvin Hagler	Bobby Chacon–Cornelius Boza-Edwards	Bobby Chacon	Las Vegas
1984	Thomas Hearns	Jose Luis Ramirez–Edwin Rosario	Jose Luis Ramirez	San Juan
1985	Donald Curry / Marvin Hagler	Marvin Hagler–Tommy Hearns	Marvin Hagler	Las Vegas
1986	Mike Tyson	Stevie Cruz–Barry McGuigan	Stevie Cruz	Las Vegas
1987	Evander Holyfield	Ray Leonard–Marvin Hagler	Ray Leonard	Las Vegas
1988	Mike Tyson	Tony Lopez–Rocky Lockridge	Tony Lopez	Inglewood, CA
1989	Pernell Whitaker	Roberto Duran–Iran Barkley	Roberto Duran	Atlantic City
1990	Julio César Chávez	Julio César Chávez–Meldrick Taylor	Julio César Chávez	Las Vegas
1991	James Toney	Robert Quiroga–Kid Akeem Anifowoshe	Robert Quiroga	San Antonio
1992	Riddick Bowe	Riddick Bowe–Evander Holyfield	Riddick Bowe	Las Vegas
1993	Michael Carbajal	Michael Carbajal–Humberto Gonzalez	Michael Carbajal	Las Vegas
1994	Roy Jones	Jorge Castro–John David Jackson	Jorge Castro	Monterrey, Mex.
1995	Oscar De La Hoya	Saman Sor Jaturong–Chiquita Gonzalez	Saman Sor Jaturong	Inglewood, CA
1996	Evander Holyfield	Evander Holyfield–Mike Tyson	Evander Holyfield	Las Vegas
1997	Evander Holyfield	Arturo Gatti–Gabriel Ruelas	Arturo Gatti	Atlantic City
1998	Floyd Mayweather	Ivan Robinson–Arturo Gatti	Ivan Robinson	Atlantic City
1999	Paulie Ayala	Paulie Ayala–Johnny Tapia	Paulie Ayala	Las Vegas
2000	Felix Trinidad	Erik Morales–Marco Antonio Barrera	Erik Morales	Las Vegas
2001	Bernard Hopkins	Micky Ward–Emanuel Burton	Micky Ward	Las Vegas
2002	Vernon Forrest	Micky Ward–Arturo Gatti	Micky Ward	Uncasville, CT

U.S. Olympic Gold Medalists

LIGHT FLYWEIGHT
1984 ....Paul Gonzales

FLYWEIGHT
1904 ....George Finnegan
1920 ....Frank Di Gennara
1024 ....Fidel LaBarba
1952 ....Nathan Brooks
1976 ....Leo Randolph
1984 ....Steve McCrory

BANTAMWEIGHT
1904 ....Oliver Kirk
1988 ....Kennedy McKinney

FEATHERWEIGHT
1904 ....Oliver Kirk
1924 ....John Fields
1984 ....Meldrick Taylor

LIGHTWEIGHT
1904 ....Harry Spanger
1920 ....Samuel Mosberg
1968 ....Ronald W. Harris
1976 ....Howard Davis
1984 ....Pernell Whitaker
1992 ....Oscar De La Hoya

LIGHT WELTERWEIGHT
1952 ....Charles Adkins
1972 ....Ray Seales
1976 ....Ray Leonard
1984 ....Jerry Page

WELTERWEIGHT
1904 ....Albert Young
1932 ....Edward Flynn
1984 ....Mark Breland

LIGHT MIDDLEWEIGHT
1960 ....Wilbert McClure
1984 ....Frank Tate
1996 ....David Reid

MIDDLEWEIGHT
1904 ....Charles Mayer
1932 ....Carmen Bath
1952 ....Floyd Patterson
1960 ....Edward Crook
1976 ....Michael Spinks

LIGHT HEAVYWEIGHT
1920 ...:...........Eddie Eagan
1952 ....Norvel Lee
1956 ....James Boyd
1960 ....Cassius Clay
1976 ....Leon Spinks
1988 ....Andrew Maynard

HEAVYWEIGHT
1984 ....Henry Tillman
1988 ....Ray Mercer

SUPER HEAVYWEIGHT
1904 ....Samuel Berger
1952 ....H. Edward Sanders
1956 ....T. Peter
                   Rademacher
1964 ....Joe Frazier
1968 ....George Foreman
1984 ....Tyrell Biggs

YET ANOTHER SIGN OF THE APOCALYPSE

Mike Tyson was considering a fight with Bob (the Beast) Sapp, a 6' 4", 375-pound mixed martial artist.

Lineal Heavyweight Champions

Champion	Reign	Age*	Career	W-L-D (KO)	Successful Defenses
John L. Sullivan	1885–92	26	1878–92	38-1-3 (33)	0
James J. Corbett	1892–97	26	1884–03	11-4-2 (7)	1
Bob Fitzsimmons	1897–99	33	1880–16	74-8-3 (67)	0
James J. Jeffries†	1899–05	24	1896–10	18-1-2 (15)	7
Marvin Hart	1905–06	28	1899–10	28–7–4 (19)	0
Tommy Burns	1906–08	24	1900–20	46-5-8 (37)	11
Jack Johnson	1908–15	30	1894–28	77-13-14 (48)	9
Jess Willard	1915–19	33	1911–23	23-6-1 (20)	1
Jack Dempsey	1919–26	24	1914–27	60-6-8 (50)	5
Gene Tunney†	1926–28	29	1915–28	61-1-1 (45)	2
Max Schmeling	1930–32	24	1924–48	56-10-4 (39)	1
Jack Sharkey	1932–33	29	1924–36	38-13-3 (14)	0
Primo Carnera	1933–34	26	1928–37	88-14-0 (69)	2
Max Baer	1934–35	25	1929–41	72-12-0 (53)	0
James J. Braddock	1935–37	29	1926–38	51-26-7 (26)	0
Joe Louis†	1937–49	23	1934–51	68-3-0 (54)	25
Ezzard Charles	1949–51	27	1940–59	96-25-1 (59)	8
Jersey Joe Walcott	1951–52	37	1930–53	53-18-1 (33)	1
Rocky Marciano†	1952–56	29	1947–56	49-0-0 (43)	6
Floyd Patterson	1956–59	21	1952–72	55-8-1 (40)	4
Ingemar Johansson	1959–60	26	1952–63	26-2-0 (17)	0
Floyd Patterson	1960–62	25	1952–72	55-8-1 (40)	2
Sonny Liston	1962–64	30	1953–70	50-4-0 (39)	1
Muhammad Ali	1964–71	22	1960–81	56-5-0 (37)	9
Joe Frazier	1971–73	27	1965–81	32-4-1 (27)	2
George Foreman	1973–74	24	1969–97	76-5-0 (68)	2
Muhammad Ali	1974–78	32	1960–81	56-5-0 (37)	10
Leon Spinks	1978	24	1977–95	26-17-3 (14)	0
Muhammad Ali†	1978–79	36	1960–81	56-5-0 (37)	0
Larry Holmes	1980–85	29	1973–	69-6-0 (44)	20
Michael Spinks	1985–88	29	1977–88	32-1-0 (21)	3
Mike Tyson	1988–90	21	1985–	49-4-0 (43)	2
Buster Douglas	1990	29	1981–99	38-6-1 (25)	0
Evander Holyfield	1990–92	28	1984–	38-5-2 (26)	3
Riddick Bowe	1992–93	25	1989–96	40-1-0 (32)	2
Evander Holyfield	1993–94	31	1984–	38-5-2 (26)	0
Michael Moorer	1994	26	1988–97	39-2-0 (31)	0
George Foreman	1994–97	45	1969–97	76-5-0 (68)	3
Shannon Briggs	1997–98	25	1992–00	32-3-1 (25)	0
Lennox Lewis	1998–01	32	1989–	40-2-1 (31)	5
Hasim Rahman	2001	28	1994–	35-4-0 (29)	0
Lennox Lewis	2001–	36	1989–	41-2-1 (32)	2

*Age when boxer won world championship.
† Boxer retired or relinquished world title.

Horse Racing

Kentucky Derby and
Preakness winner
Funny Cide

Only In Hollywood

Funny Cide and box-office hero Seabiscuit followed a similar script—until the ending

BY STEPHEN CANNELLA

RACEHORSES ARE hardly the most stable investments, which is why it was easy to assume that six friends from tiny Sackets Harbor, N.Y., were making the mistake of their middle-class lives when they decided to get into the thoroughbred game eight years ago. Fueled by the cold beer and dreamy conversation that flowed at a Memorial Day weekend gathering, the high-school buddies decided to kick in $5,000 each to form a racing syndicate. The group, which called its enterprise the Sackatoga Stable, included a construction company owner, a retired schoolteacher and an optician—not a Saudi prince or a Kentucky blueblood among them. By society's standards they were men of average means. By the high-rent standards of horse racing they were paupers, commoners crashing the sport of kings.

Thanks to the heroics of an unheralded three-year-old bred in that racing backwater, New York, their paltry initial investment nearly became a down payment on history in 2003. Funny Cide, purchased by the Sackatogans for the bargain-basement price of $75,000 one year earlier, came from nowhere to win both the Kentucky Derby and the Preakness. A run at the Triple Crown wasn't particularly shocking in and of itself—eight horses have entered the Belmont with a shot at glory since Affirmed won the last Crown in 1978—but a long-shot gelding with such modest backing and a chance to clinch immortality at his home barn? This was the stuff of Hollywood.

Coincidentally, a similar rags-to-riches tale became one of the summer's box office hits. Multiplexes were packed with railbirds and racing dilettantes alike for screenings of *Seabiscuit*, the film adaptation of Laura Hillenbrand's bestseller about the undersized, broken-down thoroughbred that took the racing world by storm and captured the hearts of a Depression-addled nation in 1938.

It may have been clichéd to call Funny Cide a modern-day Seabiscuit, but the parallels between the two long shots were difficult to ignore. Both had less-than-stellar pedigrees. Both were piloted by jockeys thought to be broken down or washed up. Jose Santos was one of the sport's most successful and sought-after riders during the 1980s, but the Chilean fell on hard times—divorce, injury and a noticeable decrease in trip's to

Santos was unfairly accused after his upset win in the Derby.

Santos was unfairly accused after his upset win in the Derby.

BILL FRAKES

the winner's circle—in the 1990s. He re-emerged with a victory in the 2002 Breeders Cup Classic aboard 43–1 long shot Volponi. Santos took Funny Cide's reins early in 2003.

Most of the hype in the days before the Kentucky Derby focused on Empire Maker, the three-year-old colt with a royal pedigree and more than his share of compelling storylines. Empire Maker sprang from the womb of Toussaud, one of the world's most sought-after mares. He was ridden by Jerry Bailey, one of the sport's elite jockeys, and trained by Bobby Frankel, who had won four Eclipse Awards and more than $135 million in purses, but never a Triple Crown race.

Many observers considered Empire Maker the horse with the best chance in years to claim the Triple Crown. Frankel and owner Khalid Abdullah, a Saudi prince, prepared the colt for the Derby as if they had three victories, not one, in mind. Their horse blew away the field in the Florida Derby in March. Rather than rest the colt for Churchill Downs, Frankel ran him right back out for the Wood Memorial less than a month later. "If I was only trying to win the Derby I wouldn't run the Wood," Frankel explained, with more than a touch of cocksureness. "But if we're going to try to win the Triple Crown with this horse we need to get him used to running every couple of weeks."

A victory in the Wood confirmed Empire Maker as the Derby favorite. Funny Cide, entered the Run for the Roses as an afterthought, if that. He did finish second in the Wood, but few handicappers gave much weight to the performance. Trainer Barclay Tagg kept Funny Cide in New York until three days before the Derby, so most race fans were oblivious to the fact that the horse had ripped through his workout rides at blistering paces.

On a clear afternoon on the first Saturday in May, Funny Cide bumped with Offlee Wild out of the gate, but recovered quickly and motored into the backstretch in third place, behind Brancusi and Peace Rules. He grabbed the lead on the far turn and never looked back, winning by 1¾ lengths. While the vaunted Empire Maker finished second, almost two lengths behind, the unheralded gelding blazed the 1¼-mile course in 2:01.19, the 10th-fastest time in the 129-year history of the Derby. He was the first New York-bred horse to win the Kentucky Derby and the first gelding in 74 years. After the race, Santos's eight-year-old son, Jose, Jr., dashed across the infield and shrieked at his father, "I can't believe we won the Kentucky Derby."

No one could, which may help explain the chaos that followed. The day after the Derby, the *Miami Herald* published a race photo in which a dark spot is visible in San-

Empire Maker, with Jerry Bailey up, dashed Funny Cide's Triple Crown dreams.

tos's whip (right) hand. A follow-up story suggested that Santos carried a foreign object during the Derby, perhaps a battery or buzzer that could jolt extra effort out of his mount. The story, which was light on facts and sloppily written, also contained some apparently damaging words from Santos himself. The jockey told the paper in a phone interview that he wore something called a "Q-ray" bracelet on his left wrist to help ease the pain of arthritis. The interviewer, misunderstanding Santos's accented English, wrote instead that Santos admitted to carrying a "cue ring" (something no one had ever heard of) to call "outriders"(which were equally mysterious entities).

Suddenly, Santos found himself tossed in a tempest. Several members of the jockey fraternity rushed to his defense, and media organizations around the country ran enlarged photos that showed Santos carried a whip in his right hand and nothing else. After several days of scrutiny, Santos was exonerated at a May 12 hearing at Churchill Downs, just five days before the Preakness.

All of Santos's post-Derby frustration evaporated on that cool and misty day at Pimlico. Funny Cide tore from the gate and moved alongside Peace Rules, the field's second betting choice, on the backside. As they turned for home, the gelding nudged ahead, and down the stretch Funny Cide simply obliterated the competition. He won by nearly 10 lengths, the largest margin of victory since the Preakness was first run in 1873. As he crossed the finish line the defiant Santos raised two fingers on his right hand—one for each of the first two Triple Crown legs—and then flashed open his fist to reveal an empty palm.

An exuberant crowd of 101,864 packed Belmont Park on June 7 for a much-anticipated coronation. Alas, Triple Crown glory eluded Funny Cide's grasp, as it has for every horse during the last 25 years. Running on his home track, which was made sloppy by heavy rain, the gelding dashed to the lead in the first turn. With half a mile to go the regal Empire Maker, who had skipped the Preakness, appeared beside him. Funny Cide had been fighting Santos for the entire race, and he wilted under Empire Maker's challenge. While Frankel's colt cruised to victory, Funny Cide fell to third place, behind Ten Most Wanted, more than five lengths behind the winner.

The loss was a reality check for the three-year-old, his workaday ownership and the sport, which desperately needs a Triple Crown winner to create the sort of buzz that *Seabiscuit* did at the box office. During the summer, racing officials sought to invigorate the sport by breathlesssly promoting a showdown between Funny Cide and Empire Maker at the Aug. 23 Travers, but the rivalry proved to be short lived. Empire Maker lost to Strong Hope at Saratoga on Aug. 3. The same day, Funny Cide was trounced in the Haskell Invitational at Monmouth, where he ran third to Peace Rules and Sky Mesa. Santos said the gelding spit the bit six furlongs into the race.

As it turned out both horses fell ill and neither ran the Travers. Funny Cide's future was cloudy: Is the gelding destined for greatness, or did he merely overachieve on the grandest stage of all? Unfortunately for the Sackatoga Stable, *Seabiscuit* provided the year's only Hollywood ending.

THOROUGHBRED RACING

The Triple Crown

129th Kentucky Derby

May 3, 2003. Grade I, 3-year-olds; 10th race, Churchill Downs, Louisville. All 126 lbs. Distance: 1¼ miles. Purse: $1,000,000 guaranteed. Track: Fast. Off: 6:08 p.m. Winner: Funny Cide (By Distorted Humor out of Belle's Good Cide); Times: 0:22.78, 0:46.23, 1:10.48, 1:35.75, 2:01.19. Won: Driving. Breeder: Winstar Farm, LLC.

Horse	Finish-PP	Margin	Jockey/Owner
Funny Cide	1–5	1³/₄	Jose Santos/Sackatoga Stable Jackson W. Knowlton
Empire Maker	2–11	head	Jerry Bailey/Juddmonte Farms, Inc.
Peace Rules	3–4	head	Edgar Prado/Edmund A. Gann
Atswhatimtalkinbout	4–3	2³/₄	David Flores/B. Wayne Hughes & Biscuit Stables, LLC
Eye of the Tiger	5–12	1	Eibar Coa/John D. Gunther
Buddy Gil	6–7	³/₄	Gary Stevens/Desperado Stables Inc.
Outta Here	7–14	1	Kent Desormeaux/William Currin & Al Eisman
Ten Cents a Shine	8–13	neck	Calvin Borel/Ramsey, Kenneth L. & Sarah K.
Ten Most Wanted	9–10	1³/₄	Pat Day/James Chisholm, Michael Jarvis & J. Paul Reddam
Domestic Dispute	10–10	1	Alex Solis/David Bienstock & Chuck Winner
Scrimshaw	11–16	1	Cornelio Velasquez/Lewis, Robert B. & Beverly J.
Offlee Wild	12–6	5¹/₂	Robbie Albarado/Azalea Stables, LLC
Supah Blitz	13–1	1³/₄	Rosemary Homeister Jr./Beebee Stables, Inc.
Indian Express	14–8	1¹/₄	Tyler Baze/Chess, Phil & Sheva
Lone Star Sky	15–9	1	Shane Sellers/Walter L. New
Brancusi	16–2	—	Tony Farina/Michael B. Tabor

128th Preakness Stakes

May 17, 2003. Grade I, 3-year-olds; 12th race, Pimlico Race Course, Baltimore. All 126 lbs. Distance: 1³⁄₁₆ miles; Stakes value: $1,000,000; Winner: $650,000; Second: $200,000; Third: $100,000; Fourth: $50,000. Track: Good. Off: 6:14 p.m. Winner: Funny Cide (By Distorted Humor out of Belle's Good Cide); Times: 0:23.37, 0:47.14, 1:11.62, 1:36.42, 1:55.61. Won: Driving. Breeder: Winstar Farm, LLC.

Horse	Finish-PP	Margin	Jockey/Owner
Funny Cide	1–9	9³/₄	Jose Santos/Sackatoga Stable Jackson W. Knowlton
Midway Road	2–6	³/₄	Robbie Albarado/William S. Farish
Scrimshaw	3–2	nose	Gary Stevens/Lewis, Robert B. & Beverly J.
Peace Rules	4–7	2	Edgar Prado/Edmund A. Gann
Senor Swinger	5–10	head	Pat Day/Lewis, Robert B. & Beverly J.
New York Hero	6–8	3¹/₄	Jorge Chavez/Paraneck Stable
Foufa's Warrior	7–3	1¹/₄	Ramon Dominguez/Sondra D. Bender
Cherokee's Boy	8–1	5³/₄	Ryan Fogelsonger/ZWP Stable
Ten Cents a Shine	9–5	1	Jerry Bailey/Ramsey, Kenneth L.& Sarah K.
Kissin Saint	10–4	—	Richard Migliore/Peter Karches & Michael Rankowitz

135th Belmont Stakes

June 7, 2003. Grade I, 3-year-olds; 11th race, Belmont Park, Elmont, NY. All 126 lbs. Distance: 1½ miles. Stakes value: $1,000,000; Winner: $600,000; Second: $200,000; Third: $110,000; Fourth: $60,000; Fifth: $30,000 Track: Sloppy. Off: 6:40 p.m. Winner: Empire Maker (By Unbridled out of Toussaud); Times: 0:23.85, 48.70, 1:13.51, 1:38.05, 2:02.62, 2:28.26. Won: Driving. Breeder: Juddmonte Farms, Inc.

Horse	Finish-PP	Margin	Jockey/Owner
Empire Maker	1–1	³/₄	Jerry Bailey/Juddmonte Farms, Inc.
Ten Most Wanted	2–6	4¹/₄	Pat Day/James Chisholm, Michael Jarvis & J. Paul Reddam
Funny Cide	3–4	5¹/₄	Jose Santos/Sackatoga Stable Jackson W. Knowlton
Dynever	4–5	15¹/₄	Edgar Prado/Peter F. Karches and Catherine Wills
Supervisor	5–2	4¹/₂	John Velazquez/Rodney G. Lundock
Scrimshaw	6–3	—	Gary Stevens/Lewis, Robert B. & Beverly J.

Major Stakes Races

Late 2002

Date	Race	Track	Distance	Winner	Jockey/Trainer	Purse ($)
Sept 21	Vosburg Stakes	Belmont Park	7 furlongs	Bonapaw	G. Melancon/ N. Miller	300,000
Sept 21	Super Derby XXIII	Louisiana Downs	1⅛ miles	Essence of Dubai	Jorge Chavez S. bin Suroor	500,000
Sept 21	Kentucky Cup Handicap	Turfway Park	1½ miles	Rochester	Mike Martin Jr/ J. Sheppard	300,000
Sept 28	Flower Bowl Invitational Handicap	Belmont Park	1¼ miles	Kazzia	Jorge Chavez/ S. bin Suroor	750,000
Sept 28	The Jockey Club Gold Cup	Belmont Park	1¼ miles	Evening Attire	Shaun Bridgmohan/ P. Kelly	1,000,000
Sept 29	Turf Classic Invitational	Belmont Park	1½ miles	Denon	Edgar Prado/ Robert Frankel	750,000
Sept 29	E.P. Taylor Stakes	Woodbine	1¼ miles	Fraulein	Kevin Darley/ E. Dunlop	837,750
Oct 4	Meadowlands Cup Handicap	Meadowlands	1⅛ miles	Burning Roma	E. Coa/ H. Giglio	400,000
Oct 4	Winstar Galaxy Stakes	Keeneland	1 3/16 miles	Owsley	Edgar Prado/ R. Schulhofer	544,500
Oct 5	Yellow Ribbon Stakes	Santa Anita Park	1¼ miles	Golden Apples	Pat Valenzuela/ B. Cecil	500,000
Oct 5	Beldame Stakes	Belmont Park	1⅛ miles	Imperial Gesture	Jerry Bailey/ S. bin Suroor	750,000
Oct 5	Champagne Stakes	Belmont Park	1 1/16 miles	Toccet	Jorge Chavez/ J. Scanlon	500,000
Oct 5	Frizette Stakes	Belmont Park	1 1/16 miles	Storm Flag Flying	John Velazquez/ C. McGauhey	500,000
Oct 5	Lane's End Breeders' Futurity	Keeneland	1 1/16 miles	Sky Mesa	Edgar Prado/ J. Ward	434,800
Oct 5	Hollywood B.C. Handicap	Santa Anita	1⅛ miles	Pleasantly Perfect	Alex Solis/ R. Mandela	500,000
Oct 5	Keeneland Turf Mile	Keeneland	1 mile	Landseer	Edgar Prado/ A. O'Brien	600,000
Oct 5	Keeneland Turf Mile	Keeneland	1 mile	Landseer	Edgar Prado/ A. O'Brien	600,000
Oct 6	Spinster Stakes	Keeneland	1⅛ miles	Take Charge Lady	Edgar Prado/ K. McPeek	546,000
Oct 12	Queen Elizabeth II Challenge Cup	Keeneland	1⅛ miles	Riskaverse	Mark Guidry/ P.J. Kelly	500,000
Oct 26	Breeders' Cup Classic	Arlington Park	1¼ miles	Volponi	Jose Santos/ P.G. Johnson	4,000,000
Oct 26	Breeders' Cup Turf	Arlington Park	1½ miles	High Chaparral	Mick Kinane/ A. O'Brien	2,420,000
Oct 26	Breeders' Cup Sprint	Arlington Park	6 furlongs	Orientate	Jerry Bailey/ D. Wayne Lukas	1,140,000
Oct 26	Breeders' Cup Mile	Arlington Park	1 mile	Domedriver	T. Thulliez/ P. Bary	1,070,000
Oct 26	Breeders' Cup Juvenile Fillies	Arlington Park	1⅛ miles	Storm Flag Flying	John Velazquez/ C. McGaughey	1,000,000
Oct 26	Breeders' Cup Distaff	Arlington Park	1⅛ miles	Azeri	Mike Smith/ L. de Seroux	2,000,000
Oct 26	Breeders' Cup Juvenile	Arlington Park	1⅛ miles	Vindication	Mike Kinane/ Bob Baffert	1,000,000
Oct 26	Breeders' Cup Filly & Mare Turf	Arlington Park	1¼ miles	Starine	John Velazquez Robert Frankel	1,280,000
Nov 29	Clark Handicap	Churchill Downs	1⅛ miles	Ledo Palace	Jorge Chavez Robert Frankel	457,200
Nov 30	Cigar Mile Handicap	Aqueduct	1 mile	Congaree	Jerry Bailey/ Bob Baffert	350,000
Nov 30	Citation Handicap	Hollywood Park	1 1/16 miles	Good Journey	Pat Day/ W. Dollase	500,000
Dec 1	Matriarch Stakes	Hollywood Park	1⅛ miles	Dress To Thrill	P. Smullen/ D. Weld	500,000
Dec 1	Hollywood Derby	Hollywood Park	1⅛ miles	Johar	Alex Solis/ R. Mandela	500,000
Dec 14	Hollywood Starlet	Hollywood Park	1 1/16 miles	Elloluv	Pat Valenzuela/ C. Dollase	366,500

Major Stakes Races (Cont.)

2003 (Through September 14)

Date	Race	Track	Distance	Winner	Jockey/Trainer	Purse ($)
Jan 11	San Fernando B.C. Sprint	Santa Anita	1 1/16 miles	Pass Rush	Corey Nakatani/ P. Burne	219,600
Jan 25	Santa Monica Handicap	Santa Anita	7 furlongs	Affluent	Alex Solis/ R. McAnally	200,000
Feb 1	Strub Stakes	Santa Anita	1 1/8 miles	Medaglia D'Oro	Jerry Bailey/ Robert Frankel	400,000
Feb 22	Donn Handicap	Gulfstream Park	1 1/8 miles	Harlan's Holiday	John Velazquez T. Pletcher	500,000
Mar 1	Santa Anita Handicap	Santa Anita Park	1 1/4 miles	Milwaukee Brew	Edgar Prado/ Robert Frankel	1,000,000
Mar 2	New Orleans Handicap	Fair Grounds	1 1/8 miles	Mineshaft	Robbie Albarado N. Howard	500,000
Mar 8	Fair Grounds Oaks	Fair Grounds	1 1/16 miles	Lady Tak	Don Meche/ S. Asmussen	350,000
Mar 9	Santa Margarita Handicap	Santa Anita Park	1 1/8 miles	Starrer	Pat Valenzuela/ J. Shirreffs	300,000
Mar 9	Louisiana Derby	Fair Grounds	1 1/16 miles	Peace Rules	Edgar Prado/ Robert Frankel	750,000
Mar 15	Florida Derby	Gulfstream Park	1 1/8 miles	Empire Maker	Jerry Bailey/ Robert Frankel	1,000,000
Mar 22	Lane's End Stakes	Turfway Park	1 1/8 miles	New York Hero	Norberto Arroyo/ J. Pedersen	500,000
Mar 23	Explosive Bid Handicap	Fair Grounds	1 1/8 miles	Candid Glen	E. Perrodin/ A. Leggio	650,000
Mar 29	Dubai World Cup	Nad Al Sheba	1 1/4 miles	Moon Ballad	Frankie Dettori/ S. bin Suroor	6,000,000
Mar 30	Winstar Derby	Sundland Park	1 1/16 miles	Excessive-pleasure	Pat Day/ D. O'Neil	500,000
Apr 5	Santa Anita Derby	Santa Anita Park	1 1/8 miles	Buddy Gil	Gary Stevens/ J. Mullins	750,000
Apr 5	Ashland Stakes	Keeneland	1 1/16 miles	Elloluv	Robbie Albarado/ C. Dollase	551,750
Apr 5	Illinois Derby	Hawthorne	1 1/8 miles	Ten Most Wanted	Pat Day/ W. Dollase	500,000
Apr 5	Apple Blossom Handicap	Oaklawn Park	1 1/16 miles	Azeri	Mike Smith/ L. de Seroux	500,000
Apr 5	Oaklawn Handicap	Oaklawn Park	1 1/8 miles	Medaglia D'Oro	Jerry Bailey/ R. Frankel	500,000
Apr 12	Arkansas Derby	Oaklawn Park	1 1/8 miles	Sir Cherokee	T. Thompson/ M. Tomlinson	500,000
Apr 12	Bluegrass Stakes	Keeneland	1 1/8 miles	Peace Rules	Edgar Prado/ Robert Frankel	750,000
Apr 12	Wood Memorial Stakes	Aqueduct	1 1/8 miles	Empire Maker	Jerry Bailey/ Robert Frankel	750,000
Apr 20	San Juan Capistrano Handicap	Santa Anita	1 3/4 miles	Passinetti	B. Blanc/ B. Cecil	400,000
May 2	Kentucky Oaks	Churchill Downs	1 1/8 miles	Bird Town	Edgar Prado/ Nick Zito	573,800
May 3	Kentucky Derby	Churchill Downs	1 1/4 miles	Funny Cide	Jose Santos/ Barclay Tagg	1,100,200
May 10	Lone Star Derby	Lone Star Park	1 1/8 miles	Dynever	Edgar Prado/ C. Clement	500,000
May 18	Preakness Stakes	Pimlico	1 3/16 miles	Funny Cide	Jose Santos/ Barclay Tagg	1,000,000
May 26	Metropolitan Handicap	Belmont Park	1 mile	Aldevaran	Jerry Bailey/ Robert Frankel	750,000
May 26	Gamely Breeders' Cup Handicap	Hollywood Park	1 1/8 miles	Tates Cree	Pat Valenzuela/ Robert Frankel	421,000
May 26	Shoemaker Breeders' Cup Mile	Hollywood Park	1 mile	Redattore	Alex Solis/ R. Mandela	415,000
June 7	Belmont Stakes	Belmont Park	1 1/2 miles	Empire Maker	Jerry Bailey/ Robert Frankel	1,000,000
June 14	Stephen Foster Handicap	Churchill Downs	1 1/8 miles	Perfect Drift	Pat Day M. Johnson	856,500
June 22	Queen's Plate Stakes	Woodbine	1 1/4 miles	Wando	Todd Kabel M. Keogh	1,000,000

2003 (Through September 14) (Cont.)

Date	Race	Track	Distance	Winner	Jockey/Trainer	Purse ($)
July 5	Suburban Handicap	Belmont Park	1¼ miles	Mineshaft	Robbie Albarado/ N. Howard	500,000
July 5	United Nations Handicap	Monmouth Park	1⅜ miles	Balto Star	J. Velez/ T. Pletcher	750,000
July 5	American Oaks	Hollywood Park	1¼ miles	Dimitrova	David Flores/ D. Weld	750,000
July 13	Hollywood Gold Cup	Hollywood Park	1¼ miles	Congaree	Jerry Bailey/ Bob Baffert	750,000
July 20	Delaware Handicap	Delaware Park	1¼ miles	Wild Spirit	Jerry Bailey/ Robert Frankel	750,000
Aug 3	Whitney Handicap	Saratoga	1⅛ miles	Medaglia D'Oro	Jerry Bailey/ Robert Bailey	750,000
Aug 3	Jim Dandy Stakes	Saratoga	1⅛ miles	Strong Hope	John Velazquez/ Todd Pletcher	500,000
Aug 3	Haskell Invitational	Monmouth Park	1⅛ miles	Peace Rules	Edgar Prado/ Robert Frankel	1,100,000
Aug 9	W Virginia Derby	Mountaineer Park	1⅛ miles	Soto	R. Dominguez/ M. Dickinson	600,000
Aug 16	Arlington Million	Arlington	1¼ miles	Sulamani	David Flores/ S. bin Suroor	1,000,000
Aug 16	Alabama Stakes	Saratoga	1¼ miles	Island Fashion	John Velazquez/ Barclay Tagg	750,000
Aug 23	Travers Stakes	Saratoga	1¼ miles	Ten Most Wanted	Pat Day/ W. Dollase	1,000,000
Aug 24	Pacific Classic	Del Mar	1¼ miles	Candy Ride	Julie Krone/ R. Mandela	1,000,000
Sept 1	Pennsylvania Derby	Philadelphia Park	1⅛ miles	Grand Hombre	Joe Bravo/ D. Manning	750,000
Sept 14	Atto Mile Stakes	Woodbine	1 mile	Touch of the Blues	Kent Desormeaux/ N. Drysdale	1,000,000

2002 Statistical Leaders

Horses

Horse	Starts	1st	2nd	3rd	Purses ($)
War Emblem	10	5	0	0	3,455,000
Volponi	8	3	3	1	2,389,200
Medaglia d'Oro	9	4	3	0	2,260,600
Azeri	9	8	1	0	2,181,540
Came Home	8	6	0	0	1,624,500
Harlan's Holiday	10	3	2	1	1,606,000
Milwaukee Brew	7	2	0	3	1,590,000
With Anticipation	8	3	3	0	1,507,700
Beat Hollow	8	4	2	1	1,437,150
Orientate	10	6	1	0	1,412,970

Jockeys

Jockey	Mounts	1st	2nd	3rd	Purses ($)	Win Pct	$ Pct*
Jerry Bailey	832	213	139	118	19,271,814	.26	.56
Edgar Prado	1527	289	246	218	18,024,429	.19	.49
John R. Velasquez	1394	289	221	185	16,361,445	.21	.50
Pat Day	1155	258	193	138	15,904,396	.22	.51
Jorge Chavez	1196	223	180	166	13,721,254	.19	.48
Victor Espinoza	1143	188	160	163	12,590,646	.16	.45
Pat Valenzuela	1297	221	225	195	12,544,098	.17	.49
Alex Solis	1123	217	194	182	12,027,315	.19	.53
Jose Santos	1161	176	165	164	11,917,955	.15	.43
Kent Desormeaux	977	160	168	143	11,676,407	.16	.48

*Percentage in the Money (1st, 2nd, and 3rd).

Trainers

Trainer	Starts	1st	2nd	3rd	Purses ($)	Win Pct	$ Pct*
Robert Frankel	480	117	82	74	17,748,340	.24	.57
Bob Baffert	686	133	113	98	12,029,115	.19	.50
Steven Asmussen	1810	407	320	281	10,248,260	.22	.56
Todd Pletcher	699	147	118	88	8,702,228	.21	.51
Scott Lake	1790	400	303	254	8,307,347	.22	.53
William Mott	710	149	105	104	7,521,998	.21	.50
Kenneth McPeek	469	81	69	57	6,647,289	.17	.44
D. Wayne Lukas	474	82	53	47	5,996,362	.17	.38
Jerry Hollendorfer	1119	265	193	150	5,909,710	.24	.54
Mark Hennig	478	79	71	57	5,814,441	.17	.43

*Percentage in the Money (1st, 2nd, and 3rd).

Owners

Owner	Starts	1st	2nd	3rd	Purses ($)
Stronach Stable	656	122	104	81	8,349,249
The Thoroughbred Corporation	313	69	52	43	7,887,915
Richard Englander	1599	279	258	220	7,530,362
Michael Gill	1424	228	215	171	5,639,292
Juddmonte Farms, Inc.	153	41	29	23	5,172,287
Edward P. Evans	239	52	35	30	4,472,047
Gary Tanaka	154	19	25	16	4,078,701
Edmund A. Gann	85	19	14	19	4,015,522
Sam-Son Farms	202	46	27	29	4,003,749
John Franks	946	150	141	137	3,905,246

HARNESS RACING

Major Stakes Races

Late 2002

Date	Race	Location	Winner	Driver/Trainer	Purse ($)
Oct 19	BC Two-year-old Colt Trot	Woodbine	Broadway Hall	John Campbell/ Jim Campbell	475,000
Oct 19	BC Two-year-old Filly Pace	Woodbine	Armbro Amoretto	Luc Ouellette/ David Smith	522,300
Oct 19	BC Two-year-old Colt Pace	Woodbine	Totally Western	Mario Baillargeon/ Ben Wallace	594,600
Oct 19	BC Two-year-old Filly Trot	Woodbine	Pick Me Up	Luc Ouellette/ Darren McCall	484,600
Oct 19	BC Three-year-old Colt Trot	Woodbine	Kadabra	David S. Miller/ Jimmy Takter	542,500
Oct 19	BC Three-year-old Filly Trot	Woodbine	Cameron Hall	Trevor Ritchie/ Bob Stewart	542,500
Oct 19	BC Three-year-old Filly Pace	Woodbine	Allamerican Nadia	Chris Christoforou/ John W. Burns	500,000
Oct 19	BC Three-year-old Colt Pace	Woodbine	Art Major	John Campbell/ Bill Robinson	500,000
Dec 7	Three Diamonds Filly Pace	Meadowlands	Dream of Mimi	Jack Moiseyev/ Bob McIntosh	370,000
Dec 7	Governor's Cup Colt Pace	Meadowlands	Allamerican Native	John Campbell/ Mark Capone	520,000

2003 (Through September 18)

Date	Race	Location	Winner	Driver/Trainer	Purse ($)
May 31	New Jersey Classic	Meadowlands	Artesian	Mike Lachance Cosmo DePinto	500,000
June 21	North America Cup	Woodbine	Yankee Cruiser	Dean Magee/ Tim Pinske	987,200
July 5	William Haughton Memorial	Meadowlands	McArdle	Mike Lachance/ Chris Ryder	650,000

2003 (Through September 18) (Cont.)

Date	Race	Location	Winner	Driver/Trainer	Purse ($)
July 12	Meadowlands Pace	Meadowlands	Allamerican Theory	Mike Lachance/ Des Tackoor	1,000,000
July 31	Peter Haughton Memorial	Meadowlands	Tom Ridge	Ron Pierce/ Jimmy Takter	440,000
Aug 1	Woodrow Wilson	Meadowlands	Modern Art	David S. Miller Joe Holloway	640,000
Aug 1	Sweetheart Pace	Meadowlands	So Artsi	John Campbell/ Bill Robinson	430,000
Aug 2	Hambletonian	Meadowlands	Amigo Hall	Mike Lachance/ Blair Burgess	1,000,000
Aug 2	Hambletonian Oaks	Meadowlands	Southwind Allaire	Ron Pierce/ Jimmy Takter	500,000
Aug 2	Nat Ray	Meadowlands	Rotation	Trevor Ritchie/ Harald Lunde	450,000
Aug 30	BC Three and up Open Trot	Woodbine	Fool's Goal	Jack Moiseyev/ Jim Doherty	800,000
Aug 30	BC Three and up Mare Pace	Woodbine	Eternal Camnation	Eric Ledford/ Jeff Miller	300,000
Aug 30	BC Three and up Open Pace	Woodbine	Art Major	John Campbell/ Bill Robinson	540,000
Sept 18	Little Brown Jug	Delaware, OH	No Pan Intended	David S. Miller/ Ivan Sugg	605,050

Major Races

The Hambletonian

Raced at The Meadowlands, East Rutherford, NJ, on August 2, 2003

Horse	Driver	PP	¼	½	¾	Stretch	Finish
Amigo Hall	Mike Lachance	6	1/2T	2/1H	3/1H	4/1	1/1
Sugar Trader	Luc Oeullette	5	4/7H	4/7	2°/1Q	1/Q	2/1
Mac's Crown K	Ron Pierce	8	5/9	5/8H	4°/2H	3/T	3/1Q
Incredible Hulk	George Brennan	10x	6/12H	6/10Q	6°/4	5/2Q	4/4Q
Power to Charm	John Campbell	4	3/5	1/1H	1/1Q	2/Q	5/4H
Malabar Millennium	David Miller	3	2/2T	3/3Q	5/4	6x/3	x6x/5H
Bebop	Jimmy Takter	1x	9/dis	8/dis	8/dis	7/25	7/33H
Penn Pronto	Jack Moiseyev	2x	8/dis	7/dis	7/23H	x8x/dis	8/dis
Smooth Glide	James Morrill	x7	7/dis	9/dis	9/dis	9/dis	9/dis
Muscle King	Brian Sears	9x	10/dis	10/dis	10/dis	10/dis	10/dis

Times: 0:28.2, 0:55.4, 1:25.0, 1:54.0.

The Little Brown Jug

Raced at the Delaware County Fairgrounds, in Delaware, OH, on September 18, 2003

Horse	Driver	PP	¼	½	¾	Stretch	Finish
No Pan Intended	David Miller	1	1/1H	1/1H	1/Q	1/NS	1/1
Make It Brief	Ron Pierce	9	2/1H	2/1H	3/1Q	3/1	2/1
Armbro Animate	John Campbell	2	4/5	3°/3H	2°/Q	2/NS	3/1
Whatanartist	Brian Sears	6	7/9Q	7°/6H	5°°/3Q	4/1H	4/1H
Pronger	Keith Oliver	3	3/3H	4/3T	4/2T	5/2H	5/2T
First Foxy	Raymond Paver	5	6/7T	6/6Q	7/4	6/4	6/3T
Yankee Cruiser	Andy Miller	4	5/6H	5°/4T	6°/3T	7/4H	7/5H
Gone West	Jack Moiseyev	7	8/10T	8/7H	8°/4	8/6H	8/6

Time: 0:28.0, 0:57.1, 1:24.4, 1:53.0.

2002 Statistical Leaders

2002 Leading Moneywinners by Age, Sex and Gait

Division	Horse	Starts	1st	2nd	3rd	Earnings ($)
2-Year-Old Pacing Colts	Allamerican Native	14	8	1	1	948,017
2-Year-Old Pacing Fillies	Loyal Opposition	15	14	1	0	886,230
3-Year-Old Pacing Colts	Art Major	31	20	3	2	1,562,779
3-Year-Old Pacing Fillies	Worldly Beauty	15	12	3	0	905,742
Aged Pacing Horses	Real Desire	13	10	1	1	1,059,790
Aged Pacing Mares	Eternal Camnation	21	7	3	3	521,741
2-Year-Old Trotting Colts	Tom Ridge	6	6	0	0	362,500
2-Year-Old Trotting Fillies	Funny Malentine	8	5	2	0	223,750
3-Year-Old Trotting Colts	Amigo Hall	9	4	3	2	596,123
3-Year-Old Trotting Fillies	Southwind Allaire	10	5	2	2	542,871
Aged Trotting Horses	Fool's Goal	11	3	1	5	639,363
Aged Trotting Mares	Hoosier Jewel	13	5	4	1	83,000

Drivers

Driver	Earnings ($)	Driver	Earnings ($)
John Campbell	11,943,027	Chris Christoforou	6,816,393
David Miller	10,578,711	Randall Waples	5,189,526
Luc Ouelette	9,440,669	Mario Baillargeon	5,120,629
Michel Lachance	8,549,281	Anthony Morgan	5,112,006
Ronald Pierce	6,892,780	George Brennan	4,940,181

THEY SAID IT

Barclay Tagg, trainer of Funny Cide, after the horse finished third in the Belmont Stakes, thus failing to complete the Triple Crown: "I don't know what happened, and he won't tell me."

FOR THE RECORD · Year by Year

THOROUGHBRED RACING

Kentucky Derby

Run at Churchill Downs, Louisville, KY, on the first Saturday in May.

Year	Winner (Margin)	Jockey	Second	Third	Time
1875	Aristides (1)	Oliver Lewis	Volcano	Verdigris	2:37¾
1876	Vagrant (2)	Bobby Swim	Creedmoor	Harry Hill	2:38¼
1877	Baden-Baden (2)	William Walker	Leonard	King William	2:38
1878	Day Star (2)	Jimmie Carter	Himyar	Leveler	2:37¼
1879	Lord Murphy (1)	Charlie Shauer	Falsetto	Strathmore	2:37
1880	Fonso (1)	George Lewis	Kimball	Bancroft	2:37½
1881	Hindoo (4)	Jimmy McLaughin	Lelex	Alfambra	2:40
1882	Apollo (½)	Babe Hurd	Runnymede	Bengal	2:40¼
1883	Leonatus (3)	Billy Donohue	Drake Carter	Lord Raglan	2:43
1884	Buchanan (2)	Isaac Murphy	Loftin	Audrain	2:40¼
1885	Joe Cotton (Neck)	Erskine Henderson	Bersan	Ten Booker	2:37¼
1886	Ben Ali (½)	Paul Duffy	Blue Wing	Free Knight	2:36½
1887	Montrose (2)	Isaac Lewis	Jim Gore	Jacobin	2:39¼
1888	MacBeth II (1)	George Covington	Gallifet	White	2:38¼
1889	Spokane (Nose)	Thomas Kiley	Proctor Knott	Once Again	2:34½
1890	Riley (2)	Isaac Murphy	Bill Letcher	Robespierre	2:45
1891	Kingman (1)	Isaac Murphy	Balgowan	High Tariff	2:52¼
1892	Azra (Nose)	Alonzo Clayton	Huron	Phil Dwyer	2:41½
1893	Lookout (5)	Eddie Kunze	Plutus	Boundless	2:39¼
1894	Chant (2)	Frank Goodale	Pearl Song	Sigurd	2:41
1895	Halma (3)	Soup Perkins	Basso	Laureate	2:37½
1896	Ben Brush (Nose)	Willie Simms	Ben Eder	Semper Ego	2:07¼
1897	Typhoon II (Head)	Buttons Garner	Ornament	Dr. Catlett	2:12½
1898	Plaudit (Neck)	Willie Simms	Lieber Karl	Isabey	2:09
1899	Manuel (2)	Fred Taral	Corsini	Mazo	2:12
1900	Lieut. Gibson (4)	Jimmy Boland	Florizar	Thrive	2:06¼
1901	His Eminence (2)	Jimmy Winkfield	Sannazarro	Driscoll	2:07¾
1902	Alan-a-Dale (Nose)	Jimmy Winkfield	Inventor	The Rival	2:08¾
1903	Judge Himes (¾)	Hal Booker	Early	Bourbon	2:09
1904	Elwood (½)	Frankie Prior	Ed Tierney	Brancas	2:08½
1905	Agile (3)	Jack Martin	Ram's Horn	Layson	2:10¾
1906	Sir Huon (2)	Roscoe Troxler	Lady Navarre	James Reddick	2:08⅕
1907	Pink Star (2)	Andy Minder	Zal	Ovelando	2:12⅗
1908	Stone Street (1)	Arthur Pickens	Sir Cleges	Dunvegan	2:15⅕
1909	Wintergreen (4)	Vincent Powers	Miami	Dr. Barkley	2:08⅕
1910	Donau (½)	Fred Herbert	Joe Morris	Fighting Bob	2:06⅖
1911	Meridian (¾)	George Archibald	Governor Gray	Colston	2:05
1912	Worth (Neck)	Carroll H. Schilling	Duval	Flamma	2:09⅖
1913	Donerail (½)	Roscoe Goose	Ten Point	Gowell	2:04⅘
1914	Old Rosebud (8)	John McCabe	Hodge	Bronzewing	2:03⅖
1915	Regret (2)	Joe Notter	Pebbles	Sharpshooter	2:05⅖
1916	George Smith (Neck)	Johnny Loftus	Star Hawk	Franklin	2:04
1917	Omar Khayyam (2)	Charles Borel	Ticket	Midway	2:04⅗
1918	Exterminator (1)	William Knapp	Escoba	Viva America	2:10⅘
1919	Sir Barton (5)	Johnny Loftus	Billy Kelly	Under Fire	2:09⅘
1920	Paul Jones (Head)	Ted Rice	Upset	On Watch	2:09
1921	Behave Yourself (Head)	Charles Thompson	Black Servant	Prudery	2:04⅕
1922	Morvich (½)	Albert Johnson	Bet Mosie	John Finn	2:04⅗
1923	Zev (1½)	Earl Sande	Martingale	Vigil	2:05⅖
1924	Black Gold (½)	John Mooney	Chilhowee	Beau Butler	2:05⅕
1925	Flying Ebony (1½)	Earl Sande	Captain Hal	Son of John	2:07⅗
1926	Bubbling Over (5)	Albert Johnson	Bagenbaggage	Rock Man	2:03⅗
1927	Whiskery (Head)	Linus McAtee	Osmond	Jock	2:06
1928	Reigh Count (3)	Chick Lang	Misstep	Toro	2:10⅖
1929	Clyde Van Dusen (2)	Linus McAtee	Naishapur	Panchio	2:10⅘
1930	Gallant Fox (2)	Earl Sande	Gallant Knight	Ned O.	2:07⅗
1931	Twenty Grand (4)	Charles Kurtsinger	Sweep All	Mate	2:01⅘
1932	Burgoo King (5)	Eugene James	Economic	Stepenfetchit	2:05⅕
1933	Brokers Tip (Nose)	Don Meade	Head Play	Charley O.	2:06⅘
1934	Cavalcade (2½)	Mack Garner	Discovery	Agrarian	2:04
1935	Omaha (1½)	Willie Saunders	Roman Soldier	Whiskolo	2:05
1936	Bold Venture (Head)	Ira Hanford	Brevity	Indian Broom	2:03⅗

Kentucky Derby *(Cont.)*

Year	Winner (Margin)	Jockey	Second	Third	Time
1937	War Admiral (1¾)	Charles Kurtsinger	Pompoon	Reaping Reward	2:03⅕
1938	Lawrin (1)	Eddie Arcaro	Dauber	Can't Wait	2:04⅘
1939	Johnstown (8)	James Stout	Challedon	Heather Broom	2:03⅗
1940	Gallahadion (1½)	Carroll Bierman	Bimelech	Dit	2:05
1941	Whirlaway (8)	Eddie Arcaro	Staretor	Market Wise	2:01⅖
1942	Shut Out (2½)	Wayne Wright	Alsab	Valdina Orphan	2:04⅖
1943	Count Fleet (3)	John Longden	Blue Swords	Slide Rule	2:04
1944	Pensive (4½)	Conn McCreary	Broadcloth	Stir Up	2:04⅕
1945	Hoop Jr. (6)	Eddie Arcaro	Pot o' Luck	Darby Dieppe	2:07
1946	Assault (8)	Warren Mehrtens	Spy Song	Hampden	2:06⅗
1947	Jet Pilot (Head)	Eric Guerin	Phalanx	Faultless	2:06⅘
1948	Citation (3½)	Eddie Arcaro	Coaltown	My Request	2:05⅖
1949	Ponder (3)	Steve Brooks	Capot	Palestinian	2:04⅕
1950	Middleground (1¼)	William Boland	Hill Prince	Mr. Trouble	2:01⅗
1951	Count Turf (4)	Conn McCreary	Royal Mustang	Ruhe	2:02⅗
1952	Hill Gail (2)	Eddie Arcaro	Sub Fleet	Blue Man	2:01⅗
1953	Dark Star (Head)	Hank Moreno	Native Dancer	Invigorator	2:02
1954	Determine (1½)	Ray York	Hasty Road	Hasseyampa	2:03
1955	Swaps (1½)	Bill Shoemaker	Nashua	Summer Tan	2:01⅘
1956	Needles (¾)	Dave Erb	Fabius	Come On Red	2:03⅖
1957	Iron Liege (Nose)	Bill Hartack	Gallant Man	Round Table	2:02⅕
1958	Tim Tam (½)	Ismael Valenzuela	Lincoln Road	Noureddin	2:05
1959	Tomy Lee (Nose)	Bill Shoemaker	Sword Dancer	First Landing	2:02⅕
1960	Venetian Way (3½)	Bill Hartack	Bally Ache	Victoria Park	2:02⅖
1961	Carry Back (¾)	John Sellers	Crozier	Bass Clef	2:04
1962	Decidedly (2¼)	Bill Hartack	Roman Line	Ridan	2:00⅖
1963	Chateaugay (1¼)	Braulio Baeza	Never Bend	Candy Spots	2:01⅘
1964	Northern Dancer (Neck)	Bill Hartack	Hill Rise	The Scoundrel	2:00
1965	Lucky Debonair (Neck)	Bill Shoemaker	Dapper Dan	Tom Rolfe	2:01⅕
1966	Kauai King (½)	Don Brumfield	Advocator	Blue Skyer	2:02
1967	Proud Clarion (1)	Bobby Ussery	Barbs Delight	Damascus	2:00⅗
1968	Forward Pass (Disq.)	Ismael Valenzuela	Francie's Hat	T.V. Commercial	2:02⅕
1969	Majestic Prince (Neck)	Bill Hartack	Arts and Letters	Dike	2:01⅘
1970	Dust Commander (5)	Mike Manganello	My Dad George	High Echelon	2:03⅖
1971	Canonero II (3¾)	Gustavo Avila	Jim French	Bold Reason	2:03⅕
1972	Riva Ridge (3¼)	Ron Turcotte	No Le Hace	Hold Your Peace	2:01⅘
1973	Secretariat (2½)	Ron Turcotte	Sham	Our Native	1:59⅖
1974	Cannonade (2¼)	Angel Cordero Jr.	Hudson County	Agitate	2:04
1975	Foolish Pleasure (1¾)	Jacinto Vasquez	Avatar	Diabolo	2:02
1976	Bold Forbes (1)	Angel Cordero Jr.	Honest Pleasure	Elocutionist	2:01⅗
1977	Seattle Slew (1¾)	Jean Cruguet	Run Dusty Run	Sanhedrin	2:02⅕
1978	Affirmed (1½)	Steve Cauthen	Alydar	Believe It	2:01⅕
1979	Spectacular Bid (2¾)	Ronald J. Franklin	General Assembly	Golden Act	2:02⅖
1980	Genuine Risk (1)	Jacinto Vasquez	Rumbo	Jaklin Klugman	2:02
1981	Pleasant Colony (¾)	Jorge Velasquez	Woodchopper	Partez	2:02
1982	Gato Del Sol (2½)	Eddie Delahoussaye	Laser Light	Reinvested	2:02⅕
1983	Sunny's Halo (2)	Eddie Delahoussaye	Desert Wine	Caveat	2:02⅕
1984	Swale (3¼)	Laffit Pincay Jr.	Coax Me Chad	At the Threshold	2:02⅖
1985	Spend A Buck (5)	Angel Cordero Jr.	Stephan's Odyssey	Chief's Crown	2:00⅕
1986	Ferdinand (2¼)	Bill Shoemaker	Bold Arrangement	Broad Brush	2:02⅘
1987	Alysheba (¾)	Chris McCarron	Bet Twice	Avies Copy	2:03⅖
1988	Winning Colors (Neck)	Gary Stevens	Forty Niner	Risen Star	2:02⅕
1989	Sunday Silence (2½)	Pat Valenzuela	Easy Goer	Awe Inspiring	2:05
1990	Unbridled (3½)	Craig Perret	Summer Squall	Pleasant Tap	2:02
1991	Strike the Gold (1¾)	Chris Antley	Best Pal	Mane Minister	2:03
1992	Lil E. Tee (1)	Pat Day	Casual Lies	Dance Floor	2:03
1993	Sea Hero (2½)	Jerry Bailey	Prairie Bayou	Wild Gale	2:02⅖
1994	Go for Gin (2½)	Chris McCarron	Strodes Creek	Blumin Affair	2:03⅗
1995	Thunder Gulch (2¼)	Gary Stevens	Tejano Run	Timber Country	2:01⅕
1996	Grindstone (Nose)	Jerry Bailey	Cavonnier	Prince of Thieves	2:01
1997	Silver Charm (Head)	Gary Stevens	Captain Bodgit	Free House	2:02⅖
1998	Real Quiet (½)	Kent Desormeaux	Victory Gallop	Indian Charlie	2:02⅒
1999	Charismatic (Neck)	Chris Antley	Menifee	Cat Thief	2:03⅕
2000	Fusaichi Pegasus (1½)	Kent Desormeaux	Aptitude	Impeachment	2:01.12
2001	Monarchos (4¾)	Jorge Chavez	Invisible Ink	Congaree	1:59.97
2002	War Emblem (4)	Victor Espinoza	Proud Citizen	Perfect Drift	2:01.13
2003	Funny Cide (1¾)	Jose Santos	Empire Maker	Peace Rules	2:01.19

Note: Distance: 1½ miles (1875–95), 1¼ miles (1896–present).

Preakness

Run at Pimlico Race Course, Baltimore, Md., two weeks after the Kentucky Derby.

Year	Winner (Margin)	Jockey	Second	Third	Time
1873	Survivor (10)	G. Barbee	John Boulger	Artist	2:43
1874	Culpepper (¾)	W. Donohue	King Amadeus	Scratch	2:56½
1875	Tom Ochiltree (2)	L. Hughes	Viator	Bay Final	2:43½
1876	Shirley (4)	G. Barbee	Rappahannock	Algerine	2:44¾
1877	Cloverbrook (4)	C. Holloway	Bombast	Lucifer	2:45½
1878	Duke of Magenta (6)	C. Holloway	Bayard	Albert	2:41¾
1879	Harold (3)	L. Hughes	Jericho	Rochester	2:40½
1880	Grenada (¾)	L. Hughes	Oden	Emily F.	2:40½
1881	Saunterer (½)	T. Costello	Compensation	Baltic	2:40½
1882	Vanguard (Neck)	T. Costello	Heck	Col Watson	2:44½
1883*	Jacobus (4)	G. Barbee	Parnell		2:42½
1884*	Knight of Ellerslie (2)	S. Fisher	Welcher		2:39½
1885	Tecumseh (2)	Jim McLaughlin	Wickham	John C.	2:49
1886	The Bard (3)	S. Fisher	Eurus	Elkwood	2:45
1887	Dunboyne (1)	W. Donohue	Mahoney	Raymond	2:39½
1888	Refund (3)	F. Littlefield	Judge Murray	Glendale	2:49
1889*	Buddhist (8)	W. Anderson	Japhet	*	2:17½
1890*	Montague (3)	W. Martin	Philosophy	Barrister	2:36¾
1894	Assignee (3)	Fred Taral	Potentate	Ed Kearney	1:49¼
1895	Belmar (1)	Fred Taral	April Fool	Sue Kittie	1:50½
1896	Margrave (1)	H. Griffin	Hamilton II	Intermission	1:51
1897	Paul Kauvar (1½)	C. Thorpe	Elkins	On Deck	1:51¼
1898	Sly Fox (2)	C. W. Simms	The Huguenot	Nuto	1:49⅗
1899	Half Time (1)	R. Clawson	Filigrane	Lackland	1:47
1900	Hindus (Head)	H. Spencer	Sarmation	Ten Candles	1:48⅖
1901	The Parader (2)	F. Landry	Sadie S.	Dr. Barlow	1:47⅕
1902	Old England (Nose)	L. Jackson	Major Daingerfield	Namtor	1:45⅘
1903	Flocarline (½)	W. Gannon	Mackey Dwyer	Rightful	1:44⅘
1904	Bryn Mawr (1)	E. Hildebrand	Wotan	Dolly Spanker	1:44⅕
1905	Cairngorm (Head)	W. Davis	Kiamesha	Coy Maid	1:45⅘
1906	Whimsical (4)	Walter Miller	Content	Larabie	1:45
1907	Don Enrique (1)	G. Mountain	Ethon	Zambesi	1:45⅖
1908	Royal Tourist (4)	E. Dugan	Live Wire	Robert Cooper	1:46⅖
1909	Effendi (1)	Willie Doyle	Fashion Plate	Hilltop	1:39⅘
1910	Layminster (½)	R. Estep	Dalhousie	Sager	1:40⅗
1911	Watervale (1)	E. Dugan	Zeus	The Nigger	1:51
1912	Colonel Holloway (5)	C. Turner	Bwana Tumbo	Tipsand	1:56⅗
1913	Buskin (Neck)	J. Butwell	Kleburne	Barnegat	1:53⅖
1914	Holiday (¾)	A. Schuttinger	Brave Cunarder	Defendum	1:53⅘
1915	Rhine Maiden (1½)	Douglas Hoffman	Half Rock	Runes	1:58
1916	Damrosch (1½)	Linus McAtee	Greenwood	Achievement	1:54⅘
1917	Kalitan (2)	E. Haynes	Al M. Dick	Kentucky Boy	1:54⅖
1918*	War Cloud (¾)	Johnny Loftus	Sunny Slope	Lanius	1:53⅗
1918*	Jack Hare, Jr (2)	C. Peak	The Porter	Kate Bright	1:53⅖
1919	Sir Barton (4)	Johnny Loftus	Eternal	Sweep On	1:53
1920	Man o' War (1½)	Clarence Kummer	Upset	Wildair	1:51⅗
1921	Broomspun (¾)	F. Coltiletti	Polly Ann	Jeg	1:54⅕
1922	Pillory (Head)	L. Morris	Hea	June Grass	1:51⅗
1923	Vigil (1¼)	B. Marinelli	General Thatcher	Rialto	1:53⅗
1924	Nellie Morse (1½)	J. Merimee	Transmute	Mad Play	1:57⅕
1925	Coventry (4)	Clarence Kummer	Backbone	Almadel	1:59
1926	Display (Head)	J. Maiben	Blondin	Mars	1:59⅘
1927	Bostonian (½)	A. Abel	Sir Harry	Whiskery	2:01⅗
1928	Victorian (Nose)	Sonny Workman	Toro	Solace	2:00⅕
1929	Dr. Freeland (1)	Louis Schaefer	Minotaur	African	2:01⅗
1930	Gallant Fox (¾)	Earl Sande	Crack Brigade	Snowflake	2:00⅗
1931	Mate (1½)	G. Ellis	Twenty Grand	Ladder	1:59
1932	Burgoo King (Head)	E. James	Tick On	Boatswain	1:59⅘
1933	Head Play (4)	Charles Kurtsinger	Ladysman	Utopian	2:02
1934	High Quest (Nose)	R. Jones	Cavalcade	Discovery	1:58⅕
1935	Omaha (6)	Willie Saunders	Firethorn	Psychic Bid	1:58⅖
1936	Bold Venture (Nose)	George Woolf	Granville	Jean Bart	1:59
1937	War Admiral (Head)	Charles Kurtsinger	Pompoon	Flying Scot	1:58⅖
1938	Dauber (7)	M. Peters	Cravat	Menow	1:59⅘
1939	Challedon (1¼)	George Seabo	Gilded Knight	Volitant	1:59⅘
1940	Bimelech (3)	F. A. Smith	Mioland	Gallahadion	1:58⅗

Preakness (Cont.)

Year	Winner (Margin)	Jockey	Second	Third	Time
1941	Whirlaway (5½)	Eddie Arcaro	King Cole	Our Boots	1:58⅘
1942	Alsab (1)	B. James	Requested Sun Again	(dead heat for second)	1:57
1943	Count Fleet (8)	Johnny Longden	Blue Swords	Vincentive	1:57⅖
1944	Pensive (¾)	Conn McCreary	Platter	Stir Up	1:59⅕
1945	Polynesian (2½)	W. D. Wright	Hoop Jr.	Darby Dieppe	1:58⅘
1946	Assault (Neck)	Warren Mehrtens	Lord Boswell	Hampden	2:01⅖
1947	Faultless (1¼)	Doug Dodson	On Trust	Phalanx	1:59
1948	Citation (5½)	Eddie Arcaro	Vulcan's Forge	Boyard	2:02⅖
1949	Capot (Head)	Ted Atkinson	Palestinian	Noble Impulse	1:56
1950	Hill Prince (5)	Eddie Arcaro	Middleground	Dooley	1:59⅕
1951	Bold (7)	Eddie Arcaro	Counterpoint	Alerted	1:56⅖
1952	Blue Man (3½)	Conn McCreary	Jampol	One Count	1:57⅖
1953	Native Dancer (Neck)	Eric Guerin	Jamie K.	Royal Bay Gem	1:57⅘
1954	Hasty Road (Neck)	Johnny Adams	Correlation	Hasseyampa	1:57⅖
1955	Nashua (1)	Eddie Arcaro	Saratoga	Traffic Judge	1:54⅗
1956	Fabius (¾)	Bill Hartack	Needles	No Regrets	1:58⅖
1957	Bold Ruler (2)	Eddie Arcaro	Iron Liege	Inside Tract	1:56⅕
1958	Tim Tam (1½)	I. Valenzuela	Lincoln Road	Gone Fishin'	1:57⅕
1959	Royal Orbit (4)	William Harmatz	Sword Dancer	Dunce	1:57
1960	Bally Ache (4)	Bobby Ussery	Victoria Park	Celtic Ash	1:57⅗
1961	Carry Back (¾)	Johnny Sellers	Globemaster	Crozier	1:57⅗
1962	Greek Money (Nose)	John Rotz	Ridan	Roman Line	1:56⅕
1963	Candy Spots (3½)	Bill Shoemaker	Chateaugay	Never Bend	1:56⅕
1964	Northern Dancer (2¼)	Bill Hartack	The Scoundrel	Hill Rise	1:56⅘
1965	Tom Rolfe (Neck)	Ron Turcotte	Dapper Dan	Hail to All	1:56⅕
1966	Kauai King (1¾)	Don Brumfield	Stupendous	Amberoid	1:55⅖
1967	Damascus (2¼)	Bill Shoemaker	In Reality	Proud Clarion	1:55⅕
1968	Forward Pass (6)	I. Valenzuela	Out of the Way	Nodouble	1:56⅘
1969	Majestic Prince (Head)	Bill Hartack	Arts and Letters	Jay Ray	1:55⅗
1970	Personality (Neck)	Eddie Belmonte	My Dad George	Silent Screen	1:56⅕
1971	Canonero II (1½)	Gustavo Avila	Eastern Fleet	Jim French	1:54
1972	Bee Bee Bee (1¼)	Eldon Nelson	No Le Hace	Key to the Mint	1:55⅗
1973	Secretariat (2½)	Ron Turcotte	Sham	Our Native	1:54⅖
1974	Little Current (7)	Miguel Rivera	Neapolitan Way	Cannonade	1:54⅗
1975	Master Derby (1)	Darrel McHargue	Foolish Pleasure	Diabolo	1:56⅖
1976	Elocutionist (3)	John Lively	Play the Red	Bold Forbes	1:55
1977	Seattle Slew (1½)	Jean Cruguet	Iron Constitution	Run Dusty Run	1:54⅖
1978	Affirmed (Neck)	Steve Cauthen	Alydar	Believe It	1:54⅖
1979	Spectacular Bid (5½)	Ron Franklin	Golden Act	Screen King	1:54⅕
1980	Codex (4¾)	Angel Cordero Jr.	Genuine Risk	Colonel Moran	1:54⅕
1981	Pleasant Colony (1)	Jorge Velasquez	Bold Ego	Paristo	1:54⅗
1982	Aloma's Ruler (½)	Jack Kaenel	Linkage	Cut Away	1:55⅖
1983	Deputed Testamony (2¾)	Donald Miller Jr.	Desert Wine	High Honors	1:55⅖
1984	Gate Dancer (1½)	Angel Cordero Jr.	Play On	Fight Over	1:53⅗
1985	Tank's Prospect (Head)	Pat Day	Chief's Crown	Eternal Prince	1:53⅖
1986	Snow Chief (4)	Alex Solis	Ferdinand	Broad Brush	1:54⅘
1987	Alysheba (½)	Chris McCarron	Bet Twice	Cryptoclearance	1:55⅘
1988	Risen Star (1¼)	E. Delahoussaye	Brian's Time	Winning Colors	1:56⅕
1989	Sunday Silence (Nose)	Pat Valenzuela	Easy Goer	Rock Point	1:53⅘
1990	Summer Squall (2¼)	Pat Day	Unbridled	Mister Frisky	1:53⅗
1991	Hansel (Head)	Jerry Bailey	Corporate Report	Mane Minister	1:54
1992	Pine Bluff (¾)	Chris McCarron	Alydeed	Casual Lies	1:55⅗
1993	Prairie Bayou (½)	Mike Smith	Cherokee Run	El Bakan	1:56⅗
1994	Tabasco Cat (¾)	Pat Day	Go For Gin	Concern	1:56⅖
1995	Timber Country (½)	Pat Day	Oliver's Twist	Thunder Gulch	1:54⅖
1996	Louis Quatorze (3¼)	Pat Day	Skip Away	Editor's Note	1:53⅖
1997	Silver Charm (Head)	Gary Stevens	Free House	Captain Bodgit	1:54⅖
1998	Real Quiet (2¼)	Kent Desormeaux	Victory Gallop	Classic Cat	1:54⅗
1999	Charismatic (1½)	Chris Antley	Menifee	Badge	1:55⅕
2000	Red Bullet (3¾)	Jerry Bailey	Fusaichi Pegasus	Impeachment	1:56.04
2001	Point Given (2¼)	Gary Stevens	A P Valentine	Congaree	1:55.51
2002	War Emblem (¾)	Victor Espinoza	Magic Weisner	Proud Citizen	1:56.36
2003	Funny Cide (9¾)	Jose Santos	Midway Road	Scrimshaw	1:55.61

*Preakness was a two-horse race in 1883, '84 and '89. It was not run 1891–1893; and in 1918, it was run in two divisions.

Note: Distance: 1½ miles (1873–88), 1¼ miles (1889), 1½ miles (1890), 1¹⁄₁₆ miles (1894–1900), 1 mile and 70 yards (1901–1907), 1¹⁄₁₆ miles (1908), 1 mile (1909–10), 1⅛ miles (1911–24), 1³⁄₁₆ miles (1925–present).

Belmont

Run at Belmont Park, Elmont, NY, three weeks after the Preakness Stakes. Held previously at two locations in the Bronx (NY): Jerome Park (1867–1889) and Morris Park (1890–1904).

Year	Winner (Margin)	Jockey	Second	Third	Time
1867	Ruthless (Head)	J. Gilpatrick	De Courcy	Rivoli	3:05
1868	General Duke (2)	R. Swim	Northumberland	Fannie Ludlow	3:02
1869	Fenian (Unknown)	C. Miller	Glenelg	Invercauld	3:04¼
1870	Kingfisher (½)	E. Brown	Foster	Midday	2:59½
1871	Harry Bassett (3)	W. Miller	Stockwood	By-the-Sea	2:56
1872	Joe Daniels (¾)	James Rowe	Meteor	Shylock	2:58¼
1873	Springbok (4)	James Rowe	Count d'Orsay	Strachino	3:01¾
1874	Saxon (Neck)	G. Barbee	Grinstead	Aaron Pennington	2:39½
1875	Calvin (2)	R. Swim	Aristides	Milner	2:40¼
1876	Algerine (Head)	W. Donahue	Fiddlestick	Barricade	2:40½
1877	Cloverbrook (1)	C. Holloway	Loiterer	Baden-Baden	2:46
1878	Duke of Magenta (2)	L. Hughes	Bramble	Sparta	2:43½
1879	Spendthrift (5)	S. Evans	Monitor	Jericho	2:42¾
1880	Grenada (½)	L. Hughes	Ferncliffe	Turenne	2:47
1881	Saunterer (Neck)	T. Costello	Eole	Baltic	2:47
1882	Forester (5)	James McLaughlin	Babcock	Wyoming	2:43
1883	George Kinney (2)	James McLaughlin	Trombone	Renegade	2:42½
1884	Panique (½)	James McLaughlin	Knight of Ellerslie	Himalaya	2:42
1885	Tyrant (3½)	Paul Duffy	St. Augustine	Tecumseh	2:43
1886	Inspector B (1)	James McLaughlin	The Bard	Linden	2:41
1887*	Hanover (28-32)	James McLaughlin	Oneko		2:43½
1888*	Sir Dixon (12)	James McLaughlin	Prince Royal		2:40¼
1889	Eric (Head)	W. Hayward	Diable	Zephyrus	2:47
1890	Burlington (1)	S. Barnes	Devotee	Padishah	2:07¾
1891	Foxford (Neck)	E. Garrison	Montana	Laurestan	2:08¾
1892*	Patron (Unknown)	W. Hayward	Shellbark		2:17
1893	Comanche (Head)	Willie Simms	Dr. Rice	Rainbow	1:53¼
1894	Henry of Navarre (2-4)	Willie Simms	Prig	Assignee	1:56½
1895	Belmar (Head)	Fred Taral	Counter Tenor	Nanki Pooh	2:11½
1896	Hastings (Neck)	H. Griffin	Handspring	Hamilton II	2:24½
1897	Scottish Chieftain (1)	J. Scherrer	On Deck	Octagon	2:23¼
1898	Bowling Brook (8)	P. Littlefield	Previous	Hamburg	2:32
1899	Jean Bereaud (Head)	R. R. Clawson	Half Time	Glengar	2:23
1900	Ildrim (Head)	N. Turner	Petrucio	Missionary	2:21½
1901	Commando (½)	H. Spencer	The Parader	All Green	2:21
1902	Masterman (2)	John Bullmann	Ranald	King Hanover	2:22½
1903	Africander (2)	John Bullmann	Whorler	Red Knight	2:23⅕
1904	Delhi (3½)	George Odom	Graziallo	Rapid Water	2:06⅗
1905	Tanya (1/2)	E. Hildebrand	Blandy	Hot Shot	2:08
1906	Burgomaster (4)	L. Lyne	The Quail	Accountant	2:20
1907	Peter Pan (1)	G. Mountain	Superman	Frank Gill	Unknown
1908	Colin (Head)	Joe Notter	Fair Play	King James	Unknown
1909	Joe Madden (8)	E. Dugan	Wise Mason	Donald MacDonald	2:21⅗
1910*	Sweep (6)	J. Butwell	Duke of Ormonde		2:22
1913	Prince Eugene (½)	Roscoe Troxler	Rock View	Flying Fairy	2:18
1914	Luke McLuke (8)	M. Buxton	Gainer	Charlestonian	2:20
1915	The Finn (4)	G. Byrne	Half Rock	Pebbles	2:18⅖
1916	Friar Rock (3)	E. Haynes	Spur	Churchill	2:22
1917	Hourless (10)	J. Butwell	Skeptic	Wonderful	2:17⅘
1918	Johren (2)	Frank Robinson	War Cloud	Cum Sah	2:20⅖
1919	Sir Barton (5)	Johnny Loftus	Sweep On	Natural Bridge	2:17⅖
1920*	Man o' War (20)	Clarence Kummer	Donnacona		2:14⅕
1921	Grey Lag (3)	Earl Sande	Sporting Blood	Leonardo II	2:16⅘
1922	Pillory (2)	C. H. Miller	Snob II	Hea	2:18⅘
1923	Zev (1½)	Earl Sande	Chickvale	Rialto	2:19
1924	Mad Play (2)	Earl Sande	Mr. Mutt	Modest	2:18⅘
1925	American Flag (8)	Albert Johnson	Dangerous	Swope	2:16⅘
1926	Crusader (1)	Albert Johnson	Espino	Haste	2:32⅕
1927	Chance Shot (1½)	Earl Sande	Bois de Rose	Flambino	2:32⅖
1928	Vito (3)	Clarence Kummer	Genie	Diavolo	2:33⅕
1929	Blue Larkspur (¾)	Mack Garner	African	Jack High	2:32⅘
1930	Gallant Fox (3)	Earl Sande	Whichone	Questionnaire	2:31⅗

Belmont (Cont.)

Year	Winner (Margin)	Jockey	Second	Third	Time
1931	Twenty Grand (10)	Charles Kurtsinger	Sun Meadow	Jamestown	2:29⅗
1932	Faireno (1½)	T. Malley	Osculator	Flag Pole	2:32⅘
1933	Hurryoff (1½)	Mack Garner	Nimbus	Union	2;32⅗
1934	Peace Chance (6)	W. D. Wright	High Quest	Good Goods	2:29⅕
1935	Omaha (1½)	Willie Saunders	Firethorn	Rosemont	2:30⅗
1936	Granville (Nose)	James Stout	Mr. Bones	Hollyrood	2:30
1937	War Admiral (3)	Charles Kurtsinger	Sceneshifter	Vamoose	2:28⅗
1938	Pasteurized (Neck)	James Stout	Dauber	Cravat	2:29⅖
1939	Johnstown (5)	James Stout	Belay	Gilded Knight	2:29⅗
1940	Bimelech (¾)	F. A. Smith	Your Chance	Andy K	2:29⅗
1941	Whirlaway (2½)	Eddie Arcaro	Robert Morris	Yankee Chance	2:31
1942	Shut Out (2)	Eddie Arcaro	Alsab	Lochinvar	2:29⅕
1943	Count Fleet (25)	Johnny Longden	Fairy Manhurst	Deseronto	2:28⅕
1944	Bounding Home (½)	G. L. Smith	Pensive	Bull Dandy	2:32⅕
1945	Pavot (5)	Eddie Arcaro	Wildlife	Jeep	2:30⅕
1946	Assault (3)	Warren Mehrtens	Natchez	Cable	2:30⅘
1947	Phalanx (5)	R. Donoso	Tide Rips	Tailspin	2:29⅖
1948	Citation (8)	Eddie Arcaro	Better Self	Escadru	2:28⅕
1949	Capot (½)	Ted Atkinson	Ponder	Palestinian	2:30⅕
1950	Middleground (1)	William Boland	Lights Up	Mr. Trouble	2:28⅗
1951	Counterpoint (4)	D. Gorman	Battlefield	Battle Morn	2:29
1952	One Count (2½)	Eddie Arcaro	Blue Man	Armageddon	2:30⅕
1953	Native Dancer (Neck)	Eric Guerin	Jamie K.	Royal Bay Gem	2:38⅗
1954	High Gun (Neck)	Eric Guerin	Fisherman	Limelight	2:30⅘
1955	Nashua (9)	Eddie Arcaro	Blazing Count	Portersville	2:29
1956	Needles (Neck)	David Erb	Career Boy	Fabius	2:29⅘
1957	Gallant Man (8)	Bill Shoemaker	Inside Tract	Bold Ruler	2:26⅗
1958	Cavan (6)	Pete Anderson	Tim Tam	Flamingo	2:30⅕
1959	Sword Dancer (¾)	Bill Shoemaker	Bagdad	Royal Orbit	2:28⅖
1960	Celtic Ash (5½)	Bill Hartack	Venetian Way	Disperse	2:29⅗
1961	Sherluck (2¼)	Braulio Baeza	Globemaster	Guadalcanal	2:29⅕
1962	Jaipur (Nose)	Bill Shoemaker	Admiral's Voyage	Crimson Satan	2:28⅘
1963	Chateaugay (2½)	Braulio Baeza	Candy Spots	Choker	2:30⅕
1964	Quadrangle (2)	Manuel Ycaza	Roman Brother	Northern Dancer	2:28⅖
1965	Hail to All (Neck)	John Sellers	Tom Rolfe	First Family	2:28⅖
1966	Amberold (2½)	William Boland	Buffle	Advocator	2:29⅗
1967	Damascus (2½)	Bill Shoemaker	Cool Reception	Gentleman James	2:28⅘
1968	Stage Door Johnny (1¼)	Hellodoro Gustines	Forward Pass	Call Me Prince	2:27⅕
1969	Arts and Letters (5½)	Braulio Baeza	Majestic Prince	Dike	2:28⅘
1970	High Echelon (¾)	John L. Rotz	Needles N Pins	Naskra	2:34
1971	Pass Catcher (¾)	Walter Blum	Jim French	Bold Reason	2:30⅖
1972	Riva Ridge (7)	Ron Turcotte	Ruritania	Cloudy Dawn	2:28
1973	Secretariat (31)	Ron Turcotte	Twice a Prince	My Gallant	2:24
1974	Little Current (7)	Miguel A. Rivera	Jolly Johu	Cannonade	2:29⅕
1975	Avatar (Neck)	Bill Shoemaker	Foolish Pleasure	Master Derby	2:28⅕
1976	Bold Forbes (Neck)	Angel Cordero Jr.	McKenzie Bridge	Great Contractor	2:29
1977	Seattle Slew (4)	Jean Cruguet	Run Dusty Run	Sanhedrin	2:29⅗
1978	Affirmed (Head)	Steve Cauthen	Alydar	Darby Creek Road	2:26⅘
1979	Coastal (3¼)	Ruben Hernandez	Golden Act	Spectacular Bid	2:28⅗
1980	Temperence Hill (2)	Eddie Maple	Genuine Risk	Rockhill Native	2:29⅘
1981	Summing (Neck)	George Martens	Highland Blade	Pleasant Colony	2:29
1982	Conquistador Cielo (14½)	Laffit Pincay, Jr.	Gato Del Sol	Illuminate	2:28⅕
1983	Caveat (3½)	Laffit Pincay Jr.	Slew o'Gold	Barberstown	2:27⅘
1984	Swale (4)	Laffit Pincay Jr.	Pine Circle	Morning Bob	2:27⅕
1985	Creme Fraiche (½)	Eddie Maple	Stephan's Odyssey	Chief's Crown	2:27
1986	Danzig Connection (1¼)	Chris McCarron	Johns Treasure	Ferdinand	2:29⅘
1987	Bet Twice (14)	Craig Perret	Cryptoclearance	Gulch	2:28⅕
1988	Risen Star (14¾)	Eddie Delahoussaye	Kingpost	Brian's Time	2:26⅖
1989	Easy Goer (8)	Pat Day	Sunday Silence	Le Voyageur	2:26
1990	Go and Go (8¼)	Michael Kinane	Thirty Six Red	Baron de Vaux	2:27⅕
1991	Hansel (Head)	Jerry Bailey	Strike the Gold	Mane Minister	2:28
1992	A.P. Indy (¾)	Eddie Delahoussaye	My Memoirs	Pine Bluff	2:26
1993	Colonial Affair (2¼)	Julie Krone	Kissin Kris	Wild Gale	2:29⅘

Belmont (Cont.)

Year	Winner (Margin)	Jockey	Second	Third	Time
1994	Tabasco Cat (2)	Pat Day	Go For Gin	Strodes Creek	2:26⅘
1995	Thunder Gulch (2)	Gary Stevens	Star Standard	Citadeed	2:32
1996	Editor's Note (1)	Rene Douglas	Skip Away	My Flag	2:28⅘
1997	Touch Gold (¾)	Chris McCarron	Silver Charm	Free House	2:28⅘
1998	Victory Gallop (Nose)	Gary Stevens	Real Quiet	Thomas Jo	2:28⅘
1999	Lemon Drop Kid (Head)	Jose Santos	Vision and Verse	Charismatic	2:27⅘
2000	Commendable (1½)	Pat Day	Aptitude	Unshaded	2:31.19
2001	Point Given (12¼)	Gary Stevens	A P Valentine	Monarchos	2:26.56
2002	Sarava (½)	Edgar Prado	Medaglia d'Oro	Sunday Break	2:29.71
2003	Empire Maker (¾)	Jerry Bailey	Ten Most Wanted	Funny Cide	2:28.26

*Belmont was a two-horse race in 1887, '88, '92, 1910 and '20; and was not held in 1911–1912.

Note: Distance: 1 mile 5 furlongs (1867–89), 1¼ miles (1890–1905), 1⅜ miles (1906–25), 1½ miles (1926–present).

Triple Crown Winners

Year	Horse	Jockey	Owner	Trainer
1919	Sir Barton	John Loftus	J. K. L. Ross	H. G. Bedwell
1930	Gallant Fox	Earle Sande	Belair Stud	James Fitzsimmons
1935	Omaha	William Saunders	Belair Stud	James Fitzsimmons
1937	War Admiral	Charles Kurtsinger	Samuel D. Riddle	George Conway
1941	Whirlaway	Eddie Arcaro	Calumet Farm	Ben Jones
1943	Count Fleet	John Longden	Mrs J. D. Hertz	Don Cameron
1946	Assault	Warren Mehrtens	King Ranch	Max Hirsch
1948	Citation	Eddie Arcaro	Calumet Farm	Jimmy Jones
1973	Secretariat	Ron Turcotte	Meadow Stable	Lucien Laurin
1977	Seattle Slew	Jean Cruguet	Karen L. Taylor	William H. Turner Jr.
1978	Affirmed	Steve Cauthen	Harbor View Farm	Laz Barrera

Legends of the Fall

The Hall of Fame riding careers of Laffit Pincay Jr., 56, and Julie Krone, 39, were threatened in March 2003, when both riders suffered seperate falls at Santa Anita. incay, the winningest jockey in history with 9,531 victories, was placed in a halo cast for eight weeks; he sustained two fractures to a bone in his neck when his mount, Trampus Too, clipped heels with another horse and went down on March 1. "I wouldn't count him out, said his agent, Bob Meldahl. "He heals better than anyone." Krone, the winningest female jockey ever, returned to riding in November after a 3½-year hiatus. She was thrown on March 8 when her horse, Sublet, stumbled and sent he tumbling over his head. She sustained two broken bones in her lower back and two fractured vertebrae, and was out of action for close to three months.

In the aftermath of his injuries, Pincay announced his retirement, but in the world of horse racing, like boxing, retirements have a way of being short lived. Just ask Krone, who had announced her retirement in 1999.

Horse of the Year

Year	Horse	Owner	Trainer	Breeder
1936	Granville	Belair Stud	James Fitzsimmons	Belair Stud
1937	War Admiral	Samuel D. Riddle	George Conway	Mrs. Samuel D. Riddle
1938	Seabiscuit	Charles S. Howard	Tom Smith	Wheatley Stable
1939	Challedon	William L. Brann	Louis J. Schaefer	Branncastle Farm
1940	Challedon	William L. Brann	Louis J. Schaefer	Branncastle Farm
1941	Whirlaway	Calumet Farm	Ben Jones	Calumet Farm
1942	Whirlaway	Calumet Farm	Ben Jones	Calumet Farm
1943	Count Fleet	Mrs. John D. Hertz	Don Cameron	Mrs. John D. Hertz
1944	Twilight Tear	Calumet Farm	Ben Jones	Calumet Farm
1945	Busher	Louis B. Mayer	George Odom	Idle Hour Stock Farm
1946	Assault	King Ranch	Max Hirsch	King Ranch
1947	Armed	Calumet Farm	Jimmy Jones	Calumet Farm
1948	Citation	Calumet Farm	Jimmy Jones	Calumet Farm
1949	Capot	Greentree Stable	John M. Gaver Sr.	Greentree Stable
1950	Hill Prince	C.T. Chenery	Casey Hayes	C.T. Chenery
1951	Counterpoint	C.V. Whitney	Syl Veitch	C.V. Whitney
1952	One Count	Mrs. W. M. Jeffords	O. White	W M. Jeffords
1953	Tom Fool	Greentree Stable	John M. Gaver Sr.	D.A. Headley
1954	Native Dancer	A.G. Vanderbilt	Bill Winfrey	A.G. Vanderbilt
1955	Nashua	Belair Stud	James Fitzsimmons	Belair Stud
1956	Swaps	Ellsworth-Galbreath	Mesh Tenney	R. Ellsworth
1957	Bold Ruler	Wheatley Stable	James Fitzsimmons	Wheatley Stable
1958	Round Table	Kerr Stables	Willy Molter	Claiborne Farm
1959	Sword Dancer	Brookmeade Stable	Elliott Burch	Brookmeade Stable
1960	Kelso	Bohemia Stable	C. Hanford	Mrs. R.C. duPont
1961	Kelso	Bohemia Stable	C. Hanford	Mrs. R.C. duPont
1962	Kelso	Bohemia Stable	C. Hanford	Mrs. R.C. duPont
1963	Kelso	Bohemia Stable	C. Hanford	Mrs. R.C. duPont
1964	Kelso	Bohemia Stable	C. Hanford	Mrs. R.C. duPont
1965	Roman Brother	Harbor View Stable	Burley Parke	Ocala Stud
1966	Buckpasser	Ogden Phipps	Eddie Neloy	Ogden Phipps
1967	Damascus	Mrs. E. W. Bancroft	Frank Y. Whiteley Jr.	Mrs. E. W. Bancroft
1968	Dr. Fager	Tartan Stable	John A. Nerud	Tartan Farms
1969	Arts and Letters	Rokeby Stable	Elliott Burch	Paul Mellon
1970	Fort Marcy	Rokeby Stable	Elliott Burch	Paul Mellon
1971	Ack Ack	E.E. Fogelson	Charlie Whittingham	H.F. Guggenheim
1972	Secretariat	Meadow Stable	Lucien Laurin	Meadow Stud
1973	Secretariat	Meadow Stable	Lucien Laurin	Meadow Stud
1974	Forego	Lazy F Ranch	Sherrill W. Ward	Lazy F Ranch
1975	Forego	Lazy F Ranch	Sherrill W. Ward	Lazy F Ranch
1976	Forego	Lazy F Ranch	Frank Y. Whiteley Jr.	Lazy F Ranch
1977	Seattle Slew	Karen L. Taylor	Billy Turner Jr.	B.S. Castleman
1978	Affirmed	Harbor View Farm	Laz Barrera	Harbor View Farm
1979	Affirmed	Harbor View Farm	Laz Barrera	Harbor View Farm
1980	Spectacular Bid	Hawksworth Farm	Bud Delp	Mmes. Gilmore and Jason
1981	John Henry	Dotsam Stable	Ron McAnally and Lefty Nickerson	Golden Chance Farm
1982	Conquistador Cielo	H. de Kwiatkowski	Woody Stephens	L.E. Landoli
1983	All Along	Daniel Wildenstein	P.L. Biancone	Dayton
1984	John Henry	Dotsam Stable	Ron McAnally	Golden Chance Farm
1985	Spend a Buck	Hunter Farm	Cam Gambolati	Irish Hill & R.W. Harper
1986	Lady's Secret	Mr. & Mrs. Eugene Klein	D. Wayne Lukas	R.H. Spreen
1987	Ferdinand	Mrs. H.B. Keck	Charlie Whittingham	H.B. Keck
1988	Alysheba	D. & P. Scharbauer	Jack Van Berg	Preston Madden
1989	Sunday Silence	Gaillard, Hancock, & Whittingham	Charlie Whittingham	Oak Cliff Thoroughbreds
1990	Criminal Type	Calumet Farm	D. Wayne Lukas	Calumet Farm
1991	Black Tie Affair	Jeffrey Sullivan	Ernie Poulos	Stephen D. Peskoff
1992	A.P. Indy	Tomonori Tsurumaki	Neil Drysdale	W.S. Farish & W.S. Kilroy
1993	Kotashaan	La Presle Farm	Richard Mandella	La Presle Farm
1994	Holy Bull	Jimmy Croll	Jimmy Croll	Pelican Stable
1995	Cigar	Allen E. Paulson	William Mott	Allen E. Paulson
1996	Cigar	Allen E. Paulson	William Mott	Allen E. Paulson
1997	Favorite Trick	Joseph LaCombe	William Mott	Mr. & Mrs. M.L. Wood

Horse of the Year (Cont.)

Year	Horse	Owner	Trainer	Breeder
1998	Skip Away	Carolyn Hine	Hubert Hine	Anna Marie Barnhart
1999	Charismatic	Robert & Beverly Lewis	D. Wayne Lukas	William Farish/Partners
2000	Tiznow	Michael Cooper and Cecilia Straub-Rubens	Jay M. Robbins	Cecilia Straub-Rubens
2001	Point Given	The Thoroughbred Corp.	Bob Baffert	The Thoroughbred Corp.
2002	Azeri	Allen Paulson Living Trust	Laura de Seroux	Allen Paulson

Note: From 1936 to 1970, the *Daily Racing Form* annually selected a "Horse of the Year." In 1971 the *Daily Racing Form*, with the Thoroughbred Racing Association and the National Turf Writers Association, jointly created the Eclipse Awards.

Eclipse Award Winners

2-YEAR-OLD COLT

1971	Riva Ridge
1972	Secretariat
1973	Protagonist
1974	Foolish Pleasure
1975	Honest Pleasure
1976	Seattle Slew
1977	Affirmed
1978	Spectacular Bid
1979	Rockhill Native
1980	Lord Avie
1981	Deputy Minister
1982	Roving Boy
1983	Devil's Bag
1984	Chief's Crown
1985	Tasso
1986	Capote
1987	Forty Niner
1988	Easy Goer
1989	Rhythm
1990	Fly So Free
1991	Arazi
1992	Gilded Time
1993	Dehere
1994	Timber Country
1995	Maria's Mon
1996	Boston Harbor
1997	Favorite Trick
1998	Answer Lively
1999	Anees
2000	Macho Uno
2001	Johannesburg
2002	Vindication

2-YEAR-OLD FILLY

1971	Numbered Account
1972	La Prevoyante
1973	Talking Picture
1974	Ruffian
1975	Dearly Precious
1976	Sensational
1977	Lakeville Miss
1978	Candy Eclair, It's in the Air
1979	Smart Angle
1980	Heavenly Cause
1981	Before Dawn
1982	Landaluce
1983	Althea
1984	Outstandingly
1985	Family Style
1986	Brave Raj
1987	Epitome
1988	Open Mind
1989	Go for Wand
1990	Meadow Star
1991	Pleasant Stage
1992	Eliza
1993	Phone Chatter
1994	Flanders
1995	Golden Attraction
1996	Storm Song
1997	Countess Diana
1998	Silverbulletday
1999	Chilukki
2000	Caressing
2001	Tempera
2002	Storm Flag Flying

3-YEAR-OLD COLT

1971	Canonero II
1972	Key to the Mint
1973	Secretariat
1974	Little Currant
1975	Wajima
1976	Bold Forbes
1977	Seattle Slew
1978	Affirmed
1979	Spectacular Bid
1980	Temperence Hill
1981	Pleasant Colony
1982	Conquistador Cielo
1983	Slew o' Gold
1984	Swale
1985	Spend A Buck
1986	Snow Chief
1987	Alysheba
1988	Risen Star
1989	Sunday Silence
1990	Unbridled
1991	Hansel
1992	A.P. Indy
1993	Prairie Bayou
1994	Holy Bull
1995	Thunder Gulch
1996	Skip Away
1997	Silver Charm
1998	Real Quiet
1999	Charismatic
2000	Tiznow
2001	Point Given
2002	War Emblem

CHAMPION TURF HORSE

1971	Run the Gantlet (3)
1972	Cougar II (6)
1973	Secretariat (3)
1974	Dahlia (4)
1975	Snow Knight (4)
1976	Youth (3)
1977	Johnny D (3)
1978	Mac Diarmida (3)

CHAMPION MALE TURF HORSE

1979	Bowl Game (5)
1980	John Henry (5)
1981	John Henry (6)
1982	Perrault (5)
1983	John Henry (8)
1984	John Henry (9)
1985	Cozzene (4)
1986	Manila (3)
1987	Theatrical (5)
1988	Sunshine Forever (3)
1989	Steinlen (6)
1990	Itsallgreektome (3)

CHAMPION MALE TURF HORSE (Cont.)

1991	Tight Spot (4)
1992	Sky Classic (5)
1993	Kotashaan (5)
1994	Paradise Creek (5)
1995	Northern Spur (4)
1996	Singspiel (4)
1997	Chief Bearhart (4)
1998	Buck's Boy (5)
1999	Daylami (5)
2000	Kalanisi (4)
2001	Fantastic Light (5)
2002	High Chaparral (3)

CHAMPION FEMALE TURF HORSE

1979	Trillion (5)
1980	Just a Game II (4)
1981	De La Rose (3)
1982	April Run (4)
1983	All Along (4)
1984	Royal Heroine (4)
1985	Pebbles (4)
1986	Estrapade (6)

CHAMPION FEMALE TURF HORSE (Cont.)

1987	Miesque (3)
1988	Miesque (4)
1989	Brown Bess (7)
1990	Laugh and Be Merry (5)
1991	Miss Alleged (4)
1992	Flawlessly (4)
1993	Flawlessly (5)
1994	Hatoof (5)
1995	Possibly Perfect (5)
1996	Wandesta (5)
1997	Ryafan (3)
1998	Fiji (4)
1999	Soaring Softly (4)
2000	Perfect Sting (4)
2001	Banks Hill (3)
2002	Golden Apples (4)

Eclipse Award Winners (Cont.)

3-YEAR-OLD FILLY

1971	Turkish Trousers
1972	Susan's Girl
1973	Desert Vixen
1974	Chris Evert
1975	Ruffian
1976	Revidere
1977	Our Mims
1978	Tempest Queen
1979	Davona Dale
1980	Genuine Risk
1981	Wayward Lass
1982	Christmas Past
1983	Heartlight No. One
1984	Life's Magic
1985	Mom's Command
1986	Tiffany Lass
1987	Sacahuista
1988	Winning Colors
1989	Open Mind
1990	Go for Wand
1991	Dance Smartly
1992	Saratoga Dew
1993	Hollywood Wildcat
1994	Heavenly Prize
1995	Serena's Song
1996	Yank's Music
1997	Ajina
1998	Banshee Breeze
1999	Silverbulletday
2000	Surfside
2001	Xtra Heat
2002	Farda Amiga

OLDER COLT, HORSE OR GELDING

1971	Ack Ack (5)
1972	Autobiography (4)
1973	Riva Ridge (4)
1974	Forego (4)
1975	Forego (5)
1976	Forego (6)
1977	Forego (7)
1978	Seattle Slew (4)
1979	Affirmed (4)
1980	Spectacular Bid (4)
1981	John Henry (6)
1982	Lemhi Gold (4)
1983	Bates Motel (4)
1984	Slew o'Gold (4)
1985	Vanlandingham (4)
1986	Turkoman (4)
1987	Ferdinand (4)
1988	Alysheba (4)
1989	Blushing John (4)
1990	Criminal Type (5)
1991	Black Tie Affair (5)
1992	Pleasant Tap (5)
1993	Bertrando (4)
1994	The Wicked North (5)
1995	Cigar (5)
1996	Cigar (6)
1997	Skip Away (4)
1998	Skip Away (5)
1999	Victory Gallop (4)
2000	Lemon Drop Kid (4)
2001	Tiznow (4)
2002	Left Bank (5)

OLDER FILLY OR MARE

1971	Shuvee (5)
1972	Typecast (6)
1973	Susan's Girl (4)
1974	Desert Vixen (4)
1975	Susan's Girl (6)
1976	Proud Delta (4)
1977	Cascapedia (4)
1978	Late Bloomer (4)
1979	Waya (5)
1980	Glorious Song (4)
1981	Relaxing (5)
1982	Track Robbery (6)
1983	Ambassador of Luck (4)
1984	Princess Rooney (4)
1985	Life's Magic (4)
1986	Lady's Secret (4)
1987	North Sider (5)
1988	Personal Ensign (4)
1989	Bayakoa (5)
1990	Bayakoa (6)
1991	Queena (5)
1992	Paseana (5)
1993	Paseana (6)
1994	Sky Beauty (4)
1995	Inside Information (4)
1996	Jewel Princess (4)
1997	Hidden Lake (4)
1998	Escena (5)
1999	Beautiful Pleasure (4)
2000	Riboletta (6)
2001	Gourmet Girl (6)
2002	Azeri (4)

STEEPLECHASE OR HURDLE HORSE

1971	Shadow Brook (7)
1972	Soothsayer (5)
1973	Athenian Idol (5)
1974	Gran Kan (8)
1975	Life's Illusion (4)
1976	Straight & True (6)
1977	Cafe Prince (7)
1978	Cafe Prince (8)
1979	Martie's Anger (4)
1980	Zaccio (4)
1981	Zaccio (5)
1982	Zaccio (6)
1983	Flatterer (4)
1984	Flatterer (5)
1985	Flatterer (6)
1986	Flatterer (7)
1987	Inlander (6)
1988	Jimmy Lorenzo (6)
1989	Highland Bud (4)
1990	Morley Street (7)
1991	Morley Street (8)
1992	Lonesome Glory (4)
1993	Lonesome Glory (5)
1994	Warm Spell (6)
1995	Lonesome Glory (7)
1996	Corregio (5)
1997	Lonesome Glory (9)
1998	Flat Top (5)
1999	Lonesome Glory (11)
2000	All Gong (6)
2001	Pompeyo (7)
2002	Flat Top (9)

SPRINTER

1971	Ack Ack (5)
1972	Chou Croute (4)
1973	Shecky Greene (3)
1974	Forego (4)
1975	Gallant Bob (3)
1976	My Juliet (4)
1977	What a Summer (4)
1978	Dr. Patches (4)
	J.O. Tobin (4)
1979	Star de Naskra (4)
1980	Plugged Nickel (3)
1981	Guilty Conscience (5)
1982	Gold Beauty (3)
1983	Chinook Pass (4)
1984	Eillo (4)
1985	Precisionist (4)
1986	Smile (4)
1987	Groovy (4)
1988	Gulch (4)
1989	Safely Kept (3)
1990	Housebuster (3)
1991	Housebuster (4)
1992	Rubiano (5)
1993	Cardmania (7)
1994	Cherokee Run (4)
1995	Not Surprising (5)
1996	Lit de Justice (6)
1997	Smoke Glacken (3)
1998	Reraise (3)
1999	Artax (4)
2000	Kone Gold (6)
2001	Squirtle Squirt (3)
2002	Orientate (4)

OUTSTANDING OWNER

1971	Mr. & Mrs. E. E. Fogleson
1974	Dan Lasater
1975	Dan Lasater
1976	Dan Lasater
1977	Maxwell Gluck
1978	Harbor View Farm
1979	Harbor View Farm
1980	Mr. & Mrs. Bertram
1981	Dotsam Stable
1982	Viola Sommer
1983	John Franks
1984	John Franks
1985	Mr. & Mrs. Eugene Klein
1986	Mr. & Mrs. Eugene Klein
1987	Mr. & Mrs. Eugene Klein
1988	Ogden Phipps
1989	Ogden Phipps
1990	Frances Genter
1991	Sam-Son Farm
1992	Juddmonte Farms
1993	John Franks
1994	John Franks
1995	Allen E. Paulson
1996	Allen E. Paulson
1997	Carolyn Hine
1998	Frank Stronach
1999	Frank Stronach
2000	Frank Stronach
2001	Richard Englander
2002	Richard Englander

Note: Number in parentheses is horse's age.

Eclipse Award Winners (Cont.)

OUTSTANDING TRAINER

1971	Charlie Whittingham
1972	Lucien Laurin
1973	H. Allen Jerkens
1974	Sherrill Ward
1975	Steve DiMauro
1976	Lazaro Barrera
1977	Lazaro Barrera
1978	Lazaro Barrera
1979	Lazaro Barrera
1980	Bud Delp
1981	Ron McAnally
1982	Charlie Whittingham
1983	Woody Stephens
1984	Jack Van Berg
1985	D. Wayne Lukas
1986	D. Wayne Lukas
1987	D. Wayne Lukas
1988	Claude R. McGaughey III
1989	Charlie Whittingham
1990	Carl Nafzger
1991	Ron McAnally
1992	Ron McAnally
1993	Bobby Frankel
1994	D. Wayne Lukas
1995	William Mott
1996	William Mott
1997	Bob Baffert
1998	Bob Baffert
1999	Bob Baffert
2000	Robert Frankel
2001	Robert Frankel
2002	Robert Frankel

OUTSTANDING JOCKEY

1971	Laffit Pincay Jr.
1972	Braulio Baeza
1973	Laffit Pincay Jr
1974	Laffit Pincay Jr
1975	Braulio Baeza
1976	Sandy Hawley
1977	Steve Cauthen
1978	Darrel McHargue
1979	Laffit Pincay Jr.
1980	Chris McCarron
1981	Bill Shoemaker
1982	Angel Cordero Jr
1983	Angel Cordero Jr
1984	Pat Day
1985	Laffit Pincay Jr
1986	Pat Day
1987	Pat Day
1988	Jose Santos
1989	Kent Desormeaux
1990	Craig Perret
1991	Pat Day
1992	Kent Desormeaux
1993	Mike Smith
1994	Mike Smith
1995	Jerry Bailey
1996	Jerry Bailey
1997	Jerry Bailey
1998	Gary Stevens
1999	Jorge Chavez
2000	Jerry Bailey
2001	Jerry Bailey
2002	Jerry Bailey

OUTSTANDING APPRENTICE JOCKEY

1971	Gene St. Leon
1972	Thomas Wallis
1973	Steve Valdez
1974	Chris McCarron
1975	Jimmy Edwards
1976	George Martens
1977	Steve Cauthen
1978	Ron Franklin
1979	Cash Asmussen
1980	Frank Lovato Jr.
1981	Richard Migliore
1982	Alberto Delgado
1983	Declan Murphy
1984	Wesley Ward
1985	Art Madrid Jr.
1986	Allen Stacy
1987	Kent Desormeaux
1988	Steve Capanas
1989	Michael Luzzi
1990	Mark Johnston
1991	Mickey Walls
1992	Jesus A. Bracho
1993	Juan Umana
1994	Dale Beckner
1995	Ramon Perez
1996	Neil Pozansky
1997	Phil Teator
	Roberto Rosado
1998	Shaun Bridgmohan
1999	Ariel Smith
2000	Tyler Baze
2001	Jeremy Rose
2002	Ryan Fogelsonger

Eclipse Award Winners (Cont.)

OUTSTANDING BREEDER

1974.....John W. Galbreath
1975.....Fred W. Hooper
1976.....Nelson Bunker Hunt
1977.....Edward Plunket Taylor
1978.....Harbor View Farm
1979.....Claiborne Farm
1980.....Mrs. Henry D. Paxson
1981.....Golden Chance Farm
1982.....Fred W. Hooper
1983.....Edward Plunket Taylor
1984.....Claiborne Farm
1985.....Nelson Bunker Hunt
1986.....Paul Mellon
1987.....Nelson Bunker Hunt
1988.....Ogden Phipps
1989.....North Ridge Farm
1990.....Calumet Farm
1991.....John and Betty Mabee
1992.....William S. Farish III
1993.....Allen Paulson
1994.....William T. Young
1995.....Juddmonte Farms
1996.....Fansworth Farms

OUTSTANDING BREEDER *(Cont.)*

1997.....Golden Eagle Farm
1998.....John and Betty Mabee
1999.....William Farish/Partners
2000.....Frank Stronach/Adena Springs
2001.....Juddmonte Farms
2002.....Juddmonte Farms

AWARD OF MERIT

1976.....Jack J. Dreyfus
1977.....Steve Cauthen
1978.....Ogden Phipps
1979.....Frank E. Kilroe
1980.....John D. Schapiro
1981.....Bill Shoemaker
1984.....John Gaines
1985.....Keene Daingerfield
1986.....Herman Cohen
1987.....J. B. Faulconer
1988.....John Forsythe
1989.....Michael P. Sandler
1991.....Fred W. Hooper
1994.....Alfred G. Vanderbilt
1996.....Allen E. Paulson
2002.....Howard Battle
.............Ogden Phipps

SPECIAL AWARD

1971.....Robert J. Kleberg
1974.....Charles Hatton
1976.....Bill Shoemaker
1980.....John T. Landry
         Pierre E. Bellocq (Peb)
1984.....C. V. Whitney
1985.....Arlington Park
1987.....Anheuser-Busch
1988.....Edward J. DeBartolo Sr.
1989.....Richard Duchossois
1994.....John Longden
         Edward Arcaro
1998.....Oak Tree Racing Association
2002   Keeneland Library

Note: Special Award and Award of Merit, for long-term and/or outstanding service to the industry, not presented annually.

Libido Lost

When it comes to the fairer sex, four-year-old stallions are usually not discriminating. Yet for reasons that elude War Emblem's new owners in Hokkaido, Japan, the 2002 Kentucky Derby champ has been a cool customer in the shed. Uninterested in most mares presented to him in his first season at stud, War Emblem had covered only six of them in two months of 2003. Other high-profile stallions easily cover 60 mares in a month. Said Eisuke Tokutake, a spokesperson for the Yoshida Family, which purchased War Emblem in September 2002 for more than $17 million, "Clearly, this is not a good situation."

War Emblem's standoffishness isn't unheard of. "We call it 'bird-watching,' because the horse will look away and pretend not to see the mares," said University of Pennsylvania equine behavorial scientist Sue McDonnell, who estimates that 5% of new stallions exhibit similar behavior. "Sometimes the horses prefer a certain color mare or don't trust a handler. Often they are affected by the pressure to perform."

That it happens to other horses is small comfort to the Yoshidas. As they negotiate with Lloyds of London for what compensation they would receive if the sire doesn't pan out, the family has called in two veterinarians to help. With more than 200 broodmares booked to him this year—at a reported fee of between $66,000 and $75,000—this stud will have plenty of chances to prove himself.
—Kelley King

Breeders' Cup

Location: Hollywood Park 1984, '87, '97; Aqueduct Racetrack 1985; Santa Anita Park 1986, '93; Churchill Downs 1988, '91, '98,'00; Gulfstream Park (FL) 1989, '92, '99; Belmont Park 1990, '95, '01; Woodbine (Toronto) 1996; Arlington Park 2002.

Juveniles

Year	Winner (Margin)	Jockey	Second	Third	Time
1984	Chief's Crown (¾)	Don MacBeth	Tank's Prospect	Spend a Buck	1:36⅕
1985	Tasso (Nose)	Laffit Pincay Jr.	Storm Cat	Scat Dancer	1:36⅕
1986	Capote (1¼)	Laffit Pincay Jr.	Qualify	Alysheba	1:43⅘
1987	Success Express (1¾)	Jose Santos	Regal Classic	Tejano	1:35⅕
1988	Is It True (1¼)	Laffit Pincay Jr.	Easy Goer	Tagel	1:46⅗
1989	Rhythm (2)	Craig Perret	Grand Canyon	Slavic	1:43⅗
1990	Fly So Free (3)	Jose Santos	Take Me Out	Lost Mountain	1:43⅖
1991	Arazi (4¾)	Pat Valenzuela	Bertrando	Snappy Landing	1:44⅗
1992	Gilded Time (¾)	Chris McCarron	It'sali'lknownfact	River Special	1:43⅖
1993	Brocco (5)	Gary Stevens	Blumin Affair	Tabasco Cat	1:42⅘
1994	Timber Country (½)	Pat Day	Eltish	Tejano Run	1:44⅖
1995	Unbridled's Song (Neck)	Mike Smith	Hennessy	Editor's Note	1:41⅗
1996	Boston Harbor (Neck)	Jerry Bailey	Acceptable	Ordway	1:43⅖
1997	Favorite Trick (5½)	Pat Day	Dawson's Legacy	Nationalore	1:41⅗
1998	Answer Lively (Head)	Jerry Bailey	Aly's Alley	Cat Thief	1:44
1999	Anees (2½)	Gary Stevens	Chief Seattle	High Yield	1:42.29
2000	Macho Uno (Nose)	Jerry Bailey	Point Given	Street Cry	1:42.05
2001	Johannesburg (1¼)	Michael Kinane	Repent	Siphonic	1:42.27
2002	Vindication (2¾)	Mike Smith	Kafwain	Hold That Tiger	1:49.61

Note: One mile (1984–85, '87), 1 1/16 miles (1986 and 1988–2001), 1⅛ miles (2002).

Juvenile Fillies

Year	Winner (Margin)	Jockey	Second	Third	Time
1984	Outstandingly*	Walter Guerra	Dusty Heart	Fine Spirit	1:37⅘
1985	Twilight Ridge (1)	Jorge Velasquez	Family Style	Steal a Kiss	1:35⅘
1986	Brave Raj (5½)	Pat Valenzuela	Tappiano	Saros Brig	1:43⅕
1987	Epitome (Nose)	Pat Day	Jeanne Jones	Dream Team	1:36⅖
1988	Open Mind (1¾)	Angel Cordero Jr.	Darby Shuffle	Lea Lucinda	1:46⅗
1989	Go for Wand (2¾)	Randy Romero	Sweet Roberta	Stella Madrid	1:44⅕
1990	Meadow Star (5)	Jose Santos	Private Treasure	Dance Smartly	1:44
1991	Pleasant Stage (Neck)	Eddie Delahoussaye	La Spia	Cadillac Women	1:46⅖
1992	Eliza (1½)	Pat Valenzuela	Educated Risk	Boots 'n Jackie	1:42⅘
1993	Phone Chatter (Head)	Laffit Pincay	Sardula	Heavenly Prize	1:43
1994	Flanders (Head)	Pat Day	Serena's Song	Stormy Blues	1:45⅕
1995	My Flag (½)	Jerry Bailey	Cara Rafaela	Golden Attraction	1:42⅖
1996	Storm Song (4½)	Craig Perret	Love That Jazz	Critical Factor	1:43⅗
1997	Countess Diana (8½)	Shane Sellers	Career Collection	Primaly	1:42⅕
1998	Silverbulletday (½)	Gary Stevens	Excellent Meeting	Three Ring	1:43⅗
1999	Cash Run (1¼)	Jerry Bailey	Chilukki	Surfside	1:43.31
2000	Caressing (½)	John Velazquez	Platinum Tiara	Shes a Devil Due	1:42.72
2001	Tempera (1½)	David Flores	Imperial Gesture	Bella Bellucci	1:41.49
2002	Storm Flag Flying (½)	John Velazquez	Composure	Santa Catarina	1:49.60

*In 1984, winner Fran's Valentine was disqualified for interference in the stretch and placed 10th.
Note: One mile (1984–85, '87), 1 1/16 miles (1986 and 1988–2001), 1⅛ miles (2002).

Sprint

Year	Winner (Margin)	Jockey	Second	Third	Time
1984	Eillo (Nose)	Craig Perret	Commemorate	Fighting Fit	1:10⅕
1985	Precisionist (¾)	Chris McCarron	Smile	Mt. Livermore	1:08⅖
1986	Smile (1¼)	Jacinto Vasquez	Pine Tree Lane	Bedside Promise	1:08⅖
1987	Very Subtle (4)	Pat Valenzuela	Groovy	Exclusive Enough	1:08⅘
1988	Gulch (¾)	Angel Cordero Jr	Play the King	Afleet	1:10⅖
1989	Dancing Spree (Neck)	Angel Cordero Jr	Safely Kept	Dispersal	1:09
1990	Safely Kept (Neck)	Craig Perret	Dayjur	Black Tie Affair	1:09⅗
1991	Sheikh Albadou (Neck)	Pat Eddery	Pleasant Tap	Robyn Dancer	1:09⅕
1992	Thirty Slews (Neck)	Eddie Delahoussaye	Meafara	Rubiano	1:08⅕
1993	Cardmania (Neck)	Eddie Delahoussaye	Meafara	Gilded Time	1:08⅗
1994	Cherokee Run (Head)	Mike Smith	Soviet Problem	Cardmania	1:09⅖
1995	Desert Stormer (Neck)	Kent Desormeaux	Mr. Greeley	Lit de Justice	1:09
1996	Lit de Justice (1¼)	Corey Nakatani	Paying Dues	Honour and Glory	1:08⅗
1997	Elmhurst (½)	Corey Nakatani	Hesabull	Bet on Sunshine	1:08
1998	Reraise (2)	Corey Nakatani	Grand Slam	Kona Gold	1:09
1999	Artax (½)	Jorge Chavez	Kona Gold	Big Jag	1:07.89
2000	Kona Gold (½)	Alex Solis	Honest Lady	Bet on Sunshine	1:07.77
2001	Squirtle Squirt (½)	Jerry Bailey	Xtra Heat	Caller One	1:08.41
2002	Orientate (½)	Jerry Bailey	Thunderello	Crafty C.T.	1:08.89

Note: Six furlongs (since 1984).

Breeders' Cup (Cont.)

Mile

Year	Winner (Margin)	Jockey	Second	Third	Time
1984	Royal Heroine (1½)	Fernando Toro	Star Choice	Cozzene	1:32⅗
1985	Cozzene (2¼)	Walter Guerra	Al Mamoon*	Shadeed	1:35
1986	Last Tycoon (Head)	Yves St-Martin	Palace Music	Fred Astaire	1:35⅕
1987	Miesque (3½)	Freddie Head	Show Dancer	Sonic Lady	1:32⅘
1988	Miesque (4)	Freddie Head	Steinlen	Simply Majestic	1:38⅗
1989	Steinlen (¾)	Jose Santos	Sabona	Most Welcome	1:37⅕
1990	Royal Academy (Neck)	Lester Piggott	Itsallgreektome	Priolo	1:35⅕
1991	Opening Verse (2¼)	Pat Valenzuela	Val de Bois	Star of Cozzene	1:37⅖
1992	Lure (3)	Mike Smith	Paradise Creek	Brief Truce	1:32⅘
1993	Lure (2¼)	Mike Smith	Ski Paradise	Fourstars Allstar	1:33⅖
1994	Barathea (Head)	Frankie Dettori	Johann Quatz	Unfinished Symph	1:34⅖
1995	Ridgewood Pearl (2)	John Murtagh	Fastness	Sayyedati	1:43⅗
1996	Da Hoss (1½)	Gary Stevens	Spinning World	Same Old Wish	1:35⅘
1997	Spinning World (2)	Cash Asmussen	Geri	Decorated Hero	1:32⅘
1998	Da Hoss (Head)	John Velazquez	Hawksley Hill	Labeeb	1:35⅕
1999	Silic (Neck)	Corey Nakatani	Tuzla	Docksider	1:34.26
2000	War Chant (Neck)	Gary Stevens	North East Bound	Dansili	1:34.67
2001	Val Royal (1¾)	Jose Valdivia	Forbidden Apple	Bach	1:32.05
2002	Domedriver (¾)	Thierry Thulliez	Rock of Gibraltar	Good Journey	1:36.92

*2nd place finisher Palace Music was disqualified for interference and placed 9th.

Distaff

Year	Winner (Margin)	Jockey	Second	Third	Time
1984	Princess Rooney (7)	Eddie Delahoussaye	Life's Magic	Adored	2:02⅖
1985	Life's Magic (6¼)	Angel Cordero Jr.	Lady's Secret	Dontstop Themusic	2:02
1986	Lady's Secret (2½)	Pat Day	Fran's Valentine	Outstandingly	2:01⅕
1987	Sacahuista (2¼)	Randy Romero	Clabber Girl	Oueee Bebe	2:02⅘
1988	Personal Ensign (Nose)	Randy Romero	Winning Colors	Goodbye Halo	1:52
1989	Bayakoa (1½)	Laffit Pincay Jr.	Gorgeous	Open Mind	1:47⅖
1990	Bayakoa (6¾)	Laffit Pincay Jr.	Colonial Waters	Valay Maid	1:49⅕
1991	Dance Smarty (½)	Pat Day	Versailles Treaty	Brought to Mind	1:50⅘
1992	Paseana (4)	Chris McCarron	Versailles Treaty	Magical Maiden	1:48
1993	Hollywood Wildcat (Nose)	Eddie Delahoussaye	Paseana	Re Toss	1:48⅕
1994	One Dreamer (Neck)	Gary Stevens	Heavenly Prize	Miss Dominique	1:50⅗
1995	Inside Information (13½)	Mike Smith	Heavenly Prize	Lakeway	1:46
1996	Jewel Princess (1½)	Corey Nakatani	Serena's Song	Different	1:48⅖
1997	Ajina (2)	Mike Smith	Sharp Cat	Escena	1:47⅕
1998	Escena (Nose)	Gary Stevens	Banshee Breeze	Keeper Hill	1:49⅘
1999	Beautiful Pleasure (¾)	Jorge Chavez	Banshee Breeze	Heritage of Gold	1:47.56
2000	Spain (1½)	Victor Espinoza	Surfside	Heritage of Gold	1:47.66
2001	Unbridled Elaine (head)	Pat Day	Spain	Too Item Limit	1:49.21
2002	Azeri (5)	Mike Smith	Farda Amiga	Imperial Gesture	1:48.64

Note: 1¼ miles (1984–87), 1⅛ miles (since 1988).

Turf

Year	Winner (Margin)	Jockey	Second	Third	Time
1984	Lashkari (Neck)	Yves St. Martin	All Along	Raami	2:25⅕
1985	Pebbles (Neck)	Pat Eddery	Strawberry Rd II	Mourjane	2:27
1986	Manila (Neck)	Jose Santos	Theatrical	Estrapade	2:25⅖
1987	Theatrical (½)	Pat Day	Trempolino	Village Star II	2:24⅖
1988	Great Communicator (½)	Ray Sibille	Sunshine Forever	Indian Skimmer	2:35⅕
1989	Prized (Head)	Eddie Delahoussaye	Sierra Roberta	Star Lift	2:28
1990	In the Wings (½)	Gary Stevens	With Approval	El Senor	2:29⅗
1991	Miss Alleged (2)	Eric Legrix	Itsallgreektome	Quest for Fame	2:30⅘
1992	Fraise (Nose)	Pat Valenzuela	Sky Classic	Quest For Fame	2:24
1993	Kotashaan (½)	Kent Desormeaux	Bien Bien	Luazar	2:25
1994	Tikkanen (1½)	Mike Smith	Hatoof	Paradise Creek	2:26⅖
1995	Northern Spur (Neck)	Chris McCarron	Freedom Cry	Carnegie	2:42
1996	Pilsudski (1¼)	Walter Swinburn	Singspiel	Swain	2:30⅕
1997	Chief Bearhart (¾)	Jose Santos	Borgia	Flag Down	2:23⅘
1998	Buck's Boy (1¼)	Shane Sellers	Yagli	Dushyantor	2:28⅗
1999	Daylami (2½)	Frankie Dettori	Royal Anthem	Buck's Boy	2:24.73
2000	Kalanisi (½)	John Murtagh	Quiet Resolve	John's Call	2:26.96
2001	Fantastic Light (¾)	Frankie Dettori	Milan	Timboroa	2:24.36
2002	High Chaparral (1¼)	Michael Kinane	With Anticipation	Falcon Flight	2:30.14

Note: 1½ miles.

Breeders' Cup (*Cont.*)

Classic

Year	Winner (Margin)	Jockey	Second	Third	Time
1984	Wild Again (Head)	Pat Day	Slew o' Gold*	Gate Dancer	2:03⅖
1985	Proud Truth (Head)	Jorge Velasquez	Gate Dancer	Turkoman	2:00⅘
1986	Skywalker (1¼)	Laffit Pincay Jr.	Turkoman	Precisionist	2:00⅖
1987	Ferdinand (Nose)	Bill Shoemaker	Alysheba	Judge Angelucci	2:01⅖
1988	Alysheba (Nose)	Chris McCarron	Seeking the Gold	Waquoit	2:04⅘
1989	Sunday Silence (½)	Chris McCarron	Easy Goer	Blushing John	2:00⅕
1990	Unbridled (1)	Pat Day	Ibn Bey	Thirty Six Red	2:02⅕
1991	Black Tie Affair (1¼)	Jerry Bailey	Twilight Agenda	Unbridled	2:02⅘
1992	A.P. Indy (2)	Eddie Delahoussaye	Pleasant Tap	Jolypha	2:00⅕
1993	Arcangues (2)	Jerry Bailey	Bertrando	Kissin Kris	2:00⅘
1994	Concern (Neck)	Jerry Bailey	Tabasco Cat	Dramatic Gold	2:02⅖
1995	Cigar (2½)	Jerry Bailey	L'Carriere	Unaccounted For	1:59⅖
1996	Alphabet Soup (Nose)	Chris McCarron	Louis Quatorze	Cigar	2:01
1997	Skip Away (6)	Mike Smith	Deputy Commander	Dowty	1:59⅕
1998	Awesome Again (¾)	Pat Day	Silver Charm	Swain	2:02
1999	Cat Thief (1¼)	Pat Day	Budroyale	Golden Missile	1:59.52
2000	Tiznow (Neck)	Chris McCarron	Giant's Causeway	Captain Steve	2:00.75
2001	Tiznow (Nose)	Chris McCarron	Sakhee	Albert the Great	2:00.62
2002	Volponi (6½)	Jose Santos	Medaglia d'Oro	Milwaukee Brew	2:01.39

*2nd place finisher Gate Dancer was disqualified for interference and placed 3rd.

Note: 1¼ miles.

England's Triple Crown Winners

England's Triple Crown consists of the Two Thousand Guineas, held at Newmarket; the Epsom Derby, held at Epsom Downs; and the St. Leger Stakes, held at Doncaster.

Year	Horse	Owner
1853	West Australian	Mr. Bowes
1865	Gladiateur	F. DeLagrange
1866	Lord Lyon	R. Sutton
1886	*Ormonde	Duke of Westminster
1891	Common	†F. Johnstone
1893	Isinglass	H. McCalmont
1897	Galtee More	J. Gubbins
1899	Flying Fox	Duke of Westminster
1900	Diamond Jubilee	Prince of Wales
1903	*Rock Sand	J. Miller
1915	Pommern	S. Joel
1917	Gay Crusader	Mr. Fairie
1918	Gainsborough	Lady James Douglas
1935	*Bahram	Aga Khan
1970	‡Nijinsky II	C. W. Engelhard

*Imported into United States. †Raced in name of Lord Alington in Two Thousand Guineas. ‡Canadian-bred.

Horse—Money Won

Year	Horse	Age	Starts	1st	2nd	3rd	Winnings ($)
1919	Sir Barton	3	13	8	3	2	88,250
1920	Man o' War	3	11	11	0	0	166,140
1921	Morvich	2	11	11	0	0	115,234
1922	Pillory	3	7	4	1	1	95,654
1923	Zev	3	14	12	1	0	272,008
1924	Sarzen	3	12	8	1	1	95,640
1925	Pompey	2	10	7	2	0	121,630
1926	Crusader	3	15	9	4	0	166,033
1927	Anita Peabody	2	7	6	0	1	111,905
1928	High Strung	2	6	5	0	0	153,590
1929	Blue Larkspur	3	6	4	1	0	153,450
1930	Gallant Fox	3	10	9	1	0	308,275
1931	Gallant Flight	2	7	7	0	0	219,000
1932	Gusto	3	16	4	3	2	145,940
1933	Singing Wood	2	9	3	2	2	88,050
1934	Cavalcade	3	7	6	1	0	111,235
1935	Omaha	3	9	6	1	2	142,255
1936	Granville	3	11	7	3	0	110,295
1937	Seabiscuit	4	15	11	2	2	168,580
1938	Stagehand	3	15	8	2	3	189,710
1939	Challedon	3	15	9	2	3	184,535
1940	Bimelech	3	7	4	2	1	110,005
1941	Whirlaway	3	20	13	5	2	272,386
1942	Shut Out	3	12	8	2	0	238,872
1943	Count Fleet	3	6	6	0	0	174,055
1944	Pavot	2	8	8	0	0	179,040
1945	Busher	3	13	10	2	1	273,735
1946	Assault	3	15	8	2	3	424,195
1947	Armed	6	17	11	4	1	376,325
1948	Citation	3	20	19	1	0	709,470
1949	Ponder	3	21	9	5	2	321,825
1950	Noor	5	12	7	4	1	346,940
1951	Counterpoint	3	15	7	2	1	250,525
1952	Crafty Admiral	4	16	9	4	1	277,225
1953	Native Dancer	3	10	9	1	0	513,425
1954	Determine	3	15	10	3	2	328,700
1955	Nashua	3	12	10	1	1	752,550
1956	Needles	3	8	4	2	0	440,850
1957	Round Table	3	22	15	1	3	600,383
1958	Round Table	4	20	14	4	0	662,780
1959	Sword Dancer	3	13	8	4	0	537,004
1960	Bally Ache	3	15	10	3	1	445,045
1961	Carry Back	3	16	9	1	3	565,349
1962	Never Bend	2	10	7	1	2	402,969
1963	Candy Spots	3	12	7	2	1	604,481
1964	Gun Bow	4	16	8	4	2	580,100
1965	Buckpasser	2	11	9	1	0	568,096
1966	Buckpasser	3	14	13	1	0	669,078
1967	Damascus	3	16	12	3	1	817,941
1968	Forward Pass	3	13	7	2	0	546,674
1969	Arts and Letters	3	14	8	5	1	555,604
1970	Personality	3	18	8	2	1	444,049
1971	Riva Ridge	2	9	7	0	0	503,263
1972	Droll Role	4	19	7	3	4	471,633
1973	Secretariat	3	12	9	2	1	860,404
1974	Chris Evert	3	8	5	1	2	551,063
1975	Foolish Pleasure	3	11	5	4	1	716,278
1976	Forego	6	8	6	1	1	401,701
1977	Seattle Slew	3	7	6	0	1	641,370
1978	Affirmed	3	11	8	2	0	901,541
1979	Spectacular Bid	3	12	10	1	1	1,279,334
1980	Temperence Hill	3	17	8	3	1	1,130,452
1981	John Henry	6	10	8	0	0	1,798,030
1982	Perrault	5	8	4	1	2	1,197,400
1983	All Along	4	7	4	1	1	2,138,963
1984	Slew o'Gold	4	6	5	1	0	2,627,944
1985	Spend A Buck	3	7	5	1	1	3,552,704

Horse—Money Won *(Cont.)*

Year	Horse	Age	Starts	1st	2nd	3rd	Winnings ($)
1986	Snow Chief	3	9	6	1	1	1,875,200
1987	Alysheba	3	10	3	3	1	2,511,156
1988	Alysheba	4	9	7	1	0	3,808,600
1989	Sunday Silence	3	9	7	2	0	4,578,454
1990	Unbridled	3	11	4	3	2	3,718,149
1991	Dance Smartly	3	8	8	0	0	2,876,821
1992	A.P. Indy	3	7	5	0	1	2,622,560
1993	Kotashaan	3	10	6	3	0	2,619,014
1994	Paradise Creek	5	11	8	2	1	2,610,187
1995	Cigar	5	10	10	0	0	4,819,800
1996	Cigar	6	8	5	2	1	4,910,000
1997	Skip Away	4	11	4	5	2	4,089,000
1998	Silver Charm	4	9	6	2	0	4,696,506
1999	Almutawakel	4	4	1	1	1	3,290,000
2000	Dubai Millennium	4	1	1	0	0	3,600,000
2001	Captain Steve	4	6	2	1	1	4,201,200
2002	War Emblem	4	10	5	0	0	3,455,000

Trainer—Money Won

Year	Trainer	Wins	Winnings ($)	Year	Trainer	Wins	Winnings ($)
1908	James Rowe, Sr.	50	284,335	1956	Willie Molter	142	1,227,402
1909	Sam Hildreth	73	123,942	1957	Jimmy Jones	70	1,150,910
1910	Sam Hildreth	84	148,010	1958	Willie Molter	69	1,116,544
1911	Sam Hildreth	67	49,418	1959	Willie Molter	71	847,290
1912	John F. Schorr	63	58,110	1960	Hirsch Jacobs	97	748,349
1913	James Rowe, Sr.	18	45,936	1961	Jimmy Jones	62	759,856
1914	R. C. Benson	45	59,315	1962	Mesh Tenney	58	1,099,474
1915	James Rowe, Sr.	19	75,596	1963	Mesh Tenney	40	860,703
1916	Sam Hildreth	39	70,950	1964	Bill Winfrey	61	1,350,534
1917	Sam Hildreth	23	61,698	1965	Hirsch Jacobs	91	1,331,628
1918	H. Guy Bedwell	53	80,296	1966	Eddie Neloy	93	2,456,250
1919	H. Guy Bedwell	63	208,728	1967	Eddie Neloy	72	1,776,089
1920	L. Feustal	22	186,087	1968	Eddie Neloy	52	1,233,101
1921	Sam Hildreth	85	262,768	1969	Elliott Burch	26	1,067,936
1922	Sam Hildreth	74	247,014	1970	Charlie Whittingham	82	1,302,354
1923	Sam Hildreth	75	392,124	1971	Charlie Whittingham	77	1,737,115
1924	Sam Hildreth	77	255,608	1972	Charlie Whittingham	79	1,734,020
1925	G. R. Tompkins	30	199,245	1973	Charlie Whittingham	85	1,865,385
1926	Scott P. Harlan	21	205,681	1974	Pancho Martin	166	2,408,419
1927	W. H. Bringloe	63	216,563	1975	Charlie Whittingham	93	2,437,244
1928	John F. Schorr	65	258,425	1976	Jack Van Berg	496	2,976,196
1929	James Rowe, Jr.	25	314,881	1977	Laz Barrera	127	2,715,848
1930	Sunny Jim Fitzsimmons	47	397,355	1978	Laz Barrera	100	3,307,164
1931	Big Jim Healey	33	297,300	1979	Laz Barrera	98	3,608,517
1932	Sunny Jim Fitzsimmons	68	266,650	1980	Laz Barrera	99	2,969,151
1933	Humming Bob Smith	53	135,720	1981	Charlie Whittingham	74	3,993,900
1934	Humming Bob Smith	43	249,938	1982	Charlie Whittingham	63	4,587,457
1935	Bud Stotler	87	303,005	1983	D. Wayne Lukas	78	4,267,261
1936	Sunny Jim Fitzsimmons	42	193,415	1984	D. Wayne Lukas	131	5,835,921
1937	Robert McGarvey	46	209,925	1985	D. Wayne Lukas	218	11,155,188
1938	Earl Sande	15	226,495	1986	D. Wayne Lukas	259	12,345,180
1939	Sunny Jim Fitzsimmons	45	266,205	1987	D. Wayne Lukas	343	17,502,110
1940	Silent Tom Smith	14	269,200	1988	D. Wayne Lukas	318	17,842,358
1941	Plain Ben Jones	70	475,318	1989	D. Wayne Lukas	305	16,103,998
1942	John M. Gaver Sr.	48	406,547	1990	D. Wayne Lukas	267	14,508,871
1943	Plain Ben Jones	73	267,915	1991	D. Wayne Lukas	289	15,942,223
1944	Plain Ben Jones	60	601,660	1992	D. Wayne Lukas	230	9,806,436
1945	Silent Tom Smith	52	510,655	1993	Robert Frankel	79	8,883,252
1946	Hirsch Jacobs	99	560,077	1994	D. Wayne Lukas	147	9,247,457
1947	Jimmy Jones	85	1,334,805	1995	D. Wayne Lukas	194	12,842,865
1948	Jimmy Jones	81	1,118,670	1996	D. Wayne Lukas	192	15,966,344
1949	Jimmy Jones	76	978,587	1997	D. Wayne Lukas	175	10,338,957
1950	Preston Burch	96	637,754	1998	Bob Baffert	139	15,000,870
1951	John M. Gaver Sr.	42	616,392	1999	Bob Baffert	169	16,934,607
1952	Plain Ben Jones	29	662,137	2000	Bob Baffert	146	11,831,605
1953	Harry Trotsek	54	1,028,873	2001	Bob Baffert	138	16,354,996
1954	Willie Molter	136	1,107,860	2002	Robert Frankel	117	17,748,340
1955	Sunny Jim Fitzsimmons	66	1,270,055				

Jockey—Money Won

Year	Jockey	Mts	1st	2nd	3rd	Pct	Winnings ($)
1919	John Loftus	177	65	36	24	.37	252,707
1920	Clarence Kummer	353	87	79	48	.25	292,376
1921	Earl Sande	340	112	69	59	.33	263,043
1922	Albert Johnson	297	43	57	40	.14	345,054
1923	Earl Sande	430	122	89	79	.28	569,394
1924	Ivan Parke	844	205	175	121	.24	290,395
1925	Laverne Fator	315	81	54	44	.26	305,775
1926	Laverne Fator	511	143	90	86	.28	361,435
1927	Earl Sande	179	49	33	19	.27	277,877
1928	Pony McAtee	235	55	43	25	.23	301,295
1929	Mack Garner	274	57	39	33	.21	314,975
1930	Sonny Workman	571	152	88	79	.27	420,438
1931	Charles Kurtsinger	519	93	82	79	.18	392,095
1932	Sonny Workman	378	87	48	55	.23	385,070
1933	Robert Jones	471	63	57	70	.13	226,285
1934	Wayne D. Wright	919	174	154	114	.19	287,185
1935	Silvio Coucci	749	141	125	103	.19	319,760
1936	Wayne D. Wright	670	100	102	73	.15	264,000
1937	Charles Kurtsinger	765	120	94	106	.16	384,202
1938	Nick Wall	658	97	94	82	.15	385,161
1939	Basil James	904	191	165	105	.21	353,333
1940	Eddie Arcaro	783	132	143	112	.17	343,661
1941	Don Meade	1,164	210	185	158	.18	398,627
1942	Eddie Arcaro	687	123	97	89	.18	481,949
1943	John Longden	871	173	140	121	.20	573,276
1944	Ted Atkinson	1,539	287	231	213	.19	899,101
1945	John Longden	778	180	112	100	.23	981,977
1946	Ted Atkinson	1,377	233	213	173	.17	1,036,825
1947	Douglas Dodson	646	141	100	75	.22	1,429,949
1948	Eddie Arcaro	726	188	108	98	.26	1,686,230
1949	Steve Brooks	906	209	172	110	.23	1,316,817
1950	Eddie Arcaro	888	195	153	144	.22	1,410,160
1951	Bill Shoemaker	1,161	257	197	161	.22	1,329,890
1952	Eddie Arcaro	807	188	122	109	.23	1,859,591
1953	Bill Shoemaker	1,683	485	302	210	.29	1,784,187
1954	Bill Shoemaker	1,251	380	221	142	.30	1,876,760
1955	Eddie Arcaro	820	158	126	108	.19	1,864,796
1956	Bill Hartack	1,387	347	252	184	.25	2,343,955
1957	Bill Hartack	1,238	341	208	178	.28	3,060,501
1958	Bill Shoemaker	1,133	300	185	137	.26	2,961,693
1959	Bill Shoemaker	1,285	347	230	159	.27	2,843,133
1960	Bill Shoemaker	1,227	274	196	158	.22	2,123,961
1961	Bill Shoemaker	1,256	304	186	175	.24	2,690,819
1962	Bill Shoemaker	1,126	311	156	128	.28	2,916,844
1963	Bill Shoemaker	1,203	271	193	137	.22	2,526,925
1964	Bill Shoemaker	1,056	246	147	133	.23	2,649,553
1965	Braulio Baeza	1,245	270	200	201	.22	2,582,702
1966	Braulio Baeza	1,341	298	222	190	.22	2,951,022
1967	Braulio Baeza	1,064	256	184	127	.24	3,088,888
1968	Braulio Baeza	1,089	201	184	145	.18	2,835,108
1969	Jorge Velasquez	1,442	258	230	204	.18	2,542,315
1970	Laffit Pincay Jr.	1,328	269	208	187	.20	2,626,526
1971	Laffit Pincay Jr.	1,627	380	288	214	.23	3,784,377
1972	Laffit Pincay Jr.	1,388	289	215	205	.21	3,225,827
1973	Laffit Pincay Jr.	1,444	350	254	209	.24	4,093,492
1974	Laffit Pincay Jr.	1,278	341	227	180	.27	4,251,060
1975	Braulio Baeza	1,190	196	208	180	.16	3,674,398
1976	Angel Cordero Jr.	1,534	274	273	235	.18	4,709,500
1977	Steve Cauthen	2,075	487	345	304	.23	6,151,750
1978	Darrel McHargue	1,762	375	294	263	.21	6,188,353
1979	Laffit Pincay Jr.	1,708	420	302	261	.25	8,183,535
1980	Chris McCarron	1,964	405	318	282	.20	7,666,100
1981	Chris McCarron	1,494	326	251	207	.22	8,397,604
1982	Angel Cordero Jr.	1,838	397	338	227	.22	9,702,520
1983	Angel Cordero Jr.	1,792	362	296	237	.20	10,116,807
1984	Chris McCarron	1,565	356	276	218	.23	12,038,213
1985	Laffit Pincay Jr.	1,409	289	246	183	.21	13,415,049
1986	Jose Santos	1,636	329	237	222	.20	11,329,297
1987	Jose Santos	1,639	305	268	208	.19	12,407,355
1988	Jose Santos	1,867	370	287	265	.20	14,877,298

Jockey—Money Won (Cont.)

Year	Jockey	Mts	1st	2nd	3rd	Pct	Winnings ($)
1989	Jose Santos	1,459	285	238	220	.20	13,847,003
1990	Gary Stevens	1,504	283	245	202	.19	13,881,198
1991	Chris McCarron	1,440	265	228	206	.18	14,441,083
1992	Kent Desormeaux	1,568	361	260	208	.23	14,193,006
1993	Mike Smith	1,510	343	235	214	.23	14,008,148
1994	Mike Smith	1,484	317	250	196	.21	15,979,820
1995	Jerry Bailey	1,265	287	193	144	.23	16,308,230
1996	Jerry Bailey	1,187	298	189	165	.25	19,465,376
1997	Jerry Bailey	1,143	272	186	178	.26	18,260,553
1998	Gary Stevens	869	178	145	122	.20	19,358,840
1999	Pat Day	1,265	254	209	209	.20	18,092,845
2000	Pat Day	1,219	267	206	186	.22	17,479,838
2001	Jerry Bailey	912	227	194	137	.25	22,597,720
2002	Jerry Bailey	832	213	139	118	.26	19,271,814

Jockey—Races Won

Year	Jockey	Mts	1st	2nd	3rd	Pct
1895	J. Perkins	762	192	177	129	.25
1896	J. Scherrer	1,093	271	227	172	.24
1897	H. Martin	803	173	152	116	.21
1898	T. Burns	973	277	213	149	.28
1899	T. Burns	1,064	273	173	266	.26
1900	C. Mitchell	874	195	140	139	.23
1901	W. O'Connor	1,047	253	221	192	.24
1902	J. Ranch	1,069	276	205	181	.26
1903	G.C. Fuller	918	229	152	122	.25
1904	E. Hildebrand	1,169	297	230	171	.25
1905	D. Nicol	861	221	143	136	.26
1906	W. Miller	1,384	388	300	199	.28
1907	W. Miller	1,194	334	226	170	.28
1908	V. Powers	1,260	324	204	185	.26
1909	V. Powers	704	173	121	114	.25
1910	G. Garner	947	200	188	153	.20
1911	T. Koerner	813	162	133	112	.20
1912	P. Hill	967	168	141	129	.17
1913	M. Buxton	887	146	131	136	.16
1914	J. McTaggart	787	157	132	106	.20
1915	M. Garner	775	151	118	90	.19
1916	F. Robinson	791	178	131	124	.23
1917	W. Crump	803	151	140	101	.19
1918	F. Robinson	864	185	140	108	.21
1919	C. Robinson	896	190	140	126	.21
1920	J. Butwell	721	152	129	139	.21
1921	C. Lang	696	135	110	105	.19
1922	M. Fator	859	188	153	116	.22
1923	I. Parke	718	173	105	95	.24
1924	I. Parke	844	205	175	121	.24
1925	A. Mortensen	987	187	145	138	.19
1926	R. Jones	1,172	190	163	152	.16
1927	L. Hardy	1,130	207	192	151	.18
1928	J. Inzelone	1,052	155	152	135	.15
1929	M. Knight	871	149	132	133	.17
1930	H.R. Riley	861	177	145	123	.21
1931	H. Roble	1,174	173	173	155	.15
1932	J. Gilbert	1,050	212	144	160	.20
1933	J. Westrope	1,224	301	235	166	.25
1934	M. Peters	1,045	221	179	147	.21
1935	C. Stevenson	1,099	206	169	146	.19
1936	B. James	1,106	245	195	161	.22
1937	J. Adams	1,265	260	186	177	.21
1938	J. Longden	1,150	236	168	171	.21
1939	D. Meade	1,284	255	221	180	.20
1940	E. Dew	1,377	287	201	180	.21
1941	D. Meade	1,164	210	185	158	.18
1942	J. Adams	1,120	245	185	150	.22
1943	J. Adams	1,069	228	159	171	.21

Jockey—Races Won *(Cont.)*

Year	Jockey	Mts	1st	2nd	3rd	Pct
1944	T. Atkinson	1,539	287	231	213	.19
1945	J.D. Jessop	1,085	290	182	168	.27
1946	T. Atkinson	1,377	233	213	173	.17
1947	J. Longden	1,327	316	250	195	.24
1948	J. Longden	1,197	319	233	161	.27
1949	G. Glisson	1,347	270	217	181	.20
1950	W. Shoemaker	1,640	388	266	230	.24
1951	C. Burr	1,319	310	232	192	.24
1952	A. DeSpirito	1,482	390	247	212	.26
1953	W. Shoemaker	1,683	485	302	210	.29
1954	W. Shoemaker	1,251	380	221	142	.30
1955	W. Hartack	1,702	417	298	215	.25
1956	W. Hartack	1,387	347	252	184	.25
1957	W. Hartack	1,238	341	208	178	.28
1958	W. Shoemaker	1,133	300	185	137	.26
1959	W. Shoemaker	1,285	347	230	159	.27
1960	W. Hartack	1,402	307	247	190	.22
1961	J. Sellers	1,394	328	212	227	.24
1962	R. Ferraro	1,755	352	252	226	.20
1963	W. Blum	1,704	360	286	215	.21
1964	W. Blum	1,577	324	274	170	.21
1965	J. Davidson	1,582	319	228	190	.20
1966	A. Gomez	996	318	173	142	.32
1967	J. Velasquez	1,939	438	315	270	.23
1968	A. Cordero Jr.	1,662	345	278	219	.21
1969	L. Snyder	1,645	352	290	243	.21
1970	S. Hawley	1,908	452	313	265	.24
1971	L Pincay Jr.	1,627	380	288	214	.23
1972	S. Hawley	1,381	367	269	200	.27
1973	S. Hawley	1,925	515	336	292	.27
1974	C.J. McCarron	2,199	546	392	297	.25
1975	C.J. McCarron	2,194	458	389	305	.21
1976	S. Hawley	1,637	413	245	201	.25
1977	S. Cauthen	2,075	487	345	304	.23
1978	E. Delahoussaye	1,666	384	285	238	.23
1979	D. Gall	2,146	479	396	326	.22
1980	C.J. McCarron	1,964	405	318	282	.20
1981	D. Gall	1,917	376	305	297	.20
1982	Pat Day	1,870	399	326	255	.21
1983	Pat Day	1,725	454	321	251	.26
1984	Pat Day	1,694	399	296	259	.24
1985	C.W. Antley	2,335	469	371	288	.20
1986	Pat Day	1,417	429	246	202	.30
1987	Kent Desormeaux	2,207	450	370	294	.28
1988	Kent Desormeaux	1,897	474	295	276	.25
1989	Kent Desormeaux	2,312	598	385	309	.25
1990	Pat Day	1,421	364	265	222	.26
1991	Pat Day	1,405	430	256	213	.31
1992	Russell Baze	1,691	433	296	237	.25
1993	Russell Baze	1,579	410	297	225	.26
1994	Russell Baze	1,588	415	301	266	.26
1995	Russell Baze	1,531	445	310	232	.29
1996	Russell Baze	1,482	415	297	200	.28
1997	Edgar S. Prado	2,037	533	384	308	.26
1998	Edgar S. Prado	1,969	470	377	285	.23
1999	Edgar S. Prado	1,902	402	307	276	.21
2000	Ramon Dominguez	1,586	361	293	238	.23
2001	Ramon Dominguez	1,864	431	368	278	.23
2002	Russell Baze	1,508	431	302	219	.29

Leading Jockeys—Career Recordstktktk

Jockey	Years Riding	Mts	1st	2nd	3rd	Win Pct	Winnings ($)
Laffit Pincay Jr. (2003)	39	48,487	9,530	7,784	6,650	.197	237,420,625
Bill Shoemaker (1990)	42	40,350	8,833	6,136	4,987	.219	123,375,524
Pat Day	31	39,137	8,543	6,650	5,544	.218	282,555,933
Russell Baze	30	38,673	8,410	6,522	5,501	.218	123,864,804
Dave Gall (1999)	41	41,775	7,396	6,525	6,131	.177	24,547,584
Chris McCarron (2002)	28	34,244	7,141	5,670	4,673	.209	264,351,679
Angel Cordero (1992)	31	38,656	7,057	6,136	5,359	.183	164,561,227
Jorge Velasquez (1998)	35	40,852	6,795	6,178	5,755	.166	125,544,379
Sandy Hawley (1998)	31	31,455	6,449	4,825	4,159	.205	88,681,292
Larry Snyder (1994)	35	35,681	6,388	5,030	3,440	.179	47,207,289
Eddie Delahoussaye (2002)	32	39,213	6,384	5,676	5,585	.163	195,881,170
Carl Gambardella (1994)	39	39,018	6,349	5,953	5,353	.163	29,389,041
Earlie Fires	39	43,476	6,276	5,355	5,175	.144	80,956,153
John Longden (1966)	40	32,413	6,032	4,914	4,273	.186	24,665,800
Jerry Bailey	30	29,437	5,543	4,310	3,724	.188	259,643,820
Mario Pino	24	32,641	5,252	4,791	4,466	.161	81,557,904
Jacinto Vasquez (1998)	38	37,337	5,228	4,714	4,510	.140	82,754,115
Ron Ardoin	31	32,335	5,226	4,298	3,793	.162	58,908,059
Edgar Prado	20	25,603	4,911	4,150	3,635	.192	127,057,402
Rick Wilson	32	24,410	4,897	4,205	3,428	.201	76,143,985
Rodolfo Baez (1999)	26	28,609	4,875	4,291	4,103	.170	30,474,225
Eddie Arcaro (1961)	31	24,092	4,779	3,807	3,302	.198	30,039,543
Gary Stevens	29	26,812	4,741	4,260	3,854	.177	211,565,174
Anthony Black	27	30,933	4,671	4,058	3,966	.151	51,945,673
Don Brumfield (1989)	37	33,223	4,573	4,076	3,758	.138	43,567,861

Note: Records go through October 2, 2003, and include available statistics for races ridden in foreign countries. Figures in parentheses after jockey's name indicate last year in which he rode.

Leading jockeys courtesy of *National Thoroughbred Racing Association*.

THEY SAID IT

Bill Shoemaker, Hall of Fame jockey, on 1979 Kentucky Derby and Preakness winner Spectacular Bid, who passed away on June 9, 2003: "He is the best horse I ever sat on."

HORSES

Ack Ack (1986, 1966)
Affectionately (1989, 1960)
Affirmed (1980, 1975)
All Along (1990, 1979)
Alsab (1976, 1939)
Alydar (1989, 1975)
Alysheba (1993, 1984)
American Eclipse (1970, 1814)
A.P. Indy (2000, 1989)
Armed (1963, 1941)
Artful (1956, 1902)
Arts and Letters (1994, 1966)
Assault (1964, 1943)
Battleship (1969, 1927)
Bayakoa (1998, 1984)
Bed o' Roses (1976, 1947)
Beldame (1956, 1901)
Ben Brush (1955, 1893)
Bewitch (1977, 1945)
Bimelech (1990, 1937)
Black Gold (1989, 1921)
Black Helen (1991, 1932)
Blue Larkspur (1957, 1926)
Bold 'n Determined (1997, 1977)
Bold Ruler (1973, 1954)
Bon Nouvel (1976, 1960)
Boston (1955, 1833)
Broomstick (1956, 1901)
Buckpasser (1970, 1963)
Busher (1964, 1942)
Bushranger (1967, 1930)
Cafe Prince (1985, 1970)
Carry Back (1975, 1958)
Cavalcade (1993, 1931)
Challedon (1977, 1936)
Chris Evert (1988, 1971)
Cicada (1967, 1959)
Cigar (2002, 1990)
Citation (1959, 1945)
Coaltown (1983, 1945)
Colin (1956, 1905)
Commando (1956, 1898)
Count Fleet (1961, 1940)
Crusader (1995, 1923)
Dahlia (1981, 1970)
Damascus (1974, 1964)
Dance Smartly (2003, 1988)
Dark Mirage (1974, 1965)
Davona Dale (1985, 1976)
Desert Vixen (1979, 1970)
Devil Diver (1980, 1939)
Discovery (1969, 1931)
Domino (1955, 1891)
Dr. Fager (1971, 1964)
Easy Goer (1997, 1986)
Eight Thirty (1994, 1936)

Elkridge (1966, 1938)
Emperor of Norfolk (1988, 1885)
Equipoise (1957, 1928)
Exceller (1999, 1973)
Exterminator (1957, 1915)
Fairmount (1985, 1921)
Fair Play (1956, 1905)
Fashion (1980, 1837)
Firenze (1981, 1884)
Flatterer (1994, 1979)
Foolish Pleasure (1995, 1972)
Forego (1979, 1970)
Fort Marcy (1998, 1964)
Gallant Bloom (1977, 1966)
Gallant Fox (1957, 1927)
Gallant Man (1987, 1954)
Gallorette (1962, 1942)
Gamely (1980, 1964)
Genuine Risk (1986, 1977)
Go For Wand (1996, 1987)
Good and Plenty (1956, 1900)
Grandville (1997, 1933)
Grey Lag (1957, 1918)
Gun Bow (1999, 1960)
Hamburg (1986, 1895)
Hanover (1955, 1884)
Henry of Navarre (1985, 1891)
Hill Prince (1991, 1947)
Hindoo (1955, 1878)
Holy Bull (2001, 1991)
Imp (1965, 1894)
Jay Trump (1971, 1957)
John Henry (1990, 1975)
Johnstown (1992, 1936)
Jolly Roger (1965, 1922)
Kelso (1967, 1957)
Kentucky (1983, 1861)
Kingston (1955, 1884)
Lady's Secret (1992, 1982)
La Prevoyante (1995, 1970)
L'Escargot (1977, 1963)
Lexington (1955, 1850)
Longfellow (1971, 1867)
Luke Blackburn (1956, 1877)
Majestic Prince (1988, 1966)
Man o' War (1957, 1917)
Maskette (2001, 1908)
Miesque (1999, 1984)
Miss Woodford (1967, 1880)
Myrtlewood (1979, 1932)
Nashua (1965, 1952)
Native Dancer (1963, 1950)
Native Diver (1978, 1959)
Needles (2000, 1953)
Neji (1966, 1950)
Noor (2002, 1945)

Northern Dancer (1976, 1961)
Oedipus (1978, 1946)
Old Rosebud (1968, 1911)
Omaha (1965, 1932)
Pan Zareta (1972, 1910)
Parole (1984, 1873)
Paseana (2001, 1987)
Personal Ensign (1993, 1984)
Peter Pan (1956, 1904)
Precisionist (2003, 1981)
Princess Doreen (1982, 1921)
Princess Rooney (1991, 1980)
Real Delight (1987, 1949)
Regret (1957, 1912)
Reigh Count (1978, 1923)
Riva Ridge (1998, 1969)
Roamer (1981, 1911)
Roseben (1956, 1901)
Round Table (1972, 1954)
Ruffian (1976, 1972)
Ruthless (1975, 1864)
Salvator (1955, 1886)
Sarazen (1957, 1921)
Seabiscuit (1958, 1933)
Searching (1978, 1952)
Seattle Slew (1981, 1974)
Secretariat (1974, 1970)
Serena's Song (2002, 1992)
Shuvee (1975, 1966)
Silver Spoon (1978, 1956)
Sir Archy (1955, 1805)
Sir Barton (1957, 1916)
Slew o' Gold (1992, 1980)
Spectacular Bid (1982, 1976)
Stymie (1975, 1941)
Sun Beau (1996, 1925)
Sunday Silence (1996, 1986)
Susan's Girl (1976, 1969)
Swaps (1966, 1952)
Sword Dancer (1977, 1956)
Sysonby (1956, 1902)
Ta Wee (1994, 1967)
Ten Broeck (1982, 1872)
Tim Tam (1985, 1955)
Tom Fool (1960, 1949)
Top Flight (1966, 1929)
Tosmah (1984, 1961)
Twenty Grand (1957, 1928)
Twilight Tear (1963, 1941)
Two Lea (1982, 1946)
War Admiral (1958, 1934)
Whirlaway (1959, 1938)
Whisk Broom II (1979, 1907)
Winning Colors (2000, 1985)
Zaccio (1990, 1976)
Zev (1983, 1920)

Note: Years of election and foaling in parentheses.

HARNESS RACING

Hambletonian

Year	Winner	Driver	Year	Winner	Driver
1926	Guy McKinney	Nat Ray	1965	Egyptian Candor	Del Cameron
1927	Iosola's Worthy	Marvin Childs	1966	Kerry Way	Frank Ervin
1928	Spenser	W. H. Leese	1967	Speedy Streak	Del Cameron
1929	Walter Dear	Walter Cox	1968	Nevele Pride	Stanley Dancer
1930	Hanover's Bertha	Tom Berry	1969	Lindy's Pride	H. Beissinger
1931	Calumet Butler	R. D. McMahon	1970	Timothy T.	J. Simpson Jr.
1932	The Marchioness	William Caton	1971	Speedy Crown	H. Beissinger
1933	Mary Reynolds	Ben White	1972	Super Bowl	Stanley Dancer
1934	Lord Jim	Doc Parshall	1973	Flirth	Ralph Baldwin
1935	Greyhound	Sep Palin	1974	Christopher T.	Bill Haughton
1936	Rosalind	Ben White	1975	Bonefish	Stanley Dancer
1937	Shirley Hanover	Henry Thomas	1976	Steve Lobell	Bill Haughton
1938	McLin Hanover	Henry Thomas	1977	Green Speed	Bill Haughton
1939	Peter Astra	Doc Parshall	1978	Speedy Somolli	H. Beissinger
1940	Spencer Scott	Fred Egan	1979	Legend Hanover	George Sholty
1941	Bill Gallon	Lee Smith	1980	Burgomeister	Bill Haughton
1942	The Ambassador	Ben White	1981	Shiaway St. Pat	Ray Remmen
1943	Volo Song	Ben White	1982	Speed Bowl	Tom Haughton
1944	Yankee Maid	Henry Thomas	1983	Duenna	Stanley Dancer
1945	Titan Hanover	H. Pownall Sr.	1984	Historic Freight	Ben Webster
1946	Chestertown	Thomas Berry	1985	Prakas	Bill O'Donnell
1947	Hoot Mon	Sep Palin	1986	Nuclear Kosmos	Ulf Thoresen
1948	Demon Hanover	Harrison Hoyt	1987	Mack Lobell	John Campbell
1949	Miss Tilly	Fred Egan	1988	Armbro Goal	John Campbell
1950	Lusty Song	Del Miller	1989	Park Ave. Joe/Probe*	R. Waples/B. Fahy
1951	Mainliner	Guy Crippen	1990	Harmonious	John Campbell
1952	Sharp Note	Bion Shively	1991	Giant Victory	Jack Moiseyev
1953	Helicopter	Harry Harvey	1992	Alf Palema	Mickey McNichol
1954	Newport Dream	Del Cameron	1993	American Winner	Ron Pierce
1955	Scott Frost	Joe O'Brien	1994	Victory Dream	Michel Lachance
1956	The Intruder	Ned Bower	1995	Tagliabue	John Campbell
1957	Hickory Smoke	J. Simpson Sr.	1996	Continentalvictory	Michel Lachance
1958	Emily's Pride	Flave Nipe	1997	Malabar Man	Mal Burroughs
1959	Diller Hanover	Frank Ervin	1998	Muscles Yankee	John Campbell
1960	Blaze Hanover	Joe O'Brien	1999	Self Possessed	Michel Lachance
1961	Harlan Dean	James Arthur	2000	Yankee Paco	T.J. Ritchie
1962	A. C.'s Viking	Sanders Russell	2001	Scarlet Knight	Stefan Melander
1963	Speedy Scot	Ralph Baldwin	2002	Chip Chip Hooray	Eric Ledford
1964	Ayres	J. Simpson Sr.	2003	Amigo Hall	Mike Lachance

*Park Avenue Joe and Probe dead-heated for win. Park Avenue finished first in the summary 2-1-1 to Probe's 1-9-1 finish.
Note: Run at 1 mile since 1947.

Little Brown Jug

Year	Winner	Driver	Year	Winner	Driver
1946	Ensign Hanover	Wayne Smart	1975	Seatrain	Ben Webster
1947	Forbes Chief	Del Cameron	1976	Keystone Ore	Stanley Dancer
1948	Knight Dream	Frank Safford	1977	Governor Skipper	John Chapman
1949	Good Time	Frank Ervin	1978	Happy Escort	William Popfinger
1950	Dudley Hanover	Del Miller	1979	Hot Hitter	Herve Filion
1951	Tar Heel	Del Cameron	1980	Niatross	Clint Galbraith
1952	Meadow Rice	Wayne Smart	1981	Fan Hanover	Glen Garnsey
1953	Keystoner	Frank Ervin	1982	Merger	John Campbell
1954	Adios Harry	Morris MacDonald	1983	Ralph Hanover	Ron Waples
1955	Quick Chief	Bill Haughton	1984	Colt Fortysix	Chris Boring
1956	Noble Adios	John Simpson Sr.	1985	Nihilator	Bill O'Donnell
1957	Torpid	John Simpso Sr.	1986	Barberry Spur	Bill O'Donnell
1958	Shadow Wave	Joe O'Brien	1987	Jaguar Spur	Dick Stillings
1959	Adios Butler	Clint Hodgins	1988	B. J. Scoot	Michel Lachance
1960	Bullet Hanover	John Simpson Sr.	1989	Goalie Jeff	Michel Lachance
1961	Henry T. Adios	Stanley Dancer	1990	Beach Towel	Ray Remmen
1962	Lehigh Hanover	Stanley Dancer	1991	Precious Bunny	Jack Moiseye
1963	Overtrick	John Patterson	1992	Fake Left	Ron Waples
1964	Vicar Hanover	Bill Haughton	1993	Life Sign	John Campbell
1965	Bret Hanover	Frank Ervin	1994	Magical Mike	Michel Lachance
1966	Romeo Hanover	George Sholty	1995	Nick's Fantasy	John Campbell
1967	Best of All	James Hackett	1996	Armbro Operative	Jack Moiseyev
1968	Rum Customer	Bill Haughton	1997	Western Dreamer	Michel Lachance
1969	Laverne Hanover	Bill Haughton	1998	Shady Character	Ron Pierce
1970	Most Happy Fella	Stanley Dancer	1999	Blissful Hall	Ron Pierce
1971	Nansemond	Herve Filion	2000	Astreos	Chris Christoforou
1972	Strike Out	Keith Waples	2001	Bettor's Delight	Michel Lachance
1973	Melvin's Woe	Joe O'Brien	2002	Million Dollar Cam	Luc Ouellette
1974	Armbro Omaha	Bill Haughton	2003	No Pan Intended	David S. Miller

Playing the Ponies

No doubt hoping that life would imitate art, Steven Spielberg and Gary Ross joined a group of show-business investors who bought a 10% stake in Kentucky Derby hopeful Atswhatimtalknbout from owner B. Wayne Hughes. Spielberg, whose Dreamworks studio handled international distribution for the movie *Seabiscuit*, and Ross, who directed the film, were brought to the investment group by Hall of Fame jockey (and Santa Anita general manager) Chris McCarron, who was a consultant on *Seabiscuit*. At the March 2003 San Felipe Stakes, the 3-year-old Atswhatimtalknbout—who was sired by 1992 Horse of the Year A.P. Indy—closed like a shot to finish second. He had a promising run-up to the Kentucky Derby but ended up finishing fourth in the Run for the Roses on May 3. Alas, there was no Hollywood ending for the Tinseltown moguls.

Breeders' Crown

1984

Div	Winner	Driver
2PC	Dragon's Lair	Jeff Mallet
2PF	Amneris	John Campbell
3PC	Troublemaker	Bill O'Donnell
3PF	Naughty But Nice	Tommy Haughton
2TC	Workaholic	Berndt Lindstedt
2TF	Conifer	George Sholty
3TC	Baltic Speed	Jan Nordin
3TF	Fancy Crown	Bill O'Donnell

1985

Div	Winner	Driver
2PC	Robust Hanover	John Campbell
2PF	Caressable	Herve Filion
3PC	Nihilator	Bill O'Donnell
3PF	Stienam	Buddy Gilmour
2TC	Express Ride	John Campbell
2TF	JEF's Spice	Mickey McNichol
3TC	Prakas	John Campbell
3TF	Armbro Devona	Bill O'Donnell
AP	Division Street	Michel Lachance
AT	Sandy Bowl	John Campbell

1986

Div	Winner	Driver
2PC	Sunset Warrior	Bill Gale
2PF	Halcyon	Ray Remmen
3PC	Masquerade	Richard Silverman
3PF	Glow Softly	Ron Waples
2TC	Mack Lobell	John Campbell
2TF	Super Flora	Ron Waples
3TC	Sugarcane Hanover	Ron Waples
3TF	JEF's Spice	Bill O'Donnell
APM	Samshu Bluegrass	Michel Lachance
ATM	Grades Singing	Herve Filion
APH	Forrest Skipper	Lucien Fontaine
ATH	Nearly Perfect	Mickey McNichol

1987

Div	Winner	Driver
2PC	Camtastic	Bill O'Donnell
2PF	Leah Almahurst	Bill Fahy
3PC	Call For Rain	Clint Galbraith
3PF	Pacific	Tom Harmer
2TC	Defiant One	Howard Beissinger
2TF	Nan's Catch	Berndt Lindstedt
3TC	Mack Lobell	John Campbell
3TF	Armbro Fling	George Sholty
APM	Follow My Star	John Campbell
ATM	Grades Singing	Olle Goop
APH	Armbro Emerson	Walter Whelan
ATH	Sugarcane Hanover	Ron Waples

1988

Div	Winner	Driver
2PC	Kentucky Spur	Dick Stillings
2PF	Central Park West	John Campbell
3PC	Camtastic	Bill O'Donnell
3PF	Sweet Reflection	Bill O'Donnell
2TC	Valley Victory	Bill O'Donnell
2TF	Peace Corps	John Campbell
3TC	Firm Tribute	Mark O'Mara
3TF	Nalda Hanover	Mickey McNichol
APM	Anniecrombie	Dave Magee
ATM	Armbro Flori	Larry Walker
APH	Call For Rain	Clint Galbraith
ATH	Mack Lobell	John Campbell

1989

Div	Winner	Driver
2PC	Till We Meet Again	Mickey McNichol
2PF	Town Pro	Doug Brown
3PC	Goalie Jeff	Michel Lachance
3PF	Cheery Hello	John Campbell
2TC	Royal Troubador	Carl Allen
2TF	Delphi's Lobell	Ron Waples
3TC	Esquire Spur	Dick Stillings
3TF	Pace Corps	John Campbell
APM	Armbro Feather	John Kopas
ATM	Grades Singing	Olle Goop
APH	Matt's Scooter	Michel Lachance
ATH	Delray Lobell	John Campbell

1990

Div	Winner	Driver
2PC	Artsplace	John Campbell
2PF	Miss Easy	John Campbell
3PC	Beach Towel	Ray Remmen
3PF	Town Pro	Doug Brown
2TC	Crysta's Best	Dick Richardson Jr.
2TF	Jean Bi	Jan Nordin
3TC	Embassy Lobell	Michel Lachance
3TF	Me Maggie	Berndt Lindstedt
APM	Caesar's Jackpot	Bill Fahy
ATM	Peace Corps	Stig Johansson
APH	Bay's Fella	Paul MacDonell
ATH	No Sex Please	Ron Waples

Note: 2=Two-year-old; T=Trotter; C=Colt; 3=Three-year-old; P=Pacer; F=Filly; A=Aged; H=Horse; M=Mare.

Breeders' Crown (Cont.)

1991

Div	Winner	Driver
2PC	Digger Almahurst	Doug Brown
2PF	Hazleton Kay	John Campbell
3PC	Three Wizzards	Bill Gale
3PF	Miss Easy	John Campbell
2TC	King Conch	Bill Gale
2TF	Armbro Keepsake	John Campbell
3TC	Giant Victory	Ron Pierce
3TF	Twelve Speed	Ron Waples
APM	Delinquent Account	Bill O'Donnell
ATM	Me Maggie	Berndt Lindstedt
APH	Camluck	Michel Lachance
ATH	Billyjojimbob	Paul MacDonell

1992

Div	Winner	Driver
2PC	Village Jiffy	Ron Waples
2PF	Immortality	John Campbell
3PC	Kingsbridge	Roger Mayotte
3PF	So Fresh	John Campbell
2TC	Giant Chill	John Patterson Jr.
2TF	Winky's Goal	Cat Manzi
3TC	Baltic Striker	Michel Lachance
3TF	Imperfection	Michel Lachance
APM	Shady Daisy	Ron Pierce
ATM	Peace Corps	Torbjorn Jansson
APH	Artsplace	John Campbell
ATH	No Sex Please	Ron Waples

1993

Div	Winner	Driver
2PC	Expensive Scooter	Jack Moiseyev
2PF	Electric Scooter	Mike Lachance
3PC	Life Sign	John Campbell
3PF	Immortality	John Campbell
2TC	Westgate Crown	John Campbell
2TF	Gleam	Jimmy Takter
3TC	Pine Chip	John Campbell
3TF	Expressway Hanover	Per Henriksen
APM	Swing Back	Kelly Sheppard
ATM	Lifetime Dream	Paul MacDonell
APH	Staying Together	Bill O'Donnell
ATH	Earl	Chris Christoforou Jr.

1994

Div	Winner	Driver
2PC	Jenna's Beach Boy	Bill Fahy
2PF	Yankee Cashmere	Peter Wrenn
3PC	Magical Mike	Michel Lachance
3PF	Hardie Hanover	Tim Twaddle
2TC	Eager Seelster	Teddy Jacobs
2TF	Lookout Victory	John Patterson
3TC	Incredible Abe	Italo Tamborrino
3TF	Imageofa Clear Day	Bill O'Donnell
APM	Shady Daisy	Michel Lachance
ATM	Armbro Keepsake	Stig Johansson
APH	Village Jiffy	Paul MacDonell
ATH	Pine Chip	John Campbell

1995

Div	Winner	Driver
2PC	John Street North	Jack Moiseyev
2PF	Paige Nicole Q	John Campbell
3PC	Jenna's Beach Boy	Bill Fahy
3PF	Headline Hanover	Doug Brown
2TC	Armbro Officer	Steve Condren
2TF	Continentalvictory	Michel Lachance
3TC	Abundance	Bill O'Donnell
3TF	Lookout Victory	Sonny Patterson
APM	Ellamony	Mike Saftic
ATM	CR Kay Suzie	Rod Allen
APH	That'll Be Me	Roger Mayotte
ATH	Panifesto	Luc Ouellette

1996

Div	Winner	Driver
2PC	His Mattjesty	Doug Brown
2PF	Before Sunrise	Steve Condren
3PC	Armbro Operative	Michel Lachance
3PF	Mystical Maddy	Michel Lachance
2TC	Malabar Man	Mal Burroughs
2TF	Armbro Prowess	Jimmy Takter
3TC	Running Sea	Wally Hennessey
3TF	Personal Banner	Peter Wrenn
APM	She's A Great Lady	John Campbell
APH	Jenna's Beach Boy	Bill Fahy
AT	CR Kay Suzie	Rod Allen

1997

Div	Winner	Driver
2PC	Artiscape	Michel Lachance
2PF	Take Flight	Luc Ouellette
3PC	Village Jasper	Paul McDonnell
3PF	Stienam's Place	Jack Moiseyev
2TC	Catch As Catch Can	Wally Hennessey
2TF	My Dolly	Wally Hennessey
3TC	Malabar Man	Malvern Burroughs
3TF	No Nonsense Woman	Jim Doherty
APM	Jay's Table	John Campbell
APH	Red Bow Tie	Luc Ouellette
AT	Moni Maker	Wally Hennessey

1998

Div	Winner	Driver
2PC	Badlands Hanover	Ron Pierce
2PF	Juliet's Fate	George Brennan
3PC	Artiscape	Michel Lachance
3PF	Galleria	George Brennan
2TC	CR Commando	Carl Allen
2TF	Musical Victory	Luc Ouellette
3TC	Muscles Yankee	John Campbell
3TF	Lassie's Goal	Mark O'Mara
APM	Shore By Five	Daniel Dube
APH	Red Bow Tie	Luc Ouellette
AT	Supergrit	Ron Pierce

Breeders' Crown *(Cont.)*

1999

Div	Winner	Driver
2PC	Tyberwood	Richard Silverman
2PF	Eternal Camnation	Eric Ledford
3PC	Grinfromeartoear	Chris Christoforou
3PF	Odies Fame	David Wall
2TC	Master Lavec	Daniel Daley
2TF	Dream of Joy	James Meittinis
3TC	CR Renegade	Rodney Allen
3TF	Oolong	Ronald Pierce
APM	Shore By Five	Daniel Dube
APH	Red Bow Tie	Luc Ouellette
AT	Supergrit	Ronald Pierce

2001

Div	Winner	Driver
2PC	Western Shooter	John Campbell
2PF	Cam Swifty	Jim Meittinis
3PC	Real Desire	John Campbell
3PF	Bunny Lake	John Stark Jr.
2TC	Duke Of York	Paul MacDonnell
2TF	Cameron Hall	Michel Lachance
3TC	Liberty Balance	Randall Waples
3TF	Syrinx Hanover	John Campbell
APM	Eternal Camnation	Eric Ledford
APH	Goliath Bayama	Sylvain Filion
AT	Varenne	G. Minnucci

2000

Div	Winner	Driver
2PC	Bettor's Delight	Michel Lachance
2PF	Lady MacBeach	Luc Ouellette
3PC	Gallo Blue Chip	Daniel Dube
3PF	Popcorn Penny	Ryan Anderson
2TC	Banker Hall	Trevor Ritchie
2TF	Syrinx Hanover	Trevor Ritchie
3TC	Fast Photo	Michel Lachance
3TF	Aviano	Trevor Ritchie
APM	Ron's Girl	Michel Lachance
APH	Western Ideal	Michel Lachance
AT	Magician	David Miller

2002

Div	Winner	Driver
2PC	Totally Western	Mario Baillargeon
2PF	Armbro Amoretto	Luc Ouellette
3PC	Art Major	John Campbell
3PF	Allamerican Nadia	Chris Christoforou
2TC	Broadway Hall	John Campbell
2TF	Pick Me Up	Luc Ouellette
3TC	Kadabra	David S. Miller
3TF	Cameron Hall	Trevor Ritchie
APM	Molly Can Do It	Jack Moiseyev
APH	Real Desire	John Campbell
AT	Fool's Goal	Jack Moiseyev

Note: 2=Two-year-old; T=Trotter; C=Colt; 3=Three-year-old; P=Pacer; F=Filly; A=Aged; H=Horse; M=Mare.

Triple Crown Winners

Trotting

Trotting's Triple Crown consists of the Hambletonian (first run in 1926), the Kentucky Futurity (first run in 1893) and the Yonkers Trot (known as the Yonkers Futurity when it began in 1955).

Year	Horse	Owner	Breeder	Trainer & Driver
1955	Scott Frost	S.A. Camp Farms	Est of W.N. Reynolds	Joe O'Brien
1963	Speedy Scot	Castleton Farms	Castleton Farms	Ralph Baldwin
1964	Ayres	Charlotte Sheppard	Charlotte Sheppard	John Simpson Sr
1968	Nevele Pride	Nevele Acres & Lou Resnick	Mr & Mrs E.C. Quin	Stanley Dancer
1969	Lindy's Pride	Lindy Farm	Hanover Shoe Farms	Howard Beissinger
1972	Super Bowl	Rachel Dancer & Rose Hild Breeding Farm	Stoner Creek Stud	Stanley Dancer

Pacing

Pacing's Triple Crown consists of the Cane Pace (called the Cane Futurity when it began in 1955), the Little Brown Jug (first run in 1946) and the Messenger Stakes (first run in 1956).

Year	Horse	Owner	Breeder	Trainer/Driver
1959	Adios Butler	Paige West & Angelo Pellillo	R.C. Carpenter	Paige West/Clint Hodgins
1965	Bret Hanover	Richard Downing	Hanover Shoe Farms	Frank Ervin
1966	Romeo Hanover	Lucky Star Stables & Morton Finder	Hanover Shoe Farms	Jerry Silverman/ William Meyer (Cane) & George Sholty (Jug & Messenger)
1968	Rum Customer	Kennilworth Farms & L. C. Mancuso	Mr. & Mrs. R.C. Larkin	Bill Haughton
1970	Most Happy Fella	Egyptian Acres Stable	Stoner Creek Stud	Stanley Dancer
1980	Niatross	Niagara Acres, C. Galbraith & Niatross Stables	Niagara Acres	Clint Galbraith
1983	Ralph Hanover	Waples Stable, Pointsetta Stable, Grant's Direct Stable & P. J. Baugh	Hanover Shoe Farms	Stew Firlotte/Ron Waples
1997	Western Dreamer	Daniel and Matthew Daly and Patrick Daly Jr.	Kentuckiana Farms	Bill Robinson/Michel Lachance
1999	Blissful Hall	Daniel Plouffe	Walnut Hall Limited	Ben Wallace/Ron Pierce

Awards

Horse of the Year

Year	Horse	Gait	Owner	Year	Horse	Gait	Owner
1947	Victory Song	T	Castleton Farm	1979	Niatross	P	Niagara Acres, Clint Galbraith
1948	Rodney	T	R.H. Johnston	1980	Niatross	P	Niatross Syndicate, Niagara Acres, Clint Galbraith
1949	Good Time	T	William Cane				
1950	Proximity	T	Ralph and Gordon Verhurst				
1951	Pronto Don	T	Hayes Fair Acres Stable	1981	Fan Hanover	P	Dr. J. Glen Brown
1952	Good Time	P	William Cane	1982	Cam Fella	P	Norm Clements, Norm Faulkner
1953	Hi Lo's Forbes	P	Mr. and Mrs. Earl Wagner	1983	Cam Fella	P	JEF's Standardbred, Norm Clements, Norm Faulkner
1954	Stenographer	T	Max Hempt				
1955	Scott Frost	T	S.A. Camp Farms				
1956	Scott Frost	T	S.A. Camp Farms	1984	Fancy Crown	T	Fancy Crown Stable
1957	Torpid	P	Sherwood Farm	1985	Nihilator	P	Wall Street-Nihilator Syndicate
1958	Emily's Pride	T	Walnut Hall and Castleton Farms	1986	Forrest Skipper	P	Forrest L. Bartlett
1959	Bye Bye Byrd	P	Mr. and Mrs. Rex Larkin	1987	Mack Lobell	T	One More Time Stable and Fair Wind Farm
1960	Adios Butler	P	Adios Butler Syndicate	1988	Mack Lobell	T	John Erik Magnusson
1961	Adios Butler	P	Adios Butler Syndicate	1989	Matt's Scooter	P	Gordon and Illa Rumpel, Charles Jurasvinski
1962	Su Mac Lad	T	I.W. Berkemeyer				
1963	Speedy Scot	T	Castleton Farm	1990	Beach Towel	P	Uptown Stables
1964	Bret Hanover	P	Richard Downing	1991	Precious Bunny	P	R. Peter Heffering
1965	Bret Hanover	P	Richard Downing	1992	Artsplace	P	George Segal
1966	Bret Hanover	P	Richard Downing	1993	Staying Together		Robert Hamather
1967	Nevele Pride	T	Nevele Acres	1994	Cam's Card Shark	P	Jeffrey S. Snyder
1968	Nevele Pride	T	Nevele Acres, Louis Resnick	1995	CR Kay Suzie	T	Carl & Rod Allen Stable, Inc.
1969	Nevele Pride	T	Nevele Acres, Louis Resnick	1996	Continental-victory	T	Continentalvictory Stables
1970	Fresh Yankee	T	Duncan MacDonald	1997	Malabar Man	T	Malvern Burroughs
1971	Albatross	P	Albatross Stable	1998	Moni Maker	T	Moni Maker Stable
1972	Albatross	P	Amicable Stable	1999	Moni Maker	T	Moni Maker Stable
1973	Sir Dalrae	P	A La Carte Racing Stable	2000	Gallo Blue Chip	P	Dan Gernatt Farms
1974	Delmonica Hanover	T	Delvin Miller, W. Arnold Hanger	2001	Bunny Lake	P	W. Springtime Racing Stable
1975	Savoir	T	Allwood Stable				
1976	Keystone Ore	P	Mr. and Mrs. Stanley Dancer, Rose Hild Farms, Robert Jones				
1977	Green Speed	T	Beverly Lloyds				
1978	Abercrombie	P	Shirley Mitchell, L. Keith Bulen	2002	Real Desire	P	Brittany Farms

Driver of the Year

Year	Driver	Year	Driver	Year	Driver
1968	Stanley Dancer	1980	Ron Waples	1992	Walter Case Jr.
1969	Herve Filion	1981	Herve Filion	1993	Jack Moiseyev
1970	Herve Filion	1982	Bill O'Donnell	1994	Dave Magee
1971	Herve Filion	1983	John Campbell	1995	Luc Ouellette
1972	Herve Filion	1984	Bill O'Donnell	1996	Tony Morgan
1973	Herve Filion	1985	Michel Lachance		Luc Ouellette
1974	Herve Filion	1986	Michel Lachance	1997	Tony Morgan
1975	Joe O'Brien	1987	Michel Lachance	1998	Walter Case Jr.
1976	Herve Filion	1988	John Campbell	1999	Dave Palone
1977	Donald Dancer	1989	Herve Filion	2000	Dave Palone
1978	Carmine Abbatiello Herve Filion	1990	John Campbell	2001	Stephane Bouchard
1979	Ron Waples	1991	Walter Case Jr.	2002	Tony Morgan

Note: Balloting is conducted by the U.S Trotting Association for the U.S. Harness Writers Association.

Annual Leaders

Leading Drivers—Money Won

Year	Driver	Winnings ($)	Year	Driver	Winnings ($)
1946	Thomas Berry	121,933	1975	Carmine Abbatiello	2,275,093
1947	H.C. Fitzpatrick	133,675	1976	Herve Filion	2,278,634
1948	Ralph Baldwin	153,222	1977	Herve Filion	2,551,058
1949	Clint Hodgins	184,108	1978	Carmine Abbatiello	3,344,457
1950	Del Miller	306,813	1979	John Campbell	3,308,984
1951	John Simpson Sr.	333,316	1980	John Campbell	3,732,306
1952	Bill Haughton	311,728	1981	Bill O'Donnell	4,065,608
1953	Bill Haughton	374,527	1982	Bill O'Donnell	5,755,067
1954	Bill Haughton	415,577	1983	John Campbell	6,104,082
1955	Bill Haughton	599,455	1984	Bill O'Donnell	9,059,184
1956	Bill Haughton	572,945	1985	Bill O'Donnell	10,207,372
1957	Bill Haughton	586,950	1986	John Campbell	9,515,055
1958	Bill Haughton	816,659	1987	John Campbell	10,186,495
1959	Bill Haughton	771,435	1988	John Campbell	11,148,565
1960	Del Miller	567,282	1989	John Campbell	9,738,450
1961	Stanley Dancer	674,723	1990	John Campbell	11,620,878
1962	Stanley Dancer	760,343	1991	Jack Moiseyev	9,568,468
1963	Bill Haughton	790,086	1992	John Campbell	8,202,108
1964	Stanley Dancer	1,051,538	1993	John Campbell	9,926,482
1965	Bill Haughton	889,943	1994	John Campbell	9,834,139
1966	Stanley Dancer	1,218,403	1995	John Campbell	9,469,797
1967	Bill Haughton	1,305,773	1996	Michel Lachance	8,408,231
1968	Bill Haughton	1,654,463	1997	Michel Lachance	9,215,388
1969	Del Insko	1,635,463	1998	John Campbell	10,768,771
1970	Herve Filion	1,647,837	1999	Luc Ouellette	10,841,495
1971	Herve Filion	1,915,945	2000	John Campbell	11,160,462
1972	Herve Filion	2,473,265	2001	John Campbell	14,184,863
1973	Herve Filion	2,233,303	2002	John Campbell	11,967,597
1974	Herve Filion	3,474,315			

Motor Sports

**Winston Cup
leader Matt Kenseth**

Winning Isn't Everything

Just ask Ryan Newman, who won more than anyone but still trailed Matt Kenseth in the NASCAR points race

BY MARK BECHTEL

NASCAR's announcement that starting in 2003–04 Nextel would replace Winston as the sponsor of its top series didn't just mean big bucks for the sport. (The ten-year deal with Nextel is worth $700 million.) It also meant that 2003 would provide the last Winston Cup points race. And it turned out to be one of the strangest.

While Ryan Newman was winning eight races—the most in the series since 1999—Matt Kenseth found Victory Lane just once. But Kenseth had a firm command on the points race for most of the season thanks to his preternatural knack for finishing in the Top 15, which he 26 times in the first 28 races. He was far from spectacular, but he always seemed to be lurking near the front, avoiding trouble and amassing a war chest of points.

Seeing Kenseth run away with the points race while Newman—who, through 28 races, had 11 Top Fives to Kenseth's 10—languished several spots behind him, well out of reach of the top spot, sparked calls for an overhaul of the points system, which rewards consistency more than wins. "The bad finishes shouldn't decide championships," Roush Racing president Geoff Smith said. "I've looked at what the points race might look like in October, if we could discard a team's three worst finishes. Suddenly, over a four- or five-year period, October was a five-car race instead of a two-car race."

Kenseth's only poor finish in the first half of the season came in his first start, at the Daytona 500. He was never a factor at a Speedweeks that seemed dominated by the ghost of Dale Earnhardt. The team he founded in 1996, Dale Earnhardt, Inc. (DEI), and Richard Childress Racing (RCR), for which he won six Winston Cup titles, spent the fortnight fighting it out for superspeedway supremacy. "This was Dale's playground," said DEI executive vice president Ty Norris. "And if we weren't competitive here, he'd be embarrassed for us. We're not going to embarrass him. That's why we put so much effort into it."

Earnhardt's influence is also still felt

After a poor start, Schumacher put himself in position to win a record sixth F1 title.

strongly at RCR, for whom he drove the last 17 years of his life. The RCR team has become so accustomed to success at the superspeedway by the shore that crew members were moping around after Kevin Harvick, driving Earnhardt's former car, qualified sixth for the 500. Childress was stunned by their reaction. In addition to the Earnhardt legacy, the rivals share information such as wind-tunnel data and body position. "It's like Larry Bird and Magic Johnson in their prime," said Norris. "Even though they had a rivalry and were driven to beat each other, they had a friendship. That's where RCR and DEI are when it comes to these races."

Dale Earnhardt Jr., however, made sure the relationship between the two teams didn't get too warm and fuzzy. After RCR's Jeff Green unexpectedly nipped Junior for the pole on Feb. 10 and teammate Robby Gordon won the first 125-mile qualifying race three days later, Junior talked a little smack. "You've got Richard Childress over there busting his ass for all these years to get what he's got, and I don't think those guys appreciate what the man is in this sport and the opportunity they have in his race cars." (Green's retort: "That's chickens---.")

The "family" rivalry aside, Junior started Speedweeks in top form, winning the Bud Shootout, his 125-mile qualifying race and the Busch race on the eve of the 500, giving him the chance to become the first driver to win four races at one Speedweeks. But alternator problems early in the 500 forced him

to change his battery, which put him two laps down.

He played a part in deciding the race, though. After a rain delay, and with more rain on the horizon, Earnhardt assumed his position at the front of the field thanks to a rule that allows cars a lap down to start alongside the lead lap cars. That enabled him to slide in behind his teammate Waltrip, who was running second to Jimmie Johnson, and push him to the lead. Shortly thereafter, the skies opened and Waltrip had his second Daytona 500 win.

Kenseth finished 20th in the race, but the next week he finished third at Rockingham and won the following race, in Las Vegas. That vaulted him to second place in points, and he took the lead the following week. By hanging onto the lead into October, Kenseth looked to become the first of NASCAR's "Young Guns" to win a championship, and several of his fellow newbies were set to finish near the top as well. In addition to Newman, Earnhardt, Harvick, Johnson and Kurt Busch were all in the Top 10.

Busch was in the spotlight for reasons other than his racing, however. The Las Vegas native has been brash since breaking into the Winston Cup series in 2001. A series of on-track incidents with Jimmy Spencer—last year Busch called Spencer an "old decrepit has-been" after they tangled on track at Indianapolis—led to a simmering rivalry that exploded after the race in Michigan on Aug. 17. Spencer believed Busch tried to wreck him, and after the race approached Busch's car in the garage. After some jawing, he punched Busch in the face, earning himself a one-race suspension and prompting a police investigation. (No charges were filed.) But Busch was not viewed as the victim—several drivers said he had it coming, and a few even offered to pay Spencer's fine. Busch won the following week, much to the chagrin of 150,000 or so fans in Bristol, who booed lustily.

The win in Bristol was Busch's fourth, but he was never going to catch Kenseth, whose steely resolve and calm demeanor were reminiscent of another champion, Michael Schumacher. Despite getting off to a terrible start, the German put himself in position to wrap up his record sixth F1 championship by winning the United States Grand Prix on Sept. 28, meaning he needed to finish seventh in the season's final race to win the title.

Schumacher's poor start was made all the more surprising by the fact that it wasn't bad luck that was hampering him—it was driver error. In the season-opening race in Australia, he tried to pass Kimi Raikkonen for the lead and sailed over the curb into the grass, damaging his car. Two weeks later in Malaysia, he made an overly aggressive move and wound up in the gravel, taking Jarno Trulli with him and earning a penalty that ruined his chances of winning. Another silly mistake cost him in the third race in Brazil. Suddenly the driver who always acted suspiciously like a machine looked all too human. "I do think that Michael shows weakness under pressure, and he does make mistakes in those situations," said David Coulthard. "Because of Ferrari's dominance last season it wasn't always apparent, but this season it has been so."

Fans began sending in suggestions: *Take up milking cows to improve the touch in your fingers; have another child; put a picture of your family in the cockpit of your car.* He finally turned things around at Imola, the site of his most bittersweet victory. After qualifying on the pole, he and his younger brother, Ralf, flew home to see their dying mother, Elisabeth, who used to work in the canteen at the Kerpen cart track where the brothers raced as teens. She passed away the night before the event, and both of her sons raced wearing black arm bands. Michael won, but did not celebrate.

The win put Schumacher on track, though. He took the following two races, including a frightening one in Austria in which flames engulfed his car on pit road. "Seeing the fire was not nice," Schumacher said with typical understatement. He returned to form during the rest of the season, holding off Kimi Raikkonen and Colombian Juan Pablo Montoya, a former CART champ, in the championship race.

Montoya's former series had a rough year. CART lost $43.5 million during the first six months of 2003, and even its purchase and privatization by a group led by team owner Paul Gentilozzi did little to improve its prospects. CART lost eight top drivers from the 2002 season, including series champ Cristiano da Matta and all-time wins leader Michael Andretti (who retired after the 2003 Indy 500), as well as big names in Dario Franchitti, Tony Kanaan, and Kenny Brack. The series' woes overshadowed the performance of Paul Tracy, a notorious slow starter who won the first three races of the year and led the standings wire to wire.

Things weren't as bad in the IRL, where Scott Dixon and Helio Castroneves waged one of the great title races in motor sports history. They went into the season's final race in a flat-footed tie for the lead, with Kanaan lurking seven points back. Castroneves came up just short in his attempt to win an unprecedented third straight Indy 500 championship. The Brazilian was edged out by teammate and countryman Gil de Ferran, who until a month before the race wasn't sure if he would even be in the field. On March 23 he suffered a concussion and two broken vertebrae when he hit the wall during a race at Phoenix International Raceway. For the next month he did little but spend time submerged in his backyard pool. "I was afraid my career might be over," he said. Three months later, it was. De Ferran called it quits at the age of 35, at the apex of his career. Said de Ferran, one of the most thoughtful, introspective drivers in the sport, "Right now, I feel I'm as good as I ever was and I'm enjoying myself, so I'd rather get out now, while the party's still cooking."

Indy Racing League

Indianapolis 500

Results of the 87th running of the Indianapolis 500 and fifth race of the 2002 Indy Racing League season. Held Sunday, May 25, 2003, at the 2.5-mile Indianapolis Motor Speedway in Indianapolis.

Distance, 500 miles; starters, 33; time of race, 3 hours, 11 mins. 56.9891 seconds; average speed, 156.291 mph; margin of victory, 0.2990 seconds; caution flags, 9 for 49 laps; lead changes, 14 among eight drivers.

TOP 10 FINISHERS

Pos.	Driver (start pos.)	Chassis-Engine	Qual. Speed	Laps	Status
1	Gil de Ferran (10)	Panoz–Toyota	228.633	200	running
2	Helio Castroneves (1)	Dallara–Toyota	231.725	200	running
3	Tony Kanaan (2)	Dallara–Honda	231.006	200	running
4	Tomas Scheckter (12)	Panoz–Toyota	227.769	200	running
5	Tora Takagi (7)	Panoz–Toyota	229.358	200	running
6	Alex Barron (25)	Panoz–Toyota	227.274	200	running
7	Tony Renna (8)	Dallara–Toyota	228.765	200	running
8	Greg Ray (14)	Panoz–Honda	227.288	200	running
9	Al Unser Jr. (17)	Dallara–Toyota	226.285	200	running
10	Roger Yasukawa (11)	Dallara–Honda	228.577	199	running

2003 Indy Racing League Results

Date	Race	Winner (start pos.)	Chassis-Engine	Qual. Speed
Mar 2	Grand Prix of Miami	Scott Dixon (12)	Panoz–Toyota	199.942
Mar 23	Phoenix 200	Tony Kanaan (1)	Dallara–Honda	178.512
Apr 13	Japan 300	Scott Sharp (7)	Dallara–Toyota	n/a
May 25	Indianapolis 500	Gil de Ferran (10)	Panoz–Toyota	228.633
June 7	Texas 500	Al Unser Jr. (7)	Dallara–Toyota	216.043
June 15	Pikes Peak 225	Scott Dixon (6)	Panoz–Toyota	150.059
June 28	Richmond 250*	Scott Dixon (1)	Panoz–Toyota	168.138
July 6	Kansas 300	Bryan Herta (11)	Dallara–Honda	215.154
July 19	Nashville 200	Gil de Ferran (4)	Dallara–Toyota	205.010
July 27	Michigan 400	Alex Barron (6)	Panoz–Toyota	221.387
Aug 10	Gateway 250	Helio Castroneves (1)	Dallara–Toyota	175.965
Aug 17	Kentucky 300	Sam Hornish Jr. (1)	Dallara–Chevrolet	219.614
Aug 24	Nazareth 225	Helio Castroneves (2)	Dallara–Toyota	170.849
Sept 7	Chicago 300	Sam Hornish Jr. (8)	Dallara–Chevrolet	221.265
Sept 21	California 400	Sam Hornish Jr. (10)	Dallara–Chevrolet	224.088

Note: Distances are in miles unless followed by K (kilometers) or * (laps).

2002 Final Championship Standings

Driver	Pts
Sam Hornish Jr.	531
Helio Castroneves	511
Gil de Ferran	443
Felipe Giaffone	432
Alex Barron	366
Scott Sharp	332
Al Unser Jr.	311
Buddy Lazier	305
Airton Dare	304
Eddie Cheever Jr.	280

Championship Auto Racing Teams

2003 CART Championship Series Results (through September 28)

Date	Event	Winner (start pos.)	Car	Avg Speed
Feb 23	Grand Prix of St. Petersburg	Paul Tracy (2)	Lola-Ford	91.401
Mar 23	Grand Prix of Monterrey	Paul Tracy (2)	Lola-Ford	87.184
Apr 13	Grand Prix of Long Beach	Paul Tracy (2)	Lola-Ford	91.590
May 5	London Champ Car Trophy	S. Bourdais (2)	Lola-Ford	105.412
May 11	German 500	S. Bourdais (1)	Lola-Ford	170.903
May 31	Milwaukee Mile 250	Michael Jourdain Jr. (2)	Lola-Ford	113.190
June 15	Grand Prix of Monterey	Patrick Carpentier (1)	Lola-Ford	107.986
June 22	G.I. Joe's 200	A. Fernandez (3)	Lola-Ford	101.602
July 5	Grand Prix of Cleveland	S. Bourdais (1)	Lola-Ford	117.315
July 13	Molson Indy Toronto	Paul Tracy (1)	Lola-Ford	96.189
July 27	Molson Indy Vancouver	Paul Tracy (1)	Lola-Ford	90.632
Aug 3	Mario Andretti Grand Prix	Bruno Junqueira (1)	Lola-Ford	29.869
Aug 10	Grand Prix of Mid-Ohio	Paul Tracy (1)	Lola-Ford	106.74
Aug 24	Molson Indy Montreal	Michael Jourdain Jr. (4)	Lola-Ford	106.573
Aug 31	Grand Prix of Denver	Bruno Junqueira (1)	Lola-Ford	85.044
Sept 28	Grand Prix Americas	M. Dominguez (8)	Lola-Ford	75.533

2002 Championship Standings

Driver	Overall	Road	Oval
Cristiano da Matta	237	196	41
Bruno Junqueira	164	110	54
Patrick Carpentier	157	117	40
Dario Franchitti	148	95	53
Christian Fittipaldi	122	103	19
Kenny Brack	114	101	13
Jimmy Vasser	114	83	31
Alex Tagliani	111	84	27
Michael Andretti	110	85	25
Michael Jourdain Jr.	105	80	25

National Association for Stock Car Auto Racing

Daytona 500

Results of the 45th Daytona 500, the opening round of the 2002 Winston Cup series. Held Sunday, February 16, 2003, at the 2.5-mile high-banked Daytona International Speedway.

Distance, 500 miles; starters, 43; time of race, 2:02:08; average speed, 133.87 mph; margin of victory, under caution; caution flags, five for 23 laps; lead changes, 11 among eight drivers.

TOP 10 FINISHERS

Pos.	Driver (start pos.)	Car	Laps	Winnings ($)
1	Michael Waltrip (4)	Chevrolet	109	1,419,406
2	Kurt Busch (36)	Ford	109	1,027,101
3	Jimmie Johnson (10)	Chevrolet	109	707,526
4	Kevin Harvick (31)	Chevrolet	109	569,630
5	Mark Martin (26)	Ford	109	444,609
6	Robby Gordon (3)	Chevrolet	109	362,807
7	Tony Stewart (8)	Chevrolet	109	315,454
8	Jeremy Mayfield (20)	Dodge	109	245,026
9	Mike Wallace (18)	Dodge	109	220,051
10	Dale Jarrett (11)	Ford	109	256,098

Late 2002 Winston Cup Series Results

Date	Track/Distance	Winner (start pos.)	Car	Laps	Winnings ($)
Oct 6	Talladega 500	Dale Earnhardt Jr. (13)	Chevrolet	188	166,040
Oct 13	Lowe's 500	Jamie McMurray (5)	Dodge	334	215,717
Oct 20	Martinsville 500	Kurt Busch (36)	Ford	500	142,175
Oct 27	Atlanta 500	Kurt Busch (8)	Ford	248	212,100
Nov 3	N Carolina 400	Johnny Benson (26)	Pontiac	393	162,965
Nov 10	Phoenix 500	Matt Kenseth (28)	Ford	312	211,895
Nov 17	Miami 400	Kurt Busch (1)	Ford	267	297,100

2003 Winston Cup Series Results (through October 5)

Date	Track/Distance	Winner (start pos.)	Car	Laps	Winnings ($)
Feb 16	Daytona 500	Michael Waltrip (4)	Chevrolet	109	1,419,406
Feb 23	N Carolina 400	Dale Jarrett (9)	Ford	393	177,828
Mar 2	Las Vegas 400	Matt Kenseth (17)	Ford	267	365,875
Mar 9	Atlanta 500	Bobby Labonte (4)	Chevrolet	325	209,233
Mar 16	Darlington 400	Ricky Craven (31)	Pontiac	293	172,150
Mar 23	Bristol 500*.	Kurt Busch (9)	Ford	500	162,790
Mar 30	Texas 500	Ryan Newman (3)	Dodge	334	406,500
Apr 6	Talladega 499	Dale Earnhardt Jr. (13)	Chevrolet	188	204,367
Apr 13	Martinsville 500	Jeff Gordon (1)	Chevrolet	500	219,143
Apr 27	California 500	Kurt Busch (16)	Ford	250	213,150
May 3	Richmond 400	Joe Nemechek (2)	Chevrolet	393	159,375
May 25	Lowe's 600	Jimmie Johnson (32)	Chevrolet	276	271,900
June 1	Dover Downs 400	Ryan Newman (1)	Dodge	400	199,325
June 8	Pocono 500	Tony Stewart (4)	Chevrolet	200	214,253
June 15	Michigan 400	Kurt Busch (4)	Ford	200	172,650
June 22	California 350K	Robby Gordon (2)	Chevrolet	110	204,512
July 5	Daytona 400	Greg Biffle (30)	Ford	160	187,975
July 13	Chicagoland 400	Ryan Newman (14)	Dodge	267	191,000
July 20	New Hampshire 300	Jimmie Johnson (6)	Chevrolet	300	200,225
July 27	Pocono 500	Ryan Newman (1)	Dodge	200	180,575
Aug 3	Brickyard 400	Kevin Harvick (1)	Chevrolet	160	418,253
Aug 10	Watkins Glen 90*	Robby Gordon (14)	Chevrolet	90	156,272
Aug 17	Michigan 400	Ryan Newman (2)	Dodge	200	155,505
Aug 23	Bristol 500*	Kurt Busch (5)	Ford	500	237,565
Aug 31	Southern 500	Terry Labonte (3)	Chevrolet	367	204,736
Sept 6	Richmond 400*	Ryan Newman (4)	Dodge	400	160,970
Sept.14	New Hampshire 300*	Jimmie Johnson (8)	Chevrolet	300	200,225
Sept 21	Dover 400*	Ryan Newman (5)	Dodge	400	160,460
Sept 28	Talladega 500	Michael Waltrip (18)	Chevrolet	188	157,090
Oct 5	Kansas 400	Ryan Newman (11)	Dodge	267	191,000

Note: Distances are in miles unless followed by K (kilometers) or * (laps).

2002 Winston Cup Final Standings

Driver	Pts	Starts	Wins	Top 5	Top 10
Tony Stewart	4,800	36	3	15	21
Mark Martin	4,762	36	1	12	22
Kurt Busch	4,641	36	4	12	20
Jeff Gordon	4,607	36	3	13	20
Jimmie Johnson	4,600	36	3	6	21
Ryan Newman	4,593	36	1	14	22
Rusty Wallace	4,574	36	0	7	17
Matt Kenseth	4,432	36	5	11	19
Dale Jarrett	4,415	36	2	10	18
Ricky Rudd	4,323	36	1	8	12

2002 Winston Cup Driver Winnings

Driver	Winnings ($)
Mark Martin	5,279,400
Jeff Gordon	4,981,170
Ward Burton	4,849,880
Tony Stewart	4,695,150
Dale Earnhardt Jr.	4,570,980
Ryan Newman	4,373,830
Rusty Wallace	4,090,050
Ricky Rudd	4,009,380
Dale Jarrett	3,935,670
Matt Kenseth	3,888,850

Formula One Grand Prix Racing

2003 Formula One Results (through September 28)

Grand Prix	Date	Winner	Car	Laps	Time
Australian	Mar 9	David Coulthard	McLaren-Mercedes	58	1:34:42.124
Malaysian	Mar 23	Kimi Räikkönen	McLaren-Mercedes	56	1:32:22.195
Brazilian	Apr 6	Giancarlo Fisichella	Jordan-Ford	54	1:31:17.748
San Marino	Apr 20	Michael Schumacher	Ferrari	62	1:28:12.058
Spanish	May 4	Michael Schumacher	Ferrari	65	1:33:46.933
Austrian	May 18	Michael Schumacher	Ferrari	69	1:24:04.888
Monaco	June 1	Juan Pablo Montoya	Williams-BMW	78	1:42:19.010
Canadian	June 15	Michael Schumacher	Ferrari	70	1:31:13.591
European	June 29	Ralf Schumacher	Williams-BMW	60	1:34:43.622
French	July 6	Ralf Schumacher	Williams-BMW	70	1:30:49.213
British	July 20	Rubens Barrichello	Ferrari	60	1:28:37.554
German	Aug 3	Juan Pablo Montoya	Williams-BMW	67	1:28:48.769
Hungarian	Aug 24	Fernando Alonso	Renault	70	1:39:01.460
Italian	Sept 14	Michael Schumacher	Ferrari	53	1:14:19.838
U.S.	Sept 28	Michael Schumacher	Ferrari	73	1:33:35.997

2002 World Championship Final Standings

Drivers compete in Grand Prix races for the title of World Driving Champion. Below are the top 10 drivers from the 2001 season. Points are awarded for places 1–6 as follows: 10-6-4-3-2-1.

Driver	Country	Team	Pts
Michael Schumacher	Germany	Ferrari	144
Rubens Barrichello	Brazil	Ferrari	77
Juan Pablo Montoya	Colombia	Williams-BMW	50
Ralf Schumacher	Germany	Williams-BMW	42
David Coulthard	Great Britain	McLaren-Mercedes	41
Kimi Räikkönen	Finland	McLaren-Mercedes	24
Jenson Button	Great Britain	Renault	14
Jarno Trulli	Italy	Renault	9
Eddie Irvine	Great Britain	Jaguar-Cosworth	8
Nick Heidfeld	Germany	Sauber-Petronas	7

Professional Sports Car Racing, Inc.

The 24 Hours of Daytona

Held at the Daytona International Speedway on February 1–2, 2003, the 24 Hours of Daytona serves as the opening round of Grand American Road Racing Association's season.

Place	Drivers	Car (Class)	Distance
1	Kevin Buckler, Michael Schrom, Timo Bernhard, Jorg Bergmeister	Porsche GT3 RS	694 laps (114.068, top mph)
2	Anthony Lazzaro, Ralf Kelleners, Johnny Mowlem	Ferrari 360GT	685
3	Dave Standridge, Richard Steranka, Johannes Van Overbeck, David Murry	Porsche GT3 RS	683
4	Scott Maxwell, David Brabham, David Empringham	Ford Multimatic	678
5	Hurley Haywood, JC France, Scott Goodyear, Scott Sharp	Porsche Fabcar	660

2003 American Le Mans Series—Prototype Class (through September 27)

Date	Race	Winners	Car
Mar 15	12 Hours at Sebring	Frank Biela, Marco Werner, Phillip Peter	Audi R8
June 29	Grand Prix of Atlanta	J.J. Lehto, Johnny Herbert	Audi R8
July 27	Grand Prix of Sonoma	Frank Biela, Marco Werner	Audi R8
Aug 8	Grand Prix de Trois-Rivières	Frank Biela, Marco Werner	Audi R8
Aug 17	Grand Prix of Mosport	Frank Biela, Marco Werner	Audi R8
Aug 24	Road America 500	Johnny Herbert, J.J. Lehto	Audi R8
Sept 7	Laguna Seca	Frank Biela, Marco Werner	Audi R8
Sept 27	Grand Prix Americas	J.J. Lehto, Johnny Herbert	Audi R8

2003 American Le Mans Series—GTS Class (through September 27)

Date	Race	Winners	Car
Mar 15	12 Hours at Sebring	Fredy Leinhard, Ron Fellows, Johnny O'Connell	Corvette C5-R
June 29	Grand Prix of Atlanta	Kelly Collins, Oliver Gavin	Corvette C5-R
July 27	Grand Prix of Sonoma	Ron Fellows, Johnny O'Connell	Corvette C5-R
Aug 8	Grand Prix de Trois-Rivières	Oliver Gavin, Kelly Collins	Corvette C5-R
Aug 17	Grand Prix of Mosport	Ron Fellows, Johnny O'Connell	Corvette C5-R
Aug 24	Road America 500	Jan Magnussen, David Brabham	Ferrari 550
Sept 7	Laguna Seca	Jan Magnussen, David Brabham	Ferrari 550
Sept 27	Grand Prix Americas	Darren Turner, David Brabham	Ferrari 550

2003 American Le Mans Series—GT Class (through September 27)

Date	Race	Winners	Car
Mar 15	12 Hours at Sebring	Sascha Maassen, Lucas Luhr	Porsche 911 GT3RS
June 29	Grand Prix of Atlanta	Jorg Bergmeister, Timo Bernhard	Porsche 911 GT3RS
July 27	Grand Prix of Sonoma	Lucas Lehr, Sascha Maassen	Porsche 911 GT3RS
Aug 8	Grand Prix de Trois-Rivières	Sascha Maassen, Lucas Lehr	Porsche 911 GT3RS
Aug 17	Grand Prix of Mosport	Jorg Bergmeister, Timo Bernhard	Porsche 911 GT3RS
Aug 24	Road America 500	Mowlem, Petersen, Stanton	Porsche 911 GT3RS
Sept 7	Laguna Seca	Sascha Maassen, Lucas Lehr	Porsche 911 GT3RS
Sept 27	Grand Prix Americas	Sascha Maassen, Lucas Lehr	Porsche 911 GT3Rs

2002 American Le Mans Series Championship Final Standings

PROTOTYPE CLASS	Pts	GTS CLASS	Pts	GT CLASS	Pts
Tom Kristensen	232	Ron Fellows	254	Lucas Luhr	245
Rinaldo Capello	230	Johnny O'Connell	231	Sascha Maassen	245
Frank Biela	209	Kelly Collins	225	Kevin Buckler	193
Emanuele Pirro	206	Andy Pilgrim	225	Timo Bernhard	186
Johnny Herbert	206	Terry Borcheller	174	Jorg Bergmeister	185
David Brabham	177	Marc Bunting	154	Peter Baron	167
Stefan Johansson	175	Emanuele Naspetti	147	Leo Hindery	159
Jan Magnussen	171	Franz Conrad	139	Brian Cunningham	126
Bill Auberlen	161	M. Schiattarella	125	Michael Schrom	121
Bryan Herta	153	Marino Franchitti	102	Tony Kester	108

24 Hours of Le Mans

Held at Le Mans, France, on June 14–15, 2003, the 24 Hours of Le Mans is the most prestigious international event in endurance racing.

Place	Drivers	Car	Laps
1	Rinaldo Capello, Tom Kristensen, Guy Smith	Bentley EXP Speed 8	377 (3,995.0 mi)
2	Mark Blundell, Johnny Herbert, David Brabham	Audi R8	375
3	J.J. Lehto, Emanuele Pirror, Stefan Johansson	Audi R8	372
4	Seiji Ara, Jan Magnussen, Marco Werner	Audi R8	370
5	Olivier Beretta, Gunnar Jeanette, Max Papis	Panoz Elan (LMP-01)	360

National Hot Rod Association

2003 Results (through October 5)

TOP FUEL

Date	Race, Site	Winner	Time	Speed
Feb 6–9	Winternationals, Pomona, CA	Larry Dixon	4.541	322.04
Feb 20–23	Kragen Nationals, Phoenix	Brandon Bernstein	4.574	322.58
Mar 13–16	Mac Tools Gatornationals, Gainesville, FL	Brandon Bernstein	4.594	326.67
Apr 3–6	Las Vegas Nationals	Larry Dixon	4.608	312.57
Apr 10–13	O'Reilly Spring Nationals, Baytown, TX	Doug Kalitta	4.580	323.43
Apr 25–27	Thunder Valley Nationals, Bristol, TN	Brandon Bernstein	4.625	320.13
May 1–4	Southern Nationals, Atlanta, GA	Larry Dixon	4.569	323.89
May 15–18	Matco Supernationals, Englishtown, NJ	Doug Kalitta	4.494	328.54
May 22–25	O'Reilly Summer Nationals, Topeka, KS	Larry Dixon	4.534	327.82
May 29–June 1	Chicagoland Nationals, Chicago, IL	Tony Schumacher	4.530	321.50
June 12–15	Pontiac Nationals, Columbus, OH	Larry Dixon	4.655	313.58
June 27–29	Sears Craftsman Nationals, Madison, IL	Doug Kalitta	4.602	312.35
July 18–20	Mile High Nationals, Morrison, CO	Larry Dixon	4.737	313.15
July 25–27	Northwest Nationals, Kent, WA	Larry Dixon	4.672	316.82
Aug 1–3	Fram Autolite Nationals, Sonoma, CA	Larry Dixon	4.640	319.67
Aug 14–17	Lucas Oil Nationals, Brainerd, MN	Doug Kalitta	4.698	311.20
Sept 5–7	U.S. Nationals, Clermont, IN	Tony Schumacher	4.498	328.54
Sept 18–21	Mid-South Nationals, Millington, TN	Tony Schumacher	4.581	317.79
Sept 25–28	NHRA Nationals, Chicago, IL	Kenny Bernstein	4.503	328.46
Oct 3–5	Lucas Oil Nationals, Reading, PA	Tony Schumacher	4.584	315.56

FUNNY CAR

Date	Race, Site	Winner	Time	Speed
Feb 6–9	Winternationals, Pomona, CA	Tony Pedregon	4.765	324.44
Feb 20–23	Kragen Nationals, Phoenix	Ron Capps	4.858	310.13
Mar 13–16	Mac Tools Gatornationals, Gainesville, FL	Gary Densham	4.876	320.85
Apr 3–6	Las Vegas Nationals	Tony Pedregon	4.916	283.07
Apr 10–13	O'Reilly Spring Nationals, Baytown, TX	Tony Pedregon	4.963	313.07
Apr 25–27	Thunder Valley Nationals, Bristol, TN	Del Worsham	4.924	310.41
May 1–4	Southern Nationals, Atlanta, GA	Tony Pedregon	4.874	318.77

2003 Results (through October 5) *(Cont.)*

FUNNY CAR *(CONT.)*

Date	Race, Site	Winner	Time	Speed
May 15–18	Matco Supernationals, Englishtown, NJ	Whit Bazemore	4.869	306.81
May 22–25	O'Reilly Summer Nationals, Topeka, KS	Tony Pedregon	4.848	320.66
May 29–June 1	Chicagoland Nationals, Chicago, IL	Whit Bazemore	4.872	319.67
June 12–15	Pontiac Nationals, Columbus, OH	Tony Pedregon	8.449	134.81
June 27–29	Sears Craftsman Nationals, Madison, IL	Del Worsham	4.884	313.00
July 18–20	Mile High Nationals, Morrison, CO	John Force	5.044	289.45
July 25–27	Northwest Nationals, Kent, WA	John Force	5.036	300.80
Aug 1–3	Fram Autolite Nationals, Sonoma, CA	Gary Scelzi	4.958	312.21
Aug 14–17	Lucas Oil Nationals, Brainerd, MN	Gary Densham	5.009	298.01
Sept 5–7	U.S. Nationals, Clermont, IN	Tim Wilkerson	4.841	321.19
Sept 18–21	Mid-South Nationals, Millington, TN	Whit Bazemore	4.894	309.42
Sept 25–28	NHRA Nationals, Chicago, IL	Tony Pedregon	4.769	316.52
Oct 3–5	Lucas Oil Nationals, Reading, PA	Tim Wilkerson	4.869	317.94

PRO STOCK

Date	Race, Site	Winner	Time	Speed
Feb 6–9	Winternationals, Pomona, CA	Warren Johnson	6.788	204.01
Feb 20–23	Kragen Nationals, Phoenix	Greg Anderson	6.865	201.61
Mar 13–16	Mac Tools Gatornationals, Gainesville, FL	Kurt Johnson	6.825	202.65
Apr 3–6	Las Vegas Nationals	Greg Anderson	6.907	200.95
Apr 10–13	O'Reilly Spring Nationals, Baytown, TX	Kurt Johnson	6.780	204.79
Apr 25–27	Thunder Valley Nationals, Bristol, TN	Kurt Johnson	6.899	200.92
May 1–4	Southern Nationals, Atlanta, GA	Warren Johnson	6.853	201.46
May 15–18	Matco Supernationals, Englishtown, NJ	Greg Anderson	6.724	205.98
May 22–25	O'Reilly Summer Nationals, Topeka, KS	Greg Anderson	6.808	202.94
May 29–June 1	Chicagoland Nationals, Chicago, IL	Kurt Johnson	6.791	203.40
June 12–15	Pontiac Nationals, Columbus, OH	Greg Anderson	6.883	199.88
June 27–29	Sears Craftsman Nationals, Madison, IL	Ron Krisher	6.843	201.64
July 18–20	Mile High Nationals, Morrison, CO	Warren Johnson	7.225	191.05
July 25–27	Northwest Nationals, Kent, WA	Greg Anderson	6.858	202.09
Aug 1–3	Fram Autolite Nationals, Sonoma, CA	Jeg Coughlin	6.839	201.07
Aug 14–17	Lucas Oil Nationals, Brainerd, MN	Greg Anderson	6.917	200.05
Sept 5–7	U.S. Nationals, Clermont, IN	Greg Anderson	6.803	203.40
Sept 18–21	Mid-South Nationals, Millington, TN	Greg Anderson	6.814	202.67
Sept 25–28	NHRA Nationals, Chicago, IL	Jeg Coughlin	6.749	203.22
Oct 3–5	Lucas Oil Nationals, Reading, PA	Warren Johnson	6.755	204.76

2002 Final Standings

TOP FUEL			FUNNY CAR			PRO STOCK		
Driver	Wins	Pts	Driver	Wins	Pts	Driver	Wins	Pts
Larry Dixon		1914	John Force		1658	Jeg Coughlin Jr.		1592
Kenny Bernstein		1724	Tony Pedregon		1627	Jim Yates		1380
Tony Schumacher		1397	Del Worsham		1407	Greg Anderson		1292
Doug Kalitta		1369	Gary Densham		1376	Warren Johnson		1218
Cory McClenathan		1310	Whit Bazemore		1175	Ron Krisher		1134

Indianapolis 500

First held in 1911, the Indianapolis 500—200 laps of the 2.5-mile Indianapolis Motor Speedway Track (called the Brickyard in honor of its original pavement)—grew to become the most famous auto race in the world. Though the Memorial Day weekend event lost participants and prestige in the mid-1990s due to feuding in the world of U.S. open-wheel racing, it annually attracts crowds of over 100,000.

Year	Winner (start pos.)	Chassis-Engine	Avg Speed	Pole Winner	Speed
1911	Ray Harroun (28)	Marmon-Marmon	74.590	Lewis Strang	First entered
1912	Joe Dawson (7)	National-National	78.720	Gil Anderson	First entered
1913	Jules Goux (7)	Peugeot-Peugeot	75.930	Caleb Bragg	Drew pole
1914	Rene Thomas (15)	Delage-Delage	82.470	Jean Chassagne	Drew pole
1915	Ralph DePalma (2)	Mercedes-Mercedes	89.840	Howard Wilcox	98.90
1916	Dario Resta (4)	Peugeot-Peugeot	84.000	John Aitken	96.69
1917–18	No race				
1919	Howard Wilcox (2)	Peugeot-Peugeot	88.050	Rene Thomas	104.78
1920	Gaston Chevrolet (6)	Frontenac-Frontenac	88.620	Ralph DePalma	99.15
1921	Tommy Milton (20)	Frontenac-Frontenac	89.620	Ralph DePalma	100.75
1922	Jimmy Murphy (1)	Duesenberg-Miller	94.480	Jimmy Murphy	100.50
1923	Tommy Milton (1)	Miller-Miller	90.950	Tommy Milton	108.17
1924	L.L. Corum	Duesenberg-Duesenberg	98.230	Jimmy Murphy	108.037
	Joe Boyer (21)				
1925	Peter DePaolo (2)	Duesenberg-Duesenberg	101.130	Leon Duray	113.196
1926	Frank Lockhart (20)	Miller-Miller	95.904	Earl Cooper	111.735
1927	George Souders (22)	Duesenberg-Duesenberg	97.545	Frank Lockhart	120.100
1928	Louis Meyer (13)	Miller-Miller	99.482	Leon Duray	122.391
1929	Ray Keech (6)	Miller-Miller	97.585	Cliff Woodbury	120.599
1930	Billy Arnold (1)	Summers-Miller	100.448	Billy Arnold	113.268
1931	Louis Schneider (13)	Stevens-Miller	96.629	Russ Snowberger	112.796
1932	Fred Frame (27)	Wetteroth-Miller	104.144	Lou Moore	117.363
1933	Louis Meyer (6)	Miller-Miller	104.162	Bill Cummings	118.524
1934	Bill Cummings (10)	Miller-Miller	104.863	Kelly Petillo	119.329
1935	Kelly Petillo (22)	Wetteroth-Offy	106.240	Rex Mays	120.736
1936	Louis Meyer (28)	Stevens-Miller	109.069	Rex Mays	119.664
1937	Wilbur Shaw (2)	Shaw-Offy	113.580	Bill Cummings	123.343
1938	Floyd Roberts (1)	Wetteroth-Miller	117.200	Floyd Roberts	125.681
1939	Wilbur Shaw (3)	Maserati-Maserati	115.035	Jimmy Snyder	130.138
1940	Wilbur Shaw (2)	Maserati-Maserati	114.277	Rex Mays	127.850
1941	Floyd Davis	Wetteroth-Offy	115.117	Mauri Rose	128.691
	Mauri Rose (17)				
1942–45	No race				
1946	George Robson (15)	Adams-Sparks	114.820	Cliff Bergere	126.471
1947	Mauri Rose (3)	Deidt-Offy	116.338	Ted Horn	126.564
1948	Mauri Rose (3)	Deidt-Offy	119.814	Rex Mays	130.577
1949	Bill Holland (4)	Deidt-Offy	121.327	Duke Nalon	132.939
1950	Johnnie Parsons (5)	Kurtis-Offy	124.002	Walt Faulkner	134.343
1951	Lee Wallard (2)	Kurtis-Offy	126.244	Duke Nalon	136.498
1952	Troy Ruttman (7)	Kuzma-Offy	128.922	Fred Agabashian	138.010
1953	Bill Vukovich (1)	KK500A-Offy	128.740	Bill Vukovich	138.392
1954	Bill Vukovich (19)	KK500A-Offy	130.840	Jack McGrath	141.033
1955	Bob Sweikert (14)	KK500C-Offy	128.209	Jerry Hoyt	140.045
1956	Pat Flaherty (1)	Watson-Offy	128.490	Pat Flaherty	145.596
1957	Sam Hanks (13)	Salih-Offy	135.601	Pat O'Connor	143.948
1958	Jim Bryan (7)	Salih-Offy	133.791	Dick Rathmann	145.974
1959	Rodger Ward (6)	Watson-Offy	135.857	Johnny Thomson	145.908
1960	Jim Rathmann (2)	Watson-Offy	138.767	Eddie Sachs	146.592
1961	A.J. Foyt (7)	Trevis-Offy	139.130	Eddie Sachs	147.481
1962	Rodger Ward (2)	Watson-Offy	140.293	Parnelli Jones	150.370
1963	Parnelli Jones (1)	Watson-Offy	143.137	Parnelli Jones	151.153
1964	A.J. Foyt (5)	Watson-Offy	147.350	Jim Clark	158.828
1965	Jim Clark (2)	Lotus-Ford	150.686	A.J. Foyt	161.233
1966	Graham Hill (15)	Lola-Ford	144.317	Mario Andretti	165.899
1967	A.J. Foyt (4)	Coyote-Ford	151.207	Mario Andretti	168.982
1968	Bobby Unser (3)	Eagle-Offy	152.882	Joe Leonard	171.559
1969	Mario Andretti (2)	Hawk-Ford	156.867	A.J. Foyt	170.568
1970	Al Unser (1)	PJ Colt-Ford	155.749	Al Unser	170.221
1971	Al Unser (5)	PJ Colt-Ford	157.735	Peter Revson	178.696
1972	Mark Donohue (3)	McLaren-Offy	162.962	Bobby Unser	195.940
1973	Gordon Johncock (11)	Eagle-Offy	159.036	Johnny Rutherford	198.413
1974	Johnny Rutherford (25)	McLaren-Offy	158.589	A.J. Foyt	191.632

Year	Winner (start pos.)	Chassis-Engine	Avg speed	Pole Winner	Speed
1975	Bobby Unser (3)	Racers Eagle-Offy	149.213	A.J. Foyt	193.976
1976	Johnny Rutherford (1)	McLaren-Offy	148.725	Johnny Rutherford	188.957
1977	A.J. Foyt (4)	Coyote-Ford	161.331	Tom Sneva	198.884
1978	Al Unser (5)	Lola-Cosworth	161.361	Tom Sneva	202.156
1979	Rick Mears (1)	Penske-Cosworth	158.899	Rick Mears	193.736
1980	Johnny Rutherford (1)	Chaparral-Cosworth	142.862	Johnny Rutherford	192.256
1981	Bobby Unser (1)	Penske-Cosworth	139.084	Bobby Unser	200.546
1982	Gordon Johncock (5)	Wildcat-Cosworth	162.026	Rick Mears	207.004
1983	Tom Sneva (4)	March-Cosworth	162.117	Teo Fabi	207.395
1984	Rick Mears (3)	March-Cosworth	163.612	Tom Sneva	210.029
1985	Danny Sullivan (8)	March-Cosworth	152.982	Pancho Carter	212.583
1986	Bobby Rahal (4)	March-Cosworth	170.722	Rick Mears	216.828
1987	Al Unser (20)	March-Cosworth	162.175	Mario Andretti	215.390
1988	Rick Mears (1)	Penske-Chevrolet	144.809	Rick Mears	219.198
1989	Emerson Fittipaldi (3)	Penske-Chevrolet	167.581	Rick Mears	223.885
1990	Arie Luyendyk (3)	Lola-Chevrolet	185.981*	Emerson Fittipaldi	225.301
1991	Rick Mears (1)	Penske-Chevrolet	176.457	Rick Mears	224.113
1992	Al Unser Jr (12)	Galmer-Chevrolet	134.477	Roberto Guerrero	232.482
1993	Emerson Fittipaldi (9)	Penske-Chevrolet	157.207	Arie Luyendyk	223.967
1994	Al Unser Jr (1)	Penske-Mercedes	160.872	Al Unser Jr	228.011
1995	Jacques Villeneuve (5)	Reynard-Ford	153.616	Scott Brayton	231.616
1996	Buddy Lazier (5)	Reynard-Ford	147.956	Tony Stewart	233.100†
1997	Arie Luyendyk (1)	G Force-Oldsmobile	145.827	Arie Luyendyk	231.468
1998	Eddie Cheever (17)	Dallara-Oldsmobile	145.155	Billy Boat	223.503
1999	Kenny Brack (8)	Dallara-Oldsmobile	153.176	Arie Luyendyk	225.179
2000	Juan Montoya (2)	G Force-Oldsmobile	167.607	Greg Ray	223.471
2001	Helio Castroneves (11)	Dallara-Oldsmobile	153.601	Scott Sharp	226.037
2002	Helio Castroneves (13)	Dallara-Chevrolet	166.499	Bruno Junqueira	231.342
2003	Gil de Ferran	Panoz-Toyota	156.291	Helio Castroneves	231.725

Indianapolis 500 Rookie of the Year Award

*Track record, winning speed.
†Track record, qualifying speed.

Year	Rookie of the Year
1952	Art Cross
1953	Jimmy Daywalt
1954	Larry Crockett
1955	Al Herman
1956	Bob Veith
1957	Don Edmunds
1958	George Amick
1959	Bobby Grim
1960	Jim Hurtubise
1961	Parnelli Jones*
	Bobby Marshman
1962	Jimmy McElreath
1963	Jim Clark*
1964	Johnny White
1965	Mario Andretti*
1966	Jackie Stewart
1967	Denis Hulme
1968	Billy Vukovich
1969	Mark Donohue*
1970	Donnie Allison
1971	Denny Zimmerman
1972	Mike Hiss
1973	Graham McRae
1974	Pancho Carter
1975	Bill Puterbaugh
1976	Vern Schuppan
1977	Jerry Sneva
1978	Rick Mears*
	Larry Rice
1979	Howdy Holmes
1980	Tim Richmond
1981	Josele Garza
1982	Jim Hickman
1983	Teo Fabi
1984	Michael Andretti
	Roberto Guerrero
1985	Arie Luyendyk*
1986	Randy Lanier
1987	Fabrizio Barbazza
1988	Billy Vukovich III
1989	Bernard Jourdain
	Scott Pruett
1990	Eddie Cheever*
1991	Jeff Andretti
1992	Lyn St. James
1993	Nigel Mansell
1994	Jacques Villeneuve*
1995	Gil de Ferran
1996	Tony Stewart
1997	Jeff Ward
1998	Steve Knapp
1999	Robby McGehee
2000	Juan Montoya*
2001	Helio Castroneves*
2002	Alex Barron
	Tomas Scheckter
2003	Tora Tagaki

*Future winner of Indy 500.

CART Championship Series Champions

From 1909 to 1955, this championship was awarded by the American Automobile Association (AAA), and from 1956 to 1979 by the United States Auto Club (USAC). Since 1979, Championship Auto Racing Teams (CART) has conducted the championship. Known as PPG CART World Series until 1998.

Year	Champion	Year	Champion	Year	Champion
1909	George Robertson	1940	Rex Mays	1974	Bobby Unser
1910	Ray Harroun	1941	Rex Mays	1975	A.J. Foyt
1911	Ralph Mulford	1942–45	No racing	1976	Gordon Johncock
1912	Ralph DePalma	1946	Ted Horn	1977	Tom Sneva
1913	Earl Cooper	1947	Ted Horn	1978	Tom Sneva
1914	Ralph DePalma	1948	Ted Horn	1979	A.J. Foyt
1915	Earl Cooper	1949	Johnnie Parsons	1979	Rick Mears
1916	Dario Resta	1950	Henry Banks	1980	Johnny Rutherford
1917	Earl Cooper	1951	Tony Bettenhausen	1981	Rick Mears
1918	Ralph Mulford	1952	Chuck Stevenson	1982	Rick Mears
1919	Howard Wilcox	1953	Sam Hanks	1983	Al Unser
1920	Tommy Milton	1954	Jimmy Bryan	1984	Mario Andretti
1921	Tommy Milton	1955	Bob Sweikert	1985	Al Unser
1922	Jimmy Murphy	1956	Jimmy Bryan	1986	Bobby Rahal
1923	Eddie Hearne	1957	Jimmy Bryan	1987	Bobby Rahal
1924	Jimmy Murphy	1958	Tony Bettenhausen	1988	Danny Sullivan
1925	Peter DePaolo	1959	Rodger Ward	1989	Emerson Fittipaldi
1926	Harry Hartz	1960	A.J. Foyt	1990	Al Unser Jr.
1927	Peter DePaolo	1961	A.J. Foyt	1991	Michael Andretti
1928	Louis Meyer	1962	Rodger Ward	1992	Bobby Rahal
1929	Louis Meyer	1963	A.J. Foyt	1993	Nigel Mansell
1930	Billy Arnold	1964	A.J. Foyt	1994	Al Unser Jr.
1931	Louis Schneider	1965	Mario Andretti	1995	Jacques Villeneuve
1932	Bob Carey	1966	Mario Andretti	1996	Jimmy Vasser
1933	Louis Meyer	1967	A.J. Foyt	1997	Alex Zanardi
1934	Bill Cummings	1968	Bobby Unser	1998	Alex Zanardi
1935	Kelly Petillo	1969	Mario Andretti	1999	Juan Montoya
1936	Mauri Rose	1970	Al Unser	2000	Gil de Ferran
1937	Wilbur Shaw	1971	Joe Leonard	2001	Gil de Ferran
1938	Floyd Roberts	1972	Joe Leonard	2002	Cristiano da Matta
1939	Wilbur Shaw	1973	Roger McCluskey		

Alltime CART Leaders

WINS		POLE POSITIONS	
A.J. Foyt	67	Mario Andretti	67
Mario Andretti	52	A.J. Foyt	53
Michael Andretti	42	Bobby Unser	49
Al Unser	39	Rick Mears	40
Bobby Unser	35	Michael Andretti	32
Al Unser Jr	31	Al Unser	27
Rick Mears	29	Johnny Rutherford	23
Johnny Rutherford	27	Gordon Johncock	20
Rodger Ward	26	Rex Mays	19
*Paul Tracy	25	Danny Sullivan	19
Gordon Johncock	25	Bobby Rahal	18
Bobby Rahal	24	*Paul Tracy	18
Ralph DePalma	24	Emerson Fittipaldi	17
Tommy Milton	23	*Gil de Ferran	16
Tony Bettenhausen	22	Tony Bettenhausen	14
Emerson Fittipaldi	22	Juan Montoya	14
Earl Cooper	20	Don Branson	14
Jimmy Bryan	19	Tom Sneva	14
Jimmy Murphy	19	Parnelli Jones	12
Danny Sullivan	17	Rodger Ward	11
Ralph Mulford	17	Danny Ongais	11
		Dario Franchitti	11

*Active driver. Note: Leaders through September 2003.

Stock Car Racing's Major Events

In 1985, Winston began offering a $1 million bonus to any driver to win three of the top four NASCAR events in the same season. A fifth event, the Brickyard 400 (in Indianapolis) was added in 1994. As of 1998 the Winston million was awarded to any driver who won three of the five events. The other four races are the richest (Daytona 500), the fastest (Talladega 500), the longest (Charlotte 600) and the oldest (Southern 500 at Darlington). Only five drivers, Lee Roy Yarbrough (1969), David Pearson (1976), Bill Elliott (1985), Dale jarrett (1996) and Jeff Gordon (1997, '98) have scored the three-track hat trick.

Daytona 500

Year	Winner	Car	Avg Speed	Pole Winner	Speed
1959	Lee Petty	Oldsmobile	135.520	Cotton Owens	143.198
1960	Junior Johnson	Chevrolet	124.740	Fireball Roberts	151.556
1961	Marvin Panch	Pontiac	149.601	Fireball Roberts	155.709
1962	Fireball Roberts	Pontiac	152.529	Fireball Roberts	156.995
1963	Tiny Lund	Ford	151.566	Johnny Rutherford	165.183
1964	Richard Petty	Plymouth	154.345	Paul Goldsmith	174.910
1965	Fred Lorenzen	Ford	141.539	Darel Dieringer	171.151
1966	Richard Petty	Plymouth	160.627	Richard Petty	175.165
1967	Mario Andretti	Ford	149.926	Curtis Turner	180.831
1968	Cale Yarborough	Mercury	143.251	Cale Yarborough	189.222
1969	Lee Roy Yarbrough	Ford	157.950	David Pearson	190.029
1970	Pete Hamilton	Plymouth	149.601	Cale Yarborough	194.015
1971	Richard Petty	Plymouth	144.462	A.J. Foyt	182.744
1972	A.J. Foyt	Mercury	161.550	Bobby Isaac	186.632
1973	Richard Petty	Dodge	157.205	Buddy Baker	185.662
1974	Richard Petty	Dodge	140.894	David Pearson	185.017
1975	Benny Parsons	Chevrolet	153.649	Donnie Allison	185.827
1976	David Pearson	Mercury	152.181	A.J. Foyt	185.943
1977	Cale Yarborough	Chevrolet	153.218	Donnie Allison	188.048
1978	Bobby Allison	Ford	159.730	Cale Yarborough	187.536
1979	Richard Petty	Oldsmobile	143.977	Buddy Baker	196.049
1980	Buddy Baker	Oldsmobile	177.602*	A.J. Foyt	195.020
1981	Richard Petty	Buick	169.651	Bobby Allison	194.624
1982	Bobby Allison	Buick	153.991	Benny Parsons	196.317
1983	Cale Yarborough	Pontiac	155.979	Ricky Rudd	198.864
1984	Cale Yarborough	Chevrolet	150.994	Cale Yarborough	201.848
1985	Bill Elliott	Ford	172.265	Bill Elliott	205.114
1986	Geoff Bodine	Chevrolet	148.124	Bill Elliott	205.039
1987	Bill Elliott	Ford	176.263	Bill Elliott	210.364†
1988	Bobby Allison	Buick	137.531	Ken Schrader	193.823
1989	Darrell Waltrip	Chevrolet	148.466	Ken Schrader	196.996
1990	Derrike Cope	Chevrolet	165.761	Ken Schrader	196.515
1991	Ernie Irvan	Chevrolet	148.148	Davey Allison	195.955
1992	Davey Allison	Ford	160.256	Sterling Marlin	192.213
1993	Dale Jarrett	Chevrolet	154.972	Kyle Petty	189.426
1994	Sterling Marlin	Chevrolet	156.931	Loy Allen Jr	190.158
1995	Sterling Marlin	Chevrolet	141.710	Dale Jarrett	193.498
1996	Dale Jarrett	Ford	154.308	Dale Earnhardt	189.510
1997	Jeff Gordon	Chevrolet	148.295	Mike Skinner	189.813
1998	Dale Earnhardt	Chevrolet	172.712	Bobby Labonte	192.415
1999	Jeff Gordon	Chevrolet	161.551	Jeff Gordon	195.067
2000	Dale Jarrett	Ford	155.669	Dale Jarrett	191.091
2001	Michael Waltrip	Chevrolet	161.783	Bill Elliott	183.570
2002	Ward Burton	Dodge	142.971	Jimmie Johnson	185.831
2003	Michael Waltrip	Chevrolet	133.87	Jeff Green	186.606

*Track record, winning speed. †Track record, qualifying speed. Note: The Daytona 500, held annually in February, now opens the NASCAR season with 200 laps around the high-banked Daytona International Speedway.

Charlotte 600

Year	Winner	Car	Avg Speed	Pole Winner
1960	Joe Lee Johnson	Chevrolet	107.752	Joe Lee Johnson
1961	David Pearson	Pontiac	111.634	Richard Petty
1962	Nelson Stacy	Ford	125.552	Fireball Roberts
1963	Fred Lorenzen	Ford	132.418	Junior Johnson
1964	Jim Paschal	Plymouth	125.772	Junior Johnson
1965	Fred Lorenzen	Ford	121.772	Fred Lorenzon
1966	Marvin Panch	Plymouth	135.042	Paul Goldsmith
1967	Jim Paschal	Plymouth	135.832	Cale Yarborough
1968	Buddy Baker	Dodge	104.207	Donnie Allison
1969	Lee Roy Yarbrough	Mercury	134.631	Donnie Allison
1970	Donnie Allison	Ford	129.680	Bobby Isaac
1971	Bobby Allison	Mercury	140.442	Charlie Glotzbach
1972	Buddy Baker	Dodge	142.255	Bobby Allison
1973	Buddy Baker	Dodge	134.890	Buddy Baker
1974	David Pearson	Mercury	135.720	David Pearson
1975	Richard Petty	Dodge	145.327	David Pearson
1976	David Pearson	Mercury	137.352	David Pearson
1977	Richard Petty	Dodge	137.636	David Pearson
1978	Darrell Waltrip	Chevrolet	138.355	David Pearson
1979	Darrell Waltrip	Chevrolet	136.674	Neil Bonnet
1980	Benny Parsons	Chevrolet	119.265	Cale Yarborough
1981	Bobby Allison	Buick	129.326	Neil Bonnett
1982	Neil Bonnett	Ford	130.508	David Pearson
1983	Neil Bonnett	Chevrolet	140.406	Buddy Baker
1984	Bobby Allison	Buick	129.233	Harry Gant
1985	Darrell Waltrip	Chevrolet	141.807	Bill Elliott
1986	Dale Earnhardt	Chevrolet	140.406	Geoff Bodine
1987	Kyle Petty	Ford	131.483	Bill Elliott
1988	Darrell Waltrip	Chevrolet	124.460	Davey Allison
1989	Darrell Waltrip	Chevrolet	144.077	Alan Kulwicki
1990	Rusty Wallace	Pontiac	137.650	Ken Schrader
1991	Davey Allison	Ford	138.951	Mark Martin
1992	Dale Earnhardt	Chevrolet	132.980	Bill Elliott
1993	Dale Earnhardt	Chevrolet	145.504	Ken Schrader
1994	Jeff Gordon	Chevrolet	139.445	Jeff Gordon
1995	Bobby Labonte	Chevrolet	151.952	Jeff Gordon
1996	Dale Jarrett	Ford	147.581	Jeff Gordon
1997	Jeff Gordon	Chevrolet	136.745	Jeff Gordon
1998	Jeff Gordon	Chevrolet	136.424	Jeff Gordon
1999	Jeff Burton	Ford	151.367	Bobby Labonte
2000	Matt Kenseth	Ford	142.640	Dale Earnhardt Jr
2001	Jeff Burton	Ford	138.107	Ryan Newman
2002	Mark Martin	Ford	137.729	Jimmie Johnson
2003	Jimmie Johnson	Chevrolet	126.198	Ryan Newman

Note: Held at the 1.5-mile high-banked Lowe's Motor Speedway in Charlotte on Memorial Day weekend.

Brickyard 400

Year	Winner	Car	Avg Speed	Pole Winner	Speed
1994	Jeff Gordon	Chevrolet	131.977	Rick Mast	172.414
1995	Dale Earnhardt	Chevrolet	155.206	Jeff Gordon	172.536
1996	Dale Jarrett	Ford	139.508	Jeff Gordon	176.419
1997	Ricky Rudd	Ford	130.814	Ernie Irvan	177.736
1998	Jeff Gordon	Chevrolet	126.772	Ernie Irvan	179.394
1999	Dale Jarrett	Ford	148.194	Jeff Gordon	179.612
2000	Bobby Labonte	Pontiac	155.912	Ricky Rudd	181.068
2001	Jeff Gordon	Chevrolet	130.790	Jimmy Spencer	179.666
2002	Bill Elliott	Dodge	125.033	Tony Stewart	182.960
2003	Kevin Harvick	Chevrolet	134.554	Kevin Harvick	184.343*

*Track record.

Talladega 500

Year	Winner	Car	Avg Speed	Pole Winner	Speed
1970	Pete Hamilton	Plymouth	152.321	Bobby Isaac	199.658
1971	Donnie Allison	Mercury	147.419	Donnie Allison	185.869
1972	David Pearson	Mercury	134.400	Bobby Isaac	192.428
1973	David Pearson	Mercury	131.956	Buddy Baker	193.435
1974	David Pearson	Mercury	130.220	David Pearson	186.086
1975	Buddy Baker	Ford	144.94	Buddy Baker	189.947
1976	Buddy Baker	Ford	169.887	Dave Marcis	189.197
1977	Darrell Waltrip	Chevrolet	164.887	A.J. Foyt	192.424
1978	Cale Yarborough	Oldsmobile	155.699	Cale Yarborough	191.904
1979	Bobby Allison	Ford	154.770	Darrell Waltrip	195.644
1980	Buddy Baker	Oldsmobile	170.481	David Pearson	197.704
1981	Bobby Allison	Buick	149.376	Bobby Allison	195.864
1982	Darrell Waltrip	Buick	156.697	Benny Parsons	200.176
1983	Richard Petty	Pontiac	135.936	Cale Yarborough	202.650
1984	Cale Yarborough	Chevrolet	172.988	Cale Yarborough	202.692
1985	Bill Elliott	Ford	186.288	Bill Elliott	209.398
1986	Bobby Allison	Buick	157.698	Bill Elliott	212.229
1987	Davey Allison	Ford	154.228	Bill Elliott	221.809
1988	Phil Parsons	Oldsmobile	156.547	Davey Allison	198.969
1989	Davey Allison	Ford	155.869	Mark Martin	193.061
1990	Dale Earnhardt	Chevrolet	159.571	Bill Elliott	199.388
1991	Harry Gant	Oldsmobile	165.620	Ernie Irvan	195.186
1992	Davey Allison	Ford	167.609	Ernie Irvan	192.831
1993	Ernie Irvan	Chevrolet	155.412	Dale Earnhardt	192.355
1994	Dale Earnhardt	Chevrolet	157.478	Ernie Irvan	193.298
1995	Mark Martin	Ford	178.902	Terry Labonte	196.532
1996	Sterling Marlin	Chevrolet	149.999	Ernie Irvan	192.855
1997	Mark Martin	Ford	188.354	John Andretti	193.627
1998	Dale Jarrett	Ford	159.318	Ken Schrader	196.153
1999	Dale Earnhardt	Chevrolet	166.632	Joe Nemechek	198.331
2000	Dale Earnhardt	Chevrolet	165.681	Joe Nemechek	190.279
2001	Dale Earnhardt Jr.	Chevrolet	164.185	Stacy Compton	185.240
2002	Dale Earnhardt Jr.	Chevrolet	183.665	qualifying cancelled	—
2003	Michael Waltrip	Chevrolet	156.045	Elliot Sadler	189.943

Note: Formerly the Winston 500, held at the 2.66-mile Talladega Superspeedway.

Southern 500

Year	Winner	Car	Avg Speed	Pole Winner
1950	Johnny Mantz	Plymouth	76.260	Wally Campbell
1951	Herb Thomas	Hudson	76.900	Marshall Teague
1952	Fonty Flock	Oldsmobile	74.510	Dick Rathman
1953	Buck Baker	Oldsmobile	92.780	Fonty Flock
1954	Herb Thomas	Hudson	94.930	Buck Baker
1955	Herb Thomas	Chevrolet	92.281	Tim Flock
1956	Curtis Turner	Ford	95.067	Buck Baker
1957	Speedy Thompson	Chevrolet	100.100	Paul Goldsmith
1958	Fireball Roberts	Chevrolet	102.590	Fireball Roberts
1959	Jim Reed	Chevrolet	111.836	Fireball Roberts
1960	Buck Baker	Pontiac	105.901	Cotton Owens
1961	Nelson Stacy	Ford	117.880	Fireball Roberts
1962	Larry Frank	Ford	117.965	Fireball Roberts
1963	Fireball Roberts	Ford	129.784	Fireball Roberts
1964	Buck Baker	Dodge	117.757	Richard Petty
1965	Ned Jarrett	Ford	115.924	Junior Johnson
1966	Darel Dieringer	Mercury	114.830	Lee Yarborough
1967	Richard Petty	Plymouth	131.933	David Pearson
1968	Cale Yarborough	Mercury	126.132	Charlie Glotzbach
1969	Lee Roy Yarbrough	Ford	105.612	Cale Yarborough
1970	Buddy Baker	Dodge	128.817	David Pearson
1971	Bobby Allison	Mercury	131.398	Bobby Allison
1972	Bobby Allison	Chevrolet	128.124	David Pearson
1973	Cale Yarborough	Chevrolet	134.033	David Pearson
1974	Cale Yarborough	Chevrolet	111.075	Richard Petty
1975	Bobby Allison	Matador	116.825	David Pearson
1976	David Pearson	Mercury	120.534	David Pearson
1977	David Pearson	Mercury	106.797	Darrell Waltrip
1978	Cale Yarborough	Oldsmobile	116.828	David Pearson
1979	David Pearson	Chevrolet	126.259	Bobby Allison
1980	Terry Labonte	Chevrolet	115.210	Darrell Waltrip
1981	Neil Bonnett	Ford	126.410	Harry Gant
1982	Cale Yarborough	Buick	126.703	David Pearson
1983	Bobby Allison	Buick	123.343	Neil Bonnett
1984	Harry Gant	Chevrolet	128.270	Harry Gant
1985	Bill Elliott	Ford	121.254	Bill Elliott
1986	Tim Richmond	Chevrolet	121.068	Tim Richmond
1987	Dale Earnhardt	Chevrolet	115.520	Davey Allison
1988	Bill Elliott	Ford	128.297	Bill Elliott
1989	Dale Earnhardt	Chevrolet	135.462	Alan Kulwicki
1990	Dale Earnhardt	Chevrolet	123.141	Dale Earnhardt
1991	Harry Gant	Oldsmobile	133.508	Davey Allison
1992	Darrell Waltrip	Chevrolet	129.114	Sterling Marlin
1993	Mark Martin	Ford	137.932	Ken Schrader
1994	Bill Elliott	Ford	127.915	Geoff Bodine
1995	Jeff Gordon	Chevrolet	121.231	John Andretti
1996	Jeff Gordon	Chevrolet	135.757	Dale Jarrett
1997	Jeff Gordon	Chevrolet	121.149	Bobby Labonte
1998	Jeff Gordon	Chevrolet	139.031	Dale Jarrett
1999	Jeff Burton	Ford	100.816	Kenny Irwin
2000	Bobby Labonte	Pontiac	108.275	Jeremy Mayfield
2001	Ward Burton	Dodge	122.773	Kurt Busch
2002	Jeff Gordon	Chevrolet	118.617	Sterling Marlin
2003	Terry Labonte	Chevrolet	120.744	Ryan Newman

Note: Held at the 1.366-mile Darlington (S.C.) Raceway on Labor Day weekend.

Winston Cup NASCAR Champions

Year	Driver	Car	Wins	Poles	Winnings ($)
1949	Red Byron	Oldsmobile	2	1	5,800
1950	Bill Rexford	Oldsmobile	1	0	6,175
1951	Herb Thomas	Hudson	7	4	18,200
1952	Tim Flock	Hudson	8	4	20,210
1953	Herb Thomas	Hudson	11	10	27,300
1954	Lee Petty	Dodge	7	3	26,706
1955	Tim Flock	Chrysler	18	19	33,750
1956	Buck Baker	Chrysler	14	12	29,790
1957	Buck Baker	Chevrolet	10	5	24,712
1958	Lee Petty	Oldsmobile	7	4	20,600
1959	Lee Petty	Plymouth	10	2	45,570
1960	Rex White	Chevrolet	6	3	45,260
1961	Ned Jarrett	Chevrolet	1	4	27,285
1962	Joe Weatherly	Pontiac	9	6	56,110
1963	Joe Weatherly	Mercury	3	6	58,110
1964	Richard Petty	Plymouth	9	8	98,810
1965	Ned Jarrett	Ford	13	9	77,966
1966	David Pearson	Dodge	14	7	59,205
1967	Richard Petty	Plymouth	27	18	130,275
1968	David Pearson	Ford	16	12	118,824
1969	David Pearson	Ford	11	14	183,700
1970	Bobby Isaac	Dodge	11	13	121,470
1971	Richard Petty	Plymouth	21	9	309,225
1972	Richard Petty	Plymouth	8	3	227,015
1973	Benny Parsons	Chevrolet	1	0	114,345
1974	Richard Petty	Dodge	10	7	299,175
1975	Richard Petty	Dodge	13	3	378,865
1976	Cale Yarborough	Chevrolet	9	2	387,173
1977	Cale Yarborough	Chevrolet	9	3	477,499
1978	Cale Yarborough	Oldsmobile	10	8	530,751
1979	Richard Petty	Chevrolet	5	1	531,292
1980	Dale Earnhardt	Chevrolet	5	0	588,926
1981	Darrell Waltrip	Buick	12	11	693,342
1982	Darrell Waltrip	Buick	12	7	873,118
1983	Bobby Allison	Buick	6	0	828,355
1984	Terry Labonte	Chevrolet	2	2	713,010
1985	Darrell Waltrip	Chevrolet	3	4	1,318,735
1986	Dale Earnhardt	Chevrolet	5	1	1,783,880
1987	Dale Earnhardt	Chevrolet	11	1	2,099,243
1988	Bill Elliott	Ford	6	6	1,574,639
1989	Rusty Wallace	Pontiac	6	4	2,247,950
1990	Dale Earnhardt	Chevrolet	9	4	3,083,056
1991	Dale Earnhardt	Chevrolet	4	0	2,396,685
1992	Alan Kulwicki	Ford	2	6	2,322,561
1993	Dale Earnhardt	Chevrolet	6	2	3,353,789
1994	Dale Earnhardt	Chevrolet	4	2	3,400,733
1995	Jeff Gordon	Chevrolet	7	9	4,347,343
1996	Terry Labonte	Chevrolet	2	4	4,030,648
1997	Jeff Gordon	Chevrolet	10	1	4,201,227
1998	Jeff Gordon	Chevrolet	13	7	6,175,867
1999	Dale Jarrett	Ford	4	0	3,608,829
2000	Bobby Labonte	Pontiac	4	2	4,041,750
2001	Jeff Gordon	Chevrolet	6	8	6,649,076
2002	Tony Stewart	Pontiac	3	4	4,695,150

Alltime NASCAR Leaders

WINS		POLE POSITIONS	
Richard Petty	200	Richard Petty	126
David Pearson	105	David Pearson	113
Bobby Allison	84	Cale Yarborough	70
Darrell Waltrip	84	Darrell Waltrip	59
Cale Yarborough	83	Bobby Allison	57
Dale Earnhardt	76	Bobby Isaac	51
*Jeff Gordon	62	*Bill Elliott	50
Lee Petty	54	Junior Johnson	47
*Rusty Wallace	54	*Jeff Gordon	45
Ned Jarrett	50	Buck Baker	44
Junior Johnson	50	*Mark Martin	41
Herb Thomas	48	Buddy Baker	40
Buck Baker	46	Tim Flock	39
*Bill Elliott	43	Herb Thomas	39
Tim Flock	40	Geoff Bodine	37

*Active drivers. Note: NASCAR leaders through 2002 NASCAR season.

Formula One Grand Prix Racing

World Driving Champions

Year	Winner	Car	Year	Winner	Car
1950	Guiseppe Farina, Italy	Alfa Romeo	1974	Emerson Fittipaldi, Brazil	McLaren-Ford
1951	Juan-Manuel Fangio, Argentina	Alfa Romeo	1975	Niki Lauda, Austria	Ferrari
1952	Alberto Ascari, Italy	Ferrari	1976	James Hunt, Grt Britain	McLaren-Ford
1953	Alberto Ascari, Italy	Ferrari	1977	Niki Lauda, Austria	Ferrari
1954	Juan-Manuel Fangio, Argentina	Maserati-Mercedes	1978	Mario Andretti, U.S.	Lotus-Ford
1955	Juan-Manuel Fangio, Argentina	Mercedes	1979	Jody Scheckter, S Africa	Ferrari
			1980	Alan Jones, Australia	Williams-Ford
1956	Juan-Manuel Fangio, Argentina	Ferrari	1981	Nelson Piquet, Brazil	Brabham-Ford
			1982	Keke Rosberg, Finland	Williams-Ford
1957	Juan-Manuel Fangio, Argentina	Maserati	1983	Nelson Piquet, Brazil	Brabham-BMW
			1984	Niki Lauda, Austria	McLaren-Porsche
1958	Mike Hawthorn, Grt Britain	Ferrari	1985	Alain Prost, France	McLaren-Porsche
1959	Jack Brabham, Australia	Cooper-Climax	1986	Alain Prost, France	McLaren-Porsche
1960	Jack Brabham, Australia	Cooper-Climax	1987	Nelson Piquet, Brazil	Williams-Honda
1961	Phil Hill, U.S.	Ferrari	1988	Ayrton Senna, Brazil	McLaren-Honda
1962	Graham Hill, Grt Britain	BRM	1989	Alain Prost, France	McLaren-Honda
1963	Jim Clark, Scotland	Lotus-Climax	1990	Ayrton Senna, Brazil	McLaren-Honda
1964	John Surtees, Grt Britain	Ferrari	1991	Ayrton Senna, Brazil	McLaren-Honda
1965	Jim Clark, Scotland	Lotus-Climax	1992	Nigel Mansell, Grt Britain	Williams-Renault
1966	Jack Brabham, Australia	Brabham-Repco	1993	Alain Prost, France	Williams-Renault
1967	Denny Hulme, New Zealand	Brabham-Repco	1994	Michael Schumacher, Ger	Benetton-Ford
			1995	Michael Schumacher, Ger	Benetton-Renault
1968	Graham Hill, Grt Britain	Lotus-Ford	1996	Damon Hill, Grt Britain	Williams-Renault
1969	Jackie Stewart, Scotland	Matra-Ford	1997	Jacques Villeneuve, Can	Williams-Renault
1970	Jochen Rindt, Austria*	Lotus-Ford	1998	Mika Hakkinen, Finland	McLaren-Mercedes
1971	Jackie Stewart, Scotland	Tyrell-Ford	1999	Mika Hakkinen, Finland	McLaren-Mercedes
1972	Emerson Fittipaldi, Brazil	Lotus-Ford	2000	Michael Schumacher, Ger	Ferrari
1973	Jackie Stewart, Scotland	Tyrell-Ford	2001	Michael Schumacher, Ger	Ferrari
			2002	Michael Schumacher, Ger	Ferrari

*The championship was awarded posthumously, after Rindt was killed during practice for the Italian Grand Prix.

Alltime Grand Prix Winners

Driver	Wins	Driver	Wins
*Michael Schumacher, Germany	63	Jim Clark, Great Britain	25
Alain Prost, France	51	Niki Lauda, Austria	25
Ayrton Senna, Brazil	41	Juan Manuel Fangio, Argentina	24
Nigel Mansell, Great Britain	31	Nelson Piquet, Brazil	23
Jackie Stewart, Great Britain	27	Damon Hill, Great Britain	22

*Active driver. Note: Grand Prix winners through Oct. 10, 2003.

Alltime Grand Prix Pole Winners

Driver	Poles	Driver	Poles
Ayrton Senna, Brazil	65	Juan Manuel Fangio, Argentina	29
*Michael Schumacher, Germany	48	Mika Hakkinen, Finland	26
Alain Prost, France	33	Niki Lauda, Austria	24
Jim Clark, Great Britain	33	Nelson Piquet, Brazil	24
Nigel Mansell, Great Britain	32	Damon Hill, Great Britain	20

*Active driver. Note: Pole winners through Oct. 10, 2003.

Professional Sports Car Racing, Inc.

The 24 Hours of Daytona

Year	Winner	Car	Avg Speed	Distance
1962	Dan Gurney	Lotus 19-Class SP11	104.101 mph	3 hrs (312.42 mi)
1963	Pedro Rodriguez	Ferrari-Class 12	102.074 mph	3 hrs (308.61 mi)
1964	Pedro Rodriguez/Phil Hill	Ferrari 250 LM	98.230 mph	2,000 km
1965	Ken Miles/Lloyd Ruby	Ford	99.944 mph	2,000 km
1966	Ken Miles/Lloyd Ruby	Ford Mark II	108.020 mph	24 hrs (2,570.63 mi)
1967	Lorenzo Bandini/Chris Amon	Ferrari 330 P4	105.688 mph	24 hrs (2,537.46 mi)
1968	Vic Elford/Jochen Neerpasch	Porsche 907	106.697 mph	24 hrs (2,565.69 mi)
1969	Mark Donohue/Chuck Parsons	Chevy Lola	99.268 mph	24 hrs (2,383.75 mi)
1970	Pedro Rodriguez/Leo Kinnunen	Porsche 917	114.866 mph	24 hrs (2,758.44 mi)
1971	Pedro Rodriguez/Jackie Oliver	Porsche 917K	109.203 mph	24 hrs (2,621.28 mi)
1972*	Mario Andretti/Jacky Ickx	Ferrari 312/P	122.573 mph	6 hrs (738.24 mi)
1973	Peter Gregg/Hurley Haywood	Porsche Carrera	106.225 mph	24 hrs (2,552.7 mi)
1974	(No race)			
1975	Peter Gregg/Hurley Haywood	Porsche Carrera	108.531 mph	24 hrs (2,606.04 mi)
1976†	Peter Gregg/Brian Redman/ John Fitzpatrick	BMW CSL	104.040 mph	24 hrs (2,092.8 mi)
1977	John Graves/Hurley Haywood/ Dave Helmick	Porsche Carrera	108.801 mph	24 hrs (2,615 mi)
1978	Rolf Stommelen/ Antoine Hezemans/Peter Gregg	Porsche Turbo	108.743 mph	24 hrs (2,611.2 mi)
1979	Ted Field/Danny Ongais/ Hurley Haywood	Porsche Turbo	109.249 mph	24 hrs (2,626.56 mi)
1980	Volkert Meri/Rolf Stommelen/ Reinhold Joest	Porsche Turbo	114.303 mph	24 hrs
1981	Bob Garretson/Bobby Rahal/ Brian Redman	Porsche Turbo	113.153 mph	24 hrs
1982	John Paul Jr/John Paul Sr/ Rolf Stommelen	Porsche Turbo	114.794 mph	24 hrs
1983	Preston Henn/Bob Wollek/ Claude Ballot-Lena/A.J. Foyt	Porsche Turbo	98.781 mph	24 hrs
1984	Sarel van der Merwe/ Graham Duxbury/Tony Martin	Porsche March	103.119 mph	24 hrs (2,476.8 mi)
1985	A.J. Foyt/Bob Wollek/ Al Unser/Thierry Boutsen	Porsche 962	104.162 mph	24 hrs (2,502.68 mi)
1986	Al Holbert/Derek Bell/Al Unser Jr.	Porsche 962	105.484 mph	24 hrs (2,534.72 mi)
1987	Chip Robinson/Derek Bell/ Al Holbert/Al Unser Jr.	Porsche 962	111.599 mph	24 hrs (2,680.68 mi)

The 24 Hours of Daytona *(Cont.)*

Year	Winner	Car	Avg Speed	Distance
1988	Martin Brundle/John Nielsen/ Raul Boesel	Jaguar XJR-9	107.943 mph	24 hrs (2,591.68 mi)
1989	John Andretti/Derek Bell/ Bob Wollek	Porsche 962	92.009 mph	24 hrs (2,210.76 mi)
1990	Davy Jones/ Jan Lammers/ Andy Wallace	Jaguar XJR-12	112.857 mph	24 hrs (2,709.16 mi)
1991	Hurley Haywood/ John Winter/ Frank Jelinski/ Henri Pescarolo/ Bob Wollek	Porsche 962C	106.633 mph	24 hrs (2,559.64 mi)
1992	Massahiro Hasemi/ Kazuoyshi Hoshino/ Toshio Suzuki/ Anders Olofsson	Nissan R91CP	112.987 mph	24 hrs (2,712.72 mi)
1993	P.J. Jones/Mark Dismore/ Rocky Moran	Toyota Eagle MK III	103.537 mph	24 hrs (2,484.88 mi)
1994	Paul Gentilozzi/ Scott Pruett/ Butch Leitzinger/ Steve Millen	Nissan 300 ZX	104.80 mph	24 hrs (2,693.67 mi)
1995	Jurgen Lassig/ Christophe Buochut/ Giovanni Lavaggi/ Marco Werner	Porsche Spyder K8	102.28 mph	690 laps (2,456.4 mi)
1996	Wayne Taylor/ Scott Sharp/ Jim Pace	Oldsmobile Mark III	103.32 mph	697 laps (2,481.32 mi)
1997	Elliot Forbes-Robinson/ John Schneider/Rob Dyson/ John Paul Jr/Butch Leitzinger/ James Weaver/Andy Wallace	Ford R & S MK III	102.292 mph	690 laps (2,456.4 mi)
1998	Arie Luyendyk/Didier Theys/ Mauro Baldi	Ferrari 333 SP	105.565 mph	711 laps (2,531.16 mi)
1999	Elliott Forbes-Robinson/ Butch Leitzinger/ Andy Wallace	Ford R & S MK III	104.9 mph	708 laps (2,520.48 mi)
2000	Olivier Beretta/Karl Wendlinger/ Dominique Dupuy	Dodge Viper	107.207 mph	723 laps (2,573.88 m)
2001	Ron Fellows/Chris Kneifel/Franck Freon/Johnny O'Connell	Corvette	97.293 mph	656 laps (2,335.360 mi)
2002	Didier Theys/Fredy Lienhard/ Max Papis/Mauro Baldi	Dallara-Judd (SRP)	106.143 mph	716 laps (2,548.96 mi)
2003	Kevin Buckler/Michael Schrom Timo Bernhard/Jorg Bergmeister	Porsche GT3 RS	114.068† mph	694 laps (2,470.64 mi)

*Race shortened due to fuel crisis. †Course lengthened from 3.81 miles to 3.84 miles. † Top speed.

World SportsCar Champions*

Year	Winner	Car	Year	Winner	Car
1978	Peter Gregg	Porsche 935	1989	Geoff Brabham	Nissan GTP
1979	Peter Gregg	Porsche 935	1990	Geoff Brabham	Nissan GTP
1980	John Fitzpatrick	Porsche 935	1991	Geoff Brabham	Nissan NPT
1981	Brian Redman	Chevy Lola	1992	Juan Fangio II	Toyota EGL MKIII
1982	John Paul Jr	Chevy Lola	1993	Juan Fangio II	Toyota EGL MKIII
1983	Al Holbert	Chevy March	1994	Wayne Taylor	Mazda Kudzu
1984	Randy Lanier	Chevy March	1995	Fermin Velez	Ferrari 333 SP
1985	Al Holbert	Porsche 962	1996	Wayne Taylor	Mazda Kudzu
1986	Al Holbert	Porsche 962	1997	Butch Leitzinger	Ford R&S MKIII
1987	Chip Robinson	Porsche 962	1998	Butch Leitzinger	Ford R&S MKIII
1988	Geoff Brabham	Nissan GTP			

Year	Prototype	GTS	GT
1999	Elliott Forbes-Robinson	Olivier Beretta	Cort Wagner
2000	Allan McNish	Olivier Beretta	Sascha Maassen
2001	Emanuele Pirro	Terry Borcheller	Jörg Müller
2002	Tom Kristensen	Ron Fellows	Lucas Luhr

*1978–93 champions raced in the GT series, which in 1994 was replaced by the World SportsCar series. Beginning in 1999, racing was reclassified according to the American Le Mans Series. The Series is comprised of two different types of race cars divided into two categories and five separate classes. The Prototype category features open-cockpit prototype World Sports Cars (WSC) and Le Mans Prototypes (LMP), as well as Grand Touring Prototype (GTP) class cars. The Grand Touring category features the Grand Touring S (GTS) class cars, formerly known as GT2, and Grand Touring (GT) cars, formerly known as GT3. Both classes feature purpose-built race cars with an emphasis on spectator car identification.

Alltime SportsCar Leaders

PROTOTYPE WINS (WSC/GTP ERA: 1994–2003)

James Weaver	14
Butch Leitzinger	13
Frank Biela	11
Rinaldo Capello	9
J.J. Lehto	9
Wayne Taylor	8
David Brabham	8
Gianpiero Moretti	7
Allan McNish	6
Emanuele Pirro	6

Seven tied with five.

GTS AND GT WINS (IMSA GT: 1971–1993)

Al Holbert	49
Peter Gregg	41
Hurley Haywood	31
Geoff Brabham	26
Parker Johnstone	25
Jim Downing	23
Irv Hoerr	23
Jack Baldwin	22
Don Devendorf	22
Bob Earl	22
Tommy Riggins	22

Note: Leaders through September 27, 2003.

24 Hours of Le Mans

Year	Winning Drivers	Car
1923	André Lagache/René Léonard	Chenard & Walker
1924	John Duff/Francis Clement	Bentley
1925	Gérard de Courcelles/André Rossignol	La Lorraine
1926	Robert Bloch/André Rossignol	La Lorraine
1927	J. Dudley Benjafield/Sammy Davis	Bentley
1928	Woolf Barnato/Bernard Rubin	Bentley
1929	Woolf Barnato/Sir Henry Birkin	Bentley Speed 6
1930	Woolf Barnato/Glen Kidston	Bentley Speed 6
1931	Earl Howe/Sir Henry Birkin	Alfa Romeo 8C-2300 sc
1932	Raymond Sommer/Luigi Chinetti	Alfa Romeo 8C-2300 sc
1933	Raymond Sommer/Tazio Nuvolari	Alfa Romeo 8C-2300 sc
1934	Luigi Chinetti/Philippe Etancelin	Alfa Romeo 8C-2300 sc
1935	John Hindmarsh/Louis Fontés	Lagonda M45R
1936	Race cancelled	
1937	Jean-Pierre Wimille/Robert Benoist	Bugatti 57G sc
1938	Eugene Chaboud/Jean Tremoulet	Delahaye 135M
1939	Jean-Pierre Wimille/Pierre Veyron	Bugatti 57G sc
1940–48	Races cancelled	
1949	Luigi Chinetti/Lord Selsdon	Ferrari 166MM
1950	Louis Rosier/Jean-Louis Rosier	Talbot-Lago
1951	Peter Walker/Peter Whitehead	Jaguar C
1952	Hermann Lang/Fritz Reiss	Mercedes-Benz 300 SL
1953	Tony Rolt/Duncan Hamilton	Jaguar C
1954	Froilan Gonzales/Maurice Trintignant	Ferrari 375
1955	Mike Hawthorn/Ivor Bueb	Jaguar D
1956	Ron Flockhart/Ninian Sanderson	Jaguar D
1957	Ron Flockhart/Ivor Bueb	Jaguar D
1958	Olivier Gendebien/Phil Hill	Ferrari 250 TR58
1959	Carroll Shelby/Roy Salvadori	Aston Martin DBR1
1960	Olivier Gendebien/Paul Frère	Ferrari 250 TR59/60
1961	Olivier Gendebien/Phil Hill	Ferrari 250 TR61
1962	Olivier Gendebien/Phil Hill	Ferrari 250P
1963	Lodovico Scarfiotti/Lorenzo Bandini	Ferrari 250P
1964	Jean Guichel/Nino Vaccarella	Ferrari 275P
1965	Jochen Rindt/Masten Gregory	Ferrari 250LM
1966	Chris Amon/Bruce McLaren	Ford Mk2
1967	Dan Gurney/A.J. Foyt	Ford Mk4
1968	Pedro Rodriguez/Lucien Bianchi	Ford GT40
1969	Jacky Ickx/Jackie Oliver	Ford GT40
1970	Hans Herrmann/Richard Attwood	Porsche 917
1971	Helmut Marko/Gijs van Lennep	Porsche 917
1972	Henri Pescarolo/Graham Hill	Matra-Simca MS670
1973	Henri Pescarolo/Gérard Larrousse	Matra-Simca MS670B

Year	Winning Drivers	Car
1974	Henri Pescarolo/Gérard Larrousse	Matra-Simca MS670B
1975	Jacky Ickx/Derek Bell	Mirage-Ford MB
1976	Jacky Ickx/Gijs van Lennep	Porsche 936
1977	Jacky Ickx/Jurgen Barth/Hurley Haywood	Porsche 936
1978	Jean-Pierre Jaussaud/Didier Pironi	Renault-Alpine A442
1979	Klaus Ludwig/Bill Whittington/Don Whittington	Porsche 935
1980	Jean-Pierre Jaussaud/Jean Rondeau	Rondeau-Ford M379B
1981	Jacky Ickx/Derek Bell	Porsche 936-81
1982	Jacky Ickx/Derek Bell	Porsche 956
1983	Vern Schuppan/Hurley Haywood/Al Holbert	Porsche 956-83
1984	Klaus Ludwig/Henri Pescarolo	Porsche 956B
1985	Klaus Ludwig/Paolo Barilla/John Winter	Porsche 956B
1986	Derek Bell/Hans-Joachim Stuck/Al Holbert	Porsche 962C
1987	Derek Bell/Hans-Joachim Stuck/Al Holbert	Porsche 962C
1988	Jan Lammers/Johnny Dumfries/Andy Wallace	Jaguar XJR9LM
1989	Jochen Mass/Manuel Reuter/Stanley Dickens	Sauber-Mercedes C9-88
1990	John Nielsen/Price Cobb/Martin Brundle	TWR Jaguar XJR-12
1991	Volker Weidler/Johnny Herbert/Bertrand Gachof	Mazda 787B
1992	Derek Warwick/Yannick Dalmas/Mark Blundell	Peugeot 905B
1993	Geoff Brabham/Christophe Bouchut/Eric Helary	Peugeot 905
1994	Yannick Dalmas/Hurley Haywood/Mauro Baldi	Porsche 962
1995	Yannick Dalmas/J.J. Lehto/Masanori Sekiya	McLaren BMW
1996	Manuel Reuter/Davy Jones/Alexander Wurz	TWR Porsche
1997	Michele Alboreto/Stefan Johansson/Tom Kristensen	TWR Porsche
1998	Allan McNish/Laurent Aiello/Stephane Ortelli	Porsche GT One
1999	Yannick Dalmas/Joachim Winkelhock/Pierluigi Martini	BMW V12 LMR
2000	Frank Biela/Tom Kristensen/Emanuele Pirro	Audi R8
2001	Frank Biela/Tom Kristensen/Emanuele Pirro	Audi R8
2002	Frank Biela/Tom Kristensen/Emanuele Pirro	Audi R8
2003	Rinaldo Capello/Tom Kritensen/Guy Smith	Bentley EXP Speed 8

High-Octane Bad Blood

NASCAR has a long history of Hatfield-McCoy–like feuds. (Richard Petty vs. David Pearson was the nastiest of 'em all.) Here's a look at the big three of '03:

1. Jeff Gordon vs. Robby Gordon
The battle of the Gordons—who are related only by their mutual antipathy—flared again after June 2003's Dodge/Save Mart 350 at Infineon Raceway in Sonoma, Calif., when Jeff, who took second, said Robby won only because of a pass made under yellow. "If Robby was as fast under green as he was under caution," said Jeff, "he'd win a lot of these things."

2. Kurt Busch vs. Jimmy Spencer
Though one-sided, this rivalry remains white-hot because Busch and Spencer simply can't stand each other. In 2002, Busch said Spencer had "the brain of a peanut"; in 2003, Mr. Excitement asserted that Busch "has a lot of problems mentally."

3. Dale Earnhardt Inc. vs. Richard Childress Racing
The team that Dale Earnhardt founded (DEI) and the team he raced for (RCR) say they have a "friendly rivalry" but often descend into smack talk over who rules restrictor-plate tracks. Adding to the intrigue: In May 2003, Jeff Green, fired by RCR, was hired by DEI, and Steve Park, fired by DEI, was hired by RCR.

Top Fuel

ELAPSED TIME

Time (Sec.)	Driver	Date	Site
9.00	Jack Chrisman	Feb 18, 1961	Pomona, CA
8.97	Jack Chrisman	May 20, 1961	Empona, VA
7.96	Bobby Vodnick	May 16, 1964	Bayview, MD
6.97	Don Johnson	May 7, 1967	Carlsbad, CA
5.97	Mike Snively	Nov 17, 1972	Ontario, CA
5.78	Don Garlits	Nov 18, 1973	Ontario, CA
5.698	Gary Beck	Oct 10, 1975	Ontario, CA
5.573	Gary Beck	Oct 18, 1981	Irvine, CA
5.484	Gary Beck	Sept 6, 1982	Clermont, IN
5.391	Gary Beck	Oct 1, 1983	Fremont, CA
5.280	Darrell Gwynn	Sept 25, 1986	Ennis, TX
5.176	Darrell Gwynn	April 4, 1987	Ennis, TX
5.090	Joe Amato	Oct 1, 1987	Ennis, TX
4.990	Eddie Hill	April 9, 1988	Ennis, TX
4.881	Gary Ormsby	Sept 28, 1990	Topeka, KS
4.799	Cory McClenathan	Sept 19, 1992	Mohnton, PA
4.762	Cory McClenathan	Oct 3, 1993	Topeka, KS
4.690	Michael Brotherton	May 20, 1994	Englishtown, NJ
4.595	Joe Amato	July 5,1996	Topeka, KS
4.539	Joe Amato	Mar 21, 1998	Baytown, TX
4.525	Gary Scelzi	Oct 23, 1998	Ennis, TX
4.503	Mike Dunn	Feb 5, 1999	Pomona, CA
4.486	Larry Dixon	Apr 9, 1999	Houston
4.480	Gary Scelzi	Oct 31, 1999	Houston
4.477	Kenny Bernstein	June 2, 2001	Joliet, IL

SPEED

MPH	Driver	Date	Site
180.36	Connie Kalitta	Sept 3, 1962	Indianapolis
190.26	Don Garlits	Sept 21, 1963	East Haddam, CT
201.34	Don Garlits	Aug 1, 1964	Great Meadows, NJ
211.26	Donny Milani	May 15, 1965	Sacramento, CA
223.32	Don Cook	Apr 24, 1965	Fremont, CA
230.17	James Warren	Apr 10, 1967	Fresno, CA
243.24	Don Garlits	Mar 18, 1973	Gainesville, FL
250.69	Don Garlits	Oct 11, 1975	Ontario, CA
260.11	Joe Amato	Mar 18, 1984	Gainesville, FL
272.56	Don Garlits	Mar 23, 1986	Gainesville, FL
282.13	Joe Amato	Sept 5, 1987	Clermont, IN
291.54	Connie Kalitta	Feb 11, 1989	Pomona, CA
301.70	Kenny Bernstein	Mar 20, 1992	Gainesville, FL
311.86	Kenny Bernstein	Oct 30, 1994	Pomona, CA
319.82	Joe Amato	Mar 21, 1998	Baytown, TX
323.50	Joe Amato	May 17, 1998	Englishtown, NJ
326.44	Gary Scelzi	Nov 2, 1998	Houston
326.91	Tony Schumacher	Oct 22, 1999	Dallas
330.55	Mike Dunn	June 2, 2001	Joliet, IL
332.18	Kenny Bernstein	Oct. 7, 2001	Richardson, TX
332.75	Larry Dixon	Apr 3, 2003	Las Vegas

Funny Car

ELAPSED TIME

Time (sec.)	Driver	Date	Site
6.92	Leroy Goldstein	Sept 3, 1970	Clermont, IN
5.987	Don Prudhomme	Oct 12, 1975	Ontario, CA
5.868	Raymond Beadle	July 16, 1981	Englishtown, NJ
5.799	Tom Anderson	Sept 3, 1982	Clermont, IN
5.637	Don Prudhomme	Sept 4, 1982	Clermont, IN
5.588	Rick Johnson	Feb 3, 1985	Pomona, CA
5.425	Kenny Bernstein	Sept 26, 1986	Ennis, TX
5.397	Kenny Bernstein	April 5, 1987	Ennis, TX
5.255	Ed McCulloch	April 17, 1988	Ennis, TX
5.193	Don Prudhomme	Mar 2, 1989	Baytown, TX
5.077	Cruz Pedregon	Sept 20, 1992	Mohnton, PA
4.987	Chuck Etcholis	Oct 2, 1993	Topeka, KS
4.819	Cruz Pedregon	Mar 21, 1998	Baytown, TX
4.807	Cruz Pedregon	Nov 1, 1998	Houston
4.788	John Force	Apr 11, 1999	Houston
4.763	John Force	June 2, 2001	Joliet, IL
4.750	William Bazemore	Sept 28, 2001	Joliet, IL
4.731	John Force	Oct. 7, 2001	Yorba Linda, CA

SPEED

MPH	Driver	Date	Site
200.44	Gene Snow	Aug, 1968	Houston
250.00	Don Prudhomme	May 23, 1982	Baton Rouge
260.11	Kenny Bernstein	Mar 18, 1984	Gainesville, FL
271.41	Kenny Bernstein	Aug 30, 1986	Indianapolis
280.72	Mike Dunn	Oct 2, 1987	Ennis, TX
290.13	Jim White	Oct 11, 1991	Ennis, TX
291.82	Jim White	Oct 25, 1991	Pomona, CA
300.40	Jim Epler	Oct 3, 1993	Topeka, KS
303.64	John Force	Sept 2, 1995	Indianapolis
308.74	John Force	Sept 28, 1997	Topeka, KS
317.46	John Force	Mar 21, 1998	Baytown, TX
323.89	John Force	May 17, 1998	Englishtown, NJ
324.05	John Force	Mar 19, 1999	Gainesville, FL
325.45	William Bazemore	Sept 28, 2001	Joliet, IL
326.87	Gary Densham	Feb. 9, 2002	Bellflower, CA

Pro Stock

ELAPSED TIME

Time (sec.)	Driver	Date	Site
7.778	Lee Shepherd	Mar 12, 1982	Gainesville, FL
7.655	Lee Shepherd	Oct 1, 1982	Fremont, CA
7.557	Bob Glidden	Feb 2, 1985	Pomona, CA
7.497	Bob Glidden	Sep 13, 1985	Maple Grove, PA
7.377	Bob Glidden	Aug 28, 1986	Clermont, IN
7.294	Frank Sanchez	Oct 7, 1988	Baytown, TX
7.184	Darrell Alderman	Oct 12, 1990	Ennis, TX
7.099	Scott Geoffrion	Sept 19, 1992	Mohnton, PA
6.988	Kurt Johnson	May 20, 1994	Englishtown, NJ
6.873	Warren Johnson	Mar 14, 1998	Gainesville, FL
6.867	Warren Johnson	Oct 23, 1998	Ennis, TX
6.866	Warren Johnson	Mar 19, 1999	Gainesville, FL
6.843	Warren Johnson	Apr 30, 1999	Dinwiddie, VA
6.840	Kurt Johnson	May 1, 1999	Dinwiddie, VA
6.822	Warren Johnson	Oct 23, 1999	Dallas
6.801	Kurt Johnson	Sept 29, 2001	Joliet, IL
6.750	Jeg Coughlin	Oct. 7, 2001	Delaware, OH

Pro Stock (Cont.)
SPEED

MPH	Driver	Date	Site
181.08	Warren Johnson	Oct 1, 1982	Fremont, CA
190.07	Warren Johnson	Aug 29, 1986	Clermont, IN
191.32	Bob Glidden	Sept 4, 1987	Clermont, IN
192.18	Warren Johnson	Oct 13, 1990	Ennis, TX
193.21	Bob Glidden	July 28, 1991	Sonoma, CA
194.51	Warren Johnson	July 31, 1992	Sonoma, CA
195.99	Warren Johnson	May 21, 1993	Englishtown, NJ
196.24	Warren Johnson	Mar 19, 1993	Gainesville, FL
197.15	Warren Johnson	Apr 23, 1994	Commerce, GA
199.15	Warren Johnson	Mar 10, 1995	Baytown, TX
201.20	Warren Johnson	Mar 14, 1998	Gainesville, FL
201.34	Warren Johnson	Oct 23, 1998	Ennis, TX
201.37	Warren Johnson	Mar 19, 1999	Gainesville, FL
202.24	Warren Johnson	Apr 30,1999	Dinwiddie, VA
202.33	Warren Johnson	Oct 23, 1999	Dallas
202.36	Warren Johnson	Oct 31, 1999	Houston
202.70	Kurt Johnson	Sept 29, 2001	Joliet, IL
204.35	Mark Osborne	Oct. 6, 2001	Abdingdon, VA

Alltime Drag Racing Leaders
NHRA CAREER WINS

*John Force	108
*Warren Johnson	92
Bob Glidden	85
*Kenny Bernstein	66
Joe Amato	52
Don Prudhomme	49
David Schultz	45
Don Garlits	35
John Myers	33
Larry Dixon	33

*Active driver. Note: Leaders through 2002 season.

THEY SAID IT

Michael Schumacher, Formula 1 driver, after winning the Grand Prix of Austria, during which his car was engulfed in flames on pit road: "Seeing the fire was not nice."

Bowling

A Bang and A Whimper

While the men's tour ended with a flourish from its No. I player, the PWBA was forced to cancel its fall tour

BY HANK HERSCH

He had already moved into second on the alltime victory list, winning his 35th title at the PBA Greater Detroit Open. He had already seized his fourth major, the 2003 U.S. Open in Fountain Valley, Calif., where he also became the first pro bowler to surpass $3 million in career PBA prize money. He had all but clinched the highest average for 2002–03, broke the season record for earnings set in 1989 and was a virtual lock for his sixth PBA Player of the Year award. With those weighty accomplishments under his belt, in the final of the championship match of the tour's final stop, the 43-year-old righthander known as Deadeye took dead aim at a finish worthy of his record-packed season.

The format of the PBA World Championship in March served to heighten the drama. Some 300 bowlers vied to qualify for the round of 16, where the eight survivors would face the PBA's top eight scorers for the season in best-of-five matches. Once that field was reduced to four, the telecast semifinals would consist of one-game, elimination showdowns in an arena setting at the Taylor (Mich.) Sportsplex, where many of the more than 2,000 spectators sat not behind the competitors, but along the length of the four lanes.

The prize at week's end: $120,000, tied for the largest first-place check in the history of bowling. That tidy amount would lift the season earnings of Walter Ray Williams Jr., a.k.a. Deadeye, to the unheard-of sum of $419,700—$121,463 more than Mike Aulby's single-season earnings record. A few months earlier, PBA president and CEO Steve Miller had told Williams he could be the first bowler to break not only the $300,000 barrier, but the $400,000 threshold as well. "I kind of laughed at him," said Williams of that conversation.

But the prospect was no more ludicrous than the notion that a prodigy at horseshoes from Chino, Calif., would graduate from Cal Poly Pomona with a degree in physics and almost 20 years later stand on

AP PHOTO/JOHN F. MARTIN

A second-year pro, Kretzer reached the final in Taylor, where he fell to Williams.

the verge of his sixth Player of the Year title—to go with his six world horseshoes championships—spanning an unprecedented three decades. Yet here was Williams, having defied probability and rewritten history, trying to cap an incredible season with a record-shattering win and a fifth major title.

In the semis at Taylor, Williams edged the feisty Pete Weber 217–207, while sixth-seed Brian Kretzer of Dayton, Ohio, dispatched Parker Bohn III, 248–222. No matter that Kretzer had bowled more than 40 games to make the finals, and Williams only a handful; they matched each other shot-for-shot through the first four frames. Spares by Williams in the next two frames created an opening, but Kretzer, a second-year pro, left a 7–10 split in the sixth.

Williams took over the match from there, rolling to a 226–205 win that placed him four behind Earl Anthony's 41 on the career victories list. Kretzer blamed the loss on the split as well as a poor throw in the ninth, when he counted seven pins before sparing. "That gave [Williams] the chance to step up and shut me out, which he did," Kretzer said. "You expect that from the Number 1 bowler in the world, if not the Number 1 bowler ever."

"If the aches and pains keep to a minimum, I think I'd be able to compete fairly well into my late 40s or early 50s," Williams said. "I'm going to keep doing it as long as I can do it well."

While the PBA season ended with a bang, the women's tour ended with a press conference. On Aug. 11 the Rockford, Ill.–based organization announced that it was canceling all four of its fall tour events, which would have completed its 13-event season. Though the television ratings of 0.64 represented an increase in viewership for the fifth straight year—and a record 45% increase from 2002—a lack of sponsorship left the PWBA short of operating funds. The association's founder and chairman John Sommer, who has reportedly lost about $4 million during the past five years, said that he would explore all options to revive the tour for 2004. "Today's announcement does not mean this is the end," said PWBA president John Falzone, "only the end this year."

The Majors

MEN

2002 Tournament of Champions

	Games	Total	Earnings ($)
Jason Couch	2	478	100,000
Ryan Shafer	2	458	50;000
Patrick Healy Jr.	1	230	25,000
Robert Smith	1	201	15,000

Playoff Results: Shafer def. Healey 234–230; Couch def. Smith 212–201; Couch def. Shafer 266–224.

Held at the Mohegan Sun in Uncasville, CT, Dec 12–15, 2002.

2003 ABC Masters
CHAMPIONSHIP ROUND

Bowler	Games	Total	Earnings ($)
Bryon Smith	1	236	100,000
Walter Ray Williams Jr.	3	709	50,000
Jason Williams	1	178	25,000
Norm Duke	1	234	15,000

Playoff Results: Williams def. Duke 264–234; W.R. Williams def. J. Williams, 225–178; Smith def. Williams, 236–220.

Held at National Bowling Stadium in Reno, NV, Jan 14–19, 2003.

2003 U.S. Open

	Games	Total	Earnings ($)
Walter Ray Williams Jr.	1	236	100,000
Michael Haugen Jr.	2	404	50,000
Pete Weber	2	439	25,000
Mika Koivuniemi	1	220	15,000

Playoff Results: Weber def. Koivuniemi 233–220; Haugen def. Weber 206–202; Williams def. Haugen 236–198.

Held at the Fountain Bowl in Fountain Valley, CA, Jan 27–Feb 2, 2003

2003 PBA World Championship
CHAMPIONSHIP ROUND

Bowler	Games	Total	Earnings ($)
Walter Ray Williams Jr.	2	443	120,000
Brian Kretzer	2	453	50,000
Parker Bohn III	1	222	20,000
Pete Weber	1	207	20,000

Playoff Results: Kretzer def. Bohn, 248–222; Williams def. Weber, 217–207; Williams def. Kretzer 226–205.

Held at Taylor Sportsplex in Taylor, MI, Mar 3–9, 2003.

WOMEN

2002 Miller High Life National Players Championship

CHAMPIONSHIP ROUND

Bowler	Games	Total	Earnings ($)
Marianne DiRupo	3	689	13,000
Leanne Barrette	1	158	7,000
Michelle Feldman	1	191	4,600
Kelly Kulick	1	152	4,200
Tammy Turner	1	190	3,700

Playoff Results: DiRupo def. Turner and Kulick, 266–190–152; DiRupo def. Feldman, 243–191; DiRupo def. Barrette 180–158.

Held at Funquest Lanes, Collierville, TN, July 21–25, 2002.

2003 WIBC Queens

CHAMPIONSHIP ROUND

Bowler	Games	Total	Earnings ($)
Wendy Macpherson	1	218	14,000
Kendra Gaines	2	415	11,000
Tish Johnson	2	457	8,500
Robin Romeo	1	218	6,500
Lisa Bishop	1	180	5,500

Playoff Results: Johnson def. Romeo and Bishop 242–218–180; Gaines def. Johnson 222–215; Macpherson def. Gaines 218–193.

Held at the National Bowling Stadium in Reno, NV, April 7–11, 2003.

2003 U.S. Open

CHAMPIONSHIP ROUND

Bowler	Games	Total	Earnings ($)
Kelly Kulick	4	951	30,000
Carolyn Dorin-Ballard	1	195	15,000
Michelle Feldman	1	174	11,000
Wendy Macpherson	1	179	9,000
Leanne Barrette	1	213	7,000

Playoff Results: Kulick def. Barrette 213–213 with rolloff 39–35; Kulick def. Macpherson 221–179; Kulick def. Feldman 256–174; Kulick def. Dorin-Ballard 261–195.

Held in Sterling Heights, MI, May 26–June 1, 2003.

Men

2002–03 Tour

Date	Event	Winner	Earnings ($)	Runner-Up
Aug 30-Sep 2,2002	Dream Bowl 2002	Hugh Miller	40,000	Yamazaki
Sep 5–8	Japan Cup	Robert Smith	50,000	Chris Barnes
Oct 9–13	Wichita Open	D'Entremont	40,000	Chris Barnes
Oct 16–20	Greater Kansas City Classic	Patrick Healey Jr.	40,000	Michael Gaither
Oct 23–27	Memphis Open	Brian Voss	40,000	Danny Wiseman
Oct 30–Nov 3	Miller High Life Open	Danny Wiseman	40,000	Walter Ray Williams Jr.
Nov 6–10	Greater Detroit Open	Walter Ray Williams Jr.	40,000	Brian Voss
Nov 13–17	PBA Banquet Classic	Eugene McCune	50,000	Walter Ray Williams Jr.
Nov 20–24	PBA Pepsi Open	Randy Pedersen	40,000	Chris Barnes
Nov 27–Dec 1	Cambridge Credit Classic	Norm Duke	40,000	David Traber
Dec 4–8	Empire State Open	Doug Kent	25,000	Chris Barnes
Dec 12–15	Tournament of Champions	Jason Couch	100,000	Ryan Shafer
Jan 1–5, 2003	Earl Anthony Classic	Mike DeVaney	40,000	Norm Duke
Jan 8–12	Medford Open	Bryan Goebel	40,000	Danny Wiseman
Jan 14–19	ABC Masters	Bryon Smith	100,000	Walter Ray Williams Jr.
Jan 19–23	PBA Storm Las Vegas Classic	Lonnie Waliczek	40,000	Patrick Allen
Jan 27–Feb 2	U.S. Open	Walter Ray Williams Jr.	100,000	Michael Haugen Jr.
Feb 5–9	Days Inn Open	Chris Barnes	40,000	Parker Bohn III
Feb 12–16	VIA Bowling Open	Chris Hayden	40,000	Jason Couch
Feb 19–23	Tar Heel Open	Pete Weber	25,000	Brian Voss
Feb 26–Mar 2	Odor-Eaters Open	Lonnie Waliczek	40,000	Tommy Jones
Mar 3–9	PBA World Championship	Walter Ray Williams Jr.	120,000	Brian Kretzer

2003 Senior Tour

Date	Event	Winner	Earnings ($)	Runner-Up
May 3–6	Chillicothe Open	Steve Neff	8,000	Mark Roth
May 10–13	Greater Detroit Open	John Bennett	8,000	Dale Eagle
May 25–30	ABC Senior Masters	Dale Eagle	20,000	Bob Glass
May 31–Jun 6	Storm U.S. Open	Dave Soutar	20,000	Gary Dickinson
Jun 8–11	Northern California Classic	Ernie Schlegel	8,000	Norb Wetzel
Jun 15–18	Epicenter Classic	Lee Snow	8,000	Henry Gonzalez
Jun 22–25	Northwest Classic	Bob Handley	8,000	John Bennett
Aug 2–5	Manassas Open	Don Sylvia	8,000	Gary Hiday
Aug 9–12	Clarksville Open	Ron Winger	8,000	Gene Stus
Aug 17–20	Lake County Open	Vince Mazzanti	8,000	Charlie Tapp
Aug 23–27	Days Inn Open	Bob Chamberlain	9,000	Sal Bongiorno

†PWBA Tour Results

2002 Fall Tour

Date	Event	Winner	Earnings ($)	Runner-Up
Sep 15–22	Three Rivers Open	Leanne Barrette	9,000	Marianne DiRupo
Sep 22–26	Burlington Open	Carolyn Dorin-Ballard	9,000	Kendra Gaines
Sep 29–Oct 3	Lady Ebonite Classic	Liz Johnson	12,000	Leanne Barrette
Oct 7–10	Greater Pasadena Open	Tish Johnson	9,000	Liz Johnson
Oct 20–24	Wheelchair Awareness Classic	Tiffany Stanbrough	9,000	Kelly Kulick
Oct 27–Nov 1	Greater San Diego Open	Michelle Feldman	9,000	Wendy Macpherson
Nov 3–8	Storm Las Vegas Challenge	Tiffany Stanbrough	12,000	Kendra Gaines

2003 Tour

Date	Event	Winner	Earnings ($)	Runner-Up
April 7–11	WIBC Queens	Wendy Macpherson	14,000	Kendra Gaines
May 29–Jun 1	U.S. Open	Kelly Kulick	30,000	Carolyn Dorin-Ballard
Jun 5–8	Greater Terre Haute Open	Tiffany Stanbrough	15,000	Lisa Bishop
Jun 11–15	Greater Rockford Classic	Tiffany Stanbrough	15,000	Michelle Feldman
Jun 19–22	Greater Cincinnati Open	Carolyn Dorin-Ballard	15,000	Liz Johnson
Jun 26–29	Greater Harrisburg Open	Dede Davidson	15,000	Cara Honeychurch
July 3–6	Greater Memphis Open	Tennelle Milligan	15,000	Cara Honeychurch
July 9–13	Dallas Open	Michelle Feldman	15,000	Kendra Gaines

Note: Remainder of 2003 tour cancelled.

†Known as LBPT until 1998.

Tour Leaders

PBA: 2002–2003

MONEY LEADERS

Name (Titles)	Tournaments	Earnings ($)
Walter Ray Williams Jr. (3)	21	419,700
Chris Barnes (1)	22	183,930
Jason Couch (1)	21	150,470
Norm Duke (1)	22	145,000
Bryon Smith (1)	21	136,700

AVERAGE

Name	Games	Average
Walter Ray Williams Jr.	569	224.94
Chris Barnes	564	222.91
Norm Duke	517	221.78
Pete Weber	419	220.73
Ryan Shafer	461	220.29

Seniors: 2003

MONEY LEADERS

Name	Tournaments	Earnings ($)
Dale Eagle (1)	11	33,900
Dave Soutar (1)	11	31,310
Bob Handley (1)	5	25,200
Bob Chamberlain (1)	11	24,350
Robert Glass (0)	11	23,700

AVERAGE

Name	Games	Average
George Pappas	247	216.98
Gary Dickinson	157	216.07
Henry Gonzalez	297	216.00
Dale Eagle	283	215.92
Bob Chamberlian	321	215.32

PWBA: 2002

MONEY LEADERS

Name (Titles)	Tournaments	Earnings ($)
Michelle Feldman (3)	19	82,405
Leanne Barrette (3)	18	72,960
Kim Terrell (1)	19	69,487
Kendra Gaines (1)	19	68,800
Carolyn Dorin-Ballard (2)	19	65,672

AVERAGE

Name	Games	Average
Leanne Barrette	717	216.45
Carolyn Dorin-Ballard	738	215.46
Wendy Macpherson	741	214.39
Michelle Feldman	745	213.93
Kendra Gaines	743	213.93

Men's Majors

BPAA United States Open

Year	Winner	Score	Runner-Up	Site
1942	John Crimmins	265.09–262.33	Joe Norris	Chicago
1943	Connie Schwoegler	not available	Frank Benkovic	Chicago
1944	Ned Day	315.21–298.21	Paul Krumske	Chicago
1945	Buddy Bomar	304.46–296.16	Joe Wilman	Chicago
1946	Joe Wilman	310.27–305.37	Therman Gibson	Chicago
1947	Andy Varipapa	314.16–308.04	Allie Brandt	Chicago
1948	Andy Varipapa	309.23–309.06	Joe Wilman	Chicago
1949	Connie Schwoegler	312.31–307.27	Andy Varipapa	Chicago
1950	Junie McMahon	318.37–307.17	Ralph Smith	Chicago
1951	Dick Hoover	305.29–304.07	Lee Jouglard	Chicago
1952	Junie McMahon	309.29–305.41	Bill Lillard	Chicago
1953	Don Carter	304.17–297.36	Ed Lubanski	Chicago
1954	Don Carter	308.02–307.25	Bill Lillard	Chicago
1955	Steve Nagy	307.17–303.34	Ed Lubanski	Chicago
1956	Bill Lillard	304.30–304.22	Joe Wilman	Chicago
1957	Don Carter	308.49–305.45	Dick Weber	Chicago
1958	Don Carter	311.03–308.09	Buzz Fazio	Minneapolis
1959	Billy Welu	311.48–310.26	Ray Bluth	Buffalo
1960	Harry Smith	312.24–308.12	Bob Chase	Omaha
1961	Bill Tucker	318.49–309.11	Dick Weber	San Bernardino, CA
1962	Dick Weber	299.34–297.38	Roy Lown	Miami Beach
1963	Dick Weber	642–591	Billy Welu	Kansas City, MO
1964	Bob Strampe	714–616	Tommy Tuttle	Dallas
1965	Dick Weber	608–586	Jim St. John	Philadelphia
1966	Dick Weber	684–681	Nelson Burton Jr.	Lansing, MI
1967	Les Schissler	613–610	Pete Tountas	St. Ann, MO
1968	Jim Stefanich	12,401–12,104	Billy Hardwick	Garden City, NY
1969	Billy Hardwick	12,585–11,463	Dick Weber	Miami
1970	Bobby Cooper	12,936–12,307	Billy Hardwick	Northbrook, IL
1971	Mike Limongello	397 (2 games)	Teata Semiz	St. Paul, MN
1972	Don Johnson	233 (1 game)	George Pappas	New York City
1973	Mike McGrath	712 (3 games)	Earl Anthony	New York City
1974	Larry Laub	749 (3 games)	Dave Davis	New York City
1975	Steve Neff	279 (1 game)	Paul Colwell	Grand Prairie, TX
1976	Paul Moser	226 (1 game)	Jim Frazier	Grand Prairie, TX
1977	Johnny Petraglia	279 (1 game)	Bill Spigner	Greensboro, NC
1978	Nelson Burton Jr.	873 (4 games)	Jeff Mattingly	Greensboro, NC
1979	Joe Berardi	445 (2 games)	Earl Anthony	Windsor Locks, CT
1980	Steve Martin	930 (4 games)	Earl Anthony	Windsor Locks, CT
1981	Marshall Holman	684 (3 games)	Mark Roth	Houston
1982	Dave Husted	1011 (4 games)	Gil Sliker	Houston
1983	Gary Dickinson	214 (1 game)	Steve Neff	Oak Lawn, IL
1984	Mark Roth	244 (1 game)	Guppy Troup	Oak Hill, IL
1985	Marshall Holman	233 (1 game)	Wayne Webb	Venice, FL
1986	Steve Cook	467 (2 games)	Frank Ellenburg	Venice, FL
1987	Del Ballard Jr.	525 (2 games)	Pete Weber	Tacoma, WA
1988	Pete Weber	929 (4 games)	Marshall Holman	Atlantic City
1989	Mike Aulby	429 (2 games)	Jim Pencak	Edmond, OK
1990	Ron Palombi Jr.	269 (1 game)	Amleto Monacelli	Indianapolis
1991	Pete Weber	956 (4 games)	Mark Thayer	Indianapolis
1992	Robert Lawrence	667 (3 games)	Scott Devers	Canandaigua, NY
1993	Del Ballard Jr.	505 (2 games)	Walter Ray Williams Jr.	Canandaigua, NY
1994	Justin Hromek	267 (1 game)	Parker Bohn III	Troy, MI
1995	Dave Husted	266 (1 game)	Paul Koehler	Troy, MI
1996	Dave Husted	730 (3 games)	George Brooks	Indianapolis
1997	No event—tournament rescheduled to April, beginning in 1998.			
1998	Walter Ray Williams Jr.	466 (2 games)	Tim Criss	Fairfield, CT
1999	Bob Learn Jr.	231 (1 game)	Jason Couch	Uncasville, CT
2000	Robert Smith	202 (1 game)	Norm Duke	Phoenix
2001	Mika Koivuniemi	247 (1 game)	Patrick Healey Jr	Fountain Valley, CA
2003	Walter Ray Williams Jr.	236 (1 game)	Michael Haugen Jr.	Fountain Valley, CA

Note: From 1942 to 1970, the tournament was called the BPAA All-Star. Peterson scoring was used from 1942 through 1962. Under this system, the winner of an individual match game gets one point, plus one point for each 50 pins knocked down. From 1963 through 1967, a three-game championship was held between the two top qualifiers. From 1968 through 1970 total pinfall determined the winner. From 1971 to the present, five qualifiers compete for the championship.

Touring Players Championship

Year	Winner	Score	Runner-Up	Site
1996	Mike Aulby	268 (1 game)	Parker Bohn III	Harmarville, PA
1997	Steve Hoskins	932 (4 games)	Danny Wiseman	Harmarville, PA
1998	Dennis Horan	481 (2 games)	Parker Bohn III	Akron, OH
1999	Steve Hoskins	503 (2 games)	Parker Bohn III	Akron, OH
2000	Dennis Horan	924 (4 games)	Pete Weber	Akron, OH
2001	Tournament discontinued.			

PBA World Championship

Year	Winner	Score	Runner-Up	Site
1960	Don Carter	6512 (30 games)	Ronnie Gaudern	Memphis
1961	Dave Soutar	5792 (27 games)	Morrie Oppenheim	Cleveland
1962	Carmen Salvino	5369 (25 games)	Don Carter	Philadelphia
1963	Billy Hardwick	13,541 (61 games)	Ray Bluth	Long Island, NY
1964	Bob Strampe	13,979 (61 games)	Ray Bluth	Long Island, NY
1965	Dave Davis	13,895 (61 games)	Jerry McCoy	Detroit
1966	Wayne Zahn	14,006 (61 games)	Nelson Burton Jr.	Long Island, NY
1967	Dave Davis	421 (2 games)	Pete Tountas	New York City
1968	Wayne Zahn	14,182 (60 games)	Nelson Burton Jr.	New York City
1969	Mike McGrath	13,670 (60 games)	Bill Allen	Garden City, NY
1970	Mike McGrath	660 (3 games)	Dave Davis	Garden City, NY
1971	Mike Limongello	911 (4 games)	Dave Davis	Paramus, NJ
1972	Johnny Guenther	12,986 (56 games)	Dick Ritger	Rochester, NY
1973	Earl Anthony	212 (1 game)	Sam Flanagan	Oklahoma City
1974	Earl Anthony	218 (1 game)	Mark Roth	Downey, CA
1975	Earl Anthony	245 (1 game)	Jim Frazier	Downey, CA
1976	Paul Colwell	191 (1 game)	Dave Davis	Seattle
1977	Tommy Hudson	206 (1 game)	Jay Robinson	Seattle
1978	Warren Nelson	453 (2 games)	Joseph Groskind	Reno
1979	Mike Aulby	727 (3 games)	Earl Anthony	Las Vegas
1980	Johnny Petraglia	235 (1 game)	Gary Dickinson	Sterling Heights, MI
1981	Earl Anthony	242 (1 game)	Ernie Schlegel	Toledo, OH
1982	Earl Anthony	233 (1 game)	Charlie Tapp	Toledo, OH
1983	Earl Anthony	210 (1 game)	Mike Durbin	Toledo, OH
1984	Bob Chamberlain	961 (4 games)	Dan Eberl	Toledo, OH
1985	Mike Aulby	476 (2 games)	Steve Cook	Toledo, OH
1986	Tom Crites	190 (1 game)	Mike Aulby	Toledo, OH
1987	Randy Pedersen	759 (3 games)	Amleto Monacelli	Toledo, OH
1988	Brian Voss	246 (1 game)	Todd Thompson	Toledo, OH
1989	Pete Weber	221 (1 game)	Dave Ferraro	Toledo, OH
1990	Jim Pencak	900 (4 games)	Chris Warren	Toledo, OH
1991	Mike Miller	450 (2 games)	Norm Duke	Toledo, OH
1992	Eric Forkel	833 (4 games)	Bob Vespi	Toledo, OH
1993	Ron Palombi Jr.	237 (1 game)	Eugene McCune	Toledo, OH
1994	David Traber	196 (1 game)	Dale Traber	Toledo, OH
1995	Scott Alexander	246 (1 game)	Wayne Webb	Toledo, OH
1996	Butch Soper	442 (2 games)	Walter Ray Williams Jr.	Toledo, OH
1997	Rick Steelsmith	888 (4 games)	Brian Voss	Toledo, OH
1998	Pete Weber	277 (1 game)	David Ozio	Toledo, OH
1999	Tim Criss	238 (1 game)	Dave Arnold	Toledo, OH
2000	Norm Duke	492 (2 games)	Jason Couch	Toledo, OH
2001	Walter Ray Williams Jr.	258 (1 game)	Jeff Lizzi	Toledo, OH
2002	Doug Kent	417 (2 games)	Lonnie Waliczek	Toledo, OH
2003	Walter Ray Williams Jr.	443 (2 games)	Brian Kretzer	Taylor, MI

Note: Totals from 1963–66, 1968–69 and 1972 include bonus pins.

Tournament of Champions

Year	Winner	Score	Runner-Up	Site
1965	Billy Hardwick	484 (2 games)	Dick Weber	Akron, OH
1966	Wayne Zahn	595 (3 games)	Dick Weber	Akron, OH
1967	Jim Stefanich	227 (1 game)	Don Johnson	Akron, OH
1968	Dave Davis	213 (1 game)	Don Johnson	Akron, OH
1969	Jim Godman	266 (1 game)	Jim Stefanich	Akron, OH
1970	Don Johnson	299 (1 game)	Dick Ritger	Akron, OH
1971	Johnny Petraglia	245 (1 game)	Don Johnson	Akron, OH
1972	Mike Durbin	775 (3 games)	Tim Harahan	Akron, OH
1973	Jim Godman	451 (2 games)	Barry Asher	Akron, OH
1974	Earl Anthony	679 (3 games)	Johnny Petraglia	Akron, OH
1975	Dave Davis	448 (2 games)	Barry Asher	Akron, OH
1976	Marshall Holman	441 (2 games)	Billy Hardwick	Akron, OH
1977	Mike Berlin	434 (2 games)	Mike Durbin	Akron, OH
1978	Earl Anthony	237 (1 game)	Teata Semiz	Akron, OH
1979	George Pappas	224 (1 game)	Dick Ritger	Akron, OH
1980	Wayne Webb	750 (3 games)	Gary Dickinson	Akron, OH
1981	Steve Cook	287 (1 game)	Pete Couture	Akron, OH
1982	Mike Durbin	448 (2 games)	Steve Cook	Akron, OH
1983	Joe Berardi	865 (4 games)	Henry Gonzalez	Akron, OH
1984	Mike Durbin	950 (4 games)	Mike Aulby	Akron, OH
1985	Mark Williams	616 (3 games)	Bob Handley	Akron, OH
1986	Marshall Holman	233 (1 game)	Mark Baker	Akron, OH
1986	Marshall Holman	233 (1 game)	Mark Baker	Akron, OH
1987	Pete Weber	928 (4 games)	Jim Murtishaw	Akron, OH
1988	Mark Williams	237 (1 game)	Tony Westlake	Fairlawn, OH
1989	Del Ballard Jr.	490 (2 games)	Walter Ray Williams Jr.	Fairlawn, OH
1990	Dave Ferraro	226 (1 game)	Tony Westlake	Fairlawn, OH
1991	David Ozio	476 (2 games)	Amleto Monacelli	Fairlawn, OH
1992	Marc McDowell	471 (2 games)	Don Genalo	Fairlawn, OH
1993	George Branham III	227 (1 game)	Parker Bohn III	Fairlawn, OH
1994	Norm Duke	422 (2 games)	Eric Forkel	Fairlawn, OH
1995	Mike Aulby	502 (2 games)	Bob Spaulding	Lake Zurich, IL
1996	Dave D'Entremont	971 (4 games)	Dave Arnold	Lake Zurich, IL
1997	John Gant	446 (2 games)	Mike Aulby	Reno
1998	Bryan Goebel	245 (1 game)	Steve Hoskins	Overland Park, KS
1999	Jason Couch	427 (2 games)	Chris Barnes	Overland Park, KS
2000	Jason Couch	198 (1 game)	Ryan Shafer	Lake Zurich, IL
2001	Not held			
2002	Jason Couch	478 (2 games)	Ryan Shafer	Uncasville, CT

ABC Masters Tournament

Year	Winner	Scoring Avg	Runner-Up	Site
1951	Lee Jouglard	201.8	Joe Wilman	St. Paul, MN
1952	Willard Taylor	200.32	Andy Varipapa	Milwaukee
1953	Rudy Habetler	200.13	Ed Brosius	Chicago
1954	Eugene Elkins	205.19	W. Taylor	Seattle
1955	Buzz Fazio	204.13	Joe Kristof	Ft. Wayne, IN
1956	Dick Hoover	209.9	Ray Bluth	Rochester, NY
1957	Dick Hoover	216.39	Bill Lillard	Ft. Worth, TX
1958	Tom Hennessy	209.15	Lou Frantz	Syracuse, NY
1959	Ray Bluth	214.26	Billy Golembiewski	St. Louis
1960	Billy Golembiewski	206.13	Steve Nagy	Toledo, OH
1961	Don Carter	211.18	Dick Hoover	Detroit
1962	Billy Golembiewski	223.12	Ron Winger	Des Moines, IA
1963	Harry Smith	219.3	Bobby Meadows	Buffalo
1964	Billy Welu	227	Harry Smith	Oakland, CA
1965	Billy Welu	202.12	Don Ellis	St. Paul, MN
1966	Bob Strampe	219.80	Al Thompson	Rochester, NY
1967	Lou Scalia	216.9	Bill Johnson	Miami Beach
1968	Pete Tountas	220.15	Buzz Fazio	Cincinnati
1969	Jim Chestney	223.2	Barry Asher	Madison, WI
1970	Don Glover	215.10	Bob Strampe	Knoxville, TN
1971	Jim Godman	229.8	Don Johnson	Detroit
1972	Bill Beach	220.27	Jim Godman	Long Beach, CA
1973	Dave Soutar	218.61	Dick Ritger	Syracuse, NY
1974	Paul Colwell	234.17	Steve Neff	Indianapolis
1975	Eddie Ressler	213.51	Sam Flanagan	Dayton, OH
1976	Nelson Burton Jr.	220.79	Steve Carson	Oklahoma City
1977	Earl Anthony	218.21	Jim Godman	Reno
1978	Frank Ellenburg	200.61	Earl Anthony	St. Louis
1979	Doug Myers	202.9	Bill Spigner	Tampa
1980	Neil Burton	206.69	Mark Roth	Louisville
1981	Randy Lightfoot	218.3	Skip Tucker	Memphis
1982	Joe Berardi	207.12	Ted Hannahs	Baltimore
1983	Mike Lastowski	212.65	Pete Weber	Niagara Falls
1984	Earl Anthony	212.5	Gil Sliker	Reno
1985	Steve Wunderlich	210.4	Tommy Kress	Tulsa
1986	Mark Fahy	206.5	Del Ballard Jr.	Las Vegas
1987	Rick Steelsmith	210.7	Brad Snell	Niagara Falls
1988	Del Ballard Jr.	219.1	Keith Smith	Jacksonville
1989	Mike Aulby	218.5	Mike Edwards	Wichita
1990	Chris Warren	231.6	David Ozio	Reno
1991	Doug Kent	226.8	George Branham III	Toledo, OH
1992	Ken Johnson	230.0	Dave D'Entremont	Corpus Christi, TX
1993	Norm Duke	245.68	Patrick Allen	Tulsa
1994	Steve Fehr	213.09	Steve Anderson	Greenacres, FL
1995	Mike Aulby	230.7	Mark Williams	Reno
1996	Ernie Schlegel	221.2	Mike Aulby	Salt Lake City
1997	Jason Queen	225.5	Eric Forkel	Huntsville, AL
1998	Mike Aulby	224.0	Parker Bohn III	Reno
1999	Brian Boghosian	246.0	Parker Bohn III	Syracuse, NY
2000	Mika Koivuniemi	241.0	Pete Weber	Albuquerque
2001	Parker Bohn III	224.0	Jason Couch	Reno
2002	Brett Wolfe	222.3	Dennis Horan Jr.	Reno
2003	Bryon Smith	236.0	W. R. Williams Jr.	Reno

BPAA United States Open

Year	Winner	Score	Runner-Up	Site
1949	Marion Ladewig	113.26–104.26	Catherine Burling	Chicago
1950	Marion Ladewig	151.46–146.06	Stephanie Balogh	Chicago
1951	Marion Ladewig	159.17–148.03	Sylvia Wene	Chicago
1952	Marion Ladewig	154.39–142.05	Shirley Garms	Chicago
1953	Not held			
1954	Marion Ladewig	148.29–143.01	Sylvia Wene	Chicago
1955	Sylvia Wene	142.30–141.11	Sylvia Fanta	Chicago
1955	Anita Cantaline	144.40–144.13	Doris Porter	Chicago
1956	Marion Ladewig	150.16–145.41	Marge Merrick	Chicago
1957	Not held			
1958	Merle Matthews	145.09–143.14	Marion Ladewig	Minneapolis
1959	Marion Ladewig	149.33–143.00	Donna Zimmerman	Buffalo
1960	Sylvia Wene	144.14–143.26	Marion Ladewig	Omaha
1961	Phyllis Notaro	144.13–143.12	Hope Riccilli	San Bernardino, CA
1962	Shirley Garms	138.44–135.49	Joy Abel	Miami Beach
1963	Marion Ladewig	586–578	Bobbie Shaler	Kansas City, MO
1964	LaVerne Carter	683–609	Evelyn Teal	Dallas
1965	Ann Slattery	597–550	Sandy Hooper	Philadelphia
1966	Joy Abel	593–538	Bette Rockwell	Lansing, MI
1967	Gloria Bouvia	578–516	Shirley Garms	St. Ann, MO
1968	Dotty Fothergill	9,000–8,187	Doris Coburn	Garden City, NY
1969	Dotty Fothergill	8,284–8,258	Kayoka Suda	Miami
1970	Mary Baker	8,730–8,465	Judy Cook	Northbrook, IL
1971	Paula Carter	5,660–5,650	June Llewellyn	Kansas City, MO
1972	Lorrie Nichols	5,272–5,189	Mary Baker	Denver
1973	Millie Martorella	5,553–5,294	Patty Costello	Garden City, NY
1974	Patty Costello	219–216	Betty Morris	Irving, TX
1975	Paula Carter	6,500–6,352	Lorrie Nichols	Toledo, OH
1976	Patty Costello	11,341–11,281	Betty Morris	Tulsa
1977	Betty Morris	10,511–10,358	Virginia Norton	Milwaukee
1978	Donna Adamek	236–202	Vesma Grinfelds	Miami
1979	Diana Silva	11,775–11,718	Bev Ortner	Phoenix
1980	Pat Costello	223–199	Shinobu Saitoh	Rockford, IL
1981	Donna Adamek	201–190	Nikki Gianulias	Rockford, IL
1982	Shinobu Saitoh	12,184–12,028	Robin Romeo	Hendersonville, TN
1983	Dana Miller-Mackie	247–200	Aleta Sill	St. Louis
1984	Karen Ellingsworth	236–217	Lorrie Nichols	St. Louis
1985	Pat Mercatani	214–178	Nikki Gianulias	Topeka, KS
1986	Wendy Macpherson	265–179	Lisa Wagner	Topeka, KS
1987	Carol Norman	206–179	Cindy Coburn	Mentor, OH
1988	Lisa Wagner	226–218	Lorrie Nichols	Winston-Salem, NC
1989	Robin Romeo	187–163	Michelle Mullen	Addison, IL
1990	Dana Miller-Mackie	190–189	Tish Johnson	Dearborn Heights, MI
1991	Anne Marie Duggan	196–185	Leanne Barrette	Fountain Valley, CA
1992	Tish Johnson	216–213	Aleta Sill	Fountain Valley, CA
1993	Dede Davidson	213–194	Dana Miller-Mackie	Garland, TX
1994	Aleta Sill	229–170	Anne Marie Duggan	Wichita
1995	Cheryl Daniels	235–180	Tish Johnson	Blaine, MN
1996	Liz Johnson	265–236	Marianne DiRupo	Indianapolis
1997	No event—tournament rescheduled to April, beginning in 1998.			
1998	Aleta Sill	276–151	Tammy Turner	Milford, CT
1999	Kim Adler	213–195	Lynda Barnes	Uncasville, CT
2000	Tennelle Grijalva	239–155	Kelly Kulick	Phoenix
2001	Kim Terrell	234–220	Wendy Macpherson	Laughlin, NV
2003	Kelly Kulick	261–195	Carolyn Dorin-Ballard	Sterling Heights, MI

Note: From 1942 to 1970, tournament was called the BPAA All-Star. Peterson scoring used from 1949 to '62. Under this system, the winner of an individual match game gets one point, plus one point for each 50 pins. From 1963 to '67, a three-game championship was held between the two top qualifiers. From 1968 to '73, 1975 to '77, 1979 and 1982, total pinfall determined the winner. In the other years, five qualifiers competed in a playoff for the championship, with the final listed above.

AMF Gold Cup *(Discontinued)*

Year	Winner	Score	Runner-Up	Site
1997	Aleta Sill	221–179	C. Gianotti-Block	Richmond, VA
1998	Dana Miller-Mackie	278–170	Dede Davidson	Richmond, VA
1999	Dana Miller-Mackie	236–222	Cara Honeychurch	Richmond, VA

WIBC Queens

ear	Winner	Score	Runner-Up	Site
1961	Janet Harman	794–776	Eula Touchette	Fort Wayne, IN
1962	Dorothy Wilkinson	799–794	Marion Ladewig	Phoenix
1963	Irene Monterosso	852–803	Georgette DeRosa	Memphis
1964	D. D. Jacobson	740–682	Shirley Garms	Minneapolis
1965	Betty Kuczynski	772–739	LaVerne Carter	Portland, OR
1966	Judy Lee	771–742	Nancy Peterson	New Orleans
1967	Millie Ignizio	840–809	Phyllis Massey	Rochester, NY
1968	Phyllis Massey	884–853	Marian Spencer	San Antonio
1969	Ann Feigel	832–765	Millie Ignizio	San Diego
1970	Millie Ignizio	807–797	Joan Holm	Tulsa
1971	Millie Ignizio	809–778	Katherine Brown	Atlanta
1972	Dotty Fothergill	890–841	Maureen Harris	Kansas City, MO
1973	Dotty Fothergill	804–791	Judy Soutar	Las Vegas
1974	Judy Soutar	939–705	Betty Morris	Houston
1975	Cindy Powell	758–674	Patty Costello	Indianapolis
1976	Pam Buckner	214–178	Shirley Sjostrom	Denver
1977	Dana Stewart	175–167	Vesma Grinfelds	Milwaukee
1978	Loa Boxberger	197–176	Cora Fiebig	Miami
1979	Donna Adamek	216–181	Shinobu Saitoh	Tucson
1980	Donna Adamek	213–165	Cheryl Robinson	Seattle
1981	Katsuko Sugimoto	166–158	Virginia Norton	Baltimore
1982	Katsuko Sugimoto	160–137	Nikki Gianulias	St. Louis
1983	Aleta Sill	214–188	Dana Miller-Mackie	Las Vegas
1984	Kazue Inahashi	248–222	Aleta Sill	Niagara Falls
1985	Aleta Sill	279–192	Linda Graham	Toledo, OH
1986	Cora Fiebig	223–177	Barbara Thorberg	Orange County, CA
1987	Cathy Almeida	850–817	Lorrie Nichols	Hartford, CT
1988	Wendy Macpherson	213–199	Leanne Barrette	Reno/Carson City, NV
1989	Carol Gianotti	207–177	Sandra Jo Shiery	Bismarck-Mandan, ND
1990	Patty Ann	207–173	Vesma Grinfelds	Tampa
1991	Dede Davidson	231–159	Jeanne Maiden	Cedar Rapids, IA
1992	Cindy Coburn-Carroll	184–170	Dana Miller-Mackie	Lansing, MI
1993	Jan Schmidt	201–163	Pat Costello	Baton Rouge, LA
1994	Anne Marie Duggan	224–177	Wendy Macpherson-Papanos	Salt Lake City
1995	Sandra Postma	226–187	Carolyn Dorin	Tucson
1996	Lisa Wagner	231–226	Tammy Turner	Buffalo
1997	S.J. Shiery-Odom	209–185	Audry Allen	Reno
1998	Lynda Norry	213–157	Karen Stroud	Davenport, IA
1999	Leanne Barrette	256–174	Dede Davidson	Indianapolis
2000	Wendy Macpherson	227–202	Marianne DiRupo	Reno
2001	Carolyn Dorin-Ballard	213–197	Kelly Kulick	Ft. Lauderdale, FL
2002	Kim Terrell	227–214	Kim Adler	Wauwatosa, WI
2003	Wendy Macpherson	218–193	Kendra Gaines	Reno

Sam's Town Invitational (Discontinued)

Year	Winner	Score	Runner-Up	Site
1984	Aleta Sill	238 (1 game)	Cheryl Daniels	Las Vegas
1985	Patty Costello	236 (1 game)	Robin Romeo	Las Vegas
1986	Aleta Sill	238 (1 game)	Dina Wheeler	Las Vegas
1987	Debbie Bennett	880 (4 games)	Lorrie Nichols	Las Vegas
1988	Donna Adamek	634 (3 games)	Robin Romeo	Las Vegas
1989	Tish Johnson	210 (1 game)	Dede Davidson	Las Vegas
1990	Wendy Macpherson	900 (4 games)	Jeanne Maiden	Las Vegas
1991	Lorrie Nichols	469 (2 games)	Dana Miller-Mackie	Las Vegas
1992	Tish Johnson	279 (1 game)	Robin Romeo	Las Vegas
1993	Robin Romeo	194 (1 game)	Tammy Turner	Las Vegas
1994	Tish Johnson	178 (1 game)	Carol Gianotti	Las Vegas
1995	Michelle Mullen	202 (1 game)	Cheryl Daniels	Las Vegas
1996	C. Gianotti-Block	892 (4 games)	Leanne Barrette	Las Vegas
1997	Kim Adler	953 (4 games)	Wendy Macpherson	Las Vegas
1998	Julie Gardner	961 (4 games)	Dede Davidson	Las Vegas
1999	Wendy Macpherson	209 (1 game)	Marianne DiRupo	Las Vegas
2000	Dede Davidson	183 (1 game)	Tiffany Stanbrough	Las Vegas

PWBA Championships (Discontinued)

1960...Marion Ladewig	1966...Joy Abel	1972...Patty Costello	1978...Toni Gillard
1961...Shirley Garms	1967...Betty Mivalez	1973...Betty Morris	1979...Cindy Coburn
1962...Stephanie Balogh	1968...Dotty Fothergill	1974...Pat Costello	1980...Donna Adamek
1963...Janet Harman	1969...Dotty Fothergill	1975...Pam Buckner	
1964...Betty Kuczynski	1970...Bobbe North	1976...Patty Costello	
1965...Helen Duval	1971...Patty Costello	1977...Vesma Grinfelds	

A Face in the Crowd

Matt Robinson, a senior at El Cerrito High in Richmond, Calif., averaged 261 over six games and rolled a 300 game while winning the Northern California Junior Bowlers Tour title in Brentwood. He also won the title at Fremont, the next stop on the tour, with a high game of 279.

BWAA Bowler of the Year

Year	Winner
1942	Johnny Crimmins
1943	Ned Day
1944	Ned Day
1945	Buddy Bomar
1946	Joe Wilman
1947	Buddy Bomar
1948	Andy Varipapa
1949	Connie Schwoegler
1950	Junie McMahon
1951	Lee Jouglard
1952	Steve Nagy
1953	Don Carter
1954	Don Carter
1955	Steve Nagy
1956	Bill Lillard
1957	Don Carter
1958	Don Carter
1959	Ed Lubanski
1960	Don Carter
1961	Dick Weber
1962	Don Carter
1963	Dick Weber
	Billy Hardwick*
1964	Billy Hardwick
	Bob Strampe*
1965	Dick Weber
1966	Wayne Zahn
1967	Dave Davis
1968	Jim Stefanich
1969	Billy Hardwick
1970	Nelson Burton Jr.
1971	Don Johnson
1972	Don Johnson
1973	Don McCune
1974	Earl Anthony
1975	Earl Anthony
1976	Earl Anthony
1977	Mark Roth
1978	Mark Roth
1979	Mark Roth
1980	Wayne Webb
1981	Earl Anthony
1982	Earl Anthony
1983	Earl Anthony
1984	Mark Roth
1985	Mike Aulby
1986	Walter Ray Williams Jr.
1987	Marshall Holman
1988	Brian Voss
1989	Mike Aulby
	Amleto Monacelli*
1990	Amleto Monacelli
1991	David Ozio
1992	Dave Ferraro
1993	Walter Ray Williams Jr.
1994	Norm Duke
1995	Mike Aulby
1996	Walter Ray Williams Jr.
1997	Walter Ray Williams Jr.
1998	Walter Ray Williams Jr.
1999	Parker Bohn III
2000	Norm Duke
2001	Parker Bohn III
2002	Walter Ray Williams Jr.

PBA Bowler of the Year. The PBA began selecting a player of the year in 1963. Its selection has been the same as the BWAA's in all but three years.

Women's Awards

BWAA Bowler of the Year

Year	Winner
1948	Val Mikiel
1949	Val Mikiel
1950	Marion Ladewig
1951	Marion Ladewig
1952	Marion Ladewig
1953	Marion Ladewig
1954	Marion Ladewig
1955	Marion Ladewig
1956	Sylvia Martin
1957	Anita Cantaline
1958	Marion Ladewig
1959	Marion Ladewig
1960	Sylvia Martin
1961	Shirley Garms
1962	Shirley Garms
1963	Marion Ladewig
1964	LaVerne Carter
1965	Betty Kuczynski
1966	Joy Abel
1967	Millie Martorella
1968	Dotty Fothergill
1969	Dotty Fothergill
1970	Mary Baker
1971	Paula Sperber Carter
1972	Patty Costello
1973	Judy Soutar
1974	Betty Morris
1975	Judy Soutar
1976	Patty Costello
1977	Betty Morris
1978	Donna Adamek
1979	Donna Adamek
1980	Donna Adamek
1981	Donna Adamek
1982	Nikki Gianulias
1983	Lisa Wagner
1984	Aleta Sill
1985	Aleta Sill/Patty Costello*
1986	Lisa Wagner/Jeanne Madden*
1987	Betty Morris
1988	Lisa Wagner
1989	Robin Romeo
1990	Tish Johnson/Leanne Barrette*
1991	Leanne Barrette
1992	Tish Johnson
1993	Lisa Wagner
1994	Anne Marie Duggan
1995	Tish Johnson
1996	Wendy Macpherson
1997	Wendy Macpherson
1998	Carol Gianotti-Block
1999	Wendy Macpherson
2000	Wendy Macpherson
2001	Carolyn Dorin-Ballard
2002	Leanne Barrette

*PWBA Bowler of the Year. The PWBA began selecting a player of the year in 1983. Its selection has been the same as the BWAA's in all but three years.

Career Leaders

Earnings

MEN

Walter Ray Williams Jr. $3,004,432
Pete Weber $2,378,951
Parker Bohn III $2,172,951
Mike Aulby $2,097,253
Brian Voss.................................$1,971,637

WOMEN

Wendy Macpherson....................$1,194,535
Aleta Sill $1,071,194
Tish Johnson..............................$1,063,062
Leanne Barrette $1,010,343
Anne Marie Duggan......................$936,421

Titles

MEN

Earl Anthony..41
Walter Ray Williams Jr.................................37
Mark Roth..34
Parker Bohn III 29
Pete Weber 29

WOMEN

Lisa Wagner 32
Aleta Sill 31
Leanne Barrette 26
Patty Costello 25
Tish Johnson 25

Note: Leaders through Sept 22, 2003.

Perfectly Ambidextrous

In August 2003, Lesley Boczar, a 39-year-old from Hollywood, Fla., became the first woman to bowl sanctioned 300 games as both a lefthander and a righty.

On July 22nd, Boczar rolled 12 consecutive strikes—southpaw style—at the South Florida Masters Trios League in Sunrise, Fla., to complete the unprecedented double. She rolled her righthanded 300 game on May 5, 1997. The Women's International Bowling Congress sanctioned Boczar's feat in early August.

Boczar became a lefthander soon after rolling her righthanded gem back in '97. An improperly drilled ball created a nerve injury in right ring finger, eventually causing her so much pain she decided to switch hands. "I worked on the footwork walking around the house," Boczar told *USA Today*. In time, she became proficient enough to make the switch a permanent one—and to strive for perfection from both sides of the lane.

Soccer

Mia Hamm of
the United States

New Day Dawning

While the U.S. women saw the end of an era of dominance, the men welcomed an unprecedented crop of talented youth

BY HANK HERSCH

FOR THE FANS, theater seating at all 27,000 seats, a Teflon-coated Fiberglas roof covering ticket holders along the sidelines, 42 luxury boxes with walls of marble and cherry wood, a 12,000-square foot restaurant (complete with wine cellar) and 15 refreshment stands. For the players, a 3,000-square foot weight room, five training fields, 10 locker rooms and an immaculate pitch of Hybrid Bullseye Bermuda seeded over with Perennial rye. And for soccer in the U.S., a multimillion-dollar act of faith by patron Philip Anschutz, owner of five of MLS's 10 franchises: *If I build it, they will come.*

When Anschutz's Los Angeles Galaxy opened the Home Depot Center in Carson, Calif., with a 2–1 victory over the Kansas City Wizards on June 7, a sport associated with foreign lands and minivans finally had demonstrable roots in the States. "If you call yourself a soccer fan and don't make a pilgrimage to come out here," said Galaxy coach Sigi Schmid, "then you are not a soccer fan."

And if you are a soccer fan, you had much to savor, all over the globe, in 2003. A 14-year-old from Maryland made European scouts wide-eyed during his debut for the U.S. in Finland. The planet's most popular team jettisoned the planet's most popular player, then during its transatlantic barnstorming tour unveiled an American goalkeeper in front of his old home crowd. After awarding the 2003 Women's World Cup to China, FIFA was forced by the outbreak of the deadly SARS epidemic to relocate the tournament to the U.S. four months before kickoff. And the new host, hoping that its top-ranked national team would play in the finals at the country's new soccer Xanadu—and simultaneously revive interest in its recently abandoned women's professional league—had those dreams disassembled by a band of *fraüleins*.

The portents of change were in the air at the under-17 world championship in Finland. "In every other form of art—music, dance, painting—history throws up a phenomenon," Barry Whitbread, Liverpool's director of youth recruitment, told SPORTS ILLUSTRATED's Grant Wahl. "He may be

Donovan may one day pair with Adu in the U.S. attack.

one of them." That high praise of Freddy Adu, however, paled in comparison to another scout's: "He's going to be the best player in the world someday."

The bird dogs from Europe's preeminent teams who descended on the under-17 tournament in August left with a song in their hearts and the number of Adu's agent on their speed dials. The 14-year-old American striker known to his teammates as Pheen (for Phenomenon) opened the tournament with a hat trick against South Korea, then scored a decisive last-second goal in a 2–1 win over Sierra Leone despite being constantly and brutally fouled during that game. "You're getting hit the whole game, not getting any calls, and the opposing players are talking all this trash," Adu said. "The only way to shut them up is to get a goal. It just breaks them." Though Brazil ended the U.S.'s run in the quarterfinals, the 5'8", 140-pound Adu, who had already inked a $1 million endorsement deal with Nike, left Finland weighing more options than Jennifer Lopez's wedding planner.

After bringing her two sons to Potomac, Md., from her native Ghana in 1997, Emelia Adu had turned down a six-figure deal for Freddy from Inter Milan, citing her son's age. He was 11 at the time the Italian club made its offer. But Adu's coming-out party in Finland only increased the number of suitors from overseas—Manchester United, AC Milan, Barcelona, PSV Eindhoven. Major League Soccer, too, made its pitch for the teenager who is fast-tracking through high school, and who has a Q-rating exceeding that of almost any player in the U.S. league. And Adu wasn't the only promising youngster in the U.S. MLS rookies such as Ricardo Clark, Eddie Gaven, Justin Mapp and Mike Magee represented a new level of talent in U.S. soccer. "Our development programs are improving at a pace that is unrivaled," said deputy commissioner Ivan Gazidis. "I think we have some things to teach the English."

One prominent product of the English development system, David Beckham, survived an eventful year in 2003. The captain of England, the husband of Posh Spice, the midfielder worshiped as far away as Thailand—where Buddhist monks kneel before his gold-plated image—he had spent almost half of his 28 years in the Manchester United system. As Man U's popularity rose (the Red Devils have more than 200 official fan clubs worldwide and an estimated fan base of 50 million) so did the striking profile of Beckham. His free-kick wizardry inspired

ELIOT J. SCHECHTER/GETTY IMAGES

the movie *Bend It Like Beckham* while his pop-star persona attracted adulation from fans of all creeds, colors and sexual orientations. Said British writer and devout soccer fan Nick Hornby, "There's no doubt he's the biggest sports star in the world now."

But in June, only days before Manchester United began its barnstorming preseason tour of the U.S., the club transferred Beckham to Real Madrid for $41 million. The financial windfall partly drove the deal, but mainly Beckham had become a victim of his own celebrity: Sir Alex Ferguson, the Man U manager, feared that the glitz surrounding Becks and his celebrated wife—"this fashion thing," he called it—would undermine him as a footballer. That concern apparently wasn't shared by Real Madrid, which rivals Man U for the title of World's Biggest club. Real paid heavily to put another star in its crowded constellation that already included Brazil's Ronaldo and Roberto Carlos, Luis Figo of Portugal, Raul of Spain and Zinedine Zidane of France.

At roughly the same time Beckham was exiting United, a far less famous Yank was completing a $2.6 million transfer to the fabled club. "It's kind of unfathomable, really," said 24-year-old Tim Howard of North Brunswick, N.J., who had emerged with the MetroStars as MLS's strongest goalkeeper. Ferguson promised that Howard would be given a shot at joining countrymen Brad Friedel and Kasey Keller as a starting keeper in the English Premier League, and during the Red Devils' four-game U.S. tour, Howard made his debut at Giants Stadium, making 11 saves—some of them of the spectacular variety—against Juventus of Turin in a 4–1 victory. When the EPL season began, Howard, stunningly, had unseated 1998 World Cup star Fabien Barthez as the starter on the world's marquee club. The early returns were encouraging, as the former MetroStar produced five shutouts in his first eight games with United. "I have the physical ability," Howard said. "It's just a matter of putting it all together."

That sort of self-belief characterized the U.S. Soccer Federation, which staged the Women's World Cup with an absolute minimum of lead time, due to the late venue change. The federation hosted the '99 WWC in grand style, but this time, the USSF staged the games in smaller stadiums, bypassing the 90,000-seat Rose Bowl as the site of the final in favor of the cozier Toolbox—a.k.a. the new Home Depot Center. During the opening round there seemed to be little doubt that the hosts would be defending their championship there. Behind the brilliant playmaking of Mia Hamm the Americans defeated Sweden, Nigeria and North Korea to conquer the most demanding of the four four-team groups.

Beyond a third Cup title lingered another hope among players and fans: that a riveting, heavily-attended victory by the U.S. would revive corporate interest in the Women's United Soccer Association (WUSA), which only days before the tournament had announced that the failure to attract sufficient sponsorship meant the three-year-old league would cease operations. A header by bruising striker Abby Wambach—whose two goals in the WUSA championship game in August had sealed a 2–1 victory for the Washington Freedom over the Atlanta Beat—gave the Yanks a 1–0 victory over archrival Norway in the quarterfinals. But in the semifinals in Portland the Yanks bowed 3–0 to Germany, which had benefited in large part from battling U.S. players in—that's right—the WUSA. "We knew that they were not better than we are," said forward Birgit Prinz. "We knew we could play one-on-one and beat them."

With that landmark victory, Germany advanced to the final to face Sweden, and all but dropped the curtain on an era of U.S. dominance. American players like Mia Hamm, Julie Foudy and Joy Fawcett, all of whom played in four Women's World Cups, will probably have just one more shot at international glory: at the 2004 Olympics in Athens. Unlike the U.S. men, who are catching up to their international counterparts, the U.S. women can see the rest of the world gaining on them.

Women's World Cup 2003

Group Standings

GROUP A						
Country	GP	W	L	T	GF	GA	Pts
*United States	3	3	0	0	11	1	9
*Sweden	3	2	1	0	5	3	6
N Korea	3	1	2	0	3	4	3
Nigeria	3	0	3	0	0	11	0

GROUP C						
Country	GP	W	L	T	GF	GA	Pts
*Germany	3	3	0	0	13	2	9
Canada	3	2	1	0	7	5	6
Japan	3	1	2	0	7	6	3
Argentina	3	0	3	0	1	15	0

GROUP B						
Country	GP	W	L	T	GF	GA	Pts
*Brazil	3	2	0	1	8	2	7
*Norway	3	2	1	0	10	5	6
France	3	1	1	1	2	3	4
S Korea	3	0	3	0	1	11	0

GROUP D						
Country	GP	W	L	T	GF	GA	Pts
*China	3	2	0	1	3	1	7
*Russia	3	2	1	0	5	2	6
Ghana	3	1	2	0	2	5	3
Australia	3	0	2	1	3	5	1

*Advanced to second round.

Note: In group play, teams are awarded three points for a victory, one for a tie. The top two in each group advance to the Round of 16.

Group Play Scores

GROUP A

N Korea 3, Nigeria 0
U.S. 3, Sweden 1
Sweden 1, N Korea 0
U.S. 5, Nigeria 0
Sweden 3, Nigeria 0
U.S. 3, N Korea 0

GROUP B

Norway 2, France 0
Brazil 3, S Korea 0
Brazil 4, Norway 1
France 1, S Korea 0
Norway 7, S Korea 1
France 1, Brazil 1

GROUP C

Germany 4, Canada 1
Japan 6, Argentina 0
Germany 3, Japan 0
Canada 3, Argentina 0
Canada 3, Japan 1
Germany 6, Argentina 1

GROUP D

Russia 2, Australia 1
China 1, Ghana 0
Russia 3, Ghana 0
China 1, Australia 1
Ghana 2, Australia 1
China 1, Russia 0

2003 Women's World Cup—Knockout Rounds

WOMEN'S WORLD CUP FINAL

Brazil

Sweden

Sweden (2-1)

Sweden (2-1)

Germany 2-1 (ot)

U.S.A. (1-0)

United States

Norway

Germany (3-0)

Germany

China

Canada (1-0)

Germany (7-1)

Russia

Canada

Group Standings

GROUP A

Country	GP	W	L	T	GF	GA	Pts
*Denmark	3	2	0	1	5	2	7
*Senegal	3	1	0	2	5	4	5
Uruguay	3	0	1	2	4	5	2
France	3	0	2	1	0	3	1

GROUP B

Country	GP	W	L	T	GF	GA	Pts
*Spain	3	3	0	0	9	4	9
*Paraguay	3	1	1	1	6	6	4
S Africa	3	1	1	1	5	5	4
Slovenia	3	0	3	0	2	7	0

GROUP C

Country	GP	W	L	T	GF	GA	Pts
*Brazil	3	3	0	0	11	3	9
*Turkey	3	1	1	1	5	3	4
Costa Rica	3	1	1	1	5	6	4
China	3	0	3	0	0	9	0

GROUP D

Country	GP	W	L	T	GF	GA	Pts
*S Korea	3	2	0	1	4	1	7
*United States	3	1	1	1	5	6	4
Portugal	3	1	2	0	6	4	3
Poland	3	1	2	0	3	7	3

GROUP E

Country	GP	W	L	T	GF	GA	Pts
*Germany	3	2	0	1	11	1	7
*Ireland	3	1	0	2	5	2	5
Cameroon	3	1	1	1	2	3	4
Saudi Arabia	3	0	3	0	0	12	0

GROUP F

Country	GP	W	L	T	GF	GA	Pts
*Sweden	3	1	0	2	4	3	5
*England	3	1	0	2	2	1	5
Argentina	3	1	1	1	2	2	4
Nigeria	3	0	2	1	3	7	1

GROUP G

Country	GP	W	L	T	GF	GA	Pts
*Mexico	3	2	0	1	4	2	7
*Italy	3	1	1	1	4	3	4
Croatia	3	1	2	0	2	3	3
Ecuador	3	1	2	0	2	4	3

GROUP H

Country	GP	W	L	T	GF	GA	Pts
*Japan	3	2	0	1	5	2	7
*Belgium	3	1	0	2	6	5	5
Russia	3	1	2	0	4	4	3
Tunisia	3	0	2	1	1	5	1

*Advanced to second round.

Note: In group play, teams are awarded three points for a victory, one for a tie. The top two in each group advance to the Round of 16.

Group Play Scores

GROUP A

Senegal 1, France 0
Denmark, 2, Uruguay 1
France 0, Uruguay 0
Denmark 1, Senegal 1
Denmark 2, France 0
Senegal 3, Uruguay 3

GROUP B

Paraguay 2, S Africa 2
Spain 3, Slovenia 1
Spain 3, Paraguay 1
S Africa 1, Slovenia 0
Spain 3, S Africa 2
Paraguay 3, Slovenia 1

GROUP C

Brazil 2, Turkey 1
Costa Rica 2, China 0
Brazil 4, China 0
Costa Rica 1, Turkey 1
Brazil 5, Costa Rica 2
Turkey 3, China 0

GROUP D

S Korea 2, Poland 0
U.S. 3, Portugal 2
U.S. 1, S Korea 1
Portugal 4, Poland 0
S Korea 1, Portugal 0
Poland 3, U.S. 1

GROUP E

Ireland 1, Cameroon 1
Germany 8, S. Arabia 0
Germany 1, Ireland 1
Cameroon 1, S. Arabia 0
Germany 2, Cameroon 0
Ireland 3, Saudi Arabia 0

GROUP F

Sweden 1, England 1
Argentina 1, Nigeria 0
Sweden 2, Nigeria 1
England 1, Argentina 0
Sweden 1, Argentina 1
Nigeria 0, England 0

GROUP G

Mexico 1, Croatia 0
Italy 2, Ecuador 0
Croatia 2, Italy 1
Mexico 2, Ecuador 1
Mexico 1, Italy 1
Ecuador 1, Croatia 0

GROUP H

Japan 2, Belgium 2
Russia 2, Tunisia 0
Japan 1, Russia 0
Tunisia 1, Belgium 1
Japan 2, Tunisia 0
Belgium 3, Russia 2

Round of 16

England 3, Denmark, 0
Brazil 2, Belgium 0
Senegal 2, Sweden 1 (ot)
Turkey 1, Japan 0

Germany 1, Paraguay 0
United States 2, Mexico 0
Spain 1, Ireland 1 (Spain advanced on penalties)
S Korea 2, Italy 1 (ot)

Quarterfinals

Brazil 2, England 1
Turkey 1, Senegal 0 (ot)

Germany 1, United States 0
S Korea 0, Spain 0 (S Korea advanced on penalties)

Semifinals

Brazil 1, Turkey 0

Germany 1, S Korea 0

Final

Brazil 2, Germany 0

2002 Final Standings

EASTERN CONFERENCE								WESTERN CONFERENCE						
Team	GP	W	L	T	Pts	GF	GA	Team	GP	W	L	T	Pts	GF	GA
†New England	.28	12	14	2	38	49	49	†Los Angeles	...28	16	9	3	51	44	33
*Columbus	28	11	12	5	38	44	43	*San Jose	28	14	11	3	45	45	35
*Chicago	28	11	13	4	37	43	38	*Dallas	28	12	9	7	43	44	43
MetroStars	28	11	15	2	35	41	47	*Colorado	28	13	11	4	43	43	48
D.C. United	28	9	14	5	32	31	40	*Kansas City	28	9	10	9	36	37	45

Note: Three points for a win. One point for a tie. †Conference champion. *Qualified for playoffs

SCORING LEADERS

Player, Team	GP	G	A	Pts
Taylor Twellman, NE	28	23	6	52
Carlos Ruiz, Los Angeles	26	24	1	49
Jeff Cunningham, Columbus	...27	16	5	37
Ante Razov, Chicago	25	14	8	36
Ariel Graziani, San Jose	28	14	5	33

ASSISTS LEADERS

Player, Team	GP	A
Steve Ralston, New England	27	19
Carlos Valderrama, Colorado	27	16
Andy Williams, NE/MetroStars	24	15
Cobi Jones, Los Angeles	19	13

Four tied with 10.

GOALS LEADERS

Player, Team	GP	G
Carlos Ruiz, Los Angeles	26	24
Taylor Twellman, NE	28	23
Jeff Cunningham, Columbus	27	16
Ante Razov, Chicago	25	14
Ariel Graziani, San Jose	28	14
Jason Kreis, Dallas	27	13

GOALS-AGAINST-AVERAGE LEADERS

Player, Team	GAA
Kevin Hartman, Los Angeles	..............1.09
Jon Busch, Columbus	........................1.09
Joe Cannon, San Jose	.......................1.10
Zach Thornton, Chicago	....................1.23
Adin Brown, New England	................1.23

2002 PLAYOFFS

Los Angeles
Kansas City → Los Angeles (6-3)
→ Los Angeles (6-0)
Dallas
Colorado → Colorado* (4-4)

→ **Los Angeles 1-0 (ot)** ←

→ New England (5-2)
New England → New England (6-3)
Chicago
→ Columbus (6-0)
San Jose
Columbus

New England

*Won tiebreaking minigame. Note: Except for the final, which was a single game, scores in parentheses are points earned (three for a win, one for a tie) in a three-game series, the winner being the first team to accumulate five points.

MLS Cup 2002

FOXBORO, MASS., OCTOBER 20, 2002

Los Angeles	0	0	0	1	—1
New England	0	0	0	0	—0

Goal: Ruiz (Marshall, Albright) 113.

New England—Brown, Llamosa (Pierce, 92), Franchino, Kante, Heaps, Cullen, Kamler (Griffiths, 90), Hernandez, Ralston, Twellman, Harris (Pineda Chacon).

Los Angeles—Hartman, Lalas, Califf, Marshall, Hendrickson, Victorine, Cienfuegos (Vagenas 61), Elliott, Jones, Moreno (Albright, 67), Ruiz.

Att: 61,316.

Women's United Soccer Association

2003 Final Standings

Team	GP	W	L	T	Pts	GF	GA	Diff.	Home	Road
Boston	21	10	4	7	37	33	29	4	5-2-4	5-2-3
Atlanta	21	9	4	8	35	34	19	15	7-2-2	2-2-6
San Diego	21	8	6	7	31	27	26	1	6-2-3	2-4-4
Washington	21	9	8	4	31	40	31	9	6-2-2	3-6-2
New York	21	7	9	5	26	33	43	-10	3-4-3	4-5-2
San Jose	21	7	10	4	25	23	30	-7	4-3-3	3-7-1
Carolina	21	7	10	4	25	31	33	-2	3-6-2	4-4-2
Philadelphia	21	5	11	5	20	30	40	-10	3-4-3	2-7-2

Note: Top four teams made the playoffs; Boston and Atlanta clinched semifinal home games.

2003 PLAYOFFS

SEMIFINALS

*Washington 0, Boston 0
Atlanta 2, San Diego 1 (ot)

2003 FOUNDERS CUP, AUGUST 24, SAN DIEGO

Washington 2, Atlanta 1 (ot)

*Washington advanced on penalty kicks.

International Club Competition

Intercontinental Cup

Competition between winners of European Cup and Libertadores Cup.

TOKYO: DECEMBER 3, 2002

Real Madrid (Esp) 1   1—1
Olimpia (Par) 0   0—0

Goal: Ronaldo 14, Guti 84.

Att: 66,070.

Real Madrid: Casillas, Salgado, Carlos, Hierro, Helguera, Cambiasso (Pavon 90), Makelele, Zidane (Solari 86), Figo, Gonzares, Ronaldo (Guti 82).
Olimpia: Tavarelli, Isasi, Zelaya, Jara, Caceres, Benitez, Enciso, Cordoba (Baez 65), Orteman, Lopez, Benitez (Caballero 81).

UEFA Cup

Competition between teams other than league champions and cup-winners from UEFA.

SEVILLE: MAY 21, 2003

Celtic (Scot) 0   2   0—2
FC Porto (Por) 1   1   1—3

Goals: Larsson 47, 57; Alenitchev 54, Silva 45, 115.

Att: 52,972.

Celtic: Douglas, Valgaeren (Laursen 64), Balde, Mjallby, Agathe, Lennon, Lambert (McNamara 76), Petrov (Maloney 105), Thompson, Sutton, Larsson.

FC Porto: Baia, P. Ferreira, Costa (Emanuel 71), Carvalho, Valente, Costinha (Ricardo Costa 9), Alenitchev, Souza, Ribeiro, Capucho (M. Ferreira 98), Silva.

European Cup

League champions of the countries belonging to UEFA (Union of European Football Associations).

MANCHESTER, ENGLAND: MAY 28, 2003

AC Milan (Ita) 0   0   0—0
Juventus (Ita) 0   0   0—0

Goals: None.

AC Milan won 3—2 on penalty kicks.

Att: 63,215.

AC Milan: Dida, Costacurta (Junior 66), Nesta, Maldini, Kaladze, Gattuso, Pirlo (Serginho 71), Seedorf, Costa (Ambrosini 87), Shevchenko, Inzaghi.

Juventus: Buffon, Thuram, Ferrara, Tudor (Birindelli 42), Montero, Camoranesi (Conte 46), Davids (Zalayeta 65), Tacchinardi, Zambrotta, Del Piero, Trezeguet.

Libertadores Cup

Competition between champion clubs and runners-up of 10 South American National Associations.

(2ND LEG) SAO PAULO, BRAZIL: JULY 3, 2003

Boca Juniors* (Arg) 1   2—3
Santos (Bra) 0   1—1

Goals: Tevez 21, Delgado 84, Schiavi 95; Alex 75

* Two-game aggregate: 5–1 to Boca.

Att: 73,103.

Boca Juniors: Abbondancieri, Ibarra, Schiavi, Burdisso, Rodriguez, Villareal (Jerez 89), Cagna (Caneo 88), Battaglia, Cascini, Tevez (Cangele 91), Delgado.

Santos: Costa, Wellington (Nene 30), Luiz, Alex, Leo, Almeida, Renato, Diego, Fabiano, Robinho, Oliveira (Douglas 68).

Country	League Champion	League Scoring Leader, Club	Cup Winner
Albania	SK Tirana	Mahir Halili, SK Tirana	Dinamo Tirane
Andorra	Santa Coloma	n/a	Santa Coloma
Armenia	Pyunik Yerevan*	Arman Karamian, Pyunik Yerevan*	Mika Ashtarak*
Austria	Austria Vienna	Lawaree, Bregenz	Austria Vienna
Azerbaijan	No league championship due to conflict between clubs and FA.		
Belarus	BATE Barysau*	Valeryi Stripeikis, Belshyna	FK Homel
Belgium	Club Brugge KV	n/a	R.AA. Louviérouise
Bosnia	FK Leotar	n/a	Zeljeznicar
Bulgaria	CSKA Sofia	G. Chilikov, Levski Sofia	Levski Sofia
Croatia	Dinamo Zagreb	Ivica Olic, Dinamo Zagreb	Hajduk Split
Cyprus	Amonia Nicosia	n/a	A. Famagusta
Czech Republic	AC Sparta Prague	Jiri Kowalik, Synot Stare Mesto	FK Teplice
Denmark	FC Copenhagen	n/a	Brøndby
England	Manchester United	Ruud van Nistelrooy, Man Utd	Arsenal
Estonia	FC Flora Tallinn*	Andrei Krolov, TVMK*	FC Levadia Tallinn
Faroe Islands	HB Tórshavn*	Andrew av Fløtum, HB Tórshavn*	NSf Runavik*
Finland	HJK Helsinki*	Mika Kottila, HJK Helsinki*	Haka Valkeakoski
France	Lyon	Shabani Nonde, Monaco	Auxerre
Georgia	Dinamo Tbilisi	Zurab Ionanidze, Torpedo	Dinamo Tbilisi
Germany	Bayern Munich	Marcio Amoroso, Borussia Dortmund	Bayern Munich
		Martin Max, 1860 Munich	
Greece	Olympiakos	n/a	PAOK
Hungary	MTK Hungaria FC	n/a	Ferencváros
Iceland	KR Reykjavik	Björgólfur Takefusa, Frottur	fA Akranes
Ireland	Bohemians	Glen Crowe, Bohemians	Derry City
Israel	Maccabi Tel-Aviv	Yaniv Abarjil, Hapoel Kfar-Saba	Hapoel Ramat-Gan
		Shai Holtzman, H.I. Rishon	
Italy	Juventus	Christian Vieri, Inter Milan	AC Milan
Kazakhstan	Irtysh Pavlodar*	Evgeni Lunev, Shakhter Karagandy*	Zhenis Astana*
Latvia	Skonto Riga*	Mihails Miholaps, Skonto Riga*	Skonto Riga*
Lithuania	FBK Kaunas*	Audrius Slekys, FBK Kaunus*	FBK Kaunus*
Luxembourg	CS Grevenmacher	n/a	CS Grevenmacher
Macedonia	Vardar Skopje	Savil, Bregalnica/Sloga	Cementarnica Skopje
Malta	Sliema Wanderers	Adrian Mifsud, Hibernians	Birkirkara
		Danilo Doncic, Sliema	
		Michael Galea, Birkirkara	
Moldova	Sheriff Tiraspol	Serghei Dadu, FC Tiraspol/Sheriff	Zimbru Chisinau
Netherlands	PSV Eindhoven	Mateja Kezman, PSV Eindhoven	FC Utrecht
Northern Ireland	Glentoran FC	Vinny Arkins, Portadown	Coleraine
Norway	Rosenborg*	n/a	Vålerenga*
Poland	Wisla Kraków	n/a	Wisla Kraków
Portugal	FC Porto	n/a	FC Porto
Romania	Rapid Bucharest	Claudiu Nicu Raducanu, Steaua Bucharest	Dinamo Bucharest
Russia	Lokomitiv Moscow*	Roland Gusev, CSKA*	CSKA Moscow*
		Dmitriy Kirichenko, CSKA*	
San Marino	SP Domagnano	n/a	SP Domagnano
Scotland	Glasgow Rangers	n/a	Glasgow Rangers
Serbia and Montenegro	Partizan Belgrad	Zvonimir Vukic, Partizan Belgrade	Sartid Smederovo
Slovakia	MSK Zilina	Marek Mintal, MSK Zilina	Matador Púchov
		Martin Fabus, Trencin/Zilina	
Slovenia	Maribor Branik	Marko Kmetic, Olimpija Ljubljana	Olimpija Ljubljana
Spain	Real Madrid	Roy Makaay, Deportivo	Mallorca
Sweden	Djurgårdens IF	n/a	Djurgårdens IF
Switzerland	Grasshopper	Richard Nuñez, Grasshopper	FC Basel
Turkey	Besiktas	Okan Yilmaz, Bursaspor	Trabzonspor
Ukraine	Dinamo Kiev	Maxim Shatskikh, Dinamo Kiev	Dinamo Kiev
Wales	Barry Town	n/a	Barry Town

Note: Results are from 2002 unless followed by *.

The World Cup

Results

Year	Champion	Score	Runner-Up	Winning Coach
1930	Uruguay	4–2	Argentina	Alberto Supicci
1934	Italy	2–1	Czechoslovakia	Vittorio Pozzo
1938	Italy	4–2	Hungary	Vittorio Pozzo
1950	Uruguay	2–1	Brazil	Juan Lopez
1954	W Germany	3–2	Hungary	Sepp Herberger
1958	Brazil	5–2	Sweden	Vicente Feola
1962	Brazil	3–1	Czechoslovakia	Aymore Moreira
1966	England	4–2	W Germany	Alf Ramsey
1970	Brazil	4–1	Italy	Mario Zagalo
1974	W Germany	2–1	Netherlands	Helmut Schoen
1978	Argentina	3–1	Netherlands	César Menotti
1982	Italy	3–1	W Germany	Enzo Bearzot
1986	Argentina	3–2	W Germany	Carlos Bilardo
1990	W Germany	1–0	Argentina	Franz Beckenbauer
1994	Brazil	0–0 (3–2)	Italy	Carlos Alberto Parreira
1998	France	3–0	Brazil	Aime Jacquet
2002	Brazil	2–0	Germany	Luis Felipe Scolari

Alltime World Cup Participation

Of the 69 nations that have taken part in the World Cup Finals, only Brazil has competed in each of the 17 tournaments held to date. West Germany or an undivided Germany (1934, '38, '94 and '98) has played in 15 World Cups. Ranked by victories.

Nation	Matches	W	T	L	Goals For	Goals Against
Brazil	87	60	14	13	191	82
*Germany	85	50	18	17	176	106
Italy	70	39	17	14	110	67
Argentina	60	30	11	19	102	70
England	50	22	15	13	68	45
France	44	21	7	16	86	61
Spain	45	19	12	14	71	53
Yugoslavia	37	17	6	14	60	46
†Russia	37	17	6	14	64	44
Uruguay	40	15	10	15	65	57
Hungary	32	15	3	14	87	57
Netherlands	31	14	9	8	55	34
Poland	28	14	5	9	42	36
Sweden	41	14	9	18	67	65
Austria	29	12	4	13	42	48
Czechoslovakia	30	11	5	14	44	45
Belgium	36	10	9	17	46	63
Mexico	41	10	11	20	43	79
Romania	21	8	5	8	30	32
Chile	25	7	6	12	31	40
Portugal	12	7	0	5	25	16
Denmark	13	7	2	4	24	18
Switzerland	22	6	3	13	33	51
United States	22	6	2	14	25	45
Paraguay	19	5	7	7	25	34
Turkey	10	5	1	4	20	17
Croatia	9	5	0	4	11	7
Scotland	23	4	7	12	25	41
Peru	15	4	3	8	19	31
Cameroon	17	4	7	6	16	28
Nigeria	11	4	1	6	14	16
Bulgaria	25	3	8	14	22	49
S Korea	21	3	6	12	19	49
Colombia	13	3	2	8	14	23
Northern Ireland	13	3	5	5	13	23
Costa Rica	7	3	1	3	9	12
Wales	5	2	6	1	10	7
Morocco	10	2	4	4	10	13
Senegal	5	2	2	1	7	6
Norway	8	2	3	3	7	8
Saudi Arabia	10	2	1	7	7	25
Algeria	6	2	1	3	6	10
Japan	7	2	1	4	6	7
E Germany	6	2	2	2	5	5
S Africa	6	1	3	2	8	11
N Korea	4	1	1	2	5	9
Tunisia	9	1	3	5	5	11
Cuba	3	1	1	1	5	12
Republic of Ireland	13	1	5	3	4	7
Iran	6	1	1	4	4	12
Jamaica	3	1	0	2	3	9
Ecuador	3	1	0	2	2	4
Israel	3	1	0	2	1	3
Egypt	4	0	2	2	3	6
Honduras	3	0	2	1	2	3
Kuwait	3	0	1	2	2	6
Slovenia	3	0	0	3	2	7
United Arab Emirates	3	0	0	3	2	11
New Zealand	3	0	0	3	2	12
Haiti	3	0	0	3	2	14
Iraq	3	0	0	3	1	4
Bolivia	6	0	1	5	1	20
El Salvador	6	0	0	6	1	22
Australia	3	0	1	2	0	5
Dutch East Indies	1	0	0	1	0	6
Canada	3	0	0	3	0	5
Zaire	3	0	0	3	0	14
Greece	3	0	0	3	0	8
China	3	0	0	3	0	9

*Includes West Germany 1950–90. †Includes USSR 1930–1990.
Note: Matches decided by penalty kicks are shown as drawn games.

World Cup Final Box Scores

URUGUAY 1930

Uruguay 1	3	—4
Argentina 2	0	—2

FIRST HALF

Scoring: 1, Uruguay, Dorado (12); 2, Argentina, Peucelle (20); 3, Argentina, Stabile (37).

SECOND HALF

Scoring: 4, Uruguay, Cea (57); 5, Uruguay, Iriarte (68); 6, Uruguay, Castro (89).

Argentina: Botosso, Della Toree, Paternoster, J. Evaristo, Monti, Suarez, Peucelle, Varallo, Stabile, Ferreira, M. Evaristo.

Uruguay: Ballesteros, Nasazzi, Mascheroni, Andrade, Fernandez, Gestido, Dorado, Scarone, Castro, Cea, Iriarte.

Referee: Langenus (Belgium).

ITALY 1934

Italy 0	1	1 —2
Czechoslovakia....0	1	0 —1

SECOND HALF

Scoring: 1, Czech., Puc (70); 2, Italy, Orsi (80).

OVERTIME

Scoring: 3, Italy, Schiavio (95).

Italy: Combi, Monzeglio, Allemandi, Ferraris Monti, Monti, Bertolini, Guaita, Meazza, Schiavio, Ferrari, Orsi.

Czechoslovakia: Planicka, Zenisek, Ctyroky, Kostalek, Cambal, Cambal, Krcil, Junek, Svoboda, Sobotka, Nejedly, Puc.

Referee: Eklind (Sweden).

FRANCE 1938

Italy 3	1	—4
Hungary 1	1	—2

FIRST HALF

Scoring: 1, Italy, Colaussi (5); 2, Hungary, Titkos (7); 3, Italy, Piola (16); 4, Italy, Piola (35).

SECOND HALF

Scoring: 5, Hungary, Sarosi (70); 6, Italy, Colaussi (82).

Italy: Olivieri, Foni, Rava, Serantoni, Andreolo, Locatelli, Biavati, Meazza, Piola, Ferrari, Colaussi.

Hungary: Szabo, Polger, Biro, Szalay, Szucs, Lazar, Sas, Vincze, Sarosi, Zsengeller, Titkos.

Referee: Capdeville (France).

BRAZIL 1950

Uruguay 0	2 —2	
Brazil 0	1 —1	

SECOND HALF

Scoring: 1, Brazil, Friaca (47); 2, Uruguay, Schiaffino (66); 3, Uruguay, Ghiggia (79).

Uruguay: Maspoli, Gonzales, Tejera, Gambretta, Varela, Andrade, Ghiggia, Perez, Miguez, Schiffiano, Moran.

Brazil: Barbosa, Augusto, Juvenal, Bauer, Banilo, Bigode, Friaca, Zizinho, Ademir, Jair, Chico.

Referee: Reader (England).

SWITZERLAND 1954

W Germany 2	1 —3	
Hungary 2	0 —2	

FIRST HALF

Scoring: 1, Hungary, Puskas (6); 2, Hungary, Czibor (8); 3, W Germ., Morlock (10); 4, W Germ., Rahn (18).

SECOND HALF

Scoring: 5, W Germany, Rahn (84).

W Germany: Turek, Posipal, Kohlmeyer, Eckel, Liebrich, Mai, Rahn, Morlock, O.Walter, F. Walter, Schaefer.

Hungary: Grosics, Buzansky, Lantos, Bozsik, Lorant, Zakarias, Czibor, Kocsis, Hidegkuti, Puskas, Toth.

Referee: Ling (England).

SWEDEN 1958

Brazil 2	3 —5	
Sweden 1	1 —2	

FIRST HALF

Scoring: 1, Sweden, Liedholm (3); 2, Brazil, Vava (9); 3, Brazil, Vava (32).

SECOND HALF

Scoring: 4, Brazil, Pelé (55); 5, Brazil, Zagalo (68); 6, Sweden Simonsson (80); 7, Brazil, Pelé (90).

Brazil: Glymar, D. Santos, N. Santos, Zito, Bellini, Orlando, Garrincha, Didi, Vava, Pelé, Zagalo.

Sweden: Svensson, Bergmark, Axbom, Boerjesson, Gustavsson, Parling, Hamrin, Gren, Simonsson, Liedholm, Skoglund.

Referee: Guigue (France).

CHILE 1962

Brazil 1	2 —3	
Czechoslovakia 1	0 —1	

FIRST HALF

Scoring: 1, Czech., Masopust (15); 2, Brazil, Amarildo (17).

SECOND HALF

Scoring: 3, Brazil, Zito (68); 4, Brazil, Vava (77).

Brazil: Glymar, D. Santos, N. Santos, Zito, Mauro, Zozimo, Garrincha, Didi, Vava, Amarildo, Zagalo.

Czechoslovakia: Schroiff, Tichy, Novak, Pluskal, Popluhar, Masopust, Pospichal, Scherer, Kvasnak, Kadraba, Jelinek.

Referee: Latychev (USSR).

World Cup Final Box Scores *(Cont.)*

ENGLAND 1966

England.............1	1	2 —— 4
W Germany 1	1	0 —— 2

FIRST HALF

Scoring: 1, W Germany, Haller (12); 2, England, Hurst (18).

SECOND HALF

Scoring: 3, England, Peters (78); 4, W. Germany, Weber (90).

OVERTIME

Scoring: 5, England, Hurst (101); 6, England, Hurst (120).

England: Banks, Cohen, Wilson, Stiles, J. Charlton, Moore, Ball, Hurst, Hunt, R. Charlton, Peters.

W Germany: Tilkowski, Hottges, Schmellinger, Beckenbauer, Schulz, Weber, Held, Haller, Seeler, Overath, Emmerich.

Referee: Dienst (Switzerland).

W GERMANY 1974

W Germany 2	0 —— 2
Netherlands.....1	0 —— 1

FIRST HALF

Scoring: 1, Netherlands, Neeskens, PK (1); 2, W Germany, Breitner, PK (26); 3, W Germany, Müller (44).

W Germany: Maier, Vogts, Beckenbauer, Schwarzenbeck, Breitner, Hoeness, Bonhof, Overath, Grabowski, Müller, Holzenbein.

Netherlands: Jongbloed, Suurbier, Rijsbergen (de Jong), Haan, Krol, Jansen, Neeskens, van Hanagem, Cruyff, Rensenbrink (van der Kerkhof).

Referee: Taylor (England).

ITALY 1982

Italy..................0	3 —— 3
W Germany 0	1 —— 1

SECOND HALF

Scoring: 1, Italy, Rossi (57); 2, Italy, Tardelli (68); 3, Italy, Altobelli (81); 4, W Germany, Breitner (83).

Italy: Zoff, Bergomi, Scirea, Collovati, Cabrini, Oriali, Gentile, Tardelli, Conti, Rossi, Graziani (Altobelli, Causio).

W Germany: Schumacher, Kaltz, Stielike, K. Foerster, B. Foerster, Dremmler (Hrubesch), Breitner, Briegel, Rummenigge (Müller), Fishcher (Littbarski).

Referee: Coelho (Brazil).

MEXICO 1986 *(Cont.)*

Argentina: Pumpido, Brown, Cuciuffo, Ruggeri, Olarticoecha, Bastista, Giusti, Burruchaga (Trobbiani 90), Enrique, Maradona, Valdona.

W Germany: Schumacher, Jakobs, Forster, Eder, Brehme, Matthaus, Berthold, Magath (Hoeness 62), Briegel, Rummenigge, Allofs (Voller 46).

Referee: Filho (Brazil).

MEXICO 1970

Brazil.................1	3 —— 4
Italy...................1	0 —— 1

FIRST HALF

Scoring: 1, Brazil, Pelé (18); 2, Italy, Boninsegna (32).

SECOND HALF

Scoring: 3, Brazil, Gerson (65); 4, Brazil, Jairzinho (70); 5, Brazil, Alberto (86).

Brazil: Feliz, Alberto, Brito, Wilson, Piazza, Everaldo, Clodoaldo, Gerson, Jairzinho, Tostao, Pelé, Rivelino.

Italy: Albertosi, Burgnich, Cera, Rosato, Facchetti, Bertini (Juliano), Mazzola, De Sisti, Domenghini, Boninsegna (Rivera), Riva.

Referee: Glockner (E Germany).

ARGENTINA 1978

Argentina..........1	2 —— 3
Netherlands 0	0 —— 1

FIRST HALF

Scoring: 1, Argentina, Kempes (38).

SECOND HALF

Scoring: 2, Netherlands, Nanninga (81).

OVERTIME

Scoring: 3, Arg., Kempes (104); 4, Arg., Bertoni (114).

Argentina: Fillol, Olguin, Galvan, Passarella, Tarantini, Ardiles (Larrosa), Gallego, Kempes, Bertoni, Luque, Ortiz (Houseman).

Netherlands: Jongbloed, Jansen (Suurbier), Krol, Brandts, Poortvliet, Neeskens, Haan, W. van der Kerkhoff, R. van der Kerkhoff, Rep (Nanninga), Rensenbrink.

Referee: Gonella (Italy).

MEXICO 1986

Argentina..........1	2 —— 3
W Germany 0	2 —— 2

FIRST HALF

Scoring: 1, Argentina, Brown (22).

SECOND HALF

Scoring: 2, Arg., Valdano (55); 3, W Germ., Rummenigge (73); 4, W Germ., Voller (81); 5, Arg., Burruchaga (83).

ITALY 1990

W Germany 0	1 —— 1
Argentina..............0	0 —— 0

SECOND HALF

Scoring: 1, W Germany, Brehme, PK (84).

W Germany: Illgner, Brehme, Kohler, Augenthaler, Buchwald, Berthold (Reuter), Littbarski, Haessler, Mattaeus, Voeller, Klinsmann.

Argentina: Goychoechea, Lorenzo, Serrizuela, Sensini, Ruggeri (Monzon), Simon, Basualdo, Burruchag (Calderon), Maradona, Troglio, Dezottir.

Referee: Coelho (Brazil).

World Cup Final Box Scores *(Cont.)*

UNITED STATES 1994

Italy	0	0	0—0
Brazil	0	0	0—0

Scoring: None. Shootout goals: Italy—2: Albertini, Evani; Brazil—3: Romario, Branco, Dunga.

Italy: Pagliuca, Benarrivo, Maldini, Baresi, Mussi (Apolloni 35), Albertini, D. Baggio (Evani 95), Berti, Donadoni, Baggio, Massaro.

Brazil: Taffarel, Jorginho (Cafu 21), Branco, Aldair, Santos, Silva, Dunga, Zinho (Viola 106), Mazinho, Bebeto, Romario.

Referee: Puhl (Hungary).

FRANCE 1998

Brazil	0	0—0
France	2	1—3

FIRST HALF
Scoring: 1, France, Zidane (27); 2, France, Zidane (45).

SECOND HALF
Scoring: 3, France, Petit (90).

Brazil: Taffarel, Cafu, Aldair, Baiano, Carlos, Sampaio (Edmundo 74), Dunga, Rivaldo, Leonardo, (Denilson 46), Bebeto, Ronaldo.

France: Barthez, Lizarazu, Desailly, Thuram, Leboeuf, Djorkaeff (Vieira 75) Deschamps, Zidane, Petit, Karembeu (Boghossian 57), Guivarc'h (Dugarry 66).

Referee: Belqola (Morocco).

KOREA/JAPAN 2002

Brazil	0	2 —2
Germany	0	0 —0

SECOND HALF
Scoring: 1, Brazil, Ronaldo (67); 2, Brazil, Ronaldo (79).

Brazil: Marcos, Cafu, Lucio, Roque Junior, Edmilson, Carlos, Silva, Ronaldo (Denilson, 90), Rivaldo, Ronaldinho (Juninho, 85), Kleberson.

Germany: Kahn, Linke, Ramelow, Neuville, Hamann, Klose (Bierhoff, 74), Jeremies (Asamoah, 77), Bode (Ziege, 84), Schneider, Metzelder, Frings.

Referee: Collina (Italy).

Alltime Leaders

GOALS

Player, Nation	Tournaments	Goals	Player, Nation	Tournaments	Goals
Gerd Müller, W Germany	1970, '74	14	Gary Lineker, England	1986, '90	10
Just Fontaine, France	1958	13	Ademir, Brazil	1950	9
Pelé, Brazil	1958, '62, '66, '70	12	Eusebio, Portugal	1966	9
Ronaldo, Brazil	1998, 2002	12	Jairzinho, Brazil	1970, '74	9
Sandor Kocsis, Hungary	1954	11	Paolo Rossi, Italy	1982, '86	9
Teofilo Cubillas, Peru	1970, '78	10	K.H. Rummenigge, W Ger	1978, '82, '86	9
Gregorz Lato, Poland	1974, '78, '82	10	Uwe Seeler, W Germany	1958, '62, '66, '70	9
Helmut Rahn, W Germany	1954, '58	10	Vava, Brazil	1958, '62	9

LEADING SCORER, CUP BY CUP

Year	Player, Nation	Goals	Year	Player, Nation	Goals
1930	Guillermo Stabile, Argentina	8	1966	Eusebio Ferreira, Portugal	9
1934	Oldrich Nejedly, Czechoslovakia	5	1970	Gerd Müller, W Germany	10
1938	Leonidas da Silva, Brazil	8	1974	Gregorz Lato, Poland	7
1950	Ademir de Menezes, Brazil	9	1978	Mario Kempes, Argentina	6
1954	Sandor Kocsis, Hungary	11	1982	Paolo Rossi, Italy	6
1958	Just Fontaine, France	13	1986	Gary Lineker, England	6
1962	Florian Albert, Hungary	4	1990	Salvatore Schillaci, Italy	6
	Valentin Ivanov, USSR		1994	Hristo Stoichkov, Bulgaria	6
	Garrincha, Brazil; Vava, Brazil			Oleg Salenko, Russia	
	Drazan Jerkovic, Yugoslavia		1998	Davor Suker, Croatia	6
	Leonel Sanchez, Chile		2002	Ronaldo, Brazil	8

Most Goals, Individual, One Game

Goals	Player, Nation	Score	Date
5	Oleg Salenko, Russia	Russia–Cameroon, 6–1	6-28-94
4	Leonidas, Brazil	Brazil–Poland, 6–5	6-5-38
4	Ernest Willimowski, Poland	Brazil–Poland, 6–5	6-5-38
4	Gustav Wetterstrïm, Sweden	Sweden–Cuba, 8–0	6-12-38
4	Juan Alberto Schiaffino, Uruguay	Uruguay–Bolivia, 8–0	7-2-50
4	Ademir, Brazil	Brazil–Sweden, 7–1	7-9-50
4	Sandor Kocsis, Hungary	Hungary–W Germany, 8–3	6-20-54
4	Just Fontaine, France	France–W Germany, 6–3	6-28-58
4	Eusebio, Portugal	Portugal–N Korea, 5–3	7-23-66
4	Emilio Butragueño, Spain	Spain–Denmark, 5–1	6-18-86

Note: 31 players have scored 32 World Cup hat tricks. Gerd Müller of West Germany is the only man to have two World Cup hat tricks, both in 1970. The last hat tricks were 6-1-02, Miroslav Klose (Ger) vs. Saudi Arabia; 6-21-98, Gabriel Batistuta (Arg) vs. Jamaica; 6-23-90, Tomas Skuhravy (Czech) vs. Costa Rica; and 6-17-90, Michel (Spain) vs. S Korea.

Attendance and Goal Scoring, Year by Year

Year	Site	No. of Games	Goals	Goals/Game	Attendance	Avg Att
1930	Uruguay	18	70	3.89	434,500	24,139
1934	Italy	17	70	4.12	395,000	23,235
1938	France	18	84	4.67	483,000	26,833
1950	Brazil	22	88	4.00	1,337,000	60,773
1954	Switzerland	26	140	5.38	943,000	36,269
1958	Sweden	35	126	3.60	868,000	24,800
1962	Chile	32	89	2.78	776,000	24,250
1966	England	32	89	2.78	1,614,677	50,459
1970	Mexico	32	95	2.97	1,673,975	52,312
1974	W Germany	38	97	2.55	1,774,022	46,685
1978	Argentina	38	102	2.68	1,610,215	42,374
1982	Spain	52	146	2.80	1,856,277	35,698
1986	Mexico	52	132	2.54	2,441,731	46,956
1990	Italy	52	115	2.21	2,514,443	48,354
1994	United States	52	140	2.69	3,567,415	68,604
1998	France	64	171	2.67	2,775,400	43,366
2002	Korea/Japan	64	161	2.52	2,705,216	42,269
Totals		580	1,754	3.02	25,064,655	43,215

The United States in the World Cup

URUGUAY 1930: FINAL COMPETITION

Date	Opponent	Result	Scoring
7-13-30	Belgium	3–0 W	U.S.: McGhee 2, Patenaude
7-17-30	Paraguay	3–0 W	U.S.: Patenaude 2, Florie
7-26-30	Argentina	1–6 L	Arg.: Monti 2, Scopelli 2, Stabile 2 U.S.: Brown.

ITALY 1934: FINAL COMPETITION

Date	Opponent	Result	Scoring
5-27-34	Italy	1–7 L	U.S.: Donelli Italy: Schiavio 3, Orsi 2, Meazza, Ferrari

BRAZIL 1950: FINAL COMPETITION

Date	Opponent	Result	Scoring
6-25-50	Spain	1–3 L	U.S.: Pariani Spain: Igoa, Basora, Zarra
6-29-50	England	1–0 W	U.S.: Gaetjens.
7-2-50	Chile	2–5 L	U.S.: Wallace, Maca Chile: Robledo, Cremaschi 3, Prieto

ITALY 1990: FINAL COMPETITION

Date	Opponent	Result	Scoring
6-10-90	Czechoslovakia	1–5 L	U.S.: Caligiuri Czech.: Skuhravy 2, Hasek, Bilek, Luhovy
6-14-90	Italy	0–1 L	Italy: Giannini
6-19-90	Austria	1–2 L	U.S.: Murray Austria: Rodax, Ogris

UNITED STATES 1994: FINAL COMPETITION

Date	Opponent	Result	Scoring
6-18-94	Switzerland	1–1 T	U.S.: Wynalda Switz.: Bregy
6-22-94	Colombia	2–1 W	U.S.: Escobar (own goal), Stewart Colombia: Valencia
6-26-94	Romania	1–0 L	Romania: Petrescu
7-4-94	Brazil	1–0 L	Brazil: Bebeto

FRANCE 1998: FINAL COMPETITION

Date	Opponent	Result	Scoring
6-15-98	Germany	2–0 L	Germany: Möller, Klinsmann
6-21-98	Iran	2–1 L	U.S.: McBride Iran: Estili, Mahdavikia
6-25-98	Yugoslavia	1–0 L	Yugoslavia: Komljenovic

KOREA/JAPAN 2002: FINAL COMPETITION

Date	Opponent	Result	Scoring
6-5-02	Portugal	3–2 W	U.S.: O'Brien, Costa (own goal), McBride Portugal: Beto, Agoos (own goal)
6-10-02	S Korea	1–1 T	U.S.: Mathis S Korea: Ahn
6-14-02	Poland	3–1 L	Poland: Olisadebe, Kryszalowicz, Zewlakow U.S.: Donovan
6-17-02	Mexico	2–0 W	U.S.: McBride, Donovan
6-21-02	Germany	1–0 L	Germany: Ballack

International Competition

European Championship

Official name: the European Football Championship. Held every four years since 1960.

Year	Champion	Score	Runner-up	Year	Champion	Score	Runner-up
1960	USSR	2–1	Yugoslavia	1980	W Germany	2–1	Belgium
1964	Spain	2–1	USSR	1984	France	2–0	Spain
1968	Italy	2–0	Yugoslavia	1988	Holland	2–0	USSR
1972	W Germany	3–0	USSR	1992	Denmark	2–0	Germany
1976	Czechoslovakia*	2–2	W Germany	1996	Germany†	2–1	Czech Republic
				2000	France†	2–1	Italy

*Won on penalty kicks. †Won in sudden-death overtime.

Under-20 World Championship

Year	Host	Champion	Runner-Up
1977	Tunisia	USSR	Mexico
1979	Japan	Argentina	USSR
1981	Australia	W Germany	Qatar
1983	Mexico	Brazil	Argentina
1985	USSR	Brazil	Spain
1987	Chile	Yugoslavia	W Germany
1989	Saudi Arabia	Portugal	Nigeria
1991	Portugal	Portugal	Brazil
1993	Australia	Brazil	Ghana
1995	Qatar	Argentina	Brazil
1997	Malaysia	Argentina	Uruguay
1999	Nigeria	Spain	Japan
2001	Argentina	Argentina	Ghana

Under-17 World Championship

Year	Champion
1985	Nigeria
1987	USSR
1989	Saudi Arabia
1991	Ghana
1993	Nigeria

Under-17 *(Cont.)*

Year	Champion
1995	Ghana
1997	Brazil
1999	Brazil
2001	France
2003	Brazil

Pan American Games

Year	Champion
1951	Argentina
1955	Argentina
1959	Argentina
1963	Brazil
1967	Mexico
1971	Argentina
1975	Brazil/Mexico (tie)
1979	Brazil
1983	Uruguay
1987	Brazil
1991	United States
1995	Argentina
1999	Mexico
2003	Argentina

South American Championship (Copa America)

Year	Champion	Host	Year	Champion	Host
1916	Uruguay	Argentina	1953	Paraguay	Peru
1917	Uruguay	Uruguay	1955	Argentina	Chile
1919	Brazil	Brazil	1956	Uruguay	Uruguay
1920	Uruguay	Chile	1957	Argentina	Peru
1921	Argentina	Argentina	1958	Argentina	Argentina
1922	Brazil	Brazil	1959	Uruguay	Ecuador
1923	Uruguay	Uruguay	1963	Bolivia	Bolivia
1924	Uruguay	Uruguay	1967	Uruguay	Uruguay
1925	Argentina	Argentina	1975	Peru	Various sites
1926	Uruguay	Chile	1979	Paraguay	Various sites
1927	Argentina	Peru	1983	Uruguay	Various sites
1929	Argentina	Argentina	1987	Uruguay	Argentina
1935	Uruguay	Peru	1989	Brazil	Brazil
1937	Argentina	Argentina	1990	Brazil	Argentina
1939	Peru	Peru	1991	Argentina	Chile
1941	Argentina	Chile	1993	Argentina	Ecuador
1942	Uruguay	Uruguay	1995	Uruguay	Uruguay
1945	Argentina	Chile	1997	Brazil	Bolivia
1946	Argentina	Argentina	1999	Brazil	Paraguay
1947	Argentina	Ecuador	2001	Colombia	Colombia
1949	Brazil	Brazil			

Awards

European Footballer of the Year

Year	Player	Club	Year	Player	Club
1956	Stanley Matthews	Blackpool	1975	Oleg Blokhin	Dynamo Kiev
1957	Alfredo Di Stefano	Real Madrid	1976	Franz Beckenbauer	Bayern Munich
1958	Raymond Kopa	Real Madrid	1977	Allan Simonsen	Borussia M'gladbach
1959	Alfredo Di Stefano	Real Madrid	1978	Kevin Keegan	SV Hamburg
1960	Luis Suarez	Barcelona	1979	Kevin Keegan	SV Hamburg
1961	Omar Sivori	Juventus	1980	Karl-Heinz Rummenigge	Bayern Munich
1962	Josef Masopust	Dukla Prague	1981	Karl-Heinz Rummenigge	Bayern Munich
1963	Lev Yashin	Moscow Dynamo	1982	Paolo Rossi	Juventus
1964	Denis Law	Manchester United	1983	Michel Platini	Juventus
1965	Eusebio	Benfica	1984	Michel Platini	Juventus
1966	Bobby Charlton	Manchester United	1985	Michel Platini	Juventus
1967	Florian Albert	Ferencvaros	1986	Igor Belanov	Dynamo Kiev
1968	George Best	Manchester United	1987	Ruud Gullit	AC Milan
1969	Gianni Rivera	AC Milan	1988	Marco Van Basten	AC Milan
1970	Gerd Mueller	Bayern Munich	1989	Marco Van Basten	AC Milan
1971	Johan Cruyff	Ajax	1990	Lothar Matthaeus	Inter Milan
1972	Franz Beckenbauer	Bayern Munich	1991	Jean-Pierre Papin	Olympique Marseille
1973	Johan Cruyff	Barcelona	1992	Marco Van Basten	AC Milan
1974	Johan Cruyff	Barcelona	1993	Roberto Baggio	Juventus

European Footballer of the Year (Cont.)

Year	Player	Club	Year	Player	Club
1994	Hristo Stoichkov	Barcelona	1999	Rivaldo	Barcelona
1995	George Weah	AC Milan	2000	Luis Figo	Real Madrid
1996	Matthias Sammer	Borussia Dortmund	2001	Michael Owen	Liverpool
1997	Ronaldo	Inter Milan	2002	Ronaldo	Real Madrid
1998	Zinedine Zidane	Juventus			

African Footballer of the Year

Year	Player	Club	Year	Player	Club
1970	Salif Keita	St. Etienne	1987	Rabah Madjer	FC Porto
1971	Ibrahim Sunday	Asante Kotoko	1988	Kalusha Bwalya	Cercle Bruges
1972	Chérif Soueymane	Hafia	1989	George Weah	Monaco
1973	Tshimen Bwanga	TP Mazembe	1990	Roger Milla	St. Denis
1974	Paul Moukila	CARA Brazzaville	1991	Abedi Pele Ayew	Marseille
1975	Ahmed Faras	Mohammedia	1992	Abedi Pele Ayew	Marseille
1976	Roger Milla	Canon Yaounde	1993	Rashidi Yekini	FC Zurich
1977	Tarak Dhiab	Esperance	1994	George Weah	Paris St. Germain
1978	Karim Abdul Razak	Asante Kotoko	1995	George Weah	AC Milan
1979	Thomas Nkono	Canon Yaounde	1996	Nwankwo Kanu	Inter Milan
1980	Jean Manga Onguene	Canon Yaounde	1997	Victor Ikpeba	Monaco
1981	Lakhdar Belloumi	GCR Mascara	1998	Mustapha Hadji	Deportivo Coruna
1982	Thomas Nkono	Espanol	1999	Nwankwo Kanu	Arsenal
1983	Mahmoud Al-Khatib	Al Ahli	2000	Patrick Mboma	Parma
1984	Theophile Abega	Toulouse	2001	El Hadji Diouf	Lens
1985	Mohamed Timoumi	Royal Armed Forces	2002	El Hadji Diouf	Lens
1986	Badou Ezaki	Real Mallorca			

South American Player of the Year

Year	Player	Club	Year	Player	Club
1971	Tostao	Cruzeiro	1987	Carlos Valderrama	Deportivo Cali
1972	Teofilo Cubillas	Alianza Lima	1988	Ruben Paz	Racing Buenos Aires
1973	Pelé	Santos	1989	Bebeto	Vasco da Gama
1974	Elias Figueroa	Internacional	1990	Raul Amarilla	Olimpia
1975	Elias Figueroa	Internacional	1991	Oscar Ruggeri	Velez Sarsfield
1976	Elias Figueroa	Internacional	1992	Rai	São Paulo
1977	Zico	Flamengo	1993	Carlos Valderrama	Junior Barranquilla
1978	Mario Kempes	Valencia	1994	Cafu	São Paulo
1979	Diego Maradona	Argentinos Juniors	1995	Enzo Francescoli	River Plate
1980	Diego Maradona	Boca Juniors	1996	Jose-Luis Chilavert	Velez Sarsfield
1981	Zico	Flamengo	1997	Marcelo Salas	River Plate
1982	Zico	Flamengo	1998	Martin Palermo	Boca Juniors
1983	Socrates	Corinthians	1999	Javier Saviola	River Plate
1984	Enzo Francescoli	River Plate	2000	Romario	Vasco da Gama
1985	Julio Cesar Romero	Fluminense	2001	Juan Riquelme	Boca Juniors
1986	Antonio Alzamendi	River Plate	2002	Jose Cardozo	Toluca

International Club Competition

Intercontinental Cup

Competition between winners of European Cup and Libertadores Cup.

1960...Real Madrid, Spain	1975...No tournament	1989...Milan, Italy
1961...Penarol, Uruguay	1976...Bayern Munich	1990...Milan, Italy
1962...Santos, Brazil	1977...Boca Juniors, Argentina	1991...Red Star Belgrade, Yugos.
1963...Santos, Brazil	1978...No tournament	1992...São Paulo, Brazil
1964...Inter, Italy	1979...Olimpia, Paraguay	1993...São Paulo, Brazil
1965...Inter, Italy	1980...Nacional, Uruguay	1994...Velez Sarsfield, Argentina
1966...Penarol, Uruguay	1981...Flamengo, Brazil	1995...Ajax Amsterdam, Netherlands
1967...Racing Club, Argentina	1982...Penarol, Uruguay	1996...Juventus, Italy
1968...Estudiantes, Argentina	1983...Gremio, Brazil	1997...Borussia Dortmund, Ger.
1969...Milan, Italy	1984...Independiente, Argentina	1998...Real Madrid, Spain
1970...Feyenoord, Netherlands	1985...Juventus, Italy	1999 ...Manchester United, England
1971...Nacional, Uruguay	1986...River Plate, Argentina	2000...Boca Juniors, Argentina
1972...Ajax Amsterdam, Netherlands	1987...Porto, Portugal	2001...Bayern Munich, Germany
1973...Independiente, Argentina	1988...Nacional, Uruguay	2002...Real Madrid, Spain
1974...Atletico de Madrid, Spain		

Note: Until 1968 a best-of-three-games format decided the winner. After that a two-game/total-goal format was used until Toyota became the sponsor in 1980, moved the game to Tokyo and switched the format to a one-game championship. The European Cup runner-up substituted for the winner in 1971, 1973, 1974, and 1979.

European Cup

1956...Real Madrid, Spain
1957...Real Madrid, Spain
1958...Real Madrid, Spain
1959...Real Madrid, Spain
1960...Real Madrid, Spain
1961...Benfica, Portugal
1962...Benfica, Portugal
1963...AC Milan, Italy
1964...Inter-Milan, Italy
1965...Inter-Milan, Italy
1966...Real Madrid, Spain
1967...Celtic, Scotland
1968...Manchester United, England
1969...AC Milan, Italy
1970...Feyenoord, Netherlands
1971...Ajax Amsterdam,
    Netherlands
1972...Ajax Amsterdam,
    Netherlands
1973...Ajax Amsterdam,
    Netherlands

1974...Bayern Munich,
    W Germany
1975...Bayern Munich,
    W Germany
1976...Bayern Munich,
    W Germany
1977...Liverpool, England
1978...Liverpool, England
1979...Nottingham Forest,
    England
1980...Nottingham Forest,
    England
1981...Liverpool, England
1982...Aston Villa, England
1983...SV Hamburg,
    W Germany
1984...Liverpool, England
1985...Juventus, Italy
1986...Steaua Bucharest,
    Romania
1987...Porto, Portugal

1988...PSV Eindhoven,
    Netherlands
1989...AC Milan, Italy
1990...AC Milan, Italy
1991...Red Star Belgrade, Yugoslav.
1992...Barcelona, Spain
1993...Olympique Marseille, France
1994...AC Milan, Italy
1995...Ajax Amsterdam, Netherlands
1996...Juventus, Italy
1997...Borussia Dortmund, Ger.
1998...Real Madrid, Spain
1999...Manchester United,
    England
2000...Real Madrid, Spain
2001...Bayern Munich, Germany
2002...Real Madrid, Spain
2003...AC Milan, Italy

Note: On four occasions the European Cup winner has refused to play in the Intercontinental Cup and has been replaced by the runner-up: Panathinaikos (Greece) in 1971, Juventus (Italy) in 1973, Atletico Madrid (Spain) in 1974, and Malmo (Sweden) in 1979.

Libertadores Cup

Competition between champion clubs and runners-up of 10 South American National Associations.

1960...Penarol, Uruguay
1961...Penarol, Uruguay
1962...Santos, Brazil
1963...Santos, Brazil
1964...Independiente, Argentina
1965...Independiente, Argentina
1966...Penarol, Uruguay
1967...Racing Club, Argentina
1968...Estudiantes, Argentina
1969...Estudiantes, Argentina
1970...Estudiantes, Argentina
1971...Nacional, Uruguay
1972...Independiente, Argentina
1973...Independiente, Argentina
1974...Independiente, Argentina

1975...Independiente, Argentina
1976...Cruzeiro, Brazil
1977...Boca Juniors, Argentina
1978...Boca Juniors, Argentina
1979...Olimpia, Paraguay
1980...Nacional, Uruguay
1981...Flamengo, Brazil
1982...Penarol, Uruguay
1983...Gremio, Brazil
1984...Independiente, Argentina
1985...Argentinos Juniors, Arg
1986...River Plate, Argentina
1987...Penarol, Uruguay
1988...Nacional, Uruguay
1989...Atletico Nacional, Colombia

1990...Olimpia, Paraguay
1991...Colo Colo, Chile
1992...São Paulo, Brazil
1993...São Paulo, Brazil
1994...Velez Sarsfield, Argentina
1995...Gremio, Brazil
1996...River Plate, Argentina
1997...Cruzeiro, Brazil
1998...Vasco da Gama, Brazil
1999...Palmeiras, Brazil
2000...Boca Juniors, Argentina
2001...Boca Juniors, Argentina
2002...Olimpia, Paraguay
2003...Boca Juniors, Argentina

UEFA Cup

1958...Barcelona, Spain
1959...No tournament
1960...Barcelona, Spain
1961...AS Roma, Italy
1962...Valencia, Spain
1963...Valencia, Spain
1964...Real Zaragoza, Spain
1965...Ferencvaros, Hungary
1966...Barcelona, Spain
1967...Dynamo Zagreb, Yugoslav.
1968...Leeds United, England
1969...Newcastle United, England
1970...Arsenal, England
1971...Leeds United, England
1972...Tottenham Hotspur, England
1973...Liverpool, England
1974...Feyenoord, Netherlands

1975...Borussia Monchengladbach,
    W Germany
1976...Liverpool, England
1977...Juventus, Italy
1978...PSV Eindhoven, Netherl.
1979...Borussia Monchengladbach,
    W Germany
1980...Eintracht Frankfurt,
    W Germany
1981...Ipswich Town, England
1982...IFK Gothenburg, Sweden
1983...Anderlecht, Belgium
1984...Tottenham Hotspur, England
1985...Real Madrid, Spain
1986...Real Madrid, Spain
1987...IFK Gothenburg, Sweden
1988...Bayer Leverkusen,
    W Germany

1989...Naples, Italy
1990...Juventus, Italy
1991...Inter-Milan, Italy
1992...Torino, Italy
1993...Juventus, Italy
1994...Internazionale, Italy
1995...Parma, Italy
1996...Bayern Munich, Germany
1997...Schalke 04, Germany
1998...Inter Milan, Italy
1999...Parma, Italy
2000...Galatasaray, Turkey
2001...Liverpool, England
2002...Feyenoord, Netherlands
2003...FC Porto, Portugal

European Cup-Winners' Cup

1961...AC Fiorentina, Italy	1974...Magdeburg, E Germany	1988...Mechelen, Belgium
1962...Atletico Madrid, Spain	1975...Dynamo Kiev, USSR	1989...Barcelona, Spain
1963...Tottenham Hotspur, England	1976...Anderlecht, Belgium	1990...Sampdoria, Italy
1964...Sporting Lisbon, Portugal	1977...SV Hamburg, W Germ.	1991...Manchester United, England
1965...West Ham United, England	1978...Anderlecht, Belgium	1992...Werder Bremen, Germany
1966...Borussia Dortmund, W Germany	1979...Barcelona, Spain	1993...Parma, Italy
1967...Bayern Munich, W Germ.	1980...Valencia, Spain	1994...Arsenal, England
1968...AC Milan, Italy	1981...Dynamo Tbilisi, USSR	1995...Real Zaragoza, Spain
1969...Slovan Bratislava, Czech.	1982...Barcelona, Spain	1996...Paris St. Germain, France
1970...Manchester City, England	1983...Aberdeen, Scotland	1997...Barcelona, Spain
1971...Chelsea, England	1984...Juventus, Italy	1998...Chelsea, England
1972...Glasgow Rangers, Scotland	1985...Everton, England	1999...Lazio, Italy
1973...AC Milan, Italy	1986...Dynamo Kiev, USSR	
	1987...Ajax Amsterdam, Neth.	

Note: the Cup-Winners Cup was discontinued after 1999.

Major League Soccer

MLS Cup Results

Year	Champion	Score	Runner-up	Regular Season MVP
1996	D.C. United	3–2 (ot)	Los Angeles	Carlos Valderrama, TB
1997	D.C. United	2–1	Colorado	Preki, Kansas City
1998	Chicago	2–0	D.C. United	Marco Etcheverry, D.C.
1999	D.C. United	2–0	Los Angeles	Jason Kreis, Dallas
2000	Kansas City	1–0	Chicago	Tony Meola, Kansas City
2001	San Jose	2–1 (ot)	Los Angeles	Alex Pineda Chacon, Mia
2002	Los Angeles	1–0 (ot)	New England	Carlos Ruiz, Los Angeles

A-League

Year	Champion	Score	Runner-Up	Regular Season MVP
1991	San Francisco	1–3, 2–0 (1–0 on PKs)	Albany	Jean Harbor, Maryland
1992	Colorado	1–0	Tampa Bay	Taifour Diane, Colorado
1993	Colorado	3–1 (OT)	Los Angeles	Taifour Diane, Colorado
1994	Montreal	1–0	Colorado	Paulinho, Los Angeles
1995	Seattle	1–2 (SO), 3–0, 2–1 (SO)	Atlanta	Peter Hattrup, Seattle
1996	Seattle	2–0	Rochester	Wolde Harris, Colorado
1997	Milwaukee	2–1 (SO)	Carolina	Doug Miller, Rochester
1998	Rochester	3–1	Minnesota	Mark Baena, Seattle
1999	Minnesota	2–1	Rochester	John Swallen, Minnesota
2000	Rochester	3–1	Minnesota	Vitalis Takawira, Mil
2001	Rochester	2–0	Vancouver	Paul Conway, Charleston
2002	Milwaukee	2–1 (2ot)	Richmond	Leighton O'Brien, Seattle
2003	Charleston	3–0	Minnesota	Thiago Martins, Pittsburgh

Woman's United Soccer Association

Founders Cup Results

Year	Champion	Score	Runner-up	Regular Season MVP
2001	Bay Area	3–3 (4–2 PKs)	Atlanta	Tiffeny Milbrett, New York
2002	Carolina	3–2	Washington	Marinette Pichon, Philadelphia
2003	Washington	2–1 (ot)	Atlanta	Maren Meinert, Boston

Open to all amateur and professional teams in the United States, the annual U.S. Open Cup is the oldest cup competition in the country and among the oldest in the world. The tournament is a single-elimination event running concurrent to the MLS season. The winner advances to the CONCACAF Cup, a tournament of the top club teams from North and Central America and the Caribbean.

Year	Champion
1914	Brooklyn Field Club (NYC)
1915	Bethlehem Steel FC (PA)
1916	Bethlehem Steel FC (PA)
1917	Fall River Rovers (MA)
1918	Bethlehem Steel FC (PA)
1919	Bethlehem Steel FC (PA)
1920	Ben Miller FC (St. Louis)
1921	Robbins Dry Dock FC (Brooklyn)
1922	Scullin Steel FC (St. Louis)
1923	Paterson FC (NJ)
1924	Fall River FC (MA)
1925	Shawsheen FC (Andover, MA)
1926	Bethlehem Steel FC (PA)
1927	Fall River FC (MA)
1928	New York National FC (NYC)
1929	Hakoah All Star SC (NYC)
1930	Fall River FC (MA)
1931	Fall River FC (MA)
1932	New Bedford FC (MA)
1933	Stix, Baer and Fuller FC (St. Louis)
1934	Stix, Baer and Fuller FC (St. Louis)
1935	Central Breweries FC (Chicago)
1936	German-Americans (Philadelphia)
1937	New York American FC (NYC)
1938	Sparta A and BA (Chicago)
1939	St. Mary's Celtic SC (Brooklyn)
1940	—
1941	Pawtucket FC (RI)
1942	Gallatin SC (PA)
1943	Brooklyn Hispano SC (NYC)
1944	Brooklyn Hispano SC (NYC)
1945	Brookhattan FC (NYC)
1946	Chicago Viking FC (IL)
1947	Ponta Delgada SC (Fall River, MA)
1948	Simpkins-Ford SC (St. Louis)
1949	Morgan SC (PA)
1950	Simpkins-Ford SC (St. Louis)
1951	German Hungarian SC (NYC)
1952	Harmarville SC (PA)
1953	Falcons SC (Chicago)
1954	New York Americans (NYC)
1955	Eintracht Sport Club (NYC)
1956	Harmarville SC (PA)
1957	Kutis SC (St. Louis)
1958	Los Angeles Kickers (CA)
1959	McIlvaine Canvasbacks (Los Angeles)

Year	Champion
1960	Ukrainian Nationals (Philadelphia)
1961	Ukrainian Nationals (Philadelphia)
1962	New York Hungaria (NYC)
1963	Ukrainian Nationals (Philadelphia)
1964	Los Angeles Kickers (CA)
1965	New York Hungaria (NYC)
1966	Ukrainian Nationals (Philadelphia)
1967	Greek American AA (NYC)
1968	Greek American AA (NYC)
1969	Greek American AA (NYC)
1970	Elizabeth SC (Union, NJ)
1971	Hota SC (NYC)
1972	Elizabeth SC (Union, NJ)
1973	Maccabee SC (Los Angeles)
1974	Greek American AA (NYC)
1975	Maccabee SC (Los Angeles)
1976	San Francisco AC (CA)
1977	Maccabee SC (Los Angeles)
1978	Maccabee SC (Los Angeles)
1979	Brooklyn Dodgers SC (NYC)
1980	NY Pancyprian-Freedoms (NYC)
1981	Maccabee SC (Los Angeles)
1982	NY Pancyprian-Freedoms (NYC)
1983	NY Pancyprian-Freedoms (NYC)
1984	AO Krete (NYC)
1985	Greek American AC (San Francisco)
1986	Kutis SC (St. Louis)
1987	Club Espana (Washington, D.C.)
1988	Busch SC (St. Louis)
1989	HRC Kickers (St. Petersburg, FL)
1990	AAC Eagles (Chicago)
1991	Brooklyn Italians SC (East NY)
1992	San Jose Oaks (CA)
1993	Club Deportivo Mexico (San Francisco)
1994	Greek American AC (San Francisco)
1995	Richmond Kickers (VA)
1996	D.C. United (MLS)
1997	Dallas Burn (MLS)
1998	Chicago Fire (MLS)
1999	Rochester Rhinos (A-League)
2000	Chicago Fire (MLS)
2001	Los Angeles Galaxy (MLS)
2002	Columbus Crew (MLS)
2003	Chicago Fire (MLS)

North American Soccer League

Formed in 1968 by the merger of the National Professional Soccer League and the USA League, both of which had begun operations a year earlier. The NPSL's lone champion was the Oakland Clippers. The USA League, which brought entire teams in from Europe, was won in 1967 by the L.A. Wolves, who were the English League's Wolverhampton Wanderers.

Year	Champion	Score	Runner-Up	Regular Season MVP
1968	Atlanta	0–0, 3–0	San Diego	John Kowalik, Chi
1969	Kansas City	No game	Atlanta	Cirilio Fernandez, KC
1970	Rochester	3–0, 1–3	Washington	Carlos Metidieri, Roch
1971	Dallas	1–2, 4–1, 2–0	Atlanta	Carlos Metidieri, Roch
1972	New York	2–1	St. Louis	Randy Horton, NY
1973	Philadelphia	2–0	Dallas	Warren Archibald, Mia
1974	Los Angeles	4–3*	Miami	Peter Silvester, Balt
1975	Tampa Bay	2–0	Portland	Steve David, Mia
1976	Toronto	3–0	Minnesota	Pelé, NY
1977	New York	2–1	Seattle	Franz Beckenbauer, NY
1978	New York	3–1	Tampa Bay	Mike Flanagan, NE
1979	Vancouver	2–1	Tampa Bay	Johan Cruyff, LA
1980	New York	3–0	Ft. Lauderdale	Roger Davies, Sea
1981	Chicago	1–0*	New York	Giorgio Chinaglia, NY
1982	New York	1–0	Seattle	Peter Ward, Sea
1983	Tulsa	2–0	Toronto	Roberto Cabanas, NY
1984	Chicago	2–1, 3–2	Toronto	Steve Zungul, SJ

*Shootout.

Championship Format: 1968 and 1970: Two games/total goals. 1971 and 1984: Best-of-three series. 1972–1983: One-game championship. Title in 1969 went to the regular-season champion.

Statistical Leaders

SCORING

Year	Player/Team	Pts	Year	Player/Team	Pts
1968	John Kowalik, Chi	69	1977	Steven David, LA	58
1969	Kaiser Motaung, Atl	36	1978	Giorgio Chinaglia, NY	79
1970	Kirk Apostolidis, Dall	35	1979	Oscar Fabbiani, Tampa Bay	58
1971	Carlos Metidieri, Roch	46	1980	Giorgio Chinaglia, NY	77
1972	Randy Horton, NY	22	1981	Giorgio Chinaglia, NY	74
1973	Kyle Rote, Dall	30	1982	Giorgio Chinaglia, NY	55
1974	Paul Child, San Jose	36	1983	Roberto Cabanas, NY	66
1975	Steven David, Miami	52	1984	Slavisa Zungul, Golden Bay	50
1976	Giorgio Chinaglia, NY	49			

The Royal Treatment

In May 2003, MetroStars and U.S. national team goalkeeper Tim Howard received a taste of what it would be like to be covered by the English press. In the middle of the month Manchester United made an inquiry to MLS about signing the 24-year-old, who had allowed just four goals in seven games that season—and who also has been diagnosed with Tourette's syndrome. The headline writers on Fleet Street, who delight in taking potshots at the Premier League champs, had a field day. UNITED WANT AMERICAN WITH BRAIN DISORDER, said *The Guardian* of London; *The Independent* wrote MANCHESTER UNITED TRYING TO SIGN DISABLED GOALKEEPER. The always tasteful *Mirror* went with TICK FOR TIM. Despite the less than friendly welcome from the press, Howard eventually signed with the club and won the starting goalkeeping job.

GO Cats!

Thomas Vanek of Minnesota

NCAA Sports

Risk-Reward Ratios

The national champions in soccer, hockey and baseball earned their titles by taking calculated risks

BY HANK HERSCH

SOMETIMES THE GAMBLE is in taking the job; other times, it's in a recruiting effort or a strategic decision during a game. No college coach can succeed without calculating risks correctly when it matters most. And those who roll the dice best on occasion reap the biggest jackpot of all—a national championship.

MEN'S SOCCER

Within months of his May 17, 2001, firing as coach of MLS's Columbus Crew, Tom Fitzgerald had relocated to Clearwater, Fla., and started selling beachfront property. His wife, Debi, had opened an antique store, and Tom was set to become the coach of a youth soccer program in the area. After 24 years of coaching, the last five with the Crew, he couldn't imagine an existence, however pleasant, without the sport.

In March of the following year Fitzgerald got a call from UCLA associate athletic director Betsy Stephenson. Within two weeks he and Debi had packed up their new life and headed to Los Angeles. The Bruins' third-year coach, Todd Saldana, had been forced to resign after the school learned he had a degree from an unaccredited university. After interviewing several candidates, including alum Steve Sampson, the former coach of the U.S. national team, UCLA offered the job to Fitzgerald, who had guided Tampa to the Division II title in 1994. "In life, you never know what's going to happen," he said. "You've got to be ready for just about anything."

With the players' feelings raw and uneasy after Saldana's abrupt departure, Fitzgerald entered a difficult situation. Assistant coach Jorge Salcedo, a former Bruin and Crew player, helped in the transition; so did the 51-year-old Fitzgerald's optimistic outlook and easygoing demeanor. "From one to 28, he makes the guys feel like they can run through walls for him," Salcedo told the *Los Angeles Times*. "Tom creates an environment where everybody feels good about their personal game."

Futagaki, who set up the winning goal against Stanford, celebrated the Bruins' fourth NCAA title.

AP PHOTO/TIM SHARP

The good vibes continued, from a fast start through a solid 13-3-3 regular-season finish, and then into the NCAA tournament. Adolfo Gregorio's go-ahead goal on an 81st minute penalty kick boosted the Bruins past Maryland 2–1 in the national semifinals, setting up a showdown with Pac-10 rival Stanford in Dallas for the title. The finale was a *re*-rematch; UCLA had won both previous meetings 1–0. The law of averages may have favored the Cardinal, whose defense, anchored by U.S. under-20 team stalwart Chad Marshall, had conceded only two goals in four tournament games. Fitzgerald prepared his team for another nailbiter. "It takes one little mistake, one little missed assignment and the whole game changes," he told his players. "Just concentrate all the way through and we'll get the bounces."

With the match scoreless in the 89th minute and UCLA having placed only one shot on goal, a Stanford foul about 35 yards from goal near the left sideline set up senior Ryan Futagaki's free kick. Trying to keep the ball out of the air, where Stanford's tall defenders had the advantage, Futagaki whipped in a waist-high ball to sophomore Aaron Lopez, who flicked it inside the right post to give the Bruins their third 1–0 victory over Stanford that season, and the school's fourth national soccer title. "You never think it can happen, but there's the trophy sitting there, so I guess it did," Fitzgerald said. "I'm happy to be here and plan on being around a long time."

MEN'S ICE HOCKEY

When Don Lucia arrived in Minnesota in 1999, he knew that he would have to break with a 13-year tradition and recruit outside the state's borders if he hoped to compete with the top programs and return the Golden Gophers to prominence. 'We have to have the same ability to go out and get those kids," Lucia said. "As long as they're recruiting all over North America or Europe, then we better, too."

The first of those out-of-state imports scored the game-winner in the 2002 championship game, a 4–3 overtime conquest of Maine. Not that Grant Potulny was exactly an exchange student: He hailed from Grand Forks, N.D., just across the Red River from Minnesota. But with the barrier broken and the school's fourth title secured, Lucia decided to extend his recruiting reach with the class of '07: He reeled in Thomas Vanek, a left winger from Graz, Austria.

Vanek left his country at age 14 to play with a bantam team in Red Deer, Alberta, before playing Junior A in Sioux Falls, S.D. He led the U.S. Hockey League in goals and points in 2002, then decided to attend college instead of entering the NHL draft. Lucia and Co. impressed him immediately. "People breathe hockey in Minnesota," said Vanek. "They are so into it."

Vanek joined a team in transition, and the Gophers' inexperience showed early. But they finished with a 14-1-2 flourish, thanks largely to the kid with the Schwarzenegger accent. The first Euopean in the program's 81 years, Vanek became the first freshman since 1970 to lead the Gophers in scoring, with 31 goals and 31 assists in 45 games. He had a terminator's instinct, too; 17 of those goals came in the third period or overtime, including a tough angle shot at 8:55 of sudden death that iced a 3–2 win over Michigan in the national semifinals. "He's just a great player, who seems to step up when the game is on the line," Lucia said. "But that's what great players do."

That's certainly what was needed against New Hampshire, a veteran team with a superb goaltender in Mike Ayers. Though Minnesota held a 30–16 edge in shots through the first two periods in Buffalo, the score was even at one. Then with 8:14 left in the final period, Vanek slipped the puck past Ayers, sparking a three-goal outburst by the Gophers, who went on to win 5–1. For the first time since Boston University in 1971 and '72, NCAA hockey had a back-to-back champ. "This," said Vanek, named the tournament's most outstanding player, "is what I came to Minnesota for."

BASEBALL

He was a 55-year-old coach, and it was his first big-time job. So what if it was at the smallest school in Division I-A with academic standards so high he could realistically recruit only 40% of the top prospects? Who cared if none of its teams had won a championship in any sport since the university opened in 1911? It was 1992 and he was Wayne Graham, a five-time national junior college title winner at San Jacinto College North in Houston, Texas. He had helped develop Roger Clemens and Andy Pettitte, he had never had a losing record in 10 seasons and he was going to take over at Rice, which had never won a conference championshiop or qualified for NCAA tournament play.

Within six years, the Owls had made it to the CWS under Graham, but their performances there were not encouraging; in three trips to Omaha Rice went 1–6. In 2003, though, they had run off a school record 30 straight wins and, behind a pair of all-America aces in Jeff Niemann (17–0) and Wade Townsend (11–2), had produced the nation's second-best ERA (2.74). Said Graham after arriving in Omaha, "We've always had to battle the perception that we had not gotten far here."

Rice battled all the way to the finals, a best-of-three series against Stanford. The 6'9", 260-pound Niemann was brilliant in the opener, a 4–3 win in 10 innings, but the Cardinal roughed up Townsend 8–3 to take Game 2 behind righty John Hudgins, who would be named MVP of the tournament. That left Graham to start sophomore righthander Philip Humber, who had lasted just 3⅔ innings in Rice's 5–4 win over Texas five days earlier.

Though Graham hadn't built his team for offense, Rice erupted for three runs in the first inning and a record-tying seven in the sixth. With Humber hurling a five-hitter the Owls rolled to the most lopsided victory in a CWS championship game, 14–2. Despite the margin, Graham, who had a cup of coffee as a Mets third baseman, bobbled a foul-ball grounder hit to him in the coaching box at third in the ninth inning. "My hands were shaking," he said with a smile.

After three decades of coaching, Graham was entitled to be nervous. "He's been waiting for this his whole life," said first baseman Vincent Sinisi, "and we finally gave it to him."

FOR THE RECORD · 2002–03

NCAA Team Champions

Fall 2002
Cross-Country

MEN

	Champion	Runner-Up
Division I:	Stanford	Wisconsin
Division II:	Western St (CO)	Abilene Christian
Division III:	WI-Oshkosh	Calvin

WOMEN

	Champion	Runner-Up
Division I:	Brigham Young	Stanford
Division II:	Western St (CO)	Adams St
Division III:	Williams	Middlebury

Field Hockey

WOMEN

	Champion	Runner-Up
Division I:	Wake Forest	Penn St
Division II	Bloomsburg	Bentley
Division III:	Rowan	Messiah

Football

MEN

	Champion	Runner-Up
Division I-AA:	Western Kentucky	McNeese St
Division II:	Grand Valley St	Valdosta St
Division III:	Mount Union	Trinity (TX)

Soccer

MEN

	Champion	Runner-Up
Division I:	UCLA	Stanford
Division II:	Sonoma St	Southern New Hampshire
Division III:	Messiah	Otterbein

WOMEN

	Champion	Runner-Up
Division I:	Portland	Santa Clara
Division II:	Christian Brothers	Nebraska-Omaha
Division III:	Ohio Wesleyan	Messiah

Volleyball

WOMEN

	Champion	Runner-Up
Division I:	Southern Cal	Stanford
Division II:	BYU–Hawaii	Truman
Division III:	WI-Whitewater	Washington (MO)

Water Polo

MEN

Champion	Runner-Up
Stanford	California

Winter 2002–2003

Basketball

MEN

	Champion	Runner-Up
Division I:	Syracuse	Kansas
Division II:	Northeastern St	vacated
Division III:	Williams	Gustavus Adolphus

WOMEN

	Champion	Runner-Up
Division I:	Connecticut	Tennessee
Division II:	S Dakota St	Northern Kentucky
Division III:	Trinity (TX)	Eastern Connecticut St

Fencing

Champion	Runner-Up
Notre Dame	Penn St

Gymnastics

MEN

Champion	Runner-Up
Oklahoma	Ohio St

WOMEN

Champion	Runner-Up
UCLA	Alabama

Ice Hockey

MEN

	Champion	Runner-Up
Division I:	Minnesota	New Hampshire
Division III:	Norwich	Oswego St

WOMEN

Champion	Runner-Up
MN-Duluth	Harvard

Rifle

Champion	Runner-Up
AK-Fairbanks	Xavier

Skiing

Champion	Runner-Up
Utah	Vermont

Swimming and Diving

MEN

	Champion	Runner-Up
Division I:	Auburn	Texas
Division II:	Drury	Cal St–Bakersfield
Division III:	Kenyon	Johns Hopkins

WOMEN

	Champion	Runner-Up
Division I:	Auburn	Georgia
Division II:	Truman St	Drury
Division III:	Kenyon	Williams

Wrestling

MEN

	Champion	Runner-Up
Division I:	Oklahoma St	Minnesota
Division II:	Central Oklahoma	Nebraska-Kearney
Division III:	Wartburg	Augsburg

Winter 2002–2003 *(Cont.)*
Indoor Track and Field
MEN

	Champion	Runner-Up
Division I:	Arkansas	Auburn
Division II:	Abilene Christian	Western St (CO)
Division III:	WI–La Crosse	WI-Oshkosh

WOMEN

Division I:	Louisiana St	S Carolina/Florida
Division II:	St. Augustine's	Abilene Christian
Division III:	Wheaton (MA)	Lehman

Spring 2003
Baseball

	Champion	Runner-Up
Division I:	Rice	Stanford
Division II:	Central Missouri St	Tampa
Division III:	Chapman	Christopher Newport

Golf
MEN

	Champion	Runner-Up
Division I:	Clemson	Oklahoma St
Division II:	Francis Marion	Rollins (FL)
Division III:	Averett	Wesley

WOMEN

Division I:	Southern Cal	Pepperdine
Division II:	Rollins (FL)	Florida Southern
Division III:	Methodist	Mary-Hardin Baylor

Lacrosse
MEN

	Champion	Runner-Up
Division I:	Virginia	Johns Hopkins
Division II:	New York Tech	Limestone
Division III:	Salisbury	Middlebury

WOMEN

Division I:	Princeton	Virginia
Division II	Stonehill	Longwood
Division III:	Amherst	Middlebury

Rowing
WOMEN

	Champion	Runner-Up
Division I:	Harvard	Brown
Division II	UC-Davis	Western Washington
Division III:	Colby	University of Puget Sound

Softball

	Champion	Runner-Up
Division I:	UCLA	California
Division II:	UC-Davis	Georgia College & St
Division III:	Central (IA)	Salisbury

Tennis
MEN

	Champion	Runner-Up
Division I:	Illinois	Vanderbilt
Division II:	BYU-Hawaii	Hawaii Pacific
Division III:	Emory	Williams

Spring 2003 (Cont.)
Tennis (Cont.)
WOMEN

	Champion	Runner-Up
Division I:	Florida	Stanford
Division II:	BYU–Hawaii	Barry
Division III:	Emory	Washington & Lee

Outdoor Track and Field
MEN

	Champion	Runner-Up
Division I:	Arkansas	Auburn
Division II:	Abilene Christian	St. Augustine's
Division III:	WI–La Crosse	Lincoln

WOMEN

	Champion	Runner-Up
Division I:	Louisiana St	Texas
Division II:	Lincoln	St. Augustine's
Division III:	Wheaton (MA)	Lehman

Volleyball
MEN

Champion	Runner-Up
Lewis	Brigham Young

Water Polo
WOMEN

Champion	Runner-Up
UCLA	Stanford

NCAA Division I Individual Champions

Fall 2002
Cross Country
MEN

Champion	Runner-Up
Jorge Torres, Colorado	Alistair Cragg, Arkansas

WOMEN

Champion	Runner-Up
Shalane Flanagan, N Carolina	Kate O'Neill, Yale

Winter 2002–2003
Fencing
MEN

	Champion	Runner-Up
Sabre	Adam Crompton, Ohio St	Ivan Lee, St. John's (NY)
Foil	Nontapat Panchan, Penn St	Nitai Kfir, St. John's (NY)
Épée	Weston Kelsey, Air Force	Micha Sobieraj, Notre Dame

WOMEN

	Champion	Runner-Up
Sabre	Alexis Jemal, Rutgers	Julia Gelman, St. John's (NY)
Foil	Alicja Kryczalo, Notre Dame	Iris Zimmerman, Stanford
Épée	Katarzyna Trzopek, Penn St	Jessica Burke, Penn St

Gymnastics
MEN

	Champion	Runner-Up
All-around	Daniel Furney, Oklahoma	Raj Bhavsar, Ohio St
Vault	Andrew DiGiore, Michigan	Zack Roeder, Penn St
Parallel bars	Daniel Furney, Oklahoma	Dustin Greenhill, Army
Horizontal bar	Linas Gaveika, Iowa	Kevin Tan, Penn St
Floor exercise	Josh Landis, Oklahoma	Graham Ackerman, California
Pommel horse	Josh Landis, Oklahoma	Zack Roeder, Penn St
Rings	Kevin Tan, Penn St	Marshall Erwin, Stanford

Winter 2002–2003 (Cont.)
Gymnastics (Cont.)
WOMEN

	Champion	Runner-Up
All-around	Richelle Simpson, Nebraska	Jamie Dantzscher, UCLA
Balance beam	Kate Richardson, UCLA	Richelle Simpson, Nebraska
Uneven bars	Jamie Dantzscher, UCLA/	
	Kate Richardson, UCLA	
Floor exercise	Richelle Simpson, Nebraska	Jamie Dantzscher, UCLA
Vault	Ashley Miles, Alabama	Jamie Dantzscher, UCLA

Skiing
MEN

	Champion	Runner-Up
Slalom	Bradley Wall, Dartmouth	James Cochran, Vermont
Giant slalom	Ben Thornhill, Utah	Bradley Wall, Dartmouth
10-kilometer free	Jimmy Vika, New Mexico	Lowell Bailey, Vermont
20-kilometer classic	Chris Cook, Northern Michigan	Ethan Foster, Vermont

WOMEN

	Champion	Runner-Up
Slalom	Lina Johansson, Utah	Jenny Lathrop, Colby
Giant slalom	Jamie Kingsbury, Vermont	Lina Johansson, Utah
5-kilometer free	Katrin Smigun, Utah	Mandy Kaempf, AK-Fairbanks
15-kilometer classic	Katrin Smigun, Utah	Sigrid Aas, AK-Fairbanks

Wrestling

	Champion	Runner-Up
125 lb	Travis Lee, Cornell	Chris Fleeger, Purdue
133 lb	Johnny Thompson, Oklahoma St	Ryan Lewis, Minnesota
141 lb	Teyon Ware, Oklahoma	Dylan Long, Northern Iowa
149 lb	Eric Larkin, Arizona St	Jared Lawrence, Minnesota
157 lb	Ryan Bertin, Michigan	Alex Tirapelle, Illinois
165 lb	Matt Lackey, Illinois	Troy Letters, Lehigh
174 lb	Robbie Waller, Oklahoma	Carl Fronhofer, Pittsburgh
184 lb	Jake Rosholt, Oklahoma St	Scott Barker, Missouri
197 lb	Damion Hahn, Minnesota	Jon Trenge, Lehigh
HWT	Steve Mocco, Iowa	Kevin Hoy, Air Force

Swimming and Diving
MEN

	Champion	Time	Runner-Up	Time
50-yd freestyle	Fred Bousquet, Auburn	19.31	Mike Cavic, California	19.37
100-yd freestyle	Duje Draganja, California	42.02	Anthony Ervin, California	42.11
200-yd freestyle	Simon Burnett, Arizona	1:33.69	Chris Kemp, Texas	1:34.40
500-yd freestyle	Erik Vendt, Southern Cal	4:13.63	Robert Margalis, Georgia	4:14.24
1650-yd freestyle	Erik Vendt, Southern Cal	14:29.85	Peter Vanderkaay, Michigan	14:43.73
100-yd backstroke	Peter Marshall, Stanford	45.57	Aaron Peirsoll, Texas	45.71
200-yd backstroke	Aaron Peirsol, Texas	1:39.16*#	Markus Rogan, Stanford	1:41.37
100-yd breaststroke	Brendan Hansen, Texas	51.96	Patrick Calhoun, Auburn	53.03
200-yd breaststroke	Brendan Hansen, Texas	1:52.62*#	Vladislav Polyakov, Alabama	1:55.38
100-yd butterfly	Ian Crocker, Texas	45.67	Luis Rojas, Arizona	46.01
200-yd butterfly	Stefan Gherghel, Alabama	1:42.35	Juan Veloz, Arizona	1:42.62
200-yd IM	George Bovell, Auburn	1:42.66*#	Joe Bruckhart, California	1:44.30
400-yd IM	Robert Margalis, Georgia	3:39.92	Erik Vendt, Southern Cal	3:39.95

	Champion	Pts	Runner-Up	Pts
1-meter diving	Joona Puhakka, Arizona St	395.80	Andy Bradley, S Carolina	359.00
3-meter diving	Phil Jones, Tennessee	649.70	Clayton Moss, Kentucky	646.75
Platform	Caesar Garcia, Auburn/	575.80		
	Jason Coben, Michigan			

*NCAA record. #American record.

Winter 2002–2003 (Cont.)
Swimming and Diving (Cont.)

WOMEN

	Champion	Time	Runner-Up	Time
50-yd freestyle	Maritza Correia, Georgia	21.83	Becky Short, Auburn	22.11
100-yd freestyle	Maritza Correia, Georgia	47.29*	Becky Short, Auburn	48.53
200-yd freestyle	Jessi Perruquet, N Carolina/	1:45.01		
	Heather Kemp, Auburn			
500-yd freestyle	Flavia Rigamonti, SMU	4:37.72	Kaitlin Sandeno, Southern Cal	4:39.31
1650-yd freestyle	Flavia Rigamonti, SMU	15:43.90	Cara Lane, Virginia	15:53.49
100-yd backstroke	Natalie Coughlin, California	50.92	Kirsty Coventry, Auburn	53.01
200-yd backstroke	Natalie Coughlin, California	1:50.86	Kirsty Coventry, Auburn	1:53.17
100-yd breaststroke	Tara Kirk, Stanford	58.62	Maggie Bowen, Auburn	59.86
200-yd breaststroke	Tara Kirk, Stanford	2:08.79	Ann Poleska, Alabama	2:09.13
100-yd butterfly	Natalie Coughlin, California	50.62	Mary DeScenza, Georgia	51.93
200-yd butterfly	Mary DeScenza, Georgia	1:53.51	Emily Mason, Arizona	1:54.25
200-yd IM	Maggie Bowen, Auburn	1:55.33	Alenka Kejzar, SMU	1:57.28
400-yd IM	Maggie Bowen, Auburn	4:06.15	Emily Mason, Arizona	4:07.07

	Champion	Pts	Runner-Up	Pts
1-meter diving	Yulia Pakhalina, Houston	339.70	Jamie Sanger, Tennessee	329.90
3-meter diving	Yulia Pakhalina, Houston	657.30	Blythe Hartley, Southern Cal	585.15
Platform	Natalia Diea, Ohio St	476.65	Blythe Hartley, Southern Cal	456.90

*NCAA record.   #American record.

Indoor Track and Field

MEN

	Champion	Time/Mark	Runner-Up	Time/Mark
60-meter dash	Julien Dunkley, E Carolina	6.54	Pierre Browne, Mississippi St	6.60
60-meter hurdles	Jabari Greer, Tennessee	7.55	Shamar Sands, Auburn	7.59
200-meter dash	Leo Bookman, Kansas	20.53	Marquis Davis, Mississippi St	20.70
400-meter dash	Gary Kikaya, Tennessee	45.71	Obra Hogans, Seton Hall	45.82
800-meter run	Nate Brannen, Michigan	1:47.79	Fred Sharpe, Auburn	1:48.16
Mile run	Chris Mulvaney, Arkansas	4:05.70	John Jefferson, Indiana	4:06.46
3,000-meter run	Alistair Cragg, Arkansas	7:55.68	Adrian Blincoe, Villanova	7:56.66
5,000-meter run	Alistair Cragg, Arkansas	13:28.93	Boaz Cheboiywo, Eastern Mich	13:29.26
High jump	Jerrick Holmes, Northridge	7 ft 3¾ in	Adam Shunk, N Carolina	7 ft 2½ in
Pole vault	Brad Walker, Washington	19 ft ¼ in	Eric Eshbach, Nebraska	18 ft 3¾ in
Long jump	Brian Johnson, Southern	27 ft 2 in	Frank Tolen, Nebraska	26 ft 6¼ in
Triple jump	Allen Simms, Southern Cal	56 ft 7½ in	Aarik Wilson, Indiana	55 ft 9 in
Shot put	Carl Meyerscough, Nebraska	70 ft 6¼ in	Dan Taylor, Ohio St	69 ft 11¾ in
35-pound wt throw	Thomas Freeman, Manhattan	71 ft 2½ in	Drew Loftin, Colorado St	71 ft 1½ in

WOMEN

	Champion	Time/Mark	Runner-Up	Time/Mark
60-meter dash	Muna Lee, Louisiana St	7.17	Elva Goulbourne, Auburn	7.24
60-meter hurdles	Lolo Jones, Louisiana St	8.00	Danielle Carruthers, Indiana	8.01
200-meter dash	Muna Lee, Louisiana St	22.61	Sanya Richards, Texas	22.90
400-meter dash	LeShinda Demus, S Carolina	51.79	Sanya Richards, Texas	51.87
800-meter run	Lena Nilsson, UCLA	2:05.13	Nicole Cook, Tennessee	2:05.19
Mile run	Johanna Nilsson, Northern Ariz	4:32.49	Tiffany McWilliams, Mississippi St	4:36.51
3,000-meter run	Shalane Flanagan, N Carolina	9:01.05	Lauren Fleshman, Stanford	9:01.58
5,000-meter run	Sara Gorton, Colorado	15:39.25	Kate O'Neill, Yale	15:40.88
High jump	Nevena Lendel, SMU	6 ft 2 ¼ in	Alexandra Church, Kent St	6 ft 1½ in
Pole vault	Lacy Janson, Florida St	14 ft 7¼ in	Becky Holliday, Oregon	14 ft 3¼ in
Long jump	Elva Goulbourne, Auburn	22 ft 4¼ in	Rose Richmond, Indiana	21 ft 2 in
Triple jump	Elva Goulbourne, Auburn	45 ft 2 ½ in	Nicole Toney, Louisian St	45 ft 2¼ in
Shot put	Laura Gerraughty, N Carolina	59 ft 3 in	Jillian Camarena, Stanford	57 ft 2¾ in
20-pound wt throw	Erin Gilreath, Florida	72 ft 3¾ in	Jukina Dickerson, Florida	67 ft 10¾ in

*NCAA record.

Rifle

	Champion	Pts	Runner-Up	Pts
Smallbore	Matthew Emmons, AK-Fairbanks	1191	Bradley Wheeldon, Kentucky	1183
Air rifle	Jamie Beyerle, Alaska	395	Per Sandberg, Alaska	394

*NCAA record.

NCAA Division I Individual Champions *(Cont.)*

Spring 2003

Golf

MEN

Champion	Score	Runner-Up	Score
Alejandro Canizares, Arizona St	287	Lee Williams, Auburn	289

WOMEN

Champion	Score	Runner-Up	Score
Mikaela Parmlid, Southern Cal	287	Andrea Vander Lende, Florida	297

Outdoor Track and Field

MEN

Event	Champion	Mark	Runner-Up	Mark
100-meter dash	Mardy Scales, Middle Tenn St	10.25	Pierre Browne, Mississippi St	10.34
200-meter dash	Leo Bookman, Kansas	20.47	Jerome Mathis, Hampton	20.48
400-meter dash	Adam Steele, Minnesota	44.57	Otis Harris, S Carolina	44.57
800-meter run	Sam Burley, Pennsylvania	1:46.50	Jonathan Johnson, Texas Tech	1:46.51
1,500-meter run	Grant Robinson, Stanford	3:40.39	Chris Mulvaney, Arkansas	3:40.44
5,000-meter run	Alistair Cragg, Arkansas	13:47.87	Louis Luchini, Stanford	13:49.81
10,000-meter run	Patrick Gildea, Tennessee	29:12.18	Adam Wallace, Wisconsin	29:15.21
110-meter hurdles	Ryan Wilson, Southern Cal	13.35	Chris Pinnock, Texas A&M	13.40
400-meter hurdles	Dean Griffiths, Auburn	48.55	Rickey Harris, Florida	48.83
3,000-m steeple	Dan Lincoln, Arkansas	8:26.65	Jordan Desilets, Eastern Mich	8:29.44
High jump	David Jaworski, Southern Cal	7 ft 5¾ in	Shaun Kologinczak, Nebraska	7 ft 5¾ in
Pole vault	Eric Eshbach, Nebraska	17 ft 10½ in	Trent Powell, Brigham Young	17 ft 10½ in
Long jump	Leevan Sands, Auburn	26 ft 5 in	Tony Allmond, S Carolina	26 ft 3¾ in
Triple jump	Julien Kapek, Southern Cal	56 ft 2 in	Leevan Sands, Auburn	55 ft 6¼ in
Shot put	Carl Myerscough, Nebraska	71 ft 11 in	Christian Cantwell, Missouri	70 ft 9 in
Discus throw	Hannes Hopley, SMU	200 ft 11 in	Josh Ralston, Texas A&M	198 ft 3 in
Hammer throw	Lucais MacKay, Georgia	230 ft 3 in	Drew Loftin, Colorado St	222 ft 6 in
Javelin throw	Brian Chaput, Pennsylvania	258 ft 2 in	Rob Minnitti, Boise St	246 ft 3 in
Decathlon	Stephen Harris, Tennessee	8061 pts	Will Thomas, Connecticut	7894 pts

WOMEN

Event	Champion	Mark	Runner-Up	Mark
100-meter dash	Aleen Bailey, S Carolina	11.18	Muna Lee, Louisiana St	11.22
200-meter dash	Aleen Bailey, S Carolina	22.65	Muna Lee, Louisiana St	22.76
400-meter dash	Sanya Richards, Texas	50.58	Dee Dee Trotter, Tennessee	50.66
800-meter run	Alice Schmidt, N Carolina	2:01.16	Neisha Bernard-Thomas, LSU	2:01.75
1,500-meter run	Tiffany McWilliams, Mississippi St	4:06.75	Lena Nilsson, UCLA	4:09.86
5,000-meter run	Lauren Fleshman, Stanford	15:24.06	Shalane Flanagan, N Carolina	15:30.60
10,000-meter run	Alicia Craig, Stanford	32:40.03	Kate O'Neill, Yale	32:47.07
100-meter hurdles	Perdita Felicien, Illinois	12.74	Danielle Carruthers, Indiana	12.89
400-meter hurdles	Sheena Johnson, UCLA	54.24	Raasin McIntosh, Texas	55.02
3,000-m steeple	Kassi Andersen, Brigham Young	9:44.95	Ida Nilsson, Northern Arizona	9:46.74
High jump	Whitney Evans, Wash St	6 ft 1¼ in	Jessica Johnson, Arkansas	6 ft 1¼ in
Pole vault	Becky Holliday, Oregon	14 ft 5½ in	Connie Jerz, Arizona	14 ft 1¼ in
Long jump	Elva Goulbourne, Auburn	22 ft 2¼ in	Viktoriya Rybalko, Maine	21 ft 5¼ in
Triple jump	Ineta Radovica, Nebraska	45 ft 8½ in	Shani Marks, Minnesota	45 ft ½ in
Shot put	Becky Breisch, Nebraska	58 ft 3¼ in	Laura Gerraughty, N Carolina	57 ft 10¼ in
Discus throw	Deshaya Williams, Penn St	181 ft 9 in	Stephanie Brown, Cal Poly	181 ft 5 in
Hammer throw	Candice Scott, Florida	229 ft	Julianna Tudja, Southern Cal	218 ft 9 in
Javelin throw	Irina Kharun, Indiana	202 ft 10 in	Inga Stasiulionyte, Southern Cal	171 ft 5 in
Heptathlon	Hyleas Fountain, Georgia	5999 pts	Ellannee Richardson, Wash St	5839 pts

Tennis

MEN

Event	Champion	Score	Runner-Up
Singles	Amer Delic, Illinois	6–4, 6–3	Benedikt Dorsch, Baylor
Doubles	Rajeev Ram & Brian Wilson, Illinois	6–4, 7–5, 6–1	Oliver Maiberger & Ryan Redondo, San Diego St

WOMEN

Event	Champion	Score	Runner-Up
Singles	Amber Liu, Stanford	7–6 (7–5), 6–2	Vilmarie Castellvi, Tennessee
Doubles	Christina Fusano & Raquel Kopps-Jones, California	6–1, 6–2	Sarah Witten & Amy Trefethen, Kentucky

CHAMPIONSHIP RESULTS

Baseball

DIVISION I

Year	Champion	Coach	Score	Runner-Up	Most Outstanding Player
1947	California*	Clint Evans	8–7	Yale	No award
1948	Southern Cal	Sam Barry	9–2	Yale	No award
1949	Texas*	Bibb Falk	10–3	Wake Forest	Charles Teague, Wake Forest, 2B
1950	Texas	Bibb Falk	3–0	Washington St	Ray VanCleef, Rutgers, CF
1951	Oklahoma*	Jack Baer	3–2	Tennessee	Sidney Hatfield, Tennessee, P-1B
1952	Holy Cross	Jack Barry	8–4	Missouri	James O'Neill, Holy Cross, P
1953	Michigan	Ray Fisher	7–5	Texas	J.L. Smith, Texas, P
1954	Missouri	John (Hi) Simmons	4–1	Rollins	Tom Yewcic, Michigan St, C
1955	Wake Forest	Taylor Sanford	7–6	Western Michigan	Tom Borland, Oklahoma St, P
1956	Minnesota	Dick Siebert	12–1	Arizona	Jerry Thomas, Minnesota, P
1957	California*	George Wolfman	1–0	Penn St	Cal Emery, Penn St, P-1B
1958	Southern Cal	Rod Dedeaux	8–7†	Missouri	Bill Thom, Southern Cal, P
1959	Oklahoma St	Toby Greene	5–3	Arizona	Jim Dobson, Oklahoma St, 3B
1960	Minnesota	Dick Siebert	2–1‡	Southern Cal	John Erickson, Minnesota, 2B
1961	Southern Cal*	Rod Dedeaux	1–0	Oklahoma St	Littleton Fowler, Oklahoma St, P
1962	Michigan	Don Lund	5–4	Santa Clara	Bob Garibaldi, Santa Clara, P
1963	Southern Cal	Rod Dedeaux	5–2	Arizona	Bud Hollowell, Southern Cal, C
1964	Minnesota	Dick Siebert	5–1	Missouri	Joe Ferris, Maine, P
1965	Arizona St	Bobby Winkles	2–1#	Ohio St	Sal Bando, Arizona St, 3B
1966	Ohio St	Marty Karow	8–2	Oklahoma St	Steve Arlin, Ohio St, P
1967	Arizona St	Bobby Winkles	11–2	Houston	Ron Davini, Arizona St, C
1968	Southern Cal*	Rod Dedeaux	4–3	Southern Illinois	Bill Seinsoth, Southern Cal, 1B
1969	Arizona St	Bobby Winkles	10–1	Tulsa	John Dolinsek, Arizona St, LF
1970	Southern Cal	Rod Dedeaux	2–1	Florida St	Gene Ammann, Florida St, P
1971	Southern Cal	Rod Dedeaux	7–2	Southern Illinois	Jerry Tabb, Tulsa, 1B
1972	Southern Cal	Rod Dedeaux	1–0	Arizona St	Russ McQueen, Southern Cal, P
1973	Southern Cal*	Rod Dedeaux	4–3	Arizona St	Dave Winfield, Minnesota, P-OF
1974	Southern Cal	Rod Dedeaux	7–3	Miami (FL)	George Milke, Southern Cal, P
1975	Texas	Cliff Gustafson	5–1	S Carolina	Mickey Reichenbach, Texas, 1B
1976	Arizona	Jerry Kindall	7–1	Eastern Michigan	Steve Powers, Arizona, P-DH
1977	Arizona St	Jim Brock	2–1	S Carolina	Bob Horner, Arizona St, 3B
1978	Southern Cal*	Rod Dedeaux	10–3	Arizona St	Rod Boxberger, Southern Cal, P
1979	Cal St–Fullerton	Augie Garrido	2–1	Arkansas	Tony Hudson, Cal St–Fullerton, P
1980	Arizona	Jerry Kindall	5–3	Hawaii	Terry Francona, Arizona, LF
1981	Arizona St	Jim Brock	7–4	Oklahoma St	Stan Holmes, Arizona St, LF
1982	Miami (FL)*	Ron Fraser	9–3	Wichita St	Dan Smith, Miami (FL), P
1983	Texas*	Cliff Gustafson	4–3	Alabama	Calvin Schiraldi, Texas, P
1984	Cal St–Fullerton	Augie Garrido	3–1	Texas	John Fishel, Cal St–Fullerton, LF
1985	Miami (FL)	Ron Fraser	10–6	Texas	Greg Ellena, Miami (FL), DH
1986	Arizona	Jerry Kindall	10–2	Florida St	Mike Senne, Arizona, LF
1987	Stanford	Mark Marquess	9–5	Oklahoma St	Paul Carey, Stanford, RF
1988	Stanford	Mark Marquess	9–4	Arizona St	Lee Plemel, Stanford, P
1989	Wichita St	Gene Stephenson	5–3	Texas	Greg Brummett, Wichita St, P
1990	Georgia	Steve Webber	2–1	Oklahoma St	Mike Rebhan, Georgia, P
1991	Louisiana St	Skip Bertman	6–3	Wichita St	Gary Hymel, Louisiana St, C
1992	Pepperdine	Andy Lopez	3–2	Cal St–Fullerton	Phil Nevin, Cal St–Fullerton, 3B
1993	Louisiana St	Skip Bertman	8–0	Wichita St	Todd Walker, Louisiana St, 2B
1994	Oklahoma	Larry Cochell	13–5	Georgia Tech	Chip Glass, Oklahoma, CF
1995	Cal St–Fullerton*	Augie Garrido	11–5	Southern Cal	Mark Kotsay, Cal St–Fullerton, CF-P
1996	Louisiana St*	Skip Bertman	9–8	Miami (FL)	Pat Burrell, Miami (FL), 3B
1997	Louisiana St*	Skip Bertman	13–6	Alabama	Brandon Larson, Louisiana St, SS
1998	Southern Cal	Mike Gillespie	21–14	Arizona St	Wes Rachels, Southern Cal, 2B
1999	Miami (FL)	Jim Morris	6–5	Florida St	Marshall McDougall, FSU 3B/2B
2000	Louisiana St*	Skip Bertman	6–5	Stanford	Trey Hodges, Louisiana St, P
2001	Miami (FL)*	Jim Morris	12–1	Stanford	Charlton Jimerson, Miami (FL), OF
2002	Texas	Augie Garrido	12–6	S Carolina	Huston Street, Texas, P
2003	Rice	Wayne Graham	14–2^	Stanford	John Hudgins, Stanford, P

*Undefeated teams in College World Series play. †12 innings. ‡10 innings. #15 innings. ^Score of decisive game of best-of-three series.

DIVISION II

Year	Champion	Year	Champion	Year	Champion
1968	Chapman*	1972	Florida Southern	1976	Cal Poly–Pomona
1969	Illinois St*	1973	UC–Irvine*	1977	UC–Riverside
1970	Cal St–Northridge	1974	UC–Irvine	1978	Florida Southern
1971	Florida Southern	1975	Florida Southern	1979	Valdosta St

DIVISION II *(Cont.)*

Year	Champion	Year	Champion	Year	Champion
1980	Cal Poly–Pomona*	1990	Jacksonville St	1999	Cal St–Chico
1981	Florida Southern*	1991	Jacksonville St	2000	SE Oklahoma St
1982	UC–Riverside*	1992	Tampa*	2001	St. Mary's (TX)
1983	Cal Poly–Pomona*	1993	Tampa	2002	Columbus St
1984	Cal St–Northridge	1994	Central Missouri St	2003	Central Missouri St
1985	Florida Southern*	1995	Florida Southern*		
1986	Troy St	1996	Kennesaw St*		
1987	Troy St*	1997	Cal St–Chico*		
1988	Florida Southern*	1998	Tampa*		
1989	Cal Poly–SLO				

DIVISION III

Year	Champion	Year	Champion	Year	Champion
1976	Cal St–Stanislaus	1986	Marietta	1996	William Paterson
1977	Cal St–Stanislaus	1987	Montclair St	1997	Southern Maine
1978	Glassboro St	1988	Ithaca	1998	Eastern Connecticut St
1979	Glassboro St	1989	NC Wesleyan	1999	N Carolina Wesleyan
1980	Ithaca	1990	Eastern Connecticut St	2000	Montclair St
1981	Marietta	1991	Southern Maine	2001	St. Thomas (MN)
1982	Eastern Connecticut St	1992	William Paterson	2002	Eastern Connecticut St
1983	Marietta	1993	Montclair St	2003	Chapman
1984	Ramapo	1994	WI–Oshkosh		
1985	WI–Oshkosh	1995	La Verne		

*Undefeated teams in final series.

Cross-Country

Men
DIVISION I

Year	Champion	Coach	Pts	Runner-Up	Pts	Individual Champion	Time
1938	Indiana	Earle Hayes	51	Notre Dame	61	Greg Rice, Notre Dame	20:12.9
1939	Michigan St	Lauren Brown	54	Wisconsin	57	Walter Mehl, Wisconsin	20:30.9
1940	Indiana	Earle Hayes	65	Eastern Michigan	68	Gilbert Dodds, Ashland	20:30.2
1941	Rhode Island	Fred Tootell	83	Penn St	110	Fred Wilt, Indiana	20:30.1
1942	Indiana	Earle Hayes	57			Oliver Hunter, Notre Dame	20:18.0
	Penn St	Charles Werner	57				
1943	No meet						
1944	Drake	Bill Easton	25	Notre Dame	64	Fred Feiler, Drake	21:04.2
1945	Drake	Bill Easton	50	Notre Dame	65	Fred Feiler, Drake	21:14.2
1946	Drake	Bill Easton	42	NYU	98	Quentin Brelsford, Ohio Wesleyan	20:22.9
1947	Penn St	Charles Werner	60	Syracuse	72	Jack Milne, N Carolina	20:41.1
1948	Michigan St	Karl Schlademan	41	Wisconsin	69	Robert Black, Rhode Island	19:52.3
1949	Michigan St	Karl Schlademan	59	Syracuse	81	Robert Black, Rhode Island	20:25.7
1950	Penn St	Charles Werner	53	Michigan St	55	Herb Semper Jr, Kansas	20:31.7
1951	Syracuse	Robert Grieve	80	Kansas	118	Herb Semper Jr, Kansas	20:09.5
1952	Michigan St	Karl Schlademan	65	Indiana	68	Charles Capozzoli, Georgetown	19:36.7
1953	Kansas	Bill Easton	70	Indiana	82	Wes Santee, Kansas	19:43.5
1954	Oklahoma St	Ralph Higgins	61	Syracuse	118	Allen Frame, Kansas	19:54.2
1955	Michigan St	Karl Schlademan	46	Kansas	68	Charles Jones, Iowa	19:57.4
1956	Michigan St	Karl Schlademan	28	Kansas	88	Walter McNew, Texas	19:55.7
1957	Notre Dame	Alex Wilson	121	Michigan St	127	Max Truex, Southern Cal	19:12.3
1958	Michigan St	Francis Dittrich	79	Western Michigan	104	Crawford Kennedy, Michigan State	20:07.1
1959	Michigan St	Francis Dittrich	44	Houston	120	Al Lawrence, Houston	20:35.7
1960	Houston	John Morriss	54	Michigan St	80	Al Lawrence, Houston	19:28.2
1961	Oregon St	Sam Bell	68	San Jose St	82	Dale Story, Oregon St	19:46.6
1962	San Jose St	Dean Miller	58	Villanova	69	Tom O'Hara, Loyola (IL)	19:20.3
1963	San Jose St	Dean Miller	53	Oregon	68	Victor Zwolak, Villanova	19:35.0
1964	W Michigan	George Dales	86	Oregon	116	Elmore Banton, Ohio	20:07.5
1965	W Michigan	George Dales	81	Northwestern	114	John Lawson, Kansas	29:24.0
1966	Villanova	James Elliott	79	Kansas St	155	Gerry Lindgren, Washington St	29:01.4
1967	Villanova	James Elliott	91	Air Force	96	Gerry Lindgren, Washington St	30:45.6
1968	Villanova	James Elliott	78	Stanford	100	Michael Ryan, Air Force	29:16.8
1969	UTEP	Wayne Vandenburg	74	Villanova	88	Gerry Lindgren, Wash St	28:59.2
1970	Villanova	James Elliott	85	Oregon	86	Steve Prefontaine, Oregon	28:00.2

Men (Cont.)

DIVISION I (Cont.)

Year	Champion	Coach	Pts	Runner-Up	Pts	Individual Champion	Time
1971	Oregon	Bill Dellinger	83	Washington St	122	Steve Prefontaine, Oregon	29:14.0
1972	Tennessee	Stan Huntsman	134	E Tennessee St	148	Neil Cusack, E Tenn St	28:23.0
1973	Oregon	Bill Dellinger	89	UTEP	157	Steve Prefontaine, Oregon	28:14.0
1974	Oregon	Bill Dellinger	77	Western Kentucky	110	Nick Rose, Western Ky	29:22.0
1975	UTEP	Ted Banks	88	Washington St	92	Craig Virgin, Illinois	28:23.3
1976	UTEP	Ted Banks	62	Oregon	117	Henry Rono, Washington St	28:06.6
1977	Oregon	Bill Dellinger	100	UTEP	105	Henry Rono, Washington St	28:33.5
1978	UTEP	Ted Banks	56	Oregon	72	Alberto Salazar, Oregon	29:29.7
1979	UTEP	Ted Banks	86	Oregon	93	Henry Rono, Washington St	28:19.6
1980	UTEP	Ted Banks	58	Arkansas	152	Suleiman Nyambui, UTEP	29:04.0
1981	UTEP	Ted Banks	17	Providence	109	Mathews Motshwarateu, UTEP	28:45.6
1982	Wisconsin	Dan McClimon	59	Providence	138	Mark Scrutton, Colorado	30:12.6
1983	Vacated			Wisconsin	164	Zakarie Barie, UTEP	29:20.0
1984	Arkansas	John McDonnell	101	Arizona	111	Ed Eyestone, Brigham Young	29:28.8
1985	Wisconsin	Martin Smith	67	Arkansas	104	Timothy Hacker, Wisconsin	29:17.88
1986	Arkansas	John McDonnell	69	Dartmouth	141	Aaron Ramirez, Arizona	30:27.53
1987	Arkansas	John McDonnell	87	Dartmouth	119	Joe Falcon, Arkansas	29:14.97
1988	Wisconsin	Martin Smith	105	Northern Arizona	160	Robert Kennedy, Indiana	29:20.0
1989	Iowa St	Bill Bergan	54	Oregon	72	John Nuttall, Iowa St	29:30.55
1990	Arkansas	John McDonnell	68	Iowa St	96	Jonah Koech, Iowa St	29:05.0
1991	Arkansas	John McDonnell	52	Iowa St	114	Sean Dollman, Western Ky	30:17.1
1992	Arkansas	John McDonnell	46	Wisconsin	87	Bob Kennedy, Indiana	30:15.3
1993	Arkansas	John McDonnell	31	Brigham Young	153	Josephat Kapkory, Wash St	29:32.4
1994	Iowa St	Bill Bergan	65	Colorado	88	Martin Keino, Arizona	30:08.7
1995	Arkansas	John McDonnell	100	Northern Arizona	142	Godfrey Siamusiye, Arkansas	30:09
1996	Stanford	Vin Lananna	46	Arkansas	74	Godfrey Siamusiye, Arkansas	29:49
1997	Stanford	Vin Lananna	53	Arkansas	56	Mebrahtom Keflezighi, UCLA	28:54
1998	Arkansas	John McDonnell	97	Stanford	114	Adam Goucher, Colorado	29:26
1999	Arkansas	John McDonnell	58	Wisconsin	185	David Kimani, S Alabama	30:06.6
2000	Arkansas	John McDonnell	83	Colorado	94	Keith Kelly, Providence	30:14.5
2001	Colorado	Mark Wetmore	90	Stanford	91	Boaz Cheboiywo, E Michigan	28:47
2002	Stanford	Andrew Gerard	47	Wisconsin	107	Jorge Torres, Colorado	29:04.7

DIVISION II

Year	Champion	Year	Champion	Year	Champion
1958	Northern Illinois	1973	S Dakota St	1988	Edinboro/ Mankato St
1959	S Dakota St	1974	SW Missouri St	1989	S Dakota St
1960	Central St (OH)	1975	UC–Irvine	1990	Edinboro
1961	Southern Illinois	1976	UC–Irvine	1991	MA–Lowell
1962	Central St (OH)	1977	Eastern Illinois	1992	Adams St
1963	Emporia St	1978	Cal Poly–SLO	1993	Adams St
1964	Kentucky St	1979	Cal Poly–SLO	1994	Adams St
1965	San Diego St	1980	Humboldt St	1995	Western St
1966	San Diego St	1981	Millersville	1996	S Dakota St
1967	San Diego St	1982	Eastern Washington	1997	S Dakota
1968	Eastern Illinois	1983	Cal Poly–Pomona	1998	Adams St
1969	Eastern Illinois	1984	SE Missouri St	1999	Western St
1970	Eastern Michigan	1985	S Dakota St	2000	Western St
1971	Cal St–Fullerton	1986	Edinboro	2001	Western St
1972	N Dakota St	1987	Edinboro	2002	Western St

DIVISION III

Year	Champion	Year	Champion	Year	Champion
1973	Ashland	1984	St. Thomas (MN)	1994	Williams
1974	Mount Union	1985	Luther	1995	Williams
1975	North Central	1986	St. Thomas (MN)	1996	WI–La Crosse
1976	North Central	1987	N Central	1997	N Central
1977	Occidental	1988	WI–Oshkosh	1998	N Central
1978	N Central	1989	WI–Oshkosh	1999	N Central
1979	N Central	1990	WI–Oshkosh	2000	Calvin
1980	Carleton	1991	Rochester	2001	WI–La Crosse
1981	N Central	1992	N Central	2002	WI–Oshkosh
1982	N Central	1993	N Central		
1983	Brandeis				

Women
DIVISION I

Year	Champion	Coach	Pts	Runner-Up	Pts	Individual Champion	Time
1981	Virginia	John Vasvary	36	Oregon	83	Betty Springs, N Carolina St	16:19.0
1982	Virginia	Martin Smith	48	Stanford	91	Lesley Welch, Virginia	16:39.7
1983	Oregon	Tom Heinonen	95	Stanford	98	Betty Springs, N Carolina St	16:30.7
1984	Wisconsin	Peter Tegen	63	Stanford	89	Cathy Branta, Wisconsin	16:15.6
1985	Wisconsin	Peter Tegen	58	Iowa St	98	Suzie Tuffey, N Carolina St	16:22.5
1986	Texas	Terry Crawford	62	Wisconsin	64	Angela Chalmers, N Arizona	16:55.49
1987	Oregon	Tom Heinonen	97	N Carolina St	99	Kimberly Betz, Indiana	16:10.85
1988	Kentucky	Don Weber	75	Oregon	128	Michelle Dekkers, Indiana	16:30.0
1989	Villanova	Marty Stern	99	Kentucky	168	Vicki Huber, Villanova	15:59.86
1990	Villanova	Marty Stern	82	Providence	172	Sonia O'Sullivan, Villanova	16:06.0
1991	Villanova	Marty Stern	85	Arkansas	168	Sonia O'Sullivan, Villanova	16:30.3
1992	Villanova	Marty Stern	123	Arkansas	130	Carole Zajac, Villanova	17:01.9
1993	Villanova	Marty Stern	66	Arkansas	71	Carole Zajac, Villanova	16:40.3
1994	Villanova	John Marshall	75	Michigan	108	Jennifer Rhines, Villanova	16:31.2
1995	Providence	Ray Treacy	88	Colorado	123	Kathy Butler, Wisconsin	16:51
1996	Stanford	Beth Alford-Sullivan	101	Villanova	106	Amy Skieresz, Arizona	17:04
1997	BYU	Patrick Shane	100	Stanford	102	Carrie Tollefson, Villanova	16:58
1998	Villanova	Marcus O'Sullivan	106	BYU	110	Katie McGregor, Michigan	16:47.21
1999	BYU	Patrick Shane	72	Arkansas	125	Erica Palmer, Wisconsin	16:39.50
2000	Colorado	Mark Wetmore	117	Brigham Young	167	Kara Grgas-Wheeler, Colorado	20:30.5
2001	BYU	Patrick Shane	62	N Carolina St	148	Tara Chaplin, Arizona	20:24
2002	BYU	Patrick Shane	85	Stanford	113	Shalane Flanagan	19:36.0

DIVISION II

Year	Champion	Year	Champion	Year	Champion
1981	S Dakota St	1989	Cal Poly–SLO	1996	Adams St
1982	Cal Poly–SLO	1990	Cal Poly–SLO	1997	Adams St
1983	Cal Poly–SLO	1991	Cal Poly–SLO	1998	Adams St
1984	Cal Poly–SLO	1992	Adams St	1999	Adams St
1985	Cal Poly–SLO	1993	Adams St	2000	Western St
1986	Cal Poly–SLO	1994	Adams St	2001	Western St
1987	Cal Poly–SLO	1995	Adams St	2002	Western St
1988	Cal Poly–SLO				

DIVISION III

Year	Champion	Year	Champion	Year	Champion
1981	Central (IA)	1988	WI–Oshkosh	1996	WI–Oshkosh
1982	St. Thomas (MN)	1989	Cortland St	1997	Cortland St
1983	WI–La Crosse	1990	Cortland St	1998	Calvin
1984	St. Thomas (MN)	1991	WI–Oshkosh	1999	Calvin
1985	Franklin & Marshall	1992	Cortland St	2000	Middlebury
1986	St. Thomas (MN)	1993	Cortland St	2001	Middlebury
1987	St. Thomas (MN)/	1994	Cortland St	2002	Williams
	WI–Oshkosh	1995	Cortland St		

Fencing

Men's and Women's Combined
TEAM CHAMPIONS

Year	Champion	Coach	Pts	Runner-Up	Pts
1990	Penn St	Emmanuil Kaidanov	36	Columbia–Barnard	35
1991	Penn St	Emmanuil Kaidanov	4700	Columbia–Barnard	4200
1992	Columbia–Barnard	G. Kolombatovich/A. Kogler	4150	Penn St	3646
1993	Columbia–Barnard	G. Kolombatovich/A. Kogler	4525	Penn St	4500
1994	Notre Dame	Michael DeCicco	4350	Penn St	4075
1995	Penn St	Emmanuil Kaidanov	440	St. John's (NY)	413
1996	Penn St	Emmanuil Kaidanov	1500	Notre Dame	1190
1997	Penn St	Emmanuil Kaidanov	1530	Notre Dame	1470
1998	Penn St	Emmanuil Kaidanov	149	Notre Dame	147
1999	Penn St	Emmanuil Kaidanov	171	Notre Dame	139
2000	Penn St	Emmanuil Kaidanov	175	Notre Dame	171
2001	St. John's (NY)	Yuri Gelman	180	Penn St	172
2002	Penn St	Emmanuil Kaidanov	195	St. John's (NY)	190
2003	Notre Dame	Janusz Bednarski	182	Penn St	179

Men
TEAM CHAMPIONS

Year	Champion	Coach	Pts	Runner-Up	Pts
1941	Northwestern	Henry Zettleman	28½	Illinois	27
1942	Ohio St	Frank Riebel	34	St. John's (NY)	33½
1943–46	No tournament				

Men (Cont.)
TEAM CHAMPIONS (Cont.)

Year	Champion	Coach	Pts	Runner-Up	Pts
1947	NYU	Martinez Castello	72	Chicago	50½
1948	CCNY	James Montague	30	Navy	28
1949	Army/Rutgers	S. Velarde/D. Cetrulo	63		
1950	Navy	Joseph Fiems	67½	NYU/Rutgers	66½
1951	Columbia	Servando Velarde	69	Pennsylvania	64
1952	Columbia	Servando Velarde	71	NYU	69
1953	Pennsylvania	Lajos Csiszar	94	Navy	86
1954	Columbia	Irving DeKoff	61		
	NYU	Hugo Castello	61		
1955	Columbia	Irving DeKoff	62	Cornell	57
1956	Illinois	Maxwell Garret	90	Columbia	88
1957	NYU	Hugo Castello	65	Columbia	64
1958	Illinois	Maxwell Garret	47	Columbia	43
1959	Navy	Andre Deladrier	72	NYU	65
1960	NYU	Hugo Castello	65	Navy	57
1961	NYU	Hugo Castello	79	Princeton	68
1962	Navy	Andre Deladrier	76	NYU	74
1963	Columbia	Irving DeKoff	55	Navy	50
1964	Princeton	Stan Sieja	81	NYU	79
1965	Columbia	Irving DeKoff	76	NYU	74
1966	NYU	Hugo Castello	5–0	Army	5–2
1967	NYU	Hugo Castello	72	Pennsylvania	64
1968	Columbia	Louis Bankuti	92	NYU	87
1969	Pennsylvania	Lajos Csiszar	54	Harvard	43
1970	NYU	Hugo Castello	71	Columbia	63
1971	NYU/Columbia	Hugo Castello/Louis Bankuti	68		
1972	Detroit	Richard Perry	73	NYU	70
1973	NYU	Hugo Castello	76	Pennsylvania	71
1974	NYU	Hugo Castello	92	Wayne St (MI)	87
1975	Wayne St (MI)	Istvan Danosi	89	Cornell	83
1976	NYU	Herbert Cohen	79	Wayne St (MI)	77
1977	Notre Dame	Michael DeCicco	114*	NYU	114
1978	Notre Dame	Michael DeCicco	121	Pennsylvania	110
1979	Wayne St (MI)	Istvan Danosi	119	Notre Dame	108
1980	Wayne St (MI)	Istvan Danosi	111	Pennsylvania/MIT	106
1981	Pennsylvania	Dave Micahnik	113	Wayne St (MI)	111
1982	Wayne St (MI)	Istvan Danosi	85	Clemson	77
1983	Wayne St (MI)	Aladar Kogler	86	Notre Dame	80
1984	Wayne St (MI)	Gil Pezza	69	Penn St	50
1985	Wayne St (MI)	Gil Pezza	141	Notre Dame	140
1986	Notre Dame	Michael DeCicco	151	Columbia	141
1987	Columbia	George Kolombatovich	86	Pennsylvania	78
1988	Columbia	G. Kolombatovich/A. Kogler	90	Notre Dame	83
1989	Columbia	G. Kolombatovich/A. Kogler	88	Penn St	85

*Tie broken by a fence-off. Note: Beginning in 1990, men's and women's combined teams competed for the national championship.

INDIVIDUAL CHAMPIONS

	Foil	Sabre	Épée
1941	Edward McNamara, Northwestern	William Meyer, Dartmouth	G.H. Boland, Illinois
1942	Byron Kreiger, Wayne St (MI)	Andre Deladrier, St. John's (NY)	Ben Burtt, Ohio St
1943–46	No tournament		
1947	Abraham Balk, NYU	Oscar Parsons, Temple	Abraham Balk, NYU
1948	Albert Axelrod, CCNY	James Day, Navy	William Bryan, Navy
1949	Ralph Tedeschi, Rutgers	Alex Treves, Rutgers	Richard C. Bowman, Army
1950	Robert Nielsen, Columbia	Alex Treves, Rutgers	Thomas Stuart, Navy
1951	Robert Nielsen, Columbia	Chamberless Johnston, Princeton	Daniel Chafetz, Columbia
1952	Harold Goldsmith, CCNY	Frank Zimolzak, Navy	James Wallner, NYU
1953	Ed Nober, Brooklyn	Robert Parmacek, Penn	Jack Tori, Pennsylvania
1954	Robert Goldman, Pennsylvania	Steve Sobel, Columbia	Henry Kolowrat, Princeton
1955	Herman Velasco, Illinois	Barry Pariser, Columbia	Donald Tadrawski, Notre Dame
1956	Ralph DeMarco, Columbia	Gerald Kaufman, Columbia	Kinmont Hoitsma, Princeton
1957	Bruce Davis, Wayne St (MI)	Bernie Balaban, NYU	James Margolis, Columbia
1958	Bruce Davis, Wayne St (MI)	Art Schankin, Illinois	Roland Wommack, Navy
1959	Joe Paletta, Navy	Al Morales, Navy	Roland Wommack, Navy
1960	Gene Glazer, NYU	Mike Desaro, NYU	Gil Eisner, NYU
1961	Herbert Cohen, NYU	Israel Colon, NYU	Jerry Halpern, NYU
1962	Herbert Cohen, NYU	Barton Nisonson, Columbia	Thane Hawkins, Navy
1963	Jay Lustig, Columbia	Bela Szentivanyi, Wayne St (MI)	Larry Crum, Navy

Men (Cont.)

INDIVIDUAL CHAMPIONS (Cont.)

Foil	Sabre	Épée
1964 ....Bill Hicks, Princeton	Craig Bell, Illinois	Paul Pesthy, Rutgers
1965 ....Joe Nalven, Columbia	Howard Goodman, NYU	Paul Pesthy, Rutgers
1966 ....Al Davis, NYU	Paul Apostol, NYU	Bernhardt Hermann, Iowa
1967 ....Mike Gaylor, NYU	Todd Makler, Pennsylvania	George Masin, NYU
1968 ....Gerard Esponda, San Francisco	Todd Makler, Pennsylvania	Don Sieja, Cornell
1969 ....Anthony Kestler, Columbia	Norman Braslow, Penn	James Wetzler, Pennsylvania
1970 ....Walter Krause, NYU	Bruce Soriano, Columbia	John Nadas, Case Reserve
1971 ....Tyrone Simmons, Detroit	Bruce Soriano, Columbia	George Szunyogh, NYU
1972 ....Tyrone Simmons, Detroit	Bruce Soriano, Columbia	Ernesto Fernandez, Penn
1973 ....Brooke Makler, Pennsylvania	Peter Westbrock, NYU	Risto Hurme, NYU
1974 ....Greg Benko, Wayne St (MI)	Steve Danosi, Wayne St (MI)	Risto Hurme, NYU
1975 ....Greg Benko, Wayne St (MI)	Yuri Rabinovich, Wayne St (MI)	Risto Hurme, NYU
1976 ....Greg Benko, Wayne St (MI)	Brian Smith, Columbia	Randy Eggleton, Pennsylvania
1977 ....Pat Gerard, Notre Dame	Mike Sullivan, Notre Dame	Hans Wieselgren, NYU
1978 ....Ernest Simon, Wayne St (MI)	Mike Sullivan, Notre Dame	Bjorne Vaggo, Notre Dame
1979 ....Andrew Bonk, Notre Dame	Yuri Rabinovich, Wayne St (MI)	Carlos Songini, Cleveland St
1980 ....Ernest Simon, Wayne St (MI)	Paul Friedberg, Pennsylvania	Gil Pezza, Wayne St (MI)
1981 ....Ernest Simon, Wayne St (MI)	Paul Friedberg, Pennsylvania	Gil Pezza, Wayne St (MI)
1982 ....Alexander Flom, George Mason	Neil Hick, Wayne St (MI)	Peter Schifrin, San Jose St
1983 ....Demetrios Valsamis, NYU	John Friedberg, N Carolina	Ola Harstrom, Notre Dame
1984 ....Charles Higgs-Coulthard, Notre Dame	Michael Lofton, NYU	Ettore Bianchi, Wayne St (MI)
1985 ....Stephan Chauvel, Wayne St (MI)	Michael Lofton, NYU	Ettore Bianchi, Wayne St (MI)
1986 ....Adam Feldman, Penn St	Michael Lofton, NYU	Chris O'Loughlin, Pennsylvania
1987 ....William Mindel, Columbia	Michael Lofton, NYU	James O'Neill, Harvard
1988 ....Marc Kent, Columbia	Robert Cottingham, Columbia	Jon Normile, Columbia
1989 ....Edward Mufel, Penn St	Peter Cox, Penn St	Jon Normile, Columbia
1990 ....Nick Bravin, Stanford	David Mandell, Columbia	Jubba Beshin, Notre Dame
1991 ....Ben Atkins, Columbia	Vitali Nazlimov, Penn St	Marc Oshima, Columbia
1992 ....Nick Bravin, Stanford	Tom Strzalkowski, Penn St	Harald Bauder, Wayne St
1993 ....Nick Bravin, Stanford	Tom Strzalkowski, Penn St	Ben Atkins, Columbia
1994 ....Kwame van Leeuwen, Harvard	Tom Strzalkowski, Penn St	Harald Winkman, Princeton
1995 ....Sean McClain, Stanford	Paul Palestis, NYU	Mike Gattner, Lawrence
1996 ....Thorstein Becker, Wayne St (MI)	Maxim Pekarev, Princeton	Jeremy Kahn, Duke
1997 ....Cliff Bayer, Pennsylvania	Keith Smart, St. John's (NY)	Alden Clarke, Stanford
1998 ....Ayo Griffin, Yale	Luke LaValle, Notre Dame	George Hentea, St. John's (NY)
1999 ....Felix Reichling, Stanford	Keeth Smart, St. John's (NY)	Alex Roytblat St. John's (NY)
2000 ....Felix Reichling, Stanford	Gabor Szelle, Notre Dame	Daniel Landgren, Penn St
2001 ....William Jed Dupree, Columbia	Ivan Lee, St. John's (NY)	Soren Thompson, Princeton
2002 ....Nontapat Panchan, Penn St	Ivan Lee, St. John's (NY)	Arpád Horváth, St. John's (NY)
2003 ....Nontapat Panchan, Penn St	Adam Crompton, Ohio St	Weston Kelsey, Air Force

Women

TEAM CHAMPIONS

Year	Champion	Coach	Rec	Runner-Up	Rec
1982 ....Wayne St (MI)	Istvan Danosi	7–0	San Jose St	6–1
1983 ....Penn St	Beth Alphin	5–0	Wayne St (MI)	3–2
1984 ....Yale	Henry Harutunian	3–0	Penn St	2–1
1985 ....Yale	Henry Harutunian	3–0	Pennsylvania	2–1
1986 ....Pennsylvania	David Micahnik	3–0	Notre Dame	2–1
1987 ....Notre Dame	Yves Auriol	3–0	Temple	2–1
1988 ....Wayne St (MI)	Gil Pezza	3–0	Notre Dame	2–1
1989 ....Wayne St (MI)	Gil Pezza	3–0	Columbia-Barnard	2–1

Note: Beginning in 1990, men's and women's combined teams competed for the national championship.

INDIVIDUAL CHAMPIONS

Foil	Foil (Cont.)	Sabre (Cont.)
1982 ....Joy Ellingson, San Jose St	1995 ....Olga Kalinovskaya, Penn St	2002 ....Sada Jacobson, Yale
1983 ....Jana Angelakis, Penn St	1996 ....Olga Kalinovskaya, Penn St	2003 ....Alexis Jemal, Rutgers
1984 ....Mary Jane O'Neill, Penn	1997 ....Yelena Kalkina, Ohio St	**Épée**
1985 ....C. Bilodeaux, Columbia-Barn.	1998 ....F. Zimmermann, Stanford	1995 ....Tina Loven, St. John's (NY)
1986 ....M. Sullivan, Notre Dame	1999 ....Monique DeBruin, Stanford	1996 ....N. Dygert, St. John's (NY)
1987 ....C. Bilodeaux, Columbia-Barn.	2000 ....Eva Petschnigg, Princeton	1997 ....Magda Krol, Notre Dame
1988 ....M. Sullivan, Notre Dame	2001 ....Iris Zimmerman, Stanford	1998 ....Charlotte Walker, Penn St
1989 ....Yasemin Topcu, Wayne St (MI)	2002 ....Alicja Kryczalo, Notre Dame	1999 ....F. Zimmermann, Stanford
1990 ....Tzu Moy, Columbia-Barn.	2003 ....Alicja Kryczalo, Notre Dame	2000 ....Jessica Burke, Penn St
1991 ....Heidi Piper, Notre Dame	**Sabre**	2001 ....E. Takács, St. John's (NY)
1992 ....Olga Cheryak, Penn St	2000 ....Caroline Purcell, MIT	2002 ....Stephanie Eim, Penn St
1993 ....Olga Kalinovskaya, Penn St	2001 ....Sada Jacobson, Yale	2003 ....Katarzyna Trzopek, Penn St
1994 ....Olga Kalinovskaya, Penn St		

Field Hockey

DIVISION I

Year	Champion	Coach	Score	Runner-Up
1981	Connecticut	Diane Wright	4–1	Massachusetts
1982	Old Dominion	Beth Anders	3–2	Connecticut
1983	Old Dominion	Beth Anders	3–1 (3 OT)	Connecticut
1984	Old Dominion	Beth Anders	5–1	Iowa
1985	Connecticut	Diane Wright	3–2	Old Dominion
1986	Iowa	Judith Davidson	2–1 (2 OT)	New Hampshire
1987	Maryland	Sue Tyler	2–1 (OT)	N Carolina
1988	Old Dominion	Beth Anders	2–1	Iowa
1989	N Carolina	Karen Shelton	2–1 (3 OT)*	Old Dominion
1990	Old Dominion	Beth Anders	5–0	N Carolina
1991	Old Dominion	Beth Anders	2–0	N Carolina
1992	Old Dominion	Beth Anders	4–0	Iowa
1993	Maryland	Missy Meharg	2–1 (3 OT)*	N Carolina
1994	James Madison	Christy Morgan	2–1 (3 OT)*	N Carolina
1995	N Carolina	Karen Shelton-Scroggs	5–1	Maryland
1996	N Carolina	Karen Shelton-Scroggs	3–0	Princeton
1997	N Carolina	Karen Shelton	3–2	Old Dominion
1998	Old Dominion	Beth Anders	3–2	Princeton
1999	Maryland	Missy Meharg	2–1	Michigan
2000	Old Dominion	Beth Anders	3–1	N Carolina
2001	Michigan	Marcia Pankratz	2–0	Maryland
2002	Wake Forest	Jennifer Averill	2–0	Penn St

*Penalty strokes.

DIVISION II *(Discontinued, then renewed)*

Year	Champion	Coach	Score	Runner-Up
1981	Pfeiffer	Ellen Briggs	5–3	Bentley
1982	Lock Haven	Sharon E. Taylor	4–1	Bloomsburg
1983	Bloomsburg	Jan Hutchinson	1–0	Lock Haven
1992	Lock Haven	Sharon E. Taylor	3–1	Bloomsburg
1993	Bloomsburg	Jan Hutchinson	2–1 (2 OT)	Lock Haven
1994	Lock Haven	Sharon E. Taylor	2–1	Bloomsburg
1995	Lock Haven	Sharon E. Taylor	1–0	Bloomsburg
1996	Bloomsburg	Jan Hutchinson	1–0	Lock Haven
1997	Bloomsburg	Jan Hutchinson	2–0	Kutztown
1998	Bloomsburg	Jan Hutchinson	4–3 (OT)	Lock Haven
1999	Bloomsburg	Jan Hutchinson	2–0	Bentley
2000	Lock Haven	Pat Rudy	2–0	Bentley
2001	Bentley	Kell McGowan	4–2	E Stroudsburg
2002	Bloomsburg	Jan Hutchinson	5–0	Bentley

DIVISION III

Year	Champion	Year	Champion	Year	Champion
1981	Trenton St	1989	Lock Haven	1997	William Smith
1982	Ithaca	1990	Trenton St	1998	Middlebury
1983	Trenton St	1991	Trenton St	1999	College of New Jersey*
1984	Bloomsburg	1992	William Smith	2000	William Smith
1985	Trenton St	1993	Cortland St	2001	Cortland St
1986	Salisbury St	1994	Cortland St	2002	Rowan
1987	Bloomsburg	1995	Trenton St		*Formerly Trenton St.
1988	Trenton St	1996	College of New Jersey*		

Golf

Men

DIVISION I

Results, 1897–1938

Year	Champion	Site	Individual Champion
1897	Yale	Ardsley Casino	Louis Bayard Jr, Princeton
1898	Harvard (spring)		John Reid Jr, Yale
1898	Yale (fall)		James Curtis, Harvard
1899	Harvard		Percy Pyne, Princeton
1900	No tournament		
1901	Harvard	Atlantic City	H. Lindsley, Harvard
1902	Yale (spring)	Garden City	Charles Hitchcock Jr, Yale
1902	Harvard (fall)	Morris County	Chandler Egan, Harvard
1903	Harvard	Garden City	F.O. Reinhart, Princeton
1904	Harvard	Myopia	A.L. White, Harvard
1905	Yale	Garden City	Robert Abbott, Yale
1906	Yale	Garden City	W.E. Clow Jr, Yale
1907	Yale	Nassau	Ellis Knowles, Yale
1908	Yale	Brae Burn	H.H. Wilder, Harvard
1909	Yale	Apawamis	Albert Seckel, Princeton

Men (Cont.)
DIVISION I (Cont.)
Results, 1897–1938 (Cont.)

Year	Champion	Site	Individual Champion
1910	Yale	Essex County	Robert Hunter, Yale
1911	Yale	Baltusrol	George Stanley, Yale
1912	Yale	Ekwanok	F.C. Davison, Harvard
1913	Yale	Huntingdon Valley	Nathaniel Wheeler, Yale
1914	Princeton	Garden City	Edward Allis, Harvard
1915	Yale	Greenwich	Francis Blossom, Yale
1916	Princeton	Oakmont	J.W. Hubbell, Harvard
1917–18	No tournament		
1919	Princeton	Merion	A.L. Walker Jr, Columbia
1920	Princeton	Nassau	Jess Sweetster, Yale
1921	Dartmouth	Greenwich	Simpson Dean, Princeton
1922	Princeton	Garden City	Pollack Boyd, Dartmouth
1923	Princeton	Siwanoy	Dexter Cummings, Yale
1924	Yale	Greenwich	Dexter Cummings, Yale
1925	Yale	Montclair	Fred Lamprecht, Tulane
1926	Yale	Merion	Fred Lamprecht, Tulane
1927	Princeton	Garden City	Watts Gunn, Georgia Tech
1928	Princeton	Apawamis	Maurice McCarthy, Georgetown
1929	Princeton	Hollywood	Tom Aycock, Yale
1930	Princeton	Oakmont	G.T. Dunlap Jr, Princeton
1931	Yale	Olympia Fields	G.T. Dunlap Jr, Princeton
1932	Yale	Hot Springs	J.W. Fischer, Michigan
1933	Yale	Buffalo	Walter Emery, Oklahoma
1934	Michigan	Cleveland	Charles Yates, Georgia Tech
1935	Michigan	Congressional	Ed White, Texas
1936	Yale	North Shore	Charles Kocsis, Michigan
1937	Princeton	Oakmont	Fred Haas Jr, Louisiana St
1938	Stanford	Louisville	John Burke, Georgetown

Results, 1939–2003

Year	Champion (Score)	Coach	Runner-Up (Score)	Host or Site	Individual Champion
1939	Stanford (612)	Eddie Twiggs	Northwestern (614) Princeton (614)	Wakonda	Vincent D'Antoni, Tulane
1940	Princeton (601) Louisiana St (601)	Walter Bourne Mike Donahue		Ekwanok	Dixon Brooke, Virginia
1941	Stanford (580)	Eddie Twiggs	Louisiana St (599)	Ohio St	Earl Stewart, Louisiana St
1942	Louisiana St (590) Stanford (590)	Mike Donahue Eddie Twiggs		Notre Dame	Frank Tatum Jr, Stanford
1943	Yale (614)	William Neale Jr	Michigan (618)	Olympia Fields	Wallace Ulrich, Carleton
1944	Notre Dame (311)	George Holderith	Minnesota (312)	Inverness	Louis Lick, Minnesota
1945	Ohio St (602)	Robert Kepler	Northwestern (621)	Ohio St	John Lorms, Ohio St
1946	Stanford (619)	Eddie Twiggs	Michigan (624)	Princeton	George Hamer, Georgia
1947	Louisiana St (606)	T.P. Heard	Duke (614)	Michigan	Dave Barclay, Michigan
1948	San Jose St (579)	Wilbur Hubbard	Louisiana St (588)	Stanford	Bob Harris, San Jose St
1949	N Texas (590)	Fred Cobb	Purdue (600) Texas (600)	Iowa St	Harvie Ward, N Carolina
1950	N Texas (573)	Fred Cobb	Purdue (577)	New Mexico	Fred Wampler, Purdue
1951	N Texas (588)	Fred Cobb	Ohio St (589)	Ohio St	Tom Nieporte, Ohio St
1952	N Texas (587)	Fred Cobb	Michigan (593)	Purdue	Jim Vickers, Oklahoma
1953	Stanford (578)	Charles Finger	N Carolina (580)	Broadmoor	Earl Moeller, Oklahoma St
1954	SMU (572)	Graham Ross	N Texas (573)	Houston Hillman	Robbins, Memphis St
1955	Louisiana St (574)	Mike Barbato	N Texas (583)	Tennessee	Joe Campbell, Purdue
1956	Houston (601)	Dave Williams	N Texas (602) Purdue (602)	Ohio St	Rick Jones, Ohio St
1957	Houston (602)	Dave Williams	Stanford (603)	Broadmoor	Rex Baxter Jr., Houston
1958	Houston (570)	Dave Williams	Oklahoma St (582)	Williams	Phil Rodgers, Houston
1959	Houston (561)	Dave Williams	Purdue (571)	Oregon	Dick Crawford, Houston
1960	Houston (603)	Dave Williams	Purdue (607) Oklahoma St (607)	Broadmoor	Dick Crawford, Houston
1961	Purdue (584)	Sam Voinoff	Arizona St (595)	Lafayette	Jack Nicklaus, Ohio St
1962	Houston (588)	Dave Williams	Oklahoma St (598)	Duke	Kermit Zarley, Houston
1963	Oklahoma St (581)	Labron Harris	Houston (582)	Wichita St	R.H. Sikes, Arkansas
1964	Houston (580)	Dave Williams	Oklahoma St (587)	Broadmoor	Terry Small, San Jose St
1965	Houston (577)	Dave Williams	Cal St–LA (587)	Tennessee	Marty Fleckman, Houston
1966	Houston (582)	Dave Williams	San Jose St (586)	Stanford	Bob Murphy, Florida
1967	Houston (585)	Dave Williams	Florida (588)	Shawnee, PA	Hale Irwin, Colorado

Men (Cont.)
DIVISION I (Cont.)
Results, 1939–2003 (Cont.)

Year	Champion (Score)	Coach	Runner-Up (Score)	Host or Site	Individual Champion
1968	Florida (1154)	Buster Bishop	Houston (1156)	New Mexico St	Grier Jones, Oklahoma St
1969	Houston (1223)	Dave Williams	Wake Forest (1232)	Broadmoor	Bob Clark, Cal St–LA
1970	Houston (1172)	Dave Williams	Wake Forest (1182)	Ohio St	John Mahaffey, Houston
1971	Texas (1144)	George Hannon	Houston (1151)	Arizona	Ben Crenshaw, Texas
1972	Texas (1146)	George Hannon	Houston (1159)	Cape Coral	Ben Crenshaw, Texas
					Tom Kite, Texas
1973	Florida (1149)	Buster Bishop	Oklahoma St (1159)	Oklahoma St	Ben Crenshaw, Texas
1974	Wake Forest (1158)	Jess Haddock	Florida (1160)	San Diego St	Curtis Strange, Wake Forest
1975	Wake Forest (1156)	Jess Haddock	Oklahoma St (1189)	Ohio St	Jay Haas, Wake Forest
1976	Oklahoma St (1166)	Mike Holder	Brigham Young (1173)	New Mexico	Scott Simpson, USC
1977	Houston (1197)	Dave Williams	Oklahoma St (1205)	Colgate	Scott Simpson, USC
1978	Oklahoma St (1140)	Mike Holder	Georgia (1157)	Oregon	David Edwards, Oklahoma St
1979	Ohio St (1189)	James Brown	Oklahoma St (1191)	Wake Forest	Gary Hallberg, Wake Forest
1980	Oklahoma St (1173)	Mike Holder	Brigham Young (1177)	Ohio St	Jay Don Blake, Utah St
1981	BYU (1161)	Karl Tucker	Oral Roberts (1163)	Stanford	Ron Commans, USC
1982	Houston (1141)	Dave Williams	Oklahoma St (1151)	Pinehurst	Billy Ray Brown, Houston
1983	Oklahoma St (1161)	Mike Holder	Texas (1168)	Fresno St	Jim Carter, Arizona St
1984	Houston (1145)	Dave Williams	Oklahoma St (1146)	Houston	John Inman, N Carolina
1985	Houston (1172)	Dave Williams	Oklahoma St (1175)	Florida	Clark Burroughs, Ohio St
1986	Wake Forest (1156)	Jess Haddock	Oklahoma St (1160)	Wake Forest	Scott Verplank, Oklahoma St
1987	Oklahoma St (1160)	Mike Holder	Wake Forest (1176)	Ohio St	Brian Watts, Oklahoma St
1988	UCLA (1176)	Eddie Merrins	UTEP (1179)	Southern Cal	E.J. Pfister, Oklahoma St
			Oklahoma (1179)		
			Oklahoma St (1179)		
1989	Oklahoma (1139)	Gregg Grost	Texas (1158)	Oklahoma Oklahoma St	Phil Mickelson, Arizona St
1990	Arizona St (1155)	Steve Loy	Florida (1157)	Florida	Phil Mickelson, Arizona St
1991	Oklahoma St (1161)	Mike Holder	N Carolina (1168)	San Jose St	Warren Schutte, UNLV
1992	Arizona (1129)	Rick LaRose	Arizona St (1136)	New Mexico	Phil Mickelson, Arizona St
1993	Florida (1145)	Buddy Alexander	Georgia Tech (1146)	Kentucky	Todd Demsey, Arizona St
1994	Stanford (1129)	Wally Goodwin	Texas (1133)	McKinney, TX	Justin Leonard, Texas
1995	Oklahoma St* (1156)	Mike Holder	Stanford (1156)	Ohio St	Chip Spratlin, Auburn
1996	Arizona St (1186)	Randy Lein	UNLV (1189)	Chattanooga	Tiger Woods, Stanford
1997	Pepperdine (1148)	John Geiberger	Wake Forest (1151)	Evanston, IL	Charles Warren, Clemson
1998	UNLV (1118)	Dwaine Knight	Clemson (1121)	Albuquerque	James McLean, Minnesota
1999	Georgia (1180)	Chris Haack	Oklahoma St (1183)	Chaska, MN	Donald Luke, Northwestern
2000	Oklahoma St* (1116)	Mike Holder	Georgia Tech (1116)	Opelika, AL	Charles Howell, Oklahoma St
2001	Florida (1126)	Buddy Alexander	Clemson (1144)	Durham, NC	Nick Gilliam, Florida
2002	Minnesota (1134)	Brad James	Georgia Tech	Ohio St	Troy Matteson, Ga. Tech
2003	Clemson (1191)	Larry Penley	Oklahoma St	Oklahoma St	A. Canizares, Arizona St

*Won sudden death playoff. Notes: Match play, 1897–1964; par-70 tournaments held in 1969, 1973 and 1989; par-71 tournaments held in 1968, 1981 and 1988; all other championships par-72 tournaments. Scores are based on 4 rounds instead of 2 after 1967.

DIVISION II

Year	Champion	Year	Champion	Year	Champion
1963	SW Missouri St	1977	Troy St	1991	Florida Southern
1964	Southern Illinois	1978	Columbus St	1992	Columbus St
1965	Middle Tennessee St	1979	UC–Davis	1993	Abilene Christian
1966	Cal St–Chico	1980	Columbus St	1994	Columbus St
1967	Lamar	1981	Florida Southern	1995	Florida Southern
1968	Lamar	1982	Florida Southern	1996	Florida Southern
1969	Cal St–Northridge	1983	SW Texas St	1997	Columbus St
1970	Rollins	1984	Troy St	1998	Florida Southern
1971	New Orleans	1985	Florida Southern	1999	Florida Southern
1972	New Orleans	1986	Florida Southern	2000	Florida Southern
1973	Cal St–Northridge	1987	Tampa	2001	W Florida
1974	Cal St–Northridge	1988	Tampa	2002	Rollins
1975	UC–Irvine	1989	Columbus St	2003	Francis Marion
1976	Troy St	1990	Florida Southern		

Note: Par-71 tournaments held in 1967, 1970, 1976–78, 1985, 1988 and 2001; par-70 tournament held in 1996; all other championships par-72 tournaments.

Men (Cont.)

DIVISION III

Year	Champion	Year	Champion	Year	Champion
1975	Wooster	1985	Cal St–Stanislaus	1995	Methodist (NC)
1976	Cal St–Stanislaus	1986	Cal St–Stanislaus	1996	Methodist (NC)
1977	Cal St–Stanislaus	1987	Cal St–Stanislaus	1997	Methodist (NC)
1978	Cal St–Stanislaus	1988	Cal St–Stanislaus	1998	Methodist (NC)
1979	Cal St–Stanislaus	1989	Cal St–Stanislaus	1999	Methodist (NC)
1980	Cal St–Stanislaus	1990	Methodist (NC)	2000	Greensboro
1981	Cal St–Stanislaus	1991	Methodist (NC)	2001	WI–Eau Claire
1982	Ramapo	1992	Methodist (NC)	2002	Guilford
1983	Allegheny	1993	UC–San Diego	2003	Averett
1984	Cal St–Stanislaus	1994	Methodist (NC)		

Note: All championships par-72 except for 1986, 1988 and 2001, which were par-71; fourth round of 1975 championships canceled as a result of bad weather; first round of 1988 championships canceled as a result of rain.

Women

DIVISION I

Year	Champion	Coach	Score	Runner-Up	Score	Individual Champion
1982	Tulsa	Dale McNamara	1191	Texas Christian	1227	Kathy Baker, Tulsa
1983	Texas Christian	Fred Warren	1193	Tulsa	1196	Penny Hammel, Miami (FL)
1984	Miami (FL)	Lela Cannon	1214	Arizona St	1221	Cindy Schreyer, Georgia
1985	Florida	Mimi Ryan	1218	Tulsa	1233	Danielle Ammaccapane, Arizona St
1986	Florida	Mimi Ryan	1180	Miami (FL)	1188	Page Dunlap, Florida
1987	San Jose St	Mark Gale	1187	Furman	1188	Caroline Keggi, New Mexico
1988	Tulsa	Dale McNamara	1175	Georgia	1182	Melissa McNamara, Tulsa
				Arizona	1182	
1989	San Jose St	Mark Gale	1208	Tulsa	1209	Pat Hurst, San Jose St
1990	Arizona St	Linda Vollstedt	1206	UCLA	1222	Susan Slaughter, Arizona
1991	UCLA*	Jackie Steinmann	1197	San Jose St	1197	Annika Sorenstam, Arizona
1992	San Jose St	Mark Gale	1171	Arizona	1175	Vicki Goetze, Georgia
1993	Arizona St	Linda Vollstedt	1187	Texas	1189	Charlotta Sorenstam, Texas
1994	Arizona St	Linda Vollstedt	1189	Southern Cal	1205	Emilee Klein, Arizona St
1995	Arizona St	Linda Vollstedt	1155	San Jose St	1181	Kristel Mourgue d'Algue, Arizona St
1996	Arizona*	Rick LaRose	1240	San Jose St	1240	Marisa Baena, Arizona
1997	Arizona St	Linda Vollstedt	1178	San Jose St	1180	Heather Bowie, Texas
1998	Arizona St	Linda Vollstedt	1155	Florida	1173	Jennifer Rosales, USC
1999	Duke	Dan Brooks	895	Arizona St/Georgia	903	Grace Park, Arizona St
2000	Arizona	Todd McCorkle	1175	Stanford	1196	Jenna Daniels, Arizona
2001	Georgia	Todd McCorkle	1176	Duke	1179	Candy Hannemann, Duke
2002	Duke	Dan Brooks	1164	Arizona/Auburn/Texas	1160	Virada Nirapathpongporn, Duke
2003	Southern Cal	Andrea Gaston	1197	Pepperdine	1212	Mikaela Parmlid, Southern Cal

*Won sudden death playoff. Note: Par-74 tournaments held in 1983 and 1988; par-72 tournament held in 1990, 2000 and 2001; all other championships par-73 tournaments.

DIVISIONS II AND III

Year	Champion	Year	Champion
1996	Methodist (NC)	1998	Methodist (NC)
1997	Lynn	1999	Methodist (NC)

DIVISION II

Year	Champion
2000	Florida Southern
2001	Florida Southern
2002	Florida Southern
2003	Rollins

DIVISION III

Year	Champion
2000	Methodist (NC)
2001	Methodist (NC)
2002	Methodist (NC)
2003	Methodist (NC)

Gymnastics

Men

TEAM CHAMPIONS

Year	Champion	Coach	Pts	Runner-Up	Pts
1938	Chicago	Dan Hoffer	22	Illinois	18
1939	Illinois	Hartley Price	21	Army	17
1940	Illinois	Hartley Price	20	Navy	17
1941	Illinois	Hartley Price	68.5	Minnesota	52.5
1942	Illinois	Hartley Price	39	Penn St	30
1943–47	No tournament				
1948	Penn St	Gene Wettstone	55	Temple	34.5
1949	Temple	Max Younger	28	Minnesota	18
1950	Illinois	Charley Pond	26	Temple	25
1951	Florida St	Hartley Price	26	Illinois	23.5
				Southern Cal	23.5
1952	Florida St	Hartley Price	89.5	Southern Cal	75
1953	Penn St	Gene Wettstone	91.5	Illinois	68
1954	Penn St	Gene Wettstone	137	Illinois	68
1955	Illinois	Charley Pond	82	Penn St	69
1956	Illinois	Charley Pond	123.5	Penn St	67.5
1957	Penn St	Gene Wettstone	88.5	Illinois	80
1958	Michigan St	George Szypula	79		
	Illinois	Charley Pond	79		
1959	Penn St	Gene Wettstone	152	Illinois	87.5
1960	Penn St	Gene Wettstone	112.5	Southern Cal	65.5
1961	Penn St	Gene Wettstone	88.5	Southern Illinois	80.5
1962	Southern Cal	Jack Beckner	95.5	Southern Illinois	75
1963	Michigan	Newton Loken	129	Southern Illinois	73
1964	Southern Illinois	Bill Meade	84.5	Southern Cal	69.5
1965	Penn St	Gene Wettstone	68.5	Washington	51.5
1966	Southern Illinois	Bill Meade	187.200	California	185.100
1967	Southern Illinois	Bill Meade	189.550	Michigan	187.400
1968	California	Hal Frey	188.250	Southern Illinois	188.150
1969	Iowa	Mike Jacobson	161.175	Penn St	160.450
	Michigan*	Newton Loken		Colorado St	
1970	Michigan	Newton Loken	164.150	Iowa St	164.050
				New Mexico St	
1971	Iowa St	Ed Gagnier	319.075	Southern Illinois	316.650
1972	Southern Illinois	Bill Meade	315.925	Iowa St	312.325
1973	Iowa St	Ed Gagnier	325.150	Penn St	323.025
1974	Iowa St	Ed Gagnier	326.100	Arizona St	322.050
1975	California	Hal Frey	437.325	Louisiana St	433.700
1976	Penn St	Gene Wettstone	432.075	Louisiana St	425.125
1977	Indiana St	Roger Counsil	434.475		
	Oklahoma	Paul Ziert	434.475		
1978	Oklahoma	Paul Ziert	439.350	Arizona St	437.075
1979	Nebraska	Francis Allen	448.275	Oklahoma	446.625
1980	Nebraska	Francis Allen	563.300	Iowa St	557.650
1981	Nebraska	Francis Allen	284.600	Oklahoma	281.950
1982	Nebraska	Francis Allen	285.500	UCLA	281.050
1983	Nebraska	Francis Allen	287.800	UCLA	283.900
1984	UCLA	Art Shurlock	287.300	Penn St	281.250
1985	Ohio St	Michael Willson	285.350	Nebraska	284.550
1986	Arizona St	Don Robinson	283.900	Nebraska	283.600
1987	UCLA	Art Shurlock	285.300	Nebraska	284.750
1988	Nebraska	Francis Allen	288.150	Illinois	287.150
1989	Illinois	Yoshi Hayasaki	283.400	Nebraska	282.300
1990	Nebraska	Francis Allen	287.400	Minnesota	287.300
1991	Oklahoma	Greg Buwick	288.025	Penn St	285.500
1992	Stanford	Sadao Hamada	289.575	Nebraska	288.950
1993	Stanford	Sadao Hamada	276.500	Nebraska	275.500
1994	Nebraska	Francis Allen	288.250	Stanford	285.925
1995	Stanford	Sadao Hamada	232.400	Nebraska	231.525
1996	Ohio St	Peter Kormann	232.150	California	231.775
1997	California	Barry Weiner	233.825	Oklahoma	232.725
1998	Caliornia	Barry Weiner	231.200	Iowa	229.675
1999	Michigan	Kurt Golder	232.550	Ohio St	230.850
2000	Penn St	Randy Jepson	231.975	Michigan	231.850
2001	Ohio St	Miles Avery	218.125	Oklahoma	217.775
2002	Oklahoma	Mark Williams	219.300	Ohio St	218.650
2003	Oklahoma	Mark Williams	222.600	Ohio St	220.700

*Trampoline.

Men *(Cont.)*

INDIVIDUAL CHAMPIONS

ALL-AROUND	HORIZONTAL BAR	PARALLEL BARS
1938.....Joe Giallombardo, Illinois	1938.....Bob Sears, Army	1938.....Erwin Beyer, Chicago
1939.....Joe Giallombardo, Illinois	1939.....Adam Walters, Temple	1939.....Bob Sears, Army
1940.....Joe Giallombardo, Illinois	1940.....Norm Boardman, Temple	1940.....Bob Hanning, Minnesota
Paul Fina, Illinois	1941.....Newt Loken, Minnesota	1941.....Caton Cobb, Illinois
1941.....Courtney Shanken, Chicago	1942.....Norm Boardman,.Temple	1942.....Hal Zimmerman, Penn St
1942.....Newt Loken, Minnesota	1948.....Joe Calvetti, Illinois	1948.....Ray Sorenson, Penn St
1948.....Ray Sorenson, Penn St	1949.....Bob Stout, Temple	.1949.....Joe Kotys, Kent
1949.....Joe Kotys, Kent	1950.....Joe Kotys, Kent	Mel Stout, Michigan St
1950.....Joe Kotys, Kent	1951.....Bill Roetzheim, Florida St	1950.....Joe Kotys, Kent
1951.....Bill Roetzheim, Florida St	1952.....Charles Simms, USC	1951.....Jack Beckner, USC
1952.....Jack Beckner, Southern Cal	1953.....Hal Lewis, Navy	1952.....Jack Beckner, USC
1953.....Jean Cronstedt, Penn St	1954.....Jean Cronstedt, Penn St	1953.....Jean Cronstedt, Penn St
1954.....Jean Cronstedt, Penn St	1955.....Carlton Rintz, Michigan St	1954.....Jean Cronstedt, Penn St
1955.....Karl Schwenzfeier, Penn St	1956.....Ronnie Amster, Florida St	1955.....Carlton Rintz, Michigan St
1956.....Don Tonry, Illlinois	1957.....Abie Grossfeld, Illinois	1956.....Armando Vega, Penn St
1957.....Armando Vega, Penn St	1958.....Abie Grossfeld, Illinois	1957.....Armando Vega, Penn St
1958.....Abie Grossfeld, Illinois	1959.....Stanley Tarshis, Mich St	1958.....Tad Muzyczko, Mich St
1959.....Armando Vega, Penn St	1960.....Stanley Tarshis, Mich St	1959.....Armando Vega, Penn St
1960.....Jay Werner, Penn St	1961.....Bruno Klaus, Southern Ill	1960.....Robert Lynn, Southern Cal
1961.....Gregor Weiss, Penn St	1962.....Robert Lynn, USC	1961.....Fred Tijerina, Southern Ill
1962.....Robert Lynn, Southern Cal	1963.....Gil Larose, Michigan	Jeff Cardinalli, Springfield
1963.....Gil Larose, Michigan	1964.....Ron Barak, USC	1962.....Robert Lynn, Southern Cal
1964.....Ron Barak, Southern Cal	1965.....Jim Curzi, Michigan St	1963.....Arno Lascari, Michigan
1965.....Mike Jacobson, Penn St	Mike Jacobsen, Penn St	1964.....Ron Barak, Southern Cal
1966.....Steve Cohen, Penn St	1966.....Rusty Rock, Cal St–	1965.....Jim Curzi, Michigan St
1967.....Steve Cohen, Penn St	Northridge	1966.....Jim Curzi, Michigan St
1968.....Makoto Sakamoto, USC	1967.....Rich Grigsby, Cal St–	1967.....Makoto Sakamoto, USC
1969.....Mauno Nissinen, Wash	Northridge	1968.....Makoto Sakamoto, USC
1970.....Yoshi Hayasaki, Wash	1968.....Makoto Sakamoto, USC	1969.....Ron Rapper, Michigan
1971.....Yoshi Hayasaki, Wash	1969.....Bob Manna, New Mexico	1970.....Ron Rapper, Michigan
1972.....Steve Hug, Stanford	1970.....Yoshi Hayasaki, Wash	1971.....Brent Simmons, Iowa St
1973.....Steve Hug, Stanford	1971.....Brent Simmons, Iowa St	Tom Dunn, Penn St
Marshall Avener, Penn St	1972.....Tom Lindner, Souhern Ill	1972.....Dennis Mazur, Iowa St
1974.....Steve Hug, Stanford	1973.....Jon Aitken, New Mexico	1973.....Steve Hug, Stanford
1975.....Wayne Young, BYU	1974.....Rick Banley, Indiana St	1974.....Steve Hug, Stanford
1976.....Peter Kormann,	1975.....Rich Larsen, Iowa St	1975.....Yoichi Tomita,
Southern Conn St	1976.....Tom Beach, California	Long Beach St
1977.....Kurt Thomas, Indiana St	1977.....John Hart, UCLA	1976.....Gene Whelan, Penn St
1978.....Bart Conner, Oklahoma	1978.....Mel Cooley, Washington	1977.....Kurt Thomas, Indiana St
1979.....Kurt Thomas, Indiana St	1979.....Kurt Thomas, Indiana St	1978.....John Corritore, Michigan
1980.....Jim Hartung, Nebraska	1980.....Philip Cahoy, Nebraska	1979.....Kurt Thomas, Indiana St
1981.....Jim Hartung, Nebraska	1981.....Philip Cahoy, Nebraska	1980.....Philip Cahoy, Nebraska
1982.....Peter Vidmar, UCLA	1982.....Peter Vidmar, UCLA	1981.....Philip Cahoy, Nebraska
1983.....Peter Vidmar, UCLA	1983.....Scott Johnson, Nebraska	Peter Vidmar, UCLA
1984.....Mitch Gaylord, UCLA	1984.....Charles Lakes, Illinois	Jim Hartung, Nebraska
1985.....Wes Suter, Nebraska	1985.....Dan Hayden, Arizona St	1982.....Jim Hartung, Nebraska
1986.....Jon Louis, Stanford	Wes Suter, Nebraska	1983.....Scott Johnson, Nebraska
1987.....Tom Schlesinger, Nebraska	1986.....Dan Hayden, Arizona St	1984.....Tim Daggett, UCLA
1988.....Vacated†	1987.....David Moriel, UCLA	1985.....Dan Hayden, Arizona St
1989.....Patrick Kirsey, Nebraska	1988.....Vacated†	Noah Riskin, Ohio St
1990.....Mike Racanelli, Ohio St	1989.....Vacated†	Seth Riskin, Ohio St
1991.....John Roethlisberger, Minn	1990.....Chris Waller, UCLA	1986.....Dan Hayden, Arizona St
1992.....John Roethlisberger, Minn	1991.....Luis Lopez, New Mexico	1987.....Kevin Davis, Nebraska
1993.....John Roethlisberger, Minn	1992.....Jair Lynch, Stanford	Tom Schlesinger, Nebraska
1994.....Dennis Harrison, Nebraska	1993.....Steve McCain, UCLA	1988.....Kevin Davis, Nebraska
1995.....Richard Grace, Nebraska	1994.....Jim Foody, UCLA	1989.....Vacated†
1996.....Blaine Wilson, Ohio St	1995.....Rick Kieffer, Nebraska	1990.....Patrick Kirksey, Nebraska
1997.....Blaine Wilson, Ohio St	1996.....Carl Imhauser, Temple	1991.....Scott Keswick, UCLA
1998.....Travis Romagnoli, Illinois	1997.....Marshall Nelson,Nebraska	John Roethlisberger, Minn
1999.....Justin Hardabura, Nebraska	1998.....Todd Bishop, Oklahoma	1992.....Dom Minicucci, Temple
2000.....Jamie Natalie, Ohio St	1999.....Todd Bishop, Oklahoma	1993.....Jair Lynch, Stanford
2001.....Jamie Natalie, Ohio St	2000.....Michael Ashe, California	1994.....Richard Grace, Nebraska
2002.....Raj Bhavsar, Ohio St	2001.....Michael Ashe, California	1995.....Richard Grace, Nebraska
2003.....Daniel Furney, Oklahoma	2002.....Daniel Diaz-Luong, Mich.	1996.....Jamie Ellis, Stanford
	2003.....Linas Gaveika, Iowa	Blaine Wilson, Ohio St
		1997.....Marshall Nelson, Nebraska
		1998.....Marshall Nelson, Nebraska

Men (Cont.)
INDIVIDUAL CHAMPIONS (Cont.)

PARALLEL BARS (CONT.)
1999.....Justin Toman, Michigan
2000.....Kris Zimmerman, Michigan
Justin Toman, Michigan
2001 ....Raj Bhavsar, Ohio St
2002 ....Cody Moore, California
2003 ....Daniel Furney, Oklahoma

VAULT
1938.....Erwin Beyer, Chicago
1939.....Marv Forman, Illinois
1940.....Earl Shanken, Chicago
1941.....Earl Shanken, Chicago
1942.....Earl Shanken, Chicago
1948.....Jim Peterson, Minnesota
1962.....Bruno Klaus, Southern Ill
1963.....Gil Larose, Michigan
1964.....Sidney Oglesby, Syracuse
1965.....Dan Millman, California
1966.....Frank Schmitz, S Illinois
1967.....Paul Mayer, S Illinois
1968.....Bruce Colter, Cal St–
Los Angeles
1969.....Dan Bowles, California
Jack McCarthy, Illinois
1970.....Doug Boger, Arizona
1971.....Pat Mahoney, Cal St–
Northridge
1972.....Gary Morava, Southern Ill
1973.....John Crosby, S Conn St
1974.....Greg Goodhue, Oklahoma
1975.....Tom Beach, California
1976.....Sam Shaw, Cal St-Fullerton
1977.....Steve Wejmar, Wash
1978.....Ron Galimore, Louisiana St
1979.....Leslie Moore, Oklahoma
1980.....Ron Galimore, Iowa St
1981.....Ron Galimore, Iowa St
1982.....Randall Wickstrom, Cal
Steve Elliott, Nebraska
1983.....Chris Riegel, Nebraska
Mark Oates, Oklahoma
1984.....Chris Riegel, Nebraska
1985.....Derrick Cornelius, Cort. St
1986.....Chad Fox, New Mexico
1987.....Chad Fox, New Mexico
1988.....Chad Fox, New Mexico
1989.....Chad Fox, New Mexico
1990.....Brad Hayashi, UCLA
1991.....Adam Carton, Penn St
1992.....Jason Hebert, Syracuse
1993.....Steve Wiegel, N Mexico
1994.....Steve McCain, UCLA
1995.....Ian Bachrach, Stanford
1996.....Jay Thornton, Iowa
1997.....Blaine Wilson, Ohio St
1998.....Travis Romagnoli, Illinois
1999.....Guard Young, BYU
2000.....Guard Young, BYU
2001.....Daren Lynch, Ohio St
2002.....Dan Gill, Stanford
2003.....Andrew DiGiore, Michigan

POMMEL HORSE
1938.....Erwin Beyer, Chicago
1939.....Erwin Beyer, Chicago
1940.....Harry Koehnemann, Illinois
1941.....Caton Cobb, Illinois
1942.....Caton Cobb, Illinois
1948.....Steve Greene, Penn St
1949.....Joe Berenato, Temple
1950.....Gene Rabbitt, Syracuse

POMMEL HORSE (CONT.)
1951.....Joe Kotys, Kent
1952.....Frank Bare, Illinois
1953.....Carlton Rintz, Michigan St
1954.....Robert Lawrence, Penn St
1955.....Carlton Rintz, Michigan St
1956.....James Brown, Cal St–L.A.
1957.....John Davis, Illinois
1958.....Bill Buck, Iowa
1959.....Art Shurlock, California
1960.....James Fairchild, California
1961.....James Fairchild, California
1962.....Mike Aufrecht, Illinois
1963.....Russ Mills, Yale
1964.....Russ Mills, Yale
1965.....Bob Elsinger, Springfield
1966.....Gary Hoskins, Cal St–L.A.
1967.....Keith McCanless, Iowa
1968.....Jack Ryan, Colorado
1969.....Keith McCanless, Iowa
1970.....Russ Hoffman, Iowa St
John Russo, Wisconsin
1971.....Russ Hoffman, Iowa St
1972.....Russ Hoffman, Iowa St
1973.....Ed Slezak, Indiana St
1974.....Ted Marcy, Stanford
1975.....Ted Marcy, Stanford
1976.....Ted Marcy, Stanford
1977.....Chuck Walter, New Mexico
1978.....Mike Burke, Northern Ill
1979.....Mike Burke, Northern Ill
1980.....David Stoldt, Illinois
1981.....Mark Bergman, California
Steve Jennings, New Mexico
1982.....Peter Vidmar, UCLA
Steve Jennings, New Mexico
1983.....Doug Kieso, Northern Ill
1984.....Tim Daggett, UCLA
1985.....Tony Pineda, UCLA
1986.....Curtis Holdsworth, UCLA
1987.....Li Xiao Ping, Cal St-Fullerton
1988....Vacated†
Mark Sohn, Penn St
1989.....Mark Sohn, Penn St
Chris Waller, UCLA
1990.....Mark Sohn, Penn St
1991.....Mark Sohn, Penn St
1992.....Che Bowers, Nebraska
1993.....John Roethlisberger, Minn
1994.....Jason Bertram, California
1995.....Drew Durbin, Ohio St
1996.....Drew Durbin, Ohio St
1997.....Drew Durbin, Ohio St
1998.....Josh Birckelbaw, California
1999.....Brandon Stefaniak, Penn St
2000.....Brandon Stefaniak, Penn St
Don Jackson, Iowa
2001 ....Clay Strother, Minnesota
2002 ....Clay Strother, Minnesota
2003 ....Josh Landis, Oklahoma

FLOOR EXERCISE
1941.....Lou Fina, Illinois
1953.....Bob Sullivan, Illinois
1954.....Jean Cronstedt, Penn St
1955.....Don Faber, UCLA
1956.....Jamile Ashmore, Florida St
1957.....Norman Marks, Cal St–
Los Angeles
1958.....Abie Grossfeld, Illinois
1959.....Don Tonry, Illinois

FLOOR EXERCISE (CONT.)
1960.....Ray Hadley, Illinois
1961.....Robert Lynn, Southern Cal
1962.....Robert Lynn, Southern Cal
1963.....Tom Seward, Penn St
Mike Henderson, Michigan
1964.....Rusty Mitchell, S Illinois
1965.....Frank Schmitz, S Illinois
1966.....Frank Schmitz, S Illinois
1967.....Dave Jacobs, Michigan
1968.....Toby Towson, Michigan St
1969.....Toby Towson, Michigan St
1970.....Tom Proulx, Colorado St
1971.....Stormy Eaton, New Mexico
1972.....Odessa Lovin, Oklahoma
1973.....Odessa Lovin, Oklahoma
1974.....Doug Fitzjarrell, Iowa St
1975.....Kent Brown, Arizona St
1976.....Bob Robbins, Colorado St
1977.....Ron Galimore, Louisiana St
1978.....Curt Austin, Iowa St
1979.....Mike Wilson, Oklahoma
Bart Conner, Oklahoma
1980.....Steve Elliott, Nebraska
1981.....James Yuhashi, Oregon
1982.....Steve Elliott, Nebraska
1983.....Scott Johnson, Nebraska
David Branch, Arizona St
Donnie Hinton, Arizona St
1984.....Kevin Ekburg, Northern Ill
1985.....Wes Suter, Nebraska
1986.....Jerry Burrell, Arizona St
Brian Ginsberg, UCLA
1987.....Chad Fox, New Mexico
1988.....Chris Wyatt, Temple
1989.....Jody Newman, Arizona St
1990.....Mike Racanelli, Ohio St
1991.....Brad Hayashi, UCLA
1992.....Brian Winkler, Michigan
1993.....Richard Grace, Nebraska
1994.....Mark Booth, Stanford
1995.....Jay Thornton, Iowa
1996.....Ian Bachrach, Stanford
1997.....Jeremy Killen, Oklahoma
1998.....Darin Gerlach, Temple
1999.....Jason Hardabura, Nebraska
2000.....Jamie Natalie, Ohio St
2001.....Clay Strother, Minnesota
2002.....Clay Strother, Minnesota
2003.....Josh Landis, Oklahoma

RINGS
1959.....Armando Vega, Penn St
1960.....Sam Garcia, Southern Cal
1961.....Fred Orlofsky, Southern Ill
1962.....Dale Cooper, Michigan St
1963.....Dale Cooper, Michigan St
1964.....Chris Evans, Arizona St
1965.....Glenn Gailis, Iowa
1966.....Ed Gunny, Michigan St
1967.....Josh Robison, California
1968.....Pat Arnold, Arizona
1969.....Paul Vexler, Penn St
Ward Maythaler, Iowa St
1970.....Dave Seal, Indiana St
1971.....Charles Ropiequet, S Illinois
1972.....Dave Seal, Indiana St
1973.....Bob Mahorney, Indiana St
1974.....Keith Heaver, Iowa St
1975.....Keith Heaver, Iowa St

Men (Cont.)
INDIVIDUAL CHAMPIONS (Cont.)

RINGS (CONT.)

1976.....Doug Wood, Iowa St	1988.....Paul O'Neill, New Mexico	1998.....Dan Fink, Oklahoma
1977.....Doug Wood, Iowa St	1989.....Vacated†	1999.....Cortney Bramwell, BYU
1978.....Scott McEldowney, Oregon	Paul O'Neill, New Mexico	2000.....Cortney Bramwell, BYU
1979.....Kirk Mango, Northern Ill	1990.....Wayne Cowden, Penn St	2001.....Chris Lakeman, Penn St
1980.....Jim Hartung, Nebraska	1991.....Adam Carton, Penn St	2002.....Marshall Erwin, Stanford
1981.....Jim Hartung, Nebraska	1992.....Scott Keswick, UCLA	2003.....Kevin Tan, Penn St
1982.....Jim Hartung, Nebraska	1993.....Chris LaMorte, N Mexico	
1983.....Alex Schwartz, UCLA	1994.....Chris LaMorte, N Mexico	
1984.....Tim Daggett, UCLA	1995.....Dave Frank, Temple	
1985.....Mark Diab, Iowa St	1996.....Scott McCall, Will. & Mary	
1986.....Mark Diab, Iowa St	Blaine Wilson, Ohio St	
1987.....Paul O'Neill, Hou. Baptist	1997.....Blaine Wilson, Ohio St	

†Championships won by Miguel Rubio (All Around, 1988; Horizontal Bar, 1988–89) and Alfonso Rodriguez (Pommel Horse, 1988; Rings, 1989; Parallel Bars, 1989) were vacated by action of the NCAA Committee on Infractions.

DIVISION II (Discontinued)

Year	Champion	Coach	Pts	Runner-Up	Pts
1968	Cal St–Northridge	Bill Vincent	179.400	Springfield	178.050
1969	Cal St–Northridge	Bill Vincent	151.800	Southern Connecticut St	145.075
1970	Northwestern Louisiana	Armando Vega	160.250	Southern Connecticut St	159.300
1971	Cal St–Fullerton	Dick Wolfe	158.150	Springfield	156.987
1972	Cal St–Fullerton	Dick Wolfe	160.550	Southern Connecticut St	153.050
1973	Southern Connecticut St	Abe Grossfeld	160.750	Cal St–Northridge	158.700
1974	Cal St–Fullerton	Dick Wolfe	309.800	Southern Connecticut St	309.400
1975	Southern Connecticut St	Abe Grossfeld	411.650	IL–Chicago	398.800
1976	Southern Connecticut St	Abe Grossfeld	419.200	IL–Chicago	388.850
1977	Springfield	Frank Wolcott	395.950	Cal St–Northridge	381.250
1978	IL–Chicago	C. Johnson/A. Gentile	406.850	Cal St–Northridge	400.400
1979	IL–Chicago	Clarence Johnson	418.550	WI–Oshkosh	385.650
1980	WI–Oshkosh	Ken Allen	260.550	Cal St–Chico	256.050
1981	WI–Oshkosh	Ken Allen	209.500	Springfield	201.550
1982	WI–Oshkosh	Ken Allen	216.050	E Stroudsburg	211.200
1983	E Stroudsburg	Bruno Klaus	258.650	WI–Oshkosh	257.850
1984	E Stroudsburg	Bruno Klaus	270.800	Cortland St	246.350

Women
TEAM CHAMPIONS

Year	Champion	Coach	Pts	Runner-Up	Pts
1982	Utah	Greg Marsden	148.60	Cal St–Fullerton	144.10
1983	Utah	Greg Marsden	184.65	Arizona St	183.30
1984	Utah	Greg Marsden	186.05	UCLA	185.55
1985	Utah	Greg Marsden	188.35	Arizona St	186.60
1986	Utah	Greg Marsden	186.95	Arizona St	186.70
1987	Georgia	Suzanne Yoculan	187.90	Utah	187.55
1988	Alabama	Sarah Patterson	190.05	Utah	189.50
1989	Georgia	Suzanne Yoculan	192.65	UCLA	192.60
1990	Utah	Greg Marsden	194.900	Alabama	194.575
1991	Alabama	Sarah Patterson	195.125	Utah	194.375
1992	Utah	Greg Marsden	195.650	Georgia	194.600
1993	Georgia	Suzanne Yoculan	198.000	Alabama	196.825
1994	Utah	Greg Marsden	196.400	Alabama	196.350
1995	Utah	Greg Marsden	196.650	Alabama	196.425
				Michigan	196.425
1996	Alabama	Sarah Patterson	198.025	UCLA	197.475
1997	UCLA	Valorie Kondos	197.150	Arizona St	196.850
1998	Georgia	Suzanne Yoculan	197.725	Florida	196.350
1999	Georgia	Suzanne Yoculan	196.850	Michigan	196.55
2000	UCLA	Valorie Kondos	197.300	Utah	196.875
2001	UCLA	Valorie Kondos	197.575	Georgia	197.400
2002	Alabama	Sarah Patterson	197.575	Georgia	197.25
2003	UCLA	Valorie Kondos Field	197.825	Alabama	197.275

Women (Cont.)
INDIVIDUAL CHAMPIONS

ALL-AROUND

1982.....Sue Stednitz, Utah
1983.....Megan McCunniff, Utah
1984......Megan McCunniff-Marsden, Utah
1985......Penney Hauschild, Alabama
1986......Penney Hauschild, Alabama
      Jackie Brummer, Arizona St
1987.....Kelly Garrison-Steves, Oklahoma
1988.....Kelly Garrison-Steves, Oklahoma
1989....Corrinne Wright, Georgia
1990....Dee Dee Foster, Alabama
1991.....Hope Spivey, Georgia
1992.....Missy Marlowe, Utah
1993.....Jenny Hansen, Kentucky
1994.....Jenny Hansen, Kentucky
1995.....Jenny Hansen, Kentucky
1996.....Meredith Willard, Alabama
1997.....Kim Arnold, Georgia
1998.....Kim Arnold, Georgia
1999....Theresa Kulikowski, Utah
2000.....Mohini Bhardwaj, UCLA
      Heather Brink, Nebraska
2001 ....Onnis Willis, UCLA
      Elise Ray, Michigan
2002 ....Jamie Dantzscher, UCLA
2003 ....Richelle Simpson, Neb.

VAULT

1982.....Elaine Alfano, Utah
1983.....Elaine Alfano, Utah
1984.....Megan Marsden, Utah
1985.....Elaine Alfano, Utah
1986.....Kim Neal, Arizona St
      Pam Loree, Penn St
1987.....Yumi Mordre, Washington
1988.....Jill Andrews, UCLA
1989.....Kim Hamilton, UCLA
1990.....Michele Bryant, Nebraska
1991.....Anna Basaldva, Arizona
1992.....Tammy Marshall, Mass.
      Heather Stepp, Georgia
      Kristein Kenoyer, Utah
1993.....Heather Stepp, Georgia
1994.....Jenny Hansen, Kentucky
1995.....Jenny Hansen, Kentucky
1996.....Leah Brown, Georgia
1997.....Susan Hines, Florida
1998.....Susan Hines, Florida
1999.....Heidi Moneymaker, UCLA
2000.....Heather Brink, Nebraska
2001.....Cory Fritzinger, Georgia

VAULT (Cont.)

2002.....Jamie Dantzscher, UCLA
2003.....Ashley Miles, Alabama

BALANCE BEAM

1982.....Sue Stednitz, Utah
1983.....Julie Goewey, Cal St–Fullerton
1984.....Heidi Anderson, Oregon St
1985.....Lisa Zeis, Arizona St
1986.....Jackie Brummer, Arizona St
1987.....Yumi Mordre, Washington
1988.....Kelly Garrison-Steves, Oklahoma
1989.....Jill Andrews, UCLA
      Joy Selig, Oregon St
1990.....Joy Selig, Oregon St
1991.....Missy Marlowe, Utah
1992.....Missy Marlowe, Utah
1992   Dana Dobransky, Alabama
1993.....Dana Dobransky, Alabama
1994.....Jenny Hansen, Kentucky
1995.....Jenny Hansen, Kentucky
1996.....Summer Reid, UUtah
1997.....Summer Reid, Utah
      Elizabeth Reid, Arizona St
1998   Larissa Fontaine, Stanford
      Susan Hines, Florida
1999.....Theresa Kulikowski, Utah
2000.....Lena Degteva, UCLA
2001.....Theresa Kulikowski, Utah
2002.....Elise Ray, Michigan
2003.....Kate Richardson, UCLA

FLOOR EXERCISE

1982.....Mary Ayotte-Law, Oregon St
1983.....Kim Neal, Arizona St
1984.....Maria Anz, Florida
1985...,.Lisa Mitzel, Utah
1986.....Lisa Zeis, Arizona St
      P. Hauschild, Alabama
1987.....Kim Hamilton, UCLA
1988.....Kim Hamilton, UCLA
1989.....Corrinne Wright, Georgia
      Kim Hamilton, UCLA
1990.....Joy Selig, Oregon St
1991.....Hope Spivey, Georgia
1992.....Missy Marlowe, Utah

FLOOR EXERCISE (Cont.)

1993.....Heather Stepp, Georgia
      Tammy Marshall, Mass.
      Amy Durham, Oregon St
1994......Hope Spivey-Sheeley, UGA
1995.....Jenny Hansen, Kentucky
      Stella Umeh, UCLA
      Leslie Angeles, Georgia
1996.....Heidi Hornbeek, Arizona
      Kim Kelly, Alabama
1997.....Leah Brown, Georgia
1998.....Kim Arnold, Georgia
      Jenni Beathard, Georgia
      Betsy Hamm, Florida
1999.....Marny Oestreng, BGSU
2000.....Suzanne Sears, Georgia
2001.....Mohini Bhardwaj, UCLA
2002.....Jamie Dantzscher, UCLA
      Nicole Arnstad, LSU
2003.....Richelle Simpson, Neb.

UNEVEN BARS

1982.....Lisa Shirk, Pittsburgh
1983.....Jeri Cameron, Arizona St
1984.....Jackie Brummer, Arizona St
1985......Penney Hauschild, Alabama
1986.....Lucy Wener, Georgia
1987.....Lucy Wener, Georgia
1988.....Kelly Garrison-Steves, Oklahoma
1989.....Lucy Wener, Georgia
1990.....Marie Roethlisberger, Minnesota
1991.....Kelly Macy, Georgia
1992.....Missy Marlowe, Utah
1993.....Agina Simpkins, Georgia
      Beth Wymer, Michigan
1994.....Sandy Woolsey, Utah
      Beth Wymer, Michigan
      Lori Strong, Georgia
1995.....Beth Wymer, Michigan
1996.....Stephanie Woods, Alabama
1997.....Jenni Beathard, Georgia
1998.....Karin Lichey, Georgia
      Stella Umeh, UCLA
1999.....Angie Leionard, Utah
2000.....Mohini Bhardwaj, UCLA
2001.....Yvonne Tousek, UCLA
2002.....Andree' Pickens, Alabama
2003.....Jamie Dantzscher, UCLA
      Kate Richardson, UCLA

Ice Hockey

Men

DIVISION I

Year	Champion	Coach	Score	Runner-Up	Most Outstanding Player
1948	Michigan	Vic Heyliger	8–4	Dartmouth	Joe Riley, Dartmouth, F
1949	Boston College	John Kelley	4–3	Dartmouth	Dick Desmond, Dartmouth, G
1950	Colorado College	Cheddy Thompson	13–4	Boston University	Ralph Bevins, Boston University, G
1951	Michigan	Vic Heyliger	7–1	Brown	Ed Whiston, Brown, G
1952	Michigan	Vic Heyliger	4–1	Colorado College	Kenneth Kinsley, Colorado Coll, G
1953	Michigan	Vic Heyliger	7–3	Minnesota	John Matchefts, Michigan, F
1954	Rensselaer	Ned Harkness	5–4 (OT)	Minnesota	Abbie Moore, Rensselaer, F
1955	Michigan	Vic Heyliger	5–3	Colorado College	Philip Hilton, Colorado College, D
1956	Michigan	Vic Heyliger	7–5	Michigan Tech	Lorne Howes, Michigan, G
1957	Colorado College	Thomas Bedecki	13–6	Michigan	Bob McCusker, Colorado Coll, F
1958	Denver	Murray Armstrong	6–2	N Dakota	Murray Massier, Denver, F
1959	N Dakota	Bob May	4–3 (OT)	Michigan St	Reg Morelli, N Dakota, F
1960	Denver	Murray Armstrong	5–3	Michigan Tech	Bob Marquis, Boston University, F
1961	Denver	Murray Armstrong	12–2	St. Lawrence	Barry Urbanski, Boston Univ, G
1962	Michigan Tech	John MacInnes	7–1	Clarkson	Louis Angotti, Michigan Tech, F
1963	N Dakota	Barney Thorndycraft	6–5	Denver	Al McLean, N Dakota, F
1964	Michigan	Allen Renfrew	6–3	Denver	Bob Gray, Michigan, G
1965	Michigan Tech	John MacInnes	8–2	Boston College	Gary Milroy, Michigan Tech, F
1966	Michigan St	Amo Bessone	6–1	Clarkson	Gaye Cooley, Michigan St, G
1967	Cornell	Ned Harkness	4–1	Boston University	Walt Stanowski, Cornell, D
1968	Denver	Murray Armstrong	4–0	N Dakota	Gerry Powers, Denver, G
1969	Denver	Murray Armstrong	4–3	Cornell	Keith Magnuson, Denver, D
1970	Cornell	Ned Harkness	6–4	Clarkson	Daniel Lodboa, Cornell, D
1971	Boston University	Jack Kelley	4–2	Minnesota	Dan Brady, Boston University, G
1972	Boston University	Jack Kelley	4–0	Cornell	Tim Regan, Boston University, G
1973	Wisconsin	Bob Johnson	4–2	Vacated	Dean Talafous, Wisconsin, F
1974	Minnesota	Herb Brooks	4–2	Michigan Tech	Brad Shelstad, Minnesota, G
1975	Michigan Tech	John MacInnes	6–1	Minnesota	Jim Warden, Michigan Tech, G
1976	Minnesota	Herb Brooks	6–4	Michigan Tech	Tom Vanelli, Minnesota, F
1977	Wisconsin	Bob Johnson	6–5 (OT)	Michigan	Julian Baretta, Wisconsin, G
1978	Boston University	Jack Parker	5–3	Boston College	Jack O'Callahan, Boston Univ, D
1979	Minnesota	Herb Brooks	4–3	N Dakota	Steve Janaszak, Minnesota, G
1980	N Dakota	John Gasparini	5–2	Northern Michigan	Doug Smail, N Dakota, F
1981	Wisconsin	Bob Johnson	6–3	Minnesota	Marc Behrend, Wisconsin, G
1982	N Dakota	John Gasparini	5–2	Wisconsin	Phil Sykes, N Dakota, F
1983	Wisconsin	Jeff Sauer	6–2	Harvard	Marc Behrend, Wisconsin, G
1984	Bowling Green	Jerry York	5–4 (OT)	MN–Duluth	Gary Kruzich, Bowling Green, G
1985	Rensselaer	Mike Addesa	2–1	Providence	Chris Terreri, Providence, G
1986	Michigan St	Ron Mason	6–5	Harvard	Mike Donnelly, Michigan St, F
1987	N Dakota	John Gasparini	5–3	Michigan St	Tony Hrkac, N Dakota, F
1988	Lake Superior St	Frank Anzalone	4–3 (OT)	St. Lawrence	Bruce Hoffort, Lake Superior St, G
1989	Harvard	Bill Cleary	4–3 (OT)	Minnesota	Ted Donato, Harvard, F
1990	Wisconsin	Jeff Sauer	7–3	Colgate	Chris Tancill, Wisconsin, F
1991	N Michigan	Rick Comley	8–7 (3OT)	Boston University	Scott Beattie, N Michigan, F
1992	Lake Superior St	Jeff Jackson	4–2	Wisconsin	Paul Constantin, Lake Superior St, F
1993	Maine	Shawn Walsh	5–4	Lake Superior St	Jim Montgomery, Maine, F
1994	Lake Superior St	Jeff Jackson	9–1	Boston University	Sean Tallaire, Lake Superior St, F
1995	Boston University	Jack Parker	6–2	Maine	Chris O'Sullivan, Boston Univ, F
1996	Michigan	Red Berenson	3–2 (OT)	Colorado College	Brendan Morrison, Michigan, F
1997	N Dakota	Dean Blais	6–4	Boston University	Matt Henderson, N Dakota, F
1998	Michigan	Red Berenson	3–2 (OT)	Boston Coll	Marty Turco, Michigan, G
1999	Maine	Shawn Walsh	3–2 (OT)	New Hampshire	Alfie Michaud, Maine, G
2000	N Dakota	Dean Blais	4–2	Boston College	Lee Goren, N Dakota, F
2001	Boston College	Jerry York	3–2 (OT)	N Dakota	Chuck Kobasew, Boston College, F
2002	Minnesota	Don Lucia	4–3 (OT)	Maine	Grant Potulny, Minnesota, F
2003	Minnesota	Don Lucia	5–1	New Hampshire	Thomas Vanek, Minnesota, F

DIVISION II (Discontinued)

Year	Champion	Coach	Score	Runner-Up
1978	Merrimack	Thom Lawler	12–2	Lake Forest
1979	Lowell	Bill Riley Jr	6–4	Mankato St
1980	Mankato St	Don Brose	5–2	Elmira
1981	Lowell	Bill Riley Jr	5–4	Plattsburgh St
1982	Lowell	Bill Riley Jr	6–1	Plattsburgh St
1983	RIT	Brian Mason	4–2	Bemidji St
1984	Bemidji St	R.H. (Bob) Peters	14–4*	Merrimack
1993	Bemidji St	R.H. (Bob) Peters	15–6*	Mercyhurst
1994	Bemidji St	R.H. (Bob) Peters	7–6*	AL–Huntsville
1995	Bemidji St	R.H. (Bob) Peters	11–6*	Mercyhurst

DIVISION II (Cont.)

Year	Champion	Coach	Score	Runner-Up
1996	AL–Huntsville	Doug Ross	10–1*	Bemidji St
1997	Bemidji St	R.H. (Bob) Peters	7–4*	AL–Huntsville
1998	AL–Huntsville	Doug Ross	11–4*	Bemidji St
1999	St. Michael's (VT)	Lou DiMasi	12–9*	New Hamp. Coll

*Two-game, total-goal series.

DIVISION III

Year	Champion	Coach	Score	Runner-Up
1984	Babson	Bob Riley	8–0	Union (NY)
1985	RIT	Bruce Delventhal	5–1	Bemidji St
1986	Bemidji St	R.H. (Bob) Peters	8–5	Vacated
1987	Vacated			Oswego St
1988	WI–River Falls	Rick Kozuback	7–1, 3–5, 3–0	Elmira
1989	WI–Stevens Point	Mark Mazzoleni	3–3, 3–2	RIT
1990	WI–Stevens Point	Mark Mazzoleni	10–1, 3–6, 1–0	Plattsburgh St
1991	WI–Stevens Point	Mark Mazzoleni	6–2	Mankato St
1992	Plattsburgh St	Bob Emery	7–3	WI–Stevens Point
1993	WI–Stevens Point	Joe Baldarotta	4–3	WI–River Falls
1994	WI–River Falls	Dean Talafous	6–4	WI–Superior
1995	Middlebury	Bill Beaney	1–0	Fredonia St
1996	Middlebury	Bill Beaney	3–2	RIT
1997	Middlebury	Bill Beaney	3–2	WI–Superior
1998	Middlebury	Bill Beaney	2–1	WI–Stevens Point
1999	Middlebury	Bill Beaney	5–0	WI–Superior
2000	Norwich	Michael McShane	2–1	St. Thomas (MN)
2001	Plattsburgh	Bob Emery	6–2	RIT
2002	WI–Superior	Dan Stauber	3–2	Norwich
2003	Norwich	Michael McShane	2–1	Oswego St

Women
DIVISION I

Year	Champion	Coach	Score	Runner-Up
2001	Minnesota-Duluth	Shannon Miller	4–2	St. Lawrence
2002	Minnesota-Duluth	Shannon Miller	3–2	Brown
2003	Minnesota-Duluth	Shannon Miller	4–3 (2ot)	Harvard

Lacrosse

Men
DIVISION I

Year	Champion	Coach	Score	Runner-Up
1971	Cornell	Richie Moran	12–6	Maryland
1972	Virginia	Glenn Thiel	13–12	Johns Hopkins
1973	Maryland	Bud Beardmore	10–9 (2 OT)	Johns Hopkins
1974	Johns Hopkins	Bob Scott	17–12	Maryland
1975	Maryland	Bud Beardmore	20–13	Navy
1976	Cornell	Richie Moran	16–13 (OT)	Maryland
1977	Cornell	Richie Moran	16–8	Johns Hopkins
1978	Johns Hopkins	Henry Ciccarone	13–8	Cornell
1979	Johns Hopkins	Henry Ciccarone	15–9	Maryland
1980	Johns Hopkins	Henry Ciccarone	9–8 (2 OT)	Virginia
1981	N Carolina	Willie Scroggs	14–13	Johns Hopkins
1982	N Carolina	Willie Scroggs	7–5	Johns Hopkins
1983	Syracuse	Roy Simmons Jr	17–16	Johns Hopkins
1984	Johns Hopkins	Don Zimmerman	13–10	Syracuse
1985	Johns Hopkins	Don Zimmerman	11–4	Syracuse
1986	N Carolina	Willie Scroggs	10–9 (OT)	Virginia
1987	Johns Hopkins	Don Zimmerman	11–10	Cornell
1988	Syracuse	Roy Simmons Jr	13–8	Cornell
1989	Syracuse	Roy Simmons Jr	13–12	Johns Hopkins
1990	Syracuse	Roy Simmons Jr	21–9	Loyola (MD)
1991	N Carolina	Dave Klarmann	18–13	Towson St
1992	Princeton	Bill Tierney	10–9	Syracuse
1993	Syracuse	Roy Simmons Jr	13–12	N Carolina
1994	Princeton	Bill Tierney	9–8 (OT)	Virginia
1995	Syracuse	Roy Simmons Jr	13–9	Maryland
1996	Princeton	Bill Tierney	13–12 (OT)	Virginia
1997	Princeton	Bill Tierney	19–7	Maryland
1998	Princeton	Bill Tierney	15–5	Maryland
1999	Virginia	Dom Starsia	12–10	Syracuse

Men (Cont.)

DIVISION I (Cont.)

Year	Champion	Coach	Score	Runner-Up
2000	Syracuse	John Desko	13–7	Princeton
2001	Princeton	Bill Tierney	10–9 (OT)	Syracuse
2002	Syracuse	John Desko	13–12	Princeton
2003	Virginia	Dom Starsia	9–7	Johns Hopkins

DIVISION II (Discontinued, then renewed)

Year	Champion	Coach	Score	Runner-Up
1974	Towson St	Carl Runk	18–17 (OT)	Hobart
1975	Cortland St	Chuck Winters	12–11	Hobart
1976	Hobart	Jerry Schmidt	18–9	Adelphi
1977	Hobart	Jerry Schmidt	23–13	Washington (MD)
1978	Roanoke	Paul Griffin	14–13	Hobart
1979	Adelphi	Paul Doherty	17–12	MD–Baltimore County
1980	MD–Baltimore County	Dick Watts	23–14	Adelphi
1981	Adelphi	Paul Doherty	17–14	Loyola (MD)
1993	Adelphi	Kevin Sheehan	11–7	LIU–C.W. Post
1994	Springfield	Keith Bugbee	15–12	New York Tech
1995	Adelphi	Sandy Kapatos	12–10	Springfield
1996	LIU–C.W. Post	Tom Postel	15–10	Adelphi
1997	New York Tech	Jack Kaley	18–11	Adelphi
1998	Adelphi	Sandy Kapatos	18–6	LIU–C.W. Post
1999	Adelphi	Sandy Kapatos	11–8	LIU–C.W. Post
2000	Limestone	Mike Cerino	10–9	LIU–C.W. Post
2001	Adelphi	Sandy Kapatos	14–10	Limestone
2002	Limestone	T.W. Johnson	11–9	New York Tech
2003	New York Tech	Jack Kaley	9–4	Limestone

DIVISION III

Year	Champion	Coach	Score	Runner-Up
1980	Hobart	Dave Urick	11–8	Cortland St
1981	Hobart	Dave Urick	10–8	Cortland St
1982	Hobart	Dave Urick	9–8 (OT)	Washington (MD)
1983	Hobart	Dave Urick	13–9	Roanoke
1984	Hobart	Dave Urick	12–5	Washington (MD)
1985	Hobart	Dave Urick	15–8	Washington (MD)
1986	Hobart	Dave Urick	13–10	Washington (MD)
1987	Hobart	Dave Urick	9–5	Ohio Wesleyan
1988	Hobart	Dave Urick	18–9	Ohio Wesleyan
1989	Hobart	Dave Urick	11–8	Ohio Wesleyan
1990	Hobart	B.J. O'Hara	18–6	Washington (MD)
1991	Hobart	B.J. O'Hara	12–11	Salisbury St
1992	Nazareth (NY)	Scott Nelson	13–12	Hobart
1993	Hobart	B.J. O'Hara	16–10	Ohio Wesleyan
1994	Salisbury St	Jim Berkman	15–9	Hobart
1995	Salisbury St	Jim Berkman	22–13	Nazareth
1996	Nazareth	Scott Nelson	11–10 (OT)	Washington (MD)
1997	Nazareth	Scott Nelson	15–14 (OT)	Washington (MD)
1998	Washington (MD)	John Haus	16–10	Nazareth
1999	Salisbury St	Jim Berkman	13–6	Middlebury
2000	Middlebury	Erin Quinn	16–12	Salisbury St
2001	Middlebury	Erin Quinn	15–10	Gettysburg
2002	Middlebury	Erin Quinn	14–9	Gettysburg
2003	Salisbury	Jim Berkman	14–13	Middlebury

Women*

DIVISION I

Year	Champion	Coach	Score	Runner-Up
2001	Maryland	Cindy Timchal	14–13 (OT)	Georgetown
2002	Princeton	Chris Sailer	12–7	Georgetown
2003	Princeton	Chris Sailer	8–7 (OT)	Virginia

DIVISION II

Year	Champion	Coach	Score	Runner-Up
2001	LIU–C.W. Post	Karen MacCrate	13–9	W Chester
2002	Westchester	Ginny Martino	11–6	Stonehill
2003	Stonehill	Michael Daly	9–8	Longwood

*Divisions I and II competed for a single championship until 2001.

Women (Cont.)
DIVISIONS I AND II

Year	Champion	Coach	Score	Runner-Up
1982	Massachusetts	Pamela Hixon	9–6	Trenton St
1983	Delaware	Janet Smith	10–7	Temple
1984	Temple	Tina Sloan Green	6–4	Maryland
1985	New Hampshire	Marisa Didio	6–5	Maryland
1986	Maryland	Sue Tyler	11–10	Penn St
1987	Penn St	Susan Scheetz	7–6	Temple
1988	Temple	Tina Sloan Green	15–7	Penn St
1989	Penn St	Susan Scheetz	7–6	Harvard
1990	Harvard	Carole Kleinfelder	8–7	Maryland
1991	Virginia	Jane Miller	8–6	Maryland
1992	Maryland	Cindy Timchal	11–10	Harvard
1993	Virginia	Jane Miller	8–6 (OT)	Princeton
1994	Princeton	Chris Sailer	10–7	Virginia
1995	Maryland	Cindy Timchal	13–5	Princeton
1996	Maryland	Cindy Timchal	10–5	Virginia
1997	Maryland	Cindy Timchal	8–7	Loyola (MD)
1998	Maryland	Cindy Timchal	11–5	Virginia
1999	Maryland	Cindy Timchal	16–6	Virginia
2000	Maryland	Cindy Timchal	16–8	Princeton

DIVISION III

Year	Champion	Score	Runner-Up	Year	Champion	Score	Runner-Up
1985	Trenton St	7–4	Ursinus	1995	Trenton St	14–13	William Smith
1986	Ursinus	12–10	Trenton St	1996	Trenton St	15–8	Middlebury
1987	Trenton St	8–7 (OT)	Ursinus	1997	Middlebury	14–9	College of NJ*
1988	Trenton St	14–11	William Smith	1998	Coll of NJ	14–9	Williams
1989	Ursinus	8–6	Trenton St	1999	Middlebury	10–9	Amherst
1990	Ursinus	7–6	St. Lawrence	2000	Coll of NJ	14–8	Williams
1991	Trenton St	7–6	Ursinus	2001	Middlebury	11–10	Amherst
1992	Trenton St	5–3	William Smith	2002	Middlebury	12–6	College of NJ*
1993	Trenton St	10–9	William Smith	2003	Amherst	11–9	Middlebury
1994	Trenton St	29–11	William Smith				

*Formerly Trenton St

Rifle

						Individual Champions	
Year	Champion	Coach	Score	Runner-Up	Score	Air Rifle	Smallbore
1980	Tennessee Tech	James Newkirk	6201	W Virginia	6150	Rod Fitz-Randolph, Tennessee Tech	Rod Fitz-Randolph, Tennessee Tech
1981	Tennessee Tech	James Newkirk	6139	W Virginia	6136	John Rost, W Virginia	Kurt Fitz-Randolph, Tennessee Tech
1982	Tennessee Tech	James Newkirk	6138	W Virginia	6136	John Rost, W Virginia	Kurt Fitz-Randolph, Tennessee Tech
1983	W Virginia	Edward Etzel	6166	Tennessee Tech	6148	Ray Slonena, Tennessee Tech	David Johnson, W Virginia
1984	W Virginia	Edward Etzel	6206	E Tennessee St	6142	Pat Spurgin, Murray St	Bob Broughton, W Virginia
1985	Murray St	Elvis Green	6150	W Virginia	6149	Christian Heller, W Virginia	Pat Spurgin, Murray St
1986	W Virginia	Edward Etzel	6229	Murray St	6163	Marianne Wallace, Murray St	Mike Anti, W Virginia
1987	Murray St	Elvis Green	6205	W Virginia	6203	Rob Harbison, TN–Martin	Web Wright, W Virginia
1988	W Virginia	Greg Perrine	6192	Murray St	6183	Deena Wigger, Murray St	Web Wright, W Virginia
1989	W Virginia	Edward Etzel	6234	S Florida	6180	Michelle Scarborough, S Florida	Deb Sinclair, AK–Fairbanks
1990	W Virginia	Marsha Beasley	6205	Navy	6101	Gary Hardy, W Virginia	M. Scarborough, S Florida
1991	W Virginia	Marsha Beasley	6171	AK–Fairbanks	6110	Ann Pfiffner, W Virginia	Soma Dutta, UTEP
1992	W Virginia	Marsha Beasley	6214	AK–Fairbanks	6166	Ann Pfiffner, W Virginia	Tim Manges, W Virginia
1993	W Virginia	Marsha Beasley	6179	AK–Fairbanks	6169	Trevor Gathman, W Virginia	Eric Uptagrafft, W Virginia
1994	AK–Fairbanks	Randy Pitney	6194	W Virginia	6187	Nancy Napolski, Kentucky	Cory Brunetti, AK–Fairbanks
1995	W Virginia	Marsha Beasley	6241	Air Force	6187	Benji Belden, Murray St	Oleg Seleznov, AK–Fairbanks

Individual Champions

Year	Champion	Coach	Score	Runner-Up	Score	Air Rifle	Smallbore
1996	W Virginia	Marsha Beasley	6179	Air Force	6168	Trevor Gathman, W Virginia	Joe Johnson, Navy
1997	W Virginia	Marsha Beasley	6223	Kentucky	6175	Marra Hastings, Murray St	Marcos Scrivner, W Virginia
1998	W Virginia	Marsha Beasley	6214	AK–Fairbanks	6175	Emily Caruso, Norwich	Karen Juzinuk, Xavier
1999	AK-Fairbanks	Randy Pitney	6276	Navy	6168	Kelly Mansfield, AK-Fairbanks	Kelly Mansfield, AK-Fairbanks
2000	AK-Fairbanks	Randy Pitney	6285	Xavier	6156	Kelly Mansfield, AK-Fairbanks	Nicole Allaire, Nebraska
2001	AK-Fairbanks	David Johnson	6283	Kentucky	6175	Matthew Emmons, AK-Fairbanks	Matthew Emmons, AK-Fairbanks
2002	AK-Fairbanks	Randy Pitney	6241	Kentucky	6209	Ryan Tanoue, Nevada	Matthew Emmons, AK-Fairbanks
2003	AK-Fairbanks	Glenn Dubis	6287	Xavier	6187	Jamie Beyerle, AK-Fairbanks	Matthew Emmons, AK-Fairbanks

Skiing

Year	Champion	Coach	Pts	Runner-Up	Pts	Host or Site
1954	Denver	Willy Schaeffler	384.0	Seattle	349.6	NV–Reno
1955	Denver	Willy Schaeffler	567.05	Dartmouth	558.935	Norwich
1956	Denver	Willy Schaeffler	582.01	Dartmouth	541.77	Winter Park
1957	Denver	Willy Schaeffler	577.95	Colorado	545.29	Ogden Snow Basin
1958	Dartmouth	Al Merrill	561.2	Denver	550.6	Dartmouth
1959	Colorado	Bob Beattie	549.4	Denver	543.6	Winter Park
1960	Colorado	Bob Beattie	571.4	Denver	568.6	Bridger Bowl
1961	Denver	Willy Schaeffler	376.19	Middlebury	366.94	Middlebury
1962	Denver	Willy Schaeffler	390.08	Colorado	374.30	Squaw Valley
1963	Denver	Willy Schaeffler	384.6	Colorado	381.6	Solitude
1964	Denver	Willy Schaeffler	370.2	Dartmouth	368.8	Franconia Notch
1965	Denver	Willy Schaeffler	380.5	Utah	378.4	Crystal Mountain
1966	Denver	Willy Schaeffler	381.02	Western Colorado	365.92	Crested Butte
1967	Denver	Willy Schaeffler	376.7	Wyoming	375.9	Sugarloaf Mountain
1968	Wyoming	John Cress	383.9	Denver	376.2	Mount Werner
1969	Denver	Willy Schaeffler	388.6	Dartmouth	372.0	Mount Werner
1970	Denver	Willy Schaeffler	386.6	Dartmouth	378.8	Cannon Mountain
1971	Denver	Peder Pytte	394.7	Colorado	373.1	Terry Peak
1972	Colorado	Bill Marolt	385.3	Denver	380.1	Winter Park
1973	Colorado	Bill Marolt	381.89	Wyoming	377.83	Middlebury
1974	Colorado	Bill Marolt	176	Wyoming	162	Jackson Hole
1975	Colorado	Bill Marolt	183	Vermont	115	Fort Lewis
1976	Colorado	Bill Marolt	112			Bates
	Dartmouth	Jim Page	112			
1977	Colorado	Bill Marolt	179	Wyoming	154.5	Winter Park
1978	Colorado	Bill Marolt	152.5	Wyoming	121.5	Cannon Mountain
1979	Colorado	Tim Hinderman	153	Utah	130	Steamboat Springs
1980	Vermont	Chip LaCasse	171	Utah	151	Lake Placid and Stowe
1981	Utah	Pat Miller	183	Vermont	172	Park City
1982	Colorado	Tim Hinderman	461	Vermont	436.5	Lake Placid
1983	Utah	Pat Miller	696	Vermont	650	Bozeman
1984	Utah	Pat Miller	750.5	Vermont	684	New Hampshire
1985	Wyoming	Tim Ameel	764	Utah	744	Bozeman
1986	Utah	Pat Miller	612	Vermont	602	Vermont
1987	Utah	Pat Miller	710	Vermont	627	Anchorage
1988	Utah	Pat Miller	651	Vermont	614	Middlebury
1989	Vermont	Chip LaCasse	672	Utah	668	Jackson Hole
1990	Vermont	Chip LaCasse	671	Utah	571	Vermont
1991	Colorado	Richard Rokos	713	Vermont	682	Park City, UT
1992	Vermont	Chip LaCasse	693.5	New Mexico	642.5	New Hampshire
1993	Utah	Pat Miller	783	Vermont	700.5	Steamboat Springs
1994	Vermont	Chip LaCasse	688	Utah	667	Sugarloaf, ME
1995	Colorado	Richard Rokos	720.5	Utah	711	New Hampshire
1996	Utah	Pat Miller	719	Denver	635.5	Montana St
1997	Utah	Pat Miller	686	Vermont	646.5	Vermont
1998	Colorado	Richard Rokos	654	Utah	651.5	Montana St
1999	Colorado	Richard Rokos	650	Denver	636	Bates College
2000	Denver	Kurt Smitz	720	Colorado	621	Park City, UT
2001	Denver	Kurt Smitz	649	Vermont	605	Middlebury, VT
2002	Denver	Kurt Smitz	656	Colorado	612	Anchorage
2003	Utah	Kevin Sweeney	682	Vermont	551	Hanover, NH

Men
DIVISION I

Year	Champion	Coach	Score	Runner-Up
1959	St. Louis	Bob Guelker	5–2	Bridgeport
1960	St. Louis	Bob Guelker	3–2	Maryland
1961	West Chester	Mel Lorback	2–0	St. Louis
1962	St. Louis	Bob Guelker	4–3	Maryland
1963	St. Louis	Bob Guelker	3–0	Navy
1964	Navy	F.H. Warner	1–0	Michigan St
1965	St. Louis	Bob Guelker	1–0	Michigan St
1966	San Francisco	Steve Negoesco	5–2	LIU–Brooklyn
1967	Michigan St / St. Louis	Gene Kenney / Harry Keough	0–0	Game called due to inclement weather
1968	Maryland / Michigan St	Doyle Royal / Gene Kenney	2–2 (2 OT)	
1969	St. Louis	Harry Keough	4–0	San Francisco
1970	St. Louis	Harry Keough	1–0	UCLA
1971	Vacated		3–2	St. Louis
1972	St. Louis	Harry Keough	4–2	UCLA
1973	St. Louis	Harry Keough	2–1 (OT)	UCLA
1974	Howard	Lincoln Phillips	2–1 (4 OT)	St. Louis
1975	San Francisco	Steve Negoesco	4–0	SIU–Edwardsville
1976	San Francisco	Steve Negoesco	1–0	Indiana
1977	Hartwick	Jim Lennox	2–1	San Francisco
1978	Vacated		2–0	Indiana
1979	SIU–Edwardsville	Bob Guelker	3–2	Clemson
1980	San Francisco	Steve Negoesco	4–3 (OT)	Indiana
1981	Connecticut	Joe Morrone	2–1 (OT)	Alabama A&M
1982	Indiana	Jerry Yeagley	2–1 (8 OT)	Duke
1983	Indiana	Jerry Yeagley	1–0 (2 OT)	Columbia
1984	Clemson	I.M. Ibrahim	2–1	Indiana
1985	UCLA	Sigi Schmid	1–0 (8 OT)	American
1986	Duke	John Rennie	1–0	Akron
1987	Clemson	I.M. Ibrahim	2–0	San Diego St
1988	Indiana	Jerry Yeagley	1–0	Howard
1989	Santa Clara / Virginia	Steve Sampson / Bruce Arena	1–1 (2 OT)	
1990	UCLA	Sigi Schmid	1–0 (OT)	Rutgers
1991	Virginia	Bruce Arena	0–0*	Santa Clara
1992	Virginia	Bruce Arena	2–0	San Diego
1993	Virginia	Bruce Arena	2–0	S Carolina
1994	Virginia	Bruce Arena	1–0	Indiana
1995	Wisconsin	Jim Launder	2–0	Duke
1996	St. John's (NY)	Dave Masur	4–1	Florida International
1997	UCLA	Sigi Schmid	2–1	Virginia
1998	Indiana	Jerry Yeagley	3–1	Stanford
1999	Indiana	Jerry Yeagley	1–0	Santa Clara
2000	Connecticut	Ray Reid	2–0	Creighton
2001	N Carolina	Elmar Bolowich	2–0	Indiana
2002	UCLA	Tom Fitzgerald	1–0	Stanford

*Under a rule passed in 1991, the NCAA determined that when a score is tied after regulation and overtime, and the championship is determined by penalty kicks, the official score will be 0–0.

DIVISION II

Year	Champion	Year	Champion	Year	Champion
1972	SIU–Edwardsville	1983	Seattle Pacific	1993	Seattle Pacific
1973	MO–St. Louis	1984	Florida International	1994	Tampa
1974	Adelphi	1985	Seattle Pacific	1995	Southern Connecticut St
1975	Baltimore	1986	Seattle Pacific	1996	Grand Canyon
1976	Loyola (MD)	1987	Southern Connecticut St	1997	Cal St-Bakersfield
1977	Alabama A&M	1988	Florida Tech	1998	Southern Connecticut St
1978	Seattle Pacific	1989	New Hampshire College	1999	Southern Connecticut St
1979	Alabama A&M	1990	Southern Connecticut St	2000	Cal St–Dominguez Hills
1980	Lock Haven	1991	Florida Tech	2001	Tampa
1981	Tampa	1992	Southern Connecticut St	2002	Sonoma St
1982	Florida International				

Men (Cont.)

DIVISION III

Year	Champion	Year	Champion	Year	Champion
1974	Brockport St	1984	Wheaton (IL)	1994	Bethany (WV)
1975	Babson	1985	NC–Greensboro	1995	Williams
1976	Brandeis	1986	NC–Greensboro	1996	College of New Jersey
1977	Lock Haven	1987	NC–Greensboro	1997	Wheaton (IL)
1978	Lock Haven	1988	UC–San Diego	1998	Ohio Wesleyan
1979	Babson	1989	Elizabethtown	1999	St. Lawrence
1980	Babson	1990	Glassboro St	2000	Messiah
1981	Glassboro St	1991	UC–San Diego	2001	Richard Stockton
1982	NC–Greensboro	1992	Kean	2002	Messiah
1983	NC–Greensboro	1993	UC–San Diego		

Women

DIVISION I

Year	Champion	Coach	Score	Runner-Up
1982	N Carolina	Anson Dorrance	2–0	Central Florida
1983	N Carolina	Anson Dorrance	4–0	George Mason
1984	N Carolina	Anson Dorrance	2–0	Connecticut
1985	George Mason	Hank Leung	2–0	N Carolina
1986	N Carolina	Anson Dorrance	2–0	Colorado College
1987	N Carolina	Anson Dorrance	1–0	Massachusetts
1988	N Carolina	Anson Dorrance	4–1	N Carolina St
1989	N Carolina	Anson Dorrance	2–0	Colorado College
1990	N Carolina	Anson Dorrance	6–0	Connecticut
1991	N Carolina	Anson Dorrance	3–1	Wisconsin
1992	N Carolina	Anson Dorrance	9–1	Duke
1993	N Carolina	Anson Dorrance	6–0	George Mason
1994	N Carolina	Anson Dorrance	5–0	Notre Dame
1995	Notre Dame	Chris Petrucelli	1–0	Portland
1996	N Carolina	Anson Dorrance	1–0	Notre Dame
1997	N Carolina	Anson Dorrance	2–0	Connecticut
1998	Florida	Becky Burleigh	1–0	N Carolina
1999	N Carolina	Anson Dorrance	2–0	Notre Dame
2000	N Carolina	Anson Dorrance	2–1	UCLA
2001	Santa Clara	Jerry Smith	1–0	N Carolina
2002	Portland	Clive Charles	2–1	Santa Clara

DIVISION II

Year	Champion
1988	Cal St–Hayward
1989	Barry
1990	Sonoma St
1991	Cal St–Dominguez Hills
1992	Barry
1993	Barry
1994	Franklin Pierce
1995	Franklin Pierce
1996	Franklin Pierce
1997	Franklin Pierce
1998	Lynn
1999	Franklin Pierce
2000	UC–San Diego
2001	UC-San Diego
2002	Christian Brothers

*Formerly Trenton St

DIVISION III

Year	Champion
1986	Rochester
1987	Rochester
1988	William Smith
1989	UC–San Diego
1990	Ithaca
1991	Ithaca
1992	Cortland St
1993	Trenton St
1994	Trenton St
1995	UC–San Diego
1996	UC–San Diego
1997	UC–San Diego
1998	Macalester
1999	UC–San Diego
2000	College of New Jersey*
2001	Ohio Wesleyan
2002	Ohio Wesleyan

Softball

DIVISION I

Year	Champion	Coach	Score	Runner-Up
1982	UCLA*	Sharron Backus	2–0†	Fresno St
1983	Texas A&M	Bob Brock	2–0‡	Cal St–Fullerton
1984	UCLA	Sharron Backus	1–0#	Texas A&M
1985	UCLA	Sharron Backus	2–1**	Nebraska
1986	Cal St–Fullerton*	Judi Garman	3–0	Texas A&M
1987	Texas A&M	Bob Brock	4–1	UCLA
1988	UCLA	Sharron Backus	3–0	Fresno St
1989	UCLA*	Sharron Backus	1–0	Fresno St
1990	UCLA	Sharron Backus	2–0	Fresno St
1991	Arizona	Mike Candrea	5–1	UCLA
1992	UCLA*	Sharron Backus	2–0	Arizona
1993	Arizona	Mike Candrea	1–0	UCLA
1994	Arizona	Mike Candrea	4–0	Cal St–Northridge
1995	Vacated	—		Arizona
1996	Arizona*	Mike Candrea	6–4	Washington
1997	Arizona	Mike Candrea	10–2***	UCLA
1998	Fresno St	Margie Wright	1–0	Arizona
1999	UCLA	Sue Enquist	3–2	Washington
2000	Oklahoma	Patty Gasso	3–1	UCLA
2001	Arizona*	Mike Candrea	1–0	UCLA
2002	California	Diane Ninemire	6–0	Arizona
2003	UCLA	Sue Enquist	1–0**	California

*Undefeated teams in final series. †Eight innings. ‡12 innings. #13 innings. **Nine innings. ***Five innings.

DIVISION II

Year	Champion	Year	Champion	Year	Champion
1982	Sam Houston St	1990	Cal St–Bakersfield	1997	California (PA)*
1983	Cal St–Northridge	1991	Augustana (SD)	1998	California (PA)
1984	Cal St–Northridge	1992	Missouri Southern	1999	Humboldt St
1985	Cal St–Northridge	1993	Florida Southern	2000	N Dakota St
1986	SF Austin St	1994	Merrimack	2001	Nebraska–Omaha
1987	Cal St–Northridge	1995	Kennesaw St	2002	St. Mary's (IA)
1988	Cal St–Bakersfield	1996	Kennesaw St	2003	UC Davis
1989	Cal St–Bakersfield				

DIVISION III

Year	Champion	Year	Champion	Year	Champion
1982	Sam Houston St	1989	Trenton St*	1997	Simpson (IA)*
1982	Eastern Connecticut St*	1990	Eastern Connecticut St	1998	WI–Stevens Point
1983	Trenton St	1991	Central (IA)	1999	Simpson (IA)
1984	Buena Vista*	1992	Trenton St	2000	St. Mary's
1985	Eastern Connecticut St	1993	Central (IA)	2001	Muskingum*
1986	Eastern Connecticut St	1994	Trenton St	2002	Williams
1987	Trenton St*	1995	Chapman	2003	Central (IA)
1988	Central (IA)	1996	Trenton St*		

*Undefeated teams in final series.

Swimming and Diving

Men

DIVISION I

Year	Champion	Coach	Pts	Runner-Up	Pts
1937	Michigan	Matt Mann	75	Ohio St	39
1938	Michigan	Matt Mann	46	Ohio St	45
1939	Michigan	Matt Mann	65	Ohio St	58
1940	Michigan	Matt Mann	45	Yale	42
1941	Michigan	Matt Mann	61	Yale	58
1942	Yale	Robert J.H. Kiphuth	71	Michigan	39
1943	Ohio St	Mike Peppe	81	Michigan	47
1944	Yale	Robert J.H. Kiphuth	39	Michigan	38
1945	Ohio St	Mike Peppe	56	Michigan	48
1946	Ohio St	Mike Peppe	61	Michigan	37
1947	Ohio St	Mike Peppe	66	Michigan	39
1948	Michigan	Matt Mann	44	Ohio St	41
1949	Ohio St	Mike Peppe	49	Iowa	35
1950	Ohio St	Mike Peppe	64	Yale	43
1951	Yale	Robert J.H. Kiphuth	81	Michigan St	60
1952	Ohio St	Mike Peppe	94	Yale	81
1953	Yale	Robert J.H. Kiphuth	96½	Ohio St	73½

Men (Cont.)
DIVISION I (Cont.)

Year	Champion	Coach	Pts	Runner-Up	Pts
1954	Ohio St	Mike Peppe	94	Michigan	67
1955	Ohio St	Mike Peppe	90	Yale/Michigan	51
1956	Ohio St	Mike Peppe	68	Yale	54
1957	Michigan	Gus Stager	69	Yale	61
1958	Michigan	Gus Stager	72	Yale	63
1959	Michigan	Gus Stager	137½	Ohio St	44
1960	Southern Cal	Peter Daland	87	Michigan	73
1961	Michigan	Gus Stager	85	Southern Cal	62
1962	Ohio St	Mike Peppe	92	Southern Cal	46
1963	Southern Cal	Peter Daland	81	Yale	77
1964	Southern Cal	Peter Daland	96	Indiana	91
1965	Southern Cal	Peter Daland	285	Indiana	278½
1966	Southern Cal	Peter Daland	302	Indiana	286
1967	Stanford	Jim Gaughran	275	Southern Cal	260
1968	Indiana	James Counsilman	346	Yale	253
1969	Indiana	James Counsilman	427	Southern Cal	306
1970	Indiana	James Counsilman	332	Southern Cal	235
1971	Indiana	James Counsilman	351	Southern Cal	260
1972	Indiana	James Counsilman	390	Southern Cal	371
1973	Indiana	James Counsilman	358	Tennessee	294
1974	Southern Cal	Peter Daland	339	Indiana	338
1975	Southern Cal	Peter Daland	344	Indiana	274
1976	Southern Cal	Peter Daland	398	Tennessee	237
1977	Southern Cal	Peter Daland	385	Alabama	204
1978	Tennessee	Ray Bussard	307	Auburn	185
1979	California	Nort Thornton	287	Southern Cal	227
1980	California	Nort Thornton	234	Texas	220
1981	Texas	Eddie Reese	259	UCLA	189
1982	UCLA	Ron Ballatore	219	Texas	210
1983	Florida	Randy Reese	238	Southern Meth	227
1984	Florida	Randy Reese	287½	Texas	277
1985	Stanford	Skip Kenney	403½	Florida	302
1986	Stanford	Skip Kenney	404	California	335
1987	Stanford	Skip Kenney	374	Southern Cal	296
1988	Texas	Eddie Reese	424	Southern Cal	369½
1989	Texas	Eddie Reese	475	Stanford	396
1990	Texas	Eddie Reese	506	Southern Cal	423
1991	Texas	Eddie Reese	476	Stanford	420
1992	Stanford	Skip Kenney	632	Texas	356
1993	Stanford	Skip Kenney	520½	Michigan	396
1994	Stanford	Skip Kenney	566½	Texas	445
1995	Michigan	Jon Urbanchek	561	Stanford	475
1996	Texas	Eddie Reese	479	Auburn	443½
1997	Auburn	David Marsh	496½	Stanford	340
1998	Stanford	Skip Kenney	594	Auburn	394½
1999	Auburn	David Marsh	467½	Stanford	414½
2000	Texas	Eddie Reese	538	Auburn	385
2001	Texas	Eddie Reese	597½	Stanford	457½
2002	Texas	Eddie Reese	512	Stanford	5011
2003	Auburn	David Marsh	609½	Texas	413

DIVISION II

Year	Champion	Year	Champion	Year	Champion
1963	SW Missouri St	1977	Cal St–Northridge	1991	Cal St–Bakersfield
1964	Bucknell	1978	Cal St–Northridge	1992	Cal St–Bakersfield
1965	San Diego St	1979	Cal St–Northridge	1993	Cal St–Bakersfield
1966	San Diego St	1980	Oakland (MI)	1994	Oakland (MI)
1967	UC–Santa Barbara	1981	Cal St–Northridge	1995	Oakland (MI)
1968	Long Beach St	1982	Cal St–Northridge	1996	Oakland (MI)
1969	UC–Irvine	1983	Cal St–Northridge	1997	Oakland (MI)
1970	UC–Irvine	1984	Cal St–Northridge	1998	Cal St–Bakersfield
1971	UC–Irvine	1985	Cal St–Northridge	1999	Drury
1972	Eastern Michigan	1986	Cal St–Bakersfield	2000	Cal St–Bakersfield
1973	Cal St–Chico	1987	Cal St–Bakersfield	2001	Cal St–Bakersfield
1974	Cal St–Chico	1988	Cal St–Bakersfield	2002	Cal St–Bakersfield
1975	Cal St–Northridge	1989	Cal St–Bakersfield	2003	Drury
1976	Cal St–Chico	1990	Cal St–Bakersfield		

DIVISION III

Year	Champion	Year	Champion	Year	Champion
1975	Cal St–Chico	1985	Kenyon	1995	Kenyon
1976	St. Lawrence	1986	Kenyon	1996	Kenyon
1977	Johns Hopkins	1987	Kenyon	1997	Kenyon
1978	Johns Hopkins	1988	Kenyon	1998	Kenyon
1979	Johns Hopkins	1989	Kenyon	1999	Kenyon
1980	Kenyon	1990	Kenyon	2000	Kenyon
1981	Kenyon	1991	Kenyon	2001	Kenyon
1982	Kenyon	1992	Kenyon	2002	Kenyon
1983	Kenyon	1993	Kenyon	2003	Kenyon
1984	Kenyon	1994	Kenyon		

Women

DIVISION I

Year	Champion	Coach	Pts	Runner-Up	Pts
1982	Florida	Randy Reese	505	Stanford	383
1983	Stanford	George Haines	418½	Florida	389½
1984	Texas	Richard Quick	392	Stanford	324
1985	Texas	Richard Quick	643	Florida	400
1986	Texas	Richard Quick	633	Florida	586
1987	Texas	Richard Quick	648½	Stanford	631½
1988	Texas	Richard Quick	661	Florida	542½
1989	Stanford	Richard Quick	610½	Texas	547
1990	Texas	Mark Schubert	632	Stanford	622½
1991	Texas	Mark Schubert	746	Stanford	653
1992	Stanford	Richard Quick	735½	Texas	651
1993	Stanford	Richard Quick	649½	Florida	421
1994	Stanford	Richard Quick	512	Texas	421
1995	Stanford	Richard Quick	497½	Michigan	478½
1996	Stanford	Richard Quick	478	SMU	397
1997	Southern Cal	Mark Schubert	406	Stanford	395
1998	Stanford	Richard Quick	422	Arizona	378
1999	Georgia	Jack Bauerle	504½	Stanford	441
2000	Georgia	Jack Bauerle	490½	Arizona	472
2001	Georgia	Jack Bauerle	389	Stanford	387½
2002	Auburn	David Marsh	474	Georgia	386
2003	Auburn	David Marsh	536	Georgia	373

DIVISION II

Year	Champion	Year	Champion	Year	Champion
1982	Cal St–Northridge	1990	Oakland (MI)	1997	Drury
1983	Clarion	1991	Oakland (MI)	1998	Drury
1984	Clarion	1992	Oakland (MI)	1999	Drury
1985	S Florida	1993	Oakland (MI)	2000	Drury
1986	Clarion	1994	Oakland (MI)	2001	Truman St
1987	Cal St–Northridge	1995	Air Force	2002	Truman St
1988	Cal St–Northridge	1996	Air Force	2003	Truman St
1989	Cal St–Northridge				

DIVISION III

Year	Champion	Year	Champion	Year	Champion
1982	Williams	1990	Kenyon	1997	Kenyon
1983	Williams	1991	Kenyon	1998	Kenyon
1984	Kenyon	1992	Kenyon	1999	Kenyon
1985	Kenyon	1993	Kenyon	2000	Kenyon
1986	Kenyon	1994	Kenyon	2001	Denison
1987	Kenyon	1995	Kenyon	2002	Kenyon
1988	Kenyon	1996	Kenyon	2003	Kenyon
1989	Kenyon				

Men

INDIVIDUAL CHAMPIONS 1883-1945

Year	Champion	Year	Champion
1883	Joseph Clark, Harvard (spring)	1914	George Church, Princeton
1883	Howard Taylor, Harvard (fall)	1915	Richard Williams II, Harvard
1884	W.P. Knapp, Yale	1916	G. Colket Caner, Harvard
1885	W.P. Knapp, Yale	1917–18	No tournament
1886	G.M. Brinley, Trinity (CT)	1919	Charles Garland, Yale
1887	P.S. Sears, Harvard	1920	Lascelles Banks, Yale
1888	P.S. Sears, Harvard	1921	Philip Neer, Stanford
1889	R.P. Huntington Jr, Yale	1922	Lucien Williams, Yale
1890	Fred Hovey, Harvard	1923	Carl Fischer, Philadelphia Osteo
1891	Fred Hovey, Harvard	1924	Wallace Scott, Washington
1892	William Larned, Cornell	1925	Edward Chandler, California
1893	Malcolm Chace, Brown	1926	Edward Chandler, California
1894	Malcolm Chace, Yale	1927	Wilmer Allison, Texas
1895	Malcolm Chace, Yale	1928	Julius Seligson, Lehigh
1896	Malcolm Whitman, Harvard	1929	Berkeley Bell, Texas
1897	S.G. Thompson, Princeton	1930	Clifford Sutter, Tulane
1898	Leo Ware, Harvard	1931	Keith Gledhill, Stanford
1899	Dwight Davis, Harvard	1932	Clifford Sutter, Tulane
1900	Raymond Little, Princeton	1933	Jack Tidball, UCLA
1901	Fred Alexander, Princeton	1934	Gene Mako, Southern Cal
1902	William Clothier, Harvard	1935	Wilbur Hess, Rice
1903	E.B. Dewhurst, Pennsylvania	1936	Ernest Sutter, Tulane
1904	Robert LeRoy, Columbia	1937	Ernest Sutter, Tulane
1905	E.B. Dewhurst, Pennsylvania	1938	Frank Guernsey, Rice
1906	Robert LeRoy, Columbia	1939	Frank Guernsey, Rice
1907	G. Peabody Gardner Jr, Harvard	1940	Donald McNeil, Kenyon
1908	Nat Niles, Harvard	1941	Joseph Hunt, Navy
1909	Wallace Johnson, Pennsylvania	1942	Frederick Schroeder Jr, Stanford
1910	R.A. Holden Jr, Yale	1943	Pancho Segura, Miami (FL)
1911	E.H. Whitney, Harvard	1944	Pancho Segura, Miami (FL)
1912	George Church, Princeton	1945	Pancho Segura, Miami (FL)
1913	Richard Williams II, Harvard		

DIVISION I

Year	Champion	Coach	Pts	Runner-Up	Pts	Individual Champion
1946	Southern Cal	William Moyle	9	William & Mary	6	Robert Falkenburg, Southern Cal
1947	William & Mary	Sharvey G. Umbeck	10	Rice	4	Gardner Larned, William & Mary
1948	William & Mary	Sharvey G. Umbeck	6	San Francisco	5	Harry Likas, San Francisco
1949	San Francisco	Norman Brooks	7	Rollins/Tulane/ Washington	4	Jack Tuero, Tulane
1950	UCLA	William Ackerman	11	California Southern Cal	5 5	Herbert Flam, UCLA
1951	Southern Cal	Louis Wheeler	9	Cincinnati	7	Tony Trabert, Cincinnati
1952	UCLA	J.D. Morgan	11	California Southern Cal	5 5	Hugh Stewart, Southern Cal
1953	UCLA	J.D. Morgan	11	California	6	Hamilton Richardson, Tulane
1954	UCLA	J.D. Morgan	15	Southern Cal	10	Hamilton Richardson, Tulane
1955	Southern Cal	George Toley	12	Texas	7	Jose Aguero, Tulane
1956	UCLA	J.D. Morgan	15	Southern Cal	14	Alejandro Olmedo, Southern Cal
1957	Michigan	William Murphy	10	Tulane	9	Barry MacKay, Michigan
1958	Southern Cal	George Toley	13	Stanford	9	Alejandro Olmedo, Southern Cal
1959	Notre Dame Tulane	Thomas Fallon Emmet Pare	8 8			Whitney Reed, San Jose St
1960	UCLA	J.D. Morgan	18	Southern Cal	8	Larry Nagler, UCLA
1961	UCLA	J.D. Morgan	17	Southern Cal	16	Allen Fox, UCLA
1962	Southern Cal	George Toley	22	UCLA	12	Rafael Osuna, Southern Cal
1963	Southern Cal	George Toley	27	UCLA	19	Dennis Ralston, Southern Cal
1964	Southern Cal	George Toley	26	UCLA	25	Dennis Ralston, Southern Cal
1965	UCLA	J.D. Morgan	31	Miami (FL)	13	Arthur Ashe, UCLA
1966	Southern Cal	George Toley	27	UCLA	23	Charles Pasarell, UCLA
1967	Southern Cal	George Toley	28	UCLA	23	Bob Lutz, Southern Cal
1968	Southern Cal	George Toley	31	Rice	23	Stan Smith, Southern Cal
1969	Southern Cal	George Toley	35	UCLA	23	Joaquin Loyo-Mayo, Southern Cal
1970	UCLA	Glenn Bassett	26	Trinity (TX) Rice	22 22	Jeff Borowiak, UCLA

Men (Cont.)

DIVISION I (Cont.)

Year	Champion	Coach	Pts	Runner-Up	Pts	Individual Champion
1971	UCLA	Glenn Bassett	35	Trinity (TX)	27	Jimmy Connors, UCLA
1972	Trinity (TX)	Clarence Mabry	36	Stanford	30	Dick Stockton, Trinity (TX)
1973	Stanford	Dick Gould	33	Southern Cal	28	Alex Mayer, Stanford
1974	Stanford	Dick Gould	30	Southern Cal	25	John Whitlinger, Stanford
1975	UCLA	Glenn Bassett	27	Miami (FL)	20	Bill Martin, UCLA
1976	Southern Cal	George Toley	21			Bill Scanlon, Trinity (TX)
	UCLA	Glenn Bassett	21			
1977	Stanford	Dick Gould		Trinity (TX)		Matt Mitchell, Stanford
1978	Stanford	Dick Gould		UCLA		John McEnroe, Stanford
1979	UCLA	Glenn Bassett		Trinity (TX)		Kevin Curren, Texas
1980	Stanford	Dick Gould		California		Robert Van't Hof, Southern Cal
1981	Stanford	Dick Gould		UCLA		Tim Mayotte, Stanford
1982	UCLA	Glenn Bassett		Pepperdine		Mike Leach, Michigan
1983	Stanford	Dick Gould		SMU		Greg Holmes, Utah
1984	UCLA	Glenn Bassett		Stanford		Mikael Pernfors, Georgia
1985	Georgia	Dan Magill		UCLA		Mikael Pernfors, Georgia
1986	Stanford	Dick Gould		Pepperdine		Dan Goldie, Stanford
1987	Georgia	Dan Magill		UCLA		Andrew Burrow, Miami (FL)
1988	Stanford	Dick Gould		Louisiana St		Robby Weiss, Pepperdine
1989	Stanford	Dick Gould		Georgia		Donni Leaycraft, Louisiana St
1990	Stanford	Dick Gould		Tennessee		Steve Bryan, Texas
1991	Southern Cal	Dick Leach		Georgia		Jared Palmer, Stanford
1992	Stanford	Dick Gould		Notre Dame		Alex O'Brien, Stanford
1993	Southern Cal	Dick Leach		Georgia		Chris Woodruff, Tennessee
1994	Southern Cal	Dick Leach		Stanford		Mark Merklein, Florida
1995	Stanford	Dick Gould		Mississippi		Sargis Sargsian, Arizona St
1996	Stanford	Dick Gould		UCLA		Cecil Mamiit, Southern Cal
1997	Stanford	Dick Gould		Georgia		Luke Smith, UNLV
1998	Stanford	Dick Gould		Georgia		Bob Bryan, Stanford
1999	Georgia	Manuel Diaz		UCLA		Jeff Morrison, Florida
2000	Stanford	Dick Gould		VA–Commonwealth		Alex Kim, Stanford
2001	Georgia	Manuel Diaz		Tennessee		Matias Boeker, Georgia
2002	Southern Cal	Dick Leach		Georgia		Matias Boeker, Georgia
2003	Illinois	Craig Tiley		Vanderbilt		Amer Delic, Illinois

Note: Prior to 1977, individual wins counted in the team's total points. In 1977, a dual-match single-elimination team championship was initiated, eliminating the point system.

DIVISION II

Year	Champion	Year	Champion	Year	Champion
1963	Cal St–LA	1977	UC–Irvine	1991	Rollins
1964	Cal St–LA/S Illinois	1978	SIU–Edwardsville	1992	UC–Davis
1965	Cal St–LA	1979	SIU–Edwardsville	1993	Lander
1966	Rollins	1980	SIU–Edwardsville	1994	Lander
1967	Long Beach St	1981	SIU–Edwardsville	1995	Lander
1968	Fresno St	1982	SIU–Edwardsville	1996	Lander
1969	Cal St–Northridge	1983	SIU–Edwardsville	1997	Lander
1970	UC–Irvine	1984	SIU–Edwardsville	1998	Lander
1971	UC–Irvine	1985	Chapman	1999	Lander
1972	UC–Irvine/ Rollins	1986	Cal Poly–SLO	2000	Lander
1973	UC–Irvine	1987	Chapman	2001	Rollins
1974	San Diego	1988	Chapman	2002	BYU-Hawaii
1975	UC–Irvine/San Diego	1989	Hampton	2003	BYU-Hawaii
1976	Hampton	1990	Cal Poly–SLO		

DIVISION III

Year	Champion	Year	Champion	Year	Champion
1976	Kalamazoo	1985	Swarthmore	1995	UC–Santa Cruz
1977	Swarthmore	1986	Kalamazoo	1996	UC–Santa Cruz
1978	Kalamazoo	1987	Kalamazoo	1997	Washington (MD)
1979	Redlands	1988	Washington & Lee	1998	UC–Santa Cruz
1980	Gustavus Adolphus	1989	UC–Santa Cruz	1999	Williams
1981	Claremont-M-S/ Swarthmore	1990	Swarthmore	2000	Trinity (TX)
1982	Gustavus Adolphus	1991	Kalamazoo	2001	Williams
1983	Redlands	1992	Kalamazoo	2002	Williams
1984	Redlands	1993	Kalamazoo	2003	Emory
		1994	Washington (MD)		

Women
DIVISION I

Year	Champion	Coach	Runner-Up	Individual Champion
1982	Stanford	Frank Brennan	UCLA	Alycia Moulton, Stanford
1983	Southern Cal	Dave Borelli	Trinity (TX)	Beth Herr, Southern Cal
1984	Stanford	Frank Brennan	Southern Cal	Lisa Spain, Georgia
1985	Southern Cal	Dave Borelli	Miami (FL)	Linda Gates, Stanford
1986	Stanford	Frank Brennan	Southern Cal	Patty Fendick, Stanford
1987	Stanford	Frank Brennan	Georgia	Patty Fendick, Stanford
1988	Stanford	Frank Brennan	Florida	Shaun Stafford, Florida
1989	Stanford	Frank Brennan	UCLA	Sandra Birch, Stanford
1990	Stanford	Frank Brennan	Florida	Debbie Graham, Stanford
1991	Stanford	Frank Brennan	UCLA	Sandra Birch, Stanford
1992	Florida	Andy Brandi	Texas	Lisa Raymond, Florida
1993	Texas	Jeff Moore	Stanford	Lisa Raymond, Florida
1994	Georgia	Jeff Wallace	Stanford	Angela Lettiere, Georgia
1995	Texas	Jeff Moore	Florida	Keri Phebus, UCLA
1996	Florida	Andy Brandi	Stanford	Jill Craybas, Florida
1997	Stanford	Frank Brennan	Florida	Lilia Osterloh, Stanford
1998	Florida	Andy Brandi	Duke	Vanessa Webb, Duke
1999	Stanford	Frank Brennan	Florida	Zuzana Lesenarova, UC-SD
2000	Georgia	Jeff Wallace	Stanford	Laura Granville, Stanford
2001	Stanford	Lele Forood	Vanderbilt	Laura Granville, Stanford
2002	Stanford	Lele Forood	Florida	Bea Bielek, Wake Forest
2003	Florida	Roland Thornqvist	Stanford	Amber Liu, Stanford

DIVISION II

Year	Champion	Year	Champion	Year	Champion
1982	Cal St–Northridge	1990	UC–Davis	1997	Lynn
1983	TN–Chattanooga	1991	Cal Poly–Pomona	1998	Lynn
1984	TN–Chattanooga	1992	Cal Poly–Pomona	1999	BYU–Hawaii
1985	TN–Chattanooga	1993	UC–Davis	2000	BYU–Hawaii
1986	SIU–Edwardsville	1994	N Florida	2001	Lynn
1987	SIU–Edwardsville	1995	Armstrong St	2002	BYU–Hawaii
1988	SIU–Edwardsville	1996	Armstrong St	2003	BYU–Hawaii
1989	SIU–Edwardsville				

DIVISION III

Year	Champion	Year	Champion	Year	Champion
1982	Occidental	1990	Gustavus Adolphus	1997	Kenyon
1983	Principia	1991	Mary Washington	1998	Kenyon
1984	Davidson	1992	Pomona-Pitzer	1999	Amherst
1985	UC–San Diego	1993	Kenyon	2000	Trinity (TX)
1986	Trenton St	1994	UC–San Diego	2001	Williams
1987	UC–San Diego	1995	Kenyon	2002	Williams
1988	Mary Washington	1996	Emory	2003	Emory
1989	UC–San Diego				

Indoor Track and Field

Men
DIVISION I

Year	Champion	Coach	Pts	Runner-Up	Pts
1965	Missouri	Tom Botts	14	Oklahoma St	12
1966	Kansas	Bob Timmons	14	Southern Cal	13
1967	Southern Cal	Vern Wolfe	26	Oklahoma	17
1968	Villanova	Jim Elliott	35	Southern Cal	25
1969	Kansas	Bob Timmons	41½	Villanova	33
1970	Kansas	Bob Timmons	27½	Villanova	26
1971	Villanova	Jim Elliott	22	UTEP	19¼
1972	Southern Cal	Vern Wolfe	19	Bowling Green/ Mich St	18
1973	Manhattan	Fred Dwyer	18	Kansas/Kent St/UTEP	12
1974	UTEP	Ted Banks	19	Colorado	18
1975	UTEP	Ted Banks	36	Kansas	17½
1976	UTEP	Ted Banks	23	Villanova	15
1977	Washington St	John Chaplin	25½	UTEP	25
1978	UTEP	Ted Banks	44	Auburn	38
1979	Villanova	Jim Elliott	52	UTEP	51
1980	UTEP	Ted Banks	76	Villanova	42
1981	UTEP	Ted Banks	76	SMU	51
1982	UTEP	John Wedel	67	Arkansas	30

Men *(Cont.)*
DIVISION I *(Cont.)*

Year	Champion	Coach	Pts	Runner-Up	Pts
1983	SMU	Ted McLaughlin	43	Villanova	32
1984	Arkansas	John McDonnell	38	Washington St	28
1985	Arkansas	John McDonnell	70	Tennessee	29
1986	Arkansas	John McDonnell	49	Villanova	22
1987	Arkansas	John McDonnell	39	SMU	31
1988	Arkansas	John McDonnell	34	Illinois	29
1989	Arkansas	John McDonnell	34	Florida	31
1990	Arkansas	John McDonnell	44	Texas A&M	36
1991	Arkansas	John McDonnell	34	Georgetown	27
1992	Arkansas	John McDonnell	53	Clemson	46
1993	Arkansas	John McDonnell	66	Clemson	30
1994	Arkansas	John McDonnell	83	UTEP	45
1995	Arkansas	John McDonnell	59	GMU/Tennessee	26
1996	George Mason	John Cook	39	Nebraska	31½
1997	Arkansas	John McDonnell	59	Auburn	27
1998	Arkansas	John McDonnell	56	Stanford	36½
1999	Arkansas	John McDonnell	65	Stanford	42½
2000	Arkansas	John McDonnell	69½	Stanford	52
2001	Louisiana St	Pat Henry	34	Texas Christian	33
2002	Tennessee	Bill Webb	62½	Louisiana St	44
2003	Arkansas	John McDonnell	52	Auburn	28

DIVISION II

Year	Champion	Year	Champion	Year	Champion
1985	SE Missouri St	1992	St. Augustine's	1998	Abilene Christian
1986	Not held	1993	Abilene Christian	1999	Abilene Christian
1987	St. Augustine's	1994	Abilene Christian	2000	Abilene Christian
1988	Abil. Christian/St. August.	1995	St. Augustine's	2001	St. Augustine's
1989	St. Augustine's	1996	Abilene Christian	2002	Abilene Christian
1990	St. Augustine's	1997	Abilene Christian	2003	Abilene Christian
1991	St. Augustine's				

DIVISION III

Year	Champion	Year	Champion	Year	Champion
1985	St. Thomas (MN)	1992	WI–La Crosse	1998	Lincoln (PA)
1986	Frostburg St	1993	WI–La Crosse	1999	Lincoln (PA)
1987	WI–La Crosse	1994	WI–La Crosse	2000	Lincoln (PA)
1988	WI–La Crosse	1995	Lincoln (PA)	2001	WI–La Crosse
1989	N Central	1996	Lincoln (PA)	2002	WI–La Crosse
1990	Lincoln (PA)	1997	WI–La Crosse	2003	WI–La Crosse
1991	WI–La Crosse				

Women
DIVISION I

Year	Champion	Coach	Pts	Runner-Up	Pts
1983	Nebraska	Gary Pepin	47	Tennessee	44
1984	Nebraska	Gary Pepin	59	Tennessee	48
1985	Florida St	Gary Winckler	34	Texas	32
1986	Texas	Terry Crawford	31	Southern Cal	26
1987	Louisiana St	Loren Seagrave	49	Tennessee	30
1988	Texas	Terry Crawford	71	Villanova	52
1989	Louisiana St	Pat Henry	61	Villanova	34
1990	Texas	Terry Crawford	50	Wisconsin	26
1991	Louisiana St	Pat Henry	48	Texas	39
1992	Florida	Bev Kearney	50	Stanford	26
1993	Louisiana St	Pat Henry	49	Wisconsin	44
1994	Louisiana St	Pat Henry	48	Alabama	29
1995	Louisiana St	Pat Henry	40	UCLA	37
1996	Louisiana St	Pat Henry	52	Georgia	34
1997	Louisiana St	Pat Henry	49	Texas/Wisconsin	39
1998	Texas	Bev Kearney	60	Louisiana St	30
1999	Texas	Bev Kearney	61	Louisiana St	57
2000	UCLA	Jeanette Bolden	51	S Carolina	41
2001	UCLA	Jeanette Bolden	53½	S Carolina	40
2002	Louisiana St	Pat Henry	57	Florida	35
2003	Louisiana St	Pat Henry	62	S Carolina/Florida	44

Women (Cont.)

DIVISION II

Year	Champion	Year	Champion	Year	Champion
1985	St. Augustine's	1992	Alabama A&M	1998	Abilene Christian
1986	Not held	1993	Abilene Christian	1999	Abilene Christian
1987	St. Augustine's	1994	Abilene Christian	2000	Abilene Christian
1988	Abilene Christian	1995	Abilene Christian	2001	St. Augustine's
1989	Abilene Christian	1996	Abilene Christian	2002	N Dakota St
1990	Abilene Christian	1997	Abilene Christian	2003	St. Augustine's
1991	Abilene Christian				

DIVISION III

Year	Champion	Year	Champion	Year	Champion
1985	MA–Boston	1992	Christopher Newport	1998	Christopher Newport
1986	MA–Boston	1993	Lincoln (PA)	1999	Wheaton (MA)
1987	MA–Boston	1994	WI–Oshkosh	2000	Wheaton (MA)
1988	Christopher Newport	1995	WI–Oshkosh	2001	Wheaton (MA)
1989	Christopher Newport	1996	WI–Oshkosh	2002	Wheaton (MA)
1990	Christopher Newport	1997	Christopher Newport	2003	Wheaton (MA)
1991	Cortland St				

Outdoor Track and Field

Men

DIVISION I

Year	Champion	Coach	Pts	Runner-Up	Pts
1921	Illinois	Harry Gill	20†	Notre Dame	16†
1922	California	Walter Christie	28†	Penn St	19†
1923	Michigan	Stephen Farrell	29†	Mississippi St	16
1924	No meet				
1925	Stanford*	R.L. Templeton	31†		
1926	Southern Cal*	Dean Cromwell	27†		
1927	Illinois*	Harry Gill	35†		
1928	Stanford	R.L. Templeton	72	Ohio St	31
1929	Ohio St	Frank Castleman	50	Washington	42
1930	Southern Cal	Dean Cromwell	55†	Washington	40
1931	Southern Cal	Dean Cromwell	77†	Ohio St	31†
1932	Indiana	Billy Hayes	56	Ohio St	49†
1933	Louisiana St	Bernie Moore	58	Southern Cal	54
1934	Stanford	R.L. Templeton	63	Southern Cal	54†
1935	Southern Cal	Dean Cromwell	74†	Ohio St	40†
1936	Southern Cal	Dean Cromwell	103†	Ohio St	73
1937	Southern Cal	Dean Cromwell	62	Stanford	50
1938	Southern Cal	Dean Cromwell	67†	Stanford	38
1939	Southern Cal	Dean Cromwell	86	Stanford	44†
1940	Southern Cal	Dean Cromwell	47	Stanford	28†
1941	Southern Cal	Dean Cromwell	81†	Indiana	50
1942	Southern Cal	Dean Cromwell	85†	Ohio St	44†
1943	Southern Cal	Dean Cromwell	46	California	39
1944	Illinois	Leo Johnson	79	Notre Dame	43
1945	Navy	E.J. Thomson	62	Illinois	48†
1946	Illinois	Leo Johnson	78	Southern Cal	42†
1947	Illinois	Leo Johnson	59†	Southern Cal	34†
1948	Minnesota	James Kelly	46	Southern Cal	41†
1949	Southern Cal	Jess Hill	55†	UCLA	31
1950	Southern Cal	Jess Hill	49†	Stanford	28
1951	Southern Cal	Jess Mortenson	56	Cornell	40
1952	Southern Cal	Jess Mortenson	66†	San Jose St	24†
1953	Southern Cal	Jess Mortenson	80	Illinois	41
1954	Southern Cal	Jess Mortenson	66†	Illinois	31†
1955	Southern Cal	Jess Mortenson	42	UCLA	34
1956	UCLA	Elvin Drake	55†	Kansas	51
1957	Villanova	James Elliott	47	California	32
1958	Southern Cal	Jess Mortenson	48†	Kansas	40†
1959	Kansas	Bill Easton	73	San Jose St	48
1960	Kansas	Bill Easton	50	Southern Cal	37

Men *(Cont.)*
DIVISION I *(Cont.)*

Year	Champion	Coach	Pts	Runner-Up	Pts
1961	Southern Cal	Jess Mortenson	65	Oregon	47
1962	Oregon	William Bowerman	85	Villanova	40†
1963	Southern Cal	Vern Wolfe	61	Stanford	42
1964	Oregon	William Bowerman	70	San Jose St	40
1965	Oregon	William Bowerman	32		
	Southern Cal	Vern Wolfe	32		
1966	UCLA	Jim Bush	81	Brigham Young	33
1967	Southern Cal	Vern Wolfe	86	Oregon	40
1968	Southern Cal	Vern Wolfe	58	Washington St	57
1969	San Jose St	Bud Winter	48	Kansas	45
1970	Brigham Young	Clarence Robison	35		
	Kansas	Bob Timmons	35		
	Oregon	William Bowerman	35		
1971	UCLA	Jim Bush	52	Southern Cal	41
1972	UCLA	Jim Bush	82	Southern Cal	49
1973	UCLA	Jim Bush	56	Oregon	31
1974	Tennessee	Stan Huntsman	60	UCLA	56
1975	UTEP	Ted Banks	55	UCLA	42
1976	Southern Cal	Vern Wolfe	64	UTEP	44
1977	Arizona St	Senon Castillo	64	UTEP	50
1978	UCLA/UTEP	Jim Bush/Ted Banks	50		
1979	UTEP	Ted Banks	64	Villanova	48
1980	UTEP	Ted Banks	69	UCLA	46
1981	UTEP	Ted Banks	70	SMU	57
1982	UTEP	John Wedel	105	Tennessee	94
1983	SMU	Ted McLaughlin	104	Tennessee	102
1984	Oregon	Bill Dellinger	113	Washington St	94½
1985	Arkansas	John McDonnell	61	Washington St	46
1986	SMU	Ted McLaughlin	53	Washington St	52
1987	UCLA	Bob Larsen	81	Texas	28
1988	UCLA	Bob Larsen	82	Texas	41
1989	Louisiana St	Pat Henry	53	Texas A&M	51
1990	Louisiana St	Pat Henry	44	Arkansas	36
1991	Tennessee	Doug Brown	51	Washington St	42
1992	Arkansas	John McDonnell	60	Tennessee	46½
1993	Arkansas	John McDonnell	69	LSU/Ohio St	45
1994	Arkansas	John McDonnell	83	UTEP	45
1995	Arkansas	John McDonnell	61½	UCLA	55
1996	Arkansas	John McDonnell	55	George Mason	40
1997	Arkansas	John McDonnell	55	Texas	42½
1998	Arkansas	John McDonnell	58½	Stanford	51
1999	Arkansas	John McDonnell	59	Stanford	52
2000	Stanford	Vin Lananna	72	Arkansas	59
2001	Tennessee	Bill Webb	50	Texas Christian	49
2002	Louisiana St	Pat Henry	64	Tennessee	57
2003	Arkansas	John McDonnell	59	Auburn	50

*Unofficial championship. †Fraction of a point.

DIVISION II

Year	Champion	Year	Champion	Year	Champion
1963	MD–Eastern Shore	1976	UC–Irvine	1990	St. Augustine's
1964	Fresno St	1977	Cal St–Hayward	1991	St. Augustine's
1965	San Diego St	1978	Cal St–LA	1992	St. Augustine's
1966	San Diego St	1979	Cal Poly–SLO	1993	St. Augustine's
1967	Long Beach St	1980	Cal Poly–SLO	1994	St. Augustine's
1968	Cal Poly–SLO	1981	Cal Poly–SLO	1995	St. Augustine's
1969	Cal Poly–SLO	1982	Abilene Christian	1996	Abilene Christian
1970	Cal Poly–SLO	1983	Abilene Christian	1997	Abilene Christian
1971	Kentucky St	1984	Abilene Christian	1998	St. Augustine's
1972	Eastern Michigan	1985	Abilene Christian	1999	Abilene Christian
1973	Norfolk St	1986	Abilene Christian	2000	Abilene Christian
1974	Eastern Illinois	1987	Abilene Christian	2001	St. Augustine's
	Norfolk St	1988	Abilene Christian	2002	Abilene Christian
1975	Cal St–Northridge	1989	St. Augustine's	2003	Abilene Christian

Men (Cont.)

DIVISION III

Year	Champion	Year	Champion	Year	Champion
1974	Ashland	1984	Glassboro St	1994	N Central
1975	Southern–N Orleans	1985	Lincoln (PA)	1995	Lincoln (PA)
1976	Southern–N Orleans	1986	Frostburg St	1996	Lincoln (PA)
1977	Southern–N Orleans	1987	Frostburg St	1997	WI–La Crosse
1978	Occidental	1988	WI–La Crosse	1998	N Central
1979	Slippery Rock	1989	N Central	1999	Lincoln (PA)
1980	Glassboro St	1990	Lincoln (PA)	2000	Nebraska Wesleyan
1981	Glassboro St	1991	WI–La Crosse	2001	WI–La Crosse
1982	Glassboro St	1992	WI–La Crosse	2002	WI–La Crosse
1983	Glassboro St	1993	WI–La Crosse	2003	WI–La Crosse

Women

DIVISION I

Year	Champion	Coach	Pts	Runner-Up	Pts
1982	UCLA	Scott Chisam	153	Tennessee	126
1983	UCLA	Scott Chisam	116½	Florida St	108
1984	Florida St	Gary Winckler	145	Tennessee	124
1985	Oregon	Tom Heinonen	52	Florida St/LSU	46
1986	Texas	Terry Crawford	65	Alabama	55
1987	Louisiana St	Loren Seagrave	62	Alabama	53
1988	Louisiana St	Loren Seagrave	61	UCLA	58
1989	Louisiana St	Pat Henry	86	UCLA	47
1990	Louisiana St	Pat Henry	53	UCLA	46
1991	Louisiana St	Pat Henry	78	Texas	67
1992	Louisiana St	Pat Henry	87	Florida	81
1993	Louisiana St	Pat Henry	93	Wisconsin	44
1994	Louisiana St	Pat Henry	86	Texas	43
1995	Louisiana St	Pat Henry	69	UCLA	58
1996	Louisiana St	Pat Henry	81	Texas	52
1997	Louisiana St	Pat Henry	63	Texas	62
1998	Texas	Bev Kearney	60	UCLA	55
1999	Texas	Bev Kearney	62	UCLA	60
2000	Louisiana St	Pat Henry	59	Southern Cal	56
2001	Southern Cal	Ron Allice	64	UCLA	55
2002	South Carolina	Curtis Frye	82	UCLA	72
2003	Louisiana St	Pat Henry	64	Texas	50

DIVISION II

Year	Champion	Year	Champion	Year	Champion
1982	Cal Poly–SLO	1990	Cal Poly–SLO	1997	St. Augustine's
1983	Cal Poly–SLO	1991	Cal Poly–SLO	1998	Abilene Christian
1984	Cal Poly–SLO	1992	Alabama A&M	1999	Abilene Christian
1985	Abilene Christian	1993	Alabama A&M	2000	St. Augustine's
1986	Abilene Christian	1994	Alabama A&M	2001	St. Augustine's
1987	Abilene Christian	1995	Abilene Christian	2002	St. Augustine's
1988	Abilene Christian	1996	Abilene Christian	2003	Lincoln
1989	Cal Poly–SLO				

DIVISION III

Year	Champion	Year	Champion	Year	Champion
1982	Central (IA)	1990	WI–Oshkosh	1997	WI–Oshkosh
1983	WI–La Crosse	1991	WI–Oshkosh	1998	Chris. Newport
1984	WI–La Crosse	1992	Chris. Newport	1999	Lincoln (PA)
1985	Cortland State	1993	Lincoln (PA)	2000	Lincoln (PA)
1986	MA–Boston	1994	Chris. Newport	2001	Wheaton (MA)
1987	Chris. Newport	1995	WI–Oshkosh	2002	Wheaton (MA)
1988	Chris. Newport	1996	WI–Oshkosh	2003	Wheaton (MA)
1989	Chris. Newport				

Volleyball

Men

Year	Champion	Coach	Score	Runner-Up	Most Outstanding Player
1970	UCLA	Al Scates	3–0	Long Beach St	Dane Holtzman, UCLA
1971	UCLA	Al Scates	3–0	UC–Santa Barbara	Kirk Kilgore, UCLA
					Tim Bonynge, UC–Santa Barbara
1972	UCLA	Al Scates	3–2	San Diego St	Dick Irvin, UCLA
1973	San Diego St	Jack Henn	3–1	Long Beach St	Duncan McFarland, San Diego St

Men (Cont.)

Year	Champion	Coach	Score	Runner-Up	Most Outstanding Player
1974	UCLA	Al Scates	3–2	UC–Santa Barbara	Bob Leonard, UCLA
1975	UCLA	Al Scates	3–1	UC–Santa Barbara	John Bekins, UCLA
1976	UCLA	Al Scates	3–0	Pepperdine	Joe Mika, UCLA
1977	Southern Cal	Ernie Hix	3–1	Ohio St	Celso Kalache, Southern Cal
1978	Pepperdine	Marv Dunphy	3–2	UCLA	Mike Blanchard, Pepperdine
1979	UCLA	Al Scates	3–1	Southern Cal	Sinjin Smith, UCLA
1980	Southern Cal	Ernie Hix	3–1	UCLA	Dusty Dvorak, Southern Cal
1981	UCLA	Al Scates	3–2	Southern Cal	Karch Kiraly, UCLA
1982	UCLA	Al Scates	3–0	Penn St	Karch Kiraly, UCLA
1983	UCLA	Al Scates	3–0	Pepperdine	Ricci Luyties, UCLA
1984	UCLA	Al Scates	3–1	Pepperdine	Ricci Luyties, UCLA
1985	Pepperdine	Marv Dunphy	3–1	Southern Cal	Bob Ctvrtlik, Pepperdine
1986	Pepperdine	Rod Wilde	3–2	Southern Cal	Steve Friedman, Pepperdine
1987	UCLA	Al Scates	3–0	Southern Cal	Ozzie Volstad, UCLA
1988	Southern Cal	Bob Yoder	3–2	UC–Santa Barbara	Jen-Kai Liu, Southern Cal
1989	UCLA	Al Scates	3–1	Stanford	Matt Sonnichsen, UCLA
1990	Southern Cal	Jim McLaughlin	3–1	Long Beach St	Bryan Ivie, Southern Cal
1991	Long Beach St	Ray Ratelle	3–1	Southern Cal	Brent Hilliard, Long Beach St
1992	Pepperdine	Marv Dunphy	3–0	Stanford	Alon Grinberg, Pepperdine
1993	UCLA	Al Scates	3–0	Cal St–Northridge	Mike Sealy/Jeff Nygaard, UCLA
1994	Penn St	Tom Peterson	3–2	UCLA	Ramon Hernandez, Penn St
1995	UCLA	Al Scates	3–0	Penn St	Jeff Nygaard, UCLA
1996	UCLA	Al Scates	3–2	Hawaii	Yuval Katz, Hawaii
1997	Stanford	Ruben Nieves	3–2	UCLA	Mike Lambert, Stanford
1998	UCLA	Al Scates	3–2	Pepperdine	George Roumain, Pepperdine
1999	Brigham Young	Carl McGown	3–0	Long Beach St	Ossie Antonetti, Brigham Young
2000	UCLA	Al Scates	3–0	Ohio St	Brandon Taliaferro, UCLA
2001	Brigham Young	Carl McGown	3–0	UCLA	Mike Wall, Brigham Young
2002	Hawaii	Mike Wilton	3–1	Pepperdine	Costas Theochardis, Hawaii
2003	Lewis	Dave Deuser	3–2	Brigham Young	Gustavo Meyer, Lewis

Women

DIVISION I

Year	Champion	Coach	Score	Runner-Up
1981	Southern Cal	Chuck Erbe	3–2	UCLA
1982	Hawaii	Dave Shoji	3–2	Southern Cal
1983	Hawaii	Dave Shoji	3–0	UCLA
1984	UCLA	Andy Banachowski	3–2	Stanford
1985	Pacific	John Dunning	3–1	Stanford
1986	Pacific	John Dunning	3–0	Nebraska
1987	Hawaii	Dave Shoji	3–1	Stanford
1988	Texas	Mick Haley	3–0	Hawaii
1989	Long Beach St	Brian Gimmillaro	3–0	Nebraska
1990	UCLA	Andy Banachowski	3–0	Pacific
1991	UCLA	Andy Banachowski	3–2	Long Beach St
1992	Stanford	Don Shaw	3–1	UCLA
1993	Long Beach St	Brian Gimmillaro	3–1	Penn St
1994	Stanford	Don Shaw	3–1	UCLA
1995	Nebraska	Terry Pettit	3–1	Texas
1996	Stanford	Don Shaw	3–0	Hawaii
1997	Stanford	Don Shaw	3–2	Penn St
1998	Long Beach St	Brian Gimmillaro	3–2	Penn St
1999	Penn St	Russ Rose	3–0	Stanford
2000	Nebraska	John Cook	3–2	Wisconsin
2001	Stanford	Don Shaw	3–0	Long Beach St
2002	Southern Cal	Mick Haley	3–1	Stanford

DIVISION II

Year	Champion	Year	Champion	Year	Champion
1981	Cal St–Sacramento	1989	Cal St–Bakersfield	1996	Nebraska–Omaha
1982	UC–Riverside	1990	West Texas A&M	1997	West Texas A&M
1983	Cal St–Northridge	1991	West Texas A&M	1998	Hawaii Pacific
1984	Portland St	1992	Portland St	1999	BYU–Hawaii
1985	Portland St	1993	Northern Michigan	2000	Hawaii Pacific
1986	UC–Riverside	1994	Northern Michigan	2001	Barry
1987	Cal St–Northridge	1995	Barry	2002	BYU–Hawaii
1988	Portland St				

DIVISION III

Year	Champion	Year	Champion	Year	Champion	Year	Champion
1981	UC–San Diego	1987	UC–San Diego	1993	Washington (MO)	1998	Central (IA)
1982	La Verne	1988	UC–San Diego	1994	Washington (MO)	1999	Central (IA)
1983	Elmhurst	1989	Washington (MO)	1995	Washington (MO)	2000	Central (IA)
1984	UC–San Diego	1990	UC–San Diego	1996	Washington (MO)	2001	La Verne
1985	Elmhurst	1991	Washington (MO)	1997	UC–San Diego	2002	WI–Whitewater
1986	UC–San Diego	1992	Washington (MO)				

Water Polo

Men

Year	Champion	Coach	Score	Runner-Up
1969	UCLA	Bob Horn	5–2	California
1970	UC–Irvine	Ed Newland	7–6 (3 OT)	UCLA
1971	UCLA	Bob Horn	5–3	San Jose St
1972	UCLA	Bob Horn	10–5	UC–Irvine
1973	California	Pete Cutino	8–4	UC–Irvine
1974	California	Pete Cutino	7–6	UC–Irvine
1975	California	Pete Cutino	9–8	UC–Irvine
1976	Stanford	Art Lambert	13–12	UCLA
1977	California	Pete Cutino	8–6	UC–Irvine
1978	Stanford	Dante Dettamanti	7–6 (3 OT)	California
1979	UC–Santa Barbara	Pete Snyder	11–3	UCLA
1980	Stanford	Dante Dettamanti	8–6	California
1981	Stanford	Dante Dettamanti	17–6	Long Beach St
1982	UC–Irvine	Ed Newland	7–4	Stanford
1983	California	Pete Cutino	10–7	Southern Cal
1984	California	Pete Cutino	9–8	Stanford
1985	Stanford	Dante Dettamanti	12–11 (2 OT)	UC–Irvine
1986	Stanford	Dante Dettamanti	9–6	California
1987	California	Pete Cutino	9–8 (OT)	Southern Cal
1988	California	Pete Cutino	14–11	UCLA
1989	UC–Irvine	Ed Newland	9–8	California
1990	California	Steve Heaston	8–7	Stanford
1991	California	Steve Heaston	7–6	UCLA
1992	California	Steve Heaston	12–11	Stanford
1993	Stanford	Dante Dettamanti	11–9	Southern Cal
1994	Stanford	Dante Dettamanti	14–10	Southern Cal
1995	UCLA	Guy Baker	10–8	California
1996	UCLA	Guy Baker	8–7	Southern Cal
1997	Pepperdine	Terry Schroeder	8–7 (OT)	Southern Cal
1998	Southern Cal	John Williams	9–8 (2 OT)	Stanford
1999	UCLA	Guy Baker	6–5	Stanford
2000	UCLA	Guy Baker/Adam Krikorian	11–2	UC–San Diego
2001	Stanford	Dante Dettamanti	8–5	UCLA
2002	Stanford	John Vargas	7–6	California

Women

Year	Champion	Coach	Score	Runner-Up
2001	UCLA	Adam Krikorian	5–4	Stanford
2002	Stanford	John Tanner	8–4	UCLA
2003	UCLA	Adam Krikorian	4–3	Stanford

Wrestling

DIVISION I

Year	Champion	Coach	Pts	Runner-Up	Pts	Most Outstanding Wrestler
1928	Oklahoma St*	E.C. Gallagher		Michigan		
1929	Oklahoma St	E.C. Gallagher	26	Michigan	18	
1930	Oklahoma St*	E.C. Gallagher	27	Illinois	14	
1931	Oklahoma St*	E.C. Gallagher		Michigan		
1932	Indiana*	W.H. Thom		Oklahoma St		Edwin Belshaw, Indiana
1933	OK St*/Iowa St*	E. Gallagher/H. Otopalik				A. Kelley, OK St/P. Johnson, Harv
1934	Oklahoma St	E.C. Gallagher	29	Indiana	19	Ben Bishop, Lehigh
1935	Oklahoma St	E.C. Gallagher	36	Oklahoma	18	Ross Flood, Oklahoma St
1936	Oklahoma	Paul Keen	14	Central St/ OK St	10	Wayne Martin, Oklahoma
1937	Oklahoma St	E.C. Gallagher	31	Oklahoma	13	Stanley Henson, Oklahoma St
1938	Oklahoma St	E.C. Gallagher	19	Illinois	15	Joe McDaniels, Oklahoma St
1939	Oklahoma St	E.C. Gallagher	33	Lehigh	12	Dale Hanson, Minnesota
1940	Oklahoma St	E.C. Gallagher	24	Indiana	14	Don Nichols, Michigan
1941	Oklahoma St	Art Griffith	37	Michigan St	26	Al Whitehurst, Oklahoma St
1942	Oklahoma St	Art Griffith	31	Michigan St	26	David Arndt, Oklahoma St
1946	Oklahoma St	Art Griffith	25	Northern Iowa	24	Gerald Leeman, Northern Iowa
1947	Cornell	Paul Scott	32	Northern Iowa	19	William Koll, Northern Iowa
1948	Oklahoma St	Art Griffith	33	Michigan St	28	William Koll, Northern Iowa
1949	Oklahoma St	Art Griffith	32	Northern Iowa	27	Charles Hetrick, Oklahoma St
1950	Northern Iowa	David McCuskey	30	Purdue	16	Anthony Gizoni, Waynesburg
1951	Oklahoma	Port Robertson	24	Oklahoma St	23	Walter Romanowski, Cornell
1952	Oklahoma	Port Robertson	22	Northern Iowa	21	Tommy Evans, Oklahoma
1953	Penn St	Charles Speidel	21	Oklahoma	15	Frank Bettucci, Cornell
1954	Oklahoma St	Art Griffith	32	Pittsburgh	17	Tommy Evans, Oklahoma
1955	Oklahoma St	Art Griffith	40	Penn St	31	Edward Eichelberger, Lehigh
1956	Oklahoma St	Art Griffith	65	Oklahoma	62	Dan Hodge, Oklahoma
1957	Oklahoma	Port Robertson	73	Pittsburgh	66	Dan Hodge, Oklahoma
1958	Oklahoma St	Myron Roderick	77	Iowa St	62	Dick Delgado, Oklahoma
1959	Oklahoma St	Myron Roderick	73	Iowa St	51	Ron Gray, Iowa St
1960	Oklahoma	Thomas Evans	59	Iowa St	40	Dave Auble, Cornell

DIVISION I *(Cont.)*

Year	Champion	Coach	Pts	Runner-Up	Pts	Most Outstanding Wrestler
1961	Oklahoma St	Myron Roderick	82	Oklahoma	63	E. Gray Simons, Lock Haven
1962	Oklahoma St	Myron Roderick	82	Oklahoma	45	E. Gray Simons, Lock Haven
1963	Oklahoma	Thomas Evans	48	Iowa St	45	Mickey Martin, Oklahoma
1964	Oklahoma St	Myron Roderick	87	Oklahoma	58	Dean Lahr, Colorado
1965	Iowa St	Harold Nichols	87	Oklahoma St	86	Yojiro Uetake, Oklahoma St
1966	Oklahoma St	Myron Roderick	79	Iowa St	70	Yojiro Uetake, Oklahoma St
1967	Michigan St	Grady Peninger	74	Michigan	63	Rich Sanders, Portland St
1968	Oklahoma St	Myron Roderick	81	Iowa St	78	Dwayne Keller, Oklahoma St
1969	Iowa St	Harold Nichols	104	Oklahoma	69	Dan Gable, Iowa St
1970	Iowa St	Harold Nichols	99	Michigan St	84	Larry Owings, Washington
1971	Oklahoma St	Tommy Chesbro	94	Iowa St	66	Darrell Keller, Oklahoma St
1972	Iowa St	Harold Nichols	103	Michigan St	72½	Wade Schalles, Clarion
1973	Iowa St	Harold Nichols	85	Oregon St	72½	Greg Strobel, Oregon St
1974	Oklahoma	Stan Abel	69½	Michigan	67	Floyd Hitchcock, Bloomsburg
1975	Iowa	Gary Kurdelmeier	102	Oklahoma	77	Mike Frick, Lehigh
1976	Iowa	Gary Kurdelmeier	123½	Iowa St	85¾	Chuch Yagla, Iowa
1977	Iowa St	Harold Nichols	95½	Oklahoma St	88¾	Nick Gallo, Hofstra
1978	Iowa	Dan Gable	94½	Iowa St	94	Mark Churella, Michigan
1979	Iowa	Dan Gable	122½	Iowa St	88	Bruce Kinseth, Iowa
1980	Iowa	Dan Gable	110¾	Oklahoma St	87	Howard Harris, Oregon St
1981	Iowa	Dan Gable	129¾	Oklahoma	100¼	Gene Mills, Syracuse
1982	Iowa	Dan Gable	131¾	Iowa St	111	Mark Schultz, Oklahoma
1983	Iowa	Dan Gable	155	Oklahoma St	102	Mike Sheets, Oklahoma St
1984	Iowa	Dan Gable	123¾	Oklahoma St	98	Jim Zalesky, Iowa
1985	Iowa	Dan Gable	145¼	Oklahoma	98½	Barry Davis, Iowa
1986	Iowa	Dan Gable	158	Oklahoma	84¼	Marty Kistler, Iowa
1987	Iowa St	Jim Gibbons	133	Iowa	108	John Smith, Oklahoma St
1988	Arizona St	Bobby Douglas	93	Iowa	85½	Scott Turner, N Carolina St
1989	Oklahoma St	Joe Seay	91¼	Arizona St	70½	Tim Krieger, Iowa St
1990	Oklahoma St	Joe Seay	117¾	Arizona St	104¾	Chris Barnes, Oklahoma St
1991	Iowa	Dan Gable	157	Oklahoma St	108¾	Jeff Prescott, Penn St
1992	Iowa	Dan Gable	149	Oklahoma St	100½	Tom Brands, Iowa
1993	Iowa	Dan Gable	123¾	Penn St	87½	Terry Steiner, Iowa
1994	Oklahoma St	John Smith	94¾	Iowa	76½	Pat Smith, Oklahoma St
1995	Iowa	Dan Gable	134	Oregon St	77½	T.J. Jaworsky, N Carolina
1996	Iowa	Dan Gable	122½	Iowa St	78½	Les Gutches, Oregon St
1997	Iowa	Dan Gable	170	Oklahoma St	113½	Lincoln McIlravy, Iowa
1998	Iowa	Jim Zalesky	115	Minnesota	102	Joe Williams, Iowa
1999	Iowa	Jim Zalesky	100½	Minnesota	98½	Cael Sanderson, Iowa St
2000	Iowa	Jim Zalesky	116	Iowa St	109½	Cael Sanderson, Iowa St
2001	Minnesota	J Robinson	138½	Iowa	125½	Cael Sanderson, Iowa St
2002	Minnesota	J Robinson	126½	Iowa St	104	Cael Sanderson, Iowa St
2003	Oklahoma St	John Smith	143	Minnesota	104½	Eric Larkin, Arizona St

*Unofficial champions.

DIVISION II

Year	Champion	Year	Champion	Year	Champion
1963	Western St (CO)	1977	Cal St–Bakersfield	1991	NE–Omaha
1964	Western St (CO)	1978	Northern Iowa	1992	Central Oklahoma
1965	Mankato St	1979	Cal St–Bakersfield	1993	Central Oklahoma
1966	Cal Poly–SLO	1980	Cal St–Bakersfield	1994	Central Oklahoma
1967	Portland St	1981	Cal St–Bakersfield	1995	Central Oklahoma
1968	Cal Poly–SLO	1982	Cal St–Bakersfield	1996	Pittsburgh–Johnstown
1969	Cal Poly–SLO	1983	Cal St–Bakersfield	1997	San Francisco St
1970	Cal Poly–SLO	1984	SIU–Edwardsville	1998	N Dakota St
1971	Cal Poly–SLO	1985	SIU–Edwardsville	1999	Pittsburgh–Johnstown
1972	Cal Poly–SLO	1986	SIU–Edwardsville	2000	N Dakota St
1973	Cal Poly–SLO	1987	Cal St–Bakersfield	2001	N Dakota St
1974	Cal Poly–SLO	1988	N Dakota St	2002	Central Oklahoma
1975	Northern Iowa	1989	Portland St	2003	Central Oklahoma
1976	Cal St–Bakersfield	1990	Portland St		

DIVISION III

Year	Champion	Year	Champion	Year	Champion
1974	Wilkes	1984	Trenton St	1994	Ithaca
1975	John Carroll	1985	Trenton St	1995	Augsburg
1976	Montclair St	1986	Montclair St	1996	Wartburg
1977	Brockport St	1987	Trenton St	1997	Augsburg
1978	Buffalo	1988	St. Lawrence	1998	Augsburg
1979	Trenton St	1989	Ithaca	1999	Wartburg
1980	Brockport St	1990	Ithaca	2000	Augsburg
1981	Trenton St	1991	Augsburg	2001	Augsburg
1982	Brockport St	1992	Brockport	2002	Augsburg
1983	Brockport St	1993	Augsburg	2003	Wartburg

INDIVIDUAL CHAMPIONSHIP
RECORDS

Swimming

Men

Event	Time	Record Holder	Date
50-yard freestyle	19.08	Neil Walker, Texas	3-27-97
100-yard freestyle	41.62	Anthony Ervin, California	3-20-02
200-yard freestyle	1:33.03	Matt Biondi, California	4-3-87
500-yard freestyle	4:08.75	Tom Dolan, Michigan	3-23-95
1,650-yard freestyle	14:26.62	Chris Thompson, Michigan	3-24-01
100-yard backstroke	45.25	Neil Walker, Texas	3-28-97
200-yard backstroke	1:39.16	Aaron Peirsol, Texas	3-29-03
100-yard breaststroke	52.32	Jeremy Linn, Tennessee	3-28-97
200-yard breaststroke	1:52.62	Brendan Hansen, Texas	3-29-03
100-yard butterfly	45.44	Ian Crocker, Texas	3-29-02
200-yard butterfly	1:41.78	Melvin Stewart, Tennessee	3-30-91
200-yard individual medley	1:42.66	George Bovell, Auburn	3-27-03
400-yard individual medley	3:38.18	Tom Dolan, Michigan	3-24-95

Women

Event	Time	Record Holder	Date
50-yard freestyle	21.69	Maritza Correia, Georgia	3-21-02
100-yard freestyle	47.29	Maritza Correia, Georgia	3-22-03
200-yard freestyle	1:43.08	Martina Moravcova, Southern Methodist	3-28-97
500-yard freestyle	4:34.39	Janet Evans, Stanford	3-15-90
1,650-yard freestyle	15:39.14	Janet Evans, Stanford	3-17-90
100-yard backstroke	49.97	Natalie Coughlin, California	3-22-02
200-yard backstroke	1:49.52	Natalie Coughlin, California	3-22-02
100-yard breaststroke	59.05	Kristy Kowal, Georgia	3-20-98
200-yard breaststroke	2:07.36	Tara Kirk, Stanford	3-22-02
100-yard butterfly	50.01	Natalie Coughlin, California	3-22-02
200-yard butterfly	1:53.36	Limin Liu, Nevada	3-20-99
200-yard individual medley	1:53.91	Maggie Bowen, Auburn	3-21-02
400-yard individual medley	4:02.28	Summer Sanders, Stanford	3-20-92

Indoor Track and Field

Men

Event	Mark	Record Holder	Date
55-meter dash	6.00	Lee McRae, Pittsburgh	3-14-86
55-meter hurdles	7.07	Allen Johnson, N Carolina	3-13-92
200-meter dash	20.26	Shawn Crawford, Clemson	3-10-00
400-meter dash	45.60	Brandon Couts, Baylor	3-10-00
800-meter run	1:45.33	Patrick Nduwimana, Arizona	3-10-01
Mile run	3:55.33	Kevin Sullivan, Michigan	3-11-95
3,000-meter run	7:46.03	Adam Goucher, Colorado	3-14-98
5,000-meter run	13:36.64	Jonah Koech, Iowa St	3-8-91
High jump	7 ft 9¼ in	Hollis Conway, SW Louisiana	3-11-89
Pole vault	19 ft 2¼ in	Jacob Davis, Texas	3-6-99
Long jump	27 ft 10 in	Carl Lewis, Houston	3-13-81
Triple jump	56 ft 9½ in	Keith Connor, Southern Methodist	3-13-81
Shot put	70 ft 1 in	Janus Robberts, Southern Methodist	3-10-01
35-pound weight throw	80 ft 11¼ in	Scott Russell, Kansas	3-9-02

Women

Event	Mark	Record Holder	Date
55-meter dash	6.56	Gwen Torrence, Georgia	3-14-87
55-meter hurdles	7.39	Tiffany Lott, BYU	3-7-97
200-meter dash	22.83	Peta-Gaye Dowdie, Louisiana St	3-6-99
400-meter dash	51.05	Maicel Malone, Arizona St	3-9-91
800-meter run	2:01.77	Hazel Clark, Florida	3-5-99
Mile run	4:30.63	Suzy Favor, Wisconsin	3-11-89
3,000-meter run	8:54.98	Stephanie Herbst, Wisconsin	3-15-86
5,000-meter run	15:39.75	Amy Skieresz, Arizona	3-7-97
High jump	6 ft 5½ in	Amy Acuff, UCLA	3-11-95
Pole vault	14 ft 10 ¼ in	Amy Linnen, Arizona	3-13-02
Long jump	22 ft 1 in	Daphne Saunders, Louisiana St	3-12-94
Triple jump	46 ft 9 in	Suzette Lee, Louisiana St	3-8-97
Shot put	60 ft 5¼ in	Teri Tunks, Southern Methodist	3-14-98
35-pound weight throw	71 ft 8¾ in	Dawn Ellerbe, S Carolina	3-7-97

Outdoor Track and Field

Men

Event	Mark	Record Holder	Date
100-meter dash	9.92	Ato Bolden, UCLA	6-1-96
200-meter dash	19.87	Lorenzo Daniel, Mississippi St	6-3-88
		John Capel, Florida	6-5-99
400-meter dash	44.00	Quincy Watts, Southern Cal	6-6-92
800-meter run	1:44.70	Mark Everett, Florida	6-1-90
1,500-meter run	3:35.30	Sydney Maree, Villanova	6-6-81
3,000-meter steeplechase	8:12.39	Henry Rono, Washington St	6-1-78
5,000-meter run	13:20.63	Sydney Maree, Villanova	6-2-79
10,000-meter run	28:01.30	Suleiman Nyambui, UTEP	6-1-79
110-meter high hurdles	13.22	Greg Foster, UCLA	6-2-78
400-meter intermediate hurdles	47.85	Kevin Young, UCLA	6-3-89
High jump	7 ft 9¾ in	Hollis Conway, SW Louisiana	6-3-89
Pole vault	19 ft 1 in	Lawrence Johnson, Tennessee	5-29-96
Long jump	28 ft	Erick Walder, Arkansas	6-3-93
Triple jump	57 ft 7¾ in	Keith Connor, Southern Methodist	6-5-82
Shot put	72 ft 2¼ in	John Godina, UCLA	6-3-95
Discus throw	220 ft	Kamy Keshmiri, Nevada	6-5-92
Hammer throw	265 ft 3 in	Balazs Kiss, Southern Cal	5-31-96
Javelin throw (new javelin)	268 ft 7 in	Esko Mikkola, Arizona	6-3-98
Decathlon	8279 pts	Tito Steiner, Brigham Young	6-2/3-81

Women

Event	Mark	Record Holder	Date
100-meter dash	10.78	Dawn Sowell, Louisiana St	6-3-89
200-meter dash	22.04	Dawn Sowell, Louisiana St	6-2-89
400-meter dash	50.18	Pauline Davis, Alabama	6-3-89
800-meter run	1:59.11	Suzy Favor, Wisconsin	6-1-90
1,500-meter run	4:08.26	Suzy Favor, Wisconsin	6-2-90
3,000-meter run	8:47.35	Vicki Huber, Villanova	6-3-88
5,000-meter run	15:37.77	Amy Skieresz, Arizona	6-5-98
10,000-meter run	32:28.57	Sylvia Mosqueda, Cal St–Los Angeles	6-1-88
100-meter hurdles	12.70	Tananjalyn Stanley, Louisiana St	6-3-89
400-meter hurdles	54.54	Ryan Tolbert, Vanderbilt	6-6-97
High jump	6 ft 5 in	Amy Acuff, UCLA	6-3-95
Pole vault	14 ft 5¼ in	Tracy O'Hara, UCLA	6-2-00
Long jump	22 ft 9¼ in	Sheila Echols, Louisiana St	6-5-87
Triple jump	46 ft ¾ in	Sheila Hudson, California	6-2-90
Shot put	61 ft 2¼ in	Tressa Thompson, Nebraska	6-4-98
Discus throw	210 ft 10 in	Seilala Sua, UCLA	6-6-99
Hammer throw	219 ft 4 in	Florence Ezah, Southern Methodist	6-2-01
Javelin throw (new javelin)	197 ft 8 in	Angeliki Tsiolakoudi, Texas–El Paso	6-3-00
Heptathlon	6527 pts	Diane Guthrie-Gresham, George Mason	6-2/3-95

Olympics

**Athens prepares
for the 2004
Summer Games**

Mixed Blessings

Many nations covet them, but the fabled Olympic Games often bring more grief than glory to aspiring cities

BY MERRELL NODEN

LIKE THE MYSTERIOUS, winking ring in a fairy tale, which everyone pursues only to discover too late its true power for mischief, the Olympic Games are a tricky thing to get hold of, and an even trickier thing to possess. Woe to the city that pursues them, for they are just as likely to bring debt, scandal and political infighting as glory and full coffers.

Of course we've known that for years. Just ask Montrealers how lucky they were to "win" the 1976 Games, which they are still paying for. Or Salt Lakers how proud they were to be hosting the 2002 Winter Games once the bribery scandal involving top officials of the Salt Lake Olympic Committee (SLOC) hit the front pages ... day after day after day.

Still, three years into the new millennium, those five Olympic rings continue to exert as strong and seductive a pull on Olympic dreamers and schemers as ever they did. Even as construction crews in next year's host city, Athens, were working desperately round the clock to stay ahead of schedule—barely—for the Opening Ceremonies on August 13, 2004, Vancouver was celebrating its narrow defeat of surprising Pyeongchang, South Korea, for the right to host the 2010 Winter Games. Time will tell which of the two cities was the luckier, the winner or the loser.

"History has taught us that the Olympic Games are a great legacy for a city," insisted Dr. Jacques Rogge, the Belgian orthopedic surgeon who took over as head of the IOC in 2001, at a press conference in Athens. No doubt some of that legacy grows out of the highest ideals, the fraternity and good will that the modern Games' founder, Baron de Coubertin, hoped the Olympics would promote. But this year offered another reminder of why everyone wants a piece of the Games: In June, the IOC announced that it had sold the U.S. television rights to the 2010 Winter Games and 2012 Summer Games to NBC and its parent company, General Electric, for $820 million and $1.181 billion, respectively.

Ward dropped the ball at the USOC, stepping down in March.

Compare those staggering sums to the $614 million the network paid for the 2006 Winter Olympics in Turin and the $894 million for the 2008 Summer Olympics in Beijing, and you begin to understand why the Olympics will survive, no matter how many scandals are exposed.

And in 2003 there seemed to be nearly as many scandals as triumphs. The fallout from last year's vote-swapping fiasco in figure skating continued, with members of the International Skating Union debating what a cheat-proof scoring system might look like. At the same time, our chances of learning what exactly did transpire during that tawdry affair were hurt by an Italian judge's decision not to extradite the alleged mastermind, reputed Russian mobster Alimzhan Tokhtakhounov, to the U.S. to stand trial. Not so fortunate were Tom Welch and Dave Johnson, the two members of the Salt Lake Organizing Committee whose 15-count indictment for bribery, racketeering and fraud had been thrown out by a Utah state court in 2001. In April, a federal appeals court in Denver reinstated charges against the pair, clearing the way for a trial.

That was far from the only embarrassment the Olympic movement suffered here in the U.S. The first half of 2003 brought little but controversy to the United States Olympic Committee. The USOC's latest shenanigans received a full airing before the U.S. Senate's Commerce Committee, which oversees the publically-funded organization, and it wasn't pretty. Ben Nighthorse Campbell, the Colorado senator who was a member of the 1964 Olympic judo team and now sits on the Senate Commerce Committee, described the goings on at the USOC as "an Olympic-sized food fight of incessant squabbles and internal dissension." By the end of the winter, six top USOC members had resigned in disgust, as had Marty Mankamyer, the body's third president in the past year. Commerce Committee chairman John McCain was proposing a comprehensive overhaul of the unwieldy, 124-member body.

Most of the controversy revolved around Lloyd Ward, the former Maytag CEO who'd taken over the USOC's top executive position in October 2001. The first African American to run the organization, Ward first drew criticism last year for his membership in the Augusta Country Club, a club which, as we were reminded repeatedly in 2003, has few minority members and no women. Ward answered that criticism with the not unreasonable explanation that he planned to work for change from inside the club.

Fair enough. Harder to explain were charges, first raised by the *Los Angeles*

Times in December 2002, that Ward had directed his staff to help a company called Energy Management Technologies win a contract to supply power generators to the organizers of the 2003 Pan American Games in the Dominican Republic. The problem was that Ward's brother, Rubert, happened to be the president of EMT, a fact that Ward at first denied to the *Dallas Morning News* before being confronted with company documents proving it. It didn't help matters when Lowell Fernandez, a member of the organizing committee in the Dominican Republic, claimed that another EMT executive, CEO Lorenzo Williams, had tried to bribe him during a meeting.

At a special meeting of the USOC's executive committee convened on Jan. 13 in Denver to discuss the situation, the organization determined that while Ward's conduct had "created the appearance of a conflict of interest" he had not actually violated the USOC's code of ethics. They gave him a formal reprimand and stripped him of a $184,000 bonus. Ward's escape from more serious punishment infuriated other committee members, six of whom resigned, including ethics compliance officer Pat Rodgers. Another casualty was Mankamyer, who, in the face of a no-confidence vote, resigned as USOC president on February 4, ending yet another conspicuously brief tenure in that position.

None of this sat well with members of the Commerce Committee, especially Senator Nighthorse Campbell, who has taken a special interest in the USOC not only because of his background as an Olympic athlete but also because the USOC's headquarters are in his home state, in Colorado Springs. After a visit to its headquarters, he and his colleague Ted Stevens of Alaska, one of the authors of the 1978 Sports Act, which had established the USOC in the first place, announced that they believed they'd found evidence of fraud when they reviewed USOC documents. That was the final blow. On March 1, Ward resigned. His resignation meant that the USOC has had four CEO's and three presidents since the 2000 Olympics.

On July 15, Senator McCain introduced legislation that would replace the USOC's 124-member board and 23-member executive committee with a nine-member elected board and four members who would have one vote combined. Those nine would be elected for a single, four-year term. Just as significantly, McCain promised closer scrutiny over USOC affairs, including its Byzantine finances.

Still, no one was under the illusion that the USOC's problems would vanish overnight. "If Jesus Christ himself were to come down to run things, it would still take years for the U.S. Olympic movement to lay claim to high ground again," declared former Olympic swimming champion John Naber.

Of course, the Olympic movement's worldwide governing body, the IOC, was in no position to criticize its U.S. underling, since it has no shortage of skeletons rattling in its own closet. Some, like the bribery and judging scandals, are merely hugely embarrassing. Others, though, like revelations about the sadistic activities of Uday Hussein, son of Saddam and the former head of Iraq's Olympic Committee, constituted an entirely different order of shame.

Appointed by his father in 1984 to run the country's Olympic and soccer programs, Uday was long thought by many to be nothing short of a full-fledged psychopath. His nickname was the Butcher's Boy. Before his death at the hands of U.S. forces on July 22, he had been known to carry an electric prod with him and to punish athletes who disappointed him—which included virtually every member of every Iraqi national team—with torture and even death. "Uday made us athletes an example," said Iraqi soccer star Sharar Haydar. "He believed that if people saw he was not afraid to beat a hero, they would live in greater fear." The building that housed the Iraqi Olympic Committee had a 30-cell prison in its basement where Uday carried out sickening acts of brutality against athletes, some of whom never returned.

Haydar described the sadistic practices of Uday Hussein's Iraqi Olympic Committee.

As U.S. and British soldiers uncovered widespread evidence of such practices, human rights organizations asked, quite reasonably, how much the IOC knew—or should have known—about Uday's gruesome antics. "That the Olympic community, which has known about the atrocities of Uday for years, has taken no action is a black eye for the organization," said Charles Forrest, CEO of INDICT, a U.S. government-funded human rights group based in London. "The IOC is in a morally indefensible position here."

For their part, IOC members did their best to diminish the revelations. Richard Pound, a powerful IOC member from Canada, cautioned that "it is important to remember these are just allegations, and you have to make sure this is not all tied to the Iraq–U.S. dispute, that we are not being used for propaganda. You never know."

You might think that these developments would make nations reluctant to join this club. But IOC membership actually increased in 2003, and a record 201 countries are expected to compete in Athens. Meeting in Prague in late June, the IOC's executive board voted to reinstate Afghanistan, which had been suspended in

October of 1999 because of the ruling Taliban's strict refusal to allow women to participate. Afghanistan, which first competed in the Olympics in 1936 but has never won a medal, last sent a team to the Atlanta Games. Its participation in the 2004 summer Games may depend on athletes from the war-torn country being awarded wild-card entries to compete. In any case, there is little doubt that they will be welcomed enthusiastically by the crowd.

Also accorded member status were two island nations in the South Pacific, East Timor and Kiribati. The East Timorese sent a largely symbolic four-member team to Sydney, where the four competed under the Olympic flag as "independent Olympic athletes." Kiribati will be competing for the first time.

The competition to host the 2010 Games featured several surprises. In the first vote Pyeongchang got 51 votes to Vancouver's 40 and Salzburg, Austria's measly 16. That removed the stunned Austrians from contention. Though Pyeongchang, a city of only 50,000 situated in the Baekdu mountains, 100 miles east of Seoul, is not known as a winter sports capital outside Asia, the Korean bid was nonetheless appealing because organizers promised to share some hosting responsibilities with North Korea. That's the sort of broader influence the IOC craves. But in the final vote, where 55 votes were needed to win, Vancouver edged Pyeongchang, 56 to 53.

This of course set off a wild celebration in Vancouver, which will spend seven years and a projected $2 billion (Canadian) to realize its "Sea to Sky Games." Some of the city's facilities, such as its General Motors Place hockey arena, already exist. But the city will have to build an Olympic village and spend an estimated $600 million to improve the only highway stretching the 78 miles from Vancouver to the resort community of Whistler, which will host the Alpine events.

And because nothing happens in the world of IOC politics that doesn't seem to cause countless ripples elsewhere, several other cities were left wondering what the

Vancouver narrowly defeated Pyeongchang, Korea, for the right to host the 2010 Games.

choice of Vancouver meant for them. After reading the Olympic tea leaves, hopefuls in Toronto withdrew that city's candidacy for the 2012 Games on the theory that the IOC probably won't award back-to-back Games to the same country, and organizers in New York City wondered glumly if the same logic didn't apply to cities on the same continent.

The other three cities already picked to host future Games seemed to be making steady progress towards readiness. In Torino, Italy, no news was probably good news, while the biggest news regarding Beijing was the IOC's decision to move the Games back two weeks, in hopes of avoiding the city's terrible summer heat, which can easily top 100° F.

And so it is on to Athens, where everything started. For all its historical and cultural claims to host these Games, it's clear that the Athens bid has produced more anxiety in IOC circles than any recent bid. Along with pollution, the threat of terrorism and the delicate task of working around the city's archeological treasures, there's the problem of what to do with the

city's estimated 10,000 to 15,000 stray dogs. "Why shouldn't the animals live among us in the streets?" asked Athens deputy mayor Tonya Kanellopoulou.

It's that kind of talk that makes the IOC honchos a bit, well, nervous. In February, IOC leaders delivered their second strong warning in three years about the importance of adhering to the timetable. "From time to time you have to give a pretty strong warning," admitted Denis Oswald, the head of the IOC's evaluation committee, which oversees each host city's progress. "We realized the situation was worse than what we had expected and that is why we shouted a little louder than on other occasions."

He and Rogge have both kept a close eye on the city's progress, and seem confident that Athens will be ready. It didn't hurt when, in July, members of the November 17 revolutionary group were arrested.

So come August 13, 2004, the Games will return to their historical birthplace for the first time since 1896. One hopes Athens will be ready, for it is certainly hard to imagine a more inspiring backdrop. The athletes are sure to be ready. They are the one part of the whole circus that never disappoints.

2000 Summer Games

TRACK AND FIELD
Men

100 METERS
1. ...Maurice Green, United States — 9.87
2. ...Ato Boldon, Trinidad and Tobago — 9.99
3. ...Obadele Thomoson, Barbados — 10.04

200 METERS
1. ...Konstadinos Kederis, Greece — 20.09
2. ...Darren Campbell, Great Britain — 20.14
3. ...Ato Boldon, Trinidad and Tobago — 20.20

400 METERS
1. ...Michael Johnson, United States — 43.84
2. ...Alvin Harrison, United States — 44.40
3. ...Gregory Haughton, Jamaica — 44.70

800 METERS
1. ...Nils Schumann, Germany — 1:45.08
2. ...Wilson Kipketer, Denmark — 1:45.14
3. ...Aissa Djabir Said-Guerni, Algeria — 1:45.16

1,500 METERS
1. ...Noah Ngeny, Kenya — 3:32.07 OR
2. ...Hicham El Guerrouj, Morocco — 3:32.32
3. ...Bernard Lagat, Kenya — 3:32.44

5,000 METERS
1. ...Millon Wolde, Ethiopia — 13:35.49
2. ...Ali Saidi-Sief, Algeria — 13:36.20
3. ...Brahim Lahlafi, Morocco — 13:36.47

10,000 METERS
1. ...Haile Gebrselassie, Ethiopia — 27:18.20
2. ...Paul Tergat, Kenya — 27:18.29
3. ...Assefa Mezgebu, Ethiopia — 27:19.75

MARATHON
1. ...Geznghe Abera, Ethiopia — 2:10:11
2. ...Eric Wainaina, Kenya — 2:10:31
3. ...Tesfaye Tola, Ethiopia — 2:11:10

110-METER HURDLES
1. ...Anier Garcia, Cuba — 13.00
2. ...Terrence Trammell, United States — 13.16
3. ...Mark Crear, United States — 13.22

400-METER HURDLES
1. ...Angelo Taylor, United States — 47.50
2. ...Hadi Souan Somalyi, Saudi Arabia — 47.53
3. ...Llewelyn Herbert, South Africa — 47.81

3,000-METER STEEPLECHASE
1. ...Reuben Kosgei, Kenya — 8:21.43
2. ...Wilson Boit Kipketer, Kenya — 8:21.77
3. ...Ali Ezzine, Morocco — 8:22.15

4 X 100-METER RELAY
1. ...United States: (Jon Drummond, Bernard Williams III, Brian Lewis, Maurice Greene) — 37.61
2. ...Brazil — 37.90
3. ...Cuba — 38.04

4 X 400-METER RELAY
1. ...United States: (Alvin Harrison, Antonio Pettigrew, Calvin Harrison, Michael Johnson) — 2:56.35
2. ...Nigeria — 2:58.68
3. ...Jamaica — 2:58.78

20-KILOMETER WALK
1. ...Robert Korzeniowski, Poland — 1:18:59
2. ...Noe Hernandez, Mexico — 1:19:03
3. ...Vladimir Andreyev, Russia — 1:19:27

50-KILOMETER WALK
1. ...Robert Korzeniowski, Poland — 3:42:22
2. ...Aigars Fadejevs, Latvia — 3:43:40
3. ...Joel Sanchez, Mexico — 3:44:36

HIGH JUMP
1. ...Sergey Kliugin, Russia — 7 ft 8¼ in
2. ...Javier Sotomayor, Cuba — 7 ft 7¼ in
3. ...Abderrahmane Hammad, Algeria — 7 ft 7¼ in

POLE VAULT
1. ...Nick Hysong, United States — 19 ft 4¼ in
2. ...Lawrence Johnson, United States — 19 ft 4¼ in
3. ...Maksim Tarasov, Russia — 19 ft 4¼ in

LONG JUMP
1. ...Ivan Pedroso, Cuba — 28 ft ¾ in
2. ...Jai Taurima, Australia — 27 ft 10¼ in
3. ...Roman Schurenko, Ukraine — 27 ft 3¼ in

TRIPLE JUMP
1. ...Jonathan Edwards, Great Britain — 58 ft 1¼ in
2. ...Yoel Garcia, Cuba — 57 ft 3¾ in
3. ...Denis Kapustin, Russia — 57 ft 3½ in

SHOT PUT
1. ...Arsi Harju, Finland — 69 ft 10¼ in
2. ...Adam Nelson, United States — 69 ft 7 in
3. ...John Godina, United States — 69 ft 6¾ in

DISCUS THROW
1. ...Virgilijus Alekna, Lithuania — 227 ft 4 in
2. ...Lars Riedel, Germany — 224 ft 9 in
3. ...Frantz Kruger, South Africa — 223 ft 8 in

HAMMER THROW
1. ...Szymon Ziolkowski, Poland — 262 ft 6 in
2. ...Nicola Vizzoni, Italy — 261 ft 3 in
3. ...Igor Astapkovich, Belarus — 259 ft 8½ in

JAVELIN
1. ...Jan Zelezny, Czech Republic — 295 ft 9½ in
2. ...Steve Backley, Great Britain — 294 ft 9½ in
3. ...Sergey Makarov, Russia — 290 ft 10½ in

DECATHLON
Pts
1. ...Erki Nool, Estonia — 8641
2. ...Roman Seberle, Czech Republic — 8606
3. ...Chris Huffins, United States — 8595

Note: OR=Olympic record. WR=world record. EOR=equals Olympic record. EWR=equals world record.

TRACK AND FIELD *(Cont.)*
Women

100 METERS

1.	...Marion Jones, United States	10.75
2.	...Ekaterini Thanou, Greece	11.12
3.	...Tanya Lawrence, Jamaica	11.18

200 METERS

1.	...Marion Jones, United States	21.84
2.	...P. Davis-Thompson, Bahamas	22.27
3.	...Susanthika Jayasinghe, Sri Lanka	22.28

400 METERS

1.	...Cathy Freeman, Australia	49.11
2.	...Lorraine Graham, Jamaica	49.58
3.	...Katharine Merry, Great Britain	49.72

800 METERS

1.	...Maria Mutola, Mozambique	1:56.15
2.	...Stephanie Graf, Austria	1:56.64
3.	...Kelly Holmes, Great Britain	1:56.80

1,500 METERS

1.	...Nouria Merah-Benida, Algeria	4:05.10
2.	...Violeta Szekely, Romania	4:05.15
3.	...Gabriela Szabo, Romania	4:05.27

5,000 METERS

1.	...Gabriela Szabo, Romania	14:40.79 OR
2.	...Sonia O'Sullivan, Ireland	14:41.02
3.	...Gete Wami, Ethiopia	14:42.23

10,000 METERS

1.	...Derartu Tulu, Ethiopia	30:17.49 OR
2.	...Gete Wami, Ethiopia	30:22.48
3.	...Fernanda Ribeiro, Portugal	30:22.88

MARATHON

1.	...Naoko Takahashi, Japan	2:23:14 OR
2.	...Lidia Simon, Romania	2:23:22
3.	...Joyce Chepchumba, Kenya	2:24:45

100-METER HURDLES

1.	...Olga Shishigina, Kazakhstan	12.65
2.	...Glory Alozie, Nigeria	12.68
3.	...Melissa Morrison, United States	12.76

400-METER HURDLES

1.	...Irina Privalova, Russia	53.02
2.	...Deon Hemmings, Jamaica	53.45
3.	...Nouza Bidouane, Morocco	53.57

4 X 100-METER RELAY

1.	...Bahamas (S. Fynes, C. Sturrup, P. Davis-Thompson, D. Ferguson)	41.95
2.	...Jamaica	42.13
3.	...United States	42.20

4 X 400-METER RELAY

1.	...United States (Jearl Miles-Clark, Monique Hennagan, Marion Jones, La Tasha Colander-Richardson)	3:22.62
2.	...Jamaica	3:23.25
3.	...Russia	3:23.46

20-KILOMETER WALK

1.	...Wang Liping, China	1:29.05
2.	...Kiersti Plaetzer, Norway	1:29.33
3.	...Maria Vasco, Spain	1:30.23

HIGH JUMP

1.	...Yelena Yelesina, Russia	6 ft 7 in
2.	...Hestrie Cloete, S Africa	6 ft 7 in
3.	...Kajsa Bergqvist, Sweden	6 ft 7 in

POLE VAULT

1.	...Stacy Dragila, United States	15 ft 1 in OR
2.	...Tatiana Grigorieva, Australia	14 ft 11 in
3.	...Vala Flosadottir, Iceland	14 ft 9 in

LONG JUMP

1.	...Heike Drechsler, Germany	22 ft 11¼ in
2.	...Fiona May, Italy	22 ft 8½ in
3.	...Marion Jones, United States	22 ft 8½ in

TRIPLE JUMP

1.	...Tereza Marinova, Bulgaria	49 ft 10½ in
2.	...Tatyana Lebedeva, Russia	49 ft 2½ in
3.	...Olena Hovorova, Ukraine	49 ft 1 in

SHOT PUT

1.	...Yanina Korolchik, Belarus	67 ft 5½ in
2.	...Laris Peleshenko, Russia	65 ft 4¼ in
3.	...Astrid Kumbernuss, Germany	64 ft 4½ in

DISCUS THROW

1.	...Ellina Zvereva, Belarus	224 ft 5 in
2.	...Anastasia Kelesidou, Greece	215 ft 7 in
3.	...Irina Yatchenko, Belarus	213 ft 11 in

JAVELIN

1.	...Trine Hattestad, Norway	226 ft ½ in OR
2.	...Mirella Maniani-Tzelili, Greece	221 ft 5½ in
3.	...Osleidys Menendez, Cuba	217 ft 1 in

HEPTATHLON

		Pts
1.	...Denise Lewis, Great Britain	6584
2.	...Yelena Prokhorova, Russia	6531
3.	...Natalya Sazanovich, Belarus	6527

HAMMER THROW

1.	...Kamila Skolimowska, Russia	233 ft 5 in OR
2.	...Olga Kuzenkova, Russia	228 ft 11 in
3.	...Kirsten Muenchow, Germany	227 ft 3 in

INDIVIDUAL ARCHERY

Men

1.	..........Simon Fairweather, Australia
2.	..........Victor Wuderle, United States
3.	..........Wietse van Alten, Netherlands

Women

1.	..........Yun Mi-Jin, S Korea
2.	..........Kim Nam-Soon, S Korea
3.	..........Kim Soo-Nyuong, S Korea

TEAM ARCHERY

Men

1.	....S Korea
2.	....Italy
3.	....United States

Women

1.	....S Korea
2.	....Ukraine
3.	....Germany

Note: OR=Olympic record. WR=world record. EOR=equals Olympic record. EWR=equals world record.

BADMINTON

Men

SINGLES

1. ...Ji Xinpeng, China
2. ...Hendra Wan, Indonesia
3. ...Xia Xuanze, China

DOUBLES

1. ...Tony Gunawan/ Candra Wijaya, Indonesia
2. ...Lee Dong-soo/ Yoo Yong-sung, S Korea
3. ...Ha Tae-kwan/ Kim Dong-moon, S Korea

Women

SINGLES

1. ...Gong Zhichao, China
2. ...Camilla Martin, Denmark
3. ...Ye Zhaoying, China

DOUBLES

1. ...Ge Fei/ Gu Jun, China
2. ...Huang Nanyan/ Yang Wei, China
3. ...Gao Ling/ Qin Yiyuan, China

MIXED DOUBLES

1. ...Zhang Jun/Gao Ling, China
2. ...Tri Kushanjanto/Minarti Timur, Indonesia
3. ...Simon Archer/Joanne Goode, Great Britain

BASEBALL

1. ...United States
2. ...Cuba
3. ...S Korea

BASKETBALL

Men

Final: United States 85, France 75
Lithuania (3rd)
United States: Shareef Abdur-Rahim, Ray Allen, Vin Baker, Vince Carter, Kevin Garnett, Tim Hardaway, Allan Houston, Jason Kidd, Antonio McDyess, Alonzo Mourning, Gary Payton, Steve Smith

Women

Final: United States 76, Australia 54
Brazil (3rd)
United States: Ruthie Bolton-Holifield, Teresa Edwards, Yolanda Griffith, Chamique Holdsclaw, Lisa Leslie, Nikki McCray, Delisha Milton, Katie Smith Dawn Staley, Sheryl Swoopes, Natalie Williams, Kara Wolters

BOXING

LIGHT FLYWEIGHT (106 LB)

1. ...Brahim Asloum, France
2. ...Rafael Lozano Munoz, Spain
3. ...Un Chol Kim, N Korea
3. ...Maikro Romero Esquirol, Cuba

FLYWEIGHT (112 LB)

1. ...Wijan Ponlid, Thailand
2. ...Bulat Jumadilov, Kazakhstan
3. ...Jerome Thomas, France
3. ...Vladimir Sidorenko, Ukraine

BANTAMWEIGHT (119 LB)

1. ...Guillermo Ortiz, Cuba
2. ...Raimkoul Malakhbekov, Russia
3. ...Serguey Daniltchenko, Ukraine
3. ...Clarence Vinson, United States

FEATHERWEIGHT (125 LB)

1. ...Bekzat Sattarkhanov, Kazakhstan
2. ...Ricardo Juarez, United States
3. ...Tahar Tamsamani, Morocco
3. ...Kamil Dzamalutdinov, Russia

LIGHTWEIGHT (132 LB)

1. ...Mario Kindelan, Cuba
2. ...Andriy Kotelnyk, Ukraine
3. ...Cristian Benitez, Mexico
3. ...Alexandr Maletin, Russia

LIGHT WELTERWEIGHT (139 LB)

1. ...Mahamadkadyz Abdullaev, Uzbekistan
2. ...Ricardo Williams, United States
3. ...Diogenes Luna Martinez, Cuba
3. ...Mohamed Allalou, Algeria

WELTERWEIGHT (147 LB)

1. ...Oleg Saitov, Russia
2. ...Sergey Dotsenko, Ukraine
3. ...Vitalii Grusac, Moldova
3. ...Dorel Simion, Romania

LIGHT MIDDLEWEIGHT (156 LB)

1. ...Yermakhan Ibraimov, Kazakhstan
2. ...Marin Simion, Romania
3. ...Pornchai Thongburan, Thailand
3. ...Jermain Taylor, United States

MIDDLEWEIGHT (165 LB)

1. ...Jorge Gutierrez, Cuba
2. ...Gaidarbek Gaidarbekov, Russia
3. ...Vugar Alekperov, Azerbaijan
3. ...Zsolt Erdei, Hungary

LIGHT HEAVYWEIGHT (178 LB)

1. ...Alexander Lebziak, Russia
2. ...Rudolf Kraj, Czech Republic
3. ...Andri Fedtchouk, Ukraine
3. ...Sergei Mikhailov, Uzbekistan

HEAVYWEIGHT (201 LB)

1. ...Félix Sávon, Cuba
2. ...Sultanahmed Ibzagimov, Russia
3. ...Sebastian Kober, Germany
3. ...Vladimir Tchantouria, Georgia

SUPERHEAVYWEIGHT (201+ LB)

1. ...Audley Harrison, Great Britain
2. ...Mukhtarkhan Dildabkov, Kazakhstan
3. ...Rustam Saidov, Uzbekistan
3. ...Paolo Vidoz, Italy

CANOE/KAYAK

Men

C-1 FLATWATER 500 METERS
1. ...Gyorgy Kolonics, Hungary — 2:24.813
2. ...Maxim Opalev, Russia — 2:25.809
3. ...Andreas Dittmer, Germany — 2:27.591

C-1 FLATWATER 1,000 METERS
1. ...Andreas Dittmer, Germany — 3:54.379
2. ...Ledys Frank Balceiro, Cuba — 3:56.071
3. ...Steve Giles, Canada — 3:56.437

C-2 FLATWATER 500 METERS
1. ...F. Novak/ I. Pulai, Hungary — 1:51.284
2. ...D. Jedraszko/ P. Baraszkiewicz, Poland — 1:51.536
3. ...F. Popescu/ M. Pricop, Romania — 1:54.260

C-2 FLATWATER 1,000 METERS
1. ...F. Popescu/ M. Pricop, Romania — 3:37.355
2. ...I. Rojas/ L. Pereira, Cuba — 3:38.753
3. ...L. Kober/ S. Utess, Germany — 3:41.129

C-1 WHITEWATER SLALOM
		Pts
1. ...Tony Estanguet, France		231.87
2. ...Michal Martikan, Slovakia		233.76
3. ...Juraj Mincik, Slovakia		234.22

C-2 WHITEWATER SLALOM
		Pts
1. ...Pavel/ Peter Hochschorner, Slovakia		237.74
2. ...K. Kolomanski/ M. Staniszewski, Poland		243.81
3. ...M. Jiras/ T. Mader, Czech Republic		249.45

K-1 FLATWATER 500 METERS
1. ...Knut Holmann, Norway — 1:57.847
2. ...Petar Merkov, Bulgaria — 1:58.393
3. ...Michael Kolganov, Israel — 1:59.563

K-1 FLATWATER 1,000 METERS
1. ...Knut Holmann, Norway — 3:33.260
2. ...Petar Merkov, Bulgaria — 3:34.640
3. ...Tim Brabants, Great Britain — 3:35.057

Men *(Cont.)*

K-2 FLATWATER 500 METERS
1. ...Z. Kammerer/ B. Storcz, Hungary — 1:47.055
2. ...D. Collins/ A. Trim, Australia — 1:47.895
3. ...R. Rauhe/ T. Wieskoetter, Germany — 1:48.771

K-2 FLATWATER 1,000 METERS
1. ...B. Bonomi/ A. Rossi, Italy — 3:14.461
2. ...M. Oscarsson/ H. Nilsson, Sweden — 3:16.075
3. ...K. Bartfai/ K. Vereb, Hungary — 3:16.357

K-4 FLATWATER 1,000 METERS
1. ...Hungary — 2:55.188
2. ...Germany — 2:55.704
3. ...Poland — 2:57.192

K-1 WHITEWATER SLALOM
	Pts
1. ...Thomas Schmidt, Germany	217.25
2. ...Paul Ratcliffe, Great Britain	223.71
3. ...Pierpaolo Ferrazzi, Italy	225.03

Women

K-1 FLATWATER 500 METERS
1. ...Josefa Idem Geurrini, Italy — 2:13.848
2. ...Caroline Brunet, Canada — 2:14.646
3. ...Katrin Borchert, Australia — 2:15.138

K-2 FLATWATER 500 METERS
1. ...B. Fischer/ K. Wagner, Germany — 1:56.996
2. ...K. Kovacs/ S. Szabo, Hungary — 1:58.580
3. ...A. Pastuszka/ B. Sokoloska, Poland — 1:58.784

K-4 FLATWATER 500 METERS
1. ...Germany — 1:34.532
2. ...Hungary — 1:34.946
3. ...Romania — 1:37.010

K-1 WHITEWATER SLALOM
	Pts
1. ...Stepanka Hilgertova, Czech Republic	247.04
2. ...Brigitte Guibal, France	251.88
3. ...Anne-Lise Bardet, France	254.77

CYCLING

Men

ROAD RACE
1. ...Jan Ullrich, Germany — 5:29:17.001
2. ...Alexander Vinokourov, Kazakhstan — 5:29:17.002
3. ...Andreas Kloeden, Germany — 5:29:29.003

INDIVIDUAL TIME TRIAL
1. ...Vyachslev Ekimov, Russia — 57:40.420
2. ...Jan Ullrich, Germany — 57:48.333
3. ...Lance Armstrong, United States — 58:14.267

1KM TIME TRIAL
1. ...Jason Queally, Great Britain — 101.609
2. ...Stefan Nimke, Germany — 102.487
3. ...Shane Kelly, Australia — 102.818

4,000-METER INDIVIDUAL PURSUIT
1. ...Robert Bartko, Germany — 4:18.515 OR
2. ...Jens Lehmann, Germany — 4:23.824
3. ...Bradley McGee, Australia — 4:19.250

4,000-METER TEAM PURSUIT
1. ...Germany (Robert Bartko, Guido Fulst, Daniel Becke, Jens Lehmann) — 3:59.710WR
2. ...Russia — 4:04.520
3. ...Great Britain — 4:01.979

Men *(Cont.)*

SPRINT
1. ...Marty Nothstein, United States — 10.874
2. ...Florian Rousseau, France — 11.066
3. ...Jens Fiedler, Germany — 10.732

40-KM POINTS RACE
1. ...Juan Llaneras, Spain — 14
2. ...Milton Wynant, Uruguay — 18
3. ...Alexey Markov, Russia — 16

KIERIN
1. ...Florian Rousseau, France — 11.020
2. ...Gary Neiwand, Australia
3. ...Jens Fiedler, Germany

MADISON
1. ...B. Aiken/ S. McGrory, Australia — 26
2. ...E. DeWilde/ M. Gilmore, Belgium — 22
3. ...S. Martinello/ M. Villa, Italy — 15

OLYMPIC SPRINT
1. ...France — 44.233
2. ...Great Britain — 44.680
3. ...Australia — 45.161

CYCLING *(Cont.)*

Women

24-KM POINTS RACE

1. ...Antonella Bellutti, Italy — 19
2. ...Leontien Zijlaard, Netherlands — 16
3. ...Olga Slioussareva, Russia — 15

INDIVIDUAL TIME TRIAL

1. ...Leontien Zijlaard, Netherlands — 42:00.781
2. ...Mari Holden, United States — 42:37.372
3. ...Jeannie Longo-Ciprelli, France — 42:52:547

3,000-METER INDIVIDUAL PURSUIT

1. ...Leontien Zijlaard, Netherlands — 3:33:360
2. ...Marion Clignet, France — 3:38:751
3. ...Yvonne McGregor, Great Britain — 3:38:850

SPRINT

1. ...Felicia Ballanger, France — 12.553
2. ...Oxana Grichina, Russia — 13.112
3. ...Irina Yanovych, Ukraine — 12.310

ROAD RACE

1. ...Leontien Zijlaard, Netherlands — 3:6:31.001
2. ...Hanka Kupfernagel, Germany — 3:6:31.002
3. ...Diana Ziliute, Lithuania — 3:6:31.003

500-M TIME TRIAL

1. ...Felicia Ballanger, France — 34.140
2. ...Michelle Ferris, Australia — 34.696
3. ...Jiang Cuihua, China — 34.768

DIVING

Men

SPRINGBOARD

	Pts
1. ....Xiong Ni, China	708.72
2. ....Fernando Platas, Mexico	708.42
3. ....Dmitri Sautin, Russia	703.20

PLATFORM

	Pts
1. ....Tian Liang, China	724.53
2. ....Hu Jia, China	713.55
3. ....Dmitri Sautin, Russia	679.26

Women

SPRINGBOARD

	Pts
1. ....Fu Mingxia, China	609.42
2. ....Guo Jingjing, China	597.81
3. ....Doerte Linder, Germany	574.35

PLATFORM

	Pts
1. ....Laura Wilkinson, United States	543.75
2. ....Li Na, China	542.01
3. ....Anne Montminy, Canada	540.15

EQUESTRIAN

3-DAY TEAM

	Pts
1. ......Australia (Phillip Dutton, Andrew Hoy, Stuart Tinney, Matt Ryan)	146.8
2. ......Great Britain	161.0
3. ......United States	175.8

3-DAY INDIVIDUAL

	Pts
1. ......David O'Connor, United States	34.00
2. ......Andrew Hoy, Australia	39.80
3. ......Mark Todd, New Zealand	42.00

TEAM DRESSAGE

	Pts
1. ......Germany (Isabell Werth, Nadine Capellmann, Ulla Salzgeber, Alexandra Simons de Ridder)	5632
2. ......Netherlands	5579
3. ......United States	5166

INDIVIDUAL DRESSAGE

	Pts
1. ......Anky van Grunsven, Netherlands	239.18
2. ......Isabell Werth, Germany	234.19
3. ......Ulla Salzberger, Germany	230.57

TEAM JUMPING

	Pts
1. ......Germany (Ludger Beerbaum, Lars Nieberg, Marcus Ehning, Otto Becker)	7.00
2. ......Switzerland	8.00
3. ......Brazil	12.00

INDIVIDUAL JUMPING

	Pts
1. ......Jeroen Dubbeldam, Netherlands	4.00
2. ......Albert Voorn, Netherlands	4.00
3. ......Khaled Al Eid, Saudi Arabia	4.00

FENCING

Men

FOIL

1. ....Kim Young Ho, S Korea
2. ....Ralf Bissdorf, Germany
3. ....Dmitri Chevtchenko, Russia

SABRE

1. ....Mihai Claudiu Covaliu, Romania
2. ....Mathieu Gourdain, France
3. ....Wiradech Kothny, Germany

ÉPÉE

1. ....Pavel Kolobkov, Russia
2. ....Hugues Obry, France
3. ....Lee Sang Ki, S Korea

TEAM FOIL

1. ....France
2. ....China
3. ....Italy

TEAM SABRE

1. ....Russia
2. ....France
3. ....Germany

TEAM ÉPÉE

1. ....Italy
2. ....France
3. ....Cuba

FENCING (Cont.)
Women

FOIL
1. ....Valentina Vezzali, Italy
2. ....Rita Koenig, Germany
3. ....Giovanna Trillini, Italy

ÉPÉE
1. ....Timea Nagy, Hungary
2. ....Gianna Habluetzel-Buerki, Switzerland
3. ....Laura Flessel-Colovic, France

TEAM FOIL
1. ....Italy
2. ....Poland
3. ....Germany

TEAM ÉPÉE
1. ....Russia
2. ....Switzerland
3. ....China

FIELD HOCKEY

Men
1. ....Netherlands
2. ....S Korea
3. ....Australia

Women
1. ....Australia
2. ....Argentina
3. ....Netherlands

GYMNASTICS

Men

ALL-AROUND
	Pts
1. ....Alexei Nemov, Russia	58.474
2. ....Wei Yang, China	58.361
3. ,..........O. Beresh, Ukraine	58.212

HORIZONTAL BAR
	Pts
1. ....Alexei Nemov, Russia	9.787
2. ....Benjamin Varonian, France	9.787
3. ....Joo-hyung Lee, S Korea	9.775

PARALLEL BARS
	Pts
1. ....Xiaopeng Li, China	9.825
2. ....Joo-hyung Lee, S Korea	9.812
3. ....Alexei Nemov, Russia	9.800

VAULT
	Pts
1. ....Gervasio Deferr, Spain	9.712
2. ....Alexei Bondarenko, Russia	9.587
3. ....Leszsk Blanik, Poland	9.475

POMMEL HORSE
	Pts
1. ....Marius Urzica, Romania	9.862
2. ....Eric Poujade, France	9.825
3. ....Alexei Nemov, Russia	9.800

RINGS
	Pts
1. ....Szilveszter Csollany, Hungary	9.850
2. ....Dimosthenis Tampakos, Kasakhstan	9.762
2. ....Iordan Iovtchev, Bulgaria	9.737

FLOOR EXERCISE
	Pts
1. ....Igors Vihrovs, Latvia	9.812
2. ....Alexei Nemov, Russia	9.800
3. ....Iordan Iovtchev, Bulgaria	9.787

TEAM COMBINED EXERCISES
	Pts
1. ....China	231.919
2. ....Ukraine	230.306
3. ....Russia	230.019

Women

ALL-AROUND
	Pts
1. ....Simona Amanar, Romania	38.642
2. ....Maria Olaru, Romania	38.581
3. ....Xuan Li, China	38.418

VAULT
	Pts
1. ....Yelena Zamolodtchikova, Russia	9.731
2. ....Andreea Raducan, Romania	9.693
3. ....Yekaterina Lobazniouk, Russia	9.674

UNEVEN BARS
	Pts
1. ....Svetlana Khorkina, Russia	9.862
2. ....Ling Jie, China	9.837
2. ....Yang Yun, China	9.787

BALANCE BEAM
	Pts
1. ....Li Xuan, China	9.825
2. ....Yekaterina Lobazniouk, Russia	9.787
3. ....Yelena Prodounova, Russia	9.775

FLOOR EXERCISE
	Pts
1. ....Yelena Zamolodtchikova, Russia	9.850
2. ....Svetlana Khorkina, Russia	9.812
3. ....Simona Amanar, Romania	9.712

TEAM COMBINED EXERCISES
	Pts
1. ....Romania	154.608
2. ....Russia	154.403
3. ....China	154.008

RHYTHMIC ALL-AROUND
	Pts
1. ....Yulia Barsukova, Russia	39.632
2. ....Yulia Raskina, Belarus	39.548
3. ....Alina Kabaeva, Russia	39.466

RHYTHMIC TEAM COMBINED EXERCISES
	Pts
1. ....Russia	39.500
2. ....Belarus	39.500
3. ....Greece	39.283

JUDO

Men

EXTRA-LIGHTWEIGHT
1. ....Tadahiro Nomura, Japan
2. ....Jung Bu-Kyung, S Korea
3. ....Manolo Poulot, Cuba
3. ....Aidyn Smagulov, Kirghyzstan

HALF-LIGHTWEIGHT
1. ....Huseyin Ozkan, Turkey
2. ....Larbi Benboudaoud, France
3. ....Giorgi Vazagashvili, Georgia
3. ....Girolamo Giovinazzo, Italy

LIGHTWEIGHT
1. ....Giuseppe Maddaloni, Italy
2. ....Tiago Camilo, Brazil
3. ....Anatoly Laryukov, Belarus
3. ....Vselvolods Zelonijs, Latvia

HALF-MIDDLEWEIGHT
1. ....Makoto Takimoto, Japan
2. ....Cho In Chul, S Korea
3. ....Nuno Delgado, Portugal
3. ....Aleksei Budolin, Estonia

MIDDLEWEIGHT
1. ....Mark Huizinga, Netherlands
2. ....Carlos Honorato, Brazil
3. ....Frederic Demontfaucon, France
3. ....Ruslan Mashurenko, Ukraine

HALF-HEAVYWEIGHT
1. ....Kosei Inoue, Japan
2. ....Nicolas Gill, Canda
3. ....Iouri Stepkine, Russial
3. ....Stéphane Traineau, France

HEAVYWEIGHT
1. ....David Douillet, France
2. ....Shinichi Shinohara, Japan
3. ....Indrek Pertelson, Estonia
3. ....Tamerlan Tmenov, Russia

Women

EXTRA-LIGHTWEIGHT
1. ....Ryoko Tamura, Japan
2. ....Lioubov Brouletova, Russia
3. ....Anna-Maria Gradante, Germany
3. ....Ann Simons, Belgium

HALF-LIGHTWEIGHT
1. ....Legna Verdecia, Cuba
2. ....Noriko Narazaki, Japan
3. ....Kye Sun Hi, N Korea
3. ....Liu Yuxiang, China

LIGHTWEIGHT
1. ....Isabel Fernández, Spain
2. ....Driulis González, Cuba
3. ....Kie Kusakabe, Japan
3. ....Maria Pekli, Australia

HALF-MIDDLEWEIGHT
1. ....Severine Vandenhende, France
2. ....Li Shufang, China
3. ....Gella Vandecaveye, Belgium
3. ....Jung Sung Sook, S Korea

MIDDLEWEIGHT
1. ....Sibelis Veranes, Cuba
2. ....Kate Howey, Great Britain
3. ....Cho Min Sun, S Korea
3. ....Ylenia Scapin, Italy

HALF-HEAVYWEIGHT
1. ....Lin Tang, China
2. ....Celine LeBrun, France
3. ....Simona Marcela Richter, Romania
3. ....Emanuela Pierantozzi, Italy

HEAVYWEIGHT
1. ....Hua Yuan, China
2. ....Daima Mayelis Beltran, Cuba
3. ....Kim Seon-Young, S Korea
3. ....Mayumi Yamashita, Japan

MOUNTAIN BIKING

Men
1. ......Miguel Martinez, France	2:09:02
2. ......Filip Meirhaeghe, Belgium	2:10.05
3. ......Christoph Sauser, Switzerland	2:11:21

Women
1. ......Paola Pezzo, Italy	1:49:24
2. ......Barbara Blatter, Switzerland	1:49.51
3. ......Margarita Fullana, Spain	1:49.57

MODERN PENTATHLON

Men
1. ......Dmitry Svatlovsky, Russia
2. ......Gabor Balogh, Hungary
3. ......Pavel Dovgal, Belarus

Women
1. ......Stephanie Cook, Great Britain
2. ......Emily deRiel, United States
3. ......Kate Allenby, Great Britain

ROWING

Men

SINGLE SCULLS
1. ...Rob Waddell, New Zealand	6:48:90
2. ...Xeno Mueller, Switzerland	6:50.55
3. ...Marcel Hacker, Germany	6:50.83

DOUBLE SCULLS
1. ...I. Cop/L. Spik, Slovenia	6:16.63
2. ...F. Beeken/O Tufte, Norway	6:17.98
3. ...G. Calabrese/N. Sartori, Italy	6:20.49

LIGHTWEIGHT DOUBLE SCULLS
1. ...T. Kucharski/R. Sycz, Poland	6:21.75
2. ...E. Liunii/L. Pettinari, Italy	6:23.57
3. ...T. Chappelle/P. Touron, France	6:24.85

QUADRUPLE SCULLS
1. ...Italy	5:45.56
2. ...Netherlands	5:47.91
3. ...Germany	5:48.64

ROWING (Cont.)
Men (Cont.)

COXLESS PAIR

1. ...M. Andrieux/ J. Rolland, France	6:32.97
2. ...S. Bea/ T. Murphy, United States	6:33.80
3. ...J. Tomkins/ M. Long, Australia	6:34.26

COXLESS FOUR

1. ...Great Britain	5:56.24
2. ...Italy	5:56.62
3. ...Australia	5:57.61

SINGLE SCULLS

1. ...Ekaterina Karsten, Belarus	7:28.14
2. ...Rumyana Neykova, Bulgaria	7:28.15
3. ...K. Rutschow-Stomporowski, Germany	7:28.99

DOUBLE SCULLS

1. ...K. Boron/ J. Thieme, Germany	6:55.44
2. ...P. Van Dishoeck/ E. Van Nes, Netherlands	7:00.36
3. ...B. Sakickiene/ K. Poplavskaya, Lithuania	7:01.71

LIGHTWEIGHT DOUBLE SCULLS

1. ...C. Burcica/ A. Alupei, Romania	7:02.64
2. ...V. Viehoff/ C. Blaserg, Germany	7:02.95
3. ...C. Collins/ S. Garner, United States	7:06.37

LIGHTWEIGHT COXLESS FOUR

1. ...France	6:01.68
2. ...Australia	6:02.09
3. ...Denmark	6:03.51

EIGHT-OARS

1. ...Great Britain	5:33.08
2. ...Australia	5:33.88
3. ...Croatia	5:34.85

Women

QUADRUPLE SCULLS

1. ...Germany	6:19.58
2. ...Great Britain	6:21.64
3. ...Russia	6:21.65

COXLESS PAIR

1. ...G. Damian/D. Ignat, Romania	7:11.00
2. ...R. Taylor/K. Slatter, Australia	7:12.56
3. ...K. Kraft/M. Ryan, United States	7:13.00

EIGHT-OARS

1. ...Romania	6:06.44
2. ...Netherlands	6:09.39
3. ...Canada	6:11.58

SHOOTING
Men

RAPID-FIRE PISTOL

	Pts
1......Serguei Alifirenko, Russia	687.6
2......Michel Ansermet, Switzerland	686.1
3......Iulian Raicen, Romania	684.6

FREE PISTOL

	Pts
1......Tanyu Kiriakov, Bulgaria	666.0
2......Igor Basinski, Belarus	663.3
3......Martin Tenk, Czech Republic	662.5

AIR PISTOL

	Pts
1......Franck Dumoulin, France	688.9
2......Yifu Wang, China	686.9
3......Igor Basinsky, Belarus	682.7

RUNNING TARGET

	Pts
1......Ling Yang, China	681.1
2......Oleg Moldovan, Moldova	681.0
3......Zhiyuan Niu, China	677.4

SMALL-BORE RIFLE, THREE-POSITION

	Pts
1......Rajmond Debevec, Slovenia	1275.1
2......Juha Hirvi, Finland	1270.5
3......Harald Stenvaag, Norway	1268.6

SMALL-BORE RIFLE, PRONE

	Pts
1......Jonas Edman, Swedem	701.3
2......Torben Grimmel, Denmark	700.4
3......Sergei Martynov, Belarus	700.3

AIR RIFLE

	Pts
1......Yalin Cai, China	696.4
2......Artem Khadjibekov, Russia	695.1
3......Evgueni Aleinikov, Russia	693.8

TRAP

	Pts
1......Michael Diamond, Australia	122.0
2......Ian Peel, Great Britain	118.0
3......David Kostelecky, Czech Republic	116.0

DOUBLE TRAP

	Pts
1......Richard Faulds, Great Britain	187.0
2......Russell Mark, Australia	187.0
3......Fehaid Al Deehani, Kuwait	186.0

SKEET

	Pts
1......Mykola Milchen, Ukraine	150.0
2......Petr Malek, Czech Republic	148.0
3......James Graves, United States	147.0

Women

SPORT PISTOL

	Pts
1......Maria Grozdeva, Bulgaria	690.3
2......Luna Tao, China	689.8
3......Lolita Evglevskaya, Belarus	686.0

AIR PISTOL

	Pts
1......Luna Tao, China	488.2
2......Jasna Sekaric, Yugoslavia	486.5
3......Annemarie Forder, Australia	484.0

SHOOTING (Cont.)

Women (Cont.)

SMALL-BORE RIFLE, THREE-POSITION

	Pts
1......Renata Mauer-Rozanska, Poland	684.6
2......Tatiana Goldobina, Russia	680.9
3......Maria Feklistova, Russia	679.9

AIR RIFLE

	Pts
1......Nancy Johnson, United States	497.7
2......Kang Cho-Hyan, S Korea	497.5
3......Jing Gao, China	497.2

DOUBLE TRAP

	Pts
1......Pia Hansen, United States	148.0
2......Deborah Gelisio, Italy	144.0
3......Kimberly Rhode, United States	139.0

TRAP

	Pts
1......Daina Gudzineviciute, Lithuania	93.0
2......Delphine Racinet, France	92.0
3......E Gao, China	90.0

SKEET

	Pts
1......Zemfira Meftakhetdinova, Azerbaijan	98.0
2......Svetlana Demina, Russia	95.0
3......Diana Igaly, Hungary	93.0

SOCCER

Men

1. ....Cameroon
2. ....Spain
3. ....Chile

Women

1. ....Norway
2. ....United States
3. ....Germany

SOFTBALL

1. ....United States
2. ....Japan
3. ....Australia

SWIMMING

Men

50-METER FREESTYLE

1. ...Gary Hall Jr., United States	21.98
1. ...Anthony Ervin, United States	21.98
3. ...Pieter van den Hoogenband, Netherlands	22.03

100-METER FREESTYLE

1. ...Pieter van den Hoogenband, Netherlands	48.30
2. ...Alexander Popov, Russia	48.69
3. ...Gary Hall Jr., United States	48.73

200-METER FREESTYLE

1. ...Pieter van den Hoogenband, Netherlands	1:45.35 EWR
2. ...Ian Thorpe, Australia	1:45.83
3. ...Massimiliano Rosolino, Italy	1:46.65

400-METER FREESTYLE

1. ...Ian Thorpe, Australia	3:40.59 WR
2. ...Massimiliano Rosolino, Italy	3:43.50
3. ...Klete Keller, United States	3:47.00

1,500-METER FREESTYLE

1. ...Grant Hackett, Australia	14:48.33
2. ...Kieren Perkins Australia	14:53.59
3. ...Chris Thompson, United States	14:56.81

100-METER BACKSTROKE

1. ...Lenny Krayzelburg, United States	53.72 OR
2. ...Matthew Welsh, Australia	54.07
3. ...Stev Theloke, Germany	54.82

200-METER BACKSTROKE

1. ...Lenny Krayzelburg, United States	1:56.76 OR
2. ...Aaron Piersol, United States	1:57.35
3. ...Matthew Welsh, Australia	1:59.59

100-METER BREASTSTROKE

1. ...Domenico Fioravanti, Italy	1:00.46 OR
2. ...Ed Moses, United States	1:00.73
3. ...Roman Sloudnov, Russia	1:00.91

200-METER BREASTSTROKE

1. ...Domenico Fioravanti, Italy	2:10.87
2. ...Terence Parkin, S Africa	2:12.50
3. ...Davide Rummolo, Italy	2:12.73

100-METER BUTTERFLY

1. ...Lars Froelander, Sweden	52.00
2. ...Michael Klim, Australia	52.18
3. ...Geoff Huegill, Australia	52.22

200-METER BUTTERFLY

1. ...Tom Malchow, United States	1:55.35 OR
2. ...Denys Sylant'yev, Ukraine	1:55.76
3. ...Justin Norris, Australia	1:56.17

200-METER INDIVIDUAL MEDLEY

1. ...Massimiliano Rosolino, Italy	1:58.98 OR
2. ...Tom Dolan, United States	1:59.77
3. ...Tom Wilkens, United States	2:00.87

400-METER INDIVIDUAL MEDLEY

1. ...Tom Dolan, United States	4:11.76 WR
2. ...Eric Vendt, United States	4:14.23
3. ...Curtis Myden, Canada	4:15.33

4 X 100-METER MEDLEY RELAY

1. ...United States (Lenny Krayzelburg, Ed Moses, Ian Crocker, Gary Hall Jr.)	3:34.84 WR
2. ...Australia	3:35.27
3. ...Germany	3:35.88

4 X 100-METER FREESTYLE RELAY

1. ...Australia (Ian Thorpe, Michael Klim, Ashley Callus, Chris Fydler)	3:13.67 WR
2. ...United States	3:13.86
3. ...Brazil	3:17.40

4 X 200-METER FREESTYLE RELAY

1. ...Australia (Ian Thorpe, Michael Klim, William Kirby, Todd Pearson)	7:07.05 WR
2. ...United States	7:12.64
3. ...Netherlands	7:12.70

Note: OR=Olympic record. WR=world record. EOR=equals Olympic record. EWR=equals world record.

SWIMMING (Cont.)
Women

50-METER FREESTYLE
1. ...Inge de Bruijn, Netherlands — 24.32
2. ...Therese Alshammar, Sweden — 24.51
3. ...Dara Torres, United States — 24.63

100-METER FREESTYLE
1. ...Inge de Bruijn, Netherlands — 53.83
2. ...Therese Alshammar, Sweden — 54.33
3. ...Dara Torres, United States — 54.43

200-METER FREESTYLE
1. ...Susie O'Neill, Australia — 1:58.24
2. ...Martina Moravcova, Slovakia — 1:58.32
3. ...Claudia Poll Ahrens, Costa Rica — 1:58.81

400-METER FREESTYLE
1. ...Brooke Bennett, United States — 4:05.80
2. ...Diana Munz, United States — 4:07.07
3. ...Claudia Poll Ahrens, Costa Rica — 4:07.83

800-METER FREESTYLE
1. ...Brooke Bennett, United States — 8:19.67 OR
2. ...Yana Klochkova, Ukraine — 8:22.66
3. ...Kaitlin Sandeno, United States — 8:24.29

100-METER BACKSTROKE
1. ...Diana Iuliana Mocanu, Romania — 1:00.21 OR
2. ...Mai Nakamura, Japan — 1:00.55
3. ...Nina Zhivanevskaya, Spain — 1:00.89

200-METER BACKSTROKE
1. ...Diana Iuliana Mocanu, Romania — 2:08.16
2. ...Roxana Maracineanu, France — 2:10.25
3. ...Miki Nakao, Japan — 2:11.05

100-METER BREASTSTROKE
1. ...Megan Quann, United States — 1:07.05
2. ...Leisel Jones, Australia — 1:07.49
3. ...Penny Heyns, S Africa — 1:07.55

200-METER BREASTSTROKE
1. ...Agnes Kovacs, Hungary — 2:24.35
2. ...Kristy Kowal, United States — 2:24.56
3. ...Amanda Beard, United States — 2:25.35

100-METER BUTTERFLY
1. ...Inge de Bruijn, Netherlands — 56.61 WR
2. ...Martina Moravcova, Slovakia — 57.97
3. ...Dara Torres, United States — 58.20

200-METER BUTTERFLY
1. ...Misty Hyman, United States — 2:05.88 OR
2. ...Susie O'Neill, Australia — 2:06.58
3. ...Petria Thomas, Australia — 2:07.12

200-METER INDIVIDUAL MEDLEY
1. ...Yana Klochkova, Ukraine — 2:10.68 OR
2. ...Beatrice Nicoleta Caslaru, Rom — 2:12.57
3. ...Cristina Teuscher, United States — 2:13.32

400-METER INDIVIDUAL MEDLEY
1. ...Yana Klochkova, Ukraine — 4:33.59 WR
2. ...Yasuko Tajima, Japan — 4:35.90
3. ...Beatrice Nicoleta Caslaru, Romania — 4:37.18

4 X 100-METER MEDLEY RELAY
1. ...United States (BJ Bedford, — 3:58.30 WR
Megan Quann, Jenny Thompson,
Dara Torres)
2. ...Australia — 4:01.59
3. ...Japan — 4:04.16

4 X 100-METER FREESTYLE RELAY
1. ...United States (Jenny Thompson, — 3:36.61 WR
Courtney Shealy, Dara Torres,
Amy Van Dyken)
2. ...Netherlands — 3:39.83
3. ...Sweden — 3:40.30

4 X 200-METER FREESTYLE RELAY
1. ...United States (Samantha Arsenault, — 7:57.80 OR
Diana Munz, Lindsay Benko,
Jenny Thompson)
2. ...Australia — 7:58.52
3. ...Germany — 7:58.64

Note: OR=Olympic record. WR=world record. EOR=equals Olympic record. EWR=equals world record.

SYNCHRONIZED SWIMMING

DUET
1. ...Russia — 99.580
2. ...Japan — 98.650
3. ...France — 97.437

TEAM
1. ...Russia — 99.146
2. ...Japan — 98.860
3. ...Canada — 97.357

SYNCHRONIZED DIVING

Men

3M SPRINGBOARD

		Pts
1.	...Xiang Ni/ Xiao Hailang, China	365.58
2.	...D. Sautin/ A. Dobroskoki, Russia	329.97
3.	...D. Pullan/ R. Newbery, Australia	322.86

10M PLATFORM

		Pts
1.	...I. Loukachine/ D. Sautin, Russia	365.04
2.	...Tian Liang/ Hu Jia, China	358.74
3.	...J.Hempel/ H. Meyer, Germany	338.88

Women

3M SPRINGBOARD

		Pts
1.	...V. Ilina/ I. Pakhalina, Russia	332.64
2.	...Guo Jing Jing/ Fu Mingxia, China	321.60
3.	...G. Sorokina/ O. Zhupina, Ukraine	290.34

10M PLATFORM

		Pts
1.	...Li Na/ Sang Zue, China	345.12
2.	...A. Montminy/ E.Heymanns, Canada	312.02
3.	...L. Tourky/ R. Gilmore, Australia	301.50

TABLE TENNIS

Men	Women
SINGLES	**SINGLES**
1. Kong Linghui, China	1. Wang Nan, China
2. Jan-Ove Wablner, Sweden	2. Li Ju, China
3. Liu Guoliang, China	3. Chen Jing, Taiwan
DOUBLES	**DOUBLES**
1. Wang Liqin/ Yan Sen, China	1. Li Ju/ Wang Nan, China
2. Kong Linghu/ Liu Guoliang, China	2. Sun Jin/ Yang Yin, China
3. Patrick Chila/ J.P. Gatien, France	3. Kim Moo Kyo/ Ji-Hye Ryu, S Korea

TAEKWONDO

Men	Women
FLYWEIGHT	**FLYWEIGHT**
1. Michail Mouroutsos, Greece	1. Lauren Burns, Australia
2. Gabriel Esparza, Spain	2. Urbia Melendez Rodriguez, Cuba
3. Chi-Hsiung Huang, China	3. Ju Chi Shu, China
FEATHERWEIGHT	**FEATHERWEIGHT**
1. Steven Lopez, United States	1. Jung Jae Eun, S Korea
2. Sin Joon Sik, S Korea	2. Hieu Ngan Tran, Vietnam
3. Hadi Saeibonehkohal, Iran	3. Hamide Bikcin, Turkey
WELTERWEIGHT	**WELTERWEIGHT**
1. Angel Valodia Matos Fuentes, Cuba	1. Sun-Hee Lee, S Korea
2. Faissal Ebnoutalib, Germany	2. Trude Gunderson, Denmark
3. Victor Estrada Garibay, Mexico	3. Yoriko Okamoto, Japan
HEAVYWEIGHT	**HEAVYWEIGHT**
1. Kyong-Hun Kim, S Korea	1. Chen Zhong, China
2. Daniel Trenton, Australia	2. Natalia Ivanova, Russia
3. Pascal Gentil, France	3. Dominique Bosshart, Canada

TEAM HANDBALL

Men	Women
1. Russia	1. Denmark
2. Sweden	2. Hungary
3. Spain	3. Norway

TENNIS

Men	Women
SINGLES	**SINGLES**
1. Yevgeni Kafelnikov, Russia	1. Venus Williams, United States
2. Tommy Haas, Germany	2. Elena Dementieva, Russia
3. Arnaud Di Pasquale, France	3. Monica Seles, United States
DOUBLES	**DOUBLES**
1. Daniel Nestor/ Sebastien Lareau, Canada	1. V. Williams/ S. Williams, United States
2. Todd Woodbridge/ Mark Woodforde, Australia	2. Kristie Boogert/ Miriam Oremans, Netherlands
3. Alex Corretja/ Albert Costa, Spain	3. Dominique van Roost/ Els Callens, Belgium

TRAMPOLINE

Men		Women	
1. Alexandre Mosalenko, Russia	41.70	1. Irina Karavaeva, Russia	38.90
2. Ji Wallace, Australia	39.30	2. Oxana Tsyhuleva, Ukraine	37.70
3. Mathieu Turgeon, Canada	39.10	3. Karen Cockburn, Canada	37.40

TRIATHLON

Men		Women	
1. Simon Whitfield, Canada	1:48.24.02	1. Brigitte McMahon, Switz.	2:00.40.52.
2. Stefan Vucovic, Germany	1:48.37.58	2. Michellie Jones, Australia	2:00.42.55
3. Jan Rehula, Czech Rep.	1:48.46,64	3. Magali Messmer, Switz.	2:01.08.83

VOLLEYBALL

Men
1. ....Yugoslavia
2. ....Russia
3. ....Italy

Women
1. ....Cuba
2. ....Russia
3. ....Brazil

BEACH VOLLEYBALL

Men
1. ....Dain Blanton/ E. Fonoimoana, United States
2. ....Ze Marco Melo/ Ricardo Santos, Brazil
3. ....Joerg Ahmann/ Axel Hager, Germany

Women
1. ....Kerri Pottharst/ Natalie Cook, Australia
2. ....Shelda Bede/ Adriana Behar, Brazil
3. ....Adriana Samuel/ Sandra Pires, Brazil

WATER POLO

Men
1. ....Hungary
2. ....Russia
3. ....Yugoslavia

Women
1. ....Australia
2. ....United States
3. ....Russia

WEIGHTLIFTING

Men

123 POUNDS
1. ....Halil Mutlu, Turkey — 671 lb WR
2. ....Wu Wenxiong, China — 631 lb
3. ....Zhang Xiangxiang, China — 631 lb

137 POUNDS
1. ....Nikolay Pechaliv, Croatia — 715 lb OR
2. ....Leonidas Sabanis, Greece — 697 lb
3. ....Gennady Oleshchuk, Belarus — 697 lb

152 POUNDS
1. ....Galabin Boevski, Bulgaria — 785 lb OR
2. ....Georgi Markov, Bulgaria — 774 lb
3. ....Sergei Lavrenov, Belarus — 680 lb

170 POUNDS
1. ....Zhan Xugang, China — 807 lb
2. ....Viktor Mitrou, Greece — 807 lb
3. ....Arsen Melikyan, Armenia — 803 lb

187 POUNDS
1. ....Pyrros Dimas, Greece — 858 lb
2. ....Marc Huster, Germany — 858 lb
3. ....George Asanidze, Georgia — 858 lb

207 POUNDS
1. ....Akakios Kakiasvilis, Greece — 891 lb
2. ....Szymon Kolecki, Poland — 891 lb
3. ....Alexei Petrov. Russia — 884 lb

231 POUNDS
1. ....Hossein Tavakoli, Iran — 935 lb
2. ....Alan Tsagaev, Bulgaria — 928 lb
3. ....Said Asaad, Qatar — 924 lb

231+ POUNDS
1. ....Hossein Rezazadeh, Iran — 1,045 lb WR
2. ....Ronny Weller, Germany — 1,025 lb
3. ....Andrei Chermerkin, Russia — 1,017 lb

Women

106 POUNDS
1. ....Tara Nott, United States — 407 lb
2. ....Raema Rumbewas, Indonesia — 407 lb
3. ....Sri Indriyani, Indonesia — 400 lb

117 POUNDS
1. ....Yang Xia, China — 495 lb WR
2. ....Li Feng ying, Taipei — 466 lb
3. ....Winarni Slamet, Indonesia — 444 lb

128 POUNDS
1. ....Soraya Mendivil, Mexico — 488 lb
2. ....Ri Song Hui, N Korea — 484 lb
3. ....Khassaraporn Suta, Thailand — 462 lb

139 POUNDS
1. ....Xiaomin Chen, China — 532 lb
2. ....Valentina Popova, Russia — 517 lb
3. ....Ioanna Chatziioannou, Greece — 488 lb

152 POUNDS
1. ....Lin Weining, China — 532 lb
2. ....Erzsebet Markus, Hungary — 532 lb
3. ....Karnam Malleswari. Indonesia — 528 lb

165 POUNDS
1. ....Maria Isabel Urrutia, Colombia — 539 lb
2. ....Ruth Ogbeifo, Nigeria — 539 lb
3. ....Kuo Yi Hang, Taipei — 539 lb

165 + POUNDS
1. ....Ding Meiyuan, China — 660 lb WR
2. ....Agata Wrobel, Poland — 649 lb OR
3. ....Cheryl Haworth, United States — 594 lb

FREESTYLE WRESTLING

119 POUNDS
1. ....Namig Abdullayev, Azerbaijan
2. ....Samuel Henson, United States
3. ....Amiran Karntanov, Greece

127.75 POUNDS
1. ....Alireza Dabir, Iran
2. ....Yevgen Buslovych, Ukraine
3. ....Terry Brands, United States

138.75 POUNDS
1. ....Mourad Oumakhanov, Russia
2. ....Serafim Barzakov, Bulgaria
3. ....Jang Jae Sung, S Korea

152 POUNDS
1. ....Daniel Igali, Canada
2. ....Arsen Gitinov, Russia
3. ....Lincoln McIlvray, United States

167.5 POUNDS
1. ....Alexander Leipold, Germany
2. ....Brandon Slay, United States
3. ....Moon Eui Jae, S Korea

187.25 POUNDS
1. ....Adam Saitiev, Russia
2. ....Yoel Romero, Cuba
3. ....Mogamed Ibragimov, Macedonia

213.75 POUNDS
1. ....Sagid Mourtasaliyev, Russia
2. ....Islam Bairamukov, Kazakhstan
3. ....Eldar Kurtanidze, Georgia

286 POUNDS
1. ....David Moussoulbes, Russia
2. ....Artur Taymazov, Uzbekistan
3. ....Alexis Rodriguez, Cuba

GRECO-ROMAN WRESTLING

119 POUNDS
1. ....Kwon Ho Sim, S Korea
2. ....Lazaro Rivas, Cuba
3. ....Young Gyun Kang, N Korea

127.75 POUNDS
1. ....Armen Nazarian, Bulgaria
2. ....Kim In Sub, S Korea
3. ....Zertian Sheng, China

138.75 POUNDS
1. ....Varteres Samourgachev, Russia
2. ....Juan Luis Maren, Cuba
3. ....Akaki Chachua, Georgia

152 POUNDS
1. ....Filiberto Azcuy, Cuba
2. ....Katsushiko Nagata, Japan
3. ....Alexei Glouchkov, Russia

167.5 POUNDS
1. ....Mourat Kardanov, Russia
2. ....Matt James Lindland, United States
3. ....M. Yli-Hannuksela, Finland

187.25 POUNDS
1. ....Hamza Yerlikaya, Turkey
2. ....Sandor Istvan Bardosi, Hungary
3. ....Mukhran Vakhtangadze, Georgia

213.75 POUNDS
1. ....Mikael Ljundberg, Sweden
2. ....Davyd Saldadze, Ukraine
3. ....Garrett Lowney, United States

286 POUNDS
1. ....Rulon Gardner, United States
2. ....Alexander Karelin, Russia
3. ....Dmitry Debelka, Belarus

YACHTING

MEN'S 470
1. ....Australia
2. ....United States
3. ....Argentina

MEN'S FINN
1. ....Iain Percy, Great Britain
2. ....Luca Devoti, Italy
3. ....Fredrik Loof, Sweden

MEN'S BOARD
1. ....Christoph Sieber, Austria
2. ....Carlos Espinosa, Argentina
3. ....Aaron McIntosh, New Zealand

WOMEN'S 470
1. ....Australia
2. ....United States
3. ....Ukraine

WOMEN'S EUROPE
1. ....Shirley Robertson, Great Britain
2. ....Margriet Matthysse, Netherlands
3. ....Serena Amato, Argentina

WOMEN'S BOARD
1. ....Alessandra Sensini, Italy
2. ....Amelie Lux, Germany
3. ....Barbara Kendall, New Zealand

SOLING
1. ....Denmark
2. ....Germany
3. ....Norway

STAR
1. ....M. Reynolds/M. Liljedahl, United States
2. ....M. Covell/ I. Walker, Great Britain
3. ....T. Grael/ M. Ferreira, Brazil

TORNADO
1. ....H. Steinacher/ R.Hagara, Austria
2. ....J. Forbes/ D. Bundock, Australia
3. ....R. Gaebler/ R. Schwall, Germany

LASER
1. ....Ben Ainslie, Great Britain
2. ....Robert Scheidt, Brazil
3. ....Michael Blackburn, Australia

49ER
1. ....T. Johnson/ J. Jarvi, Finland
2. ....I. Barker/ S. Hicksocks, Great Britain
3. ....J. McKee/ C. McKee, United States

BIATHLON

Men
10 KILOMETERS
1. ...Ole Einar Bjoerndalen, Norway   24:51.3
2. ...Sven Fisher, Germany   25:20.2
3. ...Wolfgang Perner, Austria   25:44.4

20 KILOMETERS
1. ...Ole Einar Bjoerndalen, Norway   51:03.3
2. ...Frank Luck, Germany   51:39.4
3. ...Victor Maigovrov, Russia   51:40.6

4 X 7.5-KILOMETER RELAY
1. ....Norway   1:23:42.3
2. ....Germany   1:24:27.7
3. ....France   1:24:36.6

Women
7.5 KILOMETERS
1. ...Kati Wilhelm, Germany   20:41.4
2. ...Uschi Disl, Germany   20:57.0
3. ...Magdalena Forsberg, Sweden   21:20.4

15 KILOMETERS
1. ...Andrea Henkel, Germany   47:29.1
2. ...Liv Grete Poiree, Norway   47:37.0
3. ...Magdalena Forsberg, Sweden   48:08.3

4 X 7.5-KILOMETER RELAY
1. ....Germany   1:27:55.0
2. ....Norway   1:28:25.6
3. ....Russia   1:29:19.7

BOBSLED

Men
TWO-MAN
1. ...Christoph Langen/ Markus Zimmerman, Germany I   3:10.10
2. ...Christian Reich/ Steve Anderhub, Switz.I   3:10.20
3. ...Martin Annen/ Beat Hefti, Switz II   3:10.62

FOUR-MAN
1. ....Germany II   3:07.51
2. ....USA I   3:07.81
3. ....USA II   3:07.86

Women
TWO-PERSON
1. ...Jill Bakken/ Vonetta Flowers, USA II   1:37.76
2. ...Sandra Prokoff/ Ulrike Holzner, Ger. I   1:38.06
3. ...S.L. Erdmann/ N. Herschmann, Ger II   1:38.29

CURLING

Men
1. ....Norway
2. ....Canada
3. ....Switzerland

Women
1. ....Britain
2. ....Switzerland
3. ....Canada

FIGURE SKATING

Men
1. ....Alexei Yagudin, Russia
2. ....Evgeni Plushenko, Russia
3. ....Timothy Goebel, United States

Pairs
1. ...Elena Berezhnaya/ Anton Sikharulidze, Russia
1. ...David Pelletier/ Jamie Sale, Canada
3. ...Hongbo Zhao/ Xue Shen, China

Women
1. ....Sarah Hughes, United States
2. ....Irina Slutskaya, Russia
3. ....Michelle Kwan, United States

Ice Dancing
1. ...Marina Anissina/ Gwendal Peizerat, France
2. ...Irina Lobacheva/ Ilia Averbukh, Russia
3. ...Barbara Fusar Poli/ Maurizio Margaglio, Italy

ICE HOCKEY

Men
1. ....Canada
2. ....USA
3. ....Russia

Women
1. ....Canada
2. ....USA
3. ....Sweden

LUGE

Men
SINGLES
1. ...Armin Zoeggeler, Italy   2:57.941
2. ...Georg Hackl, Germany   2:58.270
3. ...Markus Prock, Austria   2:58.283

DOUBLES
1. ...Alexander Resch/ P.F. Leitner, Ger   1:26.082
2. ...Mark Grimmette/ Brian Martin, U.S.   1:26.216
3. ...Chris Thorpe/ Clay Ives, U.S.   1:26.220

Women
SINGLES
1. ...Sylke Otto, Germany   2:52.464
2. ...Barbara Niedernhuber, Germany   2:52.785
3. ...Silke Kraushaar, Germany   2:52.865

SKELETON

Men
1. ....Jim Shea Jr., United States   1:41.96
2. ....Martin Rettl, Austria   1:42.01
3. ....Gregor Staehli, Switzerland   1:42.15

Women
1. ....Tristan Gale, United States   1:45.11
2. ....Lea Ann Parsley, United States   1:45.21
3. ....Alex Coomber, Great Britain   1:45.37

SPEED SKATING
Men

500 METERS
1. ...Casey FitzRandolph, United States   1:09.23
2. ...Hiroyasu Shimizu, Japan   1:09.26
3. ...Kip Carpenter, United States   1:09.47

1,000 METERS
1. ...Gerard Van Velde, Netherlands   1:07.18
2. ...Jan Bos, Netherlands   1:07.53
3. ...Joey Cheek, United States   1:07.61

1,500 METERS
1. ...Derek Parra, United States   1:43.95
2. ...Jochem Uytdehaage, Netherlands   1:44.57
3. ...Adne Sondral, Norway   1:45.26

5,000 METERS
1. ...Jochem Uytdehaage, Netherlands   6:14.66
2. ...Derek Parra, United States   6:17.98
3. ...Jens Boden, Germany   6:21.73

10,000 METERS
1. ...Jochem Uytdenhaage, Netherlands   12:58.92 WR
2. ...Gianni Romme, Netherlands   13:10.03
3. ...Lasse Saetre, Norway   13:16.92

500 METERS SHORT TRACK
1. ...Marc Gagnon, Canada   41.802 OR
2. ...Jonathan Guilmette, Canada   41.994
3. ...Rusty Smith, United States   42.027

1,000 METERS SHORT TRACK
1. ...Steven Bradbury, Austrialia   1:29.109
2. ...Apolo Anton Ohno, United States   1:30.160
3. ...Mathieu Turcotte, Canada   1:30.563

1,500 METERS SHORT TRACK
1. ...Apolo Anton Ohno, United States   2:18.541
2. ...Jiajun Li, China   2:18.731
3. ...Marc Gagnon, Canada   2:18.806

5,000-METER SHORT TRACK RELAY
1. ...Canada   6:51.579
2. ...Italy   6:56.327
3. ...China   6:59.633

Women

500 METERS
1. ...Catriona LeMay Doan, Canada   1:14.75
2. ...Monique Garbrecht-Enfeld, Ger   1:14.94
3. ...Sabine Voelker, Germany   1:15.19

1,000 METERS
1. ...Chris Witty, United States   1:13.83
2. ...Sabine Voelker, Germany   1:13.96
3. ...Jennifer Rodriguez, United States   1:14.24

1,500 METERS
1. ...Anni Friesinger, Germany   1:54.02
2. ...Sabine Voelker, Germany   1:54.94
3. ...Jennifer Rodriguez, United States   1:55.32

3,000 METERS
1. ...Claudia Pechstein, Germany   3:57.70
2. ...Renate Groenwold, Netherlands   3:58.94
3. ...Cindy Klassen, Canada   3:58.94

5,000 METERS
1. ...Claudia Pechstein, Germany   6:46.91 WR
2. ...Gretha Smit, Germany   6:49.22
3. ...Clara Hughes, Canada   6:53.53

500 METERS SHORT TRACK
1. ...Annie Perreault, Canada   46.568
2. ...Yang Yang, China   46.627
3. ...Chun Lee Kyung, S Korea   46.335

1,000 METERS
1. ...Yang A. Yang, China   1:36.391
2. ...Gi-Hyun Ko, Korea   1:36.427
3. ...Yang S. Yang, China   1:37.008

1,500 METERS
1. ...Gi-Hyan Ko, Korea   2:31.581
2. ...Eun-Kyung Choi, Korea   2:31.610
3. ...Evgenia Radanova, Bulgaria   2:31.723

3,000-METER SHORT TRACK RELAY
1. ...Korea   4:12.793
2. ...China   4:13.236
3. ...Canada   4:15.738

Note: OR=Olympic Record. WR=World Record. EOR=Equals Olympic Record. EWR=Equals World Record. WB=World Best.

ALPINE SKIING

Men

DOWNHILL
1. ...Fritz Strobl, Austria   1:39.13
2. ...Lasse Kjus, Norway   1:39.35
3. ...Stephan Eberharter, Austria   1:39.41

SLALOM
1. ...Jean-Pierre Vidal, France   1:41.06
2. ...Sebastien Amiez, France   1:41.82
3. ...Benjamin Raich, Austria   1:42.41

GIANT SLALOM
1. ...Stephan Eberharter, Austria   2:23.28
2. ...Bode Miller, United States   2:24.16
3. ...Lasse Kjus, Norway   2:24.32

SUPER GIANT SLALOM
1. ...Kjetil André Aamodt, Norway   1:21.58
2. ...Stephan Eberharter, Austria   1:21.68
3. ...Andreas Schifferer, Austria   1:21.83

COMBINED
1. ...Kjetil André Aamodt, Norway   3:17.56
2. ...Bode Miller, United States   3:17.84
3. ...Benjamin Raich, Austria   3:18.26

Women

DOWNHILL
1. ...Carole Montillet, France   1:39.56
2. ...Isolde Kostner, Italy   1:40.01
3. ...Renate Goetschl, Austria   1:40.39

SLALOM
1. ...Janica Kostelic, Croatia   1:46.10
2. ...Laure Pequegnot, France   1:46.17
3. ...Anja Paerson, Sweden   1:47.09

GIANT SLALOM
1. ...Janica Kostelic, Croatia   2:30.01
2. ...Anja Paerson, Sweden   2:31.33
3. ...Sonja Nef, Switzerland   2:31.67

SUPER GIANT SLALOM
1. ...Daniela Ceccarelli, Italy   1:13.59
2. ...Janica Kostelic, Croatia   1:13.64
3. ...Karen Putzer, Italy   1:13.86

COMBINED
1. ...Janica Kostelic, Croatia   2:43.28
2. ...Renate Goetschl, Austria   2:44.77
3. ...Martina Ertl, Germany   2:45.16

FREESTYLE SKIING

Men

MOGULS	Pts
1. ...Janne Lahtela, Finland	27.97
2. ...Travis Mayer, United States	27.59
3. ...Richard Gay, France	26.91

AERIALS	Pts
1. ...Ales Valenta, Czech Republic	257.02
2. ...Joe Pack, United States	251.64
3. ...Alexei Grichin, Belarus	251.19

Women

MOGULS	Pts
1. ...Kari Traa, Norway	25.94
2. ...Shannon Bahrke, United States	25.06
3. ...Tae Satoya, Japan	24.85

AERIALS	Pts
1. ...Alisa Camplin, Australia	193.47
2. ...Veronica Brenner, Canada	190.02
3. ...Deidra Dionne, Canada	189.26

NORDIC SKIING

Men

1.5 KILOMETERS SPRINT
1. ...Tor Arne Hetland, Norway — 2:56.9
2. ...Peter Schlickenrieder, Germany — 2:57.0
3. ...Cristian Zorzi, Italy — 2:57.2

10 KILOMETERS PURSUIT FREESTYLE
1. ...Johann Muehlegg, Spain — 49:20.4
2. ...Frode Estil, Norway — 49:48.9
3. ...Thomas Alsgaard, Norway — 49:48.9

15 KILOMETERS CLASSICAL
1. ...Andrus Veerpalu, Estonia — 37:07.4
2. ...Frode Estil, Norway — 37:43.4
3. ...Jaak Mae, Estonia — 37:50.8

30 KILOMETERS FREESTYLE
1. ...Johann Muelegg, Spain — 1:09:28.9
2. ...Christian Hoffman, Austria — 1:11:31.0
3. ...Mikhail Botvinov, Austria — 1:11:32.3

50 KILOMETERS CLASSICAL
1. ...Mikhail Ivanov, Russia — 2:06:20.8
2. ...Andrus Veerpalu, Estonia — 2:06:44.5
3. ...Odd-Bjoern Hjelmeset, Norway — 2:08:41.5

4 X 10-KILOMETER RELAY MIXED STYLE
1. ....Norway — 1:32:45.5
2. ....Italy — 1:32:45.8
3. ....Germany — 1:33:21.0

90-METER HILL SKI JUMPING — Pts
1. ...Simon Ammann, Switzerland — 269.0
2. ...Sven Hannawald, Germany — 267.5
3. ...Adam Malysz, Poland — 263.0

120-METER HILL SKI JUMPING — Pts
1. ...Simon Ammann, Switzerland — 281.4
2. ...Adam Malysz, Germany — 269.7
3. ...Matti Hautamacki, Finland — 256.0

120-METER HILL TEAM SKI JUMPING — Pts
1. ...Germany — 974.1
2. ...Finland — 974.0
3. ...Slovenia — 946.3

INDIVIDUAL COMBINED — Pts
1. ...Samppa Lajunen, Finland — 123.8
2. ...Jaakko Tallus, Finland — 119.9
3. ...Felix Gottwald, Austria — 110.3

INDIVIDUAL SPRINT COMBINED — Pts
1. ...Samppa Lajunen, Finland — 123.8
2. ...Ronny Ackermann, Germany — 119.9
3. ...Felix Gottwald, Austria — 110.3

TEAM COMBINED
1. ....Finland — 48:42.2
2. ....Germany — 48:49.7
3. ....Austria — 48:53.2

Women

1.5 KILOMETERS SPRINT
1. ...Julija Tchepalova, Russia — 3:10.6
2. ...Evi Sachenbacher, Germany — 3:12.2
3. ...Anita Moen, Norway — 3:12.7

5 KILOMETERS PURSUIT
1. ...Olga Danilova, Russia — 24:52.1
2. ...Larissa Lazutina, Russia — 24:59.0
3. ...Beckie Scott, Canada — 25:09.9

10 KILOMETERS CLASSICAL STYLE
1. ...Bante Skari, Norway — 28:05.6
2. ...Olga Danilova, Russia — 28:08.1
3. ...Julija Tchepalova, Russia — 28:09.9

15 KILOMETERS FREESTYLE
1. ...Stefania Belmondo, Italy — 39:54.4
2. ...Larissa Lazutina, Russia — 39:54.4
3. ...Katerina Neumannova, Czech Rep — 39:56.2

30 KILOMETERS CLASSICAL STYLE
1. ...Gabriella Paruzzi, Italy — 1:30:57.1
2. ...Stefania Belmondo, Italy — 1:31:01.6
3. ...Bente Skari, Norway — 1:31:36.3

4 X 5-KILOMETER RELAY MIXED STYLE
1. ....Germany — 49:30.6
2. ....Norway — 49:31.9
3. ....Switzerland — 50:03.6

SNOWBOARDING

Men

PARALLEL GIANT SLALOM
1. ...Philipp Schoch, Switzerland
2. ...Richard Richardsson, Sweden
3. ...Chris Klug, United States

HALF-PIPE	Pts
1. ...Ross Powers, United States	46.1
2. ...Danny Kass, United States	42.5
3. ...Jarret Thomas, United States	42.1

Women

PARALLEL GIANT SLALOM
1. ...Isabelle Blanc, France
2. ...Karine Ruby, Germany
3. ...Lidia Trettel, Italy

HALF-PIPE	Pts
1. ...Kelly Clark, United States	47.9
2. ...Doriane Vidal, France	43.0
3. ...Fabienne Reuteler, Switzerland	39.7

Olympic Games Locations and Dates

Summer

	Year	Site	Dates	Men	Women	Nations	Most Medals	US Medals
I	1896	Athens, Greece	Apr 6–15	311	0	13	Greece (10-19-18—47)	11-6-2—19 (2nd)
II	1900	Paris, France	May 20–Oct 28	1319	11	22	France (29-41-32—102)	20-14-19—53 (2nd)
III	1904	St Louis, United States	July 1–Nov 23	681	6	12	United States (80-86-72—238)	
—	1906	Athens, Greece	Apr 22–May 28	77	7	20	France (15-9-16—40)	12-6-5—23 (4th)
IV	1908	London, Great Britain	Apr 27–Oct 31	1999	36	23	Britain (56-50-39—145)	23-12-12—47 (2nd)
V	1912	Stockholm, Sweden	May 5–July 22	2490	57	28	Sweden (24-24-17—65)	23-19-19—61 (2nd)
VI	1916	Berlin, Germany	Canceled because of war					
VII	1920	Antwerp, Belgium	Apr 20–Sep 12	2543	64	29	United States (41-27-28—96)	
VIII	1924	Paris, France	May 4–July 27	2956	136	44	United States (45-27-27—99)	
IX	1928	Amsterdam, Netherlands	May 17–Aug 12	2724	290	46	United States (22-18-16—56)	
X	1932	Los Angeles, United States	July 30–Aug 14	1281	127	37	United States (41-32-31—104)	
XI	1936	Berlin, Germany	Aug 1–16	3738	328	49	Germany (33-26-30—89)	24-20-12—56 (2nd)
XII	1940	Tokyo, Japan	Canceled because of war					
XIII	1944	London, Great Britain	Canceled because of war					
XIV	1948	London, Great Britain	July 29–Aug 14	3714	385	59	United States (38-27-19—84)	
XV	1952	Helsinki, Finland	July 19–Aug 3	4407	518	69	United States (40-19-17—76)	
XVI	1956	Melbourne, Australia*	Nov 22–Dec 8	2958	384	67	USSR (37-29-32—98)	32-25-17—74 (2nd)
XVII	1960	Rome, Italy	Aug 25–Sep 11	4738	610	83	USSR (43-29-31—103)	34-21-16—71 (2nd)
XVIII	1964	Tokyo, Japan	Oct 10–24	4457	683	93	United States (36-26-28—90)	
XIX	1968	Mexico City, Mexico	Oct 12–27	4750	781	112	United States (45-28-34—107)	
XX	1972	Munich, W Germany	Aug 26–Sep 10	5848	1299	122	USSR (50-27-22—99)	33-31-30—94 (2nd)
XXI	1976	Montreal, Canada	July 17–Aug 1	4834	1251	92†	USSR (49-41-35—125)	34-35-25—94 (3rd)
XXII	1980	Moscow, USSR	July 19–Aug 3	4265	1088	81‡	USSR (80-69-46—195)	Did not compete
XXIII	1984	Los Angeles, United States	July 28–Aug 12	5458	1620	141#	United States (83-61-30—174)	
XXIV	1988	Seoul, S Korea	Sep 17–Oct 2	7105	2476	160	USSR (55-31-46—132)	36-31-27—94 (3rd)
XXV	1992	Barcelona, Spain	July 25–Aug. 9	7555	3008	172	Unified Team (45-38-29—112)	37-34-37—108 (2nd)
XXVI	1996	Atlanta, United States	July 19–Aug 4	6984	3766	197	United States (44-32-25—101)	
XXVII	2000	Sydney, Australia	Sept 15–Oct 1	6862	4254	199	United States (39-25-33—97)	

*The equestrian events were held in Stockholm, Sweden, June 10–17, 1956.

†This figure includes Cameroon, Egypt, Morocco, and Tunisia, countries that boycotted the 1976 Olympics after some of their athletes had already competed.

‡The U.S. was among 65 countries that did not participate in the 1980 Summer Games in Moscow.

#The USSR, East Germany, and 14 other countries did not participate in the 1984 Summer Games in Los Angeles.

Winter

	Year	Site	Dates	Men	Women	Nations	Most Medals	US Medals
I	1924	Chamonix, France	Jan 25–Feb 4	281	13	16	Norway (4-7-6—17)	1-2-1—4 (3rd)
II	1928	St. Moritz, Switzerland	Feb 11–19	366	27	25	Norway (6-4-5—15)	2-2-2—6 (2nd)
III	1932	Lake Placid, United States	Feb 4–13	277	30	17	United States (6-4-2—12)	
IV	1936	Garmisch-Partenkirchen, Germany	Feb 6–16	680	76	28	Norway (7-5-3—15)	1-0-3—4 (T-5th)
—	1940	Garmisch-Partenkirchen, Germany	Canceled because of war					
—	1944	Cortina d'Ampezzo, Italy	Canceled because of war					
V	1948	St. Moritz, Switzerland	Jan 30–Feb 8	636	77	28	Norway (4-3-3—10) Sweden (4-3-3—10) Switzerland (3-4-3—10)	3-4-2—9 (4th)
VI	1952	Oslo, Norway	Feb 14–25	624	108	30	Norway (7-3-6—16)	4-6-1—11 (2nd)
VII	1956	Cortina d'Ampezzo, Italy	Jan 26–Feb 5	687	132	32	USSR (7-3-6—16)	2-3-2—7 (T-4th)
VIII	1960	Squaw Valley, United States	Feb 18–28	502	146	30	USSR (7-5-9—21)	3-4-3—10 (2nd)
IX	1964	Innsbruck, Austria	Jan 29–Feb 9	758	175	36	USSR (11-8-6—25)	1-2-3—6 (7th)
X	1968	Grenoble, France	Feb 6–18	1063	230	37	Norway (6-6-2—14)	1-5-1—7 (T-7th)
XI	1972	Sapporo, Japan	Feb 3–13	927	218	35	USSR (8-5-3—16)	3-2-3—8 (6th)
XII	1976	Innsbruck, Austria	Feb 4–15	1013	248	37	USSR (13-6-8—27)	3-3-4—10 (T-3rd)
XIII	1980	Lake Placid, United States	Feb 13–24	1012	271	37	East Germany (9-7-7—23)	6-4-2—12 (3rd)
XIV	1984	Sarajevo, Yugoslavia	Feb 8–19	1127	283	49	USSR (6-10-9—25)	4-4-0—8 (T-5th)
XV	1988	Calgary, Canada	Feb 13–28	1270	364	57	USSR (11-9-9—29)	2-1-3—6 (T-8th)
XVI	1992	Albertville, France	Feb 8–23	1313	488	65	Germany (10-10-6—26)	5-4-2—11 (6th)
XVII	1994	Lillehammer, Norway	Feb 12–27	1302	542	67	Norway (10-11-5—26)	6-5-2—13 (T-5th)
XVIII	1998	Nagano, Japan	Feb 7–22	2302 (total)		72	Germany (12-9-8—29)	6-3-4—13 (6th)
XVIV	2002	Salt Lake City, United States	Feb 8–24	1513	886	77	Germany (12-16-7—35)	(10-13-11—34) (2nd)

Alltime Olympic Medal Winners

Summer

NATIONS

Nation	Gold	Silver	Bronze	Total	Nation	Gold	Silver	Bronze	Total
United States	871	659	586	2116	Finland	101	81	114	296
Soviet Union (1952–88)	395	319	296	1010	Japan	97	97	102	296
Great Britain	180	233	225	638	Romania	74	83	108	265
France	188	193	217	598	Poland	56	72	113	241
Italy	179	143	157	479	Canada	51	81	98	230
Sweden	136	156	177	469	China	80	79	64	223
E Germany (1956–88)	159	150	136	445	The Netherlands	61	67	85	213
Hungary	150	135	158	443	Bulgaria	48	82	65	195
Germany (1896–1936, 1992–)	138	138	160	436	Switzerland	47	75	61	183
Australia	102	110	138	350	Denmark	40	63	58	161
W Germany (1952–88)	77	104	120	301	Russia	59	53	47	159
					Czechoslovakia (1924–92)	49	49	44	142

Summer *(Cont.)*

INDIVIDUALS — OVERALL

Men						Women					
Athlete, Nation	Sport	G	S	B	Tot	Athlete, Nation	Sport	G	S	B	Tot
Nikolai Andrianov, USSR	Gym	7	5	3	15	Larissa Latynina, USSR	Gym	9	5	4	18
Boris Shakhlin, USSR	Gym	7	4	2	13	Vera Cáslavská, Czech	Gym	7	4	0	11
Edoardo Mangiarotti, Italy	Fen	6	5	2	13	Agnes Keleti, Hungary	Gym	5	3	2	10
Takashi Ono, Japan	Gym	5	4	4	13	Polina Astaknova, USSR	Gym	5	2	3	10
Paavo Nurmi, Finland	Track	9	3	0	12	Nadia Comaneci, Romania	Gym	5	3	1	9
Sawao Kato, Japan	Gym	8	3	1	12	Jenny Thompson, United States	Swim	7	1	1	9
Alexei Nemov, Russia	Gym	4	2	6	12	Lyudmila Tourischeva, USSR	Gym	4	3	2	9
Mark Spitz, United States	Swim	9	1	1	11	Kornelia Ender, E Germany	Swim	4	4	0	8
Matt Biondi, United States	Swim	8	2	1	11	Dawn Fraser, Australia	Swim	4	4	0	8
Viktor Chukarin, USSR	Gym	7	3	1	11	Shirley Babashoff, United States	Swim	2	6	0	8
Carl Osburn, United States	Shoot	5	4	2	11	Sofia Muratova, USSR	Gym	2	2	4	8
Ray Ewry, United States	Track	10	0	0	10	Dara Torres, United States	Swim	4	0	4	8
Carl Lewis, United States	Track	9	1	0	10	Eight tied with seven.					
Aladár Gerevich, Hungary	Fen	7	1	2	10						
Akinori Nakayama, Japan	Gym	6	2	2	10						
Vitaly Scherbo, UT/Belarus	Gym	6	0	4	10						
Aleksandr Dityatin, USSR	Gym	3	6	1	10						

INDIVIDUALS — GOLD

Men

Ray Ewry, United States 10	Sawao Kato, Japan 8	Viktor Chukarin, USSR................7
Paavo Nurmi, Finland 9	Matt Biondi, United States.........8	Aladár Gerevich, Hungary..........7
Carl Lewis, United States 9	Nikolai Andrianov, USSR 7	
Mark Spitz, United States 9	Boris Shakhlin, USSR 7	

Women

Larissa Latynina, USSR 9	Polina Astaknova, USSR 5	Janet Evans, United States........4
Jenny Thompson, U.S...............8	Krisztina Egerszegi, Hun 5	Fanny Blankers-Koen, Neth 4
Vera Cáslavská, Czech 7	Kornelia Ender, E Germany 4	Betty Cuthbert, Australia............4
Kristin Otto, E Germany............6	Dawn Fraser, Australia...............4	Pat McCormick, United States....4
Agnes Keleti, Hungary 5	Lyudmila Tourischeva, USSR 4	Bärbel Eckert Wöckel, E Ger 4
Nadia Comaneci, Romania 5	Evelyn Ashford, United States ...4	Amy Van Dyken, United States ...4

Winter

NATIONS

Nation	Gold	Silver	Bronze	Total	Nation	Gold	Silver	Bronze	Total
Norway	94	93	73	260	Finland	41	51	49	141
Soviet Union (1956–88)	78	56	59	193	E Germany (1956–88)	39	37	35	111
United States	70	70	51	191	Sweden	36	28	38	102
Austria	41	57	65	163	Switzerland	32	33	36	101
Germany	54	51	37	142	Canada	30	28	37	95

INDIVIDUALS — OVERALL

Men						Women					
Athlete, Nation	Sport	G	S	B	Tot	Athlete, Nation	Sport	G	S	B	Tot
Bjørn Dæhlie, Norway	N Ski	8	4	0	12	Raisa Smetanina, USSR/UT	N Ski	4	5	1	10
Sixten Jernberg, Sweden	N Ski	4	3	2	9	Lyubov Egorova, UT/Russia	N Ski	6	3	0	9
Seven tied with 7.						Larissa Lazutina, UT/Russia	N Ski	5	3	1	9
						Stefania Belmondo, Italy	N Ski	2	3	4	9
						Four tied with 8.					

INDIVIDUALS — GOLD

Men

Bjørn Dæhlie, Norway 8
A. Clas Thunberg, Finland 5
O. Bjoerndalen, Norway 5
Eric Heiden, United States 5

Nine tied with 4.

Women

Lyubov Egorova, UT/Russia....................6
Lydia Skoblikova, USSR...........................6
Larissa Lazutina, UT/Russia.....................5
Bonnie Blair, United States 5

Four tied with 4.

TRACK AND FIELD
Men

100 METERS

1896	Thomas Burke, United States	12.0
1900	Frank Jarvis, United States	11.0
1904	Archie Hahn, United States	11.0
1906	Archie Hahn, United States	11.2
1908	Reginald Walker, S Africa	10.8 OR
1912	Ralph Craig, United States	10.8
1920	Charles Paddock, United States	10.8
1924	Harold Abrahams, Great Britain	10.6 OR
1928	Percy Williams, Canada	10.8
1932	Eddie Tolan, United States	10.3 OR
1936	Jesse Owens, United States	10.3
1948	Harrison Dillard, United States	10.3
1952	Lindy Remigino, United States	10.4
1956	Bobby Morrow, United States	10.5
1960	Armin Hary, W Germany	10.2 OR
1964	Bob Hayes, United States	10.0 EWR
1968	Jim Hines, United States	9.95 WR
1972	Valery Borzov, USSR	10.14
1976	Hasely Crawford, Trinidad	10.06
1980	Allan Wells, Great Britain	10.25
1984	Carl Lewis, United States	9.99
1988	Carl Lewis, United States*	9.92 WR
1992	Linford Christie, Great Britain	9.96
1996	Donovan Bailey, Canada	9.84 WR
2000	Maurice Greene, United States	9.87

*Ben Johnson, Canada, disqualified.

200 METERS

1900	John Walter Tewksbury, United States	22.2
1904	Archie Hahn, United States	21.6 OR
1906	Not held	
1908	Robert Kerr, Canada	22.6
1912	Ralph Craig, United States	21.7
1920	Allen Woodring, United States	22.0
1924	Jackson Scholz, United States	21.6
1928	Percy Williams, Canada	21.8
1932	Eddie Tolan, United States	21.2 OR
1936	Jesse Owens, United States	20.7 OR
1948	Mel Patton, United States	21.1
1952	Andrew Stanfield, United States	20.7
1956	Bobby Morrow, United States	20.6 OR
1960	Livio Berruti, Italy	20.5 EWR
1964	Henry Carr, United States	20.3 OR
1968	Tommie Smith, United States	19.83 WR
1972	Valery Borzov, USSR	20.00
1976	Donald Quarrie, Jamaica	20.23
1980	Pietro Mennea, Italy	20.19
1984	Carl Lewis, United States	19.80 OR
1988	Joe DeLoach, United States	19.75 OR
1992	Mike Marsh, United States	20.01
1996	Michael Johnson, United States	19.32 WR
2000	Konstadinos Kederis, Greece	20.09

400 METERS

1896	Thomas Burke, United States	54.2
1900	Maxey Long, United States	49.4 OR
1904	Harry Hillman, United States	49.2 OR
1906	Paul Pilgrim, United States	53.2
1908	Wyndham Halswelle, Great Britain	50.0
1912	Charles Reidpath, United States	48.2 OR
1920	Bevil Rudd, South Africa	49.6
1924	Eric Liddell, Great Britain	47.6 OR
1928	Ray Barbuti, United States	47.8
1932	William Carr, United States	46.2 WR
1936	Archie Williams, United States	46.5
1948	Arthur Wint, Jamaica	46.2

400 METERS *(CONT.)*

1952	George Rhoden, Jamaica	45.9
1956	Charles Jenkins, United States	46.7
1960	Otis Davis, United States	44.9 WR
1964	Michael Larrabee, United States	45.1
1968	Lee Evans, United States	43.86 WR
1972	Vincent Matthews, United States	44.66
1976	Alberto Juantorena, Cuba	44.26
1980	Viktor Markin, USSR	44.60
1984	Alonzo Babers, United States	44.27
1988	Steve Lewis, United States	43.87
1992	Quincy Watts, United States	43.50 OR
1996	Michael Johnson, United States	43.49 OR
2000	Michael Johnson, United States	43.84

800 METERS

1896	Edwin Flack, Australia	2:11
1900	Alfred Tysoe, Great Britain	2:01.2
1904	James Lightbody, United States	1:56 OR
1906	Paul Pilgrim, United States	2:01.5
1908	Mel Sheppard, United States	1:52.8 WR
1912	James Meredith, United States	1:51.9 WR
1920	Albert Hill, Great Britain	1:53.4
1924	Douglas Lowe, Great Britain	1:52.4
1928	Douglas Lowe, Great Britain	1:51.8 OR
1932	Thomas Hampson, Great Britain	1:49.8 WR
1936	John Woodruff, United States	1:52.9
1948	Mal Whitfield, United States	1:49.2 OR
1952	Mal Whitfield, United States	1:49.2 EOR
1956	Thomas Courtney, United States	1:47.7 OR
1960	Peter Snell, New Zealand	1:46.3 OR
1964	Peter Snell, New Zealand	1:45.1 OR
1968	Ralph Doubell, Australia	1:44.3 EWR
1972	Dave Wottle, United States	1:45.9
1976	Alberto Juantorena, Cuba	1:43.50 WR
1980	Steve Ovett, Great Britain	1:45.40
1984	Joaquim Cruz, Brazil	1:43.00 OR
1988	Paul Ereng, Kenya	1:43.45
1992	William Tanui, Kenya	1:43.66
1996	Vebjoern Rodal, Norway	1:42.58 OR
2000	Nils Schumann, Germany	1:45.08

1,500 METERS

1896	Edwin Flack, Australia	4:33.2
1900	Charles Bennett, Great Britain	4:06.2 WR
1904	James Lightbody, United States	4:05.4 WR
1906	James Lightbody, United States	4:12.0
1908	Mel Sheppard, United States	4:03.4 OR
1912	Arnold Jackson, Great Britain	3:56.8 OR
1920	Albert Hill, Great Britain	4:01.8
1924	Paavo Nurmi, Finland	3:53.6 OR
1928	Harry Larva, Finland	3:53.2 OR
1932	Luigi Beccali, Italy	3:51.2 OR
1936	Jack Lovelock, New Zealand	3:47.8 WR
1948	Henri Eriksson, Sweden	3:49.8
1952	Josef Barthel, Luxemburg	3:45.1 OR
1956	Ron Delany, Ireland	3:41.2 OR
1960	Herb Elliott, Australia	3:35.6 WR
1964	Peter Snell, New Zealand	3:38.1
1968	Kipchoge Keino, Kenya	3:34.9 OR
1972	Pekkha Vasala, Finland	3:36.3
1976	John Walker, New Zealand	3:39.17
1980	Sebastian Coe, Great Britain	3:38.4
1984	Sebastian Coe, Great Britain	3:32.53 OR
1988	Peter Rono, Kenya	3:35.96
1992	Fermin Cacho, Spain	3:40.12
1996	Noureddine Morceli, Algeria	3:35.78
2000	Noah Ngeni, Kenya	3:32.07 OR

Note: OR=Olympic Record. WR=World Record. EOR=Equals Olympic Record. EWR=Equals World Record. WB=World Best.

TRACK AND FIELD (Cont.)
Men (Cont.)

5,000 METERS

1912	Hannes Kolehmainen, Finland	14:36.6 WR
1920	Joseph Guillemot, France	14:55.6
1924	Paavo Nurmi, Finland	14:31.2 OR
1928	Villie Ritola, Finland	14:38
1932	Lauri Lehtinen, Finland	14:30 OR
1936	Gunnar Höckert, Finland	14:22.2 OR
1948	Gaston Reiff, Belgium	14:17.6 OR
1952	Emil Zatopek, Czechoslovakia	14:06.6 OR
1956	Vladimir Kuts, USSR	13:39.6 OR
1960	Murray Halberg, New Zealand	13:43.4
1964	Bob Schul, United States	13:48.8
1968	Mohamed Gammoudi, Tunisia	14:05.0
1972	Lasse Viren, Finland	13:26.4 OR
1976	Lasse Viren, Finland	13:24.76
1980	Miruts Yifter, Ethiopia	13:21.0
1984	Said Aouita, Morocco	13:05.59 OR
1988	John Ngugi, Kenya	13:11.70
1992	Dieter Baumann, Germany	13:12.52
1996	Venuste Niyongabo, Burundi	13:07.96
2000	Millon Wolde, Ethiopia	13:35.49

10,000 METERS

1912	Hannes Kolehmainen, Finland	31:20.8
1920	Paavo Nurmi, Finland	31:45.8
1924	Vilho (Ville) Ritola, Finland	30:23.2 WR
1928	Paavo Nurmi, Finland	30:18.8 OR
1932	Janusz Kusocinski, Poland	30:11.4 OR
1936	Ilmari Salminen, Finland	30:15.4
1948	Emil Zatopek, Czechoslovakia	29:59.6 OR
1952	Emil Zatopek, Czechoslovakia	29:17.0 OR
1956	Vladimir Kuts, USSR	28:45.6 OR
1960	Pyotr Bolotnikov, USSR	28:32.2 OR
1964	Billy Mills, United States	28:24.4 OR
1968	Naftali Temu, Kenya	29:27.4
1972	Lasse Viren, Finland	27:38.4 WR
1976	Lasse Viren, Finland	27:40.38
1980	Miruts Yifter, Ethiopia	27:42.7
1984	Alberto Cova, Italy	27:47.54
1988	Brahim Boutaib, Morocco	27:21.46 OR
1992	Khalid Skah, Morocco	27:46.70
1996	Haile Gebrselassie, Ethiopia	27:07.34 OR
2000	Haile Gebrselassie, Ethiopia	27:18.20

MARATHON

1896	Spiridon Louis, Greece	2:58:50
1900	Michel Theato, France	2:59:45
1904	Thomas Hicks, United States	3:28:53
1906	William Sherring, Canada	2:51:23.6
1908	John Hayes, United States	2:55:18.4 OR
1912	Kenneth McArthur, S Africa	2:36:54.8
1920	Hannes Kolehmainen, Finland	2:32:35.8 WB
1924	Albin Stenroos, Finland	2:41:22.6
1928	Boughera El Ouafi, France	2:32:57
1932	Juan Zabala, Argentina	2:31:36 OR
1936	Kijung Son, Japan (Korea)	2:29:19.2 OR
1948	Delfo Cabrera, Argentina	2:34:51.6
1952	Emil Zatopek, Czechoslovakia	2:23:03.2 OR
1956	Alain Mimoun O'Kacha, France	2:25:00.0
1960	Abebe Bikila, Ethiopia	2:15:16.2 WB
1964	Abebe Bikila, Ethiopia	2:12:11.2 WB
1968	Mamo Wolde, Ethiopia	2:20:26.4
1972	Frank Shorter, United States	2:12:19.8
1976	Waldemar Cierpinski, E Germ.	2:09:55 OR
1980	Waldemar Cierpinski, E Germ.	2:11:03.0
1984	Carlos Lopes, Portugal	2:09:21.0 OR
1988	Gelindo Bordin, Italy	2:10:32
1992	Hwang Young-Cho, S Korea	2:13:23
1996	Josia Thugwane, S Africa	2:12:36
2000	Gezahgne Abera, Ethiopia	2:10:11

110-METER HURDLES

1896	Thomas Curtis, United States	17.6
1900	Alvin Kraenzlein, United States	15.4 OR
1904	Frederick Schule, United States	16.0
1906	Robert Leavitt, United States	16.2
1908	Forrest Smithson, United States	15.0 WR
1912	Frederick Kelly, United States	15.1
1920	Earl Thomson, Canada	14.8 WR
1924	Daniel Kinsey, United States	15.0
1928	Sydney Atkinson, S Africa	14.8
1932	George Saling, United States	14.6
1936	Forrest Towns, United States	14.2
1948	William Porter, United States	13.9 OR
1952	Harrison Dillard, United States	13.7 OR
1956	Lee Calhoun, United States	13.5 OR
1960	Lee Calhoun, United States	13.8
1964	Hayes Jones, United States	13.6
1968	Willie Davenport, United States	13.3 OR
1972	Rod Milburn, United States	13.24 EWR
1976	Guy Drut, France	13.30
1980	Thomas Munkelt, E Germany	13.39
1984	Roger Kingdom, United States	13.20 OR
1988	Roger Kingdom, United States	12.98 OR
1992	Mark McKoy, Canada	13.12
1996	Allen Johnson, United States	12.95 OR
2000	Anier Garcia, Cuba	13.00

400-METER HURDLES

1900	John Walter Tewksbury, U.S.	57.6
1904	Harry Hillman, United States	53.0
1906	Not held	
1908	Charles Bacon, United States	55.0 WR
1912	Not held	
1920	Frank Loomis, United States	54.0 WR
1924	F. Morgan Taylor, United States	52.6
1928	David Burghley, Great Britain	53.4 OR
1932	Robert Tisdall, Ireland	51.7
1936	Glenn Hardin, United States	52.4
1948	Roy Cochran, United States	51.1 OR
1952	Charles Moore, United States	50.8 OR
1956	Glenn Davis, United States	50.1 EOR
1960	Glenn Davis, United States	49.3 EOR
1964	Rex Cawley, United States	49.6
1968	Dave Hemery, Great Britain	48.12 WR
1972	John Akii-Bua, Uganda	47.82 WR
1976	Edwin Moses, United States	47.64 WR
1980	Volker Beck, E Germany	48.70
1984	Edwin Moses, United States	47.75
1988	Andre Phillips, United States	47.19 OR
1992	Kevin Young, United States	46.78 WR
1996	Derrick Adkins, United States	47.54
2000	Angelo Taylor, United States	47.50

3,000-METER STEEPLECHASE

1920	Percy Hodge, Great Britain	10:00.4 OR
1924	Vilho (Ville) Ritola, Finland	9:33.6 OR
1928	Toivo Loukola, Finland	9:21.8 WR
1932	Volmari Iso-Hollo, Finland	10:33.4*
1936	Volmari Iso-Hollo, Finland	9:03.8 WR
1948	Thore Sjöstrand, Sweden	9:04.6
1952	Horace Ashenfelter, U.S.	8:45.4 WR
1956	Chris Brasher, Great Britain	8:41.2 OR
1960	Zdzislaw Krzyszkowiak, Poland	8:34.2 OR
1964	Gaston Roelants, Belgium	8:30.8 OR
1968	Amos Biwott, Kenya	8:51
1972	Kipchoge Keino, Kenya	8:23.6 OR
1976	Anders Gärderud, Sweden	8:08.2 WR
1980	Bronislaw Malinowski, Poland	8:09.7
1984	Julius Korir, Kenya	8:11.8
1988	Julius Kariuki, Kenya	8:05.51 OR
1992	Matthew Birir, Kenya	8:08.84
1996	Joseph Keter, Kenya	8:07.12

TRACK AND FIELD (Cont.)
Men (Cont.)

3,000-METER STEEPLECHASE *(CONT.)*

2000	....Reuben Kosgei, Kenya	8:21.43

*About 3,450 meters; extra lap by error.

4 X 100-METER RELAY

1912	................Great Britain	42.4 OR
1920	.................United States	42.2 WR
1924	.................United States	41.0 EWR
1928	.................United States	41.0 EWR
1932	.................United States	40.0 EWR
1936	.................United States	39.8 WR
1948	.................United States	40.6
1952	.................United States	40.1
1956	.................United States	39.5 WR
1960	.................W Germany	39.5 EWR
1964	.................United States	39.0 WR
1968	.................United States	38.2 WR
1972	.................United States	38.19 EWR
1976	.................United States	38.33
1980	.................USSR	38.26
1984	.................United States	37.83 WR
1988	.................USSR	38.19
1992	.................United States	37.40 WR
1996	.................Canada	37.69
2000	.................United States	37.61

4 X 400-METER RELAY

1908	.................United States	3:29.4
1912	.................United States	3:16.6 WR
1920	.................Great Britain	3:22.2
1924	.................United States	3:16.0 WR
1928	.................United States	3:14.2 WR
1932	.................United States	3:08.2 WR
1936	.................Great Britain	3:09.0
1948	.................United States	3:10.4 WR
1952	.................Jamaica	3:03.9 WR
1956	.................United States	3:04.8
1960	.................United States	3:02.2 WR
1964	.................United States	3:00.7 WR
1968	.................United States	2:56.16 WR
1972	.................Kenya	2:59.8
1976	.................United States	2:58.65
1980	.................USSR	3:01.1
1984	.................United States	2:57.91
1988	.................United States	2:56.16 EWR
1992	.................United States	2:55.74 WR
1996	.................United States	2:55.99
2000	.................United States	2:56.35

20-KILOMETER WALK

1956	....Leonid Spirin, USSR	1:31:27.4
1960	....Vladimir Golubnichiy, USSR	1:33:07.2
1964	....Kenneth Mathews, Great Britain	1:29:34.0 OR
1968	....Vladimir Golubnichiy, USSR	1:33:58.4
1972	....Peter Frenkel, E Germany	1:26:42.4 OR
1976	....Daniel Bautista, Mexico	1:24:40.6 OR
1980	....Maurizio Damilano, Italy	1:23:35.5 OR
1984	....Ernesto Canto, Mexico	1:23:13.0 OR
1988	....Jozef Pribilinec, Czechoslovakia	1:19:57.0 OR
1992	....Daniel Plaza, Spain	1:21:45.0
1996	....Jefferson Pérez, Ecuador	1:20:07
2000	....Robert Korzeniowski, Poland	1:18:59 OR

50-KILOMETER WALK

1932	....Thomas Green, Great Britain	4:50:10
1936	....Harold Whitlock, Great Britain	4:30:41.4 OR
1948	....John Ljunggren, Sweden	4:41:52
1952	....Giuseppe Dordoni, Italy	4:28:07.8 OR
1956	....Norman Read, New Zealand	4:30:42.8
1960	....Donald Thompson, Great Britain	4:25:30 OR
1964	....Abdon Parnich, Italy	4:11:12.4 OR

50-KILOMETER WALK *(CONT.)*

1968	....Christoph Höhne, E Germany	4:20:13.6
1972	....Bernd Kannenberg, W Germany	3:56:11.6 OR
1980	....Hartwig Gauder, E Germany	3:49:24.0 OR
1984	....Raul Gonzalez, Mexico	3:47:26.0 OR
1988	....Viacheslav Ivanenko, USSR	3:38:29.0 OR
1992	....Andrey Perlov, Unified Team	3:50:13
1996	....Robert Korzeniowski, Poland	3:43:30
2000	....Robert Korzeniowski, Poland	3:42:22 OR

HIGH JUMP

1896	...Ellery Clark, United States	5 ft 11¼ in
1900	...Irving Baxter, United States	6 ft 2¾ in OR
1904	...Samuel Jones, United States	5 ft 11 in
1906	...Cornelius Leahy, Great Britain/Ireland	5 ft 10 in
1908	...Harry Porter, United States	6 ft 3 in OR
1912	...Alma Richards, United States	6 ft 4 in OR
1920	...Richmond Landon, United States	6 ft 4 in OR
1924	...Harold Osborn, United States	6 ft 6 in OR
1928	...Robert W. King, United States	6 ft 4½ in
1932	...Duncan McNaughton, Canada	6 ft 5½ in
1936	...Cornelius Johnson, United States	6 ft 8 in OR
1948	...John L. Winter, Australia	6 ft 6 in
1952	...Walter Davis, United States	6 ft 8½ in OR
1956	...Charles Dumas, United States	6 ft 11½ in OR
1960	...Robert Shavlakadze, USSR	7 ft 1 in OR
1964	...Valery Brumel, USSR	7 ft 1¾ in OR
1968	...Dick Fosbury, United States	7 ft 4¼ in OR
1972	...Yuri Tarmak, USSR	7 ft 3¾ in
1976	...Jacek Wszola, Poland	7 ft 4½ in OR
1980	...Gerd Wessig, E Germany	7 ft 8¾ in WR
1984	...Dietmar Mögenburg, W Germany	7 ft 8½ in
1988	...Gennadiy Avdeyenko, USSR	7 ft 9¾ in OR
1992	...Javier Sotomayor, Cuba	7 ft 8 in.
1996	...Charles Austin, United States	7 ft 10 in OR
2000	...Sergey Kliugin, Russia	7 ft 8¼ in

POLE VAULT

1896	...William Hoyt, United States	10 ft 10 in
1900	...Irving Baxter, United States	10 ft 10 in
1904	...Charles Dvorak, United States	11 ft 5¾ in
1906	...Fernand Gonder, France	11 ft 5¾ in
1908	...Alfred Gilbert, United States Edward Cooke Jr., United States	12 ft 2 in OR
1912	...Harry Babcock, United States	12 ft 11½ in OR
1920	...Frank Foss, United States	13 ft 5 in WR
1924	...Lee Barnes, United States	12 ft 11½ in
1928	...Sabin Carr, United States	13 ft 9¼ in OR
1932	...William Miller, United States	14 ft 1¾ in OR
1936	...Earle Meadows, United States	14 ft 3¼ in OR
1948	...Guinn Smith, United States	14 ft 1¼ in
1952	...Robert Richards, United States	14 ft 11 in OR
1956	...Robert Richards, United States	14 ft 11½ in OR
1960	...Don Bragg, United States	15 ft 5 in OR
1964	...Fred Hansen, United States	16 ft 8¾ in OR
1968	...Bob Seagren, United States	17 ft 8½ in OR
1972	...Wolfgang Nordwig, E Germany	18 ft ½ in OR
1976	...Tadeusz Slusarski, Poland	18 ft ½ in EOR
1980	...Wladyslaw Kozakiewicz, Poland	18 ft 11½ in WR
1984	...Pierre Quinon, France	18 ft 10¼ in
1988	...Sergei Bubka, USSR	19 ft 4¼ in OR
1992	...Maksim Tarasov, Unified Team	19 ft ¼ in
1996	...Jean Galfione, France	19 ft 5 ¼ in OR
2000	...Nick Hysong, United States	19 ft 4¼ in

Note: OR=Olympic Record. WR=World Record. EOR=Equals Olympic Record. EWR=Equals World Record. WB=World Best.

Summer Games Champions (Cont.)

TRACK AND FIELD (Cont.)

Men (Cont.)

LONG JUMP

1896...Ellery Clark, United States	20 ft 10 in
1900...Alvin Kraenzlein, United States	23 ft 6¾ in OR
1904...Meyer Prinstein, United States	24 ft 1 in OR
1906...Meyer Prinstein, United States	23 ft 7½ in
1908...Frank Irons, United States	24 ft 6½ in OR
1912...Albert Gutterson, United States	24 ft 11¼ in OR
1920...William Peterssen, Sweden	23 ft 5½ in
1924...DeHart Hubbard, United States	24 ft 5 in
1928...Edward B. Hamm, United States	25 ft 4½ in OR
1932...Edward Gordon, United States	25 ft ¾ in
1936...Jesse Owens, United States	26 ft 5½ in OR
1948...William Steele, United States	25 ft 8 in
1952...Jerome Biffle, United States	24 ft 10 in
1956...Gregory Bell, United States	25 ft 8¼ in
1960...Ralph Boston, United States	26 ft 7¾ in OR
1964...Lynn Davies, Great Britain	26 ft 5¾ in
1968...Bob Beamon, United States	29 ft 2½ in WR
1972...Randy Williams, United States	27 ft ½ in
1976...Arnie Robinson, United States	27 ft 4¾ in
1980...Lutz Dombrowski, E Germany	28 ft ¼ in
1984...Carl Lewis, United States	28 ft ¼ in
1988...Carl Lewis, United States	28 ft 7½ in
1992...Carl Lewis, United States	28 ft 5½ in
1996...Carl Lewis, United States	27 ft 10¾ in
2000...Ivan Pedrosa, Cuba	28 ft ¾ in

TRIPLE JUMP

1896...James Connolly, United States	44 ft 11¾ in
1900...Meyer Prinstein, United States	47 ft 5¾ in OR
1904...Meyer Prinstein, United States	47 ft 1 in
1906...Peter O'Connor, Great Britain/Ireland	46 ft 2¼ in
1908...Timothy Ahearne, Great Britain/Ireland	48 ft 11¼ in OR
1912...Gustaf Lindblom, Sweden	48 ft 5¼ in
1920...Vilho Tuulos, Finland	47 ft 7 in
1924...Anthony Winter, Australia	50 ft 11¼ in WR
1928...Mikio Oda, Japan	49 ft 11 in
1932...Chuhei Nambu, Japan	51 ft 7 in WR
1936...Naoto Tajima, Japan	52 ft 6 in WR
1948...Arne Ahman, Sweden	50 ft 6¼ in
1952...Adhemar da Silva, Brazil	53 ft 2¾ in WR
1956...Adhemar da Silva, Brazil	53 ft 7¾ in OR
1960...Jozef Schmidt, Poland	55 ft 2 in
1964...Jozef Schmidt, Poland	55 ft 3½ in OR
1968...Viktor Saneyev, USSR	57 ft ¾ in WR
1972...Viktor Saneyev, USSR	56 ft 11¾ in
1976...Viktor Saneyev, USSR	56 ft 8¾ in
1980...Jaak Uudmae, USSR	56 ft 11¼ in
1984...Al Joyner, United States	56 ft 7½ in
1988...Khristo Markov, Bulgaria	57 ft 9½ in OR
1992...Mike Conley, United States	59 ft 7½ in (w)
1996...Kenny Harrison, United States	59 ft 4¼ in OR
2000...Jonathon Edwards, G. Britain	58 ft 1¼ in

SHOT PUT

1896...Robert Garrett, United States	36 ft 9¾ in
1900...Richard Sheldon, United States	46 ft 3¼ in OR
1904...Ralph Rose, United States	48 ft 7 in WR
1906...Martin Sheridan, United States	40 ft 5¼ in
1908...Ralph Rose, United States	46 ft 7½ in
1912...Pat McDonald, United States	50 ft 4 in OR
1920...Ville Porhola, Finland	48 ft 7¼ in
1924...Clarence Houser, United States	49 ft 2¼ in
1928...John Kuck, United States	52 ft ¾ in WR
1932...Leo Sexton, United States	52 ft 6 in OR

SHOT PUT (CONT.)

1936...Hans Woellke, Germany	53 ft 1¾ in OR
1948...Wilbur Thompson, United States	56 ft 2 in OR
1952...Parry O'Brien, United States	57 ft ½ in OR
1956...Parry O'Brien, United States	60 ft 11¼ in OR
1960...William Nieder, United States	64 ft 6¾ in OR
1964...Dallas Long, United States	66 ft 8½ in OR
1968...Randy Matson, United States	67 ft 4¾ in
1972...Wladyslaw Komar, Poland	69 ft 6 in OR
1976...Udo Beyer, E Germany	69 ft ¾ in
1980...Vladimir Kiselyov, USSR	70 ft ½ in OR
1984...Alessandro Andrei, Italy	69 ft 9 in
1988...Ulf Timmermann, E Germany	73 ft 8¾ in OR
1992...Mike Stulce, United States	71 ft 2½ in
1996...Randy Barnes, United States	70 ft 11 in
2000...Arsi Harju, Finland	69 ft 10¼ in

DISCUS THROW

1896...Robert Garrett, United States	95 ft 7½ in
1900...Rudolf Bauer, Hungary	118 ft 3 in OR
1904....Martin Sheridan, United States	128 ft 10½ in OR
1906...Martin Sheridan, United States	136 ft
1908...Martin Sheridan, United States	134 ft 2 in OR
1912...Armas Taipele, Finland	148 ft 3 in OR
1920...Elmer Niklander, Finland	146 ft 7 in
1924...Clarence Houser, United States	151 ft 4 in OR
1928...Clarence Houser, United States	155 ft 3 in OR
1932...John Anderson, United States	162 ft 4 in OR
1936...Ken Carpenter, United States	165 ft 7 in OR
1948...Adolfo Consolini, Italy	173 ft 2 in OR
1952...Sim Iness, United States	180 ft 6 in OR
1956...Al Oerter, United States	184 ft 11 in OR
1960...Al Oerter, United States	194 ft 2 in OR
1964...Al Oerter, United States	200 ft 1 in OR
1968...Al Oerter, United States	212 ft 6 in OR
1972...Ludvik Danek, Czechoslovakia	211 ft 3 in
1976...Mac Wilkins, United States	221 ft 5 in OR
1980...Viktor Rashchupkin, USSR	218 ft 8 in
1984...Rolf Dannenberg, W Germany	218 ft 6 in
1988...Jürgen Schult, E Germany	225 ft 9 in OR
1992...Romas Ubartas, Lithuania	213 ft 8 in
1996...Lars Riedel, Germany	227 ft 8 in OR
2000...Virgilijus Alekna, Lithuania	227 ft 4 in

HAMMER THROW

1900...John Flanagan, United States	163 ft 1 in
1904...John Flanagan, United States	168 ft 1 in OR
1906...Not held	
1908...John Flanagan, United States	170 ft 4 in OR
1912...Matt McGrath, United States	179 ft 7 in OR
1920...Pat Ryan, United States	173 ft 5 in
1924...Fred Tootell, United States	174 ft 10 in
1928...Patrick O'Callaghan, Ireland	168 ft 7 in
1932...Patrick O'Callaghan, Ireland	176 ft 11 in
1936...Karl Hein, Germany	185 ft 4 in OR
1948...Imre Nemeth, Hungary	183 ft 11 in
1952...Jozsef Csermak, Hungary	197 ft 11 in WR
1956...Harold Connolly, United States	207 ft 3 in OR
1960...Vasily Rudenkov, USSR	220 ft 2 in OR
1964...Romuald Klim, USSR	228 ft 10 in OR
1968...Gyula Zsivotsky, Hungary	240 ft 8 in OR
1972...Anatoli Bondarchuk, USSR	247 ft 8 in OR
1976...Yuri Sedykh, USSR	254 ft 4 in OR
1980...Yuri Sedykh, USSR	268 ft 4 in WR
1984...Juha Tiainen, Finland	256 ft 2 in
1988...Sergei Litvinov, USSR	278 ft 2 in OR

TRACK AND FIELD (Cont.)
Men (Cont.)

HAMMER THROW (CONT.)

1992	Andrey Abduvaliyev, Unified Team	270 ft 9 in
1996	Balazs Kiss, Hungary	266 ft 6 in
2000	Szymon Ziolkowski, Poland	262 ft 6 in

JAVELIN

1908	Erik Lemming, Sweden	179 ft 10 in
1912	Erik Lemming, Sweden	198 ft 11 in WR
1920	Jonni Myyrä, Finland	215 ft 10 in OR
1924	Jonni Myyrä, Finland	206 ft 6 in
1928	Eric Lundkvist, Sweden	218 ft 6 in OR
1932	Matti Jarvinen, Finland	238 ft 6 in OR
1936	Gerhard Stöck, Germany	235 ft 8 in
1948	Kai Rautavaara, Finland	228 ft 10½ in
1952	Cy Young, United States	242 ft 1 in OR
1956	Egil Danielson, Norway	281 ft 2¼ in WR
1960	Viktor Tsibulenko, USSR	277 ft 8 in
1964	Pauli Nevala, Finland	271 ft 2 in
1968	Janis Lusis, USSR	295 ft 7 in OR
1972	Klaus Wolfermann, W Germany	296 ft 10 in OR
1976	Miklos Nemeth, Hungary	310 ft 4 in WR
1980	Dainis Kuta, USSR	299 ft 2⅜ in
1984	Arto Härkönen, Finland	284 ft 8 in
1988	Tapio Korjus, Finland	276 ft 6 in
1992	Jan Zelezny, Czechoslovakia	294 ft 2 in OR
1996	Jan Zelezny, Czech Republic	289 ft 3 in
2000	Jan Zelezny, Czech Republic	295 ft 9½ in OR

DECATHLON

		Pts
1904	Thomas Kiely, Ireland	6036
1912	Jim Thorpe, United States*	8412 WR
1920	Helge Lövland, Norway	6803
1924	Harold Osborn, United States	7711 WR
1928	Paavo Yrjölä, Finland	8053.29 WR
1932	James Bausch, United States	8462 WR
1936	Glenn Morris, United States	7900 WR
1948	Robert Mathias, United States	7139
1952	Robert Mathias, United States	7887 WR
1956	Milton Campbell, United States	7937 OR
1960	Rafer Johnson, United States	8392 OR
1964	Willi Holdorf, W Germany	7887
1968	Bill Toomey, United States	8193 OR
1972	Nikolai Avilov, USSR	8454 WR
1976	Bruce Jenner, United States	8617 WR
1980	Daley Thompson, Great Britain	8495
1984	Daley Thompson, Great Britain	8798 EWR
1988	Christian Schenk, E Germany	8488
1992	Robert Zmelik, Czechoslovakia	8611
1996	Dan O'Brien, United States	8824 OR
2000	Erki Nool, Estonia	8641

*In 1913, Thorpe was disqualified for having played professional baseball in 1910. His record was restored in 1982.

Women

100 METERS

1928	Elizabeth Robinson, United States	12.2 EWR
1932	Stella Walsh, Poland	11.9 EWR
1936	Helen Stephens, United States	11.5
1948	Francina Blankers-Koen, Netherlands	11.9
1952	Marjorie Jackson, Australia	11.5 EWR
1956	Betty Cuthbert, Australia	11.5 EWR
1960	Wilma Rudolph, United States	11.0
1964	Wyomia Tyus, United States	11.4
1968	Wyomia Tyus, United States	11.0 WR
1972	Renate Stecher, E Germany	11.07
1976	Annegret Richter, W Germany	11.08
1980	Lyudmila Kondratyeva, USSR	11.06
1984	Evelyn Ashford, United States	10.97 OR
1988	Florence Griffith Joyner, United States	10.54 WR
1992	Gail Devers, United States	10.82
1996	Gail Devers, United States	10.94
2000	Marion Jones, United States	10.75

200 METERS

1948	Francina Blankers-Koen, Netherlands	24.4
1952	Marjorie Jackson, Australia	23.7
1956	Betty Cuthbert, Australia	23.4 EOR
1960	Wilma Rudolph, United States	24.0
1964	Edith McGuire, United States	23.0 OR
1968	Irena Szewinska, Poland	22.5 WR
1972	Renate Stecher, E Germany	22.40 EWR
1976	Bärbel Eckert, E Germany	22.37 OR
1980	Bärbel Wöckel (Eckert), E Germ.	22.03 OR
1984	Valerie Brisco-Hooks, U.S.	21.81 OR

200 METERS (CONT.)

1988	Florence Griffith Joyner, U.S.	21.34 WR
1992	Gwen Torrence, United States	21.81
1996	Marie-José Pérec, France	22.12
2000	Marion Jones, United States	21.84

400 METERS

1964	Betty Cuthbert, Australia	52.0 OR
1968	Colette Besson, France	52.0 EOR
1972	Monika Zehrt, E Germany	51.08 OR
1976	Irena Szewinska, Poland	49.29 WR
1980	Marita Koch, E Germany	48.88 OR
1984	Valerie Brisco-Hooks, United States	48.83 OR
1988	Olga Bryzgina, USSR	48.65 OR
1992	Marie-José Pérec, France	48.83
1996	Marie-José Pérec, France	48.25 OR
2000	Cathy Freeman, Australia	49.11

800 METERS

1928	Lina Radke, Germany	2:16.8 WR
1932	Not held 1932–1956	
1960	Lyudmila Shevtsova, USSR	2:04.3 EWR
1964	Ann Packer, Great Britain	2:01.1 OR
1968	Madeline Manning, United States	2:00.9 OR
1972	Hildegard Falck, W Germany	1:58.55 OR
1976	Tatyana Kazankina, USSR	1:54.94 WR
1980	Nadezhda Olizarenko, USSR	1:53.42 WR
1984	Doina Melinte, Romania	1:57.6
1988	Sigrun Wodars, E Germany	1:56.10
1992	Ellen Van Langen, Netherlands	1:55.54
1996	Svetlana Masterkova, Russia	1:57.73
2000	Maria Mutola, Mozambique	1:56.15

Note: OR=Olympic Record. WR=World Record. EOR=Equals Olympic Record. EWR=Equals World Record. WB=World Best.

TRACK AND FIELD *(Cont.)*

Women *(Cont.)*

1,500 METERS

1972	Lyudmila Bragina, USSR	4:01.4 WR
1976	Tatyana Kazankina, USSR	4:05.48
1980	Tatyana Kazankina, USSR	3:56.6 OR
1984	Gabriella Dorio, Italy	4:03.25
1988	Paula Ivan, Romania	3:53.96 OR
1992	Hassiba Boulmerka, Algeria	3:55.30
1996	Svetlana Masterkova, Russia	4:00.83
2000	Nouria Merah-Benida, Algeria	4:05.10

3,000 METERS

1984	Maricica Puica, Romania	8:35.96 OR
1988	Tatyana Samolenko, USSR	8:26.53 OR
1992	Elena Romanova, Unified Team	8:46.04

5,000 METERS

1996	Wang Junxia, China	14:57.88
2000	Gabriela Szabo, Romania	14:40.79 OR

10,000 METERS

1988	Olga Bondarenko, USSR	31:05.21 OR
1992	Derartu Tulu, Ethiopia	31:06.02
1996	Fernanda Ribeiro, Portugal	31:01.63 OR
2000	Derartu Tulu, Ethiopia	30:17.49 OR

MARATHON

1984	Joan Benoit, United States	2:24:52 OR
1988	Rosa Mota, Portugal	2:25:40
1992	Valentin Yegorova, Unified Team	2:32:41
1996	Fatuma Roba, Ethiopia	2:26:05
2000	Naoko Takahashi, Japan	2:23.14 OR

80-METER HURDLES

1932	Babe Didrikson, United States	11.7 WR
1936	Trebisonda Valla, Italy	11.7
1948	Francina Blankers-Koen, Netherlands	11.2 OR
1952	Shirley Strickland, Australia	10.9 WR
1956	Shirley Strickland, Australia	10.7 OR
1960	Irina Press, USSR	10.8
1964	Karin Balzer, E Germany	10.5
1968	Maureen Caird, Australia	10.3 OR

100-METER HURDLES

1972	Annelie Ehrhardt, E Germany	12.59 WR
1976	Johanna Schaller, E Germany	12.77
1980	Vera Komisova, USSR	12.56 OR
1984	Benita Fitzgerald-Brown, United States	12.84
1988	Yordanka Donkova, Bulgaria	12.38 OR
1992	Paraskevi Patoulidou, Greece	12.64
1996	Lyudmila Engqvist, Sweden	12.58
2000	Olga Shishigina, Kazakhstan	12.65

400-METER HURDLES

1984	Nawal el Moutawakel, Morocco	54.61 OR
1988	Debra Flintoff-King, Australia	53.17 OR
1992	Sally Gunnell, Great Britain	53.23
1996	Deon Hemmings, Jamaica	52.82 OR
2000	Irina Privalova, Russia	53.02

4 X 100-METER RELAY

Year	Team	Time
1928	Canada	48.4 WR
1932	United States	46.9 WR
1936	United States	46.9
1948	Netherlands	47.5
1952	United States	45.9 WR
1956	Australia	44.5 WR

4 X 100-METER RELAY *(CONT.)*

Year	Team	Time
1960	United States	44.5
1964	Poland	43.6
1968	United States	42.8 WR
1972	W Germany	42.81 EWR
1976	E Germany	42.55 OR
1980	E Germany	41.60 WR
1984	United States	41.65
1988	United States	41.98
1992	United States	42.11
1996	United States	41.95
2000	Bahamas	41.95

4 X 400-METER RELAY

Year	Team	Time
1972	E Germany	3:23 WR
1976	E Germany	3:19.23 WR
1980	USSR	3:20.02
1984	United States	3:18.29 OR
1988	USSR	3:15.18 WR
1992	Unified Team	3:20.20
1996	United States	3:20.91
2000	United States	3:22.62

10-KILOMETER WALK

1992	Chen Yueling, China	44:32
1996	Elena Nikolayeva, Russia	41:49 OR

20-KILOMETER WALK

2000	Liping Wang, China	1:29.05

HIGH JUMP

1928	Ethel Catherwood, Canada	5 ft 2½ in
1932	Jean Shiley, United States	5 ft 5¼ in WR
1936	Ibolya Csak, Hungary	5 ft 3 in
1948	Alice Coachman, United States	5 ft 6 in OR
1952	Esther Brand, South Africa	5 ft 5¾ in
1956	Mildred L. McDaniel, U.S.	5 ft 9¼ in WR
1960	Iolanda Balas, Romania	6 ft ¾ in OR
1964	Iolanda Balas, Romania	6 ft 2¾ in OR
1968	Miloslava Reskova, Czech.	5 ft 11½ in
1972	Ulrike Meyfarth, W. Germany	6 ft 3½ in EWR
1976	Rosemarie Ackermann, E Germ	6 ft 4 in OR
1980	Sara Simeoni, Italy	6 ft 5½ in OR
1984	Ulrike Meyfarth, W Germany	6 ft 7½ in OR
1988	Louise Ritter, United States	6 ft 8 in OR
1992	Heike Henkel, Germany	6 ft 7½ in
1996	Stefka Kostadinova, Bulgaria	6 ft 8¾ in OR
2000	Yelena Yelesina, Russia	6 ft 7 in

LONG JUMP

1948	Olga Gyarmati, Hungary	18 ft 8¼ in
1952	Yvette Williams, New Zealand	20 ft 5¾ in OR
1956	Elzbieta Krzeskinska, Poland	20 ft 10 in EWR
1960	Vyera Krepkina, USSR	20 ft 10¾ in OR
1964	Mary Rand, Great Britain	22 ft 2¼ in WR
1968	Viorica Viscopoleanu, Romania	22 ft 4½ in WR
1972	Heidemarie Rosendahl, W Germany	22 ft 3 in
1976	Angela Voigt, E Germany	22 ft ¾ in
1980	Tatyana Kolpakova, USSR	23 ft 2 in OR
1984	Anisoara Stanciu, Romania	22 ft 10 in
1988	Jackie Joyner-Kersee, United States	24 ft 3½ in OR
1992	Heike Drechsler, Germany	23 ft 5¼ in
1996	Chioma Ajunwa, Nigeria	23 ft 4½ in
2000	Heike Drechsler, Germany	22 ft 11¼ in

Note: OR=Olympic Record; WR=World Record; EOR=Equals Olympic Record; EWR=Equals World Record; WB=World Best.

TRACK AND FIELD (Cont.)
Women (Cont.)

TRIPLE JUMP
1996...Inessa Kravets, Ukraine	50 ft 3½ in	
2000...Tereza Marinova, Bulgaria	49 ft 10½ in	

SHOT PUT
1948...Micheline Ostermeyer, France	45 ft 1½ in	
1952...Galina Zybina, USSR	50 ft 1¾ in WR	
1956...Tamara Tyshkevich, USSR	54 ft 5 in OR	
1960...Tamara Press, USSR	56 ft 10 in OR	
1964...Tamara Press, USSR	59 ft 6¼ in OR	
1968...Margitta Gummel, E Germany	64 ft 4 in WR	
1972...Nadezhda Chizhova, USSR	69 ft WR	
1976...Ivanka Hristova, Bulgaria	69 ft 5¼ in OR	
1980...Ilona Slupianek, E Germany	73 ft 6¼ in	
1984...Claudia Losch, W Germany	67 ft 2¼ in	
1988...Natalya Lisovskaya, USSR	72 ft 11¾ in	
1992...Svetlana Kriveleva, Unified Team	69 ft 1¼ in	
1996...Astrid Kumbernuss, Germany	67 ft 5½ in	
2000...Yanina Korolchik, Belarus	67 ft 5½ in	

DISCUS THROW
1928...Helena Konopacka, Poland	129 ft 11¾ in WR	
1932...Lillian Copeland, United States	133 ft 2 in OR	
1936...Gisela Mauermayer, Germany	156 ft 3 in OR	
1948...Micheline Ostermeyer, France	137 ft 6 in	
1952...Nina Romaschkova, USSR	168 ft 8 in OR	
1956...Olga Fikotova, Czechoslovakia	176 ft 1 in OR	
1960...Nina Ponomaryeva, USSR	180 ft 9 in OR	
1964...Tamara Press, USSR	187 ft 10 in OR	
1968...Lia Manoliu, Romania	191 ft 2 in OR	
1972...Faina Melnik, USSR	218 ft 7 in OR	
1976...Evelin Schlaak, E Germany	226 ft 4 in OR	
1980...Evelin Jahl (Schlaak), E Germ.	229 ft 6 in OR	
1984...Ria Stalman, Netherlands	214 ft 5 in	
1988...Martina Hellmann, E Germany	237 ft 2 in OR	
1992...Maritza Martén, Cuba	229 ft 10 in	
1996...Ilke Wyludda, Germany	228 ft 6 in	
2000...Ellina Zvereva, Belarus	224 ft 5 in	

HAMMER THROW
2000...Kamila Skolimowska, Russia	233 ft 5 in OR	

JAVELIN THROW
1932...Babe Didrikson, United States	143 ft 4 in OR	
1936...Tilly Fleischer, Germany	148 ft 3 in OR	
1948...Herma Bauma, Austria	149 ft 6 in	
1952...Dana Zatopkova, Czechoslovakia	165 ft 7 in	
1956...Inese Jaunzeme, USSR	176 ft 8 in	
1960...Elvira Ozolina, USSR	183 ft 8 in OR	
1964...Mihaela Penes, Romania	198 ft 7 in	
1968...Angela Nemeth, Hungary	198 ft	
1972...Ruth Fuchs, E Germany	209 ft 7 in OR	
1976...Ruth Fuchs, E Germany	216 ft 4 in OR	
1980...Maria Colon, Cuba	224 ft 5 in OR	
1984...Tessa Sanderson, Great Britain	228 ft 2 in OR	
1988...Petra Felke, E Germany	245 ft OR	
1992...Silke Renk, Germany	224 ft 2 in	
1996...Heli Rantanen, Finland	222 ft 11 in	
2000...Trine Hattestad, Norway	226 ft ½ in OR	

PENTATHLON
	Pts
1964...Irina Press, USSR	5246 WR
1968...Ingrid Becker, W Germany	5098
1972...Mary Peters, Great Britain	4801 WR*
1976...Siegrun Siegl, E Germany	4745
1980...Nadezhda Tkachenko, USSR	5083 WR

HEPTATHLON
	Pts
1984...Glynis Nunn, Australia	6390 OR
1988...Jackie Joyner-Kersee, U.S.	7291 WR
1992...Jackie Joyner-Kersee, U.S.	7044
1996...Ghada Shouaa, Syria	6780
2000...Denise Lewis, Great Britain	6584

*In 1971, the 100-meter hurdles replaced the 80-meter hurdles, requiring a change in scoring tables.

BASKETBALL
Men

1936
Final: United States 19, Canada 8
United States: Ralph Bishop, Joe Fortenberry, Carl Knowles, Jack Ragland, Carl Shy, William Wheatley, Francis Johnson, Samuel Balter, John Gibbons, Frank Lubin, Arthur Mollner, Donald Piper, Duane Swanson, Willard Schmidt

1948
Final: United States 65, France 21
United States: Cliff Barker, Don Barksdale, Ralph Beard, Lewis Beck, Vince Boryla, Gordon Carpenter, Alex Groza, Wallace Jones, Bob Kurland, Ray Lumpp, Robert Pitts, Jesse Renick, Bob Robinson, Ken Rollins

1952
Final: United States 36, USSR 25
United States: Charles Hoag, Bill Hougland, Melvin Dean Kelley, Bob Kenney, Clyde Lovellette, Marcus Freiberger, Victor Wayne Glasgow, Frank McCabe, Daniel Pippen, Howard Williams, Ronald Bontemps, Bob Kurland, William Lienhard, John Keller

1956
Final: United States 89, USSR 55
United States: Carl Cain, Bill Hougland, K.C. Jones, Bill Russell, James Walsh, William Evans, Burdette Haldorson, Ron Tomsic, Dick Boushka, Gilbert Ford, Bob Jeangerard, Charles Darling

1960
Final: United States 90, Brazil 63
United States: Jay Arnette, Walt Bellamy, Bob Boozer, Terry Dischinger, Jerry Lucas, Oscar Robertson, Adrian Smith, Burdette Haldorson, Darrall Imhoff, Allen Kelley, Lester Lane, Jerry West

1964
Final: United States 73, USSR 59
United States: Jim Barnes, Bill Bradley, Larry Brown, Joe Caldwell, Mel Counts, Richard Davies, Walt Hazzard, Lucius Jackson, John McCaffrey, Jeff Mullins, Jerry Shipp, George Wilson

1968
Final: United States 65, Yugoslavia 50
United States: John Clawson, Ken Spain, Jo-Jo White, Michael Barrett, Spencer Haywood, Charles Scott, William Hosket, Calvin Fowler, Michael Silliman, Glynn Saulters, James King, Donald Dee

1972
Final: USSR 51, United States 50
United States: Kenneth Davis, Doug Collins, Thomas Henderson, Mike Bantom, Bobby Jones, Dwight Jones, James Forbes, James Brewer, Tom Burleson, Tom McMillen, Kevin Joyce, Ed Ratleff

BASKETBALL (Cont.)

Men (Cont.)

1976

Final: United States 95, Yugoslavia 74
United States: Phil Ford, Steve Sheppard, Adrian Dantley, Walter Davis, Quinn Buckner, Ernie Grunfield, Kenny Carr, Scott May, Michel Armstrong, Tom La Garde, Phil Hubbard, Mitch Kupchak

1980

Final: Yugoslavia 86, Italy 77
U.S. participated in boycott.

1984

Final: United States 96, Spain 65
United States: Steve Alford, Leon Wood, Patrick Ewing, Vern Fleming, Alvin Robertson, Michael Jordan, Joe Kleine, Jon Koncak, Wayman Tisdale, Chris Mullin, Sam Perkins, Jeff Turner

1988

Final: USSR 76, Yugoslavia 63
United States (3rd): Mitch Richmond, Charles E. Smith IV, Vernell Coles, Hersey Hawkins, Jeff Grayer, Charles D. Smith, Willie Anderson, Stacey Augmon, Dan Majerle, Danny Manning, J.R. Reid, David Robinson

1992

Final: United States 117, Croatia 85
United States: David Robinson, Christian Laettner, Patrick Ewing, Larry Bird, Scottie Pippen, Michael Jordan, Clyde Drexler, Karl Malone, John Stockton, Chris Mullin, Charles Barkley, Earvin Johnson

1996

Final: United States 95, Yugoslavia 69
United States: Charles Barkley, Anfernee Hardaway, Grant Hill, Karl Malone, Reggie Miller, Hakeem Olajuwon, Shaquille O'Neal, Scottie Pippen, Mitch Richmond, John Stockton, David Robinson, Gary Payton

2000

Final: United States 85, France 75
United States: Shareef Abdur-Rahim, Ray Allen, Vin Baker, Vince Carter, Kevin Garnett, Tim Hardaway, Allan Houston, Jason Kidd, Antonio McDyess, Alonzo Mourning, Gary Payton, Steve Smith

Women

1976

Gold, USSR; Silver, United States*
United States: Cindy Brogdon, Susan Rojcewicz, Ann Meyers, Lusia Harris, Nancy Dunkle, Charlotte Lewis, Nancy Lieberman, Gail Marquis, Patricia Roberts, Mary Anne O'Connor, Patricia Head, Julienne Simpson

*In 1976 the women played a round-robin tournament, with the gold medal going to the team with the best record. The USSR won with a 5–0 record, and the USA, with a 3–2 record, was given the silver by virtue of a 95–79 victory over Bulgaria, which was also 3–2.

1980

Final: USSR 104, Bulgaria 73
U.S. participated in boycott.

1984

Final: United States 85, Korea 55
United States: Teresa Edwards, Lea Henry, Lynette Woodard, Anne Donovan, Cathy Boswell, Cheryl Miller, Janice Lawrence, Cindy Noble, Kim Mulkey, Denise Curry, Pamela McGee, Carol Menken-Schaudt

1988

Final: United States 77, Yugoslavia 70
United States: Teresa Edwards, Mary Ethridge, Cynthia Brown, Anne Donovan, Teresa Weatherspoon, Bridgette Gordon, Victoria Bullett, Andrea Lloyd, Katrina McClain, Jennifer Gillom, Cynthia Cooper, Suzanne McConnell

1992

Final: Unified Team 76, China 66
United States (3rd): Teresa Edwards, Teresa Weatherspoon, Victoria Bullett, Katrina McClain, Cynthia Cooper, Suzanne McConnell, Daedra Charles, Clarissa Davis, Tammy Jackson, Vickie Orr, Carolyn Jones, Medina Dixon

1996

Final: United States 111, Brazil 87
United States: Jennifer Azzi, Ruthie Bolton, Teresa Edwards, Lisa Leslie, Rebecca Lobo, Katrina McClain, Nikki McCray, Carla McGhee, Dawn Staley, Katy Steding, Sheryl Swoopes, Venus Lacey

2000

Final: United States 76, Australia 54
United States: Ruthie Bolton-Holifield, Teresa Edwards, Yolanda Griffith, Chamique Holdsclaw, Lisa Leslie, Nikki McCray, Delisha Milton, Katie Smith, Dawn Staley, Sheryl Swoopes, Natalie Williams, Kara Wolters

BOXING

LIGHT FLYWEIGHT (106 LB)

1968	Francisco Rodriguez, Venezuela
1972	Gyorgy Gedo, Hungary
1976	Jorge Hernandez, Cuba
1980	Shamil Sabyrov, USSR
1984	Paul Gonzalez, United States

LIGHT FLYWEIGHT (CONT.)

1988	Ivailo Hristov, Bulgaria
1992	Rogelio Marcelo, Cuba
1996	Daniel Petrov, Bulgaria
2000	Brahim Asloum, France

BOXING *(Cont.)*

FLYWEIGHT (112 LB)
1904 ....George Finnegan, United States
1906–1912......Not held
1920 ....Frank Di Gennara, United States
1924 ....Fidel LaBarba, United States
1928 ....Antal Kocsis, Hungary
1932 ....Istvan Enekes, Hungary
1936 ....Willi Kaiser, Germany
1948 ....Pascual Perez, Argentina
1952 ....Nathan Brooks, United States
1956 ....Terence Spinks, Great Britain
1960 ....Gyula Torok, Hungary
1964 ....Fernando Atzori, Italy
1968 ....Ricardo Delgado, Mexico
1972 ....Georgi Kostadinov, Bulgaria
1976 ....Leo Randolph, United States
1980 ....Peter Lessov, Bulgaria
1984 ....Steve McCrory, United States
1988 ....Kim Kwang Sun, S Korea
1992 ....Su Choi Chol, N Korea
1996 ....Maikro Romero, Cuba
2000 ....Wijan Ponlid, Thailand

BANTAMWEIGHT (119 LB)
1904 ....Oliver Kirk, United States
1906 ....Not held
1908 ....A. Henry Thomas, Great Britain
1912 ....Not held
1920 ....Clarence Walker, S Africa
1924 ....William Smith, S Africa
1928 ....Vittorio Tamagnini, Italy
1932 ....Horace Gwynne, Canada
1936 ....Ulderico Sergo, Italy
1948 ....Tibor Csik, Hungary
1952 ....Pentti Hamalainen, Finland
1956 ....Wolfgang Behrendt, E Germany
1960 ....Oleg Grigoryev, USSR
1964 ....Takao Sakurai, Japan
1968 ....Valery Sokolov, USSR
1972 ....Orlando Martinez, Cuba
1976 ....Yong Jo Gu, N Korea
1980 ....Juan Hernandez, Cuba
1984 ....Maurizio Stecca, Italy
1988 ....Kennedy McKinney, United States
1992 ....Joel Casamayor, Cuba
1996 ....István Kovács, Hungary
2000 ....Guillermo Ortiz, Cuba

FEATHERWEIGHT (125 LB)
1904 ....Oliver Kirk, United States
1906 ....Not held
1908 ....Richard Gunn, Great Britain
1912 ....Not held
1920 ....Paul Fritsch, France
1924 ....John Fields, United States
1928 ....Lambertus van Klaveren, Netherlands
1932 ....Carmelo Robledo, Argentina
1936 ....Oscar Casanovas, Argentina
1948 ....Ernesto Formenti, Italy
1952 ....Jan Zachara, Czechoslovakia
1956 ....Vladimir Safronov, USSR
1960 ....Francesco Musso, Italy
1964 ....Stanislav Stephashkin, USSR
1968 ....Antonio Roldan, Mexico
1972 ....Boris Kousnetsov, USSR
1976 ....Angel Herrera, Cuba
1980 ....Rudi Fink, E Germany
1984 ....Meldrick Taylor, United States
1988 ....Giovanni Parisi, Italy
1992 ....Andreas Tews, Germany
1996 ....Somluck Kamsing, Thailand
2000 ....Bekzat Sattarkhanox, Kazakhstan

LIGHTWEIGHT (132 LB)
1904 ....Harry Spanger, United States
1906 ....Not held
1908 ....Frederick Grace, Great Britain
1912 ....Not held
1920 ....Samuel Mosberg, United States
1924 ....Hans Nielsen, Denmark
1928 ....Carlo Orlandi, Italy
1932 ....Lawrence Stevens, S Africa
1936 ....Imre Harangi, Hungary
1948 ....Gerald Dreyer, S Africa
1952 ....Aureliano Bolognesi, Italy
1956 ....Richard McTaggart, Great Britain
1960 ....Kazimierz Pazdzior, Poland
1964 ....Jozef Grudzien, Poland
1968 ....Ronald Harris, United States
1972 ....Jan Szczepanski, Poland
1976 ....Howard Davis, United States
1980 ....Angel Herrera, Cuba
1984 ....Pernell Whitaker, United States
1988 ....Andreas Zuelow, E Germany
1992 ....Oscar De La Hoya, United States
1996 ....Hocine Soltani, Algeria
2000 ....Mario Kindelan, Cuba

LIGHT WELTERWEIGHT (139 LB)
1952 ....Charles Adkins, United States
1956 ....Vladimir Yengibaryan, USSR
1960 ....Bohumil Nemecek, Czechoslovakia
1964 ....Jerzy Kulej, Poland
1968 ....Jerzy Kulej, Poland
1972 ....Ray Seales, United States
1976 ....Ray Leonard, United States
1980 ....Patrizio Oliva, Italy
1984 ....Jerry Page, United States
1988 ....Viatcheslav Janovski, USSR
1992 ....Hector Vinent, Cuba
1996 ....Hector Vinent, Cuba
2000 ....Mahamadkadyz Abdullaev, Uzbekistan

WELTERWEIGHT (147 LB)
1904 ....Albert Young, United States
1906–1912......Not held
1920 ....Albert Schneider, Canada
1924 ....Jean Delarge, Belgium
1928 ....Edward Morgan, New Zealand
1932 ....Edward Flynn, United States
1936 ....Sten Suvio, Finland
1948 ....Julius Torma, Czechoslovakia
1952 ....Zygmunt Chychla, Poland
1956 ....Nicolae Linca, Romania
1960 ....Giovanni Benvenuti, Italy
1964 ....Marian Kasprzyk, Poland
1968 ....Manfred Wolke, E Germany
1972 ....Emilio Correa, Cuba
1976 ....Jochen Bachfeld, E Germany
1980 ....Andres Aldama, Cuba
1984 ....Mark Breland, United States
1988 ....Robert Wangila, Kenya
1992 ....Michael Carruth, Ireland
1996 ....Oleg Saitov, Russia
2000 ....Oleg Saitov, Russia

LIGHT MIDDLEWEIGHT (156 LB)
1952 ....Laszlo Papp, Hungary
1956 ....Laszlo Papp, Hungary
1960 ....Wilbert McClure, United States
1964 ....Boris Lagutin, USSR
1968 ....Boris Lagutin, USSR
1972 ....Dieter Kottysch, W Germany
1976 ....Jerzy Rybicki, Poland
1980 ....Armando Martinez, Cuba
1984 ....Frank Tate, United States

BOXING (Cont.)

LIGHT MIDDLEWEIGHT (CONT.)

1988 ....Park Si-Hun, S Korea
1992 ....Juan Lemus, Cuba
1996 ....David Reid, United States
2000 ....Yermakhan Ibraimov, Kazakhstan

MIDDLEWEIGHT (165 LB)

1904 ....Charles Mayer, United States
1908 ....John Douglas, Great Britain
1912 ....Not held
1920 ....Harry Mallin, Great Britain
1924 ....Harry Mallin, Great Britain
1928 ....Piero Toscani, Italy
1932 ....Carmen Barth, United States
1936 ....Jean Despeaux, France
1948 ....Laszlo Papp, Hungary
1952 ....Floyd Patterson, United States
1956 ....Gennady Schatkov, USSR
1960 ....Edward Crook, United States
1964 ....Valery Popenchenko, USSR
1968 ....Christopher Finnegan, Great Britain
1972 ....Vyacheslav Lemechev, USSR
1976 ....Michael Spinks, United States
1980 ....Jose Gomez, Cuba
1984 ....Shin Joon Sup, S Korea
1988 ....Henry Maske, E Germany
1992 ....Ariel Hernandez, Cuba
1996 ....Ariel Hernandez, Cuba
2000 ....Jorge Gutierrez, Cuba

LIGHT HEAVYWEIGHT (178 LB)

1920 ....Edward Eagan, United States
1924 ....Harry Mitchell, Great Britain
1928 ....Victor Avendano, Argentina
1932 ....David Carstens, S Africa
1936 ....Roger Michelot, France
1948 ....George Hunter, S Africa
1952 ....Norvel Lee, United States
1956 ....James Boyd, United States
1960 ....Cassius Clay, United States
1964 ....Cosimo Pinto, Italy
1968 ....Dan Poznyak, USSR
1972 ....Mate Parlov, Yugoslavia
1976 ....Leon Spinks, United States

LIGHT HEAVYWEIGHT (CONT.)

1980 ....Slobodan Kacer, Yugoslavia
1984 ....Anton Josipovic, Yugoslavia
1988 ....Andrew Maynard, United States
1992 ....Torsten May, Germany
1996 ....Vassili Jirov, Kazakhstan
2000 ....Alexander Lebziak, Russia

HEAVYWEIGHT (OVER 201 LB)

1904 ....Samuel Berger, United States
1906 ....Not held
1908 ....Albert Oldham, Great Britain
1912 ....Not held
1920 ....Ronald Rawson, Great Britain
1924 ....Otto von Porat, Norway
1928 ....Arturo Rodriguez Jurado, Argentina
1932 ....Santiago Lovell, Argentina
1936 ....Herbert Runge, Germany
1948 ....Rafael Inglesias, Argentina
1952 ....H. Edward Sanders, United States
1956 ....T. Peter Rademacher, United States
1960 ....Franco De Piccoli, Italy
1964 ....Joe Frazier, United States
1968 ....George Foreman, United States
1972 ....Teofilo Stevenson, Cuba
1976 ....Teofilo Stevenson, Cuba
1980 ....Teofilo Stevenson, Cuba

HEAVYWEIGHT (201* LB)

1984 ....Henry Tillman, United States
1988 ....Ray Mercer, United States
1992 ....Félix Sávon, Cuba
1996 ....Félix Sávon, Cuba
2000 ....Félix Sávon, Cuba

SUPERHEAVYWEIGHT (UNLIMITED)

1984 ....Tyrell Biggs, United States
1988 ....Lennox Lewis, Canada
1992 ....Roberto Balado, Cuba
1996 ....Vladimir Klitchko, Ukraine
2000 ....Audley Harrison, Great Britain

*Until 1984 the heavyweight division was unlimited. With the addition of the super heavyweight division, a limit of 201 pounds was imposed.

SWIMMING

Men

50-METER FREESTYLE

1904	....Zoltan Halmay, Hungary (50 yds)	28.0
1988	....Matt Biondi, United States	22.14 WR
1992	....Aleksandr Popov, Unified Team	22.30
1996	....Aleksandr Popov, Russia	22.13
2000	....Anthony Ervin, United States	21.98
	Gary Hall Jr, United States	21.98

100-METER FREESTYLE

1896	....Alfred Hajos, Hungary	1:22.2 OR
1904	....Zoltan Halmay, Hungary (100 yds)	1:02.8
1906	....Charles Daniels, United States	1:13.4
1908	....Charles Daniels, United States	1:05.6 WR
1912	....Duke Kahanamoku, United States	1:03.4
1920	....Duke Kahanamoku, United States	1:00.4 WR
1924	....John Weissmuller, United States	59.0 OR
1928	....John Weissmuller, United States	58.6 OR
1932	....Yasuji Miyazaki, Japan	58.2

100-METER FREESTLYE (CONT.)

1936	....Ferenc Csik, Hungary	57.6
1948	....Wally Ris, United States	57.3 OR
1952	....Clarke Scholes, United States	57.4
1956	....Jon Henricks, Australia	55.4 OR
1960	....John Devitt, Australia	55.2 OR
1964	....Don Schollander, United States	53.4 OR
1968	....Mike Wenden, Australia	52.2 WR
1972	....Mark Spitz, United States	51.22 WR
1976	....Jim Montgomery, United States	49.99 WR
1980	....Jörg Woithe, E Germany	50.40
1984	....Rowdy Gaines, United States	49.80 OR
1988	....Matt Biondi, United States	48.63 OR
1992	....Aleksandr Popov, Unified Team	49.02
1996	....Aleksandr Popov, Russia	48.74
2000	....P. van den Hoogenband, Neth.	48.30

Note: OR=Olympic Record. WR=World Record. EOR=Equals Olympic Record. EWR=Equals World Record. WB=World Best.

SWIMMING *(Cont.)*
Men *(Cont.)*

200-METER FREESTYLE

1900	Frederick Lane, Australia	2:25.2 OR
1904	Charles Daniels, United States	2:44.2
1906–1964	Not held	
1968	Michael Wenden, Australia	1:55.2 OR
1972	Mark Spitz, United States	1:52.78 WR
1976	Bruce Furniss, United States	1:50.29 WR
1980	Sergei Kopliakov, USSR	1:49.81 OR
1984	Michael Gross, W Germany	1:47.44 WR
1988	Duncan Armstrong, Australia	1:47.25 WR
1992	Evgueni Sadovyi, Unified Team	1:46.70 OR
1996	Danyon Loader, New Zealand	1:47.63
2000	Pieter van den Hoogenband, Netherlands	1:45.35 EWR

400-METER FREESTYLE

1896	Paul Neumann, Austria (500 yds)	8:12.6
1904	Charles Daniels, U.S. (440 yds)	6:16.2
1906	Otto Scheff, Austria (440 yds)	6:23.8
1908	Henry Taylor, Great Britain	5:36.8
1912	George Hodgson, Canada	5:24.4
1920	Norman Ross, United States	5:26.8
1924	John Weissmuller, United States	5:04.2 OR
1928	Albert Zorilla, Argentina	5:01.6 OR
1932	Buster Crabbe, United States	4:48.4 OR
1936	Jack Medica, United States	4:44.5 OR
1948	William Smith, United States	4:41.0 OR
1952	Jean Boiteux, France	4:30.7 OR
1956	Murray Rose, Australia	4:27.3 OR
1960	Murray Rose, Australia	4:18.3 OR
1964	Don Schollander, United States	4:12.2 WR
1968	Mike Burton, United States	4:09.0 OR
1972	Brad Cooper, Australia	4:00.27 OR
1976	Brian Goodell, United States	3:51.93 WR
1980	Vladimir Salnikov, USSR	3:51.31 OR
1984	George DiCarlo, United States	3:51.23 OR
1988	Uwe Dassler, E Germany	3:46.95 WR
1992	Evgueni Sadovyi, Unified Team	3:45.00 WR
1996	Danyon Loader, New Zealand	3:47.97
2000	Ian Thorpe, Australia	3:40.59 WR

1,500-METER FREESTYLE

1908	Henry Taylor, Great Britain	22:48.4 WR
1912	George Hodgson, Canada	22:00.0 WR
1920	Norman Ross, United States	22:23.2
1924	Andrew Charlton, Australia	20:06.6 WR
1928	Arne Borg, Sweden	19:51.8 OR
1932	Kusuo Kitamura, Japan	19:12.4 OR
1936	Noboru Terada, Japan	19:13.7
1948	James McLane, United States	19:18.5
1952	Ford Konno, United States	18:30.3 OR
1956	Murray Rose, Australia	17:58.9
1960	John Konrads, Australia	17:19.6 OR
1964	Robert Windle, Australia	17:01.7 OR
1968	Mike Burton, United States	16:38.9 OR
1972	Mike Burton, United States	15:52.58 OR
1976	Brian Goodell, United States	15:02.40 WR
1980	Vladimir Salnikov, USSR	14:58.27 WR
1984	Michael O'Brien, United States	15:05.20
1988	Vladimir Salnikov, USSR	15:00.40
1992	Kieren Perkins, Australia	14:43.48 WR
1996	Kieren Perkins, Australia	14:56.40
2000	Grant Hackett, Australia	14:48.33

100-METER BACKSTROKE

1904	Walter Brack, Germany (100 yds)	1:16.8
1908	Arno Bieberstein, Germany	1:24.6 WR
1912	Harry Hebner, United States	1:21.2

100-METER BACKSTROKE *(CONT.)*

1920	Warren Kealoha, United States	1:15.2
1924	Warren Kealoha, United States	1:13.2 OR
1928	George Kojac, United States	1:08.2 WR
1932	Masaji Kiyokawa, Japan	1:08.6
1936	Adolph Kiefer, United States	1:05.9 OR
1948	Allen Stack, United States	1:06.4
1952	Yoshi Oyakawa, United States	1:05.4 OR
1956	David Thiele, Australia	1:02.2 OR
1960	David Thiele, Australia	1:01.9 OR
1964	Not held	
1968	Roland Matthes, E Germany	58.7 OR
1972	Roland Matthes, E Germany	56.58 OR
1976	John Naber, United States	55.49 WR
1980	Bengt Baron, Sweden	56.33
1984	Rick Carey, United States	55.79
1988	Daichi Suzuki, Japan	55.05
1992	Mark Tewksbury, Canada	53.98 WR
1996	Jeff Rouse, United States	54.10
2000	Lenny Krayzelburg, United States	53.72 OR

200-METER BACKSTROKE

1900	Ernst Hoppenberg, Germany	2:47.0
1906–1960	Not held	
1964	Jed Graef, United States	2:10.3 WR
1968	Roland Matthes, E Germany	2:09.6 OR
1972	Roland Matthes, E Germany	2:02.82 EWR
1976	John Naber, United States	1:59.19 WR
1980	Sandor Wladar, Hungary	2:01.93
1984	Rick Carey, United States	2:00.23
1988	Igor Polianski, USSR	1:59.37
1992	Martin Lopez-Zubero, Spain	1:58.47 OR
1996	Brad Bridgewater, United States	1:58.54
2000	Lenny Krayzelburg, United States	1:56.76 OR

100-METER BREASTSTROKE

1968	Don McKenzie, United States	1:07.7 OR
1972	Nobutaka Taguchi, Japan	1:04.94 WR
1976	John Hencken, United States	1:03.11 WR
1980	Duncan Goodhew, Great Britain	1:03.44
1984	Steve Lundquist, United States	1:01.65 WR
1988	Adrian Moorhouse, Great Britain	1:02.04
1992	Nelson Diebel, United States	1:01.50 OR
1996	Fred DeBurghgraeve, Belgium	1:00.65
2000	Domenico Fioravanti, Italy	1:00.46 OR

200-METER BREASTSTROKE

1908	Frederick Holman, Great Britain	3:09.2 WR
1912	Walter Bathe, Germany	3:01.8 OR
1920	Haken Malmroth, Sweden	3:04.4
1924	Robert Skelton, United States	2:56.6
1928	Yoshiyuki Tsuruta, Japan	2:48.8 OR
1932	Yoshiyuki Tsuruta, Japan	2:45.4
1936	Tetsuo Hamuro, Japan	2:41.5 OR
1948	Joseph Verdeur, United States	2:39.3 OR
1952	John Davies, Australia	2:34.4 OR
1956	Masura Furukawa, Japan	2:34.7 OR
1960	William Mulliken, United States	2:37.4
1964	Ian O'Brien, Australia	2:27.8 WR
1968	Felipe Munoz, Mexico	2:28.7
1972	John Hencken, United States	2:21.55 WR
1976	David Wilkie, Great Britain	2:15.11 WR
1980	Robertas Zhulpa, USSR	2:15.85
1984	Victor Davis, Canada	2:13.34 WR
1988	Jozsef Szabo, Hungary	2:13.52
1992	Mike Barrowman, United States	2:10.16 WR
1996	Norbert Rózsa, Hungary	2:12.57
2000	Domenico Fioravanti, Italy	2:10.87

Note: OR=Olympic Record. WR=World Record. EOR=Equals Olympic Record. EWR=Equals World Record. WB=World Best.

SWIMMING *(Cont.)*

Men *(Cont.)*

100-METER BUTTERFLY

1968	Doug Russell, United States	55.9 OR
1972	Mark Spitz, United States	54.27 WR
1976	Matt Vogel, United States	54.35
1980	Pär Arvidsson, Sweden	54.92
1984	Michael Gross, W Germany	53.08 WR
1988	Anthony Nesty, Suriname	53.00 OR
1992	Pablo Morales, United States	53.32
1996	Denis Pankratov, Russia	52.27 WR
2000	Lars Froelander, Sweden	52.00

200-METER BUTTERFLY

1956	William Yorzyk, United States	2:19.3 OR
1960	Michael Troy, United States	2:12.8 WR
1964	Kevin Berry, Australia	2:06.6 WR
1968	Carl Robie, United States	2:08.7
1972	Mark Spitz, United States	2:00.70 WR
1976	Mike Bruner, United States	1:59.23 WR
1980	Sergei Fesenko, USSR	1:59.76
1984	Jon Sieben, Australia	1:57.04 WR
1988	Michael Gross, W Germany	1:56.94 OR
1992	Melvin Stewart, United States	1:56.26 OR
1996	Denis Pankratov, Russia	1:56.51
2000	Tom Malchow, United States	1:55.35 OR

200-METER INDIVIDUAL MEDLEY

1968	Charles Hickcox, United States	2:12.0 OR
1972	Gunnar Larsson, Sweden	2:07.17 WR
1984	Alex Baumann, Canada	2:01.42 WR
1988	Tamas Darnyi, Hungary	2:00.17 WR
1992	Tamas Darnyi, Hungary	2:00.76
1996	Attila Czene, Hungary	1:59.91 OR
2000	Massimiliano Rosolino, Italy	1:58.98 OR

400-METER INDIVIDUAL MEDLEY

1964	Richard Roth, United States	4:45.4 WR
1968	Charles Hickcox, United States	4:48.4
1972	Gunnar Larsson, Sweden	4:31.98 OR
1976	Rod Strachan, United States	4:23.68 WR
1980	Aleksandr Sidorenko, USSR	4:22.89 OR
1984	Alex Baumann, Canada	4:17.41 WR
1988	Tamas Darnyi, Hungary	4:14.75 WR
1992	Tamas Darnyi, Hungary	4:14.23 OR
1996	Tom Dolan United States	4:14.90
2000	Tom Dolan, United States	4:11.76 WR

4 X 100-METER MEDLEY RELAY

1960	United States	4:05.4 WR
1964	United States	3:58.4 WR
1968	United States	3:54.9 WR
1972	United States	3:48.16 WR
1976	United States	3:42.22 WR
1980	Australia	3:45.70
1984	United States	3:39.30 WR
1988	United States	3:36.93 WR
1992	United States	3:36.93 EWR
1996	United States	3:34.84 WR
2000	United States	3:33.73 WR

4 X 100-METER FREESTYLE RELAY

1964	United States	3:32.2 WR
1968	United States	3:31.7 WR
1972	United States	3:26.42 WR
1976–1980	Not held	
1984	United States	3:19.03 WR
1988	United States	3:16.53 WR
1992	United States	3:16.74
1996	United States	3:15.41 OR
2000	Australia	3:13.67 WR

4 X 200-METER FREESTYLE RELAY

1906	Hungary (1,000 m)	16:52.4
1908	Great Britain	10:55.6
1912	Australia/New Zealand	10:11.6 WR
1920	United States	10:04.4 WR
1924	United States	9:53.4 WR
1928	United States	9:36.2 WR
1932	Japan	8:58.4 WR
1936	Japan	8:51.5 WR
1948	United States	8:46.0 WR
1952	United States	8:31.1 WR
1956	Australia	8:23.6 WR
1960	United States	8:10.2 WR
1964	United States	7:52.1 WR
1968	United States	7:52.33
1972	United States	7:35.78 WR
1976	United States	7:23.22 WR
1980	USSR	7:23.50
1984	United States	7:15.69 WR
1988	United States	7:12.51 WR
1992	Unified Team	7:11.95 WR
1996	United States	7:14.84
2000	Australia	7:07.05 WR

Women

50-METER FREESTYLE

1988	Kristin Otto, E Germany	25.49 OR
1992	Yang Wenyi, China	24.79 WR
1996	Amy Van Dyken, United States	24.87
2000	Inge de Bruijn, Netherlands	24.32 WR

100-METER FREESTYLE

1912	Fanny Durack, Australia	1:22.2
1920	Ethelda Bleibtrey, United States	1:13.6 WR
1924	Ethel Lackie, United States	1:12.4
1928	Albina Osipowich, United States	1:11.0 OR
1932	Helene Madison, United States	1:06.8 OR
1936	Hendrika Mastenbroek, Netherlands	1:05.9 WR
1948	Greta Andersen, Denmark	1:06.3
1952	Katalin Szöke, Hungary	1:06.8
1956	Dawn Fraser, Australia	1:02.0 WR
1960	Dawn Fraser, Australia	1:01.2 OR
1964	Dawn Fraser, Australia	59.5 OR

100-METER FREESTYLE *(CONT.)*

1968	Jan Henne, United States	1:00.0
1972	Sandra Neilson, United States	58.59 OR
1976	Kornelia Ender, E Germany	55.65 WR
1980	Barbara Krause, E Germany	54.79 WR
1984	Carrie Steinseifer, United States	55.92
	Nancy Hogshead, United States	55.92
1988	Kristin Otto, E Germany	54.93
1992	Zhuang Yong, China	54.64 OR
1996	Le Jingyi, China	54.50 OR
2000	Inge de Bruijn, Netherlands	53.83 OR

200-METER FREESTYLE

1968	Debbie Meyer, United States	2:10.5 OR
1972	Shane Gould, Australia	2:03.56 WR
1976	Kornelia Ender, E Germany	1:59.26 WR
1980	Barbara Krause, E Germany	1:58.33 OR
1984	Mary Wayte, United States	1:59.23
1988	Heike Friedrich, E Germany	1:57.65 OR

Note: OR=Olympic Record. WR=World Record. EOR=Equals Olympic Record. EWR=Equals World Record. WB=World Best.

SWIMMING (Cont.)
Women (Cont.)

200-METER FREESTYLE (CONT.)

1992	Nicole Haislett, United States	1:57.90
1996	Claudia Poll, Costa Rica	1:58.16
2000	Susie O'Neill, Australia	1:58.24

400-METER FREESTYLE

1924	Martha Norelius, United States	6:02.2 OR
1928	Martha Norelius, United States	5:42.8 WR
1932	Helene Madison, United States	5:28.5 WR
1936	Hendrika Mastenbroek, Netherlands	5:26.4 OR
1948	Ann Curtis, United States	5:17.8 OR
1952	Valeria Gyenge, Hungary	5:12.1 OR
1956	Lorraine Crapp, Australia	4:54.6 OR
1960	Chris von Saltza, United States	4:50.6 OR
1964	Virginia Duenkel, United States	4:43.3 OR
1968	Debbie Meyer, United States	4:31.8 OR
1972	Shane Gould, Australia	4:19.44 WR
1976	Petra Thümer, E Germany	4:09.89 WR
1980	Ines Diers, E Germany	4:08.76 WR
1984	Tiffany Cohen, United States	4:07.10 OR
1988	Janet Evans, United States	4:03.85 WR
1992	Dagmar Hase, Germany	4:07.18
1996	Michelle Smith, Ireland	4:07.25
2000	Brooke Bennett, United States	4:05.80

800-METER FREESTYLE

1968	Debbie Meyer, United States	9:24.0 OR
1972	Keena Rothhammer, United States	8:53.68 WR
1976	Petra Thümer, E Germany	8:37.14 WR
1980	Michelle Ford, Australia	8:28.90 OR
1984	Tiffany Cohen, United States	8:24.95 OR
1988	Janet Evans, United States	8:20.20 OR
1992	Janet Evans, United States	8:25.52
1996	Brooke Bennett, United States	8:27.89
2000	Brooke Bennett, United States	8:19.67 OR

100-METER BACKSTROKE

1924	Sybil Bauer, United States	1:23.2 OR
1928	Marie Braun, Netherlands	1:22.0
1932	Eleanor Holm, United States	1:19.4
1936	Dina Senff, Netherlands	1:18.9
1948	Karen Harup, Denmark	1:14.4 OR
1952	Joan Harrison, South Africa	1:14.3
1956	Judy Grinham, Great Britain	1:12.9 OR
1960	Lynn Burke, United States	1:09.3 OR
1964	Cathy Ferguson, United States	1:07.7 WR
1968	Kaye Hall, United States	1:06.2 WR
1972	Melissa Belote, United States	1:05.78 OR
1976	Ulrike Richter, E Germany	1:01.83 OR
1980	Rica Reinisch, E Germany	1:00.86 WR
1984	Theresa Andrews, United States	1:02.55
1988	Kristin Otto, E Germany	1:00.89
1992	Krisztina Egerszegi, Hungary	1:00.68 OR
1996	Beth Botsford, United States	1:01.19
2000	Diana Iuliana Mocanu, Romania	1:00.21 OR

200-METER BACKSTROKE

1968	Pokey Watson, United States	2:24.8 OR
1972	Melissa Belote, United States	2:19.19 WR
1976	Ulrike Richter, E Germany	2:13.43 OR
1980	Rica Reinisch, E Germany	2:11.77 WR
1984	Jolanda De Rover, Netherlands	2:12.38
1988	Krisztina Egerszegi, Hungary	2:09.29 OR
1992	Krisztina Egerszegi, Hungary	2:07.06 OR
1996	Krisztina Egerszegi, Hungary	2:07.83
2000	Diana Iuliana Mocanu, Romania	2:08.16

100-METER BREASTSTROKE

1968	Djurdjica Bjedov, Yugoslavia	1:15.8 OR
1972	Catherine Carr, United States	1:13.58 WR
1976	Hannelore Anke, E Germany	1:11.16
1980	Ute Geweniger, E Germany	1:10.22
1984	Petra Van Staveren, Netherlands	1:09.88 OR
1988	Tania Dangalakova, Bulgaria	1:07.95 OR
1992	Elena Roudkovskaia, Unified Team	1:08.00
1996	Penelope Heyns, S Africa	1:07.73
2000	Megan Quann, United States	1:07.05

200-METER BREASTSTROKE

1924	Lucy Morton, Great Britain	3:33.2 OR
1928	Hilde Schrader, Germany	3:12.6
1932	Clare Dennis, Australia	3:06.3 OR
1936	Hideko Maehata, Japan	3:03.6
1948	Petronella Van Vliet, Netherlands	2:57.2
1952	Eva Szekely, Hungary	2:51.7 OR
1956	Ursula Happe, W Germany	2:53.1 OR
1960	Anita Lonsbrough, Great Britain	2:49.5 WR
1964	Galina Prozumenshikova, USSR	2:46.4 OR
1968	Sharon Wichman, United States	2:44.4 OR
1972	Beverly Whitfield, Australia	2:41.71 OR
1976	Marina Koshevaia, USSR	2:33.35 WR
1980	Lina Kaciusyte, USSR	2:29.54 OR
1984	Anne Ottenbrite, Canada	2:30.38
1988	Silke Hoerner, E Germany	2:26.71 WR
1992	Kyoko Iwasaki, Japan	2:26.65 OR
1996	Penelope Heyns, S Africa	2:25.41 OR
2000	Agnes Kovacs, Hungary	2:24.35 OR

100-METER BUTTERFLY

1956	Shelley Mann, United States	1:11.0 OR
1960	Carolyn Schuler, United States	1:09.5 OR
1964	Sharon Stouder, United States	1:04.7 WR
1968	Lynn McClements, Australia	1:05.5
1972	Mayumi Aoki, Japan	1:03.34 WR
1976	Kornelia Ender, E Germany	1:00.13 EWR
1980	Caren Metschuck, E Germany	1:00.42
1984	Mary T. Meagher, United States	59.26
1988	Kristin Otto, E Germany	59.00 OR
1992	Qian Hong, China	58.62 OR
1996	Amy Van Dyken, United States	59.13
2000	Inge de Bruijn, Netherlands	56.61 WR

200-METER BUTTERFLY

1968	Ada Kok, Netherlands	2:24.7 OR
1972	Karen Moe, United States	2:15.57 WR
1976	Andrea Pollack, E Germany	2:11.41 OR
1980	Ines Geissler, E Germany	2:10.44 OR
1984	Mary T. Meagher, United States	2:06.90 OR
1988	Kathleen Nord, E Germany	2:09.51
1992	Summer Sanders, United States	2:08.67
1996	Susan O'Neill, Australia	2:07.76
2000	Misty Hyman, United States	2:05.88 OR

200-METER INDIVIDUAL MEDLEY

1968	Claudia Kolb, United States	2:24.7 OR
1972	Shane Gould, Australia	2:23.07 WR
1976–1980	Not held	
1984	Tracy Caulkins, United States	2:12.64 OR
1988	Daniela Hunger, E Germany	2:12.59 OR
1992	Lin Li, China	2:11.65 WR
1996	Michelle Smith, Ireland	2:13.93
2000	Yana Klochkova, Ukraine	2:10.68 OR

Note: OR=Olympic Record. WR=World Record. EOR=Equals Olympic Record. EWR=Equals World Record. WB=World Best.

SWIMMING (Cont.)

Women (Cont.)

400-METER INDIVIDUAL MEDLEY

1964	Donna de Varona, United States	5:18.7 OR
1968	Claudia Kolb, United States	5:08.5 OR
1972	Gail Neall, Australia	5:02.97 WR
1976	Ulrike Tauber, E Germany	4:42.77 WR
1980	Petra Schneider, E Germany	4:36.29 WR
1984	Tracy Caulkins, United States	4:39.24
1988	Janet Evans, United States	4:37.76
1992	Krisztina Egerszegi, Hungary	4:36.54
1996	Michelle Smith, Ireland	4:39.18
2000	Yana Klochkova, Ukraine	4:33.59 WR

4 X 100-METER MEDLEY RELAY

1960	United States	4:41.1 WR
1964	United States	4:33.9 WR
1968	United States	4:28.3 OR
1972	United States	4:20.75 WR
1976	E Germany	4:07.95 WR
1980	E Germany	4:06.67 WR
1984	United States	4:08.34
1988	E Germany	4:03.74 OR
1992	United States	4:02.54 WR
1996	United States	4:02.88
2000	United States	3:58.30 WR

4 X 100-METER FREESTYLE RELAY

1912	Great Britain	5:52.8 WR
1920	United States	5:11.6 WR
1924	United States	4:58.8 WR
1928	United States	4:47.6 WR
1932	United States	4:38.0 WR
1936	Netherlands	4:36.0 OR
1948	United States	4:29.2 OR
1952	Hungary	4:24.4 WR
1956	Australia	4:17.1 WR
1960	United States	4:08.9 WR
1964	United States	4:03.8 WR
1968	United States	4:02.5 OR
1972	United States	3:55.19 WR
1976	United States	3:44.82 WR
1980	E Germany	3:42.71 WR
1984	United States	3:43.43
1988	E Germany	3:40.63 OR
1992	United States	3:39.46 WR
1996	United States	3:39.29 OR
2000	United States	3:36.61 WR

4 X 200-METER FREESTYLE RELAY

1996	United States	7:59.87
2000	United States	7:57.80 OR

DIVING

Men

SPRINGBOARD

		Pts
1908	Albert Zürner, Germany	85.5
1912	Paul Günther, Germany	79.23
1920	Louis Kuehn, United States	675.40
1924	Albert White, United States	97.46
1928	Pete DesJardins, United States	185.04
1932	Michael Galitzen, United States	161.38
1936	Richard Degener, United States	163.57
1948	Bruce Harlan, United States	163.64
1952	David Browning, United States	205.29
1956	Robert Clotworthy, United States	159.56
1960	Gary Tobian, United States	170.00
1964	Kenneth Sitzberger, United States	159.90
1968	Bernie Wrightson, United States	170.15
1972	Vladimir Vasin, USSR	594.09
1976	Phil Boggs, United States	619.05
1980	Aleksandr Portnov, USSR	905.02
1984	Greg Louganis, United States	754.41
1988	Greg Louganis, United States	730.80
1992	Mark Lenzi, United States	676.53
1996	Xiong Ni, China	701.46
2000	Xiong Ni, China	708.72

PLATFORM

		Pts
1904	George Sheldon, United States	12.66
1906	Gottlob Walz, Germany	156.0
1908	Hjalmar Johansson, Sweden	83.75
1912	Erik Adlerz, Sweden	73.94
1920	Clarence Pinkston, United States	100.67
1924	Albert White, United States	97.46
1928	Pete DesJardins, United States	98.74
1932	Harold Smith, United States	124.80
1936	Marshall Wayne, United States	113.58
1948	Sammy Lee, United States	130.05
1952	Sammy Lee, United States	156.28
1956	Joaquin Capilla, Mexico	152.44
1960	Robert Webster, United States	165.56
1964	Robert Webster, United States	148.58
1968	Klaus Dibiasi, Italy	164.18
1972	Klaus Dibiasi, Italy	504.12
1976	Klaus Dibiasi, Italy	600.51
1980	Falk Hoffmann, E Germany	835.65
1984	Greg Louganis, United States	710.91
1988	Greg Louganis, United States	638.61
1992	Sun Shuwei, China	677.31
1996	Dmitri Sautin, Russia	692.34
2000	Tian Liang, China	724.53

Women

SPRINGBOARD

		Pts
1920	Aileen Riggin, United States	539.90
1924	Elizabeth Becker, United States	474.50
1928	Helen Meany, United States	78.62
1932	Georgia Coleman, United States	87.52
1936	Marjorie Gestring, United States	89.27
1948	Victoria Draves, United States	108.74

SPRINGBOARD (CONT.)

		Pts
1952	Patricia McCormick, United States	147.30
1956	Patricia McCormick, United States	142.36
1960	Ingrid Krämer, E Germany	155.81
1964	Ingrid Engel Krämer, E Germany	145.00
1968	Sue Gossick, United States	150.77
1972	Micki King, United States	450.03

DIVING (Cont.)
Women (Cont.)

SPRINGBOARD (CONT.)

		Pts
1976	Jennifer Chandler, United States	506.19
1980	Irina Kalinina, USSR	725.91
1984	Sylvie Bernier, Canada	530.70
1988	Gao Min, China	580.23
1992	Gao Min, China	572.40
1996	Fu Mingxia, China	547.68
2000	Fu Mingxia, China	609.42

PLATFORM

		Pts
1912	Greta Johansson, Sweden	39.90
1920	Stefani Fryland-Clausen, Denmark	34.60
1924	Caroline Smith, United States	33.20
1928	Elizabeth B. Pinkston, United States	31.60
1932	Dorothy Poynton, United States	40.26
1936	Dorothy Poynton Hill, United States	33.93

PLATFORM (CONT.)

		Pts
1948	Victoria Draves, United States	68.87
1952	Patricia McCormick, United States	79.37
1956	Patricia McCormick, United States	84.85
1960	Ingrid Krämer, E Germany	91.28
1964	Lesley Bush, United States	99.80
1968	Milena Duchkova, Czechoslovakia	109.59
1972	Ulrika Knape, Sweden	390.00
1976	Elena Vaytsekhovskaya, USSR	406.59
1980	Martina Jäschke, E Germany	596.25
1984	Zhou Jihong, China	435.51
1988	Xu Yanmei, China	445.20
1992	Mingxia Fu, China	461.43
1996	Mingxia Fu, China	521.58
2000	Laura Wilkinson, United States	543.75

GYMNASTICS
Men

ALL-AROUND

		Pts
1900	Gustave Sandras, France	302
1904	Julius Lenhart, Austria	69.80
1906	Pierre Paysse, France	97
1908	Alberto Braglia, Italy	317.0
1912	Alberto Braglia, Italy	135.0
1920	Giorgio Zampori, Italy	88.35
1924	Leon Stukelj, Yugoslavia	110.340
1928	Georges Miez, Switzerland	247.500
1932	Romeo Neri, Italy	140.625
1936	Alfred Schwarzmann, Germany	113.100
1948	Veikko Huhtanen, Finland	229.70
1952	Viktor Chukarin, USSR	115.70
1956	Viktor Chukarin, USSR	114.25
1960	Boris Shakhlin, USSR	115.95
1964	Yukio Endo, Japan	115.95
1968	Sawao Kato, Japan	115.90
1972	Sawao Kato, Japan	114.65
1976	Nikolai Andrianov, USSR	116.65
1980	Aleksandr Dityatin, USSR	118.65
1984	Koji Gushiken, Japan	118.70
1988	Vladimir Artemov, USSR	119.125
1992	Vitaly Scherbo, Unified Team	59.025
1996	Li Xiaoshuang, China	58.423
2000	Alexei Nemov, Russia	58.474

HORIZONTAL BAR

		Pts
1896	Hermann Weingärtner, Germany	—
1904	Anton Heida, United States	40
1924	Leon Stukelj, Yugoslavia	19.73
1928	Georges Miez, Switzerland	19.17
1932	Dallas Bixler, United States	18.33
1936	Aleksanteri Saarvala, Finland	19.367
1948	Josef Stalfer, Switzerland	19.85
1952	Jack Günthard, Switzerland	19.55
1956	Takashi Ono, Japan	19.60
1960	Takashi Ono, Japan	19.60
1964	Boris Shakhlin, USSR	19.625
1968	Akinori Nakayama, Japan	19.55
1972	Mitsuo Tsukahara, Japan	19.725
1976	Mitsuo Tsukahara, Japan	19.675
1980	Stoyan Deltchev, Bulgaria	19.825
1984	Shinji Morisue, Japan	20.00
1988	Vladimir Artemov, USSR	19.90
1992	Trent Dimas, United States	9.875
1996	Andreas Wecker, Germany	9.850
2000	Alexei Nemov, Russia	9.787

PARALLEL BARS

		Pts
1896	Alfred Flatow, Germany	—
1904	George Eyser, United States	44
1924	August Güttinger, Switzerland	21.63
1928	Ladislav Vacha, Czechoslovakia	18.83
1932	Romeo Neri, Italy	18.97
1936	Konrad Frey, Germany	19.067
1948	Michael Reusch, Switzerland	19.75
1952	Hans Eugster, Switzerland	19.65
1956	Viktor Chukarin, USSR	19.20
1960	Boris Shakhlin, USSR	19.40
1964	Yukio Endo, Japan	19.675
1968	Akinori Nakayama, Japan	19.475
1972	Sawao Kato, Japan	19.475
1976	Sawao Kato, Japan	19.675
1980	Aleksandr Tkachyov, USSR	19.775
1984	Bart Conner, United States	19.95
1988	Vladimir Artemov, USSR	19.925
1992	Vitaly Scherbo, Unified Team	9.900
1996	Rustan Sharipov, Ukraine	9.837
2000	Xiaopeng Li, China	9.825

VAULT

		Pts
1896	Karl Schumann, Germany	—
1904	George Eyser, United States	36
1924	Frank Kriz, United States	9.98
1928	Eugen Mack, Switzerland	9.58
1932	Savino Guglielmetti, Italy	18.03
1936	Alfred Schwarzmann, Germany	19.20
1948	Paavo Aaltonen, Finland	19.55
1952	Viktor Chukarin, USSR	19.20
1956	Helmut Bantz, Germany	18.85
1960	Takashi Ono, Japan	19.35
1964	Haruhiro Yamashita, Japan	19.60
1968	Mikhail Voronin, USSR	19.00
1972	Klaus Köste, E Germany	18.85
1976	Nikolai Andrianov, USSR	19.45
1980	Nikolai Andrianov, USSR	19.825
1984	Lou Yun, China	19.95
1988	Lou Yun, China	19.875
1992	Vitaly Scherbo, Unified Team	9.856
1996	Alexei Nemov, Russia	9.787
2000	Gervasio Deferr, Spain	9.712

GYMNASTICS (Cont.)
Men (Cont.)

POMMEL HORSE

		Pts
1896	Louis Zutter, Switzerland	—
1900	Not held	
1904	Anton Heida, United States	42
1908–1920	Not held	
1924	Josef Wilhelm, Switzerland	21.23
1928	Hermann Hänggi, Switzerland	19.75
1932	Istvan Pelle, Hungary	19.07
1936	Konrad Frey, Germany	19.333
1948	Paavo Aaltonen, Finland	19.35
1952	Viktor Chukarin, USSR	19.50
1956	Boris Shakhlin, USSR	19.25
1960	Eugen Ekman, Finland	19.375
1964	Miroslav Cerar, Yugoslavia	19.525
1968	Miroslav Cerar, Yugoslavia	19.325
1972	Viktor Klimenko, USSR	19.125
1976	Zoltan Magyar, Hungary	19.70
1980	Zoltan Magyar, Hungary	19.925
1984	Li Ning, China	19.95
1988	Dmitri Bilozerchev, USSR	19.95
1992	Vitaly Scherbo, Unified Team	9.925
1996	Donghua Li, Switzerland	9.875
2000	Marius Urzica, Romania	9.862

RINGS

		Pts
1896	Ioannis Mitropoulos, Greece	—
1900	Not held	
1904	Hermann Glass, United States	45
1908–1920	Not held	
1924	Francesco Martino, Italy	21.553
1928	Leon Stukelj, Yugoslavia	19.25
1932	George Gulack, United States	18.97
1936	Alois Hudec, Czechoslovakia	19.433
1948	Karl Frei, Switzerland	19.80
1952	Grant Shaginyan, USSR	19.75
1956	Albert Azaryan, USSR	19.35
1960	Albert Azaryan, USSR	19.725
1964	Takuji Haytta, Japan	19.475
1968	Akinori Nakayama, Japan	19.45
1972	Akinori Nakayama, Japan	19.35
1976	Nikolai Andrianov, USSR	19.65
1980	Aleksandr Dityatin, USSR	19.875
1984	Koji Gushiken, Japan	19.85
1988	Holger Behrendt, E Germany	19.925
1992	Vitaly Scherbo, Unified Team	9.937
1996	Yuri Chechi, Italy	9.887
2000	Szilveszter Csollany, Hungary	9.862

FLOOR EXERCISE

		Pts
1932	Istvan Pelle, Hungary	9.60
1936	Georges Miez, Switzerland	18.666
1948	Ferenc Pataki, Hungary	19.35
1952	K. William Thoresson, Sweden	19.25
1956	Valentin Muratov, USSR	19.20
1960	Nobuyuki Aihara, Japan	19.45
1964	Franco Menichelli, Italy	19.45
1968	Sawao Kato, Japan	19.475
1972	Nikolai Andrianov, USSR	19.175
1976	Nikolai Andrianov, USSR	19.45
1980	Roland Brückner, E Germany	19.75
1984	Li Ning, China	19.925
1988	Sergei Kharkov, USSR	19.925
1992	Li Xiaoshuang, China	9.925
1996	Ioannis Melissanidis, Greece	9.850
2000	Igors Vihrovs, Latvia	9.812

TEAM COMBINED EXERCISES

		Pts
1904	Turngemeinde Philadelphia	374.43
1906	Norway	19.00
1908	Sweden	438
1912	Italy	265.75
1920	Italy	359.855
1924	Italy	839.058
1928	Switzerland	1718.625
1932	Italy	541.850
1936	Germany	657.430
1948	Finland	1358.30
1952	USSR	574.40
1956	USSR	568.25
1960	Japan	575.20
1964	Japan	577.95
1968	Japan	575.90
1972	Japan	571.25
1976	Japan	576.85
1980	USSR	598.60
1984	United States	591.40
1988	USSR	593.35
1992	Unified Team	585.45
1996	Russia	576.778
2000	China	231.919

Women

ALL-AROUND

		Pts
1952	Maria Gorokhovskaya, USSR	76.78
1956	Larissa Latynina, USSR	74.933
1960	Larissa Latynina, USSR	77.031
1964	Vera Caslavska, Czechoslovakia	77.564
1968	Vera Caslavska, Czechoslovakia	78.25
1972	Lyudmila Tousischeva, USSR	77.025
1976	Nadia Comaneci, Romania	79.275
1980	Yelena Davydova, USSR	79.15
1984	Mary Lou Retton, United States	79.175
1988	Yelena Shushunova, USSR	79.662
1992	Tatiana Gutsu, Unified Team	39.737
1996	Lilia Podkopayeva, Ukraine	39.255
2000	Simona Amanar, Romania	38.642

VAULT

		Pts
1952	Yekaterina Kalinchuk, USSR	19.20
1956	Larissa Latynina, USSR	18.833
1960	Margarita Nikolayeva, USSR	19.316
1964	Vera Caslavska, Czechoslovakia	19.483
1968	Vera Caslavska, Czechoslovakia	19.775
1972	Karin Janz, E Germany	19.525
1976	Nelli Kim, USSR	19.80
1980	Natalya Shaposhnikova, USSR	19.725
1984	Ecaterina Szabo, Romania	19.875
1988	Svetlana Boginskaya, USSR	19.905
1992	Henrietta Onodi, Hungary	9.925
	Lavinia Milosovici, Romania	9.925
1996	Simona Amanar, Romania	9.825
2000	Yelena Zamolodtchikova, Russia	9.731

GYMNASTICS (Cont.)
Women (Cont.)

UNEVEN BARS

		Pts
1952	Margit Korondi, Hungary	19.40
1956	Agnes Keleti, Hungary	18.966
1960	Polina Astakhova, USSR	19.616
1964	Polina Astakhova, USSR	19.332
1968	Vera Caslavska, Czechoslovakia	19.65
1972	Karin Janz, E Germany	19.675
1976	Nadia Comaneci, Romania	20.00
1980	Maxi Gnauck, E Germany	19.875
1984	Ma Yanhong, China	19.95
1988	Daniela Silivas, Romania	20.00
1992	Lu Li, China	10.00
1996	Svetlana Khorkina, Russia	9.850
2000	Svetlana Khorkina, Russia	9.862

BALANCE BEAM

		Pts
1952	Nina Bocharova, USSR	19.22
1956	Agnes Keleti, Hungary	18.80
1960	Eva Bosakova, Czechoslovakia	19.283
1964	Vera Caslavska, Czechoslovakia	19.449
1968	Natalya Kuchinskaya, USSR	19.65
1972	Olga Korbut, USSR	19.40
1976	Nadia Comaneci, Romania	19.95
1980	Nadia Comaneci, Romania	19.80
1984	Simona Pauca, Romania	19.80
1988	Daniela Silivas, Romania	19.924
1992	Tatiana Lisenko, Unified Team	9.975
1996	Shannon Miller, United States	9.862
2000	Xuan Li, China	9.825

FLOOR EXERCISE

		Pts
1952	Agnes Keleti, Hungary	19.36
1956	Agnes Keleti, Hungary	18.733
1960	Larissa Latynina, USSR	19.583
1964	Larissa Latynina, USSR	19.599
1968	Vera Caslavska, Czechoslovakia	19.675
1972	Olga Korbut, USSR	19.575
1976	Nelli Kim, USSR	19.85
1980	Nadia Comaneci, Romania	19.875

FLOOR EXERCISE (Cont.)

		Pts
1984	Ecaterina Szabo, Romania	19.975
1988	Daniela Silivas, Romania	19.937
1992	Lavinia Milosovici, Romania	10.00
1996	Lilia Podkopayeva, Ukraine	9.887
2000	Yelena Zamolodtchikova, Russia	9.850

TEAM COMBINED EXERCISES

		Pts
1928	The Netherlands	316.75
1932	Not held	
1936	Germany	506.50
1948	Czechoslovakia	445:45
1952	USSR	527.03
1956	USSR	444.800
1960	USSR	382.320
1964	USSR	280.890
1968	USSR	382.85
1972	USSR	380.50
1976	USSR	466.00
1980	USSR	394.90
1984	Romania	392.02
1988	USSR	395.475
1992	Unified Team	395.666
1996	United States	389.225
2000	Romania	154.608

RHYTHMIC ALL-AROUND

		Pts
1984	Lori Fung, Canada	57.95
1988	Marina Lobach, USSR	60.00
1992	A. Timoshenko, Unified Team	59.037
1996	E. Serebrianskaya, Ukraine	39.683
2000	Yulia Barsukova, Russia	39.632

RHYTHMIC TEAM COMBINED EXERCISES

		Pts
1996	Spain	38.933
2000	Russia	39.500

SOCCER
Men

1900	Great Britain	1928	Uruguay	1964	Hungary	1988	Soviet Union
1904	Canada	1936	Italy	1968	Hungary	1992	Spain
1908	Great Britain	1948	Sweden	1972	Poland	1996	Nigeria
1912	Great Britain	1952	Hungary	1976	E Germany	2000	Cameroon
1920	Belgium	1956	Soviet Union	1980	Czechoslovakia		
1924	Uruguay	1960	Yugoslavia	1984	France		

Women

1996	United States
2000	Norway

BIATHLON

Men

10 KILOMETERS

1980	Frank Ullrich, E Germany	32:10.69
1984	Eirik Kvalfoss, Norway	30:53.8
1988	Frank-Peter Rötsch, W Germany	25:08.1
1992	Mark Kirchner, Germany	26:02.3
1994	Sergei Tchepikov, Russia	28:07.0
1998	Ole Einar Bjorndalen, Norway	27:16.2
2002	Ole Einar Bjorndalen, Norway	24:51.3

20 KILOMETERS

1960	Klas Lestander, Sweden	1:33:21.6
1964	Vladimir Melyanin, Soviet Union	1:20:26.8
1968	Magnar Solberg, Norway	1:13:45.9
1972	Magnar Solberg, Norway	1:15:55.5
1976	Nikolay Kruglov, Soviet Union	1:14:12.26
1980	Anatoliy Alyabiev, Soviet Union	1:08:16.31
1984	Peter Angerer, W Germany	1:11:52.7
1988	Frank-Peter Rötsch, W Germany	56:33.3

20 KILOMETERS (Cont.)

1992	Evgueni Redkine, Unified Team	57:34.4
1994	Sergei Tarasov, Russia	57:25.3
1998	Halvard Hanevold, Norway	56:16.4
2002	Ole Einar Bjordalen, Norway	51:03.3

4 X 7.5-KILOMETER RELAY

1968	Soviet Union	2:13:02.4
1972	Soviet Union	1:51:44.92
1976	Soviet Union	1:57:55.64
1980	Soviet Union	1:34:03.27
1984	Soviet Union	1:38:51.7
1988	Soviet Union	1:22:30.0
1992	Germany	1:24:43.5
1994	Germany	1:30:22.1
1998	Germany	1:19:43.3
2002	Norway	1:23:42.3

12.5 KILOMETERS PURSUIT

2002	Ole Einar Bjorndalen	1:23:42.3

Women

7.5 KILOMETERS

1992	Antissa Restzova, Unified Team	24:29.2
1994	Myriam Bedard, Canada	26:08.8
1998	Galina Koukleva, Russia	23:08.0
2002	Kati Wilhemn, Germany	20:41.4

10 KILOMETERS PURSUIT

2002	Olga Pyleva, Russia	31:07.7

15 KILOMETERS

1992	Antje Misersky, Germany	51:47.2
1994	Myriam Bedard, Canada	52:06.6
1998	Ekaterina Dofovska, Bulgaria	54:52.0
2002	Andrea Henkel, Germany	47:29.1

3 X 7.5-KILOMETER RELAY

1992	France	1:15:55.6
1994	Russia	1:47:19.5
1998	Germany	1:40:13.6
2002	Germany	1:27:55.0

BOBSLED

4-MAN

1924	Switzerland (Eduard Scherrer)	5:45.54
1928	United States	3:20.50
	(William Fiske) (5-man)	
1932	United States (William Fiske)	7:53.68
1936	Switzerland (Pierre Musy)	5:19.85
1948	United States (Francis Tyler)	5:20.10
1952	Germany (Andreas Ostler)	5:07.84
1956	Switzerland (Franz Kapus)	5:10.44
1960	Not held	
1964	Canada (Victor Emery)	4:14.46
1968	Italy (Eugenio Monti) (2 runs)	2:17.39
1972	Switzerland (Jean Wicki)	4:43.07
1976	E Germany (Meinhard Nehmer)	3:40.43
1980	E Germany (Meinhard Nehmer)	3:59.92
1984	E Germany (Wolfgang Hoppe)	3:20.22
1988	Switzerland (Ekkehard Fasser)	3:47.51
1992	Austria (Ingo Appelt)	3:53.90
1994	Germany (Harold Czudaj)	3:27.78
1998	Germany (Christoph Langen)	2:39.41
2002	Germany (Andre Lange)	3:10.11

Note: Driver in parentheses.

2-MAN

1932	United States (Hubert Stevens)	8:14.74
1936	United States (Ivan Brown)	5:29.29
1948	Switzerland (Felix Endrich)	5:29.20
1952	Germany (Andreas Ostler)	5:24.54
1956	Italy (Lamberto Dalla Costa)	5:30.14
1960	Not held	
1964	Great Britain (Anthony Nash)	4:21.90
1968	Italy (Eugenio Monti)	4:41.54
1972	W Germany	4:57.07
	(Wolfgang Zimmerer)	
1976	E Germany (Meinhard Nehmer)	3:44.42
1980	Switzerland (Erich Schärer)	4:09.36
1984	E Germany (Wolfgang Hoppe)	3:25.56
1988	USSR (Janis Kipours)	3:53.48
1992	Switzerland (Gustav Weder)	4:03.26
1994	Switzerland (Gustav Weder)	3:30.81
1998	Canada (Pierre Lueders)	3:37.24
	Italy (Guenther Huber)	3:37.24
2002	Germany (Martin Langen)	3:10:11

WOMEN

2-PERSON

2002	United States (Jill Bakken)	1:37:76

Note: Driver in parentheses.

CURLING

Men

1998 .....Switzerland, Canada, Norway
2002 .....Norway, Canada, Switzerland
Note: Gold, silver, and bronze medals.

Women

1998 .....Canada, Denmark, Sweden
2002 .....Britain, Switzerland, Canada
Note: Gold, silver, and bronze medals.

ICE HOCKEY

Men

1920* ....Canada, United States, Czechoslovakia
1924 .....Canada, United States, Great Britain
1928 .....Canada, Sweden, Switzerland
1932 .....Canada, United States, Germany
1936 .....Great Britain, Canada, United States
1948 .....Canada, Czechoslovakia, Switzerland
1952 .....Canada, United States, Sweden
1956 .....USSR, United States, Canada
1960 .....United States, Canada, USSR
1964 .....USSR, Sweden, Czechoslovakia
1968 .....USSR, Czechoslovakia, Canada

1972 .....USSR, United States, Czechoslovakia
1976 .....USSR, Czechoslovakia, W Germany
1980 .....United States, USSR, Sweden
1984 .....USSR, Czechoslovakia, Sweden
1988 .....USSR, Finland, Sweden
1992 .....Unified Team, Canada, Czechoslovakia
1994 .....Sweden, Canada, Finland
1998 .....Czech Republic, Russia, Finland
2002 .....Canada, United States, Russia
*Competition held at Summer Games in Antwerp.
Note: Gold, silver, and bronze medals.

1998 .....United States, Canada, Finland
2002 .....Canada, United States, Sweden

Women

Note: Gold, silver, and bronze medals.

LUGE

Men

SINGLES

1964	Thomas Köhler, East Germany	3:26.77
1968	Manfred Schmid, Austria	2:52.48
1972	Wolfgang Scheidel, W Germany	3:27.58
1976	Detlef Guenther, W Germany	3:27.688
1980	Bernhard Glass, W Germany	2:54.796
1984	Paul Hildgartner, Italy	3:04.258
1988	Jens Müller, W Germany	3:05.548
1992	Georg Hackl, Germany	3:02.363
1994	Georg Hackl, Germany	3:21.571
1998	Georg Hackl, Germany	3:18.44
2002	Armin Zoeggeler, Italy	2:57.941

DOUBLES

1964	Austria	1:41.62
1968	E Germany	1:35.85
1972	E Germany	1:28.35
1976	E Germany	1:25.604
1980	E Germany	1:19.331
1984	W Germany	1:23.620
1988	E Germany	1:31.940
1992	Germany	1:32.053
1994	Italy	1:36.720
1998	Germany	1:41.105
2002	Germany	1:26.082

Women

SINGLES

1964	Ortrun Enderlein, Germany	3:24.67
1968	Erica Lechner, Italy	2:28.66
1972	Anna-Maria Müller, E Germany	2:59.18
1976	Margit Schumann, E Germany	2:50.621
1980	Vera Zozulya, USSR	2:36.537

SINGLES (Cont.)

1984	Steffi Martin, E Germany	2:46.570
1988	Steffi Walter (Martin) E Germany	3:03.973
1992	Doris Neuner, Austria	3:06.696
1994	Gerda Weissensteiner, Italy	3:15.517
1998	Silke Kraushaar, Germany	3:23.779
2002	Sylke Otto, Germany	2:52.464

YET ANOTHER SIGN OF THE APOCALYPSE

The USOC threatened to sue Nebraska Wesleyan for using the word Olympics in its annual Rat Olympics, in which trained rats compete in hurdling, long jumping, rope climbing and weightlifting.

FIGURE SKATING

Men

1908* ....Ulrich Salchow, Sweden
1920† ....Gillis Grafström, Sweden
1924 ....Gillis Grafström, Sweden
1928 ....Gillis Grafström, Sweden
1932 ....Karl Schäfer, Austria
1936 ....Karl Schäfer, Austria
1948 ....Dick Button, United States
1952 ....Dick Button, United States
1956 ....Hayes Alan Jenkins, United States
1960 ....David Jenkins, United States
1964 ....Manfred Schnelldorfer, W Germany
1968 ....Wolfgang Schwarz, Austria
1972 ....Ondrej Nepela, Czechoslovakia
1976 ....John Curry, Great Britain
1980 ....Robin Cousins, Great Britain
1984 ....Scott Hamilton, United States
1988 ....Brian Boitano, United States
1992 ....Victor Petrenko, Unified Team
1994 ....Alexei Urmanov, Russia
1998 ....Ilia Kulik, Russia
2002 ....Alexei Yagudin, Russia

*Competition held at Summer Games in London.
†Competition held at Summer Games in Antwerp.

Women

1908* ....Madge Syers, Great Britain
1920† ....Magda Julin, Sweden
1924 ....Herma Szabo-Planck, Austria
1928 ....Sonja Henie, Norway
1932 ....Sonja Henie, Norway
1936 ....Sonja Henie, Norway
1948 ....Barbara Ann Scott, Canada
1952 ....Jeanette Altwegg, Great Britain
1956 ....Tenley Albright, United States
1960 ....Carol Heiss, United States
1964 ....Sjoukje Dijkstra, Netherlands
1968 ....Peggy Fleming, United States
1972 ....Beatrix Schuba, Austria
1976 ....Dorothy Hamill, United States
1980 ....Anett Pötzsch, E Germany
1984 ....Katarina Witt, E Germany
1988 ....Katarina Witt, E Germany
1992 ....Kristi Yamaguchi, United States
1994 ....Oksana Baiul, Ukraine
1998 ....Tara Lipinski, United States
2002 ....Sarah Hughes, United States

Mixed

PAIRS

1908* ..Anna Hübler & Heinrich Burger, Germany
1920† ..Ludovika & Walter Jakobsson, Finland
1924 ....Helene Engelmann & Alfred Berger, Austria
1928 ....Andree Joly & Pierre Brunet, France
1932 ....Andree Brunet (Joly) & Pierre Brunet, France
1936 ....Maxi Herber & Ernst Baier, Germany
1948 ....Micheline Lannoy & Pierre Baugniet, Belgium
1952 ....Ria Falk and Paul Falk, W Germany
1956 ....Elisabeth Schwartz & Kurt Oppelt, Austria
1960 ....Barbara Wagner & Robert Paul, Canada
1964 ....Lyudmila Beloussova & Oleg Protopopov,
           USSR
1968 ....Lyudmila Beloussova & Oleg Protopopov,
           USSR
1972 ....Irina Rodnina & Alexei Ulanov, USSR
1976 ....Irina Rodnina & Aleksandr Zaitzev, USSR
1980 ....Irina Rodnina & Aleksandr Zaitzev, USSR
1984 ....Elena Valova & Oleg Vasiliev, USSR
1988 ....Ekaterina Gordeeva & Sergei Grinkov, USSR
1992 ....Natalia Michkouteniok & Artour Dmitriev,
           Unified Team
1994 ....Ekaterina Gordeeva & Sergei Grinkov,
           Russia
1998 ....Oksana Kazakova & Artur Dmitriev,
           Russia
2002 ....Elena Berezhnaya & Anton Sikharulidze,
           Russia/ Jamie Sale & David Pelletier, Canada

DANCE

1976 ....Lyudmila Pakhomova & Aleksandr Gorshkov,
           USSR
1980 ....Natalia Linichuk & Gennadi Karponosov,
           USSR
1984 ....Jayne Torvill & Christopher Dean, Great Britain
1988 ....Natalia Bestemianova & Andrei Bukin, USSR
1992 ....Marina Klimova & Sergei Ponomarenko,
           Unified Team
1994 ....Oksana Grishuk & Evgeny Platov,
           Russia
1998 ....Pasha Grishuk & Evgeny Platov,
           Russia
2002 ....Marina Anissina & Gwendal Peizeralt, France

*Competition held at Summer Games in London.
†Competition held at Summer Games in Antwerp.

SKELETON

Men

1928 .....Jennison Heaton, United States	3:01.8
1948 .....Nino Bibbia, Italy	5:23.2
2002 .....Jim Shea Jr., United States	1:41.96

Women

2002 .....Tristan Gale, United States	1:45.11

SPEED SKATING

Men

500 METERS

1924	Charles Jewtraw, United States	44.0
1928	Clas Thunberg, Finland	43.4 OR
	Bernt Evensen, Norway	43.4 OR
1932	John Shea, United States	43.4 EOR
1936	Ivar Ballangrud, Norway	43.4 EOR
1948	Finn Helgesen, Norway	43.1 OR
1952	Kenneth Henry, United States	43.2
1956	Yevgeny Grishin, USSR	40.2 EWR
1960	Yevgeny Grishin, USSR	40.2 EWR
1964	Terry McDermott, United States	40.1 OR
1968	Erhard Keller, W Germany	40.3
1972	Erhard Keller, W Germany	39.44 OR
1976	Yevgeny Kulikov, USSR	39.17 OR
1980	Eric Heiden, United States	38.03 OR
1984	Sergei Fokichev, USSR	38.19
1988	Uwe-Jens Mey, E Germany	36.45 WR
1992	Uwe-Jens Mey, E Germany	37.14
1994	Aleksandr Golubev, Russia	36.33
1998	Hiroyasu Shimizu, Japan	35.59 OR
	(second run)	
2002	Casey FitzRandolph, U.S.	1:09.23*

1,000 METERS

1976	Peter Mueller, United States	1:19.32
1980	Eric Heiden, United States	1:15.18 OR
1984	Gaetan Boucher, Canada	1:15.80
1988	Nikolai Gulyaev, USSR	1:13.03 OR
1992	Olaf Zinke, Germany	1:14.85
1994	Dan Jansen, United States	1:12.43 WR
1998	Ids Postma, Netherlands	1:10.64 OR
2002	Gerard van Velde, Netherlands	1:07.18

1,500 METERS

1924	Clas Thunberg, Finland	2:20.8
1928	Clas Thunberg, Finland	2:21.1
1932	John Shea, United States	2:57.5
1936	Charles Mathisen, Norway	2:19.2 OR
1948	Sverre Farstad, Norway	2:17.6 OR
1952	Hjalmar Andersen, Norway	2:20.4
1956	Yevgeny Grishin, USSR	2:08.6 WR
	Yuri Mikhailov, USSR	2:08.6 WR
1960	Roald Aas, Norway	2:10.4
	Yevgeny Grishin, USSR	2:10.4
1964	Ants Anston, USSR	2:10.3
1968	Cornelis Verkerk, Netherlands	2:03.4 OR
1972	Ard Schenk, Netherlands	2:02.96 OR
1976	Jan Egil Storholt, Norway	1:59.38 OR
1980	Eric Heiden, United States	1:55.44 OR

1,500 METERS (Cont.)

1984	Gaetan Boucher, Canada	1:58.36
1988	Andre Hoffmann, E Germany	1:52.06 WR
1992	Johann Olav Koss, Norway	1:54.81
1994	Johann Olav Koss, Norway	1:51.29 WR
1998	Aadne Sondral, Norway	1:47.87 WR
2002	Derek Parra, United States	1:43.95

5,000 METERS

1924	Clas Thunberg, Finland	8:39.0
1928	Ivar Ballangrud, Norway	8:50.5
1932	Irving Jaffee, United States	9:40.8
1936	Ivar Ballangrud, Norway	8:19.6 OR
1948	Reidar Liaklev, Norway	8:29.4
1952	Hjalmar Andersen, Norway	8:10.6 OR
1956	Boris Shilkov, USSR	7:48.7 OR
1960	Viktor Kosichkin, USSR	7:51.3
1964	Knut Johannesen, Norway	7:38.4 OR
1968	Fred Anton Maier, Norway	7:22.4 WR
1972	Ard Schenk, Netherlands	7:23.61
1976	Sten Stensen, Norway	7:24.48
1980	Eric Heiden, United States	7:02.29 OR
1984	Sven Tomas Gustafson, Sweden	7:12.28
1988	Tomas Gustafson, Sweden	6:44.63 WR
1992	Geir Karlstad, Norway	6:59.97
1994	Johann Olav Koss, Norway	6:34.96 WR
1998	Gianni Romme, Netherlands	6:22.20 WR
2002	Jochem Uytdehaage, Net	6:41.66

10,000 METERS

1924	Julius Skutnabb, Finland	18:04.8
1928	Not held, thawing of ice	
1932	Irving Jaffee, United States	19:13.6
1936	Ivar Ballangrud, Norway	17:24.3 OR
1948	Ake Seyffarth, Sweden	17:26.3
1952	Hjalmar Andersen, Norway	16:45.8 OR
1956	Sigvard Ericsson, Sweden	16:35.9 OR
1960	Knut Johannesen, Norway	15:46.6 WR
1964	Jonny Nilsson, Sweden	15:50.1
1968	Johnny Höglin, Sweden	15:23.6 OR
1972	Ard Schenk, Netherlands	15:01.35 OR
1976	Piet Kleine, Netherlands	14:50.59 OR
1980	Eric Heiden, United States	14:28.13 WR
1984	Igor Malkov, USSR	14:39.90
1988	Tomas Gustafson, Sweden	13:48.20 WR
1992	Bart Veldkamp, Netherlands	14:12.12
1994	Johann Olav Koss, Norway	13:30.55 WR
1998	Gianni Romme, Netherlands	13:15.33 WR
2002	Jochem Uytdehaage, Neth	12:58.92 WR

Women

500 METERS

1960	Helga Haase, E Germany	45.9
1964	Lydia Skoblikova, USSR	45.0 OR
1968	Lyudmila Titova, USSR	46.1
1972	Anne Henning, United States	43.33 OR
1976	Sheila Young, United States	42.76 OR
1980	Karin Enke, E Germany	41.78 OR
1984	Christa Rothenburger,	41.02 OR
	E Germany	

500 METERS (Cont.)

1988	Bonnie Blair, United States	39.10 WR
1992	Bonnie Blair, United States	40.33
1994	Bonnie Blair, United States	39.25
1998	Catriona LeMay Doan, Canada	38.21 OR
	(second run)	
2002	Catriona LeMay, Canada	1:14.75*

Note: OR=Olympic Record; WR=World Record; EOR=Equals Olympic Record; EWR=Equals World Record; WB=World Best.

*Combined time.

SPEED SKATING *(Cont.)*

Women *(Cont.)*

1,000 METERS

1960	Klara Guseva, USSR	1:34.1
1964	Lydia Skoblikova, USSR	1:33.2 OR
1968	Carolina Geijssen, Netherlands	1:32.6 OR
1972	Monika Pflug, W Germany	1:31.40 OR
1976	Tatiana Averina, USSR	1:28.43 OR
1980	Natalya Petruseva, USSR	1:24.10 OR
1984	Karin Enke, E Germany	1:21.61 OR
1988	Christa Rothenburger, E Germany	1:17.65 WR
1992	Bonnie Blair, United States	1:21.90
1994	Bonnie Blair, United States	1:18.74
1998	Marianne Timmer, Netherlands	1:16.51 OR
2002	Chris Witty, United States	1:13.83

1,500 METERS

1960	Lydia Skoblikova, USSR	2:25.2 WR
1964	Lydia Skoblikova, USSR	2:22.6 OR
1968	Kaija Mustonen, Finland	2:22.4 OR
1972	Dianne Holum, United States	2:20.85 OR
1976	Galina Stepanskaya, USSR	2:16.58 OR
1980	Anne Borckink, Netherlands	2:10.95 OR
1984	Karin Enke, E Germany	2:03.42 WR
1988	Yvonne van Gennip, Netherlands	2:00.68 OR
1992	Jacqueline Boerner, Germany	2:05.87
1994	Emese Hunyady, Austria	2:02.19
1998	Marianne Timmer, Netherlands	1:57.58 WR

1,500 METERS *(Cont.)*

2002	Anni Friesinger, Germany	1:54.02

3,000 METERS

1960	Lydia Skoblikova, USSR	5:14.3
1964	Lydia Skoblikova, USSR	5:14.9
1968	Johanna Schut, Netherlands	4:56.2 OR
1972	Christina Baas-Kaiser, Netherlands	4:52.14 OR
1976	Tatiana Averina, USSR	4:45.19 OR
1980	Bjorg Eva Jensen, Norway	4:32.13 OR
1984	Andrea Schöne, E Germany	4:24.79 OR
1988	Yvonne van Gennip, Netherlands	4:11.94 WR
1992	Gunda Niemann, Germany	4:19.90
1994	Svetlana Bazhanova, Russia	4:17.43
1998	Gunda Niemann-Stirnemann, Germany	4:07.29 OR
2002	Claudia Pechstein, Germany	3:57.70

5,000 METERS

1988	Yvonne van Gennip, Netherlands	7:14.13 WR
1992	Gunda Niemann, Germany	7:31.57
1994	Claudia Pechstein, Germany	7:14.37
1998	Claudia Pechstein, Germany	6:59.61 WR
2002	Claudia Pechstein, Germany	6:46.91 WR

SHORT TRACK SPEED SKATING

Men

500 METERS

1994	Chae Ji-Hoon, S Korea	43.54
1998	Takafumi Nishitani, Japan	42.862
2002	Marc Gagnon, Canada	41.802 OR

1,000 METERS

1992	Kim Ki-Hoon, S Korea	1:30.76
1994	Kim Ki-Hoon, S Korea	1:34.57
1998	Kim Dong Sung, S Korea	1:32.375
2002	Steve Bradbury, Australia	1:29.109

1,500 METERS

2002	Apolo Anton Ohno, United States	2:18.541

5,000-METER RELAY

1992	Korea	7:14.02
1994	Italy	7:11.74
1998	Canada	7:06.075
2002	Canada	6:51.579

Women

500 METERS

1992	Cathy Turner, United States	47.04
1994	Cathy Turner, United States	45.98
1998	Annie Perreault, Canada	46.568
2002	Yang Yang, China	44.187

1,000 METERS

1994	Chun Lee Kyung, S Korea	1:36.87
1998	Chun Lee Kyung, S Korea	1:42.776
2002	Yang A. Yang, China	1:36.391

1,500 METERS

2002	Ko Gi-Hyun, Korea	2:31.581

3,000-METER RELAY

1992	Canada	4:36.62
1994	S Korea	4:26.64
1998	S Korea	4:16.260
2002	S Korea	4:12.793

ALPINE SKIING

Men

DOWNHILL

1948	Henri Oreiller, France	2:55.0
1952	Zeno Colo, Italy	2:30.8
1956	Anton Sailer, Austria	2:52.2
1960	Jean Vuarnet, France	2:06.0
1964	Egon Zimmermann, Austria	2:18.16
1968	Jean-Claude Killy, France	1:59.85
1972	Bernhard Russi, Switzerland	1:51.43
1976	Franz Klammer, Austria	1:45.73
1980	Leonhard Stock, Austria	1:45.50
1984	Bill Johnson, United States	1:45.59
1988	Pirmin Zurbriggen, Switzerland	1:59.63
1992	Patrick Ortlieb, Austria	1:50.37
1994	Tommy Moe, United States	1:45.75
1998	Jean-Luc Crétier, France	1:50.11
2002	Fritz Strobl, Austria	1:39.13

SLALOM

1948	Edi Reinalter, Switzerland	2:10.3
1952	Othmar Schneider, Austria	2:00.0
1956	Anton Sailer, Austria	3:14.7
1960	Ernst Hinterseer, Austria	2:08.9
1964	Josef Stiegler, Austria	2:11.13
1968	Jean-Claude Killy, France	1:39.73
1972	F. Fernandez Ochoa, Spain	1:49.27
1976	Piero Gros, Italy	2:03.29
1980	Ingemar Stenmark, Sweden	1:44.26
1984	Phil Mahre, United States	1:39.41
1988	Alberto Tomba, Italy	1:39.47
1992	Finn Christian Jagge, Norway	1:44.39
1994	Thomas Stangassinger, Austria	2:02.02
1998	Hans-Petter Buraas, Norway	1:49.31
2002	Jean-Pierre Vidal, France	1:41.06

ALPINE SKIING
Men (Cont.)

GIANT SLALOM

1952	Stein Eriksen, Norway	2:25.0
1956	Anton Sailer, Austria	3:00.1
1960	Roger Staub, Switzerland	1:48.3
1964	Francois Bonlieu, France	1:46.71
1968	Jean-Claude Killy, France	3:29.28
1972	Gustav Thöni, Italy	3:09.62
1976	Heini Hemmi, Switzerland	3:26.97
1980	Ingemar Stenmark, Sweden	2:40.74
1984	Max Julen, Switzerland	2:41.18
1988	Alberto Tomba, Italy	2:06.37
1992	Alberto Tomba, Italy	2:06.98
1994	Markus Wasmeier, Germany	2:52.46
1998	Hermann Maier, Austria	2:38.51
2002	Stephan Eberharter, Austria	2:23.28

SUPER GIANT SLALOM

1988	Franck Piccard, France	1:39.66
1992	Kjetil André Aamodt, Norway	1:13.04
1994	Markus Wasmeier, Germany	1:32.53
1998	Hermann Maier, Austria	1:34.82
2002	Kjetil André Aamodt, Norway	1:21.58

COMBINED*

1936	Franz Pfnür, Germany	99.25
1948	Henri Oreiller, France	3.27
1988	Hubert Strolz, Austria	36.55
1992	Josef Polig, Italy	14.58
1994	Lasse Kjus, Norway	3:17.53
1998	Mario Reiter, Austria	3:08.06
2002	Kjetil André Aamodt, Norway	3:17.56

Women

DOWNHILL

1948	Hedy Schlunegger, Switzerland	2:28.3
1952	Trude Jochum-Beiser, Austria	1:47.1
1956	Madeleine Berthod, Switzerland	1:40.7
1960	Heidi Biebl, W Germany	1:37.6
1964	Christl Haas, Austria	1:55.39
1968	Olga Pall, Austria	1:40.87
1972	Marie-Theres Nadig, Switzerland	1:36.68
1976	Rosi Mittermaier, W Germany	1:46.16
1980	Annemarie Moser-Pröll, Austria	1:37.52
1984	Michela Figini, Switzerland	1:13.36
1988	Marina Kiehl, W Germany	1:25.86
1992	Kerrin Lee-Gartner, Canada	1:52.55
1994	Katja Seizinger, Germany	1:35.93
1998	Katja Seizinger, Germany	1:28.89
2002	Carole Montillet, France	1:39.56

SLALOM

1948	Gretchen Fraser, United States	1:57.2
1952	Andrea Mead Lawrence, United States	2:10.6
1956	Renee Colliard, Switzerland	1:52.3
1960	Anne Heggtveigt, Canada	1:49.6
1964	Christine Goitschel, France	1:29.86
1968	Marielle Goitschel, France	1:25.86
1972	Barbara Cochran, United States	1:31.24
1976	Rosi Mittermaier, W Germany	1:30.54
1980	Hanni Wenzel, Liechtenstein	1:25.09
1984	Paoletta Magoni, Italy	1:36.47
1988	Vreni Schneider, Switzerland	1:36.69
1992	Petra Kronberger, Austria	1:32.68
1994	Vreni Schneider, Switzerland	1:56.01
1998	Hilde Gerg, Germany	1:32.40
2002	Janica Kostelic, Croatia	1:46.10

GIANT SLALOM

1952	Andrea Mead Lawrence, U.S.	2:06.8
1956	Ossi Reichert, W Germany	1:56.5
1960	Yvonne Rüegg, Switzerland	1:39.9
1964	Marielle Goitschel, France	1:52.24
1968	Nancy Greene, Canada	1:51.97
1972	Marie-Theres Nadig, Switzerland	1:29.90
1976	Kathy Kreiner, Canada	1:29.13
1980	Hanni Wenzel, Liechtenstein (2 runs)	2:41.66
1984	Debbie Armstrong, United States	2:20.98
1988	Vreni Schneider, Switzerland	2:06.49
1992	Pernilla Wiberg, Sweden	2:12.74
1994	Deborah Compagnoni, Italy	2:30.97
1998	Deborah Compagnoni, Italy	2:50.59
2002	Janica Kostelic, Croatia	2:30.01

SUPER GIANT SLALOM

1988	Sigrid Wolf, Austria	1:19.03
1992	Deborah Compagnoni, Italy	1:21.22
1994	Diann Roffe-Steinrotter, U.S.	1:22.15
1998	Picabo Street, United States	1:18.02
2002	Daniela Ceccarelli, Italy	1:13.59

COMBINED*

1988	Anita Wachter, Austria	29.25
1992	Petra Kronberger, Austria	2.55
1994	Pernilla Wiberg, Sweden	3:05.16
1998	Katja Seizinger, Germany	2:40.74
2002	Janica Kostelic, Croatia	2:43.28

*Beginning in 1994, scoring was based on time.

FREESTYLE SKIING

Men

MOGULS

		Pts
1992	Edgar Grospiron, France	25.81
1994	Jean-Luc Brassard, Canada	27.24
1998	Jonny Moseley, United States	26.93
2002	Janne Lahtela, Finland	27.97

AERIALS

		Pts
1994	Andreas Schoenbaechler, Switz	234.67
1998	Eric Bergoust, United States	255.64
2002	Ales Valenta, Czech Republic	257.02

Women

MOGULS

		Pts
1992	Donna Weinbrecht, United States	23.69
1994	Stine Lise Hattestad, Norway	25.97
1998	Tae Satoya, Japan	25.06
2002	Kari Traa, Norway	25.94

AERIALS

		Pts
1994	Lina Cherjazova, Uzbekistan	166.84
1998	Nikki Stone, United States	193.00
2002	Alisa Camplin, Australia	193.47

Winter Games Champions (Cont.)

NORDIC SKIING
Men

10 KILOMETERS CLASSICAL STYLE

1992	Vegard Ulvang, Norway	27:36.0
1994	Bjørn Dæhlie, Norway	24:20.1
1998	Bjørn Dæhlie, Norway	27:24.5

15 KILOMETERS CLASSICAL STYLE

1924	Thorlief Haug, Norway	1:14:31.0*
1928	Johan Gröttumsbraaten, Norway	1:37:01.0†
1932	Sven Utterström, Sweden	1:23:07.0‡
1936	Erik-August Larsson, Sweden	1:14:38.0*
1948	Martin Lundström, Sweden	1:13:50.0*
1952	Hallgeir Brenden, Norway	1:01:34.0*
1956	Hallgeir Brenden, Norway	49:39.0
1960	Haakon Brusveen, Norway	51:55.5
1964	Eero Mantyränta, Finland	50:54.1
1968	Harald Grönningen, Norway	47:54.2
1972	Sven-Ake Lundback, Sweden	45:28.24
1976	Nikolay Bajukov, Unified Team	43:58.47
1980	Thomas Wassberg, Sweden	41:57.63
1984	Gunde Swan, Sweden	41:25.6
1988	Michael Deviatyarov, USSR	41:18.9
2002	Andrus Veerpalu, Estonia	37:07.4

*Distance was 18 km. †Distance was 19.7 km.

‡Distance was 18.2 km.

15 KILOMETERS PURSUIT FREESTYLE

1992	Bjørn Dæhlie, Norway	1:05:37.9
1994	Bjørn Dæhlie, Norway	1:00:08.8
1998	Thomas Alsgaard, Norway	1:07:01.7

30 KILOMETERS CLASSICAL STYLE

1956	Veikko Hakulinen, Finland	1:44:06.0
1960	Sixten Jernberg, Sweden	1:51:03.9
1964	Eero Mantyränta, Finland	1:30:50.7
1968	Franco Nones, Italy	1:35:39.2
1972	Viaceslav Vedenine, USSR	1:36:31.2
1976	Sergei Savelyev, USSR	1:30:29.38
1980	Nikolai Simyatov, USSR	1:27:02.80
1984	Nikolai Simyatov, USSR	1:28:56.3
1988	Alexey Prokororov, USSR	1:24:26.3
1992	Vegard Ulvang, Norway	1:22:27.8
1994	Thomas Alsgaard, Norway	1:12:26.4
1998	Mika Myllylae, Finland	1:33:55.8

50 KILOMETERS FREESTYLE

1924	Thorleif Haug, Norway	3:44:32.0
1928	Per Erik Hedlund, Sweden	4:52:03.0
1932	Veli Saarinen, Finland	4:28:00.0
1936	Elis Wiklund, Sweden	3:30:11.0
1948	Nils Karlsson, Sweden	3:47:48.0
1952	Veikko Hakulinen, Finland	3:33:33.0
1956	Sixten Jernberg, Sweden	2:50:27.0
1960	Kalevi Hämäläinen, Finland	2:59:06.3
1964	Sixten Jernberg, Sweden	2:43:52.6
1968	Olle Ellefsaeter, Norway	2:28:45.8
1972	Paal Tyldrum, Norway	2:43:14.75
1976	Ivar Formo, Norway	2:37:30.50
1980	Nikolai Simyatov, USSR	2:27:24.60
1984	Thomas Wassberg, Sweden	2:15:55.8
1988	Gunde Svan, Sweden	2:04:30.9
1992	Bjørn Dæhlie, Norway	2:03:41.5
1994	Vladimir Smirnov, Kazakhstan	2:07:20.3
1998	Bjørn Dæhlie, Norway	2:05:08.2

4 X 10-KILOMETER RELAY MIXED STYLE

1936	Finland	2:41:33.0
1948	Sweden	2:32:80.0
1952	Finland	2:20:16.0

4 X 10-KILOMETER RELAY MIXED STYLE (Cont.)

1956	USSR	2:15:30.0
1960	Finland	2:18:45.6
1964	Sweden	2:18:34.6
1968	Norway	2:08:33.5
1972	USSR	2:04:47.94
1976	Finland	2:07:59.72
1980	USSR	1:57:03.46
1984	Sweden	1:55:06.3
1988	Sweden	1:43:58.6
1992	Norway	1:39:26.0
1994	Italy	1:41:15.0
1998	Norway	1:40:55.7
2002	Norway	1:32:45.5

SKI JUMPING (NORMAL HILL)

		Pts
1964	Veikko Kankkonen, Finland	229.90
1968	Jiri Raska, Czechoslovakia	216.5
1972	Yukio Kasaya, Japan	244.2
1976	Hans-Georg Aschenbach, E Germany	252.0
1980	Toni Innauer, Austria	266.3
1984	Jens Weissflog, E Germany	215.2
1988	Matti Nykänen, Finland	229.1
1992	Ernst Vettori, Austria	222.8
1994	Espen Bredesen, Norway	282.0
1998	Jani Soininen, Finland	234.5
2002	Simon Ammann, Switzerland	269.0

SKI JUMPING (LARGE HILL)

		Pts
1924	Jacob Tullin Thams, Norway	18.960
1928	Alf Andersen, Norway	19.208
1932	Birger Ruud, Norway	228.1
1936	Birger Ruud, Norway	232.0
1948	Petter Hugsted, Norway	228.1
1952	Arnfinn Bergmann, Norway	226.0
1956	Antti Hyvärinen, Finland	227.0
1960	Helmut Recknagel, E Germany	227.2
1964	Toralf Engan, Norway	230.70
1968	Vladimir Beloussov, USSR	231.3
1972	Wojciech Fortuna, Poland	219.9
1976	Karl Schnabl, Austria	234.8
1980	Jouko Tormanen, Finland	271.0
1984	Matti Nykänen, Finland	231.2
1988	Matti Nykänen, Finland	224.0
1992	Toni Nieminen, Finland	239.5
1994	Jens Weissflog, Germany	274.5
1998	Kazuyoshi Funaki, Japan	272.3
2002	Simon Amman, Switzerland	281.4

TEAM SKI JUMPING

		Pts
1988	Finland	634.4
1992	Finland	644.4
1994	Germany	970.1
1998	Japan	933.0
2002	Germany	974.1

NORDIC SKIING (Cont.)
Men (Cont.)

NORDIC COMBINED	Pts
1924....Thorleif Haug, Norway	18.906*
1928....Johan Gröttumsbraaten, Norway	17.833*
1932....Johan Gröttumsbraaten, Norway	446.0
1936....Oddbjörn Hagen, Norway	430.30
1948....Heikki Hasu, Finland	448.80
1952....Simon Slattvik, Norway	451.621
1956....Sverre Stenersen, Norway	455.0
1960....Georg Thoma, W Germany	457.952
1964....Tormod Knutsen, Norway	469.28
1968....Frantz Keller, W Germany	449.04
1972....Ulrich Wehling, E Germany	413.34
1976....Ulrich Wehling, E Germany	423.39
1980....Ulrich Wehling, E Germany	432.20
1984....Tom Sandberg, Norway	422.595

NORDIC COMBINED (Cont.)	Pts
1988....Hippolyt Kempf, Switzerland	432.230
1992....Fabrice Guy, France	426.47
1994....Fred B. Lundberg, Norway	457.970†
1998....Bjarte Engen Vik, Norway	41:21.1†
2002....Samppa Lajunen, Finland	38:18.7

TEAM NORDIC COMBINED
1988....W Germany
1992....Japan
1994....Japan
1998....Norway
2002....Finland

SPRINT NORDIC COMBINED	
2002....Samppa Lajunen, Finland	123.8

* Different scoring system; 1924–1952 distance was 18 km; 1952–present, 15 km.

† Times in the cross-country race were not converted into points. According to the Gundersen Method, used since 1988, starting times in the race are staggered in proportion to points earned in the ski jumping segment of the event.

Women

1.5 KILOMETERS SPRINT	
2002....Julija Tchepalova, Russia	3:10.6

5 KILOMETERS PURSUIT	
2002....Olga Danilova, Russia	24:52.1

5 KILOMETERS CLASSICAL STYLE	
1964....Klaudia Boyarskikh, USSR	17:50.5
1968....Toini Gustafsson, Sweden	16:45.2
1972....Galina Kulakova, USSR	17:00.50
1976....Helena Takalo, Finland	15:48.69
1980....Raisa Smetanina, USSR	15:06.92
1984....Marja-Liisa Hamalainen, Finland	17:04.0
1988....Marjo Matikainen, Finland	15:04.0
1992....Marjut Lukkarinen, Finland	14:13.8
1994....Lyubova Egorova, Russia	14:08.8
1998....Larissa Lazhutina, Russia	17:37.9

10 KILOMETERS CLASSICAL STYLE	
1952....Lydia Widemen, Finland	41:40.0
1956....Lyubov Kosyryeva, USSR	38:11.0
1960....Maria Gusakova, USSR	39:46.6
1964....Klaudia Boyarskikh, USSR	40:24.3
1968....Toini Gustafsson, Sweden	36:46.5
1972....Galina Kulakova, USSR	34:17.8
1976....Raisa Smetanina, USSR	30:13.41
1980....Barbara Petzold, E Germany	30:31.54
1984....Marja-Lissa Hamalainen, Finland	31:44.2
1988....Vida Ventsene, USSR	30:08.3
2002....Bante Skari, Norway	28:05.6

30 KILOMETERS CLASSICAL TYLE	
2002....Gabriela Paruzzi, Italy	1:30:57.1

10 KILOMETERS PURSUIT FREESTYLE	
1992....Lyubov Egorova, Unified Team	40:07.7
1994....Lyubov Egorova, Russia	41:38.1
1998....Larissa Lazhutina, Russia	46:06.9

15 KILOMETERS FREESTYLE	
2002....Stefania Belmondo, Italy	39:54.4

15 KILOMETERS CLASSICAL STYLE	
1992....Lyubov Egorova, Unified Team	42:20.8
1994....Manuela Di Centa, Italy	39:44.5
1998....Olga Danilova, Russia	46:55.04

20 KILOMETERS FREESTYLE	
1984....Marja-Liisa Hamalainen, Finland	1:01:45.0
1988....Tamara Tikhonova, USSR	55:53.6

30 KILOMETERS FREESTYLE	
1992....Stefania Belmondo, Italy	1:22:30.1
1994....Manuela Di Centa, Italy	1:25:41.6
1998....Julija Tchepalova, Russia	1:22:01.5

4 X 5-KILOMETER RELAY MIXED STYLE	
1956....Finland	1:9:01.0
1960....Sweden	1:4:21.4
1964....USSR	59:20.0
1968....Norway	57:30.0
1972....USSR	48:46.15
1976....USSR	1:07:49.75
1980....E Germany	1:02:11.10
1984....Norway	1:06:49.7
1988....USSR	59:51.1
1992....Unified Team	59:34.8
1994....Russia	57:12.5
1998....Russia	55:13.5
2002....Germany	49:30.6

SNOWBOARDING

Men

GIANT SLALOM	
1998....Ross Rebagliati, Canada	2:03.96

PARALLEL GIANT SLALOM
2002....Philipp Schoch, Switzerland

HALF-PIPE	Pts
1998....Gian Simmen, Switzerland	85.2
2002....Ross Powers, United States	46.1

Women

GIANT SLALOM	
1998....Karine Ruby, France	2:17.34

PARALLEL GIANT SLALOM
2002....Isabella Blanc, France

HALF-PIPE	Pts
1998....Nicola Thost, Germany	74.6
2002....Kelly Clark, United States	47.9

Track & Field

TOYOTA
1174
PARIS 2003 ST-DENIS

Kelli White of the
United States

ANDY LYONS/GETTY IMAGES

Hit and Miss

There were track and field triumphs in 2003, but you had to dig through disappointment to find them

BY MERRELL NODEN

N O ONE COULD consider 2003 a good year for U.S. track and field, not unless they counted the many foreign athletes who flourished after attending American colleges. In late August, at the world championships in Paris, the U.S. won 20 medals, half of them gold, to lead all countries in both categories. That sounds impressive, but for every medal won, there seemed to be a veteran star who crashed and burned, flaming out in boorish behavior, drug accusations or just plain lousy performances.

"It's a Dickensian experience: best of times, worst of times," said a glum Craig Masback, the CEO of USA Track & Field, who surely was being optimistic in finding much of the former.

The year began with the sport's biggest star, Marion Jones, announcing that she was going to have a baby—a son as it turned out, born on June 28 and named for his world record–holding dad, Tim Montgomery. Jones missed the entire season, but is expected to return in 2004 for the Olympics.

Not expected was the post-partum lethargy that seemed to afflict proud papa. Montgomery, who set the 100-meter world record of 9.78 in his last meet of 2002, never broke 10 seconds all season and finished fifth at the world championships, behind, among others, surprise winner Kim Collins, a Texas Christian grad from St. Kitts and Nevis. Maurice Greene, the defending Olympic champion, fought injuries all year and ran grimacing in Paris, where he didn't make the final. What to expect from the pair—not to mention Jon Drummond, whose antics after being called for a false start held up the meet for more than 20 minutes—at the Athens Games is anybody's guess.

The U.S. men gained some measure of redemption in events where they are traditionally very strong, going 1–2 in the 200 (won by John Capel), the 400 (Jerome Young) and the 110 hurdles (Allen Johnson, claiming his fourth straight title). But the celebration soured when the *Los Angeles Times* revealed that Young was the athlete known to have tested positive in 1999 and then been allowed to run on the gold medal–winning U.S. 4 x 400 team in Sydney. The U.S. won the 4 x 400 in Paris too, with Young anchoring, but that wasn't the end of things. Accusations flew, and the IOC urged a reopening of the case.

Hard on the heels of that bad news came more: Kelli White, who stamped herself as the most exciting new face in U.S. track when she won the 100 and 200 at nationals and then easily won the same double in Paris, tested positive for modafinil, a drug used to treat narcolepsy. White voluntarily

PHIL COLE/GETTY IMAGES

El Guerrouj took the 1,500 for the fourth straight time at the worlds.

Edwards hurt his ankle before the worlds, finished last in Paris and announced his retirement.

But track always has young stars waiting to be rushed in to the vacuum. There was heptathlon champion Carolina Klüft of Sweden, looking, at 20, like the person who may break Jackie Joyner-Kersee's 15-year-old world record; there were the 18-year-old 5,000 champions, Tirunesh Dibaba of Ethiopia for the women and Kenya's Eliud Kipchoge for the men. The U.S. had its own precocious star, 17-year-old Allyson Felix, who ran 22.11 for 200 in May, a time which was the world's fastest until White beat it in Paris.

Four athletes were expected to dominate and did. Maria Mutola of Mozambique won her third world title at 800. Ana Guevara became the first Mexican woman to win a major track title and the first woman to break 49 seconds for the 400 since 1996, while American-born Felix Sanchez, who competes for the Dominican Republic, ran 47.25 to devastate the field in the 400 hurdles.

Above the swirl of rumor and churlish behavior one athlete stood out, as he has for nearly a decade. That is Hicham El Guerrouj of Morocco, who, like Gebrselassie and Mutola, continues to be not only one of the sport's best athletes but one of its cherished class acts. After winning his fourth straight 1500 title, in 3:31.77, El Guerrouj came back to run the 5,000 against, among others, Bekele. He did not win, lunging just inches short of Kipchoge at the tape. Tripped up in Atlanta and paralyzed by his own nerves in Sydney, he will go to Athens next year as not only a favorite to win, but also a favorite pure and simple, the sort of noble competitor Baron de Coubertin had in mind when he resurrected the Games 108 years ago.

removed herself from the U.S. 4 x 100 relay team—which lost to the French, making it the only one of the four U.S. relay teams not to win gold—and waited for the IAAF to decide what it would do with the two gold medals she'd won so convincingly.

And so it went. Regina Jacobs, Gail Devers and David Krummenacker, medal hopefuls all, failed to reach the finals of the 1500, 100 hurdles and 800, respectively. Stacy Dragila, who won the first two women's pole vault titles at the worlds, struggled all year and finished fourth in Paris.

And it wasn't only U.S. athletes who experienced a major turning of the tide: In the 10,000, Haile Gebrselassie, arguably the greatest distance runner in history, was outkicked in Paris by his young countryman, Kenenisa Bekele, in an astonishing 26:49.57. But at least the great Geb finished in the medals. Other world record holders weren't so lucky. Wilson Kipketer finished fourth in the 800. Triple jumper Jonathan

2003 IAAF World Championships

Paris, Aug 23-31

Men

100 METERS

1. Kim Collins, St. Kitts & Nevis — 10.07
2. Darrel Brown, Trinidad — 10.08
3. Darren Campbell, Great Britain — 10.08

200 METERS

1. John Capel, United States — 20.30
2. Darvis Patton, United States — 20.31
3. Shingo Suetsugu, Japan — 20.38

400 METERS

1. Jerome Young, United States — 44.50
2. Tyree Washington, United States — 44.77
3. Marc Raquil, France — 44.79

800 METERS

1. Djabir Saïd-Guerni, Algeria — 1:44.81
2. Yuriy Borzakovskiy, Russia — 1:44.84
3. Mbulaeni Mulaudzi, S Africa — 1:44.90

1,500 METERS

1. Hicham El Guerrouj, Morocco — 3:31.77
2. Mehdi Baala, France — 3:32.31
3. Ivan Heshko, Ukraine — 3:33.17

5,000 METERS

1. Eliud Kipchoge, Kenya — 12:52.79
2. Hicham El Guerrouj, Morocco — 12:52.83
3. Kenenisa Bekele, Ethiopia — 12:53.12

10,000 METERS

1. Kenenisa Bekele, Ethiopia — 26:49.57
2. Haile Gebrselassie, Ethiopia — 26:50.77
3. Sileshi Sihine, Ethiopia — 27:01.44

MARATHON

1. Jaouad Gharib, Morocco — 2:08:31
2. Julio Rey, Spain — 2:08:38
3. Stefano Baldini, Italy — 2:09:14

110-METER HURDLES

1. Allen Johnson, United States — 13.12
2. Terrence Trammell, United States — 13.20
3. Xiang Liu, China — 13.23

400-METER HURDLES

1. Felix Sánchez, Dominican Republic — 47.25
2. Joey Woody, United States — 48.18
3. Periklis Iakovákis, Greece — 48.24

3,000-METER STEEPLECHASE

1. Saif Saaeed Shaheen, Qatar — 8:04.39
2. Ezekiel Kemboi, Kenya — 8:05.11
3. Eliseo Martín, Spain — 8:09.09

HIGH JUMP

1. Jacques Freitag, S Africa — 7 ft 8½ in
2. Stefan Holm, Sweden — 7 ft 7¼ in
3. Mark Boswell, Canada — 7 ft 7¼ in

POLE VAULT

1. Giuseppe Gibilisco, Italy — 19 ft 4¼ in
2. Okkert Brits, S Africa — 19 ft 2¼ in
3. Patrik Kristiansson, Sweden — 19 ft 2¼ in

LONG JUMP

1. Dwight Phillips, United States — 27 ft 3½ in
2. James Beckford, Jamaica — 27 ft 2 in
3. Yago Lamela, Spain — 26 ft 11¾ in

TRIPLE JUMP

1. Christian Olsson, Sweden — 58 ft 1¾ in
2. Yoandri Betanzos, Cuba — 56 ft 8¼ in
3. Leevan Sands, Bahamas — 56 ft 7½ in

SHOT PUT

1. Andrei Mikahnevic, Bulgaria — 71 ft 2 in
2. Adam Nelson, United States — 69 ft 9 in
3. Yuriy Bilonog, Ukraine — 69 ft 2¾ in

DISCUS

1. Virgilijus Alekna, Lithuania — 228 ft 7¾ in
2. Róbert Fazekas, Hungary — 226 ft 5 in
3. Vasiliy Kaptyukh, Bulgaria — 218 ft 2½ in

HAMMER THROW

1. Ivan Tikhon, Bulgaria — 272 ft 5¾ in
2. Adrián Annus, Hungary — 263 ft 7¾ in
3. Koji Murofushi, Japan — 262 ft 10¼ in

JAVELIN

1. Sergey Makarov, Russia — 280 ft 3¾ in
2. Andrus Värnik, Estonia — 279 ft 5¼ in
3. Boris Henry, Germany — 278 ft ¼ in

20-KILOMETER WALK

1. Jefferson Pérez, Ecuador — 1:17:21
2. J.F. Fernandez, Spain — 1:18:00
3. Roman Rasskazov, Russia — 1:18:07

50-KILOMETER WALK

1. Robert Korzeniowski, Poland — 3:36:03
2. German Skurygin, Russia — 3:36:42
3. Andreas Erm, Germany — 3:37:46

4 x 100 RELAY

1. United States — 38.06
2. Great Britain — 38.08
3. Brazil — 38.26

4 x 400 RELAY

1. United States — 2:58.88
2. France — 2:58.96
3. Jamaica — 2:59.60

DECATHLON

1. Tom Pappas, United States — 8750 pts
2. Roman Sebrle, Czech Rep — 8634
3. Dmitry Karpov, Kazakhstan — 8374

Women

100 METERS

1. ....Kelli White, United States — 10.85
2. ....Torri Edwards, United States — 10.93
3. ....Zhanna Block, Ukraine — 10.99

200 METERS

1. ....Kelli White, United States — 22.05
2. ....Anastasiya Kapachinskaya, Russia — 22.38
3. ....Torri Edwards, United States — 22.47

400 METERS

1. ....Ana Guevara, Mexico — 48.89
2. ....Lorraine Fenton, Jamaica — 49.43
3. ....Mbacke Amy Thiam, Senegal — 49.95

800 METERS

1. ....Maria Mutola, Mozambique — 1:59.89
2. ....Kelly Holmes, Great Britain — 2:00.18
3. ....Natalya Khrushchelyov, Russia — 2:00.29

1,500 METERS

1. ....Tatyana Tomashova, Russia — 3:58.52
2. ....Süreyya Ayhan, Turkey — 3:59.04
3. ....Hayley Tullett, Great Britain — 3:59.95

5,000 METERS

1. ....Tirunesh Dibaba, Ethiopia — 14:51.72
2. ....Marta Domínguez, Spain — 14:52.26
3. ....Edith Masai, Kenya — 14:52.30

10,000 METERS

1. ....Berhane Adere, Ethiopia — 30:04.18
2. ....Werknesh Kidane, Ethiopia — 30:07.15
3. ....Yingjie Sun, China — 30:07.20

MARATHON

1. ....Catherine Ndereba, Kenya — 2:23:55
2. ....Mizuki Noguchi, Japan — 2:24:14
3. ....Masako Chiba, Japan — 2:25:09

100-METER HURDLES

1. ....Perdita Felicien, Canada — 12.53
2. ....Brigitte Foster, Jamaica — 12.57
3. ....Miesha McKelvy, United States — 12.67

400-METER HURDLES

1. ....Jana Pittman, Australia — 53.22
2. ....Sandra Glover, United States — 53.65
3. ....Yuliya Pechonkina, Russia — 53.71

HIGH JUMP

1. ....Hestrie Cloete, S Africa — 6 ft 9 in
2. ....Marina Kuptsova, Russia — 6 ft 6¾ in
3. ....Kajsa Bergqvist, Sweden — 6 ft 6¾ in

POLE VAULT

1. ....Svetlana Feofanova, Russia — 15 ft 7 in
2. ....Annika Becker, Germany — 15 ft 5 in
3. ....Yelena Isinbayeva, Russia — 15 ft 3 in

LONG JUMP

1. ....Eunice Barber, France — 22 ft 11 in
2. ....Tatyana Kotova, Russia — 22 ft 1¼ in
3. ....Bobby Anju George, India — 21 ft 11¾ in

TRIPLE JUMP

1. ....Tatyana Lebedeva, Russia — 49 ft 9½ in
2. ....Françoise E. Mbango, Cameroon — 49 ft 4½ in
3. ....Magdelín Martínez, Italy — 48 ft 10½ in

SHOT PUT

1. ....Svetlana Krivelyova, Russia — 67 ft 8 in
2. ....Nadezhda Ostapchuk, Bulgaria — 66 ft
3. ....Vita Pavlysh, Ukraine — 65 ft 10½ in

DISCUS

1. ....Irina Yatchenko, Bulgaria — 220 ft 10½ in
2. ....Anastasía Kelesídou, Greece — 220 ft 3¼ in
3. ....Ekateríni Vóggoli, Greece — 218 ft 11 in

HAMMER THROW

1. ....Yipsi Moreno, Cuba — 240 ft 7 in
2. ....Olga Kuzenkova, Russia — 235 ft 3¼ in
3. ....Manuela Montebrun, France — 232 ft 8 in

JAVELIN

1. ....Miréla Manjani, Greece — 218 ft 3 in
2. ....Tatyana Shikolenko, Russia — 207 ft 7¼ in
3. ....Steffi Nerius, Germany — 205 ft 8½ in

20-KILOMETER WALK

1. ....Yelena Nikolayeva, Russia — 1:26:52
2. ....Gillian O'Sullivan, Ireland — 1:27:34
3. ....Valentina Tsybulskaya, Bulgaria — 1:28:10

4 x 100 RELAY

1. ....France — 41.78
2. ....United States — 41.83
3. ....Russia — 42.66

4 x 400 RELAY

1. ....United States — 3:22.63
2. ....Russia — 3:22.91
3. ....Jamaica — 3:22.92

HEPTATHLON

1. ....Carolina Klüft, Sweden — 7001 pts
2. ....Eunice Barber, France — 6755
3. ....Natalya Sazanovich, Bulgaria — 6524

Palo Alto, California, June 19–22

Men

100 METERS

1. ......Bernard Williams, Nike — 10.11
2. ......Tim Montgomery, Nike — 10.15
3. ......Jon Drummond, Nike — 10.18

200 METERS

1. ......Darvis Patton, adidas — 20.15
2. ......John Capel, adidas — 20.17
3. ......Joshua Johnson, Nike — 20.22

400 METERS

1. ......Tyree Washington, Nike — 44.33
2. ......Calvin Harrison, Nike — 44.62
3. ......Jerome Young, adidas — 44.79

800 METERS

1. ......David Krummenacker, adidas — 1:45.53
2. ......Khadevis Robinson, Nike — 1:46.21
3. ......Jonathon Johnson, Texas Tech — 1:46.76

1,500 METERS

1. ......Jason Lunn, Nike — 3:44.00
2. ......Bryan Berryhill, adidas — 3:44.30
3. ......Grant Robison, Stanford — 3:44.83

5,000 METERS

1. ......Tim Broe, adidas — 13:35.23
2. ......Adam Goucher, Nike — 13:35.67
3. ......Jorge Torres, Reebok — 13:36.42

10,000 METERS

1. ......Alan Culpepper, adidas — 27:55.36
2. ......Meb Keflezighi, Nike — 27:57.59
3. ......Daniel Browne, Nike — 28:03.48

110-METER HURDLES

1. ......Allen Johnson, Nike — 13.37
2. ......Terrence Trammell, Mizuno — 13.38
3. ......Larry Wade, Nike — 13.43

400-METER HURDLES

1. ......Eric Thomas, Nike — 48.76
2. ......Bershawn Jackson, unattached — 49.01
3. ......Joey Woody, adidas — 49.22

3,000-METER STEEPLECHASE

1. ......Steve Slattery, Nike — 8:23.58
2. ......Daniel Lincoln, Nike — 8:24.10
3. ......Robert Gary, adidas — 8:24.82

HIGH JUMP

1. ......Jamie Nieto, unattached — 7 ft 6½ in
2. ......Matt Hemingway, unattached — 7 ft 5¼ in
3. ......Terrance Woods, unattached — 7 ft 5¼ in

POLE VAULT

1. ......Jeff Hartwig, Nike — 18 ft 8¼ in
2. ......Derek Miles, Nike — 18 ft 8¼ in
3. ......Timothy Mack, Nike — 18 ft 8¼ in

LONG JUMP

1. ......Dwight Phillips, Nike — 27 ft ½ in
1. ......Walter Davis, Nike — 27 ft ½ in
3. ......Savante Stringfellow, Nike — 26 ft 11¾ in

TRIPLE JUMP

1. ......Kenta Bell, Nike — 57 ft 8½ in
2. ......Walter Davis, Nike — 57 ft 7 in
3. ......Tim Rusan, Nike — 56 ft 4¾ in

SHOT PUT

1. ......Kevin Toth, Nike — 69 ft 7½ in
2. ......John Godina, adidas — 69 ft ½ in
3. ......Reese Hoffa, NYAC — 67 ft 8¾ in

DISCUS

1. ......Carl Brown, unattached — 218 ft 8 in
2. ......Adam Setliff, Nike — 206 ft 5 in
3. ......Doug Reynolds, unattached — 205 ft 9 in

HAMMER THROW

1. ......James Parker, U.S. Air Force — 239 ft 7 in
2. ......John McEwen, NYAC — 239 ft 4 in
3. ......Patrick McGrath, unattached — 236 ft 7 in

JAVELIN

1. ......Breaux Greer, adidas — 260 ft 5 in
2. ......Robert Minnitti, unattached — 253 ft 4 in
3. ......Joshua Johnson, unattached — 249 ft 10 in

DECATHLON

1. ......Tom Pappas, Nike — 8784 pts
2. ......Bryan Clay, unattached — 8482
3. ......Paul Terek, World's Greatest Athletes — 8275

20,000-METER RACE WALK

1. ......Kevin Eastler, U.S. Air Force — 1:23:52
2. ......Tim Seaman, NYAC — 1:24:47
3. ......John Nunn, U.S. Army — 1:25:15

Women

100 METERS

1. ....Kelli White, Nike	10.93
2. ....Torri Edwards, adidas	11.13
3. ....Gail Devers, Nike	11.16

200 METERS

1. ....Kelli White, Nike	22.21
2. ....Torri Edwards, adidas	22.45
3. ....Allyson Felix, unattached	22.59

400 METERS

1. ....,Sanya Richards, Texas	51.01
2. ....Demetria Washington, Nike	51.54
3. ....De'Hashia Trotter, Tennessee	51.78

800 METERS

1. ....Jearl Miles-Clark, New Balance	1:58.84
2. ....Nicole Teter, Nike	1:59.91
3. ....Jennifer Toomey, Nike	2:00.12

1,500 METERS

1. ....Regina Jacobs, Nike	4:01.63
2. ....Suzy Favor Hamilton, Nike	4:03.70
3. ....Tiffany McWilliams, Mississippi St	4:10.85

5,000 METERS

1. ....Marla Runyan, Nike	15:16.18
2. ....Shalane Flanagan, N Carolina	15:20.54
3. ....Shayne Culpepper, adidas	15:23.59

10,000 METERS

1. ....Deena Drossin, Asics	31:28.97
2. ....Elva Dryer, Nike	31:35.74
3. ....Katie McGregor, adidas	31:54.78

100-METER HURDLES

1. ....Gail Devers, Nike	12.61
2. ....Miesha McKelvy-Jones, Nike	12.62
3. ....Jenny Adams, Nike	12.68

400-METER HURDLES

1. ....Raasin McIntosh, Texas	54.62
2. ....Joanna Hayes, Nike	54.76
3. ....Sandra Glover, Nike	55.12

3,000-METER STEEPLECHASE

1. ....Brianna Shook, Toledo	9:44.71
2. ....Kathryn Andersen, Brigham Young	9:47.17
3. ....Lisa Nye, Nike	9:49.14

HIGH JUMP

1. ....Amy Acuff, Asics	6 ft 4¾ in
2. ....Gwen Wentland, Nike	6 ft 3½ in
3. ....Tisha Waller, Nike	6 ft 3½ in

POLE VAULT

1. ....Stacy Dragila, Nike	14 ft 9 in
2. ....Jillian Schwartz, Nike	14 ft 5¼ in
3. ....Mary Sauer, Asics	14 ft 3¼ in
3. ....Becky Holliday, unattached	14 ft 3¼ in

LONG JUMP

1. ....Grace Upshaw, Nike	21 ft 9½ in
2. ....Rose Richmond, Indiana	21 ft 6¼ in
3. ....Jenny Adams, Nike	21 ft 2 in

TRIPLE JUMP

1. ....Yuliana Perez, unattached	46 ft 8¼ in
2. ....Tiombe Hurd, Nike	45 ft 9¾ in
3. ....Nicole Gamble, Nike	45 ft 7¼ in

SHOT PUT

1. ....Kristin Heaston, unattached	60 ft 1¾ in
2. ....Seilala Sua, Nike	58 ft ½ in
3. ....Laura Gerraughty, unattached	57 ft 9½ in

DISCUS

1. ....Seilala Sua, Nike	196 ft 10 in
2. ....Gina LoMonico, unattached	194 ft 5 in
3. ....Roberta Collins, unattached	192 ft 5 in

HAMMER THROW

1. ....Melissa Price, unattached	230 ft 9 in
2. ....Anna Mahon, Nike	226 ft 6 in
3. ....Dawn Ellerbee, NYAC	219 ft

JAVELIN

1. ....Erica Wheeler, unattached	186 ft 6 in
2. ....Kim Kreiner, Nike	185 ft
3. ....Denise O'Connell, unattached	175 ft 1 in

HEPTATHLON

1. ....Shelia Burrell, Nike	6159 pts
2. ....Kim Schiemenz, unattached	6003
3. ....Tiffany Lott-Hogan, unattached	5843

20-KILOMETER WALK

1. ....Michelle Rohl, Moving Comfo	1:34:31
2. ....Joanne Dow, adidas	1:34:57
3. ....Teresa Vaill, Walk USA	1:36:38

2003 IAAF World Cross-Country Championships

Lausanne, Switzerland, March 29–30

MEN (12,000 METERS; 7.5 MILES)

1. ....Kenenisa Bekele, Ethiopia — 35:56
2. ....Patrick Ivuti, Kenya — 36:09
3. ....G. Gebremariam, Ethiopia — 36:17

WOMEN (8,000 METERS; 5 MILES)

1. ....Werknesh Kidane, Ethiopia — 25:53
2. ....Deena Drossin, United States — 26:02
3. ....Merima Denboba, Ethiopia — 26:28

Major Marathons

Chicago: October 13, 2002

MEN

1. ....Khalid Khannouchi, United States — 2:05:56
2. ....Daniel Njenga, Japan — 2:06:16
3. ....Toshinari Takaoka, Japan — 2:06:16

WOMEN

1. ....Paula Radcliffe, Great Britain — 2:17:18
2. ....Catherine Ndereba, Kenya — 2:19:26
3. ....Yoko Shibui, Japan — 2:21:22

New York City: November 3, 2002

MEN

1. ....Rodgers Rop, Kenya — 2:08:07
2. ....Christopher Cheboiboch, Kenya — 2:08:17
3. ....Lavan Kipkemboi, Kenya — 2:08:39

WOMEN

1. ....Joyce Chepchumba, Kenya — 2:25:56
2. ....Lyubov Denisova, Russia — 2:26:17
3. ....Olivera Jevtic, Yugoslavia — 2:26:44

Tokyo: November 17, 2002

WOMEN ONLY

1. ....Banuelia Mrashani, Tanzania — 2:24:59
2. ....Rie Matsuoka, Japan — 2:25:02
3. ....Irina Timofeyeva, Russia — 2:26:45

Tokyo: February 9, 2003

MEN ONLY

1. ....Zebedayo Bayo, Tanzania — 2:09:07
2. ....Shigeru Aburaya, Japan — 2:09:30
3. ....Noriaki Igarashi, Japan — 2:10:11

Rome: March 23, 2003

MEN

1. ....Frederick Cherono, Kenya — 2:08:47
2. ....Noah Bor, Kenya — 2:08:48
3. ....Alberico Di Cecco, Italy — 2:08:53

WOMEN

1. ....Gloria Marconi, Italy — 2:29:35
2. ....Simona Staicu, Hungary — 2:32:15
3. ....Tola Abeba, Ethiopia — 2:33:48

Paris: April 6, 2003

MEN

1. ....Mike Rotich, Kenya — 2:06:33
2. ....Benoit Zwierzchlewski, France — 2:06:36
3. ....Wilson Onsare, Kenya — 2:06:47

WOMEN

1. ....Béatrice Omwanza, Kenya — 2:27:44
2. ....Rosaria Console, Italy — 2:27:48
3. ....Banuela Mrashani, Tanzania — 2:29:13

Boston: April 21, 2003

MEN

1. ....Robert Cheruiyot, Kenya — 2:10:11
2. ....Benjamin Kimutai, Kenya — 2:10:34
3. ....Martin Lel, Kenya — 2:11:11

WOMEN

1. ....Svetlana Zakharova, Russia — 2:25:20
2. ....Lyubov Denisova, Russia — 2:26:51
3. ....Joyce Chepchumba Koech — 2:27:20

Rotterdam: April 13, 2003

MEN

1. ....William Kiplagat, Kenya — 2:07:42
2. ....Josephat Kiprono, Kenya — 2:07:53
3. ....José Manuel Martinez, Spain — 2:08:09

WOMEN

1. ....Olivera Jevtic, Yugoslavia — 2:25:23
2. ....Hiromi Ominami, Japan — 2:26:17
3. ....Maria Teresa Pulido, Spain — 2:31:56

London: April 13, 2003

MEN

1. ....Gezahegen Abera, Ethiopia — 2:07:56
2. ....Stefano Baldini, Italy — 2:07:56
3. ....Joseph Ngolepus, Kenya — 2:07:57

WOMEN

1. ....Paula Radcliffe, Great Britain — 2:15:25*
2. ....Catherine Ndereba, Kenya — 2:19:55
3. ....Deena Drossin, United States — 2:21:16

*World record.

TRACK AND FIELD

World Records

As of September 22, 2003. World outdoor records are recognized by the International Amateur Athletics Federation (IAAF).

Men

Event	Mark	Record Holder	Date	Site
100 meters	9.78	Tim Montgomery, United States	9-14-02	Paris
200 meters	19.32	Michael Johnson, United States	8-1-96	Atlanta
400 meters	43.18	Michael Johnson, United States	8-26-99	Seville
800 meters	1:41.11	Wilson Kipketer, Denmark	8-24-97	Cologne
1,000 meters	2:11.96	Noah Ngeny, Kenya	9-5-99	Rieti, Italy
1,500 meters	3:26.00	Hicham El Guerrouj, Morocco	7-14-98	Rome
Mile	3:43.13	Hicham El Guerrouj, Morocco	7-7-99	Rome
2,000 meters	4:44.79	Hicham El Guerrouj, Morocco	9-7-99	Berlin
3,000 meters	7:20.67	Daniel Komen, Kenya	9-1-96	Rieti, Italy
Steeplechase	7:53.17*	Brahim Boulami, Morocco	8-16-02	Zürich
5,000 meters	12:39.36	Haile Gebrselassie, Ethiopia	6-13-98	Helsinki
10,000 meters	26:22.75	Haile Gebrselassie, Ethiopia	6-1-98	Hengelo, Netherlands
20,000 meters	56:55.6	Arturo Barrios, Mexico	3-30-91	La Flâche, France
Hour	21,101 meters	Arturo Barrios, Mexico	3-30-91	La Flâche, France
25,000 meters	1:13:55.8	Toshihiko Seko, Japan	3-22-81	Christchurch, New Zealand
30,000 meters	1:29:18.8	Toshihiko Seko, Japan	3-22-81	Christchurch, New Zealand
Marathon	2:04:55	Paul Tergat, Kenya	9-28-03	Berlin
110-meter hurdles	12.91	Colin Jackson, Great Britain	8-20-93	Stuttgart, Germany
400-meter hurdles	46.78	Kevin Young, United States	8-6-92	Barcelona
20-kilometer walk	1:17:25	Bernardo Segura, Mexico	5-7-94	Bergen, Norway
30-kilometer walk	2:01:44.1	Maurizio Damilano, Italy	10-3-92	Cuneo, Italy
50-kilometer walk	3:40:57.9	Thierry Toutain, France	9-29-96	Héricourt, France
4 x 100-meter relay	37.40	United States (Mike Marsh, Leroy Burrell, Dennis Mitchell, Carl Lewis)	8-8-92	Barcelona
		United States (Jon Drummond, Andre Cason, Dennis Mitchell, Leroy Burrell)	8-21-93	Stuttgart, Germany
4 x 200-meter relay	1:18.68	Santa Monica TC (Mike Marsh, Leroy Burrell, Floyd Heard, Carl Lewis)	4-17-94	Walnut, CA
4 x 400-meter relay	2:54.20	United States (Jerome Young, Antonio Pettigrew, Tyree Washington, Michael Johnson)	7-22-98	New York City
4 x 800-meter relay	7:03.89	Great Britain (Peter Elliott, Garry Cook, Steve Cram, Sebastian Coe)	8-30-82	London
4 x 1,500-meter relay	14:38.8	W Germany (Thomas Wessinghage, Harald Hudak, Michael Lederer, Karl Fleschen)	8-17-77	Cologne
High jump	8 ft ½ in	Javier Sotomayor, Cuba	7-27-93	Salamanca, Spain
Pole vault	20 ft 1¾ in	Sergei Bubka, Ukraine	7-31-94	Sestriere, Italy
Long jump	29 ft 4½ in	Mike Powell, United States	8-30-91	Tokyo
Triple jump	60 ft ¼ in	Jonathan Edwards, Great Britain	8-7-95	Göteborg, Sweden
Shot put	75 ft 10¼ in	Randy Barnes, United States	5-20-90	Westwood, CA
Discus throw	243 ft 0 in	Jürgen Schult, E Germany	6-6-86	Neubrandenburg, Germany
Hammer throw	284 ft 7 in	Yuri Syedikh, USSR	8-30-86	Stuttgart, Germany
Javelin throw	323 ft 1 in	Jan Zelezny, Czech Republic	5-25-96	Jena, Germany
Decathlon	9026 pts	Roman Sebrle, Czech Republic	5-27-01	Götzis

Note: The decathlon consists of 10 events: the 100 meters, long jump, shot put, high jump and 400 meters on the first day; the 110-meter hurdles, discus, pole vault, javelin and 1,500 meters on the second.

*Pending ratification.

Women

Event	Mark	Record Holder	Date	Site
100 meters	10.49	Florence Griffith Joyner, United States	7-16-88	Indianapolis
200 meters	21.34	Florence Griffith Joyner, United States	9-29-88	Seoul
400 meters	47.60	Marita Koch, E Germany	10-6-85	Canberra, Australia
800 meters	1:53.28	Jarmila Kratochvílová, Czechoslovakia	7-26-83	Munich
1,000 meters	2:28.98	Svetlana Masterkova, Russia	8-23-96	Brussels
1,500 meters	3:50.46	Qu Yunxia, China	9-11-93	Beijing
Mile	4:12.56	Svetlana Masterkova, Russia	8-14-96	Zurich
2,000 meters	5:25.36	Sonia O'Sullivan, Ireland	7-8-94	Edinburgh
3,000 meters	8:06.11	Wang Junxia, China	9-13-93	Beijing
Steeplechase	9:08.33*	Gulnara Samitova, Russia	8-10-03	Tula
5,000 meters	14:28.09	Jiang Bo, China	10-23-97	Shanghai
10,000 meters	29:31.78	Wang Junxia, China	9-8-93	Beijing
Hour	18,340 meters	Tegla Loroupe, Kenya	8-8-98	Borgholzhausen, Germany
20,000 meters	1:05:26.6	Tegla Loroupe, Kenya	9-3-00	Borgholzhausen, Germany
25,000 meters	1:27:05.9	Tegla Loroupe, Kenya	9-21-02	Mengerskirchen
30,000 meters	1:45:50.0	Tegla Loroupe, Kenya	6-6-03	Warstein
Marathon	2:15:25*	Paula Radcliffe, Great Britain	4-13-03	London
100-meter hurdles	12.21	Yordanka Donkova, Bulgaria	8-20-88	Stara Zagora, Bulgaria
400-meter hurdles	52.34	Yuliya Pechonkina, Russia	8-8-03	Tula
5-kilometer walk	20:02.60	Gillian O'Sullivan, Ireland	7-13-02	Dublin
10-kilometer walk	41:56.23	Nadezhda Ryashkina, URS	7-24-90	Seattle
4 x 100-meter relay	41.37	East Germany (Silke Gladisch, Sabine Reiger, Ingrid Auerswald, Marlies Göhr)	10-6-85	Canberra, Australia
4 x 200-meter relay	1:27.46	United States (LaTasha Jenkins, LaTasha Colander-Richardson, Nanceen Perry, Marion Jones)	4-29-00	Philadelphia
4 x 400-meter relay	3:15.17	USSR (Tatyana Ledovskaya, Olga Nazarova, Maria Pinigina, Olga Bryzgina)	10-1-88	Seoul
4 x 800-meter relay	7:50.17	USSR (Nadezhda Olizarenko, Lyubov Gurina, Lyudmila Borisova, Irina Podyalovskaya)	8-5-84	Moscow
High jump	6 ft 10¼ in	Stefka Kostadinova, Bulgaria	8-30-87	Rome
Pole vault	15 ft 9¾ in*	Yelena Isinbayeva, Russia	7-13-03	Gateshead
Long jump	24 ft 8¼ in	Galina Chistyakova, USSR	6-11-88	Leningrad
Triple jump	50 ft 10¼ in	Inessa Kravets, Ukraine	8-10-95	Göteborg, Sweden
Shot put	74 ft 3 in	Natalya Lisovskaya, USSR	6-7-87	Moscow
Discus throw	252 ft	Gabriele Reinsch, E Germany	7-9-88	Neubrandenburg, Germany
Hammer throw	247 ft 3 in	Mihaela Melinte, Romania	8-29-99	Rüdlingen, Switzerland
Javelin throw	234 ft 8 in	Osleidys Menéndez, Cuba	7-1-01	Réthymno, Greece
Heptathlon	7291 pts	Jackie Joyner-Kersee, United States	9-23/24-88	Seoul

Note: The heptathlon consists of 7 events: the 100-meter hurdles, high jump, shot put and 200 meters on the first day; the long jump, javelin and 800 meters on the second.

*Pending ratification.

As of January 1, 2003. American outdoor records are recognized by USA Track and Field (USATF). WR=world record. EWR=equals world record.

Men

Event	Mark	Record Holder	Date	Site
100 meters	9.78 WR	Tim Montgomery	9-14-02	Paris
200 meters	19.32 WR	Michael Johnson	8-1-96	Atlanta
400 meters	43.18 WR	Michael Johnson	8-26-99	Seville
800 meters	1:42.60	Johnny Gray	8-28-85	Koblenz, Germany
1,000 meters	2:13.9	Rick Wohlhuter	7-30-74	Oslo
1,500 meters	3:29.77	Sydney Maree	8-25-85	Cologne
Mile	3:47.69	Steve Scott	7-7-82	Oslo
2,000 meters	4:52.44	Jim Spivey	9-15-87	Lausanne
3,000 meters	7:30.84	Bob Kennedy	8-8-98	Monte Carlo
Steeplechase	8:09.17	Henry Marsh	8-28-85	Koblenz, Germany
5,000 meters	12:58.21	Bob Kennedy	8-14-96	Zurich
10,000 meters	27:13.98	Mebrahtom Keflezighi	5-4-01	Palo Alto, California
20,000 meters	58:25.0	Bill Rodgers	8-9-77	Boston
Hour	20,547 meters	Bill Rodgers	8-9-77	Boston
25,000 meters	1:14:11.8	Bill Rodgers	2-21-79	Saratoga, CA
30,000 meters	1:31:49	Bill Rodgers	2-21-79	Saratoga, CA
Marathon	2:05:38	Khalid Khannouchi	4-14-02	London
110-meter hurdles	12.92	Roger Kingdom	8-16-89	Zurich
		Allen Johnson	6-23-96	Atlanta
		Allen Johnson	8-23-96	Brussels
400-meter hurdles	46.78 WR	Kevin Young	8-6-92	Barcelona
20-kilometer walk	1:23:40	Tim Seaman	8-14-00	La Jolla, CA
30-kilometer walk	2:14:31	Allen James	10-31-93	Atlanta
50-kilometer walk	3:59:41.1	Herman Nelson	6-9-96	Seattle
4x100-meter relay	37.40 WR	United States (Mike Marsh, Leroy Burrell, Dennis Mitchell, Carl Lewis)	8-8-92	Barcelona
		United States (Jon Drummond, Andre Cason, Dennis Mitchell, Leroy Burrell)	8-21-93	Stuttgart, Germany
4x200-meter relay	1:18.68 WR	Santa Monica Track Club (Mike Marsh, Leroy Burrell, Floyd Heard, Carl Lewis)	4-17-94	Walnut, CA
4x400-meter relay	2:54.20 WR	United States (Jerome Young, Antonio Pettigrew, Tyree Washington, Michael Johnson)	7-22-98	New York City
4x800-meter relay	7:06.5	Santa Monica Track Club (James Robinson, David Mack, Earl Jones, Johnny Gray)	4-26-86	Walnut, CA
4x1,500-meter relay	14:46.3	National Team (Dan Aldredge, Andy Clifford, Todd Harbour, Tom Duits)	6-24-79	Bourges, France
High jump	7 ft 10½ in	Charles Austin	8-17-91	Zurich
Pole vault	19 ft 9¼ in	Jeff Hartwig	6-14-00	Jonesboro, AR
Long jump	29 ft 4½ in WR	Mike Powell	8-30-91	Tokyo
Triple jump	59 ft 4¼ in	Kenny Harrison	7-27-96	Atlanta
Shot put	75 ft 10¼ in WR	Randy Barnes	5-20-90	Westwood, CA
Discus throw	237 ft 4 in	Ben Plucknett	7-7-81	Stockholm
Hammer throw	270 ft 9 in	Lance Deal	9-7-96	Milan
Javelin throw	285 ft 10 in	Tom Pukstys	5-25-97	Jena, Germany
Decathlon	8891 pts	Dan O'Brien	9-4/5-92	Talence, France

Women

Event	Mark	Record Holder	Date	Site
100 meters	10.49 WR	Florence Griffith Joyner	7-16-88	Indianapolis
200 meters	21.34 WR	Florence Griffith Joyner	9-29-88	Seoul
400 meters	48.83	Valerie Brisco-Hooks	8-6-84	Los Angeles
800 meters	1:56.40	Jearl Miles-Clark	8-11-99	Zurich
1,500 meters	3:57.12	Mary Slaney	7-26-83	Stockholm
Mile	4:16.71	Mary Slaney	8-21-85	Zurich
2,000 meters	5:32.7	Mary Slaney	8-3-84	Eugene, OR
3,000 meters	8:25.83	Mary Slaney	9-7-85	Rome
Steeplechase	9:41.94	Elizabeth Jackson	9-4-01	Brisbane
5,000 meters	14:45.38	Regina Jacobs	7-21-00	Sacramento, CA
10,000 meters	30:50.32	Deena Drossin	5-3-02	Palo Alto, CA
Marathon	2:21:21	Joan Samuelson	10-20-85	Chicago
100-meter hurdles	12.33	Gail Devers	7-23-00	Sacramento, CA
400-meter hurdles	52.61 WR	Kim Batten	8-11-95	Göteborg, Sweden
5,000-meter walk	20:56.88	Michelle Rohl	4-27-96	Philadelphia
10,000-meter walk	44:41.87	Michelle Rohl	7-26-94	St. Petersburg
4 x 100-meter relay	41.47	National Team (Chryste Gaines, Marion Jones, Inger Miller, Gail Devers)	8-9-97	Athens
4 x 200-meter relay	1:27.46 WR	USA Blue (LaTasha Jenkins, LaTasha Colander, Nanceen Perry, Marion Jones)	4-29-00	Philadelphia
4 x 400-meter relay	3:15.51	United States (Denean Howard, Diane Dixon, Valerie Brisco, Florence Griffith Joyner)	10-1-88	Seoul
4 x 800-meter relay	8:17.09	Athletics West (Sue Addison, Lee Arbogast, Mary Decker, Chris Mullen)	4-24-83	Walnut, CA
High jump	6 ft 8 in	Louise Ritter	7-9-88	Austin
		Louise Ritter	9-30-88	Seoul
Pole vault	15 ft 9¼ in WR	Stacy Dragila	6-9-01	Palo Alto, CA
Long jump	24 ft 7 in	Jackie Joyner-Kersee	5-22-94	New York City
			7-31-94	Sestriere, Italy
Triple jump	47 ft 3½ in	Sheila Hudson	7-8-96	Stockholm
Shot put	66 ft 2⅝ in	Ramona Pagel	6-25-88	San Diego
Discus throw	227 ft 10 in	Suzy Powell	4-27-02	La Jolla, CA
Hammer throw	236 ft 3 in	Anna Norgren-Mahon	7-28-02	Walnut, CA
Javelin throw	199 ft 1 in	Kim Kreiner	7-26-02	Rheinfeld, Germany
Heptathlon	7291 pts WR	Jackie Joyner-Kersee	9-23/24-88	Seoul

World and American Indoor Records

As of September 26, 2003. American indoor records are recognized by USA Track and Field. World Indoor records are recognized by the International Amateur Athletics Federation (IAAF).

Men

Event	Mark	Record Holder	Date	Site
50 meters	5.56	Donovan Bailey, Canada (W)	2-9-96	Reno
	5.56	Maurice Greene (A)	2-13-99	Los Angeles
55 meters*	5.99	Obadele Thompson, Barbados (W)	2-22-97	Colorado Springs
	6.00	Lee McRae (A)	3-14-86	Oklahoma City
60 meters	6.39	Maurice Greene (W, A)	3-1-98	Madrid
	6.39	Maurice Greene (W, A)	3-3-01	Atlanta
200 meters	19.92	Frankie Fredericks, Namibia (W)	2-18-96	Liévin, France
	20.26	Shawn Crawford (A)	3-11-00	Fayetteville, AR
	20.26	John Capel (A)	3-11-00	Fayetteville, AR
400 meters	44.63	Michael Johnson (W, A)	3-4-95	Atlanta
800 meters	1:42.67	Wilson Kipketer, Denmark (W)	3-9-97	Paris
	1:45.00	Johnny Gray (A)	3-8-92	Sindelfingen, Germany
1,000 meters	2:14.96	Wilson Kipketer, Denmark (W)	2-20-00	Birmingham, England
	2:17.85	David Krummenacker (A)	1-27-02	Boston

Men *(Cont.)*

Event	Mark	Record Holder	Date	Site
1,500 meters	3:31.18	Hicham El Guerrouj, Morocco (W)	2-02-97	Stuttgart, Germany
	3:38.12	Jeff Atkinson (A)	3-5-89	Budapest
Mile	3:48.45	Hicham El Guerrouj, Morocco (W)	2-12-97	Ghent, Belgium
	3:51.8	Steve Scott (A)	2-20-81	San Diego
3,000 meters	7:24.90	Daniel Komen, Kenya (W)	2-6-98	Budapest
	7:39.23	Tim Broe (A)	1-27-02	Boston
5,000 meters	12:50.38	Haile Gebrselassie, Ethiopia (W)	2-14-99	Birmingham, England
	13:20.55	Doug Padilla (A)	2-12-82	New York City
50-meter hurdles	6.25	Mark McKoy, Canada (W)	3-5-86	Kobe, Japan
	6.35	Greg Foster (A)	1-27-85	Rosemont, Illinois
55-meter hurdles*	6.89	Renaldo Nehemiah (A)	1-20-79	New York City
60-meter hurdles	7.30	Colin Jackson, Great Britain (W)	3-6-94	Sindelfingen, Germany
	7.36	Greg Foster (A)	1-16-87	Los Angeles
5,000-meter walk	18:07.08	Mikhail Shchennikov, Russia (W)	2-14-95	Moscow
	19:18.40	Tim Lewis (A)	3-7-87	Indianapolis
4 x 200-meter relay	1:22.11	Great Britain (W) (Linford Christie, Darren Braithwaite, Ade Mafe, John Regis)	3-3-91	Glasgow
	1:22.71	National Team (A) (Thomas Jefferson, Raymond Pierre, Antonio McKay Kevin Little)	3-3-91	Glasgow
4 x 400-meter relay	3:02.83	United States (W, A) (Andre Morris, Dameon Johnson, Deon Minor, Milt Campbell)	3-7-99	Maebashi, Japan
4 x 800-meter relay	7:13.94	Global Athletics & Marketing (W, A) (Rich Kenah, Joel Woody, Karl Paranya, David Krummenacker)	2-6-00	Boston
High jump	7 ft 11½ in	Javier Sotomayor, Cuba (W)	3-4-89	Budapest
	7 ft 10½ in	Hollis Conway (A)	3-10-91	Seville
Pole vault	20 ft 2 in	Sergei Bubka, Ukraine (W)	2-21-93	Donetsk, Ukraine
	19 ft 9½ in	Jeff Hartwig (A)	3-10-02	Sindelfingen, Germany
Long jump	28 ft 10¼ in	Carl Lewis (W, A)	1-27-84	New York City
Triple jump	58 ft 6 in	Alicier Urrutia, Cuba (W)	3-1-97	Sindelfingen, Germany
	58 ft 3¼ in	Mike Conley (A)	2-27-87	New York City
Shot put	74 ft 4¼ in	Randy Barnes (W, A)	1-20-89	Los Angeles
Weight throw*	84 ft 10¼ in	Lance Deal (W, A)	3-4-95	Atlanta
Pentathlon*	4478 pts	Steve Fritz, (W, A)	1-14-95	Lawrence, KS
Heptathlon	6476 pts	Dan O'Brien (W, A)	3-13/14-93	Toronto

*No recognized world record.

†Pending ratification.

YET ANOTHER SIGN OF THE APOCALYPSE

A Bucharest court ordered Romanian track star Gabriela Szabo to pay rival runner Violeta Beclea-Szekely $5,000 for calling her "ugly."

Women

Event	Mark	Record Holder	Date	Site
50 meters	5.96	Irina Privolova, Russia (W)	2-9-95	Madrid
	6.02	Gail Devers (A)	2-21-99	Liévin, France
55 meters*	6.54	Evelyn Ashford (A)	2-26-82	New York
		Jeanette Bolden (A)	2-21-86	Inglewood, CA
60 meters	6.92	Irina Privolova, Russia (W)	2-11-93	Madrid
	6.92	Irina Privolova, Russia (W)	2-9-95	Madrid
	6.95	Gail Devers (A)	3-12-93	Toronto
	6.95	Marion Jones (A)	3-7-98	Maebashi, Japan
200 meters	21.87	Merlene Ottey, Jamaica (W)	2-13-93	Liévin, France
	22.33	Gwen Torrence (A)	3-2-96	Atlanta
400 meters	49.59	Jarmila Kratochvílová, Czech. (W)	3-7-82	Milan
	50.64	Diane Dixon (A)	3-10-91	Seville
800 meters	1:55.82	Jolanda Ceplak, Slovenia (W)	3-3-02	Vienna
	1:58.71	Nicole Teter (A)	3-2-02	New York
1,000 meters	2:30.94	Maria Mutola, Mozambique (W)	2-25-99	Stockholm
	2:35.29	Regina Jacobs (A)	2-6-00	Boston
1,500 meters†	3:59.98†	Regina Jacobs, United States (W, A)	2-1-03	Boston
Mile	4:17.14	Doina Melinte, Romania (W)	2-9-90	East Rutherford, NJ
	4:20.5	Mary Slaney (A)	2-19-82	San Diego
3,000 meters	8:29.15	Berhane Adere, Ethiopia	2-3-02	Stuttgart
	8:39.14	Regina Jacobs (A)	3-7-99	Maebashi, Japan
5,000 meters	14:47.35	Gabriela Szabo, Romania (W)	2-13-99	Dortmund, Germany
	15:07.33	Marla Runyan (A)	2-18-01	New York
50-meter hurdles	6.58	Cornelia Oschkenat, E Germany (W)	2-20-88	Berlin
	6.67	Jackie Joyner-Kersee (A)	2-10-95	Reno
55-meter hurdles*	7.30	Tiffany Lott (A)	2-20-97	Air Force Academy, CO
60-meter hurdles	7.69	Lyudmila Narozhilenko, Russia (W)	2-4-90	Chelyabinsk, Russia
	7.74	Gail Devers (A)	3-1-03	Boston
3,000-meter walk	11:35.34†	Gillian O'Sullivan, Ireland	2-15-03	Belfast
	12:20.79	Debbi Lawrence (A)	3-12-93	Toronto
4 x 200-meter relay	1:32.55	SC Eintracht Hamm, W Gemany (W) (Helga Arendt, Silke-Beate Knoll, Mechthild Kluth, Gisela Kinzel)	2-20-88	Dortmund, W Germany
	1:33.24	National Team (A) (Flirtisha Harris, Chryste Gaines, Terri Dendy, Michele Collins)	2-12-94	Glasgow
4 x 400-meter relay	3:24.25	Russia (W) (Tatyanna Chebykina, Svetlana Goncharenko, Olga Kotlyarova, Natalya Nazarova)	3-7-99	Maebashi, Japan
	3:27.59	National Team (A) (Michelle Collins, Monique Hennagan, Zundra Feagin-Alexander, Shanelle Porter)	3-7-99	Maebashi, Japan
4 x 800-meter relay	8:18.71	Russia (W) (Natalya Zaytseva, Olga Kuvnetsova, Yelena Afanasyeva, Yekaterina Podkopayeva)	2-4-94	Moscow
	8:25.50	Villanova (A) (Gina Procaccio, Debbie Grant, Michelle DiMuro, Celeste Halliday)	2-7-87	Gainesville, FL
High jump	6 ft 9½ in	Heike Henkel, Germany (W)	2-8-92	Karlsruhe, Germany
	6 ft 7 in	Tisha Walker (A)	2-28-98	Atlanta
Pole vault	15 ft 9 in	Svetlana Feofanova, Russia (W)	3-16-03	Birmingham, England
	15 ft 8 in†	Stacy Dragila (A)	3-2-03	Boston
Long jump	24 ft 2¼ in	Heike Drechsler, E Germany (W)	2-13-88	Vienna
	23 ft 4¾ in	Jackie Joyner-Kersee (A)	3-5-94	Atlanta
Triple jump	49 ft 9 in	Ashia Hansen, Great Britain (W)	2-28-98	Valencia, Spain
	46 ft 8¼ in	Sheila Hudson-Strudwick (A)	3-4-95	Atlanta
Shot put	73 ft 10 in	Helena Fibingerová, Czech. (W)	2-19-77	Jablonec, Czech.
	65 ft ¾ in	Ramona Pagel (A)	2-20-87	Inglewood, CA
Weight throw*	77 ft 5 in	Dawn Ellerbe (W, A)	3-4-00	Atlanta
Pentathlon	4991 pts	Irina Byelova, CIS (W)	2-14/15-92	Berlin
	4753	Le Shundra Nathan (A)	3-4/5-99	Maebashi, Japan

*No recognized world record.
†Pending ratification.

Men

100 METERS

1983	Carl Lewis, United States	10.07
1987*	Carl Lewis, United States	9.93 WR
1991	Carl Lewis, United States	9.86 WR
1993	Linford Christie, Great Britain	9.87
1995	Donovan Bailey, Canada	9.97
1997	Maurice Greene, United States	9.86
1999	Maurice Greene, United States	9.80
2001	Maurice Greene, United States	9.82
2003	Kim Collins, St. Kitts & Nevis	10.07

200 METERS

1983	Calvin Smith, United States	20.14
1987	Calvin Smith, United States	20.16
1991	Michael Johnson, United States	20.01
1993	Frank Fredericks, Namibia	19.85
1995	Michael Johnson, United States	19.79
1997	Ato Boldon, Trinidad and Tobago	20.04
1999	Maurice Greene, United States	19.90
2001	Konstadínos Kedéris, Greece	20.04
2003	John Capel, United States	20.30

400 METERS

1983	Bert Cameron, Jamaica	45.05
1987	Thomas Schoenlebe, E Germany	44.33
1991	Antonio Pettigrew, United States	44.57
1993	Michael Johnson, United States	43.65
1995	Michael Johnson, United States	43.39
1997	Michael Johnson, United States	44.12
1999	Michael Johnson, United States	43.18 WR
2001	Avard Moncur, Bahamas	44.64
2003	Jerome Young, United States	44.50

800 METERS

1983	Willi Wulbeck, W Germany	1:43.65
1987	Billy Konchellah, Kenya	1:43.06
1991	Billy Konchellah, Kenya	1:43.99
1993	Paul Ruto, Kenya	1:44.71
1995	Wilson Kipketer, Denmark	1:45.08
1997	Wilson Kipketer, Denmark	1:43.38
1999	Wilson Kipketer, Denmark	1:43.30
2001	André Bucher, Switzerland	1:43.70
2003	Djabir Saïd-Guerni, Algeria	1:44.81

1,500 METERS

1983	Steve Cram, Great Britain	3:41.59
1987	Abdi Bile, Somalia	3:36.80
1991	Noureddine Morceli, Algeria	3:32.84
1993	Noureddine Morceli, Algeria	3:34.24
1995	Noureddine Morceli, Algeria	3:33.73
1997	Hicham El Guerrouj, Morocco	3:35.83
1999	Hicham El Guerrouj, Morocco	3:27.65
2001	Hicham El Guerrouj, Morocco	3:30.68
2003	Hicham El Guerrouj, Morocco	3:31.77

STEEPLECHASE

1983	Patriz Ilg, W Germany	8:15.06
1987	Francesco Panetta, Italy	8:08.57
1991	Moses Kiptanui, Kenya	8:12.59
1993	Moses Kiptanui, Kenya	8:06.36
1995	Moses Kiptanui, Kenya	8:04.16
1997	Wilson Boit Kipketer, Kenya	8:05.84
1999	Christopher Koskei, Kenya	8:11.76
2001	Reuben Kosgei, Kenya	8:15.16
2003	Saif Saaeed Shaheen, Qatar	8:04.39

5,000 METERS

1983	Eamonn Coghlan, Ireland	13:28.53
1987	Said Aouita, Morocco	13:26.44
1991	Yobes Ondieki, Kenya	13:14.45
1993	Ismael Kirui, Kenya	13:02.75
1995	Ismael Kirui, Kenya	13:16.77

5,000 METERS (CONT.)

1997	Daniel Komen, Kenya	13:07.38
1999	Salah Hissou, Morocco	12:58.13
2001	Richard Limo, Kenya	13:00.77
2003	Eliud Kipchoge, Kenya	12:52.79

10,000 METERS

1983	Alberto Cova, Italy	28:01.04
1987	Paul Kipkoech, Kenya	27:38.63
1991	Moses Tanui, Kenya	27:38.74
1993	Haile Gebrselassie, Ethiopia	27:46.02
1995	Haile Gebrselassie, Ethiopia	27:12.95
1997	Haile Gebrselassie, Ethiopia	27:24.58
1999	Haile Gebrselassie, Ethiopia	27:57.27
2001	Charles Kamathi, Kenya	27:53.25
2003	Kenenisa Bekele, Ethiopia	26:49.57

MARATHON

1983	Rob de Castella, Australia	2:10:03
1987	Douglas Wakiihuri, Kenya	2:11:48
1991	Hiromi Taniguchi, Japan	2:14:57
1993	Mark Plaatjes, United States	2:13:57
1995	Martín Fiz, Spain	2:11:41
1997	Abel Anton, Spain	2:13:16
1999	Abel Anton, Spain	2:13:36
2001	Gezahegne Abera, Ethiopia	2:12:42
2003	Jaouad Gharib, Morocco	2:08.31

110-METER HURDLES

1983	Greg Foster, United States	13.42
1987	Greg Foster, United States	13.21
1991	Greg Foster, United States	13.06
1993	Colin Jackson, Great Britain	12.91 WR
1995	Allen Johnson, United States	13.00
1997	Allen Johnson, United States	12.93
1999	Colin Jackson, Great Britain	13.04
2001	Allen Johnson, United States	13.04
2003	Allen Johnson, United States	13.12

400-METER HURDLES

1983	Edwin Moses, United States	47.50
1987	Edwin Moses, United States	47.46
1991	Samuel Matete, Zambia	47.64
1993	Kevin Young, United States	47.18
1995	Derrick Adkins, United States	47.98
1997	Stéphane Diagana, France	47.70
1999	Fabrizio Mori, Italy	47.72
2001	Felix Sánchez, Dominican Rep.	47.49
2003	Felix Sánchez, Dominican Rep.	47.25

20-KILOMETER WALK

1983	Ernesto Canto, Mexico	1:20:49
1987	Maurizio Damilano, Italy	1:20:45
1991	Maurizio Damilano, Italy	1:19:37
1993	Valentin Massana, Spain	1:22:31
1995	Michele Didoni, Italy	1:19:59
1997	Daniel Garcia, Mexico	1:21:43
1999	Ilya Markov, Russia	1:23:34
2001	Roman Rasskazov, Russia	1:20:31
2003	Jefferson Pérez, Ecuador	1:17.21 WR

50-KILOMETER WALK

1983	Ronald Weigel, E Germany	3:43:08
1987	Hartwig Gauder, E Germany	3:40:53
1991	Aleksandr Potashov, USSR	3:53:09
1993	Jesus Angel Garcia, Spain	3:41:41
1995	Valentin Kononen, Finland	3:43:42
1997	Robert Korzeniowski, Poland	3:44:46
1999	German Skurygin, Russia	3:44:23
2001	Robert Korzeniowski, Poland	3:42:08
2003	R. Korzeniowski, Poland	3:36:03 WR

WR=World record.   *Ben Johnson, Canada, disqualified.

World Track and Field Championships (Cont.)

Men (Cont.)

4 X 100-METER RELAY

1983	United States (Emmit King, Willie Gault, Calvin Smith, Carl Lewis)	37.86
1987	United States (Lee McRae, Lee McNeil, Harvey Glance, Carl Lewis)	37.90
1991	United States (A. Cason L. Burrell, D. Mitchell, C. Lewis)	37.50 WR
1993	United States (J. Drummond, A. Cason, D. Mitchell, L. Burrell)	37.48
1995	Canada (Robert Esmie, Glenroy Gilbert, Bruny Surin, Donovan Bailey)	38.31
1997	Canada (Robert Esmie, Glenroy Gilbert, Bruny Surin, Donovan Bailey)	37.86
1999	United States (Jon Drummond, Tim Montgomery, Brian Lewis, Maurice Greene)	37.59
2001	United States (Mickey Grimes, Bernard Williams, Dennis Mitchell, Tim Montgomery)	37.96
2003	United States (J. Capel, B. Williams D. Patton, J. Johnson)	38.06

4 X 400-METER RELAY

1983	USSR (S. Lovachev,A. Troschilo, N. Chernyetski, V. Markin)	3:00.79
1987	United States (Danny Everett Rod Haley, Antonio McKay, Butch Reynolds)	2:57.29
1991	Great Britain (Roger Black Derek Redmond, John Regis, Kriss Akabusi)	2:57.53
1993	United States (Andrew Valmon, Quincy Watts, Butch Reynolds, Michael Johnson)	2:54.29 WR
1995	United States (Marlon Ramsey, Derek Mills, Butch Reynolds, Michael Johnson)	2:57.32
1997	United States (J. Young, A. Pettigrew, C. Jones, T. Washington)	2:56.47
1999	United States (Jerome Davis, Antonio Pettigrew, Angelo Taylor, Michael Johnson)	2:56.45
2001	United States (L. Byrd, A. Pettigrew, D. Brew, A. Taylor)	2:57.54
2003	United States (C. Harrison, T. Washington, D. Brew, J. Young)	2:58.88

HIGH JUMP

1983	Gennadi Avdeyenko, USSR	7 ft 7¼ in
1987	Patrik Sjoberg, Sweden	7 ft 9¾ in
1991	Charles Austin, United States	7 ft 9¾ in
1993	Javier Sotomayor, Cuba	7 ft 10½ in
1995	Troy Kemp, Bahamas	7 ft 9¼ in
1997	Javier Sotomayor, Cuba	7 ft 9¼ in
1999	Vyacheslav Voronin, Russia	7 ft 9¼ in
2001	Martin Buss, Germany	7 ft 8¾ in
2003	Jacques Freitag, S Africa	7 ft 8½ in

POLE VAULT

1983	Sergei Bubka, USSR	18 ft 8¼ in
1987	Sergei Bubka, USSR	19 ft 2¼ in
1991	Sergei Bubka, USSR	19 ft 6¼ in
1993	Sergei Bubka, Ukraine	19 ft 8¼ in
1995	Sergei Bubka, Ukraine	19 ft 5 in
1997	Sergei Bubka, Ukraine	19 ft 8½ in
1999	Maksim Tarasov, Russia	19 ft 9 in
2001	Dmitri Markov, Australia	19 ft 10¼ in
2003	Guiseppe Gibilisco, Italy	19 ft 4¼ in

LONG JUMP

1983	Carl Lewis, United States	28 ft ¾ in
1987	Carl Lewis, United States	28 ft 5¼ in
1991	Mike Powell, U.S.	29 ft 4½ in WR

LONG JUMP (CONT.)

1993	Mike Powell, United States	28 ft 2¼ in
1995	Iván Pedroso, Cuba	28 ft 6½ in
1997	Iván Pedroso, Cuba	27 ft 7½ in
1999	Iván Pedroso, Cuba	28 ft 1 in
2001	Iván Pedroso, Cuba	27 ft 6¾ in
2003	Dwight Phillips, United States	27 ft 3½ in

TRIPLE JUMP

1983	Zdzislaw Hoffmann, Poland	57 ft 2 in
1987	Khristo Markov, Bulgaria	58 ft 9½ in
1991	Kenny Harrison, United States	58 ft 4 in
1993	Mike Conley, United States	58 ft 7¼ in
1995	Jonathan Edwards, G.B.	60 ft ¼ in WR
1997	Yoelvis Quesada, Cuba	58 ft 6¾ in
1999	Charle Michael Friedek, Ger.	57 ft 8½ in
2001	Jonathan Edwards, G. Britain	58 ft 9½ in
2003	Christian Olsson, Sweden	58 ft 1¾ in

SHOT PUT

1983	Edward Sarul, Poland	70 ft 2¼ in
1987	Werner Günthör, Switz.	72 ft 11¼ in
1991	Werner Günthör, Switz.	71 ft 1¼ in
1993	Werner Günthör, Switz.	72 ft 1 in
1995	John Godina, United States	70 ft 5¼ in
1997	John Godina, United States	70 ft 4¼ in
1999	C.J. Hunter, United States	71 ft 6 in
2001	John Godina, United States	71 ft 9 in
2003	Andrei Mikahnevic, Bulgaria	71 ft 2 in

DISCUS THROW

1983	Imrich Bugar, Czechoslovakia	222 ft 2 in
1987	Juergen Schult, E Germany	225 ft 6 in
1991	Lars Riedel, Germany	217 ft 2 in
1993	Lars Riedel, Germany	222 ft 2 in
1995	Lars Riedel, Germany	225 ft 7 in
1997	Lars Riedel, Germany	224 ft 10 in
1999	Anthony Washington, U.S.	226 ft 8 in
2001	Lars Riedel, Germany	228 ft 9 in
2003	Virgilijus Alekna, Lithuania	228 ft 7¾ in

HAMMER THROW

1983	Sergei Litvinov, USSR	271 ft 3 in
1987	Sergei Litvinov, USSR	272 ft 6 in
1991	Yuriy Sedykh, USSR	268 ft
1993	Andrey Abduvaliyev, Tajikistan	267 ft 10 in
1995	Andrey Abduvaliyev, Tajikistan	267 ft 7 in
1997	Heinz Weis, Germany	268 ft 4 in
1999	Karsten Kobs, Germany	263 ft 3 in
2001	Szymon Kiólkowski, Poland	273 ft 7 in
2003	Ivan Tikhon, Bulgaria	272 ft 5¾ in

JAVELIN

1983	Detlef Michel, E Germany	293 ft 7 in
1987	Seppo Räty, Finland	274 ft 1 in
1991	Kimmo Kinnunen, Finland	297 ft 11 in
1993	Jan Zelezny, Czech Republic	282 ft 1 in
1995	Jan Zelezny, Czech Republic	293 ft 11 in
1997	Marius Corbett, S Africa	290 ft 0 in
1999	Aki Parviainen, Finland	293 ft 8 in
2001	Jan Zelezny, Czech Republic	304 ft 5 in
2003	Sergey Makarov, Russia	280 ft 3¾ in

DECATHLON

1983	Daley Thompson, G. Britain	8666 pts
1987	Torsten Voss, E Germany	8680 pts
1991	Dan O'Brien, United States	8812 pts.
1993	Dan O'Brien, United States	8817 pts
1995	Dan O'Brien, United States	8695 pts
1997	Tomás Dvorák, Czech Rep.	8837 pts
1999	Tomás Dvorák, Czech Rep.	8744 pts
2001	Tomás Dvorák, Czech Rep.	8902 pts
2003	Tom Pappas, United States	8750 pts

WR=World record.

Women

100 METERS

1983	Marlies Gohr, E Germany	10.97
1987	Silke Gladisch, E Germany	10.90
1991	Katrin Krabbe, Germany	10.99
1993	Gail Devers, United States	10.82
1995	Gwen Torrence, United States	10.85
1997	Marion Jones, United States	10.83
1999	Marion Jones, United States	10.70
2001	Zhanna Pintusevich-Block, Ukraine	10.82
2003	Kelli White, United States	10.85

200 METERS

1983	Marita Koch, E Germany	22.13
1987	Silke Gladisch, E Germany	21.74
1991	Katrin Krabbe, Germany	22.09
1993	Merlene Ottey, Jamaica	21.98
1995	Merlene Ottey, Jamaica	22.12
1997	Zhanna Pintusevich, Ukraine	22.32
1999	Inger Miller, United States	21.77
2001	Marion Jones, United States	22.39
2003	Kelli White, United States	22.05

400 METERS

1983	Jarmila Kratochvilova, Czech.	47.99
1987	Olga Bryzgina, USSR	49.38
1991	Marie-José Pérec, France	49.13
1993	Jearl Miles, United States	49.82
1995	Marie-José Pérec, France	49.28
1997	Cathy Freeman, Australia	49.77
1999	Cathy Freeman, Australia	49.67
2001	Amy Mbacke Thiam, Senegal	49.86
2003	Ana Guevara, Mexico	48.89

800 METERS

1983	Jarmila Kratochvilova, Czech.	1:54.68
1987	Sigrun Wodars, E Germany	1:55.26
1991	Lilia Nurutdinova, USSR	1:57.50
1993	Maria Mutola, Mozambique	1:55.43
1995	Ana Quirot, Cuba	1:56.11
1997	Ana Quirot, Cuba	1:57.14
1999	Ludmila Formanová, Czech Rep.	1:56.68
2001	Maria Mutola, Mozambique	1:57.17
2003	Maria Mutola, Mozambique	1:59.89

1,500 METERS

1983	Mary Slaney, United States	4:00.90
1987	Tatyana Samolenko, USSR	3:58.56
1991	Hassiba Boulmerka, Algeria	4:02.21
1993	Dong Liu, China	4:00.50
1995	Hassiba Boulmerka, Algeria	4:02.42
1997	Carla Sacramento, Portugal	4:04.24
1999	Svetlana Masterkova, Russia	3:59.53
2001	Gabriela Szabo, Romania	4:00.57
2003	Tatyana Tomashova, Russia	3:58.52

3,000 METERS

1983	Mary Slaney, United States	8:34.62
1987	Tatyana Samolenko, USSR	8:38.73
1991	Tatyana Dorovskikh, USSR	8:35.82
1993	Qu Yunxia, China	8:28.71

5,000 METERS

1995	Sonia O'Sullivan, Ireland	14:46.47
1997	Gabriela Szabo, Romania	14:57.68
1999	Gabriela Szabo, Romania	14:41.82
2001	Olga Yegorova, Russia	15:03.39
2003	Tirunesh Dibaba, Ethiopia	14:51.72

10,000 METERS

1987	Ingrid Kristiansen, Norway	31:05.85
1991	Liz McColgan, Great Britain	31:14.31
1993	Wang Junxia, China	30:49:30
1995	Fernanda Ribeiro, Portugal	31:04.99
1997	Sally Barsosio, Kenya	31:32.92
1999	Gete Wami, Ethiopia	30:24.56
2001	Derartu Tulu, Ethiopia	31:48.81
2003	Berhane Adere, Ethiopia	30:04.18

*400 meters short.

MARATHON

1983	Grete Waitz, Norway	2:28:09
1987	Rosa Mota, Portugal	2:25:17
1991	Wanda Panfil, Poland	2:29:53
1993	Junko Asari, Japan	2:30:03
1995	Manuela Machado, Portugal	2:25:39*
1997	Hiromi Suzuki, Japan	2:29:48
1999	Jong Song-Ok, N Korea	2:26:59
2001	Lidia Simon, Romania	2:26.01
2003	Catherine Ndereba, Kenya	2:23:55

100-METER HURDLES

1983	Bettine Jahn, E Germany	12.35
1987	Ginka Zagorcheva, Bulgaria	12.34
1991	Lyudmila Narozhilenko, USSR	12.59
1993	Gail Devers, United States	12.46
1995	Gail Devers, United States	12.68
1997	Ludmila Engquist, Sweden	12.50
1999	Gail Devers, United States	12.37
2001	Anjanette Kirkland, United States	12.42
2003	Perdita Felicien, Canada	12.53

400-METER HURDLES

1983	Yekaterina Fesenko, USSR	54.14
1987	Sabine Busch, E Germany	53.62
1991	Tatyana Ledovskaya, USSR	53.11
1993	Sally Gunnell, Great Britain	52.74 WR
1995	Kim Batten, United States	52.61
1997	Nezha Bidouane, Morocco	52.97
1999	Daimi Pernia, Cuba	52.89
2001	Nezha Bidouane, Morocco	53.34
2003	Jana Pittman, Australia	53.22

10-KILOMETER WALK

1987	Irina Strakhova, USSR	44:12
1991	Alina Ivanova, USSR	42:57
1993	Sari Essayah, Finland	42:59
1995	Irina Stankina, Russia	42:13
1997	Annarita Sidoti, Italy	42:56

20-KILOMETER WALK

1999	Hongyu Liu, China	1:30:50
2001	Olimpiada Ivanova, Russia	1:27:48
2003	Yelena Nikolayeva, Russia	1:26:52

4 X 100-METER RELAY

1983	E Germany (S. Gladisch, M. Koch, I. Auerswald, M. Gohr)	41.76
1987	United States (A. Brown, D. Williams, F. Griffith, P. Marshall)	41.58
1991	Jamaica (Dalia Duhaney, Juliet Cuthbert, Beverley McDonald, Merlene Ottey)	41.94
1993	Russia (Olga Bogoslovskaya, Galina Malchugina, Natalya Voronova, Irina Privalova)	41.49
1995	United States (Celena Mondie-Milner, Carlette Guidry, Chryste Gaines, Gwen Torrence)	42.12
1997	United States (C. Gaines, M. Jones, I. Miller, G.Devers)	41.47
1999	Bahamas (S. Fynes, C. Sturrup, P. Davis-Thompson, D. Ferguson)	41.92
2001	United States (Kelli White, Chryste Gaines, Inger Miller, Marion Jones)	41.71
2003	France (P. Girard, M. Hurtis S. Félix, C. Arron)	41.78

4 X 400-METER RELAY

1983	E Germany (Kerstin Walther, Sabine Busch, Marita Koch, Dagmar Rubsam)	3:19.73

World Track and Field Championships *(Cont.)*

Women *(Cont.)*

4 X 400-METER RELAY *(CONT.)*

1987	E Germany (Dagmar Neubauer, Kirsten Emmelmann, Petra Müller, Sabine Busch)	3:18.63
1991	USSR (Tatyana Ledovskaya, Lyudmila Dzhigalova, Olga Nazarova, Olga Bryzgina)	3:18.43
1993	United States (Gwen Torrence, Maicel Malone, Natasha Kaiser-Brown, Jearl Miles)	3:16.71
1995	United States (Kim Graham, Rochelle Stevens, Camara Jones, Jearl Miles)	3:22.39
1997	Germany (A. Feller, U. Rohlander, A. Rucker, G. Breuer)	3:20.92
1999	Russia (Tatyana Chebykina, Svetlana Goncharenko, Olga Kotylarova, Natalya Nazarova)	3:21.98
2001	Jamaica (Sandie Richards, Catherine Scott, Debbie Ann Parris, Lorraine Fenton)	3:20.65
2003	United States (M. Barber, D. Washington, J. Miles-Clark, S. Richards)	3:22.63

HIGH JUMP

1983	Tamara Bykova, USSR	6 ft 7 in
1987	Stefka Kostadinova, Bulgaria	6 ft 10¼ in
1991	Heike Henkel, Germany	6 ft 8¾ in
1993	Ioamnet Quintero, Cuba	6 ft 6¼ in
1995	Stefka Kostadinova, Bulgaria	6 ft 7 in
1997	Hanne Haugland, Norway	6 ft 6¼ in
1999	Inga Babakova, Ukraine	6 ft 6¼ in
2001	Hestrie Cloete, S Africa	6 ft 6¾ in
2003	Hestrie Cloete, S Africa	6 ft 9 in

POLE VAULT

1999	Stacy Dragila, U.S.	15 ft 1 in EWR
2001	Stacy Dragila, United States	15 ft 7 in
2003	Svetlana Feofanova, Russia	15 ft 7 in

LONG JUMP

1983	Heike Daute, E Germany	23 ft 10¼ in
1987	Jackie Joyner-Kersee, U.S.	24 ft 1¾ in
1991	Jackie Joyner-Kersee, U.S.	24 ft ¼ in
1993	Heike Drechsler, Germany	23 ft 4 in
1995	Fiona May, Italy	22 ft 10¾ in
1997	Lyudmila Galkina, Russia	23 ft 1¾ in
1999	Niurka Montalvo, Spain	23 ft 2 in
2001	Fiona May, Italy	23 ft ½ in
2003	Eunice Barber, France	22 ft 11 in

WR=World record. EWR=equals world record.

TRIPLE JUMP

1993	Ana Biryukova, Russia	49 ft 6 ¼ in WR
1995	Inessa Kravets, Ukraine	50 ft 10¼ in WR
1997	S. Kasparkova, Czech Rep.	49 ft 10½ in
1999	Paraskevi Tsiamíta, Greece	48 ft 10 in
2001	Tatyana Lebedeva, Russia	50 ft ½ in
2003	Tatyana Lebedeva, Russia	49 ft 9½ in

SHOT PUT

1983	Helena Fibingerova, Czech.	69 ft ¾ in
1987	Natalya Lisovskaya, USSR	69 ft 8¼ in
1991	Zhihong Huang, China	68 ft 4¼ in
1993	Zhihong Huang, China	67 ft 6 in
1995	Astrid Kumbernuss, Germany	69 ft 7½ in
1997	Astrid Kumbernuss, Germany	67 ft 11½ in
1999	Astrid Kumbernuss, Germany	65 ft 1½ in
2001	Yanina Korolchik, Belarus	67 ft 7½ in
2003	Svetlana Krivelyova, Russia	67 ft 8 in

HAMMER THROW

1999	Mihaela Melinte, Romania	246 ft 9 in
2001	Yipsi Moreno, Cuba	231 ft 9 in
2003	Yipsi Moreno, Cuba	240 ft 7 in

DISCUS THROW

1983	Martina Opitz, E Germany	226 ft 2 in
1987	Martina Hellmann, E Germany	235 ft
1991	Tsvetanka Khristova, Bulgaria	233 ft
1993	Olga Burova, Russia	221 ft 1 in
1995	Ellina Zvereva, Belarus	225 ft 2 in
1997	Beatrice Faumuina, New Zeal.	219 ft 3 in
1999	Franka Dietzsch, Germany	223 ft 7 in
2001	Natalya Sadova, Russia	224 ft 11 in
2003	Irina Yatchenko, Bulgaria	220 ft 10½ in

JAVELIN

1983	Tiina Lillak, Finland	232 ft 4 in
1987	Fatima Whitbread, G.B.	251 ft 5 in
1991	Demei Xu, China	225 ft 8 in
1993	Trine Hattestad, Finland	227 ft
1995	Natalya Shikolenko, Belarus	221 ft 8 in
1997	Trine Hattestad, Norway	225 ft 8 in
1999	Miréla Manjani-Tzelili, Greece	220 ft 1 in
2001	Osleidys Menéndez, Cuba	228 ft 1 in
2003	Miréla Manjani, Greece	218 ft 3 in

HEPTATHLON

1983	Ramona Neubert, E Germany	6714 pts
1987	Jackie Joyner-Kersee, U.S.	7128 pts
1991	Sabine Braun, Germany	6672 pts
1993	Jackie Joyner-Kersee, U.S.	6837 pts
1995	Ghada Shouaa, Syria	6651 pts
1997	Sabine Braun, Germany	6739 pts
1999	Eunice Barber, France	6861 pts
2001	Yelena Prokhorova, Russia	6694 pts
2003	Carolina Klüft, Sweden	7001 pts

Track and Field News Athlete of the Year

Each year (since 1959 for men and since 1974 for women) *Track and Field News* has chosen the outstanding athlete in the sport.

Year	Athlete	Event
1959	Martin Lauer, W Germany	110H/Decath
1960	Rafer Johnson, United States	Decathlon
1961	Ralph Boston, United States	Long jump
1962	Peter Snell, New Zealand	800/1,500
1963	C. K. Yang, Taiwan	Decath/PV
1964	Peter Snell, New Zealand	800/1,500
1965	Ron Clarke, Australia	5K/10K
1966	Jim Ryun, United States	800/1,500
1967	Jim Ryun, United States	1,500
1968	Bob Beamon, United States	Long jump
1969	Bill Toomey, United States	Decathlon
1970	Randy Matson, United States	Shot put
1971	Rod Milburn, United States	110H
1972	Lasse Viren, Finland	5K/10K
1973	Ben Jipcho, Kenya	1,500/5K/ST
1974	Rick Wohlhuter, United States	800/1,500
1975	John Walker, New Zealand	800/1,500
1976	Alberto Juantorena, Cuba	400/800
1977	Alberto Juantorena, Cuba	400/800
1978	Henry Rono, Kenya	5K/10K/ST
1979	Sebastian Coe, Great Britain	800/1,500
1980	Edwin Moses, United States	400H
1981	Sebastian Coe, Great Britain	800/1,500
1982	Carl Lewis, United States	100/200/LJ
1983	Carl Lewis, United States	100/200/LJ
1984	Carl Lewis, United States	100/200/LJ
1985	Said Aouita, Morocco	1,500/5000
1986	Yuri Syedikh, USSR	Hammer

Track and Field News Athlete of the Year (Cont.)

MEN (CONT.)

Year	Athlete	Event
1987	Ben Johnson, Canada	100
1988	Sergei Bubka, USSR	Pole vault
1989	Roger Kingdom, United States	110H
1990	Michael Johnson, United States	200/400
1991	Sergei Bubka, CIS	Pole vault
1992	Kevin Young, United States	400H
1993	Noureddine Morceli, Algeria	1,500/mile/3K
1994	Noureddine Morceli, Algeria	1,500/mile/3K
1995	Haile Gebrselassie, Ethiopia	5K/10K
1996	Michael Johnson, United States	200/400
1997	Wilson Kipketer, Denmark	800
1998	Haile Gebrselassie, Ethiopia	5K/10K
1999	Hicham El Guerrouj, Morocco	1,500/Mile
2000	Virgilijus Alekna, Lithuania	Discus
2001	Hicham El Guerrouj, Morocco	1,500/Mile
2002	Hicham El Guerrouj, Morocco	1,500/Mile

WOMEN

Year	Athlete	Event
1974	Irena Szewinska, Poland	100/200/400
1975	Faina Melnik, USSR	Shot/Discus
1976	Tatyana Kazankina, USSR	800/1,500
1977	R. Ackermann, E Germany	High jump
1978	Marita Koch, E Germany	100/200/400
1979	Marita Koch, E Germany	100/200/400

WOMEN (CONT.)

Year	Athlete	Event
1980	Ilona Briesenick, E Germany	Shot put
1981	Evelyn Ashford, United States	100/200
1982	Marita Koch, E Germany	100/200/400
1983	J. Kratochvilova, Czechoslovakia	200/400/800
1984	Evelyn Ashford, United States	100
1985	Marita Koch, E Germany	100/200/400
1986	Jackie Joyner-Kersee, U.S.	LJ/Hept
1987	Jackie Joyner-Kersee, U.S	100H/LJ/Hept
1988	Florence Griffith Joyner, U.S.	100/200
1989	Ana Quirot, Cuba	400/800
1990	Merlene Ottey, Jamaica	100/200
1991	Heike Henkel, Germany	High jump
1992	Heike Drechsler, Germany	Long Jump
1993	Wang Junxia, China	1.5K/3K/10K
1994	Jackie Joyner-Kersee, U.S.	100H/LJ/Hept
1995	Sonia O'Sullivan, Ireland	1,500/3K/5K
1996	Svetlana Masterkova, Russia	800/1,500
1997	Marion Jones, United States	100/200/LJ
1998	Marion Jones, United States	100/200/LJ
1999	Gabriela Szabo, Romania	1,500/5,000
2000	Marion Jones, United States	100/200/LJ
2001	Stacy Dragila, United States	Pole vault
2002	Paula Radcliffe, Great Britain	Marathon

Marathon World Record Progression

Men

Record Holder	Time	Date	Site
John Hayes, United States	2:55:18.4	7-24-08	Shepherd's Bush, London
Robert Fowler, United States	2:52:45.4	1-1-09	Yonkers, NY
James Clark, United States	2:46:52.6	2-12-09	New York City
Albert Raines, United States	2:46:04.6	5-8-09	New York City
Frederick Barrett, Great Britain	2:42:31	5-26-09	Shepherd's Bush, London
Harry Green, Great Britain	2:38:16.2	5-12-13	Shepherd's Bush, London
Alexis Ahlgren, Sweden	2:36:06.6	5-31-13	Shepherd's Bush, London
Johannes Kolehmainen, Finland	2:32:35.8	8-22-20	Antwerp, Belgium
Albert Michelsen, United States	2:29:01.8	10-12-25	Port Chester, NY
Fusashige Suzuki, Japan	2:27:49	3-31-35	Tokyo
Yasuo Ikenaka, Japan	2:26:44	4-3-35	Tokyo
Kitei Son, Japan	2:26:42	11-3-35	Tokyo
Yun Bok Suh, Korea	2:25:39	4-19-47	Boston
James Peters, Great Britain	2:20:42.2	6-14-52	Chiswick, England
James Peters, Great Britain	2:18:40.2	6-13-53	Chiswick, England
James Peters, Great Britain	2:18:34.8	10-4-53	Turku, Finland
James Peters, Great Britain	2:17:39.4	6-26-54	Chiswick, England
Sergei Popov, USSR	2:15:17	8-24-58	Stockholm
Abebe Bikila, Ethiopia	2:15:16.2	9-10-60	Rome
Toru Terasawa, Japan	2:15:15.8	2-17-63	Beppu, Japan
Leonard Edelen, United States	2:14:28	6-15-63	Chiswick, England
Basil Heatley, Great Britain	2:13:55	6-13-64	Chiswick, England
Abebe Bikila, Ethiopia	2:12:11.2	6-21-64	Tokyo
Morio Shigematsu, Japan	2:12:00	6-12-65	Chiswick, England
Derek Clayton, Australia	2:09:36.4	12-3-67	Fukuoka, Japan
Derek Clayton, Australia	2:08:33.6	5-30-69	Antwerp, Belgium
Rob de Castella, Australia	2:08:18	12-6-81	Fukuoka, Japan
Steve Jones, Great Britain	2:08:05	10-21-84	Chicago
Carlos Lopes, Portugal	2:07:12	4-20-85	Rotterdam, Netherlands
Belayneh Dinsamo, Ethiopia	2:06:50	4-17-88	Rotterdam, Netherlands
Ronaldo Da Costa, Brazil	2:06:05	9-20-98	Berlin, Germany
Khalid Khannouchi, Morocco	2:05:42	10-24-99	Chicago
Khalid Khannouchi, United States	2:05:38	4-14-02	London
Paul Tergat, Kenya	2:04:55	9-28-03	Berlin

Women

Record Holder	Time	Date	Site
Dale Greig, Great Britain	3:27:45	5-23-64	Ryde, England
Mildred Simpson, New Zealand	3:19:33	7-21-64	Auckland, New Zealand
Maureen Wilton, Canada	3:15:22	5-6-67	Toronto
Anni Pede-Erdkamp, W Germany	3:07:26	9-16-67	Waldniel, W Germany
Caroline Walker, United States	3:02:53	2-28-70	Seaside, OR

Women (Cont.)

Record Holder	Time	Date	Site
Elizabeth Bonner, United States	3:01:42	5-9-71	Philadelphia
Adrienne Beames, Australia	2:46:30	8-31-71	Werribee, Australia
Chantal Langlace, France	2:46:24	10-27-74	Neuf Brisach, France
Jacqueline Hansen, United States	2:43:54.5	12-1-74	Culver City, CA
Liane Winter, W Germany	2:42:24	4-21-75	Boston
Christa Vahlensieck, W Germany	2:40:15.8	5-3-75	Dülmen, W Germany
Jacqueline Hansen, United States	2:38:19	10-12-75	Eugene, OR
Chantal Langlace, France	2:35:15.4	5-1-77	Oyarzun, France
Christa Vahlensieck, W Germany	2:34:47.5	9-10-77	Berlin, W Germany
Grete Waitz, Norway	2:32:29.9	10-22-78	New York City
Grete Waitz, Norway	2:27:32.6	10-21-79	New York City
Grete Waitz, Norway	2:25:41.3	10-26-80	New York City
Grete Waitz, Norway	2:25:29	4-17-83	London
Joan Benoit Samuelson, United States	2:22:43	4-18-83	Boston
Ingrid Kristiansen, Norway	2:21:06	4-21-85	London
Tegla Loroupe, Kenya	2:20:47	4-19-98	Rotterdam, Netherlands
Tegla Loroupe, Kenya	2:20:43	9-26-99	Berlin
Naoko Takahashi, Japan	2:19:46	9-30-01	Berlin
Catherine Ndereba, Kenya	2:18:47	10-7-01	Chicago
Paula Radcliffe, Great Britain	2:17:18	10-13-02	Chicago
Paula Radcliffe, Great Britain	2:15:25	4-13-03	London

Boston Marathon

The Boston Marathon began in 1897 as a local Patriot's Day event. Run every year but 1918 since then, it has grown into one of the world's premier marathons.

Men

Year	Winner	Time	Year	Winner	Time
1897	John J. McDermott, United States	2:55:10	1940	Gerard Cote, Canada	2:28:28
1898	Ronald J. McDonald, United States	2:42:00	1941	Leslie Pawson, United States	2:30:38
1899	Lawrence J. Brignolia, United States	2:54:38	1942	Bernard Joseph Smith, United States	2:26:51
1900	James J. Caffrey, Canada	2:39:44	1943	Gerard Cote, Canada	2:28:25
1901	James J. Caffrey, Canada	2:29:23	1944	Gerard Cote, Canada	2:31:50
1902	Sammy Mellor, United States	2:43:12	1945	John A. Kelley, United States	2:30:40
1903	John C. Lorden, United States	2:41:29	1946	Stylianos Kyriakides, Greece	2:29:27
1904	Michael Spring, United States	2:38:04	1947	Yun Bok Suh, Korea	2:25:39
1905	Fred Lorz, United States	2:38:25	1948	Gerard Cote, Canada	2:31:02
1906	Timothy Ford, United States	2:45:45	1949	Karl Gosta Leandersson, Sweden	2:31:50
1907	Tom Longboat, Canada	2:24:24	1950	Kee Yong Ham, Korea	2:32:39
1908	Thomas Morrissey, United States	2:25:43	1951	Shigeki Tanaka, Japan	2:27:45
1909	Henri Renaud, United States	2:53:36	1952	Doroteo Flores, Guatemala	2:31:53
1910	Fred Cameron, Canada	2:28:52	1953	Keizo Yamada, Japan	2:18:51
1911	Clarence H. DeMar, United States	2:21:39	1954	Veikko Karvonen, Finland	2:20:39
1912	Mike Ryan, United States	2:21:18	1955	Hideo Hamamura, Japan	2:18:22
1913	Fritz Carlson, United States	2:25:14	1956	Antti Viskari, Finland	2:14:14
1914	James Duffy, Canada	2:25:01	1957	John J. Kelley, United States	2:20:05
1915	Edouard Fabre, Canada	2:31:41	1958	Franjo Mihalic, Yugoslavia	2:25:54
1916	Arthur Roth, United States	2:27:16	1959	Eino Oksanen, Finland	2:22:42
1917	Bill Kennedy, United States	2:28:37	1960	Paavo Kotila, Finland	2:20:54
1918	No race		1961	Eino Oksanen, Finland	2:23:39
1919	Carl Linder, United States	2:29:13	1962	Eino Oksanen, Finland	2:23:48
1920	Peter Trivoulidas, Greece	2:29:31	1963	Aurele Vandendriessche, Belgium	2:18:58
1921	Frank Zuna, United States	2:18:57	1964	Aurele Vandendriessche, Belgium	2:19:59
1922	Clarence H. DeMar, United States	2:18:10	1965	Morio Shigematsu, Japan	2:16:33
1923	Clarence H. DeMar, United States	2:23:37	1966	Kenji Kimihara, Japan	2:17:11
1924	Clarence H. DeMar, United States	2:29:40	1967	David McKenzie, New Zealand	2:15:45
1925	Chuck Mellor, United States	2:33:00	1968	Amby Burfoot, United States	2:22:17
1926	John C. Miles, Canada	2:25:40	1969	Yoshiaki Unetani, Japan	2:13:49
1927	Clarence H. DeMar, United States	2:40:22	1970	Ron Hill, England	2:10:30
1928	Clarence H. DeMar, United States	2:37:07	1971	Alvaro Mejia, Colombia	2:18:45
1929	John C. Miles, Canada	2:33:08	1972	Olavi Suomalainen, Finland	2:15:39
1930	Clarence H. DeMar, United States	2:34:48	1973	Jon Anderson, United States	2:16:03
1931	James (Hinky) Henigan, United States	2:46:45	1974	Neil Cusack, Ireland	2:13:39
1932	Paul de Bruyn, Germany	2:33:36	1975	Bill Rodgers, United States	2:09:55
1933	Leslie Pawson, United States	2:31:01	1976	Jack Fultz, United States	2:20:19
1934	Dave Komonen, Canada	2:32:53	1977	Jerome Drayton, Canada	2:14:46
1935	John A. Kelley, United States	2:32:07	1978	Bill Rodgers, United States	2:10:13
1936	Ellison M. (Tarzan) Brown, United States	2:33:40	1979	Bill Rodgers, United States	2:09:27
1937	Walter Young, Canada	2:33:20	1980	Bill Rodgers, United States	2:12:11
1938	Leslie Pawson, United States	2:35:34	1981	Toshihiko Seko, Japan	2:09:26
1939	Ellison M. (Tarzan) Brown, United States	2:28:51	1982	Alberto Salazar, United States	2:08:52

Boston Marathon (Cont.)

Year	Winner	Time	Year	Winner	Time
1983	Gregory A. Meyer, United States	2:09:00	1973	Jacqueline A. Hansen, United States	3:05:59
1984	Geoff Smith, England	2:10:34	1974	Miki Gorman, United States	2:47:11
1985	Geoff Smith, England	2:14:05	1975	Liane Winter, W Germany	2:42:24
1986	Rob de Castella, Australia	2:07:51	1976	Kim Merritt, United States	2:47:10
1987	Toshihiko Seko, Japan	2:11:50	1977	Miki Gorman, United States	2:48:33
1988	Ibrahim Hussein, Kenya	2:08:43	1978	Gayle Barron, United States	2:44:52
1989	Abebe Mekonnen, Ethiopia	2:09:06	1979	Joan Benoit, United States	2:35:15
1990	Gelindo Bordin, Italy	2:08:19	1980	Jacqueline Gareau, Canada	2:34:28
1991	Ibrahim Hussein, Kenya	2:11:06	1981	Allison Roe, New Zealand	2:26:46
1992	Ibrahim Hussein, Kenya	2:08:14	1982	Charlotte Teske, W Germany	2:29:33
1993	Cosmas N'Deti, Kenya	2:09:33	1983	Joan Benoit, United States	2:22:43
1994	Cosmas N'Deti, Kenya	2:07:15	1984	Lorraine Moller, New Zealand	2:29:28
1995	Cosmas N'Deti, Kenya	2:09:22	1985	Lisa Larsen Weidenbach, United States	2:34:06
1996	Moses Tanui, Kenya	2:09:16	1986	Ingrid Kristiansen, Norway	2:24:55
1997	Lameck Aguta, Kenya	2:10:34	1987	Rosa Mota, Portugal	2:25:21
1998	Moses Tanui, Kenya	2:07:34	1988	Rosa Mota, Portugal	2:24:30
1999	Joseph Chebet, Kenya	2:09:52	1989	Ingrid Kristiansen, Norway	2:24:33
2000	Elijah Lagat, Kenya	2:09:47	1990	Rosa Mota, Portugal	2:25:24
2001	Lee Bong-Ju, Korea	2:09:43	1991	Wanda Panfil, Poland	2:24:18
2002	Rodgers Rop, Kenya	2:09:02	1992	Olga Markova, Russia	2:23:43
2003	Robert Cheruiyot, Kenya	2:10:11	1993	Olga Markova, Russia	2:25:27
			1994	Uta Pippig, Germany	2:21:45

Women

Year	Winner	Time			
			1995	Uta Pippig, Germany	2:25:11
1966	Roberta Gibb, United States	3:21:40*	1996	Uta Pippig, Germany	2:27:12
1967	Roberta Gibb, United States	3:27:17*	1997	Fatuma Roba, Ethiopia	2:26:23
1968	Roberta Gibb, United States	3:30:00*	1998	Fatuma Roba, Ethiopia	2:23:21
1969	Sara Mae Berman, United States	3:22:46*	1999	Fatuma Roba, Ethiopia	2:23:25
1970	Sara Mae Berman, United States	3:05:07*	2000	Catherine Ndereba, Kenya	2:26:11
1971	Sara Mae Berman, United States	3:08:30*	2001	Catherine Ndereba, Kenya	2:23:53
1972	Nina Kuscsik, United States	3:10:36	2002	Margaret Okayo, Kenya	2:20:43
			2003	Svetlana Zakharova, Russia	2:25:20

Note: Over the years the Boston course has varied in length. The distances have been 24 miles, 1,232 yards (1897–1923); 26 miles, 209 yards (1924–1926); 26 miles, 385 yards (1927–1952); and 25 miles, 958 yards (1953–1956). Since 1957, the course has been certified to be the standard marathon distance of 26 miles, 385 yards. (*Unofficial.)

New York City Marathon

MEN			WOMEN		
Year	Winner	Time	Year	Winner	Time
1970	Gary Muhrcke, United States	2:31:38	1970	No finisher	
1971	Norman Higgins, United States	2:22:54	1971	Beth Bonner, United States	2:55:22
1972	Sheldon Karlin, United States	2:27:52	1972	Nina Kuscsik, United States	3:08:41
1973	Tom Fleming, United States	2:21:54	1973	Nina Kuscsik, United States	2:57:07
1974	Norbert Sander, United States	2:26:30	1974	Katherine Switzer, United States	3:07:29
1975	Tom Fleming, United States	2:19:27	1975	Kim Merritt, United States	2:46:14
1976	Bill Rodgers, United States	2:10:10	1976	Miki Gorman, United States	2:39:11
1977	Bill Rodgers, United States	2:11:28	1977	Miki Gorman, United States	2:43:10
1978	Bill Rodgers, United States	2:12:12	1978	Grete Waitz, Norway	2:32:30
1979	Bill Rodgers, United States	2:11:42	1979	Grete Waitz, Norway	2:27:33
1980	Alberto Salazar, United States	2:09:41	1980	Grete Waitz, Norway	2:25:41
1981	Alberto Salazar, United States	2:08:13	1981	Allison Roe, New Zealand	2:25:29
1982	Alberto Salazar, United States	2:09:29	1982	Grete Waitz, Norway	2:27:14
1983	Rod Dixon, New Zealand	2:08:59	1983	Grete Waitz, Norway	2:27:00
1984	Orlando Pizzolato, Italy	2:14:53	1984	Grete Waitz, Norway	2:29:30
1985	Orlando Pizzolato, Italy	2:11:34	1985	Grete Waitz, Norway	2:28:34
1986	Gianni Poli, Italy	2:11:06	1986	Grete Waitz, Norway	2:28:06
1987	Ibrahim Hussein, Kenya	2:11:01	1987	Priscilla Welch, Great Britain	2:30:17
1988	Steve Jones, Great Britain	2:20:20	1988	Grete Waitz, Norway	2:28:07
1989	Juma Ikangaa, Tanzania	2:08:01	1989	Ingrid Kristiansen, Norway	2:25:30
1990	Douglas Wakiihuri, Kenya	2:12:39	1990	Wanda Panfiil, Poland	2:30:45
1991	Salvador Garcia, Mexico	2:09:28	1991	Liz McColgan, Scotland	2:27:23
1992	Willie Mtolo, S Africa	2:09:29	1992	Lisa Ondieki, Australia	2:24:40
1993	Andres Espinosa, Mexico	2:10:04	1993	Uta Pippig, Germany	2:26:24
1994	German Silva, Mexico	2:11:21	1994	Tegla Loroupe, Kenya	2:27:37
1995	German Silva, Mexico	2:11:00	1995	Tegla Loroupe, Kenya	2:28:06
1996	Giacomo Leone, Italy	2:09:54	1996	Anuta Catuna, Romania	2:28:18
1997	John Kagwe, Kenya	2:08:12	1997	Franziska Rochat-Moser, Switzerland	2:28:43
1998	John Kagwe, Kenya	2:08:45	1998	Franca Fiacconi, Italy	2:25:17
1999	Joseph Chebet, Kenya	2:09:14	1999	Adriana Fernandez, Mexico	2:25:06
2000	Abdelkhader El Mouaziz, Morocco	2:10:09	2000	Ludmila Petrova, Russia	2:25:45
2001	Tesfaye Jifar, Ethiopia	2:07:43	2001	Margaret Okayo, Kenya	2:24:21
2002	Rodgers Rop, Kenya	2:08:07	2002	Joyce Chepchumba, Kenya	2:25:56

World Cross-Country Championships

Conducted by the International Amateur Athletic Federation (IAAF), this meet annually brings together the best runners in the world at every distance from the mile to the marathon to compete in the same cross-country race.

Men

Year	Winner	Winning Team	Year	Winner	Winning Team
1973	Pekka Paivarinta, Finland	Belgium	1989	John Ngugi, Kenya	Kenya
1974	Eric DeBeck, Belgium	Belgium	1990	Khalid Skah, Morocco	Kenya
1975	Ian Stewart, Scotland	New Zealand	1991	Khalid Skah, Morocco	Kenya
1976	Carlos Lopes, Portugal	England	1992	John Ngugi, Kenya	Kenya
1977	Leon Schots, Belgium	Belgium	1993	William Sigei, Kenya	Kenya
1978	John Treacy, Ireland	France	1994	William Sigei, Kenya	Kenya
1979	John Treacy, Ireland	England	1995	Paul Tergat, Kenya	Kenya
1980	Craig Virgin, United States	England	1996	Paul Tergat, Kenya	Kenya
1981	Craig Virgin, United States	Ethiopia	1997	Paul Tergat, Kenya	Kenya
1982	Mohammed Kedir, Ethiopia	Ethiopia	1998	Paul Tergat, Kenya	Kenya
1983	Bekele Debele, Ethiopia	Ethiopia	1999	Paul Tergat, Kenya	Kenya
1984	Carlos Lopes, Portugal	Ethiopia	2000	Mohammed Mourhit, Belgium	Kenya
1985	Carlos Lopes, Portugal	Ethiopia	2001	Mohammed Mourhit, Belgium	Kenya
1987	John Ngugi, Kenya	Kenya	2002	Kenenisa Bekele , Ethiopia	Kenya
1988	John Ngugi, Kenya	Kenya	2003	Kenenisa Bekele, Ethiopia	Kenya

Women

Year	Winner	Winning Team	Year	Winner	Winning Team
1973	Paola Cacchi, Italy	England	1989	Annette Sergent, France	USSR
1974	Paola Cacchi, Italy	England	1990	Lynn Jennings, United States	USSR
1975	Julie Brown, United States	United States	1991	Lynn Jennings, United States	Kenya
1976	Carmen Valero, Spain	USSR	1992	Lynn Jennings, United States	Kenya
1977	Carmen Valero, Spain	USSR	1993	Albertina Dias, Portugal	Kenya
1978	Grete Waitz, Norway	Romania	1994	Helen Chepngeno, Kenya	Portugal
1979	Grete Waitz, Norway	United States	1995	Derartu Tulu, Ethiopia	Kenya
1980	Grete Waitz, Norway	USSR	1996	Gete Wami, Ethiopia	Kenya
1981	Grete Waitz, Norway	USSR	1997	Derartu Tulu, Ethiopia	Ethiopia
1982	Maricica Puica, Romania	USSR	1998	Sonia O'Sullivan, Ireland	Kenya
1983	Grete Waitz, Norway	United States	1999	Gete Wami, Ethiopia	Ethiopia
1984	Maricica Puica, Romania	United States	2000	Derartu Tulu, Ethiopia	Ethiopia
1985	Zola Budd, England	United States	2001	Paula Radcliffe, Great Britain	Kenya
1986	Zola Budd, England	England	2002	Paula Radcliffe, Great Britain	Ethiopia
1987	Annette Sergent, France	United States	2003	Werknesh Kidane, Ethiopia	Ethiopia
1988	Ingrid Kristiansen, Norway	USSR			

Notable Achievements

Longest Winning Streaks

MEN

Event	Name and Nationality	Streak	Years
100 meters	Bob Hayes, United States	49	1962–64
200 meters	Manfred Gemar, Germany	41	1956–60
400 meters	Michael Johnson, United States	58	1989–97
800 meters	Mal Whitfield, United States	40	1951–54
1,500 meters	Hicham El Guerrouj, Morocco	23	1996–00
1,500 meters/mile	Steve Ovett, Great Britain	45	1977–80
Mile	Herb Elliott, Australia	35	1957–60
Steeplechase	Gaston Roelants, Belgium	45	1961–66
5,000 meters	Emil Zátopek, Czechoslovakia	48	1949–52
10,000 meters	Emil Zátopek, Czechoslovakia	38	1948–54
Marathon	Frank Shorter, United States	6	1971–73
110-meter hurdles	Jack Davis, United States	44	1952–55
400-meter hurdles	Edwin Moses, United States	107	1977–87
High jump	Ernie Shelton, United States	46	1953–55
Pole vault	Bob Richards, United States	50	1950–52
Long jump	Carl Lewis, United States	65	1981–91
Triple jump	Adhemar da Silva, Brazil	60	1950–56
Shot put	Parry O'Brien, United States	116	1952–56
Discus throw	Ricky Bruch, Sweden	54	1972–73
Hammer throw	Imre Nemeth, Hungary	73	1946–50
Javelin throw	Janis Lusis, USSR	41	1967–70
Decathlon	Bob Mathias, United States	11	1948–56

Longest Winning Streaks (Cont.)

WOMEN

Event	Name and Nationality	Streak	Years
100 meters	Merlene Ottey, Jamaica	56	1987–91
200 meters	Irena Szewinska, Poland	38	1973–75
400 meters	Irena Szewinska, Poland	36	1973–78
800 meters	Ana Fidelia Quirot, Cuba	36	1987–90
1,500 meters	Paula Ivan, Romania	15	1988–91
1,500 meters/mile	Paula Ivan, Romania	19	1988–90
3,000 meters	Mary Slaney, United States	10	1982–84
10,000 meters	Ingrid Kristiansen, Norway	5	1985–87
Marathon	Katrin Dörre, E Germany	10	1982–86
100-meter hurdles	Annelie Ernhardt, E Germany	44	1972–75
400-meter hurdles	Ann-Louise Skoglund, Sweden	18	1981–83
High jump	Iolanda Balas, Romania	140	1956–67
Long jump	Tatyana Shchelkanova, USSR	19	1964–66
Shot put	Nadezhda Chizhova, USSR	57	1969–73
Discus throw	Gisela Mauermeyer, Germany	65	1935–42
Javelin throw	Ruth Fuchs, E Germany	30	1972–73
Multi	Heide Rosendahl, W Germany	15	1969–72

Most Consecutive Years Ranked No. 1 in the World

MEN

No.	Name and Nationality	Event	Years
11	Sergei Bubka, Ukraine	Pole vault	1984–94
9	Viktor Saneyev, USSR	Triple jump	1968–76
8	Bob Richards, United States	Pole vault	1949–56
8	Ralph Boston, United States	Long jump	1960–67

WOMEN

No.	Name and Nationality	Event	Years
9	Iolanda Balas, Romania	High jump	1958–66
8	Ruth Fuchs, E Germany	Javelin	1972–79
7	Faina Melnick, USSR	Discus throw	1971–77

Major Barrier Breakers

MEN

Event	Mark	Name and Nationality	Date	Site
sub 10-second 100 meters	9.95	Jim Hines, United States	Oct. 14, 1968	Mexico City
sub 20-second 200 meters	19.83	Tommie Smith, United States	Oct. 16, 1968	Mexico City
sub 45-second 400 meters	44.9	Otis Davis, United States	Sept. 6, 1960	Rome
sub 1:45 800 meters	1:44.3	Peter Snell, New Zealand	Feb. 3, 1962	Christchurch, New Zealand
sub four minute mile	3:59.4	Roger Bannister, Great Britain	May 6, 1954	Oxford
sub 3:50 mile	3:49.4	John Walker, New Zealand	Aug. 12, 1975	Göteborg, Sweden
sub 13-minute 5,000 meters	12:58.39	Said Aouita, Morocco	July 22, 1986	Rome
sub 27:00 10,000 meters	26:58.38	Yobes Ondieki, Kenya	July 10, 1993	Oslo
sub 13-second 110-meter hurdles	12.93	Renaldo Nehemiah, United States	Aug. 19, 1981	Zurich
sub 50-second 400-meter hurdles	49.5	Glenn Davis, United States	June 29, 1956	Los Angeles
7 ft high jump	7 ft ⅝ in	Charles Dumas, United States	June 29, 1956	Los Angeles
8 ft high jump	8 ft	Javier Sotomayor, Cuba	July 29, 1989	San Juan
60 ft triple jump	60 ft ¼ in	Jonathan Edwards, Great Britain	Aug. 7, 1995	Göteborg, Sweden
20 ft pole vault	20 ft	Sergei Bubka, USSR	March 15, 1991	San Sebastian, Spain
70 ft shot put	70 ft 7¼ in	Randy Matson, United States	May 5, 1965	College Station, Texas
200 ft discus throw	200 ft 5 in	Al Oerter, United States	May 18, 1962	Los Angeles
300 ft (new) javelin	300 ft 1 in	Steve Backley, Great Britain	Jan. 25, 1992	Auckland, New Zealand
9,000-pt decathlon	9026	Roman Sebrle, Czech Republic	May 27, 2001	Gotzis, Austria

Major Barrier Breakers (Cont.)

WOMEN

Event	Mark	Name and Nationality	Date	Site
sub 11-second 100 meters	10.88	Marlies Oelsner, E Germany	July 1, 1977	Dresden
sub 22-second 200 meters	21.71	Marita Koch, E Germany	June 10, 1979	Karl Marxstadt, E Germany
sub 50-second 400 meters	49.9	Irena Szewinska, Poland	June 22, 1974	Warsaw
sub 2:00 800 meters	1:59.1	Shin Geum Dan, N Korea	Nov. 12, 1963	Djakarta
sub 4:00 1,500 meters	3:56.0	Tatyana Kazankina, USSR	June 28, 1976	Podolsk, USSR
sub 4:20 mile	4:17.55	Mary Decker, United States	Feb. 16, 1980	Houston
sub 15:00 5,000 meters	14:58.89	Ingrid Kristiansen, Norway	June 28, 1984	Oslo
sub 30:00 10,000 meters	29:31.78	Wang Junxia, China	Sept. 8, 1993	Beijing
sub 2:30 marathon	2:27:33	Grete Waitz, Norway	Oct. 21, 1979	New York City
sub 2:20 marathon	2:19:46	Naoko Takahashi, Japan	Sept. 30, 2001	Berlin
sub 13-second 100-meter hurdles	12.9	Karin Balzer, E Germany	Sept. 5, 1969	Berlin
6 ft high jump	6 ft	Iolanda Balas, Romania	Oct. 18, 1958	Budapest
15 ft pole vault	15 ft ½ in	Emma George, Australia	March 14, 1998	Melbourne
70 ft shot put	70 ft 4½ in	Nadyezhda Chizhova, USSR	Sept. 29, 1973	Varna, Bulgaria
200 ft discus throw	201 ft	Liesel Westermann, W Germany	Nov. 5, 1967	Sao Paulo
200 ft javelin throw	201 ft 4 in	Elvira Ozolina, USSR	Aug. 27, 1964	Kiev
first 7,000-point heptathlon	7,148	Jackie Joyner-Kersee, U.S.	July 6–7, 1986	Moscow

Olympic Accomplishments

Oldest Olympic gold medalist—Patrick (Babe) McDonald, United States, 42 years, 26 days, 56-pound weight throw, 1920.
Oldest Olympic medalist—Tebbs Lloyd Johnson, Great Britain, 48 years, 115 days, 1948 (bronze), 50K walk.
Youngest Olympic gold medalist—Barbara Jones, United States, 15 years 123 days, 1952, 4 x 100 relay.
Youngest gold medalist in individual event—Ulrike Meyfarth, W Germany, 16 years, 123 days, 1972, high jump.

World Record Accomplishments*

Most world records equaled or set in a day—6, Jesse Owens, United States, 5-25-35, (9.4 100 yards; 26' 8¼'' long jump; 20.3 200 meters and 220 yards; and 22.6 220-yard hurdles and 200-meter hurdles.
Most records in a year—10, Gunder Hägg, Sweden, 1941–42, 1,500 to 5,000 meters.
Most records in a career—35, Sergei Bubka, 1983–94, pole vault indoors and out.
Longest span of record setting—11 years, 20 days, Irena Szewinska, Poland, 1965–76, 200 meters.
Youngest person to set a set world record—Carolina Gisolf, Holland, 15 years, 5 days, 1928, high jump, 5 ft 3⅜ in.
Youngest man to set a world record—John Thomas, United States, 17 years, 355 days, 1959, high jump, 7 ft 1¼ in.
Oldest person to set world record—Carlos Lopes, Portugal, 38 years, 59 days, marathon, 2:07:12.
Greatest percentage improvement—6.59, Bob Beamon, United States, 1968, long jump.
Longest lasting record—long jump, 26 ft 8¼ in, Jesse Owens, United States, 25 years, 79 days (1935–60).
Highest clearance over head, men—23¼ in, Franklin Jacobs, United States (5' 8"), 1978.
Highest clearance over head, woman—12¾ in, Yolanda Henry, United States (5' 6"), 1990.

*Marks sanctioned by the IAAF.

Swimming

Legend-in-Waiting

After breaking eight world records in a four-month span of 2003, Michael Phelps took aim at the Athens Olympics

BY MARK BECHTEL

IN APRIL, WHEN 17-year-old Michael Phelps became the first male swimmer to win U.S. titles in three strokes, his fellow American swimmers couldn't help themselves. They started gushing superlatives like a broken water main. "He's raising the bar in swimming the way Michael Jordan did in basketball," said Tom Wilkens, a bronze medalist in the 200 individual medley at the 2000 Sydney Olympics. Lenny Krayzelburg, who won three golds in Sydney, suggested that Phelps's performance meant the U.S. wünderkind was better than his counterpart and predecessor, Ian Thorpe of Australia, a 20-year-old with size 17 feet who won a record six golds at the 2001 world championships. "It's a mistake to call Ian Thorpe the best in the world," said Krayzelburg. "Thorpe is good in freestyle; Phelps is good across the board."

The U.S. swimmers could be forgiven for their hyperbole in assessing a talent like Phelps's, but such talk didn't go over well Down Under. In June, a month before the world championships began in Barcelona, Don Talbot, Australia's former Olympic coach, said that Phelps had accomplished "nothing in the world" compared to Thorpe. "People trying to say [Phelps] is a greater swimmer than Ian ... absolute nonsense," said Talbot. "The promise with Phelps is there, but for people saying he's going to outdo Thorpie, I live to see that day."

That day came a lot sooner than he expected. Phelps won three golds in Barcelona, as did Thorpe, but it was the dominating fashion in which Phelps won that had people talking. He set five world records—including two in less than an hour—and in his first head-to-head meeting with Thorpe at a worlds or Olympic final, he defeated the Aussie by two body lengths in the 200 individual medley, slashing his own world record by a staggering 1.48 seconds, to 1:56.04. (The United States topped the team medal table with 28, including 11 golds.)

Phelps was uninterested in talk of a budding rivalry with Thorpe. The son of a Maryland state trooper and a school teacher, Phelps is a reserved and quiet sort. After he set his first world record, in 2001,

ADAM PRETTY/GETTY IMAGES

**Though he lost to Phelps in the 200 IM,
Thorpe won three gold medals at the worlds.**

he and his sister went to the local Cheese-cake Factory to celebrate. When they learned that the wait for a table would be more than two hours, Phelps and his sis went to a pizza place rather than play up his status as a new world record holder to get earlier service.

Thorpe, by contrast, seems to embrace the spotlight more readily. Not that he's had much of a choice: While Phelps is new on the scene, Thorpe was a celebrity in Australia at age 14. The two do have one prominent feature in common, though: they are both awesome physical specimens. Thorpe's giant flipper-like feet propel him through the water with porpoise-like ease. Phelps, in the words of his coach, Bob Bowman, was simply "made to swim." His 6'4" frame and wide shoulders allow him to cover the length of a 50-meter pool in just 26 strokes, three or four fewer than most swimmers. "We both do the same thing," Phelps said of Thorpe. "It's friendly competition and I think that once we're in the pool we're both tuned in to what we want to do ourselves, and we try to accomplish that."

But no one in the past thirty years was able to accomplish what Phelps did in 2003.

In 1972, Mark Spitz set nine individual world records. From April until late August, when he lowered his own mark in the 200-meter individual medley, Phelps set eight. He also duplicated Spitz's feat of simultaneously holding world records in four individual Olympic events (the 100 and 200 butterfly and the 200 and 400 IM), leading to talk that Phelps might make a legitimate run at Spitz's Olympic record of seven golds next summer in Athens.

Even Spitz was considering the possibility. "He's going to win gold medals in the two individual medleys unless he's hit by a train," Spitz said. "Nobody is in his league in the 200 fly. In his individual program, the 100 fly is the big question mark, because of [teammate Ian] Crocker. Now, when you factor in relay participation, the complexity of trying to pull this off gets kind of weird."

For Phelps to win seven golds, in all likelihood the U.S would need to upset the Russians in the 400-meter freestyle relay and, more improbably, the Aussies in the 800-meter. While Phelps was understandably excited about the impending Games, he was not obsessed with Spitz's landmark record. "Athens is a year away," he said in August. "That's the only focus right now. I'm not trying to be the next Mark Spitz. I'm trying to be the first Michael Phelps."

2002–2003 Major Competitions

Men

U.S. Open
Minneapolis, December 5–7, 2002

50 free	Neil Walker, Circle C	22.59
100 free	Neil Walker, Circle C	49.40
200 free	Joshua Davis, Circle C	1:48.38
400 free	Rick Say, UC Swim Club	3:53.40
1,500 free	C. Thompson, Wolverine	15:22.76
100 back	Lenny Krayzelburg, Trojan SC	55.09
200 back	Keith Beavers, R O W	1:59.75
100 breast	Chad Thomsen, UASC	1:03.59
200 breast	John Stanlius, Pacific Coast	2:18.12
100 fly	Mike Mintenko, UBC Dolphins	52.44
200 fly	Tom Malchow, Wolverine	1:55.66
200 IM	Tamas Kerekjarto, Trojan SC	2:02.66
400 IM	Keith Beavers, R O W	4:24.39
400 m relay	University of Minnesota	3:46.64
400 f relay	Circle C	3:23.77
800 f relay	University of Minnesota	7:33.91

U.S. NATIONAL CHAMPIONSHIPS (SPRING)
Indianapolis, April 1–5, 2003

50 free	Neil Walker, Circle C	22.37
100 free	Scott Tucker, Novaquatics	49.43
200 free	Michael Phelps, N Baltimore	1:47.37
400 free	Klete Keller, Wolverine	3:48.15
800 free	Larsen Jensen, Mission Viejo	7:54.86
1,500 free	C. Thompson, Wolverine	15:00.00
100 back	Lenny Krayzelburg, Trojan SC	54.26
200 back	Michael Phelps, N Baltimore	1:57.04
100 breast	Glenn Moses, Curl-Burke	1:00.21
200 breast	Glenn Moses, Curl-Burke	2:11.22
100 fly	Michael Phelps, N Baltimore	51.89
200 fly	Takashi Yamamoto, R O W	1:58.18
200 IM	Tom Wilkens, Santa Clara SC	2:01.43
400 IM	Tom Wilkens, Santa Clara SC	4:16.75
400 m relay	UBC Dolphins	3:45.20
400 f relay	Circle C	3:20.03
800 f relay	UBC Dolphins	7:19.46

FINA WORLD CHAMPIONSHIPS
Barcelona, July 20–27, 2003

50 free	Alexander Popov, Russia	21.92
100 free	Alexander Popov, Russia	48.42
200 free	Ian Thorpe, Australia	1:45.14
400 free	Ian Thorpe, Australia	3:42.58
800 free	Grant Hackett, Australia	7:43.82
1,500 free	Grant Hackett, Australia	14:43.14
50 back	Thomas Rupprath, Germany	24.80WR
100 back	Aaron Peirsol, United States	53.61
200 back	Aaron Peirsol, United States	1:55.92
50 breast	James Gibson, Great Britain	27.56
100 breast	Kosuke Kitajima, Japan	59.78WR
200 breast	Kosuke Kitajima, Japan	2:09.42WR
50 fly	Matthew Welsh, Australia	23.43WR
100 fly	Ian Crocker, United States	50.98WR
200 fly	Michael Phelps, United States	1:54.35
200 IM	Michael Phelps, United States	1:56.04WR
400 IM	Michael Phelps, United States	4:09.09WR
400 m relay	United States	3:31.54WR
400 f relay	Russia	3:14.06
800 f relay	Australia	7:08.58

FINA DIVING WORLD CHAMPIONSHIPS
Barcelona July 13–20, 2003

1-m spgbd	Xiang Xu, China	431.94
3-m spgbd	Alexander Dobrosok, Russia	788.37
Platform	Alexandre Despatie, Canada	716.91
3-m sync	Alexander Dobrosok/ Dmitry Sautin, Russia	369.18
Platfm sync	Matthew Helm/ Robert Newbery, Australia	384.6

U.S. NATIONAL CHAMPIONSHIPS (SUMMER)
College Park, MD, August 5–9, 2003

50 free	Neil Walker, Circle C	23.14
100 free	Michael Phelps, N Baltimore	49.19
200 free	Michael Phelps, N Baltimore	1:45.99*
400 free	Michael Phelps, N Baltimore	3:46.73*
800 free	Larsen Jensen, Mission Viejo	7:57.35
1,500 free	Larsen Jensen, Mission Viejo	15:11.81
100 back	Randall Bal, Stanford	54.63
200 back	Michael Phelps, N Baltimore	1:56.10
100 breast	Glenn Moses, Curl-Burke	1:01.11
200 breast	Gary Marshall, Stanford	2:13.28
100 fly	Eugene Botes, Big Cat	53.20
200 fly	Brian Johns, Canada	1:59.29
200 IM	Michael Phelps, N Baltimore	1:55.94WR
400 IM	Brian Johns, Canada	4:17.04
400 m relay	Circle C	3:42.61
400 f relay	Circle C	3:21.25
800 f relay	Mission Viejo	7:24.43

*American record. WR World record.

Women

U.S. OPEN
Minneapolis, MN, December 5–7, 2002

50 free	Kara Lynn Joyce, Wolverine	25.20
100 free	Amanda Weir, Swim Atlanta	55.60
200 free	Colleen Lanne, Texas Aquatics	2:02.19
400 free	Sara McLarty, Florida	4:15.64
800 free	Diana Munz, Lake Erie Silver	8:39.71
100 back	Hayley McGregory, Circle C	1:02.47
200 back	Hayley McGregory, Circle C	2:15.75
100 breast	Masami Tanaka, Curl-Burke	1;08.89
200 breast	Masami Tanaka, Curl-Burke	2:26.52
100 fly	Audrey LaCroix, Aquatique	1:01.19
200 fly	Audrey LaCroix, Aquatique	2:12.81
200 IM	Jennifer Forster, Sharks	2:17.52
400 IM	Jennifer Forster, Sharks	4:49.87
400 m relay	Circle C	4:17.60
400 f relay	Pine Crest School	3:51.98
800 f relay	Sun Devil Aquatics	8:24.67

U.S. NATIONAL CHAMPIONSHIPS (SPRING)
Indianapolis, IN, April 1–5, 2003

50 free	Jennifer Thompson, Badger SC	25.02
100 free	Rhiannon Jeffrey, Aqua Crest	55.21
200 free	Lindsay Benko, Trojan SC	2:00.58
400 free	Lindsay Benko, Trojan SC	4:11.34
800 free	Diana Munz, Lake Erie Silver	8:32.17
1,500 free	Flavia Rigamonti, SMU	16:08.30
100 back	Haley Cope, Calif. Aquatics	1:01.37
200 back	Jennifer Fratesi, R O W	2:12.53
100 breast	Tara Kirk, Stanford	1:08.56
200 breast	Agnes Kovacs, Arizona St	2:29.48
100 fly	Misty Hyman, Ariz. Desert Fox	59.74
200 fly	Georgina Lee, SMU	2:09.48
200 IM	Amanda Beard, Tucson Ford	2:14.41
400 IM	Kaitlin Sandeno, Southern Cal	4:45.48
400 m relay	Circle C	4:11.57
400 f relay	SMU	3:48.86
800 f relay	Sun Devil Aquatics	8:13.86

FINA WORLD CHAMPIONSHIPS
Barcelona, July 20–27, 2003

50 free	Inge DeBruijn, Netherlands	24.47
100 free	Hanna-Maria Seppälä, Finland	54.37
200 free	Alena Popchanka, Bulgaria	1:58.32
400 free	Hannah Stockbauer, Germany	4:06.75
800 free	Hannah Stockbauer, Germany	8:23.66
50 back	Nina Zhivanevskaya, Spain	27.38
100 back	Antje Buschschulte, Germany	1:00.50
200 back	Katy Sexton, Great Britain	2:08.74
50 breast	Xuejuan Luo, China	30.67
100 breast	Xuejuan Luo, China	1:06.80
200 breast	Amanda Beard, United States	2:22.99WR
50 fly	Inge DeBruijn, Netherlands	25.84
100 fly	Jenny Thompson, United States	57.96
200 fly	Otylia Jedrzejczak, Poland	2:07.56
200 IM	Yana Klochkova, Ukraine	2:10.75
400 IM	Yana Klochkova, Ukraine	4:36.74
400 m relay	China	3:59.89
400 f relay	United States	3:38.09
800 f relay	United States	7:55.70

FINA DIVING WORLD CUP
Barcelona July 13–20, 2003

1-m spgbd	Irina Lashko, Australia	299.97
3-m spgbd	Jingjing Guo, China	617.94
Platform	Emilie Heymans, Canada	597.45
3-m sync	Mingxia Wu/ Jingjing Guo, China	357.3
Platfm. sync.	Lishi Lao/ Ting Li, China	344.58

U.S. NATIONAL CHAMPIONSHIPS (SUMMER)
College Park, MD, August 5–9, 2003

50 free	Malia Matella, France	25.18
100 free	Sarah Wanezek, Texas Aquatics	55.73
200 free	Brittany Reimer, Canada	2:00.62
400 free	Kalyn Keller, Trojan SC	4:10.68
800 free	Kalyn Keller, Trojan SC	8:31.54
1,500 free	Kayln Keller, Trojan SC	16:08.64
100 back	Lauren Rogers, Terrapins ST	1:02.50
200 back	Jennifer Fratesi, Canada	2:12.47
100 breast	Megan Quann, S Sound Titan	1:08.80
200 breast	Caroline Bruce, Wichita SC	2:27.88
100 fly	Emily Goetsch, N Baltimore	59.87
200 fly	Kaitlin Sandeno, Trojan SC	2:08.78
200 IM	Kaitlin Sandeno, Trojan SC	2:12.97
400 IM	Kaitlin Sandeno, Trojan SC	4:40.82
400 m relay	Novaquatics	4:12.11
400 f relay	Texas Aquatics	3:44.97
800 f relay	Trojan SC	8:10.79

*American record. WR World record.

World and American Records Set in 2003

Men

Event	Mark	Record Holder	Date	Site
200 free	1:45.99	Michael Phelps, United States (A)	8-7-03	College Park, MD
400 free	3:46.73	Michael Phelps, United States (A)	8-5-03	College Park, MD
800 free	7:48.09	Larsen Jensen, United States (A)	7-25-03	Barcelona
50 back	24.80	Thomas Rupprath, Germany (W)	7-27-03.	Barcelona
100 breast	59.78	Kosuke Kitajima, Japan (W)	7-21-03	Barcelona
	1:00.21	Ed Moses, United States (A)	4-4-03	Indianapolis
200 breast	2:09.42	Kosuke Kitajima, Japan (W)	7-24-03	Barcelona
50 fly	23.43	Matthew Welsh, Australia (W)	7-21-03	Barcelona
100 fly	50.98	Ian Crocker, United States (W, A)	7-26-03	Barcelona
200 fly	1:53.93	Michael Phelps, United States (W, A)	7-22-03	Barcelona
200 IM	1:55.94	Michael Phelps, United States (W, A)	8-9-03	College Park, MD
400 IM	4:09.09	Michael Phelps, United States (W, A)	7-27-03	Barcelona
400 medley relay	3:31.54	United States (W, A) (Michael Phelps, Aaron Peirsol, Ian Crocker, Jason Lezak)	7-27-03	Barcelona
800 free relay	7:10.26	United States (A) (Michael Phelps, Nate Dusing, Aaron Peirsol, Klete Keller)	7-23-03	Barcelona

Women

Event	Mark	Record Holder	Date	Site
100 breast	1:06.37	Leisel Jones, Australia (W)	7-21-03	Barcelona
200 breast	2:22.99	Amanda Beard, United States (EW, A)	7-25-03	Barcelona
200 free	1:57.41	Lindsay Benko, United States (A)	7-24-03	Barcelona
800 free relay	7:55.70	United States (A) (Lindsay Benko, Rachel Komisarz, Rhiannon Jeffrey, Diana Munz)		

W= world record. A= American record. EW=Equals world record.

Notes from Barcelona

Bedridden for most of the week with a 102° fever, Natalie Coughlin, the new queen of U.S. swimming, won just two relay medals at the 10th World Championships, in Barcelona: a gold on the 4 X 100-meter freestyle team and a silver as the backstroke leg in the 4 x 100-meter medley . . . Aaron and Hayley Peirsol became the first siblings to win individual event medals for the U.S. at the same worlds or Olympics when, less than 30 minutes apart, Aaron won the 100-meter backstroke and Hayley took a surprise silver in the 1,500 freestyle.

World and American Records

MEN

Freestyle

Event	Time	Record Holder	Date	Site
50 meters	21.64	Alexander Popov, Russia (W)	6-16-00	Moscow
	21.76	Gary Hall Jr. (A)	8-15-00	Indianapolis
100 meters	47.84	Pieter van den Hoogenband (W) Netherlands	9-19-00	Sydney
	48.33	Anthony Ervin (A)	7-27-01	Fukuoka, Japan
200 meters	1:44.06	Ian Thorpe, Australia (W)	7-25-01	Fukuoka, Japan
	1:45.99	Michael Phelps (A)	8-7-03	College Park, MD
400 meters	3:40.08	Ian Thorpe, Australia (W)	7-30-02	Manchester
	3:46.73	Michael Phelps (A)	8-5-03	College Park, MD
800 meters	7:39.16	Ian Thorpe, Australia (W)	7-24-03	Fukuoka, Japan
	7:48.09	Larsen Jensen (A)	7-25-03	Barcelona
1,500 meters	14:34.56	Grant Hackett, Australia (W)	7-30-01	Fukuoka, Japan
	14.56.81	Chris Thompson (A)	9-23-00	Sydney

Backstroke

Event	Time	Record Holder	Date	Site
50 meters	24.80	Thomas Rupprath, Germany (W)	7-27-03	Barcelona
	24.99	Lenny Krayzelburg (A)	8-28-99	Sydney
100 meters	53.60	Lenny Krayzelburg (W, A)	8-24-99	Sydney
200 meters	1:55.15	Aaron Peirsol (W, A)	3-20-02	Minneapolis

Breaststroke

Event	Time	Record Holder	Date	Site
50 meters	27.18	Oleg Lisogor, Ukr (W)	8-1-02	Berlin
	27.39	Ed Moses (A)	3-31-01	Austin, TX
100 meters	59.78	Kosuke Kitajima, Japan (W)	7-21-03	Barcelona
	1:00.21	Ed Moses (A)	4-4-03	Indianapolis
200 meters	2:09.42	Kosuke Kitajima, Japan (W)	7-24-03	Barcelona
	2:10.16	Mike Barrowman (A)	7-29-92	Barcelona

Butterfly

Event	Time	Record Holder	Date	Site
50 meters	23.43	Matthew Welsh, Australia (W)	7-21-03	Barcelona
	23.85	Ian Crocker (A)	7-26-01	Fukuoka, Japan
		Bryan Jones (A)	3-29-01	Austin, TX
100 meters	50.98	Ian Crocker, United States (W, A)	7-26-03	Barcelona
200 meters	1:53.93	Michael Phelps (W, A)	7-22-03	Barcelona

Individual Medley

Event	Time	Record Holder	Date	Site
200 meters	1:55.94	Michael Phelps (W, A)	8-9-03	College Park, MD
400 meters	4:09.09	Michael Phelps (W, A)	7-27-03	Barcelona

Relays

Event	Time	Record Holder	Date	Site
400-meter medley	3:31.54	United States (W,A) (Aaron Peirsol, Michael Phelps, Ian Crocker, Jason Lezak)	7-27-03	Barcelona
400-meter freestyle	3:13.67	Australia (W) (Ian Thorpe, Michael Klim, Ashley Callus, Chris Fydler)	9-16-00	Sydney
	3:13.86	United States (A) (Anthony Ervin, Neil Walker, Jason Lezak, Gary Hall Jr)	9-16-00	Sydney
800-meter freestyle	7:04.66	Australia (W) (Ian Thorpe, Michael Klim, Bill Kirby, Grant Hackett)	7-27-01	Fukuoka, Japan
	7:10.26	United States (A) (Michael Phelps, Nate Dusing, Aaron Peirsol, Klete Keller)	7-23-03	Barcelona

WOMEN

Freestyle

Event	Time	Record Holder	Date	Site
50 meters	24.13	Inge de Bruijn, Netherlands (W)	9-22-00	Sydney
	24.63	Dara Torres (A)	9-23-00	Sydney
100 meters	53.77	Inge de Bruijn, Netherlands (W)	9-20-00	Sydney
	53.99	Natalie Coughlin (A)	8-29-02	Yokohama, Japan
200 meters	1:56.64	Franziska van Almsick, Germany (W)	8-3-02	Berlin
	1:57.41	Lindsay Benko (A)	7-24-03	Barcelona
400 meters	4:03.85	Janet Evans (W, A)	9-22-88	Seoul
800 meters	8:16.22	Janet Evans (W, A)	8-20-89	Tokyo
1,500 meters	15:52.10	Janet Evans (W, A)	3-26-88	Orlando, FL

Backstroke

Event	Time	Record Holder	Date	Site
50 meters	28.25	Sandra Volker, Germany (W)	6-17-00	Berlin
	28.49	Natalie Coughlin (A)	7-23-01	Fukuoka, Japan
100 meters	59.58	Natalie Coughlin (W, A)	8-13-02	Fort Lauderdale, FL
200 meters	2:06.62	Krisztina Egerszegi, Hungary (W)	8-25-91	Athens, Greece
	2:08.53	Natalie Coughlin (A)	8-16-02	Fort Lauderdale, FL

Breaststroke

Event	Time	Record Holder	Date	Site
50 meters	30.57	Zoe Baker, Great Britain (W)	7-30-02	Berlin
	31.34	Megan Quann (A)	8-11-00	Indianapolis
100 meters	1:06.37	Leisel Jones, Australia (W)	7-21-03	Barcelona
	1:07.05	Megan Quann (A)	9-18-00	Sydney
200 meters	2:22.99	Hui Qi, China (W)	4-13-01	Hangzhou, China
	2:22.99	Amanda Beard (W, A)	7-25-03	Barcelona

Butterfly

Event	Time	Record Holder	Date	Site
50 meters	25.57	Anna-Karin Kammerling, Sweden (W)	7-30-02	Berlin
	26.50	Dara Torres (A)	8-9-00	Indianapolis
100 meters	56.61	Inge de Bruijn, Netherlands (W)	9-17-00	Sydney
	57.58	Dara Torres (A)	8-9-00	Indianapolis
200 meters	2:05.78	Otylia Jedrejczak, Poland (W)	8-4-02	Berlin
	2:05.88	Misty Hyman (A)	9-20-00	Sydney

Individual Medley

Event	Time	Record Holder	Date	Site
200 meters	2:09.72	Yanyan Wu, China (W)	10-17-97	Shanghai
	2:11.91	Summer Sanders (A)	7-30-92	Barcelona
400 meters	4:33.59	Yana Klochkova, Ukraine (W)	9-16-00	Sydney
	4:37.58	Summer Sanders (A)	7-26-92	Barcelona

Relays

Event	Time	Record Holder	Date	Site
400-meter medley	3:58.30	United States (W, A) (BJ Bedford, Megan Quann, Jenny Thompson Dana Torres)	9-23-00	Sydney
400-meter freestyle	3:36.00	Germany (W) (K. Meissner, P. Dallman, S. Vokler, F. van Almsick)	7-29-02	Berlin
	3:36.61	United States (A) (Jenny Thompson, Courtney Shealy, Dara Torres, Amy Van Dyken)	9-16-00	Sydney
800-meter freestyle	7:55.47	E Germany (W) (Manuela Stellmach, Astrid Strauss, Anke Mohring, Heike Friedrich)	8-18-87	Strasbourg, France
	7:55.70	United States (A) (Lindsay Benko, Rachel Komisarz, Rhiannon Jeffrey, Diana Munz)	7-24-03	Barcelona

World Championships

MEN

50-meter Freestyle

1986	Tom Jager, United States	22.49‡
1991	Tom Jager, United States	22.16‡
1994	Alexander Popov, Russia	22.17
1998	Bill Pilczuk, United States	22.29
2001	Anthony Ervin, United States	22.09
2003	Alexander Popov, Russia	21.92‡

100-meter Freestyle

1973	Jim Montgomery, United States	51.70
1975	Andy Coan, United States	51.25
1978	David McCagg, United States	50.24
1982	Jorg Woithe, E Germany	50.18
1986	Matt Biondi, United States	48.94
1991	Matt Biondi, United States	49.18
1994	Alexander Popov, Russia	49.12
1998	Alexander Popov, Russia	48.93‡
2001	Anthony Ervin, United States	48.33‡
2003	Alexander Popov, Russia	48.42

200-meter Freestyle

1973	Jim Montgomery, United States	1:53.02
1975	Tim Shaw, United States	1:52.04‡
1978	Billy Forrester, United States	1:51.02‡
1982	Michael Gross, W Germany	1:49.84
1986	Michael Gross, W Germany	1:47.92
1991	Giorgio Lamberti, Italy	1:47.27‡
1994	Antti Kasvio, Finland	1:47.32
1998	Michael Klim, Australia	1:47.41
2001	Ian Thorpe, Australia	1:44.06*
2003	Ian Thorpe, Australia	1:45.14

400-meter Freestyle

1973	Rick DeMont, United States	3:58.18‡
1975	Tim Shaw, United States	3:54.88‡
1978	Vladimir Salnikov, USSR	3:51.94‡
1982	Vladimir Salnikov, USSR	3:51.30‡
1986	Rainer Henkel, W Germany	3:50.05
1991	Joerg Hoffman, Germany	3:48.04‡
1994	Kieran Perkins, Australia	3:43.80*
1998	Ian Thorpe, Australia	3:46.29
2001	Ian Thorpe, Australia	3:40.17*
2003	Ian Thorpe, Australia	3:42.58

1,500-meter Freestyle

1973	Stephen Holland, Australia	15:31.85
1975	Tim Shaw, United States	15:28.92‡
1978	Vladimir Salnikov, USSR	15:03.99‡
1982	Vladimir Salnikov, USSR	15:01.77‡
1986	Rainer Henkel, W Germany	15:05.31
1991	Joerg Hoffman, Germany	14:50.36*
1994	Kieran Perkins, Australia	14:50.52
1998	Grant Hackett, Australia	14:51.70
2001	Grant Hackett, Australia	14:34.56*
2003	Grant Hackett, Australia	14:43.14

100-meter Backstroke

1973	Roland Matthes, E Germany	57.47
1975	Roland Matthes, E Germany	58.15
1978	Bob Jackson, United States	56.36‡
1982	Dirk Richter, E Germany	55.95
1986	Igor Polianski, USSR	55.58‡
1991	Jeff Rouse, United States	55.23‡
1994	Martin Lopez Zubero, Spain	55.17‡
1998	Lenny Krayzelburg, United States	55.00‡
2001	Matt Welsh, Australia	54.31‡
2003	Aaron Peirsol, United States	53.61‡

200-meter Backstroke

1973	Roland Matthes, E Germany	2:01.87‡
1975	Zoltan Varraszto, Hungary	2:05.05
1978	Jesse Vassallo, United States	2:02.16
1982	Rick Carey, United States	2:00.82‡
1986	Igor Polianski, USSR	1:58.78‡
1991	Martin Zubero, Spain	1:59.52
1994	Vladimir Selkov, Russia	1:57.42‡
1998	Lenny Krayzelburg, United States	1:58.84

200-meter Backstroke (Cont.)

2001	Aaron Peirsol, United States	1:57.13‡
2003	Aaron Peirsol, United States	1:55.92

100-meter Breaststroke

1973	John Hencken, United States	1:04.02‡
1975	David Wilkie, Great Britain	1:04.26‡
1978	Walter Kusch, W Germany	1:03.56‡
1982	Steve Lundquist, United States	1:02.75‡
1986	Victor Davis, Canada	1:02.71
1991	Norbert Rozsa, Hungary	1:01.45*
1994	Norbert Rozsa, Hungary	1:01.24‡
1998	Frederik Deburghgraeve, Belgium	1:01.34
2001	Roman Sloudnov, Russia	1:00.16
2003	Kosuke Kitajima, Japan	59.78*

200-meter Breaststroke

1973	David Wilkie, Great Britain	2:19.28‡
1975	David Wilkie, Great Britain	2:18.23‡
1978	Nick Nevid, United States	2:18.37
1982	Victor Davis, Canada	2:14.77*
1986	Jozsef Szabo, Hungary	2:14.27‡
1991	Mike Barrowman, United States	2:11.23*
1994	Norbert Rozsa, Hungary	2:12.81
1998	Kurt Grote, United States	2:13.40
2001	Brendan Hansen, United States	2:10.69‡
2003	Kosuke Kitajima, Japan	2:09.42*

100-meter Butterfly

1973	Bruce Robertson, Canada	55.69
1975	Greg Jagenburg, United States	55.63
1978	Joe Bottom, United States	54.30
1982	Matt Gribble, United States	53.88‡
1986	Pablo Morales, United States	53.54‡
1991	Anthony Nesty, Suriname	53.29‡
1994	Rafal Szukala, Poland	53.51
1998	Michael Klim, Australia	52.25‡
2001	Lars Frolander, Sweden	52.10‡
2003	Ian Crocker, United States	50.98*

200-meter Butterfly

1973	Robin Backhaus, United States	2:03.32
1975	Bill Forrester, United States	2:01.95‡
1978	Mike Bruner, United States	1:59.38‡
1982	Michael Gross, E Germany	1:58.85‡
1986	Michael Gross, E Germany	1:56.53‡
1991	Melvin Stewart, United States	1:55.69*
1994	Denis Pankratov, Russia	1:56.54
1998	Denys Sylantyev, Ukraine	1:56.61
2001	Michael Phelps, United States	1:54.58*
2003	Michael Phelps, United States	1:54.35

200-meter Individual Medley

1973	Gunnar Larsson, Sweden	2:08.36
1975	Andras Hargitay, Hungary	2:07.72
1978	Graham Smith, Canada	2:03.65*
1982	Aleksandr Sidorenko, USSR	2:03.30‡
1986	Tamás Darnyi, Hungary	2:01.57‡
1991	Tamás Darnyi, Hungary	1:59.36*
1994	Jani Sievin, Finland	1:58.16*
1998	Marcel Wouda, Netherlands	2:01.18
2001	Massimiliano Rosolino, Italy	1:59.71
2003	Michael Phelps, United States	1:56.04*

400-meter Individual Medley

1975	András Hargitay, Hungary	4:32.57
1978	Jesse Vassallo, United States	4:20.05*
1982	Ricardo Prado, Brazil	4:19.78*
1986	Tamás Darnyi, Hungary	4:18.98‡
1991	Tamás Darnyi, Hungary	4:12.36*
1994	Tom Dolan, United States	4:12.30*
1998	Tom Dolan, United States	4:14.95
2001	Alessio Boggiatto, Italy	4:13.15
2003	Michael Phelps, United States	4:09.09*

* World record. ‡Meet record.

MEN (Cont.)

400-meter Medley Relay

1973.....United States (Mike Stamm, John Hencken, Joe Bottom, Jim Montgomery) — 3:49.49

1975.....United States (John Murphy, Rick Colella, Greg Jagenburg, Andy Coan) — 3:49.00

1978.....United States (Robert Jackson, Nick Nevid, Joe Bottom, David McCagg) — 3:44.63

1982.....United States (Rick Carey, Steve Lundquist, Matt Gribble, Rowdy Gaines) — 3:40.84*

1986.....United States (Dan Veatch, David Lundberg, Pablo Morales, Matt Biondi) — 3:41.25

1991.....United States (Jeff Rouse, Eric Wunderlich, Mark Henderson, Matt Biondi) — 3:39.66‡

1994.....United States (Jeff Rouse, Eric Wunderlich, Mark Henderson, Gary Hall) — 3:37.74‡

1998.....Australia (Matt Welsh, Phil Rogers, Robin Backhaus, Rick Klatt, Jim Montgomery) — 3:37.98

2001.....Australia (Matt Welsh, Ian Thorpe, Geoff Huegill, Regan Harrison) — 3:35.35

2003.....United States (Aaron Peirsol, Brendan Hansen, Ian Crocker, ...Jason Lezak) — 3:31.54*

400-meter Freestyle Relay

1973.....United States (Mel Nash, Joe Bottom, Jim Montgomery, John Murphy) — 3:27.18

1975.....United States (Bruce Furniss, Jim Montgomery, Andy Coan, John Murphy) — 3:24.85

1978.....United States (Jack Babashoff, Rowdy Gaines, Jim Montgomery, David McCagg) — 3:19.74

1982.....United States (Chris Cavanaugh, Robin Leamy, David McCagg, Rowdy Gaines) — 3:19.26*

1986.....United States (Tom Jager, Mike Heath, Paul Wallace, Matt Biondi) — 3:19.89

1991.....United States (Tom Jager, Brent Lang, Doug Gjertsen, Matt Biondi) — 3:17.15‡

1994.....United States (Jon Olsen, Josh Davis, Ugur Taner, Gary Hall Jr.) — 3:16.90‡

1998.....United States (Bryan Jones, Jon Olsen, Bradley Schumacher, Gary Hall Jr.) — 3:16.69‡

2001.....Australia (Michael Klim, Ian Thorpe, Todd Pearson, Ashley Callus) — 3:14.10‡

2003.....Russia (Andrei Kapralov, Ivan Usov, Denis Pimankov, Alexander Popov) — 3:14.06‡

800-meter Freestyle Relay

1973.....United States (Kurt Krumpholz, Robin Backhaus, Rick Klatt, Jim Montgomery) — 7:33.22*

1975.....W Germany (Klaus Steinbach, Werner Lampe, Hans Joachim Geisler, Peter Nocke) — 7:39.44

1978.....United States (Bruce Furniss, Billy Forrester, Bobby Hackett, Rowdy Gaines) — 7:20.82

1982.....United States (Rich Saeger, Jeff Float, Kyle Miller, Rowdy Gaines) — 7:21.09

1986.....E Germany (Lars Hinneburg, Thomas Flemming, Dirk Richter, Sven Lodziewski) — 7:15.91‡

1991.....Germany (Peter Sitt, Steffan Zesner, Stefan Pfeiffer, Michael Gross) — 7:13.50‡

1994.....Sweden (Christer Waller, Tommy Werner, Lars Frolander, Anders Holmertz) — 7:17.34

1998.....Australia (Daniel Kowalski, Grant Hackett, Ian Thorpe, Anthony Rogis) — 7:12.48‡

2001.....Australia (Michael Klim, Ian Thorpe, William Kirby, Grant Hackett) — 7:04.66*

2003.....Australia (Grant Hackett, Craig, Stevens, N. Springer, Ian Thorpe) — 7:08.58

WOMEN

50-meter Freestyle

Year	Name	Time
1986	Tamara Costache, Romania	25.28*
1991	Zhuang Yong, China	25.47
1994	Le Jingyi, China	24.51*
1998	Amy Van Dyken, United States	25.15
2001	Inge de Bruijn, Netherlands	24.47
2003	Inge de Bruijn, Netherlands	24.47

100-meter Freestyle

Year	Name	Time
1973	Kornelia Ender, E Germany	57.54
1975	Kornelia Ender, E Germany	56.50
1978	Barbara Krause, E Germany	55.68‡
1982	Birgit Meineke, E Germany	55.79
1986	Kristin Otto, E Germany	55.05‡
1991	Nicole Haislett, United States	55.17
1994	Le Jingyi, China	54.01*
1998	Jenny Thompson, United States	54.95
2001	Inge de Bruijn, Netherlands	54.18
2003	Hanna-Maria Seppälä, Finland	54.37

200-meter Freestyle

Year	Name	Time
1973	Keena Rothhammer, United States	2:04.99
1975	Shirley Babashoff, United States	2:02.50
1978	Cynthia Woodhead, United States	1:58.53*
1982	Annemarie Verstappen, Netherlands	1:59.53‡
1986	Heike Friedrich, E Germany	1:58.26‡
1991	Hayley Lewis, Australia	2:00.48
1994	Franziska Van Almsick, Germany	1:56.78*
1998	Claudia Poll, Costa Rica	1:58.90
2001	Giaan Rooney, Australia	1:58.57
2003	Alena Popchanka, Bulgaria	1:58.32

400-meter Freestyle

Year	Name	Time
1973	Heather Greenwood, United States	4:20.28
1975	Shirley Babashoff, United States	4:22.70
1978	Tracey Wickham, Australia	4:06.28*
1982	Carmela Schmidt, E Germany	4:08.98
1986	Heike Friedrich, E Germany	4:07.45
1991	Janet Evans, United States	4:08.63
1994	Yang Aihua, China	4:09.64
1998	Chen Yan, China	4:06.72
2001	Yana Klochkova, Ukraine	4:07.30
2003	Hannah Stockbauer, Germany	4:06.75

* World record; ‡Meet record.

WOMEN *(Cont.)*

800-meter Freestyle

1973....Novella Calligaris, Italy   8:52.97
1975....Jenny Turrall, Australia   8:44.75‡
1978....Tracey Wickham, Australia   8:24.94‡
1982....Kim Linehan, United States   8:27.48
1986....Astrid Strauss, E Germany   8:28.24
1991....Janet Evans, United States   8:24.05‡
1994....Janet Evans, United States   8:29.85
1998....Brooke Bennett, United States   8.28.71
2001....Hannah Stockbauer, Germany   8:24.66
2003....Hannah Stockbauer, Germany   8:23.66‡

100-meter Backstroke

1973....Ulrike Richter, E Germany   1:05.42
1975....Ulrike Richter, E Germany   1:03.30‡
1978....Linda Jezek, United States   1:02.55‡
1982....Kristin Otto, E Germany   1:01.30‡
1986....Betsy Mitchell, United States   1:01.74
1991....Krisztina Egerszegi, Hungary   1:01.78
1994....He Cihong, China   1:00.57
1998....Lea Maurer, United States   1:01.16
2001....Natalie Coughlin, United States   1:00.37
2003....Antje Buschschulte, Germany   1:00.50

200-meter Backstroke

1973....Melissa Belote, United States   2:20.52
1975....Birgit Treiber, E Germany   2:15.46*
1978....Linda Jezek, United States   2:11.93*
1982....Cornelia Sirch, E Germany   2:09.91*
1986....Cornelia Sirch, E Germany   2:11.37
1991....Krisztina Egerszegi, Hungary   2:09.15‡
1994....He Cihong, China   2:07.40
1998....Roxanna Maracineanu, France   2:11.26
2001....Diana Mocanu, Romania   2:09.94
2003....Katy Sexton, Great Britain   2:08.74

100-meter Breaststroke

1973....Renate Vogel, E Germany   1:13.74
1975....Hannalore Anke, E Germany   1:12.72
1978....Julia Bogdanova, USSR   1:10.31*
1982....Ute Geweniger, E Germany   1:09.14‡
1986....Sylvia Gerasch, E Germany   1:08.11*
1991....Linley Frame, Australia   1:08.81
1994....Samantha Riley, Australia   1:07.96*
1998....Kristy Kowal, United States   1:08.42
2001....Xuejuan Luo, China   1:07.18‡
2003....Xuejuan Luo, China   1:06.80

200-meter Breaststroke

1973....Renate Vogel, E Germany   2:40.01
1975....Hannalore Anke, E Germany   2:37.25‡
1978....Lina Kachushite, USSR   2:31.42*
1982....Svetlana Varganova, USSR   2:28.82‡
1986....Silke Hoerner, E Germany   2:27.40*
1991....Elena Volkova, USSR   2:29.53
1994....Samantha Riley, Australia   2:26.87‡
1998....Agnes Kovacs, Hungary   2:25.45‡
2001....Agnes Kovacs, Hungary   2:24.90
2003....Amanda Beard, United States   2:22.99*

100-meter Butterfly

1973....Kornelia Ender, E Germany   1:02.53
1975....Kornelia Ender, E Germany   1:01.24*
1978....Joan Pennington, United States   1:00.20‡
1982....Mary T. Meagher, United States   59.41‡
1986....Kornelia Gressler, E Germany   59.51
1991....Qian Hong, China   59.68
1994....Liu Limin, China   58.98‡
1998....Jenny Thompson, United States   58.46‡
2001....Petria Thomas, Australia   58:27
2003....Jenny Thompson, United States   57.96‡

200-meter Butterfly

1973....Rosemarie Kother, E Germany   2:13.76‡
1975....Rosemarie Kother, E Germany   2:15.92
1978....Tracy Caulkins, United States   2:09.87*
1982....Ines Geissler, E Germany   2:08.66‡
1986....Mary T. Meagher, United States   2:08.41‡
1991....Summer Sanders, United States   2:09.24
1994....Liu Limin, China   2:07.25‡
1998....Susie O'Neill, Australia   2:07.93‡
2001....Petria Thomas, Australia   2:06.73‡
2003....Otylia Jedrzejczak, Poland   2:07.56

200-meter Individual Medley

1973....Andrea Huebner, E Germany   2:20.51
1975....Kathy Heddy, United States   2:19.80
1978....Tracy Caulkins, United States   2:14.07*
1982....Petra Schneider, E Germany   2:11.79
1986....Kristin Otto, E Germany   2:15.56
1991....Li Lin, China   2:13.40
1994....Lu Bin, China   2:12.34‡
1998....Wu Yanyan, China   2:10.88
2001....Martha Bowen, United States   2:11.93
2003....Yana Klochkova, Ukraine   2:10.75‡

400-meter Individual Medley

1973....Gudrun Wegner, E Germany   4:57.71
1975....Ulrike Tauber, E Germany   4:52.76‡
1978....Tracy Caulkins, United States   4:40.83*
1982....Petra Schneider, E Germany   4:36.10*
1986....Kathleen Nord, E Germany   4:43.75
1991....Lin Li, China   4:41.45
1994....Dai Guohong, China   4:39.14
1998....Chen Yan, China   4:36.66
2001....Yana Klochkova, Ukraine   4:36.98
2003....Yana Klochkova, Ukraine   4:36.74

400-meter Medley Relay

1973....E Germany (Ulrike Richter,   4:16.84
        Renate Vogel, Rosemarie Kother,
        Kornelia Ender)
1975....E Germany (Ulrike Richter,   4:14.74
        Hannelore Anke, Rosemarie Kother,
        Kornelia Ender)
1978....United States (Linda Jezek,   4:08.21‡
        Tracy Caulkins, Joan Pennington,
        Cynthia Woodhead)
1982....E Germany (Kristin Otto,   4:05.8*
        Ute Gewinger, Ines Geissler,
        Birgit Meineke)
1986....E Germany (Kathrin   4:04.82
        Zimmermann, Sylvia Gerasch,
        Kornelia Gressler, Kristin Otto)
1991....United States (Janie Wagstaff,   4:06.51
        Tracey McFarlane, Crissy
        Ahmann-Leighton, Nicole Haislett)
1994....China (He Cihong, Dai Guohong,   4:01.67*
        Liu Limin, Lu Bin)
1998....United States (Kristy Kowal, Lea   4:01.93
        Maurer, Jenny Thompson, Amy
        Van Dyken)
2001....Australia (Dyana Calub, Sarah   4:07.30
        Ryan, Petria Thomas, Leisel Jones)
2003....China (Shu Xhan, Xuejuan Luo   3:59.89‡
        Yafei Zhou, Yu Yang)

400-meter Freestyle Relay

1973....E Germany (Kornelia Ender,   3:52.45
        Andrea Eife, Andrea Huebner,
        Sylvia Eichner)
1975....E Germany (Kornelia Ender,   3:49.37
        Barbara Krause, Claudia Hempel,
        Ute Bruckner)
1978....United States (Tracy Caulkins,   3:43.43*
        Stephanie Elkins, Joan Pennington,
        Cynthia Woodhead)

WOMEN (Cont.)

400-meter Freestyle Relay (Cont.)

1982	...E Germany (Birgit Meineke, Susanne Link, Kristin Otto, Caren Metschuk)	3:43.97
1986	...E Germany (Kristin Otto, Manuela Stellmach, Sabine Schulze, Heike Friedrich)	3:40.57*
1991	...United States (Nicole Haislett, Julie Cooper, Whitney Hedgepeth, Jenny Thompson)	3:43.26
1994	...China (Le Jingyi, Ying Shan, Le Ying, Lu Bin)	3:37.91*
1998	...United States (Catherine Fox, Lindsey Farella, Melanie Valerio, B.J. Bedford)	3:42.11
2001	...Germany (Petra Dallman, Antje Buschschulter, Katrin Meissner, Sandra Volkner)	3:39.58
2003	...United States (Natalie Coughlin, Lindsay Benko, Rhiannon Jeffrey, Jenny Thompson)	3:38.09

* World record; ‡Meet record.

800-meter Freestyle Relay

1986	...E Germany (Manuela Stellmach, Astrid Strauss, Nadja Bergknecht, Heike Friedrich)	7:59.33*
1991	...Germany (Kerstin Kielgass, Manuela Stellmach, Dagmar Hase, Stephanie Ortwig)	8:02.56
1994	...China (Le Ying, Yang Alhua, Zhou Guabin, Lu Bin)	7:57.96
1998	...Germany (Silvia Szalai, Antje Buschschulte, Janina Goetz, Franziska Van Almsick)	8:02.56
2001	...Great Britain (Nicola Jackson, Janine Belton, Karen Legg, Karen Pickering)	7:58.69
2003	...United States (Lindsay Benko, Rachel Komisarz, Rhiannon Jeffrey, Diana Munz)	7:55.70‡

World Diving Championships

MEN

1-meter Springboard

		Pts
1991	........Edwin Jongejans, Netherlands	588.51
1994	........Evan Stewart, Zimbabwe	382.14
1998	........Yu Zhuocheng, China	417.54
2001	........Wang Feng, China	444.03
2003	........Xiang Xu, China	431.94

3-meter Springboard

		Pts
1973	........Phil Boggs, United States	618.57
1975	........Phil Boggs, United States	597.12
1978	........Phil Boggs, United States	913.95
1982	........Greg Louganis, United States	752.67
1986	........Greg Louganis, United States	750.06
1991	........Kent Ferguson, United States	650.25
1994	........Wu Zhuocheng, China	655.44
1998	........Dmitry Sautin, Russia	746.79
2001	........Dmitry Sautin, Russia	725.82
2003	........Alexander Dobrosok, Russia	788.37

Platform

		Pts
1973	........Klaus Dibiasi, Italy	559.53
1975	........Klaus Dibiasi, Italy	547.98
1978	........Greg Louganis, United States	844.11
1982	........Greg Louganis, United States	634.26
1986	........Greg Louganis, United States	668.58
1991	........Sun Shuwei, China	626.79
1994	........Dmitry Sautin, Russia	634.71
1998	........Dmitry Sautin, Russia	750.90
2001	........Tian Lang, China	688.77
2003	........Alexandre Despatie, Canada	716.91

3-meter Synchronized

		Pts
1998	........China (Sun Shuwei, Tian Liang)	313.50
2001	........China (Bo Peng, Kenan Wang)	342.63
2003	........Russia (A. Dobrosok, D. Sautin)	369.18

10-meter Synchronized

1998	........China (Xu Hao, Yu Zhuocheng)	326.34
2001	........China (Jian Tian, Jia Bu)	361.41
2003	........Australia (M. Helm, R. Newbery)	384.6

WOMEN

1-meter Springboard

		Pts
1991	........Gao Min, China	478.26
1994	........Chen Lixia, China	279.30
1998	........Irina Lashko, Russia	296.07
2001	........Blythe Hartley, Canada	300.81
2003	........Irina Lashko, Australia	299.97

3-meter Springboard

		Pts
1973	........Christa Koehler, E Germany	442.17
1975	........Irina Kalinina, USSR	489.81
1978	........Irina Kalinina, USSR	691.43
1982	........Megan Neyer, United States	501.03
1986	........Gao Min, China	582.90
1991	........Gao Min, China	539.01
1994	........Tan Shuping, China	548.49
1998	........Yulia Pakhalina, Russia	544.62
2001	........Jingjing Guo, China	596.67
2003	........Jingjing Guo, China	617.94

Platform

1973	........Ulrike Knape, Sweden	406.77
1975	........Janet Ely, United States	403.89
1978	........Irina Kalinina, USSR	412.71
1982	........Wendy Wyland, United States	438.79
1986	........Chen Lin, China	449.67
1991	........Fu Mingxia, China	426.51
1994	........Fu Mingxia, China	434.04
1998	........Olena Zhupyna, Ukraine	550.41
2001	........Mian Xu, China	532.65
2003	........Emilie Heymans, Canada	597.45

3-meter Synchronized

		Pts
1998	..........Russia (Irina Lashko, Yulia Pakhalina)	282.30
2001	........China (Minxia Wu, Jingjing Guo)	347.31
2003	........China (Minxia Wu, Jingjing Guo)	357.30

10-meter Synchronized

		Pts
1998	..........Ukraine (O. Zhupyna, S. Serbina)	278.28
2001	........China (Qing Duan, Xue Sang)	329.94
2003	........China (Lishi Lao, Ting Li)	344.58

Men

50-METER FREESTYLE

1988....Matt Biondi	22.14*
2000....Gary Hall Jr. and Anthony Ervin	21.98

100-METER FREESTLYE

1906....Charles Daniels	1:13.4
1908....Charles Daniels	1:05.6*
1912....Duke Kahanamoku	1:03.4
1920....Duke Kahanamoku	1:00.4
1924....John Weissmuller	59.0‡
1928....John Weissmuller	58.6‡
1948....Wally Ris	57.3‡
1952....Clarke Scholes	57.4
1964....Don Schollander	53.4‡
1972....Mark Spitz	51.22*
1976....Jim Montgomery	49.99*
1984....Rowdy Gaines	49.80‡
1988....Matt Biondi	48.63‡

200-METER FREESTYLE

1904....Charles Daniels	2:44.2
1906–1964 Not held	
1972....Mark Spitz	1:52.78*
1976....Bruce Furniss	1:50.29*

400-METER FREESTYLE

1904....Charles Daniels (440 yds)	6:16.2
1920....Norman Ross	5:26.8
1924....John Weissmuller	5:04.2‡
1932....Buster Crabbe	4:48.4‡
1936....Jack Medica	4:44.5‡
1948....William Smith	4:41.0‡
1964....Don Schollander	4:12.2*
1968....Mike Burton	4:09.0‡
1976....Brian Goodell	3:51.93*
1984....George DiCarlo	3:51.23‡

1,500-METER FREESTYLE

1920....Norman Ross	22:23.2
1948....James McLane	19:18.5
1952....Ford Konno	18:30.3‡
1968....Mike Burton	16:38.9‡
1972....Mike Burton	15:52.58‡
1976....Brian Goodell	15:02.40*
1984....Michael O'Brien	15:05.20

100-METER BACKSTROKE

1912....Harry Hebner	1:21.2
1920....Warren Kealoha	1:15.2
1924....Warren Kealoha	1:13.2‡
1928....George Kojac	1:08.2*
1936....Adolph Kiefer	1:05.9‡
1948....Allen Stack	1:06.4
1952....Yoshi Oyakawa	1:05.4‡
1976....John Naber	55.49*
1984....Rick Carey	55.79
1996....Jeff Rouse	54.10
2000....Lenny Krayzelburg	53.60‡

200-METER BACKSTROKE

1964....Jed Graef	2:10.3*
1976....John Naber	1:59.19*
1984....Rick Carey	2:00.23
1996....Brad Bridgewater	1:58.54
2000....Lenny Krayzelburg	1:56.76‡

100-METER BREASTSTROKE

1968....Donald McKenzie	1:07.7‡
1976....John Hencken	1:03.11*
1984....Steve Lundquist	1:01.65 *
1992....Nelson Diebel	1:01.50‡

200-METER BREASTSTROKE

1924....Robert Skelton	2:56.6
1948....Joseph Verdeur	2:39.3‡
1960....William Mulliken	2:37.4
1972....John Hencken	2:21.55
1992....Mike Barrowman	2:10.16*

100-METER BUTTERFLY

1968....Douglas Russell	55.9‡
1972....Mark Spitz	54.27*
1976....Matt Vogel	54.35
1992....Pablo Morales	53.32

200-METER BUTTERFLY

1956....William Yorzyk	2:19.3‡
1960....Michael Troy	2:12.8*
1968....Carl Robie	2:08.7
1972....Mark Spitz	2:00.70*
1976....Mike Bruner	1:59.23*
1992....Melvin Stewart	1:56.26
2000....Tom Malchow	1:55.35‡

200-METER INDIVIDUAL MEDLEY

1968....Charles Hickcox	2:12.0‡

400-METER INDIVIDUAL MEDLEY

1964....Richard Roth	4:45.4*
1968....Charles Hickcox	4:48.4
1976....Rod Strachan	4:23.68*
1996....Tom Dolan	4.:14.90
2000....Tom Dolan	4:11.76‡

3-METER SPRINGBOARD DIVING

1920....Louis Kuehn	675.4 points
1924....Albert White	696.4
1928....Pete Desjardins	185.04
1932....Michael Galitzen	161.38
1936....Richard Degener	163.57
1948....Bruce Harlan	163.64
1952....David Browning	205.29
1956....Robert Clotworthy	159.56
1960....Gary Tobian	170.00
1964....Kenneth Sitzberger	159.90
1968....Bernard Wrightson	170.15
1976....Philip Boggs	619.05
1984....Greg Louganis	754.41
1988....Greg Louganis	730.80

PLATFORM DIVING

1904....George Sheldon	12.66 points
1920....Clarence Pinkston	100.67
1924....Albert White	97.46
1928....Pete Desjardins	98.74
1932....Harold Smith	124.80
1936....Marshall Wayne	113.58
1948....Sammy Lee	130.05
1952....Sammy Lee	156.28
1960....Robert Webster	165.56
1964....Robert Webster	148.58
1984....Greg Louganis	576.99
1988....Greg Louganis	638.61

* World record. ‡ Meet (Olympic) record.

Women

50-METER FREESTYLE

1996	Amy Van Dyken	24.87

100-METER FREESTLYE

1920	Ethelda Bleibtrey	1:13.6*
1924	Ethel Lackie	1:12.4
1928	Albina Osipowich	1:11.0‡
1932	Helene Madison	1:06.8‡
1968	Jan Henne	1:00.0
1972	Sandra Neilson	58.59‡
1984	Carrie Steinseifer	55.92
	Nancy Hogshead	55.92

200-METER FREESTYLE

1968	Debbie Meyer	2:10.5‡
1984	Mary Wayte	1:59.23
1992	Nicole Haislett	1:57.90

400-METER FREESTYLE

1924	Martha Norelius	6:02.2‡
1928	Martha Norelius	5:42.8*
1932	Helene Madison	5:28.5*
1948	Ann Curtis	5:17.8‡
1960	Chris von Saltza	4:50.6
1964	Virginia Duenkel	4:43.3‡
1968	Debbie Meyer	4:31.8‡
1984	Tiffany Cohen	4:07.10‡
1988	Janet Evans	4:03.85*

800-METER FREESTYLE

1968	Debbie Meyer	9:24.0‡
1972	Keena Rothhammer	8:53.86*
1984	Tiffany Cohen	8:24.95‡
1988	Janet Evans	8:20.20‡
1992	Janet Evans	8:25.52
1996	Brooke Bennett	8:27.89
2000	Brooke Bennett	8:19.67

100-METER BACKSTROKE

1924	Sybil Bauer	1:23.2‡
1932	Eleanor Holm	1:19.4
1960	Lynn Burke	1:09.3‡
1964	Cathy Ferguson	1:07.7*
1968	Kaye Hall	1:06.2*
1972	Melissa Belote	1:05.78‡
1984	Theresa Andrews	1:02.55
1996	Beth Botsford	1:01.19

200-METER BACKSTROKE

1968	Pokey Watson	2:24.8‡
1972	Melissa Belote	2:19.19*

100-METER BREASTSTROKE

1972	Catherine Carr	1:13.58*
2000	Megan Quann	1:07.05

200-METER BREASTSTROKE

1968	Sharon Wichman	2:44.4‡

100-METER BUTTERFLY

1956	Shelley Mann	1:11.0‡
1960	Carolyn Schuler	1:09.5‡
1964	Sharon Stouder	1:04.7*
1984	Mary T. Meagher	59.26
1996	Amy Van Dyken	59.13

200-METER BUTTERFLY

1972	Karen Moe	2:15.57*
1984	Mary T. Meagher	2:06.90‡
1992	Summer Sanders	2:08.67
2000	Misty Hyman	2:05.88‡

200-METER INDIVIDUAL MEDLEY

1968	Sharon Wichman	2:44.4‡
1984	Tracy Caulkins	2:12.64‡

400-METER INDIVIDUAL MEDLEY

1964	Donna De Varona	5:18.7‡
1968	Claudia Kolb	5:08.5‡
1984	Tracy Caulkins	4:39.24
1988	Janet Evans	4:37.76

3-METER SPRINGBOARD DIVING

1920	Aileen Riggin	539.9 points
1924	Elizabeth Becker	474.5
1928	Helen Meany	78.62
1932	Georgia Coleman	87.52
1936	Marjorie Gestring	89.27
1948	Victoria Draves	108.74
1952	Patricia McCormick	147.30
1956	Patricia McCormick	142.36
1968	Sue Gossick	150.77
1972	Micki King	450.03
1976	Jennifer Chandler	506.19

PLATFORM DIVING

1924	Caroline Smith	33.2 points
1928	Elizabeth Becker Pinkston	31.6
1932	Dorothy Poynton	40.26
1936	Dorothy Poynton Hill	33.93
1948	Victoria Draves	68.87
1952	Patricia McCormick	79.37
1956	Patricia McCormick	84.85
1964	Lesley Bush	99.80
2000	Laura Wilkinson	543.75

* World record; ‡ Meet (Olympic) record.

Barrier Breakers
MEN

Event	Barrier	Athlete and Nation	Time	Date
100 Freestyle	1:00	Johnny Weissmuller, United States	58.6	7-9-22
100 Freestyle	:50	James Montgomery, United States	49.99	7-25-76
200 Freestyle	2:00	Don Schollander, United States	1:58.8	7-27-63
200 Freestyle	1:50	Sergei Kopliakov, USSR	1:49.83	4-7-79
200 Freestyle	1:45	Ian Thorpe, Australia	1:44.06	7-25-01
400 Freestyle	4:00	Rick DeMont, United States	3:58.18	9-6-73
400 Freestyle	3:50	Vladimir Salnikov, USSR	3:49.57	3-12-82
800 Freestyle	8:00	Vladimir Salnikov, USSR	7:56.49	3-23-79
800 Freestyle	7:40	Ian Thorpe, Australia	7:39.16	7-24-01
1500 Freestyle	15:00	Vladimir Salnikov, USSR	14:58.27	7-22-80
1500 Freestyle	14:35	Grant Hackett, Australia	14:34.56	7-29-01
100 Backstroke	1:00	Thompson Mann, United States	59.6	10-16-64
200 Backstroke	2:00	John Naber, United States	1:59.19	7-24-76
100 Breaststroke	1:00	Roman Sloudnov, Russia	59.97	6-28-01
200 Breaststroke	2:30	Chester Jastremski, United States	2:29.6	8-19-61
200 Breaststroke	2:10	Kosuke Kitajima, Japan	2:09.42	7-24-03
100 Butterfly	1:00	Lance Larson, United States	59.0	6-29-60
200 Butterfly	2:00	Roger Pyttel, E Germany	1:59.63	6-3-76

WOMEN

Event	Barrier	Athlete and Nation	Time	Date
100 Freestyle	1:00	Dawn Fraser, Australia	59.9	10-27-62
200 Freestyle	2:00	Kornelia Ender, E Germany	1:59.78	6-2-76
400 Freestyle	4:30	Debbie Meyer, United States	4:29.0	8-18-67
800 Freestyle	10:00	Jane Cederqvist, Sweden	9:55.6	8-17-60
800 Freestyle	9:00	Ann Simmons, United States	8:59.4	9-10-71
1500 Freestyle	20:00	Ilsa Konrads, Australia	19:25.7	1-14-60
	16:00	Janet Evans, United States	15:52.10	3-26-88
100 Backstroke	1:00	Natalie Coughlin, United States	59.58	8-16-02
200 Backstroke	2:30	Satoko Tanaka, Japan	2:29.6	2-10-63
100 Butterfly	1:00	Christiane Knacke, E Germany	59.78	8-28-77
400 Individual Medley	5:00	Gudrun Wegner, E Germany	4:57.51	9-6-73

Olympic Achievements
MOST INDIVIDUAL GOLDS IN SINGLE OLYMPICS
MEN

No.	Athlete and Nation	Olympic Year	Events
4	Mark Spitz, United States	1972	100, 200 Free; 100, 200 Fly

WOMEN

No.	Athlete and Nation	Olympic Year	Events
4	Kristin Otto, E Germany	1988	50, 100 Free; 100 Back; 100 Fly
3	Debbie Meyer, United States	1968	200, 400, 800 Free
3	Shane Gould, Australia	1972	200, 400 Free; 200 IM
3	Kornelia Ender, E Germany	1976	100, 200 Free; 100 Fly
3	Janet Evans, United States	1988	400, 800 Free; 400 IM
3	Krisztina Egerszegi, Hungary	1992	100, 200 Back; 400 IM
3	Michelle Smith, Ireland	1996	400 Free; 200, 400 IM
3	Inge de Bruijn, Netherlands	2000	50, 100 Free; 100 Fly

Olympic Achievements *(Cont.)*

MOST INDIVIDUAL OLYMPIC GOLD MEDALS, CAREER

MEN

No.	Athlete and Nation	Olympic Years and Events
4	Charles Meldrum Daniels, United States	1904 (220, 440 Free); 1906 (100 Free) 1908 (100 Free)
4	Roland Matthes, E Germany	1968 (100, 200 Back); 1972 (100, 200 Back)
4	Mark Spitz, United States	1972 (100, 200 Free; 100, 200 Fly)

WOMEN

No.	Athlete and Nation	Olympic Years and Events
4	Kristin Otto, E Germany	1988 (50 Free; 100 Free, Back and Fly)
4	Janet Evans, United States	1988 (400, 800 Free); 1992 (800 Free)
4	Krisztina Egerszegi, Hungary	1992 (100, 200 Back; 400 IM); 1996 (200 Back)

Most Olympic Gold Medals in a Single Olympics, Men—7, Mark Spitz, United States, 1972: 100, 200 Free; 100, 200 Fly; 4 x 100, 4 x 200 Free Relays; 4 x 100 Medley Relay.
Most Olympic Gold Medals in a Single Olympics, Women—6, Kristin Otto, E Germany, 1988: 50, 100 Free; 100 Back; 100 Fly; 4 x 100 Free Relay; 4 x 100 Medley Relay.
Most Olympic Medals in a Career, Men—11, Matt Biondi, United States: 1984 (one gold), '88 (five gold, one silver, one bronze), '92 (two gold, one silver); 11, Mark Spitz, United States: 1968 (two gold, one silver, one bronze), '72 (seven gold).
Most Olympic Medals in a Career, Women—10, Jenny Thompson, United States: 1992 (two gold, one silver), 1996 (three gold), 2000 (three gold, one bronze); 8, Dawn Fraser, Australia: 1956 (two gold, one silver), '60 (one gold, two silver), '64 (one gold, one silver); 8, Kornelia Ender, E Germany: 1972 (three silver), '76 (four gold, one silver); 8, Shirley Babashoff, United States: 1972 (one gold, two silver); '76 (one gold, four silver).
Winner, Same Event, Three Consecutive Olympics—Dawn Fraser, Australia, 100 Freestyle, 1956, '60, '64; Krisztina Egerszegi, Hungary, 200 Back, 1988, '92, '96.
Youngest Person to Win an Olympic Diving Gold—Marjorie Gestring, United States, 1936, 13 years, 9 months, springboard diving.
Youngest Person to Win an Olympic Swimming Gold—Krisztina Egerszegi, Hungary, 1988, 14 years, one month, 200 backstroke.

World Record Achievements

Most World Records, Career, Women—42, Ragnhild Hveger, Denmark, 1936–42.
Most World Records, Career, Men—32, Arne Borg, Sweden, 1921–29.
Most Freestyle Records Held Concurrently—5, Helene Madison, United States, 1931–33; 5, Shane Gould, Australia, 1972.
Most Consecutive Lowerings of a Record—10, Kornelia Ender, E Germany, 100 Freestyle, 7-13-73 to 7-19-76.
Longest Duration of World Record—19 years, 359 days, 1:04.6 in 100 Free, Willy den Ouden, Netherlands.

Skiing

CARL YARBROUGH

World Cup champion
Stephan Eberharter
of Austria

Coming Attractions

In St. Moritz, Stephan Eberharter, Bode Miller and Hermann Maier gave skiing fans a tantalizing glimpse of the future

BY MARK BECHTEL

IF THE SUPER G at the 2003 world championships is any indication, the 2003–04 season could go down as one of the tightest and best in the history of Alpine skiing. In that event, in St. Moritz on February 2, the sport's past, present and future stars staged one of the most compelling races of the year. When it was over, Austrian Stephan Eberharter, the reigning world overall champion, had won, and up-and-coming American Bode Miller and newly-returned Austrian Hermann Maier, arguably the greatest Super G skier of all-time, had finished in a dead heat for the silver.

For Maier, just being there was a remarkable feat. In August 2001 he was involved in a horrific motorcycle accident that nearly cost him his right leg. "I remember everything," he said. "I was in the best shape of my life and it was horrible. I saw the leg and it was open and all the bones were broken and they were sticking out. I saw this leg and told the doctors, 'Make it so I can walk again.'

They did, but it wasn't easy." Maier lost 37 pounds and had to take copious amounts of painkillers to get through the trying recovery period. "I became like a junkie," he said.

He returned to the slopes 17 months after his accident, and within two weeks he won his first race, the Super G in Kitzbuehel, Austria. Fighting back tears, he called it the biggest win of his storied career. Maier's foes probably were not surprised to see him return to the podium. The 30-year-old is as resilient, and talented, as they come. In 1998 he crashed spectacularly during the downhill at the Nagano Olympics, flying through two rows of safety netting—a wipeout he still hasn't watched on videotape—then got right back up and won two gold medals in the next three days.

By winning in Kitzbuehel, Maier booked a place on the Austrian team for the worlds, and his presence turned St. Moritz into a media circus. "It's almost like President Bush giving his state of the

Miller produced the best year of his career in 2002–03, and he sees room for improvement.

nation speech," Maier said. Eberharter surveyed the media horde and said, simply, "I hope they've all found a place to stay."

Maier and Miller finished 0.77 seconds behind Eberharter in the Super G at the worlds. It was a remarkable result for Maier and an encouraging one for Miller, a slalom specialist who had never finished better than sixth in a Super G in 2002–03. "Second place is great," said Miller. "But I was second twice in the Olympics. In big events like the Olympics and world championships, the only thing that matters is being on top."

Miller eventually found himself on top in the giant slalom and combined races in St. Moritz. The combined title was especially sweet, since Miller had never before paid much attention to the downhill. But as it turned out, his demeanor lent itself perfectly to the speed events. "If I ski like a wuss all year to score points and win the overall, that doesn't cut it," said Miller. "I want to ski really hard, ripping it, and show I'm the Number 1 skier in the world."

So that's what Miller did all year, and he nearly scored enough points to become the first American in 20 years to win the overall. He went to Germany the week after St. Moritz just eight points behind Eberharter—who won the 2001–02 season title with Maier on the shelf—in the overall season standings. But Miller finished

28th in the downhill and went off the course in the Super G, allowing Eberharter to pick up 177 points and essentially salt away the championship.

Miller finished second overall, and also finished second (to Switzerland's Michael von Grünigen) in the giant slalom final standings, while Eberharter won the downhill and Super G. (Kalle Palander of Finland won the slalom, edging Ivica Kostelic, whose sister, Janica, won the women's overall title in a rout.) Eberharter anointed Miller his likely successor in March, saying "He is young and he will have a great future." The he went on vacation and pondered retirement.

Miller, meanwhile, agreed with Eberharter's notion that he'd one day become a champ. "If Stephan continues, he's going to have his hands full," said Miller, "because I definitely think I can ski a lot better than I did this year." In July, Eberharter made up his mind. He decided to come back for the 2003–04 season, setting up a potentially remarkable three-way showdown: Eberharter, 34, looking for a third consecutive title; Miller, more well-rounded with another year of experience in the speed events under his belt; and a healthy Maier, who had a 14-inch metal rod, the last remnant of his motorcycle crash, removed from his leg in late February. "This, for me, is a comeback season," Maier said in the summer, referring to next year. It's shaping up to be a spectacular one for the rest of us.

FOR THE RECORD · 2002 – 2003

World Cup Alpine Racing Season Results

Men

Date	Event	Site	Winner
10-27-02	Giant Slalom	Sölden, Austria	Stephan Eberharter, Austria
11-22-02	Giant Slalom	Park City, Utah	Michael Von Grünigen, Switz
11-24-02	Slalom	Park City, Utah	Rainer Schoenfelder, Austria
11-30-02	Downhill	Lake Louise, Alberta	Stephan Eberharter, Austria
12-1-02	Super G	Lake Louise, Alberta	Stephan Eberharter, Austria
12-7-02	Downhill	Beaver Creek, Colorado	Stephan Eberharter, Austria
12-8-02	Super G	Beaver Creek, Colorado	Didier Cuche, Switzerland
12-14-02	Downhill	Val d'Isere, France	Stephan Eberharter, Austria
12-15-02	Giant Slalom	Val d'Isere, France	Michael Von Grünigen, Switz
12-16-02	Slalom	Sestriere, Italy	Ivica Kostelic, Croatia
12-20-02	Super G	Gardena, Italy	Didier Defago, Switzerland
12-21-02	Downhill	Gardena, Italy	Antoine Deneriaz, France
12-22-02	Giant Slalom	Alta Badia, Italy	Bode Miller, United States
12-29-02	Downhill	Bormio, Italy	Daron Rahlves, United States
1-4-03	Giant Slalom	Kranjska Gora, Slovenia	Bode Miller, United States
1-5-03	Slalom	Kranjska Gora, Slovenia	Ivica Kostelic, Croatia
1-11-03	Downhill	Bormio, Italy	Stephan Eberharter, Austria
1-12-03	Slalom	Bormio, Italy	Ivica Kostelic, Croatia
1-14-03	Giant Slalom	Adelboden, Switzerland	Hans Knauss, Austria
1-17-03	Downhill	Wengen, Switzerland	Stephan Eberharter, Austria
1-18-03	Downhill	Wengen, Switzerland	Bruno Kemen, Switzerland
1-19-03	Slalom	Wengen, Switzerland	Giorgio Rocca, Italy
1-19-03	Combined	Wengen, Switzerland	Kjetil André Aamodt, Norway
1-25-03	Downhill	Kitzbühel, Austria	Daron Rahlves, United States
1-26-03	Slalom	Kitzbühel, Austria	Kalle Palander, Finland
1-26-03	Combined	Kitzbühel, Austria	Michael Walchhofer, Austria
1-27-03	Super G	Kitzbühel, Austria	Hermann Maier, Austria
1-28-03	Slalom	Schladming, Austria	Kalle Palander, Finland
2-22-03	Downhill	Garmisch, Germany	Stephan Eberharter, Austria
2-23-03	Super G	Garmisch, Germany	Marco Büchel, Lichtenstein
3-1-03	Giant Slalom	Yong Pyong, S Korea	Michael von Grünigen, Switz
3-2-03	Slalom	Yong Pyong, S Korea	Kalle Palander, Finland
3-8-03	Slalom	Shigakogen, Japan	Rainer Schoenfelder, Austria/ Kalle Palander, Finland
3-12-03	Downhill	Lillehammer, Norway	Antoine Deneriaz, France
3-13-03	Super G	Lillehammer, Norway	Stephan Eberharter, Austria
3-15-03	Giant Slalom	Lillehammer, Norway	Hans Knauss, Austria
3-16-03	Slalom	Lillehammer, Norway	Giorgio Rocca, Italy

Women

Date	Event	Site	Winner
10-26-02	Giant Slalom	Sölden, Austria	A. Flemmen, Nor/ T. Maze, Slo/ N. Hosp, Austria
11-21-02	Giant Slalom	Park City, Utah	Birgit Heeb-Batliner, Lichtenstein
11-23-02	Slalom	Park City, Utah	Janica Kostelic, Croatia
11-29-02	Super G	Aspen, Colorado	Hilde Gerg, Germany
11-30-02	Slalom	Aspen, Colorado	Anja Paerson, Sweden
12-6-02	Downhill	Lake Louise, Alberta	Hilde Gerg, Germany
12-7-02	Downhill	Lake Louise, Alberta	Carole Montillet, France
12-8-02	Super G	Lake Louise, Alberta	Karen Putzer, Italy
12-12-02	Giant Slalom	Val d'Isere, France	Karen Putzer, Italy
12-13-02	Super G	Val d'Isere, France	Carole Montillet, France
12-15-02	Slalom	Sestriere, Italy	Anja Paerson, Sweden
12-21-02	Downhill	Lenzerheide, Switzerland	Michaela Dorfmeister, Austria
12-22-02	Slalom	Lenzerheide, Switzerland	Janica Kostelic, Croatia
12-22-02	Combined	Lenzerheide, Switzerland	Janica Kostelic, Croatia
12-28-02	Giant Slalom	Semmering, Austria	Karen Putzer, Italy
12-29-02	Slalom	Semmering, Austria	Janica Kostelic, Croatia
1-4-03	Giant Slalom	Bormio, Italy	Sonja Nef, Switzerland
1-5-03	Slalom	Bormio, Italy	Janica Kostelic, Croatia
1-15-03	Super G	Cortina, Italy	Carole Montillet, France
1-17-03	Super G	Cortina, Italy	Renate Götschl, Austria
1-18-03	Downhill	Cortina, Italy	Renate Götschl, Austria
1-19-03	Giant Slalom	Cortina, Italy	Anja Paerson, Sweden
1-25-03	Giant Slalom	Maribor, Slovenia	Anja Paerson, Sweden
1-26-03	Slalom	Maribor, Slovenia	Anja Paerson, Sweden
2-28-03	Super G	Innsbruck, Austria	Renate Götschl, Austria

Women *(Cont.)*

Date	Event	Site	Winner
3-1-03	Downhill	Innsbruck, Austria	Michaela Dorfmeister, Austria
3-2-03	Super G	Innsbruck, Austria	Brigitte Obermoser, Austria
3-6-03	Giant Slalom	Aare, Sweden	Anja Paerson, Sweden
3-8-03	Slalom	Aare, Sweden	Janica Kostelic, Croatia
3-12-03	Downhill	Lillehammer, Norway	Renate Götschl, Austria
3-13-03	Super G	Lillehammer, Norway	Karen Putzer, Italy
3-15-03	Slalom	Lillehammer, Norway	Kristina Koznick, United States
3-16-03	Giant Slalom	Lillehammer, Norway	Karen Putzer, Italy

World Cup Alpine Racing Final Standings

Men

OVERALL

	Pts
Stephan Eberharter, Austria	1,333
Bode Miller, United States	1,100
Kjetil André Aamodt, Nor	940
Kalle Palander, Finland	718
Didier Cuche, Switzerland	709
Daron Rahlves, United States	647
Ivica Kostelic, Croatia	632
Benjamin Raich, Austria	622
Michael Walchhofer, Austria	600
Hans Knauss, Austria	596

DOWNHILL

	Pts
Stephan Eberharter, Austria	790
Daron Rahlves, United States	593
Michael Walchhofer, Austria	430
Bruno Kernen, Switzerland	351
Hannes Trinkl, Austria	341
Antoine Deneriaz, France	337
Kjetil André Aamodt, Norway	334
Fritz Strobl, Austria	334
Didier Cuche, Switzerland	333
Klaus Kroell, Austria	317

SLALOM

	Pts
Kalle Palander, Finland	658
Ivica Kostelic, Croatia	580
Rainer Schoenfelder, Austria	473
Giorgio Rocca, Italy	438
Manfred Pranger, Austria	385
Benjamin Raich, Austria	367
Hans-Petter Buraas, Norway	280
Truls Ove Karlsen, Norway	263
Pierrick Bourgeat, France	224
Jean Pierre Vidal, France	200

GIANT SLALOM

	Pts
Michael von Grünigen, Switz	542
Bode Miller, United States	425
Hans Knauss, Austria	365
Frederic Covili, France	296
Heinz Schilchegger, Austria	249
Massimiliano Blardone, Italy	249
Christian Mayer, Austria	234
Benjamin Raich, Austria	231
Christoph Gruber, Austria	226
Joel Chenal, France	194

SUPER G

	Pts
Stephan Eberharter, Austria	356
Marco Büchel, Lichtenstein	280
Didier Cuche, Switzerland	270
Kjetil André Aamodt, Norway	251
Hannes Reichelt, Austria	194
Christoph Gruber, Austria	185
Didier Defago, Switzerland	180
Andreas Schifferer, Austria	165
Hannes Trinkl, Austria	155
Josef Ströbl, Austria	150

Women

OVERALL

	Pts
Janica Kostelic, Croatia	1,570
Karen Putzer, Italy	1,100
Anja Paerson, Sweden	1,042
Michaela Dorfmeister, Austria	972
Martina Ertl, Germany	922
Carole Montillet, France	869
Renate Götschl, Austria	830
Alexandra Meissnitzer, Austria	776
Kirsten Clark, United States	661
Nicole Hosp, Austria	558

DOWNHILL

	Pts
Michaela Dorfmeister, Austria	372
Renate Götschl, Austria	368
Kirsten Clark, United States	316
Carole Montillet, France	313
Corinne Rey Bellet, Switz	230
Hilde Gerg, Germany	196
Ingrid Jacquemod, France	153
Melanie Turgeon, Canada	149
Karen Putzer, Italy	143
Alexandra Meissnitzer, Austria	139

SLALOM

	Pts
Janica Kostelic, Croatia	710
Anja Paerson, Sweden	498
Tanja Poutiainen, Finland	367
Christel Pascal, France	359
Marlies Schild, Austria	342
Laure Pequegnot, France	341
Nicole Gius, Italy	264
Monika Bergmann, Germany	245
Martina Ertl, Germany	228
Nicole Hosp, Austria	226

GIANT SLALOM

	Pts
Anja Paerson, Sweden	514
Karen Putzer, Italy	513
Janica Kostelic, Croatia	343
Nicole Hosp, Austria	332
Sonja Nef, Switzerland	329
Denise Karbon, Italy	293
Alexandra Meissnitzer, Austria	287
Martina Ertl, Germany	280
Michaela Dorfmeister, Austria	266
Maria Jose Rienda Contreras, Spain	237

SUPER G

	Pts
Carole Montillet, France	493
Renate Götschl, Austria	458
Karen Putzer, Italy	394
Alexandra Meissnitzer, Austria	350
Michaela Dorfmeister, Austria	298
Daniela Ceccarelli, Italy	289
Janica Kostelic, Croatia	281
Hilde Gerg, Germany	281
Martina Ertl, Germany	267
Kirsten Clark, United States	252

FOR THE RECORD·Year by Year

Event Descriptions

Downhill: A speed event entailing a single run on a course with a minimum vertical drop of 500 meters (800 for men's World Cup) and very few control gates.
Slalom: A technical event in which times for runs on two courses are totaled to determine the winner. Skiers must make many quick, short turns through a combination of gates (55–75 gates for men, 40–60 for women) over a short course (140–220-meter vertical drop for men, 120–180 for women).
Combined: An event in which scores from designated slalom and downhill races are combined to determine finish order.

Giant Slalom: A faster technical event with fewer, more broadly spaced gates than in the slalom. Times for runs on two courses with vertical drops of 250–400 meters for men and 250–300 meters for women are combined to determine the winner.
Super Giant Slalom: A speed event that is a cross between the downhill and the giant slalom.
Parallel Slalom: A technical event that combines slalom and giant slalom turns.

FIS World Championships

Sites

1931 ....Mürren, Switzerland	1936 ....Innsbruck, Austria
1932 ....Cortina d'Ampezzo, Italy	1937 ....Chamonix, France
1933 ....Innsbruck, Austria	1938 ....Engelberg, Switzerland
1934 ....St. Moritz, Switzerland	1939 ....Zakopane, Poland
1935 ....Mürren, Switzerland	

Men

DOWNHILL

1931 ....Walter Prager, Switzerland
1932 ....Gustav Lantschner, Austria
1933 ....Walter Prager, Switzerland
1934 ....David Zogg, Switzerland
1935 ....Franz Zingerle, Austria
1936 ....Rudolf Rominger, Switzerland
1937 ....Émile Allais, France
1938 ....James Couttet, France
1939 ....Hans Lantschner, Germany

SLALOM

1931 ....David Zogg, Switzerland
1932 ....Friedrich Dauber, Germany
1933 ....Anton Seelos, Austria
1934 ....Franz Pfnür, Germany
1935 ....Anton Seelos, Austria
1936 ....Rudi Matt, Austria
1937 ....Émile Allais, France
1938 ....Rudolf Rominger, Switzerland
1939 ....Rudolf Rominger, Switzerland

Women

DOWNHILL

1931 ....Esme Mackinnon, Great Britain
1932 ....Paola Wiesinger, Italy
1933 ....Inge Wersin-Lantschner, Austria
1934 ....Anni Rüegg, Switzerland
1935 ....Christel Cranz, Germany
1936 ....Evie Pinching, Great Britain
1937 ....Christel Cranz, Germany
1938 ....Lisa Resch, Germany
1939 ....Christel Cranz, Germany

SLALOM

1931 ....Esme Mackinnon, Great Britain
1932 ....Rösli Streiff, Switzerland
1933 ....Inge Wersin-Lantschner, Austria
1934 ....Christel Cranz, Germany
1935 ....Anni Rüegg, Switzerland
1936 ....Gerda Paumgarten, Austria
1937 ....Christel Cranz, Germany
1938 ....Christel Cranz, Germany
1939 ....Christel Cranz, Germany

FIS World Alpine Ski Championships

Sites

1950 ....Aspen, Colorado	1985 ....Bormio, Italy
1954 ....Are, Sweden	1987 ....Crans-Montana, Switzerland
1958 ....Badgastein, Austria	1989 ....Vail, Colorado
1962 ....Chamonix, France	1991 ....Saalbach-Hinterglemm, Austria
1966 ....Portillo, Chile	1993 ....Morioka-Shizukuishi, Japan
1970 ....Val Gardena, Italy	1996 ....Sierra Nevada, Spain
1974 ....St. Moritz, Switzerland	1997 ....Sestriere, Italy
1978 ....Garmisch-Partenkirchen, W Germany	1999 ....Vail, Colorado
1982 ....Schladming, Austria	2001 ....St. Anton, Switzerland
	2003 ....St. Moritz, Switzerland

Men

DOWNHILL

1950............Zeno Colo, Italy	1985............Pirmin Zurbriggen, Switzerland
1954............Christian Pravda, Austria	1987............Peter Müller, Switzerland
1958............Toni Sailer, Austria	1989............Hansjörg Tauscher, W Germany
1962............Karl Schranz, Austria	1991............Franz Heinzer, Switzerland
1966............Jean-Claude Killy, France	1993............Urs Lehmann, Switzerland
1970............Bernard Russi, Switzerland	1996............Patrick Ortlieb, Austria
1974............David Zwilling, Austria	1997............Bruno Kernen, Switzerland
1978............Josef Walcher, Austria	1999............Hermann Maier, Austria
1982............Harti Weirather, Austria	2001............Hannes Trinkl, Austria
	2003............Michael Walchhofer, Austria

SLALOM

1950............Zeno Colo, Italy	1985............Pirmin Zurbriggen, Switzerland
1954............Christian Pravda, Austria	1987............Peter Müller, Switzerland
1958............Toni Sailer, Austria	1989............Hansjörg Tauscher, W Germany
1962............Karl Schranz, Austria	1991............Franz Heinzer, Switzerland
1966............Jean-Claude Killy, France	1993............Urs Lehmann, Switzerland
1970............Bernard Russi, Switzerland	1996............Patrick Ortlieb, Austria
1974............David Zwilling, Austria	1997............Bruno Kernen, Switzerland
1978............Josef Walcher, Austria	1999............Hermann Maier, Austria
1982............Harti Weirather, Austria	2001............Hannes Trinkl, Austria
	2003............Ivica Kostelic, Croatia

GIANT SLALOM

1950............Zeno Colo, Italy	1985............Markus Wasmaier, W Germany
1954............Stein Eriksen, Norway	1987............Pirmin Zurbriggen, Switzerland
1958............Toni Sailer, Austria	1989............Rudolf Nierlich, Austria
1962............Egon Zimmermann, Austria	1991............Rudolf Nierlich, Austria
1966............Guy Périllat, France	1993............Kjetil André Aamodt, Norway
1970............Karl Schranz, Austria	1996............Alberto Tomba, Italy
1974............Gustavo Thoeni, Italy	1997............Michael von Grünigen, Switzerland
1978............Ingemar Stenmark, Sweden	1999............Marco Büchel, Liechtenstein
1982............Steve Mahre, United States	2001............Michael von Grünigen, Switzerland
	2003............Bode Miller, United States

COMBINED

1982............Michel Vion, France	1993............Lasse Kjus, Norway
1985............Pirmin Zurbriggen, Switzerland	1996............Marc Girardelli, Luxembourg
1987............Marc Girardelli, Luxembourg	1997............Kjetil André Aamodt, Norway
1989............Marc Girardelli, Luxembourg	1999............Kjetil André Aamodt, Norway
1991............Stefan Eberharter, Austria	2001............Kjetil André Aamodt, Norway
	2003............Bode Miller, United States

SUPER G

1987............Pirmin Zurbriggen, Switzerland	1997............Atle Skaardal, Norway
1989............Martin Hangl, Switzerland	1999............Hermann Maier, Austria
1991............Stefan Eberharter, Austria	Lasse Kjus, Norway
1993............Cancelled due to weather	2001............Daron Rahlves, United States
1996............Atle Skaardal, Norway	2003............Stephan Eberharter, Austria

Women

DOWNHILL

1950............Trude Beiser-Jochum, Austria	1985............Michela Figini, Switzerland
1954............Ida Schopfer, Switzerland	1987............Maria Walliser, Switzerland
1958............Lucile Wheeler, Canada	1989............Maria Walliser, Switzerland
1962............Christl Haas, Austria	1991............Petra Kronberger, Austria
1966............Erika Schinegger, Austria	1993............Kate Pace, Canada
1970............Annerösli Zryd, Switzerland	1996............Picabo Street, United States
1974............Annemarie Moser-Pröll, Austria	1997............Hilary Lindh, United States
1978............Annemarie Moser-Pröll, Austria	1999............Renate Götschl, Austria
1982............Gerry Sorensen, Canada	2001............Michaela Dorfmeister, Austria
	2003............Melanie Turgeon, Canada

Women (Cont.)

SLALOM

1950.............Dagmar Rom, Austria	1987.............Erika Hess, Switzerland
1954.............Trude Klecker, Austria	1989.............Mateja Svet, Yugoslavia
1958.............Inger Bjornbakken, Norway	1991.............Vreni Schneider, Switzerland
1962.............Marianne Jahn, Austria	1993.............Karin Buder, Austria
1966.............Annie Famose, France	1996.............Pernilla Wiberg, Sweden
1970.............Ingrid Lafforgue, France	1997.............Deborah Compagnoni, Italy
1974.............Hanni Wenzel, Liechtenstein	1999.............Trine Bakke, Norway
1978.............Lea Sölkner, Austria	2001.............Anja Paerson, Sweden
1982.............Erika Hess, Switzerland	2003.............Janica Kostelic, Croatia
1985.............Perrine Pelen, France	

GIANT SLALOM

1950.............Dagmar Rom, Austria	1987.............Vreni Schneider, Switzerland
1954.............Lucienne Schmith-Couttet, France	1989.............Vreni Schneider, Switzerland
1958.............Lucile Wheeler, Canada	1991.............Pernilla Wiberg, Sweden
1962.............Marianne Jahn, Austria	1993.............Carole Merle, France
1966.............Marielle Goitschel, France	1996.............Deborah Compagnoni, Italy
1970.............Betsy Clifford, Canada	1997.............Deborah Compagnoni, Italy
1974.............Fabienne Serrat, France	1999.............Anita Wachter, Austria
1978.............Maria Epple, W Germany	2001.............Sonja Nef, Switzerland
1982.............Erika Hess, Switzerland	2003.............Anja Paerson, Sweden
1985.............Diann Roffe, United States	

COMBINED

1982.............Erika Hess, Switzerland	1996.............Pernilla Wiberg, Sweden
1985.............Erika Hess, Switzerland	1997.............Renate Götschl, Austria
1987.............Erika Hess, Switzerland	1999.............Pernilla Wiberg, Sweden
1989.............Tamara McKinney, United States	2001.............Martina Ertl, Germany
1991.............Chantal Bournissen, Switzerland	2003.............Janica Kostelic, Croatia
1993.............Miriam Vogt, Germany	

SUPER G

1987.............Maria Walliser, Switzerland	1997.............Isolde Kostner, Italy
1989.............Ulrike Maier, Austria	1999.............Alexandra Meissnitzer, Austria
1991.............Ulrike Maier, Austria	2001.............Regine Cavagnoud, France
1993.............Katja Seizinger, Germany	2003.............Michaela Dorfmeister, Austria
1996.............Isolde Kostner, Italy	

Note: The 1995 FIS World Alpine Ski Championships were postponed to 1996 due to lack of snow.

Unlikely Twist

Hours after winning his second bronze medal in moguls at the World Freestlye Champiionships in Deer Valley, Utah, last month, Colorado's Toby Dawson was explaining how he prepared for the risky jumps in the middle of his run. "You need to think about seven moguls ahead," he said. "Forget what you just did; know what's in front of you."

Dawson, 23, isn't one to dwell on the bumps behind him, and he's had his share. He knows almost nothing of his life before September 1981, when at roughly three years old he turned up in a basket, with a note attached, next to a police station in Seoul, South Korea. "Look after him," the note read. "We can't deal with it." Neither does he recall the ensuing six months he spent in a Korean orphanage before he was flown to Denver to meet his adoptive parents, Vail ski instructors Deb and Mike Dawson. In his two return trips to his native land, no words, sights or smells rang a bell. "My first memory of anything was playing in the snow with my [adoptive] parents, I guess because there was love," said Dawson. "Maybe I suppressed everything before that because there wasn't any."

Dawson took time to adapt to his new life.

"He woke up every night for a year screaming with nightmares," Deb saids.Toby recalled being so withdrawn as a kid that "when I'd see another person coming, I'd hide behind my mom's dress." A year after his arrival, however, the Dawsons adopted another Korean boy, whom they named K.C. He had the vibrancy Toby lacked, and Toby often asked K.C. (now a businessman) to speak to others on his behalf.

Once Toby donned skis, though, his personality emerged. Just weeks after Deb suited him up for the first time, she was dragging him off the slopes after five-hour days. He won his first trophy at age four, after repeatedly attempting to complete a child's course within an allotted time. ....

Dawson skied on his first moguls course at 12 and made his first national team six years later, quickly gaining a reputation for attempting difficult jumps. "Toby's an air bear," said Don St. Pierre, U.S. moguls coach. "I've seen him land in every possible position."

His next goal is to land on the Olympic medal stand in 2006.

—Brian Cazeneuve

Men

OVERALL

1967 ....Jean-Claude Killy, France	1986 ....Marc Girardelli, Luxembourg
1968 ....Jean-Claude Killy, France	1987 ....Pirmin Zurbriggen, Switzerland
1969 ....Karl Schranz, Austria	1988 ....Pirmin Zurbriggen, Switzerland
1970 ....Karl Schranz, Austria	1989 ....Marc Girardelli, Luxembourg
1971 ....Gustavo Thoeni, Italy	1990 ....Pirmin Zurbriggen, Switzerland
1972 ....Gustavo Thoeni, Italy	1991 ....Marc Girardelli, Luxembourg
1973 ....Gustavo Thoeni, Italy	1992 ....Paul Accola, Switzerland
1974 ....Piero Gros, Italy	1993 ....Marc Girardelli, Luxembourg
1975 ....Gustavo Thoeni, Italy	1994 ....Kjetil André Aamodt, Norway
1976 ....Ingemar Stenmark, Sweden	1995 ....Alberto Tomba, Italy
1977 ....Ingemar Stenmark, Sweden	1996 ....Lasse Kjus, Norway
1978 ....Ingemar Stenmark, Sweden	1997 ....Luc Alphand, France
1979 ....Peter Lüscher, Switzerland	1998 ....Hermann Maier, Austria
1980 ....Andreas Wenzel, Liechtenstein	1999 ....Lasse Kjus, Norway
1981 ....Phil Mahre, United States	2000 ....Hermann Maier, Austria
1982 ....Phil Mahre, United States	2001 ....Hermann Maier, Austria
1983 ....Phil Mahre, United States	2002 ....Stephan Eberharter, Austria
1984 ....Pirmin Zurbriggen, Switzerland	2003 ....Stephan Eberharter, Austria
1985 ....Marc Girardelli, Luxembourg	

DOWNHILL

1967 ....Jean-Claude Killy, France	1985 ....Helmut Höflehner, Austria
1968 ....Gerhard Nenning, Austria	1986 ....Peter Wirnsberger, Austria
1969 ....Karl Schranz, Austria	1987 ....Pirmin Zurbriggen, Switzerland
1970 ....Karl Schranz, Austria	1988 ....Pirmin Zurbriggen, Switzerland
.............................Karl Cordin, Austria	1989 ....Marc Girardelli, Luxembourg
1971 ....Bernhard Russi, Switzerland	1990 ....Helmut Höflehner, Austria
1972 ....Bernhard Russi, Switzerland	1991 ....Franz Heinzer, Switzerland
1973 ....Roland Collumbin, Switzerland	1992 ....Franz Heinzer, Switzerland
1974 ....Roland Collumbin, Switzerland	1993 ....Franz Heinzer, Switzerland
1975 ....Franz Klammer, Austria	1994 ....Marc Girardelli, Luxembourg
1976 ....Franz Klammer, Austria	1995 ....Luc Alphand, France
1977 ....Franz Klammer, Austria	1996 ....Luc Alphand, France
1978 ....Franz Klammer, Austria	1997 ....Luc Alphand, France
1979 ....Peter Müller, Switzerland	1998 ....Andreas Schifferer, Austria
1980 ....Peter Müller, Switzerland	1999 ....Lasse Kjus, Norway
1981 ....Harti Weirather, Austria	2000 ....Hermann Maier, Austria
1982 ....Steve Podborski, Canada	2001 ....Hermann Maier, Austria
.............................Peter Müller, Switzerland	2002 ....Stephan Eberharter, Austria
1983 ....Franz Klammer, Austria	2003 ....Stephan Eberharter, Austria
1984 ....Urs Raber, Switzerland	

SLALOM

1967 ....Jean-Claude Killy, France	1985 ....Marc Girardelli, Luxembourg
1968 ....Domeng Giovanoli, Switzerland	1986 ....Rok Petrovic, Yugoslavia
1969 ....Jean-Noël Augert, France	1987 ....Bojan Krizaj, Yugoslavia
1970 ....Patrick Russel, France	1988 ....Alberto Tomba, Italy
.......................Alain Penz, France	1989 ....Armin Bittner, W Germany
1971 ....Jean-Noël Augert, France	1990 ....Armin Bittner, W Germany
1972 ....Jean-Noël Augert, France	1991 ....Marc Girardelli, Luxembourg
1973 ....Gustavo Thoeni, Italy	1992 ....Alberto Tomba, Italy
1974 ....Gustavo Thoeni, Italy	1993 ....Tomas Fogdof, Sweden
1975 ....Ingemar Stenmark, Sweden	1994 ....Alberto Tomba, Italy
1976 ....Ingemar Stenmark, Sweden	1995 ....Alberto Tomba, Italy
1977 ....Ingemar Stenmark, Sweden	1996 ...,............Sebastien Amiez, France
1978 ....Ingemar Stenmark, Sweden	1997 ....Thomas Sykora, Austria
1979 ....Ingemar Stenmark, Sweden	1998 ....Thomas Sykora, Austria
1980 ....Ingemar Stenmark, Sweden	1999 ....Thomas Stangassinger, Austria
1981 ....Ingemar Stenmark, Sweden	2000 ....Kjetil André Aamodt, Norway
1982 ....Phil Mahre, United States	2001 ....Benjamin Raich, Austria
1983 ....Ingemar Stenmark, Sweden	2002 ....Ivica Kostelic, Croatia
1984 ....Marc Girardelli, Luxembourg	2003 ....Kalle Palander, Finland

Men (Cont.)

GIANT SLALOM

1967 ....Jean-Claude Killy, France	1986 ....Joël Gaspoz, Switzerland
1968 ....Jean-Claude Killy, France	1987 ....Joël Gaspoz, Switzerland
1969 ....Karl Schranz, Austria	...............Pirmin Zurbriggen, Switzerland
1970 ....Gustavo Thoeni, Italy	1988 ....Alberto Tomba, Italy
1971 ....Patrick Russel, France	1989 ....Pirmin Zurbriggen, Switzerland
1972 ....Gustavo Thoeni, Italy	1990 ....Ole-Cristian Furuseth, Norway
1973 ....Hans Hinterseer, Austria	...............Günther Mader, Austria
1974 ....Piero Gros, Italy	1991 ....Alberto Tomba, Italy
1975 ....Ingemar Stenmark, Sweden	1992 ....Alberto Tomba, Italy
1976 ....Ingemar Stenmark, Sweden	1993 ....Kjetil André Aamodt, Norway
1977 ....Heini Hemmi, Switzerland	1994 ....Christian Mayer, Austria
...............Ingemar Stenmark, Sweden	1995 ....Alberto Tomba, Italy
1978 ....Ingemar Stenmark, Sweden	1996 ....Michael von Grünigen, Switzerland
1979 ....Ingemar Stenmark, Sweden	1997 ....Michael von Grünigen, Switzerland
1980 ....Ingemar Stenmark, Sweden	1998 ....Hermann Maier, Austria
1981 ....Ingemar Stenmark, Sweden	1999 ....Michael von Grünigen, Switzerland
1982 ....Phil Mahre, United States	2000 ....Hermann Maier, Austria
1983 ....Phil Mahre, United States	2001 ....Hermann Maier, Austria
1984 ....Ingemar Stenmark, Sweden	2002 ....Frederic Covili, France
...............Pirmin Zurbriggen, Switzerland	2003 ....Michael von Grünigen, Switzerland
1985 ....Marc Girardelli, Luxembourg	

SUPER G

1986 ....Markus Wasmeier, W Germany	1995 ....Peter Runggaldier, Italy
1987 ....Pirmin Zurbriggen, Switzerland	1996 ....Atle Skaardal, Norway
1988 ....Pirmin Zurbriggen, Switzerland	1997 ....Luc Alphand, France
1989 ....Pirmin Zurbriggen, Switzerland	1998 ....Hermann Maier, Austria
1990 ....Pirmin Zurbriggen, Switzerland	1999 ....Hermann Maier, Austria
1991 ....Franz Heinzer, Switzerland	2000 ....Hermann Maier, Austria
1992 ....Paul Accola, Switzerland	2001 ....Hermann Maier, Austria
1993 ....Kjetil André Aamodt, Norway	2002 ....Stephan Eberharter, Austria
1994 ....Jan Einar Thorsen, Norway	2003 ....Stephan Eberharter, Austria

COMBINED

1979 ....Andreas Wenzel, Liechtenstein	1992 ....Paul Accola, Switzerland
1980 ....Andreas Wenzel, Liechtenstein	1993 ....Marc Girardelli, Luxembourg
1981 ....Phil Mahre, United States	1994 ....Kjetil André Aamodt, Norway
1982 ....Phil Mahre, United States	1995 ....Marc Girardelli, Luxembourg
1983 ....Phil Mahre, United States	1996 ....Günther Mader, Austria
1984 ....Andreas Wenzel, Liechtenstein	1997 ....Kjetil André Aamodt, Norway
1985 ....Andreas Wenzel, Liechtenstein	1998 ....Werner Franz, Austria
1986 ....Markus Wasmeier, W Germany	1999 ....Kjetil André Aamodt, Norway
1987 ....Pirmin Zurbriggen, Switzerland	2000 ....Kjetil André Aamodt, Norway
1988 ....Hubert Strolz, Austria	...............Lasse Kjus, Norway
1989 ....Marc Girardelli, Luxembourg	2001 ....Lasse Kjus, Norway
1990 ....Pirmin Zurbriggen, Switzerland	2002 ....Kjetil André Aamodt, Norway
1991 ....Marc Girardelli, Luxembourg	2003 ....Bode Miller, United States

Women

OVERALL

1967 ....Nancy Greene, Canada	1986 ....Maria Walliser, Switzerland
1968 ....Nancy Greene, Canada	1987 ....Maria Walliser, Switzerland
1969 ....Gertrud Gabl, Austria	1988 ....Michela Figini, Switzerland
1970 ....Michèle Jacot, France	1989 ....Vreni Schneider, Switzerland
1971 ....Annemarie Pröll, Austria	1990 ....Petra Kronberger, Austria
1972 ....Annemarie Pröll, Austria	1991 ....Petra Kronberger, Austria
1973 ....Annemarie Pröll, Austria	1992 ....Petra Kronberger, Austria
1974 ....Annemarie Moser-Pröll, Austria	1993 ....Anita Wachter, Austria
1975 ....Annemarie Moser-Pröll, Austria	1994 ....Vreni Schneider, Switzerland
1976 ....Rosi Mitermaier, W Germany	1995 ....Vreni Schneider, Switzerland
1977 ....Lise-Marie Morerod, Switzerland	1996 ....Katja Seizinger, Germany
1978 ....Hanni Wenzel, Liechtenstein	1997 ....Pernilla Wiberg, Sweden
1979 ....Annemarie Moser-Pröll, Austria	1998 ....Katja Seizinger, Germany
1980 ....Hanni Wenzel, Liechtenstein	1999 ....Alexandra Meissnitzer, Austria
1981 ....Marie-Thérèse Nadig, Switzerland	2000 ....Renate Götschl, Austria
1982 ....Erika Hess, Switzerland	2001 ....Janica Kostelic, Croatia
1983 ....Tamara McKinney, United States	2002 ....Michaela Dorfmeister, Austria
1984 ....Erika Hess, Switzerland	2003 ....Janica Kostelic, Austria
1985 ....Michela Figini, Switzerland	

Women *(Cont.)*

DOWNHILL

1967 ....Marielle Goitschel, France	1986 ....Maria Walliser, Switzerland
1968 ....Isabelle Mir, France & Olga Pall, Austria	1987 ....Michela Figini, Switzerland
1969 ....Wiltrud Drexel, Austria	1988 ....Michela Figini, Switzerland
1970 ....Isabelle Mir, France	1989 ....Michela Figini, Switzerland
1971 ....Annemarie Pröll, Austria	1990 ....Katrin Gutensohn-Knopf, Germany
1972 ....Annemarie Pröll, Austria	1991 ....Chantal Bournissen, Switzerland
1973 ....Annemarie Pröll, Austria	1992 ....Katja Seizinger, Germany
1974 ....Annemarie Moser-Pröll, Austria	1993 ....Katja Seizinger, Germany
1975 ....Annemarie Moser-Pröll, Austria	1994 ....Katja Seizinger, Germany
1976 ....Brigitte Totschnig, Austria	1995 ....Picabo Street, United States
1977 ....Brigitte Totschnig-Habersatter, Austria	1996 ....Picabo Street, United States
1978 ....Annemarie Moser-Pröll, Austria	1997 ....Renate Götschl, Austria
1979 ....Annemarie Moser-Pröll, Austria	1998 ....Katja Seizinger, Germany
1980 ....Marie-Thérèse Nadig, Switzerland	1999 ....Renate Götschl, Austria
1981 ....Marie-Thérèse Nadig, Switzerland	2000 ....Regina Haeusl, Germany
1982 ....Marie-Cecile Gros-Gaudenier, France	2001 ....Isolde Kostner, Italy
1983 ....Doris De Agostini, Switzerland	2002 ....Isolde Kostner, Italy
1984 ....Maria Walliser, Switzerland	2003 ....Michaela Dorfmeister, Austria
1985 ....Michela Figini, Switzerland	

SLALOM

1967 ....Nancy Greene, Canada	1986 ....Maria Walliser, Switzerland
1968 ....Nancy Greene, Canada	1987 ....Maria Walliser, Switzerland
1969 ....Gertrud Gabl, Austria	1988 ....Michela Figini, Switzerland
1970 ....Michèle Jacot, France	1989 ....Vreni Schneider, Switzerland
1971 ....Annemarie Pröll, Austria	1990 ....Petra Kronberger, Austria
1972 ....Annemarie Pröll, Austria	1991 ....Petra Kronberger, Austria
1973 ....Annemarie Pröll, Austria	1992 ....Petra Kronberger, Austria
1974 ....Annemarie Moser-Pröll, Austria	1993 ....Anita Wachter, Austria
1975 ....Annemarie Moser-Pröll, Austria	1994 ....Vreni Schneider, Switzerland
1976 ....Rosi Mitermaier, W Germany	1995 ....Vreni Schneider, Switzerland
1977 ....Lise-Marie Morerod, Switzerland	1996 ....Katja Seizinger, Germany
1978 ....Hanni Wenzel, Liechtenstein	1997 ....Pernilla Wiberg, Sweden
1979 ....Annemarie Moser-Pröll, Austria	1998 ....Katja Seizinger, Germany
1980 ....Hanni Wenzel, Liechtenstein	1999 ....Alexandra Meissnitzer, Austria
1981 ....Marie-Thérèse Nadig, Switzerland	2000 ....Renate Götschl, Austria
1982 ....Erika Hess, Switzerland	2001 ....Janica Kostelic, Croatia
1983 ....Tamara McKinney, United States	2002 ....Laure Pequegnot, France
1984 ....Erika Hess, Switzerland	2003 ....Janica Kostelic, Croatia
1985 ....Michela Figini, Switzerland	

GIANT SLALOM

1967 ....Nancy Greene, Canada	1986 ....Vreni Schneider, Switzerland
1968 ....Nancy Greene, Canada	1987 ....Vreni Schneider, Switzerland
1969 ....Marilyn Cochran, United States	Maria Walliser, Switzerland
1970 ....Michèle Jacot, France	1988 ....Mateja Svet, Yugoslavia
Françoise Macchi, France	1989 ....Vreni Schneider, Switzerland
1971 ....Annemarie Pröll, Austria	1990 ....Anita Wachter, Austria
1972 ....Annemarie Pröll, Austria	1991 ....Vreni Schneider, Switzerland
1973 ....Monika Kaserer, Austria	1992 ....Carole Merle, France
1974 ....Hanni Wenzel, Liechtenstein	1993 ....Carole Merle, France
1975 ....Annemarie Moser-Pröll, Austria	1994 ....Anita Wachter, Austria
1976 ....Lise-Marie Morerod, Switzerland	1995 ....Vreni Schneider, Switzerland
1977 ....Lise-Marie Morerod, Switzerland	1996 ....Martina Ertl, Germany
1978 ....Lise-Marie Morerod, Switzerland	1997 ....Deborah Compagnoni, Italy
1979 ....Christa Kinshofer, W Germany	1998 ....Martina Ertl, Germany
1980 ....Hanni Wenzel, Liechtenstein	1999 ....Alexandra Meissnitzer, Austria
1981 ....Marie-Thérèse Nadig, Switzerland	2000 ....Michaela Dorfmeister, Austria
1982 ....Irene Epple, W Germany	2001 ....Sonja Nef, Switzerland
1983 ....Tamara McKinney, United States	2002 ....Sonja Nef, Switzerland
1984 ....Erika Hess, Switzerland	2003 ....Anja Paerson, Sweden
1985 ....Maria Keihl, W Germany	
Michela Figini, Switzerland	

SUPER G

1986 ....Maria Kiehl, W Germany	1991 ....Carole Merle, France
1987 ....Maria Walliser, Switzerland	1992 ....Carole Merle, France
1988 ....Michela Figini, Switzerland	1993 ....Katja Seizinger, Germany
1989 ....Carole Merle, France	1994 ....Katja Seizinger, Germany
1990 ....Carole Merle, France	1995 ....Katja Seizinger, Germany

Women (Cont.)

SUPER G (CONT.)

1996 ....Katja Seizinger, Germany	2000 ....Renate Götschl, Austria
1997 ....Hilde Gerg, Germany	2001 ....Regine Cavagnoud, France
1998 ....Katja Seizinger, Germany	2002 ....Hilde Gerg, Germany
1999 ....Alexandra Meissnitzer, Austria	2003 ....Carole Montillet, France

COMBINED

1979 ....Annemarie Moser-Pröll, Austria	1991 ....Sabine Ginther, Austria
Hanni Wenzel, Liechtenstein	1992 ....Sabine Ginther, Austria
1980 ....Hanni Wenzel, Liechtenstein	1993 ....Anita Wachter, Austria
1981 ....Marie-Thérèse Nadig, Switzerland	1994 ....Pernilla Wiberg, Sweden
1982 ....Irene Epple, W Germany	1995 ....Pernilla Wiberg, Sweden
1983 ....Hanni Wenzel, Liechtenstein	1996 ....Anita Wachter, Austria
1984 ....Erika Hess, Switzerland	1997 ....Pernilla Wiberg, Sweden
1985 ....Brigitte Oertli, Switzerland	1998 ....Hilde Gerg, Germany
1986 ....Maria Walliser, Switzerland	1999 ....Hilde Gerg, Germany
1987 ....Brigitte Oertli, Switzerland	2000 ....Renate Götschl, Austria
1988 ....Brigitte Oertli, Switzerland	2001 ....Janica Kostelic, Croatia
1989 ....Brigitte Oertli, Switzerland	2002 ....Renate Götschl, Austria
1990 ....Anita Wachter, Austria	2003 ....Janica Kostelic, Croatia

World Cup Career Victories

Men	Women
DOWNHILL	**DOWNHILL**
25............................Franz Klammer, Austria	36............................Annemarie Moser-Pröll, Austria
19............................Peter Müller, Switzerland	17............................Michela Figini, Switzerland
15............................Franz Heinzer, Switzerland	16............................Katja Seizinger, Germany
SLALOM	**SLALOM**
40............................Ingemar Stenmark, Sweden	34............................Vreni Schneider, Switzerland
35............................Alberto Tomba, Italy	21............................Erika Hess, Switzerland
16............................Marc Girardelli, Luxembourg	16............................*Janica Kostelic, Croatia
GIANT SLALOM	**GIANT SLALOM**
46............................Ingemar Stenmark, Sweden	20............................Vreni Schneider, Switzerland
23............................*Michael Von Grünigen, Switz	16............................Annemarie Moser-Pröll, Austria
15............................Alberto Tomba, Italy	16............................Anita Wachter, Austria
SUPER G	**SUPER G**
17............................*Hermann Maier, Austria	16............................Katja Seizinger, Germany
10............................Pirmin Zurbriggen, Switzerland	12............................Carole Merle, France
7............................Marc Girardelli, Luxembourg	8............................*Renate Götschl, Austria
COMBINED	**COMBINED**
11............................Phil Mahre, United States	8............................Hanni Wenzel, Liechtenstein
Pirmin Zurbriggen, Switzerland	7............................Annemarie Moser-Pröll, Austria
Marc Girardelli, Luxembourg	Brigitte Oertli, Switzerland

*Active in 2002–03.

U.S. Olympic Gold Medalists

Men			Women		
Year	Winner	Event	Year	Winner	Event
1980 ....Phil Mahre		Combined	1948 ....Gretchen Fraser		Slalom
1984 ....Bill Johnson		Downhill	1952 ....Andrea Mead Lawrence		Slalom
1984 ....Phil Mahre		Slalom	1952 ....Andrea Mead Lawrence		Giant Slalom
1994 ....Tommy Moe		Downhill	1972 ....Barbara Ann Cochran		Slalom
			1984 ....Debbie Armstrong		Giant Slalom
			1994 ....Diann Roffe-Steinrotter		Super G
			1998 ....Picabo Street		Super G

Figure Skating

Lovely and Amazing

Favoring elegance over athleticism, Michelle Kwan won her seventh U.S. and fifth world titles

BY MERRELL NODEN

NO, YOU WEREN'T dreaming. Nor was that a hallucination you saw gliding so gracefully over the ice, first at the U.S. championships in January and then, two months later, at the world championships. It really was Michelle Kwan, whom, truth be told, most of us had written off as too old, too unathletic and too darned cautious to beat the new generation of skaters led by Kwan's Olympic conqueror, Sarah Hughes.

But beat them Kwan did, in both competitions, winning her seventh U.S. and fifth world titles by skating as expressively as she ever has in a career that now stretches all the way back to the 1994 Olympics (which she attended as an alternate). If Kwan seems, at the ripe old age of 23, to have become as fixed and predictable a part of the figure skating landscape as, say, Dick Button, well ... lucky us! Every time she skates she reminds us that no matter how acrobatic things get in this sport, there is always a place for grace, expressiveness and beauty.

Kwan herself wasn't sure what she'd do after the disappointment of taking "only" the bronze medal at the 2002 Olympics. No one would have faulted her for taking that medal, and the silver she'd won four years earlier, and skating off into the sunset—or at least to the world of ice shows, where there is more money and less pressure.

But Kwan chose the road less taken. After parting with her longtime coach, Frank Carroll, she worked briefly with her father, and then called on retired skater Scott Williams, who was surprised by her request since he considered himself more of an ice-show producer than a coach. But Kwan knew what she needed. "Scott has an aura that's relaxing and calming," she explained. At the U.S. championships in Dallas she skated calmly and beautifully to beat both Hughes and Sasha Cohen, who entered as the favorite. All three women skated so well that there was talk of a U.S. sweep at the worlds, which had not happened since 1991.

In sharp contrast to the brilliance of the U.S. women was the performance of the American men. Michael Weiss claimed his third U.S. title but in a dispiriting exhibition of ineptitude. At a time when the quad jump has become *de rigeur* for any man hoping to win a world title, Weiss became the first U.S.

With a new coach and a new attitude, 23-year-old Kwan took the U.S. and world titles.

champion in more than a decade to win without landing even a triple axel. Timothy Goebel, the Olympic bronze medalist, finished second, and Ryan Jahnke was third.

Elsewhere, the 2002 Olympic judging scandal continued to have nasty echoes. In August 2002 a grand jury indicted reputed Russian mobster Alimzhan Tokhtakhounov, the alleged "fixer" of the Olympic vote swap, on five criminal counts, including conspiracy to commit bribery. In July 2002, he was thrown in jail in Venice, after an Italian court ruled he should be extradited to the U.S. But the extradition order was overturned on appeal in June 2003—though potentially Tokhtakhounov still faced organized crime–related charges in Italy.

The International Skating Union warned its officials that if they set foot on U.S. soil they could expect to be interviewed by the FBI. One consequence of that threat was that Marina Anissina and Gwendal Peizerat, the French pairs team that is alleged to have been the beneficiary of Tokhtakhounov's efforts, decided not to skate in the 18-city Champions on Ice tour.

Also generating controversy was the scoring system the ISU concocted to replace the one used in Salt Lake City. Under the new system, the scores that count are randomly selected by computer before being posted anonymously. This did not sit well with outgoing U.S. figure skating head Phyllis Howard, who said, "The display of marks under the interim system provides no feedback to skaters or coaches and creates an environment of mistrust."

Despite all the unpleasantness, the world championships, held March 24–30 at the MCI Center in Washington, D.C., reminded us what will always bring skating fans back to the sport. Twenty-year-old Evgeni Plushenko of Russia won the men's competition, edging Goebel. (Weiss finished fifth.) Also skating magnificently were the Chinese pair of Hongbo Zhao and Xue Shen, who received four 6's.

The much hyped American sweep of the women's medals did not happen. Hughes spent the winter focusing on college admissions, which can't have helped her focus. She never skated with the same joyful abandon she'd shown at the Olympics but, after a disastrous qualifying round left her in 9th place, rebounded in the long program to improve to 6th place, two spots behind Cohen. "It's not so easy being Olympic champion," said Hughes. "I'm glad [the year] is over."

Not Kwan. This year she has surpised us and, no doubt, herself. She landed six triples at the worlds, the only wobbly landing coming on the triple toe loop. By the time she went into her straight line step at the end, the crowd was on its feet cheering so loudly the music had to be turned up.

"I never felt such energy from myself," said an exuberant Kwan, who, having medaled in eight consecutive world championships, must be ranked second only to Sonja Henie for brilliance and longevity. She would not say if the 2006 Olympics in Turin would be part of her plans, but held out that hope. "Why stop doing what you love doing?"

FOR THE RECORD 2003

World Champions

Washington, D.C., March 24–30

Women

1. ......Michelle Kwan, United States
2. ....Elena Sokolova, Russia
3. ....Fumie Suguri, Japan

Men

1. ....Evgeni Plushenko, Russia
1. ....Timothy Goebel, United States
3. ....Takeshi Honda, Japan

Pairs

1. ....Xue Shen and Hongbo Zhao, China
2. ....Tatiana Totmianina and Maxim Marinin, Russia
3. ....Maria Petrova and Alexei Tikhonov, Russia

Dance

1. ....Shae-Lynn Bourne and Victor Kraatz, Canada
2. ....Irina Lobacheva and Ilia Averbukh, Russia
3. ....Albena Denkova and Maxim Staviyski, Bulgaria

World Figure Skating Championships Medal Table

Country	Gold	Silver	Bronze	Total
Russia	1	3	1	5
United States	1	1	0	2
Japan	0	0	2	2
Canada	1	0	0	1
China	1	0	0	1
Bulgaria	0	0	1	1

Champions of the United States

Dallas, January 12–19

Women

1. ....Michelle Kwan, Los Angeles FSC
2. ....Sarah Hughes, SC of New York
3. ....Sasha Cohen, Orange County FSC

Men

1. ....Michael Weiss, Washington FSC
2. ....Timothy Goebel, Winterhurst FSC
3. ....Ryan Jahnke, Broadmoor, SC

Pairs

1. ....Tiffany Scott and Philip Dulebohn,
   Colonial FSC/Univeristy of Delaware FSC
2. ....Kathry Orscher and Garrett Lucash,
   SC of Hartford/Charter Oak FSC
3. ....Rena Inoue and John Baldwin
   All Year FSC

Dance

1. ....Naomi Lang and Peter Tchernyshev,
   American Academy FSC
2. ....Tanith Belbin and Benjamin Agosto,
   Detroit SC
3. ....Melissa Gregory and Denis Petukhov,
   Broadmoor SC/Skokie Valley SC

Kwan Do

Driving in his car when Michelle Kwan phoned him to ask if he would be her coach, former skater Scott Williams, 37, had to pull over to keep from careering off the road. Williams had only limited coaching experience, but the prospect of guiding Kwan, arguably the greatest female skater since Sonja Henie, was irresistible.

Insightful and laid back, Williams has succeeded in getting Kwan to enjoy her skating again. She still doesn't have a triple-triple combination, as most of her rivals do. What she has done is subtract the weight of the world from her shoulders. At the world championships in March 2003, it was not Kwan's six triple jumps or even her elegant signature spiral that drew the 16,116 fans at Washington's MCI Center to their feet. It was her straight-line footwork, and exquisite, Astaire-like dance of exuberance that was more like a scene of great theater than sport. The cheering audience drowned out the final 30 seconds of her music as she shimmered across the ice. Her performance, Kwan said, "tells me I should put less presure on mysefl and just go out and have fun. That's how it should have been last year [at the 2002 Olympics]."

—E.M. Swift

Skating Terminology*

Basic Skating Terms

Edges: The two sides of the skating blade, on either side of the grooved center. There is an inside edge, on the inner side of the leg; and an outside edge, on the outer side of the leg.

Free Foot, Hip, Knee, Side, etc.: The foot a skater is not skating on at any one time is the free foot; everything on that side of the body is then called "free." (See also "skating foot.")

Free Skating (Freestyle): A 4- or 5-minute competition program of free-skating components, choreographed to music, with no set elements. Skating moves include jumps, spins, steps and other linking movements.

Skating Foot, Hip, Knee, Side, etc.: Opposite of the free foot, hip, knee, side, etc. The foot a skater is skating on at any one time is the skating foot; everything on that side of the body is then called "skating."

Toe Picks (Toe Rakes): The teeth at the front of the skate blade, used primarily for certain jumps and spins.

Trace, Tracing: The line left on the ice by the skater's blade.

Jumps

Waltz: A beginner's jump, involving half a revolution in the air, taken from a forward outside edge and landed on the back outside edge of the other foot.

Toe Loop: A one-revolution jump taken off from and landed on the same back outside edge. This jump is similar to the loop jump except that the skater kicks the toe pick of the free leg into the ice upon takeoff, providing added power.

Toe Walley: A jump similar to the toe loop, except that the takeoff is from the inside edge.

Flip: A jump taken off with the toe pick of the free leg from a back inside edge and landed on a back outside edge, with one in-air revolution.

Lutz: A toe jump similar to the flip, taken off with the toe pick of the free leg from a backward outside edge. The skater enters the jump skating in one direction, and concludes the jump skating in the opposite direction. Usually performed in the corners of the rink. Named after inventor Alois Lutz, who first landed the jump in Vienna, 1918.

Salchow: A one-, two- or three-revolution jump. The skater takes off from the back inside edge of one foot and lands backwards on the outside edge of the right foot, the opposite foot from which the skater took off. Named for its originator and first Olympic champion (1908), Sweden's Ulrich Salchow.

Axel: A combination of the waltz and loop jumps, including one-and-a-half revolutions. The only jump begun from a forward outside edge, the Axel is landed on the back outside edge of the opposite foot. Named for its inventor, Norway's Axel Paulsen.

Spins

Spin: The rotation of the body in one place on the ice. Various spins are the back, fast or scratch, sit, camel, butterfly and layback.

Camel Spin: A spin with the skater in an arabesque position (the free leg at right angles to the leg on the ice).

Flying Camel Spin: A jump spin ending in the camel-spin position.

Flying Sit Spin: A jump spin in which the skater leaps off the ice, assumes a sitting position at the peak of the jump, lands and spins in a similar sitting position.

Pair Movements/Techniques

Death Spiral: One of the most dramatic moves in figure skating. The man, acting as the center of a circle, holds tightly to the hand of his partner and pulls her around him. The woman, gliding on one foot, achieves a position almost horizontal to the ice.

Lifts: The most spectacular moves in pairs skating. They involve any maneuver in which the man lifts the woman off the ice. The man often holds his partner above his head with one hand.

Throws: The man lifts the woman into the air and throws her away from him. She spins in the air and lands on one foot.

Twist: The man throws the woman into the air. She spins in the air (either a double- or triple-twist), and he catches her at the landing.

*Compiled by the United States Figure Skating Association.

World Champions

Women

1906	Madge Sayers-Cave, Great Britain
1907	Madge Sayers-Cave, Great Britain
1908	Lily Kronberger, Hungary
1909	Lily Kronberger, Hungary
1910	Lily Kronberger, Hungary
1911	Lily Kronberger, Hungary
1912	Opika von Meray Horvath, Hungary
1913	Opika von Meray Horvath, Hungary
1914	Opika von Meray Horvath, Hungary
1915–21	No competition
1922	Herma Plank-Szabo, Austria
1923	Herma Plank-Szabo, Austria
1924	Herma Plank-Szabo, Austria
1925	Herma Jaross-Szabo, Austria
1926	Herma Jaross-Szabo, Austria
1927	Sonja Henie, Norway
1928	Sonja Henie, Norway
1929	Sonja Henie, Norway
1930	Sonja Henie, Norway
1931	Sonja Henie, Norway
1932	Sonja Henie, Norway
1933	Sonja Henie, Norway
1934	Sonja Henie, Norway
1935	Sonja Henie, Norway
1936	Sonja Henie, Norway
1937	Cecilia Colledge, Great Britain
1938	Megan Taylor, Great Britain
1939	Megan Taylor, Great Britain
1940–46	No competition
1947	Barbara Ann Scott, Canada
1948	Barbara Ann Scott, Canada
1949	Alena Vrzanova, Czechoslovakia
1950	Alena Vrzanova, Czechoslovakia
1951	Jeannette Altwegg, Great Britain
1952	Jacqueline duBief, France
1953	Tenley Albright, United States
1954	Gundi Busch, W Germany
1955	Tenley Albright, United States
1956	Carol Heiss, United States
1957	Carol Heiss, United States

Women *(Cont.)*

1958	Carol Heiss, United States
1959	Carol Heiss, United States
1960	Carol Heiss, United States
1961	No competition
1962	Sjoukje Dijkstra, Netherlands
1963	Sjoukje Dijkstra, Netherlands
1964	Sjoukje Dijkstra, Netherlands
1965	Petra Burka, Canada
1966	Peggy Fleming, United States
1967	Peggy Fleming, United States
1968	Peggy Fleming, United States
1969	Gabriele Seyfert, E Germany
1970	Gabriele Seyfert, E Germany
1971	Beatrix Schuba, Austria
1972	Beatrix Schuba, Austria
1973	Karen Magnussen, Canada
1974	Christine Errath, E Germany
1975	Dianne DeLeeuw, Netherlands
1976	Dorothy Hamill, United States
1977	Linda Fratianne, United States
1978	Annett Poetzsch, E Germany
1979	Linda Fratianne, United States
1980	Annett Poetzsch, E Germany
1981	Denise Biellmann, Switzerland
1982	Elaine Zayak, United States
1983	Rosalynn Sumners, United States
1984	Katarina Witt, E Germany
1985	Katarina Witt, E Germany
1986	Debi Thomas, United States
1987	Katarina Witt, E Germany
1988	Katarina Witt, E Germany
1989	Midori Ito, Japan
1990	Jill Trenary, United States
1991	Kristi Yamaguchi, United States
1992	Kristi Yamaguchi, United States
1993	Oksana Baiul, Ukraine
1994	Yuka Sato, Japan
1995	Chen Lu, China
1996	Michelle Kwan, United States
1997	Tara Lipinski, United States
1998	Michelle Kwan, United States
1999	Maria Butyrskaya, Russia
2000	Michelle Kwan, United States
2001	Michelle Kwan, United States
2002	Irina Slutskaya, Russia
2003	Michelle Kwan, United States

Men

1896	Gilbert Fuchs, Germany
1897	Gustav Hugel, Austria
1898	Henning Grenander, Sweden
1899	Gustav Hugel, Austria
1900	Gustav Hugel, Austria
1901	Ulrich Salchow, Sweden
1902	Ulrich Salchow, Sweden
1903	Ulrich Salchow, Sweden
1904	Ulrich Salchow, Sweden
1905	Ulrich Salchow, Sweden
1906	Gilbert Fuchs, Germany
1907	Ulrich Salchow, Sweden
1908	Ulrich Salchow, Sweden
1909	Ulrich Salchow, Sweden
1910	Ulrich Salchow, Sweden
1911	Ulrich Salchow, Sweden
1912	Fritz Kachler, Austria
1913	Fritz Kachler, Austria
1914	Gosta Sandhal, Sweden
1915–21	No competition
1922	Gillis Grafstrom, Sweden
1923	Fritz Kachler, Austria
1924	Gillis Grafstrom, Sweden
1925	Willy Bockl, Austria
1926	Willy Bockl, Austria
1927	Willy Bockl, Austria
1928	Willy Bockl, Austria
1929	Gillis Grafstrom, Sweden
1930	Karl Schafer, Austria
1931	Karl Schafer, Austria
1932	Karl Schafer, Austria
1933	Karl Schafer, Austria
1934	Karl Schafer, Austria
1935	Karl Schafer, Austria
1936	Karl Schafer, Austria
1937	Felix Kaspar, Austria
1938	Felix Kaspar, Austria
1939	Graham Sharp, Great Britain
1940–46	No competition
1947	Hans Gerschwiler, Switzerland
1948	Dick Button, United States
1949	Dick Button, United States
1950	Dick Button, United States
1951	Dick Button, United States
1952	Dick Button, United States
1953	Hayes Alan Jenkins, United States
1954	Hayes Alan Jenkins, United States
1955	Hayes Alan Jenkins, United States
1956	Hayes Alan Jenkins, United States
1957	David W. Jenkins, United States
1958	David W. Jenkins, United States
1959	David W. Jenkins, United States
1960	Alan Giletti, France
1961	No competition
1962	Donald Jackson, Canada
1963	Donald McPherson, Canada
1964	Manfred Schneldorfer, W Germany
1965	Alain Calmat, France
1966	Emmerich Danzer, Austria
1967	Emmerich Danzer, Austria
1968	Emmerich Danzer, Austria
1969	Tim Wood, United States
1970	Tim Wood, United States
1971	Andrej Nepela, Czechoslovakia
1972	Andrej Nepela, Czechoslovakia
1973	Andrej Nepela, Czechoslovakia
1974	Jan Hoffmann, E Germany
1975	Sergei Volkov, USSR
1976	John Curry, Great Britain
1977	Vladimir Kovalev, USSR
1978	Charles Tickner, United States
1979	Vladimir Kovalev, USSR
1980	Jan Hoffmann, E Germany
1981	Scott Hamilton, United States
1982	Scott Hamilton, United States
1983	Scott Hamilton, United States
1984	Scott Hamilton, United States
1985	Aleksandr Fadeev, USSR
1986	Brian Boitano, United States
1987	Brian Orser, Canada
1988	Brian Boitano, United States
1989	Kurt Browning, Canada
1990	Kurt Browning, Canada
1991	Kurt Browning, Canada
1992	Viktor Petrenko, CIS
1993	Kurt Browning, Canada
1994	Elvis Stojko, Canada
1995	Elvis Stojko, Canada

Men (Cont.)

1996 ....Todd Eldredge, United States	2000 ....Alexei Yagudin, Russia
1997 ....Elvis Stojko, Canada	2001 ....Evgeni Plushenko, Russia
1998 ....Alexei Yagudin, Russia	2002 ....Alexei Yagudin, Russia
1999 ....Alexei Yagudin, Russia	2003 ....Evgeni Plushenko, Russia

Pairs

1908 ....Anna Hubler, Heinrich Burger, Germany	1963 ....Marika Kilius, Hans-Jurgen Baumler, W Germany
1909 ....Phyllis Johnson, James H. Johnson, Great Britain	1964 ....Marika Kilius, Hans-Jurgen Baumler, W Germany
1910 ....Anna Hubler, Heinrich Burger, Germany	1965 ....Ljudmila Protopopov, Oleg Protopopov, USSR
1911 ....Ludowika Eilers, Walter Jakobsson, Germany/Finland	1966 ....Ljudmila Protopopov, Oleg Protopopov, USSR
1912 ....Phyllis Johnson, James H. Johnson, Great Britain	1967 ....Ljudmila Protopopov, Oleg Protopopov, USSR
1913 ....Helene Engelmann, Karl Majstrik, Germany	1968 ....Ljudmila Protopopov, Oleg Protopopov, USSR
1914 ....Ludowika Jakobsson-Eilers, Walter Jakobsson-Eilers, Finland	1969 ....Irina Rodnina, Alexsei Ulanov, USSR
1915–21 .....No competition	1970............Irina Rodnina, Alexsei Ulanov, USSR
1922 ....Helene Engelmann, Alfred Berger, Germany	1971 ....Irina Rodnina, Sergei Ulanov, USSR
1923 ....Ludowika Jakobsson-Eilers, Walter Jakobsson-Eilers, Finland	1972 ....Irina Rodnina, Sergei Ulanov, USSR
1924 ....Helene Engelmann, Alfred Berger, Germany	1973 ....Irina Rodnina, Aleksandr Zaitsev, USSR
1925 ....Herma Jaross-Szabo, Ludwig Wrede, Austria	1974 ....Irina Rodnina, Aleksandr Zaitsev, USSR
1926 ....Andree Joly, Pierre Brunet, France	1975 ....Irina Rodnina, Aleksandr Zaitsev, USSR
1927 ....Herma Jaross-Szabo, Ludwig Wrede, Austria	1976 ....Irina Rodnina, Aleksandr Zaitsev, USSR
1928 ....Andree Joly, Pierre Brunet, France	1977 ....Irina Rodnina, Aleksandr Zaitsev, USSR
1929 ....Lilly Scholz, Otto Kaiser, Austria	1978 ....Irina Rodnina, Aleksandr Zaitsev, USSR
1930 ....Andree Brunet-Joly, Pierre Brunet-Joly, France	1979 ....Tai Babilonia, Randy Gardner, United States
1931 ....Emilie Rotter, Laszlo Szollas, Hungary	1980 ....Maria Cherkasova, Sergei Shakhrai, USSR
1932 ....Andree Brunet-Joly, Pierre Brunet-Joly, France	1981 ....Irina Vorobieva, Igor Lisovsky, USSR
1933 ....Emilie Rotter, Laszlo Szollas, Hungary	1982 ....Sabine Baess, Tassilio Thierbach, E Germany
1934 ....Emilie Rotter, Laszlo Szollas, Hungary	1983 ....Elena Valova, Oleg Vasiliev, USSR
1935 ....Emilie Rotter, Laszlo Szollas, Hungary	1984 ....Barbara Underhill, Paul Martini, Canada
1936 ....Maxi Herber, Ernst Bajer, Germany	1985 ....Elena Valova, Oleg Vasiliev, USSR
1937 ....Maxi Herber, Ernst Bajer, Germany	1986 ....Ekaterina Gordeeva, Sergei Grinkov, USSR
1938 ....Maxi Herber, Ernst Bajer, Germany	1987 ....Ekaterina Gordeeva, Sergei Grinkov, USSR
1939 ....Maxi Herber, Ernst Bajer, Germany	1988 ....Elena Valova, Oleg Vasiliev, USSR
1940–46 .....No competition	1989 ....Ekaterina Gordeeva, Sergei Grinkov, USSR
1947 ....Micheline Lannoy, Pierre Baugniet, Belgium	1990 ....Ekaterina Gordeeva, Sergei Grinkov, USSR
1948 ....Micheline Lannoy, Pierre Baugniet, Belgium	1991 ....Natalia Mishkutienok, Artur Dmitriev, USSR
1949 ....Andrea Kekessy, Ede Kiraly, Hungary	1992 ....Natalia Mishkutienok, Artur Dmitriev, CIS
1950 ....Karol Kennedy, Peter Kennedy, United States	1993 ....Isabelle Brasseur, Lloyd Eisler, Canada
1951 ....Ria Baran, Paul Falk, W Germany	1994 ....Evgenia Shishkova, Vadim Naumov, Russia
1952 ....Ria Baran Falk, Paul Falk, W Germany	1995 ....Radka Kovarikova, Rene Novotny, Czech Republic
1953 ....Jennifer Nicks, John Nicks, Great Britain	1996 ....Marina Eltsova, Andrey Buskhov, Russia
1954 ....Frances Dafoe, Norris Bowden, Canada	1997 ....Mandy Wötzel, Ingo Steuer, Germany
1955 ....Frances Dafoe, Norris Bowden, Canada	1998 ....Jenni Meno, Todd Sand, United States
1956 ....Sissy Schwarz, Kurt Oppelt, Austria	1999 ....Elena Berezhnaya, Anton Sikharulidze, Russia
1957 ....Barbara Wagner, Robert Paul, Canada	2000 ....Maria Petrova and Aleksei Tikhonov, Russia
1958 ....Barbara Wagner, Robert Paul, Canada	2001 ....Jamie Salé and David Pelletier, Canada
1959 ....Barbara Wagner, Robert Paul, Canada	2002 ....Xue Shen and Hongbo Zhao, China
1960 ....Barbara Wagner, Robert Paul, Canada	2003 ....Xue Shen and Hongbo Zhao, China
1961 ....No competition	
1962 ....Maria Jelinek, Otto Jelinek, Canada	

Dance

1950	Lois Waring, Michael McGean, United States
1951	Jean Westwood, Lawrence Demmy, Great Britain
1952	Jean Westwood, Lawrence Demmy, Great Britain
1953	Jean Westwood, Lawrence Demmy, Great Britain
1954	Jean Westwood, Lawrence Demmy, Great Britain
1955	Jean Westwood, Lawrence Demmy, Great Britain
1956	Pamela Wieght, Paul Thomas, Great Britain
1957	June Markham, Courtney Jones, Great Britain
1958	June Markham, Courtney Jones, Great Britain
1959	Doreen D. Denny, Courtney Jones, Great Britain
1960	Doreen D. Denny, Courtney Jones, Great Britain
1961	No competition
1962	Eva Romanova, Pavel Roman, Czechoslovakia
1963	Eva Romanova, Pavel Roman, Czechoslovakia
1964	Eva Romanova, Pavel Roman, Czechoslovakia
1965	Eva Romanova, Pavel Roman, Czechoslovakia
1966	Diane Towler, Bernard Ford, Great Britain
1967	Diane Towler, Bernard Ford, Great Britain
1968	Diane Towler, Bernard Ford, Great Britain
1969	Diane Towler, Bernard Ford, Great Britain
1970	Ljudmila Pakhomova, Aleksandr Gorshkov, USSR
1971	Ljudmila Pakhomova, Aleksandr Gorshkov, USSR
1972	Ljudmila Pakhomova, Aleksandr Gorshkov, USSR
1973	Ljudmila Pakhomova, Aleksandr Gorshkov, USSR
1974	Ljudmila Pakhomova, Aleksandr Gorshkov, USSR
1975	Irina Moiseeva, Andreij Minenkov, USSR
1976	Ljudmila Pakhomova, Aleksandr Gorshkov, USSR
1977	Irina Moiseeva, Andreij Minenkov, USSR
1978	Natalia Linichuk, Gennadi Karponosov, USSR
1979	Natalia Linichuk, Gennadi Karponosov, USSR
1980	Krisztina Regoeczy, Andras Sallai, Hungary
1981	Jayne Torvill, Christopher Dean, Great Britain
1982	Jayne Torvill, Christopher Dean, Great Britain
1983	Jayne Torvill, Christopher Dean, Great Britain
1984	Jayne Torvill, Christopher Dean, Great Britain
1985	Natalia Bestemianova, Andrei Bukin, USSR
1986	Natalia Bestemianova, Andrei Bukin, USSR
1987	Natalia Bestemianova, Andrei Bukin, USSR
1988	Natalia Bestemianova, Andrei Bukin, USSR
1989	Marina Klimova, Sergei Ponomarenko, USSR
1990	Marina Klimova, Sergei Ponomarenko, USSR
1991	Isabelle Duchesnay, Paul Duchesnay, France
1992	Marina Klimova, Sergei Ponomarenko, CIS
1993	Renee Roca, Gorsha Sur, United States
1994	Oksana Grishuk, Evgeny Platov, Russia
1995	Oksana Grishuk, Evgeny Platov, Russia
1996	Oksana Grishuk, Evgeny Platov, Russia
1997	Oksana Grishuk, Evgeny Platov, Russia
1998	Anjelika Krylova and Oleg Ovsyannikov, Russia
1999	Anjelika Krylova and Oleg Ovsyannikov, Russia
2000	Marina Anissina and Gwendal Peizerat, France
2001	Barbara Fusar-Poli and Maurizio Margaglio, Italy
2002	Irina Lobacheva and Ilia Averbukh, Russia
2003	Shae-Lynn Bourne and Victor Kraatz, Canada

Champions of the United States

The championships held in 1914, 1918, 1920 and 1921 under the auspices of the International Skating Union of America were open to Canadians, although the competitions were considered to be United States championships. Beginning in 1922, the championships have been held under the auspices of the United States Figure Skating Association.

Women

1914	Theresa Weld, SC of Boston
1915–17	No competition
1918	Rosemary S. Beresford, New York SC
1919	No competition
1920	Theresa Weld, SC of Boston
1921	Theresa Weld Blanchard, SC of Boston
1922	Theresa Weld Blanchard, SC of Boston
1923	Theresa Weld Blanchard, SC of Boston
1924	Theresa Weld Blanchard, SC of Boston
1925	Beatrix Loughran, New York SC
1926	Beatrix Loughran, New York SC
1927	Beatrix Loughran, New York SC
1928	Maribel Y. Vinson, SC of Boston
1929	Maribel Y. Vinson, SC of Boston
1930	Maribel Y. Vinson, SC of Boston
1931	Maribel Y. Vinson, SC of Boston
1932	Maribel Y. Vinson, SC of Boston
1933	Maribel Y. Vinson, SC of Boston
1934	Suzanne Davis, SC of Boston
1935	Maribel Y. Vinson, SC of Boston
1936	Maribel Y. Vinson, SC of Boston
1937	Maribel Y. Vinson, SC of Boston
1938	Joan Tozzer, SC of Boston
1939	Joan Tozzer, SC of Boston
1940	Joan Tozzer, SC of Boston
1941	Jane Vaughn, Philadelphia SC & HS
1942	Jane Vaughn Sullivan, Philadelphia SC & HS
1943	Gretchen Van Zandt Merrill, SC of Boston
1944	Gretchen Van Zandt Merrill, SC of Boston

Women *(Cont.)*

1945...........Gretchen Van Zandt Merrill, SC of Boston	1975 ....Dorothy Hamill, SC of New York
1946...........Gretchen Van Zandt Merrill, SC of Boston	1976 ....Dorothy Hamill, SC of New York
1947...........Gretchen Van Zandt Merrill, SC of Boston	1977 ....Linda Fratianne, Los Angeles FSC
1948...........Gretchen Van Zandt Merrill, SC of Boston	1978 ....Linda Fratianne, Los Angeles FSC
1949 ....Yvonne Claire Sherman, SC of New York	1979 ....Linda Fratianne, Los Angeles FSC
1950 ....Yvonne Claire Sherman, SC of New York	1980 ....Linda Fratianne, Los Angeles FSC
1951 ....Sonya Klopfer, Junior SC of New York	1981 ....Elaine Zayak, SC of New York
1952 ....Tenley E. Albright, SC of Boston	1982 ....Rosalynn Sumners, Seattle SC
1953 ....Tenley E. Albright, SC of Boston	1983 ....Rosalynn Sumners, Seattle SC
1954 ....Tenley E. Albright, SC of Boston	1984 ....Rosalynn Sumners, Seattle SC
1955 ....Tenley E. Albright, SC of Boston	1985 ....Tiffany Chin, San Diego FSC
1956 ....Tenley E. Albright, SC of Boston	1986 ....Debi Thomas, Los Angeles FSC
1957 ....Carol E. Heiss, SC of New York	1987 ....Jill Trenary, Broadmoor SC
1958 ....Carol E. Heiss, SC of New York	1988 ....Debi Thomas, Los Angeles FSC
1959 ....Carol E. Heiss, SC of New York	1989 ....Jill Trenary, Broadmoor SC
1960 ....Carol E. Heiss, SC of New York	1990 ....Jill Trenary, Broadmoor SC
1961 ....Laurence R. Owen, SC of Boston	1991 ....Tonya Harding, Carousel FSC
1962 ....Barbara Roles Pursley, Arctic Blades FSC	1992 ....Kristi Yamaguchi, St Moritz ISC
1963 ....Lorraine G. Hanlon, SC of Boston	1993 ....Nancy Kerrigan, Colonial FSC
1964 ....Peggy Fleming, Arctic Blades FSC	1994 ....Tonya Harding, Portland FSC
1965 ....Peggy Fleming, Arctic Blades FSC	1995 ....Nicole Bobek, Los Angeles FSC
1966 ....Peggy Fleming, City of Colorado Springs	1996 ....Michelle Kwan, Los Angeles FSC
1967 ....Peggy Fleming, Broadmoor SC	1997 ....Tara Lipinski, Detroit SC
1968 ....Peggy Fleming, Broadmoor SC	1998 ....Michelle Kwan, Los Angeles FSC
1969 ....Janet Lynn, Wagon Wheel FSC	1999 ....Michelle Kwan, Los Angeles FSC
1970 ....Janet Lynn, Wagon Wheel FSC	2000 ....Michelle Kwan, Los Angeles FSC
1971 ....Janet Lynn, Wagon Wheel FSC	2001 ....Michelle Kwan, Los Angeles FSC
1972 ....Janet Lynn, Wagon Wheel FSC	2002 ....Michelle Kwan, Los Angeles FSC
1973 ....Janet Lynn, Wagon Wheel FSC	2003 ....Michelle Kwan, Los Angeles FSC
1974 ....Dorothy Hamill, SC of New York	

Men

1914 ....Norman M. Scott, WC of Montreal	1952 ....Dick Button, SC of Boston
1915–17 .....No competition	1953 ....Hayes Alan Jenkins, Cleveland SC
1918 ....Nathaniel W. Niles, SC of Boston	1954 ....Hayes Alan Jenkins, Broadmoor SC
1919 ....No competition	1955 ....Hayes Alan Jenkins, Broadmoor SC
1920 ....Sherwin C. Badger, SC of Boston	1956 ....Hayes Alan Jenkins, Broadmoor SC
1921 ....Sherwin C. Badger, SC of Boston	1957 ....David Jenkins, Broadmoor SC
1922 ....Sherwin C. Badger, SC of Boston	1958 ....David Jenkins, Broadmoor SC
1923 ....Sherwin C. Badger, SC of Boston	1959 ....David Jenkins, Broadmoor SC
1924 ....Sherwin C. Badger, SC of Boston	1960 ....David Jenkins, Broadmoor SC
1925 ....Nathaniel W. Niles, SC of Boston	1961 ....Bradley R. Lord, SC of Boston
1926 ....Chris I. Christenson, Twin City FSC	1962 ....Monty Hoyt, Broadmoor SC
1927 ....Nathaniel W. Niles, SC of Boston	1963 ....Thomas Litz, Hershey FSC
1928 ....Roger F. Turner, SC of Boston	1964 ....Scott Ethan Allen, SC of New York
1929 ....Roger F. Turner, SC of Boston	1965 ....Gary C. Visconti, Detroit SC
1930 ....Roger F. Turner, SC of Boston	1966 ....Scott Ethan Allen, SC of New York
1931 ....Roger F. Turner, SC of Boston	1967 ....Gary C. Visconti, Detroit SC
1932 ....Roger F. Turner, SC of Boston	1968 ....Tim Wood, Detroit SC
1933 ....Roger F. Turner, SC of Boston	1969 ....Tim Wood, Detroit SC
1934 ....Roger F. Turner, SC of Boston	1970 ....Tim Wood, City of Colorado Springs
1935 ....Robin H. Lee, SC of New York	1971 ....John Misha Petkevich, Great Falls FSC
1936 ....Robin H. Lee, SC of New York	1972 ....Kenneth Shelley, Arctic Blades FSC
1937 ....Robin H. Lee, SC of New York	1973 ....Gordon McKellen Jr., SC of Lake Placid
1938 ....Robin H. Lee, Chicago FSC	1974 ....Gordon McKellen Jr., SC of Lake Placid
1939 ....Robin H. Lee, St Paul FSC	1975 ....Gordon McKellen Jr., SC of Lake Placid
1940 ....Eugene Turner, Los Angeles FSC	1976 ....Terry Kubicka, Arctic Blades FSC
1941 ....Eugene Turner, Los Angeles FSC	1977 ....Charles Tickner, Denver FSC
1942 ....Robert Specht, Chicago FSC	1978 ....Charles Tickner, Denver FSC
1943 ....Arthur R. Vaughn Jr.,	1979 ....Charles Tickner, Denver FSC
Philadelphia SC & HS	1980 ....Charles Tickner, Denver FSC
1944–45 .....No competition	1981 ....Scott Hamilton, Philadelphia SC & HS
1946 ....Dick Button, Philadelphia SC & HS	1982 ....Scott Hamilton, Philadelphia SC & HS
1947 ....Dick Button, Philadelphia SC & HS	1983 ....Scott Hamilton, Philadelphia SC & HS
1948 ....Dick Button, Philadelphia SC & HS	1984 ....Scott Hamilton, Philadelphia SC & HS
1949 ....Dick Button, Philadelphia SC & HS	1985 ....Brian Boitano, Peninsula FSC
1950 ....Dick Button, SC of Boston	1986 ....Brian Boitano, Peninsula FSC
1951 ....Dick Button, SC of Boston	1987 ....Brian Boitano, Peninsula FSC

Men (Cont.)

1988 ....Brian Boitano, Peninsula FSC
1989 ....Christopher Bowman, Los Angeles FSC
1990 ....Todd Eldredge, Los Angeles FSC
1991 ....Todd Eldredge, Los Angeles FSC
1992 ....Christopher Bowman, Los Angeles FSC
1993 ....Scott Davis, Broadmoor SC
1994 ....Scott Davis, Broadmoor SC
1995 ....Todd Eldredge, Detroit SC

1996 ....Rudy Galindo, St Moritz ISC
1997 ....Todd Eldredge, Detroit SC
1998 ....Todd Eldredge, Detroit SC
1999 ....Michael Weiss, Washington FSC
2000 ....Michael Weiss, Washington FSC
2001 ....Timothy Goebel, Winterhurst FSC
2002 ....Todd Eldredge, Los Angeles FSC
2003 ....Michael Weiss, Washington FSC

Pairs

1914 ......Jeanne Chevalier, Norman M. Scott, WC of Montreal
1915–17 .No competition
1918 ......Theresa Weld, Nathaniel W. Niles, SC of Boston
1919 ......No competition
1920 ......Theresa Weld, Nathaniel W. Niles, SC of Boston
1921 ......Theresa Weld Blanchard, Nathaniel W. Niles, SC of Boston
1922 ......Theresa Weld Blanchard, Nathaniel W. Niles, SC of Boston
1923 ......Theresa Weld Blanchard, Nathaniel W. Niles, SC of Boston
1924 ......Theresa Weld Blanchard, Nathaniel W. Niles, SC of Boston
1925 ......Theresa Weld Blanchard, Nathaniel W. Niles, SC of Boston
1926 ......Theresa Weld Blanchard, Nathaniel W. Niles, SC of Boston
1927 ......Theresa Weld Blanchard, Nathaniel W. Niles, SC of Boston
1928 ......Maribel Y. Vinson, Thornton L. Coolidge, SC of Boston
1929 ......Maribel Y. Vinson, Thornton L. Coolidge, SC of Boston
1930 ......Beatrix Loughran, Sherwin C. Badger, SC of New York
1931 ......Beatrix Loughran, Sherwin C. Badger, SC of New York
1932 ......Beatrix Loughran, Sherwin C. Badger, SC of New York
1933 ......Maribel Y. Vinson, George E. B. Hill, SC of Boston
1934 ......Grace E. Madden, James L. Madden, SC of Boston
1935 ......Maribel Y. Vinson, George E. B. Hill, SC of Boston
1936 ......Maribel Y. Vinson, George E. B. Hill, SC of Boston
1937 ......Maribel Y. Vinson, George E. B. Hill, SC of Boston
1938 ......Joan Tozzer, M. Bernard Fox, SC of Boston
1939 ......Joan Tozzer, M. Bernard Fox, SC of Boston
1940 ......Joan Tozzer, M. Bernard Fox, SC of Boston
1941 ......Donna Atwood, Eugene Turner, Mercury FSC/Los Angeles FSC
1942 ......Doris Schubach, Walter Noffke, Springfield Ice Birds
1943 ......Doris Schubach, Walter Noffke, Springfield Ice Birds
1944 ......Doris Schubach, Walter Noffke, Springfield Ice Birds
1945 ......Donna Jeanne Pospisil, Jean-Pierre Brunet, SC of New York
1946 ......Donna Jeanne Pospisil, Jean-Pierre Brunet, SC of New York

1947 ......Yvonne Claire Sherman, Robert J. Swenning, SC of New York
1948 ......Karol Kennedy, Peter Kennedy, Seattle SC
1949 ......Karol Kennedy, Peter Kennedy, Seattle SC
1950 ......Karol Kennedy, Peter Kennedy, Broadmoor SC
1951 ......Karol Kennedy, Peter Kennedy, Broadmoor SC
1952 ......Karol Kennedy, Peter Kennedy, Broadmoor SC
1953 ......Carole Ann Ormaca, Robin Greiner, SC of Fresno
1954 ......Carole Ann Ormaca, Robin Greiner, SC of Fresno
1955 ......Carole Ann Ormaca, Robin Greiner, St Moritz ISC
1956 ......Carole Ann Ormaca, Robin Greiner, St Moritz ISC
1957 ......Nancy Rouillard Ludington, Ronald Ludington, Commonwealth FSC/ SC of Boston
1958 ......Nancy Rouillard Ludington, Ronald Ludington, Commonwealth FSC/ SC of Boston
1959 ......Nancy Rouillard Ludington, Ronald Ludington, Commonwealth FSC
1960 ......Nancy Rouillard Ludington, Ronald Ludington, Commonwealth FSC
1961 ......Maribel Y. Owen, Dudley S. Richards, SC of Boston
1962 ......Dorothyann Nelson, Pieter Kollen, Village of Lake Placid
1963 ......Judianne Fotheringill, Jerry J. Fotheringill, Broadmoor SC
1964 ......Judianne Fotheringill, Jerry J. Fotheringill, Broadmoor SC
1965 ......Vivian Joseph, Ronald Joseph, Chicago FSC
1966 ......Cynthia Kauffman, Ronald Kauffman, Seattle SC
1967 ......Cynthia Kauffman, Ronald Kauffman, Seattle SC
1968 ......Cynthia Kauffman, Ronald Kauffman, Seattle SC
1969 ......Cynthia Kauffman, Ronald Kauffman, Seattle SC
1970 ......Jo Jo Starbuck, Kenneth Shelley, Arctic Blades FSC
1971 ......Jo Jo Starbuck, Kenneth Shelley, Arctic Blades FSC
1972 ......Jo Jo Starbuck, Kenneth Shelley, Arctic Blades FSC
1973 ......Melissa Militano, Mark Militano, SC of New York
1974 ......Melissa Militano, Johnny Johns, SC of New York/Detroit SC
1975 ......Melissa Militano, Johnny Johns, SC of NY/ Detroit SC

Pairs *(Cont.)*

1976 ......Tai Babilonia, Randy Gardner,
Los Angeles FSC
1977 ......Tai Babilonia, Randy Gardner, LA FSC
1978 ......Tai Babilonia, Randy Gardner,
Los Angeles FSC/Santa Monica FSC
1979 ......Tai Babilonia, Randy Gardner,
Los Angeles FSC/Santa Monica FSC
1980 ......Tai Babilonia, Randy Gardner,
Los Angeles FSC/Santa Monica FSC
1981 ......Caitlin Carruthers, Peter Carruthers,
SC of Wilmington
1982 ......Caitlin Carruthers, Peter Carruthers,
SC of Wilmington
1983 ......Caitlin Carruthers, Peter Carruthers,
SC of Wilmington
1984 ......Caitlin Carruthers, Peter Carruthers,
SC of Wilmington
1985 ......Jill Watson, Peter Oppegard, LA FSC
1986 ......Gillian Wachsman, Todd Waggoner,
SC of Wilmington
1987 ......Jill Watson, Peter Oppegard, Los Angeles FSC
1988 ......Jill Watson, Peter Oppegard,
Los Angeles FSC
1989 ......Kristi Yamaguchi, Rudy Galindo, St Moritz ISC

1990 ......Kristi Yamaguchi, Rudy Galindo, St Mortiz ISC
1991 ......Natasha Kuchiki, Todd Sand,
Los Angeles FSC
1992 ......Calla Urbanski, Rocky Marval,
U of Delaware FSC/SC of New York
1993 ......Calla Urbanski, Rocky Marval,
U of Delaware FSC/SC of New York
1994 ......Jenni Meno, Todd Sand,
Winterhurst FSC/Los Angeles FSC
1995 ......Jenni Meno, Todd Sand,
Winterhurst FSC/Los Angeles FSC
1996 ......Jenni Meno, Todd Sand,
Winterhurst FSC/Los Angeles FSC
1997 ......Kyoko Ina, Jason Dungjen, SC of New York
1998 ......Kyoko Ina, Jason Dungjen, SC of New York
1999 ......Danielle Hartsell, Steve Hartsell, Detroit SC
2000 ......Kyoko Ina, John Zimmerman, SC of New
York/Birmingham FSC
2001 ......Kyoko Ina, John Zimmerman, SC of New
York/Birmingham FSC
2002 ......Kyoko Ina, John Zimmerman, SC of New
York/Birmingham FSC
2003 ......Tiffany Scott, Philip Dulebohn, Colonial FSC/
Univ of Delaware FSC

Dance

1914 ......Waltz: Theresa Weld, Nathaniel W. Niles,
SC of Boston
1915–19..No competition
1920 ......Waltz: Theresa Weld, Nathaniel W. Niles,
SC of Boston
Fourteenstep: Gertrude Cheever Porter,
Irving Brokaw, New York SC
1921 ......Waltz and Fourteenstep: Theresa Weld
Blanchard, Nathaniel W. Niles, SC of Boston
1922 ......Waltz: Beatrix Loughran, Edward M.
Howland, New York SC/SC of Boston
Fourteenstep: Theresa Weld Blanchard,
Nathaniel W. Niles, SC of Boston
1923 ......Waltz: Mr. & Mrs. Henry W. Howe,
New York SC
Fourteenstep: Sydney Goode, James B.
Greene, New York SC
1924 ......Waltz: Rosaline Dunn, Frederick Gabel,
New York SC
Fourteenstep: Sydney Goode, James B.
Greene, New York SC
1925 ......Waltz and Fourteenstep: Virginia Slattery,
Ferrier T. Martin, New York SC
1926 ......Waltz: Rosaline Dunn, Joseph K. Savage,
New York SC
Fourteenstep: Sydney Goode, James B.
Greene, New York SC
1927 ......Waltz and Fourteenstep: Rosaline Dunn,
Joseph K. Savage, New York SC
1928 ......Waltz: Rosaline Dunn, Joseph K. Savage,
New York SC
Fourteenstep: Ada Bauman Kelly, George T.
Braakman, New York SC
1929 ......Waltz and Original Dance combined:
Edith C. Secord, Joseph K. Savage,
SC of New York
1930 ......Waltz: Edith C. Secord, Joseph K. Savage,
SC of New York
Original: Clara Rotch Frothingham, George
E. B. Hill, SC of Boston
1931 ......Waltz: Edith C. Secord, Ferrier T. Martin,
SC of New York
Original: Theresa Weld Blanchard, Nathaniel
W. Niles, SC of Boston

1932 ......Waltz: Edith C. Secord, Joseph K. Savage,
SC of New York
Original: Clara Rotch Frothingham, George
E. B. Hill, SC of Boston
1933 ......Waltz: Ilse Twaroschk, Frederick F.
Fleishmann, Brooklyn FSC
Original: Suzanne Davis, Frederick
Goodridge, SC of Boston
1934 ......Waltz: Nettie C. Prantel, Roy Hunt, SC of
New York
Original: Suzanne Davis, Frederick
Goodridge, SC of Boston
1935 ......Waltz: Nettie C. Prantel, Roy Hunt,
SC of New York
1936 ......Marjorie Parker, Joseph K. Savage,
SC of New York
1937 ......Nettie C. Prantel, Harold Hartshorne,
SC of New York
1938 ......Nettie C. Prantel, Harold Hartshorne,
SC of New York
1939 ......Sandy Macdonald, Harold Hartshorne,
SC of New York
1940 ......Sandy Macdonald, Harold Hartshorne,
SC of New York
1941 ......Sandy Macdonald, Harold Hartshorne, SCNY
1942 ......Edith B. Whetstone, Alfred N. Richards, Jr,
Philadelphia SC & HS
1943 ......Marcella May, James Lochead Jr., Skate & Ski Club
1944 ......Marcella May, James Lochead Jr., Skate & Ski Club
1945 ......Kathe Mehl Williams, Robert J. Swenning,
SC of New York
1946 ......Anne Davies, Carleton C. Hoffner Jr.,
Washington FSC
1947 ......Lois Waring, Walter H. Bainbridge Jr.,
Baltimore FSC/Washigton FSC
1948 ......Lois Waring, Walter H. Bainbridge Jr.,
Baltimore FSC/Washington FSC
1949 ......Lois Waring, Walter H. Bainbridge Jr.,
Baltimore FSC/Washington FSC
1950 ......Lois Waring, Michael McGean, Baltimore FSC
1951 ......Carmel Bodel, Edward L. Bodel, St. Moritz ISC
1952 ......Lois Waring, Michael McGean,
Baltimore FSC

Dance *(Cont.)*

1953 ......Carol Ann Peters, Daniel C. Ryan,
Washington FSC
1954 ......Carmel Bodel, Edward L. Bodel, St Moritz ISC
1955 ......Carmel Bodel, Edward L. Bodel,
St Moritz ISC
1956 ......Joan Zamboni, Roland Junso,
Arctic Blades FSC
1957 ......Sharon McKenzie, Bert Wright,
Los Angeles FSC
1958 ......Andree Anderson, Donald Jacoby, Buffalo SC
1959 ......Andree Anderson Jacoby, Donald Jacoby,
Buffalo SC
1960 ......Margie Ackles, Charles W. Phillips Jr.,
Los Angeles FSC/Arctic Blades FSC
1961 ......Diane C. Sherbloom, Larry Pierce,
Los Angeles FSC/WC of Indianapolis
1962 ......Yvonne N. Littlefield, Peter F. Betts,
Arctic Blades FSC/ Paramount, CA
1963 ......Sally Schantz, Stanley Urban,
SC of Boston/Buffalo SC
1964 ......Darlene Streich, Charles D. Fetter Jr.,
WC of Indianapolis
1965 ......Kristin Fortune, Dennis Sveum,
Los Angeles FSC
1966 ......Kristin Fortune, Dennis Sveum, Los Angeles FSC
1967 ......Lorna Dyer, John Carrell, Broadmoor SC
1968 ......Judy Schwomeyer, James Sladky,
WC of Indianapolis/Genesee FSC
1969 ......Judy Schwomeyer, James Sladky,
WC of Indianapolis/Genesee FSC
1970 ......Judy Schwomeyer, James Sladky,
WC of Indianapolis/Genesee FSC
1971 ......Judy Schwomeyer, James Sladky,
WC of Indianapolis/Genesee FSC
1972 ......Judy Schwomeyer, James Sladky,
WC of Indianapolis/Genesee FSC
1973 ......Mary Karen Campbell, Johnny Johns,
Lansing SC/Detroit SC
1974 ......Colleen O'Connor, Jim Millns, Broadmoor
SC/ City of Colorado Springs
1975 ......Colleen O'Connor, Jim Millns, Broadmoor SC
1976 ......Colleen O'Connor, Jim Millns,
Broadmoor SC
1977 ......Judy Genovesi, Kent Weigle,
SC of Hartford/Charter Oak FSC

1978 ......Stacey Smith, John Summers,
SC of Wilmington
1979 ......Stacey Smith, John Summers,
SC of Wilmington
1980 ......Stacey Smith, John Summers,
SC of Wilmington
1981 ......Judy Blumberg, Michael Seibert,
Broadmoor SC/ISC of Indianapolis
1982 ......Judy Blumberg, Michael Seibert,
Broadmoor SC/ISC of Indianapolis
1983 ......Judy Blumberg, Michael Seibert,
Pittsburgh FSC
1984 ......Judy Blumberg, Michael Seibert,
Pittsburgh FSC
1985 ......Judy Blumberg, Michael Seibert,
Pittsburgh FSC
1986 ......Renee Roca, Donald Adair,
Genesee FSC/Academy FSC
1987 ......Suzanne Semanick, Scott Gregory,
U of Delaware SC
1988 ......Suzanne Semanick, Scott Gregory,
U of Delaware SC
1989 ......Susan Wynne, Joseph Druar,
Broadmoor SC/Seattle SC
1990 ......Susan Wynne, Joseph Druar,
Broadmoor SC/Seattle SC
1991 ......Elizabeth Punsalan, Jerod Swallow,
Broadmoor SC
1992 ......April Sargent, Russ Witherby,
Ogdensburg FSC/U of Delaware FSC
1993 ......Renee Roca, Gorsha Sur, Broadmoor SC
1994 ......Elizabeth Punsalan, Jerod Swallow,
Broadmoor SC/Detroit SC
1995 ......Renee Roca, Gorsha Sur, Broadmoor SC
1996 ......Elizabeth Punsalan, Jerod Swallow, Detroit SC
1997 ......Elizabeth Punsalan, Jerod Swallow, Detroit SC
1998 ......Elizabeth Punsalan, Jerod Swallow, Detroit SC
1999 ......Naomi Lang, Peter Tchernyshev, Detroit SC
2000 ......Naomi Lang, Peter Tchernyshev, Detroit SC
2001 ......Naomi Lang, Peter Tchernyshev, Detroit SC
2002 ......Naomi Lang, Peter Tchernyshev, American
Academy FSC
2003 ......Naomi Lang, Peter Tchernyshev, American
Academy FSC

U.S. Olympic Gold Medalists

Women

1956 ....Tenley Albright	1992 ....Kristi Yamaguchi
1960 ....Carol Heiss	1998 ....Tara Lipinski
1968 ....Peggy Fleming	2002 ....Sarah Hughes
1976 ....Dorothy Hamill	

Men

1948 ....Richard Button	1960 ....David W. Jenkins
1952 ....Richard Button	1984 ....Scott Hamilton
1956 ....Hayes Alan Jenkins	1988 ....Brian Boitano

Special Achievements

Women successfully landing a triple Axel in competition:
    Midori Ito, Japan, 1988 free-skating competition at Aichi, Japan.
    Tonya Harding, United States, 1991 U.S. Figure Skating Championship.
Men successfully landing three quadruple jumps in competition:
    Timothy Goebel, United States, 1999 Skate America, Colorado Springs (two Salchows and one toe loop).

Miscellaneous Sports

Five-time Tour winner
Lance Armstrong

Drive For Five

It wasn't easy, but Lance Armstrong won a record-tying fifth consecutive Tour de France—and left Paris promising a sixth

BY MERRELL NODEN

THIS YEAR MARKED the 100th anniversary of the Tour de France, and the race—which featured dramatic reversals of fortune, gutsy rides, hairy spills and, best of all, a close finish—did its part to live up to the landmark occasion.

As late as the eve of the final stage, Chris Carmichael, coach of four-time defending champion Lance Armstrong, was still not ready to assume that his man had won. "This race will not be over until the entire peloton rolls across the finish line on the Champs Elysees," Carmichael wrote in the journal he was keeping on the Tour website. "I'm not celebrating a fifth Tour de France victory until it's really over."

In retrospect, Carmichael's caution was unnecessary. During the final Sunday ride Armstrong surrendered 15 seconds to the man he considers his chief rival, 1997 Tour champion Jan Ullrich, but managed to finish 61 seconds ahead of the German. This was the narrowest of all of Armstrong's wins, and it makes him one of two men— Miguel Indurain is the other—to win five consecutive Tours. Eddie Merckx, Bernhard Hinault and Jacques Anquetil also won five but not in succession. If Armstrong wins next summer, he will set records for both

consecutive Tour wins and overall wins.

In his four previous victories Armstrong had looked close to invincible. This year things were different. There were problems off the bike even before the Tour began. In the winter he'd separated from Kristin, his wife of six years, and their three children. In the Tour he had to survive three crashes, severe dehydration, diarrhea, a saddle sore "the size of Pike's Peak," as he put it, and a hard fall onto his crossbar, impacting what is the most tender part of any man's anatomy and is surely even more so for a survivor of testicular cancer like Armstrong.

His woes began early. As he rounded a right-hand turn some 600 yards from the finish of the first stage, he abruptly came face to face with a mass of fallen cyclists. Unable to avoid hitting them, Armstrong had to endure the terrifying certainty that other cyclists would be piling into him. He escaped with an 18-inch tire track across his back and a mixture of cuts and bruises.

Not so lucky was his countryman Tyler Hamilton, a talented 32-year-old from Marblehead, Mass., riding in his eighth Tour. Having finished second in the Giro d'Italia earlier in the season, Hamilton was viewed as a real threat to finish among the Top 3 in the Tour. But in the opening pile up

AP PHOTO/CHRISTOPHE ENA

Hamilton fell hard on his left shoulder, breaking his collarbone. At first everyone assumed he was gone from the Tour, but he gamely cycled on to the end, with his right shoulder taped.

Armstrong grabbed the yellow jersey on Stage 8, which runs through the Alps, with snow-clad Mont Blanc gleaming in the distance. He grabbed it for good, though it sure didn't look that way at the time. In Stage 9, as he pursued Alexandre Vinokourov down a steep hill in the Alps, Joseba Beloki, last year's runner-up, crashed badly, breaking his right wrist, elbow and femur. Trailing right behind him, Armstrong had to swerve hard left into a field of high grass, and then carry his bike over a ditch back onto the course.

On July 18, riding in 104° weather, Armstrong flirted dangerously with dehydration, later estimating that he lost 14 pounds in the last half hour of the stage. Six miles from the end of on Stage 15, the ascent of Luz Ardiden, a careless young spectator caught the strap of his tote bag on Armstrong's handlebars, sending the rider flying down onto the pavement. But the accident seemed to ignite a fire in Armstrong, whom Carmichael called "a man in need of a kick."

Ineed, everything seemed to be conspiring against him at this Tour—even his legendary fitness showed signs of wear. "Everyone could see he had weaknesses," said David Millar, a British rider. "He was tired. He was having to push himself, which was maybe not a new experience for Lance, but was a new experience for the rest of us to see. It gave everyone hope."

Ullrich, who was booted from the 2002 Tour for using the recreational drug Ecstasy, was in the race right up to the penultimate stage, an individual time trial running from Pornic to Nantes.

Unfortunately for the determined German, it rained that day and the pavement was perilously slick. He fell hard on a corner, skidding across the wet pavement before slamming into the bales of hay. Instead of gaining time, he lost 14 seconds and his best chance to catch Armstrong. Still, Ullrich gained confidence from seeing that Armstrong is not invincible, and he will feed off it next year's race.

Hamilton, too, will challenge Armstrong in 2004. Broken collarbone and all, he won Stage 16, crossing the line 1:55 ahead of his nearest pursuer, and he placed fourth overall, 6:17 behind Armstrong and 2:03 time behind 3rd place finisher Vinokourov.

But Armstrong vowed not to have such a close call next summer. "I'm coming back," he said. "But I'm not coming back to lose. I'm coming back to return to a level I had in the first four wins, because this year's level was unacceptable. I don't plan on being this vulnerable next year."

Late in the summer came the news that Armstrong and Kristin were divorcing. What that will mean to his preparation, no one knows. But Armstrong is a man who thrives on challenges. It's hard to imagine him not doing everything in his power to win his sixth straight Tour, having survived so much in pursuit of his fifth.

Archery

National Men's Champions

1879...Will H. Thompson	1910...Henry Richardson	1947...Jack Wilson	1978...Darrell Pace
1880...L.L. Pedinghaus	1911...Dr. Robert Elmer	1948...Larry Hughes	1979...Rick McKinney
1881...F.H. Walworth	1912...George Bryant	1949...Russ Reynolds	1980...Rick McKinney
1882...D.H. Nash	1913...George Bryant	1950...Stan Overby	1981...Rick McKinney
1883...Col. Robert Williams	1914...Dr. Robert Elmer	1951...Russ Reynolds	1982...Rick McKinney
1884...Col. Robert Williams	1915...Dr. Robert Elmer	1952...Robert Larson	1983...Rick McKinney
1885...Col. Robert Williams	1916...Dr. Robert Elmer	1953...Bill Glackin	1984...Darrell Pace
1886...W.A. Clark	1919...Dr. Robert Elmer	1954...Robert Rhode	1985...Rick McKinney
1887...W.A. Clark	1920...Dr. Robert Elmer	1955...Joe Fries	1986...Rick McKinney
1888...Lewis Maxson	1921...James Jiles	1956...Joe Fries	1987...Rick McKinney
1889...Lewis Maxson	1922...Dr. Robert Elmer	1957...Joe Fries	1988...Jay Barrs
1890...Lewis Maxson	1923...Bill Palmer	1958...Robert Bitner	1989...Ed Eliason
1891...Lewis Maxson	1924...James Jiles	1959...Wilbert Vetrovsky	1990...Ed Eliason
1892...Lewis Maxson	1925...Dr. Paul Crouch	1960...Robert Kadlec	1991...Ed Eliason
1893...Lewis Maxson	1926...Stanley Spencer	1961...Clayton Sherman	1992...Alan Rasor
1894...Lewis Maxson	1927...Dr. Paul Crouch	1962...Charles Sandlin	1993...Jay Barrs
1895...W.B. Robinson	1928...Bill Palmer	1963...Dave Keaggy Jr.	1994...Jay Barrs
1896...Lewis Maxson	1929...Dr. E.K. Roberts	1964...Dave Keaggy Jr.	1995...Justin Huish
1897...W.A. Clark	1930...Russ Hoogerhyde	1965...George Slinzer	1996...Richard (Butch) Johnson
1898...Lewis Maxson	1931...Russ Hoogerhyde	1966...Hardy Ward	1997...Richard (Butch) Johnson
1899...M.C. Howell	1932...Russ Hoogerhyde	1967...Ray Rogers	1998...Victor Wunderle
1900...A.R. Clark	1933...Ralph Miller	1968...Hardy Ward	1999...Victor Wunderle
1901...Will H. Thompson	1934...Russ Hoogerhyde	1969...Ray Rogers	2000...Richard (Butch) Johnson
1902...Will H. Thompson	1935...Gilman Keasey	1970...Joe Thornton	2001...Richard (Butch) Johnson
1903...Will H. Thompson	1936...Gilman Keasey	1971...John Williams	2002...Victor Wunderle
1904...George Bryant	1937...Russ Hoogerhyde	1972...Kevin Erlandson	2003...Joseph Bailey
1905...George Bryant	1938...Pat Chambers	1973...Darrell Pace	
1906...Henry Richardson	1939...Pat Chambers	1974...Darrell Pace	
1907...Henry Richardson	1940...Russ Hoogerhyde	1975...Darrell Pace	
1908...Will H. Thompson	1941...Larry Hughes	1976...Darrell Pace	
1909...George Bryant	1946...Wayne Thompson	1977...Rick McKinney	

National Women's Champions

1879...Mrs. S. Brown	1909...Harriet Case	1941...Ree Dillinger	1974...Doreen Wilber
1880...Mrs. T. Davies	1910...J.V. Sullivan	1946...Ann Weber	1975...Irene Lorensen
1881...Mrs. A.H. Gibbes	1911...Mrs. J.S. Taylor	1947...Ann Weber	1976...Luann Ryon
1882...Mrs. A.H. Gibbes	1912...Mrs. Witwer Tayler	1948...Jean Lee	1977...Luann Ryon
1883...Mrs. M.C. Howell	1913...Mrs. P. Fletcher	1949...Jean Lee	1978...Luann Ryon
1884...Mrs. H. Hall	1914...Mrs. B.P. Gray	1950...Jean Lee	1979...Lynette Johnson
1885...Mrs. M.C. Howell	1915...Cynthia Wesson	1951...Jean Lee	1980...Judi Adams
1886...Mrs. M.C. Howell	1916...Cynthia Wesson	1952...Ann Weber	1981...Debra Metzger
1887...Mrs. A.M. Phillips	1919...Dorothy Smith	1953...Ann Weber	1982...Luann Ryon
1888...Mrs. A.M. Phillips	1920...Cynthia Wesson	1954...Laurette Young	1983...Nancy Myrick
1889...Mrs. A.M. Phillips	1921...Mrs. L.C. Smith	1955...Ann Clark	1984...Ruth Rowe
1890...Mrs. M.C. Howell	1922...Dorothy Smith	1956...Carole Meinhart	1985...Terri Pesho
1891...Mrs. M.C. Howell	1923...Norma Pierce	1957...Carole Meinhart	1986...Debra Ochs
1892...Mrs. M.C. Howell	1924...Dorothy Smith	1958...Carole Meinhart	1987...Terry Quinn
1893...Mrs. M.C. Howell	1925...Dorothy Smith	1959...Carole Meinhart	1988...Debra Ochs
1894...Mrs. Albert Kern	1926...Dorothy Smith	1960...Ann Clark	1989...Debra Ochs
1895...Mrs. M.C. Howell	1927...Mrs. R. Johnson	1961...Victoria Cook	1990...Denise Parker
1896...Mrs. M.C. Howell	1928...Beatrice Hodgson	1962...Nancy Vonderheide	1991...Denise Parker
1897...Mrs. J.S. Baker	1929...Audrey Grubbs	1963...Nancy Vonderheide	1992...Sherry Block
1898...Mrs. M.C. Howell	1930...Audrey Grubbs	1964...Victoria Cook	1993...Denise Parker
1899...Mrs. M.C. Howell	1931...Dorothy Cummings	1965...Nancy Pfeiffer	1994...Judy Adams
1900...Mrs. M.C. Howell	1932...Ilda Hanchette	1966...Helen Thornton	1995...Jessica Carlson
1901...Mrs. C.E. Woodruff	1933...Madelaine Taylor	1967...Ardelle Mills	1996...Janet Dykman
1902...Mrs. M.C. Howell	1934...Desales Mudd	1968...Victoria Cook	1997...Janet Dykman
1903...Mrs. M.C. Howell	1935...Ruth Hodgert	1969...Doreen Wilber	1998...Janet Dykman
1904...Mrs. M.C. Howell	1936...Gladys Hammer	1970...Nancy Myrick	1999...Denise Parker
1905...Mrs. M.C. Howell	1937...Gladys Hammer	1971...Doreen Wilber	2000...Karen Scavatto
1906...Mrs. E.C. Cook	1938...Jean Tenney	1972...Ruth Rowe	2001...Kathie Loesch
1907...Mrs. M.C. Howell	1939...Belvia Carter	1973...Doreen Wilber	2002...Jessica Peterson
1908...Harriet Case	1940...Ann Weber		2003...Samantha Marino

Chess

World Champions

Curling

World Men's Champions

World Women's Champions

U.S. Men's Champions

Year	Site	Winning Club	Skip
1957	Chicago, IL	Hibbing, MN	Harold Lauber
1958	Milwaukee, WI	Detroit, MI	Douglas Fisk
1959	Green Bay, WI	Hibbing, MN	Fran Kleffman
1960	Chicago, IL	Grafton, ND	Orvil Gilleshammer
1961	Grand Forks, ND	Seattle, WA	Frank Crealock
1962	Detroit, MI	Hibbing, MN	Fran Kleffman
1963	Duluth, MN	Detroit, MI	Mike Slyziuk
1964	Utica, NY	Duluth, MN	Robert Magle Jr.
1965	Seattle, WA	Superior, WI	Bud Somerville
1966	Hibbing, MN	Fargo, ND	Joe Zbacnik
1967	Winchester, MA	Seattle, WA	Bruce Roberts
1968	Madison, WI	Superior, WI	Bud Somerville
1969	Grand Forks, ND	Superior, WI	Bud Somerville
1970	Ardsley, NY	Grafton, ND	Art Tallackson
1971	Duluth, MN	Edmore, ND	Dale Dalziel
1972	Wilmette, IL	Grafton, ND	Robert Labonte
1973	Colorado Springs, CO	Winchester, MA	Charles Reeves
1974	Schenectady, NY	Superior, WI	Bud Somerville
1975	Detroit, MI	Seattle, WA	Ed Risling
1976	Wausau, WI	Hibbing, MN	Bruce Roberts
1977	Northbrook, IL	Hibbing, MN	Bruce Roberts
1978	Utica, NY	Superior, WI	Bob Nichols
1979	Superior, WI	Bemidji, MN	Scott Baird
1980	Bemidji, MN	Hibbing, MN	Paul Pustovar
1981	Fairbanks, AK	Superior, WI	Bob Nichols
1982	Brookline, MA	Madison, WI	Steve Brown
1983	Colorado Springs, CO	Colorado Springs, CO	Don Cooper
1984	Hibbing, MN	Hibbing, MN	Bruce Roberts
1985	Mequon, WI	Wilmette, IL	Tim Wright
1986	Seattle, WA	Madison, WI	Steve Brown
1987	Lake Placid, NY	Seattle, WA	Jim Vukich
1988	St. Paul, MN	Seattle, WA	Doug Jones
1989	Detroit, MI	Seattle, WA	Jim Vukich
1990	Superior, WI	Seattle, WA	Doug Jones
1991	Utica, NY	Madison, WI	Steve Brown
1992	Grafton, ND	Seattle, WA	Doug Jones
1993	St. Paul, MN	Bemidji, MN	Scott Baird
1994	Duluth, MN	Bemidji, MN	Scott Baird
1995	Appleton, WI	Superior, WI	Tim Somerville
1996	Bemidji, MN	Superior, WI	Tim Somerville
1997	Seattle, WA	Langdon, ND	Craig Disher
1998	Bismarck, SD	Stevens Pt., WI	Paul Pustovar
1999	Duluth, MN	Superior, WI	Tim Somerville
2000	Ogden, UT	Wisconsin3	Craig Brown
2001	Madison, WI	Washington	Jason Larway
2002	Virginia, MN	Wisconsin2	Paul Pustovar
2003	Utica, NY	Minnesota3	Pete Fenson

U.S. Women's Champions

Year	Site	Winning Club	Skip
1977	Wilmette, IL	Hastings, NY	Margaret Smith
1978	Duluth, MN	Wausau, WI	Sandy Robarge
1979	Winchester, MA	Seattle, WA	Nancy Langley
1980	Seattle, WA	Seattle, WA	Sharon Kozal
1981	Kettle Moraine, WI	Seattle, WA	Nancy Langley
1982	Bowling Green, OH	Oak Park, IL	Ruth Schwenker
1983	Grafton, ND	Seattle, WA	Nancy Langley
1984	Wauwatosa, WI	Duluth, MN	Amy Hatten
1985	Hershey, PA	Fairbanks, AK	Bev Birklid
1986	Chicago, IL	St Paul, MN	Gerri Tilden
1987	St Paul, MN	Seattle, WA	Sharon Good
1988	Darien, CT	Seattle, WA	Nancy Langley
1989	Detroit, MI	Rolla, ND	Jan Lagasse
1990	Superior, WI	Denver, CO	Bev Behnke
1991	Utica, NY	Houston, TX	Maymar Gemmell
1992	Grafton, ND	Madison, WI	Lisa Schoeneberg
1993	St Paul, MN	Denver, CO	Bev Behnke
1994	Duluth, MN	Denver, CO	Bev Behnke
1995	Appleton, WI	Madison, WI	Lisa Schoeneberg
1996	Bemidji, MN	Madison, WI	Lisa Schoeneberg
1997	Seattle, WA	Arlington, WI	Patti Lank

U.S. Women's Champions (Cont.)

Year	Site	Winning Club	Skip
1998	Bismarck, SD	Wilmette, IL	Kari Erickson
1999	Duluth, MN	Madison, WI	Patti Lank
2000	Ogden, UT	Nebraska	Amy Wright
2001	Madison, WI	Illinois	Kari Erickson
2002	Virginia, MN	Madison, WI	Patti Lank
2003	Utica, NY	Illinois	Debbie McCormick

Cycling

Professional Road Race World Champions

1927 ....Alfred Binda, Italy
1928 ....George Ronsse, Belgium
1929 ....George Ronsse, Belgium
1930 ....Alfred Binda, Italy
1931 ....Learco Guerra, Italy
1932 ....Alfred Binda, Italy
1933 ....George Speicher, France
1934 ....Karel Kaers, Belgium
1935 ....Jean Aerts, Belgium
1936 ....Antonio Magne, France
1937 ....Elio Meulenberg, Belgium
1938 ....Marcel Kint, Belgium
No competition 1939–45
1946 ....Hans Knecht, Switzerland
1947 ....Theo. Middelkamp, Holland
1948 ....Alberic Schotte, Belgium
1949 ....Henri Van Steenbergen, Belgium
1950 ....Alberic Schotte, Belgium
1951 ....Ferdinand Kubler, Switzerland
1952 ....Heinz Mueller, Germany
1953 ....Fausto Coppi, Italy
1954 ....Louison Bobet, France
1955 ....Stan Ockers, Belgium
1956 ....Rik Van Steenbergen, Belg.

1957 ....Rik Van Steenbergen, Belgium
1958 ....Ercole Baldini, Italy
1959 ....Andre Darrigade, France
1960 ....Rik van Looy, Belgium
1961 ....Rik van Looy, Belgium
1962 ....Jean Stablenski, France
1963 ....Bennoni Beheyt, Belgium
1964 ....Jan Janssen, Holland
1965 ....Tommy Simpson, England
1966 ....Rudi Altig, West Germany
1967 ....Eddy Merckx, Belgium
1968 ....Vittorio Adorni, Italy
1969 ....Harm Ottenbros, Netherlands
1970 ....J.P. Monseré, Belgium
1971 ....Eddy Merckx, Belgium
1972 ....Marino Basso, Italy
1973 ....Felice Gimondi, Italy
1974 ....Eddy Merckx, Belgium
1975 ....Hennie Kuiper, Holland
1976 ....Freddy Maertens, Belgium
1977 ....Francesco Moser, Italy
1978 ....Gerri Knetemann, Holland
1979 ....Jan Raas, Holland
1980 ....Bernard Hinault, France

1981 ....Freddy Maertens, Belgium
1982 ....Giuseppe Saronni, Italy
1983 ....Greg LeMond, United States
1984 ....Claude Criquielion, Belgium
1985 ....Joop Zoetemelk, Holland
1986 ....Moreno Argentin, Italy
1987 ....Stephen Roche, Ireland
1988 ....Maurizio Fondriest, Italy
1989 ....Greg LeMond, United States
1990 ....Rudy Dhaenene, Belgium
1991 ....Gianni Bugno, Italy
1992 ....Gianni Bugno, Italy
1993 ....Lance Armstrong, United States
1994 ....Luc LeBlanc, France
1995 ....Abraham Olano, Spain
1996 ....Johan Museeuw, Belgium
1997 ....Laurent Brochard, France
1998 ....Oskar Camenzind, Switz
1999 ....Oscar Gomez Freire, Spain
2000 .....Romans Vainsteins, Latvia
2001 .....Oscar Gomez Freire, Spain
2002 .....Mario Cipollini, Italy

Tour DuPont Winners

Year	Winner	Time
1989	Dag Otto Lauritzen, Norway	33 hrs, 28 min, 48 sec
1990	Raul Alcala, Mexico	45 hrs, 20 min, 9 sec
1991	Erik Breukink, Holland	48 hrs, 56 min, 53 sec
1992	Greg LeMond, United States	44 hrs, 27 min, 43 sec
1993	Raul Alcala, Mexico	46 hrs, 42 min, 52 sec
1994	Viatcheslav Ekimov, Russia	47 hrs, 14 min, 29 sec
1995	Lance Armstrong, United States	46 hrs, 31 min, 16 sec
1996	Lance Armstrong, United States	48 hrs, 20 min, 5 sec

Note: Race not held since 1996.

Tour de France Winners

Year	Winner	Time
1903	Maurice Garin, France	94 hrs, 33 min
1904	Henry Cornet, France	96 hrs, 5 min, 56 sec
1905	Louis Trousselier, France	110 hrs, 26 min, 58 sec
1906	Rene Pottier, France	Not available
1907	Lucien Petit-Breton, France	158 hrs, 54 min, 5 sec
1908	Lucien Petit-Breton, France	Not available
1909	Francois Faber, Luxembourg	157 hrs, 1 min, 22 sec
1910	Octave Lapize, France	162 hrs, 41 min, 30 sec
1911	Gustave Garrigou, France	195 hrs, 37 min
1912	Odile Defraye, Belgium	190 hrs, 30 min, 28 sec
1913	Philippe Thys, Belgium	197 hrs, 54 min
1914	Philippe Thys, Belgium	200 hrs, 28 min, 48 sec
1915–18	No race	
1919	Firmin Lambot, Belgium	231 hrs, 7 min, 15 sec
1920	Philippe Thys, Belgium	228 hrs, 36 min, 13 sec
1921	Leon Scieur, Belgium	221 hrs, 50 min, 26 sec
1922	Firmin Lambot, Belgium	222 hrs, 8 min, 6 sec

Tour de France Winners (Cont.)

Year	Winner	Time
1923	Henri Pelissier, France	222 hrs, 15 min, 30 sec
1924	Ottavio Bottechia, Italy	226 hrs, 18 min, 21 sec
1925	Ottavio Bottechia, Italy	219 hrs, 10 min, 18 sec
1926	Lucien Buysse, Belgium	238 hrs, 44 min, 25 sec
1927	Nicolas Frantz, Luxembourg	198 hrs, 16 min, 42 sec
1928	Nicolas Frantz, Luxembourg	192 hrs, 48 min, 58 sec
1929	Maurice Dewaele, Belgium	186 hrs, 39 min, 16 sec
1930	Andre Leducq, France	172 hrs, 12 min, 16 sec
1931	Antonin Magne, France	177 hrs, 10 min, 3 sec
1932	Andre Leducq, France	154 hrs, 12 min, 49 sec
1933	Georges Speicher, France	147 hrs, 51 min, 37 sec
1934	Antonin Magne, France	147 hrs, 13 min, 58 sec
1935	Romain Maes, Belgium	141 hrs, 32 min
1936	Sylvere Maes, Belgium	142 hrs, 47 min, 32 sec
1937	Roger Lapebie, France	138 hrs, 58 min, 31 sec
1938	Gino Bartali, Italy	148 hrs, 29 min, 12 sec
1939	Sylvere Maes, Belgium	132 hrs, 3 min, 17 sec
1940–46	No race	
1947	Jean Robic, France	148 hrs, 11 min, 25 sec
1948	Gino Bartali, Italy	147 hrs, 10 min, 36 sec
1949	Fausto Coppi, Italy	149 hrs, 40 min, 49 sec
1950	Ferdi Kubler, Switzerland	145 hrs, 36 min, 56 sec
1951	Hugo Koblet, Switzerland	142 hrs, 20 min, 14 sec
1952	Fausto Coppi, Italy	151 hrs, 57 min, 20 sec
1953	Louison Bobet, France	129 hrs, 23 min, 25 sec
1954	Louison Bobet, France	140 hrs, 6 min, 5 sec
1955	Louison Bobet, France	130 hrs, 29 min, 26 sec
1956	Roger Walkowiak, France	124 hrs, 1 min, 16 sec
1957	Jacques Anquetil, France	129 hrs, 46 min, 11 sec
1958	Charly Gaul, Luxembourg	116 hrs, 59 min, 5 sec
1959	Federico Bahamontes, Spain	123 hrs, 46 min, 45 sec
1960	Gastone Nencini, Italy	112 hrs, 8 min, 42 sec
1961	Jacques Anquetil, France	122 hrs, 1 min, 33 sec
1962	Jacques Anquetil, France	114 hrs, 31 min, 54 sec
1963	Jacques Anquetil, France	113 hrs, 30 min, 5 sec
1964	Jacques Anquetil, France	127 hrs, 9 min, 44 sec
1965	Felice Gimondi, Italy	116 hrs, 42 min, 6 sec
1966	Lucien Aimar, France	117 hrs, 34 min, 21 sec
1967	Roger Pingeon, France	136 hrs, 53 min, 50 sec
1968	Jan Janssen, Netherlands	133 hrs, 49 min, 32 sec
1969	Eddy Merckx, Belgium	116 hrs, 16 min, 2 sec
1970	Eddy Merckx, Belgium	119 hrs, 31 min, 49 sec
1971	Eddy Merckx, Belgium	96 hrs, 45 min, 14 sec
1972	Eddy Merckx, Belgium	108 hrs, 17 min, 18 sec
1973	Luis Ocana, Spain	122 hrs, 25 min, 34 sec
1974	Eddy Merckx, Belgium	116 hrs, 16 min, 58 sec
1975	Bernard Thevenet, France	114 hrs, 35 min, 31 sec
1976	Lucien Van Impe, Belgium	116 hrs, 22 min, 23 sec
1977	Bernard Thevenet, France	115 hrs, 38 min, 30"sec
1978	Bernard Hinault, France	108 hrs, 18 min
1979	Bernard Hinault, France	103 hrs, 6 min, 50 sec
1980	Joop Zoetemelk, Netherlands	109 hrs, 19 min, 14 sec
1981	Bernard Hinault, France	96 hrs, 19 min, 38 sec
1982	Bernard Hinault, France	92 hrs, 8 min, 46 sec
1983	Laurent Fignon, France	105 hrs, 7 min, 52 sec
1984	Laurent Fignon, France	112 hrs, 3 min, 40 sec
1985	Bernard Hinault, France	113 hrs, 24 min, 23 sec
1986	Greg LeMond, United States	110 hrs, 35 min, 19 sec
1987	Stephen Roche, Ireland	115 hrs, 27 min, 42 sec
1988	Pedro Delgado, Spain	84 hrs, 27 min, 53 sec
1989	Greg LeMond, United States	87 hrs, 38 min, 35 sec
1990	Greg LeMond, United States	90 hrs, 43 min, 20 sec
1991	Miguel Induráin, Spain	101 hrs, 1 min, 20 sec
1992	Miguel Induráin, Spain	100 hrs, 49 min, 30 sec
1993	Miguel Induráin, Spain	95 hrs, 57 min, 9 sec
1994	Miguel Induráin, Spain	103 hrs, 38 min, 38 sec
1995	Miguel Induráin, Spain	92 hrs, 44 min, 59 sec
1996	Bjarne Riis, Denmark	95 hrs, 57 min, 16 sec

Tour de France Winners *(Cont.)*

Year	Winner	Time
1997	Jan Ullrich, Germany	100 hrs, 30 min, 35 sec
1998	Marco Pantani, Italy	92 hrs, 49 min, 46 sec
1999	Lance Armstrong, United States	91 hrs, 32 min, 16 sec
2000	Lance Armstrong, United States	92 hrs, 33 min, 8 sec
2001	Lance Armstrong, United States	86 hrs, 17 min, 28 sec
2002	Lance Armstrong, United States	82 hrs, 5 min, 12 sec
2003	Lance Armstrong, United States	83 hrs, 41 min, 12 sec

Sled Dog Racing

Iditarod

Year	Winner	Time	Year	Winner	Time
1973	Dick Wilmarth	20 days, 00:49:41	1989	Joe Runyan	11 days, 05:24:34
1974	Carl Huntington	20 days, 15:02:07	1990	Susan Butcher	11 days, 01:53:23
1975	Emmitt Peters	14 days, 14:43:45	1991	Rick Swenson	12 days, 16:34:39
1976	Gerald Riley	18 days, 22:58:17	1992	Martin Buser	10 days, 19:17:15
1977	Rick Swenson	16 days, 16:27:13	1993	Jeff King	10 days, 15:38:15
1978	Dick Mackey	14 days, 18:52:24	1994	Martin Buser	10 days, 13:02:39
1979	Rick Swenson	15 days, 10:37:47	1995	Doug Swingley	9 days, 02:42:19
1980	Joe May	14 days, 07:11:51	1996	Jeff King	9 days, 05:43:13
1981	Rick Swenson	12 days, 08:45:02	1997	Martin Buser	9 days, 08:30:45
1982	Rick Swenson	16 days, 04:40:10	1998	Jeff King	9 days, 05:52:26
1983	Dick Mackey	12 days, 14:10:44	1999	Doug Swingley	9 days, 14:31:19
1984	Dean Osmar	12 days, 15:07:33	2000	Doug Swingley	9 days, 00:58:06
1985	Libby Riddles	18 days, 00:20:17	2001	Doug Swingley	9 days, 19:55:50
1986	Susan Butcher	11 days, 15:06:00	2002	Martin Buser	8 days, 22:46:02
1987	Susan Butcher	11 days, 02:05:13	2003	Robert Sorlie	9 days, 15:47:36
1988	Susan Butcher	11 days, 11:41:40			

Fishing

Saltwater Fishing Records

Species	Weight	Where Caught	Date	Angler
Albacore	88 lb 2 oz	Gran Canaria, Canary Islands	Nov 19, 1977	Siegfried Dickemann
Amberjack, greater	155 lb 12 oz	Bermuda	Aug 16, 1992	Larry Trott
Amberjack, Pacific	104 lb	Baja California, Mexico	July 4, 1984	Richard Cresswell
Angler	126 lb 12 oz	Sognefjorden Hoyanger, Norway	July 4, 1996	Gunnar Thorsteinsen
Barracuda, great	85 lb	Christmas Island, Kiribati	April 11, 1992	John W. Helfrich
Barracuda, Mexican	21 lb	Phantom Isle, Costa Rica	Mar 27, 1987	E. Greg Kent
Barracuda, pickhandle	25 lb 5 oz	Scottburgh, Natal, South Africa	July 3, 1996	Demetrios Stamatis
Bass, barred sand	13 lb 3 oz	Huntington Beach, California	Aug 29, 1988	Robert Halal
Bass, black sea	10 lb 4 oz	Virginia Beach, Virginia	Jan 1, 2000	Allan P. Paschall
Bass, European	20 lb 14 oz	Cap d'Agde, France	Sept. 8, 1999	Robert Mari
Bass, giant sea	563 lb 8 oz	Anacapa Island, California	Aug 20, 1968	James D. McAdam Jr.
Bass, striped	78 lb 8 oz	Atlantic City, New Jersey	Sep 21, 1982	Albert R. McReynolds
Bluefish	31 lb 12 oz	Hatteras Inlet, North Carolina	Jan 30, 1972	James M. Hussey
Bonefish	19 lb	Zululand, South Africa	May 26, 1962	Brian W. Batchelor
Bonito, Atlantic	18 lb 4 oz	Faial Island, Azores	July 8, 1953	D.G. Higgs
Bonito, Pacific	21 lb 3 oz	Malibu, California	July 30, 1978	Gino M. Picciolo
Cabezon	23 lb	Juan De Fuca Strait, Washington	Aug 4, 1990	Wesley Hunter
Cobia	135 lb 9 oz	Shark Bay, Australia	July 9, 1985	Peter W. Goulding
Cod, Atlantic	98 lb 12 oz	Isle of Shoals, New Hampshire	June 8, 1969	Alphonse Bielevich
Cod, Pacific	35 lb	Unalaska Bay, Alaska	June 16, 1999	Jim Johnson
Conger	133 lb 4 oz	South Devon, England	June 5, 1995	Vic Evans
Dolphinfish	88 lb	Highbourne Cay, Bahamas	May 5, 1998	Richard D. Evans
Drum, black	113 lb 1 oz	Lewes, Delaware	Sep 15, 1975	Gerald M. Townsend
Drum, red	94 lb 2 oz	Avon, North Carolina	Nov 7, 1984	David Deuel
Eel, American	9 lb 4 oz	Cape May, New Jersey	Nov 9, 1995	Jeff Pennick
Eel, marbled	36 lb 1 oz	Durban, South Africa	June 10, 1984	Ferdie van Nooten
Flounder, southern	20 lb 9 oz	Nassau Sound, Florida	Dec 23, 1983	Larenza W. Mungin
Flounder, summer	22 lb 7 oz	Montauk, New York	Sep 15, 1975	Charles Nappi
Grouper, Warsaw	436 lb 12 oz	Destin, Florida	Dec 22, 1985	Steve Haeusler
Halibut, Atlantic	355 lb 6 oz	Valevag, Norway	Oct 20, 1997	Odd Arve Gunderstad

Saltwater Fishing Records (Cont.)

Species	Weight	Where Caught	Date	Angler
Halibut, California	58 lb 9 oz	Santa Rosa Island, California	June 26, 1999	Roger W. Borrell
Halibut, Pacific	459 lb	Dutch Harbor, Alaska	June 11, 1996	Jack Tragis
Jack, crevalle	58 lb 6 oz	Barro do Kwanza, Angola	Dec 10, 2000	Nuno A. P. da Silva
Jack, horse-eye	29 lb 8 oz	Ascencion Island, S Atlantic Ocean	May 28, 1993	Mike Hanson
Jack, Pacific crevalle	39 lb	Playa Zancudo, Costa Rica	Mar 3, 1997	Ingrid Callaghan
Jewfish	680 lb	Fernandina Beach, Florida	May 20, 1961	Lynn Joyner
Kawakawa	29 lb	Isla Clarion, Mexico	Dec 17, 1986	Ronald Nakamura
Lingcod	76 lb 9 oz	Gulf of Alaska, Alaska	Aug 11, 2001	Antwan D. Tinsley
Mackerel, cero	17 lb 2 oz	Islamorada, Florida	Apr 5, 1986	G. Michael Mills
Mackerel, king	93 lb	San Juan, Puerto Rico	Apr 18, 1999	Steve Perez Graulau
Mackerel, narrowbarred	99 lb	Natal, South Africa	Mar 14, 1982	Michael J. Wilkinson
Mackerel, Spanish	13 lb	Ocracoke Inlet, North Carolina	Nov 4, 1987	Robert Cranton
Marlin, Atlantic blue	1,402 lb 2 oz	Vitoria, Brazil	Feb 29, 1992	Paulo R.A. Amorim
Marlin, black	1,560 lb	Cabo Blanco, Peru	Aug 4, 1953	Alfred C. Glassell Jr.
Marlin, Pacific blue	1,376 lb	Kaaiwi Point, Hawaii	May 31, 1982	J.W. de Beaubien
Marlin, striped	494 lb	Tutukaka, New Zealand	Jan 16, 1986	Bill Boniface
Marlin, white	181 lb 14 oz	Vitoria, Brazil	Dec 8, 1979	Evandro Luiz Caser
Permit	56 lb 2 oz	Fort Lauderdale, Florida	June 30, 1997	Thomas Sebestyen
Pollock	50 lb	Salstraumen, Norway	Nov 30, 1995	Thor Magnus-Lekang
Pompano, African	50 lb 8 oz	Daytona Beach, Florida	Apr 21, 1990	Tom Sargent
Roosterfish	114 lb	La Paz, Mexico	June 1, 1960	Abe Sackheim
Runner, blue	11 lb 2 oz	Dauphin Island, Alaska	June 28, 1997	Stacey M. Moiren
Runner, rainbow	37 lb 9 oz	Isla Clarion, Mexico	Nov 21, 1991	Tom Pfleger
Sailfish, Atlantic	141 lb 1 oz	Luanda, Angola	Feb 19, 1994	Alfredo de Sousa Neves
Sailfish, Pacific	221 lb	Santa Cruz Island, Ecuador	Feb 12, 1947	Carl W. Stewart
Seabass, white	83 lb 12 oz	San Felipe, Mexico	Mar 31, 1953	Lyal C. Baumgardner
Seatrout, spotted	17 lb 7 oz	Ft. Pierce, Florida	May 11, 1995	Craig F. Carson
Shark, bigeye thresher	802 lb	Tutukaka, New Zealand	Feb 8, 1981	Dianne North
Shark, blue	528 lb	Montauk Point, New York	Aug 9, 2001	Joe Seidel
Shark, grter hammrhd	991 lb	Sarasota, Florida	May 30, 1982	Allen Ogle
Shark, Greenland	1,708 lb 9 oz	Trondheimsfjord, Norway	Oct 18, 1987	Terje Nordtvedt
Shark, porbeagle	507 lb	Caithness, Scotland	Mar 9, 1993	Christopher Bennet
Shark, shortfin mako	1,221 lb	Chatham, Massachusetts	July 21, 2001	Luke Sweeney
Shark, tiger	1,780 lb	Cherry Grove, South Carolina	June 14, 1964	Walter Maxwell
Shark, tope	72 lb 12 oz	Parengarenga Harbor, N.Z.	Dec 19, 1986	Melanie B. Feldman
Shark, white	2,664 lb	Ceduna, Australia	Apr 21, 1959	Alfred Dean
Skipjack, black	26 lb	Baja California, Mexico	Oct 23, 1991	Clifford K. Hamaishi
Snapper, cubera	121 lb 8 oz	Cameron, Louisiana	July 5, 1982	Mike Hebert
Snook, common	53 lb 10 oz	Parismina Ranch, Costa Rica	Oct 18, 1978	Gilbert Ponzi
Spearfish, Mediterr.	90 lb 13 oz	Madeira Island, Portugal	June 2, 1980	Joseph Larkin
Spearfish, longbill	127 lb 13 oz	Puerto Rico, Gran Canaria, Spain	May 20, 1999	Paul Cashmore
Spearfish, shortbill	74 lb 8 oz	Bay of Islands, New Zealand	Mar 16, 1999	Leonie Kai Patterson
Swordfish	1,182 lb	Iquique, Chile	May 7, 1953	Louis Marron
Tarpon	283 lb 4 oz	Sherbro Island, Sierra Leone	Apr 16, 1991	Yvon Victor Sebag
Tautog	25 lb	Ocean City, New Jersey	Jan 20, 1998	Anthony Monica
Tilapia, Mozambique	2 lb 8 oz	Delray Beach, Florida	Nov 10, 1997	Nick Cardella
Trevally, bigeye	31 lb 8 oz	Poivre Island, Seychelles	Apr 23, 1997	Les Sampson
Trevally, giant	145 lb 8 oz	Maui, Hawaii	Mar 28, 1991	Russell Mori
Tuna, Atlantic bigeye	392 lb 6 oz	Puerto Rico, Gran Canaria, Spain	July 25, 1996	Dieter Vogel
Tuna, blackfin	45 lb 8 oz	Key West, Florida	May 4, 1996	Sam J. Burnett
Tuna, bluefin	1,496 lb	Aulds Cove, Nova Scotia	Oct 26, 1979	Ken Fraser
Tuna, longtail	79 lb 2 oz	Montague Island, New South Wales, Australia	Apr 12, 1982	Tim Simpson
Tuna, Pacific bigeye	435 lb	Cabo Blanco, Peru	Apr 17, 1957	Russel Lee
Tuna, skipjack	45 lb 4 oz	Baja California, Mexico	Nov 16, 1996	Brian Evans
Tuna, southern bluefin	348 lb 5 oz	Whakatane, New Zealand	Jan 16, 1981	Rex Wood
Tuna, yellowfin	388 lb 12 oz	San Benedicto Is, Mexico	Apr 1, 1977	Curt Wiesenhutter
Tunny, little	35 lb 2 oz	Cape de Garde, Algeria	Dec 14, 1988	Jean Yves Chatard
Wahoo	158 lb 8 oz	Loreto, Baja California, Mexico	June 10, 1996	Keith Winter
Weakfish	19 lb 2 oz	Jones Beach Inlet, New York	Oct 11, 1984	Dennis Rooney
Yellowtail, California	88 lb 3 oz	Delaware Bay, Mexico	May 20, 1989	William E. Thomas
		Alijos Rocks, Baja Calif., Mexico	Jun 21, 2000	Ronald Fujii
Yellowtail, southern	114 lb 10 oz	Tauranga, New Zealand	Feb 5, 1984	Mike Godfrey

Freshwater Fishing Records

Species	Weight	Where Caught	Date	Angler
Barramundi	83 lb 7 oz	Lake Tinaroo, N Queensl'd, Aus.	Sept 23, 1999	David Powell
Bass, largemouth	22 lb 4 oz	Montgomery Lake, Georgia	June 2, 1932	George W. Perry
Bass, rock	3 lb	York River, Ontario	Aug 1, 1974	Peter Gulgin
Bass, shoal	8 lb 12 oz	Apalatchicola River, Florida	Jan 28, 1995	Carl W. Davis
Bass, smallmouth	10 lb 14 oz	Dale Hollow, Tennessee	April 24, 1969	John T. Gorman
Bass, Suwannee	3 lb 14 oz	Suwannee River, Florida	Mar 2, 1985	Ronnie Everett
Bass, white	6 lb 13 oz	Orange, Virginia	July 31, 1989	Ronald Sprouse
Bass, whiterock	27 lb 5 oz	Greers Ferry Lake, Arkansas	Apr 24, 1997	Jerald Shaum
Bass, yellow	2 lb 9 oz	Waverly, Tennessee	Feb 27, 1998	John Chappell
Bluegill	4 lb 12 oz	Ketona Lake, Alabama	Apr 9, 1950	T.S. Hudson
Bowfin	21 lb 8 oz	Florence, South Carolina	Jan 29, 1980	Robert Harmon
Buffalo, bigmouth	70 lb 5 oz	Bastrop, Louisiana	Apr 21, 1980	Delbert Sisk
Buffalo, black	63 lb 6 oz	Mississippi River, Iowa	Aug 14, 1999	Jim Winter
Buffalo, smallmouth	82 lb 3 oz	Athens Lake, Georgia	June 6, 1993	Randy Collins
Bullhead, brown	6 lb 5 oz	Lake Mahopac, New York	Sept 8, 2002	Ray Lawrence
Bullhead, yellow	4 lb 4 oz	Mormon Lake, Arizona	May 11, 1984	Emily Williams
Burbot	18 lb 11 oz	Angenmanalren, Sweden	Oct 22, 1996	Margit Agren
Carp, common	75 lb 11 oz	Lac de St. Cassien, France	May 21, 1987	Leo van der Gugten
Catfish, blue	116 lb 12 oz	Mississippi River, Arkansas	Aug 3, 2001	Charles Ashley Jr.
Catfish, channel	58 lb	Santee-Cooper Reservoir, SC	July 7, 1964	W.B. Whaley
Catfish, flathead	123 lb	Elk City Reservoir, Indep., KS	May 14, 1998	Ken Paulie
Catfish, white	21 lb 8 oz	Gorton Pond, East Lime, CT	Apr 22, 2001	Thomas Urquhart
Char, Arctic	32 lb 9 oz	Tree River, Canada	July 30, 1981	Jeffrey Ward
Crappie, white	5 lb 3 oz	Enid Dam, Mississippi	July 31, 1957	Fred L. Bright
Dolly Varden	20 lb 14 oz	Wulik River, Alaska	July 7, 2001	Raz Reid
Dorado	51 lb 5 oz	Corrientes, Argentina	Sep 27, 1984	Armando Giudice
Drum, freshwater	54 lb 8 oz	Nickajack Lake, Tennessee	Apr 20, 1972	Benny E. Hull
Gar, alligator	279 lb	Rio Grande River, Texas	Dec 2, 1951	Bill Valverde
Gar, Florida	10 lb	Florida Everglades, Florida	Jan 28, 2002	Herbert Ratner Jr.
Gar, longnose	50 lb 5 oz	Trinity River, Texas	July 30, 1954	Townsend Miller
Gar, shortnose	5 lb 12 oz	Rend Lake, Illinois	July 16, 1995	Donna K. Willmert
Gar, spotted	9 lb 12 oz	Lake Mexia, Texas	Apr 7, 1994	Rick Rivard
Grayling, Arctic	5 lb 15 oz	Katseyedie River, Northwest Territories	Aug 16, 1967	Jeanne P. Branson
Inconnu	53 lb	Pah River, Alaska	Aug 20, 1986	Lawrence Hudnall
Kokanee	9 lb 6 oz	Okanagan Lake, Vernon, BC	June 18, 1988	Norm Kuhn
Muskellunge	67 lb 8 oz	Hayward, Wisconsin	July 24, 1949	Cal Johnson
Muskellunge, tiger	51 lb 3 oz	Lac Vieux-Desert, WI, MI	July 16, 1919	John Knobla
Peacock, speckled	27 lb	Rio Negro, Brazil	Dec 4, 1994	Gerald (Doc) Lawson
Perch, Nile	230 lb	Lake Nasser, Egypt	Dec 20, 2000	William Toth
Perch, white	3 lb 1 oz	Forest Hill Park, NJ	May 6, 1989	Edward Tango
Perch, yellow	4 lb 3 oz	Bordentown, New Jersey	May 1865	C.C. Abbot
Pickerel, chain	9 lb 6 oz	Homerville, Georgia	Feb 17, 1961	Baxley McQuaig Jr.
Pike, northern	55 lb 1 oz	Lake of Grefeern, W Germany	Oct 16, 1986	Lothar Louis
Redhorse, greater	9 lb 3 oz	Salmon River, Pulaski, New York	May 11, 1985	Jason Wilson
Redhorse, silver	11 lb 7 oz	Plum Creek, Wisconsin	May 29, 1985	Neal Long
Salmon, Atlantic	79 lb 2 oz	Tana River, Norway	1928	Henrik Henriksen
Salmon, Chinook	97 lb 4 oz	Kenai River, Alaska	May 17, 1985	Les Anderson
Salmon, chum	35 lb	Edye Pass, Canada	July 11, 1995	Todd A. Johansson
Salmon, coho	33 lb 4 oz	Pulaski, New York	Sep 27, 1989	Jerry Lifton
Salmon, pink	14 lb 13 oz	Monroe, Washington	Sep 30, 2001	Alexander Minerich
Salmon, sockeye	15 lb 3 oz	Kenai River, Alaska	Aug 9, 1987	Stan Roach
Sauger	8 lb 12 oz	Lake Sakakawea, North Dakota	Oct 6, 1971	Mike Fischer
Shad, American	11 lb 4 oz	Connecticut River, Massachusetts	May 19, 1986	Bob Thibodo
Sturgeon, white	468 lb	Benicia, California	July 9, 1983	Joey Pallotta III
Sunfish, green	2 lb 2 oz	Stockton Lake, Missouri	June 18, 1971	Paul M. Dilley
Sunfish, redbreast	1 lb 12 oz	Suwannee River, Florida	May 29, 1984	Alvin Buchanan
Sunfish, redear	5 lb 7 oz	Diverson Canal, Georgia	Nov 6, 1998	Amos M. Gay
Tigerfish, giant	97 lb	Zaire River, Kinshasa, Zaire	July 9, 1988	Raymond Houtmans
Trout, Apache	5 lb 3 oz	Apache Reservation, Arizona	May 29, 1991	John Baldwin
Trout, brook	14 lb 8 oz	Nipigon River, Ontario	July 1916	W.J. Cook
Trout, brown	40 lb 4 oz	Heber Springs, Arkansas	May 9, 1992	Howard (Rip) Collins
Trout, bull	32 lb	Lake Pond Oreille, Idaho	Oct 27, 1949	N.L. Higgins
Trout, cutthroat	41 lb	Pyramid Lake, Nevada	Dec 1925	John Skimmerhorn
Trout, golden	11 lb	Cook's Lake, Wyoming	Aug 5, 1948	Charles S. Reed

Freshwater Fishing Records *(Cont.)*

Species	Weight	Where Caught	Date	Angler
Trout, lake	72 lb	Great Bear Lake, Northwest Territories	Aug 19, 1995	Lloyd Bull
Trout, rainbow	42 lb 2 oz	Bell Island, Alaska	June 22, 1970	David Robert White
Trout, tiger	20 lb 13 oz	Lake Michigan, Wisconsin	Aug 12, 1978	Pete M. Friedland
Walleye	25 lb	Old Hickory Lake, Tennessee	Aug 2, 1960	Mabry Harper
Warmouth	2 lb 7 oz	Yellow River, Holt, Florida	Oct 19, 1985	Tony D. Dempsey
Whitefish, lake	14 lb 6 oz	Meaford, Ontario	May 21, 1984	Dennis Laycock
Whitefish, mountain	5 lb 8 oz	Elbow River, Calgary, Alberta	Aug 1, 1995	Randy Woo
Whitefish, broad	9 lb	Tozitna River, Alaska	July 17, 1989	Al Mathews
Whitefish, round	6 lb	Putahow River, Manitoba	June 14, 1984	Allan J. Ristori
Zander	25 lb 2 oz	Trosa, Sweden	June 12, 1986	Harry Lee Tennison

Greyhound Racing

Annual Greyhound Race of Champions Winners*

Year	Winner (Sex)	Affiliation/Owner	Year	Winner (Sex)	Affiliation/Owner
1982	DD's Jackie (F)	Wonderland Park/ R.H. Walters Jr.	1988	BB's Old Yellow (M)	Supplemental (Southland)/ Margie Bonita Hyers
1983	Comin' Attraction (F)	Rocky Mt. Greyhound Park/ Bob Riggin	1989	Osh Kosh Juliet (F)	Tampa Greyhound Track/ William F. Pollard
1984	Fallon (F)	Tampa Greyhound Track/ E.J. Alderson	1990	Daring Don (M)	Interstate Kennel Club/ Perry Padrta
1985	Lady Delight (F)	Lincoln Greyhound Park/ Julian A. Gay	1991	Mo Kick (M)	Flagler Greyhound Track/ Eric M. Kennon
1986	Ben G Speedboat (M)	Multnomah Kennel Club/ Louis Bennett	1992	Dicky Vallie (M)	Dairyland Greyhound Track/ George Benjamin
1987	ET's Pesky (F)	Supplemental (Flagler)/ Emil Tanis	1993	Mega Morris (M)	Jacksonville Kennel Club/ Ferrell's Kennel

* The Greyhound Race of Champions has not been held since 1993.

Gymnastics

World Champions
MEN
All-Around

Year	Champion, Nation	Year	Champion, Nation	Year	Champion, Nation
1903	Joseph Martinez, France	1938	Jan Gajdos, Czechoslovakia	1983	Dimitri Bilozertchev, USSR
1905	Marcel Lalue, France	1950	Walter Lehmann, Switzerland	1985	Yuri Korolev, USSR
1907	Joseph Czada, Czechoslovakia	1954	Valentin Mouratov, USSR Victor Chukarin, USSR	1987	Dimitri Bilozertchev, USSR
1909	Marcos Torres, France	1958	Boris Shaklin, USSR	1989	Igor Korobchinsky, USSR
1911	Ferdinand Steiner, Czechoslovakia	1962	Yuri Titov, USSR	1991	Grigori Misutin, CIS
1913	Marcos Torres, France	1966	Mikhail Voronin, USSR	1993	Vitaly Scherbo, Belarus
1922	Peter Sumi, Yugoslavia F. Pechacek, Czechoslovakia	1970	Eizo Kenmotsu, Japan	1994	Ivan Ivankov, Belarus
1926	Peter Sumi, Yugoslavia	1974	Shigeru Kasamatsu, Japan	1995	Li Xiaoshuang, China
1930	Josip Primozic, Yugoslavia	1978	Nikolai Andrianov, USSR	1997	Ivan Ivankov, Belarus
1934	Eugene Mack, Switzerland	1979	Alexander Ditiatin, USSR	1999	Nicolae Krukov, Russia
		1981	Yuri Korolev, USSR	2001	Feng Jing, China
				2003	Paul Hamm, United States

Pommel Horse

Year	Champion, Nation	Year	Champion, Nation	Year	Champion, Nation
1930	Josip Primozic, Yugoslavia	1962	Miroslav Cerar, Yugoslavia	1981	Michael Mikolai, East Germany
1934	Eugene Mack, Switzerland	1966	Miroslav Cerar, Yugoslavia	1983	Dmitri Bilozertchev, USSR
1938	Michael Reusch, Switzerland	1970	Miroslav Cerar, Yugoslavia	1985	Valentin Moguilny, USSR
1950	Josef Stalder, Switzerland	1974	Zoltan Magyar, Hungary	1987	Zsolt Borkai, Hungary Dmitri Bilozertchev, USSR
1954	Grant Chaguinjan, USSR	1978	Zoltan Magyar, Hungary		
1958	Boris Shaklin, USSR	1979	Zoltan Magyar, Hungary		

World Champions (Cont.)

MEN (Cont.)

Pommel Horse (Cont.)

Year	Champion, Nation
1989	Valentin Moguilny, USSR
1991	Valeri Belenki, USSR
1992	Pae Gil Su, North Korea
	Vitaly Scherbo, CIS
	Li Jing, China

Year	Champion, Nation
1993	Pae Gil Su, North Korea
1994	Marius Urzica, Romania
1995	Li Donghua, Switzerland
1996	Pae Gil Su, North Korea
1997	Valeri Belenki, Germany

Year	Champion, Nation
1999	Alexei Nemov, Russia
2001	Marius Urzica, Romania
2003	Teng Haibin, China
	Takehiro Kashima, Japan

Floor Exercise

Year	Champion, Nation
1930	Josip Primozic, Yugoslavia
1934	Georges Miesz, Switzerland
1938	Jan Gajdos, Czechoslovakia
1950	Josef Stalder, Switzerland
1954	Valentin Mouratov, USSR
	Masao Takemoto, Japan
1958	Masao Takemoto, Japan
1962	Nobuyuki Aihara, Japan
	Yukio Endo, Japan
1966	Akinori Nakayama, Japan
1970	Akinori Nakayama, Japan

Year	Champion, Nation
1974	Shigeru Kasamatsu, Japan
1978	Kurt Thomas, United States
1979	Kurt Thomas, United States
	Roland Brucker, GDR
1981	Yuri Korolev, USSR
	Li Yuejui, Chi
1983	Tong Fei, China
1985	Tong Fei, China
1987	Lou Yun, China
1989	Igor Korobchinsky, USSR
1991	Igor Korobchinsky, USSR

Year	Champion, Nation
1993	Grigori Misutin, Ukraine
1994	Vitaly Scherbo, Belarus
1995	Vitaly Scherbo, Belarus
1996	Vitaly Scherbo, Belarus
1997	Alexei Nemov, Russia
1999	Alexei Nemov, Russia
2001	Marian Dragulescu, Rom
2003	Paul Hamm, United States
	Jordan Jovtchev, Bulgaria

Rings

Year	Champion, Nation
1930	Emanuel Loffler, Czechoslovakia
1934	Alois Hudec, Czechoslovakia
1938	Alois Hudec, Czechoslovakia
1950	Walter Lehmann, Switzerland
1954	Albert Azarian, USSR
1958	Albert Azarian, USSR
1962	Yuri Titov, USSR
1966	Mikhail Voronin, USSR
1970	Akinori Nakayama, Japan

Year	Champion, Nation
1974	N. Andrianov, USSR
	D. Grecu, Rom.
1978	Nikolai Andrianov, USSR
1979	Alexander Ditiatin, USSR
1981	Alexander Ditiatin, USSR
1983	Dimitri Bilozertchev, USSR
1985	Li Ning, China
	Yuri Korolev, USSR
1987	Yuri Korolev, USSR
1989	Andreas Aguilar, W Ger
1991	Grigory Misutin, USSR

Year	Champion, Nation
1992	Vitaly Scherbo, CIS
1993	Yuri Chechi, Italy
1994	Yuri Chechi, Italy
1995	Yuri Chechi, Italy
1996	Yuri Chechi, Italy
1997	Yuri Chechi, Italy
1999	Zhen Dong, China
2001	Jordan Jovtchev, Bulgaria
2003	Jordan Jovtchev, Bulgaria
	Dimosthénis Tampakos, Greece

Parallel Bars

Year	Champion, Nation
1930	Josip Primozic, Yugoslavia
1934	Eugene Mack, Switzerland
1938	Michael Reusch, Switzerland
1950	Hans Eugster, Switzerland
1954	Victor Chukarin, USSR
1958	Boris Shaklin, USSR
1962	Miroslav Cerar, Yugoslavia
1966	Sergei Diamidov, USSR
1970	Akinori Nakayama, Japan
1974	Eizo Kenmotsu, Japan
1978	Eizo Kenmotsu, Japan

Year	Champion, Nation
1979	Bart Conner, United States
1981	Koji Gushiken, Japan
	Alexandr Ditiatin, USSR
1983	Vladimir Artemov, USSR
	Lou Yun, China
1985	Sylvio Kroll, East Germany
	Valentin Moguilny, USSR
1987	Vladimir Artemov, USSR
1989	Li Jing, China
	Vladimir Artemov, USSR
1991	Li Jing, China

Year	Champion, Nation
1992	Li Jin, China
	Alexei Voropaev, CIS
1993	Vitaly Scherbo, Belarus
1994	Huang Liping, China
1995	Vitaly Scherbo, Belarus
1996	Rustam Sharipov, Ukraine
1997	Zhang Jinjing, China
1999	Joo-Hyung Lee, S Korea
2001	Sean Townsend, U.S.
2003	Li Xiao-Peng, China

High Bar

Year	Champion, Nation
1930	Istvan Pelle, Hungary
1934	Ernst Winter, Germany
1938	Michael Reusch, Switzerland
1950	Paavo Aaltonen, Finland
1954	Valentin Mouratov, USSR
1958	Boris Shaklin, USSR
1962	Takashi Ono, Japan
1966	Akinori Nakayama, Japan
1970	Eizo Kenmotsu, Japan
1974	Eberhard Gienger, West Germany

Year	Champion, Nation
1978	Shigeru Kasamatsu, Japan
1979	Kurt Thomas, United States
1981	Alexander Takchev, USSR
1983	Dimitri Bilozertchev, USSR
1985	Tong Fei, China
1987	Dimitri Bilozertchev, USSR
1989	Li Chunyang, China
1991	Li Chunyang, China
	R. Buechner, Germ
1992	Grigori Misutin, CIS
1993	Sergei Kharkov, Russia

Year	Champion, Nation
1994	Vitaly Scherbo, Belarus
1995	Andreas Wecker, Germany
1996	Jesús Carballo, Spain
1997	Jani Tanskanen, Finland
1999	Jesus Carballo, Spain
2001	Vlasios Maras, Greece
2003	Takehiro Kashima, Japan

World Champions (Cont.)
MEN (Cont.)

Vault

Year	Champion, Nation
1934	Eugene Mack, Switzerland
1938	Eugene Mack, Switzerland
1950	Ernst Gebendinger, Switzerland
1954	Leo Sotornik, Czechoslovakia
1958	Yuri Titov, USSR
1962	Premysel Krbec, Czechoslovakia
1966	Haruhiro Yamashita, Japan
1970	Mitsuo Tsukahara, Japan
1974	Shigeru Kasamatsu, Japan

Year	Champion, Nation
1978	Junichi Shimizu, Japan
1979	Alexander Ditiatin, USSR
1981	Ralf-Peter Hemmann, East Germany
1983	Arthur Akopian, USSR
1985	Yuri Korolev, USSR
1987	Lou Yun, China; Sylvio Kroll, East Germany
1989	Joreg Behrend, East Germany
1991	Yoo Ok Youl, South Korea

Year	Champion, Nation
1992	Yoo Ok Youl, South Korea
1993	Vitaly Scherbo, Belarus
1994	Vitaly Scherbo, Belarus
1995	G. Misutin, Ukraine; A. Nemov, Russia
1996	Alexei Nemov, Russia
1997	Sergei Fedorchenko, Kazakhstan
1999	Li Xiao-Peng, China
2001	Marian Dragulescu, Rom
2003	Li Xiao-Peng, China

WOMEN

All-Around

Year	Champion, Nation
1934	Vlasta Dekanova, Czechoslovakia
1938	Vlasta Dekanova, Czechoslovakia
1950	Helena Rakoczy, Poland
1954	Galina Roudiko, USSR
1958	Larissa Latynina, USSR
1962	Larissa Latynina, USSR
1966	Vera Caslavska, Czechoslovakia

Year	Champion, Nation
1970	Ludmilla Tourischeva, USSR
1974	Ludmilla Tourischeva, USSR
1978	Elena Mukhina, USSR
1979	Nelli Kim, USSR
1981	Olga Bicherova, USSR
1983	Natalia Yurchenko, USSR
1985	Elena Shoushounova, USSR; Oksana Omeliantchik, USSR
1987	Aurelia Dobre, Romania
1989	Svetlana Bouguinskaia, USSR

Year	Champion, Nation
1991	Kim Zmeskal, United States
1993	Shannon Miller, United States
1994	Shannon Miller, United States
1995	Lilia Podkopayeva, Ukraine
1997	Svetlana Khorkina, Russia
1999	Maria Olaru, Romania
2001	Svetlana Khorkina, Russia
2003	Svetlana Khorkina, Russia

Floor Exercise

Year	Champion, Nation
1950	Helena Rakoczy, Poland
1954	Tamara Manina, USSR
1958	Eva Bosakava, Czechoslovakia
1962	Larissa Latynina, USSR
1966	Natalia Kuchinskaya, USSR
1970	Ludmilla Tourischeva, USSR
1974	Ludmilla Tourischeva, USSR
1978	Nelli Kim, USSR; Elena Mukhina, USSR

Year	Champion, Nation
1979	Emilia Eberle, Romania
1981	Natalia Ilenko, USSR
1983	Ecaterina Szabo, Romania
1985	Oksana Omeliantchik, USSR
1987	Elena Shoushounova, USSR; Daniela Silivas, Romania
1989	Svetlana Bouguinskaia, USSR; Daniela Silivas, Romania
1991	Cristina Bontas, Romania; Oksana Tchusovitina, USSR

Year	Champion, Nation
1992	Kim Zmeskal, United States
1993	Shannon Miller, United States
1994	Dina Kochetkova, Russia
1995	Gina Gogean, Romania
1996	Gina Gogean, Romania
1997	Gina Gogean, Romania
1999	Andreea Raducan, Romania
2001	Andreea Raducan, Romania
2003	Daiane Dos Santos, Brazil

Uneven Bars

Year	Champion, Nation
1950	Gertchen Kolar, Austria; Anna Pettersson, Sweden
1954	Agnes Keleti, Hungary
1958	Larissa Latynina, USSR
1962	Irina Pervuschina, USSR
1966	Natalia Kuchinskaya, USSR
1970	Karin Janz, East Germany
1974	Annelore Zinke, East Germany
1978	Marcia Frederick, United States

Year	Champion, Nation
1979	Ma Yanhong, China; Maxi Gnauck, East Germany
1981	Maxi Gnauck, East Germany
1983	Maxi Gnauck, East Germany
1985	Gabriele Fahrnich, East Germany
1987	Daniela Silivas, Romania; Doerte Thuemmler, East Germany
1989	Fan Di, China; Daniela Silivas, Romania

Year	Champion, Nation
1991	Gwang Suk Kim, North Korea
1992	Lavinia Milosivici, Romania
1993	Shannon Miller, United States
1994	Luo Li, China
1995	Svetlana Khorkina, Russia
1996	Svetlana Khorkina, Russia
1997	Svetlana Khorkina, Russia
1999	Svetlana Khorkina, Russia
2001	Svetlana Khorkina, Russia
2003	Chellsie Memmel, U.S.; Hollie Vise, United States

World Champions (Cont.)

WOMEN (Cont.)

Balance Beam

Year	Champion, Nation	Year	Champion, Nation	Year	Champion, Nation
1950	Helena Rakoczy, Poland	1979	Vera Cerna, Czechoslovakia	1993	Lavinia Milosovici, Romania
1954	Keiko Tanaka, Japan	1981	Maxi Gnauck, East Germany	1994	Shannon Miller, United States
1958	Larissa Latynina, USSR	1983	Olga Mostepanova, USSR	1995	Mo Huilan, China
1962	Eva Bosakova, Czech.	1985	Daniela Silivas, Romania	1996	Dina Kochetkova, Russia
1966	Natalia Kuchinskaya, USSR	1987	Aurelia Dobre, Romania	1997	Gina Gogean, Romania
1970	Erika Zuchold, East Germany	1989	Daniela Silivas, Romania	1999	E. Zamolodchikova, Russia
1974	Ludmilla Tourischeva, USSR	1991	Svetlana Boguinskaia, USSR	2001	Andreea Raducan, Romania
1978	Nadia Comaneci, Romania	1992	Kim Zmeskal, United States	2003	Fan Ye, China

Vault

Year	Champion, Nation	Year	Champion, Nation	Year	Champion, Nation
1950	Helena Rakoczy, Poland	1979	Dumitrita Turner, Romania	1994	Gina Gogean, Romania
1954	T. Manina, USSR	1981	Maxi Gnauck, East Germany	1995	L. Podkopayeva, Ukraine
	Anna Pettersson, Sweden	1983	Boriana Stoyanova, Bulgaria		Simona Amanar, Rom.
1958	Larissa Latynina, USSR	1985	Elena Shoushounova, USSR	1996	Gina Gogean, Romania
1962	Vera Caslavska, Czech.	1987	Elena Shoushounova, USSR	1997	Simona Amanar, Romania
1966	Vera Caslavska, Czech.	1989	Olesia Durnik, USSR	1999	Jie Ling, China
1970	Erika Zuchold, East Germany	1991	Lavinia Milosovici, Romania	2001	Svetlana Khorkina, Russia
1974	Olga Korbut, USSR	1992	Henrietta Onodi, Hungary	2003	Oksana Chusovitina,
1978	Nelli Kim, USSR	1993	Elena Piskun, Belarus		Uzbekistan

National Champions

MEN

All-Around

Year	Champion	Year	Champion	Year	Champion
1963	Art Shurlock	1976	Kurt Thomas	1991	Chris Waller
1964	Rusty Mitchell	1977	Kurt Thomas	1992	John Roethlisberger
1965	Rusty Mitchell	1978	Kurt Thomas	1993	John Roethlisberger
1966	Rusty Mitchell	1979	Bart Conner	1994	Scott Keswick
1967	Katsuzoki Kanzaki	1980	Peter Vidmar	1995	John Roethlisberger
1968	Yoshi Hayasaki	1981	Jim Hartung	1996	Blaine Wilson
1969	Steve Hug	1982	Peter Vidmar	1997	Blaine Wilson
1970	Makoto Sakamoto	1983	Mitch Gaylord	1998	Blaine Wilson
	Mas Watanabe	1984	Mitch Gaylord	1999	Blaine Wilson
1971	Yoshi Takei	1985	Brian Babcock	2000	Blaine Wilson
1972	Yoshi Takei	1986	Tim Daggett	2001	Sean Townsend
1973	Marshall Avener	1987	Scott Johnson	2002	Paul Hamm
1974	John Crosby	1988	Dan Hayden	2003	Paul Hamm
1975	Tom Beach	1989	Tim Ryan		
	Bart Conner	1990	John Roethlisberger		

Floor Exercise

Year	Champion	Year	Champion	Year	Champion
1963	Tom Seward	1975	Peter Korman	1989	Mike Racanelli
1964	Rusty Mitchell	1977	Ron Galimore	1990	Bob Stelter
1965	Rusty Mitchell	1978	Kurt Thomas	1991	Mike Racanelli
1966	Dan Millman	1979	Ron Galimore	1992	Gregg Curtis
1967	Katsuzoki Kanzaki	1980	Ron Galimore	1993	Kerry Huston
	Ron Aure	1981	Jim Hartung	1994	Jeremy Killen
1968	Katsuzoki Kanzaki	1982	Jim Hartung	1995	Daniel Stover
1969	Steve Hug	1983	Mitch Gaylord	1996	Jay Thornton
	Dave Thor	1984	Peter Vidmar	1997	Jason Gatson
1970	Makoto Sakamoto	1985	Mark Oates	1998	Jason Gatson
1971	John Crosby	1986	Robert Sundstrom	1999	Jason Gatson
1972	Yoshi Takei	1987	John Sweeney	2000	Blaine Wilson
1973	John Crosby	1988	Mark Oates	2001	Sean Townsend
1974	John Crosby		Charles Lakes	2002	Morgan Hamm
				2003	Morgan Hamm

National Champions (Cont.)

MEN (Cont.)

Pommel Horse

Year	Champion	Year	Champion	Year	Champion
1963	Larry Spiegel	1978	Jim Hartung	1991	Chris Waller
1964	Sam Bailie	1979	Bart Conner	1992	Chris Waller
1965	Jack Ryan	1980	Jim Hartung	1993	Chris Waller
1966	Jack Ryan	1981	Jim Hartung	1994	Mihai Begiu
1967	Paul Mayer/Dave Doty	1982	Jim Hartung	1995	Mark Sohn
1968	Katsuoki Kanzaki	1983	Bart Conner	1996	Josh Stein
1969	Dave Thor	1984	Tim Daggett	1997	John Roethlisberger
1970	Mas Watanabe	1985	Phil Cahoy	1998	John Roethlisberger
1971	Leonard Caling	1986	Phil Cahoy	1999	John Roethlisberger
1972	Sadao Hamada	1987	Tim Daggett	2000	John Roethlisberger
1973	Marshall Avener	1988	Kevin Davis	2001	Brett McClure
1974	Marshall Avener	1989	Kevin Davis	2002	Paul Hamm
1975	Bart Conner	1990	Patrick Kirksey	2003	Paul Hamm
1977	Gene Whelan				

Rings

Year	Champion	Year	Champion	Year	Champion
1963	Art Shurlock	1975	Tom Beach	1989	Scott Keswick
1964	Glen Gailis	1977	Kurt Thomas	1990	Scott Keswick
1965	Glen Gailis	1978	Mike Silverstein	1991	Scott Keswick
1966	Glen Gailis	1979	Bart Conner	1992	Tim Ryan
1967	Fred Dennis	1980	Jim Hartung	1993	John Roethlisberger
	Don Hatch	1981	Jim Hartung	1994	Scott Keswick
1968	Yoshi Hayasaki	1982	Jim Hartung	1995	Paul O'Neill
1969	Fred Dennis		Peter Vidmar	1996	Kip Simons
	Bob Emery	1983	Mitch Gaylord	1997	Blaine Wilson
1970	Makoto Sakamoto	1984	Jim Hartung	1998	Jeff Johnson
1971	Yoshi Takei	1985	Dan Hayden	1999	Blaine Wilson
1972	Yoshi Takei	1986	Dan Hayden	2000	Blaine Wilson
1973	Jim Ivicek	1987	Scott Johnson	2001	Sean Townsend
1974	Tom Weeder	1988	Dan Hayden	2002	Blaine Wilson
				2003	Blaine Wilson

Vault

Year	Champion	Year	Champion	Year	Champion
1963	Art Shurlock	1977	Ron Galimore	1990	Lance Ringnald
1964	Gary Hery	1978	Jim Hartung	1991	Scott Keswick
1965	Brent Williams	1979	Ron Galimore	1992	Trent Dimas
1966	Dan Millman	1980	Ron Galimore	1993	Bill Roth
1967	Jack Kenan	1981	Ron Galimore	1994	Keith Wiley
	Sid Jensen	1982	Jim Hartung/Jim Mikus	1995	David St. Pierre
1968	Rich Scorza	1983	Chris Reigel	1996	Blaine Wilson
1969	Dave Butzman	1984	Chris Reigel	1997	Blaine Wilson
1970	Makoto Sakamoto	1985	Scott Johnson	1998	Brent Klaus
1971	Gary Morava		Mark Oates	1999	Guard Young
1972	Mike Kelley	1986	Scott Wilbanks	2000	Blaine Wilson
1973	Gary Morava	1987	John Sweeney	2001	Jason Furr
1974	John Crosby	1988	John Sweeney/Bill Paul	2002	Paul Hamm
1975	Tom Beach	1989	Bill Roth	2003	Raj Bhavsar

Parallel Bars

Year	Champion	Year	Champion	Year	Champion
1963	Tom Seward	1971	Brent Simmons	1981	Bart Conner
1964	Rusty Mitchell	1972	Yoshi Takei	1982	Peter Vidmar
1965	Glen Gailis	1973	Marshall Avener	1983	Mitch Gaylord
1966	Ray Hadley	1974	Jim Ivicek	1984	Peter Vidmar
1967	Katsuzoki Kanzaki	1975	Bart Conner		Mitch Gaylord
	Tom Goldsborough	1977	Kurt Thomas		Tim Daggett
1968	Yoshi Hayasaki	1978	Bart Conner	1985	Tim Daggett
1969	Steve Hug	1979	Bart Conner	1986	Tim Daggett
1970	Makoto Sakamoto	1980	Phil Cahoy/Larry Gerard	1987	Scott Johnson

National Champions (Cont.)

MEN (Cont.)

Parallel Bars (Cont.)

Year	Champion	Year	Champion	Year	Champion
1988	D. Hayden/K. Davis	1994	Steve McCain	2000	Trent Wells
1989	Conrad Voorsanger	1995	John Roethlisberger	2001	Sean Townsend
1990	Trent Dimas	1996	Jair Lynch	2002	Sean Townsend
1991	Scott Keswick	1997	Blaine Wilson	2003	Jason Gatson
1992	Jair Lynch	1998	Blaine Wilson		
1993	Chainey Umphrey	1999	Jason Gatson		

High Bars

Year	Champion	Year	Champion	Year	Champion
1963	Art Shurlock	1979	Yoichi Tomita	1991	Lance Ringnald
1964	Glen Gailis	1980	Jim Hartung	1992	Jair Lynch
1965	Rusty Mitchell	1981	Bart Conner	1993	Steve McCain
1966	Katsuzoki Kanzaki	1982	Mitch Gaylord	1994	Scott Keswick
1967	Katsuzoki Kanzaki	1983	Mario McCutcheon	1995	John Roethlisberger
	Jerry Fontana	1984	Peter Vidmar	1996	Bill Roth
1968	Yoshi Hayasaki		Tim Daggett	1997	Douglas Stibel
1969	Rich Grisby		Mitch Gaylord	1998	Jason Gatson
1970	Makoto Sakamoto	1985	Dan Hayden	1999	Jamie Natalie
1971	Yoshi Takei	1986	D. Hayden/D. Moriel	2000	Trent Wells
1972	Tom Lindner	1987	David Moriel		Jamie Natalie
1973	John Crosby	1988	Dan Hayden	2001	Daniel Diaz-Luong
1974	Brent Simmons	1989	Tim Ryan	2002	Blaine Wilson
1975	Tom Beach	1990	Trent Dimas	2003	Paul Hamm
1977	Kurt Thomas		Lance Ringnald		
1978	Kurt Thomas				

WOMEN

All-Around

Year	Champion	Year	Champion	Year	Champion
1963	Donna Schanezer	1976	Denise Cheshire	1991	Kim Zmeskal
1965	Gail Daley	1977	Donna Turnbow	1992	Kim Zmeskal
1966	Donna Schanezer	1978	Kathy Johnson	1993	Shannon Miller
1968	Linda Scott	1979	Leslie Pyfer	1994	Dominique Dawes
1969	Joyce Tanac	1980	Julianne McNamara	1995	Dominique Moceanu
	Schroeder	1981	Tracee Talavera	1996	Shannon Miller
1970	Cathy Rigby McCoy	1982	Tracee Talavera	1997	Vanessa Adler
1971	Joan Moore Gnat	1983	Dianne Durham		Kristy Powell
	Linda Metheny	1984	Mary Lou Retton	1998	Kristen Maloney
	Mulvihill	1985	Sabrina Mar	1999	Kristen Maloney
1972	Joan Moore Gnat	1986	Jennifer Sey	2000	Elise Ray
	Cathy Rigby McCoy	1987	Kristie Phillips	2001	Tasha Schwikert
1973	Joan Moore Gnat	1988	Phoebe Mills	2002	Tasha Schwikert
1974	Joan Moore Gnat	1989	Brandy Johnson	2003	Courtney Kupets
1975	Tammy Manville	1990	Kim Zmeskal		

Vault

Year	Champion	Year	Champion	Year	Champion
1963	Donna Schanezer	1976	Debbie Wilcox	1990	Brandy Johnson
1965	Gail Daley	1977	Lisa Cawthron	1991	Kerri Strug
1966	Donna Schanezer	1978	Rhonda Schwandt	1992	Kerri Strug
1968	Terry Spencer		Sharon Shapiro	1993	Dominique Dawes
1969	Joyce Tanac	1979	Christa Canary	1994	Dominique Dawes
	Schroeder	1980	J. McNamara/B. Kline	1995	Shannon Miller
	Cleo Carver	1981	Kim Neal	1996	Dominique Dawes
1970	Cathy Rigby McCoy	1982	Yumi Mordre	1997	Vanessa Atler
1971	Joan Moore Gnat	1983	Dianne Durham	1998	Dominique Moceanu
	Adele Gleaves	1984	Mary Lou Retton	1999	Vanessa Atler
1972	Cindy Eastwood	1985	Yolanda Mavity	2000	Kristen Maloney
1973	Roxanne Pierce	1986	Joyce Wilborn	2001	Mohini Bhardwaj
	Mancha	1987	Rhonda Faehn	2002	Elizabeth Tricase
1974	Dianne Dunbar	1988	Rhonda Faehn	2003	Annia Hatch
1975	Kolleen Casey	1989	Brandy Johnson		

Gymnastics (Cont.)

National Champions (Cont.)
WOMEN (Cont.)

Uneven Bars

Year	Champion	Year	Champion	Year	Champion
1963	Donna Schanezer	1976	Leslie Wolfsberger	1991	Elisabeth Crandall
1965	Irene Haworth	1977	Donna Turnbow	1992	Dominique Dawes
1966	Donna Schanezer	1978	Marcia Frederick	1993	Shannon Miller
1968	Linda Scott	1979	Marcia Frederick	1994	Dominique Dawes
1969	Joyce Tanac Schroeder Lisa Nelson	1980	Marcia Frederick	1995	Dominique Dawes
		1981	Julianne McNamara	1996	Dominique Dawes
1970	Roxanne Pierce Mancha	1982	Marie Roethlisberger	1997	Kristy Powell
		1983	Julianne McNamara	1998	Elise Ray
1971	Joan Moore Gnat	1984	Julianne McNamara	1999	Jamie Dantzscher Jennie Thompson
1972	Cathy Rigby McCoy	1985	Sabrina Mar	2000	Elise Ray
1973	Roxanne Pierce Mancha	1986	Marie Roethlisberger	2001	Katie Heenan
		1987	Melissa Marlowe	2002	Tasha Schwikert
1974	Diane Dunbar	1988	Chelle Stack	2003	Katie Heenan
1975	Leslie Wolfsberger	1989	Chelle Stack		
		1990	Sandy Woolsey		

Balance Beam

Year	Champion	Year	Champion	Year	Champion
1963	Leissa Krol	1978	Christa Canary	1992	Kerri Strug Kim Zmeskal
1965	Gail Daley	1979	Heidi Anderson	1993	Dominique Dawes
1966	Irene Haworth Linda Scott	1980	Kelly Garrison-Steves	1994	Dominique Dawes
1968	Linda Scott	1981	Tracee Talavera	1995	Doni Thompson Monica Flammer
1969	Lonna Woodward	1982	Julianne McNamara	1996	Dominique Dawes
1970	Joyce Tanac Schroeder	1983	Dianne Durham	1997	Kendall Beck
1971	Linda Metheny Mulvihill	1984	Pam Bileck Tracee Talavera	1998	Dominique Moceanu
1972	Kim Chace	1986	Angie Denkins	1999	Vanessa Atler
1973	Nancy Thies Marshall	1987	Kristie Phillips	2000	Alyssa Beckerman Amy Chow
1974	Joan Moore Gnat	1985	Kelly Garrison-Steves	2001	Tasha Schwikert
1975	Kyle Gayner	1988	Kelly Garrison-Steves	2002	Tasha Schwikert
1976	Carrie Englert	1989	Brandy Johnson	2003	Hollie Vise
1977	Donna Turnbow	1990	Betty Okino		
		1991	Shannon Miller		

Floor Exercise

Year	Champion	Year	Champion	Year	Champion
1963	Donna Schanezer	1979	Heidi Anderson	1993	Shannon Miller
1965	Gail Daley	1980	Beth Kline	1994	Dominique Dawes
1966	Donna Schanezer	1981	Michelle Goodwin	1995	Dominique Dawes
1968	Linda Scott	1982	Amy Koopman	1996	Dominique Dawes
1970	Cathy Rigby McCoy	1983	Dianne Durham	1997	Lindsay Wing
1971	Joan Moore Gnat Linda Metheny Mulvihill	1984	Mary Lou Retton	1998	Vanessa Atler
		1985	Sabrina Mar	1999	Elise Ray
1972	Joan Moore Gnat	1986	Yolanda Mavity	2000	Kristen Maloney
1973	Joan Moore Gnat	1987	Kristie Phillips	2001	Tabitha Yim
1974	Joan Moore Gnat	1988	Phoebe Mills	2002	Tasha Schwikert
1975	Kathy Howard	1989	Brandy Johnson	2003	Ashley Postell
1976	Carrie Englert	1990	Brandy Johnson		
1977	Kathy Johnson	1991	Kim Zmeskal Dominique Dawes		
1978	Kathy Johnson	1992	Kim Zmeskal		

Handball

National Four-Wall Champions
MEN

1919.....Bill Ranft	1941.....Joe Platak	1963.....Oscar Obert	1985.....Naty Alvarado
1920.....Max Gold	1942.....Jack Clemente	1964.....Jimmy Jacobs	1986.....Naty Alvarado
1921.....Carl Haedge	1943.....Joe Platak	1965.....Jimmy Jacobs	1987.....Naty Alvarado
1922.....Art Shinners	1944.....Frank Coyle	1966.....Paul Haber	1988.....Naty Alvarado
1923.....Joe Murray	1945.....Joe Platak	1967.....Paul Haber	1989.....Poncho Monreal
1924.....Maynard Laswe	1946.....Angelo Trutio	1968.....Stuffy Singer	1990.....Naty Alvarado
1925.....Maynard Laswe	1947.....Gus Lewis	1969.....Paul Haber	1991.....John Bike
1926.....Maynard Laswe	1948.....Gus Lewis	1970.....Paul Haber	1992.....Octavio Silveyra
1927.....George Nelson	1949.....Vic Hershkowitz	1971.....Paul Haber	1993.....David Chapman
1928.....Joe Griffin	1950.....Ken Schneider	1972.....Fred Lewis	1994.....Octavio Silveyra
1929.....Al Banuet	1951.....Walter Plakan	1973.....Terry Muck	1995.....David Chapman
1930.....Al Banuet	1952.....Vic Hershkowitz	1974.....Fred Lewis	1996.....David Chapman
1931.....Al Banuet	1953.....Bob Brady	1975.....Fred Lewis	1997.....Octavio Silveyra
1932.....Angelo Trutio	1954.....Vic Hershkowitz	1976.....Fred Lewis	1998.....David Chapman
1933.....Sam Atcheson	1955.....Jimmy Jacobs	1977.....Naty Alvarado	1999.....David Chapman
1934.....Sam Atcheson	1956.....Jimmy Jacobs	1978.....Fred Lewis	2000.....David Chapman
1935.....Joe Platak	1957.....Jimmy Jacobs	1979.....Naty Alvarado	2001.....Vince Munoz
1936.....Joe Platak	1958.....John Sloan	1980.....Naty Alvarado	2002.....David Chapman
1937.....Joe Platak	1959.....John Sloan	1981.....Fred Lewis	2003.....John Bike
1938.....Joe Platak	1960.....Jimmy Jacobs	1982.....Naty Alvarado	
1939.....Joe Platak	1961.....John Sloan	1983.....Naty Alvarado	
1940.....Joe Platak	1962.....Oscar Obert	1984.....Naty Alvarado	

WOMEN

1980.....Rosemary Bellini	1986.....Peanut Motal	1992.....Lisa Fraser	1998.....Lisa Fraser
1981.....Rosemary Bellini	1987.....Rosemary Bellini	1993.....Anna Engele	1999.....Anna Christoff
1982.....Rosemary Bellini	1988.....Rosemary Bellini	1994.....Anna Engele	2000.....Priscilla Shumate
1983.....Diane Harmon	1989.....Anna Engele	1995.....Anna Engele	2001.....Anna Christoff
1984.....Rosemary Bellini	1990.....Anna Engele	1996.....Anna Engele	2002.....Priscilla Shumate
1985.....Peanut Motal	1991.....Anna Engele	1997.....Lisa Fraser	2003.....Lisa Gilmore

National Three-Wall Champions
MEN

1950.....Vic Hershkowitz	1964.....Marty Decatur	1978.....Fred Lewis	1992.....John Bike
1951.....Vic Hershkowitz	1965.....Carl Obert	1979.....Naty Alvarado	1993.....Eric Klarman
1952.....Vic Hershkowitz	1966.....Marty Decatur	1980.....Lou Russo	1994.....David Chapman
1953.....Vic Herskkowitz	1967.....Carl Obert	1981.....Naty Alvarado	1995.....David Chapman
1954.....Vic Hershkowitz	1968.....Marty Decatur	1982.....Naty Alvarado	1996.....Vince Munoz
1955.....Vic Hershkowitz	1969.....Marty Decatur	1983.....Naty Alvarado	1997.....Vince Munoz
1956.....Vic Hershkowitz	1970.....Steve August	1984.....Naty Alvarado	1998.....Vince Munoz
1957.....Vic Hershkowitz	1971.....Lou Russo	1985.....Vern Roberts	1999.....Vince Munoz
1958.....Vic Hershkowitz	1972.....Lou Russo	1986.....Vern Roberts	2000.....Vince Munoz
1959.....Jimmy Jacobs	1973.....Paul Haber	1987.....Vern Roberts	2001.....Vince Munoz
1960.....Jimmy Jacobs	1974.....Fred Lewis	1988.....Jon Kendler	2002.....Vince Munoz
1961.....Jimmy Jacobs	1975.....Lou Russo	1989.....John Bike	2003.....Vince Munoz
1962.....Oscar Obert	1976.....Lou Russo	1990.....Vince Munoz	
1963.....Marty Decatur	1977.....Fred Lewis	1991.....John Bike	

WOMEN

1981.....Allison Roberts	1987.....Rosemary Bellini	1993.....Anna Engele	1999.....Allison Roberts
1982.....Allison Roberts	1988.....Rosemary Bellini	1994.....Anna Engele	2000.....Priscilla Shumate
1983.....Allison Roberts	1989.....Rosemary Bellini	1995.....Allison Roberts	2001.....Anna Christoff
1984.....Rosemary Bellini	1990.....Rosemary Bellini	1996.....Anna Engele	2002.....Priscilla Shumate
1985.....Rosemary Bellini	1991.....Rosemary Bellini	1997.....Allison Roberts	2003.....Lisa Gilmore
1986.....Rosemary Bellini	1992.....Anna Engele	1998.....Anna Christoff	

World Four-Wall Champions

1984...................Merv Deckert, Canada	1994...................David Chapman, United States
1986...................Vern Roberts, United States	1997...................John Bike Jr., United States
1988...................Naty Alvarado, United States	2000...................David Chapman, United States
1991...................Pancho Monreal, United States	

Lacrosse

United States Club Lacrosse Association Champions

1960 ......Mt. Washington Club	1975 ......Mt. Washington Club	1990 ......Mt. Washington Club
1961 ......Baltimore Lacrosse Club	1976 ......Mt. Washington Club	1991 ......Mt. Washington Club
1962 ......Mt. Washington Club	1977 ......Mt. Washington Club	1992 ......Maryland Lacrosse Club
1963 ......University Club	1978 ......Long Island Athletic Club	1993 ......Mt. Washington Club
1964 ......Mt. Washington Club	1979 ......Maryland Lacrosse Club	1994 ......LI-Hofstra Lacrosse Club
1965 ......Mt. Washington Club	1980 ......Long Island Athletic Club	1995 ......Mt. Washington Club
1966 ......Mt. Washington Club	1981 ......Long Island Athletic Club	1996 ......LI-Hofstra Lacrosse Club
1967 ......Mt. Washington Club	1982 ......Maryland Lacrosse Club	1997 ......LI-Hofstra Lacrosse Club
1968 ......Long Island Athletic Club	1983 ......Maryland Lacrosse Club	1998 ......LI-Hofstra Lacrosse Club
1969 ......Long Island Athletic Club	1984 ......Maryland Lacrosse Club	1999 ......New York Athletic Club
1970 ......Long Island Athletic Club	1985 ......LI-Hofstra Lacrosse Club	2000 ......Team Toyota (Baltimore)
1971 ......Long Island Athletic Club	1986 ......LI-Hofstra Lacrosse Club	2001 ......LI Lacrosse Club
1972 ......Carling	1987 ......LI-Hofstra Lacrosse Club	2002 ......Single Source Solutions
1973 ......Long Island Athletic Club	1988 ......Maryland Lacrosse Club	2003 ......Single Source Solutions
1974 ......Long Island Athletic Club	1989 ......LI-Hofstra Lacrosse Club	

National Lacrosse League Champions*

1987 ......Baltimore Thunder	1993 ......Buffalo Bandits	1999 ......Toronto Rock
1988 ......New Jersey Saints	1994 ......Philadelphia Wings	2000 ......Toronto Rock
1989 ......Philadelphia Wings	1995 ......Philadelphia Wings	2001 ......Philadelphia Wings
1990 ......Philadelphia Wings	1996 ......Buffalo Bandits	2002 ......Toronto Rock
1991 ......Detroit Turbos	1997 ......Rochester Knighthawks	2003 ......Toronto Rock
1992 ......Buffalo Bandits	1998 ......Philadelphia Wings	

*Indoor league formerly known as the Eagle Pro Box Lacrosse League, and the Major Indoor Lacrosse League.

Major League Lacrosse

2001 .....Long Island Lizards	2003 .....Long Island Lizards
2002 .....Baltimore Bayhawks	

Little League Baseball

Little League World Series Champions

Year	Champion	Runner-Up	Score	Year	Champion	Runner-Up	Score
1947	Williamsport, PA	Lock Haven, PA	16–7	1976	Tokyo, Japan	Campbell, CA	10–3
1948	Lock Haven, PA	St. Petersburg, FL	6–5	1977	Kao-Hsiung, Taiwan	El Cajun, CA	7–2
1949	Hammonton, NJ	Pensacola, FL	5–0	1978	Pin-Tung, Taiwan	Danville, CA	11–1
1950	Houston, TX	Bridgeport, CT	2–1	1979	Hsien, Taiwan	Campbell, CA	2–1
1951	Stamford, CT	Austin, TX	3–0	1980	Hua Lian, Taiwan	Tampa, FL	4–3
1952	Norwalk, CT	Monongahela, PA	4–3	1981	Tai-Chung, Taiwan	Tampa, FL	4–2
1953	Birmingham, AL	Schenectady, NY	1–0	1982	Kirkland, WA	Hsien, Taiwan	6–0
1954	Schenectady, NY	Colton, CA	7–5	1983	Marietta, GA	Barahona, D.Rep.	3–1
1955	Morrisville, PA	Merchantville, NJ	4–3	1984	Seoul, S. Korea	Altamonte Sgs, FL	6–2
1956	Roswell, NM	Merchantville, NJ	3–1	1985	Seoul, S. Korea	Mexicali, Mex.	7–1
1957	Monterrey, Mex.	LaMesa, CA	4–0	1986	Tainan Park, Taiwan	Tucson, AZ	12–0
1958	Monterrey, Mex.	Kankakee, IL	10–1	1987	Hua Lian, Taiwan	Irvine, CA	21–1
1959	Hamtramck, MI	Auburn, CA	12–0	1988	Tai-Chung, Taiwan	Pearl City, HI	10–0
1960	Levittown, PA	Ft. Worth, TX	5–0	1989	Trumbull, CT	Kaohsiung, Taiwan	5–2
1961	El Cajon, CA	El Campo, TX	4–2	1990	Taipei, Taiwan	Shippensburg, PA	9–0
1962	San Jose, CA	Kankakee, IL	3–0	1991	Tai-Chung, Taiwan	San Ramon Vly, CA	11–0
1963	Granada Hills, CA	Stratford, CT	2–1	1992*	Long Beach, CA	Zamboanga, Phil.	6–0
1964	Staten Island, NY	Monterrey, Mex.	4–0	1993	Long Beach, CA	David Chiriqui, Pan.	3–2
1965	Windsor Locks, CT	Stoney Creek, Can.	3–1	1994	Maracaibo, Venez.	Northridge, CA	4–3
1966	Houston, TX	W. New York, NJ	8–2	1995	Tainan, Taiwan	Sprint, TX	17–3
1967	West Tokyo, Japan	Chicago, IL	4–1	1996	Kao-Hsiung, Taiwan	Cranston, RI	13–3
1968	Osaka, Japan	Richmond, VA	1–0	1997	Guadalupe, Mex.	Mission Viejo, CA	5–4
1969	Taipei, Taiwan	Santa Clara, CA	5–0	1998	Toms River, NJ	Kashima, Japan	12–9
1970	Wayne, NJ	Campbell, CA	2–0	1999	Osaka, Japan	Phenix City, AL	5–0
1971	Tainan, Taiwan	Gary, IN	12–3	2000	Maracaibo, Venez.	Bellaire, TX	3–2
1972	Taipei, Taiwan	Hammond, IN	6–0	2001	Tokyo, Japan	Apopka, FL	2–1
1973	Tainan City, Taiwan	Tucson, AZ	12–0	2002	Louisville, KY	Sendai, Japan	1–0
1974	Kao-Hsiung, Taiwan	El Cajun, CA	7–2	2003	Tokyo, Japan	Boynton Beach, FL	10–1
1975	Lakewood, NJ	Tampa, FL	4–3				

*Long Beach declared a 6–0 winner after the international tournament committee determined that Zamboanga City had used players that were not within its city limits.

American Power Boat Association Gold Cup Champions

Year	Boat	Driver	Avg MPH	Year	Boat	Driver	Avg MPH
1904	Standard (June)	Carl Riotte	23.160	1955	Gale V	Lee Schoenith	99.552
1904	Vingt-et-Un II (Sep)	W. Sharpe Kilmer	24.900	1956	Miss Thriftaway	Bill Muncey	96.552
1905	Chip I	J. Wainwright	15.000	1957	Miss Thriftaway	Bill Muncey	101.787
1906	Chip II	J. Wainwright	25.000	1958	Hawaii Kai III	Jack Regas	103.000
1907	Chip II	J. Wainwright	23.903	1959	Maverick	Bill Stead	104.481
1908	Dixie II	E.J. Schroeder	29.938	1960	No race	—	—
1909	Dixie II	E.J. Schroeder	29.590	1961	Miss Century 21	Bill Muncey	99.678
1910	Dixie III	F.K. Burnham	32.473	1962	Miss Century 21	Bill Muncey	100.710
1911	MIT II	J.H. Hayden	37.000	1963	Miss Bardahl	Ron Musson	105.124
1912	P.D.Q. II	A.G. Miles	39.462	1964	Miss Bardahl	Ron Musson	103.433
1913	Ankle Deep	Cas Mankowski	42.779	1965	Miss Bardahl	Ron Musson	103.132
1914	Baby Speed Demon II	Jim Blackton & Bob Edgren	48.458	1966	Tahoe Miss	Mira Slovak	93.019
1915	Miss Detroit	Johnny Milot & Jack Beebe	37.656	1967	Miss Bardahl	Bill Shumacher	101.484
				1968	Miss Bardahl	Bill Shumacher	108.173
1916	Miss Minneapolis	Bernard Smith	48.860	1969	Miss Budweiser	Bill Sterett	98.504
1917	Miss Detroit II	Gar Wood	54.410	1970	Miss Budweiser	Dean Chenoweth	99.562
1918	Miss Detroit II	Gar Wood	51.619				
1919	Miss Detroit III	Gar Wood	42.748	1971	Miss Madison	Jim McCormick	98.043
1920	Miss America I	Gar Wood	62.022	1972	Atlas Van Lines	Bill Muncey	104.277
1921	Miss America I	Gar Wood	52.825	1973	Miss Budweiser	Dean Chenoweth	99.043
1922	Packard Chriscraft	J.G. Vincent	40.253				
1923	Packard Chriscraft	Caleb Bragg	43.867	1974	Pay 'n Pak	George Henley	104.428
1924	Baby Bootlegger	Caleb Bragg	45.302	1975	Pay 'n Pak	George Henley	108.921
1925	Baby Bootlegger	Caleb Bragg	47.240	1976	Miss U.S.	Tom D'Eath	100.412
1926	Greenwich Folly	George Townsend	47.984	1977	Atlas Van Lines	Bill Muncey	111.822
				1978	Atlas Van Lines	Bill Muncey	111.412
1927	Greenwich Folly	George Townsend	47.662	1979	Atlas Van Lines	Bill Muncey	100.765
				1980	Miss Budweiser	Dean Chenoweth	106.932
1928	No race						
1929	Imp	Richard Hoyt	48.662	1981	Miss Budweiser	Dean Chenoweth	116.932
1930	Hotsy Totsy	Vic Kliesrath	52.673				
1931	Hotsy Totsy	Vic Kliesrath	53.602	1982	Atlas Van Lines	Chip Hanauer	120.050
1932	Delphine IV	Bill Horn	57.775	1983	Atlas Van Lines	Chip Hanauer	118.507
1933	El Lagarto	George Reis	56.260	1984	Atlas Van Lines	Chip Hanauer	130.175
1934	El Lagarto	George Reis	55.000	1985	Miller American	Chip Hanauer	120.643
1935	El Lagarto	George Reis	55.056	1986	Miller American	Chip Hanauer	116.523
1936	Impshi	Kaye Don	45.735	1987	Miller American	Chip Hanauer	127.620
1937	Notre Dame	Clell Perry	63.675	1988	Miss Circus Circus	Chip Hanauer & Jim Prevost	123.756
1938	Alagi	Theo Rossi	64.340				
1939	My Sin	Z.G. Simmons Jr.	66.133	1989	Miss Budweiser	Tom D'Eath	131.209
1940	Hotsy Totsy III	Sidney Allen	48.295	1990	Miss Budweiser	Tom D'Eath	143.176
1941	My Sin	Z.G. Simmons Jr.	52.509	1991	Winston Eagle	Mark Tate	137.771
1942–45	—	No race	—	1992	Miss Budweiser	Chip Hanauer	136.282
1946	Tempo VI	Guy Lombardo	68.132	1993	Miss Budweiser	Chip Hanauer	141.195
1947	Miss Peps V	Danny Foster	57.000	1994	Smokin' Joe Camel	Mark Tate	145.260
1948	Miss Great Lakes	Danny Foster	46.845	1995	Miss Budweiser	Chip Hanauer	149.160
1949	My Sweetie	Bill Cantrell	73.612	1996	PICO American Dream	Dave Villwock	149.328
1950	Slo-Mo-Shun IV	Ted Jones	78.216	1997	Miss Budweiser	Dave Villwock	129.366
1951	Slo-Mo-Shun V	Lou Fageol	90.871	1998	Miss Budweiser	Dave Villwock	140.309
1952	Slo-Mo-Shun IV	Stan Dollar	79.923	1999	Miss PICO	Chip Hanauer	152.591
1953	Slo-Mo-Shun IV	Joe Taggart & Lou Fageol	99.108	2000	Miss Budweiser	Dave Villwock	162.850
				2001	Miss Tubby's Subs	Michael Hanson	140.519
				2002	Miss Budweiser	Dave Villwock	143.093
1954	Slo-Mo-Shun IV	Joe Taggart & Lou Fageol	92.613	2003	Miss Fox Hills	Mitch Evans	144.152

Hydro-Prop* Annual Champion Drivers

Year	Driver	Boat	Wins	Year	Driver	Boat	Wins
1947	Danny Foster	Miss Peps V	6	1976	Bill Muncey	Atlas Van Lines	5
1948	Dan Arena	Such Crust	2	1977	Mickey Remund	Miss Budweiser	3
1949	Bill Cantrell	My Sweetie	7	1978	Bill Muncey	Atlas Van Lines	6
1950	Dan Foster	Such Crust/DaphneX	2	1979	Bill Muncey	Atlas Van Lines	7
1951	Chuck Thompson	Miss Pepsi	5	1980	Dean Chenoweth	Miss Budweiser	5
1952	Chuck Thompson	Miss Pepsi	3	1981	Dean Chenoweth	Miss Budweiser	6
1953	Lee Schoenith	Gale II	1	1982	Chip Hanauer	Atlas Van Lines	5
1954	Lee Schoenith	Gale V	4	1983	Chip Hanauer	Atlas Van Lines	3
1955	Lee Schoenith	Gale V/Wha Hoppen	1	1984	Jim Kropfeld	Miss Budweiser	6
1956	Russ Schleeh	Shanty I	3	1985	Chip Hanauer	Miller American	5
1957	Jack Regas	Hawaii Kai III	5	1986	Jim Kropfeld	Miss Budweiser	3
1958	Mira Slovak	Bardah/Miss Buren	3	1987	Jim Kropfeld	Miss Budweiser	5
1959	Bill Stead	Maverick	5	1988	Tom D'Eath	Miss Budweiser	4
1960	Bill Muncey	Miss Thriftway	4	1989	Chip Hanauer	Miss Circus Circus	3
1961	Bill Muncey	Miss Century 21	4	1990	Chip Hanauer	Miss Circus Circus	6
1962	Bill Muncey	Miss Century 21	5	1991	Mark Tate	Winston/Oberto	3
1963	Bill Cantrell	Gale V	0	1992	Chip Hanauer	Miss Budweiser	7
1964	Ron Musson	Miss Bardahl	4	1993	Chip Hanauer	Miss Budweiser	7
1965	Ron Musson	Miss Bardahl	4	1994	Mark Tate	Smokin' Joe Camel	2
1966	Mira Slovak	Tahoe Miss	4	1995	Mark Tate	Smokin' Joe Camel	4
1967	Bill Schumacher	Miss Bardahl	6	1996	Dave Villwock	PICO American Dream	6
1968	Bill Schumacher	Miss Bardahl	4	1997	Mark Tate	Close Call	1
1969	Bill Sterett Sr.	Miss Budweiser	4	1998	Dave Villwock	Miss Budweiser	8
1970	Dean Chenoweth	Miss Budweiser	4	1999	Dave Villwock	Miss Budweiser	8
1971	Dean Chenoweth	Miss Budweiser	2	2000	Dave Villwock	Miss Budweiser	6
1972	Bill Muncey	Atlas Van Lines	6	2001	Dave Villwock	Miss Budweiser	1
1973	Mickey Remund	Pay 'n Pak	4	2002	Dave Villwock	Miss Budweiser	3
1974	George Henley	Pay 'n Pak	7	2003	Dave Villwock	Miss Budweiser	2
1975	Billy Schumacher	Weisfield's	2				

Hydro-Prop* Annual Champion Boats

Year	Boat	Owner	Wins	Year	Boat	Owner	Wins
1970	Miss Budweiser	Little-Friedkin	4	1987	Miss Budweiser	Bernie Little	5
1971	Miss Budweiser	Little-Friedkin	2	1988	Miss Budweiser	Bernie Little	4
1972	Atlas Van Lines	Joe Schoenith	6	1989	Miss Budweiser	Bernie Little	4
1973	Pay 'n Pak	Dave Heerensperger	4	1990	Miss Circus Circus	Bill Bennett	6
1974	Pay 'n Pak	Dave Heerensperger	7	1991	Miss Budweiser	Bernie Little	4
1975	Pay 'n Pak	Dave Heerensperger	5	1992	Miss Budweiser	Bernie Little	7
1976	Atlas Van Lines	Bill Muncey	5	1993	Miss Budweiser	Bernie Little	7
1977	Miss Budweiser	Bernie Little	3	1994	Miss Budweiser	Bernie Little	4
1978	Atlas Van Lines	Bill Muncey	6	1995	Miss Budweiser	Bernie Little	5
1979	Atlas Van Lines	Bill Muncey	7	1996	PICO Amer. Dream	Fred Leland	6
1980	Miss Budweiser	Bernie Little	5	1997	Miss Budweiser	Bernie Little	5
1981	Miss Budweiser	Bernie Little	6	1998	Miss Budweiser	Bernie Little	8
1982	Atlas Van Lines	Fran Muncey	5	1999	Miss Budweiser	Bernie Little	8
1983	Atlas Van Lines	Muncey-Lucero	3	2000	Miss Budweiser	Bernie Little	6
1984	Miss Budweiser	Bernie Little	6	2001	Miss Budweiser	Bernie Little	1
1985	Miller American	Muncey-Lucero	5	2002	Miss Budweiser	Bernie Little	3
1986	Miss Budweiser	Bernie Little	3	2003	Miss Budweiser	Joe Little	2

*Formerly known as Unlimited Hydroplane Racing Association.

Polo

United States Open Polo Champions

Year	Champion	Year	Champion	Year	Champion	Year	Champion
1904	Wanderers	1934	Templeton	1961	Milwaukee	1983	Ft. Lauderdale
1905–09	Not contested	1935	Greentree	1962	Santa Barbara	1984	Retama
1910	Ranelagh	1936	Greentree	1963	Tulsa	1985	Carter Ranch
1911	Not contested	1937	Old Westbury	1964	Concar Oak Brook	1986	Retama II
1912	Cooperstown	1938	Old Westbury			1987	Aloha
1913	Cooperstown	1939	Bostwick Field	1965	Oak Brook–Santa Barbara	1988	Les Diables Bleus
1914	Meadow Brook Magpies	1940	Aknusti	1966	Tulsa	1989	Les Diables Bleus
1915	Not contested	1941	Gulf Stream	1967	Bunntyco–Oak Brook	1990	Les Diables Bleus
1916	Meadow Brook	1942–45	Not contested	1968	Midland	1991	Grant's Farm Manor
1917–18	Not contested	1946	Mexico	1969	Tulsa Greenhill	1992	Hanalei Bay
1919	Meadow Brook	1947	Old Westbury	1970	Tulsa Greenhill	1993	Gehache
1920	Meadow Brook	1948	Hurricanes	1971	Oak Brook	1994	Aspen
1921	Great Neck	1949	Hurricanes	1972	Milwaukee	1995	Outback
1922	Argentine	1950	Bostwick	1973	Oak Brook	1996	Outback
1923	Meadow Brook	1951	Milwaukee	1974	Milwaukee	1997	Isla Carroll
1924	Midwick	1952	Beverly Hills	1975	Milwaukee	1998	Esque
1925	Orange County	1953	Meadow Brook	1976	Willow Bend	1999	Outback
1926	Hurricanes	1954	C.C.C.–Meadow Brook	1977	Retama	2000	Outback
1927	Sands Point			1978	Abercrombie & Kent	2001	Outback
1928	Meadow Brook	1955	C.C.C.			2002	Team Coca Cola
1929	Hurricanes	1956	Brandywine	1979	Retama	2003	C Spear
1930	Hurricanes	1957	Detroit	1980	Southern Hills		
1931	Santa Paula	1958	Dallas	1981	Rolex A & K		
1932	Templeton	1959	Circle F	1982	Retama		
1933	Aurora	1960	Oak Brook–C.C.C.				

Top-Ranked Players

The United States Polo Association ranks its registered players from minus 2 to plus 10 goals, with 10-Goal players being the game's best. At present, the USPA recognizes ten 10-Goal and seven 9-Goal players:

10-GOAL

Michael Azarro (San Antonio)
Martino Aguerre (Greenwich)
Adolfo Cambiaso (Palm Beach)
Memo Gracida (Palm Beach)
Marcos Heguy (Palm Beach)
Eduardo Heguy (Palm Beach)
Sebastian Merlos (Aiken)
Adam Snow (Langdon Road)

9-GOAL

Javier Novillo Astrada (Palm Beach)
Miguel Novillo Astrada (Palm Beach)
Lucas Criado (Palm Beach)
Hector Galindo (Palm Beach)
Santiago Chavanne (Everglades)
Fabio Diniz (Aspen)
Christian LaPrida (Equuleus)
Tomas Llorent (Everglades)

YET ANOTHER SIGN OF THE APOCALYPSE

A sherpa whose grandfather carried supplies on Sir Edmund Hillary's historic 1953 Everest expedition is planning to build a cybercafe on the mountain.

Professional Rodeo Cowboys Association World Champions

All-Around

1929....Earl Thode	1949....Jim Shoulders	1967....Larry Mahan	1985....Lewis Feild
1930....Clay Carr	1950....Bill Linderman	1968....Larry Mahan	1986....Lewis Feild
1931....John Schneider	1951....Casey Tibbs	1969....Larry Mahan	1987....Lewis Feild
1932....Donald Nesbit	1952....Harry Tompkins	1970....Larry Mahan	1988....Dave Appleton
1933....Clay Carr	1953....Bill Linderman	1971....Phil Lyne	1989....Ty Murray
1934....Leonard Ward	1954....Buck Rutherford	1972....Phil Lyne	1990....Ty Murray
1935....Everett Bowman	1955....Casey Tibbs	1973....Larry Mahan	1991....Ty Murray
1936....John Bowman	1956....Jim Shoulders	1974....Tom Ferguson	1992....Ty Murray
1937....Everett Bowman	1957....Jim Shoulders	1975....Tom Ferguson	1993....Ty Murray
1938....Burel Mulkey	1958....Jim Shoulders	1976....Tom Ferguson	1994....Ty Murray
1939....Paul Carney	1959....Jim Shoulders	1977....Tom Ferguson	1995....Joe Beaver
1940....Fritz Truan	1960....Harry Tompkins	1978....Tom Ferguson	1996....Joe Beaver
1941....Homer Pettigrew	1961....Benny Reynolds	1979....Tom Ferguson	1997....Dan Mortensen
1942....Gerald Roberts	1962....Tom Nesmith	1980....Paul Tierney	1998....Ty Murray
1943....Louis Brooks	1963....Dean Oliver	1981....Jimmie Cooper	1999....Fred Whitfield
1944....Louis Brooks	1964....Dean Oliver	1982....Chris Lybbert	2000....Joe Beaver
1947....Todd Whatley	1965....Dean Oliver	1983....Roy Cooper	2001....Cody Ohl
1948....Gerald Roberts	1966....Larry Mahan	1984....Dee Picket	2002....Trevor Brazile

Saddle Bronc Riding

1929....Earl Thode	1949....Casey Tibbs	1967....Shawn Davis	1985....B. Gjermundson
1930....Clay Carr	1950....Bill Linderman	1968....Shawn Davis	1986....Bud Munroe
1931....Earl Thode	1951....Casey Tibbs	1969....Bill Smith	1987....Clint Johnson
1932....Peter Knight	1952....Casey Tibbs	1970....Dennis Reiners	1988....Clint Johnson
1933....Peter Knight	1953....Casey Tibbs	1971....Bill Smith	1989....Clint Johnson
1934....Leonard Ward	1954....Casey Tibbs	1972....Mel Hyland	1990....Robert Etbauer
1935....Peter Knight	1955....Deb Copenhaver	1973....Bill Smith	1991....Robert Etbauer
1936....Peter Knight	1956....Deb Copenhaver	1974....John McBeth	1992....Billy Etbauer
1937....Burel Mulkey	1957....Alvin Nelson	1975....Mority Henson	1993....Dan Mortensen
1938....Burel Mulkey	1958....Marty Wood	1976....Monty Henson	1994....Dan Mortensen
1939....Fritz Truan	1959....Casey Tibbs	1977....Bobby Berger	1995....Dan Mortensen
1940....Fritz Truan	1960....Enoch Walker	1978....Joe Marvel	1996....Billy Etbauer
1941....Doff Aber	1961....Winston Bruce	1979....Bobby Berger	1997....Dan Mortensen
1942....Doff Aber	1962....Kenny McLean	1980....Clint Johnson	1998....Dan Mortensen
1943....Louis Brooks	1963....Guy Weeks	1981....B. Gjermundson	1999....Billy Etbauer
1944....Louis Brooks	1964....Marty Wood	1982....Monty Henson	2000....Billy Etbauer
1947....Carl Olson	1965....Shawn Davis	1983....B. Gjermundson	2001....Tom Reeves
1948....Gene Pruett	1966....Marty Wood	1984....B. Gjermundson	2002....Glen O'Neil

Bareback Riding

1932....Smoky Snyder	1951....Casey Tibbs	1968....Clyde Vamvoras	1985....Lewis Feild
1933....Nate Waldrum	1952....Harry Tompkins	1969....Gary Tucker	1986....Lewis Feild
1934....Leonard Ward	1953....Eddy Akridge	1970....Paul Mayo	1987....Bruce Ford
1935....Frank Schneider	1954....Eddy Akridge	1971....Joe Alexander	1988....Marvin Garrett
1936....Smoky Snyder	1955....Eddy Akridge	1972....Joe Alexander	1989....Marvin Garrett
1937....Paul Carney	1956....Jim Shoulders	1973....Joe Alexander	1990....Chuck Logue
1938....Pete Grubb	1957....Jim Shoulders	1974....Joe Alexander	1991....Clint Corey
1939....Paul Carney	1958....Jim Shoulders	1975....Joe Alexander	1992....Wayne Herman
1940....Carl Dossey	1959....Jack Buschbom	1976....Joe Alexander	1993....Deb Greenough
1941....George Mills	1960....Jack Buschbom	1977....Joe Alexander	1994....Marvin Garrett
1942....Louis Brooks	1961....Eddy Akridge	1978....Bruce Ford	1995....Marvin Garrett
1943....Bill Linderman	1962....Ralph Buell	1979....Bruce Ford	1996....Mark Garrett
1944....Louis Brooks	1963....John Hawkins	1980....Bruce Ford	1997....Eric Mouton
1947....Larry Finley	1964....Jim Houston	1981....J.C. Trujillo	1998....Mark Gomes
1948....Sonny Tureman	1965....Jim Houston	1982....Bruce Ford	1999....Lan LaJeunesse
1949....Jack Buschbom	1966....Paul Mayo	1983....Bruce Ford	2000....Jeffrey Collins
1950....Jim Shoulders	1967....Clyde Vamvoras	1984....Larry Peabody	2001....Lan LaJeunesse
			2002....Bobby Mote

Professional Rodeo Cowboys Association World Champions (Cont.)

Bull Riding

1929....John Schneider
1930....John Schneider
1931....Smokey Snyder
1932....John Schneider
1932....Smokey Snyder
          John Schneider
1933....Frank Schneider
1934....Frank Schneider
1935....Smokey Snyder
1936....Smokey Snyder
1937....Smokey Snyder
1938....Kid Fletcher
1939....Dick Griffith
1940....Dick Griffith
1941....Dick Griffith
1942....Dick Griffith
1943....Ken Roberts
1944....Ken Roberts
1947....Wag Blessing
1948....Harry Tompkins
1949....Harry Tompkins
1950....Harry Tompkins
1951....Jim Shoulders
1952....Harry Tompkins
1953....Todd Whatley
1954....Jim Shoulders
1955....Jim Shoulders
1956....Jim Shoulders
1957....Jim Shoulders
1958....Jim Shoulders
1959....Jim Shoulders
1960....Harry Tompkins
1961....Ronnie Rossen
1962....Freckles Brown
1963....Bill Kornell
1964....Bob Wegner
1965....Larry Mahan
1966....Ronnie Rossen
1967....Larry Mahan
1968....George Paul
1969....Doug Brown
1970....Gary Leffew
1971....Bill Nelson
1972....John Quintana
1973....Bobby Steiner
1974....Don Gay
1975....Don Gay
1976....Don Gay
1977....Don Gay
1978....Don Gay
1979....Don Gay
1980....Don Gay
1981....Don Gay
1982....Charles Sampson
1983....Cody Snyder
1984....Don Gay
1985....Ted Nuce
1986....Tuff Hedeman
1987....Lane Frost
1988....Jim Sharp
1989....Tuff Hedeman
1990....Jim Sharp
1991....Tuff Hedeman
1992....Cody Custer
1993....Ty Murray
1994....Daryl Mills
1995....Jerome Davis
1996....Terry West
1997....Scott Mendes
1998....Ty Murray
1999....Mike White
2000....Cody Hancock
2001....Blue Stone
2002....Blue Stone

Calf Roping

1929....Everett Bowman
1930....Jake McClure
1931....Herb Meyers
1932....Richard Merchant
1933....Bill McFarlane
1934....Irby Mundy
1935....Everett Bowman
1936....Clyde Burk
1937....Everett Bowman
1938....Burel Mulkey
1939....Toots Mansfield
1940....Toots Mansfield
1941....Toots Mansfield
1942....Clyde Burk
1943....Toots Mansfield
1944....Clyde Burk
1947....Troy Fort
1948....Toots Mansfield
1949....Troy Fort
1950....Toots Mansfield
1951....Don McLaughlin
1952....Don McLaughlin
1953....Don McLaughlin
1954....Don McLaughlin
1955....Dean Oliver
1956....Ray Wharton
1957....Don McLaughlin
1958....Dean Oliver
1959....Jim Bob Altizer
1960....Dean Oliver
1961....Dean Oliver
1962....Dean Oliver
1963....Dean Oliver
1964....Dean Oliver
1965....Glen Franklin
1966....Junior Garrison
1967....Glen Franklin
1968....Glen Franklin
1969....Dean Oliver
1970....Junior Garrison
1971....Phil Lyne
1972....Phil Lyne
1973....Ernie Taylor
1974....Tom Ferguson
1975....Jeff Copenhaver
1976....Roy Cooper
1977....Roy Cooper
1978....Roy Cooper
1979....Paul Tierney
1980....Roy Cooper
1981....Roy Cooper
1982....Roy Cooper
1983....Roy Cooper
1984....Roy Cooper
1985....Joe Beaver
1986....Chris Lybbert
1987....Joe Beaver
1988....Joe Beaver
1989....Rabe Rabon
1990....Troy Pruitt
1991....Fred Whitfield
1992....Joe Beaver
1993....Joe Beaver
1994....Herbert Theriot
1995....Fred Whitfield
1996....Fred Whitfield
1997....Cody Ohl
1998....Cody Ohl
1999....Fred Whitfield
2000....Fred Whitfield
2001....Cody Ohl
2002....Fred Whitfield

Steer Wrestling

1929....Gene Ross
1930....Everett Bowman
1931....Gene Ross
1932....Hugh Bennett
1933....Everett Bowman
1934....Shorty Ricker
1935....Everett Bowman
1936....Jack Kerschner
1937....Gene Ross
1938....Everett Bowman
1939....Harry Hart
1940....Homer Pettigrew
1941....Hub Whiteman
1942....Homer Pettigrew
1943....Homer Pettigrew
1944....Homer Pettigrew
1947....Todd Whatley
1948....Homer Pettigrew
1949....Bill McGuire
1950....Bill Linderman
1951....Dub Phillips
1952....Harley May
1953....Ross Dollarhide
1954....James Bynum
1955....Benny Combs
1956....Harley May
1957....Clark McEntire
1958....James Bynum
1959....Harry Charters
1960....Bob A. Robinson
1961....Jim Bynum
1962....Tom Nesmith
1963....Jim Bynum
1964....C.R. Boucher
1965....Harley May
1966....Jack Roddy
1967....Roy Duvall
1968....Jack Roddy
1969....Roy Duvall
1970....John W. Jones
1971....Billy Hale
1972....Roy Duvall
1973....Bob Marshall
1974....Tommy Puryear
1975....F. Shepperson
1976....Tom Ferguson
1977....Larry Ferguson
1978....Byron Walker
1979....Stan Williamson
1980....Butch Myers
1981....Byron Walker
1982....Stan Williamson
1983....Joel Edmondson
1984....John W. Jones
1985....Ote Berry
1986....Steve Duhon
1987....Steve Duhon
1988....John W. Jones
1989....John W. Jones
1990....Ote Berry
1991....Ote Berry
1992....Mark Roy
1993....Steve Duhon
1994....Blaine Pederson
1995....Ote Berry
1996....Chad Bedell
1997....Brad Gleason
1998....Mike Smith
1999....Mickey Gee
2000....Frank Thompson
2001....Rope Myers
2002....Sid Steiner

Professional Rodeo Cowboys Association World Champions (Cont.)

Team Roping

1929....Charles Maggini	1950....Buck Sorrels	1971....John Miller	1992....Clay O. Cooper
1930....Norman Cowan	1951....Olan Sims	1972....Leo Camarillo	1993....Bobby Hurley
1931....Arthur Beloat	1952....Asbury Schell	1973....Leo Camarillo	1994....Jake Barnes
1932....Ace Gardner	1953....Ben Johnson	1974....H.P. Evetts	Clay O. Cooper
1933....Roy Adams	1954....Eddie Schell	1975....Leo Camarillo	1995....Bobby Hurley
1934....Andy Jauregui	1955....Vern Castro	1976....Leo Camarillo	Allen Bach
1935....Lawrence Conltk	1956....Dale Smith	1977....Jerold Camarillo	1996....Steve Purcella
1936....John Rhodes	1957....Dale Smith	1978....Doyle Gellerman	Steve Northcott
1937....Asbury Schell	1958....Ted Ashworth	1979....Allen Bach	1997....Speed Williams
1938....John Rhodes	1959....Jim Rodriguez Jr.	1980....Tee Woolman	Rich Skelton
1939....Asbury Schell	1960....Jim Rodriguez Jr.	1981....Walt Woodard	1998....Speed Williams
1940....Pete Grubb	1961....Al Hooper	1982....Tee Woolman	Rich Skelton
1941....Jim Hudson	1962....Jim Rodriguez Jr.	1983....Leo Camarillo	1999....Speed Williams
1942....Verne Castro	1963....Les Hirdes	1984....Dee Pickett	Rich Skelton
Vic Castro	1964....Bill Hamilton	1985....Jake Barnes	2000....Speed Williams
1943....Mark Hull	1965....Jim Rodriguez Jr.	1986....Clay O. Cooper	Rich Skelton
Leonard Block	1966....Ken Luman	1987....Clay O. Cooper	2001....Speed Williams
1944....Murphy Chaney	1967....Joe Glenn	1988....Jake Barnes	Rich Skelton
1947....Jim Brister	1968....Art Arnold	1989....Jake Barnes	2002....Speed Williams
1948....Joe Glenn	1969....Jerold Camarillo	1990....Allen Bach	Rich Skelton
1949....Ed Yanez	1970....John Miller	1991....Bob Harris	

Steer Roping

1929....Charles Maggini	1948....Everett Shaw	1967....Jim Bob Altizer	1986....Jim Davis
1930....Clay Carr	1949....Shoat Webster	1968....Sonny Davis	1987....Shaun Burchett
1931....Andy Jauregui	1950....Shoat Webster	1969....Walter Arnold	1988....Shaun Burchett
1932....George Weir	1951....Everett Shaw	1970....Don McLaughlin	1989....Guy Allen
1933....John Bowman	1952....Buddy Neal	1971....Olin Young	1990....Phil Lyne
1934....John McEntire	1953....Ike Rude	1972....Allen Keller	1991....Guy Allen
1935....Richard Merchant	1954....Shoat Webster	1973....Roy Thompson	1992....Guy Allen
1936....John Bowman	1955....Shoat Webster	1974....Olin Young	1993....Guy Allen
1937....Everett Bowman	1956....Jim Snively	1975....Roy Thompson	1994....Guy Allen
1938....Hugh Bennett	1957....Clark McEntire	1976....Marvin Cantrell	1995....Guy Allen
1939....Dick Truitt	1958....Clark McEntire	1977....Buddy Cockrell	1996....Guy Allen
1940....Clay Carr	1959....Everett Shaw	1978....Sonny Worrell	1997....Guy Allen
1941....Ike Rude	1960....Don McLaughlin	1979....Gary Good	1998....Guy Allen
1942....King Merrit	1961....Clark McEntire	1980....Guy Allen	1999....Guy Allen
1943....Tom Rhodes	1962....Everett Shaw	1981....Arnold Felts	2000....Guy Allen
1944....Tom Rhodes	1963....Don McLaughlin	1982....Guy Allen	2001....Guy Allen
1945....Everett Shaw	1964....Sonny Davis	1983....Roy Cooper	2002....Buster Record
1946....Everett Shaw	1965....Sonney Wright	1984....Guy Allen	
1947....Ike Rude	1966....Sonny Davis	1985....Jim Davis	

Note: In 1945–46 champions were crowned only in Steer Roping.

Rowing

National Collegiate Rowing Champions

MEN

1985 ....Harvard	1991 ....Pennsylvania	1997 ....Washington
1986 ....Wisconsin	1992 ....Harvard	1998 ....Princeton
1987 ....Harvard	1993 ....Brown	1999 ....California
1988 ....Harvard	1994 ....Brown	2000 ....California
1989 ....Harvard	1995 ....Brown	2001 ....California
1990 ....Wisconsin	1996 ....Princeton	2002 ....California
		2003 ....Harvard

WOMEN

1979 ....Yale	1987 ....Washington	1995 ....Princeton
1980 ....California	1988 ....Washington	1996 ....Brown
1981 ....Washington	1989 ....Cornell	1997 ....Washington
1982 ....Washington	1990 ....Princeton	1998 ....Washington
1983 ....Washington	1991 ....Boston University	1999 ....Brown
1984 ....Washington	1992 ....Boston University	2000 ....Brown
1985 ....Washington	1993 ....Princeton	2001 ....Washington
1986 ....Wisconsin	1994 ....Princeton	2002 ....Brown
		2003 ....Harvard

Rugby Union

National Men's Club Championship

Year	Winner	Runner-Up	Year	Winner	Runner-Up
1979	Old Blues (CA)	St. Louis Falcons	1992	Old Blues (CA)	Mystic River (MA)
1980	Old Blues (CA)	St. Louis Falcons	1993	Old Mission Beach AC	Milwaukee
1981	Old Blues (CA)	Old Blue (NY)	1994	Old Mission Beach AC	Life College (GA)
1982	Old Blues (CA)	Denver Barbos	1995	Potomac Athletic Club	Old Mission Beach
1983	Old Blues (CA)	Dallas Harlequins	1996	Old Mission Beach AC	Old Blues (CA)
1984	Dallas Harlequins	Los Angeles	1997	Gentlemen of Aspen	Old Blue (NY)
1985	Milwaukee	Denver Barbos	1998	Gentlemen of Aspen	Old Blue (NY)
1986	Old Blues (CA)	Old Blue (NY)	1999	Gentlemen of Aspen	Golden Gate (CA)
1987	Old Blues (CA)	Pittsburgh	2000	Gentlemen of Aspen	Hayward Griffins
1988	Old Mission Beach AC	Milwaukee	2001	San Mateo	New York AC
1989	Old Mission Beach AC	Philly/Whitemarsh	2002	San Mateo	Austin
1990	Denver Barbos	Old Blues (CA)	2003	Boston Irish Wolfhounds	San Mateo
1991	Old Mission Beach AC	Washington			

National Men's Collegiate Championship

Year	Winner	Runner-Up	Year	Winner	Runner-Up
1980	California	Air Force	1992	California	Army
1981	California	Harvard	1993	California	Air Force
1982	California	Life College	1994	California	Navy
1983	California	Air Force	1995	California	Air Force
1984	Harvard	Colorado	1996	California	Penn St
1985	California	Maryland	1997	California	Penn St
1986	California	Dartmouth	1998	California	Stanford
1987	San Diego State	Air Force	1999	California	Penn St
1988	California	Dartmouth	2000	California	Wyoming
1989	Air Force	Long Beach	2001	California	Penn St
1990	Air Force	Army	2002	California	Utah
1991	California	Army	2003	Air Force	Harvard

World Cup Championship

Year	Winner	Runner-Up	Year	Winner	Runner-Up
1987	New Zealand	France	1995	South Africa	New Zealand
1991	Australia	England	1999	Australia	France

Rugby League

American National Rugby League Champions

Year	Winner	Runner-Up
1998	Glen Mills Bulls	Philadelphia Bulldogs
1999	Glen Mills Bulls	New Jersey Sharks
2000	Glen Mills Bulls	Philadelphia Fight
2001	Glen Mills Bulls	Media Mantarays
2002	New York Knights	Glen Mills Bulls
2003	Connecticut Wildcats	Glen Mills Bulls

World Cup Championship

Year	Winner	Runner-Up	Host
1954	Great Britain	France	France
1957	Australia	International Team	Australia
1960	Great Britain	International Team	England
1968	Australia	France	Australia–New Zealand
1970	Great Britain	Australia	England
1972	Australia	Great Britain	France
1975	Australia	England	Worldwide
1977	Australia	Great Britain	Australia–New Zealand
1985–88	Australia	New Zealand	Worldwide
1989–92	Australia	Great Britain	Worldwide
1995	Australia	England	Great Britain
2000	Australia	New Zealand	G Britain-Ireland-France

America's Cup Champions

SCHOONERS AND J-CLASS BOATS

Year	Winner	Skipper	Series	Loser	Skipper
1851	America	Richard Brown			
1870	Magic	Andrew Comstock	1–0	Cambria, Great Britain	J. Tannock
1871	Columbia (2–1)	Nelson Comstock	4–1	Livonia, Great Britain	J.R. Woods
	Sappho (2–0)	Sam Greenwood			
1876	Madeleine	Josephus Williams	2–0	Countess of Dufferin, Canada	J.E. Ellsworth
1881	Mischief	Nathanael Clock	2–0	Atalanta, Canada	Alexander Cuthbert
1885	Puritan	Aubrey Crocker	2–0	Genesta, Great Britain	John Carter
1886	Mayflower	Martin Stone	2–0	Galatea, Great Britain	Dan Bradford
1887	Volunteer	Henry Haff	2–0	Thistle, Great Britain	John Barr
1893	Vigilant	William Hansen	3–0	Valkyrie II, Great Britain	William Granfield
1895	Defender	Henry Haff	3–0	Valkyrie III, Great Britain	William Granfield
1899	Columbia	Charles Barr	3–0	Shamrock I, Great Britain	Archie Hogarth
1901	Columbia	Charles Barr	3–0	Shamrock II, Great Britain	E.A. Sycamore
1903	Reliance	Charles Barr	3–0	Shamrock III, Great Britain	Bob Wringe
1920	Resolute	Charles F. Adams	3–2	Shamrock IV, Great Britain	William Burton
1930	Enterprise	Harold Vanderbilt	4–0	Shamrock V, Great Britain	Ned Heard
1934	Rainbow	Harold Vanderbilt	4–2	Endeavour, Great Britain	T.O.M. Sopwith
1937	Ranger	Harold Vanderbilt	4–0	Endeavour II, Great Britain	T.O.M. Sopwith

12-METER BOATS

Year	Winner	Skipper	Series	Loser	Skipper
1958	Columbia	Briggs Cunningham	4–0	Sceptre, Great Britain	Graham Mann
1962	Weatherly	Bus Mosbacher	4–1	Gretel, Australia	Jock Sturrock
1964	Constellation	Bob Bavier & Eric Ridder	4–0	Sovereign, Australia	Peter Scott
1967	Intrepid	Bus Mosbacher	4–0	Dame Pattie, Australia	Jock Sturrock
1970	Intrepid	Bill Ficker	4–1	Gretel II, Australia	Jim Hardy
1974	Courageous	Ted Hood	4–0	Southern Cross, Australia	John Cuneo
1977	Courageous	Ted Turner	4–0	Australia	Noel Robins
1980	Freedom	Dennis Conner	4–1	Australia	Jim Hardy
1983	Australia II	John Bertrand	4–3	Liberty, United States	Dennis Conner
1987	Stars & Stripes	Dennis Conner	4–0	Kookaburra III, Australia	Iain Murray

60-FOOT CATAMARAN vs 133-FOOT MONOHULL

Year	Winner	Skipper	Series	Loser	Skipper
1988	Stars & Stripes	Dennis Conner	2–0	New Zealand	David Barnes

75-FOOT MONOHULL (IACC)

Year	Winner	Skipper	Series	Loser	Skipper
1992	America[3]	Bill Koch	4–1	Il Moro di Vinezia, Italy	Paul Cayard
1995	Black Magic I	Russell Coutts	5–0	Young America, United States	Dennis Conner
2000	New Zealand	Russell Coutts	5–0	Luna Rossa, Italy	Francesco de Angelis
2003	Swiss Alinghi	Russell Coutts	5–0	New Zealand	Dean Barker

Note: Winning entries have been from the United States every year but three: In 1983 an Australian vessel won, and in 1995 and 2000 a vessel from New Zealand won.

Shooting World Champions

Men

50M FREE RIFLE PRONE

1947 ....O. Sannes, Norway
1949 ....A.C. Jackson, U.S.
1952 ....A.C. Jackson, U.S.
1954 ....G. Boa, Canada
1958 ....M. Nordquist
1962 ....K. Wenk, W Germany
1966 ....D. Boyd, U.S.
1970 ....M. Fiess, S. Africa
1974 ....K. Bulan, Czechoslovakia
1978 ....A. Allan, Great Britain
1982 ....V. Danilschenko, USSR
1986 ....S. Bereczky, Hungary
1990 ....V. Bochkarev, USSR
1994 ....Venjie Li, China
1998 ....Thomas Tamas, U.S.
1999 ....Thomas Tamas, U.S.
2000 ....Siarhei Martynau, Belarus
2001 ....Matthew Emmons, U.S.
2002 ....Matthew Emmons, U.S.

AIR RIFLE

1966 .....G. Kümmet, W Germany
1970 .....G. Kusterman, W Germ.
1974 .....E. Pedzisz, Poland
1978 .....O. Schlipf, W. Germany
1979 .....K. Hillenbrand
1981 .....F. Bessy, France
1982 .....F. Rettkowski, E Germ.
1983 .....P. Heberle, France
1985 .....P. Heberle, France
1986 .....H. Riederer, W Germany
1987 .....K. Ivanov, USSR
1989 .....J. P. Amet, France
1990 .....H. Riederer, W Germany
1994 .....Boris Polak, Israel
1998 .....Artem Khadjibekov, Russia
1999 .....Jozef Gonci, Slovakia
2000 .....Artem Khadjibekov, Russia
2001 ......Jason Parker, U.S.
2002 ......Jason Parker, U.S.

THREE POSITION RIFLE

1966 .....M. Thompson, U.S.
1970 ......M. Thompson Murdock, U.S.
1974 .....A. Pelova, Bulgaria
1978 .....W. Oliver, U.S.
1982 .....M. Helbig, E Germany
1986 .....V. Letcheva, Bulgaria
1990 .....V. Letcheva, Bulgaria
1994 .....A. Maloukhina, Russia
1998 .....Sonja Pfeilschifter, Germany
1999 ......Sonja Pfeilschifter, Germany
2000 .....Hong Shan, China
2001 .....Petra Horneber, Germany
2002 .....Petra Horneber, Germany

AIR RIFLE

1970 .....V. Cherkasque, USSR
1974 .....T. Ratkinova, USSR
1978 .....W. Oliver, U.S.
1979 .....K. Monez, U.S.
1981 .....S. Romaristova, USSR
1982 .....S. Lang, W Germany
1983 .....M. Helbig, E Germany
1985 .....E. Forian, Hungary
1986 .....V. Letcheva, Bulgaria
1987 .....V. Letcheva, Bulgaria
1989 .....V. Letcheva, Bulgaria
1990 .....E. Joc, Hungary

MEN'S TRAP

1929 .....De Lumniczer, Hungary
1930 .....M. Arie, U.S.
1931 .....Kiszkurno, Poland
1933 .....De Lumniczer, Hungary
1934 .....A. Montagh, Hungary
1935 .....R. Sack, W Germany
1936 .....Kiszkurno, Poland
1937 .....K. Huber, Finland
1938 .....I. Strassburger, Hungary
1939 .....De Lumniczer, Hungary
1947 .....H. Liljedahl, Sweden
1949 .....F. Rocchi, Argentina
1950 .....C. Sala, Italy
1952 .....P.J. Grossi, Argentina
1954 .....C. Merlo, Italy
1958 .....F. Eisenlauer, U.S.
1959 .....H. Badravi, Egypt
1961 .....E. Mattarelli, Italy
1962 .....W. Zimenko, USSR
1965 .....J.E. Lire, Chile
1966 .....K. Jones, U.S.
1967 .....G. Rennard, Belgium
1969 .....E. Mattarelli, Italy
1970 .....M. Carrega, France
1971 .....M. Carrega, France
1973 .....A. Andrushkin, USSR
1974 .....M. Carrega, France
1975 .....J. Primrose, Canada
1977 .....E. Azkue, Spain
1978 .....E. Vallduvi, Spain
1979 .....M. Carrega, France
1981 .....A. Asanov, USSR
1982 .....L. Giovonnetti, Italy
1983 .....J. Primrose, Canada
1985 ....M. Bednarik,
         Czechoslovakia
1986......M. Bednarik,
         Czechoslovakia
1987 .....D. Monakov, USSR

Women

AIR RIFLE (Cont.)

1994 .....Sonja Pfeilschifter, Germany
1998 .....Sonja Pfeilschifter, Germany
1999......Sonja Pfeilschifter, Germany
2000.......Sonja Pfeilschifter, Germany
2001.......Katerina Kurkova, Czech.
2002.......Katerina Kurkova, Czech.

SPORT PISTOL

1966 .....N. Rasskazova, USSR
1970 .....N. Stoljarova, USSR
1974 .....N. Stoljarova, USSR
1978 .....K. Dyer, U.S.
1982 .....P. Balogh, Hungary
1986 .....M. Dobrantcheva, USSR
1990 .....M. Logvinenko, USSR
1994 .....Soon Hee Boo, S Korea
1998 .....Yieqing Cai, China
1999 .....Soon Hee Boo, S Korea
2000 .....Lalita Vauhleuskaya,
         Belarus
2001 .....Munkhbayar Dorjsuren,
         Germany
2002 .....Munkhbayar Dorjsuren,
         Germany

AIR PISTOL

1970 .....S. Carroll, U.S.
1974 .....Z. Simonian, USSR

MEN'S TRAP (Cont.)

1989 .....M. Venturini, Italy
1990 .....J. Damne, E Germany
1994 ....Dmitriy Monakov, Ukraine
1995 .....Giovanni Pellielo, Italy
1998 .....Giovanni Pellielo, Italy
1999 .....Joao Rebelo, Portugal
2000 .....Michael Diamond, Australia
2001.......Michael Diamond, Australia
2002.......Khaled Almudhaf, Kuwait

THREE POSITION RIFLE

1929 ....O. Ericsson, Sweden
1930 ....Petersen, Denmark
1931 ....Amundson, Norway
1933 ....De Lisle, France
1935 .....Leskinnen, Finland
1937 .....Mazoyer, France
1939 .....Steigelmann, Germany
1947 .....I.H. Erben, Sweden
1949 .....P. Janhonen, Finland
1952 .....Kongshaug, Norway
1954 .....A. Bugdanov, USSR
1958 .....Itkis, USSR
1962 .....G. Anderson, U.S.
1966 .....G. Anderson, U.S.
1970 .....Parkhimovitch, USSR
1974 .....L. Wigger, U.S.
1978 .....E. Svensson, Sweden
1982 .....K. Ivanov, USSR
1986 .....P. Heinz, W Germany
1990 .....E. C. Lee, S Korea
1994 .....P. Kurka, Czech Republic
1998 .....Jozef Gonci, Slovakia
1999 .....Jozef Gonci, Slovakia
2000 .....Jozef Gonci, Slovakia
2001 .....Marcel Bürge, Switz
2002 .....Marcel Bürge, Switz

AIR PISTOL (Cont.)

1978 .....K. Hansson, Sweden
1979 .....R. Fox, U.S.
1981 .....N. Kalinina, USSR
1982 .....M. Dobrantcheva, USSR
1983 .....K. Bodin, Sweden
1985 .....M. Dobrantcheva, USSR
1986 .....A. Völker, E Germany
1987 .....J. Brajkovic, Yugoslavia
1989 .....N. Salukvadse, USSR
1990......Jasna Sekaric, Yugoslavia
1994 .....Jasna Sekaric, IOP
1998 ....Dorisuren Munkhbayar,
         Mongolia
1999 .....Nino Salukvadze,
         Georgia
2000 .....Luna Tao, China
2001 .....Olena Kostevych, Ukraine
2002 .....Olena Kostevych, Ukraine

U.S. Champions—Men
MAJOR FAST PITCH

1933..........J.L. Gill Boosters, Chicago	1969..........Raybestos Cardinals, Stratford, CT
1934..........Ke-Nash-A, Kenosha, WI	1970..........Raybestos Cardinals, Stratford, CT
1935..........Crimson Coaches, Toledo, OH	1971..........Welty Way, Cedar Rapids, IA
1936..........Kodak Park, Rochester, NY	1972..........Raybestos Cardinals, Stratford, CT
1937..........Briggs Body Team, Detroit	1973..........Clearwater (FL) Bombers
1938..........The Pohlers, Cincinnati	1974..........Gianella Bros, Santa Rosa, CA
1939..........Carr's Boosters, Covington, KY	1975..........Rising Sun Hotel, Reading, PA
1940..........Kodak Park, Rochester, NY	1976..........Raybestos Cardinals, Stratford, CT
1941..........Bendix Brakes, South Bend, IN	1977..........Billard Barbell, Reading, PA
1942..........Deep Rock Oilers, Tulsa	1978..........Billard Barbell, Reading, PA
1943..........Hammer Air Field, Fresno	1979..........McArdle Pontiac/Cadillac, Midland, MI
1944..........Hammer Air Field, Fresno	1980..........Peterbilt Western, Seattle
1945..........Zollner Pistons, Fort Wayne, IN	1981..........Archer Daniels Midland, Decatur, IL
1946..........Zollner Pistons, Fort Wayne, IN	1982..........Peterbilt Western, Seattle
1947..........Zollner Pistons, Fort Wayne, IN	1983..........Franklin Cardinals, Stratford, CT
1948..........Briggs Beautyware, Detroit	1984..........California Kings, Merced, CA
1949..........Tip Top Tailors, Toronto	1985..........Pay'n Pak, Seattle
1950..........Clearwater (FL) Bombers	1986..........Pay'n Pak, Seattle
1951..........Dow Chemical, Midland, MI	1987..........Pay'n Pak, Seattle
1952..........Briggs Beautyware, Detroit	1988..........TransAire, Elkhart, IN
1953..........Briggs Beautyware, Detroit	1989..........Penn Corp, Sioux City, IA
1954..........Clearwater (FL) Bombers	1990..........Penn Corp, Sioux City, IA
1955..........Raybestos Cardinals, Stratford, CT	1991..........Guanella Brothers, Rohnert Park, CA
1956..........Clearwater (FL) Bombers	1992..........Natl Health Care Disc, Sioux City, IA
1957..........Clearwater (FL) Bombers	1993..........Natl Health Care Disc, Sioux City, IA
1958..........Raybestos Cardinals, Stratford, CT	1994..........Decatur Pride, Decatur, IL
1959..........Sealmasters, Aurora, IL	1995..........Decatur Pride, Decatur, IL
1960..........Clearwater (FL) Bombers	1996..........Green Bay All-Car, Green Bay, WI
1961..........Sealmasters, Aurora, IL	1997..........Green Bay All-Car, Green Bay, WI
1962..........Clearwater (FL) Bombers	1998..........Meierhoffer-Fleeman, St. Joseph, MO
1963..........Clearwater (FL) Bombers	1999..........Decatur Pride, Decatur, IL
1964..........Burch Tool, Detroit	2000..........Meierhoffer, St. Joseph, MO
1965..........Sealmasters, Aurora, IL	2001..........Frontier Players Casino, St. Joseph, MO
1966..........Clearwater (FL) Bombers	2002..........Frontier Players Casino, St. Joseph, MO
1967..........Sealmasters, Aurora, IL	2003..........Farm Tavern, Madison, WI
1968..........Clearwater (FL) Bombers	

SUPER SLOW PITCH

1981..........Howard's/Western Steer, Denver, NC	1992..........Ritch's Superior, Windsor Locks, CT
1982..........Jerry's Catering, Miami, FL	1993..........Ritch's Superior, Windsor Locks, CT
1983..........Howard's/Western Steer, Denver, NC	1994..........Bell Corp, Tampa, FL
1984..........Howard's/Western Steer, Denver, NC	1995..........Lighthouse/Worth, Stone Mt.., GA
1985..........Steele's Sports, Grafton, OH	1996..........Ritch's Superior, Windsor Locks, CT
1986..........Steele's Sports, Grafton, OH	1997..........Ritch's Superior, Windsor Locks, CT
1987..........Steele's Sports, Grafton, OH	1998..........Lighthouse/Worth, Stone Mt.., GA
1988..........Starpath, Monticello, KY	1999..........Team Easton, Wilmington, NC
1989..........Ritch's Salvage, Harrisburg, NC	2000..........Team TPS, Louisville, KY
1990..........Steele's Silver Bullets, Grafton, OH	2002..........Long Haul/Taylor Bros./Shen Corp./TPS, Albertville, MN
1991..........Sunbelt/Worth, Centerville, GA	2003..........Resmondo/Hagae/Sunbelt/Taylor, Canal Winchester, OH

Nice Catch

In June 2003, Ron Roland, a 39-year-old software salesman from Plano, Texas, hooked a 1,152-lb. bluefin tuna in the Gulf of Mexico. The biggest fish ever caught on a rod and reel, the bluefin battled Roland from 3:45 p.m until 9. "Imagine doing squats with 300-pound weights on your back for five hours," the 5'8", 190-pound Roland said. When the fish finally quit, it was too big to fit aboard the 50-foot sport fishing vessel, *Miss Cathy*. The men tied a rope through each gill and, much like Santiago in *The Old Man and the Sea*, towed the tuna to shore, where it was carved up for whomever felt like taking home a steak.

Softball (Cont.)

U.S. Champions—Men (Cont.)

MAJOR SLOW PITCH

1953..........Shields Construction, Newport, KY	1980..........Campbell Carpets, Concord, CA
1954..........Waldneck's Tavern, Cincinnati	1981..........Elite Coating, Gordon, CA
1955.........Lang Pet Shop, Covington, KY	1982.........Triangle Sports, Minneapolis
1956..........Gatliff Auto Sales, Newport, KY	1983..........No. 1 Electric & Heating, Gastonia, NC
1957..........Gatliff Auto Sales, Newport, KY	1984..........Lilly Air Systems, Chicago
1958.........East Side Sports, Detroit	1985.........Blanton's, Fayetteville, NC
1959..........Yorkshire Restaurant, Newport, KY	1986..........Non-Ferrous Metals, Cleveland
1960..........Hamilton Tailoring, Cincinnati	1987..........Starpath, Monticello, KY
1961.........Hamilton Tailoring, Cincinnati	1988..........Bell Corp/FAF, Tampa, FL
1962.........Skip Hogan A.C., Pittsburgh	1989..........Ritch's Salvage, Harrisburg, NC
1963.........Gatliff Auto Sales, Newport, KY	1990..........New Construction, Shelbyville, IN
1964.........Skip Hogan A.C., Pittsburgh	1991.........Riverside Paving, Louisville, KY
1965.........Skip Hogan A.C., Pittsburgh	1992.........Vernon's, Jacksonville, FL
1966..........Michael's Lounge, Detroit	1993..........Back Porch/Destin Roofing, Destin, FL
1967..........Jim's Sport Shop, Pittsburgh	1994..........Riverside RAM/Taylor Bros., Louisville, KY
1968..........County Sports, Levittown, NY	1995..........Riverside/RAM/Taylor/TPS, Louisville, KY
1969.........Copper Hearth, Milwaukee	1996..........Bell 2/Robert's/Easton, Orlando, FL
1970...........Little Caesar's, Southgate, MI	1997..........Long Haul/TPS, Albertville, MN
1971..........Pile Drivers, Virginia Beach, VA	1998..........Chase Mortgage/Easton, Wilmington, NC
1972.........Jiffy Club, Louisville, KY	1999..........Gasoline Heaven/Worth, Commack, NY
1973..........Howard's Furniture, Denver, NC	2000..........Long Haul/TPS, Albertville, MN
1974..........Howard's Furniture, Denver, NC	2001..........New Construction, Shelbyville, IN
1975.........Pyramid Cafe, Lakewood, OH	2002..........Twin States/Worth, Montgomery, AL
1976..........Warren Motors, Jacksonville, FL	2003......,...New Construction/B&J/Snap-On,
1977...........Nelson Painting, Oklahoma City	Metamora, IL
1978..........Campbell Carpets, Concord, CA	
1979..........Nelco Mfg Co., Oklahoma City	

Child's Play

Don't let his bashful smile fool you. Hunched over a chessboard, 15-year-old Hikaru Nakamura is one of the most ruthless competitors you'll ever see. "He goes right after the best guys in the game," said the U.S. Chess Federation's Tom Brownscombe. "In a world full of cautious chess players, Hikaru plays to win." A tennis-playing Tennessee Titans fan from White Plains, N.Y., Hikaru became the youngest U.S. grandmaster by scoring 7 ½ points in 11 games at the Bermuda International Chess Festival. (Bobby Fischer was four months, four days older when he became a grandmaster in 1958.) "This takes some pressure off," said Hikaru, who is homeschooled by his mother Carolyn Weeramantry, a renowned chess teacher. "I felt like I had been so close for a while." Nakamura picked up the game at age seven from his older brother, Asuka; by 10 he was the youngest U.S. master ever. He's always been aggressive, sacrificing pieces to earn technical advantage. "What amazes me is his willingness to try new systems in the most crucial situations," said Sunil, an international master. "Such fearlessness, it can't be taught."

—Kelley King

U.S. Champions—Women

MAJOR FAST PITCH

1933..........Great Northerns, Chicago	1969..........Orange (CA) Lionettes
1934..........Hart Motors, Chicago	1970..........Orange (CA) Lionettes
1935..........Bloomer Girls, Cleveland	1971..........Raybestos Brakettes, Stratford, CT
1936..........Nat'l Screw & Mfg., Cleveland	1972..........Raybestos Brakettes, Stratford, CT
1937..........Nat'l Screw & Mfg., Cleveland	1973..........Raybestos Brakettes, Stratford, CT
1938..........J.J. Krieg's, Alameda, CA	1974..........Raybestos Brakettes, Stratford, CT
1939..........J.J. Krieg's, Alameda, CA	1975..........Raybestos Brakettes, Stratford, CT
1940..........Arizona Ramblers, Phoenix	1976..........Raybestos Brakettes, Stratford, CT
1941..........Higgins Midgets, Tulsa	1977..........Raybestos Brakettes, Stratford, CT
1942..........Jax Maids, New Orleans	1978..........Raybestos Brakettes, Stratford, CT
1943..........Jax Maids, New Orleans	1979..........Sun City (AZ) Saints
1944..........Lind & Pomeroy, Portland, OR	1980..........Raybestos Brakettes, Stratford, CT
1945..........Jax Maids, New Orleans	1981..........Orlando (FL) Rebels
1946..........Jax Maids, New Orleans	1982..........Raybestos Brakettes, Stratford, CT
1947..........Jax Maids, New Orleans	1983..........Raybestos Brakettes, Stratford, CT
1948..........Arizona Ramblers, Phoenix	1984..........Los Angeles Diamonds
1949..........Arizona Ramblers, Phoenix	1985..........Hi-Ho Brakettes, Stratford, CT
1950..........Orange (CA) Lionettes	1986..........Southern California Invasion, Los Angeles
1951..........Orange (CA) Lionettes	1987..........Orange County Majestics, Anaheim, CA
1952..........Orange (CA) Lionettes	1988..........Hi-Ho Brakettes, Stratford, CT
1953..........Betsy Ross Rockets, Fresno	1989..........Whittier (CA) Raiders
1954..........Leach Motor Rockets, Fresno	1990..........Raybestos Brakettes, Stratford, CT
1955..........Orange (CA) Lionettes	1991..........Raybestos Brakettes, Stratford, CT
1956..........Orange (CA) Lionettes	1992..........Raybestos Brakettes, Stratford, CT
1957..........Hacienda Rockets, Fresno	1993..........Redding Rebels, Redding, CA
1958..........Raybestos Brakettes, Stratford, CT	1994..........Redding Rebels, Redding, CA
1959..........Raybestos Brakettes, Stratford, CT	1995..........Redding Rebels, Redding, CA
1960..........Raybestos Brakettes, Stratford, CT	1996..........California Commotion, Woodland Hills, CA
1961..........Gold Sox, Whittier, CA	1997..........California Commotion, Woodland Hills, CA
1962..........Orange (CA) Lionettes	1998..........California Commotion, Woodland Hills, CA
1963..........Raybestos Brakettes, Stratford, CT	1999..........California Commotion, Woodland Hills, CA
1964..........Erv Lind Florists, Portland, OR	2000..........Phoenix Storm, Phoenix
1965..........Orange (CA) Lionettes	2001..........Phoenix Storm, Phoenix
1966..........Raybestos Brakettes, Stratford, CT	2002..........Stratford Brakettes, Stratford, CT
1967..........Raybestos Brakettes, Stratford, CT	2003..........Stratford Brakettes, Stratford, CT
1968..........Raybestos Brakettes, Stratford, CT	

MAJOR SLOW PITCH

1959..........Pearl Laundry, Richmond, VA	1982..........Richmond (VA) Stompers
1960..........Carolina Rockets, High Pt, NC	1983..........Spooks, Anoka, MN
1961..........Dairy Cottage, Covington, KY	1984..........Spooks, Anoka, MN
1962..........Dana Gardens, Cincinnati	1985..........Key Ford Mustangs, Pensacola, FL
1963..........Dana Gardens, Cincinnati	1986..........Sur-Way Tomboys, Tifton, GA
1964..........Dana Gardens, Cincinnati	1987..........Key Ford Mustangs, Pensacola, FL
1965..........Art's Acres, Omaha	1988..........Spooks, Anoka, MN
1966..........Dana Gardens, Cincinnati	1989..........Canaan's Illusions, Houston
1967..........Ridge Maintenance, Cleveland	1990..........Spooks, Anoka, MN
1968..........Escue Pontiac, Cincinnati	1991..........Kannan's Illusions, San Antonio, TX
1969..........Converse Dots, Hialeah, FL	1992..........Universal Plastics, Cookeville, TN
1970..........Rutenschruder Floral, Cincinnati	1993..........Universal Plastics, Cookeville, TN
1971..........Gators, Ft. Lauderdale, FL	1994..........Universal Plastics, Cookeville, TN
1972..........Riverside Ford, Cincinnati	1995..........Armed Forces, Sacramento, CA
1973..........Sweeney Chevrolet, Cincinnati	1996..........Spooks, Anoka, MN
1974..........Marks Brothers Dots, Miami	1997..........Taylor's Major Slow Pitch, Glendale, MD
1975..........Marks Brothers Dots, Miami	1998..........Lakerettes, Conneaut Lake, PA
1976..........Sorrento's Pizza, Cincinnati	1999..........Lakerettes, Conneaut Lake, PA
1977..........Fox Valley Lassies, St. Charles, IL	2000..........Premier Motor Sports, Pittsboro, NC
1978..........Bob Hoffman's Dots, Miami	2001..........Shooters/Nike, Orlando, FL
1979..........Bob Hoffman's Dots, Miami	2002..........Diamond Queens, Nashville, TN
1980..........Howard's Rubi-Otts, Graham, NC	2003..........No Tournament
1981..........Tifton (GA) Tomboys	

All-Around World Champions

MEN

1891 .....Joseph F. Donoghue, U.S.	1935 .....Michael Staksrud, Nor.	1973 .....Göran Claeson, Sweden
1893 .....Jaap Eden, Netherlands	1936 .....Ivar Ballangrud, Norway	1974 .....Sten Stensen, Norway
1895 .....Jaap Eden, Netherlands	1937 .....Michael Staksrud, Nor.	1975 .....Harm Kuipers, Netherlands
1896 .....Jaap Eden, Netherlands	1938 .....Ivar Ballangrud, Norway	1976 .....Piet Kleine, Netherlands
1897 .....Jack K. McCulloch, Can.	1939 .....Birger Wasenius, Finland	1977 .....Eric Heiden, U.S.
1898 .....Peder Ostlund, Norway	1947 .....Lassi Parkkinen, Finland	1978 .....Eric Heiden, U.S.
1899 .....Peder Ostlund, Norway	1948 .....Odd Lundberg, Norway	1979 .....Eric Heiden, U.S.
1900 .....Edvard Engelsaas, Nor.	1949 .....Kornel Pajor, Hungary	1980 .....Hilbert van der Duin, Neth.
1901 .....Franz F. Wathan, Finland	1950 .....Hjalmar Andersen, Nor.	1981 .....Amund Sjobrand, Norway
1904 .....Sigurd Mathisen, Norway	1951 .....Hjalmar Andersen, Nor.	1982 .....Hilbert van der Duin, Neth.
1905 .....C. Coen de Koning, Neth.	1952 .....Hjalmar Andersen, Nor.	1983 .....Rolf Falk-Larssen, Nor.
1908 .....Oscar Mathisen, Norway	1953 .....Oleg Goncharenko, USSR	1984 .....Oleg Bozhev, USSR
1909 .....Oscar Mathisen, Norway	1954 .....Boris Shilkov, USSR	1985 .....Hein Vergeer, Netherlands
1910 .....Nikolai Strunnikov, Russia	1955 .....Sigvard Ericsson, Swe.	1986 .....Hein Vergeer, Netherlands
1911 .....Nikolai Strunnikov, Russia	1956 .....Oleg Goncharenko, USSR	1987 .....Nikolai Guliaev, USSR
1912 .....Oscar Mathisen, Norway	1957 .....Knut Johannesen, Nor.	1988 .....Eric Flaim, U.S.
1913 .....Oscar Mathisen, Norway	1958 .....Oleg Goncharenko, USSR	1989 .....Leo Visser, Netherlands
1914 .....Oscar Mathisen, Norway	1959 .....Juhani Järvinen, Finland	1990 .....Johann Olav Koss, Nor.
1922 .....Harald Strom, Norway	1960 .....Boris Stenin, USSR	1991 .....Johann Olav Koss, Nor.
1923 .....Klas Thunberg, Finland	1961 .....Henk van der Grift, Neth.	1992 .....Roberto Sighel, Italy
1924 .....Roald Larsen, Norway	1962 .....Viktor Kosichkin, USSR	1993 .....Falko Zandstra, Neth.
1925 .....Klas Thunberg, Finland	1963 .....Jonny Nilsson, Sweden	1994 .....Johann Olav Koss, Nor.
1926 .....Ivar Ballangrud, Norway	1964 .....Knut Johannesen, Nor.	1995 .....Rintje Ritsma, Netherlands
1927 .....Bernt Evensen, Norway	1965 .....Per Ivar Moe, Norway	1996 .....Rintje Ritsma, Netherlands
1928 .....Klas Thunberg, Finland	1966 .....Kees Verkerk, Neth.	1997 .....Ids Postma, Netherlands
1929 .....Klas Thunberg, Finland	1967 .....Kees Verkerk, Neth.	1998 .....Ids Postma, Netherlands
1930 .....Michael Staksrud, Nor.	1968 .....Fred Anton Maier, Nor.	1999 .....Rintje Ritsma, Netherlands
1931 .....Klas Thunberg, Finland	1969 .....Dag Fornaes, Norway	2000.......Gianni Romme, Netherlands
1932 .....Ivar Ballangrud, Norway	1970 .....Ard Schenk, Netherlands	2001.......Rintje Ritsma, Netherlands
1933 .....Hans Engnestangen, Nor.	1971 .....Ard Schenk, Netherlands	2002.......Jochem Uytdehaage, Neth.
1934 .....Bernt Evensen, Norway	1972 .....Ard Schenk, Netherlands	2003.......Gianni Romme, Netherlands

WOMEN

1936 .....Kit Klein, U.S.	1964 .....Lidia Skoblikova, USSR	1985 .....Andrea Schöne, GDR
1937 .....Laila Schou Nilsen, Nor.	1965 .....Inga Artamonova, USSR	1986 .....Karin Kania-Enke, GDR
1938 .....Laila Schou Nilsen, Nor.	1966 .....Valentina Stenina, USSR	1987 .....Karin Kania, GDR
1939 .....Verné Lesche, Finland	1967 .....Stien Kaiser, Netherlands	1988 .....Karin Kania, GDR
1947 .....Verné Lesche, Finland	1968 .....Stien Kaiser, Netherlands	1989 .....Constanze Moser, GDR
1948 .....Maria Isakova, USSR	1969 .....Lasma Kauniste, USSR	1990 .....Jacqueline Börner, GDR
1949 .....Maria Isakova, USSR	1970 .....Atje Keulen-Deelstra, Neth.	1991 .....Gunda Kleemann, Ger.
1950 .....Maria Isakova, USSR	1971 .....Nina Statkevich, USSR	1992 .....Gunda Niemann-Kleemann, Germany
1951 .....Eevi Huttunen, Finland	1972 .....Atje Keulen-Deelstra, Neth.	
1952 .....Lidia Selikhova, USSR	1973 .....Atje Keulen-Deelstra, Neth.	1993 .....Gunda Niemann, Germany
1953 .....Khalida Shchegoleeva, USSR	1974 .....Atje Keulen-Deelstra, Neth.	1994 .....Emese Hunyady, Austria
1954 .....Lidia Selikhova, USSR	1975 .....Karin Kessow, GDR	1995 .....Gunda Niemann, Germany
1955 .....Rimma Zhukova, USSR	1976 .....Sylvia Burka, Canada	1996 .....Gunda Niemann, Germany
1956 .....Sofia Kondakova, USSR	1977 .....Vera Bryndzej, USSR	1997 .....Gunda Niemann, Germany
1957 .....Inga Artamonova, USSR	1978 .....Tatiana Averina, USSR	1997 .....Gunda Niemann, Germany
1958 .....Inga Artamonova, USSR	1979 .....Beth Heiden, U.S.	1998 .....Gunda Niemann, Germany
1959 .....Tamara Rylova, USSR	1980 .....Natalia Petruseva, USSR	1999 .....Gunda Niemann, Germany
1960 .....Valentina Stenina, USSR	1981 .....Natalia Petruseva, USSR	2000 .....Claudia Pechstein, Ger.
1961 .....Valentina Stenina, USSR	1982 .....Karin Busch, GDR	2001 .....Anni Friesinger, Germany
1962 .....Inga Artamonova, USSR	1983 .....Andrea Schöne, GDR	2002 .....Anni Friesinger, Germany
1963 .....Lidia Skoblikova, USSR	1984 .....Karin Enke-Busch, GDR	2003 .....Cindy Klassen, Canada

National Men's Champions

HARD BALL		HARD BALL *(Cont.)*		SOFT BALL	
Year	**Champion**	**Year**	**Champion**	**Year**	**Champion**
1907	John A. Miskey	1959	Benjamin H. Heckscher	1983	Kenton Jernigan
1908	John A. Miskey	1960	G. Diehl Mateer Jr.	1984	Kenton Jernigan
1909	William L. Freeland	1961	Henri R. Salaun	1985	Kenton Jernigan
1910	John A. Miskey	1962	Samuel P. Howe III	1986	Darius Pandole
1911	Francis S. White	1963	Benjamin H.	1987	Richard Hashim
1912	Constantine Hutchins		Heckscher	1988	John Phelan
1913	Morton L. Newhall	1964	Ralph E. Howe	1989	Will Carlin
1914	Constantine Hutchins	1965	Stephen T. Vehslage	1990	Syed Jafry
1915	Stanley W. Pearson	1966	Victor Niederhoffer	1991	Hector Barragan
1916	Stanley W. Pearson	1967	Samuel P. Howe III	1992	Phil Yarrow
1917	Stanley W. Pearson	1968	Colin Adair	1993	Phil Yarrow
1918–19	No tournament	1969	Anil Nayar	1994	Roberto Rosales
1920	Charles C. Peabody	1970	Anil Nayar	1995	A. Martin Clark
1921	Stanley W. Pearson	1971	Colin Adair	1996	Mohsen Mir
1922	Stanley W. Pearson	1972	Victor Niederhoffer	1997	A. Martin Clark
1923	Stanley W. Pearson	1973	Victor Niederhoffer	1998	A. Martin Clark
1924	Gerald Roberts	1974	Victor Niederhoffer	1999	David McNeely
1925	W. Palmer Dixon	1975	Victor Niederhoffer	2000	A. Martin Clark
1926	W. Palmer Dixon	1976	Peter Briggs	2001	Damian Walker
1927	Myles Baker	1977	Thomas E. Page	2002	Damian Walker
1928	Herbert N. Rawlins Jr.	1978	Michael Desaulniers	2003	Preston Quick
1929	J. Lawrence Pool	1979	Mario Sanchez		
1930	Herbert N. Rawlins Jr.	1980	Michael Desaulniers		
1931	J. Lawrence Pool	1981	Mark Alger		
1932	Beckman H. Pool	1982	John Nimick		
1933	Beckman H. Pool	1983	Kenton Jernigan		
1934	Neil J. Sullivan II	1984	Kenton Jernigan		
1935	Donald Strachan	1987	Frank J. Stanley IV		
1936	Germain G. Glidden	1988	Scott Dulmage		
1937	Germain G. Glidden	1989	Rodolfo Rodriquez		
1938	Germain G. Glidden	1990	Hector Barragan		
1939	Donald Strachan	1991	Hector Barragan		
1940	A. Willing Patterson	1992	Hector Barragan		
1941	Charles M.P. Britton	1985	Kenton Jernigan		
1942	Charles M.P. Britton	1986	Hugh LaBossier		
1943–45	No tournament	1993	Hector Barragan		
1946	Charles M.P. Britton	1994	Hector Barragan		
1947	Charles M.P. Britton	1995	W. Keen Butcher		
1948	Stanley W. Pearson Jr.	1996	W. Keen Butcher		
1949	H. Hunter Lott Jr.	1997	Rob Hill		
1950	Edward J. Hahn	1998	Rob Hill		
1951	Edward J. Hahn	1999	Rob Hill		
1952	Harry B. Conlon	2000	Thomas Harrity		
1953	Ernest Howard	2001	Rob Hill		
1954	G. Diehl Mateer Jr.	2002	Gary Waite		
1955	Henri R. Salaun	2003	Thomas Harrity		
1956	G. Diehl Mateer Jr.				
1957	Henri R. Salaun				
1958	Henri R. Salaun				

National Women's Champions

HARD BALL		HARD BALL (Cont.)		SOFT BALL	
Year	Champion	Year	Champion	Year	Champion
1928	Eleanora Sears	1965	Joyce Davenport	1983	Alicia McConnell
1929	Margaret Howe	1966	Betty Meade	1984	Julie Harris
1930	Hazel Wightman	1967	Betty Meade	1985	Sue Clinch
1931	Ruth Banks	1968	Betty Meade	1986	Julie Harris
1932	Margaret Howe	1969	Joyce Davenport	1987	Diana Staley
1933	Susan Noel	1970	Nina Moyer	1988	Sara Luther
1934	Margaret Howe	1971	Carol Thesieres	1989	Nancy Gengler
1935	Margot Lumb	1972	Nina Moyer	1990	Joyce Maycock
1936	Anne Page	1973	Gretchen Spruance	1991	Ellie Pierce
1937	Anne Page	1974	Gretchen Spruance	1992	Demer Holleran
1938	Cecile Bowes	1975	Ginny Akabane	1993	Demer Holleran
1939	Anne Page	1976	Gretchen Spruance	1994	Demer Holleran
1940	Cecile Bowes	1977	Gretchen Spruance	1995	Ellie Pierce
1941	Cecile Bowes	1978	Gretchen Spruance	1996	Demer Holleran
1942–46	No tournament	1979	Heather McKay	1997	Demer Holleran
1947	Anne Page Homer	1980	Barbara Maltby	1998	Latasha Khan
1948	Cecile Bowes	1981	Barbara Maltby	1999	Demer Holleran
1949	Janet Morgan	1982	Alicia McConnell	2000	Latasha Khan
1950	Betty Howe	1983	Alicia McConnell	2001	Shabana Khan
1951	Jane Austin	1984	Alicia McConnell	2002	Latasha Khan
1952	Margaret Howe	1985	Alicia McConnell	2003	Latasha Khan
1953	Margaret Howe	1986	Alicia McConnell		
1954	Lois Dilks	1987	Alicia McConnell		
1955	Janet Morgan	1988	Alicia McConnell		
1956	Betty Howe Constable	1986	Alicia McConnell		
1957	Betty Howe Constable	1987	Alicia McConnell		
1958	Betty Howe Constable	1988	Alicia McConnell		
1959	Betty Howe Constable	1989	Demer Holleran		
1960	Margaret Varner	1990	Demer Holleran		
1961	Margaret Varner	1991	Demer Holleran		
1962	Margaret Varner	1992	Demer Holleran		
1963	Margaret Varner	1993	Demer Holleran		
1964	Ann Wetzel	1994	Demer Holleran		

Note: Tournament not held since 1994.

THEY SAID IT

Lance Armstrong, U.S. cyclist, after suffering minor injuries in a 35-rider pileup on the first full leg of the 2003 Tour de France: "It's never good to crash."

Triathlon

Ironman World Championship

MEN			WOMEN		
Year	**Winner**	**Time**	**Year**	**Winner**	**Time**
1978	Gordon Haller	11:46	1978	No finishers	
1979	Tom Warren	11:15:56	1979	Lyn Lemaire	12:55
1980	Dave Scott	9:24:33	1980	Robin Beck	11:21:24
1981	John Howard	9:38:29	1981	Linda Sweeney	12:00:32
1982	Scott Tinley	9:19:41	1982	Kathleen McCartney	11:09:40
1982	Dave Scott	9:08:23	1982	Julie Leach	10:54:08
1983	Dave Scott	9:05:57	1983	Sylviane Puntous	10:43:36
1984	Dave Scott	8:54:20	1984	Sylviane Puntous	10:25:13
1985	Scott Tinley	8:50:54	1985	Joanne Ernst	10:25:22
1986	Dave Scott	8:28:37	1986	Paula Newby-Fraser	9:49:14
1987	Dave Scott	8:34:13	1987	Erin Baker	9:35:25
1988	Scott Molina	8:31:00	1988	Paula Newby-Fraser	9:01:01
1989	Mark Allen	8:09:15	1989	Paula Newby-Fraser	9:00:56
1990	Mark Allen	8:28:17	1990	Erin Baker	9:13:42
1991	Mark Allen	8:18:32	1991	Paula Newby-Fraser	9:07:52
1992	Mark Allen	8:09:09	1992	Paula Newby-Fraser	8:55:29
1993	Mark Allen	8:07:46	1993	Paula Newby-Fraser	8:58:23
1994	Greg Welch	8:20:27	1994	Paula Newby-Fraser	9:20:14
1995	Mark Allen	8:20:34	1995	Karen Smyers	9:16:46
1996	Luc Van Lierde	8:04:08	1996	Paula Newby-Fraser	9:06:49
1997	Thomas Hellriegel	8:33:01	1997	Heather Fuhr	9:31:43
1998	Peter Reid	8:24:20	1998	Natascha Badmann	9:24:16
1999	Luc Van Lierde	8:17:17	1999	Lori Bowden	9:13:02
2000	Peter Reid	8:21:01	2000	Natascha Badmann	9:26:17
2001	Tim DeBoom	8:31:18	2001	Natascha Badmann	9:28:37
2002	Tim DeBoom	8:29:56	2002	Natascha Badmann	9:07:54

Note: The Ironman Championship was contested twice in 1982.

Sites: Waikiki Beach (1978–79); Ala Moana Park (1980); Kailua-Kona (since 1981).

U.S. Triathlon National Champions*

MEN		MEN (CONT.)		WOMEN		WOMEN (CONT.)	
Year	**Winner**	**Year**	**Winner**	**Year**	**Winner**	**Year**	**Winner**
1984	Scott Molina	1995	Jeff Devlin	1984	Beth Mitchell	1992	Karen Smyers
1985	Scott Molina	1996	Jeff Devlin	1985	L. Buchanan	1993	Karen Smyers
1986	Scott Molina	1997	Cameron Wydoff	1986	Kirsten Hanssen	1994	Karen Smyers
1987	Mike Pigg					1995	Karen Smyers
1988	Mike Pigg	1998	Hunter Kemper	1987	Kirsten Hanssen	1996	Susan Latshaw
1989	Ken Glah	1999	Hunter Kemper			1997	Sian Welch
1990	Scott Molina	2000	Marcel Viffian	1988	Colleen Cannon Kaushansky	1998	Siri Lindley
1991	Mike Pigg					1999	Barb Lindquist
1992	Mike Pigg	2001	Hunter Kemper	1989	Jan Ripple	2000	Joanna Zeiger
1993	Bill Braun	2002	Seth Wealing	1990	Karen Smyers	2001	Karen Smyers
1994	Scott Molina			1991	Karen Smyers	2002	Barb Lindquist

*Olympic distances: 1.5 km swim, 40km bike, 10km run.

Volleyball

World Champions

MEN		
Year	**Winner**	**Runner-up**	**Site**
1949	Soviet Union	Czechoslovakia	Prague
1952	Soviet Union	Czechoslovakia	Moscow
1956	Czechoslovakia	Soviet Union	Paris
1960	Soviet Union	Czechoslovakia	Rio de Janeiro
1962	Soviet Union	Czechoslovakia	Moscow
1966	Czechoslovakia	Romania	Prague
1970	East Germany	Bulgaria	Sofia, Bulgaria
1974	Poland	Soviet Union	Mexico City
1978	Soviet Union	Italy	Rome
1982	Soviet Union	Brazil	Buenos Aires
1986	United States	Soviet Union	Paris
1990	Italy	Cuba	Rio de Janeiro
1994	Italy	Netherlands	Athens
1998	Italy	Yugoslavia	Tokyo
2002	Brazil	Russia	Buenos Aires

World Champions (Cont.)

WOMEN

Year	Winner	Runner-up	Site
1952	Soviet Union	Poland	Moscow
1956	Soviet Union	Romania	Paris
1960	Soviet Union	Japan	Rio de Janeiro
1962	Japan	Soviet Union	Moscow
1966	Japan	United States	Prague
1970	Soviet Union	Japan	Sofia, Bulgaria
1974	Japan	Soviet Union	Mexico City
1978	Cuba	Japan	Rome
1982	China	Peru	Lima, Peru
1986	China	Cuba	Prague
1990	Soviet Union	China	Beijing
1994	Cuba	Brazil	Sao Paulo, Brazil
1998	Cuba	China	Osaka, Japan
2002	Italy	United States	Berlin

U.S. Men's Open Champions—Gold Division

1928	Germantown, PA YMCA	1966	Sand & Sea Club, CA
1929	Hyde Park YMCA, IL	1967	Fresno, CA VBC
1930	Hyde Park YMCA, IL	1968	Westside JCC, Los Angeles, CA
1931	San Antonio, TX YMCA	1969	Los Angeles, CA YMCA
1932	San Antonio, TX YMCA	1970	Chart House, San Diego
1933	Houston, TX YMCA	1971	Santa Monica, CA YMCA
1934	Houston, TX YMCA	1972	Chart House, San Diego
1935	Houston, TX YMCA	1973	Chuck's Steak, Los Angeles
1936	Houston, TX YMCA	1974	UC Santa Barbara, CA
1937	Duncan YMCA, IL	1975	Chart House, San Diego
1938	Houston, TX YMCA	1976	Malibu, Los Angeles
1939	Houston, TX YMCA	1977	Chuck's, Santa Barbara
1940	Los Angeles AC, CA	1978	Chuck's, Los Angeles
1941	North Ave. YMCA, IL	1979	Nautilus, Long Beach CA
1942	North Ave. YMCA, IL	1980	Olympic Club, San Francisco
1943–44	No championships	1981	Nautilus, Long Beach CA
1945	North Ave. YMCA, IL	1982	Chuck's, Los Angeles
1946	Pasadena, CA YMCA	1983	Nautilus Pacifica, CA
1947	North Ave. YMCA, IL	1984	Nautilus Pacifica, CA
1948	Hollywood, CA YMCA	1985	Molten/SSI Torrance, CA
1949	Downtown YMCA, CA	1986	Molten, Torrance, CA
1950	Long Beach, CA YMCA	1987	Molten, Torrance, CA
1951	Hollywood, CA YMCA	1988	Molten, Torrance, CA
1952	Hollywood, CA YMCA	1989	Not held
1953	Hollywood, CA YMCA	1990	Nike, Carson, CA
1954	Stockton, CA YMCA	1991	Offshore, Woodland Hills, CA
1955	Stockton, CA YMCA	1992	Creole Six Pack, Elmhurst, NY
1956	Hollywood, CA YMCA Stars	1993	Asics, Huntington Beach, CA
1957	Hollywood, CA YMCA Stars	1994	Asics/Paul Mitchell, Hunt. Beach, CA
1958	Hollywood, CA YMCA Stars	1995	Shakter, Belagarad, Ukraine
1959	Hollywood, CA YMCA Stars	1996	POL-AM-VBC, Brooklyn, NY
1960	Westside JCC, CA	1997	Canuck Stuff VBC, Calgary
1961	Hollywood, CA YMCA	1998	T-Town, Tulsa, OK
1962	Hollywood, CA YMCA	1999	Los Angeles Athletic Club,
1963	Hollywood, CA YMCA	2000	Paul Mitchell, Huntington Beach, CA
1964	Hollywood, CA YMCA Stars	2001	Los Angeles Athletic Club,
1965	Westside JCC, CA	2002	Paul Mitchell, Huntington Beach, CA
		2003	Paul Mitchell, Huntington Beach, CA

U.S. Women's Open Champions—Gold Division

1949	Eagles, Houston
1950	Voit #1, Santa Monica, CA
1951	Eagles, Houston
1952	Voit #1, Santa Monica, CA
1953	Voit #1, Los Angeles
1954	Houstonettes, Houston, TX
1955	Mariners, Santa Monica, CA
1956	Mariners, Santa Monica, CA
1957	Mariners, Santa Monica, CA
1958	Mariners, Santa Monica, CA
1959	Mariners, Santa Monica, CA
1960	Mariners, Santa Monica, CA
1961	Breakers, Long Beach, CA
1962	Shamrocks, Long Beach, CA
1963	Shamrocks, Long Beach, CA
1964	Shamrocks, Long Beach, CA
1965	Shamrocks, Long Beach, CA
1966	Renegades, Los Angeles
1967	Shamrocks, Long Beach, CA
1968	Shamrocks, Long Beach, CA
1969	Shamrocks, Long Beach, CA
1970	Shamrocks, Long Beach, CA
1971	Renegades, Los Angeles
1972	E Pluribus Unum, Houston
1973	E Pluribus Unum, Houston
1974	Renegades, Los Angeles
1975	Adidas, Norwalk, CA
1976	Pasadena, TX
1977	Spoilers, Hermosa, CA
1978	Nick's, Los Angeles
1979	Mavericks, Los Angeles
1980	NAVA, Fountain Valley, CA
1981	Utah State, Logan, UT
1982	Monarchs, Hilo, HI
1983	Syntex, Stockton, CA
1984	Chrysler, Palo Alto, CA
1985	Merrill Lynch, AZ
1986	Merrill Lynch, AZ
1987	Chrysler, Pleasanton, CA
1988	Chrysler, Hayward, CA
1989	Plymouth, Hayward, CA
1990	Plymouth, Hayward, CA
1991	Fitness, Champaign, IL
1992	Nick's Kronies, Chicago
1993	Nick's Fishmarket, Chicago
1994	Nick's Fishmarket, Chicago
1995	Kittleman/Branfield's/Nick's, Chi.
1996	Pure Texas Nuts, Austin, TX
1997	Kittleman/Branfield's/Nick's, Chi.
1998	The Exterminators, Barrington, IL
1999	Dominican Dream Team, Santo Domingo, D.R.
2000	Dominican Dream Team II, Santo Domingo, D.R.
2001	Dominican Dream Team III, Santo Domingo, D.R.
2002	Team Trim, Long Beach, CA
2003	The Exterminators, Barrington, IL

Wrestling

United States National Champions
1983

FREESTYLE

105.5	Rich Salamone
114.5	Joe Gonzales
125.5	Joe Corso
136.5	Rich Dellagatta*
149.5	Bill Hugent
163	Lee Kemp
180.5	Chris Campbell
198	Pete Bush

FREESTYLE (Cont.)

220	Greg Gibson
Hvy	Bruce Baumgartner
Team	Sunkist Kids

GRECO-ROMAN

105.5	T.J. Jones
114.5	Mark Fuller
125.5	Rob Hermann

GRECO-ROMAN (Cont.)

136.5	Dan Mello
149.5	Jim Martinez
163	James Andre
180.5	Steve Goss
198	Steve Fraser*
220	Dennis Koslowski
Hvy	No champion
Team	Minn. Wrestling Club

1984

FREESTYLE

105.5	Rich Salamone
114.5	Charlie Heard
125.5	Joe Corso
136.5	Rich Dellagatta*
149.5	Andre Metzger
163	Dave Schultz*
180.5	Mark Schultz
198	Steve Fraser

FREESTYLE (Cont.)

220	Harold Smith
Hvy	Bruce Baumgartner
Team	Sunkist Kids

GRECO-ROMAN

105.5	T.J. Jones
114.5	Mark Fuller
136.5	Dan Mello

GRECO-ROMAN (Cont.)

149.5	Jim Martinez*
163	John Matthews
180.5	Tom Press
198	Mike Houck
220	No champion
Hvy	No champion
Team	Adirondack 3-Style, WA

1985

FREESTYLE

105.5	Tim Vanni
114.5	Jim Martin
125.5	Charlie Heard
136.5	Darryl Burley
149.5	Bill Nugent*
163	Kenny Monday
180.5	Mike Sheets
198	Mark Schultz

FREESTYLE (Cont.)

220	Greg Gibson
286	Bruce Baumgartner
Team	Sunkist Kids

GRECO-ROMAN

105.5	T.J. Jones
114.5	Mark Fuller
125.5	Eric Seward*

GRECO-ROMAN (Cont.)

136.5	Buddy Lee
149.5	Jim Martinez
163	David Butler
180.5	Chris Catallo
198	Mike Houck
220	Greg Gibson
286	Dennis Koslowski
Team	U.S. Marine Corps

United States National Champions (Cont.)

1986

FREESTYLE

105.5 ....Rich Salamone
114.5 ....Joe Gonzales
125.5 ....Kevin Darkus
136.5 ....John Smith
149.5 ....Andre Metzger*
163 ....Dave Schultz
180.5 ....Mark Schultz
198 ....Jim Scherr
220 ....Dan Severn

FREESTYLE *(Cont.)*

286 ....Bruce Baumgartner
Team ....Sunkist Kids (Div. I)
　　　　　　Hawkeye Wrestling
　　　　　　Club (Div. II)

GRECO-ROMAN

105.5 ....Eric Wetzel
114.5 ....Shawn Sheldon
125.5 ....Anthony Amado

GRECO-ROMAN *(Cont.)*

136.5 ....Frank Famiano
149.5 ....Jim Martinez
163 ....David Butler*
180.5 ....Darryl Gholar
198 ....Derrick Waldroup
220 ....Dennis Koslowski
286 ....Duane Koslowski
Team .......U.S. Marine Corps (Div. I)
　　　　　　U.S. Navy (Div. II)

1987

FREESTYLE

105.5 ....Takashi Irie
114.5 ....Mitsuru Sato
125.5 ....Barry Davis
136.5 ....Takumi Adachi
149.5 ....Andre Metzger
163 ..,......Dave Schultz*
180.5 ....Mark Schultz
198 ....Jim Scherr
220 ....Bill Scherr

FREESTYLE *(Cont.)*

286 ....Bruce Baumgartner
Team ....Sunkist Kids (Div. I)
　　　　　　Team Foxcatcher (Div. II)

GRECO-ROMAN

105.5 ....Eric Wetzel
114.5 ....Shawn Sheldon
125.5 ....Eric Seward
136.5 ....Frank Famiano

GRECO-ROMAN *(Cont.)*

149.5 ....Jim Martinez
163 ....David Butler
180.5 ....Chris Catallo
198 ....Derrick Waldroup*
220 ....Dennis Koslowski
286 ....Duane Koslowski
Team........U.S. Marine Corp (Div. I)
　　　　　　U.S. Army (Div. II)

1988

FREESTYLE

105.5 ....Tim Vanni
114.5 ....Joe Gonzales
125.5 ....Kevin Darkus
136.5 ....John Smith*
149.5 ....Nate Carr
163 ....Kenny Monday
180.5 ....Dave Schultz
198 ....Melvin Douglas III
220 ....Bill Scherr

FREESTYLE *(Cont.)*

286 ....Bruce Baumgartner
Team ....Sunkist Kids (Div. I)
　　　　　　Team Foxcatcher (Div. II)

GRECO-ROMAN

105.5 .......T.J. Jones
114.5 ....Shawn Sheldon
125.5 ....Gogi Parseghian*
136.5 ....Dalen Wasmund

GRECO-ROMAN *(Cont.)*

149.5 ....Craig Pollard
163 ....Tony Thomas
180.5 ....Darryl Gholar
198 ....Mike Carolan
220 ....Dennis Koslowski
286 ....Duane Koslowski
Team .......U.S. Marine Corps (Div. I)
　　　　　　Sunkist Kids (Div. II)

1989

FREESTYLE

105.5 ....Tim Vanni
114.5 ....Zeke Jones
125.5 ....Brad Penrith
136.5 ....John Smith
149.5 ....Nate Carr
163 ....Rob Koll
180.5 ....Rico Chiapparelli
198 ....Jim Scherr*
220 ....Bill Scherr

FREESTYLE *(Cont.)*

286 ....Bruce Baumgartner
Team ....Sunkist Kids (Div. I)
　　　　　　Team Foxcatcher (Div. II)

GRECO-ROMAN

105.5 ....Lew Dorrance
114.5 ....Mark Fuller
125.5 ....Gogi Parseghian
136.5 ....Isaac Anderson

GRECO-ROMAN *(Cont.)*

149.5 ....Andy Seras*
163 ....David Butler
180.5 ....John Morgan
198 ....Michial Foy
220 ....Steve Lawson
286 ....Craig Pittman
Team .......U.S. Marine Corps (Div. I)
　　　　　　Jets USA (Div. II)

1990

FREESTYLE

105.5 ....Rob Eiter
114.5 ....Zeke Jones
125.5 ....Joe Melchiore
136.5 ....John Smith
149.5 ....Nate Carr
163 ....Rob Koll
180.5 ....Royce Alger
198 ....Chris Campbell*
220 ....Bill Scherr

FREESTYLE *(Cont.)*

286 ....Bruce Baumgartner
Team ....Sunkist Kids (Div. I)
　　　　　　Team Foxcatcher (Div. II)

GRECO-ROMAN

105.5 ....Lew Dorrance
114.5 ....Sam Henson
125.5 ....Mark Pustelnik
136.5 ....Isaac Anderson

GRECO-ROMAN *(Cont.)*

149.5 ....Andy Seras
163 ....David Butler
180.5 ....Derrick Waldroup
198 ....Randy Couture*
220 ....Chris Tironi
286 ....Matt Ghaffari
Team ....Jets USA (Div. I)
　　　　　　California Jets (Div. II)

*Outstanding wrestler.

United States National Champions *(Cont.)*

1991

FREESTYLE

105.5	Tim Vanni
114.5	Zeke Jones
125.5	Brad Penrith
136.5	John Smith*
149.5	Townsend Saunders
163	Kenny Monday
180.5	Kevin Jackson
198	Chris Campbell
220	Mark Coleman

FREESTYLE *(Cont.)*

286	Bruce Baumgartner
Team	Sunkist Kids (Div. I)
	Jets USA (Div. II)

GRECO-ROMAN

105.5	Eric Wetzel
114.5	Shawn Sheldon
125.5	Frank Famiano
136.5	Buddy Lee

GRECO-ROMAN *(Cont.)*

149.5	Andy Seras
163	Gordy Morgan
180.5	John Morgan*
198	Michial Foy
220	Dennis Koslowski
286	Craig Pittman
Team	Jets USA (Div. I)
	Sunkist Kids (Div. II)

1992

FREESTYLE

105.5	Rob Eiter
114.5	Jack Griffin
125.5	Kendall Cross*
136.5	John Fisher
149.5	Matt Demaray
163	Greg Elinsky
180.5	Royce Alger
198	Dan Chaid
220	Bill Scherr

FREESTYLE *(Cont.)*

286	Bruce Baumgartner
Team	Sunkist Kids (Div. I)
	Team Foxcatcher (Div. II)

GRECO-ROMAN

105.5	Eric Wetzel
114.5	Mark Fuller
125.5	Dennis Hall
136.5	Buddy Lee*

GRECO-ROMAN *(Cont.)*

149.5	Rodney Smith
163	Travis West
180.5	John Morgan
198	Michial Foy
220	Dennis Koslowski
286	Matt Ghaffari
Team	NY Athletic Club (Div. I)
	Sunkist Kids (Div. II)

1993

FREESTYLE

105.5	Rob Eiter
114.5	Zeke Jones
125.5	Brad Penrith
136.5	Tom Brands
149.5	Matt Demaray
163	Dave Schultz*
180.5	Kevin Jackson
198	Melvin Douglas
220	Kirk Trost

FREESTYLE *(Cont.)*

286	Bruce Baumgartner
Team	Sunkist Kids (Div. I)
	Team Foxcatcher (Div. II)

GRECO-ROMAN

105.5	Eric Wetzel
114.5	Shawn Sheldon
125.5	Dennis Hall*
136.5	Shon Lewis

GRECO-ROMAN *(Cont.)*

149.5	Andy Seras
163	Gordy Morgan
180.5	Dan Henderson
198	Randy Couture
220	James Johnson
286	Matt Ghaffari
Team	NY Athletic Club (Div. I)
	Sunkist Kids (Div. II)

1994

FREESTYLE

105.5	Tim Vanni
114.5	Zeke Jones
125.5	Terry Brands
136.5	Tom Brands
149.5	Matt Demaray
163	Dave Schultz
180.5	Royce Alger
198	Melvin Douglas
220	Mark Kerr

FREESTYLE *(Cont.)*

286	Bruce Baumgartner*
Team	Sunkist Kids (Div. I)
	Team Foxcatcher (Div. II)

GRECO-ROMAN

105.5	Isaac Ramaswamy
114.5	Shawn Sheldon
125.5	Dennis Hall
136.5	Shon Lewis

GRECO-ROMAN *(Cont.)*

149.5	Andy Seras*
163	Gordy Morgan
180.5	Dan Henderson
198	Derrick Waldroup

GRECO-ROMAN *(Cont.)*

220	James Johnson
286	Matt Ghaffari
Team	Armed Forces (Div. I)
	NY Athletic Club (Div. II)

1995

FREESTYLE

105.5	Rob Eiter
114.5	Lou Rosselli
125.5	Kendall Cross*
136.5	Tom Brands
149.5	Matt Demaray
163	Dave Schultz
180.5	Kevin Jackson
198	Melvin Douglas
220	Kurt Angle

FREESTYLE *(Cont.)*

286	Bruce Baumgartner
Team	Sunkist Kids (Div. I)
	Team Foxcatcher (Div. II)

GRECO-ROMAN

105.5	Isaac Ramaswamy
114.5	Shawn Sheldon
125.5	Dennis Hall*
136.5	Van Fronhofer

GRECO-ROMAN *(Cont.)*

149.5	Heath Sims
163	Matt Lindland
180.5	Marty Morgan
198	Michial Foy
220	James Johnson
286	Rulon Gardner
Team	Armed Forces (Div. I)
	Sunkist Kids (Div. II)

*Outstanding wrestler.

United States National Champions *(Cont.)*

1996

FREESTYLE

105.5 ....Rob Eiter
114.5 ....Lou Rosselli
125.5 ....Kendall Cross
136.5 ....Tom Brands
149.5 ....Townsend Saunders
163 ....Kenny Monday
180.5 ....Les Gutches*
198 ....Melvin Douglas
220 ....Kurt Angle

FREESTYLE *(Cont.)*

286 ....Bruce Baumgartner
Team ....Sunkist Kids (Div. I)
            NY Athletic Club (Div. II)

GRECO-ROMAN

105.5 ....Mujaahid Maynard
114.5 ....Shawn Sheldon
125.5 ....Dennis Hall*
136.5 ....Shon Lewis

GRECO-ROMAN *(Cont.)*

149.5 ....Rodney Smith
163 ....Keith Sieracki
180.5 ....Marty Morgan
198 ....Michial Foy
220 ....John Oostendrop
286 ....Matt Ghaffari
Team ....Armed Forces (Div. I)
            Sunkist Kids (Div. II)

1997

FREESTYLE

110 ....Kanamti Soloman
119 ....Zeke Jones
127.75 ....Terry Brands
138.75 ....Carl Kolat
152 ....Lincoln McIlravy*
167.5 ....Dan St. John
187.25 ....Les Gutches
213.75 ....Melvin Douglas

FREESTYLE *(Cont.)*

275.5 ....Tom Erikson
Team ....Sunkist Kids (Div. I)
            NY Athletic Club (Div. II)

GRECO-ROMAN

110 ....Mark Yanagihara
119 ....Broderick Lee
127.75 ....Dennis Hall

GRECO-ROMAN *(Cont.)*

138.75 ....Kevin Bracken
152 ....Chris Saba
167.5 ....Miguel Spencer
187.25 ....Dan Henderson
213.75 ....Randy Couture*
275.5 ....Rulon Gardner
Team ....Armed Forces (Div. I)
            NY Athletic Club (Div. II)

1998

FREESTYLE

119 ....Sam Henson
127.75 ....Tony Purler
138.75 ....Shawn Charles
152 ....Lincoln McIlravy
167.5 ....Steve Marianetti
187.25 ....Les Gutches*
213.75 ....Melvin Douglas

FREESTYLE *(Cont.)*

286 ....Tolly Thompson
Team ....Sunkist Kids (Div. I)
            NY Athletic Club (Div. II)

GRECO-ROMAN

119 ....Shawn Sheldon
127.75 ....Dennis Hall
138.75 ....Shon Lewis

GRECO-ROMAN *(Cont.)*

152 ....Chris Saba
167.5 ....Matt Lindland
187.25 ....Dan Niebuhr*
213.75 ....Jason Klohs
286 ....Matt Ghaffari
Team ....Armed Forces (Div. I)
            Sunkist Kids (Div. II)

1999

FREESTYLE

119 ....Lou Rosselli
127.75 ....Terry Brands
138.75 ....Cary Kolat
152 ....Lincoln McIlravy
167.5 ....Joe Williams
187.25 ....Les Gutches
213.75 ....Dominic Black

FREESTYLE *(Cont.)*

286 ....Stephen Neal*
Team ....Sunkist Kids (Div. I)
            NY Athletic Club (Div. II)

GRECO-ROMAN

119 ....Steven Mays
127.75 ....Dennis Hall
138.75 ....Glen Nieradka

GRECO-ROMAN *(Cont.)*

152 ....David Zuniga
167.5 ....Matt Lindland
187.25 ....Quincey Clark
213.75 ....Randy Couture
286 ....Dremiel Byers*
Team ....Minnesota Storm (Div. I)
            Sunkist Kids (Div. II)

2000

FREESTYLE

119 ....Sammie Henson
127.75 ....Keyy Boumans
138.75 ....Cary Kolat
152 ....Lincoln McIlravy
167.5 ....Brandon Slay*
187.25 ....Les Gutches
213.75 ....Melvin Douglas

FREESTYLE *(Cont.)*

286 ....Kerry McCoy
Team ....Sunkist Kids (Div. I)
            NY Athletic Club (Div. II)

GRECO-ROMAN

119 ....Brandon Paulson
127.75 ....Dennis Hall
138.75 ....Kevin Bracken

GRECO-ROMAN *(Cont.)*

152 ....Heath Sims
167.5 ....Matt Lindland
187.25 ....Quincey Clark*
213.75 ....Jason Gleasman
286 ....Rulon Gardner
Team ....Armed Forces (Div. I)
            Sunkist Kids (Div. II)

*Outstanding wrestler.

United States National Champions (Cont.)

2001

FREESTYLE	
119	Eric Akin
127.75	Eric Guerrero
138.75	Bill Zadick
152	Ramico Blackmon
167.5	Joe Williams
187.25	Cael Sanderson*
213.75	Dominic Black

FREESTYLE (Cont.)	
286	Kerry McCoy
Team	Sunkist Kids (Div. I)
	New York AC (Div. II)

GRECO-ROMAN	
119	Jeff Cervone
127.75	Dennis Hall
138.75	Kevin Bracken

GRECO-ROMAN (Cont.)	
152	Marcel Cooper
167.5	Keith Sieracki
187.25	Matt Lindland*
213.75	Garrett Lowney
286	Rulon Gardner
Team	Army (Div. I)
	Sunkist Kids (Div. II)

2002

FREESTYLE	
121	Teague Moore
132	Eric Guerrero
145.5	Bill Zadick
163	Joe Williams*
185	Cael Sanderson
211.5	Tim Hartung
264.5	Kerry McCoy

FREESTYLE (Cont.)	
Team	Sunkist Kids (Div. I)
	New York AC (Div. II)

GRECO-ROMAN	
121	Brandon Paulson
132	Glenn Nieradka*
145.5	Kevin Bracken

GRECO-ROMAN (Cont.)	
163	Keith Sieracki
185	Ethan Bosch
211.75	Garrett Lowney
264.5	Dremiel Byers
Team	Army (Div. I)
	New York AC (Div. II)

2003

FREESTYLE	
121	Stephen Abas
132	Eric Guerrero*
145.5	Chris Bono
163	Joe Williams
185	Cael Sanderson
211.5	Daniel Cormier
264.5	Kerry McCoy

FREESTYLE (Cont.)	
Team	Sunkist Kids (Div. I)
	Gator WC (Div. II)

GRECO-ROMAN	
121	Brandon Paulson
132	James Gruenwald*
145.5	Kevin Bracken

GRECO-ROMAN (Cont.)	
163	Keith Sieracki
185	Brad Vering
211.5	Garrett Lowney
264.5	Dremiel Byers
Team	Army (Div. I)
	Air Force (Div. II)

*Outstanding wrestler.

Wade Till Next Year

The kind people who bring us the *Women in Waders* calendar—basically a year of fly models fly-fishing—have just released their newest calendar, *Beauty and the Bass*. Melinda Hoeyne and Gary Garrison, a married couple from Eugene, Ore., have built a thriving business out of a boot fetish. "We'd go fishing and he'd like to see me in the waders," said Hoeyne. "Gary's buddies always kidded him about his woman in waders. It was such a catchy title we decided to make a calendar out of it." After their debut offering sold 5,000 copies in Oregon tackle-and-bait shops three years ago, they quit their jobs running a recording studio and devoted themselves full time to their booty call. Garrison, 51, does the camera work and helps Hoeyne, 28, manage their company. Thanks to the Internet (womeninwaders.com), they sell more than 20,000 calendars a year for $12.95 each.

The Sports Market

Superstar-in-waiting
LeBron James

Heavy Trading

Big-spending owners, heavily marketed stars and best-selling books made for an eventful year in sports business

BY MERRELL NODEN

THE SPORTS BUSINESS megastar of 2003 spent the early part of the year picking on high school kids, and for that Nike awarded him a $90 million contract even before the shoe company knew where it would be mailing his monster checks. That fellow's name, as every sports fan knows, is LeBron James, and he wound up being taken by the Cleveland Cavaliers with the first pick of the NBA draft—for a measly $12.96 million over three years. While we should be careful not to infer too much from the singular case of an athlete who owned a Hummer before he had a high school diploma, suffice it to say that in 2003 there was no sign whatsoever that sports were losing their appeal as an investment opportunity.

Not that there weren't rumblings of trouble. In a handful of cities the economy proved to be soft for specific sports—for baseball in Montreal, where the Expos played most of their home games in a nearly empty stadium; for basketball in Miami,

where the Heat asked everyone on the team's payroll to take a 10% pay cut to help offset losses of $30 million; and for women's soccer in every city where the fledgling women's pro circuit has a franchise. After losing $80 million in three seasons of existence while attracting only two corporate sponsors, the Women's United Soccer Association (WUSA) went out of business in mid-September, just five days before the start of the Women's World Cup that was supposed to boost its chances of survival. On the heels of the announcement, however, a committee was formed to attract investors and save the nascent women's league. At press time it looked like the rescue attempt would be successful.

Elsewhere, Time Warner sold two of the pro franchises it owned in Atlanta, the NBA's Hawks and the NHL's Thrashers, to Atlanta Spirit, LLC for $250 million. The media conglomerate even considered selling the jewel in its crown of sports teams, the perennial National League East divi-

Brandi Chastain and Co. had little to celebrate in 2003 as WUSA folded.

way to Chukotka, in far eastern Russia. In July, Chukotkan oil billionaire Roman Abramovich purchased Chelsea, the fashionable London soccer club, for $229 million. Abramovich reportedly had considered buying Manchester United, balking in the end not at the franchise's enormous price tag but at the fact that it would be much harder to improve the already stacked Man U than it would Chelsea. He quickly went on a Steinbrennian spending spree, shelling out £110 million for international stars such as Damien Duff of Ireland, Juan Veron of Argentina and Cameroon's Geremi.

The surprise sports business story of 2003 may have been sports books. Sports fans plunked down a lot of money for a handful of sports books. *Seabiscuit*, Laura Hillenbrand's superb tale of the extraordinary life of an underdog horse, began the year on the bestseller list and by the summer, with a boost from a misty movie starring Tobey Maguire, the paperback edition was outselling almost every other book in the country. *Seabiscuit* also proved to be a godsend to the sport of thoroughbred racing. Struggling to raise its profile for some time now, horse racing enjoyed an increase in attendence at most major tracks in 2003.

And when *Seabiscuit* began dominating the paperback lists, other sports books took over the hardcover lists, including Rick Reilly's *Who's Your Caddy?*, in which the SI columnist recounts his adventures caddying for a number of well-known golfers; John Feinstein's *Open: Inside the Ropes at Bethpage Black*, about the 2002 U.S. Open; and *Moneyball*, Michael Lewis's look at how Billy Beane, GM of the Oakland Athletics, built an extremely competitive baseball team without spending a king's ransom.

sion champion Atlanta Braves, though it eventually decided against the sale.

Whether such developments are the first hints of serious trouble for other, supposedly more robust, teams and leagues, only time will tell. For now, though, sports and the people who play them continued to be pursued as an excellent investment opportunity, whether you're talking about a 13-year-old soccer prodigy like Freddy Adu of Maryland, whom Nike signed to a $1 million contract, or the increasingly popular sport of NASCAR, which left longtime sponsor Winston in favor of Nextel for $700 million and, presumably, a glossier image.

The glitter of pro sports reached all the

(The A's, with a payroll of $56.6 million, 26th in the majors, did their part to promote the book by going on a late summer tear to overtake the Seattle Mariners in the American League West division.)

But the brainy Beane was an exception. In the world of big-time sports, money is either no object . . . or the only object. The year saw the end, one fervently hopes, of the battle for legal ownership of the ball Barry Bonds hit for his record-setting 73rd homer of the 2001 season. After 17 months of legal wrangling, San Francisco Superior Court Judge Kevin McCarthy said enough already, ruling that Alex Popov, who first caught the ball, and Patrick Hayashi, who ended up with it after a melee, must sell the ball and split the proceeds. The pair agreed to do so, and handed it over to the Barnes Sports Group of St. Louis, known for brokering the sale of Mark McGwire's 70th homer ball (from 1998) for $3 million. The sale yielded $517,500. Explained Hayashi, "Not agreeing would have damaged not only our image but the image of baseball itself." Probably a little late for that, Patrick. . . .

Cablevision, a network serving the New York tri-state area, finally agreed to carry YES, the channel which broadcasts the New York Yankees, and the New Jersey Nets and Devils. Cablevision, which owns the New York Knicks and Rangers, had wanted to charge an extra $2 per cable box. Specifics of the deal weren't revealed, but those poor publicity-starved Yankees gained another 3 million viewers.

But the year's biggest feud resisted common sense all year, and still begs a solution. It pitted Martha Burk, chairwoman of the National Council of Women's Organizations, against Hootie Johnson, chairman of the Augusta National Golf Club. When Burk learned in 2002 that Augusta has no women members and no plans to admit any, she decided to pressure the club to admit a woman. She began by writing a letter to Johnson, asking him when the club planned to admit women. Johnson did not help matters by sending a huffy reply.

Burk tried several tactics: First, she tried to shame Augusta members who happened to be the CEOs of major companies by publishing their names. She also asked major corporations which in the past had bought ads during the Masters to refuse to do so. But before Coca-Cola, IBM and Citigroup could make a decision, Johnson announced that Augusta would free them from existing contracts in order to shield them from controversy. The result was the first commercial-free broadcast of a major sporting event and a loss of $7 million in revenue to the club. During Masters weekend, Burk showed up to protest down the street from the club, but attracted only about 30 supporters. Both sides then claimed victory. No one knows how long Augusta can go on losing that sort of money, but it can't be for long.

The sports business world lost two of its visionaries this year: Mark McCormack, who built the vast sports management and promotion company, International Management Group, on a handshake deal with young Arnold Palmer, and Tex Schramm, who may not have come up with the moniker "America's Team" for his Dallas Cowboys, but did all in his power to make it stick. Both men left behind a vastly different pro sports world than the one they began their careers in.

One wonders what Schramm and McCormack would have made of some of the sports business developments of 2003. In a move that essentially dismantled the wall that is supposed to exist between professional sports and gambling, the WNBA moved its Orlando franchise to Connecticut, where, as the Sun, the team played in the belly of the Mohegan Sun casino. "There's nothing that gets you media exposure, local or national, like sports," enthused Paul Munick, who doubles as the Sun's president as well as a casino executive. No doubt that's true, but the dividing line between sports and gambling has never before been flouted quite so obviously. Despite assurances from WNBA president Valerie Ackerman that there would be "limitations and prohibitions on co-promoting gaming and basketball," many observers greeted the move with raised eyebrows.

Profit certainly seemed to be one of the biggest considerations in the University of Miami's decision to leave the Big East conference for the Atlantic Coast Conference. The Big East, understandably reluctant to lose a member that has won five national championships in the past 20 years, offered Miami $45 million over five years. Apparently, that was not enough. On June 30, Miami officially joined the ACC. Virginia Tech did too, bringing the league within one team of the dozen required for a playoff.

The Montreal Expos had identity problems as well, playing 22 "home" games in San Juan, Puerto Rico, drawing an average of 14,222 fans to the city's Estadio Hiram Bithorn. That's hardly shabby, especially since the team was drawing only 12,081 a game in Montreal, but in mid-September the Expos still didn't know where they'd be playing next season. Eventually, the franchise seems bound for one of three places that are hungry for major league baseball: Washington, D.C., the north Virginia suburbs of D.C., or Portland, OR, where voters just approved a bond issue to pay for a new stadium.

Sentimentality won't get you far in the bottom-line world of pro sports. Just prior to the primetime Battle of the Bridges, Tiger Woods decided he wanted to trade in his Nike driver for his old Titleist 975D, a driver that is no longer on the market. This cannot have pleased the folks at Nike for a number of reasons, the first of which is that in 2000 Woods signed a five-year, $100 million endorsement extension. Even worse, Woods made his decision a few months after rival Phil Mickelson had embarrassed Nike's fledging golf division by saying, in effect, that only a player as good as Woods could overcome its inferior equipment. Ouch!

Vladimir Guerrero and the Expos went 52–29 at home, which, for 22 games, was San Juan, P.R.

Even Michael Jordan, who spent the past decade as the most visible symbol of sports' power to sell products, experienced a cold blast of reality this year. When Jordan met with Washington Wizards majority owner Abe Pollin to see about resuming his role as G.M. of the struggling franchise, Pollin showed neither sentimentality nor gratitude for the many bodies Jordan drew to watch the woeful Wizards. Jordan was out.

Which brings us back to the man who may or may not be the next NBA superstar. Even if LeBron James doesn't perform like Jordan on the court, he will, for a time at least, be like Mike off it. Along with Nike, James signed endorsement deals with Upper Deck trading cards (five years for $6 million in all); Coca Cola (six years at $2 million a year); and Juice batteries for an undisclosed sum.

This is the world of sports business in 2003: James hasn't played a single game yet he's already worth well over $100 million.

Baseball Directory

Major League Baseball
Address: 245 Park Avenue
            New York, NY 10167
Telephone: (212) 931-7800
Commissioner: Bud Selig
Chief Operating Officer: Robert DuPuy
Senior VP, Public Relations: Richard Levin
www.majorleague baseball.com

Major League Baseball Players Association
Address: 12 East 49th Street, 24th Floor
            New York, NY 10017
Telephone: (212) 826-0808
Executive Director: Donald Fehr
Director of Communications: Greg Bouris
Director of Licensing: Judy Heeter
www.bigleaguers.com

Anaheim Angels
Address: P.O. Box 2000
            Anaheim, CA 92803
Telephone: (714) 940-2000
Stadium (Capacity): Edison International Field of
 Anaheim (45,050)
Owner: Arturo Moreno
General Manager: Bill Stoneman
Manager: Mike Scioscia
Vice President of Communications: Tim Mead
www.angelsbaseball.com

Arizona Diamondbacks
Address: 401 East Jefferson Street
            Phoenix, AZ 85004
Telephone: (602) 462-6500
Stadium (Capacity): Bank One Ballpark (49,033)
Managing General Partner: Jerry Colangelo
General Manager: Joe Garagiola Jr.
Manager: Bob Brenly
Director of Public Relations: Mike Swanson
www.azdiamondbacks.com

Atlanta Braves
Address: P.O. Box 4064
            Atlanta, GA 30302
Telephone: (404) 522-7630
Stadium (Capacity): Turner Field (50,091)
Vice Chrmn./Sr. Advisor of Time Warner/AOL: Ted Turner
Executive VP & General Manager: John Schuerholz
Manager: Bobby Cox
Director of Public Relations: Jim Schultz
www.atlantabraves.com

Baltimore Orioles
Address: Oriole Park at Camden Yards
            333 W Camden Street
            Baltimore, MD 21201
Telephone: (410) 685-9800
Stadium (Capacity): Oriole Park at Camden Yards
 (48,876)
Chairman of the Board/CEO: Peter G. Angelos
Vice Chairman/COO: Joseph E. Foss
Manager: TBA
Director of Public Relations: Bill Stetka
www.theorioles.com

Boston Red Sox
Address: 4 Yawkey Way
            Fenway Park
            Boston, MA 02215
Telephone: (617) 267-9440
Stadium (Capacity): Fenway Park (33,993)
Principal Owner: John W. Henry
Senior VP and General Manager: Theo Epstein
Manager: Grady Little
Director of Communications/Baseball Info: Kevin Shea
www.redsox.com

Chicago Cubs
Address: Wrigley Field
            1060 West Addison
            Chicago, IL 60613
Telephone: (773) 404-2827
Stadium (Capacity): Wrigley Field (39,111)
President and CEO: Andrew B. MacPhail
Executive VP of Business Operations: Mark McGuire
Manager: Dusty Baker
Director of Media Relations: Sharon Panozzo
www.cubs.com

Chicago White Sox
Address: Comiskey Park
            333 West 35th Street
            Chicago, IL 60616
Telephone: (312) 674-1000
Stadium (Capacity): Comiskey Park (47,098)
Chairman: Jerry Reinsdorf
General Manager: Kenny Williams
Manager: TBA
Director of Publc Relations: Scott Reifert
www.whitesox.com

Cincinnati Reds
Address: 100 Main Street
            Cincinnati, OH 45202
Telephone: (513) 765-7000
Stadium (Capacity): Great American Ball Park
(42,256)
CEO/General Partner: Carl Lindner
COO: John L. Allen
General Manager: TBA
Managing Executive: John L. Allen
Manager: TBA
Director of Media Relations: Rob Butcher
www.cincinnatireds.com

Cleveland Indians
Address: Jacobs Field
            2401 Ontario Street
            Cleveland, OH 44115-4003
Telephone: (216) 420-4200
Stadium (Capacity): Jacobs Field (43,368)
President and CEO: Lawrence J. Dolan
Executive VP and General Manager: Mark Shapiro
Manager: Eric Wedge
Vice President, Public Relations: Bob DiBiasio
www.indians.com

Colorado Rockies
Address: 2001 Blake Street
            Denver, CO 80205
Telephone: (303) 292-0200
Stadium (Capacity): Coors Field (50,449)
Chairman: Jerry D. McMorris
President: Keli McGregor
General Manager and Executive VP: Dan O'Dowd
Manager: Clint Hurdle
Senior Director of Communications/PR: Jay Alves
www.coloradorockies.com

Detroit Tigers
Address: Comerica Park
            2100 Woodward Avenue
            Detroit, MI 48201
Telephone: (313) 962-4000
Stadium (Capacity): Comerica Park (40,120)
Owner: Mike Ilitch
President and GM: Dave Dombrowski
Manager: Alan Trammell
Sr. V.P. of Marketing and Comm.: Mike Veeck
www.detroittigers.com

Baseball Directory *(Cont.)*

Florida Marlins
Address:　　2267 Dan Marino Boulevard
　　　　　　Miami, FL 33056
Telephone: (305) 626-7400
Stadium (Capacity): Pro Player Stadium (36,331)
Chairman, CEO and Managing General Partner:
Jeffrey H. Loria
President: David Samson
Senior VP and General Manager: Larry Beinfest
Manager: Jack McKeon
VP of Communications/Broadcasting:P.J. Loyello
www.floridamarlins.com

Houston Astros
Address:　　P.O. Box 288
　　　　　　Houston, TX 77001
Telephone: (713) 259-8000
Stadium (Capacity): Minute Maid Park (40,950)
Chairman: Drayton McLane
General Manager: Gerry Hunsicker
Manager: Jimy Williams
Director of Media Relations: Warren Miller
www.astros.com

Kansas City Royals
Address:　　P.O. Box 419969
　　　　　　Kansas City, MO 64141
Telephone: (816) 921-8000
Stadium (Capacity): Kauffman Stadium (40,785)
Owner and Chairman of the Board: David D. Glass
General Manager: Allard Baird
Manager: Tony Peña
Vice President, Communications: Charlie Seraphin
www.kcroyals.com

Los Angeles Dodgers
Address:　　1000 Elysian Park Avenue
　　　　　　Los Angeles, CA 90012-1199
Telephone: (323) 224-1500
Stadium (Capacity): Dodger Stadium (56,000)
Managing Partner, Chairman and CEO: Robert Daly
President and COO: Bob Graziano
General Manager: Dan Evans
Manager: Jim Tracy
Director Media Relations/Publicity: John Olguin
www.dodgers.com

Milwaukee Brewers
Address:　　1 Brewers Way
　　　　　　Milwaukee, WI 53214
Telephone: (414) 902-4400
Stadium (Capacity): Miller Park (41,900)
President and CEO: Ulice Payne Jr.
General Manager: Doug Melvin
Manager: Ned Yost
Director of Media Relations: Jon Greenberg
www.milwaukeebrewers.com

Minnesota Twins
Address:　　34 Kirby Puckett Place
　　　　　　Minneapolis, MN 55415
Telephone: (612) 375-1366
Stadium (Capacity): Hubert H. Humphrey
Metrodome (48,678)
Owner: Carl Pohlad
General Manager: Terry Ryan
Manager: Ron Gardenhire
Manager of Media Relations: Sean Harlin
www.twinsbaseball.com

Montreal Expos
Address:　　P.O. Box 500 Station M
　　　　　　Montreal, Quebec H1V 3P2 Canada
Telephone: (514) 253-3434
Stadium (Capacity): Olympic Stadium (46,500)
President: Tony Tavares

Montreal Expos *(Cont.)*
Vice President and General Manager: Omar Minaya
Manager: Frank Robinson
Director, Media Services: Monique Giroux
www.montrealexpos.com

New York Mets
Address:　　Shea Stadium
　　　　　　123-01 Roosevelt Ave.
　　　　　　Flushing, NY 11368
Telephone: (718) 507-6387
Stadium (Capacity): Shea Stadium (56,749)
Owner: Fred Wilpon
Interim General Manager: Jim Duquette
Manager: Art Howe
VP of Media Relations: Jay Horwitz
www.mets.com

New York Yankees
Address:　　Yankee Stadium
　　　　　　Bronx, NY 10451
Telephone: (718) 293-4300
Stadium (Capacity): Yankee Stadium (57,746)
Principal Owner: George Steinbrenner
Chief Operating Officer: Lonn Trost
VP/General Manager: Brian Cashman
Manager: Joe Torre
Director of Media Relations: Rick Cerone
www.yankees.com

Oakland Athletics
Address:　　7000 Coliseum Way
　　　　　　Oakland, CA 94621
Telephone: (510) 638-4900
Stadium (Capacity): Network Associates Coliseum
(43,662)
Owners: Steve Schott and Ken Hofmann
President: Michael Crowley
General Manager: Billy Beane
Manager: Ken Macha
Baseball Information Manager: Mike Selleck
www.oaklandathletics.com

Philadelphia Phillies
Address:　　P.O. Box 7575
　　　　　　Philadelphia, PA 19101-7575
Telephone: (215) 463-6000
Stadium (Capacity): Citizens Bank Park (TBA)
Chairman: Bill Giles
President: David P. Montgomery
Vice President and General Manager: Ed Wade
Manager: Larry Bowa
Vice President, Public Relations: Larry Shenk
www.phillies.com

Pittsburgh Pirates
Address:　　P.O. Box 7000
　　　　　　Pittsburgh, PA 15212
Telephone: (412) 323-5000
Stadium (Capacity): PNC Park (37,898)
CEO and Managing General Partner: Kevin McClatchy
Senior VP and General Manager: Dave Littlefield
Manager: Lloyd McClendon
Director of Media Relations: Jim Trdinich
www.pirateball.com

St. Louis Cardinals
Address:　　Busch Stadium/ 250 Stadium Plaza
　　　　　　St. Louis, MO 63102
Telephone: (314) 421-3060
Stadium (Capacity): Busch Stadium (49,814)
President: Mark Lamping
Senior Vice President and GM: Walt Jocketty
Manager: Tony LaRussa
Director of Media Relations: Brian Bartow
www.stlcardinals.com

San Diego Padres
Address: P.O. Box 122000
          San Diego, CA 92112
Telephone: (619) 283-4494
Stadium (Capacity): PETCO Park (TBA)
Chairman: John Moores
General Manager: Kevin Towers
Manager: Bruce Bochy
Director of Media Relations: Luis Garcia
www.padres.com

San Francisco Giants
Address: 24 Willie Mays Plaza
          San Francisco, CA 94107
Telephone: (415) 972-2000
Stadium (Capacity): Pacific Bell Park (41,341)
President/Managing General Partner: Peter Magowan
General Manager: Brian Sabean
Manager: Felipe Alou
Manager of Media Relations: Jim Moorehead
www.sfgiants.com

Seattle Mariners
Address: P.O. Box 4100
          Seattle, WA 98104
Telephone: (206) 346-4000
Stadium (Capacity): SAFECO Field (47,116)
Chairman and CEO: Howard Lincoln
General Manager:TBA
Manager: Bob Melvin
Director of Baseball Information: Tim Hevly
www.seattlemariners.com

Tampa Bay Devil Rays
Address: One Tropicana Drive
          St. Petersburg, FL 33705
Telephone: (727) 825-3137
Stadium (Capacity): Tropicana Field (43,761)
Managing General Partner/CEO: Vincent J. Naimoli
Senior VP and General Manager: Chuck Lamar
Manager: Lou Piniella
Vice President, Public Relations: Rick Vaughn
www.devilray.com

Texas Rangers
Address: P.O. Box 90111
          Arlington, TX 76004
Telephone: (817) 273-5222
Stadium (Capacity): The Ballpark in Arlington (49,115)
Owner: Thomas O. Hicks
General Manager: John Hart
Manager: Buck Showalter
Senior VP, Communications: John Blake
www.texasrangers.com

Toronto Blue Jays
Address: SkyDome
          1 Blue Jays Way, Suite 3200
          Toronto, Ontario M5V 1J1 Canada
Telephone: (416) 341-1000
Stadium (Capacity): SkyDome (45,100)
President/CEO: Paul Godfrey
Senior Vice President/GM: J.P. Ricciardi
Manager: Carlos Tosca
Directo of Communications: Jay Stenhouse
www.bluejays.com

Pro Football Directory

National Football League
Address: 280 Park Avenue
          New York, NY 10017
Telephone: (212) 450-2000
Commissioner: Paul Tagliabue
www.nfl.com

NFL Players Association
Address: 2021 L Street, N.W.
          Washington, D.C. 20036
Telephone: (202) 463-2200
Executive Director: Gene Upshaw
Director of Communications: Carl Francis
www.nflpa.org

Arizona Cardinals
Address: P.O. Box 888
          Phoenix, AZ 85001
Telephone: (602) 379-0101
Stadium (Capacity): Sun Devil Stadium (73,377)
President and Owner: Bill Bidwill
VP of Football Operations: Rod Graves
Head Coach: Dave McGinnis
Director of Public Relations: Paul Jensen
www.azcardinals.com

Atlanta Falcons
Address: 4400 Falcon Park Way
          Flowery Branch, GA 30542
Telephone: (770) 965-3115
Stadium (Capacity): Georgia Dome (71,228)
Owner and CEO: Arthur Blank
VP of Football Operations: Ron Hill
Coach: Dan Reeves
Director of Communications: Aaron Salkin
www.atlantafalcons.com

Baltimore Ravens
Address: 11001 Owings Mills Blvd.
          Owings Mills, MD 21117
Telephone: (410) 654-6200
Stadium (Capacity): M & T Bank Stadium(69,084)
Owner/CEO: Art Modell
President/COO: David Modell
Coach: Brian Billick
VP of Public Relations: Kevin Byrne
www.baltimoreravens.com

Buffalo Bills
Address: One Bills Drive
          Orchard Park, NY 14127
Telephone: (716) 648-1800
Stadium (Capacity): Ralph Wilson Stadium (73,967)
Chairman: Ralph C. Wilson Jr.
President and General Manager: Tom Donohoe
Coach: Gregg Williams
Vice President of Communications: Scott Berchtold
www.buffalobills.com

Carolina Panthers
Address: Ericsson Stadium
          800 South Mint St.
          Charlotte, NC 28202
Telephone: (704) 358-7000
Stadium (Capacity): Ericsson Stadium (73,258)
Founder and Owner: Jerry Richardson
President: Mark Richardson
General Manager: Marty Hurney
Coach: John Fox
Director of Communications: Charlie Dayton
www.panthers.com

Chicago Bears
Address: 1000 Football Drive
Lake Forest, IL 60045
Telephone: (847) 295-6600
Stadium (Capacity): Soldier Field (61,500)
Chairman: Michael McCaskey
President/CEO: Ted Phillips
Coach: Dick Jauron
Director of Public Relations: Scott Hagel
www.chicagobears.com

Cincinnati Bengals
Address: One Paul Brown Stadium
Cincinnati, OH 45202
Telephone: (513) 621-3550
Stadium (Capacity): Paul Brown Stadium (65,327)
President: Mike Brown
Executive Vice President: Katherine Blackburn
Coach: Marvin Lewis
Director of Public Relations: Jack Brennan
www.bengals.com

Cleveland Browns
Address: 76 Lou Groza Boulevard
Berea, OH 44017
Telephone: (440) 891-5000
Stadium (Capacity): Cleveland Browns Stadium
(73,200)
Owner: Randy Lerner
VP Player Personnel/Football Dev.: Pete Garcia
Coach: Butch Davis
Exec. Director of Communications: Todd Stewart
www.clevelandbrowns.com

Dallas Cowboys
Address: One Cowboys Parkway
Irving, TX 75063
Telephone: (972) 556-9900
Stadium (Capacity): Texas Stadium (65,639)
Owner, President and General Manager: Jerry Jones
Coach: Bill Parcells
Public Relations Director: Rich Dalrymple
www.dallascowboys.com

Denver Broncos
Address: 13655 Broncos Parkway
Englewood, CO 80112
Telephone: (303) 649-9000
Stadium (Capacity): INVESCO Field at Mile High
(76,125)
President and Chief Executive Officer: Pat Bowlen
General Manager: Ted Sundquist
Coach: Mike Shanahan
VP of Public Relations: Jim Saccomano
www.denverbroncos.com

Detroit Lions
Address: 222 Republic Drive
Allen Park, MI 48101
Telephone: (313) 216-4000
Stadium (Capacity): Ford Field (65,000)
Owner/Chairman: William Clay Ford
President/CEO: Matt Millen
Coach: Steve Mariucci
Director of Media Relations: Matt Barnhart
www.detroitlions.com

Green Bay Packers
Address: 1265 Lombardi Avenue
Green Bay, WI 54304
Telephone: (920) 496-5700
Stadium (Capacity): Lambeau Field (72,515)
President: Bob Harlan
Executive VP/GM/Coach: Mike Sherman
Executive Director of Public Relations: Lee Remmel
www.packers.com

Houston Texans
Address: Two Reliant Park
Houston, TX 77054
Telephone: (832) 667-2000
Stadium (Capacity): Reliant Stadium (71,054)
Chairman and CEO: Robert C. McNair
Senior VP and General Manager: Charley Casserly
Coach: Dom Capers
Media Realtions Manager: Rocky Harris
www.houstontexans.com

Indianapolis Colts
Address: P.O. Box 535000
Indianapolis, IN 46253
Telephone: (317) 297-2658
Stadium (Capacity): RCA Dome (56,127)
Owner and Chief Executive Officer: Jim Irsay
President: Bill Polian
Senior Executive Vice President: Pete Ward
Coach: Tony Dungy
Vice President of Public Relations: Craig Kelley
www.colts.com

Jacksonville Jaguars
Address: One Alltel Stadium Place
Jacksonville, FL 32202
Telephone: (904) 633-6000
Stadium (Capacity): Alltel Stadium (73,000)
Owner: J. Wayne Weaver
Vice President and CFO: Bill Prescott
Senior VP of Football Operations: Paul Vance
Coach: Jack Del Rio
VP of Communications and Media: Dan Edwards
www.jaguars.com

Kansas City Chiefs
Address: One Arrowhead Drive
Kansas City, MO 64129
Telephone: (816) 920-9300
Stadium (Capacity): Arrowhead Stadium (79,451)
Founder: Lamar Hunt
CEO, President and General Manager: Carl Peterson
Coach: Dick Vermeil
Public Relations Director: Bob Moore
www.kcchiefs.com

Miami Dolphins
Address: 7500 S.W. 30th Street
Davie, FL 33314
Telephone: (954) 452-7000
Stadium (Capacity): Pro Player Stadium (75,540)
Chairman of the Board/Owner: H. Wayne Huizenga
Sr. VP Football Ops/Player Personnel: Rick Spielman
Head Coach: Dave Wannstedt
Senior VP Media Relations: Harvey Greene
www.miamidolphins.com

Minnesota Vikings
Address: 9520 Viking Drive
Eden Prairie, MN 55344
Telephone: (952) 828-6500
Stadium (Capacity): HHH Metrodome (64,121)
Owner: Red McCombs
President: Gary Woods
Coach: Mike Tice
Public Relations Director: Bob Hagan
www.vikings.com

New England Patriots
Address: Gillette Stadium
1 Patriot Place, Foxboro, MA 02035
Telephone: (508) 543-8200
Stadium (Capacity): Gillette Stadium (68,436)
Owner and Chairman: Robert K. Kraft
Vice Chairman: Jonathan Kraft
Coach: Bill Belichick
Director of Media Relations: Stacey James
www.patriots.com

New Orleans Saints
Address: 5800 Airline Drive
             Metairie, LA 70003
Telephone: (504) 733-0255
Stadium (Capacity): Louisiana Superdome (68,390)
Owner: Tom Benson
GM of Football Operations: Mickey Loomis
Head Coach: Jim Haslett
Director of Media Relations: Greg Bensel
www.neworleanssaints.com

New York Giants
Address: Giants Stadium
             East Rutherford, NJ 07073
Telephone: (201) 935-8111
Stadium (Capacity): Giants Stadium (80,242)
President and co-CEO: Wellington T. Mara
Chairman and co-CEO: Preston Robert Tisch
Senior VP and General Manager: Ernie Accorsi
Coach: Jim Fassel
Vice President of Communications: Pat Hanlon
www.giants.com

New York Jets
Address: 1000 Fulton Avenue
             Hempstead, NY 11550
Telephone: (516) 560-8100
Stadium (Capacity): Giants Stadium (80,062)
Owner: Robert Wood Johnson IV
General Manager: Terry Bradway
Coach: Herman Edwards
VP of Public Relations: Ron Colangelo
www.newyorkjets.com

Oakland Raiders
Address: 1220 Harbor Bay Parkway
             Alameda, CA 94502
Telephone: (510) 864-5000
Stadium (Capacity): Network Assoc. Coliseum (63,132)
Owner: Al Davis
Coach: Bill Callahan
Executive Assistant: Al LoCasale
Director of Public Relations: Mike Taylor
www.raiders.com

Philadelphia Eagles
Address: NovaCare Complex
             1 NovaCare Way
             Philadelphia, PA 19145
Telephone: (215) 463-2500
Stadium (Capacity): Lincoln Financial Field (68,532)
Chairman: Jeffrey Lurie
Exec. VP of Football Operations/Coach: Andy Reid
Director of Football Media Services: Derek Boyko
www.philadelphiaeagles.com

Pittsburgh Steelers
Address: 3400 South Water Street
             Pittsburgh, PA 15203
Telephone: (412) 432-7800
Stadium (Capacity): Heinz Field (64,350)
Chairman: Dan Rooney
Director of Football Operations: Kevin Colbert
Coach: Bill Cowher
Director of Communications: Ron Wahl
www.steelers.com

St. Louis Rams
Address: One Rams Way
             St. Louis, MO 63045
Telephone: (314) 982-7267
Stadium (Capacity): Edward Jones Dome (66,000)
Owner and Chairman: Georgia Frontiere
President: John Shaw
Coach: Mike Martz
Director of Public Relations: Duane Lewis
www.stlouisrams.com

San Diego Chargers
Address: Qualcomm Stadium
             4020 Murphy Canyon Road
             San Diego, CA 92123
Telephone: (858) 874-4500
Stadium (Capacity): Qualcomm Stadium (70,000)
Chairman: Alex G. Spanos
President and CEO: Dean A. Spanos
Executive VP and General Manager: A.J. Smith
Coach: Marty Schottenheimer
Director of Public Relations: Bill Johnston
www.chargers.com

San Francisco 49ers
Address: 4949 Centennial Boulevard
             Santa Clara, CA 95054
Telephone: (408) 562-4949
Stadium (Capacity): 3Com Park (69,734)
Owner: Denise DeBartolo-York
Owner: John York
President: Peter Harris
General Manager: Terry Donahue
Coach: Dennis Erickson
Public Relations Director: Kirk Reynolds
www.49ers.com

Seattle Seahawks
Address: 11220 N.E. 53rd Street
             Kirkland, WA 98033
Telephone: (425) 827-9777
Stadium (Capacity): Seahawks Stadium (67,000)
Owner: Paul Allen
President: Bob Whitsitt
General Manager: Bob Ferguson
Coach: Mike Holmgren
Director of Public Relations: Dave Pearson
www.seahawks.com

Tampa Bay Buccaneers
Address: One Buccaneer Place
             Tampa, FL 33607
Telephone: (813) 870-2700
Stadium (Capacity): Raymond James Stadium (66,321)
Owner: Malcolm Glazer
General Manager: Rich McKay
Coach: Jon Gruden
Communications Manager: Jeff Kamis
www.buccaneers.com

Tennessee Titans
Address: 460 Great Circle Road
             Nashville, TN 37228
Telephone: (615) 565-4000
Stadium (Capacity): The Coliseum (68,804)
President: Jeff Diamond
General Manager: Floyd Reese
Coach: Jeff Fisher
Director of Media Relations: Robbie Bohren
www.titansonline.com

Washington Redskins
Address: 21300 Redskins Park Drive
             Ashburn, VA 20147
Telephone: (703) 726-7000
Stadium (Capacity): Fedex Field (86,484)
Owner: Daniel M. Snyder
VP of Football Operations: Vinny Cerrato
Coach: Steve Spurrier
Director of Public Relations: Michelle Tessier
www.redskins.com

Other Leagues

Canadian Football League
Address: 50 Wellington Street East - 3rd Floor
            Toronto, Ontario M5E1C8 Canada
Telephone: (416) 322-9650
Commissioner: Tom E.S. Wright
Senior VP, Business Operations/Treasurer: James E. Grundy
Director of Football Media: Shawn Lackie
www.cfl.ca

NFL EUROPE
Address: 280 Park Avenue
            New York, NY 10017
Telephone: (212) 450-2000
Managing Directrors: John Beake and Jim Connolly
Chief Operating Officer: Dan Margoshes (London)
Director of Communications: David Tossel
www.nfleurope.com

Pro Basketball Directory

National Basketball Association

National Basketball Association
Address: 645 Fifth Avenue
            New York, NY 10022
Telephone: (212) 826-7000
Commissioner: David Stern
Deputy Commissioner: Russell Granik
Sr. VP of Communications: Brian McIntyre
www.nba.com

National Basketball Association Players Association
Address: 2 Penn Plaza
            Suite 2430
            New York, NY 10121
Telephone: (212) 655-0880
Executive Director: William Hunter
www.nbapa.com

Atlanta Hawks
Address: One CNN Center
            Atlanta, GA 30303
Telephone: (404) 827-3800
Arena (Capacity): Philips Arena (19,445)
Owner: Atlanta Spirit, LLC
President: Stan Kasten
General Manager: Billy Knight
Coach: Terry Stotts
VP of Communications: Arthur Triche
www.hawks.com

Boston Celtics
Address: 151 Merrimac Street
            Boston, MA 02114
Telephone: (617) 523-6050
Arena (Capacity): FleetCenter (18,624)
CEO and Managing Partner: Wyc Grousbeck
General Manager: Chris Wallace
Coach: Jim O'Brien
Director of Media Relations: Bill Bonsiewicz
www.celtics.com

Chicago Bulls
Address: 1901 W. Madison Street
            Chicago, IL 60612
Telephone: (312) 455-4000
Arena (Capacity): United Center (21,711)
Chairman: Jerry Reinsdorf
Executive VP of Basketball Operations: John Paxson
Coach: Bill Cartwright
Senior Director of Media Services: Tim Hallam
www.bulls.com

Cleveland Cavaliers
Address: One Center Court
            Cleveland, OH 44115
Telephone: (216) 420-2000
Arena (Capacity): Gund Arena (20,562)
Chairman: Gordon Gund
President and GM: Jim Paxson
Coach: John Lucas
Director of Public Relations: Bill Evans
www.cavs.com

Dallas Mavericks
Address: 2500 Victory Avenue
            Dallas, TX 75219
Telephone: (214) 665-4660
Arena (Capacity): American Airlines Center (19,200)
Owner: Mark Cuban
General Manager and Head Coach: Don Nelson
President of Basketball Operations: Donn Nelson
Sr. VP of Marketing/Communications: Matt Fitzgerald
www.dallasmavericks.com

Denver Nuggets
Address: Pepsi Center
            1000 Chopper Circle
            Denver, CO 80204
Telephone: (303) 405-1100
Arena (Capacity): Pepsi Center (19,099)
Owner: E. Stanley Kroenke
General Manager: Kiki Vandeweghe
Coach: Jeff Bzdelik
Manager of Media Relations: Eric Sebastian
www.nuggets.com

Detroit Pistons
Address: The Palace of Auburn Hills
            Two Championship Drive
            Auburn Hills, MI 48326
Telephone: (248) 377-0100
Arena (Capacity): The Palace of Auburn Hills (22,076)
Owner: William M. Davidson
President of Basketball Operations: Joe Dumars
Coach: Larry Brown
VP of Public Relations: Matt Dobek
www.palacenet.com

Golden State Warriors
Address: 1011 Broadway
            Oakland, CA 94607-4019
Telephone: (510) 986-2200
Arena (Capacity): The Arena in Oakland (19,596)
Owner and CEO: Christopher Cohan
General Manager: Garry St. Jean
Coach: Eric Musselman
Director of Public Relations: Raymond Ridder
www.gs-warriors.com

National Basketball Association *(Cont.)*

Houston Rockets
Address: Two Greenway Plaza, Suite 400
               Houston, TX 77046
Telephone: (713) 627-3865
Arena (Capacity): Toyota Center (18,500)
Owner: Leslie Alexander
Chief Operating Officer: George Postolos
General Manager: Carroll Dawson
Coach: Jeff Van Gundy
Director of Team Communications: Nelson Luis
www.rockets.com

Indiana Pacers
Address: 125 S. Pennsylvania Street
               Indianapolis, IN 46204
Telephone: (317) 917-2500
Arena (Capacity): Conseco Fieldhouse (18,345)
Owners: Melvin Simon and Herbert Simon
CEO/President: Donnie Walsh
President of Basketball Operations: Larry Bird
Head Coach: Rick Carlisle
Media Relations Director: David Benner
www.pacers.com

Los Angeles Clippers
Address: The Staples Center
               1111 S. Figueroa Street - St. 1100
               Los Angeles, CA 90015
Telephone: (213) 742-7500
Arena (Capacity): The Staples Center (18,964)
Owner: Donald T. Sterling
Vice President of Basketball Operations: Elgin Baylor
Coach: Mike Dunleavy
Vice President of Communications: Joe Safety
www.clippers.com

Los Angeles Lakers
Address: 555 North Nash Street
               El Segundo, CA 90245
Telephone: (310) 426-6000
Arena (Capacity): The Staples Center (18,997)
Owner: Dr. Jerry Buss
General Manager: Mitch Kupchak
Coach: Phil Jackson
Director of Public Relations: John Black
www.lakers.com

Memphis Grizzlies
Address: 175 Toyota Plaza - Suite 150
               Memphis TN 38103
Telephone: (901) 888-4667
Arena (Capacity): The Pyramid (19,423)
Majority Owner: Michael E. Heisley
President of Basketball Operations: Jerry West
General Manager: Dick Versace
Coach: Hubie Brown
Director of Media Relations: Kirk Clayborn
www.grizzlies.com

Miami Heat
Address: American Airlines Arena
               601 Biscayne Boulevard
               Miami, FL 33132
Telephone: (786) 777-4328
Arena (Capacity): American Airlines Arena (16,500)
Managing General Partner: Micky Arison
President and Coach: Pat Riley
President/GM of Basketball Operations: Randy Pfund
VP of Sports Media Relations: Tim Donovan
www.heat.com

Milwaukee Bucks
Address: The Bradley Center
               1001 N. Fourth Street
               Milwaukee, WI 53203
Telephone: (414) 227-0500
Arena (Capacity): The Bradley Center (18,717)
Owner: Herb Kohl
General Manager: Larry Harris
Coach: Terry Porter
Public Relations Director: Cheri Hanson
www.bucks.com

Minnesota Timberwolves
Address: 600 First Avenue North
               Minneapolis, MN 55403
Telephone: (612) 673-1600
Arena (Capacity): Target Center (19,006)
Owner: Glen Taylor
VP of Basketball Operations: Kevin McHale
Coach: Phil (Flip) Saunders
Director of Communications: Kent Wipf
www.timberwolves.com

New Jersey Nets
Address: 390 Murray Hill Parkway
               East Rutherford, NJ 07073
Telephone: (201) 935-8888
Arena (Capacity): Continental Airlines Arena (20,049)
Principal Owner: Lewis Katz
President/General Manager: Rod Thorn
Coach: Byron Scott
Director of Public Relations: Gary Sussman
www.njnets.com

New Orleans Hornets
Address: 1501 Girod Street
               New Orleans, LA 70113
Telephone: (504) 301-4000
Arena (Capacity): New Orleans Arena (18,500)
Majority Owner: George Shinn
Co-Owner: Ray Wooldridge
Coach: Tim Floyd
VP of Public Relations: Harold Kaufman
www.hornets.com

New York Knicks
Address: Madison Square Garden
               Two Pennsylvania Plaza
               New York, NY 10121
Telephone: (212) 465-5867
Arena (Capacity): Madison Square Garden (19,763)
Owner: ITT/Sheraton and Cablevision
Chairman of MSG/President and CEO of Cablevision: James Dolan
Team President/General Manager: Scott Layden
Coach: Don Chaney
Vice President of Public Relations: Joe Favorito
www.nyknicks.com

National Basketball Association (Cont.)

Orlando Magic
Address: Two Magic Place
8701 Maitland Summit Blvd.
Orlando, FL 32810
Telephone: (407) 916-2400
Arena (Capacity): TD Waterhouse Centre (17,248)
Owner: Rich DeVos
Senior Executive Vice President: Pat Williams
General Manager: John Gabriel
Coach: Glenn "Doc" Rivers
Director of Media Relations: Joel Glass
www.orlandomagic.com

Philadelphia 76ers
Address: First Union Center
3601 South Broad Street
Philadelphia, PA 19148
Telephone: (215) 339-7600
Arena (Capacity): Wachovia Center (20,444)
Chairman: Ed Snider
General Manager: Billy King
Coach: Randy Ayers
Senior Director of Communications: Karen Frascona
www.sixers.com

Phoenix Suns
Address: 201 East Jeffreson Street
Phoenix, AZ 85004
Telephone: (602) 379-7900
Arena (Capacity): America West Arena (19,023)
Chairman/CEO and Managing General Partner: Jerry Colangelo
President and General Manager: Bryan Colangelo
Coach: Frank Johnson
VP of Basketball Communications: Julie Fie
www.suns.com

Portland Trail Blazers
Address: One Center Court
Suite 200
Portland, OR 97227
Telephone: (503) 234-9291
Arena (Capacity): Rose Garden Arena (19,980)
Chairman of the Board: Paul Allen
President and General Manager: Bob Whitsitt
Coach: Maurice Cheeks
Executive Director of Communications: Mike Hanson
www.blazers.com

Sacramento Kings
Address: One Sports Parkway
Sacramento, CA 95834
Telephone: (916) 928-0000
Arena (Capacity): ARCO Arena (17,317)
Owners: Joe and Gavin Maloof
President of Basketball Operations: Geoff Petrie
Coach: Rick Adelman
Director of Media Relations: Troy Hanson
www.kings.com

San Antonio Spurs
Address: SBC Center
100 Montana
San Antonio, TX 78203
Telephone: (210) 554-7787
Arena (Capacity): SBC Center (18,500)
Chairman: Peter Holt
General Manager: R.C. Buford
Head Coach : Gregg Popovich
Director of Media Services: Tom James
www.spurs.com

Seattle SuperSonics
Address: 351 Elliott Avenue West
Suite 500
Seattle, WA 98119
Telephone: (206) 281-5847
Arena (Capacity): KeyArena (17,072)
Owner: The Basketball Club of Seattle, LLC
Chairman: Howard Schultz
President/CEO: Wally Walker
General Manager: Rick Sund
Coach: Nate McMillan
Director of Public Relations: Marc Moquin
www.supersonics.com

Toronto Raptors
Address: 40 Bay Street, Suite 400
Toronto, Ontario M5J 2X2 Canada
Telephone: (416) 815-5600
Arena (Capacity): Air Canada Centre (19,800)
Owner: Maple Leaf Sports and Entertainment, Ltd.
Senior VP and General Manager: Glen Grunwald
Coach: Kevin O'Neill
Director of Media Relations: Jim Labumbard
www.raptors.com

Utah Jazz
Address: 301 West So. Temple
Salt Lake City, UT 84101
Telephone: (801) 325-2500
Arena (Capacity): Delta Center (19,911)
Owner: Larry H. Miller
President: Dennis Haslam
VP of Basketball Operations: Kevin O'Connor
Coach: Jerry Sloan
Director of Media Relations: Kim Turner
www.utahjazz.com

Washington Wizards
Address: 601 F Street NW
Washington D.C. 20004
Telephone: (202) 661-5000
Arena (Capacity): MCI Center (20,173)
Owner: Abe Pollin
President of Basketball Operations: Ernie Grunfeld
Coach: Eddie Jordan
Director of Public Relations: Nicole Hawkins
www.nba.com/wizards

Women's National Basketball Association

Women's National Basketball Association
Address: 645 Fifth Avenue
           New York, NY 10022
Telephone: (212) 688-9622
President: Valerie B. Ackerman
Director of Sports Communications: Maureen Coyle
www.wnba.com

Charlotte Sting
Address: 100 Hive Drive
           Charlotte, NC 29217
Telephone: (704) 357-0252
Arena (Capacity): Charlotte Coliseum (12,843)
Owner Robert Johnson
Coach: Trudi Lacey
Director of Public Relations: Karen Kase
www.charlottesting.com

Connecticut Sun
Address: One Mohegan Sun Blvd.
           Uncasville, CT 06382
Telephone: (877) 786-8499
Arena (Capacity): Mohegan Sun Arena (9,341)
Governor: Michael Etess
General Manager: Chris Sienko
Coach: Mike Thibault
Media Relations Manager: Bill Tavares
www.miami-sol.com

Detroit Shock
Address: 2 Championship Drive
           Auburn Hills, MI 48326
Telephone: (248) 377-0100
Arena (Capacity): The Palace of Auburn Hills (19,000)
Managing Partner: William Davidson
President: Tom Wilson
Head Coach: Bill Laimbeer
Director of Media Relations: Dennis Sampier
www.detroitshock.com

Houston Comets
Address: Two Greenway Plaza, Suite 400
           Houston, TX 77046-3865
Telephone: (713) 627-9622
Arena (Capacity): Toyota Center (18,500)
President: Leslie L. Alexander
Coach and General Manager: Van Chancellor
Director of Media Relations: Nelson Luis
www.houstoncomets.com

Indiana Fever
Address: 125 S. Pennsylvania Street
           Indianapolis, IN 46204
Telephone: (317) 917-2500
Arena (Capacity): Conseco Field House (18,345)
President: Donnie Walsh
Chief Operating Officer: Kelly Kraus Kopf
Coach: TBA
Director of Media Relations: Kevin Messenger
www.wnba.com/fever

Los Angeles Sparks
Address: 555 Nash Street
           El Segundo, CA 90245
Telephone: (310) 330-2434
Arena (Capacity): Staples Center (19,282)
Chairman: Dr. Jerry Buss
General Manager: Virginia (Penny) Toler
Coach: Michael Cooper
Media Relations Director: Kristal Shipp
www.lasparks.com

Minnesota Lynx
Address: Target Center
           600 First Avenue North
           Minneapolis, MN 55403
Telephone: (612) 673-8400
Arena (Capacity): Target Center (19,006)
Owner: Glen Taylor
Coach: Suzie McConnell Serio
Public Relations Manager: Mike Cristaldi
www.wnba.com/lynx/

New York Liberty
Address: Two Penn Plaza
           New York, NY 10121
Telephone: (212) 465-5867
Arena (Capacity): Madison Square Garden (19,763)
GM and Vice President: Carol Blazejowski
Coach: Richie Adubato
VP of Marketing and Communications: Amy Scheer
www.nyliberty.com

Phoenix Mercury
Address: 201 East Jefferson Street
           Phoenix, AZ 85004
Telephone: (602) 514-8333
Arena (Capacity): America West Arena (10,746)
Chairman and CEO: Jerry Colangelo
President: Bryan Colangelo
Coach: John Shumate
Media Relations Director: Tami Nealy
www.phoenixmercury.com

Sacramento Monarchs
Address: One Sports Parkway
           Sacramento, CA 95834
Telephone: (916) 455-4647
Arena (Capacity): ARCO Arena (17,317)
Owner: Maloof Family
President: John Thomas
GM and Coach: John Whisenant
Manager of Media Relations: Kimberly Williams
www.sacramentomonarchs.com

San Antonio Silver Stars
Address: One SBC Center
           San Antonio, TX 78219
Telephone: (210) 444-5050
Arena (Capacity): SBC Center (18,500)
Owner: Spurs Sports & Entertainment
COO: Clarissa Davis-Wrightsil
Coach: TBA
Media Services Manager: Kris Davis

Women's National Basketball Association (Cont.)

Seattle Storm
Address: 351 Elliott Avenue West
             Suite 500
             Seattle, WA 98119
Telephone: (206) 281-5800
Arena (Capacity): Key Arena (12,000)
Owners: The Basketball Club of Seattle LLC
Chairman: Howard Schultz
Coach: Anne Donovan
Director, Public Relations: Valerie O'Neil
www.wnba.com/storm

Washington Mystics
Address: MCI Center
             601 F Street, NW
             Washington, DC 20004
Telephone: (202) 661-5000
Arena (Capacity): MCI Center (19,093)
Chairman: Abe Pollin
President: Susan O'Malley
Coach: Marianne Stanley
Director, Public Relations: Dyani Gordon
www.washingtonmystics.com

Hockey Directory

National Hockey League
Address: 1251 Avenue of the Americas
             47th floor
             New York, NY 10020-1198
Telephone: (212) 789-2000
Commissioner: Gary Bettman
President of NHL Enterprises: Ed Horne
Executive VP and Dir. of Hockey Operations: Colin Campbell
VP of Media Relations: Frank Brown
www.nhl.com

National Hockey League Players Association
Address: 777 Bay Street, Suite 2400
             Toronto, Ontario M5G 2C8 Canada
Telephone: (416) 313-2300
Executive Director: Bob Goodenow
www.nhlpa.com

Mighty Ducks of Anaheim
Address: Arrowhead Pond of Anaheim
             2695 Katella Avenue
             Anaheim, CA 92806
Telephone: (714) 940-2900
Arena (Capacity): Arrowhead Pond of Anaheim (17,174)
Chairman and Governor: Jay Rasulo
Senior VP and General Manager: Bryan Murray
Coach: Mike Babcock
Manager of Communications: Alex Gilchrist
www.mightyducks.com

Atlanta Thrashers
Address: 1 CNN Center
             P.O. Box 15538
             Atlanta, GA 30348
Telephone: (404) 827-5300
Arena (Capacity): Philips Arena (18,545)
Owner: Atlanta Spirit, LLC
President and Governor: Stan Kasten
VP and General Manager: Don Waddell
Coach: Bob Hartley
Director of Public Relations: Tom Hughes
www.atlantathrashers.com

Boston Bruins
Address: One Fleet Center Place, Suite 250
             Boston, MA 02114-1303
Telephone: (617) 624-1900
Arena (Capacity): FleetCenter (17,565)
Owner and Governor: Jeremy M. Jacobs
Alternative Governor and President: Harry Sinden
VP/General Manager and Alt. Governor: Mike O'Connell
Coach: Mike Sullivan
Director of Media Relations: Heidi Holland
www.bostonbruins.com

Buffalo Sabres
Address: HSBC Arena
             One Seymour H. Knox III Plaza
             Buffalo, NY 14203
Telephone: (716) 855-4100
Arena (Capacity): HSBC Arena (18,690)
Owner: B. Thomas Golisano
General Manager: Darcy Regier
Coach: Lindy Ruff
VP of Communications: Michael Gilbert
www.sabres.com

Calgary Flames
Address: Pengrowth Saddledome
             555 Saddledome Rise, SE
             Calgary, Alberta T2G 2W1
Telephone: (403) 777-2177
Arena (Capacity): Pengrowth Saddledome (17,409)
Owners: Harley N. Hotchkiss, N. Murray Edwards, Alvin G. Libin, Allan P. Markin, J.R. "Bud" McCaig, Byron J.Seaman, Daryl K. Seaman
President and CEO: Ken King
General Manager and Coach: Darryl Sutter
Director of Communications: Peter Hanlon
www.calgaryflames.com

Carolina Hurricanes

Address: 1400 Edwards Mill Road
             Raleigh, NC 27607
Telephone: (919) 467-7825
Arena (Capacity): RBC Center (18,730)
Owner: Peter Karmanos
CEO and General Manager: Jim Rutherford
VP/Assistant General Manager: Jason Karmanos
Coach: Paul Maurice
Media Relations Manager: Mike Sundheim
www.carolinahurricanes.com

Chicago Blackhawks

Address: United Center
             1901 W. Madison Street
             Chicago, IL 60612
Telephone: (312) 455-7000
Arena (Capacity): United Center (20,500)
President: William W. Wirtz
Senior Vice President: Robert Pulford
General Manager: Mike Smith
Coach: Brian Sutter
Executive Director of Communications: Jim DeMaria
www.chicagoblackhawks.com

Colorado Avalanche

Address: Pepsi Center
             1000 Chopper Circle
             Denver, CO 80204
Telephone: (303) 405-1100
Arena (Capacity): Pepsi Center (18,007)
Owner and Governor: E. Stanley Kroenke
Alt. Governor, President and General Manager: Pierre Lacroix
Coach: Tony Granato
VP of Communications and Team Services:
 Jean Martineau
www.coloradoavalanche.com

Columbus Blue Jackets

Address: 200 West Nationwide Boulevard
             Columbus, OH 43215
Telephone: (614) 246-4625
Arena (Capacity): Nationwide Arena (18,136)
Owner: John H. McConnell
President, GM and Coach: Doug MacLean
Coach: Dave King
Director of Communications: Todd Sharrock
www.bluejackets.com

Dallas Stars

Address: 211 Cowboys Parkway
             Irving, TX 75063
Telephone: (972) 831-2401
Arena (Capacity): American Airlines Center (18,532)
Owner: Thomas O. Hicks
General Manager: Doug Armstrong
Coach: Dave Tippett
Executive VP of Marketing/Comm.: Bryan Perez
www.dallasstars.com

Detroit Red Wings

Address: Joe Louis Arena
             600 Civic Center Drive
             Detroit, MI 48226
Telephone: (313) 396-7444
Arena (Capacity): Joe Louis Arena (20,056)
Owner and Governor: Mike Ilitch
Owner, Secretary and Treasurer: Marian Ilitch
Senior Vice President/Alt. Governor: Jim Devellano
General Manager: Ken Holland
Coach: Dave Lewis
Senior Director of Communications: John Hahn
www.detroitredwings.com

Edmonton Oilers

Address: 11230 110th Street
             Edmonton, Alberta T5G 3H7
Telephone: (780) 414-4000
Arena (Capacity): Skyreach Centre (16,839)
Owner: Edmonton Investors Group
President and CEO: Patrick LaForge
General Manager: Kevin Lowe
Coach: Craig MacTavish
VP of Public Relations, Hockey: Bill Tuele
www.edmontonoilers.com

Florida Panthers

Address: 1 Panther Parkway
             Sunrise, FL 33323
Telephone: (954) 835-7000
Arena (Capacity): Office Depot Center (19,250)
Chairman of the Board/CEO: Alan Cohen
Alternate Governor: William A. Torrey
General Manager: Rick Dudley
Coach: Mike Keenan
Director of Media Relations: Randy Sieminski
www.floridapanthers.com

Los Angeles Kings

Address: The Staples Center
             1111 South Figueroa Street
             Los Angeles, CA 90015
Telephone: (213) 742-7100
Arena (Capacity): The Staples Center (18,118)
Owners: Philip Anschutz and Edward P. Roske Jr.
President and Governor: Tim Leiweke
Vice President and GM: Dave Taylor
Coach: Andy Murray
Director of Media Relations: Mike Altieri
www.lakings.com

Minnesota Wild

Address: 317 Washington Street
             St. Paul, MN, 55102
Telephone: (651) 602-6000
Arena (Capacity): Excel Energy Center (18,064)
Chairman: Bob Naegele Jr.
General Manager: Doug Risebrough
Coach: Jacques Lemaire
VP of Communications/Broadcasting: Bill Robertson
www.wild.com

Montreal Canadiens
Address:　　Bell Centre
　　　　　　1260 de la Gauchetiere West
　　　　　　Montreal, Quebec H3B 5E8 Canada
Telephone: (514) 932-2582
Arena (Capacity): Bell Centre (21,273)
Owner: George N. Gillett Jr.
President and Governor: Pierre Boivin
Executive VP and General Manager: Bob Gainey
Coach: Claude Julien
Director of Communications: Donald Beauchamp
www.canadiens.com

Nashville Predators
Address:　　Gaylord Entertainment Center
　　　　　　501 Broadway
　　　　　　Nashville, TN 37203
Telephone: (615) 770-2300
Arena (Capacity): Gaylord Entertainment Center
(17,113)
Owner, Chairman and Governor: Craig Leipold
President, COO: Jack Diller
Executive VP of Hockey Operations/GM: David Poile
Coach: Barry Trotz
VP of Communications/Development: Gerry Helper
www.nashvillepredators.com

New Jersey Devils
Address:　　Continental Airlines Arena, PO Box 504
　　　　　　East Rutherford, NJ 07073
Telephone: (201) 935-6050
Arena (Capacity): Continental Airlines Arena (19,040)
Owners: Ray Chambers, Louis Katz and George
　Steinbrenner
CEO, President and GM: Lou Lamoriello
Coach: Pat Burns
Director of Public Relations: Jeff Altstadter
www.newjerseydevils.com

New York Islanders
Address:　　1535 Old Country Road
　　　　　　Plainview, NY 11803
Telephone: (516) 501-6700
Arena (Capacity): Nassau Coliseum (16,234)
Owners: Charles Wong and Sanjay Kumar
Senior VP of Operations and Alt. Governor: Michael J.
　Picker
General Manager/Alt. Governor: Mike Milbury
Coach: Steve Stirling
VP of Communications: Chris Botta
www.newyorkislanders.com

New York Rangers
Address:　　Madison Square Garden
　　　　　　2 Pennsylvania Plaza
　　　　　　New York, NY 10121
Telephone: (212) 465-6000
Arena (Capacity): Madison Square Garden (18,200)
Owner: Cablevision
President and General Manager: Glen Sather
Coach: Glen Sather
VP of Public Relations: John Rosasco
www.newyorkrangers.com

Ottawa Senators
Address:　　The Corel Centre
　　　　　　1000 Palladium Drive
　　　　　　Ottawa, Ontario K2V 1A5 Canada
Telephone: (613) 599-0250
Arena (Capacity): The Corel Centre (18,500)
Owner, Governor and Chairman: Eugene Melnyk

Ottawa Senators *(Cont.)*
President and Chief Executive Officer: Roy Mlakar
General Manager: John Muckler
Coach: Jacques Martin
VP of Communications: Phil Legault
www.ottawasenators.com

Philadelphia Flyers
Address:　　First Union Center
　　　　　　3601 South Broad Street
　　　　　　Philadelphia, PA 19148
Telephone: (215) 465-4500
Arena (Capacity): Wachovia Center (19,523)
Majority Owner: Comcast Spectacor
Chairman: Ed Snider
President: Ron Ryan
General Manager: Bob Clarke
Coach: Ken Hitchcock
Director of Public Relations: Zack Hill
www.philadelphiaflyers.com

Phoenix Coyotes
Address:　　Glendale Arena
　　　　　　6520 N. 91st Avenue
　　　　　　Glendale, AZ 85305
Telephone: (480) 473-5600
Arena (Capacity): Glendale Arena (TBA)
Chairman and Governor: Steve Ellman
Managing Partner and Alt. Governor: Wayne Gretzky
VP and General Manager: Michael Barnette
Coach: Bob Francis
VP of Media and Player Relations: Richard Nairn
www.phoenixcoyotes.com

Pittsburgh Penguins
Address:　　Mellon Arena
　　　　　　66 Mario Lemieux Place
　　　　　　Pittsburgh, PA 15219
Telephone: (412) 642-1300
Arena (Capacity): Mellon Arena (16,958)
Owner: Mario Lemieux (Lemieux Ownership Group)
General Manager: Craig Patrick
Coach: Eddie Olczyk
Director of Media Relations: Steve Bovino
www.pittsburghpenguins.com

St. Louis Blues
Address:　　Savvis Center
　　　　　　1401 Clark Avenue
　　　　　　St. Louis, MO 63103
Telephone: (314) 622-2500
Arena (Capacity): Savvis Center (20,022)
President and Chief Executive Officer: Mark Sauer
Senior VP and General Manager: Larry Pleau
Coach: Joel Quenneville
Director of Media Relations: Frank Buomono
www.stlouisblues.com

San Jose Sharks
Address:　　HP Pavillion at San Jose
　　　　　　525 West Santa Clara Street
　　　　　　San Jose, CA 95113
Telephone: (408) 287-7070
Arena (Capacity): HP Pavillion at San Jose (17,496)
Owner: San Jose Sports And Entertainment
　Enterprises
President and CEO: Greg Jamison
Executive VP and General Manager: Doug Wilson
Coach: Ron Wilson
Director of Media Relations: Ken Arnold
www.sjsharks.com

Hockey Directory (Cont.)

Tampa Bay Lightning
Address: 401 Channelside Drive
              Tampa, FL 33602
Telephone: (813) 301-6600
Arena (Capacity): Ice Palace (19,758)
Owner: Palace Sports & Entertainment/Bill Davidson and David Hermelin
CEO and Governor: Tom Wilson
General Manager: Jay Feaster
Coach: John Tortorella
VP of Public Relations: Bill Wickett
www.tampabaylightning.com

Toronto Maple Leafs
Address: Air Canada Centre
              40 Bay Street - St. 400
              Toronto, Ontario M5J 2X2 Canada
Telephone: (416) 815-5500
Arena (Capacity): Air Canada Centre (18,819)
Chairman of the Board: Steve A. Stavro
President and CEO: Richard Peddie
Coach: Pat Quinn
Director of Media Relations: Pat Park
GM: John Ferguson
www.mapleleafs.com

Vancouver Canucks
Address: General Motors Place/800 Griffiths Way
              Vancouver, B.C. V6B 6G1
Telephone: (604) 899-4600
Arena (Capacity): General Motors Place (18,422)
Chairman and Governor: John E. McCaw Jr.
President and CEO: Stanley McCammon
Chief Operating Officer: David Cobb
President and GM: Brian Burke
Coach: Marc Crawford
Manager of Media Relations: Chris Brumwell
www.canucks.com

Washington Capitals
Address: 401 Ninth Street, NW
              Suite 750
              Washington, DC 20004
Telephone: (202) 266-2200
Arena (Capacity): MCI Center (18,672)
Majority Owner and Chairman: Ted Leonsis
Owner and President: Richard M. Patrick
VP and General Manager: George McPhee
Coach: Bruce Cassidy
Senior VP of Business Operations: Declan J. Bolger
www.washingtoncaps.com

Olympic Sports Directory

United States Olympic Committee
Address: Olympic House
              1 Olympic Plaza
              Colorado Springs, CO 80909
Telephone: (719) 632-5551
Acting CEO: Jim Scherr
Chief Communications Officer: Darryl Seibel
www.usolympicteam.com

U.S. Olympic Training Centers
Address: 1 Olympic Plaza
              Colorado Springs, CO 80909
Telephone: (719) 632-5551
Director: John Smith
Address: 421 Old Military Road
              Lake Placid, NY 12946
Telephone: (518) 523-2600
Director: Jack Favro
Address: 2800 Olympic Parkway
              Chula Vista, CA 91915
Telephone: (619) 656-1500
Director: Patrice Milkovich
www.olympic.org

International Olympic Committee
Address: Chateau de Vidy
              Case Postale 356
              CH-1007 Lausanne, Switzerland
Telephone: 41-21-621-6111
President: Jacques Rogge
Director General: Francois Carrard
www.olympic.org

Torino Olympic Organizing Committee for the 2006 Winter Games
Address: Via Nizza 262/58
              10126 Torino (Italy)
Telephone: 39 011 63 10 511
President: Valentino Castellani
Press Operations: Cristiano Carlutti
(XX Winter Games; Feb 10–26, 2006)
www.torino2006.org

Athens Olympic Organizing Committee for the 2004 Summer Games
Address: 7 Kifissias Avenue
              115 23 Athens, Greece
Telephone: 30 1 2004 000
President: Gianna Angelopoulos-Daskalaki
Head of Communications and Media: Serafim Kotrotsos
(XXVII Summer Games; Aug 11–29, 2004)
www.athens.olympic.org

U.S. Olympic Organizations

National Archery Association (NAA)
Address: 1 Olympic Plaza
              Colorado Springs, CO 80909
Telephone: (719) 866-4576
President: Mark Miller
Executive Director: Brad Camp
Media Relations: Desiree Freiherr
www.usarchery.org

USA Badminton (USAB)
Address: 1 Olympic Plaza
              Colorado Springs, CO 80909
Telephone: (719) 866-4808
President: Don Chew
Executive Director: Dan Cloppas
Media Contact: Barb Kissick
www.usabadminton.org

U.S. Olympic Organizations (Cont.)

USA Baseball
Address: Hi Corbett Field
        3400 East Camino Campestre
        Tucson, AZ 85716
Telephone: (520) 327-9700
Chairman: Lindsay Burbage
Executive Director/CEO: Paul V. Seiler
Director of Communications: David Fanucchi
www.usabaseball.com

USA Basketball
Address: 5465 Mark Dabling Blvd.
        Colorado Springs, CO 80918
Telephone: (719) 590-4800
President: Tom Jernstedt
Executive Director: Jim Tooley
Assistant Executive Director for Public Relations:
 Craig Miller
www.usabasketball.com

U.S. Biathlon Association (USBA)
Address: 29 Ethan Allen Avenue
        Colchester, VT 05446
Telephone: (802) 654-7833
President: Lyle Nelson
Executive Director: Stephen R. Sands
Media Contact: Anita Hall
www.usbiathlon.org

U.S. Bobsled and Skeleton Federation
Address: P.O. Box 828
        Lake Placid, NY 12946
Telephone: (518) 523-1842
President: Jim Morris
Executive Director: Matt Roy
Media and PR Director Director: Julie Urbansky
www.usabobsledandskeleton.org

USA Boxing, Inc.
Address: 1 Olympic Plaza
        Colorado Springs, CO 80909
Telephone: (719) 866-4506
President: Dr. Robert Voy
Executive Director: Eric Parthen
Director of PR and Media: Julie Goldsticker
www.usaboxing.org

U.S. Canoe and Kayak Team
Address: P.O. Box 789
        Lake Placid, NY 12946
Telephone: (518) 523-1855
Interim President: Anne Blanchard
Executive Director: Lisa Fish
Public Relations Director: Doug Haney
www.usacanoekayak.org

USA Cycling
Address: 1 Olympic Plaza
        Colorado Springs, CO 80909
Telephone: (719) 866-4581
President: Jim Ochowicz
Chief Executive Officer: Gerard Bisceglia
Director of Communications: Deborah Engen
www.usacycling.org

United States Diving, Inc. (USD)
Address: Pan American Plaza, Suite 430
        201 South Capitol Avenue
        Indianapolis, IN 46225
Telephone: (317) 237-5252
President: William Walker
Executive Director: Todd Smith
Director of Communications: Kelli Servizzi
www.usdiving.org

U.S. Equestrian Team (USET)
Address: Pottersville Rd.
        Gladstone, NJ 07934
Telephone: (908) 234-1251
Executive Director: Bonnie Jenkins
Director of Communications: Marty Bauman
www.uset.org

U.S. Fencing Association (USFA)
Address: 1 Olympic Plaza
        Colorado Springs, CO 80909
Telephone: (719) 866-4511
President: Stacey Johnson
Executive Director: Michael Massik
Media Relations Director: Cynthia Bent
www.usfencing.org

U.S. Field Hockey Association (USFHA)
Address: 1 Olympic Plaza
        Colorado Springs, CO 80909-5773
Telephone: (719) 866-4567
President: Sharon Taylor
Executive Director: Amy Frankenstein
Sport and Public Information Director:
 Howard Thomas
www.usfieldhockey.com

U.S. Figure Skating Association
Address: 20 First Street
        Colorado Springs, CO 80906
Telephone: (719) 635-5200
President: Phyllis Howard
Executive Director: John LeFevre
Communications Coordinator: Bob Dunlop
www.usfsa.org

USA Gymnastics
Address: Pan American Plaza, Suite 300
        201 South Capitol Avenue
        Indianapolis, IN 46225
Telephone: (317) 237-5050
Chairman of the Board: Ron Froehlich
President: Robert Colarossi
Director of Public Relations: Steve Penny
www.usa-gymnastics.org

USA Hockey
Address: 1775 Bob Johnson Drive
        Colorado Springs, CO 80906
Telephone: (719) 576-8724
President: Walter L. Bush, Jr.
Executive Director: Doug Palazzari
Manager of Media and PR: Heather Ahearn
www.usahockey.com

U.S. Olympic Organizations *(Cont.)*

United States Judo, Inc. (USJ)
Address: 1 Olympic Plaza Suite 202
             Colorado Springs, CO 80909
Telephone: (719) 866-4730
President: Dr. Ronald Tripp
Executive Director: William Rosenberg
www.usjudo.org

U.S. Luge Association (USLA)
Address: 35 Church Street
             Lake Placid, NY 12946
Telephone: (518) 523-2071
President: Doug Bateman
Executive Director: Ron Rossi
Public Relations Manager: Jon Lundin
www.usaluge.org

U.S. Modern Pentathlon Association
Address: 5407 Bandera Road - Suite 512
             San Antonio, TX 78238
Telephone: (210) 229-2004
President: Ralph Bender
Executive Director: Robert Marbut Jr.
www.usmpa.home.texas.net

U.S. Racquetball Association
Address: 1685 West Uintah
             Colorado Springs, CO 80904
Telephone: (719) 635-5396
President: Otto Dietrich
Executive Director: Jim Hiser
Public Relations Coordinator: Ryan John
www.usra.org

USA Roller Sports
Address: 4730 South Street
             P.O. Box 6579
             Lincoln, NE 68506
Telephone: (402) 483-7551
President: George Kolibaba
Communications Director: Bill Wolf
www.usacrs.com

U.S. Rowing
Address: Pan American Plaza, Suite 400
             201 South Capitol Avenue
             Indianapolis, IN 46225
Telephone: (317) 237-5656/ 1 (800) 314-4769
Executive Director: John Dane
Press Contact: Brett Johnson
www.usrowing.org

U.S. Sailing Association
Address: 15 Maritime Drive
             P.O. Box 1260
             Portsmouth, RI 02871
Telephone: (401) 683-0800
President: Dave Rosekrans
Executive Director: Nick Craw
Communications Director: Penny Piva Rego
Olympic Yachting Director: Jonathan R. Harley
www.ussailing.org

USA Shooting
Address: 1 Olympic Plaza
             Colorado Springs, CO 80909
Telephone: (719) 866-4670
Chairman of the Board: Mike English
Executive Director: Robert K. Mitchell
Director of Marketing: Leaha Wirth
www.usashooting.com

U.S. Ski and Snowboard Association
Address: P.O. Box 100
             Park City, UT 84060
Telephone: (435) 649-9090
Chairman: Jim McCarthy
President and CEO: Bill Marolt
V.P. of Communications and Media: Tom Kelly
www.usskiteam.com

U.S. Soccer Federation (USSF)
Address: 1801-1811 South Prairie Avenue
             Chicago, IL 60616
Telephone: (312) 808-1300
President: Robert Contiguglia
Secretary General: Dan Flynn
Director of Communications: Jim Moorhouse
www.us-soccer.com

Amateur Softball Association (ASA)
Address: 2801 N.E. 50th Street
             Oklahoma City, OK 73111
Telephone: (405) 424-5266
President: H. Franklin Taylor III
Executive Director: Ron Radigonda
Director of Communications: Brian McCall
www.softball.org

U.S. Speed Skating
Address: P.O. Box 450639
             Westlake OH 44145
Telephone: (440) 899-0128
President: Fred Benjamin
Executive Director: Katie Marquard
Public Relations Director: Nick Paulenich
www.usspeedskating.org

U.S. Swimming, Inc. (USS)
Address: 1 Olympic Plaza
             Colorado Springs, CO 80909
Telephone: (719) 866-4578
President: Ron Van Pool
Executive Director: Chuck Wielgus
Public Relations Director: Mary Wagner
www.usa-swimming.org

U.S. Synchronized Swimming, Inc. (USSS)
Address: Pan American Plaza, Suite 901
             201 South Capitol Avenue
             Indianapolis, IN 46225
Telephone: (317) 237-5700
President: Betty Hazle
Executive Director: Terry Harper
Media Relations: Brian Eaton
www.usasynchro.org

U.S. Table Tennis Association (USTTA)
Address: 1 Olympic Plaza
             Colorado Springs, CO 80909
Telephone: (719) 866-4583
Executive Director: TBA
President: Sheri Pittman
Director of Media and PR: Debbie Doney
www.usatt.org

U.S. Taekwondo Union (USTU)
Address: 1 Olympic Plaza, Suite 405
             Colorado Springs, CO 80909
Telephone: (719) 866-4632
President: Sang Lee
Executive Director: R. Jay Warwick
Media and Communications Director: Chris Condron
www.ustu.org

U.S. Olympic Organizations (Cont.)

USA Team Handball
Address: 1 Olympic Plaza
             Colrado Springs, CO 80909
Telephone: (719) 866-4036
President: Bob Djokovich
Executive Director: Mike Cavanaugh
www.usateamhandball.org

U.S. Tennis Association
Address: 70 West Red Oak Lane
             White Plains, NY 10604
Telephone: (914) 696-7000
President: Mervin Heller
Executive Director: Richard D. Ferman
Director of Public Relations: Eric Handler
www.usta.com

USA Track & Field (formerly TAC)
Address: 1 RCA Dome, Suite 140
             Indianapolis, IN 46225
Telephone: (317) 261-0500
President: Bill Roe
Chief Executive Officer: Craig A. Masback
Director of Communications: Jill Geer
www.usatf.org

USA Volleyball
Address: 715 South Circle Drive
             Colorado Springs, CO 80910
Telephone: (719) 228-6800
President: Albert M. Monaco Jr.
Executive Director: Kerry Klostermann
Coordinator of Marketing and Comm.:Cecil Bleiker
www.usavolleyball.org

United States Water Polo (USWP)
Address: 1685 West Uintah
             Colorado Springs, CO 80904
Telephone: (719) 634-0699
President: Rich Foster
Executive Director: Bruce J. Wigo
Media Director: Eric Velazquez
www.usawaterpolo.com

USA Weightlifting
Address: 1 Olympic Plaza
             Colorado Springs, CO 80909
Telephone: (719) 866-4508
President: Dennis Snethen
Executive Director and Media Contact: Wesley
 Barnett
www.usaweightlifting.org

USA Wrestling
Address: 6155 Lehman Drive
             Colorado Springs, CO 80918
Telephone: (719) 598-8181
President: Bruce Baumgartner
Executive Director: Rich Bender
Director of Communications: Gary Abbott
www.usawrestling.org

Affiliated Sports Organizations

Amateur Athletic Union (AAU)
Address: Walt Disney World Resort; P.O. Box 22409
             Lake Buena Vista, FL 32830-1000
Telephone: (407) 934-7200
President: Bobby Dodd
Media Contact: Melissa Wilson
www.aausports.org

U.S. Curling Association (USCA)
Address: 1100 Center Point Drive
             P.O. Box 866
             Stevens Point, WI 54481
Telephone: (715) 344-1199
President: Jack McNelly
Executive Director: David Garber
Communications Director: Rick Patzke
www.usacurl.org

USA Karate Federation
Address: 1300 Kenmore Boulevard
             Akron, OH 44314
Telephone: (330) 753-3114
President: George Anderson
www.usakarate.org

U.S. Orienteering Federation
Address: P.O. Box 1444
             Forest Park, GA 30298
Telephone: (404) 363-2110
President: Chuck Ferguson
Executive Director: Robin Shannonhouse
Marketing and Public Relations VP: Sherry Litasi
Publicity telephone: (303) 694-4914
www.us.orienteering.org

U.S. Squash Racquets Association
Address: 23 Cynwyd Road
             P.O. Box 1216
             Bala Cynwyd, PA 19004
Telephone: (610) 667-4006
President: Eben Hardie III
Vice President: Kevin Jernigan
www.us-squash.org

USA Triathlon
Address: 616 West Monument Street
             Colorado Springs, CO 80905
Telephone: (719) 597-9090
President: Ray Plotecia
Executive Director: Steve Locke
Communications Director: B. J. Hoeptner Evans
www.usatriathlon.org

USA Waterski
Address: 1251 Holy Cow Road
             Polk City, FL 33868
Telephone: (863) 324-4341
President: Andrea Plough
Executive Director: Steve McDermeit
Public Relations Manager: Scott Atkinson
www.usawaterski.org

Championship Auto Racing Teams (CART)
Address: 5350 Lakeview Parkway South Drive
    Building 36 - Inner Park/Park 100
    Indianapolis, IN 46268
Telephone: (317) 715-4100
President and CEO: Christopher Pook
VP of Communications: Adam Saal
www.cart.com

Indy Racing League
Address: 4565 West 16th Street
    Indianapolis, IN 46222
Telephone: (317) 484-6526
President and Founder: Tony George
Director of Media Relations: Ron Green
www.indyracing.com

International Motor Sports Association
Address: 1394 Broadway Avenue
    Braselton, GA 30517
Telephone: (706) 658-2120
President: Scott Atherton
Executive Director: Doug Robinson
www.imsracing.net

National Association for Stock Car Auto Racing (NASCAR)
Address: 1801 W International Speedway Blvd.
    Daytona Beach, FL 32114-1243
Telephone: (386) 253-0611
CEO/Chairman: Brian France
President: Mike Helton
VP of Corporate Communications: Jim Hunter
www.nascar.com

National Hot Rod Association
Address: 2035 East Financial Way
    Glendora, CA 91741
Telephone: (626) 914-4761
President: Tom Compton
VP of PR and Communications: Jerry Archambeault
www.nhra.com

Professional Women's Bowling Association
Address: 7171 Cherryvale Boulevard
    Rockford, IL 61112
Telephone: (815) 332-5756
Tournament Director: Fran Deken
Media Director: Gary Kohn
www.pwba.com

Professional Bowlers Association LLC
Address: 719 Second Avenue - Suite 701
    Seattle, WA 98104
Telephone: (206) 332-9688
Commissioner: Fred Schreyer
Director of Corporate Communications: Beth Marshall
www.pba.com

U.S. Chess Federation
Address: 3054 Route 9 W
    New Windsor, NY 12553
Telephone: (845) 562-8350
President: R. John McCrary
Executive Director: George De Feis
Media Relations: Anne Ashton
www.uschess.org

International Game Fish Association
Address: 300 Gulf Stream Way
    Dania Beach, FL 33004

International Game Fish Assoc. *(Cont.)*
Telephone: (954) 927-2628
President: Rob Kramer
www.igfa.org

Ladies Professional Golf Association
Address: 100 International Golf Drive
    Daytona Beach, FL 32124
Telephone: (386) 274-6200
Commissioner: Ty Votaw
Director of Media Relations: Connie Wilson
www.lpga.com

PGA Tour
Address: 112 PGA Tour Boulevard
    Ponte Vedra Beach, FL 32082
Telephone: (904) 285-3700
President: M.G. Orender
Senior VP of Communications: Bob Combs
www.pgatour.com

Professional Golfers' Association of America
Address: 100 Avenue of the Champions
    Box 109601
    Palm Beach Gardens, FL 33410-9601
Telephone: (561) 624-8400
President: M.G. Orender
Director of Public Relations: Julius Mason
www.pgaonline.com

United States Golf Association
Address: P.O. Box 708, Golf House
    Liberty Corner Road
    Far Hills, NJ 07931-0708
Telephone: (908) 234-2300
President: Reed Mackenzie
Director of Media Relations: Craig Smith
www.usga.org

U.S. Handball Association
Address: 2333 North Tucson Boulevard
    Tucson, AZ 85716
Telephone: (520) 795-0434
President: Bob Hickman
Executive Director: Vern Roberts
Director of Public Relations: Mark Carpenter
www.ushandball.org

Breeders' Cup Limited
Address: 2525 Harrodsburg Road
    PO Box 4230
    Lexington, KY 40504
Telephone: (859) 223-5444
President: D. G. Van Clief Jr.
Media Relations Director: James Gluckson
Director of Marketing: Damon Thayer
www.breederscup.com

The Jockeys' Guild, Inc.
Address: P.O. Box 150
    Monrovia, CA 91017
Telephone: (866) 465-6257
Chairman of the Board: Tomey Swan

Thoroughbred Racing Associations of America
Address: 420 Fair Hill Drive, Suite 1
    Elkton, MD 21921
Telephone: (410) 392-9200
President: Chris Scherf
www.tra-online.com

National Thoroughbred Racing Association
Address: 800 Third Avenue - Suite 901
        New York, NY 10022
Telephone: (212) 907-9280
Senior VP/Mrkting & Industry Rels: Keith Chamblin
www.ntra.com

United States Trotting Association
Address: 750 Michigan Avenue
        Columbus, OH 43215
Telephone: (614) 224-2291
Executive Vice President: Fred J. Noe
Director of Publicity: John Pawlak
www.ustrotting.com

Iditarod Trail Committee
Address: P.O. Box 870800; Wasilla, AK 99687
Telephone: (907) 376-5155
Executive Director: Stan Hooley
Race Director: Joanne Potts
www.iditarod.com

U.S. Lacrosse
Address: 113 W University Parkway
        Baltimore, MD 21210
Telephone: (410) 235-6882
Executive Director: Steven B. Stenersen
www.lacrosse.org

Little League Baseball, Inc.
Address: P.O. Box 3485
        Williamsport, PA 17701
Telephone: (570) 326-1921
President & CEO: Stephen D. Keener
Senior Communications Executive: Lance Van Auken
www.littleleague.org

U.S. Polo Association
Address: 771 Corporate Drive, Suite 505
        Lexington, KY 40503
Telephone: (859) 219-1000
Executive Director: David Cummings
www.uspolo.org

American Powerboating Association
Address: 17640 Nine Mile Road
        Eastpointe, MI 48021
Telephone: (586) 773-9700
Executive Administrator: Gloria Urbin
www.APBA.org

Professional Rodeo Cowboys Association
Address: 101 Pro Rodeo Drive
        Colorado Springs, CO 80919
Telephone: (719) 593-8840
Commissioner: Steven J. Hatchell
Director of Communications: Leslie King
www.prorodeo.com

USA Rugby Football Union
Address: 1033 Walnut Street
        Suite 200
        Boulder, CO 80302
Telephone: (719) 637-1022
President: Neal Brendel
CEO: DougArnot
Communications Director: Deborah Engen
www.usarugby.org

The United Soccer Leagues
Address: 14497 North Dale Mabry Highway, Ste 201
        Tampa, FL 33618
Telephone: (813) 963-3909
President and A-League Commissioner: Francisco
  Marcos
Director of Public Relations:Gerald Barnhart
www.unitedsoccerleagues.com

Major League Soccer
Address: 110 East 42nd Street, Suite 1000
        New York, NY 10017
Telephone: (212) 687-1400
Commissioner: Don Garber
Director of Communications: Trey Fitzgerald
www.mlsnet.com

Major Indoor Soccer League
Address: 1175 Post Road East
        Westport, CT 06880
Telephone: (203) 222-4900
Commissioner: Steve Ryan
Director of New Media & Marketing: Kara McGovern
www.misl.net

Women's United Soccer Association
Address: 6205 Peachtree Dunwoody Road
        Atlanta, GA 30328
Telephone: (678) 645-0800
Commissioner: Tony DiCicco
Director of Public Relations: Shaun May
www.wusa.com

Association of Tennis Professionals Tour
Address: 201 ATP Tour Boulevard
        Ponte Vedra Beach, FL 32082
Telephone: (904) 285-8000
Chief Executive Officer: Mark Miles
VP of Comm. and Media Relations: Greg Sharko
www.atptour.com

COREL WTA Tour (Women's Tennis)
Address: One Progress Plaza - Suite 1500
        St. Petersburg, FL 33701
Telephone: (727) 895-5000
Chief Executive Officer: Larry Scott
Director of Corporate Communications: Darrell Fry
www.sanexwta.com

Association of Volleyball Professionals
Address: 6080 Center Drive
        Los Angeles, CA 90045
Telephone: (310) 426-8000
Public Relations: Debbie Rubio, The Robbins Group
  (818) 776-1244
www.avptour.com

MINOR LEAGUES

Baseball (AAA)

National Association of Professional Baseball Leagues
Address: 201 Bayshore Drive S.E. - P.O. Box A
        St. Petersburg, FL 33731
Telephone: (727) 822-6937
President: Mike Moore
Director of Media Relations: Jim Ferguson
www.minorleaguebaseball.com

MINOR LEAGUES (Cont.)

Baseball (AAA) (Cont.)

International League
Address: 55 South High Street, Suite 202
              Dublin, OH 43017
Telephone: (614) 791-9300
President: Randy Mobley
www.ilbaseball.com

Pacific Coast League
Address: 1631 Mesa Avenue
              Colorado Springs, CO 80906
Telephone: (719) 636-3399
President: Branch Rickey
www.pclbaseball.com

Hockey

American Hockey League
Address: 1 Monarch Place Suite 2400
              Springfield, MA 01144
Telephone: (413) 781-2030
President, CEO & Treasurer: David A. Andrews
VP of Hockey Operations: Jim Mill
Director of Media: Jason Chaimovitch
www.theahl.com

Halls of Fame Directory

National Baseball Hall of Fame and Museum
Address: P.O. Box 590/25 Main Street
              Cooperstown, NY 13326
Telephone: (607) 547-7200
President: Dale Petroskey
Senior Vice President: Bill Haase
V.P. of Communications and Education: Jeff Idelson
www.baseballhalloffame.org

Naismith Memorial Basketball Hall of Fame
Address: 1150 West Columbus Avenue
              Springfield, MA 01105
Telephone: (413) 781-6500
President and CEO: John L. Doleva
Senior Director of Marketing: Dan O'Keefe
www.hoophall.com

International Bowling Museum and Hall of Fame
Address: 111 Stadium Plaza
              St. Louis, MO 63102
Telephone: (314) 231-6340
Executive Director: Gerald Baltz
Marketing Director: Jim Baer
www.bowlingmuseum.com

National Boxing Hall of Fame
Address: 1 Hall of Fame Drive
              Canastota, NY 13032
Telephone: (315) 697-7095
President: Donald Ackerman
Executive Director: Edward Brophy
www.ibhof.com

Professional Football Hall of Fame
Address: 2121 George Halas Drive NW
              Canton, OH 44708
Telephone: (330) 456-8207
Executive Director: John Bankert
Vice President of Public Relations: Joe Horrigan
www.profootballhof.com

LPGA Hall of Fame
Address: 100 International Golf Drive
              Daytona Beach, FL 32124
Telephone: (386) 274-6200
Commissioner: Ty Votaw
Director of Media Relations: Connie Wilson
www.lpga.com

Hockey Hall of Fame
Address: 30 Yonge Street BCE Place
              Toronto, Ontario Canada M5E 1X8
Telephone: (416) 360-7735
Chairman: William Hay
President & COO: Jeff Denomme
Director of Marketing and Facility Services: Craig Baines
www.hhof.com

National Museum of Racing and Hall of Fame
Address: 191 Union Avenue
              Saratoga Springs, NY 12866
Telephone: (518) 584-0400
Executive Director: Peter Hammell
Assistant Director: Catherine Maguire
Communications Officer: Richard Hamilton
www.racingmuseum.org

National Soccer Hall of Fame
Address: Wright Soccer Campus
              18 Stadium Circle
              Oneonta, NY 13820
Telephone: (607) 432-3351
President: Will Lunn
www.soccerhall.org

International Swimming Hall of Fame
Address: 1 Hall of Fame Drive
              Fort Lauderdale, FL 33316
Telephone: (954) 462-6536
President: Dr. Samuel J. Freas
Media Contact: Preston Levi
www.ishof.org

International Tennis Hall of Fame
Address: 194 Bellevue Avenue
              Newport, RI 02840
Telephone: (401) 849-3990
CEO: Mark Stenning
Marketing Manager: Kat Anderson
www.tennisfame.com

National Track & Field Hall of Fame
Address: 216 Ft. Washington Avenue
              The Armory Foundation
              New York, NY 10032
Telephone: (317) 261-0500
Chief Executive Officer: Craig Masback
Director of Communications: Jill Geer
www.usatf.org

Sporting Venues

STADIUM MAPS COURTESY OF TICKETMASTER

BASEBALL

Anaheim Angels
P.O. Box 2000
Anaheim, CA 92803
(714) 940-2000
Stadium: Edison International
Field of Anaheim

Arizona Diamondbacks

401 East Jefferson Street
Phoenix, AZ 85004
(602) 462-6500
Stadium: Bank One Ballpark

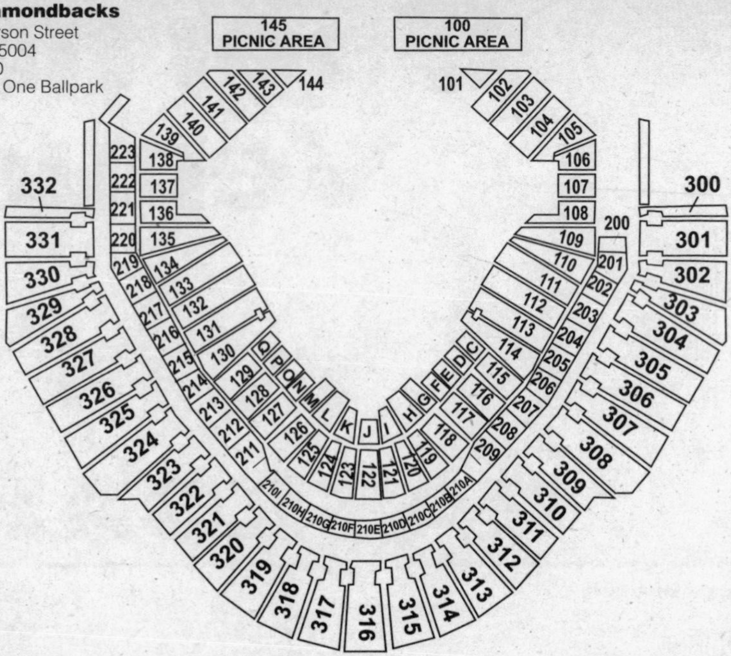

Atlanta Braves

P.O. Box 4064
Atlanta, GA 30302
(404) 522-7630
Stadium: Turner Field

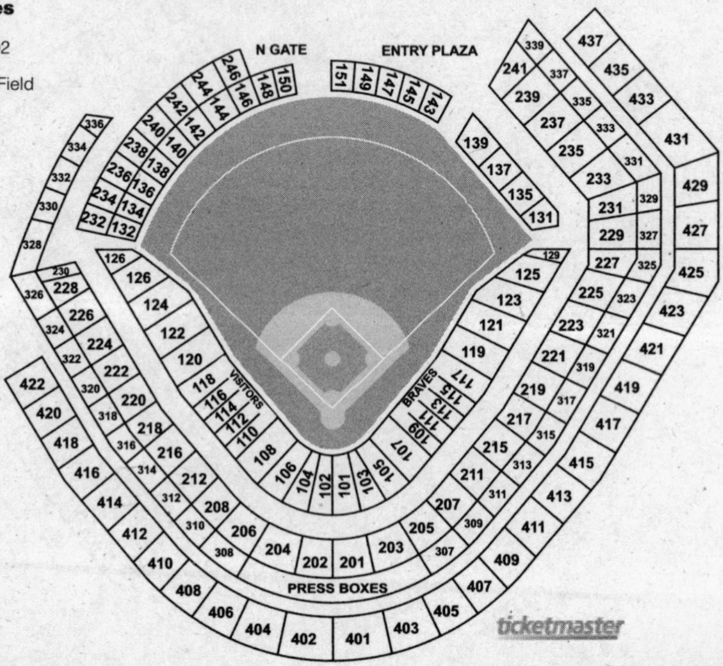

Baltimore Orioles

333 W Camden Street
Baltimore, MD 21201
(410) 685-9800
Stadium: Oriole Park
at Camden Yards

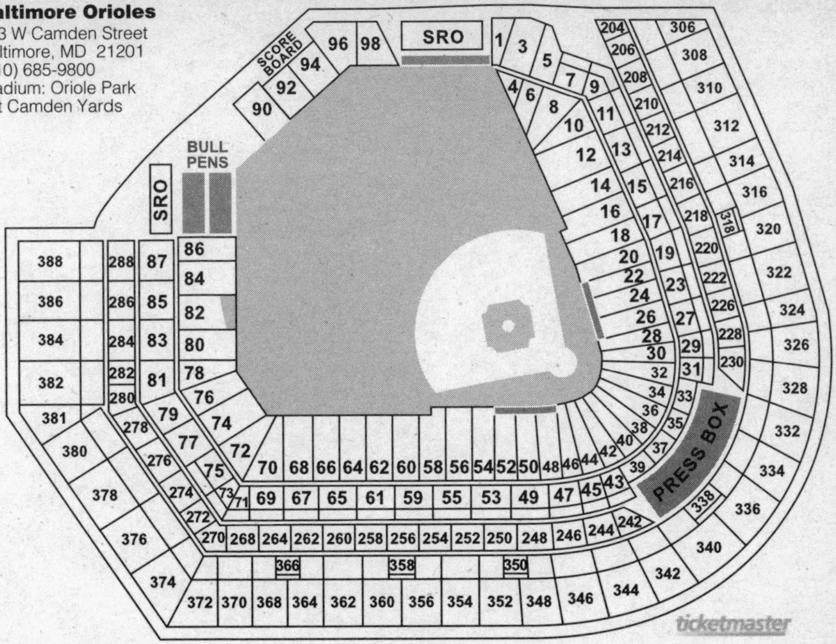

SCORE BOARD

SRO

BULL PENS

SRO

PRESS BOX

ticketmaster

Boston Red Sox

4 Yawkey Way
Boston, MA 02215
(617) 267-9440
Stadium: Fenway Park

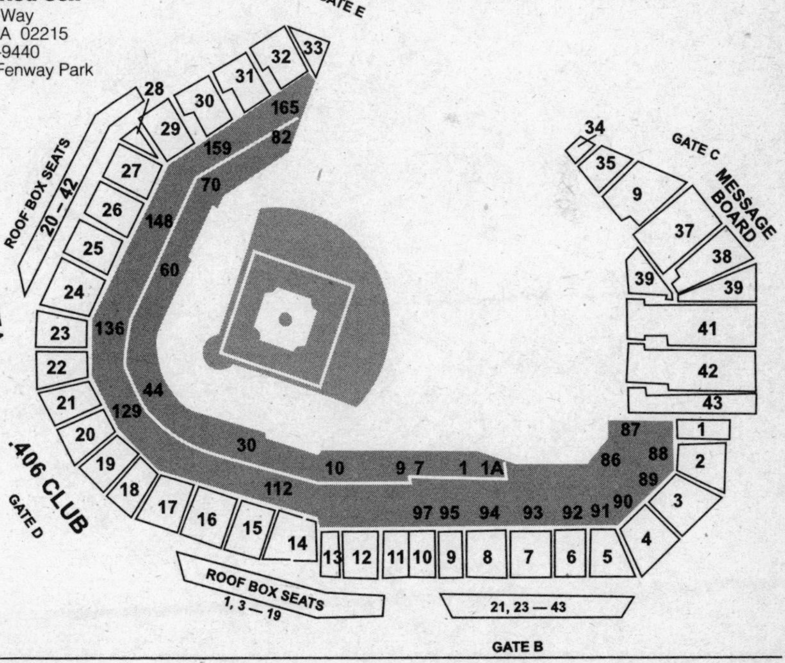

GATE E

GATE C

MESSAGE BOARD

ROOF BOX SEATS 20 — 42

GATE A

.406 CLUB

GATE D

ROOF BOX SEATS
1, 3 — 19

21, 23 — 43

GATE B

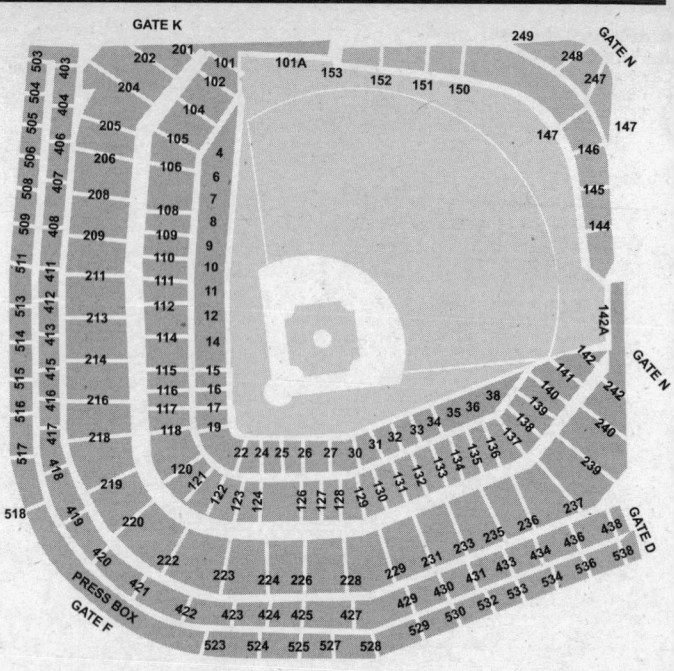

Chicago Cubs
1060 West Addison
Chicago, IL 60613
(773) 404-2827
Stadium: Wrigley Field

Chicago White Sox
333 West 35th Street
Chicago, IL 60616
(312) 674-1000
Stadium: Comiskey Park

ticketmaster

Cincinnati Reds

100 Main Street
Cincinnati, OH 45202
(513) 765-7000
Stadium: Great American Ball Park

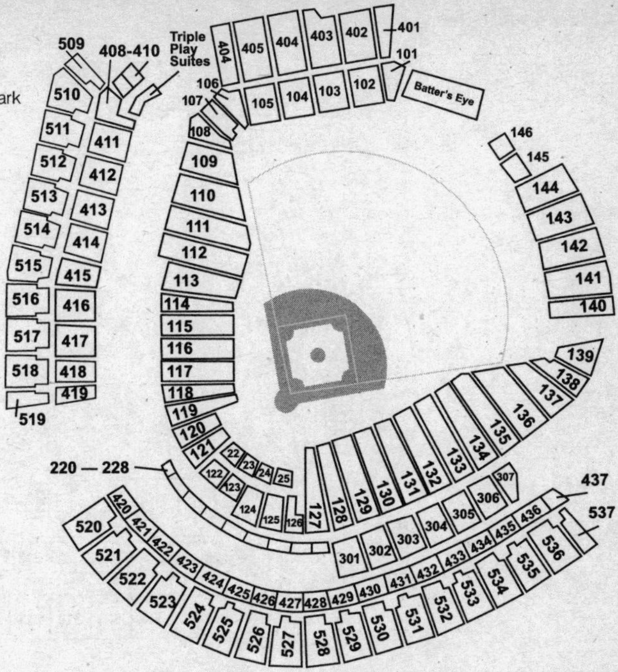

509   408-410   Triple Play Suites   404 405 404 403 402 401
510   106 107   101
511 411   108   Batter's Eye
512 412   109
513 413   110
514 414   111 112
515 415   113
516 416   114 115
517 417   116 117
518 418   118 119
519 419   120 121
146 145 144 143 142 141 140
139 138 137 136 135 134 133 132 131 130 129 128 127
220 — 228   22 23 24 25
122 123 124 125 126
307 306 305 437
520 421 422 423 424 425 426 427 428 429 430 431 432 433 434 435 436 537
521 522 523 524 525 526 527 528 529 530 531 532 533 534 535 536
301 302 303 304

Cleveland Indians

2401 Ontario Street
Cleveland, OH 44115-4003
(216) 420-4200
Stadium: Jacobs Field

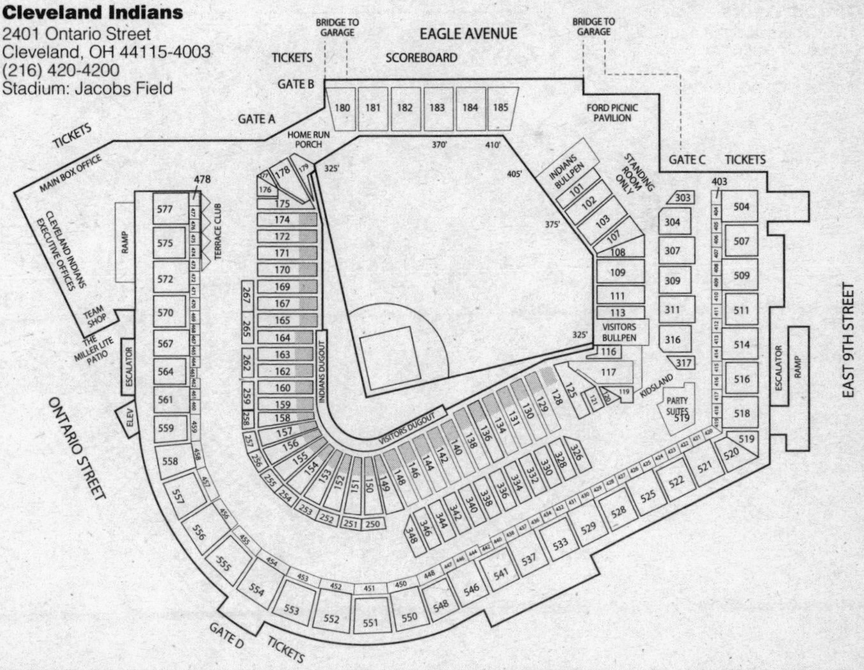

BRIDGE TO GARAGE   EAGLE AVENUE   BRIDGE TO GARAGE
TICKETS   SCOREBOARD
GATE B
GATE A   180 181 182 183 184 185   FORD PICNIC PAVILION
HOME RUN PORCH   370'   410'   GATE C   TICKETS
TICKETS   325'   405'   INDIANS BULLPEN 101   403
MAIN BOX OFFICE   178   102   303   504
478   176 175   103   304   507
577   174   107   307   509
CLEVELAND INDIANS EXECUTIVE OFFICES   575   172 171 170   108   309   511
TERRACE CLUB   572   169   109   311   514
570   167 165   111   316   516
TEAM SHOP   567   164 163   113   317   518
THE MILLER LITE PATIO   564   162   VISITORS BULLPEN   PARTY SUITES 519   519
561   160 159   116   520
ESCALATOR   559   158 157   117   RIDGLAND   521 522
558   156 155   119   EAST 9TH STREET
ONTARIO STREET   557   154   ESCALATOR   RAMP
556   153   375'   325'
555   151   STANDING ROOM ONLY
554   250 251 252 253 254   524 525 528
553 552 551 550   548 546 541 537 533 529
GATE D   TICKETS

Colorado Rockies

2001 Blake Street
Denver, CO 80205
(303) 292-0200
Stadium: Coors Field

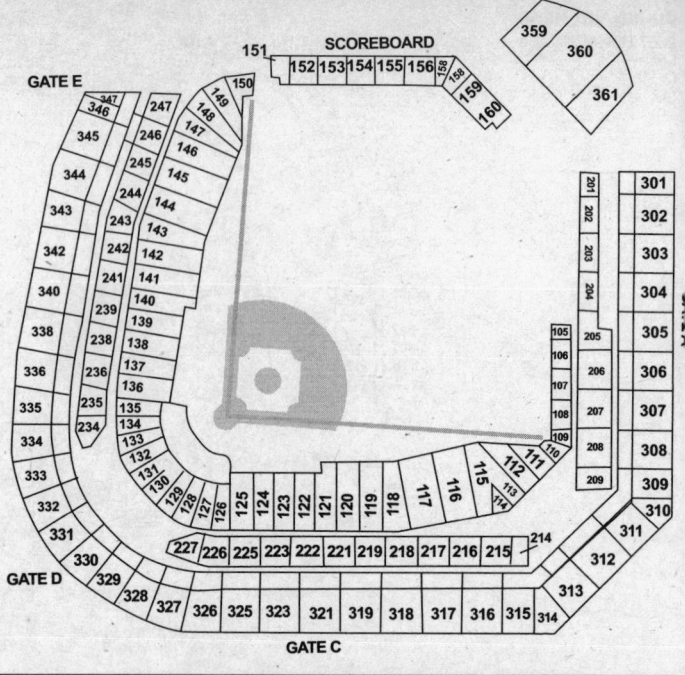

GATE E

SCOREBOARD

GATE D

GATE C

Detroit Tigers

2100 Woodward Avenue
Detroit, MI 48201
(313) 962-4000
Stadium: Comerica Park

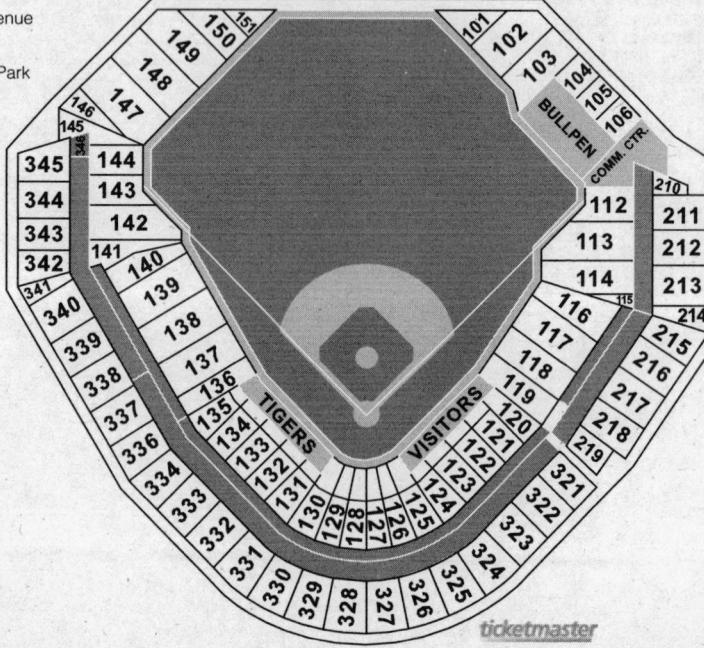

BULLPEN

COMM. CTR.

TIGERS

VISITORS

ticketmaster

Florida Marlins

2267 Dan Marino Boulevard
Miami, FL 33056
(305) 626-7400
Stadium: Pro Player
 Stadium

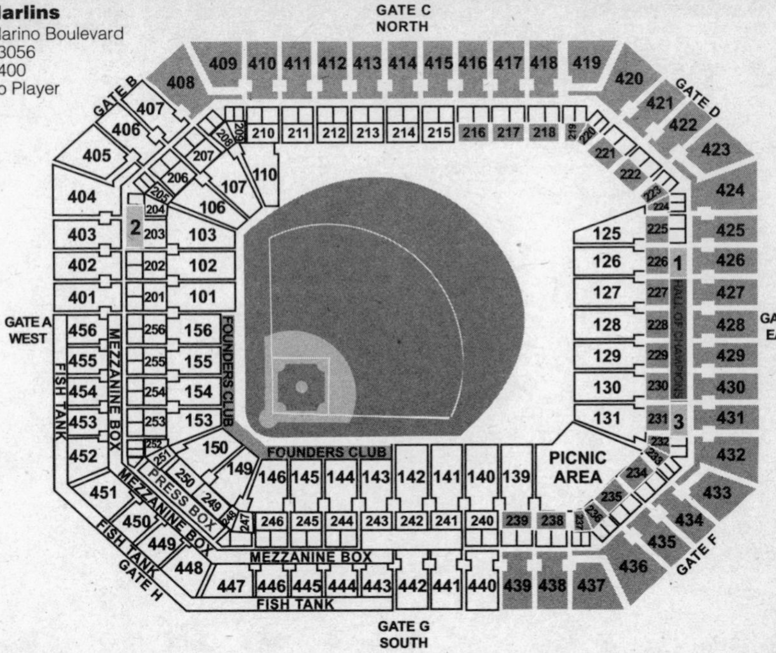

Houston Astros

P.O. Box 288
Houston, TX 77001
(713) 259-8000
Stadium:
 Minute Maid Park

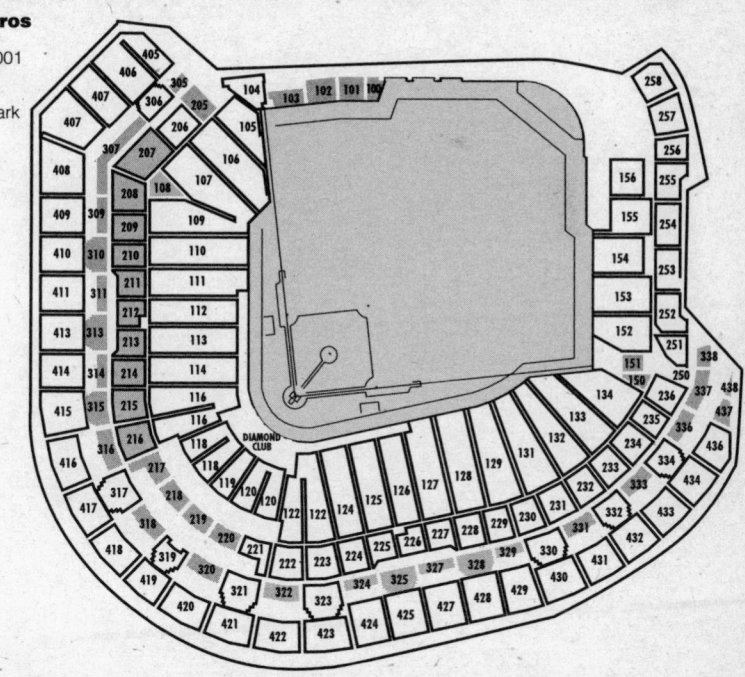

Kansas City Royals

P.O. Box 419969
Kansas City, MO 64141
(816) 921-8000
Stadium: Kauffman Stadium

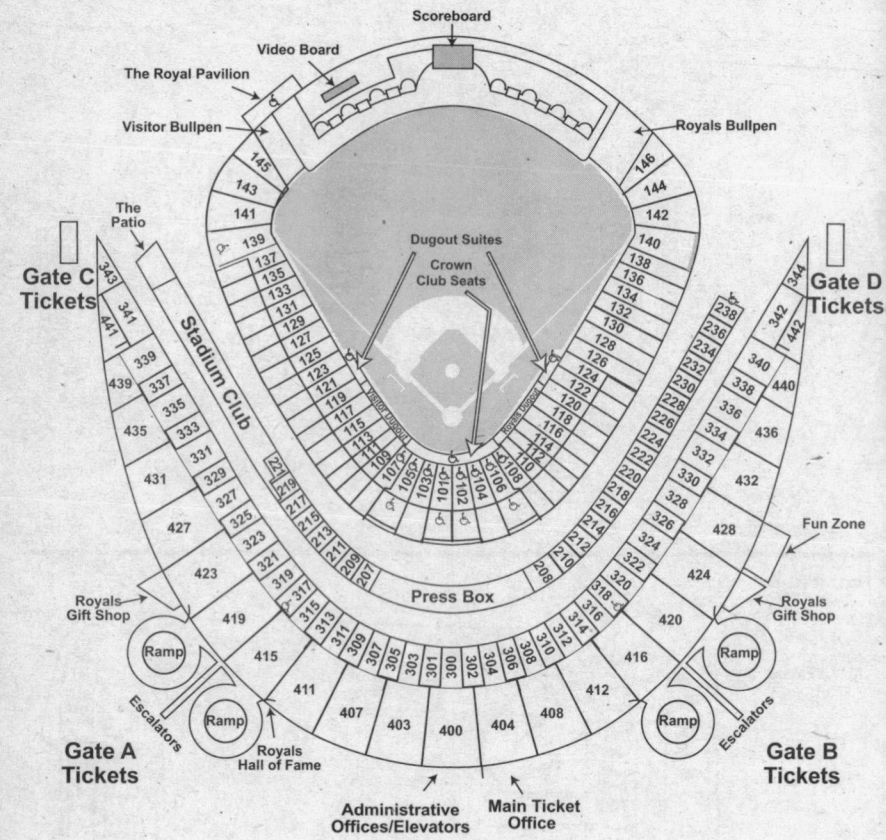

Los Angeles Dodgers

1000 Elysian Park Avenue
Los Angeles, CA 90012-1199
(323) 224-1500
Stadium: Dodger Stadium

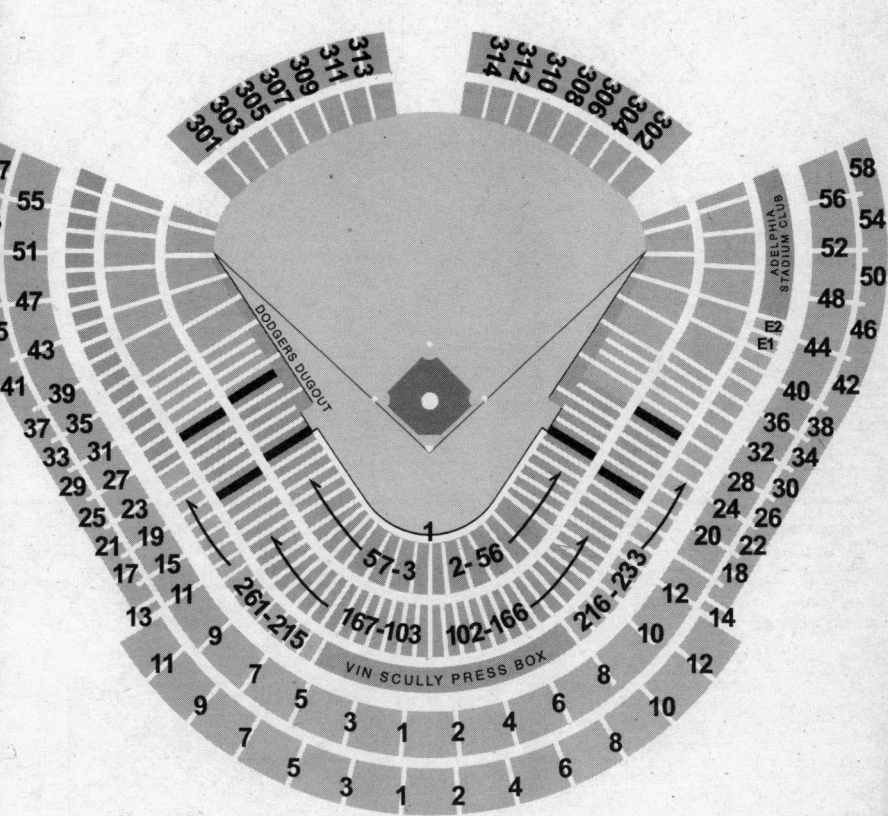

Milwaukee Brewers

1 Brewers Way
Milwaukee, WI 53214
(414) 902-4400
Stadium: Miller Park

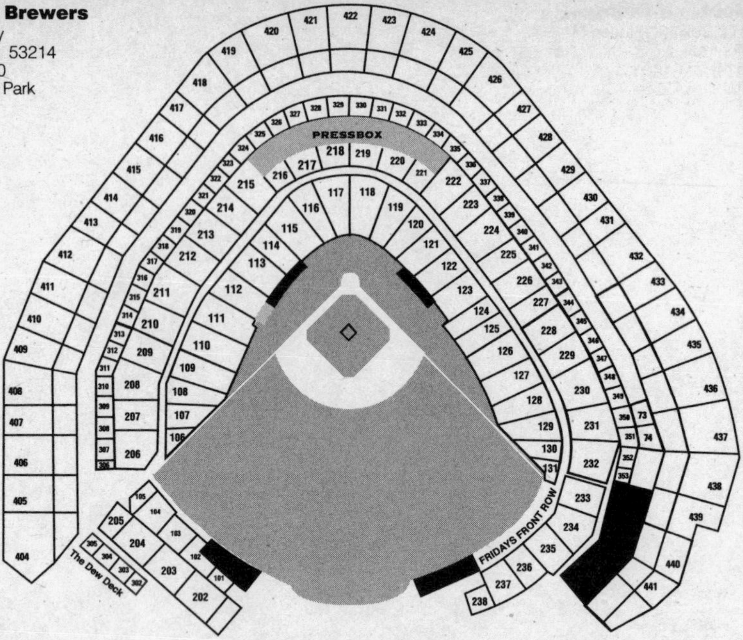

Minnesota Twins

34 Kirby Puckett Place
Minneapolis, MN 55415
(612) 375-1366
Stadium: Hubert H. Humphrey
  Metrodome

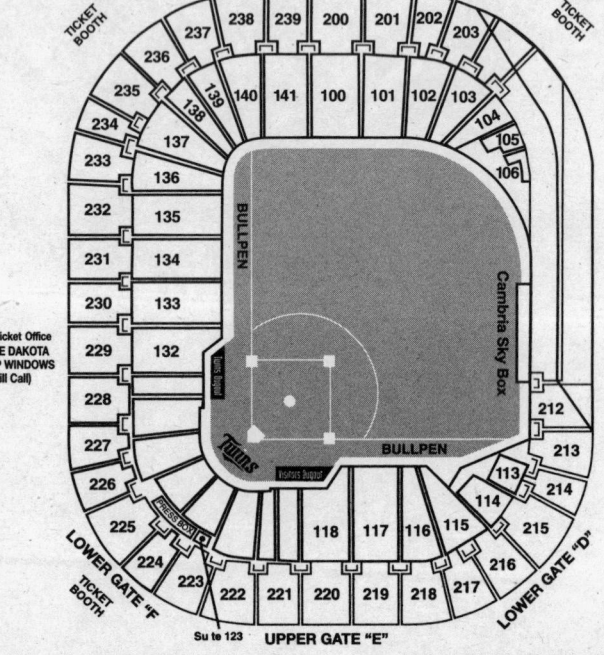

Montreal Expos

P.O. Box 500 Station M
Montreal, Quebec H1V 3P2 Canada
(514) 253-3434
Stadium:
  Olympic Stadium

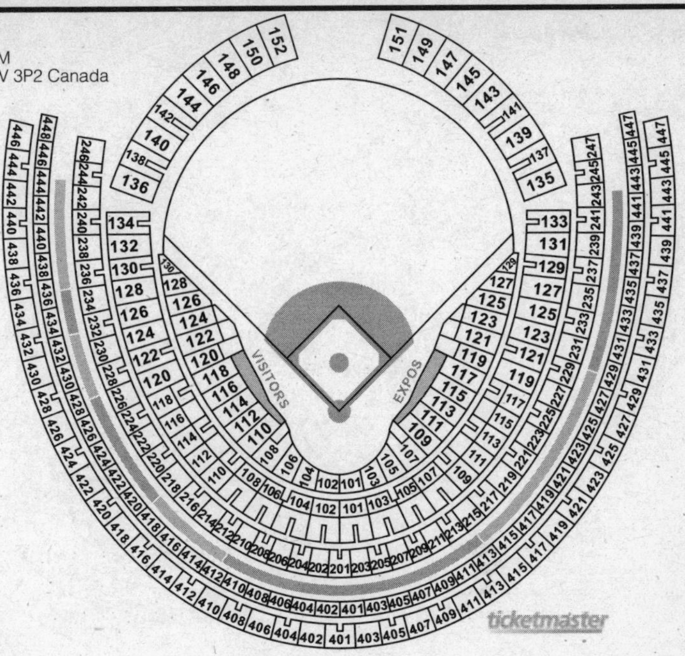

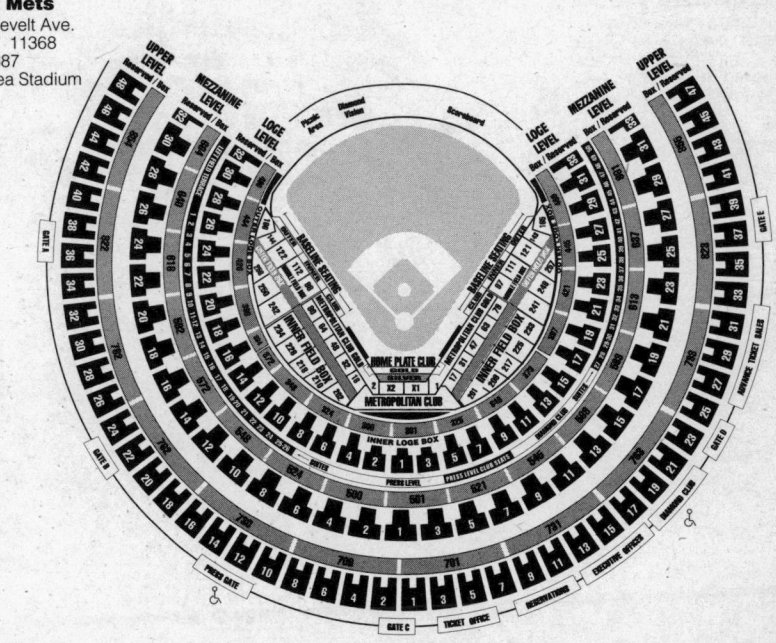

New York Mets

123-01 Roosevelt Ave.
Flushing, NY 11368
(718) 507-6387
Stadium: Shea Stadium

New York Yankees

Bronx, NY 10451
(718) 293-4300
Stadium: Yankee Stadium

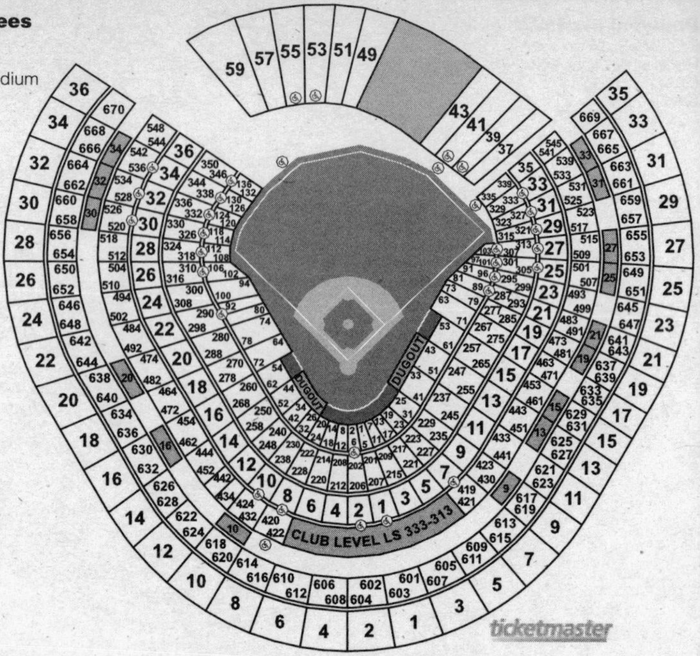

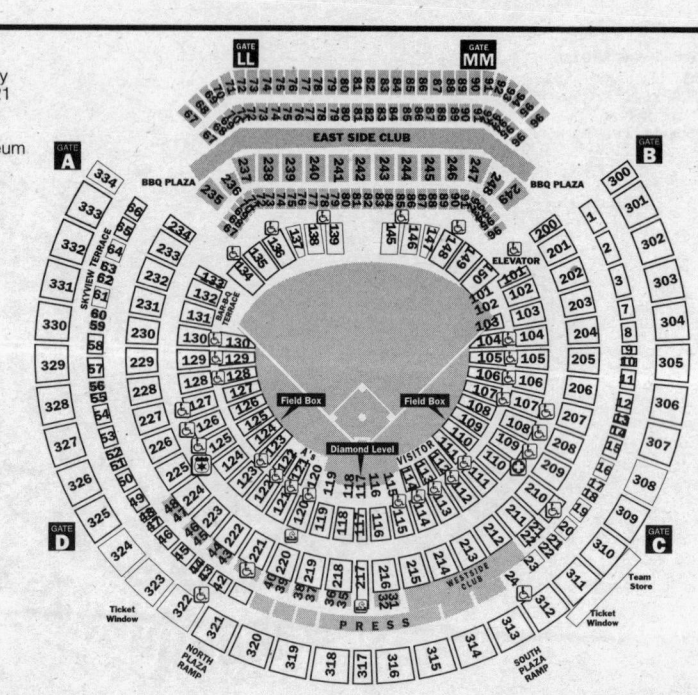

Oakland A's

7000 Coliseum Way
Oakland, CA 94621
(510) 638-4900
Stadium: Network
 Associates Coliseum

Philadelphia Phillies

P.O. Box 7575
Philadelphia, PA 19101-7575
(215) 463-6000
Stadium: Citizens Bank Park

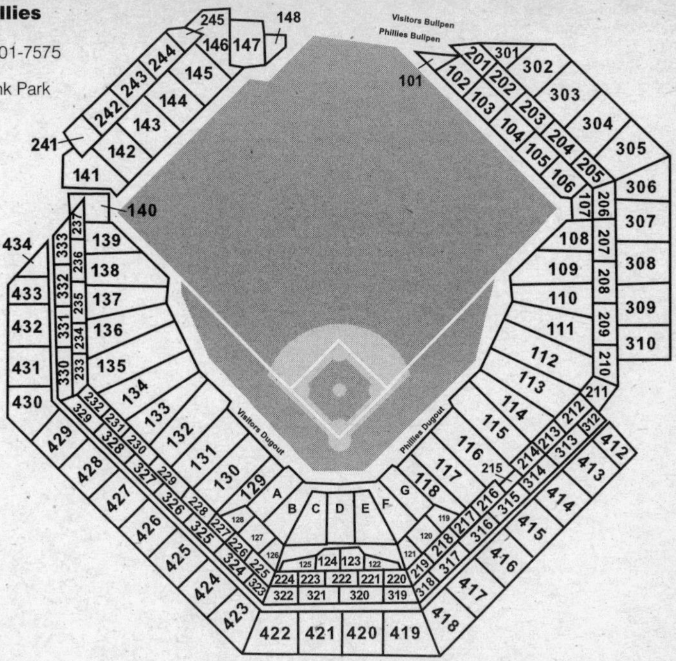

Visitors Bullpen
Phillies Bullpen

Visitors Dugout
Phillies Dugout

Pittsburgh Pirates

P.O. Box 7000
Pittsburgh, PA 15212
(412) 323-5000
Stadium: PNC Park

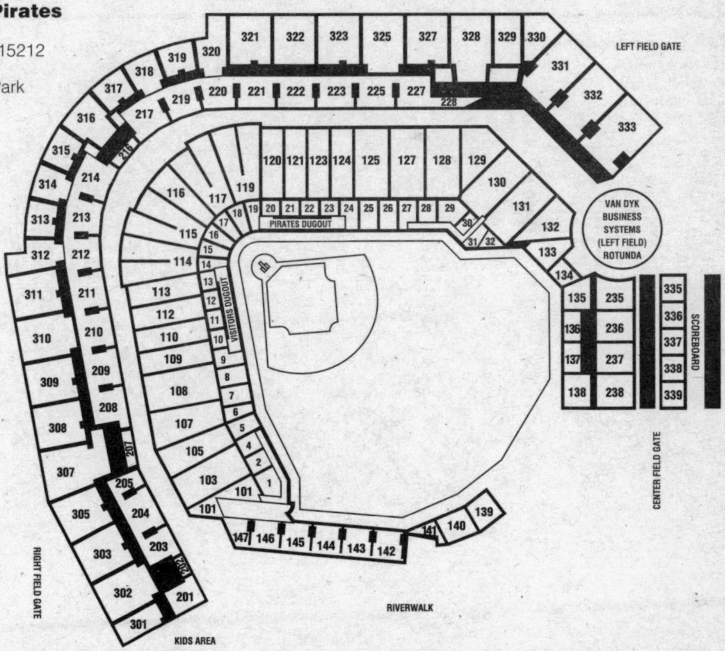

LEFT FIELD GATE

VAN DYK BUSINESS SYSTEMS (LEFT FIELD) ROTUNDA

SCOREBOARD

Pirates Dugout

VISITORS DUGOUT

CENTER FIELD GATE

RIGHT FIELD GATE

RIVERWALK

KIDS AREA

St Louis Cardinals

250 Stadium Plaza
St. Louis, MO 63102
(314) 421-3060
Stadium: Busch Stadium

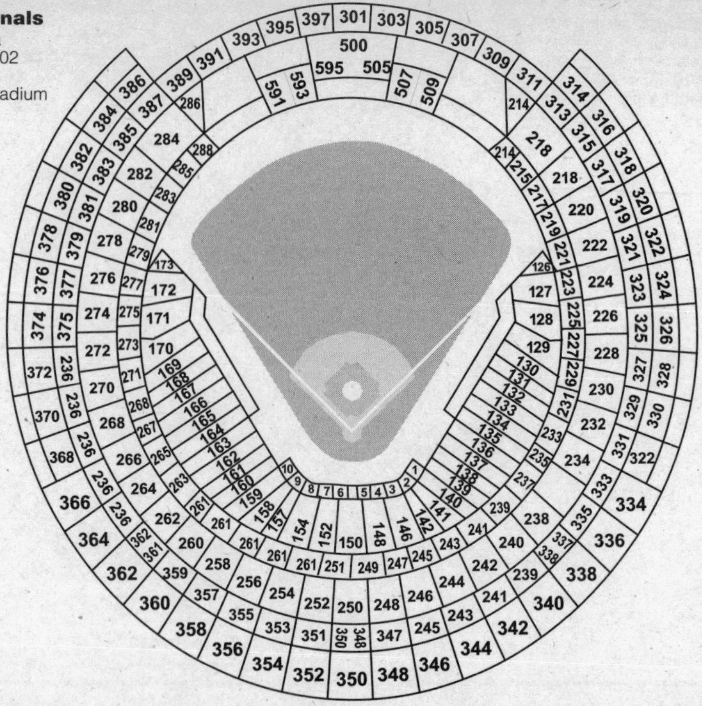

San Diego Padres

P.O. Box 122000
San Diego, CA 92112
(619) 283-4494
Stadium: Petco Park

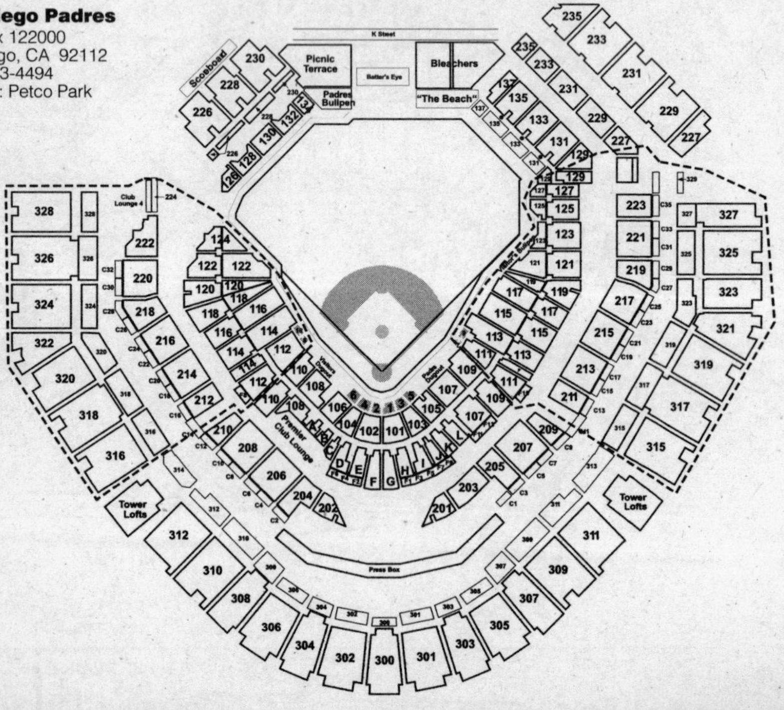

San Francisco Giants
24 Willie Mays Plaza
San Francisco, CA 94107
(415) 972-2000
Stadium: Pacific Bell Park

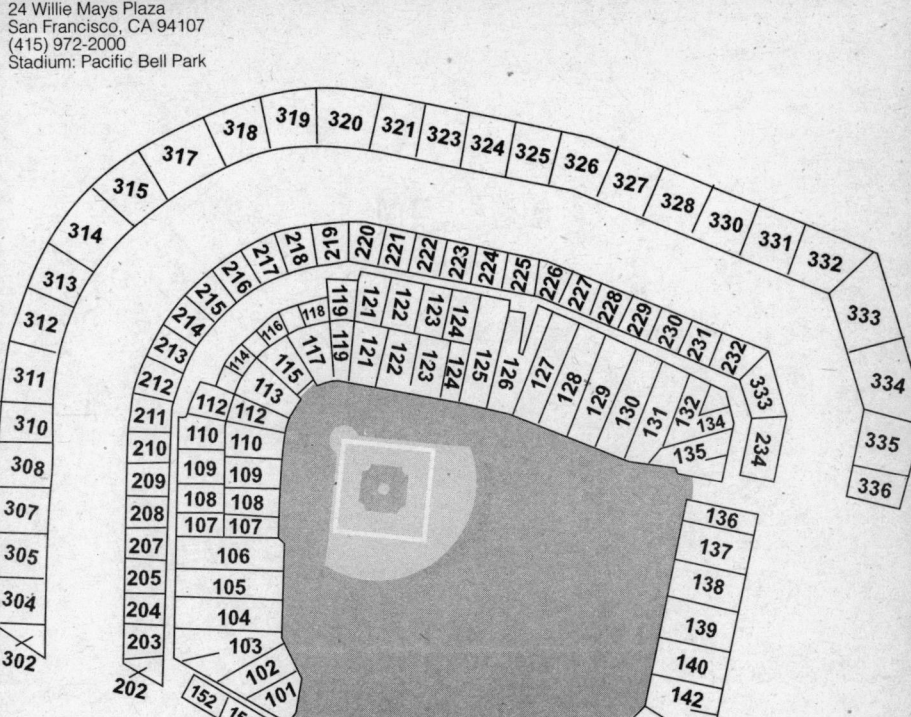

Seattle Mariners
P.O. Box 4100
Seattle, WA 98104
(206) 346-4000
Stadium: SAFECO Field

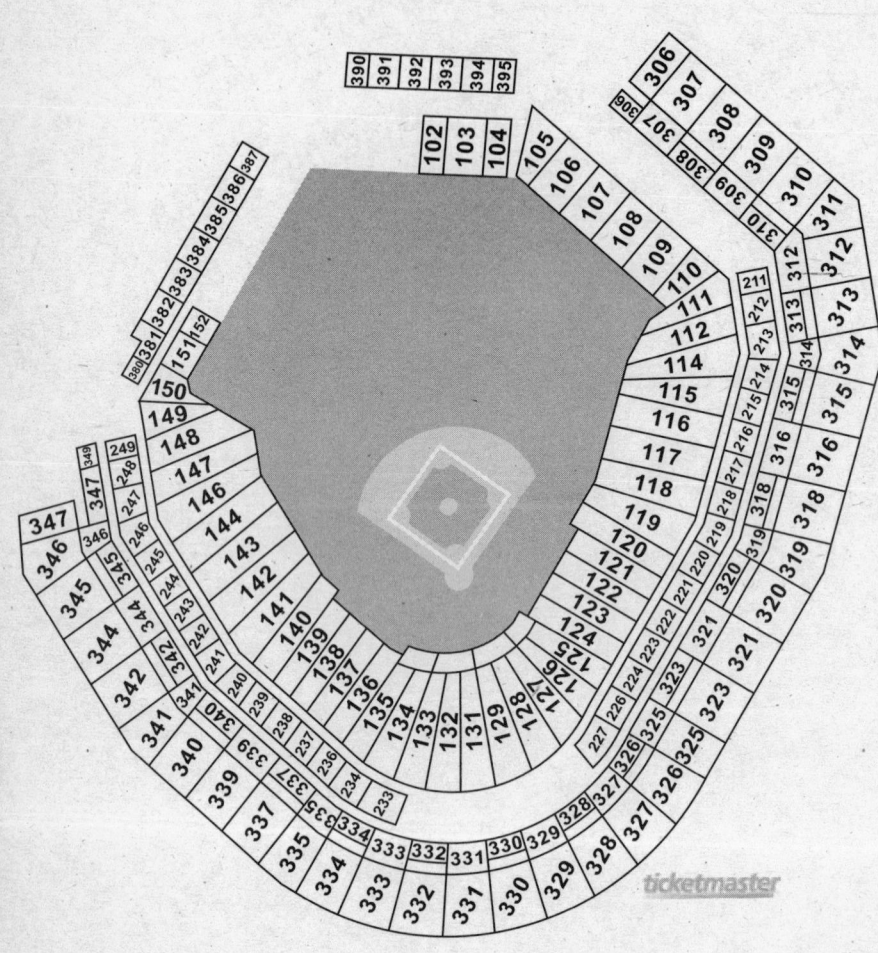

ticketmaster

Tampa Bay Devil Rays
One Tropicana Drive
St. Petersburg, FL 33705
(727) 825-3137
Stadium: Tropicana Field

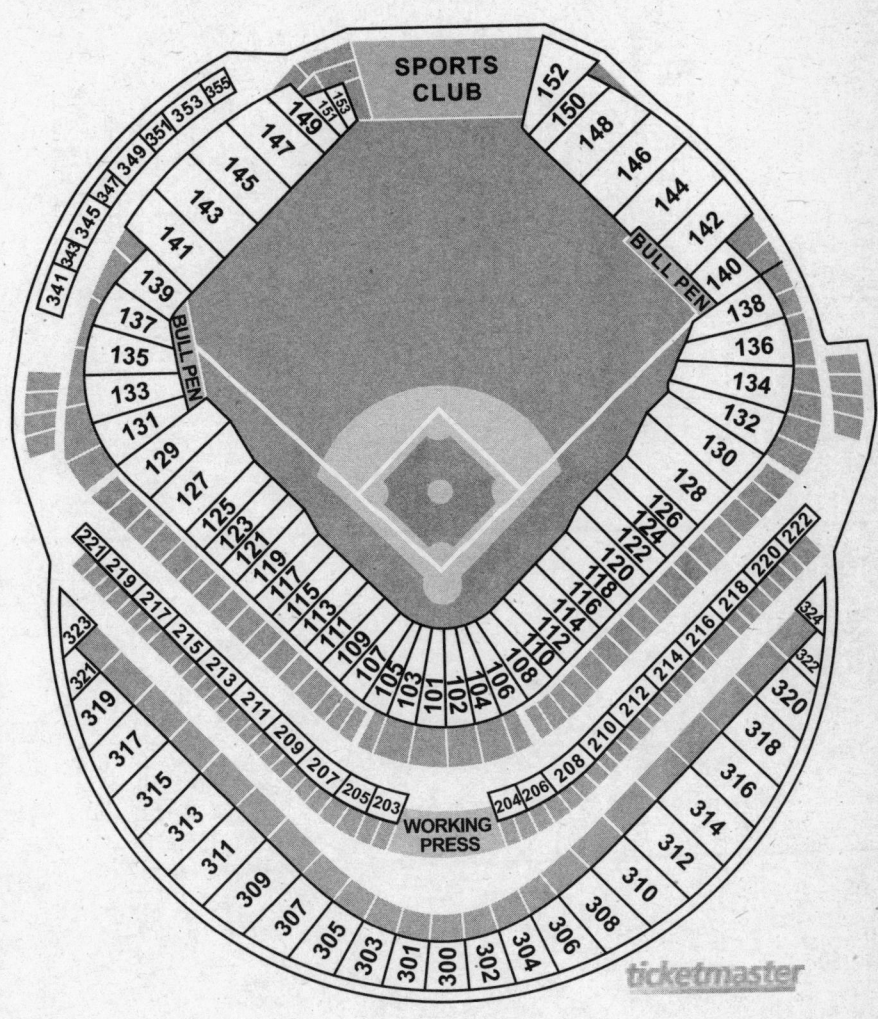

Texas Rangers

P.O. Box 90111
Arlington, TX 76004
(817) 273-5222
Stadium:
  The Ballpark in Arlington

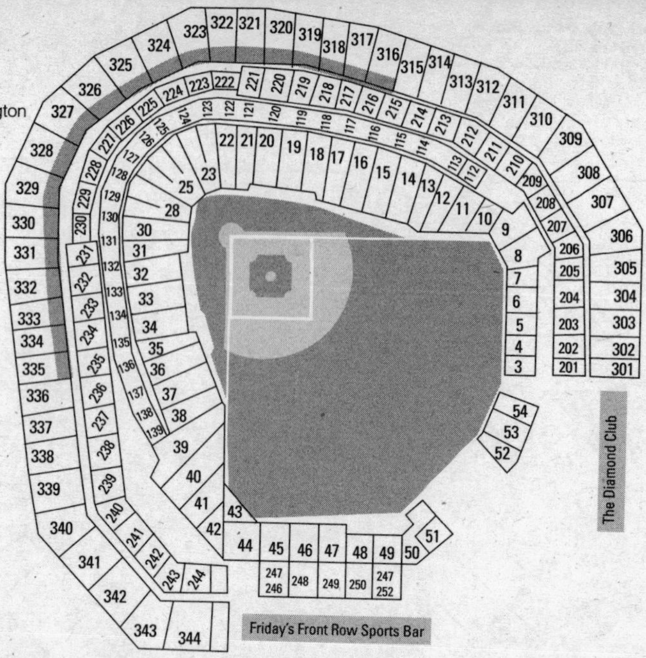

The Diamond Club

Friday's Front Row Sports Bar

Toronto Blue Jays

1 Blue Jays Way
Suite 3200
Toronto, Ontario M5V 1J1
  Canada
(416) 341-1000
Stadium: SkyDome

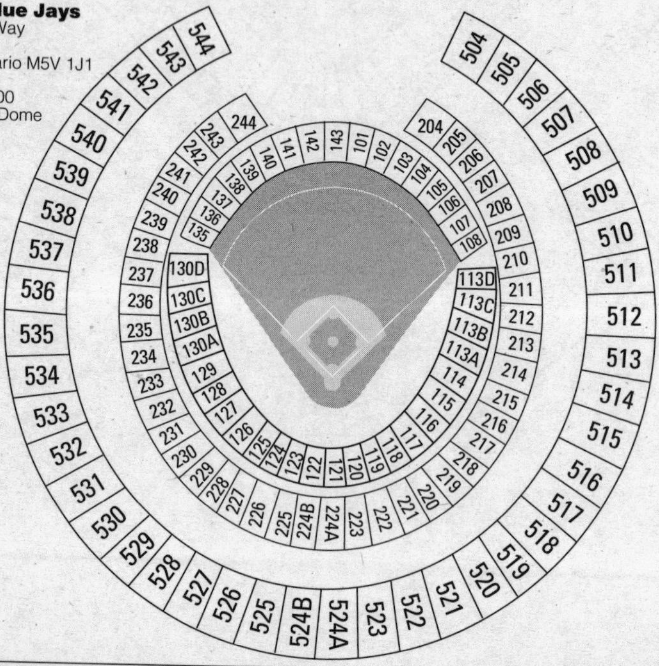

BASKETBALL

Atlanta Hawks
One CNN Center
Atlanta, GA 30303
Telephone: (404) 827-3800
Arena: Philips Arena

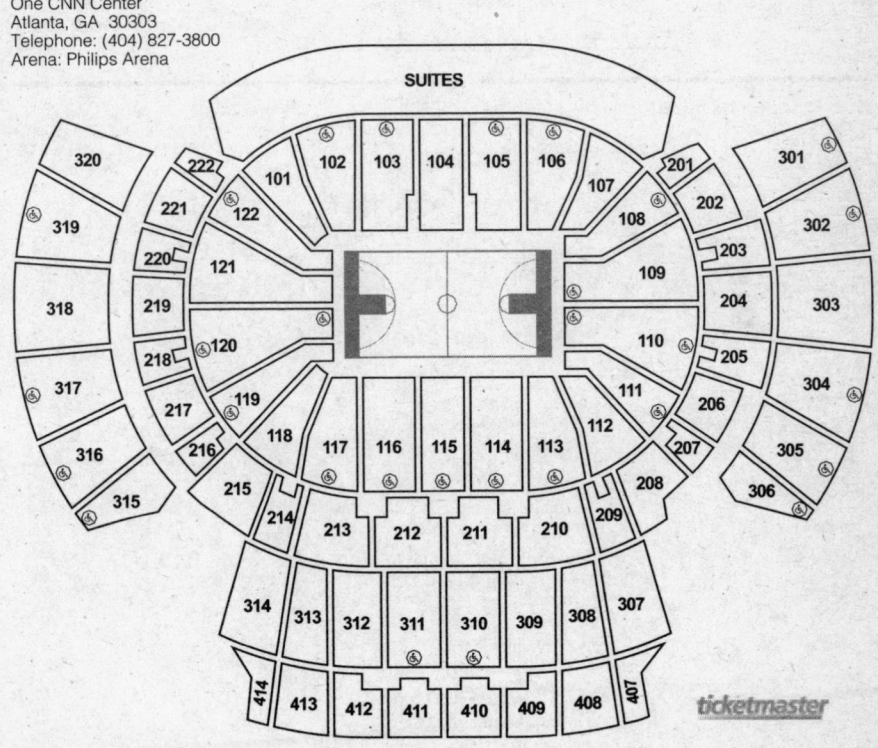

Boston Celtics

151 Merrimac Street
Boston, MA 02114
Telephone: (617) 523-6050
Arena: FleetCenter

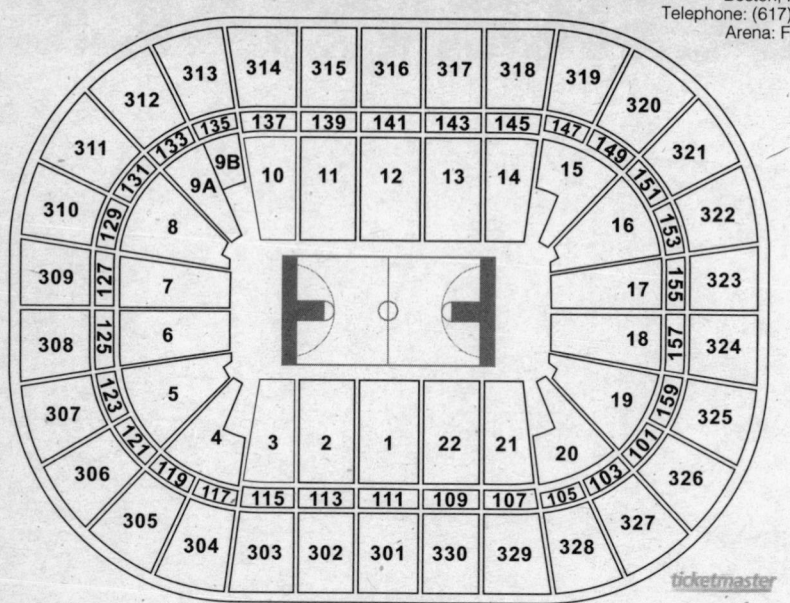

New Orleans Hornets

1501 Girod Street
New Orleans, LA 70113
Telephone: (504) 301-4000
Arena: New Orleans Arena

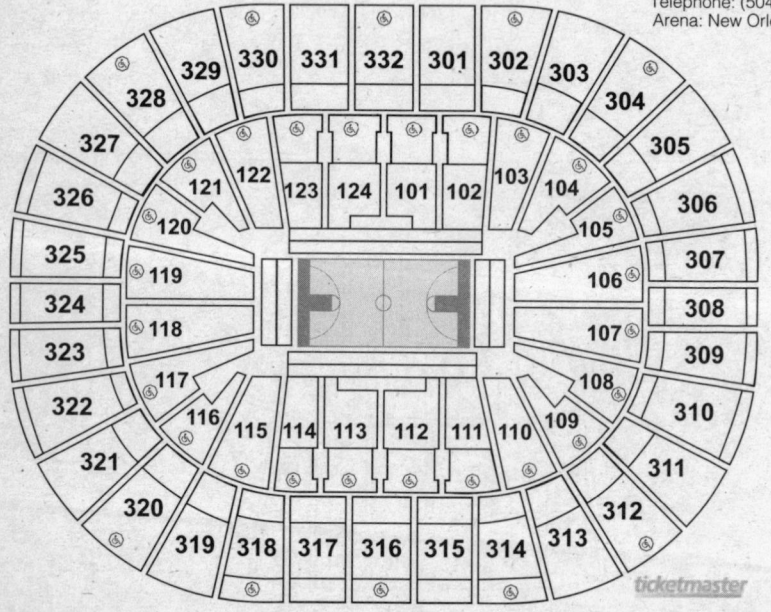

Chicago Bulls

1901 W. Madison Street
Chicago, IL 60612
Telephone: (312) 455-4000
Arena: United Center

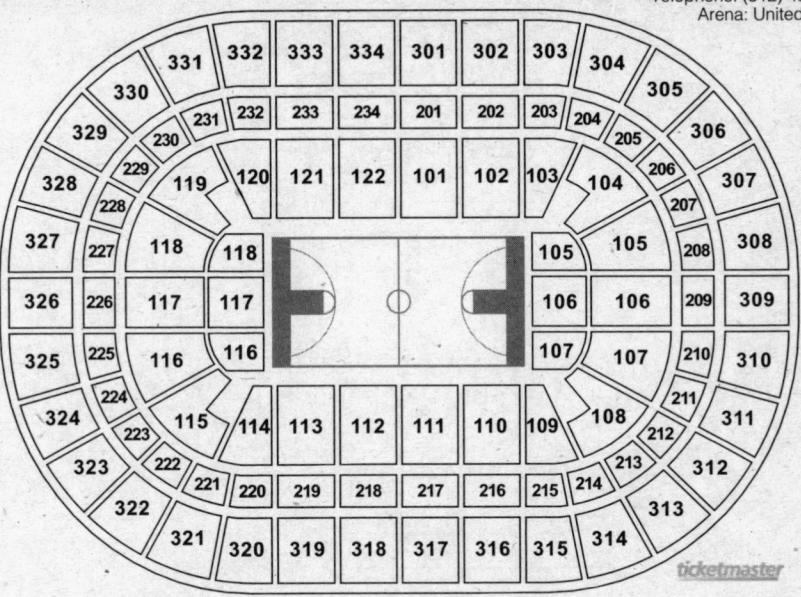

Cleveland Cavaliers

One Center Court
Cleveland, OH 44115
Telephone: (216) 420-2000
Arena: Gund Arena

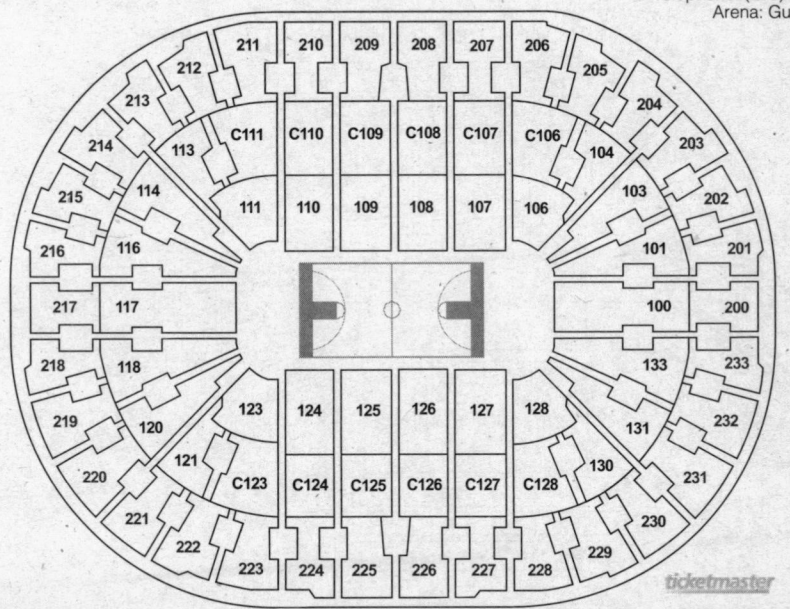

Dallas Mavericks

2500 Victory Avenue
Dallas, TX 75201
Telephone: (214) 665-4660
Arena: American Airlines Center

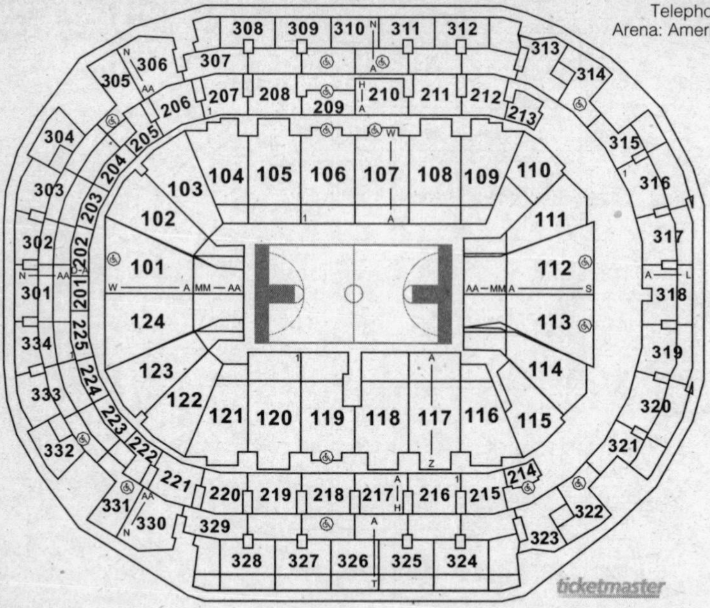

Denver Nuggets

1000 Chopper Circle
Denver, CO 80204
Telephone: (303) 405-1100
Arena: Pepsi Center

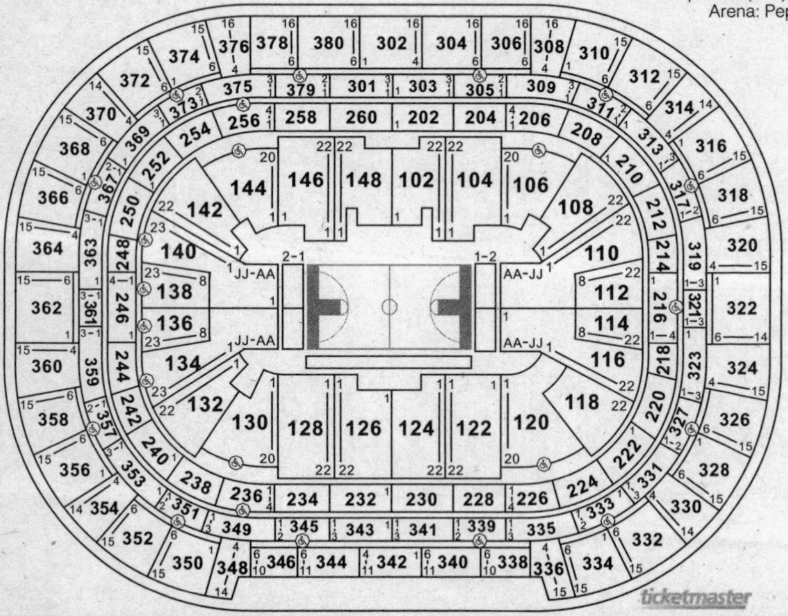

Detroit Pistons

Two Championship Drive
Auburn Hills, MI 48326
Telephone: (248) 377-0100
Arena: The Palace of Auburn Hills

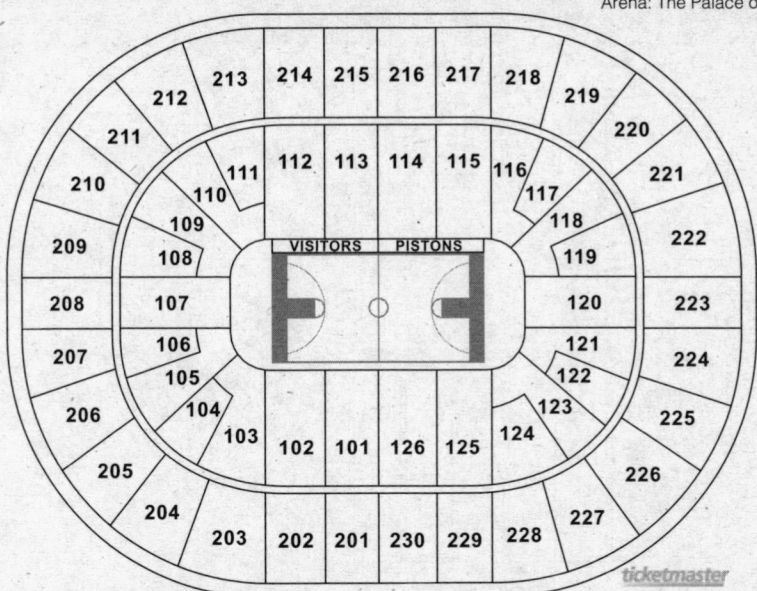

Golden State Warriors

1011 Broadway
Oakland, CA 94607-4019
Telephone: (510) 986-2200
Arena: The Arena in Oakland

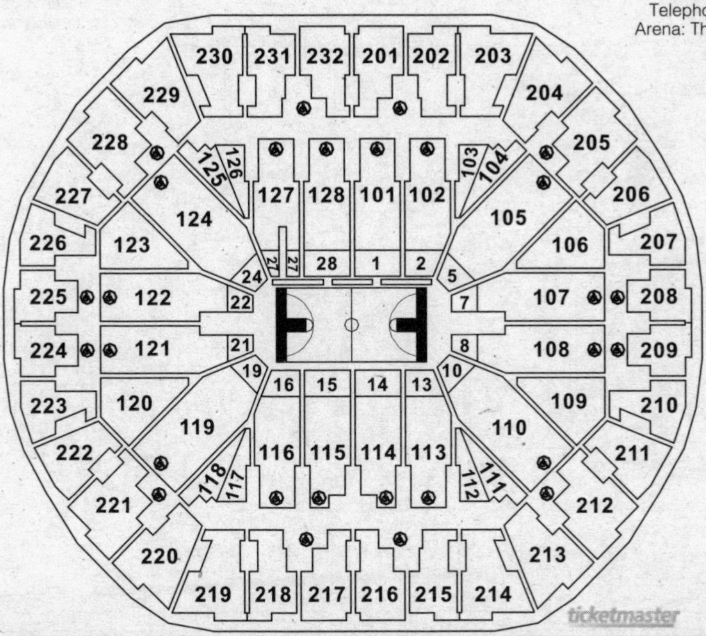

Houston Rockets

Two Greenway Plaza, Suite 400
Houston, TX 77046
Telephone: (713) 627-3865
Arena: Compaq Center

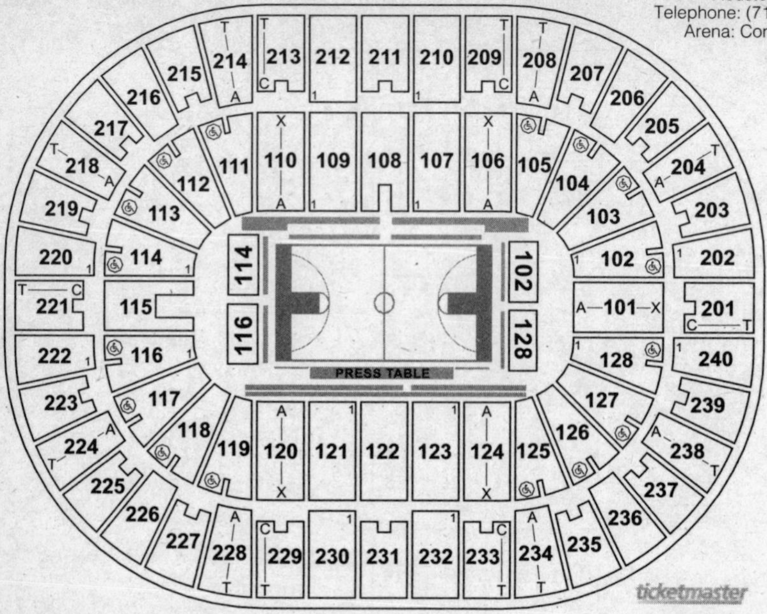

Seating chart sections: 201–240, 101–128, PRESS TABLE, 114, 116, 102, 128, 215, 214, 213, 212, 211, 210, 209, 208, 207, 206, 205, 204, 203, 202, 216, 217, 218, 219, 220, 221, 222, 223, 224, 225, 226, 227, 228, 229, 230, 231, 232, 233, 234, 235, 236, 237, 238, 239, 240, 111, 112, 113, 114, 115, 116, 117, 118, 119, 120, 121, 122, 123, 124, 125, 126, 127, 128, 110, 109, 108, 107, 106, 105, 104, 103, 102, 101

ticketmaster

Indiana Pacers

125 S. Pennsylvania Street
Indianapolis, IN 46204
Telephone: (317) 917-2500
Arena: Conseco Fieldhouse

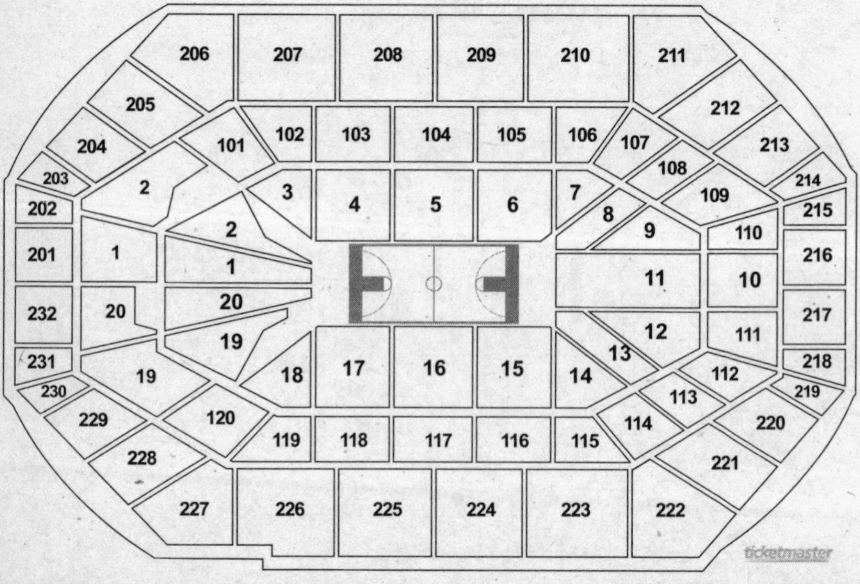

ticketmaster

Los Angeles Clippers

1111 S. Figueroa Street - St. 1100
Los Angeles, CA 90015
Telephone: (213) 742-7500
Arena: The Staples Center

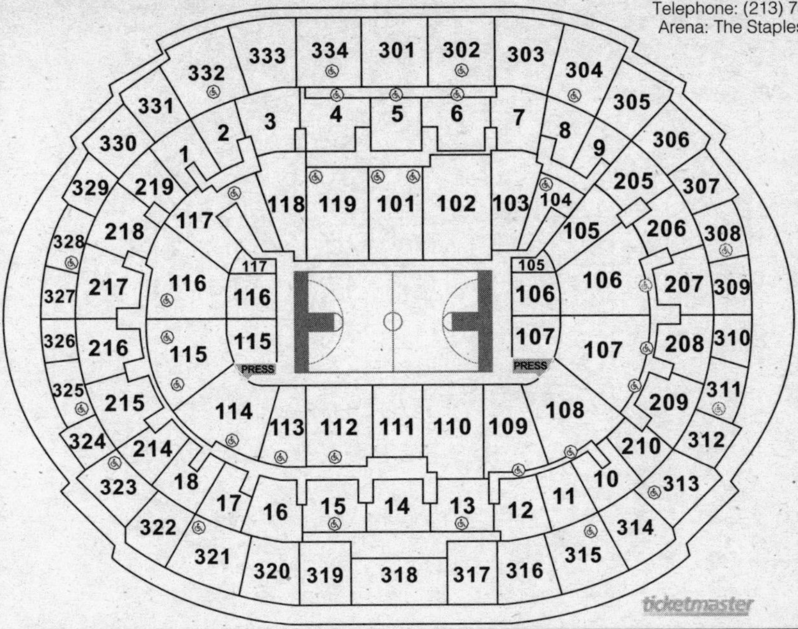

Los Angeles Lakers

555 North Nash Street
El Segundo, CA 90245
Telephone: (310) 426-6000
Arena: The Staples Center

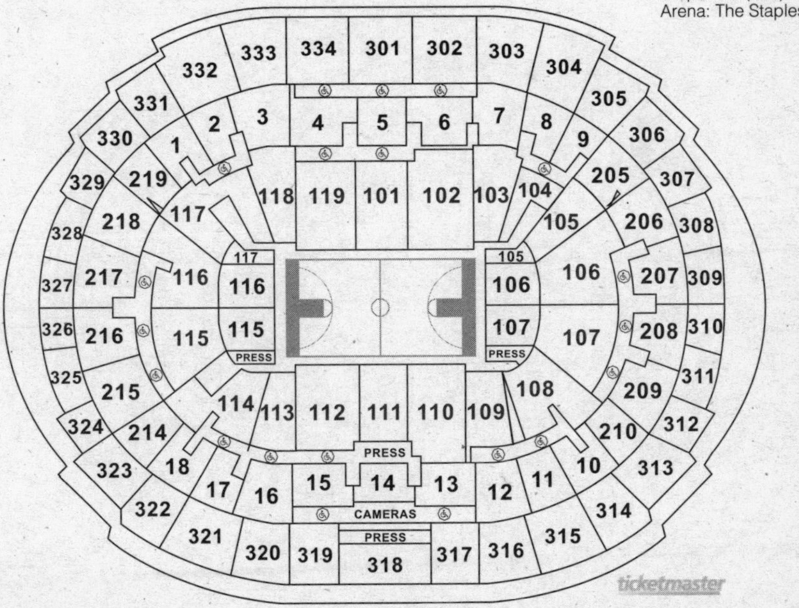

Memphis Grizzlies

60 Madison Street / 10th Floor
Memphis TN 38103
Telephone: (901) 205-1234
Arena: The Pyramid

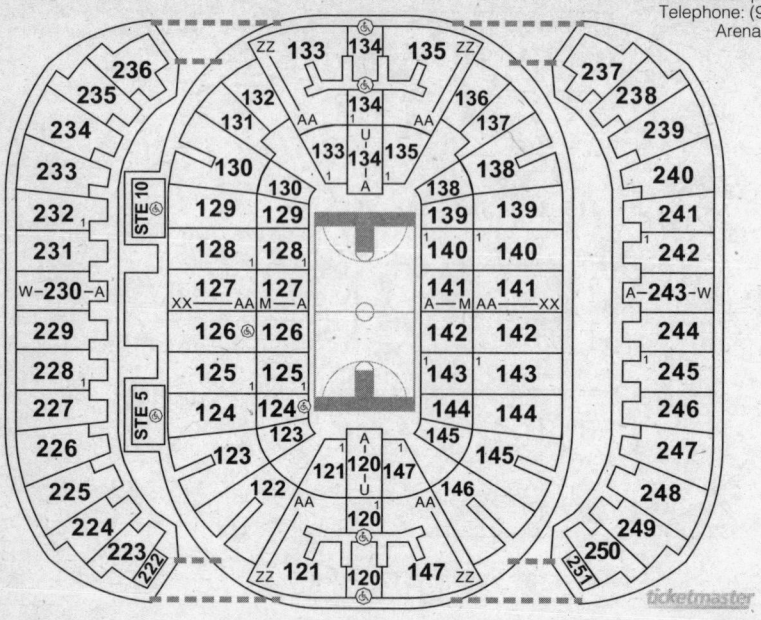

Miami Heat

601 Biscayne Boulevard
Miami, FL 33132
Telephone: (786) 777-4328
Arena: American Airlines Arena

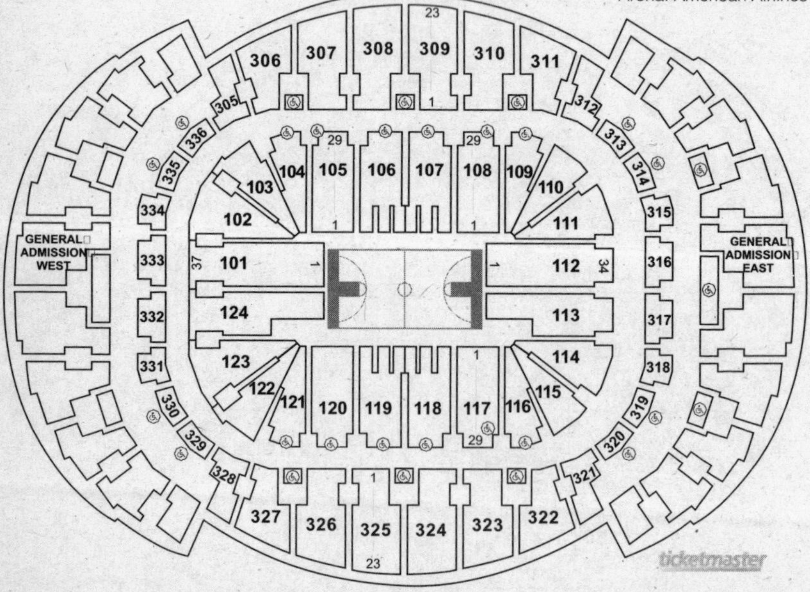

Milwaukee Bucks

1001 N. Fourth Street
Milwaukee, WI 53203
Telephone: (414) 227-0500
Arena: The Bradley Center

Minnesota Timberwolves

600 First Avenue North
Minneapolis, MN 55403
Telephone: (612) 673-1600
Arena: Target Center

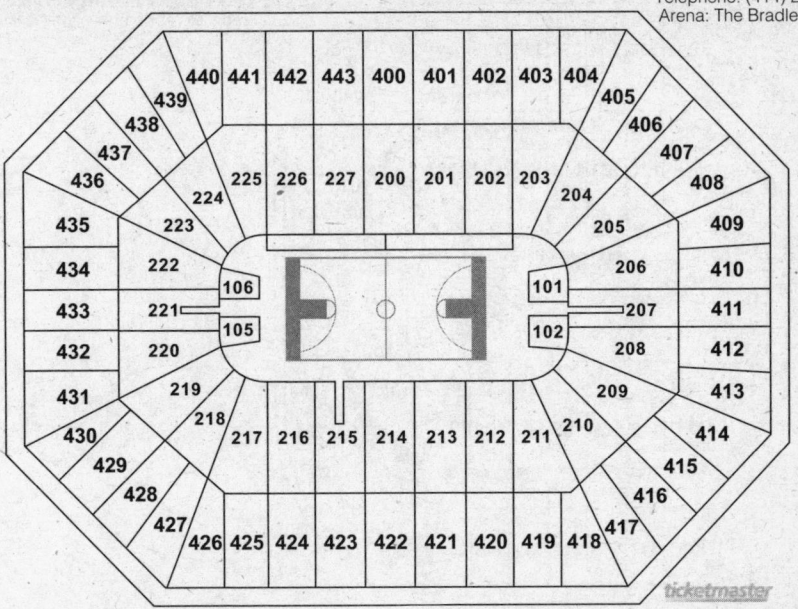

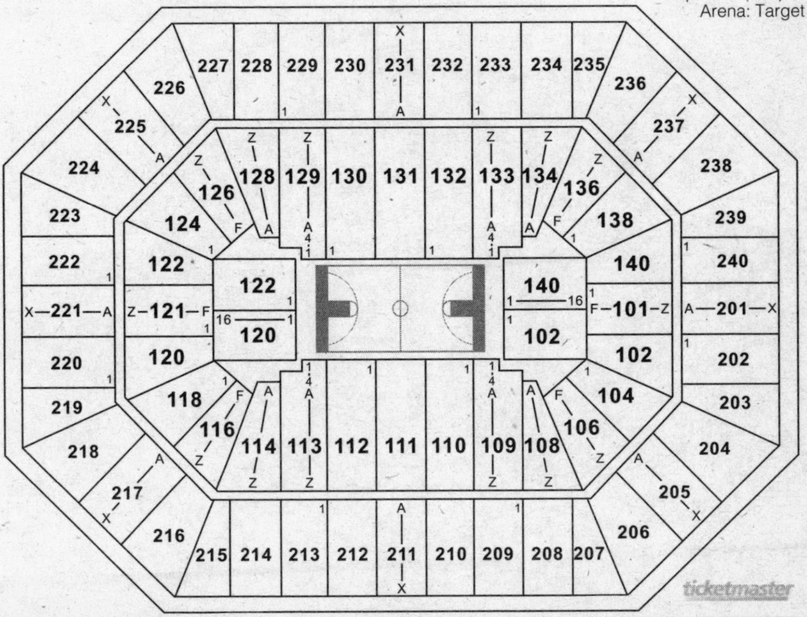

New Jersey Nets

390 Murray Hill Parkway
East Rutherford, NJ 07073
Telephone: (201) 935-8888
Arena: Continental Airlines Arena

New York Knickerbockers

Two Pennsylvania Plaza
New York, NY 10121
Telephone: (212) 465-5867
Arena: Madison Square Garden

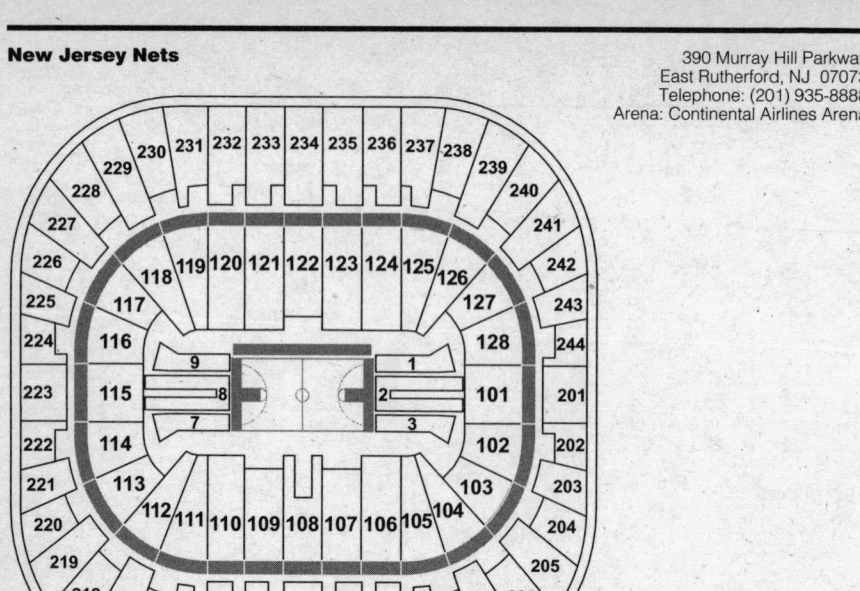

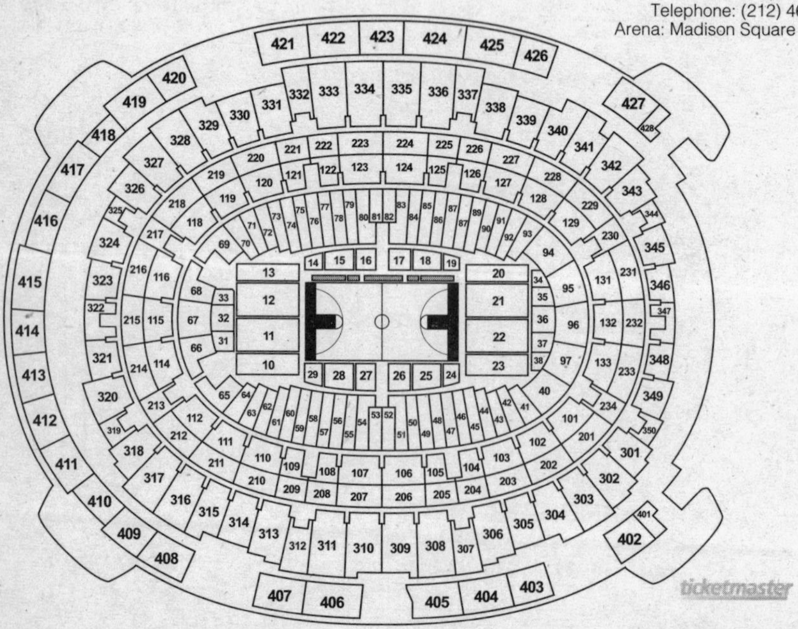

Orlando Magic

Two Magic Place
8701 Maitland Summit Blvd.
Orlando, FL 32810
Telephone: (407) 916-2400
Arena: TD Waterhouse Centre

Philadelphia 76ers

3601 South Broad Street
Philadelphia, PA 19148
Telephone: (215) 339-7600
Arena: First Union Center

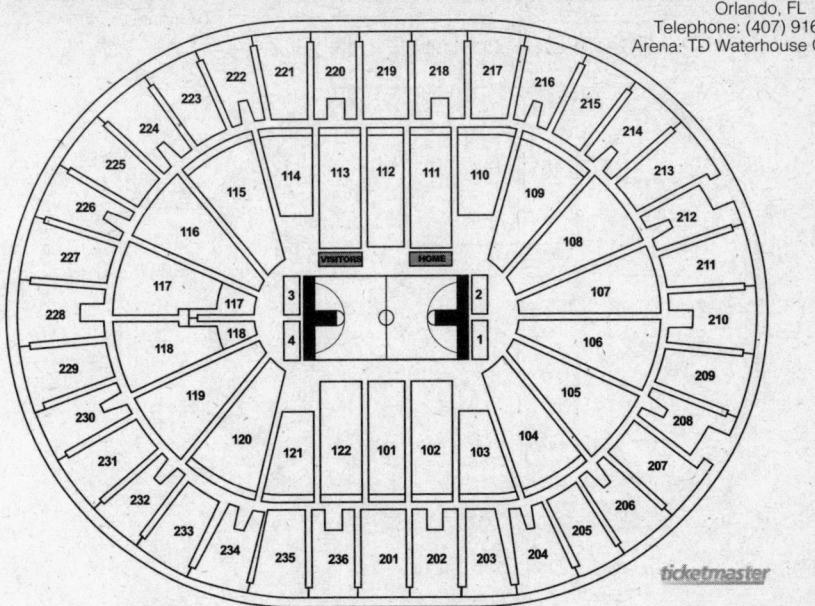

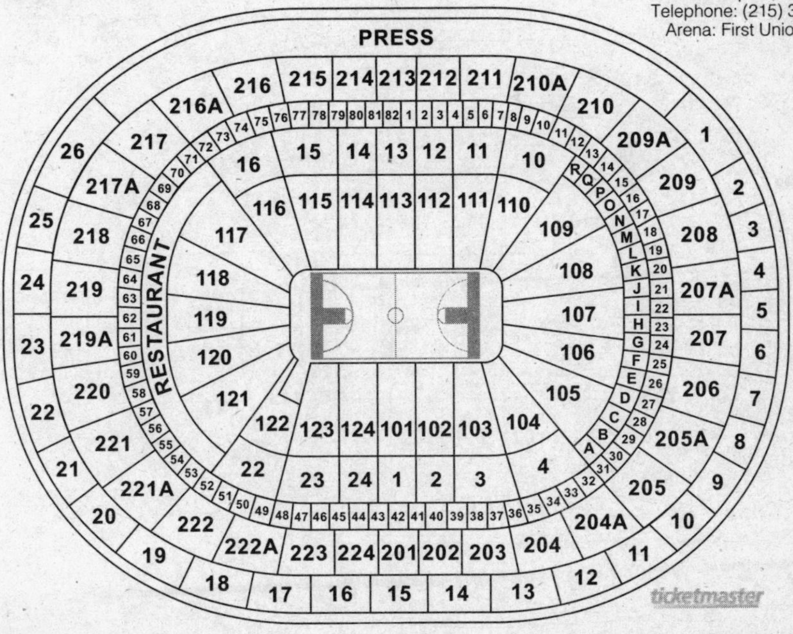

Phoenix Suns

P.O. Box 1369
Phoenix, AZ 85001
Telephone: (602) 379-7900
Arena: America West Arena

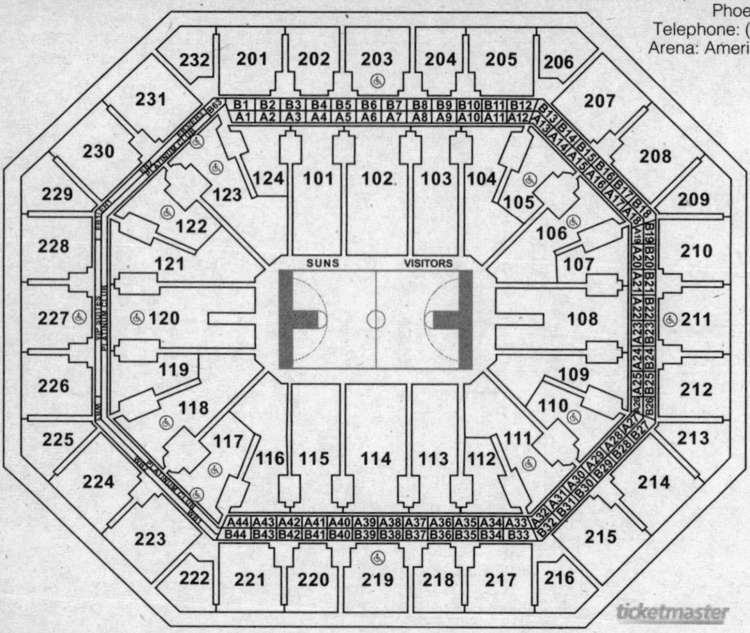

Portland Trail Blazers

One Center Court
Suite 200
Portland, OR 97227
Telephone: (503) 234-9291
Arena: Rose Garden Arena

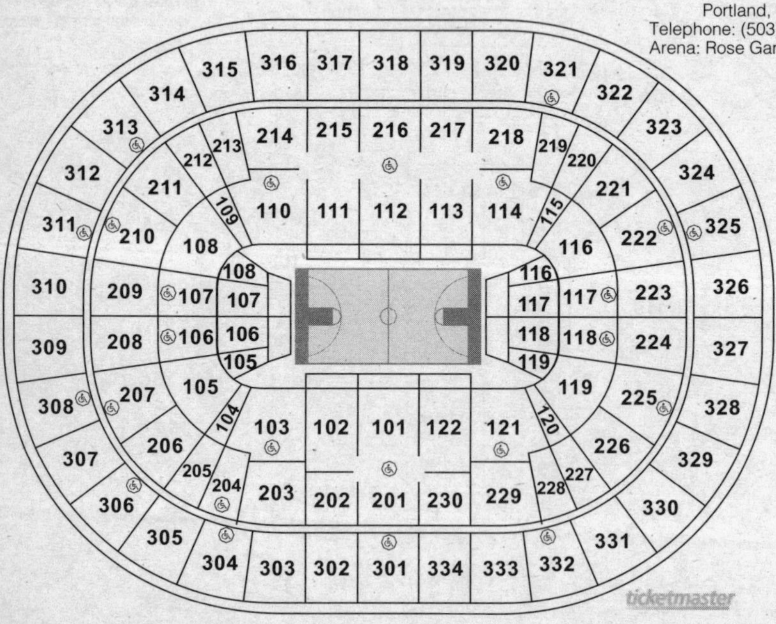

Sacramento Kings

One Sports Parkway
Sacramento, CA 95834
Telephone: (916) 928-0000
Arena: ARCO Arena

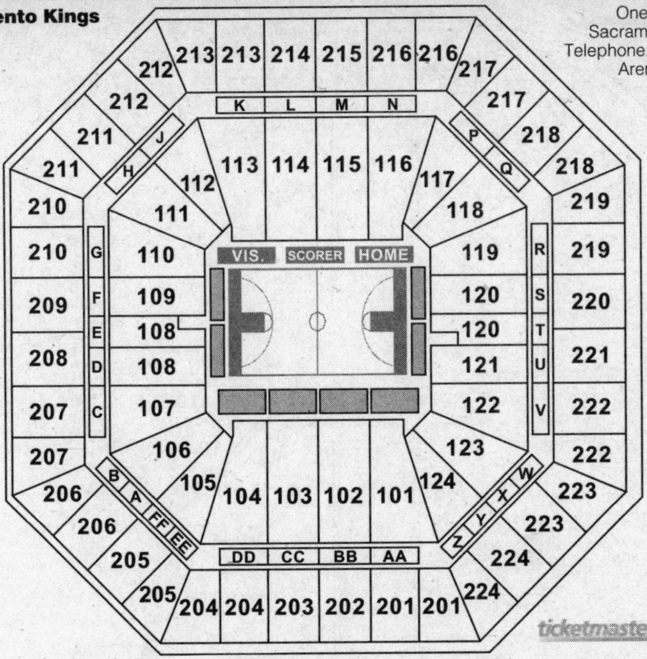

213 213 214 215 216 216 217
212
212 K L M N 217
211 J 218
211 H 113 114 115 116 218
112 117
210 111 118 219
210 G 110 VIS. SCORER HOME 119 219
209 F 109 120 220
108
208 E 108 120 221
D 121
207 C 107 122 222
106 123
207 105 124 222
206 B 104 103 102 101 223
A FF EE
206 223
205 DD CC BB AA 224
205 204 204 203 202 201 201 224

R S T U V W Z Y X

ticketmaster

San Antonio Spurs

100 Montana
San Antonio, TX 78203
Telephone: (210) 554-7787
Arena: Alamodome

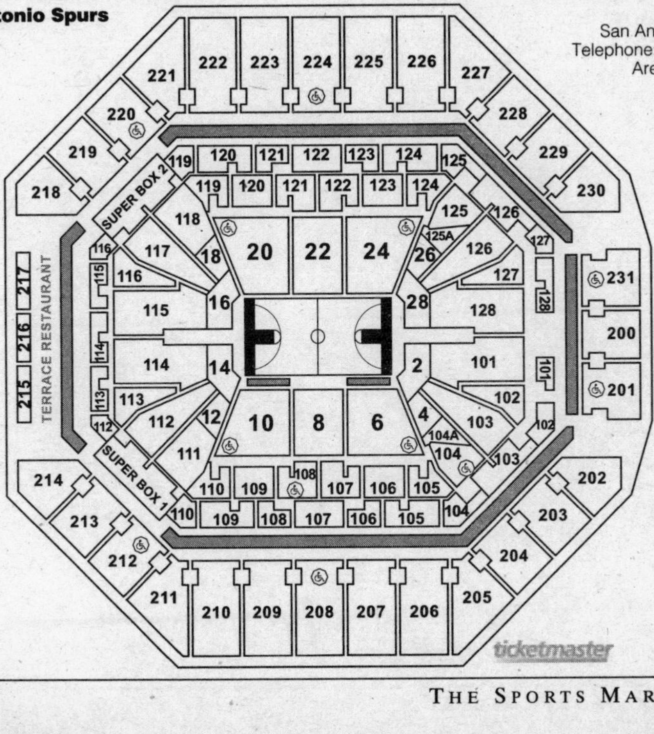

221 222 223 224 225 226 227
220 228
219 229
218 230
SUPER BOX 2 119 120 121 122 123 124 125
119 120 121 122 123 124 126
118 125 231
117 18 20 22 24 26 125A 126
116 116 127
TERRACE RESTAURANT
115 115 16 28 127 200
114 115
114 114 2 128 201
113 113 101
112 12 14 102
111 10 8 6 4 103 202
110 108 104A 104
214 110 109 107 106 105 103
213 109 108 107 106 105 104 203
SUPER BOX 1
212 204
211 210 209 208 207 206 205 202

215 216 217

ticketmaster

Seattle Supersonics

351 Elliott Avenue West
Suite 500
Seattle, WA 98119
Telephone: (206) 281-5847
Arena: KeyArena

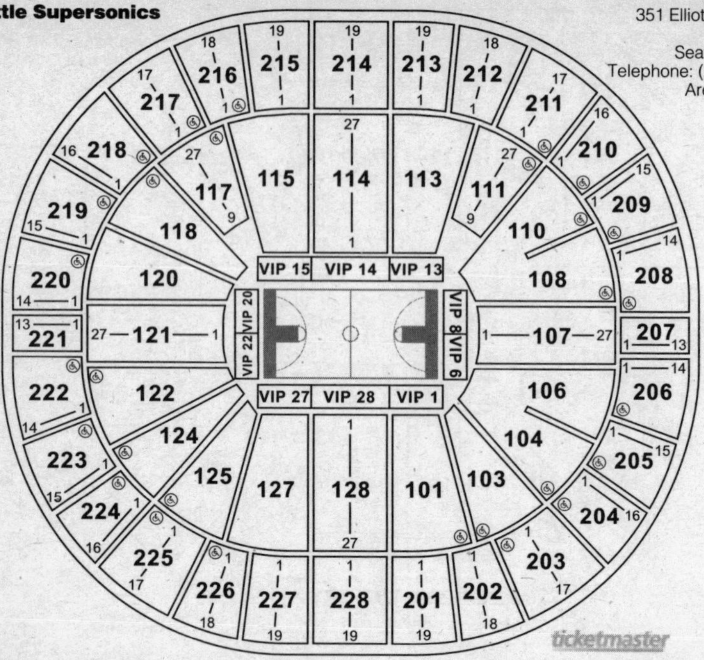

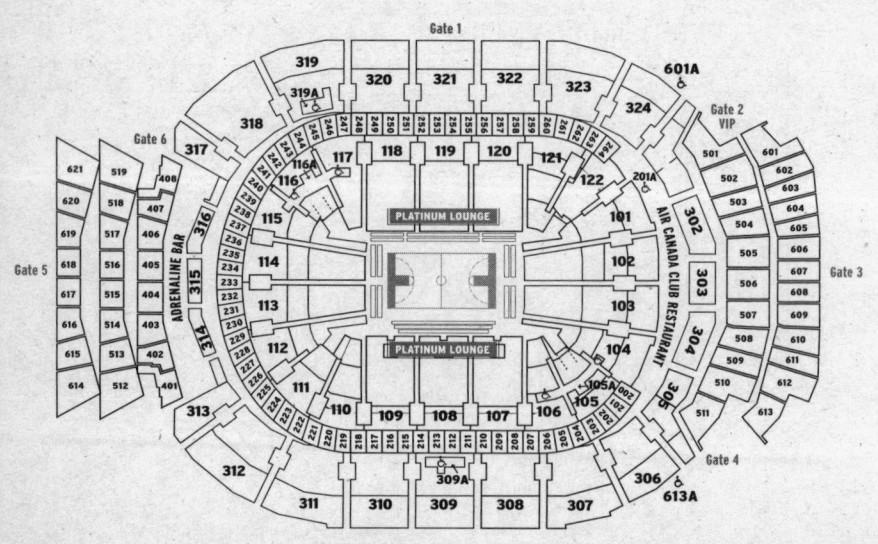

Toronto Raptors

40 Bay Street, Suite 400
Toronto, Ontario M5J 2X2 Canada
Telephone: (416) 815-5600
Arena: Air Canada Centre

Utah Jazz

301 West So. Temple
Salt Lake City, UT 84101
Telephone: (801) 575-7800
Arena: Delta Center

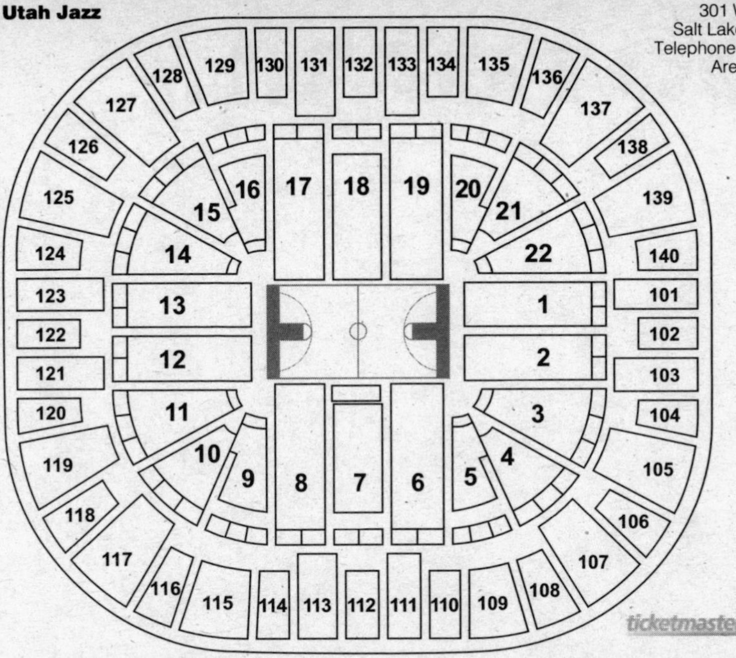

Washington Wizards

601 F Street NW
Washington D.C. 20004
Telephone: (202) 661-5000
Arena: MCI Center

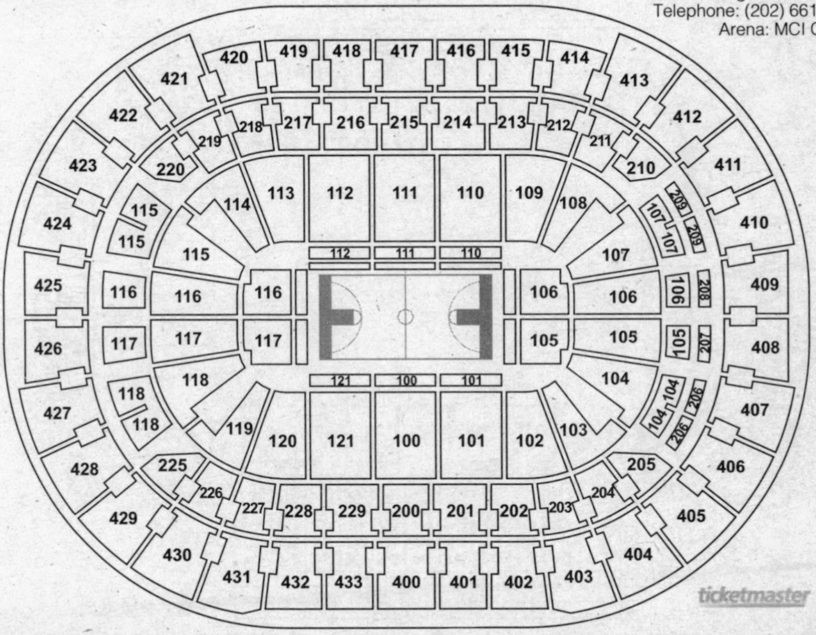

FOOTBALL

Arizona Cardinals
Sun Devil Stadium
ASU Campus Fifth Street
Tempe, AZ 85281
(602) 379-0101

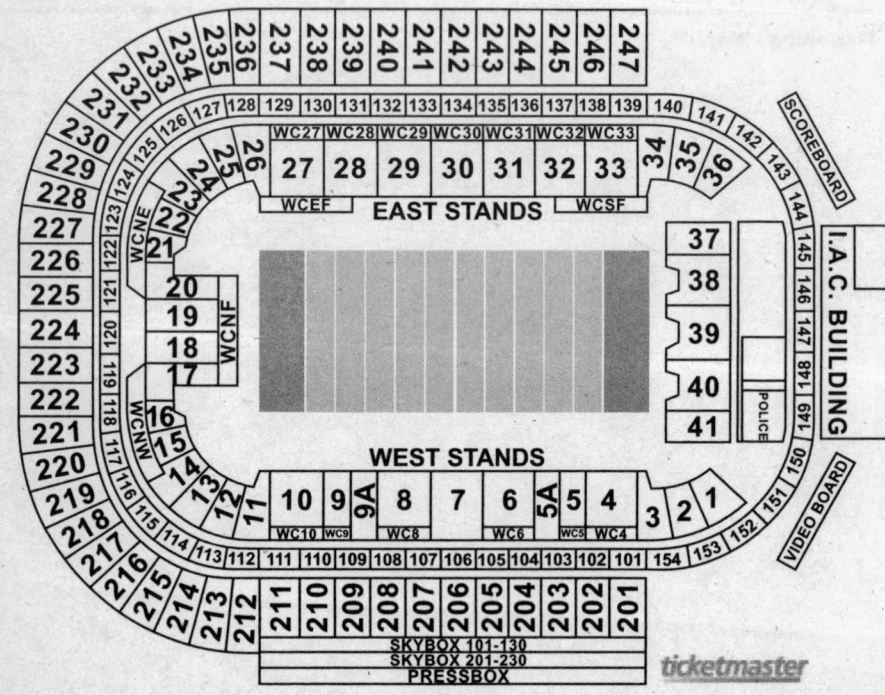

Atlanta Falcons

Georgia Dome
One Georgia Dome Dr.
Atlanta, GA 30313
(770) 965-3115

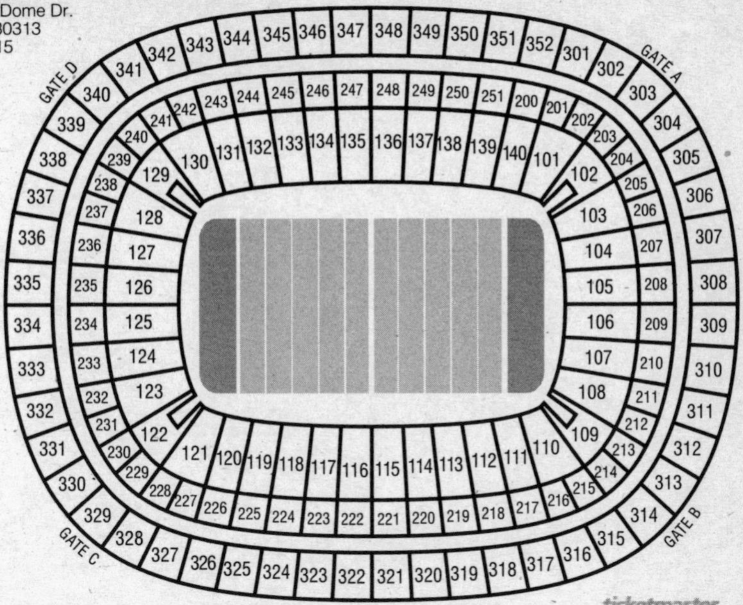

GATE D
GATE A
GATE B
GATE C

ticketmaster

Baltimore Ravens

M&T Bank Stadium
1101 Russell St.
Baltimore, MD 21230
(410) 654-6200

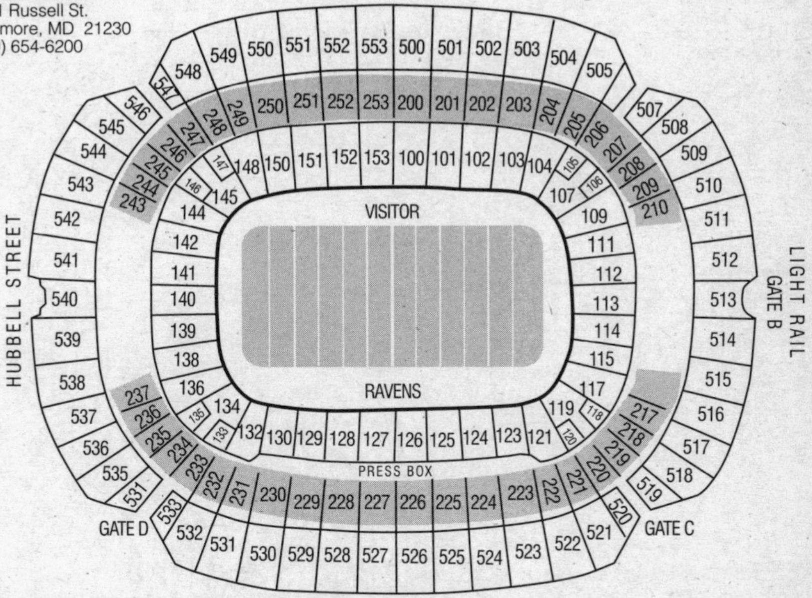

VISITOR

RAVENS

PRESS BOX

HUBBELL STREET

LIGHT RAIL
GATE B

GATE D

GATE C

OSTEND STREET

Buffalo Bills
Ralph Wilson Stadium
One Bills Drive
Orchard Park, NY 14127
(716) 648-1800

Carolina Panthers
Ericsson Stadium
800 South Mint St.
Charlotte, NC 28202
(704) 358-7000

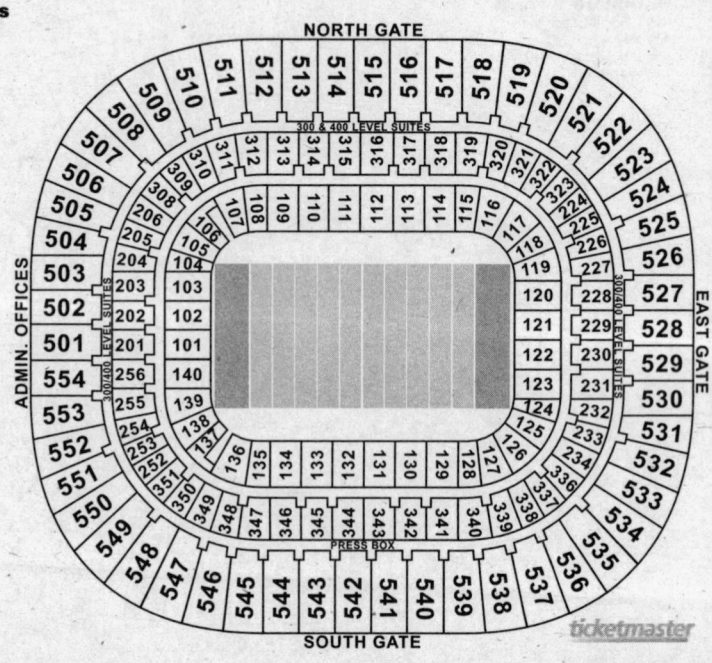

Chicago Bears
Soldier Field
16th St. at Lakeshore Dr.
Chicago, IL 60605
(847) 295-6600

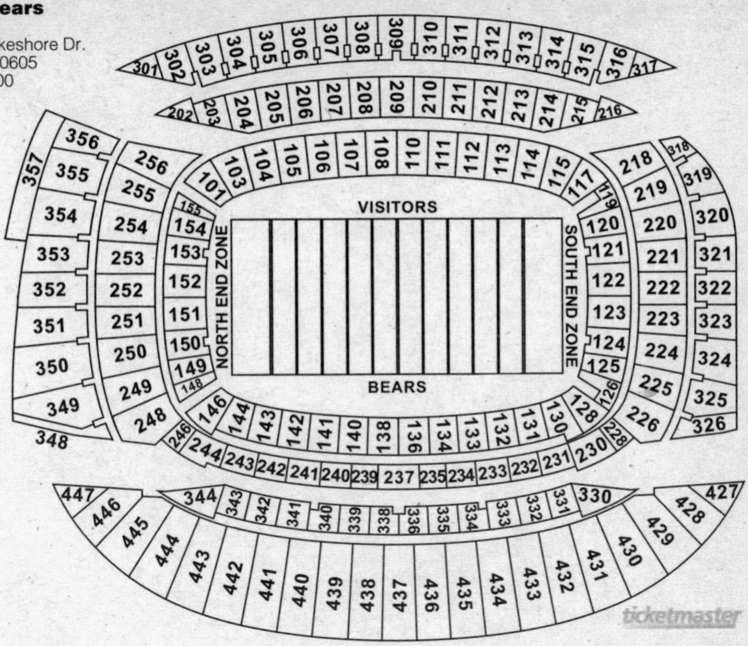

VISITORS

NORTH END ZONE

SOUTH END ZONE

BEARS

ticketmaster

Cincinnati Bengals
Paul Brown Stadium
One Paul Brown Stadium
Cincinnati, OH 45202
(513) 621-3550

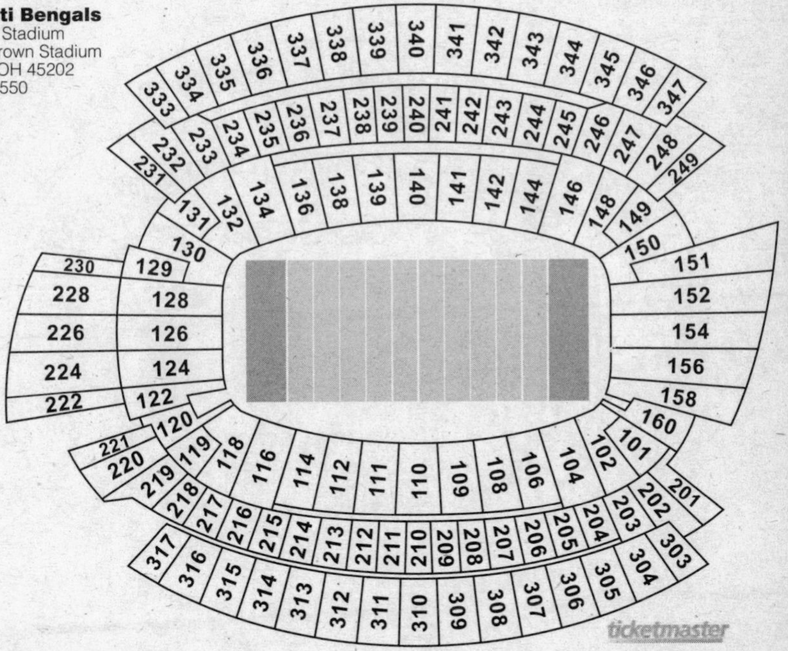

ticketmaster

Cleveland Browns
Cleveland Browns Stadium
1085 W. 3rd St.
Cleveland, OH 44114
(440) 891-5000

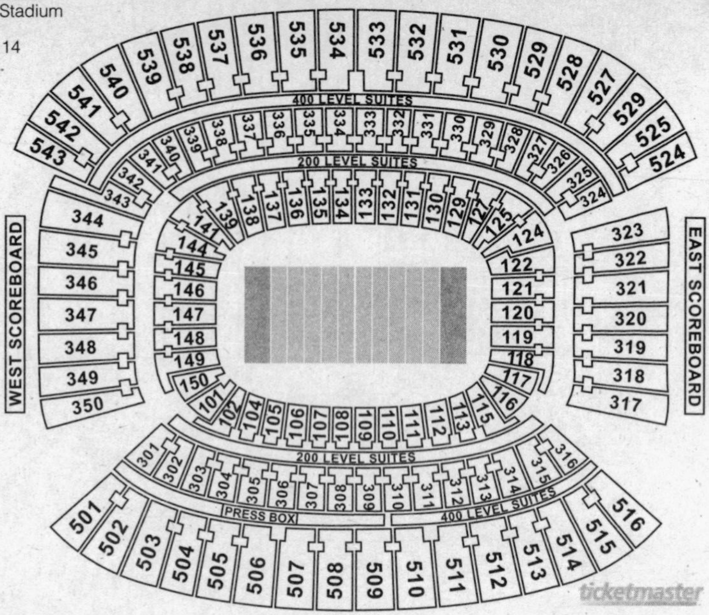

Dallas Cowboys
Texas Stadium
2401 E. Airport Freeway
Irving, TX 75062
(972) 556-9900

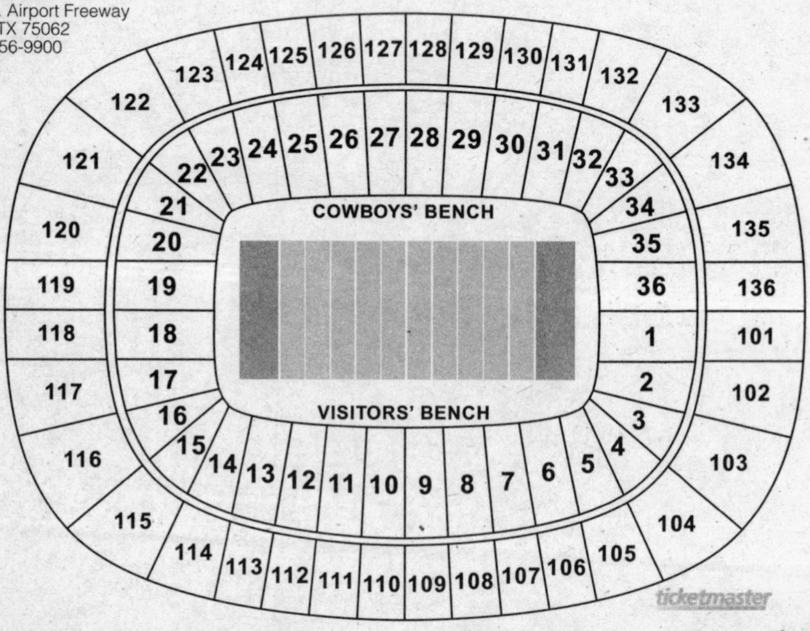

Denver Broncos
INVESCO Field at Mile High
1701 Bryant St.
Denver, CO 80204
(303) 649-9000

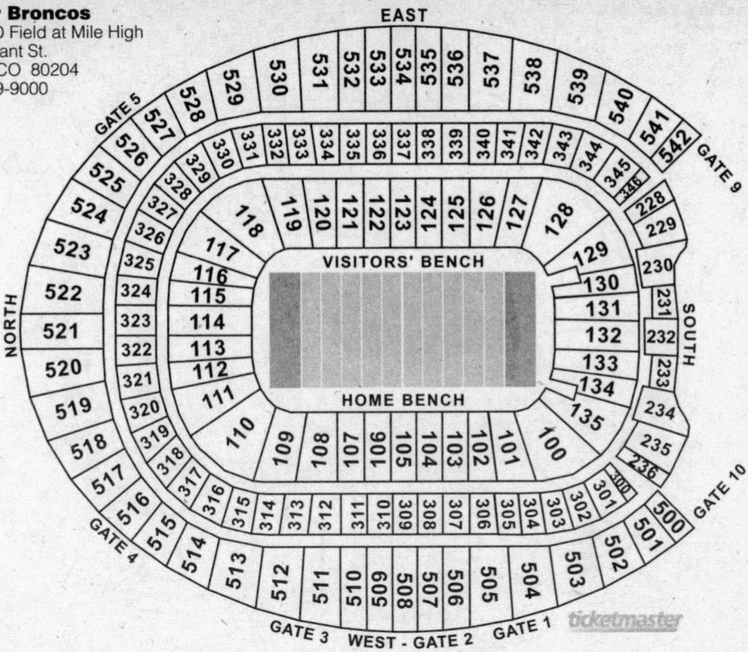

EAST

GATE 5
GATE 9
NORTH
SOUTH
GATE 10
GATE 4
GATE 3   WEST - GATE 2   GATE 1

VISITORS' BENCH

HOME BENCH

528 529 530 531 532 533 534 535 536 537 538 539 540 541 542
527 526 525 524 523 522 521 520 519 518 517 516 515 514 513 512 511 510 509 508 507 506 505 504 503 502 501 500
331 330 329 328 327 326 325 324 323 322 321 320 319 318 317 316 315 314 313 312 311 310 309 308 307 306 305 304 303 302 301 300
332 333 334 335 336 337 338 339 340 341 342 343 344 345 346
118 119 120 121 122 123 124 125 126 127 128 129 130 131 132 133 134 135
117 116 115 114 113 112 111 110 109 108 107 106 105 104 103 102 101 100
228 229 230 231 232 233 234 235 236

ticketmaster

Detroit Lions
Ford Field
2000 Brush St.
Detroit, MI 48226
(313) 216-4000

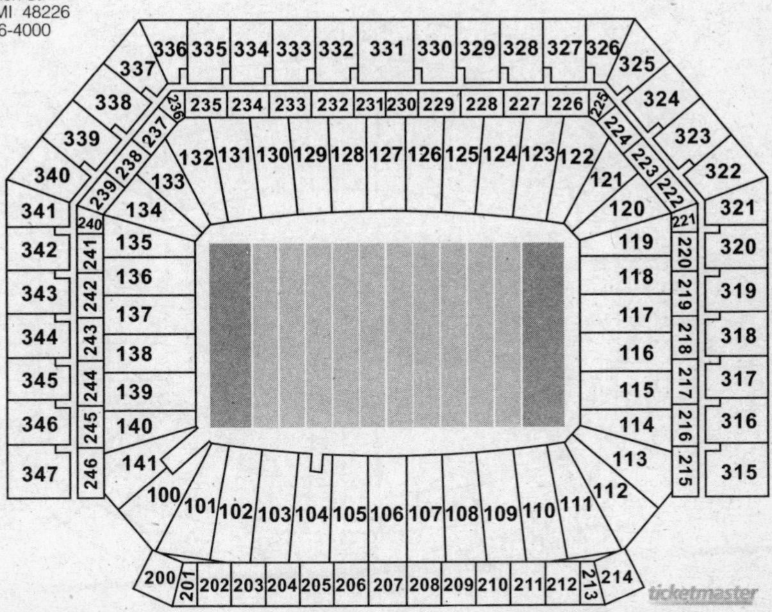

337 336 335 334 333 332 331 330 329 328 327 326 325
338 236 235 234 233 232 231 230 229 228 227 226 225 224 323
339 237 224 223 324
340 239 238 133 132 131 130 129 128 127 126 125 124 123 122 222 322
341 240 134 121 321
342 241 135 120 221 320
343 242 136 119 220 319
344 243 137 118 219 318
345 244 138 117 218 317
346 245 139 116 217 316
347 246 140 115 216 315
141 114 215
100 101 102 103 104 105 106 107 108 109 110 111 112 113
200 201 202 203 204 205 206 207 208 209 210 211 212 213 214

ticketmaster

THE SPORTS MARKET   825

Green Bay Packers

Lambeau Field
1265 Lombardi Avenue
Green Bay, WI 54304
Telephone: (920) 496-5700

ENTRANCE

ENTRANCE

403 405 407 409 411 413 415 417 419 421 423 425 427 429 431 433 435

307 305 303

301 109 111 113 115 117 119 121 123 125 127 129 131 133 135 137 138 136 134 132 130 128

105 107

103

101

100

102

104

106

108

110 112 114 116 118 120 122 126 128 130

304 306 308 310 312 314 316 318 320 322 324 326 328 330 332 334 336 338 340 342 344 346 348 350 352 354 353 351 349 347 345

ENTRANCE

ENTRANCE

Houston Texans

Reliant Stadium
One Reliant Park
Houston, TX 77054
(832) 667-2000

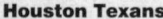

FORD GATE
(SW)

MILLER LITE
GATE (NW)

GALLERY
FURNITURE
GATE (SE)

COCA-COLA
GATE (NE)

603 604 605 606 607 608 609 610 611 612 613 614 615

602 506 508 510 514

601 502 305 306 307 308 309 310 311 312 313 314 315 316 617

643 303 304 101 102 103 104 105 106 107 108 109 110 111 112 517 518 616 618

651 552 302 140 113 320 519 619

650 551 550 549 355 354 139 114 321 520 620

649 548 353 138 115 322 521 621

648 547 352 137 116 323 522 622

647 546 351 136 117 324 523 623

646 545 350 135 118 325 524 624

645 544 349 348 134 119 326 327 525 526 625

644 543 133 120 626

643 542 345 344 132 131 130 129 128 127 126 125 124 123 122 121 330 331 627 628

641 540 343 342 341 340 339 338 337 336 335 334 333 332 528 629

640 538 534 532 630

639 638 637 636 635 634 633 632 631 629

---

826   THE SPORTS MARKET

Indianapolis Colts
RCA Dome
200 S. Capitol Ave.
Indianapolis, IN 46225
(317) 297-2658

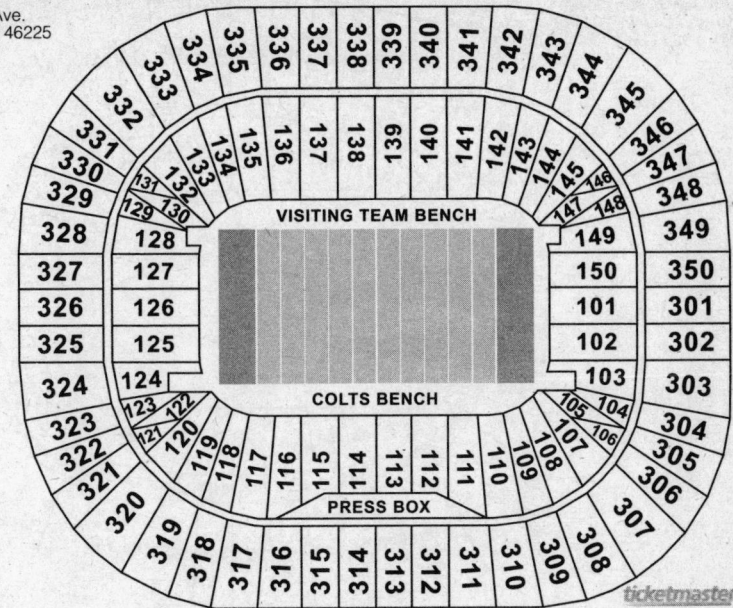

Jacksonville Jaguars
Alltel Stadium
1400 E. Duvall St.
Jacksonville, FL 32202
(904) 633-6000

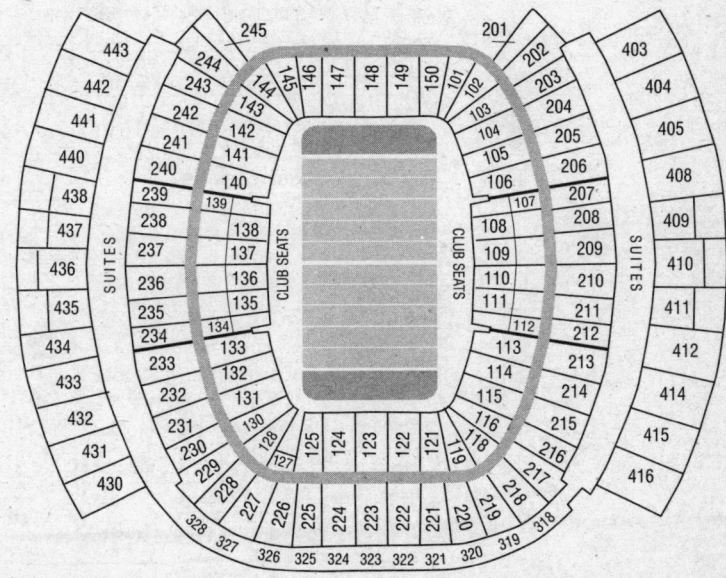

Kansas City Chiefs
Arrowhead Stadium
One Arrowhead Drive
Kansas City, MO 64129
(816) 920-9300

Miami Dolphins
Pro Player Stadium
2269 Dan Marino Blvd.
Miami, FL 33056
(954) 452-7000

GATE C NORTH

GATE B

GATE D

GATE A WEST

VISITOR SIDE

HOME SIDE

GATE E EAST

PRESS BOX

GATE H

GATE F

GATE G SOUTH

THE SPORTS MARKET

Minnesota Vikings
HHH Metrodome
900 11th Ave. South
Minneapolis, MN 55415
(952) 828-6500

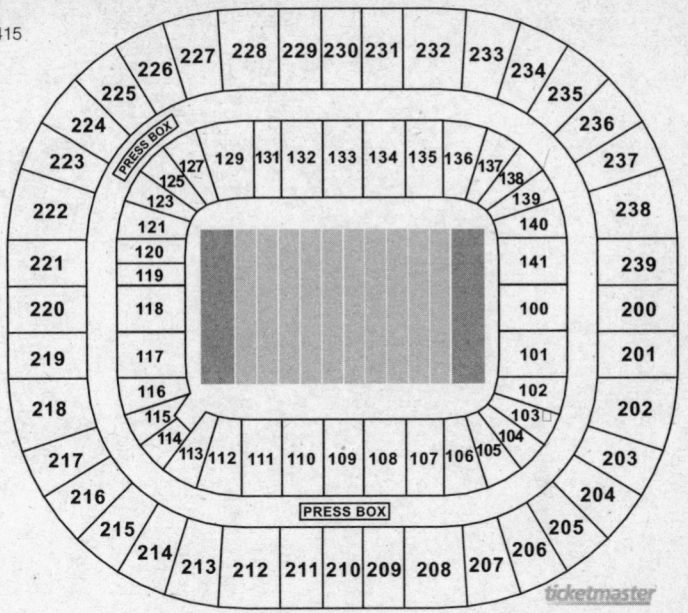

New England Patriots
Gillette Stadium
One Patriot Place
Foxborough, MA 02035
(508) 543-8200

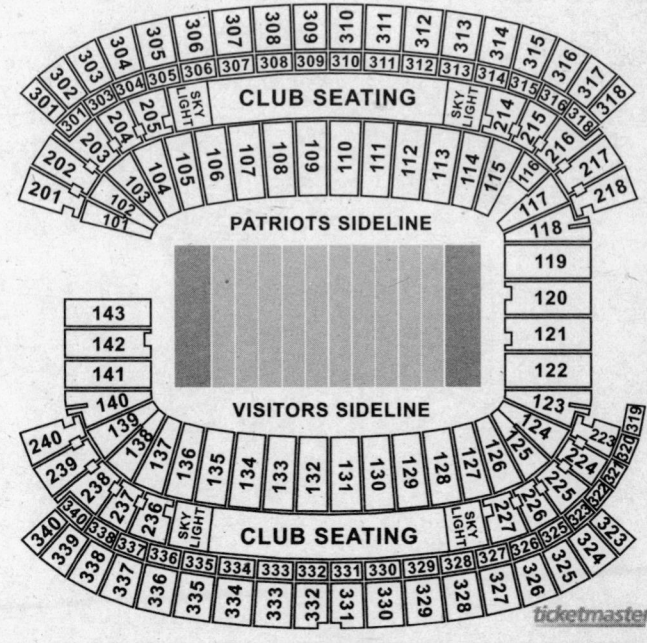

New Orleans Saints
Louisiana Superdome
1500 Podyras St.
New Orleans, LA 70112
(504) 733-0255

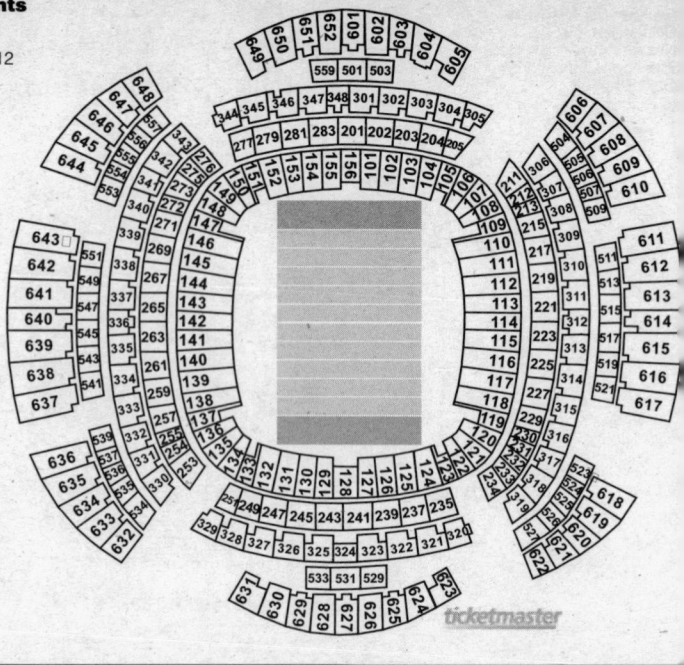

New York Giants
New York Jets
Giants Stadium
50 Route 120
East Rutherford, NJ 07073
(201) 935-8111

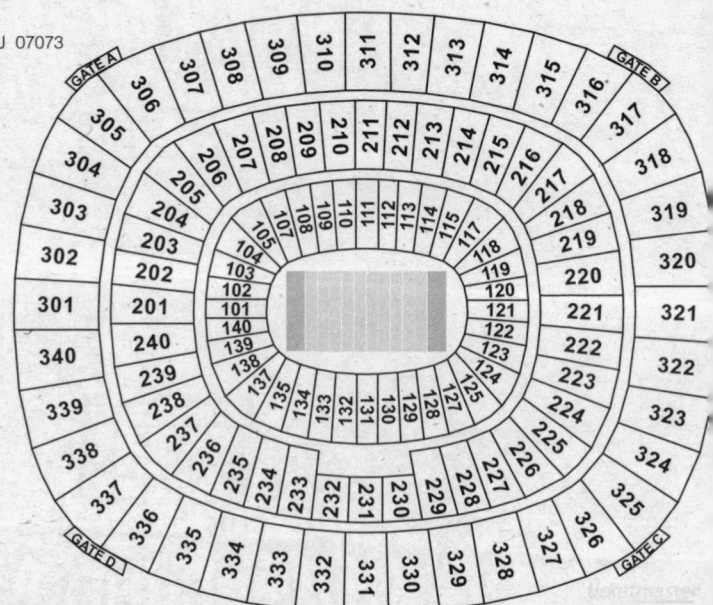

Oakland Raiders

Network Associates Coliseum
7000 Coliseum Way
Oakland, CA 94621
(510) 864-5000

Philadelphia Eagles

Lincoln Financial Field
3551 Broad St.
Philadelphia, PA 19148
(215) 463-2500

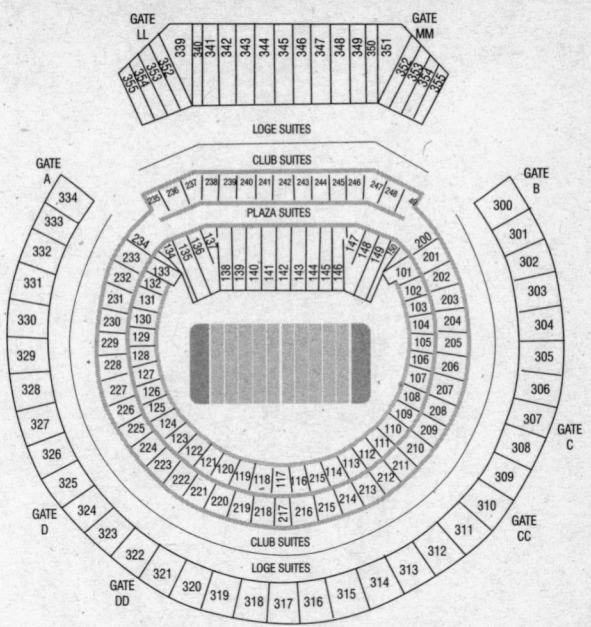

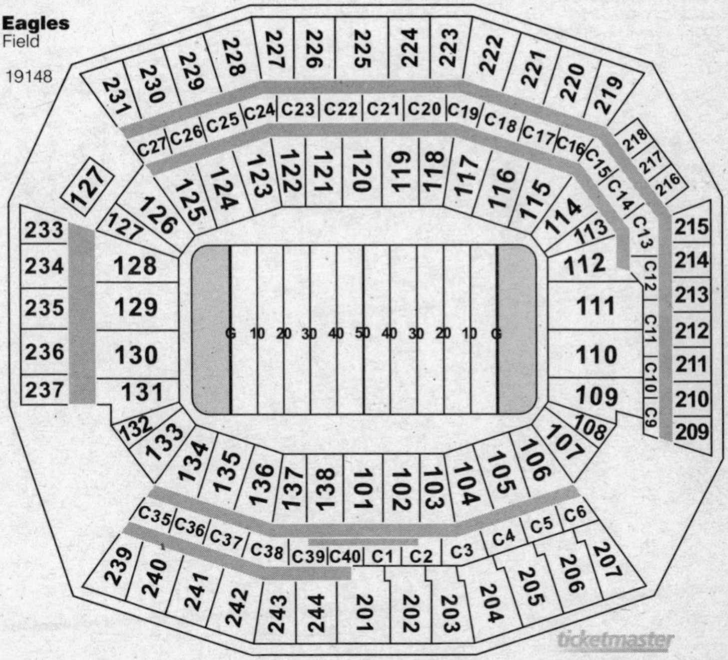

ticketmaster

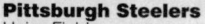

Pittsburgh Steelers

Heinz Field
100 Art Rooney Ave.
Pittsburgh, PA 15212
(412) 432-7800

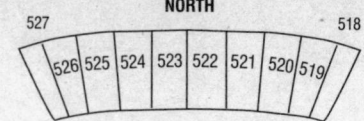

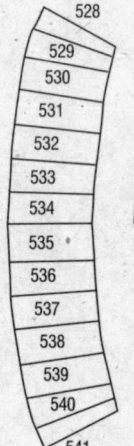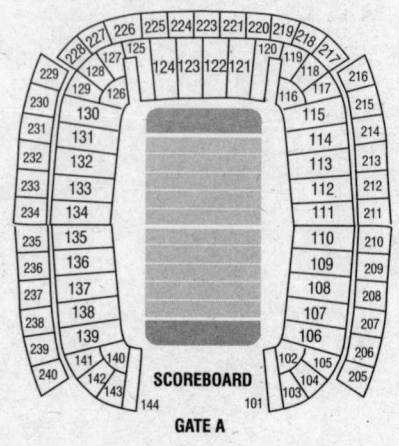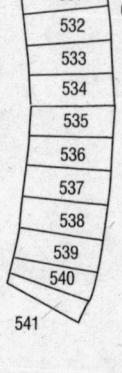

St. Louis Rams

Edward Jones Dome
701 Convention Plaza
St. Louis, MO 63101
(314) 982-7267

San Diego Chargers

Qualcomm Stadium
9449 Friars Rd.
San Diego, CA 92108
(858) 874-4500

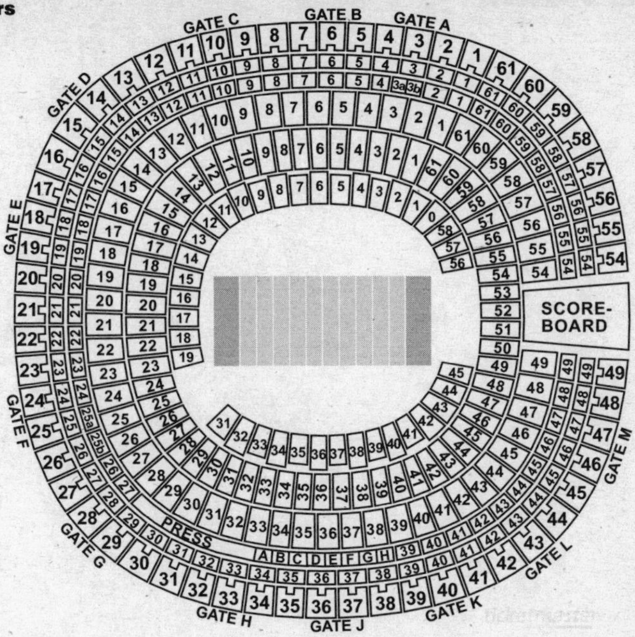

San Francisco 49ers

3Com Park
Jamestown and Harney Way
San Francisco, CA 94124
(408) 562-4949

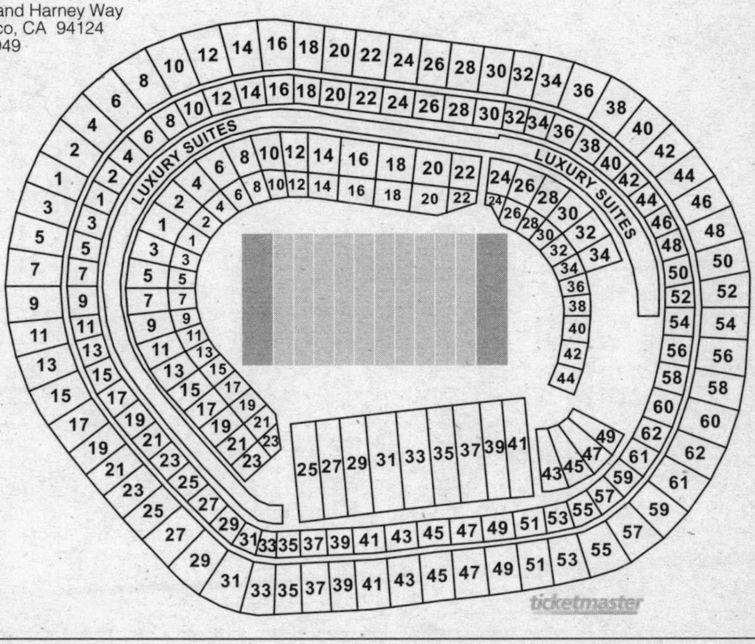

Seattle Seahawks

Seahawks Stadium
800 Occidental Ave. South
Seattle, WA 98104
(425) 827-9777

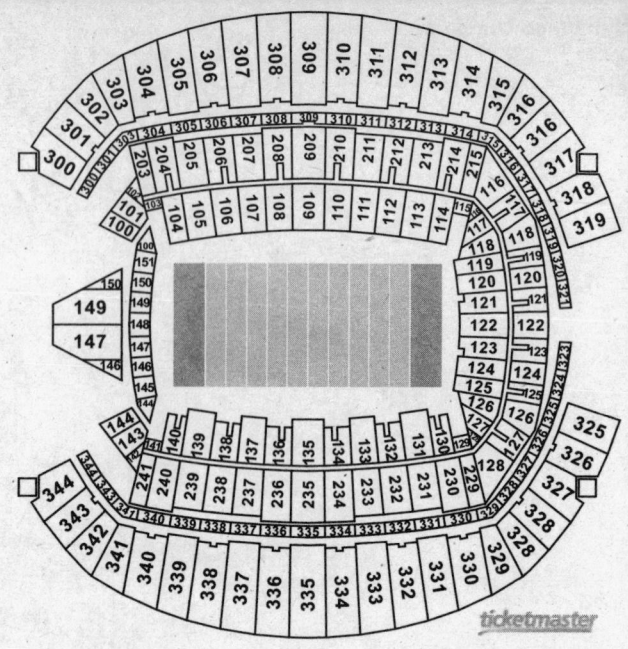

Tampa Bay Buccaneers

Raymond James Stadium
4201 N. Dale Mabry Hwy.
Tampa, FL 33607
(813) 870-2700

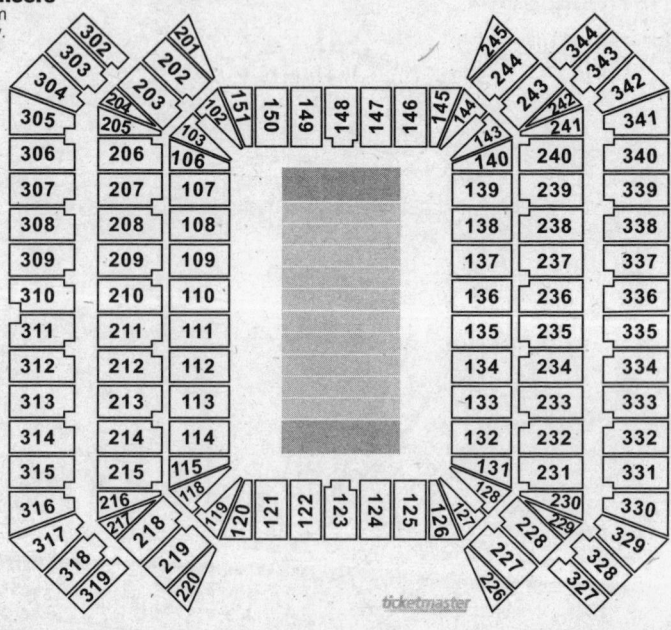

Tennessee Titans
The Coliseum
One Titans Way
Nashville, TN 37219
(615) 565-4000

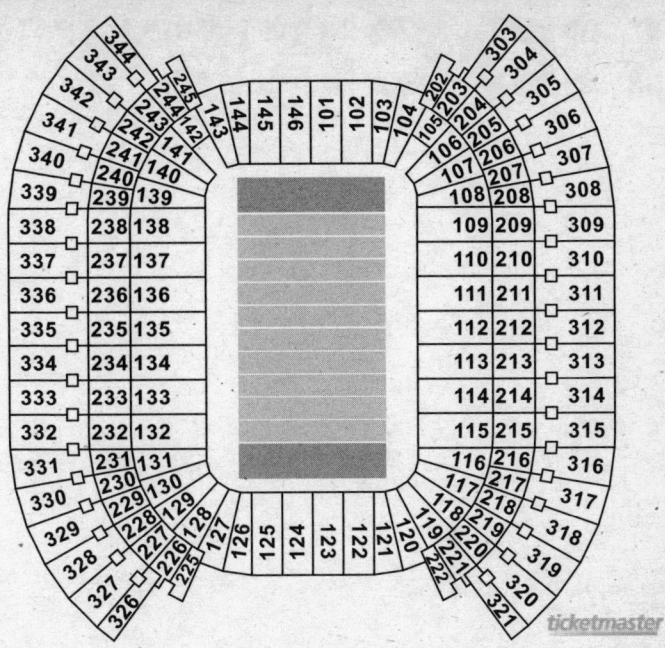

ticketmaster

Washington Redskins
Fedex Field
1600 Ralijon Rd.
Landover, MD 20785
(703) 726-7000

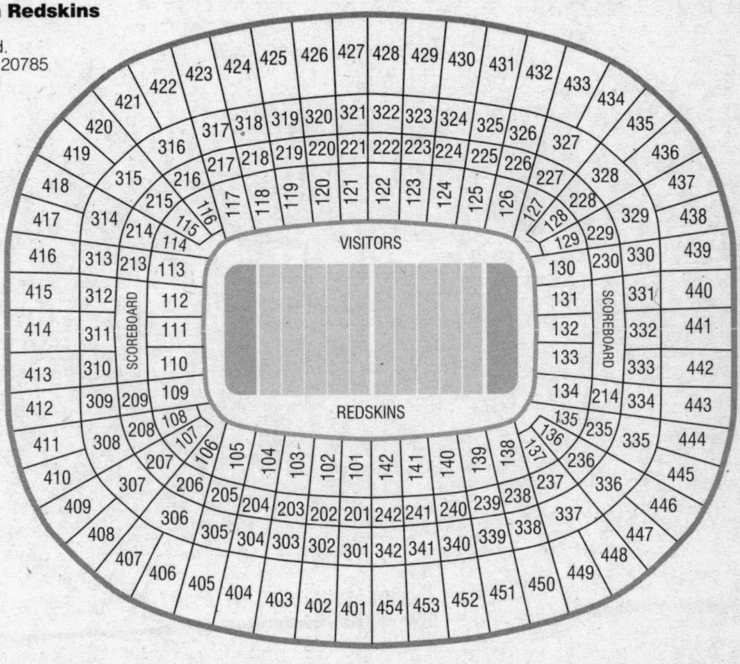

HOCKEY

Mighty Ducks of Anaheim
2695 Katella Avenue
Anaheim, CA 92806
Telephone: (714) 940-2900
Arena: Arrowhead Pond of Anaheim

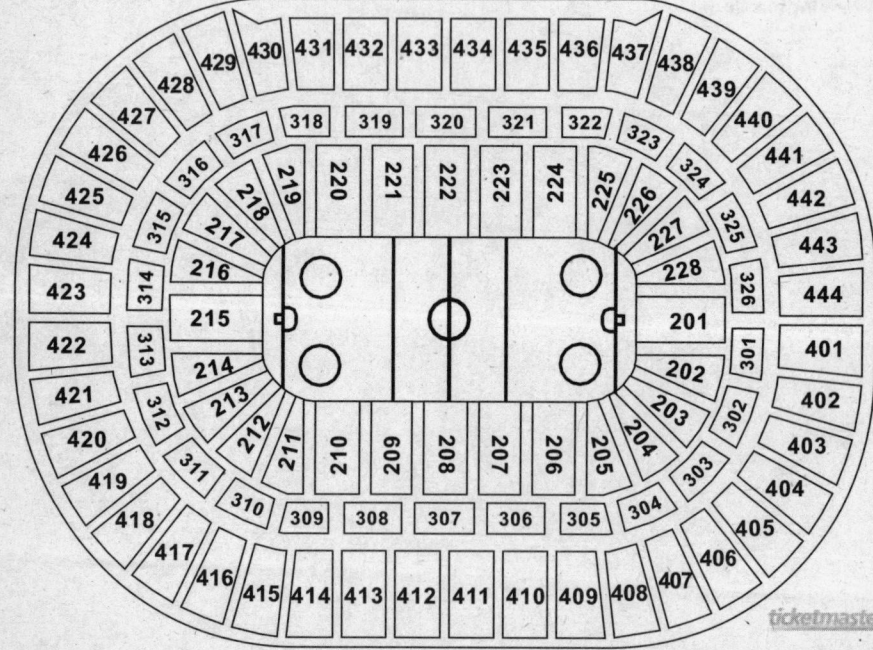

Atlanta Thrashers

1 CNN Center
P.O. Box 15538
Atlanta, GA 30348
Telephone: (404) 827-5300
Arena: Philips Arena

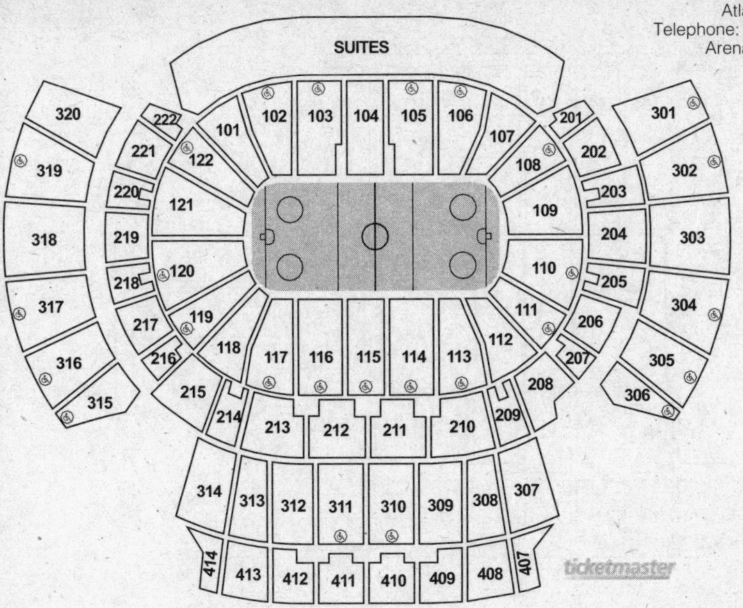

Boston Bruins

One FleetCenter, Suite 250
Boston, MA 02114-1303
Telephone: (617) 624-1900
Arena: FleetCenter

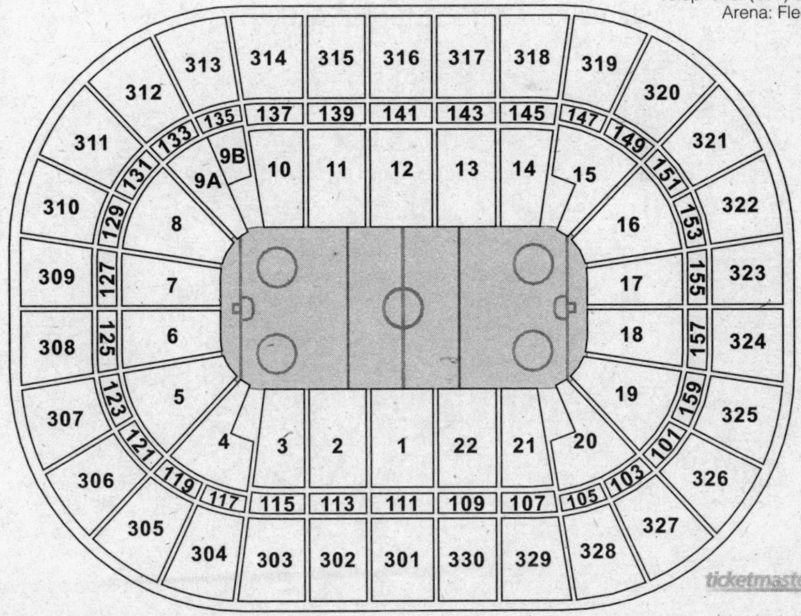

Buffalo Sabres

One Seymour H. Knox III Plaza
Buffalo, NY 14203
Telephone: (716) 855-4100
Arena: HSBC Arena

ticketmaster

Calgary Flames

555 Saddledome Rise, SE
Calgary, Alberta T2G 2W1
Telephone: (403) 777-2177
Arena: Pengrowth
Saddledome

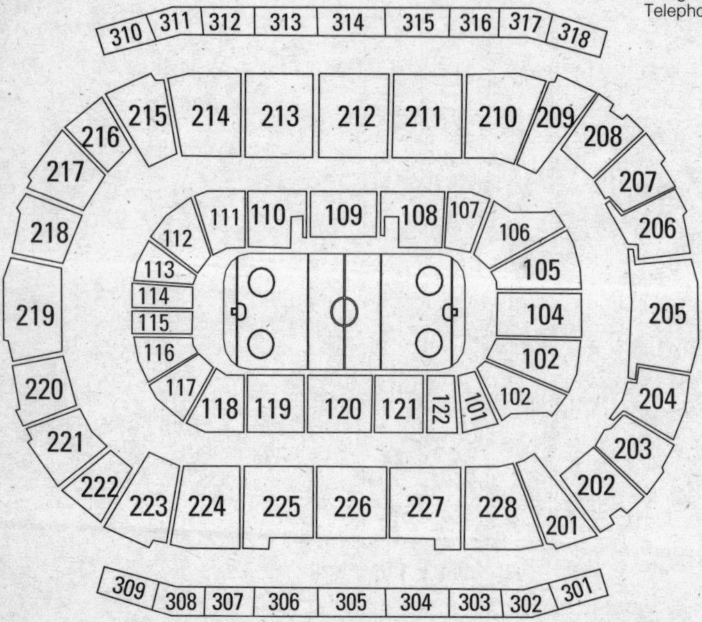

1400 Edwards Mill Road
Raleigh, NC 27607
Telephone: (919) 467-7825
Arena: Entertainment and
Sports Arena

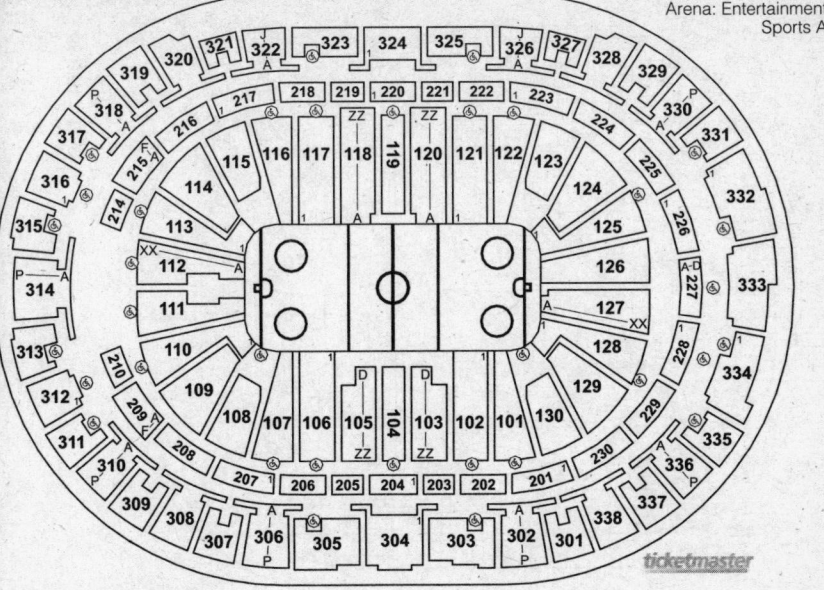

ticketmaster

1901 W. Madison Street
Chicago, IL 60612
Telephone: (312) 455-7000
Arena: United Center

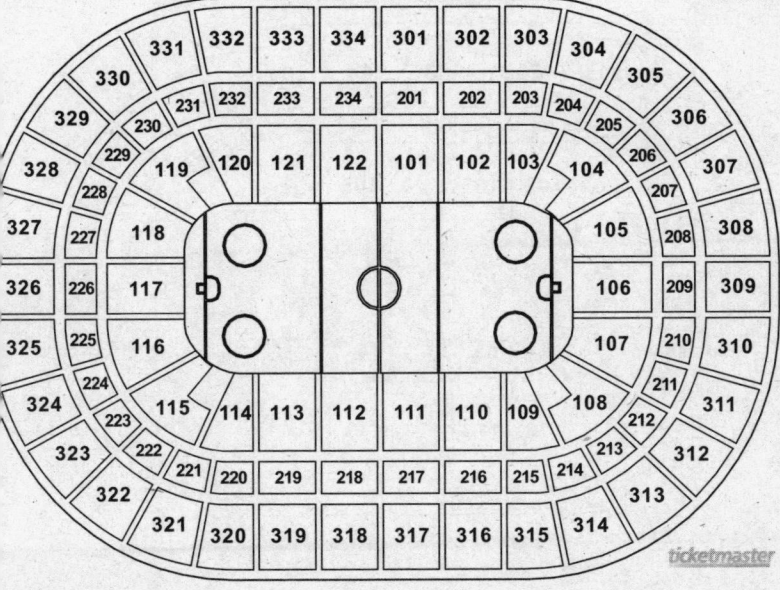

ticketmaster

Colorado Avalanche

1000 Chopper Circle
Denver, CO 80204
Telephone: (303) 405-1100
Arena: Pepsi Center

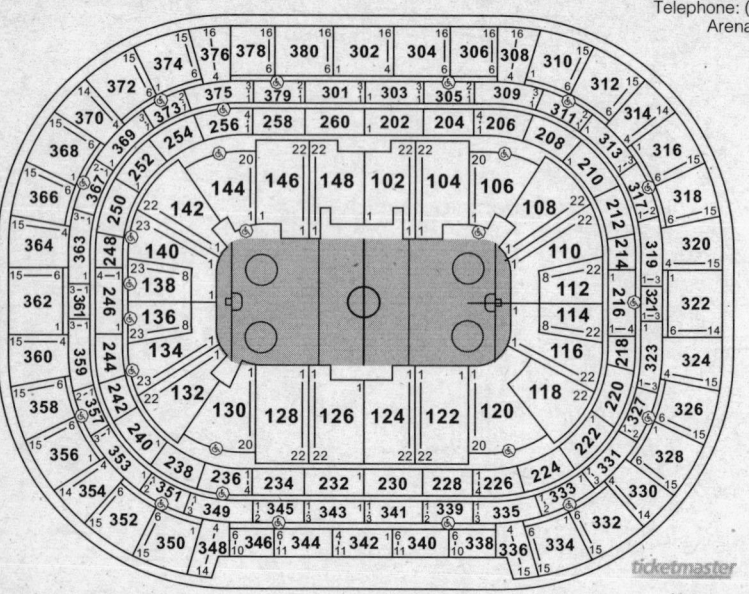

Columbus Blue Jackets

200 West Nationwide Boulevard
Columbus, OH 43215
Telephone: (614) 246-4625
Arena: Nationwide Arena

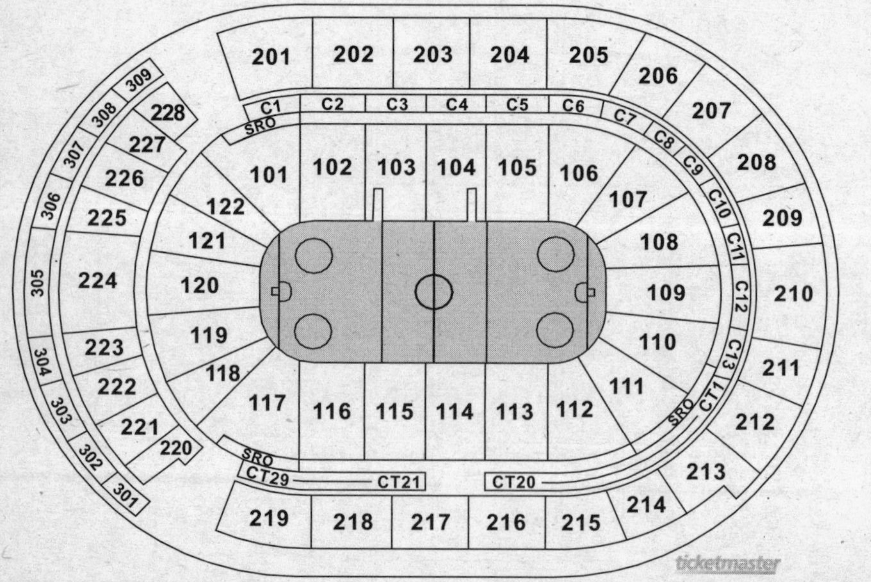

Dallas Stars

211 Cowboys Parkway
Irving, TX 75063
Telephone: (972) 831-2401
Arena: American Airlines
Center

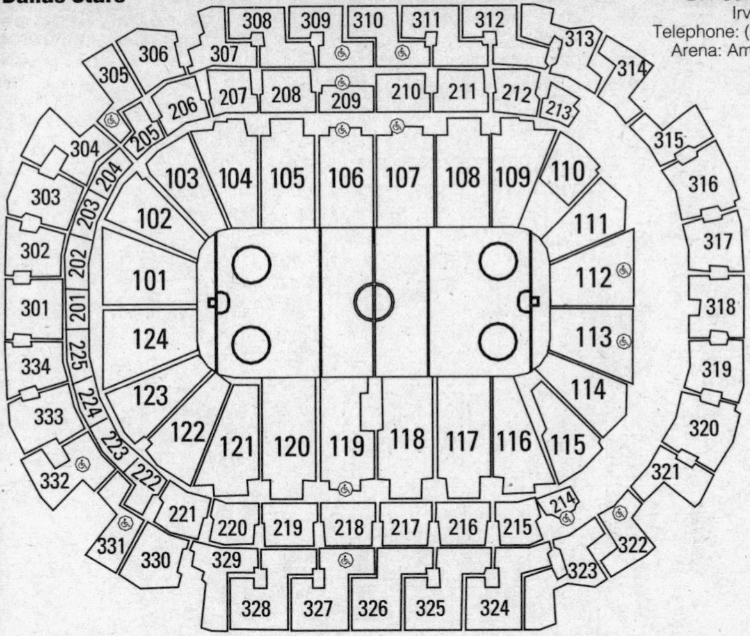

Detroit Red Wings

600 Civic Center Drive
Detroit, MI 48226
Telephone: (313) 396-7544
Arena: Joe Louis Arena

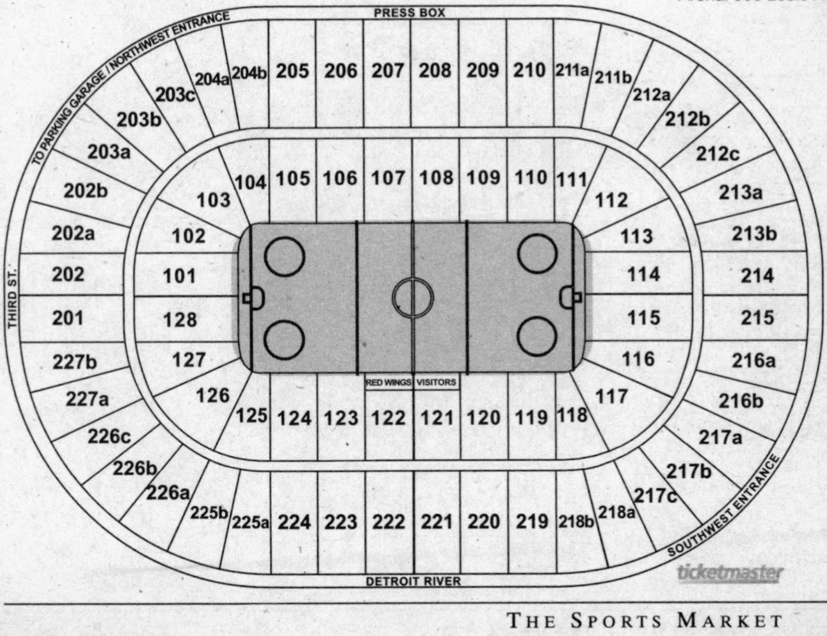

THE SPORTS MARKET   **841**

Edmonton Oilers

11230 110th Street
Edmonton, Alberta T5G 3H7
Telephone: (780) 414-4000
Arena: Skyreach Centre

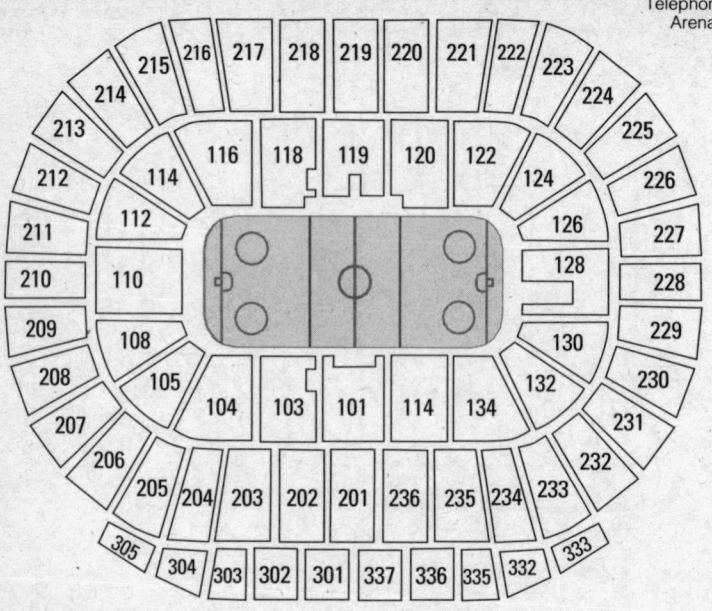

Florida Panthers

1 Panther Parkway
Sunrise, FL 33323
Telephone: (954) 835-7000
Arena: National Car Rental Center

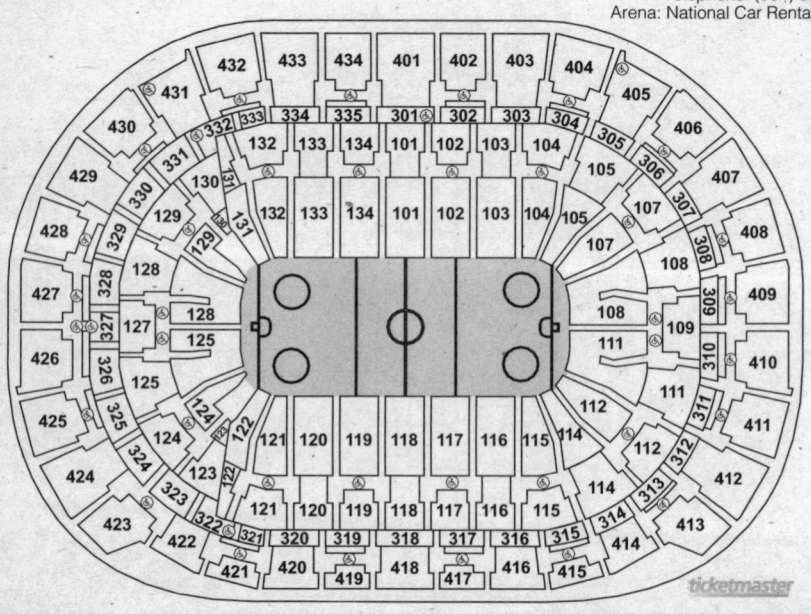

Los Angeles Kings

1111 South Figueroa Street
Los Angeles, CA 90037
Telephone: (213) 742-7100
Arena: The Staples
Center

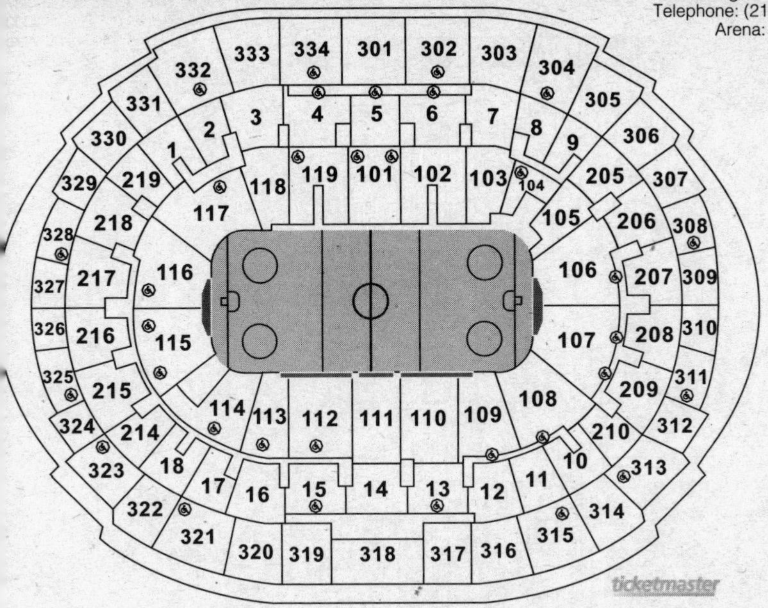

ticketmaster

Minnesota Wild

317 Washington Street
St. Paul, MN, 55102
Telephone: (651) 602-6000
Arena: Excel Energy
Center

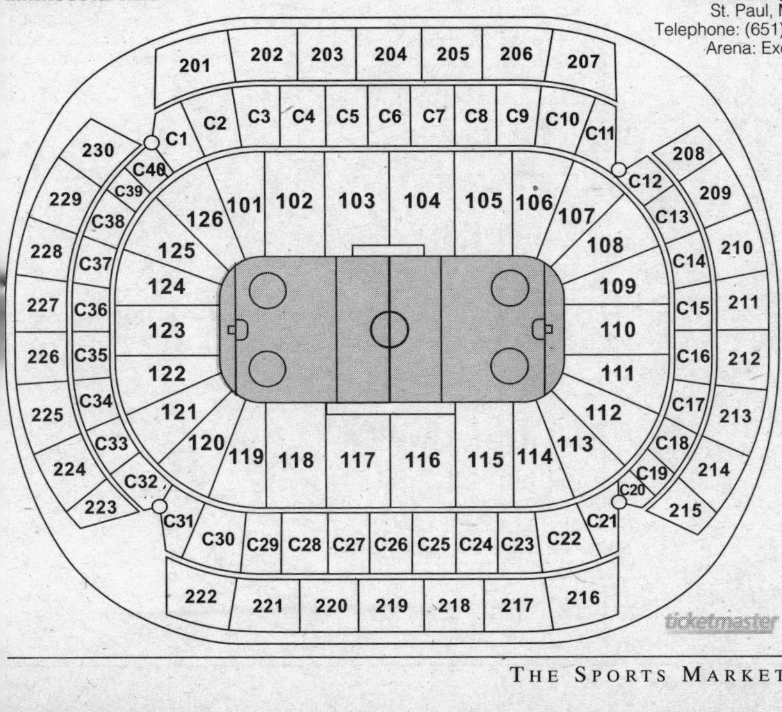

ticketmaster

Montreal Canadiens

1260 de la Gauchetiere West
Montreal, Quebec H3B 5E8 Canada
Telephone: (514) 932-2582
Arena: Molson Centre

Nashville Predators

501 Broadway
Nashville, TN 37203
Telephone: (615) 770-2300
Arena: Gaylord Entertainment
Center

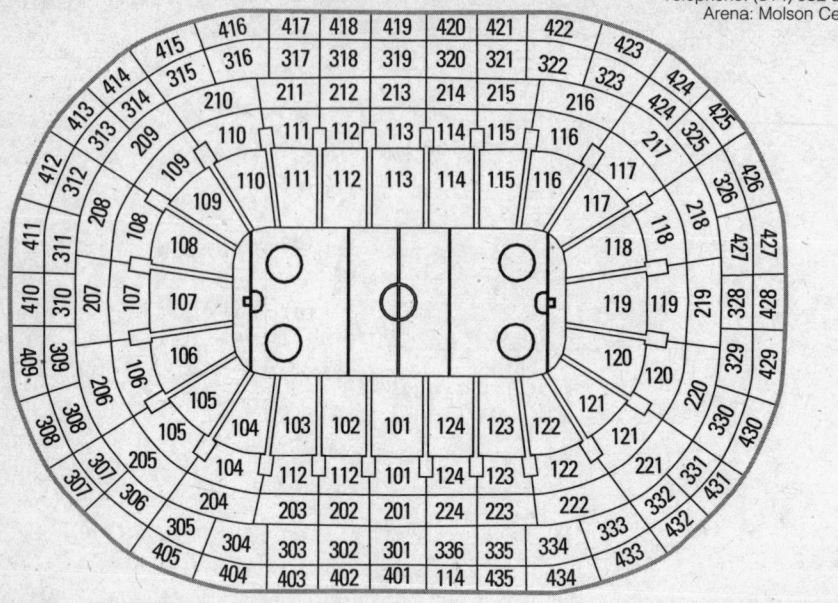

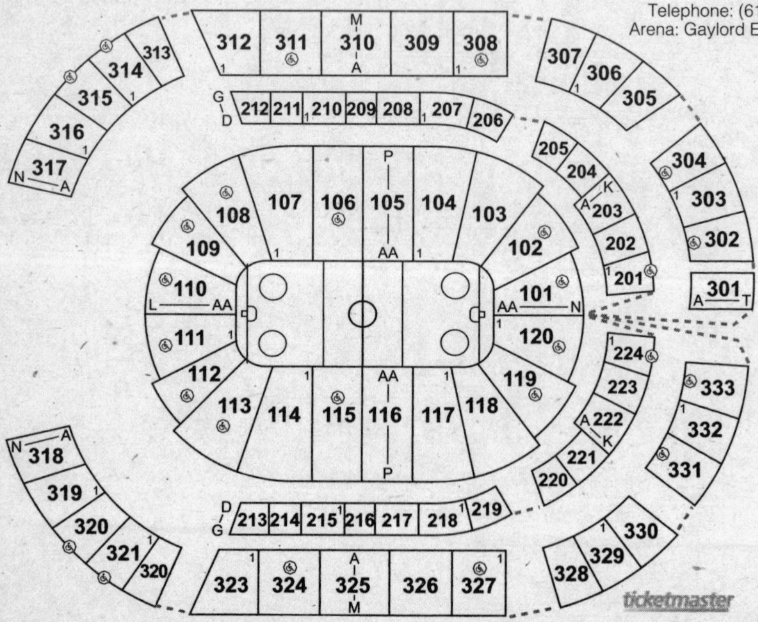

New Jersey Devils

P.O. Box 504
East Rutherford, NJ 07073
Telephone: (201) 935-6050
Arena: Continental Airlines Arena

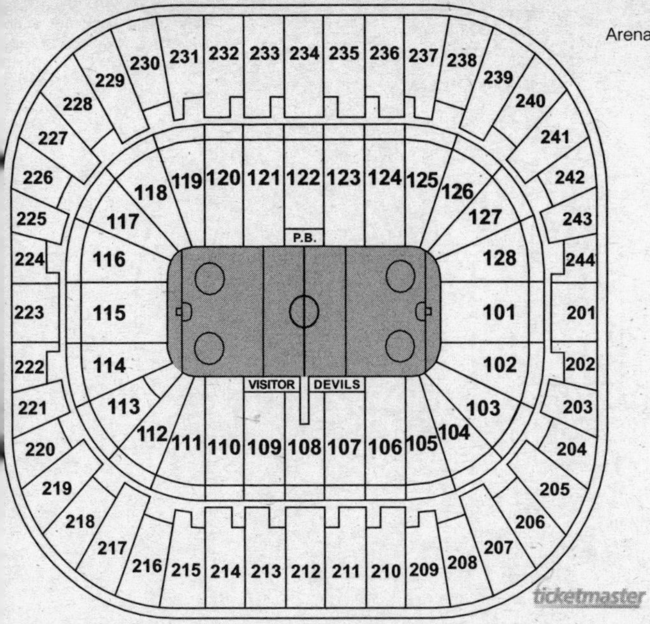

229 230 231 232 233 234 235 236 237 238 239 240 241 242 243 244

228 227 226 225 224 223 222 221 220 219 218 217 216

118 119 120 121 122 123 124 125 126 127 128 101 102 103 104 105

117 116 115 114 113 112 111 110 109 108 107 106

P.B.

VISITOR DEVILS

201 202 203 204 205 206 207 208 209 210 211 212 213 214 215

ticketmaster

New York Islanders

1535 Old Country Road
Plainview, NY 11803
Telephone: (516) 501-6700
Arena: Nassau Coliseum

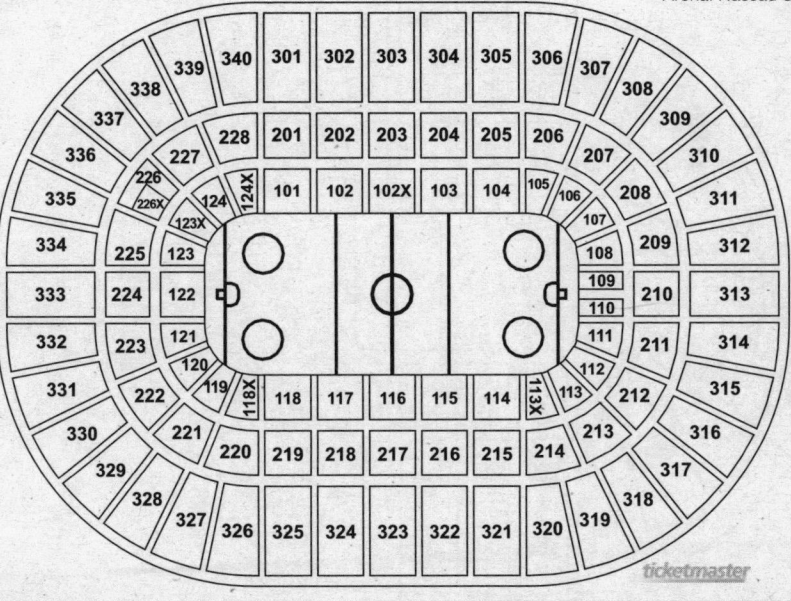

338 339 340 301 302 303 304 305 306 307 308 309 310 311

337 336 335 334 333 332 331 330 329 328 327

228 201 202 203 204 205 206 207 208 209 210 211 212 213

227 226 226X 124 124X 101 102 102X 103 104 105 106 107 108 109 110 111 112 113 113X 114 115 116 117 118 118X 119 120 121 122 123 123X 225 224 223 222 221 220 219 218 217 216 215 214

326 325 324 323 322 321 320 319 318 317 316 315 312 313 314

ticketmaster

New York Rangers

2 Pennsylvania Plaza
New York, NY 10121
Telephone: (212) 465-6000
Arena: Madison Square
Garden

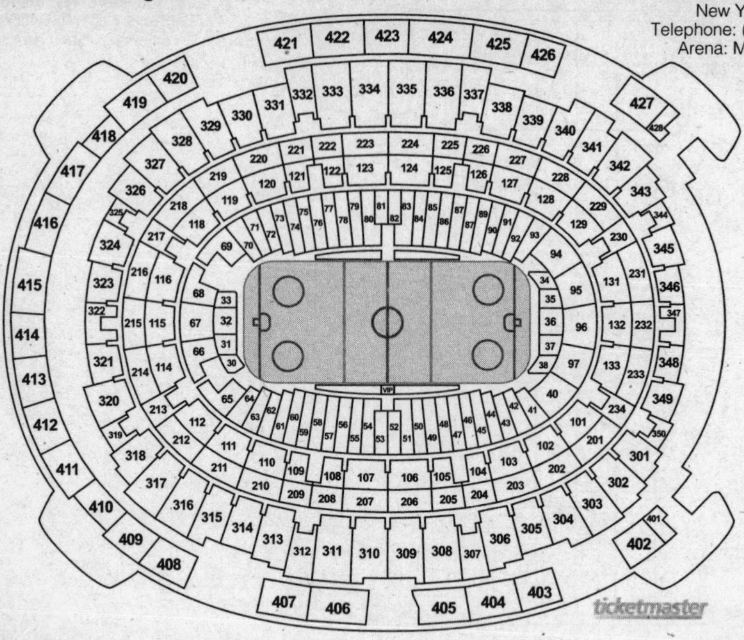

Ottawa Senators

1000 Palladium Drive
Ottawa, Ontario K2V 1A5 Canada
Telephone: (613) 599-0250
Arena: The Corel Centre

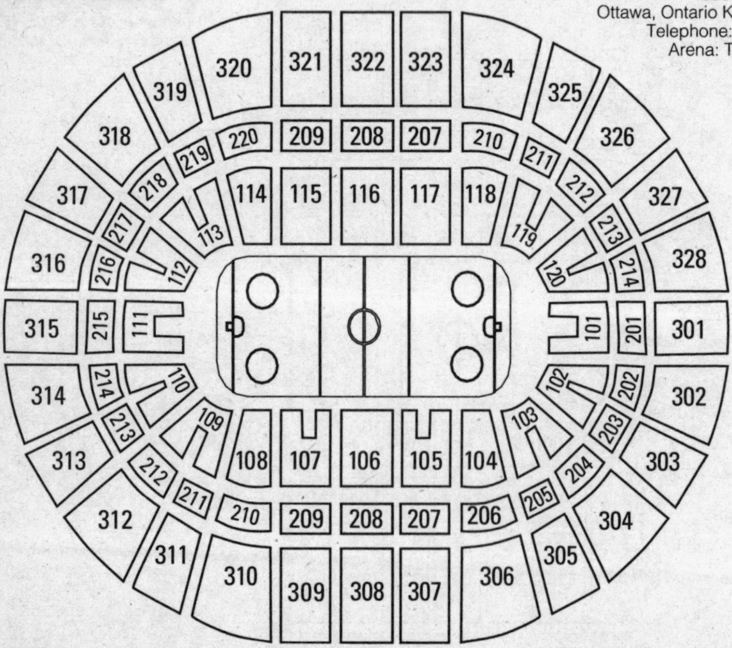

Philadelphia Flyers

3601 South Broad Street
Philadelphia, PA 19148
Telephone: (215) 465-4500
Arena: First Union Center

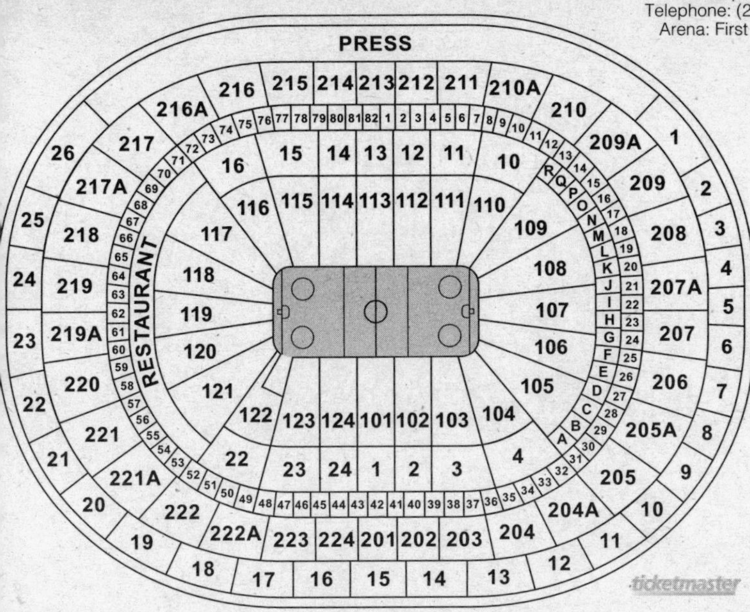

Phoenix Coyotes

ALLTEL Ice Den
9375 East Belle Road
Scottsdale, AZ 85260
Telephone: (480) 473-5600
Arena: America
West Arena

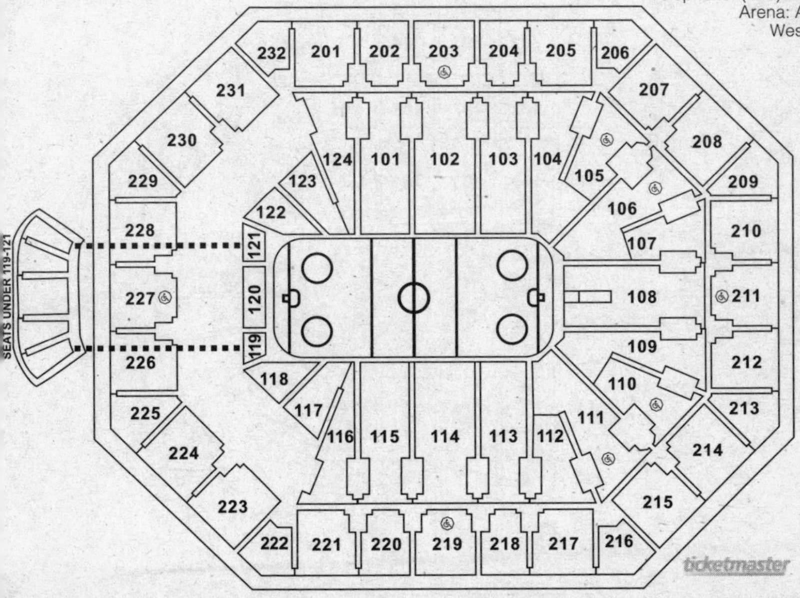

Pittsburgh Penguins

66 Mario Lemieux Place
Pittsburgh, PA 15219
Telephone: (412) 642-1300
Arena: Mellon Arena

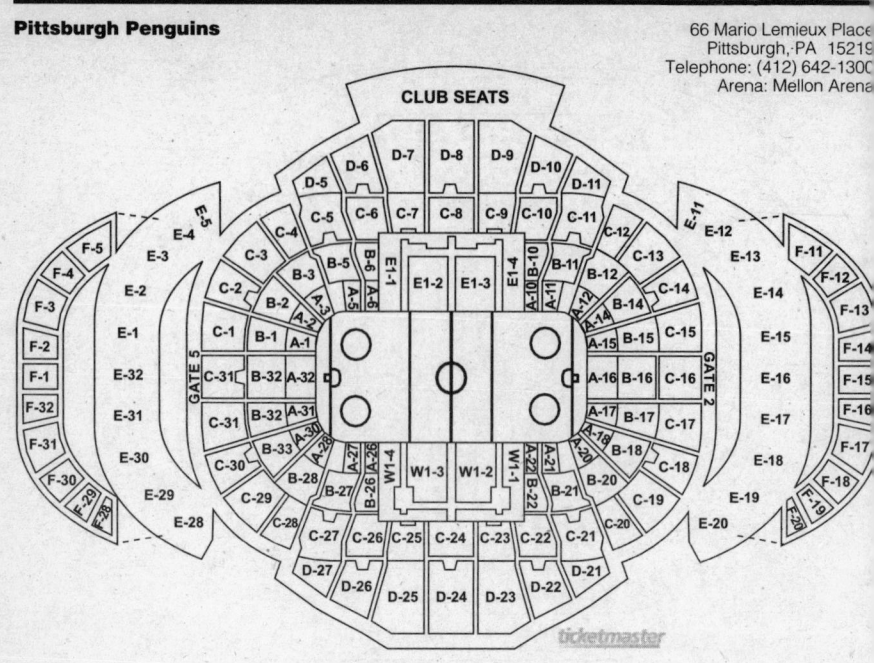

St. Louis Blues

1401 Clark Avenue
St. Louis, MO 63103
Telephone: (314) 622-2500
Arena: Savvis Center

San Jose Sharks

525 West Santa Clara Street
San Jose, CA 95113
Telephone: (408) 287-7070
Arena: Compaq Center at
San Jose

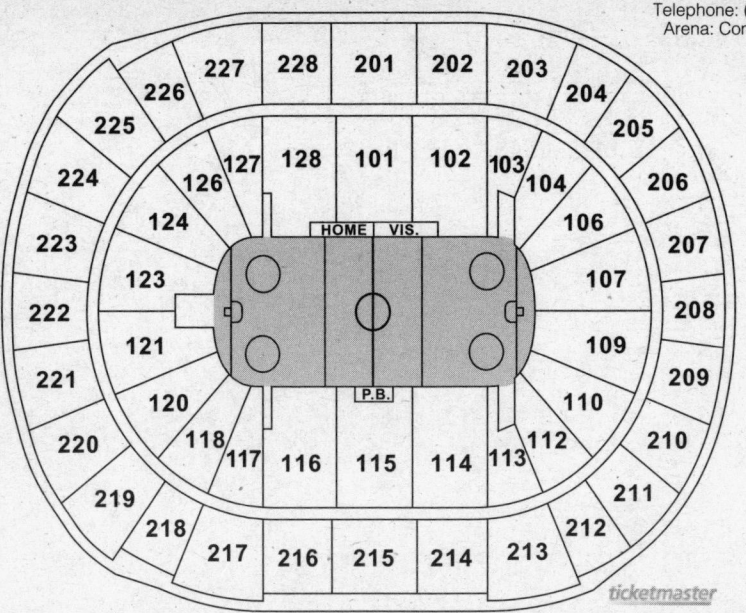

Tampa Bay Lightning

401 Channelside Drive
Tampa, FL 33602
Telephone: (813) 229-2658
Arena: Ice Palace

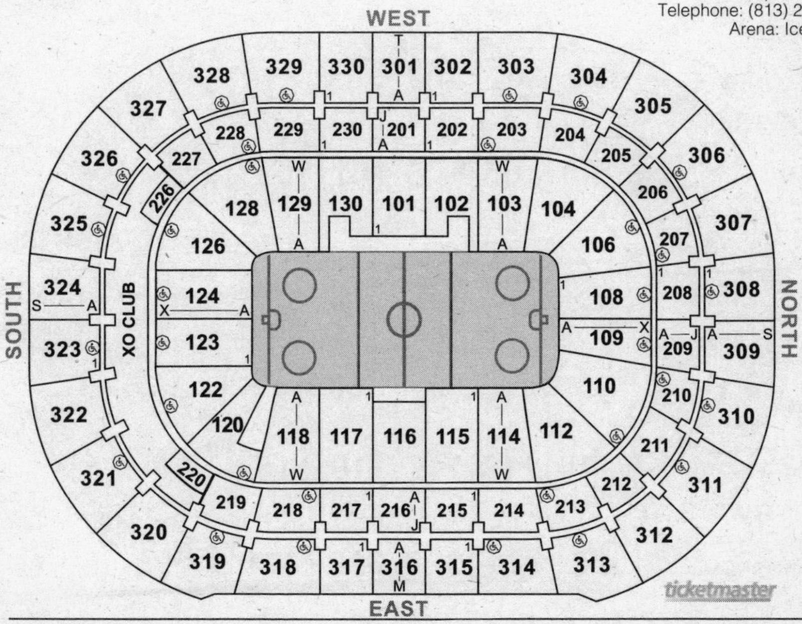

Toronto Maple Leafs

40 Bay Street - St. 400
Toronto, Ontario M5J 2X2 Canada
Telephone: (416) 815-5500
Arena: Air Canada
Centre

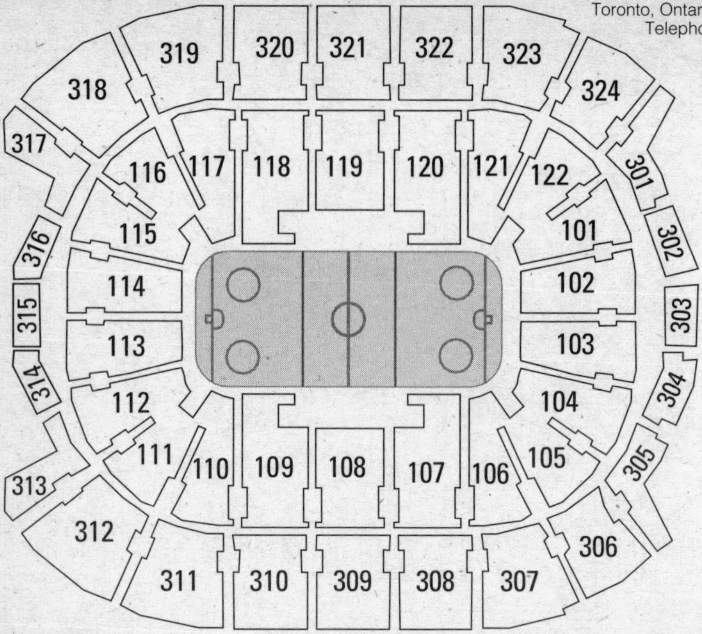

319 320 321 322 323
318 324
317 116 117 118 119 120 121 122 301
316 115 101 302
315 114 102 303
314 113 103 304
112 104
313 111 110 109 108 107 106 105 305
312 306
311 310 309 308 307

Vancouver Canucks

800 Griffiths Way
Vancouver, B.C. V6B 6G1
Telephone: (604) 899-4600
Arena: General Motors Place

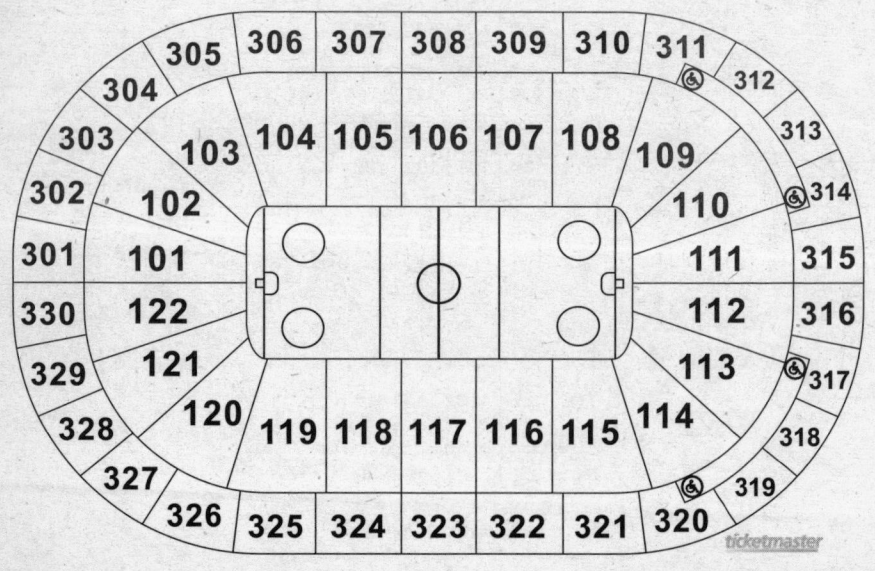

305 306 307 308 309 310 311 312
304 313
303 103 104 105 106 107 108 314
302 102 109
301 101 110 315
330 122 111 316
329 121 112 317
328 120 113 318
327 119 118 117 116 115 114 319
326 325 324 323 322 321 320

ticketmaster

Awards

Sports Illustrated

SPORTSMAN of the YEAR
Lance Armstrong
BY RICK REILLY

MONTH 00, 0000 www.cnnsi.com | AOL Keyword: Sports Illustrated

JONAS KARLSSON

Athlete Awards

Sports Illustrated Sportsman of the Year

1954	Roger Bannister, Track and Field
1955	Johnny Podres, Baseball
1956	Bobby Morrow, Track and Field
1957	Stan Musial, Baseball
1958	Rafer Johnson, Track and Field
1959	Ingemar Johansson, Boxing
1960	Arnold Palmer, Golf
1961	Jerry Lucas, Basketball
1962	Terry Baker, Football
1963	Pete Rozelle, Pro Football
1964	Ken Venturi, Golf
1965	Sandy Koufax, Baseball
1966	Jim Ryun, Track and Field
1967	Carl Yastrzemski, Baseball
1968	Bill Russell, Pro Basketball
1969	Tom Seaver, Baseball
1970	Bobby Orr, Hockey
1971	Lee Trevino, Golf
1972	Billie Jean King, Tennis
	John Wooden, Basketball
1973	Jackie Stewart, Auto Racing
1974	Muhammad Ali, Boxing
1975	Pete Rose, Baseball
1976	Chris Evert, Tennis
1977	Steve Cauthen, Horse Racing
1978	Jack Nicklaus, Golf
1979	Terry Bradshaw, Pro Football
	Willie Stargell, Baseball
1980	U.S. Olympic Hockey Team
1981	Sugar Ray Leonard, Boxing
1982	Wayne Gretzky, Hockey

1983	Mary Decker, Track and Field
1984	Mary Lou Retton, Gymnastics
	Edwin Moses, Track and Field
1985	Kareem Abdul-Jabbar, Pro Basketball
1986	Joe Paterno, Football
1987	Athletes Who Care:
	Bob Bourne, Hockey
	Kip Keino, Track and Field
	Judi Brown King, Track and Field
	Dale Murphy, Baseball
	Chip Rives, Football
	Patty Sheehan, Golf
	Rory Sparrow, Pro Basketball
	Reggie Williams, Pro Football
1988	Orel Hershiser, Baseball
1989	Greg LeMond, Cycling
1990	Joe Montana, Pro Football
1991	Michael Jordan, Pro Basketball
1992	Arthur Ashe, Tennis
1993	Don Shula, Pro Football
1994	Bonnie Blair, Speed Skating
	Johann Olav Koss, Speed Skating
1995	Cal Ripken Jr, Baseball
1996	Tiger Woods, Golf
1997	Dean Smith, College Basketball
1998	Mark McGwire, Sammy Sosa, Baseball
1999	U.S. Women's Soccer Team
2000	Tiger Woods, Golf
2001	Curt Schilling, Baseball
	Randy Johnson, Baseball
2002	Lance Armstrong, Cycling

Associated Press Athletes of the Year

	MEN	WOMEN
1931	Pepper Martin, Baseball	Helene Madison, Swimming
1932	Gene Sarazen, Golf	Babe Didrikson, Track and Field
1933	Carl Hubbell, Baseball	Helen Jacobs, Tennis
1934	Dizzy Dean, Baseball	Virginia Van Wie, Golf
1935	Joe Louis, Boxing	Helen Wills Moody, Tennis
1936	Jesse Owens, Track and Field	Helen Stephens, Track and Field
1937	Don Budge, Tennis	Katherine Rawls, Swimming
1938	Don Budge, Tennis	Patty Berg, Golf
1939	Nile Kinnick, Football	Alice Marble, Tennis
1940	Tom Harmon, Football	Alice Marble, Tennis
1941	Joe DiMaggio, Baseball	Betty Hicks Newell, Golf
1942	Frank Sinkwich, Football	Gloria Callen, Swimming
1943	Gunder Haegg, Track and Field	Patty Berg, Golf
1944	Byron Nelson, Golf	Ann Curtis, Swimming
1945	Bryon Nelson, Golf	Babe Didrikson Zaharias, Golf
1946	Glenn Davis, Football	Babe Didrikson Zaharias, Golf
1947	Johnny Lujack, Football	Babe Didrikson Zaharias, Golf
1948	Lou Boudreau, Baseball	Fanny Blankers-Koen, Track and Field
1949	Leon Hart, Football	Marlene Bauer, Golf
1950	Jim Konstanty, Baseball	Babe Didrikson Zaharias, Golf
1951	Dick Kazmaier, Football	Maureen Connolly, Tennis
1952	Bob Mathias, Track and Field	Maureen Connolly, Tennis
1953	Ben Hogan, Golf	Maureen Connolly, Tennis
1954	Willie Mays, Baseball	Babe Didrikson Zaharias, Golf
1955	Hopalong Cassidy, Football	Patty Berg, Golf
1956	Mickey Mantle, Baseball	Pat McCormick, Diving
1957	Ted Williams, Baseball	Althea Gibson, Tennis
1958	Herb Elliott, Track and Field	Althea Gibson, Tennis
1959	Ingemar Johansson, Boxing	Maria Bueno, Tennis
1960	Rafer Johnson, Track and Field	Wilma Rudolph, Track and Field
1961	Roger Maris, Baseball	Wilma Rudolph, Track and Field
1962	Maury Wills, Baseball	Dawn Fraser, Swimming
1963	Sandy Koufax, Baseball	Mickey Wright, Golf
1964	Don Schollander, Swimming	Mickey Wright, Golf
1965	Sandy Koufax, Baseball	Kathy Whitworth, Golf
1966	Frank Robinson, Baseball	Kathy Whitworth, Golf
1967	Carl Yastrzemski, Baseball	Billie Jean King, Tennis
1968	Denny McLain, Baseball	Peggy Fleming, Skating

Associated Press Athletes of the Year (Cont.)

	MEN	WOMEN
1969	Tom Seaver, Baseball	Debbie Meyer, Swimming
1970	George Blanda, Pro Football	Chi Cheng, Track and Field
1971	Lee Trevino, Golf	Evonne Goolagong, Tennis
1972	Mark Spitz, Swimming	Olga Korbut, Gymnastics
1973	O.J. Simpson, Pro Football	Billie Jean King, Tennis
1974	Muhammad Ali, Boxing	Chris Evert, Tennis
1975	Fred Lynn, Baseball	Chris Evert, Tennis
1976	Bruce Jenner, Track and Field	Nadia Comaneci, Gymnastics
1977	Steve Cauthen, Horse Racing	Chris Evert, Tennis
1978	Ron Guidry, Baseball	Nancy Lopez, Golf
1979	Willie Stargell, Baseball	Tracy Austin, Tennis
1980	U.S. Olympic Hockey Team	Chris Evert Lloyd, Tennis
1981	John McEnroe, Tennis	Tracy Austin, Tennis
1982	Wayne Gretzky, Hockey	Mary Decker, Track and Field
1983	Carl Lewis, Track and Field	Martina Navratilova, Tennis
1984	Carl Lewis, Track and Field	Mary Lou Retton, Gymnastics
1985	Dwight Gooden, Baseball	Nancy Lopez, Golf
1986	Larry Bird, Pro Basketball	Martina Navratilova, Tennis
1987	Ben Johnson, Track and Field	Jackie Joyner-Kersee, Track and Field
1988	Orel Hershiser, Baseball	Florence Griffith Joyner, Track and Field
1989	Joe Montana, Pro Football	Steffi Graf, Tennis
1990	Joe Montana, Pro Football	Beth Daniel, Golf
1991	Michael Jordan, Pro Basketball	Monica Seles, Tennis
1992	Michael Jordan, Pro Basketball	Monica Seles, Tennis
1993	Michael Jordan, Pro Basketball	Sheryl Swoopes, Basketball
1994	George Foreman, Boxing	Bonnie Blair, Speed Skating
1995	Cal Ripken Jr, Baseball	Rebecca Lobo, Basketball
1996	Michael Johnson, Track and Field	Amy Van Dyken, Swimming
1997	Tiger Woods, Golf	Martina Hingis, Tennis
1998	Mark McGwire, Baseball	Se Ri Pak, Golf
1999	Tiger Woods, Golf	U.S. Women's Soccer Team
2000	Tiger Woods, Golf	Marion Jones, Track and Field
2001	Barry Bonds, Baseball	Jennifer Capriati, Tennis
2002	Lance Armstrong, Cycling	Serena Williams, Tennis

James E. Sullivan Award

Presented annually by the AAU to the athlete who "by his or her performance, example and influence as an amateur, has done the most during the year to advance the cause of sportsmanship."

1930	Bobby Jones, Golf	1964	Don Schollander, Swimming
1931	Barney Berlinger, Track and Field	1965	Bill Bradley, Basketball
1932	Jim Bausch, Track and Field	1966	Jim Ryun, Track and Field
1933	Glenn Cunningham, Track and Field	1967	Randy Matson, Track and Field
1934	Bill Bonthron, Track and Field	1968	Debbie Meyer, Swimming
1935	Lawson Little, Golf	1969	Bill Toomey, Track and Field
1936	Glenn Morris, Track and Field	1970	John Kinsella, Swimming
1937	Don Budge, Tennis	1971	Mark Spitz, Swimming
1938	Don Lash, Track and Field	1972	Frank Shorter, Track and Field
1939	Joe Burk, Rowing	1973	Bill Walton, Basketball
1940	Greg Rice, Track and Field	1974	Rich Wohlhuter, Track and Field
1941	Leslie MacMitchell, Track and Field	1975	Tim Shaw, Swimming
1942	Cornelius Warmerdam, Track	1976	Bruce Jenner, Track and Field
1943	Gilbert Dodds, Track and Field	1977	John Naber, Swimming
1944	Ann Curtis, Swimming	1978	Tracy Caulkins, Swimming
1945	Doc Blanchard, Football	1979	Kurt Thomas, Gymnastics
1946	Arnold Tucker, Football	1980	Eric Heiden, Speed Skating
1947	John B. Kelly Jr, Rowing	1981	Carl Lewis, Track and Field
1948	Bob Mathias, Track and Field	1982	Mary Decker, Track and Field
1949	Dick Button, Skating	1983	Edwin Moses, Track and Field
1950	Fred Wilt, Track and Field	1984	Greg Louganis, Diving
1951	Bob Richards, Track and Field	1985	Joan B.-Samuelson, T & F
1952	Horace Ashenfelter, Track and Field	1986	Jackie Joyner-Kersee, T & F
1953	Sammy Lee, Diving	1987	Jim Abbott, Baseball
1954	Mal Whitfield, Track and Field	1988	Florence Griffith Joyner, Track
1955	Harrison Dillard, Track and Field	1989	Janet Evans, Swimming
1956	Pat McCormick, Diving	1990	John Smith, Wrestling
1957	Bobby Morrow, Track and Field	1991	Mike Powell, Track and Field
1958	Glenn Davis, Track and Field	1992	Bonnie Blair, Speed Skating
1959	Parry O'Brien, Track and Field	1993	Charlie Ward, Football, Basketball
1960	Rafer Johnson, Track and Field	1994	Dan Jansen, Speed Skating
1961	Wilma Rudolph, Track and Field	1995	Bruce Baumgartner, Wrestling
1962	Jim Beatty, Track and Field	1996	Michael Johnson, Track and Field
1963	John Pennel, Track and Field		

James E. Sullivan Award (Cont.)

1997 ....Peyton Manning, Football	2000 ....Rulon Gardner, Wrestling
1998 ....Chamique Holdsclaw, Basketball	2001 ....Michelle Kwan, Figure Skating
1999 ....Kelly and Coco Miller, Basketball	2002 ....Sarah Hughes, Figure Skating

The Sporting News Sportsman of the Year

1968 ....Denny McLain, Baseball	1986 ....Larry Bird, Pro Basketball
1969 ....Tom Seaver, Baseball	1987 ....No award
1970 ....John Wooden, Basketball	1988 ....Jackie Joyner-Kersee, T & F
1971 ....Lee Trevino, Golf	1989 ....Joe Montana, Pro Football
1972 ....Charles O. Finley, Baseball	1990 ....Nolan Ryan, Baseball
1973 .........................O.J. Simpson, Pro Football	1991 ....Michael Jordan, Pro Basketball
1974 ....Lou Brock, Baseball	1992 ....Mike Krzyzewski, Basketball
1975 ....Archie Griffin, Football	1993 ....Pat Gillick/Cito Gaston, Baseball
1976 ....Larry O'Brien, Pro Basketball	1994 ....Emmitt Smith, Pro Football
1977 ....Steve Cauthen, Horse Racing	1995 ....Cal Ripken Jr, Baseball
1978 ....Ron Guidry, Baseball	1996 ....Joe Torre, Baseball
1979 ....Willie Stargell, Baseball	1997 ....Michael Jordan, Basketball
1980 ....George Brett, Baseball	1998 ....Mark McGwire, Baseball
1981 ....Wayne Gretzky, Hockey	1999 ....New York Yankees, Baseball
1982 ....Whitey Herzog, Baseball	2000 ....Kurt Warner/
1983 ....Bowie Kuhn, Baseball	Marshall Faulk, Football
1984 ....Peter Ueberroth, LA Olympics	2001 ....Curt Schilling, Baseball
1985 ....Pete Rose, Baseball	2002 ....Tyrone Willingham, Football

United Press International Male and Female Athlete of the Year

	MEN	WOMEN
1974	Muhammad Ali, Boxing	Irena Szewinska, Track and Field
1975	Joao Oliveira, Track and Field	Nadia Comaneci, Gymnastics
1976	Alberto Juantorena, Track and Field	Nadia Comaneci, Gymnastics
1977	Alberto Juantorena, Track and Field	Rosie Ackermann, Track and Field
1978	Henry Rono, Track and Field	Tracy Caulkins, Swimming
1979	Sebastian Coe, Track and Field	Marita Koch, Track and Field
1980	Eric Heiden, Speed Skating	Hanni Wenzel, Alpine Skiing
1981	Sebastian Coe, Track and Field	Chris Evert Lloyd, Tennis
1982	Daley Thompson, Track and Field	Marita Koch, Track and Field
1983	Carl Lewis, Track and Field	Jarmila Kratochvilova, Track and Field
1984	Carl Lewis, Track and Field	Martina Navratilova, Tennis
1985	Steve Cram, Track and Field	Mary Decker Slaney, Track and Field
1986	Diego Maradona, Soccer	Heike Drechsler, Track and Field
1987	Ben Johnson, Track and Field	Steffi Graf, Tennis
1988	Matt Biondi, Swimming	Florence Griffith Joyner, Track and Field
1989	Boris Becker, Tennis	Steffi Graf, Tennis
1990	Stefan Edberg, Tennis	Merlene Ottey, Track and Field
1991	Michael Jordan, Pro Basketball	Monica Seles, Tennis
1992	Mario Lemieux, Hockey	Monica Seles, Tennis
1993	Michael Jordan, Pro Basketball	Steffi Graf, Tennis
1994	Nick Price, Golf	Bonnie Blair, Speed Skating
1995	Cal Ripken Jr, Baseball	Steffi Graf, Tennis

Note: Award not given since 1995.

Dial Award

Presented by the Dial Corporation to the male and female national high school athlete/scholar of the year.

	BOYS	GIRLS
1979	Herschel Walker, Football	No award
1980	Bill Fralic, Football	Carol Lewis, Track and Field
1981	Kevin Willhite, Football	Cheryl Miller, Basketball
1982	Mike Smith, Basketball	Elaine Zayak, Skating
1983	Chris Spielman, Football	Melanie Buddemeyer, Swimming
1984	Hart Lee Dykes, Football	Nora Lewis, Basketball
1985	Jeff George, Football	Gea Johnson, Track and Field
1986	Scott Schaffner, Football	Mya Johnson, Track and Field
1987	Todd Marinovich, Football	Kristi Overton, Water Skiing
1988	Carlton Gray, Football	Courtney Cox, Basketball
1989	Robert Smith, Football	Lisa Leslie, Basketball
1990	Derrick Brooks, Football	Vicki Goetze, Golf
1991	Jeff Buckey, Football, Track and Field	Katie Smith, Basketball, Volleyball, Track
1992	Jacque Vaughn, Basketball	Amanda White, Track and Field, Swimming
1993	Tiger Woods, Golf	Kristin Folkl, Basketball
1994	Taymon Domzalski, Basketball	Shannon Miller, Gymnastics
1995	Brent Abernathy, Baseball	Shea Ralph, Basketball
1996	Grant Irons, Football	Grace Park, Golf
1997	Ronald Curry, Football	Michelle Kwan, Figure Skating

Note: Award not given since 1997.

Profiles

WALTER IOOSS JR.

EVERYBODY LOVES ANNIKA

NBA FINALS Beware the Red-Hot Nets

JASON KIDD

Sports Illustrated

THE ROCKET

ROGER CLEMENS AND THE QUEST FOR

300

By Tom Verducci

JUNE 2, 2003 www.si.com | AOL Keyword: Sports Illustrated

STANLEY CUP FINALS The Ducks Take On the Devils

J.S. GIGUERE

Future Hall of Famer Roger Clemens

Henry Aaron (b. 2-5-34): Baseball OF. "Hammerin' Hank." Alltime leader in HR (755) and RBI (2,297); third in hits (3,771). 1957 MVP. Led league in HR and RBI four times each, runs scored three times, hits and batting average twice. No. 44, he had 44 homers four times. Had 40+ HR eight times; 100+ RBI 11 times; .300+ average 14 times. All-Star 24 times . Career span 1954–76; jersey number retired by Atlanta and Milwaukee.

Kareem Abdul-Jabbar (b. 4-16-47): Born Lew Alcindor. Basketball C. Alltime leader points scored (38,387), field goals attempted (28,307), field goals made (15,837); second alltime blocked shots (3,189); third alltime rebounds (17,440). Won six MVP awards (1971–72, 1974, 1976–77, 1980). Career scoring average was 24.6, rebounding average 11.2. Ten-time All-Star, All-Defensive team five times. 1970 Rookie of the Year. Played on six championship teams; was playoff MVP in 1971, 1985. Career span 1969–88 with Milwaukee, Los Angeles. Also played on three NCAA championship teams with UCLA; tournament MVP 1967–69; Player of the Year two times.

Affirmed (b. 2-21-75, d. 1-12-01): Thoroughbred race horse. Triple Crown winner in 1978 with jockey Steve Cauthen aboard. Trained by Laz Barrera.

Andre Agassi (b. 4-29-70): Tennis player. Won 1999 French Open to become fifth man in history to win all four Grand Slams. Won '92 Wimbledon, '94 and '99 U.S. Opens and '95, '00, '01 and '03 Australian Opens. Ranked No. 1 in 1995 and again in '99.

Troy Aikman (b. 11-21-66): Football QB. Quarterbacked Cowboys to three Super Bowl titles (XXVII, XXVIII, XXX). MVP of Super Bowl XXVII, in which he completed 22 of 30 passes for 273 yards and four TDs with no interceptions. Spent entire career (1989–2000) with Dallas Cowboys, passing for 32,942 yards and 171 TDs.

Michelle Akers (b. 2-1-66): Soccer player. Charter member of U.S. women's national team. Scored first goal ever for U.S. women's team on 8-21-85 against Denmark. Second alltime leading scorer in U.S. women's national team history (105 goals). Member of Women's World Cup champion team in 1991, '99, and third-place team in '95. Member of Olympic champion team in 1996. Battled chronic fatigue syndrome.

Tenley Albright (b. 7-18-35): Figure skater. Gold medalist at 1956 Olympics, silver medalist at 1952 Olympics. World champion two times (1953, 1955) and U.S. champion five consecutive years (1952–56).

Grover Cleveland Alexander (b. 2-26-1887, d. 11-4-50): Baseball RHP. Tied for third alltime in career wins (373), second in shutouts (90). Won 30+ games three times, 20+ games six other times. Set rookie record with 28 wins in 1911. Career span 1911–30 with Philadelphia (NL), Chicago (NL), St. Louis (NL).

Vasili Alexeyev (b. 1942): Soviet weightlifter. Gold medalist at two consecutive Olympics in 1972, 1976. World champion eight times.

Muhammad Ali (b. 1-17-42): Born Cassius Clay. Boxer. Heavyweight champion three times (1964–67, 1974–78, 1978–79). Stripped of title in 1967 because he refused to serve in the Vietnam War. Career record 56–5 with 37 KOs. Defended title 19 times. Also light heavyweight gold medalist at 1960 Olympics. Battles Parkinson Syndrome.

Phog Allen (b. 11-18-1885, d. 9-16-74): College baseball coach. Ninth alltime in coaching wins (746); .739 career winning percentage. Won 1952 NCAA championship. Spent most of his career from 1920 to '56 with Kansas.

Bobby Allison (b. 12-3-37): Auto racer. Third alltime in NASCAR victories (84). Won Daytona 500 three times (1978, 1982, 1988). NASCAR champion in 1983.

Naty Alvarado (b. 7-25-55): Mexican-born handball player. "El Gato (The Cat)." Won a record 11 U.S. pro four-wall handball titles, starting in 1977.

Lance Alworth (b. 8-3-40): Football WR. "Bambi" led AFL in receiving in 1966, '68 and '69. 200+ yards in a game five times in career, a record. Gained 100+ yards in a game 41 times. In 1965 gained 1,602 yards receiving. Career span 1962–70 with San Diego and 1971–72 with Dallas. Elected to Pro Football Hall of Fame 1978.

Gary Anderson (b. 7-16-59): Football K. Four-time Pro Bowl player. NFL's alltime leading scorer (2,133 pts). Made league record 40 consecutive FGs in 1997–98 season. Made every field goal and extra point attempt during the 1998–99 season.

Sparky Anderson (b. 2-22-34): Baseball manager. Only manager to win World Series in both leagues (Cincinnati, 1975–76, Detroit, 1984); only manager to win 100 games in both leagues. Elected to Hall of Fame in 2000.

Willie Anderson (b. 1880, d. 1910): Scottish golfer. Won U.S. Open four times (1901 and an unmatched three straight, 1903–05). Also won four Western Opens between 1902 and 1909.

Mario Andretti (b. 2-28-40): Auto racer. The only driver in history to win the Daytona 500 (1967), the Indy 500 (1969) and a Formula One world championship (1978). Second alltime in CART victories (52). Twelve career Formula One victories. USAC/CART champion four times (consecutively 1965–66, 1969, 1984).

Earl Anthony (b. 4-27-38, d. 8-14-01): Bowler. Won PBA National Championship six times, more than any other bowler (consecutively 1973–75, 1981–83) and Tournament of Champions two times (1974, 1978). First bowler to top $1 million in career earnings. Bowler of the Year six times (consecutively 1974–76, 1981–83). Won 41 career PBA titles.

Said Aouita (b. 11-2-60): Track and field. Moroccan set world records in 2,000 meters (4:50.81 in 1987), and 5,000 meters (12:58.39 in 1987). 1984 Olympic champion in 5,000; 1988 Olympic third place in 800.

Al Arbour (b. 11-1-32): Hockey D-coach. Led NY Islanders to four consecutive Stanley Cup championships (1980–83). Also played on three Stanley Cup champions: Detroit, Chicago and Toronto, from 1953 to 1971.

Eddie Arcaro (b. 2-19-16, d. 11-14-97): Horse racing jockey. The only jockey to win the Triple Crown two times (aboard Whirlaway in 1941, Citation in 1948). Rode Preakness Stakes winner (1941, 1948, consecutively 1950–51, 1955, 1957) and Belmont Stakes winner (consecutively 1941–42, 1945, 1948, 1952, 1955) six times each and Kentucky Derby winner five times (1938, 1941, 1945, 1948, 1952). 4,779 career wins.

Nate Archibald (b. 9-2-48): Basketball player. "Tiny" only by NBA standards at 6' 1", 160 pounds. Six-time All-Star. Led NBA in scoring (34.0) and assists (11.4) in 1972–73. First team, all-NBA in 1973, '75 and '76. MVP of NBA All-Star Game in 1981. Career span 1970–84 with six teams.

Alexis Arguello (b. 4-19-52): Nicaraguan boxer. Won world titles in three weight classes: featherweight, super featherweight and lightweight. Won first title, WBA featherweight, on 11-23-74 when he KO'd Ruben Olivares in 13. Career record: 88–8, 64 KO.

Henry Armstrong (b. 12-12-12, d. 10-24-88): Boxer. Champion in three different weight classes: featherweight, welterweight, and lightweight. Career record 145-20-9 with 98 KOs (27 consecutively, 1937–38) from 1931 to 1945.

Lance Armstrong (b. 9-18-71): Cyclist. Recovered from testicular cancer to win five straight Tour de France races (1999–03). Two-time winner of Tour DuPont (1995, '96). Won 1993 world championships.

Arthur Ashe (b. 7-10-43, d. 2-6-93): Tennis player. First black man to win U.S. Open (1968, as an amateur), Australian Open (1970) and Wimbledon singles titles (1975). 33 career tournament victories. Member of Davis Cup team 1963–78; captain 1980–85. Stadium at the United States Tennis Center, home of the U.S. Open, named in his honor.

Assault (b. 1943, d. 1971): Thoroughbred race horse. Horse of the Year for 1946 when he won the Triple Crown. Won Kentucky Derby by eight lengths, Preakness by a neck, and the Belmont by three lengths. Trained by Max Hirsch.

Red Auerbach (b. 9-20-17): Basketball coach-executive. 938 career wins. Coached Boston from 1946 to 1965, winning nine championships, eight consecutively. Had .662 career winning percentage, with 50+ wins eight consecutive seasons. Also won seven championships as general manager.

Hobey Baker (b. 1-15-1892, d. 12-21-18): Sportsman. Member of both college football and hockey Halls of Fame. College hockey and football star at Princeton, 1911–14. Fighter pilot in World War I, died in plane crash. College hockey Player of the Year award named in his honor.

Seve Ballesteros (b. 4-9-57): Spanish golfer. Notorious scrambler. Won British Opens in 1979, '84 and '88. Won Masters in 1980 and '83.

Ernie Banks (b. 1-31-31): Baseball SS-1B. "Mr. Cub." Won two consecutive MVP awards, in 1958–59. 512 career HR. League leader in HR, RBI two times each; 40+ HR five times; 100+ RBI eight times; career batting average of .274. Career span 1953–71 with Chicago.

Roger Bannister (b. 3-23-29): Track and field. British runner broke the four-minute mile barrier, running 3:59.4 on 5-6-54.

Red Barber (b. 2-17-08, d. 10-22-92): Sportscaster. TV-radio baseball announcer was the voice of Cincinnati, Brooklyn and NY Yankees. His expressions, such as "sitting in the catbird seat," "pea patch" and "rhubarb," captivated audiences from 1934 to 1966.

Charles Barkley (b. 2-20-63): Basketball F. "The Round Mound of Rebound." Eleven-time All-Star. One of only four NBA players to amass 20,000 points, 10,000 rebounds, and 4,000 assists. Named one of NBA's greatest 50 players. Leading scorer on the 1992 Olympic team. League MVP for 1992–93 season. Played for Philadelphia, Phoenix, Houston. Career averages: 22.2 ppg, 11.7 rpg.

Rick Barry (b. 3-28-44): Basketball F. Only player in history to win scoring titles in NCAA (Miami (FL), 1965), NBA (San Francisco, 1967) and ABA (Oakland, 1969). Five-time first-team All-NBA. 1966 Rookie of the Year. 1975 playoff MVP with Golden State. Eight-time NBA All-Star. Career scoring average 23.2. Career span 1966–79.

Carmen Basilio (b. 4-2-27): Boxer. Won titles as a welterweight and middleweight. Won welterweight title by TKO of Tony DeMarco in 12 rounds on 6-10-55. Won and then lost middleweight title in two 15-round fights with Ray Robinson. Made three unsuccessful bids to regain middle title. *The Ring* Fighter of the Year for 1957. Career record: 56–16–7, 27 KOs.

Sammy Baugh (b. 3-17-14): Football QB-P. Led NFL in passing six times and punting four times, a record. Holds record for highest career punting average (45.1) and highest season average (51.0 in 1940). Career span 1937–52 with Washington, passing for 21,866 yards and 186 TDs.

Elgin Baylor (b. 9-16-34): Basketball F. Fourth alltime highest scoring average (27.4) in NBA history. Averaged 30+ points three consecutive seasons (1960-63). 1959 Rookie of the Year. 11-time All-Star. Played in eight NBA Finals without winning championship. Career span 1958–71 with Lakers. MVP of 1958 NCAA Tournament with Seattle.

Bob Beamon (b. 8-29-46): Track and field. Gold medalist in long jump at 1968 Olympics with world record leap of 29' 2½" that stood until 1991.

Franz Beckenbauer (b. 9-11-45): West German soccer player. Captain of 1974 World Cup champions and coach of 1990 champions. Also played for NY Cosmos from 1977 to 1980.

Boris Becker (b. 11-22-67): German tennis player. The youngest male player (17, in 1985) to win a Wimbledon singles title. Won three Wimbledon titles (1985–86, 1989), one U.S. Open (1989) and one Australian Open title (1991). Led West Germany to consecutive Davis Cup victories (1988–89).

Chuck Bednarik (b. 5-1-25): Football C-LB. Last of the great two-way players, was named All-Pro at both center and linebacker. Missed only three games in 14 seasons with Philadelphia from 1949–62. Seven-time All-NFL. Two-time All-America at Pennsylvania.

Clair Bee (b. 3-2-1896, d. 5-20-83): Basketball coach. Originated 1-3-1 defense, helped develop three-second rule, 24-second clock. Won 82.7 percent of games as coach for Rider College and Long Island University. Coach, Baltimore Bullets, 1952–54. Author, 23-volume Chip Hilton series for children, 21 nonfiction sports books.

Jean Beliveau (b. 8-31-31): Hockey C. Won MVP award twice (1956, 1964), playoff MVP in 1965. Led league in assists three times, goals two times and points once. 507 career goals, 712 assists. All-Star six times. Played on 10 Stanley Cup champions with Montreal from 1950 to 1971.

Bert Bell (b. 2-25-1895, d. 10-11-59): Football executive. Second NFL commissioner (1946–59). Also owner of Philadelphia (1933–40) and Pittsburgh

(1941–46). Proposed the first NFL draft of college players, in 1936.

James (Cool Papa) Bell (b. 5-17-03, d. 3-7-91): Baseball OF. Legendary foot speed—according to Satchel Paige could flip light switch and be in bed before room was dark. Hit .392 in games against white major leaguers. Career span 1922–46 with many teams of the Negro Leagues, including the Pittsburgh Crawfords and the Homestead Grays. Inducted in the Hall of Fame in 1974.

Lyudmila Belousova/Oleg Protopov (no dates of birth available): Soviet figure skaters. Won Olympic gold medal in pairs competition in 1964 and 1968. Won four consecutive World and European championships (1965–68) and eight consecutive Soviet titles (1961–68).

Deane Beman (b. 4-22-38): Commissioner of the PGA Tour 1974–94. Won British Amateur title in 1959 and U.S. Amateur titles in 1960 and 1963.

Johnny Bench (b. 12-7-47): Baseball C. MVP in 1970, 1972; World Series MVP in 1976; Rookie of the Year in 1968. 389 career HR. League leader in HR two times, RBI three times. Career span 1967–83 with Cincinnati. Elected to Hall of Fame in 1989.

Patty Berg (b. 2-13-18): Golfer. Alltime women's leader in major championships (16), third alltime in career wins (57). Won Titleholders Championship and Western Open seven times each, the most of any golfer. Also won U.S. Women's Amateur (1938) and U.S. Women's Open (1946).

Yogi Berra (b. 5-12-25): Baseball C. Played on 10 World Series winners. Alltime Series leader in games, at-bats, hits and doubles. MVP in 1951 and consecutively 1954–55. 358 career HR. Career span 1946–63, '65. Managed pennant-winning Yankees (1964) and Mets (1973).

Jay Berwanger (b. 3-19-14, d. 6-26-02): College football RB. Won the first Heisman Trophy and named All-America with Chicago in 1935.

Raymond Berry (b. 2-27-33): Football WR. Led NFL in receiving 1958–60. In 13-season career, caught 631 passes, 68 for TDs. Career span 1955–67, all with Baltimore Colts. Coached New England Patriots from 1984–89 with 51–41 record.

George Best (b. 5-22-46): Northern Ireland soccer player. Led Manchester United to European Cup title in 1968. Named England's and Europe's Player of the Year in 1968. Played in North American Soccer League from 1976–81. Frequent troubles with alcohol and gambling shadowed career.

Abebe Bikila (b. 8-7-32, d. 10-25-73): Track and field. Ethiopian barefoot runner won consecutive gold medals in the marathon at Olympics, in 1960 and 1964.

Fred Biletnikoff (b. 2-23-43): Football WR. In 14 pro seasons caught 589 passes for 8,974 yards and 76 TDs. In 1971 led NFL receivers with 61 catches; in '72 led AFC with 58. Career span 1965–78, all with Raiders. Elected to Pro Football Hall of Fame in 1988.

Dmitri Bilozerchev (b. 12-22-66): Soviet gymnast. Won three gold medals at 1988 Olympics. Made comeback after shattering his left leg into 44 pieces in 1985. Two-time world champion (1983, '87). At 16, became youngest to win all-around world championship title in 1983.

Dave Bing (b. 11-24-43): Basketball G. NBA Rookie of Year in 1967. Led NBA in scoring (27.1) in 1968.

MVP NBA All-Star game in 1976. In 12-year career from 1967–78, most of it with Detroit Pistons, averaged 20.3 points. Averaged 24.8 ppg in four years at Syracuse.

Matt Biondi (b. 10-8-65): Swimmer. Won five gold medals, one silver and one bronze at 1988 Olympics. Won one gold and one silver at 1992 Games.

Larry Bird (b. 12-7-56): Basketball F. Won three consecutive MVP awards (1984–86) and two playoff MVP awards (1984, 1986). Rookie of the Year (1980) and All-Star nine consecutive seasons. Led league in free throw percentage four times. Averaged 20+ points 10 times. Career span 1979–92 with Boston. Named College Player of the Year in 1979 with Indiana State. 1997–98 NBA Coach of the Year in first year as coach of Indiana Pacers.

Bonnie Blair (b. 3-18-64): Speed skater. Won gold medal in 500 meters and bronze medal in 1,000 meters at 1988 Olympics. Swept both Olympic events in 1992 and '94. 1989 World Sprint champion. Winner of 1992 Sullivan Award. *Sports Illustrated* 1994 Sportswoman of the Year.

Toe Blake (b. 8-21-12, d. 5-17-95): Hockey LW and coach. Second alltime highest winning percentage (.634) and eighth in wins (500). Led Montreal to eight Stanley Cup championships from 1955 to 1968 (consecutively 1956–60, 1965–66, '68). Also MVP and scoring leader in 1939. Played on two Stanley Cup champions with Montreal from 1932 to 1948.

Doc Blanchard (b. 12-11-24): College football FB. "Mr. Inside." Teamed with Glenn Davis to lead Army to three consecutive undefeated seasons (1944–46) and two consecutive national championships (1944–45). Won Heisman Trophy and Sullivan Award in 1945. All-America three times.

George Blanda (b. 9-17-27): Football QB-K. Alltime leader in seasons played (26), games played (340), and PAT's (943); third in points scored (2,002); kicked 335 field goals. Passed for 26,920 career yards and 236 touchdowns. Tied record with seven touchdown passes on Nov. 19, 1961. AFL Player of the Year (1961) when he threw 36 TDs. Played until age 48. Career span 1949–75 with Chicago, Houston, Oakland.

Fanny Blankers-Koen (b. 4-26-18): Track and field. Dutch athlete won four gold medals at 1948 Olympics, in 100 meters; 200 meters; 80-meter hurdles; and 400-meter relay. She also set world records in high jump (5' 7¼" in 1943), long jump (20' 6" in 1943) and pentathlon (4,692 points in 1951).

Wade Boggs (b. 6-15-58): Baseball 3B. Won five batting titles (1983, consecutively 1985–88); had .350+ average five times, 200+ hits seven times. Won World Series with 1996 Yankees. Career span 1982–99 with Boston, New York Yankees, Tampa Bay; .328 career average, 3,010 hits.

Nick Bollettieri (b. 7-31-31): Tennis coach. Since 1976, has run Nick Bollettieri Tennis Academy in Bradenton, Fla. Former residents of the academy include Andre Agassi, Monica Seles and Jim Courier.

Barry Bonds (b. 7-24-64): Baseball OF. Baseball's single-season home run king, with 73 in 2001. Also produced .863 slugging percentage and 177 walks in 2001, breaking two of Babe Ruth's records, the first of which had stood since 1920. One of three players to top 40 homers (42) and 40 steals (40) in same season (1996). Five-time National League MVP (1990, '92, '93,

'01, '02); Career span 1986–92 with Pittsburgh; 1993– with San Francisco.

Bjorn Borg (b. 6-6-56): Swedish tennis player. Third alltime in Grand Slam singles titles (11—tied with Rod Laver). Set modern record by winning five consecutive Wimbledon titles (1976–80). Won six French Open titles (1974–75, 1978–81). Reached U.S. Open final four times, but title eluded him. 65 career tournament victories. Led Sweden to Davis Cup win in 1975.

Julius Boros (b. 3-3-20, d. 5-28-94): Golfer. Won U.S. Opens in 1952 at Northwood CC in Dallas and in 1963 at The Country Club in Brookline, Mass. Won 1968 PGA Championship at Pecan Valley CC, San Antonio, when 48 years old, making him oldest winner of a major ever. Led PGA money list in 1952 and '55.

Mike Bossy (b. 1-22-57): Hockey RW. Set NHL rookie scoring record of 54 goals in 1978. Scored 50 or more each of first nine seasons. Totaled 573 goals and 1,126 points in 10 seasons (1977–87) with New York Islanders. Elected to Hall of Fame in 1991.

Ralph Boston (b. 5-9-39): Track and field. Long jumper won medals at three consecutive Olympics: gold in 1960, silver in '64, bronze in '68.

Ray Bourque (b. 12-28-60): Hockey D. Highest scoring defenseman in NHL history (1,579 pts). Won five Norris Trophies as NHL's top defenseman. Played in 19 consecutive All-Star games. No. 77. Won first and only Stanley Cup in 2001.Career span 1979–00 with Boston; 2000–01 with Colorado.

Scotty Bowman (b. 9-18-33): Retired in 2002 after leading Detroit to his ninth Stanley Cup title. Alltime leader in regular-season wins (1,244) and playoff wins (223). Coached Montreal, St. Louis, Buffalo, and Detroit. Won Jack Adams Award, Coach of the Year, 1976–77, 1995–96.

Bill Bradley (b. 7-28-43): Basketball F. Played on two NBA championship teams with New York from 1967 to '77. Player of the Year and NCAA tournament MVP in 1965 with Princeton; All-America three times; Sullivan Award winner in 1965. Rhodes scholar. U.S. Senator (D-NJ) 1979–96.

Terry Bradshaw (b. 9-2-48): Football QB. Played on four Super Bowl champions (1974, '75, '78, '79). Named Super Bowl MVP two consecutive seasons (1978–79). 212 career touchdown passes; 27,989 yards passing. Player of the Year in 1978. Career span 1970–83 with Pittsburgh.

George Brett (b. 5-15-53): Baseball 3B-1B. Won batting titles in three different decades (1976, '80, '90). MVP in 1980 with .390 batting average. Hit .300+ 11 times. Led league in hits and triples three times. Career span 1973–93, with Kansas City. Career totals: 3,153 hits; 317 HR; 1,595 RBI; batting average .305. Elected to Hall of Fame in 1999.

Bret Hanover (b. 1962, d. 1993): Horse. Son of Adios. Won 62 of 68 harness races and earned $922,616. Undefeated as two-year-old. From total of 1,694 foals, he sired winners of $61 million and 511 horses that have recorded sub-2:00 performances.

Lou Brock (b. 6-18-39): Baseball OF. Second in career stolen bases (938); second highest single-season steals (118) of modern era. Led league in steals eight times, with 50+ steals 12 consecutive seasons. Alltime World Series leader in steals (14—tied with Eddie Collins); hit .391 in World Series play. 3,023 career hits. Career span 1961–64 Chicago (NL), 1964–79 St. Louis.

Jim Brown (b. 2-17-36): Football FB. 126 career touchdowns; 12,312 career rushing yards. Led league in rushing a record eight times. His 5.2 yards per carry average is the best ever. Player of the Year four times (1957, '58, '63, '65) and Rookie of the Year in 1957. Rushed for 1,000+ yards in seven seasons, 200+ yards in four games, 100+ yards in 54 other games. Career span 1957–65 with Cleveland; never missed a game. All-America in both football and lacrosse at Syracuse.

Paul Brown (b. 9-7-08, d. 8-5-91): Football coach. Led Cleveland to 10 consecutive championship games. Won four consecutive AAFC titles (1946–49) and three NFL titles (1950, '54, '55). Coached Cleveland from 1946 to 1962; became first coach of Cincinnati, 1968–75, and then general manager. Career coaching record 222-113-9. Also won national championship with Ohio State in 1942.

Avery Brundage (b. 9-28-1887, d. 5-5-75): Amateur sports executive. President of International Olympic Committee 1952–72. Served as president of U.S. Olympic Committee 1929–53. Also president of Amateur Athletic Union 1928–35. Member of 1912 U.S. Olympic track and field team.

Paul (Bear) Bryant (b. 9-11-13, d. 1-26-83): College football coach. Third in Division I-A football history with 323 wins. Won six national championships (1961, '64, '65, '73, '78, '79) with Alabama. Career record 323–85–17, including four undefeated seasons. Won 15 bowl games. Career span 1945–82 with Maryland, Kentucky, Texas A&M, Alabama.

Sergei Bubka (b. 12-4-63): Track and field. Ukrainian pole vaulter was gold medalist at 1988 Olympics. Only five-time world outdoor champion in any event (1983, '87, '91, '93, '95). First man to vault 20 feet, set world indoor record of 20' 2" on 2-21-93 and world outdoor record of 20' 1½" on 9-20-92.

Don Budge (b. 6-13-15, d. 1-26-00): Tennis player. First player to achieve the Grand Slam, in 1938. Won two consecutive Wimbledon and U.S. singles titles (1937, '38), one French and one Australian title (1938).

Dick Butkus (b. 12-9-42): Football LB. Regarded as greatest middle linebacker in NFL history. Selected to eight Pro Bowls. Career span 1965–73 with Chicago. All-America two times with Illinois. Award recognizing the outstanding college linebacker named in his honor.

Dick Button (b. 7-18-29): Figure skater. Gold medalist at 1948 and 1952 Olympics. World champion five consecutive years (1948–52) and U.S. champion seven consecutive years (1946–52). Sullivan Award winner in 1949.

Walter Byers (b. 3-13-22): Amateur sports executive. First director of NCAA, served from 1952 to 1987.

Frank Calder (b. 11-17-1877, d. 2-4-43): Hockey executive. First commissioner of NHL, served from 1917 to 1943. Rookie of the Year award named in his honor.

Walter Camp (b. 4-7-1859, d. 3-14-25): Football pioneer. Played for Yale in first football game vs. Harvard on Nov. 17, 1876. Proposed rules such as 11 men per side, scrimmage line, center snap, yards and downs. Founded the All-America selections in 1889.

Roy Campanella (b. 11-19-21; d. 6-26-93): Baseball C. MVP in 1951, '53, '55. Played on five pennant winners; 1955 World Series winner with

Brooklyn. Career span 1948–57, ended when paralyzed in car crash.

Earl Campbell (b. 3-29-55): Football RB. Led NFL in rushing three consecutive seasons. Rookie of the Year in 1978. Ran for 19 TDs in 1979 and 1,934 yards in 1980 when he was named league's Player of the Year twice. 9,407 career rushing yards. Career span 1978–85 with Houston, New Orleans. Won Heisman Trophy with Texas in 1977.

John Campbell (b. 4-8-55): Canadian harness racing driver. Alltime leading money winner with over $100 million in earnings. Leading money winner in 1986–90, 1992–95, '98, '00.

Billy Cannon (b. 2-8-37): Football RB. Led Louisiana State to national championship in 1958 and won Heisman Trophy in 1959. Signed contract with both NFL (Los Angeles) and AFL (Houston) teams. Houston won lawsuit for his services. Played in six AFL championship games with Houston, Oakland, Kansas City. Career span 1960–70. Served three-year jail term for 1983 conviction on counterfeiting charges.

Jose Canseco (b. 7-2-64): Baseball OF. One of three players to top 40 homers (42) and 40 steals (40) in same season (1988). AL MVP in 1988, when he also batted .307 with 124 RBI. AL Rookie of the Year in 1986. Career span 1985–01 with seven teams: 462 HRs, 1,407 RBIs, 1,942 K's.

Harry Caray (b. 3-1-17, d. 2-18-98): Sportscaster. TV-radio baseball announcer 1945–97 with St. Louis (NL), Oakland, Chicago (AL) and Chicago (NL). Achieved celebrity status on Cubs' superstation WGN by singing "Take Me Out to the Ball Game" with Wrigley Field fans.

Rod Carew (b. 10-1-45): Baseball 2B-1B. Won seven batting titles (1969, '72–75, '77, '78). Had .328 career average, 3,053 career hits, and .300+ average 15 times. 1977 MVP; 1967 Rookie of the Year. Career span 1967–85; jersey number (29) retired by Minnesota and Anaheim.

Steve Carlton (b. 12-22-44): Baseball LHP. Four Cy Young awards (1972, '77, '80, '82). Second in career strikeouts (4,136). 329 career wins; won 20+ games six times. League leader in wins four times, innings pitched and strikeouts five times each. Struck out 19 batters in one game in 1969. Career span 1965–88 primarily with St. Louis and Philadelphia.

JoAnne Carner (b. 4-21-39): Golfer. Won 42 titles, including U.S. Women's Opens in 1971 and '76 and du Maurier Classic in 1975 and '78. LPGA top earner in 1974, '82, '83. LPGA Player of the Year in 1974, '81, '82. Won five Vare Trophies (1974, '75, '81–83).

Joe Carr (b. 10-22-1880; d. 5-20-39): Football administrator. Instrumental in forming American Professional Football Association in 1920. President of AAFA from 1922 to '39.

Don Carter (b. 7-29-26): Bowler. Won All-Star Tournament four times (1952, '54, '56, '58) and PBA National Championship in 1960. Voted Bowler of the Year six times (1953, '54, '57, '58, '60, '62).

Alexander Cartwright (b. 4-17-1820, d. 7-12-1892): Baseball pioneer. Credited with setting the basic rules of baseball: bases 90 feet apart, nine men per side, three strikes per out and three outs per inning. On June 19, 1846, in what is often cited as the first baseball game, his New York Knickerbockers lost to the New York Nine 23–1 at Elysian Fields in Hoboken, NJ.

Billy Casper (b. 6-24-31): Golfer. Famed putter. Won 51 PGA tournaments. PGA Player of Year in both 1966 and '70. Won Vardon Trophy in 1960, '63, '64, '65 and '68. Won the U.S. Open twice, in 1959 at Winged Foot in Mamaronek, New York, and in 1966 in 18-hole playoff over Arnold Palmer at Olympic Club, San Francisco. Beat Gene Littler in 18-hole playoff to win 1970 Masters.

Tracy Caulkins (b. 1-11-63): Swimmer. Won three gold medals at 1984 Olympics. Won 48 U.S. national titles, more than any other swimmer, from 1978 to 1984. Also won Sullivan Award in 1978.

Steve Cauthen (b. 5-1-60): Jockey. In 1978 became youngest jockey to win Triple Crown, aboard Affirmed. First jockey to top $6 million in season earnings (1977). *Sports Illustrated* Sportsman of Year for 1977. Moved to England in 1979; rode Epsom Derby winners Slip Anchor (1985) and Reference Point (1987).

Evonne Goolagong Cawley (b. 7-31-51): Tennis player. Won four Australian Open titles from 1974 through '77; won 1971 French Open; won Wimbledon in 1971 and '80. Runner-up four straight years at U.S. Open (1973–76), which she never won.

Bill Chadwick (b. 10-10-15): Hockey referee. Spent 16 years as a referee despite vision in only one eye. Developed hand signals to signify penalties. Also former television announcer for the New York Rangers.

Wilt Chamberlain (b. 8-21-36, d. 10-12-99): Basketball C. "The Big Dipper." "The Stilt." Scored 100 points in a single game in 1962. Alltime leader in rebounds (23,924) and rebounding average (22.9). Third in career points (31,419). Alltime single-season leader in points scored (4,029 in 1962), scoring average (50.4 in 1962), rebounding average (27.2 in 1961) and field goal percentage (.727 in 1973). Set record for most rebounds in a game in 1960 (55). Four MVP awards (1960, '66–68), playoff MVP in 1972 and 1960 Rookie of the Year. 13-time All-Star. 30.1 career scoring average. Career span 1959–72 with Philadelphia/Golden State Warriors, Philadelphia 76ers, Los Angeles.

Colin Chapman (b. 1928, d. 12-16-83): Auto racing engineer. Founded Lotus race and street cars, designing the first Lotus racer in 1948. Introduced the monocoque design for Formula One cars in 1962 and ground effects in 1978.

Julio Cesar Chavez (b. 7-12-62): Mexican boxer. Held titles as junior welterweight, lightweight and super featherweight. Career record: 103-6-2 (83 KOs).

Gerry Cheevers (b. 12-7-40): Hockey goalie. Goaltender for Stanley Cup-winning Boston Bruins teams of 1970 and '72. In 12 seasons with Boston had 230-94-74 record with a goals against average of 2.89. Also coached Bruins from 1980–84, with 204-126-46 record. Elected to Hall of Fame 1985.

Cigar (b. 1990): Thoroughbred race horse. Tied Citation's American-record 16-race win-streak with a win on 7-13-96. Won $4 million Dubai World Cup on 3-27-96.

Citation (b. 4-11-45, d. 8-8-70): Thoroughbred race horse. Triple Crown winner in 1948 with jockey Eddie Arcaro aboard. Trained by Ben A. Jones.

King Clancy (b. 2-25-03, d. 11-6-86): Hockey D. Four-time All-Star. Coach, Montreal Maroons, Toronto. Also referee. Trophy named in his honor, recognizing leadership qualities and contribution to community.

Jim Clark (b. 3-4-36, d. 4-7-68): Scottish auto racer. Won 25 career Formula 1 races. Formula 1 champion two times (1963, 1965). Won Indy 500 in 1965. Named Indy 500 Rookie of the Year in 1963. Killed during competition in 1968 at age 32.

Bobby Clarke (b. 8-13-49): Hockey C. Won MVP award three times (1973, '75, '76). 358 career goals, 852 assists. Scored 100+ points three times. Played on two consecutive Stanley Cup champions (1974, '75) with Philadelphia. Career span 1969–84. Also general manager with Philadelphia 1984–90, Minnesota 1991–92, Florida 1993–94, and Philadelphia 1994–.

Roger Clemens (b. 8-4-62): Baseball RHP. Won six Cy Young awards (1986, '87, '91, '97, '98, '01), most by any pitcher. Also 1986 MVP. Has struck out a record 20 batters in one game on two occasions. League leader in ERA six times, strikeouts five times, and wins four times. Won Triple Crown of pitching in 1997 and '98. Won 300th game on June 13, 2003. Career span 1984–96 with Boston, 1997–98 with Toronto; 1999–03 with Yankees.

Roberto Clemente (b. 8-18-34, d. 12-31-72): Baseball OF. Killed in plane crash while still an active player. Had 3,000 career hits and .317 career average. Won four batting titles; .300+ average 13 times. 1966 MVP; 1971 World Series MVP. Twelve consecutive Gold Gloves; led league in assists five times. Career span 1955–72 with Pittsburgh.

Ty Cobb (b. 12-18-1886, d. 7-17-61): Baseball OF. Alltime leader in batting average (.366), second in runs scored (2,245) and hits (4,189), fourth in stolen bases (892). 1911 MVP and 1909 Triple Crown winner. Twelve batting titles. Had .400+ average three times, .350+ average 13 other times; 200+ hits nine times. Led league in hits seven times, steals six times and runs scored five times. Career span 1905–28 with Detroit and Philadelphia.

Mickey Cochrane (b. 4-6-03, d. 6-28-62): Baseball C. Second highest career batting average among catchers (.320). MVP in 1928, '34. Had .300+ average eight times. Career span 1925–37 with Philadelphia and Detroit.

Sebastian Coe (b. 9-29-56): Track and field. Two-time Olympic gold medalist in the 1,500 meters (1980, '84). Also won two gold medals in 800 meters at same two Olympics. Set world record in 800 meters (1:41.73 in 1981) and 1,000 meters (2:12.18 in 1981). Served in British Parliament after his running career.

Eddie Collins (b. 5-2-1887, d. 3-25-51): Baseball 2B. 3,311 career hits; .333 career average; .330+ average 12 times. 743 career stolen bases; alltime co-leader in World Series steals (14—tied with Lou Brock); alltime leader in single-game steals (six, twice). 1914 MVP. Career span 1906–30 with Philadelphia (AL), Chicago (AL).

Nadia Comaneci (b. 11-12-61): Romanian gymnast. First ever to score a perfect 10 at Olympics (on uneven parallel bars in 1976). Won three gold, two silver and one bronze medal at 1976 Olympics. Also won two gold and two silver medals at 1980 Olympics.

Dennis Conner (b. 9-16-42): Sailing. Captain of three America's Cup winners (1980, '87,'88).

Maureen Connolly (b. 9-17-34, d. 6-21-69): Tennis player. "Little Mo." First woman to achieve the Grand Slam, in 1953. Won the U.S. singles title in 1951 at age 16. Thereafter lost only four matches before retiring in 1954 after breaking her leg in a riding accident. Was never beaten in singles at Wimbledon, winning three consecutive titles (1952–54). Won three consecutive U.S. singles titles (1951–53) and two consecutive French titles (1953–54). Also won Australian title (1953).

Jimmy Connors (b. 9-2-52): Tennis player. Alltime men's leader in tournament victories (109). Held men's No. 1 ranking a record 160 consecutive weeks (7-29-74 through 8-16-77). Won five U.S. Open singles titles on three different surfaces (grass 1974, clay 1976, hard 1978, '82, '83). Won two Wimbledon singles titles (1974, '82) further apart than anyone since Bill Tilden. Also won 1974 Australian Open title. Reached Grand Slam final seven other times.

Jim Corbett (b. 9-1-1866; d. 2-18-33): Boxer. "Gentleman Jim." Invented jab. Won heavyweight title on 9-7-1892 with a KO of John Sullivan in 21 rounds; it was first heavyweight title fight using gloves. Lost title when KO'd by Bob Fitzsimmons in 14 on 3-17-1897, then lost two bids to regain it against Jim Jeffries. Career record: 11-4-2, 7 KOs, 2 ND.

Angel Cordero (b. 11-8-42): Jockey. Seventh alltime in wins (7,057) and earnings ($164,561,227). Led yearly earnings three times, in 1976, '82, '83, winning Eclipse Awards in the last two years.

Howard Cosell (b. 3-25-18, d. 4-23-95): Sportscaster. Lawyer–turned–TV-radio sports commentator. Best known for his work on "Monday Night Football." His nasal voice and "tell it like it is" approach made him a controversial figure.

James (Doc) Counsilman (b. 12-28-20): Swimming coach. Coached Indiana from 1957 to 1990. Won six consecutive NCAA championships (1968–73). Career record 287-36-1. Coached U.S. men's team at Olympics in 1964, '76. Swam English Channel in 1979 at age 58.

Count Fleet (b. 3-24-40, d. 12-3-73): Thoroughbred race horse. Triple Crown winner in 1943 with jockey Johnny Longden aboard. Trained by Don Cameron.

Yvan Cournoyer (b. 11-22-43): Hockey RW. "The Roadrunner" had 428 goals and 435 assists during his 15-season career with the Montreal Canadiens. Had 25 or more goals in 12 straight seasons. Played on 10 Stanley Cup championship teams. Elected to Hall of Fame in 1982.

Margaret Smith Court (b. 7-16-42): Australian tennis player. Alltime leader in Grand Slam singles titles (24) and total Grand Slam titles (62). Achieved Grand Slam in 1970 and mixed doubles Grand Slam in 1963 with Ken Fletcher. Won 11 Australian singles titles (1960–66, 1969–71, '73), five French titles (1962, '64, '69, '70, '73), 5 U.S. titles (1962, '65, '69, '70, '73) and three Wimbledon titles (1963, '65, '70). Court also won 19 Grand Slam doubles titles and 19 mixed doubles titles.

Bob Cousy (b. 8-9-28): Basketball G. Led NBA in assists eight consecutive seasons. Averaged 18+ points and named to All-Star team 10 consecutive seasons. 1957 MVP. Played on six championship teams with Boston from 1950 to 1969. Finished career with 6,955 assists; in 1958 had 28 assists in a single game. Also played on 1947 NCAA title team with Holy Cross.

Dave Cowens (b. 10-25-48): Basketball C. NBA co-Rookie of Year in 1971. NBA MVP for 1973. All-Star game MVP in 1973. Career span 1970–71 through 1982–83, all but the last year with the Boston Celtics, averaging 17.6 points and 13.6 rebounds per game. Coached Charlotte 1996–99 and Golden State 2000–01. Elected to Hall of Fame in 1991.

Ben Crenshaw (b. 1-11-52): Golfer. Legendary putter. Won Masters in 1984 and '95. Captain of 1999 U.S. Ryder Cup team.

Johan Cruyff (b. 4-25-47): Dutch soccer player. Led Ajax Amsterdam to three European Cup titles, and guided the Netherlands to the 1974 World Cup final, a 2–1 loss to Germany.

Larry Csonka (b. 12-25-46): Football RB. In 11 seasons rushed for 8,081 yards and 64 TDs. MVP of Super Bowl VIII, when he rushed 33 times for a then Super Bowl–record 145 yards in Miami's 24–7 defeat of Minnesota. Career span 1968–74, '79 with Miami; 1976–78 with New York Giants. Elected to Hall of Fame in 1987.

Billy Cunningham (b. 6-3-43): Basketball player and coach. "Kangaroo Kid." In 11 pro seasons (1965–76) with Philadelphia 76ers and Carolina Cougars, averaged 21.2 points per game. Three-time first-team All-NBA selection (1969–71). 1973 ABA MVP. Coached 76ers to three NBA Finals and the 1983 NBA title. Elected to Hall of Fame in 1985.

Bjørn Dæhlie (b.6-19-67): Norwegian skier. Legendary cross-country skier won a Winter Olympics–record eight gold medals over three Games from 1992 to '98. Won a total of 12 Olympic medals and more than 40 World Cup races.

Chuck Daly (b. 7-20-30): Basketball coach. Coached the 1992 Olympic "Dream Team." Won two consecutive NBA titles with Detroit (1989, '90). Won 50+ games four consecutive seasons. Coached Detroit 1983–92, New Jersey 1992–94, and Orlando 1997–99.

Damascus (b. 1964, d. 1995): Thoroughbred race horse. After finishing third in 1967 Kentucky Derby, won the Preakness, the Belmont, the Dwyer, the American Derby, the Travers, the Woodward and others—12 of 16 starts. Unanimous Horse of the Year in 1967.

Stanley Dancer (b. 7-25-27): Harness racing driver. Only driver to win the Trotting Triple Crown two times (Nevele Pride in 1968, Super Bowl in 1972). Also won Pacing Triple Crown driving Most Happy Fella in 1970. Won The Hambletonian four times (1968, '72, '75, '83). Driver of the Year in 1968.

Tamas Darnyi (b. 6-3-67): Hungarian swimmer. Gold medalist in 200-meter and 400-meter individual medleys at 1988 and '92 Olympics. Won both events at World Championships in 1986 and '91. Set world records in these events at 1991 Championships (1:59.36 and 4:12.36).

Al Davis (b. 7-4-29): Football executive. Owner and general manager of Raiders since 1963. Team has won three Super Bowl championships (1976, '80, '83). Served as AFL commissioner in 1966; helped negotiate AFL–NFL merger. Famously moved Raiders to Los Angeles in 1982 and back to Oakland in 1995.

Ernie Davis (b. 12-14-39, d. 5-18-63): Football RB. Won Heisman Trophy in 1961, the first black man to win the award. All-America three times at Syracuse. First selection in 1962 NFL draft, but became fatally ill with leukemia and never played professionally.

Glenn Davis (b. 12-26-24): College football HB. "Mr. Outside." Teamed with Doc Blanchard to lead Army to three consecutive undefeated seasons (1944–46) and two consecutive national championships (1944, '45). Won Heisman Trophy in 1946. Named All-America three times.

John Davis (b. 1-12-21, d. 7-13-84): Weightlifter. Gold medalist at two consecutive Olympics, 1948, '52. World champion six times.

Terrell Davis (b. 10-28-72): Football RB. One of only four players to rush for more than 2,000 yards in a season (2,008 in 1998). MVP of Super Bowl XXXII, rushing for 157 yards and three TDs for Denver. Forced to retire in 2002 after several knee injuries.

Pete Dawkins (b. 3-8-38): Football RB. 1958 Heisman Trophy winner while at Army. Never played pro football. Attended Oxford on Rhodes scholarship, won two Bronze Stars in Vietnam, rose to brigadier general before leaving Army to become investment banker. Made unsuccessful run for Senate from New Jersey in 1988.

Len Dawson (b. 6-20-35): Football QB. MVP of Super Bowl IV, a 23–7 victory against Minnesota. Threw 239 TDs in his career. Career span 1957–75, the last 13 seasons with Kansas City Chiefs. Elected to Hall of Fame in 1987.

Dizzy Dean (b. 1-16-11, d. 7-17-74): Baseball RHP. 1934 MVP with 30 wins. League leader in strikeouts, complete games four times each. 150 career wins. Arm trouble shortened career after 134 wins by age 26. Career span 1930–41 and 1947 with St. Louis and Chicago (NL).

Dave DeBusschere (b. 10-16-40, d. 5-14-03): Basketball F. NBA first-team All-Defensive Team six straight seasons, 1969–74. Member of NBA champion New York Knicks in 1970 and '73. Career span 1962–74 with Detroit and New York. Career stats: 16.1 ppg, 11.0 rpg. Youngest coach (24) in NBA history. Elected to NBA Hall of Fame in 1982.

Pierre de Coubertin (b. 1-1-1863, d. 9-2-37): Frenchman called the father of the Modern Olympics. President of International Olympic Committee from 1896 to 1925.

Oscar De La Hoya (b. 2-4-73): Boxer. Won title belts in five different weight classes between junior lightweight and junior middleweight divisions. 35–2 with 28 KOs. Won lightweight gold medal at 1992 Olympics in Barcelona.

Jack Dempsey (b. 6-24-1895, d. 5-31-83): Boxer. Heavyweight champ (1919–26), lost title to Gene Tunney and rematch in the famed "long count" bout in 1927. Career record 62-6-10 with 49 KOs from 1914–28.

Gail Devers (b. 11-19-66): Track and field sprinter-hurdler. Won 100 meters at 1992 and '96 Olympics. Successfully completed 100m/100h double at 1993 World Championships, winning 100 in 10.82 and 100 hurdles in American record 12.46. Also won '93 world indoor title in 60 (6.95). Battled Graves disease.

Klaus Dibiasi (b. 10-6-47): Italian diver. Gold medalist in platform at three consecutive Olympics (1968, '72, '76) and silver medalist at 1964 Olympics.

Eric Dickerson (b. 9-2-60): Football RB. Alltime single-season record holder in yards rushing (2,105 in 1984). Fourth in career rushing yards (13,259). Led league in rushing four times. Rushed for 1,000+ yards in seven consecutive seasons; 100+ yards in 61 games, including 12 times in 1984. Rookie of the Year in 1983. Career span 1983–93 with Los Angeles Rams, Indianapolis, Los Angeles Raiders and Atlanta.

Bill Dickey (b. 6-6-07 d. 11-12-93): Baseball C. Lifetime average .313. Hit 202 career home runs. Played on 11 AL All-Star teams. In eight World Series, hit five homers with 24 RBI. Career span 1928–43 and 1946, all with New York (AL). Inducted to Hall of Fame 1954.

Harrison Dillard (b. 7-8-23): Track and field. Only man to win Olympic gold medal in sprint (100 meters in 1948) and hurdles (110 meters in 1952). Sullivan Award winner in 1955.

Joe DiMaggio (b. 11-25-14 d. 3-8-99): Baseball OF. "The Yankee Clipper." Hit safely in record 56 straight games in 1941. MVP in 1939, '41, '47. Had .325 career batting average; .300+ average 11 times; 100+ RBI nine times. League leader in batting average, HR, and RBI two times each. Played on 10 World Series winners with New York (AL). Career span 1936–51.

Mike Ditka (b. 10-18-39): Football TE–Coach. First TE elected to Hall of Fame (1988). NFL Rookie of the Year in 1961. Named to five Pro Bowls. Made 427 catches for 5,812 yards and 43 TDs. Career span 1961–72 with Chicago, Philadelphia and Dallas. Coached Chicago to 46–10 win against New England in Super Bowl XX. Recorded 127–101 record as head coach of Chicago and New Orleans.

Tony Dorsett (b. 4-7-54): Football RB. Fifth leading rusher in NFL history (12,739 yards). Set record for longest run from scrimmage with 99-yard TD run on 1-3-83. Scored 91 career TDs. Rushed for 1,000+ yards in eight seasons. Named Rookie of the Year in 1977. Career span 1977–88 with Dallas, Denver. Graduated from Pittsburgh as alltime NCAA leader in yards rushing (6,082) and won 1976 Heisman Trophy.

Abner Doubleday (b. 6-26-1819, d. 1-26-1893): Civil War hero incorrectly credited as the inventor of baseball in Cooperstown, NY, in 1839.

Clyde Drexler (b. 6-22-62): Basketball G. Nicknamed "The Glide." Member of U.S. "Dream Team" that won 1992 Olympic gold medal. Career span 1984–1994 with Portland and 1995–98 with Houston, with whom he won his first NBA title in 1995. Career stats: 20.4 ppg, 5.6 apg. Head coach at University of Houston from 1998–00.

Ken Dryden (b. 8-8-47): Hockey G. Goaltender of the Year five times (1973, 1976–79). Playoff MVP as a rookie in 1971, maintained rookie status and named Rookie of the Year in 1972. Led league in goals against average five times. Career record 258-57-74, including 46 shutouts. Career 2.24 goals against average is the modern record. Four playoff shutouts in 1977. Played on six Stanley Cup champions with Montreal from 1970 to 1979.

Don Drysdale (b. 7-23-36, d. 7-3-93): Baseball RHP. Set the major league record—broken in 1988 by Orel Hershiser—of 58 consecutive scoreless innings in 1968. Led NL three times in strikeouts (1959, '60, '62) and once in wins (1962). Won 1962 Cy Young Award with 25–9 mark. Career record of 209–166, with 2,484 K's and 2.95 ERA. Career span 1956–69, all with Dodgers. Inducted into Hall of Fame 1984.

Tim Duncan (b. 4-25-76): Basketball C. 2001 NBA MVP. First-team All-NBA every season in the league (1998–03). 1998 Rookie of the Year. 1999 and 2003 NBA Finals MVP, when he led San Antonio to NBA titles. Also league MVP in '03 Career span 1997– with San Antonio.

Roberto Duran (b. 6-16-51): Panamanian boxer. Champion in three different weight classes: lightweight (1972–79), welterweight (1980, lost rematch to Sugar Ray Leonard in famous "no más" bout) and junior middleweight (1983–84). Career record: 104–15 (69 KOs).

Leo Durocher (b. 7-27-05, d. 10-7-91): Baseball manager. "Leo the Lip." Said "Nice guys finish last." Managed three pennant winners and 1954 World Series winner. Won 2,008 games in 24 years. Led Brooklyn 1939–48; New York (NL) 1948–55; Chicago (NL) 1966–72; and Houston 1972–73.

David Duval (b. 11-9-71): Golfer. Won 2001 British Open. Set record for tour earnings in a single season with $2.6 million in 1998, when he also won Vardon Trophy for lowest scoring average (69.13). Four-time all-America at Georgia Tech.

Tomás Dvorák (b. 5-11-72): Czech decathlete. Broke Dan O'Brien's seven-year-old decathlon world record by 103 points on 7-4-99 in Prague, amassing 8,994 points. Won decathlon bronze medal at Atlanta in '96.

Eddie Eagan (b. 4-26-1898, d. 6-14-67): Only American athlete to win gold medal at Summer and Winter Olympic Games (boxing 1920, bobsled '32).

Alan Eagleson (b. 4-24-33): Hockey labor leader. Founder of NHL Players' Association and its executive director from 1967–92. Resigned from Hall of Fame 3-25-98 and served six months of an 18-month jail sentence for three counts of fraud and theft involving players' insurance premiums.

Dale Earnhardt (b. 4-29-52, d. 2-18-01): Auto racer. "The Intimidator." NASCAR champion seven times (1980, 1986–87, 1990–91, 1993–94). Won 1998 Daytona 500 and 75 other NASCAR races. Died in crash on the final lap of the 2001 Daytona 500.

Stefan Edberg (b. 1-19-66): Swedish tennis player. Won two Wimbledon singles titles (1988, '90), two Australian Open titles (1985, '87) and two U.S. Open titles (1991, '92). Led Sweden to three Davis Cup titles (1984, '85, '87).

Gertrude Ederle (b. 10-23-06): Swimmer. First woman to swim the English Channel, in 1926. Swam 21 miles from France to England in 14:39. Also won three medals at the 1924 Olympics.

Hicham El Gerrouj (b. 9-14-74): Track and field. Morrocan runner broke world record in mile on 7-7-99, clocking 3:43.13 to trim 1.26 seconds from six-year-old previous record. Performance was his fourth world records, in addition to indoor mile, indoor 1,500 and outdoor 1,500.

Herb Elliott (b. 2-25-38): Track and field. Australian runner was gold medalist in 1960 Olympic 1,500 meters in world record 3:35.6. Also set world mile record of 3:54.5 in 1958. Undefeated at 1,500 meters/mile in international competition. Retired at 22.

Ernie Els (b.10-17-69): South African golfer. Two-time U.S. Open winner (1994, '97); first foreign-born player to win the event twice since Alex Smith in 1910. 2002 British Open champion.

John Elway (b. 6-28-60): Football QB. First player taken in 1983 NFL draft. One of two NFL QBs with more than 50,000 passing yards (51,475). 300 career TD passes. Famous for last-minute drives. Won back-to-back Super Bowls (XXXII and XXXIII) after three previous Super Bowl losses. Career span 1983–99 with Denver.

Roy Emerson (b. 11-3-36): Australian tennis player. Second alltime in Grand Slam singles titles (12). Won six Australian titles, five consecutively (1961, 1963–67), two Wimbledon titles (1964, '65), two U.S. titles (1961, '64) and two French titles (1963, '67). Also won 13 Grand Slam doubles titles.

Kornelia Ender (b. 10-25-58): East German swimmer. Won four gold medals at 1976 Olympics and three silver medals at 1972 Olympics.

Julius Erving (b. 2-22-50): Basketball F. "Dr. J." His combined ABA and NBA career points (30,026) rank fifth alltime. Career scoring average of 24.2. Won four MVP awards (1974–76, '81); playoff MVP 1974, '76. All-Star 16 times. Led ABA in scoring three times. Played on three championship teams, with New York (ABA) and Philadelphia (NBA). Career span 1971–86. Elected to Hall of Fame in 1993.

Phil Esposito (b. 2-20-42): Hockey C. "Espo." First to break the 100-point barrier (126 in 1969). Led league in goals six times, points five times and assists three times. Won MVP award two times (1969, '74). 1,590 career points, 717 goals, and 873 assists. Scored 30+ goals 13 consecutive seasons and 100+ points six times. All-Star 10 times. Career span 1963–81 with Chicago, Boston, New York Rangers.

Tony Esposito (b. 4-23-43): Hockey goalie. Brother of Phil. A six-time All-Star during 16-season NHL career, almost all of it with the Chicago Blackhawks. Career GAA of 2.92. Won or shared Vezina Trophy three times. Elected to Hall of Fame in 1988.

Janet Evans (b. 8-28-71): Swimmer. Competed in 1988, '92 and '96 Olympics, winning three gold medals in '88 and one in '92. Set world record in 400-meter freestyle (4:03.85 in 1988), 800-meter freestyle (8:16.22 in 1989) and 1,500-meter freestyle (15:52.10 in 1988). Sullivan Award winner in 1989.

Lee Evans (b. 2-25-47): Track and field. Gold medalist in 400 meters at 1968 Olympics with world record time of 43.86, which stood until 1988.

Chris Evert (b. 12-21-54): Also Chris Evert Lloyd. Tennis player. Second alltime in tournament titles (157). Tied for fourth alltime in women's Grand Slam singles titles (18). Won at least one Grand Slam singles title every year from 1974–86. Won seven French Open titles (1974, '75, '79, '80, '83, '85, '86), six U.S. Open titles (1975–77, '78, '80, '82), three Wimbledon titles (1974, '76, '81) and two Australian Open titles (1982, '84). Reached Grand Slam finals 16 other times. Reached semifinals at 52 of her last 56 Grand Slams.

Weeb Ewbank (b. 5-6-07, d. 11-17-98): Football coach. Only coach to win titles in both the NFL and AFL. Coached Baltimore Colts to classic overtime defeat of New York Giants in 1958 and New York Jets to their stunning 16–7 win over Baltimore in Super Bowl III. Career record of 134-130-7. Career span 1954–62 with Colts and 1963–73 with Jets. Elected to Hall of Fame in 1978.

Patrick Ewing (b. 8-5-62): Basketball C. First NBA "lottery" pick. 1986 Rookie of the Year. A member of two gold-medal winning Olympic teams, including the 1992 "Dream Team." Career span 1985–02 with New York, Seattle, and Orlando; averaged 21.0 ppg, 9.8 rpg. Played in three NCAA title games with Georgetown (1982, '84, '85); tournament MVP in 1984.

Nick Faldo (b. 7-18-57): British golfer. Three-time winner of Masters (1989, '90, '96) and British Open (1987, '90, '92).

Juan Manuel Fangio (b. 6-24-11, d. 7-17-95): Argentine auto racer. 24 Formula 1 victories in just 51 starts. Formula 1 champion five times, the most of any driver (1951, '54–57). Retired in 1958.

Brett Favre (b.10-10-69): Football QB. Won NFL MVP award three years in a row (1995–97). Led Packers to victory in Super Bowl XXXI. Career span 1991– with Atlanta and Green Bay.

Bob Feller (b. 11-3-18): Baseball RHP. Pitched three no-hitters and 12 one-hitters. 266 career wins; 2,581 career strikeouts. Won 20+ games six times. League leader in wins six times, strikeouts seven times, innings pitched five times. Served four years in military during career. Career span 1936–41, 1945–56 with Cleveland.

Tom Ferguson (b. 12-20-50): Rodeo. First to top $1 million in career earnings. All-Around champion six consecutive years (1974–79).

Enzo Ferrari (b. 2-8-1898, d. 8-14-88): Auto racing engineer. Team owner since 1929, he built first Ferrari race car in Italy in 1947 and continued to preside over Ferrari race and street cars until his death. In 68 years of competition, Ferrari's cars have won over 5,000 races.

Herve Filion (b. 2-1-40): Harness racing driver. Alltime leader in career wins (more than 14,000). Driver of the Year 10 times, more than any other driver (consecutively 1969–74, '78, '81, '89).

Rollie Fingers (b. 8-25-46): Baseball RHP. Won 107 games in relief in his career; 341 career saves. 1981 Cy Young and MVP winner; 1974 World Series MVP. Saved six World Series games in his career. Career span 1968–85 with Oakland, San Diego, Milwaukee.

Bobby Fischer (b. 3-9-43): Chess. World champion from 1972 to 1975, the only American to hold title. Never played competitive chess during his reign. Forfeited title to Anatoly Karpov by refusing to play him.

Carlton Fisk (b. 12-26-47): Baseball C. Alltime HR leader among catchers (352) and second in games caught (2,226). 376 career HR, including a record 75 after age 40. Rookie of the Year in 1972 and All-Star 11 times. Hit dramatic 12th-inning HR to win Game 6 of 1975 World Series. Career span 1969–93 with Boston, Chicago (AL). Elected to Hall of Fame in 2000.

Emerson Fittipaldi (b. 12-12-46): Brazilian auto racer. Won Indy 500 in 1989 and '93. Won CART championship in 1989. Formula 1 champion two times (1972, '74).

James Fitzsimmons (b. 7-23-1874, d. 3-11-66): Horse racing trainer. "Sunny Jim." Trained two Triple Crown winners (Gallant Fox in 1930, Omaha in 1935). Trained six Belmont Stakes winners (1930, '32, '35, '36, '39, '55), four Preakness Stakes winners (1930, '35, '55, '57) and three Kentucky Derby winners (1930, '35, '39).

Peggy Fleming (b. 7-27-48): Figure skater. Olympic champion 1968. World champion (1966–68) and U.S. champion (1964–68).

Curt Flood (b. 1-18-38, d. 1-20-97): Baseball OF. Challenged baseball's reserve clause by refusing to be traded after 1969 season. Supreme Court rejected his plea, but baseball was eventually forced to adopt free agency system. Won seven consecutive Gold Gloves from 1963 to 1969. Career batting average of .293. Career span 1956–69 with St. Louis.

Whitey Ford (b. 10-21-26): Baseball LHP. Alltime World Series leader in wins, losses, games started, innings pitched, hits allowed, walks and strikeouts. 236 career wins, 2.75 ERA. Led league in wins and winning percentage three times each; ERA, shutouts, innings pitched two times each. 1961 Cy Young winner and World Series MVP. Career span 1950, 1953–67 with New York Yankees.

Forego (b. 1970, d. 8-27-97): Thoroughbred race horse. Horse of the Year in 1974 (won 8 of 13 starts); '75 (won 6 of 9); and '76 (won 6 of 8). Finished fourth in 1973 Kentucky Derby. Over six years won 34 of 57 starts and $1,938,957.

George Foreman (b. 1-22-48): Boxer. Heavyweight champion (1973–74). Retired in 1977, but returned to the ring in 1987. At age 45, KO'd Michael Moorer to regain heavyweight title. Also heavyweight gold medalist at 1968 Olympics.

Dick Fosbury (b. 3-6-47): Track and field. Gold medalist in high jump at 1968 Olympics. Introduced back-to-the-bar style of high jumping, called the "Fosbury Flop."

Jimmie Foxx (b. 10-22-07, d. 7-21-67): Baseball 1B. Won three MVP awards (1932–33, '38). Fourth alltime highest slugging average (.609), with 534 career HR; hit 30+ HR 12 consecutive seasons, 100+ RBI 13 consecutive seasons. Won Triple Crown in 1933. Led league in HR four times, batting average two times. Career span 1925–45 with Philadelphia, Boston (AL).

A.J. Foyt (b. 1-16-35): Auto racer. Alltime leader in Indy Car victories (67). Won Indy 500 four times (1961, '64, '67, '77), Daytona 500 one time (1972), 24 Hours of Daytona two times (1983, '85) and 24 Hours of LeMans one time (1967). USAC champion seven times, more than any other driver (1960, '61, '63, '64, '67, '75, '79).

William H.G. France (b. 9-26-09, d. 6-7-92): Auto racing executive. Founder of NASCAR and president from 1948–72. Builder of Daytona and Talladega speedways.

Dawn Fraser (b. 9-4-37): Australian swimmer. First swimmer to win gold medal in same event at three consecutive Olympics (100-meter freestyle in 1956, '60, '64). First woman to break the one-minute barrier at 100 meters (59.9 in 1962).

Joe Frazier (b. 1-12-44): Boxer. "Smokin' Joe." Heavyweight champion (1970–73). Best known for his three epic bouts with Muhammad Ali. Career record 32-4-1 with 27 KOs from 1965 to 1976. Also heavyweight gold medalist at 1964 Olympics.

Walt Frazier (b. 3-29-45): Basketball G. "Clyde." Point guard on championship Knick teams of 1970 and '73. First team All-NBA in 1970, '72, '74 and '75. First team All-Defensive every year from 1969–'75. Averaged 18.9 points per game in 13-season NBA career. Elected to Hall of Fame in 1986.

Frankie Frisch (b. 9-9-1898, d. 3-12-73): Baseball IF. "The Fordham Flash." Led NL in hits in 1923 (223). NL MVP in 1931. Hit over .300 13 seasons. Scored 100+ runs seven times. Drove in 100+ runs three times. Career .316 batting average. Career span 1919–37 with New York (NL) and St. Louis (NL). Elected to Hall of Fame in 1947.

Dan Gable (b. 10-25-48): Wrestler. Gold medalist in 149-pound division at 1972 Olympics. Two-time NCAA champion (in 1968 at 130 pounds, in 1969 at 137 pounds). Coached Iowa to NCAA championship 15 times (1978–86, 1991–93 and 1995–97).

Clarence Gaines (b. 5-21-23): College basketball coach. "Bighouse." 828 career wins in 46 seasons at Division II Winston-Salem State from 1947–93.

John Galbreath (b. 8-10-1897, d. 7-20-88): Horse racing owner. Owner of Darby Dan Farms from 1935 until his death and of baseball's Pittsburgh Pirates from 1946 to 1985. Only man to breed and own winners of both the Kentucky Derby (Chateaugay in 1963 and Proud Clarion in 1967) and the Epsom Derby (Roberto in 1972).

Gallant Fox (b. 3-23-27, d. 11-13-54): Thoroughbred race horse. Triple Crown winner in 1930 with jockey Earle Sande aboard. Trained by James Fitzsimmons. The only Triple Crown winner to sire another Triple Crown winner (Omaha in 1935).

Don Garlits (b. 1-14-32): Auto racer. "Big Daddy." Has won 35 National Hot Rod Association Top Fuel events. Won three NHRA Top Fuel points titles (1975, 1985–86). First Top Fuel driver to surpass 190 mph (1963), 200 mph (1964), 240 mph (1973), 250 mph (1975) and 270 mph (1986). Credited with developing rear-engine dragster.

Haile Gebrselassie (b. 4-18-73): Track and field. Ethiopian distance runner has dominated long distance running since 1993. Holds world records in the 5,000 and 10,000 meters. Gold medalist in the 10,000 at the 1996 and 2000 Olympics.

Lou Gehrig (b. 6-19-03, d. 6-2-41): Baseball 1B. "The Iron Horse." Second alltime in consecutive games played (2,130), leader in grand slam HR (23), third in RBI (1,995) and slugging average (.632). MVP in 1927, '36; won Triple Crown in 1934. .340 career average; 493 career HR. 100+ RBI 13 consecutive seasons. Led league in RBI five times and HR three times. Played on seven World Series winners with New York (AL). Died of disease since named for him. Career span 1923–39.

Bernie Geoffrion (b. 2-16-31): Hockey RW. "Boom Boom" for his powerful slapshot. Won Hart Memorial Trophy for 1960–61. Scored 393 goals and 429 assists in 16 seasons (1950–68), the first 14 with Montreal, the final two with New York. Elected to Hall of Fame 1972.

Eddie Giacomin (b. 6-6-39): Hockey goalie. "Fast Eddie" led NHL goalies in wins for three straight seasons. Shared Vezina Trophy for 1970–71. Career GAA of 2.82. Career span 1965–78 with New York and Detroit.

Althea Gibson (b. 8-25-27, d. 9-28-03): Tennis player. Won two consecutive Wimbledon and U.S. singles titles (1957, '58), the first black player to win these tournaments. Also won the French Open in 1956.

Bob Gibson (b. 11-9-35): Baseball RHP. 1968 Cy Young and MVP award winner with modern National League–best ERA (1.12). Also 1970 Cy Young award winner. Pitched no-hitter in 1971. Record holder for most strikeouts in a World Series game (17); Series MVP in 1964, '67. Won 20+ games five times. 251 career wins; 3,117 strikeouts. Career span 1959–75 with St. Louis.

Josh Gibson (b. 12-21-11, d. 1-20-47): Baseball C. "The Black Babe Ruth." Couldn't play in major leagues because of racial barrier. Credited with 950 HR (75 in 1931, 69 in 1934) and .350 batting average. Had .400+ average two times. Career span 1930–46 with Homestead Grays, Pittsburgh Crawfords.

Kirk Gibson (b. 5-28-57): Baseball OF. Played on two World Series champions (Detroit in 1984 and Los Angeles in 1988). Hit dramatic pinch-hit HR to win Game 1 of 1988 series. MVP in 1988. Career span 1979–94 with Detroit, Los Angeles, Kansas City, Pittsburgh. Also starred in baseball and football at Michigan State.

Frank Gifford (b. 8-16-30): Football RB. NFL Player of Year in 1956 when he rushed for 819 yards and caught 51 passes. Played in seven Pro Bowls. Retired for one season after ferocious hit by Chuck Bednarik. Career span 1952–60 and 1962–64, all with New York (N). Elected to Hall of Fame in 1977.

Rod Gilbert (b. 7-1-41): Hockey RW. Played 16 seasons, all with the New York Rangers (1960–78), and had 406 goals and 615 assists. Elected to Hall of Fame 1982.

Sid Gillman (b. 10-26-11, d. 1-4-03): Football coach. Developed wide-open, pass-oriented style of offense, introduced techniques for situational player substitutions and the study of game films. Won AFL championship (1963) with San Diego Chargers. Career span 1955–59 Los Angeles; 1960–69 Los Angeles/San Diego Chargers; 1973–74 Houston. Lifetime record 123-104-7.

Pancho Gonzales (b. 5-9-28, d. 7-3-95): Tennis player. Won two consecutive U.S. singles titles (1948–49). In 1969, at age 41, beat Charlie Pasarell 22–24, 1–6, 16–14, 6–3, 11–9 in longest Wimbledon match ever (5:12).

Jeff Gordon (b. 8-4-71): Auto racer. NASCAR's alltime money winner. Four-time NASCAR Winston Cup champion (1995, '97, '98, '01). Youngest Winston Cup Series champion in the modern era, winning his first title at age 24. Won 1997 and '99 Daytona 500. Set NASCAR modern record with 13 wins in 1998.

Shane Gould (b. 11-23-56): Australian swimmer. Won three gold medals, one silver and one bronze at 1972 Olympics. Set 11 world records over 23-month period beginning in 1971. Held world record in five freestyle distances ranging from 100 meters to 1,500 meters in late 1971 and 1972. Retired at age 16.

Steffi Graf (b. 6-14-69): German tennis player. Achieved the Grand Slam in 1988. Won four Australian Open singles titles (1988–90, '94), seven Wimbledon titles (1988, '89, 1991–93, '95, '96), six French Open titles (1987, '88, '93, '95, '96, '99) and five U.S. Open titles (1988–89, '93, '95, '96). Held the No. 1 ranking a record 186 weeks. Gold medalist at 1988 Olympics. Second in alltime Grand Slam singles titles (22).

Otto Graham (b. 12-6-21): Football QB. Led Cleveland to 10 championship games in his 10-year career. Played on four consecutive AAFC champions (1946–49) and three NFL champions (1950, '54, '55). Combined career totals: 23,584 yards passing, 174 touchdown passes. Player of the Year two times (1953, '55). Led league in passing six times. Career span 1946–55.

Red Grange (b. 6-13-03, d. 1-28-91): Football HB. "The Galloping Ghost." All-America three consecutive seasons with Illinois (1923–25), scoring 31 touchdowns in 20-game collegiate career. Signed by George Halas of Chicago in 1925, attracted sellout crowds across the country. Established the first AFL with manager C.C. Pyle in 1926, but league folded after one year. Career span 1925–34 with Chicago, New York.

Rocky Graziano (b. 6-7-22, d. 5-22-90): Boxer. Middleweight champion from 1947–48. Career record 67–13. Endured three brutal title fights against Tony Zale, with Zale winning by KO in 1946 and 1948, and Graziano winning by KO in 1947.

Hank Greenberg (b. 1-1-11, d. 9-4-86): Baseball 1B. 331 career HR (58 in 1938). MVP in 1935, '40. League leader in HR and RBI four times each. Fifth alltime highest slugging average (.605). 100+ RBI seven times. Career span 1933-41, 1945-47 with Detroit, Pittsburgh.

Joe Greene (b. 9-24-46): Football DT. "Mean Joe." Anchored Pittsburgh's famed "Steel Curtain" defense. Selected for Pro Bowl 10 times. Played on four Super Bowl champions (1974, '75, '78, '79). Career span 1969–81 with Pittsburgh.

Maurice Greene (b. 7-23-74): Track and field. Won Olympic gold medals in Sydney in the 100 meters and the 4x100 relay. Held world record for 100 meters for three years after running 9.79 in Athens on 6-16-99.

Forrest Gregg (b. 10-18-33): Football OT/G. Played in then-record 188 straight games from 1956–71. Named all-NFL eight straight years starting in 1960. Career span 1956–71, most of it with Green Bay Packers. Played on winning Packer team in first two Super Bowls. Inducted into Hall of Fame in 1977.

Wayne Gretzky (b. 1-26-61): Hockey C. "The Great One." No. 99. Most dominant player in NHL history. Alltime scoring leader in points (2,795), assists (1,910), and goals (885). Alltime single-season scoring leader in points (215 in 1986), goals (92 in 1982) and assists (163 in 1986). Won nine MVP awards (1980-87, '89). Led league in assists 16 times, scoring 11 times, goals five times. Scored 200+ points four times, 100+ points 10 other times; 70+ goals four consecutive seasons; 50+ goals five other times; 100+ assists 11 consecutive seasons. Playoff MVP two times (1985, '88). Played on four Stanley Cup champions with Edmonton from 1978 to 1988. Career span 1978–99 with Edmonton, Los Angeles, St. Louis, and New York Rangers.

Bob Griese (b. 2-3-45): Football QB. Led Miami to three straight Super Bowls (1971–73), including the 1972 Miami team that went 17–0. Career span 1967–80 with Miami, passing for 25,092 yards and 192 TDs. Elected to Hall of Fame in 1990.

Florence Griffith Joyner (b. 12-21-59, d. 9-21-98): Track and field. Won three gold medals (100 meters, 200 meters, 4x100-meter relay) at 1988 Olympics; Set world record in 100 (10.49) in 1988 and in 200 (21.34) at the 1988 Olympics. Sullivan Award winner in 1988.

Ken Griffey Jr. (b. 11-21-69): Baseball OF. Hit 56 home runs in back-to-back seasons (1997–98). Became youngest man (31 years 261 day) to reach 450 HRs when he connected on 8-9-01. Won AL MVP award in 1997, when he hit .304 with 56 HRs and 147 RBI. 10 Gold Glove Awards. Father Ken Sr. starred with Cincinnati Reds in 1970s.

Archie Griffin (b. 8-21-54): College football RB. Only player to win the Heisman Trophy two times (1974–75), with Ohio State. Eighth alltime NCAA career yards rushing (5,177). Professional career span 1976–83 with Cincinnati; totaled 2,808 yards rushing and 192 receptions.

Lefty Grove (b. 3-6-00, d. 5-22-75): Baseball LHP. 300 career wins and fifth alltime highest winning percentage (.680). League leader in ERA nine times, strikeouts seven consecutive seasons. Won 20+ games eight times. 1931 MVP. Career span 1925–41 with Philadelphia (AL), Boston (AL).

Tony Gwynn (b. 5-9-60): Baseball OF. Won eight batting titles (1984, 1987–89, 1994–97). League leader in hits six times, with .300+ average 16 times, 200+ hits five times. Career span 1982–01 with San Diego; .338 average, 3,141 hits.

Walter Hagen (b. 12-21-1892, d. 10-5-69): Golfer. Third alltime leader in major championships (11). Won PGA Championship five times (1921, 1924–27), British Open four times (1922, '24, '28, '29) and U.S. Open two times (1914, '19). Won 40 career tournaments.

Marvin Hagler (b. 5-23-54): Boxer. "Marvelous." Middleweight champion (1980–87). Career record 62-3-2 with 52 KOs from 1973–87. Defended title 13 times.

George Halas (b. 2-2-1895, d. 10-31-83): Football owner and coach. "Papa Bear." Alltime leader in seasons coaching (40) and seasons in wins (324). Career record 324-151-31 intermittently from 1920–1967. Remained as owner until his death. Chicago won a record seven NFL championships during his tenure.

Glenn Hall (b. 10-3-31): Hockey goalie. "Mr. Goalie" was an All-Star in 11 of his 18 seasons. Set record for consecutive games played by a goaltender (502) and ended career with goals against average of 2.51. Won or shared Vezina Trophy three times. Career span 1952–71 with Detroit, Chicago and St. Louis.

Charles Haley (b. 1-6-64): Football DE. Only player in NFL history to be a member of five Super Bowl champions, two with San Francisco (1989, '90) and three with Dallas (1993, '94, '96). Career span 1986–99. Recorded 100.5 career sacks.

Mia Hamm (b. 3-17-72): Soccer player. Alltime leading scorer in U.S. women's national team history. Member of Women's World Cup champion team in 1991, '99, and third-place team in '95. Member of 1996 Olympic champion team. Debuted with national team against China on 8-3-87 as its youngest player ever, at age 15.

Arthur B. (Bull) Hancock (b. 1-24-10, d. 9-14-72): Horse racing owner. Owner of Claiborne Farm and arguably the greatest breeder in history. For 15 straight years, from 1955–69, a Claiborne stallion led the sire list. Foaled at Claiborne Farm were four Horses of the Year (Kelso, Round Table, Bold Ruler and Nashua).

Tom Harmon (b. 9-28-19, d. 3-17-90): Football RB. Won Heisman Trophy in 1940 with Michigan. Triple-threat back led nation in scoring and named All-America two consecutive seasons (1939, '40). Awarded Silver Star and Purple Heart in World War II. Played in NFL with Los Angeles (1946–47).

Franco Harris (b. 3-7-50): Football RB. Holds Super Bowl record for career rushing yards (354). Super Bowl MVP in 1974. Made the "Immaculate Reception" to win 1972 playoff game against Oakland. Played on four Super Bowl champions (1974, '75, '78, '79) with Pittsburgh. Gained 1,000+ yards in nine seasons, 100+ yards in 47 games. Played in eight Pro Bowls. Rookie of the Year in 1972. Career span 1972–84 with Pittsburgh and Seattle. Rushed for 12,120 yards and scored 100 career touchdowns. Elected to the Hall of Fame in 1990.

Leon Hart (b. 11-2-28, d. 9-24-02): Football DE. Won Heisman Trophy in 1949, the last lineman to win the award. Played on three national champions with Notre Dame (1946, '47, '49), and the Irish went undefeated during his four years (36-0-2). Also played on three NFL champions with Detroit. Career span 1950–57.

Bill Hartack (b. 12-9-32): Horse racing jockey. Rode five Kentucky Derby winners (1957, '60, '62, '64, '69), three Preakness Stakes winners (1956, '64, '69) and one Belmont Stakes winner (1960).

Doug Harvey (b. 12-19-24, d. 12-26-90): Hockey D. Defensive Player of the Year seven times (1954–57, 1959–61). Led league in assists in 1954. All-Star 10 times. Played on six Stanley Cup champions with Montreal from 1947–68.

Dominik Hasek (b. 1-29-65): Czech hockey G. Two-time NHL MVP (1997, '98) with Buffalo; six-time Vezina Trophy winner (1994, '95, 1997–99, '01) as top goalie in league. Led NHL with a 1.95 goals-against average in 1993–94, the first sub-2.00 GAA since Bernie Parent in 1974. Topped that with 1.87 GAA in 1998–99. Guided Czech Republic to Olympic gold medal in 1998 at Nagano. Career span 1990–02 with Chicago, Buffalo and Detroit; 2003– Detroit.

Billy Haughton (b. 11-2-23, d. 7-15-86): Harness racing driver. Won the Pacing Triple Crown driving Rum Customer in 1968. Won The Hambletonian four times (1974, '76, '77, '80).

John Havlicek (b. 4-8-40): Basketball F/G. "Hondo" averaged 20.8 points per game over 16-season NBA career, all with Boston. First team All-NBA (1971–74). Member of eight NBA championship teams. Playoff MVP 1974. Member of Ohio State team that won 1960 NCAA title. Elected to Hall of Fame in 1983.

Elvin Hayes (b. 11-17-45): Basketball C. Three-time first-team All-NBA selection (1975, '77, '79). 12-time All-Star (1969–80). Led NBA in scoring (1969) and in rebounding (1970, '74). Played from 1968–84 with San Diego/Houston Rockets and Baltimore/Washington Bullets, averaging 21.0 points and 12.5 rebounds per game. 1968 *Sporting News* College Player of Year as Houston senior. Elected to Hall of Fame in 1989.

Woody Hayes (b. 2-14-13, d. 3-12-87): College football coach. Won three national championship (1954, '57, '68) and four Rose Bowls. Career record 238-72-10, including four undefeated seasons, with Ohio State from 1951–1978. Forced to resign after striking an opposing player during 1978 Gator Bowl.

Marques Haynes (b. 10-3-26): Basketball G. Known as "The World's Greatest Dribbler." Beginning in 1946 barnstormed more than four million miles throughout 97 countries for the Harlem Globetrotters, Harlem Magicians, Meadowlark Lemon's Bucketeers, Harlem Wizards.

Thomas Hearns (b. 10-18-58): Boxer. "Hit Man." Champion in four weight classes: welterweight, super welterweight, middleweight and light heavyweight. Career record: 57–4–1 with 45 KOs.

Eric Heiden (b. 6-14-58): Speed skater. Won five gold medals at 1980 Olympics. World champion three consecutive years (1977–79). Won Sullivan Award in 1980.

Carol Heiss (b. 1-20-40): Figure skater. Gold medalist at 1960 Olympics, silver medalist at 1956 Olympics. World champion five consecutive years (1956–60) and U.S. champion four consecutive years (1957–60). Married 1956 gold medalist Hayes Jenkins.

Rickey Henderson (b. 12-25-57): Baseball OF. Career leader in stolen bases, walks and runs; modern single-season stolen base record holder (stole 130 bases in 1982). Led league in steals 11 times. 1990 MVP. Alltime leader in lead-off HRs. Career span 1979– with nine teams.

Sonja Henie (b. 4-8-12, d. 10-12-69): Norwegian figure skater. Gold medalist at three consecutive Olympics (1928, '32, '36). World champion 10 consecutive years (1927–36).

Orel Hershiser (b. 9-16-58): Baseball RHP. Alltime leader most consecutive scoreless innings pitched (59 in 1988). Cy Young Award winner in 1988 and World Series MVP. Career span 1983–00 with Los Angeles, Cleveland, San Francisco and New York (NL): 204–150, 3.48 ERA.

Foster Hewitt (b. 11-21-02, d. 4-22-85): Hockey sportscaster. In 1923, aired one of hockey's first radio broadcasts. Became the voice of hockey in Canada on radio and later television. Famous for the phrase, "He shoots ... he scores!"

Tommy Hitchcock (b. 2-11-00, d. 4-19-44): Polo. 10-goal rating 18 times in his 19-year career from 1922–40. Killed in plane crash in World War II.

Lew Hoad (b. 11-23-34): Australian tennis player. Won two Wimbledon singles titles (1956, '57). Also won French title and Australian title in 1956, but failed to achieve the Grand Slam when defeated at Forest Hills by countryman Ken Rosewall.

Ben Hogan (b. 8-13-12, d. 7-25-97): Golfer. Third alltime in career wins (63). Won U.S. Open four times (1948, '50, '51, '53), the Masters (1951, '53) and PGA Championship (1946, '48) two times each and British Open once (1953). PGA Player of the Year four times (1948, '50, '51, '53).

Marshall Holman (b. 9-29-54): Bowler. Won 21 PBA titles between 1975–88. Had leading average in 1987 (213.54) and was named PBA Bowler of the Year.

Nat Holman (b. 10-18-1896, d. 2-12-95): College basketball coach. Only coach in history to win NCAA and NIT championships in same season, in 1950 with CCNY; 423 career wins, a .689 winning percentage.

Larry Holmes (b. 11-3-49): Boxer. Heavyweight champion (1978–85). Career record 69–6 with 44 KOs from 1973–02. Defended title 21 times.

Lou Holtz (b. 1-6-37): Football coach. Has led four different programs to Top 20 seasons. Coached Notre Dame to national championship in 1988 and a 12–0 record with a 34–21 win over West Virginia in Fiesta Bowl. 12-8-2 career record in bowl games. Career span 1969–75 at William & Mary and N Carolina St; 1977–96 at Arkansas, Minnesota and Notre Dame; and 1999– at S Carolina.

Evander Holyfield (b. 10-19-62): Boxer. Only man to win the heavyweight title four times. Won heavyweight belt for the first time on Oct. 25, 1990, when he KO'd James (Buster) Douglas in Las Vegas. Fought three epic bouts with Riddick Bowe and two memorable clashes with Mike Tyson (Tyson was disqualified in the rematch for biting Holyfield's ears, severing one of them.)

Red Holzman (b. 8-10-20; d. 11-13-98): Basketball coach. Led New York to NBA titles in 1970 and '73. NBA Coach of the Year in 1970. After two-year coaching stints with Milwaukee and St. Louis, coached New York from 1968–82. Career record: 696–604. Elected to Hall of Fame in 1985.

Harry Hopman (b. 8-12-06, d. 12-27-85): Australian tennis coach. As nonplaying captain, led Australia to 15 Davis Cup titles between 1950–69. Mentor to Lew Hoad, Ken Rosewall, Rod Laver and John Newcombe.

Willie Hoppe (b. 10-11-1887, d. 2-1-59): Billiards. Won 51 world championship matches from 1904–52.

Rogers Hornsby (b. 4-27-1896, d. 1-5-63): Baseball 2B. Second alltime in career batting average (.358), won seven batting titles, including with .424 average in 1924. Led league in slugging nine times. Triple Crown winner in 1922, '25; MVP award winner in 1925, '29. 2,930 hits and 1,584 RBI's from 1915–37 with five teams, including St. Louis (NL).

Paul Hornung (b. 12-23-35): Football RB–K. Led league in scoring three consecutive seasons, including a record 176 points in 1960 (15 touchdowns, 15 field goals, 41 extra points). Player of the Year in 1961. Career span 1957–66 with Green Bay. Suspended for 1963 season by Pete Rozelle for gambling. Also won Heisman Trophy in 1956 with Notre Dame.

Gordie Howe (b. 3-31-28): Hockey RW. Second alltime in goals (801), first in years played (26) and games (1,767). Finished career with 1,850 points and 1,049 assists. Won MVP award six times (1952, '53, '57, '58, '60, '63). Led league in scoring six times, goals five times and assists three times. All-Star 12 times. Played on four Stanley Cup champions with Detroit from 1946–71. Teamed with sons Mark and Marty in the WHA with Houston and New England from 1973–79, in NHL with Hartford in 1980.

Carl Hubbell (b. 6-22-03, d. 11-21-88): Baseball LHP. 253 career wins. MVP in 1933, '36. League leader in wins and ERA three times each. Won 24 consecutive games from 1936–37. Struck out Ruth, Gehrig, Foxx, Simmons and Cronin consecutively in 1934 All-Star game. Pitched no-hitter in 1929. Career span 1928–43 with New York (NL).

Sam Huff (b. 10-4-34): Football LB. Made 30 interceptions. Career span 1956–69 with New York Giants and Washington. Elected to Hall of Fame in 1982.

Bobby Hull (b. 1-3-39): Hockey LW. "The Golden Jet." Led league in goals seven times and points three times. 610 career goals. Won MVP award two consecutive seasons (1965, '66). Son Brett won MVP award in 1991, the only father and son to be so honored. All-Star 10 times. Career span 1957–72 with Chicago, 1973–80 with Winnipeg of WHA.

Brett Hull (b. 8-9-64): Hockey RW. Son of Bobby Hull. Won Hart Memorial Trophy for 1990–91 season. Scored Stanley Cup–winning goal for Dallas in third overtime of Game 6 against Buffalo in 1999. Career span 1986– with Calgary, St. Louis, Dallas and Detroit.

Jim (Catfish) Hunter (b. 4-8-46, d. 9-9-99): Baseball RHP. 1974 Cy Young award winner. Won 20+ games five consecutive seasons. Led league in wins and winning percentage two times each, ERA one time. 250+ innings pitched eight times. Pitched perfect game in 1968. Member of five World Series champions for Oakland and New York (AL). Career span 1965–79.

Don Hutson (b. 1-31-13, d. 6-26-97): Football WR. Finished his career as alltime leader in touchdown receptions (99). Led league in pass receptions eight times, receiving yards seven times and scoring five consecutive seasons. Caught at least one pass in 95 consecutive games. Player of the Year two consecutive seasons (1941, '42). Career span 1935–45 with Green Bay.

Hank Iba (b. 8-6-04; d. 1-15-93): College basketball coach. Coached Oklahoma A&M (which became Oklahoma State) from 1934–70. Team won NCAA titles in 1945 and '46. 767 career wins is seventh alltime.

Jackie Ickx (b. 1-1-45): Belgian auto racer. Won the 24 Hours of LeMans a record six times (1969, 1975–77, '81, '82) before retiring in 1985.

Punch Imlach (b. 3-15-18, d. 12-1-87): Hockey coach. 467 wins. With Toronto from 1958–69. Won four Stanley Cup championships (1962–64, 1967).

Miguel Induráin (b. 7-16-64): Cyclist. Won five consecutive Tours de France (1991–95), a feat unequaled until Lance Armstrong matched in 2003.

Juli Inkster (b.6-24-60): Golfer. 28 career victories. Became only the second woman ever to win all four of the LPGA's modern majors when she won the LPGA Championship on 6-27-99. Inducted to LPGA Hall of Fame in 1999.

Bo Jackson (b. 11-30-62): Baseball OF and Football RB. Only person in history to be named to baseball All-Star game and football Pro Bowl game. 1985 Heisman Trophy winner at Auburn. 1989 MLB All-Star game MVP. Signed with football's LA Raiders in 1988. Retired 1994 following hip replacement surgery.

Joe Jackson (b. 7-16-1889, d. 12-5-51): Baseball OF. "Shoeless Joe." Third alltime highest career batting average (.356), with .300+ average 11 times. One of the "Eight Men Out" banned from baseball for throwing 1919 World Series. Career span 1908–20 with Cleveland, Chicago (AL).

Phil Jackson (b. 9-17-45): Basketball F-Coach. Coached the Lakers to their third straight NBA Championship in 2002, his ninth as a coach. Won six titles as coach of Chicago (1991–93, 1996–98). Best winning percentage in NBA history (726–258, .738). Spent 13 years as a scrappy forward in the NBA, winning an NBA title with New York in 1973.

Reggie Jackson (b. 5-18-46): Baseball OF. "Mr. October." Alltime leader in World Series slugging percentage (.755). 1977 Series MVP, hit three HR in final game on three consecutive pitches. 563 career HR total is eighth best alltime. Led league in HR four times. 1973 MVP. Alltime strikeout leader (2,597). In a 12-year period played on 10 first-place teams, five World Series winners. Career span 1967–87 with Oakland, Baltimore, New York (AL) and California. Inducted to Baseball Hall of Fame in 1993.

Bruce Jenner (b. 10-28-49): Track and Field. Set decathlon world record (8,634) in winning gold medal at 1976 Olympics. Sullivan Award winner in 1976.

John Henry (b. 1975): Thoroughbred race horse. Sold as yearling for $1,100, the gelding was Horse of the Year in 1981 and 1984 and retired with then-record $6,597,947 in winnings.

Ben Johnson (b. 12-30-61): Track and field. Canadian sprinter set world record in 100 meters (9.83 in 1987). Won event at 1988 Olympics in 9.79, but gold medal revoked for failed drug test. Both world records revoked for steroid usage. Suspended for life after testing positive for elevated testosterone level at an indoor meet in Montreal on 1-17-93.

Earvin (Magic) Johnson (b. 8-14-59): Basketball G. Retired Nov. 7, 1991 after being diagnosed with HIV, the virus that causes AIDS. Returned to Lakers Feb '96 at age 36. Finished career second alltime in assists (10,141). MVP award three times (1987, '89, '90) and playoff MVP in 1980, '82 and '87. Played on five championship teams with Los Angeles. All-Star eight consecutive seasons. League leader in assists four times, steals two times, free throw percentage once. Career stats: 19.5 ppg, 11.2 apg, 7.2 rpg. Also won NCAA championship and named tournament MVP in 1979 with Michigan State.

Jack Johnson (b. 3-31-1878, d. 6-10-46): Boxer. First black heavyweight champion (1908–15). Career record 78-8-12 with 45 KOs from 1897–28.

Jimmy Johnson (b. 7-16-43): Football coach. Won two straight Super Bowls (1993, '94) as Dallas coach. Career record of 89–66 with Dallas and Miami. Led Miami (FL) to collegiate national championship in 1987. One of only three men to win college and NFL championships.

Michael Johnson (b. 9-13-67): Track and field. First man to win gold medals in both the 200 and 400 at the Olympics (1996). Broke 17-year-old 200-meter world record (19.66) at 1996 U.S. Olympic trials, then further lowered mark to 19.32 at Atlanta. Repeated in the 400 meters at the 2000 Sydney Games. Anchored U.S. 4x400 team at 1993 World Championship to world record of 2:54.29.

Walter Johnson (b. 11-6-1887, d. 12-10-46): Baseball RHP. "Big Train." Alltime leader in shutouts (110), second in wins (416), fourth in losses (279) and third in innings pitched (5,914). His record of 3,509 career strikeouts lasted for 56 years. 2.17 career ERA. MVP in 1913, '24. Won 20+ games 12 times. League leader in strikeouts 12 times, ERA five times, wins six times. Pitched no-hitter in 1920. Career span 1907–27 with Washington.

Ben A. Jones (b. 12-31-1882, d. 6-13-61): Horse racing trainer. Trained Triple Crown winner (Whirlaway) in 1941). Trained six Kentucky Derby winners, more than any other trainer (1938, '41, '44, '48, '49, '52), two Preakness Stakes winners (1941, '44) and one Belmont Stakes winner (1941).

Bobby Jones (b. 3-17-02, d. 12-18-71): Golfer. Achieved golf's only recognized Grand Slam in 1930. Second alltime in major championships (13). Won U.S. Amateur five times, more than any golfer (1924, '25, '27, '28, '30), U.S. Open four times (1923, '26, '29, '30), British Open three times (1926, '27, '30) and British Amateur (1930). Also designed Augusta National course, site of the Masters, and founded the tournament. Winner of Sullivan Award in 1930.

K.C. Jones (b. 5-25-32): Basketball G-coach. Member of eight straight NBA-championship Boston teams in his nine season career from 1958–67. Averaged 7.4 points and 4.3 assists per game. Coached Celtics 1983–88, with 308–102 regular season record and 65–37 playoff record with NBA titles in 1984 and '86.

Robert Trent Jones (b. 6-20-06, d. 6-14-00): English-born golf course architect designed or remodeled over 500 courses, including Baltusrol, Hazeltine, Oak Hill and Winged Foot. In the mid-60s five straight U.S. Opens were played on courses designed or remodeled by Jones.

Roy Jones Jr. (b.1-16-69): Boxer. Won titles as middleweight, super middleweight and light heavyweight. Career record: 47–1, 38 KOs. Won controversial silver medal at the 1988 Olympics in Seoul despite dominating his South Korean opponent in the final. Awarded Val Barker Trophy as outstanding boxer of '88 Games.

Sam Jones (b. 6-24-33): Basketball G. Played 12 seasons with Boston (1958–69), who won NBA title every year from 1959–66, plus 1968 and '69. Averaged 17.7 points per game. Elected to Hall of Fame in 1983.

Michael Jordan (b. 2-17-63): Basketball G. "Air." Arguably greatest player of all time. Led Bulls to six NBA titles (1991–93; 1996–98). Tied with Wilt Chamberlain for lead in career scoring average (30.1 ppg), and record holder for most points scored in a playoff game (63 in 1986). Guided Bulls to an NBA-record 72 wins in 1995–96. Led league in scoring a record 10 seasons, steals three times. League MVP in 1988, '91, '92, '96 and '98; Finals MVP in 1991–93 and 1996–98; Rookie of the Year in 1985. Career span 1984–93, 1995–98 with Chicago; 2001–03 with Washington. College Player of the Year in 1984. Played on NCAA title team with North Carolina in 1982. Member of gold medal-winning 1984 and '92 Olympic teams. Played minor league baseball in 1994.

Jackie Joyner-Kersee (b. 3-3-62): Track and field. Gold medalist in heptathlon and long jump at 1988 Olympics and in the former at the 1992 Olympics. Set heptathlon world record (7,291 points) at 1988 Olympics. Also won silver medal in heptathlon at 1984 Games and bronze in long jump at 1992 and '96 Olympics. Sullivan Award winner in 1986.

Alberto Juantorena (b. 3-12-51): Track and field. Cuban was gold medalist in 400 and 800 meters at 1976 Olympics.

Wang Junxia (b. 1963): Chinese distance runner. Broke four world records in six days in Sept. 1993. Broke 10,000 (29:31.78) on Sept 8; ran 1,500 in 3:51.92 in finishing second to countrywoman Qu Yunxia's world record of 3:50.46 on Sept 11; ran 3,000 record of 8:12.19 in heats on Sept 12 and lowered it to 8:06.11 on Sept 13. Won gold in 5,000 and silver in 10,000 at 1996 Olympics.

Sonny Jurgensen (b. 8-23-34): Football QB. In 18 seasons, passed for 32,224 yards and 255 TDs. Led NFL in passing both 1967 and '69. Career span 1957–74 with Philadelphia and Washington. Elected to Hall of Fame in 1983.

Duke Kahanamoku (b. 8-24-1890, d. 1-22-68): Swimmer. Won a total of five medals (3 gold and two silver) at three Olympics in 1912, '20, '24. Introduced the crawl stroke to America. Surfing pioneer and water polo player. Later sheriff of Honolulu.

Al Kaline (b. 12-19-34): Baseball OF. 3,007 career hits and 399 career HR. As a 20-year-old in 1955, became youngest player to win batting title, with .340 average. Had .300+ average nine times. Played in 18 All-Star games. Career span 1953–74 with Detroit.

Anatoly Karpov (b. 5-23-61): Soviet chess player. First world champion to receive title by default, in 1975, when Bobby Fischer chose not to defend his crown. Champion until 1985 when beaten by Garry Kasparov. Recognized by FIDE as champion in 1994.

Garry Kasparov (b. 4-13-63): Born Garik Weinstein. Chess player. World champion from 1985 to 1993 when stripped of title by FIDE. Won six-game series against IBM computer, Deep Blue, in 1996. Lost to improved version of Deep Blue in 1997.

Kip Keino (b. 1-17-40): Track and field. Kenyan was gold medalist in 1,500 meters at 1968 Olympics and in steeplechase at 1972 Olympics.

Jim Kelly (b. 2-14-60): Football QB. Led Buffalo to four straight Super Bowls—all losses. Career passer rating of 84.4. Led NFL in passing in 1990. In 11 NFL seasons passed for 35,467 yards and 237 TDs. Career span 1983–96 with Houston (USFL) and Buffalo Bills.

Kelso (b. 1957, d. 1983): Thoroughbred race horse. Gelding was Horse of the Year five straight years

(1960–64). Finished in the money in 53 of 63 races. Career earnings $1,977,896.

Harmon Killebrew (b. 6-29-36): Baseball 3B-1B. 573 career HR total is seventh most alltime. 100+ RBI nine times, 40+ HR eight times. League leader in HR six times and RBI four times. 1969 MVP. 100+ walks and strikeouts seven times each. Career span 1954–75 with Washington and Minnesota.

Jean Claude Killy (b. 8-30-43): French skier. Won three gold medals at 1968 Olympics. World Cup overall champion two consecutive years (1967, '68).

Ralph Kiner (b. 10-27-22): Baseball OF. Led league in HR seven consecutive seasons. Third in alltime HR frequency (7.1 HR every 100 at bats). 369 career HR, with 50+ HR two times. 100+ RBI and runs scored in same season six times; 100+ walks six times. Career span 1946–55 with Pittsburgh, Chicago (NL), and Cleveland.

Billie Jean King (b. 11-22-43): Tennis player. Won a record 20 Wimbledon titles, including six singles titles (1966–68, '72, '73, '75). Won four U.S. singles titles (1967, '71, '72, '74), and singles titles at Australian Open (1968) and French Open (1972). Won 27 Grand Slam doubles titles—total of 39 Grand Slam titles is third alltime. Helped found the women's pro tour in 1970, serving as president of the Women's Tennis Association two times. Helped form Team Tennis.

Nile Kinnick (b. 7-9-18, d. 6-2-43): College football RB. Won the Heisman Trophy in 1939 with Iowa. Premier runner, passer and punter was killed in plane crash during routine Navy training flight. Stadium in Iowa City named in his honor.

Tom Kite (b. 12-9-49): Golfer. Winner of 19 career PGA Tour events, including the 1992 U.S. Open at Pebble Beach. Led PGA in scoring average in 1981 and '82. PGA Player of Year in 1989, when he won a then-record $1,395,278. Ryder Cup captain in 1997.

Franz Klammer (b. 12-3-54): Austrian alpine skier. Greatest downhiller ever. Gold medalist in downhill at 1976 Olympics. Also won four World Cup downhill titles (1975–78).

Bob Knight (b. 10-25-40): College basketball coach. Won three NCAA championships with Indiana in 1976, '81, '87. Coached U.S. Olympic team to gold medal in 1984. Fired by Indiana in 2000 after a series of disputes with the media, ex-players, students, and the university. Hired by Texas Tech in 2001, took team to 2003 NIT semifinals. Career span since 1966 with Army, Indiana and Texas Tech.

Olga Korbut (b. 5-16-55): Soviet gymnast. First ever to complete backward somersault on balance beam. Won three gold medals at 1972 Olympics.

Johann Olav Koss (b. 10-29-68): Speed Skater. Norwegian won three gold medals at 1994 Olympics in Lillehammer, with world records in the 1,500, 5,000 and 10,000 meters. Won 1,500 meter gold medal and 10,000 meter silver medal in 1992 Games at Albertville.

Sandy Koufax (b. 12-30-35): Baseball LHP. Cy Young Award winner three times (1963, '65, '66); and MVP in 1963; World Series MVP in 1963, '65. Pitched four no-hitters, including one perfect game. League leader in ERA five consecutive seasons, strikeouts four times. Won 25+ games three times. Career record 165–87, with 2.76 ERA. Career span 1955–66 with Brooklyn/Los Angeles.

Jack Kramer (b. 8-1-21): Tennis player. Won two consecutive U.S. singles titles (1946, '47) and one Wimbledon title (1947). Also won six Grand Slam doubles titles. Served as executive director of Association of Tennis Professionals from 1972–75.

Ingrid Kristiansen (b. 3-21-56): Track and field. Norwegian runner is only person—male or female—to hold world records in 5,000 meters (14:37.33 set in 1986), 10,000 meters (30:13.74 set in 1986) and marathon (2:21:06 set in 1985). Also won Boston Marathon two times (1986, '89) and New York City Marathon once (1989).

Bob Kurland (b. 12-23-24): College basketball player. 6' 10¼'' center on Oklahoma A&M teams that won NCAA titles in 1945 and '46. Consensus All-America and NCAA tournament MVP in both 1945 and '46. Led nation in scoring in 1946. His habit of swatting shots off rim led to creation of goaltending rule in 1945. Won gold medals in both 1948 and '52 Olympics. Turned down lucrative pro offers, playing instead for Phillips 66 Oilers AAU team.

Michelle Kwan (b. 7-7-80): Figure skater. Six-time U.S. champion (1996, 1998–02), four-time world champion (1996, '98, '00, '01); silver medalist in 1998 Olympics and bronze medalist in Salt Lake City in 2002.

Rene Lacoste (b. 7-2-05, d. 10-12-96): French tennis player. "The Crocodile." One of France's "Four Musketeers" of the 1920s. Won three French singles titles (1925, '27, '29), two consecutive U.S. titles (1926, '27) and two Wimbledon titles (1925, '28). Also designed casual shirt with embroidered crocodile that bears his name.

Marion Ladewig (b. 10-30-14): Bowler. Won All-Star Tournament eight times (1949–52, '54, '56, '59, '63) and WPBA National Championship once (1960). Also voted Bowler of the Year nine times (1950–54, 1957–59, '63).

Guy Lafleur (b. 9-20-51): Hockey RW. Won MVP award two consecutive seasons (1977, '78), playoff MVP in 1977. Scored 50+ goals and 100+ points six consecutive seasons. Led league in points scored three consecutive seasons, goals and assists one time each. 560 career goals, 793 assists. Played on five Stanley Cup champions with Montreal from 1971–85.

Curly Lambeau (b. 4-9-1898; d. 6-1-65): Football QB and coach. Quarterback for Packers team in early 1920s. Record of 212-106-21 in his 29 seasons (1921–49) as Packer coach, winning three NFL titles in 1929–31.

Jack Lambert (b. 7-8-52): Football LB. Anchored Pittsburgh's famed "Steel Curtain" defense. Selected for Pro Bowl nine times. Played on four Super Bowl champions (1974, '75, '78, '79) with Pittsburgh from 1974–84. Elected to Hall of Fame 1990.

Jake LaMotta (b. 7-10-21): Boxer. "The Bronx Bull." Subject of *Raging Bull*, a film by Martin Scorsese, starring Robert DeNiro. Won middleweight title by knocking out Marcel Cerdan in 10 on 6-16-49. Lost title to Ray Robinson, who KO'd him in 13 on 2-13-51. Career record: 83–19–4, 30 KOs.

Kenesaw Mountain Landis (b. 11-20-1866, d. 11-25-44): Baseball's first and most powerful commissioner from 1920–44. By banning the eight "Black Sox" involved in the fixing of the 1919 World Series, he restored public confidence in the integrity of baseball.

Tom Landry (b. 9-11-24, d. 2-12-00): Football coach. Third alltime in wins (270). The first coach in Dallas history, from 1960–88. Led team to 13 division titles, seven championship games and five Super Bowls. Won two Super Bowl championships (1971, '77). Career record 270-178-6.

Dick (Night Train) Lane (b. 4-16-28, d. 1-29-02): Football DB. Third alltime in interceptions (68) and second in interception yardage (1,207). Set record with 14 interceptions as a rookie in 1952. Career span 1952–65 with Los Angeles, Chicago Cardinals, Detroit.

Joe Lapchick (b. 4-12-00, d. 8-10-70): Basketball C–coach. One of the first big men in basketball, member of New York's Original Celtics. Coached St. John's (1936–47, 1956–65) to four NIT titles. Coached New York Knicks, 1947–56.

Steve Largent (b. 9-28-54): Football WR. Retired as alltime leader in pass receptions (819), and TD receptions (100). 177 consecutive games with reception, 10 seasons with 50+ receptions and eight seasons with 1,000+ yards receiving. Career span 1976–89 with Seattle. Oklahoma congressman from 1994–01.

Don Larsen (b. 8-7-29): Baseball RHP. Pitched only perfect game in World Series history, for New York (AL) on 10-8-56, beating the Dodgers 2–0; named World Series MVP. Career span 1953–67 for many teams.

Tommy Lasorda (b. 9-22-27): Baseball manager. Spent nearly his entire minor and major league career in Dodgers organization as a pitcher, coach and manager. Managed Dodgers 1977–96, winning four pennants and two World Series (1981, '88). Only three men managed one baseball team longer. Coached U.S. Olympic baseball team to the gold medal at the 2000 Sydney Games.

Rod Laver (b. 8-9-38): Australian tennis player. "Rocket." Only player to achieve the Grand Slam twice (as an amateur in 1962 and as a pro in 1969). Third alltime in men's Grand Slam singles titles (11—tied with Bjorn Borg). Won four Wimbledon titles (1961, '62, '68, '69), three Australian titles (1960, '62, '69), two U.S. titles (1962, '69) and two French titles (1962, '69). Also won eight Grand Slam doubles titles. First player to earn $1 million in prize money. 47 career tournament victories. Member of undefeated Australian Davis Cup team from 1959–62.

Andrea Mead Lawrence (b. 4-19-32): Skier. Gold medalist in slalom and giant slalom at 1952 Olympics.

Bobby Layne (b. 12-19-26; d. 12-1-86): Football QB. Led Detroit to NFL championships in both 1952 and '53. In 1952 led NFL in every passing category. Career span 1948–62, most with Detroit. Elected to Hall of Fame in 1967.

Sammy Lee (b. 8-1-20): Diver. Gold medalist at two consecutive Olympics (highboard in 1948, '52); bronze medalist in springboard at 1948 Olympics. Won the 1953 Sullivan Award. Also 1960 U.S. Olympic diving coach.

Jacques Lemaire (b. 9-7-45): Hockey C–Coach. As center for Montreal from 1967–79 was part of eight Stanley Cup winning teams. Over 12 seasons, all with Montreal, scored 366 goals and had 469 assists. Elected to Hall of Fame in 1984. Coached New Jersey to their first Stanley Cup in 1995.

Mario Lemieux (b. 10-5-65): Hockey C. Won MVP award in 1988, '93, '96. Playoff MVP in 1991. Led league in points five seasons and goals scored three seasons, assists one season. Rookie of the Year in 1985. Won 1992–93 scoring title despite sitting out six weeks to receive treatment for Hodgkin's disease, a form of cancer. Sat out 1994–95 season, returned in '95–96 to lead league in scoring and become second fastest player to score 500 career goals. Awarded ownership of Penguins in a settlement in 1999, and returned to the ice in 2001, when he scored 35 goals in 43 games. Career span 1984–94, 1995–97, 2001– with Pittsburgh.

Greg LeMond (b. 6-26-61): Cyclist. First American to win Tour de France; won event three times (1986, '89, '90). Recovered from hunting accident to win in 1989.

Ivan Lendl (b. 3-7-60): Tennis player. Second most alltime men's career tournament victories (94). Won three consecutive U.S. Open singles titles (1985–87) and three French Open titles (1984, '86, '87). Also won two Australian Open titles (1989, '90). Reached Grand Slam final nine other times.

Suzanne Lenglen (b. 5-24-1899, d. 7-4-38): French tennis player. Lost only one match from 1919–26. Won six Wimbledon singles and doubles titles (1919–23, '25). Won six French singles and doubles titles (1920–23, '25, '26).

Sugar Ray Leonard (b. 5-17-56): Boxer. Champion in five weight classes: welterweight, junior middleweight, middleweight, super middleweight and light heavyweight. Career record 36-3-1 with 25 KOs from 1977–97, including comeback loss to Hector Camacho at the age of 41. Also light welterweight gold medalist at 1976 Olympics.

Carl Lewis (b. 7-1-61): Track and field. Held world record for 100 meters (9.86), set at 1991 World Championships in Tokyo. Duplicated Jesse Owens's feat by winning four gold medals at 1984 Olympics (100 and 200 meters, 4x100-meter relay and long jump). Won 1996 Olympic long jump gold at age 35, giving him nine career gold medals and making him just the second track and field athlete (along with Al Oerter) to win four Olympic golds in a single event. Sullivan Award winner in 1981.

Nancy Lieberman-Cline (b. 7-1-58): Basketball G. Three-time All-America at Old Dominion. Player of the Year (1979, '80). Olympian in 1976. Promoter of women's basketball: played in WPBL, WABA. First woman to play basketball in a men's professional league (USBL, 1986). Joined WNBA in 1997, retired in '98 to become GM/coach of the Detroit Shock.

Bob Lilly (b. 7-26-39): Football DT. Dallas Cowboys' first ever draft pick, first Pro Bowl player and first all-NFL choice. Made all-NFL eight times. Career span 1961–74, all with Dallas. Elected to Hall of Fame in 1980.

Tara Lipinski (b. 6-10-82): Figure skater. In 1998 at Nagano eclipsed Sonja Henie as the youngest individual Winter Olympic champion in history when, at 15, she won the women's figure skating gold medal. Also won U.S. and world championships in 1997.

Sonny Liston (b. 5-8-32, d. 12-30-70): Boxer. Heavyweight champion from 1962–64. Won title by KO of Floyd Patterson. Lost title when TKO'd by Cassius Clay (Muhammad Ali) and then lost rematch when KO'd in first round. Career record: 50-4, 39 KOs.

Vince Lombardi (b. 6-11-13, d. 9-3-70): Football coach. Highest alltime winning percentage (.740). Career record 105-35-6. Won five NFL championships and two consecutive Super Bowl titles with Green Bay

from 1959–67. Coached Washington in 1969. Super Bowl trophy named in his honor.

Johnny Longden (b. 2-14-07, d. 2-14-03): Horse racing jockey. Rode Triple Crown winner Count Fleet in 1943. 6,032 career wins.

Nancy Lopez (b. 1-6-57): Golfer. 48 career LPGA Tour wins. LPGA Player of the Year four times (1978, '79, '85, '88). Winner of LPGA Championship three times (1978, '85, '89). Member of the LPGA Hall of Fame.

Greg Louganis (b. 1-29-60): Diver. Gold medalist in platform and springboard at two consecutive Olympics (1984, '88). World champion five times (platform in 1978, '82, '86; springboard in 1982, '86). Also Sullivan Award winner in 1984.

Joe Louis (b. 5-13-14, d. 4-12-81): Boxer. "The Brown Bomber." Longest title reign of any heavyweight champion (11 years, nine months) from 1937–49. Career record 63-3 with 49 KOs from 1934–51. Defended title 25 times.

Jerry Lucas (b. 3-30-40): Basketball F. Three-time first-team All-NBA (1965, '66, '68). Averaged 17.0 points and 15.6 rebounds per game from 1963–74 with Cincinnati, San Francisco and New York. Averaged over 20 points and 20 rebounds a game while at Ohio State. In 1960 member of both NCAA championship team and gold-medal winning U.S. Olympic team. Elected to Hall of Fame in 1979.

Sid Luckman (b. 11-21-16, d. 7-5-98): Football QB. Played on four NFL champions (1940, '41, '43, '46) with Chicago. Player of the Year in 1943. Tied record with seven touchdown passes in one game in 1943. All-Pro six times. 137 career touchdown passes. Career span 1939–50. Also All-America with Columbia.

Jon Lugbill (b. 5-27-61): Whitewater canoe racer. Won five world singles titles from 1979–89.

Hank Luisetti (b. 6-16-16, d. 12-17-02): Basketball F. The first player to use the one-handed shot. All-America at Stanford three consecutive years from 1936–38.

D. Wayne Lukas (b. 9-2-35): Horse racing trainer. Former college basketball coach and quarter horse trainer. Won six straight Triple Crown races from 1994–96, including all three Triple Crown races in 1995, the first trainer to accomplish that feat with multiple horses (Thunder Gulch and Timber County). Trained horses that have won 13 Triple Crown races—four Kentucky Derbys, five Preakness' and four Belmonts—and three Horses of the Year (Lady's Secret in 1986, Criminal Type in 1990, and Charismatic in 1999).

Connie Mack (b. 2-22-1862, d. 2-8-56): Born Cornelius McGillicuddy. Baseball manager. Managed Philadelphia for 50 years (1901–50) until age 87. All-time leader in games (7,755), wins (3,731) and losses (3,948). Won nine pennants and five World Series (1910, '11, '13, '29, '30).

Greg Maddux (b. 4-14-66): Baseball P. Won 15 or more games in 15 straight seasons (1988–02). Four-time Cy Young Award winner (1992–95). Led league in wins three times, ERA four times. 12 Gold Gloves. Career span 1986– with Chicago (NL) and Atlanta.

Larry Mahan (b. 11-21-43): Rodeo. All-around champion six times (1966–70, '73).

Frank Mahovlich (b. 1-10-38): Hockey LW. Winner of Calder Trophy for top rookie for 1957–58 season. In

8 NHL seasons with Toronto, Detroit and Montreal, had 533 goals and 570 assists. Played for six Stanley Cup winners. Elected to Hall of Fame 1981.

Phil Mahre (b. 5-10-57): Skier. Gold medalist in slalom at 1984 Olympics (twin brother Steve won silver medal). World Cup champion three consecutive years (1981–83).

Joe Malone (b. 2-28-1890, d. 5-15-69): Hockey F. "Phantom Joe." Led the NHL in its first season, 1917–18, with 44 goals in 20 games with Montreal. Led league in scoring two times (1918, '20). Holds NHL record with most goals scored, single game (7) in 1920.

Karl Malone (b. 7-24-63): Basketball F. "The Mailman." Second in NBA history in points scored (34,707). Two-time NBA MVP (1997, '99). 11-time first-team All-NBA (1989–99). All-Star MVP, 1989, 1993 (shared with John Stockton). All-Rookie team, 1986. Member of 1992 and '96 Olympic teams. Career span 1985– 2003 with Utah, 2003– with Los Angeles.

Moses Malone (b. 3-23-55): Basketball C. Three-time NBA MVP (1979, '82, '83). Playoff MVP in 1983 when he led Philadelphia to the NBA title. Second alltime in free throws made (8,531), fifth in rebounds (16,212) and fifth in points scored (27,409). Four-time first-team All-NBA. Led league in rebounding six times, five consecutively. Went directly to pros from high school. Career span 1974–95 with nine teams, including Houston and Philadelphia.

Hermann Maier (b.12-7-72): Austrian skier. Recovered from spectacular crash in the downhill to win two gold medals at 1998 Olympics in Nagano. Won 1998 Super G, Giant Slalom and overall World Cup season titles.

Man o' War (b. 1917, d. 1947): Thoroughbred race horse. Won 20 of 21 races 1919–20. Only loss was in 1919 in Sanford Stakes to Upset. Passed up Derby but won both Preakness and Belmont. Winner of $249,465. Sire of War Admiral, 1937 Triple Crown winner.

Mickey Mantle (b. 10-20-31, d. 8-13-95): Baseball OF. Won three MVP awards (1956, '57, '62); won Triple Crown in 1956. 536 career HR. Greatest switch hitter in history. Played in 20 All-Star games. Alltime World Series leader in HR (18), RBI (40) and runs scored (42). No. 7 was a member of seven World Series winners with New York (AL). Career span 1951–68.

Diego Maradona (b. 10-30-60): Argentine soccer player. Led Argentina to 1986 World Cup victory and to 1990 World Cup finals. Led Naples to Italian League titles (1987, '90), Italian Cup (1987) and to UEFA Cup title (1989). Throughout 1980s often acknowledged as best player in the world. Tested positive for cocaine and suspended by FIFA and Italian Soccer Federation for 15 months in March 1991. Failed drug test in 1994 World Cup and suspended before second round.

Pete Maravich (b. 6-22-47, d. 1-5-88): Basketball G. "Pistol Pete." Alltime NCAA leader in points scored (3,667), scoring average (44.2) and games scoring 50+ points (28, including then Division I record 69 points in 1970). Alltime single-season leader in points scored (1,381) and scoring average (44.5) in 1970. NCAA scoring leader and All-America three consecutive seasons 1968–70 with Louisiana State. Averaged 20+ points eight times as a pro, leading the league in scoring in 1977. All-Star five times. Averaged 24.2 points per game from 1970–79 with Atlanta, New Orleans/Utah and Boston.

Gino Marchetti (b. 1-2-27): Football DE. Played in Pro Bowl every year from 1955–65, except 1958 when he broke right ankle tackling Frank Gifford in Colts' 23–17 win over the Giants. Career span 1952–66, almost all with Baltimore. Inducted into Hall of Fame in 1972.

Rocky Marciano (b. 9-1-23, d. 8-31-69): Boxer. Heavyweight champion (1952–56). Career record 49–0 with 43 KOs from 1947 to 1956. Only heavyweight to retire as undefeated champion.

Juan Marichal (b. 10-24-37): Baseball RHP. 243 career wins, 2.89 career ERA. Won 20+ games six times; 250+ innings pitched eight times; 200+ strikeouts six times. Pitched no-hitter in 1963. Career span 1960–75, mostly with San Francisco. Elected to Hall of Fame in 1983.

Dan Marino (b. 9-15-61): Football QB. Set alltime single-season record for yards passing (5,084) and touchdown passes (48) in 1984. Passed for 4,000+ yards five other seasons. Career totals: 61,361 yards passing, 420 touchdown passes, first alltime in both categories. Career span 1983–00 with Miami.

Roger Maris (b. 9-10-34, d. 12-14-85): Baseball OF. Broke Babe Ruth's alltime single-season HR record with 61 in 1961. Won consecutive MVP awards and led league in RBI 1960–61. Career span 1957–68 with Kansas City, New York (AL), St. Louis.

Billy Martin (b. 5-16-28, d. 12-25-89): Baseball 2B–manager. Volatile manager was hired and fired by Minnesota, Detroit, Texas, New York (AL) (five times!) and Oakland from 1969–88. Career record: 1253–1013. Won World Series with New York as manager in 1977 and as player four times.

Pedro Martinez (b. 10-25-71): Baseball P. Three Cy Young Awards (1997, '99, '00). Became second pitcher to win Cy Young Awards in both leagues in 1999. Became first pitcher in 25 years to have more than 300 Ks and ERA below 2.00 in 1997. Led league in ERA and strikeouts three times each. Started 1999 All-Star Game and was named MVP after striking out first four batters. Career span 1992– with Los Angeles, Montreal and Boston.

Eddie Mathews (b. 10-13-31, d. 2-18-01): Baseball 3B. 512 career HR and 30+ HR nine consecutive seasons. League leader in home runs two times, walks four times. Career span 1952–68, mostly with Milwaukee.

Christy Mathewson (b. 8-12-1880, d. 10-7-25): Baseball RHP. Third alltime most wins (373, tied with Grover Alexander) and shutouts (79); career ERA 2.13. Led league in wins five times; won 30+ games four times and 20+ games nine other times. Led league in ERA and strikeouts five times each. Pitched two no-hitters. Pitched three shutouts in 1905 World Series. Career span 1900–16 with New York.

Bob Mathias (b. 11-17-30): Track and field. At age 17, youngest to win gold medal in decathlon at 1948 Olympics. First decathlete to win gold medal at consecutive Olympics (1948, '52). Also won Sullivan Award in 1948.

Ollie Matson (b. 5-1-30): Football RB. Versatile runner totalled 12,884 combined yards rushing, receiving and kick returning. Scored 73 career touchdowns, including a 105-yard kickoff return on 10-14-56, the second longest ever. Career span 1952–66 with Chicago Cardinals, Los Angeles, Detroit, Philadelphia. Also won bronze medal in 400 meters at 1952 Olympics. Elected to Hall of Fame in 1972.

Roland Matthes (b. 11-17-50): German swimmer. Gold medalist in 100-meter and 200-meter backstroke at two consecutive Olympics (1968, '72). Set 16 world records from 1967–73.

Don Maynard (b. 1-25-37): Football WR. Retired in 1973 as the NFL's alltime leading receiver. In 15 seasons, 10 with the New York Jets, caught 633 passes for 11,834 yards and 88 TDs. Averaged 18.7 yards per catch for career. Elected to Hall of Fame in 1987.

Willie Mays (b. 5-6-31): Baseball OF. "Say Hey Kid." MVP in 1954, '65; Rookie of the Year in 1951. Third alltime most HR (660), with 50+ HR two times, 30+ HR nine other times. Led league in HR four times. 100+ RBI 10 times; 100+ runs scored 12 consecutive seasons. 3,283 career hits. Led league in stolen bases four consecutive seasons. 30 HR and 30 steals in same season two times and first man in history to hit 300+ HR and steal 300+ bases. Won 11 consecutive Gold Gloves; set record for career putouts by an outfielder and league record for total chances. His catch in the 1954 World Series off the bat of Vic Wertz called the greatest ever. Career span 1951–73 with New York/San Francisco and New York (NL).

Bill Mazeroski (b. 9-5-36): Baseball 2B. Hit dramatic ninth-inning home run in Game 7 to win 1960 World Series, first of only two Series' to end on a home run. Won eight Gold Gloves. Led league in assists nine times, double plays eight times and putouts five times. Inducted to Hall of Fame in 2001. Career 1956–72 with Pittsburgh; 2,016 hits, 138 HR, .260 avg.

Joe McCarthy (b. 4-21-1887, d. 1-3-78): Baseball manager. Alltime highest winning percentage among managers for regular season (.615). First manager to win pennants in both leagues (Chicago (NL), 1929, New York (AL), 1932). From 1926–50 his teams won seven World Series and nine pennants.

Mark McCormack (b. 11-6-30, d. 5-16-03): Sports marketing agent. Founded International Management Group in 1962. Also author of best-selling business advice books.

Pat McCormick (b. 5-12-30): Diver. Gold medalist in platform and springboard at two consecutive Olympics (1952, '56). Also won Sullivan Award in 1956.

Willie McCovey (b. 1-10-38): Baseball 1B. Led NL in HRs three times (1963, '68, '69) and in RBI twice (1968, '69). 521 career homers. .270 career average. Hit 18 grand slams. Rookie of the Year 1959. NL MVP in 1969. Career span 1959–80 with San Francisco, San Diego and Oakland. Elected to Hall of Fame in 1986.

John McEnroe (b. 2-26-59): Tennis player. Third alltime men's most career tournament victories (77). Won four U.S. Open singles titles (consecutively 1979–81, '84) and three Wimbledon titles (1981, '83, '84). Also won eight Grand Slam doubles titles. Led U.S. to five Davis Cup victories (1978, '79, '81, '82, '92).

John McGraw (b. 4-7-1873, d. 2-25-34): Baseball manager. Second alltime in games (4,801) and wins (2,784). Guided New York (NL) to three World Series titles and 10 pennants from 1902–32.

Mark McGwire (b. 10-1-63): Baseball 1B. Broke Roger Maris's 37-year-old single-season HR record with 70 in 1998. Rookie of the Year in 1987, when he hit rookie record 49 home runs. Hit 30+ HR 12 times, 40+ HR six times, 50+ HR four straight years (1996–99). Member of 1984 U.S. Olympic baseball

team. Had 583 career HRs and 1,414 RBIs with Oakland and St. Louis from 1986–01.

Denny McLain (b. 3-29-44): Baseball RHP. Last pitcher to win 30+ games in a season (Detroit, 1968); won 20+ games two other times. Won two consecutive Cy Young Awards (1968 '69). Led league in innings pitched two times. Served 2½-year jail term for 1985 conviction of extortion, racketeering and drug possession. Re-entered prison in 1997 on fraud conviction. Career span 1963–72, mostly with Detroit.

Mary T. Meagher (b. 10-27-64): Swimmer. "Madame Butterfly." Won three gold medals at 1984 Olympics (100-meter butterfly, 200-meter butterfly and 400-medley relay). In 1981 set world records in 100-meter butterfly (57.93) and 200-meter butterfly (2:05.96).

Rick Mears (b. 12-3-51): Auto racer. Has won Indy 500 four times (1979, '84, '88, '91) and been CART champion three times (1979, '81, '82). Named Indy 500 Rookie of the Year in 1978.

Eddy Merckx (b. 1945): Belgian cyclist. Won five Tours de France, including four in a row (1969–72).

Mark Messier (b. 1-18-61): Hockey C. Two-time Hart Trophy (MVP) winner. Won Stanley Cups with Edmonton (1984, '85, '87, '88, '90) and New York Rangers (1994). Third alltime in scoring (1,804 pts), fourth in assists (1,146) and seventh in goals scored (658). Career span 1979– with Edmonton, New York Rangers and Vancouver.

Cary Middlecoff (b. 1-6-21, d. 9-1-98): Golfer. Won 40 PGA tournaments, including 1955 Masters and U.S. Opens in 1949 and '56. Won 1956 Vardon Trophy. Also a dentist.

George Mikan (b. 6-18-24): Basketball C. The first dominant big man in professional basketball. Averaged 20+ points per game and named to All-Star team six consecutive seasons. Led league (NBA and NBL) in scoring six times. Played on five championship teams in six years (1949–54) with Minneapolis. Also played on 1945 NIT championship team with DePaul. All-America three times. Served as ABA Commissioner from 1968–69.

Stan Mikita (b. 5-20-40): Hockey C. Won MVP award two consecutive seasons (1967, '68). 926 career assists, 1,467 career points. Led league in assists four straight seasons and points four times. 541 career goals. All-Star six times. Career span 1958–80 with Chicago.

Del Miller (b. 7-5-13; d. 8-19-96): Harness racing driver. Raced in eight decades, beginning in 1929, the longest career of any athlete. Won The Hambletonian in 1950.

Marvin Miller (b. 4-14-17): Labor negotiator. Union chief of MLB Players Association from 1966–84. Led strikes in 1972 and '81. Negotiated five labor contracts that increased minimum salary and pension fund, allowed for agents and arbitration, and brought about the end of the reserve clause and the start of free agency.

Art Monk (b. 12-5-57): Football WR. Caught 940 passed for 12,721 yards and 68 TDs during his career. Set NFL single season record with 106 catches in 1984. Career span 1980–95 with Washington, New York Jets and Philadelphia.

Earl Monroe (b. 11-21-44): Basketball G. "The Pearl" played 13 seasons (1967–80) with Baltimore and New York. NBA Rookie of Year in 1968. Four-time All-Star.

Member of 1973 NBA championship Knicks team. Averaged 18.8 points a game. Elected to Basketball Hall of Fame 1989.

Joe Montana (b. 6-11-56): Football QB. Second alltime highest-rated passer (92.3); 40,551 career passing yards and 273 TD passes. Won four Super Bowl championships (1981, '84, '88, '89) with San Francisco. Named Super Bowl MVP three times (1981, '84, '89). Player of the Year in 1989. Voted to eight Pro Bowls. Led his teams to 31 fourth-quarter comebacks. Also led Notre Dame to national championship in 1977. Career span 1979–94 with San Francisco and Kansas City. Elected to Hall of Fame in 2000.

Carlos Monzon (b. 8-7-42, d. 1-8-95): Argentine boxer. Longest title reign of any middleweight champion (6 years, nine months) from 1970–77. Career record 89-3-9 with 61 KOs from 1963–77. Won 82 consecutive bouts from 1964–77. Defended title 14 times. Retired as champion.

Helen Wills Moody (b. 10-6-05, d. 1-1-98): Tennis player. Third alltime in women's Grand Slam singles titles (19). Her eight Wimbledon titles are second most alltime (1927–30, '32, '33, '35, '38). Won seven U.S. titles (1923–25, 1927–29, '31) and four French titles (1928–30, '32). Also won 12 Grand Slam doubles titles.

Archie Moore (b. 12-13-16 d. 12-9-98): Boxer. "The Mongoose." Longest title reign of any light heavyweight champion (9 years, one month) from 1952–62. Career record 199-26-8 with an alltime record 145 KOs from 1935–65. Retired at age 52.

Davey Moore (b. 11-1-33; d. 3-23-63): Boxer. Won featherweight title by KO of Kid Bassey in 13 on 3-18-59. Five successful defenses of title, before losing it on 3-21-63 to Sugar Ramos who KO'd him in 10. Died two days after fight of brain damage suffered during fight. Career record: 58-7-1, 30 KOs.

Noureddine Morceli (b. 2-20-70). Algerian track and field middle distance runner. Set world record for mile (3:44.39) in Rieti, Italy, on 9-5-93. Set world record for 1,500 (3:28.86) on 9-5-92. World champion at 1,500 in 1991, '93 and '95. Won gold medal at 1996 Olympics in Atlanta. Only man ever to rank first in the world at 1,500/mile four straight years (1990–93).

Joe Morgan (b. 9-19-43): Baseball 2B. Sparkplug for Cincinnati's Big Red Machine in the 1970s. Won two MVP awards (1975, '76). 10-time All-Star. Fifth alltime in career walks (1,865). 689 stolen bases. 100+ walks and runs scored eight times each; 40+ stolen bases nine times. Won five Gold Gloves. Second alltime in games played by 2nd baseman (2,527). Career span 1963–84 with Houston, Cincinnati, San Francisco, Philadelphia and Oakland.

Willie Mosconi (b. 6-27-13; d. 9-16-93): Pocket billiards player. Won world title a record 15 straight times between 1941–57. Once pocketed 526 balls without a miss.

Edwin Moses (b. 8-31-55): Track and field. Gold medalist in the 400-meter hurdles at two Olympics (1976, '84); bronze medalist at 1988 Olympics. Won 122 consecutive races from 1977–87. Set four world records in 400-meter hurdles. Won the Sullivan Award in 1983.

Marion Motley (b. 6-5-20 d. 6-27-99): Football FB. All-time AAFC leader in yards rushing (3,024). Led NFL in rushing once. Combined league totals: 4,712 yards rushing, 39 touchdowns. Played for four consecutive AAFC champions (1946–49) and one NFL champion (1950). Career span with Cleveland 1946–1953.

Shirley Muldowney (b. 6-19-40): Drag racer. First woman to win the Top Fuel championship, which she won three times (1977, '80, '82).

Anthony Munoz (b. 8-19-58): Football OT. Probably the greatest offensive tackle ever. Made Pro Bowl a record-tying 11 times. Career span 1980–92 with Cincinnati. Elected to Hall of Fame 1998.

Isaac Murphy (b. 4-16-1861, d. 2-12-1896): Horse racing jockey. Top jockey of his era, Murphy, who was black, won three Kentucky Derbys (aboard Buchanan in 1884, Riley in 1890 and Kingman in 1891).

Eddie Murray (b. 2-24-56): Baseball 1B. One of greatest switch-hitters in baseball history. 100+ RBI six seasons and 30+ HRs five seasons. Retired with 3,255 hits, 504 HRs and 1,917 RBI—eighth alltime and most ever by switch hitter. Career span 1977–97 with Baltimore, Los Angeles, New York (NL), Cleveland and Anaheim. Inducted into Baseball Hall of Fame in 2003.

Jim Murray (b. 12-29-19; d. 8-16-98): Sportswriter. Won Pulitzer Prize in 1990. Named Sportswriter of the Year 14 times. Columnist for *Los Angeles Times* 1961–98.

Ty Murray (b. 10-11-69): Rodeo cowboy. All-around world champion, 1989–94. Set single-season earnings record in 1990 ($213,771). Rookie of the Year in 1988. At 20, became youngest man ever to win national all-around title in 1989.

Stan Musial (b. 11-21-20): Baseball OF–1B. "Stan the Man." Had .331 career batting average and 475 career HR. MVP award winner (1943, '46, '48). Fourth alltime in hits (3,630) and third in doubles (725). Won seven batting titles. Led league in hits six times, slugging average five times, doubles eight times. Had .300+ batting average 17 times, 200+ hits six times, 100+ RBI 10 times, and 100+ runs scored 11 times. 24-time All-Star. Career span 1941–63 with St. Louis.

John Naber (b. 1-20-56): Swimmer. Won four gold medals and one silver medal at 1976 Olympics. Sullivan Award winner in 1977.

Bronko Nagurski (b. 11-3-08, d. 1-7-90): Football FB. Punishing runner played on three NFL champions (1932, '33, '43) with Bears. 2,778 career yards with Chicago from 1930–37 and 1943.

James Naismith (b. 11-6-1861, d. 11-28-39): Invented basketball in 1891 while an instructor at YMCA Training School in Springfield, Mass. Refined the game while a professor at Kansas from 1898–37. Hall of Fame is named in his honor.

Joe Namath (b. 5-31-43): Football QB. "Broadway Joe." Super Bowl MVP in 1968 after he guaranteed victory for New York. 173 career touchdown passes. Led league in yards passing three times, including 4,007 yards in 1967. Player of the Year, 1968; Rookie of the Year, 1965. Career span 1965–77 with New York Jets and Los Angeles.

Ilie Nastase (b. 7-19-46): Romanian tennis player. "Nasty" for his unruly deportment on court. Beat Arthur Ashe to win 1972 U.S. Open title. Won 1973 French Open. Twice Wimbledon runner-up (to Stan Smith in 1972 and Bjorn Borg in 1976).

Martina Navratilova (b. 10-18-56): Tennis player. Fourth in women's Grand Slam singles titles (18—tied with Chris Evert). Won a record nine Wimbledon titles, including six consecutively (1978, '79, 1982–87, '90). Won four U.S. Open titles (1983, '84, '86, '87), three Australian Open titles (1981, '83, '85) and two French Open titles (1982, '84). Reached Grand Slam final 13 other times. Also won 40 Grand Slam doubles titles. Her total of 58 Grand Slam titles is second alltime to Margaret Court. Set mark for longest winning streak with 74 matches in 1984. Also won the doubles Grand Slam in 1984 with Pam Shriver. Won 109 consecutive doubles matches with Shriver from 1983–85.

Byron Nelson (b. 2-14-12): Golfer. Won 52 career tournaments, including 11 consecutively in 1945. Won the Masters (1937, '42) and PGA Championship (1940, '45) two times each and U.S. Open once (1939).

Ernie Nevers (b. 6-11-03, d. 5-3-76): Football FB. Set alltime pro single game record for points scored (40) and touchdowns (six) on 11-28-29. Career span 1926–31 with Duluth and Chicago. A pitcher with St. Louis (AL), surrendered two of Babe Ruth's 60 home runs in 1927. All-America at Stanford, earned 11 letters in four sports.

John Newcombe (b. 5-23-44): Australian tennis player. Won three Wimbledon singles titles (1967, '70, '71), two U.S. titles (1967, '73) and two Australian Open titles (1973, '75). Also won 17 Grand Slam doubles titles.

Pete Newell (b. 8-31-15): College basketball coach. Despite coaching only 13 seasons, 1947–60, was first coach to win NIT, NCAA and Olympic crowns. Led San Francisco to 1949 NIT title, Cal to 1959 NCAA title, and the 1960 U.S. Olympic basketball team that included Jerry Lucas, Oscar Robertson and Jerry West to gold medal. Overall collegiate coaching record of 234–123.

Jack Nicklaus (b. 1-21-40): Golfer. "The Golden Bear." Alltime leader in major championships (20). Second alltime in career wins (70). Won Masters six times, more than any golfer (1963, '65, '66, '72, '75, '86—at age 46, the oldest player to win event), PGA Championship five times (1963, '71, '73, '75, '80), U.S. Open four times (1962, '67, '72, '80), British Open three times (1966, '70, '78) and U.S. Amateur twice (1959, '61). PGA Player of the Year five times (1967, '72, '73, '75, '76). Also NCAA champion with Ohio State in 1961.

Ray Nitschke (b. 12-29-36 d. 3-8-98): Football LB. Defensive signal-caller for the great Green Bay teams of the '60s. Voted Packer MVP by teammates after 1967 season. MVP of the 1962 NFL title game. Career span 1958–72 with Green Bay.

Chuck Noll (b. 1-5-32): Football coach. Only coach to win four Super Bowls (1975, '76, '79, '80). Coaching career 1969–91 with Pittsburgh; 209-156-1.

Greg Norman (b. 2-10-55): Golfer. "The Shark" led PGA in winnings in 1986, '90, '95, '96. Won Vardon Trophy twice, 1989, '90. Won two British Opens (1986, '93) but is more famous for his heartbreaking losses. PGA Player of the Year 1996.

James D. Norris (b. 11-6-06, d. 2-25-66): Hockey executive. Owner of the Detroit Red Wings from 1933–43 and Chicago from 1946–66. Teams won four Stanley Cup championships (1936, '37, '43, '61). Defensive Player of the Year award named in his honor. Also a boxing promoter, operated International Boxing Club from 1949–58.

Paavo Nurmi (b. 6-13-1897, d. 10-2-73): Track and field. Finnish middle- and long-distance runner won a total of nine gold medals at three Olympics in 1920, '24, '28.

Matti Nykänen (b. 7-17-63): Finnish ski jumper. Three-time Olympic gold medalist. Won 90-meter jump (1984, '88) and 70-meter jump (1988). World champion on 90-meter jump in 1982. Won four World Cups (1983, '85, '86, '88).

Dan O'Brien (b. 7-18-66): Track and field decathlete. Won world decathlon title in 1991, '93, '95. Set world decathlon record of 8,891 in Talence, France, on 9-4/5-92, that stood for seven years. Heavily favored to win 1992 Olympic decathlon but missed making U.S. team when he no-heighted in pole vault at U.S. Olympic Trials. Redeemed himself with gold medal at 1996 Olympics in Atlanta.

Parry O'Brien (b. 1-28-32): Track and field. Shotputter who revolutionized the event with his "glide" technique and won Olympic gold medals in 1952 and '56, silver in '60. Set 10 world records from 1953–59, topped by a put of 63' 4" in 1959. Sullivan Award winner in 1959.

Al Oerter (b. 8-19-36): Track and field. Gold medalist in discus at four consecutive Olympics (1956, '60, '64, '68), setting Olympic record each time. First to break the 200-foot barrier, throwing 200' 5" in 1962.

Sadaharu Oh (b. 5-20-40): Baseball 1B in Japanese league. 868 career HR in 22 seasons for the Tokyo Giants. Led league in HR 15 times, RBI 13 times, batting five times and runs 13 consecutive seasons. Awarded MVP nine times; won two consecutive Triple Crowns and nine Gold Gloves.

Hakeem Olajuwon (b. 1-21-63): Basketball C. From Nigeria. Alltime NBA career leader in blocked shots (3,830). Became the first player to be named NBA MVP, NBA Defensive Player of the Year and NBA Finals MVP in the same season as Houston won its first NBA championship in 1994. Led NCAA in FG %, rebounding and blocked shots in 1984 at Houston. Member of 1996 U.S. Olympic team. Career span 1984–2002 with Houston and Toronto; 21.8 ppg, 11.1 rpg.

Merlin Olsen (b. 9-15-40): Fooball DT. Part of Los Angeles's "Fearsome Foursome" defensive line. Named to Pro Bowl 14 straight times. Career span 1962–76, all with the Los Angeles Rams. Elected to Hall of Fame 1982.

Omaha (b. 1932, d. 1959): Thoroughbred race horse. Won Triple Crown in 1935. Trained by Sunny Jim Fitzsimmons.

Mark O'Meara (b. 1-13-57): Golfer. Has 16 career PGA Tour victories, including the 1998 Masters and British Open, at age 41. Tour rookie of the year in 1981; won 1979 U.S. Amateur.

Shaquille O'Neal (b. 3-6-72): Basketball C. "Shaq." Three-time NBA Finals MVP after leading the Lakers to back-to-back-to-back NBA Finals victories (2000–02). Was named MVP of the regular season, All-Star game, and playoffs in 1999–2000. Nine-time All-Star selection (1993–98, 2000–02). Led league in scoring in 1995 and 2000, and in field goal percentage in 1994, 1998–02. Top pick of Orlando in 1992 NBA draft. NBA Rookie of the Year 1993. Member of 1996 U.S. Olympic team. Led NCAA in blocked shots in 1992 as an All-American at Louisiana State. Career span 1992– with Orlando and Los Angeles Lakers.

Bobby Orr (b. 3-20-48): Hockey D. Defensive Player of the Year more than any other player, eight consecutive seasons (1968–75). Won MVP award three consecutive seasons (1970–72), playoff MVP two

...mes (1970, '72). Also Rookie of the Year in 1967. Led league in assists five times and scoring two times. Career span 1966–77 with Boston.

Mel Ott (b. 3-2-09, d. 11-21-58): Baseball OF. 511 career HR, 1,861 RBI, .304 batting average. League leader in HR and walks six times each. 100+ RBI nine times and 100+ walks ten times. Career span 1926–47 with New York (NL).

Jim Otto (b. 1-5-38): Football C. Number 00 started every game (210) in his 15-year career (1960–74) with Oakland. Inducted to Hall of Fame in 1980.

Kristin Otto (b. 1966): German swimmer. Won six gold medals for East Germany at 1988 Olympics.

Jesse Owens (b. 9-12-13, d. 3-31-80): Track and field. Gold medalist in four events (100 meters and 200 meters; 4x100-meter relay and long jump) at 1936 Olympics. At the 1935 Big 10 championship set or equaled six world record in 70 minutes, including 100 yards, long jump, 220-yard low hurdles and 220 dash.

Alan Page (b. 8-7-45): Football DT. First defensive player to be named NFL Player of the Year, in 1972. Played in 236 straight games, including four Super Bowls. Four-time NFC Defensive Player of Year. Career span 1967–81 with Minnesota and Chicago. Now sits on Minnesota Supreme Court.

Satchel Paige (b. 7-7-06, d. 6-8-82): Baseball RHP. Alltime greatest black pitcher, didn't pitch in major leagues until 1948 at age 42 with Cleveland. Oldest pitcher in major league history at age 59 with Kansas City in 1965. Pitched in the Negro leagues from 1926–50 with Birmingham Black Barons, Pittsburgh Crawfords and Kansas City Monarchs. Estimated career record is 2,000 wins, 250 shutouts, 30,000 strikeouts, 45 no-hitters.

Se Ri Pak (b. 9-28-77): South Korean golfer. 16 career LPGA Tour victories. 1998 LPGA Rookie of the Year for winning the first two majors she ever entered, the LPGA Championship and the U.S. Open.

Arnold Palmer (b. 9-10-29): Golfer. Fourth alltime in career wins (60). Won the Masters four times (1958, '60, '62, '64), British Open two consecutive years (1961, '62) and U.S. Open (1960) and U.S. Amateur (1954) once each. PGA Player of the Year two times (1960, '62). First golfer to surpass $1 million in career earnings. Also won Seniors Championship two times (1980, '84) and U.S. Senior Open once (1981).

Jim Palmer (b. 10-15-45): Baseball RHP. 268 career wins, 2.86 ERA. Won three Cy Young Awards (1973, '75, '76). Won 20+ games eight times. Led league in wins three times, innings pitched four times, ERA two times. Never allowed a grand slam HR. Pitched on six World Series teams with Baltimore, including shutout at age 20. Pitched no-hitter in 1969. Career span 1965–84 with Baltimore.

Bernie Parent (b. 4-3-45): Hockey G. Alltime leader for wins in a season (47 in 1974). Goaltender of the Year, playoff MVP, league leader in wins, goals against average and shutouts two consecutive seasons (1974–75). Career record 270-197-121, including 55 shutouts. Career 2.55 goals against average. Tied record of four playoff shutouts in 1975. Played on two consecutive Stanley Cup champions (1974–75). Career span 1965–79 with Philadelphia.

Brad Park (b. 7-6-48): Hockey D. Seven-time All-Star. In 17 seasons with the New York Rangers, Boston and Detroit (1968–85) scored 213 goals and had 683 assists. Elected to Hall of Fame 1988.

Jim Parker (b. 4-3-34): Football T/G. All-NFL four times at guard, four times at tackle. First full-time offensive lineman inducted to Hall of Fame, in 1973. Career span 1957–67, all with Baltimore. Winner of 1956 Outland Trophy as Ohio State senior.

Joe Paterno (b. 12-21-26): College football coach. First alltime in wins in Division I-A (327). Has won two national championships (1982, '86) with Penn State since 1966. Career record 327-96-3, including five undefeated seasons. Has also won 20 bowl games.

Lester Patrick (b. 12-30-1883, d. 6-1-60): Hockey coach. Led New York Rangers to three Stanley Cup championships (1928, '33, '40). Originated the NHL's farm system and developed playoff format.

Floyd Patterson (b. 1-4-35): Boxer. Heavyweight champion two times (1956–59, 1960–62). First heavyweight to regain title, in rematch with Ingemar Johansson. Career record 55-8-1 with 40 KOs from 1952–72. Also middleweight gold medalist at 1952 Olympics.

Walter Payton (b. 7-25-54, d. 11-1-99): Football RB. "Sweetness." Alltime leader in yards rushing (16,726). Gained 1,000+ yards rushing in 10 seasons. Third alltime in rushing touchdowns (110). 125 career touchdowns. Seven-time All-Pro. Player of the Year two times (1977, '85). Led league in rushing five consecutive seasons. Career span 1975–87 with Chicago.

Pelé (b. 10-23-40): Born Edson Arantes do Nascimento. Brazilian soccer player. Soccer's great ambassador. Played on three World Cup winners with Brazil (1958, '62, '70). Helped promote soccer in U.S. by playing with New York Cosmos from 1975–77. Scored 1,281 goals in 22 years.

Willie Pep (b. 9-19-22): Boxer. Featherweight champion two times (1942–48, 1949–50). Lost title to Sandy Saddler, won it back in rematch, then lost it to Saddler again. Master tactician: legend has it he once won a round without throwing a punch. Career record 230-11-1 with 65 KOs from 1940–66. Won 73 consecutive bouts from 1940–43. Defended title nine times.

Gil Perreault (b. 11-13-50): Hockey C. NHL Rookie of the Year in 1970–71. Five-time All-Star. Scored 512 goals and had 814 assists in career from 1970–87 with Buffalo. Elected to Hall of Fame in 1990.

Fred Perry (b. 5-18-09, d. 2-2-95): British tennis player. Won three consecutive Wimbledon singles titles (1934–36), the last British man to win the tournament. Also won three U.S. titles (1933, '34, '36), one French title (1935) and one Australian title (1934).

Gaylord Perry (b. 9-15-38): Baseball RHP. First pitcher to win Cy Young Award in both leagues (Cleveland 1972, San Diego 1978). 314 career wins, 3,534 strikeouts. 20+ wins five times; 200+ strikeouts eight times; 250+ innings pitched 12 times. Pitched no-hitter in 1968. Admitted to throwing a spitter. Career span 1962–83 with eight teams.

Bob Pettit (b. 12-12-32): Basketball F. First player in history to break 20,000-point barrier (20,880 career points scored). 26.4 career scoring average; 16.2 rebound avg. MVP in 1956 and 1959; Rookie of the Year in 1955. All-Star 10 consecutive seasons. Led league in scoring two times, rebounding once. Career span 1954–64 with St. Louis.

Richard Petty (b. 7-2-37): Auto racer. Alltime leader in NASCAR victories (200). Seven-time Daytona 500 winner (1964, '66, '71, '73, '74, '79, '81) and NASCAR season points champion (1964, '67, '71, '72, '74, '75, '79), the most of any driver in both categories. First stock car racer to reach $1 million in earnings. Son of Lee Petty, three-time NASCAR champion. Retired after 1992 season.

Laffit Pincay Jr. (b. 12-29-46): Jockey. Only jockey with more than 9,000 career victories. Among the top money-winners of all time, with more than $215,000,000 in career earnings. Won five Eclipse Awards as outstanding jockey. Rode one Kentucky Derby winner (Swale), and three Belmont winners (Conquistador Cielo, Cavaet, Swale).

Scottie Pippen (b. 9-25-65): Basketball F. Won six NBA titles with Chicago (1991–93, 1996–98). Three-time first-team All-NBA (1994–96). Named to NBA's first-team All-Defensive team six times. Named MVP of the 1994 NBA All-Star Game. Member of 1992 and '96 gold medal-winning U.S. Olympic basketball teams. Career span 1987– with Chicago, Houston and Portland.

Jacques Plante (b. 1-17-29, d. 2-27-86): Hockey G. First goalie to wear a mask. Third alltime in wins (435) and second lowest modern goals against average (2.38). Goaltender of the Year seven times, more than any other goalie (consecutively 1955–59, '61, '68). Won MVP award in 1961. Led league in goals against average eight times, wins six times and shutouts four times. Was on six Stanley Cup champions with Montreal from 1952–62 and played for four other teams until retirement in 1972.

Gary Player (b. 11-1-35): South African golfer. Won the Masters (1961, '74, '78) and British Open (1959, '68, '74) three times each, PGA Championship two times (1962, '72) and U.S. Open (1965). Also won Seniors Championship three times (1986, '88, '90) and U.S. Senior Open two consecutive years (1987, '88).

Sam Pollock (b. 12-15-25): Hockey executive. As general manager of Montreal from 1964–78 won nine Stanley Cup championships (1965, '66, '68, '69, '71, '73, '76, '78).

Denis Potvin (b. 10-29-53): Hockey D. Seven-time All-Star during 15-season career (1973–88), all with New York Islanders. Won Calder Trophy for 1973–74 season. Won Norris Trophy three times. Captained Islanders to four Stanley Cup championships. Elected to Hall of Fame in 1991.

Mike Powell (b. 11-10-63): Track and field. Long jumper broke Bob Beamon's 23-year-old world record at 1991 World Championships in Tokyo with a jump of 29'4½". Won silver in 1992 Olympics.

Steve Prefontaine (b. 1-25-51, d. 5-30-75): Track and field. Distance runner killed in car accident at age 24. Held every American record from 2,000 meters to 10,000 meters at the time of his death. At age 21, finished fourth in the 5,000 meters at the 1972 Olympics in Munich after leading with less than 600 meters to go.

Annemarie Moser-Pröll (b. 3-27-53): Austrian skier. Gold medalist in downhill at 1980 Olympics. World Cup overall champion six times, more than any other skier (1971–75, '79).

Alain Prost (b. 2-24-55): French auto racer. Second alltime in Formula 1 victories (51). Formula 1 champion four times (1985–86, '89, '93).

Jack Ramsay (b. 2-21-25): Basketball coach. Coached 11 seasons at St. Joseph's University, with

234–72 record. Overall record of 864–783 as NBA coach. Coach of NBA champion 1977 Portland Trail Blazers. Elected to Hall of Fame 1992.

Jean Ratelle (b. 10-3-40): Hockey C. In 21-season career (1960–81) with the New York Rangers and Boston, scored 491 goals and had 776 assists. Twice won Lady Byng Trophy. Elected to Hockey Hall of Fame in 1985.

Willis Reed (b. 6-25-42): Basketball C. Most noted for his dramatic return to the court on 5-8-70, in the seventh and deciding game of the 1970 NBA Finals against Los Angeles. Playoff MVP of both New York championship teams, in 1970 and '73. NBA Rookie of Year in 1965. NBA MVP in 1970. Played 10 seasons (1965–74), all with New York. Career average of 18.7 points a game. Elected to Hall of Fame in 1981.

Harold Henry (Pee Wee) Reese (b. 7-23-18 d. 8-14-99): Baseball SS. Played for six pennant-winning Brooklyn teams. Led NL in runs scored in 1949, with 132. Career span 1940–58 with Brooklyn; .269 avg., 2,170 hits, 1,338 runs, 232 SB. Elected to Hall of Fame in 1984.

Mary Lou Retton (b. 1-24-68): Gymnast. Won all-around gold with a perfect 10 on her final vault at the 1984 Olympics in Los Angeles. Also won one silver and two bronze medals at those Games.

Grantland Rice (b. 11-1-1880, d. 7-13-54): Sportswriter. Legendary figure during sport's Golden Age of the 1920s. Wrote "For when the one great Scorer comes/ To write against your name/ He writes not that you won or lost/ But how you played the game." Also named the 1924–25 Notre Dame backfield the "Four Horsemen."

Jerry Rice (b. 10-13-62): Football WR. Alltime leader in touchdowns, touchdown receptions, receptions , receiving yards and in consecutive games with a TD reception (13 in 1988). Player of the Year in 1987 and led league in scoring (138 points on 23 touchdowns). Super Bowl MVP in 1989 with record 215 receiving yards on 11 catches. Also set Super Bowl record with three touchdown receptions in 1990 and in 1995. Career span 1985– with San Francisco and Oakland.

Henri Richard (b. 2-29-36): Hockey C. "The Pocket Rocket." Won 11 Stanley Cup championships with Montreal. Four-time All-Star. Career span 1955–75.

Maurice Richard (b. 8-4-21, d. 5-27-00): Hockey RW. "The Rocket." First player to score 50 goals in a season, in 1945. Led league in goals five times. 544 career goals. MVP in 1947. All-Star eight times. Tied playoff record for most goals in a game (five on March 23, 1944). Won eight Stanley Cups with Montreal 1942–59.

Bob Richards (b. 2-2-26): Track and field. The only pole vaulter to win gold medal at two consecutive Olympics (1952, '56). Also won Sullivan Award in 1951.

Branch Rickey (b. 12-20-1881, d. 12-9-65): Baseball executive. Integrated major league baseball in 1947 by signing Jackie Robinson to a contract with the Brooklyn Dodgers. Conceived of minor league farm system in 1919 at St. Louis; instituted batting cage and sliding pit.

Pat Riley (b. 3-20-45): Basketball coach. Coached Los Angeles to four NBA championships (1981, '85, '87, '88). Coach of the Year three times (1990, '93, '97) for three different teams. Led New York to NBA Finals in 1994. Coached teams to 50+ wins 13 years in a row. Coaching career 1984– with Los Angeles, New York and Miami.

Cal Ripken Jr. (b. 8-24-60): Baseball SS–3B. Broke Lou Gehrig's record for most consecutive games played (2,131) on 9-5-95; streak ended at 2,632 games on 9-20-98. Two-time AL MVP (1983, '91). Rookie of the Year in 1982. 19-time All-Star. Set record for consecutive errorless games by a shortstop (95 in 1990). Hit 20+ HRs in 10 consecutive seasons. Career span 1981–01 with Baltimore; .276 avg., 431 HR, 1,695 RBI, 3,184 hits.

Glenn (Fireball) Roberts (b. 1-20-31, d. 7-2-64): Auto racer. Won 34 NASCAR races. Died as a result of a fiery accident in the World 600 at Charlotte Motor Speedway in May 1964. At the time of his death Roberts had won more major races than any other driver in NASCAR history.

Oscar Robertson (b. 11-24-38): Basketball G. "The Big O." Only player in NBA history to average a triple-double for an entire season (1962). Rookie of the Year in 1961, MVP in 1964, and nine-time first-team All-NBA (1961–69). Led league in assists eight times. Averaged 30+ points six times in seven seasons. MVP of NBA All-Star three times (1961, '64, '69). Career span 1960–74 with Cincinnati and Milwaukee; 9,887 career assists; 26,710 points, 25.7 ppg. Also College Player of the Year, All-America and NCAA scoring leader three consecutive seasons from 1958–60 with Cincinnati. Third all-time NCAA highest scoring average (33.8).

Brooks Robinson (b. 5-18-37): Baseball 3B. Alltime leader in assists, putouts, double plays and fielding average among 3rd basemen. Won 16 consecutive Gold Gloves. Led league in fielding average a record 11 times. MVP in 1964—led league in RBI—and MVP in 1970 World Series. Career span 1955–77 with Baltimore; .267 avg, 2,848 hits, 1,357 RBI.

David Robinson (b. 8-6-65): Basketball C. "The Admiral." Three-time Olympian (1988, '92, '96), and 1995 NBA MVP. One of only two players to win an NBA rebounding title (1991), a blocked shots title (1992) and a scoring title (1994). Four-time first-team All-NBA. All-American at Navy where he led the NCAA in both rebounding (13.0) and blocked shots (5.91) in 1986. 1990 NBA Rookie of the Year. Career span 1989–2003 with San Antonio.

Eddie Robinson (b. 2-13-19): College football coach. Retired with alltime college record 408 career wins through 1941–97 at Division I-AA Grambling State.

Frank Robinson (b. 8-31-35): Baseball OF–manager. Only player to win MVP awards in both leagues (Cincinnati, 1961, Baltimore, 1966). Won Triple Crown and World Series MVP in 1966. Rookie of the Year in 1956. Fifth in career HR (586). Became first black manager in major leagues, with Cleveland in 1975. Career span 1956–76 with Cincinnati, Baltimore, Los Angeles, California and Cleveland; .294 avg., 1,812 RBI, 2,943 hits, 1,829 runs.

Jackie Robinson (b. 1-13-19, d. 10-24-72): Baseball 2B. Broke the color barrier as first black player in major leagues in 1947 with Brooklyn. 1947 Rookie of the Year; 1949 MVP with league-leading .342 batting average. Led league in stolen bases two times; stole home 19 times. Played on six pennant winners, Brooklyn, 1947–56; .311 avg., 137 HR, 947 runs, 197 SB. Elected to Hall of Fame in 1962. No. 42 retired by every team in the major leagues.

Larry Robinson (b. 6-2-51): Hockey D. Twice won Norris Trophy as NHL's top defenseman. Member of six Montreal teams that won Stanley Cup. Awarded Conn Smythe Trophy as MVP of 1978 Stanley Cup. Career span 1972–92, all but the last three with Montreal. Coached New Jersey to Stanley Cup in 2000.

Sugar Ray Robinson (b. 5-3-21, d. 4-12-89): Born Walker Smith Jr. Boxer. Called best pound-for-pound boxer ever. Welterweight champ (1946–51) and middleweight champ five times. Career record: 174-19-6 with 109 KOs from 1940–65. Won 91 consecutive bouts from 1943–51. Fifteen losses came after age 35.

Knute Rockne (b. 3-4-1888, d. 3-31-31): College football coach. Won national championship three times (1924, '29, '30). Alltime highest winning percentage (.881). Career record 105-12-5, including five undefeated seasons, with Notre Dame from 1918–30.

Bill Rodgers (b. 12-23-47): Track and field. Won the Boston and New York City marathons four times each between 1975–80.

Dennis Rodman (b. 5-13-61): Basketball F. Won seven consecutive NBA rebounding titles (1992–98). Won two NBA titles with Detroit (1989, '90) and three with Chicago (1996–98). NBA Defensive Player of the Year (1990, '91). Career span 1986–00, mostly with Detroit and Chicago; 7.3 ppg, 13.1 rpg.

Chi Chi Rodriguez (b. 10-23-35): Golfer. Led senior money list for 1987 ($509,145). Won eight events during PGA career that began in 1960.

Art Rooney (b. 1-27-01; d. 8-25-88): Owner of Pittsburgh Steelers. Bought team in 1933 and ran it until his death in 1988. Elected to Hall of Fame in 1964.

Murray Rose (b. 1-6-39) Australian swimmer. Won three gold medals (including 400- and 1,500-meter freestyle) at 1956 Olympics. Also won one gold, one silver and one bronze medal at 1960 Olympics.

Pete Rose (b. 4-14-41): Baseball OF-IF. "Charlie Hustle." Baseball's alltime hits leader (4,256), who was banned from the game for life in 1989 for his gambling activities and, thus, is ineligible for the Hall of Fame. Had 44-game hitting streak in 1978. 1963 Rookie of the Year; 1973 MVP; 1975 World Series MVP. Won three batting titles, and led the league in hits seven times, runs scored four times and doubles five times. Alltime leader in games played (3,562) and at bats (14,053); second in doubles (746); fifth in runs scored (2,165). Career span 1963–86 with Cincinnati, Philadelphia and Montreal; .303 avg., 160 HR, 1,314 RBI. Manager of Cincinnati from 1984–89. Served five-month jail term for tax evasion in 1990.

Ken Rosewall (b. 11-2-34): Australian tennis player. Won Grand Slam singles titles at ages 18 and 35. Won four Australian titles (1953, '55, '71, '72), two French titles (1953, '68) and two U.S. titles (1956, '70). Reached four Wimbledon finals, but title eluded him.

Art Ross (b. 1-13-1886, d. 8-5-64): Hockey D–coach. Improved design of puck and goal net. Manager-coach of Boston, 1924–45, won Stanley Cup, 1938–39. The Art Ross Trophy is awarded to the NHL scoring champion.

Donald Ross (b. 1873, d. 4-26-48): Scottish-born golf course architect. Trained at St. Andrews under Old Tom Morris. Designed over 500 courses, including Pinehurst No. 2 course and Oakland Hills.

Patrick Roy (b. 10-5-65): Hockey G. Retired as alltime leader in career wins for a goalie (551). Won Vezina Trophy three times. Won Conn Smythe Trophy three times (1986, '93, '01). Career span 1984–2003 with Montreal and Colorado.

Pete Rozelle (b. 3-1-26, d. 12-6-96): Football executive. Fourth NFL commissioner, served from 1960–89. During his term, league expanded from 12 to 28 teams. Created Super Bowl in 1966 and negotiated merger with AFL. Devised plan for revenue sharing of lucrative TV monies among owners. Presided during players' strikes of 1982 and '87.

Wilma Rudolph (b. 6-23-40, d. 11-12-94): Track and field. Gold medalist in three events (100 , 200 and 4 x100-meter relay) at 1960 Olympics. Also won Sullivan Award in 1961.

Adolph Rupp (b. 9-2-01, d. 12-10-77): College basketball coach. Second alltime in NCAA wins (876) and winning percentage (.822). Won four NCAA championships (1948, '49, '51, '58). Career span 1930–72 with Kentucky.

Amos Rusie (b. 5-3-1871, d. 12-6-42): Baseball RHP. Fastball was so intimidating that in 1893 the pitching mound was moved back 5' 6" to its present distance of 60' 6". Led league in strikeouts and walks five times each. Career record 246–174, 3.07 ERA with New York (NL) from 1889–1901.

Bill Russell (b. 2-12-34): Basketball C. Won MVP award five times (1958, 1961–63, '65). Played on 11 championship teams, eight consecutively, with Boston (1957, 1959–66, '68, '69). Player-coach 1968–69 (league's first black coach). Second alltime in career rebounds (21,620) and rebounding average (22.5); second-highest single-game rebounding total (51 in 1960). Led league in rebounding four times. Career span 1956–69 with Boston; 15.1 ppg, 4.3 apg. Also played on two NCAA championship teams with San Francisco in 1955–56; tournament MVP in 1955. Member of gold medal-winning 1956 Olympic team.

Babe Ruth (b. 2-6-1895, d. 8-16-48): Born George Herman Ruth. Baseball P–OF. "The Bambino," "The Sultan of Swat." Most dominant player in history. Alltime leader in slugging average (.690), HR frequency (8.5 HR every 100 at bats); retired with 714 home runs, 2,211 RBI, and 2,056 walks. Hit 54 HR in 1920, more than any other team in the American League. 1923 MVP. 60 HR in 1927, a record that stood for 34 years. Second alltime in World Series HR (15), including his "called shot" off Charlie Root in 1932. Began career as a pitcher: 94 career wins and 2.28 ERA. Won 20+ games two times; ERA leader in 1916. Played on 10 pennant winners, seven World Series winners (three with Boston, four with New York (AL)). Sold to Yankees in 1920 (Boston hasn't won World Series since). Career span 1914–35 with Boston, New York (AL) and Boston (NL); .342 avg., 2,873 hits.

Nolan Ryan (b. 1-31-47): Baseball RHP. Pitched seven no-hitters. Alltime leader in career strikeouts (5,714) and walks (2,795). League leader in strikeouts 11 times, shutouts three times, ERA two times. 300+ strikeouts six times, including season record of 383 in 1973. Career span 1966–93 with New York (NL), California, Houston and Texas; 324–292, 3.19 ERA. Elected to Hall of Fame 1999.

Jim Ryun (b. 4-29-47): Track and field. Youngest ever to run sub-four-minute mile (3:59.0 at 17 years, 37 days). Set two world records in mile (3:51.3 in 1966 and 3:51.1 in 1967) and one in 1,500 (3:33.1 in 1967). Plagued by bad luck at Olympics; won silver medal in

1968 1,500 meters despite mononucleosis; was bumped and fell in 1972. Won Sullivan Award in 1967.

Toni Sailer (b. 11-17-35): Austrian skier. Won gold medals in 1956 Olympics in slalom, giant slalom and downhill, the first skier to accomplish the feat.

Juan Antonio Samaranch (b. 7-17-20): Amateur sports executive. From 1980–01, Spaniard served as president of International Olympic Committee.

Pete Sampras (b. 8-12-71): Tennis player. Alltime leader in men's Grand Slam singles titles (14). First player in ATP rankings history to hold No. 1 ranking for six consecutive years. Won 64 tournament titles.

Joan Benoit Samuelson (b. 5-16-57): Track and field. Gold medalist in first ever women's Olympic marathon (1984). Won Boston Marathon two times (1979, '83). Sullivan Award winner in 1985.

Barry Sanders (b. 7-16-68): Football RB. Third player in NFL history to rush for over 2,000 yards (2,053 in 1997). Led league in rushing four times (1990, '94, '96, '97). Rushed for 1,000+ yards in each of his 10 pro seasons. Retired abruptly in 1999, ranked second alltime in career rushing yards (15,269). NCAA single-season leader in yards rushing (2,628 in 1988), when he won the Heisman Trophy at Oklahoma State.

Gene Sarazen (b. 2-27-02 d. 5-13-99): Golfer. Won PGA Championship three times (1922, '23, '33), U.S. Open two times (1922, '32), British Open once (1932) and the Masters once (1935). His win at the Masters included golf's most famous shot, a double eagle on the 15th hole of the final round. Won 38 career tournaments. Also won Seniors Championship two times (1954, '58). Pioneered the sand wedge in 1930.

Glen Sather (b. 9-2-43): Hockey coach and general manager. 464 regular season wins. Led Edmonton to four Stanley Cup championships (1984, '85, '87, '88) from 1979–89 and 1993–94. Also played for six teams from 1966–76.

Terry Sawchuk (b. 12-28-29, d. 5-31-70): Hockey G. Alltime leader in shutouts (103); second in wins (447). Career 2.52 goals against average. Goaltender of the Year two times (1951–52, '54, '64). Led league in wins and shutouts three times and goals against average two times. Rookie of the Year in 1950. Tied record of four playoff shutouts in 1952. Played on four Stanley Cup champions with Detroit and Toronto from 1949–69.

Gale Sayers (b. 5-30-43): Football RB. Alltime leader in kickoff return average (30.6). Scored 56 career touchdowns, including a rookie record 22 in 1965. Tied record with six touchdowns in one game on 12-12-65. Led league in rushing and gained 1,000+ yards rushing two times. Rookie of the Year in 1965. Career span 1965–71 with Chicago cut short due to knee injury. Also All-America two times with Kansas.

Dolph Schayes (b. 5-19-28): Basketball player. Retired as NBA's all-time leading scorer (19,249 pts). First-team All-NBA six times. Over stretch of 10 years played in 706 consecutive games. Career span 1948–64 with Syracuse and Philadelphia; 18.2 ppg. College star at NYU. Elected to Hall of Fame 1972.

Bo Schembechler (b. 4-1-29): Football coach. In 21 seasons at Michigan from 1969–89, had a 194-48-5 record. Overall college coaching record 234-65-8.

Mike Schmidt (b. 9-27-49): Baseball 3B. Won three MVP awards (1980, '81, '86). 548 career home runs. Led league in HR eight times, slugging average five times, and RBI and walks four times each. Won 10

Gold Gloves. Career span 1972–89 with Philadelphia; .267 avg., 1,506 runs, 1,595 RBI. Elected to the Hall of Fame in 1995.

Don Schollander (b. 4-30-46): Swimmer. Won four gold medals (including 100- and 400-meter freestyle) at 1964 Olympics; won one gold and one silver medal at 1968 Olympics. Also won Sullivan Award in 1964.

Dick Schultz (b. 9-5-29): Amateur sports executive. Second executive director of the NCAA, served from 1987–93. Also served as athletic director at Cornell (1976–81) and Virginia (1981–87).

Seattle Slew (b. 1974; d. 5-7-02): Thoroughbred race horse. Horse of the Year for 1977, when he won the Triple Crown, winning the Kentucky Derby by 1¾ lengths; the Preakness by 1½; and the Belmont by 4. In three-year career from 1976–78, won 14 of 17 starts.

Tom Seaver (b. 11-17-44): Baseball RHP. "Tom Terrific." 311 career wins, 2.86 ERA. Cy Young Award winner three times (1969, '73, '75) and Rookie of the Year 1967. Sixth alltime in career strikeouts (3,640). Led league in strikeouts five times, winning percentage four times and wins and ERA three times each. Won 20+ games five times; 200+ strikeouts 10 times. Struck out 19 batters in one game in 1970, including the final 10 in succession. Pitched no-hitter in 1978. Career span 1967–86 with New York (NL), Cincinnati, Chicago (AL), Boston.

Secretariat (b. 3-30-70, d. 10-4-89): Thoroughbred race horse. Triple Crown winner in 1973 with jockey Ron Turcotte aboard. Ran fastest Kentucky Derby and Belmont Stakes ever. Trained by Lucien Laurin.

Katja Seizinger (b. 5-10-72): German skier. Won downhill gold medals in 1994 at Lillehammer and '98 at Nagano. Won Giant Slalom bronze medal at Nagano. 1998 World Cup champion in downhill, Super G and overall. 32 World Cup victories in downhill and Super G.

Monica Seles (b. 12-2-73): Tennis player. Won three consecutive French Open singles titles (1990–92), four Australian Open titles (1991–93, '96) and two U.S. Open titles (1991, '92). Seles's 1993 season ended on 4-30 when she was stabbed in the back by Gunther Parche while seated during a changeover in a tournament in Hamburg, Germany; also missed 1994 season. Returned to tennis in 1995, reached U.S. Open final.

Bill Sharman (b. 5-25-26): Basketball G. First team All-Star four straight years 1956–59. Led NBA in free throw percentage every year from 1953–57, and in 1959 and '61. All-Star Game MVP in 1955. Career span 1950–61 with Washington and Boston; 17.8 ppg, 88.3 FT%. NBA Coach of the Year in 1972, when his Lakers won NBA title. Elected to Hall of Fame in 1974.

Wilbur Shaw (b. 10-31-02, d. 10-30-54): Auto racer. Won Indy 500 three times in four years (1937, '39, '40). AAA champion two times (1937, '39). Also pioneered the use of the crash helmet after suffering skull fracture in 1923 crash.

Patty Sheehan (b. 10-27-56): Golfer. Won back-to-back LPGA championships (1983, '84). Won 1992 and '94 U.S. Women's Opens, '93 LPGA title, '96 Nabisco. 1983 LPGA Player of Year. Vare Trophy winner in 1984. Qualified for Hall of Fame in 1993.

Fred Shero (b. 10-23-25, d. 11-24-90): Hockey coach. Fourth alltime highest winning percentage (.612). Led Philadelphia to two Stanley Cup championships (1974, '75). Former New York Rangers

defender (1947–50) coached Philadelphia and New York from 1971–81; 390-225-119.

Bill Shoemaker (b. 8-19-31 d. 10-12-03): Horse racing jockey. Second alltime in wins (8,833). Rode Belmont Stakes winner five times (1957, '59, '62, '67, '75), Kentucky Derby winner four times (1955, '59, '65, '86—at age 54, the oldest jockey to win Derby) and Preakness Stakes winner two times (1963, '67). Also won Eclipse Award in 1981.

Eddie Shore (b. 11-25-02, d. 3-16-85): Hockey D. Won MVP award four times (1933, '35, '36, '38). All-Star seven times. Played on two Stanley Cup champions with Boston from 1926–40.

Frank Shorter (b. 10-31-47): Track and field. Gold medalist in marathon at 1972 Olympics, the first American to win the event since 1908. Olympic silver medalist in 1976 marathon. Sullivan Award winner in 1972.

Jim Shoulders (b. 5-13-28): Rodeo. 16 career titles. All-Around champion five times (1949, 1956–59).

Don Shula (b. 1-4-30): Football coach. Retired as alltime NFL leader in wins (347). Won two consecutive Super Bowl championships (1972, '73) with Miami, including NFL's only undefeated season in 1972. Also reached Super Bowl four other times. Career span 1963–95 with Baltimore and Miami.

Al Simmons (b. 5-22-02; d. 5-26-56): Baseball OF. "Bucketfoot Al" for hitting stance. Named AL MVP in 1929, when he led league with 157 RBI. Led league in batting average in 1930 (.381) and '31 (.390). Career span 1924–44 with several teams, including Philadelphia (AL); .334 avg., 307 HR. Elected to Hall of Fame in 1953.

O.J. Simpson (b. 7-9-47): Born Orenthal James. Football RB. "Juice." First man to top 2,000 yards rushing in one season (2,003 in 1973). 11,236 career yards rushing. Led league in rushing four times. Gained 1,000+ yards rushing five consecutive seasons. Player of the Year three times (1972, '73, '75). Gained 200+ yards rushing in a game a record six times. Scored 61 career touchdowns, including 23 in 1975. Also won Heisman Trophy with USC in 1968.

Sir Barton (b. 1916, d. 1937): Thoroughbred. In 1919, before they were linked as the Triple Crown, became first horse to win the Kentucky Derby, the Preakness and the Belmont. Won eight of 13 starts as 3-year-old.

George Sisler (b. 3-24-1893, d. 3-26-73): Baseball 1B. Set the alltime record in 1920 with 257 hits in one season. League leader in hits two times, banged out 200+ hits six times. Won two batting titles, including the 1922 crown with a .420 average; averaged .400+ two times and .300+ 11 other times. Career span 1915–30 with St. Louis (NL); .340 avg. and 2,812 hits.

Mary Decker Slaney (b. 8-4-58): Track and field. American record holder in five events ranging from 800 to 3,000 meters. Won 1,500 and 3,000 meters at World Championships in 1983. Lost chance for medal at 1984 Olympics when she tripped and fell after contact with Zola Budd. Won Sullivan Award in 1982. Competed in 1996 Olympics at age 37.

Bruce Smith (b. 6-18-63): Football DE. Second alltime in NFL sacks (186). Played in four consecutive Super Bowls with Buffalo (1991–94), all losses. Career span 1985– with Buffalo and Washington.

Dean Smith (b. 2-28-31): College basketball coach. Alltime leader in wins (879); seventh alltime highest winning percentage (.776). Alltime most NCAA tournament appearances (27), reached Final Four 11 times. Won NCAA championship in 1982 and '93. Coached 1976 Olympic team to gold medal. Career span 1962–97 with North Carolina. 1997 *Sports Illustrated* Sportsman of the Year.

Emmitt Smith (b. 5-15-69): Football RB. Led NFL in rushing four times (1991, '92 , '93, '95). Set NFL record with 25 TDs in 1995. Named MVP of Super Bowl XXVIII, when he ran for 132 yards in a 30–13 Dallas victory over Buffalo. Career span 1990–2002 with Dallas, 2003– Arizona; in 2002, passed Walter Payton as the NFL's alltime leading rusher.

Ozzie Smith (b. 12-26-54): Baseball SS. "The Wizard of Oz." May be the best defensive shortstop in history. Holds alltime record for most assists in a season among shortstops (621 in 1980). Career double-play and assist leader among shortstops. 14-time All-Star. Won 13 consecutive Gold Gloves. Career span 1978–96 with San Diego and St. Louis; .262 avg., 2,460 hits, 580 SB.

Red Smith (b. 9-25-05, d. 1-15-82): Sportswriter. Won Pulitzer Prize in 1976. After Grantland Rice, the most widely syndicated sports columnist. His literary essays appeared in the *New York Herald Tribune* from 1945–71 and the *New York Times* from 1971–82.

Stan Smith (b. 12-14-46): Tennis. Won 39 tournaments in career, including 1972 Wimbledon in five sets over Ilie Nastase. Won 1971 U.S. Open over Jan Kodes and amateur version of U.S. Open in 1969. 1970 won inaugural Grand Prix Masters. Inducted to Tennis Hall of Fame in 1987.

Tommie Smith (b. 6-5-44): Track and field. Won 1968 Olympic 200 meters in world record of 19.83, then was expelled from Olympic Village, along with bronze medalist John Carlos, for raising black-gloved fist and bowing head during playing of national anthem to protest racism in U.S.

Conn Smythe (b. 2-1-1895, d. 11-18-80): Hockey executive. As general manager with Toronto from 1929–61 won seven Stanley Cup championships (1932, '42, '45, '47–49, '51). Award for playoff MVP named in his honor.

Sam Snead (b. 5-27-12, 5-23-02): Golfer. Alltime leader in career wins (81). Won the Masters (1949, '52, '54) and PGA Championship (1942, '49, '51) three times each and British Open (1946). Runner-up at U.S. Open four times, but title eluded him. PGA Player of the Year in 1949. Won Seniors Championship six times, more than any golfer (1964, '65, '67, '70, '72, '73).

Peter Snell (b. 12-17-38): Track and field. New Zealand runner was gold medalist in 800 meters at two consecutive Olympics (1960 and 1964). Also gold medalist in 1,500 meters at 1964 Olympics. Twice broke world mile record; broke world 800 record once.

Duke Snider (b. 9-19-26): Baseball OF. Holds NL record with 11 home runs and 26 RBI in World Series play. Played on six pennant winners with Brooklyn. Hit 40+ HR five consecutive seasons and 100+ RBI six times. Career span 1947–64 with Brooklyn/LA, New York (NL) and San Francisco; .295 average, 407 HR and 1,333 RBI.

Sammy Sosa (b. 11-12-68): Baseball RF. Followed Mark McGwire in eclipsing Roger Maris's single-season HR mark in 1998. Lost HR race to McGwire that season but won MVP with .308 average, 66 HR, 134 runs, 158 RBI. In 2001, became first man to hit 60+ home runs in three seasons. Career span 1989– with Texas, Chicago (AL) and Chicago (NL).

Javier Sotomayor (b. 10-13-67): Track and field. Cuban high jumper broke the 8-foot barrier with world record jump of 8' 0" in 1989. Set record of 8' ½" in 7-27-93 in Salamanca, Spain.

Warren Spahn (b. 4-23-21): Baseball LHP. Alltime leader in wins by a lefthander (363); 20+ wins 13 times. League leader in wins eight times, complete games nine times, strikeouts four consecutive seasons, innings pitched four times and ERA three times. 1957 Cy Young award. 63 career shutouts. Pitched two no-hitters after age 39. Career span 1942–65, all but last year with Boston/Milwaukee Braves.

Tris Speaker (b. 4-4-1888, d. 12-8-58): Baseball OF. Alltime leader in doubles (792), fifth in hits (3,514) and fifth in batting average (.345). One batting title (.386 in 1916), but .375+ average six times. League leader in doubles eight times, hits two times and HR and RBI one time each. 200+ hits four times, 40+ doubles 10 times and 100+ runs scored seven times. MVP in 1912. Career span 1907–28, mostly with Boston (AL) and Cleveland.

Michael Spinks (b. 7-13-56): Boxer. Defeated Larry Holmes for the heavyweight championship of the world on 9-22-85. Lost title to Mike Tyson in 91 seconds on 6-27-88. Won world light heavyweight title on 7-18-81 and defended it nine times before moving up to heavyweight division. 1976 Olympic middleweight champion.

Mark Spitz (b. 2-10-50): Swimmer. Won a record seven gold medals (two in freestyle, two in butterfly, three in relays) at 1972 Olympics, setting world record in each event. Also won two gold medals, one silver and one bronze medal at 1968 Olympics. Sullivan Award winner in 1971.

Amos Alonzo Stagg (b. 8-16-1862, d. 3-17-65): College football coach. 314 career wins. Won national title with Chicago in 1905. Coach of the Year with Pacific in 1943 at age 81. Five undefeated seasons. Career span 1892–46. Only person elected to both college football and basketball Halls of Fame. Played in the first basketball game in 1891.

Willie Stargell (b. 3-6-40, d. 4-9-01): Baseball OF–1B. "Pops" achieved a 1979 MVP triple crown, winning NL regular season, playoff and World Series MVP awards. Led NL in homers in 1971 and '73. Career span 1962–82 with Pittsburgh; .282 avg., 475 HR, 1,540 RBI. Elected to Hall of Fame in 1988.

Bart Starr (b. 1-9-34): Football QB. Played on three NFL champions (1961, '62, '65) and first two Super Bowl champions (1966, '67) with Green Bay. Also named MVP of first two Super Bowls. Player of the Year in 1966. League leader in passing three times. Career span 1956–71 with Green Bay; 24,718 passing yards, 152 TDs. Also coached Green Bay to 53-77-3 record from 1975–83.

Roger Staubach (b. 2-5-42): Football QB. Led Dallas to six NFC Championships, four Super Bowls and two Super Bowl titles (1971, '77). Player of the Year and Super Bowl MVP in 1971. Also led league in passing four times. Won Heisman Trophy with Navy as a junior in 1963. Served four-year military obligation before turning pro. Career span 1969–79 with Dallas; 22,700 passing yards, 153 TDs passing.

Jan Stenerud (b. 11-26-42): Football K. Scored 1,699 career NFL points. Converted 373 field goals in

558 attempts. Career span 1967–85 with Kansas City, Green Bay and Minnesota. First pure kicker inducted to Hall of Fame, 1991.

Casey Stengel (b. 7-30-1890, d. 9-29-75): Baseball manager. "The Ol' Perfesser." Managed New York (AL) to 10 pennants and seven World Series titles (five consecutively) in 12 years from 1949–60. Alltime leader in World Series games (63), wins (37) and losses (26). Platoon system was his trademark strategy, Stengelese his trademark language ("You could look it up."). Managed New York (NL) from 1962–65. Jersey number (37) retired by Yankees and Mets. Career mark: 1,905-1,842 (.508).

Ingemar Stenmark (b. 3-18-56): Swedish skier. Gold medalist in slalom and giant slalom at 1980 Olympics. World Cup overall champion three consecutive years (1976–78).

Woody Stephens (b. 9-1-13 d. 8-22-98): Horse racing trainer. Trained two Kentucky Derby winners (Cannonade, who won the 100th Derby in 1974 and Swale in 1984) and five straight Belmont winners from 1982–86, starting with 1982 Horse of the Year Conquistador Cielo.

David Stern (b. 9-22-42): Fourth NBA commissioner. Has served since 1984. Oversaw unprecedented growth of league. Owners rewarded him with five-year, $40-million contract extension in 1996.

Jackie Stewart (b. 6-11-39): Scottish auto racer. Fifth alltime in Formula 1 victories (27); Formula 1 champion three times (1969, '71, '73). Also Indy 500 Rookie of the Year in 1966. Retired in 1973.

Payne Stewart (b. 1-3-57, d. 10-25-99): Golfer. Two-time U.S. Open champion (1991, '99), also won 1989 PGA Championship. Killed in plane crash.

John Stockton (b. 3-26-62): Basketball G. Alltime leader in assists (15,177) and steals (3,128). Set single-season assist record (1,164) in 1990–91. Led NBA in assists a record nine consecutive times (1988–96). 10-time All-Star, consecutively 1989–97, 2000. Co-MVP (with Karl Malone) of 1993 All-Star Game. Member of 1992 and '96 Olympic teams. Career span 1984–2003 with Utah; 13.2 ppg, 10.7 rpg.

Picabo Street (b. 4-3-71): Skier. Won silver medal in downhill at 1994 Olympics in Lillehammer and gold in Super G at '98 Games in Nagano. World Cup downhill champion in 1995 and '96. Nine career World Cup victories.

John L. Sullivan (b. 10-15-1858, d. 2-2-18): Boxer. Last bareknuckle champion. Heavyweight title holder (1882–92), lost to Jim Corbett. Career record 38-1-3 with 33 KOs from 1878–92.

Paul Tagliabue (b. 11-24-40): Football executive. Fifth NFL commissioner, has served since 1989.

Anatoli Tarasov (b. 1918, d. 6-23-95): Hockey coach. Orchestrated Soviet Union's emergence as a hockey power. Won nine consecutive world amateur championships (1963–71) and three Olympic gold medals in 1964, '68, '72.

Fran Tarkenton (b. 2-3-40): Football QB. Hall of Famer retired with 342 touchdown passes, 47,003 yards passing, 6,467 pass attempts and 3,686 pass completions. Player of the Year in 1975. Career span 1961–78 with Minnesota, New York Giants.

Lawrence Taylor (b. 2-4-59): Football LB. Revolutionized the linebacker position. Retired as the alltime leader in sacks. Named to Pro Bowl a record 10 consecutive seasons. Player of the Year in 1986.

Played on two Super Bowl champions with New York Giants (1986, '90). Career span 1981–93 with New York. Elected to Hall of Fame 1999.

Isiah Thomas (b. 4-30-61): Basketball G. Point guard for Detroit team that won NBA title in 1989 and '90. All-NBA First Team 1984–86. NBA All-Star Game MVP in 1984 and '86. Led NBA in assists (13.9) in 1984–85. Fifth alltime in assists (9,061). Career span 1981–94 with Detroit; 19.2 ppg, 9.3 apg. GM of Toronto Raptors 1995–97. Coached Indiana Pacers 2000–03. Member of Indiana University team that won 1981 NCAA title.

Thurman Thomas (b. 5-15-66): Football RB. Rushed for 1,000+ yards eight years in a row (1989–96). Led AFC in rushing in 1990 and 1991. Career span 1988–01 with Buffalo and Miami; 12,074 yards, 88 TDs.

Daley Thompson (b. 7-30-58): Track and field. British decathlete was gold medalist at two consecutive Olympics in 1980 and '84. At 1984 Olympics set world record (8,847 points) that lasted eight years.

John Thompson (b. 9-2-41): College basketball coach. Former Boston Celtic coached at Georgetown (1973–99), where he mentored Patrick Ewing, Alonzo Mourning and Dikembe Mutombo. Won NCAA title in 1984, runner-up in '82 and '85. Career record: 596–239.

Bobby Thomson (b. 10-25-23): Baseball OF. Three-time All-Star who hit dramatic "shot heard 'round the world" off of Ralph Branca to win NL pennant for New York (NL) in 1951. The Giants had come from 13½ games behind to tie Brooklyn and force a three-game playoff. Career span 1946–60 with New York (NL), Milwaukee, Chicago (NL), Boston and Baltimore; .270, 264 HR, 1,026 RBI.

Jim Thorpe (b. 5-28-1888, d. 3-28-53): Sportsman. Gold medalist in decathlon and pentathlon at 1912 Olympics. Played pro baseball with New York (NL) and Cincinnati 1913–19, and pro football with several teams 1919–26. Stripped of gold medals when it was discovered he had played pro baseball, and they were restored only after his death. Also All-America two times with Carlisle.

Dick Tiger (b. 8-14-29; d. 12-14-71): Nigerian boxer. Born Richard Ihetu. Two-time middleweight champ, also won light heavyweight title. Fighter of the Year for 1962 and '65. Elected to Boxing Hall of Fame 1974.

Bill Tilden (b. 2-10-1893, d. 6-5-53): Tennis player. "Big Bill." Won seven U.S. singles titles, six consecutively (1920–25, '29) and three Wimbledon titles (1920, '21, '30). Also won six Grand Slam doubles titles. Led U.S. to seven consecutive Davis Cup victories (1920–26).

Ted Tinling (b. 6-23-10, d. 5-23-90): British tennis couturier. The premier source of women's tennis fashion, from Suzanne Lenglen to Steffi Graf—most notable creation: the frilled lace panties worn by Gorgeous Gussy Moran at Wimbledon in 1949.

Y.A. Tittle (b. 10-24-26): Football QB. Two-time NFL Most Valuable Player (1961, '63). Set NFL record with 36 TD passes in 1963. Career span 1948–64 with Baltimore, San Francisco and New York Giants; 33,070 yards, 242 TD. Inducted into Hall of Fame 1971.

Jayne Torvill/Christopher Dean (b. 10-7-57/ b. 7-27-58): British figure skaters. Won four consecutive ice dancing world championships (1981–84) and

Olympic ice dancing gold medal (1984). Won world professional championships in 1985. Won Olympic ice dancing bronze in 1994.

Vladislav Tretiak (b. 4-25-52): Hockey G. Led USSR to gold medals at Olympics in 1972, '76, '84. Played on 13 world amateur champions from 1970–84.

Lee Trevino (b. 12-1-39): Golfer. Won U.S. Open (1968, '71), British Open (1971, '72) and PGA Championship (1974, '84) two times each. PGA Player of the Year in 1971. Also won U.S. Senior Open in 1990. First Senior $1 million season.

Emlen Tunnell (b. 3-29-25, d. 7-23-75): Football S. Alltime leader in interception return yardage with 1,282 and second in interceptions (79). All-Pro nine times. Career span 1948–61 with New York Giants and Green Bay.

Gene Tunney (b. 5-25-1897, d. 11-7-78): Boxer. Heavyweight champion (1926–28). Defeated Jack Dempsey two times, including famous "long count" bout. Career record 65-2-1 with 43 KOs from 1915–28. Retired as champion.

Ted Turner (b. 11-19-38): Sportsman. Skipper who successfully defended the America's Cup in 1977. Also owner of the Atlanta Braves since 1976 and Hawks since '77. Founded the Goodwill Games in 1986.

Mike Tyson (b. 6-30-66): Boxer. Became boxing's youngest heavyweight champion (20 years, 144 days) by knocking out Trevor Berbick in 1986. Lost crown in devastating upset to James (Buster) Douglas in 1990. Served three years in prison (1992–95) for rape. Regained piece of heavyweight title but lost it to Evander Holyfield in 1996. He "lost it" again in their rematch in 1997, when he was disqualified for biting Holyfield's ears.

Johnny Unitas (b. 5-7-33, d. 9-11-02): Football QB. Set record by throwing TD passes in 47 consecutive games (1956–60). Three-time NFL MVP (1959, '64, '67). Led league in TD passes four consecutive seasons. Career span 1956–72 with Baltimore and San Diego; 290 TD passes, 40,239 passing yards.

Al Unser Sr. (b. 5-29-39): Auto racer. Won Indy 500 four times (1970, '71, '78, '87). Retired with 39 career CART victories. USAC/CART champion three times (1970, '83, '85). Brother of Bobby.

Bobby Unser (b. 2-20-34): Auto racer. Won Indianapolis 500 three times (1968, '75, '81). Retired with 35 career victories. USAC champion twice (1968, '74). Brother of Al Sr.

Harold S. Vanderbilt (b. 7-6-1884, d. 7-4-70): Sailor. Owner and skipper who successfully defended the America's Cup three consecutive times, in 1930, '34 and '37.

Glenna Collett Vare (b. 6-20-03, d. 2-2-89): Golfer. Won U.S. Women's Amateur six times, more than any golfer (1922, '25, '28-30, '35).

Bill Veeck (b. 2-9-14, d. 1-2-86): Baseball owner. From 1946–80, owned ballclubs in Cleveland, St. Louis (AL) and Chicago (AL). In 1948, Cleveland became baseball's first team to draw two million in attendance. That year Veeck integrated AL by signing Larry Doby and Satchel Paige. A brilliant promoter, Veeck sent midget Eddie Gaedel up to bat for St. Louis in 1951.

Guillermo Vilas (b. 8-17-52): Tennis. Argentine won 50 straight matches in 1977. In '77 won French Open, where he beat Brian Gottfried, and the U.S. Open,

where he beat Jimmy Connors. Also won Australian Open twice, 1978–79.

Lasse Viren (b. 7-22-49): Track and field. Finnish runner was gold medalist in 5,000 and 10,000 meters at two consecutive Olympics (1972, '76).

Virginia Wade (b. 7-10-45): Tennis. Beloved in Britain, Wade won three major titles, most notably Wimbledon in 1977, its centenary year, where she triumphed over Betty Stove. Also won 1968 U.S. Open, '72 Australian Open, and doubles titles in '73 at the Australian, French and U.S. Opens, all with Margaret Smith Court.

Honus Wagner (b. 2-24-1874, d. 12-6-55): Baseball SS. Had .327 career batting average, 3,415 hits and eight batting titles. Averaged .300+ 15 consecutive seasons. Led league in RBI four times, with 100+ RBI nine times. Third alltime in triples (252) and league leader in doubles eight times. 703 career stolen bases, league leader in steals five times. Career span 1897–1917 with Pittsburgh.

Grete Waitz (b. 10-1-53): Track and field. Norwegian runner won New York City Marathon a record nine times (1978–80, '82–86, '88). Won the women's marathon at the 1983 World Championship.

Jersey Joe Walcott (b. 10-31-14, d. 2-25-94): Boxer. Heavyweight champion from 1951–52. Won title at age 37 on fifth attempt before surrendering it to Rocky Marciano. Later became sheriff of Camden, NJ.

Doak Walker (b. 1-1-27, d. 9-27-98): Football HB. Led NFL in scoring two times, his first and final seasons. All-Pro five times. Played on two consecutive NFL champions (1952–53) with Detroit. Career span 1950–55. Also won Heisman Trophy as a junior in 1948. All-America three consecutive seasons with SMU.

Herschel Walker (b. 3-3-62): Football RB. 1982 Heisman Trophy winner signed with the New Jersey Generals of the USFL in '83. Gained 5,562 rushing yards and scored 61 touchdowns in three seasons before league folded. Entered NFL in 1986 with Dallas and led league in rushing yards in 1988. Career span 1983–97 with New Jersey (USFL), Dallas, Minnesota, Philadelphia and New York Giants; 13,787 rushing yards and 143 TD (both leagues).

Bill Walsh (b. 11-30-31): Football coach. Led San Francisco to three Super Bowl wins, after the 1981, '84, '88 seasons. Career record with 49ers from 1979–88, 102-63-1. Perfected short-passing offense with quarterback Joe Montana.

Bill Walton (b. 11-5-52): Basketball C. College Player of the Year three consecutive seasons (1972–74). Played on two NCAA championship teams (1972, '73) with UCLA; tournament MVP twice (1972, '73). Sullivan Award winner in 1973. NBA MVP in 1978, playoff MVP in '77. Led league in rebounding and blocks in 1977. Career span 1974–86 with Portland, San Diego and Boston; 13.3 ppg, 10.5 rpg.

War Admiral (b. 1934, d. 1959): Thoroughbred race horse. A son of Man o' War, won Triple Crown and Horse of the Year honors in 1937.

Paul Warfield (b. 11-28-42): Football WR. Five-time All-NFL, averaged sensational 20.1 yards per catch during his career. Played on two Super Bowl–winning Miami teams. Career span 1964–77 with Cleveland and Miami; 427 receptions for 8,565 yards and 85 TDs. Inducted to Hall of Fame 1983.

Glenn (Pop) Warner (b. 4-5-1871, d. 9-7-54): College football coach. Fourth alltime in wins (319). Won three national championships with Pittsburgh (1916, '18) and Stanford (1926). Career record 319-106-32 with six teams from 1896–38.

Tom Watson (b. 9-4-49): Golfer. Winner of British Open five times (1975, '77, '80, '82, '83), the Masters two times (1977, '81) and U.S. Open once (1982). PGA Player of the Year six times, more than any golfer (1977–80, '82, '84).

Dick Weber (b. 12-23-29): Bowler. Won All-Star Tournament four times (1962, '63, '65, '66). Voted Bowler of the Year three times (1961, '63, '65). Won 31 career PBA titles.

Johnny Weismuller (b. 6-2-04, d. 1-21-84): Swimmer. Won three gold medals (including 100- and 400-meter freestyle) at 1924 Olympics and two gold medals at the 1928 Olympics. Also played Tarzan in the movies.

Jerry West (b. 5-28-38): Basketball G. "Mr. Clutch." 10 time first-team All-NBA; All-Defensive Team four times; 1969 playoff MVP. Led league in assists and scoring one time each. Career span 1960–72 with Los Angeles; 27.0 ppg, 6.7 apg. All-America two times with West Virginia. Played on 1960 gold medal-winning Olympic team. Guided the Lakers to seven NBA championships as either a general manager or a consultant from 1980 to 2001.

Whirlaway (b. 4-2-38, d. 4-6-53): Thoroughbred race horse. Triple Crown winner in 1941 with jockey Eddie Arcaro aboard. Trained by Ben A. Jones.

Byron (Whizzer) White (b. 6-8-17, d. 4-15-02): Football RB. Led NFL in rushing two times (Pittsburgh in 1938, Detroit in '40). Led NCAA in scoring and rushing with Colorado in 1937; named All-America. United States Supreme Court justice 1962–93.

Reggie White (b. 12-19-62): Football DE. "Minister of Defense." Alltime leader in sacks (198). Set a Super Bowl record with three sacks against New England in Super Bowl XXXI. He played in 13 Pro Bowls. Career span: 1984–01 with Memphis Showboats (USFL), Philadelphia, Green Bay and Carolina.

Charles Whittingham (b. 4-13-13 d. 4-20-99): Thoroughbred race horse trainer. Nicknamed "Bald Eagle" after losing his hair to tropical disease in World War II. Led yearly earnings list for trainers in 1970–73, '75, '81, '82. Won three Eclipse Awards and trained two Horses of the Year (Ack Ack in 1971 and Ferdinand in 1987).

Kathy Whitworth (b. 9-27-39): Golfer. Alltime LPGA leader with 88 tour victories, including six majors. Won LPGA Championship in 1967, '71 and '75. Won Titleholders Championship (extinct major) in 1965 and '66. Won Western Open (extinct major) in 1967. Won Vare Trophy every year from 1965–72, except '68. LPGA Player of Year from 1966–69 and 1971–73.

Hoyt Wilhelm (b. 7-26-23): Baseball RHP. Hall of Famer. Threw knuckleball until age 48. Career 2.52 ERA, 227 saves. Hit home run in his first at bat (never hit another) and pitched no-hitter in 1958. Career span 1952–72 with nine teams.

Bud Wilkinson (b. 4-23-15 d. 2-9-94): Football coach. Coached Oklahoma to NCAA record 47 consecutive wins (1953–57). Won three national championships (1950, '55, '56) with Oklahoma, where he coached from 1947–1963. Won Orange Bowl four times and Sugar Bowl two times. Career record 145-

29-4, including four undefeated seasons. Also coached St. Louis of NFL in 1978–79.

Billy Williams (b. 6-15-38): Baseball OF. "Sweet Swinging." Six-time All-Star and the 1961 NL Rookie of the Year. Career span 1959–76 with Chicago (NL) and Oakland; .290 avg., 426 HR, 1,475 RBI. Elected to Hall of Fame in 1987.

Ted Williams (b. 8-30-18, d. 7-5-02): Baseball OF. "The Splendid Splinter." Last player to hit .400 (.406 in 1941). MVP in 1946, '49 and Triple Crown winner in 1942, '47. Sixth in career batting average (.344), third in walks (2,019) and second in slugging average (.634). Won six AL batting titles, and led the league in HR and RBI four times each. Had .300+ average 15 consecutive seasons; 100+ RBI and runs scored nine times each; 30+ HR eight times; and 100+ walks 11 times. Lost nearly five seasons to military service. Career span 1939–42 and 1946–60 with Boston; 521 career HR.

Hack Wilson (b. 4-26-1900; d. 11-23-48): Baseball OF. Stood 5' 6" but weighed 210. Had five astounding seasons 1926–30, before alcohol ruined his career. Best was 1930 when he hit .356, scored 146 runs, hit a NL record 56 homers and drove in 190, which is still the major league record. Career span 1923–34 with several teams. Elected to Hall of Fame in 1979.

Dave Winfield (b. 10-3-51): Baseball OF. Drafted out of Univ. of Minnesota by baseball, basketball and football teams. Drove in 100+ runs eight times, and led the NL in 1979 with 118. Derided by George Steinbrenner as "Mr. May," but hit clutch double to win 1992 World Series for Toronto. Career span 1973–95 with San Diego, New York (AL), California, Toronto, Minnesota and Cleveland; .283 avg., 465 HR, 3,110 hits, 1,833 RBI and 1,669 runs. Inducted into Hall of Fame in 2001.

Major W.C. Wingfield (b. 10-16-1833, d. 4-18-12): British tennis pioneer. Credited with inventing the game of tennis, which he called "Sphairistike" or "sticky" and patented in February 1874.

Colonel Matt Winn (b. 6-30-1861, d. 10-6-49): General manager of Churchill Downs from 1904 until his death; made Kentucky Derby premier U.S. race.

Katarina Witt (b. 12-3-65): East German figure skater. Gold medalist at 1984 and '88 Olympics. Also world champion four times (1984, '85, '87, '88).

John Wooden (b. 10-14-10): College basketball coach. Coached UCLA to 10 NCAA championships in 12 years (1964, '65, '67–73, '75). Record winning streak of 88 games (1971–74). 664 career wins and fourth highest career winning percentage (.804). First member of basketball Hall of Fame as coach and player. Career span 1949–75 with UCLA. 1932 College Player of the Year at Purdue.

Tiger Woods (b. 12-30-75): Golfer. Produced the Tiger Slam in 2000–01, an unofficial Grand Slam during which he won four consecutive professional majors. Holds the tournament record for best scores at the Masters, the U.S. Open, the PGA Championship and the British Open. Became the youngest winner of the Masters in 1997, when he shot a record-270 to win by a record 12 strokes. Became the youngest player to win all four major tournaments ('99 PGA, '00 U.S. Open, '00 British Open). Also won three straight U.S. Junior Amateur titles (1991–93) and three straight U.S. Amateur titles (1994–96). Then took the PGA tour by storm, winning six of his first 21 tournaments. Already has 34 PGA Tour victories (including eight majors) and has won more money ($32,687,252) than any golfer in history. 1996 and 2000 *Sports Illustrated* Sportsman of the Year.

Mickey Wright (b. 2-14-35): Golfer. Second alltime in career wins (82) and major championships (13; tied with Louise Suggs). Won the U.S. Open four times (1958, '59, '61, '64), the LPGA Championship four times (1958, '60, '61, '63), and the Western Open three times (1962, '63, '66).

Kristi Yamaguchi (b.7-12-71): Figure skater. Olympic champion in 1992. Back-to-back world champion (1991, '92).

Cale Yarborough (b. 3-27-40): Auto racer. Won Daytona 500 four times (1968, '77, '83, '84). 83 career victories. NASCAR champion three consecutive years (1976–78).

Carl Yastrzemski (b. 8-22-39): Baseball OF. "Yaz." 1967 MVP and Triple Crown winner. Three batting titles. Second alltime in games played (3,308) and sixth in walks (1,845). Career span 1961–83 with Boston; .285 avg., 3,419 hits, 452 HR and 1,844 RBI.

Cy Young (b. 3-29-1867, d. 11-4-55): Baseball RHP. Alltime leader in wins (511), innings pitched (7,354⅔) and complete games (749); fourth in shutouts (76). Had 2.63 career ERA. Pitched three no-hitters, including a perfect game in 1904. Career span 1890–1911 with Cleveland and Boston (AL).

Steve Young (b. 10-11-61): Football QB. Highest rated passer in NFL history, with 96.8 rating. Led the league in passing six times. Led 49ers to victory in Super Bowl XXIX of which he was MVP for tossing a record six TD passes. Two-time NFL MVP (1992 and '94). Repeated concussions forced his retirement in 2000. Career span 1984–00 with Los Angeles Express (USFL), Tampa Bay and San Francisco; 33,124 yards, 232 TD passes; rushed for 43 TD.

Robin Yount (b. 9-16-55): Baseball OF–SS. Won AL MVP as a shortstop (1982) and a centerfielder (1989). Became Milwaukee's shortstop at 18. Career span 1974–93 with Milwaukee; .285 avg., 3,142 hits, 251 HR and 583 2B. Elected to Hall of Fame 1999.

Steve Yzerman (b. 5-9-65): Hockey C. Won three Stanley Cups with Red Wings (1997, '98, '02). Won Conn Smythe trophy in 1998. Scored 100+ points six consecutive seasons (1987–93). Career span 1983– with Detroit.

Babe Didrikson Zaharias (b. 6-26-14, d. 9-27-56): Sportswoman. Commonly called the greatest female athlete of all time, Zaharias was the Gold medalist in the 80-meter hurdles and javelin throw at the 1932 Olympics; she also won the silver medal in the high jump (her gold medal jump was disallowed for using the then-illegal western roll). Became a golfer in 1935 and won 12 major titles, including U.S. Open three times (1948, '50, '54—a year after cancer surgery). Also helped found the LPGA in 1949.

Tony Zale (b. 5-29-13, d. 3-20-97): Boxer. Born Anthony Zaleski. "The Man of Steel." Two-time middleweight champ. Fought Rocky Graziano for title three times in 21 months, winning twice. 67-18-2 with 44 KOs. Elected to Boxing Hall of Fame 1958.

Emil Zatopek (b. 9-19-22): Track and field. Czech runner became only athlete to win gold medal in 5,000 and 10,000 meters and marathon, at 1952 Olympics. Also gold medalist in 10,000 meters at '48 Olympics.

Zinedine Zidane (b. 6-23-72): French soccer player. "Zizou." Led France to 1998 World Cup title; scored two goals in 3–0 win over Brazil in the final. Led Juventus to 1998 Italian League title and to '98 European Cup final. 1998 FIFA World Player of the Year. Led France to 2000 European Championship.

Obituaries

Althea Gibson
1927–2003

Roone Arledge, 71, television executive. Widely credited as the man who brought modern production techniques into the broadcasting of sports, Arledge was also the executive who pioneered the creation of *Monday Night Football*. He was for a decade the president of the sports and news divisions at ABC, during which time he created the now long-running *Nightline*. During his career, Arledge won 36 Emmy Awards and when *Sports Illustrated* named the 40 most influential people in sports in 1994, Arledge was listed third, behind only Muhammad Ali and Michael Jordan.

In New York City, of complications from cancer, December 5, 2002.

Steve Bechler, 23, baseball player. An Orioles righthander, Bechler complained of dizziness and collapsed during a running drill on a field in Fort Lauderdale, where the temperature was 81° and the humidity was 74%. He was given oxygen and intravenous fluids, then taken to a nearby medical center, where he was admitted into intensive care. He died the following morning.

In Fort Lauderdale, FL, of apparent multiple organ failure due to heatstroke, February 17, 2003.

Bobby Bonds, 57, baseball player. Bonds, a three-time All-Star and MVP of the 1973 All-Star Game, Bonds was one of the most potent combinations of power and speed in major league history. He hit at least 30 home runs and stole at least 30 stolen bases in five different seasons; the only player to accomplish the feat as many times is his son, San Francisco outfielder Barry Bonds.

In San Francisco, from lung cancer, Aug. 23, 2003.

Herb Brooks, 66, hockey coach. SI's E.M. Swift writes:

"One of the giants of U.S. hockey, Brooks was best known as the strategist behind the "Mircale on Ice" team that won a gold medal for the U.S. at the 1980 Lake Placid Olympics, a feat that SI selected as the premier athletic moment of the 20th century.

"Though calculating and demanding as any old-school coach, Brooks had a modernistic approach to the game, emphasizing speed and wide-open play. A two-time Olympian ('64 and '68) as a forward, he coached his alma mater, Minnesota, to three national titles in the 1970s. In his 1980 Olympic post he combined newfangled methods (psychological profiles to evaluate players) with an authoritarian manner that often grated on his players and his bosses at USA Hockey. Still, he molded an unheralded bunch of college kids into a team that captured the hearts of America. The U.S.'s 4–3 semifinal win over the Soviet Union, then the best team in the world, was one of the great upsets in the history of sports.

"Brooks went on to coach four NHL teams, the Rangers, North Stars, Penguins, and Devils, putting together a 219-221-66-2 record. He hated the clutch-and-grab style and was outspoken against hockey violence. His final coaching stint came during the 2002 Salt Lake City Olympics, where he guided the NHL stars from the U.S. to a silver medal, losing 5–2 to Canada in the final. 'For me it's exciting just to look at an open sheet of ice,' Brooks told SI in 1999. "All I see are possibilities.'"

Near Minneapolis, of injuries sustained in a car accident, Aug. 11, 2003.

Dave DeBusschere, 62, basketball player and executive. A key member of the New York Knicks' championship teams in 1970 and '73, DeBusschere was a forward who could score as well as dominate the boards with his tenacious style of play. Over his 12-year career, he averaged 16.1 points and 11 rebounds per game and was named to the All-Star team eight times. He was elected to the Basketball Hall of Fame in 1982 and was named one of the NBA's 50 greatest players in 1996. Teammate and fomer Senator Bill Bradley writes in SI:

"The moment I heard of Dave DeBusschere's death it was as if a lightning bolt hit my heart. In the next day's papers, one photo caught my eye: Dave driving to the basket, the ball in his left hand, shock of dark hair matted with sweat and a face full of his unique determination. It reminded me of a time when we were all younger and there was a magic about life.

"There is no other way to describe those years on our Knicks teams. How it felt to hear the Garden crowd, to know the satisfaction of a play well-executed, to feel the chills of winning a championship, to share the brotherhood of working in an environment of mutual trust, with people you respect, each of whom has the courage to take the last-second shot.

"Dave left all of himself on the court every game. He held nothing back. Once he caught an elbow in the face that broke his nose. The pain was obvious. I didn't see how he would play the next night. But there he was when the buzzer sounded—with a strip of plastic over his nose and adhesive forming an H above and below his eyes to hold it in place.

"Dave and I were roommates for six years, and he taught me a lot. In my second year in the NBA, we lost a close one in Philadelphia on a bad pass I made when the Sixers were applying full-court pressure. I was dejected. Dave put me straight: 'You can't go through a season like this. There are too many games. You blew it tonight, but when it's over, it's over. Let it go, or you won't be ready to play tomorrow.' It was NBA lesson No. 1: Don't make today's loss the enemy of tomorrow's victory....

"Championship teams share a moment few others know. The overwhelming emotion derives from more than pride. Your devotion to your teammates, the depth of your sense of belonging, is like blood kinship but without the complications. In the nonverbal world of basketball, it's like grace and beauty and ease, and it spills into all areas of your life.

"So I say, brother, goodbye; we'll miss you, number 22. May God grant you a peaceful journey."

In New York City, of a heart attack, May 14, 2003.

Larry Doby, 79, baseball player. In 1947, 11 weeks after Jackie Robinson took the field for the Dodgers and broke the major league color barrier, Doby made his debut for the Cleveland Indians, doing the same for the American League. SI's Mark Beech writes:

"Doby wasn't just the second black major leaguer; he was the first in the American League, meaning that, like Robinson, he took the field among all white peers. Doby did more than hold his own: He was a seven-time All-Star who twice led the league in homers. He hit the decisive home run off the Boston Braves' Johnny Sain to win Game 4 of the 1948 World Series. (The Indians won that Series in six games, the team's last world championship.) And in 1978 he bec[...] second black man[...]

irst, for the Indians in '75—when he took over the White Sox in mideason and managed them for the rest of the year.

"Like Robinson, Doby combined the physical skills and the strong stoic personality that [Cleveland owner Bill] Veeck thought was needed to break the color barrier. Doby was a lean lefthanded hitter with excellent power and great speed. He was also a quiet Navy veteran (he served in Guam) who married his high school sweetheart from Paterson, N.J., and was virtually vice-free. 'When I get two bottles of beer, I'm ready to go to bed,' he said in 1950.

"For Doby, Cleveland was as close to an ideal major league destination as he would find. The city's football team, the Browns, was dominating the All-America Football Conference with several black players.... Yet reaction to Doby was mixed. He received taunts and threats but also ovations. On the road some hotels barred him; the hotel Statler in Washington, D.C., accepted him as its first black guest.

"Some of Doby's teammates refused to talk to him, but others were more welcoming, especially Joe Gordon, the Indians' veteran second baseman. In one of his first games Doby struck out on three pitches, then sat down at the end of the bench with his head in his hands. Gordon was up next, and he too struck out on three pitches, flailing at the last strike. He sat next to Doby and put his head in his hands. 'I never asked Gordon then if he struck out deliberately,' said Veeck years later. '[But] after than, every time Doby went out on the field, he would pick up Gordon's glove and throw it to him. It's as nice a thing as I ever saw or heard of in sports.'

"While his teammates could sympathize with Doby, only one man could empathize. 'Jackie and I talked often,' Doby said. 'Maybe we kept each other from giving up.' Robinson, of course, became Brooklyn's catalyst and was elected to the Hall of Fame in 1962. Doby finished his career with a .283 average and 253 home runs in 13 seasons. He was elected to the Hall of Fame by the veterans committee in '98. 'Jack and I went through a lot of the same things,' said Doby in '97, 25 years after he had served as a pallbearer at Robinson's funeral. 'I'd be lying if I said I didn't want people to remember that.'"

In Montclair, NJ, of cancer, June 18, 2003.

Mark-Vivien Foe, 28, soccer player. SI's Chris Ballard writes:

"[The 28-year-old Cameroon midfielder] Foe collapsed in the 71st minute of Cameroon's 1–0 win over Colombia in the semifinals of the FIFA Confederation Cup, shortly after refusing to be substituted off the pitch. Doctors determined that his heart had stopped and tried to revive him for 45 minutes on the sidelines. Foe was a mainstay for the Indomitable Lions, playing every minute of their 2002 World Cup run, and he scored eight goals in 2002 for the Premier League's Manchester City, which is retiring his number 23 jersey. 'At halftime his last words were, 'Boys, even if it means playing on the pitch, we must win.' ' said Cameroon captain Rigobert Song. 'And he was the victim. It's terrible.'"

In Saint-Denis, France, of natural causes of cardiac origin, June 26, 2003.

Althea Gibson, 76, tennis player. SI writes:

"The first black woman to win Wimbledon and a U.S. national tennis title, Gibson also became the first of her race to on the LPGA tour in 1963. Raised in Harlem, Gibson was a 12-year-old city paddle-tennis champ before switching to a racket and winning her first tennis tournament at 14. She became the first African-American to compete at the U.S. nationals in 1950 and at Wimbledon the next year. (Boxer Joe Louis paid for her plane ticket to London.) Lithe, powerful, and raw—in 1956 SI wrote: 'She moves rangily around the court like a slightly awkward panther'—Gibson had a huge serve and, at 5' 11", extraordinary reach. Six-time Wimbledon winner Billie Jean King recalled that when she was 13 and first saw Gibson play, 'My heart was pounding.... I thought, Geez, I hope I can play like that someday.'

"Gibson, who was frustrated by her inconsistency against top players, won the first of back-to-back Wimbledons in '57. 'At last! At last!' she shouted, accepting the trophy from Queen Elizabeth II. King often notes it was Gibson, not Arthur Ashe, who broke the sport's color barrier. But Gibson's success did not lead to an influx of black women: More than 40 years passed before another, Serena Williams, won the U.S. Open in 1998. (Venus Williams was the 2000 Wimbledon champ.

"After she retired with 56 wins and five grand slam titles, Gibson, who married twice and had no children, tried singing (she recorded an album) and acted in a John Wayne movie. She was commissioner of athletics in New Jersey from 1975 to '77. In her 1968 memoir, So Much to Live For, Gibson wrote, 'I hope that I have accomplished just one thing: that I have been a credit to tennis and my country.'"

In East Orange. NJ, of respiratory failure, Sept. 28, 2003.

Kid Gavilan, 77, boxer. SI writes:

"Welterweight champ from 1951 to '54, Gavilan was born Gerardo Gonzalez in Camaguey, Cuba, where he began fighting at age 10 for purses of bread and guava paste. Gavilan turned pro in '43 and went 107-30-6 over 15 years. Famous for his samba-like shuffling and bolo punch—a quasi uppercut that mimicked the movements of Cuba's sugarcane harvesters—the flashy fighter captivated U.S. fans. Gavilan even moved up in class to beat Jake LaMotta and win the middleweight title vacated by Ray Robinson. He retired to Havana in '58 but fled to Miami 10 years later after Fidel Castro, infuriated that Gavilan preached for Jehovah's Witnesses, seized his home. Plagued by memory loss, Gavilan spent the final years of his life in an assisted-care facility in Hialeah, Fla. He was, says boxing historian Bert Sugar, 'one of the heroes in the golden era of Friday-night fights.'"

In Miami, Fla., of a heart attack, Feb. 13, 2003.

Sid Gillman, 91, football coach. Elected to the Hall of Fame in 1983, Gillman was a master innovator who created the high-powered passing-oriented West Coast offense with the Rams and the Chargers in the AFL. He later coached the NFL's Oilers and in 18 years as a pro coach went 123-104-7. SI's Paul Zimmerman writes:

"It was a December night in 1966, and Sid Gillman's Chargers had just beaten the Jets 42–27. Gillman was having dinner, as he often did, in San Diego's leading sports restaurant Pernicano's Casa di Baffi, with the owner, George Pernicano. 'I feel sorry for those New York guys,' Pernicano said, 'getting the hell beat out of them and then having that long flight home. I think I'll drive out to the airport and take them some pepperoni and cheese.' Gillman looked at Pernicano as if he were nuts. 'The hell with 'em,' he said.

That was the Gilman I knew. Tough, uncompromising. When I saw him that year at a luncheon, he strode to the podium, frowning, checking his watch, his muscular neck cramped beneath his bow tie. 'Some see football as a game,' he said. 'You know what it is to me? It's blood!'

His offense was beautiful: the deep strike to Lance Alworth, the swerving and swooping of his twin backs, Paul Lowe and Keith Lincoln. Yet there were brutal elements too. The offense was built on the vertical attack—Alworth on the deep post, a tight end splitting the hashmarks, Lowe or Lincoln pushing it down the seams. The theory was to punish the defense, and in the '63 AFL title game Gillman beat the Boston Patriots 51–10. His was the true West Coast offense (later adapted and modified by Don Coryell, Joe Gibbs and Ernie Zampese), the antithesis of Bill Walsh's horizontal approach.

"A few years ago I spent a week watching film with Gillman at his house, learning his theories. He was kind and gentle and very patient. One day I told him, 'You know, when I first met you, you scared the hell out of me.' His wife, Esther, laughed. 'He scared a lot of people,' she said. 'Until they got to know him. Then he wasn't so bad.'"

In Century City, Calif., in his sleep, Jan. 3, 2003.

Bobby Joe Hill, 59, basketball player. Hill was the point guard on the all-black Texas Western squad that defeated top-ranked—and all-white—Kentucky 72–65 for the NCAA title in 1966. Hill scored 20 points and at one point in the first half, made back-to-back steals. "Bobby Joe, he was the steering wheel to our Mack truck," said Nevil Shed, the center on Hill's championship team. "He was our leader. He was a warrior. Besides that, he was a good man."

In Fort Worth, Texas, of a heart attack, Dec. 8, 2002.

Craig Kelly, 36, snowboarder. SI's Mark Beech writes:

"Kelly, perhaps more than anyone else, was responsible for transforming snowboarding from a fringe diversion into a mainstream sport. Kelly and 20 others were trekking in the Selkirk mountain range to ski and snowboard on the Durrand Glacier, when a wall of snow 100 feet wide overwhelmed them. Kelly was swept more than 300 feet down the mountain and buried. 'We've lost a legend, a rider who set the standard for everyone,' said John Stouffer, editorial director of *Transworld Snowboarding Business* magazine. 'He made the sport significant and legitimate.'

"Because his influence extended to almost every level of the snowboarding culture, from riding styles to marketing, Kelly is often compared with Michael Jordan and is know as the godfather of his sport. A former BMX rider from Mount Vernon, Wash., Kelly began snowboarding in 1981and within a few years other riders were copying his unique knees-together stance. He dominated the world circuit in the late '80s, winning four freestyle world championships and signing a lucrative endorsement deal with Burton Snowboards. [He's the rider who put professionalism into team riding,' says Burton founder Jake Burton. After retiring from competition a decade ago, Kelly, who's survived by his girlfriend, Savina Findlay, and their infant daughter, Olivia, became a backcountry guide in Nelson, B.C. There he was a pioneer of free riding—in which snowboarders journey into the wilderness searching for virgin powder. Backcountry trekking is now one of North America's favorite forms of outdoor tourism. 'If you pick up a snowboarding magazine, you'll see 90 percent of it devoted to free riding,' says Burton. 'Craig was restless, but he always seemed a step ahead.'"

Near Revelstoke, B.C., in an avalanche, Jan. 20, 2003.

Sam Lacy, 99, sportswriter. SI writes:

"Lacy had a hand in Jackie Robinson's breaking the major league color barrier and was lauded in 2002 by Baltimore mayor Martin O'Malley as 'a teacher, historian and social scientist.' In 1944 Lacy, a writer for the Baltimore *Afro-American*, wrote to every major league owner suggesting the formation of an integration committee, which he and Dodgers owner Branch Rickey served on. Lacy and Wendell Smith, a *Pittsburgh Courier* writer, pestered Rickey to sign Robinson, who had competed against whites as a five-sport star at UCLA. When Rickey signed Robinson to a Triple A contract in 1945, Lacy traveled with him, often staying in the same 'colored-only' hotels and boarding houses. (At one such establishment in Macon, Ga., a cross was burned in the front yard.) Lacy, who was inducted into the writers' wing of the Baseball Hall of Fame in 1998, continued to write for the *Afro-American* until his death; his final column, about his generous neighbors, appeared the day after he passed away. 'I've always felt that there was nothing special about me,' Lacy said in '98. 'And I know how this may sound. But any person with a little vision, a little curiosity, a little nerve could have done what I did.'"

In Baltimore, Md., of heart and kidney failure, May 8, 2003.

Johnny Longden, 96, jockey. SI writes:

"The only man to have both ridden and trained a Kentucky Derby winner, Longden was born in England and raised in Canada, where he developed a push-pull style that earned him the nickname the Pumper. Longden rode Count Fleet to a Triple Crown in 1943. After retiring from riding in '66 with 6,032 wins—then the alltime record—Longden took up training and in '69 won the roses at Churchill Downs with Majestic Prince.

In Banning, Calif., in his sleep, Feb. 14, 2003.

Hank Luisetti, 86, basketall player. Widely credited as the man who pioneered the one-handed shot, Luisetti wowed the basketball world, gaining national notice when he scored 15 points in Stanford's 45–31 upset of heavily favored LIU in 1936. The victory ended LIU's 43-game winning streak.

In San Mateo, Calif., of an unknown illness, Dec. 17, 2002

Mark McCormack, 72, sports agent. Considered by many the father of modern sports marketing and the by some the most powerful man in sports, McCormack and International Management Group (IMG), the agency he created, cast a shadow that extended over every major professional sport. SI's S.L. Price writes:

"The silence was bad, of course, but everone was used to his silences. It was one of Mark McCormack's most famous negotiating tricks: Stay quiet, let the other guy grow uneasy, and to cover his awkwardness he'll talk, reveal himself, give you an edge before the first cup of coffee is served. Even when that tactic became a cliche—after the people across the table from him had read his books, and his words were taken as gospel by business students and by every young carnivore churned out by McCormack's colossal International Management Group—it still worked. In 1989, as Dick Ebersol, the newly minted head of NBC Sports, hurried to his first meeting with McCormack at he French Open, he kept warning himself: Don't abble, and for God's sake, don't give anything away.

"They sat, McCormack didn't say much. Within 10 minutes, Ebersol, with no authority from his bosses at General Electric, was outlining his vision of the future of sports and how NBC was going to dominate it and wondering, by the way, if there was some way NBC and IMG could merge? 'I looked in his eyes,' Ebersol says, 'and they gave me nothing back at all.'

"So, no, the fact that the 72-year-old McCormack lay speechless for four months before dying last Friday in a New York City hospital wasn't completely out of character. What most struck the friends and relatives who sat reading him e-mails, books and prayers in a vain bid to talk him out of his coma was the idea of McCormack lying there with a tube jammed into his throat, doing ... nothing. 'You're always going somewhere' a friend once complained to him. McCormack never saw the problem; this was a man, after all, who scheduled playtime with the children and set up casual phone calls months in advance. This was the agent cum entrepreneur who, after one handshake with Arnold Palmer in 1960, spent a lifetime of 18-hour days flying, meeting and scribbling endlessly on a yellow legal pad angling his way into a singular place in sports history.

" 'He did more to change the field of professional sport than anybody,' says Donald Dell, who in 1970 copied McCormack's blueprint and founded the agency ProServ (later bought by SFX Sports Group), beginning a bitter 27-year rivalry between the two companies. Who won? Put it this way: When Dell began lecturing on sports law at the University of Virginia, he asked McCormack to be his first guest lecturer. 'To my shock, he accepted,' says Dell.

"It made sense: McCormack liked victory laps. The yips had killed his ambition to be Palmer, but after signing Palmer to an exclusive represenatation deal with that handshake, McCormack singlehandedly created the field of sports marketing by attacking business with the mind-set of a jock. He never lost his adolescent pride in being the first, the best and the biggest; he kept score, needede to be No. 1 and usually was. Martk the Shark—the first agent to marry athletes to big business and the first to grasp the need to go global—built IMG into the $1.3 billion gorilla of sports (and its TV arm, TWI, into the world's biggest independent producer of sports television) and made himself and his clients very rich. Palmer, still bound to IMG by that handshake, is now worth an estimated $200 million.

"In the '70s McCormack was dubbed the most powerful man in golf; in the '80s, the most powerful in tennis. Thirteen years ago this magazine threw in the towel and declared him the most powerful man in sports. No one argued. IMG may represent talent, but it also owns or co-owns nine tennis tournaments, has a hand in marketing or televising all eight Grand Slam events in golf and China and partially financed the creation of China's pro basketball league. Even as McCormack cluttered the TV dial with trashsports such as The Superstars and World's Strongest Man, he saw the virtue of representing hoary institutions such as the All England Club at Wimbledon and the Royal and Ancient Golf Club of St. Andrew's, respecting tradition yet leaving both venues covered with his fingerprints.

"The sneaker commercial, the luxury suite, the stadium with a corporate sponsor, the athlete demanding to be shown the money, Tom Cruise begging Cuba Gooding Jr., 'Help me ... to help you'—all that, and plenty more both good and bad, came

from long-ago firings of McCormack's machine-gun mind. Yet after suffering cardiac arrest during minor surgery at a Manhattan dermatologist's office in mid-January, McCormack lay immobile, his brain choked by a lack of oxygen. 'That's what's so hard,' his wife Betsy Nagelsen, said 10 days before his death. [It's not so much the limbs; if he spent the rest of his life in a wheelchair, that wouldn't matter. But not to have his brain functioning....'

"... since the arrival of Maggie—his daughter with Nagelsen—five years ago, friends had noticed a change in McCormack. He still worked long hours, still nibbled nervously on a finger before negotiations. But he'd found religion and was spending more time in Orlando, swimming with the little girl who looked and acted just like him. He was still pulling in business: Last year Nicklaus, who left IMG in 1970 to start Golden Bear Inc., asked if McCormack would work with him again. Days before McCormack collapsed, on a January Sunday morning much like those Sundays in the '60s when Arnie was charging and you could almost smell the money coming in, McCormack met with Palmer at Bay Hill. For an hour, Palmer says, the two pioneers 'laughed and had breakfast and talked about the past and all the funny things that happened.'

"Then came fate's cruel joke: Nagelsen had brought McCormack to Christ, but they hadn't talked much about limbo. For four months he hung there, and then Friday morning, alone, with no family near, he suddenly had somewhere to go. For the last time, Mark the Shark was on the move."

In New York City, after four months in a coma following a heart attack, May 16, 2003.

Dave McNally, 60, baseball pitcher. McNally, whose legal victory in a 1975 arbitration case ended baseball's reserve clause and ushered in the era of free agency, was a key member of the sterling Orioles pitching staff that led Baltimore to four AL pennants along with World Series wins in 1966 and '70. In 1968, his best season, he went 22–10 with 202 strikeouts and an ERA of 1.95. For his career, the lefthanded McNally went 184–119 with a 3.24 ERA, 1,512 strikeouts and 33 shutouts: His 17 consecutive victories between 1968 and '69 was the alltime AL mark until it was eclipsed by Roger Clemens in 1999. McNally is also the only pitcher to hit a grand slam in the World Series.

In Billings, Mont., of cancer, Dec. 1, 2002.

Richard Meek, 79, sports photographer. SI writes:

"One of SI's original three photographers, Meek shot 45 covers for the magazine, as well as numerous photographic essays on such diverse subjects as auto racing, billiards, NFL football and a gathering of fantastically dressed Arabian horse owners in Arizona. 'His versatility was fascinating,' says longtime SI photographer Neil Leifer. 'He was a superb studio photographer, but he was equally good on the sidelines at the Olympics or at the America's Cup. His pictures ran the gamut.'

"Meek was raised in Richmond, Ind., where, in his early teens, he converted the back of his father's bakery into a darkroom. As one of his first projects he took pictures at a high school football game, raced home to develop them, then raced back to sell the prints in the stands. He came to New York City in the late 1940s to work in the photo lab at LIFE magazine, and when SI debuted on Aug. 16, 1954, he was one of a trio of photographers that included Mark Kauffman and Hy

Peskin. Meek stayed on staff until '58, then worked as a contract photographer—while also shooting covers for LIFE—until 1970. In a 1966 letter to the readers, SI publisher Garry Valk called him 'a man of genius. Meek has sampled more of sport for us than anyone else.'

"Meek had more than 550 assignments for the magazine, so many that he shot cover portraits of enduring athletes like Muhamad Ali more than once. In an era when the magazine often focused on animals—not just racehorses, but dogs, seals, bears and fish—he frequently got the call. In recent years Meek created abstract art in a darkroom at his home, where he lived with his wife, Barbara. 'I have never been able to decide whether photography is an art or a craft,' Meek once said. 'For me it doesn't really matter. I am satisfied that it is something unto itself.'"

In Huntington, N.Y., of natural causes, Jan. 19, 2003.

Roger Neilson, 69, hockey coach. SI's Michael Farber writes about the legendary Hall of Fame coach:

"Even in dying, Neilson—an innovator in the use of video as a teaching tool, the coach of eight NHL teams who went 460-381-159 and one of the great gentlemen of sports—was considerate. He died at his home in Peterborough. Ont., last Saturday, which allowed his close friends, basically the entire hockey community, to mourn him en masse at the NHL draft in Nashville. When commissioner Gary Bettman announced Neilson's passing, there was a moment of silence from men who had come to work in the sober business attire that was never Neilson's style. He preferred a russet-colored Abercrombie & Fitch baseball cap and blindingly florid five-collar ties. In the early '80s, when he was an assistant to Scotty Bowman in Buffalo and did the pioneering videotape work that earned him the nickname Captain Video, Neilson was told he needed a tie to enter the swank Aud club. So he arrived at the club wearing a tie and accompanied by his beloved dog, Mike, who swept in with him—wearing a tie of his own.

"Neilson, a man of deep Christian faith, was a lifelong bachelor with a passionate allegiance to hockey. He schooled many current coaches at his clinics, and he was the midwife of the modern neutral-zone trap, a tactic he implemented in 1990-91 with the expansion Panthers. Last year Ottawa's Jacques Martin stepped aside for two games, allowing Neilson to coach his 999th and 1,000th NHL games, a statistical shenanigans that drew hardly a protest because it was the beloved Neilson running the bench. When he was diagnosed with bone marrow cancer in '99 two oncologists said he had five years to live. The ever-optimistic Neilson told friends, 'One gave me five years and another gave me five. That means I have 10 years left.'"

In Peterborough, Ont., of cancer, June 21, 2003.

Lazslo Papp, 77, boxer. SI' writes:

"Papp was the first boxer to win a gold medal at three Olympics. The Hungarian, who sported a Clark Gable mustache and had a brutal left hook, was an Olympic champ as a middleweight in London in 1948. After getting gold as a light heavyweight in 1952 and '56—when he beat future world champion Jose Torres—Papp turned pro and won the European middleweight championship while running his record to 27-0-2 with 15 KOs. Just as he was about to get a shot at world middleweight champ Joey Giardello in '65, Papp was summoned home by the Hungarian government, which revoked his passport on the grounds that boxing for financial gain was 'incompatible with socialist principles.' Papp went on to coach Hungary's Olympic team and later ran a boxing

school. In 1989 the World Boxing Council named Papp an honorary world champion, and two years later designated him the best middleweight of all time.

In Budapest, Hungary, after a long illness, Oct. 16, 2003

George Plimpton, 76, writer. SI managing editor Terry McDonell writes:

"... In the fall of '58, with something quite unusual on his mind, Plimpton visited SI's first managing editor, Sid James, and shared what James recognized as 'a great idea.' A group of major league baseball players were staging an unofficial postseason all-star game at Yankee Stadium in a few weeks, and Plimpton thought he could write an interesting article on what it was like to participate—pitching to, say, Willie Mays and Mickey Mantle. At a pregame exhibition he would face all starters on both the National and the American League squads. The problem was, how could it be arranged?

In those days, the most influential man in sports was arguably Toots Shor, whose restaurant was only a few blocks from the SI offices. James led an expedition there and bought drinks as he and Plimpton explained the idea to the man himself. Shor said the solution was simple: Offer $1,000 to the winning team. By evening came word that Plimpton's pitching exhibition was on....

"On game day at Yankee Stadium the public-address announcer bungled Plimpton's name, calling him George Prufrock, an irony not lost on T.S. Eliot scholar Plimpton. It was agreed that George would be a facsimile batting practice pitcher and that the hitters could wait for their perfect pitch. George got Mays to pop up, but many of the hitters were making him throw a dozen or so pitches—Ernie Banks let 22 go by—and after nine National Leaguers had batted, George called timeout. He could no longer lift his arm.

"The resulting SI story was turned into the book *Out of My League.* Ernest Hemingway wired George from the Mayo Clinic, where he was being treated for depression, that it was 'beautifully observed and incredibly conceived [with] the chilling quality of a true nightmare ... the dark side of the moon of Walter Mitty.'

"Thus began George's amateur forays into professional sports for SI: Going three rounds and having his nose slightly 'collapsed' by light heavyweight champion Archie Moore at Stillman's Gym in 1959; going to training camp with the Detroit Lions in 1963. (His SI account became both a book and a movie, *Paper Lion,* about "a 36-year-old free-agent quarterback out of Harvard.")

"In reviewing these and numerous other works that followed, approving critics continued to draw on the Walter Mitty analogy, which had a surface truth, but overlooked the fact that in Mitty's daydreams he always succeeded, while in George's real-life adventures he always failed. But this truth—that his work had more to do with Everyman than Mitty—was always obscured by George's sophisticated but self-deprecating prose, which made him so easy and often hilarious to read. Likewise, far from being wholly unsuited for the sports he dove into, George was a graceful natural athlete who otherwise would never have succeeded in his failures, so to speak. He was a strong tennis player and could throw any ball he ever picked up: 'It was the first instrument of superiority I found myself owning,' he once said.

"He was also a physical presence, 6'4" and lean, and blessed with infectious energy and great physical courage. (George helped wrestle the gun from Sirhan Sirhan's hand moments after Sirhan shot Senator Robert F. Kennedy in Los Angeles in 1968.) These gifts served him well as a participatory journalist—a label he characterized as 'that ugly descriptive'—and took him from tennis with Pancho Gonzalez to the NBA with

Celtics and golf with Arnold Palmer and Jack Nicklaus to high-flying on a trapeze with the Flying Apollos. Adventure after adventure he described elegantly in nearly three dozen books but not at the expense of the most eccentric of notions, like finding out what it was like to mouth-catch a grape dropped from the top of Trump Tower.

"For April Fool's Day 1985, at the prompting of then SI managing editor Mark Mulvoy, George concocted the Buddhist pitcher, Sidd Finch, he of the 168-mile-an-hour fastball. Finch was said to be under wraps at the Mets' training camp, and the club went along, helping to stage bogus photographs. Everybody fell for it. When the prank was exposed (it had been signaled in the piece's subhead), bumper stickers appeared proclaiming SIDD FINCH LIVES, and *The Curious Case of Sidd Finch* was published as a novel in 1987....

"The world will be different without George Plimpton, less fun. Which is clear from what I have already left out: the movies, the fireworks, the expeditions. Or this: It was dusk, and we were taking a walk on a ranch road in eastern New Mexico. Actually, we were birding—on the trail of the elusive burrowing owl that lives in prairie dog holes—but we were going about it in that deeply civilized way that allows you to bring your glass of wine along on your after-dinner expedition. We had seen no owls, but George had pointed out a bat or two when suddenly he was pulling his shirt over his head and flinging it in the air. What happened next was that the shirt, peaking at perhaps 25 feet, drew at least a half-dozen bats, which tracked it to the ground like dive bombers, squeaking their shrill bat squeaks. A second throw seemed to double the number of bats. And so on until the light was completely gone.

"The trick, George explained, pulling the T-shirt back on, was to give the bats something that would come fluttering up on their sonar as potential food—like a gargantuan moth. 'These bats are *Tadarida brasiliensis mexicana*,' George said. 'Mexican free-taileds to you.' How did he know? When he was 12 George had had a very good time hunting bats and donating the "specimen skins" to museums. And it was almost predictable of him to pull something like bat expertise out of nowhere. With George, you always got something like that. *Did you know that Camus played goal for the Oran Football Club but was never moved to write about it?*

"Last year George was made a chevalier, the highest rank in France's Legion of Honor—a token of which he loved to wear in his lapel to test the alertness of new French restaurants—and was inducted into the American Academy of Arts and Letters. All the glamour and gravitas that earned him those honors rubbed off on SI, where for almost 50 years he charmed staffers, befriended writers and dedicated books to his various managing editors. The day before he died George closed the 50th anniversary issue of *The Paris Review*, and we had spoken that afternoon about how he might contribute to *Sports Illustrated*'s 50th Anniversary. As always, he had numerous ideas.

"With his passing SI loses a very good friend, and I lose my best. And it is not at all surprising to me that so many others out there feel the same way.

In New York City, of unknown causes, Sept. 25, 2003.

Tex Schramm, 83, football executive. SI writes:

"Schramm, the general manager of the Cowboys from the team's inception in 1960 until '89, transformed the Cowboys from a hapless team (they were 0-11-1 in '60) to America's team (by the 1970s their radio broadcasts were heard in 19 states and Mexico). He had a leaguewide impact, introducing computerized scouting, microphones on referees and, most memorably, in 1970, scantily clad cheerleaders. 'Fans didn't respond to cheers they way they did at college or high school,' Schramm said. 'So we said the heck with that. Let's just make it fun, make it entertainment.'

Tex Ernest Schramm—named for the state in which his parents met—had been a sportswriter in L.A. before becoming p.r. director for the Rams in 1947. He worked his way up to G.M. (and gave a young Pete Rozelle his first NFL job, in the p.r. department), then left in '56 to work for CBS Sports. During the 1960 Winter Olympics, Schramm was mesmerized by the IBM computers used to process results. When Clint Murchison hired him to run the Cowboys shortly thereafter, Schramm asked an IBM engineer—who, according to Schramm, 'didn't know if a football was full of air or full of feathers'—to create a program to evaluate players. That led to the acquisition of players such as quarterback Craig Morton and wide receiver Bob Hayes, a track star whose speed the computer loved even though Hayes had never played college football. Schramm's Cowboys had a winning record every year from 1966 until '85 and won two Super Bowls, but he left the team in '89 after new owner Jerry Jones fired coach Tom Landry, whom Schramm had hired in 1960. In '91 Schramm became the first NFL team executive to enter the Hall of Fame, fulfilling a careerlong desire. 'I never made any bones about it,' Schramm said in '78. 'I'm very conscious of history, and want to be remembered as being part of something that was great.'"

In Dallas, of undetermined causes, July 15, 2003.

Spectacular Bid, 27, thoroughbred horse. SI's William Nack writes:

"In the long annals of thoroughbred racing in America, no decade gave the sport as many surpassing horses as the 1970s. Only the 1940s, with Count Fleet and Citation leading the way, comes remotely close. The '70s were racing's golden age—a glorious stage on which Secretariat, Ruffian, Forego, Seattle Slew, Affirmed, Alydar and Spectacular Bid strutted their incomparable stuff.

"By 2003 all of them were dead but one. And then, as of last Monday, there were none. On June 9, 24 years to the day after suffering the most memorable defeat of his career, in the 1979 Belmont Stakes— a loss that prevented him from becoming the decade's fourth Triple Crown winner— 27-year-old Spectacular Bid died of old age at the farm in upstate New York to which he had been exiled after a failed career as a stallion in Kentucky. He won an astonishing 26 of 30 races—all but three of his victories came in stakes— and $2.78 million in purses. In one improbable eight-race stretch in 1979 he shttered five track records, lowering Santa Anita's seven-furlong mark to a hysterical 1:20 and its 1¼-mile record on dirt to a blistering 1:57⅘.

"In that era of champions, none was as brilliant as a 4-year-old as Spectacular Bid in 1980, and one has to go back to '53, when Tom Fool won 10 of 10 races, including New York's Triple Crown for older horses, to find an equal. In '80 Bid won all nine races he entered. He so dominated that no horse opposed him in the Woodward Stakes at Belmont, his final start. He went to the post alone and toured the grounds in a walkover, under Bill Shoemaker, a jockey who rode some of the swiftest horses in history: Swaps, Dr. Fager, Damascus and Forego. Of Spectacular Bid,

Shoemaker said simply, 'He is the best horse I ever sat on.'

"For all the lasting images of his championship seasons—his gait always steady as a drumroll, his head rising and his gray mane flying as he lit the fire off the turn for home—what we remember best is his eye-popping performance in the 1979 Florida Derby. He had been America's 2-year-old champion in '78, an easy winner in his first two races as a 3-year-old, and all jockey Ron Franklin had to do was keep Bid clear of trouble and hang on. Alas, Franklin was only 19 and unseasoned, and it remains a wonder how the horse survived the race at all. Leaving the gate, he banged hard against it, and around the first turn he nearly clipped another horse's heels as Franklin swung him outside. The jockey then rushed Bid to the inside, wher he had to steady him twice in traffic, and around the last turn he had to ease him back to find running room.

"Trainer Bud Delp watched all this in horror. There was no way Bid could win after such trouble. Yet the colt raced home first by 4½ lengths. Descending to the track in a hurry, Delp would have liked to wring the rider's neck. 'You damned idiot,' he howled as Franklin returned to the winner's circle. 'You almost got the horse killed out there!' Franklin dismounted the horse in tears.

"Other jockeys started cruising like sharks around Delp's barn, looking to get the mount, but Delp, who had an affection for the kid, kept Franklin on the colt through the Triple Crown. He had won the Kentucky Derby and the Preakness and was expected to gallop home in the Belmont when the Fates intervened. The colt stepped on an open safety pin on the morning of the Belmont, driving it a half-inch into the left front foot, and he faded in the race, finishing third. When Delp told the story of the pin, many hooted skeptically—'They called me a liar!' Delp says—but trainer Mack Miller, who had horses in the same barn as Bid, recalls that one of Delp's workers came over early that morning and, seeking help, said 'The Bid stepped on a safety pin.'

"The colt lost only once after that Belmont, when Affirmed cantered away on an easy lead in the Jockey Club Gold Cup that fall and beat him by three quarters of a lenth. That winter Bid began the 1980 campaign by which history will always remember him. Delp still chants the mantra he has been chanting for years: 'He's the greatest horse that ever looked through a bridle.' He certainly grazes in the tall grass—among the giants."

In Unadilla, N.Y., of natural causes, June 9, 2003.

Bill Shoemaker, 72, jockey. SI's Charles Leerhsen writes:

"Sometimes it's what you don't do that brings the millions, the trophies, the ladies. Bill Shoemaker didn't try to turn a horse to butter with his riding whip, He didn't rattle the reins or frantically flap his legs, even if he was behind a wall of horseflesh as he entered the homestretch. Shoemaker sat so still on a moving thoroughbred that when he first came on the scene in California in 1949, track officials worried about the impression he gave: This kid, they said, looks like he's stiffing his horses. Actually he was unstiffing them, getting them to relax and feel good about themselves, using Dale Carnegie techniques on $3,000 claimers. It was a style born of necessity—at 4' 11" and 95 pounds Shoemaker was small even for a jockey; he couldn't muscle a 1,000-pound stallion if he tried—but it worked. At the end of his first season he was the second-leading rider in the U.S. When he died in his sleep last week at age 72, after 8,833 wins and a life of ups and downs steep even by ractetrack standards, he

was the picture next to *jockey* in the dictionary. 'Horse just ran for him,' says Laffit Pincay, the only rider ahead of Shoemaker on the alltime wins list. 'He could take horses no one else could do anything with and make them go.... Ferdinand, his $17.70-to$1 shot in the 1986 Kentucky Derby was pinched back at the start behind 15 rivals, then knocked twice into the rail before the firs turn. Refusing to panic, Shoemaker convinced his colt that he was still in the hunt. Down the backstretch Ferdinand picked up momentum. When a hole suddenly opened along the rail as they turned for home, Shoemaker saw it and entered it instantly. Daylight and victory. Roses and champagne. The Shoe was 54 years old, and his beautiful third wife was shouting that she loved him.

"Not every day at the races was so glorious. Although he won four Kentucky Derbys (with Swaps, Tomy Lee, Lucky Debonair and Ferdinand), the Triple Crown eluded him, and he was outdueled by Eddie Arcaro aboard Nashua in the ballyhooed 1955 match race with Swaps. Two years later Shoemaker misjudged the Churchill Downs finish line, standing up early in the stirrups, and cost Gallant Man the Derby as Iron Liege flew by. 'I didn't make any excuses,' Shoemaker said. He called it a 'boo-boo' and moved on.

" 'Win or lose,' says Pincay of their days in California, 'we'd go out to Chasen's for drinks...' Shoemaker was legally drunk the April evening in '91 when his SUV tumbled off a highway in San Dimas, Calif., leaving him with a disloacted spine and a life as a quadriplegic...

"He rode 40,350 horses and won an astounding 21.9% of his races. Following an international farewell tour that ended in February 1990, Shoemaker retired from riding and set up shop as a trainer at Santa Anita. his gross earnings that year were $32,000. After the accident he persevered, arriving at the barn each day in his electric wheelchair, but his image in the racing community was sullied by his refusals to fess up to driving drunk and by his strategy of suing everyone in sight over the accident. (He eventually settled with Ford for $1 million.) Just when people should have been pulling for Shoe, he was out of favor on the backstretch.

"The resentment faded, though, worn away by the sight of him coming around, smiling and talking to young riders about the tricky art of getting a racehorse to run. 'A lot of people have it a lot worse than I do,' he'd say, even after his training career evaporated and his third marriage failed. Before Pincay retired with 9,530 winners last April, Shoemaker would visit his old pal in the jocks' room at Santa Anita, and when Pincay said, 'I like my horse in the eighth,' Shoe would tell his assistant to make a note. 'He liked to play the pick Six,' Pincay says, with a laugh. 'And if the horse I gave him didn't win, he would never mention it, never stop smiling. That's what being around horses taught him. You take your wins and your losses and you never give up. There's always another race.'"

In San Mateo, Calif., in his sleep, Oct. 12, 2003.

Naftali Temu, 58, runner. SI writes:

"Temu launched a Kenyan Olympic dynasty by winning the country's first gold medal, in the 10,000 meters at the 1968 Games. Temu, who as a child ran 12 miles back and forth ro school each day, raced barefoot until '62. Six years later—and properly shod—he outran the favorite, Ethiopia's Mamo Wolde, in Mexico City. Since then, Kenyan men have won 13 Olympic medals in middle-distance events."

In Nairobi, Kenya, of complications from kidney disease, March 10, 2003.

2 0 0 4 M a j o r E v e n t s

JANUARY

Major College Bowl Games	Jan 1 & 2
Sugar Bowl/National Championship	Jan 4
NFL Wild-Card Playoffs	Jan 3 & 4
NFL Divisional Playoffs	Jan 10 & 11
U.S. Figure Skating Championships	Jan 3–11
Australian Open Tennis	Jan 19–Feb 1
NFL Conference Championships	Jan 18

FEBRUARY

Super Bowl XXXVIII	Feb 1
Millrose Games	Feb 6
NHL All-Star Game	Feb 8
AFC-NFC Pro Bowl	Feb 8
NBA All-Star Game	Feb 15
Daytona 500	Feb 15

MARCH

PBA World Championship	March 15–21
The Players Championship	March 25–28

APRIL

Major League Soccer Season Begins	April 3*
NCAA Men's Basketball Final Four	April 3–5
NCAA Women's Basketball Final Four	April 4–6
Baseball Opening Day	April 5*
Stanley Cup Playoffs Begin	April 7
Masters Tournament	April 8–11
NBA Playoffs Begin	April 17
NFL Draft	April 17–18*
Boston Marathon	April 19

MAY

Kentucky Derby	May 1
Preakness	May 15
Indianapolis 500	May 30
Stanley Cup Finals Begin	May 24*

JUNE

French Open Tennis	May 24–June 6
NBA Finals Begin	June 6
Belmont Stakes	June 5
U.S. Open Golf	June 17–20
NBA Draft	June 24

JULY

Wimbledon Tennis	June 21–July 4
Baseball All-Star Game	July 13
British Open Golf	July 15–18
Tour de France	July 3–25

AUGUST

Brickyard 400	Aug 8
PGA Championship	Aug 9–15
College Football Season Begins	Aug 21

SEPTEMBER

U.S. Open Tennis	Aug 23–Sept 5
NFL Season Begins	Sept 12*
Ryder Cup	Sept 17-19

OCTOBER

NHL Season Begins	Oct 6*
World Series Begins	Oct 16*
NBA Regular Season Begins	Oct 26
Women's Tennis Tour Championships	Oct 25–31*

NOVEMBER

New York Marathon	Nov 7
MLS Cup 2004	Nov 5*
Tennis Masters Cup	Nov 8–14

DECEMBER

Heisman Trophy Presentation	Dec 13
Major College Bowl Games Begin	Dec 16*

* Approximate date.